The Penguin Companion to Classical Music

The Penguin Companion
to Classical Music

Paul Griffiths

PENGUIN BOOKS

PENGUIN BOOKS

Published by the Penguin Group
Penguin Books Ltd, 80 Strand, London WC2R 0RL, England
Penguin Group (USA) Inc., 375 Hudson Street, New York, New York 10014, USA
Penguin Group (Canada), 10 Alcorn Avenue, Toronto, Ontario, Canada MV4 3B2
(a division of Pearson Penguin Canada Inc.)
Penguin Ireland, 25 St Stephen's Green, Dublin 2, Ireland (a division of Penguin Books Ltd)
Penguin Group (Australia), 250 Camberwell Road, Camberwell, Victoria 3124,
Australia (a division of Pearson Australia Group Pty Ltd)
Penguin Books India Pvt Ltd, 11, Community Centre,
Panchsheel Park, New Delhi – 110 017, India
Penguin Group (NZ), cnr Airborne and Rosedale Roads, Albany,
Auckland 1310, New Zealand (a division of Pearson New Zealand Ltd)
Penguin Books (South Africa) (Pty) Ltd, 24 Sturdee Avenue,
Rosebank 2196, South Africa

Penguin Books Ltd, Registered Offices: 80 Strand, London WC2R 0RL, England

www.penguin.com

First published 2004
First published in the United States of America 2005
1

Copyright © Paul Griffiths, 2004
All rights reserved

The moral right of the author has been asserted

Designed by Richard Marston
Typeset in Minion and Scala Sans
Typeset by Gem Graphics, Trenance, Cornwall
Printed in England by Clays Ltd, St Ives plc

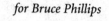

for Bruce Phillips

Contents

Preface

This book offers keys to one of the great memory banks our species has devised for itself: a store of thoughts and feelings, logical processes and fantasies, messages and enigmas, jokes and outbursts, all of which may be converted again and again from markings on paper into sound. Boundaries of time and space are crossed. Inscriptions made perhaps centuries ago become sensuous vibrations happening right now, through our voices as singers, under our fingers as players, inside our heads as listeners. From origins in a small area at a remote period – Europe in the Middle Ages – has come a universal music.

The borderlands of this music are hazy, touching on aural heritages of song, dance and sacred chant, on musical civilizations that developed independently and, since the beginning of the 20th century, on new forms of popular music transmitted round the world by electronic means. Its centre, though, is strong. Because it is notated, and because its notation is always open to interpretation, this music remains alive. Any composition is unfinished. It is not even finished when it is performed. Nor is it over when it has been heard and understood, for there will always be the possibility of a new hearing and a new understanding – a new hearing and a new understanding that some will want to put into compositions of their own.

This music, unfolding in ever-increasing richness and diversity from the development of accurate notation that began a thousand years ago, is what we know as 'classical', to use the epithet that has become unavoidable – and also unfortunate if it erects boundaries, arouses pretensions or, worst of all, suggests a shelf of works all more than a century old and irrelevant except as objects of veneration. On the contrary, the classics invite our participation, not our worship. We can all, now, be emboldened by Beethoven's hope, follow the struggles with multi-dimensional puzzles of melody, rhythm and harmony made by Machaut or Ligeti, feel the poignancy of a moment in Debussy, Schubert or Kurtág, share a joke with Haydn or Babbitt. Moreover, great works are still being written, and will go on being written. This music connects us with the past, certainly, but also with ourselves and with each other.

The classics live, too, in that they change. Half a century ago a book such as this would have barely considered music more than 300 years old: Bach and Handel marked the starting point, with Corelli, Purcell and a few others the upbeat to that beginning. A coherent view of 'the tradition' could thereby be maintained, of an evolving principle of organic form developed largely by composers in Austro-German lands – Bach's sons, Haydn, Mozart, Beethoven, Schubert, Mendelssohn, Schumann, Brahms, Bruckner, Mahler, Strauss, Schoenberg – until it was challenged by modernist outsiders: Debussy and Stravinsky.

But if this view remains central to our notion of what classical music is, much more has been added. In the concert hall and on record we can now meet the music not of three centuries but of ten, and the repertory has been amplified too in its breadth, with the emphatic arrival of, for instance, French Baroque music and the reconsideration of innumerable lesser and marginal composers. In effect the revolution of modernism, which upset all stabilities, has been completed in our relationship with the past. We now live in a much more complex musical world, in which the great river of the Austro-German tradition is only one of the waterways. To keep the image, this book is an aid to navigation.

What has also changed, especially since the introduction of the CD, is the variety of ways in which classic works can be heard. Current catalogues list, for example, over 200 available versions of Beethoven's Fifth Symphony, including 10 conducted by Wilhelm Furtwängler alone. Where recordings once served – as piano arrangements did before them – to familiarize people with works belonging in the concert hall, now they exist as achievements in their own right, to the extent that the live experience of music may seem irrelevant.

But it is not. Live music has irreplaceable virtues, not only in being unpredictable and unrecapturable but also in providing a richness of sound that no recording, still, can quite come near. Live music involves the listener, too, in an effort that joins performers and audience in concentration.

That they will go on engaging such concentration, time and again, is one of the conditions of classic works. They remain classics not just by 19th-century dictate (though indeed the notion of classical music began then) but also because generations have found them of personal and social value. Not the least of their values, in a culture of speed and the eye, is in their encouragement of sustained attention and their education of the ear. They also, in a world where the individual is primary, offer the comforts and challenges of community: the community of musicians taking part in a performance, of traditions in any score or realization, of notes in whatever the piece may project as harmony, of listeners. Our journeys through a work – or through our lives of listening and, if we will, performing – form strands in a counterpoint of millions.

For each of us the journey is an individual endeavour, part of a life of discovery and self-discovery, connection and self-connection. But we are enmeshed, too, in that multi-millionfold counterpoint, and dependent on cultural responsibilities that have to be widely shared. Music requiring performers with rare qualities, whom we naturally want to prize for their rareness, is expensive. Music whose values are not generally commercial has always needed support, from rulers or the rich.

Such music is therefore vulnerable, for all its scale and diversity, and especially vulnerable in a culture that prefers the celebrated (in this case venerated works and acclaimed recordings) to the unmeasured (new works, live music), and that has fine measures for cost but none for value. Value has to be simply affirmed, and

proved by experience. Let it be so. Listening is as important as reading. Because it comes as direct sense experience, unmediated by the analysis that words must arouse, music may even be more important than literature, addressing not only the selves we have constructed but the deepest urges of body and mind. An education that excludes music is a poor training for life. A life that excludes music is unimaginable.

Music concerns itself with memory and collective engagement, with passion and imagination, with attention and sheer sensuous pleasure. Its information cannot be stated in words, but words may carry us towards it. Hence this book, a large part of which consists of entries on composers, many with a list of works to show the scale and range of the output and provide some sense of what is most important. Here as well are outstanding performers (those who made musical history, who made historic recordings or who, now, are doing either) and some writers closely involved with music. There are also entries on instruments, on forms and genres, on cities and countries, on specific works and on other topics of musical interest, together with definitions of terms.

No book of this scope could claim to be wholly original. This one is indebted to, above all, *The New Grove*, which offers the only authoritative published information on many composers. If a few details have here been corrected, much has been gratefully gleaned, and readers are encouraged to go there for further illumination. Other suggestions for reading – books and internet sites – are given within longer entries; many of these sources were also consulted in the course of writing.

Further assistance came from persons near and far. Numerous representatives of music publishers, opera companies and orchestras responded promptly to emailed questions. On a much more general level, the book owes a vast amount to the critical readings of my editor, Nigel Wilcockson, and my wife Anne, who blessed the project as well with her eager encouragement. I have also drawn on the expertise of my sons Edmund (Russian) and Rupert (physiology). And I have dedicated the book to the one who quietly spurred me to write it. Uncountable are my further debts to musicians, readers and editors, incurred during 30 years as a professional music critic. This book comes from listening; may it help others listen.

Paul Griffiths
Los Angeles–New York–Manorbier
February–March 2004

Note on Conventions

Titles (except for generic descriptions, e.g. Symphony No.3) are given in the original language where this is English, French, German, Italian, Spanish or Latin. Titles in other languages are given in their customary English forms.

Abbreviations used in worklists (e.g. fl, s) are explained in their due alphabetical places, except for 'f.p.' (first performance), which also appears in the text. Common shortenings are used for languages, US states, English counties, months and measures.

Cross-references are indicated by SMALL CAPITALS, the reference to be found under the first word in that style. For example, *The* RITE OF SPRING is an invitation to look under 'rite'.

Worklists are selective, according to criteria of importance and popularity. The information given will normally include title and date (of composition unless otherwise stated). Between these may be mentioned the genre, the number of pieces (in the case of a cycle or collection), the author of the words (if any), the opus number or other catalogue reference (if any) and the instrumentation. Details of revisions and arrangements may be appended. The Chausson list shows most of the principles.

Oblique stroke signifies 'or'.

Superscript numbers are used for subsequent editions and reprints of books.

The Companion

A. Note name, hence A♭, A minor, etc. The naming of the notes from A upwards can be traced through Guido of Arezzo to the *Dialogus* of *c*.1000. Bass A, a 10th below middle C, was the lowest note in ordinary use and was a renaming of the *proslambanomenos* in the system inherited from Aristoxenus. Orchestras tune to the A above middle C, played by an oboe and customarily set at 440 Hz.

The key of A major is often ebullient, as in Mozart's Symphony No.29, Beethoven's Seventh and Schubert's 'Trout' Quintet (though with Mozart this could also be a key of breadth and splendour, of love music or, in the Clarinet Concerto, of seductive reflection). Its qualities come partly from how well it fits the violin (where the tonic, dominant and subdominant can all be supplied on open strings), and it is the key of many violin sonatas, by Beethoven, Schubert, etc. In Romantic music A minor is a common key for individualized emotion, as in the piano concertos of Schumann and Grieg, or Mahler's Sixth Symphony. A♭ major, warm and spacious, is rarer, but not uncommon in the piano music of Schubert (who also wrote a mass in this key) and Chopin; it is the key, too, of two Beethoven piano sonatas and Bax's Seventh Symphony. The exceedingly unusual key of A♭ minor is heard in an organ fugue by Brahms and a piano study by Moszkowski.

a. (1) (It., at, for). Used to indicate the number of parts, whether all through a composition – most often a piece of medieval or Renaissance polyphony, e.g. Browne's *Stabat mater* a 6 – or at a particular moment. In an orchestral score the instruction *a 2* may indicate that two instruments or groups play different music, or conversely that they combine. The music itself, of course, will make it clear which is the case: the instruction is an alert. The Fr. form is found, too: *à 5, à 2*, etc.

(2) The It. word also appears in the phrases A BATTUTA, A CAPPELLA, A PIACERE, A TEMPO, etc.

(3) Abbreviation for alto (i.e. contralto or male alto voice).

ab (Ger.). Off, away, as in *Dämpfer ab* (remove mutes).

ABA. Common way of denoting TERNARY form, where the first section (A) is repeated after a middle section (B).

a battuta (It., by the beat). Return to strict tempo.

Abbado, Claudio (b. Milan, 26 Jun 1933). Italian conductor. The son of a violinist and teacher, he was determined to become a conductor after hearing Debussy's *Nocturnes* as a young boy, then studied at the Milan Conservatory and with Hans Swarowsky at the Vienna Academy. In 1963 he won the Mitropoulos Prize, after which he began to make recordings and appear internationally, notably at the Salzburg Festival (1965) and Covent Garden (1968). From the first his interests were shared between opera and concerts, new music (Nono was a friend) and classics. He took leading posts with La Scala (1971–86), the LSO (1979–86), the Vienna Staatsoper (1986–91) and the Berlin Philharmonic (1990–2002), and in 1978 founded the European Community Youth Orchestra.

abbellimenti (It.). Embellishments, ornaments.

ABC. Australian Broadcasting Corporation.

Abduction from the Seraglio, The. See *Die* ENTFÜHRUNG AUS DEM SERAIL.

Abegg (i.e. A–B♭–E–G–G). Theme of piano variations by Schumann, which he dedicated to a girlfriend, Meta Abegg.

Abel, Carl Friedrich (b. Cöthen, 22 Dec 1723; d. London, 20 Jun 1787). German–British musician. The son and grandson of professional musicians, he studied with his father and possibly with J.S. Bach, a family friend. By 1743 he was playing in the Dresden court orchestra, where he stayed for a decade and a half. He then arrived in London, where he gave his first concert in 1759 and formed a musical partnership with J.C. Bach in 1764, presenting regular concerts until 1782. Another friend was Gainsborough, who painted his portrait (now at the Huntington Library, Pasadena, California). He wrote symphonies, concertos and chamber music.

abendfüllend (Ger., evening-filling). Full-length. *Das Rheingold*, for example, is *abendfüllend*, though in one act.

Abraham and Isaac. Bible story of sacrifice interrupted (Genesis 22), set by Stravinsky and Britten.

Abrahamsen, Hans (b. Copenhagen, 23 Dec 1952). Danish composer. While a student at the Royal Danish Academy of Music he had private lessons with Nørgård and Gudmundsen-Holmgreen. Associated at first with a Danish movement for new simplicity, he quickly came to an individual style of sound poetry, Schumannesque yet modern in its means. In 1982 he began teaching at his alma mater. His works include pieces for ensemble (*Winternacht*, 1976–8; *Märchenbilder*, 1984; Piano Concerto, 1999–2000), chamber music and arrangements of works by Nielsen, Ravel, Bach and Schoenberg.

Abschied (Ger.). Farewell, as in Haydn's *Abschiedsymphonie* (FAREWELL Symphony) and the finale, *Der Abschied*, of Mahler's *Das Lied von der Erde*.

Absil, Jean (Nicolas Joseph) (b. Bonsecours, Hainaut, 23 Oct 1893; d. Uccle, Brussels, 2 Feb 1974). Belgian composer. He trained as an organist before studying composition with Gilson (1920–22), whose late Romanticism he at first followed, until he discovered Berg, Milhaud and Hindemith.

A period in Paris in the 1930s encouraged his development of a Milhaudesque polytonal style; he was then professor of fugue at the Brussels Conservatory (1939–59). He wrote copiously in all non-dramatic genres.

absolute music. Term introduced by E.T.A. Hoffmann, Jean Paul Richter and other Romantic writers for music devoid of – and implicitly above – direct reference to non-musical reality. The Romantics thus introduced a distinction between absolute music and what later became known as PROGRAMME MUSIC. The instrumental works of Bach, Haydn or Mozart have often been held up as models of absolute music, though the Romantic dichotomy is not so easy to maintain: a Bach fugue may be full of expressive gestures, a Berlioz overture replete with calculation.

absolute pitch. PERFECT PITCH.

abstract music. Term having similar connotations to ABSOLUTE MUSIC, though also sometimes implying adherence to an ALGORITHM or other speculative formal device.

Abstrich (Ger.). Downbow.

Abu Hassan. One-act singspiel by Weber to a libretto by Franz Carl Hiemer after Antoine Galland's retelling of a story from the *1001 Nights*. Abu Hassan (tenor) and his wife Fatime (soprano) both try to restore the family finances by claiming the other is dead, but the resulting complications are happily resolved. Mozart's *Entführung* was a model, not least for the Turkish music. First performance: Munich, 4 Jun 1811.

abwechseln (Ger.). Change over, from one instrument to another, e.g. from oboe to cor anglais.

Abyndon, Henry (b. *c*.1420; d. 1497). English church musician, associated with Eton College (1447–51) and the Chapel Royal (1451–78), where, as master of the choristers, he may have helped to introduce the new art of polyphony involving boy singers. He is the first known recipient of the Cambridge MusB (1464).

Academic Festival Overture (*Akademische Festouvertüre*). Work Brahms wrote in recognition of the honorary doctorate conferred on him by Breslau University. With humorous academicism it uses German student songs, including 'Gaudeamus igitur'. First performance: Breslau/Wrocław, 4 Jan 1881.

academy (1) A group of artists and connoisseurs devoted to aesthetic creation and scholarly debate, founded in the late Renaissance in emulation of the school of enquiry Plato held at the grove of Academe. The Florentine CAMERATA was an example. More formal academies, still existing, include the Accademia Filarmonica of Verona (1543) and the ACCADEMIA DI SANTA CECILIA, both of which acquired functions characteristic of the next, third and last kinds.

(2) A guild. By far the most notable such academy is the Accademia Filarmonica of Bologna (1666), for whose diploma maestro Mozart successfully subjected himself to examination at 14. This academy, too, still exists, promoting scholarship and concerts, and honouring distinguished musicians.

(3) An institution for presenting opera or concerts: such academies may be organizations or theatres or both. The French Académie Royale de Musique (1669) had charge of opera, and 'Académie Nationale de Musique' was still the official title placed on the Paris Opera building of 1875. Handel wrote operas for the Royal Academy of Music in London. Other examples include the ACADEMY OF ANCIENT MUSIC and the Brooklyn Academy of Music.

(4) In 18th-century usage, a concert.

(5) A college, e.g. the RAM in London or the Liszt Academy in Budapest.

Academy of Ancient Music. London concert organization founded in 1726 (as the Academy of Vocal Music) and active for about 70 years. Its purpose was at first to bring back the sacred music and madrigals of the 16th and 17th centuries, but by the end of its existence 'ancient music' meant Handel. The name was taken in 1973 by Christopher Hogwood for an ensemble presenting Baroque music in period style.

Academy of St Martin-in-the-Fields. Chamber orchestra founded in 1959 by Neville Marriner, named after the London church in whose crypt it began giving concerts.

a cappella (It., in chapel mode). Unaccompanied. The term evolved in the 19th century to signify performance in the style of the papal chapel, without instrumental support. This remains the normal usage, though a solo singer or instrumentalist may also be said to perform *a cappella*, i.e. without piano accompaniment.

Accademia di Santa Cecilia. Roman musical institution tracing its origins to a congregation of composers (including Palestrina) formed in 1585

and currently the city's main concert organization, presenting performances since 2002 in a hall designed by Renzo Piano. In 1869 the Accademia founded a music school, which became independent in 1919 and is now known officially as the Conservatorio di Musica 'Santa Cecilia', though the old name is still often used.

Accardo, Salvatore (b. Turin, 26 Sep 1941). Italian violinist, whose breathtaking technique has made him an admired exponent of Paganini, besides inspiring composers including Xenakis (*Dikhthas*). He studied with Luigi d'Ambrosio at the Naples Conservatory and Yvonne Astruc at the Accademia Chigiana in Siena.

accelerando (It., accelerating). Get faster.

accent. Point of emphasis, placed by the composer (and indicated in music since the early 19th century by a small wedge-shaped marking: <, > or ^), to be intensified, underplayed or replaced by the performer. Accents may be achieved by dynamic change, lengthening, a slight preceding silence, attack, etc. Their judgement is essential to phrasing.

accentuation. The placing of accents.

acciacatura (It., crushing). GRACE NOTE in keyboard music, typically one scale degree above the note it precedes, or above the top note in the case of a chord (though in the 18th century it was a scale degree below). It is crushed into that note or chord, from which in general it takes an infinitesimal amount of time, though performers may play the accacciatura and the main note (or chord) simultaneously, immediately releasing the former. There are also musical contexts where the acciacatura should come before the beat. Acciacaturas, like other grace notes, are notated in small type, with or without a diagonal slash through the tail.

accidental. Pitch sign – ♯ (sharp), x (double sharp), ♭ (flat), ♭♭ (double flat) or ♮ (natural) – placed immediately before a notehead to qualify pitch. The basic signs derive from Guido, who advocated a 'b' (*rotundum*) to indicate B♭ and a square (*quadratum*) for B♮. With the rise of chromaticism in the late 16th century two forms of *quadratum* became necessary, for sharp and natural. The usual sharp sign was a twofold overlapped 'x', replaced by ♯ in the 18th century.

In music of the 18th and 19th centuries an accidental is normally meant to remain in force throughout the bar in which it finds itself, but in earlier and later music it usually affects only the one note.

accompagnato (It., accompanied). Short term for *recitativo accompagnato*, i.e. RECITATIVE accompanied by the orchestra.

accompaniment. Part of a musical composition or performance, in most cases the part that is not the solo. A singer of a Bach aria is accompanied by continuo and obbligato instruments, even if the latter have some prominence as soloists themselves. An orchestra and conductor accompany a concerto soloist, who normally has responsibility for tempos. Some members of a string quartet may at times have to accompany a solo-playing colleague. But only in very simple music is there a clear distinction between theme (solo) and accompaniment: in most cases the hierarchy is more flexible.

accompanist. Accompaniment performer. The term can be applied to a conductor of a concerto (though conductors of opera might bridle at it), but it usually signifies a pianist playing for (or with) singers or instrumentalists – especially singers. In sonatas the main role shifted from the piano to the other instrument during Beethoven's composing life, and yet generally one refers to Mozart's 'violin sonatas' and speaks of the pianist as the accompanist. In songs the demarcation may be even clearer between soloist and accompanist. Even so, sensitive listeners cannot but be aware of the importance of the piano part in the songs of Schubert or Fauré, and sensitive pianists know what fine writing for their instrument lies in the song literature. Accordingly, some (e.g. Gerald Moore) have made the art of accompanying their forte, and many solo pianists – Brendel, Richter, Schiff – have happily and rewardingly worked with singers from time to time.

Gerald Moore *The Unashamed Accompanist* (1943, ʳ1984)

accord (Fr.). Chord.

accordatura (It.). Tuning – normally the usual tuning, as opposed to SCORDATURA.

accordion (Fr. *accordéon*, Ger. *Akkordeon, Handharmonika, Ziehharmonika*, It. *fisarmonica*, Russ. *bayan*). Portable REED ORGAN having a plate for each hand with controls (normally a piano-style keyboard for the right hand and an array of buttons for the left) and pleated bellows in between. Smaller 'button accordions' are controlled largely or exclusively by buttons, and include the CONCERTINA and BAYAN. The accor-

dion and concertina were developed by several European makers in the middle decades of the 19th century, but were associated exclusively with popular music. Hindemith gave the accordion a seat at music's high table for the first time (in his *Kammermusik No.1*, 1922), and his protégé Hugo Herrmann wrote the instrument its first classical solos (1927). Later composers to have used it include Gubaidulina, Kagel, Berio (*Sequenza XIII*) and Birtwistle (*The Second Mrs Kong*). See also MELODEON.

accordo (It.). Chord.

acdn. Abbreviation for accordion.

Achtel(-Note) (Ger.). Eighth note, quaver.

Acis and Galatea. Masque by Handel to a libretto by John Gay and others, written for the country seat of James Brydges, Earl of Carnarvon, at Cannons, near London. The idyllic love of the sea nymph Galatea (soprano) for the shepherd Acis (tenor) is brutally cut short when Polyphemus (bass) kills the latter, but Galatea transforms her beloved into a fountain. In Act 2 Polyphemus has the air 'O ruddier than the cherry'. The story, from Ovid's *Metamorphoses*, was a staple of the Baroque pastoral: treatments had been made for the Duke of Vendôme at Anet (music by Lully), for Philip V of Spain (music by Antonio de Literes) and by Handel himself (cantata *Aci, Galatea e Polifemo*). Handel revived his score for London, and performances continued: Mozart made an arrangement for van Swieten. First performance: Cannons, summer 1718.

acoustic. (1) Term used of recordings made before microphones were introduced in 1925.

(2) Making sound without electric means; hence 'acoustic guitar', as opposed to 'electric guitar'.

(3) Sound quality of a room or other space.

acoustics. The science of sound: the study, therefore, of systems that generate sounds (instruments, voices), disperse it (rooms, spaces) and receive it (ears). Often, though, the term is confined to the middle part of the process, as it will be here. For sound-producing mechanisms see INSTRUMENT; SOUND; also BELL; CLARINET; FLUTE; OBOE; ORGAN; PIANO; TRUMPET; VIOLIN; VOICE; etc. For sound-receiving mechanisms see EAR.

Very little of the sound in a musical performance reaches the audience directly from the performers: most is transmitted (and modified) by reflecting surfaces and through the sympathetic vibrations of spaces and objects in the hall. Hard surfaces (polished stone, tile) tend to be highly reflective; softer materials, including audience members, will be absorbent, so that a full hall will sound quite different from an empty one. A space with a lot of sound reflection is often called 'bright' or 'lively' (at an extreme it will be 'bathroomy'), or 'warm' if it encourages lower sounds; one with very little reverberation will be described as 'dead'.

Designing a venue for music requires attention to these matters of reflection, vibration and absorption, and also to insulation from the outer and subterranean worlds. There are two chief areas of difficulty. One is that properties of reflection and sympathetic vibration will depend on the source, as will the expectations of listeners. A hall that is excellent for Romantic orchestral music (where blended sound is often a priority) may be less suited to Baroque or contemporary works, and solo singers may have different needs again, especially if one allows that their words need to be understood. Often, therefore, halls will be equipped with means of acoustic adjustment (movable reflectors, resonating spaces that can be opened or closed, electronic enhancements). Also, it was difficult, until quite recent times, to predict precisely the acoustic behaviour of spaces and materials. Even now, rather strikingly, acoustic designers often strive to reproduce the qualities of auditoria constructed long before there was much formal understanding of acoustics, such as the large halls of the Musikverein in Vienna and the Concertgebouw in Amsterdam.

Medieval cathedral builders, similarly working from standard patterns, had various ways to achieve desired acoustic effects: by gauging the ratio of height to floor area and the proportionate volumes of the main space (nave) and others (side aisles, transepts, chapels), and by inserting ceramic jars into walls and vaults to provide resonance or absorption. Long reverberations were probably considered then, as now, to enhance the contemplative aura. With the arrival of polyphony came a demand for greater clarity, which could be obtained by introducing wall hangings and wooden furnishings. It seems clear, for example, that St Mark's in Venice, presently cavernously echoing, sounded quite different with the decor it boasted in Monteverdi's time.

Baroque theatres and concert halls, being compact, offered relatively few acoustic problems; they also had the advantage that the readiest material to hand for internal use – wood – is also among the most acoustically beneficent, in its abilities to reflect and vibrate with frequencies across the audible range. But buildings of this period often included devices specifically aimed at facilitating projection: volumes of air (or, at the Teatro Argentina in Rome, water) under the stage or audience space, or resonators of wood or stone behind the orchestra.

More serious acoustic problems arose in the 19th century, with the arrival of larger buildings for music but still only a limited understanding of the physics of sound. Success might be owed more to luck than acoustics, as Charles Garnier, architect of the 1875 Paris Opera, cheerfully confessed: 'I gave myself great pains to master this bizarre science but ... nowhere did I find a positive rule to guide me; on the contrary, nothing but contradictory statements ... I must explain that I have adopted no principle, that my plan has been based on no theory, and that I leave success or failure to chance alone ... like the acrobat who closes his eyes and clings to the ropes of an ascending balloon.'

It took a century and more before architects and acoustic designers could – with the help of studies of old buildings, a deeper knowledge of the requirements of different kinds of music, acoustic analyses of materials and ever more accurate computer modelling – begin to feel some ground beneath their feet, producing such acoustically successful buildings as Symphony Hall in Birmingham (1991).

Leo Beranek *Concert and Opera Halls: How they Sound* (1996)

act. Part of an opera or ballet, as of a play. The term has also been applied to oratorios and, in 18th-century usage, concerts. Horace's recommendation of five acts was taken seriously by classicizing composers, including Monteverdi in *Orfeo* and everyone in Baroque France, but two-act and three-act forms became normal elsewhere. Wagner introduced the full-length one-acter with *Das Rheingold*. Division into acts does not necessarily imply separation by an interval: the three acts of *Wozzeck* are often performed without interruption.

acte de ballet. French rococo one-acter, often as much an opera as a ballet; e.g. Rameau's *Pigmalion*.

action. The mechanism by which information is conveyed from the fingers to the sound-producing apparatus in an organ, piano or other keyboard instrument.

action music. Music strongly motivated by the physical action of the performer. The term has been used of some of the music Cage wrote for

Tudor in the 1950s, or of Kagel's pieces for solo instrumentalists and small groups, but it could as well apply to much of Liszt and Paganini.

act tune. Instrumental piece played at the end of an act (except the last) of a Restoration play.

Actus Tragicus. Name given to Bach's funeral cantata *Gottes Zeit ist die allerbeste Zeit* (God's Time is the Best Time), BWV 106.

adagietto. Marking suggesting a relatively brief slow movement, used most famously by Mahler (Symphony No.5), but also by Bizet, Fauré and Stravinsky.

adagio (It., at ease). (1) Slow. One of the earliest tempo markings, found in Banchieri's *La battaglia* (1611) and known also to Monteverdi, Praetorius, etc. It was often taken in the Baroque period to be the second slowest speed, with *largo* slower, though this distinction was by no means universal, and for many composers and theorists *adagio*, *largo*, *lento* and *grave* were practically synonymous. Haydn and Mozart used the *adagio* marking more commonly than the by-now-equivalent *largo* for slow introductions and their slower slow movements, and in 19th-century music, from Beethoven onwards, *adagio* ruled supreme for slow music, gaining connotations of expressive gravity.

(2) A slow movement. Bruckner used the term as a movement heading (Symphonies Nos.5–9), followed by a tempo marking in German.

Adam, Adolphe (Charles) (b. Paris, 24 Jul 1803; d. Paris, 3 May 1856). French composer known principally for his ballet score GISELLE (1841). His father Louis (1758–1848) was a long-time piano teacher at the Conservatoire, but he gained more encouragement from one of his father's pupil's, Ferdinand Hérold. He studied with Boieldieu and Reicha at the Conservatoire (1820–5) with the rooted intention of composing for the stage, which he duly did, very productively, from 1824 until his death, through periods of revolution, theatrical discord and debt. *Le Chalet* (1834) and *Le Postillon de Longjumeau* (1836), both written for the Opéra-Comique, remained in the repertory through the century, the latter kept alive principally by its tenor role.

Adamberger, (Josef) Valentin (b. Rohr, near Rothenburg, Bavaria, 22 Feb 1740; d. Vienna, 24 Aug 1804). German tenor. He studied in Munich and sang there, in Italy and in London before settling in 1780 in Vienna, where Mozart wrote Belmonte in *Die Entführung* for him, as well as other music.

Adam de la Halle (b. Arras, 1245–50; d. Naples, ?1285–8). Trouvère, also known as Adam le Bossu (Adam the Hunchback), which was a family name: he was not hunchbacked. He probably studied in Paris and went to Naples in the entourage of Robert II, Count of Artois. There he is said to have died, though an Adam le Boscu who was engaged at the coronation of Edward II of England (1307) may have been him, if not his son. He was one of the last to write in the old categories of monophonic song (*chanson de geste*, *jeu-parti*), but he also composed polyphonic rondeaux and motets, as well as plays. In *Le Jeu d'Adam* he appears as a character; *Le Jeu de Robin et de Marion*, quite unusually for the period, is a play with songs, and was one of the first medieval pieces to be published anew (in 1822).

Adams, John (Coolidge) (b. Worcester, Mass., 15 Feb 1947). US composer, a post-minimalist master of exuberance and intricacy. Brought up in a musical household, he studied with Kirchner, Kim, Sessions, Shapero and del Tredici at Harvard (1965–71), then moved to San Francisco, where he taught at the conservatory (1972–82) and eagerly contributed to the adventurous search for new musical possibilities, including minimalism. He was also associated with the San Francisco Symphony (1979–85), during which time he began to diversify, bringing minimalist elements (repetition, strong beat, glowing tonal harmonies) into orchestral life as it had been left by the late Romantics and Stravinsky. His breakthrough piece was the imposing soundscape *Harmonium*, while *Grand Pianola Music* proved that humour was in his repertory, too, and a talent for pastiche. With all this, his first opera, *Nixon in China* (1985–7), was an international success, to be followed by a darker collaboration by the same team: *The Death of Klinghoffer*. Later works have included a continuing succession of *jeux d'esprit* (*Lollapalooza*) as well as the Chamber Symphony and Violin Concerto, pieces in which the lessons of modernism are intriguingly refracted, and made to combine with those of the Romantic past and the commercial present.

Stage: NIXON IN CHINA (opera), 1985–7; *The Death of Klinghoffer* (opera: Alice Goodman), f.p. Brussels, 1991; *I was looking at the ceiling and then I saw the sky* (songplay: June Jordan), f.p. Berkeley, 1995; *El niño* (Nativity oratorio), f.p. Paris, 2000; Doctor Atomic (opera: Goodman), in progress

Orchestral: *Common Tones in Simple Time*, 1979; *Harmonium* (Donne, Dickinson), ch, orch, 1980–81; *Shaker Loops*, 1983; *Harmonielehre*,

1984–5; *The Chairman Dances*, 1985; *Tromba lontana*, 1985; *Short Ride in a Fast Machine*, 1986; *Fearful Symmetries*, 1988; *The Wound Dresser* (Whitman), bar, orch, 1988; *Eros Piano*, pf, orch, 1989; *El dorado*, 1991; Violin Concerto, 1993; *Lollapalooza*, 1995; *Slonimsky's Earbox*, 1996; *Century Rolls*, pf, orch, 1996; *Naive and Sentimental Music*, 1997–8; *Guide to Strange Places*, 2001; *On the Transmigration of Souls*, ch, orch, 2002; *My Father Knew Charles Ives*, 2003; *The Dharma at Big Sur*, amplified vn, orch, 2003
Ensemble: *Christian Zeal and Activity*, 1973; *Grand Pianola Music*, 2 pf, 3 women singers, wind, perc, 1982; Chamber Symphony, 15 insts, 1992; *Scratchband*, 1996; *Gnarly Buttons*, cl, 11 insts, 1996
Chamber: *Shaker Loops*, str septet, 1978; *John's Book of Alleged Dances*, str qt, 1994; *Road Movies*, vn, pf, 1995
Piano: *Phrygian Gates*, 1977; *China Gates*, 1977; *Hallelujah Junction*, 2 pf, 1996
Electronic: *Light over Water*, 1983; *Hoodoo Zephyr*, 1992–3

Adams, John Luther (b. Meridian, Mississippi, 23 Jan 1953). US composer. Introduced to 20th-century classical music by a youthful enthusiasm for Zappa, he studied with Tenney and Leonard Stein at CalArts and in 1975 moved to Alaska as an orchestral percussionist. There he remained, deeply influenced by the landscape and culture in works such as *Earth and the Great Weather* for singers, instrumentalists and natural sounds (1990–93) and *In the White Silence* for strings and percussion (1998).

added sixth chord. Major triad with an added sixth, e.g. C–E–G–A, reading upwards. In traditional tonality this is a subdominant chord, so the example given here would have a function in G major, but jazz and Messiaen often made it a final consonance.

Addinsell, Richard (Stewart) (b. London, 13 Jan 1904; d. London, 14 Nov 1977). British composer of light music and film scores. He is known especially for his Rachmaninoffian *Warsaw Concerto* for the film *Dangerous Moonlight* (1941). Later he worked frequently with the comedian Joyce Grenfell.

Adès, Thomas (Joseph Edmund) (b. London, 1 Mar 1971). British composer. His sense for the strange poetry of harmonic, timbral or rhythmic oddity – informed by such various predecessors as Janáček, Kurtág and Nancarrow – earned him renown even while he was a student of Goehr and Holloway at Cambridge (1989–92). Besides composing, he has been active as a pianist, conductor and artistic director of the Aldeburgh Festival. In 1999 he became the youngest composer to win the Grawemeyer Award. His works include the operas

Powder her Face (f.p. Cheltenham, 1995) and *The* TEMPEST, *Asyla* for orchestra (1997) and a piano quintet (2000).

Adieux, Les. Usual name for Beethoven's Piano Sonata in E Op.81a, which his publisher entitled *Sonate caractéristique: les adieux, l'absence et le retour*. The work was indeed written as a farewell, for Archduke Rudolph on his departure from Vienna, though Beethoven preferred the simpler title *Das Lebewohl* (The Farewell).

Adler, Guido (b. Eibenschütz/Ivančice, Moravia, 1 Nov 1855; d. Vienna, 15 Feb 1941). Austrian scholar, who spent almost his whole life in Vienna and concerned himself with Austrian music from throughout history. He combined music with legal studies at the University of Vienna, where he gained his doctorate in 1880, succeeded Hanslick as professor in 1898 and established a pre-eminent school of musical scholarship.

ad libitum, ad lib. (Lat., at will). Indication of some option: a part or parts that need not be played, a place where the rhythm can be flexible, the point for a cadenza to be improvised, etc.

Adorno, Theodor (Ludwig) W(iesengrund) (b. Frankfurt, 11 Sep 1903; d. Brig, Switzerland, 6 Aug 1969). German philosopher, who took his surname from his mother's (Corsican, musical) side of the family. He pursued simultaneous studies in philosophy and music, taking lessons in Vienna from 1925 from Berg and Steuermann, and so drawing close to the Schoenberg school. He began, bizarrely, a 12-note Huckleberry Finn opera, but soon gave up composition to concentrate on philosophy, and especially on the obligations of new music. He taught for most of his life in Frankfurt, apart from a period of self-imposed exile during the Nazi years, in Oxford (1934–8) and the USA (1938–49). In his view, musical material had its inherent history, which a composer could either serve by dealing clearly, fully and logically with the current state of the musical language (Schoenberg) or deny (Stravinsky). He was suspicious of the post-war avant-garde for its understanding of musical material in a purely formal sense, divorced from the tradition and the anxieties through which that material had come into being.
Theodor W. Adorno *Philosophy of Modern Music* (1973, [2]1980), *Quasi una fantasia* (1992); Martin Jay *Adorno* (1984)

Adriana Lecouvreur. Opera by Cilea to a libretto by Arturo Colautti after a play by Scribe and Legouvé. The title character (soprano), based on a great Parisian actress of Voltaire's time, eventually reaches happiness with her beloved Maurizio (tenor), only to find she has been poisoned by her rival the Princess of Bouillon (mezzo-soprano). Most often the work has been revived as a soprano star vehicle, Adriana's numbers including her theme song 'Io son l'umile ancilla' and last-act aria 'Poveri fiori', though Maurizio also has his sweet opportunities in 'La dolcissima effigie' and 'L'anima ho stanca'. First performance: Milan, 6 Nov 1902.

Aeolian. White-note MODE on A: A–B–C–D–E–F–G–A.

Aeolian Company. New York company prominent in the PIANOLA market.

Aeolian harp (from Aeolus, Graeco-Roman keeper of the winds). Harp made to be placed outdoors and blown by the wind. Known to Homer, it had some popularity as a Romantic garden adornment in the 19th century. Chopin's Etude in A♭, Op.25:1, is sometimes called by this name.

aerophone. Formal organological term for an instrument directly creating vibrations in air; the category thus includes wind instruments and organs. The other kinds are chordophones, idiophones and membranophones.

aesthetics. See PHILOSOPHY OF MUSIC.

affect (Ger. *Affekt*). Expressive character. Several Baroque writers, including Mattheson, pursued the idea that each musical movement must have its particular affect: joy, mournfulness, etc. The source for this notion was the classical theory of RHETORIC, whereby a speech would be expected to move its hearers in a particular emotional direction.

affettuoso (It.). With affect. Also *affetuosamente, con affetto*. Markings specially common in Baroque music (e.g. Bach's Fifth Brandenburg Concerto).

affrettando (It.). Hurrying. Also *affrettato*. Both markings are associated with Italian music of the late Verdi to Puccini era.

Africa. Until the mid 20th century contacts between European–American and African musical traditions came largely in places where slaves had been settled, notably the USA, the Caribbean and Brazil. From the vigorous popular traditions that resulted – ragtime, jazz, rumba, etc. – Western classical composers from Stravinsky and Milhaud to Ligeti inherited rhythmic life and percussion instruments. More direct knowledge came from listening to recordings (Boulez), acquaintance with the work of Arom (Berio, Ligeti) and first-hand experience (Reich, Swayne – and, of course, the rather few Western-style composers born in Africa, notably Rainier and Volans).

Africaine, L' (The African Woman). Opera by Meyerbeer to a libretto by Scribe. The title character is Sélika (soprano), brought by Vasco da Gama (tenor) to Lisbon, where Inès (soprano) has been waiting for him. Other triangular relationships add to the drama, as do the acts set at sea and finally in Africa, where the basic situation is resolved by Sélika's suicide. The score includes one of the great tenor arias, 'O paradis'. First performance: Paris, 28 Apr 1865.

afterpiece. Play, often musical, given in the Georgian London theatre after the main show, e.g. Arne's 'Thomas and Sally'.

Age of Enlightenment, Orchestra of the. See ORCHESTRA OF THE AGE OF ENLIGHTENMENT.

aggregate. (1) Simultaneous or consecutive appearance of all 12 diatonic notes in a composition, each represented once. Liszt's *Faust* symphony and Webern's Concerto Op.24 are among works to open with aggregates, in both cases melodic.

(2) Simultaneous group of notes, not necessarily having any conventional harmonic function. Cage's work with the prepared piano, where each key unleashes an unchangeable (and not entirely predictable) sound, led him to consider other instrumental media as sources of defined aggregates, notably the string quartet in his Quartet in Four Parts.

Agincourt Carol. Anonymous polyphonic song celebrating the victory of Henry V (1415): 'Owre kynge went forth to Normandy/With grace and myght of chyvalry'.

agitato (It.). Agitatedly. Also the Fr. form *agité*; hence *de plus en plus agité* (more and more agitatedly), etc.

Agnus Dei. Concluding section of the ORDINARY of the MASS, a threefold acclamation in which the third part is often elaborate or otherwise culminative.

agogic. Originally a kind of accent achieved by a

short pause, as if for breath, the term broadened to include any kind of small-scale rhythmic manipulation, i.e. lengthening or shortening a value, as opposed to a longer-term flexibility, described as dynamic. A dynamic rubato will take over the whole sway of the music; an agogic one will fix on certain points of the melody.

Agon. Ballet score by Stravinsky, for choreography by Balanchine. Made to complete a classical trilogy with *Apollo* and *Orpheus*, the work takes its name from the ancient Gk for a contest that could be musical as well as athletic. This one is both: a set of 12 dances for 12 dancers, with changing combinations of instruments and bodies in play. First performance: Los Angeles, 17 Jun 1957 (concert), New York, 1 Dec 1957 (staged).

Agostini, Pietro Antonio (b. Forli, c.1635; d. Parma, 1 Oct 1680). Italian composer of robust career. He was banished from Forli for involvement in a murder, knighted for action in Crete following his musical studies with Mazzaferrata in Ferrara, and dispatched from his first professional centre, Genoa, for seducing a nun. He then spent several years in Rome writing operas, cantatas and church music before becoming chapelmaster to the Duke of Parma.

agréments (Fr.). Ornaments.

Agricola. Latinized form of Ackerman or Ackermann, the name of a Netherlandish Renaissance composer and a Bach pupil.

(1) **Alexander** (b. Ghent, c.1450; d. Valladolid, 15 Aug 1506). Nothing is known of his early life except that he and his brother Jan, also a musician, were the illegitimate sons of a wealthy businesswoman. In the early 1490s he was with the French royal chapel and in Italy; in 1500 he joined the Burgundian court, with which he travelled to Spain, where he died of fever. His music – closest to Ockeghem, but with a strangeness all its own – includes French songs, instrumental settings of songs, masses and motets (among which *Si dedero* was the most widely copied piece of the time).

(2) **Johann Friedrich** (b. Dobitschen, Saxe-Altenburg, 4 Jan 1720; d. Berlin, 2 Dec 1774). German composer. He was a pupil of Bach in Leipzig and Quantz in Berlin, where he settled in 1741. He won and lost the favour of Frederick the Great as an opera composer, and is remembered chiefly for his contributions to music theory and biography (as the author, with C.P.E. Bach, of an obituary of the latter's father).

Agrippina. Opera by Handel to a libretto by Cardinal Vincenzo Grimani. Agrippina (soprano), the wife of the emperor Claudius (bass) and mother of Nero (soprano castrato), is at the hub of complex political-sexual intrigues that involve her two lovers and the three of Poppaea (soprano). First performance: Venice, 26 Dec 1709.

Aguiari, Lucrezia (b. Ferrara, 1743; d. Parma, 18 May 1783). Italian soprano, nicknamed La Bastardina (or Bastardella). She studied in Ferrara, made her debut in Florence (1764) and rapidly gained a place among the supreme opera singers of her time, travelling around Italy, to Paris and to London in the works of Giuseppe Colla, whom she married. Leopold Mozart and his son, who heard her in 1770, confirmed her range of over three octaves, up to the C above 'top' C. Rumour had it she died as the result of slow poisoning inflicted by jealous rivals, but in fact it was tuberculosis that carried her off.

ägyptische Helena, Die (Helen in Egypt). Opera by Strauss to a libretto by Hofmannsthal. Helen (soprano) and Menelaus (tenor), reunited but separated by resentments and frustrations, come from the Trojan War to Egypt, where, thanks to the sorcery of Aithra (soprano), and to music, Menelaus learns to accept his wife again. First performance: Dresden, 6 Jun 1928, rev Salzburg, 14 Aug 1933.

Aho, Kalevi (b. Forssa, 9 Mar 1949). Finnish composer, principally of symphonies in the line of Mahler and Shostakovich. He studied with Rautavaara at the Sibelius Academy and with Blacher in Berlin (1971–2), and taught in Helsinki at the university (1974–88) and academy (1988–93). Apart from his 11 symphonies (some with instrumental soloists), his large output includes concertos, stage pieces and chamber music.

Aichinger, Gregor (b. Regensburg, 1564/5; d. Augsburg, 20/21 Jan 1628). German composer. He enrolled in 1578 at the University of Ingolstadt, where he befriended Jakob Fugger, of the Augsburg banking family. In 1584 he gained an appointment as organist at the private chapel of his friend's uncle, also Jakob Fugger, who sponsored his further studies in Venice (with Giovanni Gabrieli), Siena and Rome. He was in Rome again in 1599–1600, after which he settled in Augsburg as a musician-priest, writing and publishing sacred music influenced by the music he had heard in Italy: Gabrieli's and Viadana's.

Aida. Opera by Verdi to a libretto by Antonio Ghislanzoni after a scenario by Auguste Mariette.

The Egyptian military hero Radames (tenor), loved by the princess Amneris (mezzo-soprano) but loving Aida (soprano), from the enemy Ethiopian nation, chooses to die with his beloved. The work was written for the opening of the opera house in Cairo. Commonly heard excerpts include Aida's arias 'Ritorna vincitor!' and 'Oh, patria mia', Radames's 'Celeste Aida' and the Grand March. First performance: Cairo, 24 Dec 1871.

Aida trumpet. Straight trumpet, 6 feet 6 inches (about 2m) long, produced by Sax and later other makers to add to the spectacle of the military parade in Verdi's opera.

aigu (Fr.). High.

Aimard, Pierre-Laurent (b. Lyons, 9 Sep 1957). French pianist, who has spread back from Messiaen and modernists to engage with Beethoven and Bach. He continued with Loriod after his Paris Conservatoire training and at 19 joined the new Ensemble InterContemporain. His formidable range of touch and colour, and his aesthetic position between avant-garde and mainstream repertory, made him Ligeti's chosen interpreter from the 1990s onwards.

Aimez-vous Brahms? (Do You Like Brahms?). Novel (1959) by Françoise Sagan in which the question is a line addressed to the heroine by a younger man, a question that brings with it a cascade of other questions in her mind about what she likes and whom she loves. More generally the phrase owes its resonance to its pinpointing how human relationships are instituted and developed through intimate enquiry, and to its choosing as object a composer whose music itself invites so many questions.

air. (1) Melody of a vocal character, as in the Londonderry Air.

(2) Elizabethan-Jacobean song. Such airs (or ayres) could often be performed as lute songs or madrigals.

(3) Song, especially of theatrical provenance. Rameau's airs are Italian-style arias.

(4) In the Restoration theatre a piece of instrumental music. The suites of airs that Purcell, for example, wrote for plays generally consist of two pieces of 'first music', two of 'second music' (all for performance before the show proper), an overture and an 'act tune' to follow each of the first four acts.

air de cour (court air). French lute song of the period from 1571 to the 1650s, at its peak during the reign of Louis XIII (1610–43), when composers contribut-ing to the genre included Pierre Guédron, Antoine Boësset and Etienne Moulinié.

Air on the G String. Name given by August Wilhelmj (1845–1908) to his arrangement for violin of the slow movement from Bach's Suite No.3.

Ais (Ger.). A♯. Also *Aisis*, Ax.

Aix-en-Provence. French city, site of an annual summer music festival since 1948, with operas performed in the courtyard of the archbishop's palace.

Akkord (Ger., pl. *Akkorde*). Chord.

Alagna, Roberto (b. Clichy-sous-Bois, 7 Jun 1963). French tenor. A fine lyric artist, his romantic appeal has been enhanced by his stage partnership with his wife Angela Gheorghiu. Born to a Sicilian couple, he began his musical life as a guitar-strumming cabaret singer, won the Pavarotti Competition in Philadelphia in 1988 and, under Pavarotti's protection, made his debut with Glyndebourne Touring Opera as Rodolfo the same year. His rise then was rapid, and he married Gheorghiu backstage at the Met in 1996.

Alain, Jehan (Ariste) (b. St Germain-en-Laye, 3 Feb 1911; d. Petit-Puy, near Saumur, 20 Jun 1940). French organist-composer, whose abbreviated maturity was remarkable and poignant. The son of the organist and organ builder Albert Alain (1880–1971), he studied first with his father and then at the Paris Conservatoire (1928–39), his teachers including Dupré, Dukas and Roger-Ducasse. He married in 1935 and worked as an organist before joining the French army and dying in battle. Like his elder contemporary Messiaen, he was influenced by Debussy, non-European music (which he heard at the Exposition Coloniale in 1932) and steadfast Catholic piety. Another important fact in his life was the death of his sister Odile in a mountaineering accident in 1937. Of his other siblings, Marie-Claire (b. 1926) became a distinguished organist and Olivier (1918–94) a composer and music scholar.

Organ: Fantasy No.1, 1933; No.2, 1936; *Deux danses à Agni Yavishta*, 1933; *Le Jardin suspendu*, 1934; *Litanies*, 1937; Variations on a Theme of Clément Jannequin, 1937; *Trois danses*, 1937–9; etc.
Other works: sacred music, piano music, etc.

Alaleona, Domenico (Ottavio Felice Gaspare Maria) (b. Montegiorgio, Ascoli Piceno, 16 Nov

1881; d. Montegiorgio, 28 Dec 1928). Italian composer-scholar, trained in Rome, where he taught, did research on the Italian oratorio and postulated new harmonic possibilities, which to some degree he used: his opera *Mirra* (Rome, 1920) briefly explores a scale of five equal intervals to the octave.

Alard, (Jean) Delphin (b. Bayonne, 8 Mar 1815; d. Paris, 22 Feb 1888). French violinist-composer and teacher. He studied at the Conservatoire (1827–30) and made his debut in 1831, winning the approval of Paganini and the dedication of the latter's Op.2 sonatas. But though he maintained a career as a soloist, quartet leader and composer, he is remembered chiefly as an important link in the Italo-French school of violinists, teaching at the Conservatoire (1843–75), where his pupils included Sarasate.

alba. Type of troubadour song concerned with the parting of lovers at dawn and often placed in the mouth of a watchman: the image is present in Act 2 of *Tristan*.

Alban Berg Quartet. Austrian ensemble founded in 1970 by Günther Pichler, Klaus Mätzl (replaced by Gerhard Schulz, 1978), Hatto Beyerle (replaced by Thomas Kakuska, 1981) and Valentin Erben. Superb in the classic repertory, they have also promoted new works by Berio, Rihm and Schnittke.

Albéniz, Isaac (Manuel Francisco) (b. Camprodón, Gerona, 29 May 1860; d. Cambo-les-Bains, 18 May 1909). Spanish pianist-composer. The hopes and needs of his family pressed him into a performing career while he was a young boy, and his training was spasmodic: his most settled period as a student was with Franz Rummel and Louis Brassin at the Brussels Conservatory (1876–9). He then returned to performing and took up conducting, before going to Pedrell for composition lessons in Barcelona in 1883, the year of his marriage. By the end of 1885 he was in Madrid, effortlessly producing salon music. Amiable and obliging, he signed a contract with Henry Lowenfeld and moved to London (1890–93), where he wrote theatre music and Spanish impressions for the piano (many so infectiously Spanish that they have provided repertory for guitarists, though he wrote nothing directly for the instrument). Francis Burdett Money-Coutts next became his patron, seemingly requiring only to have a succession of his own librettos and song texts set – music history has seen few odder enterprises than that of Arthurian operas (*Merlin*, 1898–1902) being put together by a British banker and a Spanish

composer. The relationship did not stop Albéniz living in France, forming musical friendships with his French contemporaries (d'Indy, Chausson, Dukas), conducting, teaching or working on other creative projects, but he was in declining health as a result of Bright's disease. His master-piece, *Iberia*, became the last vessel for his long experience in adapting Spanish idioms to the keyboard, for his memories of the Lisztian world of virtuoso performance in which he was brought up, and for his new admiration for the pianist Joaquín Malats.

Walter Aaron Clark *Isaac Albéniz* (1998)

Piano (with publication dates): *Suite española*, Op.47, 1886–98; *Recuerdos de viaje*, 1886–7; *12 piezas características*, Op.92, 1888; *Sérénade espagnole*, Op.161, 1890; *España*, Op.165, 1890; *Mallorca*, Op.202, barcarolle, 1891; *Chants d'Espagne*, Op.232, 1892–8; *La vega*, ?1898; *Espagne: Souvenirs*, *c.*1899; IBERIA, 1906–8; etc.

Other works: Piano Concerto No.1 (*Concierto fantástico*), A minor, *c.*1887; songs, chamber music, operas, etc.

Albéniz, Mateo (Antonio) Peréz de (b. Basque region, *c.*1755; d. San Sebastián, 23 Jun 1831). Spanish church musician. He was a chapelmaster in San Sebastián for most of his life and the author of piano sonatas as well as church music. His son, Pedro Albéniz y Basanta (1795–1855), was a pianist-composer who taught at the Madrid Conservatory.

Albert, Prince Consort [Franz Karl August Albert Emanuel von Saxe-Coburg-Gotha] (b. Rosenau, Coburg, 26 Aug 1819; d. London, 14 Dec 1861). British–German prince and musical amateur. He wrote songs and some larger works, and after his marriage to Queen Victoria in 1840 organized royal performances of works by Bach, Schubert, Mendelssohn, etc.

Albert, Eugen [Eugène Francis Charles] d' (b. Glasgow, 10 Apr 1864; d. Riga, 3 Mar 1932). German–British pianist-composer. His father, Charles Louis Napoléon d'Albert (1809–86), was a popular dance composer of French origin who claimed kinship with Giuseppe Matteo and Domenico Alberti. Young d'Albert studied at the National Training School in London with Sullivan, Pauer and Prout, but was more struck by hearing *Tristan*. In 1881 he left for the continent, where he spent his whole adult life, at first as a pupil of Liszt in Weimar. Liszt rated him highly, but he was a virtuoso of a new kind, concerned with more abstract repertory (Bach, Beethoven, Brahms). He gave the first performance of Strauss's *Burleske* and wrote two concertos for himself (in B minor, 1884, and E, 1893) and a sonata (in F♯ minor, 1893). After *Tiefland* (Prague, 1903), in a Puccinified Wagner style, he devoted himself to opera, though without repeating that success.

Albert, Stephen (Joel) (b. New York, 6 Feb 1941; d. Truro, Mass., 27 Dec 1992). US composer, pioneer in reviving late Romanticism. He began composition studies with Siegmeister at 15, and continued his education at the Philadelphia Musical Academy. His works include the symphony *River-Run* (1983–4) and concertos for violin (1986) and cello (1990).

Albert Herring. Opera by Britten to a libretto by Eric Crozier after a Maupassant story, made to be taken on tour with *The Rape of Lucretia* and similarly scored. The worthies of a small town choose Albert (tenor), for his naive goodness, as their King of the May, and are bemused when he later turns up having lost his innocence. First performance: Glyndebourne, 20 Jun 1947.

Alberti. Name of two unrelated Italian composers active in the first half of the 18th century.

(1) **Domenico** (b. Venice, *c.*1710; d. Rome, 14 Oct 1746). His harpsichord sonatas gave his name limited distinction as the inventor of the Alberti bass. He was also a singer and harpsichordist, and as such served a noble family in Rome.

(2) **Giuseppe Matteo** (b. Bologna, 20 Sep 1685; d. Bologna, 18 Feb 1751). Violinist-composer, a pupil of Carlo Manzolini and prominent in Bolognese musical life as a church musician, president of the Accademia Filarmonica and composer of concertos and sonatas.

Alberti bass. Simple accompaniment, repeating arpeggios of the form C–G–E–G.

Albinoni, Tomaso (Giovanni) (b. Venice, 8 Jun 1671; d. Venice, 17 Jun 1751). Italian composer. He is most widely known for something he did not write: the adagio presented as his by the critic and music historian Remo Giazzotto (1910–98) and seemingly based only on a bass line by him. The son of a stationer and playing-card manufacturer, he had the freedom of a gentleman amateur; with whom he studied is unknown. His Op.2 collection was the first to make three-movement form, fast–slow–fast, standard for the concerto, drawing on elements from the operatic sinfonia. Also successful in this field of opera, he married an opera singer in 1705, and she continued her career between and after the births of their six children. In 1722 he was invited to produce an opera for the Munich court. (A fake Albinoni who had been touring Germany departed on the spot for Sweden.) Other operas were presented outside Italy, while his concertos were rivalled in popularity only by those of Corelli and Vivaldi, and his melodic gifts have had distinguished appreciation; Bach wrote fugues on subjects from his Op.1 sonatas.

Michael Talbot *Tomaso Albinoni* (1990)

Concertos (all volumes of 12, with publication dates): *Sinfonie e concerti a cinque*, str, con, Op.2, 1700; *Concerti a cinque*, str, con, Op.5, 1707; *Concerti a cinque*, ob/obs, str, con, Op.7, 1715; *Concerti a cinque*, ob/obs, str, con, Op.9, 1722; *Concerti a cinque*, str, con, Op.10, 1735–6; etc.
Other works: at least 50 operas, about 50 cantatas, about 100 sonatas

alborada (Sp.). Dawn song, performed on a saint's day or wedding morning.

Alborada del gracioso (The Fool's Dawn Song). Piece from Ravel's MIROIRS, orchestrated by the composer.

Albrechtsberger, Johann Georg (b. Klosterneuburg, 3 Feb 1736; d. Vienna, 7 Mar 1809). Austrian composer. He was trained as choirboy and older student at the abbeys of Klosterneuburg and Melk (1749–54), where, after further studies in Vienna and employment elsewhere, he succeeded his teacher Joseph Weiss as organist (1759–65). In 1768, by now settled in Vienna, he married. Imperial organist from 1772 and chapelmaster of St Stephen's from 1793, he was a great writer of fugues. He was also regarded as the nonpareil of organists by Mozart, and as the finest Viennese composition teacher by Haydn, who sent Beethoven to him. Apart from his keyboard preludes and fugues, he wrote church music, orchestral pieces and chamber music in abundance, though his best-remembered pieces are those that bring unusual instruments into the Viennese Classical style, such as his Trombone Concerto in B♭ (1769), Harp Concerto in C (1773) and two concertinos for jew's harp, mandora and strings.

Albright, William (Hugh) (b. Gary, Ind., 20 Oct 1944; d. Ann Arbor, Mich., 17 Sep 1998). US composer and organist, who exuberantly brought ragtime, other US vernacular forms and much else into the organ loft, while having energy for the music he commissioned for his instrument from others. He studied with Finney and Rochberg at the University of Michigan (1963–70) and with Messiaen in Paris (1968–9), and taught at his alma mater from 1970. His organ collections include *Organbook I* (1967), *II* (1971) and *III* (1977–8), and *Flights of Fancy* (1992); he also wrote church music and theatre pieces.

album. (1) Commonplace book, used as a repository for autographs, sketches and other mementoes. Hence ALBUMLEAF as a compositional form.

(2) Record release. Originally the term was applied to sets of 78 rpm records, which indeed had an album-like format, but the word was kept when such sets were replaced by single LPs. It is less commonly used of CDs.

albumleaf (Fr. *feuillet d'album*, Ger. *Albumblatt*, pl. *Albumblätter*). Short composition, normally for piano, such as a 19th-century young woman might have pasted into her album. There are albumleaves by Schumann, Smetana, Wagner, Saint-Saëns and Scriabin.

Alceste. Opera by Gluck to a libretto by Calzabigi after the play by Euripides, revised for Paris with the libretto adapted by Marie François Louis Gand Leblanc Roullet. Alcestis (soprano) resolves to die in place of her sick husband, Admetus (tenor), who thereby recovers and, once he understands why, is distraught. Their love is rewarded by Apollo, who restores them to life and each other. The Italian original was Gluck's and Calzabigi's second 'reform opera', following *Orfeo ed Euridice*. The French version, including Alcestis's defiant aria 'Divinités du Styx', is markedly different and has been repeatedly revived, for singers including Schröder-Devrient, Viardot, Callas, Baker and Norman. First performance: Vienna, 26 Dec 1767, rev Paris, 23 Apr 1776.

Other operas on the subject include Lully's *Alceste* and Handel's *Admeto*.

Alcina. Opera by Handel to an anonymous adaptation of the libretto for Broschi's opera *L'isola d'Alcina* after ARIOSTO. The powers of the sorceress Alcina (soprano) and her not entirely subservient sister Morgana (soprano) are destroyed when Ruggiero (alto castrato) recognizes his true love in Bradamante (contralto), who has both helped and confused matters by coming to Alcina's island in male attire. There are marvellous arias for Alcina, Morgana and Ruggiero. First performance: London, 16 Apr 1735.

The subject was extremely popular, throughout the Baroque period and into the early 19th century, in versions by Luigi Rossi (f.p. Rome, 1642), Campra (f.p. Paris, 1705), Albinoni (f.p. Venice, 1725), Hasse (f.p. Milan, 1771) and others.

alcuno, alcuna (It.). Some, as in *con alcune licenze* (with some liberties).

Aldeburgh. Town on the East Anglian coast where Britten took up residence in 1947 and founded an annual June festival the next year. To begin with, the festival took place in the town's tiny Jubilee Hall and in the region's churches; nevertheless, Britten wrote major works for Aldeburgh and invited distinguished friends (Fischer-Dieskau, Rostropovich, Richter). The festival's scope was broadened with the conversion of a nearby disused industrial site into the Snape Maltings, a superb concert hall, which opened in 1967 and again, after a fire, in 1970. Artistic directors of the festival since Britten's death have included Perahia, Knussen and Adès.

aleatory (from Lat. *alea*, dice). Term for music whose essential substance is not fully determined. This is quite a wide remit; it would include, for example, concertos and arias allowing room for cadenzas, as well as the long-established practice of the *ossia*. It would also include much of Ives's music, which includes exhortations to freedom (backed up by his recordings), unusually important alternatives and unrealizable notations that invite the performer to find a solution. Ives's example was important to Cowell, who used what he called 'elastic' notations, e.g. providing fragments to be put together by the players (*Mosaic Quartet*, 1934). Grainger, too, favoured 'elastic scoring'. But the term 'aleatory' is usually confined to music of around 1950–70, though acknowledging also the etymological aptness of counting as aleatory certain 18th-century musical games, which provided for dances to be composed by assembling given bars according to dice throws.

In the post-1950 period there were three distinct schools of aleatory endeavour. One sprang from Cage, and from his many diverse efforts to find, through CHANCE OPERATIONS and INDETERMINACY, ways to achieve music freed from creative will. Another was more concerned with instituting variabilities of form and movement within scores otherwise thoroughly composed (Boulez). The third emerged as a response to the different nature of electronic performance, as well as from the notion of creating a work as a giant image of a sound, requiring some equivalent for elements that could not be predicted (Stockhausen). Boulez's principal aleatory works – his Third Piano Sonata, second book of *Structures*, *Eclat* and *Pli selon pli* – were prompted partly by Asian music, partly by an understanding of serial composition as potentially endless (unlike tonal composition, which is always directed towards a cadence), and partly by Mallarmé's pursuit of ever greater ambiguity in his poetry. Stockhausen's works of this period (the late 1950s and 1960s) increasingly used electronic means, which could not be defined in the old ways, and also became increasingly open to the creative participation of performers, with a corresponding decline in notational exactitude (to the point of using plain symbols or verbal encouragements instead of regular parts). Perhaps the early-music movement, with its insistence on alternative ways of doing things, was also a stimulus to all these composers.

Stockhausen's return to traditional notation in 1970, and Boulez's successive withdrawals of the freedom of *Pli selon pli*, marked the end of a brief era. For one thing, the complexities of large-scale mobile scores could not survive a period of diminished patronage. But music gained a looseness it has not forgotten.

Aleksandrov, Aleksandr (Vasilyevich) (b. St Petersburg, 1 Apr 1883; d. Berlin, 8 Jul 1946). Russian composer, notably of the national anthem of the USSR and of songs for the Soviet Army Song and Dance Ensemble, which he founded in 1928. He was trained at the conservatories of St Petersburg (with Glazunov and Lyadov) and Moscow (with Vasilenko), and taught at the latter from 1918. His son Boris (1905–94) succeeded him in directing the army troupe.

Alexander Nevsky (*Aleksandr Nevsky*). Score by Prokofiev for Eisenstein's 1938 film on the 13th-century hero prince. Some cinematic sequences were apparently cut to the music, rather than the other way around. Prokofiev created from his score a concert work for mezzo-soprano, chorus and orchestra, with movements as follows: 1 *Russia under the Mongolian yoke*, 2 *Song about Alexander Nevsky*, 3 *The Crusaders in Pskov*, 4 *Arise, ye Russian people*, 5 *The battle on the ice*, 6 *The field of the dead*, 7 *Alexander's entry into Pskov*. First performance: Moscow, 17 May 1939 (cantata).

Alexander's Feast. Name normally associated with a concerto grosso in C by Handel, rather than with the ode, now rarely performed, with which it was first presented, and from which it took this sobriquet. That ode was based on Dryden's text for St Cecilia's Day 1697, set at a banquet given by Alexander the Great to celebrate his victory over the Persians. Its original performance included not only the new concerto grosso but also two new organ concertos (Op.4:1 and Op.4:6). First performance: London, 19 Feb 1736.

Alfano, Franco (b. Posillipo, Naples, 8 Mar 1875; d. San Remo, 27 Oct 1954). Italian composer, remembered chiefly for completing Puccini's *Turandot*, though Toscanini drastically edited his work. He studied the piano with Alessandro Longo before going on to the conservatories of Naples and Leipzig (1895–6), then scored an early success with his verismo opera *Risurrezione* (after Tolstoy; f.p. Turin, 1904). Later he was influenced by Debussy and Strauss, most importantly in *La leggenda di Sakùntala* (f.p. Bologna, 1921). It was the rich orchestration and exotic atmosphere of this opera, based on the Sanskrit play by Kalidasa, that brought him the invitation to complete Puccini's unfinished work in 1925. The rediscovery of his version in the 1980s led to some performances of his ending complete, but the standard score survived. His other works include further operas, two symphonies, three quartets and songs.

Alfonso el Sabio [the Wise] (b. Toledo, 23 Nov 1221; d. Seville, 4 Apr 1284). Spanish king and lover of the arts. Christian, Jewish and Islamic artists and thinkers were welcomed at his court, and he supervised (and possibly contributed to) a book of over 400 monophonic *Cantigas de Santa Maria*.

Alfonso und Estrella. Opera by Schubert to a libretto by Franz van Schober. Alfonso (tenor) is living in pastoral seclusion with his father Froila (baritone), the king of León ousted by Mauregato (baritone). Estrella (soprano), Mauregato's daughter, finds Alfonso and falls in love, and Mauregato cedes the young couple the throne. The work has been persistently disparaged for alleged dramatic weakness. Its overture Schubert used for *Rosamunde*. First performance: Weimar, 24 Jun 1854.

Alfred. Masque by Arne to words by David Mallett and James Thomson, source of the song 'Rule, Britannia'. First performance: Cliveden House, Bucks, 1 Aug 1740, rev as oratorio (1745) and opera (1753).

Dvořák also addressed the topic of King Alfred operatically.

Alfvén, Hugo (Emil) (b. Stockholm, 1 May 1872; d. Falun, 8 May 1960). Swedish composer, his country's great symphonic impressionist. He studied at the conservatory in Stockholm (1887–91), then privately with Lindegren, and had a long career as a choral conductor. He also loved travel, and recorded in his music his impressions of the Baltic and, in his Third Symphony, Italy.

Orchestral: Symphony No.1, F minor, Op.7, 1897;

No.2, D, Op.11, 1897–8; No.3, E, Op.23, 1905; No.4, C minor, Op.39, 1918–19; No.5, A minor, Op.54, 1942–53; Swedish Rhapsody No.1 'Midsummer Vigil', Op.19, 1903; No.2 'Uppsala Rhapsody', Op.24, 1907; No.3 'Dala Rhapsody', Op.47, 1931; *En skärgårdssägen*, Op.20, 1904; *Bergakungen* (ballet), Op.37, 1916–23 (includes *Valliflickans dans*); *Gustav II Adolf* (incidental music), Op.49, 1932 (includes Elegy)

Other works: much choral music, songs ('The forest is asleep', Op.28:6, 1908), instrumental pieces

Algarotti, Francesco (b. Venice, 11 Dec 1712; d. Pisa, 3 May 1764). Italian thinker who published a treatise on operatic reform, *Saggio sopra l'opera* (1755), which was widely circulated and debated; an English translation (Essay on the Opera) appeared in 1767. Educated in Rome and Bologna, he moved in learned circles in London, Paris and Germany before returning to Italy in 1753 on account of poor health. He published on various matters, scientific, commercial, literary and artistic. On opera, he criticized the ostentation and indiscipline of singers, advocating dominance for the poetic idea, which should be marvellous (because that was opera's nature). His example of such an idea – an *Iphigénie en Aulide* libretto presented as an appendix and showing his admiration of the Lully–Quinault operas – led to many treatments of the subject, not least Gluck's. He also had ideas for reforming theatre architecture on the Greek model.

algorithm. Rule by which a process unfolds. One musical algorithm with a long history is the ostinato, where the rule is simply to repeat a short phrase. But there are rules, too, of traditional counterpoint and harmony. Attempts to define those rules, and then apply them in order to compose in the style, say, of Palestrina, Bach or Haydn – whether those attempts are made by music students or by computers – show both how little and how much in great music can be generated mechanically. Of course, what obeys clear rules is normally uninteresting; genius lies in the exception.

Since the beginning of the 20th century many composers have been attracted to complex algorithmic processes, whether in following the rules of older music (NEOCLASSICISM) or in creating new ones. Examples of the latter include the principles of SERIALISM, the use of NUMBER systems and elaborations of the CANON idea (Messiaen, Nancarrow, Ligeti).

Al gran sole carico d'amore (In full sun charged with love). Opera by Nono to a libretto he and his director, Yuri Lyubimov, put together from Brecht and many other sources. Telling no single story, the work proceeds through protests and acclamations that are generated by real events – the Paris Commune and more recent struggles for justice – and that involve the orchestra and chorus as vociferously as the soloists. First performance: Milan, 4 Apr 1975.

Ali-Zadeh, Franghiz (Ali Aga Kïzï) (b. Baku, 28 May 1947). Azerbaijani composer, whose deft ability to let local traditions echo within a wider musical consciousness won her an international audience in the 1980s. She studied with Karayev at the Baku Conservatory (1965–72), where she remained as his assistant and then as a professor. In 1993–6 she was in Mersin, Turkey, conducting and teaching, and in 1999 she moved to Germany. Sometimes involved in her own works as a pianist, she has also written for the Kronos Quartet (*Mugam-Sajahy* with percussion and tape, 1993) and Yo-Yo Ma (*Dervish* for cello and ensemble, 2000).

Alkan, Valentin (b. Paris, 30 Nov 1813; d. Paris, 29 Mar 1888). French pianist-composer, originally Charles-Valentin Morhange. He was the son of Alkan Morhange (1780–1855), who ran a music school and produced six children who went into music, taking their father's first name as their surname. While studying at the Conservatoire (1819–34), notably with Pierre-Joseph Zimmermann, he began making a career as a salon pianist and composer, publishing his Op.1 when he was 14. As a young man he moved in fashionable circles; he knew Chopin, George Sand and Delacroix. But in 1838 he withdrew from the public, and gave only six concerts (in 1844–5 and 1853) before re-emerging in 1873. He was a devout and learned Jew, though the story that he died under a fallen bookcase, after reaching for a copy of the Talmud, is apocryphal. Elie-Miriam Delaborde (1839–1913) was his pupil and probably also his illegitimate son, a man of quite different, outgoing temperament.

Alkan's reclusive, obsessive and antiquarian nature (he kept to older fashions in dress and had an unusual respect for the Baroque masters) is reflected in his music, along with an exploratory imagination and a readiness to let virtuosity and complication lead him where they would. His set of 12 studies in all the minor keys, Op.39, includes three character pieces, a symphony (Nos.4–7), a concerto (Nos.8–10), an overture and a set of variations, *Le Festin d'Esope*. Schumann was the first to make the comparison with Berlioz, but Alkan belongs more with a pianistic fraternity of unruly alchemists that would include Busoni and Sorabji.

Ronald Smith *Alkan*, 2 Vols. (1976, 1987)

Piano (with publication dates): 3 Grand Etudes, Op.76, *c.*1838; 25 Preludes, Op.31, 1847; Grand Sonata 'Les Quatre âges', Op.33, 1848; 12 Etudes, Op.35, 1848; 12 Etudes, Op.39, 1857; Sonatina, Op.61, 1861; *48 motifs* (*Esquisses*), Op.63, 1861; etc. Other works: *Concerto da camera* No.1, A minor, Op.10, pf, orch, *c.*1832; No.2, C♯ minor, *c.*1833; *Grand duo concertant*, F♯ minor, Op.21, vn, pf, *c.*1840; Piano Trio, G minor, Op.30, pub 1841; *Sonate de concert*, E, Op.47, vc, pf, pub 1857; *Marcia funebre sulla morte d'un papagallo*, 4 solo v, 3 ob, bn, pub 1859; etc.

alla, all' (It.). To, at, by, as in ALLA BREVE; ALLA TURCA; ALLA ZINGARESE; ALLA ZOPPA; ALL'OTTAVA; ALL'UNISONO; etc.

alla breve (It., by breves). Direction to move more quickly and fluently, normally by considering a 4/4 bar as having just two beats. The term derives from medieval–Renaissance notational practice.

allant (Fr.). Going, in motion.

allargando (It., spreading). Slowing, broadening.

alla turca (It.). In Turkish style. Quite common in the later 18th century, the indication was used most famously by Mozart for the rondo finale of his Piano Sonata in A, K.331.

alla zingarese (It.). In gypsy style. A speciality of the later 19th century, the marking appears, for example, over the rondo finale of Brahms's G minor piano quartet.

alla zoppa (It., limping). 2/4 metre with the second quaver accentuated, as in some Hungarian music and ragtime.

all-combinatorial. See COMBINATORIALITY.

Alle (Ger., all). TUTTI (2).

allegramente (It.). Gaily.

allegretto. See ALLEGRO.

Allegri, Gregorio (b. Rome, 1582; d. Rome, 7 Feb 1652). Italian composer and church musician, only marginally responsible for the celebrated *Miserere* as almost ubiquitously sung in a lovely but unlikely edition from the 1950s, by the British organist and choirmaster Ivor Atkins. Gregorio and his brother Domenico (*c.*1585–1629) were choirboys under Nanino at San Luigi dei Francesi, and both became singers, composers and chapelmasters, Domenico at Santa Maria Maggiore (1610–29), Gregorio at Santo Spirito in Sassia and the papal chapel. His double-choir *Miserere* was a speciality of the latter, closely guarded – though also garlanded over the ages with high descants for the Vatican castratos. Many distinguished travellers were moved by the unique experience of hearing it in the Sistine Chapel at tenebrae in Holy Week: Mozart is said to have copied it out after a single hearing. The Atkins version draws on a copy Burney obtained from Padre Martini (who had it from the Vatican) and 19th-century sources.

allegro (It., cheerful). (1) Fairly fast. One of the earliest tempo markings, found in Banchieri's *La battaglia* (1611) and known also to Monteverdi and Frescobaldi. It was almost immediately the commonest tempo designation, and as such sprouted variant forms, such as *allegro vivace* (faster), *allegro ma non troppo* (slower), the diminutive *allegretto* (lighter, slower) or the superlative *allegrissimo* (very fast).

(2) A fairly fast movement, often a SONATA ALLEGRO.

allegro, il penseroso ed il moderato, L'. Oratorio by Handel to words by James Harris after Milton, supplemented by Jennens. Three human types are considered: the cheerful, the thoughtful and the rational. First performance: London, 27 Feb 1740.

alleluia. Lat. form of the Hebrew *halleluyah*, which was placed over 20 of the psalms and probably sung in temple worship. The word was taken up by early Christians as a response in psalm chanting, and thereby gained a place in the Latin mass, following the gradual. This mass chant consists of the word 'alleluia' – set in a melismatic style and ending with a *jubilus*, or flourish – followed by a Bible verse and a repetition of 'alleluia'. Being joyful, the alleluia is omitted from masses of penitence and mourning, including the Requiem. There is an equivalent *allēlouïa* in the Byzantine liturgy. In concert music the alleluiatic moments of Handel's *Messiah* and Mozart's *Exsultate, jubilate* take the palm.

Alleluia. Name given to Haydn's Symphony No.30, which quotes an Easter alleluia in its first movement.

allemande [allemand, almain, alman] (Fr., German dance). Moderately paced dance originating in Germany in the early 16th century, or possibly the late 15th; the term is first found in a

London dancing manual of 1521. Normally in common time, the form was favoured by English and French composers for keyboard and lute in the early 17th century, and became customary for the opening movement of a suite, as in Bach's. In the later 18th century the term was taken over by the GERMAN DANCE.

Allen, Thomas (Boaz) (b. Seaham Harbour, Co. Durham, 10 Sep 1944). British baritone, knighted in 1999, of warm lyrical voice, engaging stage personality and wide dramatic range (encompassing Billy Budd, Don Giovanni, Pelléas and Beckmesser at different periods). He studied with Hervey Alan at the RCM (1960–64), began his career with Welsh National Opera, and was appearing internationally by the mid-1970s, while remaining a particular favourite at Covent Garden.

Allende(-Sarón), Pedro Humberto (b. Santiago, 29 Jun 1885; d. Santiago, 17 Aug 1959). Chilean composer. After his studies at the Santiago Conservatory he received state support for a trip to Spain and France (1910–11), from which he returned to play an important part in Chilean life as teacher, folklorist and educator. His works include 12 *Tonadas* for piano (1918–29), three of them orchestrated. His nephew is the composer-conductor Juan Allende-Blin (b. 1928), who in 1977 made a performing version of Debussy's *La Chûte de la Maison Usher*.

all-interval row, all-interval set. 12-note row or set in which every interval from the minor second to the major seventh is represented. The simplest example is the wedge-form row C–C♯–B–D–B♭–E♭–A–E–G♯–F–G–F♯.

Allison, Richard (b. *c*.1570; d. *c*.1610). English composer, especially of pieces unusually and attractively prescribed for a mixed consort (with titles to match: *The Bachelers Delight*, *The Lady Frances Sidneys Goodmorowe*), as well as lute music and psalms.

all'ottava (It., at the octave). Term introduced by C.P.E. Bach, directing a continuo player to double a note at the octave above.

all'unisono (It., at the unison). Term introduced by C.P.E. Bach, countering *all'ottava*. It is more commonly used to negate a *divisi* marking, indicating that the instruments now join on one line.

Alma redemptoris mater (Life-giving Mother of the Redeemer). MARIAN ANTIPHON by (probably fallible) tradition ascribed to Hermannus Contractus. The beautiful melody was adorned with polyphony in settings by Du Fay, Palestrina, etc., and in paraphrase masses by Power, etc.

almain, alman. Terms found in English music of the 16th–17th centuries for ALLEMANDE.

Almeida, Francisco António de (b. *c*.1700; d. ?Lisbon, ?1755). Portuguese composer. He trained in Rome and is to be considered with the best of his Italian contemporaries, including Pergolesi. He worked in Lisbon from 1726 and perhaps died in the earthquake. His surviving works include the oratorio *La Giuditta* (1726) and the comic opera *La Spinalba* (1739).

Almglocken (Ger.). Cowbells.

Alnaes, Eyvind (b. Frederikstad, 29 Apr 1872; d. Oslo, 24 Dec 1932). Norwegian composer, especially of songs in a national late-Romantic style. He studied in Christiania and Leipzig (1892–4), then worked as an organist in Drammen (1895–1907) and Oslo (1907–32).

Alpaerts, Flor (b. Antwerp, 12 Sep 1876; d. Antwerp, 5 Oct 1954). Belgian composer, especially of orchestral music in a vivid late Romantic style (*James Ensor Suite*, 1929). He studied at the Antwerp Conservatory, where he taught from 1903, latterly as director (1934–41).

Alpensinfonie, Eine (An Alpine Symphony). Work by Strauss for enormous orchestra, describing a day in the mountains. First performance: Berlin, 28 Oct 1915.

alphorn. Long wooden trumpet, originally made from a young tree, split and hollowed out. Instruments of the kind are found not only in the Alps but across Europe; the earliest extant comes from the 9th-century Viking ship burial at Oseberg in Norway. Their uses range from herding cattle to summoning the divine. In size, too, they can be diverse, from 4 to 17 feet (1.2–5.2m) long, with a norm in Switzerland of around 11 feet (3.6m), the classic alphorn in F♯, on which a skilled player can reach up to the 12th harmonic or beyond.

al segno. See SEGNO.

Also sprach Zarathustra (Thus Spake Zarathustra). Symphony-length tone poem by Strauss after Nietzsche's book, playing continuously through nine sections: *Introduction, Of the Backworldsmen, Of the Great Longing, Of Joys and Passions, The Dirge, Of Science, The Convalescent, The Dance Song, Night Wanderer's Song*. The opening sequence, in massive triads depicting the birth of the world, was popularized by Stanley Kubrick's 1968 film *2001: A Space Odyssey*. First performance: Frankfurt, 27 Nov 1896.

Alt (Ger., pl. *Alte*). Alto, contralto.

alt, in. Pitched in the octave above the treble staff, from the F on the top line (or in some accounts the neighbouring G) to the F an octave above. The soprano's top C is thus C *in alt*. Notes in the next octave higher are *in altissimo*.

altered chord. A chord that keeps its diatonic function though one or more notes have been altered chromatically, e.g. the Neapolitan sixth chord F–A♭–D♭ in C major, which functions as the subdominant F–A–C.

alternatim (Lat., alternately). Liturgical practice of soloists singing in alternation with a choir, or the choir with the organ, etc.

alternativo (It., alternately). Word placed over one or the other of a pair of movements in an 18th-century composition, indicating that the first should be repeated after the second, producing an ABA pattern, such as became formalized in the minuet and trio.

Altflöte (Ger.). Alto flute.

altissimo, in. Pitched in the octave above F *in* ALT.

alto. (1) Used by itself the word may denote a man's voice of unusually high register, often achieved by means of FALSETTO, or a boy's, castrato's or woman's voice in the same range (though most contemporary falsettists prefer the term COUNTERTENOR and a female soloist, as opposed to a chorus member, will normally choose CONTRALTO or – these days even more normally – MEZZO-SOPRANO). The term is derived from the 15th-century *contratenor altus* (high contratenor). As an adjective it can also indicate an instrument of similar register (e.g. alto saxophone).

(2) (Fr.). Viola.

alto clarinet. Instrument in E♭ or F, a fifth or a fourth below the standard clarinet, not generally found outside bands.

alto clef. C CLEF on the middle line, used for violas.

alto flute. Larger flute, a transposing instrument in G, i.e. notated as if it were a standard flute but sounding a fourth lower. It has been common in orchestral scores since Ravel and Stravinsky.

Alto Rhapsody. Common English title for Brahms's Rhapsody for contralto, men's chorus and orchestra.

alto saxophone. See SAXOPHONE.

alto trombone. Baroque–Classical instrument revived in the 20th century. See TROMBONE.

alto viola. Ancestor of the modern viola, introduced (perhaps by the brothers Antonio and Girolamo Amati around 1600) as a smaller alternative to the TENOR VIOLA, alongside which it was sometimes given a separate part in Baroque scores.

Altposaune (Ger.). Alto trombone.

altro, altra (It., pl. *altri, altre*). Other, others, as in *con gli altri* (with the others), *altra volta* (another time), etc.

Alwyn, William (b. Northampton, 7 Nov 1905; d. Southwold, 11 Sep 1985). British composer of independent spirit, perhaps nearest to Bax in having affiliations to his native country (in his case to the metaphysical poets, the Pre-Raphaelite painters, the English landscape school of composers) but also to such early 20th-century continental masters of expanded tonality as Honegger and Nielsen. A grocer's son, he entered the RAM at 15 to study the flute and composition (with McEwen). In 1926 he returned to teach composition, and in 1927 he joined the LSO as a flautist. He left the RAM in 1955, now able to support himself from film scores, and retired to Suffolk. His works include operas (*Miss Julie*, 1972–7), five symphonies and *Naiades* for flute and harp (1971).

Alyabyev, Aleksandr (Aleksandrovich) (b. Tobolsk, Siberia, 15 Aug 1787; d. Moscow, 6 Mar 1851). Russian composer. The son of a cultured government official, he had piano lessons with Field before joining the army (1812–23). After that he began composing theatre music and songs, the latter including 'Solovey' (The Nightingale), which Viardot and later artists incorporated into the singing-lesson scene of *Il barbiere di Siviglia*. His career was soon interrupted, though, when he was imprisoned on a murder charge and sent back to

Tobolsk. He reached Moscow again in 1836, married and resumed composing for the theatre, with mixed success: his operas based on *The Tempest* and *A Midsummer Night's Dream* were not performed. He also produced symphonies and chamber music.

amabile (It.). Charmingly. Also *con amabilità* (with charm).

Amadeus Quartet. British quartet founded in 1947 by three Austrian-born musicians – Norbert Brainin, Siegmund Nissel and Peter Schidlof – and the British cellist Martin Lovett. They played until Schidlof's death in 1987, renowned for their warmth and tonal splendour. Among the few works they introduced was Britten's Third Quartet.

Amadis. Hero of an Iberian cycle of late-Renaissance chivalric fantasies (roundly challenged in print by Don Quixote) and again of miscellaneous Baroque operas:

(1) *Amadis* by Lully to a libretto by Quinault. After various trials involving an army of demons, a sorceress caught in a bind, a flaming rock and a dragon ship, Amadis (haute-contre) and Oriane (soprano) are united. Melodious airs include Amadis's monologues 'Bois épais' and 'Amour que veux-tu de moi?', and there is a big chaconne in its customary place at the end. First performance: Paris, 18 Jan 1684.

(2) *Amadis de Grèce* by Destouches to a libretto by Antoine Houdar de Lamotte. Amadis (bass) wins against the Prince of Thrace (haute-contre) the contest for the hand of Niquée (soprano), overseen by the sorceress Mélisse (soprano) and the gods. First performance: Paris, Mar 1699.

(3) *Amadigi di Gaula* by Handel to an anonymous adaptation of de Lamotte's libretto, with the names now Amadigi (mezzo-soprano castrato), Dardano (alto), Oriana (soprano) and Melissa (soprano). First performance: London, 25 May 1715.

(4) *Amadis de Gaule* by J.C. Bach to Quinault's libretto revised by Alphonse Denis Marie de Vismes du Valgay. First performance: Paris, 14 Dec 1779.

There was also a belated reflection on the subject from Massenet.

Amahl and the Night Visitors. Opera by Menotti to his own libretto, commissioned by NBC TV. Amahl (treble) is a crippled shepherd boy, visited by the Magi and cured by divine gratitude for his generosity. First performance: New York, 24 Dec 1951.

amanuensis. Scribe for a visually incapacitated composer. See BLINDNESS.

Amar Quartet. Ensemble led by Licco Amar, with Hindemith on viola, active 1921–9 largely in contemporary repertory and responsible for the first performance of Webern's Bagatelles.

amateur (Fr., lover). As introduced in the 18th century the word signified a person of gentle birth with a passion for some branch of the arts, learning or philosophy. A musical amateur would attend concerts and perhaps host them, subscribe to musical publications, be acquainted with musicians and no doubt have some performing skill. With the change from an aristocratic to a bourgeois culture, in the early 19th century, the term lost its flavour of patronage and came to mean simply a person performing for love.

A lot of music has been written for amateurs. Indeed, the vigorous music-publishing industry of the 18th, 19th and early 20th centuries could not have survived on a clientele only of professionals: piano music, quartets and songs were aimed at people performing for themselves and friends. Once that need for music at home was being supplied by recordings, the role of the amateur declined – except in the amateur chorus, a continuing necessity of musical life.

Amati, Nicolò (b. Cremona, 3 Dec 1596; d. Cremona, 12 Apr 1684). Italian violin maker, the greatest of the family that founded the Cremona school. The workshop was set up by his grandfather Andrea (d. 1577), who was making violins by 1546 and is credited with giving the instrument its lasting form. Andrea was succeeded by his sons Antonio (*c.*1540–1607) and Girolamo (*c.*1561–1630), at first working in partnership and later independently. Their instruments were much imitated, to the end of the 18th century, when Nicolò, Girolamo's son, began to be regarded as the superior maker, his violins graceful in form and noble in sound. After him came his son, another Girolamo (1649–1740), who was also an excellent maker, if without the spark that Nicolò had transmitted to two other pupils: Andrea Guarneri and Antonio Stradivari.

ambitus. Range of a plainsong chant or mode.

Ambrosian chant. Plainsong confined to Milan and surroundings. Thanks to the prestige inhering in it as the city of St Ambrose (bishop 374–397), Milan was able to maintain its own liturgical tradition and its own chant. The latter was first notated relatively late, in the 12th century, which probably accounts for its elaborateness; Gregorian chant had been fixed at an earlier point of development.

Ameling, Elly [Elisabeth Sara] (b. Rotterdam, 8 Feb 1934). Dutch soprano, much admired for her cherishable warmth in lieder and mélodies. She studied with Bodi Rapp and with Bernac in Paris, and made her formal debut in Amsterdam in 1961. For the next three decades she was one of the foremost exponents of song, retiring in 1995.

amen (Hebrew, so be it). Word used to end or respond to a prayer in Jewish, Christian and Muslim worship, a vocal gesture of concurrence and a musical gesture of cadence. In the Middle Ages, as the voice of the congregation was increasingly taken by a trained choir, so the amen (at the end of the *Gloria* and *Credo*, for example) came to be set to melismatic plainsong and rich polyphony. Baroque composers created a tradition of the fugal amen, in masses and oratorios. Later restorations of the amen to the congregation included the DRESDEN AMEN and the common singing of the word to a PLAGAL CADENCE in Protestant churches, while motifs of musical and theological confirmation echo through Messiaen's VISIONS DE L'AMEN.

American. Name given Dvořák's Quartet in F, Op.96, earlier called 'Negro' on account of its appeal to the melodic style of spirituals.

American Composers Orchestra (ACO). Organization founded by Francis Thorne, Nicholas Roussakis, Dennis Russell Davies and Paul Lustig Dunkel in 1977 to give several concerts in Carnegie Hall annually of new and recent music, chiefly from the USA but also from other American countries. Steven Sloane succeeded Davies as chief conductor in 2002.

American Federation of Musicians (AFM). Trade union founded in 1896 for musicians in the USA and, from 1900, Canada.

American Guild of Musical Artists (AGMA). Trade union founded in 1936 for performers of opera, dance and choral music.

American Guild of Organists (AGO). Professional association founded in 1896. It publishes a monthly magazine, *The American Organist*.

American Music Center. Organization founded in 1939 to promote music by US composers. It maintains a library of scores and recordings in New York.

American Musicological Society (AMS). Organization founded in 1934 to promote musical scholarship in the USA. It holds annual meetings and publishes a journal.

American organ. European term for the CABINET ORGAN.

American Symphony Orchestra. Occasional New York orchestra whose founder-conductor was Stokowski (1962–72). Under Leon Botstein (from 1992) the orchestra has made a feature of rare late-Romantic works and didactic programming.

American Symphony Orchestra League (ASOL). Organization founded in 1942 to provide advice and support to US orchestras. It publishes a bimonthly magazine, *Symphony*.

Amerindians. The first peoples of the Americas were represented on the European lyric stage in such works as Rameau's *Les Indes galantes* (1735) and Graun's *Montezuma* (1755), if with no attempt to render their music, which was largely ignored by the newer immigrant cultures, though it remained as a ferment in the mix with Iberian and African elements that produced the rich folk and popular musical traditions of Latin America. In the USA MacDowell (Indian Suite, 1891–5), Dvořák, Farwell and Cadman were among the first classical composers to interest themselves in Amerindian culture, at a time when it had almost been obliterated north of the Rio Grande. Amerindian themes and topics were tackled in the mid-20th century more often by Latin American composers (Revueltas, Chávez, Ginastera), though Varèse's *Ecuatorial* (1932–4) is this period's most extraordinary effort at creative retrieval. Towards the end of the 20th century composers of Amerindian ancestry in the USA, such as Brent Michael Davids, began to make a mark.

ametric, ametrical. Lacking a regular metre, because beats are either undifferentiated or absent.

Amfiparnasso, L' (The Lower Slopes of Parnassus). Sequence of five-part madrigals by Orazio Vecchi telling a romantic-comic-pastoral tale not meant to be staged. First performance: Modena, 1594.

Amleto. See HAMLET.

AMM. London improvisation group active from 1966. The members at the classic 1968 session were Cornelius Cardew, Lou Gare, Christopher Hobbs, Eddie Prévost and Keith Rowe.

Ammerbach, Elias Nikolaus (b. Naumburg, c.1530; buried Leipzig, 29 Jan 1597). German organist-composer, organist of St Thomas's, Leipzig (1561–95) and author of the first organ music published in Germany, *Orgel oder Instrument Tabulatur* (1571).

Amner, John (baptized Ely, 24 Aug 1579; buried Ely, 18 Jul 1641). English church musician, who studied at Oxford and was active at Ely Cathedral from 1610. He wrote services (*Cesar's Service*, named after the bishop), anthems and a set of organ variations on a psalm tune by Tallis.

amor brujo, El (That Demon Love). Ballet score by Falla to a scenario by Martínez Sierra, devised for Pastora Imperio as a piece to dance and sing. A woman is haunted by a dead lover; the climax is the Ritual Fire Dance. First performance: Madrid, 15 Apr 1915.

amoroso (It.). Lovingly. Also *con amore*.

Amphion. In Greek mythology the son of Zeus and Antiope, whom Hermes taught the lyre. When he and his twin brother Zethus were building the walls of Thebes, the stones set themelves in place, charmed by his playing. In an 18th-century opera by Naumann, the relationships are adjusted: Amphion, now a singer, is the son of Hermes, and Antiope is his beloved, whom he charms the barbarians with his singing to win. Valéry wrote a version of the story for Honegger.

amplification. Increase in volume achieved by electronic means, through the chain microphone – amplifier – loudspeaker. Amplification is necessarily involved in any kind of electronic music, including that produced by electronic instruments. It may also be used to enhance the sound of quiet instruments in ensembles (e.g. the acoustic guitar in concertos) and since the 1990s has been introduced, controversially, by some opera companies.

amplifier. Electronic device that increases the strength of a voltage input. Amplifiers are essential in sound-reproducing systems and electronic instruments.

amplitude. Range of the pressure change in a sound wave, heard as loudness.

amplitude modulation (AM). Alteration of amplitude as a means of conveying information, as in AM radio.

Amsterdam. As the capital of a nation claiming its independence in 1581 and prospering thereafter as a mercantile state, the city enjoyed a cultural boom led by a thriving middle class, and its artistic life has remained notably free and democratic. Sweelinck gave recitals and concerts, and later, in 1643, came the first public concerts presented anywhere, while opera was sometimes offered at the Schouwburg, built five years before. The city also became a leading centre of instrument building and music publishing: Vivaldi's music, for instance, was printed here. And there was a curiosity about new music, from the time of Mozart to that of Glass. Meanwhile the city gained one of the great concert halls, the Concertgebouw, inaugurated in 1888, with its own orchestra (named ROYAL CONCERTGEBOUW ORCHESTRA on the occasion of its centenary). The Netherlands Opera, founded in 1946, inaugurated its own building in 1986. There are also many other musical organizations, especially ensembles specializing in new music (Schönberg Ensemble, ASKO Ensemble) and old (Orchestra of the Eighteenth Century, Amsterdam Baroque Orchestra), contributing to one of the liveliest musical cultures in the world, with a season extended by the annual summer Holland Festival (since 1948).

Amy, Gilbert (b. Paris, 29 Aug 1936). French composer, who has travelled a great distance from the Boulezism of his 20s to the spacious works of his 50s and 60s, maturity with him bringing a wider awareness and also a greater sense of perplexity. He met Boulez in 1956, while a student at the Paris Conservatoire (1955–60), and went to Darmstadt in 1958 and 1960. His *Mouvements* for ensemble (1958) was performed by the Domaine Musical under Boulez, and his Piano Sonata (1957–60) confirmed his Boulezian orientation. He duly succeeded Boulez as director of the Domaine (1967–73), but his music was already changing: slowing, broadening. In 1984 he became director of the Lyons Conservatory. His later works include two quartets and an opera, *Le Premier Cercle* (f.p. Lyons, 1999), after Solzhenitsyn.

anacrusis. Note or notes constituting an UPBEAT. The word is borrowed from a term in poetics meaning the metrically weak beginning of a line.

analog. Technique of producing, reproducing or recording sound by means of direct transfers backwards and forwards along the line vibrations – electrical signals – storage (on disc or tape). Analog devices were generally replaced by DIGITAL means in the 1970s and 1980s.

analysis. The study of a composition's structure. Analysis is in principle absolute in its view: it is not concerned with the composition as an event in its composer's life, in music history, or in the culture of a region or period, but rather with what it is and how it works, as sound – or more realistically as score. Analytical studies may be made in order to provide help in listening to a piece, in performing it or in composing. They may therefore be made by scholars, critics and programme-note writers (publicly), by performers (informing their public presentation), by composers (privately) or by teachers of any of these. Analysis also has a life of its own, as an intellectual discipline.

It has been practised at different times in different ways and for different reasons, one of the earliest purposes being to categorize plainsong melodies according to mode. Analyses published in the Renaissance, Baroque and Classical periods were offered principally to elucidate techniques of composition; the concept of analysis as saying something about an enduring work could not exist before there was a widely held concept of the enduring work, around 1800, but then development was rapid. Jérôme Joseph de Momigny included in his *Cours d'harmonie et de composition* (1806) elaborate analyses of a first movement each by Mozart (D minor quartet) and Haydn ('Drumroll' Symphony). Four years later E.T.A. Hoffmann published an analytical review of Beethoven's Fifth Symphony that became a classic of music criticism. Both these writers were concerned equally with the materials (harmony, phrase structure, theme) and the expressive character.

Analysis in the next century tended to concentrate more on form, and especially on harmonic form, though its objects remained pre-eminently the Viennese classics, plus Bach and music evidently descended from those classics (Schubert, Schumann, Brahms). From Adolf Bernhard Marx (probably the first to analyse sonata form) in the 1830s–50s through Riemann and Adler to Schenker in the 1910s–30s, works were examined in ever closer detail, in the expectation of revealing ever fuller internal unity and greater conformity with general principles. Analysis also gained a new forum and function in the PROGRAMME NOTE, aside from its more august progress.

Concerning the latter, Schenker's approach was enormously influential, though it has subsequently been complemented or challenged by many others, understanding music in terms of thematic process (Réti), information theory, semiotics (Nattiez), pitch-class sets (Forte), the study of language (Lerdahl and Jackendoff), numerology, narrative studies and phenom-

enology. Also, a wider range of music has been analysed since the mid 20th century, including Renaissance masses, popular music and opera. Such a variety of analytical tools and sites, coupled with the influence of Derrida, has brought self-criticism into the field and made the analysis of analysis a profitable study.

Nicholas Cook *A Guide to Musical Analysis* (1987)

anche (Fr.). Reed.

ancient civilizations. See EGYPT; GREECE; MESOPOTAMIA.

ancora (It.). Still, again, yet, even, as in *ancora meno mosso* (even less motion, i.e. slower), which would normally follow *meno mosso*.

andante (It., walking). (1) Moderately slow. Late to enter the repertory of tempo markings, *andante* in the first half of the 18th century was generally an instruction to bring out the character of what is still known as a walking bass. It became a designation of speed in the Classical period, particularly for slow movements less solemn than would be implied by *adagio*. In the 19th century it became extremely common, alone or in derivative forms such as *andante con moto*, *andante molto*, *andante sostenuto*, *andantino* (in the Classical age meaning a little slower than *andante*, later a little faster), etc.

(2) A moderately slow movement.

Andante favori. Publisher's title for a movement Beethoven separated from his 'Waldstein' Sonata.

Anderson, Barry (Michael Gordon) (b. Stratford, New Zealand, 22 Feb 1935; d. Paris, 27 May 1987). New Zealand composer, especially of electronic music, in which he became interested as a teacher at Morley College (from 1969), having come to London to study the piano at the RAM (1952–6). He devoted much of his musical and technical skill to work on behalf of Stockhausen (realizations and performances) and Birtwistle (realization of electronic music for *The Mask of Orpheus*).

Anderson, Julian (David) (b. London, 6 Apr 1967). British composer, a pupil of Lambert at the RCM and Goehr at Cambridge. His scores tend to the brilliant and fantastical, with exotic tinges, as in *Alhambra Fantasy* for 15-piece ensemble (1999–2000).

Anderson, Laurie (b. Chicago, 5 Jun 1947). US performer-composer, who creates her own shows and recordings between classical music and rock, powerfully informed by her training in the fine arts, at Barnard and Columbia, and by her closeness to contemporary critical theory.

Anderson, Leroy (b. Cambridge, Mass., 29 Jun 1908; d. Woodbury, Conn., 18 May 1975). US composer of light music. He studied music and languages at Harvard (1930–34), and wrote miniatures for the Boston Pops, including *Sleigh Ride* (1948) and *The Typewriter* (1950).

Anderson, Lucy [née Philpot] (b. Bath, 12 Dec 1797; d. London, 24 Dec 1878). British pianist. The daughter of a Bath musician, she married in 1820 the violinist George Frederick Anderson (1793–1876), Master of the Queen's Music 1848–70. She was the first woman to play at a Philharmonic Society concert (1822) and after 1830 music tutor to Princess Victoria (the later queen) and her children.

Anderson, Marian (b. Philadelphia, 27 Feb 1897; d. Portland, Ore., 8 Apr 1993). US contralto who nobly faced discrimination on grounds of colour. She studied with Giuseppe Boghetti in Philadelphia, and made her debuts with the New York Philharmonic in 1925 (having won a competition) and at the Wigmore Hall, London, in 1930. In 1955 she was at last invited to sing at the Met, the first black singer to appear there.

An die ferne Geliebte (To the Distant Beloved). Song cycle by Beethoven (1816) to six poems by Alois Jeitteles. The singer is imagined amid nature, which partly hears and partly ignores songs to a love seemingly lost. The image of the distant, perhaps unattainable beloved was important to Beethoven both artistically and personally: he had written other songs 'An den fernen Geliebten' (1809) and 'An die Geliebte' (1811) and addressed a pas-sionate letter in 1812 to his 'immortal beloved' (probably Antonie Brentano).

André, Johann Anton (b. Offenbach, 6 Oct 1775; d. Offenbach, 6 Apr 1842). German publisher, whose father Johann (1741–99) founded the firm. He studied in Mannheim, notably with G.J. Vollweiler (1792–3), before entering the business. On his father's death he made a tour through Germany to Vienna, where he bought Mozart's musical estate from the composer's widow. His work on this material provided the basis for Köchel's catalogue; he also issued some exemplary editions. The publishing house continues under the direction of his great-great-great-grandson.

André, Maurice (b. Alès, 21 May 1933). French trumpeter, taught by his miner father. He, too, was a miner before studying with Sabarich at the Paris Conservatoire (1951–3). He then worked in orchestras and as his teacher's successor (1967–78) while establishing himself internationally as a soloist, with a brilliant sound and technique and an active interest in commissioning new works (concertos by Jolivet and others).

Andrea Chénier. Opera by Giordano to a libretto by Illica. Set in Revolutionary Paris, the plot concerns the real-life poet Chénier (tenor), on his way from aristocratic salon to the guillotine, joined at the last by his beloved Maddalena (soprano). Often revived for a star tenor, the score includes two arias in which the hero recites his own poetry: 'Un dì all azzuro spazio' (his Act 1 *improvviso*) and 'Come un bel dì di maggio'. Also included are Maddalena's aria 'La mamma morta' and a monologue for Gérard (baritone), the servant become judge, 'Nemico della patria'. First performance: Milan, 28 Mar 1896.

Andreae, Volkmar (b. Berne, 5 Jul 1879; d. Zurich, 18 Jun 1962). Swiss conductor and composer. He studied with Franz Wüllner in Cologne (1897–1900) and was conductor of the Zurich Tonhalle Orchestra (1906–49), with which he championed new music from Debussy, Mahler and Strauss to Stravinsky, Honegger and Schoeck.

Andreozzi, Gaetano (b. Aversa, 22 May 1755; d. Paris, 21/24 Dec 1826). Italian composer. He was a nephew and pupil of Jommelli, whence his nickname 'Jommellini', not undeserved by his operas, of which he wrote 43, mostly serious.

Andriessen. Dutch family of composers.

(1) **Hendrik (Franciscus)** (b. Haarlem, 17 Sep 1892; d. Haarlem, 12 Apr 1991). He studied the organ and composition (with Bernard Zweers) at the Amsterdam Conservatory before succeeding to his father's post as organist in Haarlem in 1913. Later he held positions at the conservatories of Amsterdam (1927–37), Utrecht (director 1937–49) and The Hague (director 1949–57). Writing in a broad symphonic style with modal features of French character, he produced much Catholic church music, besides four symphonies, concertos and other orchestral works. His brother Willem (1887–1964) was a pianist.

(2) **Jurriaan** (b. Haarlem, 15 Nov 1925; d. The Hague, 23 Aug 1996). He studied with his father in Utrecht and with Messiaen in Paris (1947). Eclectic, his works include eight symphonies and theatre music.

(3) **Louis** (b. Utrecht, 6 Jun 1939). He learned from his father and brother, then studied with Van

Baaren at the Hague Conservatory (1957–62) and Berio in Berlin and Milan (1962–5). On his return to the Netherlands he became a leader of the increasingly left-wing avant-garde, collaborating with several other Van Baaren pupils on the opera *Reconstructie* (1969), based on the life of Che Guevara. He also founded new groups to perform an aggressively new repertory: the wind-percussion ensemble De Volharding (Perseverance, 1972) and the loudly amplified Hoketus (1977). Yet in 1973 he was welcomed by his alma mater as a teacher. Strongly influenced by US minimalism, he has an ear, too, for the rhythmic, harmonic and music-historical trickery of Stravinsky.

Operas: *Reconstructie* (Reconstruction), f.p. Amsterdam, 1969 (with Reinbert de Leeuw, Mengelberg, Schat and Van Vlijmen); *De materie* (Matter; Andriessen and Robert Wilson), 1984–8, f.p. Amsterdam, 1989; *Rosa, a Horse Drama* (Peter Greenaway), 1994, f.p. Amsterdam, 1994; *Writing to Vermeer* (Greenaway), 1997–9, f.p. Amsterdam, 1999; *Inanna* (Hal Hartley), f.p. Amsterdam, 2003
Concert works: *De staat* (The Republic; Plato), 4 women's v, large ens, 1972–6; *Hoketus*, ens, 1976; *De tijd* (Time; St Augustine), women's ch, large ens, 1980–81; *De snelheid* (Velocity), large ens, 1982–4; *Trilogie van de laatste dag*, soli, children's ch, large ens, 1996–7; *La passione* (Dino Campana), s, vn, ens, 2002; etc.

Andsnes, Leif Ove (b. Karmøy, 7 Apr 1970). Norwegian pianist, of distinctively clear, aerian sound and fine intelligence. He studied with Jiří Hlinka at the Bergen Conservatory, made his debuts in Oslo in 1987 and New York in 1989, and was rapidly at the forefront. Along with Chopin, Liszt, Grieg and Rachmaninoff, he is known for less usual repertory (Haydn, Lutosławski) and for his chamber-music partnerships.

Anerio. Italian composing brothers.
(1) **Felice** (b. Rome, c.1560; d. Rome, 26/7 Sep 1614). He was a follower of Palestrina and trained under Nanino as a choirboy at Santa Maria Maggiore (1568–74). Continuing to sing, he began to compose and in 1594 succeeded Palestrina as composer to the papal choir, becoming ordained in 1607. His works include sacred and secular madrigals, masses and Holy Week responsories.
(2) **Giovanni Francesco** (b. Rome, c.1567; buried Graz, 12 Jun 1630). Much more progressive than his brother Felice, he lived most of his life in Rome, where he was associated with St Philip Neri's oratorians and eventually became a priest in 1616. Some years later he was chapelmaster to the Polish royal court; he died on his way back from Warsaw. He wrote motets and madrigals for soloists or vocal ensembles with continuo, highly expressive sacred dialogues for the oratorians, and masses in the old style.

Anfossi, Pasquale (b. Taggia, 25 Apr 1727; d. Rome, Feb 1797). Italian composer, with a place in history for having been displaced by Mozart, who wrote three glorious substitute arias for a performance of his *Il curioso indiscreto* in Vienna in 1783. He studied as a violinist at the Loreto conservatory in Naples, and played for a decade before taking composition lessons from Sacchini and Piccinni. His first opera was staged in Rome in 1763, but he was well into his 40s before he started to have much success in his new profession. Through the 1770s and 1780s he was wildly popular across Europe, producing anything up to five operas a year, serious and comic. In 1790 he retired to the life of a church musician in Rome, becoming chapelmaster of St John Lateran (1792–7). Besides operas and sacred music, he wrote symphonies.

Angel. US recording company, founded as a subsidiary of EMI in 1953.

Anglican chant. Means of singing psalms and canticles in the Anglican church, with each half-verse given a reciting tone and a cadential gesture, all to be done monophonically or harmonized. This method of chanting was introduced after the Restoration (1660), on the basis of earlier Anglican practices, themselves based on pre-Reformation psalmody.

Anglican music. The distinct musical repertory and tradition of the Anglican church, maintained not only in England and Wales but in the USA, Canada, Australia, etc. Anglican music comes in descent from the flamboyant liturgical music of the pre-Reformation Sarum rite, but with the shock injection, during the reign of Edward VI (1547–53), of the Calvinists' simple psalm singing. It tends, therefore, to hover between magnificence and restraint, and the historic importance of the mid-Tudor period (1534–59) – when the separation of the Church of England was instigated by Henry VIII, accelerated under Edward VI, repealed by Mary I and triumphantly re-established by Elizabeth I – has left an aura of authority around the music of that time, especially Tallis's, with its gentle, affirmative radiance and plaintive modal colouring, and John Marbeck's, setting the liturgy to adapted Sarum chant. Also high among the treasures of Anglicanism are the services and anthems of its glory days as a church proudly both Catholic and Protestant: the music composed for it by Byrd, Morley, Weelkes, Tomkins and Gibbons between the defeat of the Spanish Armada (1588) and the death of James I (1625) – the period when Shakespeare was writing and the King James Bible being produced.

After the interruption of civil war and a puritan republic, Anglicanism took over once again with the return of the royal house in 1660, prompting new music from Purcell and others. But, as with British music generally, there was then a lull. The settings of the long century from Tallis to Purcell provided a classic repertory for the cathedrals and colleges, joined by some works from 18th-century composers who joined their voices to that tradition (Croft, Greene, Battishill), while the music of parish churches consisted largely of metrical psalms.

In the first half of the 19th century came a renaissance. The success of the nonconformist movement led to a formidable growth of congregational hymns, and out of the principal nonconformist family came also, curiously, one of the most vigorous composers of Anglican cathedral music for many decades: Samuel Sebastian Wesley. In the last decades of the century most parish churches gained organs, and many organized choirs, enabling them to embrace at least part of the cathedral repertory, to which additions were now being made by Stanford. The traditional sound of the Anglican choir – with pure-toned boys and adult male altos – seems to date from this period.

Decline in church attendance since 1950, and liturgical changes that made much of the old repertory obsolete, led to a wide diversification (and widespread disappearance) of regular church music, while cathedrals and colleges have kept up choral evensong almost as a museum exhibit.

Peter le Huray *Music and the Reformation in England, 1549–1660* (1967, ²1978); Nicholas Temperley *The Music of the English Parish Church* (1979)

Anhalt, István (b. Budapest, 12 Apr 1919). Hungarian–Canadian composer, pupil of Kodály at the Liszt Academy (1937–41) and of Soulima Stravinsky and Nadia Boulanger in Paris (1946–9). He then moved to Canada, where he taught at McGill (1949–71) and Queen's University, Kingston (1971–84), and was one of the pioneers there of serial and electronic music. Glenn Gould recorded his Fantasia (1954); later works have included large-scale dramatic pieces to his own selections of texts.

Anhang (Ger., appendix). Term often found in catalogue numbers (abbreviated Anh.), e.g. in older editions of Köchel's Mozart catalogue.

anhemitonic. Lacking semitones, normally used

of pentatonic scales, e.g. the black-note scale F$\sharp$–G$\sharp$–A$\sharp$–C$\sharp$–D$\sharp$.

Aniara. Opera by Blomdahl to a libretto by Erik Lindegren after a poem by Harry Martinson. Renowned for its early use of a science-fiction theme and electronic music, the opera describes the decadence and decline of human life aboard the spaceship Aniara, overseen by Mimaroben (bass-baritone), operator of the computer Mima (tape). First performance: Stockholm, 31 May 1959.

anima, con (It.). With feeling.

anima del filosofo, L'. See ORPHEUS.

animal sounds. Those most often found in human music, of all times and places, came from BIRDSONG. Among other sounds noticed by Western composers are those of cats (Stravinsky's *Berceuses du chat*, Henze's *The English Cat*; see also CATS' DUET), insects (Rimsky-Korsakov's *Flight of the Bumble Bee*, Bartók's night music in *Out of Doors* and other pieces), sheep (Strauss's *Don Quixote*) and frogs. Primers of animal imitation include *Le* CARNAVAL DES ANIMAUX and *L'*ENFANT ET LES SORTILEGES.

animato (It.). Spiritedly; *animando*, *animoso* and the Fr. *animé* are also found.

Animuccia, Giovanni (b. Florence, *c*.1520; d. Rome, Mar 1571). Italian composer and church musician, the most important contemporary in Rome – where he had arrived by 1550 – of Palestrina, who served before and after his period as choirmaster of the Julian Chapel (1555–71). He was also associated with St Philip Neri's oratorians and wrote *laude* for them as well as madrigals, motets and masses. Paolo Animuccia (*c*.1500–1569), probably his brother, was also a composer and church musician.

Anna Bolena (Anne Boleyn). Opera by Donizetti to a libretto by Romani. Anne (soprano), having been trapped by her husband Henry VIII (bass) – who wants to exchange her for Jane Seymour (mezzo-soprano) – into a compromising situation involving her ex-lover Percy (tenor) and her musician Smeton (mezzo-soprano), ends the work with a solo scene of nostalgia and rage ('Al dolce guidami castel natio'). A 19th-century favourite, also including a powerful confrontation between the rival women ('Dio, che mi vedi – Sul suo capo – Va, infelice'), the work was revived for Callas in 1957 and has stayed on the fringe of the repertory. First performance: Milan, 26 Dec 1830.

Anna Magdalena. The woman for whom Bach wrote his notebooks was his wife; see BACH (5).

Années de pèlerinage (Years of Pilgrimage). Volumes of piano pieces by Liszt, as follows:

Première année, Suisse (First Year, Switzerland, 1848–55): 1 *Chapelle de Guillaume Tell* (William Tell's Chapel, after Schiller), 2 *Au lac de Wallenstadt* (By the Lake of Wallenstadt, after Byron), 3 *Pastorale*, 4 *Au bord d'une source* (Beside a Spring, after Schiller), 5 *Orage* (Storm, after Byron), 6 *Vallée d'Obermann* (Obermann's Valley, after Senancour), 7 *Eglogue* (Eclogue, after Byron), 8 *Le Mal du pays* (Homesickness), 9 *Les Cloches de Genève* (The Bells of Geneva, after Byron).

Deuxième année, Italie (Second Year, Italy, 1838–61): 1 *Sposalizio* (Betrothal, after Raphael's 'Brera' Madonna), 2 *Il penseroso* (The Contemplative, after a figure by Michelangelo), 3 *Canzonetta del Salvator Rosa*, 4 *Sonetto del Petrarca No.47*, 5 *Sonetto del Petrarca No.104*, 6 *Sonetto del Petrarca No.123*, 7 *Après une lecture de Dante, fantasia quasi sonata* (After a Reading of Dante, after Hugo; Dante Sonata).

Venezia e Napoli (supplement to *Deuxième année*, 1838–59): 1 *Gondoliera, canzone del Cavaliere Peruchini*, 2 *Canzone*, 3 *Tarantella da Guillaume Louis Cottrau*.

Troisième année (Third Year, 1877–82): 1 *Angelus!*, 2 *Aux cyprès de la Villa d'Este* (By the Cypresses of the Villa d'Este), 3 *Aux cyprès de la Villa d'Este*, 4 *Les Jeux d'eau à la Villa d'Este* (The Fountains at the Villa d'Este), 5 *Sunt lacrymae rerum* (Even things have tears [Aeneid]) 6 *Marche funèbre* (Funeral March), 7 *Sursum corda* (Lift up your hearts).

annotator. Programme-note writer, a regular position with US orchestras in the 20th century.

Anonymous IV (*fl. c.*1270–80). French theorist, author of an important treatise on NOTRE DAME SCHOOL polyphony (*De mensuris et discantu*), identified thus by Charles Edmond Henri de Coussemaker in his *Scriptorum de musica medii aevi* (1864–76). The name was taken by a US female vocal quartet specializing in medieval music (1986–2004).

Ansatz (Ger.). Embouchure; or, at the piano, touch.

Anschlag (Ger.). Ornament consisting of a leap through two notes followed by a fall to the principal note; or, at the piano, touch.

Ansermet, Ernest (b. Vevey, 11 Nov 1883; d. Geneva, 20 Feb 1969). Swiss conductor, who in his long tenure with the Orchestre de la Suisse Romande (1918–68) set the standard for the performance of Debussy, Ravel, Roussel and Stravinsky. The son of a mathematician, he followed after his father and was a professor of maths at Lausanne University (1905–9), where he had studied. Meanwhile he had lessons in composition with Bloch, and then music took over. He spent a year in Berlin, where he consulted with Nikisch and Weingartner, and returned to make his conducting debuts in Lausanne and Montreux in 1910. Soon after he met Stravinsky, who was living in Switzerland, and thereby gained the job of principal conductor to the Ballets Russes (1915–23). Noted for his clarity and care, he gave the first performances of many Stravinsky scores, from *Histoire du soldat* and *Chant du rossignol* to the Symphony of Psalms and Mass, but he was bothered by the composer's absorption of serialism – so much so that he wrote a book on 'the foundations of music in human consciousness'. He also conducted the premières of, and recorded works by, Prokofiev, Falla and Martin.

answer. In a fugue the appearance of the subject in the dominant. Normally this will come with the introduction of the second voice, a fifth above the first (or more rarely a fourth below). The subject may be unchanged (a 'real answer') or it may have required some chromatic alteration to maintain the harmony (a 'tonal answer').

antara (Quechua). Panpipes.

Antarctic. Region imaginatively explored in two symphonies: Vaughan Williams's Seventh (SINFONIA ANTARTICA) and Davies's Eighth.

antecedent. Musical idea expecting a response, the consequent. The antecedent–consequent couple – the period – is one of the foundations of the Classical style, especially at the start of a movement. Both will normally be of the same length (regularly four bars).

Antheil, George [Georg Carl Johann] (b. Trenton, NJ, 8 Jul 1900; d. New York, 12 Feb 1959). US composer. He studied with Bloch in New York (1919–21) and found a patron in Mary Louise Curtis Bok (see CURTIS INSTITUTE OF MUSIC), who supported him for 19 years even though she did not care for his music. With her help he travelled to Europe in 1922, gave a recital in London and moved on to Berlin. There he met Stravinsky, whose confirmation of his path was decisive: jazz, noise and ostinato became his specialities, worked into brutally elementary and startling designs in his early piano works. In 1923 he moved to Paris and gave a concert, which duly caused a riot and brought him support from among the avant-garde. Ezra Pound wrote a book about him, and with Fernand Léger and the film-maker Dudley Murphy he worked on the *Ballet mécanique* (1923–5), for which he wrote a score eventually performed for a reduced instrumentation of two pianos, pianola, three xylophones, electric bells, three propellers, tam tam, four bass drums and a siren. It was heavily indebted to Stravinsky's *Les Noces*.

At this point he decided to try something different: neoclassicism. Then he changed tack again and returned to Germany to work on an opera caricaturing US political life, *Transatlantic* (1927–8), using jazz and the idiom of popular song. He went back to New York in 1933, to work largely on theatre and film projects (including dance scores for Martha Graham and Balanchine), and settled in Hollywood in 1936 as a movie composer. His final self-transformation in 1942, prompted by hearing Shostakovich's music, was into a neo-Romantic symphonist. But though the language of his late works is conventional, the content is as belligerent as it had been in the 1920s.

George Antheil *Bad Boy of Music* (1945, ¹1981); Linda Whitesitt *The Life and Music of George Antheil* (1983)

Stage: *Transatlantic* (opera; Antheil), f.p. Frankfurt, 1930; *Volpone* (opera; after Jonson), Los Angeles, 1953; Capital of the World (ballet; after Hemingway), 1952; etc.

Symphonies: No.1 'Zingareska', 1920–23; Symphony for 5 Instruments, fl, tpt, va, trbn, bn, 1922–3; *A Jazz Symphony*, 1925; *Symphonie en fa*, 1925–6; No.2, 1931–8; No.3 'American', 1936–9; No.4 '1942', 1942; No.5 'Tragic', 1945–6; No.5 [*sic*] 'Joyous', 1947–8; No.6 'after Delacroix', 1947–50

Percussion ensemble: BALLET MECANIQUE, 1923–5, rev 1952–3

Chamber: String Quartet No.1, 1924–5; No.2, 1927; No.3, 1948; Violin Sonata No.1, 1923; No.2, with drums, 1923; No.3, 1924; No.4, 1947–8; Flute Sonata, 1951; Trumpet Sonata, 1951

Piano: *Airplane Sonata* (No.2), 1921; *Sonata sauvage* (No.1), 1922/3; *Jazz Sonata* (No.4), 1922/3; *Death of Machines* (Sonata No.3), 1923; Sonata No.3, 1947; No.4, 1948; No.5, 1950; *La Femme 100 têtes*, 1933; etc.

anthem. (1) Choral piece designed as an extra item in a church service, not strictly part of the liturgy – a musical adornment or homily, particularly beloved of the Anglican church. The term derives from ANTIPHON, and the post-Reformation anthem was in some respects the continuation of the earlier Tudor votive antiphon. Anthems – verse anthems with soloists and full anthems without –

were an early part of ANGLICAN MUSIC, though with no definite place in worship until the 1662 prayer book stipulated that after the third collect at Matins and Evensong 'in Quires and Places where they sing, here followeth the Anthem'.

(2) Short for NATIONAL ANTHEM.

anticipation. Dissonant note that arrives on a weak beat and will be part of the harmony on the following strong beat. In a 'rhythmic anticipation' the entire chord comes early in this way.

Antigone. In Greek mythology the daughter of Oedipus and Jocasta. She pleads with the new ruler of Thebes, her uncle Creon, for permission to bury her brother Polynices; her fate is different in the plays by Sophocles (burial alive) and Euripides (escape). Where earlier 18th-century operas had provided sequels to Euripides – and Metastasio had confused matters by treating an entirely different subject in his *Antigono* libretto – Coltellini and Traetta (*Antigona*, 1772) returned to the classic story, though with a happy ending in which Creon relents. The Sophocles version was the occasion for incidental music by Mendelssohn and Saint-Saëns and operas by Honegger and Orff.

Antill, John (Henry) (b. Sydney, 8 Apr 1904; d. Sydney, 29 Dec 1986). Australian composer, known chiefly for his evocation of aborigine ritual (and *The Rite of Spring*) in the ballet *Corroboree* (1946), though this is not typical of his tradition-oriented mentality. He was a pupil of Alfred Hill at the New South Wales Conservatorium and worked for the ABC as music editor.

antimasque. Comic-satiric interlude in a masque.

antiphon. In most cases a short text sung before a psalm and repeated after it. The term goes back at least to the 4th century and is derived from the Gk *antiphōnos* (resounding with) – as, quite separately, is 'antiphony', for there is no suggestion that antiphons have to be antiphonal. In the Western church the antiphon–psalm–antiphon unit is most often found in the offices of matins, lauds and VESPERS. Canticles such as the Magnificat can similarly be antiphon-framed, and the introit (with a vestigial psalm verse) and communion of the mass are also classed as antiphons. Other kinds, independent of psalm singing, include the processional antiphon and the MARIAN ANTIPHON.

antiphonal. (1) Exhibiting or pertaining to antiphony.

(2) Antiphoner.

antiphonary. Antiphoner.

antiphoner. Book of office chants, to be complemented by a gradual, which has the mass chants.

antiphony. Sounding of music from different positions, normally with some sense of alternation. Antiphonal performance is implicit in liturgies, most simply when an officiant is answered by a choir, though there is only an etymological connection with the ANTIPHON. Antiphony became a special feature of some church music in the late Renaissance and Baroque periods, from Gabrieli's polychoral motets and canzonas to Bach's writing for double chorus in the St Matthew Passion. In the 20th century it reappeared in many orchestral and electronic works exploiting SPACE, while the importance of the antiphonal principle is indicated in titles by Henze and Birtwistle (see also his VERSES FOR ENSEMBLES).

antique cymbals. CROTALES.

Antonello da Caserta (*fl. c.*1400). Italian composer, of polyphonic songs in French and Italian. Possibly active in northern Italy, he was a master of the ARS SUBTILIOR. His ballade *Beauté parfaite* is the unique example of a Machaut poem set by another composer.

Antunes, Jorge (de Freitas) (b. Rio de Janeiro, 23 Apr 1942). Brazilian composer, strongly active in avant-garde and electronic fields. He studied music and physics at university in Rio, and completed his training with the Groupe de Recherches Musicales in Paris (1972–3) before becoming professor of composition and director of electronic music at the University of Brasília in 1973.

anvil. Percussion instrument: normally a steel bar or tube, real anvils being too heavy. In opera it is often an illustrative effect, as in Auber's *Le Maçon* (1825, apparently the first use), Berlioz's *Benvenuto Cellini*, Verdi's *Il trovatore* and Wagner's *Das Rheingold* (requiring 18 anvils), but it also appears in Bax's Third Symphony and Varèse's *Ionisation*.

Aperghis, Georges (b. Athens, 23 Dec 1945). Greek–French composer whose works often involve theatre, unusual performing techniques and a poetic balance of strangeness with humour. He moved to France in 1963, founded his Atelier Théâtre et Musique (ATEM) in Paris in 1976, and moved with it to Nanterre in 1991.

aperto (It.). Open. Most commonly an indication to horn players to remove the hand after stopped notes (*chiuso*). Mozart several times has the rather enigmatic *allegro aperto*, e.g. for the first movement of his A major violin concerto.

a piacere (It., at pleasure). An indication that performers may please themselves, to a degree, with regard to duration or rhythm.

Aplvor, Denis (b. Collinstown, Ireland, 14 Apr 1916). British composer, of Welsh family. A chorister at Oxford and Hereford, he studied with Rawsthorne while training as a doctor in London, where he practised medicine during the war. Always alert to continental influences, he began to move towards serialism in the late 1940s. A well-received BBC performance of his cantata setting T.S. Eliot's *The Hollow Men*, in 1950, encouraged him to give up medicine and, though decades of neglect followed, he continued to compose boldly, producing four symphonies, operas, songs and chamber music.

Apocalypse. See REVELATION.

Apollo. God who, in Greek and Hellenistic traditions, gained an increasing association with the muses and with music. The dichotomy between Apollo (controlled, light, spiritual) and Dionysus (rampant, dark, corporeal) is a trope in aesthetics, introduced by Nietzsche. Works Apollonian in subject include:

(1) Mozart's first stage work, *Apollo et Hyacinthus*, written by a boy for boys to perform.

(2) Stravinsky's ballet *Apollo*, originally called *Apollon musagète* (Apollo Leader of the Muses), which shows the god being born and consorting with three of the muses, to music for strings evoking the Lullian court ballet. First performance: Washington, 27 Apr 1928.

See also Marc'Antonio PASQUALINI; Michelangelo ROSSI.

Apostel, Hans Erich (b. Karlsruhe, 22 Jan 1901; d. Vienna, 30 Nov 1972). German–Austrian composer, of the Schoenberg school. After training in Karlsruhe he went to Vienna in 1921 to study with Schoenberg and, from 1925, Berg. His developing career as a composer, pianist, conductor and teacher was cut short by the Second World War; he moved to Geneva, but was obliged to return to Vienna, where his music was almost ignored. After 1945 he returned to a sure place in the city's musical life in various official capacities and as a reader for Universal Edition. Contacts with painters (Kubin, Nolde, Kokoschka) left their mark on his music, most of which is in smaller genres.

Apostles, The. Oratorio by Elgar to his own selection from the gospels, telling the apostles' story from their calling to the Resurrection. First performance: Birmingham, 14 Oct 1903.

Appalachian Spring. Ballet score by Copland for choreography by Martha Graham, a *Les Noces* for US pioneers, musically worked around the Shaker hymn tune 'Simple Gifts'. The original score for 13-piece ensemble was subsequently arranged by the composer for symphony orchestra. First performance: Washington, 30 Oct 1944.

appassionato, appassionata. Impassionedly. Also *con passione*. 'Appassionata' has stuck as a title to Beethoven's Piano Sonata in F minor, Op.57, thanks to a publisher in 1838.

applause. Handclapping, the louder the better, is universal where Western classical music is played, but certain practices are more local. Clapping in regular rhythm is a sign of special affection and favour in eastern Europe, but in Britain the slow synchronized handclap indicates impatience. Whistling is strongly positive in the USA, but negative in Russia. Standing ovations are rare in Britain, common in the USA. Everywhere, though, calls of 'bravo' (plus, as appropriate, the feminine and plural forms, 'brava', 'brave' and 'bravi' in Italy and the USA) and demands for an ENCORE intensify the expression of appreciation.

applied dominant. Chord functioning as the dominant of some scale degree other than the tonic. Thus, in C major, an A major chord may function not as the submediant but as the dominant of the mediant (E major). In a harmonic analysis, therefore, it would be indicated not as VI but as V/III.

appoggiatura (It., leaning). Ornamental note that leans towards a main note, creating a gentle delay in the melody's arrival at an expected point. Most often the appoggiatura is a step above the note it leans towards, but it may be a step below. It is notated in small type. The appoggiatura splits the time value of the main note: the two have half each, or the appoggiatura takes two-thirds in the case of a dotted value. In some music, however, it is not notated at all, its insertion being a matter of convention: this is so, most notably, in 18th-century recitative, where a vocal descent through a third at a cadence (e.g. B–G) is to be interpreted with an appoggiatura (B–A–G). The convention

had lapsed before it was widely reintroduced in the 1950s–60s.

Apponyi. Name given to Haydn's Op.71 and Op.74 quartets, sponsored by Count Anton Georg Apponyi.

appreciation. Educated enjoyment. Music appreciation may be developed as a skill, increasing the ability to UNDERSTAND and discriminate, with the help of classes, books, programme notes and, indeed, listening.

Apprenti sorcier, L' (The Sorcerer's Apprentice). Orchestral scherzo by Dukas based on an old story as retold by Goethe. The apprentice in his master's absence casts a spell and cannot undo it: orchestral magic and power create both a firm musical design and an extraordinarily close fit to the narrative (as wonderfully demonstrated in Disney's *Fantasia* (1940), with Mickey Mouse as the apprentice). First performance: Paris, 18 May 1897.

APRA. Australasian Performing Right Association.

Après-midi d'un faune, L'. See PRELUDE A 'L'APRES-MIDI D'UN FAUNE'.

Apt. Manuscript volume of 14th-century and early 15th-century sacred polyphony from the papal court at Avignon, held in the treasury of the Basilica of St Anne at Apt, Provence.

aquarelle (Fr., water colour). Term taken into music for its sense of freshness and clear colour – first, so it would seem, by Gade (1850).

Arab music. See ISLAM.

Arabella. Opera by Strauss to a libretto by Hofmannsthal, their final collaboration and second waltz-plushed Viennese erotic comedy, after *Der Rosenkavalier*. The glamorous Arabella (soprano) and her tomboy sister Zdenka (soprano) find their respective mates in the aristocratic Mandryka (baritone) and the young officer Matteo (tenor), despite deceptions and self-deceptions. First performance: Dresden, 1 Jul 1933.

arabesque (Ger. *Arabeske*). Term borrowed from the fine arts for its sense of graceful decorative line. The earliest musical example would seem to be Schumann's (1838–9), followed by others by Heller, Gade and Debussy, all similarly piano pieces.

Araja, Francesco (b. Naples, 25 Jun 1709; d. ?Bologna, ?1770). Italian composer, the first of many to serve the Russian empresses. He had earlier success as an opera seria composer in Rome, Naples, Milan and Venice, where he probably received the summons to St Petersburg in 1735. His duties included teaching, arranging concerts and writing operas, including the first in Russian, *Tsefal i Prokris* (1755). In 1762 he left both Russia and the historical record: he probably ended his days as a singing teacher in Italy.

ARAM. Associate of the Royal Academy of Music (London).

Arányi (de Hunyadvar), Jelly (Eva) d' (b. Budapest, 30 May 1893; d. Florence, 30 Mar 1966). Hungarian violinist, a great-niece of Joachim. She and her sister Adila Fachiri (1886–1962) both studied with Hubay in Budapest and settled in England in 1913. They were noted performers of the Bach double concerto, and Holst wrote a successor for them. For the passionate and spirited Jelly alone came works from Bartók (the two sonatas of 1921–2, which he played with her) and Ravel (*Tzigane*).

Araujo, Juan de (b. Villafranca de los Barros, Extremadura, 1646; d. La Plata, now Sucre, Bolivia, 1712). Spanish church musician who went to Lima with his father and studied there. He became choirmaster at the cathedrals of Lima (until 1676) and La Plata, and wrote villancicos and church music for the lavish choirs in his charge.

Arbeau, Thoinot (b. Dijon, 17 Mar 1520; d. Langres, 23 Jul 1595). French churchman and champion of dancing, who wrote under an anagram of his real name, which was Jehan Tabourot. His *Orchéso-graphie* (1588) describes various dances with music examples and instructions. It was a source for Stravinsky when writing *Agon*.

Arcadelt, Jacques [Jakob] (b. ?near Namur, c.1505; d. 14 Oct 1568). Netherlandish composer, famed especially for the four-part madrigals he wrote in Florence in the 1530s. Following Verdelot in this genre, and showing a flair for tunefulness and suavity, his first book of madrigals (1538) was by far the most popular such collection ever: it went through 58 editions, the last in 1654. Among its contents are *Il bianco e dolce cigno* and *O felic'occhi miei*. Three further books of madrigals came out in 1539, followed by two more in the early 1540s, by which time the composer was in Rome, at the Sistine Chapel (1540–51). He then went to France, where for the rest of his life he served the Cardinal of Lorraine. Apart from madrigals he wrote sacred music and chansons, effectively madrigals in

French. One of these, *Nous voyons que les hommes*, was arranged as an *Ave Maria* by Louis Dietsch: hence the '*Ave Maria*' by Arcadelt' of which Liszt made organ and piano transcriptions.

Arcana. Orchestral work by Varèse inscribed with an arcane quotation from the Renaissance occultist Paracelsus, but supremely modern in its flinging of sound blocks. First performance: Philadelphia, 8 Apr 1927.

ARCCO. Associate of the Royal Canadian College of Organists.

Archduke. Name given Beethoven's Piano Trio in B♭, Op.97, dedicated to the Archduke RUDOLPH.

Archer, Violet (Balestreri) (b. Montreal, 24 Apr 1913; d. Ottawa, 21 Feb 2000). Canadian composer. The daughter of Italian immigrants, she studied at McGill, with Bartók in New York (1942) and with Hindemith at Yale (1947–9). Influenced by these two composers in particular, she wrote in all genres while teaching at the universities of Oklahoma (1953–61) and Alberta (1962–78).

archet (Fr.). Bow. Hence *coup d'archet* (bow-stroke).

archi (It.). Bows, also used as a term for a group of string players, as in *quartetto d'archi*.

archlute. Lute with added set of longer, unfretted courses, these often having their own pegbox on a neck bent back at right angles. The instrument arrived at the very end of the 16th century and was largely restricted to Rome until it enjoyed a period of wider popularity in the decades around 1700. An archlutenist could be a soloist, an accompanist or a continuo player. The THEORBO differs in having a larger body, with what would be the highest courses tuned down an octave.

arcicembalo. Term introduced by Nicola Vicentino (1555) for a harpsichord having split keys, or two manuals, with different tunings of the same note to facilitate performance in distant keys. Vicentino later invented an *arciorgano*.

ARCM. Associate of the Royal College of Music (London).

arco (It., pl. *archi*). Bow. Often found as a direction to return to bowing after pizzicato.

ARCO. Associate of the Royal College of Organists (London).

Ardévol (Gimbernat), José (b. Barcelona, 13 Mar 1911; d. Havana, 9 Jan 1981). Catalan–Cuban composer. Trained in Barcelona, he moved to Havana in 1930 and rapidly gained prominence in musical life as a composer and conductor, befriending Roldán and Caturla. From 1936 he taught at the national conservatory, where his disciplined introduction of atonality and neo-classicism was important to the adventurous generation graduating in the 1940s. He also held government positions after the 1959 Revolution.

Arditti Quartet. European ensemble founded in 1974 by Irvine Arditti and fellow graduates of the RAM with the explicit aim of promoting new music. It has duly presented new works by Birtwistle, Cage, Ferneyhough, Gubaidulina, Lachenmann, Stockhausen, Xenakis and many others.

Arensky, Anton (Stepanovich) (b. Novgorod, 12 Jul 1861; d. near Terioki/Zelenogorsk, 25 Feb 1906). Russian composer, best known for his Tchaikov-skian chamber music and short pieces. The son of keen musical amateurs, he studied with Rimsky-Korsakov at the St Petersburg Conservatory (1879–82) and immediately joined the teaching staff at the Moscow Conservatory, where his pupils included Rachmaninoff and Scriabin. In Moscow he came into contact with Tchaikovsky; he then succeeded Balakirev as director of the imperial chapel (1894–1901). An enthusiastic drinker and gambler, he died of tuberculosis.

Orchestral: Piano Concerto, F minor, Op.2, 1882; Violin Concerto, A minor, Op.54, 1891; Variations on a Theme of Tchaikovsky, Op.35a, str, 1894
Chamber: Piano Trio No.1, D minor, Op.32, 1894; No.2, F minor, Op.73, 1905; Suite No.1, F, Op.15, 2 pf; No.2 (*Silhouettes*), Op.23, 1892; No.3 (Variations), Op.33; No.4, Op.62; 4 Pieces, Op.30, vn, pf (No.2 Serenade)
Other works: piano solos and duets, songs, stage works, choral music

Argentina. Opera found a home in the capital Buenos Aires in the late 18th century, and was especially favoured there during the boom decades around 1900, when international stars would regularly appear at the Teatro de la Opera (1872) and its successor the Teatro Colón (1908). With Ginastera the country produced a composer of world rank; among later Argentinian composers, Davidovsky, Kagel and Golijov all sought opportunities abroad, and among performers, Argerich and Barenboim quickly embarked on international careers. Not the least of the country's musical gifts to the world is the tango.

Argento, Dominick (b. York, Penn., 27 Oct 1927). US composer, notably of operas in a determinedly Romantic vein. The son of Sicilian immigrants, he saw war service in North Africa before studying with Weisgall and Cowell at Peabody, with Dallapiccola in Florence (1951–2) and with Hanson and Hovhaness at the Eastman School (1954–7). He taught at the University of Minnesota (1958–97), where he helped found Center Opera (1964, later Minnesota Opera). Sharing the tastes of his audience, he has been able to write with total conviction in a style easily judged outmoded – though not so outmoded as to be incapable of incorporating, in the Poe opera, modernist elements of compositional technique and stagecraft.

Operas: *Christopher Sly* (John Manlove, after Shakespeare), f.p. Minneapolis, 1963; *Postcard from Morocco* (1 act: John Donahue), f.p. Minneapolis, 1971; *A Water Bird Talk* (monodrama: Argento, after Chekhov and Audobon), bar, orch, f.p. Brooklyn, 1977; *The Voyage of Edgar Allan Poe* (Charles Nolte), f.p. St Paul, 1976; *Miss Havisham's Fire* (John Olon-Scrymgeour, after Dickens), f.p. New York, 1979; *Casanova's Homecoming* (Argento), f.p. St Paul, 1985; *The Aspern Papers* (Argento, after Henry James), f.p. Dallas, 1988; *The Dream of Valentino* (Nolte), f.p. Washington, 1994; etc.
Other works: 6 Elizabethan Songs, s/t, pf, 1957, arr with Baroque ens 1962; *From the Diary of Virginia Woolf* (song cycle), mez, pf, 1974; other songs, choral music, orchestral pieces

Argerich, Martha (b. Buenos Aires, 5 Jun 1941). Argentinian pianist of urgent musicality, fierce precision and breathtaking technique. She made her debut in Buenos Aires when she was eight and left in 1955 to study with Friedrich Gulda in Vienna and with Madeleine Lipatti and Nikita Magaloff in Geneva. She won the Bolzano and Geneva competitions in 1957 and made her remarkable first DG recording in 1960, then broke off her rapidly developing career for further study with Stefan Askenase (1960–64), re-emerging to win the Chopin Competition in 1965. She was married to Dutoit from 1969 to 1973. For a while she led the life of a touring virtuoso, but, fearing exhaustion and personal dissolve, she stopped giving solo recitals in 1978 and made the last of her (rather few) solo recordings in 1984, preferring now to work regularly with a few chosen colleagues, including the duo partners Alexandre Rabino-vitch, Nelson Freire and Stephen Bishop-Kovacevich, and the cellist Mischa Maisky.

aria (It., air, pl. *arie*). Solo vocal piece, normally in an opera, though the term can also be used for opera-style pieces that exist in cantatas or oratorios, or independently (as in the CONCERT

ARIA). The aria is the occasion for a principal character to assess circumstances, make an explanation to another character or, most often, emote. It is the occasion, too, for display, from the composer and from the singer.

In Italian the word has had the general meaning of tune or melody since the late 15th century. The term gained its more restricted sense in English with the vogue for Italian opera in Handel's time, by which point the opera aria had become clearly distinguished from RECITATIVE. It had also gained a conventional form, that of the 'da capo aria', in which the first section is exactly repeated after a contrasting, usually more contemplative, second section, thus completing an ABA plan. If the singer is sent back not to the top (da capo) but to a sign part way through the first section (dal segno), the piece is known as a 'dal segno aria'.

These types ruled until the late 18th century, when the repetition of the first section began to be varied (producing varieties of ABA form) and new kinds of aria prospered, including the RONDÒ, the strophic aria (known to the 16th and 17th centuries) and the voluble patter song. The rondò model – slow–fast – became a new norm for 19th-century Italian opera, where the big solo number had two principal parts, the slow or moderate cantabile and the fast cabaletta, often separated by a *tempo di mezzo* in which some dramatic reason was given for the change of mood.

Arias of all these kinds were born in Italian music, and the term often implies delivery in Italian, with Italianate passion and formal sense. But varieties of ternary, strophic and binary (slow–fast) forms turn up occasionally in Wagner (e.g. Siegfried's Forging Song and Brünnhilde's Immolation), Strauss and Berg, as well as in Russian and French opera (though conspicuously not in *Pelléas*). Puccini's arias tend to be short, perhaps conditioned by the new recording medium. Subsequently – and indeed since the mid 19th century – many composers have sought a vocal style that would be lyrical without recourse to the symmetries and patterns that made the traditional aria.

aria con pertichini. Aria with interruptions or promptings from another character, usually lesser.

aria di sorbetto. Kind of aria written for the point in 18th-century theatres at which ices were served, as something loud was required to cover the noise of so many spoons.

Ariadne. In Greek mythology a Cretan princess who helped Theseus kill the Minotaur, left with the hero and was abandoned by him on the island of Naxos, where she died of grief or was borne away by Dionysus. Her story, with its opportunity for expressive lament in many tones, is among those that have been retold most often in music, in versions including the following:

(1) *Arianna*, lost opera by Monteverdi to a libretto by Rinuccini. Watched over by divinities and a chorus, Ariadne (soprano) and Theseus arrive on Naxos. Theseus leaves, for reasons of state. Ariadne awakes, unburdens herself of a grand lament (much admired, rescued from the rest of the score) and happily accepts Bacchus. First performance: Mantua, 28 May 1608.

(2) *Ariadne auf Naxos*, melodrama by Georg Benda with words by Johann Christian Brandes. Ariadne (speaking) awakes on Naxos in a sea of emotions and eventually throws herself from the clifftop. First performance: Gotha, 27 Jan 1775.

(3) *Arianna a Naxos*, cantata by Haydn for soprano and keyboard (?1789). A solo scena for the deserted Ariadne.

(4) *Ariadne auf Naxos*, opera by Strauss to a libretto by Hofmannsthal. Ariadne (soprano), alone from the start, has her lamentation largely ignored by three Nymphs and – worse – countered by a boisterous troupe of comedians, led by Zerbinetta (coloratura soprano), who back away at the triumphant and lengthy arrival of Bacchus (tenor). Originally the opera was preceded by a play with music, *Der Bürger als Edelmann*. In the revised version this was replaced by a sung Prologue, set backstage before the opera and featuring the Composer (mezzo-soprano). First performance: Stuttgart, 25 Oct 1912, rev Vienna, 4 Oct 1916.

(5) *Bacchus et Ariane*, ballet score by Roussel for choreography by Lifar. First performance: Paris, 22 May 1931.

(6) *Ariane*, opera by Martinů to his own libretto after Georges Neveux's play *Le Voyage de Thésée*. Theseus (baritone) arrives on Crete, falls in love with Ariadne (soprano), kills the Minotaur (bass), who is his earthier self, and leaves Ariadne. First performance: Gelsenkirchen, 2 Mar 1961.

(7) *Arianna*, opera by Goehr to Rinuccini's libretto, a late-20th-century slantwise restoration of Monteverdi's opera, incorporating his lament. First performance: London, 15 Sep 1995.

Porpora, Handel, Massenet and Milhaud also wrote Ariadne operas.

Ariane et Barbe-bleue (Ariadne and Bluebeard). Opera by Dukas to a libretto by Maeterlinck. Ariadne (mezzo-soprano), only very tangentially identified with the mythological character, is the new wife of Bluebeard (bass), whose realm is unsettled. She discovers his former wives locked away in his castle, and tries to persuade them to leave, but finally she goes without them. First performance: Paris, 10 May 1907.

arietta (It.) Short aria, though the most notable use of the term is for the theme of the variations-finale of Beethoven's last piano sonata, Op.111 in C minor.

ariette (Fr.). An adoption of the Italian *arietta*, but at first, in the operas of Campra and Rameau, with a quite different and special meaning: their *ariettes* were da capo arias on the Italian model, new to French music.

Ariettes oubliées (Forgotten Ariettas). Set of songs by Debussy, his first to poems by Verlaine, originally called *Ariettes, paysages belges et aquarelles* (1888), revised and republished under the new title 15 years later. The numbers are: 1 'C'est l'extase', 2 'Il pleure dans mon coeur', 3 'L'Ombre des arbres', 4 'Chevaux de bois', 5 'Green', 6 'Spleen'.

Ariodante. Opera by Handel to an anonymous revision of a libretto by Antonio Salvi after ARIOSTO. The prince Ariodante (mezzo-soprano castrato) and princess Ginevra of Scotland (soprano) are united after misdirections involving Dalinda (soprano, a too-clever confidante with erotic designs of her own), Polinesso (contralto, Ariodante's scheming rival) and Lurcanio (tenor, Ariodante's brother, good but confused). First performance: London, 8 Jan 1735.

The subject was a popular one, appearing in operas from Giovanni Maria Costa's *Ariodante* (f.p. Genoa, 1655) to examples in the mid-19th century, including other versions of the Salvi libretto by Vivaldi (f.p. Florence, 1736) and Wagenseil (f.p. Venice, 1745), and Méhul's *Ariodant* (f.p. Paris, 1799).

Arion (early 7th century BC). Greek poet-singer, inventor of the dithyramb, according to Herodotus, who also records the story of his being saved from drowning by a dolphin.

arioso (It., melodious). Lyrical style appearing in a recitative section; or a passage in that style. The term was used by Italian musicians from 1638, though its meaning did not settle down until the Classical period. Bach, for instance, applied it to lyrical recitative, a short aria, a chorale with recitative sections, an accompanied recitative and a quasi-vocal passage in an instrumental work (the Capriccio on the departure of a beloved brother). With the growth of accompanied recitative during the period from Mozart to Rossini, arioso came to be more strongly identified as a vocal form, though the term was still occasionally used for song-like instrumental passages (as in Beethoven's Op.110 piano sonata). There is arioso aplenty in Bellini and Verdi, and the term is also employed – ahistorically but usefully – for the fluid lyrical-reciting style of Monteverdi and his contemporaries.

Ariosti, Attilio (b. Bologna, 5 Nov 1666; d. London, 1728/9). Italian composer of flamboyant career: a monk who gained a taste for the high life of a diplomat-musician. He was an altarboy at San Petronio in Bologna and entered the Servite order there in 1688. In 1696 he moved to the Mantuan court and in 1697 to that of Sophie Charlotte, Electress of Brandenburg. She being Protestant, his order demanded he return to Bologna, but he stayed six years and then moved to Vienna, where he was appointed imperial agent in Italy (1707–11). There followed a shadowy period in which he served the future Louis XV. In 1716 he arrived in London, where he wrote operas for the Royal Academy, including most notably *Caio Marzio Coriolano* (1723), whose prison scene was admired by Rameau and Hawkins. The next year he published a volume of six cantatas and six lessons for the viola d'amore (which he played), dedicated to George I, the brother of his former employer Sophie Charlotte, with a list of subscribers including 293 peers and peeresses. But he soon ceased to be fashionable and died in poverty.

Ariosto, Ludovico (b. Reggio Emilia, 8 Sep 1474; d. Ferrara, 6 Jul 1533). Italian poet, whose principal work was the epic of chivalric fantasy *Orlando furioso*, vastly popular in the 16th century as a source of madrigal texts and in the Baroque period (and later) for opera subjects, notably those concerning ALCINA, ARIODANTE and ORLANDO.

Aristoxenus (b. Tarentum, now Taranto, Apulia, c.375–360 BC; d. ?Athens). Greek theorist, whose writings, though surviving only in fragments, provide our fullest evidence of ancient musical thinking, if not of ancient musical practice. A musician's son and follower of Aristotle, he objected to the Pythagoreans' view of musical intervals as number-determined and therefore fixed. Though he accepted the octave, fourth and fifth as primary consonances, divisions within them had sense only in the context of music as sound, and were therefore subject to subtle variability. He distinguished the three TETRACHORD genera and combined these in scales.

arithmetical durations. Note values from an arithmetical series, often up to 12; e.g. hemidemisemiquaver (1), demisemiquaver (2), dotted demisemiquaver (3), semiquaver (4), semiquaver tied to hemidemisemiquaver (5), ... dotted crotchet (12). They were introduced by Messiaen and Babbitt in the 1940s to create rhythmic serialism.

Arlésienne, L' (The Woman from Arles). Music by Bizet for Alphonse Daudet's play (in which the Arlésienne does not appear, though she produces drastic consequences), for small orchestra with chorus, using some Provençal tunes. The composer made a suite (No.1) out of four of the longer movements, rescored for full orchestra: 1 *Prélude*, 2 *Menuet*, 3 *Adagietto*, 4 *Carillon*. A second suite, by Ernest Guiraud, comprises: 1 *Pastoral*, 2 *Intermezzo*, 3 *Menuet* (from the opera *La jolie fille de Perth*), 4 *Farandole*. Besides its melodic vivacity, the score is notable for its early use of the saxophone. First performance: Paris, 1 Oct 1872.

Armida. Character from Tasso's *Gerusalemme liberata* of extraordinary operatic resilience. Tasso gives her a historical placing, as a Saracen princess at the time of the first crusade (1099), but her story on the opera stage often bends close to the sorceress Alcina's. She both loves and hates the Christian hero Rinaldo and spirits him away to a magic island. Two companions of his arrive and bring him to his senses by showing him his face in a polished shield. Relevant works include:

(1) Monteverdi's lost opera *Armida abbandonata*.

(2) Lully's opera *Armide*, to a libretto by Quinault, their last collaboration. It was specially renowned in the 18th century as a character study of Armide (soprano) and as a model of reform opera. Not only was the entire libretto (excluding the prologue) reset by Gluck, but the work also inspired versions by Traetta, Salieri, Sacchini, Naumann and Sarti, all in the 1770s–80s. First performance: Paris, 15 Feb 1686.

(3) Handel's opera *Rinaldo*, his first for London, to a libretto by Giacomo Rossi. The Saracen sorceress Armida (soprano) conjures away Almirena (soprano) from her beloved Rinaldo (mezzo-soprano castrato) but is confounded by Christian magic, beaten in battle and persuaded to convert. First performance: London, 24 Feb 1711.

(4) Gluck's opera *Armide*, to Quinault's libretto. First performance: Paris, 23 Sep 1777.

(5) Haydn's opera *Armida*, to a libretto by Nunziato Porta. Rinaldo (tenor) is in the power of Armida (soprano) from the start, but has his eyes opened by his crusader comrades and resists Armida's further magic. First performance: Eszterháza, 26 Feb 1784.

(6) Goethe's cantata text *Rinaldo* (1811), in which choral voices summon the hero to look in his shield and take up his duty. It was set at the time by Winter and later by Brahms.

(7) Rossini's opera *Armida*, to a libretto by Giovanni Schmidt. Having killed a comrade in a duel, Rinaldo (tenor) flees with Armida (soprano) to her enchanted palace, from which he is rescued by Carlo (tenor) and Ubaldo (tenor). First performance: Naples, 11 Nov 1817.

(8) Dvořák's opera *Armida*, to a libretto by Jaroslav Vrchlický. After the usual story comes the episode ascribed in Tasso to Tancredi and Clorinda (see Monteverdi's COMBATTIMENTO): Rinald (tenor) kills Armida (soprano) on the battlefield and christens her in her last moments. First performance: Prague, 25 Mar 1904.

armonica. Instrument invented by Benjamin Franklin in 1761 as an improvement on earlier methods of eliciting sounds from drinking glasses. Performance on glasses, well established in the Islamic world, gained a vogue in Europe in the 18th century: tuned with different quantities of water, the glasses would be (gently) struck with a stick or rubbed on the rim with a finger. Franklin substituted a graduated series of glasses fixed in line on a rotating spindle, operated by a pedal: the performer could then easily play chords and rapid runs with dampened hands. Later improvements included automatic wetting (by means of a trough of water through which the glasses turned) and a keyboard attachment. Mozart wrote a quintet for the armonica player Marianne Kirchgessner.

There was unease about the instrument's effect on the mind. According to some, physical contact with the ringing glasses would be psychologically damaging, yet Mesmer used the armonica's ethereal sounds to induce hypnotic trance. For Donizetti, in his original draft, the instrument was to accompany the heroine in the mad scene of *Lucia di Lammermoor* (1835), though by then its fashion was passing.

Arne, Thomas (Augustine) (b. London, 12 Mar 1710; d. London, 5 Mar 1778). British composer who worked energetically in the rumbustious world of theatre life in Hogarthian London. Born into a family of upholsterers and undertakers, he was educated at Eton and schooled in violin playing by the London violinist-composer Michael Christian Festing, who was only four years older. In 1726 he was apprenticed to an attorney, but he soon left for a life in music, which had to be also a life in the theatre, since as a Roman

Catholic he could not hold a church appointment. He presented his first opera, *Rosamond*, in 1733, and made important alliances by marriage: in 1734 his sister Susanna, the leading tragic actress in London, married the actor-manager Theophilus Cibber, and in 1737 he married Cecilia Young, an outstanding British soprano.

During the next few years he reached the height of success, with his setting of Milton's *Comus*, *Alfred* and some Shakespeare songs where his settings have become traditional. He then worked in Dublin (1742–4), collecting the future historian Burney as his apprentice on his return. His arrangement of the patriotic song 'God save the king' caught the public mood at the time of the 1745 Jacobite rebellion, and he also became a popular composer at the pleasure gardens, though by the 1750s his professional and personal fortunes were declining. During a second visit to Dublin (1755–6) he exchanged his wife for a mistress, Charlotte Brent, who starred in a new run of triumphs, among them his version of *The Beggar's Opera*, an attempt at opera seria in English (*Artaxerxes*) and the comic operas *Thomas and Sally* and *Love in a Village*. He also received an Oxford doctorate (1759). His switchback career then took another downturn before some final glories, including the ode he wrote for Garrick's 1769 Shakespeare festival in Startford. He was reconciled with his wife shortly before he died.

Michael Arne (*c*.1740–1786), seemingly his illegitimate son, was also a London theatre composer (whose most famous song was 'The lass with the delicate air', 1762), his other achievements including alchemy and the introduction of Handel's *Messiah* to Germany (1772).

Stage: COMUS, 1738; ALFRED, 1740; *Artaxerxes* (after Metastasio), f.p. London, 1762; *Thomas and Sally* (Bickerstaff), f.p. London, 1760; *Love in a Village* (Bickerstaff), f.p. London, 1762; etc.
Choral: *God save our noble king*, soli, ch, orch, 1745; *Judith* (oratorio; Bickerstaff), 1761; *An Ode upon Dedicating a Building to Shakespeare* (Garrick), soli, ch, orch, 1769; etc.
Instrumental: 8 Overtures, orch, pub 1751; 8 Sonatas or Lessons, hpd, pub 1756; 7 Trio Sonatas, pub 1757; 4 New Overtures or Symphonies, orch, pub 1767; 6 Favourite Concertos, kbd, orch, pub 1793; etc.
Songs: 'Blow, blow, thou winter's wind' (Shakespeare), 1740; 'Come away, death' (Shakespeare), 1741; 'Rule, Britannia', 1740; 'The soldier tir'd', 1762; 'Under the greenwood tree' (Shakespeare), 1740; 'Where the bee sucks' (Shakespeare), 1740; etc.

Arnell, Richard (Anthony Sayer) (b. London, 15 Sep 1917). British composer, pupil of Ireland at the RCM (1936–9) and author of ballet scores, symphonies and film music.

Arnold, Malcolm (Henry) (b. Northampton, 21 Oct 1921). British composer, knighted in 1993. He won a scholarship at 16 to the RCM, where he studied the trumpet and composition, preparatory to starting his career as an orchestral player. Receiving the Mendelssohn Scholarship (1948) persuaded him to concentrate on composition, and for a while thereafter he supported himself by writing film scores, among which that for *The Bridge on the River Kwai* (1957) won him an Oscar. Failing in health, he gave up composition in 1986, having brought to an end his cycle of nine symphonies, proud obeisances to Mahler, Vaughan Williams and Sibelius.

Symphonies: No.1, Op.22, 1949; No.2, Op.40, 1953; No.3, Op.63, 1957; No.4, Op.71, 1960; No.5, op.74, 1960; No.6, Op.95, 1967; No.7, Op.113, 1973; No.8, Op.124, 1978; No.9, Op.128, 1986
Other works: *Tam O'Shanter* (overture), Op.51, 1955; 4 Scottish Dances, Op.59, 1957; concertos, songs, film scores, chamber music (Brass Quintet No.1, Op.73, 1961; Clarinet Sonatina, Op.29, 1951), etc.

Arnold, Samuel (b. London, 10 Aug 1740; d. London, 22 Oct 1802). British musician, reputedly the child of Princess Amelia, daughter of George II. After training as a chorister in the Chapel Royal he led a busy career as a theatre composer, church musician, philanthropist and scholar.

Arom, Simha (b. Düsseldorf, 16 Aug 1930). Israeli–French music scholar, whose studies of African oral polyphony (*African Polyphony and Polyrhythm*, 1991) stimulated Berio and Ligeti. He studied the horn at the Paris Conservatoire (1951–4) and was an orchestral musician in Israel (1958–63) before working in the Central African Republic (1963–7). Since then he has been based in Paris.

arpa (It., pl. *arpe*). Harp.

arpège (Fr.). Arpeggio.

arpeggiando. Instruction to perform a chord as an arpeggio.

arpeggiation. The playing or writing of chords in arpeggio fashion.

arpeggio. Chord sounded note by note, normally from the bottom up. The term comes from the It. *arpeggiare* (to play the harp). The arpeggios most often encountered are those of the major and minor triads.

Arpeggione. Name given to the sonata Schubert wrote for a shortlived instrument that was, in retrospect, named after the work. Its 1823 inventors, J.G. Staufer of Vienna and Peter Teufelsdorfer of Pest, called it *Bogengitarre* (bowed guitar). It was, indeed, a bowed guitar, well suited to arpeggios but not, as it happened, to a continuing existence in the musical world. Schubert's sonata has become a centrepiece of the cello repertory.

arrangement. Adaptation of music from one medium to another. If the source or destination is a keyboard composition, the term TRANSCRIPTION is sometimes used. If the destination is a score for orchestra or instrumental ensemble, ORCHESTRATION and INSTRUMENTATION are alternative terms, though 'arrangement' is most common when speaking of less prestigious genres, notably the musical, where even the most adept composers (Bernstein, for example) may leave scoring to a collaborator: the arranger. Arrangement in the commercial world is a necessary and regular activity: scores may have to be adpated for new circumstances, often fast.

So things stood, too, in what might now be regarded as nobler musical realms, at least until the 20th century. Scores would be changed for different uses, whether by their composers or others. Bach and Handel frequently reworked their music and not infrequently arranged that of colleagues they admired. Also, publishers, home musicians and practical performing needs all required arrangements (in the forms of PIANO REDUCTION, VOCAL SCORE, etc.) and large works – operatic medleys, symphonies, etc. – were distributed far more widely in the 19th and early 20th centuries as piano duets than in their original dress.

With the coming of recording, the home market for arranged music virtually disappeared, and arrangement was left as a field for imagination and enterprise. Ravel presented many of his works in both orchestral and piano forms, but now the former was not necesarily an outgrowth and the latter by no means always a monochrome impression: both had equal authority and importance. Stravinsky extended the artistry of arrangement to music other than his own and created works, from *Pulcinella* onwards, in which it is hard to say what is composed and what arranged. So it is in many of Berio's scores, where – as with Stravinsky – the choice of music to be arranged is itself a creative act, and the treatment may be entirely personal to the arranger.

Arrau, Claudio (b. Chillán, 6 Feb 1903; d. Mürzzuschlag, Austria, 9 Jun 1991). Chilean–US pianist of majestic aplomb, who made his debut at five in Santiago and studied with Martin Krause at the Stern Conservatory in Berlin (1912–18). While there he absorbed much from other pianists, including Carreño and Busoni, but Krause was his only teacher, and after Krause's death in the 1918–19 flu epidemic he did not seek another. He made a return visit to South America in 1921 and a US tour two years later, then taught at his alma mater (1924–40). In 1941 he settled with his family in New York; in 1967 he renounced his Chilean citizenship in political protest, and did not revisit his country until 1984. Continuing to perform and record into his 80s, he was particularly admired in Beethoven, Brahms, Chopin and Liszt.

Arriaga (y Balzola), Juan Crisóstomo (Jacobo Antonio) de (b. Bilbao, 27 Jan 1806; buried Paris, 17 Jan 1826). Spanish composer, popularized long after his death as 'the Spanish Mozart', though what he had was more a Schubertian promise. He began composing at 11, encouraged and promoted by his father and elder brother. In 1821 he went to Paris, where he studied counterpoint and fugue with Fétis, and where he died, seemingly of exhaustion and a lung infection, leaving a symphony in D minor, the overture to a mostly lost opera (*Los esclavos felices*) and a published (1824) set of quartets in D minor, A and E♭.

Arrival of the Queen of Sheba. Short descriptive orchestral passage in Handel's SOLOMON.

ars antiqua (Lat., old practice). Term introduced by both radicals and conservatives among music theorists of the early 14th century debating the virtues of the old way and the new (ARS NOVA). Their ars antiqua went back only a few decades, covering the period around 1250–1320, when the CONDUCTUS and MOTET were dominant forms, but the term is now often understood to include as well the NOTRE DAME SCHOOL polyphony of the preceding 70 years or so.

arsis, thesis (Gk, raising, lowering). Upbeat, downbeat: the terms are derived from Greek poetry and, beyond that, dance. Zarlino confusingly introduced the term *per arsin et thesin* for the inversion of a contrapuntal subject.

ars nova (Lat., new practice). Term used at the time for the new style made possible in particular by the rhythmic innovations of Philippe de Vitry's treatise *Ars nova* (*c*.1322). This established four grades of DURATION distinguished by different signs, and not by ligatures as in earlier notation:

the long, breve, semibreve and minim, each with its own rest. The three relationships between these grades had names – modus (long-breve), tempus (breve-semibreve) and prolation (semibreve-minim) – and any of these relationships could be either perfect (three smaller units per larger one) or imperfect (two smaller units per larger one). Perfect tempus (T³) plus perfect prolation (P³) would constitute a ninefold metre: 9/8, as it were. Other combinations of tempus and prolation would generate 6/8 (T²P³), 3/4 (T³P²) and 2/4 (T²P²). Red ink would indicate a momentary change from imperfect to perfect time or vice versa. After de Vitry the dot was added as a means of making an imperfect duration perfect, i.e. adding half the value, in the way that has survived to the present. Also, it was possible for a semibreve to be divided into six, five or four parts as well as three or two: in other words, the notion of a smaller value (the future crotchet) was being introduced. All these developments allowed a greater range of metres and rhythmic values to be defined; at the same time compositions became longer and structures more intricate, within a small number of forms (the BALLADE, RONDEAU, VIRELAI and MOTET).

The term 'ars nova' began to be used for a historical period only in the early 20th century and has had varying connotations. At its widest, it could embrace all music from the early 14th century to the start of the Renaissance. Most narrowly, it has been applied just to French music from the ROMAN DE FAUVEL (?1317) to the death of Machaut (1377), though it seems unnecessary to leave out Italian music of the period (e.g. Landini's), similar in its lyrical spring, aspiration to personal feeling and formal agility.

ars subtilior (Lat., subtler practice). Term introduced by Ursula Günther in 1960 for the songs produced at Francophone courts in Provence (notably Avignon), Aragon and Cyprus c.1380–1410, pushing the rhythmic intricacy of the ars nova to a point of high refinement and even decadence. The principal sources for this repertory are the CHANTILLY and MODENA manuscripts.

Artaria. Viennese publishing firm run by the Artaria cousins: Francesco (1744–1808) and Carlo (1747–1808) from 1768, joined later by Pasquale (1755–85), Ignazio (1757–1820) and Domenico (1765–1823). They moved into music in 1778 and produced fine editions of many works by Haydn, Mozart and the young Beethoven.

Art de toucher le clavecin, L' (The Art of Playing the Harpsichord). Instructional volume by Couperin (1716), including eight preludes.

articulation. Projection in performance of individual notes or of phrases or sections. Where single notes are concerned, articulation depends on subtleties of rhythm, attack and the shaping of dynamics and colour, whether prompted by indications (STACCATO, LEGATO, the SLUR, etc.) or not. The articulation of phrase structure and form will additionally involve rubato and all the other elements of PHRASING.

artificial harmonic. HARMONIC produced on a stopped string of a string instrument.

art music. Term used in opposition to folk or religious music: Vietnamese art music, for example, would be presumed to include the traditions of royal courts and wealthy households, but not those of temples and popular music-making. In a western context, the term is awkward; 'classical music' better distinguishes the kinds considered in these pages.

Art of Fugue, The. See *Die* KUNST DER FUGE.

Artôt, (Marguerite Joséphine) Désirée (Montagney) (b. Paris, 21 Jul 1835; d. Berlin, 3 Apr 1907). Belgian soprano. Belonging to a distinguished musical family, she studied in Paris with Viardot and made her debut there in 1858. Thereafter she appeared most often in Germany. She also visited Russia, in 1868, winning a proposal from Tchaikovsky, though she married a Spanish baritone and with him had a daughter, Lola Artôt de Padilla (1876–1933), who was also a singer.

Arts Florissants, Les. Ensemble directed by William Christie, named after the Charpentier work they gave at their first concert (Paris, 1979) and specializing in French Baroque music. They have been involved in theatrical productions, beginning with a notable *Atys* (1986).

art song. Song from within the category of classical music, as opposed to a popular song or folksong – though songs of these kinds get defined as art songs when arranged by distinguished composers.

Artyomov, Vyacheslav (Petrovich) (b. Moscow, 29 Jun 1940). Russian composer concerned with the transcendent, often on a grand scale and with emanations of Scriabin. He studied with Nikolay Sidelnikov at the Moscow Conservatory (1962–8) and in 1975 began working occasionally with

Gubaidulina and Suslin in the improvisation group Astraea. His compositions include *The Way to Olympus* for orchestra (1978–84) and ritualized percussion works.

Arutiunian, Aleksandr Grigori (b. Yerevan, 23 Sep 1920). Armenian composer in the Khachaturian tradition. He studied at the conservatories of Yerevan and Moscow (1946–8) and began teaching at the former in 1965. His works include concertos for trumpet (1950) and violin (1988).

As (Ger.). A♭.

A.S. *al* SEGNO.

Asafyev, Boris (Vladimirovich) (b. St Petersburg, 29 Jul 1884; d. Moscow, 27 Jan 1949). Russian composer and, under the pseudonym of Igor Glebov, critic. He studied with Rimsky-Korsakov and Lyadov at the St Petersburg Conservatory (1904–10) and began work as a theatre répétiteur and librarian. In 1925 he started teaching at his old conservatory, and the next year he was a founder of the Leningrad branch of the Association for Contemporary Music. He wrote the first Russian book on Stravinsky (1929). In the 1930s he began devoting more time to composition (four symphonies date from 1938–42), but following his move to Moscow, in 1943, he concentrated again on scholarship and official activities.

Asas (Ger.). A♭♭.

ASCAP. American Society of Composers, Authors and Publishers, US performing rights agency.

Ascension, L' (The Ascension). Orchestral work ('symphonic meditations') by Messiaen in four movements: 1 *Majesté du Christ demandant sa gloire à son Père*, 2 *Alléluias séreins d'une âme qui désire le ciel*, 3 *Alléluia sur la trompette, alléluia sur la cymbale*, 4 *Prière du Christ montant vers son Père*. The third is replaced in the composer's organ transcription by the exultant *Transports de joie*. First performance: Paris, 9 Feb 1935 (orch), 28 May 1935 (org).

The theme of Christ's Ascension is also treated in several Bach cantatas and a Biber sonata.

Ashkenazy, Vladimir (Davidovich) (b. Gorky, 6 Jul 1937). Russian–Icelandic pianist and conductor. He studied with Anaida Sumbatyan at the Central School of Music in Moscow (1945–55) and then with Lev Oborin at the Conservatory. In 1962 he won the Tchaikovsky Competition, jointly with Ogdon, and the next year he defected to the West,

with his Icelandic wife. A player of formidable brilliance and beauty of tone, especially in his early Chopin recordings, he turned more and more to conducting, at first in Iceland, where he settled in 1969, but increasingly through the 1970s in more central locations, eventually becoming music director of the RPO (1987–94) and the Czech Philharmonic (from 1998).

Ashley, Robert (Reynolds) (b. Ann Arbor, Mich., 28 Mar 1930). US composer, especially of theatre works featuring his own downbeat narrative voice. He studied at Ann Arbor (1947–52), at the Manhattan School of Music, and then back at Ann Arbor (1957–60), where he was associated with a lively group of colleagues that included Lucier, Mumma and David Behrman. Together they founded the Sonic Arts Union (1966–73), giving live electronic performances; his most regular spot with them was *The Wolfman* (1964). With *Perfect Lives (Private Parts)* (1977–83) he brought his personal style to the unlikely medium of the television serial, a form he has gone on pursuing.

Ashwell, Thomas (b. *c*.1478; d. after 1513). English composer and church musician, a chorister at St George's Chapel, Windsor (1491–3), possibly Taverner's teacher at Tattershall in the early 1500s, and from 1513 cantor at Durham Cathedral.

Asia. See CHINA; GAGAKU; GAMELAN; INDIA; ISLAM; JAPAN; JEWISH MUSIC; ORIENTALISM; TURKEY.

Asko Ensemble. Amsterdam modern-music ensemble founded in 1966 as the Amsterdams Studenten Kamer Orkest and soon thereafter fully professional, with no permanent conductor. It has given first performances of works by Ligeti, Carter, etc.

Aspen. Colorado mountain resort, site of an annual summer festival since 1949, coming to involve student programmes as well as performances.

Asplmayr, Franz (baptized Linz, 2 Apr 1728; d. Vienna, 29 Jul 1786). Austrian violinist-composer, whose works have been mistaken for Haydn's. He worked under Haydn in Count Morzin's musical establishment (1759–61), during which time he married. Later he gained note in Vienna as a ballet composer (his father had been a dancing master), especially with *Agamemnon vengé* (1771). He also played in the quartet that first performed Haydn's Op.33 and was himself the author of around 40 quartets, as well as a similar number of symphonies.

assai (It.). Very. But though the marking *allegro assai* should therefore mean very fast, many non-Italian composers – Beethoven among them – have understood *assai* in the sense of the Fr. ASSEZ.

assez (Fr.). Rather, moderately. Hence *assez lent* (rather slowly).

Associated Board of the Royal Schools of Music. London body founded in 1889 with responsibility for examinations in music theory and performance at pre-conservatory levels. The board also publishes careful and helpful editions of classic keyboard works.

Association for Contemporary Music (Assotsiatsiya Sovremennoy Muzïki). Soviet organization active 1924–31 in promulgating new Western music.

Aston, Hugh (b. *c*.1485; buried Leicester, 17 Nov 1558). English composer and church musician. He was active in Leicester by 1525, having previously been in Coventry and perhaps London. His works include sacred works and a striking keyboard piece, *A Hornepype*.

Aston, Peter (b. Birmingham, 5 Oct 1938). British composer, especially of church music partly informed by his admiration for the exuberant lyricism of George Jeffreys. He studied at York University, and taught there (1964–74) before becoming professor at the University of East Anglia.

Astorga, Baron **Emanuele (Gioacchino Cesare Rincón) d'** (b. Augusta, Sicily, 20 Mar 1680; d. ?). Italian composer, of colourful and partly misty life. He probably studied in Palermo, where he began his career; he then went to Rome, and after 1709 visited other Italian cities, Barcelona and Vienna. In 1714 he returned home to claim his title. He married in 1717 and fathered three daughters, but in 1721 he left his lands and family to travel to Lisbon and never came back. There are uncertain traces of him later in London and Madrid, but if he wanted to vanish, he did. He left numerous cantatas, some operas and a *Stabat mater* in C minor.

asymmetry. Applied to music, the term usually denotes lack of rhythmic regularity, whether due to changing metre, cross-rhythm or absence of stable pulse.

Atalanta. Opera by Handel to an anonymous adaptation of Belisario Valeriano's libretto. The work is a pastoral, concerning the love of Meleager (soprano castrato) for Atalanta (soprano) alongside that of Amyntas (tenor) for Irene (contralto). Meleager's aria 'Care selve' is often heard alone. First performance: London, 12 May 1736.

atemlos (Ger). Breathlessly.

Atempause (Ger.). Pause as if for breath, sometimes indicated by a comma above the barline.

a tempo (It., in time). Return to strict tempo.

Athalia. Oratorio by Handel to words by Samuel Humphreys after Racine's play. Athalia (soprano), queen of Judah, has deserted Jehovah for Baal, and is supplanted by her grandson Joas (treble) at the behest of his aunt Josabeth (soprano) and her husband, the high-priest Joad (countertenor). First performance: Oxford, 10 Jul 1733.

Atmosphères. Orchestral work by Ligeti, composed of sustained sound in gradual change. First performance: Donaueschingen, 22 Oct 1961.

atonal. Not manifesting a key, mode or pitch centre.

atonality. Absence of tonality: the term only makes sense in the context of this binary opposition. Atonal music is music freed from the sense of a keynote, or of a note or chord towards which the piece must move to close. Also, the term belongs to a particular period. At a time when tonality was universal – to the extent that there was really no word for it – atonality represented a clear break. Thus Schoenberg's works of 1908–12 are very readily described as atonal, and the term also fits music that he and other composers (Berg, Webern, Varèse, Ives) produced during the next three or four decades. But after that, inevitably, the atonality–tonality dichotomy lost its relevance. For one thing, music came to move freely across the barrier, as Berg's had done since the 1920s. For another, the tonal alternative was no longer necessarily the symphonic language of the central repertory: it might be, rather, a kind of world modality embracing non-Western traditions, as in Boulez. So although 'atonality' seems to be a technical term, it is just as much a historical and cultural label. For music of the later 20th century – Ligeti's, in which diatonic-seeming thirds and other harmonic intervals wander free of tonal gravitation, or that of SPECTRAL composers, whose music may suggest a pitch centre by means of highly complex chords – the label is obsolete.

Atonal music, as usually understood, exists only in the Western tradition, where it arrived as a result of the progressive harmonic exploration of the Romantic period. In retrospect, the initial chord of Wagner's *Tristan* can be understood as opening the door, in 1858, but it took another half-century before Schoenberg stepped through. Meanwhile Liszt, in some of his late piano pieces, such as *Nuages gris* (1881) or the strikingly titled *Bagatelle sans tonalité* (1885), moved some steps nearer atonality. For long periods the music seems to float, with no harmonic anchor, or strongly dissonant chords, especially the diminished seventh, take on greater permanence and prominence. Atonality is also evoked in some of Strauss's music, especially *Elektra* (1906–8), which came so near in time to Schoenberg's first atonal works: the finale of his Second Quartet and the first songs of the cycle *Das Buch der hängenden Gärten* (1908).

Schoenberg thus founded the first and central atonal school, but there were others, notably those stemming from Scriabin's late music (especially *Vers la flamme* and other piano pieces of 1914) or propelled by a spirit of independence in the USA, where Ives's example and Charles Seeger's ideal (of dissonant counterpoint) had a strong influence on Cowell, Ruggles and others. In the same period Busoni made his own extrapolations from Liszt and Schoenberg to create a wide harmonic world in which atonality has a part.

Sometimes the term is reserved exclusively for the music produced by Schoenberg and his major pupils – Berg and Webern – between their last tonal works and their first serial ones, but it is best understood as an ideal sought (or avoided) by many composers during the eight or nine decades after *Tristan*.

attacca (It., proceed!). Instruction to go on to the next movement or section without a break, may be reinforced as *attacca subito* (proceed at once).

attack. Initiation of a note. Distinct attack is often necessary for good sound, rhythm and phrasing, but not always.

Attaingnant, Pierre (b. ?Douai, *c*.1494; d. Paris, 1551/2), French music publisher, of chansons in large numbers from 1527/8 on and also of dances and sacred music. His widow continued the business.

Atterberg, Kurt (Magnus) (b. Gothenburg, 12 Dec 1887; d. Stockholm, 15 Feb 1974). Swedish composer, in the national Romantic-impressionist manner emanating from Alfvén. He studied as a civil engineer and spent his working life in the patent office, though he also had some musical training in Stockholm with Hallén and in Germany, and was active as a conductor, administrator and critic. His Sixth Symphony (of nine) won the prize offered in 1928 by the Gramophone Company for a work to mark the centenary of Schubert's death.

Attila. Opera by Verdi to a libretto by Solera after a play by Zacharias Werner. Attila the Hun (bass), at war with the Roman forces under Aetius (EZIO, baritone), falls victim to his beloved captive Odabella (soprano), who has stayed true to Foresto (tenor). First performance: Venice, 17 Mar 1846.

Attwood, Thomas (baptized London, 23 Nov 1765; d. London, 24 Mar 1838). British composer who studied with Mozart in Vienna (1785–7). The son of a royal musician, he was a Chapel Royal chorister and in 1783 was sent abroad to study by the Prince of Wales; he went first to Naples. On his return he stayed close to the British court, and became organist of St Paul's and composer to the Chapel Royal (1796), besides other appointments. He was also a founder of the Philharmonic Society and the RAM. His works include anthems and theatre music.

Atys. Opera by Lully to a libretto by Quinault after an episode in Ovid's *Fasti*. Attis (haute-contre) is torn by his love for Sangaride (soprano), his loyalty to her betrothed Celaenus (baritone) and his duty to the goddess Cybele (soprano), who loves him. He kills Sangaride in a fit of madness induced by Cybele and, on recovering, stabs himself. First performance: St Germain-en-Laye, 10 Jan 1676.

aubade. Dawn song, from Fr. *aube* (dawn). Musical morning greetings were played for Baroque-period French kings, and the *Siegfried Idyll* is a later example, but the practice has by no means as long and varied a life as boasts the serenade. There are fancifully titled aubades by Bizet, Lalo and Poulenc.

Auber, Daniel (François Esprit) (b. Caen, 29 Jan 1782; d. Paris, 12 May 1871). French composer, who in middle age dominated the Parisian opera stage. His father, a dealer in art materials, sent him to London for commercial training (1802–3), and there he began his life as a performing musician and composer. Back in Paris he composed concertos, studied with Cherubini, befriended Ingres and made himself useful at musical salons. His father's bankruptcy caused him to focus on making his fortune in the opera world, which he duly did. His *La Muette de Portici* (1828) was significant both musically, as one of the founding works of French grand opera, and politically, for the role it played – as an opera about revolution – in Belgium's achievement of independence in 1830. From 1842 he was director of the Paris Conservatoire.

Operas: *La Muette de Portici* (Scribe and Delavigne), f.p. Paris, 1828; *Fra Diavolo* (Scribe), f.p. Paris, 1830; *Le Domino noir* (Scribe), f.p. Paris, 1837; *Les Diamants de la couronne* (Scribe and Saint-Georges), f.p. Paris, 1841; MANON LESCAUT, f.p. Paris, 1856; etc.
Other works: sacred music, cantatas, etc.

Au bord d'une source. Piano piece by Liszt, from his ANNEES DE PELERINAGE.

... au delà du hasard (... Beyond Chance). Work by Barraqué, part of his *La Mort de Virgile*, setting his own heated poetic commentary on a quotation from Broch and scored for three women's voices with wind and percussion groups. First performance: Paris, 26 Jan 1960.

Auden, W(ystan) H(ugh) (b. York, 21 Feb 1907; d. Vienna, 29 Sep 1973). British poet who worked with Britten on various projects in 1935–41 and later wrote librettos in collaboration with his lover Chester Kallman for Stravinsky (*The Rake's Progress*) and Henze (*Elegy for Young Lovers, The Bassarids*).

audience. Word sometimes used to mean not just the people at a particular event but a notional population, 'the audience', which is presumed to share likes and dislikes. However, there is no uniform audience but a variety, differing in interests, tastes, degrees of commitment and spending power. In most Western cities there are audiences for new music, for early music, for improvisation – audiences that may overlap with each other more than they do with the audience of subscribers to symphony concerts.

audition. (1) Practical trial of a musician being considered for a job. Also used as a verb: one auditions at an audition.
(2) Archaic term for hearing music at a concert or whatever (but current in Fr.).

Auer, Leopold (b. Veszprém, 7 Jun 1845; d. Loschwitz, near Dresden, 15 Jul 1930). Hungarian violinist, a strong influence on the Russian violin school through his long tenure as professor at the St Petersburg Conservatory (1868–1917): his students included Elman, Zimbalist, Milstein and Heifetz. He himself studied in Budapest, in Vienna and in Hamburg with Joachim (1863–4).

Aufforderung zum Tanze (Invitation to the Dance). Concert waltz for piano by Weber, orchestrated by Berlioz as *L'Invitation à la valse*, and used in that form for *Le Spectre de la rose* (1911), one of the early Ballets Russes successes, starring Nijinsky.

Aufführung (Ger., pl. *Aufführungen*). Performance.

aufhalten (Ger.). Hold back.

Aufstieg und Fall der Stadt Mahagonny (Rise and Fall of Mahagonny City). Opera by Weill to a libretto by Brecht, based on a 'songspiel' by the authors (1927). Mahagonny is a den of inquity where the pursuit of money besmirches and enfeebles human relationships. If these nevertheless continue, the effect and the outlook are bleak. First performance: Leipzig, 9 Mar 1930.

Aufstrich (Ger.). Upbow.

Auftakt (Ger.). Upbeat.

Auftritt (Ger., pl. *Auftritte*). Scene (of an opera, etc.).

Aufzug (Ger., pl. *Aufzugen*). Act (of an opera, etc.).

Augenmusik (Ger.). EYE MUSIC.

augment. (1) Increase an interval by a semitone: hence augmented second (e.g. D–E♯), augmented fourth (G–C♯), etc.
(2) Proportionally increase the note values of a theme. A fugue will often include towards the end a statement of the theme in augmentation, at half speed (i.e. with the values doubled) and thus imposing. An augmentation may also increase the values fourfold or by some other multiple.

augmentation. See AUGMENT (2).

augmented interval. See AUGMENT (1).

augmented sixth chord. Chord in which the tonic is heard with its flattened submediant and an augmented sixth on that note (hence A♭–C–F♯ in C major). Varieties include the FRENCH SIXTH,

GERMAN SIXTH and ITALIAN SIXTH, all these names quite arbitrary.

augmented triad. Major triad with the fifth augmented, e.g. C–E–G♯. This is a symmetrical chord, dividing the octave into three major thirds (reading enharmonically). It is therefore ambiguous in terms of its key affiliations.

aulos. Ancient Greek wind instrument, a pair of reed pipes, played by professional auletes and amateurs.

aumentata, aumentato (It.). Augmented.

aural tests. Tests of the EAR (2), a regular part of music exams.

Auric, Georges (b. Lodève, 15 Feb 1899; d. Paris, 23 Jul 1983). French composer who was a member of Les SIX in his youth and in the 1930s–50s wrote film scores for directors including René Clair (*A nous la liberté*, 1930), Cocteau (*La Belle et la bête*, 1946) and John Huston (*Moulin Rouge*, 1952). Precocious, he studied at the Paris Conservatoire (1913–14) and the Schola Cantorum, and was moving in avant-garde circles by the time he was 15. He wrote ballets for Diaghilev (*Les Fâcheux*, 1923; *Les Matelots*, 1924), and was still interesting himself in innovation half a century later, when his *Imaginées* series for small groupings (1968–76) and *Double-jeux* for two pianos (1970–71) indicated his presence at Boulez's Domaine Musical concerts. He was also head of the Paris Opera (1962–8).

Aus den sieben Tagen (From the Seven Days). Book by Stockhausen of 15 text compositions, i.e. verbal incitements to music, composed during five (not seven) days of meditative withdrawal (7–11 May 1968).

Ausdruck (Ger.). Expression. Hence *mit Ausdruck* (with expression), etc.

Ausgabe (Ger., pl. *Ausgaben*). Edition.

Austin, Larry (Don) (b. Duncan, Okla., 12 Sep 1930). US composer, specializing in electronics and improvisation. He studied at Mills College with Milhaud and at Berkeley with Imbrie, got to know Cage, Tudor and Stockhausen, and taught at the universities of South Florida (1972–8) and North Texas (1978–96). Apart from original works in diverse media he made a completion of Ives's *Universe Symphony*.

Australia. Organized musical life on the European (essentially British) model began in the mid 19th century, when choral societies were established in Melbourne, Sydney and Adelaide. For a long time professional musicians made careers largely abroad, whether as singers (Melba, Sutherland), conductors (Mackerras) or composers (Grainger, Banks, Lumsdaine), though by the 1950s–70s the country was beginning to take hold of its own musical destiny, with such signal events as the opening of the magnificent Sydney Opera House (1973) and with the arrival of numerous native and immigrant composers, including Antill, Sculthorpe, Meale, Edwards, Smalley, Yu and Dean. Institutions include the Sydney Conservatorium (1917), the symphony orchestras of Melbourne (1906) and Sydney (1908), Opera Australia (founded as Elizabethan Trust Opera in 1956) and the Perth Festival (1953).

Warren Bebbington, ed. *The Oxford Companion to Australian Music* (1997)

Austria (Österreich). Its musical history is largely that of its capital VIENNA, and of SALZBURG.

Auszug (Ger.). Reduction, especially in *Klavierauszug* (piano reduction).

authentic cadence. PERFECT CADENCE.

authenticity. Watchword of the EARLY MUSIC revival in the 1970s–80s, implying that the use of period instruments and styles would produce a more genuine performance. Contentious, the term has been generally dropped, and replaced by the more sustainable claim of HISTORICALLY INFORMED performance.

authentic mode. Church MODE in which the final is the lowest note. In a PLAGAL MODE this is not so.

autograph. SOURCE written by the composer.

auxiliary note. Momentary addition or departure, a half or full step away from the principal note to which return is immediately made, as in a trill or mordent.

avant-garde (Fr., vanguard). Term in use in France since the 1820s to signify a group or movement of artists at the head of social or cultural progress. In musical contexts the word is particularly associated with those young European composers of the 1950s–60s who embraced serialism, electronic music, new means of performance, etc. ('avant-garde techniques'), notably Boulez, Stockhausen,

Nono and their allies. At that time the term was also applied to earlier phases of MODERNISM. It is less useful in the more complex musical world that has supervened, with many diverse attitudes to innovation.

Avanti! Finnish chamber orchestra founded in 1983 by Salonen and Saraste, with a special emphasis on new music.

Ave Maria (Hail Mary). Latin prayer formulated in the 15th century, set by Josquin, Victoria, Verdi, Stravinsky, etc. Schubert's *Ave Maria* is one of his songs after Walter Scott. The ubiquitous Gounod version sets the prayer to a melody over the C major prelude from the first book of Bach's *Das wohltemperierte Clavier*.

Ave maris stella (Hail star of the sea). Vespers hymn, whose beautiful melody appears in a Victoria mass and a setting of the hymn by Monteverdi.

Aventures (Adventures). Forming with *Nouvelles aventures* (New Adventures) a pair of works by Ligeti for three singers (s, mez, bar) and seven instrumentalists (fl, hn, vc, db, hpd, pf, perc), consisting of short wordless scenes assembled in cartoon-strip fashion. First performance: Hamburg, 4 Apr 1963 (*Aventures*), 26 May 1966 (complete).

Ave regina coelorum (Hail Queen of the heavens). MARIAN ANTIPHON set polyphonically by Du Fay, Josquin, Palestrina and Victoria, of whom Du Fay and Victoria based masses on their settings.

Ave verum corpus (Hail true body). Latin hymn set by Josquin, Byrd, Mozart, etc.

Avison, Charles (baptized Newcastle upon Tyne, 16 Feb 1709; d. Newcastle upon Tyne, 9/10 May 1770). British musician who put his home town on the musical map and wrote concertos of more than local importance. Son of a wait (town musician), he probably studied in London with Geminiani before returning to Newcastle in 1735 to work as an organist and concert director. In his *An Essay on Musical Expression* (1753) he praised Geminiani and Marcello above Handel, and that preference informs his concertos (which include 12 after Scarlatti sonatas). He also wrote chamber sonatas and a little church music. His sons Edward (1747–76) and Charles (1751–95) were Newcastle musicians after him.

Avni, Tzvi (b. Saarbrücken, 2 Sep 1927). German–Israeli composer strongly marked by contact with electronic music at Columbia under Ussachevsky (1962–4). Before that he followed the 'Mediterranean style' of music in Palestine–Israel, where he had arrived with his family as a child and studied, with Ben-Haim and Abel Ehrlich. In 1971 he began teaching at the Rubin Academy in Jerusalem. His output is strong in orchestral and choral pieces.

Avshalomov, Jacob (David) (b. Qingdao, China, 28 Mar 1919). Russian–US composer, especially of choral music. The son of Aaron Avshalomoff (1894–1965), a self-taught composer who settled in China after the Russian Revolution and integrated Chinese elements into his symphonies, concertos and operas, he moved to the USA in 1937 to study with Toch in Los Angeles and Rogers at the Eastman School. He taught at Columbia (1946–54) before becoming conductor of the Portland (Oregon) Youth Philharmonic (1954–95).

Ax, Emanuel (b. Lwów/Lviv, 8 Jun 1949). Polish–US pianist, of intelligent elegance. He arrived with his family in New York in 1961, and studied with Mieczysław Munz at the Juilliard School, as well as at Columbia. Besides the regular solo repertory he has cultivated chamber music (with Ma, Stern, etc.) and new works (Adams's *Century Rolls*, Birtwistle's *The Axe Manual*).

ayre. Old spelling of 'air', sometimes used in modern writing to distinguish the lute-song repertory.

Ayrton, William (b. London, 22 Feb 1777; d. London, 8 May 1858). British musician whose multifarious achievements included the first British performance of *Don Giovanni* in full (1817) and much work, through magazines, in informing and cultivating public taste. He was the son of Edmund Ayrton (1734–1808), an organist-composer at court.

azione sacra (It., sacred action). Staged oratorio. Metastasio and Zeno used the term for their oratorio texts; works of this kind were given in Neapolitan theatres during Lent in the late 18th century and early 19th.

azione teatrale (It., theatrical action). Metastasio's term for a serenata with some staging. An example is his *Il sogno di Scipione*, set by Mozart among others.

B. Note name, hence B major, B♭, etc. In German usage, though, B indicates B♭, and B is indicated by H. B minor, therefore, is H-moll and so on.

The characters of keys are surely influenced not only by acoustic, practical and notational factors – how well particular keys suit particular instruments, how easy they are to read – but also by their histories in the literature of music. B major, for example, may owe a lot of its confident and sensuous allure to Wagner's *Tristan*, B minor much of its intimate darkness to Schubert's 'Unfinished' Symphony and Tchaikovsky's 'Pathétique', though it was already a melancholy tonality for Baroque composers. The same key is, however, rugged and magnificent at the start of Bach's B minor Mass (a misleading name, since most of the work is in D major), as in Liszt's Sonata and Borodin's Second Symphony. Haydn wrote a quartet and other works in B minor, Mozart only a keyboard adagio. B minor concertos include Dvořák's for cello and Elgar's for violin. The key of B♭, with its clarinet and trumpet connections, is quite a common choice for orches-tral music (symphonies and concertos by Haydn and Mozart, Beethoven's Fourth Symphony, Schumann's 'Spring', Bruckner's Fifth, Prokofiev's Fifth, the second piano concertos of Beethoven and Brahms) and for imposing qualities elsewhere (Beethoven's 'Hammerklavier' Sonata and Op.130 Quartet); it was also a key Schubert liked and explored typically in more private ways. B♭ minor has a passionate, dramatic aura, as in Tchaikovsky's First Piano Concerto and sonatas by Chopin and Rachmaninoff.

b. Abbreviation for bass.

Baaren, Kees van (b. Enschede, 22 Oct 1906; d. Oegstgeest, 2 Sep 1970). Dutch composer and highly influential teacher. The son of a music dealer, he studied with Friedrich Koch in Berlin (1924–9), where he worked as a jazz and cabaret pianist. He then continued studies with Pijper, whom he had met in Berlin. In his 30s he completed nothing, and when he began releasing works again, starting with the cantata *The Hollow Men* (1946), he was well advanced on the path to serialism, the first Dutch composer to take that road. By his music, and by his personality, he had an enormous impact on the young composers with whom he came into contact as director successively of the Utrecht (1953–8) and Hague (1958–70) conservatories. The subsequent leaders of the Dutch avant-garde – Schat, Andriessen, Reinbert de Leeuw, Mengelberg – were all pupils of his.

Babbitt, Milton (Byron) (b. Philadelphia, 10 May 1916). US composer, whose music has crystalline intelligence, charming humour and repose, which it maintains despite, very often, a great deal of activity. In lectures and theoretical articles he has been a vigorous proponent of serialism, and his works do not disguise the fact. But they take the battles as won, and clothe the labour in grace.

He was brought up in Jackson, Mississippi, where he started violin lessons at four and gained a taste for mathematics from his father, an actuary. In 1931 he went to the University of Pennsylvania to study mathematics, but he soon switched to New York University and music, under Marion Bauer. He became an adherent of the Schoenberg school, and continued his training with Sessions after graduating (in 1935). He then taught music at Princeton while studying for a master's degree there (1938–42), and moved to the maths faculty in 1943 before rejoining the music department in 1948. In 1973 he began teaching also at Juilliard, where he has continued to be an active member of the staff into his late 80s, just as he has remained an astonishingly productive composer.

Powerfully impressed by the new Schoenberg works of his student years, notably the Fourth Quartet, he analysed them closely, and discovered not only the principle of COMBINATORIALITY but also the use of serial relations to underpin large musical structures as coherently as diatonic relations had in the past. Taking also the idea of DERIVED SET from Webern, and having an intuition that the 12-note system should work for elements other than pitch, he wrote his first mature compositions in 1947–8. These, and their successors of the 1950s, were immediately characteristic in their quality of abstraction subverted by wit. The Second Quartet (1954) manifests an ironic pride in going through its continuous process of unfolding its series through sprouting derivatives, and *All Set* (1957) offers the appealing experience of 12-tone modern jazz, with streamlined jittery rhythm.

All his works of 1961–4 involved the RCA SYNTHESIZER, which allowed him to achieve his dense definitions with precision. The period came to end with an unusually dramatic work, a Baroque scena in modern terms: *Philomel* for soprano and tape, music of nocturnal disquiet. At the same time he was developing his ideas in articles, while in his music he more and more relinquished direct motivic connections, so that his works of the later 1960s and early 1970s are his most abstruse. His Third Quartet is an example – a half-hour continuous piece declining all effects, even pizzicato – and he has gone on writing works of similar scope. Since the late 1970s, though, he has also produced an abundance of shorter and snappier pieces, often with punning titles: *Transfigured Notes* (one of many homages to Schoenberg in his output), *Sheer Pluck*, *Whirled Series*, etc.

Playful or remote, his works generally exhibit an even pulse (essential to his TIME POINT notion) that is often rapid, and often, too, applied to highly unpredictable material: his writing for piano, in a central sequence of works, is distinguished by extreme registers, often with sudden changes, and his orchestration is similarly discontinuous. Rhetoric – the strongly urged gesture – is generally absent. Nothing matters more than anything else, and everything matters – in which respect his music not only honours its listeners but exemplifies US democratic ideals.

Milton Babbitt *Words about Music* (1987); Andrew Mead *An Introduction to the Music of Milton Babbitt* (1994)

Orchestral: *Relata II*, 1968; Piano Concerto, 1985; *Transfigured Notes*, str, 1986; Piano Concerto No.2, 1998; etc.

Ensemble: Composition for 12 Instruments, 1948; *All Set*, jazz octet, 1957; etc.

String quartets: No.1, 1948; No.2, 1954; No.3, 1969; No.4, 1970; No.5, 1982; No.6, 1993

Other chamber and instrumental works: Composition for Four Instruments, fl, cl, vn, vc, 1948; Composition for Viola and Piano, 1950; *Sextets*, vn, pf, 1966; *Arie da capo*, fl, cl, vn, vc. pf, 1973–4; *Four Play*, cl, vn, vc, pf, 1984; *Sheer Pluck*, gtr, 1984; *The Joy of More Sextets*, vn, pf, 1986; *Whirled Series*, sax, pf, 1987; *Play it again, Sam*, va, 1989; *None but the lonely flute*, fl, 1991; *Septet but Equal*, 3 cl, str trio, pf, 1992; *Triad*, va, cl, pf, 1994; Piano Quartet, 1995; Clarinet Quintet, 1996; Composition for One Instrument, cel, 1999; *Swan Song No.2*, 6 insts, 2002; etc.

Choral: *More Phonemena*, 1978; *An Elizabethan Sextette*, women's ch, 1979; etc.

Solo vocal: Three Theatrical Songs, v, pf, 1946; *The Widow's Lament in Springtime* (W.C. Williams), s, pf, 1950; *Du* (Stramm), s, pf, 1951; Two Sonnets (Hopkins), bar, cl, va, vc, 1955; Composition for Tenor and Six Instruments (Babbitt), t, fl, ob, str trio, hpd, 1960; *Sounds and Words*, s, pf, 1960; *Vision and Prayer* (Dylan Thomas), s, tape, 1961; *Philomel* (Hollander), s, tape, 1964; *Phonemena*, s, pf, 1969–70, arr s, tape 1974; *A Solo Requiem* (Shakespeare, etc.), s, 2 pf, 1976–7; *The Head of the Bed* (Hollander), s, fl, cl, vn, vc, 1982; *The Virginal Book*, a, pf, 1988; Four Cavalier Settings (Herrick, Carew), t, gtr, 1991; *Mehr 'Du'* (Stramm), s, pf, 1991; *No longer very clear*, s, fl, cl, vn, vc, 1994; etc.

Piano: Three Compositions, 1947; Partitions, 1957; Post-Partitions, 1966; Tableaux, 1972; Reflections, with tape, 1975; Playing for Time, 1977; About Time, 1982; Canonical Form, 1983; It takes twelve to tango, 1984; Lagniappe, 1985; Overtime, 1987; Emblems, 1989; Prelude, Interludes, and Postlude, 1991; Tutte le corde, 1994; Allegro penseroso, 1999; etc.

Tape: Composition for Synthesizer, 1961; *Ensembles for Synthesizer*, 1964; *Occasional Variations*, 1971

Babell, William (b. ?London, *c*.1690; d. London, 23 Sep 1723). British harpsichordist-composer, most famed for his Handel arrangements, which, in Burney's view, 'enabled the performer to astonish ignorance, and acquire the reputation of a great player at a small expence'. The son of a theatre bassoonist, he also wrote concertos.

Babi Yar. Name taken by Shostakovich's Thirteenth Symphony from one of the Yevtushenko poems it sets. Babi Yar is a ravine near Kiev, where thousands of Jews were killed soon after the Nazi occupation of the city in 1941.

baby grand. Grand piano on a smaller, domestic scale, about 5 feet (1.55m) long.

Bacarisse (Chinoria), Salvador (b. Madrid, 12 Sep 1898; d. Paris, 5 Aug 1963). Spanish composer, a proponent of Parisian neoclassicism, which he developed in more Hispanic and Romantic directions as an exile in Paris (from 1939), working for French radio's Spanish service.

bacchanal (Fr. *bacchanale*). The bacchanalia was an ancient Roman festival in honour of Bacchus (Gk Dionysos), the god associated with corporeal appetites and unrestraint. It is the tone, rather than the particular deity, that opera composers have wanted to evoke, notably Wagner at the opening of *Tannhäuser* and Saint-Saëns at the end of *Samson et Dalila*.

bacchetta (It.). Stick, whether a drumstick, a conductor's baton or the wood of a bow.

Bacewicz, Grażyna (b. Łódź, 5 Feb 1909; d. Warsaw, 17 Jan 1969). Polish violinist-composer, a neoclassicist who bravely took on new ideas in her 50s. She studied in Łódź, at the Warsaw Conservatory (composition with Kazimierz Sikorski) and in Paris (1932–4, with Boulanger and Flesch). Active as a violinist until the mid-1950s, she wrote seven concertos, seven quartets, five sonatas with piano, two solo sonatas and much else for her instrument, besides other concertos and four numbered symphonies.

Bach. German family of musicians, quite without parallel in its longevity as a musical dynasty (from the late 16th century to the mid 19th) and in producing several remarkable composers as well as one of music's greatest masters.

The first person to study the Bach family's genealogy was that central member, Johann Sebastian. According to information he gathered, he was descended from Veit Bach (c.1555–1619), who moved to Thuringia when the Counter-Reformation made life difficult for Protestants in Hungary. That history of oppression may partly explain the family's zeal and piety. The Bachs were, most of them, not just musicians but church musicians: they held appointments as organists and cantors (choirmaster-composers), and they stayed in their home region. Music was a craft, to be passed on from father to son, from uncle to nephew (a woman church musician would have been unthinkable in this culture). To the extent

that it was also an art, it was an art in the service of God.

Brief notes on members of the family are given opposite, with indentations to show descents and bold type to indicate a subject with a separate entry.

By 1700 the name Bach (Eng. Brook) was a synonym for musician in the family's home region. In 1720 there were at least 15 musical descendants of Veit Bach at work (besides other clans, possibly related further back), of whom five shared the name Johann Christoph Bach. Perhaps it is not suprising that an outstanding genius turned up – one whose genius spilled over, thanks to his aptitudes as a teacher, into the quite varied excellences of his sons.

Karl Geiringer *The Bach Family* (1954)

(1) **Johann Christoph** (baptized Arnstadt, 8 Dec 1642; buried Eisenach, 2 Apr 1703). A cousin of Johann Sebastian's father, Johann Ambrosius, and the most gifted member of the family so far, he was organist of the Arnstadt castle chapel (1663–5) before becoming a church organist and court harpsichordist in Eisenach, where Ambrosius joined him in 1671. He must have been an inspiration to the boy Johann Sebastian, who decades later performed some of his motets and sacred concertos in Leipzig, as C.P.E. Bach did later still in Hamburg.

Motets: *Der Gerechte, ob er gleich zu zeitlich stirbt*, 1676; *Sei getreu bis in den Tod*; *Der Mensch, vom Weibe geboren*; etc.
Sacred concertos: *Ach, dass ich Wassers gnug hätte*, a, str, con; *Es erhub sich ein Streit*, voices, insts, con; *Meine Freundin, du bist schön*, voices, str, con; *Wie bist du denn, o Gott*, b, str; etc.
Keyboard: *Aria Eberliniana*, hpd, 1690; org chorales, etc.

(2) **Johann Michael** (baptized Arnstadt, 9 Aug 1648; d. Gehren, 17 May 1694). Brother of Johann Christoph, whom he succeeded as Arnstadt castle organist (1665–73) before taking a post as organist in Gehren, where he was also an instrument maker and town clerk. His works include motets (*Fürchtet euch nicht, Sei lieber Tag willkommen, Unser Leben ist ein Schatten*, etc.), sacred arias and concertos, and organ chorales (including *In dulci jubilo*, once attributed to Johann Sebastian).

(3) **Johann Ludwig** (b. Thal, near Eisenach, 4 Feb 1677; buried Meiningen, 1 May 1731). Not a member of the Veit Bach clan, he was a court musician in Meiningen from 1699 and chapel-master there from 1713, writing funeral music for Duke Ernst Ludwig (1724), cantatas, motets, two masses, etc. The masses and numerous cantatas

Veit settled in Wechmar, a village near Gotha, and was a miller and baker, though also a musician, in which his son Hans took after him.

Hans (c.1580–1626) was the first professional musician in the family, trained in Gotha. He returned to Wechmar and had three notable musician sons: Johann, Christoph and Heinrich.

Johann (1604–73) was an organist-composer who settled in Erfurt, where he founded a branch of the family.

Johann Christian (1640–82) was director of the Erfurt town music.

Johann Jacob (1668–92) studied with Johann Ambrosius of Eisenach.

Johann Christoph (1673–1727) was cantor-organist in Gehren.

Johann Samuel (1694–1720) was a musician and schoolmaster.

Johann Günther (1703–56) was a musician and teacher in Erfurt.

Johann Aegidius (1645–1716) was a violinist and organist in Erfurt.

Johann Bernhard (1676–1749) succeeded Johann Christoph of Eisenach in his church and court posts, worked under Telemann there, and wrote Telemann-like orchestral suites as well as organ music.

Johann Ernst (1722–77) studied with Johann Sebastian and succeeded his father in Eisenach.

Johann Christoph (1685–1740) was an Erfurt church and town musician.

Johann Friedrich (1706–43) was schoolmaster and cantor in Andisleben, near Erfurt.

Johann Aegidius (1709–46) was cantor of Gross-Monra, near Kölleda.

Christoph (1613–61) held musical posts in Weimar, Erfurt and Arnstadt.

Georg Christoph (1642–97) studied at Leipzig University and became a cantor.

Johann Valentin (1669–1720) was a town musician and watchman in Schweinfurt.

Johann Lorenz (1695–1773) studied with Johann Sebastian (1715–17) and was from 1718 cantor-organist at Lahm im Itzgrund.

Johann Elias (1705–55) was a pupil, secretary and tutor in Johann Sebastian's Leipzig household, and later organist in Schweinfurt.

Johann Ambrosius (1645–95) was from 1671 a court and town musician in Eisenach.

Johann Christoph (1671–1721) studied with Pachelbel and spent his career as an organist in Ohrdruf, where he took in and taught his youngest brother after their parents' deaths in 1694–5.

Tobias Friedrich (1695–1768) was for nearly half a century cantor of Udestedt.

Johann Christian (1696–?) was a musician in Sondershausen.

Johann Bernhard (1700–43) studied with his uncle Johann Sebastian and became an Ohrdruf organist.

Johann Christoph (1702–56) worked at the Sondershausen court and as an organist in Ohrdruf.

Johann Heinrich (1707–83) was another pupil of his uncle Johann Sebastian, and later cantor-organist at Öhringen in Hohenlohe.

Johann Andreas (1713–79) was an Ohrdruf organist and inherited a collection of his father's (the Andreas Bach Book) that includes early pieces by Johann Sebastian.

Johann Balthasar (1673–91) was apprenticed to his father.

Johann Jacob (1682–1722) joined the Swedish army as an oboist, went with them to Constantinople, and died in Stockholm.

Johann Sebastian (1685–1750).

Catharina Dorothea (1708–74).

Wilhelm Friedemann (1710–84) was an organist and composer.

Carl Philipp Emanuel (1714–88) had a distinguished career in Berlin and Hamburg, and was one of the leading composers of his time.

Johann Gottfried Bernhard (1715–39) died of a fever soon after starting law studies in Jena.

Gottfried Heinrich (1724–63) was mentally impaired. He moved in with his married sister after their father's death.

Elisabeth Juliane Friederica (1726–81) married her father's assistant Johann Christoph Altnickol (1720–59) in 1749 and spent her widowed years in Leipzig, where her two daughters were married.

Johann Christoph Friedrich (1732–85) was a court musician in Bückeburg.

Wilhelm Friedrich Ernst (1759–1845) was a court musician in Berlin.

Johann Christian (1735–82) made his career in London, writing for the theatre and concerts.

Johanna Carolina (1737–81).

Regina Susanna (1742–1809).

Johann Christoph (1645–93) was a musician in Erfurt and Arnstadt.

Johann Ernst (1683–1739) was an organist in Arnstadt.

Johann Christoph (1689–1740) was an organist in Keula and Blankenhain.

Heinrich (1615–92) became an organist-composer in Arnstadt.

Johann Christoph (1642–1703) was a church organist and court harpsichordist in Eisenach.

Johann Nikolaus (1669–1753) was an organist-composer in Jena, and the oldest living Bach during Johann Sebastian's later years.

Johann Christoph (1676–?) went to Rotterdam and thence to England, where he disappeared from the record.

Johann Heinrich (1709–?) was noted by Johann Sebastian as a good keyboard player.

Johann Friedrich (c.1682–1730) succeeded Johann Sebastian as organist in Mühlhausen.

Johann Michael (1685–?) was an organ builder in Stockholm and another Bach who vanished from history.

Johann Michael (1648–94) was an organist-composer in Arnstadt and Gehren. His daughter Maria Barbara (1684–1720) married her second cousin Johann Sebastian.

Johann Günther (1653–83) was an organist and instrument builder.

were performed in Leipzig by Johann Sebastian, who was once believed to be the author of the cantata *Denn du wirst meine Seele*.

(4) **Johann Sebastian** (b. Eisenach, 21 Mar 1685; d. Leipzig, 28 Jul 1750). A giant not just in his family but in universal estimation, he is admired and renowned especially as the greatest master of counterpoint. Fresh in his invention and astonishing in his marshalling of contrapuntal textures, he achieved, again and again, an ideal of audible structure that has inspired and challenged composers from Mozart and Beethoven to Kurtág and Birtwistle. This clarity of design has fitted his music for media far beyond his imagining: the modern piano, the symphony orchestra, the electronic synthesizer. He also had an extraordinary range, from small keyboard pieces to some of the earliest compositions enshrined in the Western tradition as great works: compendious masterpieces that include his two Passion settings, his B minor Mass and his Goldberg Variations for harpsichord. And whether writing for the Lutheran church, the lone keyboard performer or an instrumental ensemble, he could command grief and joy, contemplation and dancing exuberance, sometimes in the same movement.

Bach started his education in Eisenach, but during his tenth year he lost both parents and moved in with his eldest brother in nearby Ohrdruf – an arrangement that lasted five years, while he studied with his brother and probably started to compose: some chorale preludes may date from his early teens. He left when he was just 15, probably to make room for his brother's growing family (Johann Bernhard, his nephew and later pupil, was born in 1700). With an older boy, Georg Erdmann, he travelled to Lüneburg, in northern Germany, where they could enrol in the school in return for singing in a church choir. While there he walked the 30 miles (50km) to hear Reincken play in Hamburg; he would also have been able to hear Georg Böhm.

He left school in 1702 and the next year found temporary employment in Weimar, back in home territory, before becoming organist of the Neue Kirche in Arnstadt, between Weimar and Ohrdruf, at the age of 18. In 1705–6 he was away for three months to hear Buxtehude in Lübeck: his employers took a dim view of this, and his relations with them did not improve, so that in 1707 he happily moved on to the post of organist of St Blasius's, Mühlhausen, again not far away. While there he married his second cousin, Maria Barbara Bach (17 October 1707), and began to attract pupils. He also had opportunities to write cantatas, including possibly *Gottes Zeit ist die allerbeste Zeit* and certainly *Gott ist mein König* (1708), his first – and for nearly two decades his only – published work. But discontent with the congregation and officials (a recurrent theme in his life) – as well as a better offer – made him return to Weimar in the summer of 1708.

By now he was 23, and his education was complete. His Ohrdruf brother, Johann Christoph, had introduced him not only to the methods of his own teacher, Pachelbel, but also to a wide range of organ music of the late 17th century, and he himself had enlarged on that grounding with his experience of leading members of the north German school (Reincken, Buxtehude, Böhm) and his study of music by their contemporaries in southern Germany, Italy and France. Even if he is, in this period of his youth, remote from us – most of his works, and his only authentic portrait, represent him in bewigged maturity – some sense of his fire, his breadth of knowledge, his ambition and his virtuosity as a performer is conveyed by compositions that date from his youth, such as the Preludes and Fugues for organ in C and E minor, the dramatic Toccata and Fugue in D minor, the sonatas for domestic keyboard and the *Capriccio sopra la lontananza del fratello dilettissimo* (Capriccio on the Departure of his Most Beloved Brother), this last piece having a quaint and rare autobiographical charm, though the occasion of its composition remains a mystery.

He stayed in his next post, as Weimar court organist, for almost a decade. There, by general reckoning, he wrote most of his organ works, and there his first six children were born, including twins who died soon after birth. He had opportunities to travel, and almost certainly got to know Telemann when the latter was in Eisenach (1708–12): Telemann stood godfather to his second surviving son, Carl Philipp Emanuel, in 1714. (On two occasions, in 1719 and 1729, his other great German contemporary, Handel, did not take the opportunity to meet him.) Also in 1714 he gained some responsibility for ensemble music, and began writing a cycle of cantatas, but this soon petered out, partly because of a feud between the two leading members of the ruling family: his employer Duke Wilhelm Ernst (1662–1728) and the head of the cadet branch, Duke Ernst August (1688–1748), whom he had served in 1703. He found a new position with this younger duke's brother-in-law, Prince Leopold of Cöthen (1694–1728), and demanded permission to go, whereupon Wilhelm Ernst – appreciative of his organist but unused to servants with plans of their own – had him jailed for a month in November–December 1717. He left as soon as he was out.

The Cöthen post, still in the same region,

brought him more money, a more congenial employer – a music-loving young man, almost a decade his junior – and a different culture. Leopold was Calvinist, so did not require elaborate church music, and though Bach wrote cantatas for the prince's birthday and New Year, he had to concentrate on instrumental music. For his Cöthen colleagues he wrote some of his greatest works of this kind, including his sets of pieces for solo violin and cello, as well as various concertos – among them the six he presented to the Marquess of Brandenburg, whose name they thereby acquired. He also accompanied Leopold to Carlsbad in 1718, journeyed to Berlin to negotiate for a new harpsichord for the court in 1719, and went with the prince again to Carlsbad in 1720. This time he returned to find his wife, not yet 36, dead and buried. The grand, impassioned chaconne of the D minor violin partita may be her memorial.

Later the same year he applied for an organist's post in Hamburg, and this time it was Reincken who came to hear and Bach who played. But though he was offered the job, he did not take it. He might have felt unsettled; he had four children in his care, aged from five to 12, and his first priority might have been to find them a stepmother, which he duly did. On 3 December 1721 he married Anna Magdalena Wilcke, a musician's daughter, with whom he had six more children who survived childhood (and seven who did not).

Just eight days later came what was, for him, a less felicitous marriage, between Prince Leopold and a cousin who did not share the princely fondness for music. With opportunities at court diminishing, Bach may have taken pleasure in being musically useful at home: a notebook for Wilhelm Friedemann, his eldest son, dates from shortly before Maria Barbara's death, and there were then two more little volumes for Anna Magdalena (1722–5), as well as the set of 24 preludes and fugues collected as *Das wohltemperirte Clavier* (The Well-Tempered Clavier, 1722) and the groups of inventions in two and three parts – all music devised as superior domestic teaching material.

Something else he could do was escape, now that his family life was well ordered again. The death of Kuhnau in 1722 left the post of cantor at St Thomas's school in Leipzig vacant. Telemann was soon appointed, but his employers in Hamburg declined to release him. Graupner seems to have been the next favoured candidate, but he was offered more money to stay in Darmstadt. So Bach got the job, and in May 1723 moved to Leipzig.

As cantor he was responsible for training the boys and young men (the age range of pupils was 12–23) who supplied choirs to St Thomas's and three other churches; he also had to supply cantatas for Sundays – for the main, three-hour service that started at 7 a.m. – and festivals during much of the liturgical year, and oversee performances. The half-hour cantatas, for a small group of choristers with instrumentalists, were musical illustrations of the day's gospel, which they immediately followed. Usually the first movement was a chorus on a biblical passage, and the last a relevant chorale, with solo recitatives and arias in between – though the set pattern, with Bach, was never a mould, more an ideal that had to be realized anew each time, with different musical ideas, textures and forms, allied to vivid expression. He himself would have played the harpsichord continuo, with other instrumental parts supplied by town musicians or by the students he had acquired through his secondary appointment as music director to the university. Working week by week with the same singers and players he could develop them in his style and congratulate the best of them with solos.

Cantatas were not performed in Advent after Advent Sunday but were required for the first three days of Christmas. Similarly, there was a gap through most of Lent, during which the cantor could prepare the Passion for Good Friday and the cantatas for Easter and Easter Monday. An annual cycle consisted of 60 cantatas and a Passion, and that was what Bach offered during his first year in Leipzig. The next year he composed another set of cantatas, but repeated the St John Passion from the year before. After that he reduced the pace, using music by other composers (cantatas by Johann Ludwig Bach, a Passion by Keiser), though he may have completed a further two sets of cantatas in 1725–9, along with the St Matthew Passion, one of many collaborations with the local poet Picander. Yet another set may then have occupied him through the next decade and more. If he did indeed produce five cycles, as his obituary notice reports, then more than 100 cantatas (plus a St Mark Passion) have been lost.

Also lost are many of the occasional cantatas he wrote for weddings and funerals, civic occasions and moments in court life (Leipzig belonged to the domains of the elector of Saxony). One such work that survives is the *Trauer Ode*, composed for a memorial service on 17 October 1727 for the electress Christiane Eberhardine, whose death kept regular music from the churches until after Christmas. Others of these extra cantatas he wrote as director – in 1729–37 and 1739–41 – of the collegium musicum that Telemann had founded; the collegium's weekly concerts, on Wednesday afternoons, also gave him opportunities to revive and revise many of his instrumental pieces from the Cöthen years, perform works by contemporaries, and meet musicians visiting the town.

There was more. During these early Leipzig years he produced other church music besides the many cantatas and Passions: the Christmas *Magnificat*, *Sanctus* settings (including the movement incorporated in the B minor Mass), motets. He also, in 1726, began a series of publications with his first partita. Having all this to do, he no doubt relished the privacy of the composing room provided for him in his lodgings at the school: with the birth of Elisabeth Juliane Friederica (5 April 1726) there were four small children in the house, and the number stayed much the same through the next several years, Anna Magdalena's annual pregnancies keeping pace with the premature harvest of infant mortality.

His children held pride of place among his pupils. In 1730 he remarked with satisfaction that he could field an entire musical consort from among his family, which at this point included Anna Magdalena (a professional singer, with whom he occasionally made expeditions to give concerts), Catharina Dorothea (21), Wilhelm Friedemann (19, a student at the university), Carl Philipp Emanuel (16, a St Thomas's scholar), Johann Gottfried Bernhard (15) and Gottfried Heinrich (6), as well as two infants. He must have been an extraordinary teacher, since all four of his sons who survived into mature adult years (as Johann Gottfried Bernhard did not) and had full mental faculties (which Gottfried Heinrich lacked) became distinguished composers.

Also in 1730, in August, he drew up a memorandum making recommendations to the town council for reforming and replenishing musical facilities. But, as usual, his advice was not heeded. In many of his tussles with local authorities he was adamant in insisting on his prerogatives, which made it easy for his enemies, or those who were merely lazy, to see as professional vanity what for him was artistic vision – and necessity. Perhaps he became discouraged. The extravagant flood of new church music thinned to a trickle, and he intensified his practice of adapting old music for new occasions, which was how the lost St Mark Passion largely came about.

The death of the Saxon elector, Friedrich August I, in 1733 led to another period of music-less national mourning, possibly ended in Leipzig on 2 July by the exultant sounds of the *Magnificat* in D. With his eldest son now working as an organist in the electoral city of Dresden, in 1736 he received the title of court composer, in recognition of

which he gave a two-hour organ recital. As Leipzig cantor his duties did not include playing the organ – all the churches had their own organists. But his fame as an organ virtuoso lived on (according to the obituary he was 'the most prodigious organist and keyboard player there has ever been'), and he would occasionally travel to give recitals or try out new organs (as in 1732 when he was called to Kassel, his furthest venture west).

Among the journeys he made in his last decade were two to Berlin, where his second son was working, in 1741 and 1747. On the latter visit he played on some of the new Silbermann pianos and on the organ, his piano recital including a three-part fugal improvisation on a theme supplied by the king, Frederick the Great. From this, once back in Leipzig, he elaborated *Das musikalische Opfer* (The Musical Offering), a collection of fugues, canons and a trio sonata, all on the same theme.

Such a work suggests he was thinking less of being useful in the present than of providing formidable messages to the future. Johann Adolph Schiebe's criticism of his style as 'bombastic and confused', published in 1737, was an indication of changing taste. Bach would let taste change, and let his music wait for it to change back. In his last years he worked on two other large projects: the B minor Mass, largely built up from earlier music, and *Die Kunst der Fuge* (The Art of Fugue), another gathering of fugues and canons. The last part of this, a quadruple fugue, he was unable to complete.

By the spring of 1749 his health was deteriorating, and his eyesight failing, because, apparently, of diabetes. He underwent two eye operations at the hands of an English specialist in March and April 1750, but these had no positive effect, and he died in the summer after suffering a stroke.

He had spent virtually his entire life in a small part of central Europe, about 125 miles (200km) west–east, from Eisenach to Dresden, by 60 miles (100km) north–south, from Cöthen to Arnstadt and Ohrdruf. His music, though, was already travelling much further afield: harpsichord works by him were in print in England, France and Italy. For the moment the music remained more in the study than the concert hall, admired for its learning and practicality, its ability to teach minds and fingers, which was how Mozart and Beethoven revered it. Mendelssohn's performance of the St Matthew Passion for the first time since the composer's death (Berlin, 1829) changed that, and Bach's music has ever since been everywhere, appreciated privately and publicly, around the world – but altering all the time, living through its own periods of Romanticism (large choirs, symphony orchestras, much rubato), neoclassicism (the harpsichord triumphant, crisp rhythms) and postmodernism (given with historically informed performance style but, inevitably, ripped from its cultural roots). No music has changed so much – or changed so many.

Still, it has its constancies. It is, in particular, music that teaches. It contains, within itself, all the information necessary for its understanding, and travellers have found that, where Beethoven or Chopin mean little in West Africa or Indonesia, a Bach invention is instantly recognized for what it is and enjoyed. In his cantatas Bach set a fair bit of the Bible to music – the Bible as translated by Luther, who was born in the same region little more than two centuries before. But he also created a many-chaptered bible of his own, treating the miracles of tonality and harmony, of melodic shapes and their relationships, of regular metres and of all these in counterpoint. He dedicated his life to the glory of God, and to the divinity that exists in sound.

Wilfrid Mellers *Bach and the Dance of God* (1980); Malcolm Boyd *Bach* (1983, ³2000); Laurence Dreyfus *Bach and the Patterns of Invention* (1996); Malcolm Boyd, ed. *J.S. Bach* (1999); Christoph Wolff *Johann Sebastian Bach* (2000)

www.jsbach.org

Works are numbered according to the Bach-Werke-Verzeichnis (BWV), which for the cantatas follows the old numbering (e.g. Cantata No.140 = BWV 140). The compositions printed during his lifetime were few: the cantata BWV 71 (1708), the four parts of the CLAVIER-ÜBUNG (1731–41), a couple of canons printed as examples by Telemann and others, numerous arrangements and possibly some melodies for a Leipzig hymnbook (1736), Das musikalische Opfer (1747), the Vom Himmel hoch *variations (1748) and the organ chorales published by Schübler, BWV 645–50 (1748–9).*

Vocal music

Passions: ST JOHN PASSION, BWV 245, 1724, rev; ST MATTHEW PASSION, BWV 244, 1727, rev; St Mark Passion, BWV 247, 1731, lost

Oratorios: CHRISTMAS ORATORIO, BWV 248, 1734–5; EASTER ORATORIO, BWV 249, 1725, rev c.1738

Latin settings: B MINOR MASS, BWV 232, 1723–c.1749; *Missa brevis* settings, F, A, G minor, G, BWV 233–6, ?1738–9; *Sanctus* settings, C, D, ?1723; *Magnificat* settings, E♭ BWV 243a, 1723 (with Christmas interpolations), D, BWV 243, c.1732–5 (rev without interpolations)

Church cantatas for more than one singer: *Also hat Gott die Welt geliebt*, BWV 68, Whit Monday, 1725; *Am Abend aber desselbigen Sabbats*, BWV 42, 1725; *Auf Christ Himmelfahrt allein*, BWV 128, Ascension, 1725; *Aus der Tiefen rufe ich*, BWV 131, 1707; *Bereitet die Wege*, BWV 132, 1715; *Bleib bei uns*, BWV 6, Easter Monday, 1725; *Christen, ätzet diesen Tag*, BWV 63, Christmas, c.1714–15; *Christ lag in Todes Banden*, BWV 4, Easter, ?before 1708; *Darzu ist erschienen*, BWV 40, Second Day of Christmas, 1723; *Erfreut euch*, BWV 66, Easter Monday, 1724; *Erschallet, ihr Lieder*, BWV 172, Whit Sunday, 1714; *Es ist euch gut*, BWV 108, 1725; *Ein feste Burg*, BWV 80, Reformation Festival, 1716, much rev; *Gottes Zeit ist die allerbeste Zeit* (ACTUS TRAGICUS), BWV 106, funeral, ?1707–8; *Gott fähret auf*, BWV 43, Ascension, 1726; *Gott ist mein König*, BWV 71, 1708; *Halt im Gedächtnis*, BWV 67, 1724; *Herz und Mund*, BWV 147, Visitation, 1723; *Der Himmel lacht!*, BWV 31, Easter, 1715; *Himmelskönig, sei willkommen*, BWV 182, Palm Sunday, 1714; *Ich hatte viel Bekümmernis*, BWV 21, 1714; *Jesu, der du meine Seele*, BWV 78, 1724; *Jesu nun sei gepreiset*, BWV 41, New Year, 1725; *Liebster Gott, wenn werd ich sterben?*, BWV 8, 1724; *Lobe den Herren*, BWV 137, 1725; *Lobet Gott* (Ascension Oratorio), BWV 11, 1735; *Meine Seel erhebt den Herrn*, BWV 10, Visitation, 1724; *Nun ist das Heil und die Kraft*, BWV 50, Michaelmas (choral fragment); *Nun komm, der Heiden Heiland*, BWV 61, Advent, 1714 ; *Nun komm, der Heiden Heiland*, BWV 62, Advent, 1724; *O ewiges Feuer*, BWV 34, Whit Sunday, c.1746/7; *Schwingt freudig*, BWV 36, c.1725–30, rev 1731; *Sie werden aus Saba*, BWV 65, Epiphany, 1724; *Unser Mund sei voll Lachens*, BWV 110, Christmas, 1725; *Wachet auf, ruft uns die Stimme*, BWV 140, 1731; *Was mein Gott will*, BWV 111, 1725; *Weinen, klagen, sorgen, zagen*, BWV 12, 1714; *Wer mich liebet*, BWV 59, Whit Sunday, 1724; *Wer nur den lieben Gott*, BWV 93, 1724; *Wer weiss, wie nahe mir mein Ende!*, BWV 27, 1726; *Wir danken dir, Gott*, BWV 29, 1731; etc.

Other cantatas for more than one singer: *Lass, Fürstin, lass noch einen Strahl* (Trauer Ode), BWV 198, 1727; *Mer Hahn en neue Oberkeet* (PEASANT CANTATA), BWV 212, 1742; *Schweigt stille, plaudert nicht* (COFFEE CANTATA), BWV 211, c.1734; *Der Streit zwischen Phoebus und Pan*, BWV 201, ?1729; etc.

Solo cantatas: *Der Friede sei mit dir*, BWV 158, b, Easter Tuesday, after 1723; *Geist und Seele*, BWV 35, a, 1726; *Gott soll allein mein Herze haben*, BWV 169, a, 1726; *Ich armer Mensch*, BWV 55, t, 1726; *Ich bin vergnügt*, BWV 84, s, 1727; *Ich habe genug*, BWV 82, b/s/a, Purification, 1727; *Ich will den Kreuzstab gerne tragen*, BWV 56, b, 1726; *Jauchzet Gott in allen Landen!*, BWV 51, s, 1730; *Mein Herze schwimmt in Blut*, BWV 199, s, 1714; *Non sa che sia dolore*, BWV 209, s, after 1729; *O holder Tag*, BWV 210, s, wedding, ?1738–41; *Vergnügte Ruh'*, BWV 170, a, 1726; *Was mir behagt* (Hunt Cantata), BWV 208, ?1713, much rev; *Weichet nur, betrübte Schatten*, BWV 202, s, wedding, before 1730; *Widerstehe doch*, BWV 54, a, 1714

Motets: *Singet dem Herren*, BWV 225, 1726/7; *Der Geist hilft*, BWV 226, with insts, 1729; *Jesu, meine Freude*, BWV 227, before 1735; *Fürchte dich nicht*, BWV 228; *Komm, Jesu, komm!*, BWV 229, before 1732; *Lobet den Herrn*, BWV 230, with org

Chorales: about 200 independent settings

Orchestral/chamber music

Violin concertos: A minor, BWV 1041, vn, str, con, c.1730; E, BWV 1042, vn, str, con, before 1730

Double violin concerto: D minor, BWV 1043, 2 vn, str, con, 1730–31

Mixed concertos: A minor, BWV 1044, fl, vn, hpd, str, con, 1729–41; BRANDENBURG CONCERTOS, BWV 1046–51

Harpsichord concertos, mostly c.1738–9: D minor, BWV 1052, hpd, str, con; E, BWV 1053, hpd, str, con; D, BWV 1054, hpd, str, con; A, BWV 1055, hpd, str, con; F minor, BWV 1056, hpd, str, con; F, BWV 1057, hpd, 2 rec, str, con; G minor, BWV 1058, hpd, str, con; D minor, BWV 1059, hpd, ob, str, con; C minor, BWV 1060, 2 hpd, str, con; C, BWV 1061, 2 hpd, str, con; C minor, BWV 1062, 2 hpd, str, con; D minor, BWV 1063, 3 hpd, str, con (arr of BWV 1043); C, BWV 1064, 3 hpd, str, con; A minor, BWV 1065, 4 hpd, str, con

Suites (Overtures): No.1, C, BWV 1066, 2 ob, bn, str, con; No.2, B minor, BWV 1067, fl, str, con; No.3, D, BWV 1068, 3 tpt, 2 ob, timp, str, con; No.4, D, BWV 1069, 3 tpt, 3 ob, bn, timp, str, con

Violin sonatas, etc.: B minor, A, E, C minor, F minor, G, BWV 1014–19, vn, hpd; G, BWV 1021, vn, con; E minor, BWV 1023, vn, con; Suite, A, BWV 1025, vn, hpd; Fugue, G minor, BWV 1026, vn, hpd

Solo violin sonatas and partitas, 1720: Sonata No.1, G minor, BWV 1001; Partita No.1, B minor, BWV 1002; Sonata No.2, A minor, BWV 1003; Partita No.2, D minor, BWV 1004; Sonata No.3, C, BWV 1005; Partita No.3, E, BWV 1006

Viola da gamba sonatas: G, D, G minor, BWV 1027–9, gamba, hpd

Solo cello suites, c.1720: G, D minor, C, E♭, C minor, D, BWV 1007–12

Flute sonatas: B minor, E♭, A, C, E minor, E, BWV 1030–35, fl, con, c.1724–41

Solo flute partita: A minor, BWV 1013, after 1723

Trio sonatas: G, BWV 1038, fl, vn, con, 1732–5; G, BWV 1039, 2 fl, con (arr of BWV 1027), c.1736–41; F, BWV 1040, vn, ob, con

Lute works: Suite, G minor, BWV 995; Suite, E minor, BWV 996; Partita, C minor, BWV 997; Prelude, Fugue and Allegro, E♭, BWV 998; Prelude, C minor, BWV 999; Fugue, G minor, BWV 1000; Partita, E, BWV 1006a (arr of BWV 1006)

Music of flexible scoring

Das MUSIKALISCHE OPFER, BWV 1079; Die KUNST DER FUGE, BWV 1080; other canons

Organ music

Most of Bach's organ works date from his Weimar period (1708–17) and earlier. Those he wrote in Leipzig (after 1723) are marked L.

Preludes and fugues: C, BWV 531; C, BWV 545; C, BWV 547; C minor, BWV 537, L; C minor, BWV 546, L; C minor, BWV 549; D, BWV 532; D minor, BWV 539; 'St Anne', E♭, BWV 552, L; E, BWV 566; E minor, BWV 533; E minor, BWV 548, L; F minor, BWV 534; G, BWV 541; G, BWV 550; G minor,

BWV 535; A, BWV 536; A minor, BWV 543; A minor, BWV 551; B minor, BWV 544, L; 8 Little Preludes and Fugues, BWV 553–60

Toccatas and fugues: 'Dorian', D minor, BWV 538; D minor, BWV 565; F, BWV 540; Toccata, Adagio and Fugue, C, BWV 564

Fantasias and fugues: C minor, BWV 562, L; G minor, BWV 542

Passacaglia and fugue: C minor, BWV 582

Fantasias: C, BWV 570; G, BWV 572; B minor, BWV 563

Fugues: C minor, BWV 574; C minor, BWV 575; G, BWV 577; 'Little G minor', BWV 578; B minor, BWV 579

Trio sonatas: E♭, C minor, D minor, E minor, C, G, BWV 525–30, L

Concertos: G, A minor, C, C, D minor, BWV 592–6 (arrs of works by Vivaldi and Prince Johann Ernst of Saxe-Weimar)

Chorale preludes: Ach bleib' bei uns, BWV 649; An Wasserflüssen Babylon, BWV 653; Ein feste Burg, BWV 720; Herzlich tut mich verlangen, BWV 727; Ich ruf' zu di, Herr Jesu Christ, BWV 639; In dulci jubilo, BWV 729; Komm, Gott, Schöpfer, BWV 667; Kommst du nun, Jesu, BWV 650; Liebster Jesu, wir sind hier, BWV 731; Meine Seele erhebt den Herren, BWV 648; Nun danket alle Gott, BWV 657; Nun freut euch, BWV 734; Nun komm, der Heiden Heiland, BWV 659; O Lamm Gottes, BWV 656; Schmücke dich, o liebe Seele, BWV 654; Wachet auf, ruft uns die Stimme, BWV 645; Wer nun den lieben Gott, BWV 647; Wo soll ich fliehen hin, BWV 646; Wir glauben all an einen Gott, BWV 680; etc.

Chorale variations: Christ, der du bist, BWV 766; O Gott, du frommer Gott, BWV 767; Sei gegrüsset, Jesu gütig, BWV 768; Vom Himmel hoch, BWV 769, L; etc.

Other works: Trio, D minor, BWV 583, L; Canzona, D minor, BWV 588; Alla breve, D, BWV 589; Pastorale, F, BWV 590; Kleines harmonisches Labyrinth, BWV 591; Duettos, E minor, F, G, A minor, BWV 802–5, L

Harpsichord/clavichord/piano music

Inventions: Two-Part Inventions, BWV 772–86; Three-Part Inventions (Sinfonias), BWV 787–801

Suites: ENGLISH SUITES, A, A minor, G minor, F, E minor, D minor, BWV 806–11; FRENCH SUITES, BWV 812–17, D minor, C minor, B minor, E♭, G, E; Partitas, BWV 825–30, B♭, C minor, A minor, D, G, E minor; French Overture, B minor, BWV 831; etc.

Preludes and fugues: Das WOHLTEMPERIRTE CLAVIER, BWV 846–93; etc.

Fantasias and fugues: CHROMATIC FANTASIA AND FUGUE, D minor, BWV 903; Fantasia and Fugue, A minor, BWV 904; Fantasia and Fugue, C minor, BWV 906; etc.

Toccatas: F♯ minor, C minor, D, D minor, E minor, G minor, G, BWV 910–16

Preludes: 6 Little Preludes, BWV 933–8; etc.

Sonatas: D, BWV 963; D minor, BWV 964; C, BWV

966; A minor, BWV 968; etc.
Concertos: Italian Concerto, BWV 971; 6 after
originals by Vivaldi etc., D, G, D minor, G minor,
C, C, BWV 972–7; etc.
Variations: GOLDBERG VARIATIONS, BWV 988
Capriccios: *Capriccio sopra la lontananza del suo
fratello dilettissimo*, B♭, BWV 992; E, BWV 993

Spurious works

*Musicians have been loth to lose some works that
scholars have discounted from the Bach catalogue.
Among these favoured rejecta are the following.*
Instrumental ensemble: Suite, G minor, BWV 1070,
str, con; Sonata, G, BWV 1037, 2 vn, hpd, by
Goldberg; Sonata, G minor, BWV 1020, vn, hpd, ?
by a son/pupil
Vocal: *Schlage doch*, BWV 53, funeral cantata, ? by
Melchior Hoffmann; *Lobe den Herrn*, BWV 143,
New Year cantata; *Bist du bei mir*, BWV 508, aria,
by Stölzel
Harpsichord: Fantasia, C minor, BWV 919, ? by
Johann Bernhard Bach; Prelude, D, BWV 925, ? by
Wilhelm Friedemann Bach

(5) **Anna Magdalena** [née Wilcke] (b. Zeitz, 22
Sep 1701; d. Leipzig, 27 Feb 1760). Second wife of
Johann Sebastian and recipient of two notebooks
from him containing keyboard pieces and songs
for her instruction and pleasure (1722–5). She was
the daughter of Johann Caspar Wilcke, a court
trumpeter at Weissenfels. How she became
acquainted with Bach is uncertain, and almost
nothing is known of her life or character, beyond
the record of 13 pregnancies in 20 years. She died in
poverty.

(6) **Wilhelm Friedemann** (b. Weimar, 22 Nov
1710; d. Berlin, 1 Jul 1784). Johann Sebastian's
second child and eldest son, he studied with his
father and, in Leipzig, at St Thomas's school and
the university, where his interests were partly
mathematical. In the summer of 1733 he left the
family home to take up a post as organist at St
Sophia's in Dresden, and from there he moved in
1746 to the Liebfrau church in Halle, where he
married rather late, in 1751. His dissatisfaction in
Halle is hard to read. He may have been under-
appreciated; he may have been over-taxed; he may
have been irresolute. In any event, he resigned in
1764 with no other position in prospect, and
though he went on applying for jobs, none came
his way. After staying on a few years in Halle he
moved to Brunswick (1771–4) and then Berlin.
Acknowledged the greatest organist of his time, he
partly supported himself and his family as a
recitalist and improviser, but he was also obliged
to sell off music he had inherited from his father.
His own works, while evidently emerging from his
father's school, have personal qualities of
emotional febrility (the solo harpsichord music,

which includes 12 polonaises and 10 fantasias from
his later years) and sometimes outlandishness (the
Sinfonia in F, *c*.1735–40). Apart from keyboard
music, sinfonias and harpsichord concertos, he
produced fugues and canons, flute duets and trio
sonatas.

(7) **Carl Philipp Emanuel** (b. Weimar, 8 Mar
1714; d. Hamburg, 14 Dec 1788). Johann Sebastian's
second surviving son, he was one of the most
prominent composers of his generation. He was
musically trained by his father and also educated
at St Thomas's school and the universities of
Leipzig (1731–4) and Frankfurt, where his subject
was law. In 1740, or thereabouts, he took an
appointment at the court of Frederick the Great in
Berlin. He married there and had three children
(of whom the youngest, Johann Sebastian, became
a painter and died at the age of 30 in Rome); he
also took care of his youngest half-brother, Johann
Christian, after their father's death. Family life, and
busy creativity, may have distracted him from not
sharing the royal favour granted Graun, Quantz
and other court musicians. But he seems, also, to
have enjoyed a philosophical disposition. He
hoped to succeed his father, and in 1755 applied for
the Leipzig post again, but had to wait until 1767
before finding an alternative appointment, in
succession to his godfather Telemann in
Hamburg. There he wrote church music, taught
and took part in concerts. For his farewell in this
last capacity, in 1786, he presented a historical
programme that included works of his own
together with movements from his father's B
minor Mass and Handel's *Messiah*.

He published many sets of keyboard sonatas,
rondos and fantasias, including six collections *für
Kenner und Liebhaber* (for cognoscenti and
amateurs, 1779–87). Often remarkable for their
technical boldness and surges of feeling, these
works were the chief source of his fame in his day,
together with his two-part *Essay on the True Art of
Playing Keyboard Instruments* (1753–62).

Hans-Günter Ottenberg *Carl Philipp Emanuel Bach*
(1987)

*Works are numbered according to the catalogue by
E. Eugene Helm.*

Vocal: *Magnificat*, H.772, 1749; *Die Israeliten in die
Wüste* (oratorio), H.238, 1769; *Die Auferstehung
und Himmelfahrt Jesu* (oratorio), H.240, 1774;
other sacred music, songs, etc.
Symphonies: G, B♭, C, A, B minor, E, H.657–62, str;
D, E♭, F, G, H.663–6, 1775–6; etc.
Concertos: D minor, H.425/484:1, hpd/fl, 1747; A
minor, H.430–32, hpd/fl/vc, str, 1750; B♭, H.434–6,
hpd/fl/vc, str, 1751; A, H.437–9, hpd/fl/vc, 1753; G,
H.444–5, kbd/fl, str, 1755; B♭, H.465–6, hpd/ob, str,
1765; E♭, H.467–8, hpd/ob, str, 1765; etc.

Woodwind sonatas: G minor, H.549, ob, con; C, H.504, fl/vn, kbd, 1745; D, H.505, fl, kbd, 1747; A minor, H.562, fl, 1747; E, H.506, fl, kbd, 1749; etc.

Organ sonatas: F, A minor, D, G minor, H.84–7, 1755; etc.

Piano/harpsichord: Sonata, A minor, H.30, pub 1744; Fantasia, C, H.284, pub 1785; Fantasia, C, H.291, pub 1787; Fantasy and Fugue, C minor, H.103; etc.

(8) **Johann Ernst** (b. Eisenach, 28 Jan 1722; d. Eisenach, 1 Sep 1777). Second cousin and pupil of Johann Sebastian. In Leipzig (1737–41) he also attended St Thomas's school and studied law at the university. He then returned to Eisenach, where, in 1749, he succeeded his father and wrote church cantatas, organ pieces and chamber music.

(9) **Johann Christoph Friedrich** (b. Leipzig, 21 Jun 1732; d. Bückeburg, 26 Jan 1795). Johann Sebastian's second youngest surviving son, he was educated by his father and at St Thomas's school. By 1751 he was at the court of Count Wilhelm of Schaumburg-Lippe in Bückeburg, where he spent all his adult life, apart from a trip to London in 1778 to see his younger brother, with whom he left his son, Wilhelm Friedrich Ernst. Much of his output was for the court – cantatas and motets, sinfonias, chamber music – and much of it was lost when the Bückeburg archives were destroyed in the Second World War. But the easy (and not so easy) sonatas he published have endeared him to generations of pianists.

(10) **Johann Christian**, 'the London Bach' (b. Leipzig, 5 Sep 1735; d. London, 1 Jan 1782). Johann Sebastian's youngest son, he was brought up in the family traditions of church and court composing – by his father in Leipzig and by his half-brother in Berlin – but moved on to seek his fortune elsewhere: in opera and in London. With his German formation, Italian airing and knowledge of French styles, he was an international figure and a natural model for Mozart.

It may have been with an Italian soprano that he travelled to Milan in 1755. He continued his education with Padre Martini and in 1760 was appointed second organist at Milan Cathedral, probably converting to Catholicism at this time. In the same year he produced his first opera seria, *Artaserse*, which led to commissions for Naples and an invitation to London, where he arrived in 1762. Within a year he had written two operas and been appointed music master to the queen; he also threw himself into the city's musical commerce, presenting concerts from 1764 with Abel, whom he may have known from boyhood, and publishing his music actively: symphonies (in the fast–slow–fast form of Italian opera overtures, including Six Symphonies, Op.6, in G, D, E♭, B♭, E♭ and G minor, and Six Grand Overtures, Op.18,

in E♭, B♭, D, D, E and D), concertos (notably the first of two for oboe in F), *symphonies concertantes* (among them one in A for violin and cello), chamber music and songs made popular at Vauxhall Gardens. Evidently he was aware as much of the risks as of the opportunities of free enterprise, for in 1773 he sued a publisher for issuing his music without permission, and he maintained contacts with publishers in Paris. Hard work won him comfort and patronage, while his friends included Gainsborough and fellow musicians, resident and visiting. Among the visitors were the Mozarts in 1764–5. He played duets with the eight-year-old Wolfgang Amadeus and left an imprint on the boy's style: several years later Mozart arranged three of his piano sonatas as concertos.

In the 1770s Bach continued writing operas for London and fulfilled commissions from Mannheim (*Temistocle*, 1772; *Lucio Silla*, 1775) and Paris (AMADIS) that testify to his international prestige. Padre Martini asked him to send a portrait, which is how a Gainsborough came to hang in the civic musical museum in Bologna. And Gainsborough also provided paintings for the Hanover Square Rooms, which Bach and Abel built for their concerts. Some time in the 1770s, too, Bach married the singer Cecilia Grassi. His death was, Mozart wrote to his father, 'a loss to the musical world'.

(11) **Wilhelm Friedrich Ernst** (b. Bückeburg, 24 May 1759; d. Berlin, 25 Dec 1845). Son and pupil of J.C.F. Bach and protégé of his uncle J.C. Bach in London (1778–82), where he had some success as a pianist and composer. He returned to Germany after his uncle's death, and from 1789 was attached to the court in Berlin. In 1843 he attended the unveiling of the monument to his grandfather in Leipzig.

(12) **P.D.Q.** Imaginary addition to the family due to Peter Schickele.

B–A–C–H. Melodic motif encoding (J.S.) Bach's name according to German note nomenclature, i.e. as B♭–A–C–B. Bach himself used the motif in *Die* KUNST DER FUGE, and his youngest son wrote a fugue on it, as did Schumann and Liszt. There are also works incorporating it by Rimsky-Korsakov, Busoni, Reger, Schoenberg and Webern.

Bach-Busoni. Imaginary persona created by BUSONI as author of Bach transcriptions and spin-offs, of which he published a seven-volume collected edition in 1920.

Bacheler, Daniel (baptized Aston Clinton, 16 Mar 1572; buried Lee, Kent, 29 Jan 1619). English lutenist-composer. Apprenticed to his lutenist uncle when he was seven, by the age of 15 he was moving in court circles and active as a composer, eventually becoming a valued servant of Elizabeth I. He wrote pavans, galliards and divisions, for his instrument and consort music.

Bachelet, Alfred (b. Paris, 26 Feb 1864; d. Nancy, 10 Feb 1944). French composer of opulent operas and songs ('Chère nuit'). He studied with Guiraud at the Paris Conservatoire, conducted at the Opera, and was head of Nancy Conservatory from 1919.

Bachianas brasileiras. Sequence of nine works by Villa-Lobos, transferring the Leipzig master's spirit to the Amazon. Most frequently heard is No.5, for soprano and cellos.

Bach trumpet. High instrument in D, introduced in the late 19th century principally for Bach's Brandenburg Concerto No.2.

Bäck, Sven-Erik (b. Stockholm, 16 Sep 1919; d. Stockholm, 10 Jan 1994). Swedish composer, a pupil of Rosenberg who took to avant-garde music in the 1950s (*A Game around a Game* for orchestra, 1959) and wrote electronic motets.

backfall. 17th-century Eng. term for a descending APPOGGIATURA.

background. In Schenkerian analysis the guiding line running behind or beneath a work or movement, as opposed to the evident foreground. But 'background music' is something else: recorded music played to be heard while doing other things, as an improvement on supposedly dull silence.

Backhaus, Wilhelm (b. Leipzig, 26 Mar 1884; d. Villach, 5 Jul 1969). German–Swiss pianist, known especially for his strength in Beethoven and Brahms, and brilliance in the Chopin Etudes. He studied at the Leipzig Conservatory and with d'Albert (1898–9), played in England in 1900–1, and won the Rubinstein Prize in Paris in 1905 (against Bartók, among others). He made the first concerto recording (Grieg, 1909) and continued his international career into his 80s.

Bacon, Ernst (b. Chicago, 26 May 1898; d. Orinda, Cal., 16 Mar 1990). US composer, especially of songs setting Dickinson, Whitman, etc., in a strong but persuasive and adaptable conservative style. He studied in Chicago and California, with Weigl and Bloch, and had a career as a college professor, notably at Syracuse University (1945–63). In 1935 he founded the Carmel Bach Festival.

badinage (Fr., banter). Early 18th-century movement of a lighthearted character. Bach's term, for the finale of his B minor orchestral suite, was *badinerie*, not found elsewhere.

Badings, Henk (b. Bandung, Java, 17 Jan 1907; d. Maarheeze, 26 Jun 1998). Dutch composer with a special interest in unorthodox scales and microtones. He was sent back from the East Indies to the Netherlands in 1915 as an orphan and obliged by his guardian to study at the technical university in Delft. But he also kept up musical studies, by himself and with Pijper, and in the mid 1930s his music began receiving performances. His acceptance of the directorship of the Hague Conservatory during the German occupation (1941–5) brought him criticism after the war, and it was a while before he gained another teaching appointment, at Utrecht University (1961–77). In the interim he developed a 31-note scale with Fokker. He also taught at the conservatory in Stuttgart (1962–72) and returned to his alma mater in Delft to work on electronic compositions. His output was colossal, including 15 symphonies, multifarious concertos, choral music, and innumerable sonatas and other instrumental pieces.

Badoaro, Giacomo (b. Venice, 1602; d. Venice, 1654). Italian poet and nobleman, whose Ulyssean librettos were set by Monteverdi and Sacrati.

Baermann, Heinrich (Joseph) (b. Potsdam, 14 Feb 1784; d. Munich, 11 Jun 1847). German clarinettist-composer, whose smooth style won him works from Weber (the concertos and concertino) and Mendelssohn. Born into a military family, he trained as a bandsman, saw action at Jena and was taken prisoner, but escaped to an appointment at the Munich court. The appealing adagio from his Third Clarinet Quintet was once attributed to Wagner. His son Carl (1810–85) followed the same profession, most importantly as a teacher and author of an influential clarinet method.

bagatelle (Fr., trifle). Miniature composition. The term was in occasional use by 18th-century publishers, but was dignified by Beethoven, whose Op.119 and Op.126 sets comprise fragmentary masterpieces of his last years. There are also bagatelles by Dvořák, Bartók and Webern.

bagpipe (Fr. *cornemuse*, Ger. *Dudelsack, Sackpfeife*, It. *cornamusa, piva, zampogna*). Instrument composed of reed pipes emanating from a bag, which the player blows into and holds firmly under one shoulder to maintain air pressure; one pipe will be a chanter, allowing melodies to be performed over a drone from the other or others. Bagpipes are particularly associated with ceremonial and folk music in Scotland, but are found throughout Europe and India in vernacular music. They appear to have been respectable in high art in the Middle Ages, but then were pushed to the fringes, bouncing back in Baroque France in the form of the MUSETTE and occasionally afterwards (as, for geographical-comic effect, in Davies's *An Orkney Wedding with Sunrise*).

baguette (Fr.). Stick, whether a drumstick, a conductor's baton or the wood of a bow. Hence *baguette d'éponge* (sponge-headed drumstick), etc.

Bahr-Mildenburg, Anna [née Mildenburg von Bellschau] (b. Vienna, 29 Nov 1872; d. Vienna, 27 Jan 1947). Austrian soprano, an artist of legendary vocal brilliance (she made only one recording) and dramatic force. After making her debut as Brünnhilde under Mahler (Hamburg, 1895), she followed him in 1898 to Vienna, where she was a member of the company until 1916. She also assisted Cosima Wagner at Bayreuth.

Baillot, Pierre (Marie François de Sales) (b. Passy, 1 Oct 1771; d. Paris, 15 Sep 1842). French violinist-composer, last representative of the classical school of Paris: Paganini's style of virtuosity dismayed him. Trained in Rome, he returned to Paris in the early 1790s and set himself to study the works of the old violinist masters, besides having composition lessons with Reicha and Cherubini. From 1795 he taught at the Conservatoire; he also played as a soloist, chamber musician (making known the quartets of Haydn, Mozart and Beethoven) and orchestra leader. His works include nine concertos.

Bainbridge, Simon (Jeremy) (b. London, 30 Aug 1952). British composer, especially of powerful and evocative orchestral music. He studied with John Lambert at the RCM (1969–72) and made his mark early with *Spirogyra* for ensemble (1970). Attendance at Tanglewood in 1973 and 1974 broadened his scope, in ways perhaps prepared by maternal genes (she being US-born, his father an Australian painter). His *Ad ora incerta* (1994), a symphonic song cycle for mezzo, bassoon and orchestra to poems by Primo Levi, won him the Grawemeyer Award in 1997. Two years later he was appointed head of composition at the RAM, having previously taught at the RCM and Guildhall School.

Baines, William (b. Horbury, Yorks., 26 Mar 1899; d. York, 6 Nov 1922). British pianist-composer,

particularly of pieces reflecting his closeness to nature and admiration for Scriabin, Debussy and Ravel. The hardship of war service (1918–19) contributed to his early death.

Baird, Tadeusz (b. Grodzisk Mazowiecki, 26 Jul 1928; d. Warsaw, 2 Sep 1981). Polish composer, who was affected by his experiences in the Second World War (during which he began serious composition studies and, still a boy, was imprisoned) and on acquaintance with Berg's music. In 1947–51 he completed his education at the music academy in Warsaw. Liberalization in Polish culture allowed him to found, with Serocki, the Warsaw Autumn Festival in 1956, and at the same time to move out of the neoclassical style represented by his *Colas Breugnon* suite (1951). His later works include the opera *Tomorrow* (f.p. Warsaw, 1968), orchestral pieces (*Four Essays*, 1958; *Psychodrama*, 1972; *Voices from Afar*, with baritone, 1981) and chamber music.

Bairstow, Edward (Cuthbert) (b. Huddersfield, 22 Aug 1874; d. York, 1 May 1946). British organist-composer, knighted in 1932. Trained as an organist at Westminster Abbey, he began his career in 1893 and held posts in Wigan and Leeds before moving to York Minster (1913–46). Everywhere he worked also with choral societies and festivals, and in 1929 he became additionally professor of music at Durham University. He wrote services and anthems fully in the Anglican tradition.

Baiser de la fée, Le (The Fairy's Kiss). Ballet score by Stravinsky to a scenario after Andersen's tale 'The Ice Maiden', choreographed by Bronislava Nijinska for Ida Rubinstein. The music is gently adapted from piano pieces and songs by Tchaikovsky, with linking material in the same hybrid style. First performance: Paris Opera, 27 Nov 1928.

Baker, Janet (Abbott) (b. Hatfield, Yorks., 21 Aug 1933). British mezzo-soprano, created dame in 1976, the foremost representative in her day of a native tradition of creamy allure combined with direct expressive intensity. She studied in London with Helene Isepp and Meriel St Clair, and made her stage debut in 1956 in Oxford (Róza in Smetana's *The Secret*). By the mid-1960s she was a regular with the Handel Opera Society, and at Aldeburgh, Glyndebourne and Covent Garden, and though she confined her opera appearances to the British Isles, she appeared widely as a Mahler soloist and song recitalist. Works written for her included Argento's *From the Diary of Virginia Woolf*, Britten's *Phaedra* and the role of Kate in his *Owen Wingrave*. She retired from opera in 1982, and from concert and recording work a few years later.

Janet Baker *Full Circle* (1982)

Bakfark, Valentin (b. Brassó/Kronstadt, Transylvania, ?1526–30; d. Padua, 22 Aug 1576). Hungarian lutenist-composer. Born into a family of lutenists, he was probably taken by his father to the Hungarian court when he was a boy and set to an Italian master. After leaving the Hungarian royal family he served the Polish court (1549–66), Emperor Maximilian II (1566–9) and the Transylvanian prince János Zsigmond (1569–71). He then moved to Padua, where he and his family were victims of plague. His works include fantasias and intabulations of vocal polyphony. In Poland his surname became a byword for virtuoso.

Balada, Leonardo (b. Barcelona, 22 Sep 1933). Spanish–US composer, with Spanish–US colours in his upbeat music (operas, concertos, chamber pieces). He studied in Barcelona and with Persichetti at Juilliard, and began teaching at Carnegie-Mellon University in 1970.

Balakauskas, (Jonas) Osvaldas (b. Miliunai, Ukmerge district, 19 Dec 1937). Lithuanian composer whose works emerge from a personal tonal system based on scales of 8–11 notes. He studied with Lyatoshynsky at the Kiev Conservatory (1964–9) and returned to Vilnius in 1972. In 1985 he began teaching at the music academy, from which he took leave to serve as his country's ambassador in Paris (1992–4). His works, mostly for instrumental and electronic resources, include five symphonies.

Balakirev, Mily (Alekseyevich) (b. Nizhny Novgorod, 2 Jan 1837; d. St Petersburg, 29 May 1910). Russian composer and encourager of others, through a creative life of fitful excitement – he combined Liszt's and Chopin's bravura with Glinka's nationalism – and abiding generosity. He grew up musically in the circle around Aleksandr Ulybyshev, a local patron and author of books on Mozart and Beethoven. In 1853 he went to study mathematics at Kazan University, though by 1855 he had settled in St Petersburg and, through Ulybyshev, met Glinka. He then started to make his name as a pianist-composer, but the course of his life was changed by his encounters with Musorgsky in 1858, Rimsky-Korsakov in 1861 and Borodin in 1862. Musorgsky and Rimsky, still in their teens, were fired by his vision; Borodin was an older man, but it was Balakirev who pushed him into a commitment to music. In 1862, too, he helped found the Free School of Music, an alternative to the conservatories not only in offering education that was indeed free but also in inclining more to Russian traditions than Westernizing influences.

A new protégé, Tchaikovsky, arrived in 1867, the year in which Stasov coined the term MIGHTY HANDFUL that came to be applied to the Balakirev group. Balakirev also became conductor of the Russian Musical Society concerts (1867–9), in which role he invited Berlioz to conduct, and during the same period he wrote one of his major works, the orientalist-virtuoso piano fantasy *Islamey*. Soon after, though, he suffered a breakdown, from which he found relief in Orthodox Christianity while working as a railway company clerk. In 1876 he resumed work on *Tamara*, his orchestral masterpiece; he also returned to the Free School as director (1881) and became joint director with Rimsky of the court chapel choir (1883–94). After that he completed several works begun decades before, during the time he had been the great igniter of Russian music.

Edward Garden *Balakirev* (1967)

Orchestral: Symphony No.1, C, 1864–6, rev 1893–7; No.2, D minor, 1900–8; Piano Concerto No.1, F♯ minor, 1855–6; No.2, E♭, 1861–2, rev 1906–9; *King Lear* (overture), 1858–61, rev 1902–5; Overture on Russian Themes No.2 (*Russia*), 1863–4, rev 1884; Overture on Czech Themes (*In Bohemia*), 1867, rev 1905; *Tamara*, 1867–82; etc.
Piano: Fantasia on Themes from Glinka's *A Life for the Tsar*, 1854–6, rev 1899; *Islamey*, 1869, rev 1902; Sonata, B♭ minor, 1900–5; etc., transcriptions
Other works: songs, choral music, folksong arrangements

balalaika. Russian lute with a long neck and a triangular body.

Balanchine, George (b. St Petersburg, 22 Jan 1904; d. New York, 30 Apr 1983). Georgian–US choreographer who brought the classic Franco–Russian style to New York and was responsible for definitive productions of Stravinsky's *Apollo*, *Jeu de cartes*, *Orpheus* and *Agon*. Trained at the imperial ballet school (1914–21), he left Russia in 1924, worked with the Ballets Russes and moved to the USA in 1934. There he founded various companies, most notably New York City Ballet, which began in 1946 as Ballet Society. His father, Meliton Balanchivadze (1862–1937), was one of the first Western-style composers in Georgia, and his brother Andria (1906–92) was similarly a composer, who spent most of his life in Tbilisi, producing operas, ballets, six symphonies and five piano concertos.

Balbastre, Claude-Bénigne (b. Dijon, 22 Jan 1727;

d. Paris, 9 May 1799). French organist-composer. The son and pupil of an organist, he moved to Paris in 1750, where he had composition lessons with Rameau. He became a virtuoso performer, at concerts and at St Roch, where he was appointed organist in 1756. So popular were his improvisations there at the Christmas midnight mass (his *Recueil de noëls* in four suites, published in 1770, may give an impression) that in 1762 the archbishop banned him from performing. But he had further outlets, at Notre Dame and at court, and he also published harpsichord pieces. After the Revolution he lived in poverty, from which he emerged to give one last performance, of his arrangement of 'La Marseillaise' in the secularized cathedral.

Baldassare, Pietro (b. ?Brescia, *c*.1683; d. after 1768). Italian composer in holy orders, long-serving chapelmaster of the oratory in Brescia, remembered for two sonatas for trumpet and strings.

Baldwin. US instrument firm founded by Dwight Hamilton Baldwin (1821–99) in Cincinnati, originally as a retail business. The company began manufacturing reed organs in 1889, upright pianos in 1891 and grands in 1895, later expanding into electric organs (1947).

Balfe, Michael (William) (b. Dublin, 15 May 1808; d. Rowney Abbey, Herts., 20 Oct 1870). Irish composer and singer, whose career and reputation were Europe-wide. After music lessons from his father, a dancing master, and a local composer, he left for London in 1823 and then moved to mainland Europe (1825–35). He completed his studies in Rome (with Paer) and Milan, where his first opera was staged, and in 1827 sang Rossini's Figaro in Paris, with the composer's encouragement. Back in Italy, singing and composing, he married a Hungarian singer, Lina Roser, with whom he appeared in his own *Enrico Quarto* (Milan, 1833). Then, following his return to London, he again won praise in both fields: for operas including *The Siege of Rochelle* (1835), *The Maid of Artois* (on the MANON LESCAUT story) and *Falstaff* (1838), and as Papageno in the first English *Zauberflöte* (1838). A venture into management failed, but he rebounded with *The* BOHEMIAN GIRL (1843), an extraordinary hit. He pursued his vocation in London and abroad without gaining the same success (except in songs, notably the Tennyson setting 'Come into the garden, Maud' of 1857), and retired to his country estate in 1864. British balladry, Rossini and Auber all informed his music; Beethoven he sometimes stole from, as he cheerfully admitted: 'Ye can't do better than to go to the fountain-head, and come away with a cupful!'

Bali. See GAMELAN.

ballabile (It.). Danceable, used especially of an opera number that is so.

ballad. Song. Derivation from the Lat. root *ball-* (dance) indicates an original association with dance songs, but the term has been used for songs and poems of diverse kinds, including:

(1) Narrative songs with a folk-like character or genuinely traditional. The ballads of Schubert (e.g. *Erlkönig*), Loewe and Schumann are of this kind; so is Senta's ballad in *Der fliegende Holländer*.

(2) Sentimental popular British and US songs, from the age of Henry Bishop ('Home, sweet home') to that of Andrew Lloyd Webber ('Memory').

ballade. (1) One of the three fixed forms (with the RONDEAU and VIRELAI) of French song in the 14th and 15th centuries. It was distinguished by having two parts to each stanza, the first repeated. Each part would have two, three or four lines of different lengths, with two or more rhymes running through the stanza (and, indeed, the song as a whole). After three stanzas there might be a shorter *envoi* (farewell). The ballade was much practised by Machaut and his ARS SUBTILIOR successors; it then fell out of favour in the 15th century, though there are examples by Du Fay and Binchois.

(2) Instrumental piece so called in allusion to the narrative kind of sung ballad. The title was first used by Chopin in the 1830s. There are also examples for piano by Liszt and Brahms, and for larger forces by Fauré and Martin.

ballad opera. English 18th-century theatrical form: a satire with vernacular-style songs linked by spoken dialogue. *The Beggar's Opera* (1728) was the prototype, much imitated in the next decade or so (by Henry Fielding among others), but unequalled. The term is sometimes applied also to 19th-century musical plays and was nostalgically revived by 20th-century composers, including Vaughan Williams and Tippett.

ballata. Italian song form of the 13th–15th centuries. The terminological closeness to the French ballade is deceptive; the VIRELAI is a much closer relative, for the ballata similarly has a basic ABBA pattern. Masters of it included Landini and Ciconia.

ballet. Rehearsed dance, by highly trained professional dancers, normally in a theatre with live music. Ballet maintains, almost uniquely, an old view of music as an accessory experience, facilitating in this case the dance, just as music facilitated poetic drama in early opera and divine worship in works for the church. In the ballet theatre a work is commonly known by the name of its choreographer rather than its composer: Balanchine's *Agon*, Ashton's *Daphnis et Chloé*. Moreover, ballet is an art full of powerful tradition and of exacting expertise having to do with keeping the body in peak performing condition. This is a world in which few musicians have felt at home. So, although most composers since the mid 18th century have been drawn into opera at least once, and although most conductors would want to tackle *Don Giovanni* or *Wozzeck*, ballet music has often been in the hands of specialist composers, arrangers and conductors.

Even so, there have been great exceptions. Ballet in France, between 1661 (when the Académie Royale de Danse was founded by Louis XIV) and the French Revolution (1789), was inseparable from opera; operas of the time – by Lully, Charpentier, Rameau and others – were partly vehicles for danced divertissements. In Italy at the same period ballet had a life of its own, already independent not only of opera but of the foremost composers. However, the great choreographer of the Classical period, Jean-Georges Noverre (1727–1810), who worked in many European cities, collaborated with composers including Gluck and the teenage Mozart (*Les Petits Riens*).

In the 19th century ballet's equivocal relation with music continued. Beethoven (*Die Geschöpfe des Prometheus*) and Tchaikovsky (*Swan Lake, Sleeping Beauty, The Nutcracker*) produced scores, but no less important in ballet history are the works danced to music by H.S. Løvenskjold (*La Sylphide*), Cesare Pugni (*Ondine*), Delibes (*Coppélia, Sylvia*) and Minkus (*Don Quixote, La Bayadère*). Throughout most of the century the main ballet centres were in Russia, where Tchaikovsky, Pugni and Minkus worked, and in Paris, where ballet's connection to opera continued – whence the ballet music in Gounod's *Faust*, Saint-Saëns's *Samson et Dalila*, Wagner's *Tannhäuser* (in the Paris Opera version), Verdi's *Les Vêpres siciliennes*, etc.

Diaghilev's BALLETS RUSSES – with the help of Stravinsky and a few others – had some lasting effect in carrying the Russian tradition west and also in making ballet composition exciting. Many of the great ballet companies of the later 20th century, in New York and western Europe, can trace some descent from the Diaghilev troupe, though

equally important has been the contribution of 'modern dance', associated principally with Martha Graham and her artistic progeny (notably Merce Cunningham), and explicitly departing from ballet tradition. Ballet companies and modern dance troupes have both freely commissioned scores, as Diaghilev did, and increasingly the lessons of modern dance have been absorbed by ballet companies, which have tended, for historical and practical reasons, to be affiliated to major opera houses and therefore have a sounder institutional base.

Debra Craine and Judith Mackrell *The Oxford Dictionary of Dance* (2000)

ballet de cour (Fr., court ballet). Genre of the French court, particularly under the young Louis XIV, who loved to dance himself in his teens and 20s, to scores provided by Lully. The form was then superseded by opera, which still had a strong dance component.

Ballet mécanique. Score by Antheil, intended to accompany a film by Fernand Léger, Man Ray and Dudley Murphy. The original version was for 16 pianolas, two pianos, three xylophones, four bass drums, tam tam, siren, seven electric bells and three aeroplane propellers; an arsenal reduced to more manageable proportions for the first performance. First performance: Paris, 19 Jun 1926.

Ballets Russes (Russian Ballet). Company managed by Diaghilev, first, from 1909, as an export business, bringing Russian artists to western Europe. Increasingly, though, it broke free of its Russian roots, which were effectively axed by the Revolution. It gave annual seasons in Paris and London, but also appeared elsewhere in Europe and even, during the First World War, in New York and South America. It disbanded in 1929, following the death of Diaghilev, and having presented the following new scores:

1910 – Stravinsky's The FIREBIRD; 1911 – Stravinsky's PETRUSHKA, Tcherepnin's *Narcisse*; 1912 – Hahn's *Le Dieu bleu*, Ravel's DAPHNIS ET CHLOE; 1913 – Debussy's JEUX, Stravinsky's The RITE OF SPRING, Schmitt's *La Tragédie de Salomé*; 1914 – Stravinsky's The Nightingale, Strauss's *Josephs-Legende*, Steinberg's *Midas*; 1917 – Tommasini's *Le donne di buon umore*, Satie's PARADE; 1919 – Respighi's *La Boutique fantasque*, Falla's El SOMBRERO DE TRES PICOS; 1920 – Stravinsky's *Chant du rossignol*, PULCINELLA; 1921 – Prokofiev's *Chout*; 1922 – Stravinsky's RENARD, MAVRA; 1923 – Stravinsky's Les NOCES; 1924 – Poulenc's *Les Biches*, Auric's *Les Fâcheux*, Milhaud's *Le Train bleu*; 1925 – Duke's *Zéphyr et*

Flore, Auric's *Les Matelots*, Rieti's *Barabau*; 1926 – Lambert's *Romeo and Juliet*, Auric's *La Pastorale*, Berners's *The Triumph of Neptune*; 1927 – Sauguet's *La Chatte*, Stravinsky's *Oedipus Rex* (see OEDIPUS), Prokofiev's *Le Pas d'acier*; 1928 – Nabokov's *Ode*; 1929 – Rieti's *Le Bal*, Prokofiev's *L'Enfant prodigue*

ballett. Variety of English madrigal produced by Morley, Weelkes and others in enthusiastic response to the Gastoldi BALLETTO, imitating its 'fa-la-la' vocalizations. These English songs were not intended for dancing.

balletto. Italian dance, played on the lute (late 16th century), sung (from the appearance of Gastoldi's first collection in 1591 for about three decades) or played by an instrumental group (17th century).

Ballif, Claude (André François) (b. Paris, 22 May 1924; d. Poissons, Haute-Marne, 24 Jul 2004). French composer, who has developed his own 'metatonality' using scales of 11 notes (i.e. with one missing). He studied in Bordeaux and at the Paris Conservatoire (with Noël Gallon, Tony Aubin and Messiaen), then in 1951 went to Berlin for further studies with Blacher, Josef Rufer and Hans Heinz Stuckenschmidt. In 1959 he returned to Paris, where he taught, notably at the Conservatoire (1971–90). His work list is particu-larly strong in chamber and solo instrumental categories but also includes a series of 'symphonic concertos' and the opera *Dracoula* (1982–4).

ballo (It., pl. *balli*). Dance, ball.

ballo in maschera, Un (A Masked Ball). Opera by Verdi to a libretto by Antonio Somma after one by Scribe. The ball scene is last, at which Renato (baritone) stabs Riccardo (tenor), partly from jealousy at the tender feelings his wife Amelia (soprano) showed this other man, though their love was blameless. The murder was predicted by the fortune-teller Ulrica (contralto) and unwit-tingly facilitated by the page Oscar (soprano). In Scribe's version the victim was Gustavus III of Sweden, whose end indeed came roughly this way. Censors obliged Verdi and Somma to give their opera an unlikely new location in colonial Boston, but often now the action is restored to Gustav's court. Arias include Amelia's 'Ma dall'arido stelo divulsa' and 'Morrò ma prima in grazia', Ulrica's 'Re dell'abisso', Riccardo's 'La rivedrà nell'estasi', 'Di' tu se fedele' and 'Ma se m'è forza perderti', and Renato's 'Alla vita che t'arride' and 'Eri tu'. First performance: Rome, 17 Feb 1859.

Baltimore. US city, a musical centre since the late 18th century, home of the PEABODY INSTITUTE and the Baltimore Symphony.

Bamberg. German city, where the Prague Deutsche Philharmonie (1939–45) was refounded in 1946 as the Bamberg Symphony. Principal conductors have included Keilberth (1950–68), Jochum (1968–73) and Jonathan Nott (from 2000).

bamboula. Caribbean dance, inspiration for one work by Gottschalk and several by Wuorinen.

Banchieri, Adriano (b. Bologna, 3 Sep 1568; d. Bologna, 1634). Italian organist-composer whose life was that of an Olivetan monk. He accordingly set psalms, masses and motets, but also produced a large number of madrigals, including the madrigal comedy *La pazzia senile* (1598), as well as pieces for instrumental ensemble (*La battaglia*, etc.) and theoretical writings.

band. Group of performers. The word can be used of almost any ensemble, but is most idiomatic in connection with wind groupings (BRASS BAND, CONCERT BAND, MILITARY BAND) and popular formations (jazz band, steel band, rock band).

banda (It.). STAGE BAND.

bandoneon. Button accordion characteristic of tango ensembles in Argentina, Uruguay and Brazil.

bandora. Bass lute of English invention, of scalloped outline, used in the late 16th and early 17th centuries in the theatre, to accompany songs and as a consort instrument.

Bangladesh. See INDIA.

Bang on a Can. Association formed in New York in 1987 by Michael Gordon, David Lang and Julia Wolfe, to present their music and that of contem-poraries. Their annual marathon concerts favour informal, rough-and-ready presentation allied with virtuoso performance. www.bangonacan.org

Banister, John (b. London, 1624/5; d. London, 3 Oct 1679). English violinist-composer. He was a member of the king's violin band from 1660, but lost royal favour and at least by 1672 was pioneering a new form, the public CONCERT, sometimes with large forces. He also wrote for the theatre.

banjo. Small guitar-like instrument, with a drum head (of skin or plastic stretched over a metal frame) for a body. It was an instrument of US Blacks until the mid 19th century, when commercial manufacturers took it up. When occasionally used by classical composers (Weill, Kagel, Peter Maxwell Davies), it has kept its low-born status.

Banks, Don(ald Oscar) (b. South Melbourne, 25 Oct 1923; d. Sydney, 5 Sep 1980). Australian composer. The son of a jazz musician, he studied at the University of Melbourne Conservatorium (1947–9), meanwhile playing jazz himself with his Don Banks Boptet. In 1950 he moved to London, and made decisive contact with Seiber, Babbitt in Salzburg (1952), Dallapiccola in Florence (1953) and Nono in Gravesano (1956). While completing his modernist training he composed rather little, but then in the 1960s came a rush of works in a style of strong gestures, lean textures and forward-urging rhythm. He kept up his interest in jazz, and in jazz–classical fusion, while supporting himself by writing film scores. In 1972 he returned to Australia to take a post at the Canberra School of Music.

Orchestral: Horn Concerto, 1965; *Assemblies*, 1966; *Intersections*, tape, orch, 1969; Violin Concerto, 1969; *Meeting Place*, jazz group, ens, elec, 1972; etc.

Chamber: *Sonata da camera*, 8 insts, 1961; *Settings from Roget*, jazz group, 1966; String Quartet, 1975; etc.

Bantock, Granville (b. London, 7 Aug 1868; d. London, 16 Oct 1946). British composer, a vigorous Romantic, knighted in 1930. A doctor's son, he studied with Corder at the RAM (1888–92) and embarked on a career as a conductor, generously promoting the work of others; he was an early champion of Sibelius, acknowledged as such with the dedication of the Finnish composer's Third Symphony. In 1900 he was appointed principal of the Birmingham School of Music, and he was then professor at Birmingham University (1908–34). He produced a vast output, especially of orchestral works, choral music and songs, often with an exotic appeal, whether Celtic or oriental.

Orchestral: *The Pierrot of the Minute* (overture), 1908; *Hebridean Symphony*, 1915; *Pagan Symphony*, 1923–8; etc.

Choral: *Omar Khayyam*, soli, ch, orch, 1906–9; *Atlanta in Corydon*, 1911; *Vanity of Vanities*, 1913; etc.

Other works: stage pieces, chamber music, songs

bar. (1) Vertical line through the staff or staves. Also, in British usage, the segment of music between two such lines, called a 'measure' in US terminology. Where there might be confusion between these two meanings of bar, the term 'barline' may be used for the former. But 'double bar' is normal for the pair of lines marking the end of a piece, movement or section.

Barlines have two functions: to clarify the vertical alignment of parts and to indicate the metre. It was the former that brought barring into being and that has continued to serve in music where the concept of metre has dissolved. The visual alignment of parts becomes an issue only when music is notated in score, and because medieval and Renaissance polyphony was generally presented in partbook form, it was not barred. Barlines were introduced for polyphony in lute or keyboard tablature in the 15th century and became universal at the start of the 17th century, when the Baroque revolution made score notation the norm. However, it was only from the mid 17th century that barring was always made to follow the metre consistently.

Music of changing metre (the finale of *The Rite of Spring* was an early example) will be notated in bars (measures) of changing length. Where there is nothing resembling a metre, composers may prefer to notate in regular 4/4 for the ease of performers, and barring becomes again simply a way of showing vertical relationships.

(2) Abbreviation for baritone.

Barber, Samuel (Osmond) (b. West Chester, Penn., 9 Mar 1910; d. New York, 23 Jan 1981). US composer, in a lyrical Romantic style close to the Tchaikovsky–Rachmaninoff tradition. He was encouraged as a boy (and later) by his aunt and uncle, the contralto Louise Homer (1871–1947) and composer Sidney Homer (1864–1953). After early piano lessons he studied at the Curtis Institute (1924–34), where Rosario Scalero was his composition teacher and where he met his life's companion, Menotti. He had rapid success. His *School for Scandal* overture was played by the Philadelphia Orchestra while he was still a student. As a baritone he sang regularly on the radio and received praise for his recording of his own *Dover Beach*. Also, while in Rome as winner of the Rome Prize (1935–7), he wrote his Symphony in One Movement, which had prestigious performances in Europe and the USA. Toscanini took up his *Essay* and Adagio for strings, the latter an arrangement of the elegiac slow movement of his quartet, and one of the few popular classics of the last 100 years.

After returning to the USA he taught at the Curtis Institute (1939–42), then moved with Menotti to Mt Kisco, NY, where he devoted himself to composing, often to prominent commissions: his piano sonata was written for Horowitz, and his opera *Antony and Cleopatra* for the opening of the new Met, in 1966. That work's poor reception hit him hard. While he worked on revising it his production of new works diminished, and there were problems of alcoholism, illness and a split with Menotti (1973). But he lived to see a successful revival of the opera (1975) and continuing public acclaim for his combination of melodiousness with fine sensibility.

Barbara B. Heyman *Samuel Barber* (1992)

Operas: *Vanessa* (Menotti), Op.32, f.p. New York, 1958; *A Hand of Bridge* (1 short act, Menotti), Op.35, f.p. Spoleto, 1959; *Antony and Cleopatra* (Zeffirelli, after Shakespeare), Op.40, f.p. New York 1966, rev New York, 1975

Ballets: MEDEA (Martha Graham), Op.23, 1946; *Souvenirs* (Todd Bolender), Op.28, 1952

Orchestral (full): Symphony No.1 in One Movement, Op.9, 1936; No.2, Op.19, 1943, rev 1947; *The School for Scandal* (overture), Op.5, 1931; *Music for a Scene from Shelley*, Op.7, 1933; *First Essay*, Op.12, 1937; Violin Concerto, Op.14, 1939; *Second Essay*, Op.17, 1942; *Commando March*, band, 1943; Cello Concerto, Op.22, 1945; *Medea's Dance of Vengeance*, Op.23a, 1953; *Toccata festiva*, Op.36, 1960; *Die natali*, Op.37, 1960; Piano Concerto, Op.38, 1961–2; *Night Flight*, Op.19a, 1964 (after Symphony No.2); *Fadograph of a Yestern Scene*, Op.44, 1971; *Third Essay*, Op.47, 1978; suites from ballets

Orchestral (strings): Serenade, Op.1, 1928; Adagio, 1938 (from String Quartet); *Capricorn Concerto*, Op.21, fl, ob, tpt, str, 1944; *Canzonetta*, Op.48, ob, str, 1978–81

Vocal orchestral: *Knoxville: Summer of 1915* (James Agee), s, orch, 1947; *Prayers of Kierkegaard*, Op.30, s, ch, orch, 1954; *Andromache's Farewell*, s, orch, 1962; *The Lovers* (Neruda), Op.43, bar, ch, orch, 1971; orchestral versions of songs

Choral: *The Virgin Martyrs* (Helen Waddell), Op.8:1, women's ch, 1935; *Let down the bars, o Death* (Dickinson), Op.8:2, 1936; *God's Grandeur* (Gerard Manley Hopkins), 1938; *A Stopwatch and an Ordnance Map* (Spender), Op.15, ch, brass, timp, 1940; *Reincarnations* (James Stephens), Op.16, 1940; *Easter Chorale* (Pack Browning), ch, brass, timp, 1965; *Agnus Dei*, 1967 (arr of Adagio); *Twelfth Night* (Laurie Lee), Op.42:1, 1968; *To be Sung upon the Water* (Louise Bogan), Op.42:2, 1968; versions of songs

Chamber: Serenade, Op.1, str qt, 1928; Cello Sonata, Op.6, 1932; String Quartet, Op.11, 1936; *Summer Music*, Op.31, wind qnt, 1955; *Canzone*, Op.38a, fl, pf, 1961 (after Piano Concerto)

Songs: 10 Early Songs, 1925–37; 3 Songs, Op.2, 1927–34; *Dover Beach* (Matthew Arnold), Op.3, mez/bar, str qt, 1931; 3 Songs (Joyce), Op.10, 1935–6; 4 Songs, Op.13, 1937–40; 2 Songs, Op.18, 1942–3; *Nuvoletta* (Joyce), Op.25, 1947; *Mélodies passagères* (5; Rilke), Op.27, 1950–51; *Hermit Songs* (10; Irish), Op.29, 1952–3; *Despite and Still* (5), Op.41, 1968–9; 3 Songs, Op.45, 1972

Piano: *Excursions*, Op.20, 1942–4; Sonata, Op.26, 1949; Nocturne, Op.33, 1959; Ballade, Op.46. 1977

Other works: Suite, carillon, 1932; *Wondrous Love*, Op.34, org, 1958

Barber of Seville, The. See *Il* BARBERE DI SIVIGLIA.

barbershop. Genre originally associated with quartets of men's voices, distinguished by homophony featuring runs of diminished seventh and other tritone-laden chords. It sprang up in the USA in the late 19th century.

Barbican Hall. London concert hall, opened in 1982.

Barbier, Jules (b. Paris, 8 Mar 1825; d. Paris, 16 Jan 1901). French librettist, active in the theatre from his teens. At the height of his career (1852–72) he was producing roughly two librettos a year, as well as plays, mostly in collaboration with Carré, his partner on *Faust* and *Roméo et Juliette* (Gounod), *Mignon* and *Hamlet* (Thomas) and *Les Contes d'Hoffmann* (the play that preceded Offenbach's opera). He also had a hand in the scenario for Delibes's *Sylvia*.

barbiere di Siviglia, Il (The Barber of Seville). Opera by Rossini to a libretto by Cesare Sterbini after the Beaumarchais play, also leaning on the libretto of the earlier operatic version by Paisiello. The barber Figaro (baritone) brings the lovers Almaviva (tenor) and Rosina (contralto) together despite the wily watchfulness of Rosina's guardian Dr Bartolo (bass) – who had planned to marry her himself – and the conniving of Don Basilio (bass). A long-standing performance tradition had Rosina's part transposed up for sopranos, who were allowed to adapt the music-lesson scene to include showy repertory of their own. Increasingly since the mid 20th century, however, the original score has been restored to currency. Rosina's 'Una voce poco fa' and Figaro's 'Largo al factotum' are among the most familiar operatic arias; other numbers include Almaviva's serenade 'Ecco, ridente', Basilio's aria 'La calunnia è un venticello' and the Figaro–Rosina duet 'Dunque io son'. First performance: Rome, 20 Feb 1816.

Barbieri, Francisco Asenjo (b. Madrid, 3 Aug 1823; d. Madrid, 17 Feb 1894). Spanish composer, associated with the zarzuela boom. He studied at the Madrid Conservatory and started his career in the theatre in his teens. Among his successes were *Jugar con fuego* (1851), *Pan y toros* (1864), *El barbarillo de Lavapiés* (1876) and *El Sr Luis el tumbón* (1891).

Barbier von Bagdad, Der (The Barber of Baghdad). Opera by Cornelius to his own libretto after the *1001 Nights*. Nureddin (tenor) is both hindered and helped by the barber Abul Hassan (bass) in his pursuit of Margiana (soprano), daughter of the wary Cadi (tenor). First performance: Weimar, 15 Dec 1858.

Barbirolli, John [Giovanni Battista] (b. London, 2 Dec 1899; d. London, 29 Jul 1970). British conductor of Italian–French descent, knighted in 1949. He studied at the RAM and began his career as a cellist before starting to conduct professionally in 1927. Soon he was appearing internationally: for five seasons (1937–42) he was permanent conductor of the New York Philharmonic-Symphony, and later he had associations with the Houston Symphony (1961–7) and the Berlin Philharmonic (1961–70). But his great joy was the Hallé, whose conductor he was from 1943. He was at his keen finest in late Romantic music, including especially Elgar, Mahler and Vaughan Williams, whose Eighth Symphony was dedicated to him. In 1939 he married the oboist Evelyn Rothwell.

Michael Kennedy *John Barbirolli* (1971)

barcarolle (Fr., It. *barcarola*). Venetian gondolier's song, or other piece evoking such, typically having a lilting 6/8 rhythm suggestive of the rocking boat and romantic possibility. The style was known in the 18th century and infiltrated some of Schubert's songs (e.g. *Der Gondelfahrer*). Of works entitled Barcarolle the most celebrated examples are Chopin's for piano (in 12/8) and Offenbach's from *Les Contes d'Hoffmann*. Fauré kept returning to the form.

Barcelona. Capital of Catalonia, Spain, having as its principal musical amenities the Gran Teatre del Liceu (1847, reopened in 1999 after a fire) and the Palau de la Música (1905–8), an oustanding example of art nouveau.

Bard, The (*Barden*). Symphonic poem by Sibelius, evocative of a bard's contemplative song while stroking his lyre. First performance: Helsinki, 27 Mar 1913.

Bardi, Giovanni de', Count of Vernio (b. Florence, 5 Feb 1534; d. Sep 1612). Italian connoisseur. A military man in his youth, by the 1570s he was the focus of the CAMERATA.

Barenboim, Daniel (b. Buenos Aires, 15 Nov 1942). Argentinian–Israeli pianist and conductor. Born to musical parents who were his first teachers, he made his debut as a pianist in Buenos Aires at seven. In 1952 the family moved to Israel, and in 1954 his parents took him to attend Markevich's conducting classes in Salzburg, where he was impressed by – and impressed – Furtwängler. The next year he was in Paris for studies with Boulanger, though by this time he was performing internationally and recording. In the 1960s and early 1970s his career was centred in Britain: he formed a close relationship with the English Chamber Orchestra as pianist-conductor (1965), married the cellist Jacqueline du Pré (1967) and made his debut as an opera conductor at the Edinburgh Festival (*Don Giovanni*, 1973). He was then music director of the Orchestre de Paris (1975–88), during which time he conducted at Bayreuth (*Tristan*, the *Ring*). After that he took charge of the Chicago Symphony (from 1991) and the Berlin Staatsoper (from 1992). He is a supremely accomplished musician, perhaps still closest to his early loves (Mozart, Beethoven), though with a repertory extending to Boulez, Birtwistle and Carter.

Bärenreiter. German music publishing firm founded in Augsburg in 1924 by Karl Vötterle, who named his company after a star in the constellation Ursa Major: Alkor, the Bear Rider. Besides music, the house publishes journals and the encyclopedia *Die Musik in Geschichte und Gegenwart*.

bar form. AAB form. The term comes from the MEISTERSINGER, and is of uncertain derivation. Wagner, in his opera *Die Meistersinger*, made reference to it, and it also seems to underlie some of the songs of Schubert, Schumann and Brahms.

Bargiel, Woldemar (b. Berlin, 3 Oct 1828; d. Berlin, 23 Feb 1897). German composer, half-brother of Clara Schumann (their mother married Adolph Bargiel, a Berlin music teacher, after divorcing Wieck). He studied at the Leipzig Conservatory (1846–50) and had a distinguished career as a composer and teacher, his works including four quartets, three piano trios, choral psalms and piano pieces.

bariolage (Fr., heterogeneity of colour). Alternation between an open string on a bowed instrument and the same note played on another string with, of course, finger stopping.

baritone (Fr. *baryton*, Ger. *Bariton*, pl. *Baritone*, It. *baritono*, pl. *baritoni*). Man's voice of middle range, a third below the tenor; or a singer with that voice. The term can also be used of an instrument or clef of similar register, e.g. the baritone saxophone or the band instrument known simply as the baritone (a member of the saxhorn family).

The derivation is from the Gk *barytonos*, deep-sounding, and indeed, when the word was introduced, in the Renaissance, it was for the lowest polyphonic voice. In the early 17th century, beginning in Italy, the baritone rose to his place between bass and tenor. However, the term 'bass' stayed in general use for all lower male voices until the 19th century, even though the baritone voice was well defined in opera roles – e.g. the Count and Figaro in *Le nozze di Figaro*. Later in the 19th century varieties of the voice came to be recognized, including the *baryton* MARTIN and the BASS-BARITONE.

baritone clef. C CLEF on the top line or F clef on the middle line (obsolete).

baritone oboe. Alternative name for bass oboe.

Barkin, Elaine [née Radoff] (b. Bronx, NY, 15 Dec 1932). US composer who moved in the late 1970s from the Babbitt orbit to a thought-filled and sophisticated exploration of semi-improvised collaboration. She studied at Brandeis and in Berlin with Blacher (1956–7), and then taught, notably at UCLA (1974–94).

barline. See BAR.

Barlow, Clarence [Klarenz] (b. Calcutta, 27 Dec 1945). Indian–German composer, who has used computers in generating his highly elaborated music, in which cherished ideals and models of the post-war avant-garde are teased. He studied sciences at Calcutta University and composition at the conservatory in Cologne (1968–73), where he settled, teaching at the conservatory from 1984 and at Darmstadt. His works include *Çogluoto-büsisletmesi* for piano (1975–9), *Im Januar am Nil* for ensemble (1981–4) and *Orchidæ Ordinariæ or The Twelfth Root of Truth* for piano and orchestra (1989).

Barnby, Joseph (b. York, 12 Aug 1838; d. London, 28 Jan 1896). British church musician, knighted in 1892. Trained as a York Minster choirboy and at the RAM, he was active at various London churches and Eton, bringing in big works from the St John Passion to *Parsifal* (British première, 1884). He wrote church music and a popular partsong, 'Sweet and low'.

Baroque (Ger. *Barock*, It. *barocco*). Term for music of the period *c*.1600–1750. Derived from the Portuguese *barroco* (a misshapen pearl), the word was first used in France disapprovingly, with regard to Rameau's HIPPOLYTE ET ARICIE (1733), and for the next several decades it continued to indicate ungainly extravagance. In the 19th century it gradually assumed its present meaning in art history, to cover a period after and distinct from the Renaissance. It was then embraced and reinterpreted by music historians, beginning with Curt Sachs in 1919.

The delay in defining Baroque music can be explained by that music's disappearance and revival. In the 19th century Bach and Handel were lone monuments, and it was not until the mid 20th century that Monteverdi, Rameau, Purcell and Vivaldi were restored to regular performance, as phenomena of the early-music movement. So although 19th-century historians had recognized the shift in musical expectations and compositional technique that took place around 1600, it was only in the 20th century, when Baroque music began to be played again in quantity, that a term for it was needed.

The shift of *c*.1600 was in several linked dimensions. What drew most comment at the time was the new expressiveness of vocal writing, which encouraged a move from polyphonic textures of several equally important voices (a style reaching its final glory in Byrd and Victoria) to music for a solo singer with instrumental accompaniment, since a soloist could both command the new virtuosity and embody the new intensity. At the same time there was pressure towards solo performance from the fresh interest in sung drama, in opera. And since the new kind of vocal expression depended not only on melodic flows and leaps but on harmonic effects and implications, it demanded a new firmness and clarity in the bass, a deeper embedding in major–minor tonality.

Keyboard instruments, which could provide full harmonic support, became more important, and keyboard-playing composers, from Frescobaldi to Scarlatti, supplied themselves and their colleagues with opportunities for virtuosity when alone. Alongside the harpsichord and its relatives, the violin gained a solo repertory, as a voice without words, and instruments of the violin family became the foundation of another Baroque invention: the orchestra. These new instrumental means could not arise without new instrumental genres (with new, and lasting, titles: concerto, sonata, symphony and sinfonia, prelude). A lot of Baroque music dances, because dance music provided a rich repertory of models for instrumental performance – models not only of metred rhythm but of regularity in phrasing and harmonic change. The principal alternative was to compose on a melodic theme, whether strictly and contrapuntally in a fugue, lyrically in a slow movement or freely in a fantasia. And instrumental melody, theme-based, flowed back into the voice, bringing a clear musical shape to the almost ubiquitous vocal form of the later Baroque: the aria.

Much changed during the course of the Baroque period, whose ending – as it gave way to the more variously paced, lighter GALANT and PRE-CLASSICAL styles – is harder to define than its beginning. Accordingly, the age is sometimes split into shorter spans, such as the early Baroque (Monteverdi), the high Baroque (from Corelli to Handel and Bach) and the late Baroque or even post-Baroque (Bach's sons, perhaps Gluck). Much clearer, though, are the geographical divisions. Bound up with language, with local dance fashions and with religious practice, Baroque music rapidly developed national or regional traditions, especially in northern and central Germany, Italy and France. Many composers drew on foreign examples, as Purcell and Bach did in their different generations, learning from French and Italian contemporaries. But the conspicuousness of such borrowings and meldings testifies to the strength and separateness of the musical cultures. Baroque music thus had a stylistic variety that was lost during the long century and more of Classical-Romantic music led from Vienna, to reappear in the early 20th century.

Claude V. Palisca *Baroque Music* (1968, [2]1981); Nicholas Anderson *Baroque Music* (1994)

Barraqué, Jean (Henri Alphonse) (b. Puteaux, near Paris, 17 Jan 1928; d. Paris, 17 Aug 1973). French composer, in a modernist style of Romantic reach and expressive charge. As a choirboy at Notre Dame he was fired with creative ambition by hearing Schubert's 'Unfinished' Symphony on record. The great masters – Bach, Beethoven, Schubert, Debussy – became his measure. He studied with Langlais and Messiaen, and absorbed Boulez's early music, but in his first important work, the Piano Sonata (1950–52), discovered a forward momentum all his own, through phases of exultation and despair.

Such phases characterized his life over the next two decades. Pleasure in friendship, and short bursts of creative work, contrasted with bleak moods and long periods of inaction. He loved the sea and the north Breton coast, where he had spent summer holidays as a child, but he lived in Paris, mostly with his parents in a wretched parody of family life, supporting himself by giving lectures and writing articles. A close comradeship with Michel Foucault, ending in a brief love affair that coincided with the completion of *Séquence* (1950–55), contributed to the intellectual development of both men.

After that he devoted himself to what he planned as a vast cycle of works, based on Hermann Broch's novel *The Death of Virgil* and set to explore its themes of death and self-destruction, of the artist's role in realizing the transcendent, and of the perils, hopelessness and necessity of taking on that responsibility. Thus boldly, even defiantly Romantic in his aims and ideals, he enfolded the discontinuity, complexity and ambiguity of his time, and developed a technique of proliferating series that allowed boundless and urgent change, up to a point of dissolve or failing.

Paul Griffiths *The Sea on Fire* (2003)

Early works: Piano Sonata, 1950–52; SEQUENCE, s, ens, 1950–55; *Etude*, tape, 1954 *La* MORT DE VIRGILE: LE TEMPS RESTITUE, s, ch, orch, 1956–68; ... AU DELA DU HASARD, 3 women's v, pf, wind, perc, 1957–9; CHANT APRES CHANT, s, pf, 6 perc, 1966; Concerto, cl, vib, 18 insts, 1962–8

Barraud, Henry (b. Bordeaux, 23 Apr 1900; d. Paris, 28 Dec 1997). French composer. Intended by his parents for the wine business, he broke away in 1926 to study at the Paris Conservatoire with Dukas and Georges Caussade. In 1933, with Rivier, he founded the Concerts du Triton to put on new repertory; he was then music director of French radio (1948–65). Sometimes severe, his music bespeaks his religious faith, and includes operas, choral works and three symphonies.

barré (Fr., barred). Application of the flat of the forefinger (usually) at a fret on a guitar, lute or banjo to stop all the strings at the same point. Also possible is the half-barré, across some but not all of the strings.

barrel organ. Organ responding, like a musical box, to a rotating drum on which the music is encoded in projecting pins. The term is commonly applied to street organs or pianos, where the music is not on a barrel at all but on perforated card or paper, as with the PIANOLA.

Barrett, Richard (b. Swansea, 7 Nov 1959). British composer of highly elaborated and expressively forceful music. Originally a science student at London University, he was spurred to compose on hearing a piece by Finnissy. He then had lessons with Peter Wiegold and, at Darmstadt in 1984, with Ferneyhough and Hans Joachim Hespos. In 1993 he settled in Amsterdam. His works include the orchestral *Vanity* (1990–94) and many pieces for solo instrument or small groupings.

Barrière, Jean (b. Bordeaux, 2 May 1707; d. Paris, 6 Jun 1747). French cellist-composer, who studied in

Italy (1736–9) and wrote sonatas that came early in his instrument's distinctive repertory.

barring. The drawing of barlines; hence how a passage is barred.

Barrios (Mangore), Agustin (Pio) (b. San Juan Bautista de la Misiones, 5 May 1885; d. San Salvador, 7 Aug 1944). Paraguayan guitarist-composer. Musically trained in Asunción, he spent long periods in other South American countries (1910–24) and in Europe (1934–6), gaining acclaim for his virtuosity. Many of his pieces entered his instrument's central repertory, including *La catedral*, the Waltz in G, *Una limosna por el amor de dios*, *Julia Florida* and *Un sueño en la foresta*.

Barron, Louis (b. Minneapolis, 23 Apr 1920; d. Los Angeles, 1 Nov 1989) and **Bebe** [née Charlotte Wind] (b. Minneapolis, 16 Jun 1927). US composers, pioneers of electronic music. They married in 1947 and set up one of the earliest electronic studios the next year in New York; Bebe had studied composition with Riegger and Cowell. Cage was among their guests, and they produced an atmospheric musical soundtrack for the science-fiction film *Forbidden Planet* (1956).

Barry, Gerald (Anthony) (b. Clarecastle, Co. Clare, 28 Apr 1952). Irish composer of music abounding in subtexts and ironies. He studied at University College, Dublin, in Amsterdam with Schat, in Cologne with Kagel and Stockhausen, and in Vienna with Cerha. Baroque music, as revealed by the early-music movement, was also important in his formation. State support has enabled him to devote himself to composition since 1986.

Operas: *The Intelligence Park* (Vincent Deane),
   1981–8; *The Triumph of Beauty and Deceit*
   (Meredith Oakes), 1991–2; *The Bitter Tears of Petra
   von Kant* (Fassbinder), 2002
Orchestral: *Chevaux-de-frise*, 1988; *The Road*, 1997;
   etc.
Chamber: *Things that Gain by Being Painted*, speaker,
   singer, vc, pf, 1977; ' — — ', ens, 1979; *Triorchic
   Blues*, pf/vn, 1990–2; etc.

Barry, John (b. York, 3 Nov 1933). British composer, mostly of film music, dropping his surname of Prendergast. The son of a cinema proprietor, he studied as an army trumpeter and by correspondence, and won fame in the late 1950s as the leader of a pop group. In the 1960s his career as a film composer took off with the James Bond movies and *Born Free* (1966), for which he won his first two Oscars (best score and best song). He moved to the USA in 1975, his later credits including

The Cotton Club (1984) and *Dances with Wolves* (1990).

Barsanti, Francesco (b. Lucca, 1690; d. London, 1772). Italian musician, who arrived in London in 1714 with Geminiani as a composer and wind player, stayed in Britain and wrote recorder sonatas and concertos.

Barshay, Rudolf (Borisovich) (b. Krasnodarsk, 1 Oct 1924). Russian conductor. After playing the viola in quartets he founded the Moscow Chamber Orchestra (1955), with which he introduced Shostakovich's Symphony No.14 and his own arrangements, notably of the same composer's Eighth Quartet. Living outside Russia between 1976 and 1993, he worked in Israel, Britain and Canada.

Bartered Bride, The (*Prodaná nevěsta*). Opera by Smetana to a libretto by Karel Sabina. Jeník (tenor) appears to sell his claims on his beloved Mařenka (soprano), but this is a cheerful subterfuge to outwit her parents and the marriage-broker Kecal, who had other plans for her, and the couple end up together. The score is full of dances and dance songs in Czech rhythms (Polka, Furiant, Dance of the Comedians). First performance: Prague, 25 Sep 1870.

Barthélemon, François Hippolyte (b. Bordeaux, 27 Jul 1741; d. Christ Church, Surrey, 20 Jul 1808). French violinist-composer who moved to London in 1764 and was variously busy composing, playing and arranging concerts. He wrote sonatas, concertos and chamber music, as well as a lot of theatre music. In later years his concerns were religious: he set the hymn 'Awake my soul' and may have put the subject of *The Creation* to Haydn, with whom he was well acquainted. His daughter Cecilia Maria published sonatas in her youth, including one she dedicated to Haydn (Op.3, 1794), but seems to have given up composing after marriage.

Bartholomée, Pierre (b. Brussels, 5 Aug 1937). Belgian composer and conductor who studied at the Brussels Conservatory as a pianist (1953–8) and gained stimulus as a composer from meeting Pousseur in 1961. He was an engineer and producer for Belgian radio (1960–70) while developing his career as a conductor and teacher.

Bartlet, John (*fl. c*.1605–10). English composer who published a *Booke of Ayres* (1606) including 'Of all the birds that I do know'.

Bartók, Béla (Victor János) (b. Nagyszentmiklós,

now Sînnicolau Mare, Romania, 25 Mar 1881; d. New York, 26 Sep 1945). Hungarian composer, folklorist and pianist. In him the modernist spirit linked up with patriotism to bring about a new musical language, but one preserving the sterling qualities of the old. Like Haydn, Beethoven and Brahms, he concentrated on instrumental genres, especially in his case the string quartet, the concerto and the solo piano piece. His music also recalls the great tradition in that its powerful expression – its anger, fierce or ebullient humour, grief and wild joy, all so contrasting with his utter composure as a person – comes not only from gesture but from form, from how the gesture is placed in a movement of solid integrity.

Until after the First World War Hungary was part of the Habsburg empire, with wider borders than now, and he grew up in its further reaches, in the company of his widowed mother (a school-teacher), his sister and aunts. His musical gifts became apparent very early: he was composing proficiently by the age of nine. He attended secondary school in Bratislava (Pozsony to Hungarians), and followed Dohnányi, an elder colleague, in going to Budapest rather than the Austro-Hungarian capital Vienna for further training. Even so, both young Hungarians began with an admiration for the echt-Viennese Brahms, though Bartók during his years at the academy (1899–1903) contracted alternative enthusiasms for Liszt and, in 1902, Richard Strauss. His teachers were István Thomán, a pupil of Liszt, for the piano and Hans Koessler, Reger's cousin, for composition.

After graduating he spent the summer with the Dohnányis in Gmunden, where he worked on the fair copy of Kossuth, a celebration of the 19th-century Hungarian statesman that leaned towards Liszt for national character and Strauss for heroic manner. Now aged 21, he wrote to his mother that he had found his life's objective: 'the good of Hungary and the Hungarian nation'. To that ideal he was true in the best way, creating music whose nationality is intrinsic and does not have to be boasted. He was deeply attached to his roots because they joined him to the world.

A year later, in July 1904, he was again away for the summer when he heard an 18-year-old nursemaid, Lidi Dósa, singing something he had not heard before: a song from the Hungarian villages, not the citified café music that Liszt and Brahms had taken as authentically Hungarian. He was thrilled. Within a few months he had formed a plan to publish a volume of Hungarian folksongs, and the next year he found a colleague to help in the work – Kodály. They went out collecting, and in 1906 published a set of 20 arrangements, 10 by

each of them. These were Hungarian songs, but Bartók also keenly collected and studied the music of other central European peoples, especially Slovaks and Romanians. Then in 1907 two things happened that made folk music not just a sideline but central. He discovered PENTATONIC music persisting in the little-visited valleys of Transylvania, and he discovered, too, a major composer who was using modes not unlike those of folksong to create a fresh and yet at the same time thoroughly sophisticated style – Debussy.

In 1907–11, after three or four years during which his music had been rhapsodic in a Liszt–Brahms manner, came a rush of works in a new voice – leaner, more angular and more chromatic, with a wide range of moods and speeds to which some of the piano titles testify: Two Elegies, Three Burlesques, Four Dirges, Allegro barbaro, this last a piece of storming ostinatos that guaranteed him a place among the modernists. Also during this time he wrote a violin concerto for his sweetheart, Stefi Geyer – a work he set aside when their romantic affair ended. He reused the first movement in Two Portraits as an image of the ideal, now followed by a contrary and exuberant caricature. His First Quartet moves from the world of the Geyer concerto to that of village festivity.

This creative surge may have been helped by the financial stability he enjoyed as Thomán's successor at the academy, where among his early students he found his first wife, Márta Ziegler (1893–1955). They were married in 1909, and their son Béla was born the next year. In 1911 he offered Márta his opera Bluebeard's Castle – an unnerving dedication, since the work's bleak message is that a husband who is forced to part with his silence cannot maintain his love. Bartók maintained his up to a point. In 1915–16 he seems to have developed tender feelings for a teenage girl he met on one of his folksong-collecting expeditions (Klára Gombossy, whose poems he set), and in 1923 he divorced Márta to marry another student, Ditta Pásztory (1903–82). They too had a son, Péter, born in 1924.

Entered for a competition, Bluebeard's Castle failed to win a performance, and, faced with resistance along other avenues, Bartók in 1912 publicly withdrew from musical life in Budapest. He stopped work on his Four Pieces for orchestra, leaving the set unorchestrated, and in 1913 he produced just some children's piano pieces. But he continued to collect folksongs in Hungary and, in June 1913, north Africa. The outbreak of war in August 1914 made travel impossible initially, but he and Kodály were able to gather folksongs from soldiers, and he got back among the Slovaks and Romanians in 1915–16. He was never restrictive in his study – and use – of folk material: what mattered was that the source 'be clean, fresh and healthy', i.e. uncorrupted by urban influences. During the war, for instance, came many Romanian arrangements, as well as a strong African thread in the weave of the Second Quartet and Suite for piano.

His biggest work of this period was the fairytale ballet *The Wooden Prince*, whose successful première at the Budapest Opera in May 1917 led to the company's staging of *Bluebeard's Castle* the next year. Soon after that he began a third theatre work, *The Miraculous Mandarin*, which again took several years to reach the stage, this time because of his slowness in finishing the score. He may have been uncertain about the post-war world, political and musical: within a year, 1918–19, Hungary veered from liberalism to communism (he served on the music directorate) to fascism, while he began moving towards his densely polyphonic and harmonically complex sonatas for violin and piano (1921–2), and wrote of his fascination with Schoenberg. (Since 1918 he had shared Schoenberg's publisher, Universal Edition.) With his orchestral Dance Suite (1923) he found ways to integrate his new, darker harmony into the lively rhythmic-tonal frames of dances, and the next year he at last completed the *Mandarin*.

He had not resumed his collecting tours after the war: he had enough material to collate and analyse at home, and he was also becoming busier as a travelling pianist. In 1922 he picked up his international career with visits to Britain, France and Germany; he also made tours of the USA (1927–8) and Russia (1928–9). For these he needed repertory: hence the flood of piano music that came in 1926, including the Sonata, the suite *Out of Doors* and the First Concerto. With his quartets he maintained his connection with compatriots, the Hungarian Quartet, who gave the premières of his Nos.1–4. But he was now known all over the Western world, and most of his first performances took place abroad. He was also receiving foreign commissions, notably from Coolidge (Fifth Quartet, played by the Kolisches, who also introduced No.6) and Sacher (Music for Strings, Percussion and Celesta, Sonata for Two Pianos and Percussion, Divertimento). The *Cantata profana* (1930) – after *Bluebeard* his biggest work with a Hungarian text – was given for the first time not in Budapest but in London, where he enjoyed an excellent relationship with the BBC.

His international rise occurred in difficult times – to which he responded. As the Nazis gained strength in Germany, he wrote about the nonsensicality of ethnic purity, pointing out what he had discovered in his own researches: that a nation's folk music gains from what it borrows. In the Dance Suite he had offered a vision of different peoples linking arms, while the *Cantata profana* inherited its language from Hungary, its textual source material from Romania (from pagan songs that Bartók, always resolutely atheist, was pleased to discover) and its musical style from both, joining two countries whose history had been one of mutual suspicion.

But the world was going another way. He gave the first performance of his Second Piano Concerto in Frankfurt just a week before Hitler assumed power. After that he withdrew himself and his music from German territory, and in 1937 he set a ban on broadcasts of his music to Germany and Italy. He also absented himself again from musical life in Budapest between 1930 and 1936, the year he made one last collecting tour, to Turkey. During this period his music became more openly diatonic: compare the Fifth Quartet with the Fourth (both in a favourite five-movement form with a symmetrical pattern, ABCBA), or the Second Piano Concerto – brilliant, engaging, Bach-like in its lucid counterpoint – with the First. The move from chromatic (dark) to diatonic (light) even became an essential part of each composition's drama, notably in the *Cantata profana* and the Music for Strings, Percussion and Celesta, where chromatic melodies, by a widening of intervals, re-emerge in diatonic form. The resurgence of clear tonal harmony was general, found in Stravinsky, Schoenberg and Prokofiev, but with Bartók it came with a particular optimism – in defiant contradiction of world events.

Musical friends were a support. There had hardly been a time when he was not working – in sonata recitals and on compositions – with one Hungarian violinist or another, including Jelly d'Arányi, Joseph Szigeti and Zoltán Székely. Now he wrote *Contrasts* (1937) for Szigeti – with himself and Benny Goodman, who commissioned the work – and his magnificent full-scale concerto (1938) for Székely.

In 1939 his mother died, and the following spring he embarked with his wife and elder son for the USA, for a concert tour that turned into permanent refuge, in New York. But he could not settle. His health was in decline, he found it impossible to compose in the great city, he was little appreciated there as a performer, and he suffered financial hardship. He was, too, separated from his beloved Hungary. In 1939–41 he arranged some of his pieces for duo recitals with Ditta, and in 1941–2 he worked at Columbia on a collection of Serbo-Croatian folk material. Only in the summer of 1943, while convalescing in the Adirondacks, did he seriously return to composition, producing the Concerto for Orchestra to a commission from Koussevitzy. Early the following year came the Solo Violin Sonata, commissioned by Menuhin, after which, in 1945, again in the Adirondacks, he worked on a concerto for Ditta (Piano Concerto No.3) and one for the viola player William Primrose. The latter had reached only a draft stage when he died.

His work as a folklorist, a monumental achievement in itself, fed into everything he produced from 1904 onwards. Not only did his music grow from the Hungarian and Romanian melodies of Transylvania (their scales, the characteristic Hungarian trochaic rhythms and melodic fourths), with touches from elsewhere (such as the Bulgarian rhythms of irregular stresses within the bar), but also his work in analysing folksongs had a direct effect on his way of composing. Examining different songs to find common motivic features gave him lessons in variation, in which his scores came to abound. Sometimes a small motif or chain of motifs would provide material for an entire composition: the Fourth Quartet and Music for Strings are classic instances, but so too is *Mikrokosmos*, which, through piano pieces graded from beginner's level to virtuoso's, is a whole world of studies also in musical invention and assembly.

The range of his output – and his capacity for irony – left plentiful room for interpretation. The Concerto for Orchestra, which rapidly entered the standard orchestral repertory (one of the last pieces to do so), has been seen as a concession, if only in comparison with the orchestral lustre and expressive richness of *The Miraculous Mandarin* or the dynamic music-making in the quartets. It has also been regarded as a triumph of creative vigour meeting popular taste – folk music becoming again folk music.

Béla Bartók *Essays*, ed. Benjamin Suchoff (1976); Malcolm Gillies, ed. *The Bartók Companion* (1993)

Theatre and orchestral music

Opera: BLUEBEARD'S CASTLE, Op.11, 1911, rev 1912, 1917–18

Ballets: *The* WOODEN PRINCE, Op.13, 1914–17; *The* MIRACULOUS MANDARIN, Op.19, 1918–19, orch 1924, rev 1926–31

Concertos: Scherzo, Op.2, pf, orch, 1904; Rhapsody, Op.1, pf, orch, 1905; PIANO CONCERTO No.1, 1926; No.2, 1930–31; No.3, 1945; Double Piano Concerto, 1940 (after 1937 Sonata); Violin Concerto No.1, 1907–8; No.2 (see Violin Concerto), 1937–8; Rhapsodies Nos.1–2, vn, orch, 1928–9; Viola Concerto, 1945 (finished by Tibor Serly)

Other orchestral works: *Kossuth*, 1903; Suite No.1, Op.3, 1905, rev *c.*1920; No.2, Op.4, 1905–7, rev 1920, 1943; 2 *Portraits*, Op.5, 1907–10; 2 *Pictures*, Op.10, 1910; 4 Pieces, Op.12, 1912, orch 1921; DANCE SUITE, 1923; CANTATA PROFANA, t, bar, ch, orch, 1930; MUSIC FOR STRINGS, PERCUSSION AND CELESTA, 1936; Divertimento, str, 1939; CONCERTO FOR ORCHESTRA, 1943, rev 1945

Orchestrations of folk pieces: Romanian Dance, 1909–11; Romanian Folk Dances, small orch, 1917; 3 *Village Scenes* (Slovak trad) women's ch, chbr orch, 1926; Transylvanian Dances, 1931; Hungarian Sketches, 1931; Hungarian Folksongs (5 from 1929 set), v, orch, 1933; Hungarian Peasant Songs, 1933

Chamber and piano music

String quartets: No.1, Op.7, 1908–9, f.p. Budapest, 19 Mar 1910; No.2, Op.17, 1914–17, f.p. Budapest, 3 Mar 1918; No.3, 1927, f.p. Philadelphia, 30 Dec 1928; No.4, 1928, f.p. Budapest, 20 Mar 1929; No.5, 1934, f.p. Washington, 8 Apr 1935; No.6, 1939, f.p. New York, 20 Jan 1941

Other chamber works: Andante, A, vn, pf, 1902; Violin Sonata, E minor, 1903; Piano Quintet, 1903–4; *From Gyergyó*, rec, pf, 1907; Violin Sonata No.1, 1921; No.2, 1922; Rhapsody No.1, vn/vc, pf, 1928; No.2, vn, pf, 1928; 44 Duos, 2 vn, 1931; *Contrasts*, vn, cl, pf, 1938; Solo Violin Sonata, 1944

Piano solo: 4 Pieces, 1903; *Marche funèbre*, 1903 (from *Kossuth*); Rhapsody, Op.1, 1904, arr as concerto and for 2 pf, 1905; 3 Hungarian Folksongs from Csík, 1907; 14 Bagatelles, Op.6, 1908; 10 Easy Pieces, 1908; 2 Elegies, Op.8b, 1908–9; *For Children* (after Hungarian and Slovak folksongs), 1908–10; 7 Sketches, Op.9b, 1908–10; 3 Burlesques, Op.8c, 1908–11; 2 Romanian Dances, Op.8a, 1909–10; 4 Dirges, Op.9a, 1909–10; *Allegro barbaro*, 1911; *First Term at the Piano*, 1913; Romanian Christmas Songs, 1915; Romanian Folk Dances, 1915; Sonatina, 1915; Suite, Op.14, 1916; 15 Hungarian Peasant Songs, 1914, 1918; 3 Hungarian Folktunes, 1914, 1918; 3 Studies, Op.18, 1918; 8 Improvisations on Hungarian Peasant Songs, Op.20, 1920; DANCE SUITE, 1925; Sonata, 1926; OUT OF DOORS, 1926; 9 Little Piano Pieces, 1926; 3 Rondos on Folktunes, 1916, 1927; MIKROKOSMOS, 1926, 1932–9; *Petite suite*, 1936 (from 44 Duos)

Piano duo: Rhapsody, Op.1, 1905; Sonata for 2 Pianos and Percussion, 1937; 7 Pieces from MIKROKOSMOS, 1939–40; Suite No.2, Op.4b, 1941

Piano duet: *The* MIRACULOUS MANDARIN, 1925

Piano arrangements: concert versions of works by Bach, Purcell and Italian Baroque masters, cadenzas, pedagogical editions, etc.

Choruses and songs

Choruses: 4 Old Hungarian Folksongs, men, 1910; 4 Slovak Folksongs, mixed, pf, *c.*1916; Slovak Folksongs, men, 1917; Hungarian Folksongs, mixed, 1930; Székely Folksongs, men, 1932; 27 Two- and Three-part Choruses (Hungarian trad), children/women, 1935–6; *From Olden Times* (Hungarian trad), men, 1935

Solo songs: 4 Songs (Lajos Pósa), 1902; *Evening* (Kálmán Harsányi), 1903; 5 Songs (Klára Gombossy, Wanda Gleiman), Op.15, 1916; 5 Songs (Ady), Op.16, 1916

Solo folksong arrangements: 'The red apple', 1904;
Hungarian Folksongs (4), c.1904–5; For the Little
'Tót', 5 children's songs, 1905; Hungarian
Folksongs (10), 1906, pub with 10 by Kodály;
Hungarian Folksongs (10), 1906–7; 2 Hungarian
Folksongs, 1907; 3 Slovakian Folksongs, 1907, 1916;
8 Hungarian Folksongs, 1907, 1917; Village Scenes
(5; Slovak trad), 1924; 5 Hungarian Folksongs
(from 1906 set), 1928; 20 Hungarian Folksongs,
1929; etc.

Bartoli, Cecilia (b. Rome, 4 Jun 1966). Italian
mezzo-soprano, she is especially famed for her
urgently persuasive and vocally alluring recordings of arias and roles by Mozart and Rossini. The
child of singers, she had a mentor for a mother,
though she also attended the Accademia di Santa
Cecilia. She made her debut in Verona in 1987 (not
counting a 1975 performance as the shepherd boy
in Tosca), and rapidly became a sensation, thanks
to support from leading conductors (Harnoncourt, Barenboim, Karajan) and from Decca
records.

Bartolozzi, Bruno (b. Florence, 8 Jun 1911; d.
Florence, 12 Dec 1980). Italian composer, known
principally as a pioneer of the MULTIPHONICS and
microtones described in his New Sounds for
Woodwind (1967). He studied at the Florence
Conservatory, where his connection with Dallapiccola was decisive. In 1964 he returned to the
conservatory to teach conducting, after two
decades as an orchestral violinist.

baryton. (1) Bass viol with, besides its bowed
strings, a set of strings on the back designed to be
plucked in the manner of a BANDORA, and also, in
the Classical period, sympathetic strings. The
skilful player would both bow and pluck, but, even
with such opportunities for virtuoso dexterity, the
instrument might have been forgotten had it not
been a favourite of Prince Nicolaus Esterházy, who
required music for it from his house composer,
Haydn. Haydn's works for it consist mostly of
trios, with viola and cello.
(2) (Fr.). Baritone.

bas-dessus (Fr., low treble). French Baroque term
implying a mezzo-soprano.

Bashmet, Yuri (Abramovich) (b. Rostov on the
Don, 24 Jan 1953). Russian viola player, a
passionate and temperamental performer. He
played the piano and violin as a child, switched to
the viola at 14 and entered the Moscow Conservatory at 18. There he studied with Vadim
Borisovsky and Fyodor Druzhinin, and soon
began teaching. His career in the West was frozen

until the late 1980s, but since then he has been
active worldwide. Works written for him include
Schnittke's concerto.

basic set. Fundamental form of the SET (2) in a
serial composition.

bass. (1) Lower part of the pitch range, as opposed
to treble, from the late Lat. bassus (low). In most
tonal music the harmony arises from the bass, and
so the term carries an implication of harmonic
foundation, especially in such locutions as 'bass
line', 'bass note'. The word can also be used of the
lowest note in a chord.
(2) (Fr. basse, Ger. Bass, It. basso). Lowest man's
voice or a singer with that voice. The normal range
is from F below the bass staff upwards through two
octaves, though lower and higher notes may be
required of soloists. The word is also used as a
qualifier in the names of low instruments, e.g. bass
trumpet.
   Medieval and Renaissance polyphony does not
generally exploit the bass register, but the arrival of
diatonic harmony thrust importance into the bass,
and bass singers were duly recognized with more
important and more florid parts from the late 16th
century onwards. There are important parts for
solo bass in Monteverdi, Purcell, Bach and
Rameau – and in Mozart, whose Don Giovanni,
with its four basses, shows a differentiation among
types, including the buffo bass (Leporello), the
serious bass (Commendatore) and the baritone
(Don Giovanni). In the 19th century all these types
were continued and developed, and joined by new
kinds: the Russian bass (the title role in Boris
Godunov, drawing on Italian opera and on the
native church tradition) and the Wagnerian bass-
baritone.
(3) Short for double bass or bass guitar.

Bassano. Italian–English family of musicians
emanating from Bassano del Grappa, in the
Veneto. Jeronimo, a wind player in early 16th-
century Venice, had six sons, of whom four –
Alvise, Gasparo, Antonio and Baptista – settled
in England during the reign of Henry VIII,
and several of their sons (notably Alvise's son
Augustine, d. 1604) and grandsons in turn were
musicians and composers in London. Jeronimo's
first son Jacomo went with them but returned to
Venice; his grandson Giovanni (1560/61–1617)
became head of the instrumentalists at St Mark's
in 1601 and published madrigals and motets.

Bassarids, The. Opera by Henze to a libretto by
Auden and Kallman after the Bacchae of Euripides.
Pentheus (baritone), attempting to repress both

the cult of Dionysus (tenor) and his own sexual desires (as revealed in a rococo intermezzo), is destroyed by his mother Agave (mezzo-soprano). First performance: Salzburg, 6 Aug 1966.

bass-bar. Internal part of a bowed string instrument: a wooden strip glued to the underneath of the belly, upwards from the point corresponding to the bridge foot on the bass side. It strengthens the belly, which can therefore be made thin and responsive.

bass-baritone. Bass voice, or singer, with a strong, lyrical baritone register. The term is particularly associated with such Wagner roles as Wotan and Hans Sachs.

bass clarinet. Instrument sounding an octave below the regular clarinet. Examples survive from the late 18th century, but the first score to include the instrument prominently is Meyerbeer's *Les Huguenots* (1836). Since Liszt and Wagner it has been in common use.

bass clef. F CLEF on the fourth line up, the standard clef for lower instruments and voices, as for the left hand at a keyboard.

bass drum (Fr. *grosse caisse*, Ger. *grosse Trommel*, It. *gran cassa*). DRUM normally 30–40 inches (80–100cm) in diameter and 15–20 inches (40–50cm) deep, and usually fixed at a slight tilt from the horizontal or played upright (as in a marching band). Inherited with the cymbals from the janissaries of Turkey, the instrument retained exotic and military associations in Gluck (*Le Cadi dupé*), Mozart (*Die Entführung*) and Beethoven (Ninth Symphony). It then gained a regular role in the orchestra – as well as a roll, introduced by Liszt (*Ce qu'on entend sur la montagne*) – and is prominent in scores by Wagner, Verdi (*Requiem*), Sibelius, Stravinsky (*The Rite of Spring*) and Adams.

basse (Fr.). Bass, hence *basse chantante* (light lyric bass), *basse chiffrée* (figured bass), *basse-contre* (Renaissance–Baroque term for double bass or low bass voice), *basse de violon* (bass violin), *basse d'harmonie* (ophicleide), *basse noble* (BASSO PROFONDO), *basse-taille* (low tenor, i.e. baritone), etc.

basse danse (Fr., low dance, It. *bassadanza*). Court dance of the 15th century and first half of the 16th, slow and followed by a faster afterdance.

basset clarinet. Modern term for the clarinet probably devised by Stadler (which he called 'bass clarinet'), with a basset-horn-like extension down through a major third. For this instrument (in A) Mozart wrote his quintet and concerto, which require certain transpositions when played on a standard clarinet. Mozart also wrote for basset clarinet in B♭ in *La clemenza di Tito*.

basset horn (Fr. *cor de basset*, Ger. *Bassethorn*, It. *corno di bassetto*). Clarinet of alto register, normally in F (occasionally G), distinguished from the alto clarinet by having an extension to take it a major third lower, and by its narrower bore and gentler (very beautiful) tone. Mozart had a soft spot for it and used it in his Requiem, *Die Zauberflöte* and other works. Beethoven (*Prometheus*) and Mendelssohn (Symphony No.3) gave it less prominence, and it disappeared in the mid 19th century to come back in Strauss's *Elektra*. That basset horns were used on hunts with basset hounds is a fiction honouring both: the dog, like the instrument, got its name from being a little low.

bassett (Ger. *Bassett*, It. *bassetto*). Little bass, etymologically. In Baroque terminology, the bass part in a high-lying passage. Also an 18th-century term for cello.

bass flute. Flute an octave below the standard instrument, U-shaped for ease of handling and uncommon. In older usage the term was applied to the alto flute.

bass guitar. Electric guitar with four strings tuned in the same way as the double bass, introduced by the Fender company in 1951 and used largely in popular music.

basso (It., pl. *bassi*). Bass, hence *basso cantante* (light lyric bass), *basso* CONTINUO, *basso numerato* (figured bass), *basso ostinato* (ground bass), BASSO PROFONDO, etc.

bass oboe. Large oboe, an octave below the standard instrument. Examples are known from the 18th and early 19th centuries, but no music. Reinvented around 1889, the instrument has been something of a British speciality, used by Delius, Tippett and Bryars.

basson (Fr.). Bassoon.

bassoon (Fr. *basson*, Ger. *Fagott*, It. *fagotto*). WOODWIND instrument, the lowest member of the family, with a double reed fitted into a metal crook attached to a U-shaped tube made from four cylindrical segments of maple. The instrument has a complex ancestry, involving in the Renaissance several different styles of manufacture and several different names – pommer, curtal, fagot and dulcian, as well as bassoon – with no clear correspondence between types and terms. Nowadays the term 'dulcian' is generally used for the obsolete instrument made from one piece of wood, the history of the bassoon beginning with the four-piece instrument introduced in France in the later 17th century. The range is from the B♭ below the bass staff up through three and a half octaves, a wide compass that enables the instrument both to reinforce the orchestral bass and to sound melodies in the alto register, as at the start of *The Rite of Spring*.

Out of several different bassoon-making traditions, the French and the German emerged as dominant in the later 19th century. The German bassoon has a mellowness that allows it to blend smoothly and firmly with horns and low strings; the French bassoon possesses a more reedy, oboe-like sound and steadily lost favour during the 20th century.

The bassoon entered the orchestra with Lully and was soon universal. It also rapidly gained a solo repertory, including concertos by Vivaldi and obbligato parts in J.S. Bach. By the mid 18th century a pair of bassoons was normal in the orchestra, increased to three or four in the late Romantic period. The solo repertory includes Mozart's concerto as well as others by J.C. Bach, Carl Stamitz, Hummel, Weber, Elgar (Romance) and Gubaidulina, concertos including additional soloists by Haydn (Sinfonia Concertante), Hindemith (Double Concerto with trumpet) and Strauss (Duett-Concertino with clarinet), obbligato parts in Bainbridge (*Ad ora incerta*) as well as Bach, and smaller works by Skalkottas (Sonata concertante) and Berio (*Sequenza XII*).

Close relatives are the DOUBLE BASSOON (contrabassoon) and TENOROON.

Lyndesay G. Langwill *The Bassoon and Contrabassoon* (1965); William Waterhouse *Bassoon* (2003)

basso ostinato (It.). GROUND bass.

basso profondo (It., deep bass). Bass voice of particular strength in the low register, as often exhibited by Russian singers.

bass trombone. Trombone pitched a fourth below the standard (tenor) TROMBONE. Originally it was a separate instrument, but modern trombones generally have a valve that effectively converts them into bass trombones.

bass trumpet. Large trumpet, trombone like in size and, therefore, range, and normally played by a trombonist.

bass viol. VIOLA DA GAMBA, or cello-like instrument made and played in New England up to the mid 19th century.

bass violin. Large violin playing in the cello register, displaced by the (smaller) cello around 1700.

Bastien und Bastienne. One-act singspiel by the 12-year-old Mozart to a libretto by several hands based on a French opéra comique, a pleasant romantic pastoral in which the love of Bastien (tenor) and Bastienne (soprano) is smoothened. The first performance was probably given at the home in Vienna of Franz Anton Mesmer, the pioneer of magnetic therapy, Sep–Oct 1768.

Bataille, Gabriel (b. *c*.1575; d. Paris, 17 Dec 1630). French lutenist-composer, who was in service to Queen Marie de' Medici from 1619, author and arranger of lute songs.

Bateson, Thomas (b. *c*.1570; d. Dublin, Mar 1630). English church musician, organist of Chester Cathedral (1599–1609) and then of Christ Church, Dublin, and author of two books of madrigals.

baton. Stick used for CONDUCTING, descendant of the cane or staff reportedly used by choirmasters since the start of the 16th century. Until around 1800, orchestras were usually coordinated by a keyboard player or the first violinist; the baton emerged with another innovation, the orchestral conductor. It is now almost universally a thin, tapering piece of whitened wood or plastic, about 12 inches (30cm) long, set in a knob of cork, to form a grip. Some conductors in the past would use much longer batons (twice as long for Münch and Boult), or more substantial ones, perhaps black or brown in colour. There are also conductors who have preferred to use their hands alone (Stokowski, Boulez). Highly ornate batons, of precious metals, enamel and jewels, were occasionally made in the 19th century: one on display at the Met was used by Levi at the première of *Parsifal*.

Batten, Adrian (baptized Salisbury, 1 Mar 1591; d. London, 1637). English church musician, probably trained at Winchester Cathedral before he became a choirman at Westminster Abbey (1614–26) and then St Paul's. He wrote services and anthems.

batterie (Fr.). (1) Percussion.

(2) Drum signal.

(3) BATTERY.

(4) RASGUEADO.

battery. Baroque practice of playing chords as arpeggios.

battimento (It.). BATTERY.

Battishill, Jonathan (b. London, May 1738; d. London, 10 Dec 1801). British composer. He was a chorister at St Paul's and stayed on as a pupil of William Savage, becoming a noted organist: he was Boyce's deputy at the Chapel Royal, held other appointments and wrote hymns and anthems. At the same time he was active in the theatre as a singer and composer. The break-up of his marriage in the mid-1770s hit him hard.

Battistelli, Giorgio (b. Albano Laziale, 25 Apr 1953). Italian composer, known for serious and ambitious theatrical works. He studied with Giancarlo Bizzi at the L'Aquila Conservatory and was artistic director of the festival in Montepulciano (1993–6) before taking a similar post with the Orchestra della Toscana.

battle. Activity lending itself to musical depiction, which will generally seize on excitement more than loss. Battle pieces formed a sub-genre in the Renaissance and commonly included imitations of shouts, fanfares, galloping horses and the clash of arms. Among examples are Janequin's *La Guerre*, Byrd's *The Battle* and *The Barley Break*, and Monteverdi's *Combattimento*, one of several works by him in which warfare and love are metaphors for each other. Battle music reappeared at the time of the Revolutionary and Napoleonic wars, notably in František Koczwara's sonata *The Battle of Prague*, Wanhal's sonata *Le Combat naval de Trafalgar et la mort de Nelson*, Beethoven's WELLINGTONS SIEG (and Ninth Symphony) and Weber's Waterloo cantata *Kampf und Sieg*. Battles of this same period are recalled in Tchaikovsky's *1812* (EIGHTEEN-TWELVE) and Prokofiev's *War and Peace*, while other battles appear in Verdi's *Macbeth*, Liszt's *Hunnenschlacht*, Wagner's *Die Walküre*, Strauss's *Ein Heldenleben*, Kodály's *Háry János*, Prokofiev's *Alexander Nevsky* and Wolpe's *Battle Piece*.

battuta (It.). Beat, hence A BATTUTA.

Baudrier, Yves (Marie) (b. Paris, 11 Feb 1906; d. Paris, 9 Nov 1988). French composer of Honeggeresque symphonic poems (*Le Musicien dans la cité*, 1937), two quartets and film scores. He trained for the law before studying music (1929–33) with Georges Loth, organist of the Sacré-Coeur. In 1935 he met Messiaen, who gave him advice, and the next year he was involved in the short-lived group La JEUNE FRANCE.

Bauer, Harold (b. Kingston-upon-Thames, 28 Apr 1873; d. Miami, 12 Mar 1951). British–US pianist. As a boy and young man he performed on both violin and piano, then was helped by Paderewski to become a pianist, while developing his technique himself. He played with the Vienna Philharmonic (1899) and in the USA (1900), and was soon established among the great virtuosos, though unusual in his serious repertory – ranging from Bach to Ravel, who dedicated *Ondine* to him – and unostentatious manner. He took US citizenship in 1917 and taught at the Manhattan School.

Bauer, Marion (Eugénie) (b. Walla Walla, Washington, 15 Aug 1882; d. South Hadley, Mass., 9 Aug 1955). US composer and teacher, who trained in Portland (Oregon), in Paris with Boulanger and Gédalge, and in Berlin. She taught at New York University (1926–51) and Juilliard (1940–55), and composed neoclassical music, although she also produced some 12-note pieces in later years.

Bauerncantate. See PEASANT CANTATA.

Bauernleier (Ger.). HURDY-GURDY.

Bauernlied (Ger.). Peasant song.

Bauld, Alison (Margaret) (b. Sydney, 7 May 1944). Australian composer, who trained as an actress and musician in Sydney and then (1969–74) in London, where she settled. Most of her works are for small combinations; many have an element of theatre.

Baumgartner, Rudolf (b. Zurich, 14 Sep 1917; d. Siena, 22 Mar 2002). Swiss violinist-conductor, who was a pupil of Stefi Geyer and Paul Müller at the Zurich Conservatory, Flesch in Paris and Schneiderhan in Vienna. In 1956 he founded the Lucerne Festival Strings, with which he performed his own Bach arrangements and works by Ligeti, Xenakis, etc.

Baur, Jürg (b. Düsseldorf, 11 Nov 1918). German composer, a pupil of Jarnach at the conservatory in Cologne (1937–48). Like Bernd Alois Zimmermann, he was slow to arrive at maturity and completely – yet cautiously – absorbed lessons (serialism, quotation) from younger composers.

His large output embraces orchestral and chamber works of diverse kinds, piano, organ and choral music, and songs. He has also worked as a church musician and teacher (notably as Zimmermann's successor at his alma mater, 1971–90).

Bavaria. For Bavarian institutions see MUNICH.

Bax, Arnold (Edward Trevor) (b. London, 8 Nov 1883; d. Cork, 3 Oct 1953). British composer, knighted in 1937. A Londoner with a love of all things Irish, especially legends and seascapes, he was a dreamer whose rhapsodic music often has a wild, dark undertow. He had independent means, and after studying with Corder at the RAM (1900–1905) he devoted himself to composition. From 1902, having read Yeats, he visited Ireland fre-quently; he also wrote poems, stories and plays on Irish subjects under the pseudonym Dermot O'Byrne. In 1910 he visited Russia, apparently in pursuit of a woman, and though he married soon afterwards, he began a long-standing affair with the pianist Harriet Cohen during the First World War and from the mid 1920s onwards also maintained a relationship with a younger woman in Scotland. The complexities of that emotional existence are perhaps reflected in his music – in its combination of luxuriance and ecstasy with bleakness, under influences that were corres-pondingly various: Debussy, Strauss, Delius, Sibelius, even Berg and Schoenberg in his Sixth Symphony, a climax of angularity and vehemence in his output, which was reduced to a trickle after 1939. In 1942 he was appointed Master of the King's Music.

Lewis Foreman *Bax* (1983, ²1988); Graham Parlett *A Catalogue of the Works of Sir Arnold Bax* (1999)

Orchestral: Symphony No.1, E♭, 1922; No.2, 1924–5; No.3, 1929; No.4, 1931; No.5, 1932; No.6, 1934; No.7, 1938–9; *In the Faery Hills*, 1909, rev 1921; *The Dance of Wild Irravel*, 1912; *Nympholept*, 1912–15, rev 1935; *The Garden of Fand*, 1913–16; *November Woods*, 1917; Symphonic Variations, E, pf, orch, 1918; *Tintagel*, 1917–19; Phantasy, va, orch, 1920; *The Happy Forest*, 1914–21; *Mediterranean*, 1920–22; *Overture to a Picareque Comedy*, 1930; *Winter Legends*, pf, orch, 1930; *Northern Ballad No.1*, 1927–31; *The Tale the Pine-trees Knew*, 1931; Cello Concerto, 1932; *Prelude for a Solemn Occasion*, 1932–3; *Northern Ballad No.2*, 1933–4; Violin Concerto, 1937–8; *Morning Song*, pf, orch, 1946; Concertante, pf left hand, orch, 1949; *Coronation March*, 1952; etc.

Film scores: *Malta G.C.*, 1942; *Oliver Twist*, 1948

Incidental music: *The Truth about the Russian Dancers* (Barrie), 1920, rev 1926

Choral: *Fatherland* (J.L. Runeberg), t, ch, orch, 1907, rev 1934; *Mater, ora filium*, ch, 1921; *This Worldes Joie*, ch, 1922; *I sing of a maiden that is makeless*, ch, 1923; *Magnificat*, ch, org, 1948; *What is it like to be young and fair?*, 1953; etc.

Chamber: Nonet, 1930; *In memoriam*, cor ang, hp, str qt, 1917; Oboe Quintet, 1922; Harp Quintet, 1919; String Quartet No.1, 1918; No.2, 1925; No.3, 1936; Piano Trio, 1946; *Elegiac Trio*, fl, va, hp, 1916; Violin Sonata No.1, 1910, rev 1914, 1920, 1945; No.2, 1914, rev 1921; No.3, 1927; in F, 1928 (arr as Nonet); Viola Sonata, 1922; Fantasy Sonata, va, hp, 1927; *Legend*, va, pf, 1929; *Folk-Tale*, vc, pf, 1920; Cello Sonata, 1923; Cello Sonatina, 1933; *Rhapsodic Ballad*, vc, 1939; *Legend-Sonata*, vc, pf, 1943; Sonata, fl, hp, 1928; Clarinet Sonata, 1934

Songs: 'The White Peacock', 1907; 'I heard a piper piping', 1921; 'Cradle Song', 1922; 'Rann of Exile', 1922; etc.

Piano solo: Sonata No.1, F♯ minor, 1910, rev 1917–21; No.2, 1919, rev 1920; No.3, 1926; No.4, 1932; 2 *Russian Tone-Pictures*, 1912; *A Mountain Mood*, 1914; *Winter Waters*, 1914; *The Princess's Rose Garden*, 1915; *In a Vodka Shop*, 1915; *The Maiden with the Daffodil*, 1915; *What the Minstrel told us*, 1919; *Whirligig*, 1919; *Lullaby*, 1920; *Burlesque*, 1920; *A Hill Tune*, 1920; *Mediterranean*, 1920; *Paean*, 1928; etc.

Piano duo: Sonata, 1929; *Moy Mell*, 1916; *Hardanger*, 1927; *The Devil that Tempted St Anthony*, 1928; *The Poisoned Fountain*, 1928; *Red Autumn*, 1931

bayan. Russian button accordion.

Bayle, François (b. Tamatave, Madagascar, 27 Apr 1932). French composer of electronic music. He studied at the Bordeaux Conservatoire (1949–54), with Messiaen at the Paris Conservatoire (1958–9), and at Darmstadt (1960–62). In 1960 he began work in the MUSIQUE CONCRETE studio of French radio, of which he became head (1966–97).

Bayreuth. Town in Germany, noted for the opera house built in 1745–8 for Margravine Wilhelmine, sister of Frederick II, but much more for the one constructed up the hill, outside the centre, by Wagner. This opened in 1876, with the first complete performances of *The Ring*. Wagner also built himself a residence in the town, Wahnfried, where he and his heirs lived until 1966, when the house became a museum. After his death (1883) the Bayreuth Festival, featuring only his operas from *Der fliegende Holländer* to *Parsifal*, was administered by his widow Cosima, succeeded by their son Siegfried (1906–30), Siegfried's widow Winifred (1930–44; a period marred by her welcoming of Hitler), their sons Wieland and Wolfgang from 1951, and Wolfgang alone after Wieland's death in 1966. *The Ring* and *Parsifal* are given nearly every year, with two of the other canonical works. Wieland Wagner's Bayreuth productions (with simply costumed figures in sparsely furnished geometrical sets, putting the emphasis on gesture and lighting) had a powerful effect on Wagner staging worldwide, an effect dissipated only by the similarly revolutionary 1976 *Ring* production by Patrice Chéreau, which re-rooted the work in 19th-century actuality, politics and fairy story.

Frederic Spotts *Bayreuth: A History of the Wagner Festival* (1994)

Bazelon, Irwin (Allen) (b. Evanston, 4 Jun 1922; d. New York, 2 Aug 1995). US composer, whose robust music draws on US avant-garde and jazz traditions. He studied at DePaul University and with Milhaud at Mills College (1946–8), then settled in New York. His works include 10 symphonies (Nos.1–9, including No.8½), various chamber works and piano pieces.

Bazin, François (Emmanuel Victor) (b. Marseilles, 4 Sep 1816; d. Paris, 2 Jul 1878). French opéra comique composer. He was a pupil of Henri Berton and Halévy at the Paris Conservatoire (1834–40), where he continued as a teacher while composing *Maître Pathelin* (1856), *Le Voyage en Chine* (1865), etc. He refused Massenet as a student – and was succeeded by him at the Conservatoire.

Bazzini, Antonio (b. Brescia, 11 Mar 1818; d. Milan, 10 Feb 1897). Italian violinist-composer, remembered chiefly for the showpiece *La Ronde des lutins* (pub 1852), though he also wrote four concertos and quartets. He was a pupil of the Brescian violinist Faustino Camisani and spent the early 1840s in Germany, where he gave the first (private) performance of Mendelssohn's concerto. He took appointments as composition professor (1873) and director (1882) at the Milan Consevatory, where Puccini was among his pupils.

BBC. British Broadcasting Corporation, a British institution, which began transmitting in November 1922 as the British Broadcasting Company, being reformed in 1927 as a national corporation, financed by licence fees from listeners. Music was essential to its programming from the first: it took over the Proms in 1927 and in 1930 founded the BBC Symphony, with Boult as permanent conductor. Edward Clark brought Bartók, Webern and others to London in the 1930s and established the BBC as an international patron of new music. In 1936 television broadcasting began, and from 1946 a new radio channel, the Third Programme, provided an evening forum for classical music, drama and talk. Radio-specific works were commissioned from writers and composers (including Britten from 1937), and an electronic studio, the Radiophonic Workshop (founded 1958), helped familiarize radio and television audiences with a new sound world. Under Glock as controller of music (1959–73) the Third Programme was joined by the Music Programme (1965), providing classical music in the daytime, and then the two services were amalgamated into Radio 3 (1970), a dawn-to-midnight (and subsequently later) classical-music station. Glock gave the BBC a leading role in disseminating new and early music, and provided the BBC Symphony Orchestra with glory days under Colin Davis (1967–71) and Pierre Boulez (1971–5). The BBC also maintains a professional choir, the BBC Singers, and other orchestras: the BBC Philharmonic (Manchester), the BBC Scottish Symphony (Glasgow) and the BBC National Orchestra of Wales (Cardiff). It remains the leading sponsor of new music in Britain.

Humphrey Carpenter *The Envy of the World: Fifty Years of the BBC Third Programme and Radio 3* (1996)

Be (Ger.). Flat sign, ♭.

Beach, Amy (Marcy) [née Cheney] (b. Henniker, NH, 5 Sep 1867; d. New York, 27 Dec 1944). US composer and pianist. Encouraged by her mother, an amateur singer and pianist, she advanced rapidly in music, and had professional teaching after the family's move to Boston in 1875. She made her debut there in 1883, and played with the Boston Symphony in 1885, though after her marriage that year to Dr Henry Harris Aubrey Beach she concentrated on composition, publishing her works as Mrs H.H.A. Beach. Following advice from the local conductor Wilhelm Gericke, she mostly taught herself with the aid of treatises and the great masters. In 1910 her husband died and in 1911 her mother; she thereupon moved to Europe to extend her reputation. She returned to the USA at the start of the First World War and for a while was more occupied with playing than composing. But from 1921 on she was regularly at the Macdowell Colony, New Hampshire, where she again wrote prolifically, now in a sparer and more astringent harmonic style.

Adrienne Fried Block *Amy Beach* (1998)

Orchestral: 'Gaelic' Symphony, E minor, Op.32, 1894–6; Piano Concerto, C♯ minor, Op.45, 1899; etc.

Chamber: Piano Quintet, F♯ minor, Op.67, 1907; String Quartet, Op.89, 1929; Violin Sonata, A minor, Op.34, 1896; *Invocation*, Op.55, vn, pf, pub 1904; etc.

Piano: *A Hermit Thrush at Eve, A Hermit Thrush at Noon*, Op.92, 1921; etc.

Other works: sacred music, cantatas, choruses, songs, etc.

beam. Line connecting the tails of consecutive quavers or smaller notes.

Beamish, Sally (b. London, 26 Aug 1956). British composer who studied at the RNCM and worked as a viola player before moving to Scotland in 1989 and concentrating on composition. Her works include the opera *Monster* (2002), two symphonies and several concertos.

Bear, The. See *L'OURS*.

Bearbeitung (Ger., pl. *Bearbeitungen*). Arrangement.

Beardslee, Bethany (b. Lansing, Mich., 25 Dec 1927). US soprano. She trained at Michigan State University and Juilliard and brought her bright, liquid tone, agility and accuracy to the service of new music in the 1950s–80s. Married first to Monod, she was remarried to the composer Godfrey Winham in 1956. Babbitt's *Philomel*, which she commissioned, includes her singing in its tape part.

Beare. British family of violin restorers and dealers founded by John Beare (1847–1928), who set up as a dealer in 1865.

Beaser, Robert (b. Boston, 29 May 1954). US composer of neo-Romantic style. He played percussion in the Greater Boston Youth Symphony before studying at Yale with Druckman and others (1973–86) and in Rome with Petrassi. In 1993 he began teaching at Juilliard.

beat. (1) Regular PULSE, the fundamental rhythmic phenomenon in metrical music, where the metre is maintained by a regular succession of strong beats (stressed) and weak beats.

(2) CONDUCTING gesture indicating the pulse and metre; or to give such a gesture. Thus a conductor may beat two in a bar, three in a bar, etc.

(3) Tremulation caused by the simultaneous sounding of two notes differing slightly in frequency. The frequency of beats is the difference between the two original frequencies – i.e., a tone of 440 Hz and one of 438 Hz will produce a beat frequency of twice a second. This phenomenon can be used in tuning.

beater. Implement used on a percussion instrument, the common types being STICK, MALLET and BRUSH.

Béatrice et Bénédict. Opera by Berlioz to his own libretto after Shakespeare's *Much Ado about Nothing*, a source he followed closely in its contrast of couples romantic and jousting: Hero (soprano) and Claudio (baritone), and Beatrice (soprano) and Benedick (tenor). Added to the cast is a buffoon music master, Somarone (bass). The work includes a spirited overture and a Duo-Nocturne for Hero and Claudio. First performance: Baden-Baden, 9 Aug 1862.

Beatriz de Dia (*fl.* late 12th century). TROBAIRITZ, of whose work only one song survives with music.

Beaumarchais, Pierre-Augustin (b. Paris, 24 Jan 1732; d. Paris, 18 May 1799). French playwright and advocate of prose naturalism, against the classical tradition of Corneille and Racine. From his Figaro trilogy – *Le Barbier de Seville* (1775), *Le Mariage de Figaro* (1784) and *La Mère coupable* (1792) – came operas by Rossini, Mozart and Milhaud. He also wrote a libretto for Salieri, *Tarare*.

Beaux Arts Trio. US piano trio formed in 1955 by the pianist Menahem Pressler, violinist Daniel Guilet (succeeded by Isidore Cohen in 1969, Ida Kavafian in 1992 and Young Uck Kim in 1998) and Bernard Greenhouse (succeeded by Peter Wiley in 1987 and Antonio Meneses in 1998). The original team made distinguished recordings of the Mozart, Beethoven and Schubert trios.

bebend (Ger., trembling). Tremolo.

Bebung (Ger., trembling). Vibrato produced on the clavichord by trembling the finger up and down, notated by a line of dots under a slur over the note.

bec (Fr.). Mouthpiece, as in *flûte à bec* (recorder).

bécarre (Fr.). Natural.

Bechstein. German piano company, founded in Berlin in 1853 by Friedrich Wilhelm Carl Bechstein (1826–1900). Von Bülow played the Liszt sonata on the first Bechstein grand in 1856, providing an example followed by many pianists in Europe during the next century, before the more robust and brilliant Steinway gained international domination.

Beck, Conrad (b. Lohn, Schaffhausen, 16 Jun 1901; d. Basle, 31 Oct 1990). Swiss composer, who worked in a neoclassical style, which he developed while living in Paris (1923–32) and associating with Roussel and Honegger. Earlier he had studied at the Zurich Conservatory; later he worked for Basle radio (1932–66) and was powerfully encouraged by Sacher. He produced seven symphonies as well as concertos, cantatas, chamber music and songs.

Beck, Franz Ignaz (b. Mannheim, 20 Feb 1734; d. Bordeaux, 31 Dec 1809). German composer, who wrote remarkable symphonies in his 20s and early 30s, after his move to France. He was the son of a Mannheim instrumentalist and pupil of Johann Stamitz, but left Mannheim under unclear circumstances for Venice. He then left Venice, whence he eloped with his master's daughter. The couple probably arrived in Paris around 1760 and settled soon after in Bordeaux, where Beck worked as an organist and concert director. His later works include a *Stabat mater* (1783) and a *Hymne à l'Etre Suprème* (1794), both for soli, chorus and orchestra, and keyboard sonatas.

Becken (Ger.). Cymbals.

Becker, Günther (b. Forbach, Baden, 1 Apr 1924). German composer and a member of the post-war avant-garde. After studies with Fortner, he taught in Athens (1956–68), while returning each summer to Darmstadt. He then taught at the conservatory in Düsseldorf (1973–89). Many of his works have an electronic component.

Becker, John (Joseph) (b. Henderson, Ky, 22 Jan 1886; d. Wilmette, Ill., 21 Jan 1961). US composer, linked with Ives, Ruggles, Cowell and Riegger among the country's early 20th-century modernists. He graduated from the Cincinnati Conservatory in 1905 with a mastery of 19th-century German style, and was radicalized by meeting Cowell in 1928. His most adventurous pieces, strong on dissonant counterpoint, came in the 1930s; later his output slackened, for reasons of declining health and neglect. A devout Catholic, he taught from 1917 to 1957 at Catholic colleges in the Midwest.

Orchestral: *Symphonia brevis*, 1929; *Abongo* (ballet), ch, perc, 1933; Horn Concerto, 1933; *A Marriage with Space* (ballet), speaking ch, orch, 1935; etc.

Chamber: *Soundpiece* No.1, pf, str, 1932–5; No.2 'Homage to Haydn', str qt, 1936; No.3, vn, pf, 1936; No.4, str qt, 1937; No.5, pf, 1937; No.6, fl, cl, 1942; No.7, 2 pf, 1949; etc.

Other works: sacred choral pieces, incidental music, songs

Beckett, Samuel (b. Dublin, 13 Apr 1906; d. Paris, 22 Dec 1989). Irish writer, whose clear force has imprinted itself on many composers since the 1950s, including Feldman, Kim, Holliger and Kurtág.

Beckwith, John (b. Victoria, BC, 9 Mar 1927). Canadian composer. Trained first as a choirboy and at the conservatory in Toronto (1945–50), he studied with Boulanger in Paris (1950–52) and returned to Toronto to teach at the university. His works cover a range of avant-garde options.

Bedyngham, John (b. ?Oxford, ?1422; d. ?Westminster, 1459/60). English composer, widely appreciated in his time. His surviving output is small – two masses (one on Binchois's ballade *Dueil angoisseux*), a few other liturgical pieces, eight songs – and parts of it have also been ascribed to Dunstable, Du Fay and Frye. The confusion betokens his stature. Similarly uncertain are the details of his life: he may have stayed in England after an education at Winchester and Oxford; certainly he died as verger of St Stephen's chapel in Westminster, a post seemingly reserved for an important composer.

Beecham, Thomas (b. St Helens, Lancs., 29 Apr 1879; d. London, 8 Mar 1961). British conductor, renowned for the crispness and buoyancy of his performances, for his energy and vision in helping revitalize British musical life, and for his wit, as shown not only in his performances but in his unrivalled command of the anecdote. The son of a successful pharmaceutical manufacturer (whose baronetcy he inherited in 1916), he had the leisure to teach himself conducting on the basis of wide experience at home and abroad. In his 30s he worked vigorously in London conducting concerts, opera (including recent works by Strauss, Delius and Sibelius) and ballet (Diaghilev's company). He took time off in 1920–23 for business, then returned to the fray, founding the LPO (1932) and in the same year becoming artistic director of Covent Garden. After spending much of the war in the USA, he returned to London in 1944. The LPO was by now self-governing, so he established another orchestra, the RPO, in 1946. Music close to him ranged from Haydn and Mozart to Sibelius and Delius, and certainly included the 'lollipops' of light classics he regularly included.

Thomas Beecham *A Mingled Chime* (1944, ʳ1987); Harold Atkins and Archie Newman, ed. *Beecham Stories* (1978, ²2001)

Beeson, Jack (Hamilton) (b. Muncie, Ind., 15 Jul 1921). US composer, especially of operas in the national naturalist tradition, his most successful such work being *Lizzie Borden* (1965). He studied at the Eastman School (1939–44), privately with Bartók in New York (1944) and at Columbia (1945–7), where his work as accompanist and conductor in the opera workshop intensified his interest in the medium and where he remained as a teacher.

Beethoven, Ludwig van (baptized Bonn, 17 Dec 1770; d. Vienna, 26 Mar 1827). German composer, the dominating presence in classical music through more than two centuries. The unprecedented dynamism of his music impressed his contemporaries, and the works in which that dynamism was expressed most emphatically – especially the symphonies, concertos and overtures – soon formed the heart of the concert repertory. There they have remained, exerting a profound influence on how music is heard and valued, and indeed on how it is written. His work had an enormous effect on composers from Schubert and Berlioz to Debussy and Mahler. The music of the 19th century is unimaginable without him: he was the creative hero the period needed, and partly created, beginning with the high critical valuations placed on him by composers and critics of the next generation: Schumann, Berlioz, Hoffmann. The more abstruse and harsh music of his final decade waited to find its audience in listeners and composers of later times, when the heroic liberator of music began to be reconsidered as a more complex, awkward and personal figure.

His paternal grandfather, also Ludwig, was a bass from Mechelen who took a post in the electoral chapel at Bonn. This Ludwig had a son Johann, a tenor, who married Maria Magdalena Keverich, daughter of a court cook. They had three children who survived infancy, of whom the composer was the first, followed by two brothers: Caspar Anton Carl (three and a half years younger) and Nikolaus Johann (six years younger). Trained by his father and other local musicians, but without much regular schooling, Beethoven made his public debut in March 1778. Soon after that he became the pupil of Christian Gottlob Neefe, who had him playing Bach's '48' at 11; his first published composition, a set of keyboard variations, dates from the same period. By now he was also playing the organ and harpsichord at court.

In 1787 he went to Vienna, where almost certainly he met Mozart. However, he came back after two weeks to be with his ailing mother before her death. His father was already drinking heavily, and Beethoven at 18 took charge of the family. He played viola in the orchestra, undertook court commissions for cantatas marking the change of emperor, and enjoyed the friendship and protection of Count Waldstein and others. Haydn was in Bonn journeying to (December 1790) and from (July 1792) London, and the two men probably met – certainly Beethoven left for Vienna in November 1792 to study with this most distinguished master of the day. As Waldstein wrote in the album he took with him: 'You shall receive Mozart's spirit from Haydn's hands.'

The relationship was not good – Beethoven was a mistrustful pupil, Haydn seemingly a complacent teacher – and both may have been glad to part when Haydn left for England again in January 1794. Beethoven then studied counterpoint with Albrechtsberger for over a year, while continuing to establish himself as a virtuoso pianist and composer in Viennese high society. Among those who gave him support were several who had been patrons of Haydn and Mozart, including Prince Lichnowsky, Baron van Swieten, Prince Lobkowitz and Count Razumovsky. He also began appearing in public concerts in March 1795, playing concertos of his own and Mozart's, and doing what earned him most astonishment: improvising.

He was slower to publish anything, because he wanted to be sure his Op.1 would be remarkable. It was: the set of three piano trios that came out in the summer of 1795, just before Haydn's return. Op.2 was a set of sonatas, dedicated to Haydn. Right from this early point he seems to have wanted to keep opus numbers for his important works, to reflect his priorities rather than publishing convenience. That was new. By 1798 he had reached, through further sonatas and chamber pieces, Op.11, while other compositions (variations, dances, songs) were published without opus number. It was perhaps also out of complete confidence in his artistic status that, in 1798, he began making his sketches in bound books, which he kept by him, providing a legacy for future scholars. The sketches help show how the urgent feeling of growth within each of his pieces reflects a painstaking process of development in the act of composition, how he would slowly build themes and forms, over months and sometimes years.

In 1796 he made a concert tour through Prague, Dresden and Berlin (where he began writing music for cello, the Prussian king's favourite instrument), and he returned to Prague in 1798. Then he set himself to completing, before the end of the century, works in the two genres Haydn had made his own: the string quartet and the symphony. His six quartets Op.18 were published in 1800, and his First Symphony was introduced at a concert he gave on 2 April that year; the programme also included his immediately popular Septet.

His ability to enjoy these triumphs was limited, for by now he was aware of increasing deafness, a condition he admitted to friends in 1801. It did not interfere with his creative work, but, as he said, it caused him to withdraw from society. Yet though the years of spectacular improvising in aristocratic salons were over, he retained his weakness for high-born young women, notably including at this time the Countess Giulietta Guicciardi. In 1802 he spent a long summer in Heiligenstadt, outside Vienna, composing his Second Symphony. There he wrote a document to his brothers, the Heiligenstadt Testament, in which he spoke of his passionate despair and of overcoming thoughts of suicide.

Soon afterwards he confronted a new challenge, as music director of the Theater an der Wien, which brought him into contact with Schikaneder, Mozart's collaborator on *Die Zauberflöte*. He took up lodgings in the theatre, and gave a concert there on 5 April 1803, including his two symphonies, C minor piano concerto and oratorio *Christus am Oelberge*. His immediate goal now was opera. In 1801–2 he had had some lessons with Salieri in vocal composition and the setting of Italian, but for Schikaneder he tackled a German libretto, *Vestas Feuer*, drawing some of the fire for his work from the recent experience of Cherubini's operas, which had brought to Vienna the sounds of the French Revolution. This project, though, gave way to further instrumental works, including a new symphony, to be named, in tribute to the saviour of the Revolution, *Bonaparte*. According to an old story, when he heard that in May 1804 Napoleon had declared himself emperor, he furiously tore out his work's title page. In 1806 he published the composition as *Sinfonia eroica*, 'to celebrate the memory of a great man'.

The 'Eroica' Symphony (1803) marks the start of a short period of intense creative energy and a new style. The progressive urge, already strong in his earlier music, comes forward with new vigour as he takes on the musical means and the human ideals of Revolution, of the Enlightenment in combat. The orchestral sound is bigger, especially in the bass, with three horns in the orchestra and an independent double-bass line, and that big sound carries its listeners along. Its appeal is universal, its formal manoeuvring out in the open; it gives the impression of a joint exercise embracing all humanity, made for the new public forum of the orchestral concert. Propulsiveness comes especially from emphatic rhythm and powerful, long-range development, in which small motifs prove to have immense capacities of transformation. Scale grows correspondingly (the work is half as long again as the First and Second symphonies), and the coda becomes a substantial part of the

form, there to ground the music after so much activity, and to be a celebration – of difficulties surmounted and expression shared, of joy and of hope.

This big, powerful and communal voice rapidly found further expression in piano sonatas (the 'Waldstein', the 'Appassionata'), opera at last (*Fidelio*), string quartets (the 'Razumovsky' set), concertos (the G major for piano, the Violin Concerto) and more symphonies (Nos.4–6), all within the next five years. Three of these works (Symphonies Nos.4 and 5, Piano Concerto No.4) he included, together with other pieces and a new Fantasia for piano, choir and orchestra as grand finale, in an extraordinary concert he gave on 22 December 1808, again at the Theater an der Wien, though Schikaneder had left before the production there of *Fidelio*. Wider dissemination (together with a livelihood) came through publishers, and by now he was dealing not only with Viennese houses but with firms in Leipzig, Zurich and London. Working at full stretch, he was an international figure.

This rush of creative achievement included the period (1804–7) when he was in love with Countess Josephine Deym, a young widow and again a noblewoman with whom he had little chance of allying himself. He could not expect romantic interest from the aristocracy, only patronage, esteem and caring friendship, which he duly received. Music addressed to everyone was thus supported by a small circle of the richly favoured, in a paradox perhaps eased for him by the solitariness to which his deafness had consigned him. In 1809 three of his patrons – Archduke Rudolph, Prince Kinsky and Prince Lobkowitz – clubbed together to guarantee him an income, as long as he remained in Vienna, and so he was freed from serious financial worries.

The pressure to compose came, rather, from within. In 1809 he wrote his last concerto (the 'Emperor'), the 'Harp' quartet and the 'Les Adieux' sonata, all works in the heroic (and 'Eroica') key of E♭. He also began music for a hero of liberation: the Egmont of Goethe's drama. This score was completed and performed the next year, during which he composed three Goethe songs and gained a distant contact with the poet through his friendship with Bettina Brentano. Then in 1812, on a visit to the spa town of Teplitz, in Bohemia, he and Goethe met. He was dismayed by Goethe's courtliness, which he found unbecoming in a poet; Goethe found him 'an utterly untamed personality', whose scorn for the world caused difficulties for himself and others.

Such comments give us the image of him as a bear of a man, unruly but lovable, and loving, though with an irascibility that deafness surely intensified. He had a passionate moral sense: he was loyal to his friends, dutiful to his brothers and intolerant of sexual frivolity. Marriage to him was an ideal as high as heroism, and similarly a sacrifice that raised human dignity. Also in 1812 he descended furiously on his brother Johann for taking a mistress. And close to the same time he wrote his letter to 'the Immortal Beloved' (probably another member of the intellectually and socially flourishing Brentano family, Antonie), a letter that is both a declaration of love and a stout resignation to celibacy. Consciously he saw music as the only partner with whom he could live.

From that relationship by now had come the Seventh Symphony (followed shortly by the Eighth), the F minor quartet and 'Archduke' trio, and scores for a theatrical double bill: *Die Ruinen von Athen* and *König Stephan*. The two symphonies seem to have been designed as a pair (with hints in the sketchbook of a third, in D minor – not pursued for another decade), and as such they help substantiate the alternation traditionally felt in his symphonies between exuberant, driven works (the odd-numbered ones) and more relaxed or classical pieces. Beyond that, though, each symphony is a type to itself. The Seventh is spacious and assured (for Wagner 'the apotheosis of the dance'), the Eighth compact, full of irony.

By another conventional way of partitioning his output, he was now near the end of his 'middle period', the period of stalwart, affirmative works initiated by the 'Eroica'. This period closed with a deceleration. Among his works of 1813–17, only two piano sonatas, two cello sonatas and the song cycle *An die ferne Geliebte* count among those most valued. Otherwise his output was rather miscellaneous, including various items of theatre and choral music, some songs, the first of several batches of folksong arrangements commissioned by the Edinburgh publisher George Thomson, an overture (*Namensfeier*) and the battle symphony *Wellingtons Sieg*, an instant hit much despised by later generations.

There were practical reasons for the paucity of major works, notably his need to earn some money, given the economic crisis and the death of one of his three patrons (Kinsky), as well as the time taken revising *Fidelio* for its 1814 revival. But he may, too, have been depressed and directionless. It was also in 1814 that, his deafness increasing, he appeared for the last time in public playing an important piano part, that of the 'Archduke' trio. And that same year he acquired parental responsibilities in caring for his nine-year-old nephew Karl, after the death of his brother Caspar Carl. His struggle for guardianship with his sister-in-law

went on until 1820, with corresponding interruptions to the boy's education, and after that there were problems from Karl himself, culminating in a suicide attempt in July 1826.

Meanwhile he cut down on occasional works (except for the arrangements for Thomson) and devoted the last 10 years of his life to piano music, string quartets and two immense scores: the *Missa solemnis* and the Ninth Symphony. The piano and the mass came first. He spent almost a year (1817–18) writing a sonata on the scale of a symphony, the 'Hammerklavier', and in 1819 began the *Missa solemnis*, intending it for performance at Archduke Rudolph's installation as archbishop of Olmütz – though the occasion came and went in 1820 with the work far from ready, partly because the score grew in scope and partly because he gave time to other projects, including the Diabelli Variations and three last piano sonatas. In 1822 he even started work on his final symphony – in part fulfilment of a commission from the Philharmonic Society of London he had accepted in 1817 – before the mass was quite finished.

In the late piano music, which also includes bagatelles written around and after the sonatas and variations, certain traits come to the fore: contrapuntal textures (including full-scale fugues in Op.106 and Op.110), musical characters strikingly defined in miniature, and a sense of vast range and potential opened up by variation form. Op.111 is in C minor, the arena of drama in earlier Beethoven (e.g. the Fifth Symphony) but now, in the variations that form the second and final movement, exuding a radiant active calm.

The Ninth Symphony was the recapitulation of a lifetime's work, characteristically a developing recapitulation. Grander in scale even than the 'Eroica' and the Seventh, lasting over an hour, it extended and elevated each of his movement categories: the sonata allegro whose conflict sets up the space and tension for the entire work, the rapt slow movement, the bounding scherzo and the culminative finale. But this time the finale includes a theme going back more than a quarter century (via the choral Fantasia to a song of 1795) and a text he had had it in mind to set for even longer, Schiller's *Ode to Joy*. Prepared by instrumental recitative, and introduced by a solo bass singing to his performing companions the composer's addition to the text ('O friends, not these sounds!'), the voices enter the work as of necessity, and express the message of liberty, equality and fraternity as much by their presence as by the words they sing.

Warmly pressed by his friends and admirers to let Vienna hear his latest works, he presented his Ninth Symphony, together with the overture *Die*

Weihe des Hauses and three segments of the *Missa solemnis* (the *Kyrie*, *Credo* and *Agnus Dei*), at a concert in the Kärntnertor theatre on 7 May 1824. Now totally deaf, he had to be alerted to the fact that behind him the audience was cheering.

After the concert he turned to a commission from a Russian prince, Nikolay Golitsyn, for quartets. Three works followed with a speed wholly out of proportion to their magnitude: Op.127 by December 1824, Op.132 by July 1825 – after his recovery from illness, commemorated within the work in a 'Heiliger Dankgesang' (Thanksgiving Hymn) – and Op.130 with its *Grosse Fuge* finale in August–November 1825. Golitsyn failed to complete the promised payments, but Beethoven went on, finishing two more quartets (Op.131 and Op.135) by October 1826, and the next month providing Op.130 with a less strenuous last movement.

These five late quartets have always been regarded as among music's Himalayas. Again they bring 19th-century drive – that essentially Beethovenian drive by means of rhythmic force and harmonic intensification – to bear on 18th-century fugue and variations. Often, and notably in the *Grosse Fuge*, the result is fiercely dissonant, befitting the clash of eras. But drive goes along, too, with an extraordinary agility, as the close-connectedness of Beethoven's earlier forms is opened out to allusiveness and abrupt change, and the music comes to switch character – almost switch style – from movement to movement. Everything about the medium is intensified: the music speaks intimately to its listeners but also, by virtue of there being four players, speaks to itself. It looks back to what was then the remotest musical past – the 'Heiliger Dankgesang' is in the Lydian mode, continuing the modal flavour of parts of the *Missa solemnis* – while chiming with the most challenging ambitions of the future.

Beethoven's funeral was a public event: an actor stood at the graveside to deliver an oration by the poet-dramatist Franz Grillparzer. The contrast with Mozart's unceremonious burial in the same city, 35 years or so before, could hardly have been more marked. A new age had come, and, as the crowd knew, this lonely man had provided its first music.

Emily Anderson, ed. *The Letters of Beethoven* (1961, ʳ1985); Maynard Solomon *Beethoven* (1977, ²1998); Lewis Lockwood *Beethoven: Studies in the Creative Process* (1992); Scott Burnham *Beethoven Hero* (1995)

Works without opus numbers are identified by WoO (Werke ohne Opuszahl) or H (Hess) numbers from standard catalogues.

Orchestral and theatre music

Symphonies (all first performances in Vienna): No.1, C, Op.21, 1800, f.p. 2 Apr 1800; No.2, D, Op.36, 1801–2, f.p. 5 Apr 1803; No.3 'EROICA', E♭, Op.55, 1803, f.p. 7 Apr 1805; No.4, B♭, Op.60, 1806, f.p. Mar 1807; No.5, C minor, Op.67, 1807–8, f.p. 22 Dec 1808; No.6 'PASTORAL', F, Op.68, 1808, f.p. 22 Dec 1808; No.7, A, Op.92, 1811–12, f.p. 8 Dec 1813; No.8, F, Op.93, 1812, f.p. 27 Feb 1814; No.9 (Schiller), D minor, Op.125, satb soli, ch, orch, 1822–4, f.p. 7 May 1824

Concertos, etc.: PIANO CONCERTO No.1, C, Op.15, 1795; No.2, B♭, Op.19, begun pre-1793, rev 1794–5, 1798; No.3, C minor, Op.37, ?1800; No.4, G, Op.58, 1805–6; No.5 'EMPEROR', E♭, 1809; Fantasia (CHORAL FANTASY), C minor, Op.80, pf, ch, orch, 1808; VIOLIN CONCERTO, D, Op.61, 1806, arr as piano concerto, 1807; Romance, F, Op.50, vn, orch, ?1798; Romance, G, Op.40, vn, orch, ?1801–2; Triple Concerto, C, pf trio, orch, 1803–4

Other concert works: WELLINGTONS SIEG, Op.91, 1813; NAMENSFEIER (overture), Op.115, 1814–15; *Gratulations-Menuet*, WoO 3, 1822

Opera: FIDELIO, Op.72, 1804–5, rev 1805–6, 1814, with OVERTURES LEONORE No.1, 1806–7, No.2, 1804–5, No.3, 1805–6, *Fidelio*, 1814

Ballets: *Ritterballett*, WoO 1, 1790–91; *Die Geschöpfe des Prometheus* (see PROMETHEUS), Op.43, 1800–1

Incidental music: CORIOLAN (overture), Op.62, 1807; EGMONT (overture, etc.), Op.84, 1809–10; *Die* RUINEN VON ATHEN (overture, etc.), Op.113, 1811; KÖNIG STEPHAN (overture, etc.), Op.117, 1811; *Tarpeja*, 1813; *Leonore Prohaska*, WoO 96, 1815; *Die* WEIHE DES HAUSES (overture, etc.), Op.124, 1822

Dances: 12 Minuets, WoO 7, 1795; 12 German Dances, WoO 8, 1795; 12 Contredanses, WoO 14, 1802

Choral orchestral: Cantata on the Death of Joseph II (S.A. Averdonk), WoO 87, with satb soli, 1790; Cantata on the Accession of Leopold II (Averdonk), WoO 88, with satb soli, 1790; CHRISTUS AM OELBERGE, Op.85, with stb soli, 1803, rev 1804; Mass, C, Op.86, 1807; *Der glorreiche Augenblick* (cantata: Alois Weissenbach), Op.136, with sstb soli, 1814; *Germania* (singspiel finale: Treitschke), WoO 94, with b solo, 1814; MEERESSTILLE UND GLÜCKLICHE FAHRT (Goethe), Op.112, 1814–15; *Es ist vollbracht* (singspiel finale: Treitschke), WoO 97, 1815; MISSA SOLEMNIS, Op.123, with satb soli, 1819–23; *Opferlied* (Friedrich von Matthisson), Op.121b, with s solo, 1823–4

Arias, etc.: 'Meine weise Mutter spricht', WoO 89, b, c.1790–92; 'Mit Mädeln', WoO 90, b, c.1790–92; 'Primo amore', WoO 92, s, c.1790–92; 'Ah! perfido' (Metastasio), Op.65, s, 1795–6; 'O welch ein Leben', WoO 91:1, t, ?1795–6; 'Soll ein Schuh', WoO 91:2, s, ?1795–6; 'No, non turbati' (Metastasio), WoO 92a, s, 1801–2; 'Ne' giorni tuoi felici' (Metastasio), WoO 93, duet (st), 1802–3; 'Tremati, empi, tremate' (Bettoni), Op.116, trio (stb), 1801–2, 1814

Wind band pieces: March, F, WoO 18, 1809; March, F, WoO 19, 1810; Polonaise, D, WoO 21, 1810; Ecossaise, D, WoO 22, 1810; Ecossaise, G, WoO 23,

?1810; March, D, WoO 24, 1816; March, C, WoO 20, before 1823

Chamber music

Numbered string quartets: Nos.1–6, F, G, D, C minor, A, B♭ Op.18, 1798–1800; Nos.7–9 'RAZUMOVSKY', F, E minor, C, Op.59, 1805–6; No.10 'Harp', E♭, Op.74, 1809; No.11, F minor, Op.95, 1810; No.12, E♭, Op.127, 1823–4, f.p. 6 Mar 1825; No.13, B♭, Op.130, 1825–6, f.p. 21 Mar 1826 (with GROSSE FUGE, Op.133), alternative finale, 1826; No.14, C♯ minor, Op.131, 1826; No.15, A minor, Op.132, 1825, f.p. 9 Sep 1825; No.16, F, Op.135, 1826

Other music for string quartet: Minuet, A♭, Hess 33, 1790–92; arr of Piano Sonata Op.14:1, 1801–2

String quintets (str qt + va): E♭, Op.4, 1795; C, Op.29, 1801; C minor, Op.104, 1817 (arr of Piano Trio Op.1:3, mostly by Kaufmann); Prelude, D minor, H.40 ?1817; Fugue, D, Op.137, 1817

String trios: No.1, E♭, Op.3, pre-1794; 12 Minuets, WoO 7, 1795; 6 Minuets, WoO 9; Serenade, D, Op.8, 1796–7; Nos.3–5, G, D, C minor, Op.9, 1797–8; 6 Ländler, WoO 15, 1801–2; 12 Contredanses, WoO 14, 1802

String duos: Duet, E♭, WoO 32, va, vc, 2 obbligato eyeglasses, 1796–7; Duet, A, WoO 34, 2 vn, 1822

Piano quartet: E♭, Op.16, pub 1801 (arr of Quintet with wind)

Piano trios: E♭, WoO 38, ?1791; Allegretto, E♭, c.1790–92; Nos.1–3, E♭, G, C minor, Op.1, 1794–5; Variations, E♭, Op.44, pub 1804; Variations on 'Ich bin der Schneider Kakadu', Op.121a, ?1803; Nos.5–6, D, E♭, Op.70, 1808; No.7 'Archduke', B♭, Op.97, 1810–11; Allegretto, B♭, WoO 39, 1812

Clarinet trios: B♭ (Piano Trio No.4), Op.11, cl/vn, vc, pf, 1797; E♭, Op.38, cl/vn, vc, pf, ?1803 (arr of Septet)

Other mixed works: Sextet, E♭, Op.81b, 2 hn, str qt, ?1795; Quintet, E♭, Op.16, pf, ob, cl, hn, bn, 1796; Septet, E♭, Op.20, cl, hn, bn, vn, va, vc, db, 1799–1800; Serenade, D, Op.25, fl, vn, va, 1801

Wind works: Allegro and Minuet, G, WoO 26, 2 fl, 1792; Octet, E♭, Op.103, ?1792–3; Rondino, E♭, WoO 25, octet, 1793; Trio, C, Op.87, 2 ob, cor ang, 1795; Variations on 'La ci darem la mano', WoO 28, 2 ob, cor ang, ?1795; Sextet, Op.71, E♭, 1796; March, B♭, WoO 29, sextet, 1798; 3 Equali, WoO 30, trbn qt, 1812

Violin sonatas: Nos.1–3, D, A, E♭, Op.12, 1797–8; No.4, A minor, Op.23, 1800; No.5 'Spring', F, Op.24, 1800–1; Nos.6–8, A, C minor, G, Op.30, 1801–2; No.9 'KREUTZER', Op.47, A minor, 1802–3; No.10, G, Op.96, 1812

Cello sonatas: Nos.1–2, F, G minor, Op.5, 1796; No.3, A, Op.69, 1807–8; Nos.4–5, C, D, Op.102, 1815

Horn sonata: F, Op.17, 1800

Pieces for mandolin and piano: Sonatina, C minor, WoO 43a, 1796; Adagio, E♭, WoO 43b, 1796; Sonatina, C, WoO 44a, 1796; Andante and Variations, D, WoO 44b, 1796

Other works for solo instrument and piano: Variations on 'Se vuol ballare', WoO 40, vn, pf, 1792–3; Rondo, G, WoO 41, vn, pf, 1793–4; 6

German Dances, WoO 42, vn, pf, 1796; Variations on 'See the Conqu'ring Hero Comes', WoO 45, vc, pf, 1796; Variations on 'Ein Mädchen ohne Weibchen', Op.66, vc, pf, 1796; Variations on 'Bei Männern, welche Liebe fühlen', WoO 46, vc, pf, 1801; Serenade, D, Op.41, fl/vn, pf, 1803 (arr of Op.25); *Notturno*, Op.42, va, pf, 1803 (arr of Op.8); 6 National Airs with Variations, Op.105, fl/vn, pf, c.1815; 10 National Airs with Variations, Op.107, fl/vn, pf, c.1818

Piano music

Sonatas: F, WoO 50, pre-1793; No.1, F minor, Op.2:1, 1793–5; No.2, A, Op.2:2, 1794–5; No.3, C, Op.2:3, 1794–5; No.4, E♭, Op.7, 1796–7; No.5, C minor, Op.10:1, ?1795–7; No.6, F, Op.10:2, 1796–7; No.7, D, Op.10:3, 1797–8; No.8 'PATHÉTIQUE', C minor, Op.13, ?1797–8; No.9, E, Op.14:1, 1798; No.10, G, Op.14:2, ?1799; No.11, B♭, Op.22, 1800; No.12, A♭, Op.26, 1800–1; No.13 (Sonata quasi una fantasia), E♭, Op.27:1, 1800–1; No.14 'MOONLIGHT' (Sonata quasi una fantasia), C♯ minor, Op.27:2, 1801; No.15 'Pastoral', D, Op.28, 1801; No.16, G, Op.31:1, 1802; No.17 'Tempest', D minor, Op.31:2, 1802; No.18, E♭, Op.31:3, 1802; No.19, G minor, Op.49:1, ?1797; No.20, G, Op.49:2, 1795–6; No.21 'WALDSTEIN', C, Op.53, 1803–4; No.22, F, Op.54, 1804; No.23 'Appassionata', F minor, Op.57, 1804–5; No.24, F♯, Op.78, 1809; No.25, G, Op.79, 1809; No.26 'Les ADIEUX', E♭, Op.81a, 1809–10; No.27, E minor, Op.90, 1814; No.28, A, Op.101, 1816; No.29 'HAMMERKLAVIER', B♭, Op.106, 1817–18; No.30, E, Op.109, 1820; No.31, A♭, Op.110, 1821–2; No.32, C minor, Op.111, 1821–2

Variations: 24 on 'Venni amore', WoO 65, 1790–91; 13 on 'Es war einmal', WoO 66, 1792; 6 on a Swiss song, WoO 64, pre-1793; 12 on the 'Menuet à la Viganò', WoO 68, 1795; 9 on 'Quant' è più bello', WoO 69, 1795; 6 on 'Nel cor più non mi sento', WoO 70, 1795; 8 on 'Un fièvre brûlante', WoO 72, ?1795; 12 on Wranitzky's Russian Dance, WoO 71, 1796–7; 10 on 'La stessa, le stessissima', WoO 73, 1799; 6 on 'Tändeln und Scherzen', WoO 76, 1799; 7 on 'Kind, willst du ruhig schlafen', WoO 75, 1799; 6 on an original theme, G, WoO 77, 1800; 6 on an original theme, F, Op.34, 1802; 15 and a fugue on an original theme (EROICA Variations), E♭, Op.35, 1802; 7 on 'God save the king', WoO 78, 1802/3; 5 on 'Rule, Britannia', WoO 79, 1803; 32 on an original theme, C minor, WoO 80, 1806; 6 on an original theme, D, Op.76, 1809; 33 on a waltz by Diabelli (DIABELLI VARIATIONS), Op.120, 1819, 1822–3

Dances: Allemande, A, WoO 81, 1793; 12 Minuets, WoO 7, 1795; 6 Minuets, WoO 10, ?1795; 7 Ländler, WoO 11, ?1798; 12 German Dances, WoO 13, ?pre-1800; 12 Contredanses, WoO 14, 1802; 6 Ländler, WoO 15, 1801–2; Minuet, E♭, WoO 82, pre-1805; 6 Ecossaises, WoO 83, ?1807; Polonaise, C, Op.89, 1814; Waltz, E♭, WoO 84, 1824; Waltz, D, WoO 85, 1825; Ecossaise, E♭, WoO 86, 1825

Other solo pieces: Preludes, Op.39, ?1789; Rondo a capriccio 'Rage over a Lost Penny', Op.129, 1795; Fugue, C, H.64, 1795; Presto, C minor, WoO 52,

?1795; Allegretto, C minor, WoO 53, 1796–7; Allegretto, C minor, H.69, 1796/7; Rondo, C, Op.51:1, ?1796–7; Rondo, G, Op.51:2, ?1798; 7 Bagatelles, Op.33, 1801–2; Bagatelle 'Lustig–Traurig', WoO 54, ?1802; Allegretto, C, WoO 56, 1803; ANDANTE FAVORI, WoO 57, 1803; Prelude, F minor, WoO 55, pre-1805; Fantasia, Op.77, 1809; Bagatelle 'Für Elise', WoO 59, 1808–10; Bagatelle, B♭, WoO 60, 1818; Allegretto, B minor, WoO 61, 1821; 11 Bagatelles, Op.119, 1820–22; 6 Bagatelles, Op.126, 1823–4; Allegretto quasi andante, G minor, WoO 61a, 1825

Duets: 8 Variations on a Theme by Count Waldstein, WoO 67, ?1792; Sonata, D, Op.6, 1796–7; 6 Variations on 'Ich denke dein', WoO 74, 1799–1803; 3 Marches, Op.45, ?1803; GROSSE FUGE, Op.134, 1826 (arr of Op.133)

Songs and miscellanea

Cycle: AN DIE FERNE GELIEBTE, Op.98, 1815–16
Sets: 6 Gellert Songs, Op.48, pub 1803; 8 Songs, Op.52, ?1790–96; 6 Songs, Op.75, 1809; 4 Ariettas and a Duet, Op.82, ?1809; 3 Goethe Songs, Op.83, 1810
Individual songs: 'Abendlied unterm gestirnten Himmel' (Heinrich Goeble), WoO 150, 1820; 'Adelaide' (Friedrich von Matthisson), Op.46, 1794–5; 'Als die Geliebte' (Stephan von Breuning), WoO 132, 1806; 'An den fernen Geliebten' (Christian Ludwig Reissig), Op.75:5; 'Andenken' (Matthisson), WoO 136, 1809; 'An die Geliebte' (Joseph Ludwig Stoll), WoO 140, 2 versions, 1811, ?1814; 'An die Hoffnung' (Christoph August Tiedge), Op.32, 1805; 'An die Hoffnung' (Tiedge, different text), Op.94, ?1815; 'Aus Goethes Faust', Op.75:3, with ch; 'Der Bardengeist' (Franz Rudolph Hermann), WoO 142, 1813; 'Der edle Mensch' (Goethe), WoO 151, 1823; 'Gedenke mein', ?1804–5, rev 1819–20; 'Gegenliebe' (Gottfried August Bürger), WoO 118:2, 1794–5; 'Das Geheimnis' (Ignaz Heinrich von Wessenberg), WoO 145, 1815; 'Der Gesang der Nachtigall' (Herder), WoO 141, 1813; 'Das Glück der Freundschaft', Op.88, 1803; 'Gretels Warnung' (Gerhard Anton von Halem), Op.75:4; 'In questa tomba oscura' (Giuseppe Carpani), WoO 133, 1807; 'Der Jüngling in der Fremde' (Reissig), WoO 138, 1809; 'Des Kriegers Abschied' (Reissig), WoO 143, 1814; 'Der Kuss' (Christian Felix Weisse), Op.128, ?1822; 'Die laute Klage' (Herder), WoO 135, ?c.1815; 'Der Liebende' (Reissig), WoO 139, 1809; 'Lied aus der Ferne' (Reissig), WoO 137, 1809; 'Der Mann von Wort' (Friedrich August Kleinschmid), Op.99, 1816; 'Mignon' (Goethe: 'Kennst du das Land?'), Op.75:1; 'Mit einem gemalten Band', Op.83:3; 'Neue Liebe, neues Leben' (Goethe), 1st setting, WoO 127, 1798/9, 2nd setting, Op.75:2; 'Resignation' (Paul von Haugwitz), WoO 149, 1817; 'Ruf vom Berge' (Treitschke), WoO 147, 1816; 'Sehnsucht' (Goethe: 'Nur wer die Sehnsucht kennt'), WoO 134, 4 settings, 1807–8; 'Sehnsucht' ('Was zieht mir?'), Op.83:2; 'Sehnsucht' (Reissig), WoO 146, 1815–16; 'So oder so' (Karl Gottlieb Lappe), WoO 148, 1817;

'Der Wachtelschlag' (Samuel Friedrich Sauter), WoO 129, 1803; 'Wonne der Wehmut', Op.83:1; 'Der Zufriedene' (Reissig), Op.75:6
Duet: 'Merkenstein' (Johann Baptist Rupprecht), Op.100, 1814–15
Choruses: *Abschiedsgesang* (J. von Seyfried), men's ch, 1814; *Cantata campestre* (Abbate Clemente Bondi), ch, pf, 1814; *Gesang der Mönche* (Schiller), men's ch, 1817; *Hochzeitslied* (Anton Joseph Stein), WoO 105, men's/mixed ch, pf, 1819; Birthday cantata for Prince Lobkowitz, WoO 106, s, ch, pf, 1823
Folksong arrangements for v, pf trio: 25 Irish, WoO 152, pub 1814; 20 Irish, WoO 153, pub 1814–16; 12 Irish, WoO 154, pub 1816; 26 Welsh, WoO 155, pub 1817; 25 Scottish, Op.108, pub 1818; 12 Scottish, WoO 156, pub 1824–5; 12 various, WoO 157, pub 1816–39; c.40 others
Other works: cadenzas for Mozart's D minor piano concerto; c.60 canons, mostly late; pieces for mechanical clock

Juvenilia and spurious works

Juvenilia: Variations on a March by Dressler, WoO 63, 1782; Rondo, C, WoO 48, 1783; Rondo, A, WoO 49, ?1783; 3 Piano Sonatas (Sonatinas), E♭, F minor, D, WoO 47, ?1783; 3 Piano Quartets, E♭, D, C, WoO 36, 1785; Trio, G, WoO 37, pf, fl, bn, 1786
The delightful Sonatina in G is not authentic.

Beethoven Quartet. Ensemble formed in 1923 by four recent graduates of the Moscow Conservatory – Dmitry Tsyganov, Vasily Shirinsky, Vadim Borisovsky and Sergey Shirinsky – who took Beethoven's name in 1931 and introduced most of Shostakovich's quartets. The group lasted through changes of personnel until 1987.

Beggar's Opera, The. Opera with ballads and airs set to a libretto by Gay; the musical arrangement is customarily attributed to Pepusch. Macheath, a notorious highwayman, is caught not so much by the law as by two of the women in his life, Polly Peachum and Lucy Lockit, together with their fathers. For its tunefulness, its unillusioned characters and its scan of the London criminal world it was immensely popular throughout the 18th century, and was diversely revived in the 20th by Brecht and Weill (*Die Dreigroschenoper*) and by Britten. First performance: London, 29 Jan 1728.

Begleitung (Ger.). Accompaniment.

Behrens, Hildegard (b. Varel, near Oldenburg, 9 Feb 1937). German soprano, vivid in her physicality, vocal warmth and passionate stagecraft. She studied in Freiburg, where she made her debut as the Countess (1971). In the 1980s she took her place among the leading Wagner singers, remarkable also as Salome, Elektra and Marie (*Wozzeck*). Berio wrote *Cronaca del luogo* for her.

Beinum, Eduard (Alexander) van (b. Arnhem, 3 Sep 1901; d. Amsterdam, 13 Apr 1959). Dutch conductor, notably of the Concertgebouw, which he joined as second conductor in 1931 and led from 1945. He was specially admired in late Romantic music (Bruckner, Elgar), though he also presented Dutch and British contemporaries.

beklemmt (Ger.). Oppressed.

Belaieff. See BELYAYEV.

bel canto (It., fine singing). Style named only when it was passing – the light, agile style of singing expected by Rossini and Bellini, replaced by a generally heavier delivery in the mid 19th century. Callas and Sutherland were at the head of a bel canto revival in the 1950s.

Belgium. The southern part of the LOW COUNTRIES, which gained its independence in 1830 in the wake of riots after the première of Auber's *La Muette de Portici* at the Théâtre de la Monnaie, the Brussels opera (founded 1700). Early Belgian composers tended to make their careers in Paris (Franck) or internationally (Ysaÿe). A local musical culture developed in the 20th century, fostering such composers as Gilson, Absil, Poot, Pousseur and Boesmans.

bell (1) (Fr. *cloche*, Ger. *Glocke*, It. *campana*). Percussion instrument of hollow metal (normally bronze, in the proportion four parts of copper to one of tin) or, less usually, ceramic or glass, in the form of an inverted cup or a ball with a slit opening. Cup-shaped (open) bells often have a swivelling clapper inside, which strikes the bell when either it or the bell is swung, or else they may be sounded by means of some external object; spherical (closed) bells have a smaller ball within and so make a sound when shaken. Open bells are found all over the world, often in connection with religious practice, and they may be large, even immense (*c*.200 tons in the case of the Tsar bell in the Moscow Kremlin), and of correspondingly low pitch. Closed bells – such as sleighbells or dancers' jingles – are nearly always small.

The sound of an open bell is complex and of long duration, containing many inharmonic partials decaying at different rates. That which gives the bell its basic pitch at first sounding is the fundamental. Around an octave below is the 'hum note', which stays long after the bell has been struck. First among the higher partials are the tierce, the quint and the nominal, close to a minor third, a fifth and an octave above the fundamental. Once the bell has been cast, these five principal partials may be tuned, by shaving off metal and so lowering the pitch. Tuning to precise octaves, thirds and fifths may not be a priority, for the bell will then lack personality.

Bronze open bells were being cast in China, India, Persia and Egypt by 1000 BC, and in Greece by the 6th century BC. Celtic missionaries, according to tradition, inherited their iron handbells from St Patrick in the 5th century, and in the 6th century the casting of bronze bells was established by the Benedictines in Italy. By the later Middle Ages bellfounders were travelling craftsmen with expertise in the pitching and tuning of bells, which now were regularly raised into towers in peals. Different bells would be used for different signals, to play tunes or, in England, in CHANGE RINGING.

Church bells are not easily transported, though their sounds may be reproduced electronically, whether from recordings (as in Harvey's *Mortuos plango*) or synthetically (as sometimes in performing *Parsifal*). The bells most commonly used in the orchestra are BELL PLATES, COWBELLS, SLEIGHBELLS and TUBULAR BELLS.

Percival Price *Bells and Man* (1983)

(2) (Fr. *pavillon*, Ger. *Schallstück, Kopfstück*, It. *campana, padiglione*). Widening end of a wind instrument.

Bell, Joshua (b. Indianapolis, 9 Dec 1967). US violinist of elegant style and serious manner, adept in the virtuoso repertory, popular traditions and chamber music. He studied with Mimi Zweig (1975–80) and Josef Gingold at the University of Indiana (1980–9) and made his concerto debut in 1981 with the Philadelphia Orchestra.

Bell Anthem. Name given in Purcell's lifetime to his *Rejoice in the Lord alway*, for the peals of its introduction.

Belle Hélène, La (Helen of Troy). Operetta by Offenbach to a libretto by Halévy and Meilhac. The great kings of Homer play games while Helen (soprano) and Paris (tenor) enjoy more physical varieties of deception, self-deception and, indeed, consummation. First performance: Paris, 17 Dec 1864.

Bellini, Vincenzo (b. Catania, 3 Nov 1801; d. Puteaux, near Paris, 23 Sep 1835). Italian composer, master of sustained, floating melody in the several operas of his short career. He was taught music by his father and grandfather, both professional musicians, and had little general education. A municipal grant took him to the Naples Conservatory (1819–25), where he studied with Zingarelli. A couple of successes, at the conservatory and the San Carlo, led to a commission for La Scala, fulfilled by *Il pirata* (1827), with which he began his collaboration with the librettist Romani and his international career. Remaining in Milan, he enjoyed aristicratic favour and a love affair, supporting himself through his operas. He made a triumphant return trip to Sicily in 1832, visited London the next year, then settled in Paris, where he became acquainted with Rossini and Chopin. Admired in true Romantic fashion for the nobility and gentleness of his soul, he died an early Romantic's early death – though post-Romantic biography revealed some claws on the dove, particularly in his attitudes to women and rivals, notably Donizetti. His operas, all serious, implied a new vocal style, emphasizing long, expressive phrasing rather than florid decoration. That style found its embodiment in a new generation of singers (Pasta, Malibran), and its lingering echo in Chopin, Verdi and Wagner.

John Rosselli *The Life of Bellini* (1996)

Operas (librettos by Romani except where stated): *Il pirata*, f.p. Milan, 1827; *La straniera*, f.p. Milan, 1829; *Zaira*, f.p. Parma, 1829; I CAPULETI E I MONTECCHI, f.p. Venice, 1830; *La* SONNAMBULA, f.p. Milan, 1831; NORMA, f.p. Milan, 1831; *Beatrice di Tenda*, f.p. Venice, 1833; I PURITANI (Pepoli), f.p. Paris, 1835
Other works: sacred music, songs, etc.

bell-lyra. GLOCKENSPIEL with the plates affixed to a lyre-shaped frame, to be held vertically for marching-band performance.

bell plates. Square or rectangular pieces of metal, hung on a frame for orchestral use.

Bells, The (*Kolokola*). Symphony by Rachmaninoff for soli (s, t, bar), choir and orchestra, setting Balmont's translation of Poe's poem in four movements. First performance: St Petersburg, 30 Nov 1913.

Bells of Zlonice, The (*Zlonické zvony*). Name Dvořák gave his First Symphony. He had grown up partly in Zlonice.

belly. Front or upper surface of a string instrument, normally made of spruce or pine and arched for bowed instruments, flat for guitars and lutes.

Belshazzar. Babylonian king whose blasphemy was punished not only by death but by death ominously foretold (see Daniel 5). Two notable choral works tell his story.

(1) Handel's oratorio *Belshazzar* to words by Charles Jennens. First performance: London, 27 Mar 1745.

(2) Walton's *Belshazzar's Feast*, for baritone, choir and orchestra, to words by Osbert Sitwell. First performance: Leeds, 8 Oct 1931.

Belyayev, Mitrofan (Petrovich) (b. St Petersburg, 22 Feb 1836; d. St Petersburg, 4 Jan 1904). Russian patron, who from 1885 supported Russian music by publishing it, organizing orchestral concerts and presenting quartet evenings. Four of his composers – Borodin, Rimsky-Korsakov, Glazunov and Lyadov – honoured him with a quartet on the notes B♭–A–F (i.e. B–La–F).

bémol (Fr.). Flat.

bemolle (It.). Flat.

ben (It.). Well, as in *ben marcato* (strongly marked).

Benda. Musical family founded by Jan Jiří Benda (1686–1757), a Czech village musician whose children included the prominent composer Georg, three violinist-composers – Franz, Johann (1713–52) and Joseph (1724–1804) – and a soprano, Anna (1728–81), all of whom pursued careers in Germany.

(1) **Franz** (baptized Staré Benátky, 22 Nov 1709; d. Nowawes, near Potsdam, 7 Mar 1786). He was a boy singer in Prague and Dresden, and then a violinist, in the service of Frederick II from 1733 until his death. Composition lessons from the Graun brothers allowed him to set down his singing line in sonatas, solo caprices and concertos. He was responsible for bringing the whole family to Prussia in 1742, and in due course had musical children himself.

(2) **Georg** (baptized Staré Benátky, 30 Jun 1722; d. Köstritz, 6 Nov 1795). Before the family's move to Prussia he attended Catholic schools in Bohemia; afterwards he joined the court orchestra as a violinist alongside his brothers Franz and Johann. In 1750 he was appointed chapelmaster at the Saxe-Gotha court, which sent him on a six-month study tour of Italy in 1765–6. What energized him more, though, was the arrival of Seyler's theatre company in 1774, giving him the chance to write German stage works. He resigned from Gotha in 1778, but returned the next year to retire. Best remembered for his melodramas *Ariadne auf Naxos* (see ARIADNE) and MEDEA, which impressed Mozart, he also wrote singspiels (*Der Jahrmarkt*, Gotha, 1775; *Romeo und Julie*, Gotha, 1776), church music, symphonies and

keyboard sonatas. Several of his children, too, became singers and violinists.

Bendl, Karel (b. Prague, 16 Apr 1838; d. Prague, 20 Sep 1897). Czech composer, in the orbit of Dvořák (a friend at the Prague Organ School) and Smetana. He wrote operas (*Lejla*, 1867) and was a choral conductor and humorist.

Benedict, Julius (b. Stuttgart, 27 Nov/24 Dec 1804; d. London, 5 Jun 1885) German–British composer and conductor, knighted in 1871. His banker father had him study with Hummel (1820–21) and Weber (1821–4), with both of whom he met Beethoven. He was then in Naples writing operas before, in 1835, he settled in London, where he worked in the theatre and later at choral festivals, besides going on tour to the USA with Jenny Lind. His most successful opera was *The Lily of Killarney* (Covent Garden, 1862); he also wrote a coloratura showpiece, *Variations de concert sur le Carnaval de Venise* (pub 1865).

Bénédiction de Dieu dans la solitude. Piano piece by Liszt, from his HARMONIES POETIQUES ET RELIGIEUSES.

Benedictus. (1) Second part of the *Sanctus* in the ORDINARY of the MASS.

(2) Canticle (the song of Zechariah, Luke 1:68–79) sung at Catholic, Orthodox and Anglican morning services.

benefit. Performance from which the proceeds went to an artist taking part, a practice of the 18th–19th centuries. Benefits now are given for charitable purposes, by performers taking no fee.

Benet, John (d. ?1458). English composer of sacred polyphony, possibly a pupil of Dunstable.

Benevoli, Orazio (b. Rome, 19 Apr 1605; d. Rome, 17 Jun 1672). Italian composer, master of polychoral music. The son of a French baker, he was trained as a choirboy at San Luigi dei Francesi in Rome (1617–23) and spent most of his life in the city as a composer and church musician, apart from a brief period in Vienna (1644–6).

Ben-Haim, Paul (b. Munich, 1 Oct 1897; d. Tel-Aviv, 14 Jan 1984). German–Israeli composer, a determining pioneer of music in Israel. He studied at the music academy in Munich and worked in Bavaria as a composer and theatre musician under his original name, Paul Frankenburger. In 1933 he moved to Palestine, took his Hebrew name and began work afresh as a teacher and composer,

absorbing local folk music into a style rooted in the great tradition from Bach to Debussy and Mahler. He wrote choral music, concertos and songs.

Benjamin, Arthur (Leslie) (b. Sydney, 18 Sep 1893; d. London, 10 Apr 1960). Australian composer resident mostly in London after he entered the RCM at 18 to study with Stanford. He began teaching there in 1926, and also travelled as an examiner – hence the Caribbean flavour of his popular *Jamaican Rumba* for two pianos or orchestra (1938), a work of characteristic amiability. In a more serious vein he wrote an opera on *The Tale of Two Cities* (1949–50).

Benjamin, George (William John) (b. London, 31 Jan 1960). British composer, contributor to the poetry of latterday modernism. He studied with Peter Gellhorn, with Messiaen and Loriod in Paris (1975–9) and with Goehr at Cambridge (1978–82). His student works won him wide attention, and he developed fast, learning from the French spectralists and Carter. Since the mid-1980s he has composed more slowly, giving each piece a markedly individual character, while also developing a career as a conductor, especially of the French post-1900 music that has been most important to him.

Renaud Machart *et al. George Benjamin* (1997)

Orchestral: *Ringed by the Flat Horizon*, 1979–80; *A Mind of Winter* (Wallace Stevens), s, orch, 1980–81; *Sudden Time*, 1989–93; *Sometime Voices* (Shakespeare), bar, ch, orch, 1996; *Palimpsest I*, 2000, *II*, 2002; etc.

Ensemble: *At First Light*, 14 insts, 1982; *Antara*, 16 insts, 1985–7; *Upon Silence* (Yeats), mez, 5 viols/7 modern str, 1989–90; 3 Inventions, chbr orch, 1993–5; etc.

Instrumental: 3 Studies, pf, 1981–5; *Viola, viola*, 2 va, 1997; etc.

Bennet, John (b. ?1575–80). English composer with northwest associations, author of madrigals (one book, 1599, including 'Weep, o mine eyes') and church music.

Bennett, Richard Rodney (b. Broadstairs, 29 Mar 1936). British composer of great fluency and wide sympathies, knighted in 1999. Encouraged by his home background, studies at the RAM with Ferguson and lessons with Boulez in Paris (1957–9), he quickly developed a style embracing the new avant-garde, the central classical tradition and jazz. His large output includes operas (*The Mines of Sulphur*, London, 1965), orchestral works (three symphonies, concertos, etc.), a wide range of vocal and choral settings, chamber music and film scores (*Far from the Madding Crowd*, 1967; *Murder on the Orient Express*, 1974). He also appears as a cabaret pianist.

Bennett, Robert Russell (b. Kansas City, Mo., 15 Jun 1894; d. New York, 18 Aug 1981). US arranger and composer, who was responsible for orchestrating *Show Boat*, *Oklahoma!*, *South Pacific*, *Camelot*, etc. Stravinsky declined his services for *Scènes de ballet*. He studied with Carl Busch in Kansas City (1912–15) and Boulanger in Paris (1926–31), and wrote symphonies, concertos and band music.

Bennett, William Sterndale (b. Sheffield, 13 Apr 1816; d. London, 1 Feb 1875). British composer, a vital figure in the early Romantic movement who became a musical worthy, knighted in 1871. Having lost both parents before he was four, he was trained by his grandfather, a Cambridge choirman, and then by Crotch and Potter at the RAM (1826–36). His First Piano Concerto (1832) came to the attention of Mendelssohn, who invited him several times to Leipzig. There he also met, and impressed, Schumann, and received the dedication of the latter's *Etudes symphoniques*. But his career as a pianist-composer gave way to a maturity in education and conducting: he taught at the RAM (1837–58, principal 1866–75), was Cambridge professor (1856–75), and conducted the Philharmonic Society concerts (1855–66).

James Robert Sterndale Bennett *The Life of William Sterndale Bennett* (1907)

Orchestral: Symphony No.1, E♭, 1832; No.2, D minor, 1832–3; No.4, A, 1833–4; No.5, G minor, 1835–6; G minor, Op.43, 1863–4; Piano Concerto No.1, D minor, Op.1, 1832; No.2, E♭, Op.4, 1833; No.3, C minor, Op.9, 1834; F minor, 1836; No.4, F minor, Op.19, 1838; A minor, 1841–3; *Parisina* (overture), Op.3, 1835; *The Naiades* (overture), Op.15, 1836; etc.
Chamber: Sextet, Op.8, pf, str, 1836; Chamber Trio, pf trio, Op.26, 1839; Sonata Duo, vc, pf, Op.32, 1852; etc.
Piano: Sonata, F minor, Op.13, 1836–7; *Fantaisie*, A minor, Op.16, 1837; *Suite de pièces*, Op.24, ?1841; *Die Jungfrau von Orleans*, sonata, Op.46, 1869–73; etc.

Benoit, Peter (Leonard Leopold) (b. Harlebeke, 17 Aug 1834; d. Antwerp, 8 Mar 1901). Belgian composer, promoter of Flemish culture. He studied with Fétis at the Brussels Conservatory (1851–4), travelled in Germany as winner of the Belgian Prix de Rome and worked as a theatre musician in Brussels and Paris before settling in Antwerp in 1867. There he founded a conservatory and the Flemish Opera, and composed works on Flemish subjects, including musical dramas for

actors speaking in rhythm to orchestral accompaniment and *De Rubenscantate* (pub 1877).

Bentzon, Nils Viggo (b., Copenhagen, 24 Aug 1919; d. Frederiksberg, 25 Apr 2000). Danish composer of extraordinary productivity (passing Op.650). He was taught the piano by his mother, a granddaughter of the composer J.P.E. Hartmann, and studied at the Copenhagen Conservatory (1938–42). Composition he taught himself, his guides being the mainstream 20th-century masters from Hindemith to Britten. He was also on the staff of the conservatories in Århus (1945–56) and Copenhagen (1950–88). His output includes 22 symphonies, numerous concertos and sonatas, 14 string quartets and an enormous cycle, *The Tempered Piano*.

Benvenuto Cellini. Opera by Berlioz to a libretto by Léon de Wailly and Auguste Barbier after the 16th-century artist's memoirs. Cellini (tenor) wins love, creative triumph and even pardon for a murder he has unwittingly committed. There is a brilliant overture; another, *Le* CARNAVAL ROMAIN, Berlioz rescued from a work he did not expect to see on the stage again (though in 1852 it was revived by Liszt at Weimar, with revisions by the composer). First performance: Paris Opera, 10 Sep 1838.

bequadro (It.). Natural.

Berberian, Cathy [Catherine] (b. Attleboro, Mass., 4 Jul 1925; d. Rome, 6 Mar 1983). US singer, who trained in New York and Milan, where she met Berio (her husband 1950–65). For him she developed a variety of voices in *Circles*, *Epifanie*, etc. She also gave the first performances of Cage's *Aria* and Stravinsky's *Elegy for J.F.K.*, sang Monteverdi and Beatles arrangements, and wrote pieces of her own.

berceuse (Fr.). LULLABY. The classic example is Chopin's; there are others by Busoni (BERCEUSE ELEGIAQUE), Debussy (*Berceuse héroïque*), Fauré, Ravel (*Berceuse sur le nom de Fauré*) and Stravinsky (in *The Firebird*).

Berceuse elégiaque (Dirge Lullaby). Work by Busoni for piano or orchestra, subtitled 'The Man's Lullaby at his Mother's Coffin'.

Berenice. Opera by Handel to an anonymous adaptation of Antonio Salvi's libretto. Based on an episode from the history of Roman Egypt, the plot concerns the sexual and great-power politics involved in the eventual marriage of Berenice (soprano) to her cousin Ptolemy Alexander II (soprano castrato). Notable numbers include the overture (with its popular minuet) and the bass aria 'Sì, tra i ceppi'. First performance: London, 18 May 1737.

Berezovsky, Maksim (Sozontovich) (b. Glukhov, Ukraine, 27 Oct 1745; d. St Petersburg, 4 Apr 1777). Russian composer, the first to write an opera. He began his career as a choirboy in the imperial chapel, also singing roles in court operas, and studied with Galuppi. Sent to Bologna to complete his education (1766–71), he stayed to write an opera, *Demofoonte* (1773), then returned to take charge of the choir he had left. His (undocumented) suicide left him a continuing mythic figure in Russian literature and, not least, film (Tarkovsky's *Nostalghia*, 1983).

Berg, Alban (Johannes Maria) (b. Vienna, 9 Feb 1885; d. Vienna, 24 Dec 1935). Austrian composer, notably of two operas, *Wozzeck* and *Lulu*, both powerful dramas about individual powerlessness. That was just one Bergian paradox. He was also a dilettante who became a composer of genius, a modernist who declined to unload his Romantic baggage, a constructivist whose music has formidable expressive sway, and a sentimentalist with a keen eye for the real.

He was born into the minor gentry: the family had a summer estate, where he took part in play readings and composed songs like any aesthetic young man of his period and background. His life changed in October 1904 when he became Schoenberg's pupil, alongside Webern. Within a few years he was not only writing big instrumental movements but also following Schoenberg – if at a little distance in time and with some reserve – into atonality. (Meanwhile he was courting Helene Nahowski, whom he married in 1910: there were no children. He had had a daughter by a household servant when he was 17.) Even when the lessons stopped, in 1911, he remained dependent on Schoenberg for approval (he dedicated four of his few mature works to his teacher) and ever willing to offer help and support.

The works he wrote under Schoenberg's tutelage included his first three with Op. numbers: a piano sonata (a first movement left to stand by itself), a nocturnal song cycle drifting off into atonality, and a fully atonal, fully developed quartet in two movements. The ensuing Altenberg Songs for soprano and orchestra (1912), like the Op.5 clarinet pieces (1914), are unusually compact. Peter Altenberg's poems combine oriental brevity with Viennese bittersweetness, and Berg's music looks both to the pure white of the whole-tone scale and to the rich confusion of atonality – to Debussy and to Schoenberg, though in this extraordinary score, his first on a large scale, he suddenly achieved independent mastery. At once erotic and spiritualized, the work also combines a zest for the new with world-weariness.

Bigger and more heavily scored, the Three Pieces Op.6 for orchestra (1914–15) lean more towards Mahler, especially the Mahler of the fateful Sixth Symphony. The first piece is a symmetrical prelude of advance from, and recession into, the hazy noise of untuned percussion, the second a dance fantasy more in the delicate and suggestive style of the Altenberg Songs, and the third an enormous march into violence and dense textural elaboration. It partly prepared the military sound-world of *Wozzeck* (1917–22), which he wrote after experiencing a soldier's life himself (1915–17). After the war he returned to Vienna, his home until his death. He stayed close to Schoenberg while they were in the same city, and travelled only to attend some of the many productions of *Wozzeck*, whose success brought him financial security.

Before embarking on a second opera he wrote a chamber concerto for piano, violin and wind (1923–5) – a celebration of the threesome he formed with Schoenberg and Webern, and a score duly filled with cryptograms and proportions based on three. The Lyric Suite for string quartet (1925–6) is similarly both highly wrought and generously expressive, its atonal features (now expressed through 12-note rows) heavy with tonal references. Just as he had refused to part company with tonal chords when he took on atonal ones, so he adapted the new serial technique to allow supple movements towards and away from tonality. Harmonies forbidden by serialism are glimpsed, but at a distance, which only heightens their allure and the corresponding effects of sensuality and nostalgia so characteristic of the composer.

Unlike that of the concerto, the Lyric Suite's programme had to be kept secret, for it concerned his love affair with Hanna Fuchs-Robettin, who was also in his mind as he wrote *Lulu*. Work on that opera was delayed by two commissions, for a concert aria (*Der Wein*) and a violin concerto, the latter conceived as an instrumental requiem for Manon Gropius, the teenage daughter of Mahler's widow, but also alluding unofficially to the affair in which he was involved – an affair in which intensity of feeling went with the knowledge there could be no consummation, for Hanna was a married woman with children. Hence, perhaps, his expression of doom in the Lyric Suite, the Violin

Concerto and *Lulu*, and his inability to finish this last work.

George Perle *The Operas of Alban Berg* , 2 Vols. (1980, 1985); Anthony Pople, ed. *The Cambridge Companion to Berg* (1997)

Operas: WOZZECK, Op.7, 1917–22; LULU, 1929–35
Orchestral: Altenberg Songs, Op.4, s, orch, 1912; 3 Pieces, Op.6, 1914–15; 3 Fragments from *Wozzeck*, s, orch, pub 1924; 3 Movements from the Lyric Suite, str, pub 1928; 7 Early Songs, s, orch, 1928; *Der Wein* (concert aria; Stefan George, after Baudelaire), s, orch, 1929; Symphonic Pieces from *Lulu*, s, orch, pub 1935; VIOLIN CONCERTO, 1935
Chamber and instrumental: Piano Sonata, Op.1, 1907–8; String Quartet, Op.3, 1910; Four Pieces, Op.5, cl, pf, 1913; CHAMBER CONCERTO, vn, pf, 13 wind, 1923–5, slow movement arr as Adagio, vn, cl, pf; LYRIC SUITE, str qt, 1925–6
Songs with piano: 7 Early Songs, 1905–8, rev 1928; *Schliesse mir die Augen beide* (Storm), 2 settings, 1907, 1925; 4 Songs (Hebbel, Mombert), Op.2, ?1909–10; numerous other early songs
Arrangement: *Wein, Weib und Gesang* (Johann Strauss II), pf, hmnm, str qt, 1921

bergamasca (It.). Harmonic scheme repeating I–IV–V–I, used as a basis for instrumental variations in the late 16th and 17th centuries. There may be some affiliation to songs and dances from Bergamo or to the COMMEDIA DELL'ARTE, which remembered the city as its home. The French 19th-century vogue for the commedia led to appropriations of the term, shorn of any musical substance, in Verlaine's poem *Clair de lune* and in works by Fauré (*Masques et bergamasques*) and Debussy (*Suite bergamasque*).

Berganza (Vargas), Teresa (b. Madrid, 16 Mar 1935). Spanish mezzo-soprano combining vocal warmth with alert precision, valued in Mozart and Rossini, and later in her career as Carmen. She trained with Lola Rodriguez Aragon and made her debut as Dorabella at Aix (1957).

Berger, Arthur (Victor) (b. New York, 15 May 1912; d. Boston, 7 Oct 2003). US composer, mostly of compact pieces abstracting neoclassical and serial elements. As a student in New York he was excited by the local avant-garde (Ives, Varèse). He studied with Piston at Harvard (1935–6), Boulanger in Paris (1937–9) and Milhaud at Mills (1939–42), where he began his long career as a teacher. After a spell as a music critic in New York, that career took him to Brandeis (from 1953) and the New England Conservatory (1979–98). Meanwhile, from the mid-1950s, he developed from a lean-textured tonal style (Babbitt wrote of 'diatonic Webern') towards greater harmonic variety and range,

though his works remained few and favoured the piano and chamber groupings.

bergerette (Fr.). Pastoral song, a term used in the 15th and 18th centuries.

Berglund, Paavo (Allan Engelbert) (b. Helsinki, 14 Apr 1929). Finnish conductor, who trained as a violinist. He was chief conductor of the Finnish Radio Symphony (1962–71), Bournemouth Symphony (1972–9), Helsinki Philharmonic (1975–9), Royal Stockholm Philharmonic (1987–91) and Royal Danish Orchestra (1993–6), and has worked also with the Chamber Orchestra of Europe, gaining acclaim in Sibelius and also in Brahms.

Bergman, Erik (Valdemar) (b. Uusikaarlepyy, 24 Nov 1911). Finnish composer, especially of choral music. He studied at the Helsinki Conservatory (1931–8), in Berlin (1937–9, 1942–3) and with Vogel in Ascona (1954). His career included periods as a choral conductor, music critic for Swedish-language papers (1945–81) and teacher at the Sibelius Academy (1963–76), while his music grew through a phase of libertarian serialism in the 1950s–60s to embrace musical and ritual traditions from around the world.

Bergonzi, Carlo (b. Vidalenzo, near Cremona, 13 Jul 1924). Italian tenor and a fine Verdi artist. Trained at the Parma Conservatory, he began as a baritone before making his debut as a tenor (Chénier, Bari, 1951). He became a regular at La Scala (from 1953), the Met (1956–88) and Covent Garden (from 1962).

Berio, Luciano (b. Oneglia, 24 Oct 1925; d. Rome, 27 May 2003). Italian composer, who, from a position in the post-war avant-garde, embraced – with fondness, fascination and extreme sophistication – a great range of other options, both historical and altogether outside the Western classical tradition (from Sicilian folk music to African polyphony). Music for him was a language of gestures in sound, and he used the full resources of his time in musically examining other languages: verbal languages in his many vocal works, languages of non-verbal communication in solo pieces, musical languages of the past (notably those of the concerto) or far away, even the languages of his own earlier works, in elaborations that carry them into new domains.

Born into a musical family (his father and grandfather were local musicians and composers), he grew up hearing and playing chamber music, then studied at the Milan Conservatory (1945–51), where his teacher Ghedini turned him towards

Stravinsky. In 1950 he met – and soon married – Cathy Berberian, and in 1952 he made his first trip to the USA, where he studied with Dallapiccola at Tanglewood and heard the first US concert of electronic music. Both experiences were crucial. *Chamber Music* (1953), written for Berberian (soon to give birth to their daughter), was a homage to Dallapiccola and also the start of an independent creative life, and that same year he made his first electronic essays. Also in 1953 he met Maderna and Stockhausen and began to take his place among the young radicals of European music: he was regularly at Darmstadt in 1956–9, the period of his hairiest scores (*Allelujah II*, *Tempi concertati*). But while he was excited by innovation, he was also encouraged by his friendship with Umberto Eco to view openness within a deeper cultural embedding. He created electronic music out of a recorded voice (Berberian's, in *Thema*), formed the first of many monologues that spring out of an instrument's nature, technique and history (*Sequenza I*), and held onto qualities of suavity and lightness not widely found among the avant-garde at this time (*Serenata I*).

He had been maintaining himself as joint head with Maderna of Italian radio's electronic music studio in Milan (1955–61), working there on *Thema* and *Visage* with Berberian, and in the concert hall with her on *Circles* and *Epifanie*. But then he shifted his centre to the USA, teaching at Mills (1962–4) and Juilliard (1965–71). Divorce, remarriage (in 1965) and the births of two more children did nothing to interrupt his creative flow, or his artistic association with his ex-wife. Still, there was a change. His collaborations with another literary friend, Edoardo Sanguineti, had been provocative, in the style of the European left of the early 1960s. Living in the USA through the Vietnam War, with the banners of protest seized by a younger generation, he became more an eager observer, concerned less with revolt than with rebirth, including the rebirth of standard media: opera and symphony. His *Sinfonia* is at once a threnody for Martin Luther King, a study of origins and destinations, and a hymn to diversity.

In 1972, soon after returning to Italy, he bought a property in a hill town near Siena, though his bucolic retirement was broken by periods in Florence, Paris (as one of Boulez's chief colleagues at IRCAM, 1974–80) and Rome (where he became director of the Accademia di Santa Cecilia in 2000). He was also married again, in 1977, to an Israeli music scholar, Talia Pecker Berio, and had two further children. And he returned to creative strength, after a few unsettled years, with *Coro* (1975–7) and the two operas that followed: *La vera storia* for La Scala and *Un re in ascolto* for Salzburg.

Coro was his boldest encounter with folk music, an abiding interest, while the operas explored new ways of creating stage narrative, their dramas being essentially musical, formed – as his music now generally was formed – from tissues of allusion, memory, cross-reference and challenge. The orchestral *Formazioni* and first version of *Ofanim*, both completed in 1988, crowned this period of supreme maturity: *Ofanim* visited a favourite site, that of the lone woman's voice, which here rears up when children and electronics have had their say.

At the same time, a new phase was opening, one of involvement with Jewish history and re-involvement with electronics. His IRCAM experience had been creatively disappointing, but in 1987 he was able to start forming his own institution in Florence, Tempo Reale, and with this team he worked on the projection and transformation of live sound in *Ofanim* and the opera *Cronaca del luogo*. He continued, though, to add to his *Sequenza* series (perhaps most spectacularly with the bassoon piece, an unbroken 20-minute span) and to display his orchestral expertise, whether in original works, in arrangements or in such self-arrangements as the *Chemins* string of *Sequenza*-based commentaries.

David Osmond-Smith *Berio* (1991)

Operas: *Opera*, 1969–70, f.p. Santa Fe, 1970, rev Florence, 1977; *La* VERA STORIA, 1977–81; *Un* RE IN ASCOLTO, 1979–84; *Outis* (Dario Del Corno), 1995–6, f.p. Milan, 1996; *Cronaca del luogo* (Talia Pecker Berio), 1998–9, f.p. Salzburg, 1999

Other vocal stage works: *Allez-Hop!* (Calvino), f.p. Venice, 1959; *Passaggio* (Sanguineti + Berio), f.p. Milan, 1963; *Recital I*, v, small orch, f.p. London, 1972

Orchestral (full): *Nones*, 1954; *Allelujah II*, 5 groups, 1957–8; EPIFANIE, s, orch, 1959–61; *Chemins I*, hp, orch, 1965; *Chemins III*, va, orch, 1968; SINFONIA, 1968–9; *Bewegung*, 1971, rev 1983; Concerto, 2 pf, orch, 1972–3; *Eindrücke*, 1973–4; CORO, ch, orch, 1975–7; *Formazioni*, 1985–6; *Concerto II (Echoing Curves)*, pf, orch, 1988–9; *Continuo*, 1989, rev as *Ekphrasis*, 1996; *Rendering*, 1989; *Récit (Chemins VII)*, a sax, orch, 1996; *Alternatim*, cl, va, orch, 1997; *Solo*, trbn, orch, 1999; *Stanze*, bar, men's ch, orch, 2003; etc.

Orchestral (smaller): *Serenata I*, fl, 14 insts, 1957; *Tempi concertati*, fl, vn, 2 pf, 4 groups, 1958–9; LABORINTUS II, 1965; *Chemins II*, va, 9 insts, 1967; *Chemins IIb*, 1969–70; *Points on the Curve to Find* ..., pf, small orch, 1974; *Calmo*, mez, small orch, 1974, rev 1989; *Chemins IV*, ob, 11 str, 1975; *Corale*, vn, 2 hn, str, 1981; *Il ritorno degli snovidenia*, vc, small orch, 1976–7; *Requies*, 1983–4; *Voci (Folk Songs II)*, va, 2 groups, 1984; *Chemins V*, gtr, chbr orch, 1992; *Kol Od (Chemins VI)*, tpt, chbr orch,

1995–6; *Ofanim* (Bible), woman's v, children's ch, insts, elec, 1988–97; etc.

Orchestrations, etc.: *Folk Songs*, s, orch, 1973; *Ritirata notturna di Madrid* (Boccherini), 1975; *Opus 120 Nr.1* (Brahms), cl/va, orch. 1984; *Contrapunctus XIV* (Bach), 23 insts, 2001; songs by Falla, Mahler, Schubert and Verdi, completion of TURANDOT, etc.

Chamber: *Opus Number Zoo*, wind qnt, 1950–51, rev 1970; *Due pezzi*, vn, pf, 1951; *Chamber Music* (Joyce), woman's v, cl, vc, hp, 1953; String Quartet, 1955–6; *Différences*, 5 insts, tape, 1958–9, rev 1967; *Circles* (cummings), woman's v, hp, 2 perc, 1960; *Sincronie*, str qt, 1963–4; *Folk Songs*, mez, 7 insts, 1964; *O King*, woman's v, 5 insts, 1967–8; *Linea*, 2 pf, vib, mar, 1973; *Duetti*, 2 vn, 1979–83; *Naturale*, va, tam tam, tape, 1985–6; *Ricorrenze*, wind qnt, 1985–7; *Notturno* (String Quartet No.3), 1993; *Korót*, 8 vc, 1998; etc.

Sequenza series: *I*, fl, 1958; *II*, hp, 1963; *III*, woman's v, 1965–6; *IV*, pf, 1965–6; *V*, trbn, 1966; *VI*, va, 1967; *VII*, ob, 1969; *VIII*, vn, 1976–7; *IX*, cl, 1980, arr sax as *IXa*, 1981; *X*, tpt, open pf, 1984; *XI*, gtr, 1987–8; *XII*, bn, 1995; *XIII* (*Chanson*), acdn, 1995–6; *XIV*, vc, 2002

Other solos: *Petite suite*, pf, 1948; *Cinque variazioni*, pf, 1952–3, rev 1966; *Rounds*, hpd, 1964–5, arr pf 1967; *Wasserklavier*, pf, 1965; *Gesti*, rec, 1966; *Erdenklavier*, pf, 1969; *Fa-si*, org, 1975; *Les Mots sont allés*, vc, 1978; *Lied*, cl, 1983; *Luftklavier*, pf, 1985; *Feuerklavier*, pf, 1989; *Psy*, db, 1989; *Leaf*, pf, 1990; *Brin*, pf, 1990; Piano Sonata, 2001

Tape: *Mutazioni*, 1955; *Perspectives*, 1957; *Thema (Omaggio a Joyce)*, 1958; *Momenti*, 1960; *Visage*, 1961; etc.

Bériot, Charles (Auguste) de (b. Louvain, 20 Feb 1802; d. Brussels, 8 Apr 1870). Belgian violinist-composer. He went to Paris in 1821, played for Viotti (who was encouraging) and was briefly a pupil of Pierre Baillot (who was not). Debuts in Paris and London were followed by a return to Belgium; he then gave concerts with Malibran (1829–36) and eventually married her, though she survived only six months. After a period of mourning he took up his career again in 1838: 'It seems as if the soul of his late wife sings through his violin,' noted Heine. He also taught – Vieux-temps among others – at the Brussels Conservatory (1843–52). In 1858 he lost his sight. He is credited with introducing Romantic qualities of virtuosity and expressiveness into the French violin school, which after him became the Franco-Belgian school. His works include 10 concertos and variation sets.

Berkeley. British composers, father and son.

(1) **Lennox (Randall Francis)** (b. Boars Hill, Oxford, 12 May 1903; d. London, 26 Dec 1989). A model Boulanger pupil, he was a fastidious neoclassicist and writer of tensile sacred music, who in his 60s bravely introduced some serial pungency into his art. The grandson of an earl, he enjoyed a childhood of privilege and travel (to France). He studied at Oxford and with Boulanger in Paris (1926–32), becoming a Catholic in 1928. Also important were his meetings with Poulenc and, in 1936, Britten. During the Second World War he worked for the BBC, and in 1946 he married. He then taught at the RAM (1946–68) and was knighted in 1974.

Peter Dickinson *The Music of Lennox Berkeley* (1988, ²2003)

Operas: *Nelson* (Alan Pryce-Jones), Op.41, f.p. London, 1954; *A Dinner Engagement* (1 act: Paul Dehn), Op.45, f.p. Aldeburgh, 1954; *Ruth* (1 act: Eric Crozier), f.p. London, 1956; *Castaway* (1 act: Dehn), Op.68, f.p. Aldeburgh, 1967

Orchestral: Symphony No.1, Op.16, 1940; No.2, Op.51, 1956–8; No.3, Op.74, 1969; No.4, Op.94, 1978; *Mont Juic*, Op.9, 1937 (with Britten); Serenade, Op.12, str, 1939; *Antiphon*, Op.85, str, 1973; Guitar Concerto, Op.88, 1974; etc.

Vocal: 4 Poems of St Teresa of Avila, Op.27, a, str, 1947; *Stabat mater*, Op.28, soli, chbr orch, 1947; *Missa brevis*, Op.57, ch, org, 1960; songs, motets, etc.

Chamber and instrumental: 3 string quartets, music for pf, org, gtr, etc.

(2) **Michael (Fitzhardinge)** (b. London, 29 May 1948). Son of Lennox and godson of Britten. He was a Westminster Cathedral chorister and musically precocious; he then studied with his father at the RAM and, in the mid-1970s, with Bennett. In 1974 he began his career as a broadcaster. His music grew more intense and challenging in the late 1980s as he moved towards his first opera, *Baa Baa Black Sheep* (Cheltenham, 1993). Artistic director of the Cheltenham Festival (1995–2004), he was appointed composer-in-residence with the BBC National Orchestra of Wales in 2001.

Berlin. Capital city of Prussia (1701–1871) and Germany, enjoying periods of musical resplendence under FREDERICK II and since the end of the 19th century. Frederick founded the opera (1742, renamed the Staatsoper in 1919) and improved the court orchestra. His successors cared much less for music. Around 1900 Nikisch, Muck and Strauss were all conducting in the city, and in the heady decade of the 1920s Kleiber was at the Staatsoper (1923–34), première of *Wozzeck* in 1925) and Klemperer at the KROLL OPERA, while Schoenberg, Busoni, Weill, Eisler, Hindemith and Schreker were all among resident composers, and there was a thriving cabaret culture. All that ended with Nazism, whose defeat in 1945 left the city divided. In East Berlin, capital of the German Democratic

Republic, the Staatsoper was rebuilt, its orchestra (the Staatskapelle) revived, and the KOMISCHE OPER founded. Meanwhile, West Berlin was home to the Berlin Philharmonic and the Städtische Oper (restyled Deutsche Oper in 1961, when it moved into a new theatre). In 1991 the city became the capital of a reunited Germany, and its three opera companies and several orchestras – including the Philharmonic, the Staatskapelle (under Barenboim from 1992) and the Deutsche Symphonie-Orchester Berlin (formerly the orchestra of West Berlin radio) – enjoyed full support, for a while.

Berlin Philharmonic Orchestra (Berliner Philharmoniker). Founded in 1882, it has been pre-eminent ever since, with principal conductors including von Bülow (1887–95), Nikisch (1895–22), Furtwängler (1923–45, 1952–4), Celibidache (1946–52), Karajan (1954–89), Abbado (1989–2002) and Rattle (from 2002). Its old hall was destroyed in 1944; the new one, designed by Hans Scharoun, opened in 1963, with a chamber auditorium added in 1987.

Berlioz, (Louis) Hector (b. La Côte-Saint-André, Isère, 11 Dec 1803; d. Paris, 8 Mar 1869). French composer, the archetypical Romantic hero in music: furiously gifted, combative, much frustrated and misunderstood, revered only after his death. Extravagantly passionate by nature (at least if his memoirs are to be believed), he brought elements of theatre into his orchestral works, several of which are concert dramas, and produced three extraordinary operas, in quite different modes. As well as being a reinventor of genre, he was a master of melody and orchestration, and though wildly at odds with the current of French music (except in his monumental classicism), he left a permanent mark in Russia and on Liszt.

He was a doctor's son and was meant for a doctor's life himself, but rebelled. As a boy he had, with his father's unwitting blessing, learned to play the flute, flageolet and guitar and started to compose. Sent to medical school in Paris in 1821, he frequented the Opera more than the anatomy theatre, and early in 1824 abandoned medicine for music. He had already started lessons with Le Sueur, been busy with an opera, and even published a set of songs. Then came the Conservatoire (1826–30), where he continued with Le Sueur and studied also with Reicha. Meanwhile there was the shock of Shakespeare. A British company brought *Hamlet* to Paris in September 1827, and he was smitten with love not only for the playwright but also for the leading actress, Harriet Smithson, whom he found it impossible to separate from

Ophelia, Juliet and Desdemona. Soon afterwards he received two further jolts when he read Goethe's *Faust* in Gérard de Nerval's translation and heard Beethoven's Third and Fifth symphonies conducted by Habeneck (March 1828). Shakespeare, Goethe and Beethoven became his household gods, along with Virgil, whose *Aeneid* had been with him since boyhood, and Gluck, discovered at the Opera. Contemporary Romantics – Scott, Byron – stood alongside. Just 24, he had all he needed.

After giving a first concert of his music (26 May 1828), he drove on through two miscellaneous collections devoted to Goethe (*Huit scènes de Faust*) and Moore's Irish poems (*Neuf mélodies*), then created the *Symphonie fantastique* early in 1830, partly out of unrequited love for Smithson. Later that year he turned his affections to a fellow musician, Marie Moke (1811–75), to whom he became engaged. Winning the Prix de Rome, however, obliged him to leave for Italy in December, and Moke found another suitor in Camille Pleyel (soon her husband), at which Berlioz started off back for Paris, but stopped himself from desperation and wrote *Lélio* instead, along with overtures on *King Lear* and *Rob Roy*.

He returned to Paris in November 1832. Smithson was there again: he courted her, and they were married 11 months later. They had a son, Louis, and though they drifted apart after a few years, Berlioz maintained affection for his wife and only child, and continued to support them, through his work as a brilliant critic and conductor and as Conservatoire librarian. He gained state commissions that sparked his sense of pomp (*Grande messe des morts*, *Grande symphonie funèbre et triomphale*), but his first opera, *Benvenuto Cellini*, was dropped after three performances in 1838. Yet he found an audience among fellow musicians and Romantics, not least Liszt (who heard the première of the *Symphonie fantastique*), Paganini (who failed to play *Harold en Italie* but still gave a generous commission fee) and Wagner (there for an early performance of the 'dramatic symphony' *Roméo et Juliette*).

In 1842–3 he made a six-month concert tour through Belgium and Germany, taking with him a singer, Marie Recio, to whom he became attached – though his emotional life was now quieter, and his creative flame too. He went on tour again in 1845–6, this time through the major cities of the Austrian empire, completing as he went *La Damnation de Faust*, which again Paris failed to comprehend. The only major works he produced during the decade after that were the *Te Deum* and the gentle oratorio *L'Enfance du Christ*. Meanwhile, he paid conducting visits to Russia

(1847) and to London for a whole season (1847–8), and that was how the pattern of his life continued. He enjoyed a close professional relationship with Liszt, who revived *Cellini* in Weimar, dedicated a work to him (the *Faust Symphony*) and encouraged him to fulfil his Virgilian dreams in *Les Troyens* (1856–8). But that work brought him further disappointment. He was eventually obliged to present just the last three acts, in 1863; of the first two he heard only a fragment.

His creative career was now over, having finished with fizz in *Béatrice et Bénédict*. After that he paid some visits to Estelle Fornier, with whom he had first fallen in love nearly half a century before. In 1867 his son, a sea captain, died of yellow fever in Havana, leaving him alone: Smithson, Recio and his two sisters had all gone before. He made a second trip to Russia (1867–8) and seemingly settled himself for death.

He was, though, a man of exuberant life – of life that lives on in his music, certainly, but also in his persona, which comes to us not only in his compositions but in his frank, vigorous writings (critical essays and memoirs) and in his physical appearance. He is the first great musician of whom there are manifold portraits: a painting by Courbet in the Musée d'Orsay, Paris, and several photographs, including striking images by Nadar and Pierre Petit. He was evidently a small, lean man, with a shock of hair (auburn in his youth), sharp features and thin, straight lips whose cast changed – perhaps as a result of the setbacks of his 30s – from youthful impetuosity and scorn to grim defiance.

In his music he impressed the image of himself. That meant choosing (or inventing) subjects that chimed with his life or his imaginings: tales of the doomed lover, the maker, the fantasist, the explorer. It also meant a dissatisfaction with rule. The resilience and excitement of his music are in the thrust of its melody, over harmony that may not be regulated according to the textbooks, through colours of unprecedented range and vividness, into forms that have a filmlike narrative drive, charged by events rather than musical development. At the time this seemed wanton. He was composing – though he may not have known it – for the late 20th century (when his magnificent Trojan epic at last became regularly performed) and beyond.

Hector Berlioz *Memoirs*, ed. David Cairns (1969, ²2002); David Cairns *Berlioz*, 2 Vols. (1989, 1999)

www.hberlioz.com

Operas: BENVENUTO CELLINI, Op.23, 1836–8; *Les* TROYENS, 1856–8; BEATRICE ET BENEDICT, 1860–62

Larger concert/sacred works: *Messe solennelle*, soli, ch, orch, 1824; *Huit scènes de Faust* (Nerval, after Goethe), soli, ch, orch, 1828–9, rev as *La Damnation de Faust* (see FAUST), Op.24, 1845–6; SYMPHONIE FANTASTIQUE, Op.14, 1830; LELIO, Op.14bis, 1831–2; HAROLD EN ITALIE, Op.16, va, orch, 1834; *Grande messe des morts* (REQUIEM), Op.5, t, ch, orch, 1837, rev 1852, 1867; *Roméo et Juliette* (ROMEO AND JULIET), Op.17, 1839; GRANDE SYMPHONIE FUNEBRE ET TRIOMPHALE, Op.15, 1840; *Tristia*, Op.18, ch, orch, 1831–48; *Te Deum*, Op.22, t, ch, orch, 1849; *L'ENFANCE DU CHRIST*, Op.25, soli, ch, orch, 1850–54

Overtures, etc.: *Les* FRANCS JUGES, 1825–6; *Waverley*, Op.1, 1827–8; *Le roi Lear*, Op.4, 1831; *Rob Roy*, 1831; *Rêverie et caprice*, Op.8, vn, orch, 1841; *Le* CARNAVAL ROMAIN, Op.9, 1844; *Le Corsaire*, Op.21, 1844

Solo cantatas and orchestral songs: *Herminie* (cantata), s, orch, 1828; *La Mort de Cléopâtre* (cantata), s, orch, 1829; *La Belle Voyageuse*, Op.2:4, mez, orch, 1829; *La Captive* (Victor Hugo), Op.12, mez/a, orch, 1832; *Le Jeune Pâtre breton*, Op.13:4, mez/t, orch, 1833; *Aubade* (de Musset), s/t, orch, 1839; *Les* NUITS D'ETE, Op.7, v, orch, 1840–41; *Le Chasseur danois*, b, orch, 1845; *Zaïde*, Op.19:1, s, orch, 1845

Orchestrations: *Hymne des marseillais* (Rouget de Lisle), ch, orch, 1830; *Chant du neuf Thermidor* (Rouget), t, ch, orch, 1830; *L'Invitation à la valse* (Weber; AUFFORDERUNG ZUM TANZE), 1841; *Marche marocaine* (de Meyer), 1845; *Plaisir d'amour* (Martini), bar, orch, 1859; *Erlkönig* (Schubert), t, orch, 1860

Smaller choral orchestral works: *La Révolution grecque*, 2 b, ch, orch, 1825–6; *La Mort d'Orphée* (cantata), t, women's ch, orch, 1827; *Chant sacré*, Op.2:6, t, ch, orch, 1829; *La Mort de Sardanapale* (cantata), s, men's ch, orch, 1830; *Quartetto e coro dei maggi*, ch, orch, 1832; *Sara la baigneuse* (Hugo), Op.11, ch, orch, 1834, rev 1850; *Le Cinq mai, chant sur la mort de l'empereur Napoléon*, Op.6, b, ch, orch, 1835; *Hélène*, Op.2:2, men's ch, orch, 1844; *Hymne à la France*, Op.20:2, ch, orch, 1844; *Le Chant des chemins de fer*, Op.19:3, t, ch, orch, 1846; *La Menace des Francs*, Op.20:1, soli, ch, orch, ?1848; *La Belle Voyageuse*, Op.2:4, women's ch, orch, 1851; *L'Impériale* (cantata), Op.26, ch, orch, 1854

Other choral works: *Le Ballet des ombres*, ch, pf, 1828; *Chant guerrier*, Op.2:3, t, men's ch, pf, 1829; *Chanson à boire*, Op.2:5, t, men's ch, pf, 1829; etc.

Songs with piano: *Neuf mélodies* (*Irlande*) (after Moore), Op.2, 1829 (6 are solo songs); *Fleurs des landes*, Op.13 (5), 1835–50; primary versions of orchestral songs, etc.

Editions: adaptations for Viardot of Gluck's *Orphée*, 1859, and *Alceste*, 1861

Berman, Lazar (Naumovich) (b. Leningrad, 26 Feb 1930; d. Florence, 6 Feb 2005). Russian pianist of supreme virtuosity and expressive fullness, pupil of Goldenweiser at the Moscow Conservatory (1948–57). In an erratic non-career, made still more erratic by official displeasure, he has produced some staggering Liszt recordings. He left Moscow in 1990 and settled in Imola, Italy.

Bermel, Derek (b. New Rochelle, NY, 14 Oct 1967). US composer and clarinettist, whose works often use small melodic patterns to loop cleanly among diverse traditions, classical, popular and ethnic. He studied at Yale and at the University of Michigan, but also in Jerusalem and Ghana. His large body of instrumental music includes a concerto he wrote for himself, *Voices* (1997).

Bernart de Ventadorn (b. Ventadorn, ?*c*.1130–40; d. Dordogne, *c*.1195–1200). Troubadour. The survival of 18 songs (especially *Quan vei la lauzeta mover*) – more than for any other 12th-century poet – suggests his repute. Of low birth, he shone at the courts of Eleanor of Castile and, later, Raimon V of Toulouse, after whose death in 1194 he is said to have entered a monastery.

Berners, Gerald Hugh Tyrwhitt-Wilson, Lord (b. Apley Park, Bridgnorth, 18 Sep 1883; d. Faringdon, 19 Apr 1950). British composer and amiable eccentric, whose talent, charm, wealth and gay sexuality he disported in Rome in the 1910s (as honorary attaché), in Paris between the wars and afterwards at his Oxfordshire house, where he entertained Stravinsky to a meal entirely pink. He had lessons with Tovey and with Edmund Kretschmer in Dresden, but found his models in Satie, Stravinsky and Casella, writing ballets (*The Triumph of Neptune* for Diaghilev, 1926; *A Wedding Bouquet* with words by Gertrude Stein, 1936), sometimes frivolous piano pieces (*Trois petites marches funèbres*, 1916) and songs.

Mark Amory *Lord Berners* (1998)

Bernstein, Leonard (b. Lawrence, Mass., 25 Aug 1918; d. New York, 14 Oct 1990). US composer and conductor, a vigorous and wholly American music-man, as much at ease writing a Broadway show as conducting Mahler or Stravinsky. The child of successful Russian Jewish immigrants, he studied composition with Piston and Edward Hill at Harvard (1935–9), and conducting with Reiner at Curtis (1939–41) and Koussevitzky at Tanglewood (1940–41). He became Koussevitzky's assistant (1942–3), then Artur Rodzinski's with the New York Philharmonic, and made a spectacular debut with that orchestra (14 Nov 1943), substituting for Walter. The next year he showed himself in public as a composer – of a symphony ('Jeremiah'), a ballet (*Fancy Free*) and a musical (*On the Town*) – and during the following decade or so his creative energy remained high and various, while he conducted widely in the USA, Israel and Europe.

In 1951 he married Felicia Montealegre, a Chilean actress, with whom he had three children; in later years he was increasingly open about his bisexuality.

Memories of him as music director of the New York Philharmonic (1958–70) are strongly cherished. He was a dynamic performer, a brilliant educator (in his televised Young People's Concerts), a great welcomer of musicians he strongly disagreed with (Gould, Cage), and a man who took seriously his role as civic figure and national ambassador. But the work drew him away from composition, and though he later moved back, he remained wedded to the podium, producing performances (*Tristan*, Mahler symphonies) of swelling expressive power. His music, of all periods, is of a piece with his conducting: eclectic, abundantly felt, and insistent on art's moral force. Beethoven, he thought, could be in his music along with jazz, Stravinskian energy with Mahlerian emotion. Ironically, his most durable creative achievement has proved to be a work that lives fully within the limits of its genre, the musical *West Side Story*.

Leonard Bernstein *The Unanswered Question* (1976); Meryle Secrest *Leonard Bernstein* (1995)

www.leonardbernstein.com

Dramatic: *Fancy Free* (ballet), 1944, enlarged as *On the Town* (musical), f.p. Boston, 1944; *Facsimile* (ballet), 1946; *Trouble in Tahiti* (1-act opera; Bernstein), f.p. Waltham, Mass., 1952, enlarged as *A Quiet Place*, f.p. Houston, 1983; *Wonderful Town* (musical), f.p. New Haven, Conn., 1953; *On the Waterfront* (film score), 1954; CANDIDE (operetta), f.p. Boston, 1956; *West Side Story* (musical), f.p. Washington, 1957; *Mass* (spectacle), f.p. Washington, 1971; *Dybbuk* (ballet), 1974; *1600 Pennsylvania Avenue* (musical), f.p. Philadelphia, 1976

Larger concert works: Symphony No.1 'Jeremiah', mez, orch, 1942; No.2 'The Age of Anxiety', pf, orch, 1949, rev 1965; No.3 'Kaddish', s, speaker, ch, orch, 1963; Serenade, vn, orch, 1954; *Chichester Psalms*, treble, ch, orch, 1965; *Songfest*, 6 v, orch, 1974

Song sets: *I Hate Music* (Bernstein), 1943; *La Bonne Cuisine* (Bernstein), 1947; Arias and Barcarolles (Bernstein, etc.), mez, bar, pf duet, 1988

Piano: 7 *Anniversaries*, 1943; 4 *Anniversaries*, 1948; 5 *Anniversaries*, 1954

Bertali, Antonio (b. Verona, Mar 1605; d. Vienna, 17 Apr 1669). Italian composer, who was resident in Vienna by 1631 and prominent among those who brought northern Italian styles to the imperial court. He wrote operas and oratorios, much sacred music and sonatas.

Berwald, Franz (Adolf) (b. Stockholm, 23 Jul 1796;

d. Stockholm, 3 Apr 1868). Swedish composer, his dashing music the finest from early Romantic Scandinavia. He belonged to a musical family of German origin. His grandfather, Johann Friedrich (1711–89), was a flautist around the Baltic; his father, Christian Friedrich Georg (1740–1825), was a violinist who settled in Stockholm; his cousin, Johan Fredrik (1787–1861), was a violinist, conductor and composer; and his brother, Christian August (1798–1869), was a violinist-composer. Presumably his father helped prepare him for his early career as a violinist in the court orchestra (1812–28); he also had lessons with J.B.E. Dupuy, the royal kapellmeister. In composition he had to make his own way, and did so. He seems to have become discouraged, though, by lack of success, and to have given up after a disappointing move to Berlin in 1829. In 1841 he married, transferred to Vienna and came alive again as a composer. He returned to Stockholm the next year and maintained his creative speed, but lost it during a second period in Austria (1846–9). From this he returned to manage a glassworks in northern Sweden, spending the summers in Stockholm, where he wrote chamber music and gained recognition. But though his first opera was at last staged, his second had to wait until the centenary of his death. His symphonies and quartets – lean, elegant, colourful – were likewise little known until the latter part of the 20th century.

Robert Layton *Franz Berwald* (1959)

Operas: *Estrella de Soria* (Otto Prechtler), c.1838–62, f.p. Stockholm, 1862; *Drottningen av Golconda* (The Queen of Golconda), 1864
Orchestral: Symphony No.1 (*Sinfonie sérieuse*), G minor, 1842; No.2 (*Sinfonie capricieuse*), D, 1842 (realized by Ellberg from draft, 1945); No.3 (*Sinfonie singulière*), C, 1845; No.4, E♭, 1845; Piano Concerto, D, 1855; Violin Concerto, C♯ minor, 1820; Double Violin Concerto, E, 1817; Concert Piece, F, bn, orch, 1827; *Elfenspiel*, 1841; *Erinnerung an die norwegischen Alpen*, 1842; *Bayaderen-fest*, 1842
Chamber: Septet, B♭, cl, hn, bn, vn, va, vc, db, ?1828; Piano Quintet No.1, C minor, 1853; No.2, A, ?1850–7; String Quartet No.1, G minor, 1818; No.2, A minor, 1849; No.3, E♭, 1849; Quartet, E♭, cl, hn, bn, pf, 1819; Piano Trio, C, 1845; Piano Trio No.1, E♭, 1849; No.2, F minor, 1851; No.3, D minor, 1851; No.4, C, ?1853; Duo concertante, A, 2 vn, ?1816–17; Duo, B♭, vc/vn, pf, ?1858; Duo, A minor, vn, pf, 1859
Other works: songs, pf pieces

Bes (Ger.). B♭♭.

Betrothal in a Monastery (*Obrucheniye v monastyre*). Opera by Prokofiev to a libretto on

which he assisted his wife Mira Mendelson, after Sheridan's *The* DUENNA. First performance: Prague, 5 May 1946.

Bevin, Elway (b. c.1554; buried Bristol, 19 Oct 1638). Welsh/English church musician, active at Bristol Cathedral from 1585. He is remembered for a service and the canons contained in his *Briefe and Short Instruction of the Art of Musicke* (1631).

bewegt (Ger.). In movement – whether agitatedly or steadily will depend on context. Also *bewegter* (faster).

Beyer, Johanna (Magdalena) (b. Leipzig, 11 Jul 1888; d. New York, 9 Jan 1944). German–US composer, close to Cowell. She moved to the USA in her mid 30s and studied with the Seegers, Rudhyar and Cowell. Her works, of dissonant counterpoint, include four quartets and pieces for percussion ensemble.

Bezifferter Bass (Ger.). Figured bass.

Bialas, Günter (b. Bielschowitz, Upper Silesia, 19 Jul 1907; d. Glonn, 7 Aug 1995). German composer. He studied at the University of Breslau/Wrocław (1926–8) and in Berlin, notably with Max Trapp at the Prussian Academy of the Arts (1936–8). After the Second World War he taught at institutions in Weimar, Detmold and Munich (1959–74), and wrote theatre works and concertos.

bianca (It.). Minim, half note.

Bianchi, (Giuseppe) Francesco (b. Cremona, c.1752; d. London, 27 Nov 1810). Italian composer, especially of opera seria, which he helped revitalize by developing the ensemble finale. He studied with Pasquale Cafaro and Jommelli in Naples, began his career in his home city, then was based in Paris (1775–8), Milan and Venice (1791–5). His last years he spent in London, collaborating with Da Ponte and travelling frequently to Paris, where he specialized in comedy. He married in London, unhappily, had a daughter who died in childhood, and killed himself.

Biber, Heinrich (Ignaz Franz von) (b. Wartenberg, near Reichenberg/Liberec, Aug 1644; d. Salzburg, 3 May 1704). Czech composer and violinist. A great player and a great imaginer of music for his instrument, he also wrote spectacular works for spaced choirs. He is said to have been in contact with Vejvanovský in Troppau/Opava, and perhaps was similarly educated by the Jesuits. In 1668 he joined Vejvanovský in

Kremsier/Kroměříž, but two years later he moved to the archbishop's court in Salzburg, where he married (1672) and rose to the rank of chapel-master (1684). He composed his most lavish polychoral scores, the *Missa salisburgensis* and *Plaudite tympana* (this in 53 parts), for the 1100th anniversary in 1682 of St Rupert's refoundation of the city. His Mystery Sonatas were also probably intended for the cathedral, as postludes to special rosary services in October. In these works, and others, he used scordatura to ease contrapuntal movement in particular keys, but the music is remarkable, too, for its keenly expressive virtuosity. While spending almost his entire adult life in the archiepiscopal city, he also gained favour (and ennoblement) from the emperor. His two sons followed him as court and cathedral musicians in Salzburg; his two daughters became nuns, one of them taking the veil to the sound of his *Missa Sancti Henrici*.

Vocal: *Missa salisburgensis*, 1682; *Plaudite tympana*, 1682; *Missa bruxellensis*, after 1696; *Missa Sancti Henrici*, 1697; other masses, 2 *Requiem* settings, school dramas, etc.

Instrumental: *Battalia*, 9 str, hpd, 1673; *Sonata Sancti Polycarpi*, 8 tpt, str, timp, 1673; MYSTERY SONATAS, vn, con, ?1674; *Sonatae tam aris quam aulis servientes*, pub 1676; *Mensa sonora* (6 partitas), 4 str, hpd, pub 1680; *Fidicinium sacro-profanum* (12 sonatas, including Serenade 'The Nightwatchman's Call' in C), 3/4 str, con, pub 1683; *Harmonia artificiosa-ariosa*, 4/5 str, con, pub 1696; etc.

Bible. Source of subjects for operas, oratorios, etc. See ABRAHAM AND ISAAC; DAVID; ESTHER; FLOOD, THE; JEPHTHA; JESUS; JOB; JOSHUA; JUDAS MACCABAEUS; JUDITH; LAMENTATIONS; MOSES; NEBUCHADNEZZAR; PSALM; REVELATION; SALOME; SAMSON; SAUL; SOLOMON.

bicinium (from Lat. roots *bi-*, two, *can-*, sing). Two-part exercise used in musical education in early Lutheran Germany. The term has been extended to cover any two-part piece or passage in Renaissance or Baroque music, and sometimes modern, too.

Biedermeier. Movement in Austro-German culture, roughly 1815–48, led by the tastes of the rising bourgeoisie for comfortable domestic art, named after a philistine character in a novel by Ludwig Eichrodt. The term, usually implying mild condescension, can be applied to music of this period by Spohr and Hummel – but certainly not to Schubert, Chopin and Schumann, who so transcended the same norms.

Biggs, E(dward George) Power (b. Westcliff, Essex, 29 Mar 1906; d. Boston, 10 Mar 1977). British–US organist, resident from 1930 in the USA, where he gave national weekly broadcasts (1942–58), made recordings and promoted new works for organ and orchestra by Copland and others.

Billings, William (b. Boston, 7 Oct 1746; d. Boston, 26 Sep 1800). Pioneer North American composer and singing teacher, self-taught son of a shop-keeper. He lived his whole life in Boston but travelled to instruct in singing schools elsewhere. His compositions – hymn tunes and other sacred songs in rugged four-part harmony (e.g. *Chester*) – were spread in a series of publications, beginning with *The New England Psalm-Singer* (1770), the earliest book of music by a composer in the future USA. Soon made obsolete by changes in musical and religious fashion, then long regarded as technically crude, his work was reassessed as vigorously independent in the mid 20th century and adapted by composers from Schuman to Cage.

David Phares McKay and Richard Crawford *William Billings of Boston* (1975)

Billington, Elizabeth [née Weichsel] (b. London, 27 Dec 1765; d. near Venice, 25 Aug 1818). British soprano, daughter of Carl Friedrich Weichsel, a German-born oboist-clarinettist working in London theatres. She thus had the benefit of lessons with J.C. Bach and Schroeter, as well as with James Billington, whom she married at 17. In 1786 she made her stage debut in London in Arne's *Love in a Village*, and went to Paris for further tuition from Michele Mortellari and Sacchini. Her memoirs, published in 1792, caused a scandal that drove the Billingtons to Dublin. They then stayed mostly on the continent, until at the start of the new century she returned to London, widowed and already separated from her second husband. Her performance as Vitellia, in the first London staging of a Mozart opera (1806), came near the end of her career. In 1817 she retired to Venice, apparently reconciled with her husband – though there were rumours he killed her.

Billy Budd. Opera by Britten to a libretto by E.M. Forster and Eric Crozier after Melville's story. Captain Vere (tenor) recalls – and the opera enacts – the time when he was obliged to sacrifice Billy (baritone), whose only crime was to have excited, by beauty and goodness, the envy and spite of Claggart (bass). Since the action takes place entirely in Vere's study and on board ship, there can be no female characters. First performance: London, 1 Dec 1951.

binary form. Pattern of two matching parts, frequently with each repeated. Generally the parts are of similar length; they may even be commensurate. Often they will share material, though not always. And the first will usually end in the dominant, as if raising a question, which the second answers, beginning in the dominant and closing back in the tonic.

Binary form was extremely common in the Baroque period – in the dance movements of suites and in the sonatas of Scarlatti and others. It survived in the minuet, to be more widely revived with 20th-century neoclassicism, which in this, as in so many other respects, was really neobaroquism.

Binchois [Gilles de Bins] (b. ?Mons, *c*.1400; d. Soignies, 20 Sep 1460). Netherlandish composer, a particular master, alongside Du Fay, of French song. He was almost certainly a choirboy and possibly also a soldier with the Duke of Suffolk's forces in France before, in the 1420s, he joined the court chapel of Philip the Good, Duke of Burgundy, whose realm included Flanders. For that court he wrote sacred music and songs, chiefly rondeaux, displaying a sweet melodic sense. In 1452 he retired to Soignies on a court pension. He was honoured in death by the two greatest composers who remained: Du Fay (*En triumphant de cruel dueil*), with whom he may have been in regular contact, and Ockeghem (*Mort tu as navré de ton dart*), who also wrote a mass on one of his songs, *De plus en plus*.

bipartite. See BINARY FORM.

Bird. Name given to Haydn's Quartet Op.33:3, for the suggestions of birdsong in the main theme of the first movement and the trio of the third.

birdsong. Natural musical source, whose imitation has had different meanings at different times. Sonic reproduction was part of the wonder of mechanical birds recorded from Hellenistic Alexandria and 9th-century Constantinople. As music, birdsong impressions have come with a certain comic bravado (Renaissance and Baroque periods), as essential to the image of the unsullied landscape (19th century) or as tokens of the divine (Messiaen).

There is variety, too, in the species chosen as models. The cuckoo enjoys a history in music stretching at least across the 700 years from 'Sumer is icumen in' to Messiaen's *Réveil des oiseaux*, thanks to its regular arrival in Europe as a harbinger of spring, and also to the simplicity of its call, normally represented by a falling third (or

fourth). Also frequently copied is the nightingale (trills, repeated notes, roulades in a context of static harmony), by virtue of its romantic associations with summer nights. It appears, for example, in Janequin's *Le Chant des oiseaux*, Couperin's *Ordre* No.14, Beethoven's 'Pastoral' Symphony, Mahler's Symphony No.2, Stravinsky's *Nightingale* and, again, Messiaen's *Réveil des oiseaux*. Quite common, too, is the lark, for its ability to float in the air (this lifting flight, not its song, being observed in Vaughan Williams's *The Lark Ascending*). Domestic fowl – hens, cockerels – are normally comedians. Parrots would also fall into this category.

Messiaen's music vastly enlarged the range and individuality of musical birdsongs. He collected his material mostly in the wild, by ear, on every continent, and wrote pieces composed very largely or even entirely of birdsong, realized for instruments, especially the piano, keyed percussion and woodwind. Alternatively, birdsongs have been imitated by means of special instruments (NIGHTINGALE, SERINETTE, SWANEE WHISTLE) and organ stops. Birds have also been brought into the concert hall by means of recordings, first by Respighi in his *Pini di Roma*. There are more generic birdsong passages in Wagner – the Forest Murmurs of *Siegfried*, where a bird (unseen) is a character – as well as Liszt and many other 19th-century composers.

Birmingham. British city musically important for its triennial festival, its conservatory (founded as the Midland Institute School of Music in 1886, becoming the Birmingham School of Music in 1949 and the Birmingham Conservatoire in 1989) and its orchestra. The festival took place from 1784 (following less regular meetings since 1759), saw the first performances of Mendelssohn's *Elijah* and Elgar's *Gerontius*, and lasted until the First World War. The orchestra then took over. Founded in 1920 as the City of Birmingham Orchestra (adding 'Symphony' to its name in 1948), it has had as its principal conductors T. Appleby Matthews (1920–24), Adrian Boult (1924–30), Leslie Heward (1930–43), George Weldon (1944–51), Rudolf Schwarz (1951–7), Andrzej Panufnik (1957–9), Hugo Rignold (1960–69), Louis Frémaux (1969–78), Simon Rattle (1980–98) and Sakari Oramo (from 1998).

Birtwistle, Harrison (Paul) (b. Accrington, 15 Jul 1934). British composer, knighted in 1987. Music is, for him, a mechanism by which time and memory sing. His own music has remained, through the decades of postmodernism since 1970, unrepentantly modern in its dissonance, its formal complexity and freedom, its continuing innovation and its mechanisms of pulse and ostinato. But at the same time it is prehistoric in its suggestions of monumental objects and ritual acts.

He was a slow starter. Though he had played the clarinet and composed from boyhood, and though he found lively colleagues at the Royal Manchester College of Music (1952–5), he was into his 30s before he produced his first works of characteristic trenchancy: *Tragoedia* for opposing wind and string chamber groups plus harp, and *Ring a Dumb Carillon*, in which numbed voice and excited clarinet pursue almost separate lines. Meanwhile he did army service, continued his clarinet studies at the RAM (but sold his instruments when he began having success as a composer) and taught at Cranborne Chase School, Dorset (1962–5). In 1966 he spent a year at Princeton, working on his first opera, *Punch and Judy*. With Davies he then established the Pierrot Players (later the FIRES OF LONDON), but he found more congenial musical homes with the London Sinfonietta, beginning with *Verses for Ensembles* (1969), and the National Theatre, where he was music director (1975–82). *Verses*, with its sectional form and its outbursts from wind groups, solo winds and percussionists, marked the quick end of his hot early style, indebted to Stravinsky, Varèse and Messiaen.

Nenia (1970) introduced a new phase of relative quiet and generative slowness, as he began to work towards a new, much bigger opera, *The Mask of Orpheus*. By the time that work was first produced, in 1986, he had completed two big symphonic pieces (*The Triumph of Time* and *Earth Dances*), a 'mechanical pastoral' – part myth, part counting game – for television (*Yan Tan Tethera*), other imposing works for brass band and modern mixed ensemble (*Silbury Air*, *Secret Theatre*) and a variety of lyrical pieces, often sensuous and ecstatic (*Meridian*). Part of this period he spent in the Hebrides, part in France, though with regular returns to London for National Theatre work (notably *The Oresteia*, 1981), teaching and performances. In 1996 he moved into an old silkworks in Wiltshire.

The eventual achievement of *The Mask of Orpheus* seems to have increased his freedom and confidence – and his range. Subsequent works have included a heroic opera about responsibility and self-knowledge (*Gawain*), another in which pervasive themes of love, loss and repetition are treated with happy lightness (*The Second Mrs Kong*), a formidable cycle of Celan songs (*Pulse Shadows*) and a symphonic meditation that introduced a new transparency to his formidable orchestral range (*The Shadow of Night*).

Jonathan Cross *Harrison Birtwistle* (2000)

Operas: PUNCH AND JUDY, 1966–7; *The Mask of Orpheus* (see ORPHEUS), 1973–83; *Yan Tan Tethera* (1 act: Tony Harrison), 1984; GAWAIN, 1990–91; *The Second Mrs Kong* (Russell Hoban), 1993–4, f.p. Glyndebourne, 1994; *The Last Supper* (Robin Blaser), 1998–9, f.p. Berlin, 2000; *The Io Passion* (Stephen Plaice), 2003, f.p. Aldeburgh, 2004

Music theatre: *Down by the Greenwood Side* (Michael Nyman), s, 5 actors, 9 insts, 1969; *Bow Down* (Harrison), 5 actors, 4 insts, 1977

Orchestral: *Chorales*, 1960–63; *3 Movements with Fanfares*, chbr orch, 1964; *Nomos*, 1968; *An Imaginary Landscape*, wind, perc, 1971; *The* TRIUMPH OF TIME, 1972; *Grimethorpe Aria*, brass band, 1973; *Melencolia I*, cl, str, hp, 1976; ... *agm* ... (Sappho), ch, 3 ens, 1978–9; *Still Movement*, str, 1984; *Words Overhead* (Birtwistle), s, chbr orch, 1985; EARTH DANCES, 1985–6; ENDLESS PARADE, tpt, vib, str, 1986–7; *Machaut à ma manière*, 1988; *Salford Toccata*, brass band, 1989; *Antiphonies*, pf, orch, 1992; *The Cry of Anubis*, tuba, orch, 1994; *Panic*, a sax, drumkit, wind, perc, 1995; *Exody*, 1996–7; *Placid Mobile*, 36 tpt, 1998; *There is something between us* (Brendel), bar, orch, 2000; *The* SHADOW OF NIGHT, 2001; *Theseus Game*, 30 insts, 2002–3; *Night's Black Bird*, 2004

Ensemble: *The World is Discovered*, 10 insts, 1960–61; *Tragoedia*, 10 insts, 1965; VERSES FOR ENSEMBLES, 1968–9; *Prologue* (Aeschylus), t, 7 insts, 1971; *The Fields of Sorrow* (Ausonius), 2 s, ch, 16 insts, 1971; *Meridian* (Logue, Wyatt), mez, women's ch, 13 insts, 1971; *Epilogue* (Shakespeare), bar, 5 brass, 2 perc, 1972; *For o, for o, the hobby-horse is forgot*, 6 perc, 1976; *Carmen arcadiae mechanicae perpetuum*, 14 insts, 1977; *Silbury Air*, 15 insts, 1977; *Secret Theatre*, 14 insts, 1984; *Songs by Myself* (Birtwistle), s, 7 insts, 1984; *An die Musik* (Rilke), s, 10 insts, 1988; *Ritual Fragment*, 14 insts, 1990; *4 Poems* (Jaan Kaplinski), s, 13 insts, 1991; PULSE SHADOWS (9 Settings of Celan + 9 Movements), 1989–96; *Slow Frieze*, pf, 13 insts, 1996; *The Woman and the Hare* (Harsent), s, speaker, 9 insts, 1999; *17 Tate Riffs*, 14 insts, 2000; *Tenebrae David*, 10 brass, 2001; *Passing Measures*, 13 insts, 2004

Choral: *Music for Sleep*, children's ch, perc, 1963; *Narration: A Description of the Passing of a Year*, 1963; *Carmen paschale*, 1964–5; *The Mark of the Goat* (school cantata), 1965–6; *On the Sheer Threshold of the Night* (Helen Waddell, after Boethius), 1980; *3 Latin Motets*, 1999; *The Ring Dance of the Nazarene* (Harsent), bar, ch, ens, 2003; *The Gleam* (Plaice), ch, 2003

Chamber: *Refrains and Choruses*, wind qnt, 1957; *Monody for Corpus Christi*, s, fl, hn, perc, 1959; *Entr'actes and Sappho Fragments*, s, 6 insts, 1962–4; *Ring a Dumb Carillon* (Logue), s, cl, perc, 1965; *Verses*, cl, pf, 1965; *Dinah and Nick's Love Song*, 4 insts, 1970; *Linoi*, cl, pf, vc, 1968–73; *Clarinet Quintet*, 1980; *Pulse Sampler*, ob, claves, 1981; *Duets for Storab*, 2 fl, 1983; *An Interrupted Endless Melody*, ob, pf, 1991; *Five Distances*, wind qnt, 1992;

Hoquetus Petrus, 2 fl, tpt, 1995; 9 Settings of Celan, s, 2 cl, va, vc, db, 1989–96; 9 Movements, str qt, 1991–6; *The Silk House Tattoo*, 2 tpt, drums, 1998; 9 Settings of Lorine Niedecker, s, vc, 1998–2000; *The Axe Manual*, pf, perc, 2000; *The Sadness of Komachi* (noh play), t, prepared pf, 2000; 26 *Orpheus Elegies*, ct, ob, hp, 2002–3; *Today Too* (Tanko), t, fl, gui, 2004
Piano: *Précis*, pf, 1960; *Harrison's Clocks*, pf, 1997–8; *Ostinato with Melody*, 2000; *Betty Freeman: Her Tango*, 2000; *Saraband: The Kings Farewell*, 2001; *Gigue*, 2002
Arrangements: *Hoquetus David* (Machaut), 6 insts, 1969; *Ut heremita solus* (Ockeghem), 6 insts, 1969; *Mercure* (Satie), 14 insts, 1980; *Bach Measures*, 14 insts, 1996

bis (Fr., twice). (1) Instruction to repeat a passage.
(2) Vocal appeal for a repetition, coming from a Francophone or Italian audience.
(3) Nicety in numbering, as in Op.32bis, distinct from Op.32.

bisbigliando (It., whispering). Rapid alternation of two harp strings sounding the same note.

biscroma (It.). Demisemiquaver, 32nd-note.

Bishop, Henry (Rowley) (b. London, 18 Nov 1786; d. London, 30 April 1855). British composer, remembered much more for one song, 'Home, sweet home' (1829), than for the crowds of operas he threw at the London stage, knighted in 1842 (the first musician so honoured). A tradesman's son, he was already in business as a composer and music seller at the age of 13, and studied harmony with Bianchi while starting to make his way in the theatre. He became musical director of Covent Garden (1810–24), for which he wrote numerous overtures, songs, dances and other items for stage pieces, later doing the same for Drury Lane and Vauxhall Gardens, until 1840, when he retired for less busy and more gentlemanly pursuits, as principal conductor of the Antient Concerts (1840–48) and Oxford professor of music (1848–55). He was married in turn to two singers, of whom the second left him after eight years and three children, though she kept her name as Anna Bishop (1810–84) through a career that included performances in Russia, Naples, the Americas both very thoroughly, the Philippines and India, and that continued almost to her death.

bitonality. Impression of being in two keys at once, an effect particularly associated with Stravinsky, Ives and others in the first half of the 20th century. The motif most associated with the puppet hero in Stravinsky's *Petrushka* (1911) is based on simultaneous arpeggios of C major and F♯ major; Ives had been writing bitonal music since his psalm settings of the 1890s. Harmony in Schoenberg's atonal and serial works has also sometimes been understood as bitonal.

Bittner, Julius (b. Vienna, 9 Apr 1874; d. Vienna, 9/10 Jan 1939). Austrian composer, notably of fairytale operas. Largely self-taught, he was a lawyer by profession, and helped Schoenberg gain exemption from military service in the First World War.

biwa. Japanese lute.

Bizet, Georges (Alexandre César Léopold) (b. Paris, 25 Oct 1838; d. Bougival, near Paris, 3 Jun 1875). French composer, whose sense for colour, sensuousness, melody and drama resulted in one great opera and a vivid miscellany of other works. The son and nephew of singing teachers, he studied with Jean François Marmontel before, still just nine, entering the Conservatoire, where his teachers included Halévy (Gounod gave him extracurricular help) and where he completed his studies in 1857 by winning the Prix de Rome. His immediate talent for high-level pastiche was astonishing: his neo-Mozartian Symphony in C (lost in the Conservatoire library until 1935) is among the most brilliant teenage compositions since Mozart himself (and Mendelssohn), while in *Le Docteur Miracle* he showed his command of Donizetti–Offenbach operatic idiocy.
Soon, though, he encountered difficulties. Exposure to Verdi (while he was in Rome, 1857–60) and Wagner (back in Paris) indicated a problem: the world was changing, and it took him a while to discover what his contribution might be. During the years 1858–62 he began and abandoned eight operas, completing just one – an Italian opera buffa, *Don Procopio* – which was not produced. He hit his stride with *Les Pêcheurs de perles* (1863), but then again fell victim to inner and outer circumstance, relinquishing projects at an early point or almost completing them in order to have them, like *Ivan IV*, rejected. The works that did reach the stage – *Les Pêcheurs de perles*, *La Jolie Fille de Perth* and later *Djamileh* – won only modest success, and he had to support himself as a publisher's arranger.
In 1869 he married Halévy's daughter Geneviève, with whom his relationship seems to have been awkward (unlike the intimate friendship he had enjoyed with the courtesan Céleste Mogador). At the time he was achieving little, aware of a coming change in his music, towards vividness and certainty. His piano duets *Jeux d'enfants* and the suite from *L'Arlésienne* at last

won him favour, but the full expression of his new style, when it came in *Carmen*, was at first less noticed than the scandalous subject matter. He grew ill within the month of the première of his greatest work and died as it was about to make its triumph.

Winton Dean *Bizet* (1948, ³1975)

Operas: *Le Docteur Miracle* (1-act operetta; Leon Battu and Halévy), 1856, f.p. Paris, 1857; *Don Procopio* (Carlo Cambiaggio), 1858–9, f.p. Monte Carlo, 1906; *Ivan IV*, 1862–5, unfinished; *Les* PECHEURS DE PERLES, 1863; *La Jolie Fille de Perth* (Jules Henri Vernoy de Saint-Georges and Jules Adenis, after Scott), 1866, f.p. Paris, 1867; *Djamileh* (1 act; Louis Gallet), 1871, f.p. Paris, 1872; CARMEN, 1873–4

Incidental music: *L'*ARLESIENNE, 1872

Orchestral: Overture, 1855; Symphony, C, 1855; *Roma*, symphony, 1860–68, rev 1871; *Marche funèbre*, 1868–9; *Petite suite*, 1871, arr from *Jeux d'enfants*; *Patrie* (overture), 1873

Piano: *Variations chromatiques de concert*, 1868; JEUX D'ENFANTS, duet, 1871; etc.

Other works: choral pieces, songs including 'Adieux de l'hôtesse arabe' (Hugo), 1866

Björling, Jussi [Johan Jonaton] (b. Stora Tuna, 5 Feb 1911; d. Stockholm, 9 Sep 1960). Swedish tenor of enchanting sweet tone and artistry, valued especially in Verdi, Puccini and Gounod. The son of a tenor, he began as a treble in the family's male quartet, then studied at the conservatory in Stockholm, where he made his formal debut as Don Ottavio in 1930. From 1937 (*Rigoletto* in Chicago) he was regularly in the USA, except during the Second World War, and he made many recordings.

Blacher, Boris (b. Niu-chang, China, 19 Jan 1903; d. Berlin, 30 Jan 1975). German composer, a neoclassicist of playful inventiveness and dark humour. He studied with Friedrich Ernst Koch and others in Berlin (1924–31), which remained his home. In the 1930s he worked there as a composer and arranger; after the Second World War he became a distinguished teacher at the conservatory, which he directed (1953–70), and as a guest abroad. At the same time he explored new constructive methods in his music. Exposure to serialism sharpened his sense of working with patterns of intervals, and in 1950 he introduced the technique of VARIABLE METRES. His *Abstrakte Oper* No.1 is abstract in having a non-verbal libretto.

Operas: *Romeo und Julia* (chbr: Blacher, after Shakespeare), Op.22, 1943, f.p. Berlin-Zehlendorf, 1947; *Abstrakte Oper* No.1 (Egk), Op.43, f.p. Hesse Radio, 1953; *Rosamunde Floris* (Gerhart von Westerman, after Georg Kaiser), Op.60, f.p. Berlin, 1960; *Zwischenfälle bei einer Notlandung* (Heinz von Cramer), f.p. Hamburg, 1966; *Zweihunderttausend Taler* (Blacher, after Sholem Aleichem), f.p. Berlin, 1969; *Yvonne, Prinzessin von Burgund* (Blacher, after Gombrowicz), f.p. Wuppertal, 1973; *Das Geheimnis des entwendeten Briefes* (chbr: after Poe), f.p. Berlin, 1975; etc.

Orchestral: *Concertante Musik*, Op.10, 1937; *Hamlet*, Op.17, 1940; Variations on a Theme of Paganini, Op.26, 1947; *Orchester-Ornament*, Op.44, 1953; concertos, etc.

Choral: *Der Grossinquisitor* (oratorio), Op.21, 1942; *Requiem*, Op.58, 1958; etc.

Other works: 5 quartets, other chamber music, various vocal pieces, piano pieces, tape music

Black, Robert (b. Dallas, 28 Apr 1950; d. Palo Alto, 14 Nov 1993). US conductor and pianist, founder of the New York New Music Ensemble (1976) and wildly demanding, wildly gifted performer of Barraqué. He studied at Oberlin and Juilliard, his teachers including Beveridge Webster, Sessions and Diamond.

Black Key. Name given Chopin's Etude in G♭, Op.10:5, in which the right hand keeps to the black keys.

Black Mass. Name Scriabin gave his Piano Sonata No.9.

Black Mountain College. North Carolina institution where Wolpe, Cage and others taught in a libertarian atmosphere in the 1940s and 1950s. Here Cage's *4′33″* was first unheard.

Blades, James (b. Peterborough, 9 Sep 1901; d. Cheam, 19 May 1999). British percussionist, an inventive and sociable musician who began in the hard school of the circus and silent cinema. He also played in dance bands and in 1935 recorded the three tam-tam strokes that introduced J. Arthur Rank films for decades afterwards. In 1940 he joined the LSO as principal, but he also worked with many other ensembles and gave his advice to composers, not least Britten. From 1960 he taught at the RAM.

Blake, David (Leonard) (b. London, 2 Sep 1936). British composer, whose communist convictions led him, after Cambridge, to study with Eisler in East Berlin. But Mahler and Messiaen are also among his sources, in a large and various output that includes two operas (*Toussaint*, London, 1977; *The Plumber's Gift*, London, 1989). He joined York University in 1963, and was appointed professor there in 1976.

blanche (Fr.). Minim, half-note.

Blaník. See MA VLAST.

Blas- (Ger.). Wind, hence *Blasinstrumente* (wind instruments), *Blasorchester* (wind orchestra), etc.

Blavet, Michel (baptized Besançon, 13 Mar 1700; d. Paris, 28 Oct 1768). French flautist-composer. He went to Paris in 1723 and was supported by various noble families while enjoying wide esteem for his playing at the Concert Spirituel (from 1726) and the Opera (from 1740). He also taught, and published sonatas and dance pieces for his instrument.

Blech (Ger.). Brass, as in *Blechbläser* (brass instruments), etc.

bleeding chunks. Excerpts, especially from Wagner. Tovey introduced the phrase when he wrote of 'bleeding chunks of butcher's meat chopped from Wagner's operas and served up on Wagner nights' (such as used to be a regular feature of the Proms).

blindness. Affliction that, whether or not it sharpens hearing, has affected several composers, including Landini, Stanley, Mercadante, Delius, Rodrigo and Langlais, and some performers (Bocelli). Composers retaining a little vision have been able to write on large staves; others have worked with an amanuensis.

Bliss, Arthur (Drummond) (b. London, 2 Aug 1891; d. London, 27 Mar 1975). British composer, knighted in 1950. He studied with Charles Wood at Cambridge, served in the First World War, and made a reputation in the immediate post-war years as the London branch of Les Six. A personal connection with Elgar soon moderated the outrageousness of such pieces as *Rout*, and, like Walton, he moved into an Elgarian style spiked with elements from Prokofiev and Ravel. Partly of US descent, he spent periods in California (1923–5, 1939–41), but he was the natural choice in 1953 as Master of the Queen's Music.

Opera: *The Olympians* (J.B. Priestley), f.p. London, 1949
Ballets: *Checkmate*, 1937; *Miracle in the Gorbals*, 1944; *Adam Zero*, 1946
Orchestral: *A Colour Symphony*, 1921–2; *Things to Come* (film score), 1934–5; *Music for Strings*, 1935; *Meditations on a Theme of John Blow*, 1955; etc.
Vocal: *Rout*, s, ens, 1920; *Pastoral: Lie Strewn the White Flocks*, mez, ch, orch, 1928; *Morning Heroes* (oratorio), 1930; cantatas, anthems, songs

Chamber and instrumental: Clarinet Quintet, 1932; etc.

Blitheman, John (b. c.1525; d. London, 23 May 1591). English organist-composer, associated with the Chapel Royal, sometimes mistakenly called William. He wrote plainsong variations and taught John Bull.

Blitzstein, Marc(us Samuel) (b. Philadelphia, 2 Mar 1905; d. Fort-de-France, Martinique, 22 Jan 1964). US composer-playwright of eclectic style and left-wing commitment. He studied at the University of Pennsylvania, with Ziloti in New York, with Rosario Scalero at Curtis (1924–6) and then in Europe for two years, with Boulanger and Schoenberg. In 1928 he witnessed *Die Dreigroschenoper*, but it was the experience of Eisler's lectures in New York, in 1935, that galvanized him as a socially active artist: the immediate result was the musical play *The Cradle will Rock*. He served in the US Air Force in 1942–5, and emerged from the war with his political commitment moderated – though not his readiness to adopt and adapt different musical styles, from the commercial to the avant-garde.

Theatre: *The Cradle will Rock*, 1936–7; *Regina*, 1946–8; *Reuben, Reuben*, 1955; etc.
Other works: *The Airborne*, soli, men's ch, orch, 1944–6; songs, film scores, etc.

Bloch, Ernest (b. Geneva, 24 Jul 1880; d. Portland, Ore., 15 Jul 1959). Swiss–US composer and teacher. He studied in Geneva with Jaques-Dalcroze, in Brussels with Ysaÿe and Rasse (1897–9) and in Frankfurt with Knorr (1899–1901), then spent periods in Munich and Paris before returning to Switzerland in 1904 to join his father's souvenir business. He also started his career as a teacher, at the Geneva Conservatory (1911–15). In 1916 he went to the USA, to conduct for the dancer Maud Allan. He stayed to teach at Mannes and, as director, at the Cleveland Institute (1920–25) and the San Francisco Conservatory (1925–30). The 1930s he spent largely in Switzerland again, but in 1941 he settled in Oregon, going down to Berkeley to give summer courses until 1952. His early works, certainly including his *Macbeth* opera, are a swirl of Romantic and post-Romantic influences, out of which he developed in strength under two guiding principles: Hebraism (*Schelomo*, etc.) and neoclassicism.

David Z. Kushner *The Ernest Bloch Companion* (2002)

Opera: *Macbeth*, 1904–9, f.p. Paris, 1910
Orchestral: *Schelomo* (see SOLOMON), vc, orch, 1915–16; Concerto Gross No.1, str, pf, 1924–5; No.2, str, str qt, 1952; *Avodath hakodesh* (Sacred Service),

bar, ch, orch, 1930–33; Violin Concerto, 1937–8; *Baal shem*, vn, orch, 1939; *Suite symphonique*, 1944; *Concerto symphonique*, pf, orch, 1947–8; *Suite hébraïque*, va/vn, orch, 1951; Symphony, E♭, 1954–5; etc.

Chamber and instrumental: Piano Quintet No.1, 1921–3; No.2, 1957; String Quartet No.1, 1916; No.2, 1945; No.3, 1952; No.4, 1953; No.5, 1956; 3 Nocturnes, pf trio, 1924; Violin Sonata No.1, 1920; No.2 (*Poème mystique*), 1924; *Baal shem*, vn, pf, 1923; *Abodah*, vn, pf, 1929; Suite, va, pf, 1919; *From Jewish Life*, vc, pf, 1924; *Méditation hébraïque*, vc, pf, 1924; *In the Night*, pf, 1922; *Poems of the Sea*, pf, 1922; Piano Sonata, 1935; etc.

Blockflöte (Ger.). Recorder.

block form. In contrasted short units, as in much of the music of Stravinsky and Messiaen.

block harmony. In chords; HOMOPHONY.

Blockwerk (Ger.). Chest of organ pipes operating together (not with separated stops), as found in 15th-century northern European instruments.

Blomdahl, Karl-Birger (b. Växjö, 19 Oct 1916; d. Kungsängen, near Stockholm, 14 Jun 1968). Swedish composer, who was seminal in bringing his colleagues and students in touch with new developments, from Hindemith in the 1940s to Ligeti in the 1960s – developments he also explored with great seriousness in his compositions, having begun as a pupil of Rosenberg. His opera *Aniara* caused particular excitement, not just for its science-fiction setting but also for its pessimism and wide musical range.

Operas: ANIARA; *Herr von Hancken* (Lindegren), f.p. Stockholm, 1965
Ballets: *Sisyphos*, 1954; *Minotauros*, 1957; *Game for Eight*, 1962
Orchestral: Symphony No.1, 1943; No.2, 1947; No.3 'Facetter', 1950; etc.
Other works: *In the Hall of Mirrors* (Lindegren), soli, ch, orch, 1951–2; 2 quartets, piano pieces, etc.

Blondel de Nesle (*fl.* 1180–1200). Trouvère, associated with Richard I, king of England, only in later legend. His songs seem to have been widely disseminated.

Blow, John (baptized Newark, 23 Feb 1649; d. London, 1 Oct 1708). English composer, outshone only by Purcell in his time. He was recruited for the restored Chapel Royal under Henry Cooke, and remained as an apprentice musician after his voice broke, in 1664, becoming organist of Westminster Abbey in 1668 and Master of the

Children of the Chapel Royal in 1674. Also in 1674 he married the daughter of a fellow royal musician; his wife died in 1683, leaving him with three daughters. He was replaced by Purcell at the abbey (1679–95), but returned afterwards, and was also organist for the Chapel Royal and St Paul's. In 1677 he received a Canterbury doctorate.

Opera: VENUS AND ADONIS
Sacred: *God spake sometime in visions* (coronation of James II), 1685; *I was glad* (opening of choir of St Paul's), 1697; many other anthems, services, etc.
Other works: *An Ode on the Death of Mr Henry Purcell* (Dryden), 2 v, 2 rec, 1696; court odes, St Cecilia's Day odes, songs, organ music, etc.

Bluebeard's Castle (*A Kékszakállú herceg vára*). Opera by Bartók to a libretto by Béla Balázs after Perrault and Maeterlinck. Bluebeard (baritone) brings his new wife Judith (soprano) into his castle and, in response to her unstoppable demands, reluctantly opens seven doors on his wealth and his sadness, orchestrally expressed. As he does so, his mood changes from anxiety to regret, though his love for Judith stays the same. Finally, her curiosity about his past obliges her to join it, with three of his former wives, and he is left alone forever. The score draws on Debussy for declamation (adapted to the trochees of Hungarian), Strauss for orchestral colour and character, and folklore for epic, emblematic story-telling. Since its action is almost entirely psychological, the piece has had a strong life in recordings and concert performances. First performance: Budapest, 24 May 1918.

Blue Danube, The (*An der schönen blauen Donau*). Waltz by Johann Strauss II.

blue note. Third or seventh (or occasionally fifth) scale degree flattened by up to a semitone, as found in the blues and related musical expressions. Blue notes probably arose from the misfit between African and European scales.

blues. US vernacular musical tradition that evolved *c.*1900 among Black people. Its basic form is the 12-bar blues, in which the singer states a line, repeats it, then adds another, rhyming, all over the harmonic progression I (4 bars)–IV (2)–I (2)–V⁷ (2)–I (2). The blues was a primary source of jazz, and has also been part of the currency of classical music since the 1920s, incorporated by Ravel (Violin Sonata, slow movement), Copland, Tippett, Turnage, etc.

Blüthner. German piano firm founded in Leipzig in 1853 by Julius Blüthner (1824–1910), who in 1873 introduced a fourth string in the treble, adding warmth and body in this register. Blüthner instruments still have this feature.

BMG. Bertelsmann Music Group, an international company with interests in recording and publishing, having acquired RCA Victor, Melodiya and Ricordi.

BMI. Broadcast Music Inc., US performing rights agency.

B minor Mass. Setting by Bach for voices with flutes, oboes, oboes d'amore, bassoons, horn, trumpets, timpani, strings and continuo. Movements with up to eight vocal parts are interspersed with numbers for one or two soloists. The *Sanctus* was first performed on Christmas Day 1724; much of the rest was adapted from cantata movements and put into final form c.1747–9.

bn. Abbreviation for bassoon.

bocca chiusa (It., closed mouth). Hummed, as in the Humming Chorus in *Madama Butterfly*.

Boccherini, (Ridolfo) Luigi (b. Lucca, 19 Feb 1743; d. Madrid, 28 May 1805). Italian composer, especially of chamber music that forms a mellifluous and imaginative Mediterranean subdepartment of the Classical style: the violinist Giuseppe Puppa called him 'Haydn's wife', an acute, if unflattering, sobriquet. The son of a professional cellist or bassist, he made his cello debut at 13 and continued his training with Giovanni Battista Costanzi in Rome (1757). He paid three visits to Vienna (1757–9, 1760–61, 1763–4) and one to Paris (1767–8) before gaining a post as composer and virtuoso to the Spanish prince, Don Luis, in Madrid (1769–85). Probably he remained in Spain after his patron's death, writing for Friedrich Wilhelm II of Prussia, for the Parisian publishing market and for Lucien Bonaparte. He wrote about 135 string quintets (almost all with two cellos) and about 90 string quartets, as well as string trios, flute quintets, piano quintets, sonatas, symphonies, cello concertos (of which the most popular are Nos.6 in D, 7 in G and 9 in B♭) and a few vocal works. Two of the quintets have descriptive titles: Op.11:6 in D 'L'uccelliera' (The Aviary), for its bird calls, and Op.30:6 in C 'La musica notturna della strade di Madrid' (Night Music in the Streets of Madrid). Another two, Op.11:5 in E and Op.13:5 in A, have popular minuets. Further string quintets and piano quintets were recycled as guitar quintets, among which No.4 in D closes with a fandango.

Germaine de Rothschild *Luigi Boccherini* (1965)

Bocelli, Andrea (b. Lajatico, 22 Sep 1958). Italian tenor, who shot to the stratosphere of stardom with his first albums in 1994 and stayed, recording Italian opera and sacred music, despite quibbles about his vocal technique. He trained as a lawyer before taking lessons with Corelli, and was discovered in 1992 when he auditioned for the Italian rock artist Zucchero. Though blind he has occasionally taken part in staged opera.

Boehm. Model of flute developed by the Munich flautist-metallurgist Theobald Boehm (1794–1881), first in 1832 and with improvements in 1847. It was distinguished from previous flutes by its bore and key system, and was manufactured by Boehm's own factory and by others.

Boehmer, Konrad (b. Berlin, 24 May 1941). German composer, emphatically critical, from a Marxist standpoint, of the modernist culture in which his music must have its being, and thereby large in his range of references, from Stockhausen through bel canto to rock music. He studied with Koenig in Cologne (1959–61), where in 1966 he gained a doctorate at the university for work on open form in music. That same year he moved to the Netherlands, working first alongside Koenig in Utrecht (1966–8), then as a music journalist and professor at the Hague Conservatory (since 1972). His works include operas (*Dr Faustus*, Paris, 1985; *Woutertje Pieterse*, Rotterdam, 1988) and piano music (*Potential*, 1961; *In illo tempore*, 1979).

Boëllmann, Léon (b. Ensisheim, Haut-Rhin, 25 Sep 1862; d. Paris, 11 Oct 1897). French organist-composer, nephew-pupil of Gigout at the École Niedermeyer (1871–81). He was organist at St Vincent-de-Paul in Paris, and wrote sacred music, songs and orchestral pieces (Symphonic Variations for cello and orchestra), besides organ works (*Douze pièces*, *Suite gothique*).

Boesmans, Philippe (b. Tongeren, 17 May 1936). Belgian composer. He studied with Froidebise and Pousseur, though his music more evokes Berio in its exploration of gestures and historical references within a fluid continuity. His works include the operas *La Passion de Gilles* (see JOAN OF ARC), *Reigen* (Brussels, 1993) and *Ein Wintermärchen* (Brussels, 1999).

Boethius (Anicius Manlius Severinus) (b. Rome, c.480; d. c.524). Roman philosopher, whose works formed the basis for education and musical thinking from the 10th century into the Renaissance. He established the quadrivium, the 'fourfold path' constituted by the mathematical disciplines of arithmetic, geometry, astronomy and music, and his musical treatise *De institutione musica* conveyed Greek knowledge (the tetrachord, the theory of consonance and of relations between pitch and vibration frequency) to the future, besides creating a deeply influential hierarchy of *musica mundana* (the MUSIC OF THE SPHERES) over *musica humana* (music produced by and acting upon the human body) over *musica instrumentalis* (instrumental music).

Boeuf sur le toit, Le (The Ox on the Roof). Ballet by Milhaud to a scenario by Cocteau, set in the eponymous Paris nightclub. First performance: Paris, 21 Feb 1920.

Bogen (Ger., pl. *Bogen*). Bow.

Bohème, La (Bohemian Life). Opera by Puccini to a libretto by Giacosa and Illica after Henry Murger's novel. The lives of four young artists sharing a Paris garret – Rodolfo (tenor), Marcello (baritone), Schaunard (baritone) and Colline (bass) – are changed when their neighbour Mimì (soprano) calls to find Rodolfo alone. These two disclose their hearts – Rodolfo in 'Che gelida manina', Mimì in 'Mi chiamano Mimì' – and sing a rapturous love duet. The rumbustious second act, set at a pavement café, contrasts their intimacy with the swaggering affair between Marcello and Musetta, who has a waltz song, 'Quando m'en vo'). Rodolfo's jealousy causes a rupture, but finally Mimì dies among them all. Brilliantly constructed and effective at every point, the work rapidly went around the world, and there it has stayed. First performance: Turin, 1 Feb 1896.

Leoncavallo's version of the subject appeared the next year.

Bohemia. See CZECH REPUBLIC.

Bohemian Girl, The. Opera by Balfe to a libretto by Alfred Bunn. The girl is Arline (soprano), a count's daughter who is brought up among gypsies (singing the immensely popular 'I dreamt that I dwelt in marble halls'), then simultaneously regains her father and gains a husband. First performance: London, 27 Nov 1843.

Böhm, Georg (b. Hohenkirchen, near Ohrdruf, 2 Sep 1661; d. Lüneburg, 18 May 1733). German organist-composer. The son of a schoolmaster-organist, he was trained in the traditions of the Bach region and graduated from Jena University in 1684, though he seems to have continued his education into his 30s in Hamburg, where he became organist of St John's in 1698. Bach may have heard him there and certainly knew his

music, especially his chorale variations. He also wrote other keyboard works (Prelude, Fugue and Postlude in G minor, 11 suites), cantatas and sacred songs.

Böhm, Karl (b. Graz, 28 Aug 1894; d. Salzburg, 14 Aug 1981). Austrian conductor, supremely effective in Austro–German opera from Mozart to Berg (decidedly by way of Wagner and Strauss). He studied law and music simultaneously, made his conducting debut in Graz (1917), and was taken on by the Munich Staatsoper under Muck and Walter (1921–7). From there he moved to chief posts in Darmstadt, Hamburg and Dresden (1934–43), where he conducted the premières of Strauss's *Die schweigsame Frau* and *Daphne*, the latter dedicated to him. After brief periods with the Vienna Staatsoper (1943–5, 1954–6), including its opening performance in the rebuilt theatre, he worked regularly in the leading centres internationally: Munich, Vienna, Bayreuth, Salzburg, London, New York.

Boieldieu, (François) Adrien (b. Rouen, 16 Dec 1775; d. Jarcy, 8 Oct 1834). French composer, whose melodic spontaneity and charm, in a style inspired by reverence for Mozart, placed him ahead of his rivals in the developing opéra comique. He studied with Charles Broche, the cathedral organist in Rouen, and found an organ post himself at 15 while also starting to make his way as a pianist-composer, but was soon seduced by the musical theatre that came to the town. His first opéra comique was produced there in 1793, and in 1796 he made for Paris. More success followed, and a brief marriage (1802–3); he then accepted an invitation to the imperial court in St Petersburg, where he led the French opera (1803–11). Back in Paris he enjoyed more mixed fortunes and virtually retired, until the craze for Rossini challenged him to respond on behalf of an older tradition, though with Romantic refinements that made *La Dame blanche* an international hit. The death of his long-estranged wife enabled him to marry his longest-serving mistress in 1827, but in 1830 he entered a period of deteriorating health.

Operas: *Le Calife de Bagdad* (1 act: Claude Godard d'Aucour), f.p. Paris, 1800; *Jean de Paris* (Godard d'Aucour), f.p. Paris, 1812; *Le Nouveau Seigneur de village* (1 act), f.p. Paris, 1813; *La Fête de village voisin*, f.p. Paris, 1816; *Le Petit Chaperon rouge*, f.p. Paris, 1818; *La Dame Blanche* (Scribe), f.p. Paris, 1825; *Les Deux Nuits* (Scribe), f.p. Paris, 1829

Other works: Harp Concerto, C, pub 1801; songs, chamber pieces, piano sonatas, etc.

bois (Fr.). Wood, as in *avec le bois* (with the wood of the bow), *bois* (woodwind instruments), etc.

Boismortier, Joseph Bodin de (b. Thionville, 23 Dec 1689; d. Roissy-en-Brie, 28 Oct 1755). French composer who sought to please. He lived in the provinces before arriving *c*.1723 in Paris, where he catered abundantly to the market for sonatas and concertos. His published collections, about 80 in number and mostly of six works apiece, include many for a pair of flutes, flute and violin, etc. The stream of operas (*Daphnis et Chloé*, 1747), cantatas and motets from him was much less.

Boîte à joujoux, La (The Toybox). Ballet score by Debussy to a scenario by André Hellé, the orchestration completed by Caplet. Among the toys are a soldier, wounded in battle, and a doll, whom he marries, producing numerous offspring. First performance: Paris, 10 Dec 1919.

Boito, Arrigo [Enrico] (b. Padua, 24 Feb 1842; d. Milan, 10 Jun 1918). Italian librettist-composer, remembered principally for his rejuvenating collaboration with the elderly Verdi. The son of an Italian miniaturist and a Polish countess, he studied at the Milan Conservatory (1853–61) and began his career writing librettos for his fellow pupil Faccio (*Amleto*) and himself (*Mefistofele*) while working as a journalist. One article, in which he spoke of the 'defiled altars' of Italian music, rankled with Verdi, for whom he had provided a cantata text, *Inno delle nazioni* (1862). *Mefistofele* was a failure at its first production (1868), and he worked on revising it. Meanwhile, Giulio Ricordi tried to get him and Verdi together, as eventually happened in 1879. The senior composer was impressed by his *Otello* libretto, but asked him first to assist in reworking *Simon Boccanegra*. Then they went on to *Otello* (1881–7) and *Falstaff* (1887–93), after which they remained friends. While working on *Falstaff* Boito also had a passionate affair with the actress Eleonora Duse. Thereafter he devoted himself to the ever-uncompleted *Nerone*.

Operas: *Mefistofele* (see FAUST), 1862–8; *Nerone*, 1877–1915
Librettos for other composers: *Amleto* (Faccio); *La falce* (Catalani); *Ero e Leandro* (Bottesini, Mancinelli); *La Gioconda* (Ponchielli); *Otello, Falstaff* (Verdi)

Bolcom, William (Elden) (b. Seattle, 26 May 1938). US composer, happily prolific in diverse styles. He studied with Verrall at the University of Washington, with Milhaud (1958–61) at Mills and in Paris (where he also attended Messiaen's classes), and with Leland Smith at Stanford (1961–4). Since then he has worked as a college professor, notably at the University of Michigan

(from 1973), while working from original extremes of luridity (*Black Host* for organ, percussion and tape, 1967), irony (*Commedia* for chamber orchestra, 1971) and vernacular frolicsomeness (several rags) towards a more settled embrace. His concert-length *Songs of Innocence and of Experience* is a compendium of his interests. He has also given recitals of US popular song with his wife, Joan Morris.

Operas: *Casino Paradise* (Arnold Weinstein), f.p. Philadelphia, 1990; *McTeague* (Weinstein and Robert Altman), f.p. Chicago, 1992; *A View from the Bridge* (Weinstein and Arthur Miller), f.p. Chicago, 1999; etc.
Orchestral: Symphony No.1, 1957; No.2, 1965; No.3, chbr orch, 1979; No.4 (Theodore Roethke), v, orch, 1986; No.5, 1989; No.6, 1996–7; Piano Concerto, 1976; *Songs of Innocence and of Experience* (Blake), soli, ch, orch, 1956–81; etc.
Other works: chamber music, piano works (*Three Ghost Rags*, 1970), choral pieces, art songs, cabaret songs

bolero. Spanish dance in moderate triple time, or Cuban one in syncopated 2/4. Manuel García helped make the Spanish model internationally known *c*.1800, prompting arrangements or imitations by Beethoven (in *Lieder verschiedener Völker*), Auber (in *La Muette de Portici*), Berlioz (in *Benvenuto Cellini*) and Chopin (Op.19), but the most famous example is Ravel's.

Boléro. Ballet score by Ravel, choreographed by Bronislava Nijinskaya for Ida Rubinstein, described by the composer as '20 minutes for orchestra without music'. First performance: Paris, 22 Nov 1928.

Bolet, Jorge (b. Havana, 15 Nov 1914; d. Mountain View, Cal., 16 Oct 1990). Cuban–US pianist, grand virtuoso. He studied at Curtis and later with Godowsky (1932–3), Rosenthal (1935) and Rudolf Serkin. War service took him to Japan, where in 1946 he conducted the local première of *The Mikado*. He then concentrated on playing, in the USA, though he was nearly 60 before he found widespread acclaim.

Bologna. Italian city where orchestral music by Cazzati, Vitali and Torelli flourished in the immense basilica of San Petronio during the high Baroque period (with the trumpet a speciality), the Accademia Filarmonica (founded 1666) survives among the most ancient musical societies and the Teatro Comunale (opened 1763) has a noble operatic tradition including the Italian première of *Tristan* (1888).

Bolshoy (Great). The principal opera and ballet theatre of Moscow, opened in 1825 and rebuilt in 1856. There was also a Bolshoy Theatre in St Petersburg (1783–1885).

bombard. As its name implies, an instrument of some size and power, whether a shawm, bagpipe or organ stop. A 'bombardon' can similarly be a tuba, shawm or organ stop.

bombo. Term used in the 17th–18th centuries for string tremolo.

Bond, Capel (baptized Gloucester, 14 Dec 1730; d. Coventry, 14 Feb 1790). British organist-composer, trained by the Gloucester Cathedral organist, Martin Smith, and active in Coventry from 1749. He helped animate musical life there, in Birmingham and around, especially by directing oratorio, and published a set of concertos (1766).

bones. Pair of marrow-bone clappers, inherited from traditional butchers' music.

bongos. Small Afro-Cuban drums with wooden shells, made in pairs of different sizes and played with the fingers. They have been a regular feature of the percussion department since Varèse's *Ionisation*.

Bonne Chanson, La (The Good Song). Song cycle by Fauré to nine poems by Verlaine. The composer made, and later withdrew, a version with piano quintet.

Bonney, Barbara (b. Montclair, NJ, 14 Apr 1956). US soprano of gilded purity, the outstanding Sophie (*Rosenkavalier*) of her time, but with the musical sense and verbal intelligence to cover a repertory from Rameau to contemporary art song. She studied at the University of New Hampshire and in Salzburg, began her career with the Darmstadt Opera in 1979, and made her debuts at Covent Garden in 1984 (Sophie) and the Met in 1988.

Bonno, Giuseppe (b. Vienna, 29 Jan 1711; d. Vienna, 15 Apr 1788). Austrian composer, son of an imperial footman from Brescia. Trained at the emperor's expense in Naples with Durante and Leo (1726–36), he returned to the Viennese court and married. In the 1750s he worked alongside Gluck and Dittersdorf for Field Marshal Joseph Friedrich von Sachsen-Hildburghausen, and in 1774 he succeeded Gassmann as imperial chapelmaster and conductor of the Tonkünstler Society. He was also responsible for court operas,

setting several of Metastasio's librettos for the first time, until in 1763 he retired to concentrate on sacred music. Leopold Mozart was a friend.

Bononcini, Giovanni (b. Modena, 18 Jul 1670; d. Vienna, 9 Jul 1747). Italian composer, whose operas and cantatas were admired across Europe as graceful, then forgotten as vapid. According to Hawkins, his 'genius was adapted to the expression of tender and pathetic sentiments' and his melodies were 'the richest and sweetest that we know of'.

He was the eldest of the three sons of Giovanni Maria Bononcini (1642–78), a Modenese composer of sonatas that may have influenced Purcell. The three boys were orphaned at an early age (the last of them was born an hour after their father's death) and all became noted musicians. Giovanni and Antonio Maria (1677–1726) were trained by Giovanni Colonna in Bologna, spent a while in Rome, worked as opera composers in Vienna (1697–1712), and returned to Italy, where Antonio settled in Modena. The posthumous Bononcini, Giovanni Maria (1678–1753), was a violin player in Rome from 1710.

Of the two older brothers, Giovanni enjoyed by far the greater vogue. After the death of his Roman patron (the Viennese ambassador) in 1719, he was snapped up by the Earl of Burlington for the Royal Academy of Music. In two seasons, 1720–22, he easily surpassed Handel in popularity and put the venture into profit for the first time. The two composers must have known one another, but left no comment. Despite his success, or because of it, he was faced with intrigues and suspicion (as a Catholic) and began spending more time in Paris, until he was brought back to London by the Duchess of Marlborough (1724–32). He then settled in Paris before returning to Vienna in 1736.

Bonporti, Francesco Antonio (baptized Trent, 11 Jun 1672; d. Padua, 19 Dec 1749). Italian composer of trio sonatas, concertos and inventions for violin and continuo, some of these last mistaken as works of Bach. He was trained at the German college in Rome, where he may have encountered Corelli, and spent his life as an unregarded priest in Trent and Padua.

Bontempi, Giovanni Andrea (b. Perugia, 21 Feb 1625; d. Brufa, near Perugia, 1 Jul 1705). Italian castrato, composer and music historian. Originally an Angelini, he adopted the surname of his patron Cesare Bontempi, who transferred him to Cardinal Francesco Barberini in Rome. There he studied with Mazzocchi before moving on to sing at St Mark's in Venice (1643–50). Most of the next three decades he spent in Dresden in various capacities: he was a stage designer, architect and historian, besides writing the operas *Il Paride* (1662) and *Dafne* (1671, jointly with his fellow Dresden musician Marco Giuseppe Peranda, the earliest German opera surviving in full score). He then retired to his villa outside Perugia and wrote his *Historia musica* (1695).

boobams. Small, tunable drums, played with fingers or mallets. Introduced in the 1950s, they were originally made from cut lengths of bamboo – hence the name.

boogie-woogie. Early 20th-century piano blues, often marked by a WALKING BASS in broken octaves.

Boosey & Hawkes. Music publishing and instrument firm formed in London in 1930 by the amalgamation of Boosey & Co. (founded *c*.1795 by Thomas Boosey) with Hawkes & Son (founded 1865). The new joint company engaged Erwin Stein and Ernst Roth to build up an extraordinary roster of living composers, including Stravinsky, Strauss, Bartók, Prokofiev, Rachmaninoff and Britten. By the end of the century it was the dominant Anglo–US music publishing corporation, with Carter, Birtwistle and Reich among those under contract.

Bordes, Charles (Marie Anne) (b. La Roche-Corbon, near Vouvray, 12 May 1863; d. Toulon, 8 Nov 1909). French musician, joint founder with Guilmant and d'Indy of the Schola Cantorum (1894), and, with his Chanteurs de St Gervais, reviver of Renaissance polyphony. He was a pupil of Franck and Jean François Marmontel, and also wrote songs, choral music and orchestral pieces on Basque themes, stimulated by the study of Basque music he made for the government.

Bordoni, Faustina (b. Venice, 30 Mar 1697; d. Venice, 4 Nov 1781). Italian mezzo-soprano. She studied with Michelangelo Gasparini and began singing in Venice, going on to dazzle Europe. In 1726–8 she was in London, singing Handel roles and engaging in rivalry with Francesca Cuzzoni: the two broke into a fist fight on stage during a performance of Bononcini's *Astianatte*. She married Hasse in 1730 and settled with him in Dresden, where she gave her last performance in 1751. The couple then moved to Vienna (1763) and Venice (1773).

Bordun (Ger.). Drone.

bore. Space inside a tube, especially a wind instrument. Its shaping – cylindrical (i.e. straight-sided) or conical (tapering) – will affect the sound, and most instruments have, through history, developed rather complex internal forms.

Boréades, Les (The Boreads, i.e. tribe of Boreas, the north-wind god). Opera by Rameau to a libretto by Louis de Cahusac. Alphise, queen of Bactria (soprano), and her beloved Abaris (haute-contre) are set in anxiety because she is obliged by tradition to marry a Boread and he is an unknown stranger. But it turns out he is indeed a grandson of Boreas – and son of Apollo. Rameau's last and most richly fantastical score, the work went unstaged until 1982 (Aix).

Boretz, Benjamin (b. New York, 3 Oct 1934). US composer-theorist, pupil of Irving Fine and Berger at Brandeis (1954–7) and of Babbitt and Sessions at Princeton (1959–60). He was music critic of *The Nation* (1962–9) and first editor of *Perspectives of New Music* (1962–82), while developing complex serial works, from which he passed to improvisatory performances with friends.

Boris Godunov. Opera by Musorgsky to his own libretto after Pushkin. No opera in the repertory has a more complicated history. Musorgsky radically changed the score in response to demands from the imperial theatres for a leading female role (the additions are indicated within brackets in the following synopsis), and after his death the work was revised again by Rimsky-Korsakov, whose version became standard, though other versions were used at the Kirov (Shostakovich) and the Met (Rathaus). Since the mid-1970s Musorgsky's own scoring, much starker than Rimsky's, has been widely preferred.

The Russian people are urged by police to beg Boris to accept the crown, which he does, singing a celebrated monologue 'I have attained the highest power'. Pimen, a monk, is coming to the end of his chronicle; his disciple Grigory asks him about the murdered tsarevich, Dmitry, then is found at an inn on his way to Lithuania. Boris reveals his guilt. (Grigory, now parading as the missing Dmitry, is in a glamorous, mutually cynical love affair with the Polish princess Marina Mniszek.) The Yurodivy, or holy fool, accuses Boris and laments the fate of Russia. Boris, hallucinating, dies. (A crowd welcomes 'Dmitry', and the Yurodivy's music is now placed here, with his lament ending the opera.) First performance: St Petersburg, 8 Feb 1874.

Borodin, Aleksandr (Porfiryevich) (b. St Petersburg, 12 Nov 1833; d. St Petersburg, 27 Feb 1887). Russian composer, member of the MIGHTY

HANDFUL and master of stirring melody, often oriental or epic in tone. He was a chemist by profession: composition was a spare-time activity he did not completely master until he was into his 30s. His output was correspondingly small.

The illegitimate son of a 60-year-old Georgian prince (Luka Stepanovich Gedianishvili), he was, following custom, registered as the child of one of his father's serfs, Porfiry Borodin. His father established him and his mother in some comfort, and he was educated at the Medico-Surgical Academy (1850–56). There he developed his passion for chemistry, while also playing piano duets and chamber music with friends. In 1858 he qualified as a physician, but he never practised, being already devoted to chemical resarch. Sent to Heidelberg the next year to continue his scientific studies, he met there in 1861 a Russian pianist, Yekaterina Protopopova, whom he married in April 1863, seven months after returning to St Petersburg.

While teaching at his alma mater (as professor from 1864) and working there on the distillation products of aldehydes, he encountered Balakirev and had his musical impulses quickened. He had composed chamber pieces as a boy and student, and more after meeting Yekaterina; now he started a symphony, which took him five years to complete. Advance with other scores was similarly slow, and on the opera *Prince Igor*, his magnum opus, he worked for nearly 20 years, without bringing the score to completion, despite encouragement from Liszt, among others. So long in progress, the opera was a background for his other important works – the Second Symphony, the two quartets and *In the Steppes of Central Asia* – which share both its tunefulness and its capacity to evoke legendary Russia (emphatic motifs like that of the symphony's first movement) or the languorous East. He died suddenly at a ball, of heart failure, leaving his opera and third sym-phony to be completed by friends.

Gerald Abraham *Borodin* (1927)

Opera: PRINCE IGOR, 1869–87, unfinished
Orchestral: Symphony No.1, E♭, 1862–7; No.2, B minor, 1869–76; No.3, A minor, 1882–7, unfinished; IN THE STEPPES OF CENTRAL ASIA, 1880
Chamber: String Quartet No.1, A, 1874–9; No.2, D, 1881; Scherzo, D, str qt, 1882; *Serenata alla spagnola*, str qt, 1886 (for B–La–F quartet honouring Belyayev); etc.
Songs: 'For the shores of thy far native land' (Pushkin), 1881; etc.

Borodin Quartet. Russian quartet founded in 1945, taking Borodin's name in 1955. The members during the next two decades, when the ensemble enjoyed relationships with Shostakovich and Richter, were Rostislav Dubinsky, Yaroslav Aleksandrov, Dmitry Shebalin and Valentin Berlinsky. Shebalin's retirement in 1996 left only Berlinsky from the classic team.

borrowing. Term for a composer's re-use of material or ideas from elsewhere, a practice well established in music from the earliest notated times up to Handel and Bach. Stravinsky, freely and often contravening the stricter proprieties of a later age, did not pretend to borrow: whatever he loved, he said, he would steal. See INTERTEXTUALITY; QUOTATION.

Bortnyansky, Dmitry (Stepanovich) (b. Glukhov, Ukraine, 1751; d. St Petersburg 10 Oct 1825). Russian composer, most importantly of sacred music, of which Tchaikovsky edited a complete collection. At the age of eight he joined the imperial chapel choir, latterly directed by Galuppi, whom he followed to Venice to study (1769–79), returning to the choir as chapelmaster and, from 1796, director. He also wrote French operas for the court, cantatas and piano sonatas.

Borup-Jørgensen, (Jens) Axel (b. Hjørring, 22 Nov 1924). Danish composer. Trained at the Copenhagen Conservatory (1946–50), he went through a Bartók–Holmboe phase before taking on board the lessons of Ligeti and Stockhausen at Darmstadt in 1959 and 1962, all the while working as a piano teacher. The bulk of his large output is in vocal and chamber genres, but he has also written orchestral pieces (*Marin*, 1963–70).

Bose, Hans-Jürgen von (b. Munich, 24 Dec 1953). German composer, notably of post-Henze opera. He studied with Hans Ulrich Engelmann at the conservatory in Frankfurt (1972–6) and lived as a composer until taking a post at the conservatory in Munich in 1992. His operas include *Die Leiden des jungen Werthers* (Schwetzingen, 1986), *63: Dream Palace* (Munich, 1990) and *Schlachthof V* (after Vonnegut, f.p. Munich, 1996). Among his many other works are orchestral and vocal orchestral pieces, and four quartets.

Bösendorfer. Viennese piano company founded in 1828 by Ignaz Bösendorfer (1796–1859) and approved by Liszt. In the 1890s the founder's son, Ludwig (1835–1919), introduced the Imperial Bösendorfer, with a bass compass extended down a sixth to C.

Bossi, Marco Enrico (b. Salò, Lake Garda, 25 Apr 1861; d. at sea in the Atlantic, 20 Feb 1925). Italian organist-composer. He studied with his organist father at the music school in Bologna (1871–3) and with Ponchielli at the Milan Conservatory (1873–81). Though he wrote operas, he threw his weight into organ, choral, orchestral and chamber music. He was also a teacher, in Naples (1890–95), Venice (1895–1902), Bologna (1902–11) and Rome (1916–23), and had a composer son, Renzo (1883–1965).

Boston. (1) US city, main centre of New England, noted for the BOSTON SYMPHONY ORCHESTRA, the HANDEL AND HAYDN SOCIETY, the Boston Early Music Festival (founded in 1980) and for educational institutions including HARVARD UNIVERSITY, MIT and the New England Conservatory.

(2) Slow waltz originating in the USA in the 1870s but not popular on mainland Europe until 50 years later, as noticed by Hindemith (*Suite 1922*) and Schulhoff (*Esquisses de jazz*).

Boston Pops. The Boston Symphony's light programmes, closely associated with Arthur Fiedler as their long-term conductor (1930–79).

Boston Symphony Orchestra. Leading US orchestra, founded in 1881 by Henry Lee Higginson, a banker in the city. Most of the original players were of Austro–German origin, and so were the first conductors: Georg Henschel, Wilhelm Gericke (1884–9), Nikisch (1889–93), Emil Paur (1893–8), Gericke again (1898–1906), Muck (1906–8), Max Fiedler (1908–12) and once more Muck, under whom this was the first US orchestra to make records (1917). In 1900 it moved into its own auditorium, Symphony Hall. The orchestra became more Francophone under Rabaud (1918–19), Monteux (1920–24), Koussevitzky (1924–49) and Münch (1949–62). It celebrated its 50th anniversary with commissions from Stravinsky (*Symphony of Psalms*), Prokofiev, Roussel, Copland, etc., and gave the first performances of Bartók's Concerto for Orchestra and Messiaen's *Turangalîla*. After short periods under Leinsdorf (1962–9) and William Steinberg (1969–72), it was Seiji Ozawa's orchestra for three decades (1973–2003), until he was succeeded by Levine.

Bostridge, Ian (Charles) (b. London, 25 Dec 1964). British tenor, an alluring, versatile and strikingly individual lyric personality. After history and philosophy at Oxford and Cambridge, he studied singing at the Britten–Pears School and with Fischer-Dieskau. He made his debut at the Wigmore Hall in 1993 and has performed formidably in recital (Schubert, Schumann), opera (Stravinsky's Rake) and oratorio (Bach's Evangelists).

Bote & Bock. German music publishing firm founded by Eduard Bote and Gustav Bock in Berlin in 1838 and acquired by Boosey & Hawkes in 1996.

Bottesini, Giovanni (b. Crema, 22 Dec 1821; d. Parma, 7 Jul 1889). Italian bassist-composer, early virtuoso of the instrument. The son of a clarinettist-composer, he quickly learned the double bass in order to gain a scholarship to the Milan Conservatory (1835–9), and made debuts in Crema and London in 1849. Inevitably dubbed 'the Paganini of the double bass', he wrote pieces that are indeed extremely difficult, but he also composed operas and a *Requiem*, and conducted (notably at the première of *Aida*).

bottles. An array of differently sized bottles, or of similar bottles filled with different amounts of water, can form a tuned percussion instrument (Fr. *bouteillophone*, Ger. *Flaschenspiel*, It. *suono di bottiglia*), as in Satie's *Parade*.

Bottrigari, Ercole (b. Bologna, 24 Aug 1531; d. San Alberto, near Bologna, 30 Sep 1612). Italian humanist of noble birth and wide education. His presence at the Ferrara court (1576–86) stimulated his musical interests, which he pursued in later years on his estate in company with Annibale Melone. In *Il desiderio* (1594) he wrote on musical life in Ferrara, on temperament and in support of the SECONDA PRATICA.

bouché (Fr.). Indication to hand-stop the horn.

bouche fermée (Fr., closed mouth). Hummed.

Boucourechliev, André (b. Sofia, 28 Jul 1925; d. Paris, 13 Nov 1997). Bulgarian–French composer best known for his *Archipel* series of mobile scores (e.g. *Archipel 2*, str qt, 1968). He studied as a pianist in Sofia and at the Ecole Normale de Musique in Paris, and started composing in 1954. He also wrote books on Beethoven and Stravinsky from a late-modern angle.

bouffe (Fr.). Comic, equivalent of It. *buffo/a*, as in opéra bouffe.

Boughton, Rutland (b. Aylesbury, 23 Jan 1878; d. London, 25 Jan 1960). British composer, a socialist visionary and Arthurian who scored a spectacular success with his opera *The Immortal Hour* between the wars. He studied briefly with Stanford and Walford Davies at the RCM, then taught at the Midland Institute (1905–11). In 1914 he founded the Glastonbury Festival, at which he gave regular performances of *The Immortal Hour*, other works of his own and pieces by Gluck, Purcell and others until 1927. Staged in London in 1922, *The Immortal Hour* had a run of 216 performances. Involvement of the chorus was a priority with him, as was closeness to folksong.

Boulanger. French musical sisters, daughters of Ernest Boulanger (1815–1900), a composer and violin teacher.

(1) **(Juliette) Nadia** (b. Paris, 16 Sep 1887; d. Paris, 22 Oct 1979). Teacher, especially at the American Conservatory at Fontainebleau (from 1921), where her pupils included Copland, Carter and Piston. She herself studied at the Paris Conservatoire with Fauré, later one of her touchstones, along with Stravinsky. In her youth she composed, but gave up after her sister's death, which affected her deeply. Instead she taught and occasionally conducted. She made pioneering Monteverdi recordings in the 1930s and was the first woman to conduct a symphony orchestra in London (4 Nov 1937).

Léonie Rosenstiel *Nadia Boulanger* (1982)

(2) **Lili (Marie Juliette Olga)** (b. Paris, 21 Aug 1893; d. Mézy, 15 Mar 1918). Composer, her sister's first protégé. Acquainted with Fauré from an early age, she also studied with Georges Caussade and Vidal at the Paris Conservatoire and was the first woman to win the Prix de Rome (1913). Given that she died at 24, having long been in poor health, her output is astonishing – and not only in its scale. Parallels with Debussy, Strauss and Dukas are less important than her quite individual strength of purpose.

Choral orchestral: Psalm 129 (*Ils m'ont assez opprimé*), 1910–16; Psalm 130 (*Du fond de l'abîme*), 1910–17; Psalm 24 (*La Terre appartient a l'Eternel*), 1916; *Vieille prière bouddhique*, 1917
Chamber: Nocturne, vn/fl, 1911; *D'un matin de printemps*, vn/fl, pf, also orch verison, 1917–18; *Pie Jesu*, s, str qt, hp, org, 1918
Songs: 'Reflets' (Maeterlinck), 1911; 'Attente' (Maeterlinck), 1912; 'Le retour', 1912; *Clairières dans le ciel* (13; Francis Jammes), 1913–14; 'Dans l'immense tristesse', 1916

Boulevard Solitude. See MANON LESCAUT.

Boulez, Pierre (b. Montbrison, 26 Mar 1925). French composer and conductor. The view he formed in his very early 20s – of modern music as an unfinished project, demanding a whole revolu-tion in musical life – has not changed. If, never-theless, he developed from the intemperate agitator of the early post-1945 years to the suave, genial figure of the new century, that was largely because he accomplished much of his mission. As a conductor, he helped clarify and establish the 20th-century canon. As the public voice of music in France, he brought to Paris a research institute (IRCAM) and a concert centre (the Cité de la Musique). As a composer, he provided startling and sometimes violent images of bold new beauty in his 20s, and was writing music of supreme mastery as he approached 80.

An industrialist's son, he broke away from family expectations in 1942 and went to Paris to pursue his musical ambitions. He absorbed what he needed rapidly – from Messiaen at the Conservatoire (1943–5) and Leibowitz outside (1945). A job as music director of the Renaud-Barrault theatre company (1945–55) gave him both practical experience and the freedom to compose, and he started bringing the disruptiveness of Schoenbergian serialism (as he understood it) into domains of rhythm, colour and form. His ideal was a perpetual turmoil, influenced partly by the compressed rage and savagery he found in his favourite poets, Artaud and René Char. Standard patterns – notably in the Second Piano Sonata (1947–8) – were there to be destroyed. Music was to be hurtling and dangerous.

But at the same time he was searching for new means of order in applying serial principles to durations, timbres and dynamic degrees. In the first section of the significantly titled *Structures* for two pianos (1951–2) he produced a model of TOTAL SERIALISM, and he explored similar possibilities of organization in two studies he created at the new musique concrète studio. Then came a return to Char, and to a more profuse musical poetry, in *Le Marteau sans maître* (1952–4), soon hailed as a masterpiece by colleagues from Stravinsky to Stockhausen. He was now the intellectual leader not just of a small circle in Paris but of a Europe-wide movement, conveying his ideas through compositions, frequent articles, teaching at Darmstadt (1955–67) and conducting.

He became a conductor as head of the DOMAINE MUSICAL which he had founded in 1954, and whose innovatory mixed programming (new music and 20th-century classics in the company of Gabrieli or Machaut) he took to his work in the late 1950s with the Concertgebouw and the German radio orchestras. He also began composing more often for large forces, while his demand for constant alertness and surprise in his music seemed to have been answered by the new ALEATORY principle, whereby small segments could be altered in performance and rearranged, as in his Third Piano Sonata and second book of *Structures*.

Yet he was finding it harder to satisfy himself creatively. Works were abandoned after a single performance (*Poésie pour pouvoir*), discarded as projects or kept in a perpetual state of incompletion. The Third Sonata, which he performed in 1957, still awaits its definitive form; other works of this time, such as the delectable *Pli selon pli* or the vigorous and brilliant orchestral invention *Figures–Doubles–Prismes*, have been repeatedly revised. Meanwhile, his conducting career began taking off, to the extent that by the end of the 1960s he had conducted at Bayreuth (*Parsifal*, 1966), at Covent Garden (*Pelléas*, 1969) and with most of the leading orchestras in Europe and the USA. His repertory now embraced Mahler and Beethoven, and he was making some highly charged recordings, notably of Debussy.

He duly became principal conductor of both the BBC Symphony (1971–4) and the New York Philharmonic (1971–7), which required him to broaden his repertory still further (if not as far as Tchaikovsky) and also meant losing some of the distinctive cold fury of his musicianship. Yet his legendary ear, the smart directness of his gestures (abjuring the baton) and his growing experience all combined to make him a superlative orchestral technician. Composition, though, was almost out of the question – though he did produce the uncharacteristically monumental and sombre *Rituel*, one of several works to emerge from a composition kit ('... *explosante-fixe* ...') he had made quickly in 1971 as a memorial to Stravinsky.

In 1967 he had set up home in Baden-Baden, having left Paris very publicly when his proposals for musical reform were ignored. At the end of his New York stint he again made Paris his professional centre, helping shape the institution the government was making for him: IRCAM. He drastically scaled down his conducting to leave just the *Ring* at Bayreuth (1976–80) and a few other engagements, and began learning the new language of computer music, spectacularly displayed in *Répons* (1980–84), for six soloists on tuned percussion (including piano and harp) with mixed ensemble. The sonic glamour of ripples and resonances went back through his music to *Eclat*, *Pli selon pli* and *Le Marteau sans maître*, but the electronic transformation and spatial redisposition of the sounds were new.

While continuing to work at IRCAM on pieces combining live and electronic means (*Dialogue de l'ombre double*, the definitive flute-concerto version of '... *explosante-fixe* ...', *Anthèmes II*), he has gone back to orchestral conducting, re-recording much of the repertory closest to him

(Debussy, Stravinsky, Webern, Ravel) and allowing himself to expand a little (Strauss, Bruckner). He has also worked on the continuing *Notations*, in which the explosive ideas of his 20-year-old self are lavishly and gorgeously reconsidered.

Pierre Boulez *Conversations with Célestin Deliège* (1976); William Glock, ed. *Pierre Boulez* (1986)

Vocal orchestral: *Le Visage nuptial* (Char), s, mez, women's ch, orch, 1946, rev 1950–51, 1986–9; *Le Soleil des eaux* (Char), s, ch, orch, 1948, rev 1958, 1965; PLI SELON PLI (Mallarmé), s, orch, 1957–62; *Cummings ist der Dichter*, small ch, small orch, 1970, rev 1986

Orchestral: *Poésie pour pouvoir* (Michaux), orch, tape, 1958; *Figures–Doubles–Prismes*, 1957–68; *Livre pour cordes*, str, 1968, rev 1988; *Rituel*, 1974–5; *Notations*, 1977–80 (I–IV), 1998 (VII)

Ensemble: *Polyphonie X*, 18 insts, 1951; *Le* MARTEAU SANS MAITRE (Char), a, 6 insts, 1952–4; ECLAT, 15 insts, 1965, extended as *Eclat/Multiples*, 24 insts, 1970; *Domaines*, cl, 21 insts, 1961–8; *Messagesquisse*, 7 vc, 1976; *Répons*, 6 perc, small orch, elec, 1980–84; *Dérive I*, 6 insts, 1984; *II*, 11 insts, 1987–91; *Mémoriale*, fl, 8 insts, 1985; *Initiale*, brass, 1987; '... *explosante-fixe* ...', fl, small orch, elec, 1971–93; *sur Incises*, 3 pf, 3 hp, 3 vib, 1995–6

Chamber: *Sonatine*, fl, pf, 1946; *Livre pour quatuor*, str qt, 1948–9; *Dialogue de l'ombre double*, cl, elec, 1982–5; *Anthèmes*, vn, 1991; *Anthèmes II*, vn, elec, 1997

Piano: *Douze notations*, 1945; *Sonata No.1*, 1946; *No.2*, 1948; *No.3*, 1955–7, unfinished; *Structures*, duo, 1951–2 (I), 1956–61 (II); *Incises*, 1994

Tape: *Etudes I–II*, 1952

Boult, Adrian (Cedric) (b. Chester, 8 Apr 1889; d. London, 22 Feb 1983). British conductor of reticent care and aplomb, knighted in 1937. After Oxford he went to Germany, where he studied at the Leipzig Conservatory (1912–13) and watched Nikisch. Back home he took on various tasks, in opera, with the Ballets Russes, with choirs, etc., while the première of *The Planets* (1918) began his long association with British music. He was then principal conductor of the Birmingham orchestra (1924–30), the new BBC SO (1930–50) and the LPO (1950–56), and went on conducting and recording to the age of 89.

Michael Kennedy *Adrian Boult* (1987)

bourdon (Fr.). Drone.

Bourgeois, Loys (b. Paris, *c*.1510–15; d. 1560 or later). French church musician, active in Geneva by 1545 setting psalms. At first all went well, but in 1551 he came under attack for introducing new tunes, and in 1553 he returned to France.

bourrée (Fr.; older Eng. forms boree, borry).

French folkdance that went to court and so became a common feature of the Baroque suite, characterized by moderate duple time and simplicity. There are bourrées in Lully and Rameau operas, all but one of Bach's orchestral suites and Handel's *Water Music*.

Bouzignac, Guillaume (b. ?St Nazaire d'Aude, near Narbonne, *c*.1587; d. after 1642). French composer and church musician, master, in his many motets, of expressive word-painting in an essentially homophonic or antiphonal style. He was trained as a chorister at Narbonne Cathedral, and held posts as master of the choirboys in various provincial cathedrals and churches.

bow (Fr. *archet*, Ger. *Bogen, Streichbogen*, It. *arco*). Device for drawing sound from a string instrument; in verb form, the drawing: one bows with a bow. The working part is a length of some material (conventionally horsehair) that will make the string vibrate, this material being held in tension by attachment at each end to a curved stick of wood (pernambuco, a variety of brazilwood, being preferred). At one end the attachment is by way of a 'frog', which may be fixed or movable, and which may allow the tension to be adjusted. The bow is normally gripped in the right hand at that end, though personal style or historical information may dictate a different place on the bow, and the posture of the hand, too, can vary with the player, instrument or style.

Bows go back to ancient times in many parts of the world as weapons of war and the hunt. As musical implements they can be traced to 10th-century Byzantium and Islam, being introduced to western Europe in the following century. Illustrations suggest a variety of shapes, lengths and grips up to the mid 18th century. The bow was then regularized by Tourte around 1785, with a slightly concave stick of standard length – about 29 inches (73–4cm) for violin bows – a little weightier than before, a movable frog with screw adjustment, and a generous width of hair, features that had emerged in the 'transitional bow' of the previous 15 years or so. Greater exposure of the hair, and greater tension, allowed more immediate attack and a widened dynamic range. The Tourte model has been reproduced for more than two centuries, latterly joined by copies of earlier styles for historically informed performance.

bowed piano. Piano in which the strings are bowed, so that tones may be continuous. The ancestor of such instruments was the *Geigenwerk* made by Hans Haiden in Nuremberg in 1575; depressing its keys caused strings to be brought up against a revolving wheel. Many instruments using this principle or others were developed during the next two and a half centuries, none of them surmounting problems of intonation and maintenance. An alternative approach – having a grand piano played by musicians with bows – has been used by Radulescu and Stephen Scott.

Bowen, (Edwin) York (b. London, 22 Feb 1884; d. 23 Nov 1961). British pianist-composer. He studied at the RAM (1898–1905) and taught there from 1909. His music, admired by Saint-Saëns, includes four symphonies and various chamber works, as well as four concertos and much else for his own instrument.

bowing. (1) Technique of using the bow, involving choice of downbow or upbow, weight and speed of stroke, and special effects (MARTELE; RICOCHET; SPICCATO; STACCATO).

(2) Marking of bowstrokes in a score or part. Such marking may be made by the composer or added by the player, conductor or leader of a section.

Bowles, Paul (Frederic) (b. New York, 30 Dec 1910; d. Tangier, 18 Nov 1999). US writer and sometime composer, who studied with Copland, Thomson and Boulanger, and produced a substantial output of song operas, ballets, songs and small instrumental pieces, mostly in the 1930s and 1940s.

Bowman, James (Thomas) (b. Oxford, 6 Nov 1941). British countertenor, whose rich voice, simultaneously ardent and plaintive, was strong in the early-music revival of the 1960s–70s. He studied at Oxford, made his stage debut as Oberon with the English Opera Group (1967), and soon had Britten writing for him (*Journey of the Magi*, Voice of Apollo in *Death in Venice*).

Boyce, William (b. London, Sep 1711; d. Kensington, 7 Feb 1779). British composer, of splendid overtures (the *Eight Symphonys* he published in 1760), church music, odes and theatre songs. Born to a City cabinet-maker, he was a chorister at St Paul's and stayed on there until 1734, apprenticed to the organist, Greene. Later he studied with Pepusch, while supporting himself as a church organist, as composer to the Chapel Royal (from 1736) and by writing theatre scores (beginning with the masque *Peleus and Thetis*, 1740). Probably in 1748 he married. In 1755 he was named Master of the King's Music, requiring him to write New Year and birthday odes, and these became virtually his whole production, in a style noble but increasingly antiquated. He also worked on editing settings of the last 200 years for his three published volumes of *Cathedral Music*, which helped carry Purcell into the 19th century. His own music, though, was largely forgotten until resuscitated by the mid-20th-century Baroque revival.

Boyd, Anne (Elizabeth) (b. Sydney, 18 Apr 1946). Australian composer, whose music often approaches an Asian spirit. She studied with Sculthorpe at Sydney University and with Mellers and Rands at York (1969–72), and has taught at the universities of Sussex (1972–7), Hong Kong (1981–90) and, thereafter, Sydney. Her works include children's operas, choral music (*As I crossed a bridge of dreams*, 1975), three quartets and piano pieces (*Angklung*, 1974).

boy soprano. TREBLE.

Bozza, Eugène (b. Nice, 4 Apr 1905; d. Valenciennes, 28 Sep 1991). French composer, trained at the Paris Conservatoire, who made a speciality of wind chamber music, though he also wrote operas, oratorios and symphonies. He was director of the Ecole Normale de Musique in Valenciennes (1951–75).

Br. Ger. abbreviation for *Bratsche* (viola).

brace. Left-edge bracket joining staves into a system. A full score often has a brace for each orchestral section, in the form of a thick vertical line with flares at top and bottom. In keyboard music the brace is thus: {.

Brade, William (b. 1560; d. Hamburg, 26 Feb 1630). English violinist who spent almost all his adult life abroad, at the courts of the Danish king and various German princes, and in Hamburg. He published several volumes of dances.

Brahms, Johannes (b. Hamburg, 7 May 1833; d. Vienna, 3 Apr 1897). German composer who carried the Classical tradition into the high Romantic period. No great composer was more aware of responsibilities to the past – especially to Beethoven, but also to Bach, Haydn and Mozart – and none was more learned. If, with him, responsibility became regret – the regret felt by a latecomer – the resulting sense of longing, of loss, of the irretrievable, he expressed with clear-eyed fullness and nobility.

Like Beethoven, he was the son of a lowly musician in northern Germany; his father was a bass player in Hamburg. As a boy of seven he began piano studies there with Otto Cossel, who in 1846 recommended him to Eduard Marxsen for theory training. In 1848 he gave his first full recital; two years later he encountered Eduard Reményi, a Hungarian violinist, and in 1853 they went on a tour, which gave him a taste for the gypsy music of Hungarian cafés, to be honoured in piano duets and in some of his finales. Afterwards he visited the Schumanns in Düsseldorf, eliciting Schumann's last article, an enthusiastic greeting to the young composer, whose works at this stage consisted of songs and piano pieces (notably three sonatas).

In 1855 he started a symphony, but more than two decades passed before the work was completed; indeed, almost all his important orchestral scores date from after his 40th birthday. Schumann's praise can only have exacerbated his self-criticism; Schumann's death created another problem, for he found himself in love with the grieving widow. Clara's response was gentle dissuasion, but she remained his friend, supporter and sounding board, and his affection for her may have interfered with any other attachment. He stayed a bachelor – though in the summer of 1858 he contemplated marriage with Agathe von Siebold, who stirred him to a succession of love songs and duets that year, and there were flirtatious relationships later. Meanwhile, in the autumns of 1857–9 he found employment at the Detmold court, for which he wrote two serenades, his first orchestral works.

Also in 1857 he and his staunch musical ally Joachim began their public separation from Liszt and the New German School. This may have dismayed the New Germans, since Brahms was so obviously gifted and clearly had the makings (in his piano ballades, for instance) of a Romantic storyteller. It also antagonized some sectors of the audience, for he and his First Piano Concerto had a rough ride in Leipzig in 1859, a few days after the successful Hanover première. But his traditionalist stance was true to him, and certainly did nothing to prevent his development. Within the next few years came a succession of chamber works, as well as virtuoso piano variations, songs and pieces for the women's choir he was directing in Hamburg.

His disagreement with the little Lisztians (more than with Liszt himself) went beyond his discomfort with programme music. The particle he most often liked to use in his musical syntax was 'and': he wanted to write new music and, emphatically, express his veneration of the past, to maintain the great 19th-century discovery of the authorial melodic voice and, most definitely, to create a rich pile of contrapuntally active harmony, to bring together distant keys in one smooth flow – even to write in duple and triple time simultaneously, creating his characteristic lilt. Extravagant in his demands of himself, he was embarrassed by outward show. His orchestration attains a kind of invisibility, just there to make the music happen. Similarly, he had problems with the virtuoso role to which his education and his gifts had led him – and which he had fulfilled in writing the sonatas, ballades and concerto of the 1850s. He went on giving concerts, but his last showpiece was the Paganini Variations (1862–3), which he wrote not for himself but for Tausig. The more frequent and characteristic works of this most companionable composer (who could also be abrupt with his friends on occasion) are those in which the piano is joined by a like-minded group – of string colleagues in the piano trios, quartets and quintet, or of orchestral musicians in his Second Piano Concerto, so different from the first in this aspect of dialogue. But a pianist did not make a fortune in the 19th century (or later) by manifesting equality.

Had he been born a century later, he would have found a waiting home for his concerns – with composition, scholarship and the fostering of the young (he was remarkable in his help to Dvořák, Dohnányi, Zemlinsky and many others) – at a university. As it was, conducting seemed the obvious way to make a living. So in 1862 he left for Vienna, in the hope of enhancing his reputation and being called back to Hamburg to conduct the philharmonic concerts. That call never came. Instead he found other posts in Vienna, though only briefly, as director of the Singakademie (1863–4) and of the Geschellschaftskonzerte (1872–5). The deaths of his mother in 1865 and of his father seven years later reduced the need to go back to Hamburg, and soon the royalties he gained, thanks to advances in copyright law, supplemented his income from winter-season concerts enough that he could live in modest comfort.

The ending of his hopes for a conducting post coincided rather neatly with the full beginning of his career as an orchestral composer, since the long-delayed First Symphony, finally completed in 1876, was followed at a rush by the Second, the Violin Concerto, a pair of overtures (Academic Festival and Tragic) and the Second Piano Concerto. He did not, however, give up performing during these busy years: he conducted widely as a guest in Germany and surrounding countries and appeared frequently at the piano. He also made holiday trips regularly from 1878 onwards to Italy, without any discernible effect on his music. One frequent stop during all his peregrinations in the 1880s was at Meiningen, where von Bülow placed the magnificent court orchestra at his disposal. This facilitated the births of his Third and Fourth symphonies, of which the latter ends

with an imposing passacaglia, bringing his symphonic output back to what he would have perceived as its origins, in Bach. After that, his only orchestral work was the Double Concerto for violin and cello (1887), also a homage to Bach.

Three years later he determined to retire, but was prevented from doing so by the artistry of the clarinettist Richard Mühlfeld, for whom he wrote a trio, a quintet and two sonatas in 1891–4 – autumnal music created during summers at the spa resort of Bad Ischl, where he would occasionally enjoy the company of the Strauss family whose waltzes he admired so much (and sometimes emulated, in his own style). After those clarinet works he did indeed stop composing, but restarted to write the *Vier ernste Lieder* and a set of 11 chorale preludes in response to Clara Schumann's death, in May 1896. He went to the funeral and was dead himself within a year.

By this point his orchestral works, chamber music, big piano pieces and songs had all moved smoothly into the places in the core repertory they might have been made for (and indeed were). Correspondingly, they irritated Mahler and Wolf as instances of Vienna-centred conformity, and little more than a decade later they seemed so old fashioned that the young modernists hardly troubled to reject them. Schoenberg, though, was to hail in an article 'Brahms the Progressive' and point to important features of his own music – irregular but satisfying phrasing, a strong motivic binding of works and movements – that had their roots in Brahms. Brahms's creative veneration of the past, too, opened a path whose ending is not yet in sight.

Jan Swafford *Johannes Brahms* (1997); Michael Musgrave *A Brahms Reader* (2000)

Orchestral music

Symphonies: No.1, C minor, Op.68, 1862–76, f.p. Karlsruhe, 4 Nov 1876; No.2, D, Op.73, 1877, f.p. Vienna, 30 Dec 1877; No.3, F, Op.90, 1883, f.p. Vienna, 2 Dec 1883; No.4, E minor, 1884–5, f.p. Meiningen, 25 Oct 1885

Concertos: PIANO CONCERTO No.1, D minor, Op.15, 1854–9; No.2, B♭, Op.83, 1881; VIOLIN CONCERTO, D, Op.77, 1878; DOUBLE CONCERTO, A minor, Op.102, vn, vc, orch, 1887

Other works without voices: Serenade No.1, D, Op.11, 1857–8; No.2, A, Op.16, 1858–9, rev 1875; VARIATIONS ON A THEME OF HAYDN, Op.56a, 1873; 3 Hungarian Dances, G minor, F, F, 1873 (from pf duets); ACADEMIC FESTIVAL OVERTURE, Op.80, 1880; Tragic Overture, Op.81, 1880

Works with voices: *Ave Maria*, Op.12, women's ch, orch, 1858; *Begräbnisgesang*, Op.13, ch, wind, timp, 1858; *Ein* DEUTSCHES REQUIEM, Op.45, s, bar, ch, orch, 1865–8; RINALDO, Op.50, t, men's ch, orch, 1863–8; Rhapsody (Goethe), Op.53, a, men's ch, orch, 1869; *Liebeslieder*, 4 solo v, orch, 1870 (from Op.52 and Op.65); *Schicksalslied* (Hölderlin), Op.54, ch, orch, 1868–71; *Triumphlied* (Revelation), Op.55, bar, ch, orch, 1870–71; *Nänie* (Schiller), Op.82, ch, orch, 1880–81; *Gesang der Parzen* (Goethe), Op.89, ch, orch, 1882

Chamber and instrumental music

String quartets: Nos.1–2, C minor, A minor, Op.51, ?1865–1873; No.3, B♭, Op.67, 1875

String quintets (str qt + va): No.1, F, Op.88, 1882; No.2, G, Op.111, 1890

String sextets: No.1, B♭, Op.18, 1859–60; No.2, G, Op.36, 1864–5

Piano quintet: F minor, Op.34, 1862

Clarinet quintet: B minor, Op.115, 1891

Piano quartets: No.1, G minor, Op.25, 1861; No.2, A, Op.26, 1861; No.3, C minor, Op.60, 1855–75

Piano trios: No.1, B, Op.8, 1853–4, rev 1889; No.2, C, Op.87, 1880–82; No.3, C minor, Op.101, 1886

Clarinet trio: A minor, Op.114, cl/va, vc, pf, 1891

Horn trio: E♭, Op.40, vn, hn, pf, 1865

Violin sonatas: No.1, G, Op.78, 1878–9; No.2, A, Op.100, 1886; No.3, D minor, Op.108, 1886–8; Scherzo, C minor, 1853 (for 'F–A–E' sonata with Schumann and Dietrich)

Cello sonatas: No.1, E minor, Op.38, 1862–5; No.2, F, Op.99, 1886

Clarinet/viola sonatas: Nos.1–2, F minor, E♭, Op.120, 1894

Piano sonatas: No.1, C, Op.1, 1852–3; No.2, F♯ minor, Op.2, 1852; No.3, F minor, Op.5, 1853

Piano variations: Variations on a Theme of Schumann, Op.9, 1854; Variations on an Original Theme, Op.21:1, 1857; Variations on a Hungarian Song, Op.21:2, 1856; Variations and Fugue on a Theme of Handel, Op.24, 1861; Variations on a Theme of Paganini, Op.35, 1862–3

Other solo piano works: Scherzo, E♭, minor, Op.4, 1851; Ballades, D minor, D, B minor, B, Op.10, 1854; Waltzes, Op.39, 1865 (from duets); Hungarian Dances, pub 1872 (from duets); 8 Pieces, Op.76, 1871–8; Rhapsodies, B minor, G minor, Op.79, 1879; Fantasias, Op.116, by 1892; 3 Intermezzos, Op.117, 1892; 6 Pieces, Op.118, by 1893; 4 Pieces, Op.119, by 1893; etc.

Piano duo: Sonata, F minor, Op.34b, 1864; Variations on a Theme of Haydn, Op.56b, 1873

Piano duet: Variations on a Theme of Schumann, Op.23, 1861; Waltzes, Op.39, 1865; Hungarian Dances, 1868 (10), 1880 (11)

Organ: 11 Chorale Preludes, Op.122, 1896; etc.

Small-scale vocal music

Motets: Psalm 13, Op.27, women's ch, org/pf, str ad lib, 1859; 2 Motets, Op.29, 1856–60; 3 Sacred Choruses, Op.37, women's ch, ?1859–63; 2 Motets, Op.74, 1863–77; 3 Motets, Op.110, by 1889

Partsongs: 4 Songs, Op.17, women's ch, 2 hn, hp, 1860; *Marienlieder*, Op.22, 1859; *Geistliches Lied*, Op.30, ch, org/pf, 1856; 5 Songs, Op.41, men's ch, 1861–2; 3 Songs, Op.42, 1859–61; 12 Songs and Romances, Op.44, women's ch, 1859–60; 7 Songs,

Op.62, 1873–4; 6 Songs and Romances, Op.93a, 1883; *Tafellied* (Eichendorff), Op.93b, ch, pf, 1884; 5 Songs, Op.104, ?1886–1888; *Fest- und Gedenksprüche*, Op.109, ?1888–9; etc.

Quartets: 3, Op.31, 1859–63; LIEBESLIEDER, Op.52, s, a, t, b, pf duet, 1868–9; 3, Op.64, 1864–74; *Neue Liebeslieder* (SEE LIEBESLIEDER), Op.65, s, a, t, b, pf duet, 1869–74; 4, Op.92, 1877–84; *Zigeunerlieder*, Op.103, 1887–8; 6, Op.112, 1888–91

Duets: 3 Duets, Op.20, 1858–60; 4 Duets, Op.28, 1860–62; 4 Duets, Op.61, 1852–74; 5 Duets, Op.66, 1873–5; 4 Ballads and Romances, Op.75, 1877–8

Song cycles/sets: Romances from Tieck's *Magelone*, 1861–?1868; *Ophelia-Lieder*, 1873; Two Songs, Op.91, a, va, pf, 1863–84; VIER ERNSTE GESÄNGE, Op.121, 1896

Songs: 'Alte Liebe' (Karl August Candidus), Op.72:1, 1876; 'An die Nachtigall' (Ludwig Hölty and Johann Heinrich Voss), Op.46:4, by 1868; 'Auf dem Kirchhofe' (Detlev von Liliencron), Op.105:4, by 1888; 'Auf dem See' (Karl Joseph Simrock), Op.59:2, 1873; 'Botschaft' (Georg Friedrich Daumer, after Hafiz), Op.47:1, 1868; 'Dein blaues Auge' (Klaus Groth), Op.59:8, 1873; 'Feldeinsamkeit' (Hermann Allmers), Op.86:2, by 1882; 'Der Gang zum Liebchen' (Josef Wenzig, after Bohemian trad), Op.48:1, 1859–62; 'Geheimnis' (Candidus), Op.71:3, 1877; 'Immer leiser wird mein Schlummer' (Hermann von Lingg), Op.105:2, 1886; 'Lerchengesang' (Candidus), Op.70:2, 1877; 'Liebestreu' (Robert Reinick), Op.3:1, 1853; 'Des Liebsten Schwur' (Wenzig, after Bohemian trad), Op.69:4, 1877; 'Das Mädchen spricht' (Otto Friedrich Gruppe), Op.107:3, 1886; 'Mädchenlied' (Heyse), Op.107.5, by 1888; 'Die Mainacht' (Hölty), Op.43:2, 1866; 'Meerfahrt' (Heine), Op.96:4, by 1885; 'Meine Liebe ist grün' (Felix Schumann), Op.63.5, 1873; 'Nicht mehr zu dir' (Daumer, after Bohemian trad), Op.32:2, 1864; 'O kühler Wald' (Brentano), Op.72:3, 1877; 'O wüsst ich doch' (Groth), Op.63:8, 1874; 'Sapphische Ode' (Hans Schmidt), Op.94:4, by 1884; 'Sonntag' (Uhland), Op.47:3, by 1860; 'Ständchen' (Franz Theodor Kugler), Op.106:1, by 1888; 'Therese' (Keller), Op.86:1, 1878; 'Der Tod, das ist die kühle Nacht' (Heine), Op.96:1, by 1885; 'Vergebliches Ständchen' (Anton von Zuccalmaglio, after Ger. trad), Op.84:4, by 1882; 'Von ewiger Liebe' (Wenzig), Op.43:1, 1864; 'In Waldeseinsamkeit' (Karl von Lemcke), Op.85:6, 1878; 'Wiegenlied' (LULLABY), Op.49:4, 1868; 'Wie bist du' (Daumer, after Hafiz), Op.32:9, 1864; 'Wie Melodien zieht es mir' (Groth), Op.105:1, 1886; 'Wie rafft ich' (August von Platen), Op.32:1, 1864; 'Wir wandelten' (Daumer, after trad), Op.96:2, by 1885

Brain, Dennis (b. London, 17 May 1921; d. Hatfield, Herts., 1 Sep 1957). British horn player, of supreme and cheerful virtuosity. His father Aubrey (1893–1955) and uncle Alfred (1885–1966) were also virtuosos of the instrument, and his father was his teacher at the RAM. He made benchmark recordings of the Mozart concertos and Britten's Serenade (written for him), and was much lamented at his early death in a car accident.

Branca, Glenn (b. Harrisburg, Penn., 6 Oct 1948). US composer who arrived in New York in 1976 after theatre studies at Emerson College, Boston, and created a stir in the early 1980s with extremely loud symphonies for electric guitars. These works led to orchestral commissions and so to further symphonies for orchestra, sometimes with chorus.

Brand, Max (b. Lemberg/Lviv, 26 Apr 1896; d. Langenzersdorf, near Vienna, 5 Apr 1980). Austrian–US composer, pupil of Schreker, Hába and Erwin Stein. He used a broad range of styles – luxurious, atonal, jazzy – to create an optimistic portrait of the technological world in *Maschinist Hopkins* (Duisburg, 1929), one of the most talked-about (and least performed) operas of its time. Banned by the Nazis, he left Europe in 1938 and settled in the USA two years later, retiring to the Vienna suburbs in 1975. His later stage works include *The Gate* (1944) and *The Astronauts* (1962, with electronics).

Brandenburg Concertos. Usual name for six works J.S. Bach dedicated in 1721 to Christian Ludwig, Margrave of Brandenburg (who may never have had them played): No.1, F, soli (ob, vn, 2 hn), 2 ob, bn, str, con; No.2, F, soli (rec, ob, tpt, vn), str, con; No.3, G, 3 vn, 3 va, 3 vc, con; No.4, G, soli (2 rec, vn), str, con; No.5, D, soli (fl, vn, hpd), str, con; No.6, B♭, 2 va, 2 va da gamba, vc, con.

branle, bransle (Fr.; older Eng. forms brawl, etc.). French country dance having many distinct kinds and local varieties – slow and fast, in duple, triple, compound and mixed metres – but always a round dance, and often with singing. Such dances, associated with rustic instruments (bagpipes, shawms), became popular at court in France in the 16th century, and the new term for them ousted the older *carole*. Bucolic and rough, they then entered the consciousness of French ballet music, as far as Rameau. Stravinsky's *Agon* includes branles of types given in Arbeau's *Orchésographie*.

Brant, Henry (Dreyfuss) (b. Montreal, 15 Sep 1913). Canadian–US composer of music for unusual combinations, often in widely separated ensembles. Having started building his own instruments as a young boy, he studied at the McGill Conservatorium (1926–9) and Juilliard (1929–34). He remained in New York as a commercial arranger and teacher, then took a post at Bennington College, Vermont (1957–80). Early examples of his non-standard instrumentation include *Angels and Devils* for solo flute with 10 other members of the flute family (1931) and *Music for a Five and Dime Store* for violin, piano and kitchen utensils (1932). His spatial conceptions began with *Antiphony 1* for five orchestral groups (1953) and often rejoice in the haphazard, sometimes involving improvisation.

brass. Family of tubular instruments made of that metal and blown into with vibrating lips and a setting of the mouth (EMBOUCHURE) that controls which harmonic is played. Natural instruments have only this method of choosing pitch; alternatives are valves (introduced *c*.1814) or a slide (trombones). The introduction of valves, making the instruments more versatile, accompanied both the evolution of harmony and the greater brass presence in the orchestra. A pair of horns was standard for Haydn and Mozart, joined sometimes by trumpets and, more rarely, trombones (for church music and opera). Beethoven introduced the new norm of a full ensemble of trumpets, horns and trombones, joined by a tuba in the mid 19th century. Resplendent by themselves, the orchestral brass also combine mightily with low strings, while often remembering their earlier lives with the hunt (horns) and fanfare ensembles (trumpets).

Trevor Herbert and John Wallace, ed. *The Cambridge Companion to Brass Instruments* (1997)

brass band. Collectivity of brass instruments or players, commonly numbering about 25. It is essentially a British amateur phenomenon, with strong roots especially in northern England, which is where many early brass bands were organized, from the 1830s onwards, as lusty expressions of particular mills or factories, e.g. the Black Dyke Mills Band, founded in 1855. Such bands perform at social events and, most assiduously, in local and national competitions. Their instruments they inherited from military bands – cornets, flugelhorns, saxhorns, euphoniums, trombones – while their music is generally a world of its own, though one explored occasionally by outside composers, notably Birtwistle.

Trevor Herbert, ed. *The British Brass Band* (2000)

brass quintet. Group of instruments consisting of two trumpets, horn, trombone and tuba or second trombone; or a group of players on those instruments; or a genre of music for that medium; or a work of that genre. Music for brass ensemble has a long history, in fanfare and TOWER MUSIC, to which more recent performing groups (beginning with the New York Brass Quintet, founded in 1954) have added a repertory of works for quintet by Carter, Davies and others.

Bratsche (Ger., from the It. *braccio*, as in *viola da braccio*, pl. *Bratschen*). Viola.

Braunfels, Walter (b. Frankfurt, 19 Dec 1882; d. Cologne, 19 Mar 1954). German composer, a late Romantic with a light touch. Trained first as a pianist (with James Kwast in Frankfurt and Leschetizky in Vienna) he later studied with Thuille and Mottl in Munich. In 1925 he became director of the Cologne conservatory, to which he returned after living in retirement during the Nazi years. His works include operas (*Die Vögel*, after Aristophanes, 1913–19), orchestral pieces and sacred cantatas (he was a Catholic convert).

bravoure (Fr.). Bravura.

bravura (It.). Bold skill, usually on the part of a solo performer. One may speak of a display of bravura, a bravura passage, etc.

Brazil. South American country settled in the 16th–19th centuries by Portuguese and African peoples. European-style church music is patchily recorded before the 18th century; opera and domestic music took off after the achievement of independence (under John VI of Portugal) in 1822. Later Brazilian composers include Gomes, Villa-Lobos and Antunes.

break. (1) Region of overlap between different vocal or instrumental registers, registers distinguished by their performance techniques and tonal qualities. Care is needed to negotiate the break.
(2) Cadenza.
(3) Change at puberty from a boy's voice to a man's.

Bream, Julian (Alexander) (b. Battersea, 15 Jul 1933). British guitarist and lutenist, and a pioneer of those instruments. Introduced to the guitar by his father, he studied at the RCM but had to find guitar lessons outside. He made his London debut in 1950 and was soon touring internationally, playing music written for him by Britten, Henze, etc.

Brecht, Bertolt (Eugen Friedrich) (b. Augsburg, 10 Feb 1898; d. Berlin, 14 Aug 1956). German playwright and poet who worked often with composers, though he was emphatically not a librettist: for him the play was the thing, strung with songs for their moral-expressive bite and realism. His major collaborations were with Weill in pre-Nazi Germany, with Dessau in East Berlin (where he settled in 1949) and with Eisler all through.

breeches part. TRAVESTI part.

breit (Ger.). Broad, grand.

Breitkopf & Härtel. German music publishing firm founded in Leipzig, probably in 1719, by Bernhard Christoph Breitkopf (1695–1777), whose son Johann Gottlob Immanuel (1719–94) modernized the music printing process and put out works by Haydn, as well as his friends C.P.E. Bach and Hiller. Gottfried Christoph Härtel (1763–1827), brought into the company by Johann's sons, bought it in 1796, introduced lithography, keenly acquired works from Beethoven (as well as from Mozart's widow) and instituted complete editions of Haydn and Mozart. The house was strong throughout the 19th century and maintained its record of complete editions into the 20th.

Brendel, Alfred (b. Wiesenberg, 5 Jan 1931). Austrian pianist, whose performances are the workings of a lively, quizzical mind. He studied in Zagreb and Graz, had composition lessons and gained from masterclasses with Edwin Fischer. In the 1950s he made many recordings, including repertory to which he has stayed close: the Beethoven and Schubert sonatas, late Liszt, Schoenberg. His international eminence in recital dates from his first complete Beethoven sonata cycle in London (1962) and first US tour (1963). He has also written poetry and musical essays (*Alfred Brendel on Music*, 2001).

Brentano. German artistic family with French–Italian forebears. Clemens Brentano (1778–1842) was a poet and co-author with Achim von Arnim of *Des* KNABEN WUNDERHORN. His sister Bettina (1785–1859), who married von Arnim, was on close terms with Beethoven, whose Immortal Beloved may have been their stepsister-in-law Antonie.

Bresgen, Cesar (b. Florence, 16 Oct 1913; d. Salzburg, 7 Apr 1988). German–Austrian composer, in the Orff line. He studied at the academy in Munich (1930–36), and in 1939 settled in Salzburg, where he taught at the Mozarteum and at his own music school. In 1945, in Mittersill, he came to know Webern, for whom he wrote a *Requiem* (1945–72). Other works include operas, children's operas and concertos.

Bresnick, Martin (b. New York, 13 Nov 1946). US composer, fertile and forceful. He studied at

Stanford (1967–72), taking a year out at the Vienna Academy under von Einem (1969–70). After three further years at Stanford on the faculty, he moved to Yale in 1976 and became one of the most sought-after composition teachers. His works include a set of 12 *Opere della music povera* (1990–99), each in a different 'key' and bouncing against limitations.

Bretón (y Hernández), Tomás (b. Salamanca, 29 Dec 1859; d. Madrid, 2 Dec 1923). Spanish composer, especially of operas with lively local colour (the farce *La verbena de la paloma*, 1894; *La Dolores*, 1895). He was earning his living as a violinist at 12, and later studied composition with Emilio Arrieta at the Madrid Conservatory and abroad, going on to a career as a composer, conductor and teacher in Madrid.

Bréval, Jean-Baptiste Sébastien (b. Paris, 6 Nov 1753; d. Colligis, Aisne, 18 Mar 1823). French cellist-composer. A pupil of Jean-Baptiste Cupis, he was active in Paris from the mid 1770s as a player, teacher and composer, producing seven cello concertos, several *symphonies concertantes*, quartets and cello sonatas, all by 1795. After that he concentrated on his cello method (1804), then played for a decade at the Opera.

breve (GB, from Lat. *brevis*, short; Fr. *brève*, It. *breve*). Double whole note (US). DURATION known from the 13th century as a division (half or third) of the long, rare in modern notation. See also ALLA BREVE.

breviary. Book with texts, and sometimes notated chants, for the DIVINE OFFICE.

Bréville, Pierre (Eugène Onfroy) de (b. Bar-le-Duc, 21 Feb 1861; d. Paris, 24 Sep 1949). French composer, who, after training as a diplomat, was a pupil of Franck. He taught, was active in the Société Nationale de Musique and wrote criticism. His works include an opera (*Eros vainqueur*, 1905), sacred and secular choral pieces, and an abundance of songs, setting choice poetry from Villon and Charles d'Orléans to Francis Jammes and Jean Moréas.

Brian, (William) Havergal (b. Dresden, Staffs., 29 Jan 1876; d. Shoreham, 28 Nov 1972). British composer, especially of 32 symphonies, of which he wrote 21 when he was past 80 and the last when he was 92. This extraordinary late harvest followed long neglect. Self-taught, he had made a break-through with a choral setting of the Shakespeare sonnet 'Shall I compare thee' (1905), but after the First World War was known almost exclusively as a

critic. Nevertheless, he went on composing, sometimes on an immense scale: his Symphony No.1 'Gothic' (1919–27) incorporates a *Te Deum* for huge choral-orchestral forces. The belated première of this work, in 1961, came as part of a revival that has, with difficulty, continued.

bridge (1) (Fr. *chevalet*, Ger. *Steg*, It. *ponticello*). Piece of wood on a string instrument, there to raise the strings and transmit their vibrations to the instrument's body.

(2) Link in a movement, most often from first to second subject in the exposition (and recapitulation) of a sonata allegro.

Bridge, Frank (b. Brighton, 26 Feb 1879; d. Eastbourne, 10 Jan 1941). British composer, who rang a distinct note in the belfry of native Romantic impressionism and in the mid-1920s moved into a punchy, harmonically sophisticated manner more in tune with Berg and Bartók. He studied with Stanford at the RCM (1899–1903) and started his career as a quartet player (on viola) and occasional conductor. In 1923 he visited the USA in the latter capacity. His most powerful and passionate – though least prolific – period came after several years of virtual silence following the First World War, when he produced the dynamic rhapsody *Enter Spring*, the stern cello *Oration* and two fine quartets. He also taught the boy Britten.

Anthony Payne *Frank Bridge* (1999)

Opera: *The Christmas Rose*, 1919–29

Orchestral: *The Sea*, 1910–11; *Summer*, 1914; *Sir Roger de Coverley*, str, 1922; *Enter Spring*, 1927; *There is a willow grows aslant a brook*, small orch, 1928; *Oration*, vc, orch, 1930; *Phantasm*, pf, orch, 1931; *Rebus* (overture), 1940; etc.

String quartets: Phantasie Quartet, F minor, 1905; 'Bologna' (No.1), E minor, 1906; (No.2), G minor, 1915; *Sally in our alley*, *Cherry ripe*, 1916; *Sir Roger de Coverley*, 1922; No.3, 1926; No.4, 1937

Other chamber works: Phantasie Piano Trio, C minor, 1907; Phantasie Piano Quartet, F♯ minor, 1910; Piano Quintet, 1904–12; String Sextet, 1906–12; Cello Sonata, 1913–17; etc.

Songs: 'Love went a-riding' (Mary Coleridge), 1914; 'Golden Hair' (Joyce), 1925; etc.

Keyboard: Piano Sonata, 1921–4; other pieces for pf, org

Bridgetower, George (Augustus) Polgreen (b. Biala, Poland, ?1779; d. London, 29 Feb 1860). British violinist. Born to an African father and European mother, he made his debut in Paris in 1789 and came under the protection of the Prince of Wales (later George IV) the next year, for lessons with the violinist-composers Barthélemon, Jarnovic, as well as with Attwood. He played in London and for the prince in Brighton, until in 1802 he went to visit his mother in Dresden. From there he went to Vienna, where he gave a concert with Beethoven (24 May 1803), introducing the Op.47 sonata that the composer later, following a disagreement, dedicated to Kreutzer. He spent the rest of his life in England, Rome and Paris.

brillante (It.), **brillant** (Fr.). Glittering, used as a marking or in titles.

brindisi (It.). Toast, in an opera, the term allegedly derived from the Ger. *bring dir's* (bring yours). There are examples in Verdi (*Macbeth, La traviata, Otello*) and Mascagni (*Cavalleria rusticana*).

brio (It.). Liveliness, as in *allegro con brio*, a favourite Beethoven marking ('Waldstein' Sonata, Symphonies Nos.3, 5, 7).

brisé (Fr.). Broken, i.e. arpeggiated or, in string playing, staccato.

Bristow, George Frederick (b. Brooklyn, 19 Dec 1825; d. New York, 13 Dec 1898). US musician, variously active as composer, violinist (New York Philharmonic 1843–79), pianist, organist, conductor and teacher. He studied with his clarinettist father, Macfarren and Bull, and wrote operas (*Rip Van Winkle*, New York, 1855), sacred music, symphonies ('Niagara', soli, ch, orch, 1893) and two quartets (1849).

Britain. See UNITED KINGDOM.

Britten, (Edward) Benjamin (b. Lowestoft, 22 Nov 1913; d. Aldeburgh, 4 Dec 1976). British composer, controversial in his brilliant youth but warmly accepted in his maturity, and given a life peerage in 1976. He became a public artist, commissioned by governments and royalty, and yet his operatic works, unlike in subject and scale, often bear on an acutely personal story of innocence, illuminated or, more often, defiled by a haunting sensuality. This collision of the naïve and childlike with the adult and experienced, worked out on a musical level, became a variable fusion between simplicity (harmonic, rhythmic, formal) and complexity, for which he found sources in Stravinsky, Schubert, Purcell and Mahler, though his voice, from a remarkably early age, was his own. Living and working on the Suffolk coast, he provided a model of a composer creating and catering to his own audience, while the resulting works went around the world.

A dentist's son, he began composing assiduously at five, started lessons with Bridge at 13, and entered the RCM in 1930 to study piano (with Samuel and Benjamin) and composition (with Ireland). At 18 he produced his Op.1, the Sinfonietta, already characteristic in its neoclassically dislocated but clear tonality and its flair. After hearing *Wozzeck* in 1934 he went to Vienna and contemplated studying with Berg, but instead took a job the next year writing music for documentary films made by the General Post Office. Auden was on the same team, and became his collaborator on concert works as well – music that caused astonishment and some dismay for its vivid awareness of continental modernism (Stravinsky, Bartók) and its satirical edge.

In 1939 he left for the USA with the tenor Peter Pears, his companion for the rest of his life and the destined singer of many of his songs and leading operatic roles. The flamboyant set of Michelangelo settings (1940), the first such creation, marked a new confidence. But though the US stay was creatively productive, he and Pears returned in 1942 to the home he had earlier acquired near Aldeburgh, the setting for his first full-scale opera, *Peter Grimes*. Given right after the war, *Grimes* was immediately hailed as a new dawn for British opera. It boasted extravagant but apt word setting in a manner descended from Purcell, plentiful atmosphere and an immense personal engagement with the central figure. That engagement, repeated in most of his subsequent operas, gives them a confessional intimacy rare in the genre.

The intimate mode of address was one he preferred. Though he wrote two further operas on a grand scale – *Billy Budd* (1951) and *Gloriana* (1953) – all the rest were composed for the smaller forces of what became the English Opera Group. And though he fulfilled commissions for the new Coventry Cathedral (*War Requiem*) and from the United Nations (*Voices of Today*), every June he and Pears were in Aldeburgh, presiding at the festival where, from 1948, many of his works had their first performances. At Aldeburgh he worked not just with distinguished musician friends (notably Rostropovich) but also with local choirs and children. He conducted there regularly as well, whereas in the wider world he preferred the role of accompanist, at recitals he gave with Pears, performing classic lieder (Schubert especially) as well as his own songs and arrangements.

Vocal music took over, too, at his writing desk. In his 20s he had produced numerous orchestral and chamber pieces, but between 1946 (*Young Person's Guide*) and 1961 (Cello Sonata) he wrote almost no purely instrumental music. His expressive shyness had grown, and taken the cover of other people's words, perhaps partly for reasons having to do with homosexual guilt. His operas largely avoid one of the genre's standard situations – frank declaration of love – which only makes more extraordinary their success in dramatizing other emotions, of fear, jealousy and deceit. When changes in the law and society at last allowed him to put homosexual attraction on stage, without the screening that had been necessary in *The Turn of the Screw* or *Billy Budd*, the result was a work in which the vision of youthful male beauty comes from a world in decay: *Death in Venice*. Even so, a door had been unlocked. Now, though in failing health, he could go back to music without words or occasion, in his Third Quartet.

Donald Mitchell *Letters from a Life*, Vols.1–2 (1991); Mervyn Cooke *The Cambridge Companion to Benjamin Britten* (1999)

www.britten-pears.co.uk

Operas: PAUL BUNYAN, Op.17, 1941; PETER GRIMES, Op.33, 1944–5; *The* RAPE OF LUCRETIA, Op.37, 1946, rev 1947; ALBERT HERRING, Op.39, 1947; *The* BEGGAR'S OPERA (realization), Op.43, 1948; *The Little Sweep* (children's opera: Eric Crozier), Op.45, 1948; BILLY BUDD, Op.50, 1951; GLORIANA, Op.53, 1953; *The* TURN OF THE SCREW, Op.54, 1954; *Noye's Fludde* (children's opera: Chester miracle play), Op.59, 1957; *A* MIDSUMMER NIGHT'S DREAM, Op.64, 1960; CURLEW RIVER (church parable), Op.71, 1964; *The Burning Fiery Furnace* (church parable: William Plomer), Op.77, 1966; *The* PRODIGAL SON (church parable), Op.81, 1968; *Owen Wingrave* (Myfanwy Piper, after Henry James), Op.85, 1970; DEATH IN VENICE, Op.88, 1973

Ballet: *The Prince of the Pagodas*, Op.57, 1956

Orchestral: Sinfonietta, Op.1, chbr orch, 1932; Simple Symphony, Op.4, str, 1933–4; *Soirées musicales*, Op.9, 1936 (after Rossini); Variations on a Theme of Frank Bridge, Op.10, str, 1937; *Mont Juic*, Op.12, 1936–7 (with Berkeley); Piano Concerto, Op.13, 1938; Violin Concerto, Op.15, 1939; *Young Apollo*, Op.16, pf, str, 1939; *Canadian Carnival*, Op.19, 1939; *Sinfonia da requiem*, Op.20, 1940; *Diversions*, Op.21, pf left hand, orch, 1940; *Matinées musicales*, Op.24, 1941 (after Rossini); *Scottish Ballad*, Op.26, 2 pf, orch, 1941; Prelude and Fugue, Op.29, 18 str, 1943; *A* YOUNG PERSON'S GUIDE TO THE ORCHESTRA, Op.34, 1946; *Occasional Overture*, Op.38, 1946; *Lachrymae*, Op.48a, va, str, arr 1976; Cello Symphony, Op.68, 1963; *The Building of the House* (overture), Op.79, 1967; Suite on English Folk Tunes 'A Time There Was', Op.90, chbr orch, 1966–75

Vocal orchestral: *Our Hunting Fathers* (Auden), Op.8, s/t, orch, 1936; *Ballad of Heroes* (Swingler, Auden), Op.14, t/s, ch, orch, 1939; *Les Illuminations* (Rimbaud), Op.18, s/t, str, 1939; Serenade, Op.31, t, hn, str, 1943; *St Nicolas* (Crozier), Op.42, soli, ch, orch, 1948; *Spring Symphony*, Op.44, soli, ch, orch, 1949; Nocturne, Op.60, t, 7 insts, str, 1958; *Cantata academica*, Op.62, soli, ch, orch, 1959; WAR REQUIEM, Op.66, 1961; *Cantata misericordium*, Op.69, soli, ch, orch, 1963; *Phaedra* (Lowell, after Racine), Op.93, mez, orch, 1975; *Welcome Ode*, Op.95, ch, orch, 1976

Choral: *A Boy was Born*, Op.3, ch, 1932–3; *Friday Afternoons*, Op.7, children's ch, pf, 1933–5; *Hymn to St Cecilia* (Auden), Op.27, ch, 1942; *A Ceremony of Carols*, Op.28, boys' ch, hp, 1942; *Rejoice in the Lamb*, Op.30, ch, org, 1943; *Festival Te Deum*, Op.32, ch, org, 1944; *A Wedding Anthem*, Op.46, ch, org, 1949; *5 Flower Songs*, Op.47, ch, 1950; *Hymn to St Peter*, Op.56a, ch, org, 1955; *Antiphon*, Op.56b, ch, org, 1956; *Missa brevis*, Op.63, boys' ch, org, 1959; Psalm 150, Op.67, children's ch, insts, 1962; *Voices for Today*, Op.75, ch, org ad lib, 1965; *The Golden Vanity*, Op.78, boys' ch, pf, 1966; *Children's Crusade*, Op.82, children's ch, insts, 1968; *Sacred and Profane*, Op.91, ch, 1974–5; etc.

Chamber: String Quartet No.1, D, Op.25, 1941; No.2, C, Op.36, 1945; No.3, Op.94, 1975; Phantasy, Op.2, ob qt, 1932; *Gemini Variations*, Op.73, fl, vn, pf duet, 1965; Suite, Op.6, vn, pf, 1934–5; *Lachrymae*, Op.48, va, pf, 1950; Cello Sonata, C, Op.65, 1961; Solo Cello Suite No.1, Op.72, 1964; No.2, Op.80, 1967; No.3, Op.87, 1972; *6 Metamorphoses after Ovid*, Op.49, ob, 1951; *Nocturnal after John Dowland*, Op.70, gtr, 1963; Harp Suite, Op.83, 1969

Canticles: *I My beloved is mine* (Quarles), Op.40, s/t. pf, 1947; *II Abraham and Isaac*, Op.51, a, t, pf, 1952; *III Still falls the rain* (Edith Sitwell), Op.55, t, hn, pf, 1954; *IV The Journey of the Magi* (T.S. Eliot), Op.86, ct, t, bar, pf, 1971; *V The Death of St Narcissus* (Eliot), Op.89, t, hp, 1974

Song cycles: *On this Island* (Auden), Op.11, s/t, pf, 1937; 7 Sonnets of Michelangelo, Op.22, t, pf, 1940; The Holy Sonnets of John Donne, Op.35, s/t, pf, 1945; *A Charm of Lullabies*, Op.41, mez, pf, 1947; *Winter Words* (Hardy), Op.52, s/t, pf, 1953; Songs from the Chinese, Op.58, s/t, gtr, 1957; *Sechs Hölderlin-Fragmente*, Op.61, v, pf, 1958; Songs and Proverbs of William Blake, Op.74, bar, pf, 1965; *The Poet's Echo* (Pushkin), Op.76, s/t, pf, 1965; *Who are these children?* (Soutar), Op.84, t, pf, 1969; *A Birthday Hansel* (Burns), Op.92, s/t, hp, 1975

Piano: *Holiday Diary*, Op.5, 1934; *Introduction and Rondo alla burlesca, Mazurka elegiaca*, Op.23, 2 pf, 1940–41

Other works: music for plays, films, radio; arrangements of folksongs, Purcell songs, etc.

Britten–Pears School. Institution at the Snape Maltings, founded by Britten and Pears in 1972 to offer short courses with visiting teachers and professionals.

Britton, Thomas (b. Rushden, Northants., 14 Jan 1644; d. London, 27 Sep 1714). British coal merchant, bibliophile and pioneer of public concerts, which he held on Thursdays above his shop from 1678.

broadcasting. See INTERNET; RADIO; TELEVISION.

Broadwood. British piano firm founded in London by John Broadwood (1732–1812), who worked with Shudi from 1761 and alone from 1782, producing instruments with improved strength, homogeneity and tonal variety. Beethoven had one. The firm maintained its output and prestige into the mid 19th century, when it was overtaken by the new technology of Steinway and Bösendorfer.

Brockes, Barthold Heinrich (b. Hamburg, 22 Sep 1680; d. Hamburg, 16 Jan 1747). German poet, whose Passion libretto (pub 1712) was set by Keiser, Telemann and Handel. He married well, lived well and also wrote nature poetry.

Brod, Max (b. Prague, 27 May 1884; d. Tel-Aviv, 20 Dec 1968). Czech–Israeli writer and composer, friend to Kafka and Janáček. Trained as a lawyer, he worked as a music critic in Prague until leaving for Palestine in 1939. There he helped develop a 'Mediterranean' style, absorbing local folk music in works including songs (*Tod und Paradies*, 1951, setting Kafka) and piano suites.

Brodsky Quartet. Two ensembles have carried this name. One was led by Adolph Brodsky (1851–1929), a Russian who became leader of the Hallé Orchestra and principal of the Royal Manchester College of Music in 1895. In homage to him, four young Manchester students revived the name in 1972.

broken chord. Chord played as an arpeggio, with the notes staggered (normally rising) rather than simultaneous, indicated by a wavy vertical line to the left (sometimes with an arrowhead to indicate whether the spread should be upward or downward).

broken consort. Renaissance–Baroque ensemble mixing instrumental families, e.g. including both recorders and viols.

broken octave. (1) Broken chord where the chord is simply two notes an octave apart.

(2) Kind of SHORT OCTAVE in which the black keys are split to accommodate two notes.

Brooklyn Academy of Music (BAM). Institution in Brooklyn, New York, founded in 1861, the present building dating from 1908. It became home to an orchestra, the part-time Brooklyn Philharmonic, in 1955, and to an annual festival, Next Wave, in 1981.

Broschi, Riccardo (b. Naples, c.1698; d. Madrid, 1756). Italian composer. He was the brother of Farinelli, for whom he wrote several operas produced in Italy in 1728–32 and the showpiece aria 'Son qual nave' (1734), and whom, after some unsuccesful years, he joined in Spain in the 1740s.

Brossard, Sébastien de (baptized Dompierre, 12 Sep 1655; d. Meaux, 10 Aug 1730). French musician-priest, musical bibliophile and author of the first French music dictionary (1703).

Brouwer, Leo (b. Havana, 1 Mar 1939). Cuban guitarist-composer. He studied with Isaac Nicola and in 1959–60 at Hartford University and Juilliard. Back in Havana he was involved in the local avant-garde and thereby came into contact with Henze, though since 1980 his works have been more mainstream. They include several guitar concertos, cantatas and other guitar music.

Brown, Earle (b. Lunenburg, Mass., 26 Dec 1926; d. Rye, NY, 2 Jul 2002). US composer, pioneer of graphic scores and mobile form. He studied at the Schillinger School (1947–50) and became associated with Cage and Tudor in 1952. His *December 1952* was the first score to dispense entirely with traditional notation, presenting an elegant array of black rectangles on a white ground. He also introduced proportional notation the same year, and mobile composition (in homage to Alexander Calder) in 1953, with *Twenty-Five Pages*, to be played in any order or assembly by up to 25 pianos. This technique he extended to orchestral forces in *Available Forms I–II* (1961–2). In later years he was a record producer and teacher, while composing in more stable form (*Tracking Pierrot* for sextet, 1992).

Brown, Rosemary (b. London, 27 Jul 1917; d. 16 Nov 2001). British psychic who in the 1970s claimed to have received works dictated by departed composers from Bach to Stravinsky.

Browne, John (*fl. c.*1490). English composer of personal obscurity but, in his music, vivid presence. His is the dominant voice in the ETON CHOIRBOOK, which includes his *Stabat mater* a 6, a work unparallelled in its superb architecture and keen expressiveness. In the same volume are other Marian antiphons by him.

Browning. 16th-century English popular tune set in variations by Byrd, etc.

Bruch, Max (Karl August) (b. Cologne, 6 Jan 1838; d. Friedenau, near Berlin, 20 Oct 1920). German composer, whose likeable, warmly Romantic music has been largely forgotten, with the signal exception of his G minor violin concerto. He studied with Ferdinand Hiller and Reinecke in his home city, where he set up as a music teacher in 1858. After several moves he settled in Berlin, teaching composition at the academy (1891–1910). In 1893 he was awarded a Cambridge honorary doctorate.

Christopher Fifield *Max Bruch* (1988)

Oratorios: *Odysseus*, Op.41, pub 1872; *Moses*, Op.67, pub 1895; etc.

Orchestral: Symphony No.1, E♭, Op.28, pub 1870; No.2, F minor, Op.36, pub 1870; No.3, E, Op.51, pub 1887; VIOLIN CONCERTO No.1, G minor, Op.26, 1866; No.2, D minor, Op.44, pub 1878; No.3, D minor, Op.58, pub 1891; Scottish Fantasy, Op.46, vn, orch, pub 1880; *Kol nidre*, Op.47, vc, orch, pub 1881; Concerto, Op.88, cl, va, orch, 1911; etc.

Other works: 3 operas, chamber music, songs, partsongs

Bruck, Arnold von (b. Bruges, ?1500; d. Linz an der Donau, Upper Austria, 6 Feb 1554). Netherlandish composer. Trained as a chorister in the chapel of Charles V, he became chapelmaster (1527–45) to the Archduke Ferdinand, later emperor, and wrote German sacred and secular songs as well as Latin church music in Josquin-descended polyphony.

Bruckner, (Joseph) Anton (b. Ansfelden, near Linz, 4 Sep 1824; d. Vienna, 11 Oct 1896). Austrian composer. His prime output was a sequence of majestic symphonies whose scale, long lines, modal features and imposingly architectural manner suggest great cathedrals in sound. Simple and modest as a person, he accepted critical advice from well-meaning friends in the editions that came out during his lifetime and soon after, but the strong international growth in estimation of him since the 1960s has been based on more authentic scores, in all their leisurely length and raw power.

The son of a village schoolmaster-organist, he began his training with his father and his cousin-godfather, Johann Baptist Weiss. In 1837, when his father died, he became a chorister in the great Baroque monastery of St Florian, which he knew from earlier visits. This became his home. His voice broke two years later, but he stayed on as a violinist, deputy organist and student, trained as a teacher in Linz (1840–41), and worked as an assistant schoolmaster in small villages before finding a similar post back at St Florian (1845–55). All the while he wrote music – almost exclusively choral music, sacred and secular – but he recognized a need for further tuition, and in 1855 visited Sechter in Vienna to begin a correspondence

course. Sechter advised him to leave St Florian, and he duly became cathedral organist in Linz (1855–67).

Rigorous instruction from Sechter lasted until 1861, when he applied for and received a diploma from the Vienna Conservatory. After he had improvised a fugue at the organ, one of the professors is said to have declared: 'He should have examined us!' But, still not satisfied with himself, he continued his studies with Linz musicians, Otto Kitzler and then Ignaz Dorn. Sechter had required him to refrain from composition; now he started writing instrumental movements, including – after the overwhelming experience of hearing and studying *Tannhäuser* in the winter of 1862–3 – a first symphony ('No.00', also known as the 'Study Symphony'), in which he suddenly moved forward from Viennese classicism to Wagnerism, without yet becoming himself. That final step he achieved in his Mass in D minor, written in his 40th year.

In 1865 he met Wagner in Munich, and in 1868 he conducted the close of *Die Meistersinger* in Linz in advance of the première. Also that year he conducted his own First Symphony in Linz, succeeded to Sechter's post at the Vienna Conservatory and became organist at the imperial chapel. He then won international acclaim as an improvising organist in Paris (1869) and London (1871), and his F minor Mass, which he conducted in Vienna in 1872, gained the unusual distinction of pleasing both the determinedly conservative, anti-Wagnerian critic Hanslick and the open-minded, pro-Wagnerian Liszt. But he had much less success with the symphonies that were taking over his artistic life. The Vienna Philharmonic was antipathetic, and had its doubts confirmed when only about two dozen people (including the teenage Mahler) stayed to the end of the first performance of the Third in 1877. Hanslick, too, joined the opponents, as perhaps was inevitable when Bruckner had dedicated the score to Wagner.

Wagner seems to have patronized this older, unworldly, organist-professor who came to Bayreuth for the première of the *Ring* in 1876, and Bruckner is said to have sat through each performance with his eyes closed, enraptured by the music and blissfully ignorant of the cheating and violence, admixed liberally with sex, taking place on stage. He seems to have gone through life protected by simplicity. In a Vienna rushing towards the 20th century, he maintained the dress and the manners of a gentleman farmer from before 1848. He took a sweet, grandfatherly delight in young women. He kept a crucifix in his studio, and a child's faith in his heart.

That refuge he needed. He had to wait almost two decades to hear his Fifth Symphony; of the

Sixth there were two movements he never heard at all; and even though the Seventh, commemorating Wagner, enjoyed a triumph – in Leipzig under Nikisch (1884), in Munich under Levi (1885) and even in Vienna under Richter (1886), where Hanslick reported, in a dismissive review, that the composer was called out for applause after every movement – the Eighth brought him problems all over again. Levi, puzzled, begged him to revise it, and he did so before moving on to his Ninth, on which he laboured for five years, to the day of his death, leaving the finale unfinished.

Meanwhile, he was repeatedly drawn back to revise earlier scores, sometimes working with younger supporters – notably Ferdinand Löwe and the brothers Franz and Josef Schalk – whose eagerness to get his works played and printed may have overcome their loyalty to what he wanted and wrote. As a result, not only are the sources manifold (there are three versions of the Third and Fourth symphonies), but their authenticity, as representing his unconstrained wishes, is debatable. Robert Haas, responsible for the collected edition that was begun in 1930, tried to discern for each symphony an ideal text, even if that sometimes meant conflating versions. Leopold Nowak, in charge of the new collected edition instituted in 1951, preferred to treat the versions as separate entities. But many questions remain about the quality of Bruckner's investment in his own and his friends' second, third and fourth thoughts. His music, seemingly so confident, so firm, is ringed with doubt.

Pfitzner seems to have been responsible for the view that he wrote the same symphony over and over again, and indeed there were models of sound and structure to which he was repeatedly drawn: the soft, tremulous opening over which an extended melody launches itself, in a return visit to the place where Beethoven's Ninth begins; the ostinato, whether used to make a static background or, in the characteristically bounding scherzo, to generate a corporeal rhythmic energy; the solemn adagio; the orchestration in distinct layers, with no unusual instruments except the Wagner tubas added from No.7 onwards; the interruption of silence, within which the music seems to reverberate within the space it is creating; the climactic contrapuntal superposing of themes; the chromaticism, an effortless link from the Renaissance to the world of Schoenberg. There is a sense in which the chromatic profusion of the slow movement of the Second is removed to leave the solider harmonic frames of Nos.7–9, but otherwise the lack of stylistic development parallels the lack of continuing thematic development within each work: instead come great plaques of statement and restatement. Bruckner took a long time getting there. Once there, he had no need to travel.

Derek Watson *Bruckner* (1975, ²1996); Crawford Howie *Anton Bruckner* (2002)

Symphonies (only major revisions are noted): No.00 'Study', F minor, 1863; No.0, D minor, 1869; No.1, C minor, 1865–6, f.p. Linz, 9 May 1868, rev 1890–91, f.p. Vienna, 13 Dec 1891; No.2, C minor, 1871–2, f.p. Vienna, 26 Oct 1873, rev 1877, 1892, f.p. Vienna, 25 Nov 1894; No.3, D minor, 1872–3, rev 1876–7, f.p. Vienna, 16 Dec 1877, rev 1887–9, f.p. Vienna, 21 Dec 1890; No.4 'Romantic', E♭, 1874, rev 1878–80, f.p. Vienna, 20 Feb 1881, rev 1888, f.p. Vienna, 22 Jan 1888; No.5, B♭, 1875–6, f.p. Graz, 8 Apr 1894, rev 1877–8; No.6, A, 1879–81, f.p. Vienna, 26 Feb 1899; No.7, E, 1881–3, f.p. Leipzig, 30 Dec 1884; No.8, C minor, 1884–7, rev 1887–90; f.p. Vienna, 18 Dec 1892; No.9, D minor, 1887–96, unfinished, f.p. Vienna, 11 Feb 1903

Other large-scale works: Requiem, D minor, soli, ch, orch, 1848–9; *Magnificat*, soli, ch, orch, 1852; Psalm 146, soli, ch, orch, *c.*1860; Overture, G minor, 1862–3; *Missa solemnis*, B♭ minor, soli, ch, orch, 1854; Mass No.1, D minor, soli, ch, orch, 1864, rev 1878, 1881–2; No.2, E minor, ch, brass, 1866, rev 1876, 1882; No.3, F minor, soli, ch, orch, 1867–8, rev 1876, 1881; *Te Deum*, soli, ch, orch, 1881–4; Psalm 150, s, ch, orch, 1892; *Das deutsche Lied*, men's ch, brass, 1892; *Helgoland*, men's ch, orch, 1893

Motets: many from 1835–56; *Ave Maria*, ch, 1861; *Afferentur regi*, ch, 3 trbn, 1861; *Asperges me*, ch, 1866–8; *Pange lingua*, ch, 1868; *Inveni David*, men's ch, 4 trbn, 1868; *In St Angelum custodem*, 1868; *Locus iste*, ch, 1869; *Tota pulchra es*, t, ch, org, 1878; *Os justi*, ch, 1879; *Christus factus est*, ch, 2 vn, 3 trbn, 1879, rev 1896, version for ch, 1884; *Ave Maria*, a, org, 1882; *Salvum fac populum*, ch, 1884; *Ecce sacerdos magnus*, ch, 3 trbn, org, 1885; *Virga Jesse floruit*, ch, 1885; *Ave regina*, ch, org ad lib, 1887; *Vexilla regis*, ch, 1892

Other works: String Quintet, F, 1879; many partsongs, few and mostly early songs, piano and organ pieces

Brüggen, Frans (b. Amsterdam, 30 Oct 1934). Dutch conductor and recorder player. He studied the recorder (with Kees Otten) and musicology in Amsterdam, and in the 1960s–70s was the outstanding virtuoso of his instrument, making many recordings and introducing works by Berio (*Gesti*), etc. In 1981 he founded the Orchestra of the Eighteenth Century and began a new career as a conductor, combining period style with potent vitality.

Bruhns, Nicolaus (b. Schwabstedt, near Husum, Nov/Dec 1665; d. Husum, 29 Mar 1697). German organist-composer and violinist, born into a family of professional musicians in Schleswig-Holstein. He studied with his father and from 1681

in Lübeck with his uncle Peter and Buxtehude. In 1689, after some years in Copenhagen, he became organist of the Stadtkirche in Husum. His small surviving output includes four preludes and fugues for organ and a dozen sacred cantatas, distinguished by expressive virtuosity in the vocal writing.

bruitism (from Fr. *bruit*, noise). Composition with noise, i.e. for percussion or by electronic means. The word unhappily suggests a style, in an area of great heterogeneity.

Brumel, Antoine (b. *c*.1460; d. *c*.1515). French composer, leading contemporary of Josquin. First heard of at Chartres in 1483 (he may have been from the locality), he moved to Geneva (1486–92) and is patchily recorded at Laon, Notre Dame in Paris (1498–1500), Chambéry (1501–2) and Ferrara (1506–10). The great weight of his output is in sacred music, including masses (*Missa de beata virgine*, a *Requiem*, a wholly canonic mass on Josquin's *A l'ombre d'ung buissant*, the Easter mass *Et ecce terrae motus* a 12), antiphons and *Magnificat* settings.

Bruneau, (Louis Charles Bonaventure) Alfred (b. Paris, 3 Mar 1857; d. Paris, 15 Jun 1934). French composer, notably of operas to librettos by his friend Zola (*Messidor*, 1894–6; *L'Ouragan*, 1897–1900; *L'Enfant Roi*, 1902) in a style combining elements from verismo, Wagner and Debussy. He was a pupil of Massenet at the Paris Conservatoire (1873–81) and also wrote other operas, vocal symphonic works and songs.

Brunelli, Antonio (b. Pisa, *c*.1575; d. Pisa, 1630 or before). Italian composer of songs and madrigals, and also of canons. He studied with Nanino in Rome, and was chapelmaster in San Miniato, Prato and Pisa (from 1614).

Bruni, Antonio Bartolomeo (b. Cuneo, 28 Jan 1757; d. Cuneo, 6 Aug 1821). Italian violinist-composer, active largely in Paris from 1780, composing and leading orchestras. He wrote comic operas, much chamber music, numerous caprices and études for violin solo, and a violin method.

Brunner, Adolf (b. Zurich, 25 Jun 1901; d. Thalwil, 15 Feb 1992). Swiss composer, especially of Protestant sacred music, including a St Mark Passion (1970–71). Given early training by his uncle, Hans Lavater, he studied with Jarnach, Schreker and Walter Gmeindl in Berlin (1921–5), where he got to know Pepping. Back in Zurich he worked for an anti-Nazi organization, for the radio and in church music.

brush. Percussion beater with wire or plastic fronds, inherited from jazz as an alternative to the stick or mallet.

Brustwerk (Ger., breast part). Small organ placed in the breast of a larger one, above the keyboards, as commonly in German and Dutch organs of the 17th–18th centuries.

Bryars, (Richard) Gavin (b. Goole, Yorks., 16 Jan 1943). British composer, who had been determinedly apart from the regular avant-garde through much of his career, though around 1990 he began to join it (or it him). He studied philosophy at Sheffield University (1961–4) and found his musical bearings by way of Cage, Satie and Busoni, admixed with jazz and the conceptual art of the period. His preferred form is the question, positing imaginary worlds in which seemingly incompatible entities coexist (e.g. US minimalism and Victorian parlour music). *The Sinking of the Titanic* (1969) is a classic of English experimental music: a documentary in sound, imagining the unimaginable. As a teacher he has enjoyed a long association with the Leicester Polytechnic.

www.gavinbryars.com

Operas: *Medea*, f.p. Lyons, 1984; *Doctor Ox's Experiment* (Blake Morrison), f.p. London, 1998; *G* (Morrison), f.p. Mainz, 2002
Concert works: *The Sinking of the Titanic*, 1969; *Jesus' blood never failed me yet*, 1971; *Allegrasco*, several versions, 1983; String Quartet No.1, 1985; No.2, 1990; No.3, 1998; *Cadman Requiem*, 4 v, str, 1989; *The Green Ray*, s sax, chbr orch, 1991; Cello Concerto, 1995; etc.

Brymer, Jack (b. South Shields, 27 Jan 1915; d. Oxted, Surrey, 16 Sep 2003). British clarinettist of smooth, engaging tone; a popularizer of his instrument. He was a schoolmaster until plucked by Beecham into the RPO (1947–63), from which he moved to the BBC SO (1963–72) and the LSO (1972–86).

Buch der hängenden Gärten, Das (The Book of the Hanging Gardens). Song cycle by Schoenberg to 15 poems by Stefan George. First performance: Vienna, 14 Jan 1910.

Buchla, Donald (Frederick) (b. Southgate, Cal., 17 Apr 1937). US designer of synthesizers. His first became available in 1964 and were used by Subotnick.

Buck, Dudley (b. Hartford, Conn., 10 Mar 1839; d. West Orange, NJ, 6 Oct 1909). US organist-composer, trained (1857–62) in Leipzig, Dresden and Paris. After periods in Chicago (1869–71) and Boston (1871–5) he settled in Brooklyn, playing the organ, conducting choirs and writing cantatas and anthems.

Budapest. Capital city of Hungary, formed in 1873 by the union of Buda, the ancient capital, with Pest, the growing city on the other side of the Danube. The 50th anniversary of that event was celebrated with a concert of new works by Dohnányi (Festival Overture), Bartók (Dance Suite) and Kodály (*Psalmus hungaricus*). Musical institutions include the LISZT ACADEMY, the opera house (inaugurated in 1884) and the Budapest Festival Orchestra (founded in 1983).

Budapest Quartet. Ensemble founded by Hungarian musicians in 1917, though by 1936 all four chairs had been taken by Russians and Ukrainians: Joseph Roisman, Alexander Schneider, Boris Kroyt and Mischa Schneider. They moved to the USA in 1938 and enjoyed great popularity and esteem before disbanding in 1967.

Buffet. French style of bassoon, as made by the French woodwind firm of Buffet-Crampon.

buffo, buffa (It.). Comic, as in opera buffa, buffo bass, etc.

buff stop. Device common on harpsichords (less so on early pianos) by which a piece of buff leather or felt is slid against a string, producing a muffled sound.

bugle (Fr. *clairon*, Ger. *Signalhorn*). Small valveless horn, used for military signals. This function distinguishes it from the post horn, as does the usual oval, trumpet-like wind of its tube. Bugle calls involve just the second to sixth harmonics – Bb–F–Bb–D–F – in the alto register for the British army bugle in Bb.

Bühnenmusik (Ger., stage music). Incidental music, or music played onstage in an opera.

buisine. Medieval herald's straight trumpet. The word lives on as the Ger. *Posaune* (trombone).

Bulgarian rhythm. Bartók's term for the kind of complex compound metre he found in Bulgarian folk music (e.g. $\frac{3+2+3}{8}$, i.e. eight quavers in the bar, in groups of three, two and three) and used in his own.

Bull, John (b. ?Old Radnor, ?1562/3; d. Antwerp, 12/13 Mar 1628). English composer and keyboard player, whose prodigious gifts as a performer, learning and bold imagination are reflected in his music. He joined the choir at Hereford Cathedral in August 1573, and within six months had been claimed by the Chapel Royal, where he was taught by Blitheman and William Hunnis, and stayed nearly 40 years. Meanwhile, he had a university education; he was awarded the BMus in 1586 at Oxford (where a portrait of him survives) and the Cambridge DMus by 1589. He was reader in music at Gresham College from 1597 to 1607, when he was obliged to leave to marry a woman he had got pregnant. Clearly he did not then change his ways, for in 1613 he fled a charge of habitual fornication. He moved to the archducal court in Brussels, until diplomatic pressure forced the archduke to release him after a year, when he found a home in Antwerp, playing at the cathedral. Apart from many keyboard pieces (*My Self*, *The King's Hunt* and other curiosities, as well as pavans, galliards, almans, corantos and plainsong settings) he wrote an In Nomine for viols, a few anthems and songs.

Walker Cunningham *The Keyboard Music of John Bull* (1984)

Bull, Ole (Bornemann) (b. Bergen, 5 Feb 1810; d. Lys en, near Bergen, 17 Aug 1880). Norwegian violinist-composer and patriot. The son of a musical apothecary, he had tuition from Viotti's pupil Poulsen and the Baillot pupil Ludholm (1820–27); he also, then and later, learned from peasant musicians. After a time based in Christiania (1828–31) he became a touring virtuoso: he heard Paganini, promoted himself as a Norwegian and began playing with a low bridge and heavy bow, facilitating contrapuntal performance. He married and in 1838 made a triumphal return to Norway, but the next year was off on his travels again, through Europe and to the USA (1843–5). During a longer period in Norway (1848–51) he established a Norwegian-language theatre in Bergen, with Ibsen as resident playwright. He then returned to the USA (1852–7), where Thackeray found him 'a mad-cap fiddler … who … charmed me still more by his oddities and character'. Later he settled again in Bergen, though he remained an unstoppable traveller and promoter of Norwegian independence. On his 66th birthday he played his *Et saeterbesøg* (A Visit to the Mountain Pasture) from the top of the Great Pyramid. His other works include pieces for violin and orchestra: concertos, variations, fantasies.

Bullant, Antoine (b. ?near Amiens, *c*.1750; d. St Petersburg, ?June 1821). French composer who settled in St Petersburg in 1780. He had published symphonies in Paris, but in Russia was known for songs and comic operas (*The Merchant of Mead*, 1783/4).

Buller, John (b. London, 7 Feb 1927; d. Sherborne, 12 Sep 2004). British composer, a late bloomer, who studied with Milner (1959–64) and became known in the early 1970s for a series of somewhat Berio-like imaginative examinations of *Finnegans Wake*. Other works include *Proença* for mezzo, electric guitar and orchestra (1977) and an operatic setting of *The Bacchae* in the original Greek (London, 1992).

Bullock, Ernest (b. Wigan, 15 Sep 1890; d. Aylesbury, 24 May 1979). British organist-professor, knighted in 1951. A pupil of Bairstow in Leeds (1907–12), he became organist-choirmaster at Exeter Cathedral (1919–27) and Westminster Abbey (1927–41), and was professor of music at Glasgow University (1941–52) and director of the RCM (1952–60). In addition to anthems, he wrote fanfares for the 1937 and 1953 coronations.

bullroarer. Ancient and widely distributed instrument, consisting of a blade of wood attached to a long string and whirled around by the player; not easily suited to concert use.

Bülow, Hans (Guido Freiherr**) von** (b. Dresden, 8 Jan 1830; d. Cairo, 12 Feb 1894). German conductor, pianist and composer. He studied with Wieck from the age of nine, and later with Louis Plaidy and Hauptmann. In 1849 he met Liszt, became an enthusiastic supporter and thereby encountered Wagner, who found him conducting work in Switzerland. He returned to Liszt for further study in 1851, and in 1853 set out on the career of a touring virtuoso, also teaching in Berlin (1855–64). In 1857 he married Liszt's daughter Cosima. As conductor of the Munich court opera he brought *Tristan* (1865) and *Die Meistersinger* (1868) into the world, and lost his wife to their composer. Shaken, he retired to Florence, but began playing internationally again in 1872 (he gave the première of Tchaikovsky's First Concerto in 1875) and had a glorious period as conductor with the Meiningen court orchestra (1880–85). Conducting, playing and teaching all occupied his later years before he died on a health trip. His works include the symphonic poem *Nirwana*.

bumbass. European folk instrument; a bowed string bass where the single string is held over an inflated pig's bladder.

Bumbry, Grace (Melzia Ann) (b. St Louis, 4 Jan 1937). US mezzo-soprano, later soprano, known for her warm strength and dramatic force. She studied with Lotte Lehmann in Santa Barbara (1955–8) and made her debut as Amneris at the Paris Opera (1960). In 1961, as Venus in *Tannhäuser*, she was the first black singer on the Bayreuth stage.

bumper. Extra orchestral player, especially a fifth horn, there to relieve the principal and increase (bump up) tutti volume.

Bund (Ger., pl. *Bunde*). Fret.

Bungert, (Friedrich) August (b. Mülheim an der Ruhr, 14 Mar 1845/6; d. Leutesdorf am Rhein, 26 Oct 1915). German composer of Wagnerian ambitions. Having spent a lengthy studentship in Cologne, Paris and Berlin, he settled at Pegli, near Genoa, and, patronized by the queen of Romania, wrote words and music for an Odyssean tetralogy: *Kirke* (Dresden, 1898), *Nausicaa* (Dresden, 1901), *Odysseus Heimkehr* (Dresden, 1896) and *Odysseus Tod* (Dresden, 1903). An Iliad pentalogy remained at the planning stage.

Buonamente, Giovanni Battista (b. Mantua; d. Assisi, 29 Aug 1642). Italian violinist-composer. First heard of in Mantua, where he may have worked under Monteverdi, he was in Vienna in the late 1620s and in Assisi from 1633. He published volumes of sonatas, etc. for string groups.

Burck, Joachim a (b. Burg, near Magdeburg, 1546; d. Mühlhausen, 24 May 1610). German composer. Perhaps self-taught, he became cantor at the grammar school in Mühlhausen when he was 17 and stayed there all his life, publishing sacred music in which Renaissance polyphony was soon replaced by a song style.

burden. Refrain, in songs and hymns of the 15th–16th centuries. The word has also been used for a shawm or a bagpipe drone.

Burghersh, Lord **John Fane,** 11th Earl of Westmorland (from 1841) (b. London, 3 Feb 1784; d. Wansford, Northants., 16 Oct 1859). British musical amateur, founder-president of the RAM, at whose concerts he insisted on hearing Italian operatic music and his own, in similar style.

Bürgmüller, (August Joseph) Norbert (b. Düsseldorf, 8 Feb 1810; d. Aachen, 7 May 1836). German composer, whose early death, from epilepsy, was regretted by Schumann and Mendelssohn. The scion of a musical family and pupil of Spohr (1826–31), he wrote two symphonies (No.2 unfinished), a piano concerto in F♯ minor, songs and chamber music.

Burgon, Geoffrey (Alan) (b. Hambledon, 15 Jul 1941). British composer. He studied with Peter Wishart and Lennox Berkeley, and set aside his trumpet in 1971 to pursue a career as a composer of both straight and applied music. His *Nunc dimittis* (1979), written for the television serial *Tinker, Tailor, Soldier, Spy*, found a wide audience.

Burgundy. Region in eastern France whose Valois dukes (1364–1477) strongly favoured the arts. Possessing most of the Low Countries and living there, Philip the Good (r. 1419–67) and Charles the Bold (r. 1467–77) had Binchois and Busnois among their musicians.

Burian, Emil František (b. Plzeň, 11 Apr 1904; d. Prague, 9 Aug 1959). Czech composer. Born into a family of singers, he was active in the avant-garde theatre in Prague before completing his studies with Foerster at the conservatory. With his Voice Band (1927–38) he pioneered speech music; he also produced stage pieces, chamber music and songs, spiked with jazz, dada and Stravinsky. During the German occupation he was imprisoned, to come back a stalwart of socialist realism.

Burkhard, Willy (b. Evilard-sur-Bienna, 17 Apr 1900; d. Zurich, 18 Jun 1955). Swiss composer, of starkly polyphonic music, often based on church modes and appealing to Bachian principles of form. He studied in Berne, in Leipzig (with Karg-Elert), in Munich and Paris. In 1924 he settled as a teacher in Berne, moving to Zurich in 1942. In addition to cantatas and other sacred choral pieces, his works include concertos, organ pieces and piano music.

burlesque. Term found in titles, whether in noun form (Strauss's *Burleske*, Bartók's *Three Burlesques*) or adjectivally (Britten's *Rondo alla burlesca*), denoting humour and irony.

burletta. Term used in London *c*.1750–1800 for a short comic opera.

Burmeister, Joachim (b. Lüneburg, 1564; d. Rostock, 5 Mar 1629). German theorist whose writings show the emergenece of a theory of major–minor tonality and an approach to understanding compositional choices (Lassus being the example) in terms of rhetorical figures. He also introduced the solmization syllables se (B) and si (B♭). Trained as a musician and humanist at school in his home town and university in Rostock (1586–93), he taught in Rostock from 1593.

Burney, Charles (b. Shrewsbury, 7 Apr 1726; d. Chelsea, 12 Apr 1814). British musical historian and traveller. The son of a dancer-violinist-portraitist, he trained as an organist, was apprenticed to Arne (1744–6) and then was house musician to Fulke Greville. In 1749 he had to leave that employment on marrying and support himself and his family as an organist and teacher. He took the Oxford DMus (1769), published an essay on comets the same year before setting out on journeys through France and Italy (1770) and Germany, Austria and the Low Countries (1772) to collect material for a history of music. Returning to his busy life as a private teacher, he wrote up his musical travel diaries and then embarked on his history, which came out in four volumes (1776–89). All these writings remain vital and engaging sources of information on contemporary musicians, styles and tastes. They also gained him access to the highest cultural and social circles. He knew Joshua Reynolds, whose portrait of him is in the National Portrait Gallery, and Samuel Johnson, who opined: 'I much question if there is in the world such another man for mind, intelligence, and manners.'

Charles Burney *A General History of Music* ([r]1957), *Music, Men and Manners in France and Italy 1770* (1969, [r]1974)

Busch. German musical brothers, sons of a musician and instrument maker.

(1) **Fritz** (b. Siegen, 13 Mar 1890; d. London, 14 Sep 1951). Conductor, who trained under Fritz Steinbach at the Cologne Conservatory (1906–9). After various minor posts and war service he became music director of the Stuttgart Opera (1918–22) and the Dresden Staatsoper (1922–33), where he was responsible for the premières of *Intermezzo*, *Doktor Faust*, *Cardillac* and *Die ägyptische Helena*. He left Germany (though he was not Jewish) and worked thereafter in Scandinavia, the Americas and at the first Glyndebourne festivals (1934–9), shaping excellent Mozart performances, as he did again there in 1950–51.

(2) **Adolf** (b. Siegen, 8 Aug 1891; d. Guilford, Vermont, 9 Jun 1952). Quartet leader, trained at the Cologne Conservatory. He formed the Busch Quartet in 1919 and played with them to the end of his life, through moves to Switzerland in 1927 and the USA in 1939; his brother Hermann (1897–1975) was cellist from 1930. The ensemble's recordings, especially of Beethoven, are deeply admired. He also worked with Rudolf Serkin, and with a larger group, the Busch Chamber Players, in concertos by Bach and Handel. A fine teacher (of Menuhin among others), he founded the Marlboro School, Vermont, in 1950.

Bush, Alan (Dudley) (b. London, 22 Dec 1900; d. Watford, 31 Oct 1995). British composer, an indomitable contrarian both as a modernist before the Second World War and as a socialist realist after. He studied with Corder at the RAM (1918–22) and Ireland privately (1921–7), had piano lessons with Moiseiwitsch and Schnabel while teaching composition at the RAM (from 1925), and went for further training in philosophy and musicology at Berlin University (1929–31). His *Dialectic* for string quartet (1929) marked an extreme point in its dissonance and quasi-serial contrapuntal elaboration from a theme, but other works of this period similarly show a confident welding of continental and English influences. Always left-wing in his views, he joined the Communist Party in 1935, and his music grew both more consonant and closer to the English folksong school.

www.alanbushtrust.org.uk

Operas (librettos by Nancy Bush except where stated): *Wat Tyler*, f.p. Leipzig, 1953; *Men of Blackmoor*, f.p. Weimar, 1956; *The Sugar Reapers*, f.p. Leipzig, 1966; *Joe Hill* (Barrie Stavis), f.p. Berlin, 1970

Orchestral: Symphony No.1, C, 1940; No.2 'Nottingham', 1949; Violin Concerto, 1948; etc.

Other works: *Dialectic*, str qt, 1929; other chamber music, much choral music, songs, piano pieces

Busnois, Antoine (b. *c*.1430; d. Bruges, 6 Nov 1492). French composer, associated with the Burgundian court from 1467 to his death. Earlier he may have studied in Paris with Ockeghem, whom he praised in a motet (*In hydraulis*); certainly his was one of the few names felt worthy at the time to be mentioned alongside that of the older master. He wrote sacred music, but seems to have devoted much more attention to songs setting his own French poems, especially rondeaux and bergerettes for two singing voices, often in imitation, over an instrumental bass. Masses based on his songs, by Obrecht, Josquin and Agricola, suggest the esteem in which he was held. So does the posthumous credit he received as the presumed composer of two of the period's ubiquitous melodies: *Fortuna desperata* and, most widely reused of all, *L'Homme armé*, on which he certainly wrote one of the earliest masses.

Paula Higgins, ed. *Antoine Busnoys* (1999)

Busoni, Ferruccio (Dante Michelangiolo Benvenuto) (b. Empoli, 1 Apr 1866; d. Berlin, 27 Jul 1924). German–Italian composer and pianist. His mixed nationality perhaps contributed to his artistic two-sidedness. He was a keyboard virtuoso, deeply versed in the literature going back to Bach, and yet his major works were operas, of which two had Italian subjects treated in German and one had an *echt*-German subject (Faust) set partly in Italy. Similarly, his profound learning, particularly in hermetic philosophy and the art of fugue, went along with a questing spirit. The complexity of his creative persona – retrogressive and adventurous, showy and shadowy, invested in strangeness and irony – surely contributed to the delayed reaction to his music, which began to gain wide renown only in the 1980s.

His father was an Italian clarinettist, his mother a pianist of partly German descent. They were his first teachers, enabling him to make his debut in Trieste when he was eight. The next year he began studies at the Vienna Conservatory, but he left after two years and in 1881 began composition lessons with Wilhelm Mayer in Graz. After further studies in Leipzig (1885–8), he began his career as a pianist and teacher in Helsinki, Russia and the USA. By his mid 20s he had met many of his great contemporaries, including Mahler and Sibelius. He married in 1890 and in 1894 settled with his wife and two sons in Berlin, where he remained, except for a time in Switzerland (1915–20). He kept up his career as a touring virtuoso, and in 1905–9 presented concerts of new orchestral music, including works by Bartók and Sibelius as well as his own massive Piano Concerto. Acquainted also with Schoenberg and Varèse, he wrote an extraordinarily forward-looking *Sketch for a New Aesthetic of Music* (1907), touching on microtones and electronics. From 1920 he taught masterclasses in composition at the Academy of the Arts, where Weill was among his pupils.

His creative output was as diverse as that of Liszt, whom he greatly admired. At first his horizons were bounded by Schumann, Mendelssohn and Brahms, but around 1890 he began to aim at neoclassicism (*junge Klassizität*, 'new classicity', was his term), taking Bach and Mozart as models of clarity. However, the 18th-century aspects of his art tend to be imposed on music that looks in many different directions: back through the Romantic 19th century, forward with Debussy and Schoenberg, across to Reger. He was interested in everything, and fittingly his greatest work emerged as a study of the thirst for knowledge in its mythic form: the figure of Faust. Many of his later works, including the almost atonal Sonatina No.2, are satellites of the troubling opera that was forming and that he did not live to complete.

Antony Beaumont *Busoni the Composer* (1985)

Operas: *Die Brautwahl* (Busoni, after Hoffmann), 1908–10, f.p. Hamburg, 1912; *Arlecchino* (Busoni), Op.50, 1914–16, f.p. Zurich, 1917; *Turandot* (Busoni, after Gozzi), 1917, f.p. Zurich, 1917; *Doktor Faust* (see FAUST), 1916–24

Orchestral: Violin Concerto, D, Op.35a, 1896–7; *Lustspielouvertüre*, Op.38, 1897, rev 1904; Piano Concerto, Op.39, with men's ch in finale (Oehlenschläger), 1903–4; BERCEUSE ELEGIAQUE, Op.42, 1909; *Nocturne symphonique*, Op.43, 1912; *Indianische Fantaisie*, Op.44, pf, orch, 1913; *Rondo arlecchinesco*, Op.46, 1915; *Indianische Tagebuch*, book 2, Op.47, 1915; Concertino, Op.48, cl, small orch, 1919; *Sarabande und Cortège*, Op.51, 1918–19; Divertimento, Op.52, fl, orch, 1920; *Tanzwalzer*, Op.53, 1920; *Romanza e scherzoso*, Op.54, pf, orch, 1921; etc.

Chamber: String Quartet No.1, C minor, Op.19, *c*.1883; No.2, D minor, Op.26, *c*.1887; Violin Sonata No.1, E minor, Op.29, *c*.1890; No.2, E minor, Op.36a, 1898–1900; etc.

Songs (Goethe), most with pf/orch: 'Lied des Mephistopheles', 1918; 'Lied des Unmuts', 1919; 'Lied des Brander', *c*.1919; 'Die Bekehrte', 1921; 'Zigeunerlied', 1923; 'Schlechter Trost', 1924

Piano solo: Variations and Fugue on Chopin's C minor Prelude, Op.22, 1884; *Elegien*, 1907; Fantasia after J.S. Bach, 1909; FANTASIA CONTRAPPUNTISTICA, 1910, 2nd version 1910, 3rd 1912; Sonatina No.1, 1910; No.2, 1912; No.3 'ad usum infantis', 1915; No.4 in die Nativitatis Christi MCMXVII, 1917; No.5 'brevis in signo Joannis Sebastiani Magni', 1918; No.6 'super Carmen', 1920; *Indianische Tagebuch*, book 1, 1915; Toccata, 1921; etc.

Piano duo: *Improvisation über Bachs Chorallied 'Wie wohl ist mir'*, 1916; *Duettino concertante*, 1919; FANTASIA CONTRAPPUNTISTICA, 4th version, pub 1922

BACH–BUSONI piano transcriptions: Prelude and Fugue, D, 1888; Prelude and Fugue 'St Anne', 1890; Chaconne (from D minor violin partita), pub ?1897; Concerto, D minor, with orch, 1899; Toccata, Adagio and Fugue, C, pub 1900; Toccata and Fugue, D minor, pub 1900; 10 chorale preludes (*Ich ruf' zu Dir; In Dir ist Freude; Nun freut euch; Nun komm, der Heiden Heiland; Wachet auf*; etc.), pub 1907–9; Goldberg Variations, 1914; *Capriccio sopra la lontananza del fratello dilettisimo*, 1915; etc.

Other works: early songs and choral pieces, other piano transcriptions

Büsser, (Paul) Henri (b. Toulouse, 16 Jan 1872; d. Paris, 30 Dec 1973). French composer and conductor. He began his training as a Toulouse Cathedral choirboy and completed it under Franck, Widor and Guiraud at the Paris Conservatoire (1889–93). There followed a long career as a composer, conductor, organist, teacher and orchestrator (notably of Debussy's *Petite Suite* and *Printemps*).

Bussotti, Sylvano (b. Florence, 1 Oct 1931). Italian composer. Born into an artistic family, he studied at the Florence Conservatory and with Max Deutsch in Paris (1956–8), where he met Boulez. In 1958 he paid his first visit to Darmstadt and became associated with Metzger. Flagrant eroticism gave a particular charge to his conception of music as a performance art and allowed him full access to what was inadmissible (in modernist terms) under the guise of high camp. Often he has designed his own productions.

Operas (all librettos by the composer): *La Passion selon Sade*, f.p. Palermo, 1965; *Lorenzaccio*, 1968–72, f.p. Venice, 1972; *Nottetempo*, f.p. Milan, 1976; *Le Racine*, f.p. Milan, 1980; *L'ispirazione*, f.p. Florence, 1988; etc.

Other works: *Pièces de chair II*, 1958–60 (includes 5 Pieces for David Tudor, pf; *voix de femme*, v, ens); *Sette fogli*, 1959 (*Couple*, fl, pf; *Coeur*, perc; *Per tre sul piano*; *Lettura di Braibanti*, v; *Mobile-stabile*, ens; *Manifesto per Kalinowksi*, ens; *Sensitivo*, solo str); *Phrase à trois*, str trio, 1960; *The Rara Requiem*, soli, orch, 1969–70; *Bergkristall* (ballet), 1974

Butt, Clara (Ellen) (b. Southwick, Sussex, 1 Feb 1872; d. North Stoke, Oxon., 23 Jan 1936). British contralto, created dame in 1920. She studied at the RCM, where her performance as Gluck's Orpheus in 1892 made her reputation – though she became almost exclusively a concert artist, tall and powerful of voice. Elgar wrote *Sea Pictures* for her.

Butterfly. Name given to Chopin's Etude in G♭, Op.25:9.

Butterley, Nigel (Henry) (b. Sydney, 13 May 1935). Australian composer, whose works chart a spiritual-creative journey that began during studies at the NSW State Conservatorium (1951–60) and received a decisive jolt with lessons from Rainier in London (1962). He worked for the Australian Broadcasting Commission and then taught at the Newcastle Conservatorium (1973–91), his output including radio pieces (*In the Head the Fire*, 1966), choral and solo settings of Dickinson, Raine, etc., and four quartets.

Butterworth, George (Sainton Kaye) (b. London, 12 Jul 1885; d. Pozières, 5 Aug 1916). British composer, vital figure in the folksong and folkdance movement (from 1906) and its creative outgrowth through both his own music and his friendship with Vaughan Williams. Brought up in Yorkshire, he studied at Eton, Oxford (1904–8) and the RCM (1910–11), and during his brief career wrote two sets of Housman songs (published in 1911 and 1912), an associated orchestral rhapsody *A Shropshire Lad* (1912) and the orchestral idyll *The Banks of Green Willow* (1913). He joined up at the start of the First World War and was killed in action.

Michael Barlow *Whom the Gods Love* (1997)

button accordion. Accordion controlled largely or wholly by buttons rather than a piano-style keyboard.

Buxheimer Orgelbuch. Important source of early keyboard music, c.1470, possibly initiated by Conrad Paumann in Munich (whence it returned after being preserved in the small Bavarian town of Buxheim, home of a Carthusian monastery).

Buxtehude, Dietrich (b. ?Helsingborg, c.1637; d. Lübeck, 9 May 1707). German organist-composer, and a pre-eminent master of the high Baroque in northern Europe. Honoured since the late 19th century as a forerunner of Bach, he became a focus of interest in his own right towards the end of the 20th century.

He must have studied with his father, whose family presumably came from the town of Buxtehude, and who from 1641 or 1642 was organist of St Olai, Elsinore. His training completed, he found posts in Helsingborg and Elsinore and in 1668 won one of the most important appointments in north Germany, to the Marienkirche in Lübeck, succeeding Franz Tunder, whose daughter he married; they raised four daughters to adulthood. There he stayed for almost 40 years, enjoying musical friendships with Reincken in Hamburg and Düben (who made a collection of his vocal works) in Stockholm. Besides playing the organ and overseeing vocal music for Sunday and festival services, he five times a year presented an *Abendmusik* (evening music) of sacred and secular pieces. Those who went to hear him included Handel (1703) and Bach (1705–6). The 20-year-old Bach's presence in Lübeck, hearing the aged master after a long journey on foot, is one of music history's great emblems of a tradition being transmitted.

Buxtehude's virtuosity and imagination as an improviser, along with his contrapuntal expertise, found lasting expression in his larger organ works: the *praeludia* (nowadays usually given such titles as 'Prelude and Fugue') and longer pieces based on chorale or plainsong melodies (customarily known now as 'chorale fantasias', e.g. BuxWV 204 and 223). Many of these survive in copies that belonged to Bach, his family members or his students. The simultaneity of fantasy and learning is also a feature of Buxtehude's chamber sonatas, of which two sets were his only major publications. His vocal works, nearly all sacred, include funeral music for his father, who had followed him to Lübeck and died in 1674 (*Fried- und Freudenreiche Hinfahrt*; Arrival in the Realm of Peace and Joy).

Kerala J. Snyder *Dietrich Buxtehude* (1987)

Vocal works: *Membra Jesu nostri*, cycle of 7 cantatas, BuxWV 75; *Fried- und Freudenreiche Hinfahrt*, funeral music, BuxWV 76; other cantatas, arias, etc.
Organ (praeludia, toccatas, chaconnes, canzonas, etc.): Prelude, Fugue and Chaconne, C, BuxWV 137; Prelude and Fugue, D, BuxWV 139; Prelude and Fugue, G minor, BuxWV 149; Toccata and Fugue, D minor, BuxWV 155; Toccata and Fugue, F, BuxWV 156; Ciacona, E minor, BuxWV 160; Passacaglia, D minor, BuxWV 161; Canzonetta, G, BuxWV 171; Fugue 'Gigue', C, BuxWV 174; about 30 others
Organ (works based on chorale/plainsong melodies): *Ach Herr, mich armer Sünder*, BuxWV 178; *Ein' feste Burg*, BuxWV 184; *Herr Christ, der einig Gottes Sohn*, BuxWV 192; *In dulci jubilo*, BuxWV 197; *Magnificat primi toni*, BuxWV 204; *Nun komm, der Heiden Heiland*, BuxWV 211; *Puer natus in Bethlehem*, BuxWV 217; *Vater unser in Himmelreich*, BuxWV 219; *Wie schön leuchtet der Morgenstern*, BuxWV 223; about 40 others
Other instrumental works: 7 Sonatas, Op.1, vn, gamba, hpd, pub ?1694; 7 Sonatas, Op.2, vn, gamba, hpd, pub 1696; other sonatas, keyboard suites and variations

BuxWV. Abbreviation for the Buxtehude catalogue *Buxtehude-Werke-Verzeichnis* (1974, ²1985).

BWV. Abbreviation for the Bach catalogue *Bach-Werke-Verzeichnis* (1950, ³1998).

Byrd, William (b. London, c.1540; d. Stondon Massey, Essex, 4 Jul 1623). English composer, revered in his time and later as the father of music in his country, for though he learned a lot from the previous generation (especially Tallis) and from continental models (by way of the elder Alfonso Ferrabosco), his synthesis was strong, adaptable to many different circumstances (sacred polyphony, consort songs and fantasies, keyboard music) and widely influential, despite the fact that much of his work was for the Roman Catholic liturgy, officially proscribed.

He is presumed to have been trained in the Chapel Royal as a choirboy and as Tallis's apprentice; he may have started to compose in his teens, under Mary I (r. 1553–8). There followed a period as organist and choirmaster of Lincoln Cathedral (1563–72), for which he seems to have written much of his English sacred music. While there he was married, in 1568, and his first children were born. In 1572 he returned to the Chapel Royal, now as Tallis's peer: he shared organ duties with the older master, and came into contact with leading poets and Catholic noblemen. Under a patent from Elizabeth I, he and Tallis published a collection of Latin motets (1575).

Soon after this the uneasy acceptance of Catholics in England began to break down. The Latin motets he continued to write were now for private, even secret worship, often setting texts of lamentation or prayer for release, yet he was able to publish these works in two volumes, protected by his eminence, his aristocratic supporters and perhaps, too, by a robust loyalty to the throne. He also composed a song celebrating the defeat of the Spanish Armada to words by the queen ('Look and bow down'), as well as other royal tributes, including the earliest example of madrigalian Elizolatry ('This sweet and merry month of May').

In general, though, the madrigal style of the younger generation (including his pupil Morley) was not to his taste. He professed the sound counterpoint of an earlier age, with musical motifs chosen not so much for their expressive qualities or colour as for their aptness as subjects for interlocking and development, in designs of superb wholeness. His preferred genre for secular vocal music was the consort song, for soloist with viols, though in publishing such works he allowed that the instrumental parts could alternatively be sung. In keyboard music he delighted in the challenge of constantly revivifying the pavan–galliard duplex structure of slow and fast movements girdered by regular phrasing, and in the other challenge of variation form. Works of these kinds – English songs and keyboard pieces – he also put in order around the time of the two books of *Cantiones sacrae* (1589, 1591). His *Psalms, Sonnets and Songs* (1588) sold out, had to be reprinted and was followed by *Songs of Sundry Natures* (1589, including the Easter anthem *Christ rising again*). In 1591 he assembled a manuscript collection of keyboard music, *My Lady Nevell's Book*.

With these compendia established he left London (probably just before Shakespeare arrived), and settled in Stondon Massey, close to Ingatestone Hall, the home of one of his Catholic patrons, Sir John Petre. There he wrote music for the Latin mass, including three settings of the ordinary and around a hundred propers: it was music of quietness but also resilience, suited to the times – and yet this music, too, he was able to publish. He also brought out a third book of anthems and songs in English, *Psalms, Songs and Sonnets* (1611), after which he may have put down his pen.

Joseph Kerman *The Masses and Motets of William Byrd* (1981); John Harley *William Byrd* (1997)

Masses: a 4, pub *c*.1592–3; a 3, pub *c*.1593–4; a 5, pub *c*.1595

Collections of motets: CANTIONES, QUAE AB ARGUMENTO SACRAE VOCANTUR, pub 1575 (with Tallis); *Cantiones sacrae I*, pub 1589 (*Ne irascaris – Civitas sancti tui* a 5, etc.); *Cantiones sacrae II*, pub 1591 (*Haec dies* a 6, *Laudibus in sanctis* a 5, *Miserere mei, Deus* a 5, etc.); *Gradualia I*, pub 1605 (*Ave verum corpus* a 4, *Iustorum animae* a 5, etc.); *Gradualia II*, pub 1607

Other motets: *Ad Dominum cum tribularer* a 8; etc.

English church music: Great Service a 6–10; *Christ rising again* a 6, *O Lord make thy servant Elizabeth* a 6, *Sing joyfully unto God our strength* a 6, etc.

Consort songs/madrigals: *Is Sidney dead?* (elegy for Philip Sidney), v, 4 viols, 1586 (also set to words *In angel's weed* as elegy for Mary Queen of Scots, 1587); *Look and bow down*, v, 4 viols, 1588; *Lullaby, my sweet little baby* a 5, pub 1588; *Rejoice unto the Lord*, v, 4 viols, 1586; *This sweet and merry month of May* a 6, pub 1590; *Ye sacred muses* (elegy for Tallis), v, 4 viols, 1585; etc.

Consort music: fantasias (3 a 3, 1 a 4, 1 a 5, 2 a 6, *Browning* a 5); In Nomines (2 a 4, 5 a 5); Pavan and Galliard a 6, Pavan a 5

Keyboard: pavans and galliards (in A minor No.2 'The Earl of Salisbury', in C No.2 'Kinborough Good', in C minor No.1, in F No.2 'Ph. Tregian', in G minor No.2 'Sir William Petre', etc.); other dances (*The Queen's Alman*, Lavolta No.1 in G minor 'Lady Morley', Jig in A minor, etc.); variations (*Callino casturame, The Carman's Whistle, Go from my window, John come kiss me now, O mistress mine, Rowland or Lord Willoughby's Welcome Home, Sellinger's Round, Walsingham, Wilson's Wild, The woods so wild*, etc.); grounds (*The Bells, Hugh Aston's Ground, The Hunt's Up, My Lady Nevell's Ground, Qui passe for My Lady Nevell*, etc.); fantasias (*Voluntary for My Lady Nevell*, etc.); descriptive pieces (*The Barley Break, The March before the Battle or The Earl of Oxford's March, The Battle*)

Byttering (*fl. c.*1410–20). English composer, of five suave pieces in the Old Hall Manuscript including *En Katerine solennia*, a wedding motet for Henry V and Catherine of France (1420). A Thomas Byteryng, recorded as a priest in Hastings and London, may have been him.

Byzantine chant. The chant of the Greek Orthodox Church, taking its name from the capital of the Eastern Empire at Byzantium/Constantinople/Istanbul. The Greek church had traditions quite distinct from Rome's long before the official schism of 1054, by which time Constantinopolitan missionaries were Christianizing the Slavs and making Byzantine chant the parent of Slavonic church music. Both Byzantine chant and Western plainsong trace their origins to the great churches of Palestine in the early Christian centuries, but many generations of oral transmission, coupled with divergences in liturgical practice, had separated the two streams by the time musical notation arrived. In both cases fully legible notation was achieved by the mid 12th century, but in different forms: Byzantine chant was notated not on staves but with sequences of signs, these indicating mode, melodic interval and accentuation.

The system of eight modes is shared with the West – indeed, was transmitted there from Byzantium in the 8th century – but otherwise Byzantine chant has its own styles and characters, even where the liturgy is similar. Often it is not: the Greek church in the age of chant composition (up to c.800), unlike the Latin, produced tens of thousands of hymns. Byzantine chant also differs in the continuing importance of the cantor soloist, often singing against a choral drone. Instruments were never permitted in the Greek church, nor was there any development of polyphony. Instead some venerated cantors from c.1300 onwards introduced florid elaborations of the chant in what became known as the kalophonic (beautiful-sounding) style. Among them was St Joannes Koukouzeles (c.1280–c.1350), who was trained in the imperial capital but left at the height of his fame to become a singing monk on Mount Athos. The further embellishments of his successors were cut short by the fall of Constantinople in 1453, after which conservation became the deeper need. In the early 19th century the chant repertory was revised and, for the first time, printed.

Egon Wellesz *A History of Byzantine Music and Hymnography* (1949, ²1961)

C. Note name, hence C♯, C major, etc. The C CLEF marks the line for middle C.

C major is the white-note key, the starting point for keyboard performers: hence its qualities of clarity and candour. It is the key of Beethoven's first symphony (and 'Waldstein' Sonata, etc.) and Schubert's last (and String Quintet, etc.), of symphonies also by Schumann, Bizet, Sibelius, Stravinsky and Shostakovich, and of the deceptively transparent *Così fan tutte*. C minor has a passionate aura, but more public than intimate, a twist it perhaps received from Beethoven, by way of his Fifth Symphony, Third Piano Concerto, several chamber works, three piano sonatas (including the last) and piano variations. Earlier C minor music includes many Bach pieces, three Haydn symphonies and various Mozart works, including a piano concerto and two masses. Among later instances are Brahms's First Symphony, Tchaikovsky's Second, Saint-Saëns's Third, Bruckner's Eighth (as well as his First and Second), Mahler's 'Resurrection' Symphony (ending in the relative major), Rachmaninoff's Second Piano Concerto and several works by Shostakovich (Symphonies Nos.4 and 8, Piano Concerto No.1, Eighth Quartet). The key of C♯, with seven sharps, is highly unusual, but C♯ minor, with four and E major as its relative, is quite common in keyboard music, examples including a Haydn sonata, Beethoven's 'Moonlight', several Chopin pieces and Rachmaninoff's popular prelude. C♯ minor is also the key of a late Beethoven quartet, Mahler's Fifth Symphony (which ends in D), Prokofiev's Seventh Symphony and Shostakovich's Second Violin Concerto.

cabaça. Gourd covered with beads on strings: a rattle inherited from Latin American bands.

cabaletta. The final part, fast and brilliant, of an aria or duet in two or more sections, as found in operas from Rossini to middle-period Verdi, e.g. 'Sempre libera' in *La traviata*. The derivation is uncertain.

Caballé, Montserrat (b. Barcelona, 12 Apr 1933). Catalan soprano, noted for her luminosity and assured virtuosity in Donizetti and Verdi. She studied at the Barcelona Conservatory and joined the Basle Opera in 1956. Her career took off in 1965, when she sang at the Met and Glyndebourne and created a sensation standing in for Horne at a New York concert performance of *Lucrezia Borgia*. She retired from opera in 1992.

Caballero, Manuel Fernández (b. Murcia, 14 Mar 1835; d. Madrid, 26 Feb 1906). Spanish composer of numerous zarzuelas, which he began writing while still a student at the Madrid Conservatory (1850–56). His biggest successes came after a visit to Cuba (1864–71) and include *El dúo de la africana* (1893). After that he went blind, but continued with the help of amanuenses to keep up his production of two or three works a year.

Cabanilles, Juan Bautista José (b. Algemesí, near Valencia, 4 Sep 1644; d. Valencia, 29 Apr 1712). Spanish organist-composer, the master in whom an independent Spanish tradition of contrapuntal keyboard music culminated. First organist at Valencia Cathedral from 1666, he left 90 tientos and other works, as well as some choral pieces.

cabaret. Song style, popular but sophisticated, with undertones of irony, satire, eroticism and sentimental pathos. The word (adopted from Fr., seemingly cognate with *chambre*) can also denote the repertory of such songs, or a place (bar or restaurant) where they are performed. Cabaret has meant different things in different places at different times, from Erik Satie at the Chat Noir in Paris around 1905 to Elvis Presley at the Hilton Hotel in Las Vegas around 1975. At its most particularly characteristic, though, it started in Paris with the opening of the Chat Noir in 1881 and closed in Berlin with the arrival of Nazism just over half a century later, having been largely confined to those two cities. It learned from operetta, waltz, art song and jazz, and left its tang on many. Schoenberg, as well as Satie, wrote cabaret songs, besides transfiguring the medium in his *Pierrot lunaire*, and it also affected Weill, Eisler and Poulenc.

Cabezón, Antonio de (b. Castrillo de Matajudíos, near Burgos, *c*.1510; d. Madrid, 26 Mar 1566). Spanish organist-composer, blind from childhood, whose mastery of counterpoint and variation form influenced composers in Spain and perhaps also England (Tallis, Byrd), which he visited in 1554–5 in the retinue of Philip II. Previously he had served the king's mother, Isabella (1526–39), probably after studies with García de Baeza at Palencia Cathedral. His works – available to keyboard or plucked-string soloists, or to ensembles – include tientos, variations (*diferencías*, *glosas*) on popular melodies and basses, plainsong settings and intabulations of pieces by Josquin and others. He was succeded as royal musician by his son Hernando (1541–1602), who published a collection of his works.

cabinet organ. REED ORGAN in which air is sucked past the reeds rather than blown (as in the harmonium).

caccia (It., hunt, pl. *cacce*). (1) Italian song of the 14th–15th centuries, equivalent to the French *chace*, usually in three parts, with the upper two canonic, i.e. chasing one another. The words may also be about hunting, or the chase may be amatory.

(2) Designation of origin or affiliation in the name of an instrument: *corno da caccia*, OBOE DA CACCIA.

Caccini. Italian musical family of the early Baroque.

(1) **Giulio Romolo** (b. Rome, 8 Oct 1551; d. Florence, Dec 1618). Composer and performer,

pioneer of expressive solo song. He sang as a treble in the Julian Chapel under Animuccia (1564–5) before being taken to perform in the intermedi for the Medici wedding in Florence in 1565. There he stayed, studying with the virtuoso singer Scipione delle Palle, joining court service, frequenting Bardi's camerata and marrying a fellow singer (in 1584). In 1586, at another Medici wedding, he was among a group of singers, costumed as angels, due to deliver a motet as they descended from the cupola of the church, but he was the only one not overcome by vertigo. Thus, in emblematic fashion, Renaissance polyphony became Baroque monody.

It was not only by accident, though, that he took a lead in the new style, but through creative artistry and professional pride. Fiercely competitive, he added music to the *Euridice* largely set by Peri for the marriage of Marie de' Medici and Henri IV of France (1600), then rushed into print with his own complete setting of Rinuccini's libretto. He followed up with the deliberately titled *Le nuove musiche* (1602), a collection of songs in which vocal melody – flowing freely above a bass line, rhythmically flexible, expressive in its contours, its harmonic journeys and its written-out embellishments – could, as he put in his preface, 'almost speak in music'. Among these 22 songs, 'Amarilli, mia bella' was an instant and continuing hit. During the next few years he enjoyed success with his family singing group, including his second wife and two daughters. He also produced a second collection of songs (1614), but gardening occupied his time as well.

(2) **Francesca** (b. Florence, 18 Sep 1587; d. Florence, after Jun 1641). Singer-composer, elder daughter of Giulio Romolo. She spent most of her life in Medici service, and wrote songs and dramatic music, including the first opera by a woman, *La liberazione di Ruggiero dall'isola d'Alcina* (1625).

cadence (Fr. *cadence*, Ger. *Kadenz*, It. *cadenza*, from the Lat. *cadere*, to fall). Closing gesture defining the end of a phrase, section, movement or work. Frequently there is indeed a melodic fall. Plainsong melodies often end with a stepwise descent (or, more rarely, ascent) to the final, setting the pattern for medieval polyphony. Renaissance music shows a move towards the major–minor system of harmonic cadences belonging to a few types, of which the PERFECT CADENCE and IMPERFECT CADENCE are the most important, followed by the PLAGAL CADENCE, PHRYGIAN CADENCE and MEDIAL CADENCE. These cadences are at the root of diatonic music's characteristic sense of directed motion: the music moves towards a perfect cadence, and continuity depends on the extension, progression through or subversion of the perfect cadence.

Composers working in other tonalities have found other cadences. Messiaen's typical cadence, for example, is a melodic-harmonic fall through a tritone. Tonal cadences also have characteristic rhythmic patterns – especially a slowing towards and in the two final chords – and these have sometimes helped distinguish cadential acts in atonal music. Some of Schoenberg's atonal works (the finale of the Second Quartet, the *Ode to Napoleon*) cadence on to tonal chords, but much more common in atonal music are alternatives to the clinching cadence, such as the cut applied to an ostinato (Berg's *Wozzeck*), the departure (Ligeti's *Melodien*), the emphatic attack, as of a book being slammed shut (Boulez's *Pli selon pli*) or the expiring in exhaustion (Barraqué's … *au-delà du hasard*).

cadenza (It., pl. *cadenze*, though in Eng. 'cadenzas'). Solo spot in a concerto, aria or other work, originally unaccompanied and improvised. The cadenza began, in 16th-century song, as a flourish at the cadence – indeed, in most languages the same term serves for both; English differentiates them with its adoptions from Italian and French.

Around 1700 the unaccompanied cadenza became a regular part of the da capo aria, placed at the end of the repeat. It might be extemporized or prepared (but then still an improvisatory manner was expected), and there was a theory it should not outstay the length of a breath, though notated examples from the period indicate there were exceptions. Instrumentalists, too, were soon expected to play cadenzas, towards the ends of concerto movements.

Concertos in the Classical period almost always have a first-movement cadenza (Mozart's Clarinet Concerto is an exception), prompted by a 6/4 chord on the dominant, after which the orchestra falls silent, to re-enter, at a dominant trill from the soloist, for the final tutti affirming the tonic: the cadenza is, therefore, still a cadence. Cadenzas may be similarly situated in Classical concerto slow movements, arias and smaller instrumental works (quartets, sonatas), while a shorter embellishment, the EINGANG, became an additional feature of the concerto first movement. Mozart's own cadenzas survive for about two-thirds of his piano concertos, and these are almost invariably played by modern performers. Where there is no original cadenza, players may prepare their own or learn someone else's: for Mozart concertos there are cadenzas by many distinguished performers, and composers from Beethoven to Stockhausen.

Beethoven completed the process by which cadenza energy was concentrated in the first movement, wrote out cadenzas for all his piano concertos and, in the last of them, the 'Emperor', made the cadenza an integral part of the score, with the orchestra taking part. This became the rule, though Brahms left room for a cadenza in the conventional place in his violin concerto. Even concertos that have very little else in common with the Classical form will often include a cadenza in its normal, semi-final position.

Cadman, Charles Wakefield (b. Johnstown, Penn., 24 Dec 1881; d. Los Angeles, 30 Dec 1946). US composer, especially of parlour songs, such as 'At dawning' (1906) and 'From the land of the sky-blue water' (1909), of which the latter was among the first of his several explorations of Amerindian music. Trained in Pittsburgh and resident in Los Angeles from 1916, he also wrote operas (*Shanewis*, Met 1918; *The Willow Tree*, NBC, 1932) and chamber music.

caesura. Pause for breath, or as if for breath, indicated by a comma or V above the staff. The term can also be used for the longer and more often sounding hold indicated by the pause sign.

Caffarelli (b. Bitonto, 12 Apr 1710; d. Naples, 31 Jan 1783). Italian castrato. Trained by Porpora in Naples, he appeared all over Italy before returning to Naples in 1734. From there he made excursions, notably to London (1737–8), where Handel wrote the title roles in *Faramondo* and *Serse* for him. His fiery pride mellowed with age and with the comforts of the dukedom he had been able to buy himself.

Cage, John (Milton) (b. Los Angeles, 5 Sep 1912; d. New York, 12 Aug 1992). US composer. By one simple step – removing what had commonly been thought an absolute essential of art, namely meaning – he radically changed how music could be thought, felt, imagined and heard. Allowing decisions to be made by chance and inviting all manner of sounds into his music, he produced a body of work of astonishing variety, and yet the very freedom of his art gave it the profile of a distinct personality: candid, open and happily disposed. His work was hugely influential, especially in the 1950s and 1960s.

He travelled in Europe in 1930–31, then studied with Cowell in New York and Schoenberg in California (1934). His first, rather abstract pieces were essays in non-serial 12-note composition. In 1937 he moved to Seattle, where he organized a percussion orchestra featuring found objects and electrical devices (tin cans, buzzers) alongside regular instruments, as he did again in San Francisco (1939–41) and Chicago (1941–2). Percussion music, by definition, could not be organized by tonal or 12-note means: for him that was one of its virtues, along with its accessibility to untrained performers. But at this time he felt it had to be organized somehow, so he developed a principle based on rhythmic proportions. The *First Construction* (1939), for example, has a rhythmic structure thus 4–3–2–3–4 units, with the whole form thus marked out in 16-bar segments (i.e. in sections of 64–48–32–48–64 bars), each similarly divided. The metal scoring, pulsation and heterophony combine to evoke gamelan music. Meanwhile, in *Imaginary Landscape No.1* he created an early example of electronic music: intended for radio performance, the score asks for frequency recordings to be manipulated on two turntables.

Having enjoyed some success with concert, dance and radio performances, he moved to New York in 1942 and continued his work with dancers and choreographers, especially Merce Cunningham, his life partner and long-standing collaborator. The prepared piano, which he had invented as a one-person percussion orchestra, became a major creative focus, not only in dance scores but also in concert pieces. It suited him well, being homemade (therefore both subject to experiment and removed from professional musical life), a gateway to oriental sounds and limited in scope, providing a gamut of particular sonorities. With it he produced his biggest venture so far, the hour-long *Sonatas and Interludes* (1946–8). At the same time he was immersing himself in Indian thought, especially the writings of Ananda K. Coomaraswamy, commencing his journey East.

In 1949 he spent some months in Paris, began a close (but brief) creative friendship with Boulez and started his String Quartet in Four Parts (for the seasons), which, like the preceding music for prepared piano, is based on a restricted set of sounds and discloses a very quiet, almost blank expressive voice. Boulez was fascinated by his objectivity but not at all by his extreme discretion. Back in New York he met young musicians much more in sympathy with him, including Feldman and Tudor. Meanwhile his oriental studies had brought him to Zen, under Daisetz Teitaro Suzuki, and to a point where he could declare: 'I have nothing to say and I am saying it and that is poetry as I need it' (1950).

He found the means to say nothing, to remove intention, by assembling the basic conditions for a musical performance and letting CHANCE OPERATIONS take over. The way to silence the will was to follow rules – but they had to be good rules, which is where creativity came into play (there and

in the beautiful, handcrafted design with which he endowed his scores). They had to be rules that would lead to openness, calm and a gentle seriousness.

In the finale of his Prepared Piano Concerto (1950–51) he let the ordering of sounds be decided by coin tosses, and he then embarked on the immense labour of tossing coins to determine every aspect of a big new piano work for Tudor, the *Music of Changes* (1951). He also discovered or invented other, less arduous ways of bringing chance into music: writing for radio receivers (*Imaginary Landscape No.4*), placing notes on imperfections in pieces of paper (Music for Piano) and removing sound altogether (*4' 33"*, 1952, realizing an idea he had been harbouring, but not daring to achieve, since 1948). Sometimes the result was flat and simple, close to silence, but it could also be fearsomely virtuoso, as in the *Music of Changes* or the 'time-length' pieces of the 1950s, which he was emboldened to create through his association with Tudor. (*Aria*, for Berberian, was another example of the joy he could take in a performer.) His European tours with Tudor in 1954 and 1958 had wide repercussions among young composers, while at home in New York an all-Cage concert in 1958 celebrated a quarter century of work, from the Sonata for clarinet to the new Concert for piano and orchestra, a compendium of determinate and indeterminate notations.

The new INDETERMINACY opened the music further, to what could produce many different results. The notation might indicate, for example, where on the piano a sound was to be made, or it might consist of a kit (often including designs on transparent sheets, as in *Variations II* and *Fontana Mix*) from which readings were to be taken. But always the interpretative action was prescribed: Cage was never interested in improvisation, which would have reintroduced intention. Indeterminacy, too, gave him access to non-traditional modes of performance, especially electronic performance, beginning with *Cartridge Music* (1960), in which the performers explore their environment and various objects with gramophone cartridges attached to amplifiers and speakers.

In 1961 he found publishers for his music (Peters) and writings, and became a figure of global renown, ridicule, puzzlement and stimulus. During the next few years he lectured widely but wrote little. His musical ideal now was not the composition but the circus, in which different performers might participate simultaneously, as in his HPSCHD. He was then drawn back to composition by a practical need, to write a piece for Cunningham with the same phrase structure as

Satie's *Socrate*, for which his friend could not get the rights – hence *Cheap Imitation* (1969). During the next two decades he worked in many different areas, producing virtuoso pieces (*Etudes australes, Freeman Etudes*) and circuses (*Roaratorio*), music following the ways of nature (using plant materials, based on tracings of rocks) or of cultural history (the *Europeras*, quilts of quotation).

Finally just one method was left, that of selecting sounds to be performed at any point within given extents of time. All these pieces, beginning with *Two* (1987), are titled with the number of performers involved, plus superscripts to distinguish those for the same number, and they embrace conventional media (solo piano, string quartet, chorus, orchestra) as well as more unusual formations (*Four*[3] for piano, rainsticks and violin or oscillator, *Two*[3] for shō and conch shells). With this simple technique and his sense for aural spacing, colour and balance, he fully revealed what his teacher Schoenberg had said he lacked: an ear for harmony.

John Cage *Silence* (1961); James Pritchett *The Music of John Cage* (1993)

www.johncage.info

Variable: *4' 33"*, 1952; *0' 00" (4' 33" No.2)*, 1962; *Variations I*, 1958; *II*, 1961; *III–IV*, 1963; *V*, 1965; *VI–VII*, 1966; *VIII*, 1978

Operas: *Europeras 1–2*, 1987; *3–4*, 1990; *5*, 1991

. Orchestral: *The Seasons*, 1947; *Concerto*, prepared pf, chbr orch, 1950–51; *16 Dances*, 9 insts, 1950–51; *Concert*, pf, insts, 1958; *Atlas eclipticalis*, 1962; *Cheap Imitation*, 1972; *Renga*, 1976; *30 Pieces*, 5 orch, 1981; etc.

Electronic: IMAGINARY LANDSCAPE *No.1*, 2 turntables, muted pf, cymbal, 1939; *No.4*, 12 radios, 1951; *No.5*, recordings, 1952; *Williams Mix*, tapes, 1952; *Fontana Mix*, tape, 1958; *Cartridge Music*, 1960; HPSCHD, 1–7 amplified hpds, tapes, 1967–9; *Roaratorio, an Irish Circus on Finnegans Wake*, 1979

Percussion ensemble: *Quartet*, 1935; *Trio*, 1936; *First Construction (in Metal)*, 1939; *Second Construction*, 1940; *Living Room Music* (Stein), 4 speakers, perc, 1940; *Double Music*, 1940 (with Harrison); *Third Construction*, 1941; *Imaginary Landscape Nos.2–3*, 1942; *Credo in Us*, 1942; *Forever and Sunsmell* (Cummings), v, 2 perc, 1942; *Amores*, 1943; *She is asleep*, v, prepared pf, 4 perc, 1943; *Child of Tree*, amplified plant materials, 1975; *Branches*, amplified plant materials, 1976; *Three*[2], 1991; *Six*, 1991; *Four*[4], 1991

Percussion solo: *27' 10.554"*, 1956; *Music for Carillon Nos.1–5*, 1952–67; *One*[2], 1990

Chamber: *Solo Clarinet Sonata*, 1933; *Nocturne*, vn, pf, 1947; *String Quartet in Four Parts*, 1949–50; *6 Melodies*, vn, kbd, 1950; *59½"*, solo str, 1953; *26' 1.1499"*, solo str, 1953–5; *Cheap Imitation*, vn, 1977; *Chorals*, vn, 1979; *Freeman Etudes*, vn, 1977–80, 1989–90; *30 Pieces*, str qt, 1983; *Haikai*, fl,

zoomoozophone, 1984; *Music for more*, any ens, 1984–7; *Two*, fl, pf, 1987; *Four*, str qt, 1989; *One*[6], vn, 1990; *One*[8], vc, 1991; *One*[10], vn, 1992; *Two*[6], vn, pf, 1992; etc.

Vocal: *5 Songs* (Cummings), a, pf, 1938; *The Wonderful Widow of Eighteen Springs* (Joyce), v, closed pf, 1942; *Four Walls* (Cunningham), v, pf, 1944; *Experiences No.2* (Cummings), v, 1948; *A Flower*, vn, closed pf, 1950; *Aria*, v, 1958; *Song Books*, 1970; *Hymns and Variations*, 12 amplified v, 1979; *Nowth upon Nacht* (Joyce), v, pf, 1984

Piano: *Metamorphosis*, 1938; *A Room*, 1943; *Experiences No.1*, 2 pf, 1945; *Ophelia*, 1946; *Two Pieces*, 1946; *The Seasons*, 1947; *Dream*, 1948; *In a landscape*, 1948; *Suite*, toy pf, 1948; MUSIC OF CHANGES, 1951; *7 Haiku*, 1951–2; *Waiting*, 1952; *For M.C. and D.T.*, 1952; *Water Music*, 1952; *Music for Piano 1–20*, 1952–3; *34' 46.776"*, 1954; *Music for Piano 21–84*, 1955–6; *Winter Music*, 1–20 pf, 1957; *Music Walk*, 1958; *Cheap Imitation*, 1969; *Etudes australes*, 1974–5; *Perpetual Tango*, 1984; *Aslsp*, 1985; *One*, 1987; *Swinging*, 1989; *Two*[2], 2 pf, 1989; *One*[2], 1989; *One*[5], 1990; etc.

Prepared piano: *Bacchanale*, 1940; *Totem Ancestor*, 1942; *And the earth shall bear again*, 1942; *Primitive*, 1942; *Tossed as it is untroubled*, 1943; *The Perilous Night*, 1944; *Prelude for Meditation*, 1944; *Root of an unfocus*, 1944; *A Valentine out of Season*, 1944; *Daughters of the lonesome isle*, 1945; *Music for Marcel Duchamp*, 1947; *Sonatas and Interludes*, 1946–8; *2 Pastorales*, 1951–2; *31' 57.9864"*, 1954; etc.

Prepared piano duo: *A Book of Music*, 1944; *3 Dances*, 1945

caisse (Fr.). Drum, as in *caisse claire* (side drum), *caisse roulante* ('rolling drum', i.e. tenor drum), *grosse caisse* (bass drum), etc.

cakewalk. Dance of US Black origin, possibly imitating the strutting of White people. It was popularized by blackface minstrel shows that went to Europe, whence Debussy's *Golliwog's Cake-Walk*. Explanations of the name (e.g. that this was a competitive dance, with the prize a cake) sound suspiciously posterior.

calando (It., dropping). Decrescendo, arguably implying also a rallentando.

Caldara, Antonio (b. Venice, ?1671; d. Vienna, 28 Dec 1736). Italian composer, hugely prolific, who carried the Venetian-Roman Baroque tradition to Vienna. A violinist's son, he may well have studied with Legrenzi, and was certainly playing cello and singing at St Mark's by the 1690s. In the same decade he established himself as a composer of sonatas, cantatas, oratorios and operas, and joined the service of the last Gonzaga duke, in Mantua and Venice until 1707. The next year he moved to Rome, working alongside Handel and the

Scarlattis under the sumptuous patronage of princes and cardinals. After an excursion to the Barcelona court of the future emperor Charles VI (1708–9), he succeeded Handel as composer to Prince Ruspoli, for whom he wrote cantatas and Lenten oratorios. In 1711 he married a singer and began petitioning for a position with Charles, now in Vienna, though this did not materialize until 1716, when he left Rome to become imperial vice-chapelmaster under Fux. Writing both for the emperor and for the prince-archbishop of Salzburg, he produced more than 60 operas (to librettos by the court poets Zeno, Metastasio and Giovanni Claudio Pasquini) and sacred compositions in abundance, and returned in 1735 to the cello, with a set of 16 sonatas. A small part of his colossal output has lived on in the affections of singers or been revived for its expressive fluency (a *Stabat mater* of 1726, an old-style *Crucifixus* a 16).

Brian W. Pritchard, ed. *Antonio Caldara* (1987)

Caldwell, Sarah (b. Maryville, Mo., 6 Mar 1924). US conductor-director, celebrated for bringing new and unusual works (*Intolleranza, Moses und Aron, War and Peace, Taverner*) to the company she founded in Boston in 1958. She trained as a violinist at the New England Conservatory and at the height of her success, in 1976, was the first woman to conduct at the Met (*La traviata*).

Callas, Maria (b. New York, 2 Dec 1923; d. Paris, 16 Sep 1977). Greek–US soprano (originally Cecilia Sophia Anna Maria Kalogeropoulou), whose recordings, combining a superb feeling for tradition with fiercely immediate personality, have kept her a living presence. Born and raised in the USA by Greek parents, she entered the Athens Conservatory in 1938 and began coloratura studies there the next year with Elvira de Hidalgo. She made her professional debut in Athens when not yet 17, sang her first Tosca at 18, and returned to New York in 1945 in the hope of furthering her career. However, she failed her Met audition and had to wait two years before gaining an engagement at Verona in *La Gioconda* under Serafin (1947). That led to a phase in heavy roles, including her first Norma (Florence, 1948), though for Serafin she also sang Elvira in *I puritani* (Venice, 1949), beginning her electrification of the bel canto repertory. In 1949, too, she married Giovanni Battista Meneghini, a businessman who became her manager. She opened the Scala season in *I vespri siciliani* in 1951, sang for the first time at Covent Garden in 1952 and made her first recordings (under an EMI contract) in 1953, including a *Tosca* under de Sabata. The next year, having lost weight dramatically, she made her US debut in Chicago. The Met

had to wait until 1956, by which time she was a superstar. Beginning to behave like one, she quarrelled with managers at the Scala and the Met in 1958, and in 1959 publicly transferred her affections from Meneghini to the shipping tycoon Aristotle Onassis. Gradually she withdrew from the stage, but was lured back by Franco Zeffirelli to take part in his productions of *Tosca* and *Norma* in 1964–5. A Covent Garden *Tosca* (5 July 1965) brought her last appearance onstage, though she starred in Pasolini's spoken *Medea* film (1969) and made a concert tour with di Stefano in 1973–4. She had blazed briefly. Her earlier recordings are the most universally admired, but though her voice later showed signs of wear, it still conveyed intense musicality and passion.

John Ardoin *The Callas Legacy* (1977, [4]1995)
www.callas.it

Calliope. The muse of heroic poetry and string playing. The US inventor Joshua C. Stoddard (1814–1902) took her name for the steam-whistle organ he devised in 1845.

calmando, calmato (It.). Calming, calmed.

Calm Sea and Prosperous Voyage. See MEERES-STILLE UND GLÜCKLICHE FAHRT.

Calvé [Calvet de Roquer], **(Rosa Noémie) Emma** (b. Decazeville, 15 Aug 1858; d. Millau, 6 Jan 1942). French soprano, acclaimed as Carmen, which she had sung 1,000 times at the Opéra-Comique by 1904. She studied in Paris, made her debut in Brussels as Marguerite (*Faust*) in 1881 and from the next decade was active internationally.

calypso. Caribbean (especially Trinidadian) song-dance form, in syncopated duple metre with upbeat character.

Calzabigi, Ranieri (Simone Francesco Maria) (b. Leghorn, 23 Dec 1714; d. Naples, 12/13 Jul 1795). Italian librettist, co-author with Gluck of REFORM OPERA. A merchant's son, he studied at the Jesuit college in Prato (1722–9) and began taking care of the family's business correspondence while also becoming a bibliophile and man of letters. He wrote his first librettos in Naples in 1745–7. Ironically, in view of the anti-Metastasian thrust of his reform operas, these early efforts won Metastasio's praise. Even more ironically, in Paris in 1755 he initiated an edition of Metastasio's librettos and wrote a supportive, if also mildly dissenting, preface. French opera had shown him an alternative – though he was just as ambivalent about that. In 1761 he arrived in Vienna, where he produced his major collaborations with Gluck: *Orfeo* (1762) and *Alceste* (1767). By this time he was openly at aesthetic war with Metastasio, a war he carried to the stage, in a satirical piece set by Gassmann (*L'opera seria*, 1769). In 1775 he retired to Pisa, where he went on writing occasional librettos, notably *Ipermestra o le Danaidi* (1784, meant for Gluck but set by Salieri, in French) and two texts for Paisiello, *Elfrida* (1792) and *Elvira* (1794).

Cambert, Robert (b. *c*.1628; d. London, Feb/Mar 1677). French composer, of the earliest full-scale opera in the language (*Pomone*, 1671). He studied with Chambonnières, was appointed organist of St Honoré in 1652 and was working with his poet collaborator, Pierre Perrin, by 1657. They prepared themselves by way of short dialogue pieces, a masque (*Pastorale*, 1659) and a more elaborate work that was not performed (*Ariane*, 1659), and moved forward when, in 1669, Perrin was granted the privilege of presenting opera. But Perrin was imprisoned for debt in 1671, and though Cambert went ahead with another writer (*Les Peines et les plaisirs de l'amour*, 1672), his venture was scuppered when Lully gained the monopoly of opera in Paris. Louis XIV arranged a consolation prize: Cambert was sent to London as music master to Louise de Kéroualle, principal mistress of Charles II. In 1674 he presented a masque for the marriage of Charles's brother James and an expanded version of *Ariane*, but the latter had no success and he did not try again. Almost all his music is lost.

cambiare (It.). Change (to another instrument, etc.), though *muta* is the instruction more often used.

cambiata (It., thing changed). In tonal harmony an unaccented dissonant note that occurs between a chord and its resolution, arriving by a melodic interval that is greater than – but in the same direction as – that taken in the resolution. For example, if the part concerned resolves from B to C, an intervening D would be a *cambiata*. If the step to the intervening note is in the opposite direction, as in D–E–C, the term is *échappée*. See also NOTA CAMBIATA.

Cambini, Giuseppe Maria (Gioacchino) (b. Leghorn, ?13 Feb 1746; d. ?Paris, ?1825). Italian violinist-composer, active in Paris from the early 1770s as a composer of symphonies, *symphonies concertantes*, chamber music and operas. Tales grew up about his origins: that he had studied in Naples (probably true) and been saved by a wealthy Venetian from enslavement to Barbary pirates (less likely). Mozart suspected him of jealous intrigue, probably wrongly: the market he was so facilely serving could have taken one more work by a visiting Austrian. By the mid-1790s, though, the musical fashions of the *ancien régime* were becoming obsolete, and he descended into obscure poverty.

Cambridge University. Music was studied from the foundation (1284), and degrees in music were awarded from 1463 to 1464. In 1684 the chair of music was founded for Staggins, whose successors have included Tudway, Greene, Walmisley, William Sterndale Bennett, Stanford and Goehr. Choral foundations include KING'S COLLEGE CHOIR.

camera (It.). Room, as in SONATA DA CAMERA, *musica da camera* (chamber music), etc.

Camerata. Gathering of artists and amateurs in Florence under Bardi's leadership (*c*.1573–87) who concerned themselves with ancient Greek music, the foundation for the new monody and incipent opera. Among musician members were Caccini, Galilei and Piero Strozzi. The term is sometimes extended to Corsi's circle, from which opera definitively emerged at the end of the 16th century.

Camilleri, Charles (b. Hamrun, 7 Sep 1931). Maltese composer, whose concern with his country's indigenous music led to a wider embrace of Mediterranean cultures, European and Islamic. Largely self-taught, he gained from contacts he made in Australia, London and North America in his 20s and early 30s. Since then he has divided his time between London and Malta, apart from a period back in North America teaching (1977–83). His many works include three symphonies and three piano concertos.

Cammarano, Salvadore (b. Naples, 19 Mar 1801; d. Naples, 17 Jul 1852). Italian librettist. From 1834 he wrote an average of two librettos a year for Neapolitan theatres, where he was also responsible for staging. He was particularly appreciated by Donizetti (*Lucia di Lammermoor*), and worked later with Mercadante, Pacini and Verdi, writing *Il trovatore* on his deathbed.

Cammerton (Ger.). Chamber pitch (in Germany in the 17th and 18th centuries), as distinct from CHORTON, the standard for organs and church music, which was higher. To match wind instruments playing in C in *Cammerton*, an organist might have to transpose to B♭ (*B-Cammerton*) or A (*A-Cammerton*).

campana (It.). Bell, hence *campane* (tubular bells), *campanelli* (tubular bells, glockenspiel), *campanette* (glockenspiel), *campanello a mano* (handbell), *campanile* (belltower), etc.

campanella, La. Third of Liszt's *Etudes d'exécution transcendentale d'après Paganini*, based on the *Rondo à la clochette* from the Genoese master's B minor violin concerto, a theme Liszt earlier used in his *Grande fantaisie di bravura sur La clochette de Paganini* (1832–4).

Campion [Campian], **Thomas** (b. London, 12 Feb 1567; d. London, 1 Mar 1620). English poet-composer, author of lute songs, masques and Latin poems. Of prosperous family, he studied at Cambridge (1581–4) and Gray's Inn, but gained no qualification at either place. Instead, by the 1590s, he was making his way as a poet. He wrote a Latin epigram for Dowland's first book (1597), and published 21 songs in a collaborative volume with his friend Rosseter (1601). Later he worked on court masques and brought out four more songbooks alone. With a few exceptions, his songs are light, lively and syllabic. They have often been regarded as perfect fusions of poetry and music, though later composers, including Imbrie, Virgil Thomson and Castiglioni (*The Lord's Masque*), have offered re-fusions of his words with music of their own.

Christopher Wilson *Words and Notes Coupled Lovingly Together* (1989)

Songs: 'All looks be pale'; 'Author of light, revive my dying sprite'; 'Fain would I wed a fair young man'; 'I care not for these ladies'; 'It fell on a summer's day'; 'Never weather-beaten sail'; 'Oft have I sighed for him'; 'O grief, o spite'; 'The peaceful western wind'; 'Shall I come?'; 'Sing a song of joy'; 'The cypress curtain of the night is spread'; etc.

Camp Meeting, The. Name Ives gave his Third Symphony.

Campo (y Zabaleta), Conrado del (b. Madrid, 28 Oct 1878; d. Madrid, 17 Mar 1953). Spanish composer, unusual in his Wagner–Strauss leanings. A pupil of Emilio Serrano at the National Music School, he earned his living as a violinist from his teens and from 1915 was an important teacher at the Madrid Conservatory. He wrote operas, sacred music and symphonic poems (*La divina commedia*, 1910).

Campra, André (baptized Aix-en-Provence, 4 Dec 1660; d. Versailles, 29 Jun 1744). French composer, outstanding in the period between Lully and Rameau. The son of a surgeon-violinist from Turin, he was a choirboy at St Sauveur in Aix and began his career as a church musician in Arles (1681–3), at Toulouse Cathedral (1683–94) and at Notre Dame in Paris (1694–1700). The success of *L'Europe galante* (1697), with which he instituted the genre of opera-ballet, encouraged him to give up his ecclesiastical career, though in 1720, with his theatrical fortunes declining, he returned to composing church music. His opera-ballets introduced a new poetic-sensuous-fantastical note into French opera, to join the nobility of the *tragédie lyrique*, and he extended Lully's style too in terms of orchestral colour, expressive harmony, boisterousness (the rigaudon from his *Idoménée* has become a wedding favourite) and Italianate vocalizing. He was also astute enough to realize, on first witnessing Rameau's *Hippolyte et Aricie*, that 'this man will eclipse us all'.

Operas: *L'Europe galante*, Paris, 1697; *Le Carnaval de Venise*, Paris, 1699; *Tancrède*, Paris, 1702; *Les Muses*, Paris, 1703; *Les Fêtes vénitiennes*, Paris, 1710; *Idoménée*, Paris, 1712; *Les Ages*, Paris, 1718
Other works: *Requiem*, c.1722; motets, cantatas, etc.

Canada. Proximately distant from the USA, the country had fewer ethnic groups until the later 20th century – essentially only Amerindian, British and French – and these had some measure of independent development. British Canada looked to London, French Canada (Quebec) to Paris for its cultural orientation. Both regions, though, had a similar history, with important bursts of energy around 1900 and again after the Second World War. Institutions founded in the first phase included the Toronto Conservatory (1886), the McGill Conservatorium in Montreal (1904) and the Toronto Symphony (1906). Among those of the second phase were the Canadian Opera Company (with antecedents going back to 1950) and the Montreal Symphony (1954). It was to this phase that the great growth of Canadian composition belonged, beginning with Anhalt, Archer, Garant, Pentland, Schafer, Somers and Weinzweig. No Canadian composer has gained more international attention than Vivier, no Canadian musician more than Gould. See also MONTREAL; TORONTO.

Timothy J. McGee *The Music of Canada* (1985)

canary. Stamping triple-time dance from Renaissance Spain (ostensibly from the Canary Islands), which developed into a kind of fast gigue in Baroque France. This later canary appears in stage music by Lully and Campra, and in instrumental suites by Louis Couperin, Telemann and Purcell.

cancan. Exuberant duple-time dance most associated with lines of high-kicking chorus girls, introduced to Paris in the 1830s, allegedly from Algeria. The best-known example is from Offenbach's *Orphée aux enfers*.

canción (Sp.). Song, hence *cancionero* (songbook).

cancrizans (Lat., crabwise). Backwards, especially of a contrapuntal line where the notes follow those of a principal or thematic line but in reverse. In fact, crabs move sideways (with respect to the direction in which their eyes are pointing), but their ability to switch direction without turning round gives the impression of backwards motion.

Candide. Operetta by Bernstein with lyrics by several hands after a tale by Voltaire. The work is best known for its brilliant overture. First performance: Boston, 29 Oct 1956.

Cannabich, (Johann) Christian (Innocenz Bonaventura) (baptized Mannheim, 12 Dec 1731; d. Frankfurt, 20 Jan 1798). German composer, a leader of the Mannheim school. He studied with his father, a Mannheim flautist-composer, and joined the court orchestra at the age of 12. Further studies followed with Johann Stamitz and, in Rome and Stuttgart, Jommelli (1752–4); he also got to know the music of Sammartini and other Italians in Milan. In 1756 he returned to Mannheim, where by 1759 he was joint concertmaster with Toeschi, directing performances from the violin and writing ballets, symphonies, concertos and chamber music. Mozart was impressed when visiting Mannheim in 1777–8 and wrote a sonata for his daughter Rosina. Cannabich in turn was clearly impressed by Mozart in the music (rather less) he wrote after the court's move to Munich in 1778. His symphonies (73 in his own numbering) are especially fine: three sets of them were published in Paris, where his music was warmly appreciated. He died while visiting his son Carl August, also a violinist and composer.

canon (from Gk *kanon*, rule). (1) Piece of music (a whole work or an element of a work) in which a melody is soon joined by one or more successive replications of itself, overlapping in counterpoint, so that the voices effectively say the same thing at different times. The word can also denote the relevant compositional technique, the art of maintaining both melodic correspondence (between one voice and another) and harmonic propriety.

These usages, however, were introduced only by theorists of the mid 16th century. Before then the term was used in its original Greek sense to denote

a rule that helped define a composition – often a rule that, applied to a melody, would produce precisely a canon (e.g. 'Repeat this melody a fifth higher after two beats'). The resulting music might be called, in different times and places, a CHACE or CACCIA (1), ROUND or ROTA (later also known as an infinite or PERPETUAL CANON), or, most commonly, *fuga* (hence FUGUE). The practice of notating a canon as a single melodic line lived on in the PUZZLE CANON, where the rule is not disclosed.

The earliest known canon, fully notated, is SUMER IS ICUMEN IN, which is so elaborate that it must have had its spring in practices that were improvised and never written down. Its canons are 'at the unison' – i.e. the melody is repeated at the same pitch level in each canonic voice. Machaut's *Ma fin est mon commencement* is an early example of the 'canon CANCRIZANS', where one voice repeats another in reverse. Then came the 'canon at the fifth', whereby the second voice starts a fifth above (or a fourth below) the first: this was introduced at the end of the 14th century by Landini, Ciconia and others, and became essential to the fugue.

Ockeghem added canons at the second, third, sixth and seventh (*Missa prolationum*), requiring chromatic alteration of the melody to keep to the mode (e.g. G–B–A–etc., starting with a major third, might be followed in a canon at the third by B–D–C–etc., starting with a minor one). He also allowed canons at the fifth and fourth to be 'diatonic', i.e. with intervals altered in this manner. Such canons are sometimes called 'free', as opposed to strict canons that follow the same intervals exactly; more often one speaks of 'free IMITATION', where later voices depart further from the original melody. The art of canon flourished alongside imitation among Franco-Netherlandish composers of the next generation: Josquin, Obrecht, etc. It was maintained by Palestrina and transferred to the instrumental domain in the fugues and ricercares of Baroque composers, culminating in the work of Bach.

The canons and fugues of *Das musikalische Opfer* and *Die Kunst der Fuge* provide a compendium of devices, including canons by inversion (with the original melody inverted in the canonic voice) and canons cancrizans, canons in which inversion and reversion are combined (i.e. the subject is repeated upside-down and backwards, producing a MIRROR canon), canons by augmentation (with the note values uniformly increased, normally twofold) and by diminution (with values uniformly decreased, again normally twofold), and instances of double canon (where two melodies are combined with a canonic voice on each in a four-part texture – a canon 'four in two', as simpler canons might be 'two in one' or 'three in one').

Bach also gave distinction and impetus to the Baroque practice of writing canons as dedications, homages and messages; he was portrayed holding such a canon. Message canons came later from Haydn and Beethoven, while the importance of canon in *Das wohltemperirte Clavier* and the Goldberg Variations stimulated Mozart and Schumann – not to mention the many subsequent composers, from Brahms to Bartók and beyond, led to canon by concerns for scholarship and tradition or by delight in abstraction. Schoenberg and, especially, Webern found canon a useful tool in atonal and serial music. Messiaen added the 'rhythmic canon', where one voice follows only the rhythm of another, possibly in augmentation or diminution. Nancarrow took those ways of slowing or speeding to extremes of sophistication, while Ligeti pursued the hidden canon. Reich's PHASING gave the ancient principle a whole new life.

Ebenezer Prout *Double Counterpoint and Canon* (1891, 'often)

(2) REPERTORY of works given privileged status. Beethoven's symphonies belong to the canon of Western classical music; Raff's do not. Such judgements have been probed and criticized since the late 20th century but by no means displaced. Strictly followed, they would lead to a closure of musical experience, while if they were totally ignored the result would be aesthetic anarchy.

canso. Troubadour term for a love song.

cantabile. Singingly, with an implication of moderate pace. The word is found in tempo markings (e.g. *andante cantabile*), as the term for the first part of an Italian 19th-century aria (to be followed by a cabaletta) and in approbations of pianists' touch and phrasing ('Zimerman's cantabile').

cantante (It., pl. *cantanti*). Singer.

cantata (It., something sung, pl. *cantate*, though in Eng. 'cantatas', Fr. *cantate*, Ger. *Kantate*). A vocal composition with at least one soloist, possibly a chorus, and instrumental accompaniment. Cantatas are customarily longer than songs or arias but shorter than oratorios, and include works written for church, domestic use or concert hall. Altogether they form a heterogeneous collection – hardly a genre at all – lacking the continuous history since the 17th century of the sonata. The term was first used by Grandi (*Cantade et arie*, before 1620).

The cantata was particularly cultivated in Baroque Rome, where it developed from a simple aria (Luigi Rossi) through various sectional forms (Carissimi, Stradella) into a sequence generally of two or three recitative–aria pairs (Alessandro Scarlatti, Handel), usually for one singer (sometimes two), with continuo or chamber ensemble. Subjects were normally amorous or pastoral, as in the larger genres of opera and serenata, though with more intimate connoisseur-appeal. French composers developed cantatas similar in form and topic in the early 18th century, while in Italy the cantata found a niche also in church.

In Germany the church cantata was paramount, from early Baroque times through Buxtehude, Telemann and Graupner to the final climax of this tradition in the works of Bach, for whom, though, the terms *Hauptmusik* (chief music) and concerto were probably more normal. Although influenced by Italian models, the German church cantata had its own strong identity, gained in part from the concluding presence of a chorale. Before this would come some selection of choruses, recitatives and arias, setting biblical texts and glosses relevant to a particular Sunday or festival.

The Roman and Lutheran cantata traditions both went into decline after 1750, and the name became affixed to works of various kinds: a scena for solo voice with piano (Haydn's *Arianna a Naxos*, 1790) and, at the same time, odes for soloists, choir and orchestra (Beethoven's cantatas for the death of one emperor and accession of the next). The French cantata, also moribund by the end of the 18th century, was revived as a test piece for the Prix de Rome. Otherwise the term has been used most often since 1800 for choral orchestral pieces, by composers including Brahms, Elgar, Debussy, Stravinsky, Bartók and Webern.

Cantata profana. Choral orchestral work by Bartók to his own words, in Hungarian, after a Romanian carol. A father (baritone) goes searching for his nine sons, who have been changed into stags. On finding them, he takes aim, but the one dearest to him, now the lead stag (tenor), explains who they are and declares they will stay in the wild forest. First performance: London, 25 May 1934.

cantatrice (Fr., It.). Female singer.

cante hondo [cante jondo] (Sp., deep song). Ancient flamenco style, distinguished by depth and intensity of expression.

Cantelli, Guido (b. Novara, 27 Apr 1920; d. Paris, 24 Nov 1956). Italian conductor, protégé of Toscanini, whose alertness and clarity he inherited. He studied at the Milan Conservatory, was imprisoned for refusing to fight for Nazism and rapidly established himself after the war for lively performances of standard orchestral repertory, coming to Toscanini's attention. His appointment as principal conductor at La Scala was announced a few days before his death in a plane crash.

Canteloube (de Malaret), (Marie) Joseph (b. Annonay, 21 Oct 1879; d. Paris, 4 Nov 1957). French composer, especially of arrangements giving a sensuous glow to folksongs from his native Auvergne. He studied the piano as a boy, and in 1902 started composition lessons with d'Indy, first by correspondence and then, from 1906, in person in Paris, where he became part of a circle around d'Indy devoted to folksong and regional identity. Accordingly he collected folksongs in the Auvergne, besides playing the piano and composing operas, songs and concert works. He produced five series of *Chants d'Auvergne* for voice with rich orchestral accompaniment (1923–54).

canticle. Biblical hymn, not including the psalms. Those most frequently used, and therefore set, include the *Benedicite* (Daniel 3), *Benedictus* (Luke 1), MAGNIFICAT (Luke 1) and *Nunc dimittis* (Luke 2). The term is often used also for the TE DEUM and some common psalms.

Canticum sacrum. Work by Stravinsky, titled in full *Canticum sacrum ad honorem Sancti Marci nominis* (Sacred Song to Honour the Name of St Mark), to words from the Latin Bible, making a homage to Venice's patron saint (and her composers Gabrieli and Monteverdi) for tenor, baritone, chorus and an orchestra comprising violas, basses, winds (no clarinets or horns) and timpani, plus organ. First performance: Venice, 13 Sep 1956.

cantiga (Sp.). Medieval monophonic song, by far the most numerous collection being Alfonso el Sabio's *Cantigas de Santa Maria*.

cantilena (1) Informal term (from It. *cantilena*, lullaby) for a smooth singing line, vocal or instrumental.

(2) Term (from Lat. *cantilena*, song) for various kinds of medieval song.

cantillation. Sacred chanting, especially that of the synagogue. See JEWISH MUSIC.

cantio (Lat.). Song. Widely used medieval term, the origin of *canso, chanson, canzone* and *canción*.

cantional. Hymnbook of early Protestant central Europe.

Cantiones, quae ab argumento sacrae vocantur (Songs called sacred because of their texts). Collection of motets published by Byrd and Tallis in 1575, 17 by each composer, for the years of the reign of the dedicatee, Elizabeth I.

cantio sacra (Lat., sacred song, pl. *cantiones sacrae*). Term for motet current in the 16th–17th centuries.

canto (It., pl. *canti*). Song, singing, the topmost string of a string instrument. Hence also *canto fermo* (CANTUS FIRMUS).

cantor (Lat., singer). Principal musician in a church or synagogue. In Jewish and many Christian traditions the cantor is a leading singer, but the Lutheran cantor was the composer-director responsible for a church's music, as Bach was responsible for St Thomas's during his time in Leipzig.

cantoris. See DECANI.

canto sospeso, Il (The Suspended Song). Work by Nono to words from letters from Nazi victims, set for soli (s, a, t), chorus and orchestra. First performance: Cologne, 24 Oct 1956.

cantus (Lat., melody). Medieval term for the top polyphonic part.

cantus firmus (Lat., fixed melody, pl. cantus firmi). Pre-existing melody around which new polyphonic lines are woven. Polyphony began this way, with the adding of voices to a line of plainsong. By the time the term was introduced, in the 13th century, it denoted a fully developed technique: the cantus firmus could be a plainsong melody or a secular tune, its words might be altered, and it would be more or less concealed in the thicket of voices around it. The technique was developed in the masses, motets and polyphonic songs of the 14th–15th centuries, with particular ingenuity in the works of Josquin and Obrecht at the end of this period. Sometimes the cantus firmus would be in the top part, paraphrased, but much more often it formed the tenor. It provided coherent continuity and stimulus to invention; it may also have been chosen as the vehicle of an implicit text or of numerical proportions. Generally without such arcana, cantus firmus technique remained important to old-style polyphony down to Monteverdi (*Sonata sopra*

'*Sancta Maria*' from the 1610 Vespers). It was then revived in the 20th century by composers again forming new compositions on plainsong melodies (Messiaen, Davies).

cantus planus (Lat.). Medieval term for plainsong.

canzona. Instrumental piece of the 16th–17th centuries. The earliest were keyboard arrangements of Franco-Netherlandish polyphonic songs. In the 1570s composers began writing canzonas for instrumental groupings (a genre spectacularly developed by Gabrieli), with keyboard canzonas following at the end of the century (Merulo, Frescobaldi). At the time such works were called by a variety of names – canzone (or canzon) da (or per) sonare, ricercare, sinfonia, sonata, concerto – but by the mid 17th century some of these had developed lives of their own. The term 'canzona', almost unknown in Italian, was coined by 20th-century scholars for the earlier kind.

canzone (It., pl. *canzoni*). Song. In opera the term may have the specific meaning of a song delivered as such within the action, e.g. Cherubino's 'Voi che sapete' in *Le nozze di Figaro*.

canzonetta (It., diminutive of *canzone*, pl. *canzonette*). Light Italian song of the 16th–18th centuries, spawning the canzonet as an English imitation. The term has also been used since for lyrical pieces, e.g. by Tchaikovsky for the slow movement of his Violin Concerto.

Caplet, André (Léon) (b. Le Havre, 23 Nov 1878; d. Neuilly-sur-Seine, 22 Apr 1925). French composer-conductor, remembered chiefly as Debussy's friend and assistant, though he had independent qualities of Romantic eeriness (*Conte fantastique*) and Catholic mysticism (*Le Miroir de Jésus*). Of poor family, he was a working musician in the theatres of his home town by the time he was 12; he then studied with Lenepveu at the Paris Conservatoire (1896–1901), continuing his theatre work as a conductor. Debussy, with whom he became close in 1907–8, entrusted him with finishing the orchestration of *Le Martyre de Saint Sébastien* and conducting the première (1911), by which time he was spending half the year away as conductor of the Boston Opera Company (1910–14) while conducting an affair with his US impresario's wife. Wounded and gassed in the First World War, he married in 1919 and, in the short while left him, entered his stride as a composer.

Vocal: *Le Miroir de Jésus*, mez, women's ch, str, hp, 1923; many songs, etc.

Instrumental: Quintet, pf, wind, 1899; *Conte fantastique*, hp, str qt, 1922–3; *Epiphanie*, vc, orch, 1923; etc.

Debussy orchestrations: *Children's Corner*, 1910; *Le Martyre de Saint Sébastien*, 1911; *La Boîte à joujoux*, 1919; etc.

capo (It.). Top, as in *da capo* (from the start) and *capotasto*, *capodastro*, etc. (top of the fingerboard). The latter term can be used for the NUT of a bowed string instrument but is more common for a movable nut on guitars and lutes, a soft-covered bar that can be fixed above a fret, effectively transposing the instrument.

cappella (It.). Chapel, hence A CAPPELLA.

capriccio (It., whim, pl. *capricci*, though in Eng. normally 'capriccios'). A genre almost defined by being undefinable, displaying fantasy and freedom. According to Praetorius's prescription: 'One takes a subject, but deserts it for another whenever it comes into one's mind to do so.' There are capriccios of this kind by many of his contemporaries and successors, for keyboard (Frescobaldi, Froberger, Bach, Handel) or violin. As instrumental forms became more standardized in the 18th century, only a cadenza or cadenza-like piece could justify being called a capriccio. Locatelli's examples prompted Paganini. Capriccios appear often enough again in the Romantic period and later, in media from solo piano (Mendelssohn, Brahms, Ligeti) to opera (Strauss), by way of picturesque orchestral piece (Rimsky-Korsakov, Tchaikovsky) and concerto (Janáček, Stravinsky).

Capriccio. Opera by Strauss to a libretto largely by Krauss, prompted by Giambattista Casti's libretto *Prima la musica e poi le parole*. A string sextet aptly opens what the authors called a 'conversation piece for music', the conversation concerning the competing claims of words and music in opera (specifically and with growing self-reference this opera itself). The debate has an amorous parallel in the rivalry between the poet Olivier (baritone) and the composer (Flamand) for the hand of the widowed Countess (soprano), in whose house the action unfolds – in Paris in 1777 according to the score, though the piece is often updated in production to the 20th century. First performance: Munich, 28 Oct 1942.

Capriccio espagnol. Orchestral piece by Rimsky-Korsakov.

Capriccio italien. Orchestral piece by Tchaikovsky.

capriccioso (It.). Capricious, in the manner of a capriccio.

caprice (Fr.). Equivalent to CAPRICCIO.

Capriol Suite. Work by Warlock most familiar in its version for string orchestra, based on dances in Arbeau's *Orchésographie* and named after a character in that book.

Caproli, Carlo (b. Rome, before 1620; d. Rome ?after 1675). Italian violinist-composer, an early master with Luigi Rossi of the Roman cantata. A greengrocer's son, he stayed in Rome, performing and composing for the Pamphili and Barberini families, except for a trip with his wife under the auspices of Cardinal Mazarin to Paris (1653–5), where his opera *Le nozze di Peleo e di Theti* was produced, with Louis XIV dancing in the divertissements.

Capuleti e i Montecchi, I (The Capulets and the Montagues). Opera by Bellini to a libretto by Romani. The story familiar from Shakespeare is retold as gorgeous extended vocalizing for Romeo (mezzo-soprano) and Juliet (soprano). First performance: Venice, 11 Mar 1830.

Caput. Piece of plainsong – the closing melisma from a Maundy Thursday antiphon in the SARUM RITE – used as cantus firmus in an anonymous 15th-century English mass that was widely admired. Ockeghem and Obrecht also wrote *Caput* masses.

Capuzzi, Giuseppe Antonio (b. Brescia, 1 Aug 1755; d. Bergamo, 28 Mar 1818). Italian violinist-composer, who is remembered for one of the rare Classical concertos for double bass (violone). He wrote most of his music in the 1780s–90s in Venice, and moved to Bergamo in 1805.

Cara, Marchetto (b. Verona, c.1465; d. Mantua, 1525). Italian singer-lutenist-composer. He was at the Mantuan court from c.1494 to his death, highly valued as a composer of frottolas. Of these, around 100 survive, showing some development towards the more textually involved and musically elaborate madrigal.

Carceri d'invenzione (Dungeons of Invention). Concert-length sequence of seven works by Ferneyhough. Named after the imaginary prisons of Piranesi's engravings, a sequence of wild escapades is weighted by the crackling *Etudes transcendentales*, which justifiably claims its place in a line from *Pierrot lunaire* and *Le Marteau sans maître*. A flautist, the composer's alter ego, is the intermittent leader: 1 *Superscriptio*, pic, 1981; 2 *Carceri d'invenzione I*, ens, 1982; 3 *Intermedio alla ciaccona*, vn, 1986; 4 *Carceri d'invenzione II*, fl, chbr orch, 1985; 5 *Etudes transcendentales*, s, fl, ob, vc, hpd, 1982–5; 6 *Carceri d'invenzione III*, 15 wind, 3 perc, 1986; 7 *Mnemosyne*, b fl, tape, 1986. First performance: Donaueschingen, 17 Oct 1986.

Cardew, Cornelius (b. Winchcombe, 7 May 1936; d. London, 13 Dec 1981). British pianist-composer, whose startling career took him from Stockhausen to Mao and beyond. A son of the potter Michael Cardew, he studied at the RAM (1953–7) before becoming Stockhausen's pupil and assistant in Cologne (1957–60), where he worked on realizing *Carré*. His first works had been in the line of Stockhausen and Boulez, but in 1958 he moved towards Cage, Brown and Feldman, and that development continued after his return to London in 1961. Taking a leading role in experimental music, he played with AMM, produced a big graphic score, *Treatise* (he was a professional graphic designer), taught at the RAM and elsewhere, and in 1969 founded the Scratch Orchestra, a libertarian group of professional and amateur musicians. His work with them became increasingly political: he repudiated the avant-garde in his book *Stockhausen Serves Imperialism* (1974) and altered his *The Great Learning* so that Confucius's message was replaced by Mao's and a gentle Cage-style anarchy by a determined adherence to revolutionary communism. He was killed by a hit-and-run driver.

Vocal: *The Great Learning* (Confucius), 7 paragraphs, various forces, 1968–70, paragraphs 1–2 rev 1972; songs
Piano: Sonatas Nos.1–3, 1955–8; *February Pieces*, 1959–61; *3 Winter Potatos*, 1961–5; Piano Album 1973; Piano Album 1974; Thälmann Variations, 1974; *We Sing for the Future*, 1981
Piano duo: 2 *Books of Study*, 1958; *Boolavogue*, 1981
Other works: *Treatise*, 1963–7; orchestral, chamber and solo pieces

Cardillac. Opera by Hindemith to a libretto by Ferdinand Lion after a Hoffmann story. Cardillac (baritone) is a Parisian goldsmith who murders his clients in order to retrieve his creations, and is eventually killed by the crowd to whom he has boasted of his crimes. The thoroughgoing revision modifies the determinedly anti-psychological nature of the original, which is generally preferred. First performance: Dresden, 9 Nov 1926; rev Zurich, 20 Jun 1952.

Cardoso, Manuel (baptized Fronteira, near Portalegre, 11 Dec 1566; d. Lisbon, 24 Nov 1650).

Portuguese composer, of Renaissance polyphony maintained with splendour and expressive intensity well into the Baroque age. He studied as a chorister at Évora Cathedral and in 1598 entered the Carmelite convent in Lisbon, where he remained as chapelmaster and subprior, famed for his musicianship and divinity. His works include a *Requiem*, several masses and motets.

Carewe, John (Maurice Foxall) (b. Derby, 17 Jan 1933). British conductor and mentor (to Rattle among others). He studied at the Guildhall School, with Walter Goehr, and in Paris with Boulez and Messiaen. Contemporary music has remained important to him: he gave the British premières of works by Boulez and Barraqué. But his enthusiasms, vividly communicated, are manifold. He held chief conductorships in Cardiff (1966–71), Brighton (1974–87) and Chemnitz (1993–6).

carillon. Set of bells played from a keyboard or automatically, in the manner of a barrel organ. The instrument is particularly a feature of church towers in the Low Countries, though it also has a life in the concert hall. Sometimes it is found as part of an organ. If the bells are small, the usual term is GLOCKENSPIEL.

Carissimi, Giacomo (baptized Marino, near Rome, 18 Apr 1605; d. Rome, 12 Jan 1674). Italian composer, crucial to the early oratorio. Nothing is known of his training. He worked in Tivoli and Assisi before his appointment as chapelmaster at the Collegio Germanico in Rome in 1629. Besides maintaining a prestigious musical establishment there, he provided music for Queen Christina (from 1656, presumably including many of his cantatas) and for the Arciconfraternità del Santissimo Crocifisso (his oratorios). The latter works, including *Jonas* and *Jephte*, set Latin narratives adapted from the Bible, and were admired at the time and later for their confluence of operatic and madrigalian principles in the interests of dramatic pacing, expressive recitative and powerful choral writing. His Europe-wide prestige, which resulted in many false attributions, also brought him private pupils (among them Charpentier and Kerll) and offers of employment elsewhere, notably as Monteverdi's successor at St Mark's. But he stayed where he was. A contemporary described him as frugal, courteous and inclined to melancholy.

Graham Dixon *Carissimi* (1986)

Carlos, Wendy [Walter] (b. Pawtucket, R.I., 14 Nov 1939). US composer-performer, whose album

Switched-on Bach (1968), recorded with a Moog synthesizer, sold over a million copies. A pupil of Luening and Ussachevsky at Columbia (1962–5), Carlos worked with Moog and remained in New York, creating film scores (*A Clockwork Orange*, *The Shining*), etc.

Carl Rosa Opera Company. British touring outfit founded in 1875 by the eponymous German-born conductor; it remained on the road until 1960.

carmen (Lat., pl. *carmina*). Song, as in CARMINA BURANA.

Carmen. Opera by Bizet to a libretto by Henri Meilhac and Halévy after Prosper Mérimée's novel. Set in Seville, with plentiful local colour in the score, the drama concerns the fatal attraction by which Carmen (mezzo-soprano), a dangerous young factory worker, draws Don José (tenor) away from his soldiering and from the tender Micaëla (soprano). Having mistaken sex for love, he is maddened when she leaves him for the bullfighter Escamillo (baritone): he challenges her and stabs her. Carmen, whose name means song, embodies not only physical passion but the spirit of music, and she seems willingly to sacrifice herself in choosing glamour over emotional candour, in an opera that has an abundance of both. Among its many vivid numbers are Carmen's Habanera, Seguidilla and Card Aria, Micaëla's aria 'Je dis que rien', José's Flower Song and Escamillo's Toreador Song. The original spoken dialogue is sometimes replaced by Guiraud's recitative setting; other alterations are also part of a complex performing tradition. First performance: Paris, 3 Mar 1875.

Carmina burana (Songs of Beuren). Work by Orff based on poems from an early 13th-century song collection once housed at the Bavarian abbey of Benedicktbeuern, a collection given this title by its editor Schmeller (1847). Orff, in his setting for soli, chorus and orchestra, made no attempt to realize the original melodies, achieving rather a rude – if endearing – vigour. First performance: Frankfurt, 8 Jun 1937.

Carnaval (Carnival). Set of 21 piano pieces by Schumann, subtitled *Scènes mignonnes sur quatre notes* (Cute Scenes on Four Notes). The four notes are A♭–E♭–C–B, spelling out in German nomenclature the home town (Asch) of the composer's girlfriend Ernestine von Fricken and jostling the musical letters in his own name: in the forms A–S–C–H and S–C–H–A, harmonized, they appear as 'sphinxes' at the head of the music. The pieces that follow suggest a masked ball, in which real people mingle with commedia dell'arte characters: 1 *Préambule*, 2 *Pierrot*, 3 *Arlequin*, 4 *Valse noble*, 5 *Eusebius* (the composer's dreamy persona), 6 *Florestan* (his active persona), 7 *Coquette*, 8 *Réplique*, 9 *Papillons*, 10 *ASCH – SCHA (Lettres dansantes)*, 11 *Chiarina* (Clara Wieck), 12 *Chopin*, 13 *Estrella* (Ernestine), 14 *Reconnaissance*, 15 *Pantalon et Colombine*, 16 *Valse allemande*, 17 *Intermezzo: Paganini*, 18 *Aveu*, 19 *Promenade*, 20 *Pause*, 21 *Marche des Davidsbündler contre les philistins*.

Carnaval des animaux, Le (The Carnival of the Animals). Work by Saint-Saëns for two pianos and ensemble (fl, cl, str qt, db, hmnm, xyl), which he made for private amusement: it was not published until after his death, except for a cello–piano adaptation of the slow movement *Le Cygne* (The Swan). Among other animals featured are fossils (with xylophone) and pianists (with scales), the complete menagerie comprising: 1 *Introduction et marche royale du lion*, 2 *Poules et coqs* (Hens and Cocks), 3 *Hémiones* (Tibetan wild asses, *presto furioso*), 4 *Tortues* (Tortoises, dancing to Offenbach's cancan ludicrously decelerated), 5 *L'Eléphant* (The Elephant, double-bass solo with allusions to Berlioz and Mendelssohn), 6 *Kangourous* (Kangaroos, with jumping pianos), 7 *Aquarium*, 8 *Personnages à longues oreilles* (Personages with Long Ears, i.e. braying donkeys), 9 *Le Coucou au fond des bois* (The Cuckoo Deep in the Woods), 10 *Volière* (Aviary), 11 *Pianistes*, 12 *Fossiles*, 13 *Le Cygne*, 14 *Finale*.

Carnaval de Venise, Le (Venetian Carnival). Popular Venetian song ('O mamma mia') varied by Paganini, Benedict, etc., also the title of operas by Campra, Errico Pretella and Ambroise Thomas.

Carnaval romain, Le (Roman Carnival). Brilliant overture by Berlioz, which he adapted from music in his opera *Benvenuto Cellini*.

Carnegie Hall. Concert hall in New York founded by the steel magnate Andrew Carnegie and until 1898 called simply Music Hall. Tchaikovsky was there on opening night (5 May 1891); many of the world's greatest musicians have made it since. In 1960 the hall was saved from demolition, largely thanks to Stern, and in 1986 it was renovated. Besides the main auditorium (seating 2,804), the building includes Weill Hall (seating 268) and Zankel Hall (opened 2003, seating 650).

Carnicer (y Batlle), Ramón (b. Tárrega, near Lérida, 24 Oct 1789; d. Madrid, 17 Mar 1855). Spanish composer, notably of the Chilean national anthem (though he never left Europe). He wrote this at the behest of the Chilean ambassador in London during one of his periods in political exile (1824–7). Before this he was active largely in Barcelona, afterwards largely in Madrid, composing, conducting and teaching. His works include operas, two *Requiem* settings and other church music, and songs.

carnival. Time of masquerade and merriment, danger and deceit, running traditionally from the day after Christmas until the day before Lent, i.e. for two months or so. Renaissance Florence had carnival songs; carnival was then the principal opera season in Catholic Europe until the later 18th century. It was remembered in Schumann's Op.9 (CARNAVAL), overtures by Berlioz, Dvořák and Glazunov, songs and operas alluding to the Venetian carnival (*Le* CARNAVAL DE VENISE), etc.

Carnival of the Animals, The. See *Le* CARNAVAL DES ANIMAUX.

carol. Protean term now denoting a traditional Christmas song, though in origin having nothing to do with Christmas. The word comes from the Fr. *carole* (whose antecedents go back through the Lat. *corolla* to the Gk *choraules*, a piper accompanying a chorus), signifying in the 12th–14th centuries a popular dance in which the dancers sang. The carol remained music in movement in the 15th–16th centuries, being associated with processions in church (at Christmas time, but also at Passiontide and to honour the Virgin) or dining halls (e.g. the Boar's Head Carol). Carols could also be patriotic (the AGINCOURT CAROL), satirical or pagan (for May Day), but whatever their purpose they generally had a verse-refrain form and a mixture of English and Latin words. Their anonymous authors, then, were educated, and could draw in sprightly fashion on both Christian and pre-Christian imagery, as in 'The Holly and the Ivy'. In a separate development, polyphonic carols were produced in the last decades before the Reformation by Browne and Cornysh. These were soon forgotten, but monophonic carols lived on in popular use at Christmas, encouraged by broadsheet publication. Just as they were starting to die out, in the early 19th century, they began to appear in volume form, with old carols (the 16th-century Coventry Carol, the 17th-century 'God rest you merry gentlemen', the 18th-century 'O come all ye faithful') joined by new ones ('Good King Wenceslas', 'Hark! The herald angels sing'). Now the carol was effectively a hymn or anthem, and so it has remained, in further contributions by Holst, Davies, Weir, etc., many of them written for KING'S COLLEGE CHOIR.

carole (Fr.). See CAROL.

Carpenter, John Alden (b. Park Ridge, Ill., 28 Feb 1876; d. Chicago, 26 Apr 1951). US composer. He studied with Paine at Harvard, and though he joined his father's firm of shipping suppliers on graduating (1897) and stayed on as vice-president (1909–36), he had further lessons from a reluctant Elgar (in Rome in 1906) and, back in Chicago, from Bernard Ziehn (1908–12). German Romanticism and French impressionism gave him his tone of voice, to which jazz, as he heard it in Chicago, added an occasional accent from the Piano Concertino (1915) onwards. His ballet *Skyscrapers* (1923–4) was intended for Diaghilev. Other works include two symphonies, the charming Ravelian suite *Adventures in a Perambulator* (1914), the symphonic poem *Sea Drift* (1933) and songs.

Carré, Michel (b. Besançon, 21 Oct 1822; d. Paris, 27 Jun 1872). French librettist, who arrived in Paris in 1840, found his métier in the theatre, and had a working partnership with Jules Barbier, though he also worked independently (Gounod's *Mireille*) or with other collaborators (Bizet's *Les Pêcheurs de perles*).

carrée (Fr.). Breve, double whole note.

Carreño, (Maria) Teresa (b. Caracas, 22 Dec 1853; d. New York, 12 Jun 1917). Venezuelan pianist. A granddaughter of the composer Cayetano Carreño (1774–1836), she was taken to New York at eight for studies with Gottschalk, then had lessons in Paris and with Anton Rubinstein. Most of her career she spent in Germany, at first a fiery virtuoso, later – after her brief marriage (1892–5) to d'Albert, third of her four husbands – a more inward one.

Carreras, José (b. Barcelona, 5 Dec 1946). Catalan tenor, most appealing in lyric roles. He began studies at the Barcelona Conservatory at eight, and at 11 was appearing as a boy soprano at the Liceo. In 1971 he sprang to international fame when he appeared with Montserrat Caballé in a concert performance of *Maria Stuarda* in London. Diagnosed with leukaemia in 1987, he recovered and returned to his career, as a soloist and one of the THREE TENORS.

Carrillo (-Trujillo), Julián (Antonio) (b. Ahualulco, San Luis Potosí, 28 Jan 1875; d. San Ángel, 9 Sep 1965). Mexican composer, a pioneer of microtonal music. He studied violin and composition in Mexico City, Ghent and Leipzig. In 1905 he returned to Mexico, where in 1924 he began working with microtones, or, to use his own term, 'sonido 13' (i.e. adding to the normal 12). Stokowski commissioned his Concertino for mixed microtonal sextet and orchestra (1927), which aroused much interest, and in the 1930s he toured Mexico with his Orquesta Sonido 13. He also made plans for pianos in third-tones, quarter-tones, etc., up to 16th-tones, and these were built for the 1958 Brussels Exposition. To the end of his long life he continued composing, in microtonal and conventional systems, tonally and atonally.

Carse, Adam (von Ahn) (b. Newcastle upon Tyne, 19 May 1878; d. Great Missenden, 2 Nov 1958). British musician, expert in the history of the orchestra and antique wind instruments, of which he gave a collection to the Horniman Museum, London. He studied at the RAM (1893–1902) and taught there from 1922, after a time as assistant music master at Winchester College.

Carter, Elliott (Cook) (b. New York, 11 Dec 1908). US composer, of ranging imagination sustained into a remarkable old age. Having established a firm place among the Copland generation of neoclassicists, he went off in a new direction in his 40s, relaxing all previous constraints of form, genre, harmony and rhythm as he let his music convey itself with driving force through polyrhythmic textures of great and increasing complexity. His music became a play of different characters, defined by speed, movement and harmony, all his own.

As a boy he travelled to Europe with his parents, whose business was importing lace. He also became acquainted with Ives, before studying with Piston at Harvard and Boulanger in Paris (1932–5). Back in New York – his base ever since – he wrote ballets, orchestral works and choral pieces, identifying with the neoclassicism he learned from Boulanger, then gradually withdrawing from it. That withdrawal became determined in and after *The Minotaur* (1947), and almost complete in his First Quartet (1950–51), written in Arizona as an effort to find his own music, independent of history and audiences. Here the four players are drawn as musical personalities, in an argument that continues across the boundaries of the underlying four movements, with an urge for constant – but coherent – change that is answered in part by METRIC MODULATION. A vestige of neoclassicism remained only in his punctiliousness, as he burst back into the modernist excitement he had felt alongside Ives a quarter-century before.

His avoidance of ingratiation brought him a new public who prized his independence. His quartet took its place within the new post-war wave that was breaking in both New York and Europe, which he visited often, sometimes for year-long stays; he found a sympathetic colleague in Boulez. Steadily, during the next quarter-century, he produced just nine big instrumental works, in which images of exuberance are conveyed within an abstract idiom. The notion of dialogue remained important: his Second Quartet (1959) is scored for four individuals, his Third (1971) for two duos, and in orchestral scores he preferred the almost inevitably dialectical genre of the concerto. At the same time he started establishing his characters more consciously than in his First Quartet, basing them on defined intervallic and metrical habits. An example is his Double Concerto (1961), where, in addition to these differences, the piano and harpsichord soloists have their own soundworlds in the pair of distinct chamber orchestras accompanying them. In his Concerto for Orchestra (1968–9) there are four such sways of sound, continuously intermingling.

His US bicentennial commission from the New York Philharmonic, *A Symphony of Three Orchestras* (1976–7), brought this period to a magnificent close. But a new one had already opened with *A Mirror on Which to Dwell* (1975), his first vocal music since 1947 and the start of a trilogy of works with compact orchestra setting poetry by US contemporaries of comparable exactitude and dash. He also began producing brilliant miniatures – expressive *jeux d'esprit* heralding the return to substantial instrumental scores that came with the Triple Duo (1982–3), perhaps the first of his pieces in which the wordless dialogue is comic. Extraordinarily he went on into his 80s and 90s creating such works, large and small, among them several concertos, a symphony, a host of condensed instrumental inventions and an opera. They express his personal qualities of courtliness and geniality, his sense of humour and his impatience; and while observant of Europe, they belong in the highest US tradition of idealism, openness and democracy.

Allen Edwards *Flawed Words and Stubborn Sounds: A Conversation with Elliott Carter* (1971); Elliott Carter, ed. Jonathan W. Bernard *Collected Essays and Lectures* (1997)

Opera: *What Next?* (1 act; Paul Griffiths), 1997–8, f.p. Berlin, 1999
Ballets: *Pocahontas*, 1936–9; *The Minotaur*, 1947
Orchestral: Symphony No.1, 1942; *Holiday Overture*, 1944; Variations, 1953–5; Double Concerto, hpd, pf, 2 chbr orchs, 1961; PIANO CONCERTO, 1964–5; Concerto for Orchestra, 1968–9; *A Symphony of 3 Orchestras*, 1976–7; *Penthode*, chbr orch, 1984–5;

Oboe Concerto, 1987; *3 Occasions* (*A Celebration of Some 100 × 150 Notes*, 1986; *Remembrance*, 1988; *Anniversary*, 1989); Violin Concerto, 1990; *Symphonia* (*Partita*, 1993; *Adagio tenebroso*, 1995; *Allegro scorrevole*, 1997); Clarinet Concerto, 1996; Asko Concerto, chbr orch, 1999–2000; Cello Concerto, 2000; Boston Concerto, 2001–2; *3 Illusions* (*More's Utopia*, 2003; *Fons juventatis*, 2003; *Micomicón*, 2002); *Reflexions*, chbr orch, 2004
Vocal with orchestra/ensemble: *Warble for Lilac-Time* (Whitman), s/t, chbr orch, 1943; 3 Poems of Robert Frost, 1943, arr s/t, orch, 1975; *Voyage* (Hart Crane), 1943, arr mez/bar, chbr orch, 1975; *The Harmony of Morning*, women's ch, chbr orch, 1944; *A Mirror on Which to Dwell* (Elizabeth Bishop), s, ens, 1975; *Syringa* (John Ashbery, ancient Gk), mez, b, ens, 1978; *In Sleep, in Thunder* (Lowell), t, ens, 1981; *Tempo e tempi* (Montale, Quasimodo, Ungaretti), s, ob, cl, vn, vc, 1998–9; *Of Rewaking* (William Carlos Williams), mez, orch, 2002
String quartets: No.1, 1950–51; No.2, 1959; No.3, 1971; No.4, 1985; No.5, 1995; *Elegy*, arr 1946; *Fragment*, 1994; *Fragment No.2*, 1999
Other works for 4–8 instruments: Canonic Suite, 4 sax/cl, 1939; Woodwind Quintet, 1948; 8 Etudes and a Fantasy, fl, ob, cl, bn, 1949–50; Sonata, fl, ob, vc, hpd, 1952; Brass Quintet, 1974; A Fantasy about Purcell's Fantasia Upon One Note, brass qnt, 1974; Triple Duo, fl, cl, vn, vc, pf, perc, 1982–3; Canon for 4, fl, b cl, vn, vc, 1984; *Birthday Flourish*, 5 brass, 1988; Quintet, pf, ob, cl, hn, bn, 1991; Quintet, pf, str qt, 1996–7; *Luimen*, tpt, trbn, vib, mand, gtr, hp, 1997; Oboe Quartet, 2001; *Mosaic*, 8 insts, 2004
Duos and trios: *Pastoral*, cor ang/va/cl, pf, 1940; *Elegy*, vc, pf, 1943; Cello Sonata, 1948; Canon for 3, 1971; Duo, vn, pf, 1974; *Esprit rude/esprit doux*, fl, cl, 1984; *Enchanted Preludes*, fl, vc, 1988; *Con leggerezza pensosa*, cl, vn, vc, 1990; *Trilogy*, ob, hp, 1992; *Esprit rude/esprit doux II*, fl, cl, mar, 1995; *Hiyoku*, 2 cl, 2001; *Au quai*, bn, va, 2002
Solos: 8 Pieces, timp, 1950–66; *Changes*, gtr, 1983; *4 Lauds*, vn (*Riconoscenza per Goffredo Petrassi*, 1974; *Fantasy*, *Statement*, 1999; *Rhapsodic Musings*, 2001); *Scrivo in vento*, fl, 1991; *Gra*, cl, 1993; *Figment*, vc, 1995; *A Six Letter Letter*, cor ang, 1996; *Shard*, gtr, 1997; *Figment No.2*, vc, 2001; *Steep Steps*, b cl, 2001; *Retracing*, bn, 2002
Piano: Sonata, 1945–6; *Night Fantasies*, 1980; *90+*, 1994; *2 Diversions*, 1999; *Retrouvailles*, 2000
Choral: *Tarantella* (Ovid), men's ch, pf duet, 1936; *Harvest Home* (Herrick), 1937; *Let's be gay* (Gay), women's ch, pf, 1937; *To Music* (Herrick), 1937; *Heart not so heavy as mine* (Dickinson), 1938; *The Defense of Corinth* (Rabelais), speaker, men's ch, pf duet, 1941; *Musicians wrestle everywhere* (Dickinson), ch, str ad lib, 1945; *Emblems* (Allen Tate), men's ch, pf, 1947
Songs: 'Tell me where is fancy bred?' (Shakespeare), a, gtr, 1938; 3 Poems of Robert Frost, mez/bar, pf, 1943; 'Voyage' (Crane), mez/bar, pf, 1943; 'Warble for Lilac-Time' (Whitman), s/t, pf, 1943; *Of Challenge and of Love* (Hollander), s, pf, 1993

Carulli, Ferdinando (M. Meinrado Francesco Pascale (Rosario) (b. Naples, 9 Feb 1770; d. Paris, 14 Feb 1841). Italian guitarist-composer, who took his instrument to Paris and into the early Romantic era. He studied the cello at first, but fixed on the guitar at 16. With his French wife and their son he settled in Paris in 1809 and won admiration for his virtuosity and poetic imagination. His 366 numbered works include instructive volumes, concertos and much chamber music, as well as solo pieces. He also wrote for a 10-string instrument of his own invention.

Caruso, Enrico (b. Naples, 25 Feb 1873; d. Naples, 2 Aug 1921). Italian tenor, whose superbly controlled and burnished voice – immediately distinct in character, yet versatile enough to move from lyric roles to the verismo repertory he helped introduce – was one of the gramophone's first discoveries. Of poor family, he began his career singing in churches as a boy, and was trained by Guglielmo Vergine and Vincenzo Lombardi. He made his opera debut in Naples in 1894, then moved to the forefront at the premières in Milan of operas by Giordano (*Fedora*, 1898) and Cilea (*L'arlesiana*, 1897; *Adriana Lecouvreur*, 1902). Also in 1902 he made his first recordings and his Covent Garden debut, in *Rigoletto*. The next year he sang for the first time at the Met (*Rigoletto* again), which became his regular and, from 1912, almost continuous home. There he took part in the première of Puccini's *La fanciulla del West* (1910) and there he gave his last performance (24 Dec 1920), before a lung condition overtook him.

Michael Scott *The Great Caruso* (1988)

Carvalho, João de Sousa (b Estremoz, 22 Feb 1745; d. Alentejo, 1799/1800). Portuguese composer. Trained in Naples on a royal grant from 1761, he returned to Lisbon to teach at the Seminário da Patriarcal (1767–98) and write operas for the royal family, to which he was also music teacher from 1778. Besides the operas, he left church and keyboard music when he retired to his country estates.

carve. Colloquial term for what a conductor does.

Carver, Robert (b. 1484–7; d. after 1567). Scottish composer, of flamboyant polyphony. He was ordained c.1503 and may have studied in Louvain around the same time; certainly his music shows an awareness of Netherlandish models, as well as of the insular tradition represented by the Eton Choirbook. Little is surely known of him. He was a canon of Scone, but probably spent more time with the Chapel Royal in Stirling. His splendid ten-part *Dum sacrum mysterium* mass, for Michaelmas, may have been sung at the coronation of James V (1513); the rapturous 19-voice cadences of *O bone Jesu* also presuppose a special occasion. Other works include the only British *L'Homme armé* mass.

Cary, Tristram (Ogilvie) (b. Oxford, 14 May 1925). British-Australian composer, pioneer of electronic music. The son of the novelist Joyce Cary, he was a naval radar officer in the Second World War, and in 1946 began experimenting with electronic composition, finishing his musical training at Trinity College, London (1948–50). He went on to produce concert and commercial pieces (including the signature tune for the TV series *Dr Who*, 1963), set up a studio at the RCM (1967), present concerts in London (1968–72) and develop the VCS3 synthesizer. A visit to Australia in 1973 led to a post at the University of Adelaide (1974–86) and permanent residence. His works range from orchestral to solo pieces, with and without electronics.

Casadesus. French musical family founded by Luis (1850–1919), a printer and amateur musician. Eight of his children entered the performing arts, including Francis (1870–1954), a composer-con-ductor who directed the American Conservatory at Fontainebleau, Henri (1879–1946), a viola player, and Marcel (1892–1981), a violinist and viol player. These three collaborated on some benign and adept forgeries, of which the most successful were a violin concerto in D ('Adélaïde') ascribed to Mozart (and duly granted its Köchel number, KAnh.294a), a viola concerto in B minor under Handel's name and a cello concerto in C minor purporting to be J.C. Bach's.

(1) **Robert (Marcel)** (b. Paris, 7 Apr 1899; d. Paris, 19 Sep 1972). Pianist-composer, nephew of the above three. Trained at the Paris Conservatoire, he was specially noted for his quiet elegance in Ravel (for whom he played) and Mozart. He also taught at the American Conservatory, which he directed from 1946, and wrote seven symphonies, much piano and chamber music, and several concertos, including a triple piano concerto for himself, his wife Gaby and his son Jean (1927–72), who died in a car accident.

(2) **Jean-Claude** (b. Paris, 7 Dec 1935). Conductor, son of Henri's daughter Gisèle. He studied at the Paris Conservatoire and began his career as a percussionist. Following studies with Pierre Dervaux in Paris (1963–5) and Boulez in Basle (1965), he started afresh as a conductor, becoming founder conductor of the Orchestre National de Lille in 1976.

Casals, Pablo [Pau] (b. Vendrell, 29 Dec 1876; d. Puerto Rico, 22 Oct 1973). Catalan cellist, whose strong singing line, wielded with exactitude and force, made him one of the foremost musicians of his time. Born to musical parents, he began cello studies at the municipal music school in his home town, where he made his debut in 1891. A royal scholarship enabled him to study further at the Madrid Conservatory (1893–5) and briefly in Brussels; he then returned to Barcelona to lead the Liceo orchestra and play chamber music. In 1899 he performed the Lalo concerto in London and Paris, beginning his long international career. Works were written for him by Fauré (*Sérénade*), Schoenberg and Tovey. He also formed a much-appreciated trio with Thibaud and Cortot in 1905, and began conducting his own orchestra in 1919. Strongly opposed to Franco, he settled in Prades, in French Catalonia, in 1936, and became as much a moral as a musical figure. He continued to perform and record as a soloist, chamber musician and conductor, especially at the festivals he organized in Prades, Perpignan and Puerto Rico, where he settled in 1956 and remarried. Surely he was the only musician to have played for both Queen Victoria (1899) and President Kennedy (1961). He also composed sacred music and a *Hymn to the United Nations* with words by Auden (1971).

David Blum *Casals and the Art of Interpretation* (1977)

Casella, Alfredo (b. Turin, 25 Jul 1883; d. Rome, 5 Mar 1947). Italian composer, a disparate creative artist and versatile performer, who did much to inject modernism into his country's music. Brought up in a musical family, he studied at the Paris Conservatoire (1896–1902), notably with Fauré, and remained in the city, excited by the artistic life and in close contact with Ravel and Stravinsky. In 1915 he moved to Rome, to teach piano and champion his contemporaries as a concert organizer. His music had just (in 1913–14) gained an energetic, dissonant and sometimes ironic edge, suggesting that, among all the composers he admired and performed, Bartók meant most to him. But while he went on playing and promoting a full range of modern music, including Schoenberg, his turn towards neoclassicism in 1920 lightened his art. A few years later his music grew heavier again, as he got caught up in fascism. Married to a French Jew, he had difficulties after 1938, exacerbated by illness.

Alfredo Casella *Music in My Time* (1955)

Opera: *La donna serpente* (Cesare Vico Lodovici, after Gozzi), Op.50, 1928–31, f.p. Rome, 1932; etc.

Orchestral: *Pupazzetti*, Op.27bis, 1920; *A notte alta*,

Op.30bis, pf, orch, 1921; *Concerto romano*, Op.43, org, orch, 1926; *Scarlattiana*, Op.44, pf, chbr orch, 1926; *Serenata*, Op.46bis, chbr orch, 1930; Triple Concerto, Op.56, pf trio, orch, 1933; *Paganiniana*, Op.65, 1942; etc.

Vocal: *Notte di maggio*, Op.20, v, orch, 1913; sacred music, songs

Chamber: *Sicilienne et burlesque*, Op.23, fl, pf, 1914; Concerto, Op.40, str qt, 1923–4; Sonata a 3, Op.62, pf trio, 1938

Piano: 9 Pieces, Op.24, 1914; *Pagine di guerra*, Op.25, duet, 1915; *Pupazzetti*, Op.27, duet, 1915; Sonatina, Op.28, 1916; *A notte alta*, Op.30, 1917; *Due ricercari sul nome B–A–C–H*, Op.52, 1932; etc.

Casken, John (Arthur) (b. Barnsley, 15 Jul 1949). British composer, capable of lustrous evocation or keen drama in his command of line and sonority. He studied at Birmingham University (1967–71) and in Warsaw (1971–2) with Andrzej Dobrowolski and Lutosławski, returning to embark on an academic career with successive appointments at Birmingham (1973), Durham (1981) and, as professor, Manchester (1992). Northern English subjects and landscapes have been important to him, but so have painters as unalike as Gauguin and Gustave Moreau.

Operas: *Golem* (Casken and Pierre Audi), f.p. London, 1989; *God's Liar* (Emma Warner and Casken, after Tolstoy), f.p. London, 2001

Orchestral: *Tableaux des trois âges*, 1976–7; *Orion over Farne*, 1984; Cello Concerto, 1990–91; *Still Mine*, bar, orch, 1991–2; *Darting the Skiff*, str, 1992–3; Violin Concerto, 1994–5; *Sortilège*, 1995–6

Vocal: *Ia orana, Gauguin*, s, pf, 1978; *Sharp Thorne*, 4 men's v, 1991–2

Chamber: *Music for the Crabbing Sun*, fl, ob, vc, hpd, 1974–5; *Music for a Tawny-Gold Day*, va, a sax, b cl, pf, 1975–6; String Quartet No.1, 1981–2; No.2, 1993–6; etc.

cassa (It.). (1) Drum, as in *cassa rullante* ('rolling drum', i.e. tenor drum), *gran cassa* (bass drum), *cassa di legno* (woodblock), etc.

(2) Box, as in *cassa dei bischieri* (pegbox).

cassation. Term current *c*.1750–75 in and around Austria for a divertimento or serenade; the terms seem to have been interchangeable for the Haydn brothers, Mozart, etc. The derivation may be from the expression *gassatim gehen* (to perform in the streets).

castanets. Clappers of Spanish origin, traditionally made of chestnut (Sp. *castaña*) wood. Flamenco dancers normally have two sets, one in each hand, the right (*hembra*, female) slightly higher in pitch than the left (*macho*, male). Orchestral castanets are usually fixed to a handle, for effects not so much visually as aurally enticing, whether in Spanish-style music (*Carmen*) or similar scenes of hedonism (in *Tannhäuser*, *Salome*).

Castelnuovo-Tedesco, Mario (b. Florence, 3 Apr 1895; d. Beverly Hills, 16 Mar 1968). Italian–US composer, productive in all fields (over 200 opus numbers), but known principally for his guitar music. He studied in Florence with Pizzetti, in Bologna and with Casella, who gave him a vigorous start. Fascism may have made him more conscious of being a Jew, and starting with his violin concerto *I profeti* (1931, for Heifetz) he began addressing Jewish subjects. At the same time his music became more frankly and old-fashionedly Romantic. He moved to the USA in the summer of 1939 and settled in southern California the next year. Devoted to Shakespeare, he wrote a *Merchant of Venice* opera (Florence, 1961), several overtures and settings of all the songs in the plays; he also wrote an opera on *The Importance of Being Earnest*. His guitar music includes a concerto in D (1939), a double concerto (1962), *24 caprichos de Goya* (1961) and songs with the instrument (*The Divan of Moses-ibn-Ezra*, 1966).

Castiglioni, Niccolò (b. Milan, 17 Jul 1932; d. Milan, 7 Sep 1996). Italian composer, a non-subscribing associate of the 1950s–60s avant-garde, who explored his own world of elaborate artifice, typically in high-treble textures. He studied at the Milan Conservatory with Ghedini and others, at the Salzburg Mozarteum (1952–3), and at Darmstadt almost annually between 1956 and 1962. After a period at US institutions (1966–70), he returned to Italy and spent most of his last 20 years teaching at his alma mater in Milan. Webern was crucial to him – but Webern as precise, delicate sound rather than serial system. His various stage and vocal works involve diverse texts from the distant and nearer past that could chime with his seductively etiolated music.

Stage: *The Lord's Masque* (1 act: Campion), 1980; *Oberon* (1 act: Jonson), 1980
Vocal: *Gyro*, ch, ens, 1963; *Dickinson-Lieder*, s, pf/orch, 1977; *Le favole di Esopo*, ch, orch, 1979; *Salmo XIX*, 2 s, ch, orch, 1979–80; *Sinfonia con rosignolo* (Grimmelshausen), s, orch, 1989; *Cantus planus* (Silesius), 2 s, 7 insts, 1990–91; *Abendlied* (Joseph Viktor von Scheffel), s, orch, 1995; *Gesang* (Hölderlin), t, orch, 1995–6; etc.
Orchestral: *Inverno in-ver*, 1973, rev 1978; *Quodlibet*, pf, chbr orch, 1976; *Sinfonia con giardino*, 1977–8; *Altisonanza*, 1992; etc.
Chamber and instrumental: *Gymel*, fl, pf, 1960; *Alef*, ob, 1965; *Tre pezzi*, pf, 1978; *Beth*, cl, 5 insts, 1979; *Daleth*, cl, pf, 1979; *Omaggio a Edvard Grieg*, 2 pf, 1981; *Como io passo l'estate*, pf, 1983; etc.

Castillon (de Saint-Victor), (Marie) Alexis, Vicomte de (b. Chartres, 13 Dec 1838; d. Paris, 5 Mar 1873). French composer. In 1863 he abandoned the military career thought appropriate to his noble birth and devoted himself to music, under the tuition of Victor Masse. Attracted above all by big instrumental forms, he wrote his fine Piano Quartet in G minor around the time of his meeting with Franck (1869), within whose circle he was influential.

Castor et Pollux. Opera by Rameau to a libretto by Pierre-Joseph Bernard. Death, observed in a grand and moving funeral scene, is overcome by the selflessness of the twins Pollux (bass) and Castor (haute-contre), each of whom is willing to sacrifice himself so that the other may enjoy life with Telaira (soprano). Their virtue brings compassion and immortality from the gods. First performance: Paris, 24 Oct 1737, rev Paris, Jun 1754.

castrato. A male voice of exceptional high range achieved by prepubertal castration, or a singer with that voice. The practice of castration for musical purposes seems to have arisen in the 1550s, possibly in Spain but soon thereafter in Italy, to which it was virtually limited. There may have been economic reasons: a boy of vocal aptitude (selected around the age of eight) would be almost guaranteed a career as a church singer. From the late 17th century to the mid 18th there was also the possibility of becoming an opera star, for during this period castratos, with opera seria their genre, were highly prized as stage heros, in almost all cities and courts where opera was given – i.e. by 1730, from Lisbon to St Petersburg, but not in France, where the heroic voice was the haute-contre.

The operation left castratos with small larynxes powered by large chests, and may have made them unusually tall, too. They would also have had continuous training from an early age. Their singing, by all reports, was powerful, refined and virtuoso, through a wide range and through tones of brilliance and magical poetry. Adding to their allure was a fascination with their sexuality: potency was as much part of their myth as vanity.

Pasqualini was among the first castratos to sing internationally in opera, followed by Siface in the late 17th century, by Senesino, Farinelli, Caffarelli and Guadagni (all of whom sang for Handel), by Rauzzini, Tenducci and Vincenzo dal Prato (among Mozart's singers) and finally by Velluti, whose retirement in 1830 brought the age of the operatic castrato to an end. Preferred to the countertenor in the 18th century as 'natural' (i.e. able to sing high without the artifice of falsetto), the voice now gave way to a different, Romantic understanding of nature, as unmodified. The role of operatic hero went first (and briefly) to cross-dressed women, who kept the vocal range, and then to tenors. Castratos retained their original place in church, but were increasingly confined to the Sistine Chapel, until banned by Pius X in 1903. One of the last, Alessandro Moreschi (1858–1921), made a few recordings, though of sentimental church music rather than splendiferous arias, so conveying only an afterglow of the voice at full power.

The revival of opera seria and associated forms – in the 1950s–60s with women in the castrato roles, latterly more often with counter-tenors – came at a time when notions of nature and normality were changing again, as reflected in the castrato's comeback now as fiction, in novels (Kingsley Amis's The Alteration, 1976; Anne Rice's Cry to Heaven, 1982) and films (Farinelli, 1994).

Angus Heriot The Castrati in Opera (1956, ʳ1975)

Castro, Juan José (b. Avellaneda, 7 Mar 1895; d. Buenos Aires, 5 Sep 1968). Argentinian composer. He and his brothers José Maria (1892–1964) and Washington (b. 1909) studied in Europe and returned to leading roles in Argentinian musical life, as composers and performers. Juan José, a pupil of d'Indy, was the most nationalist of them and the most prominent.

Castro Herrera, Ricardo (b. Nazas, Durango, 7 Feb 1864; d. Mexico City, 28 Nov 1907). Mexican pianist-composer, known for his work in small forms (impromptu, waltz), though he also wrote operas and two symphonies. He studied at the Mexico City Conservatory (1877–83) and had lessons with d'Albert during a period in Europe (1902–6).

Catalani, Alfredo (b. Lucca, 19 Jun 1854; d. Milan, 7 Aug 1893). Italian composer, who might have rivalled his fellow townsman Puccini had not persistent ill health carried him off after just one triumph, La Wally. He studied in Lucca with the same teacher, Magi, then at the Paris Conservatoire (1872–3) and with Bazzini at the Milan Conservatory (1873–5). In Milan he got caught up in the bohemian movement that aimed to renew Italian music by way of Wagner: he set a libretto by one of the movement's leaders, Boito, in the one-act La falce (f.p. Milan, 1875). His full-scale Elda (f.p. Turin, 1880), Dejanice (f.p. Milan, 1883) and Edmea (f.p. Milan, 1886) had no more than moderate success, though the first of them fared better when revised as Loreley (f.p. Turin, 1890). Illica's libretto for La Wally (f.p. Milan, 1892)

played more consistently to his strengths: poetic treatment of the supernatural and opulent melody (as laid out in the haunting popular aria 'Ebben? Ne andro lontan'). Toscanini conducted the première and was impressed enough to name his daughter after the heroine, but the composer died before he could collect the royalty payment due on the 60th performance. He also wrote orchestral pieces, piano music and songs.

Catalogue d'oiseaux (Bird Catalogue). Set of 13 piano pieces by Messiaen, each a portrait of a French bird singing in its habitat: 1 Le Chocard des alpes (Alpine Chough), 2 Le Loriot (Golden Oriole), 3 Le Merle bleu (Blue Rock Thrush), 4 Le Traquet stapazin (Black-Eared Wheatear), 5 La Chouette hulotte (Tawny Owl), 6 L'Alouette lulu (Wood Lark), 7 La Rousserolle éffarvatte (Reed Warbler), 8 L'Alouette calandrelle (Short-Toed Lark), 9 La Bouscarle (Cetti's Warbler), 10 Le Merle de roche (Rock Thrush), 11 La Buse variable (Buzzard), 12 Le Traquet rieur (Black Wheatear), 13 Le Courlis cendré (Curlew). The set is published in seven books, of 3–1–2–1–2–1–3 pieces, with those that occupy a whole book longer than the others, and the centrepiece, La rousserolle éffarvatte, playing for around 30 minutes. First performance: Paris, 15 Apr 1959.

Messiaen spoke of writing a second catalogue, but only got as far as adding one more half-hour piece, La Fauvette des jardins.

Catalonia. Region of northeast Spain, centred on Barcelona, with its own language, culture and history of independence. Its musicians have included Cererols, Valls, Soler, Sor, Pedrell, Vives, Casals, Gerhard, Mompou, Homs, Surinach, Caballé, Carreras and Savall.

Catán (Porteny), Daniel (b. Mexico City, 3 Apr 1949). Mexican composer. A student of philosophy at Sussex University, he then took a doctorate in composition under Babbitt, Randall and Boretz at Princeton (1977) and visited Japan, though his music is more lushly Romantic than such a pre-paration might imply. He won particular praise for the operas La hija de Rappaccini (Mexico City, 1991) and Florencia en el Amazonas (Houston, 1996), the first Spanish-language opera commis-sioned by a leading US company.

catch. English genre of round for three or four men to sing, current for two centuries from the end of the 16th. The subjects were such as have conventionally occupied men gathered together: drink, work problems and women. Humour and ribaldry were part of the game, often achieved by how different voices chimed in with innocent words creating together an indecency. Purcell wrote many.

Catel, Charles-Simon (b. L'Aigle, Normandy, 10 Jun 1773; d. Paris, 29 Nov 1830). French composer, of Revolutionary music (1792–7) and later of operas. He studied with Gossec as a boy, taught harmony at the Conservatoire from its foundation and, gradually after the Bourbon restoration, retired to his garden.

cathedral music. Term generally implying the more ambitious repertory of Anglican services and anthems as written and revived since the mid 19th century.

Catoire [Katuar], **Georgy (Lvovich)** (b. Moscow, 27 Apr 1861; d. Moscow, 21 May 1926). Russian composer of French descent, remembered especially, if occasionally, for his virtuoso piano music. His mixed education included piano studies with Klindworth and composition lessons with Rimsky-Korsakov, Lyadov, Arensky and Sergey Taneyev. For the last 10 years of his life he was professor of composition at the Moscow Conservatory.

Cats' Duet. Piece for meowing soprano and mezzo-soprano attributed to Rossini – probably falsely, though he would surely have accepted it gratefully. Mozart did indeed write or adapt a duet for baritone and soprano ('Nun liebes Weibchen', K.625) in which the woman can only meow. And Ravel, connoisseur of the peculiar, made sure he put a cats' duet in *L'Enfant et les sortilèges*.

Cat's Fugue, The. Name given Scarlatti's Sonata in G minor, K.30, for its suggestion of a cat prowling the keyboard.

Caturla, Alejandro García (b. Remedios, 7 Mar 1906; d. Remedios, 12 Nov 1940). Cuban composer, strongly influenced by Afro-Cuban culture, into which he married, fathering 11 children. He was equally prolific in his creative work. He studied in Havana (1926–7) and with Boulanger in Paris (1928), and pursued his Afro-Cuban style in a variety of instrumental works and songs, among which *Bembé* for chamber orchestra (1929) is particularly visceral. Also a practising lawyer, he was shot dead by a criminal.

Cavaillé-Coll, Aristide (b. Montpellier, 4 Feb 1811; d. Paris, 13 Oct 1899). French organ builder, a member of the fourth generation of an organ-building family working in southern France and

northern Spain. Rossini, visiting Toulouse, was impressed by his *poïkilorgue* (a variety of harmonium) and encouraged him to study in Paris (1833). Almost at once, though, he was not studying but busily working, alongside his father and brother. The firm eventually produced nearly 500 organs, mostly for French churches, providing immense power, tonal variety and possibilities of dynamic gradation. Their instruments made possible the great tradition of French organ music from Franck, through Widor and Vierne, Tournemire and Dupré, to Messiaen.

Fenner Douglass *Cavaillé-Coll and the French Romantic Tradition* (1999)

Cavalieri, Catarina (b. Vienna, 18 Mar 1755; d. Vienna, 30 Jun 1801). Austrian soprano. Her brilliance is memorialized in the music Mozart wrote for her: Konstanze's part in *Die Entführung*, Silberklang's in *Der Schauspieldirektor* and Elvira's 'Mi tradì' for the Vienna revival of *Don Giovanni*. Salieri was her protector.

Cavalieri, Emilio de' (b. Rome, *c*.1550; d. Rome, 11 Mar 1602). Italian composer and courtier, whose RAPPRESENTATIONE DI ANIMA, ET DI CORPO (1600) has a place in the earliest history of opera and of the new continuo style, being the first score printed with figured bass. The son of an architect close to Michelangelo, he was in Medici service from 1587, as a composer and master of ceremonies: he was in charge of the lavish 1589 intermedi, for which he wrote the madrigals *Dalle più alte sfere* and *Godi turba mortal*. He also acted as a diplomat, in dealings with Rome, and settled there in 1600 after disappointments over the handling of the festivities for the wedding of Henri IV of France to Maria de' Medici.

Cavalleria rusticana (Rustic Chivalry). Opera by Mascagni to a libretto by Giovanni Targioni-Tozzetti and Guido Menasci after Giovanni Verga's story and play. The ritual solemnity of Easter in a Sicilian village is the background for a revenge story in which Santuzza (soprano), discarded by Turiddu (tenor), brings about his death at the hands of Alfio (baritone), his new lover Lola's husband. Regarded as the archetype of verismo, the opera is almost always presented with *Pagliacci*. Its numbers include Turiddu's opening song 'O Lola', brindisi 'Viva il vino spumeggiante' and farewell 'Mamma, quel vino è generoso', the Easter Hymn led by Santuzza ('Inneggiamo') and an orchestral intermezzo. First performance: Rome, 17 May 1890.

Cavalli, (Pietro [Pier]), Francesco (b. Crema, 14

Feb 1602; d. Venice, 14 Jan 1676). Italian composer, dominant in Venetian opera and church music after Monteverdi. The son of Giovanni Battista Caletti, chapelmaster of Crema Cathedral, he had a fine voice as a boy, and in 1616 was sent to St Mark's by the town's Venetian governor, Federico Cavalli, whose surname he later took. He remained at St Mark's, a tenor and almost certainly a student of the man who became his model as a composer, Monteverdi. In 1620 he was appointed organist at San Zanipolo, in 1625 he had his first publication (a motet), and in 1630 he married a wealthy widow (who died in 1652). He became second organist at St Mark's in 1639, better paid and more highly regarded than his notional superior.

The same year saw his first opera, *Le nozze di Teti e di Peleo*, after which he produced new works more or less annually, for theatres in which he had a financial interest. He was a major participant in the development of commercial opera, still classical in subject matter but quicker paced, less lofty than the work that had come out of the poetic academies, and sometimes earthier. Touring companies took his pieces to cities elsewhere in Italy and beyond, and eventually the call came for him to travel, to Paris, to produce an opera for the marriage of Louis XIV, at the invitation of Cardinal Mazarin. He spent two years away, 1660–62, creating *Ercole amante* under fraught circumstances in an excessively large new theatre made for the occasion. Nor were his efforts rewarded: the dancing of the king and queen caused more comment than the opera, and their music was by Lully. He wrote more operas back in Venice, but after 1668, when he became chapelmaster at St Mark's, he concentrated on church music. Childless, he left his opera scores to a singer, through whom they passed to the civic library in Venice, almost untouched until the second half of the 20th century, when Raymond Leppard's elaborations were followed by more judicious versions.

Jane Glover *Cavalli* (1978)

Operas (with performance dates, in Venice unless otherwise noted): *Didone* (Giovanni Francesco Busenello), 1641; *Egisto* (Giovanni Faustini), 1643; *Ormindo* (Faustini), 1644; GIASONE, 1649; *Calisto* (Faustini), 1651; *Orione* (Francesco Melosio), 1653; *Xerse* (Nicolo Minato), 1655; *Erismena* (Aurelio Aureli), 1655; *Ercole amante* (Francesco Buti), f.p. Paris, 1662; about 25 others
Sacred: mass, psalms, canzonas, etc., pub 1656; 3 vespers settings, pub 1675; etc.
Other works: cantatas, arias

Cav and Pag. Familiar name for the traditional double bill of CAVALLERIA RUSTICANA and PAGLIACCI.

cavata (It., excavated). Baroque aria carved out from the last line or two of verse intended for recitative.

cavatina (It.). Diminutive of CAVATA, designating in the 18th century an aria without da capo repeat (e.g. 'Porgi amor' in *Le nozze di Figaro*) and in the 19th century a variety of things. Its modern usage, to denote a slow aria without cabaletta, may owe as much to Beethoven's Op.130 quartet, whose fifth movement he headed 'Cavatina', as to opera.

Cavazzoni, Marco Antonio (b. Bologna, *c*.1490; d. Venice, *c*.1560). Italian organist-composer, active from 1517 mostly in Venice, where in 1523 he published a volume of keyboard music including the first two examples of the ricercare. His son Girolamo (*c*.1525–77 or later) was also an organist-composer, whose two published books (1543) include ricercares based more on imitative polyphony.

Cavendish, Michael (b. *c*.1565; d. London, Jul 1628). English composer of lute songs and madrigals. He dedicated his single printed volume (1598) to Lady Arabella Stuart, his second cousin, and was later in service to the future Charles I.

Cavos, Catterino (b. Venice, 30 Oct 1775; d. St Petersburg, 10 May 1840). Italian–Russian composer, son of the ballet master at La Fenice. He went to St Petersburg in 1799 and was important in the early history of opera in Russian, though he lived to see his work superseded, conducting the première of Glinka's *A Life for the Tsar* (1836), on the same subject as his *Ivan Susanin* (1815). His son Alberto was the architect who rebuilt the Moscow Bolshoy and the Mariinsky.

Cazden, Norman (b. New York, 23 Sep 1914; d. Bangor, Maine, 18 Aug 1980). US composer. He graduated from Juilliard as a teacher in 1932, and picked up his studies again in the 1940s, when he took degrees in social science (City College) and musicology (Harvard). Scholarly concerns with non-diatonic consonance and folk music fed into his music. His academic career was interrupted when he refused to answer the Un-American Activities Committee, until in 1969 he gained a post at the University of Maine.

Cazzati, Maurizio (b. Lucera, near Reggio Emilia, 1616; d. Mantua, 1678). Italian composer, who established resplendent music at San Petronio in Bologna as chapelmaster (1657–71), and was influential in the early history of the chamber sonata. Before and after his time in Bologna he held posts in Mantua, Bergamo and Ferrara. He started the San Petronio tradition of music for trumpet and strings, though his command of harmony in choral works was criticized by contemporaries, resulting in a paper war (1658–64). Two-thirds of his 66 printed volumes, some of which he published himself, comprise sacred choral music; the rest contain instrumental pieces (canzonas, sonatas, dances) and vocal chamber music (cantatas, arias, canzonettas).

CBS. Columbia Broadcasting System, a US company founded in 1927 to broadcast under the auspices of COLUMBIA. It bought the recording interests of Columbia in 1938 and sold them to Sony in 1988.

CD [compact disc]. Commercial RECORDING medium introduced in 1983 and rapidly ousting its chief predecessor, the LP. A CD is a 4¾-inch (12cm) plastic disc on which sound is digitally encoded in a spiral track starting at the centre, to be read by laser means.

Cecilia. Putative saint of the early Roman church, venerated since the 5th century with November 22 as her festival, and honoured as patron saint of music and musicians since the 15th century, for reasons disputed. The earliest recorded musical celebration of her feast day took place at Evreux in 1570. Cecilian festivals on her day in London began in 1683 and were almost annual until 1703, then more irregular, replaced in modern times by a charity concert. The Baroque occasions involved a choral service followed by an ode, created by notable poets (Dryden, Pope, Congreve) and composers (Purcell, Blow, Handel). Similar commemorations and concerts took place in other British cities in the late 17th century and early 18th. In 19th-century Paris a newly composed St Cecilia's Day mass was regularly offered; Gounod wrote one. Meanwhile, in Germany there was a whole CECILIAN MOVEMENT. Composers born on St Cecilia's Day include Franz Benda and W.F. Bach (in consecutive years), Rodrigo, Britten and Schuller.

Cecilian movement. 19th-century German movement aimed at reviving sacred polyphony in the spirit of Palestrina. It began in the early years of the century from scattered 18th-century origins, and reached its peak in the 1860s–70s.

cédez (Fr., yield). Slow down, a marking particularly associated with Debussy.

cel. Abbreviation for celesta.

celesta (Fr. *céleste*). Keyboard instrument, like a small upright piano, whose hammers hit not strings but steel bars supported on felt over wooden resonators, producing sounds suggesting muted bells. It was invented by Auguste Mustel in 1886 and used soon after by Chausson (music for *The Tempest*, 1888) and Tchaikovsky (Dance of the Sugar-Plum Fairy in *The Nutcracker*, 1892). It became a frequent visitor to the orchestra in the first half of the 20th century and almost ubiquitous in the second. Bartók drew attention to its presence in his Music for Strings, Percussion and Celesta perhaps for reasons of euphony in the title, since its part in the work is certainly no greater than the unmentioned piano's. Modern instruments cover four octaves (from middle C), five (from the fifth below) or five plus a fourth (from the octave below).

Celibidache, Sergiu (Ioan) (b. Roman, 11 Jul 1912, d. Paris, 14 Aug 1996). Romanian conductor, whose fearsome demands (on players, on rehearsal time) could be matched by extraordinary performances. He studied in Iaşi, Bucharest, Paris and Berlin, where Walter Gmeindl was his conducting teacher and Martin Steinke his Zen mentor. After an illustrious start with the Berlin Philharmonic (1946–52), he conducted the Swedish Radio Symphony (1962–71), the Stuttgart Radio Symphony (1971–7) and the Munich Philharmonic (1979–96). He made no recordings, but after his death many of his broadcast performances, particularly from his Berlin and Stuttgart periods, were released on CD.

Klaus Gerke, ed. *Celibidache!* (2001)

cell. Informal term for a small group of notes used as a building block, especially by Bartók and other composers of his period. SET is a more formal alternative, but normally implies a 12-note group.

cello (Fr. *violoncelle*, Ger. *Cello, Violoncell*, pl. *Celli, Cellos, Violoncellen*, It. *violoncello*, pl. *violoncelli*). Bass violin, its name shortened from violoncello, i.e. lesser VIOLONE. Tuned an octave below the viola (C–G–D–A, from the C below the bass staff), it naturally finds itself at or near the bottom of ensembles, supplying a continuo line in Baroque music, the lowest part in a string quartet and the middle bass of an orchestral texture (with the double basses lower still). Yet its great range – of colour as well as pitch – and its capacities for intensity of phrasing and attack give it the projective power of a voice.

Its early history is a tangle of many different shapes and sizes of instrument, and even more names. Documents and pictures show that the instrument was in existence by around 1530, but no composer used the name before Giulio Cesare Arresti, in a set of sonatas published in 1665. The emergence of the standard cello at that time was made possible by the innovation of wire-wound strings, which reduced the size necessary for a bass-register violin. Stradivari's instruments, from the first decade of the 18th century, established a regular size for the instrument of about 30 inches (75–6cm), but not at once: Bach wrote not only for a five-string cello (Suite No.6) but also for a *violoncello piccolo* (tuned a fifth higher). Where the instrument was of normal size, the preferred manner of holding it was between the legs: end-pins, in use in the 18th century, became normal only at the end of the 19th.

Notable cellists of the 18th century included Caldara, Francischello (the pseudonym of Francesco Alborea, a Neapolitan virtuoso widely admired in the 1720s–30s), Barrière and, in the Classical period, Boccherini and Anton Kraft (for whom Haydn and Beethoven wrote). Among their 19th-century successors were Bernhard Romberg and Adrien François Servais, followed by Piatti and David Popper. The instrument found its late Romantic voice in concertos by Saint-Saëns, Tchaikovsky, Lalo, Brahms (Double Concerto), Dvořák and Elgar, while at the end of this period its earlier music was rediscovered by Casals, who greatly enhanced its aura and technique. After him a great many players have performed an ever-widening repertory: Rostropovich alone was responsible for works by Prokofiev, Britten, Dutilleux and Boulez. Palm (in Ligeti and Xenakis) and Uitti (in Scelsi, Kurtág and Harvey) have taken the instrument further to the edge of possibility.

William Pleeth *Cello* (1982); Robin Stowell, ed. *The Cambridge Companion to the Cello* (1999).

cello concerto. Work for solo cello and orchestra. The principal examples are by Vivaldi, C.P.E. Bach, Haydn, Boccherini, Schumann, Saint-Saëns, Lalo, Dvořák (f.p. London, 19 Mar 1896, Leo Stern), Elgar (f.p. London, 27 Oct 1919, Felix Salmond), Schoenberg (f.p. London, 3 Feb 1933, Antonio Sala), Prokofiev, Shostakovich, Ligeti and Carter.

cemb. Ger. abbreviation for CEMBALO.

cembalo (It.). Harpsichord, abbreviated from *clavicembalo*. This is the normal modern Ger. term.

Cenerentola, La. See CINDERELLA.

cent. One hundredth of a semitone, on a logarithmic scale. The term and the measure were introduced by A.J. Ellis around 1880. The interval in cents between two frequencies is the $\log_{10}$ of their ratio times $1200/\log_{10}2$.

cento (Lat., patchwork). Literary or musical work formed from passages from previous works. The term was introduced by Paolo Ferretti (1934), a high-ranking Benedictine and plainsong scholar, for chants made in this manner, by 'centonization'. It has remained essentially a term in chant studies, though the same principle is at work in the 18th-century pasticcio or, from the later 20th century, the third movement of Berio's *Sinfonia*.

Ce qu'on entend sur la montagne (What one hears on the mountain). Symphonic poem by Liszt after a poem by Victor Hugo. (Franck had written an orchestral piece on the same subject, c.1845–7.) First performance: Weimar, Feb 1850.

Cererols, Joan (b. Martorell, 9 Sep 1618; d. Montserrat, 28 Aug 1676). Catalan composer and church musician, who went to the monastery of Montserrat as a choirboy and stayed as a monk and musician. He wrote masses (*Missa de batalla*), two *Requiem* settings, vespers music and villancicos, often excitingly laid out for double choirs with continuo.

Cerha, Friedrich (b. Vienna, 17 Feb 1926). Austrian composer and conductor, most famous for completing Act 3 of Berg's *Lulu*. He studied in Vienna at both music academy (composition with Alfred Uhl) and university, and also attended the Darmstadt courses (1956–9). Around that time he started out on his triple career as teacher (at the academy, 1959–88), conductor (with the Die Reihe ensemble, which he and Schwertsik founded in 1958) and composer, developing a somewhat Ligetian concern with texture in the orchestral cycles *Mouvements I–III* (1959) and *Spiegel I–VII* (1960–61). His work on *Lulu*, begun in 1962, may have influenced his subsequent Bergian combination of stylistic diversity with expressive conviction – a feature notably of his Brecht opera *Baal* (1974–80; first performance: Salzburg, 1981). Besides two further operas and many more orchestral scores, his later works include three quartets (1989–92).

Černohorský, Bohuslav (Matěj) (baptized Nymburk, 16 Feb 1684; d. Graz, Feb 1742). Czech composer, whose few surviving works have evoked comparisons with his contemporaries Handel and Bach. The son of a schoolmaster-organist, he studied at Prague University (1700–2) and joined the Franciscans in 1704. He was, though, an unruly brother. Against the wishes of his superiors in Prague he took off for Italy, where he held posts as organist in Assisi (1710–15, Tartini being his pupil during this time) and Padua (1715–20). He was later sent into retreat (1727–30), after which he went back to Padua (1731–41) and died on his return north.

Certon, Pierre (b. ?Melun, c.1515; d. Paris, 23 Feb 1572). French composer, of sacred and secular polyphony. He joined the Sainte Chapelle as a clerk in 1532 and was master of the choristers there from 1536 until his death.

Ces (Ger.). C♭. Hence *Ceses* (C♭♭).

Cesti, Antonio [Pietro] (baptized Arezzo, 15 Aug 1623; d. Florence, 14 Oct 1669). Italian composer. Having been a choirboy in Arezzo, he joined the Franciscans in 1637, taking the name Antonio in place of his baptismal Pietro, and probably studied with Roman musicians before becoming organist of Volterra Cathedral (1644–5). He may have spent the next several years in Florence, protected by the Medici and turning from church music to opera, as a singer and subsequently composer. He produced his first two operas for Venice in 1651–2 and added more while in service at the archducal court in Innsbruck (1652–7). Of these, *Orontea* (1656) and *Dori* (1657) were among the most frequently revived operas of their time. In 1658–61 he was in Rome, partly to gain papal release from his monastic vows – though he remained a priest. A second period in Innsbruck (1662–5) was cut short by the archduke's death, after which the court musicians were transferred to Vienna. There he created *Il pomo d'oro*, a work of altogether exceptional sumptuousness and length: lasting eight hours, it was spread over two evenings when eventually performed in 1668. After that he moved back to Florence. Besides operas he composed cantatas and a small amount of church music.

ceterone (It.). Early Italian continuo instrument with bass strings, related to the cittern as the theorbo is to the lute.

cetra (It.). CITTERN. Vivaldi took the word as title for a collection of 12 concertos in two books he published in Amsterdam in 1727.

Chabrier, (Alexis) Emmanuel (b. Ambert, Puy-de-Dôme, 18 Jan 1841; d. Paris, 13 Sep 1894). French composer, whose voluptuousness and verve convey a zest for life, and whose wit simultaneously displays a lack of illusion. He studied as a boy with two Spanish musicians, and continued in Paris, after the family's move there in 1856, with the piano virtuoso Edward Wolff and various composition teachers. Legal studies and a job in the Ministry of the Interior (1861–80) did not keep him from composing or from forming friendships with poets and painters. In 1863–4 he wrote songs for two short operettas with words partly by Verlaine, and he came to own pictures by Manet (for whom he sat three times), Monet and Renoir. Also important to him was the Paris première in 1861 of *Tannhäuser*, whose full score he is said to have copied out. But his creative work consisted almost exclusively of songs for private gatherings, where Verlaine noted the amiability and ease he formed around himself.

In 1873 he married; there were two sons. Four years later came his first public triumph, *L'Etoile*, an opéra bouffe indebted to Offenbach but standing out for its orchestral finesse and its touch of poetic melancholy – its moist eye reflecting brilliance. He confessed he shed a tear of his own on hearing *Tristan* in Munich in 1880, and later that year gave up his ministry job (he had family money) to devote himself to composition. The results included his orchestral masterpiece *España*, but his sights were set on opera, and all his attempts caused him difficulties. *Gwendoline* disappeared after its first run (to be remembered for its exciting overture); complications with librettists and theatre managers left *Le Roi malgré lui* a sprawling mess; and illness intervened after the first act of *Briséïs*. But though his fully achieved works were few, their buoyancy of rhythm – racing or syncopated – and harmonic sophistication are distinctive and exhilarating.

Rollo Myers *Emmanel Chabrier and his Circle* (1969)

Operas: L'ETOILE; *Une Education manquée* (1 act: Eugène Leterrier and Albert Vanloo), pub 1879; *Gwendoline* (Mendès), 1879–85, f.p. Brussels, 1886; *Le Roi malgré lui* (Paul Burani, Emile de Najac and Jean Richepin), 1884–7, f.p. Paris, 1887; *Briséïs* (Mendès), 1888–91, unfinished; etc.

Orchestral: Larghetto, hn, orch, 1875; ESPANA, pub 1883; *La Sulamite*, mez, women's ch, orch, 1884; *Danse slave, Fête polonaise* (from *Le Roi*); *Joyeuse marche*, 1888; *Prélude pastorale*, 1888; *Suite pastorale*, 1888; *Habanera*, pub 1889; *Ode à la musique*, s, women's ch, orch, 1890; *Bourrée fantasque* (orchestration completed by Mottl)

Songs: 'L'Invitation au voyage' (Baudelaire), 1870; etc.

Piano: *Pas redoublé*, duet, 1871; *Dix pièces pitoresques*, 1880–81; *Trois valses romantiques*, 2 pf, pub 1883; *Habanera*, pub 1885; *Souvenirs de Munich*, duet, 1885–6; *Bourrée fantasque*, pub 1891; etc.

chace. Medieval term for canon (1), now applied

to 14th-century French songs parallelling the Italian CACCIA (1).

chaconne (Fr., It. *ciacona, ciaccona*). Movement based on a repeating ground bass, usually of eight bars and compelling gravity. However, its origins were otherwise. Probably arising in post-conquest Mexico, it was lively and irreverent, and became a craze in Spain at the start of the 17th century. From there it moved to Italy as an improvisatory instrumental form (Frescobaldi). Taken to Paris by Italian musicians, it became, *c.*1650, a stately instrumental piece (Louis Couperin) or ballet (Lully), and stayed as such, often having a culminative role in an opera. Thus transformed, it passed to Germany, to England and back to Italy (Corelli's Op.2:12). There remained some distinction from the PASSACAGLIA, which would generally be slower and in the minor, but Bach's examples – the Chaconne in D minor for violin from his fourth partita and Passacaglia and Fugue in C minor for organ – effectively merged the two streams. The prestige of those works made the terms interchangeable (in examples by Schoenberg, Webern and Ligeti) or unnecessary (in Beethoven's C minor Variations and the finale of Brahms's Fourth Symphony).

chacony. Older English term for chaconne, as in examples by Purcell.

Chadwick, George W(hitefield) (b. Lowell, Mass., 13 Nov 1854; d. Boston, 4 Apr 1931). US composer and teacher, second-generation New England symphonist. He learned music from his elder brother and continued at the New England Conservatory while working as an organist and teacher, then studied with Jadassohn in Leipzig (1877–9) and Rheinberger in Munich (1879–80). Back home he established a national reputation with music anticipating Dvořák's absorption of US folk elements into mainstream symphonism, increasingly as much French (Dukas-style) as German. He also taught from 1882 at his old conservatory, which he directed from 1897, his students including Parker, Mason and Still.

Orchestral: Symphony No.1, C, 1881; No.2, B♭, 1883–5; No.3, F, 1893–4; *Melpomene* (overture), 1887; Symphonic Sketches, 1895–1904; *Tam O'Shanter*, 1914–15
Other works: stage pieces, choral music, 5 string quartets, songs, etc.

Chailley, Jacques (b. Paris, 24 Mar 1910; d. Montpellier, 21 Jan 1999). French scholar and composer. He studied with Boulanger (1925–7) and at the Paris Conservatoire (1933–5), and combined an academic career (notably as professor at the Sorbonne, 1952–79) with composition. In both spheres medieval music was crucial to him.

Chailly, Riccardo (b. Milan, 20 Feb 1953). Italian conductor of broad sympathies, from Rossini to Varèse, theatrical flair and consistent diligence. The son of the composer Luciano Chailly (1920–2002), he studied with his father and at the Milan and Perugia conservatories. At 19 he became Abbado's assistant at La Scala, and in 1974 he made his US debut in Chicago (*Madama Butterfly*). He continued to conduct Italian opera while strengthening his concert repertory as chief conductor of the Berlin Radio Symphony (1982–8), from which he moved on to the Concertgebouw (1988–2004) and the Gewandhaus (from 2005).

chain. Heavy chain, to be let fall or thrown, as a percussion instrument in Schoenberg's *Gurrelieder*, etc.

chair organ (Fr. *positif*, Ger. *Rückpositiv*). Small organ in its own case, behind the organist's chair.

Chaliapin [Shalyapin, Chaliapine], **Fyodor (Ivanovich)** (b. near Kazan, 13 Feb 1873; d. Paris 12 Apr 1938). Russian bass, a byword for the strong portrayal of character in opera. He studied and began his career in Tbilisi, then joined the Mariinsky (1894–6), Savva Mamontov's company (1896–9) and the Bolshoy (1896–1914). His first foreign engagement was at La Scala as Boito's Mephistopheles (1901), a role he repeated at the Met in 1907; he also sang with Diaghilev's company (1908–10, 1913). In 1918 he returned to the Mariinsky, but in 1921 he emigrated. Recordings and photographs testify to his astonishing ability to transform himself into Boris Godunov or Philip II (*Don Carlos*), Mephistopheles (Boito's or Gounod's) or Don Quixote (Massenet's). In 1933 he played Don Quixote in Pabst's film, singing songs by Ibert. He married a dancer and had a son who became – like him, most essentially – an actor.
Victor Borovsky *Chaliapin* (1988)

chalumeau (Fr., from Lat. *calamus*, reed). Single-reed woodwind instrument, a link between recorder and clarinet, first mentioned in 1687 and only gradually displaced by the regular clarinet during the next several decades. Despite its name, it seems to have been developed by German makers and certainly was used most often by German and Austrian composers, notably Telemann. Its soft strength was in the lower range, and its name survives in the term 'chalumeau register' for this part of the clarinet's compass.

Chamber Concerto (Kammerkonzert). Work by Berg for piano, violin and 13 wind, a homage to Schoenberg's Chamber Symphony No.1, which is also for 15 musicians: Berg replaces Schoenberg's strings with (besides his soloists) another flute, trumpet and trombone. The first movement is for piano and wind, the second for violin and wind, the third for the full complement. First performance: Berlin, 27 Mar 1927.

chamber music (Fr. *musique de chambre*, Ger. *Kammermusik*, It. *musica da camera*). Music for small groups, classically of from three to five musicians. Solo pieces, accompanied or unaccompanied, are conventionally known as 'instrumental music'. As for the upper limit, that became hazy with the 20th-century development – for reasons both artistic and economic – of larger chamber ensembles as an alternative to the orchestra. Schoenberg's Chamber Symphony No.1 for 15 players (1906) is an early example, declaring in its title its encroachment on territory between chamber and symphonic repertories. But the essence of chamber music is that it is not conducted, which would discount the Schoenberg score.

Another key feature of chamber music is that it is music for a chamber, i.e. a domestic room, not a concert hall, church or theatre. This presupposes a small audience – perhaps ideally no audience at all, just a gathering of amateurs performing for their joint pleasure. Music of this kind includes the 16th-century MADRIGAL, the 17th-century CONSORT fantasy and the Classical STRING QUARTET. But there is also a great deal of chamber music demanding fully professional skills, from Machaut's ballades to Carter's quartets. Besides, the arrival of radio and recording in the early 20th century made it unnecessary for people to perform themselves in order to have music at home, and so chamber music withdrew more and more to the concert stage.

In these various poisings – between orchestral and solo music, professional and amateur, public and private, display and conversation – chamber music has its life.

W.W. Cobbett *Cobbett's Cyclopedic Survey of Chamber Music* (1929–30, ²1963); Alec Robertson, ed. *Chamber Music* (1957)

chamber opera. Term for works requiring only a small orchestra and therefore amenable to presentation in smaller theatres. *Ariadne auf Naxos* (1916) stands at the head of this 20th-century trend,

though its vocal opulence is rather that of full-scale opera. More typical are several works by Britten, e.g. *The Rape of Lucretia*. The term can also be applied to lightly scored pieces of the 17th and 18th centuries.

chamber orchestra. Phenomenon of the first (mid-20th-century) phase in the revival of 18th-century music: an orchestra of period scale, but making no attempt at period style. The maximum size would be that of Mozart's later music, i.e. double wind, timpani and around 20 strings. Examples include the English Chamber Orchestra (founded 1948) and the New York group Orpheus (founded 1972).

chamber organ. Small organ made in former times for domestic use, and since the mid 20th century for concert performances of Baroque music.

Chamber Symphony (Kammersymphonie). Title of two Schoenberg works, though the first is normally implied, a work for 15 musicians (fl, ob, cor ang, high cl, cl, b cl, bn, dbn, 2 hn, str qt, db) pushing through four symphonic movements in one continuous thrust. Webern compressed the scoring even further, for *Pierrot lunaire* quintet; Schoenberg expanded it, for full orchestra; Berg offered his tribute in a *Wozzeck* scene with the same scoring as well as in his Chamber Concerto; and Eisler wrote a chamber symphony for a different 15 players. There are also chamber symphonies by Schreker, Vainberg, Saxton and Adams.

Chambonnières, Jacques Champion Sieur de (b. Paris, 1601/2; d. Paris, 1672). French keyboard composer-performer, musical forebear of the Couperins. The son and grandson of royal keyboard musicians, he joined and gradually took over from his aged father in the 1630s and was at the height of favour in the early 1650s, when he may have been in contact with Froberger. He introduced the Couperins to royal service and not only played for Louis XIV but also danced with him – and with Lully, whose rise perhaps brought his eclipse. In 1670 he published two books of pieces, mostly in dance forms.

Chaminade, Cécile (Louise Stéphanie) (b. Paris, 8 Aug 1857; d. Monte Carlo, 13 Apr 1944). French composer, popular in her time, subsequently disparaged and latterly esteemed, all for the same reason: that, as a woman composer, her options were limited to salon music. Faced with opposition from her parents, she studied privately with Paris Conservatoire teachers, including Godard and Marmontel. From the 1880s she was publishing regularly and gaining a following in the USA, where she went on tour in 1908. She was the first woman composer admitted to the Légion d'Honneur (1913). Her works consist mostly of piano music and songs, but include a concertino with orchestra dear to flautists (*c*.1900).

Champagne, Claude (Joseph Arthur Adonai) (b. Montreal, 27 May 1891; d. Montreal, 21 Dec 1965). Canadian composer, leader of French Canadian music. Imbued with an inheritance from French Canadian and Irish grandparents, he studied with Gédalge and Koechlin in Paris (1921–8), then returned to Montreal and helped found the conservatory (1942). His works include orchestral pieces and sacred music.

chance operations. Term introduced by Cage for techniques allowing compositional decisions to be made by chance, whether by tossing coins or, later, by digital means. In the classic case of his *Music of Changes* – called after the Chinese *I Ching*, or *Book of Changes* – the results of several coin tosses determined pitches, durations and dynamic levels. Birtwistle, on a smaller scale, has used tables of random numbers to choose from among alternatives. Such procedures imply that the decision, once made, is inscribed in the score and irrevocable, unlike the case with INDETERMINACY.

Chandos anthems. 11 settings for soli, choir and instruments by Handel from 1717–18, when he was house composer to the Earl of Carnarvon (from 1719 Duke of Chandos) at Cannons, near Edgware, north of London.

change ringing. Uniquely English pursuit, datable to the late 16th century, whereby the several bells in a belltower are rung in changing succession. The various systems have venerable names: Grandsire Doubles, Cambridge Surprise Minor, Stedman Caters, etc.

changing note. See NOTA CAMBIATA.

Chanler, Theodore (Ward) (b. Newport, RI, 29 Apr 1902; d. Boston, 27 Jul 1961). US composer, especially of songs (*Eight Epitaphs*, 1939). He studied in New York, Cleveland (with Bloch), Oxford and Paris (with Boulanger), then returned to the USA in 1933 for a career as teacher and composer.

chanson (Fr.). Song. The usual French word for an art song is *mélodie*; *chanson* generally implies either a modern popular song or a polyphonic song from the period after the decline of the medieval fixed forms, i.e. from the late 15th and 16th centuries. In this latter sense it is the French madrigal, practised by Josquin, Sermisy, Janequin, Le Jeune and others.

chanson de geste (Fr.). French medieval epic, originally recited to repeated melodic formulae, e.g. the *Chanson de Roland*.

chanson de toile (Fr.). Weaving song, a class of 13th-century songs picturing a lady awaiting her true love.

chansonnier (Fr.). (1) Songbook, specifically one from the 13th–16th centuries containing polyphonic songs in French, the courtly language of western Europe. A particularly sumptuous example is the *Chansonnier cordiforme* (i.e. heart-shaped, which the book is when opened), dating from the later 15th century and including compositions by Du Fay, Binchois and Ockeghem.

(2) Popular singer.

chanson pour boire (Fr.). Drinking song, a 17th-century genre.

Chansons madécasses (Madagascar Songs). Triptych by Ravel setting prose poems by the 18th-century poet Evariste de Parny, for voice with flute, cello and piano. First performance: Rome, 8 May 1926.

chant. Liturgical singing for soloist or in unison. See BYZANTINE CHANT; PLAINSONG; RUSSIA.

Chant après chant (Song after Song). Work by Barraqué, part of his *La Mort de Virgile*, for soprano, piano and percussion sextet. First performance: Strasbourg, 23 Jun 1966.

chanter. Melody pipe of a bagpipe.

chanterelle (Fr., singing one). Top string of an instrument, usually violin or lute.

Chantilly. Manuscript volume, principal source of ARS SUBTILIOR songs, made for an unknown nobleman and held by the Musée Condé, Chantilly.

Chants d'Auvergne (Songs of the Auvergne). Sequence of five sets of folksong arrangements by Canteloube.

Chants de terre et de ciel (Songs of Earth and Heaven). Song cycle by Messiaen to his own words, in praise of the family life he was enjoying with his wife and baby son. The original title was *Prismes*. First performance: Paris, 23 Jan 1939.

chapel. In former times not so much a building as a team of people providing religious (and therefore also musical) services to a high individual: monarch or nobleman, pope or prelate. The chapel was part of the court, moving with the person it served.

The first chapel was that of the 7th-century kings of the Franks: a body of priests having as their totem the cape (*cappa*) of St Martin. Strengthened and formalized by Pippin III and his son Charlemagne, the institution was widely imitated, and came by the 14th century to be defined more by its singers and composers than by its clerical staff. In the most important Renaissance chapels, such as those of the papacy (the Sistine and Julian chapels), England (the CHAPEL ROYAL), Burgundy, Vienna and several Italian cities, there would typically be 20–30 singers under a master, a position held, at different times and places, by almost all the leading composers of the period. With the growth of instrumental and secular music at courts in the 17th century, the chapel as a musical establishment often came to include instrumentalists and gain responsibilities for opera and concert performances. In many countries this brought a change in nomenclature, but the *Kapelle* as a body of musicians remained a feature of German courts until those courts disappeared at the end of the First World War, and the word is retained in the names of two venerable orchestras, the Berlin and Dresden Staatskapellen.

chapelmaster (Fr. *maître de chapelle*, Ger. *Kapellmeister*, It. *maestro di cappella*, Sp. *maestro de capilla*). Unusual term in English, probably because the leadership of the Chapel Royal was generally more complex, but it usefully renders a post common elsewhere and is so employed in this book – except in connection with German courts c.1750–1918, where the KAPELLMEISTER was mostly a director and conductor of secular music.

Chapel Royal. Ancient term for the royal CHAPEL of England or that of Scotland. The English Chapel Royal was definitively established around 1300 and entered its great days under Henry V (r. 1413–22), who increased its size to 32 Gentlemen (singers and composers, some of them also priests) and 16 Children (choirboys), and who took it with him to France, so helping disseminate the English style. It kept roughly those numbers for two and a half centuries, to the time of Charles II (r. 1660–85), with rights to impress excellent boy singers found in other institutions. Bull and Purcell began their careers as Children of the Chapel Royal; they and many other notable composers – Abyndon, Tallis, Sheppard, Blitheman, Parsons, Byrd, Morley, Tomkins – were Gentlemen. The institution then declined in importance as well as numbers, but it still exists, singing regular Sunday services at St James's Palace and participating in royal occasions, private and public.

Chappell. British music firm founded as a publishing outfit in London in 1810 by Johann Baptist Cramer, Francis Tatton Latour and Samuel Chappell, who became sole owner c.1830. Under his son Thomas Patey Chappell (1819–1902) the company became active in concert promotion and piano manufacture and gained particular strength in light music.

character. Term used adjectivally to describe a voice type, most often a tenor. Roles for character tenor (e.g. Mime in *Siegfried*, Shuisky in *Boris Godunov*, Don Basilio in *Figaro*) will tend to require acting with the voice rather than lyrical expression.

character piece, characteristic piece (Fr. *pièce caractéristique*, Ger. *Charakterstück*). Piece having a definable character, probably compounded of mood (melancholy, energetic) and genre (waltz, march). Many keyboard pieces of the 17th–18th centuries fit this description, but the term is most characteristic of Romantic piano music, e.g. Schumann's *Davidsbündlertänze*, subtitled '18 Charakterstücke'.

charivari (Fr., US *shivaree*). Noisy music made with more or less benign intent outside the houses of persons deemed deserving of social barracking or berating.

charleston. Fast ragtime dance, for which Jimmy Johnson's *Charleston* (1922) sparked a craze. There is also one by Schulhoff (*Etudes de jazz*).

Charpentier, Gustave (b. Dieuze, Moselle, 25 Jun 1860; d. Paris, 18 Feb 1956). French composer, remembered for one opera, *Louise*, that allowed a young working-class woman to assert herself, to gorgeous music expressing affection both for her and for the city of Paris. Of humble origin himself (his father was a baker, but one who encouraged him into music), he started work in a mill in 1875. His employer and then local townspeople supported his education, at the conservatories of Lille and Paris (1881–7), where he studied with

Massenet and won the Prix de Rome. On returning from Rome in 1890, he brought with him the beginnings of *Louise*, based on his student experience of bohemian life in Montmartre. A triumph when it eventually opened 10 years later, the opera earned him a fortune, which he partly dispersed in founding a free conservatory for the real-life Louises of Paris. He wrote little else, and seems to have completed nothing after giving *Louise* a sequel, *Julien*.

Operas: LOUISE, 1889–96; *Julien* (Charpentier), f.p. Paris, 1913
Other works: *Impressions d'Italie*, orch, 1887–9; *La Vie du poète*, soli, ch, orch, 1888–92; songs, etc.

Charpentier, Marc-Antoine (b. ?Paris, 1643; d. Paris, 24 Feb 1704).

French composer, who found his musical glory largely outside the court of Louis XIV. Very little is securely known about his life or the chronology of his works, few of which were printed, though they survive in extraordinary numbers (and testify to his productivity) because they passed through his nephew into the royal library. They include nearly 500 sacred pieces (most famously a magnificent *Te Deum* in D), besides theatre music, cantatas and airs.

A scribe's son, he studied in Rome in the late 1660s, possibly with Carissimi, then returned to an appointment with the devout Marie de Lorraine, Mademoiselle de Guise. He also struck up a connection with Molière's company, served members of the royal family and in 1698 became master of music at the Sainte Chapelle, for which he wrote his Assumption mass and other works. But his chief employment was at the Jesuit church of St Louis in the Marais, where he had star singers to bring out his command of Italian and French styles, harmonic boldness, expressive powers and exciting melodic-rhythmic charge – qualities that make his music fully theatrical. The fact that he wrote so little for the stage has been blamed on Lully, but perhaps he preferred working for what a contemporary called 'the church of the opera'.

H. Wiley Hitchcock *Marc-Antoine Charpentier* (1990)

Operas: *Actéon* (1 act: Charpentier), 1683–5; *Les Arts florissants*, 1685–6; *David et Jonathas* (François Bretonneau), 1688; *Médée* (Thomas Corneille, see MEDEA), 1693; etc.
Oratorios: *Pestis mediolanensis*, soli, ch, insts; *Judicum Salomonis*, soli, ch, insts, 1702; *Le Reniement de St Pierre*, soli, ch, con; etc.
Liturgical works: *Messe de minuit pour Noël*, soi, ch, insts; *Assumpta est Maria* mass, soli, ch, insts; *Te Deum*, D, soli, ch, insts; *Motet pour une longue offrande*, soli, ch, insts, 1698–9; tenebrae lessons, soli, insts; antiphons, litanies, *Magnificat* settings, psalms, motets, etc.
Other works: *Le Malade imaginaire* (incidental

music: Molière), 1672–3; other theatre music, pastorals, cantatas, airs

Chasse, La (The Hunt).

(1) Name Haydn gave his Symphony No.73, for reason of its finale, originally the overture to his opera *La fedeltà premiata*.
(2) Name given to Haydn's Quartet Op.1:1.

Chasseur maudit, Le (The Cursed Huntsman).

Symphonic poem by Franck after Gottfried Bürger's ballad *Der wilde Jäger*.

Chausson, (Amédée) Ernest (b. Paris, 20 Jan 1855; d. Limay, near Mantes, Yvelines, 10 Jun 1899).

French composer, heir to Franck and Wagner, who composed music of resplendent valediction as he observed the arrival of a new world in his young friend Debussy. Born into the haute bourgeoisie, he was educated by a tutor (who specially furthered his artistic inclinations, taking him to salons) and had no need of paid employment. He followed his father's wishes in qualifying as a barrister (1877), but never practised; instead, the same year, he wrote his first song. Lessons with Massenet followed (1879–81), but more important were his deepening connections with Franck and his visits to Munich and Bayreuth to experience Wagner's operas (1879–83); he made the last such trip, for *Parsifal*, on honeymoon. The comforts of family life (with five children) he thereafter shared with those of composition, in a style that, no matter how Wagnerian (in his opera) or Franckist (in his chamber music), profits from an individual combination of luscious harmony with clarity of form, as well as from an unusual self-awareness. Most of his major works were written after he turned 31, which left him only 13 years of maturity before he died in a cycling accident.

Ralph Scott Grover *Ernest Chausson* (1980)

Opera: *Le* ROI ARTHUS, Op.23, 1886–95
Incidental music: *La tempête* (see *The* TEMPEST), Op.18, 1888; *La Légende de Sainte Cécile* (Bouchor), Op.22, soli, women's ch, small orch, 1891
Orchestral: *Viviane* (symphonic poem), Op.5, 1882, rev 1887; Symphony, B♭, Op.20, 1889–90; POEME, Op.25, vn, orch, 1896; *Soir de fête* (symphonic poem), Op.32, 1897–8
Larger vocal works: *Hymne védique* (Leconte de Lisle), Op.9, ch, orch, 1886; *Poème de l'amour et de la mer* (Bouchor), Op.19, s, orch, 1882–90; *Chanson perpétuelle* (Cros), Op.37, s, orch/pf qnt, 1898; motets, etc.
Chamber: Piano Trio, G minor, Op.3, 1881; Concerto, Op.21, vn, pf, str qt, 1889–91; Piano Quartet, A, Op.30, 1897; String Quartet, C minor, Op.35, 1897–9 (finished by d'Indy); Piece, Op.39, vc/va, pf, 1897
Songs: *Sept mélodies*, Op.2, 1879–82 (No.3 'Les

papillons', Gautier, No.7 'Le colibri', de Lisle);
Deux duos, Op.11, 1883; 'Le Temps des lilas', 1886
(from *Poème de l'amour et de la mer*); *Serres
chaudes* (5, Maeterlinck), Op.24, 1893–6; *Chansons
de Shakespeare* (4), Op.28, 1890–97; etc.

Piano: *Quelques danses*, Op.26, 1896; *Paysages*, Op.38, 1895

Chávez (y Ramírez), Carlos (Antonio de Padua)
(b. Mexico City, 13 Jun 1899; d. Mexico City, 2 Aug
1978). Mexican composer and conductor, who was
vigorous in his country's musical life while
enjoying connections with the USA, notably with
Copland, Varèse and Cowell. He had teachers
for piano (Ponce, 1910–14; Pedro Luis Orgázon,
1915–20) and harmony, but studied much on his
own, including the Indian culture he encountered
on family holidays. In 1921, with the Mexican
Revolution newly installed, he put on a concert
and gained a state commission for an Aztec ballet
(*El fuego nuevo*). He then visited Europe on
honeymoon (1922–3) and spent periods in New
York (1923–4, 1926–8), returning to important
positions as founder conductor of the Mexico
Symphony (1928–48) and director of the National
Conservatory (1929–33). Meanwhile, his music
entered its most vivid, Indianist phase, geared to
the primitive power of Varèsian modernism and
sometimes using ancient percussion instruments.
After the Second World War he gained a smoother
style that reflected his Romantic youth, while
continuing to write iconoclastic pieces.

Carlos Chávez *Toward a New Music* (1937, '1975)

Ballets: *El fuego nuevo*, 1921; *Los cuatro soles*, 1925;
  Caballos de vapor (*H.P.*), 1926–7; *Antigona*, 9 insts,
  1932; *La hija de Cólquide* (Martha Graham), 8
  insts, 1943
Orchestral: *Sinfonia india* (No.2), 1935–6; *Soli III*, bn,
  tpt, va, timp, orch, 1965; 6 other symphonies,
  concertos, etc.
Ensemble: *Soli I*, ob, cl, tpt, bn, 1933; *II*, wind qnt,
  1961; *IV*, tpt, hn trbn, 1966; *Xochipili*, pic, fl, cl,
  trbn, 6 perc, 1940; *Toccata*, 6 perc, 1942; 3 string
  quartets, etc.
Other works: choral pieces, songs, 6 piano sonatas,
  etc.

Chaykovsky. See TCHAIKOVSKY.

chbr. Abbreviation for chamber.

chef d'attaque (Fr., head of the attack). Leader
(UK), concertmaster (US).

chef d'orchestre (Fr.). Conductor.

cheironomy. System of hand signs used to indicate
melodic shape. Pictorial representations show that
the practice was known to Egyptians of the third

millennium BC. In Europe attempts to write down
cheironomic gestures may have helped give rise to
neumes.

Cheltenham Festival. Summer musical event
taking place in the western English spa town
annually since 1945, with an inclination towards
new British pieces. The 'Cheltenham symphony'
was a doomladen midstream genre of early years.
Under the directorships of John Manduell (1969–
94) and Michael Berkeley (1995–2004) programming became more varied.

Cherepnin. See TCHEREPNIN.

Cherkassky, Shura (b. Odessa, 7 Oct 1911; d.
London, 27 Dec 1995). Russian–US pianist, a late-
surviving exponent of the Romantic manner. He
studied with Josef Hofmann at Curtis, made his
debut at 11 and became a frequent, admired visitor
to Europe after 1945.

Cherubini, Luigi (Carlo Zanobi Salvadore Maria)
(b. Florence, Sep 1760; d. Paris, 15 Mar 1842). Italian
composer, who moved to Paris in 1786 and steered
himself into the French tradition, which he came
to dominate during the period between the
equally expatriate Gluck and Rossini. His epic
dignity and dramatization of democracy earned
Beethoven's admiration.

He studied with his father, a theatre harpsichordist, and other local musicians, then with
Sarti in Bologna and Milan (1778–81). After that he
gained increasing success as an opera composer in
Florence and London (1784–6) before his definitive move to Paris. There he was made director of a
new Italian opera company (1789–92), while with
Lodoïska (1791) he reinvented the French opéra
comique by combining Italian-style sentimental
comedy with powerful drama after Gluck's
manner. The work also exerted an appeal by
instituting a middle-class heroism in tune with the
Revolution. Returning from a judicious retirement
to Normandy (1792–3), he married and moved
forward in his career, becoming one of the
founding inspectors of the Conservatoire (1795)
and creating two more operatic successes in *Médée*
(1797) and *Les Deux Journées* (1800).

Not over-liked by Napoleon, who preferred
gentler and more malleable composers, he was
welcomed to Vienna in 1805 by Beethoven, Haydn
and others, and stayed to see the first *Fidelio*.
Back in France he became subject to melancholia,
and took up botany and painting, but the
Bourbon restoration of 1814 brought him back
into public life as superintendant of royal music
and, from 1822, director of the Conservatoire.

Stiffening with age, he irked the young Berlioz, while as a composer he largely confined himself to church music, including two *Requiem* settings – imposing (in C minor) and more darkly inward (in D minor) – and quartets. He was the first musician made a Commander of the Légion d'Honneur, and his funeral (taking place, as he had intended, to his D minor *Requiem*) was a state occasion.

Basil Deane *Cherubini* (1965)

Operas: *Lodoïska* (Claude François Fillette dit Loraux), f.p. Paris, 1791; *Eliza* (Jacques-Antoine de Révéroni Saint-Cyr), f.p. Paris, 1794; *Médée* (François Benoît, Hoffmann; see MEDEA), f.p. Paris 1797; *Les Deux journées* (Jean-Nicolas Bouilly), f.p. Paris, 1800; *Anacréon* (B. Mendouze), f.p. Paris, 1803; *Faniska* (Joseph Sonnleithner), f.p. Vienna, 1806; *Les Abencérages* (Etienne de Jouy), f.p. Paris, 1813; about 25 others, mostly earlier
Sacred: REQUIEM, C minor, ch, orch, 1816; REQUIEM, D minor, men's ch, orch, 1836; coronation mass for Charles X, other masses, motets
Other works: String Quartet No.1, E♭, 1814; No.2, C, 1829; No.3, D minor, 1834; No.4, E, 1835; No.5, F, 1835; No.6, A minor, 1837; 2 Sonatas, F, hn, str, 1804; Symphony, D, 1815; many cantatas, duets, arias, piano pieces, etc.

chest. Term for a set of viols, normally six (pairs of trebles, tenors and basses), traditionally stored together in a box.

Chester. British music publishing firm, founded by John and William Chester in Brighton in 1874. It was bought in 1915 by Otto Marius Kling, who secured works by Stravinsky. In 1989 it was acquired by Music Sales.

chest voice. Term, more evocative than anatomical, for singing that seems to come from within the chest, as opposed to the HEAD VOICE. The chest voice of a soprano or mezzo can have an earthy expressive power; tenors, in repertory from the Verdi–Wagner age on, are expected to carry the chest voice into the very highest register.

chevalet (Fr.). Bridge (on a string instrument).

Chevreuille, Raymond (b. Watermael-Boitsfort, Brussels, 17 Nov 1901; d. Montignies-le-Tilleul, 9 May 1976). Belgian composer, largely self-taught and among the first outside the Schoenberg school to write serial music, though with tonal flickerings. Working for Belgian radio as an acoustical engineer (from 1936) he produced eight symphonies, concertos, quartets, cantatas and radio music.

chiaro, chiara (It.). Clear.

chiave (It., pl. *chiavi*). Key (in either sense, of a piece, of a keyboard instrument), clef.

chiavette (It., little clefs). One of two common systems of four clefs used at the time in notating Renaissance polyphony. The *chiavette* were the G clef on the second line up (modern treble clef), the C clef on the same line, the C clef on the middle line (modern alto clef) and either the F clef on the middle line or the C clef on the fourth line (modern tenor clef). The *chiavi naturali*, the alternative foursome, were the C clef on the bottom line, the same on the middle and fourth lines (modern alto and tenor clefs) and the F clef on the fourth (modern bass clef) or middle line. Going by the vocal ranges indicated, music in *chiavette* notation was meant to be transposed down a fourth or fifth.

Chicago. US city, main centre of the Midwest. Its growth from a village in the 1830s to the nation's second city at the end of the century was accompanied by the arrival of musical facilities, including the 4,200-seat Auditorium Theater for concerts and visiting opera companies (1889). The Chicago Symphony dates from 1891, moved into Orchestra Hall in 1904 and took its present name in 1912. Its music directors have included Theodore Thomas (1893–1905), Frederick Stock (1905–42), Désiré Defauw (1943–7), Artur Rodzinski (1947–8), Kubelík (1950–53), Reiner (1953–63), Martinon (1963–8), Solti (1969–91) and Barenboim (from 1991). The Chicago Grand Opera Company (1910–32) built the Civic Opera House (1929), which was taken over by Lyric Opera of Chicago (founded 1954).

Chickering. US piano firm founded in Boston in 1823 by Jonas Chickering (1798–1853), who in 1843 made the first grand piano with an effective cast-iron frame.

chiesa (It.). Church, as in SONATA DA CHIESA.

Chihara, Paul (Seiko) (b. Seattle, 9 Jul 1938). US composer, whose feeling for sound and pace reflects his Japanese ancestry. He studied with Robert Palmer at Cornell, Boulanger in Paris (1962–3) and Pepping in Berlin (1965–6), since when he has worked in California as a composer and teacher.

Child, William (b. Bristol, 1606/7; d. Windsor, 23 Mar 1697). English composer and organist. He served his apprenticeship in his native city with

Thomas Prince, and gained the BMus (1631) and DMus (1663) at Oxford. Around the time of the former degree he became organist of St George's Chapel, Windsor, where he was reinstated after the Civil War and Commonwealth. He also joined the Chapel Royal, and played at the coronations of Charles II, James II and William and Mary. His many services and anthems probably date from the first half of his long professional life.

Child of our Time, A. Oratorio by Tippett to his own words, abstracting events leading up to the Kristallnacht attacks on Jews in Germany, with choruses based on African-American spirituals. First performance: London, 19 Mar 1944.

child prodigy. Pre-adolescent possessing remarkable skill – normally in instrumental performance, for even the works of Mozart and Mendelssohn show few great surprises before those composers were well into their teens (see PRECOCITY). Also, the spectacle of the child prodigy depends on the young star being seen and heard at work. History is full of extraordinary children (none more so than Crotch) and over-ambitious, mercenary fathers. Yet extreme talent often seems to be accompanied by great eagerness to display that talent in public, even at a very young age. And there is evidence from among present-day violinists (notably Midori) that an exceptional 10-year-old can mature, even under the spotlight, into a serious adult artist.

Children's Corner. Set of piano pieces by Debussy, which he titled in English: 1 *Doctor Gradus ad Parnassum*, 2 *Jimbo's Lullaby* (*sic*, 'Jumbo' was meant), 3 *Serenade for the Doll*, 4 *The Snow is Dancing*, 5 *The Little Shepherd*, 6 *Golliwog's Cake-Walk*. He dedicated the set to his daughter 'Chou-Chou' (b. 30 Oct 1905) and designed the cover page himself. First performance: Paris, 18 Dec 1908.

children's music. Music for children as performers or audience. Besides the vast repertory of sacred music incorporating boys' voices, some operas have TREBLE roles or scenes with children's chorus (*Carmen*), while some, challengingly, have child characters to be played by adults (*L'Enfant et les sortilèges*). Of music entirely for children to perform, school opera provides the most obvious occasion and goes back to masques put on by choristers in Elizabethan London, by way of works by Charpentier (*David et Jonathas*), Mozart (*Apollo et Hyazinthus*), Weill and Brecht (*Der Jasager*), Copland, Britten, Davies, Henze, etc. A lot of non-operatic music for child performers is

educational, though some – Bartók's *Mikrokosmos*, for instance – is also worth hearing.

The classics intended for children to hear include *Le* CARNAVAL DES ANIMAUX, HÄNSEL UND GRETEL, PETER AND THE WOLF and *A* YOUNG PERSON'S GUIDE TO THE ORCHESTRA. But, as the Disney film *Fantasia* partly showed, any music can be a child's.

Childs, Barney (Sanford) (b. Spokane, 13 Feb 1926; d. Redlands, Cal., 11 Jan 2000). US composer, a generous exponent of indeterminacy and other new techniques. He studied in the USA and at Oxford, and had Copland and Carter among his composition teachers. From 1971 he taught at the University of Redlands.

chimes (from Lat. *cymbala*, bells). Set of small bells or other resonators (of stone, bamboo, shell, etc.) made to be struck, shaken, played from a keyboard, activated by a clockwork mechanism (see CLOCK) or moved by the wind.

chimney flute. Organ pipe that is almost stopped but has a narrow tube (chimney) inserted into the cap.

Chin, Unsuk (b. Seoul, 14 Jul 1961). Korean composer with a precise sense of timbre, texture and timing. She studied with Sukhi Kang in Seoul and with Ligeti in Hamburg (1985–8), then settled in Berlin. Her works include *Akrostichon-Wortspiel* for soprano and ensemble (1991, rev 1993), and concertos for piano and violin, of which the latter won the Grawemeyer Award in 2003.

China. East Asian country, the most populous in the world, having the oldest continuous musical culture. If such items as the majestic set of Zhang dynasty bells (second millennium BC) represent traditions long lost, the pipa has been played for 1500 years, and there are songs with notation from the Song dynasty (960–1279). Beijing opera, new in Beethoven's time, is at the modern end of the Chinese musical time-scale. By then China was in trading contact with Europe, but there is little evidence of musical recognition either way before the 1920s (*Turandot* and the first Western-style Chinese composers). The communist government, fully established in 1949, encouraged music on the Soviet model, and the Central Conservatory was founded in 1950 in Tianjin, transferring to Beijing in 1958. During the Cultural Revolution (1966–76) Western music fell under interdict and the Beijing Conservatory was closed (see YELLOW RIVER CONCERTO). Its reopening brought an influx of eager students, including many who have become noted composers: Tan Dun, Zhou Long and others.

Chinese cymbal. Cymbal with an upturned rim, inherited from Chinese music, normally struck with a drumstick and making a noisier, crushed sound.

Chinese woodblock. Slab of teak or other hardwood, with one or two lengthwise slots, suspended or laid flat and struck with a beater. Such 'slit drums' are indeed known in China, but entered the Western orchestra in the 1920s by way of ragtime and jazz.

chinrest. Device fitted to the end of a violin or viola, improving the player's grip and freeing the body of the instrument to resonate. Spohr claimed to have invented it c.1822.

Ch'io mi scordi di te. Recitative and aria by Mozart, which he wrote as a concert piece for Nancy Storace and himself (at the obbligato piano) to perform with orchestra, to words from the *Idomeneo* libretto.

chitarra (It., pl. *chitarre*). Guitar.

chitarrone (It.). Alternative name for the THEORBO.

chiuso (It., closed). Indication that a horn is to be stopped with the hand, countermanded by *aperto* (open).

Chladni, Ernst (Florenz Friedrich) (b. Wittenberg, 30 Nov 1756; d. Breslau/Wrocław, 3 Apr 1827). German physicist, who provided the first visualizations of musical vibrations in patterns taken by fine sand grains or lycopodium powder on thin plates. He also invented two kinds of armonica.

Chlubna, Osvald (b. Brno, 22 Jun 1893; d. Brno, 30 Oct 1971). Czech composer, who studied with Janáček at the Brno Organ School (1914–15) and in master classes (1923–4), and created with Bakala an emended (now superseded) version of his teacher's *From the House of the Dead* for its première. He also wrote nine operas of his own and orchestral pieces, while earning his living as a bank clerk until 1953.

choeur (Fr.). Choir.

choir (Fr. *choeur*, Ger. *Chor*, It. *coro*). Group of singers. The term can also be applied to a group of instrumentalists ('brass choir', etc.), especially in antiphonal music.

Collective singing must be one of the most ancient and widely distributed musical practices. The term, in all European languages, comes from the Greek *choros* (the body of singing dancers who took part in sacred ritual and drama) and can signify anything from three to several hundred singers. English, unusually, has two words, 'choir' and 'chorus', slightly different in flavour, especially in that the latter would not normally be applied to a church group.

The size of choir appropriate to different kinds of music before the Classical period is controversial. Liturgical conventions and internal evidence suggest that some plainsong chants were meant for soloists, some for a choir of religious (gathered in what became known as the 'choir' of their church). Early polyphony was probably a specialist art, for one singer on each line, and that may have been the common way right up to the time of Bach and beyond. For example, it is hard to imagine a PART-BOOK being read by any larger group, and there is documentary support for one-to-a-part choirs as the norm in Bach's time. Such choirs, from the mid 15th century onwards, were commonly of four parts, moving towards the standard SATB format. But there was also music in five, six or more parts, rising to such exceptional occasions as Tallis's 40-part motet or Biber's 53-part mass; these prove that larger assemblies could be mustered, but they might also indicate an expectation of just one singer for each part. The sizes of choral establishments (e.g. the English Chapel Royal, set at 48 singers from the reign of Henry V to that of Charles II) can only hint at an upper limit, since by no means must all the members have sung together.

Choirs of more than one singer to a part are first firmly documented in opera, almost from the beginning – Gagliano stipulated 16–18 singers for his *Dafne* (1608). Such a complement followed what was becoming known of the chorus in Greek tragedy and may have served for opera and oratorio throughout Europe to the end of the 18th century (though Handel's operas usually have just one choral number at the end, sung by all the characters, including any deceased). Opera also introduced the mixed choir, where church choirs had been (and remained) composed of men and boys or, in nunneries, women.

Festival oratorio performances and commemorative events began to involve much larger choirs in the era of bourgeois democracy (300 singers at the first Handel festival in Westminster Abbey in 1784), and in the early 19th century choral societies and singing schools started springing up all over Germany, Britain and their culturally dependent territories, prompting a new repertory of partsongs as well as a revival of oratorio and cantata composition. Some societies, particularly in Germany and German-influenced North America, were single-sex. But though the choir was now an institution of social bonding and education, it was also an image of universal humanity – had been affirmed as such in Beethoven's Choral Symphony.

By this point there were three kinds of choir – the church choir (often of people living together in a monastic or collegiate institution), the opera choir (of professionals) and the choral society (of amateurs) – all with their own repertories, though they might come together. Mahler, for instance, wrote for boys' voices in his Third Symphony, presupposing at the time the involvement of a church choir. The needs then of radio stations – needs for singers who would be regularly available to broadcast concert programmes and acts of worship – were answered by a new kind of institution, the professional and versatile small choir, perhaps similar in size to that of Gagliano's *Dafne*. Hence the arrival of music – by Messiaen, Xenakis, Ligeti, Ferneyhough, etc. – extrapolating beyond the long, noble and continuing tradition of what regular people can achieve with a mixture of training and enthusiasm.

choke cymbals. See HI-HAT.

Chopin, Fryderyk Franciszek (b. Żelazowa Wola, near Warsaw, 1 Mar 1810; d. Paris, 17 Oct 1849). Polish pianist-composer. Almost all his works are for solo piano, and the vast majority of them are short. But in their melodic grace, their precision and variety of invention, their range of mood and immediacy of communication, their harmonic richness, their full discovery of the instrument's tones and timbres, and their subtlety in everything, they seem boundless, as if their composer, from within a domestic salon, had let fall its walls on to the universe.

He started young. The second child (of four) and only son of a French immigrant married to a Pole, he had piano lessons with Wojciech Żywny (1816–22), who usefully pointed him towards Bach and the Viennese Classics. But by all accounts the teacher's role was more that of benign, astonished bystander as Chopin took off by himself. At seven he was a published composer (of a polonaise), already known in the aristocratic salons of Warsaw and making his concert debut in a concerto by Gyrowetz (23 Feb 1818). He moved on to the high school (1823–6), where his father taught, and where he studied with Józef Elsner, director of the conservatory. At 15 he began writing more sophisticated pieces, and publishing them with opus numbers. He then continued with Elsner at the conservatory (1826–9), during which time his sights were raised by visits from Hummel and Paganini. Warsaw at this time was a provincial Russian city. Like almost all Poles of the time he was a nationalist, and he knew what national hopes were already pinned on him, but he also knew he would have to travel to further his career.

Of course, when he did so he went – and was admired as – a Pole. Soon after graduating he played in Vienna, where his *Rondo à la krakowiak* and improvisation on a Polish folksong caused a sensation, and continued his tour in Germany and Italy. Back home his Polishness was still more important. His first big concert at the National Theatre (17 Mar 1830) was rapturously received ('Chopin knows what sounds are heard in our fields and woods'), but it was soon followed by his last in the city (11 Oct 1830). At these two concerts he played his F minor and E minor concertos. Also in 1830 his Op.2 was reviewed by Schumann, who recognized him as much more than a merely local phenomenon with the celebrated words: 'Hats off, gentlemen, a genius!' He left for Vienna again, but failed to repeat his earlier triumph, and after nine months travelled on to Paris.

This was the place to be and the time to arrive. He won the admiration and friendship of fellow musicians (Berlioz, Liszt, Bellini, Meyerbeer) and the favour of the wealthy and well placed. Soon he was making a living from lessons, and possibly enjoying an affair with the Countess Delfina Potocka, to whom, with combined Romantic grandness and economy, he dedicated a work he had partly written while thinking of another young woman in Warsaw, the F minor concerto. (A subsequent work amorously recycled was the waltz 'L'Adieu' of 1835.) Welcomed in the most musical city on earth, he was able to find his particular world. The first works he wrote there were touched by the local taste for tinsel and sentiment, but after 1833 he virtually gave up public displays of virtuosity, preferring intimate gatherings. By 1832 he was fully formed as a creative artist, and his reconception of the piano as a means of voicing song – confiding and intense, across a vast range of moods and textures within a song-like or dance–song form – was opening up possibilities for himself as composer, for the many amateurs and professionals who bought and played his music, and for the instrument. A large proportion of his output dates from the next several years.

In the summers of 1834–6 he visited Germany, meeting the Schumanns, seeing his parents for the last time and forming an attachment to a young Polish woman, whose family put a stop to the relationship on the grounds of his health, now starting to deteriorate as a result of tuberculosis. No sooner had this liaison been ended than he met George Sand, and in the summer of 1838 they became lovers. The following winter they spent on Majorca with her two children. It was cold, but he was able to finish his preludes, once his Pleyel upright had made the journey. This was a necessity, for he customarily composed at the piano, working up ideas he had discovered improvising, and he preferred Pleyel's instruments, Liszt said, 'on account of their silvery and somewhat veiled sonority, and … easy touch'.

For the next eight years his life followed a regular pattern. He would spend the summer with Sand at Nohant, and the rest of the year in his Paris apartment. By now he had completely withdrawn from the concert world, earning enough from his pupils to maintain himself in modest luxury. Even his compositional output was declining, especially after 1842.

The calm was broken in 1846–7 when Sand's son and daughter, now adult, began making difficulties, bringing an end to the nine-year affair in May 1847. His health was seriously in decline, and he wrote almost nothing more. But he did return to public concerts – in Paris (16 Feb 1848, just before the revolution that sent Louis-Philippe into exile) and in Britain (Apr–Nov 1848, at the invitation of his pupil Jane Stirling). He died less than a year after his return to France, and was given a grand funeral at the Madeleine, with Mozart's *Requiem* performed.

Jeffrey Kallberg *Chopin at the Boundaries* (1996); Jim Samson *Chopin* (1996)

www.chopin.pl

Works without Op. No. are numbered according to the catalogue by Maurice J.E. Brown (B).

Piano solo

Ballades: G minor, Op.23, *c*.1833; F major/A minor, Op.38, 1839; A♭, Op.47, 1841; F minor, Op.52, 1842–3

Etudes: C, A minor, E, C♯ minor, G♭, E♭ minor, C, F, F minor, A♭, E♭, C minor, Op.10, 1830–32; A♭, F minor, F, A minor, E minor, G♯ minor, C♯ minor, D♭, G♭, B minor, A minor, C minor, Op.25, 1835–7; *Trois nouvelles études*, F minor, A♭, D♭, 1839–40

Fantasies and impromptus: Fantaisie-Impromptu, C♯ minor, Op.66, 1834; Impromptu, A♭, Op.29, *c*.1837; Impromptu, F♯, Op.36, 1839; Fantasie, F minor/A♭, Op.49, 1841; Impromptu, G♭, Op.51, 1842

Mazurkas: G, B♭, B.16, 1825–6; F♯ minor, C♯ minor, E, E♭ minor, Op.6, 1830–32; B♭, A minor, F minor, A♭, C, Op.7, 1829–32; B♭, B.73, 1832; B♭, E minor, A♭, A minor, Op.17, 1833; G minor, C, A♭, B♭ minor, Op.24, 1833; A♭, B.85, 1834; C minor, B

minor, D♭, C♯ minor, Op.30, 1837; G♯ minor, D, C, B minor, Op.33, 1838; E minor, B, A♭, C♯ minor, Op.41, 1838–9; A minor, B.140, 1840; A minor 'Notre temps', B.134, 1841; G, A♭, C♯ minor, Op.50, 1842; B, C, C minor, Op.56, 1843–4; A minor, A♭, F♯ minor, Op.59, 1845; B, F minor, C♯ minor, Op.63, 1846; G, G minor, C, A minor, Op.67, 1835 (Nos.1, 3), 1846 (No.4), 1848–9 (No.2); C, A minor, F, F minor, Op.68, *c*.1827–30 (Nos.1–3), ?1846 (No.4, completed from sketch)

Nocturnes: E minor, Op.72:1, *c*.1829; B♭ minor, E♭, B, Op.9, 1830–32; F, F♯, G minor, Op.15, 1830–32; C♯ minor, D♭, Op.27, 1835; B, A♭, Op.32, 1837; G minor, G major, Op.37, 1838–9; C minor, F♯ minor, Op.48, 1841; F minor, E♭, Op.55, 1842–4; B, E, Op.62, 1846; C minor, B.108, 1847 (completed from sketch)

Polonaises: G minor, B.1, 1817; B♭, B.3, 1817; A♭, B.5, 1821; G♯ minor, B.6, 1824; B♭ minor 'Adieu', B.13, 1826; D minor, B♭, F minor, Op.71, 1827–8; G♭, B.36, 1829; C♯ minor, E♭ minor, Op.26, 1835; A, C minor, Op.40, 1838–9; F♯ minor, Op.44, 1841; A♭, Op.53, 1842–3; Polonaise-Fantaisie, A♭, Op.61, 1846

Preludes: A♭, B.86, 1834; C, A minor, G, E minor, D, B minor, A, F♯ minor, E, C♯ minor, B, G♯ minor, F♯, E♭ minor, D♭, B♭ minor, A♭, F minor, E♭, C minor, B♭, A minor, F, D minor, Op.28, 1836–9; C♯ minor, Op.45, 1841

Rondos: C minor, Op.1, 1825; F 'à la Mazur', Op.5, 1826–7; C, 1828 (duo version Op.73); Introduction and Rondo, C minor-E♭, Op.16, 1832–3

Scherzos: B minor, Op.20, *c*.1835; D♭, Op.31, 1837; C♯ minor, Op.39, 1839; E, Op.54, 1842–3

Sonatas: No.1, C minor, Op.4, 1827–8; No.2 'Funeral March', B♭ minor, Op.35, 1837; No.3, B minor, Op.58, 1844

Variations: Introduction and Variations on a German Air, B.14, 1824; Variations brillantes on 'Je vends des scapulaires', Op.12, 1833; Variation No.6 in HEXAMERON, 1837

Waltzes: E, B.44, *c*.1829; A♭, B.21, 1830; E minor, B.56, 1830; E♭, Op.18, 1831–2; A♭, B minor, Op.69, 1829 (No.2), 1835 (No.1); A♭, A minor, F, Op.34, *c*.1834 (No.2), 1835 (No.1), 1838 (No.3); A♭, Op.42, 1840; E♭ 'Sostenuto', B.133, 1840; G♭, F minor, D♭, Op.70, 1829 (No.3), 1832 (No.1), 1842 (No.2); A minor, B.150, ?1843; D♭ 'Minute', C♯ minor, A♭, Op.64, 1847

Other pieces: *Marche funèbre*, C minor, Op.72:2, *c*.1826; 3 Écossaises, D, G, D♭, Op.72:3–5, *c*.1829; Bolero, C–A, Op.19, *c*.1833; *Andante spianato*, Op.22, 1830–35; Cantabile, B♭, B.84, 1834; Andantino, G minor, B.117, 1838 (accompaniment to song Op.74:2); *Allegro de concert*, Op.46, 1841; Tarantelle, A♭, Op.43, 1841; Fugue, A minor, B.144, *c*.1841; Albumleaf, E, B.151, 1843; Berceuse, D♭, Op.57, 1844; Barcarolle, F♯, Op.60, 1845–6; Galop, A♭, 1846; 2 Bourrées, G minor A, B.160b, 1846 (arrs); Largo, E♭, B.109, 1847

Other works

Piano and orchestra: Concerto No.1, E minor, Op.11, 1830; No.2, F minor, Op.21, 1829; Variations on 'La

ci darem', Op.2, 1827; Fantasy on Polish Airs, Op.13, 1828; *Rondo à la krakowiak*, Op.14, 1828; *Grand polonaise brillante*, Op.22, 1830–35
Chamber: Piano Trio, G minor, Op.8, 1828–9; Introduction and Polonaise brillante, Op.3, vc, pf, 1829–30; Grand Duo on Themes from *Robert le diable*, vc, pf, 1831; Cello Sonata, G minor, Op.65, 1845–6
Piano duo: Rondo, C, Op.73, 1828
Piano duet: Introduction, Theme and Variations, D, B.12a, 1826
Songs: 'The Bridegroom' (Stefan Witwicki), Op.74:15, 1831; 'Charms' (Witwicki), B.51, 1830; Dumka ('Reverie') (Bohdan Zaleski), B.132, 1840; 'The Envoy' (Witwicki), Op.74:7, 1831; 'Handsome Lad' (Zaleski), Op.74:8, 1841; 'Hymn from the Tomb'. (Wincenty Pol), Op.74:17, 1836; 'Lithuanian Song' (Ludwik Osiński), Op.74:16, 1831; 'Melody' (Zygmunt Krasiński), Op.74:9, 1847; 'Merrymaking' (Witwicki), Op.74:4, 1830; 'My Darling' (Adam Mickiewicz), Op.74:12, 1837; 'Out of my sight!' (Mickiewicz), Op.74:6, 1827; 'The Ring' (Witwicki), Op.74:14, 1836; 'The Sad Stream' (Witwicki), Op.74:3, 1831; 'Spring' (Witwicki), Op.74:2, 1838; 'There where she loves' (Witwicki), Op.74:5, *c*.1829; 2 Dumkas (Zaleski), Op.74:11, 13, 1840 ('The Double End', 'There is no need'); 'The Warrior' (Witwicki), Op.74:10, 1831; 'The Wish' (Witwicki), Op.74:1, *c*.1829

Probably spurious works

Piano: Contredanse, G♭, B.17; Mazurkas, D, B.4; D, B.71; C, B.82; Nocturne, C♯ minor, B.49; Variations 'Souvenir de Paganini', B.37; Waltz, E♭, B.46
Chamber: Variations on 'Non più mesta', fl, pf, B.9

Chopin. Opera by Giacomo Orefice (Milan, 1901) in which the composer is a tenor in a Romantic farrago only loosely related to his life and, sounding in the orchestra, his music.

Chopsticks. Elementary piano waltz, subject of paraphrases by Liszt, Rimsky-Korsakov and others, published by Belyayev (1880).

Chor (Ger., pl. *Chöre*). Choir.

choragus. Oxford University post, instituted by William Heyther in 1627 to be director of practical music. In ancient Greece the *choragos* was the chorus leader.

Choral (Ger., pl. *Choräle*). Chorale.

chorale (Ger. *Choral*). Congregational hymn of the Lutheran church. The German term refers principally to the melody and was used before the Reformation to signify plainsong. The English equivalent more commonly denotes the melody as

sung, i.e. with words (Ger. *Kirchenlied*), or a harmonization of this for four-part singing, or, less commonly, an elaboration for organ, for which the more normal terms are CHORALE PRELUDE, etc.

Sacred singing in German was not invented by Luther. German congregations from the 12th century had some possibility of singing the SEQUENCE in their everyday language, and from the 14th century there were lusty songs in mixed German and Latin for Christmas and Easter, comparable with the British carol – e.g. *In dulci jubilo*, later accepted as a chorale. Besides drawing on these repertories, Luther wrote words and perhaps also music for many new chorales, including some of the best known: *Ein' feste Burg*, *Vom Himmel hoch* and *Nun komm, der Heiden Heiland*. Others were added during his time by poet-musicians in Germany, Bohemia and Calvinist Switzerland and France. After Philipp Nicolai (*Wachet auf*) around 1600, the next great chorale composers were Paul Gerhardt (*O Haupt voll Blut und Wunden*) and Johannes Crüger (*Jesu, meine Freude*) in the mid 17th century. The tradition then tailed off and became virtually extinct in the later 18th century, as other traditions, of basing compositions on chorale tunes, moved forward.

chorale cantata. Modern term for an extension of the CHORALE CONCERTO in high-to-late Baroque style, with solo recitatives and arias between the bookends of fully scored chorale settings. The 'pure' chorale cantata, following at least the words of the chorale all through (Buxtehude), was replaced by the 'mixed' type, with new texts for the solo numbers (Kuhnau, Bach).

chorale concerto. Modern term for an extension of the CHORALE MOTET in early Baroque style, with episodes for soloists and continuo support, as practised by Praetorius, Schein and Scheidt.

chorale fantasia. Modern term for a chorale-based organ piece of some length – more substantial than a CHORALE PRELUDE, often with each phrase of the tune separately developed. There are examples by Buxtehude, Bach and Reger.

chorale fugue. Modern term for a short organ fugue on the beginning of a chorale melody, a central German genre of the late 17th century, practised by Pachelbel, as well as by members of the Bach family before and including J.S.

chorale harmonization. Setting of a chorale as the top line in four-part harmony. Arrangements go back to the same ancestral volume from which sprang the CHORALE MOTET. Bach's many examples, distributed through his cantatas and Passions, have been textbook harmony examples since the 19th century.

chorale motet. Modern term for a piece in which a chorale is to be sung with polyphonic accompaniment either sung or played. The earliest examples were published under Luther's aegis (1524), but the genre came to its full flowering in the early 17th century, in the work of Praetorius, etc. It stood at the head of the whole history of chorale settings, both vocal (developing into the CHORALE CONCERTO and CHORALE CANTATA) and for organ (through the CHORALE RICERCARE).

chorale prelude. Modern term for a short organ piece in which, most often, a whole chorale melody is entwined in counterpoint. It and its grander sibling the CHORALE FANTASIA were developed by 17th-century north German composers, from Scheidemann and Tunder to Buxtehude. Bach's notable examples stimulated a renewal of the genre by Brahms and Reger.

chorale ricercare. Modern term for an early Baroque organ piece based on a chorale, e.g. those of Praetorius.

chorale variations. Modern term for a set of organ variations based on a chorale, the whole tune normally heard as a cantus firmus in each variation, as in examples from Sweelinck to Bach.

Choral Fantasy. Work by Beethoven for solo piano with orchestra and choir (singing a poem by Christoph Kuffner), comprising variations on his song 'Gegenliebe', a theme presaging that of the last movement of the Ninth Symphony. He devised the work as grand finale for the concert at which he introduced his Fifth and Sixth symphonies. First performance: Vienna, 22 Dec 1808.

choral music. See CHOIR.

Choral Symphony. Normally Beethoven's Ninth is meant, though there are symphonies with chorus by Berlioz (Roméo et Juliette), Mahler, Vaughan Williams, Holst, Shostakovich and Berio.

Choralvorspiel (Ger.). CHORALE PRELUDE.

chord. Two or more notes sounding together and normally starting together, or almost. A polyphonic composition in which the notes C, E and G arrive successively in different voices may be said

to come to a C major harmony, but the term 'chord' is less idiomatic here than when the notes are sounded simultaneously or slightly staggered in an arpeggio. Some writers hold that the term must further be restricted to diatonic music (in which, indeed, some of the most familiar types of chord are found: the dominant seventh chord, ninth chord, etc.), with 'simultaneity' appropriate elsewhere.

chordal. Moving in chords, like a Bach chorale harmonization.

chording. The sound of a choir in chords. Chording may be good or bad, i.e. well or poorly tuned.

chordophone. Formal organological term for string instrument. The other kinds are aerophones, idiophones and membranophones.

choreographer. Practitioner of choreography.

choreography. Movements and gestures in a ballet, or the art of conceiving and communicating these.

choro. Brazilian popular ensemble music, after which Villa-Lobos named a cycle of pieces.

Chorsaite (Ger.). CHANTERELLE.

Chorton (Ger.). Pitch standard set by church organs, higher than CAMMERTON.

chorus. (1) Group of singers (see CHOIR) or composition for such a group, often a section from a larger work, such as the Hallelujah Chorus from Messiah or the Prisoners' Chorus from Fidelio.
(2) REFRAIN.

Choudens. French music publishing firm founded in Paris in 1845 by Antoine de Choudens (1825–88), who acquired many Berlioz works, Carmen, etc.

Chou Wen-chung (b. Chefoo, Yantai, 28 Jul 1923). Chinese–US composer, of cross-cultural music. He studied at the New England Conservatory (1946–9), with Luening at Columbia and with Varèse (1949–54), whose musical executor he became. In 1964 he became a professor at Columbia, and a beacon for younger Chinese composers.

Chowning, John (MacLeod) (b. Salem, NJ, 22 Aug 1934). US composer, pioneer of computer music. A pupil of Boulanger (1959–61) and of Leland Smith at Stanford, he has worked largely at that university, as head of the Center for Computer Research in Music and Acoustics since 1975. His output consists of just four computer-generated pieces: *Sabelithe* (1966–71), *Turenas* (1972), *Stria* (1977) and *Phoné* (1980–81).

Christianity. See ANGLICAN MUSIC; BYZANTINE CHANT; JEWISH MUSIC; MASS; ORATORIO; PLAINSONG; REQUIEM.

Christmas Concerto. Name given Corelli's Op.6:8 in G minor and Locatelli's Op.1:8 in F minor.

Christmas music. The ragbag of current seasonal traditions includes carols, *The Nutcracker* and *Messiah*. Various Christmases past are evoked in works by Balbastre, Biber, Fry, Gigault, Head, Padilla, Perotin, Schütz and Vaughan Williams. See also CHRISTMAS CONCERTO, CHRISTMAS ORATORIO, *La* NATIVITE DU SEIGNEUR. Several singers were born on Christmas Day: Michael Kelly, Giuseppe De Luca, Bethany Beardslee and Ian Bostridge. Christmas-birthday composers include J.A. Hiller and the Chevalier de Saint-Georges.

Christmas Oratorio. Work by Bach to words possibly by Picander, originally in six parts for services in the Christmas season: *Jauchzet, frohlocket* (25 Dec); *Und es waren Hirten* (26 Dec); *Herrscher des Himmels* (27 Dec); *Fallt mit Danken* (1 Jan); *Ehre sei dir, Gott* (2 Jan); *Herr, wenn die stolzen Feinde* (6 Jan). First performance: Leipzig, 1734–5

Christoff, Boris (Kirilov) (b. Plovdiv, 18 May 1918; d. Rome, 28 Jun 1993). Bulgarian bass, the most renowned Boris Godunov for three decades from his first assumption of the role (Covent Garden, 1949), a compelling presence on stage and a singer whose firm consistency could convey emotional complexity. He studied in Rome and Salzburg, and was no less admired in Verdi.

Christou, Jani (b. Heliopolis, Egypt, 8 Jan 1926; d. Athens, 8 Jan 1970). Greek composer, who in his last few years broke through to works of ritual atmosphere, e.g. the oratorio *Tongues of Fire* (1964) and *Enantiodrama* for orchestra (1965–8). Brought up in Alexandria, he studied philosophy with Russell and Wittgenstein at Cambridge (1945–8), music with Hans Redlich during this time and later in Italy, and Jungian psychology in Zurich. He moved to Greece in 1960 and died in a car crash.

Christus. Oratorio by Liszt to words from the Bible and Catholic liturgy, in three parts: *Oratorium in Nativitate Domini, Post Epiphaniam* and *Passio et Resurrectio*. First performance: Weimar, 29 May 1873.

Christus am Oelberge (Christ on the Mount of Olives). Short oratorio by Beethoven to words by Franz Xaver Huber. Christ prays for strength and is answered by a seraph, who remains in the action as the story moves to the arrest, with choirs of angels and disciples. First performance: Vienna, 5 Apr 1803.

chromatic (from Gk *chrōmatikos*, coloured). Involving notes other than those of a diatonic scale: thus in C major the notes C♯/D♭, D♯/E♭, F♯/G♭, G♯/A♭ and A♯/B♭ are chromatic. The chromatic SCALE includes these notes as well as the diatonic ones, i.e. proceeds by semitone steps. Chromatic harmony has plentiful chromatic notes while maintaining major–minor tonality, as in much of the music of Wagner and Scriabin. See COLOUR.

Chromatic Fantasia and Fugue. Keyboard work by Bach, from before his move to Leipzig in 1723.

chromatic harp. Harp with strings for all 12 chromatic notes. The most successful was an instrument produced by the Pleyel company from the 1890s to the 1920s, for which Debussy wrote his *Danse sacrée et danse profane*.

chromaticism. Presence of a chromatic note or notes, in the large ('Ravel's chromaticism', 'the level of chromaticism in *Manon Lescaut*') or small ('the chromaticism on the first beat in bar 67').

Chronochromie. Orchestral work by Messiaen, a study in 'chronochromy', i.e. colouring time, adapting the form of a Greek choral ode, with an epode for 18 solo strings imitating singing birds. First performance: Donaueschingen, 16 Oct 1960.

Chrysander, (Karl Franz) Friedrich (b. Lübtheen, Mecklenburg, 8 Jul 1826; d. Bergedorf, near Hamburg, 3 Sep 1901). German music scholar, a self-taught miller's son, who devoted himself to writing the life and editing the works of Handel. Both projects, interrupted by more lucrative editorial work, went unfinished.

Chung. Korean musical siblings.

(1) **Myung-Wha** (b. Seoul, 19 Mar 1944). Cellist, pupil of Rose at Juilliard (1961–5) and Piatigorsky in Los Angeles (1965–8), occasionally heard in a trio with her sister and brother.

(2) **Kyung-Wha** (b. Seoul, 26 Mar 1948). Violinist, pupil of Galamian at Juilliard (1961–71)

and an international soloist since the late 1960s, admired for her involvement and resolve. She made her London debut in 1970.

(3) **Myung-Whun** (b. Seoul, 22 Jan 1953). Conductor and pianist, trained in New York at Mannes and Juilliard. He was music director of the Opéra Bastille in Paris (1989–94).

church mode. See MODE; TONE (5).

church music. Music composed for or used in Christian worship. See ANGLICAN MUSIC; BYZAN-TINE CHANT; MASS; PLAINSONG; REQUIEM.

church sonata. SONATA DA CHIESA.

ciaccona, ciacona (It.). CHACONNE.

Ciampi, Vincenzo (Legrenzio) (b. ?Piacenza, ?1719; d. Venice, 30 Mar 1762). Italian composer, responsible for the first season of Italian comic opera in London (1748–9). He studied in Naples with Leo and Durante, and worked in Venice before, during and after his several years in London, where he published sonatas, overtures and concertos.

cibell. Gavotte-like form practised by English composers c.1690–1710 in imitation of the 'Descente de Cybelle' in Lully's *Atys* or of Purcell's imitation thereof.

Ciconia, Johannes (b. Liège, c.1370; d. Padua, Dec 1411). Netherlandish composer, who beat the path south taken by many later composers, thereby adding to his extraordinary command of French intricacy and Italian mellifluousness. Possibly a pupil of Philippe de Caserta, whose music he quoted in his song *Sus un' fontayne*, he was in Rome by 1390, working at Santa Maria in Trastevere and perhaps in contact with Antonio Zachara de Teramo. Around 1400 he settled in Padua as a priest at the cathedral, to write splendid motets in honour of Paduan and Venetian occasions. For the period, an unusually large number of his works survive, testifying to the just astonishment of ensuing generations.

Mass sections: 2 *Gloria-Credo* pairs, 5 *Gloria* settings, one *Credo*
Isorhythmic motets: *Ut te per omnes* a 3, ?1390–97; *Albane misse celitus* a 4, ?1406; *Doctorum principem* a 4, ?1406–9; *Petrum Marcello venetum* a 4, 1409
Other motets: *O felix templum jubila* a 3, 1400; *Venecie mundi splendor* a 3, 1405; *O Padua, sidus praeclarum* a 2; *O Petre Christi discipule* a 2; *O virum omnimoda* a 4
French songs: *Le ray au soleyl* ?a 3 (canon: dubious); *Sus un' fontayne* a 3 (virelai)

Italian songs: *Caçando un giorno* a 2; *Che nel servir anticho* a 3; *Gli atti col dançar* a 3; *Ligiadra donna* a 3; *Una panthera* a 3; *Per quella strada* a 2; *Poy che morir* a 2; *O rosa bella* a 3

Cid, Le. Opera by Massenet to a libretto by Adolphe d'Ennery, Edouard Blau and Louis Gallet after the play by Corneille. Rodrigue (tenor), the Cid, kills the father of Chimène (soprano) in a duel but is forgiven when he has saved Spain from the Moors. The numbers include Chimène's 'Pleurez, pleurez mes yeux', Rodrigue's Prayer ('O souverain, ô juge, ô père') and the exciting ballet. First performance: Paris, 30 Nov 1885.

Cifra, Antonio (b. near Terracina, 1584; d. Loreto, 2 Oct 1629). Italian composer, of abundant if undistinguished output. A choirboy at San Luigi dei Francesi in Rome (1594–6), he studied with Nanino and held posts in Rome before becoming chapelmaster at the Holy House in Loreto in 1609. He stayed there for the rest of his life, except for a return to Rome as chapelmaster at St John Lateran (1622–6), producing numerous volumes of motets and madrigals in traditional Roman polyphony or safe *seconda pratica*.

Cikker, Ján (b. Banská Bystrica, 29 Jul 1911; d. Bratislava, 21 Dec 1989). Slovak composer noted for his fiercely expressive operas: *Resurrection* (Prague, 1962), *Coriolanus* (Prague, 1974), etc. He studied with Novák at the Prague Conservatory and taught in Bratislava from 1939.

Cilea, Francesco (b. Palmi, 26 Jul 1866; d. Varazze, 20 Nov 1950). Italian composer, whose standing in the Puccini generation is secured by ADRIANA LECOUVREUR and some arias from *L'Arlesiana* (Milan, 1897), notably the tenor's 'E la solita storia'. He studied at the Naples Conservatory (1881–9), where a production of his first opera, *Gina*, brought him a contract with Sonzogno. The first fruit, *La Tilda* (Florence, 1892), failed to please, and he took up teaching, from which he was released by the success of *Adriana Lecouvreur* in 1902. The follow-up, *Gloria*, was introduced at La Scala in 1907 with Toscanini conducting, but dropped after two performances. He returned to conservatory life as director of the institutions in Palermo (1913–16) and Naples (1916–36).

Cimarosa, Domenico (b. Aversa, 17 Dec 1749; d. Venice, 11 Jan 1801). Italian composer, of fluency and charm, the low-calorie Mozart. He studied at a monastic school, at the Loreto conservatory in Naples (1761–71) and possibly then with Piccinni. The presence of both Piccinni and Paisiello in Naples at first overshadowed him, but he was unstoppable: from 1776 to 1786 he maintained an output of almost four operas a year on average, mostly comedies, and his reputation spread across Europe. Haydn conducted at least 12 of his operas at Eszterháza; Mozart wrote a superb replacement aria for a performance of one in Vienna; Goethe translated another. Meanwhile the busy composer married, remarried after his first wife's early death and acquired posts as chapelmaster at a girls' conservatory in Venice (c.1782) and second organist at the Neapolitan royal chapel (1785). In 1787 he was summoned to St Petersburg to take over from Sarti, but the Russian court opera was in decline, and he wrote only three new works for it before leaving in 1791.

His immediate destination was Vienna, where he was appointed kapellmeister by Leopold II, and where his *Il matrimonio segreto* so delighted the emperor that it was reprised in toto the same night. Three weeks later Leopold died. Cimarosa stayed on in Vienna another year, then returned to Naples and resumed his careers as opera composer and royal organist. In 1799 he wrote a hymn for the new republican government, which compromised him when the monarchy was restored. An adulatory cantata failed to assuage the king, and he spent four months in prison. He might have been executed had he not had friends in high places, including Lady Hamilton. On his release he went to Venice to fulfil an opera commission, but he died in less than a year. The Neapolitan government put out a medical report to quash rumours he had been poisoned at the behest of the queen.

The popular oboe concerto attributed to him is a 1942 arrangement by Arthur Benjamin of three sonatas.

Operas: *I due baroni di Rocca Azzurra* (Giuseppe Palomba), f.p. Rome, 1783; *L'impresario in angustie* (Giovanni Maria Diodati), f.p. Naples, 1786; *Il* MATRIMONIO SEGRETO, f.p. Vienna, 1792; *Gli Orazi ed i Curiazi* (Antonio Simeone Sografi), f.p. Venice, 1797; about 60 others

Other works: Concerto, G, 2 fl, orch, 1793; oratorios, masses, other sacred music, cantatas, hymns, chamber pieces, many piano sonatas

Cimarrón, El (The Runaway Slave). Recital-length work by Henze for baritone, flautist, guitarist and percussionist, to words by Hans Magnus Enzensberger after Miguel Barnet's biography of the Cuban runaway slave Esteban Montejo, who, aged 107, was still alive to meet the composer. First performance: Snape, 27 Jun 1970.

cimb. Abbreviation for cimbalom.

cimbalom. Hungarian dulcimer, a trapezoidal tray of strings struck with beaters, making an appealing clangorous–stealthy sound. The commercial instrument, much more substantial than folk prototypes, was developed by Schunda of Budapest c.1870 and has been used by Kodály (*Háry János*), Stravinsky (*Renard, Ragtime*), Bartók, Kurtág and Boulez. But see also MOSONYI.

cimbasso. Bass or contrabass valve trombone, standard in Verdi's orchestra up to *Aida*.

cimento dell'armonia e dell'inventione, Il (The Union of Harmony and Invention). Group of 12 concertos in two books Vivaldi published in Amsterdam in 1725. The first four are *Le* QUATTRO STAGIONI, followed by pieces in Eb (*La tempesta di mare*), C (*Il piacere*), D minor, G minor, D minor, Bb (*La caccia*), D and C.

Cincinnati. US city, in Ohio, which boasts the country's second oldest music festival, the May Festival, founded by Theodore Thomas in 1873 and centred on a big choral performance: only the Worcester Music Festival (1858) is older. The city's symphony orchestra was founded in 1872.

Cinderella. Heroine (from Perrault) of English pantomime and of the following:

(1) Rossini's opera *La Cenerentola*, to a libretto by Jacopo Ferretti after Perrault's tale and previous operatic versions. Don Ramiro (tenor), the prince charming of the evening, swaps places with his valet Dandini (baritone) in order to discover true love, which he finds, of course, in Cinderella (contralto), not her sisters Clorinda (soprano) and Tisbe (mezzo-soprano), ineffectually masterminded by their father Don Magnifico (baritone). Cinderella has the showpiece 'Nacqui all'affanno'. First performance: Rome, 25 Jan 1817.

(2) Massenet's opera *Cendrillon*, to a libretto by Henri Cain. Cinderella (soprano), daughter of the gentle Pandolfe (bass), meets her Prince Charming (soprano) at the palace ball, in a fairy wood, and finally at home when he arrives with the glass slipper. First performance: Paris, 24 May 1899.

(3) Prokofiev's ballet *Cinderella* (*Zolushka*), to a scenario by Nikolay Volkov for choreography by Rotislav Zakharov. Out of the score came three orchestral suites (Opp.107–9), three sets of piano pieces (Opp.95, 97, 102) and an adagio for cello and piano (Op.97bis). First performance: Moscow, 21 Nov 1945.

cinelli (It.). Cymbals.

cinema organ. Organ with many spectacular stops and effects, manufactured by Wurlitzer to accompany silent films. It became a popular feature of the evening programme, with the organ and organist rising on a lift in full view, under coloured lighting, to give a short recital.

Cinq rechants (Five Refrains). Work by Messiaen for 12 voices to his own words and syllables, evoking the French Renaissance, Arthurian myth, Peru and India. It completes his Tristan trilogy, following *Harawi* and *Turangalîla*. First performance: Paris, 1949.

cinquepace, cinque pas (Fr., five steps). Late Renaissance dance with five steps in a six-beat bar, or a synonym for 'galliard'.

cinquième (Fr., fifth). Fifth part in a French Baroque string ensemble, usually the first viola.

cipher. Systematic replacement of letters, syllables or words, used in music most often to represent names by notes. The system may depend on letter names for notes (as in the B–A–C–H motif) or on a combination of these with the syllable names of Romance languages (as in the quartet by Borodin and others honouring Belyayev in the notes B♭–A–F, i.e. B–la–F). By these means notes can be found for the letters A, B (Ger. B♭), C, D, E, F, G, H (Ger. B), L (la), M (mi), R (re), S (Ger. E♭, 'Es') and T (te). In order to cover the whole alphabet, composers have either recycled conventional letter names (e.g. I is represented by A, J by B, etc.) or made up their own systems (e.g. Messiaen's 'communicable language'). Note ciphers may also be combined with other encryptions, using EYE MUSIC or NUMBER codes.

Bach and J.C. Faber, composing when letter names were becoming accepted, were lucky in their cipherable names. Later composers signing their works have included Spohr (E♭–p–B–crotchet rest), Smetana (B♭–E♭, for his initials) and Shostakovich (D–E♭–C–B, for his monogram, representing the Russian Ш Germanically as 'Sch'). Schumann introduced the possibility of simply omitting 'nonmusical' letters (hence his E♭–C–B–A), a relaxation accepted by Brahms (B♭–A–B–E♭), Berg (B♭–E–G), etc.

Schumann, Brahms and Berg also ciphered into their music the names of girlfriends, colleagues and predecessors (notably Bach), as well as mottos: Joachim's 'Frei aber einsam' (F–A–E), Brahms's 'Frei aber froh' (F–A–F). Ciphered dedications have been particularly common in France, with the collective tributes to Haydn (A–A–D–D–G), Fauré (F–A–G–D–E) and Roussel published by the *Revue musicale*, and Boulez's honourings of Sacher (E♭–A–C–B–E–D). John Field, in 1832, thanked a hostess musically for a meal of beef and cabbage.

Messiaen was unusual among composers in enciphering whole phrases rather than single words and names. Quite outside real music, however, artificial systems representing letters by notes were in use from around 1600 by state secret services for the purposes of communicating messages in what looked like musical notation.

ciphering. Sounding of an organ pipe when no key is depressed; a fault.

circle of fifths (Ger. *Quintenzirkel*). Imaginary wheel of the 12 notes or tonalities stepping in equal-tempered fifths: C, G, D, A, E, B, F♯/G♭, C♯/D♭, A♭, E♭, B♭, F, and so back to C. Because modulation through a fifth is straightforward, passages in diatonic music often move around an arc of fifths – or even, in two early preludes by Beethoven (Op.39), the entire circle.

circular breathing. Technique, inherited from the didjeridu, of playing sustained sound on a wind instrument by inhaling through the nose while exhaling into the instrument.

Cis (Ger.). C♯. Also *Cisis* (C✕).

cistre (Fr.). Cittern.

Cité de la Musique. Building at La Villette in Paris, opened in 1995 and incorporating a medium-sized concert hall and a museum.

cithara. See KITHARA.

cithare (Fr.). Zither.

Cither (Ger.). Cittern.

Cithrinchen. Cittern whose belly has a bell-shaped outline, made and played in Hamburg from the 1670s for half a century or so.

citole. Medieval cittern.

cittern. Plucked instrument of the 16th–17th centuries, played with a plectrum, unlike the nobler (as it was thought) lute. The name, like others similar, derives from that of the KITHARA, from which the instrument also inherited functionless nodules where the neck meets the body: through the citole and the Byzantine instrument, the cittern comes in direct descent from ancient Greece. Other defining features include a scooped-out back to the neck, facilitating the left hand's speed up and down, and a pegbox less steeply angled than the lute's. The instrument was at the height of its popularity from the 1560s to the 1610s.

Ċiurlionis, Mikolajus (Konstantinas) (b. Varèna, 22 Sep 1875; d. Pustelnik, near Warsaw, 10 Apr 1911). Lithuanian painter-composer who mixed his arts in sonatas on canvas and music evoking colour. He studied with Noskowski at the Warsaw Music Institute and then, in 1901, at the Leipzig Conservatory. Among his works are symphonic poems (*In the Forest*, 1900; *The Sea*, 1903–7) as well as piano and chamber pieces, including many canons and fugues.

d. Abbreviation for clarinet.

Clair de lune (Moonlight). Popular title. Normally Debussy's piano piece is meant, a movement from his *Suite bergamasque* (*c.*1890), named after a Verlaine poem he set around the same time. The poem had earlier been set by Fauré, and there are pieces with the same title by Saint-Saëns (song to words by Catulle Mendès) and Vierne.

cláirseach (Ir.), **clàrsach** (Scots Gaelic). Celtic harp.

Clapisson, (Antoine) Louis (b. Naples, 15 Sep 1808; d. Paris, 19 Mar 1866). French composer, whose ephemeral opéras comique, songs and instrumental pieces gave him the means to amass a collection of instruments which he sold to the Conservatoire, where they became the nucleus of one of the world's great instrument museums. The son of a hornist in Neapolitan service who brought the family back to France around 1815, he studied at the Conservatoire (1830–33) and played second violin at the Opera before he began striking luck as a composer in 1838. He was elected to the Institut in 1854, handsomely defeating Berlioz.

clapper. (1) Half a percussion instrument. Pairs of clappers – of wood, bone, ivory, shell, etc. – are found all over the world. The commonest kinds in the Western orchestra are the castanets, claves and whip.

(2) Swivelling hammer-shaped part inside a bell, striking the body of the instrument during ringing.

claque. Group of audience members in an opera house motivated by the management or by a singer to applaud noisily.

Clari, Giovanni Carlo Maria (b. Pisa, 27 Sep 1677; d. Pisa, 16 May 1754). Italian composer, especially

of chamber duets and trios that rivalled Steffani's in popularity and distinction – six were appropriated by Handel for *Theodora*. He studied with his bassist father and the Pisa Cathedral chapelmaster, then in Bologna. After a time as Pistoia Cathedral chapelmaster (1703–24) he returned to take up the equivalent post in Pisa.

clarinet (Fr. *clarinette*, Ger. *Klarinette*, It. *clarinetto*, pl. *clarinetti*). Single-reed WOODWIND instrument, the most reed-like of the group. The regular clarinet is a soprano instrument in B♭, about 2 feet (60cm) long, with the 'Boehm system' of keys (a development due not to Theobald Boehm but to the clarinettist Hyacinthe Eléanore Klosé and the maker Louis-August Buffet, working in Paris around 1840 and partly guided by the Boehm flute). Other members of the family include high E♭ and D (rare) clarinets, the clarinet in A, the BASSET HORN, alto clarinets in F and E♭ (both rare), the BASS CLARINET in B♭ (an octave lower than the standard instrument) and the contrabass clarinet in B♭ (an octave lower again).

The basic parts are the mouthpiece, the barrel (a connecting element that can be pulled out a little for fine tuning), the body (usually in two 'joints') and the bell. The mouthpiece is normally of ebonite, the body – and bell, in the case of the standard instrument – of grenadilla (the black wood of an African tree, *Dalbergia melanoxylon*), though pre-modern clarinets have mouthpieces and bodies of other woods. Modern basset horns, alto clarinets and bass clarinets have upturned metal bells, and the contrabass clarinet, introduced in the late 19th century, has a metal body too.

Clarinets are TRANSPOSING INSTRUMENTS. The standard clarinet has the D (written E) below middle C as its lowest note, with an almost four-octave range to C in altissimo – and, in the hands of some virtuosos, even higher, though orchestral clarinet parts do not normally venture above a high G. The bottom 11th or so of the compass is the chalumeau register, named after the ancestral clarinet and distinguished by a soft, cool sound. Above this, from the B on the treble staff to C in alt, is the clarinet, clarion or clarino register, more brilliant. In between comes the break, throat or intermediate register, and above the extreme or acute register.

The instrument's invention is traditionally credited to Johann Christoph Denner of Nuremberg, though the earliest surviving clarinets were made by his son Jacob in 1710. Slow to take off, the clarinet was used only sporadically by Vivaldi, Handel and Rameau, normally as a second instrument for oboists. Specialist players in the

1770s–80s made it a customary member of the orchestra, and it gained magnificent music from Mozart. By now there were different schools of clarinet makers in Germany, Austria, Bohemia, England and France, and the instrument's development remained diverse in the early 19th century, when its solo repertory was enlarged again by Weber and Beethoven. The Boehm system established an international norm, and the instrument's Romantic visage was completed by Schumann and Brahms. As a common member, too, of the military band, it entered European folk music and US jazz – experiences it has retained in much of its large post-1900 repertory, which includes concertos by Debussy (*Première rapsodie*), Nielsen, Stravinsky, Boulez (*Domaines*), Barraqué, Martino (Triple Concerto for standard, bass and contrabass clarinets), Birtwistle (*Melencolia I*) and Carter, as well as chamber works by Schoenberg, Berg, Stravinsky, Webern, Bartók, Wolpe, Birtwistle and Davies. There is also a strong line of works for unaccompanied clarinet by Stravinsky, Boulez, Birtwistle, Martino, Goehr, Berio and Stockhausen.

David Pino *The Clarinet and Clarinet Playing* (1980); Colin J. Lawson, ed. *The Cambridge Companion to the Clarinet* (1995)

clarinet quintet. Group of instruments comprising clarinet plus string quartet, or work for such a line-up. There are examples by Mozart, Weber, Baermann, Brahms, Reger, Hindemith, Birtwistle, Golijov, Babbitt and Olivero.

clarinette d'amour. Rare instrument with a bulbous bell, whose stipulated presence in music is hard to ascertain.

clarino, clairon, clarion. Upper register of the trumpet, above the PRINCIPALE, or of the clarinet. The anagrammatical names come from a style of medieval trumpet that was small and brilliant.

Clark, Edward (b. Newcastle upon Tyne, 10 May 1888; d. London, 30 Apr 1962). British administrator, particularly associated with the BBC Concerts of Contemporary Music (1926–39), which included new works by Schoenberg, Bartók, Stravinsky, Webern, Hindemith and Vaughan Williams. He studied in Paris, Berlin and Vienna (with Schoenberg, 1911–14) and married Lutyens in 1944.

Clarke, James (b. London, 15 Oct 1957). British composer, of works at the edge of possibility and danger. He studied at Southampton University, at City University, London, and in Helsinki with

Usko Meriläinen. Notable compositions include *Ver-störung* for bass clarinet, cello and piano (1990), and a piano sonata comprising *Island* (1999) and *Landschaft mit Glockenturm* (2003).

Clarke, Jeremiah (b. *c*.1674; d. London, 1 Dec 1707). English composer, whose stock rose in 1953 when he was established as the author of 'Purcell's Trumpet Voluntary', which Henry Wood's arrangement had popularized. He was a Chapel Royal chorister at the coronation of James II (1685), and returned to London – to St Paul's and the Chapel Royal – after being organist of Winchester College (1692–5). His tuneful songs, anthems, odes and instrumental pieces (including the celebrated 'voluntary', which he, in versions for keyboard and for wind band, called *The Prince of Denmark's March*) do not reflect the melancholia reported of him. He shot himself.

Clarke, Rebecca (Thacher) (b. Harrow, 27 Aug 1886; d. New York, 13 Oct 1979). British composer, best known for her Viola Sonata (1919), somewhere between Vaughan Williams and Ravel. Of German–US parentage, she trained at the RAM and RCM (with Stanford), and played the viola professionally in London before settling in 1939 in New York, where she took work as a nanny. She also wrote a piano trio (1921), as well as songs and short instrumental pieces.

class. Lesson-demonstration shared by several students. See also MASTERCLASS.

classical. Protean term. At its broadest classical music embraces everything in this book. Most narrowly, with an initial capital, it is normally understood to refer to Classicism, the style of a short period, roughly 1770–1800, achieved in one city (Vienna) essentially by two composers (Haydn and Mozart), though with repercussions beyond. It can also denote orderliness, with ROMANTIC as its antonym, irrespective of period. Or it can indicate some allusion to the ancient Greek–Roman world. Or, again, it can be a marker of distinction and authority in any repertory. Thus Taneyev's *Oresteia* is classical but not Classical music, classical in its comportment and subject, yet by no means an opera classic.

Classical. Name Prokofiev gave his First Symphony, which he imagined as a work Haydn might have written a century or so on.

Classicism. The style that was at its peak in the last three decades of the 18th century – a widespread phenomenon in Western music, though centred on Vienna and with Haydn and Mozart emerging in almost immediate retrospect as its outstanding proponents. Classicism was the musical expression of the Enlightenment, in its ideals of clarity, balance and universal comprehensibility. But those ideals – and the musical priorities and procedures that supported them – lived on into the next century and long beyond, giving the music of the Classical period classic status. For many later composers, from Schumann through Brahms and Prokofiev to Henze, the Classical style was the epitome of perfection and grace. For performers and audiences, almost as soon as the period was over, Classical works provided the foundation of the repertory.

Perhaps the chief feature of Classical music is the elegant evenness with which it moves through time – an effect due to regular metre and harmonic rhythm coupled with a persuasive logic in how melodies unfold, replace one another and are developed. Along with the logic, of course, goes humour: the smile of a problem lightly solved or a promise subverted. The Classical composers invented SONATA FORM as their basic principle and the sequence of three or four movements as their recurrent type, but they also enlarged music's capacities for wit and installed, as their model of the human universe, comic opera. See also NEOCLASSICISM.

Charles Rosen *The Classical Style* (1971, ³1997)

clausula. Term that in the Middle Ages could mean a musical close (from Lat. *claudere*, to close) or a closed section of polyphony, but that now almost always denotes the latter, as created in the early 13th century. Perotin and his fellow NOTRE DAME SCHOOL polyphonists would reconceive segments of chants as music with modal rhythm, at least one added part (usually much faster than the chant, which would function as a tenor) and a decisive close. These clausulae could then take on independent lives, with different words, as motets.

clavecin (Fr.). Harpsichord.

clavecinist (Fr. *claveciniste*). Harpsichordist, especially one from the great tradition of French harpsichordist-composers that flourished from the mid 17th century to the mid 18th, embracing the Couperins, Daquin and D'Anglebert.

claves. Pair of wooden rods, of which one is held on the flat of one hand to be struck with the other, creating a sharp attack. Cuban in origin, the instrument spread through Latin-American dance combos into classical music.

clavicembalo (It., pl. *clavicembali*). Harpsichord.

clavichord. Keyboard instrument in which pressing a key brings a thin tongue of brass (a tangent) into contact with a pair of strings. The position of the tangent determines the pitch, because only the length of string between the tangent and the bridge vibrates, the remaining length beyond the tangent being damped with a piece of cloth. The resulting sound is small, confining the instrument to domestic surroundings. But because the tangent remains touching the strings (unlike the harpsichord's quills or the piano's hammers, which immediately leave) the player is able not only to gauge the sound by means of attack but to vary it during the period of resonance. The clavichord is thus unusually sensitive to touch and offers much to the solitary performer-listener.

Clavichords are documented from 1404; the earliest surviving example is from 1543. Abundant in the next two centuries, the instrument normally had the form of a rectangular box (with the strings lying perpendicular to the keys), to be placed on a table. It had a range of around four octaves and could be used for solo keyboard music, to accompany a singer or as a practice instrument for organists. Use of the BEBUNG identifies music intended specifically for the clavichord, as in a piece by C.P.E. Bach, who wrote of the instrument's 'sustaining, caressing tone'.

clavicordio (Sp.). Harpsichord.

clavicytherium. Upright harpsichord, with the soundbox now a raised wing. The earliest surviving stringed keyboard instrument is a clavicytherium of *c*.1480 held by the RCM.

clavier. General term for a stringed keyboard instrument, adopted from its use by Bach (e.g. *Das wohltemperirte Clavier*). In French the *clavier* is the keyboard of a stringed instrument (piano, harpsichord, etc.) or organ.

Clavier-Übung (Keyboard Exercise). Set of publications by Bach, borrowing a title from Kuhnau and consisting of: the six partitas (1731), the Italian Concerto and French Overture (1735), the 'St Anne' Prelude and Fugue plus 21 chorale settings (1739), and the GOLDBERG VARIATIONS (1741).

claviorgan. Harpsichord or piano having some organ pipes, an ungainly hybrid in occasional existence from the 16th century to the 19th.

Clayton, Thomas (baptized London, 28 Oct 1673; buried London, 23 Sep 1725). English composer, responsible for the first all-sung English opera, *Arsinoe, Queen of Cyprus* (1705). The son of a court violinist, he studied in Italy. An anonymous critic wrote that the success of his pioneer opera 'encouraged the author to compose another worse than the first': *Rosamond* (1707), to a libretto by Addison.

clef (from Fr. *clef*, key). Sign on a staff, indicating how the lines and spaces represent notes. The G and F clefs (familiar as treble and bass clefs) curl around the lines for the notes of their names; the C clef is centred. But the clefs work as symbols, recognized by their shapes, rather than as positioners. Those in common use are:

treble   bass   alto   tenor

These all have their origins in the Roman letters that formed the first clefs in regular musical use, beginning in the 11th century. F and C clefs were commonest in plainsong manuscripts, but all the other musical letters were also in use, including B, from which came the flat sign. By the Renaissance only F, C and G were left, now as clefs, among which composers and scribes might choose for reasons practical (to obviate leger lines and accidentals as much as possible) or arcane (to keep a cantus firmus at its original written pitch in music that transposed it), though the G clef was already associated with upper parts.

Clemens non Papa [Clement, Jacob] (b. *c.*1510–15; d. 1555/6). Netherlandish composer. Unusually prolific, he was jokingly called 'Clement not the Pope' (i.e. Clement VII, r. 1523–34) from soon after his death. Little is known of his career, apart from brief periods at Bruges Cathedral (1544–5) and with the Marian Brotherhood of 's-Hertogenbosch (1550). His works include 14 masses, a *Requiem*, 15 *Magnificat* settings, about 233 motets, metrical psalms in Dutch and about 100 secular songs (mostly in French), all in smooth, regular, imitative polyphony.

Clement, Franz (b. Vienna, 17 Nov 1780; d. Vienna, 3 Nov 1842). Austrian violinist, who led the orchestra at the Theater an der Wien (1802–11) and was honoured with Beethoven's concerto, which he played with variations of his own for which he held his instrument upside-down – on the same programme, but not necessarily between movements, as is sometimes said. Promoted by his father, he played in London in 1790, including for Haydn. He died in poverty.

Clementi, Aldo (b. Catania, 25 May 1925). Italian composer, notably of densely packed confrontations with earlier music and conventions. Of cultured family, he studied with Schoenberg's pupil Alfredo Sangiorgi, with Petrassi in Rome (1952–4) and annually at Darmstadt (1955–62). His works include the theatre pieces *ES* (Venice, 1981) and *Carillon* (Milan, 1998).

Clementi, Muzio (b. Rome, 23 Jan 1752; d. Evesham, 10 Mar 1832). Italian–British composer and musical entrepreneur. Trained in his native city, he was appointed organist of his parish church just before his 14th birthday, but within the year was snapped up by Peter Beckford, a cousin of the writer William Beckford. He spent the next seven years at Peter Beckford's Dorset estate, then went to London, where he started out as a keyboard composer and performer. A long continental tour (1780–83) included a piano contest with Mozart, on Christmas Eve 1781 in Vienna, before the emperor. Clementi is reported as saying he 'had never heard anyone play with such spirit and grace'; his rival's opinion of him was that 'he has not a kreuzer's worth of taste or feeling'. After a brief return to London, where he acquired Cramer as his pupil, he went back to the continent (1784–5), partly in unsuccessful pursuit of a young woman.

During the next, more settled phase of his life he remained in London. He was active as a performer of his own music until Haydn's arrival, after which he concentrated on teaching, ploughing the proceeds into publishing and instrument-making enterprises. His next European tour (1802–10) was as a commercial representative: he had Field with him to demonstrate his pianos and secured works by composers from Beethoven down. He also married, though his young wife died a year later in childbirth. Young Field he is said to have treated roughly, but this may be a myth. Eight years on the road, crisscrossing Europe from Italy to Russia, would have taxed anyone – not least a man in his 50s. Back in London, he took charge of his company, conducted Philharmonic Society concerts and at last had the satisfactions of family life, marrying and fathering four children. He paid further visits to the continent, much briefer and for the purposes of promoting himself as a symphonist, without lasting success. In 1830 he retired, after precisely half a century of continuous if varying absorptions with the piano as virtuoso composer-performer, publisher, manufacturer-retailer and pedagogue – a lifetime memorialized in his many sonatas, which travel from the aftermath of Scarlatti to the precincts of Beethoven, and in his three-volume collection of studies *Gradus ad Parnassum*.

Leon Plantinga *Clementi* (1977)

Piano sonatas (with publication dates): Op.12:2, E♭, 1784; Op.24:2, B♭, 1789; Op.25:3, B♭, 1790; Op.25:5, F♯ minor, 1790; Op.34:1, C, 1795; Op.40, G, B minor, D minor, 1802; Op.50:1, A, 1821; etc.

clemenza di Tito, La (The Clemency of Titus). Opera by Mozart to a libretto by Caterino Mazzolà after Metastasio. The Roman emperor Titus (tenor) displays magnanimity in releasing Servilia (soprano), his intended bride, to marry her devoted Annius (soprano), and clemency in forgiving Servilia's brother Sextus (soprano castrato), who had plotted against him at the inducement of Vitellia (soprano). The grandest arias include Sextus's 'Parto, parto' with basset clarinet obbligato and Vitellia's 'Non più di fiori' with obbligato basset horn, the latter balanced by the breath-taking candour of Servilia's 'S'altro che lagrime'. First performance: Prague, 6 Sep 1791.

Cleopatra. Egyptian queen and seductress, figure in works by Handel (GIULIO CESARE), Berlioz and Barber.

Clérambault, Louis-Nicolas (b. Paris, 19 Dec 1676; d. Paris, 26 Oct 1749). French organist-composer, esteemed also for his cantatas. Born into a musical family that had served the French crown since the 15th century, he studied with his father and other teachers, and held various organ appointments in Paris and at the royal girls' school at St Cyr, near Versailles. Meanwhile he published five volumes of *cantates françoises* (1710–26) and one of organ music (*Premier livre d'orgue*, containing two suites), besides producing other instrumental music and motets, displaying in all a fine sense for incorporating fashionable Italian qualities. His two sons became his assistants and successors; the death of the younger, in 1790, brought the line to a close.

David Tunley *The 18th-Century French Cantata* (1974, ²1997)

Cleve, Johannes de (b. Kleve, 1528/9; d. Augsburg, 14 Jul 1582). Netherlandish composer of sacred polyphony, both Catholic and Lutheran. He was a member of the imperial chapel in Vienna (1553–64), during which time masses and motets by him appeared in print. He then remained in Habsburg service in Graz and Vienna until 1579, when he moved to Augsburg Cathedral.

Cleveland. US city, in Ohio, home of the Cleveland Orchestra, which was founded in 1918 and moved into its own auditorium, Severance Hall, in 1931. Its music directors have been Nikolai Sokoloff (1918–33), Artur Rodzinski (1933–43), Leinsdorf (1943–6), Szell (1946–70), Maazel (1972–81), Christoph von Dohnányi (1984–2002) and Franz Welser-Möst (from 2002). It has also had a relationship with Boulez since 1965.

Donald Rosenberg *The Cleveland Orchestra Story* (2000)

Cliburn, Van [Harvey Lavan] (b. Shreveport, Louisiana, 12 Jul 1934). US pianist. Taught by his mother, he made his debut at four and played in Carnegie Hall at 14. He then studied with Lhévinne at Juilliard (1951–4). He created a sensation by winning the Tchaikovsky Competition in 1958, at the height of the Cold War, and was welcomed back to New York with a ticker-tape parade. Recordings testify to his grandeur at this time in the Romantic repertory, but after a few years he largely withdrew from public performance. He established the Van Cliburn International Piano Competition in Fort Worth in 1962.

Clicquot, François-Henri (b. Paris, 1732; d. Paris, 24 May 1790). French organ-builder, in succession to his father Louis-Alexandre and highly esteemed grandfather Robert (c.1645–1719). His instruments (notably that of Poitiers Cathedral) represent the acme of the French classical style.

Clio. The muse of history, sometimes shown with a kithara.

clivis. Kind of NEUME.

cloche (Fr.). Bell, hence *cloches tubes* (tubular bells), *cloche à vache* (cowbell), *clochette* (hand-bell), etc.

clock. Machine for measuring time. Clocks have a history partly parallelling that of musical compositions, which similarly exhibit determined and perceptible changes as they move through time (or as time moves through them). For example, Christiaan Huygens's first pendulum clock (1656) introduced the possibility of accurate timekeeping in every household at a time when musical pulse and metre were becoming more regular and systematic. Clocks have also had more direct musical connections. Haydn, Mozart and Beethoven are among composers who wrote pieces for organs incorporated in clocks. Birtwistle has composed works based on the sounds (*Chronometer*) or imagery (*Harrison's Clocks*) of timepieces. And the METRONOME and MUSICAL BOX are among clockwork devices specifically made for music.

Clock. Name given Haydn's Symphony No.101 (in his lifetime) on account of the tick-tock accompaniment at the start of the slow movement. First performance: London, 3 Mar 1794.

close harmony. Harmony in close position.

close position. See POSITION (3).

Club Anthem. *I will always give thanks*, as jointly set by Blow, Humfrey and William Turner (1664).

cluster. Group of adjacent notes played together. Cowell pioneered the use of clusters played on the piano with the palm or forearm, beginning with *The Tides of Manaunaun* (1912). Xenakis intro-duced orchestral clusters with *Metastasis* (1955).

C minor Mass. Setting by Mozart for two sopranos, choir and orchestra, supposedly written to fulfil a vow on his marriage to Constanze, who is presumed to have taken part in the first performance – only a partial performance, since the *Credo* was never finished and the *Agnus Dei* never started. First performance: Salzburg, 26 Oct 1783 (completed sections).

Coates, Albert (b. St Petersburg, 23 Apr 1882; d. Cape Town, 11 Dec 1953). British conductor of majestic build and style, born into a family with business in Russia. He was a pupil of, and répétiteur for, Nikisch in Leipzig, and continued his career in Germany and England before becoming principal conductor at the Mariinsky (1914–19). After that he returned to England to work with the LSO and at Covent Garden, and moved to South Africa in 1946. His opera *Pickwick* (1936) was the first seen (in part) on television.

Coates, Eric (b. Hucknall, 27 Aug 1886; d. Chichester, 23 Dec 1957). British composer of songs, marches (*Knightsbridge*, from the suite *London Everyday*, 1932; *Calling all Workers*, 1940; *The Dambusters*, 1954) and other light orchestral pieces (*By the Sleepy Lagoon*, valse-serenade, 1930). He studied with Corder at the RAM.

Cobbett, W(alter) W(ilson) (b. Blackheath, 11 Jul 1847; d. London, 22 Jan 1937). British amateur of chamber music. He is said to have devoted to business the little time he could spare from music – but so profitably that he had the means to establish prizes (especially one for a single-movement

PHANTASY) and publish a *Cyclopaedia of Chamber Music* (1929).

Cocchi, Gioacchino (b. ?Naples, *c*.1720; d. ?Venice, after 1788). Italian composer, especially of comic operas. Probably trained in Naples, he scored his biggest success with *La maestra* (1747), his entrée to a career in Venice (1749–57), London (1757–*c*.1772) and again Venice.

Coccia, Carlo (b. Naples, 14 Apr 1782; d. Novara, 13 Apr 1873). Italian composer, whose long life included two separate operatic careers, as a follower of his teacher Paisiello (1807–21: *Clotilde*, Venice, 1815) and then – after he had left Rossini-mad Italy for periods in Lisbon and London – in a more studied style (1827–41: *Caterina di Guisa*, Milan, 1833). In 1840 he succeeded Mercadante at San Gaudenzio in Novara, devoting himself now to church music – and pursued by Rossini from beyond the grave when Verdi invited his contribution to the *Requiem* he was planning.

Cocteau, (Clément Eugène) Jean (Maurice) (b. Maisons-Lafitte, Paris, 5 Jul 1889; d. Milly-la-Forêt, Seine-et-Oise, 11 Oct 1963). French writer and film maker, partly responsible for instigating a new mood in French music, sharp and smart, after the First World War. Having attached himself to Diaghilev and the Ballets Russes, he worked with Satie and Picasso on *Parade* and with Stravinsky on *Oedipus Rex*, in which he created an appropriate role for himself as master of ceremonies. His defence of *Parade*, *Le Coq et l'arlequin* (1918), provided a manifesto for the group of young composers soon to emerge under his wing, Les SIX, among whom Poulenc and Auric became his collaborators in his plays and films of the 1930s–40s.

coda (It., tail, pl. *code*, in Eng. 'codas'). End part of a tune, movement or piece, seeming at once additional and culminative. The term is particularly associated with the section succeeding the recapitulation in sonata form, a section Beethoven made imposing.

codetta (It., little tail). Link in a fugue, between one thematic statement and the next, or in a sonata movement, at the end of the exposition.

Coelho. See RODRIGUES COELHO.

Coffee Cantata. Name given to Bach's *Schweigt stille*, to words by Picander. Schlendrian's problem with his daughter Liesgen is that she prefers coffee to boys. The work was probably made for performance at Zimmermann's coffeehouse in Leipzig.

col, colla, coll' (It.). With. The term is most often found in directions for tempo and bowing. Of the former, *col basso* (with the bass), *colla parte* (with the part) and *colla voce* (with the voice) request the performer to follow the tempo of a bass line, leading part or voice. Among the latter are *coll'arco* (with the bow, after a pizzicato passage), *colla punta dell'arco* (with the point of the bow) and *col legno* (with the wood), i.e. applying the wood of the bow to the strings, either in discrete blows (*col legno battuto*) or with drawing motions (*col legno tratto*).

colascione (It.), **colachon** (Fr.). Long-necked lute of Islamic origin, made in Europe in the 16th–18th centuries but not required in any surviving music.

Colbran, Isabella (Angela) (b. Madrid, 2 Feb 1785; d. Castenaso, Bologna, 7 Oct 1845). Spanish soprano, who appeared in Italy from 1807 and whose brilliant, dramatic singing Rossini took into the roles he wrote for her. After several years together and more apart, they were legally separated in 1837; she remained where they had been married.

Coleridge-Taylor, Samuel (b. London, 15 Aug 1875; d. Croydon, 1 Sep 1912). British composer, half-African through his father, though he found his spiritual forebears among the Amerindians, as mediated through Longfellow and Dvořák, and through his training as an English choirboy. 'Coleridge' was originally his middle name, which he hyphenated to his surname – and justified by setting Samuel Taylor Coleridge's *Kubla Khan*. However, Longfellow was the poet destined for him. His cantata *Hiawatha's Wedding Feast* was enormously popular with choirs in Britain and the USA for half a century, until embarrassment at its Romanticized primitivisim overwhelmed delight in its ebullience. It came soon after his time at the RCM (1890–97), where he studied first as a violinist, then as a composer with Stanford. In 1904, 1906 and 1910 he visited the USA, making contact with Black writers and activists while observing, in his fecund output of songs and cantatas, the poetic preferences of the choral establishment.

Scenes from 'The Song of Hiawatha' (Longfellow): Overture, 1899; *Hiawatha's Wedding Feast*, t, ch, orch, 1898; *The Death of Minnehaha*, s, bar, ch, orch, 1899; *Hiawatha's Departure*, s, t, bar, ch, orch, 1900

Other works: further cantatas, orchestral, chamber and piano music, songs, partsongs, incidental scores

Colgrass, Michael (Charles) (b. Chicago, 22 Apr 1932). US composer, of evocative music proceeding coherently from Varèse, jazz and sometimes more traditional sources. A pupil of Riegger and Weber, he worked in New York as a percussionist (1956–67) and moved to Toronto in 1974.

Colista, Lelio (b. Rome, 13 Jan 1629; d. Rome, 13 Oct 1680). Italian composer whose trio sonatas prefigured Corelli's and directly influenced Purcell's, being admired in England after their composer had been forgotten in Italy. He spent almost his whole life in Rome, holding church appointments as lutenist and composer.

colla, coll'. See COL.

collaboration. All music involves collaboration between composers and performers: even recorded electronic music has to be performed by those reponsible for judging the placement of loudspeakers, levels, etc. Sometimes composers seek performers' advice during the creative process; stage works will require the collaboration of librettists, choreographers and directors. See also COLLECTIVE COMPOSITION.

collage (Fr., necklace). Term borrowed from the visual arts, denoting an arrangement of borrowed fragments that remain incompletely integrated into the new context. The festoon of tunes in a Baroque quodlibet is, therefore, excluded, being harmonically homogeneous. Collage implies, rather, the deliberate mismatch of quoted hymns and marches with new material in many of Ives's orchestral movements, or the gathering of diverse recorded elements in such a work as Varèse's *Poème électronique*. There are many other examples in pieces of the late 1960s (Berio's *Sinfonia*, Davies's *Eight Songs for a Mad King*) and later.

Collard & Collard. British piano firm tracing its origins through Clementi to Longman, and run from 1830 by Clementi's partner, Frederick William Collard. Second only to Broadwood in production 20 years later, it was overtaken by new technology, absorbed by Chappell (1929) and allowed to lapse even as a name (1971).

Collasse, Pascal (baptized Rheims, 22 Jan 1649; d. Versailles, 17 Jul 1709). French composer, Lully's assistant from 1677 and thereafter his follower. He failed to repeat the success of *Thétis et Pelée* (Paris,

1689) in later stage works, and eventually abandoned music to search for the philosopher's stone.

collective composition. The lone genius is a Romantic myth: composition is a collaborative act, a dialogue with contemporaries and with history. If, nevertheless, examples of collective composition are rare, that must be partly because music in the Western tradition generally requires a score, and the complexity of notation impedes joint action. Most collective pieces have been produced by composers working independently on different sections, whether as colleagues, planning a joint effort, or rivals, one replacing parts of another's score. Both kinds of collective effort were common in 18th-century opera: *Muzio Scevola* (London, 1721), with acts by Amadei, Bononcini and Handel, is the textbook example of the former sort, while Mozart's output includes numerous arias and a couple of ensembles written as insert pieces. Later instances of collective composition include the 'F–A–E' sonata for Joachim, the quartet, also ciphered, written for BELYAYEV and the YELLOW RIVER CONCERTO.

college band. See CONCERT BAND.

Collegium Musicum (Ger. Lat.). City institution for the performance and study of music, as found in German-speaking Europe in the 17th and 18th centuries.

col legno. See COL.

Collingwood, Lawrance (Arthur) (b. London, 14 Mar 1887; d. Killin, Perthshire, 19 Dec 1982). British conductor, accompanist to Chaliapin and Gigli in recordings. He studied at Oxford and in St Petersburg (notably as Coates's assistant), and became principal conductor of opera at Sadler's Wells (1931–47), where his *Macbeth* (1934) was presented.

Cologne (Köln). German city, home to the Gürzenich Orchestra (named after the town hall) and the WDR Symphony. Conductors of the former have included Wand (1946–74) and James Conlon (from 1991, also in charge of the opera). The Philharmonie was opened in 1986, and quickly established itself among Europe's foremost concert halls.

Colón, Teatro. The Buenos Aires opera house, founded in 1857 and rebuilt in 1908.

Colonne, Edouard (Judas) (b. Bordeaux, 23 Jul 1838; d. Paris, 28 Mar 1910). French conductor, who founded a concert series that long outlasted him. He studied at the Paris Conservatoire and began his career as a principal violinist with the Opera orchestra in 1858, starting his regular concerts as a conductor in 1873.

colophony. Rosin. The name possibly derives from that of Colophon in Asia Minor.

color. Repeating sequence of pitches in a medieval composition. The term was used in various senses at the time, but is now generally confined to the pitch sequence of a motet showing ISORHYTHM.

coloration (Lat. *coloratio*). Medieval–Renaissance notational device. 'Colored' notes – red or, later, with the noteheads filled in with black ink – had two-thirds the normal rhythmic value.

coloratura (It., colouring). Exuberant and virtuoso ornamentation, especially as displayed by a high soprano. A coloratura soprano is a singer who would undertake such work, for example as the Queen of the Night (*Zauberflöte*) or Zerbinetta (*Ariadne auf Naxos*).

colour. Music has often been seen as a play of colours – by composers, listeners, performers and theorists. Most usually the term is used metaphorically, as a synonym for timbre or tone colour, so that one may speak of the oboe's colour as distinct from the clarinet's, or the woodwind colouring of a passage, or a singer's choice of colour for a note. Harmony, too, can be coloured, i.e. CHROMATIC. But in some cases the analogy is more than a metaphor. Scriabin saw his music in specific colours, and in *Prométhée* included a part for 'light keyboard', a machine imagined as flooding the auditorium with colours appropriate to the harmony. Soon after, stage works by Schoenberg (*Die glückliche Hand*) and Bartók (*Bluebeard's Castle*) required coloured light integrated into the musical action. Messiaen, in many statements and in some of his scores, indicated the colours he inwardly saw when imagining his music: A major, most decisively, was blue, and used as such to render the colours of the sea, the sky or birds' plumage. Scriabin's blue tonality, though, was F♯. A real melding of colour and music is experienced by those suffering from synaesthesia, whereby visual and aural stimuli are confused in the brain.

Columbia. Recording company founded *c*.1890 as a subsidiary of the American Graphophone Company in the District of Columbia. It then spread to New York (1896), Paris (1897) and

London (1900). The US and British companies ran independently after the First World War, to disappear respectively into CBS (1938) and EMI (1931).

Columbus, Christopher (It. Cristoforo Colombo, Sp. Cristóbal Colón). Colonizer of the Americas in 1492, subject of operas by Franchetti (1892), Milhaud and Glass (1992), and of an overture by Wagner.

combattimento di Tancredo e Clorinda, Il (The Combat between Tancred and Clorinda). Dramatic madrigal by Monteverdi setting words from Tasso's *Gerusalemme liberata* for three singing characters: a narrator and the combattants. The work introduced not only small-scale music theatre (and was justly venerated on that count by Berio, Goehr and others in the 1960s) but also tremolo and pizzicato effects in the strings. See also ARMIDE. First performance: Venice, 1624/5.

combination tone. Tone heard as a result of two or more loud pitched sounds being experienced at once, an effect due to the acoustics of the ear or of the room in which the sounds are heard. The frequencies of combination tones may be the sums or differences of the sounding frequencies (x, y) or their multiples, i.e. $x + y$, $2x - y$, etc.

combinatoriality. Property of a set, especially a 12-note set, whereby part of one form may combine with the equivalent part of another without repetition. For example, the row of Schoenberg's Op.31 starts with a hexachord ($Bb–E–F\#–Eb–F–A$) that is combinatorial with the opening hexachord of an inversion ($G–C\#–B–D–C–Ab$). A set that has this property also with retrograde and retrograde-inversion forms is said to be all-combinatorial. Babbitt instituted the terms and has made much use of combinatorial properties in his music.

come (It.). As, hence *come prima* (as at first) and *come sopra* (as above), both prescribing a return to the previous tempo or manner of performance.

comédie larmoyante (Fr., tearful comedy). French opera genre of the late 18th century, with sentimental sadness before the happy ending.

comédie mêlée d'ariettes (Fr., comedy mixed with little songs). French opera genre of the 1750s–70s, precursor of opéra comique.

comes (Lat., count – as a rank). Entry of the subject in the dominant in a fugue, following the *dux*, the tonic entry.

Come, ye sons of art, away. Ode by Purcell, among his most splendid, for Mary II's birthday, to words possibly by Nahum Tate. Music is praised as much as the queen, not least in the alto duet 'Sound the trumpet'. The other soloists are a soprano and a bass, with choir and instruments. First performance: London, 30 Apr 1694.

comic opera. Notable examples include Mozart's *Le nozze di Figaro, Don Giovanni, Così fan tutte* and *Die Zauberflöte*, Rossini's *Il barbiere di Siviglia, La cenerentola* and other works, Donizetti's *Don Pasquale*, Verdi's *Falstaff*, Puccini's *Gianni Schicchi*, Ravel's *L'heure espagnole*, Stravinsky's *Mavra* and Carter's *What Next?* See also OPERA BOUFFE; OPERA BUFFA; OPERA COMIQUE; OPERETTA.

comma. (1) Small interval, roughly a ninth tone, encountered in misfits between intervals in natural tuning. For example, a just major third (5:4) is not quite the same as four just fifths less two octaves (81:64), and 12 fifths (531,441:4,096) make up a little more than seven octaves (128:1). These differences are respectively the 'syntonic comma' (81:80, or 21:51 cents) and the 'Pythagorean comma' (531,441:524,288, 23.46 cents).

(2) The typographical mark sometimes appears in scores – usually above the staves – to indicate a LUFTPAUSE.

commedia dell'arte (It.). Popular Italian theatre of the 16th–18th centuries featuring stock characters and situations: the dashing Harlequin (Arlecchino), his beloved Colombine (Colombina), the melancholic Pierrot (Pedrolino), the foolish Pantaloon (Pantalone), etc. Opera buffa owed a lot to them, and they reappeared in later works by Schumann (*Carnaval*), Schoenberg (*Pierrot lunaire*), Stravinsky (*Petrushka, Pulcinella*), Strauss (*Ariadne auf Naxos*) and others.

common chord. Triad, most usually major, though minor chords may also be called common.

common time. 4/4. The C time signature is not an abbreviation but an inheritance from the medieval semicircle, indicating two semibreves per breve.

communion. (1) Antiphon sung as worshippers take communion, part of the mass PROPER.

(2) In the Anglican church the term also denotes the entire eucharistic service.

comodo (It.). Comfortable, found as a tempo indication by itself or in such combinations as *allegro comodo, andante comodo*, etc.

compact disc. See CD.

Como una ola de fuerza y luz (Like a wave of force and light). Work by Nono for piano and orchestra plus soprano and tape, with words by Julio Huasi. Planned as a concerto for Pollini and Abbado, the work was galvanized by news of the death of the Chilean revolutionary Luciano Cruz. First performance: Milan, 28 Jun 1972.

compass. Range, of a voice, instrument or part.

Compère, Loyset (b. Hainaut, c.1445; d. St Quentin, 16 Aug 1518). Netherlandish composer, who was in service most of his life to the French royal court, and as such resident occasionally in Italy. His works include motets, French songs and masses.

competition. Feature of musical life from the most junior levels to the most virtuoso, where there has been an extraordinary proliferation since 1945. The most prestigious tournaments have included the Chopin (Warsaw, 1927, quinquennial; piano), Carl Flesch (London, 1945–92; violin), Reine Elisabeth (Brussels, 1951, quadrennial; violin, piano, composition and voice in rotation), Tchaikovsky (Moscow, 1958, quadrennial; piano, violin and cello coinciding), Van Cliburn (Fort Worth, 1962, quadrennial; piano), Leeds (1963, triennial; piano), Sibelius (Helsinki, 1965, quinquennial; violin), Rubinstein (Tel-Aviv, 1974, triennial; piano), Singer of the World (Cardiff, 1983, biennial) and Borciani (Reggio Emilia, 1987, triennial; string quartet).

complement. Interval that must be added to another interval in order to make an octave; thus, the complement of a major third is a minor sixth. The normal term in tonal usage is 'inversion'; 'complement' may be preferred in atonal contexts.

composer. Creator of defined music. That now customarily implies abilities to notate music as well as imagine it, though the imagining began earlier, when, in Western culture as in others, identifiable pieces of music were being made and transmitted without written means. Even so, the personal and social role of the composer is a more recent and gradual development. Nearly all composers until around 1600 were in church or court employment as singers or chapelmasters, and need not have seen their creative work as primary. Opera provided composers with a field in which they could work as independent suppliers, though very often they were valued below singers. Creativity began to rise in esteem and worth only with

the surge in music publishing in the later 18th century, allowing Haydn, Mozart and Beethoven to provide new images of what the composer might be. Since then composers have been valued largely for their capacities to discover and explore musical worlds that are both rich and new, though their place in public renown has been less consistent. The prestige and aura of the composer rose further in the early 19th century, and lasted at a high level until Stravinsky, to fall again in the second half of the 20th century.

composition. Piece of reproducible music, or the labour involved in producing such a piece, or the art of creating such pieces. Composition in Western classical music implies notation – this is what most essentially defines and characterizes the art – though in other traditions there may be no written process or memorandum. See also WORK.

compound interval. Interval greater than an octave. Thus a major 10th may be described as a compound major third.

compound time. Metre in which each beat is divided into three (usually) or more units, e.g. 6/8 (two triple beats per bar), 9/8 (three triple beats), 10/8 (two quintuple beats), etc.

compression. Electronic reduction of dynamic range.

comprimario (It.). Sub-principal (role in an opera), e.g. Frasquita and Mercédès in *Carmen* (though bit parts may also be included in the designation).

computer. Electronic device for making calculations, applying rules, etc. Computers have been used since the 1950s to assist in composition and analysis, and since the late 1960s (thanks to improvements in speed) in concert performance. Xenakis in 1956 was among the first to seek electronic help in working out complex compositional designs; Lejaren Hiller and Leonard Isaacson same year produced the first computer composition, the *ILLIAC Suite*. The use of computers to generate and transform sounds was pioneered by Mathews from the early 1960s and became normal in ELECTRONIC MUSIC studios in the mid-1970s. By the end of the next decade the spread of personal computers had placed an extremely versatile composing–performing–recording instrument in many Western homes, and the growth of the INTERNET in the 1990s enhanced the ability of digital musicians to communicate with each other and with the world of stored information.

Comte Ory, Le (Count Ory). Opera by Rossini to a libretto by Scribe and Charles Gaspard Delestre-Poirson after their own play. Count Ory (tenor) and his page Isolier (mezzo-soprano) foil each other's plans to seduce the Countess Adèle (soprano), whose husband has gone off on crusade. First performance: Paris, Opera, 20 Aug 1828.

Comus. Masque by Milton, given music by Henry Lawes (for the original production at Ludlow Castle, 1634), Arne (Dublin, 1738), Handel (Exton, Rutland, 1745) and Hugh Wood. In Graeco-Roman culture a comus was an exuberant procession with music; Milton's Comus is a magician who enters at the head of 'a rout of monsters'.

con (1) (It.). With, as in *con* BRIO, *con* SORDINO, etc. It can embrace the definite article in the forms COL, COLLA, etc.

(2) Abbreviation for continuo.

concert (1) (Fr. *concert*, Ger. *Konzert*, It. *concerto*). Musical performance with an audience. Normally a sizeable body of performers is implied – enough to warrant a conductor. Otherwise the appropriate term is 'recital'. Musicians may get together to perform without an audience, but they will not then be giving a concert: those there to listen are essential to the form, and their seating, in a CONCERT HALL, is generally fixed. The word's derivation also upholds this twofold sense of concerting (Lat. *concertare*, to contend) in consort (Lat. *consortium*, group). The importance of concerts in Western musical culture is suggested by such other terms as concert pianist, concert grand, concert singer, concert programme, concert life, concert dress, etc.

The history of the concert is inevitably bound up with that of independent music for the ORCHESTRA, which can have had no other outlet, and with the arrival of academies in the late 16th century to form a new phenomenon: the listener. Most listeners, originally, were of high birth or station, and most concerts until the later 18th century were semi-private, limited to noble households and professional gatherings. Public concerts came with bourgeois culture and came earliest where that culture was first established: in London. Growing out of tavern entertainment, the public concert traces its ancestry to John Banister's venture of 1672; by 1678 a concert hall had been built near Charing Cross, and with Handel's oratorios the concert began to gain its purpose-made repertory. These innovations then spread to other cities in Britain, Europe (Frankfurt, 1723; Paris, 1725) and the USA (Boston, 1731).

When the programme was not dominated by an oratorio or similar work, it seems generally to have been a miscellany. Playbills and descriptions of 18th-century concerts indicate a succession of ensemble pieces, usually starting with an overture and continuing with concertos or concerto movements (their genre having the same word as the event in most languages) interspersed with songs and instrumental solos. Most often there would be two parts, or acts, with an interval. New works, of course, were the norm. Handel's music remained strong in British consciousness, but Haydn wrote most of his later symphonies (the new concert genre of the later 18th century) and quartets for concerts in London and Paris, and Mozart's output of symphonies and piano concertos was similarly concert driven.

Beethoven turned the arrow of necessity the other way: he would present a concert when he had new works to offer, as with the prodigious occasion in 1808 when his programme included his Fourth and Fifth Symphonies, Fourth Piano Concerto and Choral Fantasia. The enormous prestige of his music then contrived to fix the concert in two ways: as more compact and homogeneous (with the orchestra involved throughout) and as more beholden to great works of the past. By the 1870s concerts had assumed pretty much their modern form, with a concerto often in the first half and a symphony (or equivalent work) in the second, indicating the importance of display but the greater weight of sheer musical thought. Concerts also lost their spontaneity, as listeners came to require private communion within the public space: applause between movements was discouraged, as was any noise, gesture or motion during the performance.

During the first half of the 20th century new works became increasingly rare, producing a reaction in special concert series (e.g. Schoenberg's SOCIETY FOR PRIVATE MUSICAL PERFORMANCES, Boulez's DOMAINE MUSICAL) and festivals. Further efforts to change regular patterns came from the big institutions themselves towards the end of the 20th century. When embraced out of artistic need, not desperation, new styles of concert-giving – perhaps more informal, in unusual venues or with unconventional programmes – have been widely welcomed.

(2) (Fr.). Concert, concerto.

concertante (It.). Concerto-like. The word appears in titles, especially Sinfonia Concertante, but can also be used as a term for a work or instrumental part of concerto character. Thus Berlioz's *Harold en Italie* is a concertante piece, and Mozart's concert aria *Ch'io mi scordi di te* has a concertante piano part.

concert aria. Aria made for concert performance, though many Mozart works known as such were, in fact, intended for insertion in operas in the theatre. Mozart's true concert arias (e.g. 'Bella mia fiamma') tend to begin with recitative setting the scene. Others to write such arias have included Beethoven and Berg.

concert band. US large wind ensemble with percussion. Many are attached to colleges. They have their own repertory, including not only marches but also substantial works by Schoenberg and Hindemith.

concert behaviour. To some extent the audience member, too, is a performer, from whom particular actions are expected – as well as the crucial inaction of silence and stillness during the course of the music. Applause has its fixed moments: for the arrivals of the leader (in Britain), soloists and conductor, and at the end of a work.

concert dress. Convention for performers fixed in the mid 19th century, when it was normal evening wear for the upper and middle classes: white tie and tails for men, full gowns for women (black for orchestral players; soloists can be much more flamboyant). Conductors, soloists and orchestras sometimes make efforts to modernize or democratize their attire. Ensembles for new music, especially, often have a more relaxed standard of coloured shirts with black trousers or skirts.

concerted music. (1) Music with full ensemble, as opposed, for example, to dry recitative.

(2) Music with two or more soloists on equal terms.

Concertgebouw. See AMSTERDAM; ROYAL CONCERTGEBOUW ORCHESTRA.

concert grand. Large grand piano.

concert hall. Building for musical performance. Most concert halls are orchestral auditoria, seating around 3,000 audience members; many also have one or two smaller spaces within the same structure or nearby. Among the great concert halls are the Musikverein of Vienna, the Concertgebouw of Amsterdam, Carnegie Hall, the Berlin Philharmonie and Symphony Hall in Birmingham.

concertina. Small cousin of the accordion, with button keys in its hexagonal endpieces and a pleated bellows between. Patented in 1829 by Charles Wheatstone (1802–75), the instrument soon entered folk and popular culture, and was used by Grainger as a colourful interloper in the orchestra.

concertino (It., little concerto). (1) Soloist group in a concerto grosso.

(2) Small-scale or short concerto.

concertmaster (US). LEADER (UK). A woman in the position is still a concertmaster.

concerto (1) (Fr. *concert*, Ger. *Konzert*, pl. *Konzerte*, It. *concerto*, pl. *concerti*, though in modern Eng. normally 'concertos'). Work for solo instrument and orchestra; that has been the meaning since the late 18th century. The word has been thoroughly absorbed into English (though with roughly Italian pronunciation).

For almost two centuries from c.1600 the term was more various and ambiguous, emerging with – and, in the original Italian, nominally identified with – the concert. A concerto was what was played in concert: it could be any ensemble music, therefore, vocal as well as instrumental. In modern usage, as applied to music before the Classical period, the term is usually confined to works for instrumental ensemble from the later Baroque (from Corelli to Vivaldi), or sacred vocal pieces from the earlier (Schütz).

If Corelli's concertos became the most admired, he shared responsibility for establishing the Baroque genre with other composers, including his near namesake Torelli, who published the first examples (1692). Also important was Albinoni's first concerto publication (1700), for installing three-movement form like that of the opera overture, whereas Corelli's concertos have from four to six movements, being formally modelled on the contemporary church or chamber sonata. Also, where Corelli's concertos adumbrated the group-tutti textures of the CONCERTO GROSSO, those of Torelli, Albinoni and other northern Italians featured a violin soloist. Vivaldi then took up this model and made it more exciting, with phases of solo virtuosity spurred by recurring orchestral music, the ritornello.

The chief architect of the Classical concerto was Mozart, after the model provided by J.C. Bach and others of a first movement with four main sections, melding the alternating solo-tutti tactics of the Baroque concerto with the continuous strategy of sonata form. An orchestral introduction, still called the 'ritornello', with two contrasting themes (but both in the tonic) and the soloist accompanying, prepares for the solo exposition, led by the soloist and moving into the dominant. After that a second tutti ritornello, in the style of a development section on previous themes or a fantasia without them, is capped by a recapitulation (i.e. culminating repeat of the exposition) including, near the close, a cadenza. The Mozart concerto proceeds with a slow movement, followed by a finale with rondo elements, providing altogether a form that was taken up by Haydn and vigorously adapted by Beethoven (notably in having the soloist start his Fourth Piano Concerto).

Beethoven also changed the status of the soloist, from principal conversationalist to heroic protagonist. The early Romantic concerto veered towards virtuosity and poetry, becoming effectively an accompanied solo (Chopin, Schumann, Paganini), but later a different aspect of Beethoven's heritage was absorbed, in concertos emphasizing dramatic dialogue between soloist and orchestra (Liszt, Brahms, Tchaikovsky). Meanwhile the regularities of Classical structure were eroded, though the cadenza late in the first movement remained usual, right into the 21st century. For although 20th-century composers, notably Stravinsky, brought back 18th-century forms and formats, the concerto has powerfully maintained its position as the great opportunity for solo vehemence and display.

It has also survived as a title, even in the works of composers (Barraqué, Carter, Babbitt) wary of its sister term 'symphony'. Used more loosely, the word can denote any work for solo instrument and orchestra, including those manifesting their distance from Romantic-Classical form in alternative titles, such as the concertante variations of Franck and Tchaikovsky, Stravinsky's *Movements* and Messiaen's several compositions for piano and orchestra.

See CELLO CONCERTO; DOUBLE CONCERTO; PIANO CONCERTO; VIOLIN CONCERTO.

Michael Thomas Roeder *A History of the Concerto* (1994); Michael Steinberg *The Concerto* (1998); Joseph Kerman *Concerto Conversations* (1999)

(2) (It.). Concert, concerto.

Concerto for Orchestra. 20th-century genre, implying a work in which all orchestral sections have turns in the limelight. Hindemith's was among the first and Bartók's (f.p. Boston, 1 Dec 1944) remains the most famous; later examples included works by Lutosławski, Tippett and Carter.

concerto grosso (It., big concerto, pl. concerti grossi). Work in which a small group of soloists (the concertino) is contrasted with the full ensemble (the ripieno). The principal model – a key to the whole texture of Baroque music, vocal as much as instrumental – was Corelli's Op.6 set.

There are also examples by Torelli, Albinoni, Handel, Bach (some of the Brandenburg Concertos) and Geminiani.

concert overture. Overture written as a concert piece, e.g. Berlioz's *Le Corsaire*.

concert pitch (1) The international standard: A above middle C = 440 Hz.

(2) Performers' state of full readiness, so that a musician may be said to be 'at concert pitch'.

Concert Spirituel (Fr., Sacred Concert). Parisian concert series founded by Anne Danican Philidor in 1725 and surviving until 1790, with later revivals in Paris and elsewhere. Originally only sacred works and instrumental pieces were performed, but the repertory broadened.

Concertstück, Conzertstück. See KONZERTSTÜCK.

Concierto de Aranjuez. Guitar concerto by Rodrigo. Aranjuez, south of Madrid, was a favourite resort of 18th-century Spanish kings, known therefore to Domenico Scarlatti. First performance: Barcelona, 9 Nov 1940.

concitato (It.). Excited, especially as in *stile concitato*, the style of momentary expressive excitement found in Monteverdi's *Combattimento* and other works of that period.

concord. CONSONANCE.

Concord. Name Ives gave his Second Piano Sonata – in full 'Concord, Mass., 1840–60' – after the town that was the home of New England literary life at that time, the movements honouring Emerson, Hawthorne, the Alcotts and Thoreau. There are optional obbligatos for a viola in the first movement and a flute in the last. Ives published the score privately in 1920; the commercial edition of 1947 incorporates changes. First performance: Cos Cob, Conn., Nov 1938.

concrete music. See MUSIQUE CONCRÈTE.

condensed score. Short score.

conducting. Art of stimulating and guiding the musical performance of others, normally by the silent means of hand gestures (with or without a baton), looks and body language. In the form of CHEIRONOMY that art has a long history, and there is also pictorial and documentary evidence of choirmasters using batons (staffs of office) from around 1500. With the growth of instrumental ensembles in the 17th and 18th centuries, performances came to be directed more often by a violinist or keyboard player. An alternative was to beat out the rhythm audibly, with a stick on the floor or a table, a bemusingly crude practice that is said to have survived at the Paris Opera into the age of Rameau and Gluck. Conducting – by a non-player, and noiseless – re-emerged as the norm at the start of the 19th century, now for orchestral and opera performances. Spohr, among composer-conductors of this era, recorded the use of a baton, a roll of paper or a violin bow.

Conducting became desirable around 1800 for reasons perhaps more aesthetic than practical, having to do not so much with the size of ensembles (which had sometimes been just as large before) as with the new strongly unified voice of music in Beethoven's time. The divided authority of the 18th century – possibly shared by the principal violinist, the keyboard continuo performer and a baton-waver – was no longer admissible; music needed a single source of rhythm, phrasing and flow. Given that single source, it was possible for the orchestra to grow, for metres to become more complex, for tempos to fluctuate more freely, for new combinations of sounds to be explored – indeed, for all the skills of conducting to be engaged in the development of Romantic and modern orchestral music.

Beating time is the basis of conducting, and most conductors will give the beat with the right hand, holding a baton or not and staying more or less close to conventional arm movements (straight down and up for two in a bar; down, to the right and up for three in a bar; etc.). The left hand – and indeed the rest of the body, certainly not excluding the eyes – will then be available for other signals, inducements and controls. And though the conductor's gesticulations are primarily directed to the orchestra, they may also have a direct effect on the audience. Less visibly contributing to the performance will be the conductor's preparation – studying the score, devising bowings, creating a programme – and the joint work of rehearsal.

Max Rudolf *The Grammar of Conducting* (1950, ³1993)

conductor (Fr. *chef d'orchestre*, Ger. *Dirigent*, It. *direttore d'orchestra*). Person CONDUCTING. Perhaps because they were composers (like many a conductor since), Berlioz and Wagner in the mid 19th century made the conductor a second musical creator, responsible not only for keeping the performance together at the highest level but also for communicating an interpretation through the orchestra to the audience. The status of the conductor rose again in the early 20th century,

when recording gave a lasting life to performances. Harold C. Schonberg *The Great Conductors* (1968)

conductus (Lat., guide, pl. conductus). Latin setting of the 12th and 13th centuries, usually sacred and introduced, probably in southern France, to accompany ritual movement. It became a major vehicle of creative virtuosity for composers at Notre Dame in Paris in the first half of the 13th century, distinguished by free composition in up to four parts (not on a plainsong tenor, even in the less common cases when a chant text was set rather than a new one), modal rhythm and exuberant melismatic inventions following syllabic passages. Attention turned from it to the motet in the mid 13th century.

congas. Tall, narrow, barrel-shaped Afro-Cuban drums, usually played in pairs, with the fingers.

conjunct. Term used of a melody in which the intervals are mostly scale steps (i.e. seconds) rather than disjunct leaps.

Connolly, Justin (Riveagh) (b. London, 11 Aug 1933). British composer, an adherent of a strengthening modernism. He studied law before enrolling at the RCM in 1958; there followed lessons with Mel Powell at Yale (1963–5). Since then he has worked as a teacher (at the RCM and RAM), broadcaster and composer, his works including settings of Wallace Stevens and Hölderlin (*Scardanelli Dreams*, Op.37, mez, pf, 1997–8) as well as pieces for assorted chamber groupings.

Conon de Béthune (b. *c*.1160; d. 17 Dec 1219/20). Trouvère, participant in the Third and Fourth Crusades, remaining in Constantinople after the latter.

Conradi, Johann Georg (d. Oettingen, 22 May 1699). German composer, who was active mostly at small Saxon courts, apart from a period as music director of the Hamburg opera for several years in the 1690s. His Hamburg operas were the first there to include recitative and French stylistic elements.

Consecration of the House, The. See *Die* WEIHE DES HAUSES.

consecutive intervals. Instances of the same harmonic interval – usually fifth or octave – repeated from one chord to another, because two contrapuntal parts move in parallel. For example, where the two relevant parts both move up a step, the fifth G–D would be followed by the fifth A–E, i.e. there would be a pair of consecutive fifths.

Consecutive fifths and octaves were ruled a fault by theorists from c.1300 onwards, and they virtually disappeared from Western classical music a century or so later, disliked for their bareness. But after half a millennium of ostracism, consecutive fifths – basic to the sound of ORGANUM – arrived again in the music of Debussy, Bartók and Ravel.

consequent. Musical idea answering an ANTE-CEDENT.

conservatory, conservatoire (Fr.). Music college. See CURTIS INSTITUTE OF MUSIC; EASTMAN SCHOOL OF MUSIC; JUILLIARD SCHOOL; LISZT ACADEMY; OBERLIN COLLEGE CONSERVATORY OF MUSIC; PARIS CONSERVATOIRE; PEABODY INSTITUTE; ROYAL ACADEMY OF MUSIC; ROYAL COLLEGE OF MUSIC; SIBELIUS ACADEMY; TCHAIKOVSKY CONSERVATORY.

console. Desk at which an organist sits to play, provided with keyboards, stop knobs, pedals, etc.

consonance. Sense of harmony at relative rest, the opposite of 'dissonance'. Alternatively, a chord conveying that sense, when considered either in the abstract or in a particular musical situation. Thus the C major triad is a consonance, and the C major chord at the end of Mozart's 'Jupiter' Symphony is a consonance, in a largely consonant work.

Consonance is a psychological quality. Efforts to find it a rational basis began with the Babylonians, possibly in the 4th millennium BC, when the arrival of string instruments helped show that the most consonant intervals came from simple frequency ratios: 2:1 (octave), 3:2 (fifth), 4:3 (fourth) and their compounds. But judgements of consonance seem to depend also on norms within a musical tradition, otherwise it is hard to explain why Western musicians regularly deem the major sixth more consonant than the fourth. Some mix of nature (frequency ratios) and culture (harmonic language) must be at work in defining expectations.

consort. Small ensemble for the performance of music up to the later 17th century. Such a group might be of instrumentalists (e.g. a consort of viols), singers (a consort of voices) or both, and many ensembles specializing in medieval, Renaissance or Baroque music have used the word in their names. However, when the term was introduced (in 1575, from It. *concerto*), and for some decades after, it seems to have had the specific sense of a mixed instrumental sextet comprising flute, treble viol, bass viol, lute, bandora and cittern – i.e. what is now known as a BROKEN CONSORT. Extending the modern meaning of the word, 'consort music' implies music for viols and 'consort song' a song with accompaniment for viols, a genre particularly graced by Byrd.

Constant, Marius (b. Bucharest, 7 Feb 1925). Romanian–French composer-conductor, who trained at the conservatories of Bucharest and, immediately after the Second World War, Paris. He worked with Béjart and Petit on ballets in the 1950s–60s, founded the ensemble Ars Nova (1963) and taught orchestration at the Conservatoire (1974–88).

constructivism. Term borrowed from painting, where it implies simple geometrical shapes, as in Malevich and Mondrian. In music it generally suggests structural devices such as serialism or complex canon, as applied in the same period or later.

contemporary music. Term that became current in conditions of danger, when new music seemed in need of support from new institutions, such as the International Society for Contemporary Music (founded 1922). The term has retained an association with 20th-century modernism and so become more a definer of type than of period. Thus Varèse's *Hyperprism* (1922–3) might sound contemporary – even to listeners conceived long after it was – in ways that much later works do not.

contenance angloise (Fr., English manner). Much debated term used by Martin le Franc in the 1440s with reference to what Du Fay and Binchois had taken from Dunstable, usually interpreted as suave harmony liberally dosed with thirds.

Contes d'Hoffmann, Les (The Tales of Hoffmann). Opera by Offenbach to a libretto by Barbier after his and Carré's dramatization of stories by E.T.A. Hoffmann. Hoffmann (tenor), in a tavern with his friend Nicklausse (mezzo-soprano), tells stories of blighted love affairs with Olympia, who turns out to be a doll, Antonia, who dies singing, and Giulietta, who is fickle. He has no more luck with the real-time Stella. All four love objects are sung by the same soprano, and the same baritone or bass is also Hoffmann's perpetual nemesis, appearing as Lindorf (Stella's protector), the demonic inventor Coppélius (responsible for Olympia's lifelikeness), Dr Miracle (who lures Antonia to her death) and Dapertutto (who persuades Giulietta to steal Hoffmann's reflection). The celebrated Barcarolle comes at the start of the Giulietta act, set in Venice. Other numbers include Hoffmann's 'Kleinzach Legend' and his apostrophe to Antonia ('O Dieu! de quelle ivresse'), as well as Olympia's coloratura 'Les oiseaux dans la charmille'. Dapertutto's 'Scintille diamant', though adapted from music by the composer, was the work of the composer André Bloch and the librettist's son Pierre Barbier, whose early 20th-century edition, incorporating recitatives by Guiraud, remains current. First performance: Paris, 10 Feb 1881.

Conti, Francesco Bartolomeo (b. Florence, 20 Jan 1681; d. Vienna, 20 Jul 1732). Italian composer, a theorbist and creator of operas at the imperial court in Vienna from 1701, working with the librettists Zeno and Pietro Pariati. Ignazio Maria Conti (1699–1759), his son by the first of his three marriages, was also a musician in Vienna, but gave up composing for lack of official favour.

continental fingering. System in keyboard music of numbering the digits from 1 (thumb) to 5 (little finger), adopted in Britain in the 19th century and gradually ousting English fingering (with '+' for the thumb and the fingers numbered 1–4).

continuo. Foundation of ensemble performance throughout the Baroque period and beyond, for around two centuries from c.1600. Continuo instruments might include keyboards or plucked strings (instruments capable of playing harmony), often with one or more lower bowed strings. At the simplest, in a song or sonata, a harpsichord continuo would suffice, while 17th-century court opera performances might involve a lavish and colourful assembly of harpsichord, organ, harp, guitar, theorbo, etc.

The term is an abbreviation of 'basso continuo', by origin the bass line that was all that was marked in accompanimental parts. Continuo players would have to deduce from this and, of course, from the melody the appropriate harmonies, latterly guided by a FIGURED BASS. The extent to which harmonies should be arpeggiated or otherwise embellished was, and remains, a matter of awareness and taste. So does the need for a keyboard continuo in works where it is not prescribed (e.g. Haydn symphonies of different periods) or for the soloist in a Mozart piano concerto to play continuo in orchestral sections. The continuo survived as dry recitative accompaniment in opera into the early 19th century, but now with its part written out.

contrabass. DOUBLE BASS or, used adjectivally, as in 'contrabass clarinet', an indication of similar low range.

contrabasso (It., pl. *contrabassi*). Double bass.

contrabassoon. Double bassoon.

contrafactum (pl. contrafacta). Application of new words to a vocal piece; the practice or an instance of it. The term is virtually confined to medieval and Renaissance music, where there are innumerable examples, especially of replacing secular texts with sacred. But the same principle was used by Bach and Handel and has been used again in advertising since the 1950s.

contrafagotto (It.). Double bassoon.

contralto (Ger. *Alt*). Female voice of low range (a fifth below the SOPRANO), or a solo singer with that voice, the term ALTO being more normal for members of a chorus. The contralto had a place in the solo quartet of Classical-period masses, etc., but had little chance to shine as a soloist; all Mozart's female characters, for instance, are sopranos and mezzo-sopranos. Rossini wrote important contralto roles, and in his time the contralto became a substitute for the fading castrato (a responsibility retained until the late 20th century, when countertenors acceded to this repertory). As with the bass, low sound has often been a metaphor for darkness (Ulrica in *Un ballo in maschera*) or majestic authority (Erda in the *Ring*), but the contralto's maternal resonance has also made her a bestower of balm (in Brahms, Mahler and Elgar, for instance). Current singers of this repertory often prefer to call themselves mezzos.

contrappunto (It.). Counterpoint.

contrapunctus (Lat.). Baroque German term for fugue, as used by Bach in *Die Kunst der Fuge*.

contrapuntal. Displaying counterpoint.

contrary motion. Movement of two parts in opposite directions pitchwise. For instance, keyboard scales may be played in contrary motion (hands moving apart and together again) or similar motion (hands moving in parallel). A melody may also be said to proceed in contrary motion with respect to a previous form; see INVERSION (1).

contratenor (Lat., against the tenor). Term used in the 14th century and early 15th for a part added in the range of the tenor. Later in the 15th century, when three-part writing gave way to four-part, the terms contratenor altus (hence contralto) and contratenor bassus were introduced.

contrebasse (Fr.). Double bass.

contrebasson (Fr.). Double bassoon.

contredanse (Fr., from Eng. country dance). Popular formal dance of the period of Mozart and Beethoven, both of whom wrote sets. It was in 2/4 or 6/8, in simple, tuneful phrases, and was first gentrified at the French court in the 1680s, spreading from there to Germany and Austria.

Converse, Frederick Shepherd (b. Newton, Mass., 5 Jan 1871; d. Westwood, Mass., 8 Jun 1940). US composer, a latterday New England symphonist. He studied with Paine at Harvard (1889–93), Chadwick, and Rheinberger in Munich (1896–8). A wealthy man, he taught briefly at the New England Conservatory (1898–1902) and Harvard (1903–7), then retired to his estate to compose and raise a family. His *The Pipe of Desire* (1905) was the first US opera presented by the Metropolitan, in 1910; he also wrote five symphonies and tone poems (*The Mystic Trumpeter*, 1904).

Conyngham, Barry (b. Sydney, 27 Aug 1944). Australian composer, originally a jazz musician, who studied with Raymond Hanson, with Sculthorpe and with Takemitsu in Japan (1970). His works range from oriental fragility to thoroughgoing drama.

Cooke, Arnold (Atkinson) (b. Gomersal, Yorks., 4 Nov 1906). British composer, who studied with Hindemith in Berlin after Cambridge. He taught in Manchester before wartime naval service, and in 1947 became professor at Trinity College, London. His works include four symphonies, concertos and three quartets.

Cooke, Deryck (Victor) (b. Leicester, 14 Sep 1919; d. Thornton Heath, 26 Oct 1976). British music scholar, who produced an admired 'performing version' of Mahler's Tenth Symphony on the basis of the composer's draft (1960) and a notable theory of musical expression as conveyed by melodic shape (*The Language of Music*, 1959).

Cooke, Henry (b. ?Lichfield, *c*.1615; d. Hampton Court, 13 Jul 1672). British choirmaster, trained in the Chapel Royal, which he revived on the restoration of the monarchy in 1660. As a singer he was noted for his command of the Italian style, which he communicated to his charges, Blow among them.

Cooke, John (d. ?1419). English composer, represented by nine pieces in the Old Hall manuscript. These indicate he was close to Power, possibly a pupil.

Coolidge, Elizabeth Sprague (b. Chicago, Oct 1864; d. Cambridge, Mass., 4 Nov 1953). US patron of chamber music, who commissioned works by Bartók, Stravinsky, Schoenberg, Berg and Webern.

coperti (It., covered). Instruction to cover drums (usually timpani) with cloth to damp the sound.

Copland, Aaron (b. Brooklyn, 14 Nov 1900; d. North Tarrytown, NY, 2 Dec 1990). US composer, an East Coast city boy of Jewish family who created in his music the landscape of the West, with tunes close to US folksongs and hymns, and a lean harmonic style, evocative of the open prairie. In his 20s and 30s he was a try-everything modernist, and in his 60s he ventured after Stravinsky into intensive serialism, but the central achievement of his maturity was to give pioneer heroism its music.

Born to prospering immigrant parents from western Russia, he studied in New York with Goldmark (1917–21) and in Paris with Boulanger (1921–4), one of her first US pupils. She encouraged his Stravinskian orientation (he already admired Debussy), which was useful when, back in New York, he decided to make his music more national by drawing on jazz. But after that brief episode, which produced *Music for the Theatre* and the Piano Concerto, he moved into a more personal world of hard-edged sonorities and compact form in his Piano Variations (1930), a piece almost serial in its close working of a seven-note theme.

Again he moved on, motivated now by the new national emergency of the Depression, its aftermath and war. But curiously his way to the US vernacular of his cowboy ballet *Billy the Kid* (1938) was by way of the Hispanic revelry of *El Salón México*, a lively portrait of a Mexico City bar. With *Billy* he became effectively the US composer laureate, a position he filled with extraordinary success in creating great musical occasions (*Lincoln Portrait*, Third Symphony), a supreme portrayal of the country as the land of innocent opportunity (*Appalachian Spring*) and national songbooks of Dickinson settings and folksong arrangements. Through most of this highly productive period, from 1932 to the mid-1940s, he lived with Victor Kraft, a photographer, though he necessarily kept his private life private while fulfilling his public role as a spokesman for his fellow composers and for music generally. He also remained committed to socialism.

That commitment – and the populist style that went with it – became hard to sustain as the Cold War hardened in the late 1940s, and in his Piano Quartet (1950) he began to return to serialism again; he also left Manhattan in 1947 to live in the country. He went further towards the fractured language of current Stravinsky in his Piano Fantasy and two bold orchestral scores of the 1960s: *Connotations* and *Inscape*. If thereby he abandoned his role as national composer, he continued to foster young composers at Tanglewood and conduct their music on programmes with his own, at home and abroad. After 1972 he found himself virtually unable to compose, perhaps as a first sign of the mental clouding that overtook him.

Howard Pollack *Aaron Copland* (1999)

Operas: *The Second Hurricane* (school opera: Edwin Denby), 1936, f.p. New York, 1937; *The Tender Land* (Horace Everett), 1952–4, f.p. New York, 1954, rev 1955

Ballets: *Grohg*, 1922–5; *Billy the Kid*, 1938; *Rodeo*, 1942; APPALACHIAN SPRING, 1943–4; *Dance Panels*, 1959, rev 1962

Symphonies: No.1, 1924, rev 1928; *Dance Symphony*, 1930 (after *Grohg*); No.2 (*Short Symphony*), 1932–3; No.3, 1944–6

Other orchestral works: *Music for the Theatre*, 1925; Piano Concerto, 1926; *Symphonic Ode*, 1927–9; *Statements*, 1932–5; *El Salón México*, 1933–6; *Music for Radio*, 1937; *An Outdoor Overture*, 1938; *Quiet City*, cor ang, tpt, str, 1939; *Fanfare for the Common Man*, 1942; *Lincoln Portrait*, speaker, orch, 1942; *Music for Movies*, 1942; *Danzón cubano*, 1944; Clarinet Concerto, 1947–8; *Preamble for a Solemn Occasion*, speaker, orch, 1949; Orchestral Variations, 1957 (arr of Piano Variations); *Connotations*, 1962; *Emblems*, band, 1964; *Music for a Great City*, 1964; *Inscape*, 1967; 3 Latin American Sketches, 1959–72; etc.

Film scores: *Of Mice and Men*, 1939; *Our Town*, 1940; *North Star*, 1943; *The Red Pony*, 1948; *The Heiress*, 1948; etc.

Chamber: 2 Pieces, str qt, 1923; 2 Pieces, vn, pf, 1926; *Vitebsk*, pf trio, 1928; Sextet, cl, str qt, pf, 1937 (arr of *Short Symphony*); Violin Sonata, 1942–3; Piano Quartet, 1950; Nonet, 3 vn, 3 va, 3 vc, 1960; Duo, fl, pf, 1971; *Threnodies I–II*, fl, str trio, 1971–3

Piano: Piano Variations, 1930; Sonata, 1939–41; 4 Piano Blues, 1926–48; Piano Fantasy, 1952–7; *Danza de Jalisco*, 2 pf, 1963; *Night Thoughts*, 1972; arrs of other works, etc.

Songs: 12 Poems of Emily Dickinson, 1949–50; Old American Songs, 2 sets, 1950, 1952; etc.

Other works: choral pieces, incidental music

Coppélia. Full-length ballet score by Delibes, to a scenario by Charles Nuitter and Arthur Saint-Léon (the choreographer) after Hoffmann's story *The Sandman*. First performance: Paris, 2 May 1870.

Coprario, John (b. ?c.1570–80; d. ?London, 1626). English violist-composer, who Italianized his name from the original Cowper or Cooper – possibly with the justification of having visited Italy as a young man. He served various noble and royal patrons under James I (1603–25), and wrote elegies for the Earl of Devonshire (*Funeral Tears*, 1606, including 'In darkness let me dwell') and Prince Henry (*Songs of Mourning*, 1613, to words by Campion). Charles I gave him a post, but he died barely more than a year into the new reign. The bulk of his output consists of fantasias for viols.

copyright. The right to copy text, music or images. By a long succession of national laws and international conventions, beginning with the first British copyright act (1709) and including most recently the Berne Copyright Union (1886, rev 1971) and Universal Copyright Convention (1952, rev 1971), this right has been strengthened to provide writers, composers, editors and performers with ownership of their work throughout their lifetimes, and their heirs with ownership for 75 years thereafter. Copyright in books is normally retained by the author, whose contract gives the publisher particular rights to print, sell and otherwise utilize the work. Music publishers, however, generally insist on copyright for themselves, the justification being that the musical market is international and complicated by PERFORMING RIGHTS, so that music enters a vast and complex arena of rights legislation. US law requires a copyright notice on each copy in the form of the symbol © (for printed copies) or ℗ (for sound reproductions) plus the year of first publication and the owner's name.

Photocopiers and tape or disc recorders have made it possible for almost anyone to infringe copyright, and fees are collected from manufacturers and libraries to recompense authors and publishers for private abuses. But works and recordings in copyright are regularly used without permission or charge in commercial environments (as background music in restaurants, for example), and distribution through the Internet is proving even harder to control.

Coq d'or, Le. See *The* GOLDEN COCKEREL.

cor (Fr.). Horn. Hence *cor simple* (natural horn), *cor à pistons* (valve horn), *cor de chasse* (hunting horn), *cor de basset* (basset horn), COR ANGLAIS, etc.

cor anglais (Fr.). Tenor oboe, also known in translated form as 'English horn', in use since the early 18th century. There is nothing particularly English about it, any more than there is anything French about the French horn. According to one charming if unconvincing story it was originally named (in German) for the angels, since it looked like the celestial instruments shown in medieval pictures. It is a TRANSPOSING INSTRUMENT, pitched a fifth below the oboe, and distinguished not only by its larger size but by its bulbous bell – not to mention its seductive sound, as used by Berlioz (*Symphonie fantastique*), Wagner (Act 3 of *Tristan*), Franck (in his Symphony, to the dismay of conservative critics, for whom the Berlioz example would only have intensified the outrageousness of presenting a theatre instrument in a symphony), Dvořák ('New World') and Sibelius (*The Swan of Tuonela*).

corant, coranto. COURANTE.

corda (It., pl. *corde*). String, hence UNA CORDA, TRE CORDE, *corda vuota* (open string), etc.

cordance. Place of an interval on a scale from consonance to dissonance, irrespective of musical context. Compare SONANCE.

corde (Fr.). String, hence *cordes* (snares, string orchestra), *corde à vide* (open string), etc.

Corder, Frederick (b. London, 26 Jan 1852; d. London, 21 Aug 1932). British composer and, with his wife Henrietta, translator of Wagner's librettos, including *Parsifal* (1879) and the *Ring* (1882). He wrote operas himself, notably *Nordisa* (Liverpool, 1887), and from 1888 was professor at the RAM.

cordier (Fr.). Tailpiece.

Cordier, Baude (b. Rheims, *fl.* early 15th century). French composer, some of whose works (nine rondeaux, a ballade and a *Gloria*) show ARS SUBTILIOR features while others are in the more rhythmically flowing and tuneful style of the emergent Renaissance.

cordiera (It.). Tailpiece.

Corelli, Arcangelo (b. Fusignano, 17 Feb 1653; d. Rome, 8 Jan 1713). Italian violinist-composer, whose works provided a model to his age. His output was largely and neatly confined to six volumes, each of 12 instrumental compositions: trio sonatas, solo violin sonatas and concerti grossi. These were instant classics, making him the first composer widely (and lastingly) esteemed for instrumental music.

Born into the landed gentry, he studied in Faenza, Lugo and, from 1666, Bologna, where he was admitted to the Accademia Filarmonica in 1670. By 1675 he was in Rome, becoming admired for his playing in church, and four years later joining Queen Christina's service as a chamber musician; to her he dedicated his first volume, of trio sonatas (1681). In 1682 he found his life's partner in his pupil Matteo Fornari, through whom he came into contact with Cardinal Pamphili. Two further volumes of trio sonatas, the earlier dedicated to Pamphili, must have been tried out by the house trio he formed with Fornari and the cellist-composer Giovanni Lorenzo Lulier at the concerts the cardinal gave on Sundays. As Pamphili's music master (from 1687) he also led orchestral performances. In 1690, after a return visit to Bologna, he entered the service of another music-loving cardinal, Pietro Ottoboni. He met, and performed with, Handel before, in 1708, retiring to work up his final volume, of concertos, published by Fornari posthumously. By all accounts, he was a man of serene disposition, producing music whose balance and grace fitted it for lofty status. His collections were repeatedly reprinted throughout the 18th century, to be performed, studied, imitated and honoured, notably by Couperin, in a work speaking of the veneration in which he was held: *Le Parnasse, ou l'Apothéose de Corelli*.

Peter Allsop *Arcangelo Corelli* (1999)

Works (with publication dates): 12 Trio Sonatas, Op.1, 1681; 12 Trio Sonatas, Op.2, 1685; 12 Trio Sonatas, Op.3, 1689; 12 Trio Sonatas, Op.4, 1694; 12 Violin Sonatas, Op.5, 1700; 12 Concerti Grossi, Op.6 , 1714 (No.8 'Christmas Concerto', G minor); few other sonatas

Corigliano, John (Paul) (b. New York, 16 Feb 1938). US composer, whose range runs boldly from fantasy 18th-century to a modern urban world of film, rock and hectic expression. The son of the New York Philharmonic's leader, he studied at Columbia, with Giannini at the Manhattan School and with Creston. He worked as a programmer with classical radio (1959–64) and music producer for CBS TV (1961–72); since 1968 he has taught at various New York colleges. His works include the opera *The Ghosts of Versailles* (libretto by William M. Hoffman after Beaumarchais, Met, 1991), two symphonies (1989, 2000), film scores (including *The Red Violin*, 1997, for which he won an Oscar) and concertos.

Coriolan. Overture by Beethoven for a play by his fellow Viennese Heinrich Joseph von Collin with the same hero as Shakespeare's *Coriolanus*. First performance: Vienna, Mar 1807.

cori spezzati (It., broken choirs). Groups placed in different parts of a building to perform POLY-CHORAL music.

Cornago, Johannes (b. ?Cornago, near Calahorra, c.1400; d. ?Burgos, after 1474). Spanish composer, active largely in Naples as musician and almoner to the Aragonese kings. He brought a personal touch to the international Franco-Netherlandish style in sacred music (notably the three-part mass *Ayo visto de la mappa mundi*, possibly connected with a world map made for Fernando I) and Spanish songs.

Cornelius, (Carl August) Peter (b. Mainz, 24 Dec 1824; d. Mainz, 26 Oct 1874). German composer, remembered for one opera and one song, and for his gentle and upright presence among the great Romantics: Schumann, Berlioz, Liszt, Wagner and Brahms. Born into a theatre family, he began his career as a theatre violinist in Mainz and studied in Berlin before joining Liszt's circle in Weimar in 1852. There he wrote songs, mostly to his own words, and the opera *Der Barbier von Bagdad*, for which again he wrote the text. Bizarrely, this fine, humorous and colourfully exotic piece was the spark that ignited trouble between Liszt and his Weimar enemies, ending an episode in Liszt's life – and in that of Cornelius, who went the next year to Vienna. There he enjoyed Brahms's friendship but was drawn closer to Wagner, who induced him to move to Munich in 1865 as an assistant and pet, somewhat sidelined as Cosima gained influence. He belatedly married, but achieved little more creatively.

Operas (librettos by the composer): *Der* BARBIER VON BAGDAD, 1855–8, f.p. Weimar, 1858; *Der Cid*, 1860–62, f.p. Weimar, 1865
Other works: *Weihnachtslieder*, Op.8, v, pf, 1856 (No.3 'Die Könige'); other songs and duets, mixed and male choruses, few early instrumental pieces

cornemuse (Fr.). Bagpipe. Also a shawm-like instrument alternatively known as a cornamusa.

cornet. (1) (Fr. *cornet à pistons*, Ger. *Cornett, Kornett*, It. *cornetta*). Valved brass instrument, normally in B♭, similar in form to the trumpet, but with a warmer, freer sound, thanks to the deeper mouthpiece and fuller bell. It was invented c.1828 by applying valves to the posthorn, and became a regular instrument in bands and dance orchestras, besides being employed in the symphony orchestra as a replacement for, or in conjunction with, trumpets, especially in France. Some composers have used it also for its associations with popular festivity, notably Stravinsky in *Petrushka*.
(2) Cornett.

cornett (Fr. *cornet à bouquin*, Ger. *Zink*, It. *cornetto*). Wooden trumpet of the late 15th to late 17th centuries: a carved pipe of conical bore, often slightly curved (in imitation of the animal horns from which it derived), with a mouth-piece, to be played with vibrating lips. The antique-looking name usefully distinguishes the instrument from the brass cornet; the Italian term is also borrowed.

The usual cornett is the treble, with a range from the G below middle C up to D in alt in the most brilliant music of the 17th century, when cornettists were capable of great agility. Much more rarely required are the cornettino (a fifth or fourth above the standard instrument) and the tenor cornett (a fifth below). Cornetts and trombones (sackbuts) formed a common ensemble supporting choral music in works by Gabrieli and Schütz, and also in earlier polyphonic music, such as that of Palestrina and Victoria. One of the instrument's last formal appearances was in Gluck's *Orfeo*: it was reintroduced in the 1880s for performances of that work, having recently died out as a participant in German tower music.

cornetto (It., pl. *cornetti*). Cornett.

corno (It., pl. *corna*). Horn. Hence *corno a mano* or *corno naturale* (natural horn), *corno cromatico, corno a macchina, corno a pistoni* or *corno ventile* (valve horn), *corno da caccia* (hunting horn), *corno di bassetto* (basset horn), *corno inglese* (cor anglais), etc.

Cornysh, William (d. 1523). English composer and writer, associated with Westminster Abbey, as was an earlier musician of the same name (d. c.1502), presumably his father. He was in court service by 1493 and became Master of the Children of the Chapel Royal in 1509. Plays and pageants by him were presented in London and at the Field of the Cloth of Gold (June 1520); all are lost, as is much of his music. What survives presents a patchy picture: possibly the English polyphonic songs (including 'A robin, gentle robin' and 'Woefully arrayed') were by him and the Latin church music (including flamboyant settings of the *Magnificat* and *Stabat mater*) by the elder William Cornysh.

coro (It., pl. *cori*). Chorus.

Coro (Choir). Work by Berio for 40 singers, each with an instrumentalist, proceeding through massive tuttis on words by Neruda that punctuate smaller ensembles in various ethnic styles. First performance: Donaueschingen, 24 Oct 1976.

coronation. Ceremony of crowning (normally a monarch). English coronations decked with new anthems, fanfares and marches included those of James I (1603; Tomkins), Charles I (1625; Tomkins), James II (1685; Purcell, Blow), George II (1727; Handel), Edward VII (1902; Parry, Saint-Saëns), George V (1911; Elgar), George VI (1937; Walton) and Elizabeth II (1953; Walton, Bax). Coronations have also prompted operas, among them *La clemenza di Tito*, *Il viaggio a Reims* and *Gloriana*, while *Le Prophète* has a coronation on stage.

Coronation. Name given two Mozart works performed during the celebrations around the coronation of Leopold II in Prague (1790), though neither work was new: the Mass in C, K.317 and the Piano Concerto in D, K.537.

corpo di musica (It.). Military band.

corps de rechange (Fr.). Tuning slide, crook.

Corps glorieux, Les (The Bodies in Glory). Organ work by Messiaen, subtitled 'seven brief visions of the life of the resurrected': 1 *Subtilité des corps glorieux*, 2 *Les Eaux de la grâce*, 3 *L'Ange aux parfums*, 4 *Combat de la mort et de la vie* (the big centrepiece), 5 *Force et agilité des corps glorieux*, 6 *Joie et clarté des corps glorieux*, 7 *Le Mystère de la Sainte Trinité*. First performance: Paris, 15 Nov 1943.

Correa (de Arauxo), Francisco (b. *c*.1576–7; d. Segovia, Oct 1654). Spanish organist-composer, who published a volume of 69 pieces of progressive difficulty (1626), extending from Cabezón's style into complexities of metre, harmony and figure. He was organist of San Salvador, Seville (1599–1636), Jaén Cathedral (1636–40) and Segovia Cathedral (1640–53).

Corregidor, Der (The Magistrate). Opera by Wolf to a libretto by Rosa Mayreder after Alarcón's novel *El sombrero de tres picos*. The Corregidor (tenor) sets out to seduce Frasquita (mezzo-soprano), but is foiled and himself cuckolded by her husband Lukas (baritone). First performance: Mannheim, 7 Jun 1896.

corrente (It.). (1) Flowing.

(2) COURANTE.

Corrette, Michel (b. Rouen, 1709; d. Paris, 22 Jan 1795). French organist-composer. He was a supplier and arranger of lighter style concertos, ariettes and sonatas in abundance, as well as methods, through a working life of over six decades. The son of an organist-composer, he held various positions with French churches and dignitaries.

Corri, Domenico (b. Rome, 4 Oct 1746; d. London, 22 May 1825). Italian musical businessman, active mostly in Britain. He studied in Rome and with Porpora in Naples (1763–7), after which he returned to Rome and married. A favourable mention in Burney's dispatches led to an invitation from the Musical Society of Edinburgh, where he arrived in 1771 and stayed till *c*.1790, when he took the family to London, leaving his brother Natale (1765–1822) in charge of his Edinburgh concerns. In London he formed a publishing partnership with Dussek, his son-in-law, and wrote operas as well as sonatas illustrating contemporary events. His sons Philip Anthony (?1784–1832), Montague Philip (?1784–1849) and Haydn (1785–1860) all had musical careers, as did many later descendants. Philip Anthony went to Baltimore, changed his name to Arthur Clifton and wrote an opera (*The Enterprise*, 1822), songs and piano pieces.

Corsi, Jacopo (b. Florence, 17 July 1561; d. Florence, 29 Dec 1602). Italian aristocratic amateur, in rivalry with Bardi, whose departure from Florence in 1592 left him free to encourage the development of opera. He started the setting of Rinuccini's *Dafne* that Peri completed, and it was at his house that the work was first presented (1598). The ensuing Rinuccini–Peri–Caccini *Euridice* was his wedding gift to Maria de' Medici and Henri IV.

Corteccia, (Pier) Francesco (b. Florence, 27 Jul 1502; d. Florence, 7 Jun 1571). Italian composer. The leading Florentine musician of his time, he was famed for his madrigals and was the first composer to publish a whole volume (1544). Trained as a choirboy, he held church appointments and first entered Medici service in 1531. His madrigals and intermedi for the wedding of Cosimo I (1539) were published, as were several books of madrigals and motets.

Cortot, Alfred (Denis) (b. Nyon, 26 Sep 1877; d. Lausanne, 15 Jun 1962). French pianist, especially admired for his poetic touch in Schumann, Chopin and Ravel, and for his work in a trio with Thibaud and Casals. He studied at the Paris Conservatoire with Chopin's pupil Decombes and with Diémer, completed his training in 1896, and began his career as a coach and assistant conductor at Bayreuth (1898–1901), returning to Paris to conduct the first performances there of *Götterdämmerung*, *Parsifal* and the *Missa solemnis*. From 1905, when the trio was founded, he concentrated again on the piano.

Così fan tutte. Opera by Mozart, titled in full *Così fan tutte, ossia La scuola degli amanti* (Women are All the Same, or The School for Lovers) to a libretto by Da Ponte. Ferrando (tenor) and Guglielmo (baritone) agree to a wager with Don Alfonso (bass) on the faithfulness of their sweethearts, Dorabella (mezzo-soprano) and Fiordiligi (soprano). The young men, disguised, besiege each other's beloved and, with the help of the lighthearted maidservant Despina (mezzo-soprano), both are successful in their adopted roles and therefore distraught in reality. With disguises off, the story ends happily, but uneasily. The opera was little appreciated until the later 20th century, which recognized its realism about pretence and its play-acting about reality. Its numbers include the farewell trio 'Soave sia il vento', Fiordiligi's refusal 'Come scoglio' and her poignant 'Ei parte – Per pietà', Ferrando's seductive 'Un' aura amorosa' and a garden wind serenade. First performance: Vienna, 26 Jan 1790.

Costa, Michael (Andrew Agnus) (b. Naples, 4 Feb 1808; d. Hove, 29 Apr 1884). Italian–British conductor, knighted in 1869. His teacher Zingarelli sent him to England in 1829 and he stayed. As music director from 1832 of the King's Theatre in London (subsequently Her Majesty's), he introduced conducting with the baton and was much admired. He left to found the Royal Italian Opera at Covent Garden (1846–68) and conduct the Philharmonic Society (1846–54), then returned (1871–81); he also conducted oratorio regularly in London, Birmingham and elsewhere, and made some contributions to the genre, including *Eli* (1855) and *Naaman* (1864). The former must have been the work that reached Rossini: 'Good old Costa,' the older composer reported, 'has sent me an oratorio score and a Stilton cheese; the cheese was very fine.'

Costeley, Guillaume (b. Fontanges, Auvergne, 1530/1; d. Evreux, 28 Jan 1606). French composer, almost exclusively of four-part chansons. Probably in Paris by 1554, he joined the circle around the Comtesse de Retz that included Ronsard and other poets, and participated in classicizing endeavours, exploring microtones (in *Seigneur Dieu ta pitié*) and MUSIQUE MESUREE. He became composer to the boy king Charles IX in 1560; he then published

a complete edition of his 100 chansons and three motets (1570), and retired to Evreux. Though for a while he spent winter back at court, he seems to have stopped composing.

Cottrau, Teodoro (b. Naples, 7 Dec 1827; d. Naples, 30 Mar 1879). Italian publisher and composer of Neapolitan songs (most famously 'Santa Lucia').

couac (Fr., quack). Nasty noise from a defective or mishandled clarinet.

coulé (Fr.). Flowing.

Couleurs de la Cité Céleste (Colours of the Heavenly City). Work by Messiaen for solo piano with an ensemble of clarinets, brass and percussion. First performance: Donaueschingen, 17 Oct 1964.

coulisse (Fr.). Slide of a trombone or slide trumpet. Also *coulisse à accorder* (tuning slide).

Coulthard, Jean (b. Vancouver, 10 Feb 1908; d. Vancouver, 9 Mar 2000). Canadian composer, pioneer of music from the Pacific coast. Trained first by her mother, she studied at the RCM with Vaughan Williams (1928–30) and during the next two decades had lessons with Copland, Bartók and Schoenberg. She taught at the University of British Columbia (1947–73) and wrote four symphonies and three quartets.

counter-exposition. Term from academic fugal analysis denoting a second exposition in the tonic.

counter-fugue. Fugue in which the subject is first answered in inversion.

counterpoint (from Lat. *contra punctum*, against note). Art of combining musical lines by rule, or music so produced, or a line in that music. Some examples may help clarify these linked meanings. A composer may study counterpoint (indeed, most do) in order to write counterpoint. A piece may include a counterpoint to a melody, or, to use another formulation, a line in counterpoint with a melody. Generally there is the expectation of a diatonic context, which is not so with POLYPHONY: Messiaen's birdsong choruses, for example, are more comfortably described as polyphonic than as contrapuntal (to use the standard adjectival form).

The term – and with it the start of an enormous theoretical apparatus – goes back to c.1330. Initially the art was that of writing a new line (discant) in counterpoint with an old one (tenor), and then adding another (contratenor), and perhaps another – this last being the bass part, which through the 15th century became at once normal and harmonically fundamental. At the same time contrapuntal composition became a matter not of adding one part to another but of creating all four (to give the usual case) together.

From the first the rules were primarily harmonic, concerning the appropriate placement of dissonant and consonant intervals. Less was said about speed, which could be much faster in added counterpoints than in the tenor. As modality moved towards diatonic tonality in the 15th century, though, so counterpoint became concerned with maintaining equivalent harmonic rhythm in all parts, a synchrony or gearing of movement towards the eventual cadence. Counterpoint developed, therefore, thoroughly intertwined with harmony.

The euphonious counterpoint of the later 16th century received its theoretical framework in Zarlino's treatise, and remained in esteem and development, now as 'strict counterpoint', after the new Baroque style of melody-plus-accompaniment had been introduced. This contrapuntal style, just as it was being magnificently practised by Bach, was codified by Fux, whose *Gradus ad Parnassum* provided the basis for the study of counterpoint into modern times.

With its dependence on rule and authority, counterpoint after Bach and Fux gained connotations of learning, to be displayed with humble pride (Bruckner) or swagger (Wagner), to suggest historical awareness (Mozart) or arcane knowledge (Busoni), within traditional forms (fugue, chorale prelude) or elsewhere. It lived on through the extended and avoided tonality of the 20th century – indeed, it thrived, for its rules of melodic correpondence were interpreted as applicable outside the harmonic environment they had been set to uphold. The music of Stravinsky and Ligeti also demonstrated that playfulness, as much as probity, is part of the contrapuntal ideal.

Walter Piston *Counterpoint* (1947); Kent Kennan *Counterpoint* (1959, ⁴1999)

counter-subject. A second theme introduced as a counterpoint to the subject in a fugue.

countertenor. Usual term now for the highest adult male voice, singing in the alto register by means of FALSETTO. This kind of voice survived – through centuries of neglect elsewhere – in English cathedral choirs, whence it was brought into concert halls and opera houses thanks to Deller and others in the mid 20th century. The revival of Handel's operas was assisted by the availability of countertenors to sing castrato parts,

and some have also explored unusual repertory for their voice – Schubert, Berlioz – besides adding new works.

Country Gardens. Grainger's arrangement of an English morris dance tune, in several versions: for piano (one or two players), two pianos (two or four players), descant and treble recorders, or any two instruments in C. There are numerous arrangements by other hands for forces from solo accordion to choir and orchestra.

coup d'archet (Fr.). Bowstroke, especially as in PREMIER COUP D'ARCHET.

coup de glotte (Fr., glottis stroke). Lightly percussive aspiration used to start a phrase on a vowel, advocated by the younger García and much debated since.

coup de langue (Fr., tongue stroke). Flick of the tongue required to articulate in playing a wind instrument.

Couperin. French musical family with origins in the region of Chaumes, about 30 miles (50km) southeast of Paris. Musical talents increased down the generations from Mathurin (1569–1640) through his son Charles (c.1595–1654), a local organist, to Charles's sons Louis, François and Charles. Louis established the family's hold on the organ at St Gervais in Paris, where he was succeeded by his brother Charles (1638–79), while François (c.1631–c.1710) would seem to have been a freelance performer and teacher. Charles's son François 'le Grand', the outstanding composer, took over at St Gervais and was assisted and followed by his cousin Nicolas (1680–1748), son of his uncle François. Nicolas in turn was succeeded by his son Armand Louis (1727–89), his grandsons Pierre Louis (1755–89) and Gervais François (1759–1826), and, briefly, his great-granddaughter Céleste Thérèse (1793–1860).

(1) **Louis** (b. Chaumes, c.1626; d. Paris, 29 Aug 1661). Keyboard composer-performer. In Paris by 1651, he was appointed organist at St Gervais in 1653, and lived there in the organist's lodgings with his brothers while also playing at court. His organ pieces include fugues distinguished by strong themes and fiery movement; for the harpsichord he wrote preludes, allemandes, courantes, sarabandes, chaconnes/passacailles, etc., adding to the tradition of his patron Chambonnières something from Froberger (whom he met), and something from his own bold imagination.

(2) **François 'le Grand'** (b. Paris, 10 Nov 1668; d. Paris, 11 Sep 1733). Keyboard composer-performer. In his manifold transpositions of

human expression and character into the play of fingers at a keyboard, he left images of a frivolous age given dignity by his wisdom, wistfulness and wit.

Aged 10 when his father died, he was promised the organist's post at St Gervais and taken on for training by Jacques Thomelin, while increasingly through his teens he assisted the temporary St Gervais organist, Lalande. He took over formally at 18, married at 20, and in 1690 brought out a pair of organ masses. Three years later he succeded Thomelin as one of the royal organists, beginning a productive and various life at court also as a harpsichord teacher and composer of chamber and chapel music. His success allowed him to move into larger private accommodation (his cousin Nicolas eventually moved back into the St Gervais organist's lodgings) but may have delayed him in publishing his harpsichord and chamber music, which came out in several volumes between 1713 and 1730.

Of his character and private existence very little is known. His elder daughter became a nun (and perhaps also an organist), his younger briefly a court harpsichordist and his son a soldier. Not much distracts from the image of someone whose appreciation of life went into his music. He was drawn to the new Italian sonata as represented by Corelli, but he was drawn also to the French tradition whose presiding deity was Lully: he wrote 'apotheoses' of both and professed his intention to create a *réunion des goûts* (union of tastes). Most of his harpsichord pieces fall into the rhythms and binary forms of dance movements, but many have titles that mark them out as portraits, pictures or fantasies. They remained, two centuries and more later, a model for Ravel (*Le Tombeau de Couperin*) and Richard Strauss.

Wilfrid Mellers *François Couperin and the French Classical Tradition* (1950, ²1987)

Published works are listed below, with dates of publication.

Sacred: *Leçons de Ténèbres*, 1713–17 (*Premier leçon, Seconde leçon*, s, con; *Troisième leçon*, 2 s, con); chamber-scale motets

Chamber: *Concerts royaux*, 1724 (*concerts* 1–4); *Les Goûts-réunis, ou Nouveaux concerts*, 1724 (*Le Parnasse, ou l'Apothéose de Corelli*, 2 vn, con; *concerts* 5–14); *L'Apothéose de Lully*, 1725; *Les Nations*, 2 vn, con, 1726 (4 sonata-suite pairs: *La Françoise, L'Espagnole, L'Impériale, La Piemontoise*); 2 suites, b viol, con, 1728

Harpsichord: *Premier livre*, 1713 (*ordres* 1–5); *L'ART DE TOUCHER LE CLAVECIN*, 1716; *Second livre*, 1716–17 (*ordres* 6–12); *Troisième livre*, 1722 (*ordres* 13–19); *Quatrième livre*, 1730 (*ordres* 20–27)

Organ: *Messe pour les paroisses, Messe pour les convents*, 1690

coupler. Organ device coupling one manual to another, so that one key may affect two or more pipes.

couplet. Term with two sets of meanings, formal and rhythmic:
(1) Strophe of a simple song, or episode in a French Baroque rondo.
(2) Duplet, or slurred pair of notes.

courante (Fr., running; It. *corrente*, older Eng. forms *corant, coranto*). Renaissance dance that became in the 17th century a regular ingredient of the SUITE, in one or other of its two forms: a fast type in 3/4 or 3/8 (sometimes distinguished as the corrente in Baroque and modern times) and a stately version in 3/2. Bach's suites and partitas include examples of both.

course. String on a lute, guitar or similar plucked instrument, originally a set of up to three strings tuned to the same note (or possibly including one at the upper octave, to reinforce higher partials). Instruments had multiple strings per course until the early 19th century, when thicker strings at greater tensions were introduced and provided sufficient sound alone. Still the term survived, as in '10-course guitar', for an instrument that would now have 10 strings.

court ode. See ODE.

Couture, Guillaume (b. Montreal, 23 Oct 1851; d. Montreal, 15 Jan 1915). Canadian composer, father of French Canadian music. Having begun his career as a church musician, he studied at the Paris Conservatoire (1873–7), the first Canadian to do so, and returned home to work as a composer, teacher and conductor. His works include a *Requiem* and the oratorio *Jean le Précurseur* (1907–9).

Covent Garden. Familiar name, from the area where it is situated (originally a convent garden), for the main London opera house, built in 1858 on a site that had boasted a theatre since 1732. The second theatre (1810–56) saw the première of Weber's *Oberon* and became the Royal Italian Opera in 1847, so that the present auditorium (now seating 2,186) was built as an Italian-style opera house. Having been leased and owned by a succession of managers and companies, the theatre was reorganized as a trust in 1945, and became the home of Covent Garden Opera (later the Royal Opera) and Sadler's Wells Ballet (later the Royal Ballet). The former's music directors have been Karl Rankl (1945–51), Kubelík (1955–8),

Solti (1961–71), Colin Davis (1971–86), Haitink (1988–2002) and Antonio Pappano (from 2002). Its record of premières includes works by Britten, Tippett, Henze, Davies and Birtwistle.

cover. UNDERSTUDY, ready to 'cover' a role.

cowbell. Bell of narrow aperture and characteristic clanking sound, originally made to be worn by alpine cattle. Used by Mahler (Symphony No.6) and Strauss (*Alpensinfonie*) for evocative effect, cowbells became standard percussion instruments in the 1960s.

Cowell, Henry (Dixon) (b. Menlo Park, Cal., 11 Mar 1897; d. Shady, NY, 10 Dec 1965). US composer, pioneer in his youth of experimental music, encourager of others like-minded, and later much involved with diverse US and exotic traditions. Spurred by his mother to find his own way (his father had left the family in 1902), he bought a piano in 1910, soon began working with clusters (*The Tides of Manaunaun*, ?1912) and gave a recital in San Francisco six days before his 17th birthday. Only then did he start formal training, under the guidance of Seeger, who ensured that the effect was to liberate further explorations, of dissonant counterpoint and of complex rhythms made from durations in quasi-overtone ratios (*Quartet Romantic, Quartet Euphometric*). After army service (1918–19) he extended his range of piano techniques to plucking and strumming the strings (*The Banshee*, 1925), and began giving recitals all over the USA and Europe (including in 1929 the Soviet Union, as the first US composer visitor). He also founded New Music Edition (1927), which brought out works by Ives, Ruggles, Webern, Schoenberg and Varèse. In Ives he discovered both a patron and a father figure, and he promoted Ives's music through lectures and a book. His last innovation was 'elastic form', providing fragments for performers to assemble (*Mosaic Quartet*, 1935). Imprisoned on a homosexual charge (1936–40), he devoted the second half of his creative life to works embracing the whole world of music, while travelling widely and continuing his work as a teacher (whose pupils had included Cage and Gershwin).

Henry Cowell *New Musical Resources* (1930)

Orchestral: Piano Concerto, 1929; 20 symphonies, etc.

Chamber: String Quartet No.1 (*Pedantic Quartet*), 1915–16; No.2 (Movement), 1934; No.3 (*Mosaic Quartet*), 1935; No.4 (*United Quartet*), 1936; *Quartet Romantic*, 2 fl, vn, va, 1915–17; *Quartet Euphometric*, str qt, 1916–19; *Toccanta*, v, fl, vc, pf, 1938; etc.

Piano: *The Tides of Manaunaun*, ?1912; *Anger Dance*, 1914; *Aeolian Harp*, 1923; *The Banshee*, 1925; etc.

Other works: choruses, songs

Cowen, Frederick (Hymen) (b. Kingston, Jamaica, 29 Jan 1852; d. London, 6 Oct 1935). British composer-conductor, knighted in 1911. He made an early start: trained in Leipzig (1865–6) and Berlin (1867–8), he had a symphony and a piano concerto presented in London when he was 17. His work as a composer was then overtaken by his dominating, countrywide positions as a conductor, notably with the Philharmonic Society (1888–92, 1900–7), the Liverpool Philharmonic (1896–1913) and the Handel Festival (1903–23).

cowhorn (Ger. *Stierhorn*). Ancient instrument of herding and war: a horn with its tip cut off. Wagner's request for it (in *Die Walküre, Die Meistersinger* and *Götterdämmerung*) is normally supplied by a straight conical horn of brass played with a trombone mouthpiece.

crab canon. Canon in which at least one voice goes backwards (CANCRIZANS) with respect to another.

cradle song. See LULLABY.

Craft, Robert (Lawson) (b. Kingston, NY, 20 Oct 1923). US conductor and musical assistant to Stravinsky. He studied at Juilliard and began his career as a conductor before taking up residence with Stravinsky in 1948. Besides working on numerous recordings and several conversation books (whose reflection of the composer's voice and attitudes is a matter of contention), he guided Stravinsky's move into serialism.

Cramer, Johann Baptist (b. Mannheim, 24 Feb 1771; d. London, 16 Apr 1858). German–British pianist-composer and publisher. His father, Wilhelm (1746–99), and grandfather, Jakob (1705–70), were Mannheim violinists. Wilhelm arrived in London in 1772 and called his family over soon after. His younger son, Franz (1772–1848), followed him as a violinist and became Master of the King's Music. Johann Baptist took more to the piano, and was taught by Schroeter (1780–83) and Clementi, who was a formative influence. He made his debut in 1781, and in 1788 set out as a performer, while also winning respect as a composer and teacher. After a concert tour of 1799–1800 that took him to Vienna (where Beethoven admired his playing) he married and established a more settled life in London, active in publishing from 1805. His voluminous works, all featuring the piano, reflect his enthusiasm for Mozart and his knowledge of the market. As well as 124 sonatas, nine concertos and many trifles, they include two books of studies (1804, 1810) still widely used.

craquer (Fr., to crackle). Brilliant violin effect, a fast articulation of two notes in one bowstroke, marked with dots under a slur.

crash cymbal. See CHINESE CYMBAL.

Crawford (Seeger), Ruth (Porter) (b. East Liverpool, Ohio, 3 Jul 1901; d. Chevy Chase, Md., 18 Nov 1953). US composer. She studied in Jacksonville, Florida, and Chicago before moving in 1929 to New York, where she became the pupil of Charles Seeger. A Guggenheim fellowship took her to Berlin and Paris for further study in 1930; the next year she married Seeger. She began writing music of great strength and originality, more finely made than that of other US iconoclasts. Her String Quartet (1931), in particular, displays a delight in abstract pattern-making, applying serial and numerical principles to duration as well as pitch. In other works she showed a left-wing commitment that soon led her to devote herself to working with her husband on folk music.

Joseph N. Straus *The Music of Ruth Crawford Seeger* (1995)

Creation, The (*Die Schöpfung*). Oratorio by Haydn (for s, t, b, ch, orch) to a text by Gottfried van Swieten after an anonymous English adaptation from *Paradise Lost*. Thinking of audiences in London as much as Vienna, Haydn provided both German and English versions. The first part, beginning with a Representation of Chaos and ending with the chorus 'The heavens are telling', tells of the first four days of creation, the second of the next two, and the third of Adam and Eve. First performance: Vienna, 30 Apr 1798.

Création du monde, La (The Creation of the World). Ballet by Milhaud, the music smokily redolent of jazz, to a scenario by Cendrars, originally produced with choreography by Börlin and designs by Léger. First performance: Paris, 25 Oct 1923.

Crecquillon, Thomas (b. *c*.1480–1500; d. ?Béthune, ?1557). Franco-Netherlandish composer, who was a member of the imperial chapel of Charles V and one of the creators of late Renaissance imitative polyphony. His large surviving output, testifying to the admiration he received, includes 12 masses, over 100 motets and almost 200 chansons.

Credo. Section of the ORDINARY of the mass, comprising the Nicene Creed.

Cremona. Northern Italian town, home to the violin makers Amati, Guarneri and Stradivari.

crescendo (It., growing). Direction to get louder, often abbreviated *cresc.* and even more often symbolized by a 'hairpin':

———————

The symbol can be traced to 1712 (Giovanni Antonio Piani's Op.1), the term to a little later and the practice to rather earlier: indeed, it is hard to imagine music that never included a swelling in volume. A crescendo is, indeed, a swelling and not a level of loudness: it may be a rise from *ppp* to *pp*.

Crespin, Régine (b. Marseilles, 23 Feb 1927). French soprano, later mezzo-soprano, in the grand style. She studied at the Paris Conservatoire and made her debut as Elsa at Mulhouse in 1950. For a decade after her first Kundry at Bayreuth (1958) she sang Wagner, Berlioz, Strauss (Marschallin) and Puccini (Tosca) internationally. She then retrained as a mezzo, and retired in 1989.

Creston, Paul (b. New York, 10 Oct 1906; d. San Diego, 24 Aug 1985). US composer, originally Giuseppe Guttoveggio, a child of poor Italian immigrants. Largely self-taught, he began composing seriously only in 1932. His First Symphony (1940) established his reputation and his style: ebullient and jazzy. Later works include five more symphonies, concertos, choral music and instrumental pieces.

cries. See STREET CRY.

Cristofori, Bartolomeo (b. Padua, 4 May 1655; d. Florence, 27 Jan 1731). Italian keyboard maker, inventor of the piano, in service to Prince Ferdinando de' Medici from 1690. Instruments by him are held by the Metropolitan Museum, by Leipzig University and in Rome.

critical band. Range outside which two pure tones will be perceived without roughness: approximately a minor third through much of the audible range.

criticism. Verbal description, interpretation and evaluation of music. A book-length study of, say, Beethoven's quartets may be considered a work of criticism, but the term is normally associated with newspaper, magazine and radio journalism, and with the immediate reporting of performances, by professional music critics. Criticism in that sense barely existed before the rise of daily papers at the start of the 19th century, for though there had been specialist periodicals earlier, starting with Mattheson's *Critica musica* (1722–5), their writing had generally been reflective and philosophical rather than sharpened to particular musical occasions. The first regular music critic is said to have been Johann Carl Friedrich Rellstab of the Berlin *Vossische Zeitung* (1808–13), and the first appointed to a British daily paper, Charles Lamb Kenney of *The Times* (1843–5), but the critics best remembered (and still sometimes read) tend to be those whose writings shine with the reflected glory of their creative lives: Weber, Schumann, Berlioz, Wolf, Debussy, Dukas. Among notable exceptions are Hanslick, for his unusual authority in Vienna through the half century from Brahms's youth to Mahler's maturity, and George Bernard Shaw, for his wit and decisiveness.

If newspaper criticism today is less colourful, that may be because it has lost prestige. Curiously, the arrival of computer-driven printing technology in the 1980s virtually eliminated overnight reviews, and therefore robbed criticism of its immediacy (besides robbing critics of the challenge of writing maybe 600 words in half an hour). Also, arts pages and sections became dominated not by reviews but by previews, interviews and other feature stories. It is in them – in articles that can be to some extent manipulated by public relations consultants and marketing strategists – that performers' careers are endorsed and recordings presented to the public. As for real criticism, both performers and recordings seem to be able to survive any amount of hostility or dismissal.

Criticism, like performance, demands keen musical sensitivity, acquaintance with a wide repertory as well as with the work in hand, close attentiveness, an individual response and an ability to communicate. Criticism is, of course, opinion: objective measurement and the scrutiny of evidence it includes only as part of its background. But it is opinion fired by passion and moderated by experience, cautioned by an awareness of operating in the public arena and enlivened by flair.

Harry Haskell *The Attentive Listener* (1995)

Croce, Giovanni (b. Chioggia, *c.*1557; d. Venice, 15 May 1609). Italian composer, especially of light-spirited madrigals and church music in the tradition of Andrea Gabrieli. He studied with Zarlino at St Mark's and spent much of his professional life at Santa Maria Formosa before returning to St Mark's as chapelmaster in 1603.

croche (Fr.). Quaver, eighth-note.

Croft, William (baptized Nether Ettington, Warwicks., 30 Dec 1678; d. Bath, 14 Aug 1727). British composer, of church music in late Baroque style and of hymn tunes (*St Agnes*, the tune of 'O God, our help in ages past'). He was a Chapel Royal chorister under Blow, whom he succeeded in his duties there and as organist of Westminster Abbey.

croma (It.). Quaver, eighth-note, or, in the past, crotchet, quarter-note.

crook. Length of tubing to be inserted into a wind instrument. Before the invention of valves, horns and trumpets had crooks to change the overall length and therefore the pitch. Bassoons and saxophones have crooks (curved sections connecting the mouthpiece to the body of the instrument) as part of their structure.

croon. Sing quietly, in a way made possible by the microphone.

cross-accent. Momentary instance of CROSS-RHYTHM.

Crosse, Gordon (b. Bury, 1 Dec 1937). British composer, close to Davies in his early Renaissance and serial interests, later working with a larger reach. He was a pupil of Wellesz at Oxford and Petrassi in Rome (1962), and taught at various British and US universities. His works include an operatic setting of Yeats's *Purgatory* (1966), but little since 1990.

cross-rhythm. Superimposition of different metres. A classic example is the triple dance chez Don Giovanni at the end of Act 1 of Mozart's opera, where 3/4, 2/4 and 3/8 metres are superposed. More commonly the music is notated in one metre, and the sensation of a second is produced by a different pattern of strong beats, as when 4/4, 12/8 and 3/4 merge in much of Reich's music. Where the metrical unit is shifted, so that 'strong' beats fall in 'weak' positions, the term is SYNCOPATION.

crotales. Small cymbals of definite pitch, also called 'antique cymbals', having been first made in imitation of instruments recovered from Pompeii. From contributing poetic moments to Berlioz (*Roméo et Juliette*) and Debussy (*L'Après-midi d'un faune*), they became standard in the percussion department.

Crotch, William (b. Norwich, 5 Jul 1775; d.

Taunton, 29 Dec 1847). British composer, remembered also as an unequalled musical prodigy. A carpenter's son, he is said to have begun picking out tunes on an organ at 18 months. His abilities at three and a half to perform, transpose and identify a four-note chord by ear are well attested. He toured Britain with his mother and then spent time at Cambridge (1786–8) and Oxford, where he became organist of Christ Church at 15 and professor at 21. That post he kept after leaving in 1806–7 for London, where he was founder principal of the RAM (1822–32). His works include oratorios (*Palestine*, 1805–11), anthems and organ concertos.

crotchet (UK). Quarter-note (US). See DURATION.

Crucifixus. Section of the CREDO, sometimes set separately.

Crüger, Johannes (b. Gross-Breesen, near Guben, Lower Lusatia, 9 Apr 1598; d. Berlin, 23 Feb 1662). German chorale composer and arranger. His teachers included Paul Homberger, possibly a pupil of Gabrieli, in Regensburg (1614). In 1622 he became cantor of the Nicolaikirche in Berlin, and in 1640 he brought out the first of several chorale books with figured bass. His contributions include *Herzliebster Jesu, was hast du verbrochen* and *Jesu, meine Freude*.

Crumb, George (Henry) (b. Charleston, West Virginia, 24 Oct 1929). US composer, whose music uses sonic drama and quotation to spooky effect. A doctoral pupil of Finney at the University of Michigan, he taught at the universities of Colorado (1959–65) and Pennsylvania (1965–95). His period of most intense and successful creative activity was rather brief, producing *Ancient Voices of Children* for soprano, treble, oboe and percussive ensemble (1970, the climax of a run of Lorca settings), *Black Angels* for amplified string quartet (1970) and three books of amplified piano music, *Makrkosmos I–III* (1972–4).

Don Gillespie *George Crumb* (1986)

crumhorn (from Ger. *Krummhorn*, crooked horn). Woodwind instrument with a double reed in a cap, named for its curved shape, like an upside-down walking stick. It emerged at the end of the 15th century and seems to have been used in homogeneous consorts. A limited range (a ninth), coupled with its unvarying buzzy sound, surely contributed to its rapid decline with the advent of solo instrumental writing in the early 17th century and its silence from then until the 20th-century revival of Renaissance music.

Crusell, Bernhard Henrik (b. Nystad/Uusikaupunki, 15 Oct 1775; d. Stockholm, 28 Jul 1838). Swedish clarinettist-composer. A bandboy from the age of 12, he joined the Swedish royal court in 1793 and studied composition locally and with Abbé Vogler. He wrote three concertos (E♭, Op.1; F minor, Op.5; B♭, Op.11) and other works for his instrument.

crwth. See ROTE.

cryptogram. See CIPHER.

csárdás (from Hung. *csárda*, country inn). Hungarian duple-time dance, introduced to aristocratic ballrooms in the 1830s as a folkdance, though its ancestry in fact lay in the quick part of the VERBUNKOS. There are examples by Liszt.

ct. Abbreviation for countertenor.

Cuba. Caribbean island, independent from colonial Spain since 1902. Besides its composers (Ignacio Cervantes, Roldán, Caturla, Ardévol, Brouwer), its contributions to music include the maracas, present before the Spanish conquest, and several other percussion instruments developed there from the hot fusion of African, European and indigenous cultures – the GUIRO, CLAVES and bongos – as well as the rumba, with similar origins.

cuckoo. Toy instrument imitating the birdcall. See also BIRDSONG; DAQUIN.

Cuckoo and the Nightingale, The. Name given to an organ concerto in F by Handel.

cue. Indication to start, or, as a verb, to so indicate. A conductor may cue a section of the orchestra with a hand gesture; chamber musicians will cue one another by means of nods and eye contact. A cue (i.e. tail) may also be printed in an instrumental part, showing what will be heard in someone else's part at the moment of entry. Scores and parts are normally supplied with numbered bars or occasional letters (A, B, C …) to assist in verbal cueing during rehearsal, so that a conductor may call, 'Two bars before J', etc.

Cui, César [Kyui, Tsezar Antonovich] (b. Vilnius, 18 Jan 1835; d. Petrograd, 26 Mar 1918). Russian composer-critic, a member of the MIGHTY HANDFUL. The son of a French officer who had stayed in Russia after 1812 and married a Lithuanian, he trained at the Academy of Military Engineering in St Petersburg (1855–7) and taught there as professor of fortifications while also pursuing a career as composer and critic. Though drawn into nationalist circles by Balakirev (whom he met in 1856) and a stout defender of nationalism in his reviews, his musical idol was Schumann. Of his 13 operas (including four for children), *William Ratcliff* (1861–8, St Petersburg, 1869) is remembered if not performed. Among his many songs, 'The Statue at Tsarkoye Selo' (from his Op.57 collection of 25 Pushkin settings, 1899) survives supreme and alone.

cuivré (Fr., ringing). Direction for a bright sound on the horn.

cuivres (Fr.). Brass instruments.

Cunning Little Vixen, The (*Příhody Lišky Bystroušky* [The Adventures of the Vixen Little-sharp-ears]). Opera by Janáček to his own libretto after a novel by Rudolf Těsnohlídek. The work is a magical evocation of forest sounds and forest life, its characters including – besides the Vixen (soprano) herself – Fox (soprano), Badger (bass), Cricket, Grasshopper and Frog (children), and various human animals, notably the Forester (baritone), who captures the Vixen and from whom she escapes. The radiant ending has him at peace with the natural world. First performance: Brno, 6 Nov 1924.

cup mute. Mute for the trumpet or trombone, similar to the STRAIGHT MUTE but with a cup at the wider end to cover the bell and so further reduce the sound.

cupo (It.). Gloomy.

Curlew River. Chamber opera ('parable for church performance') by Britten to a libretto by William Plomer after the noh play *Sumidagawa*. The Madwoman (tenor) has her grief released by a vision of her son, the Spirit of the Boy (treble). First performance: Orford, 12 Jun 1964.

curtal. See BASSOON; DULCIAN.

Curtis Institute of Music. Philadelphia conservatory founded in 1924 by Edward and Mary Louise Curtis Bok.

Curzon, Clifford (Michael) (b. London, 18 May 1907; d. London, 1 Jul 1982). British pianist, knighted in 1977. From the RAM he went on to study with Schnabel in Berlin (1928–30) and Landowska and Boulanger in Paris. Specially admired for his sovereign simplicity in Mozart, he was no showman, performed and recorded relatively rarely, and always kept the music before him.

Cusins, William (George) (b. London, 14 Oct 1833; d. Remouchamps, 31 Aug 1893). British conductor-composer, teacher and musical courtier, knighted in 1892. Besides work in the wider British musical world of conservatories and choral festivals, he was Victoria's private chapel organist from 1849 and her Master of Music from 1870.

cut time. Halving of durations in medieval and Renaissance music, indicated by a vertical stroke through the mensuration sign, such as survives in the time signature

¢

Cutting, Francis (*fl.* 1580s–90s). English lutenist-composer, living in London, author of fine pavans, galliards, almains, etc.

Cuzzoni, Francesca (b. Parma, 2 Apr 1696; d. Bologna, 19 Jun 1778). Italian soprano, vastly admired (and vastly paid) during her London residence of 1722–8, when she created many parts for Handel (Cleopatra in *Giulio Cesare*, Rodelinda, etc.) and caused a scandal by fighting onstage with her rival Faustina Bordoni. She continued her career largely in Italy (and away from Bordoni), but visited London again in 1734–6 and 1750, well past the time when her controlled trill, phrasing, pure intonation and sweetness had caused astonishment. Improvident and occasionally imprisoned for debt, she apparently spent her last years making buttons.

cycle. (1) Work comprising smaller items, other than the normal three or four movements of a sonata or symphony. Thus one may speak of a song cycle, piano cycle (e.g. *Carnaval*), opera cycle (the *Ring*), etc. The term is also used for the symphonies of one composer, as if those works also formed a larger entity, hence 'Abbado's Beethoven cycle', etc.

(2) Repeating unit of a vibration. Frequencies are measured in cycles per second (Herz).

cyclic form. Sequence of movements at least two of which share thematic material. Normally the term implies that all movements are so linked, creating narrative continuity, a technique adumbrated by Beethoven (Op.101 sonata), Schubert (E♭ trio) and Berlioz (*Symphonie fantastique*), extended by Schumann and Liszt, and made into a principle by Franck.

cyclic mass. Set of mass propers (at the fullest comprising *Kyrie, Gloria, Credo, Sanctus* and *Agnus Dei*) composed as a whole. The genre arose among English composers of the early 15th century (Dunstable, Power) and provided the Renaissance with its most ambitious musical form.

cymbals (Fr. *cymbales*, Ger. *Becken*, It. *piatti*). Plate-like percussion instruments of copper-tin alloy, used in pairs or alone (in one hand or suspended). The standard orchestral cymbals were imported into bands from Turkey, where they are still made – as well as in the USA – by members of the ZILDJIAN family. In the 18th and early 19th centuries they kept their Turkish and military associations (*Die Entführung*, Beethoven's Ninth Symphony); later they became more emphatic than exotic. Musicians in the 20th century introduced new effects, using different beaters and brushes on different parts of the plate, drawing sound from a suspended cymbal with a bow (Schoenberg's Op.16), or making a sizzling noise with a suspended cymbal loosely rivetted. Common, too, in the modern orchestra are antique cymbals (CROTALES) and Chinese cymbals, the latter brasher.

cymbalum. Medieval set of small bells on a frame, struck with hammers.

Cyprus. Mediterranean island remarkable in Western musical history for a rich manuscript of sacred music and songs seemingly connected with Queen Charlotte (1411–22).

Czech Philharmonic Orchestra (Orchestr České Filharmonie). Orchestra dating its history from 1896, when Dvořák conducted a concert of his music, and independent of the national opera from 1901. Its chief conductors have included Talich (1919–41), Kubelík (1942–8), Karel Ančerl (1950–68), František Neumann (1968–90) and Ashkenazy (from 1998).

Czech Quartet. Ensemble formed in 1891 by pupils of Hanuš Wihan, who became its cellist (1894–1914) as well as its mentor, while Suk played second violin until the group disbanded, in 1933. Admired for their precision and freshness, they played all over Europe and made records.

Czech Republic (Česká Republika). Central European country comprising Bohemia and Moravia, with PRAGUE as capital. The region was subordinated to the Habsburg empire from 1526 and definitively absorbed in 1620. Bohemian composers of the Baroque and Classical periods – Biber, Zelenka, the Stamitz and Benda families, Wanhal, Reicha – tended to make their careers elsewhere, but Tomášek was an exception. Smetana then initiated the roll of great Czech composers who stayed at home, among them Dvořák, Fibich, Suk and Janáček, while Martinů inherited the wanderlust of his predecessors. Bohemia, Moravia and Slovakia achieved independence in 1918 as Czechoslovakia; the name change was caused by the secession of Slovakia in 1992.

Czerny, Carl (b. Vienna, 21 Feb 1791; d. Vienna, 15 Jul 1857). Austrian pianist-composer, whose many hundreds of studies have exercised generations of students. Himself trained by his father, who was a piano teacher and all-round musician, he gained acceptance at 10 as a pupil by Beethoven, to whom he remained close for some years, gaining an inside knowledge of the piano music that he passed on in writing. He started up as a teacher at 15, and withdrew from public performance. With Liszt among his pupils, teaching is said to have occupied him 10 hours a day; much of the rest of his time he must have devoted to composition, for he reached Op.861, many of his works being whole books of studies, while he also wrote sonatas and sonatinas, symphonies, chamber works and church music. Marriage and travel were out of the question.

D. (1) Note name, hence D minor, D♭, etc.

D major has qualities of brilliance and celebration that come partly from how well it fits violin tuning and are partly inherited from the 17th–18th centuries, when trumpets were commonly in D, so that D major was often indicated when these instruments were in the orchestra. It is the key also of innumerable quartets and of many of the greatest violin concertos (those by Beethoven, Brahms, Tchaikovsky and Stravinsky). Other D major works include Beethoven's *Missa solemnis* and the second symphonies of Beethoven and Brahms. D minor is equally suited to string tuning and so equally common: it conveys drama and intensity, as in symphonies by Beethoven (No.9), Schumann, Dvořák, Bruckner, Franck, Rachmaninoff and Shostakovich, quartets by Schubert (*Death and the Maiden*), Wolf and Schoenberg, Bach's great chaconne, concertos by Mozart, Brahms and Sibelius, and Mozart's *Requiem* and *Don Giovanni*. The unusual key of D♭ is found in works by Schubert, Chopin, Fauré, Mahler (close of the Ninth Symphony), Prokofiev (First Piano Concerto) and Shostakovich (Twelfth Quartet).

(2) Abbreviation for Deutsch's catalogue of Schubert's works.

da, dal (It.). From, as in DA CAPO and *dal* SEGNO.

da capo (It.). From the top, i.e. start again, often abbreviated D.C. The reprise closes at *Fine* (It., end). The da capo thus readily produces an ABA form, as in the da capo aria or the symphonic minuet or scherzo.

dada. Those associated with the original iconoclastic movement of 1917–20 included Golïshev, Wolpe and Schwitters, whose *Sonate in Urlauten* (Sonata in Primitive Sounds) is a phonetic text for performance by speaking voices. The term has also been applied to Cage with some justification, given his sense of humour and his adoption of Duchamp, dadaist supreme, as spiritual godfather. Satie's delightful nonsense came earlier and was his own.

Dafne. See DAPHNE.

Dagincour, François (b. Rouen, 1684; d. Rouen, 30 Apr 1758). French keyboardist-composer, notable follower of Couperin in his 1733 book of harpsichord pieces. He studied in Rouen and Paris, and was from 1706 organist of Notre Dame in Rouen.

Dahl, Ingolf (b. Hamburg, 9 Jun 1912; d. Frutigen, near Berne, 6 Aug 1970). German–US composer, close to Stravinsky. He studied in Cologne (with Jarnach) and in Zurich before moving in 1938 to Los Angeles, where he had further lessons with Boulanger. His European works had been dense and fraught in the manner of German expressionism, but in California his music became clearer and more diatonic, until in his Piano Quartet (1957) he began using serial methods. He taught courses on Stravinsky at USC and assisted him as a translator, arranger, etc.

Dahlhaus, Carl (b. Hanover, 10 Jun 1928; d. Berlin, 13 Mar 1989). German music scholar, who brought compendious knowledge to bear on his dense trackings both of the creative mind and of musical culture in the broadest sense. After studies in

Freiburg (with Gurlitt) and in Göttingen he worked in the theatre and journalism before becoming head of musicology at the Technical University in Berlin (1967–89). His books include *Esthetics of Music* (1982) and *Nineteenth-Century Music* (1989).

Dalayrac, Nicolas Marie (b. Muret, Haute Garonne, 8 Jun 1753; d. Paris, 26 Nov 1809). French composer, who brought the opéra comique into a new age of tuneful sentiment and dramatic vivacity. Of noble birth, he trained in law and in 1774 joined the court at Versailles. After lessons with Honoré Langlé, and some contact with Grétry, he established himself as an opera composer before the Revolution with works that rapidly went around Europe. Beethoven played in the orchestra for *Nina*, *Azémia* and *Les Deux Petits Savoyards* in Bonn, and *Nina*, with a heroine maddened by thwarted love, prompted operas on the same subject by Paer and Paisiello. Married in 1792, he maintained his position through the turmoil of the time, partly by adapting himself to new tastes for darkness and horror (and patriotism) on stage, partly by arranging his most popular numbers as Revolutionary songs. The later *Léon* and *Léhéman* introduce reminiscence motifs and, in the latter, offstage trumpet calls that descended through Méhul's *Héléna* to *Fidelio*.

Operas: *Nina* (Benoît Joseph Marsollier des Vivetières), f.p. Paris, 1786; *Azémia* (Auguste Etienne Xavier Poisson de la Chabeaussière), f.p. Fontainebleau, 1786; *Les Deux Petits Savoyards* (Marsollier), f.p. Paris, 1789; *Camille* (Marsollier), f.p. Paris, 1791; *Léon* (François Benoît Hoffmann), f.p. Paris, 1798; *Adolphe et Clara* (Marsollier), f.p. Paris, 1799; *Maison à vendre* (Alexandre Duval), f.p. Paris, 1800; *Léhéman* (Marsollier), f.p. Paris, 1801; about 50 others

Dalbavie, Marc André (b. Neuilly-sur-Seine, 10 Feb 1961). French composer, notably of orchestral works that bring an expressive amplitude and formal largeness to the spectral tradition. He studied at the Paris Conservatoire (1980–86) and worked at IRCAM (1986–91) before establishing himself in the orchestral domain with his Violin Concerto (1995–6).

Dall'Abaco, Evaristo Felice (b. Verona, 12 Jul 1675; d. Munich, 12 Jul 1742). Italian composer, indebted to Corelli and latterly Vivaldi in his compact output of three volumes of sonatas and three of concertos. Possibly a pupil of Torelli, he went to Modena in 1696 and was in Munich by 1704, a cellist at the electoral court. He stayed with that court in exile in the Low Countries and France,

adding some Frenchness to his range, and returned with them to Munich in 1715.

Dallapiccola, Luigi (b. Pisino d'Istria, 3 Feb 1904; d. Florence, 19 Feb 1975). Italian composer. He was one of the first outside the Austro-German sphere to interest himself in Schoenberg's serialism, which he brought into a fresh context, that of Italian lyricism and a civilized mind.

Born and raised in what was part of the Habsburg Empire, he was confined with his family in Graz during the last 18 months of the First World War. There he saw *Der fliegende Holländer* in 1917 and decided he must be a composer. The family returned to Pisino, now within Italy, and he continued his musical education in Trieste with Antonio Illersberg (1919–22). He then went to Florence to study piano with Ernesto Consolo and composition with Roberto Casiraghi (1923–4). The shock of Debussy, encountered in 1921, caused him to stop composing for three years; that of *Pierrot lunaire*, in 1924, was no less disorienting, and almost a decade passed before he was writing music he wanted published. Meanwhile he attended Frazzi's composition classes at the Florence Conservatory (1929–31), where in 1934 he began teaching piano as a second study, an unpretentious post he retained until retiring, in 1967.

Helped by Casella and by travel (notably to Vienna and Berlin in 1930), he began to find his musical world – sombre but luminous, poised between modality and serialism, between the Renaissance and modernity, as also between Italian and Germanic cultures – through his Michelangelo choruses of 1933–6. Then the experience of Mussolini's Ethiopian adventure and the Spanish Civil War hardened his artistic steel, and he wrote the *Canti di prigionia* (1938–41) as protest music. He fully absorbed serial rules in his *Liriche greche* (1942–5), a trilogy of chamber settings of Sappho, Alcaeus and Anacreon, without losing the euphony and sonic poetry of the earlier *Tre laudi*. That gave him the language for *Il prigioniero* (1944–8), where the response to imprisonment is more one of humane enquiry.

After this climactic work his music became sparer in texture and more refined in its gestures, as if Berg's influence had been replaced by Webern's, though he kept his preference for all-interval series that would let diatonic features shine through. His preferred medium was vocal chamber music, his subject now of mental liberation, of contact with the divine in the beauty of thought and perception. Such textures and such ideas formed the substance and background of by far his biggest work, *Ulisse*.

Rudey Shackelford, ed. *Dallapiccola on Opera* (1987); Raymond Fearn *The Music of Luigi Dallapiccola* (2003)

Operas (all librettos by the composer): *Volo di notte* (1 act: after Saint-Exupéry), 1937–8, Florence, 1940; *Il* PRIGIONIERO, 1944–8; *Job* (1 act), Rome, 1950; *Ulisse* (see ODYSSEY), 1960–68

Orchestral: *Piccolo concerto per Muriel Couvreux*, pf, chbr orch, 1939–41; *Marsia* (ballet), 1942–3; *Due pezzi*, 1947; *Tartiniana*, vn, orch, 1951; *Variazioni*, 1954; *Piccola musica notturna*, 1954; *Tartiniana seconda*, vn, orch, 1955–6; *Dialoghi*, vc, orch, 1959–60; *Three Questions with Two Answers*, 1962

Choral: *Sei cori di Michelangelo* (Nos.1–2, ch, 1933; Nos.3–4, small boys'/women's ch, 17 insts, 1934–5; Nos.5–6, ch, orch, 1935–6); *Canti di prigionia*, ch, 2 pf, 2 hp, perc, 1938–41; *Canti di liberazione*, ch, orch, 1951–5; *Requiescant*, ch, orch, 1957–8; *Tempus destruendi – Tempus aedificandi*, ch, 1970–71

Solo vocal: *Tre laudi*, s/t, 13 insts, 1936–7; *Cinque frammenti di Saffo*, v, 15 insts, 1942; *Sei carmina Alcaei*, v, 11 insts, 1943; *Due liriche di Anacreonte*, v, 2 cl, va, pf, 1944–5; *Rencesvals*, mez/bar, pf, 1946; *Quattro liriche di Machado*, s, pf, 1948, arr s, chbr orch, 1964; *Tre poemi*, s, 14 insts, 1949; *Goethe Lieder*, s, 3 cl, 1953; *An Mathilde*, s, orch, 1955; *Cinque canti*, bar, 8 insts, 1956; *Concerto per la notte di Natale dell'anno 1956*, s, chbr orch, 1957–8; *Preghiere*, bar, chbr orch, 1962; *Parole di San Paolo*, mez/tr, 11 insts, 1964; *Sicut umbra*, mez, 12 insts, 1970; *Commiato*, s, 15 insts, 1972

Instrumental: *Musica per tre pianoforti*, 1935; *Sonatina canonica*, pf, 1942–3; *Ciaccona, intermezzo e adagio*, vc, 1945; *Due studi*, vn, pf, 1946–7; *Tre episodi* (from Marsia), pf, 1949; *Quaderno musicale di Annalibera*, pf, 1952

dal segno. See SEGNO.

Damase, Jean-Michel (b. Bordeaux, 27 Jan 1928). French composer, of ballets, concertos and chamber music in the French tradition of light, fluent elegance. A harpist's son, he was a precocious composer: at nine, after meeting Colette, he set some of her poems. He then studied with Cortot and at the Paris Conservatoire, beginning his career as a pianist-composer while still a student.

Damett, ?Thomas (b. c.1389; d. 1436/7). English composer of mass sections and motets in the Old Hall manuscript. He studied at Winchester and was associated with the Chapel Royal by 1413.

Damnation de Faust, La. See FAUST.

damp. Reduce sound volume. Damping implies an action – whether mechanical or electronic – that can be varied, whereas a mute is either on or off. The mechanism may be part of the instrument, as notably with a piano's dampers, or

may be applied from outside (a cloth on a timpanum, electronic compression).

damper. Part of a piano that comes against a string to stop it vibrating. The sustaining pedal removes the dampers.

damper pedal. SUSTAINING PEDAL.

Dämpfer (Ger., pl. *Dämpfer*). Mute.

Damrosch, Leopold (b. Posen, 22 Oct 1832; d. New York, 15 Feb 1885). German–US conductor. He abandoned a medical career to become Liszt's violinist in Weimar (1857) and a conductor in Breslau/Wrocław (1858–71) before moving with his wife and family to New York, where he founded the New York Symphony Society (1878) and German opera at the Met (1884). His younger son, Walter (1862–1950), succeeded him and became a popular broadcaster; the elder, Frank (1859–1937), was a choral conductor.

dance. Much music seems to embody or enforce, if only for the listening mind, the rhythm and movement of dancing. This is, of course, most explicit in pieces that adapt dance forms and metres (e.g. those of the pavan, minuet, waltz or charleston, whether to be danced or not), and in BALLET music.

Dance before the Golden Calf (*Tanz um das goldene Kalb*). Bacchanal in Schoenberg's opera *Moses und Aron*, a largely orchestral dance suite.

dance of death (Fr. *danse macabre*, Ger. *Totentanz*). Recurrent topic in Western culture through at least seven centuries, variously interpreted as an embrace in which Death claims his victim or as a romp of skeletons. It appealed to the Romantic imagination, examples including Liszt's *Totentanz* and Saint-Saëns's *Danse macabre*, which adds the image of Death as fiddle player. Ravel's *La Valse* is also part of this repertory.

Dance of the Blessed Spirits (*Ballet des ombres heureuses*). Episode in Gluck's *Orfeo/Orphée*, though normally the title is used for just the middle section, a graceful piece in D minor for flute and strings added in the Paris version.

Dance of the Hours (*Danza delle ore*). Divertissement from Ponchielli's *La* GIOCONDA, a ballet mounted by the patrician Alvise in his palace: the hours of dawn, day, evening and night succeed one another onstage.

Dance of the Seven Veils. Salome's dance in Strauss's opera, a luscious, exotic and partly waltzing orchestral episode. The name is authorized by Wilde's play, not the libretto or score.

Dance Suite. Orchestral work by Bartók (also a reduction for solo piano), a chain of dances drawn from different folk traditions. First performance: Budapest, 19 Nov 1923.

Dandrieu, Jean-François (b. c.1682; d. Paris, 17 Jan 1738). French keyboard composer-performer. He played the organ in the royal chapel and various Paris churches, including St Barthélemy (demolished), where he succeeded his priest uncle Pierre and was in turn succeeded by his sister Jeanne-Françoise. He revised a book of his uncle's noëls, as well as publishing several volumes of his own. One of his most popular harpsichord pieces seems to have been *Les Caractères de la guerre*.

D'Anglebert, Jean-Henri (b. Paris, 1635; d. Paris, 23 Apr 1691). French keyboard composer-performer, outstanding among those who came immediately after Chambonnières, whom he succeeded as royal harpsichordist in 1662. His single published volume (1689) includes four harpsichord suites and six organ fugues, all the music at once strengthened and animated by counterpoint.

Daniel, Arnaut (b. Riberác, ?1150–60; d. c.1200). Troubadour singled out by Dante. Two of his songs survive with music, one of them in sestina form, which he invented.

Daniel, John (baptized Wellow, near Bath, 6 Nov 1564; d. c.1626). English lutenist-composer, younger brother of the poet Samuel Daniel. He studied at Christ Church, Oxford, and was a royal musician besides being involved in theatrical ventures of his brother's. His works include lute pieces (*Mrs Anne Green her leaves be green*) and songs ('Can doleful notes').

Daniel-Lesur (b. Paris, 19 Nov 1908; d. Paris, 2 Jul 2002). French composer, originally Daniel Jean Yves Lesur. His music reflects on a French past embracing the excitement of Berlioz and the modal mystery of Tournemire, of whom – like his mother, Alice Thiboust – he was a pupil. He also studied at the Paris Conservatoire (1919–29) before embarking on a career as a teacher at the Schola Cantorum (1935–64), as organist of the Benedictine Abbey of Paris (1937–44) and with French radio in various posts. A member of *La* JEUNE FRANCE, he wrote an opera (*Andrea del Sarto*, Marseilles, 1969), orchestral pieces (*Sym-*

phonie de danses, 1958), cantatas and folksong arrangements.

Daniels, David (b. Spartanburg, S. Carolina, 12 Mar 1966). US countertenor, internationally prominent for his musicality and sensuousness. He studied as a tenor with George Shirley at the University of Michigan before discovering his countertenor self. His opera debut came in 1994 at Glimmerglass (Monteverdi's Nero).

danse macabre (Fr.). DANCE OF DEATH.

Dante (Alighieri) (b. Florence, May/Jun 1265; d. Ravenna, 14 Sep 1321). Italian poet, whose *Commedia* (often called *Divina commedia*) and other writings have been the subject of works including:

(1) Liszt's Dante Sonata, last piece in the second volume of his ANNEES DE PELERINAGE.

(2) Liszt's Dante Symphony (*Eine Symphonie zu Dantes Divina Commedia*) in two movements: *Inferno* and *Purgatorio*, the latter ending with a *Magnificat* for women's choir. (The third part of the *Commedia*, the *Paradiso*, he felt beyond him.) Wagner was the dedicatee. First performance: Dresden, 7 Nov 1857.

See also DANIEL ARNAUT; FRANCESCA DA RIMINI; PACINI; *Il* TRITTICO; TRUMPET.

Danzi, Franz (Ignaz) (b. Schwetzingen, 15 Jun 1763; d. Karlsruhe, 13 Apr 1826). German composer, whose wind quintets and concertos have survived above his numerous operas and sacred works. His parents were Innozenz Danzi, an Italian cellist in the Mannheim orchestra from 1754, and Barbara Toeschi, the composer's sister. Trained by his father, whom he joined as an orchestral cellist at 15 and succeeded in the Munich orchestra in 1783, he also studied composition with Abbé Vogler. He married a singer in 1790 and embarked on a life of travel with her, but in 1800 she died, and he eventually settled as kapellmeister in Stuttgart (1807–12) and Karlsruhe. In Stuttgart he took the young Weber under his wing.

Daphne. In Greek mythology a nymph who fled Apollo's desire and was transformed into a laurel tree. Her story is told in Ovid and opera:

(1) Rinuccini's libretto *Dafne* was set by Peri and Corsi to create the ancestral opera (Florence, 1598), by Gagliano (Mantua, 1608) and, in translation, by Schütz; only Gagliano's setting survives. There is a prologue, sung by Ovid, after which Apollo, having slain the Python, belittles Cupid, whose revenge is to make him fall in love with Daphne. She flees and is lignified; he laments.

(2) Strauss's opera *Daphne* has a libretto by Joseph Gregor. In a setting of pastoral antiquity, the chaste and solitary Daphne (soprano) loves only nature, not the shepherd Leukippos (tenor). But nature then arrives, in the imposing person of Apollo (tenor), who kills Leukippos and transforms Daphne into a tree: she finds her radiant full voice in the process. First performance: Dresden, 15 Oct 1938.

Daphnis et Chloé (Daphnis and Chloe). Ballet score by Ravel, originally choreographed by Fokine. The Arcadian story, following the Hellenistic writer Longus, concerns the erotic education of the young shepherd Daphnis and his Chloe. Of the three parts, the second (Suite No.1) concerns Chloe's abduction by pirates and the third (Suite No.2) begins with rapturous daybreak music and ends with an exultant bacchanal. First performance: Paris, 8 Jun 1912.

Da Ponte, Lorenzo (b. Ceneda, now Vittorio Veneto, 10 Mar 1749; d. New York, 17 Aug 1838). Italian librettist, famed especially for his three collaborations with Mozart: *Le nozze di Figaro*, *Don Giovanni* and *Così fan tutte*. Born a Jew, Emmanuele Conegliano, he gained a new name when he converted in 1763 so that his widower father could marry a Christian. He took the local bishop's surname and entered the seminary, but though he duly became a priest (in 1773), he also became a poet and womanizer. The latter avocation caused him to be banned from Venice in December 1779, and about 18 months later he arrived in Vienna, where Salieri gained him a post as court librettist and set his first original libretto (*Il ricco d'un giorno*, 1784). After that came a rapid sequence of three or more librettos a year in 1786–90, for composers including (besides Mozart and Salieri) Martín y Soler, Gazzaniga, Storace and Weigl. Dismissed from court in 1791, he settled in London the next year with his mistress (and eventual family), with whom he emigrated to the USA in 1805. Various business ventures in London and New York failed, but he found late success as professor of Italian at Columbia (from 1825) and as a memoirist. He was also in the audience when *Don Giovanni* reached New York 38 years after its première.

Arthur Livingston, ed. *Memoirs of Da Ponte* (1929, ʳ2000); Sheila Hodges *Lorenzo da Ponte* (1985)

Daquin, Louis Claude (b. Paris, 4 Jul 1694; d. Paris, 15 Jun 1772). French keyboard composer-performer. Godson of Jacquet de la Guerre and pupil of Marchand, he was an infant prodigy who gained his first organist's appointment, at the Petit St Antoine, when he was 12 and rose to become royal organist in succession to Dandrieu. He published a volume of harpsichord pieces, including the charmingly naïve *Le Coucou*, and also a book of noëls.

Dardanus. Opera by Rameau to a libretto by Charles-Antoine le Clerc de la Bruère. With the help of magic and dreams, Dardanus (hautecontre) slays a sea monster, thereby at once rescuing his erstwhile enemy Antenor (bass) and gaining the hand of his beloved Iphise (soprano), daughter of the Phrygian king Teucer (bass). First performance: Paris, 19 Nov 1739. The revised version (1744) makes the drama more psychological: it is now the shamed and dying Antenor who rescues Dardanus, from prison, and Dardanus wins Iphise by defeating Teucer in battle.

Dargomyzhsky, Aleksandr (Sergeyevich) (b. Troitskoye, Tula district, 14 Feb 1813; d. St Petersburg, 17 Jan 1869). Russian composer, who based his operas and songs on folk music but also on speech melody, providing impulses for the realism of Tchaikovsky and Musorgsky. Of comfortable birth, he studied the piano and had some composition lessons, but entered the civil service in 1827. An introduction to Glinka, in the winter of 1833–4, intensified his musical leanings and made him determined to write an opera, which he eventually did. Failing to get it produced, however, he resigned his government post in 1843 and spent six months in Paris in 1844–5. It was after this that he began to study folksongs and speech patterns in the interests of expressive veracity. Out of folk music came *Rusalka*; a stubborn insistence on recitative produced *The Stone Guest*, on the Don Juan story, which he did not live to finish.

Operas: *Esmeralda* (after Hugo), 1838–41, f.p. Moscow, 1847; *Rusalka* (after Pushkin), 1848–55, f.p. St Petersburg, 1856; *The Stone Guest* (Pushkin), 1866–9 (completed by Cui and Rimsky-Korsakov), f.p. St Petersburg, 1872
Songs: 'I am sad' (Lermontov), 1848; 'The Miller' (Pushkin), 1850–51; etc.
Other works: few choral, orchestral and piano pieces

Darmstadt. German city, noted for the Internationale Ferienkurse für Neue Musik (International Summer Courses for New Music) established by Wolfgang Steinecke in 1946. Stockhausen, Nono and Goeyvaerts met there in 1951, and eagerly debated Messiaen's *Mode de valeurs et d'intensités* (which its composer had planned in the same place two years earlier). Thereafter Darmstadt belonged to the new generation: Stockhausen taught there regularly from 1953 to the early 1970s; Boulez and Maderna were also regularly there in the later 1950s and 1960s, when young composers and performers came from all over the world to learn what was new – hence the term 'Darmstadt school' for the avant-garde music of this period. Since 1970 the courses have been biennial, but the commitment to modernism has not changed.

Dartington. School in Devon, site of a music summer school founded by Glock and brought there from Bryanston in 1953.

dash. (1) Short vertical line or wedge, over or under a notehead, indicating an intensified staccato: sharper in attack and more briefly sustained.

(2) Short horizontal line, over or under a notehead, indicating a full, weighty duration.

(3) Horizontal line after a figure or sign in figured bass, indicating that the same harmony is to continue.

dasian notation. Notation used in MUSICA ENCHIRIADIS and other early sources, with pitches represented by graphic symbols involving the *daesia*, the Gk accent for rough breathing.

Dauprat, Louis François (b. Paris, 24 May 1781; d. Paris, 17 Jul 1868). French hornist-composer, author of concertos, smaller pieces and a method for his instrument. He took first prize in the first horn class at the Paris Conservatoire (1797) and went back there, after serving in the army and the theatre, for composition studies with Gossec. Reicha also taught him, and wrote for him. Later he played at the Opera and taught at the Conservatoire, before retiring to Egypt in 1842.

Dauvergne, Antoine (b. Moulins, 3 Oct 1713; d. Lyons, 11 Feb 1797). French composer, notably of chamber music. A musician's son, he moved to Paris in his mid-20s, had lessons with Rameau, and became violinist (1739) and composer (1755) in the royal chamber-music establishment. He also worked at the Paris Opera as violinist, conductor and composer, and was responsible for the first French comic opera in the Italian style, *Les Troqueurs* (1753). His other works include sonatas and *concerts de simphonies* for strings and continuo.

Davaux, Jean-Baptiste (b. La Côte-St-André, 19 Jul 1742; d. Paris, 2 Feb 1822). French violinist-composer, whose appealing quartets and *symphonies concertantes* were widely published and appreciated. He pursued a career in govern-

ment service and also introduced in 1784 a device for setting tempos, the *chronomètre*.

David. Jewish king and psalmodist, commemorated in works by Tomkins, Charpentier, Handel (*Saul*), Mozart (DAVIDDE PENITENTE), Nielsen and Honegger (*Le* ROI DAVID).

David, Félicien (César) (b. Cadenet, Vaucluse, 13 Apr 1811; d. St Germain-en-Laye, 29 Aug 1876). French composer, a gentle Romantic orientalist. After training in Aix-en-Provence and at the Paris Conservatoire, he joined the Saint-Simonian community in 1831 and undertook what began as a missionary visit to Egypt but became, during the two years he spent there (1833–5), an education. On returning to Paris he wrote songs on oriental subjects, then made his name with the 'ode-symphony' *Le Désert*, for tenor, chorus and orchestra, with spoken introductions (Paris, 1844). The high point in his erratic later career was *Lalla-Roukh* (Paris, 1862), an opéra comique set in Moore's Kashmir, but better remembered is the coloratura number 'Charmant oiseau' from *La Perle du Brésil* (Paris, 1851). In 1869 he succeeded Berlioz, an erstwhile admirer, as a member of the Institut.

Dorothy Veinus Hagan *Félicien David* (1985)

David, Ferdinand (b. Hamburg, 19 Jun 1810; d. Klosters, Switzerland, 18 Jul 1873). German violinist-composer. He studied with Spohr and Hauptmann in Kassel (1823–5) and at 16 was in correspondence with Mendelssohn, for whom he became leader of the Gewandhaus orchestra (1836). There he remained, also teaching (Joachim among others) at the Leipzig Conservatory. The first exponent and dedicatee of Mendelssohn's Violin Concerto, he wrote five concertos of his own, besides much else.

David, Johann Nepomuk (b. Eferding, Upper Austria, 30 Nov 1895; d. Stuttgart, 22 Dec 1977). Austrian composer, especially of sacred choral and organ music in a style close to Hindemith. Trained at St Florian and under Marx at the Vienna Academy, he worked as a schoolteacher, church musician and professor of composition at the Stuttgart conservatory (1948–63). He also wrote eight symphonies.

Davidde penitente (David in Remorse). Oratorio by Mozart (2s, t, ch, orch) to words probably by Da Ponte, the music recycling the C minor mass with two new arias. First performance: Vienna, 13 Mar 1785.

Davidovsky, Mario (b. Buenos Aires, 4 Mar 1934).

Argentinian–US composer, noted for his vivid marshalling of instrumental ideas, with or without electronic repercussions. He studied in Buenos Aires and at Tanglewood (1958), where an encounter with Babbitt made possible a move to New York and work at the Columbia-Princeton Electronic Music Center. Remaining in New York, he held posts at Columbia (1960–93) and other teaching institutions.

Works with tape: *Synchronisms* No.1, fl, 1963; No.2, fl, cl, vn, vc, 1964; No.3, vc, 1965; No.4 (Psalm 13), ch, 1967; No.5, perc ens, 1969; No.6, pf, 1970; No.7, orch, 1973; No.8, wind qnt, 1974; No.9, vn, 1988; No.10, gtr, 1992
Other works: *Romancero*, s, fl, cl, vn, vc, 1983; orch pieces, 4 quartets, etc.

Davidsbündlertänze (David's League Dances). Sequence of 18 character pieces for piano by Schumann. The Davidsbund was the imaginary society he dreamed up to fight the Goliath of philistinism.

Davies, Fanny (b. Guernsey, 27 Jun 1861; d. London, 1 Sep 1934). British pianist, remembered especially for the dashing Schumann recordings she made late in her career. She studied in Leipzig (1882–3) and with Clara Schumann in Frankfurt (1883–5), then appeared in Britain and abroad, playing solo and with distinguished contemporaries from Joachim to Casals. Her repertory included new works and English virginal music.

Davies, Peter Maxwell (b. Manchester, 8 Sep 1934). British composer, knighted in 1987 and appointed Master of the Queen's Music in 2004. His extreme parodies of the late 1960s, his sombre reflections on the landscape and history of Orkney (his principal residence since the start of the 1970s), his symphonies and his chamber music are the products of an immensely fertile and also volatile musician, the solidity of whose later output is as uneasy and confrontational as the theatrical bravado that went before.

He studied at the Royal Manchester College of Music (1952–6), where, with his fellow students Birtwistle and Goehr, he discovered new possibilities through Indian, medieval and European avant-garde music. Pieces he wrote in his early 20s already show characteristic features of instrumental extravagance verging towards violence, and slow, troubled contemplation, as well as a melding of medieval-Renaissance techniques (producing, in particular, highly contorted rhythms) with traditional symphonic continuity. He went to Darmstadt in 1956 and studied further with Petrassi in Rome (1957–9).

A post at Cirencester Grammar School (1959–62) stimulated him to revitalize school music, by encouraging children to compose and by writing pieces specifically for them, notably *O magnum mysterium*, a sequence of modal carols interspersed with more adventurous meditations for school orchestra and capped by an organ fantasia of eerie flamboyance. He has continued to write often for children. But he learned lessons, too, himself, especially in accepting spontaneity and vivid gesture into his music. Then he went to Princeton (1962–4) to study with Sessions and Kim, and while there he began his first dramatic work, *Taverner*, on the life of the Tudor composer who was then thought to have rejected his career as a master of the old church's polyphony to become a Protestant zealot.

Work on the opera led him into areas of intense experience (madness, blasphemy, self-betrayal) and prompted an outburst of wild transformations (e.g. of Purcell) and theatre pieces (*Eight Songs for a Mad King*), many of them devised for the Pierrot Players (later FIRES OF LONDON), which he directed. Some works, like *Hymnos*, were nakedly ferocious, but many others expounded the equally disturbing triumph, after agonies and dark musings, of the foxtrot. Nothing was sacred – least of all the sacred. Yet out of this fierce and dislocated musical world he drew a monument: *Worldes Blis*.

After his move to Orkney, completed by 1975, his music became on the surface calmer. There were more music-theatre pieces, but they were now outnumbered by songs, setting the island poetry of George Mackay Brown and concerned with ancient stabilities of myth, ritual and pastoral. In 1977 he established the midsummer St Magnus Festival in Orkney. At the same time he returned to large-scale instrumental composition, with *Ave maris stella* (a one-movement symphony for the Fires ensemble) presaging whole cycles of symphonies and 'Strathclyde concertos' for Classical orchestra, besides other symphonic works and sonatas.

All these grew out of his understanding that tonal forces of long range and deep ambiguity might be created by a modal gloss on major-minor harmony. He described his Second Symphony, for instance, as being in B minor but with F as dominant, and the conflict between 'real' and traditional dominants is perhaps one source of his music's strangeness, tension and energy. Here, as in most of his compositions, the music is based on a fragment of plainsong, in a fusion of medieval and modern (serial) techniques. But the old modes of plainsong are, nearly always, deeply buried. More obvious, especially in works since the early 1980s, may be a restitution of tonality echoing Sibelius or Prokofiev, but his music has continued to form itself from doubt and disintegration.

Mike Seabrook *Max* (1994); Stewart R. Craggs *Peter Maxwell Davies* (2002)

www.maxopus.com

Full-scale operas: TAVERNER, 1962–8; *Resurrection* (Davies), 1987, Darmstadt 1988; *The Doctor of Myddfai* (David Pountney), 1995, Llandudno 1996
Smaller operas and music-theatre pieces: *Missa super L'Homme armé*, 1968, rev 1971; EIGHT SONGS FOR A MAD KING, 1969; *Vesalii icones*, 1969; *Blind Man's Buff*, 1972; *The Martyrdom of St Magnus*, 1976; *Le Jongleur de Notre Dame*, 1978; *The Lighthouse*, 1979; etc.
Symphonies: No.1, 1973–6; No.2, 1980; No.3, 1984; No.4, chbr orch, 1989; No.5, 1994; No.6, 1996; No.7, 2000; No.8 'Antarctic', 2000
Other orchestral works: Second Taverner Fantasia, 1964; *Worldes Blis*, 1966–9; *St Thomas Wake*, 1969; *Stone Litany* (runes), mez, orch, 1973; *Salome* (ballet), 1978; Violin Concerto, 1985; Trumpet Concerto, 1988; Strathclyde concertos Nos.1–10, chbr orch, 1986–96; *Caroline Mathilde* (ballet), 1990; Piccolo Concerto, 1996; Piano Concerto, 1997; Horn Concerto, 1999; etc.
Choral: *O magnum mysterium*, ch, ens, 1960; *Westerlings* (Mackay Brown), ch, 1976
Ensemble: *Leopardi Fragments*, s, a, 8 insts, 1961; 7 In Nomine, 10 insts, 1963–4; *Revelation and Fall*, v, 16 insts, 1966; *A Mirror of Whitening Light*, 14 insts, 1976–7; etc.
Fires repertory: *Antechrist*, 1967; Fantasia on a Ground and 2 Pavans (after Purcell), 1968; *From Stone to Thorn* (Mackay Brown), 1971; *Tenebrae super Gesualdo*, 1972; *Ave maris stella*, 1975; *The Blind Fiddler* (Mackay Brown), 1975; *Image, Reflection, Shadow*, 1982; etc.
Film scores: *The Devils*, 1970; *The Boy Friend*, 1971
Other works: *Alma redemptoris mater*, 6 wind, 1957; String Quartet, 1961; *Hymnos*, cl, pf, 1967; *Dark Angels* (Mackay Brown), mez, gtr, 1973; Naxos Quartets, str qt, 2002–; much children's music, etc.

Davies, (Henry) Walford (b. Oswestry, 6 Sep 1869; d. Wrington, Somerset, 11 Mar 1941). British musician, knighted in 1922 and Master of the King's Music (1934–41). Trained under Parratt at Windsor and Parry and Stanford at the RCM, he began his career as a teacher, organist and composer, but from 1926 was better known as a broadcaster on music. His works include *Solemn Melody* for organ (1908) and a popular arrangement of the carol 'O little town of Bethlehem'.

Davis, Andrew (Frank) (b. Ashridge, Herts., 2 Feb 1944). British conductor, knighted in 1999, remarkable for bringing the same exacting drive to Boulez as to Elgar, and for his dramatic skills in opera. He studied at the RCM, at Cambridge, and with Franco Ferrara in Rome, and has been music director of the Toronto Symphony (1975–88), the BBC Symphony (1988–2000), Glyndebourne (1989–2000) and the Lyric Opera of Chicago (from 2000).

Davis, Anthony (b. Paterson, NJ, 20 Feb 1951). US composer, of music resonant with the complex heritage of an African–American. Yale-trained, he began his career principally as pianist with his own jazz-classical improvisation group Episteme. The success of his first opera *X* (New York, 1986), on the Black activist Malcolm X, led to more works in the genre, notably *Amistad* (Chicago, 1997).

Davis, Colin (Rex) (b. Weybridge, 25 Sep 1927). British conductor, knighted in 1980, a full and beloved communicator of his various passions, especially for Berlioz, Tippett and Mozart. He studied at the RCM and became music director of Sadler's Wells Opera (1961–4), the BBC Symphony (1967–71) and the Royal Opera (1971–86), besides pursuing a vigorous career internationally. In 1977 he was the first British conductor at Bayreuth (*Tannhäuser*). From his sometimes stormy time at Covent Garden he emerged with boundless energy and sureness to give to his later appointments with the Bavarian Radio Symphony (1983–92) and the LSO (from 1995).

Davy, Richard (b. *c*.1465; d. 1538). English composer of fluent polyphony, best known for his four-part St Matthew Passion and other pieces in the Eton Choirbook. He probably studied at Magdalen College, Oxford, and may have served then at Exeter Cathedral and/or Fotheringhay College.

db. Abbreviation for double bass.

D.C. DA CAPO.

Dead March. Name given the funeral march in Handel's *Saul*.

deafness. Particular curse of the musician, it afflicted Beethoven and Smetana. Evelyn Glennie is an example of someone performing (on percussion) though deaf.

Dean, Brett (b. Brisbane, 23 Oct 1961). Australian composer. He studied at the Queensland Conservatorium and joined the violas of the Berlin Philharmonic (1985–2000), then returned to Australia to concentrate on composition. His works include *Carlo*, after Gesualdo, for string orchestra, sampler and CD (1997).

death. See DANCE OF DEATH; FUNERAL; LAMENT; LATE WORKS.

Death and the Maiden. See *Der* TOD UND DAS MÄDCHEN.

Death in Venice. Opera by Britten to a libretto by Myfanwy Piper after Thomas Mann's novella. Gustav von Aschenbach (tenor), the gentleman writer, sings out his passion in largely solitary scenes, while his boy idol, Tadzio (dancer), is seen always in choreographed company, with fellow dancers as his friends and family. First performance: Snape, 16 Jun 1973.

Debussy, (Achille) Claude (b. St Germain-en-Laye, 22 Aug 1862; d. Paris, 25 Mar 1918). French composer. Suggestion, for him, was more powerful than statement, and rule got in the way of both. When, in his student days, he was asked by a professor what law he followed, his answer was simple: 'My pleasure.' But the simplicity was deceptive. In pursuing pleasure – and in finding music that was indubitably his – he was obliged to invent or discover alternatives to the norms of the 19th-century French and Austro-German traditions he inherited. He subverted the major–minor system by using the old modes and the whole-tone scale, weakening the harmonic impetus to accord with forms of an improvisatory character, where subtleties of sound and orchestration took on primary importance. He wanted to reach, he said, 'the naked flesh of emotion', and did so by means of a mercuriality utterly new. But his work is precisely evocative, too, of visual phenomena: landscapes, clouds, the sea. It portrays people and nature in an ambiguous yet immediate reality.

Born into the petit bourgeoisie, he had piano lessons from Verlaine's mother-in-law before reaching the Paris Conservatoire in 1872. There he studied with Jean François Marmontel (piano) and others, and in 1880 joined Guiraud's composition class, after spending the summer as Nadezhda von Meck's house pianist in Italy, Vienna and Russia. Oddly he wrote little piano music at this time; his student compositions consist mostly of songs, one of which ('Nuit d'étoiles') was published in 1882. Two years later he won the Prix de Rome with *L'Enfant prodigue*, but he was unhappy away from Paris and from his beloved Marie-Blanche Vasnier, the destined singer of many of his youthful songs. He returned to Paris early in 1887, and balanced his enthusiasm for Wagner – ripening with visits to Bayreuth in 1888 and 1889, and the composition of the *Cinq poèmes de Baudelaire* – with a keen response to the music from Java and Indochina he encountered at the 1889 Paris Exposition. Living a bohemian life in the French capital with his new partner Gabrielle Dupont, and befriending or admiring many fellow artists (Chausson and Satie, Mallarmé and Verlaine), he produced his first important works – a varied bunch including (besides the Baudelaire songs) settings of Verlaine, the cantata *La Damoiselle élue*, *Printemps* and piano music.

A new phase opened in 1892 when he began the *Prélude à 'L'Après-midi d'un faune'*, an orchestral evocation of the hazy reverie on a warm afternoon of a tumescent faun, as described in Mallarmé's poem, and thereby a score made of stillness, seduction and dappled colour. The next year he found in Maeterlinck's play *Pelléas et Mélisande* what he had been hoping for: a kind of drama that could accommodate his new style of mingled delicacy and intensity, a waking dream. He seems to have started work at once on setting the play as his second opera (his first, *Rodrigue et Chimène*, he left unfinished). Meanwhile, his name became known through the first performances of *La Damoiselle élue* and his string quartet in 1893, then of the *Prélude* in 1894.

Creatively, though, he reached an impasse after completing the first draft of *Pelléas* in 1895. His only work of 1896 was to orchestrate a pair of Satie's *Gymnopédies*, and the next year he was shaken by Dupont's attempt at suicide. The catalogue of his works began to fill with unwritten projects, one big problem being what to contrive for the theatre after *Pelléas*. Satie's comment after the opera's première was just: 'Now one must look elsewhere.' And Debussy clearly realized that the piece was a one-off, an unprecedented and unrepeatable work in which opera characters behave quietly and in which the orchestra at once provides them with decor and expresses their unvoiced consciousness. He entertained many different plans subsequently, and kept toying with a double bill based on Poe's stories *The Devil in the Belfry* and *The Fall of the House of Usher*. But, in more than 20 years, only *Usher* went beyond the idea stage.

His refusal to accept conventional methods must also have contributed to the intermittence he experienced as a composer. After the gap of 1896 came, in 1897–8, the orchestral *Nocturnes* and the *Chansons de Bilitis*, a song cycle to languorous erotic poems by his friend Pierre Louÿs. In 1899, another creatively empty year, he married Lily Texier and ended his bachelor freedom. Then came more *Chansons de Bilitis* for reciter and ensemble, a first important piano work (the suite *Pour le piano*) and further work on *Pelléas*, leading up to the first performance in 1902. This swell of achievement continued into *La Mer* (1903–5) and other works, including several for piano: *D'un cahier d'esquisses, Estampes, L'Isle joyeuse, Masques* and the first set of *Images* – pieces all lively and full of potential. But then, once again, his output quickly dribbled almost to nothing.

The *Nocturnes* and *La Mer* were solutions to the problem of how to compose a work of symphonic scope without traditional symphonic form. *Nocturnes* drew clues from its subject matter, in the contrast of slow oscillations and diffuse textures (*Nuages*) with vivacity and brightness (*Fêtes*), and then of those qualities with wave-shape melodies sung by wordless women's voices (*Sirènes*). Only in the far background is there the sense of a symphony without a finale. In *La Mer*, which carries the subtitle 'symphonic sketches', the symphonic model is more overt, though masterfully reimagined and rejustified by the poetry of the sea, whether in the outer movements' elaboration of themes or in the spontaneity of the intervening *Jeux de vagues*. After this it took him much longer to put together another three-movement orchestral work without repeating either textbooks or himself.

But, particularly where the high creative plateau of 1903–5 is concerned, it would be hard to ignore the effect of personal circumstances. In 1903 he met Emma Bardac, a banker's wife and a singer. The next year he moved in with her, losing several friends in the process, and in 1905 she gave birth to their daughter, Claude-Emma. Now he had family responsibilities and had to earn money, which partly accounts for the relative musical dearth of 1906–8, when he started travelling regularly to play or conduct his music, and for the excessive number of theatre commissions he accepted in 1911–13 – *Le Martyre de Saint Sébastien, Khamma, Jeux, La Boîte à joujoux* – obliging him to work with assistants on all but *Jeux*. An obvious alternative route to security would have been a teaching post, but that was impossible for an artist who so much prized perception above learning and nature above art – and for one who had taken eight years to begin forgetting his own conservatory training.

If, though, financial imperatives played their part in encouraging the longer and more continuous run of compositions that began in 1909 with the first *Préludes* for piano, he may also have been writing now in the nearer awareness of death, for his cancer was diagnosed that same year. After finishing the first book of *Préludes* he moved into the most prolific phase of his career, producing the second book of *Préludes, Jeux* and the other, partly collaborative scenic works. *Jeux* – written for the Ballets Russes, and a score to which nobody else could have contributed a note – is the high spot. He had taken an interest in the Russian company,

and in their young composer Stravinsky, since their first arrival, and the company had already given a graphic visualization of the *Prélude à 'L'Après-midi d'un faune'*, with Nijinsky, that had scandalized and delighted Paris. *Jeux* went further. Its scenario concerns a tennis match that is also a sequence of amorous encounters involving a young man (Nijinsky once more) and two young women. Its score moves in sequences that dissolve almost as soon as they develop solidity and passion, the music maintaining constant fluidity with its exquisite harmonies and orchestration. Unwilling to bring back a theme unchanged, Debussy seemed also unwilling now to repeat a timbre.

Subsequently, bothered not only by his illness but by the war that broke out in August 1914, he completed only a few works, all for small forces: the Etudes for piano, *En blanc et noir* for two pianos, and the first three in a planned set of six chamber sonatas. That for flute, viola and harp employs a quintessence of his orchestra in tendrils of timbral connection, while the cello and violin sonatas have more in common with the teasing artificiality of the Verlaine and Mallarmé songs. The antique notion of a set of six sonatas, explicitly modelled on 18th-century publications, was part of a deepening fascination with the past. Evocations of ancient Greece (the Bilitis songs, *Danseuses de Delphes*), Asia (*Pagodes*), folk music (the orchestral *Images*) or the Middle Ages (*La Cathédrale engloutie*) had long provided occasions for undermining diatonic certainties by modal means. But the settings of 1910 make Villon sound as contemporary as Verlaine, and the sonatas bring into classical archetypes the free spirit of *Jeux*. The three unrealized sonatas were to have been for oboe, horn and harpsichord, for clarinet, trumpet, bassoon and piano, and for the full ensemble of piano, harpsichord, wind sextet and string trio.

As it was, the Etudes made up his last completed collection, and fittingly so. Devised in homage to Chopin, whom he revered as a master of the piano, of harmony and of delicate implication, the work became also a personal summation. Its finale, like that of *En blanc et noir*, strikingly responds to Stravinsky's recent *Petrushka*, a work that may have captivated and troubled him as revealing a genuine successor, rather than a facile imitator of the kind he was familiar with. Among its more constant and prominent features, though, the set magnificently surveys, as from a peak, the enormous range of sounds he had obtained from the piano, his extraordinary imagination, and the fluidity he had brought to how music moves.

Edward Lockspeiser *Debussy*, 2 Vols. (1962, 1965; ²1978); Richard Langham Smith, ed. *Debussy on Music* (1977); Roger Nichols *The Life of Debussy* (1998)

Theatre and orchestral music

Opera: PELLEAS ET MELISANDE, 1893–5, 1901–2

Orchestral: Intermezzo, vc, orch, 1882; *Fantaisie*, pf, orch, 1889–90; PRELUDE À 'L'APRES-MIDI D'UN FAUNE', 1891–4; *Deux* GYMNOPEDIES, 1896 (after Satie); NOCTURNES, 1897–9; *La* MER, 1903–5; *Danse sacrée et danse profane*, hp, str, 1904; *March écossaise*, 1893–1908 (after pf piece); *La Plus que lente* (café waltz), pub 1912; *Première rapsodie*, cl, orch, 1911; IMAGES, 1905–12; JEUX (ballet), 1912–13; *Berceuse héroïque*, 1914 (after pf piece)

Choral orchestral: *Invocation* (Lamartine), men's ch, orch, 1883; *L'Enfant prodigue* (Edouard Guinand), soli, ch, orch, 1884; *La Damoiselle élue* (Dante Gabriel Rossetti), s, women's ch, orch, 1887–8, rev 1902

Orchestral songs: 'La Saulaie' (Rossetti), 1896–1900; 'Le Jet d'eau', 1907 (from *Cinq poèmes de Baudelaire*); *Trois ballades de Villon*, 1910

Works with orchestration completed by others: Allegro from *Le Triomphe de Bacchus*, 1882 (Marius Gaillard); *Salut printemps* (de Ségur), women's ch, orch, 1882 (Gaillard); *Printemps*, 1887 (Büsser); *Rodrigue et Chimène* (opera: Catulle Mendès), 1890–93 (Denisov); *Fanfare d'ouverture*, *Le Sommeil de Lear* (projected incidental music), 1904 (Roger-Ducasse); *Rapsodie*, a sax, orch, 1901–8 (Roger-Ducasse); *Le* MARTYRE DE SAINT SEBASTIEN, 1911 (Caplet); KHAMMA (ballet), 1910–12 (Koechlin); *La* BOITE A JOUJOUX (ballet), 1913 (Caplet); *La Chûte de la Maison Usher* (unfinished opera; Debussy, after Poe), 1908–17 (Allende-Blin)

Chamber and piano music

Chamber: Piano Trio, G, 1880; *Nocturne et scherzo*, vc, pf, 1882; String Quartet, G minor, 1893; *Chansons de Bilitis* (Louÿs), reciter, 2 fl, 2 hp, cel, 1900–1; *Rapsodie*, cor ang/a sax, pf, 1901–8; *Première rapsodie*, cl, pf, 1909–10; *Petite pièce*, cl, pf, 1910; *Syrinx*, fl, 1913 (see PAN); Cello Sonata, 1915; Sonata for Flute, Viola and Harp, 1915; Violin Sonata, 1916–17

Piano solo: *Danse bohémienne*, 1880; *Ballade slave* (Ballade), c.1890; *Deux arabesques*, c.1890; Mazurka, c.1890; *Rêverie*, 1890; *Tarantelle styrienne* (*Danse*), c.1890; *Valse romantique*, c.1890; *Suite bergamasque* (*Prélude, Menuet*, CLAIR DE LUNE, *Passepied*), c.1890, rev 1905; Nocturne, 1892; IMAGES, 1894; *Pour le piano* (Prelude, Sarabande, Toccata), 1894–1901; ESTAMPES, 1903; *L'Isle joyeuse*, 1903–4; *Masques*, 1903–4; *D'un cahier d'esquisses*, 1904; Piece, 1904; IMAGES, set 1, 1901–5, set 2, 1907; CHILDREN'S CORNER, 1906–8; *Hommage à Haydn*, 1909; *The Little Nigar*, 1909; PRELUDES, book 1, 1909–10, book 2, 1911–13; *La Plus que lente*, 1910; *Berceuse héroïque*, 1914; *Six épigraphes antiques*, 1914 (after duets); *Elégie*, 1915; *Page d'album*, 1915; ETUDES, 1915

Piano duet: Allegro from Symphony in B minor, 1880–81; Overture to *Diane au bois*, 1883–5; *Divertissement*, 1884; *Petite suite* (*En bateau, Cortège, Menuet, Ballet*), 1886–9; *Marche écossaise*, 1890; *Six épigraphes antiques*, 1914 (after chamber *Chansons de Bilitis*)

Piano duo: *Lindaraja*, 1901; *En blanc et noir*, 1915

Songs

Choral: *Trois chansons de Charles d'Orléans*, ch, 1898–1908; 'Noël des enfants qui n'ont plus de maison', arr children, pf, 1915

Solo sets: *Ariettes oubliées* (Verlaine; 'C'est l'extase', 'Il pleure dans mon coeur', 'L'ombre des arbres', 'Chevaux de bois', 'Green', 'Spleen'), 1885–8; *Cinq poèmes de Baudelaire* ('Le Balcon', 'Harmonie du soir', 'Le Jet d'eau', 'Recueillement', 'La Mort des amants'), 1887–9; *Deux romances* (Bourget), 1891; *Trois mélodies* (Verlaine; 'La Mer est plus belle', 'Le Son du cor', 'L'Echelonnement des haies'), 1891; *Fêtes galantes* (Verlaine), set 1 ('En sourdine', 'Fantoches', CLAIR DE LUNE'), 1891, set 2 ('Les Ingénus', 'La Faune', 'Colloque sentimental'), 1904; *Proses lyriques* (Debussy), 1892–3; *Chansons de Bilitis* (Louÿs), 1897–8; *Nuits blanches* (Debussy), 1898; *Trois chansons de France* (d'Orléans, Lhermite) 1904; *Le Promenoir des deux amants* (Lhermite), 1904–10; *Trois ballades de Villon*, 1910; *Trois poèmes de Mallarmé* ('Soupir', 'Placet futile', 'Eventail'), 1913

Other solo songs: 'Nuit d'étoiles' (Banville), 1880; 'Rêverie' (Banville), 1880; 'Fleur des blés' (Girod), 1881; 'Mandoline' (Verlaine), 1882; 'Pierrot' (Banville), 1882; 'Sérénade' (Banville), 1882; 'Pantomime' (Verlaine), 1883; 'Silence ineffable' (Bourget), 1883; 'Paysage sentimental' (Bourget), 1883; 'Apparition' (Mallarmé), 1884; 'Voici que le printemps' (Bourget), 1884; 'La Belle au bois dormant' (Vincent Hyspa), 1890; 'Beau soir' (Banville), 1891; 'Les Angélus' (Grégoire le Roy), 1891; 'Dans le jardin' (Paul Gravollet), 1903; 'Noël des enfants qui n'ont plus de maison' (Debussy), 1915; etc.

Duet: 'Eglogue' (Leconte de Lisle), s, t, pf, 1881

debut. First appearance, which may be in a country, city, role, etc. Singers are particularly prone to amassing debuts. A soprano's professional debut may be followed at differing distances by her European debut, her Berlin debut, her debut as Donna Anna, her debut with the Berlin Staatsoper and so on.

decani, cantoris. The opposing sides of the choir – as an architectural structure and as a singing body – in a British cathedral or church, being 'the dean's' (south, or right from a position facing the altar) and 'the cantor's' (precentor's). Pre-Reformation and Anglican music often requires alternation between the two groups of singers.

Decaux, Abel (Marie) (b. Auffay, 1869; d. Paris, 19 Mar 1943). French composer, noted especially for his set of four late-Liszt-like piano pieces *Clairs de lune* (1900–7). He studied at the Paris Conservatoire, became organist of the Sacré Coeur in 1903 and spent the years 1926–37 teaching in Rochester, NY.

decay. Behaviour of sound after performance, dependent on the nature of the sound and on the acoustic environment. Decay characteristics often help in identifying a sound, and their removal (by editing a recording) or change (by electronic means) can be disconcerting.

Decca. British record company, which made its first releases in 1929. Technically and musically outstanding in the 1950s–70s, when it produced important recordings of new and early music as well as the first recorded *Ring*, it was absorbed by Polygram (1979) and then by the Universal Music Group (1998).

deceptive cadence. INTERRUPTED CADENCE.

decet (Fr. *dixtuor*). Piece for 10 musicians. There are examples so titled by Enescu, Claude Arrieu, Sven-Erik Bäck and few others.

déchiffrer (Fr., decipher). Sight read, especially from an orchestral score at the piano.

decibel (dB). Unit of measure for sound intensity (or other forms of energy in transmission), named after Alexander Graham Bell. The scale is logarithmic to base 10, a difference of 10 dB (or 1 bel) being equivalent to a tenfold difference in intensity, which is felt as approximately a doubling in LOUDNESS. Also, the measure is relative, with respect to a reference level (0 dB) conventionally set as the intensity of a soundwave transmitting 1 picowatt per square metre, which is below the normal threshold of audibility.

décidé (Fr.), **deciso** (It.). Decided, affirmative.

Decke (Ger.). BELLY.

decrescendo (It., decreasing). Direction to get quieter, often abbreviated *decresc.* and even more often symbolized by a 'hairpin':

decuplet. Group of 10 equal notes to be played in the time of eight or 12.

Dedekind, Constantin Christian (b. Reinsdorf, Anhalt-Cöthen, 2 Apr 1628; d. Dresden, 2 Sep 1715). German poet-composer, author of songs, sacred concertos and plays. Born into a Saxon family of churchmen and musicians – his grandfather Henning (1562–1626) and great uncle Euricius (1554–1619) were distinguished cantors – he studied at Quedlinburg Abbey and in Dresden, where he was director of the court orchestra (1666–75) before retiring to live on what he had gained as a tax collector.

De Fesch, Willem (b. Alkmaar, 1687; d. London, ?1757). Dutch violinist-composer, resident in London from the early 1730s. He trained in Bonn under Karel Rosier, whose daughter he married, and began his career in Amsterdam and Antwerp. Indebted to Vivaldi, Corelli and Handel, he published concertos, sonatas and songs. His oratorios *Judith* (1733) and *Joseph* (1745) are lost.

DeGaetani, Jan(ice) (b. Massillon, Ohio, 10 Jul 1933; d. Rochester, NY, 15 Sep 1989). US mezzo-soprano, admired for her expressive clarity and devotion to new music. She studied at Juilliard and, from 1973, taught at Eastman.

De Gamerra, Giovanni (b. Leghorn, 1743; d. Vicenza, 29 Aug 1803). Italian librettist, who began on a peak with *Lucio Silla*, for Mozart. Before that he had been a law student in Pisa and an Austrian soldier. Active in Milan (from 1771) and Vienna (from 1793), he also wrote for Paisiello, Salieri and Weigl.

De Grandis, Vincenzo. Name of two 17th-century Italian church musicians and composers. The earlier, 'il romano' (b. Montalboddo, now Ostra, 1577; d. 18 Mar 1646), became chapelmaster of the papal choir in 1625 and wrote psalms in the Palestrina tradition as well as more modern motets. The later (b. Montalboddo, 6 Apr 1631; d. Montalboddo, 4 Aug 1708) worked for the dukes of Hanover (1667–80) and Ferrara, and wrote oratorios, cantatas, etc., in which he was an early pioneer of accompanied recitative.

degree. Position on a diatonic scale, e.g. E is the third degree of the C major scale. The degrees can be numbered, as in this instance, or named: tonic (first), supertonic, mediant, subdominant, dominant, submediant, leading note (seventh).

De Koven, (Henry Louis) Reginald (b. Middletown, Conn., 3 Apr 1859; d. Chicago, 16 Jan 1920). US composer, mostly of operettas and songs ('Oh promise me' from *Robin Hood*, 1890). Educated at Oxford and in Stuttgart, Frankfurt, Florence, Vienna and Paris, he returned to the USA in 1882 and worked as a music critic in New York and Chicago. He ended his career with two operas, of which *The Canterbury Pilgrims* was given at the Met (1917) and *Rip Van Winkle* in Chicago a fortnight before he died.

Delage, Maurice (Charles) (b. Paris, 13 Nov 1879; d. Paris, 21 Sep 1961). French composer, a friend of Ravel and Stravinsky at the time of his best known work, the *Quatre poèmes hindous* for soprano and mixed nonet (1913). He was into his 20s before he started teaching himself music, and his output was small, including further songs, orchestral pieces and a string quartet.

Delibes, (Clément Philibert) Léo (b. St Germain du Val, 21 Feb 1836; d. Paris, 16 Jan 1891). French composer, almost exclusively of tuneful and deft theatre scores, including two classic ballets (*Coppélia*, *Sylvia*) and the opera *Lakmé*. Encouraged by his mother, who came from a musical family, he studied at the Paris Conservatoire, sang as a boy at the première of *Le Prophète*, and started his career as an organist and theatre accompanist in 1853. During 1856–69 he produced a succession of operettas while, as choirmaster at the Théâtre Lyrique, working on *Faust*, *Les Pêcheurs de perles* and *Les Troyens à Carthage*. In 1871 he married and gave up his jobs as organist and choirmaster in favour of composition, though in 1881 he joined the Conservatoire staff – an ironic appointment, since he had been a poor student and had learned his trade largely as a working theatre musician, modelling himself on Offenbach and later on Bizet, Gounod and Lalo.

Operas: *Le Roi l'a dit* (Edmond Gondinet), f.p. Paris, 1873; *Jean de Nivelle* (Gondinet and Philippe Gille), f.p. Paris, 1880; LAKME; *Kassya* (Meilhac and Gille), orch Massenet, f.p. Paris, 1893; 16 operettas

Ballets: *La Source*, Paris, 1866, with Minkus; COPPELIA; SYLVIA; *Le Roi s'amuse* (6 numbers), Paris, 1882

Other works: cantatas, choruses, songs (*Les Filles de Cadiz*, 1885), pf pieces

delicato (It.). Delicate. Also *delicatamente* (delicately), *delicatissimo* (very delicate).

délié (Fr., untied). With notes clearly separated, or with rhythmic freedom.

Delius, Frederick (Theodore Albert) (b. Bradford, 29 Jan 1862; d. Grez-sur-Loing, 10 Jun 1934). British composer, though of German extraction (his father was in the import-export business) and resident most of his life in France. His musical world, too, was cosmopolitan: he showed an occasional feeling for English folk music (*Brigg Fair*),

but the composers most important to him were Wagner for continuous flow, Grieg for untroubled chromaticism and Debussy for orchestral finesse. He wrote little that did not involve the orchestra nor strayed far from a manner of rhapsodic celebration undercut by elegy and nostalgia. More traditional in form than Debussy's, his pieces regularly head in sonata fashion towards resolution, and it is the exquisite delay of resolution (which may not arrive even at the end) that gives his music its poignancy.

He studied with Thomas Ward in Florida, while working there as an orange planter (1884–5), and at the Leipzig Conservatory (1886–8), where he met Grieg. Then, in Paris, he got to know Gauguin, Strindberg, Münch and another Norwegian painter, Jelka Rosen, with whom he settled at Grez-sur-Loing in 1897. Working there, often in his adored garden, he soon achieved his mature style in *Paris* and *A Village Romeo and Juliet*. These works were first given in Germany, but around 1907 he began to be more performed in England, especially by Beecham, who in 1909 presented the first complete account of his exuberant Nietzschean affirmation *A Mass of Life*. During the First World War, when he retreated to England, and for some years after, he concentrated on abstract forms. From 1923 he was virtually silent, blinded and paralysed by syphilis. The arrival of Eric Fenby as amanuensis enabled him to resume composition in his last years.

Eric Fenby *Delius as I knew him* (1936, [3]1981); Christopher Redwood *A Delius Companion* (1976, [2]1980)

Operas (librettos by the composer unless otherwise stated): *Irmelin*, 1890–92; *The Magic Fountain*, 1893–5; *Koanga* (Charles Francis Keary), 1895–7; *A Village Romeo and Juliet* (after Gottfried Keller), 1900–1, f.p. Berlin, 1907; *Margot la rouge* (Berthe Gaston-Danville), 1902; *Fennimore and Gerda* (after Jacobsen), 1909–10, f.p. Frankfurt, 1919

Orchestral: Piano Concerto, C minor, 1897; *Life's Dance*, 1899, rev 1901, 1912; *Paris: The Song of a Great City*, 1899; *Brigg Fair*, 1907; *In a Summer Garden*, 1908; Dance Rhapsody No.1, 1908; No.2, 1916; *Summer Night on the River*, 1911; *On Hearing the First Cuckoo in Spring*, 1912; *North Country Sketches*, 1913–14; Air and Dance, str, 1915; Double Concerto, vn, vc, orch, 1915–16; Violin Concerto, 1916; *Eventyr*, 1917; *A Song before Sunrise*, 1918; Cello Concerto, 1921; *Hassan* (incidental music), 1920–23; *A Song of Summer*, 1929–30; Caprice and Elegy, vc, orch, 1930; *Fantastic Dance*, 1931

Vocal orchestral: *Mitternachtslied* (Nietzsche), bar, men's ch, orch, 1898; *Appalachia* (trad.), ch, orch, 1898–1903; *Sea Drift* (Whitman), bar, ch, orch, 1903–4; *A Mass of Life* (Nietzsche), soli, ch, orch, 1904–5; *Songs of Sunset* (Dowson), mez, bar, ch, orch, 1906–7; *Cynara* (Dowson), bar, orch, 1907,

rev 1928–9; *An Arabesk* (Jacobsen), bar, ch, orch, 1911; *A Song of the High Hills* (wordless), ch, orch, 1911; *Requiem* (Simon), s, bar, ch, orch, 1914–16; *A Late Lark* (Henley), v, orch, 1925; *Songs of Farewell* (Whitman), ch, orch, 1930; *Idyll* (Whitman), s, bar, orch, 1930–32
Smaller choral works: *On Craig Dhu* (Symons), ch, pf, 1907; *2 Songs to be Sung of a Summer Night on the Water* (wordless), ch, 1917
Chamber: String Quartet, 1916; Violin Sonata No.1, 1905–14; No.2, 1923; No.3, 1930; Cello Sonata, 1916
Other works: piano pieces, songs

Della Casa, Lisa (b. Burgdorf, near Berne, 2 Feb 1919). Swiss soprano, much admired for her touching delicacy in Strauss and Mozart. She studied in Zurich, where she began her career (1943–50), going on to Salzburg (from 1947), Glyndebourne (from 1951) and the Met (1953–68).

Della Ciaia, Azzolino (Bernardino) (b. Siena, 21 May 1671; d. Pisa, 15 Jan 1755). Italian composer, resident from boyhood in Pisa. As a knight of the naval order of San Stefano, he began his career as a composer afloat (1688–1704), producing sacred music, cantatas and keyboard pieces. He was then in Rome (1713–30), where he published a notable collection of harpsichord sonatas and organ ricercares, after which he returned to Pisa, designed an elaborate organ for his order and became a priest (1734).

Deller, Alfred (George) (b. Margate, 31 May 1912; d. Bologna, 16 Jul 1979). British countertenor, vital in the revival of the voice. Spotted by Tippett in the choir of Canterbury Cathedral, he made his London debut in 1943, sang full time from 1947 and founded the Deller Consort of voices in 1950. Britten wrote the role of Oberon in *A Midsummer Night's Dream* to exploit his seductive powers.

Dello Joio, Norman (b. New York, 24 Jan 1913). US composer, of music strong in gesture and large in melody, influenced by plainsong, Italian opera and US popular music. He followed his father as a Catholic organist before studying with Wagenaar at Juilliard (1939–41) and Hindemith at Yale (1941). His works include operas (*The Triumph of St Joan*, 1959), ballets (*Seraphic Dialogue* for Martha Graham, 1948), concertos and choral music.

Del Monaco, Mario (b. Florence, 27 Jul 1915; d. Mestre, 16 Oct 1982). Italian tenor, whose thrilling ardour made him one of the stars of the decade or so after the Second World War. Trained at the Pesaro Conservatory, he sang at the Met (1951–9), etc.

Delphic hymns. Two hymns to Apollo, inscribed on stone with musical notation and found at Delphi. One, by Limenius, dates from 128 BC; the other may be of the same date or from a decade earlier. They are the earliest known compositions.

Del Tredici, David (b. Cloverdale, Cal., 16 Mar 1937). US composer, noted especially for a long series of works based on Lewis Carroll's *Alice* books, often employing large and diverse resources (*The Final Alice* – which it was not to be – for amplified soprano, folk group and orchestra, 1976) to the ends of surrealist whimsy. He studied at Berkeley (1955–9) and with Sessions at Princeton (1960, 1964).

De Luca, Giuseppe (b. Rome, 25 Dec 1876; d. New York, 26 Aug 1950). Italian baritone, much admired as a stylist. He studied at the Accademia di Santa Cecilia (1892–7), made his debut in Piacenza (1897) and was soon at the forefront; he created Sharpless in *Madama Butterfly*. From 1915 he was regularly at the Met, where he gave his farewell, as Rigoletto, in 1940.

De Lucia, Fernando (b. Naples, 11 Oct 1860; d. Naples, 21 Feb 1925). Italian tenor, whose superb technique and vivid acting gave him access both to the bel canto repertory and verismo roles. Trained in Naples, he made his debuts there in 1885 and in London two years later. He sang in the premières of Mascagni's *L'amico Fritz* and *Iris* and made important recordings in 1902–10.

Delvincourt, Claude (b. Paris, 12 Jan 1888; d. Orbetello, Tuscany, 5 Apr 1954). French composer-administrator, director of the Paris Conservatoire (1941–54), where he brought Messiaen on to the staff. Conservatoire-trained, he won the Prix de Rome jointly with Lili Boulanger, and died in a car crash returning to Rome to hear the première of his string quartet.

Demantius, (Johannes) Christoph (b. Reichenberg/Liberec, Bohemia, 15 Dec 1567; d. Freiberg, Saxony, 20 Apr 1643). German composer, of sacred and secular choral music, and author of the first alphabetical music dictionary in German (1632). After a period as cantor in Zittau (1597–1604) he spent the rest of his life in a similar position at Freiberg Cathedral. Often vividly expressive, his works include a St John Passion a 6 (1631), motets and choral songs.

Demenga, Thomas (b. Berne, 12 Jun 1954). Swiss cellist, an energetic performer in Bach and modern repertory. He studied with Walter

Grimmer at the Berne Conservatory, and with Antonio Janigro, Leonard Rose and Rostropovich. His younger brother Patrick is also a cellist.

demi-pause (Fr.). Minim (half-note) rest.

demisemiquaver (UK). 32nd-note (US). See DURATION.

demi-soupir (Fr.). Quaver (eighth-note) rest.

demiton (Fr.). Semitone.

Dench, Chris(topher) (b. London, 10 Jun 1953). Australian–British composer, self-taught virtuoso of complex intensity. Several important works since 1986 have been written for his wife, the Australian flautist Laura Chislett. He moved to Australia in 1988.

Denisov, Edison (Vasilyevich) (b. Tomsk, 6 Apr 1929; d. Paris, 24 Nov 1996). Russian composer, leaning towards the culture of France (from Boulez to Boris Vian). He studied mathematics in Tomsk before training with Shebalin at the Moscow Conservatory (1951–6), where he joined the staff in 1960. *Le Soleil des Incas* for soprano and ensemble (1964), conducted by Boulez, was one of the first works to give Western audiences a hint of the Soviet avant-garde, and established him as an important channel of communication during the Cold War. Prolific and stylistically various in his later years, he also produced completions of Schubert's *Lazarus* and Debussy's *Rodrigue et Chimène*.

Denmark (Danmark). Part of the north German sphere in the 17th and 18th centuries, the country gained musical independence in the 19th, with Gade as liberator and the foundation of the Copenhagen Conservatory (1868) a signal event. Nielsen then prepared the ground both for local symphonism (Holmboe, Bentzon) and for the exploratory modernism that passed through Nørgård to Ruders, Abrahamsen and others. In the 20th century orchestras and conservatories were established in other cities, notably Århus. The Royal Orchestra (Kongelike Kapel) traces its history to the 15th century.

density. Thickness of harmony or texture.

Density 21.5. Solo flute piece by Varèse, written to inaugurate Georges Barrère's flute of platinum (density 21·09 according to modern measurement). First performance: New York, 16 Feb 1936.

Dent, Edward (Joseph) (b. Ribston, Yorks., 16 Jul 1876; d. London, 22 Aug 1957). British music scholar. Educated at Eton and Cambridge, he taught at Cambridge from 1902, latterly as professor of music (1926–41). He was a great student and translator of opera, but also founder president of the ISCM (1923–38).

Denza, Luigi (b. Castellammare di Stabia, 24 Feb 1846; d. London, 26 Jan 1922). Italian composer, remembered for the Neapolitan-style song *Funiculì funiculà* (1880), which had the honour of being arranged by Rimsky-Korsakov, Strauss and Schoenberg. He studied with Mercadante at the Naples Conservatory and lived in London from 1887, writing parlour songs and teaching singing at the RAM.

déploration. Modern term, from the title of Guillaume Crétin's *Déploration sur le trépas de Jean Ockeghem*, for a formal elegy for a composer in the 14th–16th centuries. Besides Ockeghem, composers so memorialized include Machaut, Binchois (by Ockeghem) and Josquin.

De profundis. Psalm 130, one of the penitential psalms, associated with the appeal for mercy and the commemoration of the dead. There are settings by Josquin, Lalande and many others. As an utterance from abasement ('Out of the deep have I called to thee, O Lord') the psalm has had a modern relevance for writers and composers including Baudelaire (see LYRIC SUITE), Wilde (see RZEWSKI) and Gubaidulina.

De Reszke, Jean (b. Warsaw, 14 Jan 1850; d. Nice, 3 Apr 1935). Polish–French tenor, who held his vocal allure and good looks as he graduated from French roles at the Paris Opera to Wagner in New York and London. He began his career as a baritone, then retrained with Giovanni Battista Sbriglia and made his name in Massenet's *Hérodiade* in 1884, with his bass brother, Edouard (1853–1917), and soprano sister, Joséphine (1855–91), also in the cast. In retirement he taught.

Dering, Richard (b. *c*.1580; buried London, 22 Mar 1630). English composer and organist, who seems to have converted to Catholicism soon after taking the Oxford BMus (1610). He then spent time in Rome and Brussels before returning to London in 1625 as organist to Queen Henrietta Maria. His works include Italianate motets and madrigals, music for viols and two patchworks, *City Cries* and *Country Cries*, for singer and viols.

derived set. 12-note set derived from a smaller

motif by applying the usual serial techniques of inverting, reversing and transposing. An example is the set of Webern's Concerto Op.24, comprising a three-note idea (B–B♭–D) followed by a retrograde inversion (E♭–G–F♯), retrograde (G♯–E–F) and inversion (C–C♯–A).

Dernesch, Helga (b. Vienna, 3/13 Feb 1939). Austrian soprano, later mezzo-soprano. She studied at the Vienna Conservatory, began singing with the Berne Opera in 1961, and became widely known after her 1965 Bayreuth debut. Majestic and vocally glorious as the Marschallin, she also sang in new operas by Fortner and Reimann.

Dernier sommeil de la Vierge, Le (The Last Sleep of the Virgin). Prelude for cello and strings to the last scene of Massenet's oratorio *La Vierge*.

Des (Ger.). D♭. Hence *Deses* (D♭♭).

De Sabata, Victor (b. Trieste, 10 Apr 1892; d. Santa Margherita Ligure, 11 Dec 1967). Italian conductor, of perfectionism and intensity. After graduating from the Milan Conservatory (1910) he began to make a mark as a composer. He started conducting in 1918 and from 1930 was attached to La Scala.

descant. Countermelody taken by sopranos or trebles in a chorus, often as an enrichment in later verses of hymns or carols. See also DISCANT.

Des canyons aux étoiles ... (From the Canyons to the Stars ...). Orchestral work by Messiaen with solo piano, based on the natural wonders of Utah as places to observe and contemplate, through 12 movements making an entire concert programme: 1 *Le Désert*, 2 *Les Orioles*, 3 *Ce qui est écrit sur les étoiles*, 4 *Le Cossyphe d'Heuglin* (pf solo), 5 *Cedar Breaks et le don de crainte*, 6 *Appel interstellaire* (hn solo), 7 *Bryce Canyon et les rochers rouge-orange*, 8 *Les Ressuscités et le chant de l'étoile Aldébaran*, 9 *Le Moqueur polyglotte* (pf solo), 10 *La Grive des bois*, 11 *Omao, Leiothrix, Elepaio, Shama*, 12 *Zion Park et la Cité Céleste*. First performance: New York, 20 Nov 1974.

Déserts (Deserts). Work by Varèse for an orchestra of wind and percussion, having three 'interpolations' of 'electronically organized sound' on tape. This was probably the first use of electronics in orchestral performance. First performance: Paris, 2 Dec 1954.

desiderio (It.). Desire, as in the marking *con desiderio*.

De Silva, Andreas (b. ?Spain, c.1475–80). Composer trained in France and north Italy, active in Rome in the second decade of the 16th century. His masses and motets mark a phase between Josquin and Willaert.

deśī-tāla (Sanskrit; Fr. *deçi-tala*). Rhythmic pattern, of which Śārngadeva listed 120 in his treatise. Messiaen used them frequently.

desk. Pair of string players sharing a music stand. An orchestra may be said to include, say, eight desks of first violins, arranged in rank order.

Desmarets, Henry (b. Paris, Feb 1661; d. Lunéville, 7 Sep 1741). French composer, heir to Lalande in his psalms and motets. A treble in the royal chapel under Lully, he remained in court circles until 1699, when he eloped with a student to Brussels and then Madrid. There he married his fellow escapee and became chamber music master to the king. In 1707 he was appointed superintendent of music to the Duke of Lorraine at Lunéville, where he remained, for though he gained a royal pardon in 1720, he was unable to reestablish himself at the royal chapel. Besides church music, he wrote operas (*Iphigénie en Tauride*, Paris, 1704), divertissements and cantatas.

Désormière, Roger (b. Vichy, 13 Sep 1898; d. Paris, 25 Oct 1963). French conductor, especially associated with Debussy's *Pelléas* and with new music from Satie and Stravinsky through Milhaud and Messiaen to Boulez. Trained at the Paris Conservatoire, he made his debut in 1921 and retired in 1950 for health reasons.

Desprez. See JOSQUIN.

Dessau, Paul (b. Hamburg, 10 Dec 1894; d. Berlin, 28 Jun 1979). German composer, who worked regularly with Brecht after their meeting in New York in 1942. A synagogue cantor's grandson, he started as a boy violinist, then in 1912 began a career as a theatre conductor. He was engaged by Klemperer in Cologne (1919–23) and Walter in Berlin in 1925, and was soon making a name too as a composer. In 1933 he moved to Paris, and in 1939 to New York. His socialist ideals were sharpened by Brecht, whom he followed to southern California, and the two returned to Berlin in 1948. There he became a leading figure in East German music, developing an art of disjunct musical elements forcing attention on the text or programme. He also taught music at the upper school in his home town of Zeuthen.

Works with Brecht: *Deutsches Miserere*, soli, ch, orch, 1944–7; *Die Verurteilung des Lukullus* (opera), Berlin, 1951; memorials, songs, incidental scores (*Mutter Courage, Der gute Mensch von Sezuan, Mann ist Mann, Der kaukasische Kreidekreis*), etc.

Other operas: *Puntila* (after Brecht), f.p. Berlin, 1966; *Lanzelot* (Heiner Müller), f.p. Berlin, 1969; *Einstein* (Mickel), f.p. Berlin, 1973

Other works: choral music, songs, various theatre pieces, film scores, orchestral, chamber and piano pieces

dessous (Fr., below). French Baroque term for viola or other alto-register part.

dessus (Fr., above). French Baroque term for treble (instrument or voice), as in *dessus de violon* (or just *dessus*), *dessus de hautbois*, etc.

Destinn, Emmy (b. Prague, 26 Feb 1878; d. České Budějovice, 28 Jan 1930). Czech soprano, admired as an actress and fine singer. Originally Emmy Kittl, she took the name of her teacher, Marie Loewe-Destinn, made her debut in Berlin in 1898 and sang regularly there, at Covent Garden and at the Met (1908–16, notably as the first *Fanciulla del West*). Placed under house arrest by the Austrians during the First World War, she sang Libuše in Smetana's opera when Czechoslovakia gained its independence, and from that point used the Czech form of her name, Ema Destinnová.

Destouches, André Cardinal (baptized Paris, 6 Apr 1672; d. Paris, 7 Feb 1749). French composer. Born into a prosperous mercantile family, he may have been the first European composer to visit the East when he joined a mission to Siam (1687–8). He was then a soldier, before deciding in 1694 to devote himself to composition, at first under Campra's guidance. Connections and talent gained him rapid acceptance at court, and he held several appointments under Louis XV. His works include operas and collections of airs and dances.

destro, destra (It.). Right, as in *mano destra* (right hand, abbreviated *m.d.*).

détaché (Fr.). Detached (bowstroke), staccato.

Dettingen. Name attached to a *Te Deum* and anthem (*The King shall Rejoice*) Handel wrote for a service of thanksgiving (Chapel Royal, 27 Nov 1743) for the victory there over the French.

deutlich (Ger.). Distinct.

Deutsch, Max (b. Vienna, 17 Nov 1892; d. Paris, 22 Nov 1982). Austrian–French musician, who studied with Schoenberg in Vienna and was instrumental in communicating the music and ideas of the Second Viennese School to Paris, where he settled in 1924.

Deutsch, Otto Erich (b. Vienna, 5 Sep 1883; d. Vienna, 23 Nov 1967). Austrian scholar, responsible for documenting the lives of Handel, Mozart and Schubert, and for the standard catalogue of Schubert's works. A student of literature and art at the universities of Graz and Vienna, he made his name for his work on Schubert. He began studying Handel while in Cambridge (1939–51), after which he returned to Vienna.

Deutsche. GERMAN DANCE.

Deutsche Grammophon (DG). German record company formed in 1898, responsible for the first complete operas (*Faust* and *Carmen*, 1908) and symphony (Beethoven's Fifth conducted by Nikisch, 1913) on record. Acquired by Siemens in 1941, it became formidable in the LP era, when its artists included Karajan, Fischer-Dieskau and Stockhausen, and when it pioneered early music on its Archiv label (founded in 1948). In 1972 it was combined with Philips in Polygram, which was absorbed by the Universal Music Group in 1998.

Deutsches Requiem, Ein (A German Requiem). Work by Brahms for soprano, baritone, choir and orchestra, setting a personal choice of biblical texts in seven movements: 1 *Selig sind, die da Leid tragen*, 2 *Denn alles Fleisch ist wie Gras*, 3 *Herr, lehre doch mich*, 4 *Wie lieblich sind deine Wohnungen*, 5 *Ihr habt nun Traurigkeit*, 6 *Denn wir haben hie keine bleibende Statt*, 7 *Selig sind die Toten*. First performance: Leipzig, 18 Feb 1869 (preceded by partial performances).

deux temps (Fr.). Duple time. A *valse à deux temps* has two beats to the bar.

development. (1) Treatment of thematic material so as to extend or disturb but not lose its identity, while also maintaining continuity of thought. A theme may be changed in contour, abbreviated, taken into unfamiliar harmony, split among different instruments, combined contrapuntally with different versions of itself or with other themes, etc.

(2) Central section of a sonata form, marked by development in the more abstract sense.

Devienne, François (b. Joinville, Haute-Marne, 31 Jan 1759; d. Paris, 5 Sep 1803). French flautist-bassoonist-composer, author of much graceful music for both his instruments: concertos, quartets with strings, numerous trios for various combinations, duos, sonatas and (for flute) a method. He arrived in Paris in 1779 as a bassoonist, and played both bassoon and flute regularly at the Concert Spirituel and in theatre orchestras, besides serving from time to time in military bands. Married in his early 30s, he gained success as a composer of opéras comique (*Les Visitandines*, 1792), while from 1795 he taught at the new Conservatoire. He died in a home for the mentally ill.

devil in music. See DIABOLUS IN MUSICA.

Devil's Trill (*Le Trille du diable*). Name given a G minor sonata by Tartini when it was first published, in Jean-Baptiste Cartier's *L'Art du violon* (1798). According to legend, the trill in the last movement (or something like it) was played to the composer in a dream by the devil, to whom he had lent his violin.

Dezède [i.e. DZ], **Nicolas** (b. ?1740–45; d. Paris, 11 Sep 1792). Composer of unknown aristocratic ancestry, possibly the illegitimate son of a German prince. He studied composition in Paris, where he remained as a successful composer of pastoral operas: *Blaise et Babet* (1783) was performed as far afield as Russia, the USA and Mauritius, and Mozart wrote variations (K.264) on an air from *Julie* (1772).

Dezime (Ger.). Tenth (interval).

Dia, Comtessa de. See BEATRIZ DE DIA.

Diabelli, Anton (b. Mattsee, near Salzburg, 6 Sep 1781; d. Vienna, 7 Apr 1858). Austrian publisher. Originally a composer and church musician, he trained in Michaelbeuren and Salzburg. He arrived in Vienna in 1803 and began publishing his own sacred music in 1817, setting up a partnership with Pietro Cappi the following year. Besides a flood of music for the new bourgeois domestic market, the company issued Schubert's first publications and a volume of variations (including Beethoven's) on a waltz theme of his own that Diabelli sent to all his great contemporaries. He retired in 1851.

Diabelli Variations. Set of 33 variations by Beethoven, subjecting its simple theme to mockery and brusque dispatch, but also finding in triviality a way to vast contemplation.

diabolus in musica (Lat., devil in music). Medieval–Renaissance nickname for the tritone, regarding as usurping the place of more euphonious intervals, notably the fourth in the mode on F (F–G–A–B).

Diaghilev [Dyagilev], **Sergey (Pavlovich)** (b. Novgorod governorate, 31 Mar 1872; d. Venice, 19 Aug 1929). Russian impresario, with all the necessary qualities: bold and flighty, manipulative and loyal, cheese-paring and generous. He was responsible for the BALLETS RUSSES, and before that for bringing concerts of Russian music (1907) and *Boris Godunov* (1908) to Paris.

dialogue. (1) An exchange between characters, e.g. in opera, or, by extension, between instruments or contrapuntal parts.

(2) Specific term for a genre of verbal exchanges set as madrigals or pieces for soloists in the second half of the 16th century and first half of the 17th. The dialogue in this sense was a product of expressive recitative, and its subject could be sacred or secular.

Dialogus. Anonymous musical treatise of *c*.1000, taken up by Guido of Arezzo.

Diamond, David (Leo) (b. Rochester, NY, 9 Jul 1915). US composer, of neoclassical adroitness. He studied at Eastman, with Sessions in New York (1935) and with Boulanger in Paris (1936–7). Apart from a period in Italy (1951–65) he has lived in New York, producing 11 symphonies, 10 quartets and numerous songs.

diapason (Gk, through an octave, i.e. the octave interval or a scale). Pliable term, especially in French, where it can mean (1) pitch standard, (2) tuning fork, (3) any of various features of instrumental structure and tuning. In older English it has the sense of compass. It can also refer to a wooden bar at the back of a harpsichord or clavichord, with slots to hold the keys in place as they are pressed and released, or to organ stops.

diapente (Gk, through five). Ancient and medieval term for a fifth.

Diary of One who Disappeared (*Zápisník zmizelého*). Song cycle by Janáček to words then thought to be those of an untutored peasant, much later revealed as a composition by the Moravian poet Ozef Kalda. The one who disappeared (tenor, with piano) tells his story, how he was bewitched by a gypsy woman (mezzo-soprano), who appears in three of the 22 songs; three female singers sing as an offstage choir in two. Coming from the tense divide between recital piece and opera, the work has often been staged. First performance: Brno, 18 Apr 1921.

diastematic. Notationally indicating pitch by

means of vertical position on the page. The term is normally reserved for staffless early neumes.

diatessaron (Gk, through four). Ancient and medieval term for a fourth.

diatonic. Based on a seven-note scale, usually a major or minor one, though the term can also be applied to music in another MODE.

Dibdin, Charles (baptized Southampton, 15 Mar 1745; d. London, 25 Jul 1814). British composer, man of the theatre and popular entertainer. Largely self-taught, he was singing in London theatres by the age of 15, published a songbook at 18 and starred in his own pastoral at 19. By now he was married, but he soon left his wife for a dancer, followed by a singer, while pursuing his multifarious career. He fled his creditors to France (1776–8), was imprisoned for debt (1784), and set out on a voyage to India that he sustained as far as Torbay (1787). Success came with his one-man shows (1789–1805), which he gave in his own intimate London theatre and on tour, and for which he wrote hundreds of songs (including 'Tom Bowling'). But he died in penury.

Dichterliebe (Poet's Love). Song cycle by Schumann to 16 poems by Heine, whose poet's love turns through many moods – naive, embittered, angry – in response to an implicit narrative of joy undercut by rejection. The story begins with 'Im wunderschönen Monat Mai'.

Dickinson, Emily (b. Amherst, Mass., 10 Dec 1830; d. Amherst, 15 May 1886). US poet, whose quick images and irregular lines made her a favourite of 20th-century composers, including Farwell, Bacon, Carter, Copland, Barber, Perle, Castiglioni and Adams.

didjeridu. Australian aborigine instrument, a long pipe of hollowed, stripped eucalyptus, sounded at the fundamental with vibrating lips and traditionally played only by (all) males. Sound is maintained by circular breathing and varied in timbre by changing the shape of the mouth.

Dido. Queen of Carthage in Virgil's *Aeneid*. Her grief and suicide on being abandoned by Aeneas made her a popular opera subject, featuring in, among others:

(1) Purcell's one-act *Dido and Aeneas*, to a libretto by Nahum Tate, possibly written for a court performance c.1685. Dido sings a chaconne-lament, 'When I am laid in earth'.

(2) Metastasio's libretto *Didone abbandonata*,

from which Mozart set Dido's lament 'Basta vincesti'.

(3) Piccinni's *Didon*, to a libretto by Jean François Marmontel. First performance: Fontainebleau, 16 Oct 1783.

(4) Berlioz's *Les* TROYENS.

Diémer, Louis (Joseph) (b. Paris, 14 Feb 1843; d. Paris, 21 Dec 1919). French pianist and teacher, who studied with Marmontel at the Paris Conservatoire (1853–61), and succeeded him there in 1887. A virtuoso performer-composer, he also gave harpsichord recitals at the 1889 Paris Exposition and was co-founder of the Société des Instruments Anciens.

Diepenbrock, Alphons (Johannes Maria) (b. Amsterdam, 2 Sep 1862; d. Amsterdam, 5 Apr 1921). Dutch composer, the first of major importance since the 17th century. Born into an artistic Catholic family, he trained as a classics teacher and was self-taught in composition. Wagner and later Debussy were influences, Mahler a friend and admirer. Most of his works are vocal, among them liturgical pieces (*Te Deum*, soli, ch, orch, 1897) and tone poems with solo voice (*Zwei Hymnen an die Nacht*, 1899; *Im grossen Schweigen*, 1906; *Die Nacht*, 1911), though he also wrote incidental scores (*Marsyas*, 1909–10; *The Birds*, 1917; *Electra*, 1919–20).

Dieren, Bernard van (b. Rotterdam, 27 Dec 1887; d. London, 24 Apr 1936). Dutch–British composer of largely French ancestry, an independent admired by Warlock, the Sitwells and the sculptor Epstein, on whom he wrote a book. He settled in England in 1909 and was mostly self-taught, his works including six quartets and the *Chinese Symphony* for soli, chorus and orchestra (1914).

dièse, dièze (Fr.). Sharp, as in *fa dièse* (F♯).

Dies irae. Latin hymn of the Last Judgement attributed to Thomas of Celano (d. *c*.1250), incorporated into the *Requiem* mass in the 14th–15th centuries, and thereby set by numerous composers. Its plainsong melody became an image of death in Romantic music (Berlioz's *Symphonie fantastique*, Saint-Saëns's *Danse macabre*, Rachmaninoff's Paganini Rhapsody).

diesis (It.). Sharp, as in *do diesis* (C♯).

Dietrich, Albert (Hermann) (b. Forsthaus Golk, near Meissen, 28 Aug 1829; d. Berlin, 20 Nov 1908). German composer, protégé of Schumann and friend of Brahms, he wrote the first movement of the F–A–E violin sonata for Joachim to which the others also contributed. He had studied at the Leipzig Conservatory and became kapellmeister in Oldenburg (1861–90).

Dietsch, (Pierre) Louis (Philippe) (b. Dijon, 17 Mar 1808; d. Paris, 20 Feb 1865). French composer-conductor, who brushed twice with Wagner – first over his opera *Le Vaisseau fantôme* (Paris Opera, 1842), in which Wagner wrongly suspected plagiarism, and then over *Tannhäuser*, which he conducted at the same theatre (1861) with what Wagner thought deliberate deficiency (again wrongly: Dietsch's failings were unstudied). He studied at the Paris Conservatoire and led a career as a church musician.

Dieupart, Charles (b. ?after 1667; d. *c.*1740). French harpsichordist-composer, resident in London by 1704, when a score of his was produced at Drury Lane. Driven from the theatre by Handel's success, he made a living from lessons and concerts. His published works include suites for harpsichord or treble instrument and continuo (both versions were published), songs and flute sonatas.

diferencias (Sp.). 16th-century variations, usually for VIHUELA or keyboard.

difference tone. COMBINATION TONE produced by two loud sounds, its frequency being the difference between theirs. Its source is in the system producing (instrument), conveying (room) and hearing (ear) the sounds.

Different Trains. Work by Reich for string quartet and recordings (of quartet, speaking voices and recordings), based on train journeys of the 1940s. First performance: London, 2 Nov 1988.

digital. Style of handling information in numbers rather than, as in the ANALOG case, whole representations. See also RECORDING.

Dillon, James (b. Glasgow, 29 Oct 1950). Scottish composer, largely self-taught, who has developed in many directions from early (and diverse enough) affiliations to Ferneyhough and spectralism. His output includes orchestral pieces (*helle Nacht*, 1987), three quartets and many compositions for less regular ensembles.

diminish. (1) Decrease an interval by a semitone; hence diminished fifth (e.g. E–B♭), etc.

(2) Proportionally decrease the note values of a theme. A fugue may include faster passages where the theme appears in diminished form, normally at double speed (i.e. with the values halved).

diminished seventh chord. Chord of three minor thirds, i.e. seventh chord with diminished intervals, e.g. C–E♭–G♭–B♭♭. Being a symmetrical division of the octave (into four minor thirds), it is tonally ambiguous, and indeed can resolve on to any major or minor triad. It may therefore be useful in engineering rapid modulations to distant keys, in building new harmonic languages (as in Liszt or Messiaen) or in giving a melodramatic effect of unease.

diminished triad. Chord of two minor thirds, i.e. triad with diminished intervals, e.g. C♯–E–G.

diminuendo (It., diminishing). Direction to get quieter, often abbreviated *dim.* and even more often symbolized by a 'hairpin', like DECRESCENDO.

diminuita, diminuito (It.). Diminished.

diminution. (1) Regular shortening of time values. See DIMINISH (2).

(2) DIVISION.

d'India, Sigismondo (b. Palermo, *c.*1582; d. ?Modena, by 19 Apr 1629). Italian composer, to be mentioned with Monteverdi as a composer of songs in the new expressive style, and also one of the foremost Italian madrigalists of his time. Probably trained in Naples and itinerant through the first decade of the 17th century, he may have had contact with both Gesualdo and Monteverdi. He was then director of chamber music at the ducal court in Turin (1610–23), after which he divided his time between Rome and Modena. He published five volumes of songs and duets (1609–23) and eight of madrigals (1606–24).

d'Indy, (Paul Marie Théodore) Vincent (b. Paris, 27 Mar 1851; d. Paris, 2 Dec 1931). French composer, a staunch traditionalist for whom form was virtue. He inherited that regard for discipline from his grandmother, the Comtesse Rézia d'Indy, who brought him up, while his musical talents were fostered by his uncle, the Vicomte Wilfrid d'Indy, a pupil of Franck. After early studies with Jean François Marmontel, Diémer and Lavignac, he too became Franck's pupil, at the Conservatoire, in 1872. In the summer of 1873 he visited Liszt in Weimar and Wagner in Bayreuth, and he was back in 1876 for the first *Ring* and 1882 for *Parsifal*. Wagner became one of his personal gods, along with Franck and Beethoven, though he was also responsible for early revivals of Monteverdi and Rameau. Debussy's music he hated. In 1894, after his officially commissioned report on the

Conservatoire had been rejected, he founded the Schola Cantorum with Bordes and Guilmant. There he taught, spending the summers composing at his home in the Ardèche, ancestral d'Indy territory. He became increasingly reactionary in the new century, but in the chamber music of his last years, which he spent with his second wife, at last achieved contentment.

Andrew Thomson *Vincent d'Indy and his World* (1996)

Operas (librettos by the composer): *Fervaal*, Op.40, Brussels, 1897; *L'Etranger*, Op.53, Brussels, 1903; *La Légende de Saint Christophe*, Op.67, Paris, 1920; etc.
Orchestral: *Wallenstein*, Op.12, 3 overtures (*Le Camp, Max et Thécla, La Mort de Wallenstein*), 1879–81; *Symphonie sur un chant montagnard* (*Symphonie cévenole*), Op.25, pf, orch, 1886; *Istar*, Op.42, 1896; Symphony No.2, B♭, Op.57, 1902–3; *Jour d'été à la montagne*, Op.61, 1905; *Souvenirs*, Op.62, 1906; Symphony No.3, Op.70, 1916–18; etc.
Choral: *Le Chant de la cloche* (d'Indy, after Schiller), Op.18, soli, ch, orch, 1879–83; etc.
Chamber: String Sextet, B♭, Op.92, 1927; Piano Quintet, G minor, Op.81, 1924; String Quartet No.1, D, Op.35, 1890; No.2, E, Op.45, 1897; No.3, D♭, Op.96, 1928–9; Piano Trio No.1, B♭, Op.29, 1887; No.2, Op.98, 1929; Violin Sonata, C, Op.59, 1903–4; Cello Sonata, D, Op.84, 1924–5; *Chansons et danses*, Op.50, wind, 1898; etc.
Piano: *Tableaux de voyage*, Op.33, 1888; Sonata, E, Op.63, 1907; etc.
Other works: songs, folksong arrangements

direct. Symbol (musical note or small sawtooth line) placed at the end of a staff to indicate more follows.

direction (Fr.), **direzione** (It.), **Dirigieren** (Ger.). Conducting.

Dirigent (Ger., pl. *Dirigenten*). Conductor. Also *dirigieren* (conduct).

Diruta, Girolamo (b. ?Deruta, near Perugia, c.1554; d. after 1610). Italian organist-theorist, whose *Il transilvano* was the first exhaustive guide for organists, given in dialogue form. He joined the Franciscans at Correggio in 1574, and a few years later went to Venice, where he studied with Zarlino and Merulo; Porta was also among his teachers. The two parts of his treatise he published as cathedral organist in Chioggia (1593) and Gubbio (1609). The Transylvanian of its title was most likely Istvan de Jósika, an emissary of the prince of Transylvania.

Dis (Ger.). D♯. Also *Disis* (D✕).

discant. Word etymologically connected (at the medieval Lat. *discantus*, singing apart) and terminologically confused with DESCANT. The form 'discant' is generally preferred for a style of early polyphony in which the plainsong tenor and the added voice or voices are on the same time scale, rhythmically similar. This style is first recorded in the St Martial and other manuscripts of the early 12th century, and came to flower – and supersede ORGANUM – at Notre Dame towards the end of the century. The term remained in use until the early 15th century, i.e. until the addition of simultaneous parts to a plainsong was replaced by through-composed polyphony. In modern usage, though, it is normally restricted to compositions up to Perotin and to what treatises, especially from England, record as an improvised practice, whereby singers would follow a written plainsong in contrary motion above or below.

discography. Catalogue of commercial recordings, normally one devoted to a particular work, composer or performer. Also 'discographer', the cataloguer.

discord. DISSONANCE.

disinvolto (It.). Free, airy.

disjunct. Term used of a melody featuring leaps of a third or larger rather than conjunct scale steps.

Disklavier. Brand name of a reproducing piano introduced by Yamaha in 1986. It is played like a normal grand piano, but performances may be digitally recorded (or acquired in disc form) and played back by the instrument unaided, with nuances of touch and rhythm preserved.

dissonance. Sense of harmonic unease, the opposite of CONSONANCE.

Dissonance. Name given Mozart's Quartet in C, K.465, on account of its slow introduction.

Di Stefano, Giuseppe (b. Motta Santa Anastasia, near Catania, 24 Jul 1921). Italian tenor, who moved from elegance in lyric roles to a ringing heftiness during his brief career. He studied in Milan, made his debut in Reggio Emilia in 1946, moved into weightier repertory in the mid-1950s, and gradually withdrew from the scene in the 1960s, to return as Callas's partner (again) on her late recital tour.

Distler, Hugo (b. Nuremberg, 24 Jun 1908; d. Berlin, 1 Nov 1942). German organist-composer, latterday heir to Schütz. Studies at the Leipzig Conservatory pointed him towards Bach and earlier music. He was then organist at the Jakob-kirche in Lübeck (1931–7) and a teacher at the conservatories in Stuttgart (1937–40) and Berlin-Charlottenburg (1940–42), though he suffered official harassment and eventually committed suicide.

distratto, Il (One Distraught). Name Haydn gave his Symphony No.60, made of movements from his incidental music for *Der Zerstreute*, a version of Jean François Regnard's *Le Distrait*.

dithyramb. Ancient Greek song to Dionysus, who had the alternative name Dithyrambos, evoked by Tomášek, Schubert (*Dithyrambe*, D.801) and Stravinsky (finale of the *Duo concertant*).

ditonus, ditone. Interval of two tones, i.e. what is more commonly called a major third.

Dittersdorf, Carl Ditters von (b. Vienna, 2 Nov 1739; d. Neuhof, Pilgram, Bohemia, 24 Oct 1799). Austrian composer, one of the most gifted and fluent figures around Haydn and Mozart. The son of a court costumier, he was recommended at 11 as a violinist to the Prince of Sachsen-Hildburg-hausen, whom he served in Vienna for a decade (1751–61), during which he had composition lessons with Bonno. He then played for the court opera (1761–4) before taking kapellmeister posts with the bishops of Grosswardein (1765–9) and Breslau/Wrocław (1769–95). In 1772 he married a singer, and the next year was ennobled by Maria Theresa under the additional name of 'von Dittersdorf'. His work for the Breslau prince-bishop, at the castle of Johannisberg, near Jauernig, did not prevent him visiting Vienna from time to time – not least to present singspiels and play quartets with Haydn, Mozart and Wanhal. Apart from the singspiels (notably *Doktor und Apotheker*, to a libretto by Stephanie, Vienna, 1786), his important works include about 120 symphonies (among them 12 based on Ovid's *Metamorphoses* and one 'in the taste of five nations'). He also wrote oratorios, masses, other sacred music, concertos (including one for harpsichord in A often played by harpists), divertimentos, quartets, trios and piano duet sonatas.

A.D. Coleridge, trans. *The Autobiography of Karl von Dittersdorf* (1896, ʳ1970)

div. See DIVISI.

diva (It., goddess). Honorific bestowed on opera singers, usually women but now not always.

divertimento (It., diversion, pl. *divertimenti*, though in modern Eng. normally 'divertimentos'). (1) 18th-century term for a generally lighter instrumental composition. It originated at the end of the previous century (Giorgio Buoni's Op.1, 1693) and took off four or five decades later, becoming hard to distinguish from other titles of the time, such as 'serenade' and 'cassation'. However, the modern term 'divertimento form' is sometimes used to indicate a common sequence of allegro, minuet, andante, minuet, allegro. Mozart's Divertimento for string trio – by no means entertainment music – probably gained its title from having a form of this type (with an additional slow movement). There are also divertimentos by Mozart and many others – Haydn, Boccherini, Dittersdorf, Gassmann, the Mannheim composers – for strings (sometimes with flutes, oboes or horns), wind groups and keyboard. Bartók and Stravinsky were among 20th-century composers to revive the title and the spirit.

(2) 19th-century term for an instrumental showpiece based on an operatic tune or tunes.

divertissement (Fr., diversion). (1) Festive sequence of dances and songs, such as normally culminated each act of a French Baroque stage work or was created as an entertainment in itself.

(2) Divertimento.

Divine Office. Daily cycle of services, comprising Matins (in the early hours), Lauds, Prime, Terce, Sext, None, Vespers (at twilight) and Compline.

Divin Poème, Le (The Divine Poem, *Bozhestvennaya poema*). Title of Scriabin's Third Symphony, in three movements: *Luttes* (Struggles), *Voluptés* (Desires), *Le Jeu divin* (Divine Play). First performance: Paris, 27 May 1905.

divisi (It.) Divided. The term is used as a marking in scores (often abbreviated *div.*) to show where the players of a particular section (usually strings) must separate to play, say, the different notes of a marked chord. At such junctures one may speak of 'divisi cellos', or whatever. The indication is countermanded by *tutti* or *all'unisono* (*unisono*, *unis.*).

division. (1) 17th-century English term for variation on a ground, which is 'divided' by faster-running ornamentation or descant. It was essentially an improvisatory art for viol or violin players, who could follow guides by Simpson and Playford.

(2) Section of orchestral violins, firsts or seconds.

division viol. Kind of viola da gamba made in England for playing divisions.

Divitis, Antonius, Latinized name of Anthonius Rycke, otherwise Anthoine Le Riche (b. Louvain, *c*.1470; d. 1515–34). Netherlandish composer, associated with the Burgundian (1505–6) and French royal chapels, and thereby with Alexander Agricola and Mouton. He wrote parody masses on motets by both these colleagues, as well as other sacred works.

dixième (Fr.). Tenth.

dixtuor (Fr.). Decet.

do (It., Sp.). The note or key of C.

dodecaphony. Equal use of all 12 chromatic notes in music, normally implying serialism, a more euphonious alternative. Hence also 'dodecaphonic'.

Dodge, Charles (Malcolm) (b. Ames, Iowa, 5 Jun 1945). US composer, especially of witty computer music (*Any Resemblance is Purely Coincidental* for piano and tape, 1980, using the voice of Caruso). He studied with Luening and Ussachevsky at Columbia (1964–70) and with Godfrey Winham at Princeton (1966–7), and has taught at those and other institutions.

doh. Tonic in TONIC SOL-FA.

Dohnányi. Family including two notable musicians.

(1) **Ernő** [Ernst von] (b. Poszony/Bratislava, 27 Jul 1877; d. New York, 9 Feb 1960). Hungarian–US pianist-composer and conductor, who repeatedly helped the younger Bartók (whom he knew from school) while pursuing a more traditional course as a Romantic virtuoso. He studied with István Thomán and Hans Koessler at the academy in Budapest (1894–7), and gained Brahms's approbation for his first piano quintet (1895). By 1900 he had played around Europe and in the USA; he then taught in Berlin (1905–15) before returning to Budapest. There his compositional productivity gradually declined as he gave more attention to conducting, playing (on annual US tours, 1921–7) and teaching, his career in this last role following a switchback course as a result of political events: he joined the academy staff in 1916, became director during the brief socialist republic (1919), was dismissed on the arrival of fascism, gained reappointment in 1928, and returned to the directorship (1934–41). He moved to Austria in 1944 and crossed the Atlantic in 1949, teaching briefly in Argentina before taking a post at Florida State University. Having remained in Nazi territory through the war years, he was subject to suspicion and attack, and though his Op.25 variations could not be dislodged as a popular classic, his wider status as an Austro-Hungarian Rachmaninoff began to be recognized only at the end of the 20th century.

Ilona von Dohnányi *Ernst von Dohnányi* (2002)

Orchestral: Symphony No.1, D minor, Op.9, 1900–1; No.2, E, Op.40, 1943–4, rev 1953–6; Piano Concerto No.1, E minor, Op.5, 1897–8; No.2, B minor, Op.42, 1946–7; Violin Concerto No.1, D minor, Op.27, 1914–15; No.2, C minor, Op.43, 1949–50; VARIATIONEN ÜBER EIN KINDERLIED, Op.25, pf, orch, 1914; etc.
Chamber: Sextet, C, Op.37, cl, hn, str trio, pf, 1935; Piano Quintet No.1, C minor, Op.1, 1895; No.2, E♭ minor, Op.26, 1914; String Quartet No.1, A, Op.7, 1899; No.2, D♭, Op.15, 1906; No.3, A minor, Op.33, 1926; Violin Sonata, C♯ minor, Op.21, 1912; Cello Sonata, B♭ minor, Op.8, 1899; etc.
Piano: 6 Concert Etudes, Op.28, 1916; Variations on a Hungarian Folksong, Op.29, 1917; Pastorale, 1920; *Ruralia hungarica*, Op.32a, 1923–4; etc.

(2) **Christoph von** (b. Berlin, 8 Sep 1929). German conductor, grandson of Ernő, impressive in his thorough communication of new music (Henze, Birtwistle) as well as classic repertory. He studied at the Munich conservatory (1948–51) and in 1952 was engaged by Solti at the Frankfurt Opera. There followed posts as general music director in Lübeck (1957–63), Kassel (1963–6) and Frankfurt (1968–75), and as music director of the Hamburg Staatsoper (1977–84), the Cleveland Orchestra (1984–2002) and the Philharmonia Orchestra (from 1997).

doigté (Fr.). Fingering.

Doktor Faust. See FAUST.

dolce (It., sweet). Marking normally indicating soft, smooth projection, though sometimes more smooth than soft, as in the *f dolce* opening of the finale of Schumann's 'Rhenish' Symphony. Hence also *dolcissimo*, abbreviated *dolciss*.

dolente (It.). Doleful.

Doles, Johann Friedrich (b. Steinbach, Thuringia, 23 Apr 1715; d. Leipzig, 8 Feb 1797). German composer and church musician, a pupil of Bach (1739–43), whose lessons he mixed with those of opera. Trained first by his elder brother, who had succeeded to their father's post as cantor in

Steinbach, he was cantor in Freiberg (1744–55) before taking his former teacher's place at St Thomas's in Leipzig (1755–89). His extant works include about 160 cantatas, Passion settings, motets and songs (especially to poems by his friend Gellert).

Dolmetsch, (Eugène) Arnold (b. Le Mans, 24 Feb 1858; d. Haslemere, 28 Feb 1940). French–British reviver of the lute, harpsichord, viol, recorder and other forgotten instruments, which he both built and played, having been born into a family of instrument-makers. He studied as a violinist with Vieuxtemps, at the Brussels Conservatory (1881–3) and at the RCM (1883–4). Remaining in England, he taught at Dulwich College (1885–9) before discovering viol fantasies in the RCM library and British Museum, which led to his subsequent and intensive career. He gave his first concert of early music in 1890 and began making instruments, on his own account and also, during periods abroad, for Chickering in New York (1904–11) and Gaveau in Paris (1911–14). In 1917 he settled in Haslemere, where he turned to making recorders in 1919 and founded an annual festival in 1925. Among the children of his three marriages, Carl (1911–97) was his principal successor.

Margaret Campbell *Dolmetsch* (1975)

doloroso (It.). Dolorous, also *con dolore, dolorosamente.*

Domaine Musical. Organization founded by Boulez in Paris, originally as the Concerts du Petit Marigny, under the patronage of the Renaud-Barrault theatre company, for which Boulez was music director. The aim – to present new works in a sympathetic context of 20th-century classics and older music – was fulfilled in the very first programme (1954), which Hermann Scherchen conducted: *Das musikalische Opfer* followed by Stravinsky (*Renard*), Webern (Concerto), Nono (*Polifonia–Monodia–Ritmica*) and Stockhausen (*Kontrapunkte*). From 1957 most concerts were conducted by Boulez, who passed direction to Amy (1967–73). Besides providing a model of mixed programming, the Domaine Musical introduced works by Messiaen, Barraqué, Berio and many others.

dominant. The note or key a fifth above the tonic of a major or minor key. In C major or minor, therefore, the dominant is G and the dominant tonality G major or minor. Post-Renaissance tonality places great emphasis on the dominant as a secondary centre.

dominant seventh chord. Major triad on the dominant plus minor seventh, e.g. G–B–D–F in C major or minor. It powerfully precipitates the tonic.

Domingo, Plácido (b. Madrid, 21 Jan 1941). Spanish tenor, enjoying a career of unusual length (over 40 years) and breadth (from Rodolfo to Parsifal). He grew up with his family in Mexico, studied conducting (with Markevich) as well as singing, and made his debut as a baritone in 1957. Transferred to tenor roles in 1961 (the year of his US debut, in Dallas), his voice retained a baritonal solidity expressing itself as moral uprightness. In his careful acting, too, he inclined more to rectitude than bravura. He made his debut at the Met in 1968 and at Covent Garden in 1971, and began diversifying as a conductor (from the 1980s), company artistic director (with Washington Opera from 1996 and Los Angeles Opera from 2000) and member of the THREE TENORS.

Dominicus. Name given Mozart's Mass in C, K.66, written for the first mass celebrated by Cajetan Hagenauer, who had taken that name for his religious life. First performance: Salzburg, 15 Oct 1769.

Donato da Cascia (*fl.* Florence, 1350s–60s). Italian composer, of madrigals indebted to Jacopo da Bologna and Lorenzo da Firenze.

Donatoni, Franco (b. Verona, 9 Jun 1927: d. Milan, 17 Aug 2000). Italian composer, who in his last two decades achieved a huge number of brilliant, crisp and witty musical contrivances, mostly for small instrumental groupings (though including *Arie* for soprano and orchestra, 1978). His earlier career was a common one in the 1950s–70s of following avant-garde procedures to a point of stalemate, his introduction to Darmstadt having come by way of Maderna, whom he met in 1953. Before that he had studied in his home town, Milan, Bologna and – with Pizzetti – Rome (1952–3). Then, while taking on board lessons from Boulez, Stockhausen and Cage, he pursued a career as a teacher, notably from 1969 at the Milan Conservatory, where he had students from all over Europe.

Donaueschingen. Town in southwest Germany, home of an annual festival of contemporary music, which at first (1921–6) was patronized by Prince Max Egon zu Fürstenberg and devoted to chamber works by Hindemith, Webern, etc. In 1950 it was revived by Heinrich Strobel as an October weekend of orchestral concerts and jazz. It rapidly became one of the principal avant-garde showcases, presenting new works by Boulez, Stockhausen, Messiaen, Nono, Ligeti, Ferneyhough, etc. The death of Max Egon in 1959 was marked by memorials from Stravinsky (*Epitaphium*), Boulez and Fortner.

Don Carlo. See DON CARLOS.

Don Carlos. Opera by Verdi to a libretto by Joseph Méry and Camille du Locle after Schiller's dramatic poem. Carlos (tenor) is son and heir to Philip II of Spain (bass), and in love with his father's new wife, Elisabeth (soprano), though loved by the Princess Eboli (mezzo-soprano). Into these rivalries Carlos's friend Posa (baritone) is drawn. In a powerful scene Philip is advised by the Grand Inquisitor (bass) to sacrifice Posa; in doing so he also loses his son. Most often sung in Italian as *Don Carlo* before the late 20th century, the score includes Philip's aria 'Elle ne m'aime pas' ('Ella giammai m'amo'), Eboli's ('O don fatal') and Elisabeth's 'Toi qui sus' ('Tu, che le vanità'), as well as the Carlos–Posa cabaletta 'Dieu tu semas' ('Dio, che nell'alma infondere') First performance: Paris Opera, 11 Mar 1867, rev Milan, 10 Jan 1884.

Donemus. Foundation established in 1947 to promote new Dutch music, its name an acronym of Documentatie in Nederland voor Muziek.

Don Giovanni. Opera by Mozart, titled in full *Il dissoluto punito, ossia Il Don Giovanni* (The Libertine Punished, or Don Giovanni), to a libretto by Da Ponte, after other treatments of the Don Juan legend, including Giovanni Bertati's libretto (for Gazzaniga) and Molière's play. The rampant womanizer Don Giovanni (baritone), accompanied by his servant Leporello (bass), utterly disdains both his fellow gentlefolk – Donna Anna (soprano), her fiancé Don Ottavio (tenor) and Donna Elvira (soprano) – and the working newlyweds Zerlina (soprano) and Masetto (bass). Mocking even the dead, he meets his end when the statue of Donna Anna's father the Commendatore (bass), whom he slew at the start, accepts his dinner invitation and drags him to hell. Among the numbers are Leporello's Catalogue Aria, Giovanni's attempt on Zerlina ('Là ci darem la mano'), his serenade ('Deh vieni') and Champagne Aria ('Fin ch'han dal vino'), Zerlina's arias 'Batti, batti' and 'Vedrai, carino', Anna's aria 'Or sai chi l'onore' and recitative plus aria 'Crudele! – Non mi dir', Ottavio's aria 'Il mio tesoro', and the Act 1 quartet, in which Elvira tries to warn Anna against Giovanni's reassurances, leaving both Anna and Ottavio confused. For the 1788 Vienna revival Mozart composed Ottavio's

'Dalla sua pace' as a replacement and Elvira's 'In quali eccessi – Mi tradì' as an addition; the standard text incorporates this forceful Elvira number and both Ottavio arias. The Act 1 finale, where everyone is at a party in Don Giovanni's house, culminates in a superimposition of three different dances. The Act 2 finale quotes three popular operas (*Una cosa rara* by Martín y Soler, *Fra i due litiganti* by Sarti and *Le nozze di Figaro*) in Giovanni's supper music and ends, after the D minor storm of his punishment, with a D major sextet of continuing life and lesson-drawing for those left behind. First performance: Prague, 29 Oct 1787.

Doni, Giovanni Battista (baptized Florence, 13 Mar 1595; d. Florence, 1 Dec 1647). Italian scholar, whose thorough research into Greek music led him to advance an elaborate system of modes and to design instruments that could play in them with correct tuning. He corresponded with Mersenne.

Donizetti, (Domenico) Gaetano (Maria) (b. Bergamo, 29 Nov 1797; d. Bergamo, 8 Apr 1848). Italian composer, whose mastery of fizz and melodrama – and of tenderness with both – made him at once Rossini's natural successor in the comic genre and Verdi's most immediate model as a tragedian. If, nevertheless, he has generally been regarded more journeyman than artist, some of his works were restored to favour in the mid 20th century, and three – *L'elisir d'amore*, *Don Pasquale* and *Lucia di Lammermoor* – have never lacked an audience.

Born in great poverty, he owed his musical education to Mayr's free school, where he was one of the first pupils (1806–14). Mayr then sent him to Bologna to study counterpoint with Padre Mattei for two years, and supervised his career after his return to Bergamo in 1817. The success of *Zoraida di Granata* in 1822 led to a contract with the impresario Domenico Barbaia in Naples, where he worked as composer, conductor and teacher. Growing success enabled him to marry Virginia Vasselli in 1828, though her three pregnancies all failed to produce a child who survived.

Having scored an international triumph with *Anna Bolena*, he broke his contract with Naples in 1832 but signed another in 1834, committing him to one serious opera per year. His creative tempo was far faster. *L'elisir d'amore* had been written in under a month, and through the 1830s his annual average was three operas. Those intended for Naples after 1834 included *Lucia*, *L'assedio di Calais* and *Roberto Devereux*, while *Maria Stuarda* and *Poliuto* were banned – the former because of its sad ending (the Neapolitan queen was apocryphally said to have fainted at a rehearsal), the latter because of an onstage martyrdom.

In 1835, at Rossini's invitation, he went to Paris to stage *Marino Faliero*, gaining an exposure to French grand opera that influenced *L'assedio di Calais*. The frustration of *Poliuto*, allied with grief over his wife's death, in 1837, and disappointment on losing through politicking the directorship of the Naples Conservatory, moved him to establish himself permanently in Paris. There he hoped to earn enough to retire, as Rossini had, but he also travelled often, and in 1842 accepted a post as court kapellmeister in Vienna.

By now, though, his career was almost over. Growing signs of mental disturbance, syphilitic in origin, prevented his achieving anything after 1843. He was admitted to a sanatorium near Paris in 1846, and taken by his nephew Andrea – whose father, Giuseppe (1788–1856), was music master to the Turkish forces – to spend his last months in his native city.

William Ashbrook *Donizetti and his Operas* (1982)

Operas: *Emilia di Liverpool* (librettist unknown), f.p. Naples, 1824, rev Naples, 1828; *Le convenienze ed inconvenienze teatrali* (composer), f.p. Naples, 1827, rev Milan, 1831; *Elisabetta al castello di Kenilworth* (Andrea Leone Tottola), f.p. Naples, 1829; ANNA BOLENA; L'ELISIR D'AMORE; *Parisina* (Romani, after Byron), f.p. Florence, 1833; *Torquato Tasso* (Jacopo Ferretti), f.p. Rome, 1833; *Lucrezia Borgia* (Romani, after Hugo), f.p. Milan, 1833; *Rosmonda d'Inghilterra* (Romani), f.p. Florence, 1834; MARIA STUARDA, 1834; *Gemma di Vergy* (Giovanni Emanuele Bidera, after Dumas père), f.p. Milan, 1834; *Marino Faliero* (Bidera), f.p. Paris, 1835; LUCIA DI LAMMERMOOR; *Belisario* (Cammarano, after Marmontel), f.p. Venice, 1836; *L'assedio di Calais* (Cammarano), f.p. Naples, 1836; *Roberto Devereux* (Cammarano), f.p. Naples, 1837; *Maria de Rudenz* (Cammarano), f.p. Venice, 1838; *Poliuto* (Cammarano, after Corneille), 1838, rev as *Les Martyrs* (Scribe), f.p. Paris, 1840, original version Naples, 1848; La FILLE DU REGIMENT; *La Favorite* (Alphonse Royer and Gustave Vaëz), f.p. Paris, 1840; *Linda di Chamounix*(Gaetano Rossi), f.p. Vienna, 1842; DON PASQUALE; *Caterina Cornaro* (Giacomo Sacchero), 1842–3, f.p. Naples, 1844; *Maria di Rohan* (Cammarano), f.p. Vienna, 1843; *Dom Sébastien* (Scribe), f.p. Paris, 1843
Other works: Cor Anglais Concertino, 1817; 18 string quartets, ?1819–21; numerous songs, duets, sacred pieces, etc.

Don Juan. Profligate seducer of women and disrespecter of men; with Faust one of the great post-Renaissance mythic figures. Musical treatments include:

(1) A ballet with music by Gluck, *Don Juan, ou Le Festin de pierre*, to a scenario by Calzabigi for choreography by Gasparo Angiolini. The work was pathbreaking in creating a narrative through dance and mime. First performance: Vienna, 17 Oct 1761.

(2) Mozart's opera DON GIOVANNI.

(3) Strauss's tone poem. First performance: Weimar, 11 Nov 1889.

There are also operas on the subject by Gazzaniga, Dargomyzhsky, Pacini and Schulhoff (*Flammen*), while the serenading Don Juan is pictured in a piano piece by Szymanowski and a Tchaikovsky song, and the two Dons, Juan and Quixote, are associated in pieces by Zimmermann (*Présence*) and Sallinen.

Donna Diana. Opera by Reznicek, known almost exclusively for its overture.

Don Pasquale. Opera by Donizetti to a libretto by Giovanni Ruffini and the composer, after that of Pavesi's *Ser Marcantonio*. The elderly bachelor Don Pasquale (bass), eager to marry and so deprive his nephew Ernesto (tenor) of an inheritance, is foiled with the help of his doctor Malatesta (baritone), who arranges a mock marriage with Ernesto's beloved Norina (soprano). When she proves a wild and wilful 'wife', Don Pasquale readily agrees to Ernesto's marriage. Popular numbers include Norina's aria 'Quel guardo il cavaliere – So anch'io la virtù', Ernesto's 'Sogno soave casto' and their duet 'Tornami a dir'. First performance: Paris, 3 Jan 1843.

Don Quixote. Foolish-lovable knight whose exploits, with his squire Sancho Panza, were chronicled in the novel by Cervantes. The numerous musical treatments include:

(1) Purcell's incidental music for D'Urfey's trilogy of plays.

(2) Strauss's tone poem, with a solo cello as Quixote. First performance: Cologne, 8 Mar 1898.

(3) Massenet's opera, written for Chaliapin, to a libretto by Henri Cain. Don Quixote (bass) – disappointed as both lover, in his quest for Dulcinea (mezzo-soprano), and as hero, in his challenge to the windmills – dies with only Sancho Panza (bass-baritone). First performance: Monte Carlo, 19 Feb 1910.

(4) Songs by Ravel and Ibert, again written for Chaliapin.

There are also stage treatments by Boismortier, Telemann, Paisiello, Salieri, Mendelssohn (*Die Hochzeit des Camacho*), Minkus, Falla (*El retablo de Maese Pedro*), Gerhard and Halffter.

dopo (It.). After.

Doppel (Ger.). Double, as in *Doppel-Be* (double flat), *Doppelkreuz* (double sharp), *Doppelchor* (double choir), *Doppelschlag* (turn), *Doppelzunge* (double tongue), *Doppelganze-Note* (breve), etc.

doppio (It.). Double, as in *doppio movimento* (double speed), *doppio bemolle* (double flat), *doppio diesis* (double sharp), etc.

Dorian. Authentic MODE D–E–F–G–A–B–C–D, the first church mode/tone. A toccata and fugue in D minor by Bach, BWV 538, is commonly called 'Dorian', partly to distinguish it from the more familiar and decidedly non-Dorian BWV 565.

Dorian sixth. Raised sixth (the note or the interval it forms above the tonic) in a minor key, so called because it is a feature of the Dorian mode: e.g. D–B, rather than the minor sixth B♭.

dot. (1) Sign placed after a notehead to indicate a lengthening of the duration by half as much again. Hence 'dotted note' and 'dotted rhythm' (using dots to create 3:1 durational patterns). See DOUBLE DOT.

(2) Sign placed above a notehead as a staccato marking.

double. (1) As a noun: variation, division. Dance movements in Baroque suites often have a double.

(2) As an adjective: sounding an octave lower (being of double size), as in 'double bass' and 'double bassoon'. See also the compounds below.

(3) Also as an adjective: twofold, as in DOUBLE BAR, DOUBLE CHOIR, DOUBLE CONCERTO, DOUBLE FUGUE, DOUBLE VARIATIONS, etc.

(4) As a verb: play or sing together with. A melody may be played by violins doubled by flutes, etc. The implication may be of doubling in unison, as here, or in a different octave, as when basses are said to double cellos. One may also speak of notes in a harmony being doubled, necessarily in another octave.

(5) Also as a verb: play more than one instrument in a work or sing more than one role. An oboist may double on cor anglais; a tenor may double as Don Basilio and Don Curzio in *Le nozze di Figaro*.

(6) (Fr.). Double, as in *double bémol* (double flat), *double dièse* (double sharp), *double croche* (semiquaver, 16th-note), etc.

double bar, not 'double barline'. Pair of vertical lines marking the end of a piece, movement or section.

double bass [bass, contrabass, string bass] (Fr. *contrebasse*, Ger. *Kontrabass*, It. *contrabasso*).

Largest and lowest of the STRING instruments, normally with a body around 45 inches (1.15m) long and somewhat viol-like in shape (sloping shoulders, a flat back) – viol-like, too, in being tuned in fourths. The usual tuning for four-string basses is E–A–D–G, from the E more than an octave below the bass staff; the fifth string is tuned to the B (or C) below that, or else this lowest register may be reached by means of levers that extend the E string.

Documentary evidence of the double bass goes back to *c*.1500. The earliest surviving instrument dates from 1563, but there is very little music specifically for the double bass until the Classical period (solos in Haydn symphonies, Mozart's aria with obbligato bass 'Per questa bella mano'). In the orchestra, until Beethoven, basses would normally double the cellos at the octave below. Dragonetti and Bottesini gave the instrument a Romantic voice, and there is a concerto ascribed to Koussevitzky, who began his career as a bassist. More recent players who have advanced the repertory include Gary Karr, Bertram Turetzky and Barry Guy.

Bertram Turetzky *The Contemporary Contrabass* (1974, ²1989)

double bassoon [contrabassoon]. Double-sized BASSOON, sounding an octave below.

double canon. Four-part composition with two different melodies, each followed by a canonic imitation.

double choir, double chorus. Normally a chorus in eight parts (ssaattbb) rather than the regular four; it may be divided into two four-part groups.

double concerto. Concerto with two solo parts. The most famous work so called is Brahms's for violin and cello (f.p. Cologne, 18 Oct 1887, Joachim and Robert Hausmann). Other examples include many Vivaldi concertos, Bach's concerto for two violins, Mozart's Sinfonia Concertante for violin and viola, double piano concertos by Mozart, Martinů and Berio, Berg's Chamber Concerto, Carter's work with piano and harpsichord soloists, Ligeti's with flute and oboe, Kurtág's with piano and cello, and several composers' oboe–harp double concertos for the Holligers.

double counterpoint. INVERTIBLE COUNTERPOINT in two parts.

double dot. Sign placed after a notehead to indicate a lengthening of the duration by three-quarters as much again. Hence 'double dotting', which may be implicit, though not marked, in some French Baroque music (see NOTES INEGALES).

double escapement. Piano mechanism introduced by Erard in 1821, by which the hammers rebound immediately and only part way, so that the notes may be repeated rapidly.

double flat. Note lowered by two semitones, indicated by '♭♭'.

double fugue. Fugue on two subjects.

double harpsichord. Harpsichord with two manuals.

double note (US). Breve (UK). See DURATION.

double octave. Interval of two octaves.

double quartet. Duplication of a quartet, whether of singers or strings. Spohr wrote double string quartets.

double reed. Characteristic of oboes and bassoons; see REED.

double-ronde (Fr.). Double whole note, breve.

double sharp. Note raised by two semitones, indicated by x.

double stop. Pair of notes played simultaneously on a string instrument with two fingers on different strings, i.e. by double stopping.

double tonguing. Means of achieving detached articulation on a wind instrument by alternating the position of the tongue, as if flipping between 't' and 'k' sounds.

double variations. Variations alternately on two themes, alternately major and minor. The standard example is Haydn's set of Variations in F minor for keyboard.

double whole note (US). Breve (UK). See DURATION.

doubling. See DOUBLE (4) and (5).

doux, doucement (Fr.). Soft, softly.

douzième (Fr.). 12th.

Dowland, John (b. ?London, 1563; buried London, 20 Feb 1626). English lutenist-composer, the outstanding master of the lute song and of the art of melancholy. Converted to Catholicism in France as a teenage servant to the English ambassador, he took the Oxford BMus (1588) and was having his music heard at court by 1590. Refused a position as royal lutenist in 1594, he returned to the continent, this time to Germany and Italy. In the winter of 1596–7 he was back in London, where he published his *First Book of Songs* (1597), but he again lacked preferment and took a post at the Danish court (1598–1606), though his wife (a shadowy figure) seems to have stayed in London. Two more books of songs followed in 1600 and 1603 (laid out, like the first, with accompaniment for lute or viols), as well as the instrumental collection *Lachrimae*: all were enormously popular, and he seems to have written little more. After three years in service to Theophilus Howard, Lord Walden, he at last in 1612 gained a court appointment, in which he was succeeded by his son Robert. His songs, which in a short period left strophic frolics for blacker moods and continuity, and which astonishingly fuse verbal sense with musical sound in fluent, expressive melody, have never been forgotten or surpassed.

Diana Poulton *John Dowland* (1972, ²1982); Peter Holman *Dowland: Lachrimae* (1999)

www.johndowland.com

Songs (with publication dates): 'Awake, sweet love', 1597; 'Away with these self-loving lads', 1597; 'Can she excuse my wrongs', 1597; 'Come again, sweet love', 1597; 'Come away, come sweet love', 1597; 'Come, heavy sleep', 1597; 'Fine knacks for ladies', 1600; 'Flow, my tears', 1600; 'Go, crystal tears', 1597; 'Go, nightly cares', 1612; 'His golden locks', 1597; 'If my complaints', 1597; 'In darkness let me dwell', 1610; 'I saw my lady weep', 1600; 'Now, o, now', 1597; 'Shall I sue?', 1600; 'Sorrow, stay', 1600; 'Tell me, true love', 1612; 'Time stands still', 1603; etc.

Lute: *The Earl of Essex his Galliard* (= 'Can she excuse'); *Forlorn Hope* (fancy); *The Frog Galliard* (= 'Now, o, now'); *The King of Denmark his Galliard*; *Lady Hunsdon's Puffe* (almain); *Melancholy Galliard*; *My Lord Chamberlain his Galliard* (duet); *My Lord Willoughby's Welcome Home*; *Orlando sleepeth*; *Piper's Galliard*; *Piper's Pavan*; Prelude; *Queen Elizabeth her Galliard*; *Resolution* (pavan); *Semper Dowland semper dolens* (pavan); *The Shoemaker's Wife, a Toy* (jig); *Sir John Smith his Almain*; *Tarleton's Resurrection* (jig); *Mrs Winter's Jump* (jig); etc.

Consort: LACHRIMAE; etc.

downbeat. Gesture in a strong rhythmic position, normally the first beat in a bar, preceded by an UPBEAT. A conductor may give a downbeat, with a forceful downward movement.

downbow. Action of the bow from nut to point

(i.e. descending in the case of the violin), naturally stronger than the UPBOW.

Draeseke, Felix (August Bernhard) (b. Coburg, 7 Oct 1835; d. Dresden, 26 Feb 1913). German composer, an adherent of Liszt and Wagner (both of whom he met), during and after his studies in Leipzig with Julius Rietz. Lacking success, he moved to Switzerland (1862–76), where he achieved little but moved towards a more Classical style, in which he continued after returning to Dresden. His later works include symphonies and concertos, string quartets and other chamber music, operas, and sacred music, including *Christus* (1895–9), an oratorio trilogy to his own words. He was also composition professor at the Dresden Conservatory from 1884.

draft. Intermediate stage between sketch and finished work, with the continuity established but the detail still incomplete.

draft score. Score in DRAFT.

drag. Figure on the side drum, two grace notes into a beat. It may be combined with the PARADIDDLE in a drag paradiddle.

Draghi. Name of two 17th-century Italian composers who may have been brothers. Each found a position in a foreign capital in his mid 20s and stayed.

(1) **Antonio** (b. Rimini, 1634–5; d. Vienna, 16 Jan 1700). Recorded as a bass and librettist in Venice in 1657, he moved the next year to Vienna, where he rose to positions as kapellmeister to the dowager empress (1669–82) and then to the emperor. The vehicle of his ascent was opera in the Venetian style. He wrote, on average, seven such pieces a year as kapellmeister, nearly all in collaboration with the court poet Nicolò Minato and court architect-designer Burancini. They include operas and serenatas on mythological subjects, oratorios and sepolcros.

(2) **Giovanni Battista** (b. ?Rimini, c.1640; d. London, 1708). In London by 1667, when Pepys heard him sing and play from an opera he was devising, he was held in a perhaps uneasy alliance with Locke as organist (at the queen's chapel) and theatre musician. Both wrote for two of the most musically elaborate productions of Charles II's reign: *The* TEMPEST (1674) and Shadwell's *Psyche* (1675). Draghi's contribution consisted of act tunes and dances, but he later wrote songs for plays and set Dryden's *Song for St Cecilia's Day* (1687), before retiring on a royal pension in 1698.

Dragonetti, Domenico (Carlo Maria) (b. Venice, 10 Apr 1763; d. London, 16 Apr 1846). Italian bassist-composer, one of his instrument's first virtuosos and the author of concertos and solo pieces for it. He studied in Venice with Merini, and from 13 was principal bass in opera theatres, later succeeding his teacher at St Mark's. From 1794 he was based in London, though he toured frequently, notably to Vienna to see Haydn (1798) and Beethoven (1808). He reportedly played Beethoven's Cello Sonata Op.5:2 with the composer, who afterwards embraced both him and his instrument.

Fiona M. Palmer *Domenico Dragonetti in England* (1997)

dramatic soprano. Soprano capable of particular force and attack. The term covers a wide range of voice types and roles: few singers would attempt both Wagner's Brünnhilde and the Leonora of *Il trovatore*.

dramatic tenor. Tenor capable of particular force and attack. The term is used mainly in the context of 19th-century Italian opera, where there was a progression from the *tenore di forza* (Donizetti) to the *tenore robusto* (later Verdi). The German equivalent is HELDENTENOR.

dramaturg (borrowed from Ger.). Person employed by an opera house, especially in Germany, to assist with matters of production and text (including programme notes), working closely with invited producers.

dramma per musica (It., play for music). Usually 18th-century term for the libretto of what would now be called an OPERA SERIA.

drängend (Ger.). Pressing on.

Drdla, Franz (b. Saar/Žd'ár, 28 Nov 1868; d. Bad Gastein, 6 Sep 1944). Moravian violinist-composer, author of a popular *Souvenir* and Serenade No.1 in A. He studied at the Prague and Vienna conservatories, with Bruckner at the latter.

dream. Like Theseus in *A Midsummer Night's Dream*, many commentators have likened marvellous events (those of music or musical drama) to dreams. Works in which the analogy becomes explicit include *The Nutcracker* and *Julietta*, while dreams are recounted in *Der fliegende Holländer*, *Lohengrin*, *Manon* and *Un re in ascolto*. Dreams may also be music's source as attested by Stravinsky (Octet) and Stockhausen (*Trans*), and by legends told of Palestrina and Tartini.

Dream of Gerontius, The. Oratorio by Elgar to his own and his wife's selection of words from Cardinal Newman's poem. Gerontius (tenor) dies, and is conveyed to heaven by the Angel (mezzo-soprano). First performance: Birmingham, 3 Oct 1900.

Dreigroschenoper, Die (The Threepenny Opera). Version of The BEGGAR'S OPERA by Brecht and Elisabeth Hauptmann with songs by Weill. First performance: Berlin, 31 Aug 1928.

Dreiklang (Ger.). Three-note chord, usually more specifically a triad.

dreistimmig (Ger.). Three-part.

Dresden. German city, formerly capital of the electors and kings of Saxony. The Dresden court, long served by Schütz, became in the first half of the 18th century one of the most musically illustrious in Europe, graced by Zelenka, Lotti and Hasse. In 1817, as patronage swivelled to the bourgeoisie, a German opera company was founded under Weber's direction. It became the court opera, housed in the SEMPER OPER, where Wagner worked for an important period of his life (1843–9). Later the theatre boasted a close association with Strauss, while also presenting the premières of Doktor Faust and Cardillac. Since the First World War it has been known as the Staatsoper, and its renowned orchestra the Staatskapelle.

Dresden Amen. Magniloquent cadential formula attributed to Naumann, quoted by Mendelssohn ('Reformation' Symphony) and Wagner (Parsifal).

Drigo, Riccardo (b. Padua, 30 Jun 1846; d. Padua, 1 Oct 1930). Italian composer-conductor, last in the long line of Italian maestros who served the Russian court. Having studied in Padua and Venice, and begun to make his career in Padua, he went to Russia in 1878 and became conductor of the Italian opera in St Petersburg the next year. In 1886 he advanced to the position of composer-conductor to the imperial ballet, for which he conducted the first Sleeping Beauty and Nutcracker. Of his own scores, Harléquinade (Les Millions d'Harléquin, 1900) includes a popular serenade. He returned to Padua in 1920.

driving. Syncopation, in 17th-century English. Hence 'driving note' (syncopated note).

droit, droite (Fr.). Right, as in main droite (right hand).

drone. Sustained sound, normally of level pitch and low. Drones are built into certain instruments (bagpipes, hurdy-gurdy). They are also characteristic of Indian improvisation and Tibetan ritual music, whence in part their importance to La Monte Young and other Western composers since the 1960s.

Drottningholm. Royal palace outside Stockholm, famed for its theatre of 1766, which is unique in retaining its original machinery. Favoured by Gustavus III, it was abandoned after his assassination until 1922. Since 1953 annual summer festivals of 18th-century opera have been presented there.

Druckman, Jacob (Raphael) (b. Philadelphia, 26 Jun 1928; d. New Haven, 24 May 1996). US composer, notably of poetic-modernist orchestral music of high imaginative glide. He studied with Persichetti and Mennin at Juilliard (1949–56), with Copland at Tanglewood, and in Paris (1954). Having returned to Juilliard as a teacher, he moved in 1972 to Brooklyn College. His flair for sound and drama became manifest in his Animus series for live performers and tape, but it was Windows (1972), his first orchestral score, that firmly established his creative direction and his supreme skills as a tone painter. A Medea for the Met was sadly abandoned.

Orchestral: Windows, 1972; Lamia, s, orch, 1974; Aureole, 1979; Prism, 1980; Brangle, 1989; Counterpoise, s, orch, 1994; etc.

Chamber and instrumental: String Quartet No.2, 1966; No.3, 1981; Animus I, trbn, tape, 1966; II, woman's v, 2 perc, tape, 1968; III, cl, tape, 1969; Valentine, db, 1969; etc.

drum. PERCUSSION instrument, a hollow vessel sounded by means of fingers or an implement. Most often the vessel is covered with a membrane (of animal skin or modern synthetic material), which is tapped or beaten. Drums of such kinds are found throughout the world. Those traditional in Western classical music are the TIMPANI, BASS DRUM, SIDE DRUM and TENOR DRUM, to which the 20th century added instruments from Latin American dance bands (bongos, tom-toms) and elsewhere.

drum kit. Set-up including bass drum, side drum, cymbals and perhaps other instruments, as used in jazz, rock, etc.

Drumming. Work by Reich for his own percussion ensemble, of concert length in four sections. First performance: London, 4 Feb 1972.

Drumroll. Name given Haydn's Symphony No.103, which opens thus. First performance: London, 2 Mar 1795.

drumstick. See STICK.

D.S. *dal* SEGNO.

D–S–C–H (D–E♭–C–B). Musical monogram of Shostakovich.

Düben, Gustaf (b. Stockholm, *c.*1628; d. Stockholm, 19 Dec 1690). Swedish musician, amasser of an extraordinary collection of about 1,800 works, by Buxtehude (over 100) and others. He succeeded his father Andreas (*c.*1597–1662), a pupil of Sweelinck, as court and church organist.

Dubois, (François Clément) Théodore (b. Rosnay, Marne, 24 Aug 1837; d. Paris, 11 Jun 1924). French organist-composer. He studied at the Paris Conservatoire (1854–61) and worked under Franck at Ste Clotilde during this time and later, moving to the Madeleine in 1877. From 1871 he also taught at the Conservatoire, latterly as director (1896–1905). His works include organ and sacred choral pieces.

Du Caurroy, Eustache (baptized Beauvais, 4 Feb 1549; d. Paris, 7 Aug 1609). French composer, whose *Missa pro defunctis* a 5 (1606) was sung at the funerals of French kings from Henri IV (1610) onwards. He was in royal service from *c.*1570 and produced, in the same sober polyphonic style, other church music, besides instrumental fantasias.

ductia. Dance form mentioned by the theorist Johannes de Grocheo (*c.*1275).

Dudelsack (Ger.). Bagpipes.

due corde. Direction in piano music of the late 18th century and early 19th to depress the soft pedal halfway, so that the hammers hit only two of the three strings.

due Foscari, I (The Two Foscari). Opera by Verdi to a libretto by Piave after Byron's play. The two Foscari are Francesco (baritone), the Venetian doge, and his son Jacopo (tenor), whom Francesco sends into exile for state crimes, despite the imprecations of Lucrezia (soprano), Jacopo's wife. First performance: Rome, 3 Nov 1844.

Duenna, The. Play by Sheridan, originally produced (Covent Garden, 21 Nov 1775) with overture and songs by Thomas Linley and his son of the same name. In the best traditions of comedy, the young win their true loves, against the illusory powers of age and money. Operatic versions came from Prokofiev (BETROTHAL IN A MONASTERY) and Gerhard.

duet. Pair of similar instruments, voices or performers, or genre of music for such, or work of that genre. In opera the term implies not just a dialogue but the joining of two voices – often in thirds or tenths – that 19th-century composers used to express mutual dedication or love. The commonest instrumental form is the PIANO DUET.

Du Fay [Dufay], **Guillaume** (b. Beersel, ?5 Aug 1397; d. Cambrai, 27 Nov 1474). Brabantian composer, regarded by his contemporaries and by history as the outstanding musician of his time. With suave polyphony and vernal tonality opening a perspective through an entire composition, his music is among the glories of the early Renaissance. He spent much of his life in Cambrai, but he wrote works also for Rome, for the consecration of Brunelleschi's dome at Florence Cathedral (*Nuper rosarum flores*) and for the court of Savoy.

Born illegitimate, his father a priest, he trained as a choirboy at Cambrai Cathedral under Nicolas Malin and possibly Richard Loqueville, and began his career as musician and churchman locally before, almost certainly, joining the service of the Malatesta family in Rimini (1420–24). He returned to Cambrai and Laon, then travelled with the papal legate to Bologna (1426–8), after which he joined the papal choir in Rome (1428–33). By February 1434 he was at the court of Savoy, where that month he met Binchois, visiting with the Burgundian court. He then spent further periods with the papal chapel, now in Florence (1435–7), and at the Savoyard court (1437–9), before returning to Cambrai (1439–50). Possibly he went to Padua for the singing of his St Anthony mass at the dedication of Donatello's altar (1450), and certainly he spent another period in Savoy (1452–8). After that he was in Cambrai, where his visitors included Ockeghem, one of several composers to write *déplorations* on his death. His music continued to be copied and performed into the early 16th century, but then was forgotten until the late 19th and not fully revived until the late 20th.

David Fallows *Dufay* (1982, ²1987)

Masses: Mass for St James a 3–4, ?c.1427; *sine nomine* a 3; Mass for St Anthony of Padua a 3–4, ?1450; *Se la face ay pale* a 4, ?c.1455; L'HOMME ARME a 4, *c.*1460; *Ecce ancilla Domini* a 4, *c.*1460; *Ave regina coelorum* a 4, *c.*1470; many sections

Other sacred works: *Alma redemptoris mater* a 3 (two settings); *Flos florum* a 3; *Nuper rosarum flores* a 4 (isorhythmic motet), 1436; *Supremum est mortalibus* a 3 (isorhythmic motet), 1433; *Vergene bella* a 3 (Petrarch); etc.

Secular songs: *Adieu ces bons vins de Lannoys* a 3 (rondeau); *Ce jour de l'an* a 3 (rondeau); *Le serviteur hault guerdonné* a 3 (rondeau); *Resvelliés vous* a 3 (ballade); *Se la face ay pale* a 3 (ballade); etc.

Dufourt, Hugues (b. Lyons, 28 Sep 1943). French composer, who coined the term 'spectral music'. He studied at the Geneva Conservatory and became associated with Grisey and Murail in the group L'Itinéraire in the early 1970s. A connection with Boulez and IRCAM brought about *Antiphysis* for flute and large ensemble (1977) and *Saturne* for wind, percussion and electronics (1978–9). Later works include *Hivers* for large ensemble (1992–2001), a four-seasons cycle in which every season is winter.

Dugazon. Term for two kinds of voice named after the popular Louise-Rosalie Dugazon (1755–1821): the 'jeune Dugazon' such as she was in her youth, a light lyric soprano, and the 'mère Dugazon' such as she became, in mezzo-soprano territory.

Dukas, Paul (Abraham) (b. Paris, 1 Oct 1865; d. Paris, 17 May 1935). French composer, whose independent course was both enabled and restricted by his high standards and wide learning. He left only a handful of major works, none composed after 1912. A banker's son, he studied at the Paris Conservatoire (1881–9), where he was taught by Guiraud and struck up a friendship with Debussy. He made his public debut as a composer with the Wagnerian overture *Polyeucte* (1891) and started work as a critic the next year. His noble and resplendent Symphony (1895–6) acknowledged but enlarged French traditions (Franck, Chausson, Lalo) by its appeal to Beethoven; then came his brilliant symphonic scherzo *L'Apprenti Sorcier* (1897) and imposing Rameau Variations for piano, the latter emerging while he worked assiduously on his Maeterlinck opera *Ariane et Barbe-Bleue* (1899–1906). This is far from a re-run of *Pelléas*. A quotation from Debussy's work stands out within a score that is generally solider in harmony and darker in tone, concerned with the struggle for self-determination that was the lot of its composer as much as of its central character Ariane. It was, in a sense, a struggle he lost. His only later work on a large scale was his ballet *La Péri*, and though the deaths of his elder brother (1908) and father (1915) freed him emotionally to marry, there was no creative rebirth. Instead he settled into his work as

inspector of provincial conservatories (from 1912) and composition professor at the Paris Conservatoire (from 1928), where Messiaen was among his pupils.

Opera: ARIANE ET BARBE-BLEUE (Maeterlinck), 1899–1906

Orchestral: *Polyeucte* (overture), 1891; Symphony, C, 1895–6; L'APPRENTI SORCIER, 1897; *La Péri*, 1911–12

Songs: *Vocalise-étude*, 1909; 'Sonnet de Ronsard', 1924

Instrumental: *Villanelle*, hn, pf, 1906

Piano: Sonata, E♭ minor, 1899–1901; *Variations, interlude et final sur un thème de Rameau*, ?1899–1902; *Prélude élégiaque*, 1908; *La Plainte, au loin, du faune …*, 1920

Duke, Vernon (b. Parafyanov, now in Belarus, 10 Oct 1903; d. Santa Monica, Cal., 16 Jan 1969). Russian–US composer, originally Vladimir Alexandrovich Dukelsky. Wrested from studies at the Kiev Conservatory (1916–19), he moved with his family to Constantinople and then, in 1922, New York. There he wrote a concerto for Rubinstein (1924), which he adapted into a ballet for Diaghilev (*Zéphyr et Flore*, Monte Carlo, 1925). He began his career in musical theatre in London (1926–9), then returned to the USA to write Broadway shows and film scores while maintaining an output of choral works and chamber music.

dulcian. One of several Renaissance names for the bassoon, now preferred for the early one-piece instrument.

dulcimer. Psaltery played with hammers, commonest being the CIMBALOM.

Dumbarton Oaks. Name given to Stravinsky's Concerto in E♭, commissioned by Mr and Mrs Robert Woods Bliss for performance at their eponymous home in Washington. First performance there, 8 May 1938.

dumka (Cz., pl. *dumky*). Genre of Slavonic lament, originally Ukrainian. Dvořák addressed the style in several works, notably his piano trio *Dumky*, made of six examples.

dummy. Silent, as in 'dummy keyboard' (a practice device), 'dummy pipes' (at the front of an organ, for display).

Du Mont, Henry (b. Villers-L'Evêque, near Liège, 1610; d. Paris, 8 May 1684). French composer and church musician, originally Henry de Thier (the Walloon form), father of the *grand motet*. He was a chorister at Maastricht Cathedral from 1621 and organist there (1630–38, with a break for further study with Léonard de Hodemont in Liège). Then he went to Paris, where he was organist at St Paul in the Marais (1643–84), also holding posts as royal harpsichordist (from 1652) and chapelmaster (1663–83). Apart from his *grands motets* intended for the royal chapel (for five soli and five-part choir, with strings providing an introductory symphony and accompaniment), he wrote *petits motets* for smaller forces (two, three or four voices and continuo) and simple masses for monastic use.

dump. English lute or keyboard genre of the century from *c*.1540, having a melancholy character (as in 'down in the dumps').

Dunhill, Thomas F(rederick) (b. London, 1 Feb 1877; d. Scunthorpe, 13 Mar 1946). British composer, remembered for educational music and a Yeats song, 'The Cloths of Heaven' (Op.30:3, 1911). He studied with Stanford at the RCM (1893–9), where he taught from 1905.

Duni, Egidio (Romualdo) (baptized Matera, Basilicata, 11 Feb 1708; d. Paris, 11 Jun 1775). Italian composer, resident from 1757 in Paris, where his *opéras comique* triumphed. The son and younger brother of composers, he may have studied in Naples before beginning his career as an opera seria composer in Rome (1735), Milan (1736) and London (1737). He became chapelmaster at the Parma court, where he met Goldoni in 1756 and turned to comedy. The next year he set a French libretto, *Le Peintre amoureux de son modèle*, as a rejoinder to Rousseau's dictum that French could not be sung. Having arrived in Paris for the première, he stayed, married and enjoyed his success as a master of sentimental comedy with an Italian songfulness. He retired in 1770.

Dunstable, John (b. *c*.1390; d. 24 Dec 1453). English composer, the first (and the last until the 20th century) whose music belonged in a European environment. The survival of his works in many, widely distributed sources is a mark of his continental esteem – though conflicting ascriptions make it hard to separate his output from that of other composers from England (Power, Bedyngham, Benet) and the continent (Binchois). His music was being praised and discussed up to half a century after his death, before descending into 400 years of ignorance and misinformation, to be restored to the world of scholarship at the beginning of the 20th century and to that of vivid performance a few decades later.

Little is known of his life. He may have served the Duke of Bedford, especially during that duke's regency in France (1422–35). He certainly wrote astronomical treatises, and could have been more concerned with stars than notes in his later years. The chief glory of his music – responsible for his reputation and influence, though shared with other English composers – comes from triadic harmony and particularly from prominent thirds in the upper parts of what is normally a three-part texture. He was also a master of long melodies, again euphonious, being based on scale patterns and triads, but retaining the lively irregular rhythms of earlier generations, as well as, sometimes, the principle of isorhythm. And he was, with Power, one of the creators of the CYCLIC MASS.

Margaret Bent *Dunstaple* (1981)

Masses: *Da gaudiorum premia* a 3; *Rex seculorum* a 3; one other cycle and many sections

Isorhythmic motets: *Preco preheminencie* a 4; *Veni Sancte Spiritus* a 4; etc.

Other sacred music: *Beata Dei genitrix* a 3; *Beata mater* a 3; *Descendi in ortum meum* a 4; *Quam pulchra es* a 3; *Salve regina misericordie* a 3; *Speciosa facta es* a 3; *Sub tuam protectionem* a 3; etc.

duo. Duet, especially one for instruments or of instrumentalists. A piano duo, being a pair of duo pianists, can cover the PIANO DUO and PIANO DUET repertories.

Duparc, (Marie Eugène) Henri (Fouques) (b. Paris, 21 Jan 1848; d. Mont-de-Marsan, 12 Feb 1933). French composer, famed for just 13 songs, of which the last dates from 1884. He studied with Franck and imbibed Wagner, whose works he travelled to hear in Munich (1868) and Bayreuth (1879, with Chabrier). Their influences, though, he transcended. His hypersensitivity, which was responsible for almost half a century of creative silence, also gave him access to an intimate bond between words and music. The moment passed. He remained interested in the work of his contemporaries (especially his friend Chausson), and he drew and painted, until overcome by blindness and later paralysis.

Canonic songs (those asterisked also orchestrated): 'Au pays où se fait la guerre'* (Gautier), ?1869–70; 'Chanson triste'* (Jean Lahor, i.e. Henri Cazalis), 1868; 'Elégie' (Moore), 1874; 'Extase' (Lahor), 1874; 'L'Invitation au voyage'* (Baudelaire), 1870; 'Lamento' (Gautier), 1883; 'Le Manoir de Rosemonde'* (Robert de Bonnières), 1879; 'Phidylé'* (Leconte de Lisle), 1882; 'Sérénade florentine' (Lahor), ?1880–81; 'Soupir' (Prud-homme), 1869; 'Testament'* (Armand Silvestre), 1883; 'La Vague et la cloche'* (François Coppée), 1871; 'La Vie antérieure'* (Baudelaire), 1884

Other songs: 'La Fuite', s, t, pf, 1871; 'Le Galop' (Prudhomme), 1869; 'Romance de Mignon' (Victor Wilder), 1869; 'Sérénade' (Gabriel Marc), 1869

Other works: *Lénore*, orch, 1875; other orchestral and piano pieces

Duphly, Jacques (b. Rouen, 12 Jan 1715; d. Paris, 15 Jul 1789). French harpsichordist-composer, who inherited the Couperin tradition from his teacher Dagincour and added a strong dash of Rameau. He went to Paris in 1742, and was a sufficiently popular composer and teacher through the 1750s that he could retire (or be neglected) in comfort.

duplet. Pair of notes to be played in the time of three (i.e. momentary imposition of duple time in triple time, or of 4/4 in 6/8, etc.).

duple time. Two beats to the bar.

duplum (Lat., duple). The second voice in medieval polyphony, added to the tenor.

Dupont, Gabriel (Edouard Xavier) (b. Caen, 1 Mar 1878; d. Le Vésinet, 2 Aug 1914). French composer, pupil and follower of Massenet, victim of poor health. His verismo opera *La cabrera* (Milan, 1904) was a success in its time; he also wrote other operas, songs and instrumental pieces.

Du Pré, Jacqueline (b. Oxford, 26 Jan 1945; d. London, 19 Oct 1987). British cellist, renowned especially for her performances of Elgar's Cello Concerto, which caught both her own rhapsodic spirit and a public mood. She seized the cello at five, became a pupil of William Pleeth at 10, studied with Tortelier and Rostropovich, and made her debut in London in 1961. In 1967 she married Barenboim; in 1973 multiple sclerosis forced her to abandon her career.

Dupré, Marcel (b. Rouen, 3 May 1886; d. Meudon, 30 May 1971). French organist-composer, proponent of a virtuoso style that was taken up by his pupils Messiaen and Alain. Born into a family of organists, he had a church appointment himself at 12 and was acquainted with Cavaillé-Coll. He studied with Guilmant from that age, and with Diémer, Vierne and Widor at the Paris Conservatoire (1902–14), where in 1920 he performed all Bach's organ works. Visits to London (1920) and the USA (1921) initiated his touring career, while from 1934 he was organist at St Sulpice, Widor's successor. He also taught at the Conservatoire (1926–54).

Michael Murray *Marcel Dupré* (1985)

Organ: *Trois préludes et fugues*, B, F minor, G minor, Op.7, 1912; *Cortège et litanie*, Op.19:4, 1921; *Variations sur un noël*, Op.20, 1922; *Symphonie-Passion*, Op.23, 1924; etc.

Duprez, Gilbert (Louis) (b. Paris, 6 Dec 1806; d. Paris, 23 Sep 1896). French tenor, credited with introducing the chest-voice high C (as Arnold at the Italian première of *Guillaume Tell*, to Rossini's discomfiture) as part of the package of the *tenore di forza*. He appeared as a boy treble at the Comédie Française, and as a tenor at 18. After several years in Italy, studying and performing (notably as the first Edgardo in *Lucia di Lammermoor*), he returned to Paris as Arnold (1837), creating further roles in operas by Berlioz (*Benvenuto Cellini*), Donizetti and Verdi. He also wrote operas and memoirs.

dur (Ger.). Major. With its sister term *moll* (minor), it was introduced to print by Werckmeister (1698), being derived from the Latin *durum* (hard) and *molle* (soft), which had served to describe the notes B and B♭, and the hexachords containing them.

duramente (It.). With hardness.

Durand. French music publishing firm founded in 1869 by Auguste Durand (1830–1909), a fellow student with Franck and Saint-Saëns at the Paris Conservatoire and a professional organist, critic and composer. He and his son Jacques (1865–1928) – who also studied at the Conservatoire, alongside Debussy and Dukas – published most of the works of Saint-Saëns, Debussy, Fauré and Ravel, besides involving these composers and others in comprehensive editions of Rameau and the classic repertory. Debussy took care of the complete works of Chopin.

Durante, Francesco (b. Frattamaggiore, Aversa, 31 Mar 1684; d. Naples, 30 Sep 1755). Italian composer and renowned Neapolitan teacher, whose pupils included Pergolesi, Piccinni, Traetta, Sacchini and Paisiello. He himself studied (1699–1705) with his uncle Angelo, latterly at the San Onofrio conservatory in Naples, where he is recorded as a teacher (1710–11) during a patchily documented period of his life. A long stay in Rome is likely. He then held posts as first maestro at the leading Neapolitan conservatories: the Poveri di Gesù Cristo (1728–39), the Loreto (1742–55) and the San Onofrio (1745–55). As a composer he devoted himself almost exclusively to sacred music, appealing to the Palestrina style in some works but also keeping abreast – from within his own learned perspective – of his students.

Durastanti, Margherita (*fl.* 1700–34). Italian soprano, associated with Handel in Rome, Venice and London. She sang in his *Resurrezione* (1707) and *Agrippina* (1709), and in several operas during her London visits (1720–24, 1732–4), all suggesting a mezzo-soprano voice and versatile acting abilities.

duration. (1) Length of time, those measured in musical notation ranging from around one-twentieth of a second (in the fastest keyboard music) to several hours (for an opera).
(2) Rhythmic value. Those in common use are notated as shown, with their rests:

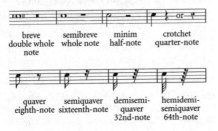

| breve | semibreve | minim | crotchet |
| double whole note | whole note | half-note | quarter-note |

quaver	semiquaver	demisemi-	hemidemi-
eighth-note	sixteenth-note	quaver	semiquaver
		32nd-note	64th-note

Of the two forms of crotchet rest, the first is normal for printed music and the (older) second for manuscript.

Durazzo, Count **Giacomo** (b. Genoa, 27 Apr 1717; d. Venice, 15 Oct 1794). Italian nobleman, who went to Vienna as Genoan ambassador in 1749 and stayed as director of the imperial theatres (1754–64). He vigorously promoted operatic reform, notably in his support of Gluck. Obliged by intrigue to resign, he was consoled by being appointed the Viennese ambassador to Venice.

durchdringend (Ger.). Piercing.

Durchführung (Ger., leading through). Development.

Durchgang (Ger.). Passing note.

durchkomponiert (Ger.). Through-composed.

Durey, Louis (Edmond) (b. Paris, 27 May 1888; d. St Tropez, 3 Jul 1979). French composer, eldest but perhaps least representative of Les Six. His music suggests his retiring nature, though in the early Cold War years (1948–52) he displayed a trenchant socialist commitment. He studied at the Schola Cantorum, and found himself enveloped in Cocteau's group through his admiration for Satie and Stravinsky. Among his works are three quartets (1917, 1922,

1928), other chamber and piano music, songs and cantatas.

durezza (It.). Hardness, as in *con durezza* (with hardness).

Durkó, Zsolt (b. Szeged, 10 Apr 1934; d. Budapest, 2 Apr 1997). Hungarian composer, typically having roots in folk (and medieval) music while enjoying the air of avant-garde freedom. He studied with Farkas at the Liszt Academy and Petrassi in Rome (1961–3), then worked as a teacher at the academy (1971–7) and with Hungarian radio (from 1982). His works include a piano concerto (1981), other orchestral music, and pieces for standard and non-standard chamber ensembles.

Duruflé, Maurice (b. Louviers, 11 Jan 1902; d. Paris, 16 Jun 1986). French composer, especially of a *Requiem* in the Fauré tradition. He studied with Tournemire from 1919 and with Gigout and Dukas at the Paris Conservatoire (1920–28). Organist at St Etienne-du-Mont from 1930, he also toured widely.

Choral: *Requiem*, Op.9, soli, ch, orch, 1947; 4 Motets, Op.10, 1960; Mass 'Cum jubilo', Op.11, bar, ch, orch, 1966; *Notre-Père*, 1977
Organ: *Scherzo*, Op.2, 1924; *Prélude, adagio et choral varié sur le 'Veni creator'*, Op.4, 1930; Suite, Op.5, 1933; *Prélude et fugue sur le nom d'Alain*, Op.7, 1942; *Prélude sur l'introit de l'Epiphanie*, 1961; *Fugue sur le carillon de Soissons*, 1962

Dusapin, Pascal (b. Nancy, 29 May 1955). French composer, astonishingly prolific with music at once cool and visceral. He studied art and art history at the Sorbonne (1974–8), and had lessons with Xenakis and Donatoni. His works include *Niobé* for soprano, small choir and wind (1982), the chamber opera *Roméo et Juliette* (Montpellier, 1989) and many bristling fragments for small instrumental groupings. See also MEDEA.

Dušek. Czech couple with Mozart associations.
(1) **František Xaver** (baptized Chotěborky, near Jaroměř, 8 Dec 1731; d. Prague, 12 Feb 1799). Composer, notably of symphonies and quartets in Classical style. Noble patronage took him from peasant origins to a Jesuit school, whence he progressed to musical studies in Prague and Vienna (with Wagenseil). Most of his professional life he spent with his wife in Prague, where Mozart visited them.
(2) **Josefa** (baptized Prague, 6 Mar 1754; d. Prague, 8 Jan 1824). Soprano. She married František Xaver, her teacher, in 1776 and took him the next year to Salzburg, her mother's home

town, where they met Mozart. The immediate result was the scena 'Ah, lo previdi', followed by 'Bella mia fiamma'. She also gave the first performance of Beethoven's 'Ah! perfido' (Leipzig, 1796).

Dushkin, Samuel (b. Suwalki, 13 Dec 1891; d. New York, 24 Jun 1976). Polish–US violinist. He was not one of the great virtuosos, but an appealing partner for Stravinsky, with whom he appeared regularly in 1931–4, especially in the first performances of the Violin Concerto and *Duo concertant*. Taken to New York as a child, he studied at the Paris Conservatoire and with Auer and Kreisler in New York.

Dussek, Jan Ladislav (b. Čáslav, 12 Feb 1760; d. St Germain-en-Laye/Paris, 20 Mar 1812). Czech pianist-composer, an early touring virtuoso and, in his music, a proto-Romantic. He was born into a musical family. His younger brother, Franz Benedikt, had a career as a composer in Italy and his younger sister, Veronica, was a singer-pianist whom in 1795 he called to London, where she married and settled. Their father, an organist-composer, was their first teacher; later Jan Ladislav was a chorister and a student at Jesuit schools. A military patron took him to the Low Countries in 1779, after which he travelled widely as a pianist and teacher before taking up residence in London in 1789. In 1792 he married the daughter of his partner in a music publishing business. When this failed in 1799, he fled, leaving behind his wife and daughter, to continue his career on the continent. He held appointments with Prince Louis Ferdinand of Prussia (1804–6) and Talleyrand in Paris (from 1807). He is reported to have been the first to play from a sideways position on stage—though at the end of his life he was not playing at all, having taken to his bed, obese and gouty. His works include 16 piano concertos, numerous sonatas for piano alone or with violin, various chamber pieces and harp music.

Dutilleux, Henri (b. Angers, 22 Jan 1916). French composer, the foremost representative of the French symphonic tradition in the age of Messaien and Boulez, though by no means opposed to learning from both. With artistic ancestors on both sides of his family, he studied at the Paris Conservatoire (1933–8), won the Prix de Rome, and worked at French radio (1943–63), also teaching at the Ecole Normale de Musique (from 1963) and the Conservatoire (from 1970). Rather like Carter, he arrived at an independent, intuitive style around 1950, having absorbed the lessons of modernism and thereby moved beyond some

sophisticated achievements in a more conventional (in his case Ravelian) manner. But though the diatonic harmony of his First Symphony was moderated in later works, its rhetorical punch was not: his music has remained firm in purpose, even while espousing an aesthetic of constant metamorphosis. That aesthetic has also limited his output to rather few works, most of them for orchestral resources, of which he is a master.

Caroline Potter *Henri Dutilleux* (1997)

Orchestral: Symphony No.1, 1949–51; No.2 'Le Double', 1956–9; *Le Loup* (ballet), 1953; *Métaboles*, 1962–5; '*Tout un monde lointain ...*', vc, orch, 1968–70; *Timbres, Espace, Mouvement*, 1977; *L'Arbre des songes*, vn, orch, 1979–85; *Mystère de l'instant*, str, cimb, perc, 1985–9; *The Shadows of Time*, 1995–7; *Sur le même accord*, vn, orch, 2001–2
Chamber: *Ainsi la nuit*, str qt, 1975–6; *Trois strophes sur le nom de Sacher*, vc, 1976–82; *Les Citations*, ob, db, hpd, perc, 1985–91
Songs: *Trois sonnets de Jean Cassou*, bar, orch, 1954; 'San Francisco Night' (Paul Gilson), s, pf, 1964
Piano: Sonata, 1947; *Résonances*, 1965; *Deux figures de résonance*, 2 pf, 1970; *Trois préludes*, 1973–88

Dutoit, Charles (b. Lausanne, 7 Oct 1936). Swiss conductor, best known for his work with the Montreal Symphony (1977–2002), especially in French music. He studied with Samuel Baud-Bovy in Geneva and Münch at Tanglewood (1959), began his career in Switzerland, and held posts in Mexico City (1973–5) and Gothenburg (1976–9). He was briefly married to Argerich.

Duvernoy, Frédéric Nicolas (b. Montbéliard, 16 Oct 1765; d. Paris, 19 Jul 1838). French hornist-composer. Self-taught, he was highly regarded as principal at the Paris Opera (1799–1817).

dux (Lat., duke). Entry of the subject in the tonic in a FUGUE, answered by the COMES, the dominant entry.

Dvořák, Antonín (Leopold) (b. Nelahozeves, near Kralupy, 8 Sep 1841; d. Prague, 1 May 1904). Czech composer. He reconciled the folk music of his native land with the symphonic tradition of nearby Vienna in the age of Brahms, and maintained in all he did an engaging natural ease, reflected above all in his superb gift for melody.

Interrupting preparation for life as a butcher (his father's and grandfather's trade), he completed his schooling in Zlonice and Česká Kamenice, then studied at the Prague Organ School (1857–9). He began his career as a viola player, in the ensemble that became the orchestra of the Provisional Theatre; as such he played under

Wagner (1863) and Smetana (from 1866), both of whom confused him. Wagner was an oppressive influence for several years, and Smetana, while providing a nationalist model to which a young artist could aspire, had little stylistically to offer a musican who cherished Classical form.

He left the orchestra in 1871 to earn his living as a teacher and (from 1874) organist, and in 1873 he married. Composing abundantly all the while, he began to gain important performances – notably of his E♭ symphony and the second version of his opera *The King and the Charcoalburner*, both in 1874 – and to draw towards an independent style, especially in his symphony in F. Winning imperial prizes, in 1874, 1876 and 1877, brought him to the attention of Brahms, who smoothed his way with publishers in Berlin, and from 1878 onwards his works were brought out and widely performed as soon as they were written. His apprenticeship was over.

It had been long. Apart from some piano pieces and songs reaching print in Prague – none before 1873 – the earliest work published in his lifetime was his A minor quartet Op.16, which he wrote when he was 33. And though preceding compositions have since been absorbed into the output (resulting in a renumbering of the symphonies), they remain little performed and little regarded. The classic Dvořák begins with the works that won him his prizes, including his symphony in F (the eventual No.5) and glorious serenade for strings.

Brahms – and Hanslick – thought that at this point he should move to Vienna, but he resisted and instead did more to encourage his audience in Britain. His first conducting engagements outside Bohemia were in London (1884), which resulted in commissions from the Philharmonic Society (Seventh Symphony) and the choral festivals of Birmingham (*The Spectre's Bride*) and Leeds (*St Ludmilla*). With these in hand, he bought a country property at Vysoká, near Příbram, where he could indulge his pastimes of walking and conversing with peasant labourers. But his British success also led to return visits once or twice a year; the two in 1891 were to receive an honorary Cambridge doctorate and to conduct the first performance of a second work for Birmingham, the *Requiem*.

That same year he started giving composition classes at the Prague Conservatory, though his time there was brief, for by the end of the year he had accepted an invitation from Jeannette Thurber to direct her National Conservatory in New York. In the first half of 1892 he made a farewell tour of Bohemia and Moravia, playing the *Dumky* trio and conducting the overture trilogy Opp.91–3. He then took up his New York appointment on 1

October 1892. One of Mrs Thurber's aims for him was to found a US school of composition, and in the first half of 1893, having heard spirituals sung by a Black student at the conservatory, he provided a model work in his 'New World' Symphony. His first summer in the USA he spent at Spillville, Iowa, which had a Czech community, besides neighbouring Amerindians; there he wrote a string quartet (in F) and quintet (in E♭) along similar lines. The following summer he returned to Bohemia, before his third and final school year in New York (1894–5), during which he wrote his Cello Concerto, partly a memorial to his sister-in-law.

Definitively, and happily, back in Bohemia in the summer of 1895, he completed a pair of quartets, arduous (in G) and sunny (in A♭). The next year he resumed his place at the Prague Conservatory, made a final trip to London for the première of the Cello Concerto and began a sequence of symphonic poems on Czech folktales. After that he was absorbed in turn by three operas – including *Rusalka*, his one big success in the form – while continuing to enjoy local and national honours and the pleasures of family life; his daughter Ottilie married his pupil Suk in 1898.

Though he worked at operas and revisions of operas through much of his life, a large proportion of his music is in standard instrumental forms and genres, and was so even before he became acquainted with Brahms. His fluency suggests that those forms and genres caused him little trouble: he took them as second nature. Similarly, and although he certainly had views about national character in music, his handling of folk material seems to have been spontaneous. Slavonic styles of dance (especially the vigorous furiant) and song (especially the melancholy dumka), along with regional accents of rhythm or modulation, were absorbed and expressed with no fuss. When he turned to US sources, in the symphony and chamber pieces of 1893 (his only full year in the USA), he discovered a pentatonic ancestry shared with central European folk music, and it is significant that he preferred the music of minorities (Blacks and Amerindians), just as he did in listening to the Czechs, Slovaks and Ukrainians within the Austro-Hungarian Empire. In his music these local, unregarded things became, with no struggle, at once international and natural.

John Clapham *Dvořák* (1979); Michael Beckerman, ed. *Dvořák and his World* (1993)

Theatre and orchestral music

Operas: *Alfred* (Karl Theodor Körner), 1870, f.p. Prague, 1938; *The King and the Charcoalburner* (Bernard J. Lobeský), Op.14, 1871, recomposed 1874 (Bernard Guldener), f.p. Prague, 1874, rev 1887

(Václav Juda Novotný), f.p. Prague, 1887; *The Stubborn Lovers* (Josef Štolba), Op.17, 1874, f.p. Prague, 1881; *Vanda* (Václav Beneš Sumavský and František Zakreis), Op.25, 1875, f.p. Prague, 1876, rev 1879–80, 1883, 1900–1; *The Cunning Peasant* (Josef Otakar Veselý), Op.37, 1877, f.p. Prague, 1878; *Dimitrij* (Marie Červinková-Riegrová), Op.64, 1881–2, f.p. Prague, 1882, rev 1883, 1885, 1894, f.p. Prague, 1894; *The Jacobin* (Červinková-Riegrová), Op.84, 1887–8, f.p. Prague, 1889, rev 1897, f.p. Prague, 1898; *The Devil and Kate* (Adolf Wenig), Op.112, 1898–9, f.p. Prague, 1899; RUSALKA, Op.114, 1900; ARMIDA, Op.115, 1902–3

Incidental music: *Josef Kajetán Tyl*, Op.62, 1881–2

Symphonies: No.1 'The BELLS OF ZLONICE', C minor, 1865; No.2, B♭, Op.4, 1865, rev 1887; No.3, E♭, Op.10, 1873, rev 1887–9; No.4, D minor, Op.13, 1874, rev 1887–8; No.5 (ex-No.3), F, Op.76, 1875, f.p. Prague, 25 Mar 1879, rev 1887; No.6 (ex-No.1), D, Op.60, 1880, f.p. Prague, 25 Mar 1881; No.7 (ex-No.2), D minor, Op.70, 1884–5, f.p. London, 22 Apr 1885; No.8 (ex-No.4), G, Op.88, 1889, f.p. Prague, 2 Feb 1890; No.9 (ex-No.5), 'From the NEW WORLD', E minor, Op.95, 1893, f.p. New York, 16 Dec 1893

Concertos: Piano Concerto, G minor, Op.33, 1876; VIOLIN CONCERTO, A minor, Op.53, 1879–80, rev 1882; CELLO CONCERTO, B minor, Op.104, 1894–5

Smaller concertante pieces (all from chamber pieces): Romance, F minor, Op.11, vn, orch, 1877; *Mazurek*, Op.49, vn, orch, 1879; Rondo, G minor, Op.94, vc, orch, 1893; *Silent Woods*, vc, orch, 1893

Overtures: *My Homeland*, 1882 (from *Josef Kajetán Tyl*); *Hussite Overture*, Op.67, 1883; *Nature, Life and Love*, trilogy (*In Nature's Realm*, Op.91, 1891; *Carnival*, Op.92, 1891; *Othello*, Op.93, 1891–2)

Symphonic poems: Symphonic Poem, Op.14, 1874; *The Water Goblin*, Op.107, 1896; *The Noon Witch*, Op.108, 1896; *The Golden Spinning-wheel*, Op.109, 1896; *The Wild Dove*, Op.110, 1896; *A Hero's Song*, Op.111, 1897

Other works: Serenade, E, Op.22, str, 1875; Nocturne, B, Op.40, str, ?1875 (from String Quartet No.4); Symphonic Variations, Op.78, 1877; Serenade, D minor, Op.44, 10 wind, vc, db, 1878; SLAVONIC RHAPSODIES, Op.45, 1878; SLAVONIC DANCES, first series, Op.46, 1878, second series, Op.72, 1886–7; Festival March, Op.54, 1879; Czech Suite, Op.39, 1879; *Legends*, Op.59, 1881 (from piano duets); *Scherzo capriccioso*, Op.66, 1883; Suite, A, Op.98b (from piano work), 1895; dances

Orchestration: Hungarian Dances Nos.17–21 (Brahms), 1880

Choral orchestral: *Hymnus*, Op.30, ch, orch, 1872, rev 1880, rev 1884; Stabat mater, Op.58, soli, ch, orch, 1876–7; Psalm 149, Op.79, men's ch, orch, 1879; *The Spectre's Bride* (cantata: Karel Erben), Op.69, soli, ch, orch, 1884; *St Ludmilla* (oratorio: Jaroslav Vrchlický), Op.71, soli, ch, orch, 1885–6; Mass, D, Op.86, soli, ch, org, 1887, orch 1892; *Requiem*, Op.89, soli, ch, orch, 1890; *Te Deum*, Op.103, soli, ch, orch, 1892; *The American Flag* (cantata: Rodman Drake), Op.102, soli, ch, orch, 1892–3;

Festival Song (Vrchlický), Op.113, ch, orch, 1900

Orchestral songs: *Evening Songs*, 1882 (from Op.3:2–3); *Biblical Songs*, 1895 (from Op.99:1–5)

Chamber and piano music

String quartets: No.1, A, Op.2, 1862; No.2, B♭, ?1868–70; No.3, D, ?1869–70; No.4, E minor, ?1870; No.5, F minor, Op.9, 1873; No.6, A minor, Op.12, 1873; No.7, A minor, Op.16, 1874; No.8, E, Op.80, 1876, rev 1888; No.9, D minor, Op.34, 1877, rev 1879; No.10, E♭, Op.51, 1878–9; Movement, F, 1881; No.11, C, Op.61, 1881; *Echo of Songs*, 1887 (12 pieces, from songs *Cypresses*); No.12 'American', F, Op.96, 1893; No.13, G, Op.106, 1895; No.14, A♭, Op.105, 1895

String sextet: A, Op.48, 1878

Piano quintets: A, Op.5, 1872; A, Op.81, 1887

String quintets: A minor, Op.1, str qt + va, 1861; G, Op.77, str qt + db, 1875, rev 1888; E♭ 'American', Op.97, str qt + va, 1893

Piano quartets: D, Op.23, 1875; E♭, Op.87, 1889

Piano trios: B♭, Op.21, 1875, rev ?1880; G minor, Op.26, 1876; F minor, Op.65, 1883; *Dumky*, Op.90, 1890–91

Violin–piano duos: Romance, F minor, Op.11, vn, pf, 1877 (from String Quartet No.5); Capriccio, vn, pf, ?1878; Nocturne, B, Op.40, vn, pf, pub 1883 (from String Quartet No.4); *Mazurek*, Op.49, vn, pf, 1879; Sonata, F, Op.57, 1880; Ballad, D minor, Op.15:1, 1884; *Romantic Pieces*, Op.75, vn, pf, 1887 (from trios Op.75a); Violin Sonatina, G, Op.100, 1893

Other chamber works: Bagatelles, Op.47, 2 vn, vc, hmnm, 1878; Terzetto, C, Op.74, 2 vn, va, 1887; *Miniatures*, Op.75a, 2 vn, va, 1887; Rondo, G minor, Op.94, vc, pf, 1891; *Silent Woods*, vc, pf, 1891 (from piano duet Op.68:5); dances

Piano solo: 8 Waltzes, Op.54, 1879–80; Humoresque, F♯, 1884; Suite, A, Op.98, 1894; 8 Humoresques, E♭ minor, B, A♭, F, A minor, B, G♭, B♭ minor, Op.101, 1894; etc.

Piano duet: SLAVONIC DANCES, first series, Op.46, 1878, second series, Op.72, 1886; *Legends*, Op.59, 1880–81; *From the Bohemian Forest*, Op.68, 1883–4

Songs

Solo songs: *Cypresses*, 1865 (18, 8 rev as *Liebeslieder*, Op.83, 1888); *Evening Songs*, 1876 (12); *Zigeunermelodien*, Op.55, 1880 (7, including 'Songs my mother taught me'); *In Folk Tone*, Op.73, 1886 (4); *Biblical Songs*, Op.99, 1894 (10); etc.

Duets: Moravian Duets, s, a, pf, Op.32, 1876 (14), Op.38, 1877 (4)

Other works: sacred pieces, v, org; partsongs

dyad. Two-note group, especially a pair of pitch classes in set theory.

dynamics. LOUDNESS, considered as a variable. The common markings are PIANO, FORTE and their gradations, as well as CRESCENDO, DECRESCENDO (DIMINUENDO) and SFORZATO (SFORZANDO).

Dyson, George (b. Halifax, 28 May 1883; d. Winchester, 28 Sep 1964). British composer and teacher, knighted in 1942. After studies with Stanford at the RCM (1900–4) he spent time in Italy. He returned to the RCM in 1921 and became director (1938–52); he also taught at Winchester. His works, principally choral, include the once-popular cantata *The Canterbury Pilgrims* (1931) and church music.

Dzerzhinsky, Ivan (Ivanovich) (b. Tambov, 9 Apr 1909; d. Leningrad, 18 Jan 1978). Russian composer, whose opera *Quiet Flows the Don* (1932–4), after the Sholokhov novel, became a positive model in the Soviet Union against the negative provided by Shostakovich's *Lady Macbeth*. He studied with progressivists, including Asafyev at the Leningrad Conservatory (1932–4), but was himself deeply traditional.

e

E. Note name, hence E♭, E major, etc.

E major has connotations of amplitude and splendour, fulfilled in Bruckner's Seventh Symphony. It is unusual in earlier orchestral music, except for violin concertos (e.g. the 'Spring' concerto in Vivaldi's *Le quattro stagioni*), though Haydn wrote two symphonies in E (as well as several other works) and Schubert drafted one. The expressiveness of E minor was specially recognized in the late Romantic period by composers including Brahms (Fourth Symphony), Tchaikovsky (Fifth Symphony), Dvořák ('New World'), Sibelius (First Symphony), Rachmaninoff (Second Symphony), Fauré and Elgar, though again there are earlier examples, notably Beethoven's second 'Razumovsky' quartet. Vaughan Williams wrote two symphonies in this key. E♭ major suits wind instruments and helps produce a full, rich orchestral sound, with an heroic air since Beethoven's 'Eroica' Symphony and 'Emperor' Concerto. Beethoven also favoured it with chamber works and sonatas, as did Schubert, and it was a common key for Haydn and Mozart. Other symphonists to have used it include Schumann ('Rhenish'), Borodin, Bruckner ('Romantic'), Stravinsky, Elgar, Sibelius and Shostakovich. E♭ minor appears in piano pieces by Schubert, Chopin and Fauré, and in quartets by Tchaikovsky, Schoenberg (third movement of No.2, where its strangeness is very much to the point) and Shostakovich (the death-daring No.15). Among the rare orchestral works placed in its shadow are Lyapunov's First Piano Concerto and Myaskovsky's Sixth Symphony.

The note E is important in Barraqué's music and Birtwistle's (e.g. *Pulse Shadows*).

ear. (1) The organ of hearing. Sound proceeds down the auditory canal to the eardrum, along a sequence of three ossicles (malleus, incus, stapes) and through a second covered aperture (the oval window) to the basilar membrane in the cochlea, the bony spiral of the inner ear. Different regions of the basilar membrane respond to different frequencies, and its movements – relative to the tectorial membrane, to which it is attached – are detected by inner hair cells. These activate neurones and so send messages to the brain. The sensation of music depends on the entire apparatus, but also on what previous experience the waiting brain has had.

(2) Power of musical discrimination. A 'good ear' implies sensitivities to tuning and timbre, and probably the ability to remember music and reproduce it accurately from memory. To 'play by ear' is to practise this latter faculty, not needing notation. People may also be said to have 'an ear for music', i.e. a desire for, and appreciation of, it.

early music. Term coined in the 1960s for music preceding what was commonly played: i.e. at that time, anything before Bach, Handel and Vivaldi. The rest was unknown territory. Munrow, in his initial Early Music Consort concerts, ranged from the troubadours to 17th-century viol music. Very soon, though, his and other groups became far more selective in their programming and increasingly sensitive to matters of performance practice, a universal concern of what became known as 'the early-music movement'. The extraordinary success of that movement overtook its name. No music is 'early' any more: the repertory regularly performed and recorded has no temporal boundary.

Yet in another sense all music is early, subject to considerations for period style that have come forward to occupy performers even of 20th-century music. See also AUTHENTICITY; HISTORICALLY INFORMED.

Early Music Consort. Ensemble founded by Munrow in 1967 to perform various pre-1700 repertories. The group's many lively recordings included thematic anthologies ('Music of the Crusades') and performances of major works by Du Fay and Purcell. Original and regular members included James Bowman (countertenor), Oliver Brookes (strings) and Christopher Hogwood (keyboards, percussion) along with Munrow on wind instruments.

Earth Dances. Orchestral work by Birtwistle, geological in its strata and as much lamenting as dancing. First performance: London, 14 Mar 1986.

ear-training. Education of the EAR (2) by means of exercises, undertaken by student musicians alone or in class.

East, Michael (b. *c.*1580; d. Lichfield, 1648). English composer of madrigals, anthems and fantasies. He worked at the cathedrals of Ely and (by 1618) Lichfield.

Easter music. The days before Easter are the time for TENEBRAE services and presentations of the PASSION. Special music for Easter itself, much less plentiful, includes settings by Brumel, Byrd and Bach (EASTER ORATORIO). See also CAVALLERIA RUSTICANA.

Easter Oratorio. Cantata by Bach. First performance: Leipzig, 1 Apr 1725; rev *c.*1738.

Eastman School of Music. Conservatory in Rochester, NY, founded by the photographic pioneer George Eastman in 1921 and forming the music department of the University of Rochester.

Eben, Petr (b. Zamberk, 22 Jan 1929). Czech organist-composer, noted for music of gothic intensity. Interned at Buchenwald in his mid-teens, he survived to study at the Prague Conservatory (1948–54). He then taught in Prague at the university (1955–90) and conservatory (1990–94) while pursuing an international career as a recitalist. His works include organ pieces (*Faust*, 1979–80), two organ concertos and Catholic church music.

Eberl, Anton (Franz Josef) (b. Vienna, 13 Jun 1765;

d. Vienna, 11 Mar 1807). Austrian pianist-composer, who was helped and possibly taught by Mozart, with whose music his was being confused (for commercial reasons) by 1788. His later works – piano sonatas, symphonies, chamber works, the opera *Die Königin der schwarzen Inseln* (1801) – are proto-Romantic. A symphony in E♭ shared the bill at the first performance of Beethoven's in the same key and was preferred.

Eberlin, Johann Ernst (baptized Jettingen, near Burgau, Bavaria, 27 Mar 1702; d. Salzburg, 19 Jun 1762). German organist-composer, resident in Salzburg from 1721 (after studies in Augsburg), and court and cathedral kapellmeister there by 1749. The Mozarts, father and son, valued his vocal works (which Leopold copied) as models of strict counterpoint. An unrelated Eberlin – Daniel (1647–*c.*1714), a gifted and irascible musician – was Telemann's father-in-law.

Eccard, Johannes (b. Mühlhausen, 1553; d. Berlin, 1611). German composer, a master of late Renaissance polyphony within the Lutheran tradition, especially in his chorale motets. He served the courts of Weimar (1567–71), Munich (1571–3, studying with Lassus, who influenced him profoundly), Königsberg (1579–1608) and Berlin (1608–11).

Eccles, John (b. ?London, *c.*1668; d. Hampton Wick, 12 Jan 1735). English composer, Purcell's chief successor as a composer of theatre music and court odes. A royal musician's son, he replaced Staggins in 1700 as Master of Music at court while working in the theatre. His operatic collaboration with Congreve, *Semele*, was not produced, and he retired to spend more time fishing.

échappée. See CAMBIATA.

echo. Reverberation in which the original sound can be identified, as when it bounces back from a distant hillside or wall. Artificial echoes appear in performed and electronic music, notably in echo songs (where, most often, the repetition of the end of a question provides the answer) and in the echo chamber (not a room but an electronic device that adds the effect of an echoing room).

Eclairs sur l'au-delà (Flashes of the Beyond). Work by Messiaen for enormous orchestra, his last completed score, in 11 movements: 1 *Apparition du Christ glorieux*, 2 *La Constellation su Sagittaire*, 3 *L'Oiseau-Lyre et la Ville-Fiancée*, 4 *Les Elus marqués de sceau*, 5 *Demeurer dans l'Amour*, 6 *Les Sept Anges avec les sept trompettes*, 7 *Et Dieu essuiera tout* *larme de leurs yeux*, 8 *Les Etoiles et la gloire*, 9 *Plusieurs oiseaux des Arbres de Vie*, 10 *Le Chemin de l'Invisible*, 11 *Le Christ, lumière du Paradis*. First performance: New York, 5 Nov 1992.

Eclat (Scintillation). Work by Boulez for nine tuned percussion (pf, glock, cel, hp, vib, cimb, mand, gtr, tubular bells) and wind-string sextet. A continuation was projected, *Eclat/Multiples*, with each of the six sustaining instruments being reinforced in turn to build a whole orchestra around the percussion group, but only the first section, mutliplying the violas, was completed. First performance: Los Angeles, 26 Mar 1965 (*Eclat*).

éclatant (Fr.). Brilliant.

ECM. German recording company, founded by Manfred Eicher in 1969. The acronym stands for Editions of Contemporary Music, and indeed the company has specialized in jazz and living composers (Reich, Pärt, Kancheli, Kurtág and others).

écossaise (Fr., Scottish). Lively dance of the early 19th century, usually in 2/4. There are sets by Beethoven, Schubert and Chopin.

Edelmann, Jean-Frédéric (b. Strasbourg, 5 May 1749; d. Paris, 17 Jul 1794). French pianist-composer. Trained as a lawyer in his home city, he arrived in Paris around 1774 and was soon in demand as a sonata composer and teacher. In 1789 he returned to a government post in Strasbourg, whence disputes and accusations led him back to Paris and the guillotine.

Eden–Tamir Duo. Israeli piano duo formed in 1952 by Bracha Eden and Alexander Tamir, both then graduating from the Jerusalem Academy.

Edinburgh Festival. Summer musical and theatrical event taking place in the Scottish capital annually since 1947.

editing. (1) Preparation of music for publication or performance. Publishing houses generally employ editors to correct errors of musical orthography or transcription and bring the music into conformity with house style. Ideally, such editors will be familiar with the composers and arrangers whose work they handle. Editing may alternatively be a task for scholars – producing authoritative editions of earlier music, complete with a discussion of sources, variant readings, etc. – or for educationists, for whom ease of reading and performance will be a primary concern.

Editing of all kinds involves decisions. An edition for performance may depart so far as to become an arrangement, as with Rimsky-Korsakov's edition of *Boris Godunov*. Scholarly editors will generally seek to intervene as little as possible, even if that means producing a text that still leaves choices, from among different versions of the score or interpretations of the notation, to be made by performers.

The great age of scholarly editing began with the institution of the first collected edition – of Bach – in 1851. Collected editions, complete or continuing, now exist for many composers, from Machaut to Bartók, and in most cases provide the most widely respected text.

James Grier *The Critical Editing of Music* (1996)

(2) Assembling of recorded fragments, normally in order to produce a complete performance from several takes.

education. Musical competence – with its blending of physical skill, imaginative ability, taste, judgement and cultural knowledge – has to be learned. Much can be gained in groups, under a choir director or class teacher, but instrumental performance has generally been felt to require individual training, and at the highest levels the teacher is often regarded as the bestower of a tradition. Perhaps even more than in medicine or law, the aspirant is brought into a well-defined culture, and the gifted teacher is one who makes that induction also a literal education, or 'drawing out' of the pupil's potential.

Learned music before the Baroque period was largely vocal. Most composers began their training as choristers, while music theory (often much closer to philosophy than to musical practice) was taught at universities: that of Salamanca was the first to boast a professor of music (1254) and perhaps the first to award music degrees. With the slow advance towards universal school education in the 16th and 17th centuries, music, at least in the form of singing, gained a place, while professional training continued as a kind of apprenticeship – which, indeed, it has remained, though formalized in the conservatories instituted from the early 19th century onwards, in imitation of those that had been developing in Naples and Venice since the Renaissance.

The notion that Classical music is everybody's – to perform, to appreciate and even to compose – was the ideal of the great age of musical education in schools, which began in the first half of the 20th century. Music clubs and children's concerts had been extending opportunities from before (George Henschel began his 'Young People's

Concerts' in London in 1890), and radio offered a new forum for educating both adults and children. By the 1950s–60s schools across the Western world boasted music classes, instrumental tuition from staff or peripatetic teachers, composition workshops, and orchestras and choirs giving regular concerts. Alas, despite the endorsement of philosophers from Plato onwards, and despite strong anecdotal and scientific evidence that making music encourages such beneficial qualities as dexterity, articulateness, responsibility and co-operativeness, school music began to lapse in the late 20th century, leaving the work of general education to be assumed more and more by orchestras, other performing groups and concert halls.

Edward. Scots ballad set by Schubert, Loewe, Brahms, Tchaikovsky and Gurney.

Edwards, Ross (b. Sydney, 23 Dec 1943). Australian composer, vigorously embracing Asian qualities of pulse into a formerly avant-garde style. He studied at the universities of Sydney and Adelaide, with Meale, Sculthorpe, Davies and Veress among his teachers; he followed Davies to England (1970–72). On returning to Australia he established himself as a largely freelance composer, his works mostly orchestral (four symphonies; the violin concerto *Maninyas*, 1988) and for chamber groupings.

également (Fr.). Equally (rhythmically).

Egge, Klaus (b. Gransherad, Telemark, 19 Jul 1906; d. Oslo, 7 Mar 1979). Norwegian composer. A folklorist in the Bartók–Prokofiev mould, author especially of symphonies, concertos and chamber works. He studied with Valen and with Walter Gmeindl in Berlin (1937–8), and worked as a critic and administrator.

Egk, Werner (b. Auchsesheim, near Donauwörth, 17 May 1901; d. Inning, near Munich, 10 Jul 1983). German composer, originally Werner Mayer, a pupil of Orff in Munich. The success he won in the Nazi era – as the author of the eclectic operas *Die Zaubergeige* (Frankfurt, 1935) and *Peer Gynt* (Berlin, 1938) and as director of the composer's section of the Reichsmusikkammer (from 1941) placed his later career under suspicion. He was essentially a theatre man, though he also produced orchestral pieces and other concert works (*La Tentation de St Antoine* for contralto and string quartet, 1947).

Egmont. Music by Beethoven for Goethe's play about the 16th-century Flemish patriot executed by the Spanish. The score comprises a heroic overture, songs, entr'actes and a final 'victory symphony' to sound Egmont's vision as he dies on the scaffold. First performance: Vienna, 15 Jun 1810.

Egorov, Youri (b. Kazan, 28 May 1954; d. Amsterdam, 15 Apr 1988). Russian pianist of spectacular weightless grace. He left the Soviet Union in 1978 and made a few recordings, notably of Debussy and Schumann, before his death from AIDS.

eguale (It.). Equal, hence *egualmente* (equally), *voci eguali* (equal voices), etc.

Egypt. Since music was among the comforts prepared for the dead under the pharaohs, numerous ancient instruments survive from tombs: trumpets and flutes, lyres and harps, clappers, cymbals and crotales, bells and drums. What they played cannot be known, but that has not stood in the way of evocations by Verdi, Debussy and Glass.

E.H. English horn, i.e. cor anglais.

Eichendorff, Joseph (Karl Benedikt) Freiherr **von** (b. Schloss Lubowitz, Upper Silesia, 10 Mar 1788; d. St Rochus, near Neisse, 26 Nov 1857). German poet, a Romantic of sensitive serenity notably set by Schumann, Mendelssohn, Brahms, Wolf and Strauss.

Eichner, Ernst (Dieterich Adolph) (baptized Arolsen, 15 Feb 1740; d. Potsdam, early 1777). German bassoonist-composer, author of 31 symphonies, which, unusually for the time, he numbered. The son of a Waldeck court musician, he played for the Zweibrücken court (1762–72), toured as a bassoonist from 1767 (including visits to Paris and London) and in 1773 joined the court of the Prussian court prince at Potsdam. His remarkable symphonies absorb Italian, German and French elements.

Eighteen-Twelve (*1812*). Overture by Tchaikovsky describing the retreat of Napoleon's forces, and of 'La Marseillaise' in the face of the Russian national hymn (assisted by bells and sometimes cannon effects). First performance: Moscow, 20 Aug 1882.

eight-foot (8'). Of 'normal' register, sounding as written. See FOOT.

eighth-note (US). Quaver (UK). See DURATION.

Eight Songs for a Mad King. Dramatic song cycle

by Davies to words by Randolph Stow. A vocalist of uncanny range presents himself as George III, on a stage occupied also by six instrumentalists. First performance: London, 22 Apr 1969.

eilend (Ger.). Hurrying.

Eimert, Herbert (b. Bad Kreuznach, 8 Apr 1897; d. Cologne, 15 Dec 1972). German composer, a pioneer of electronic music. He studied in Cologne at the conservatory (1919–24) and university (1924–30), while beginning his work in radio. An early proponent of 12-note music (Five Pieces, str qt, 1923–5) and mechanical instruments (ballet *Der weisse Schwan*, 1926), he became founder-director of the WDR electronic music studio (1951–62), where he produced *Glockenspiel* (1953) and other pieces. He was also co-editor with Stockhausen of the journal *Die Reihe*.

Einem, Gottfried von (b. Berne, 24 Jan 1918; d. Oberdurnbach, Lower Austria, 12 Jul 1996). Austrian composer, notably of operas using modernism to traditional dramatic effect. A diplomat's son, he worked as a coach in Berlin and Bayreuth before studying with Blacher (1941–3), who influenced him deeply and wrote four librettos for him. He was an important figure in post-war Austrian musical life, as a board member and administrator; he also taught at the conservatory in Vienna (1965–72).

Operas: *Dantons Tod* (Blacher and von Einem, after Büchner), Op.6, f.p. Salzburg, 1947; *Der Prozess* (Blacher, after Kafka), Op.14, f.p. Salzburg, 1953; *Der Zerrissene* (Blacher, after Nestroy), Op.31, f.p. Hamburg, 1964; *Der Besuch der alten Dame* (Dürrenmatt), Op.35, f.p. Vienna, 1971; *Kabale und Liebe* (Blacher and Lotte Ingrisch, after Schiller), Op.44, f.p. Vienna, 1976; *Jesu Hochzeit* (Ingrisch), f.p. Vienna, 1980; *Tulifant* (Ingrisch), f.p. Vienna, 1990
Other works: orchestral and chamber music, songs, etc.

einfach (Ger.). Simple.

Eingang (Ger., entrance, pl. *Eingänge*). Brief passage in a concerto (especially a Mozart piano concerto), written out or improvised.

Einklang (Ger.). Unison.

Einlage (Ger.). Interpolation.

Einleitung (Ger.). Introduction.

Einsatz (Ger.). Attack, entry.

Einsetzen (Ger.). EMBOUCHURE (in the case of reed instruments).

Einstein, Alfred (b. Munich, 30 Dec 1880; d. El Cerrito, Cal., 13 Feb 1952). German–US scholar, reviser of Köchel's catalogue and author of a popular book on Mozart. Unrelated to the revealer of relativity, he studied in Munich, left Germany in 1933, and settled in the USA in 1939.

Einstein on the Beach. Opera by Glass to a scenario and designs by Robert Wilson, a mesmeric succession of chants and dances around the image of the great physicist on a terminal shore. First performance: Avignon, 25 Jul 1976.

einstimmig (Ger.). Monophonic.

Eintritt (Ger.). Entrance.

Eis (Ger.). E♯. Also *Eisis* (E✕).

Eisler, Hanns (b. Leipzig, 6 Jul 1898; d. Berlin, 6 Sep 1962). German composer, impelled by socialist commitment. Having a liberal philosopher as father, he and his elder brother, Gerhart (later a journalist), became politically engaged while at school in Vienna before the First World War. He served in the war, then studied with Weigl at the New Vienna Conservatory and with Schoenberg (1919–23), who influenced such early works as the post-*Pierrot Palmström* (1924). But as his thinking became increasingly political, leading to his joining the Communist Party in 1926, he became critical of Schoenberg and of his own earlier work, though without repudiating either. Now in Berlin, where he had taken a post at the Klindworth–Scharwenka Conservatory in 1925, he cultivated political songs in a diatonic style and met Brecht, beginning a long collaboration with *Die Massnahme* (1930). He spent most of the Nazi period in the USA, latterly in Los Angeles teaching at USC and composing prolifically, until in 1947 he was brought before the McCarthy committee. The next year he returned to Vienna and in 1950 to Berlin, where he taught and continued to compose abundantly, following his belief that music in a socialist country must be objective, generally useful and clear in expression (hence the predominance of songs and cantatas in his output). But he met official objection when he tried to be more ambitious: his three-act libretto *Johann Faustus* was published but not set.

Albrecht Betz *Hanns Eisler* (1982)

Orchestral: *Kleine Sinfonie*, Op.29, 1932; *Kammersinfonie*, Op.69, 15 insts, 1940; suites from theatre and film scores

Choral orchestral: *Die Massnahme* (Brecht), Op.20, 1930; *Die Mutter* (Brecht), Op.25, 1931; *Deutsche Sinfonie* (Brecht), Op.50, 1935–9; etc.

Songs and such: *Palmström*, Op.5 (Morgenstern), reciter, fl, cl, vn, vc, 1924; 'Ballade von der "Jugendhure" Marie Sander' (Brecht; from the film Kuhle Wampe), 1931; 9 chamber cantatas, 1937 (No.3 Die römische Kantate, v, 2 cl, va, vc); 'Lied einer deutschen Mutter' (Brecht); 'Über den Selbstmord' (Brecht), 1939; etc.

Chamber: Divertimento, Op.4, wind qnt, 1923; String Quartet, Op.75, 1938; Nonet No.1, 1939; No.2, 1941; *Vierzehn Arten, den Regen zu beschreiben*, Op.70, fl, cl, vn, vc, pf, 1940; etc.

eisteddfod (Welsh, session). Festival of music and poetry.

Eitner, Robert (b. Breslau/Wrocław, 22 Oct 1832; d. Templin, 2 Feb 1905). German scholar. Self-taught, he is remembered for his ten-volume *Quellen-Lexikon* (1900–4), a pioneering work of musical bibliography.

Eitz, Carl (Andreas) (b. Wehrstedt, near Halberstadt, 25 Jun 1848; d. Eisleben, 18 Apr 1924). German theorist, who was a proponent of the Millioktav as the unit of interval and of a highly elaborate solmization system with syllabic names for every diatonic, chromatic and enharmonic note in the untempered 12-note system. Neither innovation took hold.

ekphonetic notation (from Gk *ekphōneō*, declaim). System of accents, dots, cheironomic figures or letters placed over sacred texts to indicate punctuation and inflection. Such systems were used in Jewish and Christian communities all over the European–Mediterranean world between the 9th and 15th centuries.

elastic. Variable. Term used by Grainger with respect to instrumentation and by Cowell with respect to form.

electric action. Transmission of signals from organ keys to pallets by electrical rather than mechanical (tracker or pneumatic) means.

electric guitar. Guitar, normally of solid construction, incorporating electric pick-ups and thereby projecting electronically amplified sound. Developed in the 1930s by Leo Fender and others, three varieties are common: the standard electric guitar (with six strings), the bass guitar (with four strings and a longer neck, going an octave lower) and the Hawaiian or steel guitar (played with a movable slide, creating glissandos). These are particularly associated with popular music, but the regular electric guitar has been used occasionally since the 1950s as an orchestral or ensemble instrument by such composers as Stockhausen (*Gruppen*), Berio and Tippett.

electric keyboard. Piano-style keyboard with a range of pre-set timbres and accompaniment patterns, a descendant of the electric pianos of the 1930s.

electric organ. Because of possible confusion with regular organs having electric action, the term ELECTRONIC ORGAN is often preferred for instruments making sound by electronic means.

electroacoustic music. Term covering either all ELECTRONIC MUSIC or hybrids of electronic and acoustic.

electronic instruments. Instruments creating sound by electronic means. The dinosaur in the field was the 200-ton telharmonium demonstrated in New York in 1906 by Thaddeus Cahill. Its more portable and long-lived successors came in three generations: first, between the world wars, the THEREMIN, ONDES MARTENOT, TRAUTONIUM, ELECTRONIC ORGAN and ELECTRIC GUITAR, then in the 1960s various kinds of SYNTHESIZER, followed in the 1980s by the SAMPLER and other computer-driven devices.

electronic music. Music made with electronic means. By the narrowest definition, it is music synthesized electronically and stored in recorded form: the *elektronische Musik* pioneered by Stockhausen and Eimert in Cologne in 1952–3 and explicitly contrasted at the time with the rival brand of MUSIQUE CONCRETE coming from Paris. The term 'electroacoustic music' is then used for the broader field of works created as recordings or requiring electronic means in performance. However, the distinction between the Cologne and Paris schools rapidly eroded, and, in any event, attempts to restrict the meaning of 'electronic music' will have to combat general usage, which is concerned less with technique than with effect: electronic music is music that sounds electronic, not acoustic.

This is not such a bad definition. It allows for the range of the field, from the thoroughly electronic (synthesized) to the totally acoustic or natural, through the vast area where most electronic music exists, using both electronic and natural resources. (The omnipresence of the electric guitar since the 1950s has perhaps brought it within the sphere of the natural, except when performed with extremes of distortion.) It also acknowledges the dismaying truth that electronic sounds can be recognized as such. The great hope for electronic music in the 20th century was that it would make available any and every possible sound. However, not only has the complexity of natural sounds proved hard to mimic, but a certain sameness in electronic material has been hard to avoid. That may partly explain why the great electronic pieces are so few, and mostly came so early.

Electronic music existed as a goal and an ideal long before it was achieved. Cahill's monster-machine telharmonium (1906) was barely practical, but it stimulated the imagination of Busoni and, through him, Varèse, who by 1915 was foreseeing great things. Fully functioning electronic instruments became available in the 1920s and 1930s, but their possibilities were limited. The bigger breakthrough was Schaeffer's creation of *musique concrète* (1948) by transforming recorded sounds of different kinds, soon followed by the spread of the tape recorder, which facilitated the changing and assembling of sounds by re-recording. The tape recorder was the basic tool of the classic electronic music studio, as it existed in the 1950s–60s: many were founded by radio stations (as in Paris and Cologne), others by universities, and they produced some remarkable pieces, notably by Varèse, Stockhausen, Berio and Babbitt.

However, studio techniques were tedious, especially in requiring a good deal of tape-splicing, and some composers shared Boulez's bafflement in a world where, notionally, anything was possible, but where in practice the results were rather meagre and predictable. One alternative was LIVE ELECTRONIC MUSIC. Also beginning in the 1960s, the synthesizer provided a machine made for musical creation, instead of the test equipment that had been used earlier, and computer programs helped control the generation and transformation of sounds in fine detail. The main centres for computer-electronic composition, since the 1970s, have been at Stanford University and at IRCAM in Paris.

With the subequent rapid advance in computer design and information technology, not only did the facilities at those places improve, but they began to be equalled, from the end of the 1990s, by what many people in the West could afford to acquire for themselves, with consequences that are as yet the stuff of further dreams.

Peter Manning *Electronic and Computer Music* (1985, ³2004); Trevor Wishart *On Sonic Art* (1985, ²1996)

electronic organ. Organ producing electronic notes: the first was manufactured by Laurens Hammond in Chicago in 1935 as a domestic instrument, though it has been elevated to concert status in works by Stockhausen.

elegy. See LAMENT.

Elegy for Young Lovers. Opera by Henze to a libretto by Auden and Kallman. Guests in an alpine hotel include a distinguished poet, Gregor Mittenhofer (baritone), a crazed widow, Hilde Mack (soprano), and two young lovers, Toni (tenor) and Elizabeth (soprano). Mittenhofer does nothing to save the last two from dying on the mountain, and makes a poem from their tragedy. First performance: Schwetzingen, 20 May 1961.

Elektra. Opera by Strauss to a libretto by Hofmannsthal (their first collaboration) after Sophocles. Elektra (soprano), unable to enlist her gentler sister, Chrysothemis (soprano), in murder, receives all she hopes when her brother, Orestes (baritone), arrives to slay their guilt-ridden mother, Clytemnaestra (mezzo-soprano), and stepfather, Aegisthus (tenor). The motif of blood-vengeance elicits Strauss's most strained and discordant score. First performance: Dresden, 25 Jan 1909.

The same mythic character appears in Mozart's *Idomeneo*.

elevator music. See MUZAK.

eleventh. Note an octave above the fourth, or interval an octave wider than a fourth.

Elfman, Danny (b. Los Angeles, 29 May 1953). US composer of eclectic and effective scores for films by Tim Burton (*Edward Scissorhands*, 1990; *Mars Attacks*, 1996) and others. His musical formation came as leading member of the rock band Oingo Boingo (1979–95).

Elgar, Edward (William) (b. Broadheath, near Worcester, 2 Jun 1857; d. Worcester, 23 Feb 1934). British composer, knighted in 1904, awarded the Order of Merit in 1911, made Master of the King's Music in 1924 and created baronet in 1931. These high honours came to a man who, as a Catholic and a shopkeeper's son, was born an outsider, and who, as a musician in a culture mistrustful of art, stayed outside. Being there he could see, and sometimes cheer, the pomp and circumstance of the British Empire. He could also hymn the passing of earthly magnificence. With his roots deep in the 19th century, especially in Brahms, Schumann and Wagner, but with his style maturing only at that century's very end, he wrote in the twilight of Romanticism.

He taught himself in his father's Worcester music shop, and from the age of 16 found work locally as a teacher, conductor and instrumentalist. Already composing, he was able to learn by practical experience, though progress was slow: by the time he was 30 he had published only a few violin miniatures, and his first important works were still a decade away. Encouragement came from his wife, Alice. She was a major-general's daughter, nine years older (40 when they married in 1889) and ambitious for him. They moved to London in 1890, and their only child, Carice, was born there. But their hopes that Elgar would achieve renown and remuneration in the capital were disappointed, and they had to return after only a year to Worcestershire, where he resumed his slower progress, now through a succession of cantatas for choral societies.

Then, as if making a second bid for recognition (but this time through music), he produced the 'Enigma' Variations for orchestra (1898–9), followed by a choral work at a level above its predecessors: *The Dream of Gerontius* (1899–1900). As this gained performances in Germany and the USA, he pressed ahead with a trilogy of oratorios, though only *The Apostles* (1902–3) and *The Kingdom* (1901–6) were finished. He also wrote more orchestral pieces – including *In the South*, stimulated by the first of several trips to Italy – and turned definitively to symphonic composition in 1907. His First Symphony, widely acclaimed, was followed rapidly by his Violin Concerto for Kreisler (secretly a portrait of Alice Stuart-Wortley, to whom he was close) and Second Symphony.

In 1912 the Elgars returned to London in triumph, and in the tone poem *Falstaff* (1913) he magnificently absorbed the colour and zestfulness of Strauss. After that, though, the output of major works dwindled, perhaps on account of the war, perhaps because he was burdened with theatre commissions. In 1918–19 came a return to productivity, but the works he then wrote – chamber pieces and, especially, his elegiac cello concerto – sound like farewells. Alice's death, in 1920, was the final blow. He retreated to Worcester in 1923, and though he was repeatedly drawn out to make recordings (he was the first composer to record a representative selection of his music), he virtually stopped composing. In 1932 he was induced to start work on an opera (*The Spanish Lady*, after Jonson's play *The Devil is an Ass*) and a symphony, but he died with both unfinished.

At his finest in his orchestral works, he preferred the standard forms, but found new ways of achieving them. Like Tchaikovsky, he interpreted the inherent dynamism of sonata form as a searching after some ideal, which may be presented at the outset in robust diatonic harmony (Symphony No.1), to be succeeded by more restless music. Another abiding characteristic is the processional beat, to which the whole world of the 19th century seems to be passing in review, one last time.

Michael Kennedy *Portrait of Elgar* (1968, [3]1987); Jerrold Northrop Moore *Edward Elgar* (1984)

www.elgar.org

Symphonies: No.1, A♭, Op.55, 1907–8; No.2, E♭, Op.63, 1909–11; No.3, C minor, Op.88, 1932–3 (completed by Anthony Payne, 1993–7)

Concertos: VIOLIN CONCERTO, B minor, Op.61, 1909–10; CELLO CONCERTO, E minor, Op.85, 1918–19

Other major orchestral works: *Sevillana*, Op.7, 1884, rev 1889; 3 Characteristic Pieces, Op.10, 1889; *Froissart* (overture), Op.19, 1890, rev 1901; Serenade, E minor, Op.20, str, 1892; 'ENIGMA' Variations, Op.36, 1898–9; *Cockaigne* (overture), Op.40, 1900–1; Funeral March from *Grania and Diarmid*, Op.42:2, 1901; *In the South (Alassio)* (overture), Op.50, 1903–4; Introduction and Allegro, Op.47, str, 1905; *Falstaff*, Op.68, 1913; *The Sanguine Fan* (ballet), Op.81, 1917

Light and minor orchestral pieces (many also available in other forms): *Salut d'amour*, Op.12, 1889; *Sursum corda*, Op.11, 1894; 3 Bavarian Dances, 1896; *Imperial March*, Op.32, 1897; Minuet, Op.21, 1897; *Sérénade lyrique*, 1899; *Chanson de nuit, Chanson de matin*, Op.15, 1899; *May Song*, 1901; Military Marches 'POMP AND CIRCUMSTANCE', Op.39, 1901–30; *Enfants d'un rêve (Dream Children)*, Op.43, 1902; *The Wand of Youth*, Op.1a–b, 2 suites, 1907, 1907–8; Elegy, Op.58, str, 1909; Romance, Op.62, bn, orch, 1910; *Coronation March*, Op.65, 1911; *Cantique*, Op.3, 1912; *Carissima*, 1913; *Sospiri*, Op.70, 1913–14; *Rosemary*, 1915; *Polonia*, Op.76, 1915; *Empire March*, 1924; Minuet from *Beau Brummel*, 1928; *Severn Suite*, Op.87, brass band/orch, 1930; *Nursery Suite*, 1930; *Soliloquy*, ob, orch, c.1930–31; *Mina*, 1932–3

Incidental scores: *Grania and Diarmid* (George Moore and Yeats), Op.42, 1901; *The Crown of India* (Henry Hamilton), Op.66, 1912; *The Starlight Express* (Violet Pearn), Op.78, 1915; *Arthur* (Binyon), 1923; *Beau Brummel* (Barry Matthews), 1928

Choral orchestral: *Spanish Serenade* (Longfellow), Op.23, 1892; *The Black Knight* (Longfellow, after Uhland), Op.25, 1889–93, rev 1898; *Scenes from the Saga of King Olaf* (H.A. Acworth, after Longfellow), Op.30, 1894–6; *Scenes from the Bavarian Highlands* (Alice Elgar), Op.27, 1896; *The Light of Life* (Capel-Cure), Op.29, 1896, rev 1899; *The Banner of St George* (Shapcott Wensley), Op.33, 1896–7; *Te Deum, Benedictus*, Op.34, 1897; *Caractacus* (Acworth), Op.35, 1898; *The* DREAM OF GERONTIUS, Op.38, 1900; *Coronation Ode* (A.C.

Benson), Op.44, 1902; *The* APOSTLES, Op.49, 1902–3; 2 Partsongs (Alice Elgar), Op.26, women's ch, orch, 1903; *The* KINGDOM, Op.51, 1901–6; *O Hearken Thou*, Op.64, 1911; *The Music Makers* (Arthur O'Shaughnessy), Op.69, 1912; *Great is the Lord*, Op.67, 1913; *Give unto the Lord*, Op.74, 1914; *The Spirit of England* (Binyon), Op.80, 1915–17; *Pageant of Empire* (Noyes), 1924

Vocal orchestral: SEA PICTURES, Op.37, a, orch, 1897–9; etc.

Orchestrations: Fantasy and Fugue (Bach), C minor, Op.86, 1921–2; *Jerusalem* (Parry), *c.*1922; Overture (Handel), D minor, 1923; Funeral March (Chopin), 1932; etc.

Chamber: String Quartet, E minor, Op.83, 1918; Piano Quintet, A minor, Op.84, 1918–19; early wind pieces

Violin and piano: Romance, Op.1, 1878; *Salut d'amour*, Op.12, 1888; *Chanson de nuit, Chanson de matin*, Op.15, 1897; Sonata, E minor, Op.82, 1918; etc.

Piano: *Salut d'amour*, Op.12, 1888; Concert Allegro, Op.46, 1901; *In Smyrna*, 1905; etc.

Organ: *Cantique*, Op.3, 1912; Sonata, G, Op.28, 1895; etc.

Other works: songs, partsongs, sacred music

Elijah (*Elias*). Oratorio by Mendelssohn to words adapted from the Bible by Julius Schubring and put into English by William Bartholomew. Elijah defeats the priests of Baal and brings an end to drought; the second part is concerned less with narrative than with hymning the prophet's righteousness. First performance: Birmingham, 26 Aug 1846.

Elision. Australian ensemble founded in 1986, having a distinctive sound by virtue of its plucked strings (guitars, koto, harp) and electronics. It has been particularly associated with Lim, Barrett and Dench.

elisir d'amore, L' (The Love Potion). Opera by Donizetti to a libretto by Romani after one by Scribe for Auber (*Le Philtre*). The potion, sold by Dulcamara (bass) to the peasant Nemorino (tenor), works not by magic but by revealing the recipient's fine qualities, which recommend him to the wealthy Adina (soprano) in preference to the soldier Belcore (baritone). The score is the source of a favourite tenor song, 'Una furtiva lagrima'. First performance: Milan, 12 May 1832.

Eller, Heino (b. Tartu, 7 Mar 1887; d. Tallinn, 16 Jun 1970). Estonian composer, pioneer of the national tradition through his works (almost all instrumental) and through his teaching in Tartu (1920–40) and at the Tallinn Conservatory (1940–70). He studied at the Petrograd Conservatory (1913–15, 1919–20).

Elman, Mischa (b. Talnoye, 20 Jan 1891; d. New York, 5 Apr 1967). Russian–US violinist, pupil of Auer at the St Petersburg Conservatory (1903–5) and rapidly acclaimed for his expressive warmth. He settled in the USA in 1911.

Eloy, Jean-Claude (b. Mont-St-Aignan, near Rouen, 15 Jun 1938). French orientalist composer. He studied at the Paris Conservatoire, at Darmstadt and at the Basle Academy with Boulez (1961–3), who helped promote such early scores as *Equivalences* for winds, keyboards and percussion (1963). A deepening concern with Asian ritual and spaciousness brought him closer to Stockhausen (*Shânti*, created at the WDR electronic studio, 1972–3) and led eventually to several works involving musicians from Japanese and other traditions.

Elsner, Józef (Antoni Franciszek) (b. Grodków, Silesia, 1 Jun 1769; d. Warsaw, 18 Apr 1854). Polish composer, Chopin's teacher. He went to school and university in Breslau/Wrocław, initially studying medicine. After a time in Lemberg/Lviv (1792–9), where he first set Polish librettos, he settled in Warsaw as director of the opera, composer and teacher. His works, following Classical precepts with a Polish folk accent, include operas, much sacred music, symphonies, chamber music and polonaises for piano.

Elvira Madigan. Film by Bo Widerberg (1967), haunted by the slow movement of Mozart's Piano Concerto in C, K.467.

embellishment. ORNAMENT.

embouchure. Posture of the mouth in playing a wind instrument. The active and controllable part of a wind instrument is a column of air extending into the player's mouth; there is no neat divide between instrument and player but rather an interface, where the sound can be affected by how the instrument is placed to the mouth and by how the mouth is held. This interface is the embouchure. It is effectively part of the instrument, and therefore of intense value and concern to the player.

EMI. British recording company, founded in 1931 as Electric and Musical Industries by the amalgamation of the British wing of Columbia with the Gramophone Company, both hit by the Depression.

Emmanuel, (Marie François) Maurice (b. Bar-sur-Aube, 2 May 1862; d. Paris, 14 Dec 1938). French composer with a particular interest in modes.

From 1880 he studied at the Paris Conservatoire, notably with Louis Albert Bourgault-Ducoudray, who encouraged his modal leanings, and Delibes, who did not. Awarded a doctorate for his work on ancient Greek dance, he returned to the Conservatoire as a teacher (1909–36) and had Messiaen among his students. His works include *Trente chansons bourguignonnes* (1913, 10 orchestrated), a cello sonata in the Phrygian mode (1887), two symphonies and two operas based on Aeschylus.

Emperor. Name given to three great works:

(1) Haydn's Quartet Op.76:3, for whose slow movement he wrote variations on his tune for the Austrian imperial hymn *Gott erhalte* (see NATIONAL ANTHEM).

(2) Beethoven's Piano Concerto No.5, the name being known only in English.

(3) Johann Strauss II's *Kaiser-Walzer*.

Empfindsamkeit (Ger.). Sensibility. The word is used as a term with respect to intimately subjective art of the mid 18th century, including works by C.P.E. Bach.

Empfindung (Ger.). Expression, hence *empfindungsvoll* (expressively).

emporté (Fr.). Transported, grand.

enchaînez (Fr.). Continue without a break.

Encina, Juan del (b. Salamanca, 12 Jul 1468; d. León, 1529–30). Spanish composer of polyphonic songs, some surely intended for his plays. Associated with the cathedral and university in his native city, he served the Duke of Alba (1492–8), after which he divided his time between Rome and Spain. He was ordained in 1519 and went to the Holy Land to celebrate his first mass on Mt Sion.

encore (Fr., again). (1) Call made by British audiences for a repetition, first recorded by Addison (1711). In France the call is 'bis' (twice); in the USA 'bravo' and its relatives are more common.

(2) Unprogrammed item played at the end of a recital or concert, or by the soloist after a concerto. Three encores are normal after a solo recital. Orchestras rarely give an encore, except when on tour.

en dehors (Fr., outside). Instruction that a line should stand out.

endless melody (*unendliche Melodie*). Wagner's

term for one of his goals: a continuity in contrast with the piecemeal approach of number opera.

Endless Parade. Work by Birtwistle for solo trumpet with strings and vibraphone, prompted by a procession winding around the streets of Lucca. First performance: Zurich, 1 May 1987.

endpin. Spike of steel or wood used to support a cello or double bass above the floor.

Enescu, George (b. Liveni Vîrnav, now George Enescu, Botoşani district, 19 Aug 1881; d. Paris, 3/4 May 1955). Romanian composer and violinist, his country's chief classical musician and an intriguing creative figure in the complex aftermath of Romanticism. He studied with Hellmesberger and Fuchs at the Vienna Conservatory (1888–94), then went on to the Paris Conservatoire (1895–9). Thereafter he divided his career between Paris and Romania, working as a composer, chamber musician, conductor and teacher. Romanian folk music was part of his creative make-up, along with tastes for Bach and a dark seriousness that align him with Busoni.

Noel Malcolm *George Enescu* (1990)

Opera: *Oedipe* (see OEDIPUS), Op.23, 1921–31

Orchestral: Symphony No.1, E♭, Op.13, 1905; No.2, A, Op.17, 1914; No.3, C, Op.21, pf, ch, orch, 1918; Suite No.1, C, Op.9, 1903; No.2, C, Op.20, 1915; No.3 'villageoise', D, Op.27, 1937–8; *Poème roumain*, Op.1, 1897; *Symphonie concertante*, B minor, Op.8, pf, orch, 1901; *Deux rhapsodies roumaines*, Op.11, 1901; Concert Overture, Op.32, 1948

Chamber: Woodwind Decet, Op.14, 1906; String Octet, Op.7, 1900; String Quartet No.1, E♭, Op.22:1, 1916–20; No.2, G, Op.22:2, 1950–53; Piano Quartet No.1, D, Op.16, 1909; No.2, D minor, Op.30, 1944; Violin Sonata No.1, D, Op.2, 1897; No.2, F minor, Op.6, 1899; No.3 'dans le caractère populaire roumain', A minor, Op.25, 1926; Cello Sonata No.1, F minor, Op.26:1, 1898; No.2, C, Op.26:2, 1935; *Impressions d'enfance*, Op.28, vn, pf, 1940; etc.

Piano: Suite No.1 'dans le style ancien', G minor, Op.3, 1897; No.2, D, Op.10, 1903; No.3 'Pièces impromptues', Op.18, 1913–16; Sonata No.1, F♯ minor, Op.24:1, 1924; (no No.2); No.3, D, Op.24:3, 1935

Enfance du Christ, L' (The Childhood of Christ). Oratorio by Berlioz to his own words, in three parts: *Le Songe d'Herod, La Fuite en Egypte, L'Arrivée à Saïs*. First performance: Paris, 10 Dec 1854.

Enfant et les sortilèges, L' (The Child and the Spells). Opera by Ravel to a libretto by Colette. The naughty Child (mezzo-soprano) is taught lessons by household objects that come to life and animals (and trees) that talk, providing opportunities for exquisite musical fantasy. First performance: Monte Carlo, 21 Mar 1925.

England. Closeness to and distance from continental Europe have affected music in England since the Middle Ages. An indigenous harmonic style, suave with thirds, had a great effect in France in the early 15th century, around the time of Dunstable and the Old Hall manuscript. After that, though, English music developed its own splendiferous sonorities, intricate rhythms and expanded forms in relative isolation, to reach a peak with Taverner, whose successors, Tallis and Byrd, moderated that style with new continental influences. Religious changes, which gave England a national Church both Catholic and Protestant, were also important in setting the country culturally apart. So was the relative unimportance of music at court, after the age of Purcell – an unimportance due partly to the distrust of opera, the genre that brought music prestige and patronage elsewhere in Europe.

See also LONDON and, for later music in England, UNITED KINGDOM.

John Caldwell, ed. *The Oxford History of English Music*, 2 Vols. (1991, 1999)

Englisches Horn (Ger.). Cor anglais.

English Cat, The. Opera by Henze to a libretto by Edward Bond. In a feline world ruled by suspiciously human self-interest, the promiscuous but loving couple Minette (coloratura soprano) and Tom (baritone), are destroyed by others' greed. First performance: Schwetzingen, 2 Jun 1983.

English fingering. See CONTINENTAL FINGERING.

English flute. Old term for the recorder.

English guitar. Cittern popular among English amateurs from the mid 18th century, when it replaced the lute, to the early 19th, when the Spanish guitar arrived and the piano gained hold.

English horn. COR ANGLAIS.

English National Opera (ENO). Name taken in 1974 by Sadler's Wells Opera, following the company's move to the London Coliseum in 1968. Distinguished from Covent Garden by singing in English, giving a new opera annually (Birtwistle's *The Mask of Orpheus* in 1986) and favouring a

house ensemble of soloists, the company established itself at the Coliseum with a *Ring* cycle and enjoyed particular success in the 1980s with Peter Jonas as general director, Mark Elder as chief conductor and David Pountney as resident producer.

English suites. Six keyboard works by Bach, who was not responsible for the title.

Englund, (Sven) Einar (b. Ljugarn, Gotland, 17 Jun 1916; d. Ljugarn, 27 Jun 1999). Finnish composer, follower of Stravinsky and Bartók. He studied with Palmgren and Bengt Carlson at the Helsinki Academy (1933–41), and was impressed by the music of Shostakovich and Prokofiev he heard in Russia after the Second World War. While making his living as a pianist in jazz and light music, he established himself creatively with the first two (1946, 1948) of his seven symphonies.

enharmonic. Term used of notes identical in sound but differently notated, e.g. B♯ and C, which are 'enharmonic equivalents'. An enharmonic modulation involves a switch between enharmonic equivalents, usually with a change of mode, as when C♯ minor turns to D♭ major in Chopin's Fantaisie-impromptu. Equivalents are strictly identical only in the equal-tempered system; in other tunings they are different pitches, though the difference may be negligible. Enharmonic keyboards, being tuned in other than equal temperament, include separate keys for enharmonic equivalents: often the black notes are split to give different keys for C♯ and D♭, etc., since the differences here are particularly large.

Enigma. Name Elgar gave to an orchestral work: Variations on an Original Theme 'Enigma'. His theme and purpose are clear: the work is a set of character studies of members of his circle. The enigma, still undecided, concerns the tune he said 'goes with' the theme. First performance: London, 19 Jun 1899.

enlevez (Fr.). Remove (a mute), lift (a pedal).

Enlightenment. Movement in 18th-century culture, guided by a rational approach to the world and a certainty in the centrality of humanity. Enlightenment ideals emerged in the 1720s–30s, but their full musical expression came more in the 1760s–80s, with the symphonies and quartets of Haydn, the operatic reform of Gluck and others, and the work of Mozart – the achievements, indeed, of early CLASSICISM.

Enriquez(-Salazar), Manuel (b. Ocotlán, Jalisco, 17 Jun 1926; d. Mexico City, 26 Apr 1994). Mexican composer, a leader in adopting 1950s avant-garde techniques and promoting them (as director of the Mexico City Conservatory). He trained as a violinist in Mexico and at Juilliard (1955–7); Wolpe steered him towards composition. Participating in European and US festivals of new music, he was one of the first Americans to receive a Donaueschingen commission (*Ixamatl* for orchestra, 1969).

ens. Abbreviation for ensemble.

En saga (A Saga). Symphonic poem by Sibelius suggesting heroic ancient times. First performance: Helsinki, 16 Feb 1893.

ensemble. (1) Togetherness. An orchestra, choir or chamber group may show good or bad ensemble, in terms of rhythmic coordination and spirit. For this meaning a French pronunciation is approximated.

(2) Group of musicians, or music for them. The term covers anything from the performing personnel of an opera house to a trio, but is most often used of an operatic number for several singers or, since the 1970s, a group of soloists specializing in contemporary music – normally a compact orchestra comprising single woodwinds and brass, string quintet, piano and percussion, i.e. 14 players in all. Examples include the ENSEMBLE INTERCONTEMPORAIN, ENSEMBLE MODERN, ENSEMBLE RECHERCHE, KLANGFORUM WIEN and LONDON SINFONIETTA. For this meaning pronunciation is anglicized or americanized.

Ensemble InterContemporain. Paris ensemble, founded by Boulez in 1976 as the house orchestra of IRCAM but latterly based at the Cité de la Musique.

Ensemble Modern. Ensemble founded in Frankfurt in 1980, with no permanent conductor.

Ensemble Recherche. Ensemble founded in Freiburg in 1985, with nine members (fl, ob, cl, vn, va, vc, 2 pf, perc).

Entartete Musik (Mutant Music). Title of an exhibition in Düsseldorf in 1938 aimed by Nazi authorities to ridicule music by Schoenberg, Stravinsky, Hindemith, etc. In the late 20th century the slogan was defiantly taken up as a banner, under which the music especially of Jewish victims of Nazism was promoted.

Entführung aus dem Serail, Die (The Abduction

from the Seraglio). Opera by Mozart to a libretto by Gottlieb Stephanie after one by Christoph Freidrich Bretzner. Belmonte (tenor) and his servant Pedrillo (tenor) plot to release Konstanze (soprano) and her maid Blonde (soprano) from confinement in the harem of the pasha Selim (actor) by getting his overseer Osmin (bass) drunk. The four Europeans are caught in the act and shamed by Selim's magnanimity. There are notable arias for Belmonte ('O wie ängstlich') and Konstanze ('Ach, ich liebte'; 'Martern aller Arten'). First performance: Vienna, 16 Jul 1782.

entr'acte (Fr.). Interlude in the theatre, perhaps an orchestral piece, as in Beethoven's *Egmont* music or Schubert's *Rosamunde*.

entrance. Entry (1).

entrée (Fr.). Baroque French term: a group of dances in a 17th-century ballet, or an entrance piece beginning a divertissement in an 18th-century stage work.

entry. (1) Point at which a musician must begin: a conductor may cue, say, a brass entry.

(2) Statement of the subject at some point in a fugue, as if the theme were in the background waiting to re-enter.

Entry of the Gladiators (*Einzug der Gladiatoren*). March by the prolific Czech bandmaster-composer Julius Fučík (1872–1916) that has found its home in circuses.

envelope. Shape of the change in a sound's amplitude over time. It is an important determinant of sound quality, and therefore of interest to creators of electronic music.

Eolides, Les (The Aeolids, daughter breezes of the wind god Aeolus). Symphonic poem by Franck after a poem by Leconte de Lisle. First performance: Paris, 13 May 1877.

éoliphone (Fr.). Wind machine.

Eötvös, Peter (b. Székelyudvarhely, 2 Jan 1944). Hungarian composer-conductor. While studying with Kardos at the Liszt Academy (1958–65) he began his career composing for theatre, films and television. He then studied with Stockhausen in Cologne (1966–8) and stayed on until 1971 as a member of Stockhausen's live electronic ensemble. After that he rapidly made a name as a conductor of contemporary music (notably at the head of the Ensemble InterContemporain, 1979–91), while more gradually building a reputation as a composer, his lively imagination, quizzical personality and sense for sound in space emerging through his sophisticated awareness of his leading colleagues.

www.eotvospeter.com

Operas: THREE SISTERS, Lyons, 1998; *Le Balcon* (after Genet), Aix, 2002.
Orchestral: *Psychokosmos*, cimb, orch, 1993; *Triangel*, perc, orch, 1993; *Replica*, va, orch, 1998; *zeroPoints*, 1999; *Jet Stream*, tpt, orch, 2002; etc.
Ensemble: *Chinese Opera*, 1986; *Shadows*, 1996; etc.

ephemera. Music's power is revealed not only in the force of its utterances, the vigour of the speculations to which it gives rise and the sureness of its consolatory touch but equally by toys and trinkets. Examples of musical ephemera range from the relatively austere (see PORTRAITS) to the edible (see MOZARTKUGEL) by way of china and glassware, items of clothing and jewellery, model musicians, playing cards, paperweights, postage stamps, works of FICTION, etc. – the inventory of gift shops regularly found at concert halls and musical museums.

Epifanie (Epiphanies). Work by Berio for female voice (Berberian) and orchestra, exploring different ways of musically communicating words in its sequences on different texts (by Proust, Machado, Joyce, Sanguineti, Claude Simon and Brecht). In the revised version (1991–2), under the English title, the composer removed the previous option to change the order of these sequences and of the orchestral interludes. First performance: Donaueschingen, 22 Oct 1961.

episode. Passage perceived as an excursion, especially in a fugue (away from the subject) or rondo (between repetitions of the principal material).

epistle sonata. Sonata covering the pause between epistle and gospel at mass. This may have been the function of the church sonatas Mozart wrote for Salzburg.

epithalamium. Wedding song.

equal. Having the same range. Music may be written for equal voices (e.g. in two soprano parts) or equal instruments (flute and violin). Beethoven's *Equali* are for trombones.

equal temperament. Tuning that divides the octave into intervals of equal size, in terms of frequency ratio and therefore of value in cents.

Overwhelmingly the most usual tuning in Western music is equal temperament with 12 semitones, which must each have the frequency ratio of the twelfth root of two to one (roughly 1·0595) and the value of 100 cents. But though this system provides a very close approximation to the perfect fifth (700 cents, as against 702 for the 3:2 frequency ratio), its major thirds are noticeably sharp (400 cents instead of 386) and its minor thirds noticeably flat (300 cents instead of 316). These deficiencies were addressed by theorists and occasionally by instrument builders almost from the time equal temperament began to be discussed – in the early 16th century. Vicentino's proposal of a scale of 31 equally tempered intervals was refined by Christiaan Huygens, his system providing almost-true fifths (697 cents), major thirds (387 cents) and minor thirds (310 cents). However, harmonic discrimination had to yield to the practical simplicity and 12-semitone equal temperament, which gradually ousted other tunings by the mid 18th century, though piano tuners, singers and instrumentalists may all deviate from it in the interests of smoother harmony.

Erard. French firm of instrument makers and music publishers, founded by Sébastien Erard around 1780. Their quiet-voiced pianos (overstringing was introduced only in 1901) were cherished as distinct from US–German instruments, and their harps were prized.

Erato. The muse of song, dance and erotic poetry, sometimes shown with a lyre. Her name was taken for a French record company founded in 1952 and acquired by Warner in 1989.

Erb, Donald (b. Youngstown, Ohio, 17 Jan 1927). US composer, of robust and characterful music in a mainstream modernist style. He studied at the Cleveland Institute, at the University of Indiana and in Paris. Some earlier works expose his jazz background.

Erber, James (b. London, 14 Feb 1951). British composer, of music at once complex, vivid in detail and sweeping. He studied at the universities of Sussex and Nottingham, worked for Peters in London (1976–9), and so came into contact with Ferneyhough, with whom he completed his training in Freiburg. Most of his works are for solo instruments or small groups.

Erdődy. Name given Haydn's Op.76 quartets, dedicated to Count Joseph Erdődy.

Erkel, Ferenc (b. Gyula, 7 Nov 1810; d. Budapest,

15 Jun 1893). Hungarian composer, father of Hungarian opera. The son of a teacher and local musician, he went to school in Pozsony/Bratislava and began work as a pianist and teacher in Kolozsvár in his late teens. By 1835 he was in Buda conducting for the Hungarian theatre company, though he was also active as a pianist-composer, until the success of his first opera, *Bátori Mária* (1840), persuaded him to concentrate on the theatre. *Hunyadi László* (1844), his second opera, was another triumph, trumped only by *Bánk Bán* (1861), in the same French–Italian style with Hungarian verbunkos zest, but boasting a patriotic story. In later works he was increasingly assisted by his four sons, among whom László taught Bartók.

erklingend (Ger.). Resounding.

Erlebach, Philipp Heinrich (baptized Esens, East Friesland, 25 Jul 1657; d. Rudolstadt, Thuringia, 17 Apr 1714). German composer, most notably of church cantatas, though fewer than 80 survive from the several hundred he wrote as chapelmaster at the Rudolstadt court from 1681. His ravaged output also included operas, arias, overtures and sonatas.

Erlkönig (Elf King). Song by Schubert to Goethe's poem, with atmospheric accompaniment and a keen invitation to the singer to characterize the voices of the night-riding father and the son who dies in his arms. There are also settings by Corona Schröter, A.J. Romberg, Reichardt, Zelter, Loewe and Spohr.

erlöschend (Ger.). Dying away.

Ernani. Opera by Verdi to a libretto by Piave after Victor Hugo's play. Ernani (tenor), the bandit chief, wins Elvira (soprano) despite having the king of Spain, Don Carlo (baritone), as his rival. But at his moment of triumph he is obliged, by an oath he swore to Elvira's uncle Silva (bass), to kill himself. The major arias are Ernani's 'Mercè, diletti amici', Elvira's 'Ernani, involami', Silva's 'Infelice!' and Carlo's 'O de' verd' anni miei'. First performance: Venice, 9 Mar 1844.

Ernst, Heinrich Wilhelm (b. Brno, 6 May 1814; d. Nice, 8 Oct 1865). Moravian violinist-composer. He entered the Vienna Conservatory in 1825 and began following Paganini around in 1829, learning pieces by ear to the astonishment of their composer. Highly regarded also by Joachim and Berlioz, he played across Europe and wrote virtuoso pieces.

Eroica. Name Beethoven gave his Third Symphony: *Sinfonia eroica* (Heroic Symphony). The same name is often applied, but without his sanction, to his Piano Variations Op.35, on the theme he was to use in the symphony's finale (and had already treated in *Die Geschöpfe des Prometheus*). Two novels have been based on the unprecedentedly imposing structure of the 'Eroica': Alejo Carpentier's *El acoso* (The Chase, 1956) and Anthony Burgess's *Napoleon Symphony* (1974).

Erstaufführung (Ger.). First performance, normally locally (e.g. *Deutsche Erstaufführung*, German première), as opposed to the URAUF-FÜHRUNG.

erste Walpurgisnacht, Die (The First Valborg's Night). Cantata by Mendelssohn setting a poem by Goethe on a clash between Druids and early Christians. First performance: Berlin, 10 Jan 1833.

ersterbend (Ger.). Dying away.

Erwartung (Awaiting). Opera by Schoenberg to a libretto by Marie Pappenheim, a 'monodrama' charting the emotions of a woman (soprano) seeking her dead or departed lover in a forest. The music responds with fervent intensity to her changing moods. First performance: Prague, 6 Jun 1924.

Es (Ger.). E♭. Also *Eses* (E♭♭).

escapement. Part of the piano's action that has the hammers rebounding away from their strings after the initial attack, so that notes can be sustained by keeping the keys held down.

Eschenbach, Christoph (b. Breslau/Wrocław, 20 Feb 1940). German conductor. Formerly a pianist, he studied as such in Cologne and Hamburg, and was the dedicatee of Henze's Second Piano Concerto. In 1973 he made his conducting debut, going on to become music director of the Houston Symphony (1988–99) and the Philadelphia Orchestra (from 2003).

Escher, Rudolf (George) (b. Amsterdam, 8 Jan 1912; d. De Koog, Texel, 17 Mar 1980). Dutch composer, half-nephew of M.C. Escher, with whose graphic work his French-leaning, clear, contrapuntal and variational music has been compared. Brought up partly in Java (1916–21), he studied at the Rotterdam Conservatory (1931–7) as a pianist and composer (with Pijper). Besides composing he taught (at Utrecht University, 1964–77), painted and published poetry. His works include orchestral pieces (*Musique pour l'esprit en deuil*, 1941–3; *Hymne du Grand Meaulnes*, 1951) and piano music (*Arcana*, 1944).

Escobar, Pedro de (b. Oporto, *c*.1465; d. ?Évora, after 1535). Portuguese composer and church musician, valued in Spain, where he was a member of Isabella's chapel (1489–99) and chapelmaster of Seville Cathedral (1507–14). Otherwise he worked in Portugal. His surviving works include a mass, a *Requiem*, motets and villancicos.

esercizio (It.). Exercise.

esitando (It.). Hesitating.

Espaces acoustiques, Les (Acoustic Spaces). Concert-length sequence of works by Grisey, based on periodic movements away from and back to an overtone spectrum on E, on sound combinations both unusual and vivid, and on a continuous expansion of resources through the six instalments, all but the last of which may be played separately: *Prologue* for viola (1976), *Périodes* for seven players (1974), *Partiels* for 18 players (1975), *Modulations* for 33 players (1976–7), *Transitoire* for orchestra (1980) and *Epilogue* for four horns and orchestra (1985).

España (Spain). Orchestral piece by Chabrier, exuberant homage to Spanish music. First performance: Paris, 6 Nov 1883.

Espansiva. Name Nielsen gave his Third Symphony.

espirando (It.). Expiring, dying away.

Esplá (y Triay), Oscar (b. Alicante, 5 Aug 1886; d. Madrid, 6 Jan 1976). Spanish composer, whose music reflects his high culture and zest for Stravinskian neoclassicism. While qualifying as an engineer on parental orders, he continued to compose, and won a prize that encouraged him to study with Reger (1912) and Saint-Saëns (1913). He exercised positions of authority in musical administration and diplomacy.

espressivo (It.). Expressive. Also *con espressione* (with expression). Both markings suggest an intimate warmth and were introduced in the early 19th century.

esquisse (Fr.). Sketch.

Estampes (Prints). Set of three piano pieces by Debussy: *Pagodes* (Pagodas), *Soirée dans Grenade* (Evening in Grenada) and *Jardins sous la pluie* (Gardens in the Rain). First performance: Paris, 9 Jan 1904.

estampie (Fr., It. *istampita*). Medieval term that can mean either a poem or a melody without text. In modern usage it is reserved for the latter, of which two groups survive in 14th-century manuscripts from France and Italy. They may have been dances.

Este. See FERRARA.

Esterházy. Hungarian princely family of enormous wealth, patrons of Haydn. His successive employers Paul Anton (1711–62) and Nikolaus (1714–90) were grandsons of Paul (1635–1713), who created a strong musical establishment at the family residence of Eisenstadt and was himself a composer. Nikolaus, on his succession, built a magnificent new summer palace, Eszterháza, with an opera house and a music building, where Haydn had an apartment. Anton (1738–94), Nikolaus's son and heir, did not share his father's musical enthusiasms, but his son, another Nikolaus (1765–1833), commissioned annual masses to celebrate his wife's name-day: Haydn wrote six and Beethoven one.

Esther. Handel's first sacred oratorio in English, to words (in which Pope may have had a hand) after Racine's play. Esther (soprano) intercedes with her husband, the Persian king Ahaseurus (tenor), to countermand the order given by Haman (bass) against the Israelites. Handel often revived the work, and often changed it. First performance: Cannons, 1718, rev London, 2 May 1732, etc.

estinguendo, estinto (It.). Extinguishing, extinguished.

estro armonico, L' (Harmonious Inspiration). Set of 12 concertos in two volumes Vivaldi published in Amsterdam in 1711, his first concerto collection. Bach transcribed six of them.

éteint (Fr., extinguished). Barely audible.

étendue (Fr.). Range.

Et exspecto resurrectionem mortuorum (And I look for the resurrection of the dead). Work by Messiaen for symphonic wind and percussion in five movements. The first two performances were given within the stained-glass-lit Sainte

Chapelle and Notre Dame de Chartres, though the composer also suggested mountaintop venues. First performance: Paris, 7 May 1965.

ethnomusicology. Term coined by Jaap Kunst in 1950 for the study of music within a particular culture or population. As a cultural product itself, ethnomusicology mostly involves Western scholars examining non-Western music. Its antecedents are therefore commonly traced in the examples of Chinese and Canadian Indian music given in Rousseau's music dictionary, or in slightly later works on Chinese music by the French missionary Joseph Amiot (1779) and on Indian music by the British judge William Jones (1784). Its techniques may, however, be applied within Western culture (Kagel's *Mare nostrum* is a creative exemplification of this) – though such studies will tend to be classed as SOCIOLOGY OF MUSIC.

Ethnomusicology has become a larger and more scientific field since the late 19th century, and its students have included notable composers, beginning with Bartók and Vaughan Williams. Others – Messiaen, Ligeti, Boulez, Berio – have drawn on studies and recordings made by professional ethnomusicologists, or have, like Stockhausen in Japan or Reich in Ghana, sought to learn directly, not as professors but as pupils. See also FOLK MUSIC.

Etoile, L' (The Star). Operetta by Chabrier to a libretto by Eugène Leterrier and Albert Vanloo. The young pedlar Lazuli (mezzo-soprano) is saved from execution because, as the court astrologer Siroco (bass) explains, his star is allied with that of the reigning monarch, Ouf (tenor). From this, delectable ridiculousness effervesces. First performance: Paris, 28 Nov 1877.

Eton Choirbook. Volume of English polyphonic music copied *c*.1490–1502 for use in Eton chapel and kept in the college library. Browne, Davy, Lambe and Wilkinson are well represented among the composers.

étouffez (Fr.). Damp. Also *étouffé* (damped).

étude (Fr.). STUDY. Used as a title, the word is often taken into English untranslated, as with the important piano collections by:

(1) Chopin: Op.10 and Op.25.

(2) Liszt: ETUDES D'EXECUTION TRANSCENDANTE, concert études.

(3) Debussy: 1 *Pour les cinq doigts*, 2 *Pour les tierces*, 3 *Pour les quartes*, 4 *Pour les sixtes*, 5 *Pour les octaves*, 6 *Pour les huit doigts*, 7 *Pour les degrés chromatiques*, 8 *Pour les agréments*, 9 *Pour les notes répétées*, 10 *Pour les sonorités opposées*, 11 *Pour les*

arpèges composées, 12 *Pour les accords*.

(4) Ligeti: Book I (1985): 1 *Désordre*, 2, *Cordes vides*, 3 *Touches bloquées*, 4 *Fanfares*, 5 *Arc-en-ciel*, 6 *Automne à Varsovie*; Book II: 7 *Galamb borong* (Melancholy Dove, 1988), 8 *Fém* (Metal, 1989), 9 *Vertige* (1990), 10 *Der Zauberlehrling* (1994), 11 *En suspens* (1994), 12 *Entrelacs* (1993), 13 *L'Escalier du diable* (1993), 14 *Coloana infinita* (1993); Book III: 15 *White on White* (1995), 16 *Pour Irina* (1996–7), 17 *A bout de souffle* (1997), 18 *Canon* (2001).

There are also sets of piano études by Schumann, Alkan, Moszkowski, Scriabin, Stravinsky, Busoni, Szymanowski, Rachmaninoff, Lyapunov, Bartók, Dohnányi, Messiaen, Ohana, Perle, Hopkins and Cage.

Etudes d'exécution transcendante. Title of two piano collections by Liszt:

(1) *Etudes d'exécution transcendante d'après Paganini* (1838–40, rev 1851): six pieces based on the caprices and the finale of the B minor concerto (No.3).

(2) *Etudes d'exécution transcendante* (Transcendental Etudes, 1851, based on 12 études published in 1839): 1 *Preludio*, 2 in A minor, 3 *Paysage*, 4 MAZEPPA, 5 *Feux follets*, 6 *Vision*, 7 *Eroica*, 8 *Wilde Jagd*, 9 *Ricordanza*, 10 *Allegro agitato molto*, 11 *Harmonies du soir*, 12 *Chasse neige*.

Eugene Onegin (*Yevgeny Onegin*). Opera by Tchaikovsky to a libretto by the composer and Konstantin Shilovsky after Pushkin's verse novel. Tatyana (soprano) writes a love letter to Onegin (baritone), who admonishes her for her lack of decorum. Later, after he has killed his friend Lensky (tenor) in a duel, he meets her again, a great society hostess and the wife of Gremin (bass). He is infatuated, but now it is his turn to be rejected. The big numbers are Tatyana's Letter Scene, Lensky's aria and Gremin's aria of warm and noble love. First performance: Moscow, 29 Mar 1879.

Eulenburg. Music publishing firm founded in Leipzig in 1874 by Ernst Eulenburg (1847–1924) and known especially for miniature scores. Their distinctive yellow livery was an inheritance from Albert Payne's editions, which Eulenburg took over. The company was acquired by Schott in 1957, with no change to its traditions.

euphonium. BRASS instrument introduced in Germany *c*.1830, a tenor tuba in C or B♭, distinguished by its velvety sound. It is common in bands, a rarity in the symphony orchestra.

euphony. Good sound, subjectively determined.

Euryanthe. Opera by Weber to a libretto by Helmina von Chezy. In a chivalric setting, Euryanthe (soprano) is subjected to extreme emotional trials by Eglantine (soprano), to whom the chief men – Lysiart (bass) and Euryanthe's beloved Adolar (tenor) – are pawns. First performance: Vienna, 25 Oct 1823.

Euterpe. The muse of lyric, sometimes shown with a double aulos.

Evangelist. The narrator in a Passion. Bach followed tradition in making this a tenor role.

Evangelisti, Franco (b. Rome, 21 Jan 1926; d. Rome, 28 Jan 1980). Italian composer, a decisive avant-garde figure who abandoned composition to explore a new future for music by means of improvisation (with Nuova Consonanza, which he founded in Rome in 1960, and which became an improvising group in 1964) and thinking. His initial training was as an engineer; also important was his long stay in Germany from 1952 and his presence at Darmstadt. His few works include *Proporzioni* for flute (1958) and *Random or Not Random* for orchestra (1956–62).

Eventail de Jeanne, L' (Jeanne's Fan). Collaborative ballet score written for the patron and ballet-school proprietress Jeanne Dubost, who allegedly took apart her fan and handed leaves to 10 composers: Ravel (*Fanfare*), Ferroud (*Marche*), Ibert (*Valse*), Roland-Manuel (*Canarie*), Marcel Delannoy (*Bourrée*), Roussel (*Sarabande*), Milhaud (*Polka*), Poulenc (*Pastourelle*), Schmitt (*Rondeau*) and Auric (*Kermesse-Valse*). First performance: Paris, 4 Mar 1929.

Excursions of Mr Brouček, The (*Výlety páně Broučkovy*). Opera by Janáček to a libretto partly by himself after novels by Svatopluk Čech. Mr Brouček (tenor), the most ordinary city fellow, has comic-fantastic adventures on the moon and in 15th-century Prague. First performance: Prague, 23 Apr 1920.

execute. Perform (archaic). Hence also 'executant', 'execution'.

exercise (Fr. *exercice*, Ger. *Übung*, It. *esercizio*). Pedagogical or technical item, designed to further and maintain proficiency, not to be heard. The term has been used, though, for pieces more in the nature of studies, where an audience is decidedly appropriate: e.g. Bach's *Clavier-Übung* or Scarlatti's volume of *Essercizi* (i.e. sonatas).

exit aria (It. *aria di sortita*). Number a character sings before going. Exit arias were the norm in opera seria, particularly for a character's first big piece.

experimental music. Innovatory music created by outsiders. The term became current in the 1960s–70s, to distinguish the work of certain, predominantly Anglo–US composers (Cage, Cardew, Bryars) from that of the official avant-garde (Boulez, Stockhausen). Experimental music in these terms is empirical, unconstrained by philosophies of progress and tradition, and happy to be simple. However, it quickly acquired a tradition of its own, with Ives and Busoni as forefathers.

Michael Nyman *Experimental Music* (1974, [2]1999)

exposition. Primary part of SONATA FORM.

expression. To perform 'with expression' is to expose nuances of tempo, rhythm, dynamic level, colour, accent, phrasing and intonation that may well not be explicit in the printed music. This meaning is quite straightforward – though a piece will, happily, be amenable to many sorts of expression. However, the word has caused problems, because it begs the question of what is being expressed. In particular, it seems to invoke the relation between music and feeling – an ancient philosophical quagmire. But there is no need to muddy one's feet there, as Edmund Gurney (1890) pointed out: 'We often call music which stirs us more *expressive* than music which does not; and we call great music *significant* ... without being able, or dreaming we are able, to connect these general terms with anything expressed or signified.' To perform with expression is to express the music – or, better, to let it express itself.

expressionism. Intensification of expression. The term was first applied to the violently coloured, virtually abstract paintings of Kandinsky, Nolde and others in 1910–11, and soon after to the music of Schoenberg (who felt an artistic kinship with Kandinsky) and his pupils. Musical expressionism is associated with free dissonance and a more or less explicit distortion of norms, as in Schoenberg's music of 1908–12 (before his elaboration of serialism) or in revisitings of that world by Davies and Henze.

Exsultate, jubilate. Motet Mozart composed for the castrato Rauzzini (who had just starred in his *Lucio Silla*), and revised in 1780, seemingly for a soprano. The last of the three movements is a brilliant alleluia. First performance: Milan, 17 Jan 1773.

extemporize. Improvise: see IMPROVISATION.

Eybler, Joseph (Leopold Edler von) (b. Schwechat, near Vienna, 8 Feb 1765; d. Vienna, 24 Jul 1846). Austrian composer, acquainted with Haydn (a distant relation) and Mozart and briefly involved in completing the latter's *Requiem*. He gained his training in the St Stephen's choir school, as a pupil of Albrechtsberger (1776–9) and through assistance from Haydn. Close to Mozart at the end, he then had a distinguished career as a choirmaster and at court, succeeding Salieri as kapellmeister in 1824. Besides much sacred music, he wrote string quintets and other chamber works.

eye music (Ger. *Augenmusik*). Musical notation having a visual appeal or significance, quite apart from its function in determining sound. Using conventional symbols (GRAPHIC NOTATION is another matter), composers and scribes have essentially three ways of creating a particular effect. First, staves may be bent to outline a shape: a heart in the CHANSONNIER *cordiforme*, a birdcage in Davies's EIGHT SONGS FOR A MAD KING. Alternatively, the design may be created by regular notes on a regular page, as when Tavener places a tutti chord along a solo line to create the form of a cross. Finally, the effect can depend on how the symbols are used, so that in this case – unlike the previous two, whose character is purely visual – the point is made through and not merely with musical notation. For example, Telemann's 'Gulliver' suite for two violins includes a Lilliputian chaconne in quasihemidemisemiquavers and a Brobdignanian gigue in semibreves.

The distinction between sight and sound, though, is not so easy to draw. A programme note may alert listeners to a peculiarity, and even if not, notational oddities that cause a performer to ponder or smile may thereby make themselves heard.

Ezio. Opera by Handel to an adaptation of Metastasio's libretto, also set by Hasse, Jommelli and Gluck. Noble behaviour from Aetius (alto castrato) and Fulvia (soprano) frustrates the machinations of the latter's father, Maximus (tenor), against the 5th-century emperor Valentinian III (contralto). Aetius also appears in Verdi's *Attila*. First performance: London, 15 Jan 1732.

F. Note name, hence F minor, F♯, etc. The F clef (bass clef) curls around the F line.

F major sometimes has pastoral associations, but by no means always: it is the key of Beethoven's compact Eighth Symphony as well as his spacious Sixth, and of two of his quartets as well as his 'Spring' Sonata. Other works in F major include Schubert's Octet, Brahms's Third Symphony, and quartets by Dvořák ('American') and Ravel. F minor, contrastingly personal and passionate, was the key Haydn chose for some of his most intense pieces, an example followed by Beethoven, Schubert, Schumann, Tchaikovsky (Fourth Symphony), Franck and Vaughan Williams (also Fourth Symphony). F♯ major is an uncommon key found in one Beethoven sonata and a good deal of Messiaen; F♯ minor is a piano-ish key, found in Chopin, Schumann, Brahms and Fauré, but also in quartets by Haydn and Schoenberg (No.2), as well as symphonies by Haydn ('Farewell') and Mahler (No.10).

f. Abbreviation for *forte* (as a dynamic marking) found in manuscript and printed music from the 17th century onwards. Hence *ff* and *fff* for increasing degrees of *fortissimo*, both established in the 18th century. Unlike the case with *p*, further intensified forms (*ffff*, etc.) are unusual.

fa (Fr., It., Sp.). The note or key of F.

Faber, Johann Christoph (*fl.* early 18th century). German composer of whom tantalizingly little is known beyond his authorship of five works containing elaborate ciphers. In two of them messages are written with a 24-letter alphabet of notes.

Faber Music. London music publishing firm founded in 1966 under the direction of Donald Mitchell, principally at first to handle Britten's music. It has maintained a strong catalogue of British composers.

faburden. British way of singing plainsong in three-part chords at sight, or, originally, the lower improvised voice (the 'fa burden'). The earliest references are English of *c*.1430, and the practice evidently remained in use in Britain until the Reformation. Beneath the plainsong the faburden would sing in thirds or, at the ends of words, fifths, while the treble, above, would sing in fourths, thus producing sequences of parallel 6–3 and 8–5 chords (by contrast with improvised DISCANT, where the motion was contrary). Continental practices of FAUXBOURDON and FALSOBORDONE may have adapted the name because they, too, are simple ways of harmonizing plainsong.

Faccio, Franc(esc)o (Antonio) (b. Verona, 8 Mar 1840; d. Monza, 21 Jul 1891). Italian composer-conductor, classmate (at the Milan Conservatory) and lifelong friend of Boito, whose HAMLET libretto he set. Winning little success as a composer, he concentrated on conducting, notably as principal conductor at La Scala (1871–89), where he was responsible for Verdi premières. He died insane.

Fach (Ger.). Category, especially of voices. A Mozart tenor might be wary of, say, Rodolfo as alien to his *Fach*.

facilement (Fr.), **facilmente** (It.). Simply.

F–A–E. Joachim's musical motto, standing for *frei abser einsam* (free but lonely). It was used in a sonata written to honour him by Dietrich, Schumann and Brahms.

F–A–F. Brahms's musical motto, partly a rejoinder to Joachim's, standing for *frei aber froh* (free but happy). It features especially in his Third Symphony.

Fagott (Ger., pl. *Fagotten*), **fagotto** (It., pl. *fagotti*). Bassoon.

fah. In tonic sol-fa the fourth degree of the scale.

Faidit, Gaucelm (b. Uzerche, near Limoges, ?c.1150; d. ?c.1220). Troubadour, possibly in the service of Richard Coeur-de-Lion, on whose death he wrote one of the most frequently copied troubadour songs, 'Fortz causa'.

Fairy-Queen, The. Semi-opera by Purcell to an adaptation of Shakespeare's *A Midsummer Night's Dream*. The music is all in masques commanded by Titania (and Oberon), one for each of the five acts. First performance: London, 2 May 1692.

Fairy's Kiss, The. See *Le* BAISER DE LA FEE.

fake. See SPURIOUS WORK.

fa-la. Colloquial English term of the time for English and Italian madrigals where the singers have to spout 'fa-la-la'.

Falco, Michele (b. Naples, ?1688; d. after 1732). Italian composer, one of the creators of opera buffa. He studied at the San Onofrio conservatory and worked as a church musician while producing his comedies, beginning with *Lo Lollo pisciaportelle* (1709). The music of all is lost.

Falcon. Term for a dramatic soprano voice in France or French opera, derived from the name of Cornélie Falcon (1812–97). She was the first Rachel in *La Juive* and Valentine in *Les Hugenots*, but by the age of 26 had lost her voice.

Falcone, Achille (b. Cosenza, c.1570–75; d. Cosenza, 9 Nov 1600). Italian composer, known for the accomplishment he displayed in contests of compositional skill to which he was challenged by the jealous Sebastián Raval (c.1550–1604), royal chapelmaster in Palermo. His rival lost and cheated, but he died of a fever and was vindicated only when his father published a volume of his madrigals and competition pieces.

Falconieri, Andrea (b. Naples, 1585/6; d. Naples, 19/29 Jul 1656). Italian lutenist-composer, whose songs, by 1619, were among the first to distinguish between recitative and arioso. He began his career in Parma (1604–14), travelled elsewhere in Italy besides visiting Spain and France, and was finally lutenist (from 1639) and chapelmaster (from 1647) at the royal Neapolitan court.

Fall, Leo(pold) (b. Olmütz/Olomouc, 2 Feb 1873; d. Vienna, 16 Sep 1925). Austrian operetta composer. He shared with Lehár the upbringing of an army bandmaster's son – indeed, they played together in Lehár's father's band. That was after his training at the Vienna Conservatory (under the Fuchs brothers) and before the run of operetta successes that began with *Die Dollarprinzessin* (1907).

Falla (y Matheu), Manuel de (b. Cadiz, 23 Nov 1876; d. Alta Gracia, Argentina, 14 Nov 1946). Spanish composer. Though he learned from close contacts with composers from France (Debussy, Ravel, Dukas) and then Russia (Stravinsky), his music only became ever more Spanish.

Musically encouraged as a boy by his mother and by teachers in Cadiz, he began to make his name there as a composer while studying piano with José Tragó at the Madrid Conservatory (1898–9). He wrote five zarzuelas (1901–3) in an unsuccessful attempt to revive the family fortunes, and in 1902 began studies with Pedrell. In 1907 he left for Paris, taking his prize-winning but unproduced opera *La vida breve*. His Spanish piano pieces and Gautier songs got him known and brought him friends (Albéniz, as well as Dukas, Debussy and Ravel), under whose encouragement he began a piano concerto (*Noches en los jardines de España*) and revised *La vida breve*.

At the outbreak of war in 1914 he returned to Spain for the most productive few years of his life, when he completed the concerto and added a solo piece for Rubinstein (*Fantasía bética*) while also writing two ballets (*El amor brujo* and *El sombrero de tres picos*) and, almost unimaginably, coming up with a comic opera based on music by Chopin (*Fuego fatuo*). Apart from this last, all these works are vividly and vigorously Spanish, drawing especially on the *cante jondo*, the passionate song from Andalusia, and also making use of what he had heard of Ravel and Stravinsky (*Petrushka* especially) in Paris. In 1919 he settled into a house in Granada.

He maintained, however, connections with Paris and with Stravinsky, and wrote his next work, *El retablo de Maese Pedro* (1919–22), for the Princesse Edmond de Polignac in a new slimmed and tangy style that owed something to Stravinsky's more recent music. That style he continued in the delectable *Psyché* and Concerto, the latter a brilliant reimagining of music in Spain from plainsong to Scarlatti. Then, from 1926 onwards, he devoted himself to *Atlántida*, a vision of South America as an Atlantis restored to life by Catholicism. Again fleeing war, he carried the project with him to Buenos Aires in 1939, but left it as a tantalizing mirage of possibilities.

Ronald Crichton *Manuel de Falla* (1976)

Stage: *La* VIDA BREVE (opera), 1904–5; *El* AMOR BRUJO (ballet), 1914–15; *El* SOMBRERO DE TRES PICOS (ballet), 1916–19; *Fuego fatuo* (opera), 1918–19; *El* RETABLO DE MAESE PEDRO (puppet opera), 1919–22; *Atlántida* (scenic cantata: Falla, after Jacinto Verdagues), 1926–46, unfinished

Orchestral: NOCHES EN LOS JARDINES DE ESPANA, pf, orch, 1911–15; *Homenajes*, 1920–39 (includes orchestrations of Debussy and Dukas tributes plus *Pedrelliana*, 1924–39)

Chamber: *Psyché* (Jean-Aubry), v, fl, hp, str trio, 1924; Concerto, hpd, fl, ob, cl, vn, vc, 1923–6

Piano/guitar: *Pièces espagnoles*, pf, 1902–8; *Fantasía bética*, pf, 1919; *Le Tombeau de Claude Debussy*, gtr, 1920; *Pour le tombeau de Paul Dukas*, pf, 1935

Songs: *Tus ojillos negros*, v, pf, 1902; *Trois mélodies* (Gautier), v, pf, 1909; *Siete canciones populares españolas*, v, pf, 1914–15; 'Soneto a Córdoba' (Góngora), v, harp/pf, 1927; *Balada de Mallorca* (Verdaguer), ch, 1933

false cadence, false close. INTERRUPTED CADENCE.

false relation. Harmonic plangency caused when two melodic parts, simultaneously or in adjacent chords, light on notes that are chromatic neighbours or a tritone apart. The relation, of discord (and resolution), is deemed false because the rules of Classical harmony require chromatic alterations to arise and be resolved within the one part.

falsetto. Higher voice available to men when, by so setting certain muscles, they cause only part of the length of their vocal cords to vibrate. The falsetto range is commonly an octave above the normal singing voice. It is used exclusively by countertenors and as part of their vocal equipment by tenors (see HEAD VOICE).

falsobordone (It., Sp. *fabordón*). Southern European way of harmonizing psalm tones extemporaneously in root-position triads, recorded from the 1480s. The name derives from FAUX-BOURDON.

Falstaff. Opera by Verdi to a libretto by Boito after Shakespeare's *The Merry Wives of Windsor* and

Henry IV plays. The amorous–pecuniary advances of Falstaff (baritone) are foiled by Alice Ford (soprano), Meg Page (mezzo-soprano) and Mistress Quickly (mezzo-soprano), while serious emotion swirls in the jealousy of Ford (baritone) and the springtime love of Nannetta (soprano) and Fenton (tenor). First performance: Milan, 9 Feb 1893.

Other operas on the subject include Salieri's *Falstaff* (Vienna, 1799), Nicolai's *Die* LUSTIGEN WEIBER VON WINDSOR, Holst's *At the Boar's Head* and Vaughan Williams's *Sir John in Love*. Elgar treated it in a symphonic poem.

fanciulla del West, La (The Girl of the Golden West). Opera by Puccini to a libretto by Guelfo Civinini and Carlo Zangarini after David Belasco's play set in gold-rush California. Minnie (soprano), almost the only woman on stage, gets her man, the outlaw Dick Johnson (tenor), by outmanoeuvring the sheriff, Jack Rance (baritone). Dick gets the hit tune, 'Ch'ella mi creda libero e lontano'. First performance: New York, 10 Dec 1910.

fancy. English term of the 16th–17th centuries for FANTASY.

fandango. Spanish courtship dance, in moderately fast 3/4. There are examples by Mozart (in *Figaro*), Boccherini and many Spanish composers.

fanfare (from Sp. *fanfa*, perhaps itself from Arabic *anfár*, trumpets). Inspiriting flourish of brass, especially trumpets, improvised or, since the 19th century, composed, and often associated with royal ceremonial. There is a majestic fanfare-introduction by Bliss to the British national anthem. Copland's, however, is a *Fanfare for the Common Man*, to which Tower responded with several *Fanfares for the Uncommon Woman*.

Fano, Michel (b. Paris, 9 Dec 1929). French composer, close to Barraqué as a student at the Paris Conservatoire (1948–53). Having written a classic of total serialism, in his Sonata for two pianos (1952), he abandoned pure composition in 1954 to make films.

fantasia, fantasy. Instrumental composition arising 'solely from the fantasy and skill of the author' (Milán, 1535), 'who taketh a point [theme] at his pleasure, and wresteth and turneth it as he list' (Morley, 1597). These principles hold good for the fantasias of Mozart and Beethoven as much as for those of the 16th century. They warn, too, that the fantasia is not a definable pattern but rather a wild flower in the garden of musical forms.

The Renaissance fantasia, fantasy or fancy, born with independent instrumental music, provided a context within which composers could understand their new freedom from words. Contrapuntal techniques provided ways of handling 'points', building logical stretches within trains of thought that would also have room for abruptness and extravagance, always moderated by a care for shape and for suggesting, by fluency, a single improvisatory gesture. The fantasia was a virtuoso conceit. And, being made for instrumentalists, it might be virtuoso, too, in its technical demands, especially if for a soloist (on plucked instrument or keyboard).

Milán and his near namesake Milano both published solo fantasias (for vihuela and lute respectively) in 1536. Keyboard fantasias were numerous in the decades around 1600, produced by Sweelinck, Byrd, Bull, Gibbons and Frescobaldi, while the consort fantasia, for viols, flourished among English composers during the century from Byrd to Purcell. With the growth elsewhere of the sonata, suite and fugue as principal instrumental genres, all of them prescribing consistency of subject and clarity of form, the fantasia diminished in the 18th century. For Bach the fantasia, like the similarly free prelude or toccata, had to be completed by a strictly ordered form: a fugue. His sons C.P.E. and W.F. wrote improvisatory fantasias, as did Mozart and Beethoven, but the idea of free-strict (fantasia-sonata) balancing persisted. Mozart's Fantasia in C minor forms an introduction to his sonata in the same key; Beethoven fused the two principles in his Op.27 pair of pieces, both called 'sonata quasi una fantasia'; and Schubert used the title *Fantasie* for works in which he enfolded the usually separate sonata movements in one sweep.

Honouring imagination as much as Renaissance lutenists had, Romantic composers took up the fantasia and gave it a miniature version, the FANTASIESTÜCK. Meanwhile, Schubert's innovation of the single-movement, sonata-style fantasia was not lost on Liszt, who also, like other virtuoso pianist-composers of his time, extrapolated from Schubert's 'Wanderer' Fantasy in making the fantasia an exploration of given themes. For Liszt and his colleagues those themes would usually be operatic, but Vaughan Williams wrote fantasias on 16th-century motifs, restoring the fantasia to its point of origin while maintaining its belated alliance with variation form. By now, though, when symphonies and sonatas could come in so many different shapes, sizes and forms, there was less need for a title implying a free imaginative act: the spirit of the fantasia was everywhere.

Fantasia. Film, released in 1940, in which Stokowski and Disney animators collaborate to give spectacular interpretations of orchestral music. Unforgettable are the brilliant and musically considerate envisionings of Dukas's *L'Apprenti Sorcier*, starring Mickey Mouse, and Ponchielli's *Dance of the Hours*, featuring ballet troupes of ostriches, hippos and crocodiles. A second instalment came out as *Fantasia 2000*, with Levine instead of Stokowski but Mickey still in place.

Fantasia contrappuntistica. Extension by Busoni of the unfinished contrapunctus from Bach's *Kunst der Fuge*, in three versions for solo piano (1910–12) and one for duo pianists (1921).

Fantasia on a Theme by Thomas Tallis. Work by Vaughan Williams for double string orchestra with solo quartet, based on the third of nine psalm tunes Tallis contributed to Archbishop Parker's psalter (1567). First performance: Gloucester, 6 Sep 1910.

fantasia-suite. Modern term for a 17th-century English genre of chamber music for violins or viols, with or without organ, where a fantasia is followed by a sequence of dances – originally, in works by Coprario, almain-galliard – and a close. The form was developed or adapted by William Lawes, Jenkins and Christopher Gibbons.

Fantasiestück (Ger., fantasy piece). Title invented by Hoffmann for a sequence of stories, *Fantasiestücke in Callots Manier* (1814–15), and first applied to music by Schumann.

farandole. Provençal folk dance for a winding chain of people holding hands, used for local colour by Bizet (*L'Arlésienne*) and Milhaud.

Farewell. Name given to Haydn's Symphony No.45. The story goes that the composer's employer, Prince Nikolaus Esterházy, was loath to leave his summer palace of Eszterháza, keeping his musicians separated from their families. So Haydn wrote this symphony with an adagio finale in which the players progressively depart, leaving just two violinists performing at the end (Haydn and Luigi Tomasini as it was originally). The prince took the hint.

Farina, Carlo (b. Mantua, *c*.1600; d. *c*.1640). Italian violinist-composer, an early master of virtuoso and characterful writing for his instrument. He moved from the Mantuan court in 1625 to Dresden, where he stayed several years and published five volumes of dances, sonatas, etc. His *Capriccio stravagante* (pub 1627), for solo violinist and three supporting players, has remarkable imitations of animal noises and other instruments. He may have returned to Italy and died of the plague.

Farinelli, professional name of Carlo Broschi (b. Andria, Apulia, 24 Jan 1705; d. Bologna, 15 Jul 1782). Italian soprano castrato, most famous of the ilk. His name he probably gained as a protégé of the Farina family. He made his debut in Naples in 1720 in *Angelica e Medoro*, singing music by his teacher Porpora and words by the young Metastasio, with whom he remained in contact. A leading singer by 1723, he appeared widely before arriving to stun audiences in London (1734–7). He was then engaged by the queen of Spain in the hope he would rescue her husband, Philip V, from depression, as indeed he did, staying on in Madrid until 1759. After that he retired to his villa in Bologna, where his own melancholy was alleviated by music, books and visitors. His brother was the composer Riccardo Broschi.

Farkas, Ferenc (b. Nagykanizsa, 15 Dec 1905; d. Budapest, 10 Oct 2000). Hungarian composer, and teacher of composers, including Kurtág and Ligeti. He studied at the Liszt Academy (1921–7) and with Respighi in Rome (1929–31); Stravinsky's influence was also important to his orchestral brilliance and international outlook. Professor at the Liszt Academy (1949–75), he wrote abundantly in all forms.

Farnaby, Giles (b. *c.*1563; buried London, 25 Nov 1640). English keyboardist-composer. He followed his father's trade of joinery and was perhaps among the few professional keyboard players who might have made their own instruments. An Oxford BMus (1592), he lived most of his life in London, except for a few years in Lincolnshire in the early 1600s. He published a book of canzonets and some psalm settings, but is best remembered for his 51 characterful pieces in the Fitzwilliam Virginal Book, including an almain for two virginals and *Tower Hill*. His son Richard was also a composer.

Farrant, Richard (b. ?1525–30; d. London, 30 Nov 1580). English composer, who was responsible for one of the earliest verse anthems (*When as we sat in Babylon*). He was master of the choristers at Windsor (from 1564) and the Chapel Royal (from 1569), and wrote (lost) plays for them.

Farrar, Ernest (Bristow) (b. Lewisham, 7 Jul 1885; d. Epéhy Ronssoy, 18 Sep 1918). British composer and organist. A promising member of the pastoral school, his fecundity was cut short when he was killed in action. He studied with Stanford and Parratt at the RCM.

Farrenc, (Jeanne) Louise [née Dumont] (b. Paris, 31 May 1804; d. Paris, 15 Sep 1875). French pianist-composer, whose marriage in 1821 to the musician-publisher Aristide Farrenc did nothing to curtail her career as a composer (admired by Schumann) and teacher (at the Conservatoire, 1842–73). Apart from piano music, she wrote three symphonies and chamber works.

farsa. Genre of comic opera, usually in one act, favoured in Venice *c.*1790–1820. Rossini wrote several.

farse. Synonymous with TROPE (1), but normally implying an insertion in an epistle or other lesson, made in the 12th–15th centuries.

Farwell, Arthur (b. St Paul, Minn., 23 Apr 1877; d. New York, 20 Jan 1952). US composer, who was at different times devoted to Amerindian music, community singing and polytonality. He graduated from the Massachusetts Institute of Technology as an electrical engineer (1893), but turned to music and took lessons from Homer Norris and Chadwick in Boston, and from Humperdinck and Pfitzner in Germany (1897–9). Concerned for his colleagues as much as himself, he founded the Wa-Wan Press (1901–12) to publish new US music. His works include orchestral, piano and chamber pieces, songs (39 to Dickinson poems) and community music.

Fasch. German composers, father and son.

(1) **Johann Friedrich** (b. Buttelstädt, near Weimar, 15 Apr 1688; d. Zerbst, 5 Dec 1758). Recruited at 13 for the choir of St Thomas's in Leipzig, he came under Telemann's influence and remained to study at the university, then went on to Darmstadt for training in composition from Graupner and Gottfried Grünewald. Various appointments followed, before, in 1722, he became kapellmeister at Zerbst. The same year he applied for the post of cantor at St Thomas's, and having lost he stayed put for the rest of his life. The large body of church music he produced has largely vanished, but his concertos, symphonies, suites and sonatas survive in quantity, even though none was published. In boldness of orchestration (bringing winds into prominence) and lively phrasing, these convey the Vivaldian style to the borders of Classicism.

(2) **Carl Friedrich Christian** (b. Zerbst, 18 Nov 1736; d. Berlin, 3 Aug 1800). He had his first lessons from his father, who sent him at 14 to study with Johann Hertel in Strelitz. Franz Benda heard him there and recommended him to the Berlin court, where he spent the whole of his professional life. Court duties were intermittent, however, and not always remunerative, so he also taught and worked as a choir director, founding the Berlin Singakademie (1791). Zelter, a pupil, was his successor.

Faschingsschwank aus Wien (Viennese Carnival Romp). Piano work by Schumann, a set of five 'fantasy pictures'.

Fauré, Gabriel (Urbain) (b. Pamiers, Ariège, 12 May 1845; d. Paris, 4 Nov 1924). French composer. Concentrating on songs, piano pieces and chamber music, heir to Schubert, Schumann and Chopin, he adapted the enriched harmony of his time to an intimate kind of expression. His songs, responsive to the verbal and rhythmic delicacy of French poetry, recreated the genre in France.

The son of a school director and a minor aristocrat, he studied at the Ecole Niedermeyer (1854–65), most notably with Saint-Saëns. That institution fitted its pupils for life as church musicians, and he duly began such a career as an organist in Rennes (1866–70) and then at various Parisian churches; from 1877 he was choirmaster at the Madeleine. Meanwhile, in 1871, he had been among the founders of the Société Nationale de Musique, which presented many of his works for the first time.

Passionate Wagnerism took him to Cologne, Munich and London for performances in 1877–82, though he seems already to have been aware that his genius was for smaller forms. By the time he brought out his first collection of 20 songs (1879, to be followed by similar volumes in 1897 and 1908), his only other published work was a violin sonata. Larger early pieces, including two symphonies and a violin concerto, were withdrawn, and yet his consolatory *Requiem* survived, if through a process of revision that took almost a quarter century. He married in 1883, and had two sons by 1889, but found a warm family life no bar to adventures outside: his affair with Emma Bardac, later Debussy's wife, led to *La Bonne Chanson* (for her) and *Dolly* (for her daughter).

In 1896 he became organist of the Madeleine and composition professor at the Conservatoire, where in 1905 he succeeded to the directorship; he was elected to the Institut in 1909. He also began giving more attention to larger works, including music for Maeterlinck's *Pelléas* (for a production in London, where he had many friends and was a regular visitor) and his opera *Pénélope*. These works have made their mark, the *Pelléas* suite as an orchestral charmer and *Pénélope* as a favourite of the few. But a certain lack of confidence remained in his creative personality. He persistently sought the advice of friends – and the help of pupils with orchestration (Koechlin in the case of *Pelléas*). Also, he maintained his devotion to private music, music whose restraint and subtlety fitted it for the salons of the time, or for the home listening of later ages. Alongside *Pelléas*, *Pénélope* and *Prométhée* (most unexpectedly for this composer, an outdoor spectacle) came his great song cycles and some of his finest piano pieces, in his preferred genres of nocturne and barcarolle.

After 1916 he returned to chamber music, and his retirement from the Conservatoire, in 1920, freed him to compose throughout the year, instead of just on summer vacations in Switzerland or the south of France. What came was a succession of masterpieces conveying a reminiscent serenity.

Jean-Michel Nectoux *Gabriel Fauré* (1991)

Songs

Cycles: *La* BONNE CHANSON, Op.61, 1892–4; *La Chanson d'Eve* (Charles Van Lerberghe), Op.95, 1906–10; *Le Jardin clos* (Van Lerberghe), Op.106, 1914; *L'Horizon chimérique* (Jean de la Ville de Mirmont), Op.118, 1921

Sets: *Poème d'un jour* (Charles Grandmougin), Op.21, 1878 ('Rencontre', 'Toujours!', 'Adieu'); *Cinq mélodies de Venise* (Verlaine), Op.58, 1891 ('Mandoline', 'En sourdine', 'Green', 'Clymène', 'C'est l'extase'); *Mirages* (de Brimont), Op.113, 1919

Individual songs: 'Après un rêve' (Romain Bussine), Op.7:1, 1877; 'Aurore' (Armand Silvestre), Op.39:1, 1884; 'Automne' (Silvestre), Op.18:3, 1878; 'Les berceaux' (Prudhomme), Op.23:1, 1879; 'Chanson d'amour' (Silvestre), Op.27:1, 1882; 'Clair de lune' (Verlaine), Op.46:2, 1887; 'Fleur jetée' (Silvestre), Op.39:2, 1884; 'Les Presents' (Villiers de l'Isle Adam), Op.46:1, 1887; 'Les Roses d'Ispahan' (Leconte de Lisle), Op.39:4, 1884; 'Lydia' (Leconte de Lisle), Op.4:2, c.1870; 'Nell' (Leconte de Lisle), Op.18:1, 1878; 'Nocturne' (Villiers de l'Isle Adam), Op.43:2, 1886; 'Noël' (Victor Wilder), Op.43:1, 1885; 'Notre amour' (Silvestre), Op.23:2, c.1879; 'Prison' (Verlaine), Op.83:1, 1894; 'Soir' (Albert Samain), Op.83:2, 1894; 'Spleen' (Verlaine), Op.51:3, 1888; 'Tristesse' (Gautier), Op.6:2, c.1873

Piano music

Barcarolles: No.1, A minor, Op.26, c.1880; No.2, G, Op.41, 1885; No.3, G♭, Op.42, 1886; No.4, A♭, Op.44, 1886; No.5, F♯ minor, Op.66, 1894; No.6, E♭, Op.70, 1896; No.7, D minor, Op.90, 1905; No.8, D♭, Op.96, 1906; No.9, A minor, Op.101, 1908; No.10, A minor, Op.104:2, 1913; No.11, G minor, Op.105, 1913; No.12, E♭, Op.106bis, 1915; No.13, C, Op.116, 1921

Impromptus: No.1, E♭, Op.25, 1881; No.2, F minor,

Op.31, 1883; No.3, A♭, ?1883; No.4, D♭, Op.91, 1905–6; No.5, F♯ minor, Op.102, 1909

Nocturnes: No.1, E♭ minor, Op.33:1, c.1875; No.2, B, Op.33:2, c.1880; No.3, A♭, Op.33:3, ?1882; No.4, E♭, Op.36, ?1884; No.5, B♭, Op.37, ?1884; No.6, D♭, Op.63, 1894; No.7, C♯ minor, Op.74, 1898; No.8, D♭, Op.84:8, 1902; No.9, B minor, Op.97, 1908; No.10, E minor, Op.99, 1908; No.11, F♯ minor, Op.104:1, 1913; No.12, E minor, Op.107, 1915; No.13, B minor, Op.119, 1921

Valse-caprices: No.1, A, Op.30, 1882; No.2, D♭, Op.38, 1884; No.3, G♭, Op.59, 1887–93; No.4, A♭, Op.62, 1893–4

Other pieces: *Trois romances sans paroles*, Op.17, ?1863; Ballade, Op.19, 1877–9; Mazurka, Op.32, c.1878; *Thème et variations*, Op.73, 1895; *Huit pièces brèves*, Op.84, 1869–1902; *Neuf préludes*, Op.103, 1909–10

Duets: *Allegro symphonique*, Op.68, c.1865; *Souvenirs de Bayreuth*, ?1888 (with Messager); *Dolly*, Op.56 (suite), 1894–7

Other music

Opera: *Pénélope* (see ODYSSEY), 1907–13

Incidental music: *Caligula* (Dumas père), Op.52, 1888 (also concert version), rev as *Jules César*, 1905 (also suite); *Shylock*, Op.57, 1890 (also suite); *Pelléas et Mélisande*, Op.80, 1898 (also suite); *Prométhée*, Op.82, 1900; *Masques et bergamasques*, Op.112, 1919 (also suite); etc.

Orchestral: Berceuse, Op.16, vn, orch, 1880; Ballade, Op.19, pf, orch, 1881; *Pavane*, Op.50, with ch ad lib (Montesquiou), 1887; *Fantaisie*, Op.111, pf, orch, 1918

Sacred: *Cantique de Jean Racine*, Op.11, ch, org, 1865, arr ch, hmnm, str qnt, 1866, orch 1906; REQUIEM, Op.48, 1877, 1887–93, rev 1900; etc.

Chamber: Piano Quintet No.1, D minor, Op.89, 1887–1905; No.2, C minor, Op.115, 1919–21; Piano Quartet No.1, C minor, Op.15, 1876–9; No.2, G minor, Op.45, ?1885–6; String Quartet, E minor, Op.121, 1923–4; Piano Trio, D minor, Op.120, 1922–3; Violin Sonata No.1, A, Op.13, 1875–6; No.2, E minor, Op.108, 1916–17; Cello Sonata No.1, D minor, Op.109, 1917; Cello Sonata No.2, G minor, Op.117, 1921; *Romance*, Op.28, vn, pf, 1877; *Berceuse*, Op.16, vn, pf, 1879; *Elégie*, Op.24, vc, pf, 1880; *Papillon*, Op.77, vc, pf, before 1885; *Petite pièce*, Op.49, vc, ?1888; *Romance*, Op.69, vc, pf, 1894; Andante, Op.75, vn, pf, 1897; *Sicilienne*, Op.78, vc/vn, pf, 1898; *Fantaisie*, Op.79, fl, pf, 1898; *Sérénade*, Op.98, vc, pf, 1908

Harp: Impromptu, Op.86, 1904; *Une Châtelaine en sa tour*, Op.110, 1918

fausset (Fr.). Falsetto.

Faust. Mythic character whose thirst for earthly life leads him to sell his soul to the devil in return for knowledge and power. His story emerged in popular stories and puppet plays in late-16th-century Germany and received a first literary fix in Marlowe's play (1604), but most of the many musical versions – strikingly various – have depended on Goethe's two-part dramatic poem (pub 1808, 1832), including all those below except the operas by Busoni and Pousseur.

(1) Spohr's opera *Faust*, to a libretto by Joseph Carl Bernard. Faust (baritone) uses his demonic powers as aids to seduction and murder, and is finally dragged to hell (compare *Don Giovanni*, first performed in the same city). First performance: Prague, 1 Sep 1816.

(2) Wagner's *Eine Faust-Ouvertüre* (A Faust Overture). First performance: Dresden, 22 Jul 1844.

(3) Berlioz's 'légende dramatique' *La Damnation de Faust*, to his own libretto with Almire Gandonnière after Gérard de Nerval's translation of Goethe. Faust (tenor), melancholic, is restored to life's pleasures by Mephistopheles (bass) and introduced to Marguerite (soprano). The cost to her turns out to be a murder charge, but Faust and Mephistopheles ride off to hell and she is saved. Among the numbers are orchestral pieces (RÁKÓCZI MARCH, Ballet of the Sylphs, Minuet of the Will-o'-the-Wisps), Marguerite's 'D'amour, l'ardente flamme', Faust's 'Nature immense' and Mephistopheles's Serenade and Song of the Flea. The score is dedicated to Liszt. Drawing on his *Huit scènes de Faust*, Berlioz intended a concert opera, but since a Monte Carlo production of 1893 the piece has often been staged. First performance: Paris, 6 Dec 1846.

(4) Liszt's *Eine Faust-Symphonie in drei Charakterbilden* (A Faust Symphony in Three Character Pictures), these being portraits of Faust, Gretchen and Mephistopheles. Faust has an unsettled, unsettlable 12-note theme; Gretchen's music is ameliorative, Mephisto's satirical. The dedication went to Berlioz. First performance: Weimar, 5 Sep 1857.

Other Faustian works by Liszt include *Zwei Episoden aus Lenaus Faust* for orchestra, of which the second is the first of his four Mephisto Waltzes.

(5) Schumann's full-length concert work *Szenen aus Goethes Faust*, the first to address Goethe's second part. First performance: Cologne, 13 Jan 1862.

(6) Gounod's opera *Faust*, to a libretto by Barbier and Carré. Faust (tenor) signs his contract with Mephistopheles (bass), who helps him seduce Marguerite (soprano) and, in an ensuing duel, kill her brother Valentin (baritone). Still she prays for her ruiner as she dies. A great favourite for almost a century, the work includes Faust's rapt cavatina 'Salut! demeure chaste et pure', Marguerite's 'Il était un roi de Thulé' and Jewel Song, Mephistopheles's Serenade and 'Le Veau d'or', and a ballet sequence added for the Paris Opera production a

decade after the première. First performance: Paris, 19 Mar 1859.

(7) Boito's opera *Mefistofele*, to his own libretto. Faust (tenor) signs his pact with Mephistopheles (bass), seduces Marguerite and Helen of Troy (the same soprano), and is at the end saved. First performance: Bologna, 4 Oct 1875; rev Venice, 13 May 1876.

(8) The second part of Mahler's Eighth Symphony, setting the celestial finale to the second part of Goethe's play. First performance: Munich, 12 Sep 1910.

(9) Busoni's opera *Doktor Faust*, to his own libretto. In a dramatic structure all the more disturbing for its ramshackle appearance, Faust (baritone) gains the companionship of Mephistopheles (tenor), is cursed by Gretchen's Brother (baritone), mesmerizes the Duchess of Parma (soprano) and dies, transferring his soul into a child. Unfinished at the composer's death, the score has been twice completed: by Philipp Jarnach and Antony Beaumont. First performance: Dresden, 21 May 1925.

(10) Pousseur's opera *Votre Faust*, to a libretto by Michel Butor. The composition of a Faust opera is played out by actors, in a layered and partly mobile connection with singers and instrumentalists. First performance: Milan, 15 Jan 1969.

There are also settings of Mephistopheles's Song of the Flea by Beethoven (Op.75:3) and Musorgsky, as well as other Faust songs by Schubert (*Szene aus Goethes Faust*, D.126) and Loewe, and further Faustian works by Eisler, Ginastera, Seiber, Rihm, Eben, Boehmer, Manzoni and Schnittke. Stravinsky's *Histoire du soldat* has the one daring God replaced by a simple soldier.

Fauvel. See ROMAN DE FAUVEL.

fauxbourdon (Fr.). Simple way of harmonizing plainsong, practised in Europe *c*.1430–1510. The harmonizing voices might be written out or indicated by a rule (e.g. sing a fourth below the top part), but either way would result in a euphony of mostly parallel chords. Both the name and the practice may derive from English FABURDEN.

Favart, Charles Simon (b. Paris, 13 Nov 1710; d. Belleville, Paris, 12 May 1792). French theatre man, who wrote opéra comique librettos and after whom the theatre of the Opéra-Comique has been named since 1783.

favola in musica (It., musical tale). Term used of early operas (Gagliano's *Dafne*, Monteverdi's *Orfeo*), acknowledging their adherence to the tradition of dramatic pastoral.

Fayrfax, Robert (b. Deeping Gate, Lincs., 23 Apr 1464; d. ?St Albans, 24 Oct 1521). English composer, a member of the Chapel Royal by 1497. Some of his earlier pieces are in the Eton Choirbook. He took the Cambridge MusB (1501) and MusD (1504), the latter awarded for his mass *O quam glorifica*, which is unusually elaborate in technique; generally he avoided the vocal virtuosity of his contemporaries. Besides six masses, two *Magnificat* settings and 10 votive antiphons, almost all in five parts, his extant works include eight songs (mostly in three parts) and two puzzle canons – a legacy whose size, above that of any other English composer of the time, may reflect the favour in which he was held by Henry VIII.

Fedora. Opera by Giordano to a libretto by Arturo Colautti after a play by Sardou. The leading characters are Russian aristocrats, seen largely in exile. Fedora (soprano) finds her ex-fiancé's murderer in Loris (tenor), to whom she emotionally succumbs when she hears the whole story – though only after she has given him away to the Russian police. They escape, but when retribution is imminent, Loris curses Fedora and she takes poison. The most celebrated number is 'Amor ti vieta' for Loris, a role first sung by Caruso. First performance: Milan, 17 Nov 1898.

feierlich (Ger.). Solemn, a marking notably used by Wagner (Siegfried's Funeral March) and Bruckner.

Feinberg, Samuel [Feynberg, Samuil Yevgenyevich] (b. Odessa, 26 May 1890; d. Moscow, 22 Oct 1962). Russian pianist-composer, of luminous singing line and mobile contrapuntal clarity in his esteemed Bach recordings, no matter how Romantic the approach. Brought up in Moscow, he studied with Goldenweiser at the conservatory and had private composition lessons with Nikolay Zhilyayev. His playing was approved by Scriabin, whose follower he was in some sense as a composer. In the 1920s he met with success on tour in western Europe, but after that he remained in Moscow, teaching at the conservatory (where he had been professor since 1922), recording and composing.

Feldman, Morton (b. New York, 12 Jan 1926; d. Buffalo, 3 Sep 1987). US composer, who in his late music combined the far limits of duration (six hours in the case of *String Quartet II*) with what had always been extremes of softness and inactivity. He studied with Riegger and Wolpe, and in 1950 met Cage, who he felt gave him permission to proceed into a sparse, near-silent music, using

GRAPH notation in his *Projection* series to indicate just the register and number of notes to be played within each time unit. Soon he returned to more conventional notation, but the nature of his music did not change: the slow, quiet drift remained his preferred form. In the early 1970s – when he turned to abstract titles from ones that had been both practical and poetic – he started to write more frequently for large forces. His scale also began to increase, especially towards the end of the decade, when he introduced a kind of irregular minimalist repetitiveness in emulation of the stitching in the oriental rugs he admired. Always drawn to visual art and viewing his music as painting with sound in time, he was also close to contemporary painters, notably Rauschenberg, Guston and Rothko. His reputation grew steadily after his death.

Morton Feldman, ed. B.H. Friedman *Give my Regards to Eighth Street* (2000)

Dramatic: NEITHER, 1977; *Words and Music* (Beckett), speaker, ens, 1987.

Orchestral: *Structures*, 1960–62; *In Search of an Orchestration*, 1967; *The Viola in my Life IV*, va, orch, 1971; *Cello and Orchestra*, 1972; *Piano and Orchestra*, 1975; *The Turfan Fragments*, 1980; *Coptic Light*, 1986; *For Samuel Beckett*, chbr orch, 1987; etc.

Vocal: *Only*, v, 1946; *Christian Wolff in Cambridge*, ch, 1963; *The Rothko Chapel*, ch, va, cel, perc, 1971–2; *3 Voices* (O'Hara), 1982; etc.

Chamber and instrumental: *Projection I*, vc, 1950; *Structures*, str qt, 1951; *The King of Denmark*, perc, 1964; *False Relationships and the Extended Ending*, 7 insts, 1968; *Between Categories*, 8 insts, 1969; *The Viola in my Life I–II*, va, 6 insts, 1970, *III*, va, pf, 1970; *Why Patterns?*, fl, glock, pf, 1978; *String Quartet*, 1979; *Crippled Symmetry*, fl, perc, kbds, 1983; *String Quartet II*, 1983; etc.

Piano: *Projection III*, 2 pf, 1951; *Intersection II*, 1951, *III*, 1953; *Extensions III*, 1952, *IV*, 3 pf, 1952; *Intermission V*, 1952, *VI*, 1953; *Vertical Thoughts I*, 2 pf, 1963, *IV*, 1964; *Triadic Memories*, 1981; *Palais de Mari*, 1986; etc.

Feldmusik (Ger., field music). Music or musicians required in battle.

Feldparthie (Ger., field partita). 18th-century genre of music for wind ensemble suggestive of *Feldmusik*.

Felix namque. Plainsong (for the offertory of a Mass of Our Lady) used as a subject for contrapuntal elaboration by English composers from the 15th century through Tallis to Tomkins.

Felsenstein, Walter (b. Vienna, 30 May 1901; d. Berlin, 8 Oct 1975). Austrian–German director,

proponent of MUSIC THEATRE as a means of making opera a parable of human beings and society. He studied as an actor, began directing in 1925, and held posts in Basle (1927–9), Freiburg (1929–32), Cologne (1932–4) and Frankfurt (1934–6) before his career was lamed by the Nazis. His most fruitful and influential period came at the Komische Oper in East Berlin, from 1947.

feminine ending. Close of a phrase on a weak beat. The term was introduced from prosody, where it distinguishes lines ending on unaccented syllables (as in 'burning') from those with accented 'masculine endings' (e.g. 'fire').

Fenice, La (The Phoenix). The Venice opera house, which opened in 1792 with Paisiello's *I giuochi d'Agrigento* and saw the first performances of works by Rossini (*Tancredi, Semiramide*), Bellini (*I Capuleti ed i Montecchi, Beatrice di Tenda*), Verdi (*Rigoletto, La traviata, Simon Boccanegra*), Stravinsky (*The Rake's Progress*), Britten (*The Turn of the Screw*) and Nono (*Intolleranza*). The theatre was destroyed by fire in 1836, rebuilt the next year, and destroyed again in 1996, to reopen in 2004.

Feo, Francesco (b. Naples, 1691; d. Naples, 28 Jan 1761). Italian composer and teacher, notably of Jommelli. He studied at the Turchini conservatory in Naples (1704–12) and then began to make his way as an opera composer. Succeeding to teaching posts at the San Onofrio conservatory (1723–39) and the Poveri di Gesù Cristo (1739–43), he also held church appointments, and produced quantities of masses, motets, psalms and oratorios, along with a few more operas.

Ferguson, Howard (b. Belfast, 21 Oct 1908; d. Cambridge, 1 Nov 1999). British composer and pianist, who was a protégé of Samuel. He studied also at the RCM, and taught at the RAM (1948–63). A Romantic but fastidious composer, he took three decades to reach his Op.19 (the cantata *The Dream of the Rood*, 1958–9), then laid aside his pen to concentrate on editing early keyboard music.

fermata. Pause.

ferne Klang, Der (The Distant Sound). Opera by Schreker to his own libretto. Fritz (tenor), a young artist, leaves his sweetheart, Grete (soprano), to find his soul, his 'distant sound'. He is appalled to rediscover Grete running a nightspot in Venice. At a performance of his opera (*Der ferne Klang*, indeed) she is overcome, while he realizes he has been on a wild goose chase. They are reconciled, but only in time for him to die in her arms. First performance: Frankfurt, 18 Aug 1912.

Ferneyhough, Brian (b. Coventry, 16 Jan 1943). British composer, of music that, in its speed and fantastical complexity of rhythm, scans a range from playfulness to ferocity. He studied at the Birmingham School of Music (1961–3), the RAM (1966–7), with Ton de Leeuw in Amsterdam (1968) and with Klaus Huber in Basle (1969–71). By 1973, when he began teaching at the Freiburg conservatory, he was making a mark in continental Europe, and he became a dominant influence at Darmstadt (1976–96) – fittingly, since the questions that were hot there for Boulez and Stockhausen in the 1950s, questions of how musical structures present themselves, have in his music remained hot. After a period when his most impressive pieces were for hard-pressed solo instrumentalist or string quartet, thrusting themselves and their listeners into areas of wild and sometimes incandescent experience, the *Carceri d'invenzione* series established him as a master on a wider plane. He took an appointment at UCSD in 1987 and moved to Stanford in 1999, by which time he was working on *Shadowtime*, an opera on the life and work of Walter Benjamin.

Brian Ferneyhough, ed. James Boros and Richard Toop *Collected Writings* (1996)

Compendia: CARCERI D'INVENZIONE, 1981–6; *Shadowtime* (opera; Charles Bernstein), 1998–2003, Munich 2004.

Other larger works: *Time and Motion Study III*, ch, perc, elec, 1974; *Transit*, 6 v, chbr orch, elec, 1972–5; *Maisons noires*, 22 insts, 1998; etc.

String quartets: Sonatas (No.1), 1967; No.2, 1980; *Adagissimo*, 1983; No.3, 1987; No.4, s, str qt, 1989–90

Other chamber works: *Funérailles*, 7 str, hp, 1969–80; *La Chute d'Icare*, cl, 6 insts, 1988; *Mort subite*, pic, cl, vib, pf, 1990; *Terrain*, vn, 8 insts, 1992; *On Stellar Magnitudes*, s, fl, cl, vn, vc, pf, 1994; String Trio, 1995; *Incipits*, va, 7 insts, 1996; *Allgebrah*, ob, 9 str, 1996; *Flurries*, 6 insts, 1997; etc.

Other solo pieces: *Cassandra's Dream Song*, fl, 1970; *Unity Capsule*, fl, 1975–6; *Time and Motion Study I*, b cl, 1971–7; *II*, vc, 1973–6; *Lemma–Icon–Epigram*, pf, 1981; *Kurze Schatten II*, gtr, 1983–9; *Trittico per G. S.*, db, 1989; *Bone Alphabet*, perc, 1991; *Unsichtbare Farben*, vn, 1997–9; etc.

feroce (It.). Fierce.

Ferrabosco. Italian–English family, in the 16th century of high servants at court in Bologna, later including several musicians.

(1) **Alfonso I** (baptized Bologna, 18 Jan 1543; d. Bologna, 12 Aug 1588). His father's appointment as a singer in the papal chapel alongside Palestrina took the family to Rome (1551–5), and he was in cardinalatial service there before and after his first visit to England, which he made in his late teens. Moving back and forth between England and the continent (c.1562–78) he may have worked as a secret agent, though certainly he was valued for his music, by Elizabeth I and by native composers (Byrd, Morley, Wilbye) impressed by his motets and madrigals. In later years he served the Duke of Savoy.

(2) **Alfonso II** (b. ?Greenwich, before 1578; buried Greenwich, 11 Mar 1628). Son of the above, he was brought up by another of Elizabeth's musicians, Gomer van Awsterwyke. From 1592 he was himself in royal service, becoming instructor to Prince Henry (1604–12) and a collaborator with Ben Jonson on masques, in which he also sang and played the lute. After Henry's death he served Charles, as prince and king. Besides church music and lute songs, he wrote a plentiful quantity of fantasias, dances and In nomines for viol consort. He married Ellen Lanier (daughter of the court musician Nicholas Lanier) and had three sons who also became musicians.

Ferrara. Italian city where music was strongly encouraged by members of the ruling Este family. Duke Ercole I (r. 1471–1505) employed Josquin and Obrecht; the former wrote a mass in his honour. His sons, Duke Alfonso I (r. 1505–34) and Cardinal Ippolito I, were also great patrons – of Brumel, Willaert and Mouton – as were his daughters, Isabella (who married Gian Francesco II Gonzaga of Mantua) and Beatrice (married to Lodovico Sforza of Milan). Of the next dukes, Ercole II (r. 1534–59) had Rore as his chapelmaster, and Alfonso II (r. 1559–97) made Ferrara an important centre of the madrigal. His composers included Luzzaschi and Wert, and he married his niece to Gesualdo.

Ferraresi, Adriana (b. Ferrara, c.1755; d. ?Venice, after 1799). Italian soprano, who studied in Venice and, in a brief and brilliant career, alighted in Vienna (1788–91), where she was Mozart's Susanna in *Figaro* (with new arias) and first Fiordiligi in *Così*. She was also Salieri's mistress.

Ferrari, Benedetto (b. Reggio Emilia, ?1603/4; d. Modena, 22 Oct 1681). Italian composer-librettist, whose partnership in Venice with Francesco Manelli produced the first commercial operas, beginning with *Andromeda* (1637; his words, Manelli's setting). The final duet of *L'incoronazione di Poppea* may have been borrowed from his *Il pastor regio* (1640), for which he wrote both words and music. Otherwise nothing of his operatic music survives, though he published three books of madrigals and arias (1633–41). He had been a choirboy at the Collegio Germanico in Rome (1617–18), and apart from his busy years in Venice (1637–44) seems to have revolved in the area of Parma, Reggio and Modena.

Ferrero, Lorenzo (b. Turin, 17 Nov 1951). Italian composer, whose unashamed use of mixed styles and pop brought him success on the opera stage with *Marilyn* (Rome, 1980) and later works.

Ferretti, Giovanni (b. c.1540; d. after 1609). Italian composer, whose Neapolitan-style villanellas were popular and influential in England. He was chapelmaster at the Holy House of Loreto (1580–82, 1596–1603) and elsewhere.

Ferrier, Kathleen (Mary) (b. Higher Walton, Lancs., 22 Apr 1912; d. London, 8 Oct 1953). British contralto, whose luscious singing – very English in being at once magniloquent and reserved – made her an internationally revered artist after her first performance with Walter of *Das Lied von der Erde* (Edinburgh, 1947). She had risen from the ranks of the chorus to be Britten's Lucretia (1946) and Gluck's Orpheus (1947) at Glyndebourne. The distanced intimacy of the gramophone suited her, and she recorded much of her repertory, which also included the Angel's part in *The Dream of Gerontius*, a gift to her balm-bestowing nobility.
Christopher Fifield, ed. *Letters and Diaries of Kathleen Ferrier* (2003)

Ferroud, Pierre Octave (b. Chasselay, near Lyons, 6 Jan 1900; d. Debrecen, 17 Aug 1936). French composer, of Bartókian leanings. He studied with Ropartz in Strasbourg (1920–22) and Schmitt in Lyons, then moved in 1923 to Paris, where, as leading co-founder of Le Triton, he mounted concerts of new chamber music. His death in a car crash prompted his friend Poulenc's first sacred work.

Fes (Ger.). F♭. Also *Feses* (F♭♭).

Festa, Costanzo (b. c.1490; d. Rome, 10 Apr 1545). Italian composer and church musician, a link between Josquin and Palestrina. By 1517 he was a member of the papal choir; before that he was employed by the Duchess of Francavilla on Ischia and perhaps by the French royal court. A master of suave imitative polyphony and sonorous cadences, he wrote motets, hymns, settings of the *Magnificat* and Lamentations, and just four masses. He was also among the early madrigalists.

Feste romane (Roman Festivals). Symphonic poem by Respighi. The festivals heard, in four sections, are those of the ancient circus, the Catholic jubilee, October (*L'Ottobrata*) and Epiphany (*La Befana*). First performance: New York, 21 Feb 1929.

Festin de l'araignée, Le (The Spider's Banquet). Ballet score by Roussel to a scenario by Gilbert de Voisins, originally choreographed by Léo Staats, a cautionary tale of insect life. The composer created a suite, or 'fragments symphoniques'. First performance: Paris, 3 Apr 1913.

festival. In music the word is associated with annual commemorations (e.g. of St Cecilia), with choral gatherings (e.g. the Three Choirs Festival, the Cincinnati May Festival), with amateur competitions and, most recently, with periods (from a weekend to a month or more) of frequent performances and an upbeat air in a particular locality. Wagner's Bayreuth (1876) and the Mozart celebrations at Salzburg (1877) were among the prototypes of this last kind, followed by the regular Salzburg Festival (1920), the Maggio Musicale in Florence (1933), Tanglewood (1937) and the Lucerne Festival (1938). Many other festivals were founded soon after the Second World War, including those of Cheltenham (1945), Prague (1946), Edinburgh (1947), Holland (1947), Ojai (1947), Aix (1948), Aldeburgh (1948), Bath (1948), Aspen (1950), Donaueschingen (1950), Marlboro (1950), Berlin (1951) and Vienna (1951). Often there will be a particular theme or an abiding local speciality, along with artists and orchestras touring from one festival to another. Festivals have played an important part, too, in the propagation of new music, and some were founded explicitly for that purpose, in Munich (Musica Viva, 1945), Warsaw (1956), Zagreb (1961), Royan (1964), Metz (1972), Huddersfield (1978), etc.

Festklänge (Festal Sounds). Symphonic poem by Liszt. First performance: Weimar, 9 Nov 1854.

Festino. Name given Haydn's Symphony No.53.

Fêtes d'Hébé, Les (Hebe's Festivities). Opera-ballet by Rameau, titled in full *Les Fêtes d'Hébé, ou Les Talents lyriques*, to a libretto by Antoine Gautier de Montdorge and others. Hebe observes separate celebrations of the arts of poetry, music and dance in a work that unites the three. First performance: Paris, 21 May 1739.

Fétis, François-Joseph (b. Mons, near Liège, 25 Mar 1784; d. Brussels, 26 Mar 1871). Belgian musical scholar, author of the encyclopedic *Biographie universelle des musiciens* (1835–44). An organist's son, he studied at the Paris Conservatoire (1800–11), then worked as an organist and teacher in Douai. During a second period in Paris (1818–33) he was variously and vigorously active as a composer, as teacher and librarian at the Conservatoire, as a critic, founding the *Revue musicale* (1827), and as an early promoter of early music (with his Concerts Historiques, given from 1832). In 1833 he was appointed director of the Brussels Conservatory. He began a *Histoire générale de la musique*, but in five volumes got only as far as the 15th century.

feuerig (Ger.). Fiery.

Feuermann, Emanuel (b. Kolomed/Kolomyya, now in Ukraine, 22 Nov 1902; d. New York, 25 May 1942). Austrian cellist, fitting partner of Heifetz and Rubinstein. He studied in Vienna and Leipzig (with the esteemed cellist, composer and teacher Julius Klengel, 1917–19), and was soon playing internationally. In 1938 he settled in the USA.

Feuersnot (Need for Fire). Opera by Strauss to a libretto by Ernst von Wolzogen. Kunrad (baritone), a sorcerer's apprentice, causes all the fires in Munich to go out; the city is relit only when he gets his way with Diemut (soprano). First performance: Dresden, 21 Nov 1901.

feuille d'album (Fr.). Albumleaf.

Févin, Antoine (b. ?Arras, *c.*1470; d. Blois, 1511/12). French composer, follower of Josquin, at the French court by 1507. He wrote masses, motets and chansons.

ff, *fff*. See F.

Fg. Ger. abbreviation for *Fagott* (bassoon).

FGSMD. Fellow of the Guildhall School of Music and Drama.

f **holes**. Soundholes in violins and similar instruments, the holes being indeed *f*-shaped.

Fiala, Joseph (b. Lochovitz/Lochovice, 2 Mar 1748; d. Donaueschingen, 31 Jul 1816). Bohemian oboist-cellist-composer, known to Mozart from 1777, when he joined the Munich court after training in Prague. He was then in Salzburg (1778–85) and, after some years of travel, Donaueschingen. His works include symphonies, concertos and chamber music.

fiato (It.). Breath, hence *stromenti a fiato* or just *fiati* (wind instruments).

Fibich, Zdeněk [Zdenko] **(Antonín Václav)** (b. Všebořice, 21 Dec 1850; d. Prague, 15 Oct 1900). Czech composer. Less obviously nationalist than his elder contemporaries Dvořák and Smetana, he was an individualist, not least in his interest in melodrama. He studied in Prague, in Leipzig with Moscheles and Jadassohn (1865–7) and in Mannheim with Vincenz Lachner (1869–70). Thereafter he lived in Prague, as a composer and teacher. He married in 1873, and after his wife had died the following year, leaving him with a baby son, he married her sister. In his last decade he maintained a passionate liaison with Anežka Schulzová, a pupil, for whom he kept a diary of *Moods, Impressions and Reminiscences*: 376 piano pieces, including the popular *Poème* (Op.41:14) and others he adapted and developed in larger works.

Operas: *The Bride of Messina* (Otakar Hostinský, after Schiller), Op.18, 1882–3; *The Tempest*, Op.40, 1893–4; *Šárka* (Schulzová), Op.51, 1896–7; etc.
Melodramas: *Hippodamia* (stage trilogy; Vrchlický), Opp.31–3, 1888–91; concert pieces
Orchestral: Symphony No.1, F, Op.17, 1877–83; No.2, E♭, Op.38, 1892–3; No.3, E minor, Op.53, 1898; *At Twilight*, Op.39, 1893; etc.
Other works: Quintet, D, Op.42, vn, cl, vc, hn, pf, 1893; *Moods, Impressions and Reminiscences*, Opp.41, 44, 47, 57, pf, 1892–9; choral music, songs, incidental scores

Fibonacci series. NUMBER sequence, each the sum of the preceding two: 1, 2, 3, 5, 8, 13, 21, 34 …. Fibonacci numbers have been used by composers (including Bartók possibly and Stockhausen certainly) to gauge formal and rhythmic proportions.

ficta. See MUSICA FICTA.

fiction. Music belongs in the realm of the non-factual (though for its believers it is as real as physics), where it has spilled over also into other fictional forms, especially literary and cinematic. Many of the results involve IMAGINARY COMPOSERS, but many, too, refract the lives and works of actual musicians, among whom the following have proved the richest sources, by virtue either of their dramatic biographies or their powerful presence in their work (some examples only are given, the novels limited to books that have appeared in English):

Saint-Colombe: film *Tous les matins du monde* (1991)
Bach: film *Chronik der Anna Magdalena Bach* (1968, with Gustav Leonhardt)
Mozart: Pushkin's play *Mozart and Salieri* (1830);

Mörike's novella *Mozart auf der Reise nach Prag*
(1856); Peter Shaffer's play *Amadeus* (1980, filmed
1984); Pupi Avati's film *Noi tre* (1984)
Beethoven: Abel Gance's film *Beethoven* (1936); John
Suchet's 3-vol. novel *The Last Master* (1996–8); see
also EROICA
Paganini: Abel Gance's film *Paganini* (1910)
Schubert: film *Blossom Time* (1934, with Richard
Tauber); Marcel Pagnol's film *La Belle Meunière*
(1948)
Chopin: film *A Song to Remember* (1945, with Cornel
Wilde and Merle Oberon)
Schumanns: film *Song of Love* (1947, with Katharine
Hepburn); film *Spring Symphony* (1983, with
Nastassja Kinski); Janice Galloway's novel *Clara*
(2002)
Liszt: Ken Russell's film *Lisztomania* (1975, with
Roger Daltrey)
Verdi: Franz Werfel's novel *Verdi* (1925)
Dvořák: Josef Skvorecký's novel *Dvořák in Love*
(1986)
Wagner: Tony Palmer's film *Wagner* (1983, with
Richard Burton)
Tchaikovsky: Klaus Mann's novel *Pathetic Symphony*
(1938); Ken Russell's film *The Music Lovers* (1970)
Elgar: James Hamilton-Paterson's novel *Gerontius*
(1989)
Mahler: Ken Russell's film *Mahler* (1974)
Gould: Thomas Bernhard's novel *The Loser* (1991);
François Girard's film *32 Short Films about Glenn
Gould* (1993)

There is also a small and special category of operas
or operettas in which composers sing, including
Pfitzner's PALESTRINA, Schnittke's *Gesualdo*,
Isouard's *Lully et Quinault*, Flotow's *Alessandro
Stradella*, Isouard's *Cimarosa*, Hahn's *Mozart*,
Rimsky-Korsakov's *Mozart and Salieri*, Lehár's
Paganini, Heinrich Berté's *Das Dreimäderlhaus*
(Vienna, 1916, filmed as *Blossom Time*) and
Orefice's CHOPIN.

fiddle. Informal term for a violin or, less usually,
other bowed string instrument. The word is
etymologically related to 'viola'. In more formal
contexts it usually implies a medieval instrument
held at the shoulder, like a modern violin. Copious
illustrations and textual references indicate that
fiddles of diverse types and tunings were widely
played across Europe from the 10th century, when
bowing entered Spain and southern Italy from
Islam and Byzantium. They faded out in the 15th
century (later in northern Europe) as viols and
violins became the bowed instruments of choice.

Fidelio. Opera by Beethoven to a libretto by Joseph
Sonnleithner based on one by Jean-Nicolas Bouilly
(set by Pierre Gaveaux, Paer and Mayr), revised by
Stephan von Breuning (1806) and Georg Friedrich
Treitschke (1814). The work was originally called

Leonore, oder Der Triumph der ehelichen Liebe
(Leonore, or The Triumph of Marital Love); now
the title LEONORE is generally reserved for the
three superseded overtures and early versions of
the score.

Leonore (soprano) is masquerading as a young
man, Fidelio, in the household of the jailer, Rocco
(bass), his daughter Marzelline (soprano) and his
assistant Jaquino (tenor), in order to get close to
her imprisoned husband, Florestan (tenor). She
begs Rocco to let the prisoners out into the light,
and he does so, precipitating a glorious chorus of
thanksgiving. But Florestan has to stay in the dark.
She finds him there, and prevents his murder at
the hands of the prison governor, Pizarro (bass-
baritone), whose rule is magniloquently over-
thrown by the minister Don Fernando (bass). The
numbers, separated by spoken dialogue, include a
soft quartet for Marzelline, Leonore, Jaquino and
Rocco ('Mir ist so wunderbar'), Florestan's recitative and aria in the darkness, his duet of reunion
with Leonore ('O namenlose Freude!') and the
whole second-act finale, a half-hour freedom
cantata.

First performance: Vienna, 20 Nov 1805; rev 29
Mar 1806; rev 23 May 1814.

Field, John (b. Dublin, Jul 1782; d. Moscow, 23 Jan
1837). Irish pianist-composer, the inventor of the
nocturne. The son and grandson of professional
musicians, he made his debut in Dublin four
months before his 10th birthday and was taken by
his father the next year to London, where he was
apprenticed to Clementi. In 1802–3 he accompanied Clementi to Paris, Vienna and St Petersburg, staying on in Russia until 1831. His health
deteriorated (apparently the fault of drink), and
he returned to London then with his illegitimate
son Leon. (His wife had left him.) In 1832 he
embarked on European travels, ending up incapacitated by illness in Naples, whence he was restored
to Moscow by Russian well-wishers in 1835.
Witnesses remarked on 'his expressive touch and
extreme delicacy', and 'the easy, heavenly "floating"
of his scales and passages' – all qualities he
transferred into his music. He settled on the title
'nocturne' in 1812 after considering other possibilities (pastorale, romance, serenade). All his
works involve the piano.

Patrick Piggott *The Life and Music of John Field* (1973)

Concertos: No.1, E♭, ?1799; No.2, A♭; No.3, E♭; No.4,
E♭; No.5 (*L'Incendie par l'orage*), C; No.6, C, ?1819;
No.7, C minor
Nocturnes (with publication dates): No.1, E♭, 1812;
No.2, C minor, 1812; No.3, E♭, 1812; No.4, A, 1817;
No.5, B♭, 1817; No.6, F, 1817; No.7, C, 1821; No.8, E
minor, 1821; No.9, C, 1827; No.10, B♭, 1829; No.11,

Eb, 1832; No.12, G, 1834; No.13, D minor, 1834; No.14, C, 1836; No.15, C, 1836; No.16, F

Other works: rondos, variations, exercises, duets, quintets, etc.

Fierrabras. Opera by Schubert to a libretto by Josef Kupelwieser. The Moorish prince Fierrabras (tenor) and the Frankish knight Eginhard (tenor) are rivals for Emma (soprano), daughter of Charlemagne (bass), while Roland (baritone), another of Charlemagne's paladins, is in love with Fierrabras's sister Florinda (soprano). The stage is set for manifold expressions of love and nobility. First performance: Karlsruhe, 9 Feb 1897.

Fiery Angel, The (*Ognenny angel, L'Ange de feu*). Opera by Prokofiev to his own libretto after Bryusov's novel. The story of religious obsession, passionate love and madness revolves around Renata (soprano), with Ruprecht (baritone) at the edge of the whirlpool. Despairing of seeing the work staged, the composer drew from it his Third Symphony, and indeed there was no production until after his death. First performance: Paris, 25 Nov 1954 (concert); Venice, 14 Sep 1955 (staged).

Fiesco, Giulio (*fl.* Ferrara, *c.*1550–70). Italian madrigalist, whose works include essays in chromaticism.

fife. Flute-type instrument, a little larger (therefore lower) than the piccolo, but narrower (therefore shriller), used in military music in company with drums.

fifteenth. Note two octaves above another, or interval of two octaves.

fifth. (1) Note in fifth position in a diatonic system, e.g. G in C major.

(2) Interval between that note and the tonic. A perfect fifth comprises seven semitones (e.g. C–G), a diminished fifth six (e.g. C–Gb). Chromatic alteration can produce an augmented fifth (e.g. C–G♯, enharmonically a minor sixth).

Fifths. Name given Haydn's Quartet Op.76:2, which opens with leaping fifths.

Figaro. Short way of referring to Mozart's *Le nozze di Figaro*.

Figner. Operatic couple of late Tsarist Russia. Nikolay Nikolayevich (b. Nikiforovka, near Kazan, 21 Feb 1857; d. Kiev, 13 Dec 1918) was a tenor who trained at the St Petersburg Conservatory and in Naples. He and his wife Medea, née Mei (b.

Florence, 4 Apr 1859; d. Paris, 8 Jul 1952) sang at the Mariinsky between 1887 and 1904, when they were divorced. They were in the premières of Tchaikovsky's *Queen of Spades* and *Iolanta*.

figural, figurate. Decorated, complicated, especially of polyphony.

figuration. Decoration of a line. The implication is that the individual notes of a relatively simple melody have been replaced by figures, which might be motifs from the composition, standard ornaments, scale patterns or arpeggios. Since the late 16th century this kind of elaboration has been a regular compositional practice, to the extent that composers may well think directly in terms of figuration to convey excitement, add interest, provide display opportunities, convey exhilarated or anxious moods, or imitate the tremulations of nature.

figure. (1) Numeral indicating an interval in a chord, used as a shorthand in FIGURED BASS and elsewhere. A first-inversion triad is represented by 6, because the notes are contained within a sixth (e.g. E–G–C); 6–4 indicates a second-inversion triad, containing a sixth and a fourth (e.g. G–C–E).

(2) MOTIF.

(3) Element in figuration.

(4) Device in RHETORIC, and thereby discernible in music created according to rhetorical principles.

figured. (1) Beset with numerals to indicate chords, as a figured bass is.

(2) Figural.

figured bass. Bass line beneath which are numerals and other symbols to indicate the harmony. Continuo players in music of the 17th–18th centuries face such parts, which imply some freedom in how the harmony is to be realized, perhaps arpeggiated or more elaborately ornamented.

figured chorale. Either meaning of FIGURED may obtain.

filar il suono (It., spin out the sound). Direction to hold a note without taking a breath or (for string instruments) changing the bow.

Fille du régiment, La (The Daughter of the Regiment). Opera by Donizetti to a libretto by Jules-Henri Vernoy de Saint-Georges and Jean-François-Alfred Bayard. Marie (soprano), nurtured by a French regiment, falls in love with a Tyrolean prisoner, Tonio (tenor), who joins up for her sake. Whisked away to a grander life by her long-lost mother the Marquise (mezzo-soprano), she is saved for Tonio by the arrival of the troops. First performance: Paris, 11 Feb 1840.

film music. Silent films were commonly accompanied by a pianist or small orchestra, usually improvising or borrowing from popular classics and light music. Sometimes, though, there would be a special score. The earliest example would seem to have been Saint-Saëns's for Henri Lavedan's *L'Assassinat du Duc de Guise* (1908); others include Strauss's unbelievable bowdlerization of *Der Rosenkavalier* (1924), Edmund Meisel's music for *Battleship Potemkin* (1925) and Honegger's for Abel Gance's *Napoléon*. There are also later composers who have enjoyed improvising (Benjamin) or composing (Mason) for silent movies.

The arrival of film soundtrack, at the end of the 1920s, greatly eased the use of original music, which now had to be rehearsed and performed just once. Soundtrack also provided a new creative medium for music, before tape, since one could draw on it and hear the result. Endeavours of that kind were made by Norman MacLaren and the Whitney brothers.

Film studios, however, have generally shown little interest in musical innovation. By the mid-1930s it was well established that feature films needed music (films entirely without remain extraordinarily rare), to jazz up the titles (often using a 'title theme'), to support or intensify chase, battle or love scenes, to suggest a mood in a place or an unspeaking head, etc. These criteria – plus the requirement for flexibility of form, following how the film is cut – have tended to keep film music within the ambit of the late-Romantic or early-modern orchestra, whether the subject be Robin Hood or intergalactic warfare.

That may seem odd, but it is no odder than the use of the same full orchestra for so many diverse situations in the opera house, and film music may be regarded as a continuation of opera scoring – with the crucial difference that the voices now are beyond the composer's reach, except in the special case of filmed musicals. Also, by limiting its stylistic range, film music appeals to a widely shared code relating music to feeling and atmosphere. Some composers have tried to open the field, in music for imaginary films (Schreker, Schoenberg) or in actual film scores (Herrmann, Birtwistle, Davies), but with little success beyond the particular instance.

Because of its special aesthetic, and because of its technical demands (notably the ability to compose to a given length of time), film music has tended to be a specialist realm, its composers including Auric, Korngold, Rózsa, Tiomkin, Alex North, Waxman, the Newman family, Michel Legrand, Maurice Jarre, John Barry, Morricone, John Williams, Kilar and Elfman. Others, with reputations elsewhere, have worked in films only occasionally (Prokofiev, Honegger, Ibert, Vaughan Williams, Walton, Bax, Bliss, Copland, Bernstein, Arnold, Henze, Corigliano, Nyman, Tan), while a very few have maintained simultaneous careers in the cinema and beyond (Shostakovich, Rota, Bennett, Takemitsu, Glass), and one has included film among his creative media (Kagel). The barrier is also crossed when a film uses existing music as background (*2001: A Space Odyssey*), foreground (FANTASIA) or subject, as in the genres of musician biography (see FICTION) and opera on film.

Roy M. Prendergast *Film Music* (1992)

filter. Electronic device that limits the range of frequencies in a source sound.

Filtz, (Johann) Anton (baptized Eichstätt, Bavaria, 22 Sep 1733; buried Mannheim, 14 Mar 1760). German composer, a leading early member of the Mannheim school. A cellist like his father, he was in the Mannheim orchestra from 1754. Upbraided by some contemporaries for the mixture of comedy and seriousness in his symphonies, he was applauded by others for his daring and folksiness. All bewailed his early death.

fin (Fr.). End.

final. Note on which a melody in a MODE is expected to end.

finale (It., pl. *finali*, though in Eng. 'finales', Fr. *final*, Ger. *Finale*). Last movement, or concluding scene or section of an opera, oratorio, etc. Haydn used the term quite often in chamber works and symphonies. With the increasing sense of wholeness and drive in music of the 19th and early 20th centuries, the symphonic or operatic finale became more culminative – a development already clear in Beethoven, and certainly maintained as far as *The Rite of Spring*. Later finales, in music where the arrow of time is felt less certainly, have often been deliberately weak or ambiguous.

Finalmusik (Ger.). Last piece in an outdoor musical entertainment of the Classical period.

Finck, Heinrich (b. ?Bamberg, 1444/5; d. Vienna, 9 Jun 1527). German composer, who helped form German Renaissance polyphony and lived to contribute to it into the age of Josquin and Isaac. He probably began his career in Poland before studying at Leipzig University, where he matriculated in 1482. Some time after that he returned to Kraków, though by 1510 he was in ducal service in Stuttgart, and he spent his last years in Salzburg and Vienna. He wrote masses, motets, hymns and German songs. His great-nephew Hermann (1527–58) was a theorist and composer at Wittenberg University.

fine (It., end). Indication that the conclusion has been reached, useful in music that seems to continue. Music in ABA form (e.g. a da capo aria) will often be printed as AB, with a repeat at the end of the B section: the marking 'Fine' is then needed at the close of the A section.

Fine, Irving (Gifford) (b. Boston, 3 Dec 1914; d. Boston, 23 Aug 1962). US composer, in a lean and elegant neoclassical style that became more venturesome through contact with serialism after 1952. He studied with Piston at Harvard (1933–8) and Boulanger in Paris, and taught at Harvard (1939–50) before moving to Brandeis. His conducting mentor was Koussevitzky, who joked about creating a programme of Fine and d'Indy. Apart from a Symphony (1960–62) and *Serious Song* for strings (1955), his modest output consists mostly of chamber music (String Quartet, 1952), choruses and songs.

Fine, Vivian (b. Chicago, 28 Sep 1913; d. Bennington, Vermont, 20 Mar 2000). US composer, whose contact with Crawford in her teens encouraged her in a style of strenuous dissonant counterpoint, moderated after she moved to New York in 1931 and studied with Sessions (1934–42). She taught at Bennington College (1964–87) and concentrated on vocal and chamber music.

Fingal's Cave (*Fingalshöhle*). Alternative title for Mendelssohn's overture *Die* HEBRIDEN.

Finger, Gottfried (b. ?Olmütz/Olomouc, c.1660; buried Mannheim, 31 Aug 1730). Moravian composer, who travelled in Italy before arriving in London in 1686 as an instrumentalist in the Catholic chapel of James II. He wrote sonatas (most notably for viola da gamba) and theatre music, including a setting of Congreve's masque *The Judgment of Paris* (1700) for a competition to find the best composer. Out of four (not three) contestants he was placed last, after Weldon, Eccles and Daniel Purcell, which may have helped move him to leave London. By 1706 his patron was Duke Karl Philipp, at Neuburg and later as Elector Palatine.

fingerboard. Part of a string instrument where the fingers of one hand touch the strings. In instruments of the violin family the fingerboard is a piece of ebony glued to the neck, curved so that the bow can act on one string at a time. In plucked instruments the fingerboard is flat and fretted, for the opposite reason: to facilitate chordal playing.

fingering. Means of deploying the fingers in playing an instrument. The fingers differ in strength, and there will often be alternative ways of adapting them to any particular pattern of notes. For keyboard and string players, therefore, fingering choices will have an effect on rhythm, accentuation and phrasing. Woodwind players can use special fingerings to produce unusual colours as well as microtones and chords.

Fingering may be indicated by numerals. The universal modern convention for keyboard music has 1–5 for the digits from thumb to little finger on either hand, though older British sources may have + (thumb) and 1–4. Bowed string music has 1–4 for the left-hand digits from index finger to little finger, plus 0 for an unstopped note. Novel woodwind fingerings, first described by Bartolozzi (1967), may be shown diagrammatically.

The importance of keyboard fingering has been widely recognized since the second half of the 16th century, when Italian and German treatises dealt with the question, and some composers marked fingerings in their works. Principles of fingering – for strings, as well as keyboard instruments – help define different historical styles and traditions. Where there is doubt, a choice will often be offered by the composer or editor – though Debussy, editing Chopin, declined to do so, implicitly recognizing that fingering is also an individual matter in his injunction: 'Cherchons nos doigtés!' ('Let us seek out our fingerings').

Finland (Suomi/Finnland). Music, especially the work of Sibelius, was one of the means by which the country asserted its independence from Russia, eventually achieved in 1917. Sibelius stopped composing soon after, but the country has produced an unusual number of prominent composers since, including Rautavaara, Sallinen, Saariaho, Lindberg and Salonen. State support has also fostered numerous festivals.

Finlandia. Orchestral work by Sibelius, a majestic national emblem immediately recognized as such. It was adapted from a movement in a theatre score for the press celebrations of 1899. First performance: Helsinki, 2 Jul 1900.

Finney, Ross Lee (b. Wells, Minn., 23 Dec 1906; d.

Carmel, Cal., 4 Feb 1997). US composer, whose music displays strong rhythmic propulsion and a passion for dialectic, rooted in 12-note principles after the 1950s. With experience in folk and jazz as well as classical music, he studied with Boulanger in Paris (1927–8), Sessions at Harvard (1928–9) and Berg in Vienna (1931–2). He produced a large output, especially of orchestral, choral and chamber music (four symphonies, several concertos, eight quartets), and was a gifted teacher, at Smith College (1929–48) and the University of Michigan (1949–74).

Finnissy, Michael (Peter) (b. London, 17 Mar 1946). British composer, of bewildering variety, from hectic virtuosity to numbed stillness, from high abstraction to elaborations of earlier music ranging from Obrecht to Gershwin. He studied at the RCM and with Vlad in Italy and has taught at various institutions in southern England. His enormous output suggests an increasing focus on the private, notably in the number and weight of works for himself (or another) as pianist, including *English Country-Tunes* (1977, rev 1982–5) and *The History of Photography in Sound* (begun 1997). Other works include *Red Earth* for orchestra (1987–8) and numerous dramatic pieces.

Henrietta Brougham, Christopher Fox and Ian Pace *Uncommon Ground: The Music of Michael Finnissy* (1997)

finta giardiniera, La (The Pretending Garden-girl). Opera by Mozart to an anonymous libretto set the previous year by Anfossi. The title character is Sandrina (soprano), who is in fact a marchioness lately stabbed by her lover Belfiore (tenor) and taking refuge in the garden of Don Anchise (tenor). The plot only gets stranger but is resolved in a triple union involving another noble couple, Arminda (soprano) and Ramiro (soprano castrato), and the servant-class Nardo (baritone) and Serpetta (soprano). Performances became more frequent after the rediscovery in 1978 of the original first act, previously known only from the singspiel version *Die verstellte Gärtnerin*. What also helped the work join the Mozart canon was a change in taste admitting contrivance and fantasy. First performance: Munich, 13 Jan 1775.

Finzi, Gerald (Raphael) (b. London, 14 Jul 1901; d. Oxford, 27 Sep 1956). British composer, especially admired for his quiet identification with English verse in songs and larger works, the sign, perhaps, of an Italian musical gene long nurtured in England, for an ancestor had immigrated from Italy in the 18th century. His private education included music lessons with Farrar (1914–16) and

with Bairstow in York (1917–22); he also studied with R.O. Morris (1925). In 1935 he moved with his wife to the country, seeking solitude, though he returned to London for war work (1941–5), during a time when he wrote little. His music was shaped by Elgarian pensiveness and Vaughan Williamsish pastoralism, but most of all by the poetry he loved and contemplated.

Stephen Banfield *Gerald Finzi* (1997)

Vocal orchestral: *Dies natalis* (Traherne), Op.8, s/t, str, 1926, 1938–9; *Intimations of Immortality* (Wordsworth), Op.29, t, ch, orch, 1936–8, 1949–50

Orchestral: Eclogue, F, Op.10, pf, str, 1920s, rev 1940s; Romance, E♭, Op.11, str, 1928; Prelude, F minor, Op.25, str, 1920s; Concerto, Op.31, cl, str, 1948–9; Cello Concerto, Op.40, 1951–5; etc.

Choral: *Lo, the full final sacrifice*, Op.26, 1946; 3 Anthems, Op.27, 1948–53; etc.

Song cycles: *Oh Fair to See*, Op.13, 1921–56; *A Young Man's Exhortation* (Hardy), Op.14, 1926–9; *Earth and Air and Rain* (Hardy), Op.15, 1928–32; *Before and After Summer* (Hardy), Op.16, 1938–49; *Let us Garlands Bring* (Shakespeare), Op.18, 1929–42; *Till Earth Outwears* (Hardy), Op.19, 1927–56; *To a Poet*, 1920s–48; *I Said to Love* (Hardy), 1928–56

Fioravanti, Valentino (b. Rome, 11 Sep 1764; d. Capua, 16 Jun 1837). Italian composer, admired by Rossini as a master of opera buffa. He studied in Rome and in Naples with Sala (1779–81). After his biggest success, *Le cantatrici villane* (Naples, 1799), he worked in Lisbon and Paris (1807) before returning to his career in Italy. In 1816 he became chapelmaster at the Sistine Chapel, and from 1824 concentrated on sacred music. His son Vincenzo (1799–1877) was also an opera buffa composer.

fioritura (It., flowering). Melodic ornamentation, especially vocal.

fipple flute. Flute blown at one end through a fipple: a plug directing the breath into a slit and against an edge. Examples include the recorder and varieties of whistle.

Fire. Name given to Haydn's Symphony No.59.

Firebird, The (*L'Oiseau de feu, Zhar-ptitsa*). Ballet score by Stravinsky for choreography by Fokine, commissioned by Diaghilev. The magical Firebird helps Prince Ivan to save his princess from a wizard monster, with help also from Russian folk music, Rimsky-Korsakov and some Scriabin in what was Stravinsky's first major work. He created a suite in 1911, another for reduced orchestra in 1919, and again another in 1945. First performance: Paris, 25 Jun 1910.

Fires of London, The. Group based on the personnel of *Pierrot lunaire* plus percussionist, founded in 1967 by Davies and Birtwistle as the Pierrot Players, and renamed in 1970 with Davies as sole music director, active until 1987. The repertory included over 50 theatre pieces, concert works and arrangements by Davies, as well as compositions by Carter (*Triple Duo*) and others.

fireworks. Perhaps the only other abstract time-based art, fireworks have often been combined with music, most notably on the occasion of Handel's MUSIC FOR THE ROYAL FIREWORKS. There are pieces descriptive of fireworks by Debussy, Stravinsky and Knussen.

first. Principal; e.g. the first clarinet in an orchestra leads the others. The first violins normally have a higher and more prominent part in orchestral music than the seconds.

first inversion. Vertical rearrangement of a triad so that the minor third is in the bass, e.g. E–G–C.

first subject. Main theme at the start of a sonata-form exposition, in the tonic key.

Fis (Ger.). F$\sharp$. Also *Fisis* (F×).

Fischer, Annie (b. Budapest, 5 Jul 1914; d. Budapest, 10 Apr 1995). Hungarian pianist of formidable moral and intellectual command, especially in Mozart and Beethoven. She studied at the Liszt Academy with Arnold Székely and Dohnányi, made her debut at eight and began an international career at 12. She recorded reluctantly.

Fischer, Edwin (b. Basle, 6 Oct 1886; d. Zurich, 24 Jan 1960). Swiss pianist, revered for his Romantic strength and deep care in Bach, Mozart, Beethoven and Brahms. He studied at the Basle Conservatory with Hans Huber and in Berlin with Krause, and became himself a valued mentor and teacher – for Brendel, among others.

Fischer, Johann Caspar Ferdinand (b. *c*.1670; d. Rastatt, 27 Mar 1746). German composer, proponent of the French (Lullian) style. He seems to have spent his entire career in service to the Baden court, which was enamoured of things French. His works include suites for strings and for keyboard, church music and a collection of 20 organ preludes and fugues published as *Ariadne musica neo-organoedum*, an influence on Bach's '48'.

Fischer, Johann Christian (b. Freiburg, 1733; buried London, 3 May 1800). German oboist and composer, resident in London by 1768. He studied with Alessandro Besozzi in Turin and appeared widely before settling in London, where he played for the Bach–Abel concerts. His marriage in 1780 to a daughter of Gainsborough was brief. Mozart, who heard him, wrote variations on the rondo from the first of his 10 published concertos for oboe or flute.

Fischer-Dieskau, Dietrich (b. Berlin, 28 May 1925). German baritone, the prime male lieder singer for a generation brought up on his many LP records. After war service (he was taken prisoner in Italy) he resumed his studies and made his debuts as an oratorio soloist (*Ein Deutsches Requiem*, Freiburg, 1947), opera singer (Posa in *Don Carlos*, Berlin, 1948) and lieder artist (Leipzig, 1948). By the early 1950s his career was international, and by the mid-1970s he had recorded a huge repertory that embraced over a thousand songs as well as operatic roles from Mozart to the 20th century, all graced by his rounded tone, smooth phrasing and love of words (of words above character). He sought out the unusual (Liszt and Schoenberg songs, parts in operas by Busoni and Hindemith), and encouraged composers including Henze, Britten and Reimann to write for him. After retiring, at the end of 1992, he devoted himself to teaching, writing and conducting.

Dietrich Fischer-Dieskau *Echoes of a Lifetime* (1989)

Fischietti, Domenico (b. Naples, *c*.1725; d. ?Salzburg, after 1810). Italian composer, who won international success with four operas to Goldoni librettos created in Venice in 1754–8. The son of a Neapolitan composer, he studied with Leo and Durante at the San Onofrio conservatory and spent his long, less illustrious later career mostly in Prague, Dresden and Salzburg (from 1772).

fischietto (It., pl. *fischietti*). Whistle.

Fisher, John Abraham (b. Dunstable or London, 1744; d. Dublin or London, May/Jun 1806). British violinist and composer of theatre music, songs for pleasure gardens and three violin concertos. A pupil of Pinto, he began his career as a London theatre musician in 1763 and was leader at Covent Garden (*c*.1769–78). He spent much of the next decade in travels from Russia to Ireland, and was married to Nancy STORACE (1783–4).

Fistelstimme (Ger.). Falsetto.

fistula (medieval–Renaissance Lat.). Pipe, flute.

Fitelberg. Polish musicians, father and son.

(1) **Grzegorz** (b. Dynaburg, Latvia, 18 Oct 1879; d. Katowice, 10 Jun 1953). Conductor. He studied at the Warsaw Conservatory and began his career as a violinist and composer, becoming a fellow member with Szymanowski of Young Poland in Music. From 1908, when he was made chief conductor of the Warsaw Philharmonic, he concentrated on conducting.

(2) **Jerzy** (b. Warsaw, 20 May 1903; d. New York, 25 Apr 1951). Composer, of neoclassical music developing from a Hindemithian to a Parisian–Polish style as he travelled from Berlin, where he stayed on after his 1922–6 studies with Schreker, to Paris (1933–9) and New York (from 1940). His works include concertos and five quartets.

Fitzenhagen, (Karl Friedrich) Wilhelm (b. Seesen, 15 Sep 1848; d. Moscow, 14 Feb 1890). German cellist, destined performer of his friend Tchaikovsky's Variations on a Rococo Theme. A professional musician's son, he began his career in Dresden in 1868 and two years later took a post at the Moscow Conservatory.

Fitzwilliam Virginal Book. Volume copied by the amateur musician Francis Tregian in 1609–19 and lodged in the Fitzwilliam Museum, Cambridge. It contains pieces by Byrd, Bull, Farnaby, etc.

Five, The. See MIGHTY HANDFUL.

five–three chord. Major or minor triad in root position – e.g. C–E–G, reading from the bottom. The chord consists of a fifth and a third over its lowest note, and is written in figured bass $\frac{5}{3}$.

fixed forms. See FORMES FIXES.

fl. Abbreviation for flute.

Flackton, William (baptized Canterbury, Mar 1709; d. Canterbury, 5 Jan 1798). British composer, notably of four viola sonatas in late Baroque style (published 1770). He was a bricklayer's son and, with his brother, a bookseller-stationer.

flageolet. Simple recorder, with from four to six holes, popular in the later 17th and 18th centuries. Handel and Rameau wrote for it.

flageolet tone. Natural HARMONIC on a string instrument, so called because its purity of sound recalls the flageolet.

Flagstad, Kirsten (Malfrid) (b. Hamar, 12 Jul 1895; d. Oslo, 7 Dec 1962). Norwegian soprano, one of the great Wagner singers. Born into a musical family, she had a varied career in Scandinavia before being spotted for Bayreuth, where she made her debut in 1933. At once grand and intimate, her singing was well suited to Wagner's great heroines, and in 1935 she sang Sieglinde, Isolde and Brünnhilde at the Met. She gave the première of Strauss's Four Last Songs, and retired from the stage after a run of performances as Purcell's Dido in London (1952–3), though she went on recording.

flam. Figure on the side drum, a grace note into a beat. It may be combined with the PARADIDDLE in a flam paradiddle.

flamenco. Term, of uncertain origin, for traditional music from the southern Spanish province of Andalusia.

flat. Lowered in pitch, normally by a semitone. Thus E♭ (to use the flat sign) is a semitone below E; a further semitone flattening produces E double flat (E♭♭). See also ACCIDENTAL.

flat key. Key with a flat or flats in its signature, e.g. A♭ major and F minor, both of which have four flats.

flatten. Lower in pitch, usually by a semitone. Thus a flattened fifth is a diminished fifth.

Flatterzunge (Ger.). FLUTTERTONGUE.

flat trumpet. English SLIDE TRUMPET, so called because it could play in flat keys. Purcell used four such instruments in his funeral music for Mary II.

flautando, flautato (It., flute-like). Instruction commonest in violin music, implying light bowing over the end of the fingerboard to produce sound of flute-like purity.

flautist (UK). Flute player, flutist (US).

flauto (It., pl. *flauti*). Flute. Hence *flauto traverso* (transverse flute, i.e. the regular instrument), *flauto a becco* or *flauto dolce* (recorder), etc.

Flavio. Opera by Handel to Haym's adaptation of an Italian libretto. Oddly set in a Britain ruled by Flavio (alto castrato), king of Lombardy, the action presents trials to the noble lovers, Emilia (soprano) and Guido (alto castrato), and the less elevated Teodata (contralto) and Vitige (soprano). First performance: London, 14 May 1723.

flebile (It.). Mournful.

Flecha, Mateo (b. Prades, ?1481; d. Poblet, ?1553). Spanish composer, notably of *ensaladas* (salads of popular melodies and other music, set out for four voices). These were posthumously published by his nephew, also Mateo (*c*.1530–1604), a musician-friar who spent much of his adult life at the Austrian court, having brought out a book of madrigals in 1568.

Fledermaus, Die (The Bat). Operetta by Johann Strauss II to a libretto by Carl Haffner and Richard Genée after Meilhac and Halévy. The bat was Falke (baritone), dressed as such and left by Eisenstein (tenor) to walk home after a masked ball. This is his jovial revenge: with the help of another masked ball, at the home of Prince Orlofsky (mezzosoprano), and further more unlikely circumstances, he exposes extramarital improprieties both on Eisenstein's part and on that of his wife Rosalinde (soprano). All ends happily, with the waltz and champagne flowing. First performance: Vienna, 5 Apr 1874.

Fleming, Renée (b. Indiana, Pa., 14 Feb 1959). US soprano, whose radiant warmth, versatile musicianship and engaging personality made her one of the opera stars of the late 20th century and early 21st. She studied at Eastman, at Juilliard and with Schwarzkopf in Frankfurt, making her debut as Konstanze in *Entführung* at the Salzburg Landestheater (1986). Her New York City Opera debut as Mimì (1989) was swiftly followed by an international career, especially singing Strauss and US music.

Flesch, Carl (b. Moson, 9 Oct 1873; d. Lucerne, 14 Nov 1944). Hungarian violinist and distinguished teacher, memorialized in a biennial violin competition run by the Guildhall School (1945–92).

flessibile (It.). Flexible.

flexatone. Percussion instrument; shaking it causes two wooden balls, one on either side, to strike a metal blade subject to thumb pressure, which thereby can produce spooky glissando effects. Patented in 1922–4, it was soon used by Honegger (*Antigone*) and Schoenberg (Variations Op.31).

flicorno (It.). Brass instrument, as in *flicorno soprano* (flugelhorn), *flicorno baritono* (tenor tuba).

fliegende Holländer, Der (The Flying Dutchman). Opera by Wagner to his own libretto after Heine. The Dutchman (bass-baritone), condemned to wander the seas until he can be redeemed by love, lands in Norway and is welcomed by Daland (bass) as a potential match for his daughter, Senta (soprano). She readily agrees: she has longed for this. Erik (tenor) protests that she had promised herself to him, and the Dutchman releases her and goes. But she plunges after him from the clifftop, and in death achieves both union with and redemption for him. Numbers include the song of the Steersman (tenor), Senta's Ballad and Erik's Dream Narration. Wagner's original plan to present the three acts continuously was first followed at Bayreuth in 1901 and has become normal. First performance: Dresden, 2 Jan 1843.

fliessend (Ger.). Flowing.

Flight of the Bumblebee, The. Episode in Rimsky-Korsakov's *The* TALE OF TSAR SALTAN, much arranged.

Flonzaley Quartet. US quartet founded in 1902 as a house ensemble by Edward J. De Coppet and named after his Swiss summer home. The group also gave public concerts and made some of the first quartet recordings, before disbanding in 1928.

Flood, The. 'Musical play' by Stravinsky for television, with words from Genesis and English miracle plays, telling the Noah story in dance, sung and spoken drama, and narration. First performance: CBS TV, 14 Jun 1962.

Floquet, Etienne Joseph (b. Aix-en-Provence, 23 Nov 1748; d. Paris, 10 May 1785). French composer, who was worsted in rivalry with Gluck during his career at the Paris Opera (1773–83). He started out as a choirboy and composer at Aix Cathedral, went to Paris in his late teens, and died perhaps from disappointment and indulgence.

Florence (Firenze). Italian city. The chief home of the Renaissance was musically distinguished by its 14th-century polyphonic songs (by Landini, etc.) and its development of opera under the Medici two centuries later. Opera theatres remained active – the Teatro della Pergola, opened in 1656, saw the premières of works by Vivaldi and Donizetti – but music was not again a Florentine priority until the 20th century, when Pizzetti and Dallapiccola were among composers working there and an annual festival, the MAGGIO MUSICALE, was founded.

Flöte (Ger., pl. *Flöten*). Flute.

Flotow, Friedrich (Adolf Ferdinand) Freiherr von (b. Teutendorf, near Neu-Sanitz, Mecklenburg-Schwerin, 27 Apr 1812; d. Darmstadt, 24 Jan 1883). German composer, whose fame rests almost entirely on his opera MARTHA (1847), influenced by the French music he heard in Paris as a student of Reicha at the Conservatoire (1828–30). He began his career back in Paris (1835–44), but from *Alessandro Stradella* (Hamburg, 1844) onwards his new works appeared mostly in the German world, where *Martha* remains in the repertory. Of the three much younger women he married after *Martha*, the first died soon after childbirth and the second he divorced to marry her sister. His other operas include scores written in collaboration, recycled or lost.

flourish. Fanfare; brief improvised introduction to an instrumental performance.

Floyd, Carlisle (Sessions) (b. Latta, S. Carolina, 11 Jun 1926). US composer, especially of operas in a conservative idiom. He studied with Bacon at Spartanburg (1943–5) and Syracuse University (1945–9), began teaching at Florida State University in 1947, and made his name with *Susannah* (Tallahassee, 1955), set in a Tennessee of hymns and folktunes. This work was presented by New York City Opera at the Brussels Exposition (1958) and staged by the Met (1999). His later operas include *Of Mice and Men* (Seattle, 1970) and others given by Houston Grand Opera after his move to the city in 1976.

flue. Kind of organ pipe made like a FIPPLE FLUTE, with air channelled to strike a lip, as distinct from the reed type. Hence 'flue-work' (the totality of stops involving this principle).

Flügel (Ger., wing, pl. *Flügel*). Grand piano.

flugelhorn. Bugle in B♭, derived from an early 18th-century German hunting instrument played by the Flügelmeister (master of the wings of the hunt). It was widely adopted by bands in the mid 19th century and has been used occasionally by classical composers (e.g. Stravinsky in *Threni*) as a warmer alternative to the trumpet.

flüssig (Ger.). Flowing.

flute (Fr. *flûte*; Ger. *Flöte*; It. *flauto*). Wind instrument sounded by air striking a sharp edge. The air may be directed by the players' lips, as in the orchestral flute, or by a built-in channel, as in the RECORDER and other kinds of FIPPLE FLUTE. Instruments of both sorts are found all over the world (see OCARINA; PANPIPES; SHAKUHACHI; WHISTLE).

Though a member of the woodwind family, the modern orchestral flute is normally of base metal or silver – or, for flamboyant soloists, gold or platinum. It is about 26 inches (66cm) long and made in three sections, with some looseness between the head (with the mouth-hole) and middle joints to allow tuning. The Boehm design of keywork, long universal, provides a range from middle C up through three octaves and more for the standard flute. Other members of the family include the PICCOLO (half-sized and so pitched an octave above), ALTO FLUTE (a fourth below) and BASS FLUTE (an octave below), all of which are transposing instruments, notated as if they were instruments of standard size: thus the piccolo sounds an octave higher than written, etc. Flutes and piccolos before the 20th century were commonly made of boxwood, ivory or ebony, providing a more rounded, less brilliant sound, which many players prefer for music of the 18th and even 19th centuries.

Until the second half of the 18th century the commonest flute was the recorder, and so such terms as 'transverse flute' or 'German flute' were necessary for the side-blown, horizontally held instrument. This instrument has, however, a history of three millennia in China and was known in the Roman world. Its spread in the Renaissance may indeed have come by way of Germany, and certainly by the early 16th century it was known throughout Europe; some instruments survive from that period. It then went into a decline, to re-emerge alongside and soon surpass the recorder in the music of Bach, Handel, Rameau and Vivaldi. By the Classical period it had ousted the recorder completely and become a normal orchestral instrument, as a pair or singleton. Mozart allegedly disliked the instrument, though he wrote quartets and concertos for it, not to mention an opera (*Die Zauberflöte*).

The Romantic period left the instrument with little important repertory, but the flute solo at the start of Debussy's *Prélude à 'L'Après-midi d'un faune'* ushered in a new age. Not only more important in the modern orchestra, the flute also drew level with the clarinet in the strength of its concertante, chamber and solo repertory, including works by Debussy, Varèse, Boulez, Berio and Ferneyhough that vastly extended its range of colour and articulation.

Ardal Powell *The Flute* (2002)

flûte (Fr.). Flute. Also *flûte à bec* (recorder).

flûte d'amour. Flute in A, a minor third below the standard instrument. Rare.

flute quartet. Group of instruments comprising flute plus string trio (vn, va, vc), or work for such a line-up. There are examples by Mozart and Tanada.

fluttertongue. Roll of the tongue while playing a wind instrument, as if sounding the letter 'R', producing a burrish sound. The technique is frequent in music since Strauss and Mahler.

Fluxus (Lat., discharge). Artistic movement founded by George Maciunas (1931–78) to produce events, objects and publications challenging bourgeois art. Active principally in Germany and New York, the movement was at its peak in the early 1960s, when La Monte Young was among the composers involved.

Flying Dutchman, The. See *Der* FLIEGENDE HOLLÄNDER.

Foerster, Josef Bohuslav (b. Prague, 30 Dec 1859; d. Vestec, near Stará Boleslav, 29 May 1951). Czech composer, adherent of the national tradition established by Smetana, Dvořák and Fibich. The son and nephew of church musicians, he studied at the Prague Organ School (1879–82) and in 1888 married the soprano Berta Lautererová, whose career took the couple to Hamburg (1893–1903) and Vienna (1903–18). They then returned to Prague, where he taught at the conservatory (1919–31). His large output includes five symphonies, orchestral suites (*Cyrano de Bergerac*, Op.55, 1903; *From Shakespeare*, Op.76, 1908–9), operas and much choral music.

Fokker, Adriaan Daniel (b. Buitenzorg, now Bogar, Java, 17 Aug 1887; d. Beckenbergen, 24 Sep 1972). Dutch physicist, diverted to tuning during the Second World War. He built an organ in Christiaan Huygen's 31-interval equal temperament.

folia. Name attached to two related melodic-harmonic outlines that were popular subjects for variations in the Baroque period. The later one has particularly notable progeny, including works by Corelli, Alessandro Scarlatti, J.S. and C.P.E. Bach, and Rachmaninoff (Corelli Variations).

folk music. 19th-century term loaded with 19th-century values. Folk music is defined with reference to Western culture, as the alternative to classical music, as the province of untrained musicians and as an essentially national phenomenon. Though thus given inferior standing, folk music was always allowed a role as a source of material, especially melodic features or dance rhythms, and recourse to folk music became a primary activity for nationalist composers from Chopin to Bartók. As local music, communicated orally and therefore limited in its spread, and as music embedded in rural life, folk music virtually disappeared from European villages during the first half of the 20th century, with improvements in transport, greater literacy, the arrival of radio and recording, and the emptying of the countryside. It was reborn, transfigured, as a medium for professional singers and composers, modelling their work on what had been collected from country people during the great age of folksong gathering, from the late 19th century to the Second World War. See also ETHNOMUSICOLOGY.

Fomin, Yevstigney (Ipatovich) (b. St Petersburg, 16 Aug 1761; d. St Petersburg, 28 Apr 1800). Russian composer, a pioneer of Russian opera. He studied at the Academy of Fine Arts in St Petersburg (1767–82) and in Bologna with Martini. Returning to St Petersburg in 1786, he wrote his first opera that year: *Boyeslayevich, the Novgorod Bogatyr*, to a libretto by Catherine II. Later works include the comic opera *The Americans* (1788; St Petersburg, 1800) and the melodrama *Orpheus and Eurydice* (St Petersburg, 1792).

Fontainebleau. Royal château south of Paris, where opera was performed under Louis XV and Louis XVI, and the dependent district, where Boulanger taught at the American Conservatory.

Fontana, Giovanni Battista (b. Brescia; d. Padua, ?1630). Italian composer known only for a volume of sonatas published in 1641, containing some of the earliest such works for solo violin and continuo.

Fontane di Roma (Roman Fountains). Symphonic poem by Respighi. The four fountains heard in succession are the Valle Giulia at dawn, the Tritone in the morning, the Trevi at midday and the Villa Medici at sunset. First performance: Rome, 11 Mar 1917.

Fontanelli, Alfonso (b. Reggio Emilia, 15 Feb 1557; d. Rome, 11 Feb 1622). Italian composer, acquainted with Gesualdo and the author of intense madrigals on a miniature scale. Of noble birth, he had joined the Ferrarese court by 1586 and was then associated with other members of the ruling d'Este family in Modena (1598–1601, being banished on a charge of murder) and Rome (1602–8, and for later periods).

Fontei, Nicolò (b. Orciano di Pesaro; d. Verona or Venice, 1647 or later). Italian organist-composer, active largely in Venice, where he published songs to words by Giulio Strozzi (1635–6) and church music.

foot. Measure of register, in terms of the length of an open pipe that would sound a C in that region. Eight-foot (approximately two octaves below middle C) is taken as the norm. Double basses may be described as 16-foot instruments, sounding an octave lower than written; a two-foot organ stop will sound two octaves higher than the given notation.

Foote, Arthur (William) (b. Salem, Mass., 5 Mar 1853; d. Boston, 8 Apr 1937). US composer, chiefly of chamber music (Nocturne and Scherzo for flute and string quartet, 1918) and songs. He studied with Paine at Harvard (1870–75), where he received the first master's degree in music accorded by a US university. Having thus completed his education without the usual period in Germany, he lived in Boston as a piano teacher, organist and composer.

Foppa, Giuseppe (Maria) (b. Venice, 12 Jul 1760; d. Venice, 1845). Italian librettist, who at the height of his career (1792–1815), was writing several comedies a year for composers including Mayr and Rossini, besides also producing plays, novels and poetry.

Force of Destiny, The. See *La* FORZA DEL DESTINO.

Ford, Thomas (buried London, 17 Nov 1648). English composer and viol player, author of songs, anthems and consort music. He was in service to Prince Henry from 1611 and subsequently to Charles, as Prince of Wales and king.

foreground. In Schenkerian analysis the main substance of a piece of music, as directly heard (though ignoring features regarded as ornamental), distinct from the BACKGROUND.

Forelle, Die. See TROUT.

Forest, John (b. *c.*1365–70; d. 25 Mar 1446). English composer in a style close to Power, likely the 'Forest' to whom works are ascribed in the Old Hall manuscript and other sources. If this is, indeed, the man, he was a member of Lincoln College, Oxford, and ended his distinguished church career as Dean of Wells (1425–46).

forgery. See SPURIOUS WORK.

Forkel, Johann Nikolaus (b. Meeder, near Coburg, 22 Feb 1749; d. Göttingen, 20 Mar 1818). German scholar, who matriculated at Göttingen University in 1769 and spent the rest of his life there as organist, teacher and concert director, while applying new standards in music history, biography (of Bach, 1802) and bibliography.

forlane (Fr., It. *forlana*). Lively dance, usually in 6/4 or 6/8, imported to France from Italy apparently by Campra (*L'Europe galante*, 1697) and reappearing in stage works and keyboard pieces for half a century: there are examples by Rameau and Couperin and also Bach. The form was revived by Chausson (*Quelques danses*) and Ravel (*Le Tombeau de Couperin*).

form. Shape of a phrase, a section, a movement, a composition. 'Form', suggesting extension in space, is a term not entirely appropriate for music, which unfolds in time; 'growth' or 'reach' might be better. All music has to grow or reach towards its ending, and many questions of form derive from how the close is to be achieved, how it may be delayed, and how it can be made satisfactory (even when abrupt) – questions that concern the performer as much as the composer. Of course, openings are important too – openings that intimate short forms or long ones (Beethoven being full of examples of both). As soon as a piece of music begins it is in process, moving with a formal purpose distinct from its tempo, though related – for example, slow movements tend to be long, as if the same consequences (probably of harmony) were limiting both speed and conclusion.

All music has form. Matters of shaping have always had to be considered by performers, improvisers and composers. But only some music displays a particular form, one of the forms that have been categorized. Of these there are remarkably few: the ABA form of repetition after a contrasting passage (the basis also of rondo form), sonata form, variations and fugue. Other 'forms' are more definitions of texture (e.g. canon) or genre (scherzo) – musical qualities with which form is entangled, as indeed it is with rhythm and harmony.

Prescribed forms held sway from the late 17th century to the early 20th, appealing to a rationalist wish for music that would follow rules, music in which listeners could confidently know where they were, even if composers would often delight in tricking or confusing that confidence. The doctrine of music appreciation became largely a study of form, at the risk of making musical experience a matter of recognition rather than communication. But the outlines of familiar form never told the whole story. By no means is sonata form always the same, from Haydn to Mahler; on the contrary, the scale, the proportions and the twists and turns of form within the regular pattern make each instance unique. Acknowledgement of that, coming with Debussy, encouraged composers to abandon the archetypes, though certain formal notions – of development and resolution, of return – seem to be deeply ingrained in what we expect music to be.

formalism. Term from Russian aesthetics, signifying a belief in art as self-sufficient. It became a standard official criticism of Shostakovich, Prokofiev and others in the 1930s and 1940s.

formant. (1) The variation of amplitude with frequency in any element concerned in the production and transmission of sound: a voice, an instrument, an electronic system, an auditorium. Such variation – such favouring of particular frequencies or bands of frequencies over others – strongly affects timbre, and is most often described as the 'formant spectrum' or 'formant characteristic'.

(2) Term applied by Boulez to mobile compositions in preference to 'movement', to avoid the implication of directedness. Thus he planned his Third Piano Sonata in five formants, playable in different orders.

formation. Group of instruments.

Formé, Nicolas (b. Paris, 26 Apr 1567; d. Paris, 27 May 1638). French composer and church musician. He was a member of the royal chapel from 1592 and Du Caurroy's successor there as composer. Said to have been so devoted to music that hearing a work of his own caused him to faint, he published a mass and two motets near the end of his life. There also survives a set of *Magnificat* settings in the eight modes.

formes fixes (Fr., fixed forms). The set forms of late medieval French song, especially ballade, rondeau and virelai.

formula (Ger. *Formel*). Stockhausen's term for the basic melody of one of his compositions from *Mantra* onwards, exemplifying a serial-variational

technique adumbrated in his earlier piece entitled *Formel*.

Forqueray. Father and son French viol players and composers.

(1) **Antoine** (b. Paris, 1671/2; d. Mantes, 28 Jun 1745). Having played before Louis XIV as a boy in 1682, he held a royal appointment from 1689.

(2) **Jean-Baptiste** (b. Paris, 3 Apr 1699; d. Paris, Aug 1782). Son of Antoine. His parents separated when he was 10, and his childhood was unhappy: it seems his father was jealous of his gifts. If, nevertheless, he devoted his only published volume (1747) largely to his father's pieces – 29 of them, against three of his own – he seems to have altered them drastically, giving the whole French viol tradition its final glory. His pupils included the Prussian prince Friedrich Wilhelm, later cellist and king.

Forster, Christoph (Heinrich) (b. Bibra, Thuringia, 30 Nov 1693; d. Rudolstadt, ?5/6 Dec 1745). German composer, who is specially remembered for a horn concerto in E♭. He studied with Heinichen in Weissenfels and Georg Friedrich Kauffmann in Merseburg, where he joined the court musical establishment. In 1743 he moved to the Rudolstadt court.

forte (It.). Loud, strong. Dynamic marking, abbreviated *f*.

Forte, Allen (b. Portland, Oreg., 23 Dec 1926). US theorist, analyst of atonal works by Schoenberg, Scriabin and others as built from sets (*The Structure of Atonal Music*, 1973). He studied at Columbia and has taught at Yale since 1959.

fortepiano. Early alternative name for the pianoforte, now usually implying an 18th-century or early-19th-century instrument (or reproduction of such).

fortissimo (It.). Very loud. Dynamic marking, the common abbreviations *ff* and *fff* allowing two degrees.

Fortner, Wolfgang (b. Leipzig, 12 Oct 1907; d. Heidelberg, 5 Sep 1987). German composer and teacher, who emerged after 1945 as a powerful force for consolidation (on the basis of the Bach tradition in which he had grown up) and regeneration (by means especially of serialism). He studied with the Reger pupil Hermann Grabner at the Leipzig Conservatory and taught at institutions in Heidelberg (1931–53), Detmold (1954–7) and Freiburg (1957–73), as well as at Darmstadt (from 1946), where Henze was among his pupils. Best known for his operas (*Die Bluthochzeit*, 1956; *Don Perlimplin*, 1962; *Elisabeth Tudor*, 1972), he also wrote orchestral pieces, songs and chamber music.

Förtsch, Johann Philipp (baptized Wertheim am Main, 14 May 1652; d. Eutin, near Lübeck, 14 Dec 1732). German composer, especially of operas for Hamburg (1684–90) and church cantatas probably from the same period, all lost. From 1692, as court doctor to the Bishop of Lübeck, he concentrated on medicine and politics.

Fortspinnung (Ger.). Term introduced by Wilhelm Fischer (1915) for the spinning-out of music from a small motif, repeated or transformed.

Fortuna desperata. Italian song, among the most popular of the Renaissance to judge from the number of polyphonic settings – by Agricola, Isaac, Busnois (possibly the tune's composer), Senfl, Greiter, Johannes Martini, etc. – and masses based on it, notably by Obrecht and Josquin.

Forty-Eight, The. See *Das* WOHLTEMPERIRTE CLAVIER.

forza del destino, La (The Force of Destiny). Opera by Verdi to a libretto by Piave after a play by Angel de Saavedra, Duke of Rigas. Leonora (soprano) elopes with Alvaro (tenor). Her brother Carlo (baritone), seeking her, meets a gypsy, Preziosilla (mezzo-soprano), who predicts a dismal future for him. Meanwhile, Leonora and Alvaro have become separated; she enters a monastery, and he bizarrely becomes Carlo's comrade. The ending, five years later, is different in the original and revised versions, but in both Carlo and Leonora die. Among the major numbers are arias for Leonora ('Me pellegrina ed orfana'; 'Madre, pietosa Vergine'; 'La Vergine degli angeli'; 'Pace, pace, mio Dio!') and Alvaro ('Oh, tu che in seno'), and duets for Alvaro and Carlo ('Solenne in quest'ora' and 'Col sangue sol cancellasi – Le minaccie'). First performance: St Petersburg, 10 Nov 1862; rev Milan, 27 Feb 1869.

forzando, forzato (It.). Forcing, forced, implying a forceful attack on a single note or chord, abbreviated *fz*.

Foss, Lukas (b. Berlin, 15 Aug 1922). German–US composer of mercurial interests and career, his works lightly quirky or humorous. He moved with his family to Paris (1933–7) and the USA, where he completed his training as a composer at Curtis (with Rosario Scalero and Thompson) and Yale (with Hindemith, 1939–40). Conducting studies with Koussevitzky at Tanglewood (1939–43) led to a post as pianist with the Boston Symphony (1944–50), during which time he established himself as a neoclassicist. While teaching at UCLA (1953–63) he opened his range, founding an improvisation quartet of clarinet, cello, piano and percussion (1957); works of this period include *Echoi* (for the quartet, 1961–3) and *Time Cycle* (for soprano with orchestra or the quartet, 1959–60). He was subsequently music director of the Buffalo Philharmonic (1963–70), since when he has lived in New York as a composer and teacher.

Foster, Stephen (Collins) (b. Lawrenceville, Penn., 4 July 1826; d. New York, 13 Jan 1864). US composer of popular songs ('Camptown Races', 'Gentle Annie', 'Jeanie with the light brown hair', 'My old Kentucky home', 'Oh! Susanna', 'Old folks at home').

Foucquet, Pierre-Claude (b. Paris, 1694/5; d. Paris, 13 Feb 1772). French organist-composer, who is known for three books of harpsichord pieces. Born into a family of organists, he acquired posts held by his grandfather (Antoine, d. 1708), father (Pierre, d. 1734/5) and uncle (Antoine), besides succeeding Dagincour at the royal chapel.

fouet (Fr.). Whip.

Foulds, John (Herbert) (b. Manchester, 2 Nov 1880; d. Calcutta, 24 Apr 1939). British composer of Busoni-like openness. The son of a bassoonist in the Hallé, he was largely self-taught and played in the orchestra himself as a cellist (1900–6). After that he supported himself by writing light music (*Keltic Lament*, 1911) while ranging from big public statement (*A World Requiem*, 1919–21, annually performed as a British Legion commemoration in the Albert Hall in the years 1923–6) to more private and innovatory music (*Quartetto intimo*). In 1935 he went to India, where the next year he took a radio post as director of European music. An opportunity to explore matters in which he had long been interested – Indian culture, microtones – was cut short by cholera.

Malcolm MacDonald *John Foulds* (1975)

fountains. Fine topic for displays of piano virtuosity, the classic examples being Liszt's *Les jeux d'eau à la Villa d'Este* and Ravel's *Jeux d'eau*.

Four Last Songs. See VIER LETZTE LIEDER.

Fournier, Pierre (Léon Marie) (b. Paris, 24 Jun

1906; d. Geneva, 8 Jan 1986). French cellist, who trained at the Paris Conservatoire and was admired for his classically elegant style in solo work and chamber music.

Four Saints in Three Acts. Opera by Virgil Thomson to a libretto by Gertrude Stein. There are, in fact, four acts, many more saints and a great many further absurdities. First performance: Hartford, Conn., 8 Feb 1934.

Four Sea Interludes. Suite of orchestral excerpts from PETER GRIMES: *Dawn*, *Sunday Morning*, *Moonlight* and *Storm*.

Four Seasons. See *Le* QUATTRO STAGIONI.

Four Serious Songs. See VIER ERNSTE GESÄNGE.

Four Temperaments, The. Ballet score by Hindemith commissioned by Balanchine, who wanted something he could also play at home with friends: hence the scoring for piano and strings. The full title is Theme with Four Variations 'The Four Temperaments', the work being based on the medieval and perhaps older notion of a quaternity of human types: melancholic (gloomy), sanguine (wildly passionate), phlegmatic (passive) and choleric (angry), to give them their traditional names, in the Hindemith–Balanchine order. First performance: New York, 20 Nov 1946.

There are also works on the topic by Nielsen (Second Symphony, with movements choleric, phlegmatic, melancholic and sanguine) and Simpson.

fourth (1) Note in fourth position in a diatonic system, e.g. F in C major.

(2) Interval between that note and the tonic. A perfect fourth comprises five semitones (e.g. C–F), a diminished fourth four (e.g. C–F♭, enharmonically a major third). Chromatic alteration can produce an augmented fourth (e.g. C–F♯).

Fox, Christopher (b. York, 10 Mar 1955). British composer, whose suspicion of subjectivity has drawn him to German and US avant-gardes. He studied with Hugh Wood at Liverpool University and Harvey at Southampton, and has taught at Darmstadt (1984–94) and Huddersfield University (from 1994).

foxtrot. Duple-time dance of ragtime origin, popular from c.1910 to the Second World War.

FRAM. Fellow of the Royal Academy of Music.

frame drum. Kind of drum with one membrane (or two) stretched over a frame, e.g. the tambourine.

Françaix, Jean (b. Le Mans, 23 May 1912; d. Paris, 25 Sep 1997). French composer, master of the suavely French, in music proceeding from Ravel and Poulenc. Both parents were teachers at the conservatory in Le Mans, and he was a published composer by his late teens, when he was studying in Paris with Isidor Philipp (at the Conservatoire) and Boulanger. Immediately appreciated abroad for the freshness of his music, he gained a German publisher (Schott) and began his career of consistent, prolific contribution to all genres. Specially valued by performers are his many concertos and chamber pieces, notably those with wind interest.

Orchestral: Piano Concertino, 1932; *L'Horloge de Flore*, ob, orch, 1959; etc.

Chamber: *Petit quatuor*, sax qt, 1935; Divertissement, bn, str qnt, 1942; Divertissement, ob, cl, bn, 1947; Wind Quintet No.1, 1948; Sonatine, C, tpt, pf, 1952; Octet, cl, hn, bn, str qnt, 1972; *Tema con variazioni*, cl, pf, 1972; *Cinque piccoli duetti*, fl, hp, 1975; Clarinet Quintet, 1977; etc.

France. Certain musical qualities – delight in timbre, a lightly accented and fluid rhythm in keeping with the language, the appeal to nature (to natural sounds and resonance or to imagery drawn from the natural world), love of order – can be found as much in Rameau as in Boulez, though the French legacy is equally one of magnificent eccentrics, including Berlioz and Messiaen. Perhaps above all, French music is defined (and has defined itself) in opposition to that of the two great neighbouring cultures, German and Italian, even if there were times when it was powerfully influenced by one or the other. A continuous French operatic tradition began with the Italian-born Lully and continued to draw in foreign composers (Gluck, Rossini, Meyerbeer); resistant alternatives to the Beethoven symphony were discovered immediately by Berlioz and later by Debussy; and there are particular styles of song (Duparc, Fauré, Debussy) and organ music (Franck, Messiaen). French music is also unlike that of Italy and Germany in having been so much centred in the principal city, PARIS, whose commercial opportunities, and whose signal importance as a capital of the free and contrary (in politics as much as in aesthetics), have made it a beacon for composers not only from the rest of the country but from abroad. So the history of French music – and not only French music – is the history of music there. See also FRENCH REVOLUTION; MELODIE.

Martin Cooper *French Music from the Death of Berlioz to the Death of Fauré* (1951, ²1984); James R. Anthony *French Baroque Music* (1973, ³1997)

Francesca da Rimini. The love between her and her brother-in-law Paolo, inhabitants of Dante's *Inferno*, is the subject of a symphonic fantasy by Tchaikovsky and operas by Zandonai and Rachmaninoff.

Francesconi, Luca (b. Milan, 17 Mar 1956). Italian composer, who began his career as Berio's assistant (1981–4) and has pursued music of comparably rich reference. He studied earlier with Azio Corghi at the Milan Conservatory, where he himself came to teach. Among his works are *Quattro studi sulla memoria* for instrumental ensembles (1989–95).

Franchetti, Baron **Alberto** (b. Turin, 18 Sep 1860; d. Viareggio, 4 Aug 1942). Italian composer. A wealthy man, who studied in Turin, Venice and Germany (with Draeseke and Rheinberger), he wrote the quatercentenary opera *Cristoforo Colombo* (Genoa, 1892).

Franchomme, Auguste (Joseph) (b. Lille, 10 Apr 1808; d. Paris, 21 Jan 1884). French cellist-composer. He completed his training at the Paris Conservatoire (1825–6), where from 1846 he taught. A founder member of the Alard Quartet, he was also a friend of Chopin, who wrote a sonata for the two of them. His own works include a concerto and many pieces with accompaniment for piano or second cello.

Franck, César (Auguste Jean Guillaume Hubert) (b. Liège, 10 Dec 1822; d. Paris, 8 Nov 1890). French composer (though of Belgian nationality for much of his life and Walloon–German by ancestry). An extraordinary late developer, he was in his mid-50s before he brought his music of 'serene anxiety' (Georges Jean-Aubry) to ripeness.

That music – passionate, sublime and heavy with Wagnerian chromaticism – ended a journey that had begun with the frilly virtuosity his father expected of him as a pianist-composer. In attempting to fulfil those paternal dreams he studied at the conservatories of Liège (1830–35) and Paris (1837–42), his teachers at the latter including the piano professor Pierre Zimmermann and Reicha. At 23 he abandoned both his career as a pianist and his parents' home, supporting himself now as a teacher and organist and marrying two years later. Less and less did he feel the urge to compose, until he was appointed organist of Ste Clotilde in 1858 and made a new start with sacred and organ music. After that his

creative flow dried up again, to begin a recovery in the late 1860s as he acquired a circle of devoted pupils, of whom Duparc was among the first (joined later by d'Indy, Chausson, Dukas, Lekeu and others). In 1871 he took French nationality to become organ professor at the Conservatoire.

His great works all came later yet, beginning with his Piano Quintet (1878–9) and continuing with orchestral, chamber and keyboard compositions in which many features of style recur: a harmonic language that is firmly tonal while allowing sudden shifts or swerves to distant keys, a consistent density of thought and texture, and tripartite form (fast–slow–fast), with stirring themes transformed from one section or movement to another. This principle of cyclic form, like much else, he inherited from Liszt and Beethoven, and passed on not only to his many pupils but also to Debussy and Messiaen.

Laurence Davies *César Franck and his Circle* (1970)

Operas: *Hulda* (Charles Grandmougin), 1879–85, Monte Carlo, 1894; *Ghiselle*, 1888–90, orchestration completed by others, Monte Carlo, 1896; etc.

Orchestral: *Les* EOLIDES, 1875–6; *Le* CHASSEUR MAUDIT, 1882; *Les Djinns*, pf, orch, 1884; Symphonic Variations, pf, orch, 1885; Symphony, D minor, 1886–8; etc.

Choral orchestral: *Ruth* (Alexandre Guillemin), soli, ch, orch, 1843–6, rev 1871; *Rédemption* (symphonic poem; Edouard Blau), soli, women's ch, orch, 1871–4; *Les Béatitudes* (oratorio; Joséphine Colomb), soli, ch, orch, 1869–79; *Rébecca* (Paul Collin), soli, ch, orch, 1880–81; *Psalm 150*, ch, orch, 1883; *Psyché* (Louis de Fourcaud; see PSYCHE), 1887–8; etc.

Chamber: Piano Quintet, F minor, 1879; String Quartet, D, 1889; Violin Sonata, A, 1886

Organ: 6 Pieces, 1860–62 (*Fantaisie*, C; *Grande pièce symphonique*; Prelude, Fugue and Variation, B minor; *Pastorale*; *Prière*; *Final*); 3 Pieces, 1878 (*Fantaisie*, A; *Cantabile*; *Pièce héroïque*); 3 Chorales, E, B minor, A minor, 1890; etc.

Piano: Prelude, Chorale and Fugue, 1884; *Danse lente*, 1885; Prelude, Aria and Finale, 1886–7; etc.

Other works: PANIS ANGELICUS, t, org, hp, vc, db, 1872; choral pieces, songs

Franck, Melchior (b. Zittau, *c*.1579; d. Coburg, 1 Jun 1639). German composer, especially of unaccompanied Lutheran motets, of which he published over 600. A painter's son, he may have studied with Demantius and surely had contact with Hassler in Nuremberg, where he arrived as a teacher in 1601. In the winter of 1602–3 he became chapelmaster at the Coburg court. He also produced secular choral music and instrumental dances in abundance.

Franco, Hernando (b. Galizuela, near Alcántara in Extremadura, 1532; d. Mexico City, 28 Nov 1585). Spanish composer, chapelmaster of Mexico City Cathedral (1575–85) and author of motets and *Magnificat* settings.

Francoeur, François (b. Paris, 21 Sep 1698; d. Paris, 5 Aug 1787). French composer, collaborator with Rebel on works for the Paris Opera from 1726 until Rebel's death nearly half a century later. His bassist father Joseph and violinist brother Louis (1692–1745) played in the Opera orchestra, as did he and Rebel, who met there as teenage violinists. The two of them were appointed joint directors of the Opera in 1757 with a 30-year contract, which they forfeited after 10. Holding positions also with the king's chamber music (1727–76), he published violin sonatas and symphonies. In addition, he brought up his nephew, Louis-Joseph (1738–1804), who similarly served the Opera as composer and administrator.

Franco of Cologne (*fl.* second half of the 13th century). German theorist, who in his *Ars cantus mensurabilis* introduced a system of prescribing durations by means of note shapes: the ligatures that had previously been used for the system of modal rhythm. His system provided for the maxima (two longs), the perfect long (three breves), the imperfect long (two breves), the breve, the altered breve (of double length), the minor semibreve (one third of a breve) and the major semibreve (two-thirds of a breve). These durations – of 18, 12, 9, 6, 3, 2 and 1 units, with rests for all but the maxima – made possible the notation of a great range of rhythmic patterns, and Franco's system was, with modification, used internationally until replaced by the innovations of ARS NOVA.

Francs Juges, Les (The Secret Judges). Opera by Berlioz (1825–6), which he revised (1829) and revised (1833), but abandoned, publishing the overture as a concert piece.

Frankel, Benjamin (b. London, 31 Jan 1906; d. London, 12 Feb 1973). British composer, notably of eight symphonies (1958–71) in which he opened his Shostakovich–Bartók style to serialism. He scraped together an education in the public library, in Germany (1922) and as a jazz player, and earned his living from the early 1930s onwards as an orchestrator and film composer. His other works include a violin concerto (1951) and five quartets.

Frankfurt. German city, whose musical institu-tions include the Museum Concerts (founded 1808), the Hoch Conservatory (1878) and the Alte Oper (1880, ruined during the Second World War and reopened as a concert hall in 1981). A particularly illustrious and adventurous time came when Gielen was music director of both the museum and the opera (1977–87).

Frankfurt group. Collectivity that may refer, in a musical context, not to German philosophers but to British composers, including Balfour Gardiner, Quilter and Scott, all of whom studied there with Knorr in the 1890s.

Franz, Robert (b. Halle, 28 Jun 1815; d. Halle, 24 Oct 1892). German composer of songs and partsongs. He studied in Halle, largely by himself, and in Dessau with Friedrich Schneider (1835–7). In 1842 he became conductor of the Halle Singakademie, and the following year his first book of songs was published, at Schumann's behest. Liszt was another admirer and even wrote a book about him. In 1851 he began teaching at Halle University, but in 1867 he had to give up his appointments on account of deafness, although he went on composing. His 280 songs, nearly all published in sets of six, were, he said, 'not meant to arouse but to create peace and tranquillity'.

Frauenchor (Ger.). Women's choir.

Frauenliebe und -leben (Womanly Love and Life). Song cycle by Schumann to eight poems by Adelbert von Chamisso.

Frauenlob (b. ? Meissen area, 1250–60; d. Mainz, 29 Nov 1318). Minnesinger, late and complex exemplar of the tradition, venerated by the Meister-singer.

Frau ohne Schatten, Die (The Woman with no Shadow). Opera by Strauss to a libretto by Hofmannsthal. The title character is the Empress (soprano), guided by her Nurse (mezzo-soprano) to the everyday world in search of the shadow she needs to save her husband, the Emperor (tenor). Barak's Wife (soprano), awkwardly married to Barak (bass-baritone), ultimately resolves to keep her shadow (and thereby have children), and in doing so salvages both marriages. First performance: Vienna, 10 Oct 1919.

FRCM. Fellow of the Royal College of Music.

FRCO. Fellow of the Royal College of Organists.

Frederick II 'the Great', King of Prussia (b. Berlin,

24 Jan 1712; d. Sanssouci, Potsdam, 17 Aug 1786). German ruler and musician, whose splendid musical establishment included Quantz, Carl Heinrich Graun and C.P.E. Bach. He founded the opera house in Berlin (1742), wrote librettos (including *Montezuma* for Graun) and dabbled in composing sonatas and concertos for the flute, his own instrument, besides contributing the theme for J.S. Bach's *Musikalisches Opfer*.

free canon. Canon in which intervals may be chromatically adjusted to suit the harmony, a thing not allowed in 'strict canon'.

free counterpoint. Counterpoint overstepping the rules of the SPECIES.

Freedman, Harry (b. Łódź, 5 Apr 1922). Polish–Canadian composer, influenced by jazz and serialism. Taken to Alberta with his family when he was three, he studied as a painter, played jazz and trained in composition with Weinzweig at the conservatory in Toronto. His works include ballets, orchestral pieces and settings of Inuit poetry.

Freeman, Betty (b. Chicago, 2 Jun 1921). US patron, for whom patronage means friendship and keen critical engagement as well as financial support. The first composer to benefit, in the 1960s, was Partch, on whom she made a film. Since then she has been responsible for commissioning works by Cage, Reich, Birtwistle, Saariaho and many others and for photographing musicians.

freemasonry. System of ethical instruction and belief having roots in medieval Europe and legendary tendrils stretching back to ancient Egypt, Judaea and Mesopotamia. It struck a particular chord during the Enlightenment, with its insistence on reason, equality and the validity of all religions fostering human decency. But though many musicians of the time were active masons (Haydn briefly, 1785–7) or sympathetic to 'the craft' (Beethoven), by far the most important music for masonic ceremonies is Mozart's, including cantatas (K.471, 619, 623), songs and the MAURERISCHE TRAUERMUSIK. Because masonic meetings are open only to initiates, such music was private. However, Mozart and Schikaneder presented masonic themes publicly in *Die Zauberflöte*, as had Rameau and de Cahusac in *Zoroastre*. Other composers of masonic music include Sibelius.

free reed. Sound-producing device in harmoniums and harmonicas. See REED.

frei (Ger.). Free.

frei aber einsam See F-A-E.

frei aber froh. See F-A-F.

Freischütz, Der (The Freeshooter). Opera by Weber to a libretto by Johann Friedrich Kind after a tale from Johann August Apel and Friedrich Laun's *Ghost Book*. Max (tenor), a forester out of luck with his shooting, is tempted by his colleague Caspar (bass) to call on the demonic help of Samiel (spoken). The price, unknown to him, is the life of his beloved Agathe (soprano), but the victim of his fatal shot, finally, is Caspar. First performance: Berlin, 18 Jun 1821.

Freitas Branco, Luís de (b. Lisbon, 12 Oct 1890; d. Lisbon, 27 Nov 1955). Portuguese composer and, as teacher and critic, invigorator of local musical life. He completed his studies abroad (1910–15), with Humperdinck in Berlin and Gabriel Grovlez in Paris, the latter city providing him with musical bearings. His output includes four symphonies, other orchestral pieces, choral music and songs.

French horn. See HORN.

French overture. Overture in two sections, slow (with dotted rhythms) and fast (fugal), a form originating in court ballets of the 1640s, definitively established by Lully with *Alcidiane* (1658) and maintained on the French stage until the early works of Rameau and beyond. It also went further: Handel wrote French overtures for his operas, and there are examples by Bach (*Ouvertüre nach französischer Art*, i.e. French Overture) and Telemann.

French Revolution. Movement generally reckoned from the fall of the Bastille (14 Jul 1789) to that of Robespierre (27 Jul 1794). During this period *Figaro* was mounted at the Opera (1793), while the deregulation of theatres brought many new houses, and new works in which liberation was enacted onstage (Cherubini's *Lodoïska*) or in the pit, in a greater orchestral vigour (Méhul's *Euphrosine*). There was also a new vogue for sentiment, answered by the operas of Dalayrac, Boieldieu and Grétry. However, the signal figure of the period was Gossec, who produced works for massed forces designed for outdoor performance at great public commemorations, such as the Fête de la Fédération on the first anniversary of the sacking of the Bastille. Something from all these innovations spilled over into the concert life that got going again when the turmoil was over, and indeed, most of the musical effects of revolutionary democratic ideals unrolled only later, like thunder after lightning, most spectacularly in the trenchancy of Beethoven and Berlioz. By shifting cultural power to the bourgeoisie, the Revolution also encouraged both the publishing and instrument-making industries that catered for music in the middle-class home and the educational industry soon represented by the new Conservatoire.

Malcolm Boyd, ed. *Music and the French Revolution* (1992)

French sixth. Dissonance useful in modulation, a variety of AUGMENTED SIXTH CHORD including an augmented fourth (i.e. A♭–C–D–F♯ in C major). This resolves to the dominant (G–B–D–G).

French suites. Six keyboard works by Bach, who was not responsible for the title.

Freni, Mirella (b. Modena, 27 Feb 1935). Italian soprano, who combined richness with purity and maintained both through a long career. She made her debut in Modena as Micaëla in 1955 and became an international figure in the mid-1960s.

frequency. Rate of vibration, measured in Hertz (Hz, cycles per second) and experienced as pitch, modern concert A being set at 440 Hz.

frequency modulation. Change to frequency. By such means information can be encoded in a radio wave; hence FM radio.

frequency ratio. The ratio between two frequencies, defining the interval between them. The simplest, involving the numbers 1, 2, 3, 5 and their compounds, are as follows (with the intervals they represent in JUST INTONATION): 1:1 (unison), 16:15 (minor second), 9:8 (major second), 6:5 (minor third), 5:4 (major third), 4:3 (fourth), 3:2 (fifth), 8:5 (minor sixth), 5:3 (major sixth), 9:5 (minor seventh), 15:8 (major seventh) and 2:1 (octave). Introducing 7 opens the way to the septimal system.

Frescobaldi, Girolamo (Alessandro) (b. Ferrara, Sep 1583; d. Rome, 1 Mar 1643). Italian organist-composer, whose music, joining contrapuntal expertise with dazzling keyboard virtuosity and expressive character, was a widely influential marvel of his time. He was brought up at the highly musical Ferrara court as a pupil of Luzzaschi, then went to Rome, probably with his teacher in 1601. After visits to Brussels (1607–8) and Milan (for the printing of his first keyboard volume), he returned to Rome as organist of St Peter's in 1608 and soon gained wider fame and patronage in the city. In 1613 he married, his bride being already pregnant with their second child. He left for posts in Mantua (1615) and Florence (1628–34), but each time went back to St Peter's, to the cardinals who favoured him, and to his pupils (who included Froberger). His fame long outlasted him – especially that of his *Fiori musicali* (published 1635), a collection of pieces for use at mass, which Bach copied out. His other post-1628 volumes mostly contain revisions of earlier ricercares (essentially contrapuntal), canzonas and capriccios (more fantastical, most of the canzonas being also printed in parts for consort performance), and toccatas (roving harmonic progressions elaborated with rapid figuration). His sacred and secular vocal music is much less important.

Frederick Hammond *Girolamo Frescobaldi* (1983)

fret. Strip on the fingerboard of a string instrument, placed perpendicular to the strings, so that they may be stopped at a certain point. Frets are set at semitone intervals on plucked instruments (lutes and guitars) and viols. They came to Europe from the East and feature on the sitar and other Indian instruments. Not only do they help the player find notes, they also provide a clearer tone, since the string is stopped by a hard edge (of metal, wood, bone or ivory). High frets, as on the sitar, allow the player to change the tension and therefore the pitch. In the violin family, however, variation of tuning is the product of not having frets.

Fricker, Peter Racine (b. London, 5 Sep 1920; d. Santa Barbara, 1 Feb 1990). British composer, remarkable in the 1950s for his European outlook: Bartók, Hindemith, Schoenberg and Berg were all taken on board, in works mostly abstract and instrumental. He studied with Morris at the RCM (1937–41) and, following war service, Seiber at Morley College (1946–8). There he was also in contact with Tippett, and there he remained as a staff member, teaching also at the RCM from 1955. In 1964 he moved to the University of California at Santa Barbara. His works include five symphonies, four quartets, keyboard music and the oratorio *The Vision of Judgement* (1957–8). His second name commemorated descent from the playwright.

friction drum. Kind of membrane drum from which sound is produced by rubbing against the skin with a hand, stick or string (see STRING DRUM).

Friderici, Daniel (b. Klein Eichstedt, near Querfurt, 1584; d. Rostock, 23 Sep 1638). German composer of numerous volumes of sacred and secular vocal music. Of lowly birth, he became a travelling scholar and spent most of his life after 1612 as a church musician in Rostock. His singing treatise *Musica figuralis* (1618) went through eight editions.

Friedenstag (Peace Day). Opera by Strauss to a libretto by Joseph Gregor. In a town under siege, the Commandant (baritone) seems set on unending war, his wife Maria (soprano) not so. Then peace comes. First performance: Munich, 24 Jul 1938.

Friml, (Charles) Rudolf (b. Prague, 7 Dec 1879; d. Los Angeles, 12 Nov 1972). Czech–US composer, mostly of operettas (*Rose Marie*, 1924; *The Vagabond King*, 1925). He studied with Dvořák and settled in the USA in 1906.

Fritz, Gaspard (b. Geneva, 18 Feb 1716; d. Geneva, 23 Mar 1783). Swiss violinist-composer, author of a set of fine early Classical symphonies, as well as chamber music. The son of a German-born music teacher, he followed a similar career himself in Geneva, after studies in Turin.

Froberger, Johann Jacob (baptized Stuttgart, 19 May 1616; d. Héricourt, near Montbéliard, 6/7 May 1667). German keyboard composer-performer, the most notable of his time, and influential into the age of the Couperins and Bach. Brought up in the richly musical Stuttgart court, where his father became chapelmaster in 1621, he was an organist at the imperial court in Vienna by 1637 and studied in Rome with Frescobaldi (1637–41) and Kircher (1645–9). Another long absence in various northern European cities (1649–53), including London, suggests involvement in diplomacy or espionage. However that may be, he ended his life out of imperial favour, supported by the dowager duchess of Montbéliard. His works – almost exclusively suites (in which he was a pioneer), ricercares, capriccios and other pieces for keyboard – unite German, Italian and French elements, and sometimes have a decided expressive or descriptive purpose, as with the *tombeau* for Blancrocher (the celebrated lutenist who died in 1652 from a fall downstairs, pictured in the music), the *lamento* for the Habsburg heir Ferdinand IV (1633–54) and an allemande 'made crossing the Rhine in a ship in great danger'.

frog. The nut of a string bow where the hair is held; in modern bows it can be moved to adjust the tension. Synonyms: heel (Fr. *talon*), nut.

Frog. Name given Haydn's Quartet Op.50:6, for the croaking theme in its finale.

Fröhlich, Friedrich Theodor (b. Brugg, 20 Feb 1803; d. Aarau, 16 Oct 1836). Swiss composer, early Romantic, he studied with Zelter in Berlin (1826–30) and met Mendelssohn, then lived in Aarau as a teacher and composer. Feeling isolated and misunderstood, he killed himself, leaving an output largely of choral works, songs and chamber music.

Fröhlich, Johannes Frederik (b. Copenhagen, 21 Aug 1806; d. Copenhagen, 21 May 1860). Danish composer, of a notable symphony (in E♭, 1829–30), quartets, violin concertos and ballets in Classical style with more modern touches. He studied in Copenhagen with his brother-in-law and in Germany, Paris and Italy (1829–31). From 1821 he was active at the Royal Theatre as a violinist and, later, conductor. His creative output slackened after an accident in 1838.

Froidebise, Pierre (Jean Marie) (b. Ohey, Namur, 15 May 1914; d. Liège, 28 Oct 1962). Belgian composer, who moved on from Stravinskian regions to keep pace with the post-1945 avant-garde – with whom he had close connections as a teacher at the Liège Conservatory from 1947, his pupils including Pousseur and Boesmans. He himself had studied at the Namur and Brussels conservatories, with Absil and Gilson, and in Paris with Tournemire.

From Bohemia's Meadows and Forests. See MA VLAST.

Fromm, Andreas (b. Pänitz, near Wusterhausen, 1621; d. Prague, 16 Oct 1683). German composer, author of an oratorio on the story of Dives and Lazarus, published in 1649 but surviving incomplete. His later life was in the Church – the Catholic Church from 1668.

From My Life (*Z mého života, Aus meinem Leben*). Name Smetana gave his First Quartet, whose most touching autobiographical feature is the high E of tinnitus in the coda to the finale.

From the House of the Dead (*Z mrtvého domu*). Opera by Janáček to his own libretto after Dostoyevsky. Cast almost entirely for men singers, the work is a sequence of narratives and episodes for inmates of a Siberian prison, framed by the arrival and release of Gorjančikov (baritone). His friendship with the Tatar boy Aljeja (mezzo-soprano) offers relief, though the keen human observation all through is also affirmative. First performance: Brno, 12 Apr 1930.

From the New World. See NEW WORLD.

Frosch (Ger.). Frog.

frottola. Italian four-part song of 1470–1530, ancestor of the more ambitious madrigal. Frottolas are generally light love songs, made by composers including Tromboncino and Josquin.

Frumerie, (Per) Gunnar (Fredrik) de (b. Nacka, 20 Jul 1908; d. Mörby, 9 Sep 1987). Swedish pianist-composer, a Scandinavian Poulenc. He studied at the conservatory in Stockholm (1923–8) and in Paris and Vienna, with Cortot and others, and from 1945 taught piano at the music high school in Stockholm. His works include concertos, songs, quartets and piano pieces.

frustra (It.). Whip.

Fry, William Henry (b. Philadelphia, 19 Aug 1813; d. Santa Cruz, Virgin Islands, 21 Dec 1864). US composer, responsible for what was probably the country's first professionally produced opera (*Leonora*, Philadelphia, 1845). He studied in Philadelphia and, as critic no less than as composer, advocated indigenity and difference in US music. Other works of his include the Christmas symphony *Santa Claus* (1853).

Frye, Walter (*fl*.1450–75). English composer, a latterday master of English consonance, who was admired by Binchois, Du Fay, Busnois and Obrecht. He wrote masses (*Flos regalis* a 4, *Nobilis et pulcra* a 3, *Summe Trinitati* a 3), motets and secular songs, though the songs have also been attributed to the English (Bedyngham) and continental (Busnois) colleagues his music brought into contact. Little is known of his life; he may have served Anne of Exeter, sister of Edward IV.

Fuchs, Robert (b. Frauenthal, Styria, 15 Feb 1847; d. Vienna, 19 Feb 1927). Austrian composer, who was admired by Brahms but is better remembered as the teacher (at the Vienna Conservatory from 1875) of Mahler, Sibelius, Wolf and Zemlinsky. His brother Johann Nepomuk (1842–99) taught at the same institution from 1888, latterly as director (1893–9), and was also an opera conductor. The younger Fuchs arrived in the capital in 1865, and studied composition at the conservatory with Felix Otto Dessoff while earning a living as a teacher and organist. His works include five symphonies, much chamber music in standard genres, choral pieces and songs.

Fuenllana, Miguel de (b. Navalcarnero, near Madrid; *fl*. 1553–78). Spanish vihuelist-composer, blind from birth. He served members of the Spanish royal family and, after 1574, the king of Portugal, possibly then returning to the Spanish court. Fantasias and other pieces are contained in the six volumes of his *Orphenica lyra* (1554).

fuga. (1) (Lat., flight) Medieval–Renaissance term for canon or canonic imitation. Zarlino distinguished between *fuga ligata* (strict canon) and *fuga sciolta* (free canon), where only the opening of a line is imitated.
    (2) (It., pl. *fuge*) Fugue.

fugal. Fugue-like.

fugato. Fugue-like passage in a non-fugue, e.g. a sonata-form development.

Fuge (Ger., pl. *Fugen*). Fugue.

Fugger. German mercantile-banking family, based in Augsburg, with a remarkable record of musical patronage from the mid 15th century to the early 17th. They collected music, built organs, employed composers, including Hofhaimer, Hassler and Aichinger, and were rewarded with dedications by Lassus, Gabrieli, etc.

fughetta (It.). Little fugue, a term used by Bach and since.

fuging-tune. See FUGUING-TUNE.

fugue (Fr. *fugue*, Ger. *Fuge*, It. *fuga*). Composition in which canonic imitation on one substantial and well-defined subject is the guiding element in a strongly unified design, or the art of writing such compositions. Fugues are nearly always in four parts or voices and customarily begin with a canon on the subject (the 'exposition' section), with the second voice (the 'answer') entering a fifth above or a fourth below (in the dominant key in a tonal fugue), the third an octave distant from the first, and the fourth an octave distant from the second. Beyond that there are no rules, only a great body of tradition and nomenclature. Tonic and dominant entries may be called DUX and COMES. A fugue will generally have a 'counter-subject', introduced by the first voice when the second takes over the subject. It may have 'episodes' between imitative passages, a second exposition of the counter-subject or a new subject (in which case it becomes a 'double fugue', and perhaps then a 'triple fugue', etc.), a STRETTO. It may also – indeed, it probably will – apply all the resources of counterpoint to its subject, including augmentation, diminution, inversion and reversion.

Fugue, as distinct from straightforward canon, emerged as instrumental music took up intimations in late Renaissance polyphony and began its own development. Fantasias by Sweelinck and his English contemporaries, and ricercares by Frescobaldi and other Italians, show the principle of canonic journeying, but without the powerful steering of one strong subject that defines fugue. That unity and strength came with Buxtehude and Pachelbel, and then outstandingly with Bach, who brought to the art immense variety and left it with immense prestige. Many of Bach's fugues are keyboard pieces in the two-part form of prelude (or toccata, or passacaglia) and fugue; others come in concertos, suites and sacred vocal music, and still others in the semi-abstract *Kunst der Fuge*. Handel's fugues are freer but no less imposing, especially those in his oratorios.

The essentially harmony-driven sonata style of the Classical period and beyond bypassed fugue. Haydn and Mozart treated it partly as tradition (especially in masses), partly as exercise, and though Beethoven brought it fully and forcibly to the centre of his world in his last years, later examples, in Mendelssohn, Brahms, Verdi (finale of *Falstaff*), Reger and Shostakovich, return to it soberly or in jocular fashion as an antiquarian device. Bartók, however, in the first movement of his Music for Strings, Percussion and Celesta, proposed a new future for monothematic counterpoint, achieving growth and resolution by other means than those of the traditional fugue, and his example has been followed by Nancarrow, Ligeti, etc.

Ebenezer Prout *Fugue* (1891, ʳoften); Roger Bullivant *Fugue* (1971)

fuguing-tune. Simple psalm or hymn setting with at least one contrapuntal passage, introduced in Britain in the mid 18th century but soon – and then overwhelmingly – a North American phenomenon.

Fukushima, Kazuo (b. Tokyo, 11 Apr 1930). Japanese composer, who was closely linked with the Western avant-garde in the 1950s–60s. A member, with Takemitsu, of the Experimental Workshop group from 1953, he gained international attention with *Ekagura* for alto flute and piano (1958), and withdrew himself again in the 1970s to teach and study at Ueno Gakuen College in Tokyo.

full anthem. Anglican form of the 16th and 17th centuries, in which the choir sings throughout (compare VERSE ANTHEM).

full cadence, full close. PERFECT CADENCE.

full orchestra. Symphony orchestra of normal strength.

full organ. Registration implying a big sound.

full score. Score of a large-scale work (symphonic, choral, operatic) showing all the parts, as distinct from a piano reduction or vocal score.

function. Role of a chord in harmony, whether as tonic, dominant or subdominant.

functional harmony. Harmony based on major-minor keys and the tonic-dominant relationship, especially as understood in the central repertory from Bach to Brahms.

fundamental. Root note of a sounding object (e.g. instrument) or space, as distinct from higher harmonics.

fundamental bass. Term introduced by Rameau for an imaginary succession of the roots of chords in a progression, as distinct from the actual bass line, which will differ where chords are inverted.

Funérailles. Piano piece by Liszt, from his *Harmonies poétiques et religieuses*. Ferneyhough recycled the title.

funeral. Ceremony preceding burial. Composers since Du Fay have written their own funeral music, helping to form the mythology of the musician defying death – a mythology particularly powerful in Mozart's case. On the public plane, many composers have been buried as great figures: Beethoven's funeral drew all Vienna; Stravinsky's was televised. Death in opera tends to come at the end, which forestalls any funeral, although *Castor et Pollux* begins with an entombment. See also FUNERAL MARCH; REQUIEM.

funeral march. Slow march appropriate for, or suggestive of, a funeral procession. Those most familiar are Chopin's (slow movement of his B♭ minor sonata) and Handel's (Dead March in *Saul*); there are also examples by Beethoven ('Eroica' Symphony and Op.26 sonata), Chopin again (Op.72:2), Berlioz, Wagner (Siegfried's Funeral March in *Götterdämmerung*) and Elgar.

funeral mass. See REQUIEM.

Funeral Music for Queen Mary II. Works by

Purcell for the royal funeral (5 Mar 1695): a march, a canzona and a setting of the funeral sentence *Thou knowest, Lord*, all with four flat trumpets. Sometimes added are earlier settings of the sentences *In the midst of life* and *Man that is born of a woman*.

fünfstimmig (Ger.). Five-part.

fuoco (It.). Fire, as in *con fuoco* (with fire).

Für Elise. Favourite easy Beethoven piece, a bagatelle bearing this inscription in another hand.

furiant. Czech dance, with the vigorous syncopations of duple patterns thrown against triple metre. There are examples by Smetana and Dvořák.

Furlanetto, Bonaventura (b. Venice, 27 May 1738; d. Venice, 6 Apr 1817). Italian composer, almost exclusively of sacred music. Born poor and barely trained, he gained confidence steadily through his 30s and 40s while serving as maestro at the Pietà hospital (from 1768). Later he held posts also at St Mark's. His works include oratorios and cantatas, solo motets, and mass and vespers music.

Furrer, Beat (b. Schaffhausen, 6 Dec 1954). Swiss–Austrian composer of music conveying extreme, abstracted psychological tension. He studied in Schaffhausen and Vienna (with Haubenstock-Ramati), where in 1985 he founded the group that became Klangforum Wien. His prodigious output includes the opera *moderato cantabile* (Zurich, 2003).

Furtwängler, (Gustav Heinrich Ernst Martin) Wilhelm (b. Berlin, 25 Jan 1886; d. Baden-Baden, 30 Nov 1954). German conductor, the greatest at a time when his country was not great, a byword for authority backed by conviction, for strength and depth of expression, and for the pursuit of music as a source of moral health. With parents an architect and a painter, he enjoyed a cultivated upbringing and had his talent for composition fostered by lessons with Rheinberger and von Schillings. Composing became important to him again later in life, when he completed three symphonies (No.1, B minor, mostly 1938–41; No.2, E minor, 1944–5; No.3, C♯ minor, 1947–54) and other works. Meanwhile, he rose through minor jobs in Breslau/Wrocław (1905–6), Zurich (1906–7), Munich (1907–9) and Stuttgart (1910–11)

to become director at the opera houses of Lübeck (1911–15) and Mannheim (1915–20). Then came a group of key appointments: with the Frankfurt Museum and Berlin Staatsoper concerts (both from 1920), and with the Leipzig Gewandhaus (1922) and Berlin Philharmonic (1923). He became particularly associated with the latter orchestra, and remained in Berlin through the Nazi years, feeling he had to maintain music's presence. That attitude caused him difficulties after the Second World War. For two years he was banned from conducting, and hostility to him in the USA continued. Then, with the growing interest in historical recordings since the 1970s, his music-making began to find a whole new audience, drawn by the powerful sway he exerted, particularly in Beethoven, Brahms and Wagner. Hugely conscientious, he studied his repertory with Schenker, which may have helped him convey the impression that the fluid, immense magma of sound he created was not just a subjective response but right.

John Ardoin and John Hunt *The Furtwängler Record* (1994)

futurism. Early 20th-century artistic movement, distinguished by a passion for technological progress, represented musically by the sonic imagery of machines and factories or by new (sometimes electronic) instruments. The original futurists were Italians, including Francesco Pratella and Russolo among musicians, but the ideology soon spread to composers in Paris (Honegger, Prokofiev) and Russia (Mosolov, Vladimir Deshevov).

Fux, Johann Joseph (b. Hirtenfeld, near St Marein, Styria, 1660; d. Vienna, 13 Feb 1741). Austrian composer, from whose treatise *Gradus ad Parnassum* (1725) Haydn and Mozart learned strict counterpoint. Of peasant stock, he gained a university education in Graz (1680–83) and Ingolstadt (1683–7), and may then have been in the service of Archbishop Kollonitsch, with whom he could have visited Rome. In 1698 he became imperial court composer in Vienna, joining a largely Italian establishment and holding the post of court kapellmeister from 1715. His output includes 95 masses, nine *Requiem* settings, much other sacred music, 22 operas, sonatas and sinfonias.

Egon Wellesz *Fux* (1965)

fz. Abbreviation for *forzando* or *forzato*.

G. Note name, hence G♯, G minor, etc. The G clef (treble clef) curls around the G line.

G major is a common and versatile key, that of Beethoven's Fourth Piano Concerto (and of four of his piano sonatas), Schubert's last quartet, Dvořák's Eighth Symphony, *Eine kleine Nachtmusik* (and classicizing suites by Tchaikovsky and Schoenberg), etc. G minor was a favourite Mozart key for passionate intimacy (Symphonies Nos.25 and 40, String Quintet K.516, etc.), gaining an aura it maintained in such different worlds as those of Brahms and Bruch. But it found a different colour through its nearness to the Phrygian mode in Debussy's quartet. G♯ minor and G♭ major, almost unthinkable outside the context of piano music (though Myaskovsky wrote a symphony in G♯ minor), are both found in Chopin, with G♭ major appearing also in Schubert, Dvořák and Fauré, and G♯ minor in Scriabin.

Gabrieli. Uncle and nephew pair of Italian composers.

(1) **Andrea** (b. Venice, ?1532/3; d. Venice, 30 Aug 1585). Apart from a visit to Germany in 1562, when a personal and musical connection with Lassus began, he seems to have stayed in his native city, though little is known of his earlier years. He was important in Venetian musical life as organist of St Mark's (1566–85) and as a composer of ceremonial music, embracing a polychoral richness he learned from Lassus. This style influenced his nephew and other composer pupils (Hassler, Aichinger), but he also produced large quantities of motets and madrigals for single choir, as well as the organ intonations (preludes), ricercares and canzonas for which he is best remembered.

(2) **Giovanni** (b. Venice, *c.*1555; d. Venice, Aug 1612). From his uncle – and from his city – he inherited a capacity for splendour, which he displayed on a scale of unparalleled sumptuousness and ostentation in his many motets and canzonas for echoing choirs. With him the dialogue of choirs became more dramatic, with simpler, more homophonic material bounced in alternation. Almost certainly he studied with his uncle, and then with Lassus in Munich in the late 1570s. In 1584 he succeeded Merulo as organist at St Mark's, joining his uncle, and the next year he became also organist to the Scuola Grande di San Rocco; works of magnificence were required by both institutions. He published books of his uncle's music and, in 1597, the first volume of his *Sacrae symphoniae*, comprising both motets and canzonas. This spread his fame, and brought him pupils from Germany and Denmark, notably Schütz. They carried his lessons northwards, while in Venice his influence was moderated by Monteverdi's. He died as a result of a kidney stone, and a second volume of *Sacrae symphoniae* came out posthumously in 1615.

Denis Arnold *Giovanni Gabrieli and the Music of the Venetian High Renaissance* (1979)

Motets (with publication dates): *O magnum mysterium* a 8, 1587; *Hodie Christus natus est* a 10, 1597; *O Jesu mi dulcissime* a 8, 1597; *Audite principes* a 16, 1615; *In ecclesiis* a 14, 1615; *Quem vidistis pastores* a 14, 1615; *Timor et tremor* a 6, 1615; etc.

Canzonas and sonatas (with publication dates): *Canzon duodecimi toni* a 10, 1597; *Canzon septimi toni* No.1 a 8, 1597; *Canzon septimi toni* No.2 a 8, 1597; *Sonata pian e forte* a 8, 1597; Canzona I 'La Spiritata' a 4, 1608; Canzona II a 4, 1608; Canzona V a 7, 1615; Canzona X a 8, 1615; Canzona XIV a 10,

1615; Canzona XVI a 12, 1615; Sonata XVIII a 14, 1615; Sonata XXI 'con tre violini' a 4/5, 1615; 32 others

Other works: organ intonations, madrigals

Gabrielli, Domenico (b. Bologna, 15 Apr 1651; d. Bologna, 10 Jul 1690). Italian cellist-composer. He studied in Venice with Legrenzi and in Bologna with Franceschini, whom he succeeded in 1680 as cellist at San Petronio. Apart from some of the earliest virtuoso cello pieces (sonatas and ricercares), he wrote operas for Venice, oratorios, cantatas and trumpet sonatas.

Gace Brulé (b. c.1160; d. after 1213). Trouvère, named after his heraldry. He seems to have moved in high literary-aristocratic circles, with Geoffrey, Count of Brittany (brother of Richard Coeur-de-Lion) among his patrons; he may also have been a crusader. His songs, maintaining the troubadour tradition, were widely admired.

Gade, Niels (Wilhelm) (b. Copenhagen, 22 Feb 1817; d. Copenhagen, 21 Dec 1890). Danish composer, who brought the early Romantic dawn to Scandinavia. An instrument-maker's son, he studied locally and joined the royal orchestra in 1834. His breakthrough as a composer came in 1840, when his overture *Echoes of Ossian* Op.1 won a prize. Mendelssohn, a strong influence, drew him to Leipzig (1844–8), after which he returned to Copenhagen and set about reforming the city's musical life. He conducted the first Danish performances of Beethoven's Ninth Symphony and Bach's St Matthew Passion, and was joint founder director of the Copenhagen Conservatory. His works include eight symphonies (No.5 with obbligato piano), two *Novelettes* for strings (Op.53 in F, 1874; Op.58 in E, 1883), operas, cantatas, string quartets, three violin sonatas, piano music and songs.

Gaffurius, Franchinus [Gafori, Franchino] (b. Lodi, 14 Jan 1451; d. Milan, 25 Jun 1522). Italian theorist. Theologically and musically trained in his native city, he spent a few years as a travelling scholar before settling in Milan in 1484 as cathedral choirmaster. Through his treatises, which were among the first published works of music theory, he passed on a compendium of practical and speculative thought, drawing on sources going back to Boethius and the Greeks. He also composed.

gagaku. Japanese imperial court music, with eighth-century origins, though the tradition was effectively re-established by the first Meiji emperor in the 1870s–80s. Its stately melody, led by the ryutēki (flute) and hichiriki (oboe), and harmonic drone, featuring the shō (mouth organ), have been imitated by Western composers, notably Varèse (*Nocturnal*) and Messiaen (*Sept haïkaï*). The imperial gagaku ensemble has also performed new works by Stockhausen (*Der Jahreslauf*), Takemitsu (*In an Autumn Garden*), etc.

Gagliano, Marco da (b. Florence, 1 May 1582; d. Florence, 25 Feb 1643). Italian composer, principal master of the early Baroque in Florence, renowned especially for one of the earliest surviving operas, *Dafne* (see DAPHNE). He studied with Luca Bati, whose assistant at San Lorenzo he became in 1602, and whom he succeeded as cathedral chapelmaster in 1608 (after some months in Mantua, during which he had presented *Dafne* and other works), adding a similar post at the Medici court the next year. In addition, he was a member of a religious confraternity, the Compagnia dell'Arcangelo Raffaello, and a leading cleric. Besides stage pieces, he wrote madrigals (from the twilight of the a cappella tradition), monodies and sacred music.

gagliarda (It.). Galliard.

Gaîté parisienne. Ballet score arranged from Offenbach by Manuel Rosenthal (1938), including the Cancan from *Orphée* and Barcarolle from *Hoffmann*.

Gál, Hans (b. Brunn, near Vienna, 5 Aug 1890; d. Edinburgh, 3 Oct 1987). Austrian composer, a late custodian of his country's great tradition (from Haydn to the earliest Schoenberg), though displaced, as a Jew, by Nazism. He studied in Vienna with Eusebius Mandyczewski and Adler, and embarked simultaneously on careers as a scholar (lecturer at Vienna University, 1919–28) and composer. His opera *Die heilige Ente* (Düsseldorf, 1923) was widely produced, but he was obliged to leave his post as director of the Mainz Conservatory (1929–33), and in 1939, thanks to Tovey's invitation, he settled in Edinburgh. His works include four symphonies, besides much choral and chamber music.

Galamian, Ivan (Alexander) (b. Tabriz, 23 Jan 1903; d. New York, 14 Apr 1981). Armenian–US violin teacher, whose pupils included Perlman, Zukerman and Chung. Trained by Konstantin Mostras in Moscow and Lucien Capet in Paris (1922–3), he moved to the USA in 1937 and taught at Curtis (from 1944) and Juilliard (from 1946).

galant (Fr.). Elegant, a musical watchword from around 1700, associated with a new melodiousness, sprightliness of rhythm and simplicity of form and texture, in contrast (or sometimes combination) with the older Baroque virtues of solid, studied, busy magnificence. The aesthetic, like the term, came from France, but was most zealously espoused in Germany and Austria, becoming endemic in the 1750s–70s, before the triumph of the Classical style, which it partly prepared.

Galanterie (Ger., from Fr.). Newer (and Frencher) kind of dance movement in an 18th-century suite, e.g. a minuet or bourrée. This is a modern usage; at the time a *Galanterie* could mean any example or aspect of galant style.

Galilei, Vincenzo (b. Santa Maria a Monte, near Florence, 1520s; buried Florence, 2 Jul 1591). Italian musician, principal theorist of sung monody on ancient Greek principles (and practitioner of that art, as a bass-voiced lutenist), though nothing of this aspect of his work survives; his published volumes are of lute music and madrigals. A protégé of Bardi, he studied with Zarlino in Venice, probably soon before the birth of his astronomer son, Galileo (in 1564). He moved from Pisa to Florence in 1572, and pursued research in acoustics that must have influenced his son.

Galimir, Felix (b. Vienna, 12 May 1910; d. New York, 10 Nov 1999). Austrian–US violinist and teacher, venerated for his musicianship and as a link with Viennese tradition. He and his sisters formed a quartet in 1927 and in 1936 recorded Berg's Lyric Suite and Ravel's quartet, with the composers in attendance. Moving to New York in 1938, he became leader of the NBC Symphony, but from the early 1950s devoted himself mostly to teaching, at Marlboro, Juilliard and Curtis.

galliard (Fr. *gaillard*, It. *gagliarda*). Late Renaissance dance in lively triple time, first mentioned *c*.1500, the earliest printed examples coming from *c*.1530. There was a vogue for the dance *c*.1590–1625 among English composers (Byrd, Dowland, Gibbons, etc.), sometimes in pairings with a preceding pavan, and it survived sporadically in England, France and Germany into the 1670s–80s, by which time it had become slow. There are 20th-century galliards by Stravinsky (*Agon*) and Vaughan Williams.

Galli-Curci, Amelita (b. Milan, 18 Nov 1882; d. La Jolla, Cal., 26 Nov 1963). Italian–US soprano, of extraordinary clear beauty in coloratura. She

studied as a pianist at the Milan Conservatory; singing she largely taught herself, and made her debut as Gilda at Trani (1906). At her peak during her time in Chicago (1916–24; recording of 'Caro nome', 1919), she sang regularly also at the Met (1921–30), and went on giving concerts until 1937. She was married twice: in 1910 to Luigi Curci, an artist-aristocrat whose name she added to her own, and in 1921 to her accompanist Homer Samuels.

Gallus. See HANDL.

galop. Lively duple-time dance that had its heyday in the 1820s–40s (Schubert, Chopin, Johann Strauss I, Liszt, finale of Rossini's *Guillaume Tell* overture) and was remembered long afterwards, especially as the ebullient close for a set of dances (Ponchielli's Dance of the Hours, several Shostakovich scores).

Galuppi, Baldassare (b. Burano, Venetian lagoon, 18 Oct 1706; d. Venice, 3 Jan 1785). Italian composer, praised in his time for the charm and vivacity of his operas and for his care as a family man. He studied with Lotti, first organist at St Mark's, and began his busy life in the Venetian theatre in 1728. By the end of the 1730s the fame of 'Il Buranello' had spread to other Italian cities, and in 1741–3 he visited London, presenting 11 operas, including four new ones. He produced 17 comic operas in partnership with Goldoni – 1749–66; including *Il mondo alla reversa* (1750), *Il filosofo di campagna* (1754), *Le nozze di Dorina* (1755), *La diavolessa* (1755) – and accepted an invitation to the Russian court (1765–8), for which he provided operas and Orthodox church music (the latter an influence on his pupil Bortnyansky). Back in Venice he abandoned opera for sacred music, notably for St Mark's, where he had been vice-chapelmaster since 1748. And he also wrote toccatas, such as Browning may have heard.

Galway, James (b. Belfast, 8 Dec 1939). British flautist, knighted in 2001, the public face of the instrument since 1975, when he began an international solo career. Earlier he had played with London orchestras and the Berlin Philharmonic (1969–75), following studies at the RCM (1956–9), the Guildhall School (1959–60) and in Paris (1960–61, with Rampal and Marcel Moyse).

gamba. Abbreviation for VIOLA DA GAMBA.

Gambler, The (*Igrok, Le Joueur*). Opera by Prokofiev to his own libretto after Dostoyevsky's novella. In a casino world where everyone is being ruined, Alexey (tenor) and Pauline (soprano) are winners, but lose each other. First performance: Brussels, 29 Apr 1929.

gamelan. Indonesian orchestra, principally of metallophones having tuned plates or gongs, but also with other percussion, flutes and voices. Gamelan instruments were known in Europe, perhaps by the 17th century: the xylophone Rameau owned may have been one. They were also played in Europe by visiting Indonesian troupes, including the Javanese ensemble Debussy heard in 1889. McPhee's studies on Bali brought further contact, increased since the 1940s by recordings and by the spread of gamelan playing in Europe and the USA. No other extra-European musical culture has been exported so successfully. Harrison wrote many works for gamelan from 1976 onwards; composers who have adapted the sound and rhythm to Western instruments include Messiaen (*Trois petites liturgies, Turangalîla*), Cage (*First Construction*), Boulez and Britten.

Neil Sorrell *A Guide to the Gamelan* (1990, ²2000)

gamma (It.), **gamme** (Fr.). Scale; for derivation see below.

gamut. The term comes from the medieval *gamma ut* (the Greek letter plus the solmization syllable), the note below the A at the bottom of the pitch system – i.e. an origin beneath the origin, G an 11th below middle C. Contraction to 'gamme' (Middle English) or 'gamut' produced a word for a hexachordal system or a scale, from which the meaning extended to cover any kind of span, making the word synonymous with 'range' or 'compass'.

Cage gave it a more specific meaning: the collection of sounds available to a composition. The prepared piano seems to have given him the idea that such collections could be limited, and he used selected gamuts in his String Quartet and other works.

Ganze-Note, Ganze-Taktnote (Ger.). Whole note, semibreve.

gapped scale. Scale with a gap where a diatonic note would be. Pentatonic scales have two, e.g. C–D(–E)–F–G–A(–B)–C.

Garant, (Albert Antonio) Serge (b. Quebec, 22 Sep 1929; d. Sherbrooke, 1 Nov 1986). Canadian composer, close to Boulez. He studied in Canada and briefly at Juilliard, largely as a clarinettist, before his year in Paris (1951–2) under Andrée Vaurabourg-Honegger and Messiaen. Contact with Boulez and Stockhausen at that time was decisive. Back in Canada he organized concerts, wrote, broadcast and, from 1966, taught at Montreal University. His works include *Anerca* for soprano and ensemble (1961), on Inuit texts.

García, Manuel (del Pópulo Vicente Rodriguez) (b. Seville, 21 Jan 1775; d. Paris, 10 Jun 1832). Spanish tenor and composer. He was the founder of an extraordinary vocal dynasty: Maria Malibran and Pauline Viardot were his daughters, and his long-lived son, also Manuel (1805–1906), taught Jenny Lind and compiled a treatise (*Traité complet de l'art du chant*, 1840–47) before devoting almost half a century to the RAM. The elder Manuel studied in Seville and married a fellow singer, Manuela Morales, in 1797. He was the Count in the first Madrid *Figaro* (1802) and scored a triumph as a composer with *El poeta calculista* (Madrid, 1805), source of the popular aria 'Yo que soy contrabandista'. In 1807 he left his wife and children in Madrid and arrived in Paris with another singer, Joaquina Briones, whom he later married. They travelled to Italy (1811–16), where he was the first Almaviva in Rossini's *Barbiere*, and also visited London. Then, with Maria, Pauline and the younger Manuel in tow, he formed a company to tour the USA and Mexico (1825–9), introducing New York to Rossini and, at Da Ponte's prompting, *Don Giovanni*. Robbed of all his takings on the way home, he returned to Paris also short on voice, and thereafter devoted himself largely to teaching. See also BOLERO; POLO.

James Radomski *Manuel García (1775–1832)* (2000)

Garden, Mary (b. Aberdeen, 20 Feb 1874; d. Inverurie, 3 Jan 1967). Scottish–US soprano, the first Mélisande. Brought up from 1883 in the USA, she studied in Chicago and Paris (from 1896), where she made her debut in 1900 as Louise, a role she was covering. This was a triumph, owed not only to her singing but to her dramatic skills, which evoked comparison with Sarah Bernhardt. She then sang with the Manhattan Opera (1908–9) and the Chicago Grand Opera (1910–31), which she directed for the 1921–2 season, introducing Prokofiev's *The Love for Three Oranges*. In 1939 she went back to Scotland.

Gardiner, (Henry) Balfour (b. London, 7 Nov 1877; d. Salisbury, 28 Jun 1950). British composer, remembered especially for his *Evening Hymn* for choir and organ (pub 1908) and an orchestral miniature, *Shepherd Fennel's Dance* (1911). He studied with Knorr in Frankfurt before, during and after his time at Oxford, and used his family wealth to help Holst, Delius and others.

Discouraged by how music was going, he abandoned composition in 1925.

Gardiner, John Eliot (b. Fontmell Magna, Dorset, 20 Apr 1943). British conductor, leading proponent of period-style performance, knighted in 1998. He studied at Cambridge and with Boulanger, and made his London debut with his Monteverdi Choir in 1966. For a while Monteverdi was the focus of his interests; he founded the Monteverdi Orchestra in 1968 and performed the Vespers at the Proms that year. But as his work extended, he refounded his group as the English Baroque Soloists (1978) and formed another ensemble, the Orchestre Révolutionnaire et Romantique (1990). He was also music director of the Lyons Opera (1983–8) and the NDR Symphony (1991–5), and has worked with the Vienna Philharmonic, his repertory extending to Stravinsky and Lehár.

Gardner, John (Linton) (b. Manchester, 2 Mar 1917). British composer. He studied at Oxford (1936–9) and taught at Morley College (1952–76) and the RAM (1956–86). His large output includes three symphonies, operas and a popular carol, 'Tomorrow shall be my dancing day' (1965).

Gaspard de la nuit (Nocturnal Gaspard). Set of three piano pieces by Ravel, drawing from the eponymous book of fantastical prose sketches by Aloysius Bertrand: *Ondine* (see UNDINE), *Le Gibet* (where Bertrand imagines the sounds of a swinging body and a distant bell) and *Scarbo* (a malevolent dwarf). First performance: Paris, 9 Jan 1909.

Gasparini, Francesco (b. Camaiore, near Lucca, 19 Mar 1661; d. Rome, 22 Mar 1727). Italian composer, who combined learning with elegance, and was the teacher of Domenico Scarlatti and Quantz. He himself probably studied with Corelli and Pasquini in Rome, where he passed most of his career, except for a time in Venice (1701–13) composing for the Ospedale della Pietà and the theatres (*Ambleto*, not after Shakespeare, 1706). Venice also brought him into contact with Vivaldi and Legrenzi. His works comprise chiefly cantatas, operas and sacred music, plus a few sonatas and sinfonias.

Some confusion has been caused by the proliferation of Gasparinis. Apart from Francesco's brothers, of whom Paolo Lorenzo was active in Rome and Michelangelo in Venice, the unrelated Quirino Gasparini (1721–78) was chapelmaster of Turin Cathedral and the author of an *Adoramus Te* once believed to be by Mozart, while Gaspare Visconti (1683–?1713) – present as a very young man in London, writing sonatas and flute airs – was also known as Gasparini.

Gassmann, Florian (Leopold) (b. Brüx/Most, 3 May 1729; d. Vienna, 20 Jan 1774). Bohemian composer, Italian-trained and famed for operas (*La contessina*, 1770) and symphonies. Taking up music against his father's wishes, he made for Italy as a boy and may have studied with Padre Martini. In 1763 he was called to Vienna to be Gluck's successor as ballet composer; on a later visit to Venice (1765–6) he recruited Salieri. He died as a result of a fall from a carriage.

Gastein. Name given to a supposedly lost symphony that Schubert's friends reported him composing during a summer holiday in 1825 that included visits to the resorts of Bad Gastein and Gmunden. This work is now believed to have been the 'Great C major'.

Gastoldi, Giovanni Giacomo (b. Caravaggio, near Cremona, c.1554; d. Mantua, 4 Jan 1609). Italian composer, known almost exclusively as the master of the BALLETTO, though he also produced a lot of sacred music, being Wert's successor as chapelmaster at the court in Mantua (1588–1609), where he had arrived by 1572.

Gaudeamus Foundation. Dutch body established by Walter Maas in 1945 to support new music. Its activities include an annual gathering of young composers and an annual competition for performers.

Gaultier. Cousins, the pre-eminent French lutenist-composers of the 17th century. Ennemond (1575–1651), known as 'le vieux' or 'de Lyon', served Marie de' Medici (1600–31) and also visited the court of Charles I and Henrietta Maria in England. Denis (1597/1603–1672), known as 'le jeune' or 'de Paris', worked independently in the capital. *La Rhétorique des dieux* is a collection of mostly dance pieces by them in the 12 classical modes.

Gautier de Coincy (b. Coincy-l'Abbé, 1177/8; d. Soissons, 25 Sep 1236). Trouvère. A monk, he wrote songs praising the Virgin, to borrowed and original melodies, for his verse compendium *Les Miracles de Nostre-Dame*. Two other trouvères had the same name (Walter): Gautier de Digues, who took part in the third crusade, and Gautier d'Espinal.

Gaveau. French firm of piano and harpsichord makers founded in 1847 by Joseph Gaveau, whose son Etienne opened the Salle Gaveau (1907).

Gaveaux, Pierre (b. Béziers, 9 Oct 1760; d. Charenton, near Paris, 5 Feb 1825). French tenor and composer, whose *Léonore, ou L'Amour conjugal* (1798) was the forerunner of *Fidelio*. As a singer he moved from the church to the theatre while in Bordeaux. He was then active in Paris as singer, composer and music seller from 1789 until his retirement to a mental asylum in 1819.

gavotte. Moderately paced duple-time dance of Breton origin, taken to French courtly circles in the late 16th century, to become widespread in ballet music and suites in the 17th and 18th. Later composers – Saint-Saëns, Prokofiev ('Classical' Symphony), Schoenberg – borrowed the term more than the form, for rococo associations.

Gawain. Opera by Birtwistle to a libretto by David Harsent after the Middle English poem *Sir Gawain and the Green Knight*. The response of Gawain (baritone) to the challenge of the magical Green Knight (bass) is a test of the notion of heroism, against the background of a decadent Arthurian court and the fixities of ritual. First performance: London, 30 May 1991.

Gawriloff, (Siegfried Jordan) Saschko (b. Leipzig, 20 Oct 1929). German violinist, proponent of Ligeti, Rihm, Schnittke, etc. The son of a Gewandhaus violinist, he studied in Leipzig and Berlin, and was an orchestra leader before embarking on a solo career in the 1960s. He taught at the Folkwanghochschule in Essen (1969–82).

Gay, John (b. Barnstaple, Jun 1685; d. London, 4 Dec 1732). British playwright, responsible for *The* BEGGAR'S OPERA and also for the libretto of Handel's *Acis and Galatea*.

Gayane (*Gayaneh*). Ballet score by Khachaturian which went through various transformations on its way from *Happiness* (Yerevan, 1939) to its final revision under the definitive title (Moscow, 1957). Gayane is an unhappily married Armenian cotton picker who finds love and fulfilment with an army commander. The final divertissement includes a Sabre Dance often heard alone; there are also three suites.

Gayer, Catherine (b. Los Angeles, 11 Feb 1937). US soprano, whose brilliant exactitude in coloratura placed her in demand for new roles. Soon after completing her studies in Berlin (where she remained with the Deutsche Oper), she was in the first *Intolleranza*; she also created Nausicaa in Dallapiccola's *Ulisse*.

gazza ladra, La (The Thieving Magpie). Opera by Rossini to a libretto by Giovanni Gherardini after a French play. The discovery of the magpie's theft of a spoon is only one element – but crucial – in the concatenation of events by which the maid Ninetta (soprano) and her father, Fernando (bass-baritone), are saved from dire consequences. The overture is one of Rossini's most dashing. First performance: Milan, 31 May 1817.

Gazzaniga, Giovanni (b. Verona, 5 Oct 1743; d. Crema, 1 Feb 1818). Italian composer, whose immensely successful *Don Giovanni* (1787) provided an impulse for Da Ponte. He served his apprenticeship with Porpora (1760–67) and Piccinni (1767–70), and spent most of the next two decades supplying theatres in Venice and elsewhere. On being appointed chapelmaster of Crema Cathedral (1791), he turned his attention largely to church music.

Gazzelloni, Severino (b. Roccasecca, Frosinone, 5 Jan 1919; d. Camino, 21 Nov 1992). Italian flautist, particularly associated with the avant-garde music of the 1950s–60s, his persuasive lyricism and agility being permanently enshrined in works by Nono (*Y su sangre*), Berio (*Sequenza I*), etc. He studied at the Accademia di Santa Cecilia.

Gebrauchsmusik (Ger.). Utility music, a term perhaps coined by the music historian Paul Nettl in 1921–2 and developed by Heinrich Besseler. It was a way of describing music as integrated into life (work, worship, entertainment), not separated as an object of aesthetic pleasure, and it originated through considerations of conditions before Bach. However, it was soon adopted to cover the work of contemporary musicians – notably Hindemith but also Weill, Eisler, etc. – who concerned themselves largely with film, theatre and radio scores, political music, and music for students and amateurs. In later usage the term has kept its German associations, particularly with Hindemith, though the ethos of usefulness was felt as much by other composers of the time, notably Prokofiev, Shostakovich, Copland and Britten.

gebunden (Ger.). Legato.

gebundener Stil (Ger., fixed style). The strict contrapuntal style of Baroque fugues, inventions, etc.

Gedackt (Ger., stopped). Organ stop, governing a rank of stopped pipes.

Gédalge, André (b. Paris, 27 Dec 1856; d. Chessy, 5

Feb 1926). French composer, best known as the teacher of Ravel, Milhaud, Honegger and many others at the Paris Conservatoire, where he remained after arriving at the age of 28, to study with Guiraud after working as a bookseller. He wrote a treatise on fugue and three symphonies, among other works.

gedämpft (Ger.). Muted, muffled.

gedehnt (Ger.). Extended, slow.

Gedda, Nicolai (Harry Gustaf) (b. Stockholm, 11 Jul 1925). Swedish tenor, a strong and engaging interpreter of lyric roles. His father was a Russian singer and choirmaster, whose surname, Ustinoff, he dropped in favour of his mother's. He studied at the conservatory in Stockholm, made his debut with the Swedish Royal Opera in 1951, and was rapidly swept into an international career, appearing at La Scala (1953), Covent Garden (1955) and the Met (1957). His wide repertory included unusual operas (*Benvenuto Cellini*, *Palestrina*) and new ones (*Vanessa*), and though he limited his appearances after the end of the 1970s, he continued singing into his 70s.

gefällig (Ger.). Pleasing.

gefühlvoll (Ger.). Expressively.

gegen- (Ger.). Counter, contrary, as in *Gegenbewegung* (contrary motion), *Gegensatz* (fugal countersubject).

gehalten (Ger.). Restrained.

geheimnisvoll (Ger.). Mysteriously.

gehend (Ger.). Andante.

Geige (Ger., pl. *Geigen*). Violin, fiddle. The word *Violine* also exists, but *Geige* is more usual.

Geigenharz (Ger.). Rosin.

Geigenwerk. See BOWED PIANO.

Geister. See GHOST.

geistlich (Ger.). Sacred. Hence also *geistliches Konzert* (sacred concerto).

gelassen (Ger.). Becalmed.

geläufig (Ger.). Fluent.

GEMA. Gesellschaft für Musikalische Aufführungs und Mechanische Vervielfältigungsrechte, German performing rights agency.

gemächlich (Ger.). Comfortable.

gemessen (Ger.). Measured.

Geminiani, Francesco (Saverio) (baptized Lucca, 5 Dec 1687; d. Dublin, 17 Sep 1762). Italian violinist-composer, who spent most of his career in the British Isles, where his playing and composing were alike highly valued. A violinist's son, he is believed to have trained in Rome with Corelli and Alessandro Scarlatti. He settled in London in 1714, and was welcomed as a pupil of Corelli, gaining aristocratic patronage and a ready supply of pupils. In 1732–3, soon after the publication of his immensely popular Op.3 concertos, he was in Paris, where he began a sideline as an art dealer. He then divided his time among the cities of Dublin, Paris and London, concerning himself after 1746 largely with pedagogical works.

Works (with publication dates): 12 Trio Sonatas, Op.1, 1716, rev 1739; 12 Concerti Grossi after Corelli's Op.5, 1726, 1729; 6 Concert Grossi, Op.2, 1732; 6 Concerti Grossi, Op.3, 1732; 6 Concerti Grossi after Corelli's Op.3, 1735; 12 Violin Sonatas, Op.4, 1739; 6 Cello/Violin Sonatas, Op.5, 1746; 6 Concerti Grossi after his own Op.4, 1743; 6 Concerti Grossi, Op.7, 1746; *The Art of Playing on the Violin*, Op.9, 1751; *The Inchanted Forrest* (originally for a pantomime), *c*.1756; etc.

gemischte (Ger.). Mixed, e.g. of voices.

gemshorn (Ger., from *Gemse*, chamois). Renaissance instrument made indeed from a chamois horn or, in modern reproductions, cowhorn.

genau (Ger.). Exact(ly).

Generalbass (Ger.). Continuo.

General Pause (Ger. *Generalpause*). Rest for all performers, abbreviated G.P.

Generalprobe (Ger.). Dress rehearsal.

Genoveva. Opera by Schumann to his own libretto after Tieck and Hebbel. The heroine is the historical eighth-century Geneviève de Brabant (soprano), who, while her husband Siegfried (baritone) is off fighting the Moors, is propositioned by Golo (tenor). She rejects him, and he exacts a malicious vengeance: by trickery he compromises her with another man. Virtue and marital love, however, are triumphant. First performance: Leipzig, 25 Jun 1850.

genre. Category of compositions. Standard genres include the symphony, lied, piano sonata, étude, *Requiem*, etc., but these are not fixed denominations. On the contrary, many great works extend the limits of a genre (Beethoven's 'Eroica' Symphony or Schubert's song cycles would be obvious examples) or mix genres, e.g. string quartet and song (Schoenberg's Second Quartet, Birtwistle's *Pulse Shadows*), piano concerto and folk music (Bartók, Ligeti), opera and concert piece (Monteverdi's *Orfeo*, Nono's *Prometeo*).

Gens, Véronique (b. Orleans, 19 Apr 1966). French soprano, captivating. She studied at the Paris Conservatoire and made her debut with Les Arts Florissants (1986), later branching out into Debussy, Ravel and Berlioz.

Genzmer, Harald (b. Blumenthal, near Bremen, 9 Feb 1909). German composer, a pupil of Hindemith in Berlin (1928–34). He taught in Freiburg (1946–56) and Munich (1957–76). His large output includes four symphonies, numerous concertos (including two for trautonium) and a wide variety of chamber pieces.

Gerald of Wales [Giraldus Cambrensis] (b. Manorbier, 1146; d. ?Lincoln, c.1223). Welsh writer and churchman, whose travelogues include information on instrumental practice in Wales, Ireland and Scotland, and vocal polyphony in Wales.

Gergiev, Valery (Abissalovich) (b. Moscow, 2 May 1953). Russian conductor, charismatic and tireless. He was brought up and began his studies in North Ossetia, then transferred to the Moscow Conservatory under Ilya Musin. In 1977 he graduated and became Yuri Temirkanov's assistant at the Kirov; in 1988 he succeeded to the artistic directorship. Under his aegis the company reverted to its former name, the Mariinsky, and became – partly under the pressure of post-Soviet economic stringency – an indefatigable touring ensemble, appearing regularly in London, New York, etc. In the performance of Russian opera and large parts of the Russian concert repertory, it set the international standard. While maintaining close control of its development, he has also appeared regularly with the Met and at Salzburg.

John Ardoin *Valery Gergiev and the Kirov* (2001)

Gerhard, Roberto (b. Valls, 25 Sep 1896; d. Cambridge, 5 Jan 1970). Catalan–British composer, who embraced both Spanish and wider European modernist traditions, to achieve a transcendent fusion in his last decade. Of German–Swiss–Alsatian parentage, he studied in Lausanne and (briefly) Munich before the First World War, then in Barcelona with Granados and Pedrell, and finally in Vienna (where he met his wife) and Berlin with Schoenberg (1923–8). His Wind Quintet (1928) was a homage to Schoenberg, whom he invited to Barcelona; he also brought the ISCM festival to the city in 1936. At the same time, he involved himself in Catalan cultural life, and his music became more vividly local.

Franco's victory in 1939 sent him into exile. Invited by Dent to Cambridge for a year (1939–40), he stayed, supporting himself through arrangements, film scores and incidental music. His dormant adherence to serialism was revitalized in his Violin Concerto (1942–3), though without displacing a Spanish feel or preventing the first signs of a vivid sense of projected sound – especially percussion sound – recalling Varèse. In his First Quartet (1950–55) he moved towards an individual kind of serialism in which hexachords become malleable sources and continuity is athematic; he also began composing electronic music. His Second Quartet shows him taking note of the new string effects introduced by Xenakis and Penderecki, and there is the same sonic exuberance in the larger chamber and orchestral works of his highly creative last decade.

Meirion Bowen, ed. *Gerhard on Music* (2000)

Opera: *The Duenna* (Gerhard and Christopher Hassall, after Sheridan), 1945–7, f.p. Madrid, 1992
Ballets: *Ariel*, 1934; *Soirées de Barcelone*, 1936–9; *Don Quixote*, 1940–41, rev 1947–9; *Alegrías*, 1942; *Pandora*, 1943–5
Orchestral: Symphony 'Homenaje a Pedrell', 1940–41; Symphony No.1, 1952–3; No.2, 1957–9; No.3 'Collages', with tape, 1960; No.4 'New York', 1967, rev 1968; Violin Concerto, 1942–3; Piano Concerto, 1951; Harpsichord Concerto, 1955–6; Concerto for Orchestra, 1964–5; *Albada, interludi i dansa*, 1936; *Epithalamium*, 1965–6, rev 1968
Choral: *L'alta naixença del rei en Jaume* (Josep Carner), s, bar, ch, orch, 1932, rev 1933; *The Plague* (Gerhard, after Camus), speaker, ch, orch, 1962–3
Songs: *L'infantament meravellós de Schahrazada* (cycle; Josep Maria López-Picó), s/t, pf, 1916–17; 7 Haïki (Josep Maria Junoy), s/t, fl, ob, cl, bn, pf, 1923, rev 1958; *Cançionero de Pedrell*, s/t, pf/ens, 1941; 'The Akond of Swat' (Edward Lear), mez/bar, 2 perc, 1954; etc.
Chamber and instrumental: 2 Sardanas, ens, 1928–9; *Hymnody*, 11 insts, 1963; *Leo*, 10 insts, 1969; Nonet, 1956–7; Concert for 8, 1962; *Libra*, 6 insts, 1968; Wind Quintet, 1928; String Quartet No.1, 1950–55; No.2, 1961–2; *Gemini*, vn, pf, 1966; Cello Sonata, 1956; *Dos apunts*, pf, 1921–2; 3 Impromptus, pf, 1950; Fantasia, gtr, 1957; Chaconne, vn, 1959; Capriccio, fl, 1949; etc.
Other works: tape pieces (*Audiomobiles I–IV*, c.1958–9); music for theatre, films, radio and TV

German (Jones), Edward (b. Whitchurch, Salop., 17 Feb 1862; d. London, 11 Nov 1936). British composer-conductor, knighted in 1928. After studies with Prout at the RAM (1880–87) he began work in the theatre, where his winning scores for *Richard III* (1889), *Henry VIII* (1892) and *Nell Gwyn* (1900) established a solid, olde-worlde style he took further in his operettas *Merrie England* (1902) and *Tom Jones* (1907). He also wrote popular songs ('Rolling Down to Rio', 'Glorious Devon') and more serious orchestral works close to Elgar, including two symphonies (No.1, E minor, 1887; No.2 'Norwich', A Minor, 1893) and a Welsh Rhapsody (1904).

German Dance (Fr. *allemande*, Ger. *Deutsche*, *Teutsche*, *Deutscher Tanz*, It. *tedesco*). Triple-time dance, precursor of the waltz, with a distinguished repertory of music written by Haydn, Mozart, Beethoven and Schubert for Viennese ballrooms and salons. The form is simple, in eight-bar phrases, but some of Mozart's examples are wild.

German flute. Old term for the transverse flute, to distinguish it from the English flute (i.e. recorder).

German radio. The authorities set up after the Second World War in West Germany were crucial supporters of new music. See SWR; WDR.

German Requiem, A. See *Ein* DEUTSCHES REQUIEM.

German sixth. Dissonance useful in modulation, a variety of AUGMENTED SIXTH CHORD including what may be read as a double-augmented fourth or perfect fifth (i.e. A♭–C–D♯/E♭–F♯ in C major). This resolves to the second inversion of the tonic chord (G–C–E–G) or to the dominant (G–B–D–G). However, it may also be read enharmonically as a dominant seventh (A♭–C–E♭–G♭), leading into the key of the flattened supertonic (D♭).

Germany (Deutschland). More a state of mind than a national territory, which it became only in 1871 with the unification of all the German kingdoms, dukedoms, bishoprics and free cities that lay outside the Austrian Empire. Mozart considered himself German, and the phrase 'German tradition' is often used airily to include other composers whose roots or residences were in Vienna. Indeed, to exclude those composers would leave a 'German tradition' that leapt from the Bachs to Weber, Mendelssohn and Schumann, and then to Strauss, Hindemith and Weill.

The justification for a larger understanding of that tradition is partly in the language, shared (more or less) by Germany and Austria, and by populations in the Czech Republic, Poland, Russia, Switzerland, etc. Not only is there a vigorous history of German song – begun by the MINNE-SINGER, democratized by the MEISTERSINGER, brought into church by the Reformation (divisive but powerfully present in German culture), brought out again by Beethoven, reborn in the Romantic LIED – but the emphatic stresses and extended phrase structures of the language may have contributed to the driving rhythm and formal cogency of so much German music. Also to be considered is a temperamental affinity for sustained abstract thought. Philosophy, from Kant (1724–1804) to Heidegger (1889–1976), was largely written by German authors, and so was instrumental music from Haydn (1732–1809) to Strauss (1864–1949).

Mention of Heidegger and Strauss must immediately recall the savage rupture brought by the Nazis in 1933. German music had never been about affirming national identity. From Beethoven onwards German composers assumed, perhaps arrogantly, that they were writing for the world, and German music had thrived not only on the native soil of folksong and local ways but from contact with surrounding cultures, especially Italian and French. In 1933–45 it lost those contacts, and its heavy indebtedness to Jewish composers (Mendelssohn, Mahler, Schoenberg) and performers was denied. German music became largely music in exile, whether a real exile (for Schoenberg, Hindemith, Weill, Eisler and Wolpe) or an interior one (for Blacher and Hartmann). There were also those who were lost: Schulhoff, Ullmann, Krása, Haas. Musicians who remained active in Nazi territories – Strauss, Furtwängler, Karajan – could justify themselves only as exemplars of music's call to a higher humanity.

Afterwards came the urge for a fresh start, vividly communicated in Stockhausen's youthful music, more earnestly sought in what Eisler and his colleagues endeavoured in the separate, communist German Democratic Republic (1949–90). There was, too, a reverse of the 1930s diaspora, bringing Kagel, Ligeti and others to the (western, capitalist) country. But more than half a century after the war there was still the sense, in such different composers as Henze and Lachenmann, of a tradition harmed.

See also BAMBERG; BERLIN; COLOGNE; DARMSTADT; DRESDEN; FRANKFURT; HAMBURG; LEIPZIG; MANNHEIM; MUNICH; PRAGUE; VIENNA.

Michael H. Kater *The Twisted Muse* (1997); John

Warrack *German Opera* (2001); David Gramit *Cultivating Music* (2002)

Gershwin, George (b. Brooklyn, 26 Sep 1898; d. Hollywood, 11 Jul 1937). US composer, the pre-eminent master of jazz-age popular song, who was determined to – and did – establish himself also as a classical composer. Originally Jacob Gershovitz, he was the second of four children born to poor Russian Jewish immigrants; his elder brother Israel (Ira) became his lyricist. In 1910 he took hold of the family piano (newly acquired for Israel), and in 1914 he started work for a song publisher, promoting the merchandise by singing and playing in the showroom. His own first published song, 'When you want 'em' (1916), led to a career on Broadway as a composer-pianist, and to his first full show, *La-la-Lucille!* (1919). At the same time he pursued classical studies with Edward Kilenyi (1915–21), though his first ostensibly classical piece was a paean to jazz, *Rhapsody in Blue* (1924), scored for him by Grofé. On Christmas Eve the same year his first show with lyrics entirely by Ira, *Lady, be Good!*, opened in New York, and from then on he pursued both lines simultaneously. He continued his studies almost to the end of his life (with Goldmark, Riegger, Cowell, Schillinger); Ravel allegedly turned him down on hearing how much he earned, suggesting the lessons should go the other way (as metaphorically they did, with results in Ravel's Piano Concerto in G). Schoenberg was another admirer, and tennis opponent after the Gershwins had moved to Hollywood in 1936. But if he gained satisfaction and prestige from his classical buddies and classical compositions (among which his long-deliberated opera *Porgy and Bess* must be included), his genius as a songwriter is unquestionable and unquenchable.

Rodney Greenberg *George Gershwin* (1998); Wayne Schneider, ed. *The Gershwin Style* (1999)

Opera: PORGY AND BESS, 1934–5
Musicals (with performance dates in New York and principal songs): *Lady, be Good!*, 1924 ('Fascinating rhythm', 'The man I love', 'Oh, lady, be good!'); *Oh, Kay!*, 1926 ('Someone to watch over me'); *Strike up the Band*, 1926, rev 1930 ('Strike up the band', 'I've got a crush on you'); *Funny Face*, 1927 ('Let's kiss and make up', ''S wonderful'); *Rosalie*, 1928 ('How long has this been going on?'); *Girl Crazy*, 1930 ('Embraceable you', 'I got rhythm', 'But not for me'); *Of thee I sing*, 1931
Films: *Shall we Dance*, 1937 ('Let's call the whole thing off', 'Shall we dance?', 'They all laughed', 'They can't take that away from me'); *A Damsel in Distress*, 1937 ('Nice work if you can get it')
Orchestral: RHAPSODY IN BLUE, 1924; Piano Concerto, F, 1925; *An American in Paris*, 1928;

Second Rhapsody, pf, orch, 1931; *Cuban Overture*, 1932; 'I got rhythm' Variations, pf, orch, 1934
Other works: *Lullaby*, str qt, *c*.1919–20; 3 Preludes, pf, *c*.1923–6; other piano pieces and arrs

Gervaise, Claude (*fl*. Paris, 1540–60). French editor and composer, notably for books of *danceries* that were published by Attaingnant in the 1550s, to give the world four centuries later a festive image of the Renaissance (and provide Stravinsky with hints for *Agon*). He also wrote polyphonic chansons.

Gervasoni, Stefano (b. Bergamo, 26 Jul 1962). Italian composer, whose pieces are simple yet individual, delicate yet sure. He studied with Lombardi, Castiglioni and Corghi at the Milan Conservatory (1980–90), and counts his meetings with Nono, Ferneyhough, Eötvös and Lachenmann as decisive. Since the late 1990s he has taught composition courses in Italy and abroad. His works include a viola concerto (1994–5) and many pieces for ensemble.

Ges (Ger.). G♭. Also *Geses* (G♭♭).

Gesamtkunstwerk (Ger., work combining arts). Term owed to Wagner (1849) for a union of theatre and music such as he imagined had been achieved by the Greeks and would be again in the future.

Gesang (Ger., pl. *Gesänge*). Song. The normal German word is *Lied*; a *Gesang* might be grander.

Gesang der Geister über den Wassern (Song of the Spirits over the Waters). Setting by Schubert of a Goethe poem for eight-part men's choir and five-part low strings (2 va, 2 vc, db). He made a first version for four-part choir in 1817 (D.538) and created the definitive score in February 1821 (D.714).

Gesang der Jünglinge (Song of the Youths). Four-track tape piece by Stockhausen created from recordings of electronic sounds and a boy singing verses from the *Benedicite*, the canticle heard from Shadrach, Meshach and Abednego in Nebuchadnezzar's burning fiery furnace. First performance: Cologne, 30 May 1956.

Gesangverein (Ger., song society). German choral organization, as founded in many cities (e.g. Lübeck, Kiel) in the 19th century; some were alternatively called *Singverein*.

gesangvoll (Ger.). Songful, cantabile.

geschleppt (Ger.). Dragged out.

Gesellschaft der Musikfreunde (Society of Music Friends). Viennese association founded in 1812 by leading philanthropists. It presents concerts and maintains an important library, with autograph scores and letters of Beethoven's bequeathed by Archduke Rudolph.

gesteigert (Ger.). Intensified.

gestopft (Ger.). Hand-stopped (of a horn).

gestrichen (Ger.). Bowed.

Gesualdo, Carlo, Prince of Venosa and Count of Conza (b. ?Naples, *c*.1561; d. Gesualdo, 8 Sep 1613). Italian composer, remarkable for his wildly veering chromatic harmonies and for the outrage he committed. He was born into a noble family, his father a prince, his mother the niece of the pope (Pius IV), who made two of his uncles cardinals: the great Carlo Borromeo and Alfonso Gesualdo. Possibly he was intended for a career in the church himself, but the death of his elder brother in 1584 left him heir, and he succeeded to the princedom in 1591. By then he was notorious, for the year before he had had both his wife and her lover killed. He retired to his castle at Gesualdo, a small hill town in the Neapolitan countryside, and to music, a lifelong passion that may have been encouraged by contact with the Netherlandish composer Giovanni de Macque, who was in the Gesualdo family's service from 1585.

In 1594 he emerged into public life again, being remarried to Leonora d'Este, of the ruling family of Ferrara. For the next two years he divided his time between Gesualdo and the intensely musical Ferrarese court, where he enjoyed the company of fellow musicians, notably Luzzaschi, and published four books of madrigals; he also visited Venice, deprecating Gabrieli. After that he returned to his solitary existence in Gesualdo. The musicians he brought with him gradually left; he seems to have been largely estranged from his wife; and his two sons, one from each marriage, both died, the death of the elder coming just three weeks before his own.

It is easy to interpret his music as fitting his melancholic disposition, though it comes too at an extreme point in a much wider late-Renaissance exploration of chromaticism. Regular chords and progressions are distorted by chromatic alteration, which results not only in a high level of dissonance but in an unstable harmonic style: the ground can seem to fall away, producing a kind of aural vertigo. All this is most alarming and poignant in the last three books of madrigals (to words generally caught up in the pain of love, the mingling of desire and frustration) and the volume of tenebrae responsories, music that for its harmonic strangeness was regarded with censure or distaste until the later 20th century, when it was keenly embraced by performers and audiences, and excited the interest of composers, from Stravinsky to Sciarrino, Schnittke and Dean.

Glenn Watkins *Gesualdo* (1973, [2]1991)

Madrigals (with publication dates, all a 5): Book 1, 1594; Book 2, 1594; Book 3, 1595; Book 4, 1596 (*Arde il mio cor*; *Che fai meco, mio cor*; *Cor mio, deh, non piangete*; *Ecco, morirò dunque*; *Io tacerò, ma nel silenzio mio*; *Luci serene e chiare*; *Or, che in gioia credea*; *Questa crudele e pia*; *Sparge la morte al mio Signor*; etc.); Book 5, 1611 (*Asciugate i begli occhi*; *Dolcissima mia vita*; *Mercè grido piangendo*; *O dolorosa gioia*; *Poichè l'avida sete*; *Tu m'uccidi, oh crudele*; etc.); Book 6, 1611 (*Beltà, poi che assenti*; *Moro, lasso, al mio duolo*; *Resta di darmi noia*; *Se la mia morte brami*); etc.
Sacred (with publication dates): Motets a 5, 1603 (*Ave, dulcissima Maria*; *O vos omnes*; *Peccantem me quotidie*); *Responsoria* a 6, 1611
Instrumental: *Canzon francese* a 4, *Gagliarda* a 4, etc.

geteilt (Ger.). Divided, i.e. divisi.

getragen (Ger.). Solemn, grand.

Gewandhaus Orchestra. Leipzig orchestra, so called because its first concerts (1781) were in the Cloth Exchange (Gewandhaus). Mendelssohn's directorship (1835–47) gave it a golden age; Reinecke (1860–95) took it into a new hall (Neues Gewandhaus, 1884–1943). Later directors included Nikisch (1895–1922), Furtwängler (1922–9), Walter (1929–33), Masur (1970–96), who led the orchestra into a new Neues Gewandhaus in 1981, Herbert Blomstedt (1988–2005) and Chailly.

gewichtig (Ger.). Weighty.

Geyer, Stefi (b. Budapest, 23 Jun 1888; d. Zurich, 11 Dec 1956). Hungarian–Swiss violinist, a pupil of Hubay and recipient of works from three composers who were successively in love with her: Bartók, Schoeck and Walter Schulthess, whom she married in 1920. She also took part in the première of Berg's Chamber Concerto.

gezogen (Ger.). Drawn out.

Ghedini, Giorgio Federico (b. Cuneo, 11 Jul 1892; d. Nervi, near Genoa, 25 Mar 1965). Italian composer, whose finest works, opening Baroque forms into a contemplative and exquisitely coloured wider musical world, came as orchestral pieces of the 1940s. They include *Architetture* (1940), the Concerto 'Il belprato' for violin and strings (1947) and most especially the *Concerto dell'albatro* (1945), with solo piano trio plus a voice speaking a passage from *Moby Dick*. Earlier he had studied in Bologna (with Bossi) and begun his career as a composer and teacher in Turin. His later appointments were at the conservatories of Parma (1938–41) and Milan (1941–62, from 1951 as director), his pupils including Berio. Among his other works are operas (*Le baccanti*, Milan, 1948; *Billy Budd*, Venice, 1949) and sacred cantatas.

Gheorghiu, Angela (b. Adjud, 7 Sep 1965). Romanian soprano, a lyric spinto of brilliance and temperament, admired in her own right and in her stage partnership with her husband, Roberto Alagna. She studied with Arta Florescu in Bucharest and made her debut as Mimì at Cluj in 1990.

Ghost. Name given Beethoven's Piano Trio Op.70:1 on account of its slow movement, which is traditionally related to the *Macbeth* opera he was planning.

Giacosa, Giuseppe (b. Colleretto Parella, Ivrea, 21 Oct 1847; d. Colleretto Parella, 2 Sep 1906). Italian playwright and librettist, already successful in the former capacity before he was drafted in by the publisher Giulio Ricordi to work for Puccini on *La Bohème*, followed by *Tosca* and *Madama Butterfly*. In each case his task was to versify Illica's dialogue.

Giannini, Vittorio (b. Philadelphia, 19 Oct 1903; d. New York, 28 Nov 1966). US composer, author of five symphonies (No.3 for band), operas and numerous songs in a blithe Romantic idiom. He studied at the Milan Conservatory (1913–17) and Juilliard, and had a career as a teacher.

Gianni Schicchi. See *Il* TRITTICO.

Giant. Name given Bach's fugue on *Wir glauben all an einen Gott*, BWV 680, on account of the giant strides in the bass.

Giardini, Felice (de) (b. Turin, 12 Apr 1716; d. Moscow, 8 Jun 1796). Italian violinist-composer, who spent most of his career in England (1751–84), as a soloist, orchestra leader (for opera in London; for the Three Choirs Festival, 1770–76), organizer and composer, notably of chamber music. Following studies in Milan and Turin (with G.B. Somis) he played in opera orchestras in Rome and Naples. He reported to Burney an encounter with Jommelli in the latter city, when his eager

ornamentation for an affecting aria was rewarded with a slap on the face. It was also to Naples that he retired, though he made an unsuccessful return to London (1790–92) before going on to Russia and penury.

Giasone (Jason). Opera by Cavalli to a libretto by Giacinto Andrea Cicognini, the most frequently performed opera of the 17th century, which it could only be, perhaps, because the story of Jason and Medea is more benignly told than in many versions. Jason (alto) has had twin sons with both Medea (soprano) and Hypsipyle (soprano). Finally he is united with the latter, while Medea happily settles for Aegeus (tenor). And the Golden Fleece is found. First performance: Venice, 5 Jan 1649.

Gibbons. Family of English musicians, clustered around Orlando. Of his elder brothers, Edward (b. 1568) moved as master of the choristers from King's College, Cambridge (1592–8) to Exeter Cathedral (1608–49), and Ellis (b.1573) had a madrigal or perhaps two in *The Triumphs of Oriana*. The woodcarver Grinling Gibbons was no relation.

(1) **Orlando** (baptized Oxford, 25 Dec 1583; d. Canterbury, 5 Jun 1625). Composer and keyboardist, outstanding in his generation. He was a chorister (1596–9) and student at King's College, and in 1603 joined the Chapel Royal, with which he remained. As a keyboardist he had Bull as his superior, and his music was included with Bull's and Byrd's in PARTHENIA (1613). After Bull's departure, that same year, he was recognized as 'the best finger' of the age, joining the select company of private musicians to the future Charles I, and becoming organist of Westminster Abbey (1623). He was taken ill and died suddenly while the court was at Canterbury to welcome the new queen, Henrietta Maria. Some of his church music has been in continuous use since the Restoration, valued for its contrapuntal majesty allied to vividness of idea, but other qualities of his work – the virtuosity of his keyboard music as an extension of Byrd's and Bull's, the melancholy of his madrigals, the exuberance of his consort music – were not rediscovered until the later 20th century.

John Harley *Orlando Gibbons and the Gibbons Family of Musicians* (1999)

Sacred: verse anthems (*See, the Word is incarnate, This is the record of John*, etc.), full anthems (*Almighty and everlasting God* a 4, *Hosanna to the Son of David* a 6, *O clap your hands* a 8, etc.), services (Short Service, Second Service in verse style, etc.), hymn tunes (*Drop, drop, slow tears*)

Other vocal works: madrigals a 5, pub 1612 (*The Silver Swan*); *The Cries of London*, 5 v, 5 viols
Consort: fantasias (6 a 2, 16 a 3, 2 a 4, 9 a 6), In Nomines (1 a 4, 3 a 5), etc.
Keyboard: *The Italian Ground*, Pavan and Galliard 'Lord Salisbury', 10 fantasias, other dances, variations, etc.

(2) **Christopher** (baptized Westminster, 22 Aug 1615; d. Westminster, 20 Oct 1676). Organist-composer, Orlando's eldest surviving son, probably trained by his uncle Edward in Exeter. He was organist of Winchester Cathedral (1638–42), then spent the Commonwealth period (1649–60) in London as a private organist and teacher. At the Restoration (1660) he was installed as organist of the Chapel Royal and Westminster Abbey, gaining also an Oxford doctorate (1664) and a reputation as a bon viveur. He wrote anthems, consort music and organ pieces.

Gibbs, Cecil Armstrong (b. Great Baddow, Essex, 10 Aug 1889; d. Chelmsford, 10 May 1960). British composer, especially of songs to poems by Walter de la Mare ('Silver', 1920). He studied with Dent and Charles Wood at Cambridge, then worked as a schoolmaster (1913–19) before completing his training under Vaughan Williams at the RCM, where he joined the staff (1921–39). Involving himself in amateur festivals as a composer and adjudicator, he also wrote more ambitious works, including three symphonies (the second choral, *Odysseus*, 1937–8).

Gideon, Miriam (b. Greeley, Col., 23 Oct 1906; d. New York, 18 Jun 1996). US composer, a classical and lyrical modernist whose finely made music came mostly in chamber forms. She trained with her organist uncle in Boston, but most importantly with Sessions (1935–43), and achieved a breakthrough with *The Hound of Heaven* for voice and oboe quartet (1945). Alongside composing she taught at the Jewish Theological Seminary (1955–91) and the Manhattan School (1967–91).

Gielen, Michael (Andreas) (b. Dresden, 20 Jul 1927). German conductor and composer, an exacting and determined communicator of older music (notably Beethoven's) as much as of the new works with which he is specially associated: his honours include the first performances of Ligeti's *Requiem* and Zimmermann's *Die Soldaten*. As Steuermann's nephew, he was born into the Schoenberg circle, and after studies with Erwin Leuchter in Buenos Aires (1942–9) he continued with the Schoenberg pupil Josef Polnauer in Vienna (1950–53). In the 1950s, while working as a répétiteur at the Vienna Staatsoper, he began conducting new music in Germany. He then held a range of appointments, notably with the Frankfurt opera (1977–87) and the SWF Symphony (1986–99). His works include larger pieces and two quartets.

Gieseking, Walter (b. Lyons, 5 Nov 1895; d. London, 26 Oct 1956). German pianist, especially valued for his sensitivity of touch and pedalling in Debussy. He studied with Karl Leimer in Hanover (1911–13) and became an international performer in the 1920s, with debuts in London (1923) and the USA (1926). Under suspicion for remaining in Germany during the Nazi period, he was able to clear his name, record Debussy's piano output virtually complete (1951–4) and return to Carnegie Hall (1955).

giga (It.). See GIGUE.

Gigault, Nicolas (b. ?Paris, *c*.1627; d. Paris, 20 Aug 1707). French organist-composer, who held appointments in Paris from 1646 and published two volumes of organ pieces, one for Christmas, including the earliest noëls with variations (1683), the other of versets in the tradition of Titelouze (1685).

Gigli, Beniamino (b. Recanati, 20 Mar 1890; d. Rome, 30 Nov 1957). Italian tenor, whose sweetness and expressive candour in lyric numbers gave him an audience far beyond that of opera connoisseurs: his recordings were immensely (and lastingly) successful, and he appeared in numerous films between 1935 and 1952. Born on the same day as Melchior, he studied in Rome, made his debut at Rovigo (1914), rose rapidly to an international career, notably at the Met (1920–32), and maintained that career almost to his death. He also published his memoirs (1957).

Gigout, Eugène (b. Nancy, 23 Mar 1844; d. Paris, 9 Dec 1925). French organist-composer, pupil of Saint-Saëns at the Ecole Niedermeyer (from 1857). He remained there as a teacher, his pupils including Boëllmann and Fauré, while also seving as organist of St Augustin (from 1863). His works include contributions to the organ's Romantic repertory (*Grand choeur dialogué*, 1881; Toccata, B minor, 1890; Scherzo, 1890) as well as pieces in neo-Baroque style.

gigue (Fr.; It. *giga*, older Eng. form *jig*). Dance apparently of low British origins, in the 15th century. The etymology is confused: in continental Europe various forms of the word could denote a violin or violinist (compare GEIGE). It is hard to discern, too, what kind of dance was associated with the term, which in Shakespeare's time seems to have implied vulgarity more than anything else; the jig was a song-and-dance routine done at the end of a play (though not at the Globe). By the late 17th century it had settled down as a court or theatrical dance in compound metre (most often 6/8), still lively, and begun to gain a customary place at the ending of a suite or church sonata. There were diverse types, the French *gigue* being contrapuntal and complex in phrasing, the Italian *giga* more simply textured and regular, though many composers, notably Bach, drew elements from both. Gigue-style 6/8 finales appear occasionally in the Classical period (e.g. in Haydn's 'Military' Symphony), and Debussy used the term in the plural in his orchestral *Images*. Otherwise post-Baroque gigues tend to be neo-Baroque in style, as in works by Reger, Schoenberg and Stravinsky.

Gilbert, Anthony (b. London, 26 Jul 1934). British composer, whose fantasy has led him in diverse directions: assertive (*9 or 10 Osannas* for five players, 1967), meditative with Indian nuances (the piano concerto *Towards Asâvari*, 1978), and playful. He came to composing late, studying with Seiber (1957–9) and with Goehr and Milner at Morley College (1959–63). As a teacher himself he moved from Goldsmiths College (1968–73) to the RNCM (1973–99).

Gilbert, Henry F(ranklin Belknapp) (b. Somerville, Mass., 26 Sep 1868; d. Cambridge, Mass., 19 May 1928). US composer, who is best known for his direct efforts to draw from Amerindian and African-American traditions (*Indian Scenes*, *Negro Dances*, both for piano, pub 1912, 1914). Born into a musical family, he had lessons with MacDowell (1889–92), but was more impressed by the musical cultures he encountered at the World's Columbian Exhibition in Chicago (1893) and by the popular touch of Charpentier's *Louise*. He worked with Farwell at the Wa-Wan Press, and in the 1920s moved into a more complex idiom.

Gilbert, Pia (b. Kippenheim, 1 Jun 1921). German–US composer, best known for her dance work. She moved with her family to New York in 1937 and studied at the New York College of Music, though as a composer she is self-taught. In 1946 she settled in Los Angeles, where she soon became close to the Schoenberg family, as later to Cage. She taught at UCLA (1947–85), then returned to New York and joined the Juilliard faculty.

Gilbert, W(illiam) S(chwenck) (b. London, 18 Nov 1836; d. Harrow Weald, 29 May 1911). British

librettist, especially in partnership with SULLIVAN, knighted in 1907.

Gilels, Emil (Grigoryevich) (b. Odessa, 19 Oct 1916; d. Moscow, 14 Oct 1985). Russian pianist, of full virtuoso strength, though admired too for his sensitive yet commanding way with Brahms, Beethoven and Grieg. He completed his studies with Neuhaus in Moscow (1935–7), and was just launched on an international career at the outbreak of war. After 1945 he remained based in Moscow, teaching at the conservatory, but he was also among the most widely travelled Soviet musicians.

Gilles, Jean (b. Tarascon, 8 Jan 1668; d. Toulouse, 5 Feb 1705). French composer and church musician, whose *Messe des morts* long outlived him, becoming the favourite *Requiem* of 18th-century France, sung at the funerals of Rameau and Louis XV. Of humble origin, he was a choirboy at Aix Cathedral (1679–87, a little after Campra), where he remained on the music staff before taking posts at the cathedrals of Agde (1695–7) and Toulouse (1697–1705). He also wrote motets and Lamentations settings.

Gillis, Don (b. Cameron, Missouri, 17 Jun 1912; d. Columbia, SC, 10 Jan 1978). US composer with a humorous bent, best known for his Symphony No.5½ (1947), with its 'Scherzofrenia'. Trained at Texas Christian University and North Texas State University, he was associated with Toscanini through his work for NBC in New York (from 1944) and spent his last decade back in university life. He wrote numerous other orchestral and chamber pieces.

Gilson, Paul (b. Brussels, 15 Jun 1865; d. Brussels, 3 Apr 1942). Belgian composer, a late-Romantic colourist whose fate was to long outlive his early triumph, the symphonic suite *La Mer* (1892). After 1906 he largely stopped composing Russo-Wagnerian operas and art-nouveau orchestral music in favour of chamber pieces, songs and teaching, his pupils including Absil and Poot. His own teacher was François Gevaert at the Brussels Conservatory (1887–9), though he is said to have learned more from studying scores.

gimel. See GYMEL.

gimping. Wrapping a string in fine wire; the string being thus gimped.

Ginastera, Alberto (b. Buenos Aires, 11 Apr 1916; d. Geneva, 25 Jun 1983). Argentinian composer, who boldly carried his colourful national style into the further reaches of modernism. He studied in Buenos Aires at the Williams (1928–35) and National (1936–8) conservatories, and made a mark while still a student when a suite from his ballet *Panambí* was performed in 1937. The ballet's first staging (1940) then resulted in a commission from Lincoln Kirstein for a second, *Estancia*. Drawing on Amerindian and gaucho music respectively, presented in a manner influenced by Bartók, Stravinsky and Falla, these scores established both his early style and his international reputation. In 1941 he met Copland at Tanglewood and began teaching at the National Conservatory, leaving for a US tour (1945–7).

In 1948, back in Argentina, he took a post as director of the National University at La Plata and founded the Argentinian section of the ISCM, for whose festivals he travelled several times to Europe in the 1950s. His music had become more subjective, more often voiced in chamber forms; his European journeys further exposed him to a wide range of new music, and in his Second Quartet (1958) he instituted serial techniques, though these were part of a rich vocabulary used to produce music of high exuberance and expressive force, a vocabulary that soon also included quarter-tones, polytonality and extreme vocal and instrumental effects. The climax came in three operas of sexuality and violence, among which *Don Rodrigo* was chosen by New York City Opera for its inaugural performance at the State Theater (1966, with Domingo) and *Beatrix Cenci* was commissioned for the opening of the Kennedy Center in Washington. Meanwhile, he remained a forceful presence back home as dean of music at the Catholic University of Argentina (1958–63) and director of music at the Di Tello Institute (1963–71). He spent the last 12 years of his life in Switzerland with his second wife, the Argentinian cellist Aurora Nátola, and his music became more lyrical.

Operas: *Don Rodrigo* (Alejandro Casona), Op.31, f.p. Buenos Aires, 1964; *Bomarzo* (Manuel Mujica Láinez), Op.34, f.p. Washington, 1967; *Beatrix Cenci* (William Shand and Alberto Girri), Op.38, f.p. Washington, 1971

Orchestral: *Panambí* (ballet), Op.1, 1934–7; *Estancia* (ballet), Op.8, 1941; *Obertura para el 'Fausto' criollo*, Op.9, 1943; *Variaciones concertantes*, Op.23, chbr orch, 1953; Harp Concerto, Op.25, 1959–65; Piano Concerto No.1, Op.28, 1961; No.2, Op.39, 1972; Violin Concerto, Op.30, 1963; Cello Concerto No.1, Op.36, 1968; No.2, Op.50, 1980–81; etc.

Larger vocal works: Psalm 150, Op.5, ch, boys' ch, orch, 1938; *Cantata para América mágica* (Amerindian), Op.27, s, perc orch, 1960; suites from operas, etc.

Chamber and instrumental: Piano Quintet, Op.29, 1963; *Impresiones de la Puna*, fl, str qt, 1934; String Quartet No.1, Op.20, 1948; No.2, Op.26, 1958, rev 1968; No.3, Op.40, with s, 1973; *Pampeana No.1*, Op.16, vn, pf, 1947; No.2, Op.21, vc, pf, 1950; Cello Sonata, Op.49, 1979; Duo, Op.13, fl, ob, 1945; *Toccata, villancico y fuga*, Op.18, org, 1947; *Pueña No.2*, Op.45, vc, 1976; Guitar Sonata, Op.47, 1976, rev 1981; etc.

Songs: *Dos canciones*, Op.3, v, pf, 1938 (No.2 *Milonga*); *Cinque canciones populares argentinas*, Op.10, v, pf, 1943; etc.

Piano: Sonata No.1, Op.22, 1952; No.2, Op.53, 1981; No.3, Op.54, 1981; *Danzas argentinas*, Op.2, 1937; 3 Pieces, Op.6, 1940; *Malambo*, Op.7, 1940; *12 preludios americanos*, Op.12, 1944; *Suite de danzas criollas*, Op.15, 1946, rev 1956; *Rondó sobre temas infantiles argentinos*, Op.19, 1947

Ginzburg, Grigory (Romanovich) (b. Nizhny Novgorod, 19 May 1904; d. Moscow, 5 Dec 1961). Russian pianist, master of fine melody in the most virtuoso music of Liszt. He studied with Goldenweiser at the Moscow Conservatory, where in 1929 he joined the staff.

Gioconda, La (The Merry Woman). Opera by Ponchielli to a libretto by Boito after Victor Hugo's play *Angélo*. La Gioconda (soprano), a singer in 17th-century Venice, enables the Genoese Enzo (tenor) to escape with his beloved Laura (mezzo-soprano) from the web woven by the spy Barnaba (baritone) – at the expense of her own life and her mother's. The score is best known for Enzo's aria 'Cielo e mar', La Gioconda's 'Suicidio!' and the DANCE OF THE HOURS. First performance: Milan, 8 Apr 1876.

giocoso (It.). Jocular, frolicsome, often as a qualifier in *allegro giocoso*. Also *giocosamente* (playfully).

gioioso (It.). Joyous. Also *con gioia* (with joy), *gioiosamente* (joyously), etc.

Giordani, Tommaso (b. Naples, *c*.1731; d. Dublin, 24 Feb 1806). Italian composer, who performed with the family opera troupe in London (1753–6) and Dublin (1764), then had an independent career in both cities as a composer for theatres and pleasure gardens. A much-sung song, 'Caro mio ben', has been attributed both to him and to Giuseppe Giordani (1751–98), a Neapolitan opera composer who stayed in Italy, but possibly neither was responsible.

Giordano, Umberto (Menotti Maria) (b. Foggia, 28 Aug 1867; d. Milan, 12 Nov 1948). Italian composer, whose place among Puccini's contemporaries is assured by ANDREA CHENIER and FEDORA. He entered the Naples Conservatory in 1882, studied with Martucci, and came sixth in Sonzogno's 1889 competition for one-act operas (*Cavalleria rusticana* won). Sonzogno was nevertheless encouraged to stick with him, through two iffy full-length pieces, and was rewarded with his two triumphs. His later operas included *Siberia* (Milan, 1903) and *La cena delle beffe* (Milan, 1924).

Giovanni da Cascia (*fl.* ?Verona, 1340s). Italian composer, important in the early history of the madrigal and possibly an older contemporary of Jacopo da Bologna at the Veronese court.

gipsy. See GYPSY.

Giraut de Bornelh (b. Bourney, near Périgueux, *c*.1140; d. *c*.1200). Troubadour, whose 'Reis glorios', one of his four poems surviving with music, is probably the most esteemed of troubadour songs. He was apparently of humble origin and a schoolmaster, whose summer travels took him all over the troubadour world – i.e. through the courts of southern France and northern Spain, and to the Holy Land on the Third Crusade.

Girl of the Golden West, The. See *La* FANCIULLA DEL WEST.

Gis (Ger.). G#. Also *Gisis* (G✗).

Giselle. Ballet score by Adam for choreography by Jean Coralli and Jules Perrot to a scenario by Théophile Gautier. Giselle, a peasant girl, is toyed with by Albrecht, a nobleman in disguise. She dies and joins the Willies, the spirits of young women betrayed, but refuses to take her revenge on Albrecht. First performance: Paris, 28 Jun 1841.

gitano, gitana (Sp.). Gypsy.

Gitarre (Ger., pl. *Gitarren*). Guitar.

gittern. Name (see KITHARA) now preferred for the small, short-necked, medieval lute, also known at the time as 'guitar'. The instrument came into Europe from Islam in the later 13th century and gave way to the lute, vihuela and guitar during the 15th.

Giuliani, Mauro (b. Bisceglie, near Bari, 27 Jul 1781; d. Naples, 8 May 1829). Italian guitarist-composer. He moved to Vienna in 1806, and while winning success as a guitar virtuoso took part as a cellist in the first performance of Beethoven's Seventh Symphony. In 1819 he returned to Italy. Of his children, Michel became a singing teacher at the Paris Conservatoire and Emilia a guitarist-composer like her father. His large output includes three concertos (No.1, A, Op.30, pub 1808; No.2, A, Op.36, pub 1812; No.3, F, Op.70), quintets and other chamber pieces, and solo music.

Giulietta e Romeo. See ROMEO AND JULIET.

Giulini, Carlo Maria (b. Barletta, 9 May 1914). Italian conductor, of superfine quality in music ranging from Verdi to Bruckner. He studied at the Accademia di Santa Cecilia, with whose orchestra he made his debut in 1944. In 1950 he formed an orchestra for the Milan radio station, came to the notice of Toscanini and De Sabata, and so was appointed principal conductor at La Scala (1953–6). During that time he also made his debuts in Britain and the USA. He became a regular in London, especially at Covent Garden (1958–67) and with the Philharmonia Orchestra; he was also music director of the Los Angeles Philharmonic (1978–84).

Giulio Cesare (Julius Caesar). Opera by Handel, titled in full *Giulio Cesare in Egitto* (Julius Caesar in Egypt), to a libretto by Haym after earlier librettos on the same subject. Caesar (alto castrato) and Cleopatra (soprano), drawn together by an unappetizing but operatically productive mix of lust, wiles and political ambition, triumph over the even more obnoxious Ptolemy (alto castrato) and the noble survivors of Pompey: his widow Cornelia (contralto) and son Sextus (soprano). Cleopatra's arias range from vocal striptease ('V'adoro, pupille') to grief ('Piangerò la sorte mia'); Caesar's include 'Va tacito', with obbligato horn. Since the 1960s the piece has been the Handel opera most often chosen by major companies. First performance: London, 20 Feb 1724.

giusto (It.). Exact, as in *tempo giusto* (strict time).

Glagolitic Mass (*Mša glagolskaja*). Work by Janáček for soli (s, a, t, b), chorus, orchestra and organ. The text is that of the Glagolitic liturgy, which had long coexisted with the Latin rite in western Slav territories: its language is Slavonic, 'Glagolitic' being the term for the alphabet. First performance: Brno, 5 Dec 1927.

Glanville-Hicks, Peggy (b. Melbourne, 29 Dec 1912; d. Sydney, 25 Jun 1990). Australian–US composer and critic, whose most productive period in both roles was in New York in the later 1940s and 1950s. From 1947 she worked on the *Herald Tribune* under Thomson while writing music influenced by her wide travels, personal history and closeness to Graeco-Latin culture. Her works include operas (*The Transposed Heads*, after Thomas Mann, 1953), songs and instrumental pieces.

Glarean, Heinrich (b. Mollis, canton of Glarus, Jun 1488; d. Freinburg, 28 Mar 1563). Swiss theorist, whose monumental *Dodecahedron* (1547) expounded a theory of 12 modes, with Greek origins, as fundamental to both plainsong and polyphony, recognizing the Ionian (major) as currently preeminent. He studied with Michael Rubellus and with Johannes Cochlaeus at Cologne University (1506–10); also important was his meeting with Erasmus in Basle, where he taught from 1514, except for a period of travel to Italy and Paris. With the advent of the Reformation in Basle, he moved in 1529 to Freiburg University.

glass harmonica. See ARMONICA.

Glass, Louis (Christian August) (b. Frederiksberg, 23 Mar 1864; d. Gentofte, 22 Jan 1936). Danish composer, notably of six symphonies close to Franck and Bruckner. He studied with his composer father, with Gade and from 1884 in Brussels with Wieniawski, then worked in Copenhagen as a composer, concert administrator and pedagogue, taking over his father's piano conservatory (1894–1932).

Glass, Philip (b. Baltimore, 31 Jan 1937). US composer, a prolific generator of large-scale works obedient to the repetitive drive of minimalism. He picked up music at home, his father being a radio repairman and record-dealer, but it took him a while to find his way. An early stint at college (the University of Chicago, 1952–6) was followed by a Juilliard education (1957–61), under Persichetti and William Bergsma. Then he studied with Boulanger in Paris (1964–6), where he took a job transcribing Ravi Shankar's music for a film company. That led him to travels through north Africa, India and the Himalayas before he returned to New York early in 1967. He soon met Reich, and the two – both of them concerned with pulsed ostinato and evident rhythmic processes – played in each other's ensembles during the next three years. He also had lessons with Alla Rakha, Ravi Shankar's tabla player.

He gave his first concerts with the Philip Glass Ensemble in spring 1968, and for the next few years worked almost exclusively with this group based on keyboards and wind instruments, whose steady beat, elementary diatonic material and heavy amplification related it to rock bands. At the same time, he virtually recapitulated the history of Western harmony, moving from unison performance (*Two Pages*) through *Music in Fifths* to the three-hour-plus *Music in 12 Parts* (1971–4), which is dodecaplex both horizontally (in having 12 sections) and vertically (in its contrapuntal count). The ensemble's collaboration with Robert Wilson, *Einstein on the Beach* (1976), turned him towards opera, more conventional forces and, on occasion, boldly expressive gestures, but without any essential change to his music's heavy machinery.

Philip Glass *Music* (1987); Richard Kostelanetz, ed. *Writings on Glass* (1997)

www.philipglass.com

Operas: EINSTEIN ON THE BEACH, 1975–6; *Satyagraha* (Glass and Constance DeJong), f.p. Rotterdam, 1980; *Akhnaten* (Glass et al.), f.p. Stuttgart, 1984; *The Fall of the House of Usher* (Arthur Yorinks, after Poe), f.p. Cambridge, Mass., 1988; *The Voyage*, f.p. New York, 1992; *Orphée* (Cocteau), f.p. Cambridge, Mass., 1993; *La Belle et la bête* (Cocteau), f.p. Gibellina, 1994; *Les Enfants terribles* (Cocteau), f.p. Zug, 1996; *Monsters of Grace* (Coleman Barks, after Rumi), f.p. Los Angeles, 1998; *Galileo Galilei* (Mary Zimmermann et al.), f.p. Chicago, 2002; etc.

Film scores: *Koyaanisquatsi*, 1982; *Powaqqatsi*, 1987; *Naqoyqatsi*, 2002; etc.

Orchestral: Symphony No.1 'Low', 1992; No.2, 1994; No.3, str, 1994; No.4 'Heroes', 1996; No.5 'Choral', soli, ch, orch, 1999; Violin Concerto, 1987; Concerto Fantasy, 2 timp, orch, 2000; etc.

Amplified ensemble: Music in Similar Motion, 1969; Music in Fifths, 1969; Music in 12 Parts, 1971–4; etc.

String quartets: No.1, 1966; No.2 'Company', 1983; No.3 'Mishima', 1985; No.4 'Buczak', 1989; No.5, 1991

Keyboard: Two Pages, 1968; Music in Contrary Motion, 1969; etc.

Glazunov, Aleksandr (Konstantinovich) (b. St Petersburg, 10 Aug 1865; d. Paris, 21 Mar 1936). Russian composer, the golden boy of the Rimsky-Korsakov circle – he studied with the master in 1880–81 and his First Symphony was conducted by Balakirev when he was still 16 – though his chief model was Tchaikovsky. Following his early successes, he gained the patronage of Belyayev, who took him to western Europe (1884). He remained hugely productive through his 20s and 30s, when he produced most of the works by which he is known, besides completing Borodin's *Prince Igor* (with Rimsky). After that his formidable energy seems to have gone largely into teaching at the St Petersburg Conservatory (1899–1930), though from 1928 he spent most of his time abroad.

Ballet scores: *Raymonda* (ballet), Op.57, 1896–7; *The Seasons* (ballet), Op.67, 1899.

Symphonies: No.1 'Slavic', E, Op.5, 1881–2, rev 1885, 1929; No.2, F# minor, Op.16, 1886; No.3, D, Op.33, 1890; No.4, E♭, Op.48, 1893; No.5, B♭, Op.55, 1895; No.6, C minor, Op.58, 1896; No.7 'Pastoral', F, Op.77, 1902; No.8, E♭, Op.83, 1906; No.9, D, 1910

Concertante works: Piano Concerto No.1, F minor, Op.92, 1910–11; No.2, B, Op.100, 1917; Violin Concerto, A minor, Op.82, 1904; *Concerto ballata*, C, Op.108, vc, orch, 1931; Saxophone Concerto, E♭, Op.109, 1934; *Sérénade espagnole*, Op.20:2, vc, orch, 1887–8; *Chant du ménéstrel*, Op.71, vc, orch, 1900

Other orchestral works: *Stenka Razin*, Op.13, 1885; *Spring*, Op.34, 1891; *Carnaval* (overture), Op.45, 1892; Concert Waltz No.1, D, Op.47, 1893; No.2, F, Op.51, 1894; *Scènes de ballet*, Op.52, 1894; *From the Middle Ages* (suite), Op.79, Op.1902; Introduction and Dance of SALOME, Op.90, 1908

Chamber and instrumental: *Méditation*, Op.32, vn, pf, 1891; *Rêverie*, Op.24, hn, pf, 1890; 7 numbered quartets, etc.

Piano: Sonata No.1, B♭ minor, Op.74, 1901; No.2, E minor, Op.75, 1901; 3 Etudes, Op.31, 1891; etc.

Other works: cantatas, songs, etc.

glee. Unaccompanied choral piece of a kind sung by amateur groups, normally of men, in Britain and the USA from the mid 18th century to the late 19th, when increasing sophistication led to a preference for the term 'partsong'. The term survives in the name of the Harvard Glee Club, founded in 1858.

gleichschwebende Temperatur (Ger.). Equal temperament.

gli (It.). The (masculine plural), as in *gli altri* (the rest, i.e. those not playing a solo).

Glière, Reinhold [Glier, Reyngold Moritsevich] (b. Kiev, 11 Jan 1875; d. Moscow, 23 Jun 1956). Russian composer, a late-Romantic follower of Borodin and Glazunov. He studied with Taneyev, Arensky and Ippolitov-Ivanov at the Moscow Conservatory (1894–1900), studied conducting with Oskar Fried in Berlin (1905–7), taught at the Kiev Conservatory (1913–20) and returned to the Moscow Conservatory as professor of composition (1920–41). His works include the much lauded ballet *The Red Poppy* (Op.70, 1926–7), operas and other works relating to Caucasian and Central Asian cultures, three symphonies (No.3 'Ilya Muromets', Op.42, 1909–11, on the hero of chivalric legend), concertos for harp (Op.74, 1938) and coloratura soprano (Op.82, 1943), and four quartets.

Glinka, Mikhail (Ivanovich) (b. Novospasskoye, near Yelnya, Smolensk district, 1 Jun 1804; d. Berlin, 15 Feb 1857). Russian composer, acclaimed by all his successors as the fountainhead of the Russian Romantic tradition, the ancestor of Tchaikovsky and Musorgsky. He enjoyed the life of a gentleman. Born and brought up on the family estate, where he had abundant opportunities to play and hear music, he later spent long periods travelling in search of medical cures and musical stimulation. Studies with Field (briefly) and Charles Mayer came when he was at school in St Petersburg (1818–22). He also had singing lessons while working in the civil service (1824–8), during which time he got to know Pushkin and other poets. In 1830 he set off for Italy with the tenor Nikolay Ivanov and stayed three years, hearing the premières of *Anna Bolena* and *La sonnambula*, and composing fantasies on these and other operas. Bel canto, whether for voice or piano, became an essential feature of his style, to be joined by a ranging harmonic imagination prompted by imagery drawn from the East, the West (Spain), and from within Russia itself. He returned to Russia in 1834 after several months studying with Siegfried Dehn in Berlin, and settled back in St Petersburg, where he failed to enjoy marriage (the alliance ended in 1839 after four and a half years) but did achieve the two operas on which his fame largely rests. Then he left again, to spend much of his time from 1844 onwards in Paris (where Berlioz was a help to him) and Berlin, apart from a period in Spain (1845–7).

David Brown *Mikhail Glinka* (1974)

Operas: *A LIFE FOR THE TSAR*, 1834–6; *RUSLAN AND LYUDMILA*, 1837–42

Orchestral: *Valse-fantaisie*, 1839, orch 1856; *Capriccio brillante* (on the *Jota aragonesa*, First Spanish Overture), 1845; *Kamarinskaya*, 1848; *Souvenir d'une nuit d'été à Madrid* (Second Spanish Overture), 1848, rev 1851; etc.

Chamber and instrumental: Viola Sonata, 1825–8; *Gran sestetto originale*, E♭, pf, str qnt, 1832; *Trio pathétique*, D minor, cl, bn, pf, 1832; numerous variation sets and other virtuoso pieces for pf, etc.

Other works: songs ('The Lark', Nestor Kukolnik, 1840), other stage music, etc.

glissando (fake It., from Fr. *glissade*, slide). Slide from one note to another, marking the chromatic or diatonic steps (as on the piano or harp), whereas the PORTAMENTO is continuous. However, usage is not quite so well defined, the term 'glissando' often being used for the continuous slides made by trombones (using the physical slide), clarinets or timpani (changing tension).

Globokar, Vinko (b. Anderny, Meurthe-et-Moselle, 7 Jul 1934). Slovenian trombonist-composer, a musician physically invested in his work. The family returned to Ljubljana for his secondary schooling and conservatory training (1947–54); he then studied at the Paris Conservatoire (1955–9), and had lessons with Leibowitz (1959–63) and Berio (1965). Berio (*Sequenza V*), Stockhausen (*Solo*) and Kagel (*Atem*) all wrote pieces for him, and influenced the music of rich reference, expanded technique and irony he began writing, while also, from 1968, working with free improvisation groups (notably his own quartet New Phonic Art, with Michel Portal on clarinet, Carlos Roqué Alsina on keyboards and Jean-Pierre Drouet on percussion). His works include *Discours II–IX* (1967–93) for groupings of like instruments and several semi-theatrical pieces for large forces.

glock. Abbreviation for glockenspiel.

Glock, William (Frederick) (b. London, 3 May 1908; d. Oxford, 28 Jun 2000). British administrator, knighted in 1970. He studied with Schnabel in Berlin (1930–33), worked as a critic and became controller of music for the BBC (1959–73), where he vigorously promoted Boulez (his choice as principal conductor of the BBC Symphony), Carter, etc.

Glocke (Ger., pl. *Glocken*). Bell.

glockenspiel (Ger., play of bells). Small instrument with tuned metal bars, which are struck either with mallets, xylophone-style, or by means of a keyboard. The normal range is from F at the top of the treble staff up through two octaves and a fifth or seventh; parts are usually notated in the treble clef two octaves lower. Two striking 18th-century uses are in Handel's *Saul* (seemingly the instrument's debut) and Mozart's *Die Zauberflöte*, both of which apparently presumed a keyboard operating a set of small bells. The mallet instrument, which may have derived from the BELL-LYRA, arrived in the mid 19th century and became almost a fixture of the late-Romantic and modern orchestra.

Gloria. Section of the ORDINARY of the mass, beginning with the words sung by the angels to the shepherds at the time of the Nativity.

Gloriana. Opera by Britten to a libretto by William Plomer. Commissioned to mark at Covent Garden the coronation of Elizabeth II, the work concerns the private life of Elizabeth I (soprano), and in particular her renunciation of her favourite Essex (tenor). First performance: London, 8 Jun 1953.

glosa (Sp., gloss). Term for variation or ornamentation in Renaissance–Baroque Spain.

glottis. Aperture in the vocal cords.

Gluck, Christoph Willibald (Ritter von) (b. Erasbach, Upper Palatinate, 2 Jul 1714; d. Vienna, 15 Nov 1787). Bohemian composer, honoured until the mid 20th century as the essential founder of opera, his telling of the Orpheus story being the oldest piece regularly performed. Since then the bounds of the operatic repertory have been thrown back, though not yet to include much of the earlier Gluck. Also important as a ballet composer, he wrote little that was not for the theatre.

His father's work as a forester in service took the family back to ancestral Bohemia in 1717, and he grew up speaking Czech. Little is known of his education. He may have gone to Prague University, and may have studied with Sammartini in Milan, where he had certainly arrived by 1737. The city was then within the Habsburg Empire, and his connections with the Lobkowitz clan, for whom his father and grandfather had worked, could have helped bring him official favour. Four operas by him were produced at the ducal theatre in 1741–5, and there were more for other northern Italian cities.

In 1745–6 he spent several months in London, where he presented two operas and earned Handel's remark, recorded by Burney: 'He knows no more of contrapunto as mein cook.' He may, though, have learned something from Handel (if not counterpoint), and from the naturalism of David Garrick's acting. After that he joined Pietro Mingotti's itinerant company, which he supplied with scores for royal occasions in Saxony (1747) and Denmark (1749), meanwhile writing a *Semiramide* for the reopening of the Viennese court theatre, the Burgtheater. Then he worked for the Kotzen Opera in Prague (1750–52) and got married in 1750 to a Viennese heiress half his age. There were no children, possibly because of a venereal disease he had contracted.

His life as a jobbing opera composer continued with a commission for Naples (1752), after which he settled in Vienna, attached first to Prince Joseph Friedrich von Sachsen-Hildburghausen and then, from 1755, to the imperial court, with particular responsibility for entertainments in the Burgtheater and other Habsburg palaces under the jurisdiction of Count Durazzo. But while answering demands for Italian operas both serious and comic, for French opéras comique and for ballets, he also wrote scores for Rome (1756), Bologna (1763), Florence (1767) and Parma (1769). In Rome he was honoured with the papal Order of the Golden Spur and ever after added the title 'knight' (*Ritter, cavaliere*) to his signature.

So far his work had been admired or censured

(by Metastasio) for irregularities, but there had been little warning of the wholesale revolution that was to come with *Orfeo ed Euridice* (1762), his second collaboration with Ranieri Calzabigi. (Their first work together had been the ballet *Don Juan*, created soon after the poet's arrival in Vienna.) With its emphasis on natural declamation and its re-invoking of a presumed Greek ideal of sung and danced drama, it achieved an undecorated vigour and solemnity for which other composers had been striving (see REFORM OPERA). This was instantly understood and acclaimed. Curiously, though, Gluck and Calzabigi did not have a chance to work together again until *Alceste* (1766–7), and the composer meanwhile went on in the Metastasian style that *Orfeo* had stood out against.

Following his dubious and calamitous financial investment in the Burgtheater (1769–70), and the cool reception accorded his and Calzabigi's third opera, *Paride ed Elena*, he turned his attention to setting odes by Klopstock and a new libretto for Paris, based on Racine's *Iphigénie*. He was part way through this when Burney encountered him again on a visit in September 1772 and found him 'like a true great genius … still in bed'. (His wife explained that he wrote all night.) He travelled to Paris in November 1773 to supervise the production of *Iphigénie en Aulide*, and saw six further operas of his presented there during the next six years, though he returned intermittently to Vienna. The first two Calzabigi settings and two earlier opéras comique he revised; the new works were *Armide*, *Iphigénie en Tauride* and *Echo et Narcisse*, in all of which he characteristically recycled music from pieces Paris had not seen. Since French lyric tragedy had been one of Calzabigi's models, in Paris Gluck was bringing reform opera home. The strengths of the Orpheus and Alcestis operas were renewed, and joined by those of the great Iphigenia dramas.

While in Paris he suffered the first in a series of strokes, and he returned to Vienna to spend his last years in virtual retirement, though alert enough to request a special performance of *Die Entführung aus dem Serail* and congratulate its composer, who was one of many to learn from him.

Patricia Howard *Gluck: An 18th-Century Portrait in Letters and Documents* (1995)

Operas: *Ipermestra* (Metastasio), f.p. Venice, 1744; *Le nozze d'Ercole e d'Ebe*, f.p. Pillnitz (Dresden), 1747; *La Semiramide riconosciuta* (Metastasio), f.p. Vienna, 1748; *La contesa de' numi* (Metastasio), f.p. Copenhagen, 1749; *Ezio* (Metastasio: first setting), f.p. Prague, 1750; *La clemenza di Tito* (Metastasio), f.p. Naples, 1752; *Le cinesi* (Metastasio), f.p. Schlosshof (Vienna), 1754; *La danza* (Metastasio),

f.p. Laxenburg, 1755; *L'innocenza justificata* (Durazzo and Metastasio), f.p. Vienna, 1755, rev as *La Vestale*, f.p. Vienna, 1768, lost; *Antigono* (Metastasio), f.p. Rome, 1756; *Il re pastore* (Metastasio), f.p. Vienna, 1756; *La Fausse Esclave* (Louis Anseaume and Pierre Augustin Lefèvre de Marcouville), f.p. Vienna, 1758; *L'Ile de Merlin* (Anseaume), f.p. Vienna, 1758; *Le Diable à quatre* (Michel-Jean Sedaine and Pierre Baurans), f.p. Laxenburg, 1759; *Cythère assiégée* (Favart), f.p. Vienna, ?1759, rev Paris 1775; *L'Arbre enchanté* (Pierre-Louis Moline), f.p. Vienna, 1759, rev Versailles, 1775; *Tetide* (Giovanni Ambrogio Migliavacca), f.p. Vienna, 1760; *L'Ivrogne corrigé* (Anseaume and Jean-Baptiste Lourdet de Santerre), f.p. Vienna, 1760; *Le Cadi dupé* (Pierre René Lemonnier), f.p. Vienna, 1761, rev as *Le Mandarin*, c.1775, not performed; *Orfeo ed Euridice* (see ORPHEUS), f.p. Vienna, 1762, rev as *Orphée et Eurydice*, f.p. Paris, 1774; *Il trionfo di Clelia* (Metastasio), f.p. Bologna, 1763; *Ezio* (Metastasio: second setting), f.p. Vienna, 1763; *La Rencontre imprévue* (Dancourt), f.p. Vienna, 1764; *Il parnaso confuso* (Metastasio), f.p. Vienna, 1765; *Telemaco* (Coltellini), f.p. Vienna, 1765; *La corona* (Metastasio), 1765; ALCESTE, f.p. Vienna, 1767, Paris 1776; *Le Feste d'Apollo*, f.p. Parma, 1769; *Paride ed Elena* (Calzabigi), f.p. Vienna, 1770; IPHIGENIE EN AULIDE, f.p. Paris, 1774; *Armide* (see ARMIDA), f.p. Paris, 1777; IPHIGENIE EN TAURIDE, f.p. Paris, 1779; *Echo et Narcisse* (Ludwig Theodor von Tschudi), f.p. Paris, 1779; 10 other early operas surviving incomplete

Ballets: DON JUAN, Vienna, 1761; etc.

Other works: symphonies, trio sonatas, settings of Klopstock's odes, few sacred pieces, prologue to Traetta's *Ifigenia in Tauride* (Florence, 1767)

glückliche Hand, Die (The Knack). One-act 'drama with music' by Schoenberg to his own libretto, a symbolist play of sexual jealousy and urgent creativity set atonally for three type-characters, men's choir and large orchestra. First performance: Vienna, 14 Oct 1924.

Glyndebourne. Opera house and company founded in 1934 by John Christie at his seat in the Sussex countryside, south of London; the new theatre opened on the 60th anniversary. From the beginning Mozart was central, though new works by Britten, Maw, Knussen, Birtwistle, etc. have also been presented. In another seeming paradox, snob appeal (formal attire, picnic suppers on the lawns) is combined with high artistic standards. Music directors have included Haitink (1978–88) and Andrew Davis (1988–2000).

Gnesin State Musical College. Moscow conservatory founded in 1895 by four Gnesin sisters, joined later by their brother Mikhail Fabianovich

(1883–1957) as composition teacher. It currently takes students aged 15 and up for four-year courses leading to a professional qualification or entry into a higher institution (such as the Tchaikovsky Conservatory).

Gnomenreigen (Gnome Dance). Concert étude by Liszt.

goblet drum. Drum of goblet shape.

Godard, Benjamin (Louis Paul) (b. Paris, 18 Aug 1849; d. Cannes, 10 Jun 1895). French composer, of fecund but mild talent, remembered especially for the often-arranged berceuse from his opera *Jocelyn* (Brussels, 1888) and for his *Suite de trois morceaux* for flute and piano (1889). Trained at the Conservatoire, he also wrote symphonies (some with programmes, and some of those with soli and choir), much piano music and songs.

Godowsky, Leopold (b. Soshly, near Vilnius, 13 Feb 1870; d. New York, 21 Nov 1938). Polish–US pianist-composer, who left incomparable challenges to his successors in studies and transcriptions where intricate polyphony meets with luminescent resonance. Largely self-taught, he left for the USA at 14 and lived a restless life thereafter on both sides of the Atlantic, besides making a tour of the Far East (1922), during which he picked up impressions of Javanese music (*Gardens of Buitenzorg*, 1925). Other works include a big Passacaglia on the opening of Schubert's 'Unfinished' Symphony (1927–8), *Triakontameron* (1919–20, 30 pieces including *Alt Wien*), 53 studies on the Chopin études (pub 1894–1914, the études having up to seven different transformations each) and arrangements of 12 Schubert songs (1926).
www.godowsky.com

God save the queen/king. National anthem of the United Kingdom, first recorded in 1744 but almost certainly older. It became popular at the time of the 1745 Jacobite rebellion, when versions by Arne and others were printed and sung in London theatres. The same tune has served not only British and former British territories but also Denmark, Russia, the USA, Germany and Liechtenstein, which still uses it. It is quoted with British affiliation in Beethoven's *Wellingtons Sieg* and US in Ives's Variations on 'America'.

Goebbels, Heiner (b. Neustadt an der Weinstrasse, 17 Apr 1952). German composer, much praised for his incursions of actuality – recorded sound, rock, the music of the street – into theatres and concert halls. He studied sociology in Frankfurt and began his career performing with rock and experimental outfits, moving into mainstream institutions in the 1990s. His works include *Surrogate Cities* for orchestra with soundtrack (1993–4) and the music-theatre piece *Hashirigaki* (Lausanne, 2000). In 1999 he began teaching at the Institute for Applied Theatre Studies of Giessen University.
www.heinergoebbels.com

Goehr. German–British musical family.
  (1) **Walter** (b. Berlin, 28 May 1903; d. Sheffield, 4 Dec 1960). Conductor, active especially at Morley College from 1943, promoting new works (*Turangalîla*, *A Child of Our Time*) and Monteverdi. He had studied with Schoenberg, and moved to London in 1933.
  (2) **(Peter) Alexander** (b. Berlin, 10 Aug 1932). Composer, Walter's son, whose generous musical sympathes and astute critical attitudes have produced works of great diversity, masterful yet often quirky. Brought to England in his first year, he grew up in a powerfully musical household and studied at the Royal Manchester College (1952–5), where his coevals included Birtwistle and Davies. He also visited Darmstadt (1954, 1956) and spent a year in Paris (1955–6), studying with Messiaen and Loriod, and meeting Boulez. Back in England he worked as a copyist and translator before gaining a job as a BBC producer (1960–68). He quickly explored a range of Schoenbergian options, from expressionism (*Sutter's Gold*) to an embrace of older patterns of form, texture and genre, all the time establishing a flexible language that allowed harmonic direction within a fully chromatic world.
  After holding visiting appointments at the New England Conservatory (1968–9), Yale (1969–70) and Southampton (1970–71), he enjoyed a new career as a university professor at Leeds (1971–6) and Cambridge (1976–99). A wise and engaging teacher, he helped form two generations of British composers, from Gilbert and Holloway to Benjamin and Adès. If there seemed some risk at first that his music, too, was becoming academic – especially in resorting to fugue and chaconne – its truly 18th-century qualities became apparent in its richness and variety, as well as its superb craftsmanship. References range from Scriabin in the orchestral *Deux études* to dream-Monteverdi in *Arianna* and askew Bach or Handel, while other pieces, such as the piano sequence ... *in real time*, are elegantly playful within their own particular worlds of harmony and metre.
Alexander Goehr, ed. Derrick Puffett *Finding the Key* (1998)

Operas: *Arden muss sterben* (Erich Fried, after 16th-century Eng. play), Op.21, f.p. Hamburg, 1967;

TRIPTYCH, 1968–70; *Behold the Sun* (John McGrath), Op.44, f.p. Duisburg, 1985; *Arianna* (see ARIADNE), Op.58, 1994–5; *Kantan and Damask Drum* (Goehr, after Zeami), Op.67, f.p. Dortmund, 1999

Orchestral: Little Symphony, Op.15, chbr orch, 1963; *Pastorals*, Op.19, 1965; Symphony in One Movement, Op.29, 1969, rev 1981; Piano Concerto, Op.33, 1972; *Metamorphosis/Dance*, Op.36, 1973–4; Fugue and Romanza on Psalm 4, Op.38b-c, str, 1976–7; *Deux études*, Op.43, 1980–81; Symphony with Chaconne, Op.48, 1985–6; *Eve Dreams in Paradise* (Milton), Op.49, mez, t, orch, 1987–8; *Colossos or Panic*, Op.55, 1991–2; *Schlussgesang*, Op.61, va, orch, 1996; ... *a second musical offering (G.F.H. 2001)*, 2001; etc.

Choral: *Sutter's Gold* (after Eisenstein), Op.10, b, ch, orch, 1959–60; Psalm 4, Op.38a, s, a, women's ch, va, org, 1976; *Babylon the Great is Fallen*, Op.40, ch, orch, 1979; *The Death of Moses* (Hollander), Op.53, soli, ch, 13 insts, 1991–2; etc.

Ensemble: *The Deluge* (after Leonardo), Op.7, s, a, 8 insts, 1957–8; ... *a musical offering (J.S.B. 1985)*, Op.46, 14 insts, 1985; *Sing, Ariel* (anthology), Op.51, mez, 2 s, 5 insts, 1989–90; etc.

Chamber and instrumental: String Quartet No.1, Op.5, 1956–7, rev 1988; No.2, Op.23, 1967; No.3, Op.37, 1975–6; No.4, Op.52, 1990; *Paraphrase on 'Il combattimento'*, Op.28, cl, 1969; etc.

Songs: *Das Gesetz der Quadrille* (Kafka), Op.41, bar, pf, 1979; etc.

Piano: *Nonomiya*, Op.27, 1969; ... *in real time*, Op.50, 1988–92; etc.

(3) **Lydia** (b. London, 10 Jan 1960). Philosopher, Alexander's daughter, who received her doctorate at Cambridge (1987) and in 1995 became a Columbia professor. See also WORK.

Goerne, Matthias (b. Karl-Marx-Stadt, now Chemnitz, 31 Mar 1967). German baritone, whose warm tone, emphatic presence and ready access to dark expression have made him one of the most admired lieder singers of his generation. He studied with Hans Beyer, Schwarzkopf and Fischer-Dieskau, and has been internationally prominent since the mid-1990s.

Goethe, Johann Wolfgang von (b. Frankfurt, 28 Aug 1749; d. Weimar, 22 Mar 1832). German writer, whose works have impinged more on music than those of any other non-scriptural author besides Shakespeare. He wrote several librettos, set by Reichardt, Schubert and others, but provided a much richer source in his two FAUST plays. Among composers to have written songs, choral pieces and operas based on other works are Beethoven, Brahms, Busoni, Dallapiccola, Henze, Liszt, Massenet, Mendelssohn, Mozart, Musorgsky, Rachmaninoff, Schoeck, Schoenberg, Schubert, Schumann, Strauss, Tchaikovsky,

Tomášek, Wagner, Webern and Wolf. See also L'APPRENTI SORCIER; ARMIDA; EGMONT; MIGNON; TASSO.

Goetz, Hermann (Gustav) (b. Königsberg, now Kaliningrad, 7 Dec 1840; d. Hottingen, near Zurich, 3 Dec 1876). German composer, a classicizing Romantic in Brahms's orbit. He studied with Julius Stern and von Bülow at the Stern Conservatory in Berlin (1860–63), then went to Winterthur for his health, but also to work as an organist and teacher. His works include an opera after *The Taming of the Shrew* (*Der widerspenstigen Zähmung*, Mannheim, 1874), orchestral pieces (Symphony, F, Op.9, 1873), chamber and piano music (Piano Trio, G minor, Op.1, 1863; Piano Duet Sonata, G minor, Op.17, 1865; Piano Quartet, E, Op.6, 1867; Piano Quintet, C minor, Op.16, 1874) and songs.

Goeyvaerts, Karel (August) (b. Antwerp, 8 Jun 1923; d. Antwerp, 3 Feb 1993). Belgian composer, closely connected with Barraqué and Stockhausen, and a crucial player in the development of total serialism. He studied in Antwerp and with Messiaen and Milhaud at the Paris Conservatoire (1947–50), also gaining much from Barraqué's friendship. Highly abstract, his early pieces had numbers rather than titles. No.1 (1950–51), a sonata for two pianos, advanced towards total serialism from Messiaen's *Mode de valeurs* and Webern's Piano Variations; it fascinated Stockhausen, with whom he played it at Darmstadt in 1951. The two composers remained in correspondence until 1956, and he created works at the Cologne electronic music studio (No.5, 1953; No.7, 1955). Never a member of the international avant-garde, he then followed his own path while working for Sabena (1957–70) and Belgian radio (1970–88), his works including choral pieces and *Litanies I–V* for forces ranging from solo piano to orchestra (1979–82).

Goldberg Variations. Work by Bach, published in 1741 as *Aria mit verschiedenen Veraenderungen* (Aria with Several Variations), written for harpsichord but happily claimed by pianists as a pinnacle of their literature. The story related by Forkel, that Bach wrote the music for Johann Gottlieb Goldberg (1727–56) to play as a soporific for Hermann Karl von Keyserlingk, may be apocryphal, though Goldberg was certainly in that nobleman's service as a boy and could have studied with Bach. There are 30 variations, of which every third is a canon, at intervals widening from the unison (variation 3) to a ninth (variation 27), the final variation being a quodlibet.

Golden. Name given the ninth, in F, of Purcell's *Sonata's in Four Parts.*

Golden Cockerel, The (*Le Coq d'or, Zolotoy petushok*). Opera by Rimsky-Korsakov to a libretto by Vladimir Belsky, after a tale by Pushkin based on stories by Washington Irving. The Astrologer (high tenor) presents King Dodon (bass) with a golden cockerel that will sound the alarm when there is danger of war. The king promises a reward, but fails to deliver when the Astrologer claims the newly arrived Queen of Shemakha (soprano). Her Hymn to the Sun is the work's vocal highlight; an orchestral suite is also often heard separately. First performance: Moscow, 7 Oct 1909.

golden section. Division into two parts, so that the smaller is to the larger as the larger is to the whole: this point comes at about the 61·8 per cent mark. Such a division seems to coincide with intuitive ideas of balance in respect of architecture, the form of paintings, etc., but it may also be interpreted durationally, e.g. dividing an eight-minute movement at the five-minute stage, approximately. There is some evidence of Debussy, Bartók and others planning movements so that the principal climax comes at this moment.

Goldenweiser, Alexander [Goldenveyzer, Aleksandr Borisovich] (b. Chişinău, 10 Mar 1875; d. Moscow, 26 Nov 1961). Russian pianist, of exquisite care. He studied at the Moscow Conservatory with Ziloti and Pavel Pabst for piano and Taneyev, Ippolitov-Ivanov and Arensky for composition. Contacts with Scriabin and Tolstoy were also important. From 1906 he taught at his alma mater, where Dmitri Bashkirov, Berman, Feinberg, Ginzburg and Nikolayeva were among his pupils. He also composed, not only piano music but a string quartet and stage pieces.

Goldmark, Karl (b. Keszthely, 18 May 1830; d. Vienna, 2 Jan 1915). Austro-Hungarian composer, of music grand, picturesque and straightforward. A Jewish cantor's son, he studied at the music school in Ödenburg/Sopron and the Vienna Conservatory (1847–8), then worked as a theatre violinist. In the 1860s he began to gain notice as a composer and to form connections (with Brahms among others), but he had to wait until the mid 1870s for his biggest successes: the opera *Die Königin von Saba*, Op.27 (The Queen of Sheba, Vienna, 1875), which was widely performed in its day, and his adjacent First Symphony, Op.26, subtitled 'Ländliche Hochzeit' (Rustic Wedding), and Violin Concerto in A minor, Op.28, both published in 1877. His later works, all over-shadowed, include five further operas, chamber music and songs. His nephew Rubin (1872–1936) was a distinguished composition professor in New York.

Goldschmidt, Berthold (b. Hamburg, 18 Jan 1903; d. London, 17 Oct 1996). German–British composer, among the most brilliantly gifted in Germany between the wars. A pupil of Schreker in Berlin (1922–5), he rapidly began making a name as both composer and conductor, his music combining Hindemithian contrapuntal energy with a brighter harmonic language and expert scoring. He had just achieved his breakthrough piece, the opera *Der gewaltige Hahnrei*, when the Nazis came to power. In 1935 he moved to London and started slowly rebuilding his career, but, discouraged, he gave up composing in 1958 to concentrate on conducting work. He advised Cooke on completing Mahler's Tenth Symphony and conducted the première (1964). Then in 1982 he returned to composition, which he pursued vigorously into his 90s, as the world began again to take notice.

Operas: *Der gewaltige Hahnrei* (Goldschmidt, after Fernand Crommelynck), Op.14, f.p. Mannheim, 1932; *Beatrice Cenci* (Martin Esslin, after Shelley), 1949–50, f.p. Magdeburg, 1994
Orchestral: Passacaglia, Op.4, 1925; *Komödie der Irrungen* (overture), Op.6, 1925; *Ciaccona sinfonica*, c.1934–6; Cello Concerto, 1953; Clarinet Concerto, 1953–4; Violin Concerto, 1951–5; *Chronica*, c.1924–86
Chamber: String Quartet No.1, Op.8, 1925–6; No.2, A minor, ?1933–6; No.3, 1988–9; No.4, 1992; etc.

goliard. Wandering scholar of the 10th–13th centuries, such as composed Latin songs of diverse kinds, none with music surviving.

Golijov, Osvaldo (b. La Plata, 5 Dec 1960). Argentinian composer of music powerfully evoking folk traditions. After studies in his home town, in Jerusalem and with Crumb at the University of Pennsylvania from 1986, he began teaching at the College of the Holy Cross, Worcester, Mass., in 1991. At Tanglewood the next year he formed connections with the St Lawrence and Kronos quartets, and for a while he wrote mostly for chamber forces (*Yiddishbbuk*, str qt, 1992; *The Dreams and Prayers of Isaac the Blind*, cl, str qt, 1994). Then came his widely acclaimed *La Pasión segun San Marcos* for soli, choir and orchestra (2000), with its irresistible rhythmic drive and braiding of Brazilian, Cuban, Spanish and Jewish styles.

www.osvaldogolijov.com

Golitsyn, Prince **Nikolay Borisovich** (b. 19 Dec 1794; d. Bogorodskoye, Kursk governorate, 3 Nov 1866). Russian patron, who, as a young officer in Vienna, got to know and admire Beethoven, and from Russia commissioned the first three of the composer's late quartets. An earlier member of the family became a character in *Khovanshchina*.

Golyshev, Yefim [Jef] (b. Kherson, Ukraine, 20 Sep 1897; d. Paris, 25 Sep 1970). Russian composer, whose single surviving work, a string trio (pub 1925), strikingly foreshadows Messiaen's application of serialism to durations. He studied with Auer and toured as a child violinist before continuing his education at the Stern Conservatory in Berlin. In 1918–19 he became involved with the Berlin dadaists as both musician and visual artist, but nearly all his work was lost when he fled in 1933. His erratic subsequent career included spells as a chemist in Barcelona, a prisoner in France, a musician in São Paulo (1956–66) and a painter in Paris.

Gombert, Nicolas (b. *c*.1495; d. *c*.1560). Netherlandish composer, highly regarded in his time for his densely worked and sonorous imitative polyphony. Possibly a pupil of Josquin, he joined the chapel of Charles V in 1526 and may have retired in his last years to Tournai. His works include 10 masses (*Tempore paschali* a 6, expanding to 12 in the *Agnus Dei*) plus a *Credo* a 8, a set of eight four-part *Magnificat* settings that he may have planned as his masterwork, over 160 motets, a tribute to Josquin (*Musae Jovis* a 6) and more than 70 chansons, where again there are references to Josquin in the music.

Gomes, (Antônio) Carlos (b. Campinas, 11 Jul 1836; d. Belém, 16 Sep 1896). Brazilian composer, who made his name with his opera *Il Guarany*. A bandmaster's son, he studied at the Imperial Conservatory in Rio and won a scholarship to the Milan Conservatory, where he was taught by Lauro Rossi from 1864. He stayed in Italy, and in *Il Guarany* (f.p. Milan, 1870) created a work that travelled not only back to Brazil but all over Europe, providing an image of Brazilian Indians, Italian-opera-style. Of his later operas, *Salvator Rosa* (f.p. Genoa, 1874) and *Lo schiavo* (f.p. Rio de Janeiro, 1889) were most successful, the latter again set in Brazil. He died soon after taking a post directing the conservatory in Belém.

gong. Circular plate or dish of bronze, with or without a central protuberance, suspended and normally struck with a beater. The name is of Javan origin, and gongs and other metallophones remain central to Indonesian music (see GAMELAN), though they had reached as far as Roman Britain by *c*.AD100. Their use in the orchestra began with the TAM TAM. Sets of tuned gongs were introduced by Puccini (*Madama Butterfly*) and became common in the 20th century; Cage added the WATER GONG. Also common are gongs from Chinese opera, which make a crashing, cymbal-like sound, with a howling resonance as the pitch slides.

Goodall, Reginald (b. Lincoln, 13 Jul 1901; d. Bridge, near Canterbury, 5 May 1990). British conductor, knighted in 1985, responsible for Wagner performances of spacious magnificence. He studied at the RCM (from 1925), eventually found a job with Sadler's Wells Opera (1944–6), for whom he conducted the première of *Peter Grimes*, and then had a largely obscure career at Covent Garden as a coach and revival conductor. Sadler's Wells brought him out of retirement for *Die Meistersinger* (1968) and the *Ring* (1970–73), and he then continued conducting Wagner in Britain into his mid-80s.

Goodman, Benny [Benjamin David] (b. Chicago, 30 May 1909; d. New York, 13 Jun 1986). US clarinettist, a superlative jazz musician who, after further studies with Reginald Kell, launched himself on a parallel classical career in 1938 when he recorded Mozart's quintet. He commissioned Bartók's *Contrasts* and Copland's concerto.

Goossens. Belgian–British musical family, founded by Eugène (1845–1906), who made his career in England, especially with the Carl Rosa company (1883–93). His son, also Eugène (1867–1956), began under him, was also the company's principal conductor (1899–1915), and had four children who became professional musicians: a third Eugene, Leon and the harpists Marie (1894–1991) and Sidonie (1899–2004).

(1) **(Aynsley) Eugene** (b. London, 26 May 1893; d. Hillingdon, 13 Jun 1962). Conductor, knighted in 1955. A pupil of Stanford at the RCM, he began his career in the early 1920s, with the Carl Rosa and with his own orchestra specializing in new scores. He was then principal conductor of the Rochester Philharmonic (1923–31), the Cincinnati Symphony (1931–47) and the Sydney Symphony (1947–56). Also a Francophile composer, he wrote a concerto for his brother Leon (1927).

(2) **Leon** (b. Liverpool, 12 Jun 1897; d. London, 12 Feb 1988). Oboist, whose sweet, expressive tone gave the instrument new appeal, and encouraged works from Bax, Vaughan Williams, Britten and many other British composers. He studied at the

RCM (1911–14) and immediately became principal of the Queen's Hall orchestra, from which he moved on to Covent Garden in 1924 and to the new LPO in 1932.

Gordon, Michael (b. Miami, 20 Jul 1956). US composer, a founder of BANG ON A CAN. He studied with Bresnick at Yale (1980–82) and began as a second-generation minimalist with strong rock affiliations. Repetition and slow change become mesmeric in his *Trance* for ensemble (1995), *Weather* for string orchestra (1997) and *Decasia* for orchestra (2001).

Górecki, Henrk (Mikołaj) (b. Czernica, near Rybnik, 6 Dec 1933). Polish composer, noted above all for slow, modal works, often religious in subject and seeming to search for models in music of the past, from chant to Chopin. He began quite otherwise – indeed, he began quite otherwise twice: first as a Paris-Warsaw neoclassicist, then, after 1956, as a modernist alongside Penderecki. But there was always a monumental simplicity about his music, and the change represented by the Three Pieces in Old Style for strings (1963) and the orchestral *Refrain* (1965) was one of vesture rather than essential personality. So far as the wider world was concerned, that change went virtually unnoticed for a quarter century, until 1992, when the Nonesuch recording of his Third Symphony came out (not a new work then, and not its first release). This 'symphony of sorrowful songs', in three slow movements, spun out gestures of lament from local sources (folk and religious), finding an international resonance. By then its composer had left (in 1979) his post as director of the Katowice Conservatory, where he had studied with Szabelski (1955–60). Among later works, *Beatus vir* was commissioned by the soon-to-be Pope John Paul II.

Adrian Thomas *Górecki* (1997)

Orchestral and vocal orchestral: Symphony No.1, Op.14, perc, str, 1959; No.2 'Copernican', Op.31, s, bar, ch, orch, 1972; No.3 'of Sorrowful Songs', Op.36, s, orch, 1976; *Scontri*, Op.17, 1960; 3 Pieces in Old Style, str, 1963; *Refrain*, Op.21, 1965; *Beatus vir*, Op.38, bar, ch, orch, 1979; Concerto, Op.40, hpd/pf, str, 1980; *Little Requiem for a Certain Polka*, Op.66, pf, 13 insts, 1993; etc.
Choral: *Amen*, Op.35, 1975; *Miserere*, Op.44, 1981, rev 1987; *Totus tuus*, Op.60, 1987; etc.
Chamber: String Quartet No.1 'Already it is Dusk', Op.62, 1988; No.2 'Quasi una fantasia', Op.64, 1991; *Lerchenmusik*, Op.53, cl, vc, pf, 1984–6; *Good Night* (Shakespeare), Op.63, s, a fl, perc, pf, 1990; etc.

Gossec, François-Joseph (b. Vergnies, 17 Jan 1734;

d. Passy, Paris, 16 Feb 1829). Walloon–French composer, who had a 30-year career in Paris writing operas, symphonies and chamber music for the *ancien régime*, then became one of the foremost composers of the Revolution. Trained as a chorister, he moved to Paris in 1751 and, through Rameau, gained a place in the orchestra of Le Riche de la Pouplinière. In his *Messe des morts* (1760) he showed a taste for the massed wind sonorities and sombre magniloquence that would serve his revolutionary music, but diversion came in his *opéras comique* and the music he wrote as founder director of the Concert des Amateurs (1769–73), influenced by Johann Stamitz and other Mannheim composers. He seems to have composed rather little in the 1780s, but then produced a great many choral and wind-band pieces under the Revolution and Directoire (1789–99), including a *Te Deum* for the first anniversary of the storming of the Bastille (1790) and a *Marche lugubre* the same year with tam tam, its first use in Europe. He also taught at the Conservatoire (1795–1816), withdrawing from creative life again after Napoleon's assumption of power. Of his large and diverse output, only some fragments remain in regular performance, including a gavotte from his opera *Rosine* (1786), another gavotte for flute and string quartet, and a tambourin from his divertissement *Le Triomphe de la République, ou Le Camp de Grandpré* (1793).

Gothic. Term imported from architecture, but normally implying a style period that, in architectural terms, is more Romanesque than Gothic, i.e. the polyphony of the 12th and 13th centuries.

Gothic Voices. British group formed by Christopher Page in 1980 to perform medieval and early Renaissance music.

Götterdämmerung (Twilight of the Gods). Opera by Wagner to his own libretto after German myth, the final part of *The Ring*. The three Norns (Fates) foretell doom. Siegfried (tenor) leaves Brünnhilde (soprano) where he found her at the end of the preceding opera and journeys down the Rhine to the wilting court of the Gibichungs, where the brother–sister pair of Gunther (baritone) and Gutrune (soprano) are lamenting their impotence in the baleful presence of Hagen (bass), Alberich's son. Drugged and amnesiac, Siegfried agrees to win Brünnhilde for Gunther; in return, he will wed Gutrune. All this duly happens, much to the dismay of Brünnhilde, who connives in Siegfried's murder but then throws herself on his funeral pyre, raising flames that reach up to Valhalla and the gods. The Rhinemaidens recapture the ring.

Often heard separately are Siegfried's Rhine Journey and Funeral Music (both orchestral interludes), and Brünnhilde's Immolation, with torchbearing soprano. First performance: Bayreuth, 17 Aug 1876.

Gottschalk, Louis Moreau (b. New Orleans, 8 May 1829; d. Tijuca, Brazil, 18 Dec 1869). US pianist-composer, whose music, while caught up in an immediate commercial world of dances and potpourris, looked ahead both to ragtime and to the rumbustious, quotation-happy side of Ives. Bifurcation was inside him. Of German-Jewish extraction on his father's side and Caribbean French on his mother's, he was sent to Paris for training just before his 12th birthday and spent the next 11½ years in France, Switzerland (1850) and Spain (1851–2). Although he became Europeanized, he did not become European: his acclaim came, especially after his 1849 debut concert at the Salle Pleyel, as an exotic, remembering what he had heard as a boy from his maternal grandmother and her Dominguan slave (Opp.2, 3, 5 and 11). He made a successful return to the USA (1853–7), touring by means of the new railroads, then drew breath in the Caribbean before resuming his US career (1862–5). All the while – as a Unionist, a democrat and a man with several siblings depending on him – he followed popular taste and made it his own. In Havana in 1860 he presented an evening that included his opera *Esceñas campestres* and *Symphonie tropicale*; for the US market he produced salon pieces and patriotic items. After that his stamping ground was South America, where an overdose of quinine, prescribed to treat malaria, may have carried him off.

S. Frederick Starr *Bamboula!* (1995), ˡ as *Louis Moreau Gottschalk* (2000)

Orchestral: *Symphonie romantique* (No.1) 'La nuit des tropiques', 1858–9; Symphony No.2 'A Montevideo', 1865–8; *Grande tarantelle*, Op.67, pf, orch, 1858–64; etc.

Vocal: *Esceñas campestres* (1-act opera), 1860; songs

Piano: *Bamboula*, Op.2, ?1846–8; *La Savane*, Op.3, pub 1849; *Le Bananier*, Op.5, ?1848; *Le Manceniller* (*La Sérénade*), Op.11, pub 1851; *Le Banjo*, Op.15, pub 1855; *The Last Hope*, Op.16, 1854; *Souvenirs d'Andalousie*, Op.22, 1851; *Tournament Galop*, pub 1854; *Ricordati*, Op.26, pub 1857; *Minuit à Seville*, Op.30, pub 1858; *Souvenir de Porto Rico* (*Marche des gibaros*), 1857–8; *Danza*, Op.33, 1857–9; *Manchega*, Op.38, pub 1860; *Souvenir de la Havane*, Op.39, 1859; *O ma charmante, épargnez-moi*, Op.44, pub 1862; *Suis-moi!*, Op.45, pub 1861; *Berceuse*, Op.47, pub 1862; *Union*, Op.48, 1852–62; *The Dying Poet*, pub 1864; *Grand scherzo*, Op.57,

1869; *Pasquinade*, Op.59, pub 1870; *Grande fantaisie triomphale sur l'hymne national brésilien*, Op.69, 1869; *Variations de concert sur l'hymne portugais*, Op.91, 1869; etc.

Piano duet: *Ojos criollos*, Op.37, 1859; *Réponds-moi*, Op.50, 1859; *La gallina*, Op.53, 1859–63; *Ses yeux*, Op.66, 1865–9; *Radieuse*, Op.72, pub 1865; etc.

Goudimel, Claude (b. Besançon, 1514–20; d. Lyons, 28–31 Aug 1572). French composer, a Huguenot who died in the St Bartholomew's Day massacre. He was living in Paris by 1549, a student at the university and busy as a composer and editor. In the former capacity he produced several volumes of psalms, setting all 150 in both harmonized and contrapuntal arrangements of the Genevan tunes, and making more elaborate motet-like versions of 67 of them. He also wrote about the same number of chansons, and some Latin church music. He moved to Metz in 1557 and to Lyons a few years later.

Gould, Glenn (Herbert) (b. Toronto, 25 Sep 1932; d. Toronto, 4 Oct 1982). Canadian pianist, who from 1964 devoted himself exclusively to recordings, in which zeal for detail, sometimes idiosyncratic, is combined with intense dynamic clarity and expressive urgency. He studied first with his mother and then with Alberto Guerrero at the conservatory in Toronto (1943–52), making his concerto debut in 1946 and giving his first public recital the next year. More significant, in view of his later career, was his early exposure to radio (1950; sonatas by Mozart and Hindemith), television (1952) and disc recording (1953; the Berg sonata and pieces with violin). In January 1955 he appeared for the first time outside Canada, in Washington and New York. The day following his New York recital he was signed by Columbia, for which his first album, devoted to the Goldberg Variations (taped in June, released the following year), was widely acclaimed. In 1957–9 he led an international career, with annual visits to Europe. He then confined his appearances to North America, reduced their frequency, and finally stopped playing in public altogether, after a recital in Los Angeles (10 Apr 1964). Thereafter, feeling the live concert to be impertinent and outmoded, he played only for microphones, basing his repertory, as he always had, on Bach (with excursions to early Baroque music and Beethoven) and Schoenberg (plus such oddities as the piano music of Strauss and Sibelius). Among his last recordings was a 25th anniversary remake of the Goldberg Variations, very different. He also expressed his love of polyphony in some exploratory radio documentaries (beginning with *The*

Idea of North, 1967) and a few compositions (notably a quartet, 1955).

Tim Page, ed. *The Glenn Gould Reader* (1984); Kevin Bazzana *Glenn Gould: The Performer in the Work* (1997), *Wondrous Strange* (2004)

www.gould.nlc-bnc.ca; glenngould.com/gg

Gould, Morton (b. New York, 10 Dec 1913; d. Orlando, Fla., 21 Feb 1996). US composer-conductor, especially of light and exuberant music for orchestra or band. He studied at the Institute of Musical Art, gained a publisher (G. Schirmer) when he was 18, and began his career in radio at 21. His most popular works are the pavane from *American Symphonette* No.2 (1935) and *American Salute* (1943).

Gounod, Charles (François) (b. Paris, 17 Jun 1818; d. Saint-Cloud, 18 Oct 1893). French composer, whose gifts for melody and a touching softness are the strengths of his best pieces and the weaknesses of so much else. The son of a painter and a music teacher, who supported her two boys after her husband's early death, he studied with Reicha and at the Conservatoire, winning the Prix de Rome in 1839. Staying in the eternal city deepened his piety; a year then in Austria and Germany brought him into contact with Beethoven's spirit and Mendelssohn in the flesh. Back in Paris from 1843, he hesitated between Church and salon, as indeed he did throughout his life, and was first claimed for opera by Pauline Viardot, whose influence won him a commission from the Opera for *Sapho* (1851). That same year he married, and took official posts as a supervisor of amateur choirs and school music. He also became a mentor to two gifted teenagers, Bizet and Saint-Saëns.

His fourth opera, *Faust* (1859), soon brought him a European reputation, enhanced by *Roméo et Juliette* (1867), as well as by the songs, salon waltzes and other minor pieces he produced in abundance. England was therefore ready for him when he arrived with his family in 1870 to escape the Franco-Prussian War and stayed on – alone – with the formidable Georgina Weldon. Their relationship may have been entirely professional; certainly it had its ups and downs, before in 1874 he returned to Paris, and soon afterwards to his wife. The triumphs of his later years, though, were not the operas he wrote for Paris but the oratorios – *La Rédemption* and *Mors et vita* – he produced for successive triennial festivals in Birmingham.

Steven Huebner *The Operas of Charles Gounod* (1990)

www.charles-gounod.com

Operas: *Sapho* (Emile Augier), f.p. Paris, 1851, rev 1858, 1884; *La Nonne sanglante* (Scribe and Delavigne, after Matthew Lewis), f.p. Paris, 1854; *Le Médecin malgré lui* (Barbier and Carré, after Molière), f.p. Paris, 1858; FAUST, 1856–9; *Philémon et Baucis* (Barbier and Carré, after La Fontaine), f.p. Paris, 1860, rev 1876; *La Colombe* (Barbier and Carré, after La Fontaine), f.p. Baden-Baden, 1860; *La Reine de Saba* (Barbier and Carré, after Nerval), f.p. Paris, 1862; *Mireille* (Carré, after Mistral), f.p. Paris, 1864; *Roméo et Juliette* (see ROMEO AND JULIET), 1865–71; *Cinq mars* (Paul Poirson and Louis Gallet, after Vigny), f.p. Paris, 1877; *Polyeucte* (Barbier and Carré, after Corneille), f.p. Paris, 1878; *Le Tribut de Zamora* (Adolphe Philippe d'Ennery), f.p. Paris, 1881

Sacred: *Messe solennelle de Sainte Cécile*, soli, ch, orch, pub 1855; *La Rédemption* (oratorio: Gounod), f.p. Birmingham, 1882; *Mors et vita* (oratorio: Gounod), f.p. Birmingham, 1885

Instrumental: Symphony No.1, D, pub 1855; No.2, E♭, pub before 1860; *Marche funèbre d'une marionette*, pf/orch, pub 1873; *Petite symphonie*, 9 wind, 1885

Songs: 'L'Absent' (Gounod), pub 1877; 'Au printemps' (Barbier), pub 1868; 'Au rossignol' (Lamartine), pub 1867; 'AVE MARIA', pub 1859; 'Chanson de printemps' (Eugène Tourneux), pub 1860; 'Où voulez-vous aller?' (Gautier), pub 1839; 'Repentir', pub 1894; 'Sérénade' (Hugo), pub 1857; 'Le soir' (Lamartine), c.1841; 'Le Temps des roses' (Roy), pub 1886; 'Le Vallon' (Lamartine), c.1841; 'Venise' (Musset), 1842; 'Viens, les gazons sont verts' (Barbier), pub 1875

Goyescas. (1) Set of piano pieces by Granados based on pictures by Goya. Book 1, 1909–11: 1 *Los requiebros*; 2 *Coloquio en la reja, duo de amor*; 3 *El fandango de candil*; 4 *Quejas, o La maja y el ruiseñor*. Book 2, 1911–12: 5 *El amor y la muerte, balada*; 6 *Epilogo, serenata del espectro*. A seventh *goyesca, El pelele* (c.1913) is normally appended, but the pieces can also be played singly, and No.4 often is.

(2) One-act opera by Granados to a libretto by Fernando Periquet, woven on to music already created out of the piano suite. Set in Madrid in Goya's time, the plot is simple: Fernando (tenor) kills Paquiro in a duel, goes to Rosario (soprano), who has been waiting in a garden (aria on *La maja y el ruiseñor*), and sings a duet with her (*Coloquio*). First performance: New York, 28 Jan 1916.

G.P. General Pause.

Grabu, Louis (b. ?c.1640; d. after 1694). Catalan violinist-composer, Master of Music to Charles II of England (1666–73). He was in London by 1665, when he was married in the queen's chapel; he then led the royal string band until forced from court as a Catholic. After that he wrote music for the theatre, including a setting of Dryden's *Albion and Albanius* (1685).

Graça, Fernando Lopes (b. Tomar, 17 Dec 1906; d. Parede, near Cascais, 27 Nov 1994). Portuguese composer, his country's Bartók. After studies in Lisbon he went to Paris (1937–9) for further training as a music scholar and composer (with Koechlin). Curiously, it was while he was in Paris that his music became distinctively Portuguese, drawing on folk music and following Bartók's example. Back in Lisbon he exerted himself in many directions, as a composer, teacher, folklorist, founder of the *Gazeta musical* and concert organizer. His works include two piano concertos, one for cello (*Concerto da camera*, 1965), four piano sonatas, two quartets, and numerous choruses and songs.

grace. Ornament.

grace note. Note intervening, usually briefly, into the main musical flow. Grace notes may come singly, in small groups or in great roulades. They are written or printed in small notes, and are notated as if of no durational value:

Those with a diagonal slash through the tail purloin time from the preceding note, otherwise they take from the note to which they lead. Growing from the 18th-century accaciatura, they attained profusion in Chopin and Liszt.

gracile (It.). Delicate.

gradevole (It.). Pleasing.

gradual. (1) Chant comprising a verse (in most cases from one of the psalms) and response, sung between the epistle and the gospel at mass, forming part of the PROPER. It was sung from a step (Lat. *gradus*), as were the lessons on either side of it.

(2) Book of mass propers.

Gradus ad Parnassum (Steps to Parnassus, i.e. to the mountain of Apollo and the muses). Title for pedagogical texts since the early 18th century, including Fux's much reprinted counterpoint book and Clementi's Op.44 collection of studies. Debussy's *Gradus ad Parnassum*, from *Children's Corner*, is a portrait of a child grappling with Clementi.

Graf. Viennese piano firm run by Conrad Graf (1782–1851), whose instruments, all dating from 1804–40, stand at the peak of the Viennese

Classical tradition and were admired by Beethoven, Chopin, Liszt, the Schumanns and Brahms.

Graham, Martha (b. Pittsburgh, 11 May 1894; d. New York, 1 Apr 1991). US choreographer, the most gifted and influential proponent of 'modern dance' as a more free and expressive alternative to traditional ballet. She founded her company in 1926, and commissioned many composers to write for it, including Riegger, Copland, Chávez, Barber and Dello Joio.

Graham, Susan (b. Roswell, New Mexico, 23 Jul 1960). US mezzo-soprano of compelling presence and rich, immediate vocal personality, especially suited to Berlioz and Gluck. She studied at the Manhattan School, made her Met debut in 1991, and was soon an international star.

Grainger, (George) Percy (Aldridge) (b. Brighton, Melbourne, 8 Jul 1882; d. White Plains, NY, 20 Feb 1961). Australian–US pianist-composer, wild boy of music. Guided first by his powerful mother, with whom he lived and travelled until her suicide when he was almost 40, he had lessons also with Louis Pabst in Melbourne (1892–4) and with James Kwast and Knorr at the Hoch Conservatory in Frankfurt (1895–1901), where he was a contemporary of the FRANKFURT GROUP. He then made his base in London (1901–14), though he returned twice to Australia for concert tours. Already in Frankfurt, still in his teens, he had wanted to liberate music, first through unstable and irregular metres. In England he became absorbed in folk music, which he appreciated as natural and forever flexible, and as a model of tunefulness. Most of his works were folksong settings (some – 'Shallow Brown' – of superb quality), pieces that folkify art music (by composers from Machaut to Strauss) or original compositions of song or dance character. Prolific under this new influence, he also remained adventurous, exploring unusual ensembles (massed single reeds in *Hill Song* No.1), unbarred rhythm, 'elastic' (i.e. variable) scoring and other innovations. At the same time he drew close to Grieg (whom he visited in Norway) and Delius.

In 1914 he moved to New York, where, apart from when serving as an army bandsman (1917–19), he enjoyed huge success as a pianist, teacher and composer. *Country Gardens*, which he came to loathe, made his fortune, and his works were taken up (and arranged) by conductors from Wood to Stokowski. He also became known for eccentric, even crankish behaviour, being an enthusiastic advocate of vegetarianism, hiking, Germanic vocabulary ('louden lots' rather than 'crescendo molto') and 'hygienic' attire (sometimes, like his music, a motley bouquet of diverse national traditions). In 1928 he married a Swedish poet onstage at the Hollywood Bowl during the course of a recital; there had been a less public ceremony five days before. He was then intermittently occupied with mechanical and electronic projects to realize his ideal of 'free music' – music that could curve and glide through time and pitch, as he had heard it in his head since childhood.

John Bird *Percy Grainger* (1976, [2]1999)

www.percygrainger.net

Works (most exist in numerous arrangements, by the composer and others): 'Near Woodstock Town' (Eng. folksong), 1899–1903; 'Mo Nighean Dubh' (Scot. folksong), pf, 1900; 'Walking Tune', 1900–5; 'Early one morning' (Eng. folksong), 1901; 'Ye banks and braes' (Scot. folksong), 1901; *Hill Song* No.1, 21 wind/2 pf, 1901–2; No.2, wind/2 pf, 1901–7; *Scotch Strathspey and Reel*, 1901–11; Irish Tune from County Derry ('Danny boy'), 1902; *In Dahomey*, pf, 1903–9; 'My Robin is to the greenwood gone' (Eng. folksong), 1904–12; 'Green bushes' (Eng. folksong), 1905–6; *Harvest Hymn*, 1905–6; 'Sussex Mummers' Christmas Carol' (Eng. folksong), 1905–11; 'Six dukes went a-fishin'' (Eng. folksong), 1905–12; 'Brigg Fair' (Eng. folksong), t, ch, 1906; 'Died for love' (Eng. folksong), 1906–7; 'Molly on the shore' (Eng. folksong), 1907; *Mock Morris*, 1910; 'Shallow Brown' (shanty), 1910; *Colonial Song*, 1911; *Handel in the Strand*, 1911–12; *The Warriors* (ballet), 3pf, orch, 1913–16; *In a Nutshell*, 1915–16 (*Arrival Platform Humlet, Gay but Wistful, Pastoral, The Gumsuckers March*); COUNTRY GARDENS (Eng. folkdance), 1918; *Shepherd's Hey* (Eng. folkdance), 1918; 'Spoon river' (US folksong), 1919–22; *Ramble on Love* (Strauss; *Der Rosenkavalier*), pf, 1922–42; *Pagodes* (Debussy), tuned perc, 1928; *Blithe Bells* (Bach; *Sheep may safely graze*), 1930–31; *The Immovable Do*, 1933–9; *Lincolnshire Posy* (Eng. folksongs), wind/2 pf, 1937; 'The Merry King' (Eng. folksong), 1938–9; *Youthful Suite*, orch, 1940–45; etc.

gramophone. See RECORDING.

Gramophone Company. British recording company founded in 1897 as an offshoot of Emile Berliner's disc operation, and joined by Fred Gaisberg as producer the next year. In 1899 it purchased Francis Barraud's picture of an attentive dog by a gramophone, 'His Master's Voice', which it registered as its trademark in 1900 and used on labels from 1909, by which time Melba and Caruso were among its stars. It became part of EMI in 1931.

Granados (y Campiña), Enrique (b. Lérida, 27 Jul 1867; d. English Channel, 24 Mar 1916). Catalan pianist-composer, in a rich vein of Iberian Romanticism. Brought up largely in Barcelona, he had piano lessons from 1880 with Joan Pujol and some training from Pedrell, though was largely self-educated as a composer. Staying with Viñes, he sat in on Bériot's lessons at the Paris Conservatoire (1887–9), then returned to Barcelona to begin a career as a pianist and composer. While not narrowly regionalist – he drew from all over Spain in the *Danzas españolas* that made his reputation – he wrote music for Catalan fantasy plays (1899–1906). And while becoming an international figure (Casals and Thibaud were among musicians he played with and wrote for), he contributed to local musical life by organizing concerts and founding a music school. He went to New York for the première of his operatic *Goyescas*, and died on the return in a vain attempt to save his wife after their ship had been torpedoed.

Operas: GOYESCAS, 1913–15; etc.

Songs: *Tonadillas en un estilo antiguo* (12; Fernando Periquet), 1910–11 (No. 7 'La maja de Goya'); *Canciones amatorias* (7), before 1915; etc.

Piano: 12 *danzas españolas*, c.1888–90 (Nos.2 *Oriental*, 4 *Villanesca*, 5 *Andaluza*, 6 *Rondalla aragonesa*, 10 *Melancólica*); *Valses poéticos* (7), pub 1894; *Allegro de concierto*, 1903–4; *Escenas románticas* (6), c.1903–4; *Cuentos de la juventud*, pub 1910; GOYESCAS, 1909–12; etc.

Other works: orchestral pieces (*Dante*, mez, orch, 1907–8), chamber music (Piano Quintet, G minor, 1894–5; Violin Sonata), etc.

gran cassa. Bass drum.

grand choeur (Fr., great choir). FULL ORGAN.

Grande-Duchesse de Gérolstein, La. Operetta by Offenbach to a libretto by Meilhac and Halévy. The Grand Duchess (soprano) supervises the rise of her good-looking protégé Fritz (tenor) from raw recruit to commander-in-chief, but the man she has to marry is Prince Paul (tenor). First performance: Paris, 12 Apr 1867.

Grande messe des morts (High Mass of the Dead). Title Berlioz gave his REQUIEM.

Grande symphonie funèbre et triomphale (Grand Funeral and Triumph Symphony). Work by Berlioz for military band (1840), commissioned by the French government for a ceremony to inter the ashes of martyrs of the 1830 revolution, then adapted for orchestra with choir ad lib (1842). There are three movements: *Marche funèbre*, *Oraison funèbre* and *Apothéose*.

Grandi, Alessandro (b. *c.*1575; d. Bergamo, 1630). Italian composer close to Gabrieli and Monteverdi. He held various posts as chapelmaster in Ferrara from 1597, except when employed as a singer at St Mark's in Venice under Gabrieli and Croce (1604–8). In 1617 he returned to the St Mark's choir, becoming Monteverdi's deputy in 1620. But he was no mere epigone. His particular talent was for the chamber-scale motet, for a small group of singers or a soloist with instruments, graced by expressive melody with which voice and violin lean towards one another in dialogue, sometimes with idiomatically different decoration. Widely distributed, his works of this kind were absorbed by Schütz and other German composers. In 1627 he became chapelmaster at Santa Maria Maggiore in Bergamo, where he died of the plague.

grand jeu (Fr.). Great registration, a standard formula in French Classical organ music, implying reed and tierce stops, often in contrast with the more homogeneous *plein jeu*.

Grand Macabre, Le (The Great Macabre). Opera by Ligeti to a libretto by Michael Meschke after Michel de Ghelderolde's play. The Great Macabre is Nekrotzar (baritone), who comes to Breughelland to announce the end of the world. But the inhabitants – including a pair of delirious young lovers called Amando (mezzo-soprano) and Amanda (soprano), another couple with maturer tastes, a toper, a boy king and Gepopo the Police Chief (coloratura soprano) – accept him as one of their own and life continues. First performance: Stockholm, 12 Apr 1978.

grand motet (Fr.). Setting of a sacred text, usually a psalm, for soli, choir and orchestra, typical of French music from Du Mont to the Revolution. The most notable examples are by Lalande, Charpentier and Rameau.

grand opera. (1) Informal term for the highbrow genre, with the implication of something smarter and perhaps snootier than an operetta or musical.

(2) Used in a stricter sense, the term denotes the kind of spectacular opera that formed the repertory of the Paris Opera from the end of the 1820s. Generally in five acts, such works included a large cast, a prominent chorus, a ballet episode and lavish scenography. Meyerbeer's operas set the norm for other composers, foreign (Verdi, Wagner in his adaptation of *Tannhäuser*) and French (Halévy); grand opera also influenced the development of opera in Italy, Russia and elsewhere. By the 1850s the form was stiffening, and slimmer styles of opera were flourishing elsewhere in Paris, but the Opera maintained its tradition into the 20th century.

grand piano. The concert instrument, 7–9 feet (2·25–2·75m) long.

Grange, Philip (Roy) (b. London, 17 Nov 1956). British composer, who brings unusual depth to a poetic darkness often announced in his titles: *Cimmerian Nocturne* for six players (1979), *In a Dark Time* for baritone and ensemble (1989), *Eclipsing* for orchestra (1996–7). He studied at York University (1976–82) and with Davies, and, after earlier academic appointments, settled at Exeter University in 1989.

Gran Partita (Great Partita). Name given Mozart's Serenade K.361, for an unually large wind ensemble of 12 players plus double bass.

gran tamburo (It.). Bass drum.

graph. Feldman's term for the kind of free notation he introduced in 1950. A score took the form of large-scale graph paper, with each square indicating what a particular instrument should do (cello low pizzicato, for example) in a given length of time.

graphic notation. Term used of non-standard symbols or visual designs with no defined meaning. In the 1960s composers as diverse as Stockhausen (*Zyklus*) and Britten (*Curlew River*) were obliged to invent new symbols to cope with new musical situations – in these particular cases the creation of a virtuoso percussion piece and the timing of ensemble music in which precise coordination was sometimes not required. Further removed from notational norms are Cage's diagram kits (e.g. his *Variations I–II*), though these always come supplied with rules of play, requiring careful and sympathetic interpretation. Other composers at this time, and a little before, presented musicians with material that was more a prompt to the imagination than a clear definition of sounds or actions: here the pioneering example was Earle Brown's *December 1952*, an elegant array of slim black rectangles on a white background, and the most imposing Cardew's *Treatise*. See also EYE MUSIC.

Graun. German brothers, both musicians for Frederick II, schooled in Dresden.

(1) **Johann Gottlieb** (b. Währenburg, 1702/3; d. Berlin, 27 Oct 1771). Violinist-composer, author of numerous solo and trio sonatas, symphonies,

concertos and French overtures. He joined Frederick's court in 1732, after studies with Tartini in Padua and a time as concert director in Merseburg – Bach sent W.F. there to be trained up as a violinist by him. For Frederick he was an orchestra leader.

(2) **Carl Heinrich** (b. Währenburg, 1703/4; d. Berlin, 8 Aug 1759). Composer, especially of operas for Frederick II (*Cleopatra e Cesare*, Berlin, 1742; *Montezuma*, libretto by the king after Voltaire, Berlin, 1755). He had begun his career in Dresden and Brunswick (1724–35), where he sang tenor, composed his first operas and wrote cantatas and church music. In Berlin his output also included the widely admired Passion oratorio *Der Tod Jesu* (1755) and concertos for flute and harpsichord.

Graupner, (Johann) Christoph (b. Kirchberg, 13 Jan 1683; d. Darmstadt, 10 May 1760). German composer, of whom history has not agreed with the Leipzig authorities who wanted him as cantor of St Thomas's in preference to Bach. He studied at St Thomas's school under Schelle and Kuhnau (1696–1704), then worked as a theatre musician in Hamburg before joining the Darmstadt court in 1709, becoming kapellmeister there in 1711. When he was chosen to succeed Kuhnau at St Thomas's, after his friend Telemann had declined the post, the Darmstadt landgrave offered him more money to stay, which he did, to the end of his life. His known output includes over 1,400 church cantatas, besides concertos, symphonies, sonatas and keyboard music.

grave. (1) (It., heavy). Slow. Tempo marking introduced by 1639, when Cavalli used it, and well established by the end of the century. It seems to have been synonymous with 'adagio', which proved to have greater staying power. Where *grave* survived in the Classical period it may have implied a connection with the Baroque past.

(2) (Fr., heavy). Low. Or slow, especially in the form *gravement*.

gravicembalo (It.). Term by which Cristofori's primeval piano was first named.

grazioso (It.). Graceful, pleasing or, sometimes in Bartók and later music, ingratiating.

Great C major. Name given Schubert's Ninth Symphony, to distinguish it from his Sixth but also on its own account.

great organ. The part of an organ controlled from the main manual, as distinct from the chair organ.

Grechaninov, Aleksandr (Tikhonovich) (b. Moscow, 25 Oct 1864; d. New York, 4 Jan 1956). Russian composer, late flower of the national Romantic tradition. His conservatory studies were with Arensky and Taneyev in Moscow (1881–90) and Rimsky-Korsakov in St Petersburg (1890–93). Back in Moscow, before the Revolution, he enjoyed success as a composer of children's piano music (associated with his work as a teacher) as well as of scores for the Arts Theatre, concert works (Symphony No.1, B minor, Op.6, 1894; No.2 'Pastoral', A, Op.27, 1902–9) and settings of the liturgy. In 1922 he left, to settle first in Paris, then (from 1940) in New York, surviving as a pianist and a composer within the émigré culture. His later works include a *Liturgia domestica* Op.79 with strings, harp and organ (1917–26), planned (because accompanied) for other than church performance, and a large-scale *Missa oeucumenica* Op.142 (1933–6) built on Russian, Gregorian and Jewish chants.

Greece. European country where the achievements of the first millennium BC, peaking in the 'classical period' (from around 500 BC to the death of Alexander the Great in 323 BC), are among the mainsprings of Western culture. On the one hand, certain Greek scientific and philosophical ideas – including, in music, the rationalization of pitch and harmony, the connection of sound with other aspects of physical and metaphysical existence, and the effect of music on people – have repeatedly stimulated later enquiry. On the other, the art of ancient Greece has been a continuing and sustaining ideal, not least for composers from the writers of plainsong through the late Renaissance inventors of opera to Birtwistle.

Only fragments survive of ancient Greek music in notation, all rather late. They include some Euripides on papyrus scraps from the 3rd century BC and the DELPHIC HYMNS. Other clues come from the instruments known from written accounts and pictures: pipes, including the AULOS and syrinx (panpipes), trumpets and horns, percussion and, most importantly, several sorts of LYRE. But altogether we have only a faint signal from a world where music was a part of ritual, theatre, epic narration, warfare, collective work and the smaller communications of social existence.

More is known of Greek musical theory, as handed down by the schools of PYTHAGORAS and ARISTOXENUS, exemplifying a dichotomy that itself has had a rich history in later music – between abstraction and physicality, music as a way of hearing numbers and music as a means of drawing sense from inchoate sound.

See also AMPHION; ANTIGONE; APOLLO; ARIADNE; ARION; DITHYRAMB; LINUS; MARSYAS; MEDEA; MUSES; ODYSSEY; OEDIPUS; ORPHEUS; PAN; PHAEDRA; PHAETON; PLATO; PROMETHEUS; TROJAN WAR. For Greek Orthodox music see BYZANTINE CHANT. Greece was largely separated from Western musical culture during the later Byzantine and Ottoman periods, to participate again in the persons of Kalomiris, Theodorakis, Christou and Xenakis.

Solon Michaelides *The Music of Ancient Greece* (1978)

Greek Passion, The (*Recké pašije*). Opera by Martinů to a libretto by him and the author after Kazantzakis's novel *Christ Recrucified*. Greek villagers, preparing for a passion play, find themselves reliving the events in actuality. The shepherd Manolios (tenor) – with followers including Katerina (soprano), a Mary Magdalen figure – is killed for his support for refugees. First performance: Zurich, 9 Jun 1961.

Greenberg, Noah (b. New York, 9 Apr 1919; d. New York, 9 Jan 1966). US pioneer of early music with his New York Pro Musica ensemble (founded in 1952), specially famed for its presentations of *The Play of Daniel*.

Greene, Maurice (b. London, 12 Aug 1696; d. London, 1 Dec 1755). British composer, notably of anthems (*Lord, let me known mine end*). A clergyman's son, he spent almost his whole life at St Paul's, as chorister, apprentice and, from 1718, organist. He also gained posts as organist and composer of the Chapel Royal (1727), Cambridge professor (1730) and Master of the King's Music (1735). Even so, Handel was treated with more favour by the royal family, which he may well have found irksome; certainly there was some dispute between the rival composers.

Greensleeves. English tune that, according to a pleasant legend, was written by Henry VIII and addressed to Anne Boleyn as the 'Lady Greensleeves' whom the singer wants to tempt back into an amorous relationship. However, the first record of the song dates from 1580, 44 years after Anne's execution. Since then the haunting melody, on the ROMANESCA bass, has sauntered on through innumerable changes of text and musical setting, appearing in cavalier songs, *The Beggar's Opera* ('Since laws were made for ev'ry degree,/To curb vice in others as well as me'), a Christmas carol ('What child is this who, laid to rest/On Mary's lap is sleeping?') and works by Vaughan Williams, Holst, etc.

greghesca (It.). Light madrigal set to verse by Antonio Molino in mixed Venetian and Greek dialects. A volume of such was published in 1564, with pieces by the leading composers in Venice at the time, including Andrea Gabrieli, Merulo, Rore and Willaert.

Gregorian chant. The most widely used chant of the Western church. See PLAINSONG.

Greiter, Matthias (b. Aichach, *c*.1494; d. Strasbourg, 20 Dec 1550). German composer and church musician, responsible for some standard psalm tunes as well as a motet on *Fortuna desperata* moving through the circle of fifths from F to F♭. He studied at the University of Freiburg and was cantor at Strasbourg Cathedral by 1522. Two years later he converted to Protestantism and kept his job; he also abandoned his monastic habit, married and fathered 10 children. In 1549 he converted back again for the same opportunist reason, but the plague soon carried him off.

grelots (Fr.). Jingles, sleighbells.

Grétry, André (Ernest Modeste) (b. Liège, 8 Feb 1741; d. Montmorency, 24 Sep 1813). Walloon–French composer, whose operas charmed Paris audiences in the two decades before the Revolution. His later reputation as 'the French Mozart' is merited by his fluency and tunefulness, though he could also be proto-Romantic in his orchestral atmosphere, formal freedom and invention of the REMINISCENCE MOTIF. In subject he embraced fairytale (Beauty and the Beast in *Zémire et Azor*), historical drama, mythology, sentimental comedy and exotic morality play.

He started as a chorister at St Denis in Liège, where his father was a musician, then had further studies from 1760 in Rome. From there he moved to Geneva (1766) and so to Paris (1767), gaining experience and contacts, the latter including Jean-François Marmontel, who had written librettos for Rameau. Collaborating with Marmontel, and bringing Italianate melody into the opéra comique, he won quick success, so that by 1770 he was writing operas for the marriage of the future Louis XVI to Marie Antoinette, who appointed him her music director when she became queen in 1774. His career flourished with hers, and declined – if less dramatically. He wrote some republican operas in the 1790s, but in the new century seems to have concentrated on a compendium of memories, thoughts and dreams, *Réflexions d'un solitaire*.

David Charlton *Grétry and the Growth of Opéra-Comique* (1986)

Operas: *Le Tableau parlant* (1 act: Louis Anseaume),

f.p. Paris, 1769; *Zémire et Azor* (Marmontel), f.p.
Fontainebleau, 1771; *Céphale et Procris*
(Marmontel), f.p. Versailles, 1773; *Le Jugement de
Midas* (Thomas d'Hèle), f.p. Paris, 1778; *Les
Fausses apparences, ou L'Amant jaloux* (d'Hèle),
f.p. Versailles, 1778; *Le Caravane du Caire* (Etienne
Morel de Chédeville), f.p. Fontainebleau, 1783;
L'Epreuve villageoise (Desforges), f.p. Paris, 1784;
Richard Coeur-de-Lion (Michel Jean Sedaine), f.p.
Paris, 1784; *Panurge dans l'île des lanternes* (de
Chédeville), f.p. Paris, 1785; *Raoul Barbe-bleue*
(Sedaine, after Perrault), f.p. Paris, 1789; *Guillaume
Tell* (Sedaine), f.p. Paris, 1791; about 55 others

Grieg, Edvard (Hagerup) (b. Bergen, 15 Jun 1843;
d. Bergen, 4 Sep 1907). Norwegian composer,
pianist and conductor. The first Nordic composer
widely known and loved – especially for his Piano
Concerto, *Peer Gynt* suites and Lyric Pieces – he
learned from Scandinavian folk music in extending harmonic possibilities while maintaining
a freshness that suggests the musicians of an
earlier generation, especially Schumann and
Mendelssohn.

He was born into a well-to-do family established by his great-grandfather, a Scottish
immigrant (originally Greig); his mother was a
professionally trained pianist who took care of his
early musical education. Sent to the Leipzig
Conservatory (1858–62), he studied with E.F.
Wenzel (who had been close to Schumann),
Moscheles and Reinecke. He then began his career
in Bergen, while making vital trips to Copenhagen,
the cultural centre of what was then the united
kingdom of Denmark and Norway. There he met
Gade (1863) and Rikard Nordraak (1864–5), a
contemporary who was more creatively precocious. He also visited Rome (1865–6), where he
encountered Ibsen. Brushing with these fellow
artists, and in love with his cousin Nina Hagerup, a
singer with whom he began giving concerts, he
found his creative voice, notably in a first
collection of Lyric Pieces (1864–7). In 1867 he and
Nina married, and the next year – during a
summer holiday in Denmark, now with a baby
daughter – he composed his Piano Concerto. Liszt,
whom he met during a second stay in Rome
(1869–70), expressed warm appreciation.

When not travelling, his base was Christiania
(the future Oslo), where he worked with the two
leading Norwegian writers of his time. For
Bjørnstjerne Bjørnson he wrote music for *Sigurd
Jorsalfar* (1872) and began an opera, from which
his attention was diverted by Ibsen's invitation to
work on *Peer Gynt* (1874–5). That collaboration
made him plainly his country's principal
musician. As conductor, pianist and accompanist
(to Nina), he engaged busily in the capital's

musical life, while going out to the country for the
stimulus of folksong and landscape. He spent
more than a year in the Hardanger district
(1877–8), whose natural beauties went into his
string quartet, and took almost annual walking
tours after that. At the same time he was a
European figure, present at the first *Ring* (1876)
and to the end of his life regularly abroad giving
concerts in the winter season. Meanwhile, each
spring and early summer, he would be at home
(the fjordside villa Troldhaugen outside Bergen
from 1885), producing mostly songs and piano
pieces.

Resembling Chopin in embracing a folk
tradition new to the classical language, he was
similarly a harmonic innovator, and his modal
features and floating chords were crucial to the
next generation of Debussy, Ravel, Delius,
Grainger and others. His clear poetry, though, was
all his own, and has endeared his music to generations of professional and home pianists.

John Horton *Grieg* (1974)

Dramatic and vocal orchestral: *Sigurd Jorsalfar*
(incidental music; Bjørnson), Op.22, 1872; PEER
GYNT, Op.23, 1874–5; *The Mountain Thrall*, Op.32,
bar, orch, 1877–8; *Bergliot* (Bjørnson), Op.42,
speaker, orch, 1871, orch 1885; *Olav Trygvason*
(opera: Bjørnson), Op.50, 1873, unfinished, rev
1888–9; etc.

Orchestral (full): Symphony, C minor, 1863–4; *In
Autumn*, Op.11, 1866, rev 1887; PIANO CONCERTO,
A minor, Op.16, 1868, rev 1907; PEER GYNT, suites,
Op.46, Op.55, 1874–5, rev 1885, 1888–92; Lyric Suite,
Op.54, orch 1904 (from pf pieces); *Sigurd Jorsalfar*
(suite), Op.56, 1872, rev 1892; Funeral March for
Rikard Nordraak, orch 1892 (from pf piece);
Symphonic Dances, Op.64, 1896–8

Orchestral (strings): 2 Elegiac Melodies, Op.34, 1880
(from songs); *From Holberg's Time* (HOLBERG
SUITE), Op.40, 1885 (from pf work); 2 Melodies,
Op.53, 1891 (from songs); 2 Nordic Melodies,
Op.63, 1895; 2 Lyric Pieces, Op.68, 1898–9 (from pf
pieces)

Choral: 4 Psalms, Op.74, bar, ch, 1906; etc.

Chamber: String Quartet, G minor, Op.27, 1877–8;
String Quartet, F, 1891, unfinished; Violin Sonata
No.1, F, Op.8, 1865; No.2, G, Op.13, 1867; No.3, C
minor, Op.45, 1886; Cello Sonata, A minor, Op.36,
1882–3; etc.

Songs: *The Heart's Melodies*, Op.5 (4; Andersen),
1864 (No.3 'I love thee'); 4 Songs from *The Fisher
Maiden* (Bjørnson), Op.21, 1870–72; 6 Poems
(Ibsen), Op.25, 1876 (No.2 'A Swan'); 5 Poems
(John Paulsen), Op.26, 1876; 12 Songs (Aasmund
Olaffson Vinje), Op.33, 1873–80; 6 Romances,
Op.39, 1869–84; 6 Songs (Ger.), Op.48, 1884–8
(No.6 'Ein Traum'); *Ave maris stella*, 1893; 5 Poems
(Vilhelm Krag), Op.60, 1893–4 (No.3 'While I
wait'); *Haugtussa* (The Mountain Maid), Op.65 (8;
Arne Garborg), 1895; etc.

Piano: Poetic Tone Pictures, Op.2, 1863; 4 Humoresques, Op.6, 1865; Sonata, E minor, Op.7, 1865; *Agitato*, 1865; Funeral March for Rikard Nordraak, 1866; LYRIC PIECES, Opp.12, 38, 43, 47, 54, 57, 62, 65, 68, 71, 1864–1901; 25 Norwegian Folktunes and Dances, Op.17, 1869; *Folkelivsbilleder* (Pictures of Folk Life), Op.19, 1869–71; Ballade, G minor, Op.24, 1875–6; 4 Album Leaves, Op.28, 1864–78; Improvisation on 2 Norwegian Folktunes, Op.29, 1878; Norwegian Dances, Op.35, duet, 1880, arr solo 1887; Waltz-Caprices, Op.37, duet, 1883, arr solo 1887; *From Holberg's Time* (HOLBERG SUITE), Op.40, 1884; 6 Pieces, Op.41, 1884 (after songs); 19 Norwegian Folktunes, Op.66, 1896–7; *Slåtter*, Op.72, 1902–3; *Stimmungen*, Op.73, 1898–1905; etc.

Griff (Ger.). Fret. Hence *Griffbrett* (fingerboard), even for instruments without frets, e.g. the violin family.

Griffes, Charles T(omlinson) (b. Elmira, NY, 17 Sep 1884; d. New York, 8 Apr 1920). US composer, a delicate orientalist who died as his music was moving into increasingly dissonant territory. He studied at Elmira College and in Berlin, at the Stern Conservatory and with Humperdinck. On his return he took a post teaching at a private school (Hackley), and seems to have composed rather little until his creative awakening after 1910, prompted first by Scriabin and then by contact with Asian art, through the Japanese dancer Michio Ito and the soprano Eva Gaulthier, who had travelled in the East. His Szymanowskiesque art has been consistently championed since his early death.
Donna K. Anderson *Charles T. Griffes* (1993)

Ballet scores (all for 7–9 insts): *The Kairn of Koridwen*, 1916; *Sho-jo*, ?1917; *Sakura-sakura*, ?1917
Orchestral: *The Pleasure Dome of Kubla-Khan*, Op.8, 1917 (from pf piece); Poem, fl, orch, 1919; *The White Peacock*, ?1919 (from pf piece); etc.
Songs: 3 Poems, Op.9, 1916; 3 Poems of Fiona MacLeod, Op.11, 1918; etc.
Piano: 3 Tone-Pictures, Op.5, 1910–12; *The Pleasure Dome of Kubla-Khan*, 1912, rev 1915; Fantasy Pieces, Op.6, 1912–15; *Roman Sketches*, Op.7, 1915–16 (No.1 *The White Peacock*); *De profundis*, 1915; *Legend*, 1915; Sonata, 1917–18; 3 Preludes, 1919; etc.

Grigny, Nicolas de (baptized Rheims, 8 Sep 1672; d. Rheims, 30 Nov 1703). French organist-composer, whose single published volume (1699) represents a culmination of the national tradition and was copied in its entirety by Bach 14 years later. The son, grandson and nephew of organists, he worked at St Denis in Paris (1693–5), then returned to Rheims and became cathedral organist. His book includes an organ mass and versets on common hymns (*Veni Creator*, etc.).

Griller Quartet. British ensemble founded in 1928 by Sidney Griller (1911–93) and fellow pupils of Tertis at the RAM. They toured internationally in the 1930s, formed a relationship with Bloch, played for British troops during the Second World War, and ended their career together in residence at the University of California at Berkeley (1949–61) and Davis (1961–3).

Grisey, Gérard (b. Belfort, 17 Jun 1946; d. Paris, 11 Nov 1998). French composer, for whom spectralism was a means toward extreme sophistication of colour and force of expression. Following training with Messiaen at the Paris Conservatoire (1965–72) and with Dutilleux (1968), he studied sound at the Faculté des Sciences (1974), and so was well placed to take a lead among the spectralists. He did so also as director, with Murail and Lévinas, of the Ensemble Itinéraire, founded in 1974. His composed concert *Les Espaces acoustiques* (1974–85) is a powerful realization of new sounds and a spiralling form. Among his later works, *Quatre chants* forms an hour-long meditation on death: sombre, with lightning bolts. He taught at Darmstadt (1976–82), Berkeley (1982–6) and the Conservatoire (1987–98).

Works: *Les* ESPACES ACOUSTIQUES, 1974–85; *Talea*, 5 insts, 1986; *L'Icône paradoxale*, 2 women's v, orch, 1993–4; *Vortex temporum*, pf, 5 insts, 1994–5; *Quatre chants pour franchir le seuil*, s, 5 insts, 1996–8

Grisi, Giulia (b. Milan, 22 May 1811; d. Berlin, 29 Nov 1869). Italian soprano, whose career, led mostly in Paris and London, straddled the period from Rossini, Bellini and Donizetti to early Verdi and Meyerbeer. Among other roles, she was the first Adalgisa in *Norma* and starred with her mezzo-soprano sister Giuditta in the same composer's *Capuleti*. Another frequent partner on stage was her lover, the tenor Giovanni Mario. Her training had come in Milan and Bologna, where she made her debut at 17, but she did not sing opera in Italy after breaking her contract with La Scala in 1832.

Grofé, Ferde [Ferdinand Rudolf von] (b. New York, 27 Mar 1892; d. Santa Monica, Cal., 3 Apr 1972). US composer and arranger. Active in commercial music from the age of 15, he was taken on by Paul Whiteman in 1920 and made his name as the arranger of *Rhapsody in Blue* (1924). He also composed original works for Whiteman's band, notably *Mississippi* (1925) and the *Grand Canyon* suite (1931), skilful and unashamedly blatant essays in local colour. In his later career, at Radio City Music Hall and the American Bandmasters'

Association, he produced much more of the same.

grosse caisse (Fr.). Bass drum.

grosse (Ger.). (1) Big, as in GROSSE FUGE, GROSSE TROMMEL.

(2) Major, as applied to intervals, e.g. *grosse Sekunde, grosse Terz*, etc.

Grosse Fuge (Big Fugue). The 15-minute movement that Beethoven intended as the finale to his Op.130 quartet, but was persuaded to replace with a more modest conclusion, his last completed movement. The original was published under this title as his Op.133, and his piano duet arrangement as Op.134.

Grosse Orgelmesse. See ORGAN SOLO MASS.

Grosse Trommel (Ger.). Bass drum.

Grossi, Andrea (*fl.* Mantua, late 17th century). Italian musician, noted especially for his Op.3 sonatas for trumpet, strings and continuo (pub 1682).

Grosskopf, Erhard (b. Berlin, 17 Mar 1934). German composer, who has developed an art of 'time-spaces', created by overlapping harmonic processes with input from minimalism and spectralism. He studied in his home city with Pepping and Blacher, and has worked there as an independent composer since 1966. Much of his work is electronic or for small instrumental forces, but he has also written larger pieces, including the Symphony 'Zeit der Windstille' (Time of Wind Calm, 1988–9).

Grotrian-Steinweg. German piano firm continuing after the Steinweg/Steinway family had moved to New York. Wilhelm Grotrian (1843–1917) was left as the leading partner, and his sons changed their name to Grotrian-Steinweg; the business remains in that family, their pianos admired for fine tone.

ground. Bass line that goes on being repeated under a sequence of variations, or a composition using this principle; the recurring line can also be called a 'ground bass'. Grounds followed soon after the institution of melody-bass composition in the Renaissance, and some ground basses became standard patterns, notably the BERGAMASCA, FOLIA, LAMENTO, PASSAMEZZO, ROMANESCA and RUGGIERO. As these names suggest, Italy was the source, and grounds were vigorously imported into England in the 16th–17th centuries with other Italian fashions. The ability to improvise on a ground became one of a musician's attainments, and composed grounds flourished as movements in larger works; examples in Purcell include Dido's lament. Elsewhere, by this time, the chaconne and passacaglia had emerged as principal ground forms.

ground bass. See GROUND.

group. (1) Ensemble.

(2) Term introduced by Stockhausen for a melodic figure or larger entity used as a building block, to get beyond the POINT mentality of 1951–2. Examples of group composition include his *Kontrapunkte* and *Gruppen*.

Groupe de Recherches Musicales. The electronic music organization of French radio, instituted as the Groupe de Recherches de Musique Concrète in 1951 under the direction of Schaeffer and Henry, and reformed under the new name in 1958. Bayle took over as director in 1966, succeeded by Daniel Teruggi in 1997.

Group for Contemporary Music. Ensemble founded at Columbia University, New York, by Harvey Sollberger and Charles Wuorinen in 1962. Since 1990 it has played only for recordings.

Grout, Donald J(ay) (b. Rock Rapids, Iowa, 28 Sep 1902; d. Skaneateles, NY, 9 Mar 1987). US music scholar, author of a standard history of music (1960). He began his career as a church musician, then pursued postgraduate studies at Harvard, leading to a doctorate in 1939. His main appointment was at Cornell (1945–70), where historiography was understandably among his interests. In retirement he turned to Alessandro Scarlatti.

Grove, George (b. Clapham, 13 Aug 1820; d. Sydenham, 28 May 1900). British lexicographer, knighted in 1883. Besides being responsible for the most comprehensive music encyclopedia in the English language – first published in 1878–89 and revised in every generation since then (1904–10, 1927–8, 1940, 1954, 1980, 2001) – he was a pioneer of the programme note (for Crystal Palace concerts), founder director of the RCM and discoverer, with Sullivan, of Schubert's *Rosamunde* music during a trip to Vienna in 1867. This is to mention only his musical accomplishments; he learned lexicography as contributing editor to a Bible dictionary (for which he visited the Holy Land twice), and he had a whole earlier career as a civil engineer.

Percy M. Young *George Grove* (1980)

Gruber. Austrian family of intermittent compositorial prowess.

(1) **Franz Xaver** (b. Unterweizburg, near Hochburg, 25 Nov 1787; d. Hallein, near Salzburg, 7 Jun 1863). Composer and church musician, known universally for a song he wrote to words by Josef Mohr on Christmas Eve 1818 and had performed at midnight mass hours later at St Nikolaus's in Oberndorf, where he was cantor-organist and Mohr was assistant priest 'Stille Nacht' (Silent Night). Not published until 1838, it then went around the world. Its composer – a weaver's son trained by a local organist – also wrote numerous masses, other church music and other songs.

(2) **H(einz) K(arl)** (b. Vienna, 3 Jan 1943). Composer-performer, great-great-grandson of Franz Xaver, master of the macabre but also of the gentle in music that reflects an exuberant and ironic personality. He sang in the Vienna Boys' Choir (1953–7) and studied at the conservatory in Vienna (1957–63), continuing composition lessons with von Einem for a year thereafter. While making a living as an orchestral bassist, he became involved with Schwertsik's concert series, where he could develop his tastes for jazz, cabaret and pop. *Frankenstein!!* (1976–7), devised for his own vampirical vocalizing of horror-comic ditties by H.C. Artmann with orchestra or ensemble, proved an extraordinary success. Besides performing this work around the world, he has sung and conducted music close to him, especially Weill's and Eisler's. Other compositions of his include concertos for violin (No.1 '… aus schatten duft gewebt', 1977–8, rev 1992; No.2 *Nebelsteinmusik*, with strings, 1988), cello (1989) and trumpet (*Aerial*, 1998–9).

Gruenberg, Louis (b. near Brest-Litovsk, 3 Aug 1884; d. Beverly Hills, 10 Jun 1964). US composer, who thrilled and sometimes alarmed audiences in the 1930s by adding jazz and extraversion to a modernism rooted in Busoni. Taken to New York the year after his birth, he studied there and with Busoni in Berlin (1908–14), and set a one-act libretto by Busoni, *The Bride of the Gods* (1913). Back in New York he conducted the US première of *Pierrot lunaire* (1923) and made his name for such works as *The Daniel Jazz* (t, cl, tpt, str qt, 1925), *Jazzettes* (vn, pf, 1926) and the piano sets *Jazzberries* (1925), *Jazz-Masks* (1929) and *Jazz Epigrams* (1929). The climax of this period was his O'Neill opera *The Emperor Jones* (Met, 1933), followed by a concerto for Heifetz (1944) that stands out among his later, more conservative works.

Grumiaux, Arthur (b. Villers, Perwin, 21 Mar 1921; d. Brussels, 16 Oct 1986). Belgian violinist, of classical bearing. He studied at the Brussels Conservatory from 1933 with Alfred Dubois, a pupil of Ysaÿe, then briefly in Paris with Enescu. Soon after the war he began his international career as a performer and recording artist, and in 1949 he succeeded his teacher at the conservatory.

Grümmer, Elisabeth [née Schilz] (b. Niederjeutz, now Basse-Yutz, Moselle, 31 Mar 1911; d. Warendorf, Westphalia, 6 Nov 1986). German soprano, of captivating tenderness. Brought up in Meiningen, she married a violinist and started a family before returning to vocal studies at Karajan's encouragement in Aachen. Under him she made her debut as Octavian (1941). Widowed after the war, she sang internationally, especially in Mozart, Strauss and Wagner (for she avoided singing in languages other than her own); her participation in Kempe's 1964 *Lohengrin* is outstanding. She retired in 1972.

Grundgestalt (Ger., basic shape). Schoenberg's term for the fundamental material of a composition, melodic, harmonic and rhythmic.

Gruppen (Groups). Work by Stockhausen for a large orchestra disposed in three groups around the audience. A classic of the 1950s avant-garde, it was conducted at its première by the composer, Boulez and Maderna, with Ligeti and Kurtág in the audience. First performance: Cologne, 24 Mar 1958.

gruppetto (It., little group, pl. *gruppetti*). TURN.

gtr. Abbreviation for guitar.

Guadagni, Gaetano (b. Lodi/Vicenza, *c.*1725; d. Padua, Nov 1792). Italian castrato, the first Orpheus in Gluck's Italian opera. His career took off in London (1748–53), where he sang for Handel and watched David Garrick, becoming, according to Burney, an incomparable actor. After that his next settled stay was in Vienna (1762–5); hence his association with Gluck, whose Orpheus he repeated in London (1770). His travels also took him to Munich and Potsdam, between appearances in Venice and Padua, where he spent his later years singing at the Santo and as Orpheus for puppet theatres, his voice now a soprano.

Guadagnini, Giovanni Battista (b. Piacenza, *c.*1711; d. 18 Sep 1786). Italian violin maker, outstanding in his time. He learned the art from his father Lorenzo (d. 1748), and practised it in Piacenza (1740–49), Milan (1749–58), Cremona

(1758), Parma (1759–71) and Turin, his Milan instruments being specially valued for their force and naturalness. Several of his descendants, down to the early 20th century, also made violins.

Guami, Gioseffo (b. Lucca, 27 Jan 1542; d. Lucca, 1611). Italian organist and composer of motets, madrigals and canzonas representative of the Venetian school. He studied in Venice with Willaert and Padovano, was taken by Lassus for service mostly at the Bavarian court (1567–79), and then was active in Genoa and Lucca. After a short period as first organist at San Marco in Venice (1588–91) he took a similar position at Lucca Cathedral (1591–1611), where he founded a dynasty slightly prefiguring the Puccinis, being succeeded by two sons. His brother Francesco (1543–1602) was also a noted musician, a trombonist-composer who was with him in Munich.

Guarneri, (Bartolomeo) Giuseppe (b. Cremona, 21 Aug 1698; d. Cremona, 17 Oct 1744). Italian violin maker, known as 'Guarneri del Gesù' (for the IHS monogram on his labels) to distinguish him from his father, and regarded as the only maker to be mentioned in the same breath as Stradivari. He had the benefit, like Stradivari, of familial and local experience. His grandfather Andrea (c.1626–98) was a pupil of Nicolò Amati, and passed on the art to two sons: Pietro (1655–1720, known as 'da Mantova', from his place of work) and Giuseppe the elder (1666–1739/40, known as 'filius Andreae'), both of whom excelled in it. So did two sons of Giuseppe: a second Pietro (1695–1762, known as 'da Venezia', since he made his home in Venice) and Guarneri del Gesù, who, even among these princes, left the most prized work.

Guarnieri, (Mozart) Camargo (b. Tietê, São Paulo, 1 Feb 1907; d. São Paulo, 13 Jan 1993). Brazilian composer, in national style. The son of a Sicilian immigrant with evident musical leanings, he studied in São Paulo and came under Mario de Andrade's nationalist influence; he also studied in Paris with Koechlin (1938–9). A vital force in Brazilian music – and welcomed, too, to the USA in the 1940s – he was chief conductor of the São Paulo Symphony from 1947 and director of the conservatory from 1960. In 1950 he wrote an open letter objecting to the German-born Hans Joachim Koellreutter's introduction of serialism, and though he modified his position a little, he stayed true to the Villa-Lobos line. His works include seven symphonies, concertos, six violin sonatas and an important body of songs.

Gubaidulina, Sofia [Göbäydullina; Gubaydulina, Sofiya Asgatovna] (b. Chistopol, 24 Oct 1931). Russian composer of works that often sheer through boundaries between sacred and secular, female and male, stylistically pure and impure. With Russian, Tatar and Jewish traditions in her background, she moves freely across a wide field of cultural references, Eastern as well as Western, while her work with the improvisation group Astraea, which she formed with Suslin and Artyomov in 1975, has further opened her experience. A visionary intensity is often present in her music, even when she is not explicitly addressing Christian subject matter.

She studied at the conservatories of Kazan (1949–54) and Moscow (1954–63), at the latter with Nikolay Peyko and Shebalin. *Night in Memphis* (1968), with some of its ancient Egyptian texts translated by Akhmatova, was among the works that established her alongside Schnittke and Denisov in the Moscow avant-garde, but she was slower than them to gain attention abroad, and did not visit the West until 1985. Her breakthrough piece was the violin concerto *Offertorium*, widely championed by Kremer and characteristic in its variety, its treatment of quotations (from Bach's *Musikalisches Opfer* via Webern's orchestration) as pregnant expressive emblems and its overall sombreness. In 1992 she moved to Germany.

Orchestral: Concerto, bn, str, 1975; *Introitus*, pf concerto, 1978; *Offertorium*, vn concerto, 1980, rev 1982, 1986; *Seven Last Words*, vc, bayan, str, 1982; *Stimmen … vertsummen …*, symphony, 1986; *Pro et contra*, 1989; *And the feast is in full progress*, vc, orch, 1993; Viola Concerto, 1996; *The Light of the End*, 2003; etc.

Choral and vocal: *Night in Memphis* (ancient Egyptian), mez, men's ch, orch, 1968; *Rubayat* (Omar Khayyam, Habiz, Chukani), bar, chbr orch, 1969; *Hour of the Soul* (Tsvetayeva), mez, perc, orch, 1976; *Perception* (Francisco Tanzer), s, bar, 7 str, 1983, rev 1986; *Hommage à T.S. Eliot*, mez, 8 insts, 1987, rev 1991; *Now always snow* (Gennady Aygi), chbr ch, ens, 1993; *Johannes-Passion*, soli, ch, orch, 2000; *Johannes-Ostern*, soli, ch, orch, 2001; etc.

Ensemble: *Concordanza*, 10 insts, 1971; *Detto II*, vc, ens, 1972; etc.

Chamber: String Quartet No.1, 1971; No.2, 1987; No.3, 1987; No.4, 1993; String Trio, 1988; *Silenzio*, bayan, vn, vc, 1991; etc.

Instrumental: Chaconne, pf, 1962; *Detto I*, org, perc, 1978; *De profundis*, bayan, 1978; *In croce*, vc, org, 1979; *Dancer on a Tightrope*, vn, pf, 1993; etc.

Gudmundsen-Holmgreen, Pelle (b. Copenhagen, 21 Nov 1932). Danish composer, whose guides have included Beckett for reduction in the late 1960s and Stravinsky, later, for range of reference. A sculptor's son, he studied at the Copenhagen Conservatory, taught at the Århus Conservatory (1967–72) and has held various administrative posts in Danish musical life. His works include orchestral pieces and eight quartets.

Guédron, Pierre (b. Normandy, c.1565; d. ?Paris, 1619/20). French singer-composer, leading practitioner of the *air de cour*, of which he published about 200. He began as a boy chorister for the Cardinal of Lorraine, moved to the royal chapel in 1588 and held increasingly important positions at court as chamber musician from 1590, contributing songs to ballets.

Guerrero, Francisco (b. Seville, ?4 Oct 1528; d. Seville, 8 Nov 1599). Spanish composer and church musician, polyphonic master whose music, like Victoria's, has an Iberian intensity. He studied with his brother Pedro, himself a distinguished composer of motets and secular songs, and with Morales, who found him his first post at an early age, as chapelmaster at Jaén Cathedral (1546–9). The next half century he spent at Seville Cathedral, where he became chapelmaster in 1574, though he also travelled as far as Rome (1581–2) and the Holy Land (1588–9). On his way back from the latter expedition he was waylaid by pirates, but he yearned to go back and was about to do so when plague struck him. His liturgical works, so expressive and fluently diatonic, went on being sung in the Hispanic world into the 18th century; they include 19 masses and numerous motets.

Guézec, Jean-Pierre (b. Dijon, 29 Aug 1934; d. Paris, 9 Mar 1971). French composer, who worked with contrasted stretches of texture, often with febrile internal movement, 'to reflect', as he put it, 'the agitation and unrest of the world in which we live' – but to do so with precision. At the Paris Conservatoire (1953–63) he was crucially influenced by Messiaen, whom he joined there as professor of analysis in 1969. Meanwhile he began making an international reputation through such pieces as *Architectures colorées* for ensemble (1964). Messiaen wrote the horn solo of *Des canyons* in his memory.

Guglielmi, Pietro Alessandro (b. Massa, 9 Dec 1728; d. Rome, 19 Nov 1804). Italian composer, among the most successful Neapolitan comic-opera composers of his time, though overtaken by Cimarosa and Paisiello. He studied with his father and uncle, then with Durante at the Loreto conservatory (1746–54). Local renown was followed by invitations from Rome, Venice and London (1767–

72), after which he returned to northern Italy and then to Naples, until his appointment in 1793 as chapelmaster of St Peter's in Rome. Among his most widely performed comedies were *La sposa fedele* (Venice, 1767), *La villanella ingentilita* (Naples, 1779), *La virtuosa di Mergellina* (Naples, 1785), *L'inganno amoroso* (Naples, 1786), *La pastorella nobile* (Naples, 1788), *La bella pescatrice* (Naples, 1789) and *La lanterna di Diogene* (Venice, 1793). He also wrote oratorios, masses and some instrumental music. Of his 10 children, his son Pietro Carlo (c.1763–1817) also composed comic operas, with much less success.

Guido of Arezzo [Aretinus] (b. c.991/2; d. after 1033). Italian theorist, one of the supreme authorities for medieval musicians, an innovator in transmitting music both in written form (with his first intimations of staff notation) and orally, through teaching based on SOLMIZATION syllables. He thereby answered the need for means by which the growing chant repertory could be preserved and taught.

Trained at the Benedictine abbey of Pomposa, near Ferrara, he remained there as a chant teacher, with success that brought him renown and envious mistrust. Around 1025 he moved to Arezzo, whose bishop asked him to write a manual, his celebrated and much recopied *Micrologus*. Perhaps three years later he was invited to Rome, to explain his methods to Pope John XIX. He then returned to the Arezzo region, possibly to the Camaldolese monastery at Avellana.

His idea of placing neumes on a system of lines and spaces marked with note letters led directly to the staff with clef. He was also probably responsible for establishing a simple code of syllables for hexachordal degrees: ut, re, mi, fa, sol, la. These two principles were included in the *Introductorium*, a primer widely used in the 16th century.

Guidonian hand. Mnemonic device, attributed to Guido, by which notes are imagined at the joints and fingertips of a hand, a melody passing from one to another.

guild. Association formed to maintain monopoly rights and other privileges for members as followers of some craft, trade or profession. Musical guilds were widespread in European cities from the 13th century and provided town musicians. They declined in prestige with the virtual extinction of civic music after the Renaissance, to be replaced by new kinds of academy, collegium musicum, professional society and, eventually, UNION.

Guildhall School of Music and Drama. London conservatory founded in 1880.

Guilhem IX, Duke of Aquitaine and Count of Poitiers (b. 1071; d. 10 Feb 1127). Troubadour, the first whose poems survive, one of them ('Pos de chantar') with incomplete music. He was a great lord, warrior and womanizer, and grandfather of Eleanor of Aquitaine (queen of Henry II of England).

Guillaume Tell (*William Tell*). Opera by Rossini to a libretto by Etienne de Jouy and Hippolyte-Louis-Florent Bis after Schiller's play. The big and stirring overture leads into a scene where the patriotic-amorous tensions of the opera are laid out: Arnold (tenor) and Tell (baritone) are united in resistance to the Austrians, but Arnold is in love with an Austrian princess, Mathilde (soprano). Arnold's position is clarified with the news that his father has been killed by the Austrians, and he joins Tell in an uprising that ends with the assassination of the Austrian governor, Gesler (bass). Arias include Mathilde's 'Sombre forêt' and Tell's 'Sois immobile', addressed to his son in the apple-on-head scene. First performance: Paris, 3 Aug 1829.

Guillelmus Monachus (*fl.* late 15th century). ?Italian theorist, author of a treatise on ways of improvising harmony to a chant: FAUXBOURDON, FALSOBORDONE and GYMEL.

Guillou, Jean (b. Angers, 18 Apr 1930). French organist-composer, follower of his Paris Conservatoire teachers Dupré, Duruflé and Messiaen. He became organist at St Eustache in Paris in 1963.

Guilmant, (Félix) Alexandre (b. Boulogne-sur-Mer, 12 Mar 1837; d. Meudon, 29 Mar 1911). French organist-composer, pioneer of the organ recital, giving which he toured Europe and North America. He studied with his organist father and briefly with Lemmens. From 1862 he was based in Paris, where he was organist of La Trinité (1871–1901), co-founder with Bordes and d'Indy of the Schola Cantorum, and Widor's successor as organ professor at the Conservatoire. His voluminous output includes eight organ sonatas (1874–1909) and two symphonies for organ and orchestra.

Guinjoán, Juan (b. Riudoms, 28 Nov 1931). Spanish composer, adding local colour to impulses from the international avant-garde. He trained at the Barcelona Liceo Conservatory (1947–52) and in Paris, and founded the Barcelona ensemble Diabolus in Musica in 1965. His works include the

opera *Gaudi* (1989–91) as well as many ensemble pieces.

Guiot de Dijon (*fl.* 1215–25). Trouvère, whose *Chanterai por mon corage* shows skilful melodic variation. The attribution of his 17 songs is contested.

Guiraud, Ernest (b. New Orleans, 23 Jun 1837; d. Paris, 6 May 1892). US–French composer, best known as the adder of recitatives to his friend Bizet's *Carmen* (Vienna, 1875) and as Debussy's teacher. His father was a French-born composer, and from the age of 12 he lived in Paris, studying with Marmontel and Halévy at the Conservatoire, whose staff he joined in 1876. Bizet found him lacking in creative ambition, which may explain his relatively small output (mostly of comic operas and orchestral pieces) and lack of conspicuous success.

guiro. Notched object (traditionally a gourd) scraped with a stick. Of Cuban origin, the instrument made its first important orchestral appearance in *The Rite of Spring*. See also RECO-RECO.

guitar (Fr. *guitare*, Ger. *Gitarre*, It. *chitarra*, Port. *violão*, Sp. *guitarra*). String instrument of waisted shape, normally fretted, and played with a plectrum or the fingers. The regular modern guitar has six strings tuned in fourths (plus one third) upwards from the E on the bass stave: E–A–D–G–B–E. Its frets, usually 19 at chromatic junctures, provide a range of three octaves plus a fifth. Parts are normally notated an octave higher.

The guitar has a long and complex history, perhaps going back to the kithara of ancient Greece and certainly interwoven with the histories of the lute, gittern and other instruments, bowed as well as plucked or strummed. If it indeed was of Greek origin, its development was surely affected by Islamic music, and it has remained associated with a country where Islam and Europe clashed and conjoined: Spain. Renaissance guitars of two kinds, small with four courses and larger with five, were played also in Italy and France. Both continued in use into the 18th century, when the six-string guitar supervened, to develop during the century's latter part further away from the lute in its construction and notation (staff replacing tablature).

In the early 19th century Sor introduced the new instrument to Paris, while Giuliani took it from Italy to Vienna. Minor vogues were initiated in both cases, but nothing like the sweep of the 20th century, when the guitar was re-established as a classical instrument (by Tárrega, Pujol, Segovia and others) and recreated in amplified form to become the instrument of choice for popular musicians. The acoustic guitar has appeared occasionally as an orchestral instrument since Mahler's Seventh Symphony, and often in mixed ensembles since Schoenberg's Serenade and Boulez's *Le Marteau sans maître*. Composers who have featured the instrument more prominently include Falla, Ponce, Villa-Lobos, Castelnuovo-Tedesco, Rodrigo, Brouwer, Henze and Berio.

Ralph Denyer and Andy Summers *The Guitar Handbook* (1982, ²1992)

Gumpelzhaimer, Adam (b. Trostberg, Upper Bavaria, 1559; d. Augsburg, 3 Nov 1625). German composer and church musician, active in the richly musical, Venetian-influenced city of Augsburg, where he studied and became cantor of St Anna's (1581–1625). He published German sacred songs, Latin motets and a music primer that remained in use for a century.

Guntram. Opera by Strauss to his own libretto, a quasi-medieval fabulation in which the titular hero (tenor) is a minstrel knight who rejects both his beloved Freihild and his chivalric order, thus allowing plentiful Wagnerian echoes. First performance: Weimar, 10 May 1894.

Guridi (Bidaola), Jésus (b. Vitoria, Alava, 25 Sep 1886; d. Madrid, 7 Apr 1961). Spanish composer, especially of zarzuelas (*El caserío*, Madrid, 1926), songs and orchestral pieces. Born into a highly musical family, he gained aristocratic support for studies in Paris (at the Schola Cantorum, 1904–6), Liège (with Jongen) and Cologne. He then returned to Bilbao to work as a church organist and choral conductor before his appointment to the new Vizcaya Conservatory in 1927.

Gurlitt, Manfred (b. Berlin, 6 Sep 1890; d. Tokyo, 29 Apr 1973). German composer, noted for piano studies and an alternative *Wozzeck* (1928). He studied with Humperdinck in Berlin, held important conducting posts in Bremen (1914–24) and Berlin (1924–39), and settled in Japan, where he taught and ran his own German opera company.

Gurney, Ivor (Bertie) (b. Gloucester, 28 Aug 1890; d. Dartford, 26 Dec 1937). British poet-composer, known for Housman settings eschewing the folk touch in favour of a lied-like sensitivity. After training as a chorister at Gloucester Cathedral he became a pupil of Stanford at the RCM, but left in 1915 to join up. Wounded and gassed, he returned to the RCM under Vaughan Williams (1918–21)

and started publishing both poetry and songs. Soon, though, he was suffering mental collapse; his last years he spent in confinement.

Gurrelieder (Gurra Songs). Concert tableaux by Schoenberg for soli, choirs and enormous ORCHESTRA, setting a German translation of poems by Jens Peter Jacobsen. The medieval Danish king Waldemar (tenor) and his beloved Tove (soprano), residing at the castle of Gurra, sing alternately of their love in almost Wagnerian style. On Tove's death Waldemar curses God and is condemned to hunt the night skies, the music becoming generally wilder and weirder. First performance: Vienna, 23 Feb 1913.

gusli. Russian folk psaltery.

Gustavus III, King of Sweden (b. Stockholm, 24 Jan 1746; d. Stockholm, 29 Mar 1792). Following his accession in 1771 he gave much of his attention to opera, at Drottningholm and at the Royal Opera, which he founded in 1782. He wrote librettos and became, through his assassination, the subject of two: for Auber's *Gustave III* and Verdi's *Un ballo in maschera*.

gusto (It.). Taste, as in *con gusto* (tastefully).

Guy, Barry (John) (b. London, 22 Apr 1947). British bassist-composer, with a special gift for novel and poetic string sounds and textures. He studied at Goldsmiths' College and the Guildhall School, and has developed parallel careers as a composer-performer in jazz and classical fields. Among his works are *After the Rain* for string orchestra (1992), *Buzz* for viol consort (1994) and *Dakryon* for Baroque violin, bass and tape (2000).

gymel. Splitting of a polyphonic part, normally the uppermost, into two simultaneous lines. The practice and the term (from Lat. *gemellus*, twin) are distinctively English of the medieval and Renaissance periods. Gymels could be improvised, one group singing a descant in thirds, or composed, examples of the latter occurring in the Eton Choirbook, Taverner, early Tallis and other music of the reigns of Henry VII and VIII (1485–1547).

Gymnopédies. Term invented by Satie for three piano pieces evoking ancient Greece in their modal simplicity. Debussy orchestrated the first and third.

gypsy (Ger. *Zigeuner*). Traditional means of referring to European nomads whose own name for themselves is *roma*. For classical musicians, especially in the late Romantic period, they provided a fascinating other: the gypsy violinist, traditionally male, with a repertoire of darkly seductive music, distinguished by a particular scale, C–D–E♭–F♯–G–A♭–B–C, with a cadence from the major second. Such bewitching players were especially to be found in the cafés of Budapest, and for visitors, including Brahms and Liszt, their music represented Hungary. Hence, for example, Brahms's Hungarian Dances, brimming with an extrovert energy that also went into many of his rondo finales. The more particular image of the piratically headclothed violinist fed into the solo violin repertory, most explicitly in Ravel's *Tzigane*.

Gypsy Rondo. Name given the finale of Haydn's piano trio in G, H.15:25

Gyrowetz, Adalbert [Jírovec, Vojtěch Matyáš] (b. České Budějovice, 20 Feb 1763; d. Vienna, 19 Mar 1850). Bohemian composer, follower of Haydn. He studied with his choirmaster father and in Prague, then gained a position as secretary and musician to Count Franz von Fünfkirchen. In 1785 he was in Vienna, and in 1786–7 in Rome with a new noble master, Prince Ruspoli. At the beginning of his stay in London (1789–93) he assisted Haydn; he also wrote symphonies, quartets and an opera, *Semiramis*, whose score was destroyed in a theatre fire. After that he returned home and soon settled in Vienna, where he became court theatre composer (1804–31), producing German operas and ballets while honouring his heritage in some Czech songs. He also befriended Beethoven, though Haydn remained his god.

H (Ger.). The note B.

Haas, Georg Friedrich (b. Graz, 16 Aug 1953). Austrian composer, of music evoking poetic and disturbing shadowlands. He studied with Neuwirth in Graz and Cerha in Vienna (1981–3), and also followed courses at Darmstadt and IRCAM. In 1998 he began teaching at the conservatory in Graz. His works include the one-act chamber opera *Nacht* (f.p. Bregenz, 1998).

Haas, Pavel (b. Brno, 21 Jun 1899; d. Auschwitz, 17 Oct 1944). Czech composer, follower of Janáček, with whom he studied at the Brno Conservatory (1920–22). He worked in his father's business and later as a music teacher, under increasingly difficult conditions before his internment as a Jew at Theresienstadt (1941–4) and eventual transfer to Auschwitz. His works include the opera *The Charlatan*, Op.14 (f.p. Brno, 1938), a wind quintet (Op.10, 1929), three string quartets and a Study for strings (1943).

Haas, Robert (Maria) (b. Prague, 15 Aug 1886; d. Vienna, 4 Oct 1960). Austrian scholar, responsible for publishing uncut versions of Bruckner's scores. He studied in Berlin, Vienna and Prague, and was head of music at the Austrian National Library (1920–45), being dismissed as a Nazi collaborator.

Hába, Alois (b. Vizovice, 21 Jun 1893; d. Prague, 18 Nov 1973). Czech composer, especially of quarter-tone music. After training as a teacher in Kroměříž he studied with Novák in Prague (1914–15) and started using quarter-tones in his Suite for strings (1917), following a newspaper report of a lecture.

He became Schreker's pupil in Vienna and Berlin (1918–22), after which he returned to Prague and taught microtonal music at the conservatory (1924–51). In his own practice microtonal intervals were an enrichment and a nuancing of regular tonal harmony, often supporting intimations of Moravian folk music, and he continued in similar style whether using these intervals (including in some pieces fifth- or sixth-tones) or not. His quarter-tone works range from pieces for a specially constructed piano to an opera, *The Mother* (1927–9).

habanera. Cuban dance or dance-song with an infectious duple rhythm, often:

$$\frac{4}{4} \; \dot{\flat} \quad \flat \flat \; \flat$$

It originated in the early 19th century, took root in Spain and, following Bizet's example in *Carmen*, was specially affected by French composers, including Chabrier, Debussy and Ravel.

Habeneck, François Antoine (b. Mézières, 22 Jan 1781; d. Paris, 8 Feb 1849). French conductor. The son of a German-born bandsman, he studied at the Paris Conservatoire and began his career as a theatre violinist, becoming principal in 1817 and director (1821–46) at the Opera, where he conducted (habitually with a bow) the first performances of *Guillaume Tell*, *Les Huguenots*, *Benvenuto Cellini*, etc. He was also important in bringing Beethoven's music to Paris, beginning with the First Symphony in 1807 and continuing from 1828 with the newly formed Société des Concerts du Conservatoire.

Hadley, Patrick (Arthur Sheldon) (b. Cambridge, 5 Mar 1899; d. King's Lynn, 17 Dec 1973). British composer, follower of Delius. He studied at Winchester, Cambridge and the RCM (with Vaughan Williams), and taught at the latter institutions, becoming Cambridge professor (1946–62). His works include *The Trees so High* (1931), a symphony-scale folksong elaboration for baritone, choir and orchestra.

Haefliger, Ernst (b. Davos, 6 Jul 1919). Swiss tenor, admired and astringent as Bach's Evangelist. A pupil of Patzak in Vienna, he made his debut in the St John Passion in 1942, sang with the Zurich Opera (1943–52), then joined the Deutsche Oper, Berlin. His son Michael became director of the Lucerne Festival in 1999.

Haendel, Ida (b. Chelm, 15 Dec 1924). Polish–British violinist, combining clean style with richness and strength, notably in the Sibelius concerto. She studied in Warsaw and with Flesch and Enescu, and settled in London in 1938.

Haffner. Prosperous Salzburg family, patrons and friends of Mozart, remembered for two works they occasioned:

(1) The 'Haffner' Serenade, K.250, written for the evening before the wedding of Marie Elisabeth. First performance: Salzburg, 21 Jul 1776.

(2) The 'Haffner' Symphony, K.385, requested by Mozart's father as a serenade to celebrate the ennoblement of Marie Elisabeth's brother, Siegmund (29 Jul 1782), though only the first movement was ready in time. If the work was completed as a serenade it probably included another minuet (of which there is no trace) and the march K.408:2.

Hahn, Reynaldo (b. Caracas, 9 Aug 1875; d. Paris, 28 Jan 1947). Venezuelan–French composer, mostly of songs and, later, operettas. Arriving in Paris at three with his German father, Venezuelan mother and multitudinous siblings, he studied with Massenet at the Conservatoire and gained an entrée to distinguished salons in his teens, singing his own songs at the piano. Proust and Sarah Bernhardt were among those who took him up. He then broadened his career into conducting and criticism, served in the First World War, and began writing more in larger forms, scoring a hit with his operetta *Ciboulette*. After the end of the Second World War he was director of the Paris Opera.

Operettas: *Ciboulette* (Robert de Flers and Francis de Croisset), f.p. Paris, 1923; *Mozart* (Sacha Guitry), f.p. Paris, 1925; *Brummell* (Robert Dieudonné and Rip), f.p. Paris. 1931; etc.

Orchestral: Violin Concerto, 1927; Piano Concerto, 1931; etc.

Songs: 'Si mes vers avaient des ailes' (Hugo), 1888; 'Chansons grises' (Verlaine), 1887–90 (No.5 'L'Heure exquise'); 'D'une prison' (Verlaine), 1892; etc.

Hail, bright Cecilia. Ode for St Cecilia's Day by Purcell to words by Nicholas Brady, scored for six soli (s, a, a, t, b, b), choir and instruments, all in a splendiferous sequence of movements praising music and musical instruments. First performance: London, 22 Nov 1692.

hairpin. Nickname for a crescendo or descrescendo sign.

Haitink, Bernard (Johann Herman) (b. Amsterdam, 4 Mar 1929). Dutch conductor, remarkable for the integrity and strength of purpose of his performances. He studied with Felix Hupka at the Amsterdam Conservatory and later with Leitner, began his career with Dutch radio and became chief conductor of the Concertgebouw (1961–88), whose Mahler–Bruckner tradition he gladly maintained. His first visit to Britain was in 1959 with the Concertgebouw, and the country became his second musical home; he was musical director of the LPO (1967–79), Glyndebourne (1977–88) and the Royal Opera (1987–2002). The central Austro-German repertory from Mozart to Mahler has remained his forte.

Hajibeyov, Uzeyir (Abdul Hussein) (b. Agjabedi, 17 Sep 1885; d. Baku, 23 Nov 1948). Azerbaijani composer, founder of his country's national school. He trained as a teacher, and with *Leyla i Majnun* (f.p. Baku, 1908) invented a new genre of 'mugam opera', marrying Western instruments and notation with the local style of improvisation on a *mugam*, or mode. After training in Moscow (1911–12) and St Petersburg (with the Rimsky-Korsakov pupil Vasily Kalafati, 1913–14), he returned to Baku, where he taught at the new conservatory and conducted folk ensembles. The most important of his later works was the opera *Kyoroglï* (f.p. Baku, 1937).

Halbe-Note (Ger.). Half-note, minim.

Halberstadt. German city whose cathedral organ of *c.*1361 has the earliest surviving keyboard of seven notes to the octave plus five more at a higher level. This arrangement, common to modern pianos, organs, harpsichords, accordions, etc., is sometimes known as a Halberstadt keyboard.

Halbton (Ger.). Semitone.

Halévy, (Jacques François) Fromental (Elie) (b. Paris, 27 May 1799; d. Nice, 17 Mar 1862). French composer, especially of grand opera and most notably of *La* JUIVE. Of Jewish parentage (the family name was changed from Levy in 1807), he entered the Paris Conservatoire at nine, became Cherubini's pupil (1811) and won the Prix de Rome (1819). He returned to the Conservatoire as a harmony teacher in 1827 and became professor of composition in 1840, his pupils including Gounod, Bizet and Saint-Saëns. Meanwhile he pursued success as an opera composer, and won it spectacularly with *La Juive*, written while he was head of singing at the Opera (1829–45). He wrote about 30 other operas, including *L'Eclair* (1835), *La Reine de Chypre* (1841) and *Charles VI* (1843). Elected to the Institut in 1836, he married an heiress in 1842, though financial security did not impair his productivity – or the skill that won him the admiration of Berlioz and Wagner. His daughter Geneviève married Bizet, for whom his nephew Ludovic (1834–1908), in partnership with Henri Meilhac, wrote the words for *Carmen* as well as librettos for Offenbach.

half-cadence, half-close. IMPERFECT CADENCE.

half-diminished seventh chord. Chord in which the top third is not minor, as in a diminished seventh chord (e.g. C–E♭–G♭–B♭♭), but major (e.g. C–E♭–G♭–B♭). The TRISTAN CHORD may be parsed as of this kind.

Halffter. Spanish family of composers, whose first two members had a German father and a Spanish mother with gifts as a pianist.

(1) **Rodolfo (Escriche)** (b. Madrid, 20 Oct 1900; d. Mexico City, 14 Oct 1987). A follower of Falla, from whom he sought advice in Granada in 1929 (being otherwise self-taught), he exiled himself first to Paris (1934–9) and then to Mexico, where he took citizenship and taught at the National Conservatory. His works include ballet scores (*Don Lindo de Almeria*, Op.7, 1935; *La madrugada del panadero*, Op.12, 1940) and a violin concerto (Op.11, 1940). After the mid-1950s he composed less.

(2) **Ernesto (Escriche)** (b. Madrid, 16 Jan 1905; d. Madrid, 5 Jul 1989). He started before his brother Rodolfo, having lessons with Falla from 1922 and seeing his first work in print the next year. His large early output comprises mostly orchestral,

chamber and piano pieces. As Falla's spiritual heir – though more briefly influenced by Parisian music of the 1920s: Stravinsky, Ravel, Les Six – he was given the task of completing his master's *Atlántida*, for which he largely forsook composition of his own during the period 1954–60, returning to produce a sequence of vocal orchestral scores and further piano works.

(3) **Cristobal (Jiménez)** (b. Madrid, 24 Mar 1930). Rodolfo's and Ernesto's nephew, he studied at the Madrid Conservatory (1947–51) and with Tansman. At first drawn to the Falla school of his uncles, he became in the 1960s the chief Spanish representative of the Darmstadt-based avant-garde. His works include the opera *Don Quijote* (f.p. Madrid, 2000), concertos, choral pieces and electronic music.

half-note (US). Minim (UK). See DURATION.

Hälfte, die (Ger., half). Marking over a part in a score, indicating that only half the instruments should play.

Hall, Richard (b. York, 16 Sep 1903; d. Horsham, 24 May 1982). British composer, though best known as the teacher of Birtwistle, Davies and Goehr. He studied at Cambridge and worked as a church musician before teaching at the Royal Manchester College (1938–56) and Dartington (1956–67). Some of his works, which include five symphonies and seven quartets, make an unusual marriage of Schoenberg with Vaughan Williams.

Hallé, Charles [Halle, Carl] (b. Hagen, Westphalia, 11 Apr 1819; d. Manchester, 25 Oct 1895). German–British conductor and pianist, resident from 1848 in Manchester (whose principal orchestra bears his name) and knighted in 1888. He studied in Darmstadt (1835–6) and Paris (1836–48), where he got to know Chopin, Liszt, Berlioz and Wagner. With so many musicians arriving in London in 1848 to escape the revolutions in mainland Europe, he settled in Manchester, founded his Hallé Concerts in 1858 and was founder principal of the Royal Manchester College of Music (1893), though he also gave recitals, especially of Beethoven, in London, Australia and South Africa.

Hallelujah Chorus. Number in *Messiah* where the choir jubilantly repeats the word 'Hallelujah'. By an old tradition the audience stands for it.

Hallé Orchestra. Hallé's Manchester band, subsequently conducted by Hans Richter (1899–1911), Harty (1920–33), Barbirolli (1943–70), Nagano (1991–2000) and Mark Elder (from 2000) among others.

Hallgrímsson, Hafliði (b. Akureyri, 18 Sep 1941). Icelandic composer and cellist, pupil of Davies. He studied in Reykjavik and London as a cellist, and worked in Britain as an orchestral musician until 1983, when he turned to composing full-time. Right away he started to make an international reputation with such works as *Poemi*, Op.7, for violin and strings (1984).

Hambraeus, Bengt (b. Stockholm, 29 Jan 1928; d. Montreal, 22 Jan 2000). Swedish composer and organist, prominent in the post-1945 avant-garde. He studied at Uppsala University (1947–56) and at Darmstadt, worked for Swedish radio, and took a post at McGill University, Montreal, in 1972. Much of his work involves his own instrument, though he was also a pioneer of tape music.

Hamburg. City in Germany, prospering since the early 17th century as a North Sea port and commercial centre, and always an independent mercantile city, with no court. Telemann spent most of his career there, as church musician and opera composer; Keiser led the opera before him, with Handel for a while as apprentice. Important institutions include the Staatsoper, whose new building opened in 1955, and the Philharmonic, founded in 1828. The city is also home to Deutsche Grammophon.

Hamelin, Marc-André (b. Montreal, 5 Sep 1961). Canadian pianist of astonishing virtuoso powers. He studied in Montreal and the USA (with Sherman), beginning his career when he won the 1985 Carnegie Hall International American Music Competition. His repertory ranges from Alkan and Sorabji to Wolpe, and includes dizzying transcriptions of his own.

Hamerik [Hammerich], **Asger** (b. Frederiksberg, near Copenhagen, 8 Apr 1843; d. Frederiksberg, 13 Jul 1923). Danish composer, reckoned his country's outstanding symphonist between Gade and Nielsen, though he spent his creative years almost entirely outside Denmark. He was related through his mother to Hartmann and Gade, both of whom gave him help before he went for further study to von Bülow in Berlin (1862–4). After that he was in Paris (1865–9), advised by Berlioz, and in Baltimore as director of the Peabody Conservatory (1871–98), where he wrote his seven numbered symphonies. He then retired to Denmark. His son, Ebbe (1898–1951), was also a composer.

Hamilton, Iain (Ellis) (b. Glasgow, 6 Jun 1922; d. London, 21 Jul 2000). Scottish composer, latterly reversing from his moderate modernist position.

Brought up largely in London, he studied with Alwyn at the RAM (1947–51) and began with abstract chamber and orchestral pieces influenced by Bartók, Berg and Hindemith, leading into a serial period that started with his Sinfonia for two orchestras (1958). Teaching at Duke University, North Carolina (1961–81), he turned more to the dramatic forms of opera (*The Royal Hunt of the Sun*, f.p. London, 1977) and concerto. From the late 1970s his music became increasingly tonal.

Hamlet. Shakespeare play in which the alienated prince, when he at last acts to avenge his father's murder, brings wholesale slaughter to the Danish court. Musical treatments include:

(1) Ambroise Thomas's opera *Hamlet* to a libretto by Carré and Barbier, which stays close to the original plot until the last act, where Hamlet (baritone) is left surviving as king. A mad scene for Ophelia (soprano) is one of the high points; Claudius is a bass and Gertrude a mezzo. The work has maintained a fingerhold on the repertory, as a vehicle for a baritone who can act. First performance: Paris, 9 Mar 1868.

(2) Franco Faccio's opera *Amleto* to a libretto by Boito, following the events of the play, with a tenor Hamlet, sopranos as Ophelia and Gertrude, and a baritone Claudius. First performance: Milan, 9 Feb 1871.

(3) Liszt's symphonic poem *Hamlet*, developed from incidental music (f.p. Weimar, 1858). First performance: Sondershausen, 2 Jul 1876.

(4) Tchaikovsky's fantasy overture *Hamlet*, predating his incidental music (f.p. St Petersburg, 1891). First performance: St Petersburg, 24 Nov 1888.

(5) Searle's opera *Hamlet* to his own libretto, again faithful, with a baritone prince. First performance: Hamburg, 4 Mar 1968.

(6) Rihm's opera on Heiner Müller's *Die Hamletmaschine*, a ruined monument to the play, with three Hamlets (old actor, young actor, baritone) and a dramatic soprano Ophelia. First performance: Mannheim, 30 Mar 1987.

Other treatments include Berlioz's funeral march for the end of the play (No.3 of his *Tristia*), overtures by Gade and Joachim, MacDowell's symphonic poems *Hamlet* and *Ophelia*, incidental scores by Wolpe and Prokofiev, Blacher's symphonic poem, Kabeláč's *Hamlet Improvisation*, Kelterborn's opera *Ophelia*, Shostakovich's double whack at the subject, in incidental music when he was a young man and in an atmospheric film score over 30 years later, and music by Walton for Olivier's film. There are also versions (Gasparini's *Ambleto* of 1706, Andreozzi's *Amleto* of 1792) that owe nothing to Shakespeare.

Hammerklavier. Name given to Beethoven's Piano Sonata Op.106, whose weight it seems to suit – though to Beethoven this was the regular German term for the piano.

Hammerschmidt, Andreas (b. Brüx, 1611/12; d. Zittau, 29 Oct 1675). Bohemian–German composer and church musician, whose prolific output of Lutheran motets and sacred concertos dominates the repertory of the generation after Schütz. Obliged, as Protestants, to leave Bohemia in 1626, his family settled in Saxony, where he presumably had his musical education. From lesser posts he moved to become organist of St Johannis's, Zwittau, in 1639, and there he remained.

Hammond organ. See ELECTRONIC ORGAN.

Hampson, (Walter) Thomas (b. Elkhart, Ind., 29 Jun 1955). US baritone of commanding expressivity and presence. He studied in Spokane and Los Angeles, began his career with the Düsseldorf company (1981–4) and was soon appearing internationally. Particularly associated with Mozart, Strauss and Mahler, he has also sung new works by Berio and others.

handbell. Small bell for ringing by hand, held by a wooden handle or loop of leather or cloth. Handbells are used all over the world as ritual instruments; in England they have for centuries also had a place in social music-making, first as practice instruments for tower bellringers and subsequently as chiming choirs in their own right. They have occasionally been used by British composers (Britten, Davies) or in performing medieval music.

Handel, George Frideric [Händel, Georg Friedrich] (b. Halle, 23 Feb 1685; d. London, 14 Apr 1759). German–British composer. Born just 19 days before Bach and in much the same region of eastern central Germany, he was in many ways his great contemporary's great opposite. With a keen sense for characters' self-presentation, he excelled at musical drama – in his English oratorios as much as in his Italian operas. He also spent most of his life far from home, unmarried and childless. Like Bach, though, he was a huge fount of creative energy, and like Bach he had to wait until the later 20th century for the full range of his output to be appreciated. For two centuries or more, regular performances of *Messiah* and a few other works, often presented by massive assemblies of singers and players, perpetuated an image of him as a composer of sturdy magnificence. In the 1920s his operas began to be performed again, but at first

only as historical curiosities. The vitality in their extravagance and the truth in their irony became much clearer as the lessons of the early-music movement filtered into opera houses in the 1970s–80s.

Born to the second wife of a 62-year-old court barber-surgeon, he lost his father before he was 12 and took his first job, as cathedral organist in Halle, when he was just 17. He probably saw opera in Berlin soon after, and in the summer of 1703 left to play second violin (later harpsichord) for the opera in Hamburg. There he came under Reinhard Keiser's influence and made friends with Johann Mattheson; he also wrote his first operas. To go further in this field, though, he had to gain experience in Italy.

Rome, where he probably arrived early in 1707, saw his startling coming-of-age. Working for the cardinals Carlo Colonna and Benedetto Pamphili, and for Prince Francesco Maria Ruspoli, he produced brilliant church music (*Dixit Dominus*), a dramatic oratorio (*La Resurrezione*) and delectable cantatas. He also wrote an opera for Florence and reputedly had an affair with a singer, though there was a homoerotic flavour to the culture in which he was moving, and the entire matter of his sexuality, whether in Italy or later, remains mysterious. Another opera (*Agrippina*), for Venice, brought his Italian period to a splendid end in the winter of 1709–10, and may have won him an invitation to Hanover, where in June 1710 he became kapellmeister to the Electress Sophia, mother of the future George I.

By early autumn he had left for London, and there he stayed until the following summer, writing *Rinaldo* for the Queen's Theatre (later King's), which had opened in 1705 as a venue for opera in Italian. Though this imported art suffered attacks in the press (notably from Joseph Addison), it enjoyed a vogue among aristocrats, who had marvelled at Italian opera when on the Grand Tour, and among the curious. Ticket prices equivalent to several months' pay for an ordinary worker effectively confined the audience to the wealthiest, of whom the theatre could accommodate 760, and performances were generally given twice a week, on Tuesdays and Saturdays, throughout a season lasting from December to June. Attempts at opera in English had been made and would continue to be made, but Italian castratos and women sopranos were the great draw, and most of them could not or would not sing in English. Opera therefore had to be made in Italian, by composers competent in the language: Handel, or one of the Italian composers who were with him in London as colleagues, rivals or both.

In October 1712, after little more than a year

back in Hanover, he returned to this world of swirling opportunity and intrigue, and this time he stayed for good. In compensation for the loss of his Hanover appointment the next year, he received a pension from Queen Anne, and he had plentiful musical opportunities, writing four more operas in 1712–15, an ode for the queen, a *Te Deum* and *Jubilate* for the service to mark the Peace of Utrecht (1713), and the *Water Music* for George I, who had succeeded both his mother and his distant cousin Anne in 1714. During this period he lived as a guest of the opera-loving Earl of Burlington.

In 1717–18 he was briefly employed as house composer by the Earl of Carnarvon (later Duke of Chandos) at Cannons, near Edgware, writing a masque (*Acis and Galatea*), a first English oratorio (*Esther*) and the 'Chandos anthems'. After that his main concern was the Royal Academy of Music – not the conservatory, which came much later, but an organization set up to secure the future of Italian opera at the King's Theatre with support from the king and nobility. He revisited Germany in 1719 to find suitable singers and wrote *Radamisto* for the opening season, working up to the glorious plateau he reached in 1724–5 with *Giulio Cesare, Tamerlano* and *Rodelinda*, though other composers, notably Bononcini, also provided scores. Some of the finest singers of the age were available, including the castrato Senesino and the sopranos Margherita Durastanti, Francesca Cuzzoni and Faustina Bordoni. Nevertheless, the academy, faced with robust competition from across London by *The Beggar's Opera*, was wound up in 1728.

This 'First Academy' period, 1720–28, established him in London society. In 1723 he moved into a house in fashionable Brook Street, his home to the end of his days, and that same year he was appointed composer to the Chapel Royal. As such, for the coronation of George II in 1727, he wrote four anthems, of which *Zadok the Priest* has been sung at every British coronation since. Also in 1727 he became a British subject.

But opera was by no means over with the collapse of the academy. Indeed, he was almost immediately back in Italy and Germany recruiting new singers for a 'Second Academy' at the King's Theatre under his independent control. For this five-year venture (1729–34) he produced works both new (*Partenope, Orlando*) and old (*Rinaldo, Giulio Cesare, Rodelinda*); he also, in the face of a pirate performance of *Esther*, presented that score in a new form and added another English oratorio, *Deborah*. In 1733 a rival company was formed with Porpora as leading composer, the Opera of the Nobility, which restored aristocratic ascendancy

and in 1734 took over the King's Theatre, having the big pull of Farinelli as star singer. Still, Handel was able to continue his operation at the new Covent Garden theatre (1734–7), where he again offered oratorios (*Athalia, Alexander's Feast*, repeats of *Esther* and *Deborah*) as well as operas (mostly new pieces, including *Ariodante* and *Alcina*).

In 1737 he suffered paralysis of the right hand, perhaps the result of a stroke, or of writing and rewriting so much: he was a great recycler of his own and others' material. A visit to the baths at Aachen happily brought complete relief. Then, as the Opera of the Nobility had gone broke, he returned to the King's Theatre, but only for a single season (1737–8), with a new castrato, Caffarelli, in *Faramondo* and *Serse*. His operatic career then sputtered out with *Imeneo* (1740) and *Deidamia* (1741), which had only two and three performances respectively. Italian opera in London continued fitfully – Gluck provided it in 1745–6 – but without its greatest creative exponent of the time, who now turned his attention wholly to English oratorio.

During three decades of writing opera for London he had produced three dozen original scores and another dozen adaptations, all belonging to the genre now known as 'opera seria' (serious opera), though having their seriousness variously speckled with ostentation, delicious mockery, fantasy or magic. By one of the form's conventions characters express themselves singly, most often in da capo arias; generally the only ensemble is a final 'chorus' uniting the principal characters, including any who might meanwhile have met their demise. But the vocalizing individual becomes, in Handel, a source of endless fascination. His music explores the pretence, collusion, deception and self-deception with which a human being will address others, whether individuals (other characters on stage) or the watching horde (the audience). The audience at the King's or Covent Garden, though, seems to have listened only to the glitter of the castratos, contention between warring sopranos and the noise of fashion.

Well, he would try another mode. In seasons at the King's Theatre (1739) and Lincoln's Inn Fields (1739–41) he presented not only his last two operas but nine oratorios or odes, including the new *Saul* and *Israel in Egypt*, of which the former and possibly also the latter had words by Charles Jennens. He worked with Jennens again in the summer of 1741 on a new oratorio for a season of concerts he was planning in Dublin (1741–2), *Messiah*, and largely completed another, *Samson*, before making the journey. This then became his usual pattern: in summer or early autumn he would work on oratorios for the coming Lenten season at Covent Garden. The form played to his strengths – to his talents for opera, in that it offered strong characters and conflicts (*Messiah* excepted), as well as to the gifts for word painting and choral vigour he had proved in his Anglican church music. In it he produced not only works of worship but pieces as secular and indeed fleshly as *Semele*, or as bellicose as those that followed the 1745 Jacobite rebellion: the *Occasional Oratorio* and *Judas Maccabaeus*. Even so, his greatest achievement came in the more explicitly sacred pieces, especially *Messiah*, where he gave the English-speaking world not just music it could take to its collective heart but a permanent slant on theology.

His oratorio performances brought him into contact with different singers, mostly British (Susanna Cibber, John Beard), though the new young castrato Guadagni also sang for him. Display was still part of the game, and there were further opportunities for it in the concertos – concerti grossi and organ concertos – he included between the acts. During this oratorio period he was therefore also busy writing and revising orchestral pieces, of which he published several volumes (notably Opp.3, 4 and 6), following on from and interleaving with books of sonatas. As one of the first composers to make his living as an independent operator, he took advantage of the newly revived publishing industry as well as of his regular oratorio performances and occasional commissions, including one for music to accompany the pyrotechnic display celebrating the Peace of Aix-la-Chapelle (Music for the Royal Fireworks, 1749). The same year he began giving annual charity concerts in the new chapel of the Foundling Hospital, usually with *Messiah* on the programme, bringing that work to the pitch of popularity it has sustained.

In the latter part of 1750 he made a final journey to Germany by way of the Netherlands. (Bach was dead now; they had never met.) He returned to start work on what would be his last concerto (Op.7:3) and last oratorio (*Jephtha*), for in February 1751 he began to lose his sight. In 1752, like Bach two years before, he underwent an operation, at the hands of the royal surgeon, but neither this nor spa visits (to Bath and Cheltenham) helped, and by January 1753 he was totally blind. Through the six years left to him he was able, nevertheless, to continue directing his oratorio performances and playing his organ concertos at them; he also wrote a few new numbers with the help of John Christopher Smith, his copyist's son, whom he had taught as a boy.

Westminster Abbey was packed for his funeral, where, according to the terms of his will, the monument by Roubiliac was installed three years later.

Donald Burrows *Handel* (1994); Donald Burrows, ed. *The Cambridge Companion to Handel* (1997); Ellen T. Harris: *Handel as Orpheus* (2001)

www.gfhandel.org

Operas, oratorios and the like
(first performances in London unless otherwise stated)

Operas: *Almira* (Friedrich Christian Feustking), f.p. Hamburg, 1705, partly lost; *Nero* (Feustking), f.p. Hamburg, 1705, lost; *Rodrigo* (after Francesco Silvani), f.p. Florence, 1707, partly lost; *Florindo and Daphne* (Hinrich Hinsch), f.p. Hamburg, 1708, mainly lost; AGRIPPINA, 1709; *Rinaldo* (see ARMIDA), 1711; *Il PASTOR FIDO*, 1712; *Teseo* (Haym, after Quinault), f.p. 1713; *Silla* (Giacomo Rossi), f.p. 1713; *Amadigi di Gaula* (see AMADIS), 1715; RADAMISTO, 1720; *Muzio Scevola* (act 3, other acts by Amadei and Bononcini), f.p. 1721; *Floridante* (Rolli), 1721; OTTONE, 1722; FLAVIO, 1723; GIULIO CESARE, 1724; TAMERLANO, 1724; RODELINDA, 1725; *Scipione* (Rolli), f.p. 1726; *Alessandro* (Rolli), f.p. 1726; *Admeto, rè di Tessaglia*, f.p. 1727; *Riccardo Primo, rè d'Inghilterra* (Rolli), f.p. 1727; *Siroe, rè di Persia* (Haym, after Metastasio), f.p. 1728; *Tolomeo, rè di Egitto* (Haym), f.p. 1728; *Lotario* (Giacomo Rossi), f.p. 1729; PARTENOPE, 1730; *Poro, rè dell'Indie* (after Metastasio), f.p. 1731; EZIO, 1732; *Sosarme, rè di Media* (after Antonio Salvi), f.p. 1732; ORLANDO, 1732; *Arianna in Creta* (after Pietro Pariati), f.p. 1734; ARIODANTE, 1734; ALCINA, 1735; ATALANTA, 1736; *Arminio* (after Salvi), f.p. 1737; *Giustino* (after Niccolo Beregan and Pariati), f.p. 1737; BERENICE, 1736–7; *Faramondo* (after Zeno), f.p. 1738; *Alessandro Severo* (after Zeno), f.p. 1738; SERSE, 1737–8; *Giove in Argo* (after Antonio Maria Lucchini), f.p. 1739; *Imeneo* (after Silvio Stampiglia), f.p. 1740; *Deidamia* (Rolli), f.p. 1741

Oratorios: *Il trionfo del tempo e del disinganno* (Cardinal Benedetto Pamphili), f.p. ?Rome, 1707, rev as *Il trionfo del tempo e della verità*, f.p. 1737, rev as *The Triumph of Time and Truth* (?Thomas Morell), f.p. 1757; La RESURREZIONE, 1708; *Brockes Passion*, f.p. ?Hamburg, 1716; ESTHER, 1718; *Deborah* (Samuel Humphreys), f.p. 1733; ATHALIA, 1733; SAUL, 1738; ISRAEL IN EGYPT, 1738; L'ALLEGRO, IL PENSEROSO ED IL MODERATO, 1740; MESSIAH, 1741, f.p. Dublin, 1742; SAMSON, 1741, rev 1742; SEMELE, 1743; *Joseph and his Brethren* (James Miller), 1743, f.p. 1744; *Hercules* (Thomas Broughton), 1744, f.p. 1745; BELSHAZZAR, 1744; *Occasional Oratorio* (Newburgh Hamilton), f.p. 1746; JUDAS MACCABAEUS, 1746; JOSHUA, 1747; *Alexander Balus* (Morell), 1747, f.p. 1748; SOLOMON, 1748; *Susanna*, 1748, f.p. 1749; THEODORA, 1749; *The Choice of Hercules* (after Robert Lowth), f.p. 1751; JEPHTHA, 1751

Masque and serenata: ACIS AND GALATEA, 1718;
Parnasso in festa, f.p. 1734
Odes: Ode for the Birthday of Queen Anne, ?1713;
Alexander's Feast (after Dryden), f.p. 1736; Ode for
St Cecilia's Day (Dryden), 1739

Other vocal music

Coronation anthems, ch, orch, 1727: *Let thy Hand be
Strengthened, My Heart is Inditing, The King shall
Rejoice, Zadok the Priest*
Other English church music: CHANDOS ANTHEMS,
1717–18; *Te Deum* 'DETTINGEN', soli, ch, orch, 1743;
other anthems, hymns
Latin church music: *Dixit Dominus*, soli, ch, insts,
1707; *Nisi Dominus*, soli, ch, insts, 1707; *Salve
regina*, s, insts, 1707; *Silete venti*, s, insts, *c.*1723–5;
etc.
Cantatas: *Dietro l'orme fuggaci* (*Armida
abbandonata*), s, 2 vn, con, 1707; *Mi palpita il cor*, v,
fl/ob, con; *Nel dolce dell'oblio* (*Pensieri notturni di
Filli*), s, rec, con; *O numi eterni* (*La Lucrezia*), s,
con, 1709; *La terra è liberata* (*Apollo e Dafne*), s, b,
insts, 1710; *Tra la fiamme*, s, insts; etc.
Other works: songs, duets, trios

Instrumental music

*Works are numbered according to the Händel-Werk-
Verzeichnis (HWV).*

Suites: WATER MUSIC, 1717; MUSIC FOR THE ROYAL
FIREWORKS, 1749; etc.
Concerti grossi: 6, Op.3, HWV 312–17, various soli,
str, con, pub 1734; 'ALEXANDER'S FEAST', C, HWV
318, 1736; 12, Op.6, HWV 319–30, 2 vn, vc, str, con,
pub 1740; etc.
Organ concertos: 6, Op.4, HWV 289–94, pub 1738
(No.6, B♭, originally for hp); 'The Cuckoo and the
Nightingale', F, HWV 295, 1739; A, HWV 296a,
1739; D minor, HWV 297, ?*c.*1738; 6, Op.7, HWV
306–11, pub 1761; etc.
Oboe concertos: 3, HWV 301–3, ob, str, con, pub 1740
Concerti a due cori: Nos.1–3, B♭, F, F, HWV 322–4,
2 wind groups, str, con, *c.*1747; Nos.1, B♭, HWV
322; No.2, F, HWV 323; No.3, F, HWV 324
Trio sonatas: 6, Op.2, HWV 386–91, pub *c.*1730; 7,
Op.5, HWV 396–402, pub 1739; etc.
Violin sonatas: G, HWV 358, *c.*1707–10; D minor,
HWV 359a, *c.*1724; A, Op.1:3, HWV 361, *c.*1725–6; G
minor, Op.1:6, HWV 364a, *c.*1724; D, HWV 371,
*c.*1749–50
Flute sonatas: E minor, Op.1:1, HWV 359b, *c.*1724; G,
Op.1:5, HWV 363b, *c.*1711–16; B minor, Op.1:9,
HWV 367b, *c.*1725–6; D, HWV 378, *c.*1707; E minor,
HWV 379, *c.*1727–8
Recorder sonatas: G minor, Op.1:2, HWV 360,
*c.*1725–6; A minor, Op.1:4, HWV 362, *c.*1725–6; C,
Op.1:7, HWV 365, *c.*1725–6; D minor, HWV 367a,
*c.*1725–6; F, Op.1:11, HWV 369, *c.*1725–6; B♭, HWV
377, *c.*1724–5
Oboe sonatas: B♭, HWV 357, *c.*1707–10; F, HWV
363a, *c.*1711–16; C minor, Op.1:8, HWV 366,
*c.*1711–12

Sonatas of dubious authenticity: HWV 368 (G
minor, vn), 370 (F, vn), 372 (A, vn), 374–6 ('Halle'
sonatas for fl)
Harpsichord: 8 suites, A, F, D minor, E minor, E
(HARMONIOUS BLACKSMITH finale), F♯ minor,
G minor, F minor, HWV 426–33, pub 1720; 9
suites, B♭, G (Chaconne), D minor, D minor, E
minor, G minor, B♭, G, G (Prelude and
Chaconne), HWV 434–42, pub 1733; other suites,
preludes, fugues, etc.
Other works: overtures, dances, marches, clock tunes

Handel and Haydn Society. Boston organization,
the oldest US oratorio society in existence,
founded in 1815. It was responsible for the US
premières of *Messiah* (1818), *The Creation* (1819),
the Verdi Requiem (1878) and Bach's B minor Mass
(1887).

hand horn. Natural horn, without valves, on
which the player can manipulate one hand in the
bell to affect intonation. It was preferred by
Brahms and used by Ligeti in his Horn Trio and
Hamburg Concerto.

Handl, Jacobus (b. ?Ribnica, 1550; d. Prague, 18 Jul
1591). Slovenian composer and church musician,
prolific author of masses and motets displaying
contrapuntal prowess and occasionally polychoral
display. Sometimes known by the Latin form of his
name, Gallus, he spent the later 1560s and 1570s
staying at monasteries from Melk to Breslau/
Wrocław. He then held posts in Olomouc (until
1585) and Prague, where he published his *Opus
musicum* (1586–90), a collection of 374 motets in
four volumes.

Handlung (Ger.). Drama. Term preferred by
Wagner, notably for *Tristan*, and adopted by later
composers in emulation of that work's dramatic
distance from operatic convention.

hand organ. Barrel organ.

Hanover Square Rooms. London concert hall,
opened by J.C. Bach and Abel in 1775. The auditorium was like a large drawing room, with sofas,
and remained in use for almost a century, until
1874.

Hänsel und Gretel (Hansel and Gretel). Opera by
Humperdinck to a libretto by his sister Adelheid
Wette after the Grimms' tale. Hänsel (mezzo-
soprano) and Gretel (soprano), protected by
angels through a night in the forest, van-
quish the Witch of the sugar house (mezzo-
soprano), to a score full of simple tunes and
irradiated by the glow of Wagner. First conducted

by Richard Strauss, the work immediately took its place internationally as a favourite winter-holiday entertainment. First performance: Weimar, 23 Dec 1893.

Hanslick, Eduard (b. Prague, 11 Sep 1825; d. Baden, near Vienna, 6 Aug 1904). Austrian critic, supporter of Brahms but not Wagner, who responded by caricaturing him as Beckmesser in *Die Meistersinger*. He studied with Tomášek in Prague, and wrote his first review in 1844. Meanwhile, he trained as a lawyer and arrived in Vienna in 1852 as a civil servant, though he was immediately active as a critic. He wrote regularly for the *Neue freie Presse* from the paper's foundation in 1864, and lectured at the university, as professor from 1870. In his treatise *Von Musikalisch-Schönen* (On the Beautiful in Music, 1854) he argued that music has aesthetic value primarily on account of its form and substance as sound, not because of its expressive connotations (which he by no means denied).
Eduard Hanslick *Music Criticisms: 1846–99*, ed. Henry Pleasants (1963).

Hanson, Howard (Harold) (b. Wahoo, Neb., 28 Oct 1896; d. Rochester, NY, 26 Feb 1981). US composer, whose Swedish ancestry may be reflected in the echoes of Grieg and Sibelius in his music. He studied with the great pedagogue Percy Goetschius in New York (1914) and at Northwestern (1915–16), and was the first composer to win a scholarship to the American Academy in Rome (1921–4), where he had orchestration lessons from Respighi. Returning to the USA to direct the Eastman School (1924–64), he was also active as a conductor.

Orchestral: Symphony No.1 'Nordic', E minor, Op.21, 1922; No.2 'Romantic', Op.30, 1930; No.3, Op.33, 1937–8; No.4 'The Requiem', Op.34, 1943; No.5 (Sinfonia sacra), Op.43, 1954; No.6, 1968; No.7 'The Sea' (Whitman), ch, orch, 1977; Serenade, Op.35, fl, hp, str, 1945; Piano Concerto, G, Op.36, 1948; Fantasy-Variations on a Theme of Youth, Op.40, pf, str, 1951; *Mosaics*, 1957; etc.
Other works: *Merry Mount* (opera; after Hawthorne), Op.31, f.p. Met, 1934; chamber music, piano pieces, cantatas

happening. Unstructured, supposedly spontaneous event characteristic especially of the FLUXUS group.

Harawi. Cycle of 12 songs for soprano and piano ('chant d'amour et de mort', song of love and death) by Messiaen to his own words after Peruvian folksongs. It was the first part of his Tristan trilogy, followed by *Turangalîla* and the *Cinq rechants*. First performance: Macôn, 24 Jun 1946.

Harbison, John (Harris) (b. Orange, NJ, 20 Dec 1938). US composer, whose considered modernist-traditional compromise has given him access to music of great variety and probity. Jazz, Bach and Stravinsky were early loves; he then studied with Piston at Harvard, Blacher in Berlin (1961) and at Princeton. Since 1969 he has taught at the Massachusetts Institute of Technology; he has also held orchestral residencies in Pittsburgh (1982–4), Los Angeles (1985–8) and St Paul (1990–92). Among his most striking pieces are chamber works, songs and his operatic one-acter after Yeats.

Operas: *Winter's Tale* (Harbison, after Shakespeare), f.p. San Francisco, 1979; *Full Moon in March* (1 act; Harbison, after Yeats), f.p. Harvard, 1979; *The Great Gatsby* (Harbison and Murray Horwitz, after Fitzgerald), f.p. New York, 1999
Orchestral: Symphony No.1, 1981; No.2, 1987; No.3, 1991; *The Most Often Used Chords*, 1993; concertos
Vocal: *Motetti di Montale*, mez, pf/ens, 1980–90; choral works; etc.
Chamber: Wind Quintet, 1979; Piano Quintet, 1981; 3 string quartets; etc.

Harfe (Ger., pl. *Harfen*). Harp.

Harmonia Mundi. French recording company, founded by Bernard Coutaz in St-Michel-de-Provence in 1958 and developing a specialization in early music and historically informed performance. A German subsidiary took on a separate existence in 1977 as Deutsche Harmonia Mundi, and was acquired successively by EMI and BMG.

harmonic. (1) Frequency that is a whole-number multiple of another, defined as the fundamental. Thus the harmonics of A = 440 Hz will be frequencies of 880 Hz (the second harmonic, A an octave above), 1320 Hz (the third harmonic, the E above that), 1760 Hz (the fourth harmonic, the next A), and so on. Such notes form a 'harmonic series', and most pitched sounds include higher harmonics as PARTIAL constituents (though there may also be INHARMONIC partials). The reason is simple. Where, for example, an instrument's pitch is decided by the length of a vibrating string or air column, the same string or air column will be experiencing vibrations that are twice as fast, three times as fast, etc., producing harmonics – or, more strictly, partials, which may deviate a little from true harmonics, depending on the instrument's materials and geometry.

Harmonics may be isolated by the performer. In the case of string instruments, a light touch some way along the length of the string will suppress the fundamental (which requires the whole string to be vibrating) and bring forward a harmonic – the second harmonic, for example, for a touch at the midway point. Instruments of the violin family are said to produce 'natural harmonics' (on open strings) or 'artificial harmonics' (on stopped strings). The former were introduced by Mondonville (*c.*1738) and became, with Paganini, an essential part of virtuoso violin writing, while artificial harmonics are more a feature of music since 1900. Harmonics are also available on the guitar and harp. Some 20th-century composers asked for harmonics on the piano, obtained by leaning into the inside and placing a finger on a string while pressing a key with the other hand.

Where brass instruments are concerned, harmonics are normal notes; the instruments work as tubes within which various harmonics can be sounded. Woodwind instruments can be persuaded to produce harmonics as special effects.

(2) Pertaining to harmony, as in 'harmonic theory', 'harmonic development', etc.

harmonica. (1) Small REED ORGAN held to the mouth; hence its alternative name, mouth organ. First produced in Vienna in the 1820s in imitation of the Chinese SHENG, it rapidly became a popular instrument for entertaining oneself and others, being easy to play. Notes of the tonic chord (generally C major) are sounded by blowing out, the other notes of the scale by sucking in, and notes can be deselected by stopping the relevant holes with the fingers or tongue. In the 1920s a fully chromatic harmonica was introduced, with a lever that would retune the instrument from C to C♯. Armed with this, two harmonica players, Larry Adler and Tommy Reilly, became virtuosos of the instrument and had works written for them by Milhaud, Vaughan Williams and others.

(2) ARMONICA.

harmonic minor. Scale with minor third and sixth, and also raised seventh (so that it provides a necessity of minor-mode harmony: the dominant triad). The harmonic minor scale on C is C–D–E♭–F–G–A♭–B–C and the same descending.

harmonic rhythm. The rhythm or speed of chord change in a piece of music, which may coincide or conflict with the rhythm or speed overtly expressed.

harmonic series. See HARMONIC (1).

harmonic seventh. Interval determined by the

seventh PARTIAL of a tone, being the gap between that partial and the fourth, i.e. expressing the frequency ratio 7:4 (1·75). This is about a sixth-tone smaller than an equal-tempered minor seventh (1·782).

Harmonie (Ger.), **harmonie** (Fr.). (1) Harmony.

(2) Wind ensemble, normally of oboes, clarinets, horns and bassoons. The German term is usefully preferred for this, partly because 'harmony' has quite enough meanings, but also because such ensembles were maintained most especially by wealthy households in the Austrian empire and Germany in the 18th century and early 19th, and graced with substantial works by Mozart.

Harmonie der Welt, Die (World Harmony). Symphony by Hindemith and opera to his own libretto. In the opera's cinematic flow of scenes and times Johannes Kepler (baritone) seeks universal coherence to a score that, in its exploration of harmony, does the same. Hindemith developed the ideas first in the symphony. First performance: Munich, 11 Aug 1957 (opera).

Harmonielehre (Ger.). Harmony as a pedagogical subject. Schoenberg wrote a treatise with this title, and John Adams an orchestral piece.

Harmoniemesse (Wind Ensemble Mass). Sixth of Haydn's late masses, with full wind instruments. First performance: Eisenstadt, 8 Sep 1802.

Harmoniemusik (Ger.). Music for HARMONIE (2).

Harmonies poétiques et religieuses. Title Liszt borrowed from two volumes of poems by Lamartine for a piano piece (1833–4) and then a whole collection (1840–48, rev 1848–53): 1 *Invocation*, 2 *Ave Maria*, 3 BENEDICTION DE DIEU DANS LA SOLITUDE, 4 *Pensée des morts*, 5 *Pater noster*, 6 *Hymne de l'enfant à son reveil*, 7 FUNERAILLES, 8 *Miserere, d'après Palestrina*, 9 *Andante lagrimoso*, 10 *Cantique d'amour*. Nos.3 and 7 are commonly excerpted.

harmonious. Agreeing and agreeable, euphonious. The usual adjective from harmony in the musical sense is HARMONIC.

Harmonious Blacksmith, The. Name given to the variation-form finale of Handel's keyboard suite in E major. There are various explanations, more or less likely: that Handel heard a tuneful smith, that the work's first publisher had turned from the horseshoe craft, etc.

harmonium. REED ORGAN operated by a keyboard and bellows, widely disseminated in the 19th century as a cheap alternative to the organ in churches and as a parlour instrument. The name, introduced by Alexandre François Debain for a small portable instrument he patented in 1842, is now used also for the commoner instruments that have the size and shape of an upright piano. Composers who wrote for this wheezing machine include Karg-Elert, Rossini and Schoenberg.

harmon mute. Metal mute for a trumpet or trombone, producing an effect of distance. The sound can be varied by means of a plunger, which alters the proportion of air entering the mute, and also by moving a hand back and forth over the bowl-shaped outer face; hence the alternative name, wa-wa mute.

harmony. Combination of pitches. The word can cover anything from a particular instance ('the first harmony in *Tristan*') to a large abstraction ('Bruckner's harmony', 'jazz harmony') – i.e. it may be simply a synonym for 'chord', or it may imply a whole world of rules and practices.

In music it does not normally have its everyday meaning of agreement ('they were in harmony on the matter'), partly because music has and needs a slightly more precise term for accord, CONSONANCE, but also because almost any music includes harmonies that are evidently disruptive. The most dissonant chord is still a harmony, for it will exist within a particular harmonic world and have harmonic consequences within that world, perhaps in implying a less dissonant chord to follow. However, one strong priority in Western aesthetics is integrity, the fit joining of parts, and there is a supposition of wholeness in the larger meaning of harmony. Indeed, works from the great period of major-minor tonality (roughly from the mid 17th to the mid 20th century) – and even those from before or after – are expected to be unified largely by harmonic means.

Harmony, in the widest sense, is accordingly accepted as one of the fundamental constituents of music and as one of the fundamental avenues of study, alongside counterpoint. Often these two are represented as music's twin dimensions, the simultaneous, or vertical, and the successive, or horizontal, but both cut across diagonally, and they are better regarded as complementary views, harmony being concerned with the union of sounds and counterpoint with the distinction of sounds. The two disciplines or views are thoroughly interdependent. Traditional counterpoint is governed by conventions that are essentially harmonic, and harmony – traditional or otherwise – is a property not only of chords (vertical) but of simple melodies (horizontal). A tune does not have to wait to be harmonized before it acquires harmony: harmony is, rather, inherent in the scale and particular intervals. The first eight notes of the *Dies irae* plainsong, to quote a much used musical theme, call up a whole harmonic world: they imply harmonies and a harmonic cadence.

They probably do so, however, only to ears conditioned by the major-minor system of harmony. That necessity for training has to be uncertain, because the ubiquity of Western music has made it hard to find ears that are innocent, but one must doubt whether those who sang the *Dies irae* in the 14th century, or made polyphonic settings in the 15th and 16th, could have anticipated – or perhaps even understood – the treatment the tune received from Berlioz or Rachmaninoff. There is also a wider relevance here. The major-minor system is to be judged by such immense, complex and persuasive achievements as Beethoven's Ninth Symphony, but that system has also overpowered alternatives – or embraced them, as with the traces of older modality revived in that very symphony. The search for new kinds of harmony, from Debussy onwards, has had to take account of – or strenuously oppose – expectations that have become, through anyone's musical experience, second nature.

Nature – first nature – is of course also involved. No musical system has developed or been devised (other than with the use of unpitched instruments) that could ignore the fundamental harmonic importance of the octave, which in Western music is so basic as to be almost not a harmony at all but rather an equivalent to the unison. Beyond that, though, raw nature's ways tend to be muddled with those of human cultures, as may be clearly heard in how the major third, from being a dissonance in the 13th and 14th centuries (when the unison, octave or fifth were the only permitted conclusions), became consonant in the 15th century, allowing the major and minor triads to begin their extraordinary several-centuries story.

One value of medieval music lies in exposing a harmonic world, rooted in the church modes, that is essentially different from the major-minor system. And where this music was thought archaic or even primitive by 19th-century historians, it seemed close by the mid 20th century, when such otherwise unlike composers as Messiaen and Partch were exploring new alternatives to major-minor tonality. Machaut's mass is an outstanding example, in frankly presenting, on strong beats, dissonances that later music would want to moderate or conceal, and in taking a cheerfully pragmatic, short-term view of harmonic progression.

From the other end of musical history, modern composers have often sought validation for their new approaches precisely in nature – so proving themselves entirely traditional, since the appeal to nature is a constant of harmonic theory, from Pythagoras through medieval and Renaissance theorists, then through Rameau (whose treatise provided the first systematic understanding of chords and functions in the major-minor system), to the spectralists of the late 20th century and early 21st. Messiaen's harmonic ideal was to imitate natural resonances, an ideal that spectralism then endorsed. Partch believed himself to be restoring and extending the Pythagorean system of intervals defined by frequency ratios, not by the equal temperament that major-minor music had required in order to establish a full array of similar chords (i.e. with the F♯ major triad having intervals of the same size as the C major).

If not nature, then culture might provide the prototype. When Schoenberg introduced atonality in 1907–8 he did so not only to flout convention but to continue it, to accept an invitation to further harmonic exploration that Liszt, Mahler, Bruckner and even Brahms had all been offering in the last two decades of the 19th century. Similarly, Stravinsky's neoclassical enterprise of the 1920s–40s was an effort to maintain connection with Bach or Delibes. Many subsequent composers, too, have tried to work with the harmonic languages of the 18th and 19th centuries, whether drawing quotations from, and references to, earlier music into a wider perspective (Berio), redefining tonal motifs and intervals in a non-tonal world (Ligeti), or fully adopting those languages (Rochberg).

One might wonder why, a century after the Debussy and Schoenberg revolutions, the major-minor system still exerts such a hold over composers – and indeed over musical life in general, to the extent that many readers of this article will expect it to be concerned only with that system. Answers must be manifold, and include social and psychological factors, but clearly of consequence is the high value that works in that system have acquired, by means of a richness – in terms of expression and structure, and variety in the interpretation of both – that has been hard to match from outside. Only a well-developed and historically founded system, it seems, could sustain the simultaneous surprise, anxiety and inevitability of, say, a modulation in Schubert. On the other hand, perhaps only a system that is newly made could uphold the exhilaration of a harmonic swerve in Carter. There is expressive purpose, too,

in the gesture unsupported by any system, as in Xenakis, or in attempts to engage with the harmony of a distant culture. Since the early 20th century, in centrifugal explosion, music has arrived at a marvellous diversity of harmonic systems and non-systems, no longer needing (perhaps, even rejecting) the agreed functions on which the major-minor language was based.

For though composers of the major-minor era are esteemed partly for their harmonic individualities, so that one may speak, for example, of a characteristically Schubertian flat sixth chord, those individualities emerge against the background of a shared language, a language formalized by Rameau and realized – in what generations of textbooks would hail as exemplary fashion – by Bach in his chorale harmonizations. This language came from long before. The elements necessary for it – triads and an understanding of the different scale degrees as having different functions (especially dominant and leading note) – had been accumulating in music since the early 15th century and been more or less fully in place since the mid 17th. But now the language was clearly stated, and the clarity of its statements – Rameau's theoretical, Bach's practical – may have contributed to its longevity. The chords of Bach's chorales, chiefly triads and their inversions plus dominant sevenths and rarer intruders whose functions were no less clear, were still the underpinning chords of Mahler's symphonies or Strauss's operas, now supporting immense structures by means of the drive conveyed by their immediate implications and command of the long range (whereby, at the simplest, tonic harmony must be the eventual goal). Their formidable power in the major-minor system made them things to be avoided by composers who, like Schoenberg in his early serial works, were intent on creating a new one.

Major-minor harmony's basic principles are simple. The fundamental consonance is the root-position tonic triad, which will generally be the final chord (at least until Mahler and Debussy in the early 20th century started ending with more complex chords or arriving at PROGRESSIVE TONALITY). Arrayed around that triad are the other functional chords. The dominant triad and the leading note may imply an imminent tonic triad, especially when they are combined in a dominant seventh chord. Subdominant, mediant and submediant chords are also neighbours, while more dissonant chords will tend to invite rapid resolution onto a consonance (until, again, early 20th-century music began to stabilize seventh chords, ninth chords and even, in Scriabin's case, more complex entities that could only have been fleeting dissonances in earlier harmony).

Good harmony traditionally involves creating chord progressions that will seem inevitable, adding twists and turns to such a simple basic formula as tonic–subdominant–dominant–tonic (I–IV–V–I; see ROMAN NUMERALS). The writing of harmony also has to take into account the melodic movement of the parts, so that each is, as far as possible, musically meaningful by itself, a pleasure to sing or play.

The increasing range of harmonic options in the 19th century and early 20th was partly brought about by composers from outside what had been music's central territories of Austria, Italy, Germany and France – composers from Poland, Russia, Spain, the Czech lands and Hungary – who brought with them affiliations to folk traditions that had not been modified by generations of major-minor thinking. Another factor was the growing interest in Renaissance music, among composers from Beethoven to Debussy, who developed harmonic styles in which modal relationships began to rival those of major and minor keys.

Also, the 19th-century engine of progress had its musical side. Beethoven installed a progressive dynamic running right through a movement, even right through a piece, a dynamic he achieved by harmonic (plus rhythmic) means, so that the balanced, regularly cadencing phrases of the Classical style began to give way to onward urgency, emphasizing not the conclusive but the motive force of internal cadences; the motto theme of the Fifth Symphony's first movement is a case in point. Progress was to occur, too, from one work to the next. Liszt floated the idea that each new composition needed to introduce a new chord, while both Brahms and Wagner were concerned to present their music as a continuation of Beethoven's – a continuation, principally, along the path of consistent harmonic enrichment. In his later music Beethoven had concerned himself more and more with the third as a harmonic relation, connecting keys as mediant and sub-mediant, and in this he was followed by Schubert and the whole of the 19th century. At the same time harmony became more chromatic and ambiguous, sometimes – especially at openings – leaving the tonic in doubt; Brahms's First Symphony exemplifies this as much as Wagner's Tristan.

From here it was only a step into atonality – a step almost taken by Liszt a generation before Schoenberg, but a step many composers since have hesitated over. Hence the great rainbow of harmonic styles in music today, and the unpredictability of harmony tomorrow.

Walter Piston Harmony (1941, ⁵1987); Jean-Philippe Rameau, trans. Philip Gossett Treatise on Harmony (1971); Arnold Schoenberg, trans. Roy E. Carter Theory of Harmony (1978)

Harnoncourt(-Unverzagt), (Johannes) Nikolaus (de la Fontaine und d') (b. Berlin, 6 Dec 1929). Austrian conductor, at first a Baroque specialist, but later carrying his historical awareness and severity into work with major orchestras, notably the Berlin and Vienna Philharmonics. He studied cello at the Vienna Academy and played in the Vienna Symphony (1952–69), meanwhile establishing his own group, Concentus Musicus Wien, which he founded in 1953. In 1972 he began teaching at the Salzburg Mozarteum. Two of his books have been translated: Baroque Music Today (1988) and The Musical Dialogue (1989).

Harold en Italie (Harold in Italy). Symphony by Berlioz with solo viola, based on Byron's Childe Harold, in four movements: 1 Harold aux montagnes, 2 Marche des pèlerins chantant la prière du soir, 3 Sérénade d'un montagnard des Abruzzes à sa maîtresse, 4 Orgie des brigands. First performance: Paris, 23 Nov 1834.

harp (Fr. harpe, Ger. Harfe, It. arpa). Plucked instrument whose strings are held in a roughly triangular frame. Harps are found all over the world, and were pictured in Egypt and Mesopotamia from the third millennium BC. The instrument was played by King David (c.1000 BC), images of whom provide it with a rich medieval iconography. At that time it was small enough to be carried, having a diatonic range of around two octaves, and already it had a special place in Celtic lands. The Renaissance harp, of which some examples survive, had a diatonic range of three and a half octaves from F below the bass staff to C above the treble. At some point the use of the fingernails, which survived in Ireland into the 18th century, began giving way to fingertip playing, while during the 16th century the instrument gained a second rank of strings (and sometimes a third), making it fully chromatic, in keeping with the increasing chromaticism of music.

In the 17th century the triple harp (i.e. with three ranks of strings) became standard in Wales, but it was an awkward instrument on which to play harmonically complex music and so was generally superseded by the single-action pedal harp. This once more had only diatonic strings, but with pedals allowing them to be sharpened: depressing, say, the G pedal would exert tension on a rod passing up through the pillar, and this would bring into action a series of hooks sharpening all the G strings. Introduced in the early 18th century, the single-action pedal harp gradually found its centre in Paris and became a popular domestic instrument for women, though professional players until the late 19th century were always men.

The next innovation was the double-action pedal harp, patented by Sébastien Erard in 1810 and having two pedal positions for each string. The open strings are tuned to the notes of the C♭ major scale through six octaves (from E♭ over an octave below the bass staff), and each can be retuned to the natural or sharp by depressing the pedal part way or fully. Near the end of the century the rival firm of Pleyel introduced the CHRO-MATIC HARP (effectively a reinvention of the 16th-century instrument), but the Erard pedal harp was not dislodged. On harps of all kinds the C (or C♭) strings are generally coloured red and the F (or F♭) strings blue or black, for the player's convenience; the chromatic harp had blue F strings and black strings for the piano's black notes.

With its bardic aura, the harp gained a place in the Orpheus operas of Monteverdi, Gluck and Haydn; Le Sueur asked for 12 in his *Ossian*. The important early concert repertory includes Mozart's concerto for flute and harp, along with pieces by Krumpholtz, Dussek and Spohr. Berlioz introduced the harp to the symphony orchestra in his *Symphonie fantastique* and wrote for six harps in *Les Troyens*, as did Wagner in the *Ring* (with a seventh in *Das Rheingold*). Glissandos and harmonics became important features of harp writing in the late 19th century, not least in Debussy. Solo pieces and concertos for the instrument have remained unusual, though there is quite a repertory for oboe and harp, created for Heinz and Ursula Holliger, and including works by Carter, Henze and Lutosławski.

Roslyn Rensch *Harps and Harpists* (1989)

Harp. Name given to Beethoven's Quartet in E♭ Op.74, for the pizzicato arpeggios in the first movement.

harpsichord (Fr. *clavecin*, Ger. *Cembalo*, It. *cembalo*, *clavicembalo*). Keyboard instrument in which the strings are plucked, not hammered as in the piano, which developed from the harpsichord at the end of the 17th century. The earliest reference dates from 1397, but the great period of the instrument, along with its cousins the SPINET and the VIRGINALS, was from the early 16th century to the later 18th, when it was ubiquitous as a solo or continuo instrument.

Depressing a key on a harpsichord causes a jack bearing a quill (originally made indeed from a crow's flight feather, usually replaced today by plastic material) to move upwards and so pluck a string. When the key is released the vibration is damped by a piece of cloth. The player can thus determine duration but has little control over loudness (since the force of plucking cannot generally be changed) or colour. However, the former deficit is often remedied by a second set of strings, which the player can bring into operation or not, while the latter may be addressed by the addition of stops. These may activate jacks placed close to the nuts of the strings, producing a nasal sound (lute stop), or bring a piece of leather or cloth into contact with the strings, damping them (buff stop), or add separate sets of strings sounding an octave above (at four-foot pitch), an octave below (16-foot) or two octaves above (two-foot).

For three generations from the 1580s the most valued harpsichords came from the Ruckers family, whose instruments generally had a range of four octaves, from C below the bass staff. Some Ruckers instruments had two keyboards, a feature that became standard with the French instruments that moved into dominance in the mid 17th century, in keeping with the dominance of French harpsichordist-composers, pre-eminently Couperin. French harpsichords from the early 18th century increased the instrument's range to five octaves, from F, and were followed in this by makers in England (Kirkman, Shudi), Germany and Flanders. Music for such instruments was coming from Bach, Handel, Rameau and Domenico Scarlatti, among many others.

The harpsichord had been ousted by the piano by 1800, after which there are only sporadic records of the instrument being played (by Moscheles in 1837) before the 1860s, when it was brought back by Ernst Pauer and Louis Diémer. Erard and Pleyel began making harpsichords in the 1880s, and the Pleyel instrument – latterly with an iron frame and always with other features more characteristic of the piano – was endorsed by the first post-Baroque virtuoso of the instrument, Landowska. Since the 1950s many other makers have been building harpsichords more closely modelled on those of the 17th and 18th centuries, leaving the Pleyel a historic instrument required for 20th-century works involving the harpsichord, such as those by Falla and Carter.

Ann Bond *A Guide to the Harpsichord* (1997); Edward L. Kottick *A History of the Harpsichord* (2003)

harpsichord-piano. Instrument combining features of the two, produced by several makers in the 1740s–80s.

Harris, Renatus (b. ?Quimper, *c*.1652; d.

Bristol/London, 1724). English organ builder, born to the craft. His father, Thomas Harris, built organs, and his mother belonged to the organ-building Dallam family. Being Catholics, Thomas and the Dallams went to Brittany in 1642, and stayed during the Civil War and the Common-wealth. The extended family returned to England after the Restoration (1660), and Renatus gradually took over from his father. An assiduous rival of 'Father' Smith, he made organs in the French style, several of which survive in altered form (St Andrew Undershaft, London; Bristol Cathedral).

Harris, (Le)Roy (Ellsworth) (b. near Chandler, Okla., 12 Feb 1898; d. Santa Monica, Cal., 1 Oct 1979). US composer, whose single-movement Third Symphony (1938) was a milestone in musical Americana, confidently pursuing a style rooted in Anglo–US folksong and hymnody. Born into a poor farming family, he worked the land himself until he began to gain success as a composer in the early 1930s. Meanwhile he undertook college studies in Los Angeles and Berkeley, and had lessons with Farwell (1924–5) and, at Copland's suggestion, Boulanger (1926–9). Between 1933 and 1976 he held various teaching posts, his pupils including Schuman, while enthusiasm for his music slipped from the 1940s onwards. Along with his US sources, Bach and Renaissance polyphony were important to him: he renamed his fourth wife Johana in honour of Bach. She, a professional pianist, helped him with his piano writing, but in his symphonies and chamber works he was robustly his own man.

Dan Stehman *Roy Harris* (1984)

Symphonies: No.1 (Symphony 1933), 1933; No.2, 1934; No.3, 1938; No.4 (Folksong Symphony), ch, orch, 1940–42; No.5, 1942; No.6 'Gettysburg', 1944; No.7, 1952, rev 1955; No.8 'San Francisco', 1962; No.9, 1962; No.10 'Abraham Lincoln', speaker, ch, brass, perc, 1965; No.11, 1967; No.12 'Père Marquette', t, orch, 1968–9; No.13 (Bicentennial Symphony), ch, orch, 1975–6
Other works: further orchestral pieces, much choral music, chamber and piano music

Harris, William H(enry) (b. London, 28 Mar 1883; d. Petersfield, 6 Sep 1973). British composer and church musician, knighted in 1954. He studied with Parratt, Wood and Walford Davies at the RCM, and held posts as organist in London, Lichfield, Oxford (1921–33) and Windsor (St George's Chapel, 1933–61). His best known work is the double-choir motet *Faire is the Heaven* (1925), to words by Spenser.

Harrison, Beatrice (b. Roorkee, India, 9 Dec 1892; d. Smallfield, Sussex, 10 Mar 1965). British cellist,

Elgar's chosen soloist for recording his concerto. She studied with W.E. Whitehouse at the RCM and played new works by Bax and Delius, including the latter's Double Concerto, written for her and her sister May (1890–1959).

Harrison, Lou (Silver) (b. Portland, Ore., 14 May 1917; d. Lafayette, Ind., 2 Feb 2003). US composer, uncomplicated in his response to tunings and traditions from around the world. Brought up in northern California, he studied with Cowell in San Francisco from 1935, starting a long friendship. In 1937 he became dance accompanist at Mills College, where Cage came to him the next year: the two composers presented percussion concerts together until 1941. Meanwhile he was also at work editing Ives scores, including the Third Symphony, whose première he conducted in 1946. By that time he was in New York, writing criticism for the *Herald Tribune* under Thomson (1944–7), but the city did not agree with him, and after a period at Black Mountain College in North Carolina (1951–3) he returned to California. Visits to Japan, Korea and Taiwan in 1961–2 were important; so was the arrival in 1967 of William Colvig as his partner in life and instrument building. They created an 'American gamelan' of metallophones made from hardware supplies and junk (1971), and in this happy, fecund part of his life he wrote much music gently supportive of non-discrimination, sexual, racial or cultural.

Leta E. Miller and Fredric Lieberman *Lou Harrison* (1998)

Chamber operas: *Rapunzel* (William Morris), 1952–3; *Young Caesar* (Robert Gordon), 1971, rev 1988
Orchestral: Symphony on G, 1947–66; Elegiac Symphony, 1975; Symphony No.3, 1982, rev 1985; Symphony No.4 (Last Symphony), 1990–95; Suite, vn, pf, chbr orch, 1951; Piano Concerto, 1985
Ensemble: Concerto No.1, fl, 2 perc, 1939; *Double Music*, 1940 (with Cage); Fugue, perc, 1942; Suite, perc, 1942; *Concerto in slendro*, vn, 5 perc, 1940–59; *La Koro Sutro*, ch, org, hp, American gamelan, 1972; Suite, vn, American gamelan, 1974; Serenade, gtr, perc, 1978; etc.
Other works: 6 Cembalo Sonatas, 1934–43; etc.

Harsányi, Tibor (b. Magyarkanisza, 27 Jun 1898; d. Paris, 19 Sep 1954). Hungarian–French composer, who studied with Kodály and settled in Paris in 1924, becoming a fully fledged member of the Parisian neoclassical school. His works include *L'Histoire du petit tailleur* for narrator and ensemble (1939), ballets, orchestral pieces and piano music.

Hart, Fritz (Bennicke) (b. London, 11 Feb 1874; d. Honolulu, 9 Jul 1949). British composer of formidable creative energy: his works include 22 operas, over 500 songs and 24 novels (unpublished). He was a Westminster Abbey chorister and then a student at the RCM (1893–6), along with Holst and Coleridge-Taylor. In 1909 he went to Australia to work as a conductor and teacher, and in 1937 he settled in Honolulu, where he was first music professor at the University of Hawaii.

Hartke, Stephen (Paul) (b. Orange, NJ, 6 Jul 1952). US composer, combining Stravinskian clarity and irony with a frank US lyricism. He studied at Yale, at the University of Pennsylvania and at Santa Barbara, and began teaching at the University of Southern California in 1987. Notable works include his piano quartet *The King of the Sun* (1988), three symphonies (No.2, 1990; No.3, 2003) and concertos for violin (1992) and clarinet (2001).

Hartmann, Johan Peter Emilius (b. Copenhagen, 14 May 1805; d. Copenhagen, 10 Mar 1900). Danish composer, whose adherence to the international Romantic movement in music was tempered by a local taste for Norse antiquity. He was born into a musical family: his German grandfather, Johann Ernst (1726–93), was active in Copenhagen from 1762 and was the author of singspiels. Johan Peter Emilius's father taught him music but advised against a career, so he studied law and was a civil servant all his working life (1828–70). He also played the organ from 1843 at Copenhagen Cathedral and taught from 1867 at the Copenhagen Conservatory, of which he was one of the founder directors. Where Gade, his son-in-law, represented Denmark to the wider world, he was more a Danish secret, writing operas (*The Raven*, with a libretto by Hans Christian Andersen, f.p. Copenhagen, 1832), overtures, chamber pieces and church music.

Hartmann, Karl Amadeus (b. Munich, 2 Aug 1905; d. Munich, 5 Dec 1963). German composer, who drew the lessons of modernism into a serious symphonic style with strong contrapuntal underpinnings and who stubbornly pursued that style through the Nazi years. He studied with Joseph Haas at the Vienna Academy (1924–9) and also consulted Scherchen. His early works, spirited and sarcastic, already show a social conscience; under the Nazis his music became darker. The end of the war unlocked his pent-up creativity, and he actively promoted new music in Munich as director of the Musica Viva festival.

Symphonies: No.1 'Versuch eines Requiems' (Whitman), a, orch, 1935–6, rev 1954–5; No.2 'Adagio', 1945–6; No.3, 1948–9; No.4, str, 1946–7; No.5 'Hommage à Stravinsky' (Symphonie concertante), 1950; No.6, 1951–3; No.7, 1957–8; No.8, 1960–62
Other orchestral works: *Miserae*, 1934; *Concerto funebre*, vn, str, 1939, rev 1959; *Sinfonia tragica*, 1940–43; *Gesangszene* (Giraudoux), bar, orch, 1963
Other works: *Simplicius simplicissimus* (chbr opera; Hartmann, Scherchen and Wolfgang Petzet), 1934–5; 2 quartets, 1933–5, 1945–6

Hartmann, Thomas [Toma Aleksandrovich] (b. Khoruzhevka, 21 Sep 1885; d. Princeton, NJ, 26 Mar 1956). Ukrainian composer, a follower during the years 1919–29 of the guru George Gurdjieff, for whom he wrote numerous piano pieces. He had trained at the St Petersburg Conservatory (1900–2) and with Arensky and Taneyev (1907).

Harty, (Herbert) Hamilton (b. Hillsborough, County Down, 4 Dec 1879; d. Brighton, 19 Feb 1941). Irish composer and conductor, knighted in 1925. Trained by his father, he started work as an organist at 12, and later had help from the Neapolitan composer Michele Esposito in Dublin. In 1900 he went to London, where he established a reputation as composer and conductor that took him to the top of the Hallé (1920–33). His works include *An Irish Symphony* (1904) and the tone poems *With the Wild Geese* (1910) and *In Ireland* (1915); orchestral panache is also a mark of his arrangements from Handel's *Water* and *Fireworks* musics.

Harvard University. The oldest US university, founded in 1636, but offering music courses only since Paine's appointment in 1862.

Harvey, Jonathan (Dean) (b. Sutton Coldfield, 3 May 1939). British composer, noted for works with electronic apparatus and an explicit spiritual dimension. After studies at Cambridge, and privately with Erwin Stein and Hans Keller, he began his career as a university teacher at Southampton (1964–77). During this period he moved from the neighbourhood of Britten to that of Stockhausen, and gained particular stimulus from reading Rudolf Steiner on meditation and studying Babbittian serialism at Princeton (1969–70). Work on exchanges between electronic (transformed) and live (natural) sounds, begun in *On Vision* and continued repeatedly at IRCAM, has given him the means to create unities and journeyings parallelling his metaphysical desires. His later university appointments were at Sussex (1977–93) and Stanford (1995–2000).

Jonathan Harvey *Music and Inspiration* (1999); Arnold Whittall *Jonathan Harvey* (1999)

Opera: *Inquest of Love* (David Rudkin and Harvey), f.p. London, 1993

Orchestral: *Inner Light III*, orch, tape, 1975; *Bhakti*, ens, tape, 1982; *Madonna of Winter and Spring*, orch, elec, 1986; Cello Concerto, 1990; *Bird Concerto with Pianosong*, pf, chbr orch, elec, 2000–1; etc.

Vocal: Cantata VII *On Vision*, s, t, ch, orch, tape, 1971; *I love the Lord*, ch, 1976; *Come, Holy Ghost*, ch, 1984; etc.

Chamber: String Quartet No.1, 1977; No.2, 1988; No.3, 1995; etc.

Tape: *Mortuos plango, vivos voco*, 1980; etc.

Harwood, Basil (b. Woodhouse Down, Olveston, Glos., 11 Apr 1859; d. London, 3 Apr 1959). British composer and church musician, remembered especially for his Service in A♭ and anthem *O how glorious is the Kingdom* (1898). He studied at Oxford and Leipzig, and held appointments as cathedral organist in Ely (1887–92) and Oxford (1892–1909) before retiring to his family estate.

Háry János (*János Háry*). Opera by Kodály to a libretto by Béla Paulini and Zsolt Harsányi after a mock epic by János Garay (1812–53). János Háry (baritone) is an army veteran boasting of his exploits, which are dramatized, and the source of a popular orchestral suite. First performance: Budapest, 16 Oct 1926.

Haskil, Clara (b. Bucharest, 7 Jan 1895; d. Brussels, 7 Dec 1960). Romanian pianist, remarkable for her unaffected inwardness with, especially, Mozart, Beethoven and Schubert. She began studies with Richard Robert in 1902 and completed her training with Lazare Lévy at the Paris Conservatoire (1905–10). Illness repeatedly interrupted her career.

Hasprois, Jehan Simon (d. 1428). French composer, master of the ars subtilior. He was a member of the Portuguese and French royal chapels, and from around 1390 was with the papal court. His four surviving songs include the ballades *Puisque je sui fumeux* and *Ma doulce amour*.

Hasse, Johann Adolf (baptized Bergedorf, near Hamburg, 25 Mar 1699; d. Venice, 16 Dec 1783). German composer, the dominant voice in opera seria in the mid 18th century, valued for his ability to let singers shine. Born into a line of organist-composers, he studied in Hamburg (1714–17) and broke with family tradition by joining the local opera as a tenor in 1718. Soon after producing his first opera, *Antioco* (f.p. Brunswick, 1721), he moved to Italy, settled in Naples and converted to Catholicism. Possibly he studied with Alessandro Scarlatti; certainly he learned from Scarlatti's scores before triumphing in 1725–9 with operas, intermezzos, serenatas and cantatas. His *Artaserse* (f.p. Venice, 1730) took his name around Europe; Farinelli sang arias from it in London (1734) and then every night while attending Philip V of Spain (1737–46). A few months after the première, still in Venice, the composer married the singer Faustina Bordoni, with whom he moved to Dresden the next year as kapellmeister.

Dresden remained his occasional base until 1756, and his second important opera, *Cleofide* (1731), was first performed there, with J.S. and W.F. Bach in the audience. But he also spent long periods in Italy, and from the early 1740s onwards he maintained connections with Berlin and Vienna, enjoying the favour of Frederick II and Maria Theresa, and the friendship of Metastasio. *Artaserse* and *Cleofide* had both been based on adaptations of Metastasio, but with *Antigono* (f.p. Dresden, 1743) and *Ipemestra* (f.p. Vienna, 1744) he began setting new librettos by the poet, henceforth his almost exclusive collaborator. He even restored the original words for *Artaserse* (f.p. Naples, 1760) and set all but one of Metastasio's earlier opera texts. In the years around 1760 he was active from Naples to Warsaw, with Vienna his principal home until 1773. Maria Theresa was a welcoming patron, and there was the stimulus of rivalry with Gluck, though Hasse and Metastasio were not immune to the spirit of reform, even if the composer was increasingly incapacitated by gout. He spent his last decade with his wife and daughters in Venice, where he taught and composed or revised church music. His voluminous output also includes sonatas and concertos.

Hassler, Hans Leo (baptized Nuremberg, 26 Oct 1564; d. Frankfurt, 8 Jun 1612). German composer, pupil of Andrea Gabrieli in Venice (1584–5) and fount of the Venetian style in Germany. His father and two younger brothers were organists, and he, too, was a highly esteemed organist, employed as such in Augsburg (1587–1601), Nuremberg (1601–4) and Dresden (1608–12). Working for the Fuggers in Augsburg, he produced masses and Latin motets (the five-part *Cantate Domino canticum novum* comes from his 1591 collection); he also wrote Lutheran psalms and sacred songs, secular songs in German and Italian, canzonas and keyboard music.

Haubenstock-Ramati, Roman (b. Kraków, 27 Feb 1919; d. Vienna, 3 Mar 1994). Polish–Austrian composer, a sprightly member of the avant-garde during the time he worked for Universal Edition as reader (1957–68). He studied with Artur Malawski in Kraków (1934–8) and Koffler in Lwów/Lviv (1939–41), left Poland for Tel-Aviv (1950–57), and was latterly a conservatory professor in Vienna (1973–89).

Hauer, Josef Matthias (b. Wiener Neustadt, 19 Mar 1883; d. Vienna, 22 Sep 1959). Austrian composer, who developed 12-note music as an objective art of speculation and design. How much he owed to Schoenberg and how much Schoenberg to him is irresoluble; certainly he impressed Hermann Hesse, who based *The Glass Bead Game* partly on him and his work. He trained as a teacher, taught himself music and only began to compose at 28. Living in Vienna from 1915, he established in 1919 a 12-note TROPE system: pieces were to be based on a division of the chromatic notes into two groups of six. At first he and Schoenberg were in wary contact, but neither would cede priority. He went his own way, until his growing success in avant-garde circles was effectively damped out after the Nazi take-over of Austria in 1938. In retirement he devoted himself exclusively to *Zwölftonspiele* (12-tone-plays), of which he produced about 1,000.

Hauptdreiklang (Ger.). Major triad.

Hauptmann, Moritz (b. Dresden, 13 Oct 1792; d. Leipzig, 3 Jan 1868). German composer, especially of choral music in the Bach tradition: he was cantor of St Thomas's, Leipzig, from 1842. Before that he was Spohr's pupil (1811) and protégé (as a violinist in the Kassel orchestra).

Hauptrhythmus (Ger., principal rhythm). Berg's term for the dominating rhythmic motif of a movement, recurring irregularly (rather than regularly as in an ostinato).

Hauptsatz (Ger., principal material). First subject group in a sonata form.

Hauptstimme (Ger., principal part). Schoenberg's term for the main line in an atonal composition, where this distinction might not be obvious. Schoenberg introduced the notational device of a horizontal bracket stemming from an H. Berg added the derivatives HR (for the *Hauptrhythmus*) and CH (to mark the chorale melody in his Violin Concerto).

Haupttonarten (Ger., principal keys). The tonic, dominant and subdominant in the major, plus, where minor keys are concerned, the relative major.

Hauptwerk (Ger., principal department). That part of an organ controlled from the main manual, also known as the great organ.

Hausmusik (Ger., home music). Music for modestly accomplished amateurs to play at home.

Hausorgel (Ger., home organ). Chamber organ.

hautbois (Fr.). Oboe.

hautbois d'amour (Fr.). Oboe d'amore.

hautboy. Older Eng. name for the oboe or shawm.

haut-dessus (Fr., high treble). French Baroque term for the top part, as distinct from the bas-dessus.

haute-contre (Fr., high against). (1) The highest man's voice as required in French music from Lully to the end of the 18th century, generally understood as essentially natural, not falsetto. At its best combining tenor-like male heroism with a countertenor's plangency and extraordinariness, it has been revived by several singers since the 1980s.

(2) French Baroque term for an instrumental part in a similar alto register, normally the highest viola line (otherwise haute-taille), unless qualified in such compounds as *haute-contre de hautbois* (oboe in A).

haute-taille (Fr., high tenor). French Baroque term for the top viola part.

Hawkins, John (b. London, 29 Mar 1719; d. London, 21 May 1789). British musical historian, knighted in 1772. A lawyer by training and profession, he also emerged as an essayist and musical amateur in his 20s, and became a member of the circle around Samuel Johnson, whose life he wrote (1787). His chief endeavour, though, was *A General History of the Science and Practice of Music* in five volumes (1776, ᴿ1963), which was outshone by Burney as decisively as his Johnson was by Boswell. His study is, though, quite different from Burney's in style, presentation and view, showing in particular a strong attachment to the 16th and 17th centuries. Fishing was another of his interests, and he contributed notes to Izaak Walton's *Compleat Angler*.

Haydn. Austrian composing brothers. Their parents, Mathias (1699–1763) and Anna Maria née Koller (1707–54), were a master wheelwright and a former cook who maintained a musical home. The three sons they reared all became professional musicians, the youngest, Johann Evangelist (1743–1805) being a tenor who joined his famous brother at the Esterházy court.

(1) **(Franz) Joseph** (b. Rohrau, Lower Austria, 31

Mar 1732; d. Vienna, 31 May 1809). Unrivalled in his time until joined by Mozart, he was the great musician of a rational epoch, expressing the ENLIGHTENMENT virtues of clarity, logic, optimism and wit. To perfect and present those virtues he took the lead in developing a new formal principle, that of sonata form, and new genres, most notably the symphony, string quartet and keyboard sonata. Though he spent much of his professional life serving the fabulously wealthy and highly cultured Esterházy family in Vienna and on their Hungarian estate, publication distributed his music widely among the growing middle classes of Europe and North America, who took him to their hearts. His symphonies, even when shifted aside by Beethoven's, were honoured as pioneering, and many of them, especially the later ones, have remained in the concert repertory since they were written. His quartets, which have never been overshadowed, established the medium's conversational nature, and he conveyed his generous spirit also in choral works, piano trios and sonatas. Only his operas have resisted attempts to bring them into regular performance – perhaps because his music has nothing to spare for dramatic characters, proceeding as it does with so much playfulness and expressivity inherent to itself (and there for the enjoyment of performers and listeners).

His education began when, at five or six, he went to live with a cousin of his father's, Johann Mathias Franck, school principal in nearby Hainburg. Two or three years later he was recruited into the choir of St Stephen's, Vienna, where he remained for a decade (c.1739–49), singing in the cathedral and at court. How much instruction he had in composition and instrumental performance is unclear, and much mythologized. Evidently he was not equipped to seek a post, since for several years he made a living as an independent teacher, player and composer, though one gaining access to the highest artistic circles. He lodged for three years with the court poet Metastasio and thereby became assistant and pupil to Nicola Porpora, a Neapolitan composer of the old school. Under Porpora's guidance, and with his own experience to draw on, he wrote church music, some of which he may have had performed on a visit to the shrine at Mariazell. Other works from his early 20s probably include divertimentos and similar household music, but, even allowing that a lot of music from this period must have been lost or destroyed, he was clearly a slow starter.

Possibly in 1757 (a date suggested by his own catalogue) he wrote his first symphony, and around the same time his first string quartets, for Baron Carl Joseph Fürnberg, who recommended him to his first permanent employer, Count Karl Joseph Franz Morzin, in 1759 or thereabouts. His life soon changed in another way: he got married. The story goes that he had fallen in love with Therese Keller, a wigmaker's daughter, but that she was obliged by her family to enter a convent, whereupon he settled for her elder sister Maria Anna Aloysia Apollonia (1729–1800). Unsurprisingly, the marriage was not happy. There were no children, and both parties sought consolation in other arms. Nor was his relationship with Morzin very productive, for the count soon ran out of money.

Nearing 30, and probably already acquiring a reputation for his symphonies, quartets and divertimentos, he was not out of work for long. In 1761 he was taken on as vice-kapellmeister (secondary music director) by Prince Paul Anton Esterházy, and he stayed with the family to the end of his life, though gaining in independence as he gained in fame. His superior as kapellmeister, Gregor Joseph Werner (1693–1766), retained control of church music for the moment, but he was responsible for all the court's other musical needs: supervising the ensemble (comprising at first roughly six violinists, one player each on viola, cello and bass, two oboists, two hornists and a bassoonist), composing symphonies and concertos for concerts, rehearsing and directing those concerts, writing divertimentos and chamber music as decor for noble life, and giving lessons. Dressed in the blue and gold uniform of a court officer, comfortably housed, head of a team that included notable virtuosos, and treated with honour in an establishment where music was highly valued, he might well have felt proud. He also recognized, at least in retrospect, his opportunity, as he told his biographer Georg August Griesinger 40 years later: 'I was cut off from the world, nobody in my vicinity could upset my self-confidence or annoy me, and so I had no choice but to become original.'

He became original, in the 1760s, chiefly in orchestral music. As vice-kapellmeister he produced approximately four symphonies and two concertos a year, writing for the outstanding musicians in his charge; he also composed occasional serenatas and cantatas. The symphonies from this period generally have the usual four movements (not three, fast–slow–fast, as in the pre-Esterházy symphonies) and make energetic demands. The three that make a diurnal cycle – 'Le Matin', 'Le Midi' and 'Le Soir' (Nos.6–8) – may have been planned as a gesture of intent, full of instrumental solos and of the tone-painting that was one aspect of the composer's naturalism.

Werner's death on 3 March 1766 left him with

full duties as kapellmeister, along tracks laid down by Prince Nikolaus, who had succeeded his brother as head of the family in 1762. More splendidly munificent and more actively musical, Nikolaus required works ranging from operas for his new palace of Eszterháza (for the purposes of which the orchestra was expanded to two dozen) to pieces for the instrument he favoured, the bass-viol-like baryton. Symphonies were also still needed, and in them Haydn continued to exercise his freedom to be original: indeed, his symphonies of 1766–72, which include several in the minor, have an unusual intensity, for which they have sometimes been connected with the STURM UND DRANG literary movement.

The 'Farewell' Symphony (1772), in F♯ minor, is emblematic of some of the tensions in a busy court. It was meant to remind the prince that his musicians wanted to leave their annual summer exile in the artificial paradise of Eszterháza and return to Vienna. Haydn may have shared that wish for his own reasons – not to rejoin a family, but to engage in metropolitan musical life. Three sets of quartets from this period (Opp.9, 17 and 20) were probably written not for the Esterházys but for Viennese patrons, and he composed an oratorio, Il ritorno di Tobia, for two concerts given in the city in April 1775 to benefit deceased musicians' widows and orphans.

Meanwhile, at Eszterháza, the pressing need was for opera. 'Summers' on the estate now stretched through 10 months of the year, with opera performances up to three or four times a week, presenting a repertory mostly of recent Italian comedies, by Cimarosa, Paisiello, Anfossi, Sarti and others. Sometimes he would write new arias for these (especially for Luigia Polzelli, a mezzo-soprano who was his mistress, and whose son Antonio, born in 1783, was probably his). And sometimes – almost annually between 1773 and 1783 – he would set one of the librettos afresh. What stopped him after that, apparently, was Mozart's arrival in Vienna, and the Mozart comparison stops his operas still, for their charm seems mild when it is couched in so similar a language. Although he failed to show his appreciation by offering a Mozart work at Eszterháza, there is ample evidence he recognized his young contemporary's genius. To Leopold Mozart he said, at a quartet party (12 February 1785): 'Before God and as an honest man I tell you that your son is the greatest composer known to me, by name or reputation.' After hearing Die Entführung (1782) he could easily have wanted to leave the opera stage silently.

He had another reason to do so, for the arrival of music publishing in Vienna offered new opportunities. Because pirate editions had been appearing since 1764, the market was ready for him. Equally, he was ready for it – ready to supply the instrumental pieces and songs it required. The first work he wrote for publication was a set of six keyboard sonatas, Nos.36–41 (H.21–6), which came out in 1774; after 1780 he continued apace, most often supplying the house of Artaria.

Publication satisfied his artistic scrupulousness and his sense of his own worth, while instrumental music suited his inexhaustible talent for presenting drama and character in terms of harmony, rhythm and line. These were his operas – the sonatas, trios, quartets and symphonies he produced for his publishers throughout the last two decades of the 18th century. These were, indeed, his comedies. He had created sonata form and quartet texture as essentially comic media, the one dominated by the basic comic-opera principles of surprise revelation and anticipated reconciliation, the other recalling the interchanges of thought and melody in a comic-opera finale. Just as his operatic career was approaching its end he published his Op.33 quartets with Artaria in 1782, warning his audience in a note that the pieces were written 'in a new way', with the four parts behaving as equals, often sportively in contest or collaboration, but also with another characteristic of the greatest comedy: depth of expression and experience, and a large capacity for resolution.

Often he would sell the same work to publishers in different countries, which sometimes involved him in fancy footwork and even legal proceedings. He could alternatively increase his income by purveying a work separately for performance and publication, as with two projects of 1785–6: the 'Paris' symphonies (Nos.82–7) and the orchestral movements commissioned for Cadiz Cathedral as interludes in a Good Friday homily on the Seven Last Words. Exploiting his assets with acumen, he arranged this otherwise singular endeavour both for string quartet and as a cantata.

The death of Nikolaus Esterházy (28 September 1790) freed him from financial worries, since he was left a generous pension. But the same event also freed him from courtly duties, for Nikolaus's son Anton, while honouring his salary at a reduced level, let the musical ensemble go and gave him a year's leave of absence. His destination was obvious: London. There he could have access to the largest musical public in Europe, increase his contacts with a thriving publishing trade, and find support from an active company of German-speaking musicians, led by Johann Peter Salomon. And in effect he had no choice. Salomon went to Vienna expressly to woo him as soon as news of Nikolaus Esterházy's passing reached London. Within seven weeks of the prince's death impresario and composer were on their way.

Haydn, who had never seen the sea before, stayed on deck all through the Channel crossing (1–2 January 1791). In London he was the talk of the town. He could have spent the whole day entertaining visitors and accepting invitations, but he had to work at the compositions stipulated in his contract with Salomon: six symphonies (Nos.93–8) and an opera (*L'anima del filosofo*, which was not in the event produced). Also he had lessons to give, and an affair to conduct with one of his pupils, Rebecca Schroeter. At the same time he found himself in friendly rivalry with a student of former years, Ignace Joseph Pleyel, who was working for another entrepreneur. As in Paris – the target not only of his 'Paris' symphonies but also of those immediately before and after (Nos.76–81 and 88–92) – so in London orchestras were of a grander size (40 or so in Salomon's band), and audiences correspondingly large. That influenced not only his scoring but also his tone of voice (as represented by the surprise of the 'Surprise' Symphony, so much bigger a gesture than his usual gentle nudges and complicit smiles) and his form, for the London concerts increased his awareness of the value of a slow introduction, whether by fascination or astonishment to silence the crowd.

When he left for Vienna again, in the early summer of 1792, it was seemingly only at the pressing urge of Prince Anton Esterházy, who, however, seems to have had little use for him. Instead – apart from giving instruction to a new pupil, Beethoven – he prepared the music he would need for a second sojourn in London, which he began in January 1794. Again he stayed a year and a half, and again he presented six new symphonies (Nos.99–104), along with a more varied repertory that included string quartets and English songs.

By the time he was back in Vienna, late in the summer of 1795, Prince Anton had been succeeded by his son, a second Nikolaus. Eszterháza was abandoned; the Austrian Empire was becoming more like a modern nation-state, administered not by quasi-feudal lords on country estates but by politicking barons at the centre. All Haydn had to provide for his uxorious new employer was a sequence of splendid masses for the princess consort's name day. There were six of these, between 1796 and 1802, and they brought the composer back to his origins half a century before as a musician serving the Church, while allowing him to embrace everything he had learned in the interim, including a breadth of design from his London visits. At the same time he produced further quartets (one including his tune for a new

Austrian national anthem), a final orchestral work in the shape of a concerto for the new KEYED TRUMPET, a *Te Deum* and the oratorios *The Creation* and *The Seasons*.

The immediate prompt for these last came from Baron Gottfried van Swieten, who had a taste for Handel, but they surely show also Haydn's own experience of hearing Handel in London, his pride in wishing to accomplish things on the same scale, and his humility in placing his art at the service of the divine. They are great hymns of praise to a rational and beneficent deity – hymns to virtues he had made his own: order, imaginative power and an ability to respond, even in age, to the delights of the everyday.

Once past 70 he began to feel his creative energy ebbing, and after the end of 1803 he lived quietly outside the city in Gumpendorf. Already he was becoming a monument. Pleyel brought out a complete edition of his quartets (1801) and initiated a new kind of publication, the miniature score, with four of his symphonies (1802), followed by all the quartets; another publisher, Härtel, issued a complete collection of solo and chamber works for piano (1800–6). From out of his vast output were being filtered the pieces that seemed to matter: the quartets, the symphonies, the piano music and, as final crown, *The Creation*. That was the image of him projected all the way to the 20th century, the image of one who, by his invention of forms and genres, was the head of a great stream – 'Papa Haydn' not only for Mozart and Beethoven, who knew him, but for Brahms and Schoenberg. As the tradition he founded recedes, and more of his work comes into play, his achievement does not grow less dumbfounding.

H.C. Robbins Landon *Haydn: Chronicle and Works*, 5 Vols. (1976–80); Hans Keller *The Great Haydn Quartets* (1986)

Where confusion might arise numbers are given from the Hoboken catalogue (H).

Vocal music

Operas (several librettos adapted by Carl Frieberth):
La canterina, (? Domenico Macchia), f.p. ?Eisenstadt, 1766; *Lo speziale* (Goldoni), f.p. Eszterháza, 1768, part lost; *Le pescatrici* (Goldoni), f.p. Eszterháza, 1770, part lost; *L'infedeltà delusa* (Marco Coltellini), f.p. Eszterháza, 1773; *Philemon und Baucis* (puppet opera: Gottlieb Konrad Pfeffel), f.p. Eszterháza, 1773; *L'incontro improvviso*, f.p. Eszterháza, 1775; *Il mondo della luna* (Goldoni), f.p. Eszterháza, 1777; *La vera costanza* (Francesco Puttini and Pietro Travaglia), f.p. Eszterháza, 1779, rev 1785; *L'isola disabitata* (Metastasio), f.p. Eszterháza, 1779; *La fedeltà premiata* (after Giambattista Lorenzi), f.p. Eszterháza, 1781; *Orlando paladino* (Nunziato

Porta), 1782; ARMIDA, 1783; *L'anima del filosofo* (see ORPHEUS), 1791; several lost

Incidental music: *Alfred, König der Angelsachsen*, 1796

Oratorios: *Il ritorno di Tobia* (Giovanni Gastone Boccherini), ssatb, ch, orch, 1774–5; *Die sieben letzten Worte*, satb, ch, orch, 1795–6; *The* CREATION, 1796–8; *The* SEASONS, 1799–1801

Masses: No.1 *Missa brevis*, F, ss, ch, orch, ?1749; No.2 *Sunt bona mixta malis*, D minor, ch, con, fragment; No.3 *Rorate coeli desuper*, G, ch, str, con, 1749; No.4 *Missa in honorem BVM* 'Grosse Orgelsolomesse', E♭, satb, ch, orch, ?*c*.1768–9; No.5 *Missa Cellensis in honorem BVM* 'Cäcilienmesse' C, satb, ch, orch, 1766; No.6 *Missa Sancti Nicolai* 'Nikolaimesse', G, satb, ch, orch, 1772; No.7 *Missa brevis Sancti Joannis de Deo* 'Kleine Orgelsolomesse', B♭, s, ch, orch, ?*c*.1773–7; No.8 *Missa Cellensis* 'Mariazellermesse', C, satb, ch, orch, 1782; No.9 *Missa in tempore belli* 'PAUKENMESSE', C, satb, ch, orch, 1796; No.10 *Missa Sancti Bernardi von Offida* 'HEILIGMESSE', B♭, satb, ch, orch, 1796; No.11 *Missa in angustiis* 'NELSON', D minor, satb, ch, orch, 1798; No.12 'THERESIENMESSE', B♭, satb, ch, orch, 1799; No.13 'SCHÖPFUNGSMESSE', B♭, satb, ch, orch, 1801; No.14 'HARMONIEMESSE', B♭, satb, ch, orch, 1802

Other sacred pieces: *Ave regina*, A, s, ch, orch, ?*c*.1750–59; *Salve regina*, E, s, ch, orch, ?1756; *Te Deum*, C, satb, ch, orch, ?*c*.1762–3; *Stabat mater*, satb, ch, orch, 1767; *Salve regina*, G minor, satb, orch, 1771; *Insanae et vanae curae*, ch, orch, by 1798, arr from chorus in *Tobia*; *Te Deum*, C, ch, orch, by 1800; etc.

Other works: *Arianna a Naxos* (cantata; see ARIADNE), s, hpd/pf, by 1790; 12 Original Canzonettas, by 1794–5 (No.10 'She never told her love'; Shakespeare); *Berenice, che fai* (*Scena di Berenice*; Metastasio), s, orch, 1795; choral cantatas, insert arias, about 400 arrs of British folksongs, etc.

Orchestral music

Symphonies: No.1, D, ?1757; No.2, C, ?by 1761; No.3, G, by 1762; No.4, D, ?by 1760; No.5, A, ?by 1760; No.6 'Le Matin', D, ?1761; No.7 'Le Midi', A, 1761; No.8 'Le Soir', G, ?1761; No.9, C, 1761; No.10, D, ?by 1761; No.11, E♭, ?by 1760; No.12, E, 1763; No.13, D, 1763; No.14, A, ?by 1762; No.15, D, ?by 1761; No.16, B♭, ?by 1765; No.17, F, ?by 1762; No.18, G, ?by 1762; No.19, D, ?by 1762; No.20, C, ?by 1762; No.21, A, 1764; No.22 'Philosopher', E♭, 1764; No.23, G, 1764; No.24, D, 1764; No.25, C, ?by 1760; No.26 'Lamentatione', D minor, ?by 1768; No.27, G, ?by 1761; No.28, A, 1765; No.29, E, 1765; No.30 'Alleluia', C, 1765; No.31 'Horn Signal', D, 1765; No.32, C, ?by 1760; No.33, C, ?by 1760; No.34, D minor-major, ?by 1765; No.35, B♭, 1767; No.36, E♭, ?*c*.1761–5; No.37, C, ?by 1758; No.38, C, ?by 1768; No.39, G minor, ?1765; No.40, F, 1763; No.41, C, ?by 1768; No.42, D, 1771; No.43 'Mercury', E♭, by 1772; No.44 'Mourning', E minor, by 1772; No.45 'Farewell', F♯ minor, 1772; No.46, B, 1772; No.47, G, 1772; No.48 'Maria Theresa', C, ?by 1769; No.49 'La Passione', F minor, 1768; No.50, C, 1773; No.51, B♭, by 1774; No.52, C minor, ?by 1772; No.53 'L'Imperiale', D, ?1778–9; No.54, G, 1774; No.55 'Schoolmaster', E♭, 1774; No.56, C, 1774; No.57, D, 1774; No.58, F, ?by 1767–8; No.59 'Fire', A, ?by 1768; No.60 'Il distratto', C, by 1774; No.61, D, 1776; No.62, D, ?1780; No.63 'La Roxelane', C, ?1779; No.64 'Tempora mutantur', A, ?by *c*.1763; No.65, A, ?*c*.1769–72; No.66, B♭, ?*c*.1775–6; No.67, F, ?*c*.1775–6; No.68, B♭, ?*c*.1774–5; No.69 'Laudon', C, ?*c*.1775–6; No.70, D, ?1778–9; No.71, B♭, ?1778–9; No.72, D, ?*c*.1763–5; No.73 'La Chasse', D, ?1781; No.74, E♭, ?1780; No.75, D, ?1779; No.76, E♭, ?1782; No.77, B♭, ?1782; No.78, C minor, ?1782; No.79, F, ?by 1784; No.80, D minor, ?by 1784; No.81, G, ?by 1784; No.82 'L'Ours', C, 1786; No.83 'La Poule', G minor, 1785; No.84, E♭, 1786; No.85 'La Reine', B♭, ?1785; No.86, D, 1786; No.87, A, 1785; No.88, G, ?1787; No.89, F, 1787; No.90, C, 1788; No.91, E♭, 1788; No.92 'Oxford', G, 1789; No.93, D, 1791; No.94 'Surprise', G, 1791; No.95, C minor, 1791; No.96 'Miracle', D, 1791; No.97, C, 1792; No.98, B♭, 1792; No.99, E♭, 1793; No.100 'Military', G, 1793/4; No.101 'Clock', D, 1793/4; No.102, B♭, 1794; No.103 'Drumroll', E♭, 1795; No.104 'London', D, 1795; No.107 (Symphony A), B♭, ?by 1761; No.108 (Symphony B), B♭, by 1765

note: Nos.82–7 are the Paris symphonies, Nos.93–104 the London symphonies. Nos.107–8 were late additions to the canon (as were Nos.105–6, subsequently discredited)

Concertos with multiple soloists: Concerto, F, kbd, vn, str, H.18:6, by 1766; Sinfonia Concertante, B♭, vn, ob, vc, bn, orch, 1792; 5 concertos, 2 lire organizzate, orch, ?1786–7; 8 notturnos, 2 lire organizzate, orch, *c*.1788–90; etc.

Keyboard concertos: D, H.18:2, by 1767; F, H.18:3, ?by *c*.1766; G, H.18:4, ?*c*.1768–70; D, H.18:11, by 1784; etc.

String concertos: Violin Concerto No.1, C, by *c*.1761–5; No.3 'Melk', ?by *c*.1765–70; No.4, G, by 1769; Cello Concerto No.1, C, ?*c*.1761–5; No.2, D, 1783; etc.

Wind concertos: Horn Concerto No.1, D, 1762; Trumpet Concerto, E♭, 1796; etc.

Other works: *The Seven Last Words*, ?1786; dances, marches

Chamber and instrumental music

String quartets: B♭, E♭, D, G, E♭, C, Op.1, ?*c*.1757–9; A, E, F, B♭, Op.2:1, 2, 4, 6, ?*c*.1760–62 (Nos.3 and 5 arr from divertimentos); C, E♭, G, D minor, B♭, A, Op.9:1–6, ?1769–70; E, F, E♭, C minor, G, D, Op.17:1–6, 1771; E♭, C, G minor, D, F minor, A, Op.20:1–6 'SUN', 1772; B minor, E♭, C, B♭, G, D, Op.33:1–6 'RUSSIAN', 1781 (E♭ 'JOKE', C 'BIRD'); D minor, Op.42, 1785; B♭, C, E♭, F♯ minor, F, D, Op.50:1–6 'Prussian', 1787 (D 'Frog'); *The Seven Last Words*, Op.51, arr of orch work; G, C, E, A, F minor, B♭, Opp.54:1–3, 55:1–3 'TOST', 1788 (F minor 'RAZOR'); C, B minor, B♭, G, D, E♭, Op.64 'Tost', 1790 (D 'LARK'); B♭, D, E♭, C, F, G minor, Opp.71:1–3, 74:1–3 'APPONYI', 1793 (G minor 'RIDER'); G, D minor, C, B♭, D, E♭, Op.76

'ERDODY', 1797 (D minor 'Fifths', C 'EMPEROR', B♭ 'Sunrise'); G, F, Op.77 'Lobkowitz', 1799; D minor, Op.103, by 1803, movts 2–3 only

Piano trios: G minor, H.15:1, ?c.1760–62; F, H.15:2, ?c.1767–71; G, H.15:5, by 1784; F, D, B♭, H.15:6–8, 1784–5; A, H.15:9, 1785; E♭, H.15:10, by 1785; E♭, E minor, C, H.15:11–13, by 1789; A♭, H.15:14, 1790; G, H.15:15, 1790; D, H.15:16, 1790; F, H.15:17, 1790; A, G minor, B♭, H.15:18–20, 1794; C, E♭, D minor, H.15:21–3, 1795; D, G, F♯ minor, H.15:24–6, 1795; C, E, E♭, H.15:27–9, ?by 1795; E♭, H.15:30, ?1796; E♭ minor, H.15:31, 1795; G, H.15:32, by 1794

Trios, 2 fl, vc: C, G, G, G, H.4:1–4, 1794–5

Piano sonatas: No.31, A♭, H.16:46, ?c.1767–70; No.32, G minor, H.16:44, c.1771–3; No.33, C minor, H.16:20, 1771; Nos.36–41, C, E, F, D, E♭, A, H.16:21–6, 1773; Nos.42–7, G, E♭, F, A, E, B minor, H.16:27–32, by 1776; No.49, C♯ minor, H.16:36, ?c.1770–75; No.50, D, H.16:37, by 1780; No.53, E minor, H.16:34, by 1784; Nos.54–6, G, B♭, D, H.16:40–2, by 1784; No.58, C, H.16:48, by 1789; No.59, E♭, H.16:49, 1789–90; No.60, C, H.16:50, c.1794–5; No.61, D, H.16:51, ?c.1794–5; No.62, E♭, H.16:52, 1794; etc.

Other piano works: Fantasia (Capriccio), C, H.17:4, 1789; Variations (Sonata), F minor, H.17:6, 1793; etc.

Other works: divertimentos, wind with/without str; string trios; over 150 trios, duets and solos for baryton; 6 duos, vn, va; pieces for mechanical clock; etc.

Doubtful/spurious works

Concertos: Keyboard Concerto, F, H.18:7, by 1766; Flute Concerto, D, H.7f:D1, by 1771, by Leopold Hofmann; Oboe Concerto, C, H.7g:C1, ?c.1800; etc.

String quartets: E, C, G, B♭, F, A, Op.3, by 1777, ?by Roman Hoffstetter; etc.

(2) (Johann) Michael (baptized Rohrau, 14 Sep 1737; d. Salzburg, 10 Aug 1806). He joined his elder brother in the choir of St Stephen's, Vienna, when he was eight, and seems to have lived a similar hand-to-mouth existence after his voice broke, around 1753, though already he had an inclination towards church music. After two years or so in Grosswardein (now Oradea, in Romania) in 1763 he gained a post as concertmaster at the archiepiscopal court in Salzburg, where his colleagues included Leopold Mozart. There he stayed. In 1768 he married a singer; their only child died in infancy. He succeeded Mozart as court organist in 1782, and became a respected teacher, his pupils including Weber. Besides about 25 surviving, fully authenticated masses and much other church music, he wrote symphonies, divertimentos and concertos (two favourite trumpet concertos, in C and D, seem to have been arranged from serenade and violin-concerto movements).

Haydn quartets. Common name for the set of quartets Mozart published as his Op.10 with a dedication to Haydn, comprising K.387, K.421, K.428, K.458, K.464 and K.465.

Haym, Nicola (Francesco) (b. Rome, 6 Jul 1676; d. London, 31 Jul 1729). Italian opera man, best remembered for the librettos he adapted for Handel in London, where he lived from 1701, though he was also a composer himself, orchestral cellist and company manager. His librettos for Handel included those of *Teseo, Ottone, Flavio, Giulio Cesare, Tamerlano, Rodelinda, Siroe, Tolomeo* and possibly *Amadigi di Gaula, Radamisto* and *Partenope*.

Hayne van Ghizeghem (b. c.1445; d. 1476–97). Netherlandish composer, connected with Charles the Bold of Burgundy and later, very possibly, with the French court. His surviving output consists entirely of rondeaux, including some of the most widely appreciated songs of the time (*Allez regretz, Amours amours, De tous biens plaine*).

head. The part of a drum that is beaten, usually membrane-covered.

Head, Michael (Dewar) (b. Eastbourne, 28 Jan 1900; d. Cape Town, 24 Aug 1976). British composer-performer, especially of his own unpretentious songs, in which he would accompany himself at the piano; 'The Little Road to Bethlehem' has become a Christmas favourite. He studied with Corder at the RAM (1919–25), where he taught from 1927.

head-motif. Idea repeated at the start of each section of a cyclic mass.

head voice. High, quiet singing that may seem to come from within the head, as distinct from the CHEST VOICE. Used of tenors, as it most often is, the term may imply FALSETTO.

hearing. See EAR; PSYCHOLOGY OF MUSIC.

Hebriden, Die (The Hebrides). Overture by Mendelssohn, which he sometimes called *The Isles of Fingal* and which his German publisher issued as *Fingals Höhle* (Fingal's Cave), a name that stuck. The composer visited the site – a sea cave on the island of Staffa, named after a legendary giant – on 8 August 1829, though he had sketched the theme the day before, in Oban. First performance: London, 14 May 1832.

Heckel. German woodwind-instrument firm, led by Johann Adam Heckel (1812–77), his son

Wilhelm (1856–1909) and subsequent generations, latterly specializing in bassoons. Its innovations include the heckel-clarina (a soprano saxophone of oboe build) and the heckelphone.

heckelphone. Tenor oboe, an octave below the standard instrument, developed by Wilhelm Heckel and first used by Strauss in *Salome*. Other composers to write for it have included Varèse and Henze.

heel. The held end of the bow, the other being the point.

heftig (Ger.). Forceful, impatient.

Heifetz, Jascha (b. Vilnius, 2 Feb 1901; d. Los Angeles, 10 Dec 1987). Russian–US violinist, widely acknowledged as the supreme virtuoso of the first age when recording could bring a musician an immense international audience. He was trained by his professional-violinist father before entering the St Petersburg Conservatory in 1910 to study with Auer. At 11 he played the Tchaikovsky concerto with the Berlin Philharmonic, and at 17 he left Russia, first for a US tour crowned by his Carnegie Hall debut (27 October 1917). He became a US citizen in 1925. Between the 1920s and the 1950s he played all over the world and recorded most of the standard repertory, as well as concertos written for him by Walton, Gruenberg and Rózsa, and some of the many transcriptions he produced as encore items (including Dinicu's *Hora staccato*, Rimsky-Korsakov's *Flight of the Bumblebee* and songs from *Porgy and Bess*). He then concentrated more on chamber music and taught at the University of Southern California (from 1962). In a choice between intensity and perfection he would always choose perfection, but his perfection was unsurpassed.

Heiligmesse. Second in the conventional order of Haydn's late masses, though first to be composed, it owes its name to its imposing setting of the opening word (Ger. *Heilig*) of the *Sanctus*. It is sometimes alternatively called after Bernard of Offrida, a friar who had been beatified in 1795.

Heiliger Dankgesang (Thanksgiving Hymn). Beethoven's name for a Lydian slow movement in his Op.132 quartet.

Heiller, Anton (b. Vienna, 15 Sep 1923; d. Vienna, 25 Mar 1979). Austrian organist-composer, esteemed as a Bach performer. He studied at the Vienna Academy (1941–2), where he taught from the end of the war. His compositions – Catholic church music, cantatas, organ pieces – are in a Hindemithian polyphonic style.

heimlich (Ger.). Secretly, secretively.

Heine, Heinrich (b. Düsseldorf, 13 Dec 1797; d. Paris, 17 Feb 1856). German poet, whose lyric Romanticism – personal, observant of nature, close to folk poetry – made him a favourite of 19th-century composers, most of whom preferred to overlook his irony. Among those who set him were Schubert (his contemporary), Schumann, Mendelssohn, Liszt, Brahms and Strauss, while his early tragedy *William Ratcliff* provided an opera subject for Cui, Mascagni and others. Living in Paris from 1831, he wrote perceptively on Chopin, Berlioz and other musicians.

Heinichen, Johann David (b. Krössuln, near Weissenfels, 17 Apr 1683; d. Dresden, 16 Jul 1729). German composer and author of an important composition treatise (*Der General-Bass in der Composition*, 1728). He studied at St Thomas's school, Leipzig, under Kuhnau, then trained at the university as a lawyer – though music soon reclaimed him, and he busied himself as a composer in Weissenfels and Leipzig before removing to Venice and other Italian cities (1710–16). In 1717 he became kapellmeister to the Saxon court in Dresden. He wrote operas, sacred music, concertos and other instrumental pieces, including a *Pastorale per la notte della nativitate Christi*.

Heininen, Paavo (Johannes) (b. Helsinki, 13 Jan 1938). Finnish composer, of Romantic rhetoric through an output of great abundance and variety. He studied with Merikanto at the Sibelius Academy (1956–60), where he has been an important teacher since 1966. His works include the one-act opera *The Damask Drum* (f.p. Helsinki, 1984), four symphonies, three piano concertos and two quartets.

Heinrich, Anthony Philip [Anton Philipp] (b. Schönbüchel/Krásný Buk, Bohemia, 11 Mar 1781; d. New York, 3 May 1861). Bohemian–US composer, pioneer of composition in his new country and of a spirit of rugged independence. After the failure of a business venture in 1817 he stayed on in the USA, and travelled widely, on foot and down the Ohio River, before setting up as a musician. Self-taught, he produced ambitious if rather ramshackle pieces, beginning with the songs and piano pieces of his Op.1 – *The Dawning of Music in Kentucky, or The Pleasures of Harmony in the Solitudes of Nature* (1820) – and continuing with a vast array of picturesque vocal, instrumental and orchestral music. Following a decade spent largely in Europe he settled in New York in 1837 and enjoyed distinguished connections, but he died poor.

Heise, Peter (Arnold) (b. Copenhagen, 11 Feb 1830; d. Tårbaek, near Copenhagen, 12 Sep 1879). Danish composer, best known for his songs, in a classicizing idiom, though he also wrote notable chamber music and the first important Danish opera, *Drot og marsk* (King and Marshal, 1878). He studied with Hauptmann in Leipzig (1852–3) and worked in Sorø as a teacher and organist (1857–65), after which a fortunate marriage enabled him to live comfortably in Copenhagen.

Heiss, Hermann (b. Darmstadt, 29 Dec 1897; d. Darmstadt, 6 Dec 1966). German composer, pupil of Hauer (1924–6) and instructor at the Darmstadt courses (1946–62), where he was the first to teach 12-note composition. His intervening works for the forces were fortunately lost.

heiter (Ger.). Cheerful.

Heldenbariton (Ger., heroic baritone). Strong and incisive voice type, defined by such roles as Telramund in *Lohengrin*.

Heldenleben, Ein (A Hero's Life). Symphony-length tone poem by Strauss, playing continuously through six sections: *The Hero, The Hero's Adversaries, The Hero's Companion, The Hero's Battlefield, The Hero's Works of Peace, The Hero's Retirement from the World and Fulfilment*. First performance: Frankfurt, 3 Mar 1899.

Heldentenor (Ger., heroic tenor). Voice type defined by (and almost limited to) Wagner's central tenor roles, especially Tannhäuser, Siegmund, Siegfried and Tristan, which require singers who can sustain force and brilliance over a long period.

Helen in Egypt. See *Die* ÄGYPTISCHE HELENA.

Helffer, Claude (b. Paris, 18 Jun 1922; d. Paris, 27 Oct 2004). French pianist, particularly associated with the sonatas of Barraqué and Boulez. He studied with Casadesus and, after the Second World War, with Leibowitz.

hell (Ger.). Bright.

Hellawell, Piers (b. Chinley, 14 Jul 1956). British composer, most typically of repetitive minimalist pieces in block form. He studied with James Wood at Oxford and later privately with Maw (1979–81),

and has been associated with Queen's University, Belfast, since 1981.

Heller, Stephen (b. Pest, 15 May 1813; d. Paris, 14 Jan 1888). Hungarian–French pianist-composer, author especially of character pieces in which he moved from Schumann's world towards Fauré and Debussy. He studied with Anton Halm in Vienna, where he met Schubert and Beethoven, and toured at his father's behest as a virtuoso (1828–30). After that, exhausted, he lived in Augsburg, before moving to Paris in 1838, making a living there as a teacher and critic. He wrote almost nothing but piano music.

Hellmesberger, Joseph (b. Vienna, 3 Nov 1828; d. Vienna, 24 Oct 1893). Austrian violinist, founder in 1849 of the Hellmesberger Quartet, which was the outstanding ensemble of its period, responsible for bringing late Beethoven and Schubert into the active repertory. He studied with his father Georg (1800–73), a great virtuoso and teacher, and led his quartet until 1891, when he was succeeded by his son Joseph, known as Pepi (1855–1907). Both Joseph Hellmesbergers also composed light music, the elder being responsible for a popular *Ballszene* (after a violin study by Joseph Mayseder).

Helmholtz, Hermann (Ludwig Ferdinand) von (b. Potsdam, 31 Aug 1821; d. Berlin, 8 Sep 1894). German scientist, responsible for fundamental work on sound and hearing. Trained in Berlin as a medical doctor, he undertook research in diverse fields but is lastingly remembered as the father of psychoacoustics. In particular, he discovered how harmonics control timbre and explored combination tones, reporting his findings in *Die Lehre von den Tonempfindungen als physiologische Grundlage für die Theorie der Musik* (1863), translated as *On the Sensations of Tone* (1875).

Hely-Hutchinson, (Christian) Victor (Noel Hope) (b. Cape Town, 26 Dec 1901; d. London, 11 Mar 1947). British composer, notably of *A Carol Symphony* (1927). He studied at Oxford and the RCM, and held posts as professor of music at Birmingham (1934–44) and director of music for the BBC (1944–7).

hemidemisemiquaver (UK). 64th-note (US). See DURATION.

hemiola. Mix of triple and duple metres, either simultaneously (as when one part has two stresses at dotted crotchet intervals in a 3/4 bar) or in alternation. The effect can be exciting, as in certain Spanish and Latin American dances, or lilting, as in many waltzes and moments in Brahms.

hemitonic. With semitones, normally used of pentatonic scales.

Hen. See *La* POULE.

Henkemans, Hans (b. The Hague, 23 Dec 1913; d. Nieuwegein, 29 Dec 1995). Dutch composer and pianist, specially associated in both roles with Debussy, whose *Préludes* he orchestrated (Book I, 1970; Book II, 1972). He studied with Pijper (1933–8) and had his Passacaglia and Gigue for piano and orchestra (1942) taken up by van Beinum; later works include several concertos, notably for viola (1955). In 1969 he retired from the concert platform, but he continued to work as a composer and (being also a qualified medical practitioner) psychiatrist.

Henle. German music publishing firm founded in Munich in 1948 by Günter Henle (1899–1979), specializing in URTEXT editions.

Henry VIII (b. Greenwich, 28 Jun 1491; d. Windsor, 28 Jan 1547). English monarch, who favoured music and wrote some songs himself, notably 'Pastime with good company' (but probably not GREENSLEEVES). His rejection of his first queen, Catherine of Aragon, and thereby of Catholic authority, had enormous musical (and other) implications, and is the subject of Saint-Saëns's opera *Henry VIII*.

Henry, Pierre (b. Paris, 9 Dec 1927). French composer of electronic music. After studies with Messiaen and others at the Paris Conservatoire (1938–48) he joined Schaeffer in 1949, collaborating with him on several works of 1950–53. He was then head of the Groupe de Recherches de Musique Concrète until 1958, when he left to go off by himself, on a fecund trajectory.

Hensel, Fanny. See MENDELSSOHN.

Henselt, (Georg Martin) Adolf von (b. Schwabach, Bavaria, 9 May 1814; d. Bad Warmbrunn, now Cieplice Śląskie-Zdrój, Poland, 10 Oct 1889). German pianist-composer, who stretched the limits of his hands (to play 11ths) and of his instrument. He completed his training with Hummel (1832) and Sechter (until 1834), then worked in retirement for two years before coming out with his *12 études caractéristiques* Op.2 (pub 1837–8: No.6 *Si oiseau j'étais*) and *12 études de salon* (pub 1838). From 1838 he was based in St Petersburg, assisting musical communication between Russia and the West through his contacts with the Schumanns and Liszt, as with Glinka and Balakirev. His later works include a concerto in F minor (Op.16, pub 1847) and many more solo pieces.

Henze, Hans Werner (b. Gütersloh, 1 Jul 1926). German composer. Born into a comfortable environment as a schoolteacher's eldest son, he developed strong feelings of attachment and apartness – apartness as an artist, as a homosexual and as one revolted by Nazism. Such feelings he has maintained in his relations with the great German tradition. Twice in his life he sided with the gainsayers – with the avant-garde centred on Darmstadt around 1950, and with the political protest movement of the late 1960s. But though he has kept post-Schoenberg procedures with him and never renounced his commitment to revolutionary socialism, most of his work reflects the range and ambiguity of a creative mind deeply embroiled in the culture of earlier epochs, from the Greeks to the late Romantics. That conserving–renewing mentality has given him unparalleled access to the great institutions internationally; in particular, his 11 full-length operas are the most widely presented additions to the repertory since Britten.

His professional training, begun at the Brunswick State Music School in 1942, was interrupted by army service (1944–5) and resumed under Fortner in Heidelberg after the war. Rapidly he acquainted himself with music the Nazis had proscribed – Stravinsky, Bartók, Schoenberg, Berg, jazz – resulting in a rush of influences; he also learned from the Darmstadt summer courses (from 1946 onwards) and from lessons with Josef Rufer and René Leibowitz. His creative life became hectic, a quick succession of theatre scores and orchestral pieces suggesting both spontaneous fertility and an artisan-like approach. In 1950 he found a job as ballet conductor in Wiesbaden, and, remaining highly productive, he took his place in the avant-garde – though while such colleagues as Boulez and Stockhausen were making music as abstract as possible, he wrote his first true opera (*Boulevard Solitude*) and made contact in the chamber cantata *Apollo et Hyazinthus* with a Mediterranean world of light, grace and elegiac beauty to which he would often return. His actual departure, then, for the Mediterranean – for Ischia, in 1953 – was both escape and homecoming.

In Italy his music became more luxuriant in harmony, richer in orchestral colour and more melodiously lyrical; from short forms he moved to the rhapsodic four-hour score of his opera *König Hirsch* (1953–6). After that he worked almost continuously on major stage works, creating five more in the next nine years, each quite distinct in dramatic style (aqueous fairytale in *Undine*, the classic stark conflict of love and duty in *Der Prinz von Homburg*, a conversation of feelings and feelinglessness in *Elegy for Young Lovers*, satire in *Der junge Lord*, the ancient riot of abandonment over repression in *The Bassarids*), and each surrounded by concert works inhabiting their particular niches, but all similar in their command of fantasy and many-layered irony. Working with colleagues of the stature of Frederick Ashton (*Undine*) and W.H. Auden (*Elegy, Bassarids*), he was an international figure. Meanwhile he began to appear widely as a teacher, lecturer and conductor of his own music, and through his operas and other commissions to reconnect himself to Germany.

This phase reached a climax in *The Bassarids*, after which he entered a period of self-questioning, charted in his Second Piano Concerto and culminating in his becoming politically engaged. In 1968 he switched his allegiance from the West Berlin Academy of Arts to the (communist) East, and in 1969–70 he spent periods teaching and studying in Cuba, where he learned new rhythms and colours as well as new forms of social combat through art. For a short period his works were fully confrontational: *Versuch über Schweine* (Essay on Pigs, 1968) has a soloist screaming at the audience, and the Hamburg première the same year of *Das Floss der Medusa*, a work he dedicated to the memory of Che Guevara, had to be abandoned when students draped a red flag over his conducting podium and the orchestra walked out. But by the time of his next, explicitly political opera, *We Come to the River* (1974–6), he had already returned to more personal realms of ripe orchestral narrative (*Tristan, Heliogabalus Imperator*) and chamber music (String Quartets Nos.3–5).

He transferred his activism into working as a community musician in Montepulciano, where from 1976 he ran an annual festival, while also drawing closer again to Germany, where he taught regularly and founded the Munich Biennale for new opera (1988). *The English Cat* (1980–83) was the last of his four English operas, followed by his Seventh Symphony (1983–4), the first of his symphonies to converse seriously with the Beethoven model. His choral Ninth (1995–7) took that conversation on, drawing also on his boyhood memories of Nazism, and a mood of retrospection and reconciliation, sometimes awkward, came to settle over his work – without at all damping the creativity that has continued in new scores, revisions and orchestrations of music by composers from Monteverdi to Wagner.

Hans Werner Henze *Bohemian Fifths* (1998)

Theatre and orchestral music

Operas: *Das Wundertheater* (1 act; Adolf von Schack after Cervantes), 1948, rev 1964, f.p. Frankfurt, 1965; *Boulevard Solitude* (see MANON LESCAUT), 1951; *Ein Landarzt* (1 act; after Kafka), 1951, rev 1964, f.p. Frankfurt, 1965, rev 1994; *Das Ende einer Welt* (1 act; Wolfgang Hildesheimer), 1953, rev 1964, f.p. Frankfurt, 1965, rev 1993; KÖNIG HIRSCH, 1953–6; *Der* PRINZ VON HOMBURG, 1958–9, rev 1991; ELEGY FOR YOUNG LOVERS, 1959–61, rev 1987; *Der* JUNGE LORD, 1964; *The* BASSARIDS, 1964–5, rev 1992; WE COME TO THE RIVER, 1974–6; *Pollicino* (children's opera; Giuseppe Di Leva), 1979–80, Montepulciano, 1980; *The* ENGLISH CAT, 1980–83; *Das* VERRATENE MEER, 1986–9; VENUS AND ADONIS, 1993–5; L'UPUPA, 2001–3

Ballets: *Das Vokaltuch der Kammersängerin Rosa Silber*, 1950, rev 1990; *Der Idiot*, 1952, rev 1990; *Tancredi*, 1962, rev 1964; *Maratona*, 1956; UNDINE, 1956–7; *L'usignolo dell'imperatore*, 1959; *Orpheus*, 1978; *Tanzstunden* (*Le disperazioni del Signor Pulcinella*, after *Jack Pudding*, 1949; *Le Fils de l'air*; *Labyrinth*, rev of 1951 score), 1995–6

Music theatre: *Der langwierige Weg in die Wohnung der Natascha Ungeheuer* (Gastón Salvatore), 1971; *La Cubana* (Hans Magnus Enzensberger), 1973

Symphonies: No.1, 1947, rev chbr orch, 1963, rev 1991; No.2, 1949; No.3, 1949–50; No.4, 1955; No.5, 1962; No.6, 1969, rev 1994; No.7, 1983–4; No.8, 1992–3; No.9 (Hans Ulrich Treichel), ch, orch, 1995–7; No.10, 1997–2000

Concertos: Chamber Concerto, fl, pf, str, 1946; Concertino, pf, wind, perc, 1947; Piano Concerto No.1, 1950; No.2, 1967; *Tristan*, pf, orch, tape, 1972–3; *Requiem*, pf, tpt, orch, 1990–92; Violin Concerto No.1, 1947; No.2 (Enzensberger), b-bar, vn, chbr orch, tape, 1971; No.3, 1996; *Il Vitalino raddoppiato*, vn, chbr orch, 1977; Music for Viola and 22 Players, 1969–70; *Ode an den Westwind*, vc, orch, 1953; *Liebeslieder*, vc, orch, 1984–5; Introduction, Theme and Variations, vc, hp, str, 1992; Double Bass Concerto, 1966; Double Concerto, ob, hp, str, 1966

Choral orchestral: *Fünf Madrigale* (Villon), ch, chbr orch, 1947; *Chor gefangener Trojer* (Goethe), ch, orch, 1948, rev 1964; *Novae de infinito laudes* (Giordano Bruno), soli, ch, chbr orch, 1962; *Cantata della fiaba estrema* (Elsa Morante), s, ch, chbr orch, 1963; *Musen Siziliens* (Virgil), ch, 2 pf, wind, timp, 1966; *Moralities* (Auden, after Aesop), soli, ch, chbr orch, 1967; *Das Floss der Medusa* (Ernst Schnabel), s, bar, speaker, ch, orch, 1968

Vocal orchestral: *Fünf neapolitanische Lieder*, bar, chbr orch, 1956; *Nachtstücke und Arien* (Bachmann), s, orch, 1957; *Ariosi* (Tasso), s, vn, orch, 1963; *Versuch über Schweine* (Salvatore), v, orch, 1968; *Aristaeus* (Henze), bar, orch, 1997–2003

Other orchestral works: *Ballett-Variationen*, 1949, rev 1992, 1998; *Quattro poemi*, 1955; *Drei sinfonische Etüden*, 1956, rev 1964; Sonata, str, 1957–8; *Drei Dithyramben*, chbr orch, 1958; *Antifone*, 1960; *Los caprichos*, 1963; *Telemanniana*, 1967; *Heliogabalus Imperator*, 1971–2; *Katharina Blum*, 1975, from film score; *Ragtimes und Habaneras*, brass band, 1975; *Aria de la folía española*, 1977; *Barcarola*, 1979; *Concerto barrocco*, 1980; *Kleine Elegien*, old insts, 1984–5; *Fandango*, 1985, rev 1992; *Cinque piccoli concerti e ritornelli*, 1987; *Seconda sonata*, str, 1995; *Voie lactée ô soeur lumineuse*, chbr orch, 1995–6; *Sieben Boleros*, 1999; *Fraternité*, 1999; *Scorribanda sinfonica*, 2001; suites and excerpts from operas and ballets

Orchestrations: *Don Chisciotte* (Paisiello), 1976; *Jephte* (Carissimi), 1976; *Wesendonck-Lieder* (Wagner), a, chbr orch, 1976; *Il ritorno d'Ulisse in patria* (Monteverdi), 1981; *I sentimenti di Carl Philipp Emanuel Bach*, chbr orch, 1982; *Il re Teodoro in Venezia* (Paisiello), 1991–2; *Richard Wagnersche Klavierlieder*, mez, bar, ch, orch, 1998–9; etc.

Other music

Choral: *Wiegenlied der Mutter Gottes*, children's ch, 9 insts, 1948; *Lieder von einer Insel* (Bachmann), ch, 7 insts, 1964; *Orpheus Behind the Wire* (Edward Bond), 1981–3

Ensemble: *Whispers from Heavenly Death* (Whitman), s/t, 8 insts, 1948; *Apollo et Hyazinthus* (Trakl), a, hpd, 8 insts, 1952–3; *Kammermusik 1958* (Hölderlin), t, gtr, 8 insts, 1958; *Being Beauteous* (Rimbaud), s, hp, 4 vc, 1963; *In memoriam: Die weisse Rose*, 12 insts, 1965; *El* CIMARRON (Enzensberger), bar, fl, gtr, perc, 1969–70; *Voices*, mez, t, 15 insts, 1973; *El rey de Harlem* (Lorca), mez, ens, 1979; *Le Miracle de la rose*, cl, 13 insts, 1981; *Sonata*, 8 brass, 1983; *Sonata*, 6 insts, 1984; *Ode an eine Äolsharfe*, gtr, 15 insts, 1985–6; *Drei Lieder über den Schnee* (Treichel), s, bar, 8 insts, 1989; *Minotauros Blues*, 6 perc, 1996; *L'Heure bleue*, 13 insts, 2001

Chamber: String Quartet No.1, 1947; No.2, 1952; No.3, 1975–6; No.4, 1976; No.5, 1976; Chamber Sonata, pf, trio, 1948; Wind Quintet, 1952; Fantasia, str sextet, 1966, from film score *Der junge Törless*; *Carillon, Récitatif, Masque*, mandolin, gtr, hp, 1974; *Amicizia!*, cl, trbn, vc, pf, perc, 1976; *L'autunno*, wind qnt, 1977; Piano Quintet, 1990–91; *Adagio adagio*, pf trio, 1993; String Trio, 1998; etc.

Instrumental: Violin Sonata, 1946; Solo Violin Sonata, 1976–7; *Fünf Nachtstücke*, vn, pf, 1990; Viola Sonata, 1979; Serenade, vc, 1949; Capriccio, vc, 1981; Flute Sonata, 1947; *Royal Winter Music*, 2 sonatas, gtr, 1975–6, 1979; *Prison Song*, perc, tape, 1971; *Five Scenes from the Snow Country*, mar, 1978; etc.

Songs: 3 Auden Songs, t, pf, 1983; *Sechs Gesänge aus dem Arabischen* (Henze), t, pf, 1997–8

Keyboard: Piano Variations, Op.13, 1949; Piano Sonata, 1959; *Six absences*, hpd, 1961; *Lucy Escott Variations*, hpd/pf, 1963; *Cherubino*, pf, 1980–81; *Scorribanda pianistica*, 2003; etc.

heptachord. Seven-note scale.

heptatonic. Term describing a scale of seven notes to the octave – like the major scale, minor scales and church modes – or music based on such modes or scales.

Herabstrich (Ger.). Downbow on violin/viola.

Heraufstrich (Ger.). Upbow on violin/viola.

Herbert, Victor (August) (b. Dublin, 1 Feb 1859; d. New York, 26 May 1924). Irish–US composer, especially of operettas (*Babes in Toyland*, 1903; *Naughty Marietta*, 1910). Brought up in London and Germany, and trained as a cellist at the Stuttgart Conservatory, he played in Eduard Strauss's orchestra for a year. In 1886 he and his wife, the operatic soprano Therese Foerster, moved to New York, where he worked as a cellist, teacher and bandmaster before gaining success in the operetta field. He was also conductor of the Pittsburgh Symphony (1898–1904), and wrote two concertos (No.1, Op.8, 1884; No.2, E minor, Op.30, 1894) and other works for his own instrument.

Herdenglocken (Ger.). Cowbells.

Héroïde funèbre (At a Hero's Funeral). Symphonic poem by Liszt.

Herold [Hérold], **(Louis Joseph) Ferdinand** (b. Paris, 28 Jan 1791; d. Paris, 19 Jan 1833). French composer, of numerous opéras comique (*Zampa*, 1831; *Le Pré aux clercs*, 1832) and ballets (*La Fille mal gardée*, 1828). The son of a pianist-composer, he completed his years at the Paris Conservatoire (1806–12) as Méhul's pupil, won the Prix de Rome and wrote his first opera in Naples (1815). Having returned to Paris via Vienna, where he met Salieri, he worked as keyboard accompanist at the Théâtre Italien (1816–26) and coach at the Opera (1826–33), while writing works whose fortunes were mixed.

Herreweghe, Philippe (b. Ghent, 2 May 1947). Belgian conductor, of manifest seriousness in repertory ranging from the Renaissance to Bruckner. He began his career as a Baroque specialist, with his choir Collegium Vocale (founded 1969) and choral-orchestral organization Chapelle Royale (1977). With the latter he has made many recordings, especially of sacred music. In 1998 he became music director of the Royal Philharmonic of Flanders.

Herrman, Bernard (b. New York, 29 Jun 1911; d. Los Angeles, 24 Dec 1975). US composer and conductor, among the greats of film music. After studies at Juilliard (1930–32) and with Grainger at

New York University (1932–3) he worked in radio theatre, then moved into movies with Orson Welles, for whom he scored *Citizen Kane* (1941). Other directors with whom he worked included Hitchcock (*The Man Who Knew Too Much*, 1956; *Vertigo*, 1958; *Psycho*, 1960), Truffaut (*Fahrenheit 451*, 1966) and Scorsese (*Taxi Driver*, 1976). He also wrote an operatic version of *Wuthering Heights* (1943–51), a cantata *Moby Dick* (1937–8) and chamber pieces.

Herschkowitz, Philip (b. Iaşi, 7 Sep 1906; d. Vienna, 5 Jan 1989). Romanian–Russian composer, pupil of Berg (1928–31) and Webern (from 1935–9). His flight from Nazi Europe to the Soviet Union, in 1940, was a leap from the frying pan into the refrigerator: his music was ignored, and he earned a living as a music editor and film-score orchestrator. In 1960, after a break of some years, he returned to composition, and took some pupils. He was able to emigrate in 1987 and settled again in Vienna, where he wrote his last work, *Drei Gesänge* for mezzo-soprano and ensemble on poems of Lorca, Rilke and Celan.

Herstrich (Ger.). Downbow on cello/bass.

hervorgehoben (Ger.). Brought forward.

hervortretend (Ger.). Stepping forward.

Herz, Henri (b. Vienna, 6 Jan 1803; d. Paris, 5 Jan 1888). Austrian pianist-composer, resident most of his life in Paris as a leading light in the city's culture of virtuoso pianism. Trained by his father and at the Paris Conservatoire, he travelled widely in the 1830s–40s in Europe and the Americas, and produced large quantities of variations and other pieces.

Herzogenberg, (Leopold) Heinrich (Picot de Peccaduc Freiherr) von (b. Graz, 10 Jun 1843; d. Wiesbaden, 9 Oct 1900). Austrian composer, friend and admirer of Brahms, whom he came to know through his teacher at the Vienna Conservatory, Felix Otto Dessoff. He moved to Leipzig in 1872 and to Berlin in 1885, and published much choral music, three symphonies, songs and chamber music.

Hes (Ger.). B♭, though this note's normal Ger. name is B.

Heseltine, Philip. British music scholar, better known under the name he took as a composer, Peter WARLOCK.

Hess, Myra (b. London, 25 Feb 1890; d. London, 25 Nov 1965). British pianist, created dame in 1941. She is remembered especially for her warmly Romantic and authoritative Beethoven, as also for her Bach transcription *Jesu, joy of man's desiring* and her participation in the National Gallery concerts that had such an effect on morale during the Second World War. A pupil of Tobias Matthay at the RAM, she made her debut in London in 1907, played regularly in mainland Europe, and returned often to the USA after her first tour there in 1922. She gave her last concert in 1960.

heterophony. (1) The presentation of the same melody simultaneously in differing rhythmic forms. This is unusual in Western music before Debussy.

(2) Sometimes the term is used more loosely to denote any kind of music existing on different simultaneous planes, e.g. much of Messiaen's.

Heuberger, Richard (Franz Joseph) (b. Graz, 18 Jun 1850; d. Vienna, 28 Oct 1914). Austrian composer, known for his operetta *Der Opernball* (f.p. Vienna, 1898). He turned to music from engineering in 1876, and worked in Vienna as a choirmaster and critic, succeeding Hanslick on the *Neue freie Presse* (1896–1901).

Heugel. French music publishing firm founded by Jacques-Léopold Heugel (1815–83), who entered the business as Jean-Antoine Meissonnier's partner in 1839. The company was acquired by Leduc in 1980.

Heure espagnole, L' (Spanish Time). Opera by Ravel, setting a play by Franc-Nohain. Introduced by a brief overture of tickings, the action takes place in a clockmaker's shop. The clockmaker's wife Concepcion (soprano) has to arrange her adulterous affair with the rhapsodic Gonsalve (tenor) by the clock; interrupted by the muleteer Ramiro (baritone), she eventually turns his presence to her advantage. First performance: Paris, 19 May 1911.

hexachord. (1) Sequence of six adjacent notes fundamental to musical theory and practice from the medieval period to the Baroque. Guido of Arezzo gave the first full description of the system, by which a tone was added at either end to a diatonic TETRACHORD, producing the sequences C–D–E–F–G–A (eventually known as the *hexachordum naturale*), G–A–B–C–D–E (*hexachordum durum*) and F–G–A–B♭–C–D (*hexachordum molle*). Also from Guido came the names ut-re-mi-fa-sol-la for the hexachordal positions, and the system of naming notes both with letters and with these syllables, to define their place. Thus G sol in a hexachord on C could become G ut in one on G or G re in one on F. Many plainsong melodies unfold within the interval of a sixth, and so can be described in terms of a single hexachord. Those with a wider range could be understood as mutating from one hexachord to another through overlapping sequences, e.g. from C–D–E–F–G–A to G–A–B–C–D–E. In the Renaissance the hexachord became not only a means of understanding melodies but also a compositional source, as in the masses on ut-re-mi-fa-sol-la by Brumel, Morales and Palestrina, or keyboard fantasias on the same motif by Byrd, Tomkins and Frescobaldi.

(2) Half a 12-note set. In Schoenberg's serial music the hexachords are often reordered transpositions or inversions of one another, a feature that helps in linking serial forms through COMBI-NATORIALITY.

Hexaméron. Set of bravura piano variations by Liszt, Thalberg, Pixis, Herz, Czerny and Chopin on the march from Bellini's *I puritani*, assembled in 1837–8 by Liszt on behalf of Princess Cristina Belgiojioso as, bizarrely, a means of agitating for Italian liberation. Besides providing the theme and second variation, Liszt added an introduction, linking material and a conclusion, in versions for solo piano and for piano and orchestra. It seems only a nice myth that the six composer-pianists got together to give the first performance. The work was named after a species of exegesis concerned with the six days (Gk *hexameron*) of the divine creation.

hexatonic. Term describing a scale of six notes to the octave, or music based on such a scale. The whole-tone scale is an example, but the term has also been used more particularly for the scale of alternating minor thirds and semitones (e.g. C–E♭–E–G–A♭–B–C), which has been detected in Liszt, Rimsky-Korsakov and Bartók.

Hf. Ger. abbreviation for *Harfe* (harp).

Hiawatha, The Song of. Amerindian epic by Longfellow (1855), from which Coleridge-Taylor took passages for three cantatas popular in the early 20th century.

hidden fifth. A harmonic interval of a fifth appearing as a result of two parts moving in similar motion from a different interval of separation (e.g. from the sixth G–E down to the fifth F–C). This is permitted by the rules of part writing, except where the outermost parts are concerned.

hidden octave. A harmonic interval of an octave appearing in the same way as a hidden fifth, and similarly permitted.

Higgins, Dick [Richard Carter] (b. Cambridge, 15 Mar 1938; d. Quebec, 25 Oct 1998). British–US composer, a proponent of 'intermedia', between music and conceptual art, poetry or theatre. He studied in New York in the late 1950s with Cowell and Cage and was associated with the FLUXUS movement.

hi-hat. Pair of cymbals supported on a vertical rod, with the upper one movable in response to pressure on a pedal, producing a somewhat muffled crash; hence the alternative name, choke cymbals. The pair may also be struck. Introduced as a drum-kit appendage in 1927, the instrument became relatively common in ensembles and orchestras after the Second World War.

Hildegard of Bingen (b. Bermersheim, near Alzey, 1098; d. Rupertsberg, near Bingen, 17 Sep 1179). German poet-composer, author of liturgical and visionary art as founder abbess of a convent and as seer. Of noble birth, she was placed in a Benedictine monastery at 14, together with the six-years-older Jutta von Spanheim. In 1136 Jutta died, and Hildegard took charge of the convent that had grown around them. During the 1150s she moved her flock to a new and independent convent, and in the next decade she travelled through Germany preaching. She was allowed to start recording her visions in 1141, but most of her writings – visionary texts, scientific studies, contributions to the liturgy and a sung mystery play, *Ordo virtutum* (The Order of the Virtues) – were set down when she was in her 50s and 60s. Her liturgical or quasi-liturgical chants resemble plainsong in their range from syllabic setting (in hymns and sequences) to floridly melismatic writing (in responds) by way of the moderately ornamental antiphons, but they are based on an individual repertory of melodic formulae, repeated and varied. Performance and scholarly appreciation of her work received a huge boost after the 800th anniversary of her death.

Barbara Newman, ed. *Voice of the Living Light* (1998)

Hymns and sequences: *Ave generosa* (Virgin Mary); *Columba aspexit* (St Maximinus); *O ecclesia oculi tui* (St Ursula); *O Euchari in leta via* (St Eucharius); *O ignis Spiritus Paraclitus* (Holy Spirit); *O Jerusalem aurea civitas* (St Rupert); *O presul vere civitatis* (St Disibod); *O virga ac diadema* (Virgin Mary); etc.

Responds: *Ave Maria o auctrix vitae* (Virgin Mary); *Favus distillans* (St Ursula); *O clarissima mater* (Virgin Mary); *Spiritui Sancto honor sit* (St Ursula); etc.

Antiphons: *Caritas abundat in omnia* (Holy Spirit); *Hodie aperuit nobis* (Incarnation); *O frondens virga* (Virgin Mary); *O gloriosissimi lux* (Angels); *O pastor animarum* (God the Father); *O quam mirabilis* (God the Father); *O rubor sanguinis* (St Ursula); *O virtus sapientiae* (God the Father); *Quia ergo femina* (Virgin Mary); *Unde quocumque* (St Ursula); etc.

Other works: *Ordo virtutum* (play); *Kyrie eleison*; *O dulcissime amator* (Virgins); *O viridissima virga* (Virgin Mary); etc.

Hilfslinie (Ger.). LEGER LINE.

Hill, Alfred (Francis) (b. Melbourne, 16 Dec 1870; d. Sydney, 30 Oct 1960). Australian composer, reckoned the father of Western music in Australasia. Brought up by musical parents largely in Wellington, New Zealand, he was heard by the violinist Eduard Reményi and dispatched to the Leipzig Conservatory (1887–91). While there he played in the Gewandhaus orchestra under Brahms and Tchaikovsky. He returned to Wellington to work as a teacher and conductor, then settled in Sydney, where he again found conducting jobs and eventually took a post at the New South Wales State Conservatorium (1916–34). Within a style rooted in the central European tradition, he incorporated elements of Maori and Australian aboriginal culture. Important works include his first three symphonies, subtitled 'Maori' (1896–1900), 'Joy of Life' (1941, with chorus) and 'Australia' (1951).

Hill, Edward Burlingame (b. Cambridge, Mass., 9 Sep 1872; d. Francetown, New Hampshire, 9 Jul 1960). US composer, a Francophile whose works include three symphonies, other orchestral pieces and chamber music. He studied with Paine at Harvard, Widor in Paris (1898) and Chadwick at the New England Conservatory (1902), and taught at Harvard from 1908 until his retirement in 1940.

Hiller, Ferdinand (von) (b. Frankfurt, 24 Oct 1811; d. Cologne, 11 May 1885). German composer and conductor, who met Beethoven (on his deathbed) and enjoyed the friendship and esteem of Mendelssohn, the Schumanns, Wagner and Brahms, though of his works – six operas, many large choral pieces, chamber music, songs – little is remembered apart from a piano concerto in F♯ minor (Op.69, pub 1861). He studied with Hummel in Weimar (1825–7), spent periods in Paris and Italy before returning permanently to Germany in 1842, and was then conductor in Leipzig (1843–4), Dresden (1844–7), Düsseldorf (1847–50) and Cologne (1850–84).

Hiller, Johann Adam (b. Wendisch-Ossig, near Görlitz, 25 Dec 1728; d. Leipzig, 16 Jun 1804). German composer, especially of modest works sparked by French and Italian comic opera, but he was also an all-round musician essential to Leipzig's musical life in the second half of the 18th century. He studied law at Leipzig University, and from 1758 was active in the city as composer, concert organizer, conductor, teacher and musical journalist (being founder editor of, and a major contributor to, the *Wöchentliche Nachrichten*). He conducted the Gewandhaus concerts (1781–5) and from 1789 was cantor of St Thomas's.

Hiller, Lejaren (Arthur) (b. New York, 23 Feb 1924; d. Buffalo, 26 Jan 1994). US composer, notably of the first score generated with computer aid, the *ILLIAC Suite* for string quartet (1957), which he created with the assistance of Leonard Isaacson and renamed the fourth of his seven quartets. He had lessons with Sessions and Babbitt while studying chemistry at Princeton, and produced his epochal piece while working in the chemistry department at the University of Illinois (1952–68). Later he was professor of composition at Buffalo. Besides various theatrical and concert works, he helped introduce Cage to computer music as collaborator on HPSCHD (1967–9).

Hilliard Ensemble. British vocal group founded in 1973 by the bass Paul Hillier in honour of his near-namesake, the miniaturist Nicholas Hilliard, and generally working as a quartet of men's voices with the countertenor David James on the top line. Besides medieval and Renaissance music, its repertory includes numerous commissions.

Hindemith, Paul (b. Hanau, near Frankfurt, 16 Nov 1895; d. Frankfurt, 28 Dec 1963). German composer. Coming to maturity during the First World War, he caught the close of pre-war expressionism, and it stayed with him, but much more important was the neoclassicism he helped form after the war. For him the return to the 18th century was not just stylistic: what he exemplified, with formidable energy, was a revival of the composer as supplier, providing music for all occasions and purposes. When his endeavours for a socially useful, instructive and constructive music were disrupted by Nazism, his search for reintegration brought him back towards symphonic continuity and tonality.

Strongly encouraged by his father, he was studying violin with Adolf Rebner at the Hoch Conservatory in Frankfurt in his early teens, and from 1912 had composition lessons there from Arnold Mendelssohn (a great-nephew of the composer) and Bernhard Sekles. In 1914 he joined the Frankfurt opera orchestra; he also played in Rebner's quartet. He returned to both positions after army service (1917–18), but now playing viola – increasingly his preferred instrument – in the quartet. There were also changes in his compositional style, from late Romanticism to an expressionism voiced in a hectic succession of stage pieces, and, almost immediately, to his own kind of neoclassicism, marked by vigorous, dissonant counterpoint and compact forms, often Baroque-like in their fugal or dance characters. The term 'Hindemithian' generally denotes this style, found in such works of the early 1920s as his Third and Fourth quartets, first solo string sonatas, *Kammermusik* No.1 and song cycle *Das Marienleben*. Rapidly making his mark, he was able to leave the opera orchestra in 1923 to concentrate on his work as a composer, as violist of the Amar Quartet and as a director of the Donaueschingen Festival. The next year he married.

While paralleling Stravinsky's, his neoclassicism was fuelled more by the German aesthetic of NEUE SACHLICHKEIT (new objectivity) and by his own intent to be useful. 'The composer today,' he averred in 1927, 'should write only if he knows for what purpose he is writing.' And his own purposes were many: bringing new objectivity to the opera house in *Cardillac* (1925–6), creating a set of modern Brandenburg concertos in his *Kammermusik* series (1922–7); or advancing GEBRAUCHS-MUSIK (utility music) – music made for contemporary media and social situations. He wrote scores for radio and films; he experimented with mechanical keyboard instruments, with the trautonium and with manipulating sounds on gramophone records; and he produced quantities of music for amateur choirs and chamber ensembles.

In 1927 he began teaching at the conservatory in Berlin, where he was briefly attracted to the socialism of Weill, Eisler and Brecht, before coming to place his faith more in art than politics. The arrival of the Nazis in 1933, however, forced politics upon him. He made a grim, finally glowing assertion of art as the artist's first duty in his opera *Mathis der Maler* (1933–5), but his work was attacked in Germany, then banned, and from 1936 onwards he spent long periods outside the country, eventually emigrating to the USA in 1940.

There he took up his teaching career at Yale (1940–53), while also becoming a useful composer in US terms through his renewed interest in the symphony orchestra. At the same time he added to his collection of sonatas, covering most of the standard instruments, and continued work on the harmonic theory that underpinned all his later

music. While he recognized a continuum through the intervals from the most consonant (octave) to the most dissonant (minor second/major seventh), and while he also embraced a generous variety of chords, his music from *Mathis* onwards was more tonally centred and diatonic, and he even adapted some of his most trenchant works of the 1920s (such as *Cardillac*) to his new manner.

After the war he made return visits to Europe and began a new career as a conductor. He settled definitively in Switzerland in 1953.

Paul Hindemith *A Composer's World* (1952); Geoffrey Skelton *Paul Hindemith* (1975)

www.hindemith.org

Dramatic, orchestral and vocal music

Operas (full-length): CARDILLAC, Op.39, 1925–6, rev 1952; *Neues vom Tage* (Marcellus Schiffer), 1928–9, f.p. Berlin, 1929, rev 1953–4; MATHIS DER MALER, 1933–5; *Die* HARMONIE DER WELT, 1956–7

Operas (1 act): *Mörder, Hoffnung der Frauen* (Kokoschka), Op.12, 1919, f.p. Stuttgart, 1921; *Das Nusch-Nuschi* (Franz Blei), Op.20, 1920, f.p. Stuttgart, 1921; *Sancta Susanna* (Stramm), Op.21, 1921, f.p. Frankfurt, 1922; *Hin und zurück* (Schiffer), Op.45a, 1927, f.p. Baden-Baden, 1927; *Wir bauen eine Stadt* (children's opera; Robert Seitz), 1930; *Das lange Weihnachtsmahl* (Thornton Wilder), 1960–61, f.p. Mannheim, 1961

Orchestral (without soloists): *Lustige Sinfonietta* (Morgenstern), Op.4, with narrator, 1916; *Nusch-Nuschi-Tänze*, 1921; *Rag Time*, 1921; *Der Dämon*, Op.28 (ballet), 1922; Concerto for Orchestra, Op.38, 1925; *Konzertmusik*, Op.41, military band, 1926; *Konzertmusik*, Op.50, brass, str, 1930; *Philharmonisches Konzert*, 1932; Symphony 'MATHIS DER MALER', 1933–4; *Symphonische Tänze*, 1937; *Nobilissima visione* (ballet), 1938; Symphony, E♭, 1940; *Amor und Psyche* (ballet overture), 1943; SYMPHONIC METAMORPHOSIS ON THEMES BY CARL MARIA VON WEBER, 1943; *Hérodiade* (ballet; after Mallarmé), 1944; *Symphonia serena*, 1946; Sinfonietta, E, 1949–50; Symphony 'Die HARMONIE DER WELT', 1951; Pittsburgh Symphony, 1958; radio and film scores, etc.

Orchestral (with soloists): Cello Concerto, E♭, Op.3, 1915–16; *Klaviermusik mit Orchester*, Op.29, pf left hand, orch, 1923; *Konzertmusik*, Op.48, va, small orch, 1930; *Konzertmusik*, Op.49, pf, brass, 2 hp, 1930; *Konzertstück*, trautonium, str, 1931; *Der Schwanendreher*, va, small orch, 1935; *Trauermusik*, va/vn/vc, str, 1936; Violin Concerto, 1939; Cello Concerto, 1940; *The* FOUR TEMPERAMENTS, str, pf, 1940; Piano Concerto, 1945; Clarinet Concerto, 1947; Concerto, woodwind quartet, hp, orch, 1949; Horn Concerto, 1949; Concerto, tpt, bn, str, 1949–52; Organ Concerto, 1962–3

Kammermusik series: No.1, Op.24a, ens, 1922; No.2, Op.36:1, pf, ens, 1924; No.3, Op.36:2, vc, ens, 1925; No.4, Op.36:3, vn, small orch, 1925; No.5, Op.36:4, va, small orch, 1927; No.6, Op.46:1, va d'amore, ens, 1927; No.7, Op.46:2, org, ens, 1927

Choral: *Das Unaufhörliche* (oratorio; Gottfried Benn), s, t, bar, b, ch, orch, 1931; WHEN LILACS LAST IN THE DOORYARD BLOOM'D, mez, bar, ch, orch, 1946; *Ite angeli veloces* (cantata; Claudel), a, t, ch, audience, orch, 1953–5; Mass, ch, 1963; etc.

Songs: *Die junge Magd* (6; Trakl), Op.23:2, a, fl, cl, str qt, 1922; *Das Marienleben* (15; Rilke), Op.27, s, pf, 1922–3, rev 1935–48; etc.

Chamber and instrumental music

String quartets: No.1, C, Op.2, 1915; No.2, F minor, Op.10, 1918; No.3, Op.16, 1920; No.4, Op.22, 1921; No.5, Op.32, 1923; No.6, E♭, 1943; No.7, E♭, 1945

Other chamber works: Octet, cl, hn, bn, 2 va, vc, db, 1957–8; Septet, fl, ob, cl, tpt, b cl, hn, bn, 1948; Clarinet Quintet, Op.30, 1923, rev 1955; *Kleine Kammermusik*, Op.24:2, wind qnt, 1922; *Morgenmusik*, brass qnt, 1932; Quartet, cl, vn, vc, pf, 1938; Sonata, 4 hn, 1952; String Trio No.1, Op.34, 1923; No.2, 1933; Trio, va, heckelphone, pf, Op.47, 1928; etc.

Duo sonatas with piano: vn, E♭, Op.11:1, 1918; vn, D, Op.11:2, 1918; vn, E, 1935; vn, C, 1939; va, Op.11:4, 1919; va, Op.25:4, 1922; va, 1939; *Kleine Sonate*, va d'amore, Op.25:2, 1922; vc, Op.11:3, 1919; vc, 1948; db, 1949; fl, 1936; ob, 1938; cor anglais, 1941; cl, 1939; a sax/hn, 1943; bn, 1938; hn, 1939; tpt, 1939; trbn, 1941; tuba, 1955

Solo string sonatas: vn, G minor, Op.11:6, 1917; vn, Op.31:1, 1924; vn, Op.31:2, 1924; va, Op.11:5, 1919; va, Op.25:1, 1922; va, Op.31:4, 1923; va, 1937; vc, Op.25:3, 1923

Piano: Suite '1922', Op.26, 1922; Sonatas Nos.1–3, A, G, B♭, 1936; Sonata, duet, 1938; *Ludus tonalis*, 1942; Sonata, 2 pf, 1942; etc.

Organ: Sonatas Nos.1–2, 1937; No.3 'nach alten Volksliedern', 1940

Other works: *A frog he went a-courting*, variations, vc, pf, 1941; 8 Pieces, fl, 1927; Harp Sonata, 1939; pieces for mechanical and electronic instruments; etc.

Hinstrich (Ger.). Upbow on cello/bass.

Hippolyte et Aricie. Opera by Rameau to a libretto by Simon-Joseph Pellegrin after the Phaedra plays of Euripides, Seneca and Racine. Theseus (bass) returns from a heroic mission in the underworld to find his wife Phaedra (soprano), desperately and hopelessly in love with his son, Hippolytus (haute-contre). Phaedra's death and Theseus's near-suicide are not expunged from memory by the happy ending in which Hippolytus is united with his beloved Aricia (soprano). First performance: Paris, 1 Oct 1733.

Hirt auf dem Felsen, Der (The Shepherd on the Rock). Song by Schubert to words by Wilhelm Müller with additional lines by Helmina von Chezy, written for Anna Milder-Hauptmann to sing with piano and obbligato clarinet. The shepherd calls forlornly and then with expectant joy to his distant beloved.

His (Ger.). B♯. Also *Hisis* (B✗).

Histoire du soldat (The Soldier's Tale). Play by C.F. Ramuz with music by Stravinsky for septet (vn, cl, cornet, trbn, bn, db, perc). Based on Russian folktales, with echoes also of the Faust and Orpheus myths, it concerns a trusting soldier to whose violin (soul) the Devil helps himself. The composer made a suite, and also a five-movement selection for violin, clarinet and piano. First performance: Lausanne, 28 Sep 1918.

historically informed. Term that superseded 'authentic' in the 1990s as the claim made by musicians performing with full regard for the instruments, notational conventions and other conditions of the music's time. See also AUTHENTICITY; EARLY MUSIC.

history. The task of music history is to draw a coherent narrative from the multifarious evidences of compositions, documented musical life and composers' biographies. Since such evidences are far more abundant for Western music than for any other, music history is essentially the history of a European-based TRADITION, to use a common term, but one loaded with implications of continuity within limits. Often the historical narrative will imply a notion of progress, whether impelled by aesthetic or social-economic forces, but historians, as students of the past, will naturally have a fondness for the old as well as a desire to explain how it turned into the new. One outcome of this tension was, by the late 19th century, the notion of PERIOD, which allowed past epochs to be valued in their own terms.

Music histories were written in German (Wolfgang Caspar Printz, 1690), Italian (Bontempi, 1695) and French (Pierre Michon Bonnet-Bourdelot, 1715) before the earliest examples in English (Hawkins, 1776; Burney, 1776–89). The later history of music history includes the works of Forkel (1788–1801), Adolf Bernhard Marx (1855), August Wilhelm Ambros (1962–8), Fétis (1869–76), Riemann (1903–13), Paul Henry Lang (1941), Grout and Dahlhaus.

hitch pin. Pin on a harp or keyboard instrument securing a string at the other end from the WREST PIN.

hmnm. Abbreviation for harmonium.

hn. Abbreviation for horn.

Hoboken, Anthony van (b. Rotterdam, 23 Mar 1887; d. Zurich, 1 Nov 1983). Dutch cataloguer of Haydn's works. He studied at the Hoch Conservatory in Frankfurt (1911) and with Schenker in Vienna (1925–34), and formed an important collection of early editions, besides preparing the definitive Haydn catalogue.

hocket. Medieval technique of breaking a contrapuntal line with a short silence, after which the line is resumed by another voice; alternatively, a composition using this technique, which was common in the 13th and 14th centuries. The term is cognate with 'hiccup', and that can indeed be the effect: the music moves in fits and starts.

Hoddinott, Alun (b. Bargoed, Glam., 11 Aug 1929). Welsh composer, who exhibits a forceful, highly chromatic but essentially tonal style in a large output that includes 10 symphonies, operas, much choral music, 12 piano sonatas and chamber pieces of many kinds. He studied at University College, Cardiff, and in London with Benjamin. In 1959 he returned to his college (later Cardiff University) as lecturer, and in 1987 he retired after 20 years there as professor.

hoedown. US dance in duple time, instanced in Copland's *Rodeo*.

Hofer, Josepha. See Josepha WEBER.

Høffding, (Niels) Finn (b. Copenhagen, 10 Mar 1899; d. Copenhagen, 3 Mar 1997). Danish composer, of the post-Nielsen school. He studied with Nielsen's pupil Knud Jeppesen in Copenhagen and Joseph Marx in Vienna (1922–3), and wrote an opera after Andersen's *The Emperor's New Clothes* (f.p. Copenhagen, 1926), orchestral pieces and numerous choral works.

Hoffmann, E(rnst) T(heodor) A(madeus) (b. Königsberg, now Kaliningrad, 24 Jan 1776; d. Berlin, 25 Jun 1822). German writer, composer and critic, important as a stimulator, exemplar and proponent of Romanticism in its first phase. His fantastic tales spurred composers as diverse as Schumann (*Kreisleriana*) and Offenbach (*Les Contes d'Hoffmann*), while his 1810 review of Beethoven's Fifth Symphony was enormously influential in forming a view of the composer as a heroic genius communicating from 'the wondrous realm of the Infinite'. He had a musical training while studying law in Königsberg (1792–5), and his work as a practising lawyer was eventually swamped by writing and composing. His compositions, suggesting his idealization of Mozart,

include the opera UNDINE, other theatre scores, sacred music and chamber pieces.

Hoffmeister, Franz Anton (b. Rothenburg am Neckar, 12 May 1754; d. Vienna, 9 Feb 1812). Austrian composer and publisher, resident in Vienna from 1768 and vigorous in the music business after completing legal training. During his time as a publisher (1784–1806) he brought out works by Haydn, Mozart (a friend, who supplied him with, among other compositions, the K.499 quartet sometimes known as the 'Hoffmeister') and Beethoven. His own works include symphonies, concertos, chamber pieces and operas.

Hoffnung, Gerard (b. Berlin, 22 Mar 1925; d. London, 28 Sep 1959). German–British humorist, known for musical cartoons and for the 'Hoffnung Music Festivals' of spoofs and jokes he organized from 1956.

Hoffstetter, Roman (b. Laudenbach, near Bad Mergentheim, 4 Apr 1742; d. Miltenberg, 21 Jun 1812). German composer, most notably of a set of quartets (Op.3) long attributed to Haydn, No.5 being the popular 'Serenade' Quartet. He was a Benedictine monk at Amorbach, and author of other quartets and masses in Haydnesque style.

Hofhaimer, Paul (b. Radstadt, 25 Jan 1459; d. Salzburg, 1537). Austrian organist-composer, much famed in his time. He joined the ducal court at Innsbruck in 1478, served Emperor Maximilian I intermittently (1489–1519) and ended his career as cathedral and archiepiscopal organist in Salzburg. Of his works, all that survive are a published volume of German polyphonic songs and a few organ pieces.

Hofkapelle (Ger.). Court CHAPEL.

Hofmann, Josef (Casimir) (b. Krákow, 20 Jan 1876; d. Los Angeles, 16 Feb 1957). Polish–US pianist. He was among the first musicians to record (at Edison's laboratory in 1887), was vastly admired (especially in Chopin), interested himself in technology (holding patents in car and piano design) but recorded little in his maturity. Promoted by his pianist father as a prodigy in Europe (from 1883) and the USA (1887), he retired for further study with Anton Rubinstein (1892–4). Rachmaninoff's Third Concerto was dedicated to him, though he never played it in public. He was also director of Curtis (1926–38), and wrote five concertos, among other works for his instrument.

Hofmann, Leopold (b. Vienna, 14 Aug 1738; d.

Vienna, 17 Mar 1793). Austrian composer, close in style to Haydn, who disliked him. Active from his youth as a violinist, organist and composer, he spent his last decade in comfortable retirement. He is credited with the slow introduction as a symphonic device. Apart from more than 40 symphonies, he also wrote concertos for flute, cello, violin and harpsichord, church music and chamber pieces.

Hofmannsthal, Hugo von (b. Vienna, 1 Feb 1874; d. Vienna, 15 Jul 1929). Austrian poet and dramatist, and one of the great librettists. Born into a cultivated Viennese family, he had made a reputation for himself as a poet by his late teens and then turned to the theatre. In 1900 he offered Strauss a ballet scenario, *Der Triumph der Zeit*, but Strauss declined it and the music was composed by Zemlinsky. Strauss then initiated their collaboration in 1906 by asking to set the *Elektra* he had written as a play in 1903; after that they proceeded to *Der Rosenkavalier*, *Ariadne auf Naxos*, *Die Frau ohne Schatten* and *Die ägyptische Helena*. *Arabella* and *Die Liebe der Danae* were completed by Strauss after his colleague's death with the help of other writers. The libretto of *Der Rosenkavalier*, with its wealth of character and incident and its consistent lyric spirit, justifies the comparisons it evokes with Da Ponte's librettos for Mozart.

Hofoper (Ger.). Court opera. In many German cities and in Vienna the opera was a court institution until the collapse of the monarchies after the First World War.

Hogwood, Christopher (Jarvis Haley) (b. Nottingham, 10 Sep 1941). British conductor, founder of the Academy of Ancient Music (1973). He studied at Cambridge and was a founder member of the Early Music Consort.

Hoher Bass (Ger.). High bass; Wagner's term for the voice type required for such roles as Wotan, more commonly known as bass-baritone.

Hohner. German firm known for harmonicas, accordions, melodicas and other instruments. It was founded in Trossingen in 1857 by Mattias Hohner (1833–1903).

Hoiby, Lee (b. Madison, Wis., 17 Feb 1926). US composer, especially of operas, songs and choral music in a lyrical Romantic vein. He studied for a career as a pianist, but was turned towards composition by lessons with Menotti at Curtis (1949–52).

Holberg Suite (*From Holberg's Time*). Work by Grieg for piano or string orchestra, written to mark the bicentenary of the Norwegian dramatist Ludvig Holberg (1684–1754), whose time was almost coterminous with Bach's; hence the movements Präludium, Sarabande, Gavotte, Air and Rigaudon.

Holborne, Antony (b. ?c.1545; d. c.30 Nov 1602). English composer of music for lute, bandora and consort, associated with prominent courtiers from the 1580s. Among his most popular pieces now are almains (*The Honeysuckle, Night Watch*), galliards and corantos.

Holbrooke, Joseph (Charles) (b. Croydon, 5 Jul 1878; d. London, 5 Aug 1958). British composer in a richly pictorial-descriptive Romantic idiom. He studied at the RAM and made his reputation with his symphonic poem *The Raven* (1900), after Poe, a favourite writer. From 1908 he enjoyed the patronage of Lord Howard de Walden, who provided him with librettos for a trilogy of operas based on the *Mabinogion*: *The Children of Don* (1912), *Dylan* (1910) and *Bronwen* (1920), known collectively as *The Cauldron of Annwn*. He also wrote five symphonies, numerous concertos and chamber music.

Hölderlin, (Johann Christian) Friedrich (b. Lauffen am Neckar, 20 Mar 1770; d. Tübingen, 7 Jun 1843). German poet. Born in the same year as Beethoven, he was more important to later generations for his closeness both to the ancient Greeks and to madness; he spent the second half of his life in an asylum. Composers to set his poetry have included Brahms, Strauss, Henze, Maderna, Holliger, Ligeti and Kurtág.

Holewa, Hans (b. Vienna, 16 May 1905; d. Stockholm, 26 Apr 1991). Austrian–Swedish composer, applying serialism with abstract rigour. He studied at the Vienna Academy and moved to Sweden in 1937, but had little success there as a composer until he was in his mid 50s. Most of his works, including his three piano concertos and many chamber pieces, come from after this breakthrough.

Holidays. See NEW ENGLAND HOLIDAYS.

Holland Festival. Annual summer festival instituted in 1948, especially active in promoting new music and dance in the major Dutch cities.

Höller, York (b. Leverkusen, 11 Jan 1944). German composer, master of a commanding language with avant-garde roots. He studied with Zimmermann and Eimert in Cologne (1963–7), and worked on electronic projects at the studios of both Stockhausen and Boulez. His works include *Arcus* for ensemble and tape (1978), one of IRCAM's early successes, and the opera *Der Meister und Margarita* (f.p. Paris, 1989).

Holliger, Heinz (b. Langenthal, 21 May 1939). Swiss composer and oboist, the outstanding oboist of his time and a composer of intense expressivity and exactitude. He studied in Berne with Emile Cassagnaud (oboe, 1950–58) and Veress (composition, 1956–60), in Paris with Pierre Pierlot (oboe, 1958–9), and in Basle with Boulez (composition, 1961–3). Remarkable as an oboist for his acute musicality, address and range of sound, he began an international career in the early 1960s, playing 18th-century music and new pieces, including solo works for him by Stockhausen, Berio and Carter, and double concertos for him and his wife, the harpist Ursula Holliger, by Henze, Lutosławski, Schnittke and Martin. Since 1965 he has taught at the conservatory in Freiburg.

As a composer he moved forward at first more slowly, absorbing the lessons of his teachers (the oboe concerto *Siebengesang* moves through Boulezian sound worlds of delicate harmony and rippling percussion), of the Second Viennese School (Berg in particular) and of favourite writers (Trakl especially). In the early 1970s he came close to Kagel and Lachenmann in exploring instrumental theatre (*Cardiophonie*) and marginal sounds, and his subsequent progress has been to restore lively inventiveness, and even humour, without betraying the ashen sensibility he had achieved in the intellectual company of Beckett, Hölderlin and Robert Walser.

Stage: *Come and Go* (Beckett), 9 s, 9 insts, 1976–7; *Not I* (Beckett), s, tape, 1978–80; *What Where*, 4 male v, 4 trbn, perc, tape (Beckett), 1988; SCHNEEWITTCHEN, 1997–8; etc.
Orchestral: *Siebengesang*, ob, orch, 7 women's v, 1966–7; *Zwei Liszt-Transkriptionen*, 1986; Violin Concerto, 1993–5; *Recicanto*, va, chbr orch, 2000–2001; *ConcErto? … cErtO!*, 2001; etc.
Choral: *Psalm* (Celan), ch, 1971; SCARDANELLI-ZYKLUS (Hölderlin), ch, fl, chbr orch, tape, 1975–91; etc.
Chamber and instrumental: *Sequenzen über Johannes I,32*, hp, 1962; *Cardiophonie*, ob, elec, 1971; String Quartet, 1973; *Trema*, va/vc/vn, 1981–3; *Lieder ohne Worte I–II*, vn, pf, 1982–3, 1985–94; *Praeludium, Arioso und Passacaglia*, hp, 1987; Quintet, pf, wind, 1989; *Beiseit* (Walser), ct, cl, acc, db, 1990–91; Partita, pf, 1999

Holloway, Robin (Greville) (b. Leamington Spa, 19 Oct 1943). British composer, of Protean variety: rhapsodist-constructivist, Romantic-modernist, at once impatient of and besotted with the past. He studied privately with Goehr (1959–63), at Cambridge (1961–4) and at Oxford (1965–7), and returned to Cambridge as a research fellow in 1969, gaining a position as lecturer in 1975. Two works after Schumann brought him attention for what was a provocative allegiance in the very early 1970s: the orchestral *Scenes* and smaller Fantasy-Pieces. But his range of resource soon proved to be immense, stirring increasing puzzlement at a creative persona seemingly in perpetual dissolve yet acting with complete assurance and perspicacity.

Orchestral: Concerto for Orchestra No.1, Op.8, 1966–9; No.2, Op.40, 1978–9; No.3, Op.80, 1981–94; *Scenes from Schumann*, Op.13, 1970, rev 1986; *Sea Surface full of Clouds* (Wallace Stevens), Op.28, soli, ch, chbr orch, 1974–5; Symphony, Op.88, 1998–9; etc.
Chamber and instrumental: Fantasy-Pieces, Op.16, 13 insts, 1971; *Gilded Goldbergs*, Op.86, 2 pf, 1992–7; etc.
Other works: operas, oratorios, choral music, song cycles

Holmboe, Vagn (Gylding) (b. Horsens, 20 Dec 1909; d. Ramløse, 1 Sep 1996). Danish composer, prolific in a sturdy, contrapuntal, tonal idiom guided by Nielsen, Sibelius and Stravinsky. His works include 13 numbered symphonies, 13 chamber concertos, numerous concertos with full orchestra and 21 numbered string quartets, besides much choral music. He studied at the Copenhagen Conservatory with Knud Jeppesen and Høffding from 1926, then briefly in Berlin with Toch. Back in Copenhagen he worked as a critic and teacher, at the Blind Institute and the conservatory (1950–65), before retiring on a state pension to his lakeside house in the north.

Holmès, Augusta (b. Paris, 16 Dec 1847; d. Paris, 28 Jan 1903). French composer of Irish parentage (though reputedly the natural child of the poet Alfred de Vigny). Brought up and trained in Versailles, she moved to Paris in her mid-20s and joined Franck's circle. She also took up with the writer Catulle Mendès, with whom she lived for 20 years and had five children. Her works include operas, choral orchestral pieces and songs.

Holst, Gustav(us Theodore von) (b. Cheltenham, 21 Sep 1874; d. London, 25 May 1934). British composer, whose other works – studies in Englishness, Indianism and the neoclassic – have been far outshone in popularity by *The Planets*. Born into a cultured family of German paternal ancestry, he studied with Stanford and Parry at the RCM (1893–8), where he began a lifelong friendship with Vaughan Williams. He earned his living as an orchestral trombonist until 1903, and then as a teacher, notably as music director of St Paul's Girls' School in Hammersmith (1905–34) and Morley College (1907–24). Much of the music he produced before his early 30s was never published. Liberation from confusion and Wagnerism came through diverse impulses, including Debussy, Strauss, British folksong and ancient Indian culture (he made some studies of Sanskrit), and his output was to remain correspondingly multiform. His Op.29, for example, includes both the 'oriental suite' *Beni Mora* (1909–10), product of a holiday in Algeria, and the spruce, very English St Paul's Suite for strings (1912–13). Other works of this period, notably the chamber opera *Sāvitri*, evoke ancient India with unusual spareness. The further influence of early Stravinsky made possible *The Planets*, but he continued to explore various possibilities: ecstatic spirituality in *The Hymn of Jesus*, comic opera, and a magical bleakness in *Egdon Heath*. His daughter, Imogen (1907–84), was a conductor, composer and joint director of the Aldeburgh Festival.

Michael Short *Gustav Holst* (1990)

Operas (all 1 act): *Sāvitri* (Holst, after the *Mahābhārata*), Op.25, 1908; *The Perfect Fool* (Holst), Op.39, 1918–22; *At the Boar's Head* (Holst, after Shakespeare), Op.42, 1924; *The Wandering Scholar* (Clifford Bax), Op.50, 1929–30

Choral ballets: *The Golden Goose*, Op.45:1, 1926; *The Morning of the Year*, Op.45:2, 1926–7

Orchestral: *A Somerset Rhapsody*, Op.21:2, 1906–7; Suites Nos.1–2, E♭, F, Op.28, military band, 1909, 1911; *Beni Mora*, Op.29:1, 1909–10; St Paul's Suite, Op.29:2, str, 1912–13; *The* PLANETS, Op.32, 1914–16; A Fugal Overture, Op.40:1, 1922; A Fugal Concerto, Op.40:2, fl, ob, str, 1923; *Egdon Heath*, Op.47, 1927; *A Moorside Suite*, brass band, 1928; Double Violin Concerto, Op.49, 1929; Prelude and Scherzo 'Hammersmith', Op.52, military band, 1930; Brook Green Suite, str, 1933; Lyric Movement, va, chbr orch, 1933; etc.

Vocal orchestral: *The Mystic Trumpeter* (Whitman), Op.18, s, orch, 1904, rev 1912; Choral Hymns from the Rig Veda (4 groups), Op.26, ch, orch, 1908–12; *The Cloud Messenger* (Kálidása), Op.30, ch, orch, 1909–10; *Christmas Day*, ch, orch, 1910; *Hecuba's Lament*, Op.31:1, a, women's ch, orch, 1911; *Hymn to Dionysus*, Op.31:2, women's ch, orch, 1913; *A Dirge for Two Veterans* (Whitman), men's ch, brass, perc, 1914; *The Hymn of Jesus* (Acts of John), Op.37, ch, orch, 1917; *Ode to Death* (Whitman), Op.38, ch, orch, 1919; *I vow to thee, my country* (Cecil Spring Rice), ch, orch, c.1921 (after *Jupiter* from *The Planets*); First Choral Symphony (Keats), Op.41, s, ch, orch, 1923–4; A Choral Fantasia (Bridges), Op.51, s, ch, orch, 1930; etc.

Smaller choral works: *Ave Maria*, Op.9b, women's ch, 1900; *In the bleak midwinter*, ch, org, 1904/5; *Nunc dimittis*, ch, 1915; *Personent hodie*, ch, ?1916–17; *Lullay my liking*, Op.34:2, s, ch, 1916; *The Evening-Watch* (Henry Vaughan), Op.43:1, ch, 1924; other carol and folksong arrs, partsongs, etc.

Other works: 12 Songs (Humbert Wolfe), Op.48, 1929; other songs, chamber music

Hölszky, Adriana (b. Bucharest, 30 Jun 1953). Romanian composer of Austro-German parentage, a proponent of latterday expressionism. She studied with Niculescu at the Bucharest Conservatory (1972–5) and moved with her family to Germany in 1976, where she has held teaching posts at the conservatories in Stuttgart (1980–89) and Rostock (from 1997). Her works include the opera *Bremer Freiheit* (f.p. Stuttgart, 1988).

Holt, Simeon ten (b. Bergen, North Holland, 24 Jan 1923). Dutch pianist-composer, notably of minimalist pieces for multiple pianos, beginning with *Canto ostinato* (1976–9). He studied in his home town with Jakob van Domselaer, who had been close to Mondrian, and in Paris with Honegger and Milhaud (1949–54), and had an earlier avant-garde phase.

Holt, Simon (b. Bolton, 21 Feb 1958). British composer, whose works are often imaginative, precise and secure journeys through dark and threatening landscapes, echoing with forebears as diverse as Birtwistle and Feldman. He studied with Anthony Gilbert at the RNCM (1978–82) and made his mark early with *Kites* for the London Sinfonietta (1983). Several of his pieces, including his opera *The Nightingale's to Blame* (f.p. Huddersfield, 1998), are based on Lorca.

Holz (Ger.). Wood; hence *Holzblasinstrumente* (woodwinds), *Holzblock* (woodblock), *Holzharmonika* (xylophone), *Holzklapper* (whip), *Holztrompete* (wooden trumpet, or alphorn), etc.

Holzbauer, Ignaz (Jakob) (b. Vienna, 17 Sep 1711; d. Mannheim, 7 Apr 1783). Austrian composer, active in Mannheim as theatre kapellmeister (1753–78). Before that he had periods in Vienna and Italy. He wrote operas, sacred music, symphonies, concertos and chamber music.

Holzmair, Wolfgang (b. Vöcklabruch, 14 Apr 1952). Austrian baritone, whose lightness and grain convey a confiding persona, admirably suited to lieder. He studied at the Vienna Music Academy and moved to the forefront internationally in the mid-1980s.

Homme armé, L' (The Armed Man). 15th-century song with enigmatic words: 'The armed man is to be feared: the cry goes out all over. Everyone should put on a hauberk of mail.' Whether by reason of this text (which has been variously interpreted as a crusading call or as a warning of Christ's coming), of its robust musical line or of symbolic and numerological connections with the labyrinth, the melody gave rise to a whole tradition of mass settings, by composers including Busnois, Du Fay, Ockeghem, Obrecht, Josquin, La Rue, Carver, Morales, Guerrero and Palestrina, with later echoes in Carissimi and Davies.

homophonic. Exemplifying HOMOPHONY.

homophony. The movement of parts together in chords, as distinct from POLYPHONY, which normally implies some differentiation of the parts in rhythm and phrasing. Textures of melody with chordal accompaniment may also be described as homophonic.

homorhythm. Sameness of rhythm in all parts, a condition of homophony in the strict sense.

Homs (Oller), Joaquim (b. Barcelona, 21 Aug 1906; d. Barcelona, 9 Sep 2003). Catalan composer, a modernist who studied with Gerhard (1931–8) after training as an engineer and cellist.

Honegger, Arthur (Oscar) (b. Le Havre, 10 Mar 1892; d. Paris, 27 Nov 1955). Swiss composer, a serious-minded artist who applied himself diligently to new media (films, radio), developed a strong contrapuntal energy to motivate dissonant – if still tonal – harmony, and addressed moral questions in his oratorios and symphonies. Brought up in Le Havre, where his parents belonged to the Swiss Protestant colony, he studied at the Zurich Conservatory (1909–11) and with Gédalge, Widor and d'Indy at the Paris Conservatoire (1911–18). When his parents returned to Switzerland, he stayed in Montmartre, though he developed contacts with Swiss writers and institutions, and indeed these produced his first big success, *Le Roi David* (1921–3), a characteristic junction of Bach, Stravinsky and dense chords – the same heavy and effective machinery found in *Pacific 231* (1923), which consolidated his reputation. Around the same time he was caught up in Les Six, though he distanced himself from the group's sporting with triviality. He had an affair with the mezzo-soprano Claire Croiza, for whom he wrote the title role in *Judith* and other works; then in 1926 he married Andrée Vaurabourg, a pianist and teacher. The surprise triumph in 1930

of an operetta, *Les Aventures du roi Pausole*, helped his finances, but he showed his awareness of the wider desperations of the time in his oratorio *Cris du monde*. From 1934 to the end of the Second World War he was regularly involved with films, while working on *Jeanne d'Arc* and other parables of resistance. After his Second Symphony he produced little in occupied Paris, returning then to full creative vigour in three further symphonies before his heart condition began to worsen.

Arthur Honegger *I am a Composer* (1946); Harry Halbreich *Arthur Honegger* (1999)

www.arthur-honegger.com

Operas: *Antigone* (Cocteau, after Sophocles), 1924–7; *Les Aventures du roi Pausole* (operetta; Arthur Willemetz, after Pierre Louÿs), 1929–30; etc.

Ballets: *Le Dit des jeux du monde*, ens, 1918; *Horace victorieux*, orch, 1920–21; *Skating Rink*, orch, 1921–2; *Amphion* (Valéry), soli, ch, orch, 1929; *Sémiramis* (Valéry), soli, ch, orch, 1933–4; *Le Cantique des cantiques*, soli, ch, orch, 1936–7; etc.

Orchestral: Symphony No.1, 1929–30; No.2, str, tpt ad lib, 1940–41; No.3 'Liturgique', 1945–6; No.4 'Deliciae basiliensis', 1946; No.5 'Di tre re', 1950; *Pastorale d'été*, 1920; *Pacific 231* (MOUVEMENT SYMPHONIQUE No.1), 1923; Piano Concertino, 1924; *Rugby* (MOUVEMENT SYMPHONIQUE No.2), 1928; Cello Concerto, 1929; MOUVEMENT SYMPHONIQUE No.3, 1932–3; *Concerto da camera*, fl, cor anglais, str, 1948; *Monopartita*, 1951; etc.

Film scores: *Napoléon*, 1926–7; *Les Misérables*, 1933–4; *Regain*, 1937; *Mermoz*, 1943; etc.

Incidental music: *La Tempête* (theatre), 1923–9; *Christophe Colomb* (radio), 1940; etc.

Choral: *Le ROI DAVID*, 1921–3; *Judith* (oratorio; Morax), 1927; *Cris du monde* (oratorio; René Bizet), 1930–31; *Jeanne d'Arc au bûcher* (JOAN OF ARC at the Stake), 1935; *La Danse des morts* (cantata; Claudel), 1938; *Une Cantate de Noël*, bar, ch, org, 1952–3; etc.

Chamber and instrumental: String Quartet No.1, 1916–17; No.2, 1934–6; No.3, 1936–7; Violin Sonata No.1, C♯ minor, 1916–18; No.2, B, 1919; Cello Sonata, D minor, 1920; Viola Sonata, 1920; *Danse de la chèvre*, fl, 1921; Clarinet Sonatina, 1921–2; *Prélude, arioso et fughette sur le nom de BACH*, pf, 1932; Solo Violin Sonata, D minor, 1940; *Intrada*, tpt, pf, 1947; *Romance*, fl, pf, 1952/3; etc.

Songs: *Six poèmes* (Apollinaire), 1915–17; *Six poésies* (Cocteau), 1920–23; *Trois poèmes* (Claudel), 1939–40; *Trois psaumes*, 1940–41; etc.

Hopkins, Bill [George William] (b. Prestbury, Ches., 5 Jun 1943; d. Newcastle upon Tyne, 10 Mar 1981). British composer, who, like his teacher Barraqué, sought an expressive truth that could withstand the storms of time. His studies with Barraqué (1965) followed tuition at Oxford (1961–4). He then worked in London, where he developed a reputation as a critic of new music, but in 1967 he removed himself to the Isle of Man to continue work on his major achievement, the *Etudes en série* for piano (1965–8, rev 1969–72), a sequence of interior conversations of superb authority, despite their often fragmented surfaces. Discouraged by neglect but not disheartened, he returned to the mainland to take university teaching posts in Birmingham and Newcastle before his death from a heart attack.

Hopkinson, Francis (b. Philadelphia, 21 Sep 1737; d. Philadelphia, 9 May 1791). US judge, signatory of the Declaration of Independence, and amateur musician, responsible for the first secular composition produced in the future USA: a song, 'My days have been so wondrous free' (1759). He also published a set of seven songs (1788).

Hoquetus David. Wordless three-part polyphonic composition by Machaut, based on the chant for the word 'David' in the alleluia for the Nativity of the Virgin. Birtwistle made an arrangement for six instruments (1969) followed by an orchestral disquisition, *Machaut à ma manière* (1988).

Horenstein, Jascha (b. Kiev, 6 May 1899; d. London, 2 Apr 1973). Russian–US conductor active mostly in western Europe. In 1911 he moved with his mother to Vienna, where in 1917 he began studies at the academy with Schreker, whom in 1920 he followed to Berlin. He was chief conductor of the Düsseldorf Opera (1928–33), then travelled widely before settling in the USA in 1940. After the Second World War he played an important part in the revival of Mahler and Bruckner, and the flame of his recorded performances (of these composers and of symphonic repertory from Mozart to Strauss) has kept his name alive.

horizontal. The linear dimension of music, as opposed to the vertical, which has to do with chords.

horn (1) (Fr. *cor*, Ger. *Horn*, It. *corno*). BRASS instrument, distinguished from the trumpet not only by its lower register and round-wound shape but also by its deeper mouthpiece (therefore warmer sound) and conical bore at the mouthpiece end. The obsolescent term 'French horn' seems to have honoured the country where the orchestral form originated, in Lully's orchestra for *La Princesse d'Elide* (1664), though instruments identifiable as horns had been widely used by huntsmen for a century and more before then. The terms *cor de chasse*, *Jagdhorn* and *corno da caccia* (Fr., Ger., It., hunting horn), and *Waldhorn* (Ger., forest horn), survive for the 'natural horn', i.e. the

instrument with no VALVE, which was the only instrument available before *c*.1814. A certain air of the hunt hangs about the horn still, and the instrument has also been used – notably by Mozart in *Figaro* – to suggest the horns of the cuckold.

The usual modern horn has four valves, of which one, operated by the thumb, moves the airflow from one to the other of the two tubes in what is a 'double horn', having a tube in F, about 12 feet (369cm) long and one in Bb, about 9 feet (270cm) long – though most players use only the Bb part. The other three valves lower the pitch by a tone, a semitone and a tone and a half respectively (so by a tritone when all are open), providing a full chromatic range. On the natural horn, where the fixed length produces the pitches of a harmonic series (normally in F), further notes can be obtained by adding a CROOK or by working the hand inside the bell, both techniques dating from the 18th century. Both change the timbre, and the different colours of the HAND HORN were expected by composers from Mozart to Brahms, who preferred the pre-valve instrument.

Also part of the instrument's tradition since hand-horn times is a distinction between higher parts, requiring a more trumpet-like technique, and lower; this survives in the modern orchestra, where first and third horns generally play above second and fourth. The practical range is from B below the bass staff (second partial on the F horn with all valves open) up through three and a half octaves. Horn parts are customarily notated in F, on the treble staff sounding a fifth lower, or on the bass staff sounding a fourth higher. Besides hand stopping, which thins or muffles the sound, mutes can be applied.

The horn was in frequent use by the end of the 17th century, and a pair was standard in the Classical orchestra, increased to three or four in the early 19th century and to eight in music from Wagner to Strauss. Works featuring solo horn or horns include Bach's First Brandenburg Concerto, Mozart's four concertos, Beethoven's sonata, Weber's Concertino, Schumann's *Conzertstück* for horn quartet, Brahms's trio with violin and piano, Strauss's two concertos, Britten's Serenade, Messiaen's *Des canyons aux étoiles* ..., and Ligeti's trio (for the same outfit as the Brahms) and concerto.

Barry Tuckwell *Horn* (1983, ʳ2002); Verne Reynolds *The Horn Handbook* (1997)

(2) In jazz terminology any wind instrument may be called a horn.

Horn, Charles Edward (b. London, 21 Jun 1786; d. Boston, 21 Oct 1849). British musician, active as composer, singer and instrumentalist on both sides of the Atlantic, and remembered above all for his song 'Cherry ripe'. He studied with his father, the German-born composer and royal musician Charles Frederick Horn (1762–1830), and with Rauzzini, and began his career in London theatres. After 1827 he spent most of his time in New York and Boston, credited with the first US oratorio (*The Remission of Sin*, 1835).

Horne, Marilyn (Bernice) (b. Bradford, Penn., 16 Jan 1929). US mezzo-soprano, famed especially for the grandeur and expressive colour she brought to serious Rossini roles. She studied at USC and dubbed the singing voice of the title character in the film *Carmen Jones* (1954). Her Covent Garden debut came in 1964 (Marie in *Wozzeck*), her Met debut in 1970 (*Norma* with Sutherland; a celebrated partnership), and she remained active internationally until retiring in 1998.

horn fifths. Kind of open fifth allowed in Classical–Romantic style for its quaint suggestion of natural horns. Horn fifths arise when the supertonic is supported by the fifth (thus D and G in C major) without the third to complete the triad (B), a note that the natural horn in the key could not produce.

hornpipe. British dance, named after the simple reed instrument used to accompany it. There are examples by Purcell and Handel.

Horn Signal. Name given to Haydn's Symphony No.31 from how the four horns in the slow movement behave.

Horowitz, Vladimir (b. ?Kiev, 1 Oct 1903; d. New York, 5 Nov 1989). Russian–US pianist, of breathtaking technique. He was taught first by his mother and then, at the Kiev Conservatory, by Vladimir Puchalsky and Sergey Tarnovsky (pupils of Leschetizky), and Felix Blumenfeld (a pupil of Anton Rubinstein). Also in Kiev he made his debut (1920); he then played throughout the Soviet Union before leaving in 1925 for Western Europe and, following his 1928 debut there, New York. Meeting Rachmaninoff was a crucial event for him: though he appeared rather little in concertos or chamber music, he made three recordings of the composer's Third Concerto (1930, 1951, 1978). In 1933 he married Toscanini's daughter Wanda, and in 1936–8 he withdrew from performing. His career thereafter was largely limited to the USA, and for long periods (1953–65, 1969–74) it was limited to recording, as he struggled with a nervous complaint. He returned to Europe in 1982

for the first time in three decades, and in 1986 he played again in Russia; a video-recording was made at this time, testifying to his still-electrifying powers. Prominent in his repertory throughout his career were (besides Rachmaninoff) Liszt, Chopin, Schumann and Scarlatti, as well as transcriptions of his own – not least a dazzling version of *The Stars and Stripes Forever*.
Harold Schonberg *Horowitz* (1992)

Hörspiel (Ger., play for hearing). Radio play, or musical piece designed for radio.

Horszowski, Mieczyslaw (b. Lemberg/Lviv, 23 Jun 1892; d. Philadelphia, 22 May 1993). Polish–US pianist, a pupil of Leschetizky from 1899 in Vienna, where he made his formal debut in 1902. At the outbreak of the Second World War he moved to the USA, and he taught at Curtis from the early 1940s until his death. Touring the world in his 90s, he was received everywhere with appreciation and astonishment, his poetic playing still fluent and unpretentious.

Hosenrolle (Ger.). TRAVESTI part.

Hosokawa, Toshio (b. Hiroshima, 23 Oct 1955). Japanese composer, of music on borderlands between frenzy and silence. He studied in Tokyo, in Berlin with Yun (1976–82) and in Freiburg with Huber and Ferneyhough (1983–6). Notable works include the *Landscape* series for chamber and orchestral groupings (1992–4).

Hotter, Hans (b. Offenbach am Main, 19 Jan 1909; d. Munich, 6 Dec 2003). German bass-baritone, the leading interpreter of Wagner's Wotan and Hans Sachs in the 1950s–60s. He studied with Matthäus Roemer and enjoyed his early maturity in Munich, where he was the first Olivier in Strauss's *Capriccio*. After the war he appeared regularly at Bayreuth (from 1952) and internationally, his resonant and authoritative voice backed by a noble bearing. He retired from opera in 1972 but went on giving recitals.

Hotteterre, Jacques (Martin) (b. Paris, 29 Sep 1673; d. Paris, 16 Jul 1763). French flautist-composer, author of the earliest method for the transverse flute (1707) and of several volumes of pieces for the instrument. Born into a family of woodwind player-makers (his grandfather, father, brother and several cousins were all active in the business in Paris), he was more artist than craftsman. In 1717–47 he was chamber flautist to Louis XV and laid the groundwork for the prominence of the flute in French musical culture.

Houston. Texan city, home to the Houston Symphony (decisively refounded in 1930 after beginnings in 1913–18) and the Houston Grand Opera (founded in 1955). Conductors of the Symphony have included Stokowski (1955–61), Barbirolli (1961–7) and Eschenbach (1988–99).

Hovhaness, Alan (b. Somerville, Mass., 8 Mar 1911; d. Seattle, 21 Jun 2000). US composer of an enormous body of music (434 Op. numbers) in which Western Renaissance-Baroque counterpoint is fused with the entranced harmonic stasis and repetition of Asian traditions and given colourful scoring. Originally Alan Vaness Chakmakjian, he dropped his Armenian father's surname in favour of the extended version of his middle name (the Armenian John). Composing from boyhood, he studied with Converse at the New England Conservatory (1932) but learned more from hearing Sibelius and Indian musicians. Contact with Armenian music, through his position from 1940 as organist of the Armenian church in Watertown, led to an Armenian period (1943–51) of works sounding 'giant melodies in simple or complex modes around stationary or movable tonal centres'. To that principle he remained true, for a while adding further Eastern elements (especially after visits to India, Japan and Korea in 1959–62). In the late 1940s he began to find favour with colleagues (Cage, Harrison, Thomson), and Stokowski's première of his Symphony No.2 'Mysterious Mountain' (1955) was a key event. His rhapsodic melody and mystical bent now won him an enthusiastic audience, while elsewhere his music earned suspicion for its naivety and overtly illustrative appeal. Unconcerned, he strode on creatively until stopped by failing health in his mid 80s. His output includes 67 symphonies, other orchestral works, sacred choral pieces, chamber music, and sonatas and other compositions for piano.
www.hovhaness.com

Hovland, Egil (b. Fredrikstad, 18 Oct 1924). Norwegian composer, a Hindemith–Stravinsky–Bartók neoclassicist who added avant-garde ideas in the 1960s. He studied at the Oslo Conservatory and returned to his home town as organist of Glemmen church (1949–94), writing sacred choral and organ works besides orchestral and chamber music.

How do you do? Name given to Haydn's Quartet Op.33:5.

Howells, Herbert (Norman) (b. Lydney, Glos., 17 Oct 1892; d. London, 23 Feb 1983). British composer, a late and long-lived scion of the national Romantic school. He studied with Brewer at Gloucester Cathedral (1910–12) and with Stanford and Charles Wood at the RCM, where he returned to teach (on into his 80s) after illness had cut short his career as a cathedral organist. He was also Holst's successor as music director of St Paul's Girls' School (1936–62). Early success as a composer of cathedral music, chamber works, songs and orchestral pieces was followed by a decade of near-silence, from which he was brutally stirred in 1935 by the death of his nine-year-old son from polio. *Hymnus paradisi* (for s, t, ch, orch, 1938, rev 1950) was the boy's memorial, followed by a large output of anthems and services.

Hoyland, Vic(tor) (b. Wombwell, Yorks., 11 Dec 1945). British composer, an assiduous modernist whose involvement with music theatre has increasingly given way to concerns with instrumental gesture and form. He studied at Hull and York (with Rands), worked as an editor for Universal Edition and joined Birmingham University in 1981.

hp. Abbreviation for harp.

hpd. Abbreviation for harpsichord.

HPSCHD. Work by Cage (with assistance from Lejaren Hiller) for up to seven harpsichords and up to 51 tapes. The work was originally presented as a 'musicircus', with slides and films, to an audience of 9,000. In keeping with the essential indeterminacy of the project, the commercial recording was issued with a score, different for each copy, proposing alterations of playback volume. First performance: Urbana, 16 May 1969.

Hubay, Jenő (b. Budapest, 15 Sep 1858; d. Budapest, 12 Mar 1937). Hungarian violinist-composer, who founded the Budapest school of violinists. A professional violinist's son, he studied with his father and with Joachim in Berlin, and became a protégé of Liszt, who had him move to Paris in 1878. There he Magyarized his name (from the original Eugen Huber) and found favour with Vieuxtemps, who was responsible for his appointment to the Brussels Conservatory in 1882. He was then head of violin studies (1886–1936) and director (1919–34) of the music academy in Budapest. His compositions, of which few were written after his mid 50s, include operas, symphonies and four violin concertos, though best remembered are two encore pieces for violin and piano from the 1880s: *Zephir* from *Blumenleben* and the csárdás *Hejre Kati*.

Huber, Klaus (b. Berne, 30 Nov 1924). Swiss composer, a modernist of esoteric inclinations. He studied with Burkhard at the Zurich Conservatory (1947–55) and Blacher in Berlin (1955–6), and taught at the academy in Basle (1964–73) and the conservatory in Freiburg (1973–90). Notable among his works are large-scale vocal pieces, such as ... *inwendig voller figur* ... on texts from Dürer and the Book of Revelation (1969–70).

Huber, Nicolaus A. (b. Passau, 15 Dec 1939). German composer, militantly engaged in contradicting bourgeois musical culture. He studied with Bialas in Munich (1964–7), with Stockhausen at Darmstadt (1967) and with Nono in Venice, and has taught since 1969 at the Folkwang-Hochschule in Essen. Where in earlier works his subversive intentions were upfront, his takes on minimalism and postmodernism since the mid 1980s have been more subtly interrogatory.

Huberman, Bronisław (b. Częstochowa, 19 Dec 1882; d. Corsier-sur-Vevey, 15 Jun 1947). Polish violinist. He studied with several teachers, among whom he valued Karol Gregorowicz most, and began his international career at 10; at 13 he played the Brahms concerto for the admiring composer. Renowned more for expressive depth and certainty than beauty of tone, he used his position as a public figure to agitate for a pan-European vision (against growing racialism) and then, after 1933, for a symphony orchestra in Palestine, which he had first visited in 1929. He is therefore remembered as a founding father of the Israel Philharmonic.

Hucbald of St Amand (b. northern France, c.850; d. St Amand, 20 Jun 930). Carolingian theorist and composer, not the author of MUSICA ENCHIRIADIS, with which he was once credited, but still an important figure for his chant compositions and for the practical guide to theory he provided in his treatise *Musica*. He probably entered the monastery of St Amand (then Elnon) as a boy and spent much of his life there, though he was called by the archbishop to Reims to help restore religious and scholastic life after Viking depredations.

Huddersfield. Northern British city noted for its choral society, founded in 1836, and contemporary music festival, founded in 1978.

Huguenots, Les (The Huguenots). Opera by Meyerbeer to a libretto by Scribe and Emile Deschamps. The Huguenots are Raoul (tenor) and his servant Marcel (bass), wending their way between the murderous mockery of Catholic noblemen – Nevers (baritone) and Saint-Bris (bass) – and the allurements of Catholic ladies: Queen Marguerite (soprano) and her lady-in-waiting Valentine (soprano), Saint-Bris's daughter. The outcome is execution for both, and for Valentine, who has joined them. Most famous of the solo pieces is Raoul's 'Plus blanche que la blanche hermine'. First performance: Paris, 29 Feb 1836.

huitième de soupir (Fr.). Demisemiquaver (32nd-note) rest.

hum. Make tuned vocal tone with lips closed, a device requested by Puccini (Humming Chorus of *Madama Butterfly*), Berio and others.

Humble, (Leslie) Keith (b. Geelong, 6 Sep 1927; d. Geelong, 23 May 1995). Australian composer and pianist, for whom modernism – including serialism – was a continuing journey of musical and social exploration. He studied at the University of Melbourne Conservatorium (1947–9), with Ferguson at the RAM (1950–51) and most crucially with Leibowitz in Paris (1953–5), where he remained as founder director of the ensemble Centre de Musique (1960–66). Back in Australia he was first head of the music department at La Trobe University, Melbourne (1974–89). His works include four piano sonatas.

Humfrey, Pelham (b. 1647/8; d. Windsor, 14 Jul 1674). English composer, one of the bright musical lights of the early Restoration. He joined the Chapel Royal as a chorister in 1660 and was composing before his voice broke (in 1664). Sent to France and Italy to continue his training (1664–6), he returned, according to Pepys, 'an absolute Monsieur, as full of form and confidence and vanity'. In some ways he was right to be pleased with himself: the verse anthems he wrote as a gentleman of the Chapel Royal (singing tenor) introduced elements from Lully and Carissimi that helped form Purcell's style. He also produced court odes and some pieces for *The* TEMPEST.

Hummel, Johann Nepomuk (b. Pressburg/Bratislava, 14 Nov 1778; d. Weimar, 17 Oct 1837). Austrian pianist-composer, the most famed virtuoso of his time. A professional musician's son, he proved a prodigy, and at eight was taken to Vienna for lessons with Mozart. His father then escorted him on a tour of Germany, Denmark, Britain and the Netherlands (1788–92), from which he returned to Vienna for further study with Albrechtsberger, Salieri and Haydn. An appointment to Prince Nikolaus Esterházy in Eisenstadt (1804–11) produced an excursion into sacred music, but he kept up his busy output of piano, chamber and orchestral music for Vienna, where he was Beethoven's chief antipode: genial, engaging, never challenging. There may also have been some rivalry between the composers for the hand of Elisabeth Röckel, whom he married in 1813. The next year he returned to the concert circuit, and he continued making annual tours while kapellmeister in Stuttgart (1816–18) and Weimar (from 1819). As both pianist and composer he was one of the big successes of the early age of musical commerce, with an abundant output of theatre, concert and domestic music. Best known now are his Trumpet Concerto in E (1803, often played in E♭) and works he wrote for himself, including the Rondo in E♭, Op.11, the Adagio, Variations and Rondo on 'Schöne Minka' with flute and cello, Op.78, the Quintet, Op.87 (1802) and several concertos.

humoresque (Ger. *Humoreske*). Short fantasy, generally for piano, portraying one or more humours (i.e. feelings, states of mind). The earliest example would appear to be Schumann's Op.20; there are others by Grieg, Tchaikovsky, Dvořák, Sibelius and Prokofiev.

humour. Happily, little music is free of it, across the range from PARODY to playfulness – the smile-effect of an unusual juxtaposition or, equally, of a motif justly placed. Humour at the latter edge, witty and dexterous, may come from a closely determined language, where exceptions to the norm – and affirmations of it – can be recognized and thereby communicated as funny by the composer (or, independently of the composer, by performers). Hence the prevalence of humour in the Classical style, and especially in Haydn and Mozart. There are, though, tight styles and forms that are rarely humorous – fugue, for example. Humour can also easily arise when reference is made to an old or debased musical language, as in neoclassicism and postmodernism. See also COMIC OPERA; VIOLA JOKE.

Humperdinck, Engelbert (b. Siegburg, 1 Sep 1854; d. Neustrelitz, 27 Sep 1921). German composer, known almost exclusively for one of the rare great works of children's music, HÄNSEL UND GRETEL. From 1872 he studied with Ferdinand Hiller at the Cologne Conservatory, where he heard his first Wagner. He continued his training with Rheinberger and Franz Lachner in Munich (1877–9), and met Wagner during a year in Italy (1879–80). For a year and a half (1881–2) he lived in Bayreuth

working as Wagner's copyist on *Parsifal*. There followed several restless years before he achieved professional and personal stability with the composition of *Hänsel und Gretel* (1890–93) and marriage (1892). The opera was an enormous success, but so in its time was another fairytale drama, *Königskinder*, which he wrote first for speaking voices (1895–7, with the earliest use of SPRECHGESANG) and adapted as a sung opera for the Met (1910). He also wrote incidental scores, orchestral pieces, chamber music and songs, and taught in Frankfurt (1890–97) and Berlin (1900–20).

hundred-and-twenty-eighth note (US). Quasi-hemidemisemiquaver (UK). See DURATION.

Hungaria. Symphonic poem by Liszt. First performance: Pest, 8 Sep 1856.

Hungarian Dances (*Ungarische Tänze*). Sets of 10 (1868) and 11 (1880) piano duets by Brahms, who arranged the first collection for piano solo and three numbers from it for orchestra.

Hungarian Quartet. Ensemble founded in Budapest in 1935 as the New Hungarian Quartet, in distinction from the group led by Imre Waldbauer, which played from 1909 to 1946 and introduced Bartók's first four quartets. The new team was led by Sándor Végh, succeeded by Zoltán Székely in 1937, and after the Second World War it dropped the 'New'.

Hungarian Rhapsodies (*Ungarische Rhapsodien*). 19 piano works by Liszt, of which the first 15 emerged in 1846–53 and the last four in 1882–5. There are also orchestral versions of six by Liszt and Franz Döppler (1857–60), and piano duet arrangements of these six (1874). No.15, one of the favoured six, is a version of the RÁKÓCZI MARCH.

Hungary (Magyarország). Occupied by Turkish forces (1541–1686), then subordinated to Vienna, the country was slow to develop independent musical voices: those came in the mid 19th century in the work of Erkel and Liszt, then still more decisively in the 20th century in that of Bartók and Kodály, followed by Seiber, Veress, Ligeti, Kurtág and Eötvös. With these distinguished examples, and with music education given high priority, Hungary has also been an impressive source of performing musicians: conductors (Reiner, Szell, Solti, Dorati), pianists (Annie Fischer, Kocsis), violinists (Auer, Hubay, Szigeti, Végh) and string quartets (Hungarian, Keller). See also BUDAPEST.

Hunnenschlacht (Battle of the Huns). Symphonic poem by Liszt after a mural by Wilhelm von Kaulbach. First performance: Weimar, 29 Dec 1857.

Hunt. Name given to Mozart's Quartet in B♭, K.458, on account of its first movement's first subject. See also *La* CHASSE.

Hunt, Lorraine. See LIEBERSON.

hüpfend (Ger., hopping). SPICCATO.

hurdy-gurdy (Fr. *vielle à roue*, Ger. *Leier*, It. *lyra tedesca*). Instrument with a handle to crank a wooden wheel and so draw sound from the strings, some of which provide a drone while others can be played by tangents applied by means of a keyboard. Usually designed to be slung around the player's neck, the instrument was widespread in the Middle Ages, and enjoyed a vogue in Baroque France, but is most often associated with folk musicians, as in the last song of Schubert's *Winterreise*.

Husa, Karel (b. Prague, 7 Aug 1921). Czech–US composer, of music in a rhythmically energized neoclassical style having links with Honegger, Bartók and the Schoenberg school. He studied with Jaroslav Řídký at the Prague Conservatory (1941–5) and with Boulanger and Honegger in Paris (1946–51). His First Quartet (1948) marked the start of a promising career in Europe, before the fastening of the Iron Curtain, which he escaped by taking a post at Cornell (1954–92). Later works, mostly instrumental, include concertos and three further quartets.

Hüsch, Gerhard (Heinrich Wilhelm Fritz) (b. Hanover, 2 Feb 1901; d. Munich, 21 Nov 1984). German baritone of delectable lyric timbre, whose operatic and lieder recordings are treasured; he was the first to record both Schubert song cycles. He studied with Hans Emge in Hanover, and in the 1930s sang in both Berlin and London.

Huygens, Constantijn (b. The Hague, 4 Sep 1596; d. The Hague, 29 Mar 1687). Dutch musical amateur, a member of a family high in political and intellectual life. He was secretary to the stadholder (1625–50) and a diplomat; he also published a book of sacred and secular songs, *Pathodia sacra et profana* (1647). His son Christiaan was the physicist who invented the pendulum clock, first saw Saturn's rings and developed the theory of 31-interval equal temperament.

Hvorostovsky, Dmitri (b. Krasnoyarsk, 16 Oct 1962). Russian baritone, whose vocal charm and sensuality match his striking silver-haired appearance. He studied in his home town and made his debut there in 1986. In 1989 he won the Cardiff Singer of the World competition, after which he was soon active internationally, especially in Tchaikovsky, Mozart and Verdi roles and as a recitalist.

hydraulis. WATER ORGAN.

Hygons, Richard (b. *c*.1435; d. Wells, *c*.1509). English composer and church musician, active at Wells Cathedral from 1458 and responsible for a *Salve regina* on CAPUT in the Eton Choirbook.

Hyla, Lee [Leon Joseph] (b. Niagara Falls, 31 Aug 1952). US composer of quirky and energetic music coming out of modernism. He studied at the New England Conservatory with Malcolm Peyton, then took a master's degree in 1978 at Stony Brook under David Lewin. In 1992 he returned to the New England Conservatory to teach. His works include four string quartets and a setting of Allen Ginsberg's 'Howl' for narrator and quartet (1993).

hymn. Sacred song to non-scriptural words, in metrical strophes and with a simple melody inviting universal participation. Some of the earliest hymns (including 'Deus Creator omnium') had words by St Ambrose, the late 4th-century patriarch of Milan, and entered the liturgy. So did others from the next half millennium or so, including 'A solis ortus cardine' (with words by the 5th-century Irish poet Sedulius), 'Pange lingua' and 'Vexilla regis' (both with words by the 6th-century Italian poet Venantius Fortunatus), 'Ave maris stella', 'Te lucis ante terminum' and 'Veni Creator Spiritus'. How long their melodies predated notation is a matter of speculation.

An innovation of the Renaissance was to alternate from strophe to strophe between chant and polyphony: Du Fay's versions were widely disseminated, then replaced in the 16th century by versions by Tallis, Lassus, Palestrina, Victoria and others. Such settings presupposed performance by a trained choir, in contrast with the emphasis in the new Reformed churches on congregational singing; whence the CHORALE in the Lutheran Church and the metrical psalm in the Calvinist and Anglican traditions.

The great British–US tradition of hymn writing was started by Nonconformists in the late 17th century (Isaac Watts) and early 18th (John and Charles Wesley). Opposition in the established

Church could not withstand the popularity of hymns, and increasing numbers of hymnbooks were published, culminating in *Hymns Ancient and Modern* (1861), which made the high Victorian language of song – in which robustness exactly balances sentiment – as central to the Anglican Church as the *Book of Common Prayer*. Meanwhile the US had its own hymnwriters, of whom the most successful were Moody and Sankey. *Hymns A&M* was supplemented, but not displaced, in Britain by the *English Hymnal* (1906) and *Songs of Praise* (1925), and came out in a revised form in 1950. Since the late 1960s various factors – the new place for the laity and vernacular language in the Roman Catholic Church, the growing success of charismatic movements and the ubiquity of rock music – have contributed to a pluriform rebirth of the hymn.

J.R. Watson *The English Hymn* (1997)

hymnary. Latin hymnbook.

Hymnen (Anthems). Two-hour electronic work by Stockhausen, bringing together national anthems from around the world with other material. The composer intended the piece (originally on tape) to be heard either alone or as a matrix for other musical or theatrical activities, and he provided two such elaborations himself: one with his own ensemble of four musicians (f.p. Cologne, 30 Nov 1967), the other with an orchestra in the third of the composition's four 'regions'.

hymnody. The singing of hymns.

Hyperaeolian. Glarean's term for the mode known later as LOCRIAN.

Hyperion. British recording company, founded in 1980 by Edward Perry to specialize in unusual repertory and compendious projects (e.g. the complete piano music of Liszt and songs of Schubert).

Hyperprism. Work by Varèse, his first for a compact ensemble of wind (fl and pic, E♭ cl, 3 hn, 2 tpt, 2 trbn) and percussion. A hyperprism is a four-dimensional object. First performance: New York, 4 Mar 1923.

Hypoaeolian. Plagal MODE E–F–G–A–B–C–D–E with A as final.

Hypodorian. Plagal MODE A–B–C–D–E–F–G–A with D as final – or, in a common Renaissance transposition, D–E–F–G–A–B♭–C–D with G as final. This is the second church mode/tone.

Hypoionian. Glarean's term for the plagal mode G–A–B–C–D–E–F–G with C as final, more usually considered at the time a transposition of the Hypolydian.

Hypolydian. Plagal MODE C–D–E–F–G–A–B♭–C with F as final, the sixth church mode/tone.

Hypomixolydian. Plagal MODE D–E–F–G–A–B–C–D with G as final, the eighth church mode/tone.

Hypophrygian. Plagal MODE B–C–D–E–F–G–A–B with E as final, the fourth church mode/tone.

i

Iberia. Collection of 12 piano pieces by Albéniz in four books (*cuadernos*): 1 *Evocation, El puerto* and *Fête-Dieu à Séville,* 2 *Rondeña, Almería* and *Triana,* 3 *El Albaicín, El polo* and *Lavapiés,* and 4 *Malaga, Jerez* and *Eritaña.* A 13th piece, *Navarra,* was completed by de Sévérac. The composer orchestrated *El puerto,* but the familiar orchestral versions are by Enrique Fernández Arbós (nine pieces) and Peter Breiner (all 12).

Debussy used the title, as *Ibéria,* for one of his orchestral IMAGES.

Ibert, Jacques (François Antoine Marie) (b. Paris, 15 Aug 1890; d. Paris, 5 Feb 1962). French composer, close to Ravel and Poulenc. His mother was a trained pianist, and he naturally studied that instrument before entering the Conservatoire in 1910, where Gédalge was an important influence. Having had his studies interrupted by service in the First World War as a nurse and naval officer, he returned to win the Prix de Rome in 1919. While in Rome he wrote the orchestral suite *Escales* (1921–2), with its movements *Rome-Palerme, Tunis-Nefta* and *Valencia* evocatively recalling a Mediterranean cruise. It made his reputation. Many of his later works, including his spirited *Divertissement,* came out of his busy output of scores for films and plays. He returned to the French academy in Rome, the Villa Médicis, as director (1937–60, except for a period in the Second World War).

Operas: *Angélique* (1 act; Nino), 1926; etc.
Orchestral: *Escales,* 1921–2; Concerto, vc, wind, 1925; *Divertissement,* chbr orch, 1929–30 (from incidental music for Eugène Labiche's *Un Chapeau de paille d'Italie*); Symphonic Suite

'Paris', 1930 (from incidental music for Jules Romains's *Donogoo*); Flute Concerto, 1932–3; *Concertino da camera,* sax, ens, 1935; *Symphonie concertante,* ob, str, 1948–9; etc.
Chamber and instrumental: 6 Pieces, hp, 1917; *Histoires,* pf, 1922 (No.2 *Le Petit Ane blanc* and 4 others for duet); *Trois pièces brèves,* wind qnt, 1930; *Entr'acte,* fl, gui/hp, 1935 (other arrs); Piece, fl, 1936; *Deux interludes suivi de Carillon,* fl, vn, hpd/hp, 1946 (from incidental music for Suzanne Lilar's *Le Burlador*); etc.
Other works: *Don Quichotte* (film score; Pabst), 1932 (includes 3 songs for Don Quixote and 1 for Sancho Panza); ballets, incidental music, choral pieces, songs

Ichiyanagi, Toshi (b. Kobe, 4 Feb 1933). Japanese composer and pianist, associated with Cage in New York (1952–61) and later a more mainstream modernist. He studied with Ikenouchi before going to New York to attend Juilliard, and has worked in Japan promoting new music.

ictus (Lat.). Term for stress in poetry, sometimes used to mean DOWNBEAT.

Ideale, Die (The Ideals). Symphonic poem by Liszt after a poem by Schiller. First performance: Weimar, 5 Sep 1857.

idée fixe (Fr., obsession). Motif that keeps recurring throughout a composition. Berlioz used the term in connection with his *Symphonie fantastique,* when it was new in both psychological and artistic parlance.

idiophone. Formal organological term for an instrument whose sound comes immediately from its body, not from a string (chordophone), wind column (aerophone) or skin (membranophone). Other than skin drums, then, percussion instruments are idiophones, further categorized according to whether they are struck, shaken, plucked, rubbed or blown upon.

Idomeneo. Opera by Mozart, titled in full *Idomeneo, re di Creta* (Idomeneus, King of Crete), to a libretto by Giovanni Battista Varesco after Antoine Danchet's for the opera by Campra. Idomeneus (tenor) has promised Neptune he will sacrifice the first creature he meets on reaching Crete. When this turns out to be his son Idamantes (soprano castrato), he is horror-struck. Idamantes, meanwhile, is loved by both a gentle Trojan, Ilia (soprano), and a wild Greek, Electra (soprano). When Neptune sends a monster to ravage the island, Idomeneus is forced to go through with the long-postponed sacrifice, but the god relents when Ilia puts herself forward to die instead, and Idamantes and Ilia are installed as the new rulers. The arias include Idomeneus's 'Fuor del mar', Ilia's 'Zeffiretti lusinghieri' and Electra's 'D'Oreste, d'Ajace'; the final ballet is normally cut from stage performances, which have become much commoner since the mid-20th-century recognition that formality could go along with grandeur, colour and expressiveness. First performance: Munich, 29 Jan 1781, rev Vienna, 13 Mar 1786 (with tenor Idamantes and two new numbers).

Ifukube, Akira (b. Kushiro, Hokkaidō, 31 May 1914). Japanese composer of colourful film scores, concert works and ballets using folk music. Trained in forestry, he was largely self-taught as a composer, though he had a few lessons from Alexander Tcherepnin in 1936. He taught at Tokyo National University of Fine Arts and Music (1946–53) and was president of the Tokyo College of Music (1975–88).

IGNM (Internationale Gesellschaft für Neue Musik). See ISCM.

Ikenouchi, Tomojirō (b. Tokyo, 21 Oct 1906; d. Tokyo, 9 Mar 1991). Japanese composer, a fastidious artist close to Ravel and the son of a noted haiku poet. He studied at the Paris Conservatoire (1927–36), and taught at Nihon University (from 1936) and the Tokyo National University of Fine Arts and Music (from 1947). His small output comprises mostly chamber pieces.

Illica, Luigi (b. Castell'Arquato, near Piacenza, 9 May 1857; d. Colombarone, 16 Dec 1919). Italian

librettist, remembered for his work for Puccini, first on *Manon Lescaut*, then with Giuseppe Giacosa on *La Bohème*, *Tosca* and *Madama Butterfly*. He also wrote librettos for Catalani (*La Wally*), Franchetti (*Cristoforo Colombo*), Giordano (*Andrea Chénier*), Mascagni (*Iris*) and others.

Images (Pictures). Title Debussy gave to four sets of pieces:

(1) Three piano pieces published long posthumously as *Images oubliées*, of which the first has no heading and the other two carry playful superscriptions: 'In saraband tempo, that is, solemn and slow, even a bit like an old portrait, souvenir of the Louvre, etc …' and 'Some aspects of the song "Nous n'irons plus au bois", because the weather is dreadful'.

(2) Three piano pieces (first set): *Reflets dans l'eau* (Reflections in Water), *Hommage à Rameau*, *Mouvement*. First performance: Paris, 14 Dec 1905 (No.2), 3 Mar 1906 (complete).

(3) Three piano pieces (second set): *Cloches à travers les feuilles* (Bells through Leaves), *Et la lune descend sur le temple qui fût* (And the moon goes down on the temple as was), *Poissons d'or* (Goldfish, referring to a piece of black Japanese lacquer). First performance: Paris, 21 Feb 1908.

(4) Three orchestral pieces: *Gigues*, *Ibéria*, *Rondes de printemps*. First performance: Paris, 20 Feb 1910 (*Ibéria*), 2 Mar 1910 (*Rondes*), 26 Jan 1913 (complete).

imaginary composers. They include:

(1) Jean-Christophe Krafft in Romain Rolland's *Jean-Christophe* (1904–12), a genius hero based partly on the author's image of Beethoven.

(2) Vinteuil, author of a violin sonata with a 'little phrase' that runs through Proust's *A la recherche du temps perdu* (1914–27). Favourite candidates for Proust's model are the Franck sonata and Saint-Saëns's first.

(3) Adrian Leverkühn in Thomas Mann's *Doctor Faustus* (1947), the product of the author's deep investment in – and pessimism about – recent German culture.

See also P.D.Q. BACH.

Imaginary Landscape. Title used by Cage for a series of five works, including electrically produced sounds (1939–52), and by Birtwistle for a piece for orchestral wind and percussion (1971).

Imbrie, Andrew (Welsh) (b. New York, 6 Apr 1921). US composer, a clear-minded follower of his teachers Boulanger and Sessions. He studied with Boulanger in 1937 and with Sessions both before the Second World War in Princeton and afterwards at Berkeley, where he soon returned as a valued teacher (1949–91). His works include three symphonies, three piano concertos, five string quartets and a *Requiem*.

imitation. Melodic echo from one part to another of a polyphonic composition. Strict imitation, with an exact match of rhythmic-intervallic shape, is an essential feature of CANON and FUGUE, but looser kinds are also frequent in polyphonic writing, and have been so since Perotin.

imitative. Term used of a texture exhibiting imitation.

imperfect cadence [half-cadence, half-close]. Cadence on to the dominant chord, normally from the tonic or subdominant, usually with both chords in root position. Conveying a sense of closure but with more to come, imperfect cadences are common at the ends of phrases, and at the ends of opening sections in binary forms (e.g. dance movements in Bach suites and symphonic minuets). In US terminology 'half-close' is sometimes preferred, leaving the formula 'imperfect cadence' for a V–I progression in which the dominant chord is inverted or the tonic lacks the keynote at the top.

imperfect consonance. The third or sixth, either one major or minor. These were distinguished in medieval times from the PERFECT CONSONANCE.

imperfect time. Division of a basic rhythmic unit into two equal parts in medieval-Renaissance music, corresponding to duple time.

Impériale, L'. Name given to Haydn's Symphony No.53.

impresario (It., entrepreneur, pl. *impresarii*, though in Eng. 'impresarios'). PRODUCER (2), agent or company manager. The first impresarios, in 17th-century Venice, were hired by theatre owners to manage opera seasons, and this system became ubiquitous. Then the arrival of the touring virtuoso in the early 19th century provided a niche for the impresario in concert life. The term implies a certain swagger.

Impresario, The. See *Der* SCHAUSPIELDIREKTOR.

impressionism. Term originating in discussion of painting and painters. Monet's title *Impression: Soleil levant* (Sunrise) caused the critic Louis Leroy to write dismissively of 'impressionists' in reviewing the first exhibition (1874) by the group, who thereupon took the label as a badge of honour. In 1887 Debussy's *Printemps* was officially reproved for 'dangerous impressionism' – with some justice as to the association with Monet, especially, for there are parallels between Debussy's fluid, colourful, improvisatory style and Monet's brushwork, and some of the composer's titles suggest impressionist canvases (*Jardins sous la pluie*, *Les Collines d'Anacapri*). Accordingly, the term has gained a place in the vocabulary of music to denote Debussy's music and works close to him in style by Ravel, Dukas, Bartók, Roussel, Ibert and others.

impromptu (Fr., improvised). Short piece, almost always for piano. The title was introduced by Voříšek (or his publisher) in 1817, then established by Schubert and Chopin. It implies a spontaneous composition, or informal variations on an idea plucked from the air.

improvisation. Performance on the spot, not backed by a composition. Most musicians will want to improvise now and again in the practice room – try out possibilities, spin out an idea, follow where imagination will take them. Improvisation must also have a part in any performance, at least in subtleties of dynamics and timing that will have to spring from the place and the occasion. And even the classic Western tradition, dominated by the score, has found room for improvisation on a fuller scale, albeit normally for improvisation on composed material and within the confines of an established practice: examples include the realization of a figured bass, ORNAMENTATION, the spontaneous elaboration of a cadenza in a concerto or aria (as seems to have happened commonly in the 18th century) and extemporization on a keyboard instrument. Beethoven was a famed improviser in his youth, and something of his capabilities may be transmitted in his Choral Fantasy and other works. (Of course, improvisation before the advent of recorded sound is essentially a lost art.) Soon after Beethoven's death improvisation became largely limited to the organ loft, where the ability to improvise on a submitted theme has remained part of a recitalist's technique.

Since the late 1960s improvisation has gained a larger role in new music as a result of various impulses: from jazz, from non-European traditions, from INDETERMINACY and the ALEATORY concept, from live electronic music, and from the pushing of instrumental and vocal possibilities beyond what could readily be notated. Improvising groups established themselves, including Globokar's quartet New Phonic Art, AMM,

Musica Elettronica Viva and Stockhausen's ensemble, while Young, Riley and others began to study with Indian masters. Through improvisation the boundaries of the Western classical tradition could thus be tested, with permanent effect even on those composers who, like Stockhausen and Rzewski, returned to the written score. Meanwhile the importance of improvisation in the Baroque and Classical ages was being increasingly recognized.

in alt, in altissimo. See ALT; ALTISSIMO.

In C. Work by Riley comprising a sequence of 53 figures that any number of musicians (35 is suggested) may travel through more or less independently, repeating and moving on, but performing to the same pulse. The result is a journey of iterations and unison canons through various modal harmonies on C, and the repetitive formula became one of the fundamentals of minimalism – not least for Reich, who took part in the first performance. First performance: San Francisco, 8 Nov 1964.

incalzando (It., pursuing). Accelerate.

incidental music. Music included in the performance of a play, normally on the stage, though the term can also cover scores for radio or television drama. Such music was called 'incidental', in the mid 19th century, not because it was inessential but on the contrary because it was necessary to the conduct of a scene, whether as a song that a character must sing, as a means to convey some supernatural act or appearance, or as a way to underline an extreme mood. Overtures and entr'actes were later included in the category.

Until Ibsen, in the late 19th century, most plays were written in expectation of music, and theatre orchestras were ubiquitous until the mid 20th century, surviving still, in the form of reduced ensembles, within companies specializing in classic repertory. Most composers since the 17th century have therefore written incidental music at least occasionally, sometimes producing substantial scores, as with Purcell (*Don Quixote* and many others), Beethoven (*Egmont*), Weber, Schubert (*Rosamunde*), Mendelssohn (*A Midsummer Night's Dream*), Schumann (*Manfred*), Bizet (*L'Arlésienne*), Tchaikovsky, Grieg (*Peer Gynt*), Fauré (*Pelléas et Mélisande*), Debussy (*Le Martyre de Saint-Sébastien*), Sibelius (*Pelléas et Mélisande*, *The Tempest*) and Shostakovich.

incipit (Lat.). Citation of the opening, as found in a thematic catalogue.

incoronazione di Poppea, L' (The Coronation of Poppaea). Opera by Monteverdi and others to a libretto by Giovanni Francesco Busenello. Poppaea (soprano) successfully schemes her way to the imperial throne alongside Nero (soprano), leaving in her wake her husband Otho (mezzo-soprano), the former empress Octavia (soprano) and the emperor's wiser counsellor Seneca (bass). Along with more regular performance since the 1960s has come recognition that parts of the score were written by younger composers: Sacrati, Ferrari and Cavalli. First performance: Venice, 1643.

Incorporated Society of Musicians (ISM). British professional organization, founded in Manchester in 1882.

incudine (It.). Anvil.

Indes galantes, Les (Exotic Courtship). Opera by Rameau to a libretto by Louis Fuzelier, a set of four love stories set on an island in the Indian Ocean, in Peru, in Persia and in North America, with European characters in three of them. Picturesque ceremonials (with dance) and delicate (or not) foreign sensibilities are persistent themes. First performance: Paris, 23 Aug 1735.

indeterminacy. Cage's term for the leeway in scores leaving fundamental matters to be decided (usually by chance) in performance. He thereby drew a distinction from CHANCE OPERATIONS, which he used in the process of composition, and also from the ALEATORY principle in European music, where choice rather than chance was operative. Chance operations could result in a more or less conventionally notated score, whereas indeterminacy implied a different kind of product: graphic notation (Concert for piano and orchestra), a kit of graphic elements (*Variations II*), verbal instructions (*Inlets*), multitudinous options (HPSCHD). Cage's lecture *Indeterminacy* consists of an unlinked sequence of anecdotes; he published it in his book *Silence* and recorded it.

India. Subcontinent, whose diverse musical cultures are not constrained by the modern boundaries separating India, Pakistan, Bangladesh and Sri Lanka. Those cultures have some of the same sources as music in modern Europe, especially Greek (before and after Alexander the Great's incursion) and Islamic (whence the dominance of string instruments in both regions). The difference is that Indian music developed as an art of solo improvisers, not one of composed collectivities, as in the West, and this fundamental divergence has limited both the spread of Western music in the subcontinent (despite the two centuries of British rule that ended in 1947) and the influence of Indian music in the West (despite regular tours by outstanding musicians, beginning with Ali Akbar Khan's visit to the USA in 1955 and Ravi Shankar's to both the USA and Europe in 1956–7). Exchange is much more apparent in popular music – open to improvisation and eager for non-classical sounds in the West, accepting of electronic technology in India – than in the cultivated traditions of either region. Even so, some Western classical composers since the end of the 19th century have learmed from Indian scales (Foulds), rhythms (Messiaen) and improvisatory practices (Young, Riley), and a few Indians have become Western-style composers, usually in Britain (Sohal, Vir).

Indiana University School of Music. Institution founded in Bloomington in 1921, though the university goes back to 1820 and has had music on its curriculum since 1893.

Indonesia. See GAMELAN.

Indy. See D'INDY.

Inextinguishable, The (*Det uudslukkelige*). Name Nielsen gave his Fourth Symphony.

infinite canon. PERPETUAL CANON.

inflection. Bending of pitch, a potentially stylish and expressive device when done by a singer or solo instrumentalist.

Ingegneri, Marc'Antonio (b. Verona, 1535/6; d. Cremona, 1 Jul 1592). Italian composer of madrigals and sacred music, but remembered more as Monteverdi's teacher. A choirboy at Verona Cathedral, he may have completed his training with Rore in Parma in the early 1560s. By 1566 he was in Cremona, where he was cathedral chapelmaster by 1580.

Inghelbrecht, Désiré-Emile (b. Paris, 17 Sep 1880; d. Paris, 14 Feb 1965). French conductor, associated especially with Debussy. The son of a viola player at the Paris Opera, but expelled from the Conservatoire, he began his conducting career in 1908 and founded the Orchestre National de la Radiodiffusion Française in 1934. Suspended for refusing to conduct 'La Marseillaise' under German occupation, he laid down his baton till the war was over. His works include orchestral and piano pieces, notably the collection *La Nursery*, presented in both forms.

inharmonic. Term used of partials not belonging to a HARMONIC series. All vibrating objects, including strings and bodies of air, present some degree of inharmonicity. Where the object is particularly massive, as in bells and other percussion instruments, this will be particularly marked.

innig (Ger.). Inward.

inno (It.). Hymn.

In Nomine. English genre of polyphonic instrumental composition, arising from the example of the 'In Nomine' section of Taverner's *Gloria Tibi Trinitas* mass and using as cantus firmus the same Trinity Sunday antiphon from the Sarum rite. There are In Nomines for consort or keyboard by, among others, Tallis, Tye, Parsons, Byrd, Bull, the younger Ferrabosco, Tomkins, Gibbons, Ward, Jenkins and Purcell, whose pair closed the tradition until the seven by Davies.

Inori (Jap., Adorations). Orchestral work by Stockhausen with a mime (or two) going through gestures of prayer in synchrony with the music's elaboration of a melody. First performance: Donaueschingen, 20 Oct 1974.

insert. Term used of a piece made to replace a number in an opera. Mozart wrote insert arias and insert ensembles.

inspiration. Preliminary idea for a composition (perhaps a theme or pattern of notes, perhaps an inkling of the whole), or the process by which composers may feel themselves to be receiving, rather than conceiving, a work. Because it unfolds through time yet has no words, music is readily understood as a transmission from some generally unperceived level of existence – especially from the divine. Particularly, therefore, in the sphere of sacred music, composers may have a strong sense of being inspired. Handel is said to have remarked, of composing *Messiah*: 'I did think I did see all Heaven before me and the great God himself.'

instrument. Sound-producing device. Often instruments and voices are thought of as separate categories – hence 'instrumental music' and 'vocal music' – but a singer may speak of 'my instrument'. And indeed, according to the classification established by E.M. von Hornbostel and Curt Sachs in 1914 and still current, voices are classed with wind instruments and organs as types of AEROPHONE, the other kinds being CHORDOPHONE (string instrument), MEMBRANOPHONE (skin drum) and IDIOPHONE (instrument whose whole body vibrates, as with most other percussion instruments). Western music, however, has traditionally grouped instruments slightly differently, as strings, woodwind, brass and percussion.

instrumentation. Term used as an alternative to ORCHESTRATION in either of two ways: instrumentation may be said to cover the choice of instruments and orchestration their use, or may be preferred where a small ensemble is concerned, in which case Stravinsky instrumented his *Histoire du soldat* but orchestrated his *Petrushka*.

Modern scores often include an instrumentation list at the front; catalogues may supply the information in shorthand form. For example, Birtwistle's *Earth Dances* asks for three flutes (of which the second also plays piccolo and the third alto flute), three oboes, three clarinets (of which the second doubles on E♭ clarinet and the third on that plus bass clarinet), three bassoons (second and third doubling on double bassoon), four horns, four trumpets, four trombones, two tubas, five percussionists, two harps, piano, 30 violins (with none classed as seconds) and nine each of violas, cellos and double basses. This can be expressed thus: 3 (2 + pic, 3 + a fl).3.3 (2 + E♭ cl, 3 + E♭ cl, b cl).3 (2 + dbn, 3 + dbn) – 4.4.4.2 – 5 perc, 2 hp, pf – 30.0.9.9.9.

intabulation. Arrangement of a vocal piece for keyboard or plucked string instrument in the 14th–16th centuries, notated in tablature.

Intégrales. Work by Varèse for wind (2 pic, ob, E♭ cl, cl, hn, high D tpt, tpt, 3 trbn) and percussion. First performance: New York, 1 Mar 1925.

Intendant (Ger.). Artistic director of an opera company, orchestra or festival.

intensity. Loudness, especially as a physical quantity; see also DECIBEL.

interlude. Movement separating the larger parts of a work, often an orchestral movement played between sections of an opera or oratorio.

intermède (Fr.). Short piece performed between acts of a play or opera in France in the 16th–17th centuries. In the 18th century the term was applied to rather longer comic operas.

intermedio (It., pl. *intermedi*, though in Eng. often 'intermedios'). Short piece performed between acts of a play or opera in Italy in the 16th century. The only intermedi surviving are those that were

published: the sets for Medici weddings in Florence in 1539 (music by Corteccia) and 1589 (music by Cristoforo Malvezzi, Marenzio and others, words largely by Rinuccini), of which the latter – classical allegories of music's powers – presaged the incipient arrival of opera.

intermezzo (It., pl. *intermezzi*, though in Eng. normally 'intermezzos'). (1) Comic opera presented in Italy in the early 18th century in instalments between acts of an opera seria. Pergolesi's *La serva padrona* is an example.

(2) The It. equivalent to interlude or entr'acte. *Cavalleria rusticana* has one.

(3) Kind of movement, more equable in tempo and gentle in mood, introduced by Mendelssohn in his Second Piano Quartet (1823) as an alternative to the scherzo. Intermezzos appear also in larger works by Schumann and Brahms, and as independent pieces by these composers and others.

Intermezzo. Opera by Strauss to his own libretto, based on an episode from his marital life. Christine (soprano), beginning a wary connection with a young Baron (tenor) on the ski slopes, erupts when she intercepts a compromising letter from a young woman to her husband, the conductor Robert Storch (baritone). Harmony is restored when it turns out that the letter was meant for another conductor, Stroh. First performance: Dresden, 4 Nov 1924.

intermission. Pause between acts in an opera or parts in a concert (US).

intermodulation. The interference of two waves or electronic signals, commonly heard when a radio is not quite tuned in. Stockhausen adapted the notion in tape and live electronic pieces from the mid-1960s to the mid-1970s; in *Telemusik*, for instance, a recording may be given the dynamic envelope of another and the rhythm of yet another.

International Musicological Society (IMS). Body set up in Basle in 1927, responsible for various publications (notably RILM and RISM) and for a congress every five years.

International Society for Contemporary Music. See ISCM.

internet [world wide web]. System of information storage and retrieval in 'cyberspace', i.e. available to anyone at a modern computer with a modem. The system originated as the NSFNET, set up in 1986 by the US National Science Foundation in order to facilitate communication among scholars. It spread rapidly and absorbed other networks, and with the similarly rapid development of home and library computers, it provided global access by the mid-1990s to a vast array of material and e-mail. Its musical effects have been to enlarge the forum for broadcasting (by regular radio and television companies, and indeed by anyone with the necessary technology) and to provide a means of disseminating recordings, which can be retained ('burnt') on recordable CDs. Loss of quality is involved in this process, but the technology is advancing all the time, and attempts to control the resulting copyright abuses may be unsustainable.

interpretation. How a piece is conveyed in performance: the process and the result. The art of interpretation presumes technical adroitness and complete familiarity with the score, the instrument and matters of performance practice. Then comes the coherent expression of the music's substance and meaning, i.e. interpretation.

interrupted cadence. Cadence in which a dominant chord is followed not by the expected tonic but by another chord.

intertextuality. Term introduced by Julia Kristeva in 1969 to cover relationships among literary texts, and applied since the 1980s to musical works. It embraces BORROWING, QUOTATION, ARRANGEMENT and connections based on similarities of form, genre or scoring.

interval. (1) The gap between two pitches, whether sensed as a rise or fall when they are heard consecutively (melodic interval) or as a particular quality when they are heard together (harmonic interval). Throughout the range of most music (as measured, say, by the extent of the piano's keyboard), an interval will sound identifiably the same no matter where it is placed.

Intervals are named according to corresponding positions in a diatonic scale, and these names have persisted even when non-diatonic music is at issue. Thus, taking C as the lower note, the following names apply for intervals of the given numbers of semitones, with those in square brackets being rare:

0 C–C: unison, [C–Dbb: diminished second]

1 [C–C♯: augmented unison], C–Db: minor second

2 C–D: major second, [C–Ebb: dimished third]

3 C–D♯: augmented second, C–Eb: minor third

4 C–E: major third, [C–Fb: diminshed fourth]

5 [C–E♯: augmented third], C–F: (perfect) fourth

6 C–F♯: augmented fourth, C–Gb: diminished fifth

7 C–G: (perfect) fifth, [C–Abb: diminished sixth]

8 [C–G♯: augmented fifth], C–Ab: minor sixth

9 C–A: major sixth, C–Bbb: diminished seventh

10 C–A♯: augmented sixth, C–Bb: minor seventh

11 C–B: major seventh, [C–Cb: diminished octave]

12 C–C: (perfect) octave, [C–Dbb: diminished ninth]

13 [C–C♯: augmented octave], C–Db: minor ninth

etc.

(2) Pause between acts in an opera or parts in a concert (UK).

interval class. Name for interval irrespective of the order and register of the notes. Thus interval class 3 includes not only minor thirds (e.g. C–Eb) but also major sixths (e.g. Eb–C), minor tenths, major 13ths, etc. Accordingly there are but seven interval classes, numbered 0–6. The term and the concept were introduced by Babbitt, in parallel with PITCH CLASS.

interversion. Algorithm applied by Messiaen to sequences of durations, whereby the same change is repeated. For example, if the sequence 1–2–3–4–5–6 is followed by 3–4–2–5–1–6 (reading from the middle outwards), then the next interversion will be 2–5–4–1–3–6, and so on.

In the Steppes of Central Asia (*V sredney Azii* [In Central Asia]). Orchestral work by Borodin, one of 12 commissioned from Russian composers for an exhibition of tableaux vivants planned to celebrate the silver jubilee of Tsar Alexander II. The show was cancelled following an attempt on the tsar's life. Borodin dedicated his score to Liszt. First performance: St Petersburg, 8 Apr 1880.

Intimate Letters (*Listy důvěrné*). Subtitle Janáček gave his Second Quartet, the letters being those he had written to Kamila Stösslová.

Intolleranza (Intolerance). Opera by Nono to his own libretto assembled from diverse sources, concerning a migrant worker (tenor) caught in the machine of police surveillance and bourgeois capitalism. First performance: Venice, 13 Apr 1961 (as *Intolleranza 1960*), rev Florence, 1974 (as *Intolleranza 1970*).

intonarumori (It., noise intoners). Russolo's term for his futurist percussion.

intonation. (1) Quality of a performer's tuning. This is a subjective measure: what is expressive inflection to one listener may be poor intonation for another.

(2) System of tuning, as in JUST INTONATION.

(3) Opening portion of a liturgical text, sung by a priest or soloist before the whole choir enters. In settings of the mass 'Gloria in excelsis Deo' and 'Credo in unum Deum' are often sung as intonations.

(4) Organ prelude to a sacred piece.

intrada. Entrance piece of the 16th–17th centuries, sometimes forming part of a suite. The title has been used again since the early 20th century, notably by Janáček for a movement in his *Glagolitic Mass*.

introduction. Opening. Music is full of openings, especially overtures and preludes. An introduction is normally a slower passage leading into an allegro first movement, or the first number of an opera, where this is an ensemble for three or more singers. The former device – probably encouraged by the growth of public concerts and the need therefore to alert and settle an audience – seems to have been introduced (as it were) in symphonies by Leopold Hofmann. It was taken up by Haydn in his 'London' symphonies, and following him by Mozart, Beethoven (Symphonies Nos.1, 2, 4 and 7), Schubert, Schumann (all four symphonies) and later composers. Introductions are also quite common in chamber music from Haydn onwards, and they occasionally appear in finales (e.g. those of the first symphonies of Beethoven and Brahms), now without their quietening function. The introduction-and-allegro became a separate form with Schumann (Op.92 and Op.134 for piano and orchestra), later examples coming from Ravel and Elgar.

introit. Chant sung during the entrance of the celebrant at mass, forming part of the PROPER.

intuitive music. Term preferred by Stockhausen in the late 1960s and early 1970s for music that performers were meant to intuit (not improvise) in response to indeterminate notation, material on tape, shortwave broadcasts or verbal texts.

invention. Term used for various short compositions in the later 16th century and the 17th, but associated above all with two sets of 15 pieces each by Bach: the two-part inventions (which he called by the Lat. form *inventiones*) and the three-part inventions (for which his term was fantasia, then sinfonia).

Inventionshorn, Inventionstrompete (Ger.). Names given divers short-lived instruments of the 17th–19th centuries mechanically adapted to provide a wider range.

inversion. The turning of a melody, chord, interval or contrapuntal texture upside-down, or the result of doing so: the process of inversion produces an inversion.

(1) In melodic inversion, each interval goes the other way. Bach's Two-Part Invention in C, for example, begins with the conjunct pattern C–D–E–F–D–E–C (in semiquavers), which is soon heard in inversion as A–G–F–E–G–F–A. The immediately following F–E–D–C–E–D–F still counts as an inversion even though the intervals have been altered to maintain the key of C major (major intervals switched to minor, and vice versa), and is still heard as an inversion. Inversions, as much as transpositions, maintain a sense of self-similarity, and are therefore common in forms where that is prevalent, notably the fugue.

(2) In inverting a chord or harmonic interval, the vertical order of the notes is changed. Thus the inversion of a major third (e.g. C–E) is a minor sixth (E–C). Chords of more than two notes will have more than one inversion. For example, any triad has a FIRST INVERSION and a SECOND INVERSION.

(3) If the lines of a contrapuntal texture can be rearranged vertically, the passage is said to be in INVERTIBLE COUNTERPOINT.

inverted cadence. MEDIAL CADENCE.

inverted mordent. See MORDENT.

invertible counterpoint. Counterpoint in which the lines can change places (e.g. two-part counterpoint in which the upper line can be transposed down to become the bass and the lower line transposed up to become the top part) without infringing the rules of harmony and part writing. The writing of such counterpoint is a technical skill – and more than that in examples by Bach in *Die Kunst der Fuge* and other works. Invertible counterpoint may be described as double, triple or quadruple counterpoint, depending on the number of parts, any of which may change places with any other. A piece of triple counterpoint will thus have six forms (with the lines in the vertical orders 1–2–3, 1–3–2, 2–3–1, 2–1–3, 3–1–2 and 3–2–1) and a quadruple counterpoint 24.

Invisible City of Kitezh. See *The* LEGEND OF THE INVISIBLE CITY OF KITEZH.

Invitation to the Dance/Waltz. See AUFFORDE-RUNG ZUM TANZE.

Iolanta. Opera by Tchaikovsky to a libretto by his brother Modest after a play by Henrik Hertz, written to form a double bill with *The Nutcracker*. Iolanta (soprano), blind daughter of King René (bass), is kept oblivious of her malady. Informed of it by Vaudémont (tenor), who has arrived by accident and immediately fallen in love with her, she can then be cured. First performance: St Petersburg, 18 Dec 1892.

Ionian. Glarean's term for the authentic mode C–D–E–F–G–A–B–C, more usually considered at the time a transposition of the Lydian.

Ionisation. Work by Varèse, among the first in the Western classical tradition for percussion alone. The composer suggested a team of 13 players, though it can be played by six. First performance: New York, 6 Mar 1933.

Iphigénie en Aulide (Iphigenia in Aulis). Opera by Gluck to a libretto by Marie François Louis Gand Leblanc Roullet after Racine's play. While Agamemnon (baritone) moves unwillingly toward sacrificing his daughter Iphigenia (soprano), following the goddess Diana's demands, rage and fury come from Clytemnestra (soprano) and Achilles (tenor). At a late stage Diana relents. Gluck cut the extraordinary final war chorus after the first run, but it tends to be restored in modern productions. Wagner made a version that held the stage in Germany into the 20th century. First performance: Paris, 19 Apr 1774.

Iphigénie en Tauride (Iphigenia in Tauris). Opera by Gluck to a libretto by Nicolas François Guillard after a play by Guymond de la Touche based on Euripides. In events long after those of *Iphigénie en Aulide*, Iphigenia (soprano) is Diana's high priestess, condemned against her will to offer sacrifices herself and urged to do so by the Scythian king Thoas (bass). The intended victim is her brother Orestes (baritone), whom she at last recognizes at the near-fatal point. His comrade Pylades (tenor) then vanquishes the Scythians. First performance: Paris, 18 May 1779.

Ippolitov-Ivanov, Mikhail (Mikhaylovich) (b. Gatchina, near St Petersburg, 19 Nov 1859; d. Moscow, 28 Jan 1935). Russian composer, a follower of Rimsky-Korsakov and Tchaikovsky. He studied with Rimsky at the St Petersburg Conservatory (1875–9) and privately (1880–82), and worked in Tbilisi and Moscow as a teacher and conductor, notably as director of the Moscow Conservatory (1905–22). His works include operas, choral music and five exotic orchestral suites, of which the first is *Caucasian Sketches*, Op.10 (1894), with its popular finale 'Procession of the Sardar'.

Iradier (y Salaverri), Sebastián de (b. Labciego, Alava, 20 Jan 1809; d. Vitoria, 6 Dec 1865). Spanish composer, notably of Hispanic songs that gained a wide and notable audience. 'La paloma' remained a favourite into the 20th century, and 'El arreglito' was heard by Bizet, who took it for a folksong and made it the model for the habanera in *Carmen* (then acknowledged the source when he discovered his error). Iradier began his career as a teenage church organist, taught at the Madrid Conservatory (1839–51) and visited Paris to teach Empress Eugénie (1855).

IRCAM (Institut de Recherche et Coordination Acoustique/Musique). Studio for computer music in Paris, opened with Boulez as founder director in 1977. Among composers to have worked there, besides Boulez, are Harvey, Saariaho, Stroppa, Dalbavie and Benjamin. The underground facility has a flexible auditorium, the Espace de Projection.

Ireland. Country where the usual stand-off between art and folk traditions was exacerbated by political-religious differences. Dublin, effectively an English colony in the 18th century, cultivated art music London-style: *Messiah* was first performed there. From early in the next century, the careers of the contemporaries Moore and Field are exemplary: both left Ireland in early youth never to return, making their names by popularizing Irish folksongs abroad (the Catholic Moore) or forgetting everything Irish (the Protestant Field). Composers who emerged later – Balfe, Wallace, Herbert, Stanford – pursued their various careers outside the country, and even since the achievement of independence in 1922 (for all but Ulster), classical music has not been strong. Barry, in the late 20th century, was the first composer to make an international career from an Irish base.

Ireland, John (Nicholson) (b. Bowdon, Ches., 13 Aug 1879; d. Rock Mill, Washington, Sussex, 12 Jun 1962). British composer, who developed a post-Elgar style drawing also on Debussy to effects at once atmospheric, introspective and nostalgic. Trained at the RCM as pianist and composer

(1893–1901), he was a pupil of Stanford. He became organist-choirmaster at St Luke's, Chelsea (1904–26), and also taught at the RCM in the 1920s–30s, before retiring first to Guernsey then to west Sussex. Even more than with most British composers, his music found its particular adherents, and a John Ireland Society was established two years before his death.

Orchestral: MAI-DUN, 1920–21; Piano Concerto, E♭, 1930; *The Overlanders* (film score), 1946–7; etc.

Chamber and instrumental: Violin Sonata No.1, D minor, 1908–9, rev 1917, 1944; No.2, A minor, 1915–17; Cello Sonata, G minor, 1923; Fantasy-Sonata, E♭–E♭ minor, cl, pf, 1943; *The Holy Boy*, pf, 1913 (various arrs); etc.

Vocal: *Greater love hath no man*, ch, org, 1911; *Love unknown* (hymn tune), 1919; songs, etc.

Irino, Yoshirō (b. Vladivostok, 13 Nov 1921; d. Tokyo, 23 Jun 1980). Japanese composer, one of the post-1945 modernists, his *Concerto da camera* (1951) counting as the first Japanese 12-note serial piece. He had private lessons with Moroi while studying economics, turned to composition full time in 1946, and taught at the Tōhō Gakuen School of Music (1952–70) and the Tokyo College of Music (from 1973). Several of his scores include Japanese instruments.

irrational. Term used of a duration or attack in conflict with the basic pulse and its expected duple or triple subdivisions. Irrational values normally appear in groups as triplets, quintuplets, etc.

irregular rhythm. Rhythm departing from its metre (e.g. in having irrational values or syncopations) or having no definable metre at all.

Isaac, Henricus [Heinrich] (b. Flanders/Brabant, *c*.1450–55; d. Florence, 26 Mar 1517). Netherlandish composer, among the leading composers around Josquin, active in Italy and Austria. He was at the ducal court in Innsbruck in 1484, and in Florence the next year in the service of Lorenzo the Magnificent. While there he married. Following Lorenzo's death in 1492 his main patron was Emperor Maximilian I, whom he served in Vienna and Innsbruck, though he maintained his house in Florence and Italian contacts. His major achievement was a collection of mass propers in four parts, apparently intended to cover all Sundays and major festivals. The 99 sets he completed – some commissioned by Konstanz Cathedral in 1508, others probably written for the imperial chapel – were published as *Choralis Constantinus* (3 Vols., 1550–55), possibly assembled by his pupil Senfl (and later edited in part by Webern). He also produced about 40 settings of the mass ordinary, other sacred works and secular songs in German ('Innsbruck, ich muss dich lassen') and Italian ('A la battaglia', 'La morra').

ISCM (International Society for Contemporary Music). Organization founded in Salzburg in 1922, following an international festival of new chamber music at the Salzburg Festival, attended by Bartók, Webern, Hindemith, Honegger and others. Edward Dent was its first president, and its headquarters were in London; now it is run from the Gaudeamus Foundation. It has national sections in most countries where Western classical music is strong, and presents an annual festival of new music, the World Music Days.

Ishii, Maki (b. Tokyo, 28 May 1936; d. Tokyo, 8 Apr 2003). Japanese composer, chiefly of orchestral and instrumental pieces fusing Western modernism with Japanese tradition. The son of a leading male ballet dancer, he studied with Ifukube and Ikenouchi, and in Berlin with Blacher and Rufer (1958–61). His brother, Kan (b. Tokyo, 30 Mar 1921), is known for operas and ballets close to Orff, with whom he studied in Munich (1952–4).

Islam. Culture existing at once in distinct separation from Europe and intimate connection. The separation is expressed in Islamic traditions of art music centred on the improvising soloist, and in the very secondary status of Western classical music in most Islamic countries. On the other hand, all bowed and plucked string instruments entered modern Europe by way of Islam, so that the Western orchestra echoes the sound of this great historical other. See also TURKEY.

isochronism (adj. isochronic). Text-setting in which each syllable occupies the same duration, no matter how many notes it covers.

isomelism. Self-similarity in the melodic openings of the top part (usually) in sections of a 15th-century motet, a phenomenon observed in works by Du Fay and others.

isoperiodicity. Inexact ISORHYTHM, where the phrase-length is the same but only some of the rhythmic detail. This is common in isorhythmic motets in parts other than the tenor.

isorhythm. Self-similarity in the rhythm of parts in a motet or mass section, a practice common in the 14th–15th centuries. An isorhythmic composition will generally be based on a tenor in which the sequence of durations (the TALEA) and the succession of pitches (the COLOR) are both rotating in strict repetition, but not synchronously. For example, Machaut's motet *Fons tocius superbie* has a tenor with a talea of eight notes and a color of 12, so that the two start together again only after three repetitions of the talea (24 notes) and two of the color (similarly 24 notes). Before that, rhythmic repetition will come to different pitches, and pitch repetition to different rhythms. At this level, though, Machaut's piece follows 13th-century practice. What properly distinguishes isorhythm, as it developed as a term in the 20th century, is the presence of self-similarity in the rhythms (but not pitch lines) of parts other than the tenor. In that same Machaut composition, for example, each of the other two parts repeats a rhythmic pattern (one of five notes, the other of eight) over the boundaries between talea statements in the tenor, these passages of sameness alternating with stretches of difference. The music thus has complete, asynchronous but interlocking self-similarities of rhythm and pitch contour in the tenor, together with intermittent self-similarity of rhythm in the other two parts, which makes it 'panisorhythmic'. Many further subtleties are possible, such as repetition of the talea in diminished values.

Isorhythm, thus defined, is frequent in French motets from the early ars nova to Du Fay, and occasional in works by English and Italian composers, as also in other genres, notably the mass. Isorhythmic features may be found as well in ballades. Stimulated by such examples of algorithmic composition by masters of half a millennium and more before, some composers of the mid 20th century worked with isorhythm, especially Messiaen, Davies and Birtwistle.

Isouard, Nicolas (b. Valletta, May 1773/6 Dec 1775; d. Paris, 23 Mar 1818). Maltese–French composer, leading rival to Boieldieu in developing opéra comique, baptized John Joachim Edward Nicholas and known also as Nicolò de Malte, the pseudonym he took to avoid embarrassing his merchant family. Schooled in Paris (until he fled the Revolution in 1790), he was able to complete his musical education in Palermo and Naples (with Sala and Guglielmi). His first opera (Florence, 1794) led to further opportunities in Italy and Malta, before his move back to Paris in 1800. There he produced two opéras comique a year on average, including *Cendrillon* (1810), whose extraordinary public success gained his father's approbation. Perhaps it was from pride in his profession that he set librettos with composer heros in *Cimarosa* (1808) and *Lully et Quinault* (1812).

Israel. Western classical music was introduced by the European Jewish migrants who came in growing numbers from the 1880s, and who founded the Palestine Opera (1923), the Palestine Orchestra (1936) and the Rubin Academy in Tel-Aviv (1945). In 1948, with the foundation of the state of Israel, the orchestra was renamed the Israel Philharmonic; Mehta has been its regular conductor since 1969. Among composers who arrived in the 1930s were Ben-Haim, Wolpe, Partos and Avni.

Israel in Egypt. Oratorio by Handel to a text possibly by Charles Jennens, in three parts: *Lamentations of the Israelites for the Death of Joseph*, *Exodus* and *Moses' Song*, of which the first is usually omitted. Prominently featuring the Children of Israel in its telling of the Exodus story, the score has much for the choir, and that balance has made it, with *Messiah*, one of Handel's most popular oratorios among choral societies. First performance: London, 4 Apr 1739.

istesso tempo, l' (It.). The same tempo, a marking most often used in music before the late 19th century to indicate constancy of beat through a change of metre, e.g. from 2/4 to 6/8, with the new dotted crotchet equal to the old crotchet. In later music, often metrically more unstable, the same message would be conveyed symbolically:

Italian. Name given to Mendelssohn's Fourth Symphony, which includes reminiscences of his 1830–31 visit, not least in its finale, headed 'Saltarello'. First performance: London, 13 May 1833.

italiana in Algeri, L' (The Italian Girl in Algiers). Opera by Rossini to a libretto adapted from that for an opera by Luigi Mosca (1808). The Italian girl is Isabella (contralto), spirited and determined, who contrives not only to outwit the bey Mustafà (bass) and escape with her beloved Lindoro (tenor) but also to reconcile the Algerian to his wife Elvira (soprano). Notable numbers include Isabella's entrance cavatina 'Cruda sorte!', her love song 'Per lui che adoro' and her rousing rondò 'Pensa alla patria'. First performance: Venice, 22 May 1813.

Italian Concerto (*Concerto nach italiänischem Gusto*). Solo keyboard work by Bach.

Italian overture (It. SINFONIA). Instrumental

movement in fast–slow–fast form, introduced by Alessandro Scarlatti (1687) and rapidly established as the standard way in which to open an opera or oratorio – except in France or among composers imitating the FRENCH OVERTURE. Detached from their contexts, Italian overtures were important to the concert repertory emerging in the early 18th century, and composers began writing them as independent pieces, i.e. as symphonies. In their original function as overtures they were replaced in the 1770s–80s by new single-movement, sonata-form types. Schubert's two 'overtures in the Italian style' belong to a later, Rossinian phase in the overture's history.

Italian sixth. Dissonance useful in modulation, the simplest sort of AUGMENTED SIXTH CHORD (A♭–C–F♯ in C major), resolving to the dominant (G–B–D–G).

Italienisches Liederbuch (Italian Songbook). Title Wolf gave to two volumes of songs, setting translations by Paul Heyse of anonymous Italian poems.

Italienische Serenade (Italian Serenade). Rondo in G by Wolf for string quartet, which he called first 'Serenade', then 'Italian Serenade' when he arranged it for a chamber orchestra of strings.

Italy (Italia). Like Germany, Italy was a cultural force long before it became a political entity (with unification in 1861). Its prosperity and artistic vigour from the late 14th century onwards drew many of the finest musicians from the north (Flanders, France, England) and west (Spain), including Ciconia, Du Fay, Josquin, Willaert, Morales, Lassus and Victoria. By the later 16th century, though, the flux was beginning to go the other way. If foreign composers had helped bring to music in Italy the Renaissance virtues of lucidity, clarity and unity, native musicians added the dash of expressive melody, whether for voices or for the violins that were coming into vogue – melody dispensed in songs, in madrigals and in the new genre of opera. For two centuries and more, almost to the end of the 18th century, music had its principal home in Italy, and was a prime export commodity. At first Italian madrigals, distributed through the new Venetian technology of music printing, spurred local traditions of song in France, Germany and, particularly, England. Then Italian composers, singers and instrumentalists were welcomed at courts from Lisbon to St Petersburg, where Italian opera was one of the aristocracy's ruling passions. And Italian terms gained a permanent place in the musical vocabulary: sonata, piano, soprano, allegro, staccato, crescendo and many more.

From the Europe-wide dominance of Italian opera came a sense, continuing to the present, of an Italian genius for song and ease, as opposed to or balanced by a German strength in form and earnestness. Thus Beethoven thought it worthwhile to study with Salieri, and many young composers, before and after him, travelled to Italy in search of musical sunshine. But though the Italian language does indeed lend itself easily to singing, being melodious in its speech patterns and overt in its expressive nuances, German can be no less songful (not least as Schubert made it sound) and the very terms 'sonata' and 'concerto' remain to prove how Italian musicians (especially Corelli) gave standard instrumental forms their beginnings. Also, Italian opera, being so widespread, became a general European concern: the greatest Italian-language operas of the 18th century were written by foreign composers – Handel, Mozart – for foreign audiences.

The Italian tradition is not only thus larger than Italy, it is also smaller, in that each of the major cities had its own musical history, at least during the period before unification (see BOLOGNA, FERRARA, FLORENCE, MANTUA, MILAN, NAPLES, ROME, VENICE). Inevitably those histories intertwined; the development of the madrigal in the 16th century, for example, was shared among composers in Florence, Ferrara, Mantua, Rome, the Neapolitan area and Venice, and the impetus for opera sprang in the first half of the 17th century from Florence to Mantua to Rome and so to Venice, with Naples then becoming the nursery of opera composers throughout the next century. Nevertheless, local conditions – and local pride – maintained distinctions.

Rossini, trained not in Naples but in Bologna, was the first truly national composer, in that he belonged to no regional school and was almost immediately acclaimed the length of the country (and beyond). He also established opera as the Italian musician's primary field, in which he was succeeded by Bellini, Donizetti and Verdi, then at the end of the 19th century by Puccini, Leoncavallo and Mascagni.

In the 20th century Italian music was less single-mindedly operatic and, not entirely coincidentally, once again pan-European, now participating in a confluence. Busoni spent much of his life in Berlin; Casella, Dallapiccola, Malipiero and Petrassi learned from the modernist masters; and Nono, Berio, Bussotti, Togni, Evangelisti and Donatoni belonged in one way or another to the post-1945 avant-garde movement. Still, local traditions may be heard surviving in Nono's

Gabrieli-like feeling for massive choral sonority or Bussotti's madrigalian sense of music as love-making.

David Kimbell *Italian Opera* (1991)

Ivan Susanin. See A LIFE FOR THE TSAR.

Ivan the Terrible. Score by Prokofiev for Eisenstein's unfinished film trilogy about the 16th-century tsar. There are concert versions for soli, choir and orchestra by Abram Stasevich (1961), Michael Lankester (1988) and Christopher Palmer (1990).

Ives, Charles (Edward) (b. Danbury, Conn., 20 Oct 1874; d. New York, 19 May 1954). US composer. The great iconoclast of Western music, he was working with polytonality, atonality, ametrical rhythms, unusual ensembles, spatial music and quotations all in the first two decades of the 20th century, evincing a New World openness and independence. Somewhat paradoxically, he used those means of the new century to express what he remembered as a boy in New England before the automobile. Resolute to the point of being crusty, he had little time for the Europe-beholden musical establishment in New York; correspondingly his music was almost unknown until the 1930s, and only began to be widely performed around the time of his centenary.

He was first taught – and taught to question and experiment – by his bandmaster father, George Ives. From the age of 14 he worked as a church organist, an activity he continued while studying at Yale (1894–8), where he had composition lessons with Parker. He then moved to New York to start in the insurance business, but went on as a church musician, and in that capacity wrote works both conventional (*The Celestial Country*) and unconventional (Psalm 67, whose five-note chords suggest two keys being heard simultaneously). In other pieces of this time, notably his first quartet and first two symphonies, he used US material (hymn tunes, popular songs) in a manner emanating from Dvořák, Brahms and Tchaikovsky.

In 1902 he gave up his church appointment; at the beginning of 1907 he founded his own insurance company; and later the same year he married (his wife's name was Harmony). Insurance in his view was a democratic institution, spreading the costs of individual hardship; profit was secondary. But since his agency became the most widely used insurer in the country, he prospered sufficiently to be able later to help fellow composers whose musical ideals he shared (especially Cowell). He also had the means to buy, in 1912, a house back near his home town, in West Redding, where he spent long summers with his wife, their adopted daughter, visiting nieces and nephews, and impoverished New Yorkers he had stay for holidays.

Meanwhile, as a composer, he moved decisively away from the norm. Because none of his music was published or performed until much later, and because he often went on revising his manuscripts (as if each piece were an open field for exploration), his works are hard to date. Still, he seems to have begun making startling excursions around 1908 (*The Unanswered Question*) and entered his stride around 1911. In his orchestral music – usually prompted by the memory of a specific image or moment from childhood or youth, as in *Three Places in New England* and the symphony *New England Holidays* – themes from popular songs, hymns and marches emerge from and dissolve into entanglings with others or mists of dissonant harmony. Often there is a cinematic sense of scene and close-up. In his many songs, words would provide the occasion for nostalgic reverie on hymn tunes (*At the River*), comic sketch (*Ann Street*), grand atonal rhetoric (*Paracelsus*), breezy Americana (*Charlie Rutlage*) or a characteristic and unparalleled mixture of the visionary and the commonplace (*General William Booth Enters into Heaven*). From literature, too, came the indoor and outdoor atmospheres, sweeping and ruminative, of his most important piano work, the 'Concord' Sonata. Rarely did he write an abstract piece; those entitled *Tone Roads* are studies in freely evolving atonality but linked with the idea of striding into unmapped territory, and his note on his Second Quartet indicates that the independence of parts was to suggest an argumentative discussion. The breeching of musical boundaries was always a priority, and he chose topics and texts that would take him there. Beyond that – and beyond even his most specific evocations of time and place – he shared the aim of 19th-century US writers and philosophers to discover eternity.

In 1918 he suffered a heart attack and was out of the office for a year. He began putting together three volumes for publication: the 'Concord' Sonata, the accompanying *Essays before a Sonata*, and a book of 114 songs, all of which he arranged to be printed and distributed in 1920–22. Next he worked at completing his Fourth Symphony, a conspectus and consummation of his musical world, after which he fell silent, his last work being a song, 'Sunrise' (1926). He retired from business in 1930. Slowly, then, his music began to be heard, notable events including the first performances of *Three Places* (1931, under Slonimsky), the 'Concord' Sonata (1938, John Kirkpatrick), the Third

Symphony (1946) and the Second Symphony (1951). In declining health, listening to the Second Symphony over the radio, he did at last hear his strenuous imagination confirmed.

Charles Ives *Essays before a Sonata*, ed. Howard Boatwright (1961); Jan Swafford *Charles Ives* (1996)

www.charlesives.org

All composition dates approximate; many works in different versions (notably as songs and scores for chamber orchestra); many edited or realized by others.

Orchestral (full): Symphony No.1, 1898–1901, rev 1907–8; No.2, 1907–9; No.3 'The Camp Meeting', 1908–11; No.4, 1912–25; *The General Slocum*, 1909–10; *Yale-Princeton Football Game*, 1910–11; *Emerson Overture*, pf, orch, 1910–14, rev 1920–21; NEW ENGLAND HOLIDAYS, 1911–20; *Robert Browning Overture*, 1912–14, rev 1936–42; THREE PLACES IN NEW ENGLAND (Orchestral Set No.1), 1912–21; Orchestral Set No.2, 1915–19; No.3, 1912–22; UNIVERSE SYMPHONY, 1915–28, unfinished

Orchestral (chamber): *From the Steeples and the Mountains*, tpt, trbn, bells, 1905–6; *Scherzo: All the Way Around and Back*, 6 insts, 1907–8; *The* UNANSWERED QUESTION, 1908, rev 1930–35; *Central Park in the Dark*, 1909, rev 1936; Overture and March '1776', 1909–10; *Scherzo: Over the Pavements*, 9 insts, 1910, rev 1926–7; 'Country Band' March, 1910–14; *Tone Roads* Nos.1 and 3, 1913–14; Set for Theatre Orchestra, 1915 (*In the Cage, In the Inn, In the Night*); Set No.1, 1915–16 (*The See'r, A Lecture, The Ruined River, Like a Sick Eagle, Calcium Light Night, Allegretto sombreoso*); 4 Ragtime Dances, 1915–21; Set No.2, 1916–17 (*The Indians, Gyp the Blood, Ann Street, The Last Reader*); Set No.3, 1918–19 (*At Sea, Luck and Work, Premonitions*); *Chromâtimelôdtune*, 1923; Suites Nos.4–10, ?1925–30 (*Afterglow, Charlie Rutlage, Evening, Mists, The New River, The Pond, The Rainbow, Swimmers*, etc.); *The Circus Band*, 1932–3; *The Gong on the Hook and Ladder*, 1934; etc.

Choral: Psalm 67, ch, 1898–9; *The Celestial Country* (cantata; Henry Alford), soli, ch, orch, 1898–1902; Psalm 24, ch, 1901, rev 1912–13; Psalm 25, ch, org, 1901, rev 1912–13; Psalm 54, 1902; Psalm 100, ch, insts ad lib, 1902; Psalm 14, 1902, rev 1912–13; Psalm 135, ch, insts, 1902, rev 1912–13; *Three Harvest Home Chorales*, ch, brass, org, 1912–15; Psalm 90, ch, bells, org, 1923–4; *General William Booth Enters into Heaven*, ch, orch, 1934, arr Becker under Ives's supervision; etc.

Chamber: String Quartet No.1 'From the Salvation Army', 1897–1900, 1909; No.2, 1913–15; A Set of 3 Short Pieces, str qt, db, pf, 1903–9; *The Gong on the Hook and Ladder*, str qt, db, pf, 1912; *Hallowe'en*, pf qnt, drum ad lib, 1914; *In re con moto et al.*, pf qnt, 1915–16, rev 1923–4; Piano Trio, 1909–10, rev 1914–15; etc.

Violin and piano: Pre-First Violin Sonata, 1908–13; Violin Sonata No.1, 1914, rev 1917–18; No.2, 1914–17, rev 1920–21; No.3, 1913–14; No.4, 1911–16; Largo, vn, pf, 1909–10; *Decoration Day*, vn, pf, 1919

Songs: 'Ann Street' (Maurice Morris), 1921; 'At the River' (Robert Lowry), 1916; 'Charlie Rutlage' (Dominick John 'Kid' O'Malley), 1920–21; 'A Christmas Carol' (Ives), before 1898; 'The Circus Band' (Ives), ?1899; 'Down East' (Ives), 1919; 'Evening' (Milton), 1921; 'General William Booth Enters into Heaven' (Vachel Lindsay), 1914; 'Like a Sick Eagle' (Keats), 1920; 'Memories' (Ives), 1897; 'Paracelsus' (Browning), 1921; 'Qu'il m'irait bien', 1897–9; 'Remembrance' (Ives), 1921; 'The See'r' (Ives), 1914–15; 'Serenity' (Whittier), 1919; 'The Side Show' (Ives), 1921; 'Sunrise' (Ives), 1926; 'Tarrant Moss' (Kipling), 1902–3; 'They are There!' (Ives), 1924; 'The Things Our Fathers Loved' (Ives), 1917; 'Thoreau' (Ives), 1920; 'Tom Sails Away' (Ives), 1917; 'Two Little Flowers' (Charles and Harmony Ives), 1921

Piano: Sonata No.1, 1915–16, 1920–22; No.2 'CONCORD', 1916–19; Set of 5 Take-Offs, 1909; Three-Page Sonata, 1910–11, rev 1925–6; Waltz-Rondo, 1911; 23 Studies (No.9 *The Anti-Abolitionist Riots*, 1912–13; No.20 March, 1917–19; No.21 *Some Southpaw Pitching*, 1918–19; No.22, 1918–23); Varied Air and Variations, 1920–22; 3 Quarter-Tone Pieces, 2 pf, 1923–4; etc.

Organ: Variations on 'America', 1891–2, rev 1909–10; etc.

jack. One of the wooden struts in a keyboard instrument on each of which a plectrum (harpsichord family) or hammer (piano) is mounted.

Jackson, Francis (Alan) (b. Malton, Yorks., 2 Oct 1917). British composer, organist and church musician, a pupil and follower of Bairstow, whom he succeeded at York Minster (1946–82). His works include organ sonatas, anthems and canticles.

Jacob, Gordon (Percival Septimus) (b. London, 5 Jul 1895; d. Saffron Walden, 8 Jun 1984). British composer, especially known for his lively and brilliant concertos and as a teacher at the RCM (1924–66), where he himself had studied with Stanford, Howells and Vaughan Williams after serving in the First World War.

Jacobi, Frederick (b. San Francisco, 4 May 1891; d. New York, 24 Oct 1952). US composer, especially of music based on Jewish subjects and musical material. He studied in New York with Goldmark and Bloch, and in Berlin with Juon. In the 1920s he made some use of Amerindian music he had studied on the spot, but from 1930 onwards he concentrated on the Jewish heritage, whether in liturgical music or concert pieces evoking biblical heros.

Jacob's Dream. Name given to the second movement of Haydn's piano trio in E♭ minor, H.15:31.

Jacobs, Paul (b. New York, 22 Jun 1930; d. New York, 25 Sep 1983). US pianist, a brilliant exponent especially of 20th-century music (Debussy, Stravinsky, Busoni). Taught and encouraged by his mother, he went to Paris in 1951 and joined Boulez's circle. Back in New York he made notable recordings for Nonesuch and was the Philharmonic's pianist. He was an early victim of AIDS.

Jacobs, René (b. Ghent, 30 Oct 1946). Belgian conductor and countertenor. He sang as a boy at Ghent Cathedral, and continued singing studies with Louis Devos and Lucie Frateur, soon becoming one of the rising countertenor stars of early music. In 1977 he founded the ensemble Concerto Vocale, with which he has performed and recorded operas by Monteverdi, Cavalli and Handel.

Jacopo da Bologna (*fl.* ?1340–60). Italian composer, whose sweetly consonant polyphony and shapely melody influenced younger compatriots, notably Landini. He was associated with the Visconti court in Milan, and wrote mostly madrigals in two or three parts, including the only known Petrarch setting from the poet's lifetime (*Non al suo amante*) and a work suggesting French music in having three simultaneous texts (*Aquila altera*).

Jacquet de la Guerre, Elisabeth (baptized Paris, 17 Mar 1665; d. Paris, 27 Jun 1729). French composer and harpsichordist, the first woman in France to write an opera (*Céphale et Procris*, f.p. Paris, 1694). Her father, Claude Jacquet, was an organist; other members of the family made harpsichords; and at 19 she married an organist, Marin de la Guerre. Before that she played and sang at court, and gained Madame de Montespan's protection. After marrying she played and taught in Paris, and published volumes of keyboard pieces, violin sonatas and cantatas.

Jacquet of Mantua (b. Vitré, 1483; d. Mantua, 2 Oct 1559). French–Italian composer, a follower of Josquin who matured to create, in his suave continuous polyphony, a model for Palestrina. His surname was Colebault, but he was known always by the diminutive form of his Christian name. In Italy by 1519, he was in Mantua from 1526, serving the cardinal-bishop Ercole Gonzaga. His works include 24 masses and motets.

Jadassohn, Salomon (b. Breslau/Wrocław, 13 Aug 1831; d. Leipzig, 1 Feb 1902). German teacher, notably at the Leipzig Conservatory from 1871. He himself had studied there and also with Liszt in Weimar (1849–52). Though he was thoroughly active as a composer, he is remembered more as the teacher of Busoni and Grieg, and for textbooks on composition and harmony.

Jaëll, Marie [née Trautmann] (b. Steinseltz, near Wissembourg, Alsace, 17 Aug 1846; d. Paris, 4 Feb 1925). French pianist-teacher, who evolved a method based on an understanding of the physiology and psychology of muscle action. She studied with Herz at the Paris Conservatoire and was, with her pianist husband Alfred (1832–82), acquainted with Liszt. She was also the first French pianist to play all the Beethoven sonatas (1893).

Jagd (Ger.). Hunt, hence *Jagdhorn*, *Jagdmusik*, etc.

Jäger (Ger.). Hunter, hence *Jägerhorn*, *Jägermusik*, etc.

Jahreszeiten, Die. See *The* SEASONS.

Jakobsleiter, Die (Jacob's Ladder). Unfinished oratorio by Schoenberg, orchestrated by Winfried Zillig. Set in heaven, it concerns the journey of the soul towards perfection. First performance: Vienna, 16 Jun 1961.

jam session. Gathering of (usually jazz) musicians to jam (i.e. improvise) together.

Janáček, Leoš [Leo Eugen] (b. Hukvaldy, Moravia, 3 Jul 1854; d. Moravská Ostrava, 12 Aug 1928). Czech composer. Though older than Mahler and groomed in the tradition of Dvořák, he belonged musically with the generation of Bartók and Stravinsky. Not only did he produce most of his greatest works – including four of his five principal operas – in the 1920s, when he was past 65, he also shared his younger contemporaries' zest for folk

music in the raw. With that went a closeness to the rhythms and intonations of Moravian speech, producing a Musorgsky-like realism – except at those equally characteristic junctures of sudden and abundant lyrical glow. His orchestral writing is similarly individual, with its energetic ostinato patterns, its strongly characterized motifs, its tangy combinations and its open spacings.

The son and grandson of village teachers and musicians, he began his long apprenticeship in the choir of the Augustinian monastery in Brno, from which he went on to the city's teacher-training college (1869–72). He remained in the city as a teacher and choirmaster, apart from brief periods of further study at the organ school in Prague (1874–5), where he got to know Dvořák, and at the conservatories of Leipzig (1879–80) and Vienna (1880). In 1881, recently married, he was appointed director of the new organ school in Brno, a post he retained until 1919. Neither his composing nor his marital life was so settled. Apart from his first, Dvořákian opera *Šárka*, not performed at the time, his creative achievements in his 20s and 30s consisted mostly of small choral pieces and folksong arrangements, and his harsh treatment of his young wife – not yet 16 when they married – resulted in a long period of separation. Even when they were back together their relationship was strained, and after the deaths of their young son (1890) and 20-year-old daughter (1903) they lived as strangers.

During the decade of work on *Jenůfa* (1894–1903) he discovered all the themes and means of his operatic maturity, not least the tight drawing of an inevitable tragedy and then, at the last moment, the outburst of optimistic hope in youth and love. But though the work was a success in Brno, it was not seen elsewhere, and its composer was left directionless again. He worked in turn on two troublesome if striking operatic projects, the semi-autobiographical *Osud* and the comic fantasy *The Excursions of Mr Brouček*, of which the latter again occupied 10 years (1908–17). Other works of this period include further choruses and a violin sonata.

Various circumstances then released his creative energy. *Jenůfa* was at last staged in Prague (1916) and began from there its international career. He was freed from administrative and teaching obligations at the organ school, though he continued to give master classes. His patriotic hopes were fulfilled with the creation of an independent Czechoslovakia in 1918. And in 1917 he fell in love with Kamila Stösslová, a married woman less than half his age. Henceforth she was his confidante (in a voluminous correspondence) and his muse. Transmuted, she became the heroines of three operas he wrote in quick succession – *Katya Kabanova*, *The Cunning Little Vixen* and *The Makropulos Case* – and the boy who radiates and reflects humanity in the prison of his last, *From the House of the Dead*. She was also the seductress of the dramatic song cycle *Diary of One who Disappeared*. He wrote the *Glagolitic Mass* for their imaginary marriage, and two string quartets that told their story with reference to a Tolstoy novella (*The Kreutzer Sonata*) and to his letters to her. In these late years he also expressed himself vividly in newspaper articles.

Hindered by Nazism and war, his works were slow to make their way into wide circulation. Charles Mackerras's recordings of the major operas in the 1970s hastened them on their way.

Jaroslav Vogel *Leoš Janáček* (1963, ²1981); Vilem and Margaret Tausky, ed. *Janáček: Leaves from his Life* (1982)

Operas: *Šárka* (Julius Zeyer), 1887, rev 1918–19, 1925, f.p. Brno, 1925; *The Beginning of a Romance* (Jaroslav Tichý, after Gabriela Preissová), 1891, f.p. Brno, 1894; JENŮFA, 1894–1903; OSUD, 1903–5; *The* EXCURSIONS OF MR BROUČEK, 1908–17; KATYA KABANOVA, 1920–21; *The* CUNNING LITTLE VIXEN, 1922–3; *The* MAKROPULOS CASE, 1923–5; FROM THE HOUSE OF THE DEAD, 1927–8

Orchestral: Suite, str, 1877; *Idyll*, str, 1878; *Jealousy*, 1895, original overture to *Jenůfa*; *The Fiddler's Child*, 1913; TARAS BULBA, 1915–18; *The Ballad of Blaník*, 1919; Lachian Dances, 1924; *The Danube*, 1923–5, completed by Chlubna, and by M. Štědroň and L. Faltus; Sinfonietta, 1926; Violin Concerto, 1926, completed by Faltus and Štědroň; *Schluck und Jau* (incidental music; Hauptmann), 1928, 2 pieces drafted; etc.

Choral: *Amarus* (cantata; Jaroslav Vrchlický), soli, ch, orch, 1896–7, rev 1901, 1906; *Our Father*, t, ch, hp, org, 1901, rev 1906; *Zdrávas Maria*, t, ch, vn, org, 1904; *Kantor Halfar*, men's ch, 1906; *Maryčka Magdónova*, men's ch, 1906, rev 1907; *70,000*, men's ch, 1909, rev 1912; Mass, E♭, soli, ch, org, 1908, unfinished; *The Čarták on Soláň* (cantata; Kurt Honolka), men's ch, orch, 1911, rev 1920; *The Eternal Gospel* (cantata; Vrchlický), soli, ch, orch, ?1913–14; GLAGOLITIC MASS, 1926–7; etc.

Chamber: Concertino, pf, 2 vn, va, cl, hn, bn, 1925; Capriccio, pf left hand, fl and pic, 6 brass, 1926; MLÁDÍ, 6 wind, 1924; String Quartet No.1 'The KREUTZER Sonata', 1923; No.2 'INTIMATE LETTERS', 1928; Violin Sonata, 1914–15, rev 1916–22; *Pohádka* (*Fairy Tale*), vc, pf, 1910, rev 1912, 1923; etc.

Chamber vocal: DIARY OF ONE WHO DISAPPEARED, 1917–20; *Říkadla* (*Nursery Rhymes*), ch, ens, 1926

Piano: *Thema con variazioni*, 1880; *On the Overgrown Path*, 1900–11; Sonata '1.X.1905', 1905–6; *In the Mists*, 1912; Three Moravian Dances, 1904–21; *Reminiscence*, 1928

Janequin [Jannequin], **Clément** (b. Châtellerault, c.1485; d. Paris, after 1558). French composer, remembered especially for his polyphonic songs imitating birdsong (*Le Chant des oiseaux*), fanfares, war cries and the clash of arms (*La Bataille de Marignan*), hunting calls (*La Chasse*), etc. He served leading clerics in Bordeaux (1505–29) and was then based in Angers and Paris (from 1549), becoming composer in ordinary to the king in his last years. Over 250 songs by him survive, most of them in four parts and many in publications by Attaingnant; even those without onomatopoeic effects are marked by short motifs and vigorous rhythms. Of sacred music he wrote rather little, and one of his two masses is based on *La Bataille*.

janissary (Turkish *jeni çeri*, new troop). Elite troop of the Ottoman Empire, founded in 1329. Their bands of shawms, trumpets, drums and cymbals made a big impression in the West, and imitations of them ('janissary music') contributed to the painting of Turkey or militarism in music from the late 17th to the early 19th century, including works by Mozart (*Die Entführung*), Haydn ('Military' Symphony) and Beethoven (Ninth Symphony).

Janko, Paul von (b. Totis/Tata, 2 Jun 1856; d. Constantinople, 17 Mar 1919). Hungarian inventor, especially in 1882 of a piano keyboard with six rows of touch points, each row sounding the notes of a whole-tone scale. With keys closer together, the player could produce wide chords, but that advantage did not outweigh the impediment of having to learn an entirely changed instrument, and the Janko keyboard soon died out.

Janowitz, Gundula (b. Berlin, 2 Aug 1937). German soprano, whose full and lovely lyric soprano specially graced Mozart and Strauss. After studies in Graz she made her debut at the Vienna Staatsoper (Barbarina, 1960), where she sang through three decades, also appearing at Salzburg and occasionally abroad.

Jansons, Mariss (b. Riga, 14 Jan 1943). Latvian conductor, among the most musically exciting of his time. The son of the conductor Arvīds Jansons (Arvid Yansons), he studied at the Leningrad Conservatory, with Hans Swarowsky in Vienna (1969–72) and with Karajan in Salzburg. His posts as music director have been with the Oslo Philharmonic (1979–2000), the Pittsburgh Symphony (from 2000), the Bavarian Radio Symphony (from 2003) and the Royal Concertgebouw (from 2004).

Japan (Nihon). No country outside the European–

American sphere has embraced Western music with anything like Japanese avidity. European-style classical music was welcomed as a sign of the Westernization sought after the country turned away from isolation in 1868, and again as a mark of the modernization proceeding after 1945. By the late 20th century Tokyo had a wealth of orchestras, concert halls, recital series and visiting companies similar to that of London or New York, as well as a big stake in the recording industry. A Japanese tradition of Western-style composition had also developed, especially after the emergence of Takemitsu, Ichiyanagi, Irino and Yuasa in the 1950s. Among composers of the next generation are Tanada, Nishimura and Hosokawa.

Western contact with Japan has brought influences the other way as well, from a rather generalized oriental pentatony in Puccini's *Madama Butterfly* through connections in the 1960s with specific instruments and traditions (Cowell's two koto concertos, Messiaen's impression of GAGAKU in *Sept haïkaï*, Britten's adaptation of Noh drama in *Curlew River*) to more continuing involvements with Japanese cultures old and new in the work of Stockhausen and Zorn.

Jaques-Dalcroze, Emile (b. Vienna, 6 Jul 1865; d. Geneva, 1 Jul 1950). Swiss pioneer of a system of music education, eurhythmics, by which musical responsiveness is encouraged and developed through bodily movement. He studied music in Geneva, Paris and Vienna, and began applying his method as a harmony teacher at the Geneva Conservatory in the 1890s. In 1914 he founded his own institute in Geneva, the centre of a rapidly developing international organization.

Járdányi, Pál (b. Budapest, 30 Jan 1920; d. Budapest, 29 Jul 1966). Hungarian composer, a follower of Kodály, his teacher at the Liszt Academy (1936–42). He taught there himself (1944–59), and wrote a 'Vörösmarty' Symphony (1952), a concertino for violin and strings (1964), choral pieces and chamber music.

Jarnach, Philipp (b. Noisy-le-Sec, near Paris, 26 Jul 1892; d. Börnsen, near Bergedorf, 17 Dec 1982). French-German composer, best known for having completed Busoni's opera *Doktor Faust*. He studied with Lavignac in Paris, and became close to Busoni in Zurich during the First World War. In 1921 he followed Busoni to Berlin; he then taught at the conservatory in Cologne (1927–49).

Jason. See GIASONE; MEDEA.

Jatékok (Games). Continuing sequence of short piano pieces by Kurtág, an extraordinary journey of instruction and fantasy incorporating inventions, homages, jokes and moments of pungent expression. The first four volumes, of which the fourth is for four hands, date from 1973–6. Three further volumes include pieces written up to 2002.

jazz. Tradition that has provided Western classical music with an alternative – rival and nourisher – since the start of the 1920s. Jazz became an international rage straight after the First World War, and though it was essentially independent of the classical tradition – in being improvised and therefore transmitted aurally, in having its roots in RAGTIME and other mixes of US, African and European elements, in existing outside the world of formal education, in developing its own styles and its characteristic ensembles – contact was inevitable.

From the classical side, Milhaud's experience is illustrative. He heard jazz in London in 1920 and Harlem in 1922, and responded in *La Création du monde* (1923), in which he at once embraced many of the aspects of jazz that would go on appealing to classical composers: compound metres, syncopation, added-note harmonies, an ensemble led by saxophones and brass, and an atmosphere of transgression. By the end of the decade jazz had entered the music of composers as different as Berg and Stravinsky, Hindemith and Copland, Weill and Ravel, Martinů and Poulenc, Schulhoff and Wolpe. Reckoned the flavour of modernity, it had also been responsible for the spectacular success of Krenek's opera *Jonny spielt auf* (1927). Meanwhile, influence was going the other way. Ellington's band worked from scores he had composed, and Gershwin created jazz-classical fusions not fundamentally different from those of Stravinsky or Ravel.

Though jazz and classical music have developed since along their own distinct and frequently bifurcating roads, instances of proximity and overlap have been frequent. Classical composers whose music has touched on jazz include, again, many disparate characters – Babbitt and Bernstein, Schuller and Henze, Banks and Globokar, Stockhausen and Turnage – while Benny Goodman and Keith Jarrett are among jazz instrumentalists to have performed compositions from the classical repertory. See also POPULAR MUSIC.
Ted Gioia *The History of Jazz* (1997)

Jeffreys, George (b. *c*.1610; d. Weldon, Northants., 4/5 Jul 1685). English composer, influenced by Grandi and other Italian contemporaries. He spent his entire adult life in service to the Hatton family, copying Italian music and writing church music together with a smaller quantity of secular songs and fantasias.

Jehannot de l'Escurel [Jehan de Lescurel] (*fl.* early 14th century). French composer, known for songs appended to the *Roman de Fauvel*, all but one of them monophonic.

Jelinek, Hanns [Johann] (b. Vienna, 5 Dec 1901; d. Vienna, 27 Jan 1969). Austrian composer, who trafficked between light music and the 12-note school. He studied briefly with Schoenberg and Berg in his late teens, but did not become an out-and-out serial composer until after the Second World War. As a younger man he played the piano in bars and cinemas, and wrote popular songs and satirical pieces.

Jeney, Zoltán (b. Szólnok, 4 Mar 1943). Hungarian composer, motivated by Cage and US minimalism. He studied with Farkas at the Liszt Academy (1961–6) and with Petrassi in Rome (1969), then was a co-founder with Sáry and Vidovszky of the New Music Studio.

Jenkins, John (b. Maidstone, 1592; d. Kimberley, Norfolk, 27 Oct 1678). English composer, principally of music for viol consort. Probably the son of a carpenter and instrument maker, he spent his life from boyhood to extreme old age as a valued musical guest of noble and gentle families, mostly in East Anglia. His numerous fantasias and fantasia-suites bring the tradition of Byrd, Coprario, the younger Ferrabosco and others to a supreme and long climax, being subtle and persuasive in their use of harmony to create form and exceptional in their understanding of viol sonorities.

Jenkins, Karl (b. Penclawdd, Gower, 17 Feb 1944). Welsh composer, of music frankly combining the driving rhythm of minimalism and rock with traditional sounds from around the world, Western classical and other. He studied at Cardiff University and the RAM (1967–8), and began his professional life in jazz and rock, notably with the Soft Machine. His first 'classical' album, *Adiemus: Songs of Sanctuary* (1995), was the start of an enormously successful new career. Later works include *The Armed Man: A Mass for Peace* (2000).

Jenůfa. Common name outside Czech lands for Janáček's opera to his own libretto after Gabriela Preissová's play, the original title for both play and opera being *Její pastorkyňa* (Her Stepdaughter). Jenůfa (soprano) is the stepdaughter of the Kostelnička (soprano), or sacristan, and is loved by two half-brothers: the macho Števa (tenor), by whom she is pregnant, and the quieter Laca (tenor). The story is one of harsh love. Laca, in a fit of jealousy, disfigures Jenůfa, and the Kostelnička, seeing no alternative, does away with the younger woman's illegitimate child. Finally Jenůfa and Laca are left at the threshold of a frank and loving future. First performance: Brno, 21 Jan 1904.

Jephtha. Oratorio by Handel to a text by Thomas Morrell after Judges 11. Jephtha has promised that, if successful in leading the Israelites in battle against the Ammonites, he will sacrifice whatever should come to greet him on his homecoming. He is horrified when this turns out to be his daughter Iphis, but at the crucial point an angel appears to release him from his vow. First performance: London, 16 Mar 1753.

Jeritza, Maria (b. Brno, 6 Oct 1887; d. Orange, NJ, 10 Jul 1982). Moravian–US soprano, admired as an actress as well as for her rich and powerful voice. Puccini intended *Turandot* for her, and she also created Strauss's Ariadne (both versions) and Empress (*Die Frau ohne Schatten*). She sang regularly at the Met and in Vienna in the 1920s–30s.

Jérusalem. See *I* LOMBARDI.

Jesus. Founder of Christianity, and therefore omnipresent in Christian liturgical music, of which most Western composers have written at least some. The comparatively rare works in which parts of Jesus's story are told outside a liturgical context include Handel's *Messiah* and Birtwistle's *The Last Supper*.

jeté (Fr., thrown). Bowstroke bouncing off the string, up to eight times.

Jeune France, La (Young France). Group of composers comprising Messiaen, Jolivet, Daniel-Lesur and Baudrier, who banded together in 1936 to present concerts and promote music as challenging and expressive, in opposition to the smart ways of Parisian neoclassicism. The group did not outlast the outbreak of the Second World War.

Jeunehomme. Name given to Mozart's Piano Concerto No.9, K.271, supposedly written for a Mlle Jeunehomme.

Jeunesses Musicales. Musical youth movement founded by Maurice Cuvelier in Belgium in 1940, and from 1945 an international organization (Fédération Internationale des Jeunesses Musicales). It promotes music among young people by means of concerts, lectures, courses, camps and exchange programmes.

Jeux (Games). Ballet score by Debussy for choreography by Nijinsky. A play of encounters for two girls and a boy on the tennis court, it is supported by the composer's most teasing and fantastical score. First performance: Paris, 15 May 1913.

Jeux d'eau à la Villa d'Este, Les (The Fountains at the Villa d'Este). Piano piece by Liszt, from the third volume of his *Années de pèlerinage*.

Jeux d'enfants (Children's Games). Set of 12 piano duets by Bizet, who orchestrated five of them as his *Petite suite*.

Jewish music. A strong ethos of appreciation for music has made Jewish families contribute more than most to the ranks of professional musicians, especially in the USA, home to Jewish composers from Irving Berlin to Milton Babbitt, as well as to violinists, conductors, pianists and jazz musicians of Jewish birth. More broadly, the entire Western tradition has important Jewish roots, in that plainsong developed partly from synagogue chant. More specifically, Jewish music includes that of synagogue practices and folk traditions, both highly diverse on account of the long history of Judaism and the wide geographical spread of Jewish communities. In the context of Western classical music, the most important stream is that of the Ashkenazim, the population that was established in Germany in the early Middle Ages and spread from there through northern Europe from Britain and France to Russia and Lithuania, as well as to the USA in the 19th and 20th centuries. The other branch of European Judaism was that of the Sephardim, the Jews of Spain, who migrated elsewhere around the Mediterranean and also to the USA.

Central to all Jewish traditions are sabbath morning and evening services, including the chanting of psalms and other sacred texts, led by a cantor (Hebrew *hazzan*). Salamone Rossi was among the few Jewish composers to publish sacred music before the 19th century, when the Reform tradition brought forth a repertory of music for choir (singing in the vernacular as well as in Hebrew) plus organ. Among composers creating this repertory were Salomon Sulzer (1804–90) in Vienna and Louis Lewandowski (1821–94) in Berlin. Among mid 20th-century composers responsible for sacred services and other liturgical music were Bloch, Milhaud and Schoenberg. Since the 1970s the emphasis has been more on bringing popular music into the synagogue and, outside, reviving popular forms, especially KLEZMER.

jig. See GIGUE. Bach's 'Jig' Fugue is the one in G, BWV 577.

jingles. Small bells, SLEIGHBELLS.

Jingling Johnny. TURKISH CRESCENT.

Jirák, K(arel) B(oleslav) (b. Prague, 28 Jan 1891; d. Chicago, 30 Jan 1972). Czech–US composer, notably of six symphonies and seven quartets. He studied with Novák and Foerster, then was active in Prague between the wars as a critic and teacher; he was also head of music for Czech radio (1930–45). In 1947 he moved to Chicago, to teach at Roosevelt College.

Joachim, Joseph (b. Kitsee/Jarovce, near Pressburg/Bratislava, 28 Jun 1831; d. Berlin, 15 Aug 1907). German violinist, composer and conductor, a friend of Brahms. Born into a Jewish family on Esterházy estates, he made his debut in Pest at seven and then studied in Vienna with Joseph Böhm. In 1843 he went to Mendelssohn and in 1847, on the latter's death, to Liszt. After serving the Hanover court (1853–68) he moved to Berlin, where he taught and conducted. Though he was himself a composer – notably of three violin concertos (No.1, G minor, Op.3, pub *c*.1855; No.2 'in ungarischer Weise', D minor, Op.11, pub 1861; No.3, G, pub 1899) and a *Hamlet* overture (Op.4) – he saw a greater duty to the greater masters, as both soloist and quartet leader. He helped bring about Brahms's Violin Concerto (for which he wrote the standard cadenza), Double Concerto and several chamber works; Schumann's Violin Concerto was also written for him.

Joan of Arc. Inspiration of France, a warrior maiden who was captured and burned at the stake in 1431, aged 19. Works based on her life and legend include a piano sonata by Sterndale Bennett and the following:

(1) Verdi's opera *Giovanna d'Arco*, to a libretto by Solera after Schiller's play. Joan (soprano) dies not at the stake but in battle, having saved the day for Charles VII (tenor), with whom she shares tender feelings; her father Giacomo (baritone) consistently voices concern. First performance: Milan, 15 Feb 1845.

(2) Tchaikovsky's opera *The Maid of Orleans* (*Orleanskaya deva*), to his own libretto after the same source. Joan (soprano/mezzo-soprano) secures the coronation of Charles VII (tenor); it is love for the Burgundian knight Lionel (baritone)

that leads to her downfall – this time indeed at the stake. First performance: St Petersburg, 25 Feb 1881.

(3) Honegger's dramatic oratorio *Jeanne d'Arc au bûcher*, to words by Claudel. Joan (speaker) is absorbed in music telling of her past, her present and her heavenly future. First performance: Basle, 12 May 1938.

(4) Boesmans's opera *La Passion de Gilles*. Joan (soprano) and her comrade-in-arms Gilles de Rais (baritone) pursue paths to sanctity and damnation. First performance: Brussels, 18 Oct 1983.

Job. Biblical model of endurance. He was adopted as a patron by Renaissance musical guilds, and has had his story told by Parry and Davies as oratorio, Vaughan Williams as ballet and Dallapiccola as opera.

Jochum, Eugen (b. Babenhausen, Bavaria, 1 Nov 1902; d. Munich, 26 Mar 1987). German conductor, most valued in Bruckner. He studied in Munich, and worked his way up through posts in Kiel, Mannheim and Duisburg to become music director for Berlin radio in 1932. From there he moved to Hamburg as principal conductor of the opera and philharmonic (1934–49), after which he was founder conductor of the Bavarian Radio Symphony (1949–60), joint chief conductor with Haitink of the Concertgebouw Orchestra (1961–4) and conductor laureate of the LSO (from 1975).

Johnson, Robert (b. London, *c*.1583; d. London, Nov 1633). English lutenist-composer, who wrote songs for plays, including Shakespeare's *The Tempest* ('Full fathom five', 'Where the bee sucks'), *The Winter's Tale* ('Get you hence') and *Cymbeline* ('Hark, hark, the lark!'). The son of the lutenist-composer John Johnson, he followed his father in royal service, and wrote almans and pavans as well as songs.

Johnson, Robert Sherlaw (b. Sunderland, 21 May 1932; d. Appleton, Oxon., 3 Nov 2000). British composer, a follower of Messiaen, whose classes he attended while in Paris as Boulanger's pupil (1957–8), after studies at Durham University (1950–53) and the RAM (1953–7). He taught at the universities of York (1965–70) and Oxford (1970–99), and wrote a book on Messiaen, besides performing and recording much of the piano music. His own works include three piano sonatas and *Green Whispers of Gold* for soprano, piano and tape (1971).

Johnson, Scott (b. Madison, Wis., 12 May 1952).

US composer, open to rock influences and a pioneer in deriving melodies from sampled speech (*John Somebody* for electric guitar and tape, 1982). He studied at the University of Wisconsin and moved to New York in 1975.

Johnson, Tom (b. Greeley, Col., 18 Nov 1939). US composer, author of *The Four Note Opera* for four singers and piano (1972), *Rational Melodies* (1982) and other works within tight constrictions, besides a masterpiece of musical humour – *Failing* for speaking bassist (1975) – and the *Bonhoeffer Oratorium* for choir and orchestra (1988–92). He studied at Yale and privately with Feldman, and followed downtown music in New York for the *Village Voice* (1972–82), then moved to Paris in 1983.

Johnston, Ben(jamin Burwell) (b. Macon, Georgia, 15 Mar 1926). US composer, an exponent of JUST INTONATION. He studied with Partch (1950–51), with Milhaud at Mills and with Cage (1959–60), and taught at the University of Illinois (1951–83). His works include 10 quartets.

Joke. Name given to Haydn's Quartet Op.33:2, for his use of silence in the finale.

Jolas, Betsy (b. Paris, 5 Aug 1926). French composer, who has created a path somewhere between Boulez and the Renaissance in pursuing both avant-garde sounds and lyrical polyphony. The daughter of Eugène and Maria Jolas, publishers of the literary review *transition*, she was brought up in Paris and New York, with Joyce and Hemingway among visitors to the house. In 1946 she returned to Paris, where she entered the Conservatoire (for studies with Messiaen and Milhaud), married (1949) and keenly followed the Domaine Musical. She succeeded Messiaen at the Conservatoire as professor of analysis (1975) and composition (1978). Her works include the opera *Schliemann* (Lyons, 1995), *Quatuor II* for wordless soprano and string trio (1964) and much other chamber music.

Jolivet, André (b. Paris, 8 Aug 1905; d. Paris, 20 Dec 1974). French composer, of music often invoking dance and magic. The son of a painter and a pianist, he trained as a teacher before taking lessons with Paul Le Flem (from 1928) and Varèse. His first important work was *Mana* (1935), a set of six piano pieces based on objects Varèse had left with him (a Balinese statue, a puppet, a bird image, three small animal sculptures by Alexander Calder). Further evocations of magic vitality followed in the *Cinq incantations* for unaccompanied flute in flexible, irregular rhythms (1936) and the *Cinq danses rituelles* for orchestra or piano (1939), both these works coming from the time he was involved with Messiaen in *La* JEUNE FRANCE. His later output includes concertos for ondes martenot (1947), trumpet (1948 and 1954) and percussion (1958), and incidental music from his time as music director of the Comédie Française (1943–59).

Jommelli, Niccolò (b. Aversa, 10 Sep 1714; d. Naples, 25 Aug 1774). Italian composer, a leading innovator in the age of REFORM OPERA. He studied at the San Onofrio conservatory in Naples from 1725, and at the Pietà dei Turchini from 1728, also learning from Hasse and Leo, who were working in the city. After early successes in Naples and Rome he moved to Bologna in 1741 and had further tuition from Padre Martini. He was then based in Venice (mid 1740s) and Rome (1747–53), writing sacred music for the Vatican during part of the latter period, but also travelling to take care of the two or three operas he was producing each year on average. His works were staged all over Italy and in Vienna, and his use in his sinfonias of expressive harmonic and dynamic effects (not least the crescendo) was widely imitated. Seemingly a man of some literary culture, he worked not only with Metastasio librettos but also with texts involving more dramatic forms and events, including onstage suicide in *Sofonisba* (1745). He was then attached to the Stuttgart court (1753–68), where he had the opportunity to go further in writing for the orchestra and incorporating French-style ballet and choral episodes. His last years he spent back in Naples. See also ANDREOZZI, GIARDINI.

Jones, Daniel (Jenkyn) (b. Pembroke, 7 Dec 1912; d. Swansea, 23 Apr 1993). Welsh composer, notably of 13 symphonies and eight quartets in a firmly tonal style with an individual kind of metrical complexity. He studied at the RAM after taking an English degree at Swansea, and was a friend from boyhood of Dylan Thomas, writing music for the original broadcast of *Under Milk Wood* (1954).

Jones, Philip (b. Bath, 12 Mar 1928; d. London, 17 Jan 2000). British trumpeter, founder of the Philip Jones Brass Ensemble (1951–86). He studied with Ernest Hall at the RCM (1944–8), held principal appointments at Covent Garden (1948–51) and then with other London orchestras until 1972, and ended his career as principal of Trinity College of Music (1988–94).

Jongen, (Marie Alphonse Nicolas) Joseph (b. Liège, 14 Dec 1873; d. Sart, 12 Jul 1953). Belgian organist-composer, heir to Franck but also to wider French (d'Indy, Fauré, Debussy) and German (Strauss) influences. He studied at the conservatory in Liège and began his career as a church organist there in 1891, though he spent periods away in Germany (where he had some lessons with Strauss), Paris, Rome and, during the First World War, England. In 1920 he became professor of fugue at the Brussels Conservatory, which he then directed (1925–39). He left a large output, including much chamber music, but is best remembered for his organ music, especially the *Sonata eroica*, Op.94 (1930), and *Symphonie concertante*, Op.81, with orchestra (1926–7). His brother Léon (1884–1969) was also a composer, and succeeded him as director of the Brussels Conservatory (1939–49).

jongleur. Wandering instrumentalist of the 12th–15th centuries (though only later did the term gain this meaning).

Joplin, Scott (b. northeast Texas, 1867/8; d. New York, 1 Apr 1917). US composer, who made the piano rag a sophisticated art form. Of African–US origin, he was a professional musician by the age of 13, then completed his education in Sedalia, Missouri, where he lived, played, composed and taught from 1894. Publication of piano rags, beginning in 1899 with *Original Rags* and the wildly successful *Maple Leaf Rag*, brought him modest financial security and acknowledgement as the 'king' of ragtime. He moved to St Louis in 1901 and New York in 1907, and devoted much effort to opera, notably *Treemonisha*, which he published in vocal score in 1911, though the work had only a few try-out performances during his lifetime. His music was then largely forgotten until 1970, when Joshua Rifkin's record brought it new life. *Treemonisha* was finally staged in full (Atlanta, 1972) and several of the rags were arranged by Marvin Hamlisch for the movie *The Sting* (1973).

All dates given are those of publication.

Piano rags: *Original Rags*, 1899; *Maple Leaf Rag*, 1899; *Swipesy Cake-Walk*, 1900; *The Easy Winners*, 1901; *Peacherine Rag*, 1901; *Sunflower Slow Drag*, 1901; *A Breeze from Alabama*, 1902; *Elite Syncopations*, 1902; *The Entertainer*, 1902; *The Strenuous Life*, 1902; *Palm Leaf*, 1903; *Something Doing*, 1903; *Weeping Willow*, 1903; *The Cascades*, 1904; *The Chrysanthemum*, 1904; *Bethena*, 1905; *Eugenia*, 1906; *The Ragtime Dance*, 1906; *Gladiolus Rag*, 1907; *Heliotrope Bouquet*, 1907; *Searchlight Rag*, 1907; *Fig Leaf Rag*, 1908; *Pine Apple Rag*, 1908; *Sugar Cane*, 1908; *Country Club*, 1909; *Euphonic Sounds*, 1909; *Paragon Rag*, 1909; *Pleasant Moments*, 1909; *Wall Street Rag*, 1909; *Scott Joplin's New Rag*, 1912; *Magnetic Rag*, 1914

Other piano pieces: *Combination March*, 1896; *Great Collision March*, 1896; *Harmony Club Waltz*, 1896; *Augustan Club Waltz*, 1901; *Cleopha*, 1902; *Binks's Waltz*, 1905; *Solace*, 1909

Other works: *Treemonisha* (opera), 1911; songs

Josephs, Wilfred (b. Newcastle upon Tyne, 24 Jul 1927; d. London, 17 Nov 1997). British composer, fecund and bountifully expressive within a basically traditional style. He trained as a dentist, and practised both before and after composition studies with Nieman at the Guildhall School (1954–6) and Deutsch in Paris (1958–9). After winning an international prize with his *Requiem* (1963), a kaddish for the Jewish dead of the Second World War, he was able to live as a composer, producing atmospheric scores for television series (*The Great War*, 1964; *I, Claudius*, 1976), operas (*Rebecca*, Op.126, f.p. Leeds, 1983) and a range of concert works including 12 symphonies and several concertos.

Joshua. Oratorio by Handel to an anonymous text after the Bible. Joshua (tenor) rallies the Israelites to victory at Jericho, backed by Caleb (bass), whose daughter Achsah (soprano) and Othniel (alto) are in love. First performance: London, 9 Mar 1748.

Josquin des Prez (b. ?near Saint Quentin, *c*.1450–55; d. Condé-sur-l'Escaut, 27 Aug 1521). French composer, the outstanding master of polyphony at the high noon of the Renaissance. Often remembered by succeeding generations, his name is found in various forms: Josquin is the diminutive of his baptismal Josse, and his family name in full was Lebloitte dit Desprez (or des Prez). It seems appropriate, however, to know him by roughly the name with which he acrostically signed his motet *Illibata Dei virgo nutrix*, IOSQVIN DES PREZ.

His achievement and his biography have also been muddled by the centuries. Since his name was a byword for excellence in the early 16th century, it was applied fairly indiscriminately by copyists and publishers. And since his range was astonishing, style alone may not readily identify what he wrote. As to his life, until the 1990s he was confused with an older Josquin, and so thought to have been born around 1440. Even now, few facts are certain. Connections in his youth or boyhood with Ockeghem and perhaps also Du Fay remain tantalizing possibilities.

The first documentary notice of him places him at Aix-en-Provence in 1477, when he was a singer in King René's chapel. He may then have served Louis XI of France, or moved directly to the service of Cardinal Ascanio Sforza; certainly he was with the cardinal in Rome in 1484–5 and Milan in 1489. In the latter year he joined the papal chapel, with which he stayed until 1495 and possibly later. He may then have returned to the Sforza cardinal or to the French court before becoming chapelmaster to Ercole d'Este in Ferrara (1503–4). A letter from one of Ercole's agents, discussing this appointment, gives an intriguing glimpse of him in a comparison with his contemporary Isaac: 'Josquin composes better, but he composes when he wants to and not when one wants him to.' Perhaps this independent spirit led him to return to ancestral territory as provost of Notre Dame, Condé-sur-l'Escaut in 1504, where he remained to the end of his life.

Living into the age of music printing, he was the first composer to have his reputation made and his music perpetuated by this medium. Most notably, Petrucci placed Josquin settings first in each of the four collections of motets he issued (1502–5) and also published three volumes of masses by the composer (1502, 1505, 1514). What appealed to contemporaries seems to have been what still appeals: lucidity in texture and harmonic form, sensitivity to words, and audible ingenuity in handling given material (plainsong, popular melody, an existing polyphonic composition) to create something new and fresh. Sometimes the polyphony will be for just two voices, limberly supporting each other, and these duets are used to formal purpose within the generally fuller setting. Formal clarity comes also from the abundant imitation, which opens the music to a listener's perception, and from a sense of harmonic flow maintained through luminous consonance.

His music was still being published and sung long after his death (until 1616 in the case of a psalm in use at the Sistine Chapel). Among those who sang it was Luther, who is reported as saying: 'Josquin is the master of the notes, which must do as he wishes, while other composers must follow what the notes dictate.'

Richard Sherr, ed. *The Josquin Companion* (2000)

Masses, all a 4: *Ad fugam, Ave maris stella, De Beata Vergine, Di dadi, D'ung aultre amer, Faisant regretz, Fortuna desperata, Gaudeamus, Hercules Dux Ferrariae, L'Ami Baudichon, L'Homme armé sexti toni, L'Homme armé super voces musicales, La Sol fa re mi, Malheur me bat, Mater Patris, Pange lingua, Sine nomine, Une Musque de Biscaye*; several separate sections

Motets: *Absalon, fili mi* a 4; *Ave Maria … benedicta tu* a 4; *Ave Maria … virgo serena* a 4; *Benedicta es* a 6; *De profundis* a 5; *Illibata Dei virgo nutrix* a 5; *Inviolata, integra et casta es* a 5; *Miserere mei Deus* a 5; *O Domine Jesu Christe* a 4; *Pater noster* a 6;

Planxit autem David a 4; *Praeter rerum seriem* a 6; *Salve regina* a 5; *Stabat mater* a 5; etc.

Lament: *Nymphes des bois* (*Déploration de Johannes Ockeghem*) a 5

Songs, all a 4: *Adieu mes amours, El grillo, Mille regretz, Scaramella*, etc.

jota. Lively Spanish dance in triple time, imitated by Glinka.

journals. Among the most distinguished in English are *The Musical Quarterly* (from 1915), *Music and Letters* (from 1920), *Notes* (from 1943), the *Journal of the American Musicological Society* (from 1948), *Nineteenth-Century Music* (from 1978), *The Opera Quarterly* (from 1983) and the *Cambridge Opera Journal* (from 1989). See also MAGAZINES.

Judas Maccabaeus. Oratorio by Handel to a text by Thomas Morrell after the Bible. The story was chosen to celebrate the defeat of the 1745 Jacobite rebellion: the title hero (tenor) leads the Jews out of servitude. Numbers include the chorus 'See the conqu'ring hero comes!' First performance: London, 1 Apr 1747.

Judenkünig, Hans (b. Schwäbisch Gmünd, *c*.1445–50; d. Vienna, Mar 1526). German lutenist-composer, who late in life published two books of lute music including teaching material and intabulations.

Judith. Biblical heroine who freed the Jews from siege by captivating and beheading the Assyrian general Holofernes. Her story has been retold in opera or oratorio form by Vivaldi, Arne, Serov, Parry and Honegger.

Juilliard Quartet. Ensemble founded in 1946 by William Schuman, then president of Juilliard, and led until 1997 by Robert Mann. The current team comprises Joel Smirnoff (second violin 1986–97), Ronald Copes, Samuel Rhodes (since 1969) and Joel Krosnick (since 1974). From its beginning the group has favoured new US works (by Babbitt, Carter and others) alongside the classic quartet repertory; it has also made a speciality of *Die Kunst der Fuge*.

Juilliard School. New York conservatory founded in 1905 by Frank Damrosch as the Institute of Musical Art. In 1924 the secretary of the Juilliard Music Foundation, set up according to the will of the self-made millionaire textile importer Augustus D. Juilliard (1836–1919), established the Juilliard Graduate School, and this merged with the Institute two years later to become the Juilliard School of Music. In 1969 the school moved to new premises at Lincoln Center, and its name was shortened to take account of the addition of dance and drama divisions.

Juive, La (The Jewess). Opera by Halévy to a libretto by Scribe. Set with mysterious precision in the Swiss city of Konstanz in 1414, the work has its title character Rachel (soprano) exonerate her beloved Léopold (tenor) but choose to die for her religion with the zealous Eléazar (tenor), whom she believes to be her father. Only after her death, and just before his own, does Eléazar reveal that she was, in fact, the daughter of Cardinal Brogni (bass). The most famous number is Eléazar's 'Rachel, quand du Seigneur'. First performance: Paris, 23 Feb 1835.

Julietta. Opera by Martinů to his own libretto after Georges Neveux's play *Juliette*. Michel (tenor) arrives in a town of people without memory, where he hears Julietta (soprano) and goes in search of her. When he finds her, he discovers they have different impressions of reality and fantasy. Finally he decides to stay in this dream world. First performance: Prague, 16 Mar 1938.

Julius Caesar. See GIULIO CESARE.

Jullien, Louis (George Maurice Adolphe Roch Albert Abel Antonio Alexandre Noé Jean Lucien Daniel Eugène Joseph-le-brun Joseph-Barême Thomas Thomas Thomas-Thomas Pierre Arbon Pierre-Maurel Barthélemi Artus Alphonse Bertrand Dieudonné Emanuel Josué Vincent Luc Michel Jules-de-la-plane Jules-Bazin Julio César) (b. Sisteron, 23 Apr 1812; d. Paris, 14 Mar 1860). French conductor, a showman on a scale to match his name, which he owed to having had as godfathers all 36 members of the Sisteron Philharmonic, his father's orchestra. He studied at the Paris Conservatoire, started out conducting dance music in Paris, and made (and lost) his fortune in England. There he was active from 1840 to 1859, conducting programmes that included quadrilles, novelty items, solo spots and Beethoven symphonies (for which he took a jewelled baton). He also toured the USA under the auspices of P.T. Barnum (1853–4).

junge Lord, Der (The Young Lord). Opera by Henze to a libretto by Ingeborg Bachmann after a story by Wilhelm Hauff. The young English gentleman, Lord Barrat (tenor), creates a sensation in a German town, until he is discovered to be a monkey. First performance: Berlin, 7 Apr 1965.

Juon, Paul [Yuon, Pavel Fyodorovich] (b. Moscow, 6 Mar 1872; d. Vevey, 21 Aug 1940). Russian–German composer, known as 'the Russian Brahms', especially for his chamber works with piano (a sextet, two quintets, two quartets and several trios with strings, a divertimento with wind quintet, and sonatas). The grandson of a confectioner who had emigrated from Switzerland, he attended the German school in Moscow. His conservatory training was with Arensky and Taneyev in Moscow (from 1889) and Bargiel in Berlin (1894–5). He then spent a year teaching at the Baku Conservatory, but in 1898 he returned to Berlin, where he taught at the conservatory (1906–34) before retiring to Switzerland.

Jupiter. Name given to Mozart's last symphony, No.41, possibly at an early London performance.

Jurinac, Sena [Srebrenka] (b. Travnik, 24 Oct 1921). Yugoslav–Austrian soprano, esteemed for the vocal radiance and expressive candour she brought to Mozart and Strauss. She studied with Milka Kostrenčić at the conservatory in Zagreb, where she made her debut in 1942 (Mimì). From 1946 (Cherubino) to 1983 (Marschallin) she was a fixed star at the Vienna Staatsoper; she also appeared at Glyndebourne.

just intonation. Tuning in simple frequency ratios, so that all fifths are 3:2, all major thirds 5:4 and so on. Argument has continued since Zarlino as to the supposed musical and metaphysical virtues of just intervals, and as to whether they may be naturally preferred by singers and string players released from the TEMPERAMENT inevitable for normal keyboard instruments. Some composers since the mid 20th century (Partch, Young, Tenney) have worked with instruments constructed or adapted to provide just intervals.

K. Abbreviation for Köchel's catalogue of Mozart's works. Often the numbering of the sixth edition (1964) – the latest to have been fully revised – replicates that of the first. Where there are divergences, the old numbering has generally proved resilient. For example, the Sinfonia Concertante for violin and viola remains known as K.364, not as K.320d. Intermediate editions include an appendix (Ger. *Anhang*); hence the abbreviation K. Anh. sometimes found.

Kabalevsky, Dmitry (Borisovich) (b. St Petersburg, 30 Dec 1904; d. Moscow, 14 Feb 1987). Russian composer, a lively traditionalist. He studied with Myaskovsky, Catoire and Goldenweiser at the Moscow Conservatory (1925–30), where he joined the staff in 1932. His opera *Colas Breugnon*, Op.24 (f.p. Leningrad, 1938) brought him to the forefront; other notable works include his suite for small orchestra *The Comedians*, Op.26 (1940, based on theatre music), concertos for violin (C, Op.48, 1948) and cello (No.1, G minor, Op.49, 1948–9; No.2, C, Op.77, 1964), and piano compositions (24 Preludes, Op.38, 1943–4; Sonata No.2, Op.45, 1945; No.3, Op.46, 1946). He also wrote appealingly for children, and in later years concentrated on that field.

Kabeláč, Miloslav (b. Prague, 1 Aug 1908; d. Prague, 17 Sep 1979). Czech composer, a steady innovator who interested himself in other musical cultures, including that of the west European avant-garde in the 1960s. He studied with Jirák, Hába and Schulhoff at the Prague Conservatory (1928–32), then worked for the radio in Prague until 1955 (except for the period 1942–5, when he

was excluded on account of having a Jewish wife). His works include eight symphonies (each for a different combination), the orchestral *Hamlet Improvisation*, Op.46 (1962–3), choral music and pieces for percussion ensemble.

Kadosa, Pál (b. Léva/Levice, now in Slovakia, 6 Sep 1903; d. Budapest, 30 Mar 1983). Hungarian composer, a pupil of Kodály at the Liszt Academy (1921–7), where he taught from 1945, following a period at the Fodor Conservatory (1927–43). His output includes eight symphonies, four piano concertos and a lot of solo piano music.

Kafka-Fragmente. Hour-plus work by Kurtág for soprano and violin setting mostly aphoristic texts from Kafka's diaries and letters. First performance: Witten, 25 Apr 1987.

Kagel, Mauricio (b. Buenos Aires, 24 Dec 1931). Argentinian–German composer, a creative anarchist who has used seductive irony to perturb both institutions and preconceptions. Born into a leftist Jewish family, he was trained as a pianist but taught himself composition, and began his variegated career in music, theatre and film when still in his teens. In 1957 he moved to Cologne, where he immediately became an enlivening, disruptive presence among the west European avant-garde. His exploration of space and unusual vocal sounds in *Anagrama* (1955–8) struck Feldman, Stockhausen, Ligeti and Berio, while his introduction of absurdist theatre in *Sur scène* (1959–60, a lecture with commentary) proved more bemusing. He taught often at Darmstadt (1960–76), and in 1975 was named professor of new music theatre at the conservatory in Cologne.

In his influential but inimitable vision, musical materials that are defunct, patchy, banal and absurd are treated to elegant techniques of composition. The medium with him is part of the subject; in the 1960s, above all, his works tend to inspect hallowed genres and situations, including the orchestra (*Heterophonie*), the string quartet, the virtuoso (*Atem*, for a wind player who is an exhausted survivor), sacred music (*Hallelujah*), period-style performance (*Musik für Renaissance-Instrumente*), musical competitions (*Match*) and opera (*Staatstheater*). At the end of this period, he registered an amused criticism of his colleague Stockhausen in *Acustica*, *Tactil* and other works for his own touring players, who concerned themselves with small sounds and decay rather than things cosmic. Later works tend to address moments in music history. *Aus Deutschland* is a dramatization of the world of 19th-century lieder, and composers are impersonated in *Ludwig van* (film), *Variationen ohne Fuge* (actors masked and costumed as Handel and Brahms), the *Sankt-Bach-Passion* and *Interview mit D.* (Debussy). Staging and gesture are often written into the scores, as is a sharp wit, expressed also in the composer's film and radio work.

Operas: *Staatstheater*, 1967–70; *Aus Deutschland*, 1977–80

Films: *Match*, 1966; *Hallelujah*, 1969; *Ludwig van*, 1969; *MM 51*, 1981; etc.

Orchestral: *Heterophonie*, 1959–61; *Musik für Renaissance-Instrumente*, 23 players, 1965–6; *Variationen ohne Fuge*, 1971–2; *Interview mit D.*, speaker, orch, 1993–4; Etudes I–III, 1992–6; etc.

Choral: *Anagrama*, soli, ch, ens, 1957–8; *Hallelujah*, ch, 1967–8; SANKT-BACH-PASSION, 1981–5; *Burleske*, bar sax, ch, 1999–2000; *Schwarzes Madrigal*, ch, ens, 2000; etc.

Chamber: String Sextet, 1953–7; *Transición II*, pf, perc, tape, 1958–9; *Match*, 2 vc, perc, 1964; String Quartet I–II, 1965–7; *Acustica*, 2–5 players, 1968–70; *Tactil*, 3 players, 1970; *Exotica*, 6 players on non-European insts, 1971–2; *Variété*, 6 insts, 1977; *Fürst Igor, Strawinsky*, b, 6 insts, 1982; String Quartet No.3, 1987; No.4, 1993; etc.

Chamber/instrumental collections: *Programm*, 1971–2; *Rrrrrr …*, 1981–2; etc.

Solos: *Improvisation ajoutée*, org, 1961–2; *Atem*, wind, 1969; *MM 51*, pf, 1976; *An Tasten*, pf, 1977; *Passé composé*, pf, 1993; etc.

Kahn, Erich Itor (b. Rimbach, 23 Jul 1905; d. New York, 5 Mar 1956). German–US composer and pianist, impressed by Schoenberg as well as by influences he picked up at the Hoch Conservatory in Frankfurt, where he trained, and in Paris, where he lived his first years of exile after 1933. In 1945 he settled in New York. His works include *Ciaccona dei tempi di guerra* (1943) and other piano pieces, a string quartet and songs.

Kaiser (Ger.). EMPEROR.

Kajanus, Robert (b. Helsinki, 2 Dec 1856; d. Helsinki, 6 Jul 1933). Finnish conductor and composer, who made way for Sibelius. He studied in Helsinki and Leipzig (1877–82), had lessons also with Svendsen in Paris, and in 1882 founded the Helsinki Orchestral Society, which in 1914 became the Helsinki Philharmonic. Though an outstanding Sibelius conductor himself, he stood aside for the composer at premières. He also virtually abandoned composition, having made an imposing start with such works as *Aino* (1885), a symphonic poem with choral finale.

Kalinnikov, Vasily (Sergeyevich) (b. Voina, Orel governorate, 13 Jan 1866; d. Yalta, 11 Jan 1901). Russian composer, notably of two Borodinesque symphonies (No.1, G minor, 1894–5; No.2, A, 1895–7) and other works. He spent the years 1884–93 in Moscow studying and scratching a living as an orchestral bassoonist, then moved to the Crimea when his fragile health began to give way. His brother Viktor (1870–1927) was a composer, conductor and teacher in the choral field.

Kalkbrenner, Frédéric [Friedrich Wilhelm Michael] (b. between Kassel and Berlin, Nov 1785; d. Enghien-les-Bains, 10 Jun 1849). German–French pianist-composer, a virtuoso from immediately before Chopin and Liszt. Born into a musical family on the move, he studied with Louis Nicodami, Louis Adam and Catel at the Paris Conservatoire (1799–1801), and also met Haydn and Clementi in Vienna (1803–4). In 1815 he settled in England, where he became more prominent; in 1824 he returned to Paris, now the public's favourite, until the arrival of a new generation in the mid-1830s. He gave assistance to Chopin, and published a method (1831) in which he advocated the use of a rail on which the forearms could rest, so that finger action independent of arm movement would be developed. His output also includes four concertos, 13 sonatas and much else for the piano.

Kalliwoda, Johann Wenzel (b. Prague, 21 Feb 1801; d. Karlsruhe, 3 Dec 1866). Bohemian composer and violinist, a prolific author of concert, sacred and salon music. He studied at the Prague Conservatory from 1811 and spent most of his adult life (1822–50, 1857–66) as kapellmeister to the Fürstenberg court at Donaueschingen, while maintaining some activity as a touring virtuoso. Schumann dedicated a work (Op.4) to him but became critical of his triviality. His *Wenn sich der Geist auf Andachtsschwingen* was the unofficial anthem of Germans in Bohemia until the Nazi period.

Kallman, Chester (Simon) (b. Brooklyn, 7 Jan 1921; d. Athens, 18 Jan 1975). US poet, who collaborated with Auden on librettos and was the author of one himself (*The Tuscan Players*, for Chávez).

Kálmán, Emmerich [Imre] (b. Siófok, 24 Oct 1882; d. Paris, 20 Oct 1953). Hungarian composer, who added paprika to the Viennese operetta in its sunset years. He studied with Hans Koessler from 1900 at the academy in Budapest, where fellow pupils included Bartók. The immense success of his first operetta, *Tatárjárás* (The Gay Hussars, 1908), took him to Vienna, where he produced *Der Zigeunerprimas* (1911), *Die Csárdásfürstin* (The Gypsy Princess, 1915), *Gräfin Mariza* (1924) and other works. Forced out in 1938, he moved to Paris, to the USA (1939–49) and back to Paris.

Kalomiris, Manolis (b. Smyrna/Izmir, 14 Dec 1883; d. Athens, 3 Apr 1962). Greek composer, his country's pre-eminent national Romantic. A doctor's son, he studied with Hermann Graedener at the conservatory in Vienna (1901–6), where hearing Wagner and Rimsky-Korsakov (*Sheherazade*) left a lasting impression. He married a Greek fellow student and went to Kharkov/Kharkiv as a piano teacher before settling in Athens in 1910. There he took his place at the forefront of musical life. He taught at the Athens Conservatory (1910–19), and was founder director of the Hellenic Conservatory (1919–26) and National Conservatory (1926–48). His works include the opera *The Mother's Ring* (1917) and three symphonies (No.1 'Levendia', 1920).

Kammer (Ger.). Chamber, hence *Kammermusik* (chamber music), *Kammersymphonie* (chamber symphony), *Kammerorgel* (chamber organ), *Kammeroper* (chamber opera), KAMMERSÄNGER, etc. See also CAMMERTON.

Kammersänger, Kammersängerin (Ger.). Honorific titles bestowed on favoured singers by opera companies in Germany and Austria.

Kancheli, Giya (b. Tbilisi, 10 Aug 1935). Georgian composer, admired above all for his expression of tragedy and lament in long, slow sound-dramas. He studied with Iona Tuskiya at the Tbilisi Conservatory and was music director of the Rustaveli

Theatre there (1971–90). Emerging from the world of Shostakovich, his voice became more powerful and confident in the late 1980s, when he began to gain recognition abroad, notably with his 'liturgy' for viola and orchestra *Mourned by the Wind* (1989). He moved to Berlin in 1991 and Antwerp in 1995.

Kantate (Ger., pl. *Kantaten*). CANTATA.

Kantor (Ger., pl. *Kantore*). Cantor. Hence also *Kantorat* (cantorate), *Kantorei* (the musicians a Lutheran cantor would direct).

Kapelle (Ger., pl. *Kapellen*). Chapel.

Kapellmeister (Ger., pl. *Kapellmeister*, though in Eng. normally 'kapellmeisters'). CHAPELMASTER, at German courts *c*.1750–1918 largely concerned with secular music and more with conducting than composition. Haydn was a kapellmeister, but the term also has adverse connotations, of a minor functionary and routine composition, especially in the compound *Kapellmeistermusik* (kapellmeister music).

Kapsperger, Giovanni Girolamo (b. ? Venice, *c*.1580; d. Rome, Jan 1651). Italian composer, who spent nearly all his adult life in Rome, mostly serving Cardinal Francesco Barberini. The son of a colonel in the Austrian army, he wrote music for lute and theorbo, consort dances, sacred music and stage pieces.

Karajan, Herbert von (b. Salzburg, 5 Apr 1908; d. Anif, 16 Jul 1989). Austrian conductor, whose compelling authority and mastery of high finish – aided by his command of supreme positions with the Berlin Philharmonic (from 1955), the Salzburg Festival (from 1956) and Deutsche Grammophon – made him a dominant figure in musical life. He studied with Frank Schalk at the Vienna Academy and began his career in Ulm (1929–34) and Aachen (1934–42). In 1938 he made his debuts in Berlin with the Philharmonic and the Staatsoper, where a performance of *Tristan* in October was his breakthrough. Having been a member of the Nazi party he was banned from conducting at the close of the war, until the end of 1947. In 1948–9 he resumed his career in Salzburg, Vienna, Lucerne and Milan, and began working with the Philharmonia Orchestra; in 1951–2 he conducted at Bayreuth. As chief conductor of the Berlin Philharmonic, he started recording with them for DG in 1959. In 1967 he founded the Salzburg Easter Festival, at first to present Wagner's *Ring* in performances he both conducted and directed.

(The irksomeness of working with directors had led him to leave a position as artistic director of the Vienna Staatsoper, 1957–64.) By the late 1970s he had recorded virtually everything in the central symphonic and opera repertory from Haydn and Mozart to Strauss and Webern, and been loaded with honours. His last years, though, were darkened by strife with the Berlin Philharmonic, ill health and the reawakened ghost of his Nazi past.

Richard Osborne *Herbert von Karajan* (1998)

Karayev, Kara (Abulfaz-oglï) (b. Baku, 5 Feb 1918; d. Baku, 25 May 1982). Azerbaijani composer, follower of Shostakovich with oriental colouring. After conservatory training in Baku and Leningrad he became Shostakovich's pupil (1942–6), then returned to Baku, where he taught at the conservatory and soon gained leading positions in the composers' union. He gained national success with his ballets *Seven Beauties* (f.p. Baku, 1952) and *In the Path of Thunder* (f.p. Leningrad, 1958), and also produced three symphonies and a cycle of 24 piano preludes (1951–63). His son Faraj (b. 1943) is also a composer, whose works include a setting of Beckett's *Waiting for Godot*.

Karel, Rudolf (b. Plzeň, 9 Nov 1880; d. Theresienstadt, 6 Mar 1945). Czech composer, who journeyed from Romanticism through expressionism to a folk-rooted simplicity. He studied at the Prague Conservatory and was Dvořák's last pupil (1903). Stranded in Russia during the First World War, he sided first with the Bolsheviks, then against them. He returned to Prague in 1920, began teaching at the conservatory in 1923, and became a leftist again in the 1930s. Arrested for resistance activities in 1943, he was transferred to the Theresienstadt camp in 1945. His works include operas (*Ilsea's Heart*, Op.10, 1906–9; *Grandmother's Death*, Op.30, 1928–32), orchestral pieces and chamber music.

Karelia. Music by Sibelius for *tableaux vivants* depicting the history of Karelia, a Finnish-speaking region that was (and has remained) part of Russia. He published the overture (Op.10) and a popular suite (Op.11: Ballade, Intermezzo, Alla marcia). First performance: Viipuri, 13 Nov 1893 (original score).

Karetnikov, Nikolay (Nikolayevich) (b. Moscow, 28 Jun 1930; d. Moscow, 10 Oct 1994). Russian composer, leading dissident of the late Soviet period. Born into a cultured family, he studied with Shebalin at the Moscow Conservatory (1948–53) and began to establish himself with symphonies and ballets. A change came in 1957 when he encountered the music of Schoenberg, Berg and Webern, with results clear in his Fourth Symphony, Op.17 (1963), which had its première in Prague in 1968. Soon after that he virtually absented himself from the public platform to work on his opera *Till Eulenspiegel*, Op.26 (1965–85) and opera-oratorio *The Mystery of the Apostle Paul*, Op.28 (1970–86), of which the former circulated in an underground recording.

Karg-Elert, Sigfrid (b. Oberndorf am Neckar, 21 Nov 1877; d. Leipzig, 9 Apr 1933). German composer and keyboard player, best known for his organ and harmonium works. Originally Siegfried Theodor Karg, he added his mother's maiden name (Ehlert, dropping the h) and Nordicized his first name. He was brought up in Leipzig, in the large family of a book-dealer, and studied at the conservatory there with Reznicek, Reinecke and Jadassohn. Grieg was an important influence, through his music and through his advice to learn from the masters of the 17th and 18th centuries. Henceforth – rather like Reger, whom he succeeded in 1919 at his alma mater – he was caught between late Romanticism and the Baroque, and he was similarly productive. But his career was more erratic. He suffered periods of collapse and uncertainty, and though in 1924 he gave weekly radio broadcasts on his Kunstharmonium (a sophisticated version of the instrument with numerous stops, developed by the French company Mustel), his 1932 US tour was a disaster. Best remembered are his organ works, not so much the picturesque impressions (*Seven Pastels from the Lake of Constance*) as the chorale-based pieces, notably two versions of *Nun danket alle Gott* (Nos.20 and 59 of the *Choral-Improvisationen*, Op.65, 1908–10, the latter headed 'Marche triomphale') and the *Drei symphonische Choräle*, Op.87.

Karłowicz, Mieczysław (b. Wiszniew/Vishnevo, Lithuania, 11 Dec 1876; d. near Zakopane, 8 Feb 1909). Polish composer, notably of symphonic poems in Wagner–Strauss mode and songs. The son of a musical philologist, he studied in Warsaw and with Heinrich Urban in Berlin (1895–1901). He then returned to Warsaw, and sympathized with the aims of Szymanowski's Young Poland movement. In 1906 he moved to Zakopane, where he indulged his love of mountain hiking.

Katerina Izmaylova. Alternative title for Shostakovich's THE LADY MACBETH OF THE MTSENSK DISTRICT, normally used to distinguish the revised version (f.p. Moscow, 8 Jan 1963), to which the original score is nearly always preferred outside Russia.

Katya Kabanova (*Kát'a Kabanová*). Opera by Janáček to his own libretto after Aleksandr Ostrovsky's play *The Storm*. As in *Jenůfa*, the principal drama is between two women, one young and passionate (Katya, soprano), the other a formidable authoritarian (Kabanicha, her mother-in-law, contralto). While her mother-cowed husband Tichon (tenor) is away, Katya gives full physical expression to her love for Boris (tenor), and is then driven by guilt to confess and throw herself into the Volga. First performance: Brno, 23 Nov 1921.

Kavatine (Ger.). Cavatina.

Kay, Ulysses (Simpson) (b. Tucson, 7 Jan 1917; d. Englewood, NJ, 20 May 1995). US composer, notably of orchestral, choral and piano music in tonal style. A nephew of the jazz musician 'King' Oliver, he studied with Rogers and Hanson at Eastman, Hindemith at Yale and Luening at Columbia. He worked for BMI, then taught at Lehman College (1968–88).

kazachok. Vigorous duple-time Cossack dance, imitated by Tchaikovsky and Dargomyzhsky.

kazoo [bazooka]. Toy instrument consisting of a simple tube with a membrane-covered hole on top. When the tube is blown or hummed into, the membrane vibrates, producing a buzzing noise. First made in the USA around 1850, the device was international by the end of the century, but its progress in serious music has been slow.

Kb. Ger. abbreviation for *Kontrabass* (double bass).

Keal, Minna [née Minnie Nerenstein] (b. London, 22 Mar 1909; d. Princes Risborough, Bucks., 14 Nov 1999). British composer, who studied with Alwyn at the RAM (1928–9), abandoned music to help in the family book business, and began studying again only after meeting Justin Connolly in 1973. She completed her Op.1, a string quartet, in 1978; her Symphony, Op.3 (1982–7) was introduced at the 1989 Proms.

Kegelstatt (Ger., skittle alley). Name given to Mozart's Trio for clarinet, viola and piano, K.498. Though it is nice to have a nickname for this wonderful piece, the label should go to the 12 Duos, K.496a, which the composer signed 'untern kegelscheiben' (during a skittles match).

Keilberth, Joseph (b. Karlsruhe, 19 Apr 1908; d. Munich, 20 Jul 1968). German conductor, admired in (mostly Austro-German) symphonic and opera repertory from Mozart to Pfitzner and Hindemith. He studied and began his career in his home town, and held appointments with the Deutsche Philharmonie of Prague (1940–45), its successor, the Bamberg Symphony (1949–68), and the Bayerische Staatsoper, Munich (1951–68). Like Mottl, he died while conducting *Tristan* there.

Keiser, Reinhard (b. Teuchern, near Weissenfels, 10/11 Jan 1674; d. Hamburg, 12 Sep 1739). German composer, the greatest exponent of German opera in his time, and the most prolific – though under a third of his output survives (19 operas of 66). His father, an organist-composer, left the family when he and his younger brother were infants, so he owed his musical education to St Thomas's school in Leipzig (1685–92), to the study of Italian music, and to experience at the Brunswick-Wolfenbüttel court, for which he wrote five operas in 1694–6. Most of his later scores were made for Hamburg, except during a period of travelling (1718–22), towards the end of which he wrote for Copenhagen. He composed little after 1728, and retired altogether following the death in 1735 of his wife (a singer, like their daughter Sophia). His sacred music includes the first setting of the Brockes Passion (1712).

Kelemen, Milko (b. Slatina, 30 Mar 1924). Croatian composer, close to the Western European avant-garde in the 1960s–70s, when he founded (1961) and directed the Zagreb Conservatory. He studied with Stjepan Šulek at the music academy in Zagreb (1945–52), with Messiaen in Paris (1954–5) and with Fortner in Freiburg (1960–61). Since then he has divided his time between Croatia and Germany, holding conservatory appointments in Düsseldorf (1970–72) and Stuttgart (1973–89). His works include operas based on Ionesco, Camus and Fernando Arrabal, and a violin concerto, *Grand jeu classique* (1982), with which he moved into postmodernism.

Keller, Hans (b. Vienna, 11 Mar 1919; d. London, 6 Nov 1985). Austrian–British critic, and critic of criticism. He fled to London in 1938, and worked as a violinist before emerging as a trenchant and provocative writer on music after the war. Passionate about Schoenberg (as also about Mozart, Gershwin and football), he was wary of the 1950s avant-garde but certain of the value and seriousness of Britten. An appointment at the BBC (1959–79) enabled him to express his breadth and his acuity in programming and broadcast talks.

Much of his work was published in volume form posthumously, notably as *The Great Haydn Quartets* (1986), *Essays on Music* (1994) and *Functional Analysis* (2001).

Kelly, Bryan (George) (b. Oxford, 3 Jan 1934). British composer, known especially for choral and other music evincing traditional craftsmanship. He was a chorister at Worcester College, Oxford, and afterwards trained with Howells and Jacob at the RCM (1951–5) and Boulanger in Paris. A period teaching at the RCM (from 1963) was followed by residence in Italy and France.

Kelly, Michael (William) (b. Dublin, 25 Dec 1762; d. Margate, 9 Oct 1826). Irish tenor, the first Don Basilio and Don Curzio in *Figaro*, and author of *Reminiscences* (1826), including impressions of Mozart. Born into a prominent Dublin family, he was taught by Rauzzini and Michael Arne, and left for further study in Naples at 16. He then began his career in Italy (1781–3) before being recruited to the Vienna company (1783–7). After that he lived in London as a singer, stage manager, composer and wine merchant (his father's trade).

Kelly, (Thomas Alexander Erskine) 6th Earl of (b. Kellie Castle, Fife, 1 Sep 1732; d. Brussels, 9 Oct 1781). Scottish composer, notably of overtures and sonatas in which he applied lessons learned in Mannheim in the early 1750s.

Kelterborn, Rudolf (b. Basle, 3 Sep 1931). Swiss composer, in international modernist style. He studied at the Basle Academy and, following further lessons with Bialas and Fortner, began teaching there in 1955. His career took him on to other institutions in Switzerland and Germany before he returned to the academy as director (1983–94). Notable works include the operas *Ein Engel kommt nach Babylon* (Dürrenmatt; f.p. Zurich, 1977), *Der Kirschgarten* (f.p. Zurich, 1984), *Ophelia* (f.p. Schwetzingen, 1984) and *Julia* (f.p. Zurich, 1990).

Kempe, Rudolf (b. Niederpoyritz, Saxony, 14 Jun 1910; d. Zurich, 12 May 1976). German conductor, renowned for a clear, calm intimacy, especially with Austro-German Romantic music from Schumann to Strauss. He had his conservatory training in Dresden and began his career as an oboist, notably with the Gewandhaus (1928–35). After that came répétiteur jobs, followed by leading positions with the opera companies of Dresden (1949–53) and Munich (1952–4). He then conducted often at Covent Garden and became principal conductor of the RPO (1961–75), the Zurich Tonhalle (1965–72), the Munich Philharmonic and the BBC Symphony (1975–6).

Kennedy, Nigel (Paul) (b. Brighton, 28 Dec 1956). British violinist, a virtuoso in the old mode of dazzlement and showmanship, though borrowing new tricks from rock musicians in his concert attire and image-projection. He studied at the Yehudi Menuhin School, and made his London concerto debut in 1977. His recording of *Le quattro stagioni*, released in 1997, was a bestseller.

Kerll, Johann Caspar (b. Adorf, Saxony, 9 Apr 1627; d. Munich, 13 Feb 1693). German composer and organist, in the tradition of Frescobaldi and Froberger. He studied with his organist father, with Giovanni Valentini in Vienna and with Carissimi in Rome; Froberger, too, he probably met there. In 1656 he joined the Munich court, whose opera house opened with his (lost) *Oronte* the next year. There he remained, apart from a decade or so in Vienna from 1673. Most important are his keyboard works, including a *Battaglia*, a *Capriccio sopra il cucu* and a passacaglia in D minor.

Kerman, Joseph (Wilfred) (b. London, 3 Apr 1924). US scholar, whose wide interests include the conduct of musical scholarship (where he has been critical of analysis but insistent on close reading). He studied at New York University and took a doctorate at Princeton (1950) as a pupil of Oliver Strunk. He was then on the faculty at Berkeley (1951–94), apart from a period as professor of music at Oxford (1971–4). His *Opera as Drama* (1956, [2]1988) caused a stir, not only for its description of *Tosca* as a 'shabby little shocker'. Other books by him include *The Beethoven Quartets* (1967), *The Masses and Motets of William Byrd* (1981) and *Concerto Conversations* (1999).

Kernis, Aaron Jay (b. Philadelphia, 15 Jan 1960). US composer of vibrant and expressively emphatic music embracing Romantic and popular elements. He studied at the San Francisco Conservatory, the Manhattan School and Yale, with Adams, Wuorinen and Druckman. His works include two symphonies and two quartets, as well as *Le quattro stagioni dalla cucina futurismo* for speaker and piano trio (1991).

Kertész, István (b. Budapest, 28 Aug 1929; d. near Tel-Aviv, 16 Apr 1973). German–Hungarian conductor, incisive in music from Mozart to Bartók (by way of Dvořák). He studied with Kodály and Leo Weiner at the Liszt Academy, and observed Klemperer and Walter with profit. In

1956 he left for Germany, finding posts in Augsburg (1958–63) and Cologne (from 1964). He was also chief conductor of the LSO (1966–8), until he walked out over disagreements with the board. He drowned in the Mediterranean.

Ketélbey, Albert W(illiam) (b. Birmingham, 9 Aug 1875; d. Cowes, 26 Nov 1959). British composer of light music, especially *In a Monastery Garden* (1915) and *In a Persian Market* (1920), pieces much liked in their time as simple piano evocations or in the composer's scoring. He studied at Trinity College, London, began his career as a pianist and organist, and was a theatre and recording conductor.

Ketting, Otto (b. Amsterdam, 3 Sep 1935). Dutch composer, drawing on Berg, Stravinsky and other streams in mainstream modernism. The son of the composer Piet Ketting (1904–84), he studied with his father, at the Hague Conservatory and with Hartmann in Munich, and has worked as a conservatory teacher and conductor. His opera *Ithaka* opened the Muziektheater in Amsterdam on 23 September 1986.

kettledrum. See TIMPANI.

Keuris, Tristan (b. Amersfoort, 3 Oct 1946; d. Amsterdam, 15 Dec 1996). Dutch composer, whose orchestral Sinfonia (1974) provocatively restored consonant harmonies. He studied with Ton de Leeuw at the Utrecht Conservatory (1962–9) and taught at the conservatories of Groningen (1974–7), Hilversum (1977–84), Utrecht (1984–96) and Amsterdam (1989–96). Later works, using tonality over a broad but still fragmented architecture, include two violin concertos and a Symphony in D (1995).

key (1) Harmonic character, from among the 24 in the major-minor system. A composition, or part of a composition, may be said to be 'in the key of C major' – or more briefly and commonly, 'in C'. A tune in C will gravitate towards that note, and a larger composition in C major will similarly move towards a resolution on the C major triad, with the other functions of diatonic tonality duly allotted to other chords (G major as dominant) and notes (B as leading note). A symphony, concerto, sonata or quartet in C will have its outer movements in that key; a slow movement may well be in the dominant (G), subdominant (F) or relative minor (A minor). Many Baroque music theorists assigned the keys different expressive qualities, and to some extent these associations have persisted in diatonic music (see A; B; C; D; E; F; G).

(2) Transposition level, for TRANSPOSING INSTRUMENTS. A trumpet in (the key of) B♭ sounds a major second below its notated music, as if transposing from C to B♭.

(3) Lever depressed to make sound on a keyboard instrument or define pitch on a keyed instrument (e.g. woodwind instruments, on which keys were introduced in the early 15th century).

(4) One of a line of pieces of tuned wood (on a xylophone or marimba) or metal (on a vibraphone) struck to make sound.

keyboard. That part of a piano, organ, accordion or similar instrument that is an array of keys (3). Hence 'keyboard instrument', often abbreviated to 'keyboard', though this short form can mean more specifically an electronic keyboard.

Used adjectivally, the term becomes general again. A keyboard player in an orchestra or ensemble might perform on piano, celesta or harpsichord, depending on the occasion, while the phrase 'Bach's keyboard partitas' avoids having to define them as harpsichord music – usefully, when they have become so much part of the piano literature. Where a composer clearly wrote for one particular instrument or another, generalization is inappropriate: Messiaen, for example, wrote piano works and organ works, and these would not normally be lumped together as 'keyboard works'.

The earliest keyboard instruments and music, both dating from the 14th century, indicate a compass in the region of two octaves, covering the comfortable range of human voices (from C on the bass staff upwards). Instruments of this period have B♭ as part of the normal range, but the other chromatic keys are already differently coloured and at a higher level, as on a modern piano or organ. Other layouts have been advanced to ease wider spans (see Paul von JANKO) or accommodate microtone tuning, but the norm stoutly remains the norm.

Early keyboard music, from the oldest surviving (the Robertsbridge Codex, c.1360, from a priory in Sussex) for the next two centuries, consisted most commonly of transcribed vocal pieces or contrapuntal elaborations of plainsong melodies. The spread of keyboard instruments in the late 16th century, coupled with the rise of secular instrumental music (at first in the form of dances and fantasies) and the rapid development of digital virtuosity responsive to the mechanics of different instruments, helped encourage a divide between church (organ) and chamber (harpsichord), though music was often composed and published indiscriminately for either kind of instrument down to Bach's time. Beyond that the HARPSICHORD, ORGAN and PIANO have their own histories.

keyed trumpet. Trumpet with keys, usually five, developed in the late 18th century to play more chromatic music. Its greatest proponent was Anton Weidinger (1766–1852), for whom Haydn and Hummel wrote concertos, but even he (and they) could not withstand the tide of the valve trumpet in the 1820s.

keynote. See TONIC.

key signature. Set of sharp or flat signs placed at the start of a composition to indicate which notes are sharpened or flattened throughout, i.e. to show the key. The practice goes back to manuscripts of the 11th–12th centuries and has been abandoned only in harmonically complex or atonal music.

The key signatures for major keys are:

C   G   D   A   E   B   F♯   C♯

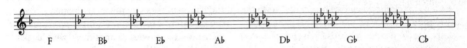

F   B♭   E♭   A♭   D♭   G♭   C♭

These have been standard since the Classical period. Minor keys have the signatures of their relative majors (e.g. three flats for C minor, two sharps for B minor). Baroque composers would sometimes use one sharp fewer for the sharper major keys (e.g. three sharps for E major) and one flat fewer for minor keys (two flats for C minor). The key signature customarily follows the time signature. A new key signature may appear later; if so, the old one may be cancelled with the appropriate natural signs immediately before the new one.

keywork. System of keys on a woodwind instrument.

Kfg. Ger. abbreviation for *Kontrafagott* (double bassoon).

Khachaturian, Aram (Ilich) (b. Tbilisi, 6 Jun 1903; d. Moscow, 1 May 1978). Armenian composer, who maintained the tradition of full-blooded Russian Romanticism to the mid 20th century by giving it a twist of regional flavour. His gifts for rapturous melody and excitement in just a few pieces – notably his two principal ballets (*Gayane* and *Spartacus*) and his Piano Concerto – gave them a lasting appeal.

Brought up in Tbilisi, he moved to Moscow in 1921, and studied biology at the university and music (cello and composition) at the Gnesin Institute before moving on to the conservatory (1929–36), where his teachers included Gnesin and Myaskovsky. The Toccata and Trio of 1932, followed by the Piano Concerto (1936), made his name, and he started writing film music; he also married a fellow student and composer, Nina Makarova (1908–76), in 1933. In 1939 he spent some time in the Armenian capital Yerevan working on his ballet *Happiness* (a score reused in *Gayane*), and that same year he became organizing secretary of the Soviet Composers' Union. He lost the position in 1948, when he was a victim of the edict against formalism (see POLITICS), but in 1950 he gained new appointments to teach composition at his old colleges: the Gnesin Institute and the Moscow Conservatory. Also that year he began life as a conductor, which allowed him to travel internationally. His nephew Karen (b. 1920) was also a composer.

Victor Yuzefovich *Aram Khachaturyan* (1985)

Ballets: *Happiness*, 1939, partly reused in GAYANE, 1942, rev 1947; SPARTACUS, 1950–54
Orchestral: Symphony No.1, 1934; No.2 'Symphony with a Bell', 1943, rev 1944; No.3 'Symphony-Poem', 1947; PIANO CONCERTO, D♭, 1936; Violin Concerto, D minor, 1940; *Masquerade* (suite), 1944; Cello Concerto, E, 1946; Violin Concerto-Rhapsody, 1961; Cello Concerto-Rhapsody, 1963; Piano Concerto-Rhapsody, 1968; etc.
Chamber and instrumental: Toccata, pf, 1932; Trio, vn, cl, pf, 1932; etc.
Other works: film scores, incidental music, songs, choruses

Khamma. Ballet score by Debussy (orchestrated by Koechlin), commissioned by Maud Allan for her to dance in what might pass for ancient Egyptian style, though she failed to use it. Partly but not entirely because of Koechlin's contribution, it has never been accepted as one of Debussy's central works.

Khovanshchina (The Khovansky Affair). Opera by Musorgsky to his own libretto from historical sources concerning events before Peter the Great's assumption of power. The rival parties on stage are as follows: Prince Ivan Khovansky (bass) and his son Andrey (tenor), who command a militia; the boyar Shaklovity (baritone), who seems to be acting for Peter; Prince Vasily Golitsyn (tenor), the lover of Peter's elder sister Sophia; and the Old Believers, led by Dosifey (bass) and Marfa (mezzo-soprano). By the end of the opera Shaklovity has killed the elder Khovansky, Golitsyn has been sent into exile, and Andrey has died with his beloved Marfa and all the Old Believers in a mass suicide by conflagration. Musorgsky had hardly started to orchestrate the score or fix the order of scenes when he died. The first performing version was Rimsky-Korsakov's, adapted by Stravinsky and Ravel for Diaghilev (1913), with the notable addition of a final chorus by Stravinsky. Shostakovich also made an orchestration. First performance: St Petersburg, 21 Feb 1886.

Khrennikov, Tikhon (Nikolayevich) (b. Yelets, 10 Jun 1913). Russian composer, although he owes his controversial reputation to having been secretary of the Soviet Composers' Union from immediately after the 1948 clampdown (see POLITICS) until the dissolution of the USSR in 1991. In his public statements – and indeed in his music – he propounded the conservatism that was understood as socialist realism. On the other hand, much more advanced music (by Schnittke, Gubaidulina and others) was published, performed and recorded under his authority, and composers were protected from the sanctions imposed on writers. He was a pupil of Shebalin and Neuhaus at the Moscow Conservatory (1932–6), where he succeeded Shebalin as head of composition in 1963. Given that he remained active as a composer into his late 80s, his output is relatively small, comprising operas, ballets, orchestral music (three symphonies, four piano concertos) and smaller items.

Kienzl, Wilhelm (b. Waizenkirchen, near Linz, 17 Jan 1857; d. Vienna, 3 Oct 1941). Austrian composer, a mild-natured Wagnerian. He studied in Graz, Prague, Leipzig and Vienna during the years up to 1879, had lessons from Liszt in Weimar and attended the first *Ring* (1876). From then on he was regularly at Bayreuth, while directing the Styrian Music Union in Graz (1886–1917) and composing operas, choral music, songs and piano pieces. By far his most successful opera was *Der Evangelimann* (f.p. Berlin, 1895), to his own libretto on the Wagnerian topic of sin and redemption in a monastery setting: its tenor aria 'Selig sind' was once a favourite. In 1917 he moved to Vienna, and the next year wrote a national anthem for the new Austrian republic, *Deutsch-Österreich*, which

remained in use until Haydn's imperial hymn was reinstated with new words in 1929. After writing three operas, with his second wife as librettist (1921–7), he concentrated on smaller works, watching as his older operas fell out of fashion.

Kilar, Wojciech (b. Lwów/Lviv, 17 Jul 1932). Polish composer, a highly successful collaborator with film directors including Coppola (*Bram Stoker's Dracula*), Polanski (*Death and the Maiden, The Ninth Gate, The Pianist*), Kieślowski, Wajda and Zanussi, as well as of orchestral and sacred music driven by the same bold ability to reproduce or replace Romanticism. He studied in Katowice with Woytowicz (1950–55), in Kraków (1955–8), at Darmstadt (1957) and in Paris with Boulanger (1959–60), and was an avant-gardist in the 1960s.

Killmayer, Wilhelm (b. Munich, 21 Aug 1927). German composer, whose journey has taken him from the region of Orff (his teacher, 1951–4) into a questioning encounter with the 19th-century Romantics, especially the great composers of lieder. Having gained some success with operas and ballets in the early 1960s, he stepped aside and began to concentrate on songs, choruses and instrumental pieces, sometimes with explicit reference to Schumann or Brahms. In 1973 he began teaching at the conservatory in Munich, the city where he has spent most of his life. His works include three volumes of *Hölderlin-Lieder* for tenor with orchestra or piano (1982–91) and several piano cycles.

Kilpinen, Yrjö (Henrik) (b. Helsinki, 4 Feb 1892; d. Helsinki, 2 Mar 1959). Finnish composer, almost exclusively of songs (said to number 767) admired in their time as continuing the German lied tradition into a Nordic bareness, for he set German poems (Morgenstern, Hesse) as well as others in Swedish and Finnish. During studies with Eric Furuhjelm in Helsinki (1908–17) he had lessons with Heuberger in Vienna (1910–11) and Juon and Otto Taubmann in Berlin (1913–14). His reputation suffered from the success of his songs in Nazi Germany.

Kim, Earl [Eul] (b. Dinuba, Cal., 6 Jan 1920; d. Cambridge, Mass., 19 Nov 1998). US composer of Korean descent, who, in a restricted output, found a sparseness through which oriental traditions could communicate with Beckett and other modern writers. He studied with Schoenberg at UCLA (1939–40), then went to Bloch at Berkeley, where he continued his education with Sessions after wartime intelligence work. There followed posts at Princeton (1952–67) and Harvard

(1967– 90). His Beckett settings include *Exercises en route* for soprano and ensemble (1963–70), presentable in dramatic form with actors and dancers. He also wrote a Violin Concerto (1979).

Kind (Ger., pl. *Kinder*). Child, hence *Kindersopran* (child soprano), *Kinderoper* (children's opera), *Kinderstück* (children's piece), etc.

Kinderscenen (Childhood Scenes). Set of 13 piano pieces by Schumann, including *Träumerei*.

Kindertotenlieder (Songs of the Death of Children). Orchestral song cycle by Mahler to five poems by Friedrich Rückert. First performance: Vienna, 29 Jan 1905.

King Arthur. Semi-opera by Purcell and Dryden, titled in full *King Arthur, or The British Worthy*, a patriotic pageant, in which the warring of Britons and Saxons is resolved in harmonious celebration of the 'fairest isle', to cite the song sung by Venus near the end. Other musical episodes, typically reserved for incantation and the supernatural, include a Frost Scene celebrated for its depiction of shivering cold. First performance: London, May/Jun 1691.

Kingdom, The. Oratorio by Elgar to his own selection from the gospels, a sequel to *The Apostles* beginning with Pentecost. First performance: Birmingham, 3 Oct 1906.

King Lear. Shakespeare play of cruelty, disappointment and a gleam of honesty. It was long considered as an opera subject by Verdi, and realized by Reimann and Sallinen. Composers to have written overtures, incidental music or film scores include Berlioz, Balakirev, Debussy and Shostakovich.

King Priam. Opera by Tippett to his own libretto. The tragedy of Priam (bass-baritone) is that of a man whose choices are frustrated or overruled by a more powerful machinery (the gods? fate? necessity?). In saving his son Paris (treble, then tenor) he precipitates the Trojan War, and thereby brings about his own death, after a chain of casualities that includes Hector (baritone) and Achilles (heroic tenor). A chorus of mezzo-soprano, tenor and bass addresses the audience from time to time. First performance: Coventry, 29 May 1962.

King Roger (*Król Roger*). Opera by Szymanowski to a libretto he adapted from Jarosław Iwasz-kiewicz's. The work transplants Euripides's *The Bacchae* to the hedonistic-hieratic world of 12th-century Sicily. Roger (baritone) is the king who has to watch as his queen, Roxana (soprano), is beguiled by the new spirituality of the Shepherd (tenor), but who finally emerges independent and alone. First performance: Warsaw, 19 Jun 1926.

King's College Choir. The choir of King's College, Cambridge, made up of men and boys, widely esteemed as the outstanding exemplar of the English cathedral-style tradition. A Christmas Eve carol service was instituted in 1918.

King's Singers, The. British group of six men singers, active since 1968 with changes of personnel: five of the original team were members of King's College Choir. To a varied repertory of Renaissance music, folksongs and pop arrangements, the sextet has added works commissioned from Ligeti and others.

Kinloch, William (*fl.* late 16th century). Scottish composer of keyboard music and possibly also a secret agent.

Kinnhalter (Ger.). Chin rest.

Kinsella, John (b. Dublin, 8 Apr 1932). Irish composer, notably of symphonies (some with voices) following an adieu to the avant-garde in the late 1970s. He studied as a viola player at the Dublin College of Music (1953–7) and worked as a computer programmer before joining Irish radio in 1968. After serving as head of music there (1983–8) he left to concentrate on composition, in which he is self-taught.

Kirche (Ger., pl. *Kirchen*). Church, hence *Kirchenmusik* (church music), *Kirchenoper* (church opera), etc.

Kircher, Athanasius (b. Geisa, near Fulda, 2 May 1601; d. Rome, 27 Nov 1680). German polymath, responsible for *Musurgia universalis* (1650), an immense conspectus of music history and theory. Trained in Jesuit schools, he joined the order and spent most of his life (from 1633) in Rome. He also invented a composing machine.

Kirchner, Leon (b. Brooklyn, 24 Jan 1919). US composer, whose rangy music adds to the Schoenberg school a distinctive Russian thrust owed to Scriabin, to Stravinsky and perhaps also to his inheritance from his Russian Jewish parents. They and he moved to Los Angeles when he was nine, and there he studied with Toch and Schoenberg. He went on to Bloch at Berkeley (1938–42) and Sessions in New York, before and after military service (1943–6). His career as a teacher then took him from USC to Mills (1954–61) and Harvard (1961–89), where he taught not only in class but conducting.

Opera: *Lily* (Kirchner, after Saul Bellow). 1973–6, f.p. New York, 1977

Orchestral: Piano Concerto No.1, 1953; No.2, 1963; Concerto, vn, vc, 10 wind, perc, 1960; Music for Orchestra I, 1969; II, 1990; Music for Cello and Orchestra, 1992; etc.

Ensemble and chamber: String Quartet No.1, 1949; No.2, 1958; No.3, 1966; Trio, pf trio, 1954; Trio II, pf trio, 1993; Music for 12, 1985; etc.

Kirchner, Theodor (Fürchtegott) (b. Neukirchen, near Chemnitz, 10 Dec 1823; d. Hamburg, 18 Sep 1903). German composer, close to Schumann, whose style he perpetuated in numerous piano miniatures, as well as in songs and chamber pieces. He studied as an organist with Knorr and Becker in Leipzig, and was taken up by the Schumanns when still in his teens. Later he was in contact with both Wagner and Brahms. Careers (as a conductor and teacher) and his marriage fell apart, and he had to be saved from penury by friends and publishers.

Kirchner, Volker David (b. Mainz, 25 Jun 1942). German composer, especially of stage and symphonic works expressive of darkness and conflict. He studied with Günter Raphael in Mainz (1956–9) and Zimmermann in Cologne (1959–63), and pursued a career as an orchestral viola player until 1988.

Kirkman. Family of harpsichord makers founded by Jacob Kirkman (1710–92), who moved to London from his native Alsace in the early 1730s and learned the craft from the Flemish-born Hermann Tabel. He married Tabel's widow in 1738, took over the business, and brought his nephew Abraham (1737–94) into partnership. Abraham was succeeded by his son Joseph as the company moved increasingly into the piano market; the last surviving Kirkman harpsichord is dated 1800.

Kirkpatrick, John (b. New York, 18 Mar 1905; d. Ithaca, NY, 8 Nov 1991). US pianist and scholar, responsible for the first performance of Ives's 'Concord' Sonata and for cataloguing the composer's manuscripts. He studied at Princeton and with Boulanger in Fontainebleau (1925–8). From 1942 he held university positions, notably at Cornell and Yale.

Kirkpatrick, Ralph (b. Leominster, Mass., 10 Jun 1911; d. Guilford, Conn., 13 Apr 1984). US harpsi-

chordist and scholar, cataloguer of Scarlatti's sonatas. He studied at Harvard, where he took up the harpsichord in 1930; later he was Landowska's pupil. From 1940 he taught at Yale.

Kirnberger, Johann Philipp (b. Saalfeld, Thuringia, 24 Apr 1721; d. Berlin, 27 Jul 1783). German theorist and composer, pupil of Bach and from 1751 employed at the Prussian court. His name is attached to 24 Bach chorale preludes (two of them spurious) he acquired from Breitkopf and to 'Kirnberger III', a temperament he advocated, based on some narrow perfect fifths (C–G–D–A–E) and the rest just.

Kirov. Name attached to the MARIINSKY theatre and companies from 1935 to 1991, and only slowly being dislodged.

Kiss, The (*Hubička*). Opera by Smetana to a libretto by Eliška Krásnohorská after a story by Karolina Světlá. The kiss is one – or more – that Vendulka (soprano) declines to accept from Lukáš (tenor) until they are married. Frustration and estrangement ensue, but at the end all is well. First performance: Prague, 7 Nov 1876.

Kissin, Evgeny (Igorevich) (b. Moscow, 10 Oct 1971). Russian pianist of formidable technique. A pupil of Anna Kantor at the Gnesin Institute, he made his debut at 10, and at 13 played both Chopin concertos in one concert with the Moscow Philharmonic, a feat he repeated in 1990 for his US debut. Since then his recitals and recordings have met with huge acclaim, and some reserve on grounds of musical blankness.

Kistner & Siegel. German music publishing firm formed in 1923 by the amalgamation of two companies with roots in the first half of the 19th century.

kit [pochette]. Diminutive fiddle, played variously by dancing masters, itinerant musicians and noble amateurs. It could be stored in a coat-tail pocket.

kitchen. Slang term for an orchestra's percussion department. But some composers, e.g. Brant, have written for real kitchenware.

kithara. Ancient Greek plucked string instrument, similar in shape and design to the lyre, but differing in being larger and having a soundbox of wood. The player stood, using a plectrum, and might also have sung. Probably introduced from Asia Minor, the instrument became central to classical Greek culture in a form with seven strings.

Kittl, Johann Friedrich [Jan Bedřich] (b. Orlík nad Vltavou, 8 May 1806; d. Lissa/Leszno, Prussia/Poland, 20 Jul 1868). Czech composer, a Mendelssohnian Romantic, who is remembered for four symphonies (especially No.2 'Jagdsymphonie', E♭, Op.9, 1837), songs, piano music and an opera to a libretto by Wagner, *Bianca und Giuseppe* (Prague, 1848), set during the French Revolutionary siege of Nice in 1793. He studied in Prague with Tomášek and was head of the Prague Conservatory (1843–65).

Kjerulf, Halfdan (b. Christiania, now Oslo, 17 Sep 1815; d. Christiania, 11 Aug 1868). Norwegian composer, first master of the Norwegian art song. Following his father's death in 1840 he had to give up law studies to support the family as a journalist, and he acquired his musical education belatedly and piecemeal, in Christiania (with Carl Arnold, 1848–9), Copenhagen (with Gade, 1849–50) and Leipzig (1850–51). After that he lived in Christiania as a piano teacher, while writing songs, choral pieces and piano miniatures, often drawing on Norwegian folk music.

Kl. Ger. abbreviation for *Klavier* (piano).

klagend (Ger.). Sorrowing.

klagende Lied, Das (The Sorrowing Song). Cantata by Mahler for soli, choir and orchestra to his own words, partly based on a story by Ludwig Bechstein and one from Grimm. Two brothers go out to find a red flower and thereby win the queen's hand. One kills the other for it, and a minstrel, finding the victim's bones, makes a flute from one – a flute that sings its own murder story at the wedding feast. The work was originally in three parts – *Waldmärchen*, *Der Spielmann* and *Hochzeitsstück* – of which the first was dropped from the definitive version but has occasionally been restored. First performance: Vienna, 17 Feb 1901.

Klami, Uuno (Kalervo) (b. Virolahti, 20 Sep 1900; d. Virolahti, 29 May 1961). Finnish composer, who refreshed the nationalist tradition with influences from Stravinsky and Ravel. He studied with Ravel in Paris (1924–5), after his years at the Helsinki College of Music under Melartin (1915–24) and before he completed his training with Gál in Vienna (1928–9). Earning his living as music critic of the daily *Helsingin Sanomat* (1932–59), he created a notable body of orchestral music, including the Kalevala Suite (1933), the Karelian Rhapsody (1927), two piano concertos, two symphonies, a violin concerto and the ballet *Whirls* (1960).

Klang (Ger.). Sound. Hence also *Klangfarbe* (tone colour, timbre), KLANGFARBENMELODIE, *Klangwelt* (sound world), *Dreiklang* (triad), etc.

Klangfarbenmelodie (Ger.). Sound-colour melody. The term was introduced by Schoenberg in his *Harmonielehre* (1911) to indicate melody defined by changes of colour rather than pitch. This is something he had tried out, more or less, in his orchestral piece Op.16:3, though the technique is associated more with Webern. At the end of Webern's orchestral piece Op.10:1 comes a particularly clear instance, where the same note is sounded four times, by flute, flute with trumpet, just trumpet, and celesta. However, the term is also used more loosely of music where changes of colour are less instantaneous but still important, e.g. Webern's orchestration of the Bach six-part ricercare.

Klangforum Wien. Ensemble founded by Beat Furrer in Vienna in 1985.

Klar. Ger. abbreviation for KLARINETTE.

Klarinette (Ger., pl. *Klarinetten*). Clarinet.

Klavarscribo. A form of piano notation invented by Cornelis Pot in 1931, showing music in graph form, with pitch on the vertical axis and time on the horizontal.

Klaviatur (Ger.). Keyboard, in the primary sense of a row of keys.

Klavier (Ger., pl. *Klaviere*). Keyboard (instrument), or more specifically (and especially in compounds), piano. Hence also *Klavierauszug* (piano score), *Klavierkonzert* (piano concerto), *Klaviermusik* (piano music), *Klavierquartett* (piano quartet), *Klavierstück* (piano piece), *Klavierunterricht* (piano training), etc.

Klavierübung. See CLAVIER-ÜBUNG.

Klebe, Giselher (Wolfgang) (b. Mannheim, 28 Jun 1925). German composer, especially known for operas in a vein of modern expressionism. He studied in Berlin with Kurt von Wolfurt (1941–3), Josef Rufer and Blacher (1946–51), and followed a path rather like Henze's, being briefly associated with the Darmstadt-centred avantgarde before finding his creative life in the theatre. His first opera was *Die Räuber*, Op.25 (f.p. Düsseldorf, 1957), after Schiller's play; others – similarly based on his own adaptations of literary classics – include *Alkmene*, Op.36 (Berlin, 1961, commissioned for the opening of the Deutsche Oper) and *Jacobowsky und der Oberst*, Op.49 (f.p. Hamburg, 1965). Further works include six symphonies. He also taught at the academy in Detmold from 1957.

Kleiber. Austrian conductors, father and son.

(1) **Erich** (b. Vienna, 5 Aug 1890; d. Zurich, 27 Jan 1956). Growing up in Vienna, he heard Mahler's performances at the opera. He then studied at the conservatory in Prague, where he began his career before moving on to appointments in Darmstadt (1912–19) and other relatively minor cities. In 1923 he made a spectacular debut in Berlin conducting *Fidelio*, which led to his taking the head position at the Staatsoper the following year. While there he was responsible for the first performance of *Wozzeck*, but in 1934 he resigned and the next year settled in Buenos Aires, returning to Europe frequently before and after the war. Passionate for precision, he did important foundational work at Covent Garden in the early 1950s.

(2) **Carlos** (b. Berlin, 3 Jul 1930; d. Konjsica, Slovenia, 13 Jul 2004). Moving with his family to Buenos Aires as a young child, he gained Argentinian nationality (but became an Austrian citizen in 1980) and studied in the city. He made his conducting debut at La Plata in 1952, then went to Europe, ostensibly to study chemistry in Zurich, though he was soon taking conducting posts in Germany. His debuts at the Vienna Staatsoper (*Tristan*, 1973), Bayreuth (*Tristan* again, 1974) and Covent Garden (*Rosenkavalier*, 1974) marked the beginning of an international career that was both spectacular and fitful. Requiring long and intensive rehearsal, he produced performances of extraordinary charisma, and made remarkable recordings of some pieces in his restricted repertory (Beethoven's Fifth, *Tristan*). But his demands limited his engagements and kept him from accepting permanent positions; he declined the conductorship of the Berlin Philharmonic in succession to Karajan. Appearing rarely after 1990, he gave his last concerts in 1999.

klein, kleine (Ger.). (1) Small, little, as in *kleine Flöte* (piccolo), *kleine Trommel* (side drum), *Eine* KLEINE NACHTMUSIK, etc.

(2) Minor, as applied to intervals, e.g. *kleine Sekunde, kleine Terz*, etc.

kleine Nachtmusik, Eine (A Little Night Music). Serenade in G for strings by Mozart, K.525. There are four movements – Allegro, Romanza, Menuet, Rondo – the original second movement (surely a minuet, in keeping with divertimento form) having been ripped from the manuscript.

Kleine Orgelmesse. See ORGAN SOLO MASS.

Kleinmeister (Ger., pl. *Kleinmeister*). Minor composer.

Klemperer, Otto (b. Breslau, 14 May 1885; d. Zurich, 6 Jul 1973). German conductor, renowned especially for his work with the KROLL OPERA (1927–31) and for the rugged grandeur he brought to Beethoven and Mahler in his 70s and 80s as principal conductor of the Philharmonia Orchestra (1955–72). He studied with James Kwast and Knorr in Frankfurt and with Pfitzner in Berlin; he also met Mahler, who helped him find his first appointments. In 1933 he moved to Los Angeles, where he became conductor of the Philharmonic (1933–9). After that ill health kept him from the podium, but he returned as conductor of the Budapest Opera (1947–50) before centring his work in London. He also composed, especially in later years, his works including six symphonies, nine quartets and a *Merry Waltz* for orchestra (1959).

Peter Heyworth *Otto Klemperer*, 2 Vols. (1983, 1996)

Klenau, Paul (August) von (b. Copenhagen, 11 Feb 1883; d. Copenhagen, 31 Aug 1946). Danish composer and conductor, for whom studies with Schoenberg soon after the First World War were decisive. His earlier training had been with Bruch in Berlin (1901–3), Thuille in Frankfurt (1903–7) and Schillings in Frankfurt (1908–9), and he had begun his creative career in late Romantic style. Notable later works include a version of Kleist's *Michael Kohlhaas* (f.p. Stuttgart, 1933) and the last three of his seven symphonies. He also held conducting posts in Germany and Copenhagen.

klezmer (Yiddish). Style of traditional Jewish music originating in Germany and eastern Europe, played by small ensembles on festive or commemorative occasions; the Yiddish word connotes a musician performing such music. Klezmer music, like jazz, can be played by any grouping, but clarinet and violin solos commonly feature. There was a revival of it in the late 20th century, affecting Saxton, Golijov and other composers.

Klindworth, Karl (b. Hanover, 25 Sep 1830; d. Stolpe, near Oranienburg, 27 Jul 1916). German pianist and conductor, a pupil of Liszt and ally of Wagner. He was with Liszt in Weimar (1852–4) and met Wagner during his time in London (1854–68). From there he moved to the Moscow Conservatory to teach (1868–82), after which he settled in Berlin and founded his own conservatory (1884), which was merged with Scharwenka's after his retirement in 1895. He made the vocal scores of the *Ring* and had an adopted daughter, Winifred Williams, whom he introduced to her future husband, Siegfried Wagner.

Knabe (Ger.). Boy, hence *Knabensopran* (treble), *Knabenchor* (boys' choir), *Sängerknaben* (singing boys), etc.

Knaben Wunderhorn, Des (The Boy's Magic Horn). Collection of German folk poetry edited by Achim von Arnim and Clemens Brentano. It was a particularly important source for Mahler, who set texts from it in numerous songs as well as in his Symphonies Nos.2–4, sometimes known collectively as his 'Wunderhorn symphonies'. His involvement began with his *Lieder und Gesänge* for voice and piano (1887–90), of which Vol.2 comprises four settings ('Um schlimmer Kinder artig zu machen', 'Ich ging mit Lust', 'Aus! Aus!', 'Starke Einbildungskraft') and Vol.3 five ('Zu Strassburg auf der Schanz', 'Ablösung im Sommer', 'Scheiden und Meiden', 'Nicht wiedersehen!', 'Selbstgefühl'). In 1899 he used the title for a volume for singer with piano or, in the case of all but No.11, orchestra: 1 'Der Schilwache Nachtlied' (1892), 2 'Verlor'ne Müh' (1892), 3 'Trost im Unglück' (1892), 4 'Wer hat dies Liedlein erdacht?' (1892), 5 'Das irdische Leben' (1892–3), 6 'Des Antonius von Padua Fischpredigt' (1893, adapted in Symphony No.2), 7 'Rheinlegendchen' (1893), 8 'Lied des Verfolgten im Turm' (1898), 9 'Wo die Schönen Trompeten blasen' (1898), 10 'Lob des hohen Verstandes' (1896), 11 'Es sungen drei Engel' (1895, adapted in Symphony No.3), 12 'Urlicht' (?1892, in Symphony No.2). Not included in the set was 'Das himmlische Leben' (1892), the finale of the Fourth Symphony. Two further settings, also with piano or orchestra, followed: 'Revelge' (1899) and 'Der Tambourg'sell' (1901), making a total of 24.

Other composers to have drawn from the collection include Schumann, Strauss, Schoenberg and Webern.

Knaifel, Aleksandr (Aronovich) (b. Tashkent, 28 Nov 1943). Russian composer. The son of professional musicians, he trained as a cellist before a hand injury diverted him to composition studies with Boris Arapov at the Leningrad Conservatory (1964–7). Some of his music maintains a style of sacred simplicity for long periods, but he has also written a burlesque opera, *The Canterville Ghost* (f.p. Leningrad, 1974), and another opera on Lewis Carroll's Alice books.

Knappertsbusch, Hans (b. Elberfeld, 12 Mar 1888; d. Munich, 25 Oct 1965). German conductor, revered for his sovereign way with Wagner (especially *Parsifal*) and Bruckner. He studied with Emil Steinbach at the Cologne Conservatory from 1908, and learned also from working as assistant to Siegfried Wagner and Richter at Bayreuth in his early 20s. Positions followed in his home town, Leipzig and Dessau; he then succeeded Walter in Munich (1922–36). Disdainful of the Nazis, he was obliged to withdraw to Vienna, but he returned to Munich after the Second World War – and to Bayreuth.

Knarre (Ger.). Ratchet.

Knipper, Lev (Konstantinovich) (b. Tbilisi, 3 Dec 1898; d. Moscow, 30 Jul 1974). Russian composer, whose satirical opera *The North Wind* (1929–30) was judiciously followed by works in a blander style. He became a composer only after military service, studying with Glière and Nikolay Zhilyayev at the Gnesin Institute from 1922, and he spent much of his later life in musical posts with the army. Soldierly themes, with appropriate choral movements, also crop up in his 21 symphonies.

Knorr, Iwan (Otto Armand) (b. Mewe, West Prussia, 3 Jan 1853; d. Frankfurt, 22 Jan 1916). German composer, most noted, though, as a teacher at the Hoch Conservatory in Frankfurt (1883–1916), to which he was recommended by Brahms. His own training had been in Leipzig at the hands of Moscheles, Richter and Reinecke. Three operas, a symphony, chamber pieces and choral items feature in his rather small and often densely contrapuntal output.

Knot Garden, The. Opera by Tippett to his own libretto, in which the psychological knots afflicting a married couple in early maturity, their ward, the wife's freedom-fighter sister, and a male homosexual couple – Dov (tenor) and Mel (bass-baritone) – are resolved with the aid of an analyst, analogues from *The Tempest* and music. First performance: London, 2 Dec 1970.

Knüpfer, Sebastian (b. Asch/Aš, 6 Sep 1633; d. Leipzig, 10 Oct 1676). German composer and church musician, among Bach's predecessors as cantor of St Thomas's in Leipzig (1657–76), where he sharply countered a period of decline. A cantor's son, he studied at the Gymnasium Poeticum in Regensburg (1646–54), then moved to Leipzig as a singer and teacher, so that he was already in the city when the previous cantor, Tobias Michael, died. He was a scholarly man as well as a fine musician. His works consist almost entirely of sacred concertos in the Schütz tradition, most to German but some to Latin texts.

Knussen, (Stuart) Oliver (b. Glasgow, 12 Jun 1952). British composer and conductor, creator of music at once surely driven and fanciful, within a harmonic world strong enough to embrace a rich range of reference, especially to late Romantic and early modern music (Musorgsky, Ravel, Stravinsky), without compromise. The son of an orchestral bass player, he studied composition with John Lambert (1963–9) and conducted the LSO in his own First Symphony when he was 15. He then studied with Schuller at Tanglewood (1970–73). Emerging in the 1980s as a conductor with striking gifts for clarity and form, especially in music from Stravinsky on, he began an association with the Aldeburgh Festival in 1983 (he later moved to the area) and became artistic director of the London Sinfonietta (1998–2002). His precocity as a composer was deceptive: many of his works have taken a long time to complete. They include two operas after children's books by Maurice Sendak – *Where the Wild Things are* (Op.20, 1979–83) and *Higglety Pigglety Pop!* (Op.21, 1984–90) – as well as a Third Symphony (Op.18, 1973–9) and concertos for horn (Op.28, 1994) and violin (Op.30, 2002).

Kobbé, Gustav (b. New York, 4 Mar 1857; d. Babylon, Long Island, 27 Jul 1918). US writer on music, active as a music critic in New York from 1880 and an author of plays and poems as well as non-fiction. His name survives thanks to his *Complete Opera Book* (1919), a standard, regularly updated work conveying synopses and first performance details for repertory operas.

Kochański, Paweł (b. Orel, Russia, 14 Sep 1887; d. New York, 12 Jan 1934). Polish violinist, close to Szymanowski. A pupil of Emil Młynarski in Warsaw, he finished his training with César Thomson in Brussels (1903), then embarked on a career as soloist and teacher, in Warsaw, Petrograd and Kiev. In 1921 he moved to the USA.

Köchel, Ludwig (Alois Ferdinand Ritter**) von** (b. Stein, near Krems, 14 Jan 1800; d. Vienna, 3 Jun 1877). Austrian gentleman scholar, universally remembered for compiling the standard catalogue of Mozart's works (1862, repeatedly revised). He had interests in botany and mineralogy; there was also a second Köchel listing he produced, of Fux's works.

Kocsis, Zoltán (b. Budapest, 30 May 1952). Hungarian pianist and conductor, who combines thoughtful musicianship with a vital élan. He studied at the Liszt Academy, where his teachers included Kadosa and Kurtág, and from which he graduated in 1973. By then he had already made his debuts in the US (1971) and Britain (1972). His favoured repertory includes Beethoven, Bartók, Debussy and Kurtág (who wrote concertante works for him). He began his second career as co-founder of the Budapest Festival Orchestra (1983) and in 1998 became music director of the Hungarian National Philharmonic.

Kodály, Zoltán (b. Kecskemét, 16 Dec 1882; d. Budapest, 6 Mar 1967). Hungarian composer and educationist. Bartók's colleague in studying folk music and creating a musical language out of it, he had a gentler artistic personality and his creativity was intermittent; most important are his early cello sonatas and a few larger scores of his middle years. He gave a lot of his attention to establishing music in the school curriculum throughout Hungary.

A stationmaster's son, he was brought up in small towns now in Slovakia, and threw himself into music – playing several instruments, singing, composing – before he left school. He then studied with Hans Koessler at the academy in Budapest (1900–6), and started collecting folksongs with Bartók in 1905. Having received a scholarship for further study in Berlin and Paris (1906–7), he returned with some of Debussy's music, which he introduced to his colleague. Later the same year (1907) he began teaching at the academy, and in 1910 he married Emma Schlesinger, a composer herself and a vital force in Budapest musical life. Thereafter the pattern of his life changed little: he taught, composed, agitated for music in schools, and worked on folk music, collecting, arranging and editing. After the Second World War he was the grand old man of Hungarian music, and his tuneful, folkish style (never as dense, harsh or analytic as Bartók's) became the model for younger composers, while his ideals for school music were implemented. Though he produced rather few large-scale works, almost all before 1940, he composed a vast quantity of choral music, especially from the mid-1920s to the 1950s, most of it close to folk sources.

Percy M. Young *Zoltán Kodály* (1964)

Singspiels: HARY JANOS, Op.15, 1925–7; *Czinka Panna*, 1946–8

Orchestral: *Summer Evening*, 1906; *Dances of Marosszék*, 1930 (from pf work); *Dances of Galánta*, 1933; Variations on a Hungarian Folksong 'The Peacock', 1938–9; Concerto for Orchestra, 1939–40; Symphony, C, 1930s–61; etc.

Vocal: *Psalmus hungaricus*, Op.13, t, ch, orch, 1923;

Budavári Te Deum, soli, ch, orch, 1936; *Missa brevis*, ch, org, 1944; many choruses, songs and folksong arrs

Chamber: String Quartet No.1, Op.2, 1908–9; No.2, Op.10, 1916–18; Serenade, Op.12, 2 vn, va, 1919–20; Cello Sonata, Op.4, 1909–10; Duo, Op.7, vn, vc, 1914; Solo Cello Sonata, Op.8, 1915; Capriccio, vc, 1915; Hungarian Rondo, vc, pf, 1917; Sonatina, vc, pf, 1921–2

Piano: Piano Music, Op.3, 1909; 7 Pieces, Op.11, 1910–18; *Dances of Marosszék*, 1927

Koechlin, Charles (Louis Eugène) (b. Paris, 27
Nov 1867; d. Le Canadel, Var, 31 Dec 1950). French composer, enormously productive, especially after the age of 50, when he worked, largely neglected, on orchestral scores that bring polyphonic density into the kind of evocative musical landscape he inherited from Debussy but that, in his case, tends to be more sombre, shadowed. Any judgement, though, has to be circumspect, of an output so large and little known.

Of a well-to-do Alsatian family, he studied with Massenet, Gédalge and Fauré at the Paris Conservatoire (1890–97), then lived on his private means. Besides dozens of orchestral works, he produced song cycles, large choral pieces and many smaller instrumental items, ranging widely in several dimensions. He had passions for Kipling's *Jungle Book* and for the screen actress Lilian Harvey; he wrote in church modes and for ondes martenot; he was a communist as well as a contrapuntalist. In earlier years he was known in Paris as a composer, critic and organizer, and Debussy called on his services for *Khamma*. He also gave private lessons, with Milhaud and Poulenc among his pupils. But in his last two decades he lived in isolation, working on his music and on textbooks. He described his life as 'a series of happy chances under a cloud of general misfortune'.

Robert Orledge *Charles Koechlin* (1989)

Works after the *Jungle Book*: Trois poèmes du 'Livre de la jungle', Op.18, soli, ch, orch, 1899–1910; *La Course de printemps*, Op.95, orch, 1908–27; *La Méditation de Purun Bhagat*, Op.159, orch, 1936; *La Loi de la jungle*, Op.175, orch, 1939–40; *Les Bandar-log*, Op.176, orch, 1939–40

Other orchestral works: *La Forêt*, 2 parts, Op.25 and Op.29, 1896–1907; SEVEN STARS' SYMPHONY, Op.132, 1933; etc.

Other works: songs ('Si tu le veux', Op.5:5, 1890s), chamber and instrumental music

Koenig, Gottfried Michael (b. Magdeburg, 5 Oct
1926). German composer, one of Stockhausen's liveliest contemporaries. He studied at the academy in Detmold with Bialas (1947–50) and at the conservatory in Cologne (1953–4), then worked alongside Stockhausen in the Cologne radio studio for electronic music (1954–64), assisting in the creation of *Gesang der Jünglinge* and *Kontakte*. In 1964 he was appointed director of the studio at Utrecht University, where he has similarly devoted himself more to younger colleagues than to his own work. His correspondingly modest output includes instrumental and electronic compositions (*Essay*, 1957–8).

Koffler, Józef (b. Stryj, 28 Nov 1896; d. near
Krosno, 1944). Polish composer, a Schoenberg pupil and early serialist. His studies with Schoenberg in Vienna (1920–24) came after a period there with Hermann Graedener (1914–16) and alongside a scholarly training under Adler. He returned to become a teacher at the Lwów/Lviv Conservatory (1929–41) and a critic, while writing mostly instrumental pieces, including three symphonies, a string trio (1929) and piano works.

Kokkonen, Joonas (b. Iisalmi, 13 Nov 1921; d.
Järvenpää, 20 Oct 1996). Finnish composer, within the modernist mainstream. He studied as a pianist at the Sibelius Academy and as a music scholar at Helsinki University, then joined the staff at the academy (1950–63). His works include symphonies, concertos, quartets and an opera, *The Last Temptations* (f.p. Helsinki, 1975).

Kolisch, Rudolf (b. Klamm am Semmering, 20 Jul
1896; d. Watertown, Mass., 1 Aug 1978). Austrian–US violinist, a pupil of Schoenberg, who married his sister, and founder of the Kolisch Quartet (1922–39), which pioneered playing from memory and introduced works by Schoenberg (Quartets Nos.3 and 4, Quartet Concerto), Bartók (No.5), Berg (Lyric Suite) and Webern (Op.20 and Op.28). The group moved to the USA in 1935. In 1942 Kolisch became leader of the Pro Arte Quartet. He also taught.

Kol nidre (All Vows). Aramaic prayer for Yom
Kippur, evoked by Bruch in a work for cello and orchestra, and set by Schoenberg in his own English version for cantor (in SPRECHGESANG), choir and orchestra (f.p. Los Angeles, 4 Oct 1938).

Koloratur (Ger.). Coloratura.

Komische Oper. Opera theatre and company in
Berlin, founded by the producer Walter Felsenstein in 1947 to renew dramatic vitality in the genre, continuing the work of the pre-Nazi Kroll. It kept to its mission under Felsenstein's disciples

and successors, Joachim Herz (1976–81) and Harry Kupfer (from 1981).

Komitas (b. Kyotaya, Turkey, 8 Oct 1869; d. Paris, 22 Oct 1935). Armenian composer, almost exclusively of choruses and songs close to folk music. Orphaned in 1881, he was sent to a seminary, from which he emerged in 1896 as priest and vardapet (doctor of theology), already noted for his gifts as a singer and musician. Studies in Western music followed with Richard Schmidt in Berlin (1896–9). He promoted Armenian music in Paris and the eastern Mediterranean, but was prostrated by the Turkish massacre of 1915 and spent his last 16 years in a hospital outside Paris.

Kondo, Jo (b. Tokyo, 28 Oct 1947). Japanese composer, influenced by US experimental music. He studied at the National University for Fine Arts and Music (1968–72) and began teaching there in 1986, moving to the Elizabeth Music University in Hiroshima in 1988.

Kondrashin, Kirill (Petrovich) (b. Moscow, 6 Mar 1914; d. Amsterdam, 7 Mar 1981). Russian conductor, notably with the Moscow Philharmonic (1960–75). Born into a musical family, he studied with Nikolay Zhilyayev and spent the earlier part of his career in opera, especially with the Maly in Leningrad (1936–43) and the Bolshoy in Moscow (1943–56). In 1978 he left for the West.

König Hirsch (King Stag). Opera by Henze to a libretto by Heinz von Cramer after Carlo Gozzi. Leandro (tenor), raised in the forest, flees back there from his new, confusing life as king, and is transformed into a stag by his chancellor, Tartaglia (bass-baritone), who assumes control. Finally, though, he is restored to his throne and to his beloved Costanza (soprano). First performance: Berlin, 23 Sep 1956, rev as *Il re cervo*, Kassel, 10 Mar 1963.

König Stephan (King Stephen). Set of pieces by Beethoven – including an overture, choruses and a victory march – for a prologue by August von Kotzebue that, with *Die Ruinen von Athen* by the same team, opened the German theatre in the Hungarian capital. Stephen was the monarch who christianized his country. First performance: Pest, 10 Feb 1812.

Kontarsky, Aloys (b. Iserlohn, 14 May 1931). German pianist, associated particularly with Stockhausen; he was a member of the composer's ensemble in the late 1960s and early 1970s, during which time he gave the first complete performance

of Piano Pieces I–XI (Darmstadt, 1966) and the world première with his brother Alfons (b. 1932) of *Mantra*. The two brothers both studied at the conservatory in Cologne and with Eduard Erdmann in Hamburg (1955–7). A third brother, Bernhard (b. 1937), is a conductor.

Kontakte (Contacts). Four-track tape piece by Stockhausen, to be heard with or without piano and percussion soloists. First performance: Cologne, 26 Oct 1961.

Kontrabass (Ger.). Double bass.

Kontrafagott (Ger.). Double bassoon.

Kontrapunkt (Ger.). Counterpoint.

Kontrapunkte (Counterpoints). Work by Stockhausen for piano with nine instruments (fl, cl, b cl, bn, tpt, trbn, hp, vn, vc) that drop out one by one. First performance: Cologne, 26 May 1953.

Kontretanz (Ger.). Contredanse.

Konwitschny, Franz (b. Fulnek, north Moravia, 14 Aug 1901; d. Belgrade, 28 Jul 1962). German conductor of Romantic taste and temperament, admired in music from Beethoven to Mahler and Strauss. He studied in Leipzig, and played violin and viola in the Gewandhaus orchestra under Furtwängler. That orchestra duly became his own (1949–62), following periods in Freiburg (from 1933) and Frankfurt (from 1938), and with it he died, during a rehearsal of Beethoven's *Missa solemnis* on tour.

Konzert (Ger.). Concert, concerto.

Konzertmeister (Ger.). Concertmaster, leader.

Konzertstück (Ger.). Concerted piece, a title often used (e.g. by Weber) for a one-movement concerto.

Koopman, Ton [Antonius] (b. Zwolle, 2 Oct 1944). Dutch conductor and keyboard player, specially distinguished in Bach. He studied with Leonhardt at the Amsterdam Conservatory (1965–70), and taught harpsichord there (1978–88) before moving to a similar post in The Hague. In 1979 he founded the Amsterdam Baroque Orchestra, with which he has made numerous recordings.

Kornett (Ger.). Cornet.

Korngold, Erich Wolfgang (b. Brno, 29 May 1897;

d. Hollywood, 29 Nov 1957). Austrian–US composer, who discovered a style of ripe Romanticism in his late teens in Vienna and held to it in the film scores and concert works he composed in Hollywood. Encouraged by his father, the music critic Julius Korngold (1860–1945), he studied with Zemlinsky as a boy and had his early music praised by Schnabel, Strauss and Puccini. Such were the expectations that his murky symbolist opera *Die tote Stadt* – with a libretto he wrote with his father after Georges Rodenbach's *Bruges la morte* – was given simultaneous first performances in Hamburg and Cologne (1920). He moved to Hollywood in 1934 and won two Oscars (for *Anthony Adverse* and *The Adventures of Robin Hood*), besides composing a concerto for Heifetz.

Brendan G. Carroll *The Last Prodigy* (1997)

www.korngold-society.org

Operas: *Der Ring des Polykrates* (1 act), Op.7, f.p. Munich, 1916; *Violanta* (1 act; Hans Müller), Op.8, f.p. Munich, 1916; *Die tote Stadt* (Paul Schott, i.e. Julius Korngold), Op.12, f.p. Hamburg and Cologne, 1920; *Das Wunder der Heliane* (Müller), Op.20, f.p. Hamburg, 1927; *Die Kathrin* (Ernst Decsey), Op.28, f.p. Stockholm, 1939

Orchestral: *Der Schneemann* (ballet), 1910; *Schauspiel Ouvertüre*, Op.4, 1911; Sinfonietta, Op.5, 1912; Left-Hand Piano Concerto, C♯, Op.17, c.1923; Violin Concerto, D, Op.35, 1945; Cello Concerto, C, Op.37, 1946; Symphonic Serenade, B, Op.39, str, c.1947; Symphony, F♯, Op.40, 1951–2; etc.

Chamber and instrumental: String Quartet No.1, A, Op.16, c.1923; No.2, E♭, Op.26, 1935; No.3, D, Op.34; Piano Sonata No.1, D minor, 1908; No.2, E, Op.2; No.3, C, Op.25, 1931; etc.

Film scores: *Anthony Adverse*, 1936; *The Adventures of Robin Hood*, 1938; etc.

Kortholt (Ger.). Name used in the 16th–17th centuries for several instruments of the bassoon type.

koto. Japanese long zither, played as a solo instrument or in ensembles.

Kotoński, Włodzimierz (b. Warsaw, 23 Aug 1925). Polish composer, avant-garde pioneer. He studied with Piotr Rytel at the Warsaw Conservatory (1945–51), with Tadeusz Szeligowski in Poznań (1950–51) and at the Darmstadt summer courses (1957–60), which led him away from a folk-neoclassical-Szymanowski area towards a keen exploitation of percussion and electronic sounds. He returned to the Warsaw Conservatory in 1967 to teach.

Koussevitzky, Serge [Kusevitsky, Sergey Aleksandrovich] (b. Vishny-Volotchok, Tver, 26

Jul 1874; d. Boston, Mass., 4 Jun 1951). Russian–US conductor. A colourful figure, he supported his composer contemporaries by means of the largesse he gained by marriage and of his not always coherent dynamism. He began his musical career as a bass player, training at the Moscow Philharmonic music school from the age of 14, playing in the Bolshoy orchestra from 1894, and touring as a soloist from 1896. In 1905, the year of his marriage, he gave the first performance of a concerto he had written with an uncertain amount of help from Glière. He then recreated himself as a conductor; he watched Nikisch in Berlin and practised with a student orchestra at the conservatory before hiring the Berlin Philharmonic for his debut (1908). The next year he formed his own orchestra and founded a publishing company, Editions Russes de Musique, to handle the scores of composers he admired, including Scriabin, Rachmaninoff, Stravinsky and Prokofiev. After the Russian Revolution he continued his activities in Paris (1917–24) and as conductor of the Boston Symphony (1924–49), whose summer residence at TANGLEWOOD he established in 1935. For the orchestra's half-centenary season of 1930–31 he commissioned works from Stravinsky, Prokofiev, Hindemith, Honegger, Roussel and others, and in 1942 he set up a foundation that has continued to commission leading composers.

Kovacevich, Stephen (Bishop) (b. San Pedro, Cal., 17 Oct 1940). US pianist, acclaimed most of all in Beethoven and Mozart, though he has also promoted concertos by Richard Rodney Bennett (written for him) and Tippett. He studied with Lev Schorr, and from 1959 with Myra Hess in London, which has remained his base.

Kovařovich, Karel (b. Prague, 9 Dec 1862; d. Prague, 6 Dec 1920). Czech conductor and composer, unfortunately remembered as the man who delayed the Prague production of Janáček's *Jenůfa* and agreed to mount it only in his own revised form, a form it kept for more than 60 years. In other respects he was a thorough and forward-looking head of opera at the National Theatre (1900–20), having reached that post by way of training at the Prague Conservatory (1873–9), private lessons with Fibich (1878–80), and experience both as a harpist at the theatre (1879–85) and as a conductor elsewhere, notably with the new Czech Philharmonic (1896–8). He wrote mostly operas and ballets, but also some orchestral pieces, three quartets, choruses and songs.

Kowalski, Jochen (b. Wachow, Brandenburg, 30

Jan 1954). German countertenor, known especially for his ardent, virile portrayal of Gluck's Orpheus. He studied in Berlin (1977–83) and joined the Komische Oper in 1983.

Kozeluch, Leopold [Koželuh, Jan Antonín] (b. Velvary, 26 Jun 1747; d. Vienna, 7 May 1818). Bohemian composer and pianist, an adept of the Viennese Classical style alongside Mozart and Beethoven. He took the name 'Leopold' to distinguish himself from his cousin Jan Antonín (1738–1814), who studied with Gluck, Gassmann and Hasse in Vienna (1763–6) but spent most of his life in Prague, where he was chapelmaster of St Vitus's Cathedral (1784–1818). Leopold studied in Prague with this cousin and also with Dušek, but when he went to Vienna, in 1778, he stayed. He became active as a publisher, and gained a court appointment in 1792. His copious output includes a large amount of piano music – about 50 solo sonatas, about 100 chamber works with one or two other instruments, about 20 concertos – as well as symphonies, operas and choral music.

Krafft, Jean-Christophe. See IMAGINARY COMPOSERS.

kräftig (Ger.). Powerful.

krakowiak. Lively folkdance from the Kraków area, in duple time and syncopated. It became a symbol of a Poland that had vanished from the map. The first published collection came out in 1816, but the most distinguished example is Chopin's Op.14.

Krása, Hans (b. Prague, 30 Nov 1899; d. Auschwitz, 18 Oct 1944). German composer, author of a children's opera, *Brundibár* (The Bumblebee, 1938–9), which had its first performance (1943) only after he and its cast had been interned at Theresienstadt. He was a pupil of Zemlinsky.

Krasner, Louis (b. Cherkassy, 21 Jun 1903; d. Boston, 4 May 1995). Russian–US violinist who commissioned the Berg concerto and introduced others by Schoenberg, Casella and Sessions. Having travelled to the USA with his family at five, he studied at the New England Conservatory and in Europe with Flesch, Lucien Capet and Otakar Ševčík. In later years he taught at the University of Syracuse.

Kraus, Alfredo (b. Las Palmas, Canary Islands, 24 Sep 1927; d. Madrid, 10 Sep 1999). Spanish lyric tenor, esteemed for his elegance in Italian and French opera. He studied with Mercedes Llopart and made his debut at Cairo (1956), followed by appearances at Covent Garden (1959), La Scala (1960) and the Met (1966). He remained at the international forefront well into his 60s.

Kraus, Joseph Martin (b. Miltenberg am Main, 20 Jun 1756; d. Stockholm, 15 Dec 1792). German composer attached (from 1781) to the court of Gustavus III of Sweden. Musically raised in Mannheim, he pursued a university legal training before moving to Stockholm at a friend's suggestion in 1778. The king sent him on a long European tour (1782–7), during which he met Gluck (an important influence) and Haydn. He wrote operas (*Aeneas i Carthago*, f.p. Stockholm, 1799), as well as cantatas and orchestral pieces that include two memorials to the king: a *Begravnings-kantata* and a *Symphonie funèbre*. Nine months after the royal assassination he died of tuberculosis.

Krauss, Clemens (b. Vienna, 31 Mar 1893; d. Mexico City, 16 May 1954). Austrian conductor, especially associated with the operas of Strauss: he conducted the premières of *Arabella*, *Friedenstag*, *Capriccio* (whose libretto he had written) and *Die Liebe der Danäe*, and was married to a leading Strauss soprano, Viorica Ursuleac. The son of an actress-singer (Clementine Krauss), he began his conducting career at 20 and rose to chief posts with the principal opera companies in Frankfurt (1924–9), Vienna (1929–35), Berlin (1935–7) and Munich (1937–43). His failure to distance himself from Nazism led to a two-year ban after the war; he then returned to his post in Vienna, and died on tour with the company.

Krebs, Johann Ludwig (baptized Buttelstedt, Weimar, 12 Oct 1713; d. Altenburg, 1 Jan 1780). German organist-composer, a pupil of J.S. Bach, to whom is attributed the double pun 'He is the only crayfish (*Krebs*) in my stream (*Bach*)'. His father, Johann Tobias (1690–1762), was also an organist-composer who had lessons with Bach (and Walther), in his native Weimar. Johann Ludwig was Bach's student at St Thomas's school in Leipzig (1726–35), where he went on to the university (1735–7). He then held posts in Zwickau (1737–43) and at the castles of Zeitz (1744–55) and Altenburg (1755–80); he applied to succeed Bach in Leipzig, but was passed over. Affection for his master is suggested by his music, though he was also open to the galant spirit. His works include fantasias for solo instrument and organ, preludes and fugues for organ, chorale preludes (*Herzlich Lieb' hab' ich dich, o Herr*) other keyboard music, chamber sonatas and a few sacred choral pieces. All three of his sons also became organist-composers. The eldest, Johann Gottfried (1741–1814), was debarred from succeeding him because of an association with 'an unacceptable female', and so – perhaps because the second, Carl Heinrich Gottfried (1747–93), already had a job at Eisen-berg – the post went to the youngest, Ehrenfried Christian Traugott (1753–1804).

Kreisler, Fritz (b. Vienna, 2 Feb 1875; d. New York, 29 Jan 1962). Austrian–US violinist. He studied first with his doctor father, then with Hellmesberger and Bruckner at the Vienna Conservatory (1882–5), where he was the youngest entrant ever, and by far the youngest to graduate with a gold medal. Two years with Joseph Massart at the Paris Conservatoire (1885–7) completed his training: he was 12. However, it was not until 1899 that he began his solo career, with the Berlin Philharmonic under Nikisch. Then he quickly became an international sensation, admired for his elegance, the fine polish of his vibrato, his total mastery. Elgar's concerto was written for him. In 1914, after a quick release from war service, he moved to the USA. He returned to Europe after the war and settled in Berlin (1924–34), but in 1939 he returned to the US. There his career ended; he played Carnegie Hall for the last time in 1947. His cadenzas for the Beethoven and Brahms concertos remain standard; he also wrote a number of short pieces he passed off as the works of minor 18th-century masters.

Kreisleriana. Set of eight piano fantasies by Schumann, prompted by Hoffmann's story collection *Kreisleriana* and its madcap kapellmeister hero, Johannes Kreisler.

Kremer, Gidon (b. Riga, 7 Feb 1947). Russian violinist, an agile virtuoso with an eager taste for new music and new ways of making music. He studied with Oistrakh and Bondarenko at the Moscow Conservatory (1965–73), and made his much awaited London debut in 1975. Though he then played the international circuit, he regularly presented works written for him by Soviet composers (Schnittke, Gubaidulina, Pärt), and his recording of the Beethoven concerto came, characteristically, with a new cadenza by Schnittke. In 1981 he founded the LOCKENHAUS festival; in 1997 he formed his own chamber orchestra, the Kremerata Baltica.

Krenek, [Křenek] **Ernst** (b. Vienna, 23 Aug 1900; d. Palm Springs, Cal., 23 Dec 1991). Austrian–US composer, who in his long life and many works spanned the distance from Busoni to Boulez. He began studies with Schreker at 16 and followed his teacher to Berlin (1920–23). His early works, including three symphonies of 1921–2, explored protracted dissonance in ways suggesting his closeness to Busoni and Mahler (whose daughter Anna he married), but a short while later he was impressed by the neoclassicism he heard in Paris. *Jonny spielt auf* (f.p. Leipzig, 1927) – already this fecund composer's third full-length opera – brought him spectacular success; the work rapidly enjoyed over 100 productions, in cities from New York to Leningrad, thanks to its (modest) jazz influence and modish contemporary setting. Able to give up menial conducting work and compose full time, he settled in Vienna and composed a slantwise Schubertian song cycle, *Reisebuch aus dem oesterreichischen Alpen* (1929), then began to use 12-note serialism, one of the first composers outside Schoenberg's circle to do so (though he was in contact with Berg and Webern). His first big serial piece was the opera *Karl V* (1930–33) – a pointed eulogy to what he saw as the benign civilization of Catholic Europe under Emperor Charles V – which was stopped in rehearsal at the Vienna Staatsoper in 1934 and given four years later in Prague. In the interim he wrote his Sixth Quartet, one of his strongest works. In the year of the *Karl V* première he moved to the USA, where he taught, theorized and went on composing abundantly, normally using the serial technique in a speculative fashion and adding ROTATION to the standard transformations.

Operas (librettos by the composer unless otherwise stated): *Der Sprung über den Schatten*, Op.17, f.p. Frankfurt, 1924; *Orpheus und Eurydike* (Kokoschka), Op.21, f.p. Kassel, 1926; *Jonny spielt auf*, Op.45, f.p. Leipzig, 1927; *Leben des Orest*, Op.60, f.p. Leipzig, 1930; *Karl V*, Op.73, f.p. Prague, 1938; *Pallas Athene weint*, Op.144, f.p. Hamburg, 1955; *Sardakai*, Op.206, f.p. Hamburg, 1970; etc. Other works: 5 symphonies, many concertos, 7 quartets (No.6, Op.78, 1937), songs (*Reisebuch aus dem oesterreichischen Alpen*, Op.62, 1929), sacred music (*Spiritus intelligentiae, sanctus*, 2 v, tape, 1955), etc.

Kreutzer. Name given to Beethoven's Violin Sonata Op.47, dedicated to Rodolphe Kreutzer. Tolstoy took the title for his novella *The Kreutzer Sonata*, to which Janáček referred in giving the same name to his first quartet – music based on literature based on music.

Kreutzer, Conradin (b. Messkirch, Baden, 22 Nov 1780; d. Riga, 14 Dec 1849). German composer, especially of operas and other theatre music, choral works and songs. Schooled at the monastery of Zwiefalten, he probably studied with Albrechtsberger in Vienna after 1804. He was court kapellmeister in Stuttgart (1812–16) and Donaueschingen (1818–22), then worked until 1840 at theatres in Vienna, where he achieved his biggest operatic successes, *Das Nachtlager in Granada* and *Der Verschwender* (both 1834).

Kreutzer, Rodolphe (b. Versailles, 16 Nov 1766; d. Geneva, 6 Jan 1831). French violinist and composer, a virtuoso praised by Beethoven for his 'modesty and natural behaviour', which the great composer rewarded with a sonata that has kept his name alive. The son of a German musician, he studied with his father and Anton Stamitz, and made his debut in Paris at 13. At 17 he played his first concerto, and at 23 began a long run of works for the stage. He taught at the newly founded Paris Conservatoire until 1826, and also played at the Opera (where he became chief conductor, 1817–24), at court under Napoleon and Louis XVIII, and abroad, not least in Vienna, where Beethoven heard him.

Kreuz (Ger.). Sharp sign.

Krieger, Adam (b. Driesen, near Frankfurt an der Oder, 7 Jan 1634; d. Dresden, 30 Jun 1666). German composer, mostly of 100 songs published in two volumes (1657, 1667). From the age of 16 or 17 he studied at Leipzig University; he also had organ lessons from Scheidt in Halle. In 1655 he became organist of St Nicholas's in Leipzig, but two years later he was called to Dresden to be keyboard teacher to the Elector's daughters. Most of his songs are strophic, and some of his melodies were adopted as chorales.

Krieger. German organist-composer brothers.

(1) **Johann Philipp** (baptized Nuremberg, 27 Feb 1649; d. Weissenfels, 6 Feb 1725). He studied in his home city, in Nuremberg in his teens, and in Italy in his mid-20s, while attached to the Bayreuth court. In 1677 he became court organist in Halle, and in 1680 he moved with the court to Weissenfels, now as chapelmaster. He wrote over 2,000 church cantatas, of which only 74 survive, along with chamber sonatas and a keyboard passacaglia.

(2) **Johann** (baptized Nuremberg, 1 Jan 1652; d. Zittau, 18 Jul 1735). After studying in Nuremberg he followed his brother to Bayreuth and perhaps also Halle before settling as organist and choirmaster in Zittau for over half a century (1682–1735). He wrote church cantatas, songs and operas, but was most admired – not least by Handel – as a writer of fugues and other keyboard music.

Krips, Josef (b. Vienna, 8 Apr 1902; d. Geneva, 13 Oct 1974). Austrian conductor, admired above all in Mozart. He studied with Eusebius Mandyczewski and Weingartner at the Vienna Academy, then worked in various German cities before returning to Vienna in 1933. In 1938, with the Nazi annexation, he was out, but in 1945 he returned, and his work with the Staatsoper and the Vienna Philharmonic was the foundation of his later career. He became chief conductor of the LSO (1950–54), the Buffalo Philharmonic (1954–63) and the San Francisco Symphony (1963–70). His brother, Henry (1912–87), became a conductor in Australia and London.

Křížkovský, (Karel) Pavel (b. Kreuzendorf/ Holasovice, Silesia, 9 Jan 1820; d. Brno, 8 May 1885). Czech choirmaster-composer, a vital figure in the musical life of Brno before his pupil Janáček. He settled in Brno in 1843, following studies in Troppau/Opava, and became choirmaster for the Augustinians in 1848. His works, almost all choral, include sacred pieces and folksong arrangements.

Krohn, Ilmari (Henrik Reinhold) (b. Helsinki, 8 Nov 1867; d. Helsinki, 25 Apr 1960). Finnish music scholar, a pioneer of folksong research; his method of classification was adopted by Bartók.

Kroll Opera. Branch of the Berlin Staatsoper set up at the Kroll Theatre (1927–31) with Klemperer in charge of a repertory that emphasized new works (by Stravinsky, Schoenberg, Janáček, Weill and Hindemith) and modern-style productions.

Krommer, Franz (Vinzenz) (b. Kamenice u Třebíče, 27 Nov 1759; d. Vienna, 8 Jan 1831). Bohemian composer, a minor Classical master remembered for his concertos and chamber music featuring woodwinds (Clarinet Concerto, E♭, Op.36, pub 1803; other concertos for clarinet, oboe, flute, two clarinets, etc.). He studied with his composer-choirmaster uncle, and after 1785 lived mostly in Vienna.

Kronos Quartet. US ensemble founded in Seattle in 1973 by David Harrington, then formally established in San Francisco in 1978 with a line-up also including Hank Dutt, John Sherba and Joan Jeanrenaud (replaced by Jennifer Culp in 1999). Playing new works almost exclusively, the group has preferred music with strong links to rock or ethnic music, by composers including Riley, Reich and Golijov. Its performances correspondingly affront the norms of the quartet world with cool attire, vivid lighting and amplification.

Krummhorn (Ger.). Crumhorn.

Krumpholtz, Jean-Baptiste (b. Budenice, near Zlonice, 3 May 1742; d. Paris, 19 Feb 1790). Bohemian harpist-composer, the great virtuoso of his time. With a bandmaster father and harpist mother, he was torn between two musical careers, but seems to have settled down as Haydn's harpist and composition pupil in 1773. He moved to Paris in 1778 and married a pupil. She eloped to London in 1788 with Dussek, and he drowned himself in the Seine two years later. His works comprise mostly harp music: concertos, sonatas and variations. His brother, Wenzel (*c*.1750–1817), was one of Beethoven's early supporters.

Kubelík. Czech musicians, father and son.

(1) **Jan** (b. Michle, near Prague, 5 Jul 1880; d. Prague, 5 Dec 1940). Violinist, a virtuoso who played all over the world. He studied with Otakar Ševčík at the Prague Conservatory, began his career in 1898, made his London debut in 1900 and first toured the USA in 1902. During these years he also helped support the Czech Philharmonic. He composed six concertos, cadenzas and other music.

(2) **Rafael (Jeronym)** (b. Býchory, near Kolin, 29 Jun 1914; d. Lucerne, 11 Aug 1996). Conductor, associated with the Bavarian Radio Symphony (principal conductor 1961–79), the Vienna Philharmonic and other orchestras in many fine recordings, before his career was ended by arthritis. He studied at the Prague Conservatory and made his debut in 1934 with the Czech Philharmonic. In 1948 he left Cezchoslovakia, settling eventually in Switzerland and taking Swiss nationality. He became music director of the Chicago Symphony (1950–53), Covent Garden Opera (1955–8) and the Met (1973–4). Also a composer, he wrote operas, three *Requiem* settings and orchestral pieces.

Kuckuck (Ger.). Avian organ stop.

Kuhlau, (Daniel) Friedrich (Rudolph) [Frederik] (b. Uelzen, near Hanover, 11 Sep 1786; d. Copenhagen, 12 Mar 1832). German–Danish composer, an early Romantic of local colour. A bandsman's son, he studied with C.F.G. Schwenke in Hamburg and moved to Copenhagen in 1810 to escape Napoleon's invasion. Once there he found work as a pianist, theatre composer and court musician. He also travelled in Sweden and to Vienna, where he met Beethoven in 1825 and exchanged canonic greetings (as was his wont), Beethoven's to him being *Kühl, nicht lau* (cool, not tepid). Otherwise his works comprise mostly flute repertory (Trio, G, Op.119, 2 fl, pf, pub 1832; 3 Quintets, D, E minor, A, Op.51, pub 1823), piano music, songs and part-songs.

Kuhnau, Johann (b. Geising, Erzgebirge, 6 Apr 1660; d. Leipzig, 5 Jun 1722). German composer and keyboard player, one of the great masters in the generation before Bach, his successor as cantor of St Thomas's in Leipzig. Musically trained in Dresden (*c*.1670–80, at court and as a chorister at the Kreuz church), he continued his education in Zittau and at Leipzig University (1682–8), where he graduated as a lawyer. Meanwhile he was beginning careers as a professional musician and as a father: married in 1689, he had 10 children. He became organist of St Thomas's in 1684 and cantor in 1701, bringing to the post a range of intellectual accomplishments. His works include church cantatas partly foreshadowing Bach's and four published volumes of keyboard music, including the *Biblische Historien* (1700), a set of six sonatas explicitly based on stories from the Hebrew Bible. He also wrote a satirical novel, *The Musical Charlatan* (1700, Eng. trans. 1997).

Kuhschelle (Ger.). Cowbells.

Kuijken. Belgian brothers, prominent in the early music movement, especially in the 1970s–80s, Wieland (b. 1938) being a virtuoso of the viola da gamba, Sigiswald (b. 1944) a violinist and conductor of his own orchestra, La Petite Bande (founded 1972), and Barthold (b. 1949) a player on the flute and recorder. They all studied at the conservatories of Bruges and Brussels, and began performing together publicly in 1972.

Kunst der Fuge, Die (The Art of Fugue). Late collection by Bach, published the year after his death, of 14 'contrapuncti' (i.e. fugues), four canons, two mirror fugues and a presumably final quadruple fugue that is incomplete, all based on the same subject. Among completions of the final fugue are those by Tovey and Busoni (in his FANTASIA CONTRAPPUNTISTICA). There is no indication of order or medium: organists, pianists and string quartets have claimed the music.

Kunstmusik (Ger.). Art music, sometimes abbreviated K-Musik, as distinct from U-Musik (Unterhaltungsmusik, entertainment music).

Kurpiński, Karol Kazimierz (b. Włoszakowice, Wielkopolska, 6 Mar 1785; d. Warsaw, 18 Sep 1857). Polish composer and conductor, a leading figure in Warsaw during the youth of Chopin, for whose first concerts he conducted. An organist's son, he began work as an organist himself at 12, then worked for noble families before settling in Warsaw in 1810 and becoming, among several other appointments, principal conductor of the opera (1824–40). He wrote operas, church music and various instrumental pieces.

Kurtág, György (b. Lugoj, Romania, 19 Feb 1926). Hungarian composer, whose works are gatherings of fragments, bound by extraordinary intensities of gesture, colour, expression and humour. He studied first in Timișoara, then at the Liszt Academy in Budapest (1946–55), with Veress, Farkas, Kadosa and Leo Weiner. In 1957 he went to Paris for further studies with Milhaud and Messiaen, though more important were the psychiatric sessions he had with Marianne Stein and the experiences he gained re-encountering his classmate Ligeti and hearing the first performance of Stockhausen's *Gruppen*. Back in Budapest he became a valued coach, and joined the staff at the Liszt Academy (1967–86), where, as professor of chamber music, he had a crucial influence on numerous outstanding performers. Previously little known outside Hungary, he became an international figure in the 1980s (Boulez's commissioning of *Messages* was a turning point) and accepted residencies with the Berlin Philharmonic (1993–5), in Vienna (1995–6), in Amsterdam (1996– 7) and in Paris (from 1999). He also began giving occasional four-hand recitals with his wife Márta, playing his own pieces and Bach transcriptions.

He remade himself as a composer after his time with Stein. Withdrawing his earlier works (apart from a viola concerto already in print), he began to work on a small, Webern-like scale, but with his own vivid rhetoric and Hungarian (Bartókian) accent. In three years (1959–61) he produced five sets of instrumental pieces; during the next seven years he completed only one work, but a formidable one, *The Sayings of Péter Bornemisza*. After that he fell almost silent. Then came the unexpected delight he found in creating wide-ranging challenges and amusements for young pianists in *Játékok* (Games), of which he has gone on producing occasional volumes since the mid-1970s. By allowing him to be earnest and playful at the same time, and to make more or less oblique references to all kinds of music, *Játékok* provided the key to his whole later output. If, nevertheless, he has remained a severely self-critical creator, writing pieces rapidly but often releasing them only after many years of thought, his world has grown to embrace larger formations (often fragmented orchestras, with soloists and groups in different positions) and to accommodate even such huge figures as Kafka and Beckett.

His son György (b. 1954) is a composer-performer of electronic music, and his collaborator on *Zwiegespräch*.

Orchestral: Viola Concerto, 1953–4; *Grabstein für Stephan*, Op.15c, gtr, ens, 1978–9, rev 1989; … QUASI UNA FANTASIA …, Op.27:1, pf, ens, 1987–8; Double Concerto, Op.27:2, pf, vc, ens, 1989–90; *Samuel Beckett: What is the Word?*, Op.30b, a, 5 v, ens, 1991; *Stele*, Op.33, 1994; *Messages*, Op.34, ch, orch, 1991–6; *New Messages*, Op.34a, 1998–; … *concertante* …, Op.42, vn, va, orch, 2003

Choral: *Omaggio a Luigi Nono* (Akhmatova, Rimma Dalos), Op.16, 1979, rev 1985; *Songs of Despair and Sorrow* (Russ. poets), Op.18, ch, ens, 1980–94; 8 Tandori Choruses, Op.23, 1981–4

Solo vocal: *The* SAYINGS OF PÉTER BORNEMISZA, Op.7, s, pf, 1963–8, rev 1976; *In memory of a winter sunset* (Pál Gulyás), Op.8, s, vn, cimbalom, 1969; 4 Capriccios (István Bálint), Op.9, s, 14 insts, 1971; 4 Songs (János Pilinszky), Op.11, b, 7 insts, 1973–5; *S.K. Remembrance Noise* (Dezső Tandori), Op.12, s, vn, 1974–5; *Herdecker Eurythmie*, Op.14a-c, speaker, fl, vn, lyre, 1979; *Messages of the Late Miss R.V. Troussova* (Dalos), Op.17, s, small orch, 1976–80; *Scenes from a Novel* (Dalos), Op.19, s, vn, cimb, db, 1979–82; *Attila József Fragments*, Op.20, s, 1981; 7 Songs (Károlyi, Tandori), Op.22, s, cimb/pf, 1981; KAFKA-FRAGMENTE, Op.24, s, vn, 1985–7; *3 Old Inscriptions*, Op.25, s, pf, 1986–7; *Requiem for the Beloved* (Dalos), Op.26, s, pf, 1982–7; *An Friedrich Hölderlin*, Op.29, t, pf, 1988–9; *Friedrich Hölderlin: Im Walde*, Op.29:2, v, 1993; *Samuel Beckett: What is the Word?*, Op.30a, s, pf, 1990; *Hölderlin-Gesänge*, Op.35, bar, vs and insts ad lib, 1993–; … *pas à pas – nulle part* … (Beckett), Op.36, b, str trio, perc, 1993–8; *Einige Sätze aus den Sudelbüchern Georg Christoph Lichtenbergs*, Op.37, s, db ad lib, 1999; *Fancsikó and Pinta* (Péter Esterházy), Op.40, s, upright pf and cel, 1999; 4 songs (Akhmatova), Op.41, s, ens, 1997–

String quartets: Op.1, 1959; *12 Microludes*, Op.13, 1977–8; OFFICIUM BREVE, Op.28, 1988–9; *Zwiegespräch*, 1999–, with elec by György Kurtág junior

Other chamber works: Wind Quintet, Op.2, 1959; 8 Duos, Op.4, vn, cimbalom, 1961; *Signs*, Op.5, va, 1961, rev 1992; *Signs*, Op.5b, vc, 1961–99; *Splinters*, Op.6c, cimb, 1973; 6 Bagatelles, Op.14d, fl, db, pf, 1981; *Tre pezzi*, Op.14e, vn, pf, 1979; *The Little Predicament*, Op.15b, pic, trbn, gtr, 1978; *Hommage à R. Sch.*, Op.15d, cl, va, pf, 1990; *Games and Messages*, wind solos/duos/ens pieces, 1984–; *Signs, Games and Messages*, str solos/duos/ens pieces, 1986–; *Ligatura*, Op.31b, vc/ens, 1989; *Életút* (Curriculum vitae), Op.32, 2 pf, 2 basset hn, 1992; *Rückblick*, tpt, db, kbd, 1993; *Tre pezzi*, Op.38, cl, cimb, 1996; *Tre altri pezzi*, Op.38a, cl, cimb, 1996; *Scenes*, Op.39, fl, 1999

Piano: 8 Pieces, Op.3, 1960; *Pre-Games*, 1973–4; JÁTÉKOK (Games), 1973–; *Splinters*, Op.6d, 1978

Kurz, Selma (b. Biala, Silesia, 15 Oct 1874; d. Vienna, 10 May 1933). Austrian soprano, famed as a coloratura artist. She made her debut in Hamburg

(1895) but spent most of her career in Vienna (1899–1927), where her roles included Zerbinetta in the première of the revised *Ariadne auf Naxos*.

Kusser, Johann Sigismund (baptized Pressburg/ Bratislava, 13 Feb 1660; d. Dublin, Nov 1727). German composer, notably of operas in the French mould. He studied with Lully for six years some time before 1682–3, when he was at the Ansbach court. Later he worked for the Bruns-wick-Wolfenbüttel court (1690–94), for the public theatre in Hamburg (1694–6), with his own tour-ing company, in London (1705–9) and then in Dublin. Suites and arias survive from his earlier operas, but almost nothing from his time in England and Ireland.

Kyburz, Hanspeter (b. Lagos, 8 Jul 1960). Swiss composer, adept at maintaining clarity and beauty of sound under conditions of high speed and complexity, developing his forms through a dialogue of computer calculation with imagina-tion. He studied with Gösta Neuwirth in Graz (1980–82) and Berlin (1982–90), where he was also a pupil of Beyer and Dahlhaus. After completing his training with Zender in Frankfurt (1990–93) he returned to Berlin, and began teaching at the Eisler Conservatory in 1997. In 2000 he took an addi-tional teaching post at the Basle Conservatory.

Works: *Cells*, sax, ens, 1993–4; *Parts*, ens, 1994–5; *The* VOYNICH CIPHER MANUSCRIPT, 1995; *Malstrom*, orch, 1998; Piano Concerto, 2000; *Noesis*, orch, 2002; etc.

Kyriale. Book of mass ordinary chants.

Kyrie eleison. Section of the ORDINARY of the mass, there at least since the 6th century: it is the only part of the common Western liturgy in Greek. Being so brief – consisting just of the words 'Kyrie eleison, Christe eleison, Kyrie eleison' (Lord have mercy, Christ have mercy, Lord have mercy), each phrase often repeated three times – it was widely elaborated with tropes in the early Middle Ages, replacing the nouns with longer invocations of the divine persons; hence the term 'troped *Kyrie*'.

l

la (Fr., It., Sp.). The note or key of A.

La Barre. French musical family founded by Pierre de la Barre (d. 1600), a Paris organist. One of his sons, another Pierre (1592–1656), held court appointments as a performer on the organ, harpsichord and spinet, and had several musical children, including Anne (1628–c.1687), a court singer who visited Queen Christina of Sweden, and Joseph (1633–c.1678), an organist who succeeded his father at the royal chapel. Most of the La Barre men were also composers, and their surviving works – airs, arias and dances – are often hard to attribute to any particular member of the family.

La Barre, Michel de (b. c.1675; d. 1743/4). French flautist-composer, seemingly not a member of the above family, responsible for the first book of suites for flute and continuo (1702), as well as several later suites for the same combination and for flute duet. He played in the royal chamber music and also wrote stage music and airs.

L'Abbé. Sobriquet of a French musical family whose surname was Saint-Sévin, the nickname acquired because both Pierre Philippe, L'Abbé l'aîné (c.1700–68), and his brother Pierre, L'Abbé le cadet (c.1710–77), took minor orders. Both were cellists. The elder's son Joseph Barnabè, L'Abbé le fils (1727–1803), was a violinist who studied with Leclair (1740–42), performed as a soloist and at the Opera, and composed sonatas and symphonies. His violin method, *Principes du violon* (1761), is an important source.

Lablache, Luigi (b. Naples, 6 Dec 1794; d. Naples, 23 Jan 1858). Italian bass, the foremost of his generation, creator of roles in operas by Bellini (*I puritani*) and Donizetti (*Don Pasquale*). He studied at the Pietà dei Turchini conservatory in Naples and began his career in the city in 1812. With his reputation growing he appeared at La Scala (1817), and in Vienna (1824), London (1830) and Paris (also 1830), maintaining his career in the last two cities into the 1850s and retiring in 1856. In 1839 Wagner wrote an extra aria for him as Oroveso in *Norma*, but he did not sing it. His son Federico was also a bass; his daughter Cecchina married Thalberg.

La Borde, Jean-Benjamin (François) de (b. Paris, 5 Sep 1734; d. Paris, 22 Jul 1794). French composer, of stage works and songs. Of aristocratic birth, he was at the court of Louis XV, had lessons from Rameau and Dauvergne, and was familiar with Voltaire. He seems to have virtually given up composition after the death of Louis XV (1774), but went on engaging in musical scholarship and controversy, and showed an unusual interest in old music; in his *Essai sur la musique ancienne et moderne* (1780) he included trouvère songs. He died on the guillotine.

Laborintus II. Work by Berio for three women singers, speaker, choir, ensemble and tape, to words by Edourdo Sanguineti, a polyvalent cantata about language and power. First performance: Paris, Feb 1965.

Lachenmann, Helmut (Friedrich) (b. Stuttgart, 27 Nov 1935). German composer, who has built a whole pristine world out of sounds normally regarded as marginal and even downright ugly: 'instrumental *musique concrète*' is his term, his aim being to maintain the creative energy and the social purpose of post-1945 modernism. After a conservatory training in his home city (1955–8) he became Nono's pupil in Venice (1958–60) – a decisive and potent experience. While his political alignment has never been as overt as Nono's, he became fully engaged in the musical revolution, and especially in the search for sounds, instrumental practices and compositional strategies that had been overlooked. Beginning with *temA* (1968), he made unconventional sonorities a priority; his first string quartet, *Gran torso* (1971–2), is an adventure in gratings, brushings and whispers. And though works since the mid-1970s have reconnected with tradition – with particular works (Mozart's Clarinet Concerto in *Accanto*) or with the problematics of a whole genre (opera in *Das Mädchen mit den Schwefelhölzern*) – they have done so in a continuing spirit of opening and refreshment. In 1981, after experience elsewhere, he returned to the conservatory in Stuttgart to become the pre-eminent composition teacher in Europe.

Opera: *Das* MÄDCHEN MIT DEN SCHWEFEL-HÖLZERN, 1990–96
Orchestral: *Schwankungen am Rand*, 1974–5; *Accanto*, cl, orch, 1975; *Ausklang*, pf, orch, 1984-5; *Staub*, 1985–7; *Nun*, fl, trbn, orch, 1998–9; *Schreiben*, 2003; etc.
Choral: *Consolation I–IV*, ch, insts, 1967–73
Ensemble: *Mouvement (– vor der Erstarrung)*, 1982–4; '… *Zwei Gefühle* …': *Musik mit Leonardo*, speaker, ens, 1991–2
Chamber: *temA*, v, fl, vc, 1968; *Gran torso*, str qt, 1971–2, rev 1976, 1988; *Salut für Caudwell*, 2 gtr, 1977; *Allegro sostenuto*, cl, vc, pf, 1987–91; *Reigen seliger Geister*, str qt, 1989; *Grido* (String Quartet No.3), 2000–1; etc.
Solo instrumental: *Interieur I*, perc, 1966; *Pression*, vc, 1969; *Dal niente*, cl, 1970; *Guero*, pf, 1970; *Serynade*, pf, 1997–8; etc.

Lachner, Franz Paul (b. Rain am Lech, 2 Apr 1803; d. Munich, 20 Jan 1890). German composer and conductor, prominent in the musical life of Munich from 1836 until Wagner's arrival in 1864. Trained by his organist father (three brothers also became professional musicians), he continued his education with Sechter and the Abbé Stadler in Vienna when he was in his early 20s, and became acquainted with Schubert and Beethoven. He also established himself there as a conductor. In a composing life of well over half a century he wrote operas, choral music, eight symphonies, seven orchestral suites, six quartets and much other chamber music.

Lachrimae (Tears). Consort collection published by Dowland in 1604 and titled in full *Lachrimae, or Seaven Teares*. It includes seven pavans – *Lachrimae antiquae* (an arrangement of the song *Flow my tears*), *Lachrimae antiquae novae*, *Lachrimae gementes*, *Lachrimae tristes*, *Lachrimae coactae*, *Lachrimae amantis*, *Lachrimae verae* – and 14 other pieces.

Lady Macbeth of the Mtsensk District, The (*Ledi Makbet Mtsenskovo uyezda*). Opera by Shostakovich to a libretto he wrote with Alexander Preys after a short story by Nikolay Leskov. Katerina Izmaylova (soprano) is the bored wife of a merchant, Zinovy (tenor), and the victim of verbal abuse from his father, Boris (high bass). While her husband is away she takes a lover in the lusty worker Sergey (tenor) and poisons her father-in-law; she and Sergey then kill the returning Zinovy, which enables them to marry. But their deeds are uncovered, they join a convoy of convicts, and Sergey betrays her with another woman. Thus are all hopes quashed and all values devalued in a score full of exaggeration and parody. First performance: Leningrad, 22 Jan 1934.

At first a huge success, the opera was officially censured in 1936 and withdrawn. It reappeared in 1963 in revised form as KATERINA IZMAYLOVA; the original version was not heard again until after the composer's death, and then only in the West, where it has remained the score of choice.

L'Affilard, Michel (b. *c*.1656; d. ?Versailles, 1708). French composer of dance songs, the first composer anywhere to supply numerical tempo markings, which he fixed with the aid of Joseph Sauveur's calibrated pendulum. He joined the choir of the Sainte Chapelle in 1679 and moved to the royal chapel at Versailles in 1683.

Lafont, Charles Philippe (b. Paris, 1 Dec 1781; d. near Tarbes, 23 Aug 1839). French violinist, pre-eminent in that tradition in his time. He studied with Kreutzer and Rode, but first with his mother, who came from a violin-playing family. In 1816 he appeared in Milan with Paganini, who praised him but said he failed to surprise. He also performed with Moscheles and other leading pianists, with whom he collaborated on duo compositions. He died in a carriage accident.

Lage (Ger.). Position, on string instrument or of chord (i.e. root position or inversion).

lah. Sixth degree of the scale (submediant) in tonic sol-fa.

La Houssaye, Pierre (Nicolas) (b. Paris, 11 Apr

1735; d. Paris, 1818). French violinist, pupil of Tartini during a long period in Italy (c.1753–68). He then worked in London and, from 1776, Paris, as an orchestra leader at theatres and in concerts. His six published sonatas (c.1774) attest his skills.

lai (Fr.). The long song of the 13th–14th centuries, having no fixed pattern of metre or rhyme. Machaut's are nearly all in 12 stanzas, diverse except in that the last resembles the first both poetically and musically. Such a song might take half an hour to sing.

laisser vibrer (Fr.). Allow to vibrate, a marking used for metal percussion instruments.

Lajtha, László (b. Budapest, 30 Jun 1892; d. Budapest, 16 Feb 1963). Hungarian composer and folk music scholar, who combined his love of Hungary with an attachment to France. He studied with the violinist Viktor Herzfeld at the academy in Budapest, briefly joined Bartók and Kodály as a folk music collector in 1910, and gained positions at the National Museum (from 1913) and the National Conservatory (1919–49). In 1952 he was appointed professor at the Liszt Academy. His works include nine symphonies, 10 quartets and choral music.

Lakmé. Opera by Delibes to a libretto by Edmond Gondinet and Philippe Gille after Pierre Loti's novel *Rarahu*. Lakmé (soprano) – fiercely opposed by her father, the Brahmin priest Nilakantha (bass-baritone), and on the point of being deserted by her beloved British officer Gérald (tenor) – swallows poison. Her Bell Song is a favourite coloratura number; she also has a Flower Duet with her servant Mallika (mezzo-soprano). First performance: Paris, 14 Apr 1883.

Lalande, Michel-Richard de (b. Paris, 15 Dec 1657; d. Versailles, 18 Jun 1726). French composer, of magnificent psalms for Louis XIV's chapel (*De profundis*, 1689) and of delightful music for the king's suppers (*Sinfonies pour les soupers du roi*). Trained as a chorister at St Germain-l'Auxerrois under François Couperin, he went on to play the organ at several Paris churches and also at court, where from 1683 he steadily accrued positions as organist and composer of chamber music. In 1684 he married Anne Rebel, sister of the composer; they had two daughters who became singers in their short lives, both dying of smallpox in 1711. In 1723, after the death of their mother the previous year, he remarried, and had a third daughter. His royal appointments enabled him to live in some style, with a town house in Paris, a country

residence and a carriage, as well as his apartment at Versailles, the palace for which most of his music was made – grand music befitting its occasion, but also harmonically expressive and quirky.

Lalo, Edouard (Victoire Antoine) (b. Lille, 27 Jan 1823; d. Paris, 22 Apr 1892). French composer, known especially for the vigorous music he produced past the age of 50. His father, a veteran of the Napoleonic wars, opposed a musical career, so he left home at 16 to make his way in Paris as a violinist and student (of Julius Schulhoff and J.E. Crèvecoeur). The first works he published, dating from his later 20s and early 30s, are chamber pieces and songs. In 1855 he was a co-founder of the Armingaud Quartet, in which he played viola and second violin. His creativity fizzled out at the end of the 1850s, and though the fire returned in his first opera, *Fiesque* (1866–7), disappointment at the lack of a production doused his spirits again. Then, in 1873, he began a strong series of orchestral compositions, interrupted by work on his second opera, *Le Roi d'Ys*. Together with the freshness of melody that has given his *Symphonie espagnole* lasting appeal, these orchestral pieces convey a brusque energy quite independent of the main lines in French music, as does *Le Roi d'Ys*. His ballet *Namouna* was admired by Debussy; his son Pierre (1866–1943), who became a critic, did not return the compliment.

Operas: *Fiesque* (Charles Beauquier, after Schiller), 1866–7; *Le* ROI D'YS, 1875–88
Orchestral: *Divertissement*, 1872; Violin Concerto, F, Op.20, 1873; SYMPHONIE ESPAGNOLE, Op.21, vn, orch, 1874; Cello Concerto, D minor, 1877; *Fantaisie norvégienne*, vn, orch, 1878; *Rapsodie norvégienne*, 1879; *Concerto russe*, Op.29, vn, orch, 1879; NAMOUNA (ballet), 1881–2; Symphony, G minor, 1886; Piano Concerto, F minor, 1888–9; etc.
Chamber: String Quartet, E♭, Op.19, 1859, rev as Op.45, 1880; Piano Trio No.1, C minor, Op.7, c.1850; No.2, B minor, c.1851; No.3, A minor, Op.26, 1880; etc.
Other works: songs, sacred pieces

Lambe, Walter (b. ?1450/1; d. 1504 or later). English composer, strongly represented in the Eton Choirbook (eight pieces, plus four more listed but lost). Possibly an Eton scholar, he was later in the choir of St George's Chapel, Windsor (1479–84/5, 1492–9). His works, showing a fine command of the floridity and full textures typical of English music at the time, include the Marian antiphon *Nesciens mater* a 5.

Lambert, (Leonard) Constant (b. London, 23 Aug 1905; d. London, 21 Aug 1951). British composer and conductor, whose liveliness and wit made him a natural ally of the Parisian neoclassicists. The son of an Australian-born painter, he studied with Vaughan Williams and Morris at the RCM from 1922, and moved into the circle of Walton and the Sitwells. His ballet *Romeo and Juliet* (f.p. Monte Carlo, 1926) was Diaghilev's first by a British composer and led to a career in ballet as composer (*Pomona*, 1926; *Horoscope*, 1937), conductor (music director of the Sadler's Wells Ballet, 1931–47) and arranger. His other works include *The Rio Grande* for solo piano, choir and orchestra (1927), an exuberant mix of the Hispanic, the jazzy and the Delian to words by Sacheverell Sitwell, and a concerto for piano and nonet (1930–31). He also published *Music Ho!* (1934), subtitled 'a study of music in decline'.

Lambert, Michel (b. Champigny-sur-Veude, near Loudun, 1610; d. Paris, 29 Jun 1696). French composer, whose airs (about 300 survive) were the most important of the second half of the 17th century. Having trained as a choirboy in Champigny, he soon arrived at court, rising to become master of the king's chamber music from 1661. The next year Lully married his daughter Madeleine.

lamellaphone. Instrument whose sound comes from the vibration of lamellae (i.e. thin strips) that are plucked or flicked. The most usual kinds are African and have metal lamellae attached to a gourd or wooden box.

lame musicale (Fr.). Musical saw.

lament. A song of mourning, such as in many cultures belongs more to the folk tradition than to formal religion. The term – or its It. equivalent *lamento* – is also used more particularly of 17th-century threnodies based on a descending tetrachord (e.g. C–Bb–A–G, or a version with chromatic infill); examples include Monteverdi's *Lamento della ninfa* and Dido's lament in Purcell's *Dido and Aeneas*. This repertory provides various musical features – the slow downward scale, minor keys, sighing vocal effects – that made the lament a continuing topic in later music.

Lamentatione. Name given to Haydn's Symphony No.26, which apparently quotes a Lamentations chant.

Lamentations. Book of the Hebrew Bible, large parts of which are heard in the lessons at tenebrae in Holy Week, with the verses enumerated by Hebrew letters. Many composers have set these texts, including Alexander Agricola, Arcadelt,

Crecquillon, Isaac, La Rue, Sermisy, Morales, Victoria, Lassus, Palestrina, Tallis, Couperin and Stravinsky (*Threni*).

lamento. (1) Italian Baroque LAMENT.
(2) Descending tetrachord bass typical of such.

Lamoureux, Charles (b. Bordeaux, 28 Sep 1834; d. Paris, 21 Dec 1899). French conductor, who founded an orchestra that keeps his name alive. He arrived in Paris as a teenager to study the violin with Narcisse Girard at the Conservatoire, supporting himself as an orchestral player and later as a chamber musician. Conducting became possible when he married into money. Impressed by what he had heard in England and Germany, he presented big choral works by Handel, Bach and others (1873–4), then worked briefly at the Opéra-Comique and the Opera before creating his own orchestra in 1881. His passion for Wagner caused controversy.

Lampe, John Frederick (b. Brunswick, 1702/3; d. Edinburgh, 25 Jul 1751). German–British composer, notably of *The Dragon of Wantley* (1737) and other operatic burlesques for the London stage mocking Handel. He arrived in London c.1724 and worked as a theatre bassoonist before being launched as a composer by Arne's father in 1732. In 1738 he married Arne's sister-in-law, Isabella Young, who had starred in *The Dragon*. They became friends of Charles Wesley, some of whose hymns Lampe set before taking his family to Dublin in 1748 and Edinburgh in 1750.

Lampugnani, Giovanni Battista (b. ?Milan, 1708; d. ?Milan, 2 Jun 1788). Italian composer, of operas (mostly serious), trio sonatas and symphonies. Apart from a season in London (1743–4), and possibly some years of travel thereafter, he was based in Milan, where he went on playing the harpsichord at the opera house until almost 80.

lancers. Square dance popular in England from the 1870s into the early 20th century. It was similar to the quadrille, and owed its name to the popular *Quadrille des lanciers* that the dancing master John Duval had introduced in Dublin in 1817.

Landi, Stefano (baptized Rome, 26 Feb 1587; d. Rome, 28 Oct 1639). Italian composer, master of the old polyphony and the new monody, both of which he practised in sacred and secular settings, most notably in his opera *Il SANT' ALESSIO*. He entered the Collegio Germanico in 1595 and moved on to the Seminario Romano (1602–7). Apart from a brief time as chapelmaster to the

Bishop of Padua (1618–20), he remained in Rome, working for members of the Borghese and Barberini families as a singer (he may have accompanied himself on the guitar) and composer. He was also a member of the papal choir from 1629.

Landini, Francesco (b. ?Fiesole, *c*.1325; d. Florence, 2 Sep 1397). Italian composer, the pre-eminent master of Italian song in the second half of the 14th century. The son of the painter Jacopo del Casentino, he lost his sight to smallpox as a child and so turned to music. He became proficient not only as a composer but also as a singer, organist and organ builder, and interested himself in philosophy. Prominent in Florentine life as an organist and adviser on organs from at least 1361, he may have spent some time in Venice and elsewhere in northern Italy. Of the more than 150 songs known to be his, the vast majority are polyphonic ballatas, for two voices or three – a form based on the French VIRELAI, and one he seems to have introduced. He also wrote some madrigals in the Italian tradition. French influence can be further detected in the rhythmic intricacy of some of the three-part songs, together with a fluent melodic expressiveness that was his own.

Ballatas: *Cara mie donna* a 3; *Ecco la primavera* a 2; *Giunta vaga biltà* a 3; *Gran pianto a gli ochi* a 3; *La bionda treccia* a 2; *Non avrà mai pietà* a 3; *Questa fanciulla, Amor* a 3, etc.
Other works: madrigals, other songs

Landini cadence. Cadence in which the top voice steps down from the leading note to the sixth before reaching the tonic. Named by the German scholar A.G. Ritter (1884), it is characteristic not only of Landini but also of much polyphony of the 15th century and early 16th.

Ländler (Ger., from Landl, an old name for Upper Austria). Slowish triple-time dance popular in Austria and southern Germany from the early 19th century, with antecedents going back two centuries before. It affected the courtly German Dances and sometimes the scherzos of Haydn, Mozart and Schubert, but is particularly associated with Mahler's music, where its low connotations are at once cherished and ironically emphasized.

Landon, H(oward) C(handler) Robbins (b. Boston, 6 Mar 1926). US scholar, author of the standard work on Haydn, in five volumes (1976–8), and of popularizing books on Beethoven, Mozart, Venetian music and other topics. He studied at Swarthmore (1943–5) and Boston University (1945–7), and worked mostly in independence from academia.

Landowska, Wanda (b. Warsaw, 5 Jul 1879; d. Lakeville, Conn., 16 Aug 1959). Polish harpsichordist, a pioneer of the instrument, to which she brought emphatic vigour and variety of colour. She played modern instruments, by Pleyel, and inspired new works by Falla, Poulenc and others, but her historic role was to reintroduce Bach on the harpsichord. Trained as a pianist in Warsaw, she moved to Berlin in 1896 to study composition and to Paris in 1900. She gave her first performance on the harpsichord in 1903, and made her first US tour (and her first records) in 1923. Two years later she founded a school and a summer festival south of Paris. In 1940, as the Germans approached, she left for the USA.

Landowski, Marcel (b. Pont l'Abbé, Finistère, 18 Feb 1915; d. Paris, 23 Dec 1999). French composer, a moderate whose appointment as music director to the government (1966) led Boulez to shun French musical life. He studied with Büsser at the Paris Conservatoire and had some advice from Honegger in the 1940s. His works include operas, symphonies and cantatas.

Landré, Guillaume (b. The Hague, 24 Feb 1905; d. Amsterdam, 6 Nov 1968). Dutch composer, notably of symphonies and other orchestral works stemming from the music of his teacher, Pijper. His father, Willem (1874–1948), was a composer and music critic, and he too worked as a critic (and as a lawyer).

Lange, Aloysia. See Aloysia WEBER.

Lange-Müller, Peter Erasmus (b. Frederiksberg, 1 Dec 1850; d. Copenhagen, 26 Feb 1926). Danish composer, especially of moody songs related to Brahms and French music, most of them dating from the period 1874–1900. He had some training as a pianist, but was essentially a self-taught composer, living on his private means. Choral pieces and incidental scores also feature in his output.

Langgaard, Rued (Immanuel) (b. Copenhagen, 28 Jul 1893; d. Ribe, 10 Jul 1952). Danish composer, a modernist-Romantic whose outsider status brought his music renewed interest in the late 20th century, by which time his extraordinary *Music of the Spheres* (1916–18) could be heard as anticipating aspects of Ligeti and minimalism. With parents both pianists, he began to compose at seven, had his first public performance at 14 and completed his first symphony at 17. This was rejected, and increasing isolation made him artistically self-reliant. A man of strong religious convictions, he was also appalled by the clean-cut

dispassion of neoclassicism and reacted by returning to Gade and Wagner. Nielsen was another influence on his symphonies, of which No.11 lasts only six minutes (but has four tubas in the orchestra). In 1940 he was appointed organist of Ribe Cathedral.
www.langgaard.dk

Opera: *Antichrist* (after Revelation), 1921–3, rev 1926–30

Symphonies: No.1 'Rock Pastorals', 1908–11; No.2 'Awakening of Spring', s, orch, 1912–14, rev 1926–33; No.3 'Flush of Youth', 1915–16, rev 1925–33; No.4 'Autumn', 1916, rev 1920; No.5, 1917–18, rev 1926, second version 'Summer Legend Drama', 1917–20, rev 1931; No.6 'The Heaven-Rending', 1919–20, rev 1928–30; No.7, 1925–6, second version 'By Tordenskjold in Holmen's Church', 1925–6, rev 1930–32; No.8 'Memories of Amalienborg', ch, orch, 1926–34; No.9 'From the City of Queen Dagmar', 1942; No.10 'Yon Hall of Thunder', 1944–5; No.11 'Ixion', 1944–5; No.12 'Hélsingeborg', 1946; No.13 'Belief in Wonders', 1946–7; No.14 'Morning', ch, orch, 1947–8, rev 1951; No.15 'Sea Storm', bar, men's ch, orch, 1949; No.16 'Sun Deluge', 1950–51

Other works: *Music of the Spheres*, s/mez, ch, orch, 1916–18; 6 quartets, choral music, piano pieces, organ pieces, etc.

Langlais, Jean (b. La Fontenelle, 15 Feb 1907; d. Paris, 8 May 1991). French organist-composer, who combined the virtuosity of Dupré with the mysticism of Tournemire. Blind from early childhood, he studied with both these masters, and with Dukas at the Conservatoire. In 1932 he became organist of St Pierre de Montrouge, moving from there in 1945 to Ste Clotilde, in succession to Franck and Tournemire. He made his first trip to the USA in 1952 and returned often. His works comprise mostly organ pieces (*Trois paraphrases grégoriennes*, Op.5, 1934) and sacred music (*Messe solennelle*, Op.67, ch, org, 1951).

langsam (Ger.). Slow. Hence also *langsamer* (slower).

Lanier, Nicholas (baptized London, 10 Sep 1588; buried London, 24 Feb 1666). English composer and singer-lutenist, prominent at court in the latter half of James I's reign and under Charles I. He belonged to a fecund family of royal musicians founded by two brothers, John and Nicholas (his grandfather, d. 1612), who arrived from Rouen in 1561. With his multifarious talents, he contributed to masques by Ben Jonson as a composer, singer and set designer. He was appointed Master of the Music to the future Charles I in 1618, and became the first Master of the King's Music, though

Charles seems to have used him more as an agent in buying pictures in Italy. Journeys there broadened his musical range, and during the Civil War and under the Commonwealth he spent more time abroad.

Lanner, Joseph (Franz Karl) (b. Vienna, 12 Apr 1801; d. Oberdöbling, near Vienna, 14 Apr 1843). Austrian composer, chief rival to Johann Strauss I in Vienna as a composer of waltzes and other dances. Largely self-taught, he joined Michael Pamer's orchestra at 12, playing alongside Strauss. In 1818 he formed his own trio, which Strauss joined to make a quartet and which grew into an orchestra. Professional disagreements led to a rupture, after which he went on purveying his own, more seductive kind of dance music. He died of typhus.

Lantins, de. Name of several early 15th-century musicians from the Liège region who may have been related, including the two below.
(1) **Arnold** (*fl. c.*1430). Mentioned in Venice in 1428 and as a member of the papal choir in 1431–2, he wrote sacred music and French songs.
(2) **Hugo** (*fl. c.*1420–30). Seemingly also active in Italy, he produced a similar output, but one distinguished by the use of imitation.

largamente (It.). Broadly.

large. The longest note value ever, equivalent to two or three longs. It was introduced in the 13th century and fell out of use in the mid-15th century.

larghetto (It.). Somewhat broad, a tempo marking introduced in the early 18th century and known to Handel.

largo (It.). (1) Broad, a tempo marking introduced in the early 17th century and normally regarded as a little faster than adagio.
(2) A broad-paced movement. 'Handel's Largo', as a title, implies an arrangement of the aria 'Ombra mai fù' from his *Serse*.

Lark. Name given to Haydn's Quartet in D Op.64:5, for its opening.

Larsson, Lars-Erik (Vilner) (b. Åkarp, Skåne, 15 May 1908; d. Helsingborg, 26 Dec 1986). Swedish composer, who began as a national Romantic and took on board neoclassicism and serialism; his 10 Two-Part Piano Pieces (1932) are said to include the first Swedish 12-note compositions. He studied with Ernst Ellberg at the conservatory in

Stockholm (1925–9), and in Vienna and Leipzig (1929–30), taking lessons with Berg and Fritz Reuter. Back in Sweden he held appointments at the radio, the Stockholm Conservatory (1947–59) and Uppsala University (1961–6). He wrote mostly orchestral and chamber works.

La Rue, Pierre de (b. ?Tournai, *c*.1452; d. Kortrijk/Courtrai, 20 Nov 1518). Netherlandish composer, among Josquin's most illustrious contemporaries. He circulated within the Low Countries and to Cologne before joining the Burgundian court chapel in 1492, and went with the court to Spain in 1501–3 and 1506, but never visited Italy. On his journeys he met Isaac and probably also Josquin. The latter part of his career he spent back in the Low Countries, at the court of the Archduchess Marguerite (from 1508), before retiring to Kortrijk/Courtrai. About 32 masses form the crown of his output; they resemble Josquin's in their two-part sections and frequent canonic features, but do not pursue verbal expressiveness so intimately. He also produced similar numbers of motets and chansons.

Masses: *Cum iocunditate* a 4–5, *L'homme armé* a 4, *Pro defunctis* a 4, etc.
Motets: *O salutaris hostia* a 4, *Vexilla regis* a 4, etc.
Chansons: *Autant en emporte le vent* a 4, *Il viendra le jour désiré* a 4, etc.

LaSalle Quartet. US ensemble founded in 1949, specializing in the Second Viennese School and works written for them by Ligeti, Lutosławski and others.

Lassus, Orlando de [Roland/Orlande de Lassus, Orlando di Lasso] (b. Mons, ?1532; d. Munich, 14 Jun 1594). Netherlandish composer, who bestrode the musical world of his time, more prolific and various than any contemporary. Works published during his life, or soon after, include many hundreds of sacred settings as well as Italian madrigals and similar works with words in German and French.

Nothing is known of his early boyhood. According to legend, he was a chorister at St Nicholas's in his home town and was kidnapped three times for the beauty of his voice. At 12 or so he joined the service of Ferrante Gonzaga, with whom he travelled to Mantua, Palermo and Milan (1546–9). He was then in Naples, Rome (chapelmaster of St John Lateran, 1553–4) and Antwerp, and may have visited France and England. In Antwerp he published what has become known as his 'Op.1' (1555), a volume of madrigals, villanellas, French songs and motets, displaying his versatility as well as his confident technique.

The following year he was recruited as a tenor to the ducal court in Munich, where he remained to the end of his days. He became chapelmaster in 1563, and so had to supervise music not only for daily services but also for banquets and other celebrations. A manuscript illustration shows him at the keyboard with a group of instrumentalists, but he went on composing in the old polyphonic tradition, if with unmatched variety of texture and robustness of expression. He married in 1558 and had a family that included two sons, Ferdinand (*c*.1560–1609) and Rudolph (*c*.1563–1625), who became court composers in Munich after him. Enjoying his house and garden, he declined an invitation to move to Dresden in 1580, even though his ensemble in Munich had been slimmed down when Albrecht V had been succeeded by his son Wilhelm V the year before; besides, he savoured his friendly relationship with Wilhelm. Also, his life was varied by journeys – to Flanders, to Paris, to Vienna and to several Italian cities – and he had the satisfaction of international renown. Honoured by both emperor and pope, and with an average of two books of his music appearing in print annually during his years in Munich, he was the most respected musician of his time, and may have included the Gabrielis among his pupils.

His very productivity dazzled history (which soon came to prefer the more poised style and restrained output of Palestrina), and has continued to dazzle performers and scholars. But if the circle of his major works has still to be defined, it certainly includes the *Prophetiae Sibyllarum*, a set of 12 very chromatic settings of humanist texts, and the late *Lagrime di San Pietro*, a cycle of 21 spiritual madrigals.

Masses: *Bell' Amfitrit' altera* a 8, *Entre vous filles* a 5, REQUIEM a 4, *Susanne un jour* a 5, etc.
Other Latin settings: *Justorum animae* a 5, Lamentations a 4, Lamentations a 5, *Prophetiae Sibyllarum* a 4, Tenebrae responsories a 4, *Timor et tremor* a 6, *Tristis est anima mea* a 5, etc.
Italian settings: *Lagrime di San Pietro* a 7, *Madonna mia pietà* a 4, *Matona mia cara* a 4, *O là o che bon eccho* a 8, *Poi che 'l mio largo pianto* (Petrarch) a 4, etc.
Other works: *Bon jour mon coeur* a 4, *La nuict froide et sombre* a 4, *Susanne un jour* a 5, other chansons, German songs

late works. Even composers approaching death in their 30s, like Mozart and Schubert, may seem to be signalling some awareness in their music, so ready are we to identify a late style. With those who live longer, the case may be more explicit, whether they create consummate works (Bach, Messiaen) or transcend previous achievements in a new style

(Beethoven, Stravinsky). Often, too, there will be an explicit engagement with themes of death and eternity – though the end may come too with comic opera (Verdi).

Latrobe, Christian Ignatius (b. Fulneck, Leeds, 12 Feb 1758; d. Fairfield, near Liverpool, 6 May 1836). British composer and churchman, responsible for publishing sacred music by Haydn, Mozart and others, adapted for use in Britain. Of Huguenot descent, he became a minister and missionary of the Moravian church, and a self-taught composer of services and anthems.

laùd (Sp.). Lute.

lauda (It., praise song, pl. *laude, laudi*). Song of a kind associated with popular religious movements in Italy. Specially important are the 13th-century monophonic examples, with their popular tunes, and the polyphonic repertory of the 14th–16th centuries.

Laudon. Name given to Haydn's Symphony No.69 in honour of Field Marshal Gideon von Laudon (1717–90), who broke the Turkish siege of Belgrade in 1789. Haydn himself is said to have given the decade-old work its name, to mark either the victory or the victor's death.

lauds. Service of the divine office, sung at dawn.

Lauri-Volpi, Giacomo (b. Rome, 11 Dec 1892; d. Valencia, 17 Mar 1979). Italian tenor, whose bright cantabile in lyric-dramatic roles (Manrico, Othello, Calaf) established him among the stars of the 1920s–30s. He studied law before training at the Accademia di Santa Cecilia and making his debut at Viterbo in 1919. Installed by Toscanini at La Scala in 1922, he also appeared at the Met (1922–33) and continued to sing until 1959.

Laute (Ger.), **lauto** (It.). Lute.

Lavallée, Calixa (b. Ste Théodosie de Verchères, renamed Calixa-Lavallée, Quebec, 28 Dec 1842; d. Boston, 21 Jan 1891). Canadian composer, who worked to promote musical life there. The son of an instrument maker and bandmaster, he took various musical jobs in Canada and the USA from the age of 14 or so, then completed his education at the Paris Conservatoire with Marmontel and others (1873–5). His efforts to found a conservatory and an opera company in Canada were unsuccessful, and soon after writing the country's national anthem (1880) he moved to Boston, where he taught, composed and directed music at the Catholic cathedral.

Lavignac, (Alexandre Jean) Albert (b. Paris, 21 Jan 1846; d. Paris, 28 May 1916). French teacher, remembered as founder-editor of a music encyclopedia. Trained at the Paris Conservatoire, he was on the staff there (1871–1915) as a teacher of SOLFÈGE and, later, harmony.

Lavrangas, Dionysios (b. Argostolion, Kefallinia, 17 Oct 1860/4; d. Razata, Kefallinia, 18 Jul 1941). Greek composer, especially of opera. He studied locally, then in Naples (1882–5) and for about four years in Paris with Delibes and Massenet, prominent influences on his mature style. In 1894 he settled in Athens, where he was founder conductor of the Helleniko Melodhrama (Greek Opera) company (1900–35) and a conservatory teacher.

Lawes. English composing brothers. Brought up in Salisbury, where their father was a lay vicar from 1602, they were probably choristers at the cathedral. They found employment with local noblemen – Henry with the Earl of Bridgwater, William with the Earl of Hertford – before coming together again at the court of Charles I. Henry was a gentleman of the Chapel Royal from 1626, and William may have been in royal service from around that time too, though his first documented court music (for a Jonson masque) dates from 1633. While Henry was primarily a singer and songwriter, William was a brilliant all-round composer, whose loss in the Civil War was much lamented. Henry edited a memorial volume of *Choice Psalms* (1648), including 30 psalm settings by each brother and elegies by other composers and poets.

(1) **Henry** (baptized Dinton, Wilts., 5 Jan 1596; d. London, 21 Oct 1662). Once arrived in London he formed a friendship with Milton, for whom he arranged the commission to write a masque, *Comus*, for his old patron Bridgwater. He lived out the Commonwealth period (1649–60) as a teacher, also presenting concerts at his house, then returned to his royal appointments at the Restoration; he set *Zadok the Priest* as a coronation anthem for Charles II. Mostly, though, he wrote songs, of which he published three books (1653–8) and left many more in manuscript, for a total of 433, setting words by Milton, Carew, Waller, Herrick and other poets of the period. Irritated by the fashion for Italian songs, he set the table of contents of a volume by Cifra and enjoyed hearing the result admired.

(2) **William** (baptized Salisbury, 1 May 1602; d. Chester, 24 Sep 1645). As a protégé of Hertford he became a pupil of Coprario, and probably also came into contact with the future Charles I. Besides contributing music to court masques and

plays, he wrote songs, anthems and consort music. His music in this last category is especially valued, on account of its boldness and scale (in fantasias for viols), its vivacity (in dance suites and sonatas featuring solo or paired violins) and altogether its excellent writing for the instruments. A manuscript collection, *The Royal Consort*, includes suites (or 'setts') in D minor (Nos.1–3), D major (Nos. 4–6), A minor (No.7), C (No.8), F (No.9) and B♭ (No.10).

Layolle, Francesco de (b. Florence, 4 Mar 1492; d. Lyons, *c*.1540). Italian composer, an early master of the Renaissance madrigal, and notable too for introducing Franco-Netherlandish features into Italian sacred music. He was a chorister and organ pupil at the Santissima Annunziata, where Andrea del Sarto included his likeness in a fresco (1511). In 1521 he settled in Lyons, whence the French form of his name, originally 'dell'Aiolle' (with variants). There he was organist at Notre Dame de Confort and a music publisher. His son Alamanne (*c*.1523–1590) returned to Florence and became known as Aiolli, working also as a music publisher and producing a manuscript volume of keyboard arrangements of popular polyphonic songs by Janequin, Lassus and others.

Lazarof, Henri (b. Sofia, 12 Apr 1932). Bulgarian–US composer, companion of the international avant-garde in his work as composer and promoter at UCLA (from 1962). He studied in Sofia, in Jerusalem (1949–52), in Rome with Petrassi (1955–7) and at Brandeis (1957–9).

Lazarus. Unfinished oratorio by Schubert, titled in full *Lazarus, oder Die Feier der Auferstehung* (Lazarus, or the Feast of the Resurrection), to words by August Hermann Niemeyer. The score breaks off partway through the second of the three acts, and was completed by Denisov (1994).

le. Sharpened sixth degree of the scale in tonic sol-fa.

leader (UK). Concertmaster (US). Principal violinist in an orchestra, ensemble or string quartet. An orchestra leader sits in the outside (audience-side) chair of the first desk of first violinists – i.e., on the conductor's immediate left. Leaders have to consult with conductors ahead of time about markings in string parts; they also have a role, in rehearsal and performance, in transmitting the conductor's intentions visually and musically to other members of their section and to the strings in general.

leading note. The seventh degree of a diatonic scale, so called because it has a strong tendency to resolve on to the tonic. That force is contained in the perfect cadence, since the third of the dominant triad (G–B–D in C major) is the tonic key's leading note.

Lear, Evelyn [née Shulman] (b. Brooklyn, 8 Jan 1928). US soprano, active largely in Germany, with a repertory including Lulu besides roles in operas from Handel to Strauss. Trained at Juilliard and in Berlin, she made her stage debut in 1959 in the latter city as the Composer in *Ariadne auf Naxos* and sang also at Covent Garden (from 1965) and the Met (from 1967).

Lebègue, Nicolas-Antoine (b. Laon, *c*.1631; d. Paris, 6 Jul 1702). French keyboard composer-performer. Though lowly born, he had a musician uncle, but nothing is definitely known of his life before 1661, by which time he was an organist in Paris. He gained appointments at St Merry (from 1664) and at court (from 1678), and published three volumes of organ pieces, two of harpsichord music and one of motets. The first organ book is remarkable in the period for its technical demands, and some of the harpsichord pieces are finely made. Grigny was a pupil.

lebendig, lebhaft (Ger.). Lively.

Lebensstürme (Storms of Life). Name given to a piano duet movement by Schubert.

Lebewohl, Das. See *Les* ADIEUX.

Le Caine, Hugh (b. Port Arthur, Ontario, 27 May 1914; d. Ottawa, 3 Jul 1977). Canadian technician-composer, an early exponent of electronic music. Trained as a physicist in Canada and England, he founded an electronic music laboratory for the National Research Council in Ottawa (1954) and created *Dripsody* (1955) from the sounds of waterdrops.

Lechner, Leonhard (b. Adige valley, *c*.1553; d. Stuttgart, 9 Sep 1606). German composer, especially of motets and German polyphonic songs in the tradition of Lassus, under whom he began his musical life as a choirboy in Munich. After a decade in Nuremberg as a composer and schoolteacher, in 1584 he was appointed chapelmaster to Count Eitelfriedrich IV von Hohenzollern-Hechingen, but his presence as a Lutheran at a Catholic court became irksome and he absconded the next year. He found sanctuary at the Stuttgart court, first as a tenor, then from 1595 as chapelmaster.

Leclair, Jean-Marie (b. Lyons, 10 May 1697; d. Paris, 22 Oct 1764). French violinist-composer, author of sonatas and concertos in which Italian models (Corelli, Vivaldi) are elegantly Frenchified. The son of a cellist-lacemaker, he learned both his father's arts (though his instrument was always the violin) as well as dancing. Most of his seven siblings also became musicians, but whereas they stayed largely in Lyons, he was an international figure. He visited Turin in 1722 and 1726–7, having lessons with the Corelli pupil, G.B. Somis, went to London, and played at the Kassel court in a competitive display with Locatelli; a witness recorded that he played like an angel (he was renowned for his sweet tone and brilliant multiple stops), Locatelli like a devil. But from 1723 his base was Paris, where he enjoyed the favour of the rich and well placed. His first wife having died, he was remarried in 1730 to Louise Roussel, the engraver of almost all his works. A court appointment (1733–7) came to an end when he declined to accept another player, Pierre Guignon, as joint leader, and he took a position at the court of Princess Anne of Orange in Amsterdam (1738–43). He then returned to Paris, wrote a single opera, and in 1748 began working for the Duke of Gramont's private theatre at Puteaux. At about the age of 60 he separated from his wife, who became one of the suspects when, a few years later, he was murdered as he returned home at night. A violinist nephew, though, is most likely to have been the assailant.

Works (with publication dates): 12 Sonatas, Op.1, vn, con, 1723; 12 Sonatas, Op.2, vn, con, c.1728; 6 Sonatas, Op.3, 2 vn, 1730; 6 Trio Sonatas, Op.4, 2 vn, con, c.1732; 12 Sonatas, Op.5, vn, con, 1734; 2 easy suites, Opp.6 and 8, 2 vn, con, 1736 and c.1737; 6 Concertos, Op.7, 1737; 12 Sonatas, Op.9, vn, con, 1743; 6 Concertos, Op.10, 1745; *Scylla et Glaucus* (opera), Op.11, 1746; 6 Sonatas, Op.12, 2 vn, c.1748; 3 Overtures and 3 Trio Sonatas, Op.13, 2 vn, con, 1753; etc.

Lecocq, (Alexandre) Charles (b. Paris, 3 Jun 1832; d. Paris, 24 Oct 1918). French composer of operettas, notably *La Fille de Madame Angot* (f.p. Brussels, 1872). Born poor and lame, he had to use crutches from early childhood, but gained facility as a pianist. At the Paris Conservatoire (1849–54) he made friends with the young Bizet and Saint-Saëns; he and Bizet were joint winners in 1856 of Offenbach's competition for settings of *Le Docteur Miracle*. More operettas followed, but none with lasting success until *Les Cent Vierges* (1872), *La Fille de Madame Angot* and *Giroflé-Girofla* (1874), all written during the few years he spent in Brussels. He then returned to Paris and gained further triumphs with *La Petite Mariée* (1875), *Le Petit Duc* (1878), *Janot* (1881), *Le Jour et la nuit* (1881), and *Le Coeur et la main* (1882). The relatively few scores he wrote after 1890 include the ballet *Le Cygne* (1899) and the operetta *La Belle au bois dormant* (1900).

leçon de ténèbre (Fr.). Tenebrae lesson, from LAMENTATIONS.

ledger line. See LEGER LINE.

Leduc. French publishing firm, founded in Paris c.1841 by Alphonse Leduc (1804–68), himself a prolific composer of piano dances and other instrumental items. It remained a family business and continued to specialize in amateur and educational music, but became Messiaen's chief publisher. There is no connection with other Leducs who were violinists and music publishers in the later 18th century and early 19th.

Leeds. City in northern England, musically renowned for its choral festival (founded 1858 and now biennial), its international piano competition (founded 1963 and triennial) and its opera company (Opera North, founded 1977).

Lees, Benjamin (b. Harbin, China, 8 Jan 1924). Russian–US composer, a mainstream modernist noted above all for his concertos (including one for string quartet, 1964) and chamber music. Arriving very young with his family, he was brought up in California, served in the Second World War and studied at USC (1945–8) with Halsey Stevens, after which he spent four years as a pupil of Antheil. He then went to Europe (1954–62), living mostly in France and choosing relative isolation in order to develop his style, then returning to the USA to work as a composer and occasional college professor.

Leeuw, Reinbert de (b. Amsterdam, 8 Sep 1938). Dutch conductor, who brings acute intensity and expressive fullness to a range of contemporary music embracing Messiaen, Ligeti, Ustvolskaya and Andriessen. A pupil of van Baaren, he had a brief and remarkable career as a composer himself before founding the Schönberg Ensemble in 1974.

Leeuw, Ton de (b. Rotterdam, 16 Nov 1926; d. Paris, 31 May 1996). Dutch composer, who found a serene balance of Western avant-garde and Asian influences. He studied with Badings (1947–9), with Messiaen and Thomas de Hartmann in Paris (1949–50), and with Jaap Kunst as a musical ethnologist (1950–54), then worked for Dutch radio before becoming head of composition at the

Amsterdam Conservatory (1959–86). Present at Darmstadt in 1953, he was one of the first Dutch composers to align himself with Boulez and Stockhausen; equally important was his first visit to India, in 1961. Works of the 1960s deploy spaced groupings and moving soloists, but from the mid-1970s on he developed a style of post-tonal modality.

Lefèvre. French family of organ builders, active from 1524 and reaching a climactic end in the career of Jean Baptiste Nicolas (1705–84), who was responsible for the biggest French classical organ, at St Martin in Tours.

Le Flem, Paul (b. Lezardrieux, Côtes-du-Nord, 18 Mar 1881; d. Trégastel, 31 Jul 1984). French composer, long-lived follower of d'Indy, but with his own Breton melancholy. He studied at the Paris Conservatoire and, from 1904, at the Schola Cantorum, where his teachers included d'Indy and Roussel, and with which he remained associated as a teacher and choirmaster until 1938. Remaining creatively active into his mid 90s, he produced four symphonies, stage works, songs and chamber music.

left hand. The one needed for agility on the violin and strength on the piano. Some composers have written (piano) pieces for left hand alone, either as exercises or for injured pianists. Examples include Scriabin's Two Pieces, Op.9, Janáček's Capriccio and the concertos written for Paul WITTGEN-STEIN.

Le Gallienne, Dorian (Leon Marlois) (b. Melbourne, 19 Apr 1915; d. Melbourne, 29 Jul 1963). Australian composer, a neoclassicist esteemed for his Symphony (1952–3) and lighter Sinfonietta (1951–6). Trained in Melbourne and London (with Jacob), he worked as a critic in Melbourne and was afflicted by a heart complaint.

legato (It., bound). Smooth linking of notes into a line, as opposed to STACCATO. The term may be used as a marking, or the linking may be indicated by a slur. With wind instruments (including the voice) legato normally implies performance in one breath; with string instruments one bowstroke. Where keyboard instruments are concerned, a similar span is customary. Legato is essential to phrasing in most music.

Legend of the Invisible City of Kitezh, The. Opera by Rimsky-Korsakov, titled in full *The Legend of the Invisible City of Kitezh and the Maiden Fevroniya (Skazaniye o nevidimom grade Kitezhe i*

deve Fevronii), to a libretto by Vladimir Belsky after old Russian sources. Fevroniya (soprano) is discovered in her forest dwelling by Prince Vsevolod (tenor), son of the ruler of Kitezh, but before their wedding can take place the Tatars attack. She is captured and he dies on the battle-field. The city, however, is saved: through her prayers it is disguised in a golden haze. Within that invisible city she finally meets Vsevolod again. First performance: St Petersburg, 20 Feb 1907.

léger, légèrement (Fr.). Light, lightly, suggesting moderately fast speed as well as lightness.

leger line. Short horizontal line placed above or below a staff in order to notate pitches beyond the staff's range. For example, middle C requires one leger line below the treble staff or above the bass, and the soprano's high C is on the second leger line above the treble staff. Leger lines have been in common use since the early 16th century.

Legge, Walter (b. London, 1 Jun 1906; d. St Jean, Cap Ferrat, 22 Mar 1979). British administrator and record producer. Self-taught, he worked for EMI and its antecedent HMV (1927–64), producing important recordings by Schnabel and Lipatti, Callas and Schwarzkopf (his second wife), Karajan and Klemperer. He also founded the Philharmonia.

leggero, leggiero, leggermente, leggiermente (It.). Equivalent to LEGER, LEGEREMENT. Beethoven's spellings 'leggeramente' and 'leggiera-mente' are his own.

leggiadro (It.). Pretty.

leggierezza, La. Concert étude by Liszt.

legno (It., wood). (1) The wood of the bow, as in *col legno*, an instruction to strike the strings with the bowstick.

(2) The wood of woodwind instruments, called *strumenti di legno* or *legni*.

Legrenzi, Giovanni (baptized Clusone, near Bergamo, 12 Aug 1626; d. Venice, 27 May 1690). Italian composer and church musician, most renowned for his sonatas, though he also wrote much sacred music and gave the 17th-century Venetian operatic tradition its sunset. A church musician's son, he moved to Bergamo as organist at Santa Maria Maggiore in 1645 and was ordained in 1651. He was then chapelmaster of the Accademia dello Spirito Santo in Ferrara (1656–65), and by 1670 was living in Venice, where he rose to become chapelmaster of St Mark's in 1685.

Lehár, Franz [Ferencz] (b. Komarón, 30 Apr 1870; d. Bad Ischl, 24 Oct 1948). Austro–Hungarian composer, who maintained the tradition of Viennese light classics, notably in his operetta *Die lustige Witwe* (The Merry Widow). His father was a bandmaster-composer who married a Hungarian and lived largely in Hungary; hence the Magyar accent on the surname, nevertheless stressed on the first syllable. At 10 the boy was sent to his uncle in Sternberg. He played the violin in a summer spa orchestra, and at 12 went to Prague, where, as a conservatory student, he came into contact with Foerster, Fibich and Dvořák. Called up in his late teens, he remained in military service as a bandmaster until 1902; by now he was in Vienna, winning success as a composer of waltzes as well as marches. That success was hugely exceeded by *Die lustige Witwe* (1905), and re-echoed in *Der Graf von Luxemburg* and *Zigeunerliebe*. In the late 1920s Tauber's artistry helped him regain popularity, and he wrote his last work for Tauber: *Giuditta* – given, in an unusual show of esteem, at the Vienna Staatsoper.

Operettas: *Die* LUSTIGE WITWE; *Der Graf von Luxemburg* (A.M. Willner and Robert Bodanzky), f.p. Vienna, 1909; *Zigeunerliebe* (Willner and Bodanzky), f.p. Vienna, 1910; *Paganini* (Paul Knepler and Bela Jenbach), f.p. Vienna, 1925; *Der Zarewitsch* (Viktor Leon and Leo Stein), f.p. Berlin, 1927; *Friederike* (Ludwig Herzer and Fritz Löhner), f.p. Berlin, 1928; *Das Land des Lächelns* (Herzer and Löhner), f.p. Berlin, 1929 (includes 'Dein ist mein ganzes Herz'); *Giuditta* (Knepler and Lehar), f.p. Vienna, 1934
Other works: waltzes (*Gold und Silber*, Op.79, 1902), marches, film scores, etc.

Lehmann, Lilli (b. Würzburg, 24 Nov 1848; d. Berlin, 17 May 1929). German soprano, appearing for over half a century (1865–1920) in a repertory that grew to include the major Wagner roles in the 1880s–90s, when she sang at the Met, Covent Garden and Bayreuth. She trained with her mother, herself a singer.

Lehmann, Liza [Elizabeth Nina Mary Frederica] (b. London, 11 Jul 1862; d. Pinner, 19 Sep 1918). British singer-composer, notably of parlour songs. Her mother was also a songwriter, her father a German painter. She studied singing and composition, with teachers including Lind and Mac-Cunn. After her marriage (1894) she concentrated on composition, though her success in that sphere brought her back to public performance, accompanying herself at the piano. She made two US tours, taught singing at the Guildhall School, and was first president of the Society of Women Musicians (1911–12). Her songs include the cycle *In a Persian Garden* (to verses from Omar Khayyam, satb soli, pf, pub 1896) and 'There are fairies at the bottom of our garden' (1917).

Lehmann, Lotte (b. Perleberg, 27 Feb 1888; d. Santa Barbara, 26 Aug 1976). German–US soprano, much admired for the richness of the voice and personality, grand yet intimate, she brought to the Marschallin in *Rosenkavalier*. She studied in Berlin with Mathilde Mallinger, the first Eva in *Die Meistersinger*, which duly became one of her own key roles. Her debut came in 1910 at Hamburg, but from 1916 her base was Vienna, where she created the Dyer's Wife in *Die Frau ohne Schatten*; she was also the first Christine in *Intermezzo*. In 1938, in the face of the Nazi takeover, she moved to the USA. She gave her last stage performance in San Francisco in 1946 as the Marschallin, and retired altogether in 1951.

Lehrstück (Ger., teaching piece). Short play with a message, as made by Brecht and composers associated with him (Eisler, Hindemith, Weill).

Leibowitz, René (b. Warsaw, 17 Feb 1913; d. Paris, 29 Aug 1972). Polish–French composer, conductor and teacher, an important transmitter of 12-note serialism through his work as a private teacher (Boulez was a pupil) and author of *Schoenberg and his School* (Fr. 1947, Eng. 1949). He arrived in Paris in 1929/30, and may have studied with Schoenberg and Webern. His compositions, Schoenbergian in technique, include operas, songs, eight quartets and other chamber pieces. As a conductor he promoted Schoenberg in Paris soon after the Second World War and in 1962 recorded the Beethoven symphonies.

Leich (Middle High Ger.). LAI.

Leider, Frida (b. Berlin, 18 Apr 1888; d. Berlin, 4 Jun 1975). German soprano, the leading exponent of the heavy Wagner roles in her 40s, when she appeared regularly at the Berlin Staatsoper, Bayreuth, Covent Garden and elsewhere, besides making notable recordings. She studied in Berlin, made her debut in Halle (1915), and became resident at the Berlin Staatsoper (1923–38), where she was able to remain even though married to a Jew (Rudolf Deman, the orchestra's ex-leader). In retirement she taught and directed.

Leier (Ger.). Lyre, hurdy-gurdy.

Leifs, Jón (b. Sólheimar, 1 May 1899; d. Reykjavík, 30 Jul 1968). Icelandic composer, known for the primeval energy he drew from the folk music and landscape of his country, especially in *Hekla*, Op.52 (1961), a choral-orchestral volcanic eruption with abundant percussion. Originally Jón Thorleifsson, he studied in Reykjavík and with Aladár Szendrei and Paul Graener at the Leipzig Conservatory (1916–21). Though he returned to Iceland to collect folk music, Germany remained his base until 1944, when declining professional opportunities, plus the fact of having a Jewish wife, drove him back home for good. Other works include the Organ Concerto, Op.7 (1917–30), the ballet *Baldr*, Op.34 (1943–7) and the choral-orchestral *Geysir*, Op.51 (1961). Little noticed in his lifetime, he became a cult composer at the end of the 20th century.

Leighton, Kenneth (b. Wakefield, 2 Oct 1929; d. Edinburgh, 24 Aug 1988). British composer of much choral, keyboard and orchestral music in mainstream modernist style. After Oxford (1947–51) he studied with Petrassi in Rome. He returned to Oxford as lecturer in 1968, and two years later was appointed professor in Edinburgh. His works include sacred settings (masses, motets, carols), concertos (three for piano) and keyboard music.

Leinsdorf, Erich (b. Vienna, 4 Feb 1912; d. Zurich, 11 Sep 1993). Austrian–US conductor. Trained at both university and academy in Vienna, he had early professional experience with Webern, Walter and Toscanini. In 1937 he joined the Met as assistant conductor, and he retained an association with the house through later appointments with the Rochester Philharmonic (1947–55) and Boston Symphony (1962–9).

Leipzig. German city, whose musical hub was first St Thomas's church, where cantors included Schein, Kuhnau and Bach, then the GEWANDHAUS ORCHESTRA. Mendelssohn was founder principal of the conservatory.

leitmotif (Ger. *Leitmotiv*, leading motif). Musical idea that is characteristic of a person, place or principle in an opera and that also, being generally quite short, can be transformed. The term was introduced by the scholar August Wilhelm Ambros (*c*.1865) in connection with Wagner and Liszt, and was given a more particular definition by Hans von Wolzogen, who published a guide (1876) to themes in the *Ring*. His names for these – Valhalla, Redemption through Love and so on – have been criticized but not displaced. Yet the essence of a leitmotif is that, while keeping an identity that makes a label valid and useful, it can recur in altered form, like a theme in a Beethoven symphony (Wagner's revered model), but with the difference that the alteration has meaning within

the context of the opera. Thus the uncertainty of the Tarnhelm motif, appearing briefly in *Das Rheingold*, comes to suffuse much of *Götterdämmerung*. This goes far beyond the simple recall of the older REMINISCENCE MOTIF.

Leitton (Ger.). Leading note.

Le Jeune, Claude (b. Valenciennes, 1528–30; buried Paris, 26 Sep 1600). French composer, known principally for MUSIQUE MESUREE. He was a Huguenot, supported by various Protestant noblemen (including Henry of Navarre, later Henry IV of France) before and after his arrival in Paris in the early 1560s. There he joined the Académie de Poésie et de Musique, established by the literary musicians Jean Antoine de Baïf and Joachim Thibault de Courville, and worked towards its renascent aims in attempting to revive not only the metres but also the modalities of ancient Greek song. The effect, far from antiquarian, is of unusual rhythmic vitality and, at times, extreme chromaticism. In keeping with the academy's principles, little of his music was published, though several volumes appeared after his death, including volumes of psalms, settings of Calvinist instructional verses (*Octonaires de la vanité et inconstance du monde*) and, most notably, *Le Printemps*, to poems by Baïf.

Lekeu, Guillaume (Jean Joseph Nicolas) (b. Heusy, near Verviers, 20 Jan 1870; d. Angers, 21 Jan 1894). Belgian composer, a disciple of Franck and d'Indy. He died of typhoid fever, having already achieved mastery without betraying his youthfulness – and a catalogue exceeding Op.100. The most admired of his works is the violin sonata in G he wrote in 1891 for Ysaÿe. Others include a cello sonata and a piano quartet, both completed by d'Indy.

Lélio. Concert work by Berlioz, the sequel to his *Symphonie fantastique*, titled in full *Lélio, ou le retour à la vie*. It comprises songs, choral pieces and an orchestral movement, intended to come from unseen musicians while an actor stands in for the composer. First performance: Paris, 9 Dec 1832 (with the *Symphonie fantastique*).

Lemmens, Jaak Nikolaas (b. Zoerle-Parwijs, Antwerp, 3 Jan 1823; d. Zemst, near Mechelen, 30 Jan 1881). Belgian organist-composer, who helped bring Bach to the Francophone world. After his time at the Brussels Conservatory (1839–45) he studied for a year in Breslau with Adolf Hesse, who had studied with Bach's pupil Forkel. He founded a school of sacred music in Mechelen, and wrote masses and motets as well as organ pieces including three sonatas. His wife was Helen Lemmens-Sherrington (1834–1906), the leading British oratorio soprano of the 1860s–70s, and their base was in London from 1869 to 1878.

Lemminkäinen Suite. Set of four orchestral pieces by Sibelius evoking episodes in the life of Lemminkäinen, hero of the *Kalevala*: 1 *Lemminkäinen and the Maidens of the Island*, 2 *Lemminkäinen in Tuonela*, 3 *The SWAN OF TUONELA*, 4 *Lemminkäinen's Homeward Journey* (though the composer later reversed the order of the internal movements). First performance: Helsinki, 13 Apr 1896.

Lemoine. French publishing firm founded in Paris in 1772 by Antoine Marcel Lemoine (1753–1817) and currently in the hands of the seventh generation.

Lemoyne, Jean Baptiste (b. Eymet, Dordogne, 3 Apr 1751; d. Paris, 30 Dec 1796). French composer of operas modelled on Gluck and Piccinni, notably *Electre* (f.p. Paris, 1782), *Phèdre* (f.p. Fontainebleau, 1786) and *Nephté* (f.p. Paris, 1789). Brought up by his chapelmaster uncle, he went to Berlin in 1770, studied there with Graun, Johann Philipp Kirnberger and Schulz, wrote his first opera for Warsaw (1775) and arrived in Paris *c.*1780. Some of his later operas have revolutionary settings.

Léner Quartet. Hungarian string quartet, founded in 1918 by Jenő Léner (1894–1948) and three of his contemporaries at the Liszt Academy. The group was active internationally in the 1920s–30s, admired for its mellow intimacy with the great quartet literature, much of which it recorded.

Lengnick. British publishing firm founded in London in 1893 by Alfred Lengnick and known principally for educational music.

Leningrad. Name given Shostakovich's Seventh Symphony, a response to the 1941 German siege of the city.

lent (Fr.), **lentement** (Fr.), **lento** (It.). Slow, slowly. Venerable tempo marking, *lento* appearing for the first time in Praetorius and *lentement* in Lully. Also found occasionally is *lentando* (slowing).

Lenya, Lotte (b. Vienna, 18 Oct 1898; d. New York, 27 Nov 1981). Austrian–US singer (originally Karoline Wilhelmine Blamauer), the wife and classic interpreter of Weill. As an aspirant dancer she studied the Dalcroze method in Zurich (1914–20), but learned more from Frank Wedekind's

ballad singing. From Zurich she moved to Berlin, where she appeared in Georg Kaiser's plays and so met Weill, whom she married in 1926. She created Jenny in *Die Dreigroschenoper*, on stage and on film, and was the destined protagonist of *Die sieben Todsünden*. After Weill's death she continued to devote herself to his works.

Leo, Leonardo (Ortensio Salvatore de) (b. San Vito degli Schiavi, now San Vito de Normanni, near Brindisi, 5 Aug 1694; d. Naples, 31 Oct 1744). Italian composer, the most prominent member of the Neapolitan school after 1730, renowned especially for Metastasio settings, comic operas and liturgical pieces – music in which he combined Alessandro Scarlatti's nobility and rich texture with the vivacity of his sooner blooming contemporaries Pergolesi and Vinci. He studied with Nicola Fago at the Turchini conservatory in Naples from 1709 and began gaining church appointments in 1713, rising to become royal chapelmaster in his last year. His sacred music includes a famed *Miserere* a 8 and oratorios to texts by Metastasio, notably *Santa Elena al Calvario* (f.p. Bologna, 1734). At the same time he became a productive opera composer, writing two scores a year on average from the early 1720s: Neapolitan comedies (*Amor vuol sofferenze*, 1739) and serious operas for the major centres (Act 3 of a collaborative *Demofoonte*, f.p. Naples, 1735; *L'Olimpiade*, f.p. Naples, 1737; *Il Ciro riconosciuto*, f.p. Turin, 1739). He was also principal teacher at two of the Neapolitan conservatories: the San Onofrio (from 1739) and his own Turchini (from 1741). His music indicates a scholarly bent, confirmed by his treatises on counterpoint and cantus firmus, and the best of it came in his later years.

Leoncavallo, Ruggero (b. Naples, 8 Mar 1857; d. Montecatini, 9 Aug 1919). Italian composer, remembered almost exclusively for his passionate short opera PAGLIACCI. He studied with Lauro Rossi at the Naples Conservatory (1866–76), took a degree in literature at Bologna in 1878 (he was to write several of his own librettos and song lyrics), and travelled as a café pianist before the singer Maurel introduced him to the publisher Ricordi. Ricordi gave him support but not performances, and, irritated by waiting and by the success of Mascagni's *Cavalleria rusticana*, he determined to outdo that score and offer the result, *Pagliacci*, to the rival firm of Sonzogno. So he did. The work was accepted and instantly acclaimed, only to be linked forever with the piece it had been made to trump. After that his career went steeply downhill. *I Medici* (f.p. Milan, 1893), intended as the first part of a quasi-Wagnerian trilogy set in the

Renaissance, was laughed off the stage, and with his next opera he knowingly challenged Puccini, for the two composers worked simultaneously on their versions of *La Bohème*; his came second (f.p. Venice, 1897), not only chronologically. In it the tenor is Marcello, who has the aria 'Testa adorata'. *Zazà* (f.p. Milan, 1900) is remembered, especially for its baritone arias 'Buona Zazà' and 'Zazà, piccola zingara'; its four successors and several operettas are not. Among his songs is the popular 'Mattinata' (1904), which he recorded at the piano with Caruso.

Leonhardt, Gustav (Maria) (b. 's Graveland, 30 May 1928). Dutch keyboard player and conductor, leading figure in the early music movement from 1950 onwards, admired for his expository directness, even severity. He studied with Eduard Müller at the Schola Cantorum in Basle (1947–50), and has combined performing (as a soloist, with distinguished colleagues and with the Leonhardt Consort, which he founded in 1955) with teaching, at the Vienna Academy (1952–5) and the Amsterdam Conservatory (from 1954).

Leoni, Michael (b. ?London, *c.*1755; d. Kingston, Jamaica, 1797). British tenor who was the first Don Carlos in Sheridan's *The Duenna* and ended his life as cantor at the synagogue in Kingston. He was also responsible for the hymn tune *Leoni*, which he based on a Hebrew melody.

Leonin [Leoninus, Léonin] (*fl.* Paris, *c.*1150s–1201). French composer, to whom Anonymous 4 ascribed the MAGNUS LIBER of NOTRE DAME SCHOOL polyphony in its earliest state. Since the book is known only in revisions of the next century and later, the nature of his contribution is disputed. The general supposition, though, is that he was responsible for adding a single voice in florid organum style over the long, drone-like notes of a plainsong. He was associated with Notre Dame from before building started, and achieved high rank in the cathedral hierarchy.

Leonore (Leonora). Title Beethoven intended for *Fidelio*. It is commonly applied to the three overtures he wrote and abandoned, and to the 1805–6 versions of the score.

Leopold I (b. Vienna, 9 Jun 1640; d. Vienna, 5 May 1705). Austrian monarch and composer. As Holy Roman Emperor (1658–1705) he strongly favoured music, bringing Bertali, Fux, Antonio Draghi, Cesti and many others to his court. He was also a notable composer himself – of festival stage pieces but more particularly of sacred music, including several oratorios and masses.

Leppard, Raymond (John) (b. London, 11 Aug 1927). British conductor, best known for the colourfully (and controversially) enriched realizations of operas by Monteverdi and Cavalli he presented in the 1960s. He studied at Cambridge (1948–52), and taught there (1957–67) as his conducting career took off. Later he was principal conductor of the BBC Northern Symphony (1973–80) and Indianapolis Symphony (1987–2001).

Le Roux, Gaspard (*fl.* Paris, 1690–1705). French keyboard composer-performer, known for a single volume (1705), which is remarkable not only for its quality but also in suggesting versions of the music for one or two melody instruments with continuo or for two harpsichords.

Le Roux, Maurice (b. Paris, 6 Feb 1923; d. Avignon, 19 Oct 1992). French composer-conductor, a part-time member of the avant-garde while working as a conductor and film composer. He studied with Messiaen at the Paris Conservatoire (1946–52) and held appointments as conductor of the Orchestre National de l'ORTF (1960–68), artistic adviser to the Opera (1969–73) and inspector general of music (1973–88).

Le Roy, Adrian (b. Montreuil-sur-mer, *c.*1520; d. Paris, 1598). French publisher, active from 1551 in partnership with his cousin Robert Ballard. He was also a composer and performer of songs with accompaniment for lute, guitar or other plucked instrument, and the author of manuals for these instruments.

Leschetizky, Theodor (b. Lańcut, Galicia, 22 Jun 1830; d. Dresden, 14 Nov 1915). Polish pianist, known especially as one of the great teachers, in a chain linking his own teacher, Czerny, to his pupils Paderewski, Schnabel and many more (of whom, in succession, he married four). A professional musician's son, he made his debut at 10 in Lemberg/Lviv and soon after was taken to Vienna by his family to study with Czerny and Sechter. He also read philosophy at the university (1845–8). In 1852 he moved to St Petersburg, where at Rubinstein's invitation he became head of piano studies at the conservatory (1862–78), then returned to Vienna. He wrote virtuoso miniatures.

lesson. (1) Session of instruction, normally involving a teacher and a single pupil, or perhaps two. Lessons, whether in performance or composition, are normally focused on exercises or pieces prepared by the student. With larger numbers the session is a CLASS.

(2) In older English usage (from Byrd to the 18th

century), a piece, most commonly for keyboard or lute.

Le Sueur, Jean François (b. Drucat-Plessiel, near Abbeville, 15 Feb 1760; d. Paris, 6 Oct 1837). French composer, who cultivated a style of grand simplicity in opera and sacred music. Of peasant origin, he was trained in choir schools in Abbeville and Amiens, and in 1776 began the life of a church choirmaster. During one of his brief spells in Paris he had further lessons with the learned abbé Nicolas Roze; during another (1786–7) he took charge of the choir at Notre Dame. His treatise *Exposé d'une musique* (1787) was, like his music, at once proto-Romantic (in defending music as representation of feelings) and neoclassical (in taking up the old French preoccupation with rhythm based on Greek metres). He reappeared in Paris as the composer of *La Caverne* (1793), a fiercely dramatic opera that suited the age, and this time he stayed. The same year he began an association with the Conservatoire that lasted until 1802, and was restored in 1818. Meanwhile, his talent for monumental choral writing appealed to Napoleon, who approved his opera *Ossian, ou Les Bardes* (1804) and made him music director of the Tuileries chapel. There he remained under the returning Bourbon monarchs.

letania (Lat.). Litany.

Leuckart. German publishing firm, founded by Constantin Sander (1826–1905), who in 1849 took over the shop in Breslau opened by his grandfather, Franz Ernst Christoph Leuckart. The firm moved to Leipzig in 1870 and Munich in 1948.

leuto (It.). Lute.

Levant, Oscar (b. Pittsburgh, 27 Dec 1906; d. Beverly Hills, 14 Aug 1972). US composer, principally of film scores and popular songs, though also of a piano concerto (1942) and other concert works. He studied in Pittsburgh and New York, and had some lessons with Schoenberg.

levé (Fr.). Upbeat.

Leverkühn, Adrian. See IMAGINARY COMPOSERS.

Levi, Hermann (b. Giessen, Upper Hesse, 7 Nov 1839; d. Munich, 13 May 1900). German conductor, remembered principally for conducting the first *Parsifal*, a work in which he apparently communicated spirituality beyond the irritation he received from the composer. A rabbi's son, he studied with Hauptmann and Julius Rietz at the Leipzig Con-

servatory (1855–8), and worked his way up to leading posts in Karlsruhe (1864–72), where performances of *Die Meistersinger* and *Rienzi* in 1869 gained him Wagner's attention, and Munich (from 1872).

Levidis, Dimitrios (b. Athens, 8 Apr 1885/6; d. Palaeon Phaleron, near Athens, 29 May 1951). Greek composer, who was touched by long residence in France (1910–32) and by his mixed education in Athens (with Lavrangas and others), Lausanne (1906–7) and Munich (1907–8, with Friedrich Klose and Mottl). His music – consisting largely of orchestral scores, with or without voices – thus speaks a Ravel–Strauss language with a Greek accent. Fascinated by new and unusual colours, he was among the first to write for the ONDES MARTENOT (1928).

Levin, Robert (David) (b. Brooklyn, 13 Oct 1947). US pianist and scholar, known especially for his improvised cadenzas to Mozart's piano concertos. Trained as a composer from an early age, with Wolpe in New York (1957–61) and Boulanger in Fontainebleau (1960–64), he has pursued a dual career as a pianist-scholar, each side informing the other. He has also taught at Curtis (1968–73), Purchase (1972–86), the Freiburg conservatory (1986–93) and Harvard (from 1993).

Lévinas, Michaël (b. Paris, 18 Apr 1949). French composer and pianist, who combines in his works a robust and fluid sense of timbre with a gentle fantasy. The son of the philosopher Emmanuel Lévinas, he studied at the Paris Conservatoire with Messiaen and Loriod, and was influenced also by Stockhausen, Ligeti, Scelsi and Lachenmann. In 1974 he was co-founder of the Ensemble Itinéraire; he also teaches analysis at the Conservatoire. His works include *Par-delà* for orchestra (1994) and the operas *GO-gol* (f.p. Strasbourg, 1996) and *Les Noirs* (f.p. Lyons, 2004).

Levine, James (b. Cincinnati, 23 Jun 1943). US conductor, admired for the breadth of his performances (expressively rich, finely detailed) and of his repertory (in which Mozart, Verdi, Wagner, Mahler and Schoenberg are major elements but Bach, Carter and Babbitt feature too). He first performed with an orchestra at 10, as piano soloist with the Cincinnati Symphony; in adult life he has gone on appearing as a pianist, but only in chamber music and, especially, to accompany singers. From his early teens he attended the Marlboro and Aspen festivals, and he entered Juilliard in 1961 as a graduate, to study with Lhévinne and Morel. He was assistant conductor to Szell in Cleveland (1964–70), made his debut with the Met in 1971 (*Tosca*), and became successively principal conductor (1973), music director (1975) and artistic director (1986), while holding posts with the Munich Philharmonic (1999–2004) and Boston Symphony (from 2003).

Levinson, Gerald (Charles) (b. New Hyde Park, NY, 22 Jun 1951). US composer of harmonically vivid and colourful music. He studied with Crumb, Richard Wernick and Rochberg at the University of Pennsylvania, with Shapey in Chicago and with Messiaen in Paris (1974–6). In 1977 he began teaching at Swarthmore, where he has remained, apart from visits to Bali (1979–80, 1982–3). His works include two symphonies, besides other orchestral and ensemble pieces.

Levy, Marvin David (b. Passaic, NJ, 2 Aug 1932). US composer, with the rare distinction of an opera commissioned by the Met (*Mourning Becomes Electra*, 1967). He studied with Philip James at NYU and Luening at Columbia, and made his mark with earlier operas in New York and Santa Fe. Later works include the Jean Genet musical *The Grand Balcony* (1978–92), deriving from a second Met commission that the company abandoned.

Lewkovitch, Bernhard (b. Copenhagen, 28 May 1927). Danish composer, especially of Catholic sacred music drawing on Stravinsky and other modernist influences. He was trained in Copenhagen as a choirboy at the (Catholic) St Ansgar's church, where he became organist (1947–63), and at the conservatory; he also studied composition with Paul Schierbeck and Jörgen Jersild.

LGSMD. Licentiate of the Guildhall School of Music and Drama.

l.h. Abbreviation for left hand in keyboard music.

Lhéritier, Jean (b. c.1480; d. 1552 or later). French composer, especially of motets in a style of imitative polyphony. He seems to have been active mostly in Italy, and was an important link from Josquin to Palestrina.

Lhévinne, Josef (b. Orel, 13 Dec 1874; d. New York, 2 Dec 1944). Russian pianist, among the titans of his time, admired especially for his musicianship in Chopin. He studied with Vasily Safonov at the Moscow Conservatory (1885–91), where his classmates included Rachmaninoff and Scriabin.

After a period teaching there (1902–6) he moved to Berlin (1907–19) and then New York, in company with his wife Rosina (1880–1976), who devoted herself to his career and then to her work as a teacher at Juilliard.

L'homme armé. See *L'HOMME ARME*.

Liadov, Anatoly. See Anatoly LYADOV.

liberamente (It.). Freely.

Liber usualis (Lat., book of common practice). Chantbook published from the monastery of Solesmes, northern France, standard in Catholic use between its first edition (1896) and the Second Vatican Council.

libitum. See AD LIBITUM.

library. Among those with outstanding collections of composers' manuscripts are the following, most of which have changing exhibitions of their holdings, besides providing facilities for researchers:

Basle:	Sacher Foundation (20th century, 21st century)
Berlin:	Deutsche Staatsbibliothek (Bach, Mozart, etc.)
Cambridge, England:	Fitzwilliam Museum (English music)
Cambridge, Mass.:	Houghton Library (general)
Chicago:	Newberry Library (Renaissance music)
London:	British Library (Mozart, English music, etc.)
Moscow:	Lenin Library (Russian music)
New York:	New York Public Library (general), Pierpont Morgan Library (general)
Oxford:	Bodleian Library (general)
Paris:	Bibliothèque Nationale (French music from the troubadours to Barraqué)
Rome:	Biblioteca Apostolica Vaticana (sacred music)
Salzburg:	Mozarteum (Mozart)
Venice:	Biblioteca Nazionale Marciana (Venetian music)
Vienna:	Gesellschaft der Musikfreunde (Beethoven, Schubert, Brahms), Österreichische Nationalbibliothek (Haydn, Mozart, Beethoven)
Washington:	Library of Congress (general)

librettist. Libretto writer. The function has been undertaken by writers of distinction in other fields (Jonson, Lope de Vega, Calderón, Corneille, Dryden, Voltaire, Rousseau, Goldoni, Sheridan, Goethe, Zola, Maeterlinck, Apollinaire, Brecht, Cocteau, Claudel, Colette, Karel Čapek, Auden,

Beckett, Bachmann, Edward Bond, Calvino), by composers themselves in many cases since the 19th century (Berlioz, Wagner, Glinka, Musorgsky, Borodin, Leoncavallo, Busoni, Janáček, Pfitzner, Schreker, Schoenberg, Prokofiev, Hindemith, Tippett, Dallapiccola, Henze, Davies), by composers' siblings (Modest Tchaikovsky, Adelheid Wette née Humperdinck), by 18th-century monarchs (Frederick II, Catherine II) and by others who are remembered principally as librettists (Rinuccini, Striggio, Badoaro, Giovanni Francesco Busenello, Quinault, Zeno, Metastasio, Haym, Calzabigi, Da Ponte, Romani, Cammarano, Scribe, Solera, Piave, Barbier and Carré, Meilhac and Halévy, Illica and Giacosa, Boito, Hofmannsthal).

The librettist is nearly always the second partner in the creation of an opera, and in modern times may even be the third, after the director as well as the composer. This hierarchy reveals itself in how operas are written, with the words fixed first, subject to the composer's advice, instruction, criticism and adjustment. Only to a much lesser degree, if at all, do composers return the favour. Correspondingly, in contemporary culture, operas are valued and understood principally as composers' works. *Don Giovanni* is placed with *Idomeneo* (by the same composer), not with *L'arbore di Diana* (by the same librettist, and even from the same year), while *Il trovatore* (by a widely revered composer) is not harmed by a ramshackle libretto, any more than *Didone abbandonata* (by a widely revered librettist), in any of its many settings, is saved by a sublime one.

Provided the librettist is not entirely supine, though, great experiences (during the collaboration and in the resulting work) can come from having the composer on top. Opera, throughout the ages, has been made by words crying out to be heard.

libretto (It., little book). The text of an opera, or the pamphlet in which that text is printed, in the manner of a play script.

A libretto is not, however, a play, and the ranks of librettists include few great playwrights. Nor do great plays infallibly make great operas: from all of Shakespeare, and out of many hundreds of attempts, few lasting operas have been born.

Those few – they barely extend beyond Berlioz's *Béatrice et Bénédict*, and Verdi's *Otello* and *Falstaff* – may help to show some of the features that make librettos different. One is concision (since sung words, except in simple recitative, will take several times longer to deliver than spoken text), and a corresponding openness to extended timescales. Another is the fact that, where characters in

a play expose and express themselves largely in dialogue, those in opera do so largely alone, whether in soliloquy, in statement to another character, or in the entwined soliloquies or statements of duets and ensembles. A further difference is the need for words that will readily take music and become singable. This affects vocabulary (the deployment of short and long vowels, the avoidance or not of 'thick' groups of consonants, in a word such as 'strengths') and form. Librettos – in this like plays – were customarily in verse until the later 19th century, and many have been since, even if metre and lineation are commonly disregarded by the composer. (Louis Gallet, himself a librettist, defined the object of his craft ruefully thus: 'A libretto is a work in verse which is entrusted to a composer to be turned into prose.') Where not overtly poetic, a libretto will still normally use a language amenable to song in its sounds, its images and its simple syntax (for, leaving aside the contentious question of whether the words should be understood by the audience, they probably should be understood by – and capable of being phrased by – the singer).

The history of the libretto – in the principal, abstract sense – is indistinguishable from that of OPERA. Operatic reform has always presupposed libretto reform, and has even been led by librettists (notably Metastasio and Calzabigi). Also, the questioning of operatic institutions since the late 19th century has involved a questioning of the libretto; hence the 'found libretto' – a pre-existing text or group of texts – in operas from Debussy and Berg to Nono and Reich.

As published items, librettos were produced principally for audiences to consult, whether during the performance (in theatres normally lit, if dimly, before the later 19th century), in advance or afterwards. Their practical function in the theatre has been taken over by SURTITLES.

P.J. Smith *The Tenth Muse* (1970)

licenza (It., licence). (1) Term found in the marking *con alcuna licenza* (with some freedom).

(2) An epilogue in a stage work of the 17th–18th centuries (an aria or a longer piece), inserted to commend the observing ruler.

Lichnowsky. Noble brothers, Prince Karl (*c.*1760–1814) and Count Moritz (1771–1837), both supporters of Beethoven, who dedicated to the former his Op.1 trios, his Second Symphony and three piano works (WoO 69, Op.13 and Op.26), and to the latter two further piano works (Op.35 and Op.90).

Licht (Light). Cycle of seven operas by Stockhausen to his own librettos, each devoted to a day of the week and to episodes in a synthetic myth involving three characters who may be represented instrumentally as well as vocally: the hero, Michael (tenor, trumpet), his mother or lover, Eva (soprano, basset horn), and their enemy, Luzifer (bass, trombone). Each opera has a different central figure or figures, as follows, and each includes many extracts available for separate performance (the details given are those of the complete theatre premières): 1 *Donnerstag* (Michael; Milan, 3 April 1981), 2 *Samstag* (Luzifer; Milan, 25 May 1984), 3 *Montag* (Eva; Milan, 7 May 1988), 4 *Dienstag* (Michael–Luzifer; Leipzig, 28 May 1993), 5 *Freitag* (Michael–Eva; Leipzig, 12 Sep 1996), 6 *Mittwoch* (Eva–Luzifer), 7 *Sonntag* (Michael–Eva–Luzifer).

Lidholm, Ingvar (Natanael) (b. Jönköping, 24 Feb 1921). Swedish composer, especially of choral and orchestral music, in which avant-garde elements are fused with a native lyricism. While playing viola in the royal chapel (1943–6) he studied with Rosenberg; later he went to Darmstadt (1949) and had lessons in London with Seiber (1954). He conducted a semi-professional orchestra, the Örebro (1947–56), then worked for Swedish radio (1956–84) and taught at the conservatory in Stockholm (1965–75). His works include an operatic setting of Strindberg's *A Dream Play* (f.p. Stockholm, 1990) as well as orchestral and choral music.

Liebe der Danae, Die (The Love of Danae). Opera by Strauss to a libretto by Joseph Gregor. Treating mythology in serio-comic vein, the opera brings together Danae, whom Jupiter ravished as a shower of golden rain, and Midas of the golden touch. Danae (soprano) prefers Midas (tenor) to Jupiter (baritone), even at the expense of abandoning divinity and moving from a glittering court to a humble abode where she and her husband can enjoy human love. First performance: Salzburg, 14 Aug 1952 (a previous production there was dropped on government orders after the dress rehearsal, 16 Aug 1944).

Liebermann, Rolf (b. Zurich, 14 Sep 1910; d. Paris, 2 Jan 1999). Swiss composer, notably of operas and orchestral works in eclectic modern style (Concerto for jazzband and orchestra, 1954), but better known as the actively commissioning intendant of the Hamburg Staatsoper (1959–73) and Paris Opera (1973–80), in which posts he virtually stopped composing. He began again in his retirement.

Lieberson. US musical family.

(1) **Goddard** (b. Hanley, Staffs., 5 Apr 1911; d. New York, 29 May 1977). Record producer and executive, working for Columbia from 1939 and responsible for Stravinsky's many recordings and re-recordings. He was taken to the USA as a child, and trained under Rogers at the Eastman School, beginning his career as a composer and critic.

(2) **Peter** (b. New York, 25 Oct 1946). Composer (son of Goddard), who has adapted a colourful modernist style to Buddhist myths and subjects. He studied privately with Babbitt, at Columbia with Wuorinen and Sollberger (1972–4), and at Brandeis with Martino and Martin Boykan (1981–4), then taught at Harvard (1984–8) and at the Shambhala centre in Halifax, Nova Scotia (until 1994). His works include two concertos for Peter Serkin (1980–83, 1999).

(3) **Lorraine Hunt** (b. San Francisco, 1 Mar 1954). Mezzo-soprano, a performer of commanding presence and utterance. Trained as a violinist and viola player, she switched to singing in 1981 and made her reputation in 18th-century opera. In the late 1990s she began broadening her repertory to embrace Berlioz's Dido and new works. She married Peter Lieberson in 1999.

Liebeslieder (Love Songs). Sets of waltz songs by Brahms for piano duet with voices ad lib, Op.52 and Op.65.

Liebestod (Love-Death). Customary title for the finale of *Tristan*: Isolde's ecstatic solo of homecoming to her dead lover. This sequence, without Isolde's voice, is often tacked on to the Prelude to make a concert item. Wagner, however, called the finale Isolde's Transfiguration and used the term Liebestod for the prelude.

Liebestraum (Love-Dream). Popular piano piece by Liszt, the last, in A♭, of his three *Liebesträume*. All were based on songs, this one on 'O lieb, o liebe, so lang du lieben kannst'.

lied. The normal Ger. word for SONG, used in Eng. (and always with the same pl., 'lieder') for any song with Ger. words, from the Middle Ages to the present. However, in both languages the term most commonly implies a song with piano from the tradition that began in the late 18th century and reached its climax in the 19th. Other terms for song were available at the time (*Romanze, Gesang*), but now 'lied' is used universally. Earlier repertories are usually qualified as the polyphonic lied (from the 14th century to madrigalesque works of the late Renaissance) and the continuo lied (the Baroque form). The history of the later lied parallels that of the Romanticism that provided its lyric impulse, from beginnings in Mozart and Beethoven, through the outbursts of Schubert, Schumann, Brahms and Wolf (and Mendelssohn, Loewe, Franz and Liszt), to repercussions in Mahler, Strauss, Schoenberg, Berg, Webern, Killmayer, Henze and Rihm.

lieder artist, lieder singer. Singer, normally German-speaking, specializing in lieder.

Liederbuch (Ger.). Songbook, normally one from the 15th–16th centuries.

Lieder eines fahrenden Gesellen (Songs of a Travelling Lad). Song cycle by Mahler to four poems of his own. Partly autobiographical, the work is a first-person narrative of disappointed love and lonely departure. First performance: Berlin, 16 Mar 1896 (with orchestra).

Liederkreis (Song Circle). Title Schumann gave two of his song cycles, setting nine poems by Heine (Op.24) and 12 by Eichendorff (Op.39). Both are voiced by male figures suffering Romantic dislocation and anguish that can be resolved only by love (Eichendorff) or death (Heine). The word has also been used as a general term, along with *Liederkranz* (song wreath) and *Liederzyklus* (song cycle).

Liederspiel (Ger., song play). Play including songs, from a German popular tradition of around 1800.

Liedertafel (Ger., song table). Amateur choral group, originally for men only. The first was founded by Zelter in Berlin (1808).

Lieder ohne Worte (Ger.). SONGS WITHOUT WORDS.

Lied von der Erde, Das (The Song of the Earth). Symphonic song cycle by Mahler (a/bar, t, orch) on Chinese poems translated by Hans Bethge and partly adapted by the composer. The exuberance of the first five songs is balanced by the effulgent leave-taking of 'Der Abschied', for the low voice. First performance: Munich, 20 Nov 1911.

Lienas, Juan de (*fl.* Mexico, ?1620–50). Mexican composer of sacred polyphony, of whose origin (Spanish or native) and life nothing is known.

lieto fine (It.). Happy ending. The term implies the tradition in the 17th–18th centuries of bringing a serious opera to a conclusion in which all conflicts are resolved.

Lieutenant Kijé (*Poruchik Kizhei*). Score by Prokofiev intended for a film by Aleksandr Faintsimmer about an officer who has to be invented because of a clerical error. The project did not go forward, but from the brilliant, satirical music the composer made a popular suite in five movements: *Kijé's Birth, Romance, Kijé's Wedding, Troika, Kijé's Burial*. First performance: Moscow, 21 Dec 1934 (suite).

Life for the Tsar, A (*Zhizn za tsarya*). Opera by Glinka to a libretto by several hands. Ivan Susanin (bass), a semi-legendary figure from the period of confusion following Boris Godunov's death, refuses to reveal to invading Poles the way to the tsar's hiding place. His sacrifice is heightened by his stature as a family man, surrounded by his daughter Antonida (soprano), new son-in-law Sobinin (tenor) and ward Vanya (contralto). First performance: St Petersburg, 9 Dec 1836.

In Soviet times the opera was given as *Ivan Susanin*, with a libretto adapted by Sergey Gorodetsky.

ligature. NEUME prescribing two or more notes and their rhythm.

Ligeti, György (Sándor) (b. Dicsöszentmárton/ Diciosânmartin, now Tîrnăveni, Transylvania, 28 May 1923). Hungarian composer, living outside the country since 1956. His arrival in the West brought something new to the new-seeking avant-garde: an extraordinary sureness of imagination and an inimitable sense of fun, both dependent on absolute precision of detail, colour and timing. Traces from throughout history and all over the globe – medieval polyphony and Caribbean popular music, Schumann and Nancarrow, gamelan and Hungarian folksong – meet in his fantastical music, whose underside is melancholy.

Born into an artistic Hungarian-Jewish family, he studied with Farkas at the Kolozsvár Conservatory (1941–3), until excluded on racial grounds, then resumed his studies with Farkas again, Veress and Járdányi at the Liszt Academy (1946–9), where in 1950 he joined the staff. Constrained as much now by Stalinism as previously by Nazism, he had to confine himself largely to folksy choruses while being aware, from reports and sporadic broadcasts, of the freedom enjoyed by composers elsewhere. He therefore took part in the exodus that followed the Russian action of 1956, and determined on recreating himself as a composer in western Europe. To that end he kept almost all his earlier music under wraps until the 1990s, by which time, in returning to choral music and folksong, he had caught up with his young self.

His first destination in the West was Vienna, and he took Austrian nationality, but he has spent almost all his time since in Germany. Feeling that the electronic medium would yield the strictly measured but unmetred polyphony of his imagination, he went to Cologne, where he learned from Koenig and produced three tape projects (1957–8). During the next decade he developed his technique of MICROPOLYPHONY in works for dense orchestral and choral formations, notably *Atmosphères*, the *Requiem*, *Lontano* and *Lux aeterna*, in all of which very gradually widening and narrowing clusters are shot through with suddenly simpler harmonies, coming as shafts of light through clouds. That first Ligeti style (as it seemed in the West) caused a commotion at the first performance of *Atmosphères*, was popularized by the film *2001: A Space Odyssey* (1968) and was widely influential. He became a valued teacher, at Darmstadt (from 1959) and at the conservatory in Stockholm (from 1961). Meanwhile, in parts of the *Requiem*, as well as in *Aventures* and its successor *Nouvelles aventures*, he created quick successions of different vivid characters, in the manner of a comic strip.

In works of the late 1960s and early 1970s he increased his range to include chamber music, to embrace harmonics among other untempered or deliberately mistuned intervals, and to restore something else the avant-garde had neglected or lost: melody, in the sense of supple, coherent line, hence his orchestral piece with the explicit and at the time controversial title *Melodien*. A visit in 1972 to California, where he was visiting professor at Stanford, led to discoveries of kinships with Partch (for novel harmonies) and with the new minimalists (for the repetitive patterning he had introduced independently in his micropolyphony). These came as the post-war European avant-garde was losing its impetus – an eventuality that troubled him for its larger implications (he was strongly opposed to the neo-Romanticism of younger German composers) as well as for its effect on his own work. He devoted himself to an opera (*Le Grand Macabre*) and to his students in Hamburg, where he joined the conservatory staff in 1973.

After the opera he took some while to find his way again. He did so partly by reawakening the Romantic past in a characteristic spirit of sceptical resignation and playfulness (Horn Trio), partly by listening avidly to Caribbean polymetres and the percussion sounds of east Asia (Piano Concerto), and partly by contemplating the connection between Nancarrow's music and the algorithmic processes suggested by computers (which, however, he has never used in composition). The biggest outcome of this period was his continuing series of piano Etudes, interleaved with further concertos and songs from the world he has created.

Richard Steinitz *György Ligeti* (2003)

Opera: *Le* GRAND MACABRE, 1974–7, rev 1996

Vocal orchestral: REQUIEM, s, mez, ch, orch, 1963–5; *Clocks and Clouds*, women's ch, orch, 1972–3; *Mysteries of the Macabre*, s, chbr orch, 1991, (from opera)

Orchestral: Old Hungarian Parlour Dances, str, fl/cl ad lib, 1949; Romanian Concerto, 1952; *Apparitions*, 1958–9; ATMOSPHERES, 1961; Cello Concerto, 1966; LONTANO, 1967; *Ramifications*, str, 1968–9; MELODIEN, 1971; Double Concerto, fl, ob, orch, 1972; *San Francisco Polyphony*, 1973–4; Piano Concerto, 1985–8; VIOLIN CONCERTO, 1989–93; Hamburg Concerto, hn, chbr orch, 1998–9, rev 2003

Ensemble: *Fragment*, 10 insts, 1961; AVENTURES, s, a, bar, 7 insts, 1962; *Nouvelles aventures* (see AVENTURES), s, a, bar, 7 insts, 1962–5; Chamber Concerto, 13 insts, 1969–70; *With Pipes, Drums, Fiddles* (Sándor Weöres), mez, 4 perc, 2000

Chamber and instrumental: Ballad and Dance, 2 vn, 1950; Andante cantabile and Allegretto poco capriccioso, str qt, 1950; Solo Cello Sonata, 1948–53; 6 Bagatelles, wind qnt, 1953, from *Musica ricercata*; String Quartet No.1 'Métamorphoses nocturnes', 1953–4; No.2, 1968; 10 Pieces, wind qnt, 1968; *Hyllning*, vn, vc, 1982; Horn Trio, vn, hn, pf, 1982; *Die grosse Schildkröten-Fanfare vom Südchinesischen Meer*, tpt, 1985; Solo Viola Sonata, 1991–4

Piano duo: *Monument, Selbstportrait, Bewegung*, 1976

Piano duet: March, 1942; Polyphonic Study, 1943; 3 Wedding Dances, 1950; Sonatina, 1950–51

Piano solo: 2 Capriccios, 1947; Invention, 1948; *Musica ricercata*, 1951–3; *Trois bagatelles*, 1961; ETUDES, 1985–2001

Organ: Ricercare, 1953, from *Musica ricercata*; *Volumina*, 1961–2, rev 1966; 2 Studies (*Harmonies, Coulée*), 1967–9

Harpsichord: *Continuum*, 1968; *Hungarian Rock, Passacaglia ungherese*, 1978

Choral (unaccompanied unless indicated): *The Magi* (Attila József), 1946; *Abroad* (4 songs; Bálint Balassa, trad), 1945–6; *Easter* (trad), 1946; *Solitude* (Weöres), 1946; *Wandering* (trad), 1946; *By the huge rock* (trad), 1946; *If I could flow like the river* (trad), 1947; *Kálló Two-step* (trad), 1950; Four Wedding Dances (trad), 3 s, pf, 1950; Wedding Dance, 1950; *Hortobágy* (trad), 1951; *Youth* (trad), 1952; *Gossip* (Weöres), 1952; Songs from Inaktelke (trad), 1953; *Widow Pápai* (trad), 1953; Songs from Mátraszentimre (trad), 1955; *Night, Morning* (Weöres), 1955; *Lux aeterna*, 1966; 3 Phantasien (Hölderlin), 1983; *Hungarian Studies* (Weöres), 1983; *Nonsense Madrigals* (William Brighty Rands, Heinrich Hoffmann, Lewis Carroll), 6 men's v, 1988–93

Songs: 3 Songs (Weöres), 1946–7; 5 Songs (János Arany), 1952; 'Der Sommer' (Hölderlin), 1989

Tape: *Glissandi*, 1957; *Pièce électronique* No.3, 1957–8, realized 1996; *Artikulation*, 1958

Miscellaneous: *Die Zukunft der Musik*, lecturer, audience, 1961; *Poème symphonique*, 100 metronomes, 1962; *Rondeau*, actor, tape, 1976; Etude XIVa, pianola, arr 1993

light. See COLOUR.

light baritone. Bright, youthful singer or role.

Light Cavalry. Popular overture by Suppé.

light classics. Term, current especially in the early and mid-20th century, for instrumental pieces that are classical in constitution (for modest orchestra, chamber group, piano) but have more the brevity and simplicity of a popular song or dance. The category would include shorter POPULAR CLASSICS (e.g. Fauré's *Pavane*), movements from classical works, dances, marches, some film music, and items by such specialist composers as Ketèlbey and Coates.

light music. Term embracing LIGHT CLASSICS and popular music a generation or more old. See also POPS.

light opera. Operetta and related forms, including opera buffa and musicals.

light orchestra. Orchestra specializing in light music.

light soprano. Bright, youthful singer or role. The SOUBRETTE is a subcategory.

light tenor. Bright, youthful singer or role.

Lilburn, Douglas (Gordon) (b. Wanganui, 2 Nov 1915; d. Wellington, 6 Jun 2001). New Zealand composer, the father of classical music there. He evolved from a national Romanticism in the mode of Vaughan Williams (with whom he studied at the RCM, 1937–40) through mainstream modernism to avant-garde pursuits from the 1960s onwards. Teaching at Victoria University in Wellington (1947–79), he established there the first Australasian electronic music studio. His works include three symphonies.

Lim, Liza (b. Perth, 30 Aug 1966). Australian composer, an impassioned modernist for whom the newest sounds and techniques link up with ancient ritual practices. She studied in Melbourne and with Ton de Leeuw in Amsterdam, and has been particularly associated with Elision. Her works include small-scale operas (*The Oresteia*, 1991–3) and orchestral scores (*The Tree of Life*, 2001).

limerick. Choice form for music criticism, e.g.:

The music of Abbé Franz Liszt
If loszt would never be miszt:
They all stood aghaszt
As he played oh-so-faszt,
But moszt of the time he was piszt.

Lincoln Center for the Performing Arts. Site in New York, so called because it was built over the former Lincoln Square, itself named after a local farmer. Neighbours there are the JUILLIARD SCHOOL, two theatres, a branch of the Public Library and four musical venues: the METROPOLITAN OPERA, the New York State Theater (opened 1964, seating 2,737), Avery Fisher Hall (opened 1962, seating 2,378) and Alice Tully Hall (opened 1969, seating 1,096).

Lind, Jenny [Lind-Goldschmidt, Johanna Maria] (b. Stockholm, 6 Oct 1820; d. Wynds Point, Herefordshire, 2 Nov 1887). Swedish soprano, 'the Swedish nightingale'. She entered the school of the Royal Opera in Stockholm in 1830, and appeared in smaller roles there before making her official debut as Agathe in *Der Freischütz* (1838). After further studies with Manuel Garcia in Paris (1841–2) she returned to the Stockholm opera, then appeared in Germany and Vienna (1843–7), Britain (1847–9) and, under the auspices of Phineas T. Barnum, the USA and Havana (1850–51). Those were her golden years, though she continued singing until 1883, when she began teaching at the RCM. For Chopin, who heard her in *La sonnambula* in 1848, she was 'surrounded not by an ordinary halo but by a kind of northern lights …. She sings with amazing purity and certainty, and her *piano* is so steady – as smooth and even as a thread of hair'.

Lindberg, Magnus (b. Helsinki, 27 Jun 1958). Finnish composer, especially of orchestral music moving from late modernism into more continuous dynamism and exuberant colour. He studied with Rautavaara and Heininen at the Sibelius Academy (1977–81), and attended courses at Darmstadt and IRCAM. With his academy classmates, including Saariaho and Salonen, he founded Toimii (Ears Open), whose members he featured in his massively powerful *Kraft* for orchestra (1983–5), the work that gained him international attention. Later orchestral works include *Aura* (1993–4) and the triptych of *Feria* (1997), *Parada* (2001) and *Cantigas* (1997–9).

line. Informal term whose meanings all have to do with continuity, as in 'melodic line' (drawing attention to the linear aspect of melody), 'bass line' (normally used for music that is essentially chordal and bass-directed), or 'contrapuntal line'. One may also speak of the line of a movement or entire composition, meaning its overall span.

linear. Having evident contrapuntal lines.

line-up. Choice of instruments.

Liniensystem (Ger.). Staff (in notation).

linke Hand (Ger.). Left hand.

Linley. British musical family.

(1) **Thomas** (b. Badminton, 17 Jan 1733; d. London, 19 Nov 1795). An all-round musician, who trained under Thomas Chilcot at Bath Abbey and Boyce in London. He made his reputation in Bath and worked for the London theatre from 1767. He became joint manager of the Drury Lane theatre with Sheridan, who had eloped with (and married) his daughter, Elizabeth Ann, a theatre and oratorio soprano. Several of his other 11 children became musicians, including his eldest son:

(2) **Thomas** (b. Bath, 5 May 1756; d. Grimsthorpe, Lincs., 5 Aug 1778). Brilliant and full of promise, he played a violin concerto in Bristol at seven, then studied with Boyce in London (1763–8) and Nardini in Florence (1768–71), where he met his close contemporary Mozart. He returned to his family in Bath and London, and led the Drury Lane orchestra from 1773, meanwhile composing both theatre music (notably for Sheridan's *The Duenna*, to which his father also contributed) and songs, choral pieces, concertos and sonatas for the family's concerts. Gainsborough painted his portrait twice (and his father's once). His death, in a boating accident, was much lamented.

Linus. Ambiguous figure in Greek mythology, evoked in ritual lament and sometimes considered the son (and rival) of Apollo and discoverer of music.

Linz. Name given to Mozart's Symphony No.36, written and first performed there.

lion's roar. See STRING DRUM.

lip. A part of the body energetically worked by brass players. A work or programme making much

use of the brass may therefore be said to be hard on the players' lips. See EMBOUCHURE.

Lipatti, Dinu [Constantin] (b. Bucharest, 19 Mar 1917; d. Geneva, 2 Dec 1950). Romanian pianist, who is keenly remembered for the poetry of his playing, the fruit of supreme technical control and a fine musical intelligence, a poetry as remarkable in Bach as in Chopin. Born into a musical family (Enescu was his godfather), he studied at the Bucharest Conservatory with Florica Musicescu and in Paris with Cortot, Münch, Boulanger and Dukas. He returned to Romania in 1939 and moved to Geneva in 1943. A progressive cancer curtailed his public career (though he went on recording as well as giving occasional recitals) and led to his early death.

lira da braccio (It.). Viola-like instrument of the Renaissance, used especially in Italy by poet-musicians to accompany themselves with music largely in chords. It had seven strings, five passing over the fingerboard and two positioned obliquely, where they could provide a drone.

lira organizzata (It.). 18th-century instrument, a hurdy-gurdy (*lira*) incorporating a miniature organ, with a mechanism to make sound from strings, pipes or both. It was a favourite of Ferdinand IV of Naples, who commissioned works for it from Haydn.

lirico spinto. See SPINTO.

lirone (It.). Cello-size adaptation of the LIRA DA BRACCIO, similarly having two drone strings, but with 9–14 strings over the fingerboard, which differed too in being fretted. First mentioned in connection with the 1565 Florentine intermedi, it probably never left Italy and fell out of use in the middle of the next century.

Lisinski, Vatroslav (baptized Zagreb, 8 Jul 1819; d. Zagreb, 31 May 1854). Croatian composer, the region's pioneer Romantic musician. Born Ignacije Fuchs, he changed his name after returning from studies with Kittl and Karl Franz Pitsch in Prague in the late 1840s. His works consist mostly of songs, piano pieces and choral items, but he also wrote two operas – *Love and Malice* (f.p. Zagreb, 1845) was the first in Croatia – and orchestral pieces.

listen. Pay heed to by ear. In the everyday world we may listen to gather information about the environment, listen to the content and delivery of a public message (from an actor, a news broadcaster), listen to someone speaking just to us, listen to the qualities of a sound that has attracted our attention, listen into a conversation not meant for us, listen out for a signal. All these modes of listening, and more, may be engaged by music. Listening implies active attention, which may lapse from time to time through a piece that is unfamiliar or over-familiar, or through a mediocre performance. A strong performance may be described as 'compelling', i.e. compelling such attention.

Liszt, Franz (b. Raiding/Doborján, 22 Oct 1811; d. Bayreuth, 31 Jul 1886). Hungarian composer and pianist. Diverse and mercurial, he was a showman and a contemplative, forward-looking and backward-yearning, enraptured by the theatre and thrilled by the Church, a man of carnal appetites and religious aspirations, of mockery and prayer. He lived his life from boyhood in the public gaze, while turning himself from a concert virtuoso into a court conductor and finally into a wandering eminence in ecclesiastical garb: 'Mephistopheles disguised as an abbé' (i.e. minor cleric), as he was described by the historian Ferdinand Gregorovius. His enormous musical output follows all the twists in his complex career and personality. Throughout was one constant: the piano.

His father, of Hungarian family (the surname is the word for flour), served the court of Prince Nikolaus Esterházy and thereby played cello in Haydn's orchestra; his mother came from southern Germany. The story goes that when he was six he became fascinated by the sound of the piano as played by his father, who began giving him lessons. By the age of eight he was composing, and at just nine he made his debut in Sopron, after which a group of notabilities provided for his education. The next year, 1821, his family took him to Vienna, where he studied with Czerny and Salieri, then made a spectacular debut on 1 December 1822. He remembered all his life that Beethoven kissed his brow at his second concert on 13 April 1823, a moment he regarded as a baptism into art. A variation for Diabelli's set (1823) was his first publication.

That same year the Liszt family moved to Paris, where he continued his studies with Reicha and Paer, and where he continued also to astonish at his concerts, given in Paris, elsewhere in France and in England, when he was still in his early teens. The Liszt frenzy even resulted in an opera, which he wrote with Paer's help. In 1827, however, no longer a child prodigy, he gave up touring to settle in Paris as a teacher, and as the honoured acquaintance of the many distinguished artists crowded in what was now the capital of European culture: Berlioz, Bellini, Donizetti and Chopin among composers, Hugo, Alfred de Musset, Alphonse de Lamartine and Heine among writers. Inclinations to the priesthood were quashed by his mother (his father died in 1827) but not eradicated. Meanwhile he seems to have been preparing himself for a new start as a composer – a new start that began in 1833–4 with a transcription of Berlioz's *Symphonie fantastique*, a fantasy for piano and orchestra after the same composer's *Lélio*, and some original pieces.

Around the time of these first mature creative and re-creative efforts he met the Countess Marie d'Agoult. Her description of him complements several photographs soon taken: he had, she wrote, 'an exceedingly tall and thin figure, a pale face with sea-green eyes which shone with rapid flashes like waves in flames … an indecisive walk in which he seemed to glide'. Having hands in proportion with his figure, he could easily stretch a 10th; reports of his playing further emphasize strength and clarity. According to Hallé, who heard him in this period: 'Liszt was all sunshine and dazzling splendour, subjugating his hearers with a power that none could withstand. For him there were no difficulties of execution, the most incredible seeming child's play under his fingers. One of the transcendent merits of his playing was the crystal-like clearness which never failed for a moment even in the most complicated and, to anybody else, impossible passages.'

In 1835 the first of these witnesses, with whom he had started an affair, left her husband and family to be with him in Geneva, where their daughter Blandine (1835–62) was born; two more children followed: Cosima (1837–1930), later Wagner's wife, and Daniel (1839–59). The growing family stayed in Switzerland and Italy, while he gained travel impressions to be reworked in the first two books of his *Années de pèlerinage*, and also made his beginnings as a song composer. Then, within months of Daniel's birth, he and Marie split up. She and the children returned to Paris, while he resumed the life of an itinerant virtuoso, crossing Europe from Portugal and Ireland to Russia and Turkey, not excluding Hungary, which he revisited in 1840. He found new mistresses in Paris (where he supervised his children's education), but much of the time he was on the road, performing an enormous repertory that stretched from Bach to Chopin and Schumann, and included transcriptions he made of Beethoven symphonies and Schubert songs. His original creative output – of piano pieces, songs and choral items – was correspondingly moderate during this time.

He settled down again in February 1848 in

Weimar, into a new career as music director to the grand ducal court; he had held the position since 1842, but now was taking it seriously. What prompted him to do so – and to take himself seriously as a composer – was his new relationship with the Princess Carolyne Sayn-Wittgenstein, whom he had met in Kiev a year before. She, like Marie, was married, and her efforts to get a divorce went on for the next dozen years, while she lived with Liszt in Weimar as his wife. There, with an orchestra and an opera house at his disposal, he became a vigorous supporter of the NEW GERMAN SCHOOL, of which he made Weimar the intellectual hub, attracting disciples who included von Bülow, Cornelius and Tausig. He conducted the première of *Lohengrin* and also presented works by Berlioz, Schumann, Donizetti and Verdi. He sketched an opera himself (after Byron's *Sardanapalus*), but preferred the orchestra, rapidly producing several essays in a new genre, the SYMPHONIC POEM, and working up his two concertos, which dated back to the 1830s. Feeling insecure at first in this unaccustomed medium, he sought help with orchestration from Raff and Conradi, but was soon scoring and rescoring his works himself. Then, as the climax of his orchestral venture, came two symphonies, on Goethe's *Faust* and Dante's *Divine Comedy*, both first performed in 1857.

The piano was not neglected. While in Weimar he produced the definitive versions of the *Etudes d'exécution transcendante*, the Paganini études, *Harmonies poétiques et religieuses*, the first two books of *Années de pèlerinage* and most of the Hungarian Rhapsodies, bringing his major piano works up to date with his thinking and with developments in piano construction. High among new works was the B minor Sonata (1852–3), remarkable not only for virtuosity but also for intensity of feeling and gripping form. In this piece he developed his technique of thematic transformation to a point where it could support an entire symphonic argument in a single movement (following intimations in late Beethoven and Schubert's 'Wanderer' Fantasy) and create a continuous dialogue of strongly expressive ideas. Placed on display here and in the symphonic poems, the technique – and the harmonic venturesomeness it encouraged and supported – was keenly noted by Wagner.

His music, his tastes and his private life also gained him opposition, and in August 1861 he left for Rome, where Carolyne had already gone to present her divorce case to the pope (the tsar having failed her). Though the Holy Father did not ultimately oblige, they stayed on in Rome, separately, and Liszt took steps that made marriage

impossible: he moved into the Oratorio della Madonna del Rosario (1863) and was ordained an abbé (1865), stopping short of the priesthood. Unusual as this ascent was for a virtuoso, it made sense within the process of thematic transformation that was his life; he had been pious from childhood, and had been expressing that piety in religious works since the mid-1850s – as he was to go on doing. He had, besides, recently lost two of his children.

The survivor was meanwhile beginning her affair with Wagner, and though she was doing exactly what her mother had done – abandon her husband for a musician – Liszt blamed Wagner and there was a rift. Characteristically, though, that did not stop him from showing his admiration for Wagner in piano arrangements, even of music from the work his daughter had grasped with its author: *Tristan*. For though he was now making only occasional appearances as a pianist at charity concerts, he never lost the old desire to transcribe music he loved, his own and others'. There were also important original pieces, including the 'Weinen, klagen, sorgen, zagen' variations (1862), written after his elder daughter's death, and the two St Francis legends (1862–3).

There were also more journeys. In 1869 he began making regular return visits to Weimar, to teach and conduct, and from 1871 he was periodically in Budapest. Reconciled with Wagner in 1872, he attended the Bayreuth festival and was with his daughter's family in Venice in 1882, when he wrote *La Lugubre Gondola* in response to a presentiment of Wagner's death. He also pursued his internal pilgrimage, to a point extraordinarily removed from showmanship. His late works – comprising mostly sacred music (*Via Crucis*), a last symphonic poem (*Von der Wiege bis zum Grabe*) and piano pieces – are grave, austere and on the furthest edge of diatonic harmony. They stare out into the future.

He died in Bayreuth eight days after the première of *Parsifal*, and since then much of his music has slept, the comparatively few works regularly performed including the concertos, the sonata, several of the flashier, more illustrative items from the *Années de pèlerinage* books and other collections, and, among the symphonic poems, *Les Préludes*. These project an exciting image, but a partial one. They leave out the complexity of an artist who could be obscure, sentimental, excessive and even trashy. They also omit the modernity of one who was not primarily an originator of masterpieces, more a reactor to occasion and opportunity (hence his constant willingness to arrange, revise and adapt), and, beyond that, a capacious space within which almost all the music of his time and culture could be found – the 19th century's record superstore.

Alan Walker *Franz Liszt*, 3 Vols. (1983–97)

Vocal, orchestral, chamber and organ music

Opera: *Don Sanche* (Théaulon de Lambert and de Rancé; music with Paer), f.p. Paris, 1825

Oratorios: *Die Legende von der heiligen Elisabeth* (Otto Roquette), 1857–62; CHRISTUS, 1866–72

Other choral works: *Missa solemnis* (Gran Mass), soli, ch, orch, 1855–8; *Cantico del sol di San Francesco d'Assisi*, bar, men's ch, orch, 2 versions, 1862, 1879–82; *Missa choralis*, ch, org, 1859–65; VIA CRUCIS, ch, org/pf, 1876–9; *Salve regina*, ch, 1885; *Psalm 129*, bar, men's ch, org, 1883–6; etc.

Orchestral with piano: PIANO CONCERTO No.1, E♭, finished 1835–56; No.2, A, 1839–61; *Malédiction*, pf, str, 1833–40; *Totentanz*, 1847–?62; Fantasia on Beethoven's *Ruins of Athens*, 1848–52; *Concerto pathétique*, 1849–50, rev 1885; Fantasia on Hungarian Folktunes, 1849–52

Symphonic poems: CE QU'ON ENTEND SUR LA MONTAGNE (No.1), 1847–56; TASSO (No.2), 1847–54; *Les* PRELUDES (No.3), 1849–55; ORPHEUS (No.4), 1853–4; PROMETHEUS (No.5), 1850–55; MAZEPPA (No.6), 1851–4; FESTKLÄNGE (No.7), 1853–61; HEROIDE FUNEBRE (No.8), 1849–56; HUNGARIA (No.9), 1854; HAMLET (No.10), 1858; HUNNENSCHLACHT (No.11), 1857; *Die* IDEALE (No.12), 1856–7; VON DER WIEGE BIS ZUM GRABE (No.13), 1881–2

Other orchestral works: FAUST Symphony, 1854–7, rev 1861 (also version with t, men's ch); DANTE Symphony, 1855–6; 6 HUNGARIAN RHAPSODIES, 1857–60; 2 Episodes from Nikolaus Lenau's *Faust*, 1857–61; *Trois odes funèbres*, 1860–66; etc.

Orchestrations: *Wandererfantaisie* (Schubert), pf, orch, by 1852; *Polonaise brillante* (Weber), pf, orch, 1849; etc.

Chamber: *Am Grabe Richard Wagners*, str qt, hp ad lib, 1883; *La Lugubre Gondola*, vn/vc, pf, 1882–5; etc.

Songs: 'Der du von dem Himmel bist' (Goethe), 4 versions, 1842–70; 'Die drei Zigeuner' (Lenau), 2 versions, 1860; 'Es muss ein Wunderbares sein' (von Redwitz), 1852; 'Freudvoll und Leidvoll' (Goethe), 3 versions, 1844–9; 'Die Loreley' (Heine), 2 versions, 1841–59; 'Oh! quand je dors' (Hugo), 2 versions, 1842–9; *Tre sonetti del Petrarca*, 2 versions, 1842–6, 1864–82; 'Über allen Gipfeln ist Ruh'' (Goethe), 2 versions, 1848–59; etc.

Recitations: *Lenore* (Gottfried August Bürger), 1857–8; etc.

Organ: Fantasy and Fugue on the Chorale 'Ad nos, ad salutarem undam', 1850; Prelude and Fugue on BACH, 1855–6, rev 1869–70; Variations on 'WEINEN, KLAGEN, SORGEN, ZAGEN', ?1862–3; etc.

Piano music

Original works: *Grand galop chromatique*, 1838; ETUDES D'EXECUTION TRANSCENDANTE *d'après Paganini*, 1838–40, rev as *Grandes études de Paganini*, 1851; *Tre sonetti del Petrarca*, 1843–6 (rev in *Années*, Vol.2); *Rhapsodie espagnole*, 1848; 3 Concert Etudes, 1845–9 (*Il lamento, La leggierezza, Un sospiro*); *Liebesträume* (3 Notturnos), 1843–50; *Consolations* (6) 1849–50; ETUDES D'EXECUTION TRANSCENDANTE, 1851; Scherzo and March, 1851; HARMONIES POETIQUES ET RELIGIEUSES, 2 versions, 1840–53; *Valse-impromptu*, 1850–52; HUNGARIAN RHAPSODIES Nos.1–15, 1846–53; Sonata, B minor, 1852–3; Ballade No.2, B minor, 1853; ANNEES DE PELERINAGE, Vol.1, 1848–55, Vol.2, 1838–61, supplement *Venezia e Napoli*, 1838–59; Prelude on 'WEINEN, KLAGEN, SORGEN, ZAGEN', 1859; Berceuse, D♭, 1854–62; First MEPHISTO WALTZ, 1856–61; 2 Concert Etudes, 1862 (*Waldesrauschen, Gnomenreigen*); Variations on 'WEINEN, KLAGEN, SORGEN, ZAGEN', 1862; *Deux légendes*, 1863 (*St François d'Assise: la prédication aux oiseaux, St François de Paule marchant sur les flots*); Fantasia and Fugue on BACH, 1870; Impromptu (Nocturne), 1872; *Weihnachtsbaum*, 1874–6; *Sancta Dorothea*, 1877; *Die Zelle in Nonnenwerth*, 4 versions, 1841–80; Second MEPHISTO WALTZ, 1878–81; *Nuages gris*, 1881; *Unstern!*, 1881; ANNEES DE PELERINAGE, Vol.3, 1877–82; *Csárdás macabre*, 1881–2; *La Lugubre Gondola*, 2 versions, 1882–5; *R.W. – Venezia*, 1883; *Am Grabe Richard Wagners*, 1883; *Schlaflos*, 1883; Third MEPHISTO WALTZ, 1883; *Csárdás obstiné*, 1884; HUNGARIAN RHAPSODIES Nos.16–19, 1882–5; *Valses oubliées* (4), 1881–4 (No.1, F♯); *Bagatelle sans tonalité*, 1885; *En rêve*, 1885; etc.

Operatic fantasies: *Réminiscences de Lucia di Lammermoor*, 1835–6; HEXAMERON, 1837–8; *Fantaisie sur La sonnambula*, 2 versions, 1839–?42; *Réminiscences de Don Juan*, 1841; *Réminiscences de Norma*, 1841; Fantasia on themes from *Figaro* and *Don Giovanni*, 1842; *Tarantelle di bravura* after *La muette de Portici*, 1846; *Rigoletto: paraphrase de concert*, ?1855; *Réminiscences de Boccanegra*, 1882; etc.

Symphony transcriptions: *Symphonie fantastique* (Berlioz), 1833, rev c.1876; Beethoven Nos.5–7 and funeral march from No.3, 1837; Beethoven Nos.1–9, 1863–4

Bach transcriptions: Prelude and Fugue, A minor, 1842–50; Fantasia and Fugue, G minor, 1869

Schubert transcriptions: 12 songs, 1837–8 ('Auf dem Wasser zu singen', 'Erlkönig', 'Meeresstille', 'Frühlingsglaube', 'Gretchen am Spinnrade', 'Ständchen "Horch, horch!"', 'Das Wandern', 'Ave Maria'); *Schwanengesang*, 1838–9 ('Liebesbotschaft', 'Ständchen "Leise flehen"'); *Winterreise*, 1838–9; other songs ('Die Forelle', 2 versions, 1844–6; 'Der Müller und der Bach', 1846; 'Wohin?', 1846); etc.

Wagner transcriptions: Overture *Tannhäuser*, 1847; 'O du mein holder Abendstern' (*Tannhäuser*), 1849; *Festspiel und Brautlied* (*Lohengrin*), 1854; *Elsas Traum und Lohengrins Verweis*, 1854; *Spinnerlied* (*Holländer*), 1860; *Isoldens Liebestod*, 1867; *Feierliche Marsch zum heiligen Gral*, 1882; etc.

Other transcriptions: 'Le Rossignol' (Alyab'yev), 1842; 6 songs (Chopin), 1857–60; Waltz from *Faust*

(Gounod), 1861; Overture to *Guillaume Tell* (Rossini), ?1838–41; *Danse macabre* (Saint-Saëns), 1876; *Widmung* (Schumann), ?1846–60s; *Frühlingsnacht* (Schumann), 1872; Polonaise from *Eugene Onegin*, 1879; 'Miserere' from *Il trovatore*, 1859; *Danza sacra e duetto final* from *Aida*, ?1876; etc.

Duo/duet: versions of orchestral and solo piano works

Liszt Academy. The principal conservatory in Budapest, founded as the Academy of Music in 1875 and given Liszt's name 50 years later.

litany. Act of praise, wherein a sacred person or object is repeatedly invoked. One such is the *Litania lauretana*, or Litany of Loreto, associated with the Holy House in that city and devoted to the Virgin Mary. There are settings by Victoria, Palestrina, Lassus, Gabrieli, Charpentier, Mozart, Schubert and Bruckner, several of whom also set other litanies.

literature. See FICTION.

Literaturoper (Ger., literature-opera). Opera closely based on an acknowledged literary text, and exemplifying a 20th-century tendency to widen operatic subject matter and form. Thus Reimann's *Lear* would qualify, but not Verdi's *Otello*.

lithophone. Instrument making sound from struck stone, or stone out-of-doors used for this purpose. Stone chimes and tuned stones have appeared in works by Stockhausen, Crumb and others.

Litolff, Henry (Charles) (b. London, 7 Aug 1818; d. Bois-Colombes, 5 Aug 1891). Franco–German pianist-composer, whose colourful life began when he was born to a Scot who had married a dance-master prisoner-of-war from Alsace. He studied with his father and Moscheles (1830–35), eloped at 17, separated from his wife a few years later, returned to England and was imprisoned (1845), escaped with the help of the jailer's daughter, at last got his divorce, married the widowed owner of a music publishing firm in Brunswick (1851), was divorced again (1858), settled in Paris, and was finally married to a 17-year-old after the death of his third wife (1873). He is remembered for this, and for the scherzo from the fourth of his five *concertos symphoniques* (Op.102, c.1852).

Little C major. Name sometimes given to Schubert's Sixth Symphony, in distinction from his Ninth.

Little G minor. Name given to Mozart's Symphony No.25, in distinction from his No.40.

Little Russian. Name given to Tchaikovsky's Second Symphony by his critic friend Nikolay Kashkin, 'Little Russia' being an affectionate term for Ukraine, whence some of the work's melodies derive.

liturgical drama. Medieval enactment of a gospel story or other sacred tale, e.g. the PLAY OF DANIEL and VISITATIO SEPULCHRI.

liturgy. Sacred service, especially in Orthodox and Catholic churches, though the term is regularly used in Jewish contexts and has been extended to cover ceremonial acts not sanctioned by any religious body (e.g. Messiaen's *Trois petites liturgies*).

liuto (It.). Lute.

live electronic music. Music whose performers work with amplified sound in unusual ways. Since the category of unusualness inevitably diminishes through time, the term applies most comfortably to music from the high noon of the post-war avant-garde, in the 1960s and early 1970s – before the use of electronics in performance was smoothened by technological advance (particularly in the availability of portable computers as well as sophisticated samplers and synthesizers) and habit. Emphatically empirical, live electronic music was an art for performer-improvisers and for groups (e.g. Musica Elettronica Viva, AMM), though Cage and Stockhausen produced open-ended scores for live electronic interpretation.

Livre d'orgue (Organbook). Organ work by Messiaen in seven movements mixing abstraction, biblical imagery and nature study: 1 *Reprises par interversion*, 2 *Pièce en trio*, 3 *Les mains de l'abîme*, 4 *Chants d'oiseaux*, 5 *Pièce en trio*, 6 *Les yeux dans les roues*, 7 *Soixante-quatre durées*. First performance: Stuttgart, 23 Apr 1952.

Livre du Saint Sacrement, Le (The Book of the Holy Sacrement). Organ work by Messiaen in 18 movements: 1 *Adoro te*, 2 *La Source de Vie*, 3 *Le Dieu caché*, 4 *Acte de foi*, 5 *Puer natus est nobis*, 6 *La Manne et le Pain de Vie*, 7 *Les Ressuscités et la Lumière de Vie*, 8 *Institution de l'Eucharistie*, 9 *Les Ténèbres*, 10 *La Résurrection du Christ*, 11 *L'Apparition du Christ ressuscité à Marie-Madeleine*, 12 *La Transubstantiation*, 13 *Les Deux Murailles d'eau*, 14 *Prière avant la Communion*, 15 *La Joie de la grâce*, 16 *Prière après la Communion*, 17 *La Présence* *multipliée*, 18 *Offrande et alleluia final*. First performance: Detroit, 1 Jul 1986.

livret (Fr.). Libretto.

Lloyd, George (Walter Selwyn) (b. St Ives, Cornwall, 28 Jun 1913; d. London, 3 Jul 1998). British composer, a belated late Romantic. Trained at the Trinity College of Music, he had early success as a symphonist and opera composer: *Iernin* had a three-week run in London (1935) and *The Serf* was staged at Covent Garden (1938). Wartime shipwreck contributed to his later troubles, and though he had a Festival of Britain commission for his third opera, *John Socman* (f.p. Bristol, 1951), his career went into decline and he survived as a grower of mushrooms and carnations. He nevertheless went on composing, and was rewarded by a revival of interest during his last two decades. His works include 12 symphonies and *The Vigil of Venus* for soli, choir and orchestra (1980).

Lloyd, Jonathan (b. London, 30 Sep 1948). British composer, provocative and sometimes disturbing in his ranges of reference and swerves of style. He studied with Edwin Roxburgh and John Lambert at the RCM (1966–9). His works include five symphonies (1983–9), of which No.2 is a version of his piquant Mass for six voices (1983) and No.5 is for chamber ensemble.

Lobgesang. Name Mendelssohn gave his Second Symphony, in which three orchestral movements are followed by a biblical cantata with soli and choir. First performance: Leipzig, 25 Jun 1840.

Lobkowitz, Joseph Franz Maximilian Fürst (b. Roudnice nad Lebem, 7 Dec 1772; d. Třeboň, 15 Dec 1816). Austrian patron. He commissioned Haydn's Op.77 quartets and lavishly supported Beethoven, being rewarded with the dedications of the Third, Fifth and Sixth symphonies, the Triple Concerto, the Op.18 and Op.74 quartets, and *An die ferne Geliebte*. His father and grandfather nurtured Gluck.

Lobo, Alonso (b. Osuna, 25 Feb 1555; d. Seville, 5 Apr 1617). Spanish composer and church musician, a learned polyphonist. He became a Seville Cathedral choirboy at 11 and studied at the university in his home town, where he remained before taking posts as Guerrero's assistant in Seville (1591–3) and chapelmaster at the cathedrals of Toledo (1593–1604) and again Seville (from 1604). His works include a published book of six masses (1602) as well as motets (*Versa est in luctum a 6*).

Locatelli, Pietro Antonio (b. Bergamo, 3 Sep 1695; d. Amsterdam, 30 Mar 1764). Italian violinist-composer, a pioneer virtuoso who left a dazzling image of his accomplishments in the 24 capriccios he included in his 12 concertos, *L'arte del violino*, Op.3 (1733). Employed at Santa Maria Maggiore in Bergamo by the age of 14, he travelled to Rome (1711–23), where he continued his studies within the Corelli school and played for Cardinal Pietro Ottoboni. His first publication was a volume of 12 concerti grossi, among them his 'Christmas Concerto' in F minor (1721). He then travelled in Italy and Germany before settling in 1729 in Amsterdam, where he became active in publishing and book dealing, now performing only for a small circle of connoisseurs at his own home.

Locke, Matthew (b. ?Exeter, 1621–3; d. London, ?Aug 1677). English composer, the foremost of his age, in every field of musical creativity. Trained as a choirboy at Exeter Cathedral, he may have gone with the future Charles II to France in 1646 and become a Catholic while abroad. He then spent time back in Exeter and in Herefordshire, where he married. During this period he probably concentrated on consort music, of which he published a volume of 10 suites (*The Little Consort*, 1656). Later collections, not published, include *The Broken Consort* (another 10 suites) and the imposing *Consort of Four Parts* (six suites). Also in 1656 he wrote his first theatre music, for The SIEGE OF RHODES, indicating he was now in London. He also revised Christopher Gibbons's music for a revival of the masque *Cupid and Death*. At the Restoration in 1660 he became one of the leading court musicians, attached to the 24 Violins and to the Catholic queen's chapel as organist, besides writing MUSIC FOR HIS MAJESTY'S SACKBUTS AND CORNETTS, keyboard music (published in his *Melothesia, or Certain General Rules for Playing upon a Continued-Bass*), anthems and more theatre music, including the masque of Orpheus in *The Empress of Morocco* (1673), string pieces for *The Tempest* (1674) and the semi-opera *Psyche* (1675). Anecdotes suggest the evident spirit of his music was matched by his own hot temper.

Lockenhaus. Austrian castle, near the Hungarian border, site of a summer festival founded in 1981 by Kremer for chamber music of mixed repertory, presented informally.

Lockwood, Annea (b. Christchurch, 29 Jul 1939). New Zealand composer, active in experimental and environmental music. She studied at the RCM (1961–3) and with Koenig in Cologne, and made her name giving performances of her *Glass*

Concert on glass instruments from 1966 to 1973, when she moved to the USA. There her works have ranged from electronic installations (*A Sound Map of the Hudson River*, 1982) to pieces for standard instruments. She also taught at Vassar (1982–2001).

loco (It., place). Marking to remind the performer, after a passage in changed register (see OTTAVA), that notes are now to be played as written.

Locrian. Mode B–C–D–E–F–G–A–B with F as final; Glarean's Hyperaeolian.

Loeffler, Charles [Karl] **Martin** (b. ?Mulhouse, 30 Jan 1861; d. Medfield, Mass., 19 May 1935). German–US composer and violinist. He claimed Alsatian origin but may have been born in the neighbourhood of Berlin, where certainly he studied with Joachim, Bargiel and the violinist Eduard Rappoldi (1874–7), before completing his education in Paris with Joseph Massart and Guiraud. In 1881 he moved to the USA, and then joined the Boston Symphony (1882–1903), afterwards retiring to his farm at Medfield and to his music, rich and colourful as it was, with French influences. He wrote operas, orchestral pieces (*A Pagan Poem*, Op.14, 1906), violin pieces and songs.

Loeillet. Flemish musical family. Pieter (1651–1735) was a violinist in Ghent and Bordeaux, and probably responsible for imparting music to his nephews as well as his sons.

(1) **John** [Jean-Baptiste] 'of London' (baptized Ghent, 18 Nov 1680; d. London, 10 Jul 1730). Composer-performer. Pieter's nephew, he is credited with introducing both the transverse flute and Corelli's concerti grossi to London, where he settled *c*.1705 and gave weekly concerts. He also published sonatas, trio sonatas and keyboard suites.

(2) **Jacques** (baptized Ghent, 7 Jul 1685; d. Ghent, 28 Nov 1748). Oboist-composer. John's brother, he was active at the courts of Munich and Versailles. He wrote sonatas and concertos.

(3) **Jean-Baptiste** 'de Gant' (baptized Ghent, 6 Jul 1688; d. Lyons, *c*.1720). Composer. Pieter's eldest son, he was in service to the Archbishop of Lyons. He published four collections of 12 recorder sonatas (several more familiar now in arrangements for trumpet and organ) and one of trio sonatas.

Loevendie, Theo (b. Amsterdam, 17 Sep 1930). Dutch composer, emerging as such in 1969 after a rich career as a jazz clarinettist. His works – chiefly chamber pieces, concertos and operas – reflect that background, and also his absorption in Turkish, African and other non-European traditions.

Loewe, (Johann) Carl (Gottfried) (b. Löbejün, near Halle, 30 Nov 1796; d. Kiel, 20 Apr 1869). German singer-composer, remembered almost exclusively for his ballads, which he performed himself and in which he maintained the tastes of his youth in terms of subject matter (the supernatural, the world of chivalry) and musical style. The son of a cantor-schoolteacher, he studied with Daniel Gottlob Türk at the Franke Institute in Halle, supported himself through university as an organist, and became music director in Stettin (1821–66). From there he travelled through Germany and abroad balladeering. Being out of fashion gained him princely favour, especially in Berlin, if it limited later appreciation.

Ballads: 'Archibald Douglas' (Fontane), Op.128, 1857; 'Edward' (Herder), Op.1:1, 1818; 'Erlkönig' (Goethe), Op.1:3, 1818; 'Der heilige Franziskus' (Heinrich von Wessenberg), Op.75:3, 1837; 'Heinrich der Vogler' (Johann Nepomuk Vogl), Op.56:1, 1836; 'Herr Oluf' (Herder), Op.2:2, 1821; 'Hochzeitlied' (Goethe), Op.20:1, 1832; 'Kleiner Haushalt' (Rückert), Op.71, 1838; 'Odins Meeresritt' (Aloys Wilhelm Schreiber), Op.118, 1851; 'Prinz Eugen' (Ferdinand Freiligrath), Op.92, 1844; 'Spirito Santo' (Emilie van der Goltz), Op.143, 1864; 'Tom der Reimer', Op.135a, *c*.1860; 'Die Uhr' (Johann Gabriel Seidl), Op.123:3, 1852; etc.

Songs: 'Heimlichkeit' (Karl Siebel), Op.145:4, *c*.1859; 'Meeresleuchten' (Siebel), Op.145:1, *c*.1859; etc.

Other works: partsongs, chamber music, piano pieces, operas, oratorios

Lohengrin. Opera by Wagner to his own libretto. Lohengrin (tenor) makes a magical arrival in medieval Brabant, on a boat drawn by a swan, to champion Elsa (soprano) in her struggle for succession against Telramund (baritone) and his sinister wife, Ortrud (mezzo-soprano). His condition: Elsa must not ask his name. He defeats Telramund in single combat, but Ortrud sows the seeds of doubt in Elsa's mind. Newly wed to Lohengrin, she cannot keep from asking who he is and so bringing about his departure. Notable extracts include the preludes to acts 1 and 3, Elsa's Dream from before Lohengrin's arrival ('Einsam in trüben Tagen'), the Bridal Chorus ('Treulich geführt', habitually played by organists at weddings for the bride's entry), Lohengrin's Narration in which he discloses he is a grail knight and son of Parsifal ('In fernem Land') and his Farewell ('Mein lieber Schwan'). First performance: Weimar, 28 Aug 1850.

Lolli, Antonio (b. Bergamo, *c*.1725; d. Palermo, 10 Aug 1802). Italian violinist-composer, the greatest virtuoso of his age. Attached to the Württemberg court from 1758, he married the sister-in-law of the French choreographer Jean Georges Noverre. On tour he played in Paris, Vienna and elsewhere, and while chamber virtuoso to Catherine II (1774–83) he seems to have spent more time away from St Petersburg, disliking the climate and being adequately compensated by other patrons. He visited London in 1785 and 1791, and spent his last years down at heel in Palermo.

lombardi, I. Opera by Verdi to a libretto by Solera, titled in full *I lombardi alla prima crociata* (The Lombards at the First Crusade). The Lombards, under Arvino (tenor), gain Jerusalem thanks to assistance from a heavenly vision of Oronte (tenor) – an Arab prince who had converted to be with his beloved Griselda (soprano) then died – and from Pagano (bass), Arvino's brother atoning for earlier misdeeds as a hermit in the Holy Land. Oronte's andante 'La mia letizia infondere' is a favourite number. First performance: Milan, 11 Feb 1843.

The composer overhauled the score to a new libretto by Alphonse Royer and Gustave Vaëz to make *Jérusalem*, in which the Lombards become Toulousians, Arvinio is now the Count and a baritone, Oronte is Gaston and not sacrificed, Griselda is Hélène and Pagano is Roger. The action is modified and a ballet is added, but the time is still that of the First Crusade and Jerusalem is still won. This version, though, has always come second. First performance: Paris, 26 Nov 1847.

Lombardic rhythm. Dotted rhythm with the short notes on the beat.

London. Capital city of England and later the United Kingdom, and, with New York, one of the musical capitals of the modern world. Since the reign of Elizabeth I (1558–1603) London has drawn musicians from throughout the country and abroad. Byrd, Tallis, Bull, Dowland, Tomkins, Gibbons, the Lawes brothers and the immigrant families of Ferrabosco and Lanier all came principally to serve the court, but since the Restoration (1660) the city's musical life has been busily commercial. The CONCERT and the concert hall were born there; theatres, churches and recording studios, in their various times, have provided further opportunities – as has an audience larger and perhaps more discriminating than any other city can boast.

Composers of the immediate post-Restoration period included Locke, Purcell and Blow, but the rage for music quickly developed into a rage exclusvely for foreign music, producing the conditions hospitable in the 18th century to

Handel and others: Geminiani, J.C. Bach, Abel and, more briefly, Haydn. The native tradition of semi-opera fizzled out as native composers did, and when all-sung opera was introduced in 1705, English (the language of Clayton's pioneering *Arsinoe*) was quickly overtaken by Italian. A pattern of rivalry, extravagance and ruin was set up, which even Handel was unable to change. Far more successful were robuster forms of musical theatre, such as *The Beggar's Opera* (1728), which continued the older indigenous scheme of songs integrated into a spoken drama and which had more to say to an urban middle-class audience.

That audience, in the first city where commerce and industry superseded the court, also preferred music combined with uplift (in oratorio), social intercourse (at pleasure gardens and concert halls) or domestic entertainment (hence the growing market for sheet music and, towards the end of the 18th century, keyboard instruments, providing opportunities for such entrepreneurs as Clementi). For concerts, the principal venues in succession were: York Buildings in Villiers Street; Hickford's Room, which moved from James Street (1714) to Brewer Street (1739); the Dean Street Room (1751); and the Hanover Square Rooms (1775). Vaster numbers could be assembled in the great churches, as for the 1784 Handel Commemoration in Westminster Abbey.

Into the early 19th century the King's Theatre in the Haymarket was the principal (indeed, usually sole) venue for full-scale opera, with ballad opera and similar forms flourishing elsewhere, but from around 1810 it was joined by the new COVENT GARDEN and Drury Lane theatres, and others. The King's Theatre (Her Majesty's after the accession of Victoria in 1837) remained the home of Italian opera, presenting Mozart, Paisiello and Rossini, while the newer theatres offered opera in English: versions of works by the same composers, along with new pieces by Bishop and Balfe. However, in 1847 the Royal Italian Opera was established at Covent Garden, which now competed with Her Majesty's for star singers and new works: French and German operas were given at both theatres in Italian translation. Composers who came to London to supervise their works included Weber (who wrote *Oberon* for Covent Garden), Verdi (who wrote *I masnadieri* for Her Majesty's) and Meyerbeer.

Concert life meanwhile was dominated by the Philharmonic Society (later Royal), which was founded in 1813, and which helped build a classic repertory founded on the symphonies of Beethoven: the Ninth it commissioned. The Royal Academy of Music opened in 1822; music publishing began to thrive; and the city became a stopping place for virtuosos, performing at the old Hanover Square Rooms or in one of the theatres. The Crystal Palace, moved from Hyde Park to Sydenham, provided a new orchestral venue from 1854, joined by St James's Hall in Piccadilly (1858–1905), and the ROYAL ALBERT HALL. The Hanover Square Rooms, visited by Haydn and Liszt, closed in 1874. Conductors active in London through these years included Jullien, Costa and Manns, while Wagner was among visitors.

The Queen's Hall (1893–1941), with its orchestral and chamber auditoria, became a new centre of concert life and was the home of the city's first permanent orchestra, conducted by Wood. Other chamber venues were built by piano and pianola manufacturers: the Steinway Hall (1878), the Bechstein Hall (1901, renamed Wigmore Hall in 1917) and the Aeolian Hall (1904). British composers made a noise again, in genres ranging from operetta (Sullivan) to oratorio and symphony (Parry, Elgar), without affecting the welcome – or at least tolerance – afforded Strauss and Schoenberg, as later Stravinsky and Janáček. By the 1930s there was a large population of British composers, conductors, singers and instrumentalists, but still a strong flux of visiting musicians, as well as a vigorous publishing industry, a new stimulus from recording (where London was the busiest centre) and radio, a range from opera (at Covent Garden and Sadler's Wells) to musical comedy, and a plenitude of orchestras and smaller ensembles.

Major institutions were founded before or just after the Second World War, including the five leading orchestras: the BBC Symphony, LSO, LPO, Philharmonia and RPO. Little has changed since then but for the decline of publishing, recording and instrument-making enterprises, the establishment of the SOUTH BANK CENTRE and BARBICAN HALL, and the widening of concert experience since the 1960s to include more new music and more old.

London College of Music (LCM). Conservatory founded in 1887.

London Mozart Players. Orchestra founded in 1949 by Harry Blech.

London Philharmonic Orchestra (LPO). Orchestra founded by Beecham in 1932, self-governing from 1939. Subsequent principal conductors have included Van Beinum (1949–51), Boult (1951–8), Haitink (1967–79), Solti (1979–81), Tennstedt (1983–7), Welser-Möst (1990–96) and Masur (from 2000).

London Sinfonietta. Modern music ensemble

founded in 1968 by David Atherton (conductor) and Nicholas Snowman (manager).

London symphonies. Name given to Haydn's Nos.93–104 (all written for London) and in particular the last (f.p. London, 4 May 1795). Vaughan Williams called his second *A London Symphony*.

London Symphony Orchestra (LSO). Orchestra founded as a self-governing body in 1904 by players breaking away from Wood's Queen's Hall Orchestra. Its principal conductors have included Richter, Nikisch, Elgar, Harty, Krips (1950–54), Monteux (1961–4), Kertesz (1966–8), Previn (1968–79), Abbado (1979–86), Tilson Thomas (1988–95) and Colin Davis (from 1995).

long. Note value, worth two or three breves. It became extinct around 1600.

Long, Marguerite (Marie Charlotte) (b. Nîmes, 13 Nov 1874; d. Paris, 13 Feb 1966). French pianist, personally associated with Debussy, Fauré and Ravel (who composed his G major concerto for her): she wrote memoirs of all three composers. She studied with Marmontel at the Paris Conservatoire, where she later taught (1906–40).

longevity. Composers to have remained creative past 80 include Schütz, Verdi, Saint-Saëns, Widor, Brian, Le Flem, Stravinsky, Ornstein, Rieti, Goldschmidt, Tippett, Matsudaira, Messiaen, Carter, Hovhaness, Babbitt and Harrison, of whom Brian, Le Flem, Ornstein, Rieti, Goldschmidt, Matsudaira and Carter were composing in their 90s. Ornstein's life of 108 years is without parallel among notable musicians. There are also cheering examples of activity at great age from pianists (Horowitz, Horszowski) and conductors (Monteux, Klemperer, Boult, Karajan, Sanderling).

Longo, Alessandro (b. Amantea, 30 Dec 1864; d. Naples, 3 Nov 1945). Italian scholar, pianist and composer. He was responsible for an edition of Domenico Scarlatti's sonatas (1906–10) and for a system of numbering them that survived until Kirkpatrick's catalogue. A member of a distinguished Neapolitan musical family, he studied (1878–85) and taught (1897–1934) at the Naples Conservatory.

lontano (It.). Distant, hence *da lontano* (from far off), *come da lontano* (as if from far off). Ligeti used the term as title for an orchestral piece (f.p. Donaueschingen, 22 Oct 1967).

Lopatnikoff, Nikolai [Lopatnikov, Nikolay Lvovich] (b. Reval/Tallinn, 16 Mar 1903; d.

Pittsburgh, 7 Oct 1976). Russian–US composer, promoted by Koussevitzky. After conservatory studies in St Petersburg and Helsinki he trained as a civil engineer in Karlsruhe (1921–7). He then lived in Berlin and London before moving to the USA in 1939. His works include two piano concertos, four symphonies and three quartets.

Lopes-Graça, Fernando. See Fernando Lopes GRAÇA.

Lorenz, Alfred (Ottokar) (b. Vienna, 11 Jul 1868; d. Munich, 20 Nov 1939). German scholar. He studied in Berlin, and worked as a conductor in Coburg and Gotha (1898–1920) before devoting himself to scholarly studies under Moritz Bauer at Frankfurt University, His influential *Die Geheimnis der Form bei Richard Wagner* (1924–33) proposed a strong overarching form in each of Wagner's operas.

Lorenzani, Paolo (b. Rome, 1640; d. Rome, 28 Nov 1713). Italian composer who spent an important time in Paris, where he wrote sacred music and challenged Lully's monopoly of opera. Trained under Benevoli as a choirboy in the Julian Chapel, Rome (1651–4), he became chapelmaster of Messina Cathedral in 1675, and fled from there to Paris when the Spanish invaded in 1678. Introducing the latest Italian fashions, he quickly gained influential support at the court of Louis XIV and from musicians, against Lully's opposition, and became superintendant of the queen's music. A nephew of Cardinal Mazarin wrote the libretto for his pastorale *Nicandro e Fileno* (f.p. Fontainebleau, 1681). The queen's death in 1683 weakened his position, though he stayed in Paris until 1694, when he was appointed director of the Julian Chapel.

Lorenzo da Firenze (d. Florence, winter 1372–3). Italian composer, working in the swirl of French musical influences and possibly Landini's teacher. His works, featuring unusually long melismas, include monophonic ballatas, two-part madrigals and a sanctus.

Loriod, Yvonne (b. Houilles, Seine-et-Oise, 20 Jan 1924). French pianist. Messiaen's chosen performer from 1943, when he encountered her in his class at the Paris Conservatoire, and his second wife. Her playing – full in sonority, rhythmically acute and bursting with colour – is partly written into Messiaen's music, and had a determining influence on her pupils and others. She also made the first recordings of Barraqué's Sonata and Boulez's second.

Lortzing, Albert (b. Berlin, 23 Oct 1801; d. Berlin, 21 Jan 1851). German composer, chiefly of comic operas in which he skilfully adapted Mozartian and French patterns to bourgeois German taste and thereby gained a lasting place in the German repertory. With parents in the theatre (his mother was to sing in his *Zar und Zimmermann*), he was encouraged to perform, study music theory and compose. He married an actress in 1823 and stayed with the family troupe until he and his wife joined the Detmold court theatre (1826–33). From there they moved to Leipzig (1833–45), where he enjoyed his first triumphs. In his unsettled later years he suffered professional disappointments and illness. He made an opera on the Meistersinger and wrote all his own librettos, but had nothing of Wagner's drive to the sublime: his business was with straightforward theatrical entertainment, nicely polished.

Operas: *Die beiden Schützen*, f.p. Leipzig, 1835; *Zar und Zimmermann*, f.p. Leipzig, 1837; *Hans Sachs*, f.p. Leipzig, 1840; *Der Wildschütz*, f.p. Leipzig, 1842; UNDINE, f.p. Magdeburg, 1845; *Der Waffenschmied*, f.p. Vienna, 1846; etc.

Los Angeles. US city, the largest on the west coast, having grown vastly in the 20th century on account of the movie industry. The Los Angeles Symphony (founded 1898) was superseded by the Philharmonic (founded 1919), whose music directors have included Artur Rodzinski (1929–33), Klemperer (1933–43), Alfred Wallenstein (1943–56), Van Beinum (1956–8), Mehta (1962–78), Giulini (1978–83), Previn (1985–92) and Salonen (from 1992). It moved into Disney Hall in 2003 from its previous home, the Dorothy Chandler Pavilion, which it shared with the Los Angeles Opera (founded 1986). Summer concerts have taken place since 1922 at the Hollywood Bowl. Schoenberg and Stravinsky both settled in the city in their late 50s.

Los Angeles, Victoria de (b. Barcelona, 1 Nov 1923). Spanish soprano, of bright, sweet voice and winning personality. She studied in her native city and made her debut there at the Liceo (1945, Countess in *Figaro*). In the 1950s she enjoyed international acclaim, not least at Covent Garden and the Met, especially as Mimì, Manon and Marguerite (*Faust*). She maintained her recital career, strongly featuring Spanish songs, into the 1990s.

Lotosflöte (Ger.). Swanee whistle.

Lotti, Antonio (b. Hanover, 1666; d. Venice, 5 Jan 1740). Italian composer, highly regarded in his time and later for his elegant mastery of the voice.

His father, Matteo, was chapelmaster in Hanover. By 1683 he was studying in Venice with Legrenzi, and by 1687 he was associated with St Mark's, where he rose to become first organist (1704–36) and then chapelmaster. Accordingly, he wrote a good deal of sacred music, some of which was still being sung at St Mark's into the early 19th century, as well as operas and cantatas. His *Crucifixus a 8*, one of several settings of the text, remains popular, as does an aria attributed to him, 'Pur dicesti', from an *Arminio* produced in Naples in 1714. He married a singer, and she went with him when he was invited to Dresden (1717–19), where he wrote *Teofane* (1719) and two other operas.

loudness. Quantity of sound, as perceived. This is affected principally by intensity, though frequency, spectrum and duration may also play a part. DECIBEL measures of intensity are often taken as measures of loudness, but more strictly the measure should be the phon, which is equivalent to the decibel for a sine wave of 1,000 Hz, or the sone, where 40 phons = 1 sone, 50 phons = 2 sones, 60 phons = 3 sones, etc.

In a musical context the more neutral term DYNAMICS is preferred, leaving loudness as something to be complained of in brass players and accompanists.

loudspeaker. Device converting electrical signals into sound waves, with a premium on fidelity.

Louise. Opera by Charpentier to a libretto probably by Saint-Pol-Roux. Louise (soprano) is a seamstress who breaks away from her working-class background (sympathetically depicted) to join the poet Julien (tenor). The big number is her 'Depuis le jour'. First performance: Paris, 2 Feb 1900.

Louis Ferdinand [Friedrich Christian Ludwig], Prince of Prussia (b. Friedrichsfelde, near Berlin, 18 Nov 1772; d. Saalfeld, 13 Oct 1806). German pianist-composer, nephew of Frederick II, whose musical and military inclinations he shared. He was fatally wounded in battle, though not before he had published several chamber pieces with piano and gained the approbation of Beethoven, marked by the dedication of the latter's Third Piano Concerto.

lourd, lourde (Fr.). Heavy.

loure. French Baroque dance, slow and in compound time. Bach adopted it in his fifth French suite and E major violin partita.

louré (Fr.). PORTATO.

Lourié, Arthur Vincent [Lurye, Artur Sergeyevich] (b. St Petersburg, 14 May 1892; d. Princeton, 12 Oct 1966). Russian–US composer, a member of the post-Scriabin avant-garde in St Petersburg before the 1917 revolution, later the author of strongly religious concert pieces and two operas after Pushkin (*The Feast During the Plague*, 1935; *The Blackamoor of Peter the Great*, 1961). He studied at the St Petersburg Conservatory and dedicated his *Formes en l'air* (1915) to Picasso. After serving as music commissar (1918–21) he moved to Berlin, Paris (1924–41) and the USA. In Paris he was close to Stravinsky, who may have been influenced by his *Sonata liturgica* for altos and chamber orchestra (1928) and *Concerto spirituale* for piano, voices and an orchestra omitting woodwinds, violins and violas (1929).

Love for Three Oranges, The (*Lyubov k trem apelsinam*). Opera by Prokofiev to his own libretto after a play by Carlo Gozzi. A satirical fantasy set in the realm of the King of Clubs, the piece involves a quest in which the Prince (tenor) and the jester, Truffaldino (tenor), make off with three oranges, each of which is discovered to contain a princess. Two of these ladies rapidly succumb to thirst, but the third is saved and duly arrives with the Prince in Clubland, despite the machinations of the sinister team Celio (bass) and Fata Morgana (soprano). The orchestral suite (Op.33a) includes the score's irresistible march. First performance: Chicago, 30 Dec 1921.

Love the Magician. See *El* AMOR BRUJO.

Low Countries. The region including the NETHERLANDS, BELGIUM and Luxembourg, with part of northeast France. The modern boundaries, formed in 1830, long postdate the Renaissance flowering of music (and painting) in the southern, Belgian–French portion, ruled for much of that time by the dukes of BURGUNDY. Among composers from this area valued abroad, notably in Italy and France, were Ciconia, Dufay, Ockeghem, Josquin, La Rue, Obrecht, Isaac, Arcadelt, Willaert and Lassus.

lower mordent. See MORDENT.

LPO. London Philharmonic Orchestra.

LSO. London Symphony Orchestra.

Lübeck, Vincent (b. Paddingbüttel, Dorum, Land Wursten, 1654; d. Hamburg, 9 Feb 1740). German organist-composer, whose few surviving works (eight preludes and fugues, two chorale settings) are stylistically close to Buxtehude but individual in their brilliance. Trained partly by his father in Flensburg, he held posts in Hamburg at Sts Cosmas and Damian (1679–1702) and then St Nicolai's, where he was succeeded by his son, also Vincent (1684–1755).

Lucerne. Swiss city. The lakeside villa Triebschen, on the outskirts, was Wagner's home for the period 1866–72. One of the leading music festivals was instituted in the city in 1938.

Lucia di Lammermoor. Opera by Donizetti to a libretto by Cammarano after Walter Scott's novel *The Bride of Lammermoor*. Enrico (baritone) needs his sister Lucia (soprano) to make a good match and is outraged to discover she is in love with Edgardo (tenor). He arranges a marriage with the more suitable Arturo (tenor), whom Lucia kills on their wedding night and descends (or ascends) into madness. Numbers include the sextet 'Che mi frena in tal momento', Lucia's larghetto 'Regnava nel silenzio', cabaletta 'Quando rapito in estasi' and Mad Scene (with solo flute), Enrico's 'Cruda, funesta smania', and Edgardo's larghetto 'Fra poco a me ricovero' and cabaletta 'Tu che in Dio spiegasti l'ali'. First performance: Naples, 26 Sep 1835.

Lucier, Alvin (b. Nashua, New Hampshire, 14 May 1931). US composer, a gentle and inventive explorer of electronic sound worlds. He studied at Yale (1950–56) and Brandeis (1958–60), and was on the Brandeis faculty (1962–70) before moving to Wesleyan University in Connecticut. Working with the live-electronic Sonic Arts Union (1966–73), he produced *Vespers* (1968), for people in the dark using echo-location devices to sound the space, and *I am sitting in a room* (1970), in which the title phrase is repeatedly played back and re-recorded, until the words dissolve in resonances from the room. His many later works include sound installations and further confluences of live and electronic resources (Music for Piano with Slow Sweep Pure Wave Oscillators, 1992).

Luci mie traditrici (My Traitorous Eyes). Opera by Sciarrino to his own libretto, after a 1664 play by Giacinto Andrea Cicognini based on Gesualdo's revenge murder. First performance: Schwetzingen, 19 May 1998.

Lucio Silla. Opera by Mozart to a libretto by Giovanni de Gamerra. Lucius Sulla (tenor),

dictator of Rome, wants to seize Junia (soprano) from her beloved Cecilius (soprano castrato). Cecilius's friend Cinna (soprano), in love with Sulla's sister Celia (soprano), compounds a plot, but finally Sulla proves magnanimous, allows both couples to marry, and retires from government. The best known aria is Cecilius's 'Il tenero momento'. First performance: Milan, 26 Dec 1772.

Ludford, Nicholas (b. *c.*1490; buried Westminster, 9 Aug 1557). English composer, especially of masses in the florid polyphony characteristic of pre-Reformation England; the two in six parts, *Videte miraculum* and *Benedicta et venerabilis*, stand with Taverner's. He seems to have spent his creative life serving St Stephen's, Westminster, a royal institution, and to have stopped composing in the 1530s, living on as a pensioner.

Ludwig, Christa (b. Berlin, 16 Mar 1928). German mezzo-soprano, much admired in Mahler, and in an operatic repertory extending from Mozart to Strauss. The child of singers, she studied with her mother and made her debut in Frankfurt in 1946 (Orlovsky in *Die Fledermaus*). In 1955 she joined the Vienna Staatsoper, though she also appeared at the Met, notably as Berlioz's Dido (1973). She retired in 1994.

Luening, Otto (Clarence) (b. Milwaukee, 15 Jun 1900; d. New York, 2 Sep 1996). US composer, notably of electronic music, though he also wrote much chamber music (especially for the flute, his own instrument) and an opera, *Evangeline* (1930, rev 1948). The child of musicians, he had formal studies in Munich (1915–17) and Zurich (1919–20), and private lessons with Jarnach and Busoni in the latter city. Soon after returning to the USA he set out on a teaching career that took him to Columbia (1944–68). His electronic pieces include *Fantasy in Space* (1952), composed from flute sounds, and *Gargoyles* for violin and tape (1960), as well as compositions made in collaboration with Ussachevsky, with whom he presented the earliest public concert of electronic music (Museum of Modern Art, New York, 28 Oct 1952).

Luftpause (Ger., air pause). Pause suggesting a quick inhalation before an outburst; the term is particularly associated with Mahler.

lugubre (It.). Gloomy.

Luisa Miller. Opera by Verdi to a libretto by Cammarano after Schiller's play *Kabale und Liebe*. The love of Luisa (soprano), daughter of the army veteran Miller (baritone), and Rodolfo (tenor), son of Count Walter (bass), is frustrated by a plot in which the count is assisted by his steward Wurm (bass). Duped by this, Rodolfo has Luisa share a poisoned cup with him, but seizes the chance to kill Wurm before the end. Much the most celebrated number is Rodolfo's 'Quando le sere al placido'. First performance: Naples, 8 Dec 1849.

lullaby. Soft song with rocking motion, usually in moderate triple time, as used down the ages, with greater or lesser success, to lull infants to sleep. The genre is recalled in songs and piano pieces by Schubert, Chopin (see BERCEUSE), Brahms (the song Op.49:4 being his celebrated example), Wolf and many others, and is enacted in Berg's *Wozzeck*.

Lully, Jean-Baptiste (b. Florence, 29 Nov 1632; d. Paris, 22 Mar 1687). Italian–French composer, originally Giovanni Battista Lulli. Having arrived in France at 13, he gained increasing prestige and power at the court of Louis XIV during his 20s and 30s, and then, with his regular librettist Quinault, effectively begat the genre of French opera: classical in its subject matter, expressively nuanced, and set to graceful dance interspersed with recitative.

A miller's son, he was taken to France as a serving boy with whom the 'Grande Mademoiselle', a cousin of Louis XIV's, could practise her Italian. He may already have had musical propensities, which he developed, and at 20 he danced in a ballet with the boy king, who appointed him royal composer of instrumental music. In 1661–2 he gained further court appointments, French nationality and a wife, Madeleine, the daughter of the composer Michel Lambert. Up to now his compositions seem to have consisted largely of dances and, later, whole scores for court ballets, but in 1663 he began writing dances and songs for comedies by Molière, and in 1672 he acquired a royal privilege granting him sole control of opera sung throughout.

Notwithstanding the king's displeasure at his homosexual conduct, as well as some clerical distress at the classical standards of morality espoused by his characters, he exercised his right with great force – in an opera almost every year, created almost always in collaboration with his chosen poet Quinault – and protected it with considerable energy. As the most vigorous personality in the team that created French opera (a team that included choreographers, designers and machinists besides Quinault and the performers), he must be credited with establishing a form that lasted almost a century and that was raised by Rameau but not overturned. Presented in the shape of an abstract prologue followed by exemplary, concrete action in five acts, each concluding with a divertissement, a Lully opera provided models – of dignity, justice and the acceptance but subjection of erotic love – to the most important person in the audience: the king. These works also established a kind of recitative suited to French, with changing metres and expressive contours.

Lully controlled his performances as assiduously as he policed his monopoly. Conducting his *Te Deum* to celebrate the king's return to health, he struck his toe with his long baton and gangrene set in. His appointments, but not his talents, devolved on his three sons.

R.H.F. Scott *Jean-Baptiste Lully* (1973)

Tragédies lyriques (with librettos by Quinault except where stated): *Cadmus et Hermione*, f.p. Paris, 1673; *Alceste*, f.p. Paris, 1674; *Thésée*, f.p. Saint-Germain, 1675; ATYS, f.p. Saint-Germain, 1676; *Isis*, f.p. Saint-Germain, 1677; *Psyché* (Thomas Corneille and Bernard le Bouyer de Fontenelle), f.p. Paris, 1678; *Bellérophon* (Thomas Corneille and de Fontenelle), f.p. Paris, 1679; *Proserpine*, f.p. Saint-Germain, 1680; *Persée*, f.p. Paris, 1682; *Phaëton*, f.p. Versailles, 1683; AMADIS, f.p. Paris, 1684; *Roland* (see ORLANDO), f.p. Versailles, 1685; *Armide* (see ARMIDA), f.p. Paris, 1686; *Achille et Polyxène* (Jean Galbert de Campistron), f.p. Paris, 1687 (completed by Collasse)

Other stage works: *Le Bourgeois Gentilhomme* (comédie-ballet; Molière), f.p. Chambord, 1670; *Psyché* (tragédie-ballet; Molière, Pierre Corneille and Quinault), f.p. Paris, 1671; *Les Fêtes de l'Amour et de Bacchus* (pastorale; Quinault), f.p. Paris, 1672; *Acis et Galatée* (pastorale héroïque; Campistron), f.p. Anet, 1686; court ballets, etc.

Motets: *Miserere*, 1663; *Te Deum*, 1677; etc.

Lulu. Opera by Berg to his own adaptation of Frank Wedekind's plays *Earth Spirit* and *Pandora's Box*. Lulu (soprano) is the embodiment of female sensuality, the still centre of a maelstrom of lovers including the cynical businessman Dr Schön (baritone), his idealistic artist son Alwa (tenor), the Countess Geschwitz (mezzo-soprano) and several more. Her rise and descent through society provide a large-scale palindromic form. Berg did not fully orchestrate the third act, and his widow blocked completion of the score in her lifetime. First performance: Zurich, 2 Jun 1937; with Act 3 finished by Cerha, Paris, 24 Feb 1979.

Lumbye, Hans Christian (b. Copenhagen, 2 May 1810; d. Copenhagen, 20 Mar 1874). Danish composer, the Johann Strauss I of Copenhagen. Having begun his career as a bugle boy at 14, he was impressed by hearing an Austrian band play music by Lanner and Strauss, and in 1840 formed his own orchestra. He wrote mostly dances, for August Bournonville's ballets and for concerts at the Tivoli Gardens (1843–72), and was succeeded by two sons.

Lumsdaine, David (b. Sydney, 31 Oct 1931). Australian composer, of music clear-cut and strong in its imagery and form. He studied in Sydney before moving in 1952 to London, where he completed his training at the RAM and with Seiber. Remaining in London as a teacher and editor, he made his mark with three works of 1964: *Annotations of Auschwitz* for soprano and sextet, a *Missa brevis* for choir and organ, and *Kelly Ground* for piano. Later works include meditations on Bach, the orchestral *Hagoromo* (1975–7), after the noh play, and tape pieces based on birdsong. He taught at Durham University (1970–81) and King's College, London (1981–93).

lungo, lunga (It., long). Marking indicating an extension, normally of a fermata. Also found is *lunga pausa* or *pausa lunga*.

luogo (It.). Alternative to LOCO.

Luonnotar. Symphonic poem by Sibelius, with a soprano singing lines from the *Kalevala* on the creation of the world, Luonnotar being the primal goddess. First performance: Gloucester, 10 Sep 1913.

Lupi, Johannes (b. c.1506; d. Cambrai, 20 Dec 1539). Netherlandish composer and church musician, notably of motets showing a confident handling of imitative polyphony in five and six parts. He was associated with Cambrai Cathedral from 1514 as choirboy, master of the choirboys (from 1527), cleric and composer. Other works by him include two masses and chansons.

Lupo. Milanese–English family of musicians serving the English court from 1540, when Ambrose Lupo (d. 1591) arrived as one of six Italian viol players. The most distinguished member of the dynasty was his nephew Thomas (1571–?1627), who was at court from 1588 and wrote over 80 consort fantasias, as well as songs and sacred music.

Lupu, Radu (b. Galaţi, 30 Nov 1945). Romanian pianist, who combines compelling authority with complete calm in a repertory centred on Mozart, Schubert and Brahms. He studied with Lipatti's teacher Florica Musicescu and from 1963 with Heinrich and Neuhaus at the Moscow Conservatory. In 1966 he won the Van Cliburn Competition, but he remained at his studies until he won the Leeds in 1969.

lusingando, lusinghiero (It.). Coaxing, charming.

lustig (Ger.). Merrily.

lustigen Weiber von Windsor, Die (The Merry Wives of Windsor). Opera by Nicolai to a libretto by Salomon Hermann Mosenthal after Shakespeare. Numbers include the romance 'Horch, die Lerche singt in Hain!' sung by Fenton (tenor). First performance: Berlin, 9 Mar 1849.

lustige Witwe, Die (The Merry Widow). Operetta by Lehár to a libretto by Victor Léon and Leo Stein after a play by Meilhac. The widow is Hanna Glawari (soprano), merry because she can tease, test and trap Danilo (tenor), who is required by the Pontevedrin ambassador to save her (and her millions) from rivals in Paris (where the action unfolds at a sequence of parties), and whose contrary behaviour only confirms his love for her. Numbers include Hanna's 'Es lebt' eine Vilja', with its refrain 'Vilja, o Vilja', and the love duet 'Lippen schweigen'. First performance: Vienna, 30 Dec 1905.

lutanist. Older term for a lute player, generally replaced by lutenist.

lute (Fr. *luth*, Ger. *Laute*, It. *lauto, leuto, liuto*, Sp. *laúd*). Plucked string instrument, introduced to Europe by the Moors of Spain, and deriving its name in European languages from the Arabic *al 'ūd*. Its earlier history goes back to Mesopotamia in the 3rd millennium BC.

The European lute has a body shaped like the first third sliced lengthwise from a plum, with a neck extending straight and a head bent back at an oblique angle. The body is made from strips of wood (sycamore and maple are commonly used) bent and glued together to support the flat soundboard (usually of pine). Punctured in the soundboard is a circular soundhole, or rose, often intricately carved. The courses (pairs of strings) extend from a bridge near the further end of the soundboard to the head, which functions as pegbox. The neck provides a fretted fingerboard.

Western lutenists at first adopted the Arab method of playing with a plectrum, but in the latter half of the 15th century plucking with the fingertips became the rule. This allowed players to sound several strings at the same time, and so to perform polyphonic music, which at once began to be notated in TABLATURE. To the original four courses were added a fifth in the 15th century and a sixth around 1500, with the tuning intervals of fourth, fourth, major third, fourth and fourth. Lutes were made in several sizes during the 16th century, the custom being to tune the top course as high as possible, almost to the point of breaking. In the case of the standard lute, this resulted in a tuning of G–C–F–A–D–G, with the top string a fifth above middle C. Also made were lutes a fourth and an octave higher, and similarly a fourth and an octave lower, as well as the adapted bass forms ARCHLUTE, THEORBO, BANDORA and MANDORA, developed as the instrument gained a new role in continuo playing. More courses were added to the standard lute in the 17th and 18th centuries, giving it a full bass range and eliminating the need for other sizes and forms.

The lute in the 16th century had a place equivalent to that of the piano in the 19th: it was the most usual instrument for amateurs and for accompanying song, besides appearing often in ensembles. The vogue for it seems to have begun in Italy at the start of the century, and spread to France, the German-speaking lands, the Low Countries and England, as represented by publications of lute music and treatises. Dowland's death in 1626 coincided with the instrument's eclipse, and though there were outstanding performer-composers throughout the next century and more, the rise of the piano in the later 18th century drove the lute into extinction, from which it was reclaimed by the early-music revival of the 20th century.

lute-harpsichord. Harpsichord with gut strings imitating the sound of the lute. Various such instruments were made, particularly in Germany in the first half of the 18th century; Bach owned two.

lute song. Song for lutenist-singer, characteristic of English music in the age of Dowland, its foremost practitioner. The cross-Channel equivalent was the AIR DE COUR.

lute stop. Rank of jacks on a harpsichord plucking close to the nut, so producing a piercing sound.

luth (Fr.). Lute.

Lutheran music. Martin Luther (1483–1546), who effectively instituted the Reformation when he nailed his 95 theses to the door of the Schlosskirche in Wittenberg (1517), himself probably composed or arranged tunes for the hymns he wrote. Sung in four-part harmony from the end of the 16th century, these and many others by Luther's contemporaries and successors gave rise to the CHORALE tradition. The importance of that tradition, and of biblical exposition in Luther's teaching, pulled Lutheran music in its

golden age – which started in the early 17th century and climaxed in Bach – towards vocal forms in which the words and melodies of chorales could be included and Bible stories contemplated, chiefly those forms now known as the SACRED CONCERTO (in the earlier part of the period) and the church CANTATA.

luthier. Originally the Fr. term for a lute maker, now used in Eng. and other languages for all string-instrument builders.

Lutosławski, Witold (b. Warsaw, 25 Jan 1913; d. Warsaw, 9 Feb 1994). Polish composer. Drawn in his youth by music coming from Paris (by Stravinsky and others), he gained an agility of rhythm and luminosity of texture he kept all his life, through a time when Bartók's influence was paramount to a sportive engagement, after 1960, with principles of freedom emanating from the new Paris of Boulez (and from Cage). He was a master of the orchestra, and most of his music, from all periods, is for this medium. His individual soundworld combines a French euphony with poetic elegance (even when the feeling is dramatic or mournful) and, in the post-1960 music, a discreet balance of measured movement with aleatory passages building a more static yet subtle web of figures.

Born into the landed gentry, he and his two brothers were brought up by their mother, following their father's execution during a family sojourn in Moscow (1915–18). He studied with Jerzy Lefeld for piano and Witold Maliszewski for composition at the Warsaw Conservatory (1932–7). The war, during which he stayed in Warsaw, restricted his activities, and he devoted himself largely to arranging music to play with Panufnik as a piano duo. After the war came constraints of another kind, with the enforcement of folklore models and tunefulness in communist Poland, to which he gamely responded with the help of Bartók's example. His *Musique funèbre* for strings (1954–8), a memorial to Bartók, was a farewell to that way of musical life. With official reins now loosened, he was able to explore more complex harmonies, and tease music out of them; he was also able to hear new music from abroad at the annual Warsaw Autumn festivals. An encounter with Cage's Concert for Piano and Orchestra introduced him to aleatory possibilities, which he introduced into his *Jeux vénitiens* (1960–61). After that his *Trois poèmes*, Second Symphony and *Livre* established him as a senior member of the avant-garde, distinguished by the ease and range of his orchestral textures and the drama of his forms. He also appeared internationally conducting his music, beginning with the première of the *Trois poèmes*. In works from the Preludes and Fugue for solo strings (1970–72) onwards he was able to recover the neoclassical spirit in a more open manner and pay allegiance especially to Bach, while his last two symphonies are rare syntheses of modernism and the great tradition.

Bálint András Varga *Lutosławski Profile* (1976); Charles Bodman Rae *The Music of Lutosławski* (1994, ²1999)

Orchestral (full): Symphony No.1, 1941–7; No.2, 1965–7; No.3, 1981–3; No.4, 1988–92; *Lacrimosa*, s, ch, orch, 1937; Symphonic Variations, 1936–8; Little Suite, 1950–51; Silesian Triptych, s, orch, 1951; Concerto for Orchestra, 1950–54; Three Postludes, 1958–63; *Trois poèmes* (Michaux), ch, orch, 1961–3; *Livre pour orchestre*, 1968; Cello Concerto, 1969–70; *Les Espaces du sommeil* (Desnos), bar, orch, 1975; *Mi-parti*, 1975–6; Paganini Variations, pf, orch, arr 1977–8; *Novelette*, 1978–9; *Chain 2*, vn, chbr orch, 1984–5; *Chain 3*, 1986; Piano Concerto, 1987–8; Partita, vn, orch, arr 1988; 20 Polish Carols, s, ch, orch, arr 1984–9; Interlude, 1989; Prelude for Guildhall School of Music, 1989

Orchestral (reduced): Overture, str, 1949; Dance Preludes, cl, chbr orch, 1955; *Musique funèbre*, str, 1954–8; 5 Songs (Iłłakowicz), mez, chbr orch, arr 1958; *Jeux vénitiens*, chbr orch, 1960–61; *Paroles tissées* (Chabrun), t, chbr orch, 1965; Preludes and Fugue, 13 str, 1970–72; Double Concerto, ob, hp, chbr orch, 1979–80; *Grave: Metamorphosis*, vc, str, 1982; *Chain 1*, 14 insts, 1983; *Slides*, 11 insts, 1989; *Chantefleurs et chantefables* (Desnos), s, chbr orch, 1989–90; fanfares, children's music

Chamber: *Recitative e arioso*, vn, pf, 1951; *Bucolics*, va, vc, arr 1952; Dance Preludes, cl, pf, 1954; String Quartet, 1964; Sacher Variation, vc, 1975; *Epitaph*, ob, pf, 1979; *Grave: Metamorphosis*, vc, pf, 1981; *Mini-Overture*, brass qnt, 1982; Partita, vn, pf, 1984; *Subito*, vn, pf, 1992

Songs: 20 Polish Carols, 1946; 5 Songs (Iłłakowicz), 1956–7; children's songs

Piano: 2 Etudes, 1941; Variations on a Theme of Paganini, 2 pf, 1941; Folk Melodies, 1945; *Bucolics*, 1952; *Miniatura*, 2 pf, 1953; Three Pieces for the Young, 1953; *An Overheard Tune*, 2 pf, 1957; Invention, 1968

Lutyens, (Agnes) Elisabeth (b. London, 6 Jul 1906; d. London, 14 Apr 1983). British composer, who lived to see her musical ideals of intensive adventure widely espoused by younger musicians in London, whom she encouraged by her teaching and by the example of her productivity: in her last 20 years she wrote over 100 works, from bizarre operas to chamber pieces of diverse kinds. A daughter of the architect Edwin Lutyens, she studied in Paris and at the RCM. Marriage to Edward Clark brought her into contact with leading continental composers, and she arrived in the late 1930s at a 12-note style with no precedent in British music.

Luzzaschi, Luzzasco (b. Ferrara, ?1545; d. Ferrara, 10 Sep 1607). Italian composer, a leading madrigalist who was also renowned in his time as a keyboard performer: he was Frescobaldi's teacher, but most of his keyboard music is lost. By his own account, he was taught as a boy by Rore. He then spent his entire career at the Ferrarese court, as a singer (from 1561), first organist (from 1564) and composer of madrigals for the delectation of the duke's inner circle. The most celebrated of these use intense chromaticism, but his harmonic language was much more usually restrained.

Lyadov, Anatoly (Konstantinovich) (b. St Petersburg, 11 May 1855; d. Polïnovka, Novgorod district, 28 Aug 1914). Russian composer, a master magician of orchestral colour in the tradition of Rimsky-Korsakov, his teacher at the St Petersburg Conservatory (1870–78). He was the son of a Mariinsky conductor, and conducted himself; he also stayed on at the conservatory to teach, was one of Belyayev's composers, and worked in folksong collection. Creatively indolent, he spent his summers on the estate he had acquired by marriage (he died there), and completed very little in his last dozen years but the orchestral pieces by which he is chiefly remembered. Of these, *Baba-Yaga* and *Kikimora* are exciting evocations of witchery, while *The Enchanted Lake* is an extraordinary creation of dappled stillness. His failure to complete (or probably even begin) *The Firebird* led Diaghilev to transfer the commission to Stravinsky.

Orchestral: Polonaise in memory of Pushkin, Op.49, 1899; Polonaise for unveiling a statue of Anton Rubinstein, Op.52, 1902; *Baba-Yaga*, Op.56, ?1891–1904; 8 Russian Folksongs, Op.58, pub 1906; *The Enchanted Lake*, Op.62, pub 1909; *Kikimora*, Op.63, 1909; *Nénie*, Op.67, pub 1914; etc.

Piano: *About Olden Times*, Op.21, 1889, orch 1906; *A Musical Snuffbox*, Op.32, 1893, arr fls, cls, hp, bells, 1897; etc.

Other works: songs, choruses, incidental scores

Lyapunov, Sergey (Mikhaylovich) (b. Yaroslavl, 30 Nov 1859; d. Paris, 8 Nov 1924). Russian pianist-composer, a nationalist Lisztian: his Op.11 studies complete the key sequence of Liszt's Transcendental Etudes. The son of a schoolmaster and a pianist, he studied at the Moscow Conservarory (1878–83) with Klindworth, Pavel Pabst, Tchaikovsky and Taneyev. He then moved to St Petersburg and became Balakirev's disciple; in 1893 he went on a folksong-collecting expedition with Balakirev and Lyadov. Besides succeeding Rimsky-Korsakov at the imperial chapel (1894–1902), he held various teaching posts, notably at the St Petersburg Conservatory (1910–17). In 1919 he was appointed to the new State Institute of Art, but he soon emigrated to Paris.

Orchestral: Symphony No.1, B minor, Op.12, 1887; No.2, B♭ minor, Op.66, 1917; Piano Concerto No.1, E♭ minor, Op.4, 1890; No.2, E, Op.38, 1909; etc.

Piano: *Douze études d'execution transcendante*, Op.11, 1897–1905; Sonata, F minor, Op.27, 1906–8; etc.

Other works: songs, choral music, piano sextet

Lyatoshynsky, Boris Mykolayovich (b. Zhitomir, 3 Jan 1895; d. Kiev, 15 Apr 1968). Ukrainian composer, the dominant force in his country's music in the mid 20th century. He studied with Glière at the Kiev Conservatory, where he taught from his graduation (1919) to the end of his life. His works include five symphonies, two operas, chamber music, piano pieces and songs.

Lydian. Authentic MODE F–G–A–B–C–D–E–F, the fifth church mode/tone.

Lympany, Moura (b. Saltash, 18 Aug 1916). British pianist, admired especially in Rachmaninoff and newer repertory (Khachaturian's concerto, Rawsthorne), created dame in 1992. She studied at the RAM, with Tobias Matthay and with several teachers abroad, and enjoyed an international career after coming second to Gilels in the 1938 Ysaÿe Competition.

lyra viol. Small bass viol popular in 17th-century England.

lyre. Plucked string instrument on which the strings are attached to a bar above (or to one side of) a resonating box, which may be made from wood or metal, or from a gourd or shell. It is an ancient type, known from Mesopotamia in the 3rd millennium BC and particularly important to the Greeks. By tradition it was invented by Hermes, who made the first example from a tortoise shell, but it was associated most strongly with Apollo. Thereby it gained prestige as a symbol of music, continuing as such long after it had died out in European culture, as it did with the Roman Empire, though it survives in Ethiopia and surrounding territories.

lyre guitar. Guitar with wings and crosspiece, so

having the form of a lyre. There was a vogue for such instruments around 1785–1815.

lyric. (1) As a noun (normally pl.), sung words, especially those of a popular song or musical.

(2) As an adjective, sung or singing, especially in a theatre context; hence such locutions as 'the lyric stage' (i.e. the operatic stage). See also below.

lyrical. In singing style. A symphony or a piano piece may include a lyrical passage.

lyricism. The condition of being lyrical.

Lyric Pieces (*Lyrische Stücke, Lyrische Stückchen, Lyriske småstykker*). 10 sets of piano pieces by Grieg. Among the most popular numbers are: 'Arietta' (Book 1:1), 'Butterfly' (3:1), 'Erotic' (3:5), 'In Springtime' (3:6), 'Notturno' (5:4), 'Wedding Day at Trolhaugen' (8:6) and 'Cradle Song' (9:5).

lyric soprano. Regular soprano voice, neither light nor heavy.

Lyric Suite (*Lyrische Suite*). String quartet by Berg in six movements, the odd-numbered ones increasingly fast, their companions increasingly slow. He dedicated it to Zemlinsky, whose Lyric Symphony is quoted, but secretly wrote it for his intimate friend Hanna Fuchs-Robettini: it has an undisclosed programme concerning their relationship, and the adagio finale is an instrumental setting of Baudelaire's 'De profundis clamavi'. First performance: Berlin, 31 Jan 1929.

Lyric Symphony (*Lyrische Symphonie*). Work by Zemlinsky, in seven movements setting poems by Tagore for soprano and baritone. First performance: Prague, 4 Jul 1924.

lyric tenor. Tenor voice on the light side.

Lysenko, Mykola Vytalyevich (b. Hrynsky, near Kremenchug, Poltava district, 22 Mar 1842; d. Kiev, 6 Nov 1912). Ukrainian composer, a patriotic nationalist. He studied in Kiev and Leipzig, collected Ukrainian folksongs and completed his training with Rimsky-Korsakov in St Petersburg (1874–6). After that he worked in Kiev, where he was briefly imprisoned (1907) for political activities. His works include operas in Ukrainian (*Taras Bulba*, 1880–90), choral music and songs.

ma (It.). But, as in *allegro ma non troppo* (fast, but not too much so).

Ma, Yo-Yo (b. Paris, 7 Oct 1955). Chinese–US cellist, enormously successful by reason of his musicianship and engaging openness. He studied with Leonard Rose at Juilliard (1964–71) and took a humanities degree at Harvard before beginning his career in 1976. Since the 1990s (by which time he had recorded most of the traditional repertory) he has worked with video artists, folk musicians and Carter.

Maazel, Lorin (Varencove) (b. Neuilly, France, 6 Mar 1930). US conductor, esteemed for his precision and command. Brought up in Los Angeles and Pittsburgh, he was trained to conduct (and play the violin) at an early age; he conducted the New York Philharmonic at the 1939 World's Fair. After further studies and a time playing in the Pittsburgh Symphony (1949–51) he went to Italy, where he made a new debut as a conductor (Catania, 1953). By the early 1960s his career was international. He was then music director of the Cleveland Orchestra (1972–81), the Vienna Staatsoper (1982–4), the Orchestre National (1988–91), the Pittsburgh Symphony (1988–96), the Bavarian Radio Symphony (1993–2002) and the New York Philharmonic (from 2002). Since the 1990s he has also been active as a composer.

Macbeth. Shakespeare play, of witchcraft and a usurper's guilt. Musical treatments include:

(1) Verdi's opera, to a libretto by Piave, with the main characters Macbeth (baritone), Lady Macbeth (soprano), Banquo (bass) and Macduff (tenor). Numbers include Lady Macbeth's aria 'Vieni, t'affretta' and Sleepwalking Scene ('Una macchia'), a ballet in the witches' cave, the chorus 'Patria oppressa' and Macduff's romanza 'Ah, la paterna mano'. First performance: Florence, 14 Mar 1847; rev Paris, 21 Apr 1865.

(2) Strauss's tone poem. First performance: Weimar, 13 Oct 1890.

(3) Bloch's opera, to a libretto by Edmond Fleg, again with baritone and soprano leads. First performance: Paris, 2 Nov 1910.

(4) Sciarrino's opera, to his own libretto, featuring once more a baritone–soprano central couple. First performance: Schwetzingen, 6 Jun 2002.

Other treatments include overtures by Spohr, Raff, Sullivan and Fry, Collingwood's opera, and pieces for piano by Smetana and guitar by Henze. Orson Welles made versions with music by Herrman (recording) and Ibert (film).

McCabe, John (b. Huyton, 21 Apr 1939). British composer, a prolific and versatile exponent of a language connecting him to Hartmann, Hindemith and Rawsthorne. He studied with Humphrey Proctor-Gregg and Thomas Pitfield in Manchester (1958–62) and with Genzmer in Munich (1964). Since then he has worked as a composer, pianist and writer. His works include ballets (*Edward II*, 1994–5), five symphonies and other orchestral works (Variations on a Theme of Hartmann, 1964; *Notturni ed alba*, s, orch, 1970), and diverse smaller pieces.

McCormack, John (b. Athlone, 14 Jun 1884; d. Dublin, 16 Sep 1945). Irish tenor, an early gramophone favourite, recording operatic arias, lieder and Irish folksongs with a particular sweetness. Briefly a member of the choir of the Catholic cathedral in Dublin, with which he made his first visit to the USA in 1904, he studied in Milan with Vincenzo Sabatini the next year and began his career in Italy. He made his Covent Garden debut in 1907 (Turiddu) and sang both there and at the Met (1910–18), then retired from the stage. His espousal of Irish nationalism affected his reputation in England, but not in the USA, where he spent most of his time during and after the First World War and took nationality (1917). He returned to Ireland and toured widely.

MacCunn, Hamish (b. Greenock, 22 Mar 1868; d. London, 2 Aug 1916). Scottish composer and conductor, of conservatively Romantic music with Scottish atmosphere. A ship-owner's son, he studied with Parry and Stanford at the RCM (1883–6) and remained in London as a teacher and opera conductor. He wrote operas, cantatas, orchestral works and songs, but is remembered almost exclusively for the overture *Land of the Mountain and the Flood*, Op.3 (1887).

MacDowell, Edward (Alexander) (b. New York, 18 Dec 1860; d. New York, 23 Jan 1908). US composer and pianist, widely acclaimed in his time, especially for his poetic piano pieces in the manner of Grieg. Born into a family enjoying comfort and culture, he was taken by his mother in 1876 to Paris, where he studied with Marmontel. He continued his education with the renowned teacher and critic Louis Ehlert in Wiesbaden (1878–9) and with Carl Heymann (piano) and Raff at the Hoch Conservatory in Frankfurt (1879–80). Liszt also offered encouragement. He remained largely in Germany until returning to the USA in 1888, with his wife of four years. They settled in Boston, and he went on composing, performing and teaching, as he had in Germany; he seems to have found the division of his time irksome but necessary. In 1896 he was appointed first professor of music at Columbia, but mental instability overtook him. He composed nothing after 1902 and resigned from the university in 1904. He was able, though, to plan turning his summer home at Peterborough, New Hampshire, into an artists' retreat – the MacDowell Colony – which endures.

Orchestral: Piano Concerto No.1, A minor, Op.15, 1882; No.2, D minor, Op.23, 1884–6; *Hamlet, Ophelia* (symphonic poems), Op.22, 1884–5; etc.
Piano: Sonata No.1 'Tragica', G minor, Op.45, 1891–2; No.2 'Eroica', G minor, Op.50, 1894–5; No.3 'Norse', D minor, Op.57, 1898–9; No.4 'Keltic', E minor, Op.59, 1900; *Zwei Fantasiestücke*, Op.17, 1883 (2: *Hexentanz*); *Woodland Sketches*, Op.51, 1896 (1: *To a Wild Rose*); *Sea Pieces*, Op.55, 1896–8; etc.
Other works: songs, partsongs

Mace, Thomas (b. ?Cambridge, 1612/13; d. ?Cambridge, ?1706). English composer, author of the compendious *Musick's Monument* (1676), an important source of information concerning taste and performance practice. He seems to have spent almost his entire life in Cambridge, from 1635 as a member of the Trinity College choir.

McEwen, John (Blackwood) (b. Hawick, 13 Apr 1868; d. London, 14 Jun 1948). Scottish composer, a nationalist late Romantic, knighted in 1931. He studied at Glasgow University and with Ebenezer Prout, Corder and Tobias Matthay at the RAM (1893–5), where he returned to teach in 1898 and became principal (1924–36). His works include a Milton setting, *Hymn on the Morning of Christ's Nativity*, for soprano, choir and orchestra (1901–5), and 17 quartets.

Macfarren, George (Alexander) (b. London, 2 Mar 1813; d. London, 31 Oct 1887). British composer, among the most notable and certainly the most productive of the high Victorian period, knighted in 1883. The son of a dancing master and theatre man, he studied with Potter at the RAM (1829–36), where he spent much of his later life as a teacher and in 1875 became principal. Blind from 1860, he continued to add to his output of operas, oratorios, symphonies (nine eventually) and other works.

McFerrin, Bobby [Robert] (b. New York, 11 Mar 1950). US jazz musician, who since 1990 (following studies with Bernstein, Ozawa and Gustav Meier) has appeared as conductor and extempore vocalist with orchestras including the San Francisco Symphony (for his debut), Chicago Symphony and Vienna Philharmonic. He also provided vocal accompaniment to Chick Corea in recordings of two Mozart piano concertos. His father, also Robert (b. 1921), was in 1955 the first African-American man to join the Met company.

Machaut, Guillaume de (b. ?Machault, Champagne, c.1300; d. Rheims, Apr 1377). French poet-composer. The survival of what is probably his complete output, in six luxury copies, testifies not only to his artistic pride but to the esteem in which he was held. That esteem faded soon after his death, but was reawakened in the second half of the 20th century, restoring him as the great musical light of his period. His mass, lively and fascinating in its harmonic-rhythmic structure, is the earliest unified setting; his songs – 141, all to his own words – cover a range from sprightly tunes to convolutions of irony and cross-reference, besides responding with consummate variety to limitations of poetic form and subject matter (in most cases courtly love, intense but chaste). He also wrote twice as many lyric poems he did not set, as well as 15 long poetic allegories. Two of his longer narratives, Le VOIR DIT and the REMEDE DE FORTUNE, include songs.

From c.1323 he was in the service of Jean de Luxembourg, king of Bohemia, who, though blind, followed an active career as a soldier knight and travelled widely. In 1340 the composer seems to have settled in Rheims, where he was a canon at the cathedral: the association went back at least to 1324, when he wrote a motet for the installation of a new bishop, and may have extended to his student days. He maintained contacts with the Luxembourg family, in particular with Jean's daughter Bonne and her sons Charles (Charles V of France) and Philip (Duke of Burgundy), of whom Charles, as dauphin, visited him in his house. In 1350 he began making compilations of his works for his patrons, who also included other members of the French royal house, Charles II of Navarre and Jean, Duke of Berry (who later commissioned the Très riches heures). Occasionally he was in Paris. His brother Jean, who had been with him at the court of the blind king, joined him as a Rheims canon, lived in the same house and died in 1372.

He drew with determination on his predecessors: an ancient tradition for his contributions to the LAI; the Roman de Fauvel as well as de Vitry (whom he may have met) in his motets; and more generally the notational innovations of de Vitry's ARS NOVA, which made possible a new rhythmic suppleness and intricacy. His uniqueness lay in his sense for how harmony, rhythm and texture could create coherent form, his care for detail, his melodic gift (linked to rhythmically and expressively subtle word-setting) and his establishment of the VIRELAI, the RONDEAU and the BALLADE as a hierarchy of increasingly imposing genres. Fittingly he was honoured after his death with a double ballade (two poems to be set in counterpoint) by his pupil Eustache Deschamps, mourning 'Machaut, le noble rethorique'.

Daniel Leech-Wilkinson Machaut's Mass (1990); Anne Walters Robertson Guillaume de Machaut and Reims (2002)

Mass: MESSE DE NOSTRE DAME a 4
Motets: Qui es promesses de Fortune a 3; Hareu, hareu, le feu a 3; Trop plus est bele a 3; 20 others
Ballades: Amours me fait desirer a 3; Honte, paour, doubtance a 3; De toutes flours a 3; Nes que on porroit a 3; Quant Theseus a 4; Phyton, le mervilleus serpent a 3; 36 others
Rondeaux: Rose, liz a 4; Ma fin est mon commencement a 3; 20 others
Virelais: Douce dame jolie a 1; Quant je suis mis au retour a 1; 31 others
Other works: 19 lais, 1 complainte and 1 chanson royal, HOQUETUS DAVID

mächtig (Ger.). Mighty.

Mackenzie, Alexander (Campbell) (b. Edinburgh, 22 Aug 1847; d. London, 28 Apr 1935). Scottish composer and administrator, knighted in 1895. The son of a violinist-composer, he studied in Sondershausen (from 1857) and at the RAM (1862–5), then returned to Edinburgh, where he began to make his mark as a composer and teacher. Escaping exhaustion, he moved to Florence (1879–85), but then took important posts in London, including that of principal of the RAM (1888–1924), which he reinvigorated. He also exerted himself as a conductor, notably with the Philharmonic Society (1892–9), and stimulated such successors as Elgar, both as a man and by his music, which includes operas, oratorios (The Rose of Sharon, Op.30, 1884), three Scottish rhapsodies and a salon charmer, Benedictus, Op.37:3, first published in 1888 for violin and piano and later orchestrated.

Mackerras, (Alan) Charles (MacLaurin) (b. Schenectady, NY, 17 Nov 1925). Australian conductor, knighted in 1979, distinguished by his selfless elegance, pleasure in performance and regard for niceties of style: he was an early exponent of ornamentation in Mozart and of learning from period instruments, besides the work he did in promoting Janáček's music and producing faithful editions. After studies at the New South Wales Conservatorium he became principal oboist of the Sydney Symphony (1945–7). He then studied with Talich in Prague, and settled in London in 1948, conducting at Sadler's Wells, where he was responsible for the British première of Katya Kabanova (1951). The same year he created a ballet score from Sullivan's music, Pineapple Poll. Seemingly impervious to glitter, he did not make his Met debut until 1972 (Gluck's Orfeo), but since then he has been active internationally, besides taking charge of the Sadler's Wells Opera as it became English National Opera (1970–77) and of Welsh National Opera (1987–92).

Mackey, Steve(n) (b. Frankfurt, 14 Feb 1956). US composer and electric guitarist, whose music mixes materials with ironic dash. He studied at Davis, at Stony Brook and with Martino at

Brandeis, where he took a doctorate in 1985. Having joined the Princeton faculty that year, he became professor in 1993. His works include the electric guitar concerto *Tuck and Roll* (2000), other pieces involving orchestra and electric guitar separately, and a full-length opera, *Ravenshead* (1997), for solo male performer and ensemble.

MacMillan, James (b. Kilwinning, 16 Jul 1959). Scottish composer, commanding an ample emotional rhetoric. He studied at the universities of Edinburgh and Durham (with Casken, PhD 1987), and soon gained attention for works combining protest with aspiration in a manner informed by Penderecki and liberation theology. Examples include *The Confession of Isobel Gowdie* (Proms, 1990), on a witch burning, and numerous other explicitly programme-based pieces.

Maconchy, Elizabeth (b. Broxbourne, Herts., 19 Mar 1907; d. Norwich, 11 Nov 1994). British composer, created dame in 1987. She gained a lasting attachment to central European currents as a student of Jirák in Prague (1929–30), following earlier studies with Wood and Vaughan Williams at the RCM (1923–9). Foremost in her output is her half-century sequence of 13 quartets (1933–83). Her daughter is the composer Nicola LeFanu (b. 1947).

McPhee, Colin (Carhart) (b. Montreal, 15 Mar 1900; d. Los Angeles, 7 Jan 1964). US composer and student of Balinese music. After studies at Peabody (1918–21), in Toronto and in Paris (with Le Flem and Isidor Philipp, 1924–6) he settled in New York, where an encounter with a recording of Balinese music led him to base himself there (1931–8). This led to his most celebrated works, notably *Tabuh-tabuhan* for an orchestra incorporating a Western gamelan of two pianos and percussion (1936) and *Balinese Ceremonial Music* for two pianos (1934–8), as well as his treatise *Music in Bali*. His life after returning to the USA in 1939 was fraught with personal and creative difficulties.

Madama Butterfly (Madam Butterfly). Opera by Puccini to a libretto by Giacosa and Illica after David Belasco's play set in Nagasaki in what were then recent times. Cio-Cio-San (soprano), the title character, is married to the US lieutenant Pinkerton (tenor), who goes away with his ship. When he returns three years later with a new wife, Cio-Cio-San, who has waited faithfully, kills herself. The score achieves a rare combination of exotic prettiness with passion, partly by rooting both in pentatonic features. Its top numbers include Cio-Cio-San's 'Un bel di', Pinkerton's 'Addio, fiorito asil', the love duet 'Viene la sera' and the Humming Chorus, evocative of evening before the final scene. The original version, letting Pinkerton off less lightly, has sometimes been revived since the 1980s. First performance: Milan, 17 Feb 1904; rev Brescia, 28 May 1904.

Mädchen mit den Schwefelhölzern, Das (The Little Match-Girl). Opera by Lachenmann to his own libretto based on Hans Christian Andersen's story and other sources. With little direct narrative, the work is an imposing organism of luminous sounds scraped from a large, fragmented assembly of instruments and voices. First performance: Hamburg, 26 Jan 1997.

Maderna, Bruno (b. Venice, 21 Apr 1920; d. Darmstadt, 13 Nov 1973). Italian composer and conductor, who worked for avant-garde goals with a rare big-heartedness. Exploited by his presumptive father as a prodigy violinist and conductor (he conducted a concert with the Scala orchestra at 12), he was rescued by Irma Manfredi, a Veronese dressmaker, and eventually taken to the Rome Conservatory, where he studied with Alessandro Bustini. He completed his training in composition with Malipiero in Venice (1941–2), and in conducting with Guarineri in Siena (1941) and Hermann Scherchen in Venice (1948), where he lived in the immediate post-war years as a conservatory teacher and commercial composer. During this time he also met and befriended Nono, followed by more contemporaries he encountered from 1949 onwards at the Darmstadt summer school. In the 1950s he divided his time between Darmstadt and Milan, where he was joint director with Berio of the electronic music studio. After that he was often on the road as a conductor, admired above all in contemporary music and Mahler; his recordings of works by Nono and Boulez were groundbreaking and remain exemplary. All these acts of musical partisanship left him little time, and the best of his music has the flair of something achieved at speed, together with a characteristic largeness of gesture. *Musica su due dimensioni* seems to have been the first composition for simultaneous live and electronic sounds. Memorials to him came from Boulez (*Rituel*) and Berio (*Calmo*).

Raymond Fearn *Bruno Maderna* (1990)

Stage: *Hyperion* (after Hölderlin), f.p. Venice, 1964, rev several times (potentially includes *Dimensioni II*, tape, 1960; *III*, fl, orch, 1963–4; *IV*, 4 fl, chbr orch, 1964; *Aria*, s, fl, orch, 1964; *Stele per Diotima*, orch, 1965; *Cadenza*, fl; *Gesti*, ch, orch, 1969); etc.
Orchestral (full): Flute Concerto, 1954; Piano Concerto, 1959; Oboe Concerto No.1, 1962–3; No.2, 1967; No.3, 1973; *Quadrivium*, 1969; Violin

Concerto, 1969; *Grande aulodia*, fl, ob, orch, 1970; *Aura*, 1972; *Biogramma*, 1972; etc.

Orchestral (chamber): *Amanda*, 1966; *Serenata per un satellite*, 1969; *Juilliard Serenade*, with tape, 1970–71; *Giardino religioso*, 1972; etc.

Smaller works: *Musica su due dimensioni*, fl, cymbals, tape, 1952, rev fl, tape, 1958; String Quartet, 1955; *Honeyrêves*, fl, pf, 1962; *Aulodia per Lothar*, ob d'amore, gui ad lib, 1965; *Widmung*, vn, 1967; etc.

Madetoja, Leevi (Antti) (b. Oulu, 17 Feb 1887; d. Helsinki, 6 Oct 1947). Finnish composer, the leading national Romantic after Sibelius, with whom he studied in Helsinki (1906–10). After further studies in Paris with d'Indy, in Vienna with Fuchs and in Berlin, he returned to Helsinki in 1912, and worked there as a conservatory teacher and critic. His works include the operas *The Ostrobothnians*, Op.45 (f.p. Helsinki, 1924) and *Juha*, Op.74 (f.p. Helsinki, 1935), the ballet *Okon Fuoko*, Op.58 (1930) and three symphonies (No.1, F, Op.29, 1915–16; No.2, E♭, Op.35, 1917–18; No.3, A, Op.55, 1926).

madness. The abilities of outstanding performers – particularly violinists and pianists – are so much at an extreme and require so much unusually intensive and even obsessive activity (i.e. practice), that insanity may seem a waiting danger if not an actual condition. But though there are many virtuosos who seem, in person or in anecdote, to be dwellers on the edge, and though there are some who lost control of their faculties, most enjoy robust mental health. Where composers are concerned, although the disciplines of notation make an orderly mind essential, music by its nature confuses the category of the rational. What to some will seem most logical – Bach, for instance, or Webern – may alternatively be viewed as manic, and radical changes in musical style, such as came with Beethoven or with 20th-century modernism, have commonly been explained by reluctant listeners as signs of derangement. Oddly, music history provides some support for that: where composers have sought to give an image of madness, they have often gone beyond the stylistic norms of the time, thus inviting performers, also, to extend the limits (whereas real madness is more a confinement and reduction of powers). There are famous mad scenes in Handel's *Orlando*, Bellini's *I puritani*, Donizetti's *Lucia di Lammermoor*, Thomas's *Hamlet* and Stravinsky's *The Rake's Progress*. Schoenberg's *Pierrot lunaire* might be understood as mad scene from beginning to end, and implicitly is so understood by Davies in compositions based on it, notably *Eight Songs for a Mad King*.

madrigal. (1) Vocal composition characteristic of the high Renaissance, usually secular and for several voices. The form seems to have arisen in Florence and Rome in the 1520s, when the influence of French polyphonic song met the newly deeper work of Italian poets at a time when cultivated amateurs could enjoy the results. The first printed volume to use the term 'madrigal' (1530) was dominated by Verdelot; other composers of the genre's early spring included Festa and Layolle, followed by Arcadelt. Willaert and Rore moved the madrigal in the 1540s–50s towards a more text-based style, which strongly influenced Lassus, de Monte and Andrea Gabrieli in the next generation. The classic madrigal, combining suave counterpoint with expressivity, then reached its apogee in the works of Marenzio in the 1580s, while Wert introduced a more dramatic note. Madrigals by Marenzio and others, published in London with their texts translated, helped stimulate the great flourishing of the English madrigal in the 1590s, with Morley, Weelkes and Wilbye the leading composers. Meanwhile, in Italy, a more intensely expressive and chromatic style was being developed by Luzzaschi and, especially, Gesualdo. After 1600 the English madrigal went into decline, but in Italy a new form arose, for voices with essential instrumental support. Madrigals from the 16th century may have been performed with instruments doubling or replacing vocal parts, especially when the context was public festivity rather than private chamber music. But Monteverdi and others after 1600 reconceived the madrigal as a medium for solo singers (in some cases only one) with instruments. From there it dissolved variously into cantata and opera, and by the time of Monteverdi's last, posthumous book (1651) the term was virtually defunct.

(2) The term was also used in the 14th century for a kind of polyphonic song in two or three parts and normally in eight-line stanzas, as practised by Jacopo da Bologna, Landini and others.

madrigal comedy. Modern term for a drama with madrigalian numbers, the clearest examples being by Vecchi and Banchieri.

madrigale spirituale (It.). Madrigal with a sacred but non-liturgical text, intended for private devotion. There are examples by most of the great madrigal composers from Rore to Gesualdo and Monteverdi.

madrigalian. Term implying one of the chief characteristics of the 16th-century madrigal, Italian or English: expressive word painting within lively counterpoint.

Madrigali guerrieri et amorosi (Madrigals Warlike and Amorous). Title of a collection by Monteverdi, his eighth madrigal book, dedicated to Emperor Ferdinand III. The feelings and actions of warriors and lovers turn out to be alike, for both have to do with detection, pursuit, struggle, victory and exhaustion. Still, the notional two types are separated in the book, and arranged as follows, each half ending with a ballo to poetry by Rinuccini and the first including also a larger theatre piece, the *Combattimento*:

Madrigali guerrieri: *Altri canti d'Amor*, 6 v, str, con; *Or che'l cielo e la terra* (Petrarch), 6 v, 2 vn, con; *Gira il nemico* (Giulio Strozzi), a, t, b, con; *Se vittorie sì belle*, 2 t, con; *Armato il cor*, 2 t, con; *Ogni amante è guerrier* (Rinuccini), 3 v, con; *Ardo, avvampo*, 8 v, 2 vn, con; *Il* COMBATTIMENTO DI TANCREDI E CLORINDA; *Volgendo il ciel* (Rinuccini)
Madrigali amorosi: *Altri canti di Marte* (Giambattista Marino), 6 v, 2 vn, con; *Vago augelletto* (Petrarch), 7 v, str, con; *Mentre vaga angioletta* (Giovanni Battista Guarini), 2 t, con; *Ardo e scoprir*, 2 t, con; *O sia tranquillo il mare*, 2 t, con; *Ninfa che scalza*, 2 t, con; *Dolcissimo uscignolo* (Guarini), 5 v, con; *Chi vole aver felice* (Guarini), 5 v, con; *Non avea Febo ancora* (*Lamento della ninfa*), 4 v, con; *Perchè t'en fuggi?* (Rinuccini), 3 v, con; *Non partir*, 3 v, con; *Su, su, su, pastorelli vezzosi*, 3 v, con; *Ballo delle ingrate* (Rinuccini)

Maelzel, Johann Nepomuk (b. Regensburg, 15 Aug 1772; d. on board ship off the South Carolina coast, 21 Jul 1838). German inventor, notably of the METRONOME. An organ builder's son, he moved to Vienna in 1792 and began his career as a musical inventor with mechanical instruments. Beethoven wrote *Wellingtons Sieg* (1813) for his panharmonicon, then instituted a legal case over ownership of the material. This was resolved, and the composer became one of the first adherents of the metronome. Maelzel sailed to New York in 1826 and spent the rest of his life touring with his inventions.

maestoso (It.). Majestic. The marking appears by itself or as a tempo qualification, e.g. *andante maestoso*.

maestro (It.). Master. In It. the term is applied to craftsmen and artists of many sorts, but in Eng. it is usually reserved for conductors.

maestro di cappella (It.). Conductor, chapelmaster.

maestro di cappella, Il (The Conductor). Comic scena by Cimarosa in which the Maestro (bass) eventually exerts himself over an initially unruly and deficient orchestra.

magazines. Several writers, notably Mattheson, issued periodical publications about music in the first half of the 18th century, but the earliest general musical magazines, open to various contributors, started at the century's end and included the *Allgemeine musikalische Zeitung* (1798–1848), in which, for example, Hoffmann published on Beethoven. Among long survivors in the field are the *Neue Zeitschrift für Musik* (founded by Schumann in 1834), *The Musical Times and Singing Class Circular* (1844, known as *The Musical Times* since 1904) and *The Strad* (1890, for string instruments). More recent are several opera magazines – *Opera News* (US, from 1936), *Opera* (UK, from 1950), *Opernwelt* (Germany, from 1960), *Das Opernglas* (Germany, from 1980), *Opera Now* (UK, from 1989) – and record reviews: *The Gramophone* (UK, from 1923), *Fanfare* (US, from 1977) and the *International Record Review* (UK, from 2000). Magazines for new music have flourished since the 1920s, including *Melos* (Germany, 1920–75), *Modern Music* (US, 1924–46), *Tempo* (UK, from 1939) and *The Score* (UK, 1949–61). Half a century later came reviews devoted to past times, notably *Early Music* (from 1973) and *Goldberg* (from 1997). See also JOURNALS.

Maggio Musicale (Musical May). Florentine music festival, instituted in 1933 and generally overspilling the boundaries of the month.

maggiore (It.). Major. Used as a marking, especially in variations, to signal a change of mode.

Magic Flute, The. See *Die* ZAUBERFLÖTE.

Magnard, (Lucien Denis Gabriel) Albéric (b. Paris, 9 Jun 1865; d. Baron, Oise, 3 Sep 1914). French composer, notably of symphonies of dour nobility. The son of the editor of *Le Figaro*, he trained in law before studying with Massenet at the Paris Conservatoire (1887–8) and then with d'Indy. From 1896 he taught at the Schola Cantorum, but depression and partial deafness kept him largely in isolation. He died when German soldiers set fire to his house, and some of his music went with him. His friend Ropartz reconstructed the parts for his opera *Guercoeur*, Op.12 (to his own medieval-meditative libretto, 1897–1901); other works include a second full-length opera *Bérénice*, Op.19 (after Racine, 1905–9), his four symphonies (No.1, C minor, Op.4, 1890; No.2, E, Op.6, 1893; No.3, B♭ minor, Op.11, 1896; No.4, C♯ minor, Op.21, 1913), chamber music and songs.

Magnificat. Canticle to words from Luke 1 (Mary's at the Annunciation), frequently set on its own, besides as the consummation of vespers in the Catholic tradition or with the *Nunc dimittis* for Anglican evensong. Most composers of the 15th and 16th centuries set it, often many times (Lassus made over 100 settings) and usually to polyphony alternating with plainsong verses. There are resplendent versions by Monteverdi and Bach, and many in a quieter style devised for Anglican worship.

Magnus liber (Great Book). Anonymous IV's term for the collection of early polyphony deriving from Notre Dame in Paris, created by Leonin and revised by Perotin. Copies travelled to England, Spain and Germany, besides elsewhere in France, and several survive, conveying the repertory in diverse states.

Mahagonny. See AUFSTIEG UND FALL DER STADT MAHAGONNY.

Mahler. Austrian composers, husband and wife.

(1) **Gustav** (b. Kalischt/Kaliště, near Iglau/ Jihlava, Bohemia, 7 May 1860; d. Vienna, 18 May 1911). The ultimate Romantic in making his music an emotional and spiritual autobiography – fierce, passionate, searching – he simultaneously broke through into the modern era by virtue of his wide-ranging harmony, his intense and highly varied palette, his formal freedom and, above all, his irony, his ability to achieve poignancy and parody together. Also one of the leading conductors of his time, he confined his creative work to songs and symphonies, genres he brought together in symphonic song cycles, symphonies with song movements and whole sung symphonies (No.8 and *Das Lied von der Erde*). There are no minor works.

So much of him is in his music that the details of his life seem curiously redundant, like the novelization of a film. For instance, the music's qualities of nostalgia and alienation – and its specific moments of tavern dance, march and fanfare – scarcely need explanation as the memories of a Jewish boy, the son of a rough-tempered innkeeper, in the small town of Iglau. He completed his education in Vienna, at the conservatory with Fuchs and Franz Krenn (1875–8), and as an adherent of Wagner's music and disciple of Bruckner, along with fellow students including Hans Rott and Hugo Wolf. Soon he was a professional. He had no early success as a composer (his cantata *Das klagende Lied* did not win a hoped-for prize, and he failed to complete his opera *Rübezahl*) – but early conducting jobs in the Austrian provinces prepared him for increasingly prominent, though junior, appointments in Kassel (1883–5), Prague (1885–6) and Leipzig (1886–8).

Love affairs with a singer in Kassel and with the granddaughter-in-law of Weber in Leipzig, where he produced a completion of the composer's comic opera *Die drei Pintos*, helped stimulate his first notable song cycle (*Lieder eines fahrenden Gesellen*) and his First Symphony, but still his reputation was largely that of a conductor – and one who made exacting demands.

He won the opportunity to exert himself fully when he became director of the Budapest opera (1888–91), where he restored recitative in *Don Giovanni* (traditionally performed at the time with spoken dialogue) and introduced *Cavalleria rusticana*. Also in Budapest he conducted his symphony and began a successor (though at first he considered both works as symphonic poems), while the deaths of his parents in 1889 left him with responsibilities for his two brothers and, especially, his two sisters. Both young women moved in with him during his time in Hamburg (1891–7), where he was principal conductor at the opera and, in succession to von Bülow from 1894, of the symphony concerts. In 1892 he led the opera company on his only visit to London, where he gave the first complete performance of the *Ring* in Britain.

From the following year, to the end of his life, he returned to the Austrian countryside for the summer to devote himself to composition, his first regular holiday home being at Steinbach in the Salzkammergut, where he worked in a detached studio. His main projects now were his Second and Third symphonies, overlapping with each other and with songs to poems from the collection *Des Knaben Wunderhorn*, whose faux-naif character provided one key to his music's ambivalence – its childlike simplicity and aspiration, and its very adult complexity and doubt. Both symphonies are narratives. The Second begins with a funeral march and arrives at a promise of resurrection, forcefully affirmed in the choral finale. The Third, in its search for answers to the existential questions asked by its long and turbulent first movement, moves beyond paradise (fifth movement, with angel choirs) to an adagio of love music. In both works traditional patterns are still present; they include the sonata-style opposition of dynamic and lyrical music, and the multi-movement scheme in which slow movement and scherzo are balancing interludes. But although the transformation of these patterns by inserting extra movements and voices had Beethoven's blessing, Mahler made his music unavoidably personal in its intensity of utterance and of memory. Like Bruckner, he reconceived the symphony as credo, but as the credo of one always struggling to find belief.

His acceptance of Catholic baptism in 1897 was

merely a necessity for him to be employed as director of the court opera in Vienna. Work there, bouts of ill health and the revision of *Das klagende Lied* interrupted the succession of symphonies, which picked up again with No.4, a work whose comparative closeness to the norms (it is in four movements and has certain classical gestures) only heightens its irony; this time a child's vision of heaven is the goal. The score was completed in 1900 in a new 'composing hut' near the Wörthersee, in Carinthia, and little more than a year later he achieved stability in another dimension when he met Alma Schindler (see below), whom he married on 9 March 1902. Their first daughter, Maria, was born nine months later, their second, Anna, in June 1904. As for his sisters, they had found matches in his orchestra, with the leader Arnold Rosé and his cellist brother, Eduard.

A new creative phase was opening. Having made his last *Wunderhorn* setting in 1901, he turned to poems by Friedrich Rückert, including those of the *Kindertotenlieder*, while his next three symphonies, Nos.5–7 (1901–6), were purely orchestral. In that respect – and formally, and texturally – they adhere more to the great tradition, and certainly the Fifth (another symphony beginning with a funeral march) reaches a conclusion unusually positive and high-spirited for this composer. Nevertheless, the language of melody and gesture remains highly individual, and the expressive character ambiguous: depending on the performance (and no doubt also on the listener), the Fifth Symphony's interior adagietto, for strings and harp, can sound like warm love music or a farewell. About the meaning of the Sixth there may be less doubt, though its deathward urge, continuing into a last movement of savage gloom, produces a powerful image of negativity, and the Seventh has always been a puzzle, with its nocturnal intermezzos and its open-ended finale. Meanwhile, at the opera, he was leading a succession of innovatory productions designed and lit by Alfred Roller. He was also receiving and accepting more invitations to conduct his own music elsewhere, especially after the belated première of the Third Symphony in 1902. Perhaps from these invitations he drew the confidence to write for expanded choral orchestral forces with multiple soloists in his Eighth Symphony (1906–7), where a hymn of spiritual girding, the *Veni Creator Spiritus*, is followed by a musical realization of the close of Goethe's *Faust* – another final moment in paradise.

In 1907 his life changed. His elder daughter, suffering simultaneously from scarlet fever and diphtheria, could not be saved, and he himself was found to have heart trouble. Difficulties at the opera – the usual wrangles of singers at odds with a rigorous conductor, coupled with endemic antisemitism – led to his departure, and he spent the early months of 1908 conducting at the Met. New York became his second home. He returned again for the 1908–9 season, and then for those of 1909–10 and 1910–11 at the head of the New York Philharmonic. As always, during summers by the Wörthersee, he composed. The last two works he completed, *Das Lied von der Erde* (a symphony in six songs) and the Ninth Symphony, both end with slow movements in which the atmosphere of leave-taking is unmistakable. The Tenth, of which two movements were virtually finished and three only drafted (to be realized by Deryck Cooke and others), might have been more affirmative, though its opening movement reaches a dissonant climax of extraordinary bareness and ferocity.

Das Lied and the Ninth Symphony had their posthumous premières under Bruno Walter; Mengelberg was another early supporter. Then for nearly half a century after his death he was a marginal figure. But in time his complex absorption of cheap music, Romantic stereotypes and violent modernism – of everything from schmalz to shrieks – began to seem emphatically central. A symphony, he is alleged to have said in discussion with Sibelius, must be a world. Since the 1960s the world has been ready to hear him.

Kurt and Herta Blaukopf, ed. *Mahler: His Life, Work and World* (1991); Donald Mitchell and Andrew Nicholson, ed. *The Mahler Companion* (1999)

www.gustav-mahler.org

Symphonies (first performances conducted by the composer unless otherwise stated): No.1 'Titan', D, ?1884–1888, f.p. Budapest, 20 Nov 1889, rev 1893–6, *c*.1906 (without original second movement *Blumine*); No.2 'Resurrection', with s, a, ch (Des Knaben Wunderhorn; Mahler, after Klepstock), C minor–E♭, 1888–94 (first movement originally self-sufficient *Todtenfeier*), f.p. Berlin, 13 Dec 1895 (complete), rev 1903; No.3, with a, women's ch, boys' ch, D minor–major, 1893–6 (Nietzsche, Des Knaben Wunderhorn), f.p. Krefeld, 9 Jun 1902 (complete), rev 1906 ; No.4, with s (Des Knaben Wunderhorn), G–E, 1892, 1899–1900, f.p. Munich, 25 Nov 1901, rev 1901–10; No.5, C♯ minor–D, 1901–2, f.p. Cologne, 18 Oct 1904; No.6, A minor, 1903–4, rev 1906, f.p. Essen, 27 May 1906; No.7, E minor–C, 1904–5, f.p. Prague, 19 Sep 1908; No.8 'Symphony of a Thousand', with soli, ch, boys' ch, (Veni Creator Spiritus, II; Goethe *Faust*, Part 2), E♭,1906–7, f.p. Munich, 12 Sep 1910; *Das* LIED VON DER ERDE, 1908–9; No.9, D–D♭, 1908–9, f.p. Vienna, 26 Jun 1912 (Walter); No.10, F♯ minor, 1910, unfinished, performing versions by Deryck Cooke, Clinton Carpenter, Joe Wheeler, Remo Mazzetti, Rudolf Barshai, and Nicola Samale and Giuseppe Mazzuca

Cantata: *Das* KLAGENDE LIED, 1878–80, rev 1892–3, 1898–9

Chamber: Piano Quartet, A minor, ?1876–8, first movement only

Songs: *Lieder* (3; Mahler), t, pf, 1880; LIEDER EINES FAHRENDEN GESELLEN, 1883–5, rev ?1891–6; *Lieder und Gesänge* (5), Vol.1, v, pf, 1880–87; *Des* KNABEN WUNDERHORN settings, 1887–1901; *Rückert-Lieder* (5), v, pf/orch, 1901–2; KINDERTOTENLIEDER, 1901–4

Orchestrations: *Die drei Pintos* (Weber), pub 1888; Suite from the Orchestral Works of Bach, pub 1910; arrs for str of quartets by Beethoven (Op.95) and Schubert (D.819), reorchestrations of symphonies by Beethoven and Schumann, etc.

(2) **Alma (Maria)** [née Schindler] (b. Vienna, 31 Aug 1879; d. New York, 11 Dec 1964). A painter's daughter, she studied composition with Zemlinsky, the first of several foremost artists with whom she was romantically involved. She was subsequently married to Mahler, who demanded she abandon composition, then to the architect Walter Gropius and the writer Franz Werfel. Her total output comprises 14 songs.

Maid of Pskov, The (*Pskovityanka*). Opera by Rimsky-Korsakov to his own libretto after a play by Lev Mey. Ivan the Terrible (bass) saves the city of Pskov for the sake of his natural daughter Olga (soprano), but she is killed in the conflict unleashed by her sweetheart Tucha (tenor). First performance: St Petersburg, 13 Jan 1873.

Mai-Dun. Tone poem by Ireland ('symphonic rhapsody') evoking life at the Iron Age hill fort better known as Maiden Castle, in Dorset.

main (Fr.). Hand, hence *main droite* (right hand), *main gauche* (left hand).

Maisky, Mischa (b. Riga, 10 Jan 1948). Soviet–Israeli cellist, a fervent explorer of traditional and non-traditional repertory. He studied in Riga, Leningrad and Moscow (with Rostropovich), and emigrated to Israel in 1972 after 14 months in prison. Since then he has worked with Argerich and others.

maître. Master, an honorific equivalent to the It. maestro.

maître de chapelle (Fr.). Chapelmaster.

maîtrise (Fr.). Choir school, boys' choir.

majeur (Fr.). Major.

major. Term descriptive of a mode, scale, key or interval.

(1) The major MODE is the diatonic mode with semitone intervals in third and seventh places.

(2) The major SCALE is that of the major mode, e.g. C–D–E–F–G–A–B–C (C major), D–E–F♯–G–A–B–C♯–D (D major), B♭–C–D–E♭–F–G–A–B♭ (B♭ major), etc.

(3) Music in the major mode will be in one or another of the major keys, named after the keynote, e.g. C major, D major, B♭ major, etc.

(4) A major interval is a semitone larger than the corresponding minor interval, e.g. the major second (C–D), major third (C–E), major sixth (C–A), major seventh (C–B), major ninth (C–D), etc.

Makropulos Case, The (*Věc Makropulos*). Opera by Janáček to his own libretto after Karel Čapek's play. The acclaimed singer Emilia Marty (soprano) is both siren and sphinx: she fascinates men – including Gregor (tenor) and Prus (baritone), combatants in a legal battle – and she has an uncanny knowledge of the past, which is eventually explained as due to her longevity. She is really Elina Makropulos, the daughter of a Greek physician and over 300 years old. Wearied by an existence that has become meaningless, she achieves radiance in embracing death. First performance: Brno, 18 Dec 1926.

mal (Ger.). Times, as in *dreimal* or *3mal*, marking a passage to be performed three times.

malagueña. Slowish Spanish dance; there is one in Ravel's *Rapsodie espagnole*.

Malibran, Maria (Felicia) [née García] (b. Paris, 24 Mar 1808; d. Manchester, 23 Sep 1836). French mezzo-soprano, daughter of Manuel García and sister of Pauline Viardot. Intensively trained by her father, she began her career in *Il barbiere di Siviglia* in London in 1825, repeating her performance in New York later that year. There she married François Eugène Malibran, a banker who was 43 years older and fell on hard times. After staying a year with him she returned to Europe and her career, in London, Paris and Italy, singing Rossini heroines, Leonora in *Fidelio* and the title role in Donizetti's *Maria Stuarda*, which she created. Her vocal power and brilliance caused wonderment, and her legend was bolstered by her early death. In March 1836 she married the violinist Charles de Bériot, with whom she had been living for several years, but the following month she fell from her horse, and though she continued to sing on crutches, her health was broken.

malinconia (It.). Melancholy. Also *malinconico* (melancholic), etc.

Malipiero, Gian Francesco (b. Venice, 18 Mar 1882; d. Treviso, 1 Aug 1973). Italian composer, who went through many changes in a composing career of over 60 years, his best works distinguished by a surrealist atmosphere related to Debussy and older Venetian music. He made a groundbreaking edition of Monteverdi's complete works (1926–42). Born into a musical and aristocratic family, he studied with Bossi in Venice and Bologna, and worked as amanuensis to Smareglia. He was in Paris for the first performance of *The Rite of Spring*, a shock that unleashed his most remarkable works, including *Sette canzoni* (1918–19), a sequence of seven tiny operas, and the rather less compressed *Tre commedie goldoniane* (1920–22). In 1932 he began teaching at the conservatory in Venice, where he became director (1939–52). Besides many other operas his works include 11 symphonies, concertos, choral music, eight quartets and piano pieces. His nephew Riccardo (1914–2003) also became a composer.

Mallarmé, Stéphane (b. Paris, 18 Mar 1842; d. Valvins, near Fontainebleau, 9 Sep 1898). French poet, whose dazzling lines desert the middle time of sense for the immediacy of sound and the adagio of contemplation. Debussy, who frequented his salon, made song settings and an orchestral translation (*Prélude à 'L'Après-midi d'un faune'*). There are also settings by Ravel, Milhaud, Hindemith and Boulez (whose *Pli selon pli* is a portrait of the poet).

mallet. Percussion beater having a distinct head. The glockenspiel, marimba, vibraphone and xylophone are commonly played with mallets and may be collectively described as mallet instruments.

Ma mère l'oye (Mother Goose). Music by Ravel illustrating fairytales by Perrault, written first as a set of piano duets, then orchestrated and expanded to make a ballet.

Mamlok, Ursula (b. Berlin, 1 Feb 1928). German–US composer, in the Schoenberg tradition. Arriving in New York in 1941, she studied at Mannes College, the Manhattan School and privately with Sessions, Wolpe, Shapey and Steuermann. She has taught at various New York institutions while producing an output strong in chamber music.

Manchester school. Term used of Birtwistle, Davies and Goehr, who were students together in Manchester in the mid-1950s.

mand. Abbreviation for mandolin.

mandolin. Small pear-shaped, guitar-like instrument, with four strings tuned like those of a violin. Descended from the gittern and mandore, it has lived mostly in the shadows of light music, and carried that aura with it into works by Mozart (*Don Giovanni*) and Mahler (Symphonies Nos.7–8, *Das Lied von der Erde*). Mahler's example impressed Schoenberg and Webern, who in turn had an effect on Stravinsky (*Agon*), Boulez and Henze.

Manfred. Verse drama by Byron, concerning a doomed soul wandering the Alps. There are two notable musical extrapolations:

(1) Overture and incidental music by Schumann. First performance: Weimar, 13 Jun 1852.

(2) Symphony by Tchaikovsky. First performance: Moscow, 23 Mar 1886.

mandora. German bass lute.

mandore. French treble lute of the late 16th and 17th centuries.

Manhattan School of Music. New York conservatory founded in 1917 by Janet D. Schenck.

Mann, Thomas. See IMAGINARY COMPOSERS.

Männerchor (Ger.). Men's choir, alternatively *Männergesangverein*.

mannerism. (1) Trait found in a composer's or performer's work, by implication regrettable.

(2) Term used in art history to denote the decadence of Renaissance innovations in the middle and later 16th century. It is sometimes applied to music, especially to Gesualdo's.

Mannes College of Music. New York conservatory founded in 1916 by David and Clara Mannes, since 1989 part of New School University.

Mannheim. German city, musically important as the seat of the Palatine Electors Carl Philipp (1720–42) and his nephew Carl Theodor, who in 1778, having succeeded to the Bavarian electorate, moved his court to Munich. The Mannheim orchestra was a testing ground for the emergent symphony, as practised by Johann Stamitz and his sons, as well as by Holzbauer, Cannabich, Toeschi, Filtz and Beck. Other composers who worked there included J.C. Bach, Traetta, F.X. Richter and Vogler.

Manns, August (b. Stolzenberg, 12 Mar 1825; d.

Norwood, London, 1 Mar 1907). German–British conductor, knighted in 1903. Of poor family, he was a working musician from a young age and spent most of his 20s in Prussian army bands. In 1854 he moved to London. Grove supported him as conductor of the Crystal Palace concerts (1855–1901), which had a determining role in popularizing the classics.

mano (It.). Hand, hence *mano destra* (right hand), *mano sinistra* (left hand).

Manon Lescaut. Novel by the Abbé Prévost (1731), about the survival capacity of desire. Manon, bound for a convent, falls in love with the Chevalier Des Grieux. Soon she moves on to a wealthy protector, but she comes down in the world, is deported and dies in the arms of her first lover, who has remained fascinated by her. At least five operas ensued, all with a soprano Manon and tenor Des Grieux:

(1) Balfe's *The Maid of Artois*. First performance: London, 27 May 1836.

(2) Auber's *Manon Lescaut* to a libretto by Scribe. First performance: Paris, 23 Feb 1856.

(3) Massenet's *Manon* to a libretto by Meilhac and Philippe Gille. Numbers include Manon's farewell to her domestic happiness with Des Grieux ('Adieu, notre petite table'), Des Grieux's dream ('En fermant les yeux'), Manon's gavotte ('Obéissons quand leur voix appelle') and Des Grieux's prayer ('Ah! fuyez, douce image'). First performance: Paris, 19 Jan 1884.

(4) Puccini's *Manon Lescaut* to a libretto by Domenico Oliva and Illica. Numbers include Des Grieux's 'Donna non vidi mai', and Manon's 'In quelle trine morbide' and 'Sola, perduta, abbandonata'. First performance: Turin, 1 Feb 1893, rev Milan, 7 Feb 1894.

(5) Henze's *Boulevard Solitude* to a libretto by Grete Weil, a work that updates and diversifies the story, mixing satire with sentiment. First performance: Hanover, 17 Feb 1952.

Manoury, Philippe (b. Tulle, 19 Jun 1952). French composer, working often with mixed live-electronic resources and over relatively large expanses of time. He studied with Max Deutsch at the Ecole Normale de Musique and with Michel Philippot, Ivo Malec and Ballif at the Conservatoire (1974–8). In 1987, after several years at IRCAM, he began teaching at the Lyons Conservatory. His works include the operas *60e parallèle* (f.p. Paris, 1996) and *K …* (f.p. Paris, 2003).

Mansurian, Tigran (b. Beirut, 27 Jan 1939). Armenian composer, whose works convey nostalgia both for his country's ancient traditions and for the departing Romantic style. He studied at the Yerevan Conservatory (1960–67), followed a common path from serialism to older ways and began to be noticed abroad in the 1990s. His works consist mostly of orchestral, chamber and piano music.

Mantua (Mantova). Italian city where music was favoured under Gonzaga rule during the Renaissance and early Baroque. The first great patron was Isabella d'Este, who married Gian Francesco II in 1490 and died in 1539; her musicians included Tromboncino and Cara. Her son Ercole (cardinal bishop 1527–63) employed Jacquet at the cathedral, and his nephew Guglielmo (duke 1550–87) was the patron of Wert and Striggio. Guglielmo's son Vincenzo (duke 1587–1612) mounted weekly concerts and had Monteverdi's first two operas staged.

manual. Keyboard played by the hands (unlike a PEDALBOARD). The term is most often used when there is more than one, as on organs and harpsichords.

manualiter. Marking on music to be played on manuals only, countermanding PEDALITER.

Manuel, Roland. See ROLAND-MANUEL.

Manzoni, Giacomo (b. Milan, 26 Sep 1932). Italian composer, pursuing a path from Schoenberg and Adorno into a surprising lyricism. He studied in Milan, where he began teaching at the conservatory in 1962. His works include *Masse* for piano and orchestra (1977), written for Pollini, and the opera *Doktor Faust* (f.p. Milan, 1988).

Manzoni Requiem. Name sometimes given to Verdi's Requiem, which was first performed at a memorial service for the writer Alessandro Manzoni (1785–1873).

maqām (Arabic). Mode.

maracas. Pair of rattles, traditionally made from dried gourds, the rattling elements being the seeds, but also constructed artificially from wood, metal, plastic and other materials. Originating in northern South America before the arrival of Europeans, they became an essential component of the Latin American dance ensemble and entered the symphonic percussion section in Varèse's *Ionisation*. Because they are nearly always played in pairs, the singular form 'maraca' is rare.

Marais, Marin (baptized Paris, 31 May 1656; d. Paris, 15 Aug 1728). French composer and outstanding master of the viol. He was a fellow chorister with the young Lalande at St Germain-l'Auxerrois, and studied the viol with Sainte-Colombe. Before reaching 20 he was performing in Paris and at court, and though so much associated with the viol as a virtuoso performer, composer and teacher (several of his 19 children became musicians), he also made a notable contribution to French opera between Lully and Rameau – much more with *Alcyone* than with *Sémélé* (1709), whose failure hastened his eclipse.

Operas: *Alcyone*, f.p. Paris, 1706; etc.
Chamber: *Pièces de viole*, book 1, pub 1686; book 2, pub 1701 (Suite No.1 'Les Folies d'Espagne', A minor, etc.); book 3, pub 1711 (Suite No.2, D); book 4, pub 1717 (Suite No.7 'd'un goût étranger'); book 5, pub 1725; *La Gamme et autres morceaux de simphonie*, vn, viol, hpd, pub 1723 (*La Sonnerie de Sainte Geneviève du Mont à Paris*, etc.); etc.

Marbeck [Merbecke], **John** (b. ?Windsor, *c*.1505; d. ?Windsor, *c*.1585). English composer, the originator of Anglican chant in *The Book of Common Prayer Noted* (1550). He seems to have spent virtually all his life as a musician of St George's Chapel, Windsor.

Marcabru (*fl. c*.1129–50). Troubadour, active in Provence and Spain. Of his four songs surviving in notation, *Pax in nomine Domini!* aligns itself with the Christian reconquest of Spain.

marcato (It., marked). Stressed, clearly articulated.

Marcello. Italian composing brothers, both nobly born and practising music as dilettantes.

(1) **Alessandro** (b. Venice, 24 Aug 1669; d. Venice, 19 Jun 1747). A government official, he had varied artistic interests, and his compositional output was relatively small. Besides his Oboe Conerto in D minor (pub *c*.1717) – famous for its adagio, and transcribed by Bach – he wrote other concertos, sonatas and cantatas.

(2) **Benedetto** (**Giacomo**) (b. Venice, 24 Jun/Jul 1686; d. Brescia, 24 Jul 1739). Seemingly less distinguished than his brother in the government, he was more active musically. He published settings of the first 50 psalms (*Estro poetico-armonico*, 2 Vols., 1724–6) remarkable for their attempts to reawaken Classical and ancient Hebrew practices, and at times for their expressive tenacity. Other works by him include cantatas, sonatas (for cello, recorder and keyboard), sinfonias and concertos.

march. Piece of music normally in regular common or duple time, suitable for an orderly procession of people in step. This means a tempo of 60–80 beats per minute for a slow march and 100–140 for a quick march; faster yet is the double-quick march, for soldiers in attack. Besides their military uses, marches are played to engineer and dignify ceremonials, whether in real life or onstage. The march is also a type – implying no more than imaginary movement – that has often appeared in piano and symphonic music since the early 19th century.

The use of a steady drumbeat to synchronize marching is documented only from the late 16th century. Military marches are known from the 17th century, not long before marches began appearing onstage. There are examples in theatre works by Lully, Handel, Mozart, Beethoven, Mendelssohn, Berlioz, Meyerbeer, Verdi, Wagner, Stravinsky, Prokofiev and many others, while marches for the purpose of marching were made by composers including Beethoven, the Strausses, Sousa and Elgar. Often the categories intersect. The march in Handel's *Scipione* was written for (and is still used by) the Grenadier Guards, while the nuptial marches in Mendelssohn's *Midsummer Night's Dream* music and Wagner's *Lohengrin* have graced innumerable actual weddings. 20th-century stage marches, though, tend to have an ironic edge that would suit actual ceremonies less well, examples including those in Stravinsky's *Nightingale* and Prokofiev's *Love for Three Oranges*. Schubert wrote marches for 20 fingers at the piano, and there are march movements in symphonic works by Mozart, Beethoven, Berlioz and Berg. See also CORONATION; FUNERAL MARCH.

Marchand, Louis (b. Lyons, 2 Feb 1669; d. Paris, 17 Feb 1732). French organist-composer, admired by Rameau and others as a virtuoso. He was in Paris by 1689, when he contracted a marriage that ended in acrimony 12 years later. Meanwhile, he found posts at several churches and became a court organist in 1708. In 1717 he failed to show up at a planned trial of strengh with Bach. Most of his organ pieces are in four manuscript volumes, of which the second includes an imposing *Grand jeu* and a harmonically weird and meandering *Fond d'orgue*.

marche (Fr.), **marcia** (It.). March.

Märchenoper (Ger.). Romantic fairytale opera, e.g. *Hänsel und Gretel*.

Marco (Aragón), Tomás (b. Madrid, 12 Sep 1942). Spanish composer, notably of symphonies and concertos having to do with memory, not least memory of musical hispanicism. Largely self-taught, though he went to Darmstadt in 1962, he has been prominent in Spanish musical life as a critic and radio producer.

Marenzio, Luca (b. Coccaglio, near Brescia, 1553/4; d. Rome, 22 Aug 1599). Italian composer, among the leading madrigalists. Possibly a pupil of Giovanni Contino in Brescia and Mantua, he came to the fore as household musician to Cardinal Luigi d'Este in Rome (1578–86), during which time he published 13 volumes of madrigals and villanellas. He remained largely in Rome, serving other princes of the church, though he also spent time in Florence and Warsaw. During this post-Este period he produced 10 more books of secular songs, besides motets inspirited with the same madrigalian sense of imagery. He favoured settings for five voices (10 books, including one of *madrigali spirituali*) or six (six books), and his music's vitality, as well as its word-painting, gained him an international audience. His more serious, dark and complex later music was not so widely disseminated.

Marian antiphon. Prayer sung in honour of the Blessed Virgin Mary, often at the evening service of compline. Some of the most glorious music of the Renaissance was produced for such occasions. The great Marian antiphons are ALMA REDEMPTORIS MATER, AVE REGINA COELORUM, REGINA COELI and SALVE REGINA.

Maria Stuarda (Mary Stuart). Opera by Donizetti to a libretto by Giuseppe Bardari after Schiller's play. The power play between Elizabeth I (soprano) and Mary Stuart (soprano) is spurred by their rivalry over Leicester (tenor). In the opera, as in the play, they meet, which in life they did not. First performance: Milan, 30 Dec 1835.

Maria Theresa [Maria Theresia]. Name given to Haydn's Symphony No.48 in honour of the Austrian empress who reigned 1740–80.

Mariinsky. Premier opera and ballet theatre of St Petersburg, opened in 1860. It saw the premières of *Boris Godunov*, *Khovanshchina*, *The Queen of Spades*, *The Sleeping Beauty* and *Prince Igor*. In the 1920s it became the State Academic Theatre for Opera and Ballet; Stalin renamed it the Kirov in 1935. It reverted to its old name in 1991, under Gergiev, its music director since 1988.

marimba. Percussion instrument of the xylophone type, but with broader, thicker keys (hence a mellower sound), resonators of wood or metal, and a five-octave range from C below the bass clef. Its timbre and range make it one of the most adaptable percussion instruments, though it was not much used before 1945. Grainger's *In a Nutshell* (1915–16) belongs to its scarce ancient repertory. The term comes from southeast Africa, where marimbas are of the LAMELLAPHONE type; they became larger and stick-beaten in South and Central America, and were first manufactured in the USA in 1910.

marimbaphone. Obsolete steel marimba, one of the many inventions of John Calhoun Deagan (1853–1934).

Marini, Biagio (b. Brescia, 5 Feb 1594; d. Venice, 1663). Italian composer and violinist, author of fine sonatas, sinfonias and suites. Possibly trained by a composer uncle, he was appointed to St Mark's in Venice as a violinist in 1615. There he would have worked alongside Monteverdi, who followed his innovation (1618) of making a madrigal in the form of a love letter. After that he travelled, mostly in Italy and Germany.

marionette opera. See PUPPET OPERA.

Markevitch, Igor (b. Kiev, 27 Jul 1912; d. Antibes, 7 Mar 1983). Ukrainian–French conductor and composer, who, having been the rising star of Stravinsky-age modernism, gave up his creative ambitions to become an electric interpreter. The family (his father was a pianist) left Kiev for Switzerland when he was two, and he studied with Cortot and Boulanger in Paris from the age of 13. Diaghilev commissioned his Piano Concerto (1929), after which came his conducting debut (1930), ballet *L'Envol d'Icare* (1932), oratorio *Le Paradis perdu* (1933–5) and the beginnings of a collaboration with C.F. Ramuz on a concert of assorted works. In 1935 he married Nijinsky's daughter Kyra, and with her he moved to Florence at the outbreak of war. He revised his ballet as *Icare* (1943), then abandoned composition to become one of the outstanding international conductors of the 1950s–60s, keenly admired for his recordings of Tchaikovsky and Stravinsky. Increasingly deaf, he devoted his later years to his memoirs.

markiert (Ger.). Marcato.

markig (Ger.). Vigorous.

Marlboro. Town in Vermont, USA, where a summer school for chamber music was founded in 1951 by Rudolf Serkin and others. Regular participants included Casals, Galimir and Horszowski.

Marmontel, Jean François (b. Bort les Orgues, Haute-Corrèze, 11 Jul 1723; d. Abloville, 31 Dec

1799). French writer, notably of librettos for Rameau, Grètry and Piccinni, not to be confused with Antoine François Marmontel (1816–98), who was piano professor at the Paris Conservatoire for four decades (1848–87), his pupils including Bizet and Debussy.

Marriage (*Zhenit'ba*). Unfinished opera by Musorgsky setting Gogol's play. Just as one character hops out of a window to avoid wedlock, so the composer jilted his work, leaving just the first act in vocal score. This has been orchestrated by Aleksandr Gauk (1917) and others, of whom Ippolitov-Ivanov completed the piece (1931). There are also settings of the play by Grechaninov (f.p. Paris, 1950) and Martinů.

Marriage of Figaro, The. See *Le* NOZZE DI FIGARO.

Marsch (Ger.). March.

Marschner, Heinrich August (b. Zittau, 16 Aug 1795; d. Hanover, 14 Dec 1861). German composer, most importantly of Romantic operas. A craftsman's son, he had a piecemeal education, picked up partly under the patronage of Hungarian noblemen, one of whom introduced him to Beethoven. Weber presented his opera *Heinrich IV und d'Aubigné* in 1820 in Dresden, which became briefly his home (1821–6). He then made his name with DER VAMPYR, to a libretto by his actor brother-in-law Wilhelm August Wohlbrück. They collaborated again on *Der Templer und die Judin* (f.p. Leipzig, 1829), after Scott's *Ivanhoe*, and he worked with another theatre man, Eduard Devrient, on *Hans Heiling* (f.p. Berlin, 1833), a second tale of the supernatural. Based for much of the rest of his life in Hanover with his third and fourth wives, both singers, he had no similar success again. His other works include further operas, choruses and songs.

Marseillaise, La. National anthem of France, written by Rouget de l'Isle as a marching song, 'Chant de guerre pour l'armée du Rhin', on 25 April 1792. In July it was sung by volunteers from Marseilles entering Paris, who established its national popularity and its new name. An attempt to replace it under Napoleon III was instantly abandoned on his fall. Works quoting it include Schumann's *Faschingsschwank aus Wien*, Tchaikovsky's *1812* and Debussy's *Feux d'artifice*.

Marshall, Ingram (Douglass) (b. Mont Vernon, NY, 10 May 1942). US composer, a minimalist incorporating recordings of natural sounds. He studied with Paul Henry Lang and Ussachevsky at Columbia (1965–7) and Subotnick at CalArts; visits to Bali and Sweden were also important. His *Fog Tropes* for brass sextet and electronics (1982) came from observation of the San Francisco Bay. In 1989 he moved to Connecticut.

Marsyas. Satyr associated with the aulos in Greek mythology. Apollo, beating him in musical contest, had him flayed.

Marteau sans maître, Le (The Hammer with no Master). Work by Boulez interlocking settings of three poems by René Char with wordless commentaries, using different combinations from the ensemble of contralto, alto flute, viola, guitar, vibraphone, xylophone and percussion. First performance: Baden-Baden, 18 Jun 1955.

martelé (Fr., hammered). Bowstroke, using heavy pressure and sudden release to create a *sforzando*.

martellando, martellato (It., hammering, hammered). An extreme *sforzato*.

Martenot. See ONDES MARTENOT.

Martha. Opera by Flotow to a libretto by W. Friedrich, titled in full *Martha, oder Der Markt zu Richmond* (Martha, or Richmond Market). The title character is Lady Harriet Durham (soprano) in disguise. She and her maid Nancy (mezzo-soprano) accoutre themselves as peasants in order to escape the ennui of court life and win true love – which they do, with Lyonel (tenor) and Plunkett (bass). Numbers include 'Ach so fromm' (Lyonel) and 'Letzte Rose', a version of the Irish folksong 'The Last Rose of Summer' sung by 'Martha'. First performance: Vienna, 25 Nov 1847.

Martin. Style of French baritone with almost a full tenor range: the *baryton Martin*, named after Jean-Blaise Martin (1768–1837). The voice type was used by Gounod (Valentin in *Faust*), Bizet, Debussy (Pelléas) and others.

Martin, Frank (b. Geneva, 15 Sep 1890; d. Naarden, 21 Nov 1974). Swiss composer, who had to wait until the age of 50 before achieving his judicious and feeling balance of Bach, Debussy, Bartók and Schoenberg. The tenth and youngest child of a Calvinist minister, he was deeply impressed by hearing the St Matthew Passion when he was 12. He studied with Joseph Lauber, worked with Jaques-Dalcroze, and listened with interest to the French music Ansermet conducted in Geneva, but not until his 30s was he writing music that satisfied him, and his mature style only began to form in 1933, when he started to work with Schoenberg's 12-note method in a way that allowed him to preserve a sense of 'gliding tonality'. Then came his first masterpiece, *Le Vin herbé* (1938–41), a choral retelling of the Tristan story that released a relative flood of major works, including the delightful and intriguing *Petite symphonie concertante*. In 1946 he moved to the Netherlands, and from his home in Naarden he taught at the conservatory in Cologne (1950–57), where Stockhausen was one of his pupils.

www.frankmartin.org

Operas: *Der Sturm* (see The TEMPEST), 1952–5; *Monsieur de Pourceaugnac* (Molière), 1960–62, f.p. Geneva, 1963

Orchestral: Ballade, a sax, str, perc, pf, 1938; Ballade, pf, orch, 1939; Ballade, fl, str, pf, 1941; Ballade, trbn/t sax, chbr orch, 1941; PETITE SYMPHONIE CONCERTANTE, 1944–5; Ballade, vc, chbr orch, 1949; Concerto, 7 wind, perc, str, 1949; Violin Concerto, 1950–51; Etudes, str, 1955–6; Cello Concerto, 1965–6; *Trois danses*, ob, hp, str, 1970; Ballade, va, wind, hp, hpd, timp, 1972; *Polyptyque*, vn, str, 1973; etc.

Choral: Mass, double ch, 1922–6; *Le Vin herbé* (secular oratorio; Joseph Bédier), 12 v, 7 str, pf, 1938–41; *In terra pax* (oratorio; Bible, in Fr.), 1944; *Golgotha* (oratorio; Gospels and St Augustine, in Fr.), 1945–8; *Pilate* (cantata; Arnoul Gréban), 1964; *Requiem*, soli, ch, orch, 1971–2; *Et la vie l'emporta* (chbr cantata; Maurice Zundel, Luther, Fra Angelico), 1974; etc.

Solo vocal: *Der Cornet* (Rilke), a, chbr orch, 1942–3; *Sechs Monologe aus Jedermann* (Hofmannsthal), bar, pf, 1943–4, orch 1949; *Trois chants de noël* (Albert Rudhart), s, fl, pf, 1947; *Maria-Triptychon* (Ave Maria, Magnificat, Stabat mater), s, vn, orch, 1967–8; *Poèmes de la mort* (Villon), t, bar, b, 3 elec gtr, 1969–71; etc.

Chamber and instrumental: *Trio sur des mélodies populaires irlandaises*, pf trio, 1925; Ballade, fl, pf, 1939; Ballade, trbn/t sax, pf, 1940; *Passacaille*, org, 1944; 8 Preludes, pf, 1947–8; Ballade, vc, pf, 1949; etc.

Martini, Padre (Giovanni Battista) (b. Bologna, 24 Apr 1706; d. Bologna, 3 Aug 1784). Italian teacher and composer. A musician's son, he had a musical training and spent his whole life after 1722 attached to San Francesco in Bologna as organist and chapelmaster; he gained the latter post in 1725 and lived there as a monk and (from 1729) priest. He assembled an enormous music library (17,000 books by 1770 and 300 portraits by the end of his life), mostly preserved in the Civico Museo Bibliografico Musicale in Bologna. Renowned for his learning, he was sought out as a teacher by Mozart, J.C. Bach, Jommelli, Grétry and many

others, and was an active correspondent, though he rarely left home. Burney remarked also on his geniality: 'Upon so short an acquaintance I never liked any man more.' He published on music theory and history (three volumes, not reaching beyond the Greeks), and though the rules of the Bolognese Accademia Filarmonica excluded monks, he was admitted in 1758. His compositions include sinfonias and concertos, sonatas and other keyboard music, stage pieces, arias and duets, as well as sacred music.

Martini, Jean Paul Gilles (b. Freystadt, Bavaria, 31 Aug 1741; d. Paris, 10 Feb 1816). German–French composer, originally Johann Paul Aegidius Martin and known in Paris, where he arrived in 1764, as 'Martini il Tedesco' to distinguish him from Padre Martini. An organist's son, he moved to Lorraine in 1760 and gained the patronage of the fashionable Marchioness of Desarmoises and ex-king Stanislas I of Poland. His closeness then with the royal family in Paris did not prevent him, after a judicious retirement to Lyons (1792–4), from continuing his career under changing governments. He wrote operas, sacred music and songs, of which 'Plaisir d'amour' keeps his name alive.

Martini, Johannes (b. Leuze, *c.*1430–40; d. Ferrara, 1497). Netherlandish composer, resident by 1473 in Ferrara, where he wrote masses, psalms and secular songs.

Martino, Donald (James) (b. Plainfield, NJ, 16 May 1931). US composer, of works at once scrupulous in their workmanship, fluent in gesture, and rich in expression and wit. He played the clarinet as a boy, then studied at Syracuse, at Princeton with Sessions and Babbitt (1952–4) and in Florence with Dallapiccola (1954–6). His subsequent career as a teacher included appointments at Yale (1959–69), the New England Conservatory (1969–81) and Harvard (1983–92). *Notturno* – a classic of the repertory for *Pierrot* quintet and percussionist, evoking many nocturnal atmospheres – won him the 1974 Pulitzer Prize. Some later works judiciously bring forward tonal and jazz references that were always there under the skin.

Orchestral: Triple Concerto, cl, b cl, db cl, 1977; Violin Concerto, 1996; etc.

Vocal: *Paradiso Choruses* (Dante), soli, ch, orch, tape, 1974; *The White Island* (Herrick), ch, chbr orch, 1985; etc.

Chamber and instrumental: Concerto, wind qnt, 1964; *Parisonatina al' dodecafonica*, vc, 1964; *B,A,B,B,I,T,T*, cl, 1966; *Notturno*, 6 insts, 1973; *Quodlibets II*, fl, 1979; String Quartet No.4, 1983; *From the Other Side*, fl, vc, per, pf, 1988; *3 Sad*

Songs, va, pf, 1993; *Serenata concertante*, 8 insts, 1999; *Romanza*, vn, 2000

Piano: *Pianississimo*, pf, 1970; Fantasies and Impromptus, pf, 1978; 12 Preludes, 1991

Martinon, Jean (b. Lyons, 10 Jan 1910; d. Paris, 1 Mar 1976). French conductor, admired for his clarity, especially in Debussy, Ravel and Prokofiev. After graduating from the Paris Conservatoire (1928) he continued his studies with Münch and Desormière. He became one of the most prominent French conductors after the Second World War, and held posts with the Lamoureux orchestra (1951–7), the Chicago Symphony (1963–9) and others. Also a composer, trained by Roussel, he wrote four symphonies, concertos and chamber music.

Martinů, Bohuslav (Jan) (b. Polička, 8 Dec 1890; d. Liestal, Switzerland, 28 Aug 1959). Czech composer. Among the most productive and versatile composers of the 20th century, he perhaps chose speed as a route to fantasy: much of his music has to do with imagining his homeland (from which he was separated for most of his adult life), his desires or the past. Layers of reminiscence and regret came to overlay the spikiness of his first mature works, written when he was in his 30s.

He spent the first 12 years of his life with his family in a church tower, where his father was bellringer and firewatcher. Studies at the Prague Conservatory (1906–10) ended in expulsion for 'incorrigible negligence', and he spent the war years teaching and composing back in Polička. The influence of a fellow student then allowed him to play from 1918 with the Czech Philharmonic, with which he visited Paris for the first time the next year. In 1922 a concert given by an English madrigal group left him with a lasting ideal of polyphony, and he returned to the conservatory for composition lessons with Suk. But his father's death the next year released him to the pull of Paris, and he moved there to study with Roussel.

Stravinsky and jazz also impressed him; so too, more unusually, did literary surrealism, opening him to dreamlike atmospheres. Yet he also retained contact with Czech folk music, and most of his dramatic works were written for Czechoslovakia. In 1931 he married, though he remained prone to affairs. Particularly intense were his feelings for his pupil Vítězslava Kaprálová, who may have represented to him the lost heroine of his recent opera *Julietta*; she may also have seemed the embodiment of Czechoslovakia, annexed to the Nazi empire in 1939. He wrote his *Field Mass* for the Free Czech troops, before having to flee to the south of France in 1940 and from there to New York early in 1941.

He now wrote symphonies for US orchestras and *Madrigal Stanzas* for the violin of Albert Einstein. Once the war was over he made plans to return to Czechoslovakia, but a serious fall in 1946, the doubtful political situation in Prague and a new affair with a student composer held him back, and he took posts at the Mannes School (1947) and Princeton (1948). When he returned to Europe in 1952, it was not to Czechoslovakia but to Paris, where he completed his lustrous, unsettled yet sinewy Sixth Symphony. Then he settled in Nice (1953–5), before travelling on to New York (1955–6), Rome (at the American Academy, 1956–7) and Switzerland, where his long-term supporter Sacher found him a final home.

Brian Large *Martinů* (1975)

www.martinu.cz

Operas (full-length): *The Soldier and the Dancer* (Jan Löwenbach), 1926–7, f.p. Brno, 1928; JULIETTA, 1936–7; *Mirandolina* (Martinů, after Goldoni), 1953–4, f.p. Prague, 1959; *The* GREEK PASSION, 1954–9

Operas (shorter): *Les Larmes du couteau* (Georges Ribemont-Dessaignes), 1929; *Les Trois Souhaits* (film; Ribemont-Dessaignes), 1928–9; *The Miracles of Our Lady* (Vítězslav Nezval, Henri Ghéon, Julius Zeyer), 1933–4, f.p. Brno, 1935; *The Voice of the Forest* (radio; Nezval), 1935, f.p. Prague, 1935; *The Comedy on the Bridge* (radio; Martinů, after Václav Kliment Klicpera), 1935; *Suburban Theatre* (Martinů), 1935–6, f.p. Brno, 1936; *Alexandre bis* (André Wurmser), 1937, f.p. Mannheim, 1964; *What men live by* (television; Martinů), 1951–2, f.p. New York, 1953; *The Marriage* (television; Martinů, after Gogol), 1952, f.p. New York, 1953; *Ariane* (see ARIADNE), 1958

Orchestral (full, without soloists): Symphony No.1, 1942; No.2, 1943; No.3, 1944; No.4, 1945; No.5, 1946; *Fantaisies symphoniques* (No.6), 1951–3; *Half-Time*, 1924; *La Bagarre*, 1926; *Le Jazz*, 1928; Sinfonia Concertante, 1932; *Memorial to Lidice*, 1943; *Thunderbolt P-47*, 1945; *The Frescoes of Piero della Francesca*, 1955; *The Parables*, 1957–8; *Estampes*, 1958; etc.

Orchestral (full, with soloists): Piano Concerto No.1, 1925; No.2, 1934; No.3, 1948; No.4 'Incantations', 1955–6; No.5 (*Fantasia concertante*), 1957–8; Double Piano Concerto, 1943; Violin Concerto No.1, 1932–3; No.2, 1943; *Suite concertante*, vn, orch, 1938–9; Rhapsody-Concerto, va, orch, 1952; Cello Concerto No.1, 1938; No.2, 1944–5; etc.

Orchestral (chamber): Jazz Suite, 1928; Divertimento (Serenade No.4), vn, va, chbr orch, 1932; Harpsichord Concerto, 1935; Concerto grosso, 1937; Double Concerto, str, pf, timp, 1938; *Tre ricercari*, 1938; *Toccata e due canzoni*, 1946; Sinfonietta 'La Jolla', pf, chbr orch, 1950; Oboe Concerto, 1955; etc.

Choral: *Špaliček* (ballet; Martinů, after trad), ch, orch, 1931–2, rev 1940; *Field Mass* (Jiří Mucha), bar, men's ch, orch, 1939; *The Epic of Gilgamesh* (Martinů, after Babylonian), soli, ch, orch, 1954–5; *Mikeš of the Mountains* (cantata; Miloslav Bureš), s, t, ch, 4 insts, 1959; *The Prophecy of Isaiah* (Isaiah), s, a, bar, ch, 4 insts, 1959; etc.

Chamber (5–9 insts): *La Revue de cuisine* (ballet), vn, cl, vc, bn, trbn, pf, 1927; Sextet, pf, wind, 1929; Serenade No.1, 3 vn, va, cl, hn, 1932; No.3, 4 vn, ob, cl, vc, 1932; String Sextet, 1932; Fantasia, theremin, ob, str qt, pf, 1944; Nonet, wind qnt, vn, va, vc, db, 1959; etc.

Chamber (3–4 insts): String Quartet No.1, 1918; No.2, 1925; No.3, 1929; No.4, 1937; No.5, 1938; No.6, 1947; No.7 (*Concerto da camera*), 1947; Quartet, cl, hn, vc, side drum, 1924; Sonata, 2 vn, pf, 1932; Serenade No.2, 2 vn, va, 1932; Piano Quartet, 1942; etc.

Chamber (2 insts): Violin Sonata No.1, 1929; No.2, 1931; No.3, 1944; 4 Intermezzos, vn, pf, 1937; 5 *Madrigal Stanzas*, vn, pf, 1943; Czech Rhapsody, vn, pf, 1945; 3 *Madrigals*, vn, va, 1947; Duo No.1, vn, vc, 1927; No.2, 1958; Cello Sonata No.1, 1939; No.2, 1941; No.3, 1952; 4 Nocturnes, vc, pf, 1930; 6 Pastorales, vc, pf, 1930; 7 *Arabesques*, vc, pf, 1931; Variations on a Theme of Rossini, vc, pf, 1942; Variations on a Slovak Folksong, vc, pf, 1959; Flute Sonata, 1945; Clarinet Sonatina, 1956; etc.

Piano duo: *Fantaisie*, 1929; 3 Czech Dances, 2 pf, 1940

Piano: 3 Czech Dances, 1926; *Fantaisie et toccata*, 1940; Etudes and Polkas, 1945; Sonata, 1954

Other works: film scores, songs, harpsichord pieces, etc.

Martín y Soler, Vicente (b. Valencia, 2 May 1754; d. St Petersburg, 10 Feb 1806). Spanish composer, of comic operas made of simple and charming songs. He wrote his first opera for the Spanish court in 1775, then moved to Italy and so to Vienna (1785–8), where he produced *Il burbero di buon cuore* (1785), *Una cosa rara* (1786) and *L'arbore di Diana* (1787), all to librettos by Da Ponte. The last two were big successes, *L'arbore di Diana* being performed more often than any other Italian opera at the Viennese court during Mozart's time. Very soon, though, all that was heard of them was Mozart's quotation from *Una cosa rara* in *Don Giovanni*, while their composer seems to have lost his flair. He spent most of his later life in St Petersburg, where he wrote ballets, though he teamed up with Da Ponte again for two operas in London (1794–5). He also wrote canzonettas and cantatas.

Martland, Steve (b. Liverpool, 10 Oct 1959). British composer, who studied with Andriessen at the Hague Conservatory (1982–5) and has, in more extreme fashion, used rock-edged minimalism as a form of political expression.

Martucci, Giuseppe (b. Capua, 6 Jan 1856; d. Naples, 1 Jun 1909). Italian composer, pianist and conductor, his country's outstanding proponent of late-Romantic music without words. Promoted as a young virtuoso by his father (a bandsman turned teacher), he had an abbreviated training at the Royal College of San Pietro a Majella in Naples (1868–71), then was on the road again before settling in Naples as conductor of the Orchestra Napoletana (from 1881) and a teacher at his alma mater. He moved to Bologna as conductor and conservatory director (1886–1902) and returned to Naples in similar positions. In Bologna in 1888 he met his idol Brahms, and since neither could speak the other's language, they communicated in song. That was not, though, the Italian's preferred form; he wrote little but piano, chamber and orchestral music (Symphony No.1, D minor, Op.75, 1889–95; No.2, F, Op.81, 1899–1904; Piano Concerto, B♭ minor, Op.66, 1884–5; Notturno, Op.70:1, 1901).

Martyre de Saint Sébastien, Le (The Martyrdom of St Sebastian). Music by Debussy for a play by Gabriele d'Annunzio. The beautiful young saint holds to Christianity against a decadent paganism that wants to see him as Adonis. The orchestral suite has five movements: *La Cour de lys*, *La Chambre magique*, *Le Concile des faux dieux*, *Le Laurier blessé*, *Le Paradis*. First performance: Paris, 22 May 1911.

Marx, Joseph (b. Graz, 11 May 1882; d. Graz, 3 Sep 1964). Austrian composer, especially of lieder maintaining the Romantic tradition. His settings of poems from the Giraud–Hartleben *Pierrot lunaire* (e.g. 'Valse de Chopin', 1910) show his distance from Schoenberg. Yet he too had to fight – against family insistence on a legal career, from which he freed himself in an outburst of over 100 songs in 1908–12. Wolf was a model; he set Paul Heyse's translations omitted from his hero's *Italienisches Liederbuch*. Orchestral and chamber works came later, and he also taught at the Vienna Academy from 1922.

marziale (It.). Martial.

Masaniello. Alternative title for Auber's *La Muette de Portici*.

Mascagni, Pietro (Antonio Stefano) (b. Leghorn, 7 Dec 1863; d. Rome, 2 Aug 1945). Italian composer, known especially as the author of the brief village drama of jilting and revenge *Cavalleria rusticana*. A baker's son, he studied in Leghorn with Alfredo Soffredini and at the Milan Conservatory (1882–5), where he met Puccini. He left without graduating to take work as an operetta conductor and teacher, then wrote *Cavalleria rusticana* in response to the publisher Sonzogno's announcement in July 1888 of a competition for one-act operas. Early the next year he got married; his first child was born the following day. The première of his opera a few months later was a triumph, and within a year the piece had been staged all over Italy and beyond – in Germany, Budapest (under Mahler), Vienna, St Petersburg and Buenos Aires. Its success brought him many invitations to conduct, and many commissions, but though he wrote 15 further operas, only the sentimental comedy *L'amico Fritz* and the Japanese tragedy *Iris* (anticipating *Madama Butterfly*) have had much continuing echo. Both boast inspiring tenor arias ('Ed anche Beppe amò' and 'Apri la tua fenestra'); *L'amico Fritz* is notable also for the Cherry Duet sung by the amiable Fritz (tenor) and his unexpected consort Suzel (soprano). Meanwhile Mascagni also directed music schools in Pesaro (1895–1903) and Rome (1903–11). He virtually stopped composing after *Il piccolo Marat* and retired to a Roman hotel in 1927, from which he emerged with high hopes for his *Nerone*, partly aimed at pleasing Mussolini. Its failure silenced him, though he returned again to *Cavalleria rusticana* to make a 50th-anniversary recording in Milan in 1940.

Alan Mallach *Pietro Mascagni and his Operas* (2002) www.mascagni.org

Operas: CAVALLERIA RUSTICANA, 1888–9; *L'amico Fritz*, f.p. Rome, 1891; *Guglielmo Ratcliff*, f.p. Milan, 1895; *Zanetto*, f.p. Pesaro, 1896; *Iris*, f.p. Rome, 1898; *Isabeau*, f.p. Buenos Aires, 1911; *Lodoletta*, f.p. Rome, 1917; *Il piccolo Marat*, f.p. Rome, 1921; *Nerone*, f.p. Milan, 1935
Songs: *Ave Maria*, 1880; 'La tua stella', 1882; 'Pena d'amore', 1883; 'Serenata', 1883

Mason. US musical family.

(1) **Lowell** (b. Medfield, Mass., 8 Jan 1792; d. Orange, NJ, 11 Aug 1872). Educator and hymn compiler, 'Joy to the World' being ascribed to him. Brought up in the New England of choirs, singing schools and bands, he became a leader of musical benevolence in Savannah (1812–27), and made a national reputation with his first collection of hymn tunes (1822). He then moved to Boston, where he was active in school music, and in 1853 to the New York area. Of his sons, Daniel Gregory (1820–69) and Lowell (1823–85) were music publishers, William (1829–1908) was a pianist who studied with Liszt, and Henry (1831–90) was a founder of the MASON & HAMLIN firm of organ and piano makers.

(2) **Daniel Gregory** (b. Brookline, Mass., 20 Nov 1873; d. Greenwich, Conn., 4 Dec 1953). Composer,

a belated member of the New England school, son of Henry. He studied with Paine at Harvard (1891–5) and with Chadwick and Percy Goetschius. In 1905 he began teaching at Columbia, where he became professor (1929–42). Though he went to Paris for further lessons with d'Indy in 1913, his style was essentially formed in the Brahmsian mould. His works include three symphonies (No.1, C minor, Op.11, 1913–14; No.2, A, Op.30, 1928–9; No.3 'Lincoln', Op.35, 1935–6), chamber music (String Quartet on Negro Themes, Op.19, 1918–19) and songs.

Mason, Benedict (b. London, 21 Jun 1955). British composer, notably of scores approaching Ligeti in fascination and playfulness, and latterly of site-specific pieces. After Cambridge (1971–5) he studied film-making at the Royal College of Art (1975–8); composition came several years later. His reproducible works include *Lighthouses of England and Wales* for orchestra (1988) and *ChaplinOperas*, music for two singers and small orchestra to acompany silent films (1988).

Mason & Hamlin. US keyboard-instrument firm, founded in Boston in 1854 by Henry Mason and Emmons Hamlin to manufacture reed organs for Sunday schools and homes. Piano production began in 1883 and until the 1920s remained at a high level of excellence. The company then was taken over, but its name has been retained.

masonic music. See FREEMASONRY.

masque. Allegorical entertainment in spoken poetry, song and dance, associated especially with the English royal court under the Tudors and early Stuarts (i.e. 1485–1649). It developed from earlier English forms, with influence from the French *ballet de cour* and Italian intermedio, and reached its height under James I (1603–25), in collaborations involving Ben Jonson, Alfonso Ferrabosco II and – for the sets, costumes and machines – Inigo Jones. Among other composers who contributed to Stuart masques were Robert Johnson, Campion, Lanier and the Lawes brothers. Masques were also written for the public theatre, beginning with the betrothal masque in *The Tempest* (1611) and culminating in SEMI-OPERA, while the tradition of the masque as state or aristocratic-pastoral diversion persisted in works by Locke, Handel and Arne. Ideals that have accrued to the masque – of moral instruction, of Englishness, of marrying poetry and music on a high plane – are responsible for nods to it in works by Vaughan Williams ('*Job*, a masque for dancing'), Tippett (*The Mask of Time*) and Birtwistle (*The Mask of Orpheus*).

mass (Lat. *missa*, Fr. *messe*, Ger. *Messe*, It. *messa*, Sp. *misa*). Service in commemoration of Christ's Last Supper, especially as embodied in the Catholic tradition. In musical contexts the term generally refers to settings of the ORDINARY, of which there are innumerable examples by composers from Machaut to the 21st century. Such settings are often regarded (and performed and recorded) as continuous musical forms, though most, having been made for use in the liturgy, are forms to be dispersed within other forms, since the sections of the ordinary are separated by other material in any celebration of mass. Josquin – or Mozart – wrote masses as allied segments of great splendour to punctuate a generally plainer and more heterogeneous ceremony.

The mass was the most important musical product of western Europe in the 15th and 16th centuries – that to which composers seem to have brought special care in achieving technical feats and paying homage to colleagues and patrons. The masses of Du Fay, Ockeghem, Obrecht and Josquin, of Taverner, and of Palestrina, Byrd and Victoria are among the triumphs of their respective ages. Later times had other genres, even within the sphere of church music, and the mass lost artistic prestige. Even so, masses have gone on being written, whether as liturgical settings in the old way, as more personal documents of faith and doubt, praise and prayer, or as studies in style. Indeed, no text has been set more often or more variously. Among the most notable post-1600 settings are those of Bach (B MINOR MASS), Mozart, Haydn, Beethoven (MISSA SOLEMNIS), Schubert, Liszt, Bruckner, Janáček (GLAGOLITIC MASS) and Stravinsky. See also REQUIEM.

Massenet, Jules (Emile Frédéric) (b. Montaud, St Etienne, 12 May 1842; d. Paris, 13 Aug 1912). French composer, essentially of operas, dealing with sensuality and often also with religion in a variety of settings: historical, exotic, fairytale, biblical, mythological. Long dismissed (or adored) as decadent and sentimental, his music began to enjoy a general revival in the late 20th century. *Manon* and *Werther* had remained in the repertory all through; perhaps not coincidentally, they are his most naturalistic pieces.

The youngest child of an ironmaster, he was brought up with seven siblings, of whom two died while he was a boy. In 1848 the family moved to Paris, and in 1853, having had initial instruction from his mother, he entered the Conservatoire. He had to leave when the family made another move the next year, to Chambéry, but he was then able to rejoin the institution (1855–63), staying with his sister and eventually studying in Thomas's composition class. The Prix de Rome took him to Italy (1863–5), where he was introduced by Liszt to his future wife, Ninon. Married in 1866, the couple set up home in Paris; their only child Juliette was born in 1868. Meanwhile the composer was making a professional start: orchestral pieces and a one-act opera were performed, songs published.

He became much better known after the first performance of his oratorio *Marie-Magdeleine*, in 1873, with Viardot. Two years later, with Bizet's death, he lost both a friend and his only serious rival, and the première at the Opera of *Le Roi de Lahore*, in 1877, secured his international reputation; productions soon followed in Turin, London, Rio de Janeiro and elsewhere. He was also, in 1878, made professor at the Conservatoire and a member of the Institut. However, his position was not fully assured. *Hérodiade* was turned down by the Opera (as sacrilegious); so was *Werther* by the Opéra-Comique (as morbid), despite the immense success there of *Manon*. The two works were duly introduced abroad and reached Paris soon afterwards. In 1887 their composer met the US soprano Sybil Sanderson, for whom he revised *Manon* and wrote *Esclarmonde* and *Thaïs* to exploit her enormous range and physical beauty. *Thaïs*, at the Opera, was one of three premières in the spring of 1894, followed by *Le Portrait de Manon* at the Opéra-Comique and *La Navarraise* at Covent Garden.

On the death of Thomas in 1896 he was offered the directorship of the Conservatoire, but he took the opportunity instead to stop teaching and concentrate on composition, interrupted only by travels to see his works performed. He persevered without much change to his style, industrious as ever, though he lost his normal fluency with *Amadis*, in progress for two decades. Many of his later works were written for Monte Carlo, and all from *Ariane* onwards included major roles for a new favourite singer, the French mezzo-soprano Lucy Arbell. There were failures (*Bacchus*, as earlier *Le Mage*), apparently accepted as such, but despite declining health he went on producing an opera almost every year, a composer whose aim was to please.

Jules Massenet *My Recollections* (1919); Demar Irvine *Massenet* (1974, ¹1994)

www.jules-massenet.com

Operas (full-length): *Don César de Bazan* (Philippe Dumanoir, Adolphe d'Ennery and Jules Chantepie), f.p. Paris, 1872, rev Geneva, 1888; *Le Roi de Lahore* (Louis Gallet), f.p. Paris, 1877; *Hérodiade* (Paul Milliet, Henri Grémont, i.e. Georges Hartmann, and Angelo Zanardini, after Flaubert), f.p. Brussels, 1881, rev, Paris 1884; *Manon* (see MANON LESCAUT), 1882–3; *Le* CID, 1884–5;

WERTHER, 1885–7; *Esclarmonde* (Alfred Blau and Louis de Gramont), f.p. Paris, 1889; *Le Mage* (Jean Richepin), f.p. Paris, 1891; THAÏS, 1892–3, rev 1897; *Cendrillon* (see CINDERELLA), 1894–6; *Sapho* (Henri Cain and Arthur Bernède, after Alphonse Daudet), f.p. Paris, 1897, rev Paris, 1909; *Grisélidis* (Armand Silvestre and Eugène Morand), f.p. Paris, 1901; *Le Jongleur de Notre-Dame* (Maurice Léna), f.p. Monte Carlo, 1902; *Chérubin* (Francis de Croisset and Cain), f.p. Monte Carlo, 1905; *Ariane* (Catulle Mendès), f.p. Paris, 1906; *Bacchus* (Mendès), f.p. Paris 1909; *Don Quichotte* (see DON QUIXOTE); *Roma* (Cain, after Alexandre Parodi), f.p. Monte Carlo, 1910; *Panurge* (Georges Spitzmuller and Maurice Boukay, after Rabelais), f.p. Paris, 1913; *Cléopâtre* (Louis Payen), f.p. Monte Carlo, 1914; *Amadis* (Jules Claretie), f.p. Monte Carlo, 1922

Operas (shorter): *La Grand'tante* (Jules Adenis and Charles Grandvallet), f.p. Paris, 1867; *Le Portrait de Manon* (Georges Boyer), f.p. Paris, 1894; *La Navarraise* (Claretie and Cain), f.p. London, 1894; *Thérèse* (Claretie), f.p. Monte Carlo, 1907

Incidental music: *Les Erinnyes* (Leconte de Lisle), f.p. Paris, 1873 (*Elégie* arr vc, pf, and as song); etc.

Oratorios: *Marie-Magdeleine* (Gallet), 1871–2; *Eve* (Gallet), 1874; *La Vierge* (Charles Grandmougin), 1877–8 (includes *Le* DERNIER SOMMEIL DE LA VIERGE); *La Terre promise* (Vulgate), 1897–9

Orchestral: Suite No.1, 1865; No.2 (*Scènes hongroises*), 1870; No.3 (*Scènes dramatiques*), 1874; No.4 (*Scènes pittoresques*), 1872; No.5 (*Scènes napolitaines*), 1875; No.6 (*Scènes de féerie*), 1880–81; No.7 (*Scènes alsaciennes*), pub 1882; Piano Concerto, E♭, 1902; etc.

Other works: ballets, smaller choral works, songs, piano music, etc.

mässig (Ger.). Measured, moderately paced.

Mass in B minor. See B MINOR MASS.

Mass in C minor. See C MINOR MASS.

Mass in D minor. See NELSON.

master class. Lesson given by a distinguished performer to a group of advanced students. Since distinguished performers remain performers even when teaching, master classes are sometimes given with an audience and televised, and some distinguished performers (e.g. Schwarzkopf) have found a whole new career this way. Callas's alightings at Juilliard in 1971–2 prompted Terrence McNally's play *Master Class* (1995).

Master of the King's/Queen's Music. English court appointment, normally dated from Lanier's period in office. His successors were Grabu (1666–73), Staggins (1674–1700), Eccles (1700–35), Greene (1735–55), Boyce (1755–79), Stanley (1779–86), William Parsons (1786–1816), Shield (1817–29), Franz Cramer (1829–48), George Frederick Anderson (1848–70), William George Cusins (1870–93), Parratt (1893–1924), Elgar (1924–34), Walford Davies (1934–41), Bax (1942–53), Bliss (1953–75), Williamson (1975–2003) and Davies (2004–).

Masterpiece Theatre. See MOURET.

Mastersingers. See MEISTERSINGER.

Masur, Kurt (b. Brieg/Brzeg, Silesia, 18 Jul 1927). German conductor, a vigorously physical exponent of 19th-century Austro–German repertory and Shostakovich. He studied in Breslau and at the conservatory in Leipzig (1946–8), and worked his way up to appointments with the Dresden Philharmonic (1955–8, 1965–72) and the Komische Oper (1960–64). His later posts have been with the Leipzig Gewandhaus (1970–96), the New York Philharmonic (1991–2002) and the LPO (from 2002).

mathematics. See NUMBER (1).

Mathews, Max (Vernon) (b. Columbus, Nebraska, 13 Nov 1926). US cyberneticist, a developer of programs for sound generation and composition. He studied at CalTech and MIT, and worked at Bell Labs (1955–87), where he created the programs MUSIC I–V and GROOVE. In 1987 he joined Stanford University's Center for Computer Research in Music and Acoustics.

Mathias, William (James) (b. Whitland, Carmarthenshire, 1 Nov 1934; d. Menai Bridge, 29 Jul 1992). Welsh composer, having a decisive style forged out of Bartók, Hindemith and Britten. He studied at Aberystwyth and with Berkeley at the RAM (1956–9), then taught at Bangor until 1987. His works include three symphonies, concertos, three quartets and a large quantity of choral music, including an anthem commissioned for the marriage of the Prince of Wales (*Let the People Praise Thee, O God*, Op.87, 1981).

Mathis der Maler (Mathis the Painter). Opera by Hindemith to his own libretto based on the life of Matthias Grünewald. Mathis (baritone) travels from hope through disgust to bitter wisdom, appalled both by the venality of the churchmen he serves as a painter and by the cruelty of the peasants with whom he allies himself as a man of action. Before the opera came a symphony of three movements related to panels from Grünewald's

Isenheim altarpiece: *Engelkonzert* (Angel Concert), *Grablegung* (Entombment) and *Versuchung des heiligen Antonius* (Temptation of St Anthony). First performance: Berlin, 12 Mar 1934 (symphony); Zurich, 28 May 1938 (opera).

Matin, Le. Name given to Haydn's Symphony No.6, which forms a trilogy with No.7 'Le Midi' and No.8 'Le Soir'.

matrimonio segreto, Il (The Clandestine Marriage). Opera by Cimarosa to a libretto by Giovanni Bertati after a play by David Garrick and George Colman. Paolino (tenor) and Carolina (soprano), who are the ones secretly married, want to avert the wrath of her father, Geronimo (bass), by engineering a match between her sister Elisetta (mezzo-soprano) and Count Robinson (bass). Of course there are mischances along the way, and of course all comes out right in the end. First performance: Vienna. 7 Feb 1792.

Matsudaira, Yoritsune (b. Tokyo, 5 May 1907; d. Tokyo, 30 Oct 2001). Japanese composer, influenced by French music and gagaku. A pupil of Kōsuke Komatsu, he had an international reputation by the 1930s and was creative into his 90s. His son Yori-aki (b. 1931) is also a composer.

Matteis, Nicola (b. Naples, ?1640s; d. Colkirk, Norfolk, after 1713). Italian violinist-composer who arrived in England *c*.1670 and caused amazement as representing a new species: the violin virtuoso. He published books of violin solos and songs.

Matteo da Perugia (*fl. c.*1400–20). Italian composer, remarkable for the rhythmic complexity of some of his songs, notably the ballade *Le Greygnour bien*: another ballade, *Se je me plaing*, quotes two ballades by Machaut. The scanty historical records of him show an association with Milan Cathedral, perhaps at first as the protégé of the learned and worldly archbishop Filargo.

Mattheson, Johann (b. Hamburg, 28 Sep 1681; d. Hamburg, 17 Apr 1764). German musical writer and composer, who in his books addressed the professionals and amateurs of his time, thus communicating much to later generations. His early career with the Hamburg opera carried him from treble to tenor (1690–1705) and brought him into contact with Handel. A warm friendship developed, but not without signs of rivalry. According to his own account he was singing Mark Antony in his own *Cleopatra* in 1704 to Handel's keyboard accompaniment, expecting to take over

when, as Antony, he had committed suicide in the third act. But Handel refused to shift, and the argument led to a duel, in which the younger composer was saved by a heavy button on his coat. From 1706 he was secretary to the English ambassador in Hamburg while also working as a church musician and writing voluminously. At his funeral the 83-year-old Telemann conducted the 'cheerful death-song' his 82-year-old colleague had written for the occasion.

Matthews. British composing brothers, both of whom became assistants to Deryck Cooke on his realization of Mahler's Tenth Symphony and studied classics at Nottingham University.

(1) **David** (**John**) (b. Walthamstow, 9 Mar 1943). He was Britten's assistant (1966–9) and studied composition with Milner and Maw. Positioning himself with respect to a tonal tradition from Beethoven to Tippett, he has produced five symphonies, nine quartets and much else.

(2) **Colin** (b. London, 13 Feb 1946). Following his brother as Britten's assistant (1971–6), he simultaneously undertook doctoral studies in Mahler at Sussex University. His works show an engagement with international modernism from Schoenberg to Carter, and a particular gift for channelling musical energy in instrumental forms, whether for orchestra (*Broken Symmetry*, 1991–2), mixed ensemble (*Suns Dance*, 1984–5) or soloist. He has also been active on behalf of the Britten and Holst estates, and wrote an eighth movement for *The* PLANETS.

Matthus, Siegfried (b. Mallenuppen, East Prussia, 13 Apr 1934). German composer, the most notable modernist to emerge in East Germany. After conservatory studies in East Berlin (1952–8) he joined Eisler's class at the Academy of the Arts (1958–60). His works include concertos, chamber pieces and operas.

Mattila, Karita (b. Somero, 5 Sep 1960). Finnish soprano, vocally radiant and agile, and a performer of keen dramatic energy. She studied at the Sibelius Academy and with Vera Rozsa in London, and won the Cardiff Singer of the World competition in 1983. The growth of her voice brought her to the front rank internationally in the mid 1990s in a wide range of operatic roles, including Katya Kabanova, Salome, Elsa (*Lohengrin*) and Elisabeth (*Don Carlos*).

Matyushin, Mikhail Vasilyevich (b. Nizhniy Novgorod, 1861; d. Leningrad, 14 Oct 1934). Russian composer and painter, who entered the avant-garde in his late 40s. He then worked with quarter-tones and produced a partly futurist score for the drama *Victory over the Sun* (1913), with designs by Malevich. He had studied at the Moscow Conservatory (1875–80).

Maurel, Victor (b. Marseilles, 17 Jun 1848; d. New York, 22 Oct 1923). French baritone, the first Iago (*Otello*), Falstaff and Tonio (*Pagliacci*). He studied at the Paris Conservatoire, made his debut in Marseilles (1867), and was soon active internationally, his association with Verdi beginning when he created the title role in the revised *Simon Boccanegra*. Singing into the new century, he then turned to teaching in New York.

Maurerische Trauermusik (Masonic Funeral Music). Work in C minor by Mozart for a sombre, reed-rich orchestra (2 ob, cl, 3 basset horns, 2 hn, dbn, str), composed in July 1785. Apparently it was first performed at the installation of a masonic lodge master and later reused at a memorial ceremony.

Má vlast (My Homeland). Set of six symphonic poems by Smetana: 1 *Vyšehrad* (ancient citadel of the Czech kings), *c*.1872–4; 2 *Vltava* (The Moldau), 1874; 3 *Šárka* (warrior woman of Czech legend), 1875; 4 *Z českých luhů a hájů* (From Bohemia's Meadows and Forests), 1875; 5 *Tábor* (Hussite town), 1878; 6 *Blaník* (mountain refuge of the Hussites), 1879. First performance: Prague, 4 Apr 1875 (2); Prague, 17 Mar 1877 (3); Prague, 4 Jan 1880 (5–6).

Mavra. One-act opera by Stravinsky to a libretto by Boris Kochno after Pushkin. Sketched in short numbers with wind-led orchestra, the piece is a comedy whose title character is a hussar hired as a maidservant by his beloved to outwit her mother. First performance: Paris, 1 Jun 1922.

Maw, (John) Nicholas (b. Grantham, 5 Nov 1935). British composer, supremely sophisticated restorer of late Romanticism. He studied with Berkeley and Paul Steinitz at the RAM (1955–8), and with Boulanger and Max Deutsch in Paris (1958–9). *Scenes and Arias* (1962) was his breakthrough piece, channelling an almost Straussian rhapsodic flood with intricate manoeuvres. With *The Rising of the Moon* he produced a comic opera played out by rich characters. Then came the unparalleled *Odyssey*, a 90-minute unbroken symphony that is a journey in itself and also the record of a creative journey towards more clearly avowed tonality. Since 1984 he has divided his time between Britain and the USA, where he has taught at Yale, Bard and Peabody.

Operas: *One Man Show* (Arthur Jacobs), f.p. London, 1964; *The Rising of the Moon* (Beverley Cross), f.p. Glyndebourne, 1970; *Sophie's Choice* (Maw, after William Styron), f.p. London, 2002
Orchestral: *Life Studies*, str, 1973–6; *Odyssey*, 1972–87; Violin Concerto, 1993; etc.
Vocal: *Scenes and Arias* (medieval), s, mez, a, orch, 1962, rev 1966; *La vita nuova* (It. Renaissance), s, ens, 1979; *The Ruin* (Michael Alexander, after Old English), ch, hn, 1980; etc.
Chamber and instrumental: 3 string quartets, piano pieces, etc.

Maxfield, Richard (Vance) (b. Seattle, 2 Feb 1927; d. Los Angeles, 27 Jun 1969). US composer, principally of electronic music. He studied with Sessions at Berkeley, Babbitt at Princeton, Dallapiccola in Italy (1955–7) and Cage. Bringing to his music the skills of a sound engineer, he produced pieces for tape alone or with solo instrumental performance. He died when he jumped from a window under the influence of drugs.

maxima. LARGE.

Mayer, Robert (b. Mannheim, 5 Jun 1879; d. London, 8 Jan 1985). German–British philanthropist, founder of regular children's concerts in London (1923), knighted in 1939. He studied at the Mannheim Conservatory as a boy and was encouraged by Brahms, but instead moved to England in 1896 and made a fortune in business. After the Second World War he was instrumental in founding Youth and Music, the British arm of Jeunesses Musicales.

Mayr, (Giovanni) Simone [Johann Simon] (b. Mendorf, near Ingolstadt, 14 Jun 1763; d. Bergamo, 2 Dec 1845). German composer, who moved to Italy when he was in his mid 20s and became the prime mover of Italian 19th-century opera: Donizetti was his pupil, Rossini and Bellini learned at greater distance. The son of a schoolmaster-organist, he began university studies in 1781 in Ingolstadt, where he also started out as a musician and composer. He continued his musical training in Bergamo, where he arrived in 1789, and with Ferdinando Bertoni in Venice, where he produced his first opera, *Saffo* (1794). Of its 67 successors, almost half were written for Venice, but he made his home in Bergamo, where he founded a free music school in 1805, and where he lived with his second wife, his first, her sister, having died in childbirth. A quiet provincial existence evidently suited him. His operas were esteemed – and emulated – for their harmonic vigour, their multimovement aria patterns and their other moves towards continuous dramatic thrust. They include

Ginevra di Scozia (f.p. Trieste, 1801), *L'amor coniugale* (f.p. Padua, 1805, on the same subject as *Fidelio*) and *Medea in Corinto* (see MEDEA). In 1824 he retired from the theatre to devote himself to church music and essays.

Mayuzumi, Toshirō (b. Yokohama, 20 Feb 1929; d. Kawasaki, 10 Apr 1997). Japanese composer, whose adoption of Western avant-garde techniques was a route to engaging with ancient Japanese music and Buddhist thought. After studies with Ikenouchi and Ifukube at the Tokyo National University of Fine Arts and Music he completed his training in Paris (1951–2). His varied output includes electronic and orchestral pieces, musicals and operas.

Mazeppa. Stalwart hero who, as a page in Poland discovered to have amorous designs on his lady, was tied naked to a horse and sent charging into the forest. He survived to become a cossack leader who turned against Peter the Great over Ukrainian sovereignty and against a friend whose daughter he wanted to marry. His story, or part of it, was told by Pushkin, Byron and Hugo, and in the following works.

(1) Liszt's fourth Transendental Etude, after Hugo.

(2) Liszt's symphonic poem, based partly on the étude. First performance: Weimar, 16 Apr 1854.

(3) Tchaikovsky's opera, to a libretto by Victor Burenin, after Pushkin, concentrating on the mature man's ruthless love. The score includes a popular Cossack Dance. First performance: Moscow, 15 Feb 1884.

mazurka (Pol. *mazur*). Polish dance from Mazovia, the region including Warsaw. The folk tradition includes several kinds, distinct in tempo but sharing a shift of accent to the second or third beat in triple time. Chopin drew on this tradition in his mazurkas, capturing features easily associated with national pride and melancholy, and providing models for later composers, notably Szymanowski.

Mazzochi, Domenico (baptized Civita Castellana, 8 Nov 1592; d. Rome, 21 Jan 1665). Italian composer, mostly of vocal chamber music both secular and sacred. He went to Rome in 1614, became a priest in 1619, and soon afterwards joined the entourage of Cardinal Ippolito Aldobrandini. His music arose within the cultivated circles of the Aldobrandini, Pamphili and Barberini families, and his influence may have helped his brother Virgilio (1597–1646), also a priest-composer, who became chapelmaster of the Julian Chapel (1629–46).

Mazzolà, Caterino (b. Longarone, 18 Jan 1745; d. Venice, 16 Jul 1806). Italian librettist, who adapted Metastasio's *La clemenza di Tito* for Mozart. He was court Italian poet in Dresden (1780–96), where he received Da Ponte en route from Venice to Vienna. Most probably Da Ponte returned the favour in gaining him, briefly, a post in Vienna (1791).

m.d. Abbreviation for the It. *mano destra* or Fr. *main droite* (right hand).

Meale, Richard (Graham) (b. Sydney, 24 Aug 1932). Australian composer, moving in the 1970s from a poetic avant-garde style to a firmly symphonic one. He abandoned conservatory studies in Sydney to educate himself while working in a record shop. His Flute Sonata (1960) won him a grant to study Japanese music at UCLA; he then worked for Australian radio. His works include orchestral pieces (… *clouds now and then*, 1969; *Viridian*, 1979), operas (*Voss*, f.p. Adelaide, 1986; *Mer de glace*, on the Shelleys, Byron and the Frankenstein story, f.p. Sydney, 1991) and three quartets.

mean. Eng. term for the lower boys' line in Tudor polyphony.

mean-tone. Temperament in which the major third is divided into two equal whole tones. If the major third is pure, i.e. tuned to the frequency ratio 5:4, the more precise term is '¼-comma mean-tone', as fifths will be that much smaller and fourths that much larger than pure. Other mean-tone tunings are based on impure major thirds.

measure. (1) US equivalent to bar.

(2) Rhythmic character of a dance.

mechanical instruments. Musical instruments operated by programmed mechanical apparatus, normally of one of the following kinds:

(1) Flowing water. See WATER ORGAN.

(2) A cylinder, carrying the program in the form of pins and rotated either manually or, more commonly, by a clockwork mechanism. See BARREL ORGAN; CARILLON; CLOCK; MUSICAL BOX.

(3) A length of paper or other material, perforated with the program. The most notable examples are the PIANOLA and the fairground organ.

Medea. Mythological princess of Colchis who helped Jason gain the golden fleece, bore him two sons and, in the play by Euripides, killed them in response to his promise of marriage with Glauke, daughter of Creon, king of Corinth. She has been the subject of several works:

(1) Cavalli's opera GIASONE.

(2) Charpentier's opera *Médée*, to a libretto by Thomas Corneille after Euripides, with the main characters Medea (soprano), Jason (haute-contre), Creusa (soprano) and Creon (bass). First performance: Paris, 4 Dec 1693.

(3) Georg Benda's melodrama *Medea*, to words by Friedrich Wilhelm Gotter. Medea (speaking) moves through regret and vengefulness to murderous violence and bitter triumph. First performance: Leipzig, 1 May 1775.

(4) Cherubini's opera *Médée*, to a libretto by François-Benoît Hoffman after Euripides, with the main characters Medea (soprano), Jason (tenor), Dirce (i.e. Glauke) and Creon (bass). First performance: Paris, 13 Mar 1797.

(5) Mayr's opera *Medea in Corinto*, to a libretto by Romani after Euripides, with the disposition as in Cherubini–Hoffman and the characters' names as in Charpentier–Corneille. First performance: Naples, 28 Nov 1813.

(6) Barber's ballet score *Medea* for Martha Graham, later renamed *The Cave of the Heart*. First performance: New York, 10 May 1946.

(7) Pasolini's film starring Callas (1970).

(8) Dusapin's one-act opera *Medeamaterial*, setting Heiner Müller's text for soprano, choir, Baroque orchestra and tape. First performance: Brussels, 11 Mar 1992.

Other treatments include operas by Gazzaniga (*Gli Argonauti in Colco*), Pacini, Milhaud and Bryars. Medea is also a character in Lully's *Thésée* and Handel's *Teseo*.

medesimo tempo (It.). The same speed.

medial cadence. (1) Cadence in which the penultimate chord is in inversion, as distinct from a RADICAL CADENCE.

(2) Modal cadence ending on a note other than the final.

mediant. The note or key a third above the tonic of a major or minor key, so called because it is between tonic and dominant. The mediant relationship is crucial in the minor mode, for the mediant major (E♭ in C minor) is also the relative major. In major-key music the mediant had increasing importance from Beethoven onwards.

Méditations sur le mystère de la Sainte Trinité (Meditations on the Mystery of the Holy Trinity). Organ work by Messiaen in nine movements. First performance: Washington, 20 Mar 1972.

medieval. Belonging to the Middle Ages, a period defined – almost as soon as it could be, by Filippo Villani in 1382 – as intermediate between classical antiquity and modern times (i.e. what would subsequently be known as the RENAISSANCE). This span of a thousand years can hardly be viewed as a single style period in music, for even if the late development of notation and the paucity of surviving sources have helped give it some uniformity, it saw phenomena as diverse as PLAINSONG, TROUBADOUR song and the polyphony of the NOTRE DAME SCHOOL, ARS ANTIQUA, ARS NOVA and ARS SUBTILIOR, to use terms that became labels of manner and technique only in the later 20th century. The usefulness of these terms – and even of 'medieval' itself – has been questioned, and in particular the notion of a partition at the Renaissance has been undermined. The medieval–Renaissance dichotomy was developed in the 19th and 20th centuries with reference principally to visual art and architecture, above all in Florence, and its relevance to music in, say, northern France is debatable. But composers from the 12th century to the 15th had much in common: a background in plainsong, since all were trained as choristers and held responsibilities for church music in later life; contrapuntal techniques involving the addition of parts to a tenor; a way of thinking that was essentially vocal; a sense for intricate detail that was lost with the smoother and more euphonious polyphony of the 16th century. Living, too, in an age before print, medieval composers can have reached only very small numbers of patrons and connoisseurs – an audience vastly different from that which has, since the 1970s, found their music fascinatingly distant and close.

Richard H. Hoppin *Medieval Music* (1978); Daniel Leech-Wilkinson *The Modern Invention of Medieval Music* (2003)

medium. Performing means, as in 'the orchestral medium'.

medley. String of tunes. Some lighter opera and operetta overtures – by Auber, Hérold, Sullivan – have this form.

Medtner, Nicolas [Metner, Nikolay Karlovich] (b. Moscow, 5 Jan 1880; d. London, 13 Nov 1951). Russian pianist-composer, whose music blends Russian and Austro–German Romantic idioms on a supreme level. Born into a Scandinavian–German family thoroughly settled in Russia, he studied with his uncle Fyodor Goedicke, and with Vasily Safonov at the Moscow Conservatory (1892–1900). In composition he had no formal training, yet almost from the first his emphasis as a performer was on his own works. He also returned to the conservatory to teach (1908, 1915–21), before leaving with his wife for Berlin. Little understood there – for his conservative Romanticism was out of tune with the times – he fared no better in Paris, where he settled after his 1924–5 US tour. He made further tours of Russia (1927) and the USA (1929–30), and also visited Britain, where he found a more sympathetic audience. Accordingly, in 1935 he moved to the London suburb of Golders Green, though his material existence remained hazardous until he acquired a patron in the Maharajah of Mysore, who financed a series of recordings.

Barrie Martyn *Nicolas Medtner* (1995)

Piano concertos: No.1, C minor, Op.33, 1914–18; No.2, C minor, Op.50, *c*.1920–27; No.3, E minor, Op.60, *c*.1940–43

Piano sonatas: F minor, Op.5, 1895–1903; Sonata Triad, A♭, D minor, C, Op.11, 1904–7; G minor, Op.22, 1901–10; Sonata-Fairytale, C minor, Op.25:1, 1910–11; E minor, Op.25:2, 1910–11; Sonata-Ballade, F♯, Op.27, 1912–14; A minor, Op.30, 1914; *Sonata romantica*, B♭ minor, Op.53:1, ?1929–31; *Sonata minacciosa*, F minor, Op.53:2, ?1929–31; Sonata-Idylle, G, Op.56, ?1935–7

Other piano works: *Fairytales*, Op.8, 1904–5 (2); Op.9, 1904–5 (3); Op.14, 1905–7 (2); Op.20, 1909 (2); Op.26, ?1910–12 (4); Op.34, ?1916–17 (4); Op.35, ?1916–17 (4); Op.42, ?1921–4 (4); Op.48, 1925 (2); Op.51, 1928 (6); *Forgotten Melodies*, Opp.38–40, ?1919–22; *Trois morceaux*, Op.31, *c*.1914; etc.

Other works: songs, chamber music

Meeresstille und glückliche Fahrt (Calm Sea and Prosperous Voyage). Paired poems by Goethe, subject of a cantata by Beethoven and an overture by Mendelssohn.

Mefistofele. See FAUST.

Mehrstimmigkeit (Ger.). Polyphony.

Mehta, Zubin (b. Bombay, 29 Apr 1936). Indian conductor, who has struggled with the problems of routine following his spectacular early career. Abandoning medical studies, he trained with Hans Swarowsky in Vienna and in 1958 won a year's posting with the Royal Liverpool Philharmonic. He then held posts with the Montreal Symphony (1961–7), the Los Angeles Philharmonic (1962–78), the Israel Philharmonic (from 1969), the New York Philharmonic (1978–91) and the Staatsoper in Munich (1998–2006).

Méhul, Etienne-Nicolas (b. Givet, Ardennes, 22 Jun 1763; d. Paris, 18 Oct 1817). French composer, grounded in the Viennese Classical style, to which he added a liveliness of colour that suited Napoleonic as much as revolutionary France. The son of a count's major domo, he studied locally and, from 1778/9, in Paris with Edelmann. His reputation, already climbing, was sealed by *Euphrosine* (1790), his operatic debut, and while maintaining his career in the theatre he emerged as one of the leading composers of revolutionary hymns and songs. In 1795 he became both a founder member of the Institut and an inspector at the Conservatoire. Under Napoleon he wrote big public works and court cantatas, comedies (*L'irato*, 1801, dedicated to the First Consul) and further serious operas, including *Uthal* (1806) and *Joseph* (1807). The former, with a violin-less orchestra to explore sombre tone colours in keeping with the misty subject from Ossian, is remembered in histories if not in the theatre; *Joseph*, with its biblical subject, includes a harp. His marriage failed, and he set up home with the sister-in-law of his friend Cherubini. After the Bourbon restoration he stayed in favour, though in declining health.

Operas (all first performed in Paris): *Euphrosine* (François-Benoît Hoffman), f.p. 1790; *Stratonice* (Hoffman), f.p. 1792; *Horatius Coclès* (Antoine-Vincent Arnault), f.p. 1794; *Mélidore et Phrosine* (Arnault), f.p. 1794; *Le Jeune Henri* (Jean-Nicolas Bouilly), f.p. 1797 (overture *La Chasse du jeune Henri*); *Ariodant* (Hoffman), f.p. 1799; *Bion* (Hoffman), f.p. 1800; *L'irato*, f.p. 1801; *Héléna*, f.p. 1803; *Les Deux Aveugles de Tolède* (Benoît-Joseph Marsollier des Vivetières), f.p. 1806; *Uthal* (Jacques-Maximilien Benjamin Bins de Saint-Victor, after Ossian), f.p. 1806; *Joseph* (Alexandre Duval), f.p. 1807; etc.

Symphonies: No.1, G minor, 1808; No.2, D, 1809; No.3, C, 1809; No.4, E, 1810; No.5, A, 1810

Other works: choral music, songs, ballets, etc.

Meilhac, Henri (b. Paris, 21 Feb 1831; d. Paris, 6 Jul 1897). French librettist, working mostly in collaboration with Ludovic Halévy.

Meistergesang (Ger.). Mastersong, the art of the Meistersinger.

Meistersinger (Ger., pl. *Meistersinger*). Master-singers, German poet-composers belonging to bourgeois guilds. Their activity was strong from the late 15th century to the early 17th, though the last acknowledged Meistersinger (from Memmingen) died in 1922. The Meistersinger tradition reached its pinnacle, as Wagner well knew, in Nuremberg under Hans Sachs in the mid 16th century. That tradition, though fundamentally middle class, looked to the princely MINNESINGER as models, and many of the Meistersinger's approved melodies (always in BAR FORM) came from that source. Their melodies also remained monophonic, to be sung normally by a soloist, while the poetic subject matter was most often religious. In Nuremberg there was a competition every month – a competition essentially in performance, not (as in Wagner's opera) composition.

Meistersinger, Die (The Mastersingers). Opera by Wagner, titled in full *Die Meistersinger von Nürnberg*, to his own libretto. The knight Walther von Stolzing (tenor) sets himself to become a Meistersinger in order to win Eva (soprano), promised by her father, Pogner (bass), to the winner of a mastersong competition. Sachs (bassbaritone) offers wise supervision, and his apprentice David (tenor) eager advice, but Beckmesser (tenor) is spurred to a ridiculous rivalry. Walther of course wins, but the hero – restraining the young man from scorning his Meistersinger chain – is Sachs. Orchestral excerpts include the Prelude (in majestic C major polyphony), the brooding prelude to the third act and the Dance of the Apprentices. Among the songs and mastersongs are Sachs's Flieder Monologue, noisy second-act song ('Jerum! Jerum!'), third-act meditation ('Wahn! Wahn!') and admonishment to Walther ('Verachtet mir die Meister'), Walther's introduction of himself ('Am stillen Herd'), Trial Song ('Fanget an!') and Prize Song ('Morgenlich leuchtend'), Beckmesser's serenade ('Den Tag seh' ich') and the radiant quintet for Eva and Walther, David and his sweetheart Magdalene, and Sachs ('Selig, wie die Sonne'). First performance: Munich, 21 Jun 1868.

mel. Measure of pitch as subjectively experienced, described by Stevens and Volkman in 1940. Defining a frequency of 1,000 Hz as 1,000 mels, they established a scale that was roughly linear below this point (i.e. 500 Hz = 500 mels, etc.) but not above: 2,000 Hz, for instance, was perceived as less than a 'doubling' of pitch level (whatever that might mean). However, pitch perception depends on contexts provided by harmony, temperament and musical tradition, quite apart from training, and the mel scale has proved of limited use.

Melartin, Erkki [Erik Gustaf] (b. Käkisalmi/ Priozersk, 7 Feb 1875; d. Pukinmäki, near Helsinki, 14 Feb 1937). Finnish composer, in lyrical-wistful late Romantic style. He studied with Martin Wegelius at the Helsinki Music Institute (1892–9) and Fuchs in Vienna (1899–1901), then returned to the institute, whose director he became (1911–36). His works include six symphonies (No.1, C minor,

Op.30:1, 1902; No.2, E minor, Op.30:2, 1904; No.3, F, Op.40, 1906–7; No.4 'Summer', E, Op.80, 1912; No.5 (*Sinfonia brevis*), A minor, Op.90, 1916; No.6, Op.100, 1924), the opera *Aino* (1907), incidental music for *The Sleeping Beauty* (1904), and numerous songs and piano pieces.

Melba, Nellie (b. Richmond, Victoria, 19 May 1861; d. Sydney, 23 Feb 1931). Australian soprano, a star of the early gramophone, created dame in 1918. Born Helen Porter Mitchell, she used the familiar form of her first name and invented 'Melba' from the name of her native city, Richmond being a suburb of Melbourne. In due course this pseudonym became attached to a dessert (peach melba) and crisp, thin-sliced bread (melba toast), both created by Escoffier. To achieve the eminence such distinctions betokened, she travelled to London in 1886 with her father, husband and son, and so to Paris, where Mathilde Marchesi prepared her for her debut (Brussels, 1887). Thereafter her career was based at Covent Garden, until her farewell appearance there in 1926, though she also sang at the Met. She excelled in Italian and French roles that would show off her bright melodiousness.

Melchior, Lauritz (Lebrecht Hommel) (b. Copenhagen, 20 Mar 1890; d. Santa Monica, Cal., 18 Mar 1973). Danish–US tenor, the paradigmatic Wagner tenor. Born on the same day as Gigli, he studied at the Royal Opera School in Copenhagen as a baritone, and so began his career. He then retrained as a tenor with Vilhelm Herold (1917–18), but was enjoying only moderate success before being taken up by the British novelist Hugh Walpole, who enabled him to study with Anna Bahr-Mildenburg and others. In 1924 he sang Siegmund at Covent Garden and Bayreuth (where he was also Parsifal). He then maintained his supremacy on stage and on record until 1950, when he gave his farewell performance at the Met (though he sang the first act of *Walküre* in Copenhagen 10 years later).

melisma (Gk, song, pl. *melismata*, though 'melismas' is acceptable in Eng.). Run of notes to a syllable, usually without the display that characterizes coloratura.

melismatic. Term used of music distinguished by melismata.

Mellers, Wilfrid (Howard) (b. Leamington, 26 Apr 1914). British composer and scholar, his work in both fields exuberant and all-embracing. He was a pupil of F.R. Leavis at Cambridge and of Wellesz and Rubbra in Oxford, after which he remained in academic life. His time as visiting professor at Pittsburgh (1960–63) widened him, and gave him a lasting love of the USA and its tangled musical traditions. He was then able to introduce a new vision of music education as founder professor of the music department at York University (1964–81). His acknowledged compositions, chiefly choral pieces and songs of diverse kinds, date mostly from the 1960s and early 1970s, but he has gone on writing prose with the same lively passion. Among his books are *Music in a New Found Land* (1964), *Caliban Reborn* (1967) and monographs on Couperin, the Beatles, Bach, Beethoven and Vaughan Williams.

Mellnäs, Arne (b. Stockholm, 30 Aug 1933). Swedish composer, a delicate avant-gardist. He studied at the conservatory in Stockholm (1953–63) and stayed there to teach (1963–86); he also had lessons with Blacher, Max Deutsch, Ligeti and Koenig. His output is particularly strong in choral and chamber music.

mellophone. Brass instrument, a simplified French horn most often found in US college bands.

melodeon. General name for several kinds of button accordion generally used in folk music.

melodic. Having to do with melody in an abstract sense, as in 'melodic line' (a term that is almost tautologous, but useful as an alternative to 'melody' emphasizing the abstractness.) Compare MELODIOUS.

melodica. Harmonica with a keyboard, introduced by Hohner in 1958. Generally a simple school instrument, it has been used occasionally by composers.

mélodie (Fr.). Melody, song. The term is used in Eng. for classic French song, the repertory that began with Berlioz, was enlarged by Lalo, Liszt, Gounod, Saint-Saëns and Bizet, reached its apogee in the settings of Fauré, Duparc, Debussy, Chabrier, Chausson and Ravel, and received a postscript from Poulenc. The mélodie developed later than the lied; indeed, Schubert's lieder, in translation, were an important influence.

Melodie (Ger.). Melody in the particular.

Melodien. Orchestral work by Ligeti, its advertisement of melody provocative at the time. It contains, indeed, a profusion of melodies emerging from, and folding into, harmonic-timbral textures. First performance: Nuremberg, 10 Dec 1971.

Melodik (Ger.). Melody in the abstract.

melodious. Tuneful. Compare MELODIC.

Melodiya. Soviet recording company, founded in 1964, when it took over all previous Soviet recordings. It failed to survive the dismantling of the Soviet Union, and its catalogue was acquired in 1994 by BMG.

melodrama. The combination of speech and music, or a section or whole work so written, almost always for a soloist. In this sense the term (from Gk MELOS), has no melodramatic (from Gk *melas* = black) connotations. Indeed, the form may not even be dramatic, though most examples are, outside the 19th-century art of RECITATION and its curious progeny in Schoenberg's works with SPRECHGESANG.

Where straight acting with music is concerned, almost any kind of drama before late 19th-century naturalism would have brought the two into association, but theatrical melodrama implies a quite specific interlocking, in which the music is almost another character in dialogue with the actor: prompting, punctuating, responding. The outstanding pioneer example was Rousseau's *Pygmalion* (1770), which was reset by other composers including Georg Benda (f.p. Gotha, 1779), whose *Ariadne auf Naxos* and *Medea* had already caused a stir – not least in Mozart, who tried out the form in *Thamos* and *Zaide*. This was to be part of melodrama's mixed future, in special scenes within plays (*Egmont*) and operas (*Fidelio*, *Der Freischütz*), alongside whole works having an actor protagonist (Berlioz's *Lélio*, Stravinsky's *Perséphone*, Honegger's *Jeanne d'Arc au bûcher*).

melodramma (It.). 19th-century term for opera.

melody. Term whose meaning seems closely familiar but recedes at any attempt to define it, largely because it is both a neutral, abstract element and a label of approval, to be granted or withheld; hence the distinct adjectival forms MELODIC and MELODIOUS. What makes music melodious is personal judgement, which will depend on familiarity. It may be hard at first to recognize melody in Boulez; one of the original critics heard no melody in *Carmen*.

Also, the term takes on a different meaning when prefaced, actually or implicitly, with the indefinite article. A melody has to arrive at some point of closure, to be a unit detachable from its context. Where Wagner's melody is a language spoken through all his mature music, Walther's Prize Song melody is a theme. But again, the matter of what makes a melody is contentious, and probably most people would reserve the term for something they could remember.

Melody in the abstract is, in principle, the flowing of notes one after another and is thus a component of almost all music. Because the flow goes through time, melody is inseparable from rhythm: a line in music is always a line in motion. And because that motion is powered in most cases by harmonic forces, melody is also inseparable from harmony, as is clear from the prominence of triadic notes in melodies within the major-minor system. But melody does not have to be so constrained. The history of the last thousand years has been a history of constant expansion of the notion of melody, from the sung to the imitation of the sung and on to the unsung and unsingable.

melologue. Piece of melodrama.

melos (Gk, song, limb). Melodic character of a repertory, as in 'the melos of Russian chant'.

Melpomene. The muse of tragedy, poetry in the Aeolic dialect and threnody.

membranophone. Formal organological term for an instrument drawing sound from a skin (membranophone); the category includes drums and also kazoos. The other kinds are AEROPHONES, CHORDOPHONES and IDIOPHONES.

memory. The medium within which music largely operates. Even sight reading and improvisation are arts of memory, in which the performer draws on experience. To perform from memory is to perform without looking at the music, but musicians performing from a score are also in a sense performing from memory, since what they play or sing will be the projection of what they remember (from previous performances by themselves and others, from study, from rehearsal), revivified by instantaneous forces of imagination and nervous energy that make it effectively a new memory, a memory never heard before. And because music unfolds through time, the act of listening also depends heavily on memory – on stored remembrances of style, tradition, the work and the composer, and on the immediate recognition of how the piece and the performance are proceeding.

Mendelssohn(-Bartholdy). German composing

siblings, grandchildren of Moses Mendelssohn (1729–86), who, in the spirit of the Enlightenment, led his fellow Jews on an exodus from the ghetto and his fellow Germans on a journey into tolerance. Two of his sons, Abraham and Joseph, founded a bank in Hamburg, and moved to Berlin in 1811. There in 1816 Abraham gave his four children – Fanny, Felix, Rebecka and Paul – for baptism as Lutherans and added Bartholdy (from a family farm) to their name, though he and his wife Lea did not convert until 1822. The children were therefore brought up in a mixed culture, with Catholics as well as Jews and Protestants in the family, and with many high achievers: their aunt Dorothea was married to the writer Friedrich von Schlegel, while her son from her first marriage, Philipp Veit, became a distinguished painter. Lea supervised her children's rapid musical development; they also had lessons in Paris in 1816–17 with Marie Bigot, who had played for Haydn and Beethoven. By 1819 Fanny and Felix were studying with Zelter and attending his Singakademie rehearsals; his reverence for Bach affected them both. Soon afterwards Karl Ludwig Heyse was engaged as family tutor; he was to become a philologist of note and father of Paul Heyse, first German winner of the Nobel Prize for literature. Rebecka married the mathematician Lejeune Dirichlet; Paul went into the bank and later became a partner in an aniline-dye firm that gave rise to the AGFA company.

(1) **Fanny (Cäcilie)** (b. Hamburg, 14 Nov 1805; d. Berlin, 14 May 1847). She composed steadily from the age of 14, though – understandably in awe of her beloved brother and deferent to the culture of the time – she at first published nothing but six numbers included without separate attribution in his Opp.8–9 sets of songs (including her Grillparzer song 'Italien', 1825). Most of her music was meant for the salon she maintained, following her marriage in 1829 to Wilhelm Hensel; Sebastian, their only child, was to publish a Mendelssohn-Bartholdy family history. Trips with her husband to Italy in 1839–40 and 1845 delighted her, and in 1846 she at last found the confidence to start publishing her music, but she died of a stroke the next year. Apart from numerous songs and piano pieces she wrote choral works (*Oratorium nach den Bildern der Bibel*, 1831) and chamber music (Piano Trio, Op.11, 1846).

(2) **(Jacob Ludwig) Felix** (b. Hamburg, 3 Feb 1809; d. Leipzig, 4 Nov 1847). Showing huge creative gifts from early in his second decade – plus a great capacity for study – he became the most classically minded of the great early Romantics. His music is full of immediate responses to poetry and the natural scene – often he composed at great

speed – but he was also the first important composer to have a modern sense of the power of the past, as conveyed in the music of Beethoven, Mozart and Bach.

His facility and his studiousness were strongly encouraged by his parents, with Fanny, too, an early support and testing board. He was playing in public at nine and composing at 10. A one-act singspiel by him was performed with orchestra at home on his 12th birthday; later that year he was at the première of *Der Freischütz* and was taken to visit Goethe, the first of several obeisances to the poet. At 13 he was performing at the family's Sunday musicales, for which he produced symphonies for strings, concertos and other works, and at 14 he was a published composer, with his Op.1 a piano quartet. Also when he was 14 he received a copy of Bach's St Matthew Passion as a present from his grandmother. The next year, on his 15th birthday, Zelter declared his apprenticeship over, though he had lessons with Moscheles a few months later.

At 16 he visited Paris with his father and came into contact with musicians from Liszt to Cherubini. Back home in Berlin he composed his Octet for strings – his first masterpiece and one of his most brilliant, already fully characteristic in its fineness of texture, its sense of ease and its athletic joy in movement. The following year came another piece combining complete assurance with freshness, his *Midsummer Night's Dream* overture. He then took courses in law, geography and aesthetics (with Hegel) at the University of Berlin (1827–9), while in his spare time continuing to compose and preparing a performance of the St Matthew Passion, the first since Bach's lifetime, taking place on 11 March 1829. Conducting from the piano, he was just 20.

The next month he made his first visit to Britain, where he stayed until November. He took part in London musical life, then travelled to Scotland (gaining impressions that sparked the overture *Die Hebriden* and the 'Scottish' Symphony) and Wales. The following year his continuing journeys took him to Vienna and on to Italy, where again his stay was long – from November 1830 to July 1831 – and divided between making artistic acquaintances (Berlioz, Donizetti) and opening himself to sights and sounds that would generate music. His indefatigable travelling in his early 20s, seemingly driven by a thirst for new experiences and new friends, may have helped him maintain the eager creative freshness he had known as a boy. But his appreciation of his more adventurous contemporaries (Berlioz, Liszt, Wagner) was tempered with a caution inherited from his studies.

Between December 1831 and June 1832 he was in Paris and London again. In London he prepared for the press a volume of 'Original Melodies for the Pianoforte', later retitled as the first of several books of Songs without Words, pieces with an immense and lasting appeal to amateur pianists. In 1833 he made two more trips to London, in the spring to conduct his 'Italian' Symphony for the Philharmonic Society, which had commissioned it, and in the summer with his father on holiday. He returned to Germany to take up an appointment as director of music in Düsseldorf, where he had to conduct at the theatre and for monthly church services. His contract was for three years, but in September 1835 he moved to Leipzig as director of the Gewandhaus orchestra, which he conducted in an annual winter season of 20 concerts, raising standards, helping to establish a classic repertory (Bach, Handel, Haydn, Mozart, Beethoven) and introducing new works, including Schubert's Ninth Symphony, which Schumann, one of the first friends he made in Leipzig, had unearthed. With the support of Schumann and other contemporaries, notably Ferdinand David and Gade, he made Leipzig the capital of a new Romantic music that had vital 18th-century roots.

His father's death during his first season was a blow, from which he recovered partly by pressing on to complete his first oratorio, St Paul. This was soon being given widely in western Europe and the USA, for he had found a form in which he could answer both his own neo-Baroque aspirations and a public wish for music that combined aesthetic experience with religious. This infusion of the sacred is to be found also in two of his symphonies: the 'Reformation' (1830) and 'Lobgesang' (1840). Soon after the first performance of St Paul in the summer of 1836 he fell in love with Cécile Jeanrenaud, whom he married the following March. They spent a blissful honeymoon in southwestern Germany, before he had to make a quick visit to England in August–September 1837, presenting both St Paul and his new D minor piano concerto in Birmingham.

To a continuing schedule of winter concerts in Leipzig and summer festivals elsewhere, he added in 1841 regular obligations in Berlin, as royal kapellmeister, writing music for theatre productions by Ludwig Tieck (*Antigone* and *A Midsummer Night's Dream*, in which he had to live up to the youthful magic of his overture) and supervising church music. His London visit in the summer of 1842 brought invitations to Buckingham Palace. Queen Victoria sang songs of his and his sister's to his accompaniment and later accepted the dedication of his 'Scottish' Symphony. But Leipzig remained the centre of his musical world, and there in 1843 he was responsible for founding the conservatory, with Schumann and the violinist Ferdinand David among his colleagues on the staff. Work, again, provided relief from grief at the loss of a parent, his mother having died in December 1842.

In September 1844, after another short working excursion to London, he completed for David his Violin Concerto, the great work of this period. The next year he declined an invitation to the USA, and in 1846 came the first performance of his second oratorio, *Elijah*, commissioned for the Birmingham festival. In April 1847 he was back in England, conducting further performances of *Elijah* in London and Manchester as well as Birmingham, and appearing again at court. He was in Frankfurt when he received news the following month of his sister's death. Shattered and silenced, he only gradually returned to composition, producing his F minor quartet, beginning a third oratorio, *Christus*, and starting out too on the Romantic fairytale opera he had long wanted to write. But in October he began to suffer from strokes, and he died within six months of Fanny.

His music is full of paradoxes. Manifest exuberance and facility in creation went along with passionate anxieties about measuring up to the masters of the past. His urgent reverence for Beethoven, in particular, prompted some of his most intense pieces, including his A minor quartet and *Variations sérieuses* for piano. Like any Romantic he valued improvisatory freedom and direct lyric utterance (more in his Songs without Words than in those with), but formal integrity was important to him too, and in his symphonies and concertos he found novel ways to create a sense of wholeness in multi-movement designs. He exerted himself ably in the working world of commissions, concert promotion and publication, but he had learned his art in the bosom of a loving family, whose disappearance he could not survive. One thing he had that enabled him to negotiate these opposing pulls, and he made it his triumph: infectious charm.

Peter Mercer-Taylor *The Life of Mendelssohn* (2000)

Orchestral and theatre music

Symphonies: No.1, C minor, Op.11, 1824; No.2 'LOBGESANG', Bb, Op.52, with s, ch in finale, 1840; No.3 'SCOTTISH', Op.56, A minor, 1842; No.4 'ITALIAN', A, Op.90, 1833, rev 1834; No.5 'REFORMATION', D, Op.107, 1830, rev 1832

Overtures: 'Trumpet', C, Op.101, *c*.1825, rev 1833; *A MIDSUMMER NIGHT'S DREAM*, Op.26, 1826; MEERESSTILLE UND GLÜCKLICHE FAHRT, Op.27, 1828; *Die* HEBRIDEN, Op.26, 1830, rev 1832; *Die schöne Melusine*, Op.32, 1833; *Ruy Blas*, Op.95, 1839

Concertos: A minor, pf, str, 1822; Piano Concerto No.1, G minor, Op.25, 1831; No.2, D minor, Op.40, 1837; *Capriccio brillant*, Op.22, pf, orch, 1832; *Rondo brillant*, Op.29, pf, orch, 1834; *Serenade und Allegro giocoso*, Op.43, pf, orch, 1838; Double Piano Concerto, E, 1823; Double Piano Concerto, Ab, 1824; D minor, vn, str, 1822; VIOLIN CONCERTO, E minor, Op.64, 1844; Concerto, D minor, vn, pf, orch, 1823

Symphonies for strings: Nos.1–13, C, D, E minor, C minor, Bb, Eb, D minor, D, C, B minor, F, G minor (Fugue), C minor, 1821–3

Other orchestral works: Overture, C, Op.24, wind, 1824, rev 1826, 1838; *Trauermarsch*, Op.103, wind, 1836; March, Op.108, 1841

Operas: *Die Hochzeit des Camacho* (?Friedrich Voigt, after *Don Quixote*), Op.10, 1825, f.p. Berlin, 1827; *Heimkehr aus der Fremde* (1 act; Karl Klingemann), Op.89, 1829, f.p. Berlin, 1829; *Die Lorelei* (Emanuel Geibel), Op.98, 1847 (unfinished)

Incidental music: *Antigone* (Sophocles), Op.55, 1841; *A MIDSUMMER NIGHT'S DREAM*, Op.61, 1843; *Oedipus at Colonus* (Sophocles), Op.93, 1845; *Athalie* (Racine), Op.74, 1845

Choral and vocal music

Oratorios: ST PAUL, Op.36, 1836; ELIJAH, Op.70, 1846, rev 1847; *Christus*, Op.97, 1847 (unfinished)

Smaller choral works: 3 Sacred Pieces, Op.23, 1830 (*Aus tiefer Noth*, t, ch, org; *Ave Maria*, soli, ch, con; *Mitten wir in Leben sind*, ch); *Die* ERSTE WALPURGISNACHT, Op.60, ch, orch, 1832, rev 1842–3; Psalm 42, Op.42, soli, ch, orch, 1837, rev 1838; *Festgesang*, men's ch, brass, timp, 1840 (for the Gutenberg Festival, No.2 set to Charles Wesley's 'Hark! The herald angels sing' by William H. Cummings); *Hear my prayer*, s, ch, org, 1844; *Sechs Sprüche*, Op.79, ch, 1843–6; *Die deutsche Liturgie*, ch, 1846; 3 Psalms, Op.78; 3 Motets, Op.69, soli, ch, 1847; etc.

Concert arias: 'Infelice' (Metastasio), Op.94, 1834; 'On Lena's Gloomy Heath' (Ossian), 1846

Songs: 'Allnächtlich im Traume' (Heine), Op.86:4, pub 1850; 'Altdeutsches Frühlingslied' (Friedrich von Spee), Op.86:6, 1847; 'Auf Flügeln des Gesanges' (Heine), Op.34:2, 1835; 'Bei der Wiege' (Klingemann), Op.47:6, 1833; 'Das erste Veilchen' (Karl Egon Ebert), Op.19a:2, 1832; 'Frühlingslied' (Ulrich von Lichtenstein), Op.19a:1, 1830; 'Frühlingslied' (Klingemann), Op.71:2, 1845; 'Grüss' (Heine), Op.19a:5, pub 1833; 'Der Mond' (Geibel), Op.86:5, pub 1850; 'Nachtlied' (Eichendorff), Op.71:6, 1847; 'Neue Liebe' (Heine), Op.19a:4, pub 1833; 'Reiselied' (Ebert), Op.19a:6, 1830; 'Suleika' (Marianne von Willemer), Op.34:4, pub 1837; 'Venetianisches Gondellied' (Ferdinand Freigrath, after Moore), Op.57:5, 1842; 'Winterlied', Op.19a:3, pub 1833; etc.

Duets: 3 Folksongs, 1836–8; 6 Duets, Op.63, 1836–44; 3 Duets, Op.77, 1836–47

Chamber and keyboard music

String quartets: No.1, Eb, Op.12, 1829; No.2, A minor, Op.13, 1827; Nos.3–5, D, E minor, Eb, Op.44,

1837–8; No.6, F minor, Op.80, 1847; 4 Pieces, Op.81 (Andante and Variations, E, 1847; Scherzo, A minor, 1847; Capriccio, E minor, 1843; Fugue, E♭, 1827)

String quintets (str qt and va): No.1, A, Op.18, 1826; No.2, B♭, Op.87, 1845

Piano quartets: No.1, C minor, Op.1, 1822; No.2, F minor, Op.2, 1823; No.3, B minor, Op.3, 1825

Piano trios: No.1, D minor, Op.49, 1839; No.2, C minor, Op.66, 1845

Other chamber works: Octet, E♭, Op.20, 2 str qt, 1825; Sextet, D, Op.110, pf, str qt, db, 1824; Concert Piece No.1, F, Op.113, cl, basset hn, pf, 1832; No.2, D minor, Op.114, cl, basset hn, pf, 1833; etc.

Duos: Violin Sonata, F minor, Op.4, 1823; Violin Sonata, F, 1838; Viola Sonata, C minor, 1824; Cello Sonata No.1, B♭, Op.45, 1838; No.2, D, Op.58, 1843; *Variations concertantes*, D, Op.17, vc, pf, 1829; Song without Words, D, Op.109, vc, pf, 1845; Clarinet Sonata, E♭, ?1824; etc.

Piano: SONGS WITHOUT WORDS, Vol.1, Op.19b, 1829–30; Vol.2, Op.30, 1830–34; Vol.3, Op.38, 1835–7; Vol.4, Op.53, 1835–41; Vol.5, Op.62, 1841–4; Vol.6, Op.67, 1839–45; Vol.7, Op.85, 1834–45; Vol.8, Op.102, 1841–5; Sonata, G minor, Op.105, 1821; E, Op.6, 1826; B♭, Op.106, 1827; Fantasia on 'The Last Rose of Summer', Op.15, ?1827; 3 Fantasies/Caprices, Op.16, 1829; Rondo capriccioso, Op.14, 1830; Fantasia (*Sonate écossaise*), Op.28, 1828–33; 3 Caprices, Op.33, 1833–5; 3 Etudes, Op.104b, 1834–6; 6 Preludes and Fugues, Op.35, 1832–7; *Gondellied*, 1837; *Variations sérieuses*, D minor, Op.54, 1841; *Sechs Kinderstücke*, Op.72, 1842; etc.

Organ: 3 Preludes and Fugues, Op.37, 1833–7; Andante and Variations, D, 1844; 6 Sonatas, F minor, C minor, A, B♭, D, D minor, Op.65, 1844–5; etc.

Mengelberg, (Josef) Willem (b. Utrecht, 28 Mar 1871; d. Zuort, Switzerland, 22 Mar 1951). Dutch conductor, a champion of Mahler and Strauss. He studied in Utrecht and Cologne, began his career in Lucerne and in 1895 was appointed conductor of the Concertgebouw, a position he held for half a century. Strauss dedicated *Ein Heldenleben* to him; Mahler he invited to Amsterdam to conduct, himself giving a complete Mahler cycle in 1920. Among other appointments, he conducted the Frankfurt Museum concerts (1907–20) and appeared annually with the New York Philharmonic (1921–9). As he went on conducting in the Netherlands under Nazi occupation, and even appeared in Germany, he was obliged after the war to retire to Switzerland. Other musicians in the family have included his nephews Rudolf (1892–1959) and Karel (1902–84), and Karel's son Misha (b. 1935), all of them composers.

Mennin, Peter (b. Erie, Penn., 17 May 1923; d. New York, 17 Jun 1983). US composer, notably of symphonies in conservative mould. He studied with Hanson and Bernard Rogers at Eastman, achieved early success with his Second Symphony (1944), which Bernstein took up, and became director successively of Peabody (1958–62) and Juilliard (1962–83).

meno (It.). Less, as in *meno mosso* (less moved, i.e. slower).

Menotti, Gian Carlo (b. Cadegliano, 7 Jul 1911). Italian–US composer, unashamed of theatrical immediacy and tonal melody, two features that won him a string of operatic successes in the few years after the Second World War. A businessman's son, he entered the Milan Conservatory at 13, then moved to Curtis (1928–33). Barber was a fellow student, and the two became a couple. Menotti remained largely in the USA, but maintained links with Italy and exercised those links in founding the Spoleto Festival in 1958. Long before that he had established himself as a composer of operas, always to his own librettos. *Amelia al ballo* (1937), his last work in Italian, was his first US triumph and led to an association with NBC. After the war *The Medium* (with a comedy, *The Telephone*, as curtain-raiser) and *The Consul* both enjoyed Broadway runs of several months. *The Medium* is the tragedy of a woman caught between impenetrable reality and an incredible world beyond; *The Consul* is a police-state drama. Then in 1951 he wrote the first television opera, the hugely successful and repeatedly produced *Amahl and the Night Visitors*. Later works include the libretto for Barber's *Vanessa*.

Operas (all librettos by the composer): *Amelia al ballo*, f.p. Philadelphia, 1937; *The Old Maid and the Thief* (1 act), f.p. NBC, 1939; *The Medium*, f.p. New York, 1946; *The Telephone* (1 act), f.p. New York, 1947; *The Consul*, f.p. Philadelphia, 1950; AMAHL AND THE NIGHT VISITORS (1 act), f.p. NBC TV, 1951; *The Saint of Bleecker Street*, f.p. New York, 1954; *The Unicorn, the Gorgon and the Manticore*, f.p. Washington, 1956; etc.

Other works: *Sebastian* (ballet), 1944; Piano Concerto, F, 1945; Violin Concerto, A minor, 1952; etc.

mensural. Term used of rhythmic notation in distinct values, as arose in the mid 13th century.

mensuration. System of proportions among rhythmic values, introduced by FRANCO OF COLOGNE. See also MODUS; PROLATION; TEMPUS.

mensuration canon. Canon in which one voice has rhythmic values proportionately different from another's, a device from the age of mensuration.

menuet (Fr.), **menuetto** (It.). Minuet.

Menuhin, Yehudi (b. New York, 22 Apr 1916; d. Berlin, 12 Mar 1999). US–British violinist, who was hugely influential, too, in his work on behalf of music education and transcending barriers: he settled in London in 1959, was knighted in 1985, and was granted a peerage, becoming Lord Menuhin in 1993. He began his career in San Francisco in 1924 and completed his training with Enescu after his Paris debut at 10. Besides showing a complete command of the traditional repertory at an early age, he recorded Elgar's concerto with the composer (1932) and was the destined performer of Bartók's solo sonata. In later years, bravely combatting technical problems, he became the public voice of music in Britain, respected for his calm and authority. He performed with Indian and jazz musicians, founded a school for musically gifted children (the Menuhin School, Stoke d'Abernon), and became a conductor and festival director.

Mephisto Waltz (*Mephisto Walz*). Title Liszt gave to three piano pieces, of which the first is the best known, being a transcription of the second of his orchestral Two Episodes from Nikolaus Lenau's *Faust*. The scene is in an inn, where Mephistopheles seizes a violin and creates, by his playing, an orgy.

Mer, La (The Sea). Orchestral work by Debussy, a set of 'symphonic sketches' amounting almost to a symphony in D♭, with a scherzo surrounded by two allegros of emphatic statement swayed by mutability. The movements, in order, are: *De l'Aube à midi sur la mer* (From Dawn to Noon on the Sea), *Jeux de vagues* (Waveplays) and *Dialogue du vent et de la mer* (Dialogue of the Wind and the Sea). First performance: Paris, 15 Oct 1905.

Merbecke. See John MARBECK.

Mercadante, (Giuseppe) Saverio (Raffaele) (baptized Altamura, near Bari, 17 Sep 1795; d. Naples, 17 Dec 1870). Italian composer, who enjoyed a 40-year career alongside Rossini, Bellini, Donizetti and Verdi, producing works that were widely performed and influential, but are now all but forgotten – ironically his most frequently performed piece is a student composition, his Flute Concerto No.2 in E minor, Op.57 (1814). Of illegitimate birth, he studied at the Collegio di San Sebastiano in Naples (1808–20), notably with

Zingarelli. *Elisa e Claudio* (1821) brought him international success, and he spent the years 1826–31 writing operas in Spain and Portugal. In 1832, having resumed his Italian career, he married. Three years later Rossini invited him to compose an opera for Paris, where he was impressed by Meyerbeer, with results to come in *Il giuramento* (1837) and later works. Striving to remove operatic conventions and emphasize drama, he was briefly at the forefront of Italian opera, until overtaken by Verdi. He became head of his alma mater in 1840, and his output slackened. In 1862 he lost his sight, though he continued to compose instrumental pieces by dictation.

Operas: *Elisa e Claudio* (Luigi Romanelli), f.p. Milan, 1821; *Amleto* (Romani), f.p. Milan, 1822; *Il giuramento* (Gaetano Rossi), f.p. Milan, 1837; *Orazi e Curiazi* (Cammarano), f.p. Naples, 1846; 57 others
Other works: sacred music, cantatas, orchestral pieces, etc.

Mercure, Pierre (b. Montreal, 21 Feb 1927; d. Avallon, 29 Jan 1966). Canadian composer, who worked chiefly for ballets, films and radio. He studied with Champagne at the Quebec Conservatory and Boulanger in Paris (1949–50). Return visits there helped his move towards modernist techniques around 1960. He also worked on music programmes for the French-language television service in Canada from 1952 until his death in a car accident.

Mercury. Name given to Haydn's Symphony No.43, for reasons unknown.

Merikanto, Aarre (b. Helsinki, 29 Jun 1893; d. Helsinki, 29 Sep 1958). Finnish composer, notably of the opera *Juha* (1922), which was not performed until after his death, but has since been installed as the foundation stone of Finnish opera, comparable with Janáček in its delineation of character and locale. The son of Oskar Merikanto (1868–1924), who composed the first Finnish-language opera, *The Maid of the North* (1899), he studied in Helsinki with Melartin, in Leipzig with Reger (1912–14) and in Moscow with Sergey Vasilenko (1915–16). Apart from *Juha*, he produced orchestral music (three symphonies, three piano concertos, four violin concertos, etc.) and chamber pieces. Neglect drove him to adopt a more conventional style while teaching at the Sibelius Academy (1936–58).

Merry Wives of Windsor, The. See FALSTAFF; *Die LUSTIGEN WEIBER VON WINDSOR*.

Mersenne, Marin (b. La Soultière, near Oizéí,

Maine, 8 Sep 1588; d. Paris, 1 Sep 1648). French savant, important to the history of music for his work on the physics of sound, compositional theory and the classification of instruments. Educated at a Jesuit school and the Sorbonne, he entered the Order of Minims and spent most of his life serving that order in Paris. He was the first to recognize that the pitch of a vibrating string is related not only to its length but also to its thickness and mass; he also understood how harmonics arise.

Merula, Tarquinio (b. Cremona, 1594/5; d. Cremona, 10 Dec 1665). Italian composer, alert to Venetian influences in his madrigals, motets, psalms, masses and canzonas. He enters the record as an organist in Lodi (1616–21), after which he worked in Warsaw. From 1626 he was chapelmaster for the *laudi della madonna* at the cathedral in his home town, except when he was engaged in Bergamo (1631–3 and 1638–46).

Merulo, Claudio (b. Correggio, 8 Apr 1533; d. Parma, 4 May 1604). Italian organist-composer, the greatest of his time. He probably studied in his native city and possibly in Venice: he was briefly organist of Brescia Cathedral (1556–7) before gaining a similar post at St Mark's in Venice (1557–84). From 1586 he held various positions in Parma, which is where he was buried, alongside Rore. Much of his music was published in Venice, and he was involved in the trade himself during the decade 1566–75. Chief among his works are his organ toccatas, which interleave counterpoint with fantasy and had an influence on Frescobaldi. He also wrote ricercares and canzonas for organ, motets and madrigals, these vocal works being close in style to Andrea Gabrieli.

Mesomedes (b. Crete, late 1st century). Greek poet-composer and kithara player, the emperor Hadrian's chief musician. A few settings by him, including hymns to Helios and Nemesis, survive with notated melodies, if of an unremarkable sort.

Mesopotamia. Early centre of civilization. The Sumerians of the 3rd millennium BC had harps, lyres and clappers, all known from inscriptions and rare survivals; there are reconstructions of a harp and a lyre in the British Museum. Reliefs from the Babylonian and Assyrian cultures of the next millennium and a half show harps, lyres, lutes, drums, cymbals and the ancestor of the aulos. Music throughout this period seems to have been essentially religious.

messa (It.). Mass. Hence also *messa per i defunti* (mass for the dead. i.e. *Requiem*).

messa di voce (It., placing the voice). Crescendo and diminuendo on a sustained note, first mentioned by Caccini at the very beginning of the 17th century and surviving as an essential part of the opera singer's technique. It has also been applied to instrumental performance.

Messager, André (Charles Prosper) (b. Montluçon, Allier, 30 Dec 1853; d. Paris, 24 Feb 1929). French composer – especially of operettas – and conductor. He studied with Fauré and Saint-Saëns at the Ecole Niedermeyer (1869–74), and remained friendly with both men. With Fauré he collaborated on a set of Wagner skits, *Souvenirs de Bayreuth* for piano duet: as with Chabrier, author of a similar entertainment, mockery went along with admiration, and he became the leading Wagner conductor in France. Meanwhile, he began his career as an organist and as a composer of operettas and ballets. His successes in the latter role came mostly before and after his heyday as a conductor, when he held principal posts at the Opéra-Comique (1898–1903, 1919–20), Covent Garden (1901–7) and the Paris Opera (1907–14). He was responsible for the première of *Pelléas*.

Operettas: *Madame Chrysanthème* (Georges Hartmann and André Alexandre, after Pierre Loti), f.p. Paris, 1893; *Véronique* (Albert Vanloo and Georges Duval), f.p. Paris, 1898; *Fortunio* (Gaston-Arman de Caillavet and Robert de Flers, after de Musset), f.p. Paris, 1907; *Monsieur Beaucaire* (Frederick Lonsdale and Adrian Ross, after Booth Tarkington), f.p. Birmingham, 1919; *La Petite Fonctionnaire* (Xavier Roux, after Alfred Capus), f.p. Paris, 1921; *L'Amour masqué* (Sacha Guitry), f.p. Paris, 1923; *Passionnément* (Maurice Hennequin and Albert Willemetz), f.p. Paris, 1926; *Coups de roulis* (Willemetz, after Maurice Laurroy), f.p. Paris, 1928
Other works: *Les Deux Pigeons* (ballet), 1886; *Souvenirs de Bayreuth*, pf duet, ?1888 (with Fauré); songs; etc.

messe (Fr.). Mass. Hence also *messe des morts* (mass of the dead, i.e. *Requiem*).

Messe (Ger.). Mass.

Messe de Nostre Dame. Four-part setting by Machaut, the earliest polyphonic treatment of the mass ordinary by a single composer, comprising *Kyrie, Gloria, Credo, Sanctus, Agnus Dei* and, less usually, *Ite missa est*.

Messiaen, Olivier (Eugène Prosper Charles) (b. Avignon, 10 Dec 1908; d. Paris, 28 Apr 1992). French composer, teacher and organist. Unlike almost everything in the Western tradition before, his music makes no attempt at progressive continuity. Its time is rather that of sudden shift, stasis and repetition – the eternal time of ecstasy and enlightenment, or the once-and-for-all time of vision and change. Colour is its other essential attribute: he imagined colours when he heard or composed music, and sometimes he marked in his scores effects of his favourite blues, purples and reds, vividly present as contrasting qualities of harmony and timbre. A devout Catholic all his life, he wrote many works devoted to sacred stories and articles of faith, but musically he was ecumenical, drawing from Debussy and Stravinsky, from the French organ tradition, from the rhythmic theory of ancient Greece and India, from the Indonesian gamelan and Peruvian folksong, and not least from the birds, whose songs he notated with scrupulous if idiosyncratic care. As a teacher he guided many composers of the next two generations, including Boulez, Barraqué, Stockhausen, Goehr and Benjamin. As a person he conveyed a complete serenity, which shines through his music.

It was a matter of pride to him that his mother, Cécile Sauvage, had addressed a cycle of poems to him in the womb; his father was an English teacher. After an early childhood in Grenoble and Nantes, he studied at the Paris Conservatoire (1919–30), where his teachers included Dukas, Dupré and Emmanuel. His earliest acknowledged works were written before he completed his studies and are already characteristic in their use of his MODES OF LIMITED TRANSPOSITIONS and of rhythms that are either strongly pulsed or not pulsed at all. The very slow organ meditation Le Banquet céleste exemplifies the latter kind and treats a favourite theme, that of divine, eternal presence in the everyday world, as represented in this case by the eucharist.

In 1930 he became organist of La Trinité, a church in northern central Paris equipped with a Cavaillé-Coll instrument; he remained in that post until his death, while appearing elsewhere occasionally as a recitalist. Organ works featured prominently in his output of the next decade, but so did music about his family. In 1931 he married Claire Delbos, a composer and violinist, for whom he wrote a Theme and Variations for violin and piano, followed by his first big song cycle, a celebration of marital love: Poèmes pour Mi (1936), 'Mi' being his pet name for her. Two years later came Chants de terre et de ciel, in which their infant son Pascal also features. Such private offerings required that he write his own texts, as he did for later vocal works, blending the styles of Christian liturgy and surrealist poetry.

Meanwhile, in the larger world, he was active in the group La JEUNE FRANCE, along with others who rejected the urbane Parisian music of the immediate pre-war years, represented by Poulenc. He also found ways to refresh his fundamentally homophonic early style by means of rhythmic irregularity (inherited from ancient Indian formulae and from birds) and a kind of dislocated counterpoint in which the parts are harmonically and rhythmically independent. His musical progress is charted in his first three organ cycles, on the Ascension, the Nativity and the nature of bodies in resurrected glory (Les Corps glorieux), though these works show as well his essential stability of language and purpose. His personal modes are all-pervasive, as are colourful harmonies, vigorous rhythms (sometimes NON-RETROGRADABLE), moments of utter calm, verse-refrain forms and subjects concerning the meeting of the human and the divine.

In 1939 he was called up for army service. Captured in the confusion when France fell the next year, he was sent to a prisoner-of-war camp in eastern Germany, along with other musicians. He wrote his most important chamber piece, Quatuor pour la fin du temps, to be played to camp inmates in the depth of the bleakest winter of the war; its eight movements, prompted by images from Revelation, form a catalogue of his musical manners hitherto: exuberant dance and luminous, slow, purely consonant song, a bizarre piece of contrapuntal machinery in which the four instruments go their own ways ('Liturgie de cristal') and a clarinet solo picturing birds as a symbol of hope in the abyss of hopelessness.

Released in 1941 he returned to Paris and in 1942 was appointed to teach harmony at the Conservatoire. As he had more to impart than the curriculum allowed, in 1943 he began giving private classes for his pupils, who included Boulez and the pianist Yvonne Loriod. She became his musical inspiration and helpmeet, the destined performer of all his works of 1943–4: the Visions de l'Amen (with him at the other piano), Trois petites liturgies and Vingt regards. The première of the second of these – for chanting women's choir with strings, percussion, ondes martenot (an electronic instrument he favoured for its celestial voice) and solo piano – was fiercely controversial, and its composer was castigated not only for placing religious music in the concert hall but also for including in his divine praise chords from the popular music of the time (especially the added sixth).

At the same time, contact with a new generation, eager for change, seems to have spurred his development, especially in increasing his openness to the exotic and abstract: Balinese music, rhythmic and formal patterns based on number sequences. As he turned 40 he produced a further summation in a disparate trilogy based on the same story of love and death as Wagner's *Tristan*: the song cycle *Harawi*, the *Turangalîla* symphony and *Cinq rechants* for small choir. *Turangalîla*, ranging from the unashamedly vulgar to the deeply strange or esoteric, became his most popular piece. In it he picked up on his students' interest in serialism, before going further to create a composition with rows of durations and dynamic levels, *Mode de valeurs et d'intensités* (1949).

That degree of abstraction he did not want to repeat, but nor did he want to go back to former ways of working. Instead, throughout the 1950s, he devoted himself to creative imitations of bird-songs, including a piano concerto in which the instruments form a dawn chorus (*Réveil des oiseaux*), another piano concerto with an ensemble of wind and percussion enunciating the brilliant and raucous calls of tropical species (*Oiseaux exotiques*) and a set of solo piano pieces each of which portrays a French bird in its habitat, with appropriate effects of colour, light and ambience (*Catalogue d'oiseaux*). At the end of this period came the joyous outburst of *Chronochromie*, for a full orchestra whose birdsongs are exultant and at times implacable.

In 1962, following the death of his first wife after an illness of two decades, he married Loriod. The pattern of his life was now settled: the academic year he would spend in Paris, teaching at the Conservatoire and playing at La Trinité, while the summers were for composition, at a second home beneath the French Alps. That regime was broken only by invitations to teach, lecture or attend performances around the world – invitations he accepted partly from pleasure and gratitude, partly because they gave him opportunities to hear and notate new birdsongs. For example, his first visit to Japan, undertaken with Loriod soon after their marriage, resulted in *Sept haïkaï*, which includes impressions of the country's human and avian music.

He then returned to religious subjects, after a gap of almost 20 years since the *Vingt regards* (excepting organ works), and produced the kaleidoscopic *Couleurs de la Cité Céleste* and the sombre *Et exspecto resurrectionem mortuorum*. Elements of his earlier music – frankly tonal harmonies, melodies suggesting or even quoting plainsong – were starting to reappear, preparing for a further effort in creative consummation, *La Transfiguration*. Like the *Trois petites liturgies*, this is an act of worship devised for the concert hall, but monumental in its resources (seven instrumental soloists plus large orchestra and chanting choir) and two-hour duration. The subject was made for him, with its imagery of light, of high mountain places (such as he could see and visit from his summer home, and which he had awesomely evoked in *Chronochromie* and other works) and of eternity's intervention at a specific moment in human history.

More conspectuses followed: a cycle of meditations on the Trinity for organ (1969), a concert-length celebration of the birds, rocks and stars of the Utah deserts (*Des canyons aux étoiles …*, 1971–5), and an opera depicting scenes from the life and death of St Francis, written on a scale exceeding even that of *La Transfiguration*. Asked why his *Saint François d'Assise* needed such an enormous choral-orchestral apparatus to portray a life of poverty and self-abnegation, he replied that St Francis was rich in spiritual gifts and that it was these he wanted to set forth, hence the powerful sound of the angel knocking at the monastery door, the tumult of birds attending the saint's sermon and the magnificent affirmation of the closing chorale.

Saint François d'Assise was first performed shortly before his 75th birthday and seemed a completion. He produced a further, lengthy organ volume to gather up the fruits of his improvising (*Livre du Saint Sacrement*) and afterwards just a couple of pieces for 80th birthday concerts. But then came a final, hour-plus work for expanded orchestra, *Eclairs sur l'au-delà*: a vision of the beyond, revisiting and transcending previous scenes of musical glory, with a culminating benignity. Like all his music, it is equally a re-vision of what is earthly and present: birdsongs, and also – through the range of his harmony from the added-sixth chord to far more complex formations – qualities of natural resonance that produce effects of bursting colour and light.

Olivier Messiaen *Music and Color* (1994); Peter Hill, ed. *The Messiaen Companion* (1995)

Opera: SAINT FRANÇOIS D'ASSISE, 1975–83
Orchestral (full): *Les Offrandes oubliées*, 1930; *Le Tombeau resplendissant*, 1931; *Hymne au Saint-Sacrement*, 1932; L'ASCENSION, 1932–3; TURANGALILA Symphony, 1946–8; REVEIL DES OISEAUX, pf, orch, 1953; CHRONOCHROMIE, 1959–60; *La Ville d'En-haut*, pf, orch, 1987; *Un Sourire*, 1989; ECLAIRS SUR L'AU-DELA, 1988–92; *Concert à quatre*, pf, fl, ob, vc, orch, 1990–92 (completed by Loriod, Holliger and Benjamin)
Orchestral (reduced): OISEAUX EXOTIQUES, pf, 11 wind, 7 perc, 1955–6; SEPT HAIKAI, pf, 13 wind, 6 perc, 8 vn, 1962; COULEURS DE LA CITE CELESTE, pf, 13 wind, 6 perc, 1963; ET EXSPECTO RESURRECTIONEM MORTUORUM, 34 wind, 3 perc, 1964; DES CANYONS AUX ETOILES …, pf, 43

insts, 1971–5; *Un Vitrail et des oiseaux*, pf, 18 wind, 8 perc, 1986

Vocal orchestral: POEMES POUR MI, s, orch, arr 1937; TROIS PETITES LITURGIES DE LA PRESENCE DIVINE, women's ch, pf, ondes martenot, perc, str, 1943–4; *Chant des desportés* (Messiaen), ch, orch, 1945; *La* TRANSFIGURATION DE NOTRE SEIGNEUR JESUS-CHRIST, ch, 7 insts, orch, 1965–9

Other vocal works: *Trois mélodies* (Sauvage, Messiaen), v, pf, 1930; *La Mort du nombre* (Messiaen), s, t, vn, pf, 1930; Vocalise, s, pf, 1935; POEMES POUR MI (Messiaen), s, pf, 1936; *O sacrum convivium!*, satb, 1937; CHANTS DE TERRE ET DE CIEL (Messiaen), s, pf, 1938; HARAWI, s, pf, 1945; CINQ RECHANTS, 12 v, 1949

Chamber: Theme and Variations, vn, pf, 1932; QUATUOR POUR LA FIN DU TEMPS, cl, vn, vc, pf, 1940–41; *Le Merle noir*, fl, pf, 1952; Piece, pf qnt, 1991

Organ: *Le Banquet céleste*, 1928; *Diptyque*, 1930; *Apparition de l'église éternelle*, 1932; L'ASCENSION, 1933–4; *La* NATIVITE DU SEIGNEUR, 1935; *Les* CORPS GLORIEUX, 1939; *Messe de la Pentecôte*, 1949–50; LIVRE D'ORGUE, 1951; *Verset pour la Fête de la Dédicace*, 1960; MEDITATIONS SUR LE MYSTERE DE LA SAINTE TRINITE, 1969; *Le* LIVRE DU SAINT SACREMENT, 1984

Piano: Preludes, 1928–9; *Fantaisie burlesque*, 1932; *Pièce pour le tombeau de Paul Dukas*, 1935; *Rondeau*, 1943; VISIONS DE L'AMEN, 2 pf, 1943; VINGT REGARDS SUR L'ENFANT-JESUS, 1944; *Cantéyodjayâ*, 1949; *Quatre études de rythme* (*Ile de feu* I, MODE DE VALEURS ET D'INTENSITES, *Neumes ryhtmiques*, *Ile de feu* 2), 1949–50; CATALOGUE D'OISEAUX, 1956–8; *La Fauvette des jardins*, 1970; *Petites esquisses d'oiseaux*, 1985

Electronic: *Fêtes des belles eaux*, 6 ondes martenot, 1937

Messiah. Oratorio by Handel to words from the Bible and Book of Common Prayer assembled by Charles Jennens to tell, in three parts, of the coming of the Messiah, his work of redemption and humanity's gratitude. Handel composed the score in little more than three weeks (22 August to 14 September 1741) and revised it for performances that took place in 1743, 1745 and annually from 1749. Thus established as a favourite during his lifetime, the work has majestically held its appeal, through performances by many hundreds of singers that began at the Handel centenary commemoration in Westminster Abbey in 1784 and continued to the early 20th century, up to present ways of reproducing the original modest scale, adapting the score to more modern tastes, fondly repeating it annually as a Christmas celebration for church choirs, or inviting the audience to sing along with music that has become part of the heritage of the English language. First performance: Dublin, 13 Apr 1742.

Donald Burrows *Handel: Messiah* (1991)

Part 1: Overture, 'Comfort ye – Ev'ry valley shall be exalted' (t/s), 'And the glory of the Lord' (ch), 'Thus saith the Lord' (b), 'But who may abide?' (a), 'And he shall purify the sons of Levi' (ch), 'Behold, a virgin shall conceive – O thou that tellest good tidings to Zion' (a, ch), 'For behold – The people that walked in darkness' (b), 'For unto us a child is born' (ch), Pastoral Symphony, 'There were shepherds – And lo, the angel of the Lord' (s), 'And the angel said unto them – And suddenly there was with the angel' (s), 'Glory to God in the highest' (ch), 'Rejoice greatly' (t/s), 'Then shall the eyes – He shall feed His flock' (s), 'His yoke is easy' (ch)

Part 2: 'Behold the Lamb of God' (ch), 'He was despised' (a), 'Surely he hath borne our griefs' (ch), 'And with His stripes' (ch), 'All we, like sheep' (ch), 'All they that see Him' (t/s), 'He trusted in God that He would deliver Him' (ch), 'Thy rebuke hath broken His heart – Behold, and see if there be any sorrow' (t/s), 'He was cut off – But Thou didst not leave' (t/s), 'Lift up your heads' (ch), 'Unto which of the angels?' (t/s), 'Let all the angels' (ch), 'Thou art gone up' (a), 'The Lord gave the word' (ch), 'How beautiful are the feet' (s), 'Their sound is gone out' (ch), 'Why do the nations?' (b), 'Let us break their bonds' (ch), 'He that dwelleth in Heaven – Thou shalt break them' (t), 'Hallelujah!' (ch)

Part 3: 'I know that my redeemer liveth' (s), 'Since by man came death' (ch), 'Behold, I tell you a mystery – The trumpet shall sound' (b), 'Then shall be brought to pass – O death, where is thy sting?' (a, t), 'But thanks be to God' (ch), 'If God be for us' (s), 'Worthy is the Lamb' (ch)

mesto (It.). Sad.

mesuré (Fr., measured). A direction for strict rhythm, perhaps after a free episode, found in 18th-century French music.

Met. Common abbreviation for the METROPOLITAN OPERA.

metallophone. Percussion instrument with a row or rows of tuned metal bars, the metal equivalent to a xylophone. The principal examples in the Western orchestra are the glockenspiel and vibraphone, belated inheritances from the rich metallophone cultures of Turkey, China and Indonesia.

Metamorphosen (Metamorphoses). Work by Strauss for 23 strings (10 vn, 5 va, 5 vc, 3 db), begun in response to the bombing of the Munich opera house. First performance: Zurich, 25 Jan 1946.

Metastasio, Pietro (b. Rome, 3 Jan 1698; d. Vienna, 12 Apr 1782). Italian librettist, whose gift for simple but telling images in elegant forms made his texts the chief foundation of opera seria for almost a century. His first independent opera libretto – and one of his biggest successes, *Didone abbandonata*, first set by Domenico Sarro – was reinterpreted by composers including Albinoni, Porpora, Galuppi, Hasse, Jommelli, Traetta, Sarti, Piccinni, Sacchini, Paisiello, Paer and, in 1823, Mercadante.

Born Antonio Domenico Bonaventura Trapasi, he was adopted and renamed by a scholar-lawyer, whose death left him financially secure at the age of 20. He soon began writing words for music in Naples, then from 1724 was active in Rome and Venice before moving to Vienna in 1730 as court poet in succession to Zeno. His operas concern monarchs from antiquity, whether real, mytho-logical or imagined, caught between erotic passion and noble, rational behaviour, with the victory of the latter producing a happy ending after numer-ous occasions for outbursts of love, jealousy, ven-geance, lamentation, self-sacrifice and other musically fruitful situations. He also wrote texts for oratorios and serenatas.

Librettos (with dates of first performance): *Didone abbandonata* (see DIDO), 1724; *Siroe re di Persia*, 1726; *Catone in Utica*, 1728; EZIO, 1728; *Semiramide*, 1729; *Alessandro nell'Indie*, 1729; *Artaserse*, 1730; *Demetrio*, 1731; *Adriano in Siria*, 1732; L'OLIMPIADE, 1733; *Demofoonte*, 1733; *La* CLEMENZA DI TITO, 1734; *Antigono*, 1743; *Il RE PASTORE*, 1751; *La Nitteti*, 1756; etc.

method. Book of graduated lessons in playing an instrument or singing.

metre. The organization of rhythm in regular patterns of strong and weak beats, or an example of such organization (e.g. common time, with its pattern of strong–weak–moderate–weak). The term comes from poetry (e.g. iambic metre: weak–strong, weak–strong), but musical metres them-selves are mostly inheritances from dances (pavane, minuet, gavotte, waltz, etc.). One may speak of metre as defined by the time signature, e.g. '2/4 metre', but that is not the whole story. The rhythmic shapes of bars and phrases will deter-mine whether the 2/4 is a march, a dance or neither. Nearly all music from *c*.1600 to the early 20th century has a consistent metre throughout a section or movement.

metrical psalm. Psalm rewritten in a poetic metre for the ease of communal singing in the Calvinist church, notably in Scotland.

metric modulation. Term introduced by Carter for a technique of changing the pulse from one passage to the next and usually changing the metre, too, by introducing the new rhythmic char-acter as a cross-rhythm within the old. For instance, in bars 22ff of his First Quartet the cello defines a 4/4 metre at crotchet = 120; the viola then enters in triplet crotchets and establishes a new movement in 3/2 at minim = 90.

metronome. Device producing a regular sound at a variable prescribed speed, used by composers to set tempos and by performers in rehearsal to realize those expectations. After a history of theorizing and experiment going back to Galileo, Maelzel successfully created and marketed a clockwork metronome from 1815. The device survived virtually unchanged for a century and a half before being replaced by electronic forms.

Metropolitan Opera [Met]. The chief opera company of New York, founded by stockholders – including J.J. Astor, Cornelius Vanderbilt and J. Pierpont Morgan – who could not gain admission to what was previously the city's main opera house, the Academy of Music. Its first theatre, on Broadway between 39th and 40th streets, opened on 22 Oct 1883 with *Faust*, in Italian. The next season it became a German-language company, which it largely remained until Maurice Grau took over as manager in 1891 and instituted the house's lasting love affair with outstanding singers. Subsequent administrators have included Giulio Gatti-Casazza (1908–35), Edward Johnson (1935–50), Rudolf Bing (1950–72) and Joseph Volpe (from 1990), with James Levine in increasingly com-manding positions since 1973. Bing supervised the move to new premises – with an auditorium seating 3,788 – at Lincoln Center, where the opening production was Barber's specially composed *Antony and Cleopatra* (16 September 1966). The Met's short record of premières also includes *La fanciulla del West*. Until 1986 the company made annual tours to other US cities. It owes its status as a national institution also to regular radio broadcasts, which began with *Hänsel und Gretel* (Christmas Day 1931).

Metzger, Heinz-Klaus (b. Konstanz, 6 Feb 1932). German writer on music. He studied at the conservatory in Freiburg (1949–52) and Tübingen University (1952–4), and also took composition lessons from Deutsch in Paris. Closely associated in the 1950s with the Darmstadt circle, he played a role of philosophical apologist similar to Adorno's for the Second Viennese School. In the 1960s he began to find US experimental music more inviting to his Hegelian-Marxist analysis, but he has written on a wide range of topics in the journal

Musik-Konzepte, which he founded with Rainer Riehn in 1977.

Mewton-Wood, Noel (b. Melbourne, 20 Nov 1922; d. London, 5 Dec 1953). Australian pianist, highly acclaimed for his musical sensitivity in a repertory extending from Beethoven and Chopin to Stravinsky and Tippett. He committed suicide.

Mexico. Country with the longest history of Western music in the New World. Sacred polyphony was composed and printed there from the 16th century, early composers including Lienas and Padilla. In the 18th and 19th centuries Italian opera was the driving force, replaced by a nationalism of Romantic or modernist inclination. Notable composers of this later phase included Carrillo, Ponce, Revueltas and Chávez.

Meyer, Ernst Hermann (b. Berlin, 8 Dec 1905; d. Berlin, 8 Oct 1988). German composer, a committed socialist who took a leading role in the music of the German Democratic Republic after the Second World War. He studied in Berlin and Heidelberg, his teachers including Hindemith and Eisler. In 1933 he went into exile in England, where he continued composing and worked on a study of English chamber music from the period up to Purcell. He returned to Berlin in 1948 as a composer and university professor.

Meyerbeer, Giacomo (b. Vogelsdorf, near Berlin, 5 Sep 1791; d. Paris, 2 May 1864). German composer, most especially of four works that dominated the repertory of the Paris Opera in the middle decades of the 19th century, that excited Verdi's emulation and Wagner's profoundly mixed feelings, and that remained in the international repertory until the decline, after the First World War, of the society and the wealth that had sustained them.

Known originally as Jakob Liebmann Meyer Beer, he owed those names to his father Jakob Herz Beer and his maternal grandfather Liebmann Meyer Wulf, both prosperous Jewish businessmen. The family home was accordingly highly cultured, and the future composer was able to study with Zelter (1805–7) and with Abbé Vogler in Darmstadt (1810–11), where his fellow pupils included Weber. At this stage he was planning a career as a piano virtuoso, but during a stay in Italy (1816–25), where he Italianized his first name, he wrote six operas, of which *Il crociato in Egitto* (f.p. Venice, 1824) was successfully revived in London and Paris. A new career beckoned – though first he got married, to his cousin Minna Mosson.

Aiming now for the Paris Opera, he achieved a tremendous hit with *Robert le diable* (1831), a triumph exceeded only by that of *Les Huguenots* (1836). In these works, as later in *Le Prophète* and *L'Africaine* (both planned in the mid-1830s but long delayed, *L'Africaine* being produced only after his death), he offered sonic spectacle expanding over a five-act evening, with plentiful opportunities not only for solo passion and crowd magnificence but also for an engagement with the age's consciousness of social and personal forces creating history. It was a formula that worked – backed by his careful selection of singers and astute handling of the press. Instead of moving to Paris, though, he kept his principal home in Berlin, where he was Prussian general music director (1842–8) and court composer. See also *Les* PATINEURS.

Heinz and Gudrun Becker *Giacomo Meyerbeer* (1989)

Grand operas: *Robert le diable* (Scribe and Delavigne), f.p. Paris, 1831; *Les* HUGUENOTS, f.p. Paris, 1836; *Le* PROPHÈTE, f.p. Paris, 1849; *L'*AFRICAINE, f.p. Paris, 1865
Other operas: *L'Étoile du nord* (Scribe), f.p. Paris, 1854; *Le Pardon de Ploërmel* (Barbier and Carré), f.p. Paris, 1859; 10 early pieces
Other works: songs, choral music, instrumental pieces

mez. Abbreviation for mezzo-soprano.

mezzo, mezza (It.). Half, as in *mezza voce* (with half voice, at a restrained level), *mezzoforte* (medium loud), *mezzopiano* (medium soft), MEZZO-SOPRANO.

mezzo-contralto. 19th-century term for a low mezzo-soprano.

mezzoforte. Medium loud, abbreviated *mf*.

mezzopiano. Medium soft, abbreviated *mp*.

mezzo-soprano [mezzo]. Woman's voice of middle range, a third below the soprano, or a singer with that voice. Quantz introduced the term (1754–5), but it did not become widely current until after 1800, even though Mozart clearly distinguished between soprano and mezzo roles, notably in writing for the sisters in *Così fan tutte*. The mezzo type was further developed through the 19th century, not least by Verdi (Eboli in *Don Carlos*, Amneris in *Aida*) and Wagner (Brangäne in *Tristan*, Fricka in the *Ring*), but nomenclature has remained hazier for women's voices than for men's. Many sopranos have sung mezzo parts, while present-day mezzos have absorbed the territory of the almost extinct contralto.

mezzo-soprano clef. C clef on the second line up; rare.

mf. Mezzoforte.

m.g. Abbreviation for the Fr. *main gauche* (left hand).

mi (Fr., It., Sp.). The note or key of E.

Miaskovsky, Nicolai. See Nikolay MYASKOVSKY.

Michelangeli, Arturo Benedetti (b. Brescia, 5 Jan 1920; d. Lugano, 12 Jun 1995). Italian pianist, of superlative technique and exceedingly scrupulous in his choice of repertory and occasions to play: he made few recordings. He studied with Giuseppe Anfossi at the Milan Conservatory, from which he graduated in 1933, though his international reputation was delayed by war until after 1945, and he then retired to teach before re-emerging in the 1960s.

microphone. Device converting sound waves into electric signals that retain the original information. Those signals can then be reconverted into sound by an amplifier and loudspeakers or be used to generate a recording or broadcast. Introduced in the early 1920s, the microphone was rapidly adopted for recording purposes. See also AMPLIFICATION.

microphone voice. A 'good microphone voice' is one that sounds smoothly integrated and expressive in a recording or broadcast. Singers with relatively small voices, disappointing in the theatre or concert hall, may yet sound immediate and thrilling when performing for the microphone. Popular singers will also need to have 'microphone technique' – i.e. the ability to suit their voices to the amplification system – but this is not normally required of singers in the classical tradition, where natural sound has a place of honour.

micropolyphony. Term coined by Ligeti for his textures of numerous parts.

microtonal. Concerning microtones.

microtone. Interval smaller than a semitone, or pitch from the gaps between the notes of an equal-tempered chromatic scale. Microtones arise under either or both of two sets of circumstances: as alternatives to equal-tempered intervals and notes within a traditional kind of diatonic harmony, and as essential components of some new harmonic system.

As alternatives to the fixed 12-note scale they have been considered by theorists – and no doubt practised by performers – from as far back as such scales began to exert their hegemony, with the rise of keyboard instruments in the late Renaissance. Subtle adjustments of intonation may easily be made by singers and by string and wind players, whether for expressive purposes or to accord with the harmonic context, so that, for example, a D♭ will be different from a C♯. Microtonal deviations of the latter kind are instituted in JUST INTONATION.

The first quarter-tones recorded in a score are in the string parts of Halévy's *Prométhée enchaîné* (1849). But pitch systems with more than 12 notes to the octave were not practised intensively until the early 20th centry, as extensions either of just intonation (adding more complex ratios) or of equal temperament (splitting the gaps to make quarter-tones, sixth-tones, etc.). Early exponents included Partch on the one hand and Carrillo, Foulds, Ives (Fourth Symphony), Bartók (*The Miraculous Mandarin*, Sonata for solo violin), Wyschnegradsky and Hába on the other. With the introduction of electronic music, microtonal intervals and alternative scales became readily available, but many composers have continued to demand quarter-tones and other fine discriminations from performers, whether as part of a saturation of musical possibilities (Ferneyhough), in the creation of complex harmonic strata (Grisey), or in pursuit of non-standard tunings (Johnston). The most usual signs are:

‡	♯♯	↓♭	♭♭♭
quarter-tone sharp	three quarter-tones sharp	quarter-tone flat	three quarter-tones flat

Middle Ages. See MEDIEVAL.

middle C. The note roughly in the middle of the human vocal range (high for a man, low for a woman or child).

Midi, Le. Name given to Haydn's Symphony No.7, which forms a trilogy with No.6 'Le Matin' and No.8 'Le Soir'.

MIDI. Musical Instrument Digital Interface; specifications concerning the electronic transfer of musical information from one device (e.g. an electronic keyboard or an acoustic instrument) to another (e.g. a computer). The standard was established in 1983, has been continuously modified and is universal. A work requiring, say, electronic modification of a cello part is likely to specify 'MIDI cello'.

Midsummer Marriage, The. Opera by Tippett to his own libretto. Jenifer (soprano) and Mark (tenor) are the couple about to be married, in an England blending the contemporary with the prehistoric. Their union can be completed, though, only after each has been psychically educated. The score includes a set of Ritual Dances separately available for orchestra (without the opera's choir). First performance: London, 27 Jan 1955.

Midsummer Night's Dream, A. Shakespeare play, set largely in a fairy wood, where lovers' tiffs are resolved while workmen put their efforts into a play. Musical treatments include:

(1) The FAIRY-QUEEN, little related to the play in its sung parts.

(2) Mendelssohn's overture and incidental music (*Ein Sommernachtstraum*). First performance: Stettin, 20 Feb 1827 (overture); Potsdam, 14 Oct 1843 (incidental music).

(3) Britten's opera, to his and Pears's adaptation of the play. First performance: Aldeburgh, 11 Jun 1960.

Mighty Handful (*Moguchaya kuchka*). Term invented by Stasov in a concert review of 1867, designating the group led by Balakirev, also including Musorgsky, Rimsky-Korsakov, Borodin and Cui, and alternatively known as 'The Five'. At the time they were united by adherence both to old Russian culture and to the incisive Romanticism of Berlioz and Liszt, but they went their own ways.

Mignon. Opera by Thomas to a libretto by Barbier and Carré after Goethe. Mignon (mezzo-soprano), abducted as a child, undergoes trials by fire and jealousy – her rival being a glamorous actress, Philine (soprano) – before being united with her father, Lothario (bass), and her true love, Wilhelm (tenor). Numbers include Mignon's 'Connais-tu le pays?', Philine's 'Je suis Titania' and Wilhelm's 'Adieu, Mignon' and 'Elle ne croyait pas'. First performance: Paris, 17 Nov 1866.

Mignone, Francisco (Paulo) (b. São Paulo, 3 Sep 1897; d. Rio de Janeiro, 2 Feb 1986). Brazilian composer, in a national Romantic style in the 1930s–50s, after which he absorbed avant-garde techniques. He studied with his Italian-born father and at the conservatories of São Paulo and Milan, preparing for a career in opera. Diverted by his vigorous identification with the diverse musical cultures of Brazil, from 1929 until the early 1940s he produced orchestral pieces (four *Fantasias brasileiras* for piano and orchestra; *Festa das igrejas*, 1940), ballets, piano music and songs. Later works include concertos, chamber works and sacred music.

Migot, Georges (b. Paris, 27 Feb 1891; d. Levallois, near Paris, 5 Jan 1976). French composer, in an elevated style emanating from late Fauré. The son of a pastor-doctor, he studied with Widor, d'Indy and Emmanuel at the Paris Conservatoire, where he became keeper of the instrument collection (1949–61). His works, often on religious themes, include cantatas and oratorios, 13 symphonies, songs and instrumental pieces.

Mihalovich, Ödön (Péter József de) (b. Feričance, Slovenia, 13 Sep 1842; d. Budapest, 22 Apr 1929). Hungarian composer, a follower of Wagner, whose first Pest concert decided him to pursue music (though he had already been a pupil of Mosonyi as a boy). He then studied with Hauptmann in Leipzig (1865) and Cornelius in Munich (1866). In 1887 he succeeded Liszt as head of the music academy in Budapest. His works include operas, four symphonies and other orchestral pieces, including a *Timon of Athens* overture.

Mihály, András (b. Budapest, 7 Nov 1917; d. Budapest, 19 Sep 1993). Hungarian composer. He studied as a cellist at the Liszt Academy, but had composition lessons privately with Kadosa. As a communist from 1941 he was involved in political and aesthetic struggles, from which he emerged wise and generous. He gave much of his energy to teaching (as professor of chamber music at the academy from 1950) and conducting new music (with the Budapest Chamber Ensemble he founded in 1968). Meanwhile he advanced from a Bartókian style in the 1950s to embrace avant-garde features.

Miki, Minoru (b. Tokushima, Shikoku, 16 Mar 1930). Japanese composer of cross-cultural music including many operas and works for the Ensemble Nipponia, a group of Japanese instruments of which he was founder director (1964–84). He studied with Ifukube and Ikenouchi at the Tokyo National University of Fine Arts and Music (1951–5), and has supported himself as a film composer.

Mikrokosmos. Six books of progressive piano pieces by Bartók, conveying the performer from beginner level to concert pitch. The last book ends with Six Dances in Bulgarian Rhythm (Nos.148–53). Bartók also arranged seven numbers for two pianos.

Milan (Milano). Italian city, first prominent as the western capital of the Roman Empire in the late 4th century, when St Ambrose was bishop (see AMBROSIAN CHANT). More than a millennium later music thrived under the Sforzas (1450–1535), whose musicians included Josquin. The city and region then fell under Spanish and, from 1708, Austrian dominion, enjoying a rich musical life in the 18th century, thanks to native composers (Sammartini) and visitors (J.C. Bach, Mozart). With the foundation of La SCALA (1778) it was confirmed as a leading operatic centre. Its conservatory (1807) took over from those of Naples as a principal training ground for operatic composers and singers, and the local publishing firms of RICORDI and SONZOGNO divided the spoils.

Milán, Luys (b. c.1500; d. after 1560). Spanish composer, notably of pavans and 40 fantasias for the vihuela published in his collection El maestro (1536), which also includes villancicos, and which was composed when he was at the ducal court in Valencia.

Milhaud, Darius (b. Marseilles, 4 Sep 1892; d. Geneva, 22 Jun 1974). French composer. A byword for creative fruitfulness, he produced 443 works with Op. numbers, including full-length operas, numerous orchestral pieces, cantatas, ballets, 18 string quartets and smaller compositions of every description. His vast output, so far unsifted by history, defies brisk description. Commentators remark on his abiding attachment to his dual heritage as a Provençal Jew, but also on his willingness to experiment, with speaking chorus and percussion (Les Choéphores, 1915–16), with bitonality (prompted perhaps by connections with Stravinsky and Koechlin), with jazz (La Création du monde, 1923) and with non-consecutive theatre (Christophe Colomb, 1928).

Brought up in Aix-en-Provence within a prosperous and musical family, he studied with Gédalge at the Paris Conservatoire from 1909. Equally important was his meeting in 1912 with the writer and diplomat, Paul Claudel: Les Choéphores was among their early collaborations, and at the beginning of 1917 he left to join Claudel's embassy staff in Brazil, where he stayed almost two years. He returned to find Paris in a torrent of musical activity, to which he gladly contributed. His ballet Le Boeuf sur le toit gave its name to an artists' café, and his election into the miscellaneous group Les Six was at least justified by some samples of urbanity, including a song cycle setting descriptions from a catalogue of farm machinery (Machines agricoles, 1919). But he remained an irrepressible traveller (even in later life, when

confined to a wheelchair), and his continuing journeys both exposed him to new influences (jazz in London in 1920 and Harlem in 1922) and spread his reputation (to the Schoenberg school when he visited Vienna in 1921). In 1925 he married his cousin Madeleine, who became his stalwart travelling companion.

The performance of Christophe Colomb at the Kroll Opera in Berlin (1930), and a percussion concerto finished the same year, effectively completed his time as a member of the international avant-garde. In the more difficult ensuing decade he wrote a lot of music for plays and films; then in 1940, obliged to leave France once the Nazis were in power, he moved to the USA, where he taught at Mills and Aspen. In 1947 he returned to Paris, and to a position at the Conservatoire, but he remained on the Mills faculty until 1971, shuttling between continents and writing freely for orchestras and ensembles on both.

Darius Milhaud Notes without Music (1952, ¹1967)

Operas: Les Malheurs d'Orphée (Armand Lunel), Op.85, 1925, f.p. Brussels, 1926; Le Pauvre Matelot (Cocteau), Op.92, 1926, f.p. Paris, 1927; Trois opéras minutes (Henri Hoppenot), 1927 (L'Enlèvement d'Europe, Op.94, f.p. Baden-Baden, 1927; L'Abandon d'Ariane, Op.98, f.p. Wiesbaden, 1928; La Délivrance de Thésée, Op.99, f.p. Wiesbaden, 1928); Christophe Colomb (Claudel), Op.102, 1928, f.p. Berlin, 1930; La Mère coupable (after Beaumarchais), Op.412, 1964–5, f.p. Geneva, 1966; etc.

Ballets: L'Homme et son désir, Op.48, 1918; LE BOEUF SUR LE TOIT, Op.58, 1919; La CREATION DU MONDE, Op.81, 1923; Le Train bleu, Op.84, 1924; etc.

Incidental music: Orestie (Claudel, after Aeschylus: Agamemnon, Op.14, 1913–14; Les Choéphores, Op.24, 1915–16; Les Euménides, Op.41, 1917–22); etc.

Orchestral: Saudades do Brasil, Op.67b, 1920–21; Le Carnaval d'Aix, Op.83b, pf, orch, 1926; Concerto, perc, chbr orch, Op.109, 1929–30; Suite provençale, Op.152c, 1936; Suite française, Op.248, brass band/orch, 1944; Concerto, Op.278, mar, vib, orch, 1947; etc.

Chamber: Le Printemps, Op.18, vn, pf, 1914; Flute Sonatina, Op.76, 1922; Clarinet Sonatina, Op.100, 1927; Suite, Op.157b, vn, cl, pf, 1936; La Cheminée du roi René, Op.205, wind qnt, 1939; Duo concertante, Op.351, cl, pf, 1956; 18 string quartets, etc.

Songs: Poèmes juifs, Op.34, v, pf, 1916; Machines agricoles, Op.56, v, 7 insts, 1919; Catalogue de fleurs, (Alphonse Daudet), Op.60, v, pf/7 insts, 1920; etc.

Piano: Saudades do Brasil, Op.67, 1920–21; 3 Rag Caprices, Op.78, 1922; Scaramouche, Op.165b, 2 pf, 1937; etc.

Military. Name given to two works:
(1) Haydn's Symphony No.100, for the bass

drum, triangle and cymbals in its second and fourth movements. First performance: London, 31 Mar 1794.

(2) Chopin's Polonaise in A, Op.40:1.

military band. UK term for what is known in the USA as a college or concert band: a large wind ensemble with percussion.

Millöcker, Carl (b. Vienna, 29 Apr 1842; d. Baden, near Vienna, 31 Dec 1899). Austrian composer, chiefly of operettas. He studied as a flautist at the Vienna Conservatory (1855–8), joined the Theater in der Josefstadt, and became Suppé's pupil and protégé. Conducting from 1864, he gained a position as second conductor at the Theater an der Wien (1869–83). The success of *Der Bettelstudent* (1882) allowed him to concentrate on composition, his later works including *Gasparone* (1884) and *Der arme Jonathan* (1890).

Milner, Anthony (Francis Dominic) (b. Bristol, 13 May 1925; d. Alfaz del Pí, Alicante, 22 Sep 2002). British composer of music affirming traditional continuity in a time of change. He studied with R.O. Morris at the RCM and privately with Seiber, and was active as a teacher in London and the USA. Many of his works are choral, to religious texts of Roman Catholic bearing.

Milnes, Sherrill (Eustace) (b. Downers Grove, Ill., 10 Jan 1935). US baritone, leading Verdi singer at the Met for a quarter-century from his 1965 debut. He studied with Ponselle and made his debut in Boston (Masetto, 1960).

Milstein, Nathan (b. Odessa, 31 Dec 1904; d. London, 21 Dec 1992). Russian–US violinist, noted for his purity of tone and line. After studies with Auer at the St Petersburg Conservatory he made his debut in Odessa in 1920. In 1925 he emigrated with Horowitz, his regular recital partner at the time. He took advice from Ysaÿe in Brussels (1926), then settled in the USA.

mime. See PANTOMIME.

miniature score. Full score of reduced dimensions, made for listeners and students rather than performers. See also PLEYEL.

minim. (UK). Half-note (US). See DURATION.

minimalism. Term normally applied not to music whose sounds really are minimal (with Cage's *4′ 33″* at the extreme) but rather to that based on the repetition in regular rhythm of chords or simple figures, as in the work of Reich, Riley and Glass. There are adumbrations of this in Satie and earlier Cage, and indeed in Baroque music (the C major prelude from the first book of Bach's '48', Handel's *Zadok the Priest*), but the immediate source was the music created by Young and Riley in the mid-1960s, to which Reich and Glass added a notion of gradual harmonic or rhythmic process within ostinato textures. Early minimalist works, such as Reich's *Four Organs* and Glass's *Music in Fifths* (both 1969), have the beauty of streamlined simplicity, soon replaced by elaboration and an accommodation with the norms of concert life (notably in Adams's contributions). Essentially US in origin, and surely related to rock music as well as to non-European traditions, minimalism has nevertheless found European adherents (Louis Andriessen, Bryars) and observers (Ligeti).

Minkus, Léon (b. Vienna, 23 Mar 1826; d. Vienna, 7 Dec 1917). Czech/Polish composer, mostly of ballets for the Russian imperial stage. Having probably studied in Vienna, he wrote his first ballet for Paris in 1846 and went to Russia a few years later. He joined the Bolshoy in Moscow as a violinist (1861) and became its conductor (1862–72) before being appointed ballet composer to the imperial theatres (1872–91). Then he seems to have returned to Vienna and to an obscure retirement. His scores for *Don Quixote* (1869) and *La Bayadère* (1877), though musically unremarkable, remain in the ballet repertory.

Minneapolis. US city on the upper Mississippi; St Paul, on the other side of the river, is its twin. Musical institutions include the Minnesota Orchestra (originally the Minneapolis Symphony, 1903–68, whose conductors included Ormandy, Mitropoulos and Dorati), the St Paul Chamber Orchestra (founded in 1959) and Minnesota Opera (1962).

Minnesinger (Ger., pl. *Minnesinger*). Medieval German poet-composer, of a tradition comparable with, and dependent on, that of the troubadours. *Minne* – love for an unattainable lady, intense but unfulfilled – was the classic subject. The tradition began in the late 12th century, quickly rose to full flame in the work of Walther von der Vogelweide, remained strong through the 13th century and then subsided. Other notable Minnesinger included Hartmann von Aue, Tannhäuser and Frauenlob.

minor. Term descriptive of a mode, scale, key or interval.

(1) The minor MODE is the diatonic mode with semitone intervals in second and fifth places.

(2) The natural minor SCALE is that of the minor mode, e.g. A–B–C–D–E–F–G–A (A minor). It has two variants: the harmonic minor (A–B–C–D–E–F–G♯–A) and the melodic minor (rising A–B–C–D–E–F♯–G♯–A and falling as the natural minor).

(3) Music in the minor mode will be in one or another of the minor keys, named after the keynote, e.g. C minor, D minor, F♯ minor, etc.

(4) A minor interval is a semitone smaller than the corresponding major interval, e.g. the minor second (C–D♭), minor third (C–E♭), minor sixth (C–A♭), minor seventh (C–B♭), minor ninth (C–D♭), etc.

minore (It.). Minor, used as a marking to advertise a change to the minor, normally in a set of variations.

minstrel. Performing musician of the 13th–15th centuries. In the late 19th century the term came to imply an itinerant songster ('A wandering minstrel I'), but at the time it seems to have been applied mostly to instrumentalists, many of whom would certainly travel, though many also spent long periods at one court. The word was replaced by 'musician' in the 16th century.

minuet. Dance in moderate triple time, normally in two segments, of which the second answers the first. It was a standard movement of the 18th-century symphony, string quartet and sonata, generally placed third and in ABA form, with a contrasting trio as middle section. However, there are also minuet finales (notably in some Haydn sonatas and Mozart concertos) and minuet slow movements (in Beethoven's sonatas Op.30:3 and Op.31:3).

The minuet seems to have been introduced at the French court a little before Lully, who included many examples in his ballets and operas. At this point it consisted of just two eight-bar phrases, and in that form it both entered instrumental music and spread rapidly to England, Italy and Germany. Its phrases, particularly the second, became more elaborate, but it kept its essential graceful simplicity. The Italian minuet, which was faster, increased the range of options internationally, so that Bach, for instance, wrote both slowish French minuets and livelier Italian ones. People went on dancing minuets – but not other Baroque dances – until the end of the 18th century, which may explain why it alone survived to become so frequent in instrumental music. The scherzo, introduced as an alternative in the second half of the century, came to replace it, and the minuet of Beethoven's Eighth Symphony is already retrospective. In a similar spirit are the revivals by Brahms (Serenade No.1), Debussy (*Suite bergamasque*), Ravel, Schoenberg (Opp.24–5) and Bartók (Nine Little Pieces).

Minute. Name given to Chopin's Waltz Op.64:1, which is certainly brief, but practicable in a minute only at a racing tempo.

Miracle. Name given to Haydn's Symphony No.96 (f.p. London, 1791). But the story – that the audience, drawn by the music at its first performance, moved nearer the platform and so escaped harm from the fall of a chandelier at the back of the hall – apparently belongs to No.102 (f.p. London, 2 Feb 1795).

Miraculous Mandarin, The (*A csodálatos mandarin*). Ballet score by Bartók (also a reduction for piano duet) to a scenario by Menyhért Lengyel. A prostitute, pressed by ruffians, lures men from a busy street below. The third she attracts is a mandarin, whom the men set upon, but he does not die until his lust has been assuaged. First performance: Cologne, 27 Nov 1926.

Miroirs (Mirrors). Book of five piano pieces by Ravel: *Noctuelles*, *Oiseaux tristes*, *Une Barque sur l'océan*, ALBORADA DEL GRACIOSO, *La Vallée des cloches*. First performance: Paris, 6 Jan 1906.

mirror. Term denoting inversion, retrograde motion or both in a piece of counterpoint. Mirror canons have voices displaying these relations; mirror fugues have a second section inverting the first.

misa (Sp.). Mass.

missa (Lat.). Mass, hence *missa brevis* (short mass, either a *Kyrie-Gloria* pair or an abbreviated setting of the whole ordinary), *missa pro defunctis* (mass for the dead, i.e. *Requiem*), MISSA SOLEMNIS.

missal. Book of mass texts (sometimes with plainsong settings) for the liturgical year.

missa pro defunctis (Lat.). Mass for the dead, i.e. *Requiem*.

Missa solemnis (Solemn Mass). Work by Beethoven for soli, choir and orchestra, from his last years, one of music's great monuments, originally planned for the consecration of Archduke Rudolph in Olmütz (9 March 1820) but not completed until three years later. The composer's patron-admirer Prince Nikolay Golitsyn arranged the first performance (St Petersburg, 7 Apr 1824), preceding by exactly a month a performance in Vienna of just the *Kyrie*, *Credo* and *Agnus Dei*, in the composer's presence.

misura (It.). Measure, bar, time, as notably in *senza misura* (unbarred, outside the prevailing metre and tempo). The return to measured time is signalled by *a tempo*, *tempo giusto* or just *giusto*.

Mitridate, re di Ponto (Mithridates, King of Pontus). Opera by Mozart to a libretto by Vittorio Amedeo Cigna-Santi derived from Racine's play. Mithridates (tenor) has two sons: the loyal Xiphares (soprano castrato) and the erratic Pharnaces (alto castrato). After various frictions both turn out to be worthy heirs, united respectively with Aspasia (soprano) and Ismene (soprano). First performance: Milan, 26 Dec 1770.

Mitropoulos, Dimitri (b. Athens, 1 Mar 1896; d. Milan, 2 Nov 1960). Greek–US conductor, an inspiring if erratic head of the New York Philharmonic (1949–58) who helped instal Mahler, Schoenberg and Berg in the repertory. He studied as a pianist at the Odeion Conservatory in Athens and with Busoni in Berlin (1921–4), and also had composition lessons with Gilson in Brussels (1920–21). In 1924 he returned to his conservatory in Athens, to teach and conduct. With his reputation growing he conducted the Berlin Philharmonic (1930) and the Boston Symphony (1936, his US debut), and became conductor of the Minneapolis Symphony (1937–49). He died of a heart attack while rehearsing Mahler's Third with the Scala orchestra.

mixed media. Term applied to works combining media (music, dance, film, speech) in ways nonstandard and heterogeneous. The ethos was that of the 1960s–70s, examples including Cage's HPSCHD.

mixolydian. Authentic MODE G–A–B–C–D–E–F–G, the seventh church mode/tone.

mixture. Organ stop sounding several notes, usually in octaves or fifths.

MLA. MUSIC LIBRARY ASSOCIATION.

Mlada. Opera subject from Slav mythology, about the love of Prince Yaromir for the murdered Mlada, and his union with her beyond death. Borodin, Cui, Musorgsky and Rimsky-Korsakov collaborated in 1872 on a treatment with dances by Minkus. This never reached the stage, and Rimsky

then completed his own version alone, with a tenor Yaromir and mime Mlada. First performance: St Petersburg, 1 Nov 1892.

Mládí (Youth). Four-movement suite by Janáček for wind sextet (fl and pic, ob, cl, b cl, hn, bn).

MM. Abbreviation of the Ger. *Metronom Maelzel*, prefacing metronome markings.

mobile form. Term, probably stimulated by Alexander Calder's mobile sculptures, for a concept of form as variable, with elements that may be differently ordered. The classic examples, by Boulez, Stockhausen, Berio and Earle Brown, date from the 1950s–60s. See also ALEATORY.

modal. Having the melodic-harmonic attributes of a MODE (1). One may thus speak of modal harmony in Debussy's quartet, with its Phrygian colouring, or in works by Bartók or Vaughan Williams that spring from folksong.

modality. The musical use of a particular MODE (1), as in 'Dorian modality', or of modes more generally ('Bartókian modality', 'Hungarian modality').

modal rhythm. Practice found in music from around 1200 – especially that of the NOTRE DAME SCHOOL – of keeping throughout a composition or section to one of six rhythmic modes, or repeating patterns of durations. The 13th-century theorist Johannes de Garlandia defined six rhythmic modes, indicated by means of ligatures: long-breve, long-breve, etc. (1); breve-long, breve-long, etc. (2); long-breve-breve, long-breve-breve, etc. (3); breve-breve-long, breve-breve-long, etc. (4); long, long, long, etc. (5); and breve, breve, breve, etc. (6).

mode. Term derived from the Lat. *modus* (measure, manner), current in western European music theory from before Boethius, normally with reference to the first meaning below.

(1) Diatonic scale of a kind found in plainsong and much European folk music. The commonest examples – with names derived from ancient Greece, the source of modal theory – are the PHRYGIAN, DORIAN, LYDIAN and MIXOLYDIAN. These are the four authentic modes, each of which has a plagal relative, forming a system of eight modes (or tones) that was the basis for plainsong, for the folk music that surrounded it and for the music that developed from it: the polyphony of the Middle Ages and Renaissance. Glarean (1547) added the IONIAN and AEOLIAN modes, with

their plagal forms, partly for completeness, partly with reference to ancient authors, but perhaps partly also to accord with musical practice, to give names to the emerging major and minor scales.

As classically described for plainsong in Guido's *Micrologus* (*c.*1026) and in an anonymous *Dialogus* that came slightly earlier, each of the original eight modes was defined by its final (the note on which melodies in it would come to rest) and its ambitus (range). The finals are D (Dorian, Hypodorian), E (Phrygian, Hypophrygian), F (Lydian, Hypolydian) and G (Mixolydian, Hypomixolydian), and the authentic modes range through the white notes from the final, or a second or third below, up to the ninth or tenth, while the plagal modes tend to embrace a fifth on either side of the final, with perhaps an additional note above.

Unlike the 12 keys of later music, therefore, the eight modes set out different worlds of melodic movement, because of their different placings of tones (T) and semitones (S). The Dorian mode, for instance, rises from the final T–S–T–T–T–S–T–T, whereas in the Lydian mode this pattern in T–T–T–S–T–T–S–T. The third is – to use later terms – major in the modes with F and G finals (F–A, G–B) but minor in those with D and E (D–F, E–G). To give another example, the Lydian and Hypolydian modes have only an augmented fourth above the final (F–B) and the Hypolydian would have a diminished fifth below (B–F). However, because the unsettling TRITONE was abhorred in medieval practice, the Hypolydian mode went down only to the fourth below the final, and the upper fourth in both modes would often be flattened (F–B♭). Some of the other modes, too, could have the B flattened, to avoid tritones in the melody. Thus altered, the Lydian and Dorian modes would become transpositions of the modes with finals C (T–T–S–T–T–T–S–T) and A (T–S–T–T–S–T–T–T), which is presumably why these 'Ionian' and 'Aeolian' modes were not needed.

They were not needed, that is, until they became the major and minor scales, an evolution that was completed during the 17th century, though traces of the old modes would often survive in minor-key music. The modes were then consciously revived in the late 19th century and early 20th, often by composers – Debussy, Bartók, Vaughan Williams – who were intrigued as much by the distant past as by the future.

(2) Any pattern of intervals providing a musical source, including the eight described in MODE (1). Major and minor may be considered alternative modes ('the next variation is in the minor mode'). Other modes occur in folk music, such as the 'Romanian scale' that fascinated Bartók (C–D–E–

F♯-G–A–B♭-C) or the host of pentatonic and heptatonic scales found in musical cultures around the world. Further modes emerged from the more dissonant harmony of the late 19th century (e.g. the OCTATONIC and WHOLE TONE scales, and Messiaen's MODES OF LIMITED TRANSPOSITIONS).

Note that the use here of the terms 'scale' and 'mode' interchangeably follows loose common practice. Strictly, a scale is a way of dividing the octave (there is therefore a 'Dorian scale', a 'Mixolydian scale', etc.), whereas 'mode' implies patterns of intervals above and below a final, through ranges that may be less than or more than an octave. Attached to the term, too, are notions of melodic shapes and expressive attributes specific to each mode – notions associated not only with the modal system of western Europe up to the Renaissance but also with the Middle Eastern *maqām*, Indian raga and Indonesian *paṭĕt*.

(3) Mensural proportion in early notation, usually designated by the Lat. form MODUS to avoid confusion with the above.

(4) Pattern in MODAL RHYTHM.

(5) Term for interval type introduced by Hucbald, who identified nine such modes in plainsong, from semitone to nine semitones (i.e. modern minor sixth). With variations this system was maintained through Guido and beyond, and the term persisted intermittently to the early 18th century.

Mode de valeurs et d'intensités (Mode of values and intensities). Piano piece by Messiaen using an array of 36 notes, each with its unvarying duration, volume and manner of attack – the ne plus ultra in its composer's pursuit of mechanical composition but a starting point for his pupils Boulez and Stockhausen. The composer gave the première in Tunis in 1950.

Modena. Manuscript volume of sacred and secular pieces by Matteo da Perugia and others, held at the Biblioteca Estense e Universitaria, Modena.

moderato (It.), **modéré** (Fr.). (1) At moderate pace, a marking introduced at the end of the 17th century.

(2) A moderately paced movement.

moderator pedal. A device on certain pianos to mute the tone by sliding a length of cloth between hammers and strings.

modernism. A term that has become more current, because more useful, since the arrival around

1970 of challenges to what one may call the modernist tradition – challenges that came most immediately from minimalism and from efforts to reinstall the styles and the rhetoric of Romanticism, but that may have had their deeper motivation in the abiding success of rock music. Modernism implies a dissatisfaction with traditional means of expression (tonal harmony, metrical rhythm, the symphony orchestra as conventionally set up, and standard genres and forms) and a questing for new ones, continuously. This is a mentality with a long history in music, but the term is generally reserved for music since 1900 and for such composers as Schoenberg and Varèse, Boulez and Stockhausen, Birtwistle and Lachenmann. See CONTEMPORARY MUSIC.

Modern Psalm (*Moderner Psalm*). Work by Schoenberg to his own text, for speaker, choir and orchestra, left off at the words 'and still I pray'. First performance: Cologne, 29 May 1956.

modes of limited transpositions. Term coined by Messiaen for scales that contain repeating units and that therefore can be transposed only a limited number of times before the same set of pitches is produced, unlike the non-repeating major and minor scales, each of which has 12 different transpositions in 12-note equal temperament. For instance, the 'first mode' is the whole-tone scale (repeating unit of two semitones), which has but two transpositions: C–D–E–F♯–G♯–A♯–C and C♯–D♯–F–G–A–B–C♯. A further upward transposition simply restores the notes of the first form: D–E–F♯–G♯–A♯–C–D. The 'second mode' has a repeating unit of two-one semitones (C–D–D♯–F–F♯–G♯–A–B–C, i.e. the OCTATONIC scale), the 'third mode' one of two-one-one semitones (C–D–D♯–E–F♯–G–G♯–A♯–B–C), the 'fourth mode' one of three-one-one-one semitones (C–D♯–E–F–F♯–A–A♯–B–C) and the 'sixth mode' one of two-two-one-one semitones (C–D–E–F–F♯–G♯–A♯–B–C). All divide the octave symmetrically, the symmetry being that of the diminished seventh chord (second mode), augmented triad (first and third) or TRITONE (all but the third). They therefore lend themselves to static harmony.

modulation. (1) Smooth transition from one key to another. The transition is usually effected by means of a pivot chord or note, i.e. a chord that belongs to the key being left and takes on a new function in the key being entered (e.g. G–B♭–E♭ appearing as a first inversion in E♭ major and resolving, as the Neapolitan sixth, into D minor), or a note that is held or repeated from one chord to

another (e.g. G as the third degree of an E♭ major chord and the tonic of a G major or minor chord).

(2) Imposition of information on a wave. Radio programmes, for example, are transmitted by modulating either the amplitude of a radio wave (hence AM, for amplitude modulation) or its frequency (FM). Sound waves too may be modulated, and often are in electronic music. See also RING MODULATOR.

modus. The relationship between breve and long in early notation: 3:1 (*modus perfectus*) or 2:1 (*modus imperfectus*).

Moeck. German firm, founded by Hermann Moeck in Celle in 1925 and specializing in recorders and recorder music.

Moeran, E(rnest) J(ohn) (b. Heston, 31 Dec 1894; d. near Kenmare, Ireland, 1 Dec 1950). British composer of music generally reflective and pastoral. A clergyman's son, he studied at Uppingham, at the RCM (1913–14) and, after war service, with Ireland. Through the 1920s he established a place for himself within the British school, but his Symphony in G minor (1934–7), created after his retirement to the Cotswolds, revealed a new individuality and sense of purpose, with Sibelius in the background as well as Delius and Vaughan Williams. Other notable works include a set of seven Joyce songs (1929) and a violin concerto (1942). He drowned in a river, having fallen after a heart attack.

möglich (Ger.). Possible, as in *so schnell wie möglich* (as fast as possible).

Moiseiwitsch, Benno (b. Odessa, 22 Feb 1890; d. London, 9 Apr 1963). Russian–British pianist, admired especially for the passion and poetry he brought to a virtuoso repertory, including Rachmaninoff and Medtner. He studied in Odessa and, from the age of 14, with Leschetizky in Vienna, then settled with his family in England, where he began his career in Reading (1908) and London (1909). After the First World War he travelled worldwide and made many recordings of solo and chamber music.

moll (Ger.). Minor, as in *C moll* (C minor), *Mollklang* (minor chord).

Molter, Johann Melchior (b. Tiefenort, near Eisenach, 10 Feb 1696; d. Karlsruhe, 12 Jan 1765). German composer, a product of the same environment as J.S. Bach but alert to new fashions. The son of a teacher-cantor, he studied at Bach's old school in Eisenach and joined the margravial court at Karlsruhe in 1717. He went on a study tour to Venice and Rome (1719–21), and revisited Italy in 1737–8, now in service to the duke in Eisenach (1734–41). In 1742 he returned to Karlsruhe, where the young new margrave supported a lavish orchestra. Sinfonias, concertos and other orchestral and chamber pieces accordingly dominate his later output.

molto (It.). Much, very, as in *andante molto*, *molto adagio*.

moment. Stockhausen's term for a self-standing unit of form. Moments, in a work in 'moment form', may be rearranged and reinterpreted, as in the composer's versions of his paradigmatic MOMENTE.

Momente (Moments). Work by Stockhausen, a celebration of love and time for soprano, choir, brass, percussion and electronic organs. First performance: Cologne, 21 May 1962; Bonn, 8 Dec 1972 (final version).

Moments musicaux. Titled invented by the Viennese publisher Marcus Leidesdorf (in the erroneous form *Momens musicals*) for six pieces by Schubert.

Mompou, Federico (b. Barcelona, 16 Apr 1893; d. Barcelona, 30 Jun 1987). Catalan composer, almost exclusively of piano pieces and songs, in which he created a magical simplicity related to Satie, to earlier Spanish music and to the work of his friend Joan Miró. Of Catalan–French parentage, he studied as a pianist in Barcelona and Paris (1911–14), where he turned definitively to composition under the influence of Satie and Debussy. Apart from another, more extended period in Paris (1921–41), he lived quietly in his native city, playing his music only for friends or occasional recordings. He often worked long, perfecting his pieces, and reduced notation to the minimum, omitting barlines. After completing the four books of *Música callada* (Music Silenced) in his early 70s, he wrote little more.

Wilfrid Mellers *Le Jardin retrouvé* (1987)

Piano: *Impresiones intimas*, 1911–14, rev 1959; *Pessebres*, 1914–17; *Suburbis*, 1916–17; *Scènes d'enfants*, 1915–18; *Cants màgics*, 1917–19; *Fêtes lointaines*, 1920; *Charmes*, 1920–21; *Trois variations*, 1921; *Dialogues I–II*, 1923; *Souvenirs de l'exposition*, 1937; *Variations sur un thème de Chopin*, 1938–57; *Paisajes*, 1942–60; *Cançons i danses*, 1918–28 (Nos.1–4), 1942–62 (Nos.5–12), 1948–62 (No.14); *Preludes*, 1927–60 (12); *Canción de cuna*, 1951; *Música callada*, 1959–67; etc.

Guitar: *Suite compostelana*, 1962; *Cançó i dansa* No.13, 1972

Songs: *Combát del somni* (3; Janés), 1942–8; etc.

Other works: choral, orchestral and chamber pieces

Mondonville, Jean-Joseph Cassanéa de (baptized Narbonne, 25 Dec 1711; d. Belleville, 8 Oct 1772). French composer, notably of violin sonatas admired for their vitality and variety. His father was an organist, and both he and his younger brother Jean became violinists in the royal chapel. In his time and later he was celebrated for his chamber music and *grands motets*, most of which predated his marriage in 1748 to Anne-Jeanne Boucon, a harpsichordist and pupil of Rameau. Subsequently he concentrated more on stage works and oratorios.

Moniot d'Arras (*fl*. 1213–39). Trouvère, best known for the delightful pastoral song *Ce fut en mai* (quoted by Hindemith in *Nobilissima visione*), which may, however, not be his. His name means 'little monk'.

Moniuszko, Stanisław (b. Ubiel, near Minsk, 5 May 1819; d. Warsaw, 4 Jun 1872). Polish composer, whose opera *Halka* (1846–7), about the tragedy of a village girl abandoned by a young nobleman, is a national monument. Schooled in Warsaw and Minsk, he completed his musical training with C.F. Rungenhagen in Berlin (1837–40) and became organist of St John, Vilnius. A return visit to Warsaw in 1846 sparked his creativity: he met the poet Włodzimierz Wolski, his librettist for *Halka*, as well as others who shared his patriotic enthusiasm. In 1858 a revised *Halka* was staged in Warsaw to great acclaim, and the following year he moved to the city with his family, to work as opera conductor at the Grand Theatre and, from 1864, as a teacher at the music institute. He scored another success with the ebullient comedy *The Haunted Manor* (f.p. Warsaw, 1865). Wholly devoted to the nationalist cause, he also produced choral music and 12 'songbooks for home use', and often based numbers on Polish dances. In other respects his style came out of Auber and Rossini.

Monk, Meredith (Jane) (b. New York, 20 Nov 1942). US composer-performer, who has worked principally with her own ensemble on projects combining light-voiced chant and dance. After graduating from Sarah Lawrence College (1964) she established herself in the experimental culture of downtown Manhattan with solo pieces and larger theatrical endeavours. Tours and recordings then took her work worldwide from the 1980s, and she wrote *Atlas* for the Houston Grand Opera (1991).

www.meredithmonk.org

Monn. Austrian composing brothers.

(1) **Matthias Georg** [Georg Matthias] (b. Vienna, 9 Apr 1717; d. Vienna, 3 Oct 1750). One of the leading Viennese galant figures, he composed a lot in a short time (21 symphonies, numerous chamber and keyboard pieces, sacred music), but is best remembered for a cello concerto outrageously and magnificently adapted two centuries later by Schoenberg. He seems to have been trained as a choirboy, then worked as organist of St Charles in Vienna. One of his symphonies (1740) is the earliest in the later ubiquitous four-movement form with a minuet in third place.

(2) **Johann Christoph** (b. 1726; d. Vienna, 24 Jun 1782). Of obscure life, he produced eight piano sonatas of note.

monochord. Instrument consisting of a single string stretched between bridges on a table or box. It was used in the Middle Ages as a means of discovering, verifying and teaching relationships between intervals and string lengths.

Monod, Jacques (Louis) (b. Asnières, Paris, 25 Feb 1927). French conductor and composer, resident since 1951 in the New York area and keenly admired for his astute idealism in the cause of new music. He was a pupil with Boulez of Messiaen (1944) and Leibowitz (1944–50), then studied with Wagenaar at Juilliard and Rudolf Thomas at Columbia. Publicly active in the 1950s–60s, sometimes with his wife Bethany Beardslee, he has latterly concentrated on teaching.

monodrama. MELODRAMA or opera for one character. The term was invented in the 18th century for cases of the former, but Schoenberg gave it operatic currency with *Erwartung*.

monodic. Exemplifying monody.

monody. (1) Unaccompanied melody, MONOPHONY.

(2) More particularly the term is applied to early Baroque Italian song, in which the solo vocal line is paramount. Relevant composers include Caccini, Grandi and, in a few works, Monteverdi.

monophonic. Exemplifying monophony.

monophony. Music comprising a single line, e.g. plainsong.

monothematic. Having one theme, where two or more would be normal. Haydn was a master of the monothematic sonata allegro, in which the second subject is derived from the first.

monotone. Chanting of several words on a single note, as in the recitation of a prayer, psalm or lesson in church. The technique appears occasionally in opera (finale of *Così fan tutte*) and concert music (Barraqué).

Monsigny, Pierre-Alexandre (b. Fauquembergues, near St Omer, 17 Oct 1729; d. Paris, 14 Jan 1817). French composer, almost exclusively of comic operas. Born into the dilapidated nobility, he had to support his family from the time of his father's death in 1748, and so went to Paris, where he became major domo to the Duke of Orleans. Spurred by the duke's love of theatre, and briefly prepared by lessons with the double bass player Gianotti, he began his composing career with *Les Aveux indiscrets* (1759). More comedies followed at an annual rate, as well as a single work for the Opera, *Aline, reine de Golconde* (1766). After *Félix ou l'enfant trouvé* (1777), however, he gave up composition, and in 1784 he married. He survived the French Revolution on pensions, living on to see his works return to the stage and to gain election to the Institut (1813). His music is tuneful and sometimes strikingly scored.

Monte, Philippe de (b. Mechlin/Mechelen, 1521; d. Prague, 4 Jul 1603). Netherlandish composer, notably of more than 1,100 madrigals. Probably trained as a choirboy in his home town, he then spent time in Naples (1542–51), Rome and, briefly in 1555, England, in the chapel of Philip of Spain. Around this time he was described as 'a quiet, reticent person' who spoke Italian like a native. In 1568 he became chapelmaster to the Habsburg imperial court, and there he remained, writing masses and motets as well as the abundant supply of madrigals, in a style of fluent contrapuntal mastery.

Montéclair, Michel Pignolet de (baptized Andelot, Haute-Marne, 4 Dec 1667; d. Aumont, 22 Sep 1737). French composer, especially of stage works and cantatas. Born Michel Pignolet, a weaver's son, he took the name of a fortress in his home town. His training came as a choirboy at Langres Cathedral, and he moved to Paris in 1687, visiting Italy as music master to the prince of Vaudéamont. By the end of the century he was playing in the Opera orchestra, where he was among the first to perform on the double bass. He was also a respected teacher. Besides two works for the Opera – *Les Festes de l'été* (1716) and *Jephté* (1732) – he produced three volumes of cantatas, several books of airs, a little sacred music and chamber pieces.

Montemezzi, Italo (b. Vigasio, near Verona, 31 May 1875; d. Vigasio, 15 May 1952). Italian composer, remembered for his opera *L'amore di tre re* (f.p. Milan, 1913), a heady brew of Wagner and Puccini. He studied at the Milan Conservatory, and had some success with other operas – *Giovanni Gallurese* (f.p. Turin, 1905), *Hellera* (f.p. Turin, 1909) and *La Nave* (f.p. Milan, 1918) – after which he wrote rather little. He spent the years 1939–49 largely in California.

Monteux, Pierre (b. Paris, 4 Apr 1875; d. Hancock, Maine, 1 Jul 1964). French–US conductor, of sagacity and distinction. He studied at the Paris Conservatoire as a string player from the age of nine, and joined the Opéra-Comique as a violist at 15. Though he conducted his first concert when he was 12, he remained principally a viola player until he became conductor of the casino orchestra in Dieppe (1908–11). He then conducted for Diaghilev (1911–14), giving the premières of *Petrushka*, *The Rite of Spring* and *Jeux*. In 1916 he went to the USA, where he was conductor of French opera at the Met (1917–19) and principal conductor of the Boston Symphony (1920–24). His long, later maturity he spent with the Concertgebouw (1924–34), his own Orchestre Symphonique de Paris (1929–38), the San Francisco Symphony (1936–52) and, finally, the LSO, with which he signed a 25-year contract in 1961, aged 86.

Monteverdi, Claudio (Giovanni Antonio) (b. Cremona, 15 May 1567; d. Venice, 29 Nov 1643). Italian composer. Though he was certainly famed in his time and remembered by history, his music went out of circulation until the mid 20th century, and only since his quatercentenary has he been acknowledged the pre-eminent master of his age – the creator of the first viable operas, of keenly expressive madrigals and of glorious church music. There is something athletic in his manner, in his eager venturing all over the fresh continent of music that could represent how people feel and how their feelings show.

The son of a doctor-apothecary, he made an early start as a composer, publishing a volume of three-part motets when he was 15. In it he described himself as a pupil of Ingegneri, whom he went on acknowledging as his master in other collections up to 1590. That year or the next he found employment at the Gonzaga court in Mantua, where he joined a rich musical establishment led by Wert, a strong influence on his second and third madrigal books. His rising prestige is signalled by his travels with the duke, to Hungary (1595), to Flanders (1599) and probably to Florence (1600), for the royal wedding at which Peri's

Euridice was performed. (In 1599 he was himself married, to a court singer, Claudia Cattaneo.) Further evidence of the esteem he had gained by his 30s comes from the attacks launched at him in print by Giovanni Maria Artusi of Bologna (1600–3). He was defended by his younger brother, Giulio Cesare, also a composer at the Mantuan court, as exemplifying a 'seconda pratica' distinct from the PRIMA PRATICA of older masters.

Evidently the controversy caused no concern to his Gonzaga employers. In 1601 he was appointed master of the court music; the duke accepted the dedication of his fifth book of madrigals (1605); and his first opera, *Orfeo* (1607), was commissioned by the duke's son Francesco. A few months after the première he went back to his father in Cremona; his wife was ill, and she died in September 1607, leaving him with three children, of whom the eldest was just six. He had to return promptly to Mantua to compose music for Francesco's wedding, including a second opera, *Arianna*, whose music is lost, except for its celebrated lament, but a year later he was back in Cremona, discontented with his prospects and recompense under the Gonzagas. He may have published his magnificent *Vespers* in 1610 as self-advertisement; the original purpose and possible liturgical usefulness of such an elaborate and particular setting have been much debated. Then, although his Mantuan frustrations were answered partly by the award of a pension, he seems to have been further unsettled by Francesco's accession and death in the same year, 1612. In the summer of 1613 he applied to succeed Giulio Cesare Martinengo as state chapelmaster in the city to which he had been sending music for publication for more than 30 years: Venice. Almost at once he was appointed.

Venice was bursting with musical opportunities. His principal responsibilities were at St Mark's, the state church, but he also wrote for other churches, for secular state occasions and for private patrons. He produced the compact opera *Combattimento di Tancredi e Clorinda* (1624/5) for a patrician, Girolamo Mocenigo, and a mass for the ending of the 1630–31 plague. At the same time he continued to supply music to the court of Mantua, whose subject he remained: one such commissioned work was *Andromeda* (1619/20), another lost opera. After 1622, when Eleonora Gonzaga married the Habsburg emperor, he composed also for the imperial court in Vienna.

Much of what he created, for ecclesiastical ceremonies as for court entertainments, has failed to survive, but happily he went on publishing madrigals, through a sea-change in the genre. Where his first six volumes had all comprised pieces for five voices, his seventh book (1619) and a second collection of *Scherzi musicali* (1632) are devoted largely to solos and duets, while the magnificent eighth book (1638) again includes duets, along with more sumptuously scored pieces. The duet form, which he also exploited in sacred music, allowed him to show how two similar voices can race with one another, or wrap themselves intimately together. Many of the other madrigals of these later books are solo expressions, or poetic depictions. They suggest what the operas missing from this period (some lost, others abandoned) might have been like – but they leave little room for regret. They display his remarkable ability to sustain formal shape and beauty while making music do what he often, in his letters, insisted it must do: paint the passions.

Of his children, his elder son Francesco became a singer at St Mark's, and the younger son, Massimiliano, a doctor. He did not remarry and in 1632 entered the priesthood, for reasons unclear. Perhaps he felt his age; there is a sense of summation in the eighth madrigal book, as in the collection of church music *Selva morale e spirituale* (1640–41). But just at this time, in his 70s, he embarked on a new career in the Venetian opera houses, writing three works in quick succession: *Il ritorno d'Ulisse in patria*, *Le nozze d'Enea con Lavinia* (yet another lost opera) and *L'incoronazione di Poppea*. The public theatres of Venice could not support instrumental ensembles as lavish as that available at the Mantuan court for *Orfeo*, but his central preoccupation had always been with the voice, as a vehicle at once for melodious grace and full expression, and both *Ulisse* and *Poppea* show his exemplary style of operatic writing, by which verbal phrases, always audible, come to flower.

He was buried in the great Venetian church of I Frari, where his memorial stone may still be seen, after so long a time when he was only a name.

Denis Stevens and Nigel Fortune, ed. *The New Monteverdi Companion* (1985); Gary Tomlinson *Monteverdi and the End of the Renaissance* (1987); Tim Carter *Monteverdi's Musical Theatre* (2002)

Operas: *Orfeo* (see ORPHEUS), f.p. Mantua, 1607; *Arianna* (see ARIADNE), f.p. Mantua, 1608 (lost); *Il ritorno d'Ulisse in patria* (see ODYSSEY), f.p. Venice, 1640; *L'INCORONAZIONE DI POPPEA*, f.p. Venice, 1642; several others lost
Smaller stage works: *De la bellezza le dovute lodi*, pub 1607; *Ballo delle ingrate* (Rinuccini), f.p. Mantua, 1608; *Tirsi e Clori* (Striggio), f.p. Mantua, 1616; COMBATTIMENTO DI TANCREDI E CLORINDA, f.p. Venice, 1624/5; *Volgendo il ciel* (Rinuccini), f.p. Vienna, 1636
Madrigals (with publication dates):

Book 1, 5 v, pub 1587: *Baci soavi e cari* (Giovanni Battista Guarini); etc.
Book 2, 5 v, pub 1590: *Ecco mormorar l'onde* (Tasso); etc.
Book 3, 5 v, pub 1592: *Lumi, miei cari lumi* (Guarini); etc.
Book 4, 5 v, pub 1603: *A un giro sol* (Guarini); *Io mi son giovinetta* (Guarini); *La piaga c'ho nel core* (Aurelio Gatti); *Sfogava con le stelle*; *Sí ch'io vorrei morire* (Mauritio Moro); etc.
Book 5, 5 v, con, pub 1605: *Ecco, Silvio* (Guarini); etc.
Scherzi musicali I, pub 1607: *Damigella tutta bella*; etc.
Book 6, 5 v, con, pub 1614: *Lasciatemi morire* (*Lamento d'Arianna*; Rinuccini); *Sestina* (*Lagrime d'amante al sepolcro dell'amata*; Scipione Agnelli); etc.
Book 7, pub 1619: *Con che soavità* (Guarini), s, str, kbds; *Non è di gentil core*, 2 s, con; *O come sei gentile* (Guarini), 2 s, con; *Ohimé, dov'è il mio ben?* (Tasso), 2 s, con; *Se i languidi miei sguardi* (*Lettera amorosa*; Claudio Achillini), s, con; *Tempro la cetra* (Giambattista Marino), t, insts, con; etc.
Scherzi musicali II, pub 1632: *Eri già tutta mia*, s, con; *Et è per dunque vero*, s, con; *Maledetto*, s, con; *Quel sguardo sdegnosetto*, s, con; *Zefiro torna* (Rinuccini), 2 t, con; etc.
Book 8, MADRIGALI GUERRIERI ET AMOROSI, pub 1638
Others: *Ohimé ch'io cado*, s, con, pub 1624; etc.
Sacred (with publication dates): VESPERS, 1610; Mass 'In illo tempore', 6 v, con, 1610; *Adoramus te, Christe*, 6 v, con, 1620; *Cantate Domino*, 6 v, con, 1620; *Ego flos campi*, a, con, 1624; *O quam puchra es*, t, con, 1625; *Exulta filia Sion*, s, con, 1629; Mass, 4 v, con, 1641; *Jubilet tota civitas*, s, con, 1641; *Laudate Dominum*, 8 v, 2 vn, con, 1641; Mass, 4 v, con, 1650; etc.

Montpellier. Manuscript volume of 13th-century polyphony, including over 300 pieces, held at the Bibliothèque Inter-Universitaire in Montpellier.

Montreal. Canadian city, home of the Montreal Symphony (Orchestre Symphonique de Montréal), which was founded in 1934, and whose music directors have included Markevitch (1957–60), Mehta (1961–7) and Dutoit (1977–2002).

Montsalvatge, Xavier (b. Gerona, 11 Mar 1912; d. Barcelona, 7 May 2002). Spanish composer, who broadened the national tradition to embrace Caribbean music and a certain modernism from Stravinsky and inter-war Paris. He studied at the Barcelona Conservatory (1922–36) and made his living in the city as a music critic and teacher. Besides his popular *Cinco canciónes negras* for voice with piano (1945–6) or orchestra (1949), he wrote other songs, instrumental pieces, concertos and stage works.

Moog, Robert A(rthur) (b. New York, 23 May 1934). US instrument designer, known for the first commercial synthesizer (1964). He paid his way through Columbia and Cornell by building electronic instruments and has remained active in the field.

Moonlight. Name given to Beethoven's Piano Sonata Op.27:2, for its rippling first movement.

Moore, Douglas (Stuart) (b. Cutchogue, NY, 10 Aug 1893; d. Greenport, NY, 25 Aug 1969). US composer, especially of operas rooted in folksong and the US scene. Born into a family resident on Long Island since the 17th century, he studied with Parker at Yale and, after wartime naval service (1917–19), with d'Indy in Paris. He was resident musician at the art museum in Cleveland (1921–5), where he also had lessons with Bloch and appeared as a professional actor. Then he taught at Columbia (1926–62). His operas *The Devil and Daniel Webster* (f.p. New York, 1939) and, particularly, *The Ballad of Baby Doe* (f.p. Central City, Col., 1956) have a place in the US repertory. Among his other works is the orchestral suite *The Pageant of P.T. Barnum* (1924).

Moore, Gerald (b. Watford, 30 Jul 1899; d. Penn, Bucks., 13 Mar 1987). British ACCOMPANIST, the first anywhere to devote himself to that art. He studied in England and Canada (1913–19), his family having moved there, and began recording in 1921. By the time of his retirement in 1967, he had worked with the great recital singers of half a century, including Elisabeth Schumann, Schwarzkopf, Fischer-Dieskau and Baker.

Moore, Thomas (b. Dublin, 28 May 1779; d. Sloperton Cottage, near Devizes, 26 Feb 1852). Irish poet and song arranger, best known for his oriental fantasy *Lalla Rookh* and several volumes of Irish melodies, to which he contributed words and tunes. His visions of both the East and Ireland were part of the essential library of the Romantic age: among composers who made settings were Berlioz, Schumann, Mendelssohn and Duparc.

Morales, Cristóbal de (b. Seville, c.1500; d. ?Marchena, Sep/Oct 1553). Spanish composer and church musician, the first of his country to win international prestige, widely regarded then and since as both a true heir of Josquin and the source of a new verbal expressiveness. He was probably a chorister at Seville Cathedral, where he may have begun his career and, in 1526, encountered Gombert in the suite of Charles V. Posts as chapelmaster at the cathedrals of Ávila (1526–9) and Plasencia (1529–31) followed, after which he possibly left for Naples. Next he was based in Rome, as a tenor in the papal chapel (1535–45); in 1544 he published two books of masses (16 altogether) in the city, and dedicated them to Cosimo de' Medici and Pope Paul III. He spent the rest of his life in Spain, as chapelmaster at Toledo Cathedral (1545–7), in Marchena (1548–51) and at Málaga Cathedral (1551–3). His music was being sung in Rome and throughout the Iberian empires (so in the Americas and Africa) until the 18th century. Apart from his masses, he wrote two *Requiem*, eight *Magnificat* and several Lamentations settings, motets (*Jubilate Deo* a 6, *Lamentabatur Jacob* a 5, *O sacrum convivium* a 5) and a few secular pieces.

Moravia. See CZECH REPUBLIC.

Morceau (Fr.). Piece.

Mordent. Quick slip down to the note below and back again. This may also be called a 'lower mordent' to distinguish it from the upper or inverted mordent, in which the displacement is upwards. Notations and realizations are as follow:

Morel, Jacques (*fl. c.*1710–30). French composer and viol player. He was a pupil of Marais, to whom he dedicated his *Premier livre* (c.1710), a book of four suites for bass viol including a *chaconne en trio*.

Morel, Jorge (b. Buenos Aires, 9 May 1931). Argentinian guitarist-composer, author of virtuoso pieces on South American rhythms. He studied with his father and with Pablo Escobar at the music academy in Buenos Aires, and from 1969 had composition lessons with Rudolf Schramm in New York, where he has remained.

morendo (It.). Dying, i.e. falling gradually into silence.

moresca (It., Moorish). Dance especially popular in the 15th–16th centuries in western Europe, supposedly in Moorish style. English Morris dancing, which goes back to the 14th century, seems to be part of the same pattern.

Moreschi, Alessandro (b. Monte Compatri, near Rome, 11 Nov 1858; d. Rome, 21 Apr 1921). Italian soprano castrato, seemingly the last to possess that voice and the only one to make recordings (in

1902–3). He was a member of the papal choir (1883–1913).

Moret, Norbert (b. Ménières, Fribourg, 20 Nov 1921; d. Fribourg, 17 Nov 1998). Swiss composer, a poetic loner who received attention in his 60s when his music was taken up by Rostropovich (Cello Concerto, 1985) and Mutter (*En rêve*, vn, chbr orch, 1988). He studied with Honegger, Messiaen and Leibowitz in Paris (1948–50) and with Furtwängler and Kraus in Vienna (1950–51), then lived quietly as a teacher before emerging as a composer in his 50s.

Morlacchi, Francesco (Giuseppe Baldassare) (b. Perugia, 14 Jun 1784; d. Innsbruck, 28 Oct 1841). Italian composer, lucklessly a contemporary of Rossini: he produced a version of *Il barbiere di Siviglia* the same year, in Dresden, where he was among the last Italian musicians to be employed at German courts. He studied with his uncle, who was organist of Perugia Cathedral, as well as with Zingarelli at Loreto and Stanislao Mattei in Bologna. Active as an opera composer from 1807, he moved to Dresden in 1810, and there became Weber's arch-rival. He wrote operas, oratorios and sacred music, but is best known now for a virtuoso flute piece, *Il pastore svizzero*.

Morley, Thomas (b. Norwich, 1557/8; d. London, Oct 1602). English composer and editor, the source principally of light madrigals and instruction for amateurs. A pupil of Byrd, he may have studied with that master before returning to Norwich as cathedral organist (1583–7). By 1589 he was living in London with his wife and family; he became organist of St Paul's and, from 1592, a member of the Chapel Royal. From 1593 he was busy in the publishing business. He was largely responsible for the vogue for the lighter sort of Italian madrigal, putting out volumes of arrangements, of original contributions and, finally, of pieces collected from his English contemporaries (*The* TRIUMPHS OF ORIANA, which itself had an Italian model). Other publications include a book of lute songs, one of consort music comprising mostly arrangements of pieces by Dowland and others (*The First Book of Consort Lessons*, 1599), and *A Plain and Easy Introduction to Practical Music* (1597). Two popular Shakespeare songs are ascribed to him: 'It was a lover and his lass' he indeed wrote, though whether he did so for the play (*As You Like It*) is not known, but 'O mistress mine' is an adaptation of Shakespeare's words (from *Twelfth Night*) to his song 'Mistress mine, well may you fare'.

Madrigals: *April is in my mistress's face*; *Fire, fire* (after Marenzio); *My bonny lass, she smileth* (after Gastoldi); *Now is the month of maying* (after Vecchi); *Sing we and chant it* (after Gastoldi); *Though Philomela lost her love*; etc.

Other works: lute songs ('It was a lover and his lass'), services, anthems (*Nolo mortem peccatoris*), consort pieces (*Joyne hands*), keyboard pieces

Moroi, Makoto (b. Tokyo, 17 Dec 1930). Japanese composer, who is engaged with the Western avant-garde and latterly with Japanese traditions. The son of the German-schooled composer Saburō Moroi (1903–77), he studied with Ikenouchi at the Tokyo National University of Fine Arts and Music. International prizes established him in his mid 20s, and he worked at the electronic studio in Cologne (1955–6). In 1964 he began writing for the shakuhachi (bamboo flute), and later for other Japanese instruments, this aspect of his work taking over in the early 1990s after a long period of near silence.

Morricone, Ennio (b. Rome, 10 Nov 1928). Italian composer, whose all-embracing grasp of style, and stylishness, has made him one of the most sought-after film composers, working with directors including Leone (*Per un pugno di dollari*, 1964), Pasolini, Bertolucci, Joffé (*The Mission*, 1986), De Palma (*The Untouchables*, 1987) and Almodóvar. The son of a trumpeter in light music, he studied the instrument himself at the Accademia di Santa Cecilia, where he was also a composition pupil of Petrassi. Besides contributing to around 10 films or television programmes annually, he has maintained a steady output of concert music.

Morris, R(eginald) O(wen) (b. York, 3 Mar 1886; d. London, 15 Dec 1948). British composer, but better known as the teacher of others at the RCM (where he had himself studied, after Harrow and Oxford) and as an author of textbooks.

Mort de Virgile, La (The Death of Virgil). Life's work of Barraqué, after Hermann Broch's novel.

Morton, Robert (b. *c*.1430; d. ?1497). English composer, at the Burgundian court (1457–76) and possibly identifiable with the Robert Morton who became Bishop of Worcester. His small surviving output of songs includes two of the finest of the time: *Le Souvenir de vous me tue* and *N'aray je jamais mieulx que j'ay*.

Moscheles, Ignaz (Isaac) (b. Prague, 23 May 1794; d. Leipzig, 10 Mar 1870). Bohemian pianist-composer, a virtuoso and a classicist. Of Jewish family, he studied with B.D. Weber in Prague (1804–8), then moved to Vienna, drawn by admiration for Beethoven. He continued his studies with Albrechtsberger and Salieri, and in 1815 set out as a touring virtuoso. Soon after his marriage (1825) he settled in London, where he conducted the local première of Beethoven's *Missa solemnis* (1832) and developed his friendship with Mendelssohn, whom he had known since giving the boy some lessons in 1824. Doubtful about the new generation of Chopin and Liszt, he was curious about older music (even Purcell) and, most unusually at the time, played the harpsichord. In 1846 he accepted Mendelssohn's invitation to join the staff of the new Leipzig Conservatory. He was a kindly teacher, with Grieg and Sullivan among his pupils, and the influence of his studies has been felt by ensuing generations. Among his other works are six concertos (No.3, G minor, Op.60, 1820), sonatas and chamber pieces.

Moscow (Moskva). Russian city, the capital before 1703 and since 1918. The principal opera house is the BOLSHOY; the conservatory was founded in 1864. Orchestras of the Soviet period included the Moscow Philharmonic, the Moscow Radio Symphony and the USSR State Symphony. Latterly the Russian National Orchestra, founded by Pletnev in 1990, has been supreme.

Moses. Biblical leader of the Israelites on their exodus from Egypt. He features in choral works by Handel (*Israel in Egypt*), Bruch and Goehr, and in two notable operas, both of which have him a bass and his brother Aaron a tenor:

(1) Rossini's *Mosè in Egitto*, to a libretto by Andrea Leone Tottola. Moses sings his prayer 'Dal tuo stellato soglio' before the parting of the Red Sea. First performance: Naples, 5 Mar 1818; rev as *Moïse et Pharaon* (Luigi Balochi and Etienne de Jouy), Paris, 26 Mar 1827.

(2) Schoenberg's *Moses und Aron*, to his own libretto. Moses (in sprechgesang) speaks with God (unseen chorus), but it is his brother who can speak to the people – though his softening of Moses's austere vision leads to the orgy of the Dance before the Golden Calf. Schoenberg wrote the text for the short third act but did not set it. First performance: Hamburg, 12 Mar 1954.

Mosolov, Aleksandr (Vasilyevich) (b. Kiev, 11 Aug 1900; d. Moscow, 12 Jul 1973). Russian composer, noted for his avant-garde works of the 1920s. He fought in the civil war (1918–20), then studied with Glière and Myaskovsky at the Moscow Conservatory (1921–5). A leading member of the Association for Contemporary Music, he wrote songs of a Musorgskian intensity and satirical edge (*Three Children's Scenes*, Op.18; *Four Newspaper An-*

nouncements, Op.21a) as well as futurist machine music (*The Foundry*, Op.19, for an orchestra including a struck steel sheet, 1926–8). He then came under criticism, studied folk music and turned to more conventional pieces, including symphonies and choral music.

Mosonyi, Mihály (b. Boldogasszonyfalva, now Frauenkirchen, Austria, 4 Sep 1815; d. Pest, 31 Oct 1870). Hungarian composer, a nationalist who in 1859 Magyarized his Christian name and called himself after the county of his birth, Moson. Born into a family of furriers, he was largely self-taught. He managed, though, to make a living as a piano teacher, first with a noble family in Rétfalu, then from 1844 in Pest. There he began to establish himself as a composer, moving from a Beethovenian style to incorporate Hungarian elements around the time he met Liszt in 1856. Among his later works are Hungarian songs, operas and cantatas, as well as *Homage to Ferenc Kazinczy* (1860, on the centenary of the man who had restored Hungarian as a literary language), the first orchestral piece to include a CIMBALOM.

mosso (It., moved). Marking usually found in the forms *più mosso* (faster) and *meno mosso* (slower).

Moszkowski, Moritz (b. Breslau/Wrocław, 23 Aug 1854; d. Paris, 4 Mar 1925). German composer, almost exclusively of piano music for virtuoso and amateur. Of Polish-Jewish family, he studied in Berlin with Eduard Frank and at Theodore Kullak's academy, whose staff he joined when he was 17. In 1897 he moved to Paris, his wife being a sister of Cécile Chaminade, and there he took pupils, including Landowska and Beecham. His music was immensely popular, and pieces were recorded by Horowitz, Hofmann, Rachmaninoff and many others. But he went out of fashion until the end of the century. Most frequently encountered are his Serenata (Op.15:1) *Etincelles* (No.6 from *Huit morceaux caractéristiques*, Op.36), *Caprice espagnol* (Op.37), *Guitare* (Op.45:2, usually as a violin piece), *Jongleuse* (from the Etudes, Op.52) and *Quinze études de virtuosité* 'Per aspera ad astra' (Op.72, especially No.6 in F and No.11 in A♭), his *Fünf spanische Tänze* for piano duet (Op.12) and his Piano Concerto in E (Op.59, 1898).

motet. Term having different meanings with respect to different periods, as outlined in chronological order below.

(1) Polyphonic composition of the 13th–15th centuries, cultivated especially in France and typically having two very active melodic lines, each with its own text, over a slow tenor. It was not

especially a liturgical form; indeed, 14th-century motet texts could be in French as well as Latin, and could express courtly love (Machaut), animal satire (*Roman de Fauvel*) or political antipathy (Vitry). The motet also became an arena for musical conceits, notably ISORHYTHM. The Lat. term MOTETUS was a derivation from the Fr. *mot*, meaning 'stanza' at the time, and so the motet had a name that answered its origin: it began as words, not music – words added to a CLAUSULA in the early 13th century. Soon it became an independent form, but still with a tenor taken from plainsong.

(2) Sacred piece to a single Latin text – i.e. not a mass, but including pieces with diverse liturgical functions: antiphons, psalms, sequences, hymns, prayers. Composers began setting such texts to polyphony, without the strict architecture of the isorhythmic motet, in the mid 15th century, and for their successors from Josquin to Palestrina the motet was a principal form alongside the mass, to which it was related, since composers would often make a mass a PARODY of a motet of their own or a colleague.

The prestige of Renaissance polyphony has tended to confine the term to that period, where Latin sacred music is concerned. Composers after 1600 would conceive music in terms of instrumental accompaniment and distinct sections with different vocal textures, and for such works the term is not normally used (except in the case of French music, with its traditions of the GRAND MOTET and PETIT MOTET). Thus the *Stabat mater* settings of Josquin and Palestrina are commonly described as motets, but those of Pergolesi, Vivaldi, Rossini or Schubert are not.

(3) Lutheran piece of sacred choral polyphony, unaccompanied or with organ, the most notable examples being Bach's.

(4) Short sacred setting, unaccompanied or with organ, as composed by Mendelssohn, Bruckner and later composers. Some composers since the mid 19th century (e.g. Schumann, Strauss, Lutyens) have used the term for non-liturgical pieces, with reference to the style or seriousness of earlier motet traditions.

motet-chanson. Modern term for a late-15th-century chanson on a plainsong tenor. There are examples by Josquin, Compère and Agricola.

motetus (Lat.). Motet, or the voice in such a piece immediately above the tenor.

motif. Small element, distinguished as having some importance within a larger entity, whether a tune or a large-scale composition. For example, the first three notes of the British national anthem

('God save our') represent a motif that soon reappears in altered form ('Long live our'). Beethoven's music provides examples of motifs raised to the status of themes, a conspicuous instance being the first movement of his Fifth Symphony. Most often a motif will be, as in these examples, melodic, but one may speak also of a harmonic motif; the *Tristan* chord would be one such.

motive. Obsolescent equivalent of motif.

moto (It.). Motion, as in the tempo designations *con moto* (with motion) and *allegro con moto*.

moto perpetuo (It., perpetual motion). See PERPETUUM MOBILE.

motor rhythm. Rhythm of equal accented beats, as in much Stravinsky and Hindemith of the 1920s.

Mottl, Felix (Josef) (b. Unter-St Veit, Vienna, 24 Aug 1856; d. Munich, 2 Jul 1911). Austrian conductor, associated with Wagner's music from the first *Ring*, when he was not yet 20. He studied with Bruckner at the Vienna Conservatory and held conducting posts in Karlsruhe (1881–1903) and the Munich opera (1903–11), appearing also at Bayreuth and Covent Garden. Also a composer, he wrote theatre works, songs and a quartet, and orchestrated Wagner's *Wesendonck-Lieder*. He died after collapsing while conducting *Tristan*.

motto. Musical idea whose recurrences give it weight. The term may be used of a head-motif in a polyphonic mass or of a psychologically endowed theme in a Romantic symphony, e.g. the IDEE FIXE in Berlioz's *Symphonie fantastique* or the similar ideas in Tchaikovsky's Fourth and Fifth.

Moulinié, Etienne (b. Languedoc, *c*.1600; d. Languedoc, 1669 or later). French composer, most importantly of AIRS DE COUR, though he also wrote sacred music. He moved to Paris in 1624 in the wake of his elder brother, and four years later became music director to the king's brother, Gaston of Orleans. In 1661, after Gaston's death, he returned to Languedoc.

Moulu, Pierre (b. ?1484; d. *c*.1550). French composer, associated with the French royal court in his early maturity, possibly having studied with Josquin. His works include four masses, motets and chansons.

Mouret, Jean-Joseph (b. Avignon, 11 Apr 1682; d. Charenton, 20 Dec 1738). French composer, respected for his work for the theatre and the

Concert Spirituel (which he directed, 1728–33). The son of an Avignon silk merchant, he moved to Paris in his early 20s and gained employment with the Duke of Maine, an illegitimate son of Louis XIV. He died insane – not knowing that two and a half centuries later the opening rondeau from the first of his orchestral suites (1729), with prominent trumpet, would provide the signature tune for the US television series 'Masterpiece Theatre'.

Mourning. Name given to Haydn's Symphony No.44, for its expressive character. According to legend, the composer wanted it played at his funeral.

Moussorgsky, Modest. See Modest MUSORGSKY.

mouth organ. See HARMONICA.

mouthpiece. Section of a wind instrument, of the brass or clarinet families, made to receive the player's lips. The mouthpieces of different instruments differ in internal shape: the trumpet's is Y-shaped, with a shallow bowl at the mouth end, a sudden narrowing and then a widening bore, whereas the horn's tapers gradually. These differences have much to do with how the instrument sounds and how it behaves.

Mouton, Jean (b. ?Samer, before 1459; d. St Quentin, 30 Oct 1522). French composer and church musician, whose calmly flowing polyphony seems of a piece with the humility reported of him. He followed the life of a provincial choirmaster in Nesle (near Péronne), St Omer, Amiens and Grenoble, before being acquired by Anne of Brittany, wife of Louis XII, early in the 16th century. Remaining the chief musician of the French royal court to the end of his life, he journeyed with Francis I to Bologna to meet the pope (1515) and possibly also to the parley with Henry VIII at the Field of the Cloth of Gold (1520). His works include 15 masses, about 100 motets and chansons.

mouvement (Fr.). Movement, motion.

Mouvement symphonique. Title of three orchestral works by Honegger. *Pacific 231* describes a locomotive of this class, the numbers referring to pairings of wheels (f.p. Paris, 8 May 1924). *Rugby* illustrates the sport (f.p. Paris, 19 Oct 1928). Bill Hopkins suggested that the undisclosed subject of *Mouvement symphonique* No.3 is a sexual encounter (f.p. Berlin, 26 Mar 1933).

movement. Section of a work – in principle one that comes to a close and is followed by a break.

Symphonies, sonatas, concertos and suites are typically multi-movement works, and where such a work has no breaks – examples include Sibelius's Seventh Symphony and Barraqué's Sonata – it may be said to be 'in one movement', a designation that would not be applied to an overture or a continuous ballet score. In music of the 17th–18th centuries each movement generally had its own tempo, or at least its own metre, but by Mahler's time a movement could embrace many different kinds of motion. Carter's First Quartet introduced the notion of a movement that could span a break, and so of a cleft between the two natures of a movement: as a separated length of time and as a distinct way of moving through time.

The term is also regularly applied to masses (though here the sections were conceived to be divided not by pauses but by other parts of the litrgy), but for operas and other vocal works divided into segments the term 'number' is preferred.

Movements. Compact piano concerto by Stravinsky. First performance: New York, 10 Jan 1960.

movie music. See FILM MUSIC.

Mozarabic chant. Plainsong of the Mozarabic rite, the ancient liturgy of Spain, which is still used in Toledo. The original chant, however, is recorded only in notation that cannot be fully deciphered.

Mozart. German-Austrian musical family, clustered around one member. Those considered below include also his father, his sister, his wife and their two sons.

(1) **(Johann Georg) Leopold** (b. Augsburg, 14 Nov 1719; d. Salzburg, 28 May 1787). Composer and guide, whose own career virtually stopped as soon as he recognized the talents of his son. He had lost his own father, a bookbinder, at 16, and gone the next year to study philosophy and law at Salzburg University. In 1739 he was expelled for truancy, but he stayed in the city as a household musician, joining the archiepiscopal court in 1743. There he stayed to the end of his life, never rising above deputy kapellmeister. Meanwhile, in 1747 he married Anna Maria Pertl, with whom he raised two children to adulthood. He devoted himself to their education, and soon to their presentation in public, which began when they were 11 (Nannerl) and six (Wolfgang Amadeus). Nobody at the time would have regarded such early exposure as exploitation, and there is every evidence that the children enjoyed their opportunities to travel and astonish the courts of Europe, while the boy certainly profited from the range of musical experiences he thereby acquired. If, later, father

and son came to irk each other at times, their attachment remained strong, and Leopold's anxieties were all for his son to gain the position in the world he deserved (which never came). After 1762 he wrote very little, perhaps nothing. Earlier he had produced quantities of church and instrumental music, though the only works much played now are his Trumpet Concerto in D (1762) and two novelty items that make an ironic legacy for one of history's most famous fathers: the divertimento in F *Das musikalische Schlittenfahrt* (The Musical Sleighride, 1755) and a cassation with toy instruments in G, possibly not by him at all, three movements of which are commonly excerpted as the 'Toy Symphony'. He also published a treatise on violin playing, *Versuch einer gründlichen Violinschule* (1756).

(2) **Maria Anna (Walburga Ignatia)**, known to the later world by her family name **Nannerl** (b. Salzburg, 30/31 Jul 1751; d. Salzburg, 29 Oct 1829). Mozart's sister: his childhood companion and warm friend in adulthood. She too composed, though nothing of her work survives. She also played the piano, both on their early travels and in later life. In 1784, at her father's behest, she married a magistrate 15 years her senior, Johann Baptist von Berchtold zu Sonnenburg. Their only child to reach adulthood was Leopold (1785–1840), with whom she returned to Salzburg after her husband's death in 1801. With interest in her brother increasing, she provided information and helped trace manuscripts.

(3) **(Johann Chrysostom) Wolfang Amadeus** (b. Salzburg, 27 Jan 1756; d. Vienna, 5 Dec 1791). Composer. The first wonder is his music's naturalness, the way melodies flow like water, and whole movements (which may be over 20 minutes long in the case of opera finales) unfold with every harmonic turn placed at the right moment, to leave, at the end, a sense of perfect finish and unity. This naturalness presents the performer with a challenge: that of letting the music achieve the fluency, grace and clarity that are its own. And the listener too is challenged, for the music's naturalness is, like nature itself, inexhaustible. This is the second wonder, that music sounding so simple can convey such complexity and ambiguity, so many shades of tenderness and anxiety and mischief in a throwaway gesture.

Mozart spent his life having to react spontaneously to changing circumstances. Between the ages of seven and 17 he was most of the time on the road with his family, visiting the principal musical centres of Europe – Vienna, Munich, Paris, London, Milan, Venice – and absorbing all he heard. By the age most musicians were starting their professional training, he had gained first-hand experience of the new symphonic style of Austria and south Germany, of opera in northern Italy, of the French mix of drama, colour and lightness in instrumental music and, indeed, of his own powers, which included abilities to assimilate, combine and, in everything, outdo.

Having made the difficult transition from child prodigy, he was a working musician by the start of his teens, producing symphonies and operas, extravagant arias and elementary exercises, music for the church and music for evening parties. The creative abundance never stopped. In 1786 alone, for instance, he completed not only one of the greatest operas, *Le nozze di Figaro*, but also three marvellous piano concertos, the 'Prague' symphony, a string quartet, the 'Kegelstatt' trio and much else. Though based now in Vienna, he still had to take what opportunities he could, having no steady employment. He seems generally to have lived quite well, and he certainly had renown and respect. It is also hard to know how much the speed at which he worked was pressed on him by need, and how much it was self-generated, the *allegro molto* of a racing mind. Like so much in his life, his hectic and uncertain pattern of work left no mark on his music's sublime ease, while its moments of disquiet express things far deeper.

With his father his only tutor, in music and also in other subjects, he began his public career aged five, when he took part in a theatrical presentation in Salzburg. Around his sixth birthday he played the harpsichord for the Elector of Bavaria in Munich; perhaps he included the minuet in G that stands as the first item in Köchel's standard catalogue of his output (K.1), and that dates from close to this time. Within the year he had performed for Empress Maria Theresa in Vienna, winning accolades that may have encouraged Leopold to take the family on further travels. In June 1763 they left. After visiting various German courts and cities, they spent the winter of 1763–4 in Paris (where two little volumes of keyboard sonatas with violin were published – the boy Mozart's first music in print), then stayed right through until the summer of 1765 in London. There Mozart wrote his first symphonies and his first choral piece (*God is our refuge*, K.20), all at the age of eight or nine. On the homeward journey through the Netherlands, Paris, Switzerland and Germany he again performed and composed (and had three bouts of illness).

This period away had taken him from the age of seven and a half to almost 11 (Nov 1766), a vitally impressionable phase, during which he had learned to delight again and again, and had become more than proficient as a composer. Leopold, who probably helped shape his infant compositions, was now there only to offer him occasional correction, and during almost a year back in Salzburg he embarked on musical drama with *Apollo et Hyacinthus*, besides writing sacred music and divertimentos. There was then another long excursion, this time to Vienna, where the family stayed until Mozart was nearly 13 (September 1767 to January 1769). A plan to present an opera by him (*La finta semplice*) was frustrated, but the court did hear him direct his first, grand setting of the mass (the 'Waisenhausmesse'). Then, once more back in Salzburg, he wrote more for the church and for pleasure (minuets, cassations), and received an unpaid post at the court of the prince-archbishop, his father's employer.

Leopold's sights were now on opera again, and Italy. Opera offered the highest prospects of reward to an 18th-century composer; Italy was its home, and Italian its language. So father and son set out again, the month before he turned 14, and this time went south. They were not disappointed. In Milan, which was still within the Austrian Empire, they gained the promise of a commission. They then went on to Rome (where Mozart transcribed Allegri's eight-part *Miserere* after one hearing), Naples and Pompeii, before coming to rest for the summer near Bologna. Back in Milan the new opera, *Mitridate*, was written, performed and applauded, and they took themselves to Venice before returning to Salzburg in March 1771. By August they were back again in Milan, so that Mozart could write another dramatic work – not an opera this time but a serenata, a court entertainment for the marriage of the ruling Archduke Ferdinand, Maria Theresa's son: *Ascanio in Alba*. And they were back yet again in the winter of 1772–3 for a second full-scale opera, *Lucio Silla*.

By this time Mozart was nearly 17 and a thoroughly mature composer. Besides reaching powerful moments in *Silla*, he had proved himself further in masses and symphonies for Salzburg. His father by now was no more than his travelling companion and agent – in which latter role his success was mixed. He failed to gain his son a permanent appointment at the Milanese court, at least partly because his strategy of touring had backfired: Maria Theresa, who had been charmed by the six-year-old a decade before, advised Ferdinand not to engage people who were going around Europe 'like beggars'. Instead Mozart had his position in Salzburg confirmed, with a salary. He went with his father to Vienna for two and a half months in the summer of 1773, but now as a young man seeking employment (again unsuccessfully), not a child marvel. Those days were over, and for the rest of his teens, to the age of 21, he was a professional musician in Salzburg. There

was just one more journey during these four years, to Munich for the composition and performance of a bizarre comic opera, *La finta giardiniera*.

Salzburg, with its princely court, its Baroque churches and its wealthy mercantile families, offered multitudinous opportunities to a composer, and Mozart explored them all: opera (*Il re pastore*, plus arias for other shows), symphony (including two stirring works, Nos.25 and 29, dating from either side his 18th birthday), serenade (notably the 'Haffner', written when he was 20), concerto (especially the five violin concertos and the 'Jeunehomme' for piano) and church composition. Nevertheless, he seems to have felt himself in a backwater and unappreciated, and in September 1777 he set out again, this time with his mother, as his father could not afford to be away.

Their principal destinations were Mannheim (winter 1777–8) and Paris (spring–summer 1778), and though he did not gain the hoped-for position or opera commission in either place, he took another step forward as a composer and wrote some important works: arias, concertos, flute quartets, violin sonatas, piano sonatas and the 'Paris' symphony. Mannheim also held other attractions in the form of Aloysia Weber, a 16-year-old soprano. (He was 21.) To Leopold's horror, he announced a plan to take her to Italy and write operas for her, and though that did not happen, he left a portrait of her in the arias he composed for her, both at this time and years later. Following Leopold's firm insistence, he and his mother continued to Paris, whence he had to convey the news to his father of his mother's death. Leopold then asked him to return to Salzburg, to a post as cathedral organist, and was further annoyed when he stopped for weeks in Mannheim and Munich on the way. He arrived shortly before his 23rd birthday.

But the time in Mannheim and Munich – two cities ruled by the same prince – had not been wasted. In Mannheim he had heard the finest orchestra in Europe and met its chief composers, with telling effect on the enriched harmonies and timbres of the works he wrote back in Salzburg: liturgical settings (including the splendid *Vesperae solennes de confessore*), symphonies, the Sinfonia Concertante in Eb (a concerto-in-dialogue for violin and viola), and the unfinished opera known as *Zaide*. Then from Munich, in the summer of 1780, came an opera commission, which resulted in the majestic and moving *Idomeneo*, his contribution to widespread endeavours at the time to make *opera seria* more vigorously dramatic, more thrusting in form, more natural and, at the same time, truer to notions of antique grandeur – in a word, more French, in the tradition taken up from Lully and Rameau by Gluck and Piccinni. He spent late autumn and winter in Munich, completing and supervising the opera (which had its première two days after his 25th birthday), and this time he travelled alone.

From Munich he went in March 1781 not back to Salzburg but to Vienna, summoned by the archbishop, who, with other notables, was there to celebrate the accession of Joseph II as emperor. This archbishop, Hieronymus Count Colloredo, is remembered as the man who treated Mozart as his servant (placed at the dinner table above the cooks but below the valets) and who, when the composer asked to be released from his service, had his steward provide a departing kick on the backside. The pain did not last. Mozart had spent less than three months with the archbishop's entourage in Vienna – enough to convince him he could make his own way in the city. He first found lodgings with the Webers. Aloysia was married now, but slowly he fell in love with her younger sister, Constanze, which made it fitting for him to leave the house. Supporting himself as a teacher and performer (he played the violin and viola in chamber music, but preferred the piano for concerts and private parties), he also worked on an opera for the new German-language company Joseph had instituted at the court theatre (*Die Entführung aus dem Serail*, 1781–2) and began his connection with the Viennese music publishing industry (Six Violin Sonatas, Op.2, 1781). When the opera reached the stage, in the summer of 1782, the emperor observed that it contained 'very many notes' – a complaint, in all probability, not about length or vocal virtuosity (of which 18th-century rulers could not get enough) but about complexities of harmony and texture. 'Exactly as many as are necessary,' Mozart is alleged to have replied.

Also that summer, on 4 August, he and Constanze were married, in St Stephen's Cathedral. Soon afterwards he began composing a mass as a thank-offering, but this, the C minor Mass, he failed to finish – not, it would seem, out of any marital misgivings, for his relationship with his wife was evidently both passionate and affectionate. All their difficulties came from a shared inability to handle money, the downside of a shared sense of fun. They went to see Leopold in Salzburg for the summer of 1783, and on the way back Mozart wrote a symphony hurriedly for a concert in Linz. A first child died at two months, but the second, Carl Thomas, throve.

For the moment the new household was buoyed along by the Mozart vogue, for in 1782–5 the composer was intensely in demand as a performer (hence the dozen piano concertos of this period), while publishers in Vienna and Paris brought out his sonatas, some of his concertos and the set of quartets he dedicated to Haydn. These quartets – 'the fruits of long and laborious endeavour,' he called them – testify to the esteem in which he held his senior contemporary: it was highly unusual to dedicate an edition to a colleague, rather than to a noble patron who would have been flattered into providing monetary support. The admiration went both ways. When Leopold visited Vienna in 1785, Haydn confessed as much, affirming that 'your son is the greatest composer known to me', and the story of the string quartet through the next several years is one of a creative conversation between the form's first two supreme practitioners, rivalling, evoking and encouraging one another. At least on occasion they would meet to play quartets. For Haydn, of course, the medium was a native language. For Mozart it was not; he worked more easily with richer arrays of colour (as in the Quintet for piano and wind, the flute and oboe quartets, the 'Kegelstatt' trio and the Clarinet Quintet) or at least with the second viola present in his string quintets. The quartet, as a form, responded to Haydn's endless fascination with reinventing the rudimentary: four-part writing, short triadic themes, a straightforward assignment of equal roles. Mozart required more space, more depth of sound, and more variable hierarchies.

He required, in essence, theatre. After the curious *L'oca del Cairo*, abandoned in 1783, two years passed before he found another libretto, but it was worth the wait, for what he now produced, together with the court poet Da Ponte, was *Le nozze di Figaro* (1785–6). Nothing in his previous output was a preparation for this, unless his piano concertos, with their similar flickering between intensity and self-mockery. (Indeed, his piano concertos – utterly characteristic of his music in how an instrument is made to sing, and to display itself – have much of the form and character of operatic arias in their first and slow movements.) Based on a play by Beaumarchais that had thrilled and scandalized Europe, *Figaro* contains a dangerous edge of satire at the expense of the aristocracy: the Count – forceful, not least in pressing his sexual claims on his servant Susanna – is outwitted by his valet (and her betrothed) Figaro. But Mozart was seemingly untouched by the spirit of the French Revolution. His adherence to freemasonry (from December 1784) was an adherence to the Enlightenment virtues of fraternity and reason, virtues he perhaps expected would refresh, but certainly not overturn, the old system of Catholic, imperial Vienna. Besides, the main values of *Figaro* lie elsewhere than in its politics – in the evoking of a little community, with all its intricate relationships established right away, and in the extraordinary closeness with which the music follows what the characters say, do and mean.

A few months after the première, in the autumn of 1786, Constanze gave birth to a third child, another son who soon died. Then in the new year Mozart went to Prague, where *Figaro* seems to have been an even bigger success than in Vienna, resulting in a commission for a new opera to be produced in the coming autumn. Once back in Vienna he made contact with Da Ponte again, and they began a second collaboration, *Don Giovanni*. This cannot have been very far along when, in the spring of 1787, his father fell ill and died. Whatever feelings he may have had are hard to deduce from the works he was writing at the time: two string quintets (though they include the troubled G minor) and a sequence of songs. He could also keep pieces separate in his mind, for in the summer he was at work simultaneously on *Don Giovanni* and *Eine kleine Nachtmusik*. At the start of October he left for the second time that year to oversee an opera in Prague, where he completed the overture two days before the first performance.

Before the end of 1787 he had gained a position at the Viennese court as chamber musician, which required him to supply dances. In the four years left him he produced over a hundred, remarking on one payslip that the money was 'too much for what I did, too little for what I could do'. What he could do, in 1788, he demonstrated in three symphonies, all grand and sonorous works, but diverse in character and seeming to form a deliberate trilogy: expansive (No.39), driven (No.40) and culminatory (No.41). He also wrote new music for the Vienna revival of *Don Giovanni* and made the first of several adaptations of Handel scores, modernizing the orchestration for performances mounted by Baron van Swieten. In the summer he lost, at six months, his first daughter. And his finances were taking a dive: he sought and received help from a fellow mason, Michael Puchberg, whose reward was the powerfully mistitled 'divertimento' for string trio, one of the composer's most searching chamber works.

Another patron, Prince Karl Lichnowsky, took him on a trip to Berlin in the spring of 1789. He played for the Prussian king, and in the carriage on the way home started writing quartets giving prominence to that monarch's beloved cello. *Figaro* was revived in Vienna in late summer, and he wrote two replacement arias for it, after which his main projects were his Clarinet Quintet and his third opera in partnership with Da Ponte, *Così fan tutte*. A second daughter, in November, did not outlast the day of her birth. The death of the emperor three months later caused an interruption in the *Così* run but also opened opportunities.

Mozart went to Frankfurt in September 1790 for the coronation of Leopold II, and while there played his 'Coronation' concerto. But this was not new, and indeed 1790 was by far his least productive year: he finished his last two (of three) 'Prussian' quartets, arranged more Handel for van Swieten and wrote a string quintet.

In contrast, 1791 was astoundingly fruitful. While working on a German fantasy opera with the impresario Emanuel Schikaneder (*Die Zauberflöte*) he received two important commissions: for the opera to be given in Prague when Leopold was crowned king of Bohemia (*La clemenza di Tito*), and for a *Requiem* to be written secretly for Count Walsegg-Stuppach, who wanted it performed in his late wife's memory as his own composition. Mozart went to Prague for the première of *Tito* (6 September, 'a piece of German piggery' was the Italian-born empress's verdict) and returned to Vienna for that of *Die Zauberflöte* (30 September), in a playhouse outside the city centre, not the court theatre that had seen the premières of *Die Entführung*, *Figaro* and *Così*. To one of the subsequent performances he took his seven-year-old son Carl – among the first of many children to enjoy this universal marriage of philosophy and clown show. (Franz Xaver – his second child to survive, just two months old – remained at home.) Then, with the *Requiem* still in progress, he composed a clarinet concerto and a masonic cantata (*Laut verkünde*).

The *Requiem* remained unfinished. What happened next has, not surprisingly, acquired much myth and misinterpretation. Mozart was not poisoned by his fellow composer Antonio Salieri out of jealousy or anger at God, as proposed in influential works by Pushkin and Peter Shaffer. It seems unlikely that friends gathered to sing with him parts of his *Requiem* as he lay dying, or that he felt doomed by this work, writing it under sentence of death. And it was not unusual for a person of modest rank to be buried in an unmarked grave with no mourners.

The mourning came afterwards, and soon. Constanze, with two young children to support, helped launch her husband's rapidly rising posthumous career by mounting performances in which the *Requiem* (completed by his pupil Süssmayr) and *Tito* took pride of place. She released an edition of *Idomeneo* and sold other works to a publisher. The first biography, by Franz Xaver Niemetschek, came out in 1798. Music that had puzzled emperors and empresses only a decade or so before, and that had been less successful at the Viennese court theatre than that of Cimarosa or Martín y Soler, was coming to exert an immense hold over the emergent bourgeois audience. Had

Mozart lived to be 45, he would have found his music being performed across the western world in the new century. Had he reached 70, he could have heard the first of Beethoven's late quartets. As to what he himself might have been composing by then, imagination reels.

Emily Anderson, ed. *The Letters of Mozart and his Family* (1938, ³1985); H.C. Robbins Landon, ed. *The Mozart Compendium* (1990); Maynard Solomon *Mozart* (1995)

The traditional numbering stems from the first edition of Köchel's catalogue (K) and its appendix (K. Anh.), but the occasional number from the sixth edition (K⁶) has gained currency.

Theatre music

Operas: *Apollo et Hyacinthus* (Rufinus Widl), K.38, f.p. Salzburg, 1767; BASTIEN UND BASTIENNE, K.50, f.p. Vienna, 1768; *La finta semplice* (Marco Coltellini, after Carlo Goldoni), K.51, f.p. Salzburg, 1769; MITRIDATE, RE DI PONTO, K.87, f.p. Milan, 1770; *Ascanio in Alba* (Giuseppe Parini), K.111, f.p. Milan, 1771; *Il sogno di Scipione* (Metastasio), K.126, f.p. Salzburg, 1772; LUCIO SILLA, K.135, f.p. Milan, 1772; *La* FINTA GIARDINIERA, K.196, f.p. Munich, 1775; *Il* RE PASTORE, K.208, f.p. Salzburg, 1775; IDOMENEO, K.366, 1780–81; *Die* ENTFÜHRUNG AUS DEM SERAIL, K.384, 1782; *Le* NOZZE DI FIGARO, K.492, 1786; DON GIOVANNI, K.527, 1787; COSI FAN TUTTE, K.588, 1789–90; *Die* ZAUBERFLÖTE, K.620, 1791; *La* CLEMENZA DI TITO, K.621, 1791

Unfinished operas: ZAIDE, K.344, 1780; *L'oca del Cairo* (Varesco), K.422, 1782; *Lo sposo deluso* (?Giuseppe Petrosellini), K.430, ?1785

Other theatre scores: THAMOS, KÖNIG IN ÄGYPTEN (play with music), K.345, ?1773–9; *Les Petits Riens* (ballet), K. Anh.10, 1778; *Der* SCHAUSPIELDIREKTOR (1-act singspiel), K.486, 1786

Insert numbers for operas: *L'astratto*, 1775–6 (arias K.210, 256); *Le nozze di Dorina*, 1775 (aria K.217); *Il curioso indiscreto*, 1783 (arias K.418–20); *La villanella rapita*, 1785 (quartet K.479, trio K.480); *Le gelosie fortunate*, 1788 (aria K.541); *I due baroni di Rocca Azzurra*, 1789 (aria K.578); *Il burbero di buon core*, 1789 (arias K.582–3); *Der Stein des Weisen*, 1790 (see CATS' DUET)

Arias and songs

Arias (v, orch): 'Si mostra la sorte', K.209, t, 1775; 'Con ossequio' (Petrosellini), K.210, t, 1775; 'Voi avete un cor fedele', K.217, s, 1775; 'Ombra felice' (Giovanni de Gamerra), K.255, a, 1776; 'Clarice cara' (Petrosellini), K.256, t, 1776; 'Ah, lo previdi' (Vittorio Amedeo Cigna-Santi), K.272, s, 1777; 'Alcandro, lo confesso' (Metastasio), K.294, s, 1778; 'Se al labbro', K.295, t, 1778; 'Basta vincesti' (Metastasio), K.486a/K⁶.295a, 1778; 'Popoli di Tessaglia' (Calzabigi), K.316, s, 1778–9; 'Ma che vi fece' (Metastasio), K.368, s, 1779–80; 'Misera! dove son' (Metastasio), K.369, s, 1781; 'A questo seno'

(De Gamerra), K.374, s, 1781; 'Nehmt meinen Dank', K.383, s, 1782; 'Mia speranza adorata' (Gaetano Sertor), K.416, s, 1783;' Vorrei spiegarvi', K.418, s, 1783; 'Non, che non sei capace', K.419, s, 1783; 'Per pietà', K.420, t, 1783; 'Misero! o sogno' (Mazzolà), K.431, t, 1783; 'Così dunque tradisci' (Metastasio), K.432, b, ?1783; CH'IO MI SCORDI DI TE (Varesco), K.505, s, pf obbligato, 1786; 'Alcandro, lo confesso' (Metastasio), K.512, b, 1787; 'Mentre ti lascio' (Duca Sant'Angioli-Morbilli), K.513, b, 1787; 'Bella mia fiamma' (Michele Sarcone), K.528, s, 1787; 'Ah se in ciel' (Metastasio), K.538, s, 1788; 'Ich möchte wohl' (Johann Wilhelm Ludwig Gleim), K.539, b, 1788; 'Un bacio di mano' (?Da Ponte), K.541, b, 1788; 'Alma grande' (Giuseppe Palomba), K.578, s, 1789; 'Chi sa qual sia' (?Da Ponte), K.582, s, 1789; 'Vado, ma dove?' (?Da Ponte), K.583, s, 1789; 'Per questa bella mano', K.612, b, db obbligato, 1791; etc.

Songs (v, pf): 'Abendempfindung' (?Joachim Campe), K.523, 1787; 'Die Alte' (Friedrich von Hagedorn), K.517, 1787; 'An Chloe' (Johann Georg Jacobi), K.524, 1787; 'Dans un bois solitaire' (Antoine Houdar de la Motte), K.308, 1777–8; 'Im Frühlingsanfang' (Christoph Sturm), K.591, 1791; 'Ich würd' auf meinem Pfad '(Johann Timotheus Hermes), K.390, 1781–2; 'Das Kinderspiel' (Christian Adolf Overbeck), K.592, 1791; 'Die kleine Spinnerin', K.531, 1787; 'Komm, liebe Zither', K.351, 1780–81; 'Das Lied der Trennung' (Klamer Eberhard Karl Schmidt), K.519, 1787; 'Als Luise die Briefe' (Gabriele von Baumberg), K.520, 1787; 'Oiseaux, si tous les ans' (Antoine François Claude Ferrand), K.307, 1777–8; 'Sehnsucht nach dem Frühling' (Overbeck), K.590, 1791; 'Sei du mein Trost '(Hermes), K.391, 1781–2; 'Das Traumbild' (Ludwig Hölty), K.530, 1787; 'Das Veilchen' (Goethe), K.476, 1785; 'Die Verschweigung' (Weisse), K.518, 1787; 'Der Zauberer' (Christian Felix Weisse), K.472, 1785; 'Die Zufriedenheit' (Johannes Martin Miller), K.473, 1785; etc. (see Catholic and masonic songs below)

Catholic and masonic music

Requiem: REQUIEM, D minor, K.626, satb soli, ch, orch, 1791

Masses (satb soli, ch, orch): *Missa solemnis* 'Waisenhausmesse', C minor, K.139, 1768; *Missa brevis*, D, K.194, 1774; *Missa brevis* 'SPARROW', K.220, 1775–7; C, K.262, 1775; 'Credo', C, K.257, 1776; *Missa brevis* 'SPAUR', C, K.258, 1775/6; *Missa brevis* 'Organ Solo', C, K.259, 1776; *Missa brevis*, B♭, K.275, ?1777; 'CORONATION', C, K.317, 1779; C, K.337, 1780; C MINOR MASS, K.427, 1782; etc.

Vespers: Vesperae de Dominica, K.321, 1779; Vesperae solennes de confessore, K.339, 1780

Other liturgical settings: *Grabmusik*, K.42, s, b, ch, orch, 1767; *Inter natos mulierum*, K.72, ch, orch, ?1771; *Regina coeli*, K.127, s, ch, orch, 1772; *Ergo interest*, K.143, s, orch, 1772–3; EXSULTATE, JUBILATE, K.165, s, orch, 1773; *Litaniae de venerabili altaris sacramento*, K.243, satb soli, ch, orch, 1776; *Sancta Maria, mater Dei*, K.273, ch, orch, 1777; *Regina coeli*, K.276, satb soli, ch, orch, late 1770s; *Alma Dei creatoris*, K.277, satb soli, ch, orch, by 1781; *Kyrie*, D minor, K.341, ch, orch, ?1780–81; *Ave verum corpus*, K.618, ch, orch, 1791; etc.

Church sonatas (for org, str): No.1, E♭, K.67, 1771–2; No.2, B♭, K.68, 1771–2; No.3, D, K.69, 1771–2; No.4, D, K.144, 1774; No.5, F, K.145, 1774; No.6, B♭, K.212, 1775; No.7, F, K.224, 1779–80; No.8, A, K.225, 1779–80; No.9, G, K.241, 1776; No.10, F, K.245, 1776; No.11, D, K.246 1776; No.12, C, K.263, plus 2 tpt, 1776; No.13, G, K.274, 1777; No.14, C, K.278, plus wind, timp, 1777; No.15, C, K.328, 1779; No.16, C, K.329, plus wind, timp, 1779; No.17, C, K.336, 1780

Oratorios: *La Betulia liberata* (Metastasio), K.118, 1771; DAVIDDE PENITENTE, K.469, 1785

Song: 'O Gottes Lamm', 'Als aus Aegypten', K.343, s, con, ?1787–8

Masonic music: 'Lobgesang auf die feierliche Johannisloge' (Ludwig Friedrich Lenz), K.148, v, pf, 1773; 'Lied zur Gesellenreise' (Joseph Franz von Ratschky), K.468, v, pf, 1785; *Dir, Seele des Weltalls* (Lorenz Leopold Haschka), K.429, t, men's ch, orch, 1785 (unfinished); *Die Maurerfreude* (Franz Petran), K.471, t, men's ch, orch, 1785; MAURERISCHE TRAUERMUSIK, K.477, orch, 1785; 'Die ihr des unermesslichen Weltalls Schöpfer ehrt' (*Kleine deutsche Kantate*; Franz Heinrich Ziegenhagen), K.619, s, pf, 1791; *Laut verkünde unsre Freude* (Schikaneder), K.623, 2t, b, orch, 1791; etc.

Orchestral music

Symphonies (the numbering has been muddled by discoveries and reattributions): No.1, E♭, K.16, 1764–5; No.4, D, K.19, 1765; F, K. Anh.223/K⁶.19a, 1765–6; No.5, B♭, K.22, 1765; No.6, F, K.43, 1767; No.7, D, K.45, 1768; No.7a, G, K. Anh.221/K⁶.45a, 1766; No.55, B♭, K. Anh.214/K⁶.45b, 1768; No.8, D, K.48, 1768; No.9, C, K.73, 1769–70; No.10, G, K.74, 1770; No.42, F, K.75, 1771; No.44, D, K.81, ?1770; No.11, D, K.84, ?1770; No.45, D, K.95, ?1770; No.46, C, K.96, ?1771; No.47, D, K.97, ?1770; D, 1775 (overture and aria from *Il re pastore* and finale K.102); No.12, G, K.110, 1771; No.13, F, K.112, 1771; No.14, A, K.114, 1771; No.48, D, ?1771 (overture to *Ascanio in Alba* and finale K.120); D, 1774–5 (overture to *La finta giardiniera* and finale K.121); No.15, G, K.124, 1772; No.16, C, K.128, 1772; No.17, G, K.129, 1772; No.18, F, K.130, 1772; No.19, E♭, K.132, 1772; No.20, D, K.133, 1772; No.21, A, K.134, 1772; No.22, C, K.162, 1773; No.50, D, 1773–4 (overture to *Il sogno di Scipione* and finale K.163); No.23, D, K.181, 1773; No.24, B♭, K.182, 1773; No.25, G minor, K.183, 1773; No.26, E♭, K.184, 1773; No.28, C, K.200, 1773/4; No.29, A, K.201, 1774; No.30, D, K.202, 1774; D, 1775 (from Serenade K.204); D, 1776 (from 'Haffner' Serenade); No.31 'Paris', D, K.297, 1778; No.32, G, K.318, 1779 (first movement only); No.33, B♭, K.319, 1779; D, 1779 (from 'Posthorn' Serenade); No.34, C, K.338, 1780; No.35 'HAFFNER', D, K.385, 1782; Minuet, C, K.409, 1782; No.36 'LINZ', C, K.425, 1783; No.37, G, K.444, 1783/4

(introduction to symphony by Michael Haydn); No.38 'Prague', D, K.504, 1786; No.39, E♭, K.543, 1788; No.40, G minor, K.550, 1788; No.41 'Jupiter', C, K.551, 1788

Piano concertos: Nos.1–4, F, E♭, D, G, K.37, 39–41, 1767 (after kbd pieces by others); No.2, K.39, 1767; No.3, K.40, 1767; No.4, K.41, 1767; K.107:1–3, D, G, E♭, 1772 (after kbd sonatas by J.C. Bach); No.5, D, K.175, 1773 (new finale, K.382, 1782); No.6, B♭, K.238, 1776; No.8 'Lützow', C, K.246, 1776; No.9 'JEUNEHOMME', E♭, K.271, 1777; No.11, F, K.413, 1782–3; No.12, A, K.414, 1782; No.13, C, K.415, 1782–3; No.14, E♭, K.449, 1784; No.15, B♭, K.450, 1784; No.16, D, K.451, 1784; No.17, G, K.453, 1784; No.18, B♭, K.456, 1784; No.19, F, K.459, 1784; No.20, D minor, K.466, 1785; No.21, C, K.467, 1785; No.22, E♭, K.482, 1785; No.23, A, K.488, 1786; No.24, C minor, K.491, 1786; No.25, C, K.503, 1786; No.26 'CORONATION', D, K.537, 1788; No.27, B♭, K.597, 1791

Double piano concerto: No.10, E♭, K.365, ?1780

Triple piano concerto: No.7, F, K.242 'Lodron', 1776 (also for 2 pf)

Violin concertos: No.1, B♭, K.207, 1773; No.2, D, K.211, 1775; No.3, G, K.216, 1775; No.4, D, K.218, 1775; No.5, A, K.219, 1775 (alternative slow movement, K.261, 1776); Rondo, B♭, K.269, 1776; Rondo, C, K.373, 1781

Woodwind concertos: Bassoon Concerto, B♭, K.191, 1774; Flute Concerto, G, K.313, 1778; Oboe Concerto, C, K.314, 1778; Andante, C, K.315, fl, orch, 1780; Clarinet Concerto, A, K.622, 1791

Horn concertos: No.1, D, K.412, 1791; No.2, E♭, K.417, 1783; No.3, E♭, K.447, ?1787; No.4, E♭, K.495, 1786

Multiple concertos: Concertone, C, K.190, 2 vn, 1774; Sinfonia Concertante, E♭, K.Anh.9/K⁶.297b, ob, cl, hn, bn (probably not authentic, but based on a lost sinfonia concertante for fl, ob, hn, bn, 1778); Concerto, C, K.299, fl, hp, 1778; Concerto, D, K. Anh.20, vn, pf, 1778 (completed by Robert Levin); Sinfonia Concertante, E♭, K.364, vn, va, 1779–80; Sinfonia Concertante, G, 2 fl, 2 ob, 2 bn, 1783 (from 'Posthorn' Serenade)

Divertimentos, serenades and cassations for orchestra: *Gallimathius musicum*, K.32, 1766; Cassation, D, K.100, 1769; Cassation, G, K.63, 1769; Divertimento, E♭, K.113, 1769; Divertimento, D, K.131, 1772; Divertimento, D, K.205, ?1773 (plus March K.290); Serenade, D, K.185, 1773 (plus March K.189); Serenade, D, K.203, 1774 (plus March K.237); Serenade, D, K.204, 1775 (plus March K.215); *Serenata notturna*, D, K.239, 1776; Divertimento, F, K.247, 1776 (plus March K.248); Serenade 'HAFFNER', D, K.250, 1776 (plus March K.249); Divertimento, D, K.251, 1776; Notturno, D, K.286, 4 ens 1776–7; Divertimento, B♭, K.287, 1777; Serenade 'Posthorn', D, K.320, 1779 (plus March K.335); Divertimento, D, K.334, 1779–80 (plus March K.445); *Ein* MUSIKALISCHER SPASS, F, K.522, 1787; *Eine* KLEINE NACHTMUSIK, G, K.525, 1787

Separate marches: K.214, 1775; K.408:1–3, 1782

Dances: 6 German Dances, K.571, 1789; 3 German Dances, K.605, 1791; numerous other German dances, minuets, contredanses

Divertimentos and serenades for wind: Divertimento, B♭, K.186, 1773; Divertimento, E♭, K.166, 1773; Divertimento, F, K.213, 1775; Divertimento, B♭, K.240, 1776; Divertimento, E♭, K.252, 1776; Divertimento, C, K.188, 1776; Divertimento, F, K.253, 1776; Divertimento, B♭, K.270, 1777; Serenade, E♭, K.375, 1781, rev 1782; Serenade, C minor, K.388, 1782/3; Serenade 'Gran Partita', B♭, K.361, 1783–4

Chamber music

String quartets: 'Lodi', G, K.80, 1770; 3 Divertimentos, D, B♭, F, K.136–8, 1772; 6, D, G, C, F, B♭, E♭, K.155–60, 1772–3; 6, F, A, C, E♭, B♭, D minor, K.168–73, 1773; 5 fugues, K.405, 1782 (arr of J.S. Bach); 6 'Haydn', 1782–5 (G, K.387, 1782; D minor, K.421, 1783; E♭, K.428, 1783; B♭, K.458, 1784; A, K.464, 1785; C, K.465, 1785); 'Hoffmeister', D, K.499, 1786; Adagio and Fugue, C minor, K.546, 1788; 3 'Prussian', 1789–90 (D, K.575, 1789; B♭, K.589, 1790; F, K.590, 1790)

String quintets (str qt and va): B♭, K.174, 1773; C minor, K.406, 1788 (from Serenade K.388); C, K.515, 1787; G minor, K.516, 1787; D, K.593, 1790; E♭, K.614, 1791

String duos and trio: 2 Duos, G, B♭, K.423–4, vn, va, 1783; Divertimento, E♭, K.563, str trio, 1788

Piano quartets: G minor, K.478, 1785; E♭, K.493, 1786

Piano trios: Divertimento, B♭, K.254, 1776; G, K.496, 1786; B♭, K.502, 1786; E, K.542, 1788; C, K.548, 1788; G, K.564, 1788

Works for 2–5 instruments with wind: Flute Quartet, D, K.285, 1777; Flute Quartet, G, K.285a, 1778; Duo, B♭, K.292, bn, vc (possibly spurious); Flute Quartet, A, K.298, 1786–7; Oboe Quartet, F, K.370, 1781; Horn Quintet, E♭, K.407, 1782; Quintet, E♭, K.452, pf, ob, cl, hn, bn, 1784; Trio 'KEGELSTATT', E♭, K.498, cl, va, pf, 1786; Allegro, F, K. Anh. 90/K⁶.580b, cl, basset hn, str trio; Allegro, B♭, K. Anh.91/K⁶.516c, cl, str qt; Clarinet Quintet, A, K.581, 1789; Adagio and Rondo, C minor, K.617, armonica, fl, ob, va, vc, 1791

Works for 2–5 wind instruments: Adagio, F, K.410, 2 basset hn, bn, 1782; Adagio, B♭, K.411, 2 cl, 3 basset hn, 1782; 12 Duos, K.487, 2 hn, 1786

Violin sonatas: 6, G, E♭, C, E minor, A, D, K.301–6, 1778; 6, 1778–81 (C, K.296, 1778; B♭, K.378, 1779–80; F, K.376, 1781; F, K.377, 1781; G, K.379, 1781; E♭, K.380, 1781); B♭, K.454, 1784; E♭, K.481, 1785; A, K.526, 1787; F, K.547, 1788; 16 others, 1762–6; 2 sets of variations, K.359–60, 1781

Piano music

Sonatas: 6, C, F, B♭, E♭, G, D, K.279–84, 1775; C, K.309, 1777; A minor, K.310, 1778; D, K.311, 1777; 3, C, A, F, K.330–32, 1781; B♭, K.333, 1783–4; C minor, K.457, 1784; F, K.533, 1788; C, K.545, 1788; B♭, K.570, 1789; D, K.576, 1789

Variations: 'Ah vous dirai-je, maman', K.265, pf, 1781–2; 'Les Hommes pieusement', K.455, pf, 1784; Minuet by Duport, K.573, pf, 1789; etc.

Other solo pieces: Prelude and Fugue, C, K.394, 1782; Capriccio, C, K.395, 1777; Funeral March, C minor, K⁶.453a, 1784; Fantasia, C minor, K.475, 1785; Rondo, D, K.485, 1786; Rondo, F, K.494, 1786; Minuet, D, K.355, ?1786–7; Rondo, A minor, K.511, 1787; Adagio, B minor, K.540, 1788; *Kleine Gigue*, G, K.574, 1789; etc.

Duos: Fugue, C minor, K.426, 1783; Sonata, D, K.448, 1781

Duets: Sonata, C, K⁶.19d, 1765; Sonata, B♭, K.358, 1773–4; Sonata, D, K.381, 1772; Sonata, F, K.497, 1786; Andante and Variations, G, K.501, 1786; Sonata, C, K.521, 1787

Kindred pieces: Adagio, C, K.356, armonica, 1791; Adagio and Allegro, F minor, K.594, mechanical organ, 1790; Fantasia, F minor, K.608, mechanical organ, 1791; Andante, F, K.616, mechanical organ, 1791

Miscellanea

Other works: 5 notturnos, K.346, 436–9, 3 v, wind, 1786; few other ensembles, numerous canons, teaching material

Arrangements of Handel scores: *Acis and Galatea*, K.566, 1788; *Messiah*, K.572, 1789; *Alexander's Feast*, K.591, 1790; Ode for St Cecilia's Day, K.592, 1790

Spurious works: Symphony No.2, K.17, by Leopold Mozart; Symphony No.3, K.18, by C.F. Abel; Symphony 'Odense', K. Anh. 220; TWELFTH MASS, G, K. Anh. 232; Violin Concerto 'Adelaïde', D, K. Anh.294a (see CASADESUS); etc.

(4) (Maria) Constanze (Caecilia Josepha Johanna Aloisia) (b. Zell, 5 Jan 1762; d. Salzburg, 6 Mar 1842). She married Mozart in 1782 and probably sang in a partial performance of his C minor mass the next year. After his death she supported herself and their two sons by arranging performances and publications of his music. She remarried only in 1809, her second husband being a Danish diplomat, Georg Nikolaus Nissen, who retired to write Mozart's biography.

(5) Carl Thomas (b. Vienna, 21 Sep 1784; d. Milan, 31 Oct 1858). Mozart's elder surviving child, who became a civil servant in Milan. In 1842 he and his brother were in Salzburg for the unveiling of the memorial to their father. Neither of them had children, and so the direct line ended with him.

(6) Franz Xaver (Wolfgang) (b. Vienna, 26 Jul 1791; d. Carlsbad, 29 Jul 1844). Mozart's younger surviving child, a pianist-composer who spent most of his adult life in Lemberg/Lviv. He studied with Dušek in Prague and with Hummel, Albrechtsberger and Salieri in Vienna. His works include two piano concertos (C, Op.14, pub 1809; E♭, Op.25, pub 1818), chamber pieces, piano variations, choral music and songs.

Mozart and Salieri. Opera by Rimsky-Korsakov setting Pushkin's 'little tragedy', a dialogue on art between the graceful Mozart (tenor) and the demonic Salieri (baritone), with piano accompaniment. First performance: Moscow, 7 Dec 1898.

Mozart fifths (Ger. *Mozartquinten*). Consecutive fifths arising when a German sixth chord resolves on to the dominant (e.g. A♭–E♭–C–F♯ goes to G–D–B–G). The term, though, is a misnomer, as Mozart would normally decorate such a progression in order to avoid the effect.

Mozartkugel. Confectionery item – a chocolate ball filled with nougat, marzipan and pistachio paste – seemingly invented by the Salzburg café proprietor Paul Fürst in 1890.

mp. Mezzopiano.

Mravinsky, Yevgeny (Aleksandrovich) (b. St Petersburg, 4 Jun 1903; d. Leningrad, 19 Jan 1988). Russian conductor, whose intensive work with the orchestra he directed for half a century, the Leningrad Philharmonic (1938–88), resulted in intense and scrupulously detailed performances. He studied biology at university before training at the Leningrad Conservatory with Vladimir Shcherbachev and Aleksandr Gauk, graduating in 1931. There followed some years at the Kirov, as it was called by the time he left, in 1938, having won the All-Union Conductors' Competition. He gave the first performances of Prokofiev's Symphony No.6 and of Shostakovich's Nos.5, 6, 8 (dedicated to him), 9, 10, 11 and 12 (the last two in their official premières).

m.s. Abbreviation for the It. *mano sinistra* or Fr. *main sinistre* (right hand).

Muck, Carl (b. Darmstadt, 22 Oct 1859; d. Stuttgart, 3 Mar 1940). German conductor, especially esteemed in Wagner and Bruckner. Studies at the universities of Heidelberg and Leipzig led him to a doctorate in 1880. Then, though having no conservatory training, he launched himself as a conductor, rising to principal posts at the opera houses of Prague (1886) and Berlin (1892). He conducted *Parsifal* at Bayreuth regularly from 1901, and had periods with the Boston Symphony (1906–8, 1912–18), as well as at Covent Garden and latterly with the Hamburg Philharmonic (1922–33).

Mudarra, Alonso (b. c.1510; d. Seville, 1 Apr 1580). Spanish vihuelist-composer, author of important music for his instrument and of the earliest pieces explicitly notated for guitar. His *Tres libros de*

musica en cifras para vihuela (1546) probably contain the fruits of his work as a musician at the ducal court in Guadalajara; among the 77 pieces is a *Fantasía que contrahaze la harpa en la manera de Ludovico*, an impression of the royal harpist of Aragon. The books were published when he had just taken office as a canon of Seville Cathedral, where he remained to the end of his life.

Muffat. German organist-composers, father and son, having Scottish ancestry.

(1) **Georg** (baptized Mégève, Savoy, 1 Jun 1653; d. Passau, 23 Feb 1704). A stout hybridizer of styles, he studied with Lully and others in Paris (1663–9), had his Jesuit college and university education in Alsace and Bavaria, and went to Rome (early 1680s), where he took further lessons from Pasquini and encountered Corelli. This Italian excursion came when he was organist and chamber musician to the Salzburg archbishop (from 1678), after which, from 1690, he was chapelmaster to the bishop of Passau. Almost all his surviving music comes in five published volumes: *Armonico tributo* (1682), a set of five sonatas for strings and continuo written under the immediate impression of Corelli's concerti grossi; *Apparatus musico-organisticus* (1690), a book of organ music including 12 toccatas; two collections entitled *Florilegium* (1695, 1698), containing orchestral dance suites in the Lullian mould; and *Ausserlesene Instrumental-Music* (1701), 12 concerti grossi of which some are revisions of those in the 1682 set. Early and late in his career he failed to gain a post at the imperial court in Vienna, but three of his sons did.

(2) **Gottlieb** (baptized Passau, 25 Apr 1690; d. Vienna, 9 Dec 1770). He spent most of his adult life as an organist to the Viennese imperial court (1717–63), to which he had become attached in 1711 as a pupil of Fux. Virtually his entire, substantial output was of organ music: suites and partitas, toccatas and canzonas, capriccios and preludes, ricercares and fugues.

Mühlfeld, Richard (Bernhard Herrmann) (b. Salzungen, 28 Feb 1856; d. Meiningen, 1 Jun 1907). German clarinettist and Brahms's chosen exponent. Born into a musical family, he was principal clarinettist in the Meiningen court orchestra from 1879 to his death. Brahms heard him there in 1891, and wrote for him the Clarinet Trio, Clarinet Quintet and two sonatas.

Muldowney, Dominic (b. Southampton, 19 Jul 1952). British composer, who has learned from Brecht in his projection of music through theatre and concerto form. He studied with Harvey and Birtwistle, and with Rands and Blake at York

University (1970–74), then joined Birtwistle at the National Theatre, and succeeded him there as music director (1981–97). Besides theatre and ballet scores, his works include song cycles and the series of concertos begun with those for piano (1983) and saxophone (1984).

Müller, Iwan (b. Reval/Tallinn, 3 Dec 1786; d. Bückeburg, 4 Feb 1854). German clarinettist-composer, whose studies remain in use. After years as a touring virtuoso he became a court musician in Bückeburg.

Müller, Wenzel (b. Tyrnau/Trnava, 26 Sep 1767; d. Baden, near Vienna, 3 Aug 1835). Austrian composer, mostly of light opera. Taught in his native Moravia by a local schoolmaster and at a monastery, he became a pupil of Dittersdorf in Johannisberg and arrived in Vienna in 1786 as conductor of the Leopoldstadt theatre. He spent most of his life there.

Müller-Siemens, Detlev (b. Hamburg, 30 Jul 1957). German composer, whose path has taken him from dream-like urban imagery (*Under Neonlight I,* chbr orch, 1981) to chaos theory. He studied with Ligeti at the conservatory in Hamburg, from which he graduated at 17, then with Messiaen in Paris. In 1991 he began teaching at the Basle Academy.

Mulliner Book. Collection of mid-16th-century English keyboard music, assembled by Thomas Mulliner (of whom little is known) and including pieces by Blitheman, Redford and Tallis. It rests in the British Library.

Mullova, Viktoria (b. Moscow, 27 Nov 1959). Russian violinist, an intense communicator of the great Romantic concertos. She studied with Leonid Kogan at the Moscow Conservatory, and won a string of international prizes: the Wieniawski (1981), the Sibelius (1981) and the Tchaikovsky (1982). In 1983 she defected to the West.

multiphonics. Multiple notes sounding from a wind instrument. Multiphonics can be obtained by means of unusual fingerings (which allow the air inside the instrument to vibrate in two different ways), by appropriately fashioning the embouchure or by singing into the instrument. They feature prominently in works of the 1960s–80s by such composers as Berio, Boulez and Henze.

multi-piece. Term proposed by the scholar Jonathan Dunsby in 1983 for a collection of miniatures complementing one another. His example was Brahms's Fantasies, Op.116, but the category could also include works by composers from Schumann to Kurtág.

multiple stop. Multiplicity of notes sounding simultaneously on a string instrument. See also DOUBLE STOP; TRIPLE STOP; QUADRUPLE STOP.

multitracking [multitrack recording]. Technique by which recordings are made separately and then combined. Thus, for instance, a pianist may perform a four-hand work, recording the second player's part while listening to the previously recorded first part on headphones.

Mumford, Jeffrey (b. Washington, 22 Jun 1955). US composer of poetic and colourful pieces resembling cloudscapes. He studied at UCSD with Rands and also had lessons with Carter, and has taught at the Washington Conservatory (1989–99) and Oberlin.

Mumma, Gordon (b. Framingham, Mass., 20 Mar 1935). US composer and performer of electronic music. He studied at Ann Arbor, where his connection with Ashley led to the Sonic Arts Union (1966–73), his most celebrated piece of this period being *Hornpipe* (1967), in which he performed on a French horn with a double reed mouthpiece and electronics. Also a composer for Merce Cunningham's company (1966–74), he later taught, notably at UC Santa Cruz (1975–94). He has also written experimental pieces for standard instruments.

Münch [Munch], **Charles** (b. Strasbourg, 26 Sep 1891; d. Richmond, Virginia, 6 Nov 1968). French conductor, a fine exponent not only of French and modern repertories but also of the Austro–German classics. His Alsatian origin may have helped give him that breadth, as may his period as leader of the Gewandhaus orchestra under Furtwängler (1926–33). Trained as a violinist at the Strasbourg Conservatory, where his father taught organ, he successfully set himself up as a conductor in Paris in 1933. Later he was music director of the Boston Symphony (1949–62).

Mundy. English composers and church musicians, father and son.

(1) **William** (b. *c.*1529; d. ?London, ?1591). Head chorister at Westminster Abbey in 1543, he held appointments at various London churches before joining the Chapel Royal in 1564. His output includes many works that may be his son's, but the

big votive antiphons (*Vox Patris caelestis* a 6) are definitely his.

(2) John (b. *c*.1555; d. Windsor, 29 Jun 1630). He was for 40 years organist of St George's Chapel, Windsor, and wrote anthems, songs, keyboard pieces and In Nomines.

Mundry, Isabel (b. Schlüchtern, Hessen, 20 Apr 1963). German composer, whose music poetically evokes a complexity of different temporal streams. She studied in Berlin with Frank Michael Beyer and Gösta Neuwirth (1983–91), and in Frankfurt with Zender (1991–4), reaching international attention with her string quartet *No one* (1994–5). In 2003 she began an opera, *Ein Atemzug – Odyssee*.

Mundstück (Ger.). Mouthpiece.

Munich (München). German city, the capital of Bavaria. Senfl and Lassus worked at the ducal court in the 16th century. The court opera was founded there in the mid-17th century and saw the premières of two Mozart works: *La finta giardiniera* (1775) and *Idomeneo* (1781). Almost a century later King Ludwig II imported Wagner's works, including *Tristan*, *Die Meistersinger*, *Das Rheingold* and *Die Walküre* in their first performances. During this period the city also became a centre of music education: the principal conservatory was founded as the Royal Music School (1846) and was known as the Music Academy (1892–1946). The opera, now known as the Munich Staatsoper, had its theatre rebuilt after the Second World War. Of orchestras, the Munich Philharmonic (founded in 1924) has been directed by Rosbaud, Kempe and Levine, the Bavarian Radio Symphony (founded in 1945) by Jochum, Kubelík, Colin Davis, Maazel and Jansons.

Munrow, David (John) (b. Birmingham, 12 Aug 1942; d. Chesham Bois, 15 May 1976). British musician, an energetic and versatile wind instrumentalist who, as the motivating spirit of the Early Music Consort (1967–76), was a leading player in the revival of music from the 12th–17th centuries. He spent a year in South America, and came back impressed by folk performance, before his Cambridge studies (1961–4). His brilliant personality was extinguished by suicide.

Muradeli, Vano (Ilich) (b. Gori, 6 Apr 1908; d. Tomsk, 17 Aug 1970). Georgian composer, whose opera *The Great Friendship* (f.p. Perm, 1947) sparked the 1948 official censure of such mightier creative figures as Shostakovich and Prokofiev. He studied at the conservatories of Tbilisi and, with

Shekhter and Myaskovsky (another to feel the heat in 1948), Moscow.

Murail, Tristan (b. Le Havre, 11 Mar 1947). French composer, associated particularly with the spectral movement. Only after studies of Arabic and politics did he enter the Conservatoire, in 1967, to learn from Messiaen. The Prix de Rome took him to the Italian capital (1971–3), where he encountered Scelsi. Back in Paris, he was a founder member of the group L'Itinéraire, performing on keyboards. He also taught at the Conservatoire and at IRCAM before taking an appointment at Columbia, New York, in 1997. His large output is predominantly of instrumental music, from solos to orchestral pieces.

muses. Tutelary deities of the arts and sciences in ancient Greece. According to Hesiod (8th century BC) they were the daughters of Mnemosyne (Memory) and were nine in number: CALLIOPE, CLIO, ERATO, EUTERPE, MELPOMENE, POLYHYMNIA, TERPSICHORE, THALIA and URANIA.

Muset, Colin (*fl. c*.1200–50). Trouvère, probably also a jongleur, to go by the references to instruments in his songs and by their folk-like style (e.g. *En mai, quant il rossignolet*).

musette. (1) Small bagpipe, which enjoyed a vogue in high culture in France in the 17th century and, particularly, the first half of the 18th century. It appeared in chamber music, as a concerto soloist, and in the theatre orchestras of Lully and Rameau.

(2) Dance suggestive of the instrument, having a drone and often a wistful pastoral character. There are examples not only by French 18th-century composers but also by Handel (*Alcina*), Bach (English Suite No.3), Mozart (*Bastien und Bastienne*) and indeed Schoenberg (Suite Op.25).

(3) Fr. term for a button accordion.

Musgrave, Thea (b. Barnton, Midlothian, 27 May 1928). Scottish composer, especially of music in which instruments become characters and players sometimes actors. She studied with Gál at Edinburgh University, with Boulanger in Paris (1949–54) and in the USA. In 1959 she became an extramural lecturer at London University, and her music entered its most radical phase. Notable works include her Concerto for Orchestra (1967) and concertos for clarinet (1968), horn (1971) and viola (1973), in all of which performers are required to stand up or move around in execution of musical combats. The Viola Concerto was written for her husband, Peter Mark, who became artistic director of the Virginia Opera Association in 1975, and with whom she moved to Norfolk, Virginia. There she has gone on writing dramatic and poetic instrumental works (*Narcissus* for flute and digital delay, 1987) while adding to an operatic output that includes *The Decision* (f.p. London, 1967), *The Voice of Ariadne* (f.p. Snape, 1974), *Mary, Queen of Scots* (f.p. Edinburgh, 1977), *A Christmas Carol* (f.p. Norfolk, 1979), *Harriet, the Woman Called Moses* (f.p. Norfolk, 1985) and *Simón Bolívar* (f.p. Norfolk, 1995).

music. The subject of this book, and of very much more besides. The term derives from the Gk *mousikē*, by way of Lat. *musica* and Fr. *musique*. Originally it designated everything the muses superintend, but by the time it arrived in Eng. in the 13th century it meant the art of sound and time. The same word has been borrowed by many other languages, suggesting a previous lack of such a general term, even in highly musical cultures, such as that of Indonesia.

The term's inclusiveness, though, has changed and been contended. With the idea of music goes the idea of not-music, which for most people in modern Western cultures would embrace sounds heard in the street or kitchen – though many might want to include birdsongs as music, and perhaps also the sounds of waves or of the wind through trees. Equally, some people's music may be not-music to others.

If any definition has to be determined, therefore, not by the thing itself but by an attitude to it (listening with pleasure or interest), Berio's is the best: 'Music is what someone listens to with the intention of listening to music.' Music as a noun vanishes in the circularity of this definition. It is not a particular repertory or set of repertories (though with qualification it may be such, as in 'Beethoven's music', or 'Indonesian music', or indeed 'my music'). It is almost a verb: a way of listening, a way of life.

musica da camera (It.). Chamber music.

Musica Elettronica Viva. Live electronic ensemble founded in Rome in 1966 by US musicians including Rzewski, performing until 1970.

Musica enchiriadis. 9th-century treatise, which, with the associated *Scolica enchiriadis*, includes the earliest melodies that can be read – chants in DASIAN NOTATION – and information about early organum. The title, not original, probably means 'music handbook'.

musica ficta (Lat., false music). Practice of flattening or sharpening notated pitches in polyphony of the 12th–16th centuries in order to regularize chords or cadences whose notation had been constrained by the system of hexachords upholding *musica recta*. Scholars and performers dispute where such alterations are desirable.

musica figurata (Lat.). Renaissance term for FIGURAL polyphony.

musical. (1) As a noun, a modern popular theatrical entertainment with songs and continuous narrative, the term being an abbreviation of 'musical comedy'. The form, associated particularly with New York and London, had origins in the 1890s, but the first lasting example was *Show Boat* (1927), with music by Jerome Kern and 'book' (playscript) and lyrics by Oscar Hammerstein II. These two verbal components are often distinguished thus, and may be supplied by different writers or even by the composer, as in the case of Frank Loesser's *Guys and Dolls* (1950). Other works from the classic period of the Broadway musical – whose termini are widely considered *Oklahoma!* (1943) and *The Sound of Music* (1960), both by Rodgers and Hammerstein – include the same team's *Carousel* (1945), *South Pacific* (1949) and *The King and I* (1951), Cole Porter's *Kiss Me, Kate* (1948), Loewe's *My Fair Lady* (1956) and Bernstein's *West Side Story* (1957).

(2) As an adjective, possessing a feeling for music, a responsiveness to musical form and expression. This is not the same as talent: a virtuoso pianist may be unmusical and a totally untrained listener highly musical – probably because of innate tastes and aptitudes, though these can certainly be developed.

musical box. Mechanical instrument in which tunes are encoded on rotating drums with projecting pins, the drums normally powered by wind-up mechanisms and the pins generally striking the prongs of a comb to sound the desired notes. Musical boxes have been produced as novelty items since the late 18th century, especially in Switzerland, and have occasionally become a creative tool, whether as a point of departure (Davies's *Eight Songs for a Mad King*, sparked off by the organ-type musical box with which George III tried to train singing birds) or as a sounding resource (Stockhausen's *Tierkreis*).

musical clock. See CLOCK.

musical comedy. See MUSICAL (1).

musical glasses. See ARMONICA.

musicality. Quality of being musical.

Musical Joke, A. See *Ein* MUSIKALISCHER SPASS.

Musical Offering, The. See *Das* MUSIKALISCHE OPFER.

Musica Nova. Contemporary music festival held every two or three years in Glasgow from 1971 to 1990, revived in 2004.

musica reservata (Lat., reserved music). Late Renaissance term of mutable meaning. In some sources it indicates music strongly and expressively bound to the words; in others, it seems to involve matters of rhythm or performance.

Musica Viva. Annual contemporary music festival in Munich, founded by K.A. Hartmann in 1946.

music box. See MUSICAL BOX.

music drama. Term associated with Wagner's *Ring*, *Tristan* and *Parsifal*, and with other works in which 'operatic' elements (distinct arias, closed scenes) are subordinated to a continuous theatrical narrative, especially one having a mythic dimension.

Music for His Majesty's Sackbuts and Cornetts. Pair of suites by Locke, 'five part tthings for His Majestys Sagbutts and Cornetts'.

Music for Strings, Percussion and Celesta (*Musik für Saiteninstrumente, Schlagzeug und Celesta*). Work by Bartók for antiphonal string orchestras and a percussion group that includes – in addition to the celesta – piano, harp, xylophone, timpani and untuned instruments. A single theme runs through the four movements, which follow a slow–fast–slow–fast pattern. First performance: Basle, 21 Jan 1937.

Music for the Royal Fireworks. Suite by Handel, made to accompany a pyrotechnic display in Green Park to celebrate the Peace of Aix-la-Chapelle (1748): 1 Overture, 2 Bourrée, 3 La Paix, 4 La Réjouissance, 5 Menuet. The music was originally played by a wind band (24 ob, 12 bn, 9 tpt, 9 hn, 3 timp), possibly with strings. First performance: London, 27 Apr 1749.

Musici, I. String ensemble formed in 1952 by 12 students at the Accademia di Santa Cecilia, and continuing through changes of membership.

musician. Musical practitioner; normally an instrumentalist is meant.

Musicians Benevolent Fund. British charity founded in 1921 by the voice teacher Victor Beigel, caring for elderly and sick musicians.

Musicians' Union. British trade union founded in 1921 by the merging of two unions going back to the early 1890s.

Music Library Association. US institution founded in 1931 to provide services to music libraries, including the publication of the quarterly *Notes*.

musico (It.). Musician, especially a castrato in the 17th and 18th centuries.

Music of Changes. Piano work by Cage, early classic of chance operations, in four books, composed for and dedicated to Tudor. First performance: Boulder, Col., Aug 1951 (Book I); New York, 1 Jan 1952 (complete).

music of the spheres. Harmony present in the motions of heavenly bodies and in their distances from the sun, which was central in ancient cosmologies. Of Mesopotamian origin, the idea was known to Jews and Greeks. Plato, in *The Republic*, imagined a siren in each ring of the heavens, and some later writers proposed that the sirens' celestial song resounded throughout the universe. People on earth, living with it constantly, remained oblivious.

musicology. The scholarly study of music, embracing matters of history, theory, analysis, editing and textual criticism. Most musicologists teach at universities, training their successors, though some work as archivists or librarians.

Music Sales. Music publishing firm founded in 1935. Its acquisitions of G. Schirmer, Chester, Novello and other companies in the 1980s made it a leading force in classical music.

music stand. Item essential for all but keyboard performers: a contraption of wood or metal, adjustable in height to hold the music where it can be read.

music theatre. (1) Term introduced by Felsenstein for a kind of opera production in which the drama of character, situation and social setting is foremost.

(2) Small-scale musical-theatrical work, intentionally divorced from the traditions of opera. It had its brief heyday from the mid-1960s to the early 1970s, when pieces of this kind were created

by Berio (*Laborintus II*), Birtwistle (*Down by the Greenwood Side*), Davies (*Eight Songs for a Mad King*), Henze, Kagel and others, and when earlier examples were recognized in works by Stravinsky (*Renard, Histoire du soldat*), Schoenberg (*Pierrot lunaire*), Falla, Weill and even Monteverdi (*Il combattimento*). It faltered when regular opera companies became more open to new work, and composers more open to tradition.

music therapy. The use of sound and music in healing, either directly as a way of effecting physical or psychological change, or as a means of inducing a curative atmosphere. Music therapy has ancient roots all over the world, but has gained respect within Western medicine only since the 1950s.

Musikalien (Ger.). A music shop's stock: sheet music, music books, ephemera.

Musikalische Exequien (Musical Exequies). Lutheran funeral music by Schütz, written for the interment of Heinrich Posthumus of Reuss (1572–1635), in whose domains the composer had been born. Set for nine voices and continuo, the work comprises a funeral mass, a motet and a *Nunc dimittis*, all in German.

musikalische Opfer, Das (The Musical Offering). Work by J.S. Bach, based on a theme with a descending chromatic scale fragment that Frederick II gave him as a challenge. He is said to have improvised the three-part ricercare on the spot, then added the six-part ricercare, 10 canons and a trio sonata. The sonata is laid out for flute, violin and continuo, but the instrumentation of the other items is not specified. They have been realized by keyboard players, chamber groups and orchestral conductors (including Webern in the case of the six-part ricercare).

musikalischer Spass, Ein (A Musical Joke). Divertimento by Mozart full of deliberate awkwardness and ineptitude.

Musikant, Musikantin (Ger.). Musician, normally of a lowlier sort.

Musiker, Musikerin (Ger.). Musician.

Musikforschung, Musikwissenschaft (Ger.). Musicology.

Musiklehre, Musikunterricht (Ger.). Music education.

musique concrète (Fr., concrete music). Term introduced by Schaeffer in 1948 for music made with concrete sounds, i.e. from recordings, and still used for this technique and its products. Varèse's *Poème électronique* is an example. Lachenmann coined the term 'instrumental *musique concrète*' for his use of non-standard sounds on conventional instruments.

musique de chambre (Fr.). Chamber music.

musique mesurée (à l'antique) (Fr., music in ancient measures). Music following the rhythmic patterns of late-16th-century French verse based on classical metres, normally with double values for long syllables. The brief vogue was led by the poet Jean-Antoine de Baïf and the composer Le Jeune.

Musique Vivante. Paris ensemble, founded by the conductor Diego Masson in 1966.

Musorgsky, Modest Petrovich (b. Karevo, Pskov district, 21 Mar 1839; d. St Petersburg, 28 Mar 1881). Russian composer, one of music's few great realists in his preference for truth over beauty. Though he became impatient not only with musical convention but with his own care, he achieved masterpieces of characterization in the genres of opera (*Boris Godunov*), piano showpiece (*Pictures at an Exhibition*) and song cycle.

Born into the landed gentry and schooled accordingly (in St Petersburg from 1849), he took to the piano and composition as gentlemanly pursuits and ways to entertain fellow students. That attitude began to change when, through Dargomyzhsky and Cui, he met Balakirev, from whom he began taking lessons in December 1857. Six months later he resigned his army commission to concentrate on music, though for several years he wrote little more than exercises and salon miniatures, while proceeding through what seems to have been a difficult late adolescence. His encounter with ancient Russia, on a first visit to Moscow in 1859, provided a stimulus. Though he learned from Verdi, the great cosmopolitan, his effort increasingly was to create works grounded in the history, language and folklore of his own country.

In 1863 the family's financial situation forced him into the civil service, and he moved into a communal apartment in St Petersburg until 1865, when he joined his brother's household. He began larger projects: an opera on Flaubert's *Salammbô*, which he abandoned, and the tone poem *Night on the Bare Mountain*. Completed in 1867, this vibrant essay in the musical macabre marked his creative coming of age, and Balakirev's criticisms caused a rift. Meanwhile he was learning realism from Dargomyzhsky, setting words as heightened speech. That pursuit, together with his emerging gifts for character and irony, supported his essay in recitative opera, *Marriage* (1868), and songs of the same period, culminating in the cycle *The Nursery*.

Setting *Marriage* aside (and also setting marriage aside, for he moved in with friends again as his civil service career advanced), he moved on to Pushkin's historical play *Boris Godunov*, which became the only opera he completed. Indeed, he completed it twice, for when it was turned down by the Mariinsky on the grounds that it lacked a major female role, he made a new version. The first *Boris* (1868–9) is a magnificent balance of realism with Russian melody and a decisive study of the central character; the second (1871–2) broadens the view and adds some striking scenes as well as some Romantic amplitude.

He immediately started another historical opera, with a larger sweep from the beginning and to his own libretto: *Khovanshchina*. In the summer of 1874, though, he turned to a Ukrainian village comedy, *Sorochintsy Fair*, and wrote *Pictures at an Exhibition* and the song cycle *Sunless*, to poems by Arseny Golenishchev-Kutuzov, a young relative with whom he briefly shared an apartment. Around this time, too, youthful problems of neurosis and drinking began to recur. Henceforth he alternated between *Khovanshchina* and *Sorochintsy Fair*, of which he almost completed the former, except for the orchestration. Friends continued to provide support, including the singer Darya Leonova, whom he accompanied in 1879 on tour and later in St Petersburg. But his drinking was getting the better of him.

Rimsky-Korsakov not only finished *Khovanshchina* but well-meaningly revised most of the other major works, on the grounds of technical deficiency. But gradually through the 20th century the composer's own bold harmony (often coming from his use of modes characteristic of Russian folksong) and stark orchestration came to be valued as the marks of an original.

Richard Taruskin *Musorgsky* (1992)

Operas: *Salammbô* (Musorgsky, after Flaubert), 1863–6, unfinished; MARRIAGE, 1868, unfinished; BORIS GODUNOV, 1868–9, rev 1871–2; MLADA, 1872 (items for Acts 2–3); KHOVANSHCHINA, 1872–80, unfinished; SOROCHINTSY FAIR, 1874–80, unfinished
Other large-scale works: NIGHT ON THE BARE MOUNTAIN, 1866–7; choral and orch pieces
Song sets: *The* NURSERY, 1868–72; SUNLESS, 1874; SONGS AND DANCES OF DEATH, 1875–7
Individual songs (those obelisked orchestrated by the composer): 'Darling Savishna' (Musorgsky), 1866; 'Hopak' (Lev Mey, after Shevchenko), 1866[†]; 'King Saul' (Pavel Kozlov, after Byron), 1863, rev 1866–71; 'Lullaby' (Ostrovsky), 1865; 'The Magpie' (Pushkin), 1867; 'Mephistopheles's Song in Auerbach's Cellar' (Aleksandr Strugovshchikov, after Goethe), 1879; 'Night' (after Pushkin), 1864[†], rev 1868–71; 'The Ragamuffin' (Musorgsky), 1867; 'Where art thou, little star?' (Nikolay Grekov), 1857[†], rev 1863–6; 'The Wild Winds Blow' (Aleksey Koltsov), 1864; etc.
Piano: Scherzo, B♭, 1858, also orch; PICTURES AT AN EXHIBITION, 1874; *On the Southern Shore of the Crimea*, 1879; *Une larme*, 1880; etc.

muta (It.). Change, as in *muta in si♭* (change to the instrument in B♭).

mutation. Organ stop sounding a note different from that of the key, normally used in groups to parallel the sound of a mixture stop.

mute. Contrivance applied to an instrument to muffle the sound.

String mutes are clamps attached to the bridge, made of metal, wood or other material, generally with three prongs. They were known to Mersenne, and first specified in scores by Lully and Purcell.

Brass mutes include the STRAIGHT MUTE, PRACTICE MUTE, CUP MUTE, HARMON MUTE and others. Their use was vastly encouraged by jazz. Brass and woodwind players can also mute their instruments with a hand or cloth placed in the bell.

Keyboard instruments have had various kinds of muting devices, including the BUFF STOP and UNA CORDA pedal, as well as the ad hoc mutes used to create the PREPARED PIANO. Harps, timpani and percussion instruments can be muted by a hand or cloth.

Muti, Riccardo (b. Naples, 28 Jul 1941). Italian conductor, of supreme command. He studied at the Naples and Milan conservatories, taking composition with Rota and Bruno Bettinelli and conducting with Antonio Votti. His debut (RAI orchestra, 1967) was rapidly followed by principal appointments in Florence at the Maggio Musicale (1968) and the opera (1969), and by appearances with the Philadelphia Orchestra, New Philharmonia and Berlin Philharmonic (all 1972). He then became music director of the Philharmonia (1973–82), the Philadelphia Orchestra (1980–92) and La Scala (from 1986).

Mutter, Anne Sophie (b. Rheinfelden, 29 Jun 1963). German violinist, of strong presence. She studied with Erna Honigberger and Aïda Stucki, and began her career at 13 as a protégée of Karajan. Rapidly launched then on an international career, she has tended to concentrate on a particular area of the repertory each season, besides introducing new works by Lutosławski, Rihm, Penderecki and others. In 2002 she married Previn.

muzak. Piped music intended to provide a soothing background. The word comes from the name of the company founded by General George Squier in the early 1920s, a name he formed by analogy with Kodak. Early clients included department stores, wishing to allay the anxieties of customers travelling in lifts; hence the alternative term 'elevator music'.

Myaskovsky, Nikolay Yakovlevich (b. Novo-Georgiyevsk/Modlin, Poland, 20 Apr 1881; d. Moscow, 8 Aug 1950). Russian composer, especially of symphonies charting a generally introspective extension of Russian late Romanticism. The son of a military engineer, he had a military education, but music was important to him from an early age and belatedly he studied at the St Petersburg Conservatory with Lyadov, Rimsky-Korsakov and Jazeps Vītols (1906–11). He served at the front during the First World War, then in 1921 began teaching at the Moscow Conservatory. Thenceforth his career was that of an honoured composer and professor, though he was among those criticized for formalism in 1948.

Symphonies: No.1, C minor, Op.3, 1908; No.2, C♯ minor, Op.11, 1910–11; No.3, A minor, Op.15, 1914; No.4, E minor, Op.17, 1917–18; No.5, D, Op.18, 1918; No.6, E♭ minor, Op.23, 1922–3; No.7, B minor, Op.24, 1922; No.8, A, Op.26, 1924–5; No.9, E minor, Op.28, 1926–7; No.10, F minor, Op.30, 1927; No.11, B♭ minor, Op.34, 1931–2; No.12, G minor, Op.35, 1931–2; No.13, B♭ minor, Op.36, 1933; No.14, C, Op.37, 1933; No.15, D minor, Op.38, 1933–4; No.16, F, Op.39, 1935–6; No.17, G♯ minor, Op.41, 1936–7; No.18, C, Op.42, 1937; No.19, E♭, Op.46, band, 1939; No.20, E, Op.50, 1940; No.21, F♯ minor, Op.51, 1940; No.22, B minor, Op.54, 1941; No.23, A minor, Op.56, 1941; No.24, F minor, Op.63, 1943; No.25, D♭, Op.69, 1946; No.26, C, Op.79, 1948; No.27, C minor, Op.85, 1949–50

Other works: 13 string quartets, 9 piano sonatas, other orch pieces, etc.

Mysliveček, Josef (b. Prague, 9 Mar 1737; d. Rome, 4 Feb 1781). Czech composer, who became one of the leading founts of opera seria and oratorio in Italy. He and his twin brother joined their father's profession as millers, but in his mid 20s he turned to music, taking lessons in Prague and Italy with support from his brother and others. Their confidence was rewarded by the success of *Il Bellerofonte* (f.p. Naples, 1767), followed by 25 more serious operas in the next 14 years, most of them to librettos by Metastasio, though the later ones incorporated aspects of reform. He also wrote oratorios (*Isacco figura del redentore*, f.p. Florence, 1776), symphonies, concertos, three wind octets and other chamber music. In the 1770s he was in touch with the Mozart family, whose letters are the source for the myth of the composer-rake celebrated in Stanislav Suda's opera *Il divino boemo* (1912). Mozart was once thought to have arranged an aria of his as a canzonetta, 'Ridente la calma', K.152.

Mystery Sonatas [Rosary Sonatas]. Set of 15 sonatas for violin and continuo by Biber for the mysteries of the rosary – the joyful (1 *The Annunciation*, 2 *The Visitation*, 3 *The Nativity*, 4 *The Presentation*, 5 *The Finding in the Temple*), the sorrowful (6 *The Agony in the Garden*, 7 *The Scourging of Jesus*, 8 *The Crowning of Jesus with Thorns*, 9 *Jesus Carries his Cross*, 10 *The Crucifixion*) and the luminous (11 *The Resurrection*, 12 *The Ascension*, 13 *The Descent of the Holy Ghost*, 14 *The Assumption of Our Lady*, 15 *The Coronation of the Blessed Virgin Mary*) – plus a final passacaglia.

Nabokov, Nicolas [Nikolay] (b. Lyubcha, Novogrudok, near Minsk, 17 Apr 1903; d. New York, 6 Apr 1978). Russian–US composer, animator of prestigious festivals and memoirist. A cousin of the novelist Vladimir Nabokov, he studied in Russia with Rebikov (1913–20), in Stuttgart (1920–22) and in Berlin with Juon and Busoni (1922–4). Diaghilev commissioned his ballet-oratorio *Ode: méditation sur la majesté de Dieu* (1928); his later works include further ballets, orchestral works and operas based on Rasputin (*The Holy Devil*, f.p. Louisville, 1958) and Shakespeare's *Love's Labour's Lost* (f.p. Brussels, 1973, libretto by Auden and Kallman). In 1939 he became a US citizen, but he was active internationally as a festival organizer and associate of the great (including Stravinsky).

Nabucco. Opera by Verdi, originally called *Nabucodonosor*, to a libretto by Solera. Hostility between the title character (baritone), king of Babylon, and his Jewish captives, led by the prophet Zaccaria (bass), is resolved when he accepts their faith. Resolution comes also to a love triangle involving Ishmael (tenor), the Babylonian princess Fenena (soprano) and her formidable rival Abigaille (soprano). Notable numbers include prayers for Zaccaria ('Vieni, o Levita') and Nabucco ('Dio di Giuda'), Abigaille's 'Ben io t'invenni – Anch'io dischiuso un giorno', and, most celebrated of all, the sturdy chorus of Hebrew slaves 'Va pensiero'. First performance: Milan, 9 Mar 1842.

Nachlass (Ger.). What an artist leaves behind unpublished.

Nachschlag (Ger., afterstroke). Ornament in Austro–German music of the 18th and early 19th centuries, a variety of appoggiatura.

Nachtanz (Ger., afterdance). The second in a pair of dances from the 14th–17th centuries.

Nachtigall (Ger., nightingale). Organ stop imitating the bird.

Nachtmusik, Nachtstück (Ger.). Nocturne.

Nagano, Kent (George) (b. Morro Bay, Cal., 22 Nov 1951). US conductor, who is noted for his luminous clarity and keen appreciation of 20th-century music, Messiaen especially. He studied at UC Santa Cruz, with Laszlo Varga at San Francisco State University (1974–6) and at the University of Toronto (1977–9). In 1978 he began his career with the Berkeley Symphony, to which he has remained faithful while accepting appointments with the Lyons Opera (1989–98), the Hallé (1991–2000), the Deutsches Sinfonieorchester (from 2000), the Los Angeles Opera (from 2001), the Montreal Symphony (from 2006) and the Bavarian State Opera (from 2006).

nakers. Small, portable kettledrums played in pairs, introduced to Europe at the time of the crusades.

Namensfeier (Name-day). Overture by Beethoven, so called because he completed it in 1814 on the name-day of the emperor (St Francis's day, 4 Oct). First performance: Vienna, 25 Dec 1815.

Namouna. Ballet score by Lalo, to a scenario after

Alfred de Musset's oriental tale, also the source of Bizet's *Djamileh*. Debussy admired the music, from which the composer drew two suites. First performance: Paris, 6 Mar 1882.

Nancarrow, (Samuel) Conlon (b. Texarkana, Ariz., 27 Oct 1912; d. Mexico City, 10 Aug 1997). US composer, resident from 1940 in Mexico City, where he devoted himself to fascinating and entertaining counterpoint using the rhythmic precision and mechanical oddity of the pianola. He studied at Cincinnati College Conservatory (1929–32), fought in the Spanish Civil War and moved to Mexico City in response to anti-communist feeling in the US. In 1947 he returned briefly to New York to buy a pianola, and from then on he composed exclusively for that instrument until the 1980s, when growing interest in his music, not least from performers, led him to return to the regular piano and chamber media of his youth (String Quartet No.3, 1987; Two Canons for Ursula, pf, 1989). His 51 numbered 'studies for player piano' feature canons with voices at different speeds, simultaneous accelerandos and ritardandos, and a sense of music as process. Some use a jazz vocabulary, others are abstract. Their influence has been acknowledged by composers from Ligeti to Adès.

Kyle Gann *The Music of Conlon Nancarrow* (1995)

Nanino, Giovanni Maria (b. Tivoli, 1543/4; d. Rome, 11 Mar 1607). Italian composer, a follower of Palestrina, whose tradition he conveyed to the Allegri brothers, Felice Anerio and many others. He may have studied with (and succeeded) Palestrina at Santa Maria Maggiore; from 1575 he was associated with San Luigi dei Francesi and from 1577 with the papal choir. His works include madrigals as well as motets, as did those of his brother Giovanni Bernardino (*c.*1560–1618), who also spent his career in Rome.

Naples (Napoli). Italian city. It was a major centre of music education in the 17th–18th centuries, boasting four conservatories: those of Santa Maria di Loreto (founded 1537), Santa Maria della Pietà dei Turchini (1583), the Poveri di Gesù Cristo (1599) and San Onofrio (early 17th century). The prestige of Alessandro Scarlatti helped to make the city an opera factory, with distinguished teachers at the conservatories – Provenzale, Porpora, Durante, Feo and Leo – training composers including Vinci, Pergolesi, Jommelli, Traetta, Piccinni, Paisiello, Cimarosa and Spontini, as well as hosts of singers. The chief product was opera seria, though Neapolitan composers also took a lead in developing the comic tradition. As for performance, the Teatro San Carlo was opened as the principal opera house in 1737 and remained a leading force in Italian opera into the 20th century, even though composers were now being schooled in the north. The conservatories were amalgamated in 1807. In the late 19th century and early 20th there flourished a tradition of popular Neapolitan song, whose practitioners included Denza, Tosti and Pasquale Mario Costa.

Nápravník, Eduard (b. Býšť, near Hradec Králové, 24 Aug 1839; d. Petrograd, 23 Nov 1916). Czech–Russian conductor, chief at the Mariinsky from 1869. He studied in Prague and went to St Petersburg in 1861. A thorough professional, he conducted the first performances of operas by Musorgsky, Rimsky-Korsakov and Tchaikovsky, as well as his own *Harold* (1886, on the Norman conquest of England) and *Dubrovsky* (1895, to a libretto by Modest Tchaikovsky after Pushkin).

Nardini, Pietro (b. Leghorn, 12 Apr 1722; d. Florence, 7 May 1793). Italian violinist-composer, famed especially for his cantabile. He studied with Tartini in Padua from 1734 and became a touring virtuoso, continuing to travel after settling at the Florentine court in 1768. His works include concertos and sonatas.

narrative. The idea of music as story, independent of words, is an old one. It was essential to PROGRAMME MUSIC as expounded by composers from Berlioz and Liszt to Strauss and Stravinsky. More generally, emerging perhaps from the application of principles from RHETORIC, it underlay the development of tonality from the 17th century to the 20th, whereby matters of continuity, directedness, surprise and resolution became crucial. On another level, music history and biography are narrative expressions. Students of narratology are concerned with these questions, as also with the nature in music of the narrating voice or voices. If music is story, who sings it?

Nasard. Kind of organ stop especially typical of French instruments.

Nash Ensemble. London ensemble founded by Amelia Freedman in 1964 to perform classic and modern pieces for mixed chamber groups.

Nathan, Isaac (b. Canterbury, 1790; d. Sydney, 15 Jan 1863). British–Australian composer, a pioneer of European music in Australia. He studied at Cambridge and with Corri in London, and supplied settings for Byron's *Hebrew Melodies*. Involvements in the theatre and at court did not save him from ruin, whereupon, in 1841, he emigrated, to write patriotic songs and the first

Australian opera (*Merry Freaks in Troublous Times*, 1843). His descendant Harry Nathan (1866–1906) is one candidate for the composer of *Waltzing Matilda*.

national anthem. Song or tune adopted by a country as its musical ensign. GOD SAVE THE QUEEN/KING took on that purpose for the United Kingdom from 1745 onwards; other 18th-century examples include La MARSEILLAISE and the imperial hymn Haydn wrote for Austria (see EMPEROR; this anthem was dropped by Austria on the fall of the monarchy in 1917, and in 1922 the tune was adopted by Germany). Other composers to have written anthems include Aleksandrov, Carnicer, Kienzl, Lavallée. See also HYMNEN; STAR-SPANGLED BANNER.

National Federation of Music Societies. British organization founded by Dyson in 1935 to support amateur orchestras, choirs and music clubs.

nationalism. Term denoting, in musical contexts, the presence of traits that can be identified as deliberately expressing the composer's national affiliation. This often involves gestures both positive and negative – positive in projecting national material (of language, folklore, history, myth or landscape) and negative in avoiding or undermining the norms of more dominant cultures. Commentators have placed the origins far back in music history, as far as the Carolingian Empire, in which plainsong was moulded. But nationalism became explicit and crucial from the mid 19th century to the mid 20th, when the Austro–German and Italian traditions had established their shared hegemony, prompting alternative voices from Poland (Chopin), followed by Bohemia (Smetana, Dvořák), Russia (Tchaikovsky, Musorgsky, Balakirev, Rimsky-Korsakov, Borodin), Norway (Grieg), Finland (Sibelius), England (Elgar, Vaughan Williams), Russia again (Stravinsky, Prokofiev, Shostakovich), Hungary (Bartók), the USA (Copland, Harris) and elsewhere. This was also the period when several of these countries – Poland, Bohemia, Norway, Finland, Hungary – were achieving independence from powerful neighbours, while others (Russia, England, the USA) were seeking to adjust their cultural weight to their new political importance.

Composers may, of course, draw on national sources other than their own, as Chabrier, Lalo, Debussy and Ravel did in their Spanish works, creating an imaginary nationalism. Other examples include Copland in Mexico, Elgar in Italy and Bavaria, and Bartók in Slovakia, Romania and north Africa. Bartók's intention in his Dance Suite

was to convey the idea of 'the brotherhood of nations', and indeed most nationalism in music can be read as doing the same. As much as Sibelius may have been proud of his status as a national figure, his music depends on stylistic features from Russian and Austro–German traditions, on an institution developed in Italian Baroque opera (the orchestra), and on instruments having antecedents in the Islamic and ancient Mediterranean worlds.

National Youth Orchestra of Great Britain. Organization founded in 1947 by the conductor and composer Ruth Railton to provide training and concert experience in school holidays for teenagers not enrolled at conservatories.

Nativité du Seigneur, La (The Nativity of Our Lord). Organ work by Messiaen in nine movements: 1 *La Vierge et l'Enfant*, 2 *Les Bergers*, 3 *Desseins éternels*, 4 *Le Verbe*, 5 *Les Enfants de Dieu*, 6 *Les Anges*, 7 *Jésus accepte la souffrance*, 8 *Les Mages*, 9 *Dieu parmi nous*. First performance: Paris, 27 Feb 1936.

natural. The regular pitch, neither sharp nor flat, identified by the sign ♮ when there might be some doubt, or to cancel a ♯ or ♭ that came previously or was indicated in the key signature. See also ACCIDENTAL.

natural harmonic. HARMONIC produced on an open string of a string instrument.

natural horn. HAND HORN.

naturalism. The imitation in art of natural behaviour and events. This is not generally how music works, though there are instances, such as the bird calls in Beethoven's 'Pastoral' Symphony. Opera, too, can be naturalistic (*Le nozze di Figaro*). See also REALISM.

natural notes. Notes playable on a natural brass instrument, i.e. those of a harmonic series.

Naumann, Johann Gottlieb (b. Blasewitz, near Dresden, 17 Apr 1741; d. Dresden, 23 Oct 1801). German composer, notably of operas, in which he moved from Metastasio's world closer to Gluck and French music. From 1757 he was in Italy, where he came into contact with Tartini, Padre Martini and Hasse, who helped him return to Dresden to a court appointment in 1764. Further Italian visits followed in 1765–8 and 1772–4; he was then attached to the royal courts in Stockholm and Copenhagen, writing *Cora och Alonzo* (1778) and *Gustaf Wasa* (1786) for the former and *Orpheus og*

Eurydike (1786) for the latter. In 1786 he was made chief kapellmeister in Dresden. Besides operas he wrote sacred music, songs and chamber pieces with armonica, an instrument said to have jangled his nerves. Two of his grandsons became music scholars and composers.

NBC. National Broadcasting Company, US company founded by RCA in 1926. It broadcast musical performances from its first year and maintained an orchestra conducted by Toscanini (1937–54).

Neapolitan school. Opera composers of the 17th–18th centuries trained or active in Naples, from Provenzale and Alessandro Scarlatti to Paisiello and Cimarosa.

Neapolitan sixth. First inversion of the major triad on the flattened second degree of the scale, e.g. in C major or minor F–A♭–D♭, normally preceding the dominant in a perfect cadence. It was much used by members of the Neapolitan school, but also by composers earlier (Purcell) and later (Beethoven).

Nebendreiklang (Ger.). Minor triad.

Nebensatz (Ger., secondary material). Second subject group in a sonata form.

Nebenstimme (Ger., secondary part). Schoenberg's term for the line secondary to the hauptstimme, indicated by a horizontal bracket stemming from an N.

Nebentonarten (Ger., secondary keys). Those other than the haupttonarten, principally the mediant, submediant and supertonic.

Nebuchadnezzar. King of Babylon (see Daniel 1–4) featuring in works by Verdi (NABUCCO) and Britten (*The Burning Fiery Furnace*).

neck. Narrow, elongated part of a string instrument over which the strings extend beyond the body.

Nedbal, Oskar (b. Tábor, 26 Mar 1874; d. Zagreb, 24 Dec 1930). Czech composer and conductor, a follower of Dvořák, with whom he studied at the Prague Conservatory (1885–92). He played viola in the Czech Quartet (1891–1906), while also conducting the Czech Philharmonic and producing his ballet *Legend of Honza* (f.p. Prague, 1902), with its popular *Valse triste*. Later works include operettas for Vienna, from his time as founder conductor of the Tonkünstlerorchester (1907–18). He killed himself by jumping from a window of the Zagreb Opera.

Neefe, Christian Gottlob (b. Chemnitz, 5 Feb 1748; d. Dessau, 26 Jan 1798). German composer, best remembered as Beethoven's early teacher. After law studies at Leipzig University (1769–71) he became Hiller's pupil and a theatre musician, notably in Bonn, where he was also court organist (1782–96). He wrote operas, songs and sonatas.

Neel, (Louis) Boyd (b. Blackheath, London, 9 Jul 1905; d. Toronto, 30 Sep 1981). British conductor, especially of his own Boyd Neel Orchestra, an 18-piece string group that made its debut in London in 1933. He was then dean of the conservatory in Toronto and head of the university music faculty (1953–71).

Neidhart (b. ?*c*.1190; d. 1236 or later). Minnesinger, later called 'von Reuental' (of the Vale of Tears) for the lachrymose nature of some of his songs. Others are more optimistic and dance-like, but both kinds were popular, to judge by the imitations made at the time.

neighbour note. AUXILIARY NOTE.

Neither. Opera by Feldman to a near-minimal libretto by Beckett, his only text made for singing. The sole vocal performer is a soprano, with orchestra. First performance: Rome, 13 May 1977.

Nelson. Name given to the third of Haydn's late masses, allegedly because it was performed before the great admiral and Lady Hamilton when they visited Eszterháza in 1800.

Nenna, Pomponio (baptized Bari, 13 Jun 1556; d. ?Rome, ?1613). Italian composer, principally of madrigals (eight books), though he also published two books of responsories. The son of a Bari city official, he served as governor of neighbouring Andria before moving to Naples in the mid-1590s. There he drew close to Gesualdo, though he was never so extreme. He emerged into the daylight of the Roman madrigal, and settled in that city in 1607/8.

neoclassicism. The revival of older (especially 18th-century) aspects of style, language and form in a distinctly different context, especially in music of the 1920s–30s – an instance of what was later termed POSTMODERNISM. The separate presence of old and new is crucial, and the source of neoclassicism's essential irony, its spirit of mocking celebration. Brahms's passacaglia (in his Fourth Symphony) does not have this – the music emphasizes closeness to the past and continuity with it – but Stravinsky's (in his Septet) does: the old and the new are like oil and vinegar in the same bottle. The contemporary term 'wrong-note music' drew attention to that, in suggesting how old forms and patterns were being put together with deliberate mistakes. But, of course, the wrong notes are right.

Neoclassicism may be found in much of the music of the late 19th century and early 20th, by composers from Mahler to Satie, but its first full, sharp appearances are in Prokofiev's 'Classical' Symphony (1916–17) and Stravinsky's *Pulcinella* (1919–20), the one made to an old model, the other deliberately distorting old music. For Stravinsky, *Pulcinella* was his 'passport' to a new style, and it was a passport eagerly borrowed by other composers in Paris between the wars: Ravel, Roussel, Poulenc, Martinů and many more. Stravinsky's neoclassicism also had a strong effect outside France, notably on Hindemith. Schoenberg disapproved, and made public his disapproval in his cantata *Der neue Klassizismus* (1925), which ridicules 'little Modernsky' for wanting to don Papa Bach's wig. In doing so, though, the piece becomes neoclassical itself, and indeed much of the music produced by Schoenberg, Berg and Webern in this period shows a neoclassical disparity between traditional form and non-traditional material.

Such disparity is hard to sustain. With time the two separating fluids of old and new began to form stable emulsions, often in a renewed Romanticism, as in the music produced in the 1930s–40s by Prokofiev and Hindemith – though Stravinsky went on creating such evidently neoclassical pieces as his Mozartian opera *The Rake's Progress* (1948–51), and even his later serial works can be seen as neoclassical in their mix of the modern with the monumentally antique.

neoromanticism. The revival of 19th-century kinds of expression, particularly in the 1930s–50s (Prokofiev, Hindemith, Shostakovich, Vaughan Williams) and the 1970s–90s (Penderecki, Adams, Schnittke, Davies).

Nepomuceno, Alberto (b. Fortaleza, 6 Jul 1864; d. Rio de Janeiro, 16 Oct 1920). Brazilian composer, a pioneer of European-style music there. He studied in Recife and Rio, and in Europe (1888–95), at conservatories in Rome, Berlin and Paris. Back home he directed the Rio Conservatory and used Brazilian material in orchestral, chamber and piano pieces.

nera (It.). Crotchet, quarter-note.

Netherlandish. Term used in this book for the many composers who came from the LOW COUNTRIES in the 15th–16th centuries, mostly from Hainaut, Brabant and Flanders.

Netherlands (Nederland). The northern part of the LOW COUNTRIES, with its capital in AMSTERDAM. As in Britain, music was largely an import commodity between the 17th century (Sweelinck) and the late 19th, since when the roll of Dutch composers has included Diepenbrock, Wagenaar, Vermeulen, Pijper, Van Baaren, de Leeuw, Schat and the Andriessens.

Netherlands Opera. See AMSTERDAM.

Netherlands Wind Ensemble. Group formed in 1959, specializing in new music and new ways of presenting music.

Neue Sachlichkeit (Ger., new objectivity). Buzz word of the second half of the 1920s, drawing attention to the rejection of extravagant personal emotion in favour of elements from before Romanticism (Baroque-style counterpoint, clear form) and after (jazz, new sounds from mechanical and electronic instruments, radio). The term is generally restricted to artists in Germany, including Hindemith, Weill and Wolpe among composers.

Neuhaus, Heinrich (b. Elizavetgrad/Yelizavetgradka, 12 Apr 1888; d. Moscow, 10 Oct 1964). Russian pianist and teacher, whose pupils included Richter and Gilels. He was born into a musical family, including a piano teacher (his father, Gustav), a distinguished pianist (Felix Blumenfeld) and a composer (his cousin, Szymanowski). Having started his career in his teens (on one occasion playing with the 11-year-old Elman), he completed his training in Vienna with Godowsky and at the Petrograd Conservatory. But though he was admired for his poetry in Chopin, Scriabin and Debussy, he was a dedicated teacher, notably at the Moscow Conservatory from 1922.

Neukomm, Sigismund Ritter von (b. Salzburg, 10 Jul 1778; d. Paris, 3 Apr 1858). Austrian composer. Extraordinarily productive, his own catalogue, begun in 1804, lists 1,265 works, preponderantly in vocal genres (sacred music, choruses, quartets, trios, duets, songs). He studied with both Haydn brothers, and as Joseph's pupil (1797–1804) made numerous arrangements. After Haydn's death he settled in Paris, but he also travelled widely – to Rio de Janeiro (1816–21), Italy, Britain and north Africa.

neume. Sign representing a segment of melody. Such signs appeared in chant books in western Europe in the 9th century and in the Byzantine Empire in the 10th century; there are also neumatic systems of similar age from Japan and Tibet. Western European neumes were adapted to four-line staves in the later 11th century, and this kind of notation remains standard for plainsong, among the commonest neumes being the punctum, virga, pes, clivis, torculus and porrectus. Their shapes and meanings are shown below

punctum porrectus   clivis   torculus   pes

Neusidler, Hans (b. Pressburg/Bratislava, c.1508–9; d. Nuremberg, 2 Feb 1563). German lutenist-composer, who published several books of lute music, for beginners and for experienced players, including intabulations and original pieces. *Ein newes Lautenbüchlein mit vil schonen Liedern* (1540) includes *Der hupf auff* and *Juden-Tanz*. He lived in Nuremberg from 1530 and had 17 children, among whom Melchior (1531–90) and Conrad (1541–1603) followed his profession.

neutralization. (1) Smoothing-out of chromatic notes in diatonic music, whereby sharpened ones move up and flattened ones down.
(2) Removal of a motif's features, so that they become fragments of scales or arpeggios.

neuvième (Fr.). Ninth (interval).

Neuwirth. Austrian composers, father and daughter.
(1) **Gösta** (b. Vienna, 6 Jan 1937). Interweaving times and styles, his music includes a cycle of mostly instrumental pieces after Proust, *Gestern und Morgen* (1953–96). He studied with Karl Schiske in Vienna (1954–62), completed a doctorate on Schreker in Berlin (1968), and became a valued teacher of composition, in Graz (from 1973) and at the Academy of the Arts in Berlin (from 1983).
(2) **Olga** (b. Graz, 4 Aug 1968). Her music features sharp contrasts in an atmosphere of expressivet tension, film-like in its referential force and projection of light into darkness. She studied at conservatories in San Francisco (1986–7) and Vienna (1987–93), and at IRCAM (1993–4), by which time she was internationally known.

Neveu, Ginette (b. Paris, 11 Aug 1919; d. San Miguel, Azores, 28 Oct 1949). French violinist, whose brilliant career was cut short by a plane crash. Born into a musical family, she made her debut at seven, completed her training with Enescu and Flesch, and was launched by winning the 1935 Wieniawski Competition.

Nevin, Ethelbert (Woodbridge) (b. Edgeworth, near Pittsburgh, 25 Nov 1862; d. New Haven, 17 Feb 1901). US composer of parlour songs and piano pieces. Born into a comfortable and musical family, he was educated at home, in Boston (1881–3) and with Klindworth and others in Berlin (1884–6). He played his own music in recitals, his most popular pieces including the songs 'The Rosary' (1897) and 'Mighty lak' a rose' (1901), and *Narcissus* from his *Water Scenes* for piano (Op.13, 1891). His brother, Arthur (1871–1943), was a more ambitious composer, notably of the Amerindian opera *Poia*, the first US work to be performed at a European court opera (f.p. Berlin, 1910).

new complexity. Term current in the late 1980s and 1990s for the music of Ferneyhough, Finnissy and other composers, mostly British, pursuing notational refinement and extremes of textural activity.

New England Holidays. Symphony by Ives comprising *Washington's Birthday*, *Decoration Day*, *The Fourth of July* and *Thanksgiving and Forefather's Day*.

New German School. Term introduced by the Leipzig music historian Franz Brendel in 1859 to embrace decisively progressive composers – chiefly Wagner and Liszt, though Berlioz was also included. Among younger composers associated with the school were von Bülow, Cornelius and Raff. The group soon lost any coherence, but the term has stayed in use to denote the contra-Brahms tendency of the time.

Newman, Alfred (b. New Haven, 17 Mar 1900; d. Los Angeles, 17 Feb 1970). US composer, mostly of film scores. Born in poverty, he worked his way up from theatre pianist to conductor, and went to Hollywood in 1930, becoming head of music for Universal Artists and then for 20th-Century Fox (1940–60). Among the many films he scored were *The Prisoner of Zenda* (1937), *The Hunchback of Notre Dame* (1939), *Wuthering Heights* (1939), *The Song of Bernadette* (1943), *Captain from Castile* (1947) and *The Robe* (1953). His brothers, Emil (1911–84) and Lionel (1916–89), followed him into the world of film music, as did his nephew, Randy (b. 1943), and his sons, David (b. 1954) and Thomas (b. 1955).

Newman, Chris(topher) (b. London, 1958). British composer and singer, active also as a visual artist and writer, the transgression of boundaries being his one constancy. After studying music at King's College, London, he went to Cologne in 1979 as Kagel's pupil and has remained largely in Germany.

new music. Term used pretty consistently in the 1950s–70s for the music of Boulez, Cage, Stockhausen and their contemporaries. Latterly its meaning has varied with the user.

New World. Name by which Dvořák's Ninth Symphony, composed in the USA, is generally known. He called it 'From the New World' (*Z nového světa*).

New York. US city, joint capital with London of the musical world. Its history is, of course, shorter: the first known concert was given by Carl Theodor Pachelbel in 1736, and it was not until half a century later that the appurtenances of musical life – regular concerts, music shops – were established. Even then, efforts were sporadic, and much dependent on visiting stars: full-scale opera arrived in 1825–6 with García's troupe, backed by da Ponte. Bigger, more lasting institutions came in the mid 19th century, as the population rose to over half a million in 1850 (from 33,000 in 1790). Music, for this largely immigrant citizenry, was a link with the home culture, and the repertory cultivated was overwhelmingly European. The Philharmonic Symphony Society (ancestor of the NEW YORK PHILHARMONIC ORCHESTRA), founded in 1842, emphasized Austro–German music, the Academy of Music – opened in 1854 as the world's biggest opera house, seating 4,600 – Italian. From 1867 the Philharmonic Symphony concerts were given at the Academy of Music, from which they moved successively to the new METRO-POLITAN OPERA in 1886 and CARNEGIE HALL six years later.

By 1920 the population was over five million, and the city was finding its own musical voices, from Irving Berlin to Edgard Varèse. The liveliness of jazz and the MUSICAL during the next four decades – coupled with a belief in classical music as elevating and socially integrating – stimulated more composers, and into the stir of native creativity came refugees from Nazi Europe. Composers working in the city in 1950 included – besides Berlin and Varèse – Carter, Copland, Rodgers, Cage, Babbitt, Loesser, Wolpe and, spanning much of the range, Bernstein. With ups and downs, the city has maintained this vitality of difference, aided by continuing immigration and continuing interactions. However, commercial and non-commercial music have drifted apart, and the opening of LINCOLN CENTER in the 1960s may have helped to foster a divide, too, between 'uptown' music – traditional repertory, big-name soloists, conventional concert-giving – and a 'downtown' culture having its home in clubs, galleries and other small venues in the southern districts of Greenwich Village and SoHo. To some extent the latter gap is bridged by Merkin Hall (an independent recital hall near Lincoln Center) and Miller Theater (an auditorium attached to Columbia University, presenting much contemporary music).

New York Philharmonic Orchestra. Institution dating its origins from the founding of the Philharmonic Symphony Society of New York by Ureli Corelli Hill in 1842. Principal conductors in early years included Theodore Thomas (1877–91), Mahler (1909–11) and Josef Stransky (1911–23). After that the orchestra worked with Mengelberg (1921–9), Toscanini (1928–36), Barbirolli (1937–42), Rodzinski (1943–7), Walter (1947–9), Mitropoulos (1949–58), Bernstein (1958–70), Boulez (1971–7), Mehta (1978–91), Masur (1991–2002) and Maazel (from 2002).

New Zealand. The New Zealand Symphony was founded as the National Orchestra in 1946. Composers from the country have included Douglas Lilburn, Annea Lockwood, Barry Anderson and Dennis Smalley.

Niccolò da Perugia (*fl.* Florence, second half of the 14th century). Italian composer, whose works comprise mostly two-part ballatas and madrigals.

Nicolai, Otto (b. Königsberg, now Kaliningrad, 9 Jun 1810; d. Berlin, 11 May 1849). German composer, remembered for one of the German-speaking world's most popular comic operas, *Die* LUSTIGEN WEIBER VON WINDSOR. A composer's son, he fell out with his father and had to fend for himself for two years in his late teens as a travelling pianist. He then came under Zelter's protection in Berlin, where he continued his training (with Bernhard Klein and others) and had contact with the Mendelssohns. Further lessons, with Giuseppe Baini, followed when he was organist of the Prussian embassy in Rome (1834–6). His goal now was to make a career as a composer of Italian opera, and this he pursued both in Italy and while serving as assistant conductor at the Kärntnertor theatre in Vienna (1837–9). Success came with *Il templario* (after Scott's *Ivanhoe*, f.p. Turin, 1840), one of four Italian operas from this period, but he turned down the *Nabucco* libretto that Verdi quickly took up and in 1841 returned to Vienna as conductor of both the Kärtnertor and the court opera. His world changed. In 1842 he instituted philharmonic concerts favouring the works of Beethoven and Mozart, and he put two of his Italian operas into German for the Kärtnertor. He returned to Berlin in 1847, as conductor of the royal opera, and there *Die lustigen Weiber* was presented. Its fluent mix of Italian elements (Bellini, Donizetti) and Austro–German (Mozart, Beethoven, Weber) gave it lasting appeal, and it remained unique: two months after the première its composer died. Besides his operas he left choral music and songs, as well as orchestral, chamber and piano pieces.

Niculescu, Ştefan (b. Moreni, Dâmboviţa, 31 Jul 1927). Romanian composer, who has used mathematical models and artificial scales in exploring music that is neither diatonic nor chromatic. He studied in Bucharest with the composer Michel Andricu and, already a leading modernist in his country, attended the Darmstadt courses (1966–9). His output includes five symphonies and choral music.

Niedermeyer, (Abraham) Louis (b. Nyon, 27 Apr 1802; d. Paris, 14 Mar 1861). Swiss composer, but better remembered as the founder of the Ecole Niedermeyer (1853), a school for church musicians. He lived in Paris from 1823 and wrote operas and songs before devoting himself to church music in his last years.

Nielsen, Carl (August) (b. Sortelung, Funen, 9 Jun 1865; d. Copenhagen, 3 Oct 1931). Danish composer, noted especially for his six symphonies and other works in which he pursued a personal path out from late Romanticism, helped by a strong feeling for harmonic drive. His alliances of keys are often unusual (though justified by modal relationships), with a push from one tonality into another.

He grew up with music in a village on the island of Funen: his mother would sing to him, and his housepainter father was an amateur musician. His own talents were enough to win him support from local worthies for conservatory training in Copenhagen (1884–6), where his teachers included J.P.E. Hartmann and Orla Rosenhoff. In 1889 he became a violinist in the opera orchestra, though he was soon off on a nine-month journey funded by a scholarship (1890–91). In Paris he met a sculptress compatriot, Anne Marie Brodersen, and they were married in Florence. On their return he took up his orchestral job again and began making a

name as a composer. In 1903 they visited Athens, where the overture *Helios* was composed; soon after he arrived at a different, 18th-century kind of classicism in his comic opera *Maskarade*. While writing that work, in 1905, he resigned from the orchestra, only to rejoin it soon after as a conductor.

In 1914 came crises in his career and in his personal life. Disappointed not to receive the position of principal conductor, he left the opera, and at the same time his extramarital affairs caused a rift with his wife. It is hard not to read these events into the resolution of his Fourth Symphony and the compact, vigorous style in which he composed so abundantly in his last decade.

Robert Simpson *Carl Nielsen, Symphonist* (1952, [2]1979)

Operas: *Saul og David* (see SAUL) 1898–1901; *Maskarade* (Vilhelm Andersen, after Ludvig Holberg), 1904–6, f.p. Copenhagen, 1906

Incidental music: *Aladdin* (Adam Oehlenschläeger), Op.34, 1918–19; *Mother* (Helge Rode), Op.41, 1920; *Amor og dikteren* (Karin Michaëlis), Op.54, 1930; etc.

Symphonies: No.1, G minor, Op.7, 1891–2; No.2 '*The* FOUR TEMPERAMENTS', Op.16, 1901–2; No.3 'Sinfonia espansiva', Op.27, 1910–11; No.4 'The Inextinguishable', Op.29, 1914–16; No.5, Op.50, 1921–2; No.6 'Sinfonia semplice', 1924–5

Other orchestral works: Little Suite, A minor, Op.1, str, 1888–9; *Helios*, Op.17, overture, 1903; *Saga-Dream*, Op.39, 1907–8; Violin Concerto, Op.33, 1911; Paraphrase on 'Nearer my God to Thee', wind, 1913; *Pan and Syrinx*, Op.49, 1917–18; Flute Concerto, 1926; *An Imaginary Journey to the Faroes*, 1927; Clarinet Concerto, Op.57, 1928

Other vocal works: *Hymnus amoris* (Axel Olrik, Lat. trans Johan Ludvig Heiberg), Op.12, soli, ch, orch, 1896–7; *Springtime on Funen* (Aage Bernsten), Op.42, soli, ch, orch, 1921; 3 Motets, Op.55, ch, 1929; other cantatas, songs, etc.

String quartets: No.1, F minor, Op.5, 1890; No.2, G minor, Op.13, 1887–8, rev 1897–8; No.3, E♭, Op.14, 1897–8, rev 1899–1900; *Piacevolezza*, Op.19, 1906, rev as No.4, F, Op.44, c.1919

Other chamber works: *At the Bier of a Young Artist*, str qt, db, 1910; *Serenata in vano*, cl, hn, vc, bn, db, 1914; Wind Quintet, Op.43, 1922; Violin Sonata No.1, A, Op.9, 1895; No.2, Op.35, 1912; Prelude and Theme with Variations, Op.48, vn, 1928; *Preludio e presto*, Op.52, vn, 1927–8; Fantasy Pieces, Op.2, ob, pf, 1889; *Canto serioso*, hn, pf, 1913; etc.

Piano: 5 Pieces, Op.3, 1890; Symphonic Suite, Op.8, 1894; Humoresque-Bagatelles, Op.11, 1894–7; Chaconne, Op.32, 1916–17; Theme with Variations, Op.40, 1917; Suite 'The Luciferian', Op.45, 1919–20; Piano Music for Young and Old, Op.53, 1929–30; 3 Pieces, Op.59, 1927–8; etc.

Organ: 29 Little Preludes, Op.51, 1929; *Commotio*, Op.58, 1930–31; etc.

Nielsen, (Karl Henrik) Ludolf (b. Nørre Tvede, near Naestved, 29 Jan 1876; d. Copenhagen, 16 Oct 1939). Danish composer, a late Romantic with impressionist inclinations. He studied at the conservatory in Copenhagen as an instrumentalist (on violin and piano); as a composer he was self-taught. While working variously as a chamber musician and teacher he wrote three symphonies, three quartets, choral music and songs.

Niemetschek, Franz Xaver (b. Sadska, 24 Jul 1766; d. Vienna, 19 Mar 1849). Czech critic, the author of the first biography of Mozart (1798), which was based partly on materials supplied by Constanze. He studied in Prague and taught at the university there (1802–20) before moving to Vienna.

Nietzsche, Friedrich (Wilhelm) (b. Röcken, near Leipzig, 15 Oct 1844; d. Weimar, 25 Aug 1900). German philosopher, whose writings stimulated composers from Mahler to Barraqué. His early enthusiasm for Wagner turned into a caustic dissatisfaction. He was also an amateur composer, of songs, choral items and piano pieces.

Nigg, Serge (b. Paris, 6 Jun 1924). French composer, an ally of Boulez in his youth, later more connected to their shared teachers, Messiaen and Leibowitz, in his exuberant surrealism and contrastingly staunch left-wing commitment. His works include orchestral scores (*Visages d'Axel*, 1967), vocal pieces and chamber music.

night. Though winter-season concerts and opera performances generally take place after dark, music meets the night explicitly only when it is given outdoors (see NOTTURNO, SERENADE, SERENATA). More frequently the encounters are as image or metaphor. Many operas include noctural scenes, not least *Figaro* and *Don Giovanni*, whose composer also imagined a Queen of the Night (in *Die Zauberflöte*). Moonlit serenity is reflected by tradition in a favourite Beethoven piano sonata and affirmedly in the early Romantic nocturne, while other 19th-century composers (Berlioz, Musorgsky) heard witchery and devilment after dusk. There are also pieces that incorporate night-time sounds, whether animal (Bartók) or human (Biber). But the poetry of night – of gloom, uncertainty, melancholia and death – belongs most especially to music since 1900, by composers such as Mahler, Varèse, Barraqué, Carter, Birtwistle and Lachenmann. Even in these dark times, though, there have been some who looked up and heard the stars (Cage in *Atlas eclipticalis*, Stockhausen in *Sternklang*) and planets (Holst).

Night at the Chinese Opera, A. Opera by Weir to her own libretto after a play from Yuan-dynasty China. Chao Lin (bar) finds his life uncannily mirrored in a play he sees. First performance: Cheltenham, 8 Jul 1987.

nightingale. Whistle supposedly imitating the bird's song. See also BIRDSONG.

Nightingale, The (*Le Rossignol, Solovey*). Short opera by Stravinsky to a libretto by Stepan Mitusov after Hans Christian Andersen's tale. The Emperor of China (baritone) prefers a Japanese mechanical nightingale to the real thing (soprano), which nevertheless returns to save him from death. First performance: Paris, 2 Feb 1920.

Night on the Bare Mountain (*Noch na lysoy gore*). Orchestral piece by Musorgsky, which he originally titled *St John's Night on the Bare Mountain* and based on a scene in Baron Georgy Mengden's play *The Witch* in which Satan is summoned to a witches' sabbath. He then adapted it to form an episode in the collaborative opera *Mlada* and, after that, in his own *Sorochintsy Fair*, neither of which came off. Rimsky-Korsakov made a spectacular revision of the third version, but the first, in Musorgsky's own scoring, is often preferred. First performance: St Petersburg, 27 Oct 1886 (Rimsky treatment); London, 3 Feb 1932 (original).

Nightride and Sunrise (*Öinen ratsastus ja auringonnousu*). Symphonic poem by Sibelius, following the programme suggested by the title. First performance: St Petersburg, 23 Jan 1909.

Nikisch, Arthur (b. Lébényszentmiklós, 12 Oct 1855; d. Leipzig, 23 Jan 1922). Hungarian conductor, the most admired of his time for his total yet undemonstrative command. He studied with Hellmesberger and Felix Otto Dessoff at the Vienna Conservatory from 1866 and entered the court orchestra as a violinist in 1874, playing under Brahms, Liszt, Wagner, Verdi and Bruckner. In 1878 he became second conductor of the Leipzig opera, and the next year principal. Then in 1895, after periods with the Boston Symphony (1889–93) and the Budapest opera (1893–5), he took charge simultaneously of the Leipzig Gewandhaus and the Berlin Philharmonic. He remained with both to the end of his life, while also working regularly for periods with the LSO and other orchestras. A few recordings capture his work in Berlin, where he extended the repertory to include Berlioz, Liszt, Bruckner, Mahler, Reger and Strauss.

Nikolayeva, Tatyana (Petrovna) (b. Bezhitza, 4

May 1924; d. San Francisco, 22 Nov 1993). Russian pianist, commanding in Bach. She studied with Goldenweiser at the Moscow Conservatory until 1947 and established herself in 1950 by winning the Bach Competition in Leipzig. Shostakovich, who was on the jury, thereupon wrote his 24 Preludes and Fugues for her. By the 1980s, when she first appeared in the West, she was a legend.

Nilsson, (Märta) Birgit (b. Västra Karups, 17 May 1918). Swedish soprano, the outstanding Wagnerian soprano of her time. She studied with Joseph Hislop at the conservatory in Stockholm and made her debut at the opera there as Agathe (*Freischütz*) in 1946. From the mid 1950s to the early 1970s she was internationally supreme as Isolde, Brünnhilde, Elektra and Turandot, possessing an enormous voice of thrilling brightness and thrust.

Nilsson, Bo (b. Skellefteå, 1 May 1937). Swedish composer, a precocious avant-gardist whose subsequent career has been erratic. Self-taught, and taking Boulez and Stockhausen as models, he won a performance by Cologne radio of his *Zwei Stücke* (fl, b cl, pf, perc) when he was 18. By his mid 20s he had left Darmstadt for other shores, including film music, Turkish traditions and jazz.

Nin (y Castellanos), Joaquín (b. Havana, 29 Sep 1878; d. Havana, 24 Oct 1949). Cuban composer, mostly of popular Spanish songs and piano pieces dating from after he was 40. Before that he was active in Spain and Paris as a pianist, especially in French and Spanish Baroque music. He was the father of the writer Anaïs Nin and the composer Joaquín Nin-Culmell (1908–2004).

Ninot le Petit (*fl. c.*1500). French composer of chansons, motets and a mass. He may have been associated with the French royal chapel and later with Langres Cathedral.

ninth. Note an octave above the second, or interval an octave wider than a second.

ninth chord. A triad with added ninth and probably also seventh, i.e. in close position a tower of thirds (e.g. C–E–G–B–D). Such chords became quite normal in the early 20th century, notably in Ravel and jazz.

Ninth Symphony. In the absence of a composer's name, Beethoven's is implied. The fatefulness of No.9 was felt by Mahler: Schubert's last symphony had that number, as well as Beethoven's, and Bruckner had died with his Ninth incomplete. Mahler sought to escape by giving his ninth

symphony, *Das Lied von der Erde*, no number, so that his ensuing No.9 was really his tenth. But then he died with No.10 in draft. Among other composers who failed to get beyond No.9 were Dvořák (whose symphonies were differently numbered in Mahler's time), Glazunov, Vaughan Williams, Sessions, Arnold and Schnittke. Though Harris, Henze, Langgaard, Myaskovsky, Panufnik, Pettersson, Rubbra, Schuman, Shostakovich and Tubin all leapt the hurdle, Davies was perhaps wise to announce in 2000 that he would stop at No.8.

Nishimura, Akira (b. Osaka, 8 Sep 1953). Japanese composer, whose music's radiance derives from Western-modernist and Japanese-traditional sources. He studied at the Tokyo National University of Fine Arts and Music, and became internationally known in the late 1970s. His output includes many orchestral works and three quartets.

Nixon in China. Opera by Adams to a libretto by Alice Goodman. Based on recent history, and prompted by the stage director Peter Sellars, the work shows Nixon (baritone) and his wife Pat (soprano) as small people in big roles. Chou En-Lai (baritone) sings a concluding lament as light fails. First performance: Houston, 22 Oct 1987.

nobilmente (It.), **noblement** (Fr.). Nobly.

Noces, Les (*Svadebka*, The Wedding). Ballet score by Stravinsky for choreography by Bronislava Nijinska. It is in four choral tableaux: *At the Bride's House, At the Bridegroom's House, The Bride's Departure, The Wedding Feast*. Stravinsky took a while to find the right medium for his ceremonial machine, sung by soli and chorus, and composed in 1914–17. First he gave it orchestral accompaniment (1917); then he scored the first two scenes for pianola, two cimbaloms, harmonium and percussion (1919) before settling on an ensemble of four pianos and percussion (1921–3). First performance: Paris, 13 Jun 1923.

Noches en los jardines de España (Nights in the Gardens of Spain). Piano concerto by Falla, in three movements: *En el Generalife, Danza lejaña, En las jardines de la sierra de Córdoba*. First performance: Madrid, 9 Apr 1916.

nocturne. Piece – normally for piano – evoking night, usually by tranquillity. The first nocturnes came from Field, the greatest from Chopin, for whom the nocturnal image was that of a solitary dreamer or insomniac. Bartók offered a more objective vision in *The Night's Music* from his suite *Out of Doors*.

Nocturnes. Orchestral triptych by Debussy, comprising *Nuages* (Clouds), *Fêtes* (Festivities) and *Sirènes* (Sirens), the last movement with wordless women's choir. First performance: Paris, 9 Dec 1900 (without *Sirènes*), 27 Oct 1901 (complete).

noël. French Christmas carol.

noire (Fr.). Crotchet, quarter-note.

Nona (Ger.), **nona** (It.). Ninth (interval).

Nonesuch. US record label, founded in 1964. With Teresa Sterne at its head (1965–79) it gained an unparallelled reputation for music new, ancient, neglected and traditional from around the world.

nonet (Fr. *nonette*, Ger. *Nonett*, It. *nonetto*). Group of nine instruments or voices, or group of nine performers on such, or genre of music for that medium, or work of that genre. The classic example is Spohr's Nonet for one each of the orchestral strings and woodwinds plus horn.

non-harmonic note. In tonal music a note creating a dissonance and therefore requiring resolution.

non-harmonic relation. FALSE RELATION.

Nono, Luigi (b. Venice, 29 Jan 1924; d. Venice, 8 May 1990). Italian composer, the most radical among the leaders of the post-1945 European generation and perhaps, in the long term, the most influential. With him the splintered, assertive sounds of the new music expressed a fierce participation in the combat for social justice. In the mid-1970s his sound world became quieter but also stranger as he cherished extreme (in register), marginal and electronically transformed sonorities over extended durations, increasingly aware that the struggle would be long and that it would have to begin with a calm unwinding of old assumptions.

The son of a civil engineer and grandson of a Venetian painter, he attended Malipiero's classes at the city's conservatory before studying law at Padua University (1942–6). In 1946 he met Maderna, with whom two years later he studied with Scherchen in Venice. On that occasion contact with Eunice Catunda, a Brazilian musician and communist, was decisive; so were encounters at Darmstadt with Varèse (1950) and Stockhausen (1951). He now had all his means: political commitment (he joined the Italian Communist Party in 1952), sonic exuberance and analytical

precision, along with a passionate native lyricism that came through as much in his orchestral works of the 1950s as in the pieces for small vocal groupings from the next decade. Often the style is uncompromising, but he was also capable of such gentle originals as the *Liebeslied* he wrote for Schoenberg's daughter, Nuria, whom he met in 1954 at the first performance of *Moses und Aron*. They married the next year, set up home on the Giudecca in Venice in 1956, and had two daughters. Meanwhile he travelled in both eastern and western Europe, teaching and lecturing. In 1964 he began giving lecture-concerts in Italian factories, for which he moved away from normal avant-garde genres to concentrate on documentary pieces incorporating texts, live music and electronic sound. Visits to Latin America in 1967–8 further intensified his immersion in current reality – though one result, encouraged by Abbado and Pollini, was a return to the concert hall with *Como una ola* (1971–2).

A solo piece for Pollini, ... *sofferte onde serene* ... (1976), initiated the more inward, meditative style, which he thoroughly expressed in his quartet *Fragmente-Stille*. In 1978 he began to work on his third opera, *Prometeo*, from which he removed action and characters to concentrate on the essential: listening. Several smaller pieces of the *Prometeo* period are satellites; many involved live electronics, on which he worked at the Südwestfunk studios in Freiburg. In 1985 he noticed an inscription on the wall of the Franciscan monastery in Toledo: 'Wayfarers, there are no ways, only the faring on.' To these words he devoted most of his last works.

Operas: INTOLLERANZA, 1960; AL GRAN SOLE CARICO D'AMORE, 1972–4; *Prometeo* (see PROMETHEUS), 1978–84

Orchestral (without voices): *Variazioni canoniche sulla serie dell'op.41 di A. Schönberg*, 1949; *Composizione No.1*, 1951; *Y su sangre ya viene cantando* (*Epitaffio per Federico García Lorca No.2*), fl, chbr orch, 1952; *Due espressioni*, 1953; *Incontri*, 24 insts, 1955; *Varianti*, vn, orch, 1957; *Composizione No.2* (*Diario polacco '58*), 1958–9; *Per Bastiana Tai-Yang Cheng*, orch, tape, 1967; *A Carlo Scarpa architetto, ai suoi infiniti possibili*, 1984; *No hay caminos, hay que caminar ... Andrej Tarkowskij*, 1987

Orchestral (with voices): *Il* CANTO SOSPESO, soli, ch, orch, 1956; COMO UNA OLA DE FUERZA Y LUZ (Julio Huasi), s, pf, orch, tape, 1971–2; *Caminantes ... Ayacucho* (Giordano Bruno), a, fl, org, ch and orch in groups, 1986–7; etc.

Smaller vocal works: *Liebeslied* (Nono), ch, insts, 1954; *Cori di Didone* (Ungaretti), ch, perc, 1958; *Ha venido* (Antonio Machado), s, 6 women's v, 1960; *Sarà dolce tacere* (Pavese), 8 solo v, 1960; *Djamila*

Boupachà (*Canti di vita e d'amore No.2*), s, 1962; *Canciones a Guiomar* (Machado), s, 6 women's v, insts, 1962–3; *Da un diario italiano*, 2 ch, 1964; *La fabbrica illuminata* (Giuliano Scabia, Pavese), mez, tape, 1964; *A floresta è jovem e cheja de vida* (Giovanni Pirelli), s, 3 speakers, cl, perc, tape, 1966; *Das atmende Klarsein* (Rilke), ch, b fl, elec, 1981; *¿Donde estàs, hermano?*, 4 women's v, 1982; *Quando stanno morendo*, 4 women's v, b fl, vc, elec, 1982; *Omaggio a György Kurtág*, a, fl, cl, tuba, elec, 1983; *Risonanze erranti*, mez, fl, tuba, 5 perc, elec, 1986; etc.

Ensemble and instrumental: *Polifonica – monodia – ritmica*, 5 wind, pf, perc, 1951; *Canti per 13*, 1955; … *sofferte onde serene* …, pf, tape, 1976; *Con Luigi Dallapiccola*, 6 perc, elec, 1979; *Fragmente-Stille, an Diotima*, str qt, 1979–80; *A Pierre*, b fl, db cl, elec, 1985; *Post-prae-ludium No.1*, tuba, elec, 1987; *La lontananza nostalgica utopica futura*, vn, tape, 1988; *'Hay que caminar' soñando*, 2 vn, 1989; etc.

Tape: *Omaggio a Emilio Vedova*, tape, 1960; etc.

non-quartal harmony. Harmony in three-part music of the later 15th century where fourths can appear only as discords.

non-retrogradable rhythm. Messiaen's term for a palindromic rhythm (e.g. quaver–semiquaver–quaver–semiquaver–quaver), such as he enjoyed using. Such figures are 'non-retrogradable' because they do not change when reversed. See also PALINDROME.

Nordheim, Arne (b. Larvik, 20 Jun 1931). Norwegian composer, his country's most important in the later 20th century. He studied at the Oslo Conservatory (1948–52), then took electronic music courses in Paris (1955) and Bilthoven (1959). His luminous, colourful style developed under the influences of Lutosławski and Ligeti, displaced a little since the mid 1970s by a revival of Romantic gesture. Among his works are ballets (*The Tempest*, 1979), orchestral scores (*Greening*, 1973) and big choral pieces (*Eco*, 1968; *Nidaros*, 1997).

Nørgård, Per (b. Gentofte, 13 Jul 1932). Danish composer. He has been phenomenally productive and open in his response to the diverse influences – post-1945 modernism, Buddhist thought, abstract pattern and process, the unhinged art of the Swiss schizophrenic Adolf Wölfli – he has brought into a style at once Nordic and airy. He studied with Holmboe, privately from 1949 and then at the Copenhagen Conservatory (1952–5), completing his training with Boulanger in Paris (1956–7). In the 1960s, without quite losing his Sibelian hold on steady form, he began to learn from the music of Boulez, Cage and Stockhausen. This evolution quickened his impatience with the

conservatism of the Copenhagen Conservatory, where he had joined the staff in 1960, and in 1965 he moved to the similar institution in Århus, which he made a thriving centre of new music. In his own work he developed the 'infinity row', a kind of musical genetic principle, designed to create parallels with organic and fractal forms in nature. He married for a second time in 1966, and his music entered its most laid-back phase (*Voyage into the Golden Screen*, Second Symphony). But this did not last long. His Third Symphony (1972) is more disruptive, and his opera *Siddharta* centres on the necessity of alertness and experience to the achievement of bliss. As if to shake his own assumptions, he then based several works, including his Fourth Symphony and opera *The Divine Circus*, on the art of Wölfli. His music since then has been an extended working-out of earlier themes, of chaos and continuity.

Anders Beyer, ed. *The Music of Per Nørgård* (1996)

www.pernoergaard.dk

Operas: *The Labyrinth* (Bent Nørgård), 1963, f.p. Copenhagen, 1967; *Gilgamesh* (Nørgård), 1971–2; *Siddharta* (Nørgård and Ole Sarvig) , 1974–9, f.p. Stockholm, 1983; *The Divine Circus* (Nørgård, after Wölfii), 1982, f.p. Århus, 1983; *Nuit des hommes* (Nørgård and Jacob Schocking, after Apollinaire), 1996, f.p. Copenhagen, 1996

Orchestral: Symphony No.1 'Sinfonia austera', Op.13, 1953–5; No.2, 1970; No.3, 1972; No.4 'Indian Rose Garden and Chinese Witch's Lake', 1981; No.5, 1990–91; No.6 'At the End of the Day', 1997–9; *Voyage into the Golden Screen*, 1968; etc.

Other works: 9 string quartets, much else of all kinds

Nørholm, Ib (b. Copenhagen, 24 Jan 1931). Danish composer, who, like his friend and colleague Nørgård, is prolific and multifaceted in his extensions of Nordic symphonism. He studied at the Copenhagen Conservatory (1950–56), where he began teaching in 1961. His works include symphonies, concertos, operas, much vocal music and string quartets.

Norma. Opera by Bellini to a libretto by Romani after a verse drama by Alexandre Soumet. Norma (soprano), a Gaulish druidess, cannot relinquish her love for the Roman proconsul Pollione (tenor), despite his enemy status and his abandonment of her for her acolyte Adalgisa (soprano). Finally she takes him with her to the funeral pyre. The title role, demanding force and agility, includes the aria 'Casta diva'. First performance: Milan, 26 Dec 1831.

Norman, Jessye (b. Augusta, Georgia, 15 Sep 1945). US soprano, of rich sound, superb flow and majestic presence. She studied at Peabody and the

University of Michigan, and made her opera debut in Berlin in 1969 as Elisabeth in *Tannhäuser*. By the early 1980s she was appearing internationally, finding her métier especially in late Romantic music (Mahler, Strauss, Berg).

Norrington, Roger (b. Oxford, 16 Mar 1934). British conductor, known especially for his compelling attunement to period performance styles; he was knighted in 1997. He studied at Cambridge and with Boult at the RCM, and began as a conductor with his own Heinrich Schütz Choir (1962) and Kent Opera (1969–82). With the London Classical Players (1978–97), also founded by him, he moved from late 18th-century to 19th-century music, which led to engagements with major orchestras in Europe and the USA.

North, Alex (b. Chester, Penn., 4 Dec 1910; d. Los Angeles, 8 Sep 1991). US composer, chiefly for films. He studied at Curtis and Juilliard, and also at the Moscow Conservatory (1933–5), which resulted in his becoming the only US member ever of the Soviet Composers' Union. Later he had lessons with Copland and Toch in New York and Revueltas in Mexico. His first feature film score, for *A Streetcar Named Desire* (1951), caused excitement in using jazz and led to a productive career (*Spartacus*, 1960; *Cleopatra*, 1963; *Who's Afraid of Virginia Woolf?*, 1966). He also wrote two symphonies and other concert pieces.

North, Roger (b. Tostock, Suffolk, 1651; d. Rougham, Norfolk, Mar 1734). English thinker about music, the author of voluminous unpublished writings concerning the philosophy and psychology of music, diatonic harmony, tuning, style, performance practice and other matters. In some respects he prefigured Rameau and even Helmholtz. He also continued the work of his elder brother Francis, Lord Guilford (1637–85), who published *A Philosophical Essay of Music* (1677), one of the first attempts at a scientific understanding of consonance. Like Francis he was in public life, serving as a Member of Parliament. After the ousting of James II (1688), though, he retired to pursue his musical investigations.

Norway (Norge). Its musical history, in the classical sense, effectively began with Grieg and Svendsen in the 1860s–70s. Later Norwegians of note include Sinding, Valen, Saeverud and Nordheim. Among important institutions are the Oslo Philharmonic, the Bergen Festival (founded 1953) and the Ultima festival of contemporary music in Oslo.

Nose, The (*Nos*). Opera by Shostakovich to a libretto by himself and others after Nicolai Gogol. The title character (tenor) is separated from – and after many fantastical-ironic episodes reunited with – the face of Kovalev (baritone). Of several orchestral interludes, the first is for unpitched percussion, an early example of such scoring in Western music. First performance: Leningrad, 18 Jan 1930.

nose flute. Flute played with the nose, as found in Southeast Asia and the Pacific.

Noskowski, Zygmunt (b. Warsaw, 2 May 1846; d. Warsaw, 23 Jul 1909). Polish composer, a Romantic with yearnings for Classicism and counterpoint. He studied with Moniuszko at the music institute in Warsaw (1864–7) and with Friedrich Kiel in Berlin (1872–5). In 1881 he returned to Warsaw, where he taught (at the music institute from 1888), conducted and wrote criticism. His works include the first Polish symphonic poem (*The Steppe*, Op.66, 1896), operas and chamber music.

nota cambiata (It., changed note). In Renaissance polyphony an unaccented dissonant note resolved by a downward leap of a third. See also CAMBIATA.

notation. The representation of music in graphic symbols. Notation arose in ancient Mesopotamia and China almost four thousand years ago, and was maintained by various cultures in the Middle East, the Far East and the Mediterranean, but there is no parallel elsewhere for the precise indication of pitch and rhythm that developed in western Europe in the 11th–14th centuries. Much that is unique to Western music followed from this: the possibility of repeating the same composition, the elevated status of the work and the composer, the feasibility of long and complex pieces, the genesis of a tradition and notions of progress within that tradition.

One thing that changed over time was the nature of notation itself. At first a mnemonic device to remind singers of chants they had learned orally, it became a system of instructions to performers, by which they could execute music they had not heard or seen. The temporal precedence sound→sign was thus reversed, with huge implications. Performance instructions could be interpreted by others with no thought of presenting the music as sound: scholars, students and, not least, fellow composers. Notation thus became essential to music theory, music education and intertextuality, and the written or printed form began to seem more central and more authoritative than the performed result. We speak of *a* performance of a Beethoven symphony but of *the* score, even though there will be many different editions and manuscript sources. And this score, only notionally unique, is regarded as the arbiter of questions of interpretation.

Still, the fact that there are indeed questions of interpretation – even and not least in such heavily notated music as that of Ferneyhough – points to the fallibility of notation. To some degree notated signs are still mnemonics – not prescriptions of the unknown but reminders of the heard and practised. Notation of all periods therefore needs to be read with an understanding of the musical conventions obtaining.

Western notation began its development with the staff, in the 11th century, used first for neumes. Many different dialects emerged, in different places and among different religious orders, but the material was the same: plainsong. The notation of polyphony began in the later 12th century, sometimes with modal rhythm; distinct note values and rests appeared in the mid 13th century. Very few secular songs were notated before the 14th century (though the repertory then set down extended back to the 12th), when, too, the finer indication of rhythmic values was one of the innovations of ars nova. But still rhythmic notation had to be read in relation to the prevailing mensuration. By the later 14th century notational subtleties, in matters of rhythm, were starting to drive creative intentions, instituting a protracted dialectic in Western composition between notating what can be heard and hearing what can be notated.

Practices – especially rhythmic practices – remained local and changeable until the early 16th century, when two developments made for stability. One was the spread of music printing, the other the fact that, increasingly, notated music was addressed not to singers but to keyboard players, lutenists and chamber groups. The easy communication of eye to mouth was therefore replaced by a more complex network involving both interactions with machines (instruments) and tightly co-ordinated polyphony; hence the introduction of barlines and time signatures (15th century), together with unambiguous rhythmic values. And though there was still considerable variety in the forms of notes, 16th-century staff notation can be read without difficulty.

With the introduction of tempo and dynamic markings around 1600, and the increasing standardization of note forms, music by the mid 17th century had settled into the visual aspect it has largely retained. However, typographical conventions continued to change, as did composers' personal habits, and a serious performer might want to consult not only a modern edition but printed versions the composer could oversee and, indeed, any autograph manuscripts.

The rapid evolution of music during the period 1905–55 was achieved in many respects by extrapolations from notational norms – for example, in the writing of irrational rhythms. However, there were also innovations, including symbols for microtones and clusters, indications for more extreme non-standard sounds, and notations for electronic music.

See also ACCIDENTAL; CLEF; DURATION; DYNAMICS; EYE MUSIC; GRAPHIC NOTATION; KEY SIGNATURE; MICROTONE; ORNAMENT; PAUSE; REPEAT; SCORE; SEGNO; STACCATO; STAFF; TABLATURE; TEMPO; TIME SIGNATURE; TIME-SPACE NOTATION.

Gardner Read *Music Notation* (1978)

note. (1) A single sound, or its graphic representation: 'She played the note as written.'

(2) Pitch or pitch class in an abstract sense: 'The note E has a special place in Barraqué's music.'

note-against-note. Term used of counterpoint in which relationships are between simultaneous notes, rather than between staggered lines, as in a canon or other kind of imitative texture.

note row. See ROW.

notes inégales (Fr., unequal notes). Phenomenon in French Baroque music, whereby pairs of notes in running figuration are to be performed alternately long and short, though they may be written in equal values. The difference may be slight, or equivalent to dotting (¾:¼) or overdotting, normally interpreted as double dotting (⅞:⅛): the application of these inequalities is a matter of taste and discernment. Also unclear – and highly controversial – is the relevance of the French practice to other music of the period, notably Bach's.

note values. See DURATION.

Notker (b. near St Gallen, present-day Switzerland, *c.*840; d. St Gallen, 6 Apr 912). Monk and poet, the author of hymns and sequences, and of valuable remarks about musical notation. Nicknamed *balbulus* (stammerer), he was canonized in 1513.

Notre Dame school. Modern term for the composers active at or around the cathedral of Notre Dame in Paris in the second half of the 12th and first half of the 13th centuries. See also LEONIN; MAGNUS LIBER; PEROTIN.

notturno (It.). 18th-century piece for outdoor performance at night. There are examples by Haydn and Mozart.

Nourrit, Adolphe (b. Montpellier, 3 Mar 1802; d. Naples, 8 Mar 1839). French tenor, who succeeded his father Louis (1780–1831) at the Opera in 1826 and created roles in operas by Rossini, Auber, Halévy and Meyerbeer. He lost his voice in 1836, left the Opera and went to Italy to recover. Having given a performance that worried him but pleased his audience, he leapt to his death from his hotel the following morning.

Nouvelles aventures. See AVENTURES.

Novák, Vítězslav (Augustín Rudolf) (b. Kamenice nad Lipou, 5 Dec 1870; d. Skuteč, 18 Jul 1949). Czech composer, a Moravian late Romantic, sharply distinguished from Janáček by his later conservatism. He studied at the Prague Conservatory with Dvořák and others (1889–92), and from 1896 onwards spent periods in Moravia, returning to the conservatory to teach (1909–39). His works include orchestral pieces (Serenade, F, small orch, 1894–5; *In the Tatras*, Op.26, 1902, rev 1905–7; Moravian-Slovak Suite, Op.32, small orch. 1903), cantatas (*The Storm*, Op.42, 1908–10), chamber music, songs and operas.

Novello. British family of musicians and publishers.

(1) **Vincent** (b. London, 6 Sep 1781; d. Nice, 9 Aug 1861). The son of an Italian pastry-cook, he trained with Webbe and at 16 became organist and choirmaster of the Portuguese embassy chapel. His performances there of Haydn and Mozart masses excited attention, and he began publishing them in vocal score (though his collection included spurious items; see TWELFTH MASS). He was also a founder member of the Philharmonic Society. In 1829 he and his wife visited Mozart's sister in Salzburg.

(2) (**Joseph**) **Alfred** (b. London, 12 Aug 1810; d. Genoa, 16 Jul 1896). Vincent's eldest son, he was apprenticed to a music publisher in York and set up his own shop from the family home in London when he was 19. From this evolved the firm of Novello, with its overwhelming command of the choral market throughout the British Empire. He also founded the *Musical Times* (1844).

(3) **Clara (Anastasia)** (b. London, 10 Jun 1818; d. Rome, 12 Mar 1908). Vincent's fourth daughter, who was renowned as an oratorio singer from 1851, when she returned to Britain after pursuing an operatic career in Italy. Named after her, Clara Novello Davies (1861–1943) was a Welsh singing

teacher and choirmistress whose son, Ivor Novello (1893–1951), became a popular actor and composer of musicals (*Perchance to Dream*, 1945; *King's Rhapsody*, 1949).

nozze di Figaro, Le (The Marriage of Figaro). Opera by Mozart to a libretto by Da Ponte after a play by Beaumarchais. Figaro (baritone) and his betrothed Susanna (soprano), servants of the Count (baritone), succeed not only in preventing him exercise the feudal 'right of the first night' but in embarrassing him in front of the Countess (soprano). Meanwhile, love smiles for the ageing Bartolo (bass), as for the adolescent Cherubino (mezzo-soprano). There are extraordinary finales to the second and fourth acts, where music empowers every turn of events, but the work is full, too, of characterful solos: Figaro's 'Se vuol ballare', 'Non più andrai' and 'Aprite un po' quegl'occhi', Susanna's lively 'Venite, inginocchiatevi' and seductive 'Deh vieni', the Count's 'Vedrò, mentre io sospiro', the Countess's affecting 'Porgi, Amor' and 'Dove sono', Bartolo's mockpowerful 'La vendetta', and Cherubino's expressions of youthful ardour in 'Non so più' and 'Voi che sapete'. Mozart wrote new arias for Ferraresi as Susanna in a 1789 Vienna revival: 'Un moto di gioia' and 'Al desio'. But the original score is widely preferred. First performance: Vienna, 1 May 1786.

Nuits d'été, Les (Summer Nights). Song cycle by Berlioz, with orchestra, to words by Théophile Gautier. There are six numbers, originally intended for different voice types (though now the work is most often taken by a soprano or mezzosoprano): 1 'Villanelle' (mez/t), 2 'Le Spectre de la rose' (a), 3 'Sur les lagunes' (mez/a/bar), 4 'Absence' (mez/t), 5 'Au cimitière' (t), 6 'L'Ile inconnue' (mez/t).

number. (1) Musicians have to count: rhythm is sounding number. Beyond that, lengths (in bars) and speeds are often numerically measured, notes and intervals are named by numbering the diatonic scale, big pieces often have numbers of movements, and numbers are inherent in the phenomena of pitch (as frequency), spectrum (as bundle of frequencies) and interval (as frequency ratio). There are thus many ways in which music may be made to assert or encode specific numbers, and these have been pursued avidly since the early 20th century as part of a more analytical approach to composition and scholarship. Relevant composers include Berg (units of 30 bars in his Chamber Concerto; his personal number 23 in other works), Messiaen (ARITHMETICAL DURATIONS; rhythmic patterns based on prime numbers; sevenfold form in *Les Corps glorieux, La Transfiguration* and other works), Cage (rhythmic structures drawn from number sequences), Nancarrow (canons in voices at numerically geared speeds) and Xenakis (textures and shapes modelled on probability distributions). Working with computers may also encourage composers to think in numbers. At the same time, since the 1940s, several scholars have looked for number patterns in older music, especially that of Bach, who some speculate used numbers derived from the alphabetical positions of letters in a word (e.g. BACH = 2 + 1 + 3 + 8 = 14). See also ALGORITHM; FIBONACCI SERIES; GOLDEN SECTION.

(2) Item in a longer work, especially an opera or oratorio, where numbers (arias, duets, ensembles) are connected by recitative or spoken dialogue. Numbers may also be discerned where the music is more continuous, e.g. Siegmund's 'Winterstürme' in *Die Walküre*.

(3) Song, with connotations of popular music.

number opera. Opera made of self-contained units; see NUMBER (2). This kind of form is particularly associated with the 18th century. Opera in the 19th century became more continuous, but some 20th-century composers (Stravinsky, Birtwistle) recreated number opera.

Nunes, Emanuel (Tito Ricoca) (b. Lisbon, 31 Aug 1941). Portuguese composer, among the most respected latterday modernists, working with complex textures (*Quodlibet* for instruments and groups in a large auditorium, 1990–91) and electronic interactions (*Wandlungen* for chamber orchestra, 1986). He studied in Lisbon, at Darmstadt (1963–5), with Pousseur, Spek and Stockhausen at the conservatory in Cologne (1965–7), and at the Paris Conservatoire. Cologne and Paris have remained his two places of residence; he has also taught since 1986 in Freiburg.

Nuova Consonanza. Organization for new music founded in Rome by Evangelisti in 1960. It now presents concerts under radio auspices.

Nursery, The (*Detskaya*). Cycle of seven songs by Musorgsky to his own words, largely in the voice of a child addressing nanny and mother.

nut. (1) Small ridge fixed at the top of the fingerboard on a violin, to raise the strings.

(2) See FROG.

Nutcracker, The (*Casse-noisette, Shchelkunchik*). Ballet score by Tchaikovsky for choreography by Petipa after a tale by Hoffmann. The original work was made to form a double bill with *Iolanta*. Clara's best Christmas gift, a nutcracker, is transformed into a prince, who takes her to the Kingdom of Sweets for an entertainment staged by the Sugar-Plum Fairy. This latter sequence forms the bulk of the popular suite, comprising Miniature Overture, March, Dance of the Sugar-Plum Fairy, Russian Dance (*Trepak*), Arabian Dance, Chinese Dance, Dance of the Mirlitons, Waltz of the Flowers. First performance: St Petersburg, 19 Mar 1892 (suite), 18 Dec 1892 (ballet).

Nyireghází, Ervin (b. Budapest, 19 Jan 1903; d. Los Angeles, 13 Apr 1987). Hungarian–US pianist, an intensely personal musician who lived much of his life in obscurity. He studied with Dohnányi from 1914 and played Liszt's Second Concerto under Nikisch in Berlin when he was 15. By the 1930s he was in Los Angeles playing for films, until he was rediscovered in 1974. Among the works he then recorded were several of his own operatic paraphrases.

Nyman, Michael (Laurence) (b. London, 23 Mar 1944). British composer, a minimalist whose music refers equally to rock and the 18th century. After studies with Bush at the RAM (1961–4) and Thurston Dart at King's College, London (1964–7), he began his career as a writer: he wrote the text for Birtwistle's *Down by the Greenwood Side* and an influential book on EXPERIMENTAL MUSIC. Not until his early 30s did he emerge as a composer, but he rapidly made up for lost time. His works include operas (*The Man who Mistook his Wife for a Hat*, 1986), film scores (*The Draughtsman's Contract*, 1982; *The Piano*, 1992), chamber music and pieces for his own Michael Nyman Band.

Nymphs and Shepherds. Song by Purcell, for Thomas Shadwell's *The Libertine*.

Nystroem, Gösta (b. Silvberg, Dalarna, 13 Oct 1890; d. Särö, 9 Aug 1966). Swedish composer, who rediscovered Nordic symphonism after encountering the music of Debussy, Ravel and Stravinsky in Paris (1920–32). The son of a musician and amateur painter, he pursued both arts himself, learning first from his father and then, through a fitful training, with Andreas Hallén and others. His major compositions, most dating from after he turned 40, include six symphonies.

O

ob. Abbreviation for oboe.

obbligato (It., obligatory). In the most general sense, the opposite of AD LIBITUM. More specifically, and more usually, the term is applied to an instrumental solo or solo instrument standing out from the orchestra accompanying a voice. The aria 'Erbarme Dich' in the St Matthew Passion may be described as having a violin obbligato or obbligato violin.

Oberlin College Conservatory of Music. Conservatory in Oberlin, near Cleveland, founded in 1865.

Oberon. Opera by Weber to a libretto by James Robinson Planché. Oberon (tenor) and Puck (mezzo-soprano) lend assistance to Huon (tenor) in winning the hand of Reiza (soprano), daughter of Harun al Rashid. Numbers include Reiza's 'Ozean! du Ungeheuer' ('Ocean, thou mighty monster'). First performance: London, 12 Apr 1826.

oboe (Fr. *hautbois*, Ger. *Oboe*, It., *oboe*). Double-reed WOODWIND instrument, the civilized descendant of the SHAWM. Its name comes from the Fr. *haut bois* (high/main wood). The regular oboe is a soprano instrument in C, having a range from the B♭ below middle C up through three octaves (or more in the hands of a virtuoso). Other members of the family include the OBOE D'AMORE (in A, a third lower), the COR ANGLAIS (in F, a fifth lower) and the rare bass or baritone oboe (an octave lower).

From many different traditions of oboe making,

the Conservatoire-system oboe became almost universal during the early 20th century. It arrived in 1872 as the last stage in a collaboration between the maker Frédéric Triébert and the player Apollon Barret, and was adopted by the Paris Conservatoire nine years later. The body of the instrument is a narrow-bore tube of grenadilla (the African black wood also used for clarinets), about 24 inches (60cm) long and made in three sections. Into it is fitted a double reed, i.e. a pair of thin pieces of cane, shaved thin at the mouth end and, at the other, set in a tubular metal 'staple'. Placed between the lips and blown through, the reed vibrates and transmits impulses to the air column in the body. This places great strain on a fragile mechanism, and oboists need to replace their reeds frequently.

As is suggested by the ubiquity of the Fr. name in various forms, the oboe arose in France in the mid 17th century, its main point of difference from the shawm being the absence of the pirouette and therefore a more delicate sound. Its first clearly documented use was in Lully's *Les Plaisirs de l'île enchantée* (1664); by the end of the century it was being heard across Europe in orchestras, ensembles and military bands. Made often of boxwood or rosewood (sometimes ivory), it was played with the fingers directly on the holes, having only one or two keys to produce D♯; not until the beginning of the 19th century did it begin to acquire more keys and move towards its modern form.

Since the 1970s interest in period performance styles has stimulated many makers to reproduce 'Baroque oboes', i.e. instruments of 18th-century type. Such instruments have an enormous repertory, especially of music from the first third of the century: obbligatos in Bach, concertos by Handel, Vivaldi and Albinoni, choice passages in Rameau, chamber music by other French and German composers. Works of the Classical period include Mozart's concerto and quartet (with strings). In the 19th century the oboe was almost exclusively an orchestral instrument, if granted important solos by composers from Beethoven to Mahler. It then became an instrument for concertos, chamber music and solo pieces again in the 20th century, thanks partly to outstanding performers, principally Goossens and Holliger. There are notable works by Strauss, Poulenc, Britten, Yun, Maderna, Berio, Ligeti, Holliger himself and Carter.

Geoffrey Burgess and Bruce Haynes *The Oboe* (2004)

oboe da caccia. Alto oboe in F, with a curved, leather-bound body. Never widespread, it has been reintroduced in modern times thanks to Bach's use of it in the St Matthew Passion and other works.

oboe d'amore. Mezzo-soprano oboe in A, used by Bach and Telemann. Bach's parts for it led to the production from the late 19th century of modern-style instruments, which have been used occasionally by composers, notably Mahler (*Um Mitternacht*), Debussy (*Gigues*) and Ligeti (Double Concerto).

oboe quartet. Group of instruments comprising oboe plus string trio (vn, va, vc), or work for such a line-up. There are examples by Mozart and Carter.

Obouhow, Nicolas [Obukhov, Nikolay] (b. Olshanka, Kursk, 22 Apr 1892; d. St Cloud, 13 Jun 1954). Russian composer, for whom music was divine revelation, demanding blood on the page in the case of his *Kniga zhizni* or *Le livre de la vie*, for voices, two pianos, electronic instruments and orchestra (1918–c.1925). He studied at the conservatories of Moscow and St Petersburg (with William Steinberg and Tcherepnin), and left Russia in 1918, to settle the next year in Paris. There he developed his own style, out of Scriabin, with his own electronic instruments, notably the *croix sonore* (sounding cross). He continued producing massive mystical works to the end of his life, but also published some piano pieces (*Adorons Christ*, 1945).

Obrecht, Jacob (b. Ghent, 1457/8; d. Ferrara, Jun/Jul 1505). Netherlandish composer, the most enigmatic of Renaissance masters, revered at one time for his ingenious artifice but latterly more for his strength of movement, immediacy and variety. The son of Willem Obrecht, a Ghent city trumpeter, he may have come into contact with Busnois at the Burgundian court. Certainly his early masses show a response to Busnois, as to, still more so, Ockeghem. His first documented position was at St Gertrude's in Bergen op Zoom (1480–84), after which he moved often, from Cambrai Cathedral (1484–5) to St Donatian's in Bruges (1485–91, during which time he was absent for a year, 1487–8, mostly at the Ferrara court), then to Our Lady's in Antwerp (1492–7), and so back to Bergen op Zoom (1497–8) and the churches he had served in Bruges (1498–1500) and Antwerp (1500–1503). During this switchback progress, probably soon after 1490, he developed a new style, in which cadence, phrasing, triadic melodies, imitation and repetition combine to produce a firm sense of harmonic direction. In September 1504 he became chapelmaster back in Ferrara, but he lost the post four months later when Duke Ercole I died, and he himself died in the summer.

Rob C. Wegman *Born for the Muses* (1994)

Masses (a 4 unless otherwise stated): *Caput, Fortuna desperata, L'Homme armé, Libenter gloriabor, Malheur me bat, Maria zart, Petrus apostolus, Rose playsante, Salve diva parens, de Sancto Donatiano, de Sancto Martino, Sicut spina rosam, Sub tuum presidium* a 3–7; 16 others extant
Motets: *Salve crux arbor vitae* a 5; *Salve regina* a 6; etc.
Songs: *Tsat een cleyn meeskin* a 4; etc.

ocarina (It., little goose). Small wind instrument, normally oval in shape and made of terracotta or plastic, with holes for mouth and fingers. It is found worldwide, but only in a very few classical scores (e.g. Ligeti's Violin Concerto).

occasional piece. A composition made for an occasion, e.g. a birthday, often with no thought of survival.

Oceanides, The (*Aallottaret*). Symphonic poem by Sibelius, his Finnish title meaning 'the spirits of the waves'. First performance: Norfolk, Conn., 4 Jun 1914.

Ockeghem, Jean de (b. St Ghislain, near Mons, c.1410; d. ?Tours, 6 Feb 1497). Netherlandish composer, of music moving with serene complexity through polyphony of long lines. His date of birth is extremely uncertain, and indeed nothing is recorded of him before 1443, when he was at Our Lady's in Antwerp; in his youth he may have come across Binchois. He later served the Bourbon court at Moulins, before joining the

French royal chapel, probably in 1451. There he remained until the 1480s, when he seems to have retired to Tours, to take charge of lucrative ecclesiastical interests he had held since the late 1450s. In the 1460s he went to Cambrai at least twice and visited Du Fay, whom he may have encountered earlier; during the same decade he probably met Busnois in Tours, and he accompanied one or both of two French embassies to Spain in 1469–70.

There is a tradition – perhaps supported by nothing more than the bass-heaviness of his music – that he had a low voice. He also had a long life, though the chronology of his output is irrecoverable, partly because of his seeming wish to make each work unique. The *Missa prolationum* is an extraordinary instance of contrapuntal virtuosity (in the form of mensuration canons at different intervals), while other masses are based on diverse cantus firmus treatments or else freely composed. In all cases the impression is of smooth ease, yet also of melodic movement that is unpredictable, suggesting a constant rumination. Somewhat unusual is the working with compact motifs in the possibly instrumental *Ut heremita solus*, which may have been a reply to Busnois's encomium *In hydraulis*. After his death he was eulogized by Guillaume Crétin, Jean Molinet (*Nymphes des bois*, set by Josquin) and Erasmus. His *Requiem* is the earliest extant.

Ernst Krenek *Johannes Ockeghem* (1953)

Masses: *Au travail suis* a 4; *Caput* a 4; *Cuiusvis toni* a 4; *De plus en plus* a 4; *Ecce ancilla Domini* a 4; *Fors seulement* a 5; *L'Homme armé* a 4; *Ma maitresse* a 4 (*Kyrie–Gloria* only); *Mi-mi* a 4; *Missa prolationum* a 4; *Missa quinti toni* a 3; *Missa sine nomine* a 3; *Missa sine nomine* a 5; *Requiem* 3–4; lone *Credo* a 4
Motets: *Alma redeptoris mater* a 4; *Ave Maria* a 4; *Intemerata Dei mater* a 5; *Salve regina* a 4; *Ut heremita solus* a 4
Chansons: *Au travail suis* a 3; *Fors seulement l'attente* a 3; *Ma maitresse* a 3; *Mort, tu as navré* a 4 (on death of Binchois); etc.

Octandre (Octandrous, i.e. having eight stamens). Work by Varèse for wind (wind qnt, tpt, trbn) and double bass. First performance: New York, 13 Jan 1924.

octatonic. Term describing a scale of eight notes to the octave, normally with alternating semitones and whole tones, e.g. C–C♯–D♯–E–F♯–G–A–A♯–C or C–D–E♭–F–G♭–A♭–A–B–C. Such scales are found in Beethoven (Diabelli Variations), Liszt, Musorgsky, Rimsky-Korsakov and, especially, Stravinsky, as well as Messiaen, for whom this was the second mode of limited transpositions.

octave. (1) Interval that is a basic element of similarity in most pitch systems, representing a frequency ratio of 2:1. Because of this connection, notes an octave apart sound alike; in the Western system they have the same letter name and are regarded as functionally identical in most respects. Besides this perfect octave (e.g. C–C) musical terminology recognizes a diminished octave (C–B) and an augmented octave (C–C♯).

(2). Register: 'B appears in several different octaves.'

octet (Fr. *octuor*, Ger. *Oktett*, It. *ottetto*). Group of eight instruments or voices, or group of eight performers on such, or genre of music for that medium, or work of that genre. Notable examples include Schubert's (cl, hn, bn, str qt, db) and Mendelssohn's (2 str qt), written in consecutive years, as well as Stravinsky's (fl, cl, 2 tpt, 2 trbn, 2 bn).

ode. An ancient Greek and Roman song form, though in musical contexts the term is most associated with a celebratory form invented at the English court under Charles II, but with precedents from the reigns of his father and grandfather. Court odes were written for monarchs' birthdays and returns to London, and for New Year, in the form of cantatas for soli, choir and orchestra. They provided models for odes for St CECILIA's Day and for university ceremonials. By far the most interesting composer of odes was Purcell, followed by Handel and a long decline.

Odington, Walter (*fl. c.*1300). English theorist, an Evesham monk whose *Summa de speculatione musica* covers questions of number and harmony, and of polyphonic composition.

Odyssey. Epic by Homer of the wanderings of Odysseus (Ulysses), the tales he tells and tricks he pulls, his return home to his wife Penelope and son Telemachus, and his dispatching of Penelope's suitors. Musical treatments include:

(1) Monteverdi's opera *Il ritorno d'Ulisse in patria* (Ulysses' Return to his Homeland) to a libretto by Badoaro. Ulysses (tenor) is brought back to his lamenting wife, Penelope (soprano), by the assistance of gods and mortals against the efforts of the vain and foolish. First performance: Venice, 1640.

(2) Rebel's opera *Ulysse*, also concerned with the hero's return, though with Circe as antagonist. First performance: Paris, 1703.

(3) Keiser's opera *Ulysses*, based on a German translation of the libretto set by Rebel. First performance: Copenhagen, 1722.

(4) John Christopher Smith's opera *Ulysses*, again on the subject of the return. First performance: London, 1733.

(5) Gluck's opera *Telemaco*, to a libretto by Marco Coltellini, once more with Circe as agent of magic and malevolence, now working on her island, where Ulysses is captive and Telemachus shipwrecked. First performance: Vienna, 1765.

(6) Cimarosa's opera *Penelope*, wresting from the story a classic opera seria scenario of nobility triumphant. First performance: Naples, 1794.

(7) August Bungert's tetralogy *Die Odyssee*. First performance: Dresden, 1898–1903.

(8) Fauré's opera *Pénélope*, to a libretto by René Fauchois, returning to the return of Ulysses (tenor). First performance: Monte Carlo, 4 Mar 1913.

(9) Skalkottas's overture *The Return of Ulysses* (1942–3).

(10) Dallapiccola's opera *Ulisse*, with scenes from throughout the epic. First performance: Berlin, 29 Sep 1968.

Oedipus. Mythic king of Grecian Thebes, whose tragedy began when he unknowingly killed his father and married his mother. Their daughter ANTIGONE has her own drama; aspects of his, as related in Sophocles's *King Oedipus* and *Oedipus at Colonus*, are treated in the following:

(1) Stravinsky's opera-oratorio *Oedipus Rex* to a libretto by Cocteau after the first Sophocles play, the sung portion translated into Lat. by Jean Daniélou. Oedipus (tenor), determined to rid the city of pestilence, and in defiance of dire warning from Jocasta (soprano), learns the truth of his parentage, blinds himself and leaves. First performance: Paris, 30 May 1927 (concert), 23 Feb 1928 (staged).

(2) Enescu's opera *Oedipe* to a libretto by Edmond Fleg, following both Sophocles plays and their background, with Oedipus a bass-baritone. First performance: Paris, 13 Mar 1936.

There are also Oedipal works by Purcell, Sacchini, Mendelssohn, Partch and Rihm.

Oelze, Christiane (b. Cologne, 9 Oct 1963). German soprano, whose engaging brightness and precision suit music from Bach and Handel to Webern and Ligeti. She studied with Klesie Kelly-Moog, won the Hugo Wolf Competition in 1987 and made her opera debut as Despina in Ottawa in 1990.

oeuvre (Fr.). Work. The term is used in Eng. to signify a corpus of works, as in 'Handel's oeuvre', 'Handel's operatic oeuvre'.

off-beat. Any beat other than the first in the bar.

Offenbach, Jacques [Jacob] (b. Cologne, 20 Jun 1819; d. Paris, 5 Oct 1880). German–French composer, the inventor and exuberant master of operetta. His father, a synagogue cantor, took him and his elder brother Julius (Jules) to Paris in 1833 and left them there for further musical study. Jacob, soon Jacques, was already a published composer, but principally a cellist, and after playing in the Opéra-Comique orchestra (1834–8) he began making his name as a virtuoso. Along the way he had some composition lessons with Fromental Halévy, whose nephew Ludovic was to become one of his principal librettists. In 1844 he converted to Catholicism and married, and in 1850 he was appointed music director of the Comédie-Française. Creative fulfilment, though, did not come until July 1855, when he took over a theatre, renamed it the Bouffes Parisiens, put on a triple bill of one-acters and filled the house. By the end of the year he had moved to a larger theatre, on rue Monsigny, still known now as the Bouffes Parisiens. There, with his brother leading the orchestra, he continued his success with one-act pieces and also promoted young composers, including Lecocq and Bizet, whose settings of *Le Docteur Miracle* he presented on consecutive days in April 1857. *Orphée aux enfers*, the next year, was his first attempt at a longer piece, and a triumph. In 1862 he stepped down as director of the Bouffes Parisiens, but creatively there was no let-up. After the Franco-Prussian War (1870–71) and the fall of the Second Empire came a period of eclipse, yet by the time he died he was in favour again and preparing his first serious drama, *Les Contes d'Hoffmann*.

Left incomplete, *Hoffmann* is an elusive piece, full of the composer's dream and aspiration. In his most celebrated operettas, by contrast, he has his feet firmly on the ground, endorsing the wit and satire of his librettists while fully conveying the joy of life.

Peter Gammond *Offenbach* (1980)

www.offenbach.org

Opera: *Les* CONTES D'HOFFMANN, 1877–80

Operettas: *Orphée aux enfers* (see ORPHEUS), 1858; *La* BELLE HELENE, 1864; *Barbe-bleue* (Meilhac and Halévy), f.p. Paris, 1866; *La Vie parisienne* (Meilhac and Halévy), f.p. Paris, 1866; *La* GRANDE-DUCHESSE DE GEROLSTEIN, 1866–7; *Robinson Crusoé* (Eugène Cormon and Hector Crémieux), f.p. Paris, 1867; *Madame Favart* (Alfred Duru and Henri Chivot), f.p. Paris, 1868; *La* PERICHOLE, 1868; *La Fille du tambour-major* (Chivot and Duru), f.p. Paris, 1879; 32 other full-length pieces, over 50 one-acters

Other works: incidental scores, ballets, cello music

offertory. Chant in verse-refrain form, in most

cases to words from one of the psalms, sung during the preparation of the bread and wine at mass, and forming part of the PROPER.

Officium breve. String quartet by Kurtág, titled in full *Officium breve in memoriam Andreae Szervánsky*, in 15 movements, of which the 10th is a transcription of the chorale-canon from Webern's Second Cantata and the last quotes from the remembered colleague. First performance: Witten, 22 Apr 1988.

off key. Out of tune.

offstage. Invisible to the audience, as a stage band may be in an opera. Offstage instruments are used in the concert hall to produce dramatic effects in works by, for example, Beethoven (trumpet call in *Leonore* overtures Nos.2–3), Berlioz (oboe echoing onstage cor anglais in the *Symphonie fantastique*), Mahler (posthorn in the Third Symphony, etc.), Ives (strings in *The Unanswered Question*) and Kurtág (... *quasi una fantasia* ... and other works).

Ogdon, John (Alexander Howard) (b. Mansfield Woodhouse, Notts., 27 Jan 1937; d. London, 1 Aug 1989). British pianist, much valued for strength of hand and mind – a strength he maintained at intervals even through the schizophrenia that overtook him in the 1970s. He studied at the Royal Manchester College from 1945, and had pieces written for him by Goehr and Davies. His debut as a substitute in Brahms's Second Concerto (Liverpool, 1958) made his national reputation, which became international when he was joint winner, with Ashkenazy, of the 1962 Tchaikovsky Competition. Unusually, he championed Alkan, Busoni and, later, Sorabji; he was also a composer.

Ohana, Maurice (b. Casablanca, 12 Jun 1913; d. Paris, 13 Nov 1992). Gibraltarian–French composer, of music afloat in a Mediterranean world, where Arab and African sources are as important as others from Spain and France. Having been brought up in Morocco and Spain, he studied as a pianist, with Lazare-Lévy and Frank Marshall, while undergoing formal training in architecture in Paris (1932–6). He then abandoned architecture for the piano and composition, studying with Daniel-Lesur at the Schola Cantorum (1937–40). During this time he also worked with the flamenco artist La Argentinita, who had been close to Lorca. He served in the British army during the Second World War (he abandoned British nationality for French only in 1976), then settled in Paris, where, working independently, he gradually developed the mature style that emerged in his 'sigma series' of 11 works, all with titles beginning with the letter S. His continuing contact with non-European cultures gave him an unusual breath and breadth, a familiarity with percussion and microtones, and a sense of music as magic.

Caroline Rae *The Music of Maurice Ohana* (2000)
www.mauriceohana.com

Dramatic: *Syllabaire pour Phèdre* (chbr opera; Raphaël Cluzel, after Euripides), 1966–7; *La Célestine* (opera, after Fernando de Rojas), 1982–6, f.p. Paris, 1988; etc.

Orchestral: *Trois graphiques*, gtr, 4 perc, orch, 1950–57; *Synaxis*, 2 pf, 4 perc, orch, 1966; *Chiffres de clavecin*, hpd, orch, 1968; *Silenciaire*, 6 perc, str, 1969; *T'Harân-Ngô*, 1974; *Anneau du Tamarit*, vc, orch, 1976; *Livre des prodiges*, 1978–9; *Crypt*, str, 1980; Piano Concerto, 1981; Cello Concerto No.2 'In Dark and Blue', vc, orch, 1989–90

Vocal: *Llanto por Ignacio Sánchez Mejías* (oratorio; Lorca), 1950; *Cantigas* (Renaissance Sp.), s, mez, ch, ens, 1953–4; *Tombeau de Claude Debussy*, s, ⅓-tone zither, pf, chbr orch, 1962; *Sibylle*, s, perc, tape, 1968; *Cris*, ch, 1968–9; *Stream*, b, str trio, 1970; *Office des oracles*, soli, ch, ens, 1974; *Lys de madrigaux*, women's ch, ens, 1975–6; Mass, s, mez, ch, ens, 1977; *Swan Song* (Ohana, after Pierre de Ronsard), 12 v, 1987–8; *Avoaha*, ch, 2 pf, perc, 1990–91; etc.

Ensemble: *Etudes chorégraphiques*, 4–6 perc, 1955–61; *Signes*, fl, 2 zithers, pf, 4 perc, 1965

Chamber and instrumental: *Cinq séquences*, str qt, 1963; String Quartet No.2, 1978–80; No.3 'Sorgin-Ngô', 1989; *Kypris*, ob, va, db, pf, 1985; *Sacral d'Ilx*, ob, hn, hpd, 1975; *Neumes*, ob, pf, 1965; *Syrtes*, vc, pf, 1970; *Noctuaire*, vc, pf, 1976; *Satyres*, 2 fl, 1976; *Quatre improvisations*, fl, 1960; *Sarc*, ob, 1972

Keyboard: *Sonatine monodique*, pf, 1945; *Trois caprices*, pf, 1944–54; *Carillons*, hpd, 1960; *Sorôn-Ngô*, 2 pf, 1969–70; 24 Preludes, pf, 1972–3; *Wamba*, carillon, 1980; 2 Pieces, hpd, 1983; *Douze études d'interprétation*, pf, 1982–5 (Nos.11–12 with perc); *Miroir de Célestine*, hpd, perc, 1989–90; *So Tango*, hpd, 1991

Guitar: *Tiento*, 1957; *Si le jour paraît*, 1963–4; *Cadran lunaire*, 1981–2; *Anonyme XXème siècle*, 2 gtr, 1988

Oiseaux exotiques (Exotic Birds). Work by Messiaen made almost entirely from avian songs and calls, brightly projected by solo piano and an orchestra of wind and percussion. First performance: Paris, 10 Mar 1956.

Oiseau-Lyre, L'. Publishing and record company founded in Paris in 1932 by Louise Dyer, who named it after the lyrebird of her native Australia. A strong tradition in early music was maintained by Decca, which took over the record label in 1970.

Oistrakh, David (Fyodorovich) (b. Odessa, 30 Sep 1908; d. Amsterdam, 24 Oct 1974). Russian violinist, a commanding musician. He graduated from Petr Stolyarsky's class at the Odessa Conservatory in 1926, and in 1928 moved to Moscow. Successes in the 1935 Wieniawski Competition (second to Neveu) and the 1937 Ysaÿe (first) made him an international figure, but his travels were limited before his 1955 New York debut, after which he became one of the Soviet Union's pre-eminent musical ambassadors. He also, from 1934, taught at the Moscow Conservatory, where his pupils included his son, Igor (b. 1931). Concertos were written for him by Shostakovich (both), Khachaturian and Myaskovsky.

Oktave (Ger.). Octave. Hence also *Oktavflöte* (piccolo).

Oktett (Ger.). Octet.

Old Hall. Manuscript volume of English sacred polyphony copied *c*.1415–21 with additions during the next decade, including music by Power, Pycard, Bytteryng, Damett, Cooke, Forest, Dunstable and others. It may have been produced for the chapel of Thomas, Duke of Clarence, brother of Henry V. Acquired by John Stafford Smith in 1813, it passed to St Edmund's College in Old Hall, Herts., in 1893, and was sold to the British Library in 1973.

Old Hundredth [Old Hundred]. Tune for Psalm 100 that was 'old' by 1696, when Nahum Tate and Nicholas Brady called it so in their psalter. Indeed, it had first appeared in Geneva in 1551, as Loys Bourgeois's melody for Psalm 134. There are organ versions by Purcell, Pachelbel and J.C. Bach, and one for full choral-orchestral forces by Vaughan Williams.

Old Roman chant. Tradition preserved in a few Roman sources of the 11th–13th centuries, whose chants are often more melismatic than the Gregorian equivalents.

Olimpiade, L' (The Olympiad). Libretto by Metastasio, in which tests to love and friendship unfold from a contest at the Olympic Games. One of his most popular, it was set by Caldara, Vivaldi, Pergolesi, Leo, Galuppi, Hasse, Jommelli, Piccinni, Sacchini, Mysliveček, Cherubini, Cimarosa and Paisiello. Mozart set the aria 'Alcandro, lo confesso' twice.

oliphant (Old Fr., elephant). Intricately carved ivory horn of the 10th–11th centuries, more a display item than a musical instrument, though mentioned in the latter capacity in the *Chanson de Roland*.

Oliver, Stephen (b. Chester, 10 Mar 1950; d. London, 29 Apr 1992). British composer, fecund with operas. He studied with Leighton and R.S. Johnson at Oxford, where a student production of his *The Duchess of Malfi* (1971) made his name. Among later works are *Tom Jones* (1976), *Timon of Athens* (1991) and a version of Mozart's *L'oca del Cairo* (1991), besides many scores for films, plays and television.

Olivero, Betty (b. Tel-Aviv, 16 May 1954). Israeli composer, achieving a Berio-like embrace of traditional materials, including Jewish folksong and KLEZMER. She studied at the Rubin Academy in her home city (1972–9), with Druckman at Yale, and with Berio at Tanglewood and in Italy (1982–6). Notable works include *Bakashot* (Supplications) for clarinet, choir and orchestra (1996), and music for clarinet quintet for Paul Wegener's film *Der Golem* (1997).

Oliveros, Pauline (b. Houston, 30 May 1932). US composer-performer, whose concept of 'deep listening' involves contact with both personal musical intuition and the space in which performance is to take place. Following studies at the University of Houston (1949–52), privately with Robert Erickson and at San Francisco State College, she was a founder director of the tape music centre at Mills College (1966–7) and then taught at UCSD (1967–81). Increasingly she became concerned with improvisation, performing herself on an accordion with special tunings, and in 1985 she set up the Pauline Oliveros Foundation to foster her work.
www.deeplistening.org

Olsen, Poul Rovsing (b. Copenhagen, 4 Nov 1922; d. Copenhagen, 2 Jul 1982). Danish composer, for whom serialism, acquired through an encounter with Babbitt in 1952, was a path to interactions with the folk music he studied in Greenland and the Persian Gulf. He studied with Knud Jeppesen at the Copenhagen Conservatory (1943–6) and with Boulanger and Messiaen in Paris (1948–9). Besides his work as a composer and researcher, he was a regular music critic and administrator. His works include operas after García Lorca (*Belisa*, Op.50, f.p. Copenhagen, 1966) and Poe (*Usher*, Op.83, f.p. Århus, 1982), as well as chamber and piano pieces.

ombra (It., shade). Term used of scenes in opera where supernatural beings appear or are summoned. There are ombra scenes in works from Monteverdi's *Orfeo* to Wagner's *Ring* (Erda's arrivals) and beyond.

ondeggiando (It., waving). ONDULE.

ondes martenot (Fr., Martenot waves). Electronic instrument invented by Maurice Martenot (under the name *ondes musicales*) as an improvement on the THEREMIN, and introduced in Levidis's *Poème symphonique* (1928). It can produce only one note at a time, in response to a keyboard or the sliding of a ring along a ribbon (to generate glissandos), and can offer some variety of colour thanks to its different speakers: a 'palm' with sympathetic strings and others containing a tam tam and springs. Much in vogue in Paris in the 1930s–40s, it gained repertory from Honegger (*Jeanne d'Arc au bûcher*), Varèse (*Ecuatorial*) and Messiaen (*Trois petites liturgies*, *Turangalîla*), enough to keep it alive.

Ondine. See UNDINE.

ondulé (Fr., wavy). String technique by which the bow is made to waver from one string to another.

one-work composer. See UNICA.

Onslow, (André) Georges (Louis) (b. Clermont-Ferrand, 27 Jul 1784; d. Clermont-Ferrand, 3 Oct 1853). French composer, a gentleman amateur of fine chamber music. Of British–French parentage, he studied piano with Dussek in Hamburg (1799–1800) and Cramer in England, and is said to have had just three composition lessons with Reicha to perfect himself. Central to his output are 34 string quintets and 37 quartets.

onzième (Fr.). 11th.

Op. See OPUS NUMBER.

Op.1. Term sometimes used figuratively of a composer's first work even if no number is attached.

open. (1) Vibrating naturally. String players may perform on 'open strings', i.e. strings not stopped and therefore sounding their fundamental tones, or harmonics thereof. Similarly, brass instrumentalists have 'open notes', i.e. notes from the instrument's natural harmonic series, not using keys.

(2) The opposite of muted or stopped on brass instruments. The word may therefore appear in a part as an instruction to remove the mute.

open pedal. SUSTAINING PEDAL.

open position. See POSITION (3).

open score. Score of contrapuntal music with each part on its own staff. See also SCORE.

opera (Fr. *opéra*, Ger. *Oper*, It. *opera*). Drama with music. The term is used for an individual example ('Bartók's single opera'), a genre ('French Baroque opera'), a performance ('tonight's opera'), a kind of performance ('we're going to the opera'), or a theatre or company set up to present such works ('the Netherlands Opera'). Meaning simply 'work' in It., it had gained the specific connotation in Eng. of musical drama by 1644, when John Evelyn used it this way.

Opera is multiform. It brings together the skills of singer and instrumentalist, director and designer, theatre architect and impresario, conductor and stage hand, dancer and choreographer (in many cases), and, of course, composer and librettist, all to present a piece of theatre that is, most essentially, sung – and sung with force, given that opera customarily takes place in a large theatre, with an orchestra whose power must be matched. Singing this way does many things. Being a special kind of vocal behaviour, it gives people – the singers themselves, and their audience – access to experiencing extremes of heroic resolve, sexual ardour, divine inspiration and madness. It gives them access, also, to a fluidity of time, whereby a brief moment (a surge of love, a gasp of recognition, a dying breath) can be extended to several minutes. And it can be funny; hence comic opera. Its demands on those who do it are equalled by the prestige they thereby acquire, and their sense of belonging to a tradition, almost a guild. It also means – in a culture where opera is nearly always performed from a score, not improvised or developed in rehearsal – that the composer largely controls the drama, which is why operas in the Western tradition are generally known as the works of their composers rather than their librettists, singers or companies.

Sung drama is common human property – common because of its elevation from everyday speech – and existed, for example, in classical Greece (5th century BC) and Song dynasty China (10th–13th centuries AD). However, the term 'opera' is normally confined to Western culture from after c.1600, when various aspects conjoined to create a new form. One was the recognition that, indeed, Greek drama was sung. Another was the development of musical pageantry as court entertainment in the 16th century (INTERMEDIO; MASQUE), out of a humanist impulse to educate monarchs while celebrating them. Yet another was the arrival of a musical style, RECITATIVE, which made it possible for individual singers to express themselves as characters.

It is not surprising that opera arose in Italy, where these questions of aesthetics, of the nature of humanity and of musical expression were being vigorously debated and explored. Opera became there the ultimate achievement of the Renaissance, on the threshold of the Baroque. The earliest examples were produced in Florence, still the headquarters of Renaissance humanism, in settings of poetic dramas by Rinuccini: *Dafne* (1598, music by Peri) and *Euridice* (1600, rival scores by Peri and Caccini). Simultaneously in Rome – from a different impulse, to have music empower spiritual instruction – came oratorio and sacred opera (*Rappresentatione di anima, et di corpo*, 1600, music by Cavalieri). Then in Mantua appeared a first masterpiece, the work that can fittingly be designated not its poet's but its composer's: Monteverdi's *Orfeo* (1607).

Happily Monteverdi lived to write more operas in Venice after 1637, when a visit by a company from Rome – where opera had become sumptuous spectacle – had sparked off the world's first opera craze, followed rapidly by the world's first opera houses, open to a ticket-buying public for the short CARNIVAL season. Venetian and Roman opera then spread in the 1640s–60s to Milan, Naples, Paris, Innsbruck, Vienna and Dresden, conveyed in almost every instance by Italian singers and Italian composers (including Luigi Rossi, Cavalli and Cesti). There were only sporadic attempts to establish opera in other languages: German (Schütz's lost *Dafne*, 1627), English (*The* SIEGE OF RHODES, 1656) and Spanish. Perhaps it seemed already that Italian was the natural language of opera, by virtue of its easy rhymes, its melodiousness in speech and the readiness with which it can express both poetic fancy and urgent passion (though it could be, conversely, that the nature of the language has been changed by national exposure to opera). Lasting traditions of non-Italian opera were not established until the 1670s in Paris (Lully), London (SEMI-OPERA) and Hamburg (Theile).

Lully's operas formed the foundation for a continuing repertory, being revived in France well into the 18th century, but little else survived the sea change of the late 17th century, when early opera was pruned of its variousness – its multiplicity of short numbers, its intermingling of solos, ensembles and choruses, its inclusion of comic episodes amid scenes of grandeur – to produce OPERA SERIA, leaving comedy for OPERA BUFFA. As a result of this revolution in taste and practice, 17th-century opera became unperformable (to remain so until the later 20th century), and the survival of so many scores from the period can be attributed only to the number of copies made of successful pieces, coupled with a lucky laziness on the part of theatres in clearing out their archives.

Opera seria in the 18th century spread all over Europe, carried on the librettos of Metastasio from Lisbon to St Petersburg – but not to Paris, where the home tradition was developed by Rameau. That French tradition then became one of the models for those who, in the 1760s, sought to reform opera seria. Dependent on star singers engaged at high, sometimes huge, cost, opera seria required the support of courts or, as in London, consortia of wealthy subscribers, and it established opera as a luxury commodity (which the art has largely remained). Meanwhile, opera buffa was only one of the new genres made for a bourgeois audience, along with BALLAD OPERA in Britain, OPERA COMIQUE in France, SINGSPIEL in Germany and ZARZUELA in Spain, all of which offered more naturalistic personages: tenor young swains instead of the castratos who lorded it in opera seria (and would not stoop to the buffa variety). In the growth of these genres in the 1760s – alongside REFORM OPERA, and the ousting at the Paris Opera of Rameau and Lully in favour of Gluck, Sacchini and Piccinni – may be seen another big change in opera, away from serving as a mirror for princes to forming one at which all spectators could feel themselves involved, having their fantasy lives indulged even while their morality was being affirmed.

Meanwhile, the composer's stock was rising. The great opera creators of the later 18th century were often great travellers: Traetta, for example, in a working life of under three decades (1751–79) was called to present operas in Naples, Rome, several northern Italian cities, Vienna, Mannheim, Munich, St Petersburg and London. Moreover, where Metastasian opera seria had depended on the constancy of the libretto (set again and again, and often performed with music by different composers, to accommodate singers' preferences), reform opera and opera buffa increasingly vested integrity in the score. This development led naturally to the beginnings of an operatic repertory, which started to form in the very early 19th century around the works of Gluck and Mozart. The latter's success in his lifetime was limited. *Le nozze di Figaro* (1786) enjoyed revivals in Prague and Vienna, but its composer had nothing to compare with the international hit scored a generation before by Piccinni with *La buona figliuola* (a piece that may even have reached Beijing), or indeed with the acclaim that greeted the operas by Sarti and Martín y Soler he quoted in Don Giovanni's supper music. Two decades after his death, though, his later comedies were central to a newly stable operatic life, at least in London and Germany.

The repertory was congealing everywhere by the 1820s, with Rossini's comedies essential to it, followed during the next half century by selected works of Donizetti, Bellini and Meyerbeer, most of Verdi, Wagner's music dramas as special occasions, *Faust* and *Carmen*, and perhaps *Der Freischütz* and *Martha*. To some extent the Paris Opera retained its independence, as the home of GRAND OPERA, though its products were imported and emulated by theatres in Italy and Russia. (Berlioz was widely overlooked.) There were also new national traditions that developed in the 1860s–70s in Russia (Serov, Tchaikovsky, Musorgsky, Rimsky-Korsakov, Rubinstein) and Prague (Smetana, Dvořák). Nevertheless, by the end of that time the repertory was broadly international, being played in opera houses in New York and Naples, Berlin and Buenos Aires.

This standardization could have happened only because the audience for opera was rather the same in every country. Opera houses in much of Europe remained court bodies, but they were independently operated, and their patrons came from the upper middle class, a class that respected, in opera as in other arts, naturalism and tradition, and that rated the edifying above the entertaining (even if it might secretly prefer the latter). Opera buffa virtually disappeared after Donizetti's *Don Pasquale* (1843), though OPERETTA arrived in the next decade. As for serious opera, the inevitable happy ending (*lieto fine*) of the 18th century was decisively dropped in Rossini's *Otello* (1816). Since the opera stage was no longer a mirror but rather a window into another world – with all the invitations to voyeurism and *schadenfreude* as well as imaginative sympathy – what happened there could be gruesome, as in such favourite works as Verdi's *Rigoletto* (1851). But, to prevent obscenity, stories would have to be validated by acclaimed treatment in some other form; hence the great number of 19th-century operas based on the works of Scott, Schiller, Hugo, Pushkin (in Russia) and Shakespeare, or on episodes from history.

Naturalism affected not only opera's plots but its texture. Opera seria had been generally indifferent as to whether its heroes were enacted by castratos or women (Handel could easily switch from one to the other in reviving a piece); what mattered was that the voice be high, not to imitate a real hero but to convey excitement and be exciting. Even Mozart's *La clemenza di Tito* (1791), late in the history of opera seria, had given its two young male leads to soprano voices. That was unacceptable in the 19th century (which was one reason for the work's sudden eclipse, despite the

Mozart provenance). From Rossini onwards, male characters were given evidently male voices, as tenors, baritones or basses, while women sang only female roles (or boys) and castratos disappeared. Bellini's mezzo Romeo (1830) was a late exception. By the time of Donizetti's operas, in the 1830s–40s, the voice types were becoming associated with particular kinds of character. The romantic leads would normally be a soprano and a tenor; women with lower voices would have to be mothers, friends, sybils or witches, and similarly baritones and basses got used to enacting fathers, confidants, rivals or priests. At the same time, with the orchestra growing in size, a different kind of vocal virtuosity was being required: a virtuosity of power rather than agility, with corresponding changes in melodic style.

Wagner's operas, which seem to counter 19th-century naturalism in their subject matter, abundantly endorse it in other respects. His treatment of voice types was thoroughly in keeping with 19th-century practice, as was his enlargement of the orchestra and consequent demand for voices of force. Also, in his operas as much as Verdi's, the dramas are those of romantic love and family life.

By the time Verdi presented his last opera, *Falstaff* (1893), a new generation had come forward with such works as *Cavalleria rusticana* (Mascagni), *Pagliacci* (Leoncavallo) and *Manon Lescaut* (Puccini), which continued the tradition of naturalism, drawing on Verdi and *Carmen*. Outside Italy Wagner's was the more potent influence, less on a musical level (though there too) than in persuading composers that opera could plunge into the heart of things through fantasy, taking the guise of fairytale (Rimsky-Korsakov's works from *The Snow Maiden* to *The Golden Cockerel*, Humperdinck's *Hänsel und Gretel*, Dvořák's *Rusalka*, Dukas's *Ariane et Barbe-Bleue*, Zemlinsky's *Der Zwerg*), Arthurian romance (Debussy's *Pelléas et Mélisande*, Chausson's *Le Roi Arthus*) or mythic family psychodrama (Strauss's *Salome* and *Elektra*). Yet all these new works were struggling to enter a repertory that was continuing almost unchanged since the 1870s. Mahler's record is striking here. As director of the Vienna opera (1897–1907) he won admiration for his command of singers, orchestra and stagecraft in a repertory from Mozart to Mascagni, but all his creative work went elsewhere.

After the First World War the court operas of Germany, Austria and Russia became state institutions, and the new spirit of democracy was marked in operas that, with rude immediacy, discovered the heroism of the ordinary while deploring social corruption in pictures of more or less contemporary life (Berg's *Wozzeck*, the Brecht–Weill

Dreigroschenoper, Janáček's *From the House of the Dead,* Shostakovich's *The Lady Macbeth of the Mtsensk District,* Gershwin's *Porgy and Bess*), that took a sharply satirical view of previous pretensions (Stravinsky, Shostakovich) and that introduced elements of jazz and popular music (Brecht–Weill, Gershwin). However, the deeper implications of modernism were disturbing for the genre. Opera had originated with the new bass-led harmonic style that could underpin continuous, progressive spans suited to conventional Western drama. Such spans were being questioned or disintegrated in the most adventurous music of the 1920s – Varèse's music, for example, would have required a very different kind of narrative from Verdi's – but opera companies, weighted with a predominantly 19th-century repertory and hiring singers trained for that repertory, could rarely countenance radical change, so that composers either ignored the genre or tried alternatives, as Stravinsky did in *Histoire du soldat.* Innovation, in the big opera houses, became restricted to design and production – aspects of opera that looked critically at 19th-century naturalism.

Gradually the advance of the active opera repertory came to a total halt. Berg's *Lulu* (1937) and Stravinsky's *The Rake's Progress* (1951) are, still, the last works internationally regarded by leading companies as essential to their programming. Where growth has come, since the 1950s, it has been in the acknowledgement of Janáček, the addition of *Idomeneo* and *La clemenza di Tito* to the Mozart canon, and a tentative venturing into Baroque opera – though the early music revolution of the 1970s effectively confined this repertory to specialist ensembles. Yet this has also been a period of great operatic creativity, from composers appreciating contact with an essentially 19th-century form (Tippett, Britten, Henze), and from others – Nono, Berio, Birtwistle, Messiaen, Carter – who have had other tales to tell.

Roger Parker, ed. *The Oxford Illustrated History of Opera* (1994); Amanda Holden, ed. *The New Penguin Opera Guide* (2001)

1607–99: *Orfeo* (1607), *Il ritorno d'Ulisse in patria* (1640), *L'incoronazione di Poppea* (1643), *Giasone* (1649), *Atys* (1676), *Roland* (1685), *Dido and Aeneas* (c.1685), *Armide* (1686), *King Arthur* (1691), *The Fairy-Queen* (1692), *Médée* (1693)

1700–59: *Agrippina* (1709), *Rinaldo* (1711), *Il pastor fido* (1712), *Radamisto* (1720), *Flavio* (1723), *Giulio Cesare* (1724), *Tamerlano* (1724), *Rodelinda* (1725), *Partenope* (1730), *Orlando* (1732), *La serva padrona* (1733), *Hippolyte et Aricie* (1733), *Ariodante* (1735), *Alcina* (1735), *Les Indes galantes* (1735), *Castor et Pollux* (1737), *Serse* (1738), *Dardanus* (1739), *Platée* (1745), *Zoroastre* (1749)

1760–99: *Orfeo ed Euridice* (1762), *Les Boréades* (1763), *Alceste* (1767), *Iphigénie en Aulide* (1774), *La finta giardiniera* (1775), *Iphigénie en Tauride* (1779), *Idomeneo* (1781), *Die Entführung aus dem Serail* (1782), *Le nozze di Figaro* (1786), *Don Giovanni* (1787), *Così fan tutte* (1790), *La clemenza di Tito* (1791), *Die Zauberflöte* (1791), *Il matrimonio segreto* (1792), *Médée* (1797)

1800–40: *Fidelio* (1805), *La vestale* (1807), *L'italiana in Algeri* (1813), *Il turco in Italia* (1814), *Il barbiere di Siviglia* (1816), *Otello* (1816), *La Cenerentola* (1817), *La gazza ladra* (1817), *Mosè in Egitto* (1818), *Der Freischütz* (1821), *Euryanthe* (1823), *Il viaggio a Reims* (1825), *Oberon* (1826), *Guillaume Tell* (1829), *I Capuleti e i Montecchi* (1830), *Anna Bolena* (1830), *La sonnambula* (1831), *L'elisir d'amore* (1832), *I puritani* (1835), *La Juive* (1835), *Lucia di Lammermoor* (1835), *Maria Stuarda* (1835), *Les Huguenots* (1836), *A Life for the Tsar* (1836), *Benvenuto Cellini* (1838), *La Fille du régiment* (1840)

1841–65: *Nabucco* (1842), *Ruslan and Lyudmila* (1842), *Don Pasquale* (1843), *Der fliegende Holländer* (1843), *Tannhäuser* (1845), *Macbeth* (1847), *Martha* (1847), *Die lustigen Weiber von Windsor* (1849), *Le Prophète* (1849), *Genoveva* (1850), *Lohengrin* (1850), *Rigoletto* (1851), *Il trovatore* (1853), *La traviata* (1853), *Les Vêpres siciliennes* (1855), *Un ballo in maschera* (1859), *Faust* (1859), *Béatrice et Bénédict* (1862), *La forza del destino* (1862), *Les Pêcheurs de perles* (1863), *Les Troyens* (1863), *L'Africaine* (1865)

1865–89: *Tristan und Isolde* (1865), *Don Carlos* (1867), *Roméo et Juliette* (1867), *Hamlet* (1868), *Die Meistersinger* (1868), *Das Rheingold* (1869), *Die Walküre* (1870), *The Bartered Bride* (1870), *Aida* (1871), *The Maid of Pskov* (1873), *Boris Godunov* (1874), *Carmen* (1875), *Mefistofele* (1875), *La gioconda* (1876), *Siegfried* (1876), *Götterdämmerung* (1876), *Samson et Dalila* (1877), *Eugene Onegin* (1879), *Les Contes d'Hoffmann* (1881), *Simon Boccanegra* (1881), *The Snow Maiden* (1882), *Parsifal* (1882), *Lakmé* (1883), *Manon* (1884), *Le Cid* (1885), *Khovanshchina* (1886), *Otello* (1887), *Le Roi d'Ys* (1888)

1890–1914: *Cavalleria rusticana* (1890), *Prince Igor* (1890), *The Queen of Spades* (1890), *Werther* (1892), *Pagliacci* (1892), *Iolanta* (1892), *Manon Lescaut* (1893), *Falstaff* (1893), *Hänsel und Gretel* (1893), *La Bohème* (1896), *Cendrillon* (1899), *Tosca* (1900), *Louise* (1900), *Rusalka* (1901), *Pelléas et Mélisande* (1902), *Le Roi Arthus* (1903), *Jenůfa* (1904), *Madama Butterfly* (1904), *Salome* (1905), *The Legend of the Invisible City of Kitezh* (1907), *Ariane et Barbe-bleue* (1907), *Elektra* (1909), *The Golden Cockerel* (1909), *Don Quichotte* (1910), *La fanciulla del West* (1910), *Der Rosenkavalier* (1911), *L'Heure espagnole* (1911), *Der ferne Klang* (1912), *Francesca da Rimini* (1914)

1915–37: *Ariadne auf Naxos* (1916), *Palestrina* (1917), *Bluebeard's Castle* (1918), *Die Frau ohne Schatten* (1919), *The Nightingale* (1920), *The Excursions of Mr Brouček* (1920), *Katya Kabanova* (1921), *The*

Love for Three Oranges (1921), Der Zwerg (1922), Padmâvatî (1923), Erwartung (1924), The Cunning Little Vixen (1924), L'Enfant et les sortilèges (1925), Doktor Faust (1925), Wozzeck (1925), Turandot (1926), King Roger (1926), Cardillac (1926), The Makropulos Case (1926), Oedipus Rex (1927), Die Dreigroschenoper (1928), The Nose (1930), Aufstieg und Fall der Stadt Mahagonny (1930), From the House of the Dead (1930), Arabella (1933), The Lady Macbeth of the Mtsensk District (1934), Mathis der Maler (1934), Porgy and Bess (1935), Lulu (1937)

1938–76: Julietta (1938), Semyon Kotko (1940), Capriccio (1942), Peter Grimes (1945), Betrothal in a Monastery (1946), Il prigioniero (1950), The Rake's Progress (1951), Billy Budd (1951), Moses und Aron (1954), The Turn of the Screw (1954), The Midsummer Marriage (1955), Aniara (1959), War and Peace (1959), Intolleranza (1961), Elegy for Young Lovers (1961), King Priam (1962), Die Soldaten (1965), The Bassarids (1966), Punch and Judy (1968), Ulisse (1968), The Knot Garden (1970), Taverner (1972), Death in Venice (1973), Al gran sole carico d'amore (1975), We Come to the River (1976)

1976–: Einstein on the Beach (1976), Le Grand Macabre (1978), La vera storia (1982), Saint François d'Assise (1983), Un re in ascolto (1984), Prometeo (1984), The Mask of Orpheus (1986), Die Hamletmaschine (1987), Nixon in China (1987), Gawain (1991), Medeamaterial (1992), The Second Mrs Kong (1994), Arianna (1995), Das Mädchen mit Schwefelhölzern (1997), Luci mie traditrici (1998), Schneewittchen (1998), Three Sisters (1998), What Next? (1999), Macbeth (2002), The Tempest (2004), The Io Passion (2004)

Opéra. See PARIS OPERA.

opera ball. Grand dance given in an opera house, often at New Year.

opera-ballet. Term used especially of French Baroque works in which the main purpose of the opera component seems to be to provide occasions for danced divertissements, e.g. Rameau's Les Indes galantes. Roussel applied it to his Padmâvatî.

Opéra Bastille. See PARIS OPERA.

opéra bouffe (Fr.). French OPERETTA, especially that of Offenbach.

opéra bouffon (Fr.). 18th-century Fr. term for It. opera buffa.

opera buff. Knowledgeable connoisseur, especially of the standard repertory and singers' performances.

opera buffa (It.). Term used then (with others) and now for comic opera in It. of the 18th century and early 19th. The tradition started in Naples at the beginning of the 18th century and gave rise to masterpieces by Pergolesi, Galuppi, Mozart, Rossini and Donizetti, with Verdi a sunset observer in Falstaff and Wolf-Ferrari a belated follower. Developing in contrast with opera seria, it emphasized low-born characters in stories not far removed from everyday life. Whereas a Metastasio libretto might be placed in ancient Phrygia, an opera buffa took place in contemporary Naples or Seville. The comic genre was also cynical about the advantages of social standing and age – though not about love, whose free blossoming would provide the motive force. Because it depended at least as much on action and relationships as on interior states, it offered much more space than opera seria did to ensembles and elaborate finales. It also required fast music to be not just a depiction of excitement but a means of progress through the plot, and indeed the Classical style of the 1770s–80s learned its paces from opera buffa.

opera cloak. Garment worn over evening clothes, as by opera-goers of the second half of the 19th century and early 20th. Now the item – normally a man's is meant, in black – has become fancy dress.

opéra comique (Fr.). Term applied since the late 19th century to French opera with spoken dialogue, not necessarily comic in the Eng. sense; Carmen is an example. In earlier times many different terms were used, though as a company name Opéra-Comique was instituted in 1714 and has lasted, with interruptions, to the present. Notable composers of opéra comique when it was indeed a light genre included Philidor, Grétry, Dalayrac, Cherubini, Boieldieu and Isouard. With Gounod's Roméo et Juliette (1867) the Opéra-Comique moved into all-sung works, having already made its repertory more serious, and it introduced most of the lasting French operas of the next half century, including – besides Carmen – Les Contes d'Hoffmann, Lakmé, Manon, Le Roi d'Ys, Cendrillon, Louise, Pelléas et Mélisande, Ariane et Barbe-bleue and L'Heure espagnole. Only this last is most definitely a comic opera, but not, though produced at the Opéra-Comique, an opéra comique, being sung throughout.

opera composer. Most composers have written operas alongside other works, but some have taken opera as their métier, their other works being secondary: Lully, Rameau, Gluck, Rossini, Bellini, Donizetti, Verdi, Wagner, Mascagni, Leoncavallo and Puccini. The converse group is that of composers who eschewed the genre: Bach, Chopin, Brahms, Bruckner, Mahler, Ives, Babbitt and Boulez.

opéra féerie (Fr.). Fairy opera, a genre of the 18th and early 19th century, e.g. Grétry's *Zémire et Azor*, a Beauty and the Beast tale set in Persia.

opera glasses. Small binoculars taken to the theatre by patrons or supplied by the management on payment (frequently in the later 20th century by placing a coin in a slot). They became common in the mid 19th century; before that people used small telescopes.

opera house. Theatre devoted to opera and, in most cases, ballet. Many of the great examples date from 1850–75, including the BOLSHOY (1856), COVENT GARDEN (1858), the MARIINSKY (1860), the Vienna Staatsoper (1869) and the Palais Garnier (PARIS OPERA, 1875). Earlier designs are preserved at Berlin (Staatsoper, 1742), Munich (Cuvilliés Theatre, 1753; Staatsoper, 1825), DROT- TNINGHOLM (1766), *La* SCALA (1778), Prague (Estates Theatre, 1783), Naples (San Carlo, 1816), Venice (*La* FENICE, 1837), Dresden (SEMPER OPER, 1841) and Barcelona (Liceu, 1847), all totally rebuilt except those at Drottningholm, Prague and Naples. Among newer models are the METRO- POLITAN OPERA (1966), the Sydney Opera House (1973), the Opéra Bastille (Paris, 1990) and GLYN- DEBOURNE (1994).

Opera North. British company founded in 1977 in Leeds.

Opera Pacific. US company founded in 1987 in Costa Mesa, Cal.

opera semiseria. Early 19th-century kind of opera buffa with an extra charge of sentiment, there being examples by Rossini (*La gazza ladra*) and Donizetti.

opera seria (It., serious opera). Term introduced in the late 18th century for a genre that was dying out: dramatic opera in It., stylized in its musical forms (with the da capo aria paramount), charac- ter types and situations. Instituted at the begin- ning of the century, opera seria – or 'dramma per musica', to use the term of the time – was the most prestigious form of drama in Italy and the German-speaking lands throughout the period, and enjoyed moments of triumph, too, in England, the Iberian peninsula, Scandinavia and eastern Europe (including Russia), but not in France, where the native tradition and local scepticism withstood its allure.

That allure it owed partly to star singers (chiefly women and castratos), partly to its heroic charac- ters, partly to the images it unfailingly presented of virtue rewarded, benevolence shown and mis- understandings resolved, partly to fine poetry in its librettos, and, of course, partly to the work of its composers, who included Alessandro Scarlatti, Handel, Vinci, Leo, Porpora, Pergolesi, Hasse, Jommelli, Galuppi, Traetta, Piccinni, Sarti, Sacchini, Salieri, Haydn, Paisiello, Cimarosa and Mozart.

An opera seria libretto (Metastasio's were the most favoured from the 1730s onwards, repeatedly reset) provided strings of arias linked by recitative, each aria expressing an extreme emotional condi- tion that normally required the character to leave at the end. Composers had to deal, therefore, not only with a very compartmented structure (arias would receive orchestral accompaniment, recita- tives be supported by continuo only) but with a switchback of expressive types. And no matter what had happened, all problems would have to be resolved in the conventional *lieto fine*, or happy ending. Many great works were written under these constraints, making from formality a proud sense of show. By the 1760s, though, there was pressure for an operatic form more in keeping with developing ideas of the 'natural', leading to REFORM OPERA and the decline of the genre.

Reinhard Strohm *Dramma per musica* (1997)

opera singer. Some singers perform regularly as recitalists, soloists with orchestras and on stage in opera, but many are principally opera singers. Leaving aside questions of fame and reward, they may have made that choice because they under- stand operatic acting (which is quite different from any style of acting in the contemporary spoken theatre) and enjoy stage work, or because they have powerful voices, suited to the traditional repertory in traditional theatres. But there are many different sorts of opera singer, as there are many sorts of opera in the contemporary world. Some make careers in opera of the 17th–18th cen- turies, others in new works.

operetta. Light comic opera of the period from the 1850s, when Offenbach effectively invented the form, to the 1930s. Born from one kind of popular music – the waltz, polka, cancan and other mid- 19th-century dances – it folded into a new form, the MUSICAL, on the arrival of jazz, blues and associated song styles. Its dominant practitioners were – besides Offenbach – Chabrier, Lecocq, Johann Strauss II, Sullivan, Millöcker, Messager, Lehár, Straus, Fall and Kálmán. Bernstein belatedly used the term of his *Candide*. Offenbach seized his moment when the repertory of the Opéra-Comique was becoming more serious. Saint-Saëns was, therefore, historically accurate, as well as wise and witty in his view: 'Operetta is the daughter of opéra comique – a daughter who turned out badly, but then: daughters who turn out badly are often not without charm.'

ophicleide. Keyed wind instrument patented by the Parisian maker Halary in 1821, generally made of brass and usually in a bass register, though smaller varieties exist. It replaced the serpent, and was itself replaced in the 1860s–70s by the euphonium and tuba – but not before parts had been written for it in orchestral scores by Berlioz, Verdi and Wagner.

Oppens, Ursula (b. New York, 2 Feb 1944). US pianist, a formidable exponent of new US music (Carter, Nancarrow, Rzewski), which she often confronts with more traditional repertory (Beethoven, Rachmaninoff). She studied at Radcliffe and Juilliard, her teachers including her mother Edith Oppens, Rosina Lhévinne and Felix Galimir, and made her debut in New York in 1970.

opus (Lat., work, pl. *opera*, though in Eng. normally 'opuses'). Composition, publication.

opus number [Op.]. Number given to a work or group of works by the composer or publisher on publication. Works within a group are given individual numbers, as with Haydn's 'Joke' Quartet, Op.33 No.2 (or, in this book, Op.33:2).

Examples go back to Viadana (*Motecta festorum*, Op.10, Venice, 1597) but did not become frequent until the late 17th century. Corelli's neat output of just six opuses, each of 12 works, provided an example to Leclair and others. Beethoven seems to have been the first composer to use Op. numbers consistently for a larger and more various output, so that they have become part of how his works are known ('the Op.18 quartets') and provide information about dates: opus numbers in the 70s, for instance, are likely to come from 1808–9, though some will be earlier pieces whose publication was delayed. On the other hand, Weber's Op. numbers, more subject to the vagaries of publication, are no guide to chronology.

Beethoven's model may have been Haydn, whose quartet sets all bear Op. numbers and are still distinguished thus. In turn, Beethoven provided an example of coherent opus numbering to Schumann, Brahms, Saint-Saëns, Tchaikovsky, Dvořák, Grieg, Fauré, Chausson, Elgar, Scriabin, Strauss, Nielsen, Sibelius, Reger, Rachmaninoff, Schoenberg, Szymanowski, Webern, Prokofiev, Hindemith, Shostakovich, Britten and Kurtág. Stockhausen calls his works simply by number, e.g. *Gruppen*, Nr.6. Stravinsky, Berg and Bartók all

gave up using Op. numbers, Berg allegedly because they pointed up how small his output was. Those whose Op. numbers might appear, by contrast, proud manifestations of creative energy include Hovhaness (434), Milhaud (443), Johann Strauss II (479), Bentzon (beyond 650), Czerny (861) and Zajc (1202).

oratorio. The term now usually denotes a large-scale work on a sacred subject given in a concert hall, but the original oratorios of the 1620s–40s were smaller, shorter and designed for the kind of building from which they took their name: the oratories founded in Rome by St Philip Neri and his followers. The first use of the term to mean a musical work was in Italy in 1640, and the word was taken into other languages as the form travelled.

Oratorians placed great emphasis on spiritual exercises, for themselves and their congregations, and it was from these that the oratorio emerged, as a scene on a biblical topic, set quasi-operatically for soli, choir and instruments, but performed without decor or costumes. Carissimi's enjoyed special favour. After him, virtually any composer spending time in Rome in the later 17th century and early 18th would be obliged to contribute to the genre; the list includes Stradella, Alessandro Scarlatti, Handel and Caldara. At the same time the oratorio spread with the oratorian movement to other Italian cities, notably Florence, Bologna and Modena (Cazzati, Vitali), and Venice (Legrenzi, Caldara, Lotti, Vivaldi), as well as to Vienna, where it enjoyed not only imperial patronage but participation, by the composer emperor Leopold I. Other composers writing oratorios under him and his immediate successors included Caldara (again) and Fux, setting texts by the court poets Zeno and Metastasio.

As these names might suggest, the oratorio evolved in parallel with opera. In Vienna it even had a distinctly operatic offshoot, the SEPOLCRO. Moreover, as with opera, there were efforts to transplant it into other cultures, notably French (Charpentier) and German. In Germany it took vigorous root, for the Lutheran church had developed its own tradition of sacred musical narration that arrived at much the same time as oratorio, and for similar reasons: to divert the persuasive passion of opera to pious ends. There are examples in Schütz, many more in the history of the PASSION, and others in the oratorios produced by Keiser, Mattheson and Telemann in opera-loving Hamburg, or in opera-deprived Leipzig by Bach, who advanced the mass to oratorio scale in his B minor setting.

Meanwhile in England, where there had been

oratorio-like short pieces in the 17th century by Purcell (*In guilty night*) and others, the genre was definitively and magnificently established by Handel, beginning with *Esther* (1718) and going on to the run of great works with which he consoled himself in 1738–52 for the collapse of opera. Among these, *Saul*, *Israel in Egypt*, *Messiah* and *Solomon* have been cherished in Anglophone countries from then on, providing a model for later composers. The continuing English suspicion that music had better come from abroad benefited Mendelssohn (*Elijah*, 1846), Gounod (*Redemption*, 1882) and Dvořák (*St Ludmilla*, 1886), but there were also home-grown works, by Parry, Elgar (*Gerontius*, 1900) and others, succeeded in the 20th century by Walton (*Belshazzar's Feast*, 1931), Tippett (*A Child of our Time*, 1944) and Davies, still with Handel strongly in the background.

At first Handel had nothing to say to composers in Italy, Vienna, Germany and France (Paisiello, Cimarosa, Graun, C.P.E. Bach, Mondonville), who went on developing local customs, but by the end of the 18th century his amalgam of imaginary opera and choral monument was unavoidable. Haydn's two examples, *Die Schöpfung* (1798) and *Die Jahreszeiten*, endorsed it; then came Beethoven's *Christus am Oelberge* (1803) and oratorio-style *Missa solemnis* (1819–23), and Schubert's unfinished *Lazarus* (1820). *Die Jahreszeiten* further validated the secular oratorio, taken up with enthusiasm by Schumann (*Das Paradies und die Peri*, 1843) and Berlioz (*La Damnation de Faust*, 1845–6).

But such works remained rare (Bruch's *Odysseus*, Schoenberg's *Gurrelieder* and Martin's *Le Vin herbé* are later examples). By now escaped into the concert hall, oratorio was the province not of church choirs but of amateur choral societies, one of the oldest being the significantly named Handel and Haydn Society of Boston (1815). Attachment to those two composers, soon joined by Bach and Beethoven, was an attachment to singing divine glory, and this was the subject of the oratorio boom of the later 19th century. Besides those written for the English festivals, there were oratorios from Berlioz in properly sacred mode (*L'Enfance du Christ*), Liszt (*St Elizabeth*, *Christus*) and Franck (*Les Béatitudes*), as well as settings of liturgical texts (the mass, *Requiem*, *Te Deum* and *Stabat mater*) intended primarily as concert pieces.

The works of Gounod and Franck went out of fashion, and Liszt was never in, leaving choral societies to go on with an essential repertory of Handel, Bach, Haydn and Beethoven, a repertory they have happily maintained against a scholarly tide for trimmer performances of such music.

Though new works stand little chance of entering this obdurate world, composers from Schoenberg (in his later *Die Jakobsleiter*) to Messiaen (*La Transfiguration*) and beyond have gone on being drawn to a genre in which ultimate questions can be addressed.

Howard E. Smither *A History of the Oratorio*, 4 vols. (1977–2000)

oratorio volgare (It.). 17th-century term for oratorio in Italian, as opposed to *oratorio latino*. Henze called his *Das Floss der 'Medusa'* an 'oratorio volgare e militare'.

orch. Abbreviation for 'orchestra'.

orchestra (Fr. *orchestre*, Ger. *Orchester*, It. *orchestra*). Body of players or instruments. Normally the term denotes the standard mixed body of Western music since the late 18th century, with a preponderance of strings and much smaller numbers of woodwinds, brass and percussion (including timpani and harp). The most usual seating plan for such an ensemble is shown opposite.

But the word can also be used of musical collectivities from other traditions (GAGAKU orchestra), or of such unusual formations as the percussion orchestra of Varèse's *Ionisation* or the 40-flute orchestra of Radulescu's *Byzantine Prayer*.

Professional orchestras of the more customary type are at work in most great cities. They normally number around 80 regular players, supported by a smaller administrative staff. Usually they have two heads – the chief conductor or music director, and the managing director – sharing responsibility for programming and policy. They give concerts throughout a season from September to May/June, with the addition of festival performances at home or on tour in the summer; some also play regularly for opera. They may be employed by the city or national government, or by a radio authority, or they may be self-governing – in effect, medium-sized not-for-profit companies, answerable to a board representing major donors. Because orchestras cannot support themselves by what they earn at the box office and through recordings, finance has to come from individuals, foundations and companies, or from public funds. Among leading orchestras are the BERLIN PHILHARMONIC ORCHESTRA, BOSTON SYMPHONY ORCHESTRA, CHICAGO Symphony Orchestra, CLEVELAND Orchestra, LONDON PHILHARMONIC ORCHESTRA, LONDON SYMPHONY ORCHESTRA, LOS ANGELES Philharmonic Orchestra, MARIINSKY, NEW YORK PHILHARMONIC ORCHESTRA, PHILADELPHIA Orchestra, ROYAL CONCERTGEBOUW ORCHESTRA and VIENNA PHILHARMONIC ORCHESTRA.

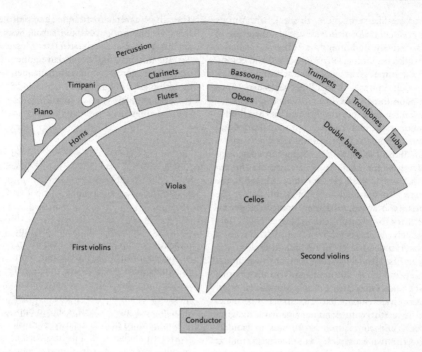

The term comes from the ancient Greek theatre, where the orchestra (dancing place) was the arena for the chorus, in front of the stage. Because the instrumentalists in an opera performance occupied a similar position, the word was applied to their station (by the mid 17th century) and soon to them.

This connection with the opera theatre was not accidental. In the 17th–18th centuries the orchestra developed largely as the matrix supporting opera, and the regularity with which big instrumental ensembles before the later 18th century were assembled elsewhere – in performing church music, in giving concerts – has become a matter of dispute since the early music revival of the 1970s. It may be, for instance, that Bach's concertos, cantatas and larger sacred works involved no more than one player to each part, in which case his 'orchestra' may have comprised only a dozen or so instrumentalists. Strikingly, this realization came about at a time when composers were again writing for a group of a similar size: the mixed EN-SEMBLE.

But between Bach and, say, Birtwistle, lies a long period during which the regular orchestra was on a larger scale – a period when, indeed, there became such a thing as a regular orchestra. And regularity, of constitution and performance, is important, for an orchestra is a social body, needing to exert itself as a body in order to maintain its skills, morale and identity.

The earliest such institution was the VINGT-QUATRE VIOLINS DU ROI, established at the French court in the early 17th century. Groups of similar or greater size came together before that; the published score of Monteverdi's *Orfeo* (1607), for instance, proudly lists 39 players. But such 'orchestras' were gatherings of small ensembles, brought together for unique occasions. The French king's 24 strings, by contrast, formed a stable body, performing as such in the royal chapel, at dinner and for theatrical entertainments, including, by the 1670s, Lully's operas, for which the string band would be joined by keyboard, percussion and a few wind instruments.

With the widespread creation of court opera companies around the same time, and the frequent travels of composers and singers from one court to another, standardization was inevitable, and by the 1730s–40s an orchestra similar in scale to Lully's – with two parts for oboes (doubling on flutes), bassoons and horns playing consistently with the strings, and trumpets and trombones brought in for special effects – had become the European norm, playing for opera and beginning to feel its independence in the new genre of the symphony. This was still Haydn's orchestra in the 1770s, though in the next two decades it grew to become what is now known as the 'Classical orchestra', the orchestra of Haydn's 'London' symphonies and Mozart's operas: strings with two parts each for flutes, oboes, clarinets, bassoons, horns and trumpets, plus timpani, with trombones remaining occasional extras, not for use in symphonies until Beethoven's Fifth.

Beethoven's other additions to the Classical orchestra were relatively modest. Besides trombones (and piccolo) in his Fifth, Sixth and Ninth symphonies, he asked for a third horn in Nos.3, 5, 7 and 8, and a fourth in the Ninth, as well as a double bassoon in the Fifth and Ninth, and military-band percussion in the Ninth. More than six decades later, Brahms in his Fourth Symphony (1885) was still writing for much the same ensemble, the set-up that was by now a century old, preserved by the constancy of Haydn, Mozart and Beethoven in the repertory. The sameness may, though, be deceptive. Reports suggest that orchestras could vary markedly in size; Beethoven had 14 strings for a concert in 1813 but 79 for one the next year, with exactly the same wind complement of 14. Sometimes wind parts were doubled (two players to a part), sometimes not. Composers – even Beethoven – had to deal with circumstances they could not control, and so documentary evidence is of limited help to modern performers in gauging correct sound. Most today would want around 24 strings in Beethoven (therefore an orchestra of around 40) and perhaps half as many again in Brahms, always with just one player to each wind part. The reasons for this have at least as much to do with taste and tradition as historical accuracy.

In the opera house there are much clearer signs of expansion immediately after Beethoven, and for most orchestras the opera house was still home, with concerts an occasional activity. The brass section gained a bass member in the serpent or ophicleide, soon replaced by the tuba, and new woodwind instruments were introduced: the cor anglais, and E♭ and bass clarinets. Wind sections might now have three parts, or four, and a harp or two and percussion became standard. As the orchestra grew, so a conductor became essential because the players could no longer maintain contact with a leading keyboard or string player. In concert works by composers close to opera these innovations were incorporated and even pioneered. Berlioz's *Symphonie fantastique* (1830) boasts, besides its eloquent cor anglais solo and multiple timpani, a pair of harps and the first orchestral use of the E♭ clarinet. The composer, his own conductor, also wrote of trying this score out with an orchestra of 130.

Certainly a hundred or so players were mustered by Wagner for his *Ring* in 1876. For the first time the size of the string body was specified (16 each of first violins and seconds, 12 each of violas and cellos, eight double basses), and there were also to be four in most of the wind departments, but eight

horns, as well as six harps, timpani and percussion. Even while Brahms, Dvořák and Tchaikovsky were continuing to imagine an orchestra of little more than half this size, the Wagnerian apparatus was brought into the symphony by Bruckner. It was then expanded still further by Mahler and Strauss, and by Schoenberg, whose *Gurrelieder*, completed in 1911, requires an orchestra of around 135 (8.5.7.5 – 10.7.7.1 – 6 timp, cel, xyl, perc, 4 hp – strings; see INSTRUMENTATION).

Economic changes after the First World War – coupled with the establishment of regular symphony concerts all over the Western world, their repertory based on symphonic music from Haydn to Brahms – brought a new standard at a more modest level of triple wind (an orchestra therefore of around 75), rising if need be to quadruple (implying around 90 players). This is the kind of formation for which most composers have written since the 1920s, though with a range of other options, including the STRING ORCHESTRA, CHAMBER ORCHESTRA and various kinds of reduced ensemble, in which Schoenberg was also an explorer with his first CHAMBER SYMPHONY (1906).

Further efforts on the part of composers to change the nature of the orchestra have continued since the 1950s, including placing groups in different parts of the hall or changing the seating plan (see SPACE), adding new instruments or electronics, or basing the texture not on the strings but on wind instruments (Birtwistle's *The Mask of Orpheus*) or percussion (Boulez's *Pli selon pli*), following suggestions in the wind-percussion textures of *The Rite of Spring* or the different kinds of orchestra to be found in east Asia and Africa.

Most established orchestras, however, find it hard to accommodate innovation, with its demands on organizational expertise and rehearsal scheduling. Since the 1970s they have lost the bulk of their 18th-century repertory to specialist groups coming together for occasional concerts (very much, therefore, in an 18th-century spirit), while other specialist groups working on a similar basis (and sometimes with the same players) have taken responsibility for new music. The symphony orchestra is itself becoming a period ensemble, devoted to the repertory from Beethoven to Shostakovich.

Colin Lawson, ed. *The Cambridge Companion to the Orchestra* (2003)

orchestral. Adjective from orchestra, as in 'orchestral musician', 'orchestral chimes' (tubular bells), etc.

Orchestra of St Luke's. Chamber orchestra

founded in 1978 as an outgrowth from the active music programme at St Luke's, Chelsea, New York. Its principal conductors have included Norrington (1990–94), Mackerras (1998–2001) and Donald Runnicles (from 2001).

Orchestra of the Age of Enlightenment. London-based, period-practice ensemble founded in 1986 and working frequently with Brüggen, Mackerras, Rattle and others.

Orchestra of the Eighteenth Century. Amsterdam-based period-practice ensemble founded by Brüggen in 1981.

orchestrate. To score for orchestra.

orchestration. Scoring for orchestra, either the process of doing so or the result. It is an art dependent on knowledge of instrumental ranges, their timbres and dynamic capabilities in different registers, their blending and balance, the acoustic relationships that come from orchestral layout, and other relationships with voices or solo instruments, where present. There are no rules, though many treatises. Practical experience in leading or conducting orchestras may seem to have helped such composers as Bach, Haydn, Mendelssohn, Berlioz, Wagner, Mahler and Boulez; on the other hand, there are many who became expert orchestrators without any involvement in orchestral performance, such as Debussy, Ravel, Stravinsky and Berg.

Orchestration has traditionally been regarded as coming separately and later in the creation of music. Composers would draft a composition in something like keyboard form or SHORT SCORE, then orchestrate it. Even with the growing importance of timbre since the late 19th century, composition directly into full score has remained unusual. The resulting two-stage process makes it perfectly natural to take fully achieved keyboard works and orchestrate them, as Ravel did with his own and others' piano pieces, or as many composers did with Bach, including Mahler, Elgar, Schoenberg, Webern and Stravinsky, all making orchestration a creative activity. Conversely, some composers (Liszt in early versions, Stockhausen in *Carré*) have seen it as a task that could be left to associates.

But even if orchestration comes subsequently, and even if it is achieved by other hands, it has to be regarded as representing the composer's ultimate intentions, until proved otherwise (by a revision, for instance). Conductors and fellow composers in the 19th century and first half of the 20th were wont to adapt scorings they deemed

deficient; classic examples include Rimsky-Korsakov's editions of Musorgsky and Mahler's reorchestration of Schumann's 'Rhenish' Symphony. Latterly, though, the original scores have been preferred, and Schumann–Mahler (though not yet Musorgsky–Rimsky) revived as a historical curiosity.

Alfred Blatter *Instrumentation and Orchestration* (1980, ²1997)

Orchestre de la Suisse Romande. Body formed by Ansermet in Geneva in 1918.

Orchestre de Paris. Premier French orchestra, founded in 1967 in succession to that of the SOCIETE DES CONCERTS DU CONSERVATOIRE. Its principal conductors have included Münch (1967–8), Karajan (1969–71), Solti (1972–5), Barenboim (1975–88) and Eschenbach (from 2000).

Orchestre Révolutionnaire et Romantique. London-based period-practice ensemble founded in 1990 by Gardiner.

ordinary. That part of the mass which is the same whatever the occasion, including the KYRIE ELEISON, GLORIA, CREDO, SANCTUS and AGNUS DEI, as distinct from the proper, which is specific to a particular Sunday or feast day.

Ordonez, (Johann) Karl (Rochus) von [Carlo d'] (baptized Vienna, 16 Aug 1734; d. Vienna, 6 Sep 1786). Austrian composer, notably of symphonies. He had a double life as civil servant and professional violinist.

ordre (Fr.). Term used by Couperin and others for a suite.

Orfeo, Orfeo ed Euridice. See ORPHEUS.

Orff, Carl (b. Munich, 10 Jul 1895; d. Munich, 29 Mar 1982). German composer, best known for the propulsive energy of his *Carmina burana*. He studied at the academy in his native city (1912–14), worked in the theatre, and then returned to his studies, with Heinrich Kaminski (1920–21). In 1924 he joined Dorothee Günther in founding a school, where he developed an influential method of music education through performance, movement and vocalizing: Orff-Schulwerk. His goal was 'elemental music', which he achieved in a different way with *Carmina burana* (1936), a vulgarization of the motor-rhythm incantation of Stravinsky's *Les Noces*. Remaining in Germany throughout the Nazi era, he produced several more works of the same kind, based on an understanding of the primitive in medieval, peasant and ancient worlds, as well as a *Midsummer Night's Dream* score (f.p. Frankfurt, 1939), which he allowed, probably naively, to be accepted as a replacement for Mendelssohn's. All this brought him criticism after the war (and more posthumously), but he was given a chair in composition at the conservatory in Munich (1950–60) and had further stage works performed.

Stage: CARMINA BURANA, 1936; *Der Mond* (Orff, after the Brothers Grimm), 1936–8, f.p. Munich, 1939; *Catulli Carmina* (Orff, after Catullus), 1941–3, f.p. Leipzig, 1943; *Trionfo di Afrodite* (Catullus, Sappho, Euripides), 1949–51, f.p. Milan, 1953 (as third part of *Trionfi*, with *Carmina burana* and *Catulli carmina*); etc.
Other works: choral pieces, school music

organ (Fr. *orgue*, *orgues*, Ger. *Orgel*, It. *organo*). Keyboard instrument producing sound from pipes. The organ is a church instrument in Western Christianity (though eschewed in the Orthodox tradition), and most organists are church men (leaving women to excel as virtuoso recitalists), committed to accompanying choir and congregation, improvising during waiting periods, and playing a preludial or postludial voluntary. Virtually the entire organ literature is of music connected to church life, and it comes in two great crescendos: one of German Baroque music culminating in Bach, the other of French Romantic music climaxing in Messiaen. Each wave coincided, unsurprisingly, with phases of high artistry in organ building, a craft endowed with great expertise and as great mystique. Bach's contemporaries included the original Silbermann brothers, and French organ music from Franck to Messiaen was written for the splendours of Cavaillé-Coll's instruments. Organs are also found in many concert halls (not all: Carnegie Hall lacks one), where they are used not so much for recitals as for big choral works.

The essential parts of any organ are four: a keyboard (or, more usually, keyboards; two or three manuals and an array of pedals, all allowing the player to work simultaneously with different kinds of ORGAN STOP); a 'chest' of pipes; a constant supply of air to be blown through the pipes; and a mechanism by which the actions of the player can take effect. Of these, the first two have not changed in essence since the WATER ORGAN of 2,000 years ago. Means of maintaining air pressure, though, have advanced, with flowing water giving way to people working bellows, to steam power and then, in the late 19th century, to electric motors. Around the same time electric

circuits with switches were made to link the pipes to the keyboard, replacing the mechanical TRACKER action of earlier organs. However, the resulting loss of control over articulation led to a reversal of that trend in the mid 20th century. By the end of the century questions were being raised, too, about the usefulness of steady wind pressure (and therefore steady timbre, volume and intonation) in music conceived, like Bach's, for a certain respiration in the air supply, though the result has been to investigate ways of reproducing that effect automatically rather than to restore job opportunities for organ blowers.

Most organ pipes are of the flue type, producing sound the way flutes do: air passes through a narrow aperture to hit a lip, setting up vibrations in the column of air within the pipe. Second most common are reed pipes, in which the principle is that of oboes and bassoons: incoming air sets a reed (of brass) in vibration, and so induces sympathetic vibrations in the air in the pipe above. In regals, inherited from an early type of portable organ of that name, the reeds vibrate but there is no pipe. Other kinds, such as the free reeds introduced in the 19th century, were mere blips in the instrument's history-conscious progress.

From beginnings in the 1st century AD (and perhaps earlier), that progress seems to have been maintained for several centuries in the Byzantine world, taken up by the Arabs, and transferred to western Europe. The word comes from the Gk *organon* (tool), cognate with *ergon* (work). Early Western mentions of an *organum* (the Lat. form) may therefore refer to an engine of some sort, even an imaginary engine, and not a sound-producing apparatus at all. But from the 10th century the organ as an instrument – already a sacred instrument, which it had not been for the Byzantines or Arabs – is clearly documented, and a few actual instruments survive, though altered, from the 14th century, notably that of the cathedral of Halberstadt in northwest Germany (c.1361). The earliest important source of organ music, the BUXHEIMER ORGELBUCH, comes from about a century later, by which time builders were beginning to express their ingenuity in stops.

Several organs are extant from the 16th century, and many survive from the 17th century onwards, testifying to the growing power and range of colours achieved especially by German, Dutch, Italian and French makers. Composers in those countries took note, among them Frescobaldi, Froberger, Titelouze and Sweelinck, though the English school of organist-composers, from Redford to Bull, predated the great organs installed by Renatus Harris and 'Father' Smith. Among German masters of the generation or two before Bach were Buxtehude, Pachelbel, Reincken, Muffat and Bruhns. After Bach it is hard to avoid an impression of stagnation and decline, until the revival of the early 19th century, which was prompted in part by the rediscovery of his music. A signal event was the building of a new organ in his church of St Thomas's, Leipzig, by Wilhelm Sauer (1831–1916), a disciple of Cavaillé-Coll and exponent therefore of the grand style that made possible the music of Franck, Widor, Vierne, Tournemire and, eventually, Messiaen. Builders since his time have struggled with how to create instruments suited to two such different repertories as those of Bach and Messiaen, and composers, such as Ligeti and Kagel, with how to write for an instrument so rich in lore.

Nicholas Thistlethwaite and Geoffrey Webber, eds. *The Cambridge Companion to the Organ* (1998)

organetto a manovella. BARREL ORGAN.

organ mass. Set of organ replacements for alternate verses of plainsong in the mass.

organology. The study of musical instruments.

organo pleno (It.). Full organ, i.e. a prompt for a full registration.

organ point. Ambiguous term, having the meanings of both POINT D'ORGUE and ORGELPUNKT.

organ score. Organ reduction of a larger work, such as an oratorio.

Organ Solo Mass. Name given Mozart's Mass in C, K.259. Two Haydn masses are similarly named for the same reason, his *Grosse Orgelmesse* (or *Orgelsolomesse*) and *Kleine Orgelmesse* (or again *Orgelsolomesse*).

organ stop. A row of organ pipes, which can be opened by the organist at the console pulling on a knob, so changing the register or timbre. The term can also refer to the knob. It is recorded in English from the time of Henry VIII (r. 1509–47), for reasons unclear; other languages prefer 'register' (Fr. *registre*, Ger. *Register*, It. *registro*). By using stops the organist can make a note sound on any of several pipes – differing in tone by virtue of their materials and geometry, by whether they are open, stopped (closed at the top) or almost stopped (see CHIMNEY FLUTE), and by their construction as flues or reeds – or on combinations of pipes.

The polyglot names of organ stops record the instrument's long and mixed history. Some indicate resemblances to other instruments: Bassoon

(Fagotto, Basson), Carillon, Clarinet, Cornetto (Cornet, Zink), Cromorne (Cremona, Krummhorn), Flageolet, Flute (Flöte, Flauto), Gamba (Viola da Gamba), Geigen, Gemshorn, Hautbois, Piffaro (Fiffaro), Posaune, Querflöte, Recorder (Blockflöte), Schalmei, Sordun, Theorbe, Trumpet (Trompette, Trommet, Trompeta, Clarín), Zimbel (Cymbale). Others convey the interval at which the stop sounds: Contrabass, Tierce, Quint, Quintadena, Octave, Twelfth, Sesquialtera, Fifteenth (Quintadecima, Superoctave), Nineteenth (Decimanona), Twenty-second. Still others are more fanciful (KUCKUCK, Nachthorn, NACHTIGALL, SALICET, UNDA MARIS, Vogelgesang, VOX HUMANA, ZIMBELSTERN), or technologically descriptive (GEDACKT, Tremulant), or etymologically obscure (NASARD, Portunal, Rauschpfeife, Regal, Tolkaan).

organum. Term used since the 9th century for one of the earliest recorded forms of polyphony, in which a plainsong melody (*vox principalis*) is joined by a second voice proceeding with it note by note at intervals up to a fifth (*vox organalis*). By the 12th century the term was being applied to a new style, in which the plainsong proceeded very slowly, with a festoon of melody in the *vox organalis* greeting each note. Examples of this exuberant but also solemn style survive from ST MARTIAL and from music attributable to LEONIN. The older kind of note-against-note polyphony continued as DISCANT, and survived the more florid organum.

Orgel (Ger.). Organ.

Orgel-Büchlein, Das (The Organ Booklet). Collection of chorale preludes assembled by J.S. Bach to provide instruction and usefulness throughout the church year. A total of 164 were planned, but only 45 completed, during his time in Weimar.

Orgelmesse, Orgelsolomesse. See ORGAN SOLO MASS.

Orgelpunkt (Ger., organ point). PEDAL (2).

orgue à manivelle, orgue de Barbarie. BARREL ORGAN.

orientalism. Presence of Asian (or sometimes north African) qualities in Western music, often as modes, microtones or instruments (especially gongs and other metal percussion). Western music developed in company with that of other cultures: plainsong, for example, has roots in Jewish liturgical singing, while most string instruments came to Europe from the Islamic world. However, the term usually implies a deliberate reference to the other culture, such as can hardly be detected before the JANISSARY music and other Turkish features sported in the 18th century and a little before. Romantic orientalism is often opulent, as in the Sheherazade works of Rimsky-Korsakov and Ravel, Saint-Saëns's *Samson et Dalila* or Puccini's *Madama Butterfly* and *Turandot*, whereas a more precise attention to Asian musical techniques and philosophies is evident in the music of such later composers as Cowell, Cage, Messiaen, Harrison and Stockhausen.

Orlando. Hero of ARIOSTO's epic *Orlando furioso*, and of operas by Piccinni, Vivaldi and Haydn as well as the following:

(1) Lully's opera *Roland*, to a libretto by Quinault. Roland (baritone) goes mad when he learns that his beloved Angélique (soprano) has absconded with Médor (haute-contre), but recovers when assured by Glory and Fame of his future as a warrior hero. First performance: Versailles, 8 Jan 1685.

(2) Handel's opera *Orlando*, to an anonymous adaptation of Carlo Sigismondo Capece's libretto. The plot is essentially the same but vastly more complicated. Orlando (alto castrato) has a powerful mad scene, and the characters around him include, besides Angelica (soprano) and Medoro (alto), a hapless bystander in the shepherdess Dorinda (soprano) and a magician, Zoroastro (bass), who saves the day. First performance: London, 27 Jan 1733.

Ormandy, Eugene (b. Budapest, 18 Nov 1899; d. Philadelphia, 12 Mar 1985). Hungarian–US conductor, originally Jenő Blau, famed for the silkiness he drew from the Philadelphia strings as the orchestra's long-standing music director (1938–80). Trained as a violinist by Hubay at the academy in Budapest, he moved to New York in 1921, and joined the Capitol Theatre orchestra, of which he became leader and then conductor (1926). In 1931 a first engagement in Philadelphia led to a post as music director of the Minneapolis Symphony (1931–6), from which he returned to Philadelphia as joint conductor with Stokowski before taking over.

ornament. Momentary figure regarded as an embellishment of a note. Ornamentation must have been an improvised practice before there were any signs for it; those signs appeared in the late 15th century, associated particularly with keyboard music. They proliferated in the 17th century and first half of the 18th among German and French keyboard composers, whose usages were often personal and therefore ambiguous. Some, however, survived in more or less standardized form into later periods, including the ACCIACCATURA, APPOGGIATURA, GLISSANDO, GRACE NOTE, MORDENT, TREMOLO, TRILL, TURN and VIBRATO. See also ANSCHLAG; NACHSCHLAG; SLIDE (1); SPRINGER.

ornamentation. The improvised addition of ornaments in performance. This is rarely required in music since the mid 19th century, but seems to have been widely expected of singers in opera from Monteverdi to Bellini, and of instrumentalists performing songful music. Musicians since the late 20th century have recognized its importance again, especially in the repeats of da capo forms and in slow music.

Ornstein, Leo (b. Kremechug, 2 Dec 1893; d. Green Bay, Wisconsin, 24 Feb 2002). Russian–US composer of modernist works in his 20s, which he so long outlived. A cantor's son, he studied as a pianist at the St Petersburg Conservatory and, after emigrating in 1907, with Bertha Fiering Tapper at the Institute of Musical Art in New York, where he gave his debut recital in 1911. His *Wild Men's Dance*, Op.13:2 (*c.*1913) and other works of that period created a sensation with their clusters and, indeed, wildness, and he was acclaimed both in the USA and on tour in Europe. In other moods he was more nostalgic. He virtually gave up performing in 1920, but taught in Philadelphia until 1953 and composed into his 90s.

orpharion. Lute of bandora shape, invented in England in the late 16th century and named after Orpheus and Arion.

Orpheus. Legendary singer of Thrace. Many stories are told of him in Greek and Latin poetry: how his music held the magical power to move even animals, how he outsang the sirens and so saved the Argonauts, how, when he had been torn to pieces by women worshippers of Bacchus, his head went on singing as it floated across the sea to Lesbos. But the episode that has repeatedly been remembered in music, drama and poetry since the Middle Ages is that of his grief at the death of his wife, Eurydice, his journey to the underworld after her, his successful musical pleading with Hades/Pluto and Persephone/Proserpine for her return, and his fatal inability to keep the bargain and not look back. Musical treatments go back to the dawn of opera, in the settings of Rinuccini's *Euridice* by Peri and Caccini, and include:

(1) Monteverdi's opera *Orfeo*, to a libretto by

Alessandro Striggio. After a prologue sung by Music (soprano), Orpheus (tenor) and Eurydice (soprano) are married. With her away he sings of love and memory ('Vi ricorda, o boschi ombrosi') before Sylvia (soprano) brings news of her death ('Ahi caso acerbo'). He then appeals to Charon for entry to the underworld ('Possente spirito'), regains Eurydice thanks to Proserpine's pleasure in his singing, but loses her. Finally he is summoned to the skies by his father Apollo (tenor). First performance: Mantua, 24 Feb 1607.

(2) Gluck's opera *Orfeo ed Euridice*, to a libretto by Calzabigi, revised as *Orphée et Eurydice* with words rewritten by Pierre Louis Moline. The beginning is at Eurydice's funeral, to which Orpheus (alto castrato in the It. version, tenor in the Fr.) responds with a lament ('Chiamo il mio ben così'/'Objet de mon amour'). Cupid (soprano) brings news that he can descend to the underworld, where he is threatened by Furies before reaching the Elysian Fields, evoked in the DANCE OF THE BLESSED SPIRITS. After the catastrophe comes a second lament, one of the most popular arias ('Che farò senza Euridice?'/'J'ai perdu mon Eurydice'), especially among mezzos and contraltos taking the It. version. First performance: Vienna, 5 Oct 1762; rev Paris, 2 Aug 1774.

(3) Haydn's opera *L'anima del filosofo, ossia Orfeo ed Euridice*, to a libretto by Carlo Francesco Badini. Creon (baritone) is perhaps the philosopher, blessing the marriage of his daughter Eurydice (soprano) to Orpheus (tenor), and reacting again to Eurydice's death and the anguish of Orpheus, who travels to Hades, retrieves Eurydice, looks back, and takes poison. Written for the composer's 1791 London visit, the work was not performed. First performance: Florence, 9 May 1951.

(4) Liszt's symphonic poem, first performed as an introduction to Gluck's opera. First performance: Weimar, 16 Feb 1854.

(5) Offenbach's operetta *Orphée aux enfers* (Orpheus in the Underworld), to a libretto by Hector Crémieux and Ludovic Halévy. Orpheus and Eurydice have seen too much of one another. He, however, is obliged by Public Opinion to fulfil his mythic destiny, and to meet virtually the entire population of Mount Olympus, later seen doing the CANCAN. First performance: Paris, 21 Oct 1858, rev 7 Feb 1874.

(6) Stravinsky's ballet score *Orpheus*, for choreography by Balanchine. The story is told in orchestral chiaroscuro, with a harp leading the way. First performance: New York, 28 Apr 1948. (Elements of the myth also appear in his *Histoire du soldat* and *The Rake's Progress*.)

(7) Birtwistle's opera *The Mask of Orpheus*, to a libretto by Peter Zinovieff, with electronic music made in collaboration with Barry Anderson. Coming late in the myth's history, the work also seems to be the matrix from which so many stories could have emerged. Moments are told and retold, with the roles of Orpheus, Eurydice and Aristaeus each taken by two singers and a mime. First performance: London, 21 May 1986.

There are other operatic treatments by Luigi Rossi, Locke, Charpentier, Campra (in *Le Carnaval de Venise*), Naumann, Malipiero, Milhaud, Krenek, Casella and Glass, as well as cantatas by Clérambault, Rameau, Rossini and Berlioz, concert pieces by Musgrave and a ballet score by Henze.

Orpheus Britannicus (The British Orpheus). Title of a collection of Purcell's songs published by Playford in 1698.

Orrego-Salas, Juan (Antonio) (b. Santiago, 18 Jan 1919). Chilean composer, a neoclassicist with a large output of chamber music and songs, as well as symphonies, concertos and choral pieces. He studied in Chile, and in the USA with Thomson and Copland (1944–6), after which he returned to work as a teacher and critic, then settled as founder director of the Latin American Music Center at the University of Indiana (1961–87).

Ortiz, Diego (b. Toledo, *c*.1510; d. ?Naples, *c*.1570). Spanish composer, whose *Trattado de glosas* (pub. Rome, 1553) provides instruction to string players, with some pieces. By the time of its publication he was in Naples, where he became viceregal chapelmaster. He also published a book of sacred music.

Orto, Marbrianus de (b. Tournai, *c*.1460; d. Nivelles, Jan/Feb 1529). Netherlandish composer, noted for a polyphonic setting of Dido's lament to Virgil's words, *Dulces exuviae*. A priest's son, he bore the name Dujardin but preferred the Latin form. He went from Tournai to Rome in 1482 in the bishop's retinue and stayed there, as a singer in the papal chapel, joined by Josquin. Later his base was Nivelles, where he was dean of St Gertrude's, but he also served the Burgundian dukes, travelling with Philip the Fair to Spain in 1506.

Osborne, Nigel (b. Manchester, 23 Jun 1948). British composer, for whom expressionist modernism works hand in glove with social lament and protest. He studied at Oxford and in Warsaw with the composer Witold Rudziński (1970–71), and has taught at the universities of Nottingham (1978–90) and Edinburgh (as professor, from 1990), working also for the charity War Child in Bosnia Herzegovina. His compositions include the opera *The*

Electrification of the Soviet Union (f.p. Glyndebourne, 1987).

ossia (It., or). Marking indicating an alternative, often a less arduous passage or less difficult note, or contrariwise a more decorated version.

ostinato (It., obstinate). Short repeating element, usually only a bar or two long, though the term may also be applied to such longer repetitions as occur in a chaconne or passacaglia. The element may be a rhythm (Ravel's *Boléro*), a broken chord (Handel's *Zadok the Priest*) or a melodic figure (Ligeti's *Continuum*), and it may, as these examples suggest, be either the scaffolding for other material or the whole piece. Though common in Baroque music and endemic in minimalist scores, ostinatos occur in all periods. In music from the great age of industrialization, from the early 19th to the early 20th century, they often suggest machinery: spinning wheels (*Der fliegende Holländer*), a mill wheel (*Jenůfa*), a steam locomotive (*Pacific 231*).

Ostrčil, Otakar (b. Prague, 25 Feb 1879; d. 20 Aug 1935). Czech conductor and composer, remembered more for introducing Janáček's operas to Prague, where he was music director at the National Theatre from 1920, than for his own works, which include operas, cantatas and orchestral pieces. His formal studies were of languages (and he was to work as a college teacher of Czech and German before establishing himself as a conductor), but he was also Fibich's pupil and amanuensis.

Osud (Fate). Opera by Janáček to a libretto by Fedora Bartošová based on a scenario by him. Autobiography disguised as autobiography, the piece shows the doomed love of the composer Zivný (tenor) and Míla Válková (soprano) as an image of Janáček's attraction to Kamila Urválková, and as a correction to Ludvik Čelanský's portrait of the same lady in his opera *Kamila* (1897). First performance: Brno, 18 Sep 1934 (broadcast).

ôtez (Fr.). Remove, as in *ôtez les sourdines* (remove mutes).

Othello. Shakespeare play, of how the title character, insecure as a Moor among Venetians, is driven into a jealous frenzy by his lieutenant Iago, and kills his beloved, faithful wife Desdemona. It is the subject of two major operas, both with a tenor Otello (though very different kinds of tenor: bel canto and heroic) and, inevitably, soprano Desdemona:

(1) Rossini's *Otello*, to a libretto by Francesco Berio di Salsa closing asymptotically towards Shakespeare. It notably includes three big tenor roles, with those of Iago and Rodrigo, and has two choice numbers for Desdemona in the last act: her Willow Song ('Assisa a piè d'un salice') and her prayer ('Deh calma'). First performance: Naples, 4 Dec 1816.

(2) Verdi's *Otello*, to a libretto by Boito closer to the original, though with such striking additions as the nihilistic creed for Iago (baritone), 'Credo in un Dio crudel'. Among other powerful moments are, again, Desdemona's Willow Song ('Piangea cantando') and prayer ('Ave Maria'), the love duet 'Già nella notte densa', the Othello–Iago oath-taking duet 'Si, pel ciel marmoreo giuro!', Iago's drinking song 'Inaffia l'ugola' and fatal narrative 'Era la notte', and Othello's entrance aria 'Esultatae!', his regretful 'Ora e per sempre addio', his overwhelmed 'Dio! mi potevi scagliar' and his final testament 'Niun mi tema'. Verdi added a third-act ballet for Paris in 1894. First performance: Milan, 5 Feb 1887.

ottava (It.). Octave. Hence the markings *ottava alta/sopra* (an octave higher than written), *ottava bassa/sotta* (an octave lower than written) and ALL'OTTAVA. Hence also *ottava battuta* (struck octave), a fault in part writing whereby an octave is accented having been approached by two parts moving in opposite directions.

ottavino (It.). Piccolo, having this name because it plays an octave above the regular flute. Also called thus is a small spinet playing an octave above normal.

Otter, Anne Sofie von (b. Stockholm, 9 May 1955). Swedish mezzo-soprano, who is much admired for her combination of creamy vocal richness with cool demeanour, and for her expressive way with words. She began her career, after studies in Stockholm and London, as Cherubino at Covent Garden (1985) and the Met (1988), and could have been typecast as a Mozart–Strauss cross-dresser had she not gone on broadening her repertory, even to Carmen (2002).

ottetto (It.). Octet.

Ottone. Opera by Handel to a libretto by Haym after one by Stefano Benedetto Pallavicino. Ottone (alto castrato), king of Germany, is united with the Byzantine princess Teofane (soprano) after plots and mischances involving the usurper Adalberto (alto), his mother Gismonda (soprano) and the pirate captain Emireno (bass), who turns out to be

Teofane's brother and therefore eastern emperor. Gismonda has two notable arias: 'Vieni, o figlio' and 'La speranza è giunta'. First performance: London, 12 Jan 1723.

ottoni (It.). Brass.

Ours, L' (The Bear). Name given to Haydn's Symphony No.82 on account of one or other (or both) of two features in the finale: a bagpipe tune suggesting a bear dance and a gruff melody.

Out of Doors (*Szabadban*). Set of five piano pieces by Bartók: *With Drums and Pipes, Barcarolla, Musettes, The Night's Music, The Chase*.

outdoor music. There are acoustic problems of dispersal and disturbance, but a good deal of 18th-century music was written for outdoor performance (see MUSIC FOR THE ROYAL FIREWORKS, NOTTURNO, SERENADE, SERENATA, WATER MUSIC), and many summer festivals stage opera and concerts outside.

overblow. To increase pressure and adjust embouchure so that a wind instrument sounds in a higher register than normal. Open cylindrical tubes (flutes) and closed conical ones (oboes and bassoons) overblow at the octave, closed cylindrical tubes (clarinets), at the 12th. Overblowing is a fault in beginners, but can be tamed to expand the instrument's range – even stratospherically by going into higher and higher octaves.

overdotting. Performance of a rhythm with an inequality exceeding that of dotting. See NOTES INEGALES.

overspun string. String of gut, plastic or metal wound round with wire, as used in string and keyboard instruments.

overstrung. Kind of keyboard construction in which bass strings pass diagonally over those of middle register, so that the body of the instrument has a less attenuated shape.

overtone. Frequency constituent of a sound, other than the fundamental (the first PARTIAL). In the case of a relatively pure sound, therefore, the octave above will be the first overtone but the second partial.

overtone singing. Producing overtones, audibly distinct from the fundamental, by use of facial muscles. This is especially characteristic of the music of east Asian peoples, notably Mongolians and Tuvans. It was probably first used in Western music by Stockhausen (*Stimmung*).

overture (Fr. *ouverture*, Ger. *Ouvertüre*, It. *sinfonia*). Introduction to an opera, play or other large work, or a concert piece of similar character. From simple beginnings two kinds evolved during the 17th century: the FRENCH OVERTURE and the ITALIAN OVERTURE. In the early 18th century the latter gave birth to the symphony (still sometimes called 'overture' at the end of the century), and that gift to the concert hall was redoubled in the 19th century when the theatre overture spawned first the concert overture and then the symphonic poem.

In the opera house, the overture as a separate and separable number was almost universal in the 18th century and up to the end of Rossini's career, but after that it could be replaced by a short introduction, recreated as an entry into the musical-dramatic world that would flow from it without interruption (as with Wagner's preludes), or dropped altogether. The concert hall gave it a new existence. Beethoven's *Leonore* overtures became concert pieces without planning, but he, Schubert and Weber all produced concert overtures in the period around 1810. Mendelssohn and Berlioz followed suit, but then, with Liszt, works made as overtures (*Tasso, Prometheus, Orpheus*, all in the years 1847–55) began to have the extra length that warranted a new description: symphonic poem. Brahms's pursuit of the concert overture into the 1880s is one symptom of his sublime conservatism.

Oxford University. Among the oldest choirs in continuous existence anywhere is that of New College (1379). There are musical treatises by Oxford scholars from around the same time, and music was being taught, from Boethius, by the early 15th century, followed by the granting of degrees in music from the late 15th century onwards. In 1626 William Heather endowed the chair in music still named after him; its occupants have included Crotch, Stainer, Parry and Parratt. Oxford University Press, dating back to 1478, began publishing music regularly in 1922.

Oxyrhynchos hymn. Hymn to the Trinity, recovered on a papyrus of around 300 from the Eqyptian city (modern Al-Bahnasah).

Ozawa, Seiji (b. Fenytien, now Shenyang, China, 1 Sep 1935). Japanese–US conductor, the long-serving music director of the Boston Symphony (1973–2002), from which he moved to the Vienna Staatsoper. He studied with Hideo Saito in Tokyo, made his professional debut there in 1954 while a student, and completed his training with Münch and Monteux at Tanglewood and Karajan in Berlin. After a further period as Bernstein's assistant with the New York Philharmonic (1961–5) he gained principal posts in Toronto (1965–9) and San Francisco (1970–76). His gifts to Boston were lithe energy and a careful openness to new music; in Paris he conducted the première of Messiaen's *Saint François*.

P. Abbreviation for pedal.

p. Abbreviation for *piano* (as a dynamic marking) found in manuscript and printed music from the 17th century onwards. Hence *pp* and *ppp* for increasing degrees of pianissimo, both established in the 18th century. Verdi introduced *pppp* in his *Requiem*, Tchaikovsky *ppppp* in his 'Pathétique' Symphony, and Ligeti upped (or downed) the scale to *pppppppp* in his Cello Concerto.

Pablo (Costales), Luis de (b. Bilbao, 28 Jan 1930). Spanish composer, vigorous and industrious in assimilating avant-garde ideas of the 1950s–60s. He trained as a lawyer and worked as such for the airline Iberia before quickly establishing himself as a composer in the early 1960s, following some lessons with Ohana and Deutsch. At the same time he did much to promote new music in Madrid, where he was appointed professor at the conservatory in 1971. His works include four operas (*Kiu*, f.p. Madrid, 1983) and many other large-scale pieces.

Pachelbel, Johann (baptized Nuremberg, 1 Sep 1653; buried Nuremberg, 9 Mar 1706). German organist-composer. His name is most often associated with a much arranged canon, marked by a haunting downward scale theme over a re-peating bass and bright, straightforward harmony (Canon and Gigue in D for three violins and continuo, date uncertain, the gigue customarily ignored in performance). In his time, though, he was one of the principal German organist-composers and as such an influence on Bach.

After academic and musical studies in Altdorf and Regensburg, he was deputy organist at St Stephen's Cathedral in Vienna (1673–7), a Catholic side-step in his career as a Lutheran church musician. He was then briefly in Eisenach before becoming organist at the Predigerkirche in Erfurt (1678–90). Bach was born in Erfurt during this period, and an elder brother, Johann Christoph, had lessons with Pachelbel, who was also god-father to their sister Johanna Juditha. In Erfurt, too, Pachelbel started a family of his own. He married in 1681: two years later his wife and their baby son were victims of plague. The next year he married again, and from this union came two daughters and five sons, among whom Wilhelm Hieronymus (1686–1764) and Carl Theodor (1690–1750) became successful organist-com-posers, the latter spending his last two decades in North America.

Pachelbel took his family briefly to Stuttgart and Gotha before returning in 1695 to St Sebald's in his home town. He produced a large quantity of chorales, fantasias, toccatas, fugues (including 95 on the *Magnificat*) for the organ, other keyboard music (suites, variation sets), sacred concertos and *Magnificat* settings for choir with instruments and continuo, and motets.

Pachmann, Vladimir de (b. Odessa, 27 Jul 1848; d. Rome, 6 Jan 1933). Russian pianist, especially admired in Chopin. Sorabji remarked on 'the almost unlimited range of his gradations of tone within a mezzo-forte and an unbelievable *quasi niente*' – or near silence, the celebrated 'Pach-mannissimo' – as well as other qualities of touch and colour. But he was a vain and eccentric performer, and one who played up his eccentricities, grimacing and even talking to the audience while playing. He had studied with his violinist father and at the Vienna Conservatory, and made his début in Odessa in 1869, but then spent most of the next decade in retirement, perfecting his technique. After that he led the life of a touring virtuoso, playing regularly in New York from 1891 onwards, and making a few recordings of small pieces by Chopin, Liszt, Raff and Schumann. He married several times.

Mark Mitchell *Vladimir de Pachmann* (2003)

Pacific 231. See MOUVEMENT SYMPHONIQUE.

Pacini, Giovanni (b. Catania, 11 Feb 1796; d. Pescia, 6 Dec 1867). Italian composer. The son of a distinguished tenor (and later buffo bass), he studied in Venice and began his career in his teens, rivalling Rossini in operas both comic and, later, serious (including *Niobe*, on which Liszt wrote a fantasy). He wrote fast and, by his own admission, without much thought. 'God help us,' Rossini remarked, 'if he knew music: no one could resist him.' Still, his facility helped when it came to the quick closing section of an aria, and he got the name of 'the master of the cabaletta'. Several of his operas have English or, especially, Scottish settings, following the vogue for Sir Walter Scott.

In Rome, in 1821, he contracted a liaison with Princess Pauline Borghese, Napoleon's sister, from whom he extricated himself by marrying in 1825. His wife died three years later, and he became the lover of Countess Samoylov, a Russian émigrée in Milan. Their relationship survived his second marriage, and the countess used her influence in his interests. Nevertheless, he came to recognize that he had been overtaken by Bellini and Donizetti, and in 1833 he retired from composition to found a music school in Viareggio, which he moved to Lucca in 1837 on becoming director of the ducal chapel there.

The next year, though, he returned to the theatre to work in a new style, embracing elements from Bellini, who had died in the interim. Now came some of his biggest successes, notably *Saffo* and two works produced during a triumphant visit to Palermo in 1843: *Maria, regina d'Inghilterra* and *Medea*. His second period of success was brief, for Verdi was overtaking him as Bellini and Donizetti had before, but still there were intermittent successes in his later career. He was thrice married and had nine children.

Operas: *Adelaide e Comingio* (Gaetano Rossi), f.p. Milan, 1817; *Il barone di Dolsheim* (Romani), f.p. Milan, 1818; *L'ultimo giorno di Pompei* (Andrea Leone Tottola, after Bulwer-Lytton), f.p. Naples, 1825; *Niobe* (Tottola), f.p. Naples, 1826; *Ivanhoe* (Rossi, after Scott), f.p. Venice, 1832; *Il convitato di pietra* (Giovanni Bertati), f.p. Viareggio, 1832; *Saffo* (Cammarano, after Pietro Beltrane), f.p. Naples, 1840; *Maria, regina d'Inghilterra* (Leopoldo Tarantini), f.p. Palermo, 1843; *Medea* (Benedetto Castiglia), f.p. Palermo, 1843; around 80 others

Sacred music: *Requiem*, C minor, pub 1843; oratorios, masses, vespers settings

Other works: *Dante Symphony*, orch, pf, 1863; 6 string quartets, songs, etc.

Paderewski, Ignacy Jan (b. Kuryłówka, Podolia, 18 Nov 1860; d. New York, 29 Jun 1941). Polish pianist-composer and national figurehead. He studied at the Warsaw Conservatory (1872–8), where he stayed on as a teacher. In 1880 he married a fellow graduate, Antonia Korsakowna, who died within the year, soon after the birth of their son Alfred (1880–1901). Dissatisfied with conservatory life, he tried to find ways to gain further training, and eventually left for study with Leschetizky in Vienna (1884–7). He began his international career in Paris (1888) and played at the concerts inaugurating Carnegie Hall (1891), after which he was regularly in the US. In 1899 he was remarried, to Helena Groska, and they set up home on Lake Geneva.

Performance diverted him from composition, most of his many piano pieces dating from the 1880s (including his celebrated Minuet in G, a Mozartian miniature). In the first decade of the 20th century he produced a few more works, mostly on a big scale. His opera *Manru*, set among the peasants of the Tatra mountains, had a production at the Met in 1902, and his Symphony, also distinctly Polish in tone, was first heard in Boston in 1909.

After that his expressions of patriotism became actual rather than musical. In 1910 he spoke at the unveiling in Kraków (then Russian territory) of a monument he had commissioned to mark the 500th anniversary of the Battle of Grunwald, at which the Teutonic Knights had been defeated by King Władysław Jagiełło, and during the First World War he campaigned strenuously for Polish causes in the US. (He also set up prizes for US composers.) When, at the end of the war, Poland re-emerged as a state, he was appointed its first prime minister and foreign minister on 16 Jan 1919. But he was ill suited to political wrangling and resigned in December, though he was briefly involved again in state affairs the next year. He went back to his concert career; he also appeared in a British film, *Moonlight Sonata* (1937). Following the invasion of Poland in 1939 he turned his attention again to politics, but he was now nearing 80. By presidential decree he was buried in the Arlington National Cemetery, whence his remains were transferred to Poland in 1992. His recordings – of Chopin, inevitably, but also of music from Haydn to Debussy – convey his free rubato, but not the proud demeanour and the patriotic aura that made him so admired.

Adam Zamoyski *Paderewski* (1982)

Piano: *Humoresques de concert*, Op.14, 1886–7 (No.1 Minuet, G); Concerto, A minor, Op.17, 1882–8; Sonata, E♭, Op.21, 1887–1903; *Variations et fugue*, E♭, Op.23, 1885–1903

Other works: *Manru* (opera; Alfred Nossig), f.p. Dresden, 1901; Symphony, B minor, Op.24, 1903–8; songs, etc.

Padilla, Juan Gutiérrez de (b. Málaga *c.*1590; d. Puebla, Mexico, Mar/Apr 1664). Spanish composer, active in Puebla by 1622. He trained as a choirboy at Málaga Cathedral and held posts there and in Cádiz before sailing for New Spain. In 1629 he was appointed chapelmaster of Puebla Cathedral, where he was responsible for a lavish musical establishment and for composing both liturgical music (in Renaissance-style polyphony, often for double choir) and entertainments for Christmas and other festivals.

Padmâvatî. Opera by Roussel to a libretto by Louis Laloy based on the story of an Indian queen who lived around 1300. Padmâvatî (contralto) kills her husband, Ratan-Sen (tenor), and herself rather than submit to the moghul sultan, Aladdin (baritone). Much of the action is ceremonial and danced. First performance: Paris, 1 June 1923.

Padovano, Annibale (b. Padua, 1527; d. Graz, 15 Mar 1575). Italian composer. He was organist at St Mark's in Venice (1555–65) before joining the archducal court in Graz. He wrote masses (including a polychoral setting in 24 parts), madrigals, ricercares and toccatas for organ, and a battle piece for wind octet.

Paer, Ferdinando (b. Parma, 1 Jun 1771; d. Paris, 3 May 1839). Italian composer, also known under the French form of his name, Paër. He studied in his native city, where he began his career as an opera composer before moving with his wife in 1797 to Vienna. There he learned to emulate Mozart and produced *Achille* (1801), whose funeral march impressed Beethoven. He moved on briefly to Prague before settling in Dresden, where his *Leonora* (1804) preceded Beethoven's opera on the same subject. Napoleon drew him to Poland in 1806 and to Paris the next year, and there he remained. He wrote the bridal march for Napoleon's second wedding in 1810 and maintained his position as a singing teacher, theatre director and

opera composer after the emperor's fall – though not after Rossini's rise. The work of his that best survived was his light comedy *Le Maître de chapelle* (1821).

Paganini, Nicolò (b. Genoa, 27 Oct 1782; d. Nice, 27 May 1840). Italian violinist-composer, the model of the virtuoso whose charisma and command suggest supernatural, even demonic powers. Strenuously encouraged by a zealous father, he studied in his native city and had composition lessons with Paer in Parma in 1795–6. In 1801 he escaped from his father and settled in Lucca with his brother Carlo (1778–1830), also a violinist. From 1805 to 1809 the two were in the service there of Napoleon's sister Elisa Baciocchi.

The younger Paganini started on the life of a touring soloist in 1810, but for a long while he confined his appearances to Italy. In 1824 he began an affair with Antonia Bianchi, a singer, by whom he had a son, Achille (b. 1825). They legally separated when he left for Vienna in 1828 to begin his international career, and he gained custody of Achille. His life then was one of travel and acclaim. During the next six years he toured widely throughout Europe, from Scotland to Poland, astonishing audiences that included Chopin, Schumann and Liszt, all of whom found their notions of virtuosity changed. He was able – possibly by virtue of a medical condition that made his fingers unusually pliable – to push violin technique into new domains: high harmonics, pizzicatos played with either hand, double stops, extreme velocity. He also liked to show off his prowess by playing on just the G string, perhaps tuned a third higher. His expertise, coupled with his cadaverous appearance, gave rise to many stories – notably that he had entered into a pact with the devil – and he cultivated his myth by his reckless gambling and womanizing.

In 1835, exhausted and subjected to jealous attacks, he had retired to his villa in Parma, where he was invited by the ex-empress Marie-Louise to take charge of the court orchestra. His later projects included a casino in Paris, a violin method, a quartet (to play late Beethoven) and an instrument dealership, but his health was in decline and nothing of these plans materialized. Because he refused the last rites, believing them premature, he was forbidden Christian burial by the Archbishop of Nice, and his body set out on a career of delayed interment and repeated exhumation. He left his treasured Guarneri del Gesù violin to the city of his birth.

His legacy to violinists includes pre-eminently his 24 unaccompanied caprices, made to surpass Locatelli's in astonishing difficulty; he delayed their publication until 1820 to prevent anyone else trying to play them. Also of extraordinary brilliance are his concertos and sets of variations for violin and orchestra; tackled by few, on account of their extreme technical challenges, they can be awesome in performance, suggesting what it might have been like to hear their creator. He taught himself to play the guitar, allegedly to pursue a love affair, whence his works for that instrument. He also wrote for the viola in 1832–4, which is when he asked Berlioz to write him a concerto. Though dissatisfied with the result (*Harold en Italie*), he sent Berlioz a large cheque, unprompted, in 1838 and was rewarded with the dedication of *Roméo et Juliette*.

The last of the violin caprices, in A minor, was the subject of variations by Brahms, Rachmaninoff, Lutosławski and others. His music and mystique also prompted a set of études by Liszt and an operetta by Lehár.

Geraldine I.C. de Courcy *Paganini, the Genoese* (1957)

Violin concertos: No.1, E♭ (usually played in D), 1816; No.2, B minor, 1826 (with *Rondo la clochette* finale); No.3, E, 1826; No.4, D minor, ?1830; No.5, A minor, 1830; 'No.6', E minor, c.1815; *Le Streghe*, variations, 1813; etc.
Other works: 24 caprices, vn, c.1805; 12 sonatas, vn, gtr, c.1805; 15 quartets, vn, va, vc, gtr, 1806–20; etc.

page turner. Assistant to a pianist or other keyboard player performing from music on paper. Soloists generally perform from memory. If not, they will usually have a student turn pages, from a chair to the left of the piano bench. Page turning is a minor art in itself, requiring not only dexterity and decent reading skills but an ability to know just when to act, though the player may help with a nod.

Pagliacci (Clowns). Opera by Leoncavallo to his own libretto, traditionally given as the second half of a double bill with *Cavalleria rusticana*, 'Cav and Pag'. Tonio (baritone) stands in front of the curtain to introduce the action. He belongs to a troupe of players, and his unrequited love for Nedda (soprano), wife of the company manager Canio (tenor), leads him on a path of vengeance and destruction. Canio sings his emotional aria 'Vesti la giubba' as he puts on his costume, unable to leave behind the tragedy of his real life. First performance: Milan, 21 May 1892.

Pahud, Emmanuel (b. Geneva, 27 Jan 1970). French–Swiss flautist, a master of the instrument's range of sound, shape and colour. Following his graduation in 1990 from the Paris Conservatoire, he studied further with Aurèle Nicolet, and in 1993

took the principal's chair with the Berlin Philharmonic, from which he resigned in 2000 to pursue a solo career.

Paik, Nam June (b. Seoul, 20 Jul 1932). Korean artist. He studied in Tokyo and, between 1956 and 1962, in Munich, Freiburg and Cologne. In this last city he encountered Stockhausen and was part of the team for the latter's *Originale*, but he was already under the influence of Cage and the FLUXUS movement (see his *hommage à john cage* for two pianos that are destroyed during the performance, three tape recorders, projections and live actions involving eggs, toy cars and motorbikes, 1959). He moved to New York in 1964 and became better known as a video artist.

Paine, John Knowles (b. Portland, Maine, 9 Jan 1839; d. Cambridge, Mass., 25 Apr 1906). US composer and teacher, New England symphonist. The son of a music-store owner and grandson of an organ builder, he studied in his home town with the German-born organist Hermann Kotzschmar and completed his education under Karl Haupt in Berlin (1858–61). In 1862 he was invited to Harvard, where he expanded his duties from those of choir training and organ playing until he had formed a music department and been appointed to a chair in 1875 – the first US professor of music. He retired in 1905. Among his compositions, the best in a style of Schumannesque openness, are large-scale choral works (Mass in D, Op.10, 1865; the oratorio *St Peter*, Op.20, 1870–72), two symphonies (No.1 in C minor, Op.23, 1875; No.2 'In the Spring' in A, Op.34, 1879), piano pieces and organ music. He devoted his last 15 years to an opera, *Azara*, whose promised Met production failed to materialize.

John C. Schmidt *The Life and Works of John Knowles Paine* (1980)

Paisiello, Giovanni (Gregorio Cataldo) (b. Roccaforzata, Taranto, 9 May 1740; d. Naples, 5 Jun 1816). Italian composer. Blessed with a fine voice as a boy, he studied in Taranto and from 1754 was a pupil of Durante at the San Onofrio conservatory in Naples, the forming ground for Neapolitan composers. There he wrote a good deal of church music but also a comic intermezzo that won him a commission to compose an opera for Bologna (1764), after which he maintained his luck in northern Italian cities before returning to Naples to produce a string of further successes, serious and comic, including the sharply satirical *Socrate immaginario*.

In 1776 he accepted an invitation from Catherine II to come to St Petersburg as court Italian opera composer in succession to Traetta, and there he again wrote both serious operas and comedies. Among the latter were *La serva padrona*, on the same libretto as Pergolesi's opera, and *Il barbiere di Siviglia*, which was so widely played and admired it prompted a sequel from Mozart (*Le nozze di Figaro*) and for a while stood in the way of Rossini's remake. He also wrote a setting of Metastasio's passion oratorio for the Catholic cathedral in St Petersburg.

The following year he returned to Naples by way of Vienna, where he composed *Il re Teodoro in Venezia*. Back in Naples he produced *Nina*, in a new vein of sentimental comedy, and *L'amor contrastato*, which was produced in Vienna as *La molinara* (Beethoven wrote variations on an aria from it). In 1799 he accepted an appointment from the brief republican government in Naples, which made his position difficult when the monarchy was restored. Napoleon invited him to Paris in 1802, and he wrote a mass for the emperor, whose favour can be explained by the engaging tunefulness of his music and perhaps also by the fact that the ceremonial grandeur he had evoked in his serious operas he could now lay on for the new imperial court. However, after the tepid reception of his *Proserpine* he returned to Naples.

Once more he was the victim of political change. Having welcomed the patronage of Joseph Bonaparte and Joachim Murat, successive Napoleonic kings, and written a *Te Deum* for the coronation of Napoleon's son as King of Rome, he fell into disgrace at the Bourbon restoration, lost his pension and died in poverty, his death hastened by that of his beloved wife in 1815.

Operas: *L'idolo cinese* (Giambattista Lorenzi), f.p. Naples, 1767; *Don Chisciotte della Mancia* (Lorenzi), f.p. Naples, 1769; *Socrate immaginario* (Lorenzi), f.p. Naples, 1775; *Nitteti* (Metastasio), f.p. St Petersburg, 1777; *La serva padrona* (Federico), f.p. Tsarkoye Selo, 1781; *Il barbiere di Siviglia* (Giuseppe Petrosellini, after Beaumarchais), f.p. St Petersburg, 1782; *Il re Teodoro in Venezia* (Giovanni Battista Casti, after Voltaire), f.p. Vienna, 1784; *Fedra* (Innocenzo Frugoni), f.p. Naples, 1788; *L'amor contrastato* (*La molinara*; Giuseppe Palomba), f.p. Naples, 1789; *Nina, o sia La pazza per amore* (Giuseppe Carpani, after Marsollier; see DALAYRAC), f.p. Caserta, 1789; *Proserpine* (Nicolas François Guillard, after Quinault), f.p. Paris, 1803; more than 70 others
Other works: *La passione di Gesù Cristo* (Metastasio), 1783; several masses, other church music, quartets, keyboard concertos, etc.

Pakistan. See INDIA.

Paladilhe, Emile (b. Hérault, near Montpellier, 3 Jun 1844; d. Paris, 8 Jan 1926). French composer, best remembered for songs. He was just 16 when he won the Prix de Rome, and 17 when his fifth opera, *Le Passant*, was staged at the Opéra-Comique with his mistress starring; it includes his most popular song, 'La mandolinata'.

Palais Garnier. Historic venue of the PARIS OPERA.

Palester, Roman (b. Śniatyn/Snyatyn, 28 Dec 1907; d. Paris, 25 Aug 1989). Polish composer. A pupil of Sikorski at the Warsaw Conservatory (1925–31), he spent time in Paris in the 1930s and settled there in 1947, emerging from a national-neoclassical style close to the later Szymanowski into a mature manner of firm individuality and technical assurance. His output is dominated by chamber and orchestral pieces, including five symphonies.

Palestrina, Giovanni Pierluigi da (b. ?Palestrina, near Rome, 1525/6; d. Rome, 2 Feb 1594). Italian composer and church musician, the ultimate master of Renaissance polyphony at its most suave and dignified. According to legend, his voice was discovered when he came to Rome to sell produce from his parents' farm – though he may not have been a country boy at all, but born in Rome to a family hailing from Palestrina. Rome, in any event, was where he spent almost all his professional life, starting as a choirboy at Santa Maria Maggiore by 1537. His one excursion was to be organist and choirmaster at the cathedral in Palestrina (1544–51), where he married Lucrezia Gori. Their three sons, Rodolfo (1549–72), Angelo (1551–75) and Iginio (1558–1610), all became musicians.

The bishop of Palestrina was elected pope as Julius III in 1550 and the next year called his musician to Rome as master of the Julian Chapel, a Vatican establishment for training Italian singers. (Foreigners dominated the older Sistine Chapel.) In 1554 Julius sponsored the publication of Palestrina's first book of masses, the earliest such collection printed in Rome, and in 1555, shortly before his death, he advanced the composer to the Sistine Chapel. The next pope – briefly – was Marcellus II, commemorated in the *Missa Papae Marcelli* from Palestrina's second book (1567). Another legend, dramatized by Pfitzner in his opera *Palestrina*, has it that the composer received this classic work by angelic dictation in a single night and thereby saved polyphony, showing how the old style could be adapted to the Counter-Reformation desires Marcellus had expressed, to have the liturgy intelligible. But though the piece is indeed beautifully clear and radiant, it represented only one possibility for Palestrina: other works have a cooler minor-mode tone or more involved counterpoint.

Marcellus's successor, Paul IV, removed from the Sistine Chapel all composers who had disgraced themselves by either marrying or writing madrigals. Palestrina, guilty on both counts, took posts at St John Lateran (1555–60) and Santa Maria Maggiore (1561–5). He also taught at a seminary, organized summer musical festivities at Cardinal Ippolito d'Este's new villa in Tivoli, and wrote music for St Philip Neri's oratory. In 1568 he refused the offer of a post in Vienna from Emperor Maximilian II; also that year he began a long connection with the Mantuan court, for which he wrote several masses.

In 1571 he was restored to his position at the Julian Chapel under Pius V. Acknowledged as the outstanding composer in Rome, he helped to found a professional organization, the Vertuosa Compagnia dei Musici. This was, however, also a time of travail, for he lost not only two of his sons but also his brother and, in 1580, his wife, all victims of plague. He briefly considered ordination, but chose early in 1581 to marry Virginia Dormoli, a widow, and join her in her lucrative fur business. This enabled him to complete the publication of his music. In 1592 he received the remarkable homage of a printed volume of 16 vesper psalms set by his colleagues. He was buried in St Peter's, but all trace of his grave was soon lost during building works.

His masses exemplify the main techniques of the period: some have a cantus firmus (*L'homme armé*, *Ut-re-mi-fa-sol-la*, plainsong in several others), others are freely composed (*Missa Papae Marcelli*, *Missa brevis*), but the majority are parody masses – works, that is, based on polyphonic compositions, in most cases the composer's own motets and hymns (*Assumpta est Maria*, *Hodie Christus natus est*, *Dum complerentur*, *Aeterna Christi munera*), but sometimes madrigals or motets by composers of the preceding generation or two (e.g. Rore, Primavera, Josquin, Morales and the Mantua composer Jachet). Most are in four, five or six parts.

As the renowned, if apocryphal, saviour of Renaissance polyphony, and as the outstanding practitioner of it in its ultimate stage, Palestrina remained known and admired, and some of his music has been continuously in the ecclesiastical repertory since it was created. In the 19th century certain features of his style – mellifluous melody avoiding wide intervals, a clear relationship of parts moving consistently through triadic harmonies with evenly flowing rhythm – were codified to create a model in the teaching of music.

Jerome Roche *Palestrina* (1971)

Masses (with publication dates): *Ecce sacerdos magnus* a 4, 1554; *Missa Papae Marcelli* a 6, 1567;

Missa brevis a 4, 1570; *L'Homme armé* a 5, 1570; *Ut-re-mi-fa-sol-la* a 6, 1570; *L'Homme armé* a 4, 1582; *Aeterna Christi munera* a 4, 1590; *Dum complerentur* a 6, 1599; *Assumpta est Maria* a 6; *Benedicta es* a 6; *Hodie Christus natus est* a 8; 93 others

Motets a 5 from the Song of Songs, pub 1584: *Nigra sum, Pulchra es, Surge, amica mea, Tota pulchra es*, 25 others

Other motets: *Dum complerentur* a 6, *Exsultate Deo* a 5, *Hodie Chrisrus natus est* a 8, *O bone Jesu* a 6/8, *O magnum mysterium* a 6, *Peccantem me* a 5, *Sicut cervus* a 4, *Stabat mater* a 8, *Super flumina Babylonis* a 4/5, about 500 others

Other works: Lamentations, *Magnificat* settings, about 100 madrigals

Palestrina. Opera by Pfitzner to his own libretto. Palestrina (tenor) – confused by the new music of Florence and disconsolate over his wife's death, but prompted by Cardinal Borromeo (baritone) – composes his Pope Marcellus mass in a night of angelic communion. Conflicting cardinals are in turmoil at the Council of Trent, but Palestrina is given his destiny – to continue composing – by the grateful pope. Pfitzner here dramatized his passionate belief in the tradition (of German Romanticism) he felt to be under attack, and created his masterpiece. First performance: Munich, 12 Jun 1917.

Paliashvili, Zakharia (b. Kutaisi, 16 Aug 1871; d. Tbilisi, 6 Oct 1933). Georgian composer, one of the founders of modern art music in his country. He studied at the Tbilisi Music College and with Taneyev at the Moscow Conservatory (1900–3), then returned to Tbilisi to work energetically as a composer, teacher, choirmaster and folk music collector. His works include the prototype of Georgian opera, *Abesalom da Eteri* (1909–18).

palindrome. Just as a verbal palindrome is a sequence of words whose letters read the same backwards as forwards, a classic example in English being 'Madam, I'm Adam', so a musical palindrome can be composed with reversible elements. This is hard in tonal music, which is by nature progressive and therefore irreversible – though Haydn produced an example in the minuet and trio of his 'Palindrome' Symphony, No.47. Palindromes became commoner in the 20th century, when more deliberate and sometimes playful compositional attitudes enhanced their possibility and allure. Examples include the A–B–C–B–A forms Bartók liked to design (as in his Fourth and Fifth quartets), Messiaen's NON-RETROGRADABLE RHYTHMS and whole movements by Berg (Chamber Concerto: Adagio) and Webern

(Symphony: Variations) in which events are recapitulated backwards after a midpoint. Hindemith's *Hin und zurück* is a rare, brief instance of a palindromic opera; Berg's *Lulu* goes through a looser reversal after the midpoint.

Pallavicino, Benedetto (b. Cremona, *c.*1551; d. Mantua, 26 Nov 1601). Italian composer. In service at the Mantuan court by 1583, he was a prominent madrigalist, influenced by Wert and influencing Monteverdi.

Pallavicino, Carlo (b. Salò, Lake Garda, *c.*1640; d. Dresden, 29 Jan 1688). Italian musician. He was active in Dresden, Padua and Venice as an opera composer and organist, winning a Europe-wide reputation in the former capacity.

pallet. Flap that opens and closes an organ pipe.

Palm, Siegfried (b. Wuppertal, 25 Apr 1927). German cellist. He studied with his cellist father of the same name and began a career as an orchestral player in 1945. As a member of the Hamann Quartet (1951–62) he gained experience in playing new music, and many composers wrote solo works and concertos for him, including Zimmermann, Penderecki, Xenakis and Ligeti. In 1962 he began teaching at the conservatory in Cologne.

Palmgren, Selim (b. Pori, 16 Feb 1878; d. Helsinki, 13 Dec 1951). Finnish composer, especially of songs, choruses and lyric piano pieces in a Romantic vein.

Pan. Greek god of fertility, represented as a mature, bearded man with horns. He chased the nymph Syrinx, whose companion nymphs changed her into a reed before he could catch her, and he then played on the reed, or panpipes (Gk *syrinx*). The story is recalled in Ravel's *Daphnis et Chloé* and Debussy's *Syrinx* (its publisher's title for the piece he called *La Flûte de Pan*). Birtwistle's *Panic* also invokes him.

pan. See STEEL PAN.

pandiatonicism, pandiatonic. Term coined by Slonimsky in 1937 to indicate the use of additional notes to the tonic, third and fifth in non-resolving chords, e.g. the sixth in jazz and Messiaen or the seventh and ninth in Debussy and Ravel.

Panic. Work by Birtwistle for alto saxophone and drum kit with an orchestra of wind and percussion. Commissioned to cause a stir at the Last Night of the Proms, it did. First performance: London, 16 Sep 1995.

Panis angelicus (Bread of the Angels). Sacred favourite by Franck, to words by St Thomas Aquinas, originally for tenor with organ, harp, cello and double bass, much arranged.

panisorhythm. Self-similarity of rhythm, at least intermittently, in all polyphonic parts of a composition.

panpipes. Instrument comprising a row of several pipes – wooden, cane or ceramic – bound together in ascending or descending order of length and therefore of pitch. They have no mouthpieces and are stopped, their open ends aligned. The player blows across them and may sound one or more at a time. Sometimes they are arranged by length in a V shape, so as to produce two whole-tone scales. In Greek mythology the invention of panpipes was credited to Pan, but the instrument may have originated in China and spread both to Europe and across the Pacific to Peru, to take its important place in Andean folk music. In *Die Zauberflöte* Papageno plays panpipes, and the original Papageno really did so, though generally the music is supplied by a flute in the orchestra pit.

pantomime (Gk *pantomimos*, one who mimics everything). (1) Representation of action in mime, or dumb show. Ballets often have pantomime separating formal dances, as recitative separates arias in an opera. Pantomime can also be a feature of opera, as in the third act of *Die Meistersinger*, where Beckmesser, alone on stage, purloins Walther's prize song.

(2) British Christmas show, with a fairytale plot, comedy routines and songs.

pantonality, pantonal. Term preferred to 'atonality' or 'atonal' by Schoenberg and used by the music analyst Rudolph Réti with reference to 20th-century music that is tonal but where the key is constantly fluctuating or compromised (that of Bartók or Stravinsky, for instance).

Panufnik, Andrzej (b. Warsaw, 24 Sep 1914; d. Twickenham, 27 Oct 1991). Polish–British composer and conductor, knighted in 1991. He studied at the Warsaw Conservatory (1934–6), had further training as a conductor with Weingartner in Vienna (1937–8), and completed his education in Paris and London (1938–9). During the Second World War he gave two-piano recitals in Warsaw with Lutosławski; he then conducted the Kráków Philharmonic (1945–6) and the Warsaw Philharmonic (1946–7). In 1954 he left Poland for Britain, where he was principal conductor of the City of Birmingham Symphony Orchestra (1957–9), after which he concentrated on composition. Starting out from the international mid-century neo-classical mainstream, he went his own way, creating music seemingly self-generated from small motifs.

Andrzej Panufnik *Composing Myself* (1987)

Symphonies: *Sinfonia rustica* (No.1), 1948, rev 1955; *Sinfonia elegiaca* (No.2), 1957, rev 1966; *Sinfonia sacra* (No.3), 1963; *Sinfonia concertante* (No.4), fl, hp, str, 1973; *Sinfonia di sfere* (No.5), 1974–5; *Sinfonia mistica* (No.6), 1977; *Metasinfonia* (No.7), org, str, timp, 1978; *Sinfonia votiva* (No.8), 1981, rev 1984; *Sinfonia della speranza* (No.9), 1986, rev 1987; No.10, 1988, rev 1990

Other works: concertos, choral music, chamber pieces, etc.

Panzéra, Charles (Auguste Louis) (b. Geneva, 16 Feb 1896; d. Paris, 6 Jun 1976). Swiss baritone, especially admired for his performance as Pelléas and recording of *Dichterliebe* with Cortot.

Paolo da Firenze (b. Florence, c.1355; d. Florence, 1436 or later). Italian composer. He was known as Paolo Tenorista, suggesting that he was a singer besides being responsible for polyphonic songs drawing on Landini and the French post-Machaut tradition of rhythmic complexity. A Benedictine, he was abbot of San Martino al Pino, near Arezzo (1401–33), then rector of the Orbatello in Florence.

Papillons (Butterflies). Set of 12 piano pieces by Schumann, based on a masked ball in Jean-Paul Richter's *Flegeljahre*. The title was also used by Couperin and Grieg for keyboard pieces.

Parade. Ballet score by Satie to a scenario by Cocteau, designed by Picasso and choreographed by Massine. The score includes parts for pistol and typewriter, this being a 'realist ballet' with modern characters (strongly influenced too by circus). First performance: Paris, 18 May 1917.

paradiddle. Onomatopoeic term for a side-drum roll of four short, even notes.

Paradies und die Peri, Das (Paradise and the Peri). Oratorio by Schumann (1843) to an adaptation of the second part of Moore's *Lalla Rookh*. A peri is an earthbound angel in Persian mythology. This one is promised return to paradise if she can bring with her earth's dearest gift, which she finds in the tears of a penitent malefactor. First performance: Leipzig, 4 Dec 1843.

Paradis, Maria Theresia von (baptized Vienna, 15 May 1759; d. Vienna, 1 Feb 1824). Austrian composer and pianist. The daughter of a promi-nent court official, she was named after the empress and, having lost her sight in early child-hood, was given a thorough musical education by Salieri, Vogler, Kozeluch and others. Concertos were written for her by Salieri, Mozart (probably K.456) and Haydn (in G). A lengthy concert tour (1783–6) took her to Paris and London; after that she concentrated on composition (songs, stage works, piano pieces, almost all lost) and teaching.

parallel. Harmonic relationship of transposition without change. Parallel thirds and sixths are customary in diatonic harmony; parallel (or consecutive) fifths and octaves were regarded as faults, though they had provided the harmony of ORGANUM. Parallel triads and other chords, sometimes suggesting a medieval flavour, appear in Debussy and later music. Piano scales may be played in parallel motion (with the hands aligned, producing parallel double octaves) or contrary motion (with one hand rising as the other falls).

parameter. Aspect of a sound event, the four most usual being pitch, duration, loudness and timbre. The term gained currency in Europe in the 1950s, when, in efforts at total serialism, principles of serial control were applied not only to pitch but to the other parameters.

paraphrase. (1) Technique in Renaissance mass composition of taking a melody, usually from plainsong, as a cantus firmus. By contrast with earlier practice, the given melody may move from part to part, at the same speed as the other parts. Frequently it is paraphrased, i.e. new notes are inserted; hence the term.

(2) Term used by Liszt for a piano version of an operatic aria or medley of arias.

pardessus (Fr.). Treble, as in *pardessus de viole* (treble viol).

Paris. Cultural and government centre of France since the time of Clovis (6th century). Among the musicians working at the churches and university in the 12th and 13th centuries were Peter Abelard, Leonin and Perotin (who provided music for the new Notre Dame, consecrated in 1182). In the early 14th century the city was the source of the Ars Nova that spread across Europe, and de Vitry, one of the new art's foremost practitioners, was in royal service.

A couple of centuries later, in the decades around 1500, the royal chapel was led by several important composers, including Ockeghem, Mouton and de Sermisy. At this time Paris was the biggest city in Europe, with a population of around 300,000, and music of all kinds flourished there, Rabelaisian and refined. In the mid 16th century the poetry of Ronsard and Marot – and the printing press of Pierre Attaingnant – fostered a new spring in French song (Certon, Janequin, Le Jeune). Attaingnant also published dances, and was succeeded in the business of music printing by the Ballard family. The first half of the 17th century was the age of the *air de cour* (Guédron, Moulinie).

The long reign of Louis XIV (1643–1715) brought a great musical enrichment, even though Paris had to share the riches with Versailles after the king moved there in 1682. Cavalli came, and the Académie Royale de Musique, the royal opera company, was formed under Lully's direction in 1672; this was the ancestor of the PARIS OPERA. Charpentier and Lalande also lived and worked in the city, followed by Couperin. Composers under Louis XV (r. 1715–74) included Rameau and – working for the new concert organizations, notably the CONCERT SPIRITUEL – Leclair and Gossec. Among visitors during the 1770s and 1780s were Mozart, Haydn and Gluck, all promoted by the new music-publishing industry led from the city. As much as at the medieval university, musical practice was subjected to theoretical speculation, resulting in doctrinal battles between, for example, Lully's followers and Rameau's, or between amateurs of French music and admirers of Italian.

Cherubini, Méhul and Spontini were leading composers during the FRENCH REVOLUTION and the Napoleonic Empire; Cherubini was on the staff at the new PARIS CONSERVATOIRE, the principal teaching institution for musicians. Another immigrant, Pleyel, became Erard's main competitor in the building of pianos. After Napoleon's fall in 1815 and through the Second Empire, under Napoleon III (r. 1852–70), the city was an international musical capital, its opera theatres, salons and concert halls invigorated by residents (Berlioz, Habeneck, Gounod, Bizet, Lalo, Delibes), visitors (Liszt, Bellini, Donizetti, Wagner, Verdi) and visitors who became residents (Chopin, Rossini, Meyerbeer, Offenbach). Several new music-publishing houses were established (Choudens, Durand, Heugel, Leduc), and there was abundant production of pianos, wind instruments (Sax) and organs (Cavaillé-Coll). The opening of the Palais Garnier in 1875 gave the city the grandest opera house in the world.

Towards the end of the 19th century came an avant-garde (Satie, Debussy) reacting against the city's institutions and receiving encouragement from the arrival of new visitors in the early 20th century, notably Stravinsky. Between 1918 and 1939 Paris was again home to an extraordinary number of composers, native (Ravel, Roussel, Poulenc, Milhaud, Messiaen) and foreign (Stravinsky, Prokofiev, Martinů, Honegger). Nadia Boulanger taught Copland, Carter and many others. Messiaen's pupils included the dominant figures of the next generation, Boulez, Barraqué and Xenakis, of whom Boulez was responsible for two of the great musical projects of the late 20th century: an electronic music studio (IRCAM) and a new concert hall, the CITE DE LA MUSIQUE. Orchestras in the city include the ORCHESTRE DE PARIS and the ENSEMBLE INTERCONTEMPORAIN.

Nigel Simeone *Paris – A Musical Gazetteer* (2000)

Paris Conservatoire. Institution founded in 1795, and since then the principal music college in France. Its first home was where the old royal music school had been, in what is now the rue du Conservatoire. In 1811 a concert hall was opened there (see SOCIETE DES CONCERTS DU CONSERVATOIRE). In 1911 the Conservatoire moved to new premises in the rue de Madrid, and in 1990 it moved again, to La Villette, across the plaza from the Cité de la Musique.

Paris Opera. The institution dates back to the foundation of the Académie Royale de Musique (1672) by Louis XIV for Lully. For almost a century (until 1763) the Académie gave performances in the theatre within the royal palace, presenting the works of Lully, Rameau, etc. Fires and changes of government then sent it hurrying from one theatre to another before it settled into a new permanent home in the rue Le Peletier (1821), where Parisian GRAND OPERA was nurtured and the epoch-making 1861 revival of *Tannhäuser* took place. That house was succeeded by the Palais Garnier (1875), named after its architect (see ACOUSTICS); this was the Opera haunted by Gaston Leroux's Phantom. In 1990 the Opéra Bastille was opened (seating 2,703 in the main auditorium), and opera performances have subsequently been shared between this new theatre and the Palais Garnier (now seating 1,979).

Lully's original arrangement gave him a monopoly of opera in Paris, but since then the Paris Opera has normally had rivals. Italian companies opened several times, and had their own house, the Théâtre Italien, in Rossini's time. The Opéra-Comique has a continuous history since 1801; it specialized at first in opera with spoken dialogue, the genre known as OPERA COMIQUE, but increasingly took on all-sung works on a less lavish scale (e.g. *Pelléas*) and today presents a broad repertory from Baroque opera to musicals. Opera is also presented regularly at the Théâtre du Châtelet.

Paris Orchestra. See ORCHESTRE DE PARIS.

Paris symphonies. Name given to Mozart's No.31 and Haydn's Nos.82–7, all of which were written for the city. Mozart's work was for the Concert Spirituel (f.p. 18 Jun 1778); Haydn's commission came from Count d'Orgny for the Concert de la Loge Olympique.

Parker, Horatio (William) (b. Auburndale, Mass., 15 Sep 1863; d. Cedarhurst, Long Island, 18 Dec 1919). US composer and teacher. A pupil of Rheinberger in Munich (1882–5), he was then a church musician in New York (1885–93), organist of Trinity Church, Boston (1893–1904), and first head of the school of music at Yale (1894–1919), where Ives was among his students. His most successful work was his oratorio *Hora novissima* (1893), whose performance at the 1899 Three Choirs Festival led to English commissions. He also wrote an opera, *Mona*, set in ancient Britain, which won a prize and so was given at the Met in 1912.

parlando (It., speaking). Kind of delivery imitating the rhythm and phrasing of speech. It may be required of an instrument as much as a voice.

parlour song. Kind of song intended for amateur performance at home, in a parlour (sitting room). The genre flourished in the late 19th century and early 20th, especially in Britain and the USA, its proponents including Balfe, Sullivan, Foster and Tosti.

parody. (1) Mimicry with exaggeration to the point of mockery, as in the normal use of the word. Musical parodies go back at least to the Renaissance, but became routine in the 18th century. Mozart parodied compositional incompetence in *A Musical Joke* and created a more subtle interplay of parody and sincerity in *Così fan tutte*. These remained major butts of musical parody: feeble music (at moments of parodic explosion in Beethoven's Diabelli Variations or all through Beckmesser's song in Wagner's *Die Meistersinger*) and operatic ostentation (as in many parodies of Wagner or Strauss's parodies of Italian singing in *Der Rosenkavalier* and *Capriccio*). More insidious are occasions where parody invades the whole musical substance, as in Schoenberg's *Pierrot lunaire*, or the many works by Davies that lean into self-parody.

(2) Practice in Renaissance composition, whereby the music of one piece (commonly a motet or madrigal) is reworked to make another (a mass); hence the term 'parody mass', with its unwarranted suggestions. The technique certainly does not imply ridicule but, quite the reverse, pride of workmanship and, where another composer's music is used, homage. Palestrina's *Benedicta es* mass is a parody on Josquin's motet setting that text.

Parratt, Walter (b. Huddersfield, 10 Feb 1841; d. Windsor, 27 Mar 1924). British organist, teacher and composer, knighted in 1892. He studied with his organist father and rose through other posts to become organist of Magdalen College, Oxford (1872–82). As such he featured in Holman Hunt's picture of May Day carolling atop the college tower; he also wrote music for an Oxford presentation of the Aeschylus *Agamemnon* in 1880. In 1882 he moved to St George's Chapel, Windsor, and in 1893 was appointed Master of the Queen's Music. He taught, too, at the RCM (1883–1923, his pupils including Vaughan Williams and Stokowski), at Oxford (as professor of music, 1908–18) and at London University (as dean of music, 1905–24). It is said that he could play a Beethoven sonata blindfold and conduct two games of chess at the same time. He wrote church music.

Parrott, Andrew (Haden) (b. Walsall, 10 Mar 1947). British conductor, proponent of historically informed performance from his time as an Oxford undergraduate in the late 1960s. In 1973 he formed the Taverner Choir (followed by the Taverner Consort and Taverner Players) to perform Baroque and Renaissance music, but he was always involved also with contemporary music (Tippett, Weir). He became principal conductor of the London Mozart Players in 2000 and of the New York Collegium in 2002.

Parry, (Charles) Hubert (Hastings) (b. Bournemouth, 27 Feb 1848; d. Rustington, Sussex, 7 Oct 1918). British composer and teacher, knighted in 1898, created baronet in 1903, and best remembered for his stirring setting of Blake's *Jerusalem*. He studied at Eton and Oxford, and in accord with family wishes became an underwriter at Lloyd's. In 1872 he married Maude Herbert, an earl's daughter, and the next year he started lessons with the pianist and writer Edward Dannreuther in London, who encouraged him to espouse the classical forms as mediated by the German Romantics – principally Brahms, though Wagner was also on the agenda. To that tradition Parry added an Englishness, imbibed from church music, to create a style foreshadowing Elgar. Much of his sizeable output of chamber and piano music dates from the few years following his encounter with

Dannreuther, for whom he also wrote his Piano Concerto. Later he concentrated on symphonic and vocal music. He also taught at the RCM from 1883 (as director from 1895), where Vaughan Williams and Holst were among his pupils, and was professor of music at Oxford (1900–8). Photographs of him as an Edwardian worthy belie the youthful Romanticism he retained, and the warmth and generosity of spirit he showed his students.

Jeremy Dibble *C. Hubert H. Parry* (1992)

Orchestral: Symphony No.1, G, 1880–82, No.2 'Cambridge', F, 1882–3, No.3 'English', C, 1887–9, No.4, E minor, 1889, No.5 (Symphonic Fantasia '1912'), B minor, 1912; *Elegy for Brahms*, 1897; Symphonic Variations, E minor, 1897; *From Death to Life*, 1914; etc.

Choral: Evening Service, D, 1881; *Blest pair of sirens* (Milton), ch, orch, 1887; *I was glad* (coronation anthem), ch, orch, 1902; *The Soul's Ransom*, s, b, ch, orch, 1906; *Jerusalem*, ch, orch, 1916; *Songs of Farewell*, ch, 1916–18 (No.1 'My soul, there is a country'); oratorios (*Judith*, 1888; *Job*, 1892; *King Saul*, 1894), anthems, hymns ('Dear Lord and Father'), partsongs

Other works: Toccata and Fugue 'The Wanderer', org, 1912–18; chamber music, piano pieces, songs

Parry, John (b. Bryn Cynan, *c.*1710; d. Ruabon, 7 Oct 1782). Blind Welsh harpist, admired in his younger years by Handel and the Prince of Wales (later George III). With Evan Williams he published the earliest collection of Welsh melodies (1742).

Parry, Joseph (b. Merthyr Tydfil, 21 May 1841; d. Penarth, 17 Feb 1903). Welsh composer. When he was 13 his family moved to the USA, where his musical skills won him financial support to study at the RAM. He then spent his adult life in Wales, teaching at the university colleges in Aberystwyth (1873–9) and Cardiff (1888–1903). Though he wrote operas (including the first in Wales: *Blodwen*, 1878) and oratorios, he is best remembered for his hymn tunes, especially *Aberystwyth* (1879, sung to the words 'Jesu, Lover of my Soul').

Parsifal. Opera by Wagner to his own libretto after the romances by the German medieval poet Wolfram von Eschenbach. In an action prepared by the narration of Gurnemanz (bass), Parsifal (tenor) succeeds, despite the efforts of the magician Klingsor (bass) and his creature Kundry (mezzo-soprano), in replacing the sacred spear in the chapel of the grail knights, so setting right the error of the grail king, Amfortas (baritone), whom he replaces. Wagner wrote the work for his Bayreuth theatre and called it a *Bühnenweihfestspiel*

(Stage Dedication Festival Play). His widow Cosima placed an embargo on performances elsewhere that was almost universally respected for three decades. The prelude and Good Friday Music (delicate but sombrely weighted, representing the blossoming, suffering earth) are often heard as orchestral concert items. First performance: Bayreuth, 26 Jul 1882.

Parsley, Osbert (b. 1511; d. Norwich, 1585). English composer of church music (for Norwich Cathedral, where he sang) and ingenious contrapuntal pieces for viols.

Parsons, Robert (b. Exeter, *c.*1530; d. Newark, 25 Jan 1572). English composer of church music (to Latin and Anglican texts), consort music and songs. He was master of a full, sonorous style prefiguring Byrd's, and in 1563 was appointed a Gentleman of the Chapel Royal. His death came as he was crossing the swollen River Trent.

part. (1) Line in a polyphonic composition: hence 'fugue in four parts', etc.

(2) Contribution made by one performer to a group, and therefore the printed music from which that performer plays or sings. Orchestral musicians play their parts from parts. Chamber works are often published in the form of score and parts.

(3) Section of a large work. For example, Mahler's Third Symphony is in two parts, the second consisting of all but the first movement.

Pärt, Arvo (b. Paide, 11 Sep 1935). Estonian composer, famed since the late 1970s for his music of contemplation and cool consonance. He studied with the composer Heino Eller at the Tallinn Conservatory (1957–63) while working as a radio producer, writing film scores and starting to make a name as a composer. At that time he was one of the first in the Soviet Union to explore serialism, which he did in an unusually abstract, rule-based manner (*Perpetuum mobile* for orchestra, 1963). He went on to introduce quotations and other references to older music, especially Bach's, but the provocative *Credo* for chorus, piano and orchestra (1968) was his last such work before he withdrew from composition to reconsider and study early polyphony, from the organum of the 12th-century Notre Dame school through Machaut to the Flemish composers of the 15th century. His Third Symphony (1971) was an interim report; then came his decisive discovery of a new style in a little piano piece, *Für Alina* (1976). In this style, which he called 'tintinnabulation', the notes of a triad (often A minor) are maintained in slow arpeggios or drones while other voices unfold melodies on the notes of the scale. *Fratres* (1977), arranged for several different instrumental combinations, is the classic example and was included on a record ('Tabula Rasa', 1977) that brought him international attention. In 1980 he left the Soviet Union and soon after settled in Berlin. Most of his later works have sacred texts, whether in Latin (St John Passion), Church Slavonic (*Kanon Pokajanen*) or modern languages.

Paul Hillier *Arvo Pärt* (1997)

Choral: *An den Wassern zu Babel sassen wir und weinten*, ch, ens/org, 1976; *Summa*, ch, 1977; *Missa syllabica*, ch, org ad lib, 1977; ST JOHN PASSION, soli, ch, ens, 1982; *Te Deum*, ch, str, prepared pf, tape, 1984–5; *7 Magnificat Antiphons*, ch, 1988; *Miserere*, soli, ch, ens, 1989; *Berliner Messe*, ch, str/org, 1990; *Litany*, soli, ch, orch, 1994; *Kanon Pokajanen*, ch, 1997; *Triodion*, ch, 1998; *Cecilia, vergine romana*, ch, orch, 2000; *In principio*, ch, orch, 2003; etc.

Solo vocal: *Stabat mater*, s,a,t, str trio, 1985; *Como cierva sedienta*, s, orch, 1998; 'My heart's in the highlands' (Robert Burns), ct, org, 2000; etc.

Orchestral: *Wenn Bach Bienen gezüchtet hätte*, str, 1976; *Cantus in Memory of Benjamin Britten*, str, bell, 1977; *Tabula rasa*, str, 1977; *Festina lente*, str, 1988; *Trisagion*, str, 1992; *Orient & Occident*, str, 1999–2000; *Lamentate*, pf, orch, 2002–3; etc.

Ensemble/Instrumental: *Für Alina*, pf, 1976; *Arbos*, brass/recs, perc, 1977; *Fratres*, various, 1977; *Spiegel im Spiegel*, vn/va/vc, pf, 1978; *Annum per annum*, org, 1980; etc.

partbook. Volume in which the parts of a polyphonic composition for voices were laid out in different regions of a double-page spread, so that the performers could all sing from one open book. Partbooks were in regular use from the early 13th to the mid 16th century.

Partch, Harry (b. Oakland, 24 Jun 1901; d. San Diego, 3 Sep 1974). US composer. Largely self-taught, he developed his own theory of music during the 1920s. Authority came from the Greeks, seconded by the rather few composers he approved (Musorgsky for one) as endorsing his view of music as a 'corporeal' rather than an intellectual art, which should act on spectators at theatrical presentations and use the natural intervals of just intonation. (Seeing a Beijing opera performance in San Francisco when he was 13 was a crucial experience.) He began by adapting standard instruments (a viola in 1928–30, later a guitar), writing at this stage only for his own voice and accompaniment. In 1934 he visited the British Museum on a grant; on his return to the USA he led a hobo existence while starting to build

percussion and wind instruments tuned to simple frequency ratios in a 43-note scale. Often given evocative names (Cloud Chamber Bowls, Marimba Eroica, Spoils of War), these instruments are as spectacular to look at as to hear, and their layout on the platform made a contribution to the music, creating stage sets for the theatre pieces that were his principal works. A Guggenheim fellowship for 1943–4 allowed him to complete and present a group of works, and so gain some recognition. But performances inevitably remained infrequent, most of them being sponsored by universities, and he disseminated his music more widely by means of private recordings, all of which have been reissued. After his death the instruments were maintained by the group Newband.

Harry Partch *Genesis of a Music* (1949, ʼ1974); Bob Gilmore *Harry Partch* (1998)

www.corporeal.com

Theatre works: *King Oedipus* (Partch, after W.B. Yeats, after Sophocles), 1933–51, f.p. Oakland, 1952; *The Bewitched*, 1955–6, f.p. Urbana, 1957; *Revolution in the Courthouse Square* (Partch, after Euripides *The Bacchae*), 1959–60, f.p. Urbana, 1961; *Water! Water!* (Partch), 1961, f.p. Urbana, 1962; *Delusion of the Fury* (Partch), 1965–6, f.p. Los Angeles, 1969

Other works: *17 Lyrics of Li-Po*, 1930–33; *Barstow* (hitchhiker inscriptions), 1941; *Dark Brother* (Thomas Wolfe), 1942–3; *The Letter* (Partch), 1943; *San Francisco* (Partch), 1943; *U.S. Highball* (Partch), 1943; *2 Settings from 'Finnegans Wake'*, 1944; *Intrusions*, 1946–50; *Plectra and Percussion Dances*, 1952, rev 1968; *2 Settings from Lewis Carroll*, 1952–4; *Ulysses at the Edge of the World* (Partch), 1955; *Windsong*, 1958, rev as *Daphne of the Dunes*, 1967; *And on the Seventh Day Petals Fell on Petaluma*, 1963–6

Partenope. Opera by Handel to a libretto possibly by Haym. Arsace (alto castrato) has deserted Rosmira (contralto) for Partenope (soprano), but is daunted when circumstances oblige him to fight a duel with his former partner, who has arrived in male attire. He extricates himself, his love restored, and Partenope has Armindo (contralto) to fall back on. First performance: London, 24 Feb 1730.

Parthenia (Gk, maidenhood). Title of the first book of keyboard music printed in Britain (1613), with pieces by Byrd, Bull and Orlando Gibbons. A second volume, of music for keyboard and bass viol, appeared as *Parthenia inviolata* (i.e. inviolate and, punningly, for viol).

partial. Frequency constituent of a sound. Any pitched sound has a fundamental (the first partial), corresponding to the sounding pitch, and a number of higher partials, which contribute to the timbre or colour. In the case of a relatively pure sound, such as that of the flute, the upper partials will be the harmonics of the first partial: i.e., the second partial will be an octave higher (frequency ratio 2:1), the third a fifth above that (frequency ratio 3:1), etc. Other sounds, such as those of bells, have INHARMONIC partials.

Particell (Ger.), **particella** (It.). Short score.

Partie (Fr., Ger., Ger. pl. *Partien*). Part.

partita (It., game, pl. *partite*, though in Eng. normally 'partitas'). Term introduced in Germany in the late 17th century in various forms (*Partie, Parthie, Parthia, Partia*) to denote a SUITE. The most notable examples are Bach's six keyboard partitas and three for unaccompanied violin. Carter's *Partita* uses the term for its original Italian meaning.

partitino. Score for extra or offstage performers.

partition. (1) (Fr.) Score.
　(2) Term coined by Babbitt to denote a division of the 12-note set, hence his *Partitions* and *Post-Partitions* for piano.

Partitur (Ger.) Score.

partitura (It.). Score.

Partos, Oedoen (b. Budapest, 1 Oct 1907; d. Tel-Aviv, 6 Jul 1977). Hungarian–Israeli composer. He studied at the academy in Budapest with Hubay and Kodály, and moved to Tel-Aviv in 1938. There he played the viola, taught and composed, adapting his Budapest training to new circumstances by exploring the possibilities of eastern Jewish folk music. Later he added serialism to his repertory. His works include three viola concertos and chamber music.

partsong. Short choral setting with the tune in the top part, harmonized by the other voices. The genre developed with the growth of amateur singing societies in the 19th century, principally in Germany and Austria and in England. There are examples for women's, men's and mixed choirs, usually without accompaniment, by Schumann, Brahms, Elgar and many others.

part writing. The art of interweaving parts in a composition, whether or not those parts stand out as contrapuntal lines; the texture may equally be essentially homophonic. The US term is 'voice leading'.

pas (Fr., step). Ballet term, as in *pas de deux* (sequence for two dancers, commonly a love duet and often having several subsections allowing the couple to dance singly and together), *pas seul* (solo), *pas d'action* (action sequence), etc. Sections so called may thus be found in ballet scores.

pasodoble (Sp., double step). Lively Hispanic dance generally in 6/8, instanced in Stravinsky's *Soldier's Tale*.

Pasqualini, Marc'Antonio (baptized Rome, 25 Apr 1614; d. Rome, 3 Jul 1691). Italian castrato, known as Malagigi. He sang for Monteverdi in 1628 and the next year became a protégé of Cardinal Antonio Barberini, for whom he performed in opera while also a member of the Sistine Chapel choir. In 1647 he sang in Rossi's *Orfeo* in Paris. A large painting by Andrea Sacchi showing him crowned by a nude, non-castrate Apollo hangs in the Metropolitan Museum, New York.

Pasquini, Bernardo (b. Massa Valdinievole, now Massa e Cozzile, Pistoia, 7 Dec 1637; d. Rome, 21 Nov 1710). Italian composer and keyboard player. He arrived in Rome in 1650 and remained as a church organist (Santa Maria in Aracoeli, 1664–1710) and harpsichordist for princes, cardinals and an exiled queen (Christina of Sweden), performing alongside Corelli. He was the author of operas and oratorios but most abundantly of keyboard music, including suites, sonatas, toccatas and variation sets.

passacaglia (Fr. *passacaille*). Old dance in slow triple time, and more particularly the musical form that emerged, in which a repeating eight-bar bass supports variations. Repetition and slow speed convey an aura of solemnity, often augmented by the minor mode. 20th-century revivals include Webern's Op.1, Wolpe's and movements in *Pierrot lunaire*, *Wozzeck* and Stravinsky's Septet. See also CHACONNE.

passage. Informal term for any small section in a composition: 'the passage in D minor', 'the awkward passage'.

passage work. Development of a figure in rapid flow, especially in virtuoso piano writing. Thus a passage in a concerto might be distinguished by passage work for the soloist.

passamezzo (**pass'e mezzo**) (It., step and a half). Renaissance dance in moderate tempo, source of two common eight-bar bass themes: the *passamezzo antico* (to which 'Greensleeves' goes) and the *passamezzo nuovo*. There are keyboard passa-mezzos by Byrd and other composers of his time; the passamezzo also occurs as a movement in a suite.

passepied (Fr., pass foot). Dance in quick triple or sextuple time characteristic of French Baroque music, including that by non-French composers (e.g. Bach's French Overture). Debussy's slow, duple-time example in *Pour le piano* is not in any strict sense a passepied at all, but uses the name for historical resonance.

passing note. Note that connects two chords without belonging to either.

Passion. Work narrating the Passion of Christ – i.e. the events leading up to and including the Crucifixion – as told in one of the four gospels. Such works stem from an ancient tradition, traceable to Jerusalem in the 4th century, of reciting the gospel Passions at masses in Holy Week. By the 13th century the recitation was being dramatized by dividing the text into roles, and the rule began to be established of having the evan-gelist narrator a tenor and Christ a bass. In some places the dramatization went further and the Passion was acted out as a play. An alternative development was to have parts of the Passion sung in polyphony; there are settings by Obrecht and Davy from around 1500.

The Passion survived the Reformation, and in Germany gained in importance, the text now being delivered in Luther's translation. With the arrival of the Baroque style, Passions could be accompanied by strings and keyboard, or else sung unaccompanied, as in the examples by Schütz. Sometimes the gospel wording was replaced by a metrical paraphrase (such as the popular Brockes text), and there might also be accretions to the text, in the way of contemplative arias and chorales. Thus appeared the 'oratorio Passion', of which the earliest example is Thomas Selle's St John (1643), followed by the works of Handel, Telemann and outstandingly Bach. The practice of singing a full-scale Passion in church on Good Friday fell into disuse soon after Bach, and was revived only with the revival of Bach's music in the 19th century.

The 18th-century Catholic tradition is repre-sented by Metastasio's oratorio version, set by Caldara, Paisiello, etc. Passions also began to be written much later as concert works. Penderecki's St Luke Passion is a modernization of the Bach model, which is also variously recalled in four works commissioned for Stuttgart in the Bach year of 2000, from Golijov, Gubaidulina, Rihm and Tan, though the most poignant homage to Bach is provided by Kagel's SANKT-BACH-PASSION. Pärt's St John Passion connects more with the pre-Reformation tradition.

Basil Smallman *The Background of Passion Music* (1957, ²1970)

passione (It.). Passion, as in *con passione* (with passion).

Passione, La. Name given to Haydn's Symphony No.49 in F minor, for the affect of its adagio first movement.

Pasta, Giuditta (Angiola Maria Costanza) [née Negri] (b. Saronno, near Milan, 26 Oct 1797; d. Como, 1 Apr 1865). Italian soprano, one of the great dramatic singers of her time. She studied in Milan with Giuseppe Scappa and in 1815 made her debut there in his *Le tre Eleonore*. After her marriage to the tenor Giuseppe Pasta she appeared in Paris (1816) and London (1817) before retiring for a short while to give birth to her daughter Clelia. She then sang throughout Italy, and again in Paris and London, one of her best roles being Desdemona in Rossini's *Otello*. For the same composer she was Corinna in the first *Viaggio a Reims*. She also created the principal soprano roles in Bellini's *La sonnambula*, *Norma* and *Beatrice di Tenda*, and Donizetti's *Anna Bolena* and *Ugo conte di Parigi*, all in 1830–33. After that she sang less frequently, and gave her final stage appearances in Poland and Russia in 1840–41.

pasticcio (It., pie, mess). Dramatic entertainment whose elements are taken from different works. In the 18th century opera singers would often replace their arias with ones taken from other pieces or newly composed for them. The *pasticcio* took this a step further, in that all the music came from elsewhere, being adapted to a new (or old) libretto. The custom fell out of favour early in the 19th century but was revived in *The Jewel Box* (Opera North, 1991, music by Mozart). The term has also sometimes been extended to works freshly composed by several hands, such as *Muzio Scevola* (f.p. London, 1721, music by Amadei, Bononcini, Handel), and including concert pieces and instrumental collections.

pastiche. Imitation. The task of making some-thing in the style of another composer (e.g. a Bach chorale harmonization) is a regular exercise for music students. Pastiche as a fully creative act may be motivated by irritation with the original (in which case it tends towards parody) or affection for it. Such affection, admixed with some irritation, was abundantly displayed by Stravinsky in many works, such as his Concerto for piano and winds (pastiche Bach) or opera *The Rake's Progress* (pastiche Mozart, etc.). Other composers of the period also engaged in pastiche, Poulenc a great deal. Stravinsky and Poulenc, of course, knew what they were doing and were able to maintain their own musical personalities while copying others'. Where the imitation is less artful, the effect will be less fortunate.

Pastoral. Name Beethoven gave his Sixth Symphony, with corresponding movement titles: 1 *Erwachen heiterer Gefühle bei der Ankunft auf dem Lande* (Awakening of cheerful feelings on arriving in the country), 2 *Szene am Bach* (Brookside scene), 3 *Lustiges Zusammensein der Landleute* (Merry gathering of country people), 4 *Gewitter, Sturm* (Thunderstorm), 5 *Hirtengesang – Frohe und dankbare Gefühle nach dem Sturm* (Shepherd song – Happy and thankful feelings after the storm). There are also pastoral symphonies by Glazunov, Grechaninov, Vaughan Williams and Rawsthorne.

pastoral, pastorale. Terms used of music referring to the countryside – or more specifically, and etymologically, to the life of the shepherd (Lat. *pastor*). Pastoral music has certain conventions – imitation of a shepherd's pipe, the key of F major (that of Beethoven's 'Pastoral' Symphony), lilting 6/8 time – but these are not invariable. Beethoven's symphony and Vaughan Williams's (No.3) were both called 'pastoral' by their composers; Beethoven's 'Pastoral' Sonata for piano, Op.28, gained that name from a publisher.

The pastoral as a dramatic genre is older and relates to an understanding of pastoral life gleaned from the Greek and Roman poets rather than, as with Beethoven and Vaughan Williams, walking the fields. Examples of this idyllic, idealized pastoral include innumerable cantatas, serenatas and operas of the Baroque period, e.g. Monteverdi's *Orfeo* or Handel's *Acis and Galatea*. The shepherds of Christmas could also be evoked by pastoral symphonies (Bach's Christmas Oratorio, Handel's *Messiah*) and *pastorale* movements (Christmas concertos by Corelli and Tartini).

pastorella. Form of Christmas music based on the shepherds' visit to the manger, popular in Austria, Bohemia and Moravia from the second half of the 17th century into the 20th century.

pastor fido, Il (The Faithful Shepherd). Opera by Handel to a libretto by Giacomo Rossi after Battista Guarini's play of 1585. The constant pastoralist in Arcadia is Mirtillo (soprano castrato), who is of course eventually united with his beloved Amarilli (soprano), despite the scheming of Eurilla (soprano) and the diversions of a secondary love interest involving Dorinda (contralto) and Silvio (alto castrato). Handel revised the score twice in 1734. First performance: London, 22 Nov 1712.

Beecham gave the title *The Faithful Shepherd* to a suite of movements from various works by Handel.

pathétique (Fr.). Passionate. The first edition of Beethoven's C minor piano sonata Op.13 has the title *Grande sonate pathétique*, possibly his own. Tchaikovsky took up the term for his Sixth Symphony.

Patineurs, Les (The Skaters). Two works are so called:

(1) A waltz by Waldteufel.

(2) A ballet score adapted by Lambert from the skaters' ballet in Meyerbeer's *Le Prophète* with the addition of music from the same composer's *L'Etoile du nord*.

patron. Professional music in Western culture has nearly always depended on patronage, whether from kings, princes and cardinals, rich individuals, state organizations, foundations, businesses or broadcasting authorities. Individual patrons with a particular devotion to music have included a succession of Baroque Roman cardinals, FREDERICK II, the ESTERHÁZY family, a circle who supported the Viennese Classical composers (including LOBKOWITZ, RAZUMOVSKY and VAN SWIETEN) the Princesse de POLIGNAC, Elizabeth Sprague COOLIDGE and Betty FREEMAN.

patter song. Song with a lot of words to be rapidly enunciated, e.g. Mozart's insert aria 'Clarice cara', Figaro's 'Largo al factotum' from *Il barbiere di Siviglia*, or many numbers in Gilbert and Sullivan operettas.

Patti, Adelina (Juana Maria) (b. Madrid, 19 Feb 1843; d. Craig-y-Nos Castle, near Brecon, Wales, 27 Sep 1919). Italian soprano. The daughter of singers, she started her career as a child in the US and made her opera debuts in New York, Paris and London while still in her teens. Hugely successful, she toured the world, but sang most regularly at Covent Garden. She retired to her Welsh castle in 1906, having made some recordings.

Patzak, Julius (b. Vienna, 9 Jul 1898; d. Rottach-Egern, Bavaria, 26 Jan 1974). Austrian tenor, self-taught, based in Munich (1928–45) and later Vienna. He was noted for his performances of Mozart roles, the Evangelist in Bach's Passions and Florestan in *Fidelio*.

Pauken (Ger.). Timpani.

Paukenmesse. First in the conventional order of Haydn's late masses, though composed second, it has PAUKEN prominent and is also known as the *Missa in tempore belli*. First performance: Vienna, 26 Dec 1796.

Paul Bunyan. Opera by Britten to a libretto by Auden, the composer's first stage work, made in and for the USA. Bunyan, a giant logger of US folklore, leads a team of pioneers in preparing the ground – moral and political – for the new country. Britten kept the score under wraps until revising it near the end of his life. First performance: New York, 5 May 1941.

Paulus. See ST PAUL.

Paulus, Stephen (Harrison) (b. Summit, NJ, 24 Aug 1949). US composer. He studied at the University of Minnesota (PhD 1978), with Argento, and became the master of a gentle Romantic lyricism that won him many commissions for operas (*The Postman Always Rings Twice*, 1982; *The Woodlanders*, 1985; *The Woman at Otowi Crossing*, 1995; *Héloise and Abelard*, 2002), orchestral works and choral music.

Paumann, Conrad (b. Nuremberg, *c*.1410; d. Munich, 24 Jan 1473). Prototypical German organist-composer, the forerunner also of a long line of organists who have been blind. In the 1440s he came into important positions in his home city, but his reputation was already nationwide, and in 1450 he absconded to Munich to take a post as court organist. There he remained, while travelling widely. He was succeeded in Munich by his son Paul. Little of his music survives.

pausa (It., pl. *pause*). Rest.

pause. Extension of a note, chord or rest beyond its notated value – perhaps for half as much again, depending on the context. It is indicated by

$$\frown$$

which is sometimes found placed over a barline to indicate a short silence. Barraqué's scores adapt the pause sign in discrete ways to signify holds of up to 15 seconds.

Pause (Ger., pl. *Pausen*). Pause, rest or interval (in a concert).

Pauset, Brice (b. Besançon, 17 Jun 1965). French composer, of music subtly infusing his experiences of early music, as a keyboard player, into a modern world. He studied with Philippot and Grisey at the Paris Conservatoire (1988–92) and also followed courses under Ferneyhough and Donatoni. His works include *Huit Canons* for oboe d'amore and ensemble (1998).

pavan (Fr. *pavane*, It. *pavana*). Late Renaissance dance in slow duple time with a long–short–short pulse, perhaps taking its name from Paduan (It. *padovana*) associations. It is particularly associated with English music of the late 16th and early 17th centuries, there being noble examples by Byrd, Dering, Gibbons, Philips and Dowland. Byrd and Gibbons paired the pavan with the much more upbeat and extrovert galliard. Purcell's Pavan in G minor looked back to the tradition from a time when the dance had long gone out of fashion. Further retrospective pavans came much later from Fauré and Ravel.

Pavane pour une infante défunte (Pavan for a Deceased Infanta). Piano piece by Ravel, which he later orchestrated. He chose the title for its euphony. First performance: Paris, 5 Apr 1902 (pf), 25 Dec 1910 (orch).

Pavarotti, Luciano (b. Modena, 12 Oct 1935). Italian tenor, one of the most successful (with Domingo) of the later 20th century. He made his debut as Rodolfo in *La Bohème* at Reggio Emilia in 1961 and was soon in demand all over the world, making his debuts in the same role at Covent Garden (1963), La Scala (1964) and the Met (1968). Possessed of a glorious voice, radiant yet beguiling, he enjoyed the role of superstar (at outdoor amplified recitals given before enormous crowds, by himself and as one of the THREE TENORS) while maintaining his artistry for most of his long career.

Jürgen Kesting *Luciano Pavarotti* (1996)

Pavesi, Stefano (b. Casaletto Vaprio, near Crema, 22 Jan 1779; d. Crema, 28 Jul 1850). Italian composer. Expelled from the San Onofrio conservatory in Naples in 1799 on account of his republicanism, he went to Dijon and returned to Italy as a soldier in Napoleon's army. He finished his studies with Gazzaniga, then embarked on an immediately successful and prolific career as an opera composer. *Ser Marcantonio* (1810) played all over Italy, and he was renowned abroad, too, succeeding Salieri as director of the court opera in Vienna (1826–30). He also wrote symphonies.

pavillon (Fr., pavilion, or in this case the bell-shaped end of a brass instrument or clarinet). The marking *pavillons en l'air* indicates that players are to raise their instruments in order to enhance volume and penetration.

Payne, Anthony (Edward) (b. London, 2 Aug 1936). British composer, who is married to the soprano Jane Manning. He studied at Durham University and began work as a critic while developing a way to honour his commitments at once to Schoenbergian modernism and the British late Romantic tradition. His works include *Time's Arrow* for orchestra (1990) and a markedly successful completion of Elgar's Third Symphony.

Peabody Institute. Music school in Baltimore, Maryland, founded in 1857 by George Peabody, though it did not start operating until 1866, on account of the Civil War. The institute comprises a preparatory division (embraced in 1898) and a conservatory, of which the latter is part of Johns Hopkins University.

Pearlfishers, The. See *Les* PECHEURS DE PERLES.

Pears, Peter (Neville Luard) (b. Farnham, 22 Jun 1910; d. Aldeburgh, 3 Apr 1986). British tenor, companion of Britten, knighted in 1978. He studied at the RCM and had begun making a reputation as a soloist before meeting Britten in 1937. The two were a couple from that time on, and Britten wrote roles for Pears in all his operas, as well as in many other works, exploiting an unusual high tessitura and complex expressive tone, at once anxious and seductive. Britten and Pears also gave recitals together all over the world.

Pearsall, Robert Lucas (b. Clifton, 14 Mar 1795; d. Wartensee, Switzerland, 15 Aug 1856). British composer. Born into a family of means, he left England in 1825 for Germany and spent his last decade and more at Schloss Wartensee, above Lake Constance. He is remembered especially for his madrigals of 1836–42, rare instances of the Romantic Gothic revival in music.

Peasant Cantata (*Bauerncantate*). Name given to J.S. Bach's *Mer Hahn en neue Oberkeet*, to words by Picander, a comic peasantly paean to Carl Heinrich von Dieskau as new squire of Klein-Zschocher, near Leipzig. First performance: Klein-Zschocher, 30 Aug 1742.

péchés de vieillesse (sins of old age). Rossini's term for unpretentious pieces he wrote long after retiring from opera, from his mid-60s to mid-70s.

Pêcheurs de perles, Les (The Pearlfishers). Opera by Bizet to a libretto by Eugène Cormon and Michel Carré. Among the pearlfishers, in Ceylon, are Zurga (baritone) and Nadir (tenor), whose duet of friendship, 'Au fond du temple saint', is the opera's most famous item. Nadir commits a sacrilege in engaging the priestess Leïla (soprano) in a love duet; both are condemned to death, but Zurga eventually saves them. First performance: Paris, 30 Sep 1863.

Ped. Abbreviation for 'pedal' or 'pedals' in keyboard music. In piano music, the sustaining pedal is signified. The type is normally curly, thus: 𝄢.

pedal (from Lat. *pedalis*, of the foot). (1) Foot-operated lever found on various instruments. Pedals on the piano and harpsichord affect tone and sustaining power, while those on the harp and timpani change tuning and the organ's play notes in the manner of a keyboard. Drums and cymbals can also be pedal-operated.

(2) Sustained note – often, in tonal music, the dominant or tonic of the key in operation. The term may also be pedal note, pedal tone, pedal point or pedal bass. If the pedal is not in the bass but above, it is an inverted pedal.

(3) Fundamental of a brass instrument. Valves or a slide may provide various pedals, or pedal notes.

pedal bass. PEDAL (2).

pedalboard. Foot-operated keyboard, a regular part of an organ.

pedaliter. Marking on music to be played on manuals and pedalboard, countermanded by MANUALITER.

pedal note. PEDAL (2).

pedal piano. Piano with pedalboard; an organist's practice instrument, though there is also music written specifically for it by Schumann.

pedal point, pedal tone. PEDAL (2).

Pedrell, Felipe (b. Tortosa, 9 Feb 1841; d. Barcelona, 9 Aug 1922). Catalan composer, scholar and teacher. The father of the Spanish musical renaissance around 1900 – his pupils including

Albéniz, Granados, Falla and Gerhard – he had little success himself as a composer; his operas were mostly unperformed and his other works mostly early. He also edited the complete works of Victoria.

Peebles, David (d. ?1579). Scottish composer, an Augustinian canon at St Andrews, author of a fine motet, *Si quis diligit me* (*c*.1530), possibly of a *Felix namque* mass in similar style, and of post-Reformation psalm settings.

Peer Gynt. Play by Ibsen, first performed in its revised version with music by Grieg. First performance: Christiania, now Oslo, 24 Feb 1876.

There are two orchestral suites: No.1, Op.46 (1 *Morning*, 2 *Death of Aase*, 3 *Anitra's Dance*, 4 *In the Hall of the Mountain King*) and No.2, Op.55 (1 *Abduction of the Bride* and *Ingrid's Lament*, 2 *Arabian Dance*, 3 *Peer Gynt's Homecoming*, 4 *Solvejg's Song*). Later composers attracted to the subject include Egk, Saeverud and Schnittke.

Peerson, Martin (b. ?March, Cambridgeshire, *c*.1572; buried London, 15 Jan 1651). English composer of sacred and secular songs, consort music and keyboard pieces (*The Fall of the Leafe*), choirmaster of St Paul's under Charles I.

Peeters, Flor (b. Tielen, 4 Jul 1903; d. Antwerp, 4 Jul 1986). Belgian organist-composer, a private pupil of Dupré and friend of Tournemire, who was an influence on his output of organ pieces and music for the Catholic liturgy.

peg. Wooden screw used to adjust the tension of a string on a string instrument. Several of them are set in a pegbox at the far end of the neck.

peine entendu, à (Fr.). Barely heard.

Peirol (b. Peirol, Auvergne, *c*.1160; d. *c*.1222). Troubadour. A poor knight of the Auvergne, he probably died soon after taking part in the Fifth Crusade.

Pelléas et Mélisande. Opera by Debussy, setting the play by Maurice Maeterlinck. The plot is a love triangle involving Pelléas (high baritone), Mélisande (soprano) and her husband – also Pelléas's half-brother – Golaud (baritone), expressed in music of great delicacy and power to insinuate. First performance: Paris, 30 Apr 1902.

Fauré and Sibelius wrote incidental scores for the play, Schoenberg a symphonic poem on it (f.p. Vienna, 25 Jan 1905).

Peñalosa, Francisco de (b. Talavera de la Reina, *c*.1470; d. Seville, 1 Apr 1528). Spanish composer of sacred polyphony, outstanding in his generation, active largely in Seville, though he was also in Rome (1517–21).

Penderecki, Krzysztof (b. Dębica, 23 Nov 1933). Polish composer, known in the 1960s for his dramatic use of avant-garde effects. He studied with Malawski at the Kráków Conservatory (1955–8), where he stayed on as a teacher. In 1959 he won three first prizes in a national competition. Soon afterwards he gained international attention for his *Threnody* for strings (1960), in which he derived raw emotional power from sonorities that had been more abstractly deployed by Xenakis and Stockhausen, notably clusters, microtones and unusual string effects. It was a language he used with great panache in his St Luke Passion and other works up to his First Symphony (1972–3) – a turning point that led him into a world of sombreness and thematic continuity somewhat recalling Bruckner. That work also marked the start of his second career as a conductor.

Wolfram Schwinger *Krzysztof Penderecki* (1989)

Operas: *Die Teufel von Loudun* (Penderecki, after John Whiting), 1968–9, f.p. Hamburg, 1969; *Paradise Lost* (Christopher Fry, after Milton), 1975–8, f.p. Chicago, 1978; *Die schwarze Maske* (Harry Kupfer and Penderecki, after Gerhart Hauptmann), 1984–6, f.p. Salzburg, 1986; *Ubu Rex* (Jerzy Jarocki and Penderecki, after Jarry), 1990–91, f.p. Munich, 1991

Orchestral: Symphony No.1, 1972–3; No.2, 1979–80; No.3, 1988; No.4 (Adagio), 1989; No.5, 1991–2; Piano Concerto, 2002; Violin Concerto No.1, 1976–7; No.2, 1992–5; Viola Concerto, 1983–4; Cello Concerto No.1, 1972; No.2, 1982; *Anaklasis*, str, perc, 1960; *Threnody*, str, 1960; Sonata, vc, orch, 1964; Capriccio, ob, str, 1965; *De natura sonoris I*, 1966, *II*, 1971; Capriccio, vn, orch, 1967; *Partita*, 1971; *Als ich Jakob erwachte*, 1974; etc.

Choral orchestral: *Dimensions of Time and Silence*, 1960; St Luke Passion, 1963–5; *Dies irae*, 1967; *Utrenja*, 1969–71; *Kosmogonia*, 1970; *Canticum canticorum Salomonis*, 1970–73; *Magnificat*, 1973–4; *Te Deum*, 1979–80; *Polish Requiem*, 1980–84; *Seven Gates of Jerusalem*, 1996; *Credo*, 1997–8

Other works: 2 string quartets (1960, 1968), etc.

penny whistle. See WHISTLE.

pentagramma (It.). Five-line staff.

pentatonic. Term describing a scale of five notes to the octave – often a scale without semitones (e.g. C–D–E–G–A–C, or alternatively the black-note scale on the piano) – or music based on such a scale. Pentatonic scales are found all over the world: Dvořák was happy to discover them in the music of North American Indians and Blacks as much as in that of Czech peasants. 'Auld Lang Syne' is a pentatonic tune, and pentatonic music can also easily be evocative of the Far East, as in works by Debussy (*Pagodes*), Stravinsky (*The Nightingale*), Puccini (*Madama Butterfly*), Mahler (*Das Lied von der Erde*) and Messiaen (*Visions de l'Amen*).

Pentland, Barbara (Lally) (b. Winnipeg, 2 Jan 1912; d. Vancouver, 5 Feb 2000). Canadian composer. She made steady progress from a post-Franckian world to – following a trip to Europe in 1955 – a post-Webernian one. Her works include four symphonies, five string quartets, choral music and educational piano pieces.

Pepping, Ernst (b. Duisburg, 12 Sep 1901; d. Berlin, 1 Feb 1981). German composer of Lutheran church music in a Hindemithian style, and teacher at the Spandau Church Music School from 1934.

Pepusch, Johann Christoph (b. Berlin, 1667; d. London, 20 Jul 1752). German composer, who was resident in London from 1704 and variously active as composer, arranger, performer and writer of theory books. He is remembered for *The Beggar's Opera*, with which he probably had little to do beyond possibly writing the overture and conducting the first performance.

Perahia, Murray (b. New York, 19 Apr 1947). US pianist distinguished by his quiet seriousness, coupled to lucidity, grace and colour. Taught by Artur Balsam and Horszowski, he made his debut in New York in 1968 and was launched on an international career by winning the Leeds Competition in 1972. He was always especially valued in Mozart and Chopin, and in the 1990s added to his range an exceptional aptitude in Bach.

perc. Abbreviation for percussion.

percussion (Fr. *batterie*, Ger. *Schlagwerk*, It. *percussione*). Heterogeneous family of instruments that make sounds when struck. But this definition is imprecise: it would include the piano – which, when it appears as an orchestral instrument is placed apart from the percussion and played by a specialist performer (to wit, a pianist) – and exclude certain instruments that are commonly the province of percussionists but not struck, such as the wind machine or various kinds of whistle.

The multifariousness of the percussion department is partly a product of its rapid growth, during the period from the 1890s to the 1960s. Yet percussion instruments must go back to the very earliest human music, perhaps the human body itself being among the first, with its facilities for hand clapping, stamping, thigh slapping, etc. Purpose-made instruments exist in all parts of the world, and the development of the orchestral percussion was partly a process of assimilation. The xylophone, for example, had its origins in sub-Saharan Africa; other imports came more directly from China (gongs) or Latin America (congas, maracas). Instruments much longer established in Europe include bells and clappers found in churches, military drums, and small instruments used to accompany dancing (tabor, nakers). But these were slow to enter notated music. Bach, for instance, used no percussion apart from timpani, though opera composers of his time all over Europe could have expected theatres to use percussive machines to add sound effects (thunder, rain) independently of the score.

Timpani took a regular place in the orchestra in the 17th century, and have remained the province of experts distinct from the rest of the percussion. The tiny seed of the latter department was provided by the occasional glockenspiel, tambourine or pair of cymbals. Other instruments added by the Romantics include triangle, celesta, xylophone and bells, but in most cases these instruments were still used for special effects and for their evocative powers: bells, for instance, would be associated with church scenes in operas or descriptive symphonies. Debussy's handling of antique cymbals at the close of his prelude to *L'Après-midi d'un faune* presages a new parity of the percussion with other sections of the orchestra.

That parity was fully achieved, if not exceeded, in several works of the 20th century's second decade: Berg's Op.6:1, Webern's Op.6:4, Milhaud's *Les Choéphores* (for voices and percussion) and Stravinsky's *Rite of Spring*, dominated by winds and drumming. *The Rite*, with its successor *Les Noces* for voices, pianos and percussion (1923), had a massive influence on, for example, Bartók (Sonata for two pianos and percussion), Antheil and Varèse, the last of whom wrote elaborately for percussion alone, as did Shostakovich in *The Nose* (1927–8). Varèse's *Ionisation* (1929–31) was among the earliest scores exclusively for percussion, along with works by Roldán and, a little later, Cage, who gave percussion-only concerts in 1937–42, often using found materials (tin cans, etc.). Partch, soon after, began building his own percussion instruments. What propelled these developments was partly an increased awareness of non-European music (especially Caribbean and Balinese), partly the modernist urge to innovate and partly a dissatisfaction with the established tradition.

After the Second World War, expanded percussion sections of six players or more became common, found in scores by Barraqué, Carter, Messiaen, Stockhausen, Xenakis and many others – not least Boulez, who made the percussion central in his *Pli selon pli* (1957–65). New instruments came again from extra-European sources and domestic objects (glasses filled with water, crockery to be smashed). A percussion sextet, *Les* PERCUSSIONS DE STRASBOURG, was followed by many similar ensembles, all actively commissioning composers when they were not led by a composer (as in the case of Reich's group). The core repertory, though, has remained limited to a few works by Varèse, Cage and Reich, as may be inevitable, given the abundant variety of percussion instruments and therefore the opportunities for players to pursue their own inclinations and create their own sound worlds. That may also explain why no percussion concerto (Milhaud's was the first, in 1947) has established itself, though there are important solo pieces by Stockhausen, Xenakis, Feldman and Ferneyhough.

Percussion instruments are often divided into two groups, the tuned (or pitched) and the untuned (or unpitched), but this rather brutally cuts through the spectrum that exists from instruments whose notes are pitched as clearly as those of the piano (celesta, marimba) through the muffled or uncertain (timpani, woodblock) to the thoroughly opaque (cymbals, tam tam). An alternative classification is in terms of the sounding material:

Wood: xylophone, marimba, woodblock, drums, clappers, whip, castanets, hammer
Metal: vibraphone, glockenspiel, celesta, jingles, bells, gongs, triangle, cymbals, brake drums, anvil
Skin: timpani, drums

The tambourine, of course, belongs in two of these groups, and there are also instruments that pertain to none: the cimbalom, wind machine, glasses, whistles, toy instruments, etc. Plucked-string instruments (harp, lute, guitar, zither, etc.) may be allied with the percussion but are not normally regarded as members.

James Blades *Percussion Instruments and their History* (1970, ³1984; James Holland *Percussion* (1978); John H. Beck, ed. *Encyclopedia of Percussion* (1995)

Percussions de Strasbourg, Les. French percussion sextet formed in 1962, varying since then in personnel. Promoted by Boulez, the group took part in the first performances of works by Messiaen (*Sept haïkaï*, *Couleurs de la Cité Céleste*,

Et exspecto) and Barraqué (*Chant après chant*). Since 1965 the players have generally appeared by themselves, in works written for them by Xenakis (*Persephassa*, *Pléïades*) and others.

perdendo, perdendosi (It., losing). Dying away.

Perényi, Miklós (b. Budapest, 5 Jan 1948). Hungarian cellist, of intimate seriousness. He studied at the Liszt Academy, with Enrico Mainardi in Rome, and with Casals (1965–72). In 1974 he returned to the Liszt Academy to teach, while building an important solo career that has included collaborations with Kurtág.

Perez, David (b. Naples, 1711; d. Lisbon, 30 Oct 1778). Italian composer of Spanish descent. He studied at the Loreto conservatory in Naples and soon made a name for himself as a composer of both serious and comic operas. In 1752 he moved to Lisbon as music master to the royal princesses, and there he remained, though his music was known, published and admired beyond Portugal.

perfect cadence [authentic cadence, full close]. Cadence from the dominant chord (or dominant seventh) to the tonic, both normally in root position. For complete finality, as at the end of a work or movement, the tonic chord must also have the keynote at the top.

perfect consonance, perfect interval. The fifth, octave and their compounds (e.g. 12th, double octave) are so called, being the oldest consonances recognized in Western music. The fourth (plus compounds) was admitted to the club by medieval theorists as the inversion of the fifth.

perfect pitch. The ability – also known as absolute pitch – to name the pitch of a sound and, conversely, to play or sing a named pitch by ear. It is an ability that seems to be innate, but with varying degrees of acuity. Some people can, without reflection, name the pitches of sounds as coarse as those of a fan or buzzer; some can distinguish quarter-tones or smaller intervals. On the other hand, people not born with perfect pitch may well be able to learn, for example, tuning A and thereby be able to pitch other sounds around that. Perfect pitch is not necessary for a musician, though it may be helpful, especially for singers.

perfect time. Division of a basic rhythmic unit into three equal parts in medieval–Renaissance music, corresponding to triple time.

performance. The act of singing or playing music,

in general (as in 'the art of performance') or on a particular occasion ('that performance of the Ligeti *Requiem*'). There are several synonyms: interpretation, presentation, execution – not to mention some that are more archaic or stuffy, such as reading, rendering, rendition, production.

Until the invention of recording, music could be experienced only in performance. Then it was gone. Even now, though electronically created music has a history going back to 1948, most composers still write for live performance, and most recordings are more or less faithful representations of performances. There has even been a shift, since the 1970s, away from studio manipulation towards live recording, i.e. capturing a complete, unedited performance.

In the Western classical tradition performance is nearly always based on a score, though performers will be drawing too on their experience and understanding of the work and its composer (biographical, critical and analytical information, other performances they have given or heard), on their knowledge of the performance practice of the time, on their tastes and intuitions, etc. Performers are collaborators with the composer, and it is a paradox that often the most highly defined and expressively nuanced music (Beethoven's outstandingly) is also the most open to varieties of approach, endlessly.

performance art. Term originating in the 1970s in the world of visual art, where performance – live action by an artist – was unusual, even (or especially) if it was taking place in a gallery. In music, performance is the almost universal norm, but the term may be useful in thinking about musicians and composers who arrived by this route, such as Laurie Anderson.

performance practice. How music was performed in earlier times and other places. This has been a subject of interest to performers only since the early 20th century. Until the early 19th century performers generally made do with the music of their own time and, in most cases, their own place. During the next century, although music was now remembered longer and sought from further afield, musicians would apply much the same approach to Bach as to Brahms, to Tchaikovsky as to Verdi. For various reasons having to do with historical awareness and cultural humility, performers then began to learn extinct instruments (harpsichord, lute, recorder) and study other ways of doing things, finding their evidence in treatises, in accounts or pictures of performances, in archives documenting musical establishments, and, for the period since around 1910, in recordings, in order to produce HISTORICALLY INFORMED performance.

Stanley Sadie and Howard Mayer Brown *Performance Practice*, 2 Vols. (1990)

performing rights. Money due to composers, writers (of song lyrics or opera librettos) and publishers for the performing or broadcasting of music. Collection and distribution is in the hands of professional associations: the Performing Right Society (PRS) in Britain, in the USA the American Society of Composers, Authors and Publishers (ASCAP) and Broadcast Music, Inc. (BMI), and comparable bodies elsewhere (e.g. APRA, GEMA, SACEM, SOCAN).

Pergament, Moses (b. Helsinki, 21 Sep 1893; d. Gustavsberg, near Stockholm, 5 Mar 1977). Finnish–Swedish composer of unusually varied background. Jewish by family, he studied in Russia as a violinist and in Berlin at the Stern Conservatory. He worked in all genres and favoured Jewish subjects.

Pergolesi, Giovanni Battista (b. Iesi, Marche, 4 Jan 1710; d. Pozzuoli, near Naples, 16 Mar 1736). Italian composer, furiously popular in his (brief) time and just after for his lively tunefulness. His paternal grandfather came from the village of Pergola, in the province of Pesaro; hence the family name. Sickly as a child yet evidently musical, he gained aristocratic support for his studies at the Poveri conservatory in Naples, where he was a pupil of Durante, father of the Neapolitan school. He won a modest success with his comedy *Lo frate 'nnamorato* (1732), in Neapolitan dialect, then capped that with his opera buffa *La serva padrona*, inserted as an intermezzo in his *Il prigioner superbo* (1733), the music brilliant and vivacious. He followed up with a similar double bill and a setting of Metastasio's *L'Olimpiade* for Rome, where his Mass in F had caused excitement the year before. Early in 1736 he moved into the Franciscan monastery in Pozzuoli, where he may have written his *Stabat mater* for two castratos, strings and organ – a work more frequently printed in the 18th century than any other. He died of a chronic illness, perhaps tuberculosis, and publishers were obliged to supply the huge posthumous demand for his music with false attributions. Much of the 'Pergolesi' arranged by Stravinsky in *Pulcinella* is fake.

Operas: *Li prodigi della divina grazia nella conversione di San Guglielmo Duca d'Aquitania*, f.p. Naples, 1731; *Salustia* (after Zeno), f.p. Naples, 1732; *Lo frate 'nnamorato* (Gennaro Antonio Federico), f.p. Naples, 1732; *Il prigioner superbo* (after Francesco Silvani), f.p. Naples, 1733, with intermezzo La SERVA PADRONA; *Adriano in Siria* (Metastasio), f.p. Naples, 1734, with intermezzo *La contadina astuta* (*Livietta e Tracolo*); *L'Olimpiade* (Metastasio), f.p. Rome, 1735; *Il Flaminio* (Federico), f.p. Naples, 1735

Church music: Mass, D, soli, ch, orch, ?1731; Mass, F, soli, ch, orch, ?1732; *Stabat mater*, s, a, str, org, 1736; etc.

Other works: cantatas, duets, some instrumental pieces

Peri, Jacopo (b. Rome/Florence, 20 Aug 1561; d. Florence, 12 Aug 1633). Italian composer, one of the founders of opera. After studies with Cristoforo Malvezzi he served the Medicis, composing and singing in the new style of expressive monody. His and Corsi's setting of Rinuccini's *Dafne*, performed in 1598, is the earliest recorded opera; nearly all its music is lost. He set a second such piece for the marriage in 1600 of Henry IV of France and Marie de' Medici, *Euridice*, to which Caccini added music. Both composers then completed their own versions. His later music includes further dramatic works and oratorios, of which little survives, and songs.

Péri, La (The Peri). Ballet score by Dukas (1911), to which he added an opening fanfare (1912). Prince Iskander foreswears immortality for the sake of a kiss from the Peri (compare *Das* PARADIES UND DIE PERI). Commissioned by Diaghilev, the score passed to the dancer Natasha Trouhanova (and later to Pavlova). First performance: Paris, 22 Apr 1912.

Périchole, La. Operetta by Offenbach to a libretto by Meilhac and Ludovic Halévy. La Périchole (soprano) and Piquillo (tenor) are Lima street musicians, brought to a happy end when the Viceroy (baritone) withdraws his claim on the first of them. First performance: Paris, 6 Oct 1868.

period. (1) Short musical segment ending with a completion. The classical model comprises antecedent and consequent phrases.

(2) Part of music HISTORY with some consistency of style. The periods generally recognized are those of the ARS NOVA (*c*.1320–1400), the RENAISSANCE (*c*.1400–1600), the BAROQUE (*c*.1600–1750), CLASSICISM (*c*.1770–1800) and ROMANTICISM (*c*.1820–1920). But the styles have a tendency to spill out of their time frames; for example, many Baroque composers wrote occasional works in *stile antico* (i.e. according to principles of Renaissance polyphony) and the flood of Romantic music did not stop in the early 20th century. The heterogeneity of music since 1920 makes it impossible to

distinguish periods; MODERNISM is more a state of mind than a length of time.

periodicals. See JOURNALS; MAGAZINES.

period instrument. Instrument of earlier times – e.g. lute, Baroque oboe, Classical-period clarinet – or long-established instrument set up and played as in former times, such as a violin restored to its 17th-century form and played with a Baroque bow. Most period instruments in use are in fact copies of period instruments, the latter generally being found in museums or beyond the budget of working musicians.

period style. Performance manner of an earlier epoch, as studied or reinterpreted by proponents of HISTORICALLY INFORMED performance.

Perle, George (b. Bayonne, New Jersey, 6 May 1915). US composer and theorist, lucid and thorough in both domains. He studied at De Paul University (1934–8) and was at that time one of the first in the USA to explore Schoenberg's music deeply. The outcome was a theory of 12-note tonality, drawing principally on the music of Berg and Bartók – a theory developed in practice in music at once euphonious and sophisticated in its harmonic relations, clear in design and propelled by an irregular pulse. He taught in Louisville, in Davis (California) and, from 1961, at Queens College, New York. His works include nine string quartets, four wind quintets and a lot of piano music (including concertos).

George Perle *The Listening Composer* (1990), *The Right Notes* (1995)

Perlman, Itzhak (b. Tel-Aviv, 31 Aug 1945). Israeli violinist. Having started training in Tel-Aviv, he won a contest in 1958 that took him to New York. There he stayed, studying further with Galamian at the Juilliard School and making his debut in 1963 at Carnegie Hall. His supremely accomplished and expressively immediate playing brought him widespread acclaim, and as a person surpassing disability (polio at four had left him unable to walk without crutches) he has been an inspiration.

Perosi, Lorenzo (b. Tortona, 20 Dec 1872; d. Rome, 12 Dec 1956). Italian composer and priest, choirmaster of the Sistine Chapel from 1898 until his death (with interruption 1915–23). His oratorios – *La risurrezione di Cristo* (1898), *Il natale del Redentore* (1899), *Il giudizio universale* (1904) and others – adapted the new operatic language of Puccini and Mascagni to sacred subjects and were extraordinarily successful in their time. He also wrote numerous masses and string quartets.

Perotin [Perotinus, Pérotin] (*fl.* Paris, *c.*1200). French composer, musically vital but dimly documented. He is credited with revising and updating the MAGNUS LIBER of polyphonic compositions compiled at Notre Dame by Leonin, whose pupil he might have been. Works ascribed to him include the two most majestic pieces of early polyphony: *Sederunt principes* and *Viderunt omnes*, both for the Christmas season. The tenor in both sings out the plainsong in long notes, supporting three-part polyphony that shows a vigorous use of repeating rhythmic patterns and a confident harmonic control. These are the earliest surviving pieces in four parts.

perpetual canon. Canon in which, as in a round, the whole thing can start again as it is ending.

perpetuum mobile (Lat., in constant motion). Movement or passage in which rapid even notes convey an impression of perpetual motion. The equivalent It. term is *moto perpetuo*.

Perrault, Charles (b. Paris, 12 Jan 1628; d. Paris, 15/16 May 1703). French writer. He supported Lully, but is best remembered, even by musicians, for his fairytales, including *Cinderella*, *Sleeping Beauty* and *Bluebeard*, from which sprang works by Grétry, Rossini, Tchaikovsky, Dukas, Ravel (*Ma mère l'oye*), etc.

Persichetti, Vincent (b. Philadelphia, 6 Jun 1915; d. Philadelphia, 14 Aug 1987). US composer. He studied in Philadelphia and had a long career, from 1947, as a teacher at the Juilliard School. His vast output includes works of all kinds, including many for student performers.

Persimfans. Conductorless orchestra, its name abbreviated from Pervïy Simfonicheskiy Ansambl bez Dirizhora (First Symphony Ensemble without Conductor), active in Moscow, 1922–32.

persona. Sense of a human individual present in non-human material, e.g. music. A great deal of Romantic music conveys such a sense. In Beethoven's Third and Fifth symphonies, or in the symphonies by Berlioz, Tchaikovsky and Mahler that were so much influenced by those works, one seems to hear voiced the aspirations, sufferings and sometimes the triumphs of a human being, and it may be hard not to take these persona symphonies as autobiographical. Richard Strauss, by contrast, provides many examples of persona music where the view is external. These are stories being told about someone else – even when, as in the *Symphonia domestica*, that 'someone else' is explicitly the composer in his day-to-day existence. The unified persona had been a compelling victory of the Romantic movement; subsequent music – Strauss's as much as Schoenberg's or Stravinsky's – has generally found its personae split or otherwise compromised.

pes (Lat., foot). (1) Kind of NEUME.
(2) Slower voice accompanying a round.

pesante (It., weighing). Heavily.

Peter and the Wolf (*Petya i volk*). Tale for narrator and orchestra with words and music by Prokofiev, charmingly made to introduce children to the orchestra, the characters being identified by themes assigned to different instruments or groups. First performance: Moscow, 2 May 1936.

Peter Grimes. Opera by Britten to a libretto by Montagu Slater after George Crabbe's poem *The Borough*. The title character (tenor) is an intemperate misfit within a small, narrow-minded and hypocritical community in a fishing town on the English east coast. Crabbe based his work on Aldeburgh, where Britten took up residence. First performance: London, 7 Jun 1945.

Peters. Music publishing firm tracing its origins to 1800 in Leipzig, and taking its name from Carl Friedrich Peters (1779–1827), who acquired the company in 1814. It owes its success, though, to Max Abraham (1831–1900), who in 1863 initiated the Edition Peters, a library of classic scores distinguished by scholarly care, excellent printing and a uniform cover design in lime green and black. In the 1930s and 1940s offshoots of the company were opened in London, New York and Frankfurt, largely in response to Nazi and communist takeovers of the Leipzig house.
Irene Lawford-Hinrichsen *Music Publishing and Patronage* (2000)

Peterson-Berger, Wilhelm (b. Ullånger, Ångermanland, 27 Feb 1867; d. Östersund, 3 Dec 1942). Swedish composer. He studied at the conservatory in Stockholm (1886–9) and in Dresden (1889–90), then spent more than 30 years as a music critic in Stockholm. A leading figure in the national Romantic school, he wrote five symphonies, songs, piano pieces, much choral music and operas.

petite flûte (Fr., little flute). Piccolo.

Petite Messe solennelle (Little Solemn Mass). Mass by Rossini (for 12 v, 2 pf, hmnm, later orchestrated), not so small and not so solemn.

Petite Suite (Little Suite). Set of four piano duets by Debussy, orchestrated by Henri Büsser in 1907.

Petite Symphonie (Little Symphony). Work by Gounod for wind nonet, written for the flautist Paul Taffanel to play with pairs of oboes, clarinets, horns and bassoons.

Petite Symphonie concertante (Little Concertante Symphony). Work by Martin for harp, harpsichord and piano soloists with double string orchestra. First performance: Zurich, 17 May 1946.

petit maître (Fr., minor master). See KLEIN-MEISTER.

petit motet (Fr., little motet). Setting of a sacred text for up to three soloists with continuo, as practised in France by Du Mont and his successors.

Petrarch [Francesco Petrarca] (b. Arezzo, 20 Jul 1304; d. Arquà, 18 Jul 1374). Italian poet, especially famed for his sonnets. He had musician friends, but the great vogue for his poetry among composers came two centuries later, when Willaert and Rore were among those who made madrigals with his words. Liszt set three sonnets as songs, and revised them as piano solos in the second volume of his *Années de pèlerinage*; Schoenberg set a sonnet in his *Serenade*.

Petrassi, Goffredo (b. Zagarolo, near Palestrina, 16 Jul 1904; d. Rome, 2 Mar 2003). Italian composer. He studied with the composer Alessandro Bustini at the Conservatorio di Santa Cecilia (1928–33) and taught there (1939–59) before transferring to the Accademia di Santa Cecilia. His early works were neoclassical, and he was encouraged by Casella, but after the Second World War he increasingly modernized his style in response to Bartók, the later Stravinsky and Webern. Abiding qualities of dynamism and instrumental virtuosity are well shown in his eight concertos for orchestra.

One-act operas: *Il cordovano* (Montale, after Cervantes), 1944–8, f.p. Milan, 1949; *Morte dell'aria* (Toti Scialoja), 1949–50, f.p. Rome, 1950

Ballets: *La follia di Orlando*, 1942–3; *Ritratto di Don Chisciotte*, 1945

Concertos for Orchestra: No.1, 1933–4; No.2, 1951; No.3 'Récréation concertante', 1952–3; No.4, str, 1954; No.5, 1955; No.6 'Invenzione concertata',

1956–7; No.7 'Prologo e cinque invenzioni', 1961–2, rev 1964; No.8, 1970–72

Choral and vocal: Psalm 9, ch, orch, 1934–6; *Magnificat*, s, ch orch, 1939–40; *Coro di morti* (Leopardi), men's ch, chbr orch, 1940–41; *Quattro inni sacri*, t, bar, org, 1942, orchd 1950; *Noche oscura* (St John of the Cross), ch, orch, 1950–51; *Orationes Christi*, ch, brass, low str, 1974–5; *Tre cori sacri*, 1980–83; *Kyrie*, ch, str, 1990; etc.

Chamber: String Quartet, 1958; String Trio, 1959; *per sette*, wind trio, 1964; *Estri*, 15 insts, 1966–7; *Quattro odi*, str qt, 1973–5; *Grand septuour*, cl, sextet, 1977–8; *Sestina d'autunno*, sextet, 1981–2; etc.

Petrucci, Ottaviano (dei) (b. Fossombrone, 18 Jun 1466; d. ?Venice, 7 May 1539). Italian music printer who set up in Venice the first press producing polyphonic music from movable type. His initial volume, *Harmonice musices odhecaton A* (100 Harmonic Songs A, 1501), was a collection predominantly of Franco-Netherlandish polyphonic songs, by composers including Josquin and Busnois. It was followed during the next 14 years by more songbooks, lute music and collections of masses and motets, constituting the most impressive body of printed music from the period.

Petrushka (Pétrouchka). Ballet by Stravinsky and Alexandre Benois, designed by Benois and choreographed by Fokine. The love agonies of the puppet hero are presented within the mechanical bustle of a shrovetide fair in St Petersburg. The score is for large orchestra (reduced by the composer in 1946) with prominent piano. Stravinsky also arranged Three Movements from *Petrushka* as a virtuoso piece for Arthur Rubinstein. First performance: Paris, 13 Jun 1911.

Pettersson, (Gustaf) Allan (b. Västra Ryd, 19 Sep 1911; d. Stockholm, 20 Jun 1980). Swedish composer, most notably of symphonies. Of poor family, he taught himself to play the violin before gaining admission to the conservatory in Stockholm (1930–39). He worked as an orchestral violist in the 1940s while having composition lessons from Blomdahl, and then, at the start of the 1950s, went to Paris for further lessons with Honegger, Milhaud and Leibowitz. In 1952 he stopped playing in order to devote himself to composition; he also began experiencing the effects of rheumatoid arthritis. Still success was slow in coming: not until 1968 did he make a breakthrough, with the première of his Seventh Symphony. He died while working on his 17th, symphonies constituting the bulk of his mature output. Most of those after No.7 are in one movement projecting psychological conflict in a search for euphonious release from raging dissonance.

Symphonies: No.1, 1950–51; No.2, 1952–3; No.3, 1954–5; No.4, 1958–9; No.5, 1960–62; No.6, 1966; No.7, 1966–7; No.8, 1968–9; No.9, 1970; No.10, 1971–2; No.11, 1971–3; No.12 'The Dead in the Square' (Pablo Neruda), ch, orch, 1973–4; No.13, 1976; No.14, 1978; No.15, 1978; No.16, a sax, orch, 1979; No.17, 1980 (unfinished)
Other works: concertos, chamber pieces, songs

peu (Fr.). Little, slightly, as in *un peu animé* (a little animated), *un peu en dehors* (a little in relief).

Pezel, Johann Christoph (b. Glatz, Silesia, 1639; Bautzen, 13 Oct 1694). German town bandsman and composer of TOWER MUSIC, who was active in Leipzig and, from 1681, Bautzen.

pezzo (It., pl. *pezzi*). Piece.

pf. Abbreviation for pianoforte (i.e. piano).

Pfitzner, Hans (Erich) (b. Moscow, 5 May 1869; d. Salzburg, 22 May 1949). German composer, a committed Romantic. He studied with James Kwast and Knorr at the Hoch Conservatory in Frankfurt (1886–90), and began to make a name with his first opera, securing an appointment at the Stern Conservatory in Berlin (1897–1907). While there he eloped with Kwast's daughter. He then moved to Strasbourg as a teacher and conductor, reviving early Romantic German operas while working on his own magnum opus, *Palestrina*. Deeply marked by the defeat of Germany in the First World War (and not only by the loss thereby of his positions in Strasbourg, which returned to France), he became a cantankerous polemicist. He was fiercely opposed to Schoenberg, Berg and Strauss, all of whom he felt were betraying the great German tradition, and he was just as irascible and adversarial in his dealings with the Nazis. His wife's death in 1926 did not help. The end of the Second World War found him destitute in Munich, and he was given a pension by the Vienna Philharmonic. His sense of himself as a preserver, guarding the gates of culture, may have kept him from continuing the imaginative richness of his opera *Palestrina*, where the theme of the artist's moral responsibility is pursued with abundant humanity and humour.

John Williamson *The Music of Hans Pfitzner* (1992)

www.pfitzner-gesellschaft.de

Operas: *Der arme Heinrich* (James Grun) 1891–3, f.p. Mainz, 1895; *Die Rose vom Liebesgarten* (Grun) 1897–1900, f.p. Elberfeld, 1901; *Das Christ-Elflein*, Op.20, 1906, f.p. Munich, 1906; PALESTRINA, 1912–15; *Das Herz* (Hans Mahner-Mons and Pfitzner), Op.39, 1930–31, f.p. Munich and Berlin, 1931

Cantatas: *Vom deutscher Seele* (Eichendorff), Op.28, 1921; *Das dunkle Reich* (Michelangelo, Goethe, Meyer, Dehmel), Op.38, 1929
Other works: chamber music, symphonies, concertos, over 90 songs

Phaedra. In Greek mythology the wife of Theseus, destroyed by her love for her stepson Hippolytus. The story is told in works by Rameau, Paisiello, Britten, etc.

Phaeton. In Greek mythology the son of Helios, the sun god. He borrows his father's chariot to ride across the sky and is struck down by Zeus. The story is the subject of an opera by Lully and a symphonic poem by Saint-Saëns.

Phalèse. Family of music printers active in Louvain (1545–76) and then for another century in Antwerp. The business was founded by Pierre Phalèse (*c*.1510–*c*.1576) and continued by his son, also Pierre (*c*.1550–1629), and granddaughters, Madeleine (1586–1652) and Marie (1589–*c*.1674). They published lute music, madrigals and church music, mostly by Italian composers.

Phantasie (Ger., pl. *Phantasien*). Fantasy.

Phantasy. Fantasy. Cobbett instituted a prize in 1905 for works with this title; hence the examples by Bridge, Vaughan Williams, etc. Schoenberg also preferred this spelling.

phase. Term used in stating whether two sound or electrical waves are synchronous ('in phase', their peaks and troughs coinciding) or asynchronous ('out of phase', staggered).

phasing. Repeating the same motif in two or more parts at slightly different speeds, so that the repetitions become out of phase with one another, then eventually move back in phase again. The technique was introduced by Reich.

Philadelphia. US city with a history of concerts and opera going back to the mid 18th century. Its main musical institutions now are the CURTIS INSTITUTE OF MUSIC and the Philadelphia Orchestra, traditionally famed for its strings, and conducted successively by Fritz Scheel (1900–7), Karl Pohlig (1907–12), Stokowski (1912–38), Ormandy (1938–80), Muti (1981–92), Sawallisch (1993–2003) and Eschenbach (from 2003).

John Ardoin, ed. *The Philadelphia Orchestra* (1999)

Philharmonia Orchestra. London orchestra founded by Legge in 1945 principally for recording, briefly known after his regime as the New Philharmonia Orchestra (1964–77). It became a permanent and distinguished concert orchestra under Klemperer (1959–73), whose successors have included Muti (1973–82), Giuseppe Sinopoli (1984–94) and Christoph von Dohnányi (from 1997).

philharmonic (from Gk *philos*, beloved, *harmonikos*, of harmony). Term commonly found in the names of orchestras (e.g. Vienna Philharmonic), musical societies (Royal Philharmonic Society) and halls (Philharmonic Hall). Often abbreviated to Phil. In older usage a philharmonic is a music lover.

Philidor, François André Danican (b. Dreux, 7 Sep 1726; d. London, 31 Aug 1795). French composer and chess virtuoso. The son of a royal musician, André Danican Philidor (*c.*1647–1730), he learned both his arts as a boy at Versailles. By the age of 18 he was the leading chess player in Paris, able to play and win two simultaneous matches blindfold. From 1745 he was in London regularly, more as a chessman than as a musician, though he did hear Handel operas. Back in Paris he had some success as a composer of comic operas, notably *Tom Jones* (f.p. Paris, 1765), after Fielding's novel. He died stranded in England by the outbreak of war.

Philippe (b. Paris, *c.*1170; d. Paris, 1236). French scholar. The bastard son of an archdeacon of highly distinguished family, he was known as Philippe the Chancellor for the position he held at Notre Dame from 1218. He wrote the words and possibly also the music for at least two dozen Latin songs, most of them monophonic.

Philippus de Caserta (*fl. c.*1370–80). Musician active at the papal court in Avignon, author of theoretical treatises and a few compositions of rhythmic complexity.

Philips. Dutch electrical company, which made its first recordings in 1950. It became part of Polygram with Deutsche Grammophon in 1972, and of the Universal Music Group in 1998.

Philips, Peter (b. *c.*1561; d. Brussels, 1628). English composer and organist. He was a choirboy at St Paul's, then fled the country as a Catholic in 1582. After a while at the English college in Rome, in 1585 he joined the retinue of Lord Thomas Paget, with whom he visited Madrid and Paris before settling in Brussels. Following Paget's death in 1590, he moved to Antwerp and married. In 1593 he was arrested on suspicion of plotting against Queen Elizabeth, but released, having written a pavan and galliard 'Dolorosa' in prison. He published his first book of madrigals in 1596, and became an organist at the archducal court in Brussels the next year. His later works include two more madrigal collections and several volumes of sacred music, besides keyboard and consort music.

Philomel. In classical mythology a young woman who, escaping a man, is transformed into a nightingale; hence a poetic name for that bird. Babbitt's *Philomel* for soprano and tape tells the story.

Philosopher, The (*Der Philosoph*). Name given to Haydn's Symphony No.22 (in his lifetime) on account of its pensive opening adagio.

philosophy of music. The study of what music is and how it has meaning. Attendant on these large and abstract matters are questions that have to do with composition, performance and listening: What is beauty in music? What are the effects of music on individuals, groups and whole societies? What relationships does music have with the nature of sound and with that of the cosmos? Is music a language, and if so what kind are its messages and who is their source? What are the grounds for judging compositions and performances (i.e. CRITICISM)? Are some musical traditions superior to others? What is a musical WORK? These are topics that have exercised philosophers from (in the Western tradition) the Greeks onwards, and though music and philosophy have both been through many changes during that period, the essential theories about the nature of music have remained remarkably durable, which means also that they have proved remarkably hard to vindicate or discredit.

Some of those theories have to do with EXPRESSION. If we say (and by no means all philosophers do say) that music expresses feelings, still there is large room for argument as to what this means. Do composers deliberately translate into notes on paper feelings that performers then translate into sounds and listeners translate back into feelings? Or does this all happen inadvertently, while the people concerned are concentrating on other matters, of form, performance and comprehension? In either event, how do these translations occur? Is there some code? If there is, does it depend on the nature of the ear and sound or on convention? Does music mimic the speech and gesturing of an agitated person, or does it have an expressive language all its own? Should we regard its expression as belonging to it rather than to its composer? Does it arouse feelings in us, encourage sympathy with the feelings of others, or provide an understanding of those feelings in a more general way?

Alternatives or complements to the expressive theory of music come in essentially three forms, asserting variously that music's meanings are to do with the nature of sound and time, that it is a means of communication with higher forces (perhaps divine, perhaps within the mind), or that it is an instrument of thought about the constitution of the universe. Theories of the last sort often depend on links between music and mathematics, as in the notion of the MUSIC OF THE SPHERES, holding that human music is an image of the grand proportions of the planetary orbits, or in the application of NUMBER systems to music. Such theories rarely concern themselves with the means by which the numbers, hermetically sealed into harmony or rhythm, convey their associations and meanings to the listening ear.

Contrariwise, formalist theories of music as self-sufficient received support and encouragement in the 17th, 18th and 19th centuries from increased understanding of sound and of musical form. Indeed, the elaboration of musical form in the works of Brahms, Wagner and Mahler demonstrates the strength of these theories, even in an age keenly attuned to music's expressiveness – which only goes to show it is possible for musicians to hold divergent opinions about their art simultaneously. For Wagner at least, the theory of music as drawing the numinous into the area of the immediately perceptible was evidently no less powerful.

The ability of music to speak in many different voices – the manifest voices of polyphony or the more submerged voices of different participants (composer, performer, character or persona, to which one might add the voices of instrumental, formal and national traditions) – is essential to what has made it so fascinating and perplexing a subject of philosophical debate. See also PSYCH-OLOGY OF MUSIC.

Philip Alperson, ed. *What is Music?* (1987, ²1994); Edward A. Lippman *Musical Aesthetics: A Historical Reader*, 3 Vols. (1986–90)

phonograph. Edison's term for his RECORDING machine, a term that survived in US English to the time of the LP (but not the CD).

phrase. Segment of music, analogous to a phrase in language: a short sequence that conveys some sense of completion together with (unless it be the final phrase, and possibly even then) the expectation of more. Phrases can be short. They may equally be so circuitous and capacious as not to leave any pause for breath or space for mental assimilation until quite some course has been run. The norm, though, is the four-bar phrase.

Phrases will often be defined by some combination of melodic, harmonic and rhythmic features providing a sense of rise and fall, or of departure and return. Such features, at least in the melodic sense, are as old as plainsong. But in some music that is strongly pulsed (Messiaen) or totally pulseless (Stockhausen) phrases may be hard to discern.

The notation of phrases by long ligatures, above or below the notes, began in the 17th century.

phrasing. The art of bringing out phrases and assuring continuity. This is no paradox: the just distinction and weighting of phrases contributes to music's onwardness as well as to its expressive power.

Phrygian. Authentic MODE E–F–G–A–B–C–D–E, the third church mode/tone.

Phrygian cadence. Malleable term, most often denoting a cadence on to the dominant of the relative minor (e.g. E major in C major).

piacere. See A PIACERE.

piacevole (It.). Pleasingly.

piangendo, piangente, piangevole, piangevol-mente (It.). Plaintive.

pianino. Upright piano.

pianissimo (It.). Very soft. Dynamic marking, the common abbreviations *pp* and *ppp* allowing two degrees.

piano (It., soft). The word is given something like It. pronunciation for the first meaning below (*pee-AH-no*) but is thoroughly absorbed into Eng. for the second (*pee-AN-no*).

(1) Soft, quiet. Dynamic marking, abbreviated *p*.

(2) (Fr. *piano*, Ger. *Klavier*, It. *pianoforte*, pl. *pianoforti*). Keyboard instrument, its name shortened from pianoforte (It., soft-loud), a reminder of what distinguished this instrument when it was new: unlike members of the harpsichord family it could provide different levels of volume. The German term alludes instead to what it inherited from the harpsichord: the keys.

Bartolomeo Cristofori built the ancestral piano at the very end of the 17th century, and the first published description called it *gravicembalo con piano e forte* (harpsichord with soft and loud).

Cristofori achieved that capacity by combining features of the harpsichord (the keyboard and case of strings) with the hammers of the dulcimer.

Pressing a key on the piano keyboard causes a hammer to fall on a string (or on two or three strings in most cases) and rebound, by a mechanism known as 'escapement'; this is necessary to allow the string or strings to vibrate freely. Speed and force at the keyboard will transmit themselves to the hammer, producing greater loudness and intensity. At the same time, the action of the key releases a damper from the string, allowing that string to vibrate for as long as the key is depressed, while other strings remain damped and so cannot vibrate in sympathy.

A lot in the nature of the piano flows from this simple matter of the instrument's mechanical action, for the control of volume is not just useful in itself but a vital tool in phrasing, and especially in allowing the piano to imitate a singing voice; *cantabile* (songful) is a common marking on piano music and a common term of approbation with reference to pianists.

The sustaining pedal, normally played with the right foot, raises all the dampers, so that notes will sound on after the fingers have left the keys; sympathetic vibrations will also arise. A second pedal – the soft pedal, played with the left foot – shifts the hammers to one side so that they hit only one of the two or three strings. Pianos in the 18th century commonly had two or three strings per note. Modern pianos normally have one string per note in the extreme bass (and so the soft pedal has no effect there), two in the low-middle register and three above that, to counteract the lesser volume produced by shorter (higher) strings. Finally, the sound is made rounder and fuller by the wooden sounding board, placed below the strings in the case of a grand piano, behind them on an upright.

The earliest pianos – those of Cristofori and then Silbermann – followed the wing shape of the harpsichord. C.P.E. Bach, writing for the Silbermann piano, produced some of the first important music to take account of the piano's capabilities, and gradually, during the third quarter of the 18th century, pianos replaced harpsichords in concert rooms, theatres and domestic settings. The square piano (in fact rectangular, after the pattern of the clavichord), more suitable for middle-class homes, was introduced by Johannes Zumpe in 1761 in London, which soon became the leading centre of piano production and piano music publication, with Clementi and Broadwood active in the business. There were also important piano factories in the 1770s and 1780s in Augsburg (Stein), Vienna (Walter), Paris (Erard) and Philadelphia.

At the same time the piano took a central place in the art of composition. The last quarter of the 18th century saw the concertos, sonatas and variations of Mozart and Haydn, as well as of Dussek, one of the first touring virtuosos. Haydn, Mozart and Carl Stamitz also included the piano in chamber music. Composers for the piano in the first three decades of the 19th century included – besides Beethoven and Schubert – Hummel and Moscheles. New piano-making firms opened – Pleyel in Paris, Graf and Bösendorfer in Vienna – and the upright was developed by Hawkins in Philadelphia and Wornum in London, supplanting the square piano, which could not keep pace with the demands for increased range and strength. The last essential change to the instrument's action was the double escapement introduced by Erard (1821), a mechanism of springs and levers that had the hammers rebound immediately and only part way, so that notes could be repeated rapidly, before the keys had risen completely. Soon after, US makers introduced the cast-iron (instead of wooden) frame, obtaining a bigger sound from thicker strings at correspondingly greater tension. To distribute the increasingly powerful tensions evenly, makers in the 1830s started overstringing – placing one set of strings over another at an angle. As for range, the span increased from the five octaves of Mozart's time through the six Beethoven exploited in his last sonatas to over seven, pianos since the 1830s regularly having 88 keys (96 in the case of the Imperial Bösendorfer).

These developments in reach and power coincided with the touring careers of Liszt and Chopin, in the 1830s and 1840s, the period also of Schumann's important piano music (including chamber music). In 1859 the firm of Steinway in New York introduced a piano that effectively completed the instrument's technological development, with even more robustness and a third pedal, the sostenuto pedal or middle pedal, allowing the performer to sustain particular notes without raising all the dampers.

Nearly all composers in the 19th century were pianists of some sort (Berlioz being a notable exception), but the tradition of the virtuoso composer-pianist was broken. Brahms and Grieg wrote a lot for the piano and gave concerts, but not regularly: the virtuosos of the age included, rather, Tausig, Thalberg, von Bülow and Leschetizky, who found their repertory pre-eminently in Chopin and Liszt. Around the turn of the century, though, there arrived a new generation of creator-practitioners, including Busoni, Scriabin and Rachmaninoff, followed a little later by Bartók and Prokofiev. Busoni was among the first concert pianists to offer Bach, whose music had earlier been felt most suitable for private study. Other pre-piano music entered the piano repertory in the early 20th century, notably Scarlatti's and Rameau's. Debussy and Ravel wrote importantly for the instrument at this time but were not primarily performers; Godowsky, who was, pushed virtuosity to an extreme.

Meanwhile, composers began using the piano in non-traditional ways: as a prominent but subsoloist member of the orchestra (Stravinsky's *Petrushka*), as part of a mixed ensemble (Schoenberg's *Pierrot lunaire*), as a percussive instrument, reversing the 19th-century primacy of cantabile playing (Stravinsky, Bartók), as a resonating body (Schoenberg, with his technique of silently depressing keys to let them vibrate sympathetically) and as a source of unexpected sounds (Cowell, Cage). All these developments took piano music out of the hands of the amateur, who had still been served by Brahms and Tchaikovsky.

The same tide, less necessarily, took new piano music out of the hands of the most distinguished performers; hesitation in expanding the repertory was about the only trait connecting Horowitz, Schnabel (though he was himself a composer) and Gould (though he venerated Schoenberg), to recall three pianists highly valued for their recordings. Thus while the technology of the instrument has remained essentially the same since the early 20th century – through a period dominated by Steinway instruments – the piano has gained two almost separate histories: one of great performers (additionally Cortot, Rubinstein, Gieseking, Richter, Arrau, Argerich, Berman, Uchida, Perahia, Sokolov, Zimerman, Pogorelich and many more), the other of great music (by Messiaen, Barraqué, Stockhausen, Babbitt, Carter, Kurtág, Ligeti, Ferneyhough and Sciarrino, among others). Yet sometimes – in Pollini's advocacy of Boulez and Nono, or Kocsis's of Kurtág – these magnificent traditions fuse.

Harold C. Schonberg *The Great Pianists* (1963, ²1987); David Rowland, ed. *The Cambridge Companion to the Piano* (1998)

piano accordion. See ACCORDION.

piano concerto. Work for solo piano and orchestra, usually titled thus (e.g. Grieg's Piano Concerto), though the term may be used generically, as in 'Birtwistle's piano concerto *Antiphonies*'. The idea of pitting a keyboard soloist against an instrumental ensemble appears to have been one of Bach's inventions, developed by the next generation and brought to sudden maturity in Mozart's 21 non-childhood solo piano con-

certos. The subsequent central repertory includes works by:

Beethoven: No.1, f.p. Vienna, 18 Dec 1795, Beethoven; No.2, f.p. Vienna, 29 Mar 1795, Beethoven; No.3, f.p. Vienna, 5 Apr 1803, Beethoven; No.4, f.p. Vienna, Mar 1807, Beethoven; No.5, f.p. Vienna, ?28 Nov 1811, Beethoven

Chopin: No.1, f.p. Warsaw, 11 Oct 1830, Chopin; No.2, f.p. Warsaw, 17 Apr 1830, Chopin

Schumann: f.p. Leipzig, 1 Jan 1846, Clara Schumann

Liszt: No.1, f.p. Weimar, 17 Feb 1855, Liszt, Berlioz conducting; No.2, f.p. Weimar, 7 Jan 1857, Hans Bronsart von Schellendorf, Liszt conducting

Brahms: No.1, f.p. Hanover, 22 Jan 1859, Brahms; No.2, f.p. Budapest, 9 Nov 1881, Brahms

Grieg: f.p. Copenhagen, 3 Apr 1869, Grieg

Tchaikovsky: No.1, f.p. Boston, 25 Oct 1875, von Bülow

Franck: SYMPHONIC VARIATIONS

Rachmaninoff: No.2, f.p. Moscow, 9 Nov 1901, Rachmaninoff, Ziloti conducting; No.3, f.p. New York, 28 Nov 1909, Rachmaninoff, Damrosch conducting

Prokofiev: No.1, f.p. Moscow, 7 Aug 1912, Prokofiev; No.2, f.p. Pavlovsk, 23 Aug 1913, Prokofiev; No.3, f.p. Chicago, 16 Dec 1921, Prokofiev; No.4, f.p. Berlin, 5 Sep 1956, Paul Rapp; No.5, f.p. Berlin, 31 Oct 1932, Prokofiev

Stravinsky: Concerto, f.p. Paris, 22 May 1924, Stravinsky, Koussevitzky conducting; Capriccio, f.p. Paris, 6 Dec 1929, Stravinsky, Ansermet conducting; MOVEMENTS

Bartók: No.1, f.p. Frankfurt, 1 Jul 1927, Bartók, Furtwängler conducting; No.2, f.p. Frankfurt, 23 Jan 1933, Bartók, Rosbaud conducting; No.3, f.p. Philadelphia, 8 Feb 1946, György Sándor, Ormandy conducting

Ravel: Left Hand, f.p. Vienna, 6 Jan 1932, Wittgenstein; G major, f.p. Paris, 14 Jan 1932, Long, Ravel conducting

Khachaturian: f.p. Moscow, 12 Jul 1937, Lev Oborin

Schoenberg: f.p. New York, 6 Feb 1944, Steuermann, Stokowski conducting

Carter: f.p. Boston, 6 Jan 1967, Jacob Lateiner, Leinsdorf conducting

Nono: COMO UNA OLA DE FUERZA Y LUZ

Kurtág: ... QUASI UNA FANTASIA

Ligeti: f.p. Graz, 23 Oct 1986, Anthony di Bonaventura

Berio: *Concerto II (Echoing Curves)*, f.p. Paris, 3 Nov 1988, Barenboim, Boulez conducting

Birtwistle: *Antiphonies*, f.p. Paris, 5 May 1993, Joanna MacGregor, Boulez conducting

Sciarrino: *Il clima dopo Harry Partch*, f.p. Paris, 8 Nov 2000, Nicolas Hodges

There are also piano concertos by Haydn, Mendelssohn (2), Saint-Saëns (5, No.3 being the most popular), Scriabin, Busoni, Shostakovich (2), Henze (2), Messiaen (several), Kirchner (2), Cage (Concert), Goehr, Lachenmann (*Ausklang*),

Babbitt (2) and Lutosławski. See DOUBLE CON-CERTO and TRIPLE CONCERTO for works with more than one soloist.

piano duet. Pair of pianists at one piano, or genre of music for such a combination, or work of that genre. Domestic and companionable, the piano duet made it possible for two amateurs of different capabilities to play together, the more gifted at the treble end of the piano (primo), the other at the bass (secondo). The earliest duet sonatas were written in the 1770s and 1780s, by composers including Mozart and Clementi. Then, from around 1800 until the arrival of the gramophone, duet arrangements became the principal means by which orchestral music was disseminated. Schubert gave the genre a quite different seriousness; other composers who added important original works to the repertory include Schumann, Brahms, Dvořák, Grieg, Bizet, Fauré, Debussy and Ravel.

piano duo. Pair of pianists, or genre of music for them at two pianos, or work of that genre. Not so domestic by nature (since only the homes of professional musicians would be likely to boast two pianos), the piano duo has a repertory including important concert pieces by Mozart, Schumann, Brahms, Reger, Debussy, Stravinsky, Bartók, Rachmaninoff and Messiaen. Commonly played piano concertos are published in piano duo versions for rehearsal purposes, one pianist taking the orchestral part.

pianoforte. Full name of the piano.

pianola. Mechanical piano in which the action responds not to the player's fingers but to a recording in the form of a roll of paper, with perforations representing notes and durations. Several instruments of this kind were developed in the last two decades of the 19th century, including what the US organ builder Edwin Scott Votey invented as the pianola in 1895. At its most sophisticated, the pianola roll could also register subtleties of dynamics, pedalling and tempo, and so record pianists' performances at a time when the gramophone was in its infancy: the first such 'reproducing piano' was the Welte-Mignon (1904), produced by Edwin Welte in Freiburg, and rolls for the instrument were recorded by Debussy and Mahler, neither of whom made any gramophone recordings. Votey's Aeolian Company responded with the Duo-Art machine, for which Rachmaninoff and Gershwin recorded. Stravinsky in 1917 wrote an Etude for pianola; he also planned to include a pianola in *Les Noces*, besides arranging other pieces for the Aeolian instrument. But the pianola's ecological niche was being taken over by the gramophone – though not for Nancarrow, who found a new virtuosity in it after the Second World War. Nancarrow exploited the pianola not for its reproducing accuracy but for what it could do that was unprecedented: perform at extreme velocity, project many lines at once in different tempos, exceed the reach of hands. With Nancarrow as example, other composers subsequently created pieces for pianola, including Ligeti. Strictly the name 'pianola' is the property of the Aeolian Company, the more general term for the instrument being 'player piano'. Its successor as a reproducing piano was the DISKLAVIER.

Arthur W.J.G. Ord-Hume *Pianola* (1984)

piano quartet. Group of instruments comprising piano plus string trio (vn, va, vc), or group of players on those instruments, or genre of music for that medium, or work of that genre. There are examples by Mozart, Mendelssohn, Brahms, Dvořák, Strauss, Fauré, Chausson, Enescu, Copland, Schnittke and Babbitt.

piano quintet. Group of instruments comprising piano plus string quartet, or group of players on those instruments, or genre of music for that medium, or work of that genre. There are examples by Schumann, Brahms, Dvořák, Franck, Fauré, Dohnányi, Bartók, Bloch, Elgar, Shostakovich, Martin, Schnittke, Feldman, Carter and Adès. The term may also include other groupings, notably that of piano, violin, viola, cello and double bass (Schubert's 'Trout' Quintet) or piano, oboe, clarinet, horn and bassoon (works by Mozart, Beethoven, Holliger and Carter).

piano reduction [piano score]. Manuscript or printed music in which orchestral (and sometimes vocal) parts are condensed into something readable at the piano. Publishers in the 19th and early 20th centuries commonly offered piano reductions of symphonic works for delectation at home; the practice ended with the arrival of recordings, which fulfilled the same function. But piano reductions are still needed for other purposes when only a pianist is to hand, to accompany dancers rehearsing ballets or soloists learning concertos. In the case of operas, and other vocal works with orchestra, the appropriate term is VOCAL SCORE.

piano roll. Roll of paper having perforations to operate a PIANOLA.

piano sonata. SONATA for piano alone. The

capabilities of the lone keyboard player were observed and explored by many composers (notably Domenico Scarlatti and Soler) before Haydn, Mozart and their contemporaries brought forward the Classical piano sonata in three movements. Beethoven and Schubert, simultaneously and independently, made this one of the most important instrumental genres, on a level with the string quartet and the symphony. Beethoven's example, in particular, established it as an enduring challenge to composers – a challenge taken up by Schumann, Chopin, Liszt, Brahms, Medtner, Scriabin, Dukas, Szymanowski, Janáček, Rachmaninoff, Berg, Ives, Stravinsky, Bartók, Prokofiev, Tippett, Copland, Carter, Dutilleux, Boulez, Ustvolskaya, Barraqué, Henze, Sciarrino, Schnittke and Berio.

piano trio. Group of instruments comprising piano, violin and cello, or group of players on those instruments, or genre of music for that medium, or work of that genre. There are examples by Haydn, Beethoven (whose Triple Concerto also features the grouping), Schubert, Mendelssohn, Schumann, Smetana, Tchaikovsky, Brahms, Dvořák, Fauré, Chausson, Ives, Ravel, Copland, Shostakovich and Rihm.

piano tuner. See TUNE (2).

Piatigorsky, Gregor (b. Ekaterinoslav, 17 Apr 1903; d. Los Angeles, 6 Aug 1976). Russian–US cellist. He studied at the Moscow Conservatory, left Russia in 1921 and was principal cellist of the Berlin Philharmonic under Furtwängler (1924–8) before becoming a prominent soloist, chamber musician and teacher. Hindemith and Walton wrote concertos for him.

piatti (It.). Cymbals.

Piatti, Alfredo (Carlo) (b. Bergamo, 8 Jan 1822; d. Crocetto di Mozzo, 18 Jul 1901). Italian cellist. Born into a musical family, he studied at the Milan Conservatory, started out as a touring soloist in 1838, and gained encouragement from Liszt. In 1846 he settled in London, to enjoy a long career as a soloist, chamber musician and teacher.

Piave, Francesco Maria (b. Murano, 18 May 1810; d. Milan, 5 Mar 1876). Italian librettist, son of a glass maker. In Rome he became acquainted with the librettist Jacopo Ferretti; he wrote his first libretto in 1842. Two years later he began an association with Verdi that lasted through 10 operas, including *Rigoletto* and *La traviata*. His connection with Verdi also won him a post as poet

and stage director at La Scala from 1859 to 1867, when he suffered a stroke that left him incapacitated.

Piazzolla, Astor (Pantaleon) (b. Mar del Plata, 11 Mar 1921; d. Buenos Aires, 5 Jul 1992). Argentinian composer. He spent his childhood in New York, where his father was a hairdresser, and began playing the bandoneon. In the 1940s, back in Mar del Plata, he heard Aníbal Troilo's tango orchestra, which he joined as a performer, arranger and composer. A scholarship took him to Paris for studies with Boulanger (1954–5), and after his return he formed his own ensembles, especially the Quinteto Tango Nuevo (from 1976), while also writing concert pieces, songs and film scores in which he combined tango and classical traditions.

Maria Susana Azzi and Simon Collier *Le Grand Tango* (2000)

Picander. Pseudonym of Christian Friedrich Henrici (b. Stolpen, near Dresden, 14 Jan 1700; d. Leipzig, 10 May 1764), who worked in Leipzig as a poet and tutor. In 1725 he began a long collaboration with Bach, which produced the St Matthew Passion and numerous cantatas.

Picardy third. See TIERCE DE PICARDIE.

Piccinni, (Vito) Niccolò (Marcello Antonio Giacomo) (b. Bari, 16 Jan 1728; d. Passy, 7 May 1800). Italian composer, best remembered for operas he wrote for the French court. He studied with Durante at the San Onofrio conservatory in Naples before producing his first success there, *Le donne dispettose* (1754). Among his many operas of the next two decades, serious and comic, was the wildly successful *La buona figliuola*, but despite this and other triumphs in Rome, he remained in Naples with his wife – a singing pupil he had married in 1756 – and seven children. Burney, who met him there, called him 'a lively agreeable little man, rather grave for an Italian so full of fire and genius'.

His gravity may have helped in the competitive world of 18th-century opera. The Roman public switched their enthusiasm from him to Anfossi, and in 1776 he moved to Paris, where he was the victim of adverse comparisons with Gluck and, later, Sacchini – though he was as innovative as either. Having lost his pension following the French Revolution, he returned to Naples in 1791 and was ironically placed under house arrest from 1794 to 1798 on suspicion of revolutionary leanings. He then went back to Paris.

Operas: *La buona figliuola* (*La Cecchina*; Goldoni, after Richardson *Pamela*), f.p. Rome, 1760; *La*

pescatrice, f.p. Rome, 1766; *Roland* (Marmontel, after Quinault), f.p. Paris, 1778; *Atys* (Marmontel, after Quinault), f.p. Paris, 1780; *Iphigénie en Tauride* (Alphonse Ducongé Dubreuil), f.p. Paris, 1781; *Didon* (Marmontel, after Metastasio), f.p. Fontainebleau, 1783; *Pénélope*, f.p. Fontainebleau, 1785; *La Griselda*, f.p. Venice, 1793; over 100 others
Other works: sacred music, cantatas, sinfonias

piccolo. (1) (from It. *flauto piccolo*, little flute, though the usual It. name for the instrument is *ottavino*). Small flute pitched an octave above the standard flute. Parts for it are normally notated an octave below the sounding pitch. In an orchestra, flautists (except the principal) may be required to double on piccolo in many works written since the early 19th century, Beethoven's *Egmont* overture being among the first examples. The piccolo is also an instrument in the military band. Its tiny solo and chamber repertory includes pieces by Ferneyhough.

The term can also be used adjectivally in designating other small, high instruments, e.g. piccolo clarinet (in E♭), piccolo trumpet.

(2) 1' or 2' flute stop on an organ.

Picker, Tobias (b. New York, 18 Jul 1954). US composer. After studies with Wuorinen, Carter and Babbitt he moved into a large Romantic style, and gained particular success with his first opera, *Emmeline* (1996). Other works include further operas (*Thérèse Raquin*, 2001), three symphonies and concertos.

pick-up. (1) Ad hoc. A pick-up orchestra is made up of freelance musicians coming together for an occasional concert or recording.

(2) Electrical device that reads an analogue disc.

Pictures at an Exhibition (*Kartinki s vystavki*, *Tableaux d'une exposition*). Piano work by Musorgsky, suggesting a visit to a memorial show of work by his friend Viktor Hartmann. Linking music (*Promenade*) introduces and occasionally connects the 10 pictures: 1 *Gnomus*, 2 *Il vecchio castello* (The Old Castle), 3 *Tuileries*, 4 *Bydlo* (a Polish cart), 5 *Ballet of the Unhatched Chicks*, 6 *Samuel Goldberg and Schmuyle*, 7 *Limoges: The Market*, 8 *Catacombae*, 9 *Baba-yaga (The Hut on Fowls' Legs)*, 10 *The Great Gate of Kiev*. The standard orchestration is by Ravel (f.p. Paris, 19 Oct 1922), but there are also versions by Mikhail Tushmalov (1886, 7 pictures), Henry Wood (1915), Leo Funtek (1922), Leonidas Leonardi (1924), Lucien Cailliet (1937), Stokowski (1938, cutting Nos.3 and 7), Walter Goehr (1942), Sergey Gorchakov (1955), Lawrence Leonard (1977, as a piano concerto), Ashkenazy (1982) and Thomas Wilbrandt (1992). Among many other realizations are Giuseppe Becce's for salon orchestra (1922) and piano trio (1930), that of Emerson, Lake and Palmer for rock group (1971), Isao Tomita's for synthesized sounds (1975), Elgar Howarth's for brass band (1978), Thomas Bauer's for accordion orchestra (2000) and adaptations by several organists and guitarists.

piece (Fr. *pièce*, *morceau*, Ger. *Stück*, It. *pezzo*). Composition – anything from a one-page piano miniature to a full-length opera, though it is not normal to refer to a song as a piece. In titles the term was first used by French clavecinists of the 17th and 18th centuries, and became more widespread in the Romantic period to denote lyrical miniatures (e.g. Schumann's several sets of *Fantasiestücke*). It embarked on a new career in the early 20th century when Schoenberg and his pupils used it for sets of movements not adhering to any established form.

pièce de circonstance (Fr.). See OCCASIONAL PIECE.

Pierné, (Henri Constant) Gabriel (b. Metz, 16 Aug 1863; d. Ploujean, Finistère, 17 Jul 1937). French composer-conductor. He studied at the Conservatoire with Frank and Massenet, and inherited the thoughtfulness of the one as much as the colour and emotion of the other. His works include comic operas and oratorio-like pieces (*La Croisade des enfants*, 1902). He was also conductor of the Concerts Colonne (1910–33).

Pierrot lunaire (Moonstruck Pierrot). Set of 21 songs by Schoenberg for sprechgesang voice and quintet (fl and pic, cl and b cl, vn and va, vc, pf), setting poems from Otto Erich Hartleben's German translation of the volume by the Belgian poet Albert Giraud. Keyless harmony, eruptive gestures and reminiscences express alienation, violence and nostalgia. The work was commissioned by an actress, Albertine Zehme, who first gave it in costume with Schoenberg conducting. It had a deep influence, not least on the composers who described it as 'the solar plexus of 20th-century music' (Stravinsky) and 'a superior cabaret' (Boulez). First performance: Berlin, 16 Oct 1912.

Pierrot Players. See FIRES OF LONDON.

Pierrot quintet. The instrumental ensemble of PIERROT LUNAIRE.

Pierson, Henry Hugo (b. Oxford, 12 Apr 1815; d. Leipzig, 28 Jan 1873). British–German composer. After Harrow and Cambridge he continued his studies in Germany and Prague, and settled in Germany. He wrote, with Romantic audacity, almost exclusively in vocal genres, producing operas, oratorios and smaller choral works, and nearly 100 songs.

piffaro. SHAWM, especially as played by shepherds from the Abruzzi in Italian cities at Christmas time. Handel imitated the effect in the pastoral symphony of *Messiah*.

Pijper, Willem (Frederik Johannes) (b. Zeist, 8 Sep 1894; d. Leidschendam, 18 Mar 1947). Dutch composer. He studied with Johan Wagenaar in Utrecht (1911–16), then taught at the conservatories of Amsterdam (1918–30) and Rotterdam (1930–47). In 1920 he introduced a technique of composing works or movements out of cells of three or four notes in a somewhat Bartókian manner. His works include an opera (*Halewijn*, 1933), three symphonies (1917, 1921, 1926), songs and chamber pieces.

Pilkington, Francis (b. c.1570; d. Chester, 1638). English composer. He took the Oxford BMus at Lincoln College in 1595 and from 1602 was associated with Chester Cathedral as a musician and, latterly, priest. His works, though, are overwhelmingly secular: madrigals, lute songs ('Rest sweet nimphes'), instrumental pieces.

Pini di Roma (Pines of Rome). Symphonic poem by Respighi, including a recording of a nightingale. The pines heard, in four sections, are those of the Villa Borghese, near the catacombs, on the Janiculum hill and on the Appian Way. First performance: Rome, 14 Dec 1924.

Pinto, George Frederick (b. Lambeth, 25 Sep 1785; d. Chelsea, 23 Mar 1806). British composer, the great-grandson of a Neapolitan immigrant. He studied the violin with Salomon and packed quite a career as a violinist, pianist and composer into his brief life. His works include piano and violin music, and songs.

Pintscher, Matthias (b. Marl, 29 Jan 1971). German composer, a pupil of Klebe and Trojahn, and protégé of Henze. His opera *Thomas Chatterton* (f.p. Dresden, 1998) and other works show a compelling manner of making the orchestra speak with an intensity and subtlety recalling Berg.

Pinza, Ezio (Fortunato) (b. Rome, 18 May 1892; d. Stamford, Conn., 9 May 1957). Italian lyric bass of warmly appealing sound and fine address, noted in Verdi and as Mozart's Figaro and Don Giovanni. He studied at the Bologna Conservatory and began his career in Italy, before becoming a regular at the Met (1926–48) and afterwards on Broadway (notably in *South Pacific*, 1949).

pipa. Chinese lute.

pipe. (1) Simple woodwind instrument, a reed or wooden tube with holes.

(2) Sounding element of an organ.

Pipelare, Matthaeus (b. c.1450; d. c.1515). Netherlandish composer of masses, motets and secular songs, based in Antwerp. He made lively use of esoteric techniques, and of exciting syncopation in some works. His name indicates that he or an ancestor was a piper.

Pique Dame. See *The* QUEEN OF SPADES.

piston. The moving part of a valve in a brass instrument. In French the term applies to the whole valve: hence *cor à pistons* (valve horn), etc.

Piston, Walter (Hamor) (b. Rockland, Maine, 20 Jan 1894; d. Belmont, Mass., 12 Nov 1976). US composer whose works have the ease and fluency of US–Parisian neoclassicism. He started out in architecture before studying at Harvard (1919–24) and with Boulanger and Dukas in Paris (1924–6). After that he returned to Harvard, where he taught until 1960. He wrote textbooks on *Harmony* (1941), *Counterpoint* (1947) and *Orchestration* (1955), and numbered Carter and Bernstein among his pupils.

Howard Pollack *Harvard Composers* (1992)

Orchestral: Symphony No.1, 1937; No.2, 1943; No.3, 1947; No.4, 1950; No.5, 1954; No.6, 1955; No.7, 1960; No.8, 1965; Double Piano Concerto, 1959; Violin Concerto No.1, 1939; No.2, 1960; Viola Concerto, 1957; Flute Concerto, 1971; Clarinet Concerto, 1967; Concerto, str qt, wind, perc, 1976; *The Incredible Flutist* (ballet), 1938; etc.

Chamber: String Sextet, 1964; Piano Quintet, 1949; Flute Quintet, 1942; Wind Quintet, 1956; String Quartet No.1, 1933; No.2, 1935; No.3, 1947; No.4, 1951; No.5, 1962; Piano Quartet, 1964; etc.

pit. Part of a theatre, especially an opera house, that is before, below and usually partly beneath the stage, to accommodate the orchestra and conductor. Wagner's Bayreuth Festspielhaus (1876) helped make the pit almost ubiquitous; previously the orchestra had been seated at the same level as the stalls audience.

pitch. Quality of a sound dependent on its FREQUENCY of vibration. For example, in modern concert tuning a vibration of 440 Hz corresponds to A on the treble staff, though the sensation of pitch can be slightly affected by timbre, loudness and context. The faster the vibration, the higher the pitch.

The correlation between frequency and pitch has been different at different times and places, as may be determined by measuring the frequencies produced by old organs and tuning forks, or by consulting documents, such as the diagram in Praetorius's *De organographia* (1619) showing the lengths of organ pipes that would give specified pitches. Evidence of these kinds suggests a range of pitch standards covering fully a tritone, from an organ of 1610 in Worcester Cathedral (A at about 360 Hz) to a medieval example in Halberstadt Cathedral (A at about 510 Hz).

Standardization became inevitable with the rise of string instruments (which could not be tuned too high, or else the strings would break) and of ensemble music (requiring, for example, strings and a keyboard to have the same tuning). Those developments happened in the 17th century, but still the pitch level varied from place to place, being particularly low in 18th-century Rome and France. The A at 440 Hz was adopted by the International Organization for Standardization in 1955.

pitch class. Name for pitch irrespective of register. For example, 'pitch class C' means any C. This octave equivalence is implicit in tonal music: a piece in C major can cadence on to a C major chord in any register (within limits). But the term was not introduced until the 1950s, and then by Babbitt, with reference to 12-note serial music. The concept had been implicit in such music from the first, since the 12-note series was for Schoenberg a series of pitch classes rather than of distinct pitches.

pitchpipe. Wooden pipe with a plunger, marked to give specific pitches. Such pipes were used in Britain to give choirs their starting notes in churches lacking an organ or band.

Pittsburgh. US city musically renowned for its symphony orchestra, which was founded in 1896, though inoperative in 1910–26. Its music directors have included Herbert (1898–1904), Reiner (1938–48), William Steinberg (1952–76), Previn (1976–85), Maazel (1988–96) and Jansons (from 1997).

più (It.). More, as in *più andante*.

Pixis, Johann Peter (b. Mannheim, 10 Feb 1788; d.

Baden-Baden, 22 Dec 1874). German pianist-composer. His father, an organist, took him and his brother, a violinist, on a concert tour in 1796. The family moved in 1806 to Vienna, where he studied with Albrechtsberger and met Beethoven and Schubert. He settled in Paris in 1824 as one of the supreme virtuosos, spinning off brilliant variation sets and chamber pieces. In 1840 he retired to Baden-Baden.

Pizzetti, Ildebrando (b. Parma, 20 Sep 1880; d. Rome, 13 Feb 1968). Italian composer, who reacted against Puccinian emotional rhetoric. He studied at the Parma Conservatory (1895–1901), where Giovanni Tebaldini encouraged him in the direction of Renaissance music. This duly influenced the arioso style of his operas and of his fine unaccompanied *Requiem*. His long career as a teacher took him from the conservatories of Florence (1908–24) and Milan (1924–36) to the Accademia di Santa Cecilia in Rome (1936–58).

Guido M. Gatti *Ildebrando Pizzetti* (1951, '1979)

Operas: *Fedra* (Gabriele d'Annunzio), 1909–12, f.p. Milan, 1915; *Dèbora e Jaéle* (Pizzetti), 1917–21, f.p. Milan, 1922; *Assassinio nella cattedrale* (Pizzetti, after T.S. Eliot), 1956–7, f.p. Milan, 1958; etc.
Other works: *Messa di requiem*, ch, 1922; other choral music, orchestral pieces, chamber music, songs, etc.

pizzicato (It.), abbreviated *pizz.* Plucked; a direction for string instruments that are normally bowed. The effect was first notated in Monteverdi's *Combattimento di Tancredi e Clorinda* (1624). Paganini introduced left-hand pizzicato, in combination with right-hand bowing. Bartók added pizzicato glissandos and a snap pizzicato in which the string is plucked so hard it bounces back against the fingerboard. Cowell pioneered pizzicato on the piano.

plagal cadence [amen cadence]. Cadence from the sudominant chord to the tonic, both normally in root position.

plagal mode. MODE with an AMBITUS from a fourth below to a fifth above the final, where the corresponding 'authentic mode' will have the final as its lowest note. For example, the Dorian mode (D–E–F–G–A–B–C–D, with D as final) has as its plagal relative the Hypodorian (A–B–C–D–E–F–G–A, but still with D as final).

plainsong. The ancient music of the Christian church; the corpus of unaccompanied melodies to which nearly all parts of the liturgy were sung.

Often the term is applied more specifically to the 'Gregorian' chant of the Western church.

Like Christianity itself, plainsong emerged from the synagogue and was marked by the cultures through which it passed: Greek, Roman and barbarian (Gothic, Frankish, etc.). But its history is hard to reconstruct, for there was no notation until c.900, and none that can now be read unambiguously until the 11th century. By that time many different ecclesiastical traditions had developed, each with its own liturgy and corresponding chant: Byzantine, Georgian, Armenian, Coptic (in Egypt), Russian and – in Western Europe – Gregorian, with some local forms (notably Ambrosian in Milan and Mozarabic in Toledo). Other traditions, such as Celtic, had come and gone.

Gregorian chant owes its name to the legend that it was dictated directly to Pope Gregory the Great (r. 590–604) by the Holy Ghost, but it is both older, in having origins that recede into the unrecorded early centuries of Christian worship, and newer, in that it did not become the almost universal language of the Western church until two centuries later, when much of the territory came under the control of Charlemagne. The achievement of musical uniformity probably began in 754, when Charlemagne's father, Pippin III, received a lengthy visit from Pope Stephen II, though it is not at all clear how much of the eventually standard chant came from Rome, how much from the Franks, and how much from the century and a half before notation began to give the music a fixed form.

The texts of chants, and later the notes as well, are found in liturgical books of various kinds, including mass books, antiphonals and tropers. Classed by usage, chants include mass propers (the items PROPER to a particular Sunday or festival), antiphons, litanies and hymns. In terms of musical style, they fall into other categories. At the simplest, texts may be sung to a reciting note (collects, lessons) or intoned to simple formulae (psalms). Hymns generally have syllabic tunes, repeated from verse to verse. Other chants have small groupings as well as single notes for their syllables; a group of two or three notes may be represented by a NEUME in chant notation. Many graduals take highly elaborate melodies, in which a syllable may be stretched over a long and brilliant flow of notes, numbering up to several hundred.

Chants also varied in how they were performed, whether by a soloist or restricted ensemble of highly trained singers (as would be implied by the most ornate melodies), by a full monastic choir, by a choir in two parts singing antiphonally, or in the 'question-answer' form of responsorial singing between a soloist and a choir. Antiphonal and responsorial forms were both taken over from Jewish practice, as, of course, was the chanting of psalms, from which so many mass propers derived. At the same time the modes of plainsong may be an inheritance from the Greek world.

The body of plainsong transmitted around the empire under Charlemagne was possibly restricted to 650 chants, mostly mass propers. Though it was the desire for homogeneity that prompted notation, the ability to write music down paradoxically stimulated an extremely non-homogeneous flowering of composed music, beginning with an abundance of new chants in the 9th, 10th and 11th centuries and continuing with polyphony. There was a practical reason for adding chants, for the offices of new and local saints as Latin Christianity spread northwards and eastwards, but at the same time existing offices were being expanded in various ways: by troping (inserting parenthetic lines in a chant, sometimes to the overwhelming of the original), adding musical flourishes or introducing new items, especially sequences.

Such luxuriant growths were fiercely pruned as a result of the musical pronouncements coming from the later sessions of the Council of Trent in 1562–3, and since music could now be printed, this second phase of homogenizing moved rapidly and decisively. But it was a homogenizing only within one branch of the church, for Protestants were already developing their own kinds of chant and hymn.

From the anonymous chant compilers and devisers of the Carolingian period to Mozart and Haydn at the end of the 18th century, a great many composers worked in the service of the church, were exposed routinely to plainsong, had to write in the context of it and often would incorporate plainsong melodies. Polyphonic music began with the addition of new lines above chants, and fragments of chant were still being incorporated into sacred music by Palestrina and Monteverdi. Even in the 20th century plainsong could be a source of musical material (Davies) or a model of unaccompanied melody (Messiaen).

By then a further reform of plainsong had taken place, starting in the late 19th century, when scholar monks at the Abbey of Solesmes in northern France began to issue new editions. The renovations of the Second Vatican Council (1962–5), which displaced Latin as the universal language of the Catholic Church, compromised the position of plainsong in the liturgy, but perhaps contributed to making it an object of musical and spiritual contemplation in its own right.

See also AMBROSIAN CHANT; MOZARABIC CHANT; OLD ROMAN CHANT.

David Hiley *Western Plainchant: A Handbook* (1993); Richard L. Crocker *An Introduction to Gregorian Chant* (2000)

Planets, The. Orchestral suite by Holst comprising movements for the planets then known, with their astrological attributes, arranged in order of distance from the earth: 1 *Mars, the Bringer of War*, 2 *Venus, the Bringer of Peace*, 3 *Mercury, the Winged Messenger*, 4 *Jupiter, the Bringer of Jollity*, 5 *Saturn, the Bringer of Old Age*, 6 *Uranus, the Magician*, 7 *Neptune, the Mystic*. First performance: London, 29 Sep 1918.

Colin Matthews added a *Pluto* in 2000. Mattheson records a lost suite of planet suites – seven, one for each heavenly body – for keyboard by Buxtehude.

Planquette, (Jean) Robert (b. Paris, 31 Jul 1848; d. Paris, 28 Jan 1903). French composer. He trained at the Paris Conservatoire and was responsible for one of the most successful French operettas, *Les Cloches de Corneville* (1877).

Platée. Comic opera by Rameau to a libretto by Adrien-Joseph Le Valois d'Orville. Jupiter (bass) prepares for a marriage with the ill-favoured marsh nymph Platae (haute-contre; a drag role) and has his wife Juno (soprano) interrupt the proceedings, so bringing mockery on herself for her jealousy. The work was incongruously given as a wedding entertainment for the dauphin Louis and his Spanish princess bride. First performance: Versailles, 31 Mar 1745.

platform. Raised part of a concert venue, equivalent to the stage in a theatre, on which the performance takes place.

Plato (b. Athens, *c*.429 BC; d. Athens, 347 BC). Greek philosopher. He was influential on later generations for his views of music as a civilizing influence on the individual and in society – but also as a potentially harmful one, therefore requiring careful judgement in the choice of modes and musicians.

Platti, Giovanni Benedetto (b. ?Venice, ?*c*.1690; d. Würzburg, 11 Jan 1763). Italian composer and instrumentalist, the son of a musician at St Mark's in Venice. Attached from 1722 to the prince-bishop's court in Würzburg, he was a striking master of the pre-Classical style, writing church music, concertos (notably for harpsichord and cello) and sonatas exploiting the new piano.

playbill. Printed sheet giving details of a concert or theatrical performance, published daily by the management and available both outside and inside the auditorium. The playbill was in existence before operas and public concerts, and survived to the 1860s, when it began to turn into the PROGRAMME (2).

player piano. See PIANOLA.

Playford, John (b. Norwich, 1623; d. London, 1686/7). English music publisher, active in the trade in London from 1651. He published instructional volumes (notably *The English Dancing Master*, with tunes for country dances), devotional books and collections of songs and instrumental pieces. The business was continued by his son, Henry Playford (*c*.1657–*c*.1707), who brought out the posthumous Purcell collection *Orpheus Brittanicus*.

playing score. Score from which a musician plays in a chamber composition, instead of using a part. Pianists in Classical–Romantic quartets and quintets customarily play from the score. Many chamber works written since the mid 20th century would be impracticable unless all the musicians did so.

Play of Daniel, The (*Ludus Danielis*). Early 13th-century liturgical drama for Christmastide, with music, from Beauvais Cathedral.

pleasure gardens. Places of recreation in London, where music would be among the entertainments on offer. The most famous were Marylebone (*c*.1659–1778), Vauxhall (in Lambeth, 1661–1859), Ranelagh (in Chelsea, 1741–1803) and SADLER'S WELLS.

plectrum. Object of natural material (wood, ivory, bone, quill, etc.) or plastic made to pluck a string or strings. Plectra are often used in playing lutes, guitars, mandolins and zithers, and are part of the action of harpsichords. They are seldom applied to instruments of the violin and viol families or to harps.

plein jeu (Fr.). Full registration, a standard formula in French Classical organ music, implying main and mixture stops, often in contrast with the more spectacular *grand jeu*.

Pletnev, Mikhail (b. Archangel, 14 Apr 1957). Russian pianist. Born of musical parents, he studied from 1974 at the Moscow Conservatory with Yakov Flier and Lev Vlasenko, and won the

Tchaikovsky Competition in 1978. In 1990, with government support, he formed the Russian National Orchestra, with which he embarked on a new career as a conductor, touring internationally and making outstanding recordings of Russian music. At the same time he maintained and even enlarged his great strengths as a pianist, in particular, his dazzling technical skill and musical decisiveness. His repertory ranges from Scarlatti and Bach to Prokofiev and transcriptions of his own.

Pleyel, Ignace Joseph (b. Ruppersthal, 18 Jun 1757; d. Paris, 14 Nov 1831). Austrian composer, piano maker and publisher, active in Paris from 1795. He studied with Haydn from around 1772, and worked in Austria and Naples before settling in Strasbourg in the mid 1780s. There he married and produced a quantity of string quartets and quintets. The French Revolution drove him to London (1791–2), his visit bringing him back into contact with his teacher: the two men dined together and attended each other's concerts. He then returned to Strasbourg, where he was able to buy a large country house with the profits from his London concerts, before moving to Paris to open a music shop, piano-making firm and publishing house. His publications included the earliest miniature scores (1802, four Haydn symphonies) and a complete edition of Haydn's quartets. In 1805 he and his son, Camille (1788–1855), his successor in the business, returned to Vienna to see Haydn and hear Beethoven. His works, enormously popular in their time, are almost entirely instrumental: symphonies, concertos, chamber pieces.

Pleyel. French firm of instrument makers founded by Ignace Pleyel in 1807. Chopin favoured their pianos. Later they also made harps (see CHROMATIC HARP), percussion instruments and harpsichords.

Pli selon pli (Fold by Fold). Work by Boulez for soprano, singing words by Mallarmé, with an orchestra tilted towards tuned percussion. There are five movements, performable separately or in different combinations: *Don* (1960–62, rev 1989–90), *Improvisations sur Mallarmé I–III* (*I–II* 1957, *I* orchd 1962, *III* 1959, rev 1983–4) and *Tombeau* (1959). Some of the revisions are documented in the composer's recordings (1969, 1981, 2001). First performance: Cologne, 13 Jun 1960.

pluralism. The appearance of different styles within a work, sometimes simultaneously. This was Bernd Alois Zimmermann's term for COLLAGE.

pneumatic action. Style of organ building in which the connection from key to pallet is by means of a tube of air.

pochette. KIT.

poco (It.). Little, slightly, as in *un poco più mosso* (a little more movement). There are diminutive forms *pochetto* and *pochettino*, and, at the bottom of the scale, the superlative *pochissimo*.

podium. Dais on which a conductor stands, elevated a foot or two, the better to be seen by the musicians (and audience). Some works since the 1960s with innovatory seating plans may require podia for instrumentalists; Birtwistle's *Verses for Ensembles* is an example.

Podles, Ewa (b. Warsaw, 26 April 1952). Polish–US mezzo-soprano, formidably deep, strong and immediate in her utterance. She trained and started singing in Warsaw, made her debut at the Met in *Rinaldo* in 1984, and has appeared widely in Handel and Rossini, though her forceful projection is perhaps most extraordinary in recital.

Poe, Edgar Allan (b. Boston, 19 Jan 1809; d. Baltimore, 7 Oct 1849). US writer, whose tales expose darkness with clarity. Translated by Baudelaire and Mallarmé, his writings enjoyed a vogue in Paris, admirers including Debussy (who planned a pair of Poe operas) and Ravel. Others attracted to the cold flame have included Rachmaninoff, Holbrooke, Argento, Glass and Staud.

poem. Term introduced into music by Liszt, as part of his formulation 'symphonic poem', and used in titles of works by Chausson, Scriabin, Varèse, etc.

Poème. Work for violin and orchestra by Chausson, which he wrote for Ysaÿe and which was based on Turgenev's story *The Song of Triumphant Love*. First performance: Paris, 4 Apr 1897.

Poème de l'amour et de la mer (Poem of Love and the Sea). Work for mezzo and orchestra by Chausson, setting three poems by Maurice Bouchor.

Poème de l'extase, Le (The Poem of Ecstasy). Orchestral work by Scriabin, expressing his growing faith in art's power to cause spiritual exhilaration. First performance: New York, 10 Dec 1908.

Poème électronique (Electronic Poem). Tape piece by Varèse, made from recordings of percussion instruments, a solo voice, a musical performance (of the composer's *Etude pour 'Espace'*), electronic tones and natural sounds. It was commissioned to be heard within the Philips pavilion designed by Le Corbusier for the 1958 Exposition. First performance: Brussels, 2 May 1958.

Poèmes pour Mi. Song cycle by Messiaen to his own words, a hymn to marital love, Mi being his pet name for his wife. The work is for a big dramatic soprano with piano or orchestra. First performance: Paris, 28 Apr 1937 (pf version).

Poet and Peasant. Popular overture by Suppé.

Poglietti, Alessandro (b. ?Tuscany; d. Vienna, Jul 1683). Italian organist-composer. Resident in Vienna by 1661, he was highly esteemed and honoured by both emperor and pope. He excelled in strict counterpoint and the imitation at the keyboard of other sounds (birds, wind and string instruments, battles), both talents being on display in his extended suite *Rossignolo* (1677). He died in the Turkish siege.

Pogorelich, Ivo (b. Belgrade, 20 Oct 1958). Yugoslav pianist, who trained in Moscow from 1970. His principal teacher at the conservatory (1975–8) was Aliza Kezeradze, whom he married. His elimination before the finals of the 1980 Chopin Competition caused Argerich to resign from the jury. It also brought him worldwide publicity and some controversy, since his renewed Romantic style was seen by some as narcissism, by others as formed by spectacular technique. His appearances and recordings have, since the early 1990s, been infrequent.

Pohjola's Daughter (*Pohjolan tytär*). Symphonic fantasia by Sibelius, depicting an episode from the Kalevala, the Finnish national epic. The magician Väinämöinen makes vain attempts on the impossible tasks set him by Pohjola's heartless daughter, and eventually goes on his way. First performance: St Petersburg, 29 Dec 1906.

poi (It.). Then, as in *poi la coda* (then the coda).

point. (1) Term used in England in the 16th and 17th centuries for a motif suitable for contrapuntal imitation.

(2) The end of the bow away from the hand.

(3) Isolated note in a musical composition. The example of Webern encouraged many young European composers around 1950 to work with single notes, serially organized. Total serialism, in particular, tended to produce such textures, as in Messiaen's *Mode de valeurs et d'intensités*, Boulez's *Structures Ia* and Stockhausen's significantly titled *Punkte* (Points, 1952).

point d'orgue (Fr., organ point). PAUSE.

pointillism. Term borrowed from art history, where it is used of Seurat's technique of covering areas with dots of primary colour, and applied to the 1950s style of composition in points – though Ligeti's micropolyphony is closer to Seurat in effect, creating a generalized radiance from many tiny jostling contrasts.

polacca (It.). Polish. The marking *alla polacca* may indicate polonaise rhythm (Bach's Brandenburg Concerto No.1) or, more generally, an exuberant delivery (finale of Sibelius's Violin Concerto).

Poland. The country was Christianized in the 10th century and remained Catholic after the Renaissance. Marenzio was among the Italian composers who visited in the Renaissance and Baroque periods, when native talent also flourished. But the first Polish composers to make an international reputation did not come until the first half of the 19th century: Moniuszko, Wieniawski and, of course, Chopin. By that time Poland had ceased to exist as a state, having been partitioned by Russia, Prussia and Austria. The restoration of an independent Poland in 1918 owed much to a musician, Paderewski, even at a time when he and his colleagues were being musically challenged by a new generation, led by Szymanowski. Subsequent Polish composers have included Koffler, Lutosławski, Panufnik and Penderecki. The sound of Poland can also be heard in Polish dances – especially polonaises and mazurkas – written by composers having no connection with the country.

Polignac, Princesse Edmond de (b. Yonkers, NY, 8 Jan 1865; d. London, 26 Nov 1943). US–French patron, originally Winnaretta Singer, daughter of the sewing-machine manufacturer Isaac Singer. She married Prince Edmond de Polignac (1834–1901) in 1893, and lived on in Paris after his death, supporting Stravinsky, Falla, Satie, Rubinstein, Horowitz and many other musicians. Proust attended her salons.

Polish. Name given to Tchaikovsky's Third Symphony.

politics. Music may have served a function in enhancing the prestige of chieftains, warriors and priests right from the distant past, but its overt use to convey political messages had to await the public discussion and availability (albeit restricted) of political choices, which came about in the 18th century. Morale-boosting songs were important in the conduct of the American Revolution, and still more so the French ('La Marseillaise', 1792). French Revolutionaries also appreciated the continuing usefulness of music to consolidate changes in society and mentality. New ceremonials and celebrations used elements of military music – march rhythm, wind bands – to marshal the people, and though such events only briefly replaced Christian worship, their influence persisted in the music of Beethoven and Berlioz. Beethoven's ideals of human freedom and collegiality, as expressed in *Fidelio* and the Ninth Symphony, were an adaptation of revolutionary principles at their finest. Yet those ideals were readily redirected in the interests of the bourgeois parties that assumed power in many European countries in the 1830s and 1840s, when Beethoven's works were beginning to be installed as cornerstones of the repertory.

Wagner's career, from being an active supporter of the 1849 Dresden revolution to becoming pronely supported by Ludwig II of Bavaria 15 years later, is typical of the defusing of musicians' political engagement around the mid 19th century. Socialist ideals were replaced by nationalist ones, especially in Italy (with Verdi a standard-bearer for unification), Russia and the Austro-Hungarian territories.

That changed during the catastrophe of nationalism that was the First World War. Marx had little to prescribe for the cultural life of revolutionary societies, and so Russia, after 1917, had to find its own way. There was one certainty: things would be different. Beyond that, two views emerged, and two organizations to promote them were established. The Association for Contemporary Music (ACM) welcomed anything new in music as appropriate to a new society; hence the opportunities available in the 1920s to the futurists and the young Shostakovich. For the Russian Association for Proletarian Music (RAPM), on the other hand, music in a socialist state would have to be comprehensible to everyone, which meant favouring choral songs and a musical language rooted in the age of Borodin and Tchaikovsky. In 1931 the ACM collapsed, and though the success of the RAPM was moderated by the foundation the next year of the Union of Soviet Composers, earlier adventurousness was suppressed in the interests of SOCIALIST REALISM. In 1936

Shostakovich was criticized for formalism (in Russian terms the opposite of realism), and the charge was repeated in 1948, when Andrey Zhdanov, the Central Committee official responsible for ideological work, instituted a period of severe artistic repression that lasted until after Stalin's death in 1953 and applied as much to other countries in Russia's sphere of influence.

Nazi Germany's cultural policy was founded on racial rather than aesthetic and social considerations, yet the effect was much the same, since the most advanced music in 1933–45 was associated with Schoenberg, a Jew. Many musicians left Germany and its satellites, including not only Schoenberg but also Bartók and Hindemith. Those who remained, such as Strauss, Webern, Furtwängler and Karajan, could claim to be trying to ameliorate the situation in which they found themselves.

Curiously, a need for political alignment was felt in the 1930s and 1940s by composers outside those countries where engagement or obedience was enforced. In the USA, for example, the left-leaning philosophy and musical practice of Copland would have fitted him quite well for membership in the Union of Soviet Composers. After the Second World War, though, the communist and capitalist countries developed musically in quite separate ways. The western European and US avant-garde movements of the 1950s and 1960s, as represented by such composers as Boulez, Stockhausen, Xenakis, Cage, Babbitt and Carter, had very little echo on the other side of the Iron Curtain, except when an accommodation to liberal capitalism was in progress, as in Poland in the 1960s (Lutosławski, Penderecki). Yet many avant-garde composers were leftist or anarchist, and some of them took the ACM line that music could espouse political ideals by its form and nature, without taking on an explicit verbal message. Nono, whose communist sympathies sustained him in consistent exploration from the 1950s to the 1980s, found his audience in western Europe (where communism was a dream still held), not in the Soviet Union (where it had become a cynical mask). The precipitate collapse of communism in 1989–91 left voices of musical and political dissent largely directionless.

polka (probably from the Czech *polska*, a Polish girl). A lively dance in 2/4, which originated in Bohemia and became one of the most popular ballroom dances of the 19th century. There are examples by the Strauss family, Smetana and Stravinsky.

Pollini, Maurizio (b. Milan, 5 Jan 1942). Italian

pianist, remarkable for the thoughtfulness of his playing – for his ability to show how a composition is made, and to make music of the showing. His technique is extraordinary, but he can be impatient with surface beauty. Since winning the Chopin Competition in 1960 (he had left the Milan Conservatory the year before) he has been at the international forefront, with a repertory extending from Beethoven, Schumann and Chopin through Debussy and Schoenberg to Boulez's Second Sonata, some Stockhausen pieces and works written for him by Nono (*Como una ola, ... sofferte onde serene ...*) and Sciarrino. He has also conducted Rossini operas and organized concert series for the Salzburg Festival (1997, 1999) and Carnegie Hall (1999–2000), involving himself and other musicians in programmes ranging from medieval or Renaissance music through standard repertoire to the present.

polo. Spanish song-dance in moderate triple time, marked by syncopations and shouts. Bizet quoted an example by García in *Carmen*, and there are polos by Falla and other Spanish composers.

polonaise. Polish dance in stately triple time, exemplified in compositions by W.F. Bach, Schubert, Chopin and Tchaikovsky (*Sleeping Beauty* and *Eugene Onegin*).

Polovtsian Dances. Ballet in the second act of Borodin's *Prince Igor*, dynamic and sensuous, with chorus, and with oriental flavours appropriate to the encampment of people from Central Asia. The music's exotic sex appeal conquered Paris during the first (1909) Ballets Russes season.

polychoral. Having more than one group of singers or (since a choir can be instrumental) players. Such music was introduced by Willaert and others in Venice in the first half of the 16th century and spread from there during the next several decades, being specially prized in Germany and Austria in the early Baroque. Music for double chorus, implying two four-part groups facing one another, was an inevitable outcome of antiphonal plainsong and, indeed, of chancel architecture. The Venetian–Baroque tradition often implied several groups disposed in different parts of the building, as in works by Giovanni Gabrieli, Monteverdi, Michael Praetorius and Biber.

Polyhymnia [Polymnia]. The muse of hymns, dance and mime, sometimes shown with a barbitos (type of lyre).

polymetre. The simultaneous presence of different metres in different musical lines. This is not uncommon in 14th-century song, but it then disappeared – apart from such special cases as the Act I finale of *Don Giovanni*, where three different dances are in progress – until the 20th century. There are many instances in Ives, Carter, Messiaen, Stockhausen, etc.

polyphonic. Exemplifying polyphony.

polyphonic song. Secular vocal composition of the 14th and 15th centuries, normally for three or four voices and in one of the fixed forms: BALLADE, RONDEAU and VIRELAI in France, BALLATA in Italy. The almost invariable subject was courtly love, i.e. a love that is experienced as intense physical desire that cannot be satisfied and that therefore remains pure. The term can also be applied more loosely to later forms, such as the MADRIGAL.

polyphony (from the Gk *polyphonia*, that which has many sounds or voices). Music in many parts, or the art of writing such music, or an example of such music. The term has been in continuous use since 1536, though it has come to be restricted to music in which the parts have some aural independence (as they do not in homophony) but work together in a necessary fashion (as they do not in heterophony). The distinction in meaning from 'counterpoint' is imprecise; the latter term tends to be associated with diatonic harmony (Bach, Brahms), whereas polyphony is more likely to be earlier (Machaut) or later, from the period when the word began to be used in titles (Boulez's *Polyphonie X*, Ligeti's *San Francisco Polyphony*). Polyphony is also found in non-Western cultures, including African and Georgian.

polyrhythm. Term embracing POLYMETRE and the more traditional momentary conflict with the prevailing metre, i.e. CROSS-RHYTHM.

polystylistic. Incorporating different styles of composition. The term was introduced by Schnittke to describe his COLLAGE practice in the early 1970s.

polytextual, polytextuality. Terms for music with two or more simultaneous texts, normally restricted to medieval motets, though the phenomenon is common in operatic ensembles.

polytonality. Term for music adhering to more than one key at a time. Music in two simultaneous keys exhibits BITONALITY, and while tritonality and further sorts are hard to contemplate, a more fluctuating and kaleidoscopic sense of tonalities in play can be described as polytonal.

Pommer (Ger.). Bass shawm.

Pomp and Circumstance. Subtitle of a set of five marches by Elgar, quoting from *Othello* ('pride, pomp, and circumstance of glorious war', Act 3, scene 3): No.1, D, 1901; No.2, A minor, 1901; No.3, C minor, 1904; No.4, G, 1907; No.5, C, 1929–30. He arranged the middle section of the first to words by A.C. Benson, 'Land of Hope and Glory'.

Ponce (Cuéllar), Manuel (María) (b. Fresnillo, Zacatecas, 8 Dec 1882; d. Mexico City, 24 Apr 1948). Mexican composer. Brought up in Aguascalientes, he was supported by his brother Antonio while studying in Mexico City, Bologna and Berlin. He returned to Mexico to teach, compose and study folk music, apart from a period when he had lessons with Dukas in Paris (1925–33). His works consist mostly of songs and pieces for piano or guitar, in Hispanic style.

Ponchielli, Amilcare (b. Paderno, near Cremona, 31 Aug 1834; d. Milan, 17 Jan 1886). Italian composer, second only to Verdi as a master of opera in his time. He studied at the Milan Conservatory (1843–54), spent most of the next two decades in Cremona and returned to his alma mater as professor of composition in 1880, his pupils including Puccini. He owed his fame to four works produced in Milan in the 1870s: *I promessi sposi* (1872, a revision of his first opera, which had been presented in Cremona 16 years before), the ballet *Le due gemelle* (f.p. La Scala, Milan, 1872), the opera *I lituani* (f.p. La Scala, 1874); and, most especially, *La* GIOCONDA. Boito's libretto for this last work provided for an ironic return to grand opera, though the piece has almost dropped from the repertory. He also wrote church music, songs, band pieces and piano duets.

Pons, Lily (Alice Joséphine) (b.. Draguignan, 12 Apr 1898; d. Dallas, 13 Feb 1976). French–US coloratura soprano of pure tone and agility. She studied the piano at the Paris Conservatoire and singing in New York with Giovanni Zenatello. After starting her career in France she joined the Met, where she gave her debut (1931) and farewell (1958) performances as Lucia.

Ponselle, Rosa (Melba) (b. Meriden, Conn., 22 Jan 1897; d. Green Spring Valley, Maryland, 25 May 1981). US soprano, vocally splendid, expressive and polished. Born to Italian immigrants and originally surnamed Ponzillo, she and her mezzo sister Carmela were encouraged by their mother and began singing in movie theatres and vaudeville. She was brought to the Met's attention by her coach, made an early and spectacular debut in *La forza del destino* with Caruso and De Luca (1918), and stayed with the company until 1937, singing a wide variety of roles from Donna Anna to Norma.

ponticello (It.). Bridge, on a string instrument. The marking *sul ponticello* indicates playing close to the bridge to produce an acid sound, an effect often found in music from Schoenberg onwards.

Poot, Marcel (b. Vilvoorde, near Brussels, 7 May 1901; d. Brussels, 12 Jun 1988). Belgian composer, a pupil of Gilson and an exponent of a lively, Prokofiev-like style. He worked as a music critic before becoming director of the Brussels Conservatory (1949–66). His compositions include six symphonies, concertos, other orchestral pieces (*Charlot*, 1926, suggested by Chaplin films; *Vrolijke Ouverture*, 1935) and chamber music.

Popov, Gavriil (Nikolayevich) (b. Novocherkassk, 12 Sep 1904; d. Repino, 17 Feb 1972). Russian composer, a radical in his youth, during and after his time at the Leningrad Conservatory (1922–30), where he studied with Shcherbachev. Works of this period include his Septet (1927) and First Symphony (1927–34); his Third, 'Heroic' Symphony for strings (1939–46) he dedicated to Shostakovich. In 1948 he was among those officially castigated (see POLITICS), and he accordingly drew in his horns in three more symphonies and other works.

Popp, Lucia (b. Uhorská Ves, 12 Nov 1939; d. Munich, 16 Nov 1993). Slovak–Austrian soprano, much esteemed for her silvery voice and charm. She studied at the conservatory in Bratislava, where she made her debut in 1962 as the Queen of the Night – the role that, the following year, made her a sensation at the Staatsoper in Vienna. Soon an international star, she sang for the first time at Covent Garden in 1966 and the Met in 1967. In the mid 1980s she began singing weightier roles, such as the Marschallin (*Rosenkavalier*); she was also a valued recitalist.

pops. LIGHT CLASSICS, as performed on BOSTON POPS and other programmes.

popular classics. Category supposing immediacy as well as breadth of appeal. Such works can usefully serve to introduce new listeners, and tend accordingly to be popular in terms more of record sales and radio playings than concert performances, as with Mozart's *Eine kleine Nachtmusik*, Tchaikovsky's *1812* and Serenade for strings, Rimsky-Korsakov's *Sheherazade* and Sibelius's *Karelia* suite.

popular music. Music generally modest in its aims – whether of amiability or rude force – as it is also in its dimensions, which are those of the song and the dance. The term arose in the 19th century, along with others of similar meaning: LIGHT MUSIC, SALON MUSIC, entertainment music (*Unterhaltungsmusik*).

Popular music is perhaps best identified not in aesthetic but in economic terms, as music that is expected to make a profit, unlike classical music (which has nearly always required financial support or amateur enthusiasm) and folk music (which exists outside the monetary economy). Accordingly, it did not exist before the rise of capitalist societies in Europe between the late 16th and the early 19th century. Its early forms, during this transitional period, would have to include the songs and dances of street and theatre musicians, and also the music to be heard in pleasure gardens. The most populous cities, Paris and London, naturally had such music first.

During the Classical period in Vienna, dance music was written by the most esteemed composers – Mozart, Haydn, Beethoven – but in the 1820s that changed, and specialist composers began to emerge, notably the Strauss family. Later in the century there were similar developments in London (Sullivan), Paris (Offenbach) and the USA (Foster), and by the 1890s a wide range of musical entertainment was available in dance halls, variety theatres, parks and operetta houses, the more genteel kind being spread much further in the form of sheet music. Still, serious composers kept pace: Brahms wrote waltzes, and the sounds of café and band music were overheard in the music of Mahler and Ives.

The triumph of recording after the First World War changed the game, and the new popular music grew from the ragtime of the early 1900s until it had reached, 50 years later, a global audience. Someone who heard Sousa's band as a child in New York, London or Paris could easily have witnessed this expansion, living through the entire careers of George Gershwin and Cole Porter to observe the enormous popularity of Elvis Presley and the Beatles in the 1960s.

Some reciprocity between art and entertainment persisted. Stravinsky and Barraqué were among composers to learn from JAZZ, while Frank Zappa admired Varèse. Also, various kinds of popular music developed qualities of artistic expertise and exploration coupled with audience connoisseurship – qualities characteristic of high art. Conversely, some composers rooted in the classical tradition won fame and fortune in the popular field, especially through scoring films, while others felt compelled (or really were compelled; see POLITICS) to find a simpler style in the hope of a wider audience. To some extent, these trends blurred the distinction between the popular music and classical, and occasional classical recordings have achieved sales on the scale of rock bands.

Nevertheless, classical music has retained its integrity and its importance largely by ignoring the criterion of commercial success that gives popular music its stimulus and its vitality. The challenge then becomes that of finding audiences outside the conditions of the marketplace.

Colin Larkin, ed. *The Virgin Encyclopedia of Popular Music* ('2002)

Porgy and Bess. Opera by Gershwin to a libretto by DuBose Heyward and Ira Gershwin after Heyward's novel. Among the poor blacks of Charleston, South Carolina, Porgy (bass-baritone) is a noble, generous man, tempest-tossed by the fickleness of his Bess (soprano), the male pride of Crown (baritone) and the tricks of Sportin' Life (tenor). Segregation is part of the story – and of the work's fate, for it falls between the categories of opera and Broadway show, being through-composed but having a string of hit numbers: 'Summertime'; 'I got plenty o' nuttin''; 'Bess, you is my woman'; 'It ain't necessarily so'; 'I loves you, Porgy'; etc. First performance: New York, 10 Oct 1935.

Porpora, Nicola (Antonio) (b. Naples, 17 Aug 1686; d. Naples, 3 Mar 1768). Italian composer. He studied at the Poveri conservatory in Naples from 1696, and set out on his career as an opera composer with *Agrippina* (f.p. Naples, 1708). His fame spread to Vienna, his works performed there including the serenata *Angelica* (1720); the words were by the young Metastasio, whose first important libretto this was. Porpora also began to make a name as a singing teacher, first at the San Onofrio conservatory in Naples (1715–21), where his pupils included Farinelli, then in Venice (1726–33). An invitation from the Opera of the Nobility, a new company planning to rival Handel, took him to London, where in two and a half years he wrote five operas and other works. He then shuttled between Venice and Naples for a decade and took posts in Dresden (1747–51) and Vienna before returning to Naples in 1760. His works consist almost exclusively of operas, oratorios and church music.

porrectus. Kind of NEUME.

portamento (It., carryingly). Continuous slide from one note to another, normally by a singer or string player. This is often a special effect, being introduced as such by Farina in his *Capriccio stravagante*. But it may also be a style generally applied to wider intervals, as recordings show it was among violinists of the early 20th century. The term GLISSANDO often implies a discontinuous slide, which string players may also achieve.

portative organ. Instrument that could be carried around strapped to the body, the right hand playing the keyboard while the left worked bellows. Depictions of such instruments are common in 15th-century art.

portato (It., carried). A bowstroke implying a re-emphasis of each note within a slur, producing a dragging effect.

Porter, (William) Quincy (b. New Haven, 7 Feb 1897; d. Bethany, Conn., 12 Nov 1966). US composer of smooth melodies moving purposefully through chromatic polyphony. He studied at Yale (1915–20), with d'Indy in Paris (1920) and with Bloch in New York and Cleveland, where he remained as a viola player and teacher before returning to Paris in 1928. From 1932 to 1965 he taught successively at Vassar College, the New England Conservatory and Yale.

Orchestral: Symphony No.1, 1934; No.2, 1962; Viola Concerto, 1948; Ukrainian Suite, str, 1925; Music for Strings, 1941; *The Desolate City*, bar, orch, 1950; *New England Episodes*, 1958
Other works: String Sextet on Slavic Folk Tunes, 1947; 9 string quartets, 2 violin sonatas, songs, incidental music

Porter, Walter (b. *c*.1590; buried London, 30 Nov 1659). English composer, possibly a pupil of Monteverdi. He was associated with the Chapel Royal under James I and Charles I, and indeed showed up-to-date Italian influence in his madrigals and sacred music.

portraits. The most widely reproduced visual images of musicians have less to do with their look than with their sound – or with the popular encapsulation of their sound: Beethoven determined and unkempt, Mozart gently smiling, Chopin gently melancholy, Stravinsky frontal and clear. Such images feature in many musical households, and certainly in the studios of performers and composers, as icons of tutelary deities: framed engravings, postcards pinned to a board, plaster busts on the piano. See also VISUAL ART.

Portugal (Portogal). Here, at the far west edge of Europe, Renaissance polyphony enjoyed a 17th-century sunset in the music of Manuel Cardoso and his contemporaries, who included the musician king João (John) IV. In the next century

Italian influence was strong, and Domenico Scarlatti and David Perez spent time in Lisbon, while Seixas was the most important native composer. Visitors in the later 20th century, commissioned by the Gulbenkian Foundation in the city, included Messiaen, Xenakis and Stockhausen.

Posaune (Ger., pl. *Posaunen*). Trombone. Also a 16' or 32' reed stop on an organ.

position. (1) Placement of the left hand on the fingerboard of a string instrument so as to reach certain notes. Positions are numbered from first (simplest and lowest) upwards. Fourth position on the violin was in use by the 1630s, seventh by the century's end.

(2) Placement of the trombone slide, which is progressively further extended from first position to seventh.

(3) Registral placement of notes in a chord. In close position they are maximally near, normally – in the case of diatonic harmony – with thirds between the notes. Chords in open position cover more registral space.

positive. A movable, but not portable, organ, or a comparable manual of a larger instrument (i.e. a CHAIR ORGAN).

posthorn. Brass instrument used by postillions on mail coaches to sound signals. Early examples were simple coiled horns, which could play only notes of the harmonic series. In the early 19th century crooks and valves were introduced. British posthorns (brass) and coach horns (copper) of that time were straight; the Sunday mail was still conveyed from London to Oxford by coach, plus coach horn, until 1914. There are parts for posthorn in Mozart's 'Posthorn' Serenade, in German dances by Mozart and Beethoven, and in Mahler's Third Symphony.

postlude. Closing movement or section.

postmodernism. Term introduced in the 1970s to denote a state of mind in which modernism no longer had to be accepted or countered but could be relegated, ironically, to the past. Postmodernist music could therefore reinstall tonality, as well as traditional forms and media, while remaining playfully ambiguous about their meaning. It could also combine elements from different traditions and periods. Once defined, postmodernism could be seen as a current in music that took in the neoclassicism of Stravinsky, and perhaps also that of Reger, even Brahms – even Mozart. It turned out to have been embraced, too, by such latterday modernists as Ligeti and Berio.

Glenn Watkins *Pyramids at the Louvre* (1994)

potentiometer. Electronic device allowing voltage (and so, for example, sound level) to be regulated.

potpourri (Fr.). Literally a rotten pot; a jar containing miscellaneous spices, vegetables, etc. The term was applied in 18th-century France to collections of songs, and later to gatherings of tunes from operas or other sources presented as light music for piano, band or orchestra.

Potter, (Philip) Cipriani (Hambly) (b. London, 3 Oct 1792; d. London, 26 Sep 1871). British composer and pianist, who was born into a musical family. He studied with Attwood, Crotch and Joseph Woelfl, and visited Beethoven in Vienna (1817–18). In 1819 he returned to England, where he gave the local premières of concertos by Mozart and Beethoven; he also taught and conducted. His compositions, almost all instrumental and completed before he was 45, include symphonies, piano concertos, Shakespeare overtures (*Antony and Cleopatra, Cymbeline, The Tempest*) and piano pieces (including 'Enigma' Variations, 'in the style of five eminent artists').

Poule, La (The Hen). Name given to Haydn's Symphony No.83, the second of his Paris symphonies, for the oboe's clucking in the first movement.

Poulenc, Francis (Jean Marcel) (b. Paris, 7 Jan 1899; d. Paris, 30 Jan 1963). French composer who, with superb talent, turned Stravinsky's irony into distinctly French modes of chic and charm. The scion of a wealthy family, he discovered how to do so when still a boy. Having heard *The Rite* in its first season, he began lessons with Ricardo Viñes in 1915, and through his teacher came into contact with Satie, Auric and others prominent in the Parisian avant-garde. Formal training in composition came only in 1921–4, when he had lessons with Koechlin. His early sonatas show him alert to Stravinsky's rapid development during the time of the Symphony of Wind Instruments and the Octet, while simultaneously he was following Cocteau's aesthetic in pouring popular references and sophisticated wit into his songs, notably *Cocardes*. He was a natural member of Les Six, and he kept up a Cocteauesque regard for style, elegance, classicism and suave modernity in his music of the 1920s and early 1930s. A sophisticated harmonic palette gave him the means for characteristic shifts that can be sly and seductive.

Shaken by the death of his fellow composer Ferroud in 1936, he made a pilgrimage to the shrine of Notre-Dame de Rocamadour and recovered his Catholic faith. The creative result was a sequence of sacred works, but without an essential change of voice. Gravity may even be, as in the Organ Concerto, a gambit to be tried on, playfully. Also notable among his later works are two short operas: the surreal comedy *Les Mamelles de Tirésias* and *La Voix humaine*, an extended solo scena in which the protagonist is talking on the telephone to her lover, discovering him to be, in fact, her ex-lover. Here Poulenc could explore his understanding of the heart; he had problems with the homosexual life, wanted to marry at one point, and fathered a child in 1946. The work further expresses his longstanding appreciation of Cocteau and his gift for fluent and touching vocal writing. He was the most applauded exponent of the *mélodie* after Debussy and Fauré, and appeared internationally in recital with Pierre Bernac, his companion from the mid 1930s to the end of the 1950s.

Benjamin Ivry *Francis Poulenc* (1996); Sidney Buckland and Myriam Chimenes, ed. *Francis Poulenc* (1999)

Operas: *Les Mamelles de Tirésias* (Poulenc, after Apollinaire), 1944, f.p. Paris, 1947; *Dialogues des carmélites* (Poulenc, after Bernanos), 1953, f.p. Milan, 1957; *La Voix humaine* (Cocteau), 1958, f.p. Paris, 1959

Other dramatic works: *Les Biches* (ballet), ch, orch, 1923; *Les Animaux modèles* (ballet), 1940–42; incidental music, film scores

Orchestral: *Pastourelle* for L'EVENTAIL DE JEANNE, 1927; *Concert champêtre*, hpd, orch, 1927–8; *Aubade*, pf, chbr orch, 1929; Concerto, D minor, 2 pf, orch, 1932; Concerto, G minor, org, timp, str, 1938; *Les Biches* (suite), 1939–40; Sinfonietta, 1947–8; Piano Concerto, 1949; occasional pieces

Vocal orchestral: *Sécheresses* (James), ch, orch, 1937; *Chansons villageoises* (Maurice Fombeure), v, chbr orch, 1942; *Litanies à la vierge noire*, arr women's ch, str, timp, 1947; *Stabat mater*, s, ch, orch, 1950; *Gloria*, s, ch, orch, 1959; *La Dame de Monte Carlo* (Cocteau), s, orch, 1961; *Sept répons de ténèbres*, child s, ch, orch, 1961–2

Smaller choral works: *Chanson à boire*, men, 1922; *Sept chansons*, mixed, 1936; *Litanies à la vierge noire*, women, org, 1936; *Petites voix*, children, 1936; Mass, G, mixed, 1937; *Quatre motets pour un temps de pénitence*, mixed, 1938–9; *Exultate Deo*, mixed, 1941; *Salve regina*, mixed, 1941; *Figure humaine* (Paul Eluard), 12 soli, 1943; *Un Soir de neige* (Eluard), mixed, 1944; *Quatre petites prières de Saint François d'Assise*, men, 1948; *Quatre motets pour le temps de noël*, mixed, 1951–2; *Ave verum corpus*, women, 1952; *Laudes de Saint Antoine de Padoue*, men, 1957–9

Chamber: *Rapsodie nègre*, bar, fl, cl, str qt, pf, 1917; Sonata, 2 cl, 1918; *Le Bestiaire*, v, fl, cl, bn, str qt, 1919; *Cocardes*, v, vn, cornet, trbn, perc, 1919; Sonata, cl, bn, 1922; Sonata, hn, tpt, trbn, 1922; Trio, ob, bn, pf, 1926; *Le Bal masqué* (Max Jacob), bar/mez, ob, cl, bn, vn, vc, pf, perc, 1932; *Villanelle*, pipe, pf, 1934; *Suite française*, 9 wind, perc, hpd,

1935; Sextet, pf, wind qnt, 1932–9; Sonata, vn, pf, 1942–3; Sonata, vc, pf, 1940–48; Sonata, fl, pf, 1956–7; *Elégie*, hn, pf, 1957; Sarabande, gtr, 1960; Sonata, cl, pf, 1962; Sonata, ob, pf, 1962

Song sets: *Le Bestiaire* (Apollinaire), 1919; *Cocardes* (Cocteau), 1919; *Chansons gaillardes* (17th century), 1925–6; *Trois poèmes de Louise Lalanne* (Apollinaire), 1931; *Quatre chansons pour enfants* (Jaboune), 1934; *Tel jour, telle nuit* (Eluard), 1936–7; *Deux poèmes* (Apollinaire), 1938; *Miroirs brulants* (Eluard), 1938–9; *Fiançailles pour rire* (Louise de Vilmorin), 1939; *Banalités* (Apollinaire), 1940; *Chansons villageoises*, 1942; *Deux poèmes* (Louis Aragon), 1943; *Métamorphoses* (de Vilmorin), 1943; *La Fraîcheur et le feu* (Eluard), 1950; *Le Travail du peintre* (Eluard), 1956; *La Courte Paille* (Maurice Carème), 1960; etc.

Individual songs: 'Toréador' (Cocteau), 1918; 'A sa guitare' (Ronsard), 1935; 'Priez pour paix' (d'Orléans), 1938; 'Bleuet' (Apollinaire), 1939; 'Ce doux petit visage' (Eluard), 1939; 'Les Chemins de l'amour' (Anouilh), 1940; 'Montparnasse' (Apollinaire), 1941–5; 'Le Disparu' (Desnos), 1947; 'Main dominée par le cœur' (Eluard), 1947; 'Dernier poème' (Desnos), 1956; 'Fancy' (Shakespeare), 1959; etc.

Narration with piano: *L'Histoire de Babar* (Jean de Brunhoff), 1940–45

Piano: Sonata, duet, 1918; *Trois mouvements perpétuels*, 1918; *Valse*, 1919; Suite, C, 1920; *Six impromptus*, 1920; *Napoli*, 1925; *Deux novelettes*, 1927–8; *Trois pièces*, 1918–28; *Pièce brève sur le nom d'Albert Roussel*, 1929; Nocturnes Nos.1–8, 1930–38; *Valse-improvisation sur le nom de Bach*, 1932; *Villageoises*, 1933; Improvisations Nos.1–15, 1933–59; Presto, 1934; Intermezzos, C, D♭, 1934; Humoresque, 1934; *Les Soirées de Nazelles*, 1930–36; *Suite française*, 1935; *Française*, 1939; *Mélancolie*, 1940; Intermezzo, A♭, 1943; *L'embarquement pour Cythère*, 2 pf, 1951; *Thème varié*, 1951; Sonata, duo, 1952–3; *Elégie*, duo, 1959; *Novelette sur un thème de M. de Falla*, 1959; etc.

Pousseur, Henri (Léon Marie Thérèse) (b.
Malmédy, 23 Jun 1929). Belgian composer. He studied at the Liège and Brussels Conservatories, and with Froidebise, who introduced him to Webern's music. Also important were his meetings with Boulez in 1951 and Stockhausen in 1954. He became a regular teacher at Darmstadt (1957–67) and participant in the avant-garde movement. Later he taught in Liège. During his Darmstadt years he was particularly concerned with aleatory form, and in his opera *Votre Faust* (see FAUST) he allowed eventualities to be decided by the audience. This libertarian attitude led to a Utopian view of music as a model of a free society, with diverse results in his later output.

Powell, Mel (b. New York, 12 Feb 1923; d. Los
Angeles, 24 Apr 1998). US composer, originally Melvin Epstein. He was a noted jazz arranger and pianist, working with Benny Goodman and Glenn Miller before his studies with Hindemith at Yale, where he graduated in 1952. For some years he followed Hindemith into neoclassicism, but around the time he joined the Yale faculty, in 1958, he took up Webernian serialism, whose delicacy he emulated while adding a strong, flexible pulse that showed his jazz sense still very much alive. In 1969 he became founding dean of music at CalArts. Most of his works are on a chamber scale, sometimes with voice; several have electronic music on tape. A striking and vital exception in size is his double piano concerto *Duplicates* (1987–90).

Power, Leonel (b. c.1375; d. Canterbury, 5 Jun
1445). English composer, second only to the probably younger Dunstable at a time when English music was at a peak of attainment and prestige. With Dunstable he pioneered the musically integrated mass, notably in an example with four sections (no *Kyrie*), all having the plainsong *Alma redemptoris mater* in the tenor. Earlier music of his appears in the Old Hall manuscript, where he was represented by more pieces than any other composer when the collection was first put together. These compositions show an awareness of continental music that he could have picked up in France as a member of the household of Henry V's brother, Thomas, Duke of Clarence. French rhythmic subtlety is combined with English harmonic mastery in a way that excited widespread admiration. He also wrote a treatise on DISCANT. Though he was attached from 1423 to the priory of Christ Church, Canterbury, his later music circulated abroad. His works, mostly in three parts, are all settings of parts of the mass ordinary or other liturgical texts.

pp, ppp, etc. See P.

prächtig (Ger.). Grand.

practice. Physical routine undertaken to maintain and develop instrumental or vocal expertise, or, as a verb (practise), to engage in that routine. Practice sessions normally begin with exercises to WARM UP, then continue with favourite pieces, pieces to be performed in the near future, improvisation, etc. The distinction from rehearsal is that the latter is directed more particularly towards a forthcoming performance. Musicians normally practise alone, though the term can be extended to regular groups, e.g. string quartets. Most serious musicians would want to devote some time to practice almost daily, that time varying from a few minutes to several hours.

practice mute. STRAIGHT MUTE for brass instruments, thickly corked to reduce sound to a trickle.

praeludium. Prelude. Latinized form of the word used by Bach and Stravinsky.

praetorius, Michael (b. Creuzburg an der Werra, near Eisenach, ?15 Feb 1571; d. Wolfenbüttel, 15 Feb 1621). German composer-theorist, a major force in establishing the Baroque in Germany. The name Praetorius was a Latinization of 'Schultze' (variously spelled) and was borne by several other musicians of around the same time. Among them, Hieronymus (1560–1629) was a Hamburg organist-composer whose works include some important polychoral motets (*Cantate Domino, Decantabat populus Israel, Ein Kindelein so löbelich, Herr Gott dich loben war*). His sons, Jacob (1586–1651) and Johannes (*c*.1595–1660), studied with Sweelinck and were also composers and organists in Hamburg; both wrote wedding cantatas, and Jacob some notable organ works.

Michael met Hieronymus at Gröningen in 1596, when both were there to play the new organ in the castle chapel, but he came from a different family, of theologians from Silesia. He studied at the Latin school in Torgau and university in Frankfurt an der Oder, where he began his career as an organist. Shortly before the Gröningen organ trials he joined the ducal court in Wolfenbüttel, where he remained until his death – though with frequent and sometimes lengthy stays away. He married in 1603 and had two sons.

Despite his rather short life and abundant travelling, he produced an enormous quantity of music, consisting mostly of choral arrangements of Protestant hymns, which he published in several volumes, among which *Polyhymnia caduceatrix et panegyrica* (1619) includes a full range of solo, choral and polychoral settings with continuo. He also published a book of French dances (*Terpsichore*, 1612) and the first three volumes of an exhaustive musical survey, *Syntagma musicum* (1614–18), covering religious music, instruments and forms.

Prague (Praha). Cultural centre of the Czechs since the Middle Ages. Its court, churches and university (founded 1348, the first in central Europe) made for a rich musical life, muted by the Habsburg conquest of 1620. But then the Jesuits, brought in to re-establish Catholicism in a city that had been waywardly Protestant since the time of Jan Hus (early 15th century), encouraged education, and their pupils at the Clementinum included Zelenka, Gluck (possibly) and Johann Stamitz. Meanwhile, the flourishing of opera in the 18th century led to the establishment of a permanent company at the Estates Theatre in 1783; there Mozart conducted the first performances of *Don Giovanni* (1786) and *La clemenza di Tito* (1791). He stayed with Dussek and also wrote his 'Prague' Symphony for the former visit. The local vogue for his music survived him, and in 1794–5 *Die Zauberflöte* was the first opera to be given in Czech.

Beethoven made six trips to the city, and Weber was conductor of the opera (1813–16); visitors during the next three decades included Paganini, Chopin, Wagner, Liszt and Berlioz. Rising nationalism brought the foundation of a conservatory (1811), an organ school (1830) and orchestras, as well as an increasing supply of operas, songs and choruses in Czech. In 1862 the opera company moved to a new home, the Provisional Theatre, which gained an important repertory in the works of Smetana, Dvořák and Janáček. The Estates Theatre continued as a German-language house, replaced in 1888 by the Neues Deutsches Theater. In 1901 the Czech Philharmonic achieved an independent existence from the Czech opera company, and in 1911 a new home, Smetana Hall; early visiting conductors included Mahler and Varèse.

In 1918 Prague became the capital of independent Czechoslovakia, but remained bicultural. Zemlinsky (1911–27) and Szell conducted the German opera, Ostrčil and Talich the Czech, while composers active in the city included Czechs (Martinů, Hába) and people who belonged, like Kafka, to the German Jewish population (Schulhoff). This mix was devastated when the Czechs were once more absorbed, now by Hitler (1939–45). Musical institutions were revitalized after 1945, since when opera has been given in the Smetana Theatre, Tyl Theatre and National Theatre, and concerts in the Smetana Museum, Smetana Hall and villa Bertramka (Dussek's home).

Pralltriller (Ger.). Short trill played with a snap of the fingers.

precentor. Cleric or lay musician responsible for the choir in an Anglican cathedral.

precipitato, precipitoso, precipitando (It.). Precipitately.

pre-Classical. Belonging to the period before the Classical style of Haydn and Mozart but after the Baroque of Handel and Bach. Yet 'period' is not quite the word: Haydn wrote his first symphonies when Handel was still living, and Pergolesi – a classic pre-Classical composer – was dead long before Bach began *Die Kunst der Fuge*.

Pre-Classical music comes not so much from a time as from a mentality, of change.

precocity. Schoenberg's advice to composers was to start at 26. Some, though, have achieved remarkable works at much younger ages:

12: Mozart's *Bastien und Bastienne*; Rossini's string sonatas (?); Mendelssohn's first six string symphonies

13: Mendelssohn's C minor piano quartet

14: Mozart's *Mitridate*; Korngold's *Schauspiel Ouvertüre*

15: Chopin's C minor rondo; Cowell's *The Tides of Manaunaun* (?); Knussen's Symphony No.1

16: Mozart's *Lucio Silla*; Mendelssohn's octet; Glazunov's Symphony No.1

17: Purcell's elegy for Locke; Mozart's 'Little G minor' symphony, violin concerto in B♭, *Exsultate, jubilate*; Schubert's 'Gretchen am Spinnrade'; Mendelssohn's *Midsummer Night's Dream* overture; Chopin's *Rondo à la mazur*; Bizet's Symphony in C; Strauss's wind serenade

18: Alessandro Scarlatti's first opera; Mozart's symphony in A (No.29); Arriaga's quartets; Schubert's Symphony No.3, 'Erlkönig', 'Heidenröslein'; Mendelssohn's A minor quartet; Chopin's C minor sonata; Dohnányi's C minor piano quintet; Prokofiev's Piano Sonata No.1

19: Mozart's *La finta giardiniera*, other violin concertos; Beethoven's imperial cantatas; Schubert's Symphonies Nos.4–5, first three violin sonatas; Donizetti's cor anglais concertino; Chopin's F minor concerto; Brahms's F♯ minor piano sonata; Debussy's 'Mandoline'; Strauss's first horn concerto; Rachmaninoff's C♯ minor prelude; Poulenc's sonata for two clarinets; Shostakovich's Symphony No.1; Messiaen's *Le banquet céleste*; Markevitch's Partita

20: Mozart's 'Haffner' Serenade; Rossini's *La scala di seta*; Schubert's 'Die Forelle', 'Der Tod und das Mädchen'; Schumann's 'Abegg' Variations; Chopin's E minor concerto; Brahms's F minor piano sonata; Mahler's *Das klagende Lied*; Boulez's *Douze notations*; Benjamin's *Ringed by the Flat Horizon*; Adès's *Catch*

preghiera (It., prayer). Aria delivered by an opera character in need, as by Desdemona in both Rossini's *Otello* and Verdi's.

prelude. In origin and etymology a piece played before something else. The origin was practical: instrumental players needed to warm up before performing, and check the tuning of their instruments. Preambles and preludes for that purpose go back to the mid 15th century. Baroque composers discovered the usefulness of the prelude as a contrasting, freer introduction to a fugue or to a set of dances, in a suite or partita, as in the incomparable examples of Bach. The Baroque-style suite recurred seldom in later music, but the prelude-fugue form was taken up by Liszt and Shostakovich among others. Meanwhile, the prelude had become an independent form in the sets written by Hummel and, more influentially, Chopin (1836–9) – a form, indeed, that was scarcely a form at all, for Chopin's preludes vary greatly in length, shape and character. That was the point: the term aroused no particular expectations. Chopin's example was followed, always in the sphere of piano music, by Alkan, Busoni, Scriabin, Debussy, Rachmaninoff and many others. Wagner preferred the term – as *Vorspiel* – to overture in his later operas.

Prélude à 'L'Après-midi d'un faune' (Prelude to 'The Afternoon of a Faun'). Orchestral work by Debussy referring to a poem by Stéphane Mallarmé, sensuously suggestive – the poem and the music – of erotic reverie in an idyllic landscape. In 1912 Nijinsky brought the image to the ballet stage. First performance: Paris, 23 Dec 1894.

Préludes. Two books of piano pieces by Debussy. Their titles, placed after the music, are as follows:

Book I: 1 *Danseuses de Delphes* (Women Dancers of Delphi), 2 *Voiles* (Sails/Veils), 3 *Le Vent dans la plaine* (The Wind over the Plain), 4 *Les Sons et les parfums tournent dans l'air du soir* (Sounds and Scents Turn in the Evening Air, a line by Baudelaire), 5 *Les Collines d'Anacapri* (The Hills of Anacapri), 6 *Des pas sur la neige* (Footsteps on Snow), 7 *Ce qu'a vu le vent d'ouest* (What the West Wind Saw), 8 *La Fille aux cheveux de lin* (The Flaxen-Haired Girl, the title of a poem by Leconte de Lisle), 9 *La Sérénade interrompue* (The Interrupted Serenade), 10 *La Cathédrale engloutie* (The Submerged Cathedral), 11 *La Danse de Puck* (Puck's Dance), 12 *Minstrels* (i.e. black-face minstrels in a music-hall).

Book II: 1 *Brouillards* (Mists), 2 *Feuilles mortes* (Dead Leaves), 3 *La Puerta del Vino* (gate of the Alhambra), 4 *Les Fées sont d'exquises danseuses* (Fairies are Exquisite Dancers), 5 *Bruyères* (Heaths), 6 *General Lavine – eccentric* (a music-hall performer), 7 *La Terrasse des audiences du clair de lune* (The Terrace for Moonlit Audiences, a scene from George V's visit to Delhi), 8 *Ondine* (see UNDINE), 9 *Hommage à S. Pickwick Esq., P.P.M.P.C.*, 10 *Canope* (Canopus, a Hellenistic-Roman city on the Nile delta, or a funerary urn from there), 11 *Les Tierces alternées* (Alternating Thirds), 12 *Feux d'artifice* (Fireworks).

Préludes, Les (The Preludes). Symphonic poem by Liszt taking its title from a poem by Lamartine, seeing life as a sequence of preludes to the hereafter. First performance: Weimar, 23 Feb 1854.

premier coup d'archet (first bowstroke). Vaunted as a speciality of the Parisian Concert Spirituel in the late 18th century, the first entry of the strings together en masse. But Mozart was not impressed.

première (Fr., first). First performance. The word is misborrowed, since the French term is *création*. The very first performance of a work is its world première, which may be followed by a US première, London première, etc.

preparation. (1) The lessening of the dissonant effect of a note in tonal music by making it part of a consonant chord. A passing note may thus be prepared or unprepared.

(2) Procedure resulting in a prepared piano.

prepared piano. Grand piano prepared with extraneous objects between or on the strings: bolts, screws, pieces of rubber or plastic, etc. The effect is radically to alter the pitches, timbres and dynamic responses of the affected notes, creating a one-person percussion orchestra. Cage did this first, in *Bacchanale* (1940), and again in many later works. The effects of preparation, though minutely specified in many of Cage's scores, will vary with the build of the instrument. For Cage, always open to the unpredictable, that uncertainty was not a problem, but it may account for the paucity of such enterprises later, outside a few works by composers close to Cage (Harrison, Wolff).

presser (Fr.). Accelerate. Also found in the It. forms *pressando, pressante*.

Presser. US music publishing firm founded by Theodore Presser (1848–1925) in Philadelphia in 1883, though with a history going back to 1783 through Ditson, acquired in 1931. In 1949 the company moved to Bryn Mawr, Pennsylvania.

prestissimo. See PRESTO.

presto (It., ready). (1) Fast. One of the earliest tempo markings, found in Banchieri's *La battaglia* (1611) and soon after in works by Monteverdi, Michael Praetorius and Schütz. Throughout the 17th century and into the 18th it seems to have implied a moderately fast speed, in contrast with *tardo* or *adagio*. But from the very early 18th century it was also used for a speed faster than *allegro*, and in the Classical period it became the regular marking for finales, as opposed to (and surely faster than) the *allegro* of first movements. That has remained the scale of values.

The superlative *prestissimo* was used occasionally in the 18th century and early 19th ('For he is like a refiner's fire' in *Messiah*, Beethoven's sonatas Opp.10:2 and 109), becoming a little more common later. But *presto* since the Classical period generally indicates as fast as possible.

(2) A fast movement.

Previn, André (George) (b. Berlin, 6 Apr 1929). German–US conductor and composer, resident in the USA from 1939, his name changed from the original Andreas Ludwig Priwin. His family settled in Los Angeles, where his great-uncle Charles was music director for Universal pictures, and where he had lessons from Castelnuovo-Tedesco and Toch. He was working as a jazz pianist and film composer-arranger before he was out of his teens. Then, having won four Oscars for music direction (1958–64), he set out on a new career as a concert conductor, taking charge of the Houston Symphony (1967–70), the LSO (1968–79), the Pittsburgh Symphony (1976–85), the Los Angeles Philharmonic (1985–90) and the RPO (1985–7). His compositions include an opera after Tennessee Williams's play *A Streetcar Named Desire* (f.p. San Francisco, 1998) and a concerto for Mutter (2003), newly his wife.

André Previn *No Minor Chords* (1991)

Prey, Hermann (b. Berlin, 11 Jul 1929; d. Krailling vor München, 23 Jul 1998). German baritone. Trained in Berlin, he made his stage debut in Wiesbaden in 1952, and was soon appearing internationally in Mozart roles and as a lieder singer. His manner was sunny, his voice engaging and finely focused.

Price, (Mary Violet) Leontyne (b. Laurel, Miss., 10 Feb 1927). US soprano. She won a scholarship to the Juilliard School in 1949. Her sensuous intensity made her internationally in demand for Verdi roles; she made her debuts at Covent Garden (1958) and La Scala (1960) as Aida, and at the Met (1961) as Leonora in *La forza del destino*. Barber wrote the female lead in *Antony and Cleopatra* for her, and she made her farewell at the Met, again as Aida, in 1985.

Price, Margaret (Berenice) (b. Blackwood, Mon., 13 Apr 1941). Welsh soprano, esteemed for her purity and musicality in Mozart, created dame in 1993. She studied in London and made her debuts as Cherubino with Welsh National Opera (1962) and at Covent Garden (1963). From the early 1970s she was singing internationally, until retiring from the stage in 1994 and the concert platform in 1999.

prick-song. Tudor English term for music pricked, i.e. notated, rather than being aurally transmitted:

polyphonic music rather than plainsong. Mercutio (*Romeo and Juliet*, Act 2, scene 4) says of Tybalt that he 'fights as you sing prick-song, keeps time, distance, and proportion; rests me his minim rest, one, two, and the third in your bosom'. A prick could also be a dot after a note.

prigioniero, Il (The Prisoner). One-act opera by Dallapiccola to his own libretto. The Prisoner (baritone), seemingly befriended by the Gaoler (tenor) and supported from a distance by his Mother (soprano), discovers freedom, but discovers it to be an illusion. First performance: Florence, 20 May 1950.

prima (It.). (1) First, as in *come prima* (as at first), *prima volta* (first time), etc.
(2) Unison.

prima donna (It., first lady). The principal soprano in an opera or opera company. The term goes back to the first public opera houses, those of mid 17th-century Venice. Rivalries between singers led to amended forms – *altra prima donna, prima donna assoluta, prima donna assoluta e sola* – and to the common use of the term for anyone difficult to work with, male or female.

prima la musica e poi le parole (It.). First the music and then the words. Phrase taken from the title of an entertainment with words by Giovanni Battista Casti and music by Salieri, and often used to refer to the eternal argument about the rival claims of text and score – especially since Strauss's *Capriccio*, for which the Salieri–Casti piece was a source. In almost all cases the libretto comes first chronologically. The argument concerns its artistic place.

prima pratica (It., first practice). Term originating in Italy in the very early 17th century to denote Renaissance polyphony, as distinct from the new text-led style, *seconda pratica*. Giulio Cesare Monteverdi, in a note printed with his brother Claudio's *Scherzi musicali* (1607), mentions composers from Ockeghem to Willaert as masters of the *prima pratica*, and from Rore to Peri and Caccini as representatives of the *seconda*.

primavera (It., spring). See SEASONS.

prime. (1) Monastic service.
(2) Bottom note of a scale or chord.
(3) Fundamental form of the SET in a serial composition.

Prime (Ger.). Unison.

primo (It.). First, as in *tempo primo* or the marking on the upper part of a piano duet.

primo uomo (It., first man). The principal man in an opera or opera company. The term, or the alternative *primo musico* (first musician), arrived soon after *prima donna* when castratos demanded similar distinction. In the 18th century it began to be applied to tenors.

Primrose, William (b. Glasgow, 23 Aug 1903; d. Provo, Utah, 1 May 1982). British–US viola player. He studied in Glagow, in London and in Belgium with Ysaÿe (1925–7), who advised him to concentrate on the viola. Toscanini made him principal viola of the NBC Orchestra (1937–42), after which he concentrated on solo and quartet work; he commissioned Bartók's concerto. Following a heart attack in 1963 he concentrated on teaching.

Prince Igor (*Knyaz Igor*). Opera by Borodin to his own libretto after a medieval Russian epic. The Russian prince, Igor (baritone), and his son, Vladimir (tenor), are prisoners of the Polovtsians, under their magnanimous khan, Konchak (bass), who provides entertainment (POLOVTSIAN DANCES) and blesses Vladimir's marriage to his daughter Konchakovna (contralto) after Igor has escaped to rejoin his lamenting wife, Yaroslavna (soprano). Borodin failed to complete the score, after working on it for nearly 20 years, and it was finished by Rimsky-Korsakov and Glazunov. First performance: St Petersburg, 4 Nov 1890.

principal. First player in an orchestral group, e.g. principal cello, principal clarinet. The principal first violin is known as the LEADER (UK) or CONCERTMASTER (US). A principal will take solos, lead the group and have some hand in recruitment.

principale. Register of the natural trumpet, from middle C or the G below, as opposed to the CLARINO register starting an octave above middle C. The register was a professional speciality in the Baroque period, when a trumpet ensemble would include principale and clarino players, the former needing lung power and, on the battlefield, bravery.

printemps (Fr., spring). See SEASONS.

printing. Music could circulate in manuscript copies once there was adequate notation, and such copies were still being made for sale into the 19th century, long after the writing of literary texts by hand had ceased to be a commercial proposition.

This delay in the completion of technological advance was due largely to the extra complexity of musical notation over textual, and the initial need, when type was used, of at least two impressions: one for the staves, one for the notes. The earliest surviving printed music, a gradual from about 1473, makes elegant use of type. Several printers in the next decade introduced an alternative technique, using a block of wood or metal cut with the music to provide a forme from which impressions could be taken. That method, too, survived into the 19th century. Meanwhile, the printing of music from type was developed by Petrucci, who in 1501 published the first polyphonic music to be produced this way. In the 1520s Rastell and Attaingnant managed to print music from type at one impression, and others around the same time started printing music from engraved copper plates. The use of type (letterpress) dominated music printing until the end of the 17th century, and continued thereafter, while engraving became the preferred method for fine music printing from then until the 1860s. It was replaced by offset lithography – printing from etched stone, the image transferred from an engraved plate or a photograph. Engraving began to die out after the Second World War, and photolithography rapidly became obsolete, except for special purposes, in the wake of the computer revolution of the 1980s. See also PUBLISHING.

Prinz von Homburg, Der (The Prince of Homburg). Opera by Henze to a libretto by Ingeborg Bachmann after Heinrich von Kleist's play. The Prince (high baritone) escapes from a military world of warfare and irresistible duty into a fantasy life with his beloved Princess Natalie (soprano). First performance: Hamburg, 22 May 1960.

Prioris, Johannes (b. ?Brabant, c.1460; d. c.1514). Composer, choirmaster to Louis XII of France. He wrote masses (including one of the earliest Requiem settings, possibly written for Anne of Brittany in 1514), Magnificat settings, motets and songs.

Priuli, Giovanni (b. Venice, c.1575; d. Vienna, 1629). Italian composer, a pupil and follower of Giovanni Gabrieli, latterly active in Austria. He published five volumes of sacred music (masses, motets, canzonas) and five of madrigals.

Prix de Rome (Fr., Rome Prize). Award given each year from 1803 to 1968 by the Académie des Beaux-Arts in Paris, enabling a young composer to spend four years at the Villa Médicis in Rome with colleagues practising other arts. Entrants had to write a cantata in isolation. The roll of winners included Halévy (1819), Berlioz (1830), Thomas (1832), Gounod (1839), Bizet (1857), Massenet (1863), Debussy (1884), Charpentier (1887), Schmitt (1900), Caplet (1901), Lili Boulanger (1913) and Dutilleux (1938). But there is also a distinguished list of those who failed, including Ravel and Messiaen. Prizes of the same name are awarded in Belgium and the USA.

Probe (Ger.). Rehearsal.

processional. Hymn sung by a choir while in procession, normally within a church but possibly outdoors. The practice is old; there are plainsong processionals.

Prodigal Son. Character in one of the parables of Christ who leaves his father for a life of irresponsibility but then returns (Luke 15). His story has been musically told by Debussy, Prokofiev and Britten.

prodigy. See CHILD PRODIGY.

producer. (1) Person responsible for staging an opera, equivalent to the director in the spoken theatre. The function could be assumed in the 17th, 18th and 19th centuries by the librettist, composer, designer, conductor, choreographer, theatre manager or any combination of these. Specialist directors emerged haphazardly over a long period, most notably in Paris in the 1820s, not becoming the widespread norm until after the Second World War.

(2) Person with overall responsibility for the financing and artistic direction of an event.

production. Staging of an opera (or other theatre work), an art intimately linked at all periods with design – less intimately, on many occasions, with musical components.

The traditions of courtly entertainments, surviving into early opera, required grace, simplicity and eloquence from singers in their movements and gestures: there is evidence of this from treatises, from prefaces to scores and from engravings. Also important were the stage machines, scenic transformations, sumptuous costumes and ranks of supernumeraries provided by mid-17th-century public opera.

The formalization of Italian opera in the later 17th century rendered production secondary. Singers would find themselves in much the same situations, expressing much the same sentiments, from opera to opera – they had all they needed in the music, and in the elementary stage directions printed in the libretto. In Paris, though, dramatic variety and complexity continued, and production was one of the responsibilities Lully assumed in his control of French opera. However, it was not Parisian *tragédie lyrique* but Neapolitan opera buffa that helped to introduce a more vital style of operatic acting in the later 18th century, in keeping with an Enlightenment taste for naturalness. Singers in the new style included Guadagni and Sophie Arnoud, and Mozart's operas – whose first productions are not well documented – seem to play to this trend, their characters being so individual.

Production books, fixing the placings, movements and gestures, began to be published in Paris in the 1820s, and the innovation was enthusiastically taken up by Verdi. It fell out of use with the arrival of the 20th-century producer, a specialist in stagecraft and a person expected to bring a particular vision to a production. No longer would opera productions conform to a definitive pattern (except in the case of a few works, such as *La Bohème* and *Wozzeck*, where the production is virtually written into the score and ungainsayable). No longer would they have to present, straightforwardly, the settings and actions described in the libretto, as if an opera were a play with music.

Opera production since the First World War has been concerned rather with creating conditions for the exceptional thing that opera is: theatre in which people sing, in which there is a constant unseen presence (the orchestra), in which rival messages may be at play in words and music, in which qualities judged obsolete in the day-to-day world – grandeur, heroism, divinity – are still current, in which extremes of artistry and vulgarity exist side by side.

Mark A. Radice, ed. *Opera in Context : Essays on Historical Staging* (1998)

profession. Performing musicians sometimes speak of 'the profession' as if it were a medieval guild, and indeed music has retained (longer than medicine, say) a method of preparation in which the master–pupil relationship is paramount. Membership in the profession – being a professional – depends more on this locking into a tradition than on charging a fee. Among composers, though, there is room for the self-taught, whose professional status is underpinned by the respect of professional performers.

programme. (1) The choice and order of works performed in a CONCERT, recital or recording. This will be in the hands of performers in collaboration with the producing institution, which might be a hall, festival, broadcasting authority or record company. Concert programming is an essential part of the art of performance, and a balancing of various considerations, both practical (e.g. the need to warm up) and artistic. Record programming is generally based on homogeneity rather than imaginative combination.

(2) Booklet offered for sale or free at a performance, usually including a list of the works to be heard, a PROGRAMME NOTE on each, short biographies and photographs of the performers, notices of future events, and advertising. For opera performances in the 18th and 19th centuries the printed libretto fulfilled the functions of a programme, containing a cast list, note and other information. Audiences could also refer to the PLAYBILL. Programmes of the modern sort began slowly to supervene in the later decades of the 19th century.

(3) Meaning of a piece of PROGRAMME MUSIC. Often this was written out, to be printed as a preface to the score (Liszt) or leaflet to be sold or handed out at concerts (Berlioz). Scriabin's poetic programmes for *Le Poème de l'extase* and *Prométhée* are quite elaborate.

programme music. Music that conveys the feelings of a person involved in a scene or story, whether as participant or observer. The term was introduced by Liszt, but the genre was well established before him, examples including Beethoven's 'Pastoral' Symphony and Berlioz's *Symphonie fantastique*. Such works, so powerfully subjective, are fully Romantic conceptions, and different in kind from, for example, the birdsong impressions and other pictorial episodes of the clavecinists. They are different, too, from later music (Messiaen's music especially) in which there may be a minute illustration of natural phenomena, but without a palpable human presence. The era of programme music was, indeed, the era of Romanticism, from Beethoven, Berlioz and Weber through Liszt, Rimsky-Korsakov, Tchaikovsky and Musorgsky to Scriabin, Debussy, Strauss and Sibelius. Yet there were Romantics – Schubert, Schumann, Chopin, Brahms – who wrote very little of it.

The most characteristic genres of programme music are those that were invented specifically for it: the symphonic poem (or tone poem) and the illustrative piano piece. But there are also many programme symphonies (Tchaikovsky's Nos.4–6 and *Manfred* as well as those of Beethoven and Berlioz) and a few programme concertos (Berlioz's *Harold en Italie*). Chamber music is poorly represented, perhaps partly because of its relatively private character (for programme music tends to the heroic and spacious), but by reason, too, of its prestige (for programme music was felt to be inferior to ABSOLUTE MUSIC). Opera and song, where the voice makes a real human presence unmistakable, cannot command the virtual subjectivity of programme music.

Leslie Orrey *Programme Music* (1975)

programme note. Commentary on a work, printed in the PROGRAMME (2). The note may be anything from a sentence to an essay of several pages, to be read before, after or during the performance (a matter over which the author has little control, though the three prepositions would indicate different approaches to programme-note writing). Arne in London (1768) and Reichardt in Berlin (1783) are among late 18th-century musicians who provided some printed introduction to their concerts. Programme notes of a fuller kind, with music examples, were instituted by John Ella at his Musical Union concerts in London (1845–80), his explicit aim being to prepare his audience. In the last quarter of the 19th century his innovation became ubiquitous.

US orchestras in the 20th century commonly employed an annotator. Alternatively programme notes may be written by critics or scholars. Composers often write their own notes, but very few performers do so outside the field of early music (where they might feel a similar need to justify their approach), presumably on grounds of the self-sufficiency of performance. A programme note presented with a recording is more commonly called a 'sleeve note' or 'liner note' (terms originating in the days of 78 rpm records, when they had a physical meaning, but surviving into the time of CDs, when they do not), 'disc note' or 'booklet note'.

progression. A succession of chords having some harmonic coherence, and often also conveying a sense of movement or gesture.

progressive tonality. Process by which a work aptly concludes in a key on a tonic different from that of its opening, as Mahler's Fifth Symphony does, moving from C♯ minor to D major. The ending of a minor-mode work in the major on the same tonic (e.g. moving from F minor to F major) had been commonplace since the Classical period, when, indeed, few minor-key works were without such a happy ending. Progressive tonality involves a change of tonic.

Prokofiev, Sergey (Sergeyevich) [Prokofieff, Serge] (b. Sontsovka, Yekaterinoslav district, Ukraine, 23 Apr 1891; d. Moscow, 5 Mar 1953). Russian composer. A master of irony and hugely productive, he raced from topic to topic, style to style, ranging from bitter sarcasm to the lushest Romanticism, or from, in one short period, the artful fantasy of *The Love for Three Oranges* to the hysteria of *The Fiery Angel*. His restlessness expressed itself also in travelling. He emigrated soon after the 1917 revolution, then lived in the USA and Paris, but in the 1930s gradually returned to assume an uncomfortable place in Russia under Stalin.

Born into a well-to-do family and precocious, he began composing when he was five and wrote his first opera at the age of nine. He then had lessons from Glière before his studies at the St Petersburg Conservatory (1904–14), where courses with Lyadov, Rimsky-Korsakov and Tcherepnin were less important than the friendships he made with Myaskovsky and Asafyev. In 1908 he played some of his own pieces at one of the contemporary music evenings in St Petersburg. He then made his Moscow debut in 1910 with his First Piano Sonata, published the next year, and burst on to the larger scene with the premières of his first two piano concertos (1912, 1913). In 1914 he visited London and met Diaghilev, who commissioned a ballet. However, his first effort came to nothing (its music went into the *Scythian Suite*) and his second, *Chout*, was held up by the war. He returned to Petrograd (St Petersburg) and wrote *The Gambler*, as well as his first exercise in neoclassicism – his 'Classical' Symphony, an attempt to imagine Haydn in the 20th century – and his lyrical First Violin Concerto.

In May 1918 he left for the USA, where he quickly wrote *Three Oranges* for the Chicago Lyric Opera and began *The Fiery Angel*. He returned to Paris (1920–21), in the first place to revise *Chout* for Diaghilev but then to continue work on various fronts. There was his outgoing, virtuoso Third Piano Concerto, which he wrote for himself, and which made a contrast with the complex Second Concerto and enjoyably bumptious First. In the winter of 1921–2 he was back in Chicago for the staging of *Oranges*, but after that Paris was his centre for the next dozen years. His works remained diverse, ranging from the machine-age futurism of the Second Symphony and ballet *Le Pas d'acier* to the grace of another ballet, *L'Enfant prodigue* (again for Diaghilev), and the fevered excitement of another symphony, his Third, drawn from *The Fiery Angel*.

In 1927 he made his first return trip to Russia since leaving, and increasingly he began to write for Soviet audiences; *Romeo and Juliet* was commissioned by the Leningrad ballet in 1934. Meanwhile Western commissions led to his Fourth

Symphony (for Koussevitzky and the Boston Symphony, the music based on *L'Enfant prodigue*), his ballet *Sur le Borysthène* (for the Paris Opera) and, finally, his Second Violin Concerto. In 1936 he took up residence in Moscow with his wife and two boys. The time was not propitious; Shostakovich had just been condemned for writing *The Lady Macbeth*, and *Romeo and Juliet* was rejected. During his early years in Moscow he accordingly concentrated on music that could be deemed useful: patriotic cantatas, theatre scores, film music (for Eisenstein's *Alexander Nevsky*) and the instructive *Peter and the Wolf*. His first Soviet opera, *Semyon Kotko*, was dropped after its first season; his second, *The Duenna*, was not staged for several years; his third, *War and Peace*, had no complete performance until after his death.

In 1940 he began a liaison with a young writer, Mira Mendelson, which led to the break-up of his marriage. (His wife, under wartime suspicion as a Spaniard, was sent to a labour camp.) During the war he worked on his Tolstoy opera and with Eisenstein again, on *Ivan the Terrible*, while returning to concert music: his Piano Sonatas Nos.7–8 and imposing Fifth Symphony (1944). A fall in 1945, shortly after he had conducted the symphony's première, left him permanently weakened. He was a principal target of the criticism meted out to composers in 1948, and the works of his last years have generally been regarded as anodyne responses to an impossible situation, made by a man ailing. He died a few hours before Stalin.

Sergey Prokofiev *Autobiography, Articles, Reminiscences*, ed. Semyon Isaakevich Shlifshteyn (*c*.1960); Harlow Robinson *Sergei Prokofiev* (1987)
www.prokofiev.org

Dramatic and orchestral music

Operas: *Maddalena* (Prokofiev), Op.13, 1911–13, unfinished; *The* GAMBLER, Op.24, 1915–17, rev 1927–8; *The* LOVE FOR THREE ORANGES, Op.33, 1919; *The* FIERY ANGEL, Op.37, 1919–23, rev 1926–7; SEMYON KOTKO, Op.81, 1939; BETROTHAL IN A MONASTERY, Op.86, 1940–41; WAR AND PEACE, Op.91, 1941–52; *The Story of a Real Man* (Prokofiev and Mira Mendelson), Op.117, 1947–8, f.p. Leningrad, 1948

Ballets: *Chout*, Op.20, 1915, rev 1920; *Le Pas d'acier*, Op.41, 1925–6; *L'Enfant prodigue*, Op.46, 1928–9; *Sur le Borysthène*, Op.51, 1930–31; ROMEO AND JULIET, Op.64, 1935–6; CINDERELLA, Op.87, 1940–44; *The Tale of the Stone Flower*, Op.118, 1948–53

Film scores: ALEXANDER NEVSKY, 1938; IVAN THE TERRIBLE, Op.116, 1942–5; etc.

Incidental music: *Egyptian Nights*, 1934; *Boris Godunov*, Op.70bis, 1936; *Eugene Onegin*, Op.71, 1936; *Hamlet*, Op.77, 1937–8

Choral orchestral: 2 Poems (Konstantin Balmont),

Op.7, women's ch, orch, 1909–10; *They are Seven* (Balmont), Op.30, t, ch, orch, 1917–18, rev 1933; Cantata for the 20th Anniversary of the October Revolution, Op.74, 1936–7; *Songs of Our Times*, Op.76, 1937; ALEXANDER NEVSKY (cantata after film score), Op.78, mez, ch, orch, 1939; *Hail to Stalin*, Op.85, 1939; *Ballad of an Unknown Boy*, Op.93, 1942–3; *Flourish, Mighty Homeland*, Op.114, 1947; *Winter Bonfire*, Op.122, 1949–50; *On Guard for Peace*, Op.124, 1950

Symphonies: No.1 'CLASSICAL', D, Op.25, 1916–17; No.2, D minor, Op.40, 1924–5; No.3, C minor, 1928; No.4, C, Op.47, 1929–30, rev as Op.112, 1947; No.5, B♭, Op.100, 1944; No.6, E♭, Op.111, 1945–7; No.7, C♯ minor, Op.131, 1951–2

Concertos: PIANO CONCERTO No.1, D♭, Op.10, 1911–12; No.2, G minor, Op.16, 1912–13, rev 1923; No.3, C, Op.26, 1917–21; No.4, B♭, Op.53, left hand, 1931; No.5, G, Op.55, 1931–2; VIOLIN CONCERTO No.1, D, Op.19, 1916–17; No.2, G minor, Op.63, 1935; Symphony-Concerto, E minor, Op.125, vc, 1933–8, rev 1950–52; Cello Concertino, G minor, Op.132, 1952

Other orchestral works: *Autumnal Sketch*, Op.8, 1910, rev 1915, 1934; *Scythian Suite*, Op.20, 1914–15; Overture, B♭, Op.42, chbr orch, 1926, arr full orch 1928; Divertissement, Op.43, 1925–9; Sinfonietta, A, Op.48, 1929; *Chant symphonique*, Op.57, 1933; Overture on Hebrew Themes, Op.34bis, arr 1934; LIEUTENANT KIJE (suite), 1934; PETER AND THE WOLF, Op.67, with narrator, 1936; Russian Overture, 1936; *A Summer Day*, Op.65bis, small orch, arr 1941; *The Year 1941* (suite), Op.90, 1941; *Ode to the End of the War*, Op.105, 1945; *Thirty Years*, Op.113, 1947; *The Meeting of the Volga and the Don*, Op.130, 1951; suites from stage works, marches

Chamber music and songs

String quartets: No.1, B minor, Op.50, 1930; No.2, F, Op.92, 1941

Other chamber works: Overture on Hebrew Themes, Op.34, cl, str qt, pf, 1919; Quintet, G minor, Op.39, ob, cl, vn, va, db, 1924; Humoresque Scherzo, Op.12bis, 4 bn, 1915

Duos: 5 Melodies, Op.35bis, vn, pf, 1925; Sonata, C, Op.56, 2 vn, 1932; Sonata No.1, F minor, Op.80, vn, pf, 1938–46; Sonata, D, Op.94, fl/vn, pf, 1943; Sonata, D, Op.115, vn/vns, 1947; Ballade, C minor, Op.15, vc, pf, 1912; Adagio (from CINDERELLA), Op.97bis, vc, pf, 1944; Sonata, C, Op.119, vc, pf, 1949

Songs: 2 Songs (Balmont, Apukhtin), Op.9, 1910–11; *The Ugly Duckling*, Op.18, 1914, orchd; 5 Poems (Balmont), Op.23, 1915; 5 Poems (Anna Akhmatova), Op.27, 1916; 5 Songs without Words, Op.35, 1920; 5 Poems (Balmont), Op.36, 1921; 2 Songs from *Lieutenant Kijé*, Op.60bis, 1934; 6 Mass Songs, 1935; 3 Romances (Pushkin), Op.73, 1936; 3 Children's Songs, Op.68, 1936; 3 Songs from *Alexander Nevsky*, Op.78bis, 1938–9; 7 Songs, Op.79, 1939; 12 Russian Folksongs, Op.104, 1944; 2 Duets (Russ. trad), Op.106, 1945

Piano music

Sonatas: No.1, F minor, Op.1, 1907–9; No.2, D minor, Op.14, 1912; No.3 'From Old Notebooks', A minor, Op.28, 1907–17; No.4 'From Old Notebooks', C minor, Op.29, 1908–17; No.5, C, Op.38, 1923, rev as Op.135, 1952–3; No.6, A, Op.82, 1939–40; No.7, B♭, Op.83, 1939–42; No.8, B♭, Op.84, 1939–44; No.9, C, Op.103, 1945–7

Other works: 4 Etudes, Op.2, 1909; 4 Pieces, Op.3, 1911; 4 Pieces, Op.4, 1910–12 (No.4 *Suggestion diabolique*); Toccata, D minor, Op.11, 1912; 10 Pieces, Op.12, 1906–13; *Sarcasmes*, Op.17, 1912–14; *Visions fugitives*, Op.22, 1915–17; *Contes de la vieille grand'mère*, Op.31, 1918; Divertissement, Op.43bis, 1938; *Choses en soi*, Op.45, 1928; 6 Pieces, Op.52, 1930–31; 2 Sonatinas, E minor, G, Op.54, 1931–2; 3 Pieces, Op.59, 1933–4; *Pensées*, Op.62, 1933–4; *Musiques d'enfants*, Op.65, 1935; arrangements from stage and orchestral works

prolation. In ARS NOVA notation the division of the semibreve into three minims (major prolation) or two minims (minor prolation).

proliferating series (Fr. *séries proliférantes*). Term introduced by Barraqué for his technique of creating whole families of rows out of two by applying Messiaen's principle of INTERVERSION.

prologue. Part of an opera distinct from, and before, the main business. The earliest operas, including Monteverdi's *Orfeo*, were equipped with prologues, which served principally to justify the innovation of sung drama and then to introduce the action. Prologues in mid-17th-century Venetian opera tend to feature deities whose rivalries are to be acted out in the human drama to come. In French opera, from Lully to Rameau, this kind of Olympian prologue might also serve to flatter the monarch. Prologues then disappeared, to be restored in many operas from the 1890s onwards, including *Pagliacci*, *Bluebeard's Castle* (spoken prologue), *The Love for Three Oranges*, *Lulu* and *Punch and Judy*. In all these diverse cases the prologue is a direct statement to the audience, as it had been at first.

prolongation. Term in Schenkerian analysis for the extension of a background model. A piece or movement is understood as having a through line, the URLINIE, in which a very basic harmonic progression is prolonged by various excursions.

promenade concerts. Concerts at which some audience members stand – though they probably should not walk about, as the word 'promenade' suggests, in a reminiscence of PLEASURE GARDENS. There were promenade concerts in Paris and London in the 1830s, but the term is generally associated with the London summer concerts – the Proms – initiated by Henry Wood in 1895 and maintained since 1927 by the BBC.

Prometheus. In classical mythology the Titan who gave human beings fire and was punished. Among Promethean works are the following:

(1) Goethe's poem (1773), set by Schubert and Wolf.

(2) Beethoven's ballet score, *Die Geschöpfe des Prometheus* (The Creatures of Prometheus), for choreography by Salvatore Viganò. Beethoven provided an overture, introduction and 16 dance numbers, for a narrative in which Prometheus requires the help of other gods and demigods in humanizing a pair of statues. Only the overture is at all often performed; the other music unusually requires harp and basset horn. First performance: Vienna, 28 Mar 1801.

(3) Liszt's symphonic poem *Prometheus*, originally the overture to Johann Gottfried Herder's *Prometheus Unbound*. First performance: Weimar, 24 Aug 1850, rev as symphonic poem Brunswick, 18 Oct 1855.

(4) Scriabin's *Prométhée, le poème du feu* (Prometheus, the Poem of Fire) for piano, orchestra and coloured light. First performance: Moscow, 2 Mar 1911.

(5) Nono's *Prometeo*, not an opera but a 'tragedy of listening', for the ear. For the original performances a wooden structure by Renzo Piano was installed in a disused church. First performance: Venice, 29 Sep 1984.

prompter. Person who supplies verbal and musical reminders to singers in an opera performance, traditionally from a prompt box tucked beneath the centre of the stage, its roof undisguised – though prompters may also be placed in the wings. The standard practice is for the prompter or prompters (a wide stage may require two, one at each side) to cue singers throughout the performance.

proms. See PROMENADE CONCERTS.

proper. That part of the mass which is specific – proper – to a particular Sunday or feast day, invariably including the INTROIT, GRADUAL, OFFERTORY and COMMUNION (the propers), as distinct from the ORDINARY.

Prophète, Le (The Prophet). Opera by Meyerbeer to a libretto by Scribe. Jean (tenor), venerated by the Anabaptists of 16th-century Holland as a god on earth, does not have the power to unite with his beloved Berthe (soprano, a part created by

Viardot), whose suicide precipitates an explosion that carries him off with his mother Fidès (mezzo-soprano) and everyone else in the opera. Often heard separately are the Coronation March and Fidès's 'Mon fils'. First performance: Paris Opera, 16 Apr 1849.

proportional notation. See TIME–SPACE NOTATION.

Proprium missae (Lat.) Mass PROPER.

Protopopov, Sergey Vladimirovich (b. Moscow, 2 Apr 1893; d. 14 Dec 1954). Russian composer, a modernist with roots in Scriabin. He graduated from Boleslav Yavorsky's class at the Kiev Conservatory in 1921 and became active in the Association for Contemporary Music, producing three piano sonatas and vocal pieces. Very little is known of him after 1928, except that he taught at the Moscow Conservatory (1938–43).

Proust, Marcel. See IMAGINARY COMPOSERS.

Provenzale, Francesco (b. Naples, c.1626; d. Naples, 6 Sep 1704). Italian composer, whose *Il Ciro* (?1653) has claims as the first Neapolitan opera; it was revived by Cavalli in Venice in 1654. Provenzale went on to a distinguished career in his native city as opera composer, church musician and conservatory teacher.

PRS. Performing Right Society (UK).

Prussian. Name given to two sets of quartets commissioned in the late 1780s by Frederick William II of Prussia: Haydn's Op.50 and Mozart's K.575, K.589 and K.590.

psalm. Sacred song, especially as recorded in the biblical Book of Psalms. The Greek term *psalmos* – originally meaning a striking or plucking, especially of string instruments – was adopted by Jewish translators of the Bible two centuries before Jesus, presumably on account of the tradition that the psalms were first sung by King David to the accompaniment of his harp. Psalms were sung in the temple at Jerusalem by a choir with instruments. They continued into synagogue worship and so into the liturgy of the Christian Church, where they appear fragmentarily in many mass propers and whole in other services, notably VESPERS and comparable Protestant evening services. Psalms are thus ubiquitous in liturgical music, including that of Josquin, Monteverdi, Schütz, Sweelinck, Purcell, Buxtehude, Bach (motets *Singet dem Herrn* and *Lobet dem Herrn*),

Handel and Mozart. Post-Reformation metrical paraphrases, encouraged by Calvin, were set for congregational use in France, Switzerland, the Low Countries, England, Scotland and North America. The psalms also survived into the concert music of a more secular age, set by Schubert, Mendelssohn, Schumann, Liszt, Bruckner, Brahms, Dvořák, Roussel, Lili Boulanger, Zemlinsky, Kodály and Stravinsky. Some writers, notably Schoenberg and Celan (set by Holliger), have used the word for new poems.

psalmody. The chanting or composition of psalms.

psalter. Liturgical book containing psalms and possibly other texts.

psaltery. Plucked string instrument. The strings are set in a rectangular, triangular, trapezoidal or wing-shaped wooden box and plucked with the fingers or plectra. Beause of its mention in the Bible, the psaltery may have enjoyed a richer existence in medieval art – in the hands of King David and innumerable angels – than in life, at least until the Islamic form of the instrument entered Europe through Spain. Its use, though, is mentioned by Chaucer in 'The Miller's Tale': 'He kiste hire sweete and taketh his sawtrie, / And pleyeth faste and maketh melodie.' Because that melody (losing the metaphor) could only be diatonic, the psaltery became obsolete in the Renaissance, to be reborn with chromatic tuning and hammers as the dulcimer or with a keyboard as the harpsichord or virginals.

Psyche. Princess beloved of Cupid, whom she loses for lack of trust, subject of works by Lully, Locke and others, Franck, Falla and Hindemith. Franck's symphonic poem with chorus is performed much less often than four orchestral extracts: *Le Sommeil de Psyché, Psyché enlevée par les zéphyrs, Les Jardins d'Eros, Eros et Psyché.*

psychoacoustics. The means by which SOUND is sensed. See also PSYCHOLOGY OF MUSIC.

psychology of music. The study of how music is heard, understood and enjoyed, as distinct from what and how it means. An inquiry into musical listening was proposed by Aristoxenus around 320 BC, but was delayed for almost two millennia, until Mersenne, who began the experimental study of timbre. Pre-eminent among 19th-century scientists who worked on SOUND and the EAR was Helmholtz, but research was beginning just at the moment when the basic subject matter – music –

was becoming much more diverse, as a result of the advent of modernism in Western music and the greater awareness of non-European cultures. And though much was learned about the perception of sound, the means by which sounds register themselves as musical entities – motifs, varieties of motion, harmonies, expressive gestures – remain obscure.

No doubt this is partly because several processes are at work simultaneously. Melodic utterance seems geared to the apparatus of speech recognition: melodies in a musical culture tend to bear some relation, especially of rhythm, to the spoken language of that culture. Metre and tempo connect rather with the pulsations of the body at rest (heartbeat, breathing) and moving (walking, running). Harmony and timbre may be experienced as moments of delight (or pain); they may also trigger interpretative machineries expecting progression and closure. Contrapuntal music may be appreciated as self-similar pattern, or provide a matrix on which these other processes can unfold.

Also, because the language of musical description is hazy, so that people cannot give precise reports to psychological tests, and because musical judgements will vary with culture and taste, experimental evidence covers only the basics. Among the conclusions to be drawn from such evidence are:

1. Recognition of pitch or interval is easier with complex tones than with simple sine waves, tails off radically above 5,000 Hz (a few steps above the standard piano's top note), and depends on the subject's musical culture. Training can help, though few people will ever be able to discriminate intervals smaller than an eighth-tone.
2. Consonances are not quite exactly geared to pure frequency ratios: the psychological octave represents a ratio a little above 2:1 (as was already known to the Greeks).
3. The ear can distinguish much shorter intervals of time than can the eye, down to two milliseconds. Yet the present can be a sensation lasting much longer, to an extent. Sounds separated by more than about a second and a half will no longer be felt to belong to one continuity.
4. Perception of pitch is minimal for sounds lasting under 10 milliseconds. Lower pitches require more time, seemingly so that a minimal two or three cycles of vibration can be experienced (a tenth of a second, then, for the bottom A on the piano).
5. Rhythmic perception draws on both memory and expectation, yet the perceiver knows very well which is which: rhythmic sequences

sounded in reverse are by no means easily perceived as such.
6. Regular undifferentiated pulses tend to be heard as grouped in twos or threes.

The psychology of musical performance has been studied as a model of learning, self-correction, skill acquisition, teamwork and public presentation. In its developing of all these qualities, which have applications right outside music, performance cannot but have a beneficial effect on the individual. Whether listening does so, though, is a question as old as Plato. See also PHILOSOPHY OF MUSIC.

Diana Deutsch, ed. *The Psychology of Music* (1982, [2]1999); Anthony Storr *Music and the Mind* (1992)

publisher. See this book's dedication.

publishing. The sale of music in copies on paper began with the rise of capitalist economies around 1500, the first music publishers being also printers, in Venice (Petrucci, 1501), Paris (Attaingnant, 1528), Nuremberg, and the Low Countries (Susato, 1543; Phalèse, 1545). In England the trade was pioneered by Thomas Vautrollier (1570), who printed music for Tallis and Byrd after they had gained a monopoly of music publishing in the country in 1575. In the 17th century music publishing waned, to be revived with the social change that was the Industrial Revolution. Significantly, the business took off again in places where that Revolution was felt first: London around 1700 (Walsh), Paris in the 1740s, Leipzig in the 1750s (Breitkopf), Vienna around 1780 (Artaria, Hoffmeister) and various US cities in the 1790s. Many leading firms trace their origins to the early 19th century, including Ricordi (1808), Novello (1811), Peters (1814) and Boosey (c.1816). See also PRINTING.

Music publishers produce printed music for sale to performers, libraries and music lovers (served by the MINIATURE SCORE). But this is only part of what they do, for the close connection with performance makes the publishing of music very different from that of books. 19th-century music publishers fostered the notion of copyright, and performing rights became a more important part of their income than sales. Music could be performed only from an authorized edition, for whose use a fee would have to be paid to the publisher (and shared with the composer, arranger or editor). It might therefore be disadvantageous to place all the performing materials for a work on sale – except in the case of older music in which copyright had lapsed (so that any publishing company would want to push its own edition by all possible means) or of music for which there was a strong demand from amateurs, who would generate no performing rights. Much of a publisher's catalogue – and music publishers were offering promotional catalogues in the 19th century, long before book publishers were – will therefore consist of classics and pedagogical material. Otherwise the general principle is to print scores and parts for hire only, and only to put on sale forms that cannot be used for a performance: piano reductions, vocal scores, miniature or study scores. The dependence on performing rights was intensified by the rise of radio and recordings in the 1920s, encouraging publishers to place their composers under contract. By the 1970s, with incomes thus secured from the great mid-century composers, as well as from classics and pedagogic editions, some publishers were able to begin playing an important role in the promotion of contemporary music beyond any immediate commercial advantage. Others, without such impressive back catalogues, were absorbed by the larger houses.

Important publishers in the field now include Bärenreiter, Boosey & Hawkes, Breitkopf, Durand, Faber Music, Leduc, Music Sales, Peters, Presser, Ricordi, Schott and Universal Edition.

Kate Van Orden *Music and the Cultures of Print* (2000)

Puccini, Giacomo (Antonio Domenico Michele Secondo Maria) (b. Lucca, 22 Dec 1858; d. Brussels, 29 Nov 1924). Italian composer, one of the last and most successful contributors to the central operatic repertory, a master of musical-dramatic continuity and unforgettable tunes.

He was also the last member of an extraordinary dynasty of musicians: his ancestors through five generations were composers – all represented in his long roll of baptismal names – and the post of cathedral organist was in the family continuously from 1739 for a century and a quarter. His great-great-grandfather, Giacomo (1712–81), and great-grandfather, Antonio (1747–1832), wrote sacred music and local pageants, as did his grandfather, Domenico (1772–1815), who studied with Paisiello in Naples and gained some notice for his operas. Domenico's early death, possibly from poisoning, left his son Michele (1813–64) to be taught by Antonio, and though Michele also had lessons in Naples, with Donizetti and Mercadante, he is remembered more as a teacher and chronicler of Lucchese musical history. Two of his sons became musicians: the celebrated Giacomo and Michele (1864–91), who went to South America.

Giacomo was five when his father died, whereupon his uncle, Fortunato Magi, was deputed to take over at San Martino and teach the boy, pending his being old enough to assume the family job.

At 14 he began work as an organist in and around Lucca, but three years later he saw *Aida* in Pisa and his life was changed. He completed his studies in Lucca, at the musical institute, then went to the Milan Conservatory (1880–83), where his teachers were Antonio Bazzini and Ponchielli.

While still a student he started his first opera, *Le villi*, which was presented in May 1884 as a one-acter. The publisher Giulio Ricordi heard it, advised him to lengthen it to two acts (in which form it was staged in Turin before the year was out) and commissioned a new opera, *Edgar*. While working on this, Puccini began a liaison with a married woman, Elvira Gemignani. Their son Tonio was born in 1886, and after Elvira's husband's death in 1904 they were married. Meanwhile, *Edgar* failed, and revisions could not save it.

In 1891 Puccini and his family moved into a lakeside house at Torre del Lago, where they remained until 1921. There he completed *Manon Lescaut*, which scored a triumph at its first performance in 1893 and took his name around the world. Despite an incoherent plot (on which five librettists worked, besides Ricordi and the composer himself), the piece has radiant central roles, together with moments of orchestral and harmonic boldness comparable with contemporary works by Strauss and Mahler.

After this, in under a decade, came his three most popular operas: *La Bohème*, *Tosca* and *Madama Butterfly* (though this last was not an immediate success), all written in collaboration with the librettists Illica and Giacosa. These operas' settings are very different: the mid-century Paris of young artists, the Napoleonic Rome of people both older and more cynical, and Japan in the early days of contact with the West. Moreover, those settings are scrupulously reflected in the music, with gorgeous and atmospheric use of the orchestra. Yet the three works are similar in that their central characters have access to strong, vital melodic expressions of emotion. Out of their diverse contexts, they sing with the frankness of popular song of the period.

Subsequently Puccini's productivity slowed, partly because he was eager for new challenges, which he had difficulty finding. Also, there was a domestic catastrophe. One of his servants, Doria Manfredi, killed herself in January 1909 after Elvira had accused her of having an affair with him. *La fanciulla del West* (1908–10) and, especially, *La Rondine* (1914–16, written for Vienna, with an approach to waltzing operetta mode) did not meet with the success of their predecessors, nor did the first two parts of the triple bill *Il trittico* (1913–18), though its comic finale, *Gianni Schicchi*, is perhaps the composer's most brilliant score.

In 1921, now into his last opera *Turandot*, he moved with his family to Viareggio. The new work's legendary exotic setting allowed him to profit from Schoenberg and Stravinsky as well as Debussy (already an influence), while its violent subject matter intensified the cruelty that had always been essential to his expressive tone, along with sentimentality. He squeezed a lot out of his characters, his singers and ultimately himself. He travelled to Brussels for X-ray treatment for throat cancer and died there with *Turandot* unfinished.

Julian Budden *Puccini* (2002)

Operas: *Le villi* (Ferdinando Fontana, after Alphonse Karr *Les Willis*), 1883–4, f.p. Milan, 1884; *Edgar* (Fontana, after Alfred de Musset *La Coupe et les lèvres*), 1884–8, f.p. Milan, 1889, rev 1891–2, 1901, 1905; MANON LESCAUT, 1890–92; *La* BOHEME, 1894–5; TOSCA, 1898–9; MADAMA BUTTERFLY, 1901–3, rev 1904–6; *La* FANCIULLA DEL WEST, 1908–10; *La* RONDINE, 1914–16; *Il* TRITTICO, 1913–18; TURANDOT, 1920–24

Other works: *Preludio sinfonico*, 1876; Mass (*Messa da Gloria*), t, bar, b, ch, orch, 1880; *Capriccio sinfonico*, 1883; *Crisantemi*, str qt, pub 1890; etc.

Pugnani, (Giulio) Gaetano (Gerolamo) (b. Turin, 27 Nov 1731; d. Turin, 15 Jul 1798). Italian violinist-composer, who was taught by a pupil of Corelli (G.B. Somis) and was the teacher of Viotti. He spent his life in service to the Turin court, with occasional and much-acclaimed trips abroad, notably to Paris (1754), London (1767–9) and Switzerland, Germany and Russia (1780–82). Besides a lot of violin music, he wrote symphonies, quartets and operas, including an opera buffa during his London period. Kreisler passed off a piece as by him.

Pulcinella. Ballet score by Stravinsky, for a production designed by Picasso and choreographed by Léonide Massine. The music, for three singers (s, t, b) and chamber orchestra, is a brightened distortion of pieces attributed to Pergolesi. The suite includes 11 of the 18 numbers and omits the soloists. First performance: Paris, 15 May 1920.

pulse. Rhythmic quantity, normally regular, and thereby equivalent to the beat in metrical music. But music may be strongly pulsed without having a consistent metre, as often in Stravinsky and Messiaen. Also possible is an irregular pulse, as in Barraqué. Music's pulse rate generally marks out the speed at which one moment of time, one 'now', is succeeded by another. This is rarely slower than once every second and a half (beyond that, the sense of an unbroken 'now' breaks down) or faster than 10 times a second (for practical reasons).

Pulse Shadows. Work by Birtwistle interleaving his Nine Settings of Celan and Nine Movements for string quartet. First performance: London, 29 Apr 1996.

Punch and Judy. Opera by Birtwistle to a libretto by Stephen Pruslin after the old English puppet show, with chamber-scale accompaniment. Punch (high baritone) kills Judy (mezzo-soprano), the Lawyer (high tenor) and the Doctor (low bass), escapes execution by adding the hangman (baritone) to his victims, and is united with Pretty Polly (high soprano). First performance: Aldeburgh, 8 Jun 1968.

punctum. Kind of NEUME.

punta d'arco (It.). With the point of the bow. Also *a punta d'arco*.

punteado (Sp.). Plucked. Indication in guitar music, as opposed to *rasgueado* (strummed).

Punto, Giovanni (b. Zehušice, near Čáslav, 28 Sep 1746; d. Prague, 16 Feb 1803). Czech horn virtuoso, who Italianized his name from the original Johann Wenzel Stich. Widely travelled, he was the outstanding horn player of the age, performing on a silver instrument made for him in Paris. Composers who wrote for him included Mozart (Sinfonia Concertante for wind quartet) and Beethoven (Horn Sonata). He himself produced a large quantity of horn music, including 11 concertos, mixed chamber pieces, trios and duos.

pupitre (Fr.). Music stand, desk.

puppet opera. Opera presented by puppets with the singers normally unseen. First recorded in Paris and Venice in the late 1670s, the genre enjoyed a vogue in the 18th century – Haydn wrote at least two puppet operas for Esterháza. There was a revival in the early 20th century, when puppet theatres presenting opera were set up in Salzburg (1913) and other places, and when new operas with puppets began to be written. Examples include Falla's *El retablo de Maese Pedro* and Birtwistle's *The Mask of Orpheus*, both of which combine puppets with human characters.

Purcell, Henry (b. ?Westminster, ?10 Sep 1659; d. Westminster, 21 Nov 1695). English composer, the musical luminary of his age. Extraordinary in his range – theatre music (including the outstanding English-language opera before Stravinsky), anthems, court odes, songs and chamber pieces – he brought to everything a keen expressive vitality and delight in surprise. Henry Playford, publishing a collection of his songs three years after his death, provided a comment that endures beyond its need as a commercial puff: 'The Author's extraordinary Talent in all sorts of Musick is sufficiently known, but he was especially admir'd for the *Vocal*, having a peculiar Genius to express the Energy of *English* Words, whereby he mov'd the Passions of all his Auditors.'

His parentage is uncertain. Probably the son of another Henry Purcell, a Chapel Royal singer who died in 1664, he was brought up by Thomas Purcell, who also sang in the Chapel Royal and was very likely his uncle. Inevitably he himself joined the Chapel Royal as a boy. He also started very early as a composer: a three-part song by him was included in an anthology published in 1667. In 1673 his voice broke and he was apprenticed to John Hingeston, keeper of the king's keyboard and wind instruments. He progressed fast to become composer for the royal violins in succession to Locke (1677), organist of Westminster Abbey in succession to Blow (1679), organist of the Chapel Royal (1682) and instrument keeper after Hingeston's death (1683).

During this period he got married and rapidly moved to the forefront among London composers. While still in his early twenties he was writing anthems regularly for the Chapel Royal and helping to fulfil the obligation on royal musicians to provide odes celebrating monarchs' birthdays and returns to London. At the same time, in his purely instrumental compositions, he was looking back over the English tradition (his two In Nomines were the last until the 20th century) and out to the continent. Something of French music had already been absorbed by his predecessors Locke, Blow and Humfrey. To this he added, in the 12 *Sonnata's of III Parts* he published in 1683, a tinge of Italian bravura. Eight years later John Dryden, in the dedication to *Dioclesian*, noted that English music was 'now learning *Italian*, which is its best Master, and studying a little of the *French* Air, to give it more of Gayety and Fashion'.

He wrote an anthem, *My Heart is Inditing* for the coronation of James II in 1685, and was confirmed in his posts. But the Chapel Royal entered into a period of decline, and he seems to have written relatively little liturgical music after James's accession, concentrating instead on songs, on the continuing court odes and – following the arrival of William III and Mary II in 1688 – on theatre music. His one fully sung opera, the one-act *Dido and Aeneas*, probably comes from an earlier period, but his four semi-operas (spoken dramas with lengthy musical episodes) and most of his incidental scores date from after 1690. For some plays he provided just songs; others gained movements for strings and, in some cases, big scenes with soloists and chorus. Dryden's approbation – sealed by *King Arthur* – may have been crucial.

From this period, too, come his most striking odes: those for the birthdays of Mary II (especially *Come, ye sons of art, away*) and *Hail, bright Cecilia*. These are imposing cantatas, with songs, duets and choruses, the piece for Saint CECILIA's Day a splendiferous display of music's powers and majesty, the 1694 birthday ode indicating a sweet affection for the monarch. At her funeral, in January 1695, music by him was performed. His own funeral took place later that year, in the same place (Westminster Abbey, where he was buried) and with some of the same music.

Not much is recorded of his personality. Despite the swaggering conviviality suggested by his catches, he must have spent most of his time at work, especially in his last few years, when, in addition to his court duties, he was so busy in the theatre. Changes in the theatre, the Church and society rapidly rendered much of his music obsolete, but a number of songs and some anthems lived on, to be joined again by the rest of his extraordinary output in a revival that followed the Second World War.

His brother Daniel (*c.*1664–1717), took over from him as a composer of theatre music, songs, sonatas and court odes, unremarkably. His son Edward (1689–1740) was an organist.

J.A. Westrup *Purcell* (1937, [8]1980, [1]1995); Maureen Duffy *Henry Purcell* (1995); Jonathan Keates *Purcell* (1995)

Theatre music and odes

Opera: *Dido and Aeneas* (see DIDO), ?1689

Semi-operas: *Dioclesian* (Thomas Betterton, after Fletcher and Massinger *The Prophetess*), 1690; KING ARTHUR, 1691; *The* FAIRY-QUEEN, 1692; *The Indian Queen* (after John Dryden and Robert Howard), 1695

Substantial incidental scores: *Theodosius*, 1680; *The Double Marriage*, ?1682–5; *A Fool's Preferment*, 1688; *Circe*, ?1689; *Amphitryon*, 1690; *Distress'd Innocence*, 1690; *The Gordian Knot Unty'd*, 1690; *Sir Anthony Love*, 1690; *Oedipus*, ?1692; *The Double Dealer*, 1693; *The Old Bachelor*, 1693; *The Married Beau*, 1694; *Timon of Athens*, 1694; *The Virtuous Wife*, ?1694; *The Comical History of Don Quixote*, parts 1–3, 1694–5; *Abdelazer*, 1695; *Bonduca*, 1695; *The Rival Sisters*, 1695; *The Libertine*, ?1695

Court odes: *Welcome, viceregent of the mighty king*, 1680; *Swifter, Isis, swifter flow*, 1681; *What, What shall be done in behalf of the man?*, 1682; *The Summer's absence unconcerned we bear*, 1682; *From hardy climes and dangerous toils of war*, 1683; *Fly, bold rebellion*, 1683; *From those serene and rapturous joys*, 1684; *Why, why are all the muses mute?*, 1685; *Ye tuneful muses*, 1686; *Sound* the trumpet, 1687; *Now does the glorious day appear* (birthday of Mary II; Thomas Shadwell), 1689; *Arise, my muse* (birthday of Mary II; Thomas D'Urfey), 1690; *Welcome, welcome, glorious morn* (birthday of Mary II), 1691; *Love's goddess sure was blind* (birthday of Mary II; Charles Sedley), 1692; *Celebrate this festival* (birthday of Mary II; Nahum Tate), 1693; COME, YE SONS OF ART, AWAY (birthday of Mary II), 1694; *Who can from joy refrain?*, 1695

Other odes: *Welcome to all the pleasures* (St Cecilia's Day; Charles Fishburn), 1683; *Raise, raise the voice* (St Cecilia's Day), c.1685; *Celestial music did the gods inspire* (Maidwell's School), 1690; *Of old when heroes thought it base* (Yorkshire Feast; D'Urfey), 1690; HAIL, BRIGHT CECILIA, 1692; *Great parent, hail* (Trinity College Dublin; Tate), 1694; *Te Deum and Jubilate* (St Cecilia's Day), 1694

Church music

Anthems with strings: *I was glad when they said unto me*; *In Thee, O Lord, do I put my trust*; *My beloved spake*; *My heart is inditing*; *O give thanks unto the Lord*; *O praise God in His Holiness*; *O sing unto the Lord*; *Praise the Lord, O Jerusalem*; *Rejoice in the Lord alway* (BELL ANTHEM); *They that go down to the sea in ships*; etc.

Other anthems: *Blessed is he whose unrighteousness is forgiven*; *Blow up the trumpet in Sion*; *Hear my prayer, O God*; *Hear my prayer, O Lord*; *Hosanna to the Highest*; *I will love Thee, O Lord*; *I will sing unto the Lord*; *Jehova, quam multi sont hostes*; *Let mine eyes run down with tears*; *Lord, how long wilt Thou be angry?*; *The Lord is King, be the people never so impatient*; *O God, Thou art my God*; *O God, Thou hast cast us out*; *O Lord God of hosts*; *O Lord our Governor*; *Out of the deep have I called*; *Remember not, Lord, our offences*; *Who hath believed our report?*; *Thy word is a lantern unto my feet*; *Turn Thou us, O good Lord*; etc.

Services: Morning and Evening Service, B♭; *Magnificat* and *Nunc dimittis*, G minor; FUNERAL MUSIC FOR QUEEN MARY II

Domestic music

Devotional cantatas (for 2–4 voices and continuo): *Awake, ye dead*; *Beati omnes qui timent Dominum*; *Close thine eyes and sleep secure*; *Hear me, O Lord, the great support*; *Hosanna to the Highest*; *In guilty night*; *Lord, I can suffer Thy rebukes*; *Let the night perish* (Job's Curse); *We sing to him whose wisdom form'd the ear*; etc.

Devotional songs: 'Awake and with attention hear'; 'The earth trembled'; 'In the black dismal dungeon of despair'; 'Lord, what is man?'; 'Now that the sun hath veiled his light' ('An Evening Hymn on a Ground'); 'Tell me, some pitying angel' ('The Blessed Virgin's Expostulation'); 'Thou wakeful shepherd' ('A Morning Hymn'); 'With sick and famish'd eyes'

Elegies: *What hope for us remains now he is gone?* (for Matthew Locke), 1677; *Gentle shepherds* (for John Playford), 1686–7; *O dive custos Auriacae domus* (for Mary II), 1695

Secular songs: 'Ah! cruel nymph'; 'Beneath the poplar's shadow'; 'Fairest isle'; 'The fatal hour'; 'Fly swift, ye hours'; 'From silent shades (Bess of Bedlam)'; 'From rosy bow'rs'; 'Hark, the ech'ing air'; 'How blest are shepherds'; 'I attempt from love's sickness'; 'I came, I saw, and was undone'; 'If grief has any power to kill'; 'If music be the food of love', 3 settings; 'If prayers and tears'; 'I'll sail upon the dog-star'; 'I lov'd fair Celia'; 'Incassum Lesbia rogas' ('The Queen's Epicedium'); 'I take no pleasure in the sun's bright beams'; 'Let each gallant heart'; 'Let formal lovers still pursue'; 'Let the dreadful engines'; 'Let us dance'; 'Love in their little veins'; 'Love, thou can'st hear'; 'Man is for the woman made'; 'Music for a while'; 'Not all my torments'; 'No, to what purpose'; 'Nymphs and shepherds'; 'O! fair Cedaria'; 'O lead me to some peaceful gloom'; 'On the brow of Richmond Hill'; 'O solitude, my sweetest choice'; 'Pious Celinda'; 'Retir'd from any mortal's sight'; 'She loves and she confesses too'; 'Since from my dear'; 'Stript of their green'; 'Sweeter than roses'; 'Sylvia, now your scorn'; 'Take not a woman's anger ill'; 'Turn then thine eyes'; 'Urge me no more'; 'Ye gentle spirits of the air'; etc.

Secular duets: 'Dulcibella, when e'er I sue for a kiss'; 'I spy Celia'; 'Lost is my quiet for ever'; 'No, no resistance is but vain'; 'Shepherd, leave decoying'; 'What can we poor females do?'; 'When Myra sings'; etc.

Music for strings: Chacony, G minor, a 4, c.1678; Three Parts upon a Ground, ?1678; Fantasia upon One Note, a 5, c.1680; Fantasias a 3, D minor, F, G minor, c.1680; Fantasias a 4, G minor, B♭, F, C minor, D minor, A minor, E minor, G, D minor, 1680; In Nomine a 6, c.1680; In Nomine a 7, c.1680; Pavan, G minor, 3 viol/vn, con, after 1678; Pavans, A, A minor, B♭, G minor, 2 viol/vn, con, c.1680; 22 Sonatas, 2 vn, b viol, con, (pub as 12 *Sonnata's of III Parts*, 1683, and *Ten Sonata's in Four Parts*, 1697); Overtures, G, D minor, G minor, c.1682; Prelude, vn/rec; Sonata, G minor, vn, con, ?1683–4; Sonata, D minor, tpt, str, c.1690–95

Other works: suites, dances, marches, arrangements, hpd; voluntaries, org; catches, 3/4 voices

puritani, I (The Puritans). Opera by Bellini to a libretto by Carlo Pepoli deriving from Walter Scott's *Old Mortality*. Elvira (soprano), belonging to a Puritan family, is in love with Arturo (tenor), a cavalier on the opposing side in the English Civil War. Their wedding is approved by her uncle Giorgio (bass) but derailed by the jealous Riccardo (baritone), sending her mad. Arturo comes back, gets captured and is about to be executed, but the cessation of hostilities makes possible a happy ending. Bellini wrote the work for four outstanding singers – Grisi, Rubini, Tamburini, Lablache – with numbers including Arturo's cavatina 'A te, o cara', Elvira's polacca 'Son vergin vezzosa' and her mad scene 'Qui la voce'. First performance: Paris, 25 Jan 1835.

Pushkin, Aleksandr (Sergeyevich) (b. Moscow, 26 May 1799; d. St Petersburg, 29 Jan 1837). Russian poet, of extraordinary fecundity, brilliance and variety. His place in Russian literature might be compared with that in English of Byron (for Romanticism and style, in art as in life) plus Shakespeare (as a universally revered founding figure). Many Russian composers have set his poems as songs, while his tales and dramas have provided the basis for a significant part of the Russian operatic repertory, including Glinka's *Ruslan and Lyudmila*, Dargomyzhsky's *The Stone Guest*, Musorgsky's *Boris Godunov*, Tchaikovsky's *Eugene Onegin, Mazeppa* and *The Queen of Spades*, Rimsky-Korsakov's *Mozart and Salieri, Tsar Saltan* and *The Golden Cockerel*, Rachmaninoff's *Aleko* and *The Miserly Knight*, and Stravinsky's *Mavra*.

puzzle canon. Canon notated just as one line, leaving the others to be deduced – as they may be, by considering the harmonies that will be produced.

Pycard (*fl. c.*1410). English composer whose exciting settings of mass sections in the Old Hall manuscript, for four and five voices, include remarkable canonic ingenuity.

Pygott, Richard (b. *c.*1485; d. autumn 1549). English composer, attached to Cardinal Wolsey's private chapel and after 1530 to the Chapel Royal. Less spectacular than Taverner's, his music is sure in movement; a *Veni Sancte Spiritus* mass and a few other pieces (notably *Quid petis o fili*) survive.

Pythagoras (6th century BC). Greek philosopher credited with discovering that strings of particular length ratios produce particular intervals: 2:1 for the octave, 3:2 for the fifth, etc. This was known, however, to the Babylonians, perhaps three millennia before. See CONSONANCE; FREQUENCY RATIO; TEMPERAMENT.

Pythagorean comma. See COMMA.

qnt. Abbreviation for quintet.

qt. Abbreviation for quartet.

Quadrat (Ger.). Natural, as in 'C natural'.

quadrille (from It. *squadriglia* or Sp. *cuadrilla*, a small cavalry troop). 19th-century dance for well regulated groups of couples, its music in bouncy and repetitive phrases of duple rhythm. Parodies of Wagner were written in quadrille form by Chabrier (*Souvenirs de Munich*, themes from *Tristan*) and Fauré and Messager (*Souvenirs de Bayreuth*, themes from *The Ring*).

quadruple counterpoint. INVERTIBLE COUN-TERPOINT in four parts.

quadruple croche (Fr.). 64th-note, hemidemi-semiquaver.

quadruple stop. Foursome of notes played simultaneously on a string instrument with thumb and three fingers on different strings, i.e. by quadruple stopping. Most often the notes will be arpeggiated.

quadruplet. Group of four equal notes to be played in the time of some other number, most usually three.

quadruple time. Four beats to the bar, more commonly known, when these are crotchet beats, as common time.

quadruple wind. Four each of flutes, oboes, clarinets and bassons, the standard line-up in Bruckner, Mahler and Strauss.

Quantz, Johann Joachim (b. Oberscheden, Hanover, 30 Jan 1697; d. Potsdam, 12 Jul 1773). German flautist-composer. He grew up as a town musician, apprenticed first to his uncle, and in 1717 had counterpoint lessons with Zelenka in Vienna. The next year he joined the Polish court in Dresden and Warsaw as an oboist, but turned to the flute and began composing for the instrument. He then spent the years 1724–7 in Italy (studying with Gasparini), Paris and London (where he met Handel). Soon after returning to Dresden he began making regular visits to Berlin, to give flute lessons to the crown prince, who, now Frederick II, invited him to court in 1741. There he remained, supervising the regular evening concerts and adding to an output of hundreds of flute sonatas and concertos. In 1752 he published a treatise on playing the flute, full of important evidence of period style.

quarta (It.). Fourth (interval).

quartal. Term used of harmony based on fourths.

quart de soupir (Fr.). Semiquaver (16th-note) rest.

quarte (Fr.). Fourth (interval), hence *quarte juste* (perfect fourth), *quarte augmenté*.

Quarte (Ger.). Fourth (interval).

Quarte de nasard. French organ stop a fourth above the Nasard.

quarter-note (US). Crotchet (UK). See DURA-TION.

quarter-tone. Half a semitone. See MICROTONE.

quartet (Fr. *quatuor*, Ger. *Quartett*, pl. *Quartette*, It. *quartetto*, pl. *quartetti*). Group of four instruments or voices, or group of performers on such, or genre of music for that medium, or work of that genre. In the sphere of vocal music, the term is generally confined to the 19th-century tradition represented by Brahms's *Liebeslieder* waltzes, to sections for four singers in operas (there are notable examples in *Don Giovanni*, *Fidelio* and *Rigoletto*) and to the group of soloists often required in a mass, oratorio or similar composition: soprano, contralto, tenor and bass. Far and away the most important instrumental form is the STRING QUARTET, followed a long way after by the PIANO QUARTET, FLUTE QUARTET and OBOE QUARTET. There are also quartets for other groupings by Webern, Messiaen and Wolpe.

Quartett (Ger.). Quartet, often string quartet.

quartetto (It.). Quartet, often string quartet (more formally *quartetto d'archi*).

Quartetto Italiano. Ensemble founded in Reggio Emilia in 1945 and active internationally until 1987, comprising Paolo Borciani, Elisa Pegreffi, Piero Farulli and Franco Rossi. They played from memory and made many magnificent recordings.

quasihemidemisemiquaver (UK). 128th note (US). See DURATION.

... quasi una fantasia .... Work by Kurtág for piano and dispersed instrumental groups, written for Kocsis in homage also to Beethoven and his Op.27 pair of sonatas 'quasi una fantasia'. Similarly Kurtág's Op.27 comprises this work along with another concerto. First performance: Berlin, 16 Oct 1988.

Quattro pezzi sacri (Four Sacred Pieces). Set of miscellaneous pieces by Verdi comprising: *Ave Maria* (satb, 1889), *Laudi alla Vergine Maria* (ssaa, c.1890), *Te Deum* (soli, ch, orch, 1895–6), *Stabat mater* (ch, orch, 1896–7).

quattro stagioni, Le (The Four Seasons). Set of four violin concertos by Vivaldi: *La primavera* (Spring) in E, *L'estate* (Summer) in G minor, *L'autunno* (Autumn) in F and *L'inverno* (Winter) in F minor. They include impressions of weather (heat haze, frost) and seasonal activities (hunting), and in the above order opened his published set of 12 concertos *Il* CIMENTO DELL'ARMONIA E DELL'INVENTIONE.

quatuor (Fr.). Quartet, often string quartet (more formally *quatuor à cordes*).

quatuor concertant (Fr., concertante quartet). String quartet with a solo part for the leader, as favoured by Parisian publishers in the 1770s and 1780s, and written by Carl Stamitz and others.

Quatuor pour la fin du temps (Quartet for the End of Time). Work by Messiaen for clarinet, violin, cello and piano, based on images from the Apocalypse, in eight movements: 1 *Liturgie de cristal*, 2 *Vocalise pour l'ange qui annonce la fin du temps*, 3 *Abîme des oiseaux* (cl), 4 *Intermède*, 5 *Louange à l'éternité de Jésus* (vc, pf), 6 *Danse de la fureur, pour les sept trompettes*, 7 *Fouillis d'arcs-en-ciel, pour l'ange qui annonce la fin du temps*, 8 *Louange à l'immortalité de Jésus* (vn, pf). Messiaen wrote it for himself to play with fellow inmates in a prisoner-of-war camp. First performance: Görlitz, 15 Jan 1941.

quaver (UK). Eighth note (US). See DURATION.

Queen of Spades, The (*Pikovaya Dama*, *Pique Dame*). Opera by Tchaikovsky to a libretto by his brother Modest after Pushkin's novella. Hermann (tenor), an officer, determines to win Lisa (soprano) by making his fortune at cards, but his desperation leads to the deaths of both of them. The second act includes a rococo pastoral divertissement. First performance: Mariinsky, St Petersburg, 19 Dec 1890.

Querelle des bouffons (Fr., Quarrel of the Comedians). Dispute aroused by the presentation of Pergolesi's *La serva padrona* and other Italian comedies at the Paris Opera in 1752. For two years the rival supporters of Italian music (including Rousseau) and French fired off pamphlets at each other.

Querflöte (Ger.). Transverse flute, as opposed to *Blockflöte* (recorder).

quill. Plucking part of a harpsichord or similar instrument. Traditionally the shafts of crow feathers were used; modern plastic replacements are still called 'quills'.

Quilter, Roger (Cuthbert) (b. Hove, 1 Nov 1877; d. London, 21 Sep 1953). British composer, a pupil of Knorr in Frankfurt, who is known especially for his elegant songs setting Shakespeare-age and Romantic lyrics, among which are 'Now sleeps the crimson petal' (Tennyson, 1897) and 'Love's Philosophy' (Shelley, pub 1905). He also wrote light orchestral music.

Quinault, Philippe (baptized Paris, 5 Jun 1635; d. Paris, 26 Nov 1688). French poet. A protégé of Tristan l'Hermite, he was the author of librettos for Lully, some of which were set a century later by composers including Gluck and J.C. Bach.

quint. Fifth (interval). Also an organ stop, for chorus ranks sounding a fifth above.

quinta (It.). Fifth (interval), hence *quinta giusta* (perfect fifth), *quinta diminuita, quinta eccedente* (augmented fifth).

quinte (Fr.). Fifth (interval), hence *quinte juste* (perfect fifth), *quinte diminué, quinte augmenté.*

Quinte (Ger.). Fifth (interval), also used as a prefix in the name of an instrument, e.g. *Quintposaune*, sounding a fifth lower than normal.

Quinten. See FIFTHS.

quintet (Fr. *quintette*, Ger. *Quintett*, pl. *Quintette*, It. *quintetto*, pl. *quintetti*). Group of five instruments or voices, or group of performers on such, or genre of music for that medium, or work of that genre. In the sphere of vocal music, the term is generally confined to sections for five singers in operas (there is a notable example in *Die Meistersinger*). The important instrumental forms are the STRING QUINTET, WIND QUINTET, CLARINET QUINTET and PIANO QUINTET. There are also quintets for other groupings by Mozart, Beethoven, Prokofiev, Carter, etc.

quintole. QUINTUPLET.

quintuplet. Group of five equal notes to be played in the time of some other number, most usually three or four.

quintuple time. Five beats to a bar, unusual as a regular metre and generally subdivided as 2 + 3 (i.e. secondary stress on the third beat) or 3 + 2 (secondary stress on the fourth beat). In the context of more normal metres it may convey mental disturbance (mad scene of Handel's *Orlando*, Act 3 of *Tristan*), a distinctive lilt (second movement of Tchaikovsky's 'Pathétique' Symphony, first of *The Planets*) or a suave barbarism (finale of Ravel's *Daphnis*).

quodlibet (Lat., what you please). Medley of popular melodies, named after a humorous kind of disputation in 16th-century Germany. The most famous example is Bach's in the Goldberg Variations.

quotation. Excerpt from one work placed in another. Most medieval and Renaissance polphony is based on quotation, of plainsong, popular tune or other polyphony. The busy composers of the Baroque, including Bach and Handel, would readily re-use earlier material, whether their own or others'. Quotations in Classical and Romantic music generally take the form of subjects for variations. Schumann, however, introduced a different, momentary use of quotations and self-quotations, taken up by Berg in his Lyric Suite (*Tristan* prelude) and Violin Concerto (Bach chorale). Ives, meanwhile, had used quotations exuberantly and plentifully. For a brief period around 1970 quotation was ubiquitous: the middle movement of Berio's *Sinfonia* is a tissue of borrowings within the frame of the scherzo from Mahler's Second Symphony.

r

Raaff, Anton (baptized Gesdorf, near Bonn, 6 May 1714; d. Munich, 28 May 1797). German tenor, active all over western Europe, creator of roles in operas by Jommelli, J.C. Bach and Mozart (Idomeneo).

Rabaud, Henri (b. Paris, 10 Nov 1873; d. Paris, 11 Sep 1949). French composer. Born into a musical family, he studied at the Conservatoire and in the classic way was converted to Wagnerism by a trip to Bayreuth. He wrote operas (*Marouf, savetier du Caire*, 1914) and orchestral works, and was director of the Conservatoire (1922–41).

Rabinovitch(-Barakovsky), Alexandre [Aleksandr Ilyich] (b. Baku, 30 Mar 1945). Russian composer, pianist and conductor, a frequent partner of Argerich and fecund source of minimalist tonal music imbued with metaphysical notions from many cultures. He studied at the Moscow Conservatory with Nathan Fischmann and Kabalevsky, and emigrated in 1974, eventually settling in Switzerland. Many of his works are for amplified instruments, with or without orchestra.

Rachmaninoff, Serge [Rachmaninov; Rakhmaninov, Sergey Vasilyevich] (b. Oneg, 1 Apr 1873; d. Beverly Hills, 28 Mar 1943). Russian pianist-composer. Distinctly dour as an individual, he had a radiant lyrical gift that made him the last great master of Russian Romanticism, in the tradition especially of Tchaikovsky.

Born into a bourgeois family in reduced circumstances, he studied in St Petersburg and then – from 1885, after his sister had died from diphtheria and his parents had separated – in Moscow. He was set on a career as a concert pianist, and to that end, from 1889 he lodged with his teacher, Nikolay Zverev. Meanwhile he attended classes at the conservatory with Ziloti, Taneyev and Arensky, gaining the skills that would enable him to fulfil his second goal: that of becoming a composer. (He had begun writing music in 1886.) In 1892 he graduated from the conservatory, signed a publishing contract with Karl Gutheil, and wrote his popular Prelude in C♯ minor. Right away his works were not just those of a regular composing virtuoso; his early compositions include symphonic poems (*Prince Rotislav, The Rock*) and a one-act opera – *Aleko*, staged at the Bolshoy in 1893 – as well as a trio in memory of Tchaikovsky. But the première of his First Symphony in 1896 was a failure. His confidence gone, he turned to conducting, in which capacity he made his first trip abroad, to London in April 1899, for a performance of *The Rock*.

In 1900 he undertook a course of psychiatric treatment at the hands of Nikolay Dahl, and very soon he was composing again on a large scale. His Second Suite for two pianos, Cello Sonata and Second Piano Concerto all emerged in 1900–1, and the success of the concerto – which he introduced in Moscow with Ziloti conducting on 9 November 1901 – fully restored his belief in himself. The next year he got married, to his cousin Natalya Satina. They had two daughters, Irina and Tatyana, and travelled a good deal as a family, spending time in Dresden and Rome, though Natalya's family estate of Ivanovka, which they inherited, was a regular base.

The flurry of compositional work went on, with the Chopin Variations and other piano music in

1901–3, followed in 1903–5 by two more one-act operas, *The Miserly Knight* and *Francesca da Rimini*, which he introduced during two seasons when he was conducting at the Bolshoy (1904–6). He considered further opera subjects, but turned instead to orchestral scores (including his grand and passionate Second Symphony) and piano music. In 1909 he made his first US tour, during which he gave the first performance of his Third Piano Concerto, at Carnegie Hall on 28 November, again with immediate success. The following years were devoted to concert tours in Europe and composition at Ivanovka, including work on two big liturgical settings, the choral symphony *The Bells* and the two volumes of *Etudes-Tableaux*.

This busy period came to an abrupt end in 1917. He and his family left Russia just before Christmas, soon after the Bolshevik Revolution, and went first to Stockholm, then Copenhagen, before travelling in November 1918 to New York. There he abandoned composition, at least partly so that he could support his family as a concert pianist. Famed for the music he was no longer writing, he travelled widely in the USA, with a repertory largely of his own works, Chopin and Liszt. Meanwhile, at home, he and his family continued to live as they had at Ivanovka, with Russian meals served to them by their Russian servants.

In 1926 he returned to composition, producing his Fourth Piano Concerto, which was badly received. Though later revised, it has remained the poor relation of its two predecessors, and the setback surely contributed to a further five-year creative silence. Then came a string of late masterpieces, which he composed either during summers at his villa in Switzerland or in the USA: the Corelli Variations, Paganini Rhapsody, Third Symphony and Symphonic Dances. The last three works, written for US orchestras, brought a new outwardness and lustre to his style.

Sergei Bertensson and Jay Leyda *Sergei Rachmaninoff* (1956, ²2001); Geoffrey Norris *Rachmaninoff* (1976, ²1993)

Dramatic and orchestral music

One-act operas: *Aleko* (Vladimir Nemirovich-Danchenko, after Pushkin), 1892, f.p. Moscow, 1893; *The Miserly Knight* (Pushkin), Op.24, 1903–5, f.p. Moscow, 1906; *Francesca da Rimini* (Modest Tchaikovsky, after Dante), Op.25, 1904–5, f.p. Moscow, 1906

Symphonies: No.1, D minor, Op.13, 1895; No.2, E minor, Op.27, 1906–7; No.3, A minor, Op.44, 1935–6, rev 1938

Concertante works: PIANO CONCERTO No.1, F♯ minor, Op.1, 1890–91, rev 1917; No.2, C minor, Op.18, 1900–1; No.3, D minor, Op.30, 1909; No.4, G minor, Op.40, 1926, rev 1941; Rhapsody on a Theme of Paganini, Op.43, 1934

Symphonic poems: *Prince Rotislav*, 1891; *The Rock*, Op.7, 1893; *The Isle of the Dead*, Op.29, 1909

Other orchestral works: *Caprice bohémien*, Op.12, 1892, 1894; *Spring* (cantata; Nikolay Nekrasov), Op.20, bar, ch, orch, 1902; *The* BELLS (choral symphony), Op.35, 1913; 3 Russian Songs, Op.41, ch, orch, 1926; Symphonic Dances, 1940

Chamber and piano music

Chamber: *Trio élégiaque*, G minor, pf trio, 1892; 2 Pieces, Op.2, vc, pf, 1892; 2 Pieces, Op.6, vn, pf, 1893; *Trio élégiaque*, D minor, Op.9, pf, trio, 1893, rev 1907, 1917; Cello Sonata, G minor, Op.19, 1901; Hopak from *Sorochintsy Fair* (Musorgsky), vn, pf, arr 1926

Piano: *Morceaux de fantaisie*, Op.3, 1892 (No.2 Prelude, C♯ minor); *Morceaux de salon*, Op.10, 1893–4; *Moments musicaux*, Op.16, 1896; *Morceau de fantaisie*, G minor, 1899; Fughetta, 1899; Variations on a Theme of Chopin, Op.22, 1902–3; 10 Preludes, Op.23, 1901–3; Sonata No.1, D minor, Op.28, 1907; 13 Preludes, Op.32, 1910; *Etudes-Tableaux*, book 1, Op.33, 1911; Sonata No.2, B♭ minor, Op.36, 1913, rev 1931; *Etudes-Tableaux*, book 2, Op.39, 1916–17; *Oriental Sketch*, 1917; Piece, D minor, 1917; Fragments, 1917; Variations on a Theme of Corelli, Op.42, 1931

Arrangements for piano: *Polka VR* (Behr), 1911; *The Star-Spangled Banner*, 1918; Minuet from *L'Arlésienne* (Bizet), 1922; Hopak from *Sorochintsy Fair* (Musorgsky), 1924; *Wohin?* (Schubert), 1925; *Liebesfreud* (Kreisler), 1925; *Liebeslied* (Kreisler), 1931; *Flight of the Bumblebee* (Rimsky-Korsakov), 1931; Prelude, Gavotte and Gigue from the Violin Partita in E (Bach), 1933; Scherzo from *A Midsummer Night's Dream* (Mendelssohn), 1933; *Daisies* (own song), 1940; *Lilacs* (own song), 1941

Piano duo: *Russian Rhapsody*, 1891; *Fantaisie-Tableaux* (Suite No.1), Op.5, 1893; Suite No.2, Op.17, 1900–1; Prelude in C♯ minor, arr 1938

Piano duet: Romance, duet, 1893; 6 Duets, Op.11, 1894; *Polka italienne*, duet, ?1906

Sacred music and songs

Sacred: *Liturgy of St John Chrysostom*, Op.31, ch, 1910; *All-Night Vigil*, Op.37, ch, 1915

Songs: 'Again I am alone' (Shevchenko), Op.26:9, 1906; 'All things pass by' (Daniil Rathaus), Op.26:15, 1906; 'Arion' (Pushkin), Op.34:5, 1912; 'Before my window' (Glafira Galina), Op.26:10, 1906; 'Believe it or not' (A.K. Tolstoy), Op.14:7, 1896; 'Beloved, let us fly' (Arseny Golenishchev-Kutuzov), Op.26:5, 1906; 'By the fresh grave' (Semyon Nadson), Op.21:2, 1902; 'Christ is risen' (Dmitry Merezhovsky), Op.26:6, 1906; 'Daisies' (Igor Severyanin), Op.38:3, 1916; 'The Dream' (Aleksey Pleshcheyev, after Heine), Op.8:5, 1893; 'A Dream' (Sologub), Op.38:5, 1916; 'Fate' (Apukhtin), Op.21:1, 1900; 'The Fountain' (Tyutchev), Op.26:11, 1906; 'He took all from me' (Tyutchev), Op.26:2, 1906; 'How fair this spot' (Galina), Op.21:7, 1902; 'How long, my friend' (Golenishchev-Kutuzov), Op.4:6, 1893; 'How painful for me' (Galina),

Op.21:12, 1902; 'I have grown fond of sorrow' (Shevchenko), Op.8:4, 1893; 'I wait for thee', Op.14:1. 1894; 'I was with her' (Aleksey Koltsov), Op.14:4, 1896; 'In my garden at night' (Blok, after Isaakian), Op.38:1, 1916; 'In the silence of the secret night' (Fet), Op.4:3, ?1892; 'The Isle' (Balmont, after Shelley), Op.14:2, 1896; 'Lilacs' (Ekaterina Beketova), Op.21:5, 1902; 'Loneliness' (Apukhtin, after De Musset), Op.21:6, 1902; 'Melody' (Nadson), Op.21:9, 1902; 'Morning', Op.4:2, ?1891–2; 'Night is mournful' (Bunin), Op.26:12, 1906; 'No prophet I' (Aleksandr Kruglov), Op.21:11, 1902; 'Oh, do not grieve' (Apukhtin), Op.14:8, 1896; 'Oh no, I beg you' (Merezhkovsky), Op.4:1, 1892; 'Prayer' (Pleshcheyev, after Goethe), Op.8:6, 1893; 'She is as lovely as the noon' (Nikolay Minsky), Op.14:9, 1896; 'Sing not to me' (Pushkin), Op.4:4, ?1892–3; 'Spring Waters' (Tyutchev), Op.14:11, 1896; 'The Storm' (Pushkin), Op.34:3, 1912; 'These summer nights' (Rathaus), Op.14:5, 1896; 'They answered' (Mey, after Hugo), Op.21:4, 1902; ''Tis time' (Nadson), Op.14:12, 1896; 'Twilight' (Ivan Tkhorzhevsky, after Guyot), Op.21:3, 1902; 'Vocalise', Op.34:14, 1912, rev 1915; 'The Waterlily' (Pleshcheyev, after Heine), Op.8:1, 1893; 'When yesterday we met' (Yakov Polonsky), Op.26:13, 1906; etc.

racket. Wind instrument, a squashed and stopped shawm or bassoon, current in the decades around 1600 and, in modified form, in the 18th century.

Radamisto. Opera by Handel to a libretto possibly by Haym. Radamisto (soprano) and his wife, Zenobia (soprano), are subjected to many vicissitudes at the hands of fate and of the tyrant Tiridate (tenor), unassisted by his virtuous wife Polissena (contralto). The good triumph and pardon the wicked. First performance: London, 27 Apr 1720.

raddoppiato (It.). Redoubled, i.e. twice as fast.

Radetzky March. Piece by Johann Strauss I, not to be confused with RÁKÓCZI MARCH.

radical cadence. Cadence in which both chords are in root position, as distinct from a MEDIAL CADENCE.

radio. Telegraphy and wireless communication – with their descendants TELEVISION and the INTERNET – made it possible for music to be disseminated to large, potentially limitless audiences. Sporadic experiments in broadcasting through the telephone system began in the 1880s. Using technology accelerated by war, regular public radio started during the years 1920–25 in the USA, Europe, India and elsewhere. In most European countries broadcasting was soon placed in the control of a single authority (though Germany had several, in major cities), with state support and varying degrees of independence, while the USA developed a large network of local stations, drawing revenue from advertising. Programming, though, was much the same on both sides of the Atlantic. Prompted by a widely shared belief in the value of great art – and a widely shared confidence that radio could transmit that art to everyone – radio corporations took part in the great educational enterprise of the interwar years. Radio orchestras were founded (beginning with the Danish Radio Symphony in 1926), studio concerts promoted, recordings aired, live events transmitted (including in the USA Saturday afternoon broadcasts from the Met, instituted on Christmas Day 1931), instructive programmes developed, and works commissioned specifically for radio, among the earliest being the Brecht–Weill cantata *Das Berliner Requiem* (1928) and Cadman's *The Willow Tree* (f.p. NBC, 1932), seemingly the first radio opera. In the later 1930s and early 1940s Britten and Auden collaborated on radio features for the BBC in London and CBS in New York; other composers to write specifically for radio during this period included Copland (*Saga of the Prairie*, 1937) and Walton (*Christopher Columbus*, 1942).

The radio environment remained propitious for classical music after the Second World War, when in most countries there was a splitting of programming into channels for talk and news, light and popular music, and high culture. There came a splitting, too, in conditions for music on radio around the globe, in response to the boom in popular music and the arrival of television as the new universal medium. In the USA commercial recordings came to dominate airtime (though with broadcasts continuing from the Met and major orchestras), and the NBC Symphony was disbanded in 1954, though National Public Radio, funded by donations and state grants, was founded in 1971 to maintain a place for classical music. Meanwhile in Europe, on both sides of the Iron Curtain, radio organizations were taking greater responsibility for musical performance and, particularly, creation. The avant-garde music of the 1950s–70s was strongly promoted by radio stations, especially in Germany, as was the new genre of electronic music; Stockhausen recognized his debt to the medium in using radio receivers as performing instruments in 1968–9 (though Cage had preceded him, in his *Imaginary Landscape No.4* of 1951). In the 1980s–90s, however, there came a change of mood, everywhere. The sense of moral and educational mission began to waver; programming was now dictated less by a producer's judgement of worth than by an accountant's estimate of popularity. Nevertheless, many of the institutions remained in place, to develop slowly in the more beneficent atmosphere of the 21st century. See also BBC; CBS; NBC; SWR; WDR.

Gilbert Chase, ed. *Music in Radio Broadcasting* (1946)

Radulescu, Horatiu (b. Bucharest, 7 Jan 1942). Romanian–French composer of daring imagination. After studies with Tiberiu Olah, Niculescu and Aurel Stroe at the Bucharest Conservatory, he moved to Paris in 1969, threw himself into the avant-garde musical world and became an influential if wild figure in the early history of spectral music. In 1970–72 he studied with Kagel and Ferrari in Cologne and with Stockhausen at Darmstadt. In 1974 he began working with the 'sound icon': a grand piano placed on its side, with its strings undamped, and played with bows, producing extraordinary resonant sounds. Other works are for more normal instruments, though often in abnormal formations.

Large-scale: *Clepsydra*, 16 sound icons, 1983; *Awakening* ∞, chbr orch, 1983; *Byzantine Prayer*, 40 fl, 1988; *Angolo divino*, orch, 1993–4; etc.
Ensemble: *Sensual Sky*, 9 insts, 1985; *Inner Time II*, 7 cl, 1993; etc.
String quartets: No.5 'before the universe was born', 1990–95; No.6 'practising eternity', 1992; etc.
Piano sonatas: No.1 'being and non-being create each other', 1991; No.2 'you will endure forever', 1992–9; No.3 'like a well … older than God', 1993; etc.

Raff, (Joseph) Joachim (b. Lachen, near Zurich, 27 May 1822; d. Frankfurt, 24/5 Jun 1882). German composer, notably of programme symphonies. While working as a schoolteacher (1840–44) he had help from Mendelssohn in getting some piano pieces published. Later he was taken up by von Bülow and by Liszt, whose assistant he became in Weimar (1850–56). He then moved to Wiesbaden, where he married, and in 1877 to Frankfurt, where he directed the Hoch Conservatory. A hugely energetic and ambitious composer who hoped to integrate diverse styles, old and new, he was much admired in his time, then not so much.

www.raff.org

Symphonies: No.1 'An das Vaterland', D, Op.96, 1859–61; No.2, C, Op.140, 1866; No.3 'Im Walde', F, Op.153, 1869; No.4, G minor, Op.167, 1871; No.5 'Lenore', E, Op.177, 1872; No.6, D minor, Op.189, 1873; No.7 'In den Alpen', Bb, Op.201, 1875; No.8 'Frühlingsklänge', A, Op.205, 1876; No.9 'Im Sommer', E minor, Op.208, 1878; No.10 'Zur Herbstzeit', F minor, Op.213, 1879; No.11 'Der Winter', A minor, Op.214, 1876
Other works: *Dame Kobold* (opera; Reber), 1870;

Weltende, Gericht, Neue Welt (oratorio), Op.212, 1879–81; concertos, overtures, suites, chamber music (*Cavatina*, D, Op.85:3, vn, pf), partsongs, solo songs, numerous piano compositions, etc.

raga. Melodic formula, basis of improvisation, central to the music of INDIA.

ragtime. Musical style distinguished by syncopated and often pentatonic melodies set against rhythmically regular basses in square, symmetrical forms. Its heyday was the period from the late 1890s to around 1915, and its main practitioners were black pianist-composers in Missouri (Scott Joplin) and on the east coast (James P. Johnson). Unlike jazz, which largely replaced it, ragtime circulated in print (Joplin's *Maple Leaf Rag* of 1899 soon sold a million copies), and it was in print form that Stravinsky encountered it, to respond in his *Rag-time* (1918). Ragtime also appears in Ives's First Piano Sonata and other works. There was a revival in the 1970s, when Bolcom and others began writing rags.

Raimbaut de Vaqeiras (b. Vacqueiras, near Orange, ?1150–60; d. ?near Messiople, Greece, 4 Sep 1207). Troubadour, who probably died in battle under the flag of his patron Boniface, Marquis of Monferrat. Seven songs by him survive with music, all dating from his last decade, including the ESTAMPIE *Kalenda maya*.

Raimon de Miraval (*fl.* 1185–1229). Troubadour, the author of 22 songs surviving with music.

Raindrop. Name given Chopin's Prelude in Db Op.28:15 on account of its raining repeated Ab.

Rainier, (Ivy) Priaulx (b. Howick, Natal, 3 Feb 1903; d. Besse-en-Chandesse, 10 Oct 1986). South African composer. She won a violin scholarship to the RAM in 1920, and was in her 30s before she started concentrating on composition, which she studied with Boulanger in Paris. Her works are compact and relatively few, with some influence from Bartók and African music, but a distinctive force and frankness.

Vocal: *Cycle for Declamation* (Donne), v, 1953–4; *Requiem* (Gascoyne), t, ch, 1955–6; etc.
Instrumental: *Barbaric Dance Suite*, pf, 1949; *Quanta*, ob qt, 1961–2; *Ploërmel*, wind, perc, 1972–3; *Concertante*, ob, cl, orch, 1980–81; etc.

Raitio, Väinö (Eerikki) (b. Sortavala, 15 Apr 1891; d. Helsinki, 10 Sep 1945). Finnish composer. He studied at the Helsinki Conservatory (1911–16), then broadened his horizons in Moscow (1916–17), Berlin (1921) and Paris (1925–6), absorbing influences from Scriabin and Debussy that were new to Finnish music. His works include tone poems and operas.

Rake's Progress, The. Opera by Stravinsky to a libretto by Auden and Kallman, after Hogarth's series of paintings. Tom Rakewell (tenor), led by his devilish alter ego Nick Shadow (bass), turns against natural virtue as represented by Anne Trulove (soprano). The work is scored for Mozartian forces, including harpsichord continuo, and also gathers Monteverdi, Donizetti and Verdi into its recollections. First performance: Venice, 11 Sep 1951.

Rákóczi March. Anonymous Hungarian march of the early 19th century bearing the name of the patriot Prince Ferenc Rákóczi II (1676–1735), used by Berlioz in *The Damnation of Faust* and Liszt in his Hungarian Rhapsody No.15. It is not to be confused with the march named after Radetzky, who was on the other side (and at another time).

rallentando (It.). Slowing down, abbreviated *rall.*, the same as *ritardando*.

RAM. Royal Academy of Music, London.

Rameau, Jean-Philippe (baptized Dijon, 25 Sep 1683; d. Paris, 12 Sep 1764). French composer, remarkable for the expressive verve, wit and colour he re-introduced to opera in Paris and Versailles. Among opera composers between Monteverdi and the late 18th century, he can be ranked only with Handel. As a composer of dances, he bewilders comparison.

He started late, producing no important composition until he was 50. Instead, he began by following in the footsteps of his organist father, and became organist of Clermont Cathedral in 1702. He moved to Paris around 1706, then took over from his father in Dijon in 1709, moving on to Lyons by 1713 and back to Clermont in 1715. This modest career as a provincial organist came to an end in 1722, when he published his *Traité de l'harmonie*, an enormously influential text that applied to music the analytical keenness and comprehensiveness of the French *encyclopédistes* who were his contemporaries. Tonal harmony was placed on a rational basis in nature, its chords related to simple frequency proportions. Rameau was the first to classify inversions, and to show progressions and cadences as formed from two essential kinds of harmony: the triad and the seventh chord. What mattered to him as much as the system, though, was the expressive effect of each chord or inversion.

He had moved to Paris again to see his book through the press and to witness the excitement and controversy it provoked. He decided to stay. In 1726 he married the 19-year-old Marie-Louise Mangot, a singer who took part in his performances, and with whom he had four children. His wife, so it was said, learned nothing of his earlier life, because he was so unforthcoming about himself. He also seems to have engaged more energetically in intellectual debate with distant correspondents than in close friendships. His tall, thin physique was the mirror of his aloofness, a Voltaire-like smile that of his sharp curiosity.

During his first years in Paris he seems to have composed little, but then at last he found the opportunity to launch himself as an opera composer, with *Hippolyte et Aricie*, staged six days after his 50th birthday. It established him as more than a theoretician, but it was not universally admired. Some, devoted to Lully's works, found it overelaborate and contrived; it was the first musical work to be called 'Baroque' as a term of opprobrium. Others, though, appreciated its expressive vigour, colour and creative abundance. Soon he was working with Voltaire on *Samson* – a project that came to nothing, though the two men later collaborated successfully on *La Princesse de Navarre* and *Le Temple de la gloire* – and then with other writers on an extraordinary string of works for the Paris Opera from *Les Indes galantes* (1735) to *Dardanus* (1739), each new piece exacerbating the controversy between supporters and detractors.

His innovations were not in operatic form, but in accepting the traditional alternation of narrative episodes with dance sequences he invigorated both. He was a master of irresistible rhythmic gestures in his dances, of poignant melody in his songs (with some Italian influence; he had spent a few months in Milan when he was 18) and of rich harmony and brilliant orchestration all through. Those works in which the narrative has some importance include the five serious operas – *Hippolyte*, *Castor et Pollux*, *Dardanus*, *Zoroastre* and *Les Boréades* – as well as the comedy *Platée* and the one-act *Pigmalion*. Other works are more masque-like, with dance to the fore and situations fantastical.

In the early 1740s there was an interruption in his output, followed by a flood of works in 1745–9, some for the Paris Opera again, others commissioned as court entertainments to celebrate royal weddings or state triumphs. After that his productivity declined once more, though he went on assisting with the frequent revivals of his older pieces. *Castor*, *Dardanus* and *Zoroastre* all exist in two radically different versions. He also continued his theoretical work and became involved in further disputes, now not as the innovator but as the champion of the old guard, to be challenged by admirers of Italian opera in the QUERELLE DES BOUFFONS. His supreme achievement in *Les Boréades*, which he produced when he was close on 80, was evidently not recognized, for the piece was rehearsed at Versailles but not performed.

His works went on being played at the Paris Opera for two decades after his death before they were displaced by those of Gluck, Piccinni and Sacchini. They began to be published and performed again at the end of the 19th century, to be welcomed by new audiences that included Debussy.

Cuthbert Girdlestone *Jean-Philippe Rameau* (1957, ²1969); Charles William Dill *Monstrous Opera* (1998)

Stage works, with performance dates: HIPPOLYTE ET ARICIE, 1733; *Les* INDES GALANTES, 1735; CASTOR ET POLLUX, 1737; *Les Fêtes d'Hébé* (Antoine Gautier de Montdorge), 1739; DARDANUS, 1739; *La Princesse de Navarre* (Voltaire), 1745; PLATEE, 1745; *Les Fêtes de Polymnie* (Louis de Cahusac), 1745; *Le Temple de la gloire* (Voltaire), 1745; *Les Fêtes de l'Hymen et de l'Amour* (Cahusac), 1747; *Zaïs* (Cahusac), 1748; *Pigmalion* (1 act; Antoine Houdar de la Motte), 1748; *Les Surprises de l'Amour* (Pierre Joseph Bernard), 1748; *Naïs* (Cahusac), 1749; ZOROASTRE, 1749; *La Guirlande* (1 act; Marmontel), 1751; *Acante et Céphise* (Marmontel), 1751; *Daphnis et Eglé* (1 act; Charles Collé), 1753; *Les Sibarites* (1 act; Marmontel), 1753; *La Naissance d'Osiris* (1 act; Cahusac), 1754; *Anacréon* (1 act; Bernard), 1754; *Les Paladins*, 1760; *Les* BOREADES, rehearsed 1763; *Nélée et Myrthis* (1 act); *Zéphyre* (1 act)
Cantatas (most before 1722): *Les Amants trahis, Aquilon et Orinthie, Le Berger fidèle, Cantate pour la Saint Louis, L'Impatience, Orphée, Thétis*
Grands motets (all before 1722): *Deus noster refugium, In convertendo, Quam dilecta*
Instrumental works: *Pièces de clavecin en concert*, hpd, vn/fl, viol/vn, 5 suites, pub 1741; solo harpsichord pieces

Rampal, Jean-Pierre (Louis) (b. Marseilles, 7 Jan 1922; d. Paris, 20 May 2000). French flautist. Trained at the Paris Conservatoire (1943–6), he played in the opera orchestras of Vichy (1946–50) and Paris (1956–62) while starting his career as a soloist and chamber musician. A player of unusual smoothness, he introduced concertos by Jolivet and others, though generally preferring Baroque and Classical music.

Randall, James K(irtland) (b. Cleveland, 16 Jun 1929). US composer. He studied at Columbia, at Harvard and with Babbitt and Sessions at Princeton (1956–8), where he taught (1959–91) while working as a pioneer of computer music. Later he devoted himself to traditional instruments again, with a quietness that was always characteristic.

Rands, Bernard (b. Sheffield, 2 Mar 1934). British–US composer. He studied at Bangor (1953–8) and in Italy (1959–62) with Vlad, Dallapiccola and Berio. After a period teaching at York University, he settled in the USA in 1975, and has taught at Harvard since 1988. Berioesque at first, his music in the USA became more relaxed but no less poetic. Important works include a triptych of song cycles for voice and orchestra: *Canti lunatici* for soprano (1980–81), *Canti del sole* for tenor (1983–4) and *Canti dell'eclisse* for bass (1992).

range. The span of notes attainable by an instrument, a voice or a particular performer, or the span required by a part.

Rangström, (Anders Johan) Ture (b. Stockholm, 30 Nov 1884; d. Stockholm, 11 May 1947). Swedish composer. He studied with Pfitzner in Berlin (1905–6) and worked in Sweden as a critic, conductor and singing teacher. His works include four symphonies, chamber music and songs.

rank. Row of organ pipes.

rank-and-file. Adjectival term descriptive of orchestral musicians other than principals.

ranz des vaches (Swiss Fr., procession of cows). Genre of melody played on the alphorn by Swiss cowherds, imitated by Beethoven ('Pastoral' Symphony, last movement), Berlioz (*Symphonie fantastique*, third movement) and Wagner (*Tristan*, Act 3).

Rape of Lucretia, The. Opera by Britten to a libretto by Ronald Duncan after André Obey's play. Lucretia (contralto, a part written for Ferrier) stabs herself rather than live on after being raped by Tarquinius (baritone). Scored for 12 instruments, this was the first of the composer's chamber operas. First performance: Glyndebourne, 12 Jul 1946.

Rappresentatione di anima, et di corpo (Play of the Soul and the Body). Sacred opera by Emilio de' Cavalieri to a libretto probably by Agostino Manni, the first opera to be published and the first to survive in score intact. Body (tenor) and Soul (soprano) are protected by a Guardian Angel (soprano) from the blandishments of The World (tenor) and Worldly Life (soprano), with other allegorical figures featuring. First performance: Rome, Feb 1600.

rappresentativo (It., representing). Term sometimes used, normally in the form *stile rappresentativo*, for the expressive recitative of Monteverdi and other early Baroque composers, in distinction from later and more formal recitative.

rasch, rascher (Ger.). Fast, faster.

rasgueado (Sp.). Strummed. Indication in guitar music, as distinct from *punteado* (plucked).

rastrum (Lat., rake). Writing instrument with several parallel nibs, used for inscribing staves. The use of such instruments can be detected in some 14th-century manuscripts, and they by no means disappeared when staved paper became available in the 16th century: Stravinsky regularly used one.

ratamacue. Onomatopoeic term for a side drum roll of three triplets and a beat.

rataplan. Onomatopoeic rendering of the sound of a military drum, the 'rata' being a pair of grace notes, so that a 4/4 bar might go 'rataplan, rataplan, rataplan-plan-plan'. Such syllabic concoctions appear in opera, sung or in the title of a number (as in *La forza del destino*).

ratchet. Percussion instrument making a sound when a cog wheel is turned, its cogs striking strips of wood or metal, as in Leopold Mozart's 'Toy Symphony' and the Ravel orchestration of Musorgsky's *Pictures at an Exhibition*.

Rathaus, Karol (b. Tarnopol, 16 Sep 1895; d. New York, 21 Nov 1954). Polish–US composer. A pupil of Schreker in Vienna and Berlin, he enjoyed a lively success in the latter city from 1920 as a composer for orchestra, theatre and film (*The Brothers Karamazov*, 1931). He then moved successively to Paris (1932), London (1934) and the USA (1938), where he taught at Queens College. His orchestration of *Boris Godunov* was used at the Met from 1952 until the 1970s.

rattle. Percussion instrument making a sound when shaken, usually because small objects (seeds, shells) are contained in a box (wooden, woven, gourd). Commonest are the MARACAS.

Rattle, Simon (Denis) (b. Liverpool, 19 Jan 1955). British conductor, knighted in 1994. He was principal conductor of the City of Birmingham Symphony Orchestra (1979–98) and took a similar position in 2002 with the Berlin Philharmonic, with which he had been appearing as a guest since 1987. Exceptional always in early 20th-century music (Mahler, Debussy, Janáček) and new works amenable to his dynamic approach, he achieved an unusual understanding of Classical music and Beethoven through his work with period-style performers in the 1980s.

Nicholas Kenyon *Simon Rattle* (1987, ²2001)

Rautavaara, Einojuhani (b. Helsinki, 9 Oct 1928). Finnish composer. He studied with Merikanto at the Sibelius Academy, graduating in 1959, and completed his education in the USA and at Ancona and Cologne. In 1966 he returned to his alma mater to teach. A common path from neoclassicism through post-1945 modernism led in his case to a luminous style that won him much acclaim around the turn of the century. His works include eight symphonies.

Rauzzini, Venanzio (baptized Camerino, near Rome, 19 Dec 1746; d. Bath, 8 Apr 1810). Italian castrato and composer. He was Cecilio in the first performance of Mozart's *Lucio Silla*, and the composer wrote the display piece *Exsultate, jubilate* for him. In 1774 he moved to London and in 1777 to Bath, where he arranged concerts and received guests, including Haydn. His works include operas and other vocal music but also quartets and sonatas.

Ravel, (Joseph) Maurice (b. Ciboure, Basses Pyrénées, 7 Mar 1875; d. Paris, 28 Dec 1937). French composer. So seductively sensuous, his music can be brilliant or darkly menacing – or, most often, both at once. It is also scrupulously and masterfully crafted. He loved fairytales, faraway places and Gothic fantasies, all of which he worked into his music. He loved, too, the mechanisms of his art – dance rhythms, archaic forms, interlocking orchestral colours – and often delighted in making alternative versions of the same piece for piano and for orchestra, neither one inferior.

His family moved from his mother's home territory in the Basque country to Paris when he was a baby. With the encouragement of his father, a well-to-do engineer of Swiss origins, he started piano lessons with Henri Ghys in 1882 and harmony lessons five years later. He continued his studies at the Conservatoire (1889–95) while learning a lot beyond its walls – from the Javanese gamelan and concerts given by Rimsky-Korsakov at the 1889 Exposition, from a friendship with his pianist classmate Ricardo Viñes, and from contacts with Chabrier and Satie. Within months of leaving the Conservatoire he had produced his first characteristic pieces, including the *Menuet antique* for piano and *Habanera* for two pianos, but he then returned for further training with Fauré and Gédalge (1897–1903).

For whatever reason, he was unable to concentrate. He was beyond student exercises and repeatedly failed to win the Prix de Rome, despite going on trying until 1905. The matter became something of a scandal, given the remarkable successes he was achieving outside the Conservatoire. By 1900 several of his works had been published (including the *Pavane pour une infante défunte*) or performed (including the *Shéhérazade* overture, his first orchestral composition). By the time of the 1905 débacle he was known for his bravura piano piece *Jeux d'eau*, his String Quartet and a different *Shéhérazade*, a song cycle of sophisticated opulence. He also had the support of his friends, among whom he led the existence of a bohemian dandy. (His love life seems to have remained a blank.)

During the next few years he pressed ahead, creating one of the masterpieces of operatic comedy (*L'Heure espagnole*), an orchestral suite (also Spanish, *Rapsodie espagnole*), songs and virtuoso piano pieces (*Gaspard de la nuit*). When Diaghilev's Ballets Russes arrived in 1909, he was a natural choice for a commission, and the result was his longest work, *Daphnis et Chloé*, in which he adopted the Satie–Debussy conceit of using Greek modes to evoke an Arcadian past, but added tones of sumptuousness and languour all his own. By the time the score was finished in 1912 he had composed two other ballets, *Ma mère l'oye* and *Valses nobles et sentimentales*.

With the Ballets Russes came Stravinsky, and Ravel was quickly one of the Frenchmen closest to him, personally and musically. They exchanged dedications, Stravinsky offering one of his Japanese songs and Ravel one of his gorgeous Mallarmé settings of 1913, though not the harmonically abstruse third song, which perversely he inscribed to Satie. The outbreak of war excited his musical patriotism, expressed in *Le Tombeau de Couperin* and the *Trois chansons* for chorus, and he served as a driver. But his life was turned upside down by the death in 1917 of his mother, for whom he probably cared more than for any other human being.

His output slowed. He orchestrated *Le Tombeau* for a ballet, and returned to an old project for another: *La Valse*, the waltz to end all waltzes, for Diaghilev, who did not use it. After that he left Paris, and in 1921 acquired a home in Montfort-l'Amaury, a doll's house he furnished with treasures. His first occupations there were the childhood fantasy opera *L'Enfant et les sortilèges* (1920–25) and the orchestration of Musorgsky's *Pictures at an Exhibition* that rapidly became a standard of the repertory.

In 1928 he made a US tour, from which he returned to write two piano concertos of different

temperaments, bright (in G) and sombre (for the left hand). A set of songs intended for a film, *Don Quichotte à Dulcinée* (1932–3), was his last new composition, written during the onset of the disease that progressively incapacitated him. Towards the end of his life he asked a friend's assurance that not everything he had written was totally without worth.

Arbie Orenstein *Ravel: Man and Musician* (1975), *A Ravel Reader* (1990)

www.maurice-ravel.net

Operas: L'HEURE ESPAGNOLE, 1907–9; L'ENFANT ET LES SORTILEGES, 1920–25
Ballets and orchestral works: *Shéhérazade* (overture), 1898; *Une Barque sur l'océan*, 1906; *Rapsodie espagnole*, 1907–8; PAVANE POUR UNE INFANTE DEFUNTE, 1910; MA MERE L'OYE, 1911, also suite; DAPHNIS ET CHLOE, with ch, 1909–12, 2 suites; *Valses nobles et sentimentales* (see VALSE), 1912; ALBORADA DEL GRACIOSO, 1918; *Le* TOMBEAU DE COUPERIN, 1919; *La* VALSE, 1919–20; TZIGANE, vn, orch, 1924; *Fanfare* for L'EVENTAIL DE JEANNE, 1927; BOLERO, 1928; *Menuet antique*, 1929; PIANO CONCERTO for the Left Hand, 1929–30; PIANO CONCERTO, G, 1929–31
Orchestrations: excerpts from *Carnaval* (Schumann), *c*.1914; *Menuet pompeux* (Chabrier), 1918; *Sarabande* and *Danse* (Debussy), 1922; PICTURES AT AN EXHIBITION (Musorgsky), 1922
Songs with orchestra: 'Manteau de fleurs'; *Shéhérazade* (SHEHERAZADE), 1903; 'Noël des jouets', 1905, rev 1913; 'Le Réveil de la mariée', 'Tout gai' (from *Cinq mélodies populaires grecques*); *Deux mélodies hébraïques*, 1919; 'Chanson hébraïque' (from *Chants populaires*), 1923–4; *Don Quichotte à Dulcinée* (Paul Morand), 1932–3; 'Ronsard à son âme', 1935
Songs with ensemble: *Trois poèmes de Stéphane Mallarmé*, v, 2 fl, 2 cl, str qt, pf, 1913; CHANSONS MADECASSES, v, fl, vc, pf, 1925–6
Songs with piano: 'Ballade de la reine morte d'aimer' (Roland de Marès), *c*.1893; 'Un grand sommeil noir' (Verlaine), 1895; 'Sainte' (Mallarmé), 1896; 'Chanson du rouet' (Leconte de Lisle), 1898; 'Si morne!' (Verhaeren), 1898; *Deux épigrammes de Clément Marot*, 1896–9; 'Manteau de fleurs' (Paul Gravollet), 1903; 'Fascination' (Maurice de Féraudy), 1904; 'Noël des jouets' (Ravel), 1905; *Cinq mélodies populaires grecques*, 1904–6; *Histoires naturelles* (5, Jules Renard), 1906; 'Les Grands vents venus d'outremer' (Henri de Régnier), 1907; 'Sur l'herbe' (Verlaine), 1907; *Vocalise-étude en forme de habanera*, 1907; 'Tripatos', 1909; *Chants populaires* (5), 1910; *Deux mélodies hébraïques*, 1914; 'L'Enigme éternelle' (anon.), 1914; 'Ronsard à son âme', 1923–4; 'Rêves' (Fargue), 1927
Choral: *Trois chansons* (Ravel), unaccompanied, 1914–15
Chamber: Sonata, vn, pf, 1897; String Quartet, F, 1902–3; Introduction and Allegro, hp, sextet, 1905; Piano Trio, 1914; Sonata, vn, vc, 1920–22; *Berceuse*

sur le nom de Gabriel Fauré, vn, pf, 1922; TZIGANE, vn, pf, 1924; Sonata, vn, pf, 1923–7

Piano solo: *Sérénade grotesque*, c.1893; *Menuet antique*, 1895; PAVANE POUR UNE INFANTE DEFUNTE, 1899; *Jeux d'eau*, 1901; Sonatine, 1903–5; MIROIRS, 1904–5; GASPARD DE LA NUIT, 1908; *Menuet sur le nom d'Haydn*, 1909; *Valses nobles et sentimentales* (see VALSE), 1911; *A la manière de Borodine*, 1913; *A la manière de Chabrier*, 1913; Prelude, 1913; *Le* TOMBEAU DE COUPERIN, 1914–17

Piano duo: *Sites auriculaires*, 1895–7 (*Habanera, Entre cloches*); *Frontispice*, 5 hands, 1918 ; *La* VALSE, 1920

Piano duet: MA MERE L'OYE, 1908–10; *Boléro*, 1929

Prix de Rome cantatas: *Myrrha*, 1901; *Alcyone*, 1902; *Alyssa*, 1903

Ravenscroft, Thomas (b. c.1592; d. c.1635). English compiler, notably of *Pammelia* (1609), the first English collection of rounds and catches, and *The Whole Booke of Psalmes* (1621).

ravvivando (It., reviving). Quickening.

Rawsthorne, Alan (b. Haslingden, Lancs., 2 May 1905; d. Cambridge, 24 Jul 1971). British composer, unusually continental in his outlook. He studied at the Royal Manchester College of Music (1925–30) and abroad, notably as a piano pupil of Egon Petri, before settling in London in 1932. While supporting himself as a film composer, he developed a spruce style with something of the English north country in it, despite evident links to Hindemith.

John McCabe *Alan Rawsthorne* (1999)

Orchestral: Symphony No.1, 1950; No.2 'A Pastoral Symphony', s, orch, 1959; No.3, 1964; Piano Concerto No.1, 1939, rev 1942; No.2, 1951; Violin Concerto No.1, 1948; No.2, 1956; Cello Concerto, 1965; *Street Corner* (overture), 1944; *Practical Cats* (T.S. Eliot), speaker, orch, 1954; *Carmen vitale*, s, ch, orch, 1963; etc.

Other works: choral pieces, songs, chamber music, film scores

Razor. Name given to Haydn's Quartet in F minor Op.55:2 on account of the work's original price: the composer told the English publisher Bland that he would give his best quartet for a good razor.

Razumovsky, Count Andrey Kirillovich (b. St Petersburg, 2 Nov 1752; d. Vienna, 23 Sep 1836). Russian patron of Beethoven, resident in Vienna from 1792 as ambassador. He played the violin himself, and Beethoven honoured him with the dedication of the quartets that thenceforth bore his name, the three published as Op.59 (1806). A quartet led by Schuppanzigh was supported by him from 1808 until 1814, when his palace caught fire and he was obliged to economize.

RCA Victor. US recording company, operating as Victor from early in the 20th century, before it became part of the Radio Corporation of America. It was acquired by BMG in 1986.

RCM. Royal College of Music, London.

re. In tonic sol-fa the second degree of the scale. In It. and Sp. the note or key of D; see SOLMIZATION.

ré (Fr.). The note or key of D; see SOLMIZATION.

real answer. An ANSWER in a FUGUE where no alteration of the subject is necessary, as it is in a tonal answer.

realism. The penetration in art to the real. Probably all art is realist, reality being so versatile a concept. In music the term is most often applied to expressive diction as found in the vocal writing of Dargomyzhsky and Musorgsky. See also NATURALISM; SOCIALIST REALISM; VERISMO.

realization. Completion of music only partly notated, a term used especially with respect to Baroque music where a FIGURED BASS or skeletal CONTINUO part remains to be realized.

rebec (from the Arabic *rabāb*). Medieval bowed instrument with three strings, inherited from the Arab world.

Rebel, François (b. Paris, 19 Jun 1701; d. Paris, 7 Nov 1775). French composer, born into a family of musicians. His father, Jean Féry (1666–1747), was a court violinist and composer of sonatas and dance symphonies. His aunt, Anne Renée (1663–1722), was a singer who married de Lalande. And his grandfather Jean had also been a singer.

He joined the Paris Opera orchestra when he was 13 years old and rose to become co-director of the institution from 1757 to 1767 with his friend François Francoeur, with whom he had been collaborating since they were in their early twenties. They produced 18 stage works together, and supported Rameau in the QUERELLE DES BOUFFONS.

Rebikov, Vladimir (Ivanovich) (b. Krasnoyarsk, Siberia, 31 May 1866; d. Yalta, 4 Aug 1920). Russian composer. A pupil of Nicolai Klenovsky at the Moscow Conservatory, he began as a composer under Tchaikovsky's influence but became a modernist, introducing whole-tone harmony and, in his 'musico-psycholographic dramas', vocal expressionism.

recapitulation. Section of a composition bringing back earlier material, especially the latter part of a movement in sonata form, where the exposition is repeated with harmonic change.

reception. How a work is received and understood, especially on first appearance, though scholars of reception history will also interest themselves in later views. Beethoven's Fifth Symphony, for instance, is a work that has grown, developed and diversified through two centuries of performance and criticism – not a score created once and for all in 1804–8 – and so its reception may be deemed no less important than its construction.

rechte Hand (Ger.). Right hand.

recit. Abbreviation for recitative.

recital. Term often preferred to 'concert' where a soloist or small group is concerned; hence 'piano recital', 'song recital'. Its use in a musical context seems to date from a performance Liszt gave in London on 9 June 1840. At that time it was unusual for a soloist to give a complete programme; there would be supporting artists. Liszt changed that, and was soon followed by other musicians, such as Ole Bull. At first the solo recital was novel for the audience and heady for the performer. By the 1870s it was the norm.

recitation. The delivery of text, in particular, in a musical context, on a RECITING NOTE or spoken with piano accompaniment, as in works by Liszt and Strauss made for domestic storytellers.

recitative (Fr. *récitatif*, Ger. *Rezitativ*, pl., *Rezitative*, It. *recitativo*). Kind of vocal declamation in which transmitting the words is paramount: the singer, literally, recites. Recitative therefore lacks independent melodic shape, except at cadences. Melodic movement is prompted by the melody inherent in the words or is a momentary expressive response to them. Several syllables will often be sung at the same pitch, with movements up or down only for accent or emphasis, allowing a rhythmic flexibility with which singers can deliver the music as tuned speech.

Thus defined, recitative is at least as old as plainsong and the practice of chanting long texts on a reciting tone. But the term is generally used for a style that came out of the Italian late-Renaissance desire for greater naturalness and immediacy of vocal expression, in conformity, so it was thought, with ancient Greek drama. That style emerged around 1600 in the first operas, and

also in solo songs. Monteverdi in 1619 referred to it as *genere* RAPPRESENTATIVO, and Ben Jonson remarked that the music of his masque *Lovers Made Men* was 'sung after the Italian manner, *stylo recitativo*'. Recitative was also introduced to Germany by Schütz. At this point giving the words an expressive contour was at least as important as getting them across.

That changed with the stylization of opera and other vocal forms in the later 17th century, when recitative became more a matter of reciting, within various conventions. It became the rule that recitative was accompanied only by the continuo (*recitativo secco*, or *semplice*, dry or simple recitative), with the orchestra reserved for the arias, although recitative with orchestra (*recitativo accompagnato*: accompanied recitative) was also possible, particularly for expressive purposes. Approximating to the pace of speech, dry recitative was the norm for dialogue, and its cadences became important signals. Half cadences would indicate one character stopping for another to begin; a full cadence, on the continuo alone, would follow the last couplet of the recitative, usually rhymed. These were the norms from before Handel to early Rossini, though with different solutions to the problems of balancing effective delivery with expressive moulding.

Recitative during this long period also appeared in different contexts: in operas, in cantatas, oratorios and Passions, and in concert pieces for singers that often took the form of an accompanied recitative and aria (e.g. Mozart's 'Basta! Vincesti'). The form was common wherever Italian was the language of singing – which meant pretty much throughout Europe from Lisbon to St Petersburg – but was also regularly adapted to German, and to English after Handel. The French language, with its more even stresses, developed its own styles of recitative, more rhythmically varied and flexible in metre, in opera from Lully to Rameau.

Dry recitative died out not long after *Il barbiere di Siviglia* (1816), and operas and oratorios became orchestrally accompanied all through. In opera the distinction between recitative sections and arias, choruses or ensembles faded. It was rejected by Wagner as a matter of artistic principle, since what had begun in Monteverdi's time as a liberation of the word had become an imprisonment. Even so, recitative-like passages occur in Wagner as they do in most subsequent operas, and the convention may even be explicitly revived, as by Stravinsky in *The Rake's Progress*.

There is also a tradition of recitative style in instrumental works, to give an impression of speech. Relevant pieces include Haydn's

Symphony No.7, two Beethoven sonatas (Op.31:2 and Op.110) and the finale of his Ninth Symphony (where the cellos and basses are instructed to play 'in the manner of a recitative, but in tempo'), as well as Schoenberg's Variations on a Recitative and Barraqué's Concerto.

Recitative. Name given to Haydn's Quartet Op.17:5.

reciting note. Note on which several syllables (at least) are intoned, as in the chanting of prayers, psalms and lessons.

recorder (Fr. *flûte à bec*, Ger. *Blockflöte*, It. *flauto diretto*). Reedless woodwind instrument, end-blown (unlike the orchestral flute) through a whistle mouthpiece and with holes stopped by the fingers. The mouthpiece is almost closed by a plug, or 'fipple': hence the term 'fipple flute' for this class of instrument. As for the name 'recorder', it seems to be derived from a verb meaning to sing like a bird. The word is found in English in the 15th century, and the instrument itself may not be much older. Renaissance recorders had a range of an octave plus a sixth and were made in sets of different sizes to play dances or polyphonic music in consort. Instrumentation then was free: the first pieces specifying recorders did not appear until the early 17th century.

Around 1680 the instrument, now with a range of two octaves and a note, became popular with amateurs, especially in England. Pepys bought one and grumbled about the 'ridiculous and trouble-some way' of notating its music, in tablature indicating the fingerings. Purcell wrote for recorders in several works, as did Handel, Bach, Vivaldi and Telemann, but then the instrument vanished. It was brought back in the early 20th century, notably by Dolmetsch, as a means of playing early music and also, for children, an early means of playing music. A new repertory for it began to emerge in works by Britten, Berio, etc.

The usual recorder is the descant (UK) or soprano (US), starting on C on the treble staff. Successively larger recorders are pitched a fifth below (treble or alto), an octave below (tenor) and an octave and a fifth below (bass). Also to be found are the sopranino, a fourth above the descant, and the great bass, a fourth below the bass.

John Mansfield Thomson *The Cambridge Companion to the Recorder* (1995)

recording. Storage of sound, so that it may be re-heard. The first basic technique was invented independently in 1877 by Thomas Edison (1847–1931) and Charles Cros (1842–88): sound waves were converted into grooves cut into some substance, and then converted back again by an apparatus tracking the grooves. In 1898 Valdemar Poulsen (1869–1942) invented a method of recording sounds as magnetic fields on a length of wire – a technique that eventually led to tape recording immediately after the Second World War. A third way of recording sounds – digitally, as numbers of electric pulses – was developed in the late 1970s.

Edison's invention did not become commercially viable until the 1890s, when the market was immediately divided between cylinders, following his design, and flat discs, introduced by Emile Berliner and made of shellac, a product derived from insects. These flat discs, more easily manufactured in quantity, had supplanted cylinders by 1920. In 1925 'acoustic recording' – channelling the sound directly to the point of a stylus cutting the record – was replaced by 'electric recording', using a microphone. Around the same time, the original multiplicity of disc sizes and speeds gave way to the standard 12-inch 78 rpm record. Such records could accommodate only about four minutes of music on each side, which was one reason for the success of operatic arias and songs as material, another being the relative fidelity of vocal recordings, in both acoustic and electric eras. But symphonic works and whole operas were being recorded on numerous sides from the first decade of the 20th century.

The record business suffered badly in the Depression, and did not recover until after the Second World War, helped by a further technical innovation, the long-playing record (LP). Introduced by Columbia Records in 1948, this increased the capacity of a side to close on half an hour, by replacing shellac with polyethylene ('vinyl'), whose smoother texture allowed narrower grooves, and by reducing the turntable speed to 33⅓ rpm. Stereo records were first produced in 1957, by which time records and radio were the major means of access to music for most people in the modernized world. Within a few more years the great classics of Western music had all been recorded (a marker was the first recording of the *Ring*, 1958–65), along with sprinklings of early and avant-garde music. No longer was it necessary to gain some instrumental facility in order to enjoy music at home, and amateur music-making declined – not to mention more far-reaching changes in taste and response that came from the fact that the choice of repertory was now in the hands of the listener (prompted by the record companies), along with choice of time and place.

There were changes, too, for performers. Nearly all, under contract to record companies, began making records regularly; Glenn Gould decided to do so exclusively, using the opportunities to edit. (The alternative – recording at one take, whether in a studio or at a public performance – similarly has its proponents.) Yet there have also been artists wary of recording, and others not deemed suitable by the major companies, whose important contribution to the musical economy brought them great power.

With the successful arrival (after several attempts) of miniature tape machines in 1963, record companies began to release many recordings on cassette. A bigger change came in 1983 with the first compact disc (CD), which used digital recording and could accommodate up to 75 minutes or so on a smaller format. Records rapidly became much cheaper to produce, stimulating a huge growth in the recorded repertory and bringing back into circulation recordings going back to the earliest days. Meanwhile, audio-visual recordings – made specially or retrieved from television archives – were introduced in different videotape formats (in the early 1980s) and on laser disc (1991), the latter being superseded by DVD at the end of the century. In 2000–2001 new cousins of the DVD appeared, offering 'surround sound' from several loudspeakers in place of the stereo (two-speaker) system that had been normal since the early 1960s.

Roland Gelatt *The Fabulous Phonograph* (1955, ²1977); Anthony Pollard *Gramophone: The First 75 Years* (1998)

reco-reco. Scraped metal tube, with Brazilian origins.

recte et retro (Lat., right way and backwards). Contrapuntal combination of a theme with its reversal, as in a canon CANCRIZANS.

Redford, John (d. autumn 1547). English composer, active at St Paul's, author of some of the earliest organ compositions, consisting of elaborations on plainsong melodies. Some are included in the MULLINER BOOK.

reduction. Arrangement for fewer performers, usually a PIANO REDUCTION.

reed. Thin object made to vibrate in a wind instrument or organ. Reeds are made from 'cane' (actually a kind of grass grown in the Mediterranean region and the USA), metal or plastic. In the construction of the instrument they may be 'beating' (hitting against the edge of the aperture in which they are placed) or 'free' (unrestricted). Beating reeds may be single (as in clarinets and saxophones) or double (i.e. two reeds bound together, or one bent round so that its ends touch,

with in either case a space between that widens and narrows in response to blowing, as in oboes and bassoons). Both beating and free reeds are used in most church organs, free reeds being found also in reed organs.

reed organ. Instrument with free reeds, a principle used anciently in east Asia for mouth organs (Chinese sheng, Japanese shō) but not until the late 18th century in the West, where instruments of this kind include the harmonica, accordions, harmoniums and cabinet organs.

reel. Scottish dance of ancient ancestry, its music marked by flowing quavers in 2/2 time. Across the Atlantic it became the HOEDOWN.

Reformation. Name Mendelssohn gave to his Fifth Symphony, written for the 300th anniversary of the Augsburg Confession but not performed until two years later. It includes the DRESDEN AMEN and the chorale *Ein' feste Burg*. First performance: Berlin, 15 Nov 1832.

reform opera. Opera has survived many periods of reform, but the term 'reform opera' generally signifies one of the later works of Gluck, especially his first two collaborations with Calzabigi: *Orfeo* (1762) and *Alceste* (1767). These works had orchestral accompaniment all through (i.e. no dry recitative), characters expressing themselves directly (i.e. without the flowery language, vocal display and da capo form of the conventional aria) and a chorus closely involved – all features inherited from French *tragédie lyrique* or, to give the more venerable model much invoked at the time, Greek drama. Other composers – Traetta, Jommelli, Sacchini, Piccinni – were working in a similar direction, but Gluck and Calzabigi got the historical credit, with their *Orfeo* the textbook and repertory example.

refrain. Part of a song that recurs after each verse, also called a chorus. The term can also be applied to similar patterns in instrumental music, as in Birtwistle's *Refrains and Choruses*.

regal, regals. Small organ of the 16th and 17th centuries, with beating reeds and no pipes.

Reger, (Johann Baptist Joseph) Max(imilian) (b. Brand, Upper Palatinate, Bavaria, 19 Mar 1873; d. Leipzig, 11 May 1916). German composer of formidable productivity. The son of a Catholic schoolteacher of peasant and artisan origins, he studied as a boy with Adalbert Lindner, the local musician in his home town of Weiden, and became a prolific composer and an organist. When he was 15 a visit to Bayreuth confirmed his vocation, and soon after he went for further study to Riemann, whom he followed to Wiesbaden in 1890. In 1898 he returned home to write much of his important organ music. He moved to Munich in 1901 and married the next year; he and his wife adopted two children. He was then professor of composition at Leipzig University (1907–11) and conductor of the Meiningen court orchestra (1911–14), after which his base was Jena. Composing abundantly all the while, he still found time for visits abroad, notably to St Petersburg (1906), where he earned the admiration of Prokofiev though not of Stravinsky.

His determination to continue on from Brahms and Wagner, but to remember Bach, may be responsible for a certain bifocal quality in his music, where a rich, unstoppable surge of harmony risks eluding contrapuntal control. This music was widely admired, by composers as different as Schoenberg and Bartók, and only its sheer volume stopped the best of it from entering the repertory. His self-characterization, in a letter to Busoni, was acute: 'You'll probably be rather surprised at the "turgidity" in my works; one always wants to do too much at first. But I was always in earnest!'

Orchestral: Sinfonietta, Op.90, 1904–5; Variations and Fugue on a Theme of J.A. Hiller, Op.100, 1907; Symphonic Prologue to a Tragedy, Op.108, 1908; Piano Concerto, F minor, Op.114, 1910; A Comedy Overture, Op.120, 1911; A Romantic Suite, Op.125, 1912; 4 Tone Poems after Arnold Böcklin, Op.128, 1913; Variations and Fugue on a Theme of Mozart, Op.132, 1914; etc.

Vocal: 2 Songs ('Der Einsiedler', Eichendorff; 'Requiem', Hebbel), Op.144, v, ch, orch, 1915; cantatas, choruses, lieder

String quartets: D minor, 1888–9, with db in finale; G minor, Op.54:1, 1900; A, Op.54:2, 1900; D minor, Op.74, 1903–4; E♭, Op.109, 1909; F♯ minor, Op.121, 1911

Other chamber music: Clarinet Quintet, A, Op.146, 1915; 2 pf qnts, 2 pf qts, str sextet, 6 trios, 9 vn sonatas, 4 vc sonatas, 3 cl sonatas, 11 unacc. vn sonatas, preludes and fugues for unacc. vn, suites for unacc. vc, suites for unacc. va, etc.

Piano: Variations and Fugue on a Theme of J.S. Bach, Op.81, 1904; Variations and Fugue on a Theme of Beethoven, Op.86, 2 pf, 1904; duet arrs of Brandenburg Concertos; etc.

Organ: Fantasia and Fugue on B–A–C–H, Op.46, 1900; Variations and Fugue on an Original Theme, Op.73, 1903; chorale fantasias, chorale preludes, etc.

Regina coeli (Queen of Heaven). MARIAN ANTIPHON, the words dating from the 12th century and the older surviving chant from the mid 13th. This was the basis for polyphonic settings by Dunstable, Victoria, Philips, etc.

register. (1) Part of the pitch range. Different registers of voices and instruments are normally identified by a difference of quality as well as of range, as with the head voice of singers or the chalumeau register of the clarinet. More abstractly, the term can be applied to different levels in a piece of music, so that a chord may be said to span different registers or a melody skip from one register to another.

(2) Stop on a keyboard instrument. See ORGAN STOP.

registration. The choice of stops to create different effects on an organ or harpsichord.

regular rhythm. Rhythm closely bound by a metre.

rehearsal. Preparation leading immediately up to a performance, as distinct from day-to-day PRACTICE. Opera productions may be rehearsed over a period between two and seven weeks, depending on the company and on whether the production is new or a revival. In the case of a new or unfamiliar work, the chorus, soloists and even the orchestra may have been rehearsing for much longer, in gaps from other activities. At the start of the full-scale rehearsal period, staging rehearsals led by the producer (in a studio within the theatre and with piano accompaniment), coaching sessions for the soloists and rehearsals for the orchestra will proceed independently. Then the elements will be brought together, at piano-stage rehearsals (with the production now on stage but no orchestra), a sitzprobe (sit-down rehearsal, for the singers and orchestra but no staging), orchestra-stage rehearsals (not in costume) and finally dress rehearsals. The last dress rehearsal may be open to a non-paying public, perhaps including critics.

Rehearsals for orchestral concerts are commonly measured in three-hour sessions, of which there may be only two for any particular programme. Chamber groups and soloists, of course, may rehearse as much or as little as they please, but nearly all musicians would want some time in a hall to practise on the day of a concert or the day before.

rehearse. Prepare for performance. See REHEARSAL.

Reich, Steve [Stephen Michael] (b. New York, 3 Oct 1936). US composer who has consistently developed the pulsed repetitions of minimalism into music of intricacy and excitement. He studied philosophy at Cornell (1953–7), then composition at the Juilliard School (1958–61) and with Milhaud and Berio at Mills (1962–3). After working at the San Francisco Tape Music Center (1964–5) he returned to New York, set up his own studio and began giving performances in museums and galleries. He based his music on ostinatos in exceedingly slow canon, an idea that sprang from the effect of loops being played on two tape recorders that gradually got out of phase; hence his use of the word 'phasing' for processes of this kind. Another kind of long-range process he used was that of gradually adding notes to a repeating figure, or taking them away, as in *Four Organs*. In 1970 he visited Ghana to study drumming, and returned to found his own ensemble based on tuned percussion instruments, Steve Reich and Musicians, with whom he toured internationally. The ensemble grew in size and the music in timbral and harmonic splendour – a long-range process in itself that began with the classic *Drumming* (1970–71) and culminated in *Music for 18 Musicians* (1974–6).

The spectacular success of the latter work, in concert and on record, encouraged him to publish his music, which hitherto had been confined to his own group. He also began to receive commissions to write for other formations, including symphony orchestra and string quartet, which brought an increasing subtlety of sound and design within his personal style of repeating modal figures that gain a consistent rhythmic vitality from metric ambiguity (generally about the grouping of 12 beats in threes or fours). At the same time, Jewish music and subjects became more important to him. In some works, notably *Different Trains*, he also brought back a technique from his first tape pieces, of using fragments of recorded speech, now as melodic formulae to be imitated by instruments. He went on to work with video recordings (by his wife Beryl Korot) in combination with recorded and live music.

Steve Reich, ed. Paul Hillier *Writings on Music, 1965–2000* (2002)

www.stevereich.com

Video operas: *The Cave*, 1990–93; *Three Tales*, 1998–2002 (*Hindenburg, Bikini, Dolly*)

Orchestral: *Variations for Winds, Strings and Keyboards*, 1979; *Eight Lines*, chbr orch, 1983; *Three Movements*, 1986; *The Four Sections*, 1987; *Duet*, 1993; *City Life*, chbr orch, 1995; *Different Trains*, str orch version, 2000

Vocal: *Tehillim* (Psalms), 4 women's v, small orch, 1981; *The Desert Music* (William Carlos Williams), ch, orch, 1983; *Proverb* (Wittgenstein), 5 v, 4 kbd, 1995; *Know What is Above You*, 4 women's v, perc, 1999; *You Are (Variations)*, ch, orch, 2004

Large ensemble: DRUMMING, 1970–71; *Music for Mallet Instruments, Voices and Organ*, 1973; *Music for 18 Musicians*, 1974–6; *Music for a Large Ensemble*, 1978

Small ensemble: *Piano Phase*, 2 pf, 1967; *Violin Phase*, 1–4 vn, 1967; *Four Organs*, 4 elec org, maracas, 1970; *Phase Patterns*, 4 elec org, 1970; *Clapping Music*, 2 players, 1972; *Music for Pieces of Wood*, 5 players, 1973; *Six Pianos*, 1973; Sextet, kbds, 1984; DIFFERENT TRAINS, str qt, elec, 1988; *Nagoya Marimbas*, 2 mar, 1994; *Triple Quartet*, str qt, elec, 1998; *Dance Patterns*, 2 xyl, 2 vib, 4 pf, 2002

Solo instrumental: *Vermont Counterpoint*, fl, elec, 1982; *New York Counterpoint*, cl, elec, 1985; *Electric Counterpoint*, elec gtr, elec, 1987; *Cello Counterpoint*, vc, elec, 2003

Tape: *It's Gonna Rain*, 1965; *Come Out*, 1966; *Melodica*, 1966

Reicha, Antoine (Joseph) (Antonín, Anton) (b. Prague, 26 Feb 1770; d. Paris, 28 May 1836). Czech–French composer, of disparate life and output. He studied with his composer-cellist uncle Josef (1752–95), who adopted him. In 1785 the family moved to Bonn, where he was a friend of Beethoven and met Haydn. On the French invasion of the city he moved to Hamburg (1794–9), and devoted himself to readings in music, mathematics and philosophy that encouraged his speculative turn of mind and interest in canon and other formal procedures. He then went to Paris, but lack of opportunity in the theatre led him to Vienna (1801–8). There he renewed his contacts with Beethoven and Haydn, published a volume of 36 fugues for piano (1803, dedicated to Haydn and possibly an influence on Beethoven) and produced a lot of other music, for all kinds of combinations. Back in Paris he became a noted teacher, and in 1818 was appointed professor of counterpoint and fugue at the Conservatoire, where his pupils included Berlioz and Liszt; Berlioz recalled that he always gave reasons for rules and was open to innovation. His treatises, published in Vienna (by Czerny) as well as Paris, spread his methods more widely. Also in 1818 he married; he and his wife had two daughters. His 24 wind quintets (1811–19) established a new genre and have been continuously admired, while most of the rest of his large and various output was soon lost to view.

Reichardt, Johann Friedrich (b. Königsberg, now Kaliningrad, 25 Nov 1752; d. Giebichenstein, near Halle, 27 Jun 1814). German composer, the author of 1,500 songs. He was Schubert's most important predecessor, as Schubert recognized, and his published travel sketches and musical notes show the Romantic sensibility found also in his music. He studied with his lutenist father, Johann, and other teachers, and learned much on his travels through northern Germany and Bohemia in 1771–4. As court composer in Berlin (1775–90) he wrote operas, including the first of four to texts by Goethe. He also married a daughter of Franz Benda in 1776, and remarried after her death in 1783; his daughter, Louise (1779–1826), became a choral director and composer in Hamburg. Following a visit to Paris in 1792, he published letters sympathetic to the French Revolution, and was obliged to retire to Giebichenstein, where his guests included Goethe, Hoffmann, Tieck and Novalis. Fleeing Napoleon's invasion in 1806, he returned the next year to find his house in ruins, his glory days over.

Reihe (Ger., pl. *Reihen*). Row.

Reimann, Aribert (b. Berlin, 4 Mar 1936). German composer and pianist, a pupil of Blacher and Pepping at the music academy in Berlin (1955–9) and exponent of a neo-expressionist style. An association with Fischer-Dieskau as accompanist led to the composition of several songs as well as the opera *Lear* (f.p. Munich, 1978). His other operas include *Ein Traumspiel* (1965), *Melusine* (1971), *Die Gespenstersonate* (1984), *Troades* (1986), *Das Schloss* (1992) and *Bernarda Albas Haus* (2000).

Reinagle, Alexander (baptized Portsmouth, 23 Apr 1756; d. Baltimore, 21 Sep 1809). British–US composer and pianist, the son of the Austrian-born trumpeter Joseph Reinagle. He spent much of his early life in Scotland, but with visits to C.P.E. Bach in Hamburg and to Lisbon. In 1786 he sailed to New York. He wrote music for the theatre in Philadelphia and Baltimore, and also piano pieces (including *A Selection of the Most Favorite Scots Tunes with Variations*, 1787, the first secular music published in the USA).

re in ascolto, Un (A King Listening). Opera by Berio to his own libretto incorporating texts by Italo Calvino, Auden, *et al*. Prospero (bass-baritone) is dreaming and dying in the theatre of his imagination – a theatre in which a version of *The Tempest* is being rehearsed, with monitory intrusions from the world outside. First performance: Salzburg, 7 Aug 1984.

Reincken, Johann Adam (b. ?c.1640; d. Hamburg, 24 Nov 1722). German organist-composer. He arrived in Hamburg in 1654 to study with Sweelinck's pupil Heinrich Scheidemann, whom

he succeeded in 1663 as organist of St Catharine's. Bach in his teens walked to hear the old master, and paid his respects in arranging for organ some chamber pieces by Reincken.

Reine, La. Name given to Haydn's Symphony No.85, fourth of his Paris symphonies, on the grounds that it was admired by Marie Antoinette.

Reinecke, Carl (Heinrich Carsten) (b. Altona, 23 Jun 1824; d. Leipzig, 10 Mar 1910). German composer, teacher and conductor, the son of the author of musical textbooks, J.P. Rudolf Reinecke (1795–1883), who gave him a thorough grounding. He spent time in various cities as a pianist, teacher and conductor, and was warmly received by Mendelssohn, the Schumanns and Liszt. Then, in 1860, he joined the Leipzig Conservatory, where he finished his career as director (1897–1902). He wrote abundantly in all forms, his list of Op. numbers reaching almost 300, but is remembered chiefly for his piano music.

Reiner, Fritz (b. Budapest, 19 Dec 1888; d. New York, 15 Nov 1963). Hungarian–US conductor. Trained at the academy in Budapest, he worked his way up to become principal conductor at the Dresden Staatsoper in 1914, where he came into contact with Nikisch, Muck and Strauss. He then moved to the US, where he headed the symphony orchestras of Cincinnati (1922–31), Pittsburgh (1938–48) and Chicago (1953–63), and in the 1930s taught at Curtis, with Bernstein among his pupils. His insistence on rhythmic precision and clarity from his players was unmoderated by any wish to be loved.

Reizenstein, Franz (Theodor) (b. Nuremberg, 7 Jun 1911; d. London, 15 Oct 1968). German–British composer and pianist. A pupil of Hindemith in Berlin (until 1934) and Vaughan Williams in London, he wrote mostly piano and chamber music.

réjouissance (Fr., rejoicing). Kind of movement found in Baroque suites, notably the fourth of Bach's orchestral suites and Handel's *Royal Fireworks Music*.

relative key. One of two keys with the same key signature. E♭ major is the relative major of C minor, and D minor is the relative minor of F major. In minor-key sonata movements the relative major is usually the key of the second subject, so fulfilling the function of the dominant in a major-key movement.

religious music. See LITURGY; SACRED MUSIC.

Reliquie. Name given to Schubert's unfinished sonata in C, D.840.

relish. English Baroque ornament, a turn or trill (single relish, indicated by a triangle of dots), or a lengthier combination of these (double relish, shown by more dots).

Remede de Fortune (Fortune's Remedy). Allegory by Machaut concerning a young man's education in the art of love. It includes songs that are also examples of diverse poetic forms: lai (*Qui n'auroit autre deport*), complainte (*Tels rit au main qui au soir pleure*), chanson royal (*Joie, plaisence et douce nourriture*), ballade (*En amer a douce vie, Dame de qui toute ma joie vient*), virelai (called *chanson balladée* in the manuscript; *Dame, a vous sans retollir*) and rondeau (*Dame, mon cuer en vous remaint*).

reminiscence motif. In an opera, a theme recalled from an earlier point. Figaro in *The Marriage of Figaro* recalls the threat to the Count he had voiced in 'Se vuol ballare', but the term is particularly associated with French examples, such as the recollection of Blondel's song in Grétry's *Richard Coeur-de-Lion*. The reminiscence motif is effective because of its unusualness; not so the Wagnerian LEITMOTIF.

Renaissance (Fr., rebirth). Term coined by the French historian Jules Michelet (1855) and soon widely applied to the period of cultural change that started in Italy (especially Florence) in the early 15th century and spread more or less rapidly through western Europe.

The rebirth was felt at the time: artists and philosophers saw themselves as making a fresh start on the basis of natural observation and a new understanding of the ancient Greeks. These were linked foundations, in that the Greeks had made nature their model. Theorists of the 16th century, notably Zarlino, were impressed by the connection between consonance and simple ratios of vibration, as transmitted by Pythagoras. However, music had started to become more smoothly consonant, more rooted in triads, from early in the previous century, as again the theorists recognized. In 1477 Tinctoris noted that a new beginning had been made by Dunstable and continued by Du Fay and others. (Indeed, the epicentre for early Renaissance music was not Florence but the region around the English Channel: southern England, northern France and the Low Countries.) The emphasis on consonance and the emergence of diatonic harmony gave music something comparable with the laws of perspective in visual art: a new depth, and a new familiarity.

As in visual art, too, the church provided the greatest opportunities, and most Renaissance composers, from Dunstable and Du Fay through Ockeghem and Josquin to Byrd, Lassus, Palestrina and Victoria, spent their lives applying the new sense of harmony to polyphonic masses and motets. In polyphonic songs – French chansons, Italian and English madrigals – a similar style could be used with a lighter touch, an ear for illustrative detail (imitating bird songs or battle cries, for example) and a keener expressiveness.

The idea of song as expressive came again from the Greeks, from an attempt to understand how the ancient dramas were performed. It also gained a lift from the higher valuation of individual experience that followed (and perhaps fuelled) the Reformation. A new repertory evolved of solo songs with accompaniment for lute (Dowland) or keyboard, and then came – right at the end of the period, back in Florence – opera. Instrumental music also grew in importance, in the form of dances or solo pieces, as music left the hands (and voices) of a highly trained guild to enter the practical lives of the aristocracy and burgeoning bourgeoisie, for everything could be quickly and widely disseminated thanks to the new publishing industry.

Tess Knighton and David Fallows, ed. *Companion to Medieval and Renaissance Music* (1992); Leeman L. Perkins *Music in the Age of the Renaissance* (1999)

Renaissance instruments. Cornett, crumhorn, dulcian, lute, recorder, regals, sackbut, shawm, viol, virginals, etc. Since the 1960s, in the wake of the early-music revival, these instruments have occasionally been used again by composers, notably Kagel and Davies.

Renard. 'A burlesque in song and dance' by Stravinsky, setting Russian popular rhymes to make a farmyard fable of four animal characters 'to be played by clowns, dancers or acrobats'. The music is for four singers (2 t, 2 b) and a 14-piece band (including cimbalom). First performance: Paris, 18 May 1922.

render. Perform (archaic). Hence also 'rendering' (a term given new life by Berio's work based on symphonic sketches by Schubert), 'rendition'.

re pastore, Il (The Shepherd King). Libretto by Metastasio, in which the shepherd Aminta is revealed as the true king of Sidon and is given his throne and his love at the behest of Alexander the Great. The text was set first by Giuseppe Bonno

(1756), and after by Gluck and Mozart. Gluck's version was written for the birth of the Archduke Maximilan Franz (1756), Mozart's for the same person's visit to Salzburg (First performance: Archiepiscopal Palace, 23 Apr 1775).

repeat. The repetition of passages has been indicated in music since the 17th century by the signs

$$\|:$$

at the beginning and

$$:\|$$

at the end. In the absence of a sign at the start of the passage, the repetition is to be from the opening of the piece or movement. Normally only one repetition is implied; greater numbers may be indicated by '× 3', etc., above the staff at the end of the repeating section, a usage particularly occasioned by minimalism since the late 1960s.

Repeats were commonly expected in Baroque suites and Classical sonata movements, minuets and rondos. In sonata movements repeats were marked for two sections – the exposition and the development plus recapitulation – until around 1800, though the latter part was probably not repeated in performance. Expositions went on being repeated well into the Romantic period, as is proved by the frequent provision of two different links from the end of the section: one back to its start, the other into the development. Even where this different music does not provide a reason to observe the repeat, a sense of proportion may do so – though many musicians in the first half of the 20th century held a different view.

The repetition of figures may be indicated by paired diagonal lines with a dot on each side.

repertory, repertoire. Collection of works in general performance. Repertories may be owned by musicians ('Pollini's repertory'), by instruments or voices ('the clarinet repertory'), by theatres or other performing institutions ('Covent Garden's repertory'), by forms or genres ('the song repertory') by countries or cities ('the Welsh repertory', which might, according to context, mean music performed in Wales or music created by Welsh composers) or by the world at large. There is also a specialized meaning in opera practice; theatres may run a 'repertory system', presenting many different works for occasional performances throughout their calendar, as distinct from the STAGIONE system of bunched performances.

The repertory in the largest sense – that of a canon of classics, to which occasional new works might be admitted – is a notion due to the mid 19th century, when it grew around the symphonies of Beethoven, soon 'core repertory' for any permanent orchestra. That notion reached its practical limits after about a century: Bartók's Concerto for Orchestra (1945) is the last work in the universal orchestral repertory – though the symphonies of Mahler and Bruckner were added in the 1960s – and *The Rake's Progress* (1951) is the last repertory opera.

répétiteur (Fr., rehearser). Musician engaged by an opera company to coach singers and perhaps lead rehearsals and prompt. Traditionally the job was one for an apprentice conductor.

répétition (Fr.). Rehearsal. The *répétition générale* is the dress rehearsal.

repetitive music. See MINIMALISM.

reprise. Repeat or recapitulation.

reproducing piano. Instrument capable of reproducing performances from analog (PIANOLA) or digital (DISKLAVIER) information.

Requiem (Mass for the Dead, Lat. *Missa pro defunctis, Missa defunctorum*, Fr. *Messe des morts*, Ger. *Totenmesse*). Commemoration of the departed, normally in the form of the Latin mass for the dead. Most musical settings may be performed liturgically, or as commemorative acts outside the church, or as concert items – though some may resist one or other of these circumstances. The term comes from the introit to the mass, *Requiem aeternam dona eis, Domine* (Eternal rest grant unto them, O Lord).

The history of the *Requiem* is the history of death, treated with solemnity in the Renaissance, then in the Romantic period a cause for passionate drama (Cherubini, Berlioz, Verdi) or consolation (Fauré), to become black comedy (Ligeti) or mystery (Stravinsky). Closely connected with that history are commemorative works from other religious traditions (Schütz's MUSIKALISCHE EXEQUIEN, Purcell's FUNERAL MUSIC FOR QUEEN MARY II, Brahms's *Ein* DEUTSCHES REQUIEM).

As a liturgy the *Requiem* has varied in form with time and place, but since the Council of Trent (1545–63) it has usually included the following items: Introit (*Requiem aeternam*), *Kyrie*, Gradual (*Requiem aeternam*), Sequence (*Dies irae*, often divided into several sections by composers),

Offertory (*Domine Jesu Christe*), *Sanctus*, *Benedictus*, *Agnus Dei*, Communion (*Lux aeterna*) and Responsory (*Libera me, Domine*).

In his will Du Fay asked for his *Requiem* to be sung at his funeral, and his may have been the earliest polyphonic setting. But it is lost. Among its successors are the following:

(1) Ockeghem: Introit, *Kyrie*, Tract, Gradual, Offertory.

(2) Morales: Introit, *Kyrie*, Gradual, Offertory, *Sanctus*, *Benedictus*, *Agnus Dei*, Communion.

(3) Lassus: Responsory (*Memento mori*), Introit, *Kyrie*, Gradual, Offertory, *Sanctus*, *Benedictus*, *Agnus Dei*, Communion, Antiphon (*In paradisum*).

(4) Victoria: Introit, *Kyrie*, Gradual, Offertory, *Sanctus*, *Benedictus*, *Agnus Dei*, Communion, Motet (*Versa est in luctum*), Responsory.

(5) Mozart: Introit, *Kyrie*, Sequence (*Dies irae – Tuba mirum – Rex tremendae – Recordare – Confutatis maledictis – Lacrimosa*), Offertory (*Domine Jesu – Hostias et preces*), *Sanctus*, *Benedictus*, *Agnus Dei*, Communion; satb soli, ch, orch. Left unfinished at the composer's death, the score was worked on by Joseph Eybler and completed by Franz Xaver Süssmayr. Others, dissatisfied with Süssmayr's solutions, have put forward competing completions. First performance: Vienna, 2 Jan 1793.

(6) Cherubini: C minor. Introit – *Kyrie*, Gradual, Sequence, Offertory, *Sanctus*, *Pie Jesu*, *Agnus Dei*; ch, orch. First performance: St Denis, 21 Jan 1817.

(7) Berlioz: Introit – *Kyrie*, Sequence (*Dies irae – Quid sum miser – Rex tremendae – Quaerens me – Lacrimosa*), Offertory (*Domine Jesu – Hostias et preces*), *Sanctus*, *Agnus Dei*; t, ch, orch. First performance: Paris, 5 Dec 1837.

(8) Cherubini: D minor. Introit – *Kyrie*, Gradual, Sequence, Offertory, *Sanctus*, *Pie Jesu*, *Agnus Dei*; men's ch, orch. First performance: Paris, 23 Mar 1838.

(9) Verdi: Introit – *Kyrie*, Sequence (*Dies irae – Tuba mirum – Liber scriptus – Quid sum miser – Rex tremendae – Recordare – Ingemisco – Confutatis maledictis – Lacrimosa*), Offertory, *Sanctus*, *Agnus Dei*, Communion, Responsory; satb soli, ch, orch. First performance: Milan, 22 May 1874.

(10) Fauré: Introit – *Kyrie*, Gradual, Offertory, *Sanctus*, *Pie Jesu*, *Agnus Dei*, Responsory, *In paradisum*; s, bar, orch. The original score had accompaniment for chamber orchestra and organ, an ensemble enlarged in revisions up to 1900. First performance: Paris, 16 Jan 1888.

(11) Ligeti: Introit, *Kyrie*, Sequence (*De die judicii sequentia – Lacrimosa*); s, mez, ch, orch. First performance: Stockholm, 14 Mar 1965.

(12) Stravinsky: *Requiem Canticles*. Prelude, Exaudi, Dies irae, Tuba mirum, Interlude, Rex tremendae, Lacrimosa, Libera me, Postlude; a, b, ch, orch. First performance: Princeton, 8 Oct 1966.

Alec Robertson *Requiem* (1967)

rescue opera. Operatic genre in which the drama hinges on a rescue effected by human agency. Anticipated by Grétry's *Richard Coeur-de-Lion* (1784), it was reinforced by the French Revolution, and a French libretto gave rise to the noblest example, Beethoven's *Fidelio*.

resolution. Ending, by the restoration of the keynote or tonic harmony, 'resolving' earlier discord.

resonance. (1) Vibration in response to some input. The resonance may be natural, as when the air in an organ pipe vibrates in sympathy with the reed, or when a glass or other household item vibrates in response to some music. It may also be that the resonating body cannot but vibrate, being in direct contact with the stimulus, as with the bodies of string instruments or the sounding boards of pianos. In all these cases the body is resonating with something else: a reed, other sounds, strings.

(2) The word can also be applied to vibrations that go on after the stimulus has stopped, so that one may speak of the resonance of bells, etc.

(3) Reverberation.

Respighi, Ottorino (b. Bologna, 9 Jul 1879; d. Rome, 18 Apr 1936). Italian composer, a master of orchestral colour. He studied in Bologna as a string player, and took the opportunity on concert trips to Russia in 1900–1903 to take lessons with Rimsky-Korsakov. The result was a decisive influence on his spectacular orchestral style, which was also informed by the music of Strauss and Ravel. In his youth he continued to work as a violinist and viola player; then in 1913 he settled in Rome as a composer and teacher. *Fontane di Roma* made him famous, and was followed by several more symphonic poems and suites, some based on older music. After his time as director of the Santa Cecilia conservatory (1923–6) he travelled widely on both sides of the Atlantic with his wife Elsa Olivieri-Sangiacomo (1894–1996), a singer and composer.

Elsa Respighi *Ottorino Respighi* (1962)

Operas: *La bella dormente nel bosco* (puppet opera; Gian Bistolfi, after Perrault), f.p. Rome, 1922; *Belfagor* (Claudio Guastalla, after Ercole Luigi Morselli), f.p. Milan, 1923; *La campana sommersa* (Guastalla, after Gerhart Hauptmann), f.p.

Hamburg, 1927; *Maria egiziaca* (Guastalla, after Frà Domenico Cavalca), f.p. New York, 1932; *La fiamma* (Guastalla, after Anne Pedersdotter), f.p. Rome, 1934; etc.
Orchestral: FONTANE DI ROMA, 1914–16; *Antiche danze et arie per liuto*, 3 suites, 1917, 1923, 1931; *La Boutique fantasque* (after Rossini), 1919; Violin Concerto 'Gregoriano', 1921; PINI DI ROMA, 1923–4; *Vetrate di chiesa*, 1925; *Trittico botticelliano*, 1927; FESTE ROMANE, 1928; *Gli uccelli*, 1928; etc.
Other works: *Il tramonto* (Shelley), v, str qt, 1914; etc.

respiro (It., sigh, pl. *respiri*). Rest, pause.

responsory. Chant sung in alternation by a leader and choir, or congregation.

rest. Cessation of activity on the part of the performer. Rest signs entered music in the 13th century, and have not been significantly altered since the 15th century; see DURATION.

resultant tone. See COMBINATION TONE.

Resurrection. Name given to Mahler's Second Symphony, on account of the words by Friedrich Klopstock set in its finale.

resurrezione, La. Oratorio by Handel, titled in full *Oratorio per la Resurrezione di Nostro Signor Gesù Cristo*, to words by Carlo Sigismondo Capece. An Angel (soprano castrato) disputes Christ's eternal fate with Lucifer (bass), while Mary Magdalen, Mary Cleophas and St John lament then exult. Corelli led the orchestra at the first performance. First performance: Rome, 8 Apr 1708.

retablo de Maese Pedro, El (Master Peter's Puppet Show). Short theatre piece by Falla to his own libretto after an episode in *Don Quixote*. The Trujáman (treble), or narrator, describes a chivalric puppet show, on which Don Quixote (bass-baritone) also comments. First performance: Seville, 23 Mar 1923; Paris, 25 Jun 1923 (staged).

retenant, retenu (Fr.). Holding back, held back, i.e. decelerating.

retransition. Closing part of the development in a sonata form, preparing for the recapitulation.

retrograde. Reversal of a musical line or passage. Rare examples of such reversal before the 20th century appear in Machaut's 'Ma fin est mon commencement' and the finale of Beethoven's 'Hammerklavier' Sonata. Retrograding was instituted as a basic element of serialism by Schoenberg. It is also, of course, essential to any PALINDROME.

Reubke, (Friedrich) Julius (b. Hausneindorf, near Quedlinburg, 23 Mar 1834; d. Pillnitz, near Dresden, 3 Jun 1858). German composer. The son of the organ builder Adolf Reubke (1805–75), he was a graduate of the Berlin Conservatory and pupil of Liszt in Weimar (1856). He is remembered for two works he completed in 1857: his Piano Sonata in Bb minor and, especially, his Organ Sonata on Psalm 94. Weak health carried him off so young.

Réveil des oiseaux (Awakening of the Birds). Piano concerto by Messiaen composed entirely of birdsong transcriptions and compressing a 24-hour cycle (beginning with nightingales) into 20 minutes. First performance: Donaueschingen, 11 Oct 1953.

Revelation. Last book of the Bible, a source for Brahms (*Triumphlied*), Vaughan Williams (*Sancta civitas*), Langgaard, Schmidt, Rosenberg, Messiaen (QUATUOR POUR LA FIN DU TEMPS), Huber and others.

reverberation. Response of a room to sound played within it. The reverberation time is a measure of that response: the time taken for a loud sound to decay to inaudibility. That time will be short in a room furnished with absorbent materials, and such a room will be said to be acoustically dry. A relatively small room in which hard surfaces dominate – stone, glass, ceramic – will have repeated reverberations and will be said to be acoustically lively. Large churches have long reverberation times on account of their scale, and their sound is more confused than lively.

Revolutionary. Name given to Chopin's Etude in C minor Op.10:12, on the apocryphal grounds that it expressed his fury at the Russian occupation of Warsaw.

revolutionary music. See FRENCH REVOLUTION; POLITICS; RUSSIA.

Revueltas, Silvestre (b. Santiago Papasquiaro, Durango, 31 Dec 1899; d. Mexico City, 5 Oct 1940). Mexican composer. He studied in Mexico City (1913–16), Austin, Texas (1916–18) and Chicago (1918–20), and spent much of the 1920s in the USA, until Chávez made him assistant conductor of the Mexico Symphony Orchestra (1929–35). After that he taught at the Mexico City Conservatory, and died an early death from alcoholism. His diverse output includes fascinating studies in polymetre (*Ocho por radio*), delightfully laid-back string quartets and neo-primitive blockbusters (*Sensemayá, La noche de los mayas*).

Orchestral: *Ventanas*, 1931; *Planos*, chbr orch, 1934, rev full orch as *Danza geometrica*; *Homenaje a Federico García Lorca*, chbr orch, 1935; *Redes*, 1938; *Sensemayá*, 1938; *La noche de los mayas*, 1939
Chamber: String Quartets Nos.1–4, 1930–32; *Ocho por radio*, 8 insts, 1933; *Dos pequeñas piezas serias*, wind qnt, 1938

Reyer, (Louis Etienne) Ernest (b. Marseilles, 1 Dec 1823; d. Le Lavandou, Var, 15 Jan 1909). French composer and critic, originally Rey. Largely self-taught, he admired Gluck, Weber, Schumann and Berlioz (who returned the compliment). He was further from Wagner, though he wrote an opera on the Siegfried myth (*Sigurd*, 1884), as well as another after Flaubert's *Salammbô* (1890).

Reynolds, Roger (Lee) (b. Detroit, 13 Jul 1934). US composer, chiefly of works using electronic means to create sound in movement. He studied at the University of Michigan, joined the staff at the University of California, San Diego, in 1969, and has worked at IRCAM.

Rezniček, Emil Nikolaus von (b. Vienna, 4 May 1860; d. Berlin, 2 Aug 1945). Austrian composer-conductor. A pupil of Reinecke and Jadassohn at the Leipzig Conservatory, he is known principally if not uniquely for the spirited overture to his opera *Donna Diana* (1894). He wrote other operas, symphonies and quartets.

rf, rfz. Abbreviations for *rinforzando* or *rinforzato*.

r.h. Abbreviation for right hand in keyboard music.

rhapsody (from the Gk *rapsodia*, a singing of epic poetry). The term was introduced to music by Tomašek with his Six Rhapsodies for piano (*c*.1803) and popularized by the Hungarian Rhapsodies of Liszt (1846–85), since when it has often been applied to works with a strong national character, as in examples by Dvořák, Bartók, Ravel and Gershwin. But Brahms's Alto Rhapsody is a rhapsody more in the Greek sense and Rachmaninoff's example rhapsodizes on Paganini, in 24 variations.

Rhapsody in Blue. Work by Gershwin for piano and jazz band or symphony orchestra, both versions scored by Grofé. It was first performed by the composer with Paul Whiteman and his Palais Royal Orchestra, on a programme headed 'An Experiment in Modern Music'. First performance: New York, 12 Feb 1924.

Rheinberger, Joseph (Gabriel) (b. Vaduz, Liechtenstein, 17 Mar 1839; d. Munich, 25 Nov 1901). German composer. He studied at the Munich Conservatory (1851–4) and taught there from 1859, his pupils including Humperdinck, Wolf-Ferrari and Furtwängler. Solidly traditional, his works include music for the Catholic church and 20 organ sonatas.

Rheingold, Das (The Rhinegold). Opera by Wagner to his own libretto after German myth, the first part of *The Ring*. Alberich (bass-baritone) steals the eponymous gold and makes it into a ring, which is stolen from him by Wotan (bass-baritone) to pay off the giants who have built Valhalla for the gods. Notable moments include the warning addressed to Wotan by the goddess Erda (contralto), the music, clattering with anvils, where Alberich has his fellow Nibelungs (dwarves) working for him, and the glorious-menacing Entrance of the Gods into Valhalla. First performance: Munich, 22 Sep 1869.

Rhenish. Name given to Schumann's Third Symphony, which he wrote soon after moving to Düsseldorf, on the Rhine, and in whose slow movement he recalled seeing the enthronement of the archbishop in Cologne Cathedral.

rhetoric. The art of persuasion. Rhetoric was taught in late Renaissance and Baroque schools, and contemporary theorists noted its application to the new style of music presented by a soloist (whether singer or instrumentalist) as expressive declamation. Classical rhetoric proposed that a speech should have six sections: *exordium* (introduction), *narratio* (factual statement), *divisio* or *propositio* (outline of points to be affirmed), *confirmatio* (confirmation), *confutatio* (rebuttal) and *peroratio* or *conclusio* (conclusion). Musical treatises in the Baroque period would often advise composers to plan their works in a similar way and to intensify their music with figures analogous to those of rhetoric, such as *anaphora* (repetition of a motif on a different degree of the scale) or *catabasis* (descending line).

rhythm. Moment-to-moment movement through time – or perhaps movement *of* time, since music generally seems not so much to be proceeding against some other temporal measure as to be working as the measure itself. Music is thus, for as long as it is attended to, the way time moves.

The experience of one sound creates the expectation of another. (Music consisting of just one sound would belong to a domain in which rhythm does not meaningfully exist.) The interval of time between the two creates expectations about how time will continue – but not only the time interval, for accentuation may also be crucial and may be achieved in any of several ways. An accent may come from greater volume or harder tone (the usual meaning of accentuation), from a melodic rise or fall, or from a change of harmony or colour.

Once more than two sounds have been heard, it may be possible to distinguish between periodic movement, marked by regular pulses, and aperiodic movement, in which pulse is either irregular or absent. Most music behaved in the former manner until the 20th century. If there are regular pulses, or beats, they may then be gathered in metrical units, nearly always comprising two beats, three beats or some combination (two plus three, two times three, three times two, etc.). On the next level of scale, metrical units (notated as bars, or measures) will be linked in phrases. Higher levels of organization belong to the sphere of form rather than of rhythm.

All the components of sound – timing of attack, duration, melodic movement, harmony, timbre – may be used (and undoubtedly will in interesting music) to endorse, distort or counter the rhythmic frame of pulses, beats, bars and phrases in operation at any time. And these endorsements, distortions and counterings may not be notated but left to the taste and discretion of performers. In almost any music, rhythms notated as undifferentiated pulsations (a run of semiquavers, say) will sound better for the unevenness that will come from sensitivity. On a higher level, dance measures (waltz, tango) and references to more or less distant styles (Bach, reggae) will have rhythmic implications. A feeling for rhythm, in all such circumstances, is part of knowing a tradition and being a musician.

rhythmic. Having to do with rhythm, not necessarily regular (though this is sometimes implied).

rhythmic anticipation. Chord arriving on a weak beat, to be repeated on the following strong beat.

rhythmic modes. See MODAL RHYTHM.

rhythmic values. See DURATION.

ribattuta (It.). Beat.

Ricci. Italian composing brothers, who wrote operas both independently and in collaboration.

(1) **Luigi** (b. ?Naples, 8 Jun/Jul 1805; d. Prague, 31 Dec 1859). He studied at the Naples Conservatory from the age of nine, and began his career in the city in 1824 before moving on. His most successful works included *Chiara di Rosembergh* (1831) and the long-popular *Crispino e la comare* (1850, with Federico). In between he worked in Trieste, where he lived in a ménage-à-trois with the teenage twin singers Fanny and Lidia Stolz, whose younger sister Teresa was to become a leading Verdi soprano. He married Lidia – their daughter Adelaide (1850–71) started a career as a singer – but he also had a son by Fanny, the composer and conductor Luigi Ricci-Stolz (1852–1906). He died insane.

(2) **Federico** (b. Naples, 22 Oct 1809; d. Conegliano, near Treviso, 10 Dec 1877). He joined his brother at the Naples Conservatory at a similarly tender age, and left early to follow Luigi to Rome in 1829. His independent successes included *La prigione di Edimburgo* (1838), after Walter Scott's *Heart of Midlothian*, and a comedy for Vienna, *Il marito e l'amante* (1852). The failure of a second Viennese piece the next year persuaded him to go to St Petersburg to supervise singing studies at the conservatory for 16 years, but he returned to find favour in Paris with more comedies, including *Une folie à Rome* (1869).

ricercare, ricercar (It., to seek out). A contrapuntal composition on one theme. The term was revived by Bach for movements in three and six parts in *Das musikalische Opfer* after long neglect: it had been employed by Italian composers of keyboard music in the later 16th and 17th centuries (e.g. Andrea Gabrieli and Frescobaldi). When first used by Cavazzoni (1523), though, it signified an improvisatory prelude.

Richafort, Jean (b. ?Hainaut, c.1480; d. ?Bruges, c.1547). Netherlandish composer, a follower and possible pupil of Josquin. He was connected with the French royal chapel in the 1510s, and wrote masses, motets, *Magnificat* settings and French songs.

Richter, Franz Xaver (b. ?Holleschau/Holešov, 1 Dec 1709; d. Strasbourg, 12 Sep 1789). German composer, emerging in 1740 at the court of the Prince-Abbot Anselm von Reichlin-Meldegg in Kempten, Allgäu, where in 1743 he was married. From 1746 to 1769 he served the Mannheim court as composer and bass; afterwards he was at Strasbourg Cathedral. He wrote sacred music, symphonies, concertos and chamber music, generally in a conservative manner, though his six string quartets (published in 1768) are among the forerunners of the Classical style.

Richter, Hans [Johann Baptist Isidor] (b. Raab/ Györ, 4 Apr 1843; d. Bayreuth, 5 Dec 1916). Austro-Hungarian conductor, associated with Wagner from 1866. He played the trumpet in the first performance of the *Siegfried Idyll* and conducted the first *Ring*, returning regularly to Bayreuth. He was also active in England, notably as conductor of the Hallé Orchestra (1897–1911), with which his repertory of new music included Elgar and Bartók.

Richter, Sviatoslav (Teofilovich) (b. Zhitomir, Ukraine, 20 Mar 1915; d. Moscow, 1 Aug 1997). Russian pianist of extraordinary narrative power, his performances seizing attention from the first note. Though the son of an organist-composer, he was self-taught before he went to the Moscow Conservatory in 1937 to complete his training under Neuhaus. He made his debut in Moscow in 1940 with a new Prokofiev sonata, No.6, on the programme. Later he gave the premières of the Seventh and Ninth sonatas. Poetic and commanding, he was an individual performer – and an unpredictable one, sometimes cancelling or changing a programme at short notice. His repertory was immense, ranging from Bach to Hindemith, and his musical interests wider still: Boulez was among those he invited to the annual festivals he gave in a converted barn near Tours from 1964.

Bruno Monsaingeon *Sviatoslav Richter: Notebooks and Conversations* (2001)

ricochet. String effect in which the bow bounces on the string several times, usually with changes of stopping to produce a rapid falling or rising figure.

Ricordi. Music-publishing firm founded in Milan in 1808 by Giovanni Ricordi (1785–1853), whose grandson, Giulio (1840–1912), had important relationships with Verdi and Puccini. There was an independent branch in Munich.

Ride of the Valkyries, The (*Walkürenritt*). Introduction to Act 3 of Wagner's *Die Walküre*.

Rider. Name given to Haydn's Quartet Op.74:3 on account of the cantering rhythm of its finale.

Riegger, Wallingford (Constantin) (b. Albany, Georgia, 29 Apr 1885; d. New York, 2 Apr 1961). US composer, a traditionalist who changed direction

and then rather changed back again. Brought up in a musical family, he played the piano, violin and cello as a boy. His family moved to New York in 1900, and he studied at the Institute of Musical Art, becoming one of the first graduates, in 1907. He spent much of the next decade in Germany, studying with Bruch and starting out as a conductor; during this period he also got married. After a while teaching in Iowa – where he had made a fresh start as a composer with his Piano Trio Op.1 while still writing tonally – he returned to New York in 1922 and became acquainted with Ives, Varèse, Cowell and Ruggles. The result was a period of creative silence, 1923–6, followed by such works as *Study in Sonority* and *Dichotomy*, exploiting dissonant counterpoint and driving rhythms. He also worked frequently in the 1930s with modern dance companies, including Martha Graham's. Later works, in large, abstract instrumental forms, tend to be more conventional in style.

Orchestral: *Study in Sonority*, Op.7, 10 vn, 1926–7; Fantasy and Fugue, Op.10, 1930–31; *Dichotomy*, Op.12, chbr orch, 1931–2; Symphony No.3, Op.42, 1946–7; *Music for Brass Choir*, Op.45, 1948–9; Symphony No.4, Op.63, 1956; etc.

Chamber: Piano Trio, B minor, Op.1, 1919–20; Suite, Op.8, fl, 1929; 3 Canons, Op.9, wind qt, 1931; *Bacchanale* (dance for Martha Graham), Op.11, septet, 1930; Divertissement, Op.15, fl, vc, hp, 1933; *Music for Voice and Flute*, Op.23, 1936–7; String Quartet No.1, Op.30, 1938–9; No.2, Op.43, 1948; Wind Quintet, Op.51, 1952; Concerto, Op.53, pf, wind qnt, 1953; etc.

Piano: *Blue Voyage*, Op.6, pf, 1927; *4 Tone Pictures*, Op.14, pf, 1932; *New and Old* (12 pieces), pf, 1941; etc.

Riemann, (Karl Wilhelm Julius) Hugo (b. Gross-Mehlra, near Sondershausen, 18 Jul 1849; d. Leipzig, 10 Jul 1919). German scholar. He studied at Leipzig University from 1871 and began his career as a teacher five years later, returning to Leipzig in 1895. Harmonic theory gained much of his attention; he also wrote a music dictionary (1882).

Rienzi. Opera by Wagner, titled in full *Rienzi, der Letzte der Tribunen* (Rienzi, the Last of the Tribunes), to his own libretto after Edward Bulwer-Lytton's novel. Rienzi (tenor) triumphs over the feuding Colonna and Orsini families, but falls victim to a popular uprising that also claims his sister Irene (soprano) and her beloved Adriano Colonna (mezzo-soprano, a part written for Schröder-Devrient). The fifth act includes Rienzi's prayer 'All'mächtger Vater'. First performance: Dresden, 20 Oct 1842.

Ries, Ferdinand (baptized Bonn, 28 Nov 1784; d. Frankfurt, 13 Jan 1838). German pianist-composer, the son and grandson of Bonn musicians. His father, Franz Anton (1755–1846), was one of Beethoven's teachers, and he too studied with his father, before going to Vienna in 1801. There he was Beethoven's piano pupil and protégé, and in 1804, at his debut, he played his master's Third Piano Concerto with his own cadenza. After that he travelled widely before settling in London (1813–24), where he got married in 1814. He then returned to Germany, and worked with F.G. Wegeler on one of the most important early Beethoven biographies. Of him Beethoven is said to have remarked: 'He imitates me too much.' His works, many of them featuring solo piano, include concertos, chamber pieces, sonatas and numerous rondos on songs and operatic airs.

Rieti, Vittorio (b. Alexandria, Egypt, 28 Jan 1898; d. New York, 19 Feb 1994). Italian–US composer. He studied with Giuseppe Frugatta in Milan (1912–17) and Casella in Rome, and became internationally known between the wars, forging contacts with Schoenberg, Stravinsky, Diaghilev, etc. In 1940 he moved to the USA, where he worked as a college teacher and continued, into his mid 90s, to add to a large, consistently neoclassical output that eventually included 11 symphonies and 11 string quartets.

rigaudon. Lively French dance in common time, included by Rameau in nearly all his operas and also to be found in suites by François Couperin, Fux, Muffat, Pachelbel, Grieg (*Holberg*) and Ravel (*Le Tombeau de Couperin*).

Rigoletto. Opera by Verdi to a libretto by Piave after Victor Hugo's play *Le Roi s'amuse*. Rigoletto (baritone), jester to the Duke of Mantua (tenor), pays to have his master killed for seducing his daughter Gilda (soprano), but the nearly extinct body in the bag at the end is hers. The Duke's cynical recklessness is expressed in his arias 'Questa o quella' and 'La donna è mobile', his deeper feeling in 'Parmi veder le lagrime' and 'È il sol dell'anima' (duet with Gilda). In the quartet 'Bella figlia dell'amore', a masterpiece of operatic emotional polyphony, he conducts a love affair while Gilda and Rigoletto draw their own conclusions. Other numbers include Gilda's aria 'Caro nome', Rigoletto's soliloquy 'Pari siamo' and his outburst 'Cortigiani, vil razza dannata'. First performance: Venice, 11 Mar 1851.

Rihm, Wolfgang (b. Karlsruhe, 13 Mar 1952). German composer, of hectic creative speed. He studied at the conservatory in his home town (1968–72), with Stockhausen in Cologne (1972–3) and with Klaus Huber in Freiburg (1973–6). Enormous and various, his output defies compact description. Some of his early works were composed in contradiction of the prevailing modernism in Germany in the 1970s, but he has also aligned himself with the austerity and compunction of late Nono. His music can be playful; it can equally embrace the fierce poetics of Artaud. Through his teaching, in Karlsruhe (as professor at the conservatory since 1985) and at Darmstadt, he has been important to younger composers.

Operas: *Faust und Yorick* (after Jean Tardieu), f.p. Mannheim, 1977; *Jakob Lenz* (after Büchner), f.p. Hamburg, 1979; *Die Hamletmaschine* (see HAMLET), 1983–6; *Oedipus* (after Sophocles, Hölderlin, Nietzsche, Heiner Müller), f.p. Berlin, 1987; *Die Eroberung von Mexiko* (after Artaud), f.p. Hamburg, 1992; *Séraphin* (textless; after Artaud), f.p. Frankfurt, 1994

Oratorio: *Deus passus* (St Luke Passion), 1999–2000

Orchestral: *Frau/Stimme* (Müller), s, orch, 1989; *Gesungene Zeit*, vn, orch, 1991–2; *In-Schrift*, 1995; etc.

Ensemble: *Chiffre-Zyklus*, 1982–8; *Kein Firmament*, 1988; etc.

Chamber: String Quartet No.1, 1970; No.2, 1970; No.3 'Im Innersten', 1976; No.4, 1980; No.5 'Ohne Titel', 1981; No.6 'Blaubuch', 1984; No.7 'Veränderungen', 1985; No.8, 1987–8; No.9 'Quartettsatz', 1992–3; No.10, 1997; No.12, 2000–2001; *Musik für Drei Streicher*, str trio, 1977; *Fremde Szenen I–III*, pf trio, 1982–4; etc.

Songs: *Wölfli-Liederbuch*, 1980–81; etc.

Piano: Piece No.1, 1970; No.5 'Tombeau', 1975; No.7, 1980; etc.

Riisager, Knudåge (b. Port Kunda, Estonia, 6 Mar 1897; d. Copenhagen, 26 Dec 1974). Danish composer, a proponent of Parisian neoclassicism in his ballets and five symphonies. After studying political science in Copenhagen, he went to Paris for lessons with Roussel and Le Flem (1921–3), then returned to Denmark to work as a civil servant.

Riley, Terry (Mitchell) (b. Colfax, Cal., 24 Jun 1935). US composer-improviser. He studied in San Francisco and Berkeley, and moved to New York, where he continued his connection with his Berkeley classmate La Monte Young. Working then at the French radio studios (1962–4), he became interested in the effects of overlapping repeating tonal motifs. The spectacular outcome was his IN C (1964), which was crucial to the early history of minimalism. After that, he made deep studies of Indian music (under Pandit Pran Nath, 1970–96) and – while releasing occasional composed works – became principally a solo improviser on electronic keyboards.

www.terryriley.com

RILM (Répertoire International de Littérature Musicale). Bibliography of scholarly writings, published since 1967 in periodical volumes and latterly also in CD-ROM form and online.

rim shot. Stroke on the side drum so that the stick hits the rim as well as the head, producing an echoing crack.

Rimsky-Korsakov, Nikolay (Andreyevich) (b. Tikhvin, Novgorod government, 18 Mar 1844; d. Lyubensk, St Petersburg government, 21 Jun 1908). Russian composer. A master of the orchestra and a thorough self-educator, he devoted himself energetically to revising and polishing not only his own works but those of his colleagues Musorgsky and Borodin. Whether under his own name or theirs, he produced lustrous scores, absorbing harmonic lessons from Liszt and clothing them in brilliant colour. Subjects for his operas and orchestral works he suitably found in seductive storybook realms.

Born into the minor aristocracy, he set out on a naval career in emulation of his brother Voin, who was 22 years older. When he graduated from the naval cadet college in St Petersburg in 1862 Voin was its director. By now he had met Balakirev, Cui and Musorgsky, all a little older, and felt the pull of music. But Voin insisted he fulfil his duties as a new midshipman and embark on a tour that lasted two and a half years, taking him to England, the Americas and the Mediterranean. On his return to St Petersburg he made contact with Balakirev again and completed the symphony he had started before his voyage. He went on composing, and in the winter of 1867–8 heard Berlioz conduct. Then he wrote his first opera, *The Maid of Pskov* (1868–72), completing the score alongside Musorgsky, who was at work on *Boris Godunov*; they shared a room and a piano, Musorgsky working in the mornings, Rimsky in the afternoons.

The two operas cover adjacent historical periods, and at this point the two composers were close musically, colleagues in the MIGHTY HANDFUL. But Rimsky grew dissatisfied with his lack of technical background and in 1873 started out on a programme of study. By now he was married to an accomplished pianist, Nadezhda Purgold, and working as inspector of naval bands. In 1876–7 he made a first revision of *The Maid of Pskov*, and in 1878 returned to serious composition with *May Night*, his first essay in the fantastical, which was soon followed by a second, *The Snow Maiden*. He

then devoted himself for almost two years to editing and correcting (as he saw it) the scores of the recently deceased Musorgsky.

After that, in the mid 1880s, came another creatively blank period, during which he became associated with Belyayev, and thereby with an altogether more classicizing aesthetic. Then he produced his most exciting orchestral works: the *Capriccio espagnol*, the rapturous oriental fantasy *Sheherazade* and the *Russian Easter Festival Overture*. In 1889 he heard *The Ring* in St Petersburg, with fascination, and went to Paris to conduct two concerts of Russian music at the Exposition. But a period of depression, partly occasioned by illness and death in his family, led him to set his works in order (revising *The Maid of Pskov* again) before largely abandoning composition.

He got going once more with *Christmas Eve* (1894–5), after which he was occupied to the end of his life with one opera after another, including his high-gloss version of *Boris*. Meanwhile, he divided his life between St Petersburg and his beloved country estate, between his family and his pupils, who included Stravinsky and Prokofiev. His son, Andrey (1878–1940), became a music scholar.

Nikolay Rimsky-Korsakov *My Musical Life* (1942, ʳ1989); Gerald Abraham *Rimsky-Korsakov* (1945)

Operas: *The* MAID OF PSKOV, 1868–72, rev 1876–7, 1891–2, 1898; *May Night* (after Nikolai Gogol), 1878–9, f.p. St Petersburg, 1880; *The* SNOW MAIDEN, 1880–81; MLADA, 1889–90; *Christmas Eve* (after Gogol), 1894–5, f.p. St Petersburg, 1895; SADKO, 1895–6; MOZART AND SALIERI (1 act), Op.48, 1897; *The Tsar's Bride* (Rimsky and Ilya Tyumenev, after Mey), 1898, f.p. Moscow, 1899; *The* TALE OF TSAR SALTAN, 1899–1900; *Servilia* (Rimsky, after Mey), 1900–1901, f.p. St Petersburg, 1902; *Kashchey the Immortal* (1 act; Rimsky and daughter Sofiya), 1901–2, f.p. Moscow, 1902; *Pan Voyevoda* (Tyumenev), 1902–3, f.p. St Petersburg, 1904; *The* LEGEND OF THE INVISIBLE CITY OF KITEZH, 1903–4; *The* GOLDEN COCKEREL, 1906–7

Orchestral: Symphony No.1, E minor, Op.1, 1861–5, rev 1884; No.2 'Antar', Op.9, 1868, rev 1875, 1897, 1903; No.3, C, Op.32, 1866–73, rev 1886; *Sadko*, Op.5, 1867, rev 1869, 1892; Concerto, B♭, trbn, band, 1877; Overture on Russian Themes, Op.28, 1866, rev 1879–80; *Skazka*, Op.29, 1879–80; Piano Concerto, C♯ minor, Op.30, 1882–3; *Capriccio espagnol*, Op.34, 1887; SHEHERAZADE, Op.35, 1888; *Russian Easter Festival Overture*, Op.36, 1888; *From Homer*, Op.60, women's ch, orch, 1901; suites from operas, etc.

Songs: 'Enslaved by the rose, the nightingale' (Aleksey Koltsov), Op.2:2, 1865–6; 'The clouds begin to scatter' (Pushkin), Op.42:3, 1897; 'The Prophet' (Pushkin), Op.49:2, 1897, orch; etc.

Chamber music: Quintet, B♭, pf, fl, cl, hn, bn, 1876; str qt movements, etc.

Other works: folksong arrangements, choruses, piano pieces

Editions: KHOVANSHCHINA (Musorgsky), 1881–3; NIGHT ON THE BARE MOUNTAIN (Musorgsky), 1886; BORIS GODUNOV (Musorgsky), 1892–6, rev 1906–7; PRINCE IGOR (Borodin), 1887–8 (with Glazunov)

Rimsky-Korsakov Conservatory. Formal name of the St Petersburg Conservatory.

Rinaldo. See ARMIDA.

rinforzando, rinforzato (It.). Reinforcing, reinforced, implying a forceful attack on a single note or chord, generally less forceful than a *sforzando* or *sforzato*, abbreviated *rf*, *rfz*.

Ring, The. Common short name for Wagner's operatic tetralogy *Der Ring des Nibelungen* (The Nibelung's Ring), comprising *Das Rheingold*, *Die Walküre*, *Siegfried* and *Götterdämmerung*. Complete performances are normally spread over the Monday, Tuesday, Thursday and Saturday evenings of a week, as on the first occasion. First performance: Bayreuth, 13–17 Aug 1876.

ring modulator. Electronic device, so called from its ring of four diodes, producing from two sound inputs an output of sum and difference frequencies. For example, if the inputs are pure tones of 400 Hz and 500 Hz, the outputs will be tones of 100 Hz and 900 Hz. In musical uses one input is normally an instrumental or vocal sound and the other a pure frequency, creating a distorting effect somewhat like that of a radio slightly out of tune. Stockhausen used ring modulators both in tape pieces (*Telemusik*) and concert works (*Mantra*).

Rinuccini, Ottavio (b. Florence, 20 Jan 1562; d. Florence, 28 Mar 1621). Italian librettist, one of the founders of opera. Of noble birth, he began writing poetry as a youth and joined one of the Florentine academies in 1586. He wrote most of the words for the intermedi performed to celebrate the grand duke's wedding in 1589, and the libretto for *Dafne* (1598, music by Peri and Corsi), the first drama sung throughout. His great innovation here was a kind of verse appropriate to recitative, with changing metres and free rhymes that allowed speech-like declamation. He later wrote *Euridice* (1600, Peri and Caccini) and *Arianna* (1608, Monteverdi), as well as other texts set by Monteverdi.

ripieno (It., replenished). Full ensemble. The term is associated with Baroque music, especially the concerto grosso and allied forms, where passages for a small group (the concertino or concertante) will alternate with others for all the musicians.

Riquier, Guiraut (b. Narbonne, c.1230; d. c.1300). Troubadour, last in the line, servant of Alfonso X of Castile in the 1270s. A total of 48 of his songs survive with music, many more than for any other troubadour.

Rise and Fall of Mahagonny City. See AUFSTIEG UND FALL DER STADT MAHAGONNY.

riser. Movable large box on which musicians may be placed on the concert platform. A soloist – particularly a cellist, because seated – may play from a riser, or podium. And unless the platform has structural rising levels at the back, wind players, percussionists and choral singers will normally be stationed on risers to improve their view and projection.

RISM (Répertoire International des Sources Musicales). Inventory of musical sources, presented in a continuing series of catalogues initiated in 1961.

risoluto (It.). Resolute.

Risset, Jean-Claude (b. Le Puy, 13 Mar 1938). French composer, a pupil of Jolivet in Paris (1961–4) before he moved to the USA to study computer technology with Mathews (1964–9). He has worked at IRCAM and in his own department at the University of Marseilles-Luminy. His music for the Hiroshima play *Little Boy* (1968) is one of the early classics of computer music, followed by *Songes* (1979), *Sud* (1985), etc.

ritardando (It.). Slowing down, abbreviated *rit.*, the same as *rallentando*.

Rite of Spring, The (*Le Sacre du printemps*, *Vesna svyashchennaya* [Sacred Spring]). Ballet by Stravinsky, 'scenes of pagan Russia', to a scenario worked out with Nikolay Rerikh, choreographed originally by Nijinsky. Scored for large orchestra, the music is in two parts, each moving from a slow and hesitant introduction to a loudly pulsing finale: Dance of the Earth in the first part, Sacrificial Dance in the second. The first performance was vociferously challenged from the audience; the work's status as one of the great avatars of modernism was at once affirmed. First performance: Théâtre des Champs-Elysées, Paris, 29 May 1913.

ritenuto (It.). Held back quite suddenly, as opposed to the gradual deceleration of a *ritardando*.

ritmo di tre battute, **ritmo di quattro battute** (It., rhythm of three/four bars). Indication of a supermetre in which each bar counts as a beat, as in the scherzo of Beethoven's Ninth Symphony.

ritornello (It., little return, pl. *ritornelli*, though in Eng. often 'ritornellos'). Refrain. The term has been in musical use since the 14th century, but normally applies to a recurring passage for full instrumental ensemble marking off sections in an aria (e.g., to cite an early instance, the prologue to Monteverdi's *Orfeo*) or, in the later Baroque and Classical concerto, to orchestral passages separating solo excursions.

ritorno d'Ulisse in patria, Il. See ODYSSEY.

Ritual Fire Dance (*Danza ritual del fuego*). Climactic sequence in Falla's opera *El amor brujo*.

rivers. Flowing water – so picturesque, and so easily assimilable to music's passage through time – is a common subject in music, especially Romantic music. Rivers that have been depicted include the Rhine (Wagner), Danube (Johann Strauss II), Moldau (Smetana) and Housatonic (Ives), as well as the unnamed streams of *Die schöne Müllerin* and many another Schubert song. Rivers have also been the sites of musical festivities, especially the Elbe at Dresden (see SERENATA) and the Thames at London (Handel).

Rivier, Jean (b. Villemomble, Seine, 21 Jul 1896; d. Paris, 6 Nov 1987). French composer. His education delayed by war service and convalescence, he was a pupil of Georges Caussade at the Paris Conservatoire (1922–6) and wrote symphonies, concertos and chamber music.

RNCM. Royal Northern College of Music, Manchester.

Rochberg, George (b. Paterson, NJ, 5 Jul 1918). US composer. He studied at the Mannes School and at the Curtis Institute (1945–7, with Scalero and Menotti). In 1950 he met Dallapiccola in Rome and was impressed by the expressive power of 12-note music. He then worked as a publisher's editor before joining the University of Pennsylvania in 1960. Meanwhile, around 1957, he took on Webernian serialism, and in the early 1960s he began to work with collage, quoting from Boulez, Berio, Varèse and Ives in his quartet *Contra mortem et*

tempus. His Third String Quartet and later works go beyond quotation to a full-scale attempt at the revival of older styles, especially those of Mahler and the later Beethoven, and an emphatic rejection of the modernism he had once embraced.

George Rochberg *The Aesthetics of Survival* (1984)

Orchestral: Symphony No.1, 1948–57, No.2, 1955–6, No.3, with soli and ch, 1966–9, No.4, 1976, No.5, 1984, No.6, 1986–7; concertos for vn, 1974, ob, 1983, cl, 1996; *Music for the Magic Theater*, chbr orch, 1965–9; etc.

Chamber: String Quartet No.1, 1952, No.2, with v, 1959–61, No.3, 1972, Nos.4–6 'Concord', 1977–8, No.7, with bar, 1979; *Contra mortem et tempus*, fl, cl, vn, pf, 1965; *50 Caprice Variations*, vn, 1970; etc.

Other works: piano music, songs, choral works, opera

rococo. Term borrowed from architecture (in which context it was derived from Fr. *rocaille*, shellwork) and applied to 18th-century painting and music, especially French, implying decorativeness. It tends to be pejorative, or at least diminishing, unlike the alternatives PRE-CLASSICAL and GALANT.

Rode, (Jacques) Pierre (Joseph) (b. Bordeaux, 16 Feb 1774; d. Château de Bourbon, near Damazon, 25 Nov 1830). French violinist-composer, a pupil of Viotti in Paris. He gave the premières of his teacher's concertos Nos.17 and 18, and in 1795 was appointed professor at the new Conservatoire. Concert tours took him all over Europe, from Madrid to St Petersburg, and not least to Vienna, where he gave the first performance of Beethoven's Op.96 sonata, written for him. In 1814 he settled in Berlin and married. Five years later he returned to Bordeaux, his playing days over. His works include 13 concertos, sets of 24 solo caprices and duos, a violin method and quartets.

Rodelinda. Opera by Handel to a libretto by Haym. The central character is not Rodelinda (soprano) but her husband, Bertarido (alto castrato), who is restored to his wife and throne with the help of his sister Eduige (soprano), overcoming the ambitious Grimoaldo (tenor) and Garibaldo (bass). Bertarido also has the most exciting arias, including 'Dove sei, amato bene?' and 'Vivi, tiranno!'. First performance: King's Theatre, London, 13 Feb 1725.

Rodrigo (Vidre), Joaquín (b. Sagunto, 22 Nov 1901; d. Madrid, 6 Jul 1999). Spanish composer, most famously of the guitar concerto *Concierto de Aranjuez*, redolent of 18th-century palace courtyards. King Juan Carlos I created him Marqués de los Jardines de Aranjuez in 1991.

Blind from the age of three, he studied with Francisco Antich in Valencia (1917–22) and with Dukas at the Schola Cantorum during a period in Paris (1927–32) when he also met Falla. He returned to Valencia and married (his only child, Cecilia, was born in 1941), then left during the Civil War to live in Paris, Salzburg and Freiburg (1936–8). The *Concierto de Aranjuez* was written on another visit to Paris, in 1939, after which he settled in Madrid as head of the artistic section of the national organization for the blind, also working as a critic, broadcaster and teacher.

www.joaquin-rodrigo.com

Concertos: CONCIERTO DE ARANJUEZ, gtr, 1939; *Concierto heroico*, 1933–42, rev 1995 as Piano Concerto; *Concierto de Estío*, vn, 1943; *Concierto in modo galante*, vc, 1949; *Concierto serenata*, hp, 1952; *Fantasía para un gentilhombre*, gtr, 1954; *Concierto madrigal*, 2 gtr, 1966; *Concierto Andaluz*, 4 gtr, 1967; *Concierto pastoral*, fl, 1978; *Concierto como un divertimento*, vc, 1981; *Concierto para una fiesta*, gtr, 1982
Other works: pieces for orchestra, piano, guitar, songs, etc.

Rodrigues Coelho, Manuel (b. Elvas, *c.*1555; d. ?Lisbon, *c.*1635). Portuguese organist-composer, who served at Elvas Cathedral (where he had probably trained) and the royal chapel (1602–33). His *Flores de musica* (1620) is the earliest surviving book of keyboard music printed in Portugal, and shows him conversant with Cabezón, Sweelinck and English music.

Rodríguez, Vicente (b. Ontoniente, near Valencia; buried Valencia, 16 Dec 1760). Spanish composer, notably of 30 keyboard sonatas in the Scarlatti–Soler tradition.

Rodríguez de Ledesma, Mariano (b. Saragossa, 14 Dec 1779; d. Madrid, 28 Mar 1847). Spanish composer, who sang as a tenor in the royal chapel except during periods of political exile in London (1811–15, 1823–31). He was influenced by Haydn, Mozart (whose music he promoted in Madrid) and latterly Weber. In earlier years he wrote piano sonatas and arias, but after his appointment as court choirmaster (1836) he devoted himself to sacred music, including a Lamentations (1838).

Roger-Ducasse, Jean (Jules Aimable) (b. Bordeaux, 18 Apr 1873; d. Taillan-Médoc, Gironde, 19 Jul 1954). French composer. He studied with Fauré at the Conservatoire, and in 1910 took a post as inspector of singing teaching in Paris schools. His works, displaying a conscientious, independent mind influenced by Fauré and Debussy, include an

opera, a ballet (*Orphée*, 1912–13), choral tableaux, orchestral pieces, two quartets (in D minor, 1900–9, and major, 1912–53), piano pieces, motets and organ music. He also finished and orchestrated Debussy's saxophone *Rapsodie*.

Rohrflöte (Ger.), **Rohr flute**. CHIMNEY FLUTE.

Roi Arthus, Le (King Arthur). Opera by Chausson to his own libretto, a noble and personal work from the post-Wagnerian twilight concerning the ending of the rule of Arthur (baritone), as predicted by Merlin (baritone) after an adulterous liaison between Guinevere (soprano) and Lancelot (tenor). First performance: Brussels, 30 Nov 1903.

Roi David, Le (King David). Oratorio ('symphonic psalm') by Honegger to words by René Morax, written originally as incidental music to a play (1921), adapted to the concert hall (1922) and rescored for full orchestra (1923). The work follows the biblical king's life from being chosen by Samuel to death. First performance: Mézières, 11 Jun 1921.

Roi d'Ys, Le (The King of Ys). Opera by Lalo to a libretto by Edouard Blau. Rivalry between the sister princesses Margared (mezzo-soprano) and Rozenn (soprano) for the hand of Mylio (tenor) almost leads to the inundation of the Breton city of Ys. The overture takes its exhilarating main theme from Margared's aria 'Lorsque je t'ai vu soudain'; another fine number is Mylio's aubade 'Vainement, ma bien aimée'. First performance: Paris, 7 May 1888.

Roland. See ORLANDO.

Roland-Manuel (b. Paris, 22 Mar 1891; d. Paris, 2 Nov 1966). French composer and critic, whose full name was Roland Alexis Manuel Lévy. He studied with Roussel and with Ravel, whose follower he became; his Ravel biography was translated (1947). Also close to Stravinsky, he contributed a good deal to the latter's *Poetics of Music*, proclaiming an aesthetic of objectivity and restraint he followed in his own compositions: operas (including *Jeanne d'Arc*, 1955, to words by Charles Péguy), ballets, oratorios, songs, orchestral and chamber works.

Roldán (Gardes), Amadeo (b. Paris, 12 Jul 1900; d. Havana, 2 Mar 1939). Cuban composer. He studied with del Campo in Madrid, and in 1921 settled in Havana, where he revived musical life through his activities as composer, quartet leader, conductor and teacher. A mulatto, he drew on Afro-Cuban music as well as on the dynamism of *The Rite of*

Spring, and was part of a lively artistic scene in Havana, collaborating with Alejo Carpentier (ballet *La rebambaramba*, 1927–8) and Nicolas Guillén (*Curujey* for ch, 2 pf, 2 perc, 1931). Other works include the *Rítmicas* series (1930), of which *I–IV* are for piano with wind quintet and *V–VI* were among the first Western works for percussion ensemble.

roll. Succession of very fast drumbeats, obtained, for example, by alternating strokes with hands or sticks. A drum roll can be a call to attention (e.g. alerting an audience to stand for a national anthem), an impression of thunder, etc. See also DRAG; FLAM; PARADIDDLE; RATAMACUE; RUFF.

Rolla, Alessandro (b. Pavia, 6 Apr 1757; d. Milan, 14 Sep 1841). Italian violinist-composer. He served the ducal court in Parma (1782–1802) and was then leader and director of the orchestra at La Scala (1803–33), while also teaching violin at the Milan Conservatory (1808–35) and adding to a large output of violin music: concertos, chamber works and solo pieces. His son, Giuseppe Antonio Rolla (1798–1837), followed him as a violinist (notably with the Italian opera in Dresden) and composer.

Rolland, Romain. See IMAGINARY COMPOSERS.

Roman, Johan Helmich (b. Stockholm, 26 Oct 1694; d. Haraldsmåla, near Kalmar, 20 Nov 1758). Swedish composer, the first of importance. He followed his father as a court musician (by 1711), and was sent for further training in England (1716–21). In 1735–7 he made another journey, through England, France and Italy. His works include concertos, sinfonias, sonatas, church music and songs.

romance. The Spanish *romance* was a folk ballad, with origins in the 15th century and perhaps earlier; a book of such songs would be a *romancero*. Around the middle of the 18th century the term spread to France, where it soon meant a sentimental drawing-room song. That usage was taken up in Germany and Russia, being maintained in the latter country into the 20th century; there are romances by Shostakovich. The term was also transferred rapidly to instrumental music for slow movements with a song-like theme, perhaps the first example appearing in Gossec's Symphony in E♭, Op.5:2. Successors include movements in Mozart's *Eine kleine Nachtmusik* and Piano Concerto in D minor, Beethoven's two Romances for violin and orchestra, and Schumann's sets for piano and oboe.

Roman de Fauvel. Romance in French verse. Fauvel is an ass with every possible personality defect, who nevertheless climbs to the summit of power and prestige in a world turned upside-down – a world tellingly like the real one. The second version – written probably in 1317 and most likely by Gervès de Bus, a clerk in French royal circles – includes 34 polyphonic motets and other musical items. With some of its motets ascribable to Philippe de Vitry, the *Roman* is a crucial source of early ARS NOVA polyphony.

romanesca. Common harmonic frame for Italian songs and instrumental pieces of the 16th–17th centuries: III–VII–I–V–III–VII–I–V–I.

Romani, (Giuseppe) Felice (b. Genoa, 31 Jan 1788; d. Moneglia, 28 Jan 1865). Italian librettist, the most distinguished and prolific of his age. He began writing librettos in 1813 for his friend Mayr and within the next two decades completed around 80, for composers including Rossini (*Il turco in Italia, Bianca e Faliero*), Donizetti (*Anna Bolena, L'elisir d'amore*) and Bellini (*Il pirata, La sonnambula, Norma*).

Roman numerals. Used as a shorthand for triads or tonalities based on the degrees of a scale. Thus in the key of C major II represents D major, ii D minor, III E major, iii♭ E♭ minor, and so on. Added notes are indicated by superscript Arabic numbers, so that V^7 represents G major plus B, i.e. the dominant seventh.

Romantic. Adhering to Romanticism – or, more generally (and without the initial capital), vaunting spontaneity and expression above form and order; in this sense the opposite is CLASSICAL in one of its senses. Thus one might describe Dowland's songs as romantic and Byrd's as classical. Bruckner called his Fourth Symphony 'Romantic'.

Romanticism. Artistic movement emphasizing personal feeling. Its origins may be traced to the late 18th century, but in music it refers especially to the paradigmatically varied generation of composers born in or around the period 1800–10: Schubert, Berlioz, Mendelssohn, Schumann, Chopin, Liszt and Wagner. For all of them the example of Beethoven was crucial, and many of Beethoven's works and pronouncements evince a Romantic temperament, though he is too big to be seen as part of a movement.

A lot of Romantics died young, and by 1850, when the great burst of Romantic energy and enthusiasm was ebbing, only Berlioz, Schumann,

Liszt and Wagner remained. There was, however, a second wave of Romanticism that lasted much longer, from the 1850s to the time of the First World War and beyond, represented by Brahms, Tchaikovsky, Dvořák, Verdi, Bruckner, Mahler, Strauss and Schoenberg. In a sense it was superseded by modernism, which challenged such essential foundations of Romanticism as key-based harmony and symphonic continuity. But in another sense modernism was a continuation of Romanticism by other means, maintaining the Romantic search for authentic personal expression. Barraqué was a self-avowed Romantic.

In the music of the early Romantics, especially, lyric expression is paramount. There was a great renewal of song, which had been a virtually dormant genre since the mid 17th century, and a great reinvention of the song-like instrumental miniature in the piano music of the period. But composers of that same generation were highly conscious of the magnitude of their predecessors, particularly Mozart and Beethoven. They therefore repeatedly assailed the larger forms of sonata, string quartet and symphony, but they reinterpreted those forms as personal NARRATIVE. That predilection for story-telling also had effects in bringing about more continuous forms of opera as well as a new genre: the SYMPHONIC POEM.

The word's history goes back through 'romance' to the Roman language from which those of Iberia, France and Italy (the Romance languages) evolved. 'Romantic' in the English of the later 17th and 18th centuries meant extravagant or fanciful – meanings it took from the romance. The use of Romanticism as a noun may stem from Hoffmann's 1813 essay in which he indeed claimed Beethoven as a Romantic.

Leon Plantinga *Romantic Music* (1984); Charles Rosen *The Romantic Generation* (1995)

Romberg. German musician cousins. **Bernhard Heinrich** (b. Dinklage, Oldenburg, 13 Nov 1767; d. Hamburg, 13 Aug 1841) was a cellist and composer, who in his youth led a much-travelled existence with **Andreas Jakob** (b. Vechta, near Münster, 27 Apr 1767; d. Gotha, 10 Nov 1821), a violinist. They spent time in Paris, Bonn, Hamburg, Italy and Vienna (where they were acquainted with Haydn and Beethoven). Andreas then settled in Hamburg, but Bernhard continued his journeyings – to Spain, Paris again, Berlin, Russia and England, before himself settling in Hamburg in 1820. He wrote concertos and much else for his instrument, but also symphonies and operas. His daughter, Bernhardine (1803–78), became a singer and his son, Karl (1811–97), was a cellist with the German

opera in St Petersburg in the 1830s, in a section led by Andreas's son, Ciprian Friedrich (1807–65), while another of Andreas's sons, Heinrich Maria (1802–59), led the imperial opera in the same city.

Rome (Roma). City with a leading importance in European culture as the centre of the Roman Empire and then of the papacy. Music had a place in ancient Roman religious ritual (singing, playing on the double reed pipe, flute, lyre and percussion instruments), military life (trumpet and horn signals), drama and domestic entertainment (songs to the harp or other string instrument, organ playing). In Christian Rome choirs and choir schools go back at least as far as the 7th century; their importance in the composition and teaching of plainsong is likely to have been great. The city again became an important musical centre at the end of the 15th century, when Josquin was there. After that, its record was prodigious. Palestrina and Victoria were contemporaries in the city; Frescobaldi and Allegri were both working in the Vatican in the 1620s and 1630s; and Baroque Rome heard extraordinary musical magnificence: the oratorio flourished in the works of Carissimi and Stradella, while Corelli and Pasquini played for Queen Christina and wealthy cardinals promoted the sensuous genres of cantata and opera, the latter with all-male casts, in obedience to a papal ban on female stage performers. After a sleepy later 18th century, Rome saw the premières of many significant operas from *Il barbiere di Siviglia* (1816) to *Tosca* (1900), and the music school founded by the ACCADEMIA DI SANTA CECILIA became one of the leading conservatories in Italy.

Romeo and Juliet. Shakespeare play – about two young lovers, doomed as the scions of warring families – with a rich history of musical adaptations:

(1) Dramatic symphony by Berlioz for soli (mez, t, b), chorus and orchestra. Romeo and Juliet do not sing: the only characters who do are Mercutio (briefly) and Friar Laurence. There are three purely orchestral movements: *Roméo seul* (Romeo Alone), *La Reine Mab* (Queen Mab Scherzo), *Roméo au tombeau des Capulets* (Romeo at the Capulets' Tomb). First performance: Paris, 24 Nov 1839.

(2) Opera by Gounod to a libretto by Barbier and Carré. The plot stays close to Shakespeare except in adapting the end so that Romeo (tenor) and Juliet (soprano) can sing in duet. Favourite numbers from earlier points are Juliet's valse-ariette 'Je veux vivre' and Romeo's cavatina 'Ah! lève-toi, soleil!' In 1888 the composer added a

ballet for a production at the Paris Opera. First performance: Paris, 27 Apr 1867.

(3) Fantasy overture by Tchaikovsky. First performance: Moscow, 16 Mar 1870.

(4) Full-length ballet score by Prokofiev to a scenario by Leonid Lavrovsky, Adrian Pitrovsky, Sergey Radlov and the composer, choreographed by Vanya Psota. Besides a piano volume (Op.75) Prokofiev drew three orchestral suites from his score (Op.64bis, Op.64ter, Op.101); some conductors have also made their own selections of numbers. First performance: Brno, 30 Dec 1938.

There are other operatic versions by Georg Benda, Steibelt, Sutermeister, Blacher and Kelterborn. Italian contributions – not only Bellini's *I* CAPULETI E I MONTECCHI (1830) but also the *Giulietta e Romeo* operas of Zingarelli (1796), Zaccai (1825) and Zandonai (1922) – tell the same story from within an Italian tradition going back to Shakespeare's sources. Delius's *A Village Romeo and Juliet* has a parallel plot.

ronde (Fr.). Semibreve, whole note.

rondeau. One of the three fixed forms (with the BALLADE and VIRELAI) of French song in the 14th and 15th centuries, apparently so called because of a circulating movement in the dances for which rondeaux were first sung, in the early 13th century. The simple classic rondeau is in eight lines, with the scheme A–B–A'–A–A'–B'–A–B – i.e. the fourth and seventh lines are the same as the first (A), the third and fifth have the same rhyme (A'), the last is the same as the second (B) and the sixth has the same rhyme (B'). More elaborate forms in 11, 13, 16 and 21 lines were also possible and were taken up by later poets, particularly around 1900. The Giraud–Hartleben poems set in Schoenberg's *Pierrot lunaire* are 13-line rondeaux.

rondes (Fr.). ROUND DANCE.

Rondine, La (The Swallow). Opera by Puccini to words by Giuseppe Adami after a Viennese libretto. Magda (soprano), a woman with a past, lets herself fall in love with Ruggero (tenor) before sadly withdrawing from his life. First performance: Monte Carlo, 27 Mar 1917.

rondo (Fr. *rondeau*). Musical form in which the first section comes back to frame episodes. The simplest such form would therefore have the pattern ABACA or, still more simply, ABABA, though much more usual is a combination of these: ABACABA. There is no connection with the medieval *rondeau*; the rondo developed in French music in the later 17th century, surely out of ritornello and verse-refrain forms. Composers elsewhere remembered its origin in using the French form of the word, as Bach did and sometimes Mozart. But by Mozart's time the rondo had transformed itself from French stateliness into a lively and tuneful movement, suitable for comic operas and the finales of instrumental works. In Mozart's rondos, as in those of Haydn and Beethoven, there is some influence from sonata form, so that the B section functions as second subject (brought into the tonic key at its return) and the C part as development. One or other of the later A sections would then be omitted: Mozart preferred the ABACBA form, Haydn and Beethoven the ABACAB plus coda. These sonata rondo forms remained models, especially for concerto finales, followed and adapted by composers from Brahms to Bartók.

rondò. Aria form of the late 18th century, barely related to the regular rondo, with the pattern AABB, where A is slow and B is fast. There are examples by Mozart, including two arias he wrote for insertion in Anfossi's *Il curioso indiscreto*, 'Per pietà, non ricercate' and 'Vorrei spiegarvi'.

Rondo alla turca. Finale of Mozart's Piano Sonata in A, K.331.

Röntgen, Julius (b. Leipzig, 9 May 1855; d. Bilthoven, 13 Sep 1932). Dutch composer, son of Engelbert Röntgen (1823–97), a violinist in the Gewandhaus orchestra. He studied in Leipzig and Munich, and in 1877 moved to Amsterdam, where he taught. His large output – 21 symphonies, seven piano concertos, 19 string quartets – spans musical history and geography from Brahms to Debussy.

root. Lowest note of a chord. A chord in the major-minor system is said to be in root position if its root is also its tonic; otherwise it is in INVERSION.

Ropartz, Joseph Guy (Marie) (b. Guingamp, 15 Jun 1864; d. Lanloup, 22 Nov 1955). French composer. He entered the Paris Conservatoire in 1885 but left the next year to study with Franck, whose circle of devoted admirers he joined. After directing the conservatories in Nancy (1894–1919) and Strasbourg (1919–29) he retired to his native Brittany to continue composing in a Franckian style of rich, wandering tonality. His works include five symphonies (No.3 with chorus, 1905), six quartets, religious music (masses, motets, large-scale psalm settings, organ pieces), songs, piano pieces and useful music for wind and brass players.

Rore, Cipriano da (b. Ronse, 1515/16; d. Parma, Sep

1565). Netherlandish composer. Almost nothing is known of his life before 1542–6, when he was in Brescia and may also have been a singer at St Mark's in Venice under Willaert. His first book of madrigals (1542) attracted attention, and in 1546 he was appointed chapelmaster to Duke Ercole II of Ferrara. His brother's death drew him back to Flanders for the winter of 1558–9, and he was there again in 1559–60, after which he became chapelmaster in Parma, a post he left for a brief return to St Mark's as Willaert's successor (1563–4). He wrote five masses and numerous motets, but his richest contribution was to the madrigal, in which he combined Flemish imitative counterpoint with Italian lyricism in ways that were to be powerfully influential on composers from Palestrina to Monteverdi. He looked for texts of weight, preferring sonnets, above all those of Petrarch.

Rorem, Ned (b. Richmond, Ind., 23 Oct 1923). US composer, especially of songs. Brought up in Chicago, he studied in New York, at the Juilliard School (1945–8) and privately with Virgil Thomson and Diamond. From 1949 to 1958 he lived largely in Paris and Morocco, his charm, intelligence, good looks and gay sexuality leading him to adventures that provided material for the first of several published diaries. Meanwhile, the French–US ambience of Thomson and Poulenc determined his style, at once sentimental and ironic. His output of songs and choral music is enormous, but he has also written orchestral and chamber music, and an opera (*Miss Julie*, 1965).

Ned Rorem *A Ned Rorem Reader* (2001)

Rosa, Carl. See CARL ROSA OPERA COMPANY.

Rosamunde. Music by Schubert for Helmina von Chezy's lost play *Rosamunde, Fürstin von Zypern* (Rosamund, Princess of Cyprus), the score comprising entr'actes, ballet numbers and vocal items, but no overture. The overture for the occasion was taken from *Alfonso und Estrella*; oddly, the work known as the *Rosamunde* overure was written for *Die Zauberharfe*. First performance: Vienna, 20 Dec 1823.

Rosary Sonatas. See MYSTERY SONATAS.

Rosbaud, Hans [Johannes] (b. Graz, 22 Jul 1895; d. Lugano, 29 Dec 1962). Austrian conductor. Keenly but not solely devoted to contemporary music, his record of premières ran from Bartók's Second Piano Concerto (1933) to Boulez's *Le Marteau sans maître* (1955) and included Schoenberg's *Moses und Aron*. He held posts in Frankfurt (1928–37),

Münster (1937–41), Strasbourg (1941–4), Munich (1945–8) and Baden-Baden (1948–62).

rose. Soundhole in a Renaissance–Baroque lute, guitar or keyboard instrument, with florid tracery befitting its name.

Rosé [Rosenblum], **Arnold (Josef)** (b. Iaşi, 24 Oct 1863; d. London, 25 Aug 1946). Austrian violinist. He studied at the Vienna Conservatory and led the Vienna Philharmonic for over half a century, 1881–1938. His Rosé Quartet, founded in 1882, gave the first performances of works by Brahms, Schoenberg, Reger, etc. He and his brother Eduard, the quartet's original cellist, were married to Mahler's sisters.

Roseingrave, Thomas (b. Winchester, 1690/91; d. Dunleary, 23 Jun 1766). British composer, son of Daniel Roseingrave, then organist of Winchester Cathedral. Daniel's career took him to Salisbury and Dublin (1698–1727), where his sons Daniel and Ralph remained as organists. Thomas, though, went to Italy in 1709 and was dazzled by Domenico Scarlatti. He returned to England around 1715 and put on a performance of a Scarlatti opera in 1720; he also published an edition of 42 Scarlatti sonatas in 1739. Meanwhile, in 1725 he had become organist of St George's, Hanover Square, Handel's parish church, where he might have remained had it not been for a disappointment in love. Subject to fits of madness, he retired in 1753 to the Dublin house of his nephew William, Ralph's son. He wrote anthems, songs and keyboard items.

Rosen, Charles (Welles) (b. New York, 5 May 1927). US pianist and scholar. He studied with Moriz Rosenthal and at Princeton, where his principal interests were literary. As a pianist he is renowned for his lucid approach to Bach, late Beethoven and new works, especially those of Carter and Boulez. His book *The Classical Style* (1971) is itself a classic.

Rosenberg, Hilding (Constantin) (b. Bosjökloster, Ringsjön, Skåne, 21 Jun 1892; d. Stockholm, 19 May 1985). Swedish composer. He studied at the conservatory in Stockholm with Ernst Ellberg (1915–16), was encouraged by Stenhammar (who gave him counterpoint lessons) and gained, too, from trips to Vienna and Paris in the early 1920s, meeting Schoenberg and Stravinsky. Under their influence he began as an acerbic neoclassicist, and he had an important role in the Swedish inter-war avant-garde as a theatre composer, chamber musician and organizer, quite apart from his steady output of concert music. In the late 1930s his music became smoother and more consonant, allowing him to take a place within the Nordic symphonic tradition, while renewing that tradition (for instance, with his Stravinsky-like choral writing).

Stage: *Marionettes* (opera), 1938; *Orpheus in Town* (ballet), 1938; *Joseph and his Brothers* (opera-oratorio, after Thomas Mann), 1946–8

Orchestral: Symphony No.1, 1917; No.2 'Sinfonia grave', 1928–35; No.3 'The Four Ages of Man', 1939; No.4 'The Revelation of St John', with bar, ch, 1940; No.5 'Hortulanus', with a, ch, 1944; No.6 'Sinfonia semplice', 1951; No.7, 1968; No.8 'In candidum', with ch, 1974; concertos for str orch (4), pf (2), vn (2), vc (2), va, tpt; etc.

Chamber: String Quartet No.1, 1920, No.2, 1924, No.3 'Quartetto pastorale', 1926, No.4, 1939, No.5, 1949, No.6, 1954, Nos.7–12, 1956

Rosenkavalier, Der (The Rose Chevalier). Opera by Strauss to a libretto by Hofmannsthal, set in rococo Vienna though suffused with sublime anachronism by the 19th-century waltz. (Strauss drew from the score two orchestral 'waltz sequences' as well as a suite.) Feeling her age, the Marschallin (soprano) encourages a match between her young lover, Octavian (mezzo-soprano), and Sophie (soprano), frustrating the hopes of her buffoon cousin Baron Ochs (bass). There is a vivid abundance of minor characters, but at the end the stage clears for a gorgeous trio for the principal women's voices. First performance: Dresden, 26 Jan 1911.

Rosenmüller, Johann (b. Oelsnitz, near Zwickau, *c.*1619; buried Wolfenbüttel, 12 Sep 1684). German composer. He studied in Oelsnitz and Leipzig, and was teaching at St Thomas's school in the latter city by 1642. In 1655 he was arrested on grounds of pederasty. He fled jail and turned up in 1658 as a trombonist at St Mark's, Venice, in which city he stayed until, near the end of his life, he took an appointment as chapelmaster to the Wolfenbüttel court. His works include a large quantity of sacred music, to Latin and German texts, and sonatas. Bach's Cantata No.27 incorporates one of his funeral hymns.

Rosenthal, Moriz (b. Lemberg/Lviv, 18 Dec 1862; d. New York, 3 Sep 1946). Ukrainian pianist. He studied from 1872 at the local conservatory with Karol Mikuli, a pupil of Chopin, and in 1875 the family moved to Vienna so that he could continue his training with the esteemed virtuoso Rafael Joseffy. Two years later he met Liszt, with whom he stayed for the remaining nine years of the elder musician's life, while also studying philosophy at Vienna University. After that his playing was acclaimed by Brahms and Tchaikovsky, among others. His sensitivity, intelligence and access to the two great 19th-century traditions – Chopin's, distinguished principally by legato, and Liszt's, more brilliant – made him one of the outstanding pianists of his time. He married a pupil and in 1938 emigrated from Vienna to New York.

rosin. Substance rubbed on bowhair to increase friction on the strings. It is obtained by distilling oil of turpentine and was first recorded in a German manual of 1532.

Roslavets, Nikolay (Andreyevich) (b. Dushatino, Chernihiv region, Ukraine, 5 Jan 1881; d. Moscow, 23 Aug 1944). Russian composer. He studied at the Moscow Conservatory (1902–12) but was more impressed by what he heard at that time of Debussy and Scriabin. Their music led him along 12-note paths, confirmed when he encountered Schoenberg's music in 1923. He was also active in the Association for Contemporary Music, representing the more radical wing in Soviet music, and when that organization was eclipsed in the early 1930s his name disappeared from concert programmes and dictionaries. His works include a violin concerto (1925), quartets, sonatas for solo strings with piano, piano pieces and songs.

Rosseter, Philip (b. 1567/8; d. London, 5 May 1623). English composer, a friend to Campion. He was appointed a court lutenist in 1603 and helped to manage a company of boy actors, the Children of the Queen's Revels (1609–17). His works include lute pieces in the old contrapuntal style and lute songs in which he specifically avoided that style, 'intricate, bated with fuge'.

Rossi, Lauro (b. Macerata, 19 Feb 1812; d. Cremona, 5 May 1885). Italian composer. He studied at the Naples Conservatory and began a properly Neapolitan career as a composer of comic operas. Reaching a degree of eminence, he was induced by Malibran to write an opera in which she could dance a pas de deux with a ballerina; *Amelia* (1834), the result, was not a success, and Rossi left for Mexico City at the head of a touring company that presented his *Giovanna Shore* (1836). In 1841–2 he was involved with another company that appeared in Havana and New Orleans, and whose young soprano, Isabella Obermeyer, he married. The two of them returned to Europe in 1843 to recover from yellow fever, and Rossi had renewed success during the next few years, notably with a revival of one of his earlier operas as *I falsi monetari* (1844), regarded as his *Barbiere*. He was later director of the conservatories in Milan and Naples.

Rossi, Luigi (b. Torremaggiore, ?1597/8; d. Rome, 19 Feb 1653). Italian composer. Most likely he studied in Naples before moving to Rome by 1620, probably summoned by the Borgheses. In 1627 he married Costanza de Ponte, a celebrated harpist, and in 1633 was appointed organist of San Luigi dei Francesi. He moved from the Borgheses to the household of Cardinal Antonio Barberini in 1641, and his reputation and opportunities increased. Already famed as a composer of cantatas, a master of decorous sentiment, he produced his first opera for the Palazzo Barberini, the spectacular seven-hour *Il palazzo incantato* (1642), on the Alcina topic. In 1645 the Barberinis left for France, and the next year Rossi was called to Paris by Cardinal Mazarin. While away, he learned of his wife's sudden death, and his grief may have delayed the completion of the opera he was writing, *Orfeo*. This was presented in March–May 1647, and then he returned to Rome, only to be invited back for a further stay (1648–9), though this time with no opera commission. Apart from his two operas and around 300 cantatas (most of them solo songs with continuo, some more elaborate in scoring and form), he produced a small quantity of church music. His brother, Giancarlo (c.1617–92), was also a musician and cantata composer in Rome, and deputized for him at San Luigi dei Francesi during his absences.

Rossi, Michelangelo (b. Genoa, 1601/2; buried Rome, 7 Jul 1656). Italian composer, known in his time as 'the Michelangelo of the violin' for his supremacy as a performer, but remembered chiefly for his keyboard compositions, which follow those of his teacher Frescobaldi. His career also partly intertwined with that of the unrelated Luigi Rossi, especially in that he wrote an opera for the Palazzo Barberini, *Erminia sul Giordano* (1633), which had spectacular sets by Bernini, and in which he took part as Apollo, playing his violin.

Rossi, Salomone (b. ?Mantua, ?19 Aug 1570; d. ?Mantua, c.1630). Italian composer of Jewish faith, associated with the ducal court of Mantua and probably with the city's Jewish theatre companies. He published madrigals, settings of psalms and other sacred texts in Hebrew, and instrumental pieces. These last show a move away from the canzona, with its equal parts, towards the Baroque trio sonata, in which two voice-like lines play above a continuo.

Rossini, Gioachino (Antonio) (b. Pesaro, 29 Feb 1792; d. Passy, 13 Nov 1868). Italian composer, the greatest master of pure operatic comedy and an artist of engaging cheerfulness too in his serious works. Vivid and brilliant, his music owed little to the more cautious and expository manner of his Italian predecessors, and created a basis for Bellini, Donizetti and Verdi.

His father was a horn player who secured the future composer's legitimacy by marrying his mother, a singer, when she was four months pregnant. In his early years the boy was often left with his grandmother while his parents were on tour, but then a throat condition forced his mother to retire and the family set up residence in Bologna. There the young all-round musician made his stage debut, as the boy Adolfo in Paer's *Camilla* in 1805, having already begun playing keyboard in theatres and composing; six charming and highly skilled sonatas for strings date from around 1804. He was then given a thorough training at the music school in Bologna, which he entered in April 1806 and where he was exposed to the music of Mozart, 'the admiration of my youth, the desperation of my mature years, the consolation of my old age'.

While still at the school he was commissioned by the tenor Domenico Mombelli to set a serious libretto, *Demetrio e Polibio*, but this was performed only after he had started to make his name as a composer of comedies. His first in this vein was *La cambiale di matrimonio*, written in 1810 for the Teatro San Moisè in Venice, the theatre for which he was to provide four more comic operas in 1812–13, including one of his most successful early works, *L'inganno felice*, and one of his best, *Il Signor Bruschino*. With five other operas to write during those two years, he began the practice of recycling numbers, using a duet from *Demetrio* in five later pieces. More surprising was his ability to project into his music the speed and freshness with which it was written, not least in the overtures, normally written last and perhaps most speedily.

The creative presto was in part compelled by his need to support himself and his parents. But it was also the expression of fluency, and perhaps a personal embodiment of the early industrial age – Rossini as a factory, producing pieces with perfectly turning cogwheels of rhythm, tune, form and plot. Yet even these early works show his sense of fun, his increasing zest for characterization (instrumental as much as vocal, an example of the former being the bow-tapping for the strings on their candle holders in the *Bruschino* overture) and his touch for expressing feeling in simple melody.

Two of the 1813 operas sprang him to international attention: the serious *Tancredi* and the comic *L'italiana in Algeri* – though, with his abundant good humour, he was dealing with heroic drama and farce in very similar musical terms. Then came another serious-comic pair for La Scala in Milan: *Aureliano in Palmira* and *Il turco in Italia*. The former of these included a part for the last great castrato, Velluti, at a time when the role of hero was more normally allotted to a woman in male attire (as in *Tancredi*) and would soon be assumed by a tenor (as in *Armida*). After these works, neither a spectacular success at the time, Rossini was most closely associated with Naples for several years, his works there being almost exclusively serious, from the piece about Elizabeth I (1815) to *Zelmira* (1822). During the earlier part of this period, though, he was called to other cities for comedies, including *Il barbiere di Siviglia* and *La Cenerentola*.

His conquest of Naples was significant. Italian opera in the 18th century, from Pergolesi to Paisiello and Cimarosa, had been almost a Neapolitan preserve. But that age was over, and anyway, Rossini's inventiveness was irresistible. So was Isabella Colbran, the leading lady he found in Naples. She was just one of the brilliant Neapolitan singers who inevitably marked the music he wrote for them (*Otello*, for instance, has three extravagantly demanding tenor roles), but she also marked him personally, and he her. When he arrived she was probably the mistress of the theatre director, Domenico Barbaia; in 1822 she and Rossini were married. Meanwhile, his music was changing. *Elisabetta*, his first work for Colbran, was also his first in which all the recitatives are accompanied by strings, not just keyboard. Simultaneously the separate numbers of 18th-century opera were being welded into longer sequences, with more duets and ensembles, though still leaving plentiful room for solo display, and with the chorus more vigorously present in the musical drama. Soon this new style was being heard all over the Western world.

In 1822 he was in Vienna when Barbaia mounted six of his operas there. He may have met Beethoven, and certainly his music gave Schubert equivocal feelings of fascination and mistrust. But that was the end of his association with Barbaia, and after *Semiramide* (1823) he left Italy for Paris and London.

Paris was where he settled, first as director of the Italian theatre and then as a composer for the Opera, for which he began by providing versions of older pieces – *Le Siège de Corinthe*, *Moïse* and *Le Comte Ory* (based on *Il viaggio a Reims*, which had been produced at the Italian theatre as an ebullient footnote to the last French coronation, that of Charles X) – and then produced a new work, *Guillaume Tell* (1829). He agreed to write at least four more pieces for the Opera, in alternate years,

but that project was derailed by the revolution of 1830 that toppled Charles X.

By now, too, his relationship with his wife was strained, and he began an affair with Olympe Pélissier, whom he was to marry in 1846, after Colbran's death. Paris remained his home for a few years, but in 1836 he returned to Italy, and Pélissier followed him. During the next two decades he achieved rather little, except for the definitive version of his *Stabat mater* and remarriage. Poor health was partly to blame. Perhaps, too, material comfort dulled his incentive, and he preferred to leave the field to a new generation (though Meyerbeer was older than him and Donizetti only a few years younger). Then in 1855, when he and his wife went back to Paris, his creative vitality returned. There were no more operas; instead he devoted himself largely to piano pieces, songs and other small-scale frolics (with the exception of the *Petite messe solennelle*), which were performed at the Saturday salons he and his wife held, and which he called his 'péchés de vieillesse' (sins of old age).

Some of his operas – *Il barbiere di Siviglia*, of course – have been continuously in performance since the moment they were written. Others began to be appreciated (and published in reliable editions) only during the second half of the 20th century, in an age that could again understand tragedy being given the vim of comedy. Still others have remained forgotten – and not always because they contain little that the eminently practical composer had not used in earlier works.

Stendhal *Life of Rossini* (1956, ²1970); Richard Osborne *Rossini* (1986)

Comic operas: *La cambiale di matrimonio* (1 act; Gaetano Rossi), f.p. Venice, 1810; *L'equivoco stravagante* (Gaetano Gasbarri), f.p. Bologna, 1811; *L'inganno felice* (1 act: Giuseppe Foppa, after Giuseppe Palomba), f.p. Venice, 1812; *La* SCALA DI SETA (1 act); *La pietra del paragone* (Luigi Romanelli), f.p. Milan, 1812; *L'occasione fa il ladro* (1 act; Luigi Prividali, after Scribe), f.p. Venice, 1812; *Il* SIGNOR BRUSCHINO (1 act); *L'*ITALIANA IN ALGERI; *Il* TURCO IN ITALIA; *Il* BARBIERE DI SIVIGLIA; *La gazzetta* (Palomba, after Goldoni), f.p. Naples, 1816; *La Cenerentola* (see CINDERELLA); *Il* VIAGGIO A REIMS; *Adina* (1 act; Gherardo Bevilacqua Aldobrandini, after Romani), f.p. Lisbon, 1826; *Le* COMTE ORY

Semiserious operas: *Torvaldo e Dorliska* (Cesare Sternini), f.p. Rome, 1815; *La* GAZZA LADRA; *Matilde di Shabran* (Jacopo Ferretti, after libretto of Méhul's *Euphrosine*), f.p. Rome, 1821

Serious operas: *Demetrio e Polibio* (Vincenzina Viganò Mombelli), f.p. Rome, 1812; *Ciro in Babilonia* (Francesco Aventi), f.p. Ferrara, 1812; TANCREDI; *Aureliano in Palmira* (Romani), f.p. Milan, 1813; *Sigismondo* (Foppa), f.p. Venice, 1814;

Elisabetta, regina d'Inghilterra (Giovanni Schmidt), f.p. Naples, 1815; *Otello* (see OTHELLO); ARMIDA; *Adelaide di Borgogna* (Schmidt), f.p. Rome, 1817; *Mosè in Egitto* (see MOSES); *Ricciardo e Zoraide* (Francesco Berio di Salsa), f.p. Naples, 1818; *Ermione* (Tottola, after Racine), f.p. Naples, 1819; *Eduardo e Cristina* (pastiche of *Adelaide*, *Ricciardo* and *Ermione*; Tottola and Aldobrandini, after Schmidt), f.p. Venice, 1819; *La donna del lago* (Tottola, after Scott), f.p. Naples, 1819; *Bianca e Faliero* (Romani), f.p. Milan, 1819; *Maometto II* (Cesare della Valle), f.p. Naples, 1820, rev as *Le Siège de Corinthe* (Luigi Balocchi and Alexandre Soumet), f.p. Paris, 1826; *Zelmira* (Tottola), f.p. Naples, 1822; *Semiramide* (see SEMIRAMIS); GUILLAUME TELL

Other vocal works: *Messa di gloria*, soli, ch, orch, 1820; *Tantum ergo*, soli, orch, 1824; *Il pianto delle muse in morte di Lord Byron*, t, ch, orch, 1824; *Giovanna d'Arco*, cantata, s, pf, 1832; *Stabat mater*, soli, ch, orch, 1832, rev 1841; *Les Soirées musicales* (12 songs and duets), *c*.1830–35; *Tantum ergo*, soli, orch, 1847; PETITE MESSE SOLENNELLE, 12 soli, 2 pf, hmnm, 1863, orch 1867; numerous other cantatas, sacred works, songs

Instrumental: 6 Sonatas, 2 vn, vc, db, *c*.1804; Variations, F, cl, str qt, orch, 1809; Variations, C, cl, orch, 1809; *Andante e Tema con variazioni*, wind qt, 1812; *Andante con variazioni*, hp, va, *c*.1820; Serenade, septet, 1823; etc.

Péchés de vieillesse: songs, vocal ensembles, piano and instrumental pieces, 1857–68

Rostropovich, Mstislav (Leopoldovich) (b. Baku, 27 Mar 1927). Russian cellist and conductor. He studied as a cellist with Semyon Kozolupov at the Moscow Conservatory, where he also had composition lessons with Shostakovich and Shebalin. An immediate star, he was still in his early 20s when he worked with Prokofiev on two concertos (Symphony-Concerto, Concertino). Other composers to write for him included Shostakovich and, following a visit to Britain in 1960, Britten. In 1955 he married the soprano Galina Vishnevskaya, with whom he began his conducting career. Increasingly critical of the Soviet government, he left the country with his wife and family in 1974. Once abroad, he turned more to conducting, displaying the same big, eager musical personality he had shown as a cellist. He was music director of the National Symphony Orchestra of Washington (1977–94).

rostrum. PODIUM.

rota (It., wheel). Medieval term for ROUND.

Rota, Nino (b. Milan, 3 Dec 1911; d. Rome, 10 Apr 1979). Italian composer. Born into a musical family, he began to compose when he was eight and had an oratorio performed when he was 11. Training followed with Pizzetti (1925–6), with Casella in Rome and with Rosario Scalero at the Curtis Institute (1931–2). In 1939 he began teaching at the Bari Conservatory, where he became director (1950–77). He is known chiefly for his opera *Il cappello di paglia di Firenze* (The Italian Straw Hat, 1946) and the scores he wrote for films by Fellini (*I vitelloni*, *Le notti di Cabiria*, 8½, *Amarcord*, etc.) and others, matching both the sophistication and the emotional immediacy of the Italian cinema in the 1950s and 1960s, the fantasy and the realism. He also wrote concertos, chamber pieces and choral music.

rotation. Recycling of notes in serial technique, normally applied to a hexachord, as when C–B–F♯–A–A♭–E gives rise to B–F♯–A–A♭–E–C.

rote (Ger. *Rotte*, Welsh *crwth*). Ancient and early medieval lyre, as known from excavations and manuscript illustrations to have been used by Celtic and Germanic peoples.

roto-toms. Small skin drums fixed to a stand. Rotation by hand will change their tuning within the range of an octave.

Rott, Hans (b. Vienna, 1 Aug 1858; d. Vienna, 25 Jun 1884). Austrian composer. He was a pupil of Bruckner at the Vienna Conservatory and a friend of Mahler, whose music his Symphony in E (1878–80) prefigures. In 1880 he became insane.

Rouet d'Omphale, Le (Omphale's Spinning Wheel). Symphonic poem by Saint-Saëns representing Hercules's labour in disguise as a female slave, spinning wool for Queen Omphale.

Rouget de Lisle, Claude-Joseph (b. Lons-le-Saunier, 10 May 1760; d. Choisy-le-Roi, 26/27 Jun 1836). French song writer, author of 'La MARSEILLAISE'.

roulade (Fr., roll). Informal term for a fast run performed by a singer or instrumentalist especially in the upper register.

round. Song in which three or more voices make staggered entries with the same words and music. In a simple example, such as 'London's Burning', there are four phrases. As the first singer reaches each new phrase, so the second, third and fourth singers begin. The first singer can then return to the first phrase, so that the song can continue indefinitely – hence the term, which was introduced in the early 16th century (though the first notated example is SUMER IS ICUMEN IN, from three centuries earlier). The round is a peculiarly English form, with its bawdy Baroque relative the CATCH. But there are canons by Haydn and Beethoven that follow the same principle.

round dance. One in which the participants form a circle, an old English example being 'Sellinger's Round'. The French term, *rondes*, appears in Stravinsky's *Rite of Spring* and Debussy's *Images*, the German *Reigen* in Berg's Op.6.

Rouse, Christopher (Chapman) (b. Baltimore, 15 Feb 1949). US composer. He studied at the Oberlin Conservatory and Cornell University, with Crumb and Husa, and has taught at the Eastman School since 1981. His works use conventional forms, especially the concerto, to contain music that is strongly urged and passionate.

Rousseau, Jean-Jacques (b. Geneva, 28 Jun 1712; d. Ermenonville, 2 Jul 1778). Swiss philosopher and composer, a proponent of a return to nature. His scant musical training was adequate to his purpose, which was to bring music back to the supposedly natural form of melody with basic accompaniment. Impressed by the music he heard in Venice in 1743–4, he settled then in Paris and campaigned for his ideal, antagonizing Rameau. His chief practical effort was the short opera *Le Devin du village* (f.p. Fontainebleau, 1752), close to the folk songs and dances he collected. He later came to think that opera should be replaced by melodrama, of which he provided an example in *Pygmalion* (f.p. Lyons, 1770), with music by himself and Horace Coignet.

Roussel, Albert (Charles Paul Marie) (b. Tourcoing, 5 Apr 1869; d. Royan, 23 Aug 1937). French composer. Like his near contemporary Ravel, he took an independent path around two successive giants, Debussy and Stravinsky, distinguishing himself from all three composers by the robust yet poetic vigour of his music.

Born into a wealthy family, he lost both his parents when he was very young and was brought up by relatives. He was schooled for the navy and saw service in the Far East and elsewhere before resigning his commission in 1894 to study music in Paris. He became a pupil of d'Indy at the Schola Cantorum in 1898, and was invited by d'Indy in 1902 to stay on as a counterpoint teacher. At the same time he began making a name for himself. He married in 1908, and the next year went with his wife on a tour of India and Southeast Asia, from which he returned with impressions that went into his orchestral *Evocations* and opera

Padmâvatî; composition of the latter work, set in legendary India, was interrupted by his service in the First World War as an artillery officer. He also produced an intriguing ballet of insect life, *Le Festin de l'araignée*, typically tart and characterful. In 1922 he retired to the Normandy coast, where he entered a new phase with a rapid succession of big scores exhibiting formal strength within a neoclassical style powered by polytonal harmony and, often, a rugged rhythmic impetus. Important works of this period include his Third Symphony and ballet *Bacchus et Ariane*.

Basil Deane *Albert Roussel* (1961)

Opera: PADMAVATI, Op.18, 1913–18; *La Naissance de la lyre* (1 act; Théodore Reinach), Op.24, 1922–4, f.p. Paris, 1925; *Le Testament de la tante Caroline* (opéra bouffe; Nino), 1932–3, f.p. Olomouc, 1936

Ballets: LE FESTIN DE L'ARAIGNEE, Op.17, 1912–13; *Bacchus et Ariane* (see ARIADNE), Op.43, 1930; *Aenéas*, Op.54, ch, orch, 1935

Orchestral: Symphony No.1 (*Le Poème de la forêt*), op.7, 1904–6; No.2, B♭, Op.23, 1919–21; No.3, G minor, Op.42, 1929–30; No.4, A, Op.53, 1934; Piano Concerto, G, Op.36, 1927; Cello Concertino, Op.57, 1936; *Pour un fête de printemps*, Op.22, 1920; Suite, F, Op.33, 1926; Concerto, Op.34, chbr orch, 1926–7; *Petite suite*, Op.39, 1929; Sinfonietta, Op.52, str, 1932; etc.

Choral orchestral: *Evocations* (M.D. Calvocoressi). Op.15, soli, ch, orch, 1910–11; Psalm 80, Op.37, t, ch, orch, 1928

Songs: 'Jazz dans la nuit' (René Dommange), Op.38, 1928; 'A Flower Given to my Daughter' (Joyce), 1931; etc.

Chamber: Divertissement, Op.6, wind qnt, pf, 1906; Serenade, Op.30, fl, hp, str trio, 1925; String Quartet, D, Op.45, 1931–2; Piano Trio, E♭, Op.2, 1902, rev 1927; String Trio, Op.58, 1937; Trio, Op.40, fl, va, vc, 1929

Instrumental: Violin Sonata No.1, D minor, Op.11, 1907–8; No.2, A, Op.28, 1924; Suite, F♯ minor, pf, Op.14, 1909–10; Impromptu, Op.21, hp, 1919; *Joueurs de flûte*, Op.27, fl, pf, 1924; *Ségovia*, Op.29, gtr, 1925; Prelude and Fughetta, Op.41, org, 1929; Andante and Scherzo, Op.51, fl, pf, 1934; etc.

rovescio (It., in reverse). Inversion. A canon *al rovescio* is one in which the second voice is an inversion of the first – i.e., if the first voice were to begin with a rise through a third, the second would start with an equivalent fall. The term may also be applied to a passage that can be played backwards.

Rovetta, Giovanni (b. ?Venice, c.1595; d. Venice, 23 Oct 1668). Italian composer, son of a musician at St Mark's, where he spent his whole life as an instrumentalist, bass and composer under Monteverdi and, from 1644, as chapelmaster in succession to his master.

row [series, SET]. Sequence of the 12 notes of the chromatic scale in a particular order, as used in SERIALISM.

Roxelane, La [Roxolana]. Name Haydn gave his Symphony No.63, apparently thinking its allegretto a portrait of the beautiful, scheming Ottoman sultana.

Royal Academy of Music. (1) Club of noblemen formed to support Italian opera in London under Handel.

(2) (RAM). London conservatory founded in 1822. First housed in Tenterden Street, it moved in 1911 to the Marylebone Road.

Royal Albert Hall. Auditorium in Kensington, London, opened by Queen Victoria in 1871, named after her late husband, and accommodating an audience of 7,000 (now 5,500). It became home to the Proms in 1941, after the bombing of the Queen's Hall.

Royal College of Music (RCM). London conservatory opened in 1883 at Prince Consort Road, near the Royal Albert Hall.

Royal Concertgebouw Orchestra (Koninklijk Concertgebouworkest). Founded in 1888 as the orchestra of the new Concertgebouw (Concert Hall) in Amsterdam, it has had only seven principal conductors: Willem Kes (1888–95), Mengelberg (1895–1945), Van Beinum (1938–59), Jochum (1961–4), Haitink (1961–88), Chailly (1988–2004) and Jansons (from 2004), of whom Mengelberg established it as one of the finest orchestras in the world, with a strong tradition in Mahler (whom he invited to conduct) and Bruckner. It received the appellation 'Royal' in honour of its centenary.

Royal Festival Hall. See SOUTH BANK CENTRE.

Royal Fireworks Music. See MUSIC FOR THE ROYAL FIREWORKS.

Royal Hunt and Storm (Chasse royale et orage). Ballet in Berlioz's Les Troyens, effectively a tone poem depicting the hunt of Dido and Aeneas disrupted by a storm and continuing in another fashion as they take shelter in a cave.

Royal Northern College of Music (RNCM). Manchester conservatory founded in 1972, in succession to the Royal Manchester College of Music, founded in 1893.

Royal Philharmonic Orchestra (RPO). London orchestra founded by Beecham in 1946, originally for recordings and Royal Philharmonic Society concerts. Later principal conductors have included Kempe (1961–75), Dorati, Previn (1985–91), Ashkenazy (1987–94) and Daniele Gatti (from 1996).

Royal Philharmonic Society (RPS). London concert organization founded in 1813 as the Philharmonic Society, made Royal in 1911. To be remembered for commissioning Beethoven's Ninth Symphony, it has also granted its gold medal to distinguished musicians since 1871 while continuing to promote concerts.

Royal Scottish Academy of Music and Drama (RSAMD). Glasgow conservatory founded in 1929 as the Scottish National Academy of Music.

Rózsa, Miklós (b. Budapest, 18 Apr 1907; d. Los Angeles, 27 Jul 1995). Hungarian–US composer. Born into a prosperous family, he trained in Budapest and Leipzig before settling in Paris (1931) and then London (1935), where he began writing film music for Alexander Korda, whom in 1940 he accompanied to Hollywood. Expert in the luxuriant Romantic style that was the norm for film music, he scored – among many other movies – *The Thief of Baghdad* (1940), *Spellbound* (1945), *A Double Life* (1948) and *Ben-Hur* (1959), and won Oscars for the last three. His concert works, which include a Violin Concerto (1953), have more a Bartókian accent.

Miklós Rózsa *Double Life* (1982)

RPO. Royal Philharmonic Orchestra.

RPS. Royal Philharmonic Society.

RSAMD. Royal Scottish Academy of Music and Drama.

rubato (It., robbed). What is stolen is time, from one note, bar or sequence to another – i.e. the tempo fluctuates. This is necessary to a degree in almost all music, for expressive and structural purposes, but it may be marked as a special requirement.

Rubbra, (Charles) Edmund (b. Northampton, 23 May 1901; d. Gerrards Cross, 14 Feb 1986). British composer, a noted symphonist. Brought up in a musical working-class family, he left school at 14 but came to the attention of Cyril Scott, who taught him. He then won scholarships to Reading University and the RCM, and began to support himself as a teacher, pianist and critic. Not until the mid-1930s did he begin to get going as a composer, but then he became solidly productive. His symphonies won particular admiration for their cogent growth through polyphonic textures, lack of display, formal rectitude and noble expressive power. He also wrote a good deal of sacred music, especially after his conversion to the Roman Catholic faith in 1948. From 1947 to 1968 he taught at Oxford and from 1961 also at the Guildhall School, beloved for his care and honesty even by pupils who went in radically different directions from his.

Ralph Scott Grover *The Music of Edmund Rubbra* (1993)

Symphonies: No.1, Op.44, 1935–7; No.2, Op.45, 1937, rev 1950; No.3, Op.49, 1939; No.4, Op.53, 1941; No.5, B♭, Op.63, 1947–8; No.6, Op.80, 1953–4; No.7, Op.88, 1957; No.8, Op.132, 1966–8; No.9 (*Sinfonia sacra*), Op.140, soli, ch, orch, 1971–2; No.10 (*Sinfonia da camera*), Op.145, 1974; No.11, Op.153, 1977–9
Other orchestral works: Sinfonia Concertante, Op.38, pf, orch, 1934–6; Piano Concerto, G, Op.85, 1956; Violin Concerto, Op.103, 1959; Viola Concerto, A, Op.75, 1952; *Soliloquy*, Op.57, vc, orch, 1943–4; *Improvisations on Virginal Pieces by Giles Farnaby*, Op.50, 1939; *Festival Overture*, Op.62, 1947; *Resurgam* (overture), Op.149, 1975
Choral: *Missa cantuariensis*, Op.59, 1945; *Missa in honorem Sancti Dominici*, Op.66, 1948; etc.
Other works: String Quartet No.1, F minor, Op.35, 1933, rev 1946; No.2, E♭, Op.73, 1950; No.3, Op.112, 1962–3; No.4, Op.150, 1976–7; Oboe Sonata, Op.100, 1958; songs; etc.

Rubini, Giovanni Battista (b. Romano, near Bergamo, 7 Apr 1794; d. Romano, 3 Mar 1854). Italian tenor, a prototype of the Romantic hero on the opera stage. A horn player's son, he studied singing as a boy and later in Naples, after he had embarked on his career. From the mid 1820s he appeared internationally, creating roles in works by Bellini (*Il pirata, La sonnambula, I puritani*) and Donizetti (*Anna Bolena, Marino Faliero*). He retired to his home town in 1845.

Rubinstein. Russian musician brothers, both pianists and leaders of musical life, the elder being also a noted composer.
   (1) **Anton (Grigoryevich)** (b. Vikhvatintsï, Ukraine, 28 Nov 1829; d. Peterhof, now Petrodvorets, 20 Nov 1894). A child virtuoso, he made a protracted tour of western Europe in 1840–43 with his teacher, met Chopin and Liszt, then continued his training in Berlin and Vienna. Back in Russia he gained the patronage of the Grand Duchess Elena Pavlovna, who supported him in founding the St Petersburg Conservatory in 1862. After five years he embarked on two further decades of spectacular international success as a pianist, admired for his spontaneous and inspiring performances. He then returned to his office as director of the conservatory. A prolific composer throughout his busy life, he wrote six symphonies, five piano concertos, 10 string quartets and so on, all outshone in memory by a little piano piece, the Melody in F (1852). Of his 20 operas, the melodrama *The Demon* (1871) survives shakily alone.

Anton Rubinstein *Autobiography* (1890)

   (2) **Nikolay (Grigoryevich)** (b. Moscow, 14 Jun 1835; d. Paris, 23 Mar 1881). His career paralleled his brother's in all respects except composition: his brother, he said, composed enough for three. He founded the Moscow Conservatory (1864) and invited the young Tchaikovsky on to the staff. Though he later dismissed his colleague's First Piano Concerto, he retracted his position and played the work. He also gave the first performance of Balakirev's *Islamey*, and altogether promoted Russian music much more than did his brother, besides being, by all accounts, a more sober, analytical performer.

Rubinstein, Arthur [Artur] (b. Łódź, 28 Jan 1887; d. Geneva, 20 Dec 1982). Polish–US pianist. At the age of three, already showing huge promise, he was introduced to Joseph Joachim, whose protégé he became. He made his debuts in Berlin aged 12 and Paris aged 17, and from this point had no regular teacher, though he occasionally consulted Paderewski in Switzerland. Alacritous and brilliant – and decisively different from his Romantic predecessors – he interested himself in new music; he commissioned Stravinsky to write a solo digest of *Petrushka*, and took up contemporary music from Spain (Falla, Albéniz, Granados) and South America following a tour in 1916–17. Szymanowski, Ravel and Prokofiev were other composers whose works he played.

In 1932 he married Aniela Mlynarski, the daughter of a Polish conductor and in due course the mother of his four children. Soon after marrying he retired for a period of rethinking and consolidation, after which he showed a new maturity along with all his old technical accomplishment. He gained immense and continuing acclaim in the USA after his return there in 1937. He also changed in his enthusiasm for new music, concentrating now on Chopin, Brahms and the great concertos and chamber works of the 19th century, though continuing to include Debussy and Ravel in his repertory. His domicile, too, was different, for he had moved to Beverly Hills at the outbreak of the Second World War; he was therefore on hand to make soundtrack recordings for Hollywood movies and so appeared unseen in cinemas as Schumann, Liszt and Brahms. He took US citizenship in 1946 and played again in Poland in 1958, but refused to appear in Germany after the Second World War. He went on playing internationally, and recording, almost to the end of his life.

Arthur Rubinstein *My Young Years* (1973), *My Many Years* (1980)

Ruckers. Netherlandish family of makers of harpsichords and virginals, active in Antwerp from around 1580 until the 1650s. The founder of the firm was Hans Ruckers (*c*.1545–98), who was followed by his sons Johannes and Andreas, and by Andreas's son Andreas, all building instruments valued for their unusually rich sound.

Rückkehrung (Ger.). Retrograde.

Rudel, Jaufre (*fl.* 1120–47). Troubadour, of whose poems seven survive, four with music. He took part in the Second Crusade (1147) and addressed poems to an 'amor de lonh' (distant love). Eight and a half centuries later his story was the subject of Saariaho's opera *L'Amour de loin*.

Ruders, Poul (b. Ringsted, 27 Mar 1949). Danish composer. He trained as an organist at the conservatory in Copenhagen; as a composer he is self-taught. A versatile, prolific and expressively vigorous artist, his range embraces spiritual darkness and high wit, explored with references and resources drawn from throughout musical history.

www.poulruders.net

Opera: *The Handmaid's Tale* (Paul Bentley, after Margaret Atwood), f.p. Copenhagen, 2000; *The Trial* (Bentley, after Kafka), in progress
Orchestral: Symphony No.1, 1989; No.2, 1995–6; Piano Concerto, 1994; Violin Concerto No.1, 1981, No.2, 1990–91; Viola Concerto, 1994; Oboe Concerto, 1998; Concerto for Clarinet and Double Orchestra, 1985; Paganini Variations, gtr, orch, 1999–2000; *Concerto in Pieces*, 1994–5; *Listening Earth*, 2001; etc.
Other works: ensemble, chamber, instrumental, choral and vocal works

Rudhyar, Dane (b. Paris, 23 Mar 1895; d. San Francisco, 13 Sep 1985). French–US composer, originally Daniel Chennevière. Largely self-taught in music, he emigrated in 1916, settled in southern California in 1919 and was naturalized in 1926 under a new Hindu name that went with his esoteric interests. His works, proceeding from Scriabin, are mostly for orchestra (five 'syntonies', 1920–59) or piano (*Moments*, 1924–6; *Paeans*, 1927; *Granites*, 1929). He composed little after the 1930s, moving on to other areas of thought, especially astrology.

Rudolph (Johann Joseph Rainer), Archduke of Austria, Cardinal Archbishop of Olmütz (b. Florence, 8 Jan 1788; d. Baden, near Vienna, 24 Jul 1831). Austrian patron and amateur of music, the youngest son of Emperor Leopold II. He first went to Beethoven for lessons when he was 15, and continued doing so through two decades, while becoming also the composer's principal patron and, thanks to a gentle disposition, close friend. Beethoven dedicated to him two piano concertos (Nos.4 and 5), three piano sonatas ('Les Adieux', the 'Hammerklavier' and Op.111), the Violin Sonata Op.96, the 'Archduke' Trio and, not least, the *Missa solemnis*, intended for his enthronement in Olmütz (in 1820) but not ready in time. His own compositions include a clarinet sonata, a set of 40 variations for piano on a Beethoven theme (his Op.1, 1818–19), and a Diabelli variation.

ruff. Figure on the side drum, triplet grace notes into a beat.

Rugby. See MOUVEMENT SYMPHONIQUE.

Ruggiero. Bass melody that was a popular foundation for variations in late Renaissance and Baroque Italy, e.g. by Frescobaldi. It probably took its name from a line of Ariosto no doubt set in an early version.

Ruggles, Carl [Charles Sprague] (b. East Marion, Mass., 11 Mar 1876; d. Bennington, Vt, 24 Oct 1971). US composer. He studied the violin and in his teens began work in theatre orchestras. Later came lessons in composition, with Paine, and work as a music engraver and critic. In 1907 he moved to Winona, Minnesota, where he formed an orchestra and started writing an opera. Partly to promote that project, he moved to New York in 1917 and met Varèse. His modernist inclinations were now released and, past 40, he wrote his first acknowledged composition, *Toys* (1919), a song addressed to his four-year-old son. During the next 12 years he added to his output, developing a style of unabashed dissonance and strong, angular melody, a music of quiet exclamations and rampant challenges. He also came into contact with Cowell, who published him, and Ives. His masterpiece *Sun-treader* was performed in Europe in the 1930s but not in the USA until 1966, by which time he had ceased work as a composer, settled in Vermont and devoted himself to painting.

Marilyn J. Ziffrin *Carl Ruggles* (1994)

Orchestral: *Men and Mountains*, 1924, rev 1936–41; *Portals*, str, 1925, rev 1929–53; *Sun-treader*, 1926–31; *Evocations*, 1942 and later; *Organum*, 1944–7

Vocal: *Toys* (Ruggles), v, pf, 1919; *Vox clamans in deserto* (Browning, C.H. Meltzer, Whitman), s, small orch, 1923; *Exaltation*, ch, 1958

Chamber and instrumental: *Angels*, 6 tpt, 1920–21, rev for 4 tpt, 3 trbn, 1938; *Evocations*, pf, 1937–43

ruhig (Ger.). Peaceful.

Rührtrommel (Ger.). Tenor drum.

Ruinen von Athen, Die (The Ruins of Athens). Set of pieces by Beethoven – including an overture, choruses and a Turkish march – for an epilogue by August Kotzebue that, with *König Stephan* by the same team, opened the German theatre in the Hungarian capital. In 1924 Strauss and Hofmannsthal made an adaptation. First performance: Pest, 10 Feb 1812.

Rule, Britannia! Song by Arne to words by James Thomson, included in the masque *Alfred* (1740). The tune appears in works by Handel (*Occasional Oratorio*), Beethoven (a set of variations and *Wellingtons Sieg*) and Wagner (overture).

rumba. Dance of Afro-Cuban cultic origin, desensualized for US and European ballroom society in the 1930s while retaining its highly syncopated duple metre and its accompanying rhythmic ostinato on maracas, claves or other Afro-Cuban percussion instrument. Milhaud caught it before this process had taken place, in his *La Création du monde*.

run. Rapid rising or falling scale.

Rusalka. Opera by Dvořák to a libretto by Jaroslav Kvapil. Rusalka (soprano) is a water nymph who takes human form so that she can be with her beloved Prince (tenor), but has to return to her lake when he rejects her. She has a silvery 'Song to the Moon'. First performance: Prague, 31 Mar 1901.

There is a different *Rusalka* opera by Dargomyzhsky, to his own libretto after Pushkin, for the name belongs to the whole genus of Slav water nymphs.

Ruslan and Lyudmila. Opera by Glinka to a libretto by Valerian Shirkov after Pushkin's mock epic. Ruslan (baritone) is a knight and Lyudmila (soprano) a princess in a fairytale Russia of magicians and exotic princes, heroic exploits and choral tableaux, a dwarf and a giant head. First performance: St Petersburg, 27 Nov 1842.

Russia (Rossiya). The origins of the country's music are in chant and folksong, which were potent influences on composers in the 19th and 20th centuries. As in other European countries, indigenous music was sought out to provide sources for a national style, but in Russia this process began earlier and lasted longer. That was at least partly because composers in Russia regularly took their country as their subject. And that in turn was, perhaps, because music in Russia was a state enterprise, through the two centuries from the reign of Catherine II to the collapse of the Soviet Union.

Russian chant at first followed Constantinopolitan, gaining independence after the fall of the Eastern Empire in 1453. The earliest manuscripts that can be deciphered date from the late 16th century and show traits that would remain characteristic of Russian Orthodox music in their wide intervals and cadences. Instruments were not permitted in the Russian Church, and the arrival of polyphony, in the 17th century, was not universally welcomed. Besides, having lacked a Renaissance, Russia could not now have a Baroque. In the 19th century Russian church music settled into a tradition of harmonized chant sung by unaccompanied chorus, a tradition that Tchaikovsky and later Rachmaninoff dignified.

Meanwhile, Western music had entered by another door: opera. The form was encouraged by the empresses Anna (1730–40), Elizabeth (1741–62) and Catherine II (1762–96), but almost exclusively as an import. Catherine called Galuppi, Traetta, Paisiello, Sarti, Cimarosa and Martín y Soler to St Petersburg, occasionally to set Russian librettos (by her) but mostly to write as they would have done for Naples or Vienna. She also sent Berezovsky, Bortnyansky and Fomin to study in Italy and so become the first Russian composers of more than amateur capability. During her reign, too, there was a vogue for Russian folksong.

Early in the next century music took a deeper hold, through the work of an Italian who became a permanent immigrant, Catterino Cavos, of native composers, notably Glinka, and of aristocratic patrons who founded the St Petersburg Philharmonic Society in 1802. Liszt, Berlioz and the Schumanns visited. In 1859 Anton Rubinstein founded the Russian Musical Society, the umbrella organization for orchestral concerts and conservatories, and the great age of Russian music began, supported by a new generation of Russian capitalists.

It remained typical of Russian culture that there was antagonism between Westernizers (outstandingly Tchaikovsky) and isolationists (the MIGHTY HANDFUL of Balakirev, Musorgsky, Borodin, Rimsky-Korsakov and Cui), and typical, too, that the antagonism was exaggerated: Tchaikovsky owed as much to folksong and chant as Musorgsky did, and Verdi's music was observed keenly by both. Another continuing feature of Russian musical life was the high value placed on works for the imperial theatres: the Mariinsky in St Petersburg and the Bolshoy in Moscow. But there were now many more opportunities for orchestral and chamber music, and for publication. Balakirev wrote no operas, nor did Scriabin, whose harmonic venturesomeness encouraged a school of modernists in the early 20th century.

The Bolshevik Revolution of 1917 brought radical changes to musical life, though in some senses its effect was to restore older patterns of central state control, now over orchestras, concert agencies, conservatories and creative musicians (see POLITICS). Some composers – Rachmaninoff, Stravinsky and at first Prokofiev – stayed in exile. Within the new Soviet Union the choice in the 1920s was between revolutionary futurism and populist stability, though Shostakovich, the preeminent Soviet composer, took a course in between. The doctrine of SOCIALIST REALISM, dogmatically enforced from the 1930s until after Stalin's death in 1953, produced few masterpieces and perhaps was not intended to. Relaxation of official constraints then allowed such composers as Schnittke, Gubaidulina, Volkonsky and Silvestrov to emulate in some respects their avant-garde colleagues in the West, though still with a distinctively Russian moral anxiety. Following the disintegration of the Soviet Union in 1991, many of the country's musicians chose to emigrate.

Gerald Abraham *On Russian Music* (1939); Boris Schwarz *Music and Musical Life in Soviet Russia, 1917–70* (1972); Richard Taruskin *Defining Russia Musically* (1997)

Russian. Name given to Haydn's Quartets Op.33, dedicated to the Grand Duke Paul of Russia.

Russolo, Luigi (b. Portogruaro, 30 Apr 1885; d. Cerro di Laveno, Varese, 6 Feb 1947). Italian composer. A painter associated with the futurists, he published a manifesto *The Art of Noises* (1913) and backed it up by designing a series of 'intonarumori' (noise intoners), built into large boxes with operating levers and horn-shaped speakers. These he demonstrated in 1913–14 in Milan, Genoa and London, and again in Paris in 1921 and later, attracting the interest of Ravel, Stravinsky and, especially, Varèse. He left Paris in 1932 and eventually returned to Italy. His instruments, remaining behind, were destroyed during the Second World War: all that remains of them is a foggy recording.

Rustic Wedding (*Ländliche Hochzeit*). Symphony by Goldmark.

Rustle of Spring (*Frühlingsrauschen*). Popular piano piece by Sinding.

Rutini, Giovanni Marco (b. Florence, 25 Apr 1723; d. Florence, 22 Dec 1797). Italian composer. He studied in Naples at the Turchini conservatory, with Leo for composition and Nicola Fago for the harpsichord. Apart from short periods at the courts of Prague and St Petersburg (where he was harpsichord teacher to the future Catherine II), he spent most of his later life in his native city. He was married there in 1761, taught himself counterpoint and wrote operas, mostly comic, as well as harpsichord sonatas that left a mark on Haydn and Mozart.

Rutter, John (Milford) (b. London, 24 Sep 1945). British composer-conductor. He studied at Cambridge and remained there as a choral director. His compositions include a *Requiem* (1985) and much else for chorus.

Ruzicka, Peter (b. Düsseldorf, 3 Jul 1948). German composer and administrator. He studied at the conservatory in Hamburg (1963–8) and then at the universities of Munich, Hamburg and Berlin before becoming artistic director of the Berlin Radio Symphony Orchestra (1979–87), the Hamburg Staatsoper (1988–97), the Munich Biennale (from 1996) and the Salzburg Festival (from 2002). His music exposes a keen expressive voice in a language developed from such Romantic modernists as Henze, Webern and Mahler. Among his works are the opera *Celan* (1999), various other works based on Celan poems (... *Inseln randlos* ... for violin, chamber choir and orchestra, 1994–5), orchestral pieces and string quartets.

Rysanek, Leonie (b. Vienna, 14 Nov 1926; d. Vienna, 7 Mar 1998). Austrian soprano, of exciting vocal and dramatic power. After training at the Vienna Academy, she made her debut in 1949 in Innsbruck as Agathe in *Der Freischütz* and her reputation two years later in Bayreuth as Sieglinde.

Formidable in the stronger roles of Wagner, Strauss, Verdi and Puccini, she maintained her career into the 1990s.

Rzewski, Frederic (Anthony) (b. Westfield, Mass., 13 Apr 1938). US pianist-composer. He studied at Harvard (1954–8) and Princeton (1958–60), his teachers including Piston, Sessions and Babbitt, then was active as a pianist in Europe. He gave the first performance of Stockhausen's Piano Piece X in 1962. From 1966 to 1971 he was in Rome, a founder member of MUSICA ELETTRONICA VIVA, with which his work became increasingly open and increasingly political. Engagement became more important than personal style: *Coming Together* (1972) uses minimalist repetition to give enforced and moving delivery to words from a prisoner's letter, while *The People United will Never be Defeated!* (1975) is a set of piano variations on a Chilean song, embracing late Romantic techniques with some modern elements. Later works include Four North American Ballads for piano (1979), a setting of Oscar Wilde's *De profundis* for speaking pianist (1992) and *The Road*, a four-and-a-half-hour 'novel' for piano. In 1977 he took an appointment at the Liège Conservatory, but he has gone on performing on both sides of the Atlantic.

S

s. Abbreviation for soprano.

Saariaho, Kaija (Anneli) (b. Helsinki, 14 Oct 1952). Finnish composer. She studied with Heininen at the Sibelius Academy (1976–81) and with Ferneyhough and Huber at the conservatory in Freiburg (1981–2). Immediately following, she began work at IRCAM and settled in Paris, marrying her IRCAM colleague Jean Baptiste Barrière. Influenced by Grisey and Murail, her first Paris compositions gained a lot of attention for their flair and sense of adventure, modulated by a subtle ear for timbre. Later works tend to be more static, exploring rich and resonant reserves of harmony.

www.petals.org

Opera: *L'Amour de loin* (Amin Maalouf), f.p. Salzburg, 2000
Orchestral: *Verblendungen*, with tape, 1982–4; *Du cristal*, 1989–90; *... à la fumée*, 1990; *Graal théâtre*, vn, orch, 1994; *Château de l'âme*, s, women's ch, orch, 1995; *Aile du songe*, fl, orch, 2000–1
Other works: *Lichtbogen*, 9 insts, elec, 1985–6; *Nymphaea*, str qt, elec, 1987; *Lonh*, s, elec, 1996; etc.

Sabaneyev, Leonid (Leonidovich) (b. Moscow, 1 Oct 1881; d. Antibes, 3 May 1968). Russian scholar and composer, trained as both physical scientist and musician. A champion of Scriabin, he was prominent in early Soviet times as music editor of *Pravda* and *Izvestiya* and president of the progressive Association for Contemporary Music. After 1926 he lived abroad.

Sacchini, Antonio (Maria Gasparo Gioacchino) (b. Florence, 14 Jun 1730; d. Paris, 6 Oct 1786). Italian composer, of operas warmly received in Paris and London as well as Italy. His father's work as a cook took the family to Naples, and there he entered the Loreto conservatory when he was 10. Highly regarded by his teacher Durante, he stayed on at the conservatory to teach, but left to compose. Rome was then his base for a few years, until in 1768 he moved to Venice, where he became a noted teacher of singing. The output of operas (and oratorios) continued. His next move, in 1772, was to London, where he presented revisions of earlier scores as *Il Cid* and *Tamerlano* (both 1773). These Burney described as 'so entire, so masterly, yet so new and natural, that there was nothing left for criticism to censure, though innumerable beauties to point out and admire'. Such judgements – widely voiced at the time, and probably prompted by the composer's gift for melody – have been modified by history. He remained London's favourite opera composer for several years, but his dissolute ways caught up with him, and in 1781 he moved to Paris, where his operas had already generated enthusiasm. Under the patronage of Marie Antoinette, he wrote *Dardanus* (1784) and *Oedipe à Colone* (1786), adapting his style to the recently Gluckified French tradition. That failed to save him from criticism from both sides in the dispute between Gluck's supporters and Piccinni's, though *Oedipe* remained in the Paris repertory until 1830.

SACEM. Société des Auteurs, Compositeurs et Editeurs de Musique, French performing rights agency.

Sacher, Paul (b. Basle, 28 Apr 1906; d. Basle, 26

May 1999). Swiss patron and conductor. For the Basle Chamber Orchestra, which he founded in 1926, he commissioned an extraordinary succession of composers, from Bartók (Music for Strings, Percussion and Celesta), Stravinsky (Concerto in D) and Strauss (*Metamorphosen*) to Birtwistle (*Endless Parade*). His munificence was assisted by his marriage in 1934 to Maja Hoffmann-Stehlin, sole heir to the pharmaceutical firm Hoffmann–La Roche. He also established the Basle Academy and the Sacher Foundation, which holds collections of manuscripts by these composers and many other 20th-century luminaries, including Boulez, Nancarrow, Carter and Berio.

Sachs, Hans (b. Nuremberg, 5 Nov 1494; d. Nuremberg, 19 Jan 1576). MEISTERSINGER and opera character, in Lortzing's *Hans Sachs* and Wagner's *Die Meistersinger*.

sackbut. English term for the trombone (with a less flared bell) that was in use from the 15th to the 18th century.

Sacrati, Francesco (baptized Parma, 17 Sep 1605; d. ?Modena, 20 May 1650). Italian composer, especially of operas for Venice in the 1640s. Badoaro, who wrote Ulyssean librettos for both him (*L'Ulisse errante*) and Monteverdi, called him the moon to the other's sun. In 1642 he turned down a job at St Mark's as unworthy a person of his reputation. His one surviving opera, *La finta pazza* (1641), strengthens the suspicion that he had a hand in L'INCORONAZIONE DI POPPEA.

sacred concerto. German Baroque church composition for one or more singers with instrumental ensemble. Bach used the term 'concerto' for several of his cantatas, but generally now it is reserved for 17th-century pieces.

sacred music. Besides music written for some LITURGY, the category is generally held to include settings of liturgical texts for the concert hall, such as Verdi's *Requiem*, but not operas on the lives of saints (from *Sant' Alesssio* to *Saint François d'Assise*), concert oratorios (Handel's for instance) or songs with religious texts (such as those by Purcell, Brahms and Webern).

Sacre du printemps, Le. See The RITE OF SPRING.

Sadko. Opera by Rimsky-Korsakov to his own libretto after old Russian ballads and tales. Sadko (tenor), a bard of Novgorod, impresses foreign traders and has adventures under the sea. The score includes songs for the traders, Indian (tenor), Venetian (baritone) and Varangian (bass). First performance: Moscow, 26 Dec 1897.

Sadler's Wells. London pleasure garden. A theatre opened on the site in 1765, was reconstructed in 1931 and gave its name to Sadler's Wells Opera, which played there from 1935 to 1968. The company then moved to the Coliseum and became ENGLISH NATIONAL OPERA.

Saeverud, Harald (Sigurd Johan) (b. Bergen, 17 Apr 1897; d. Bergen, 27 Mar 1992). Norwegian composer, a pupil of Borghild Holmsen at the Bergen Conservatory (1915–20) and of Erland Koch in Berlin (1920–21). He began slowly: by 1940 he had produced only 13 works, though most of these were orchestral (including four symphonies) and showed a stylistic growth from late Romanticism through greater dissonance to neoclassicism. Later he became more prolific, having settled into a style of rhythmic strength and thematic metamorphosis through polyphony. His works include nine symphonies, concertos, piano pieces and incidental music for *Peer Gynt* (1947) decisively contrary to Grieg's Romantic score. His son is the composer Ketil Hvoslef (b. 1939).

saga, En. See EN SAGA.

St Anne. Hymn tune, normally sung to the words 'O God, our help in ages past'. A Bach organ fugue in E♭ opens similarly and is therefore known as the 'St Anne' Fugue.

St Antoni. See VARIATIONS ON A THEME OF HAYDN.

Sainte-Colombe, Jean de (second half of the 17th century). French bass viol player and composer, of whom little is known except that he lived in Paris, wrote viol solos and duets, taught Marais and was brought to popular attention by the film *Tous les matins du monde* (1991).

Saint François d'Assise (St Francis of Assisi). Opera by Messiaen to his own libretto after old Franciscan texts. Eight scenes project the spiritual growth of St Francis (baritone) in his dealings with his brother monks, a leper (tenor) and an angel (soprano). Chant-like vocal lines are accompanied by an immense orchestra of birdsongs and dazzling harmonies, plus a large chorus at culminative moments. First performance: Paris Opera, 28 Nov 1983.

Saint-Georges, Joseph Boulogne, Chevalier de

(b. near Basse Terre, Guadeloupe, 25 Dec 1745; d. Paris, 9 Jun 1799). French–Caribbean violinist-composer. He had a French father and black Guadeloupe mother, and the family moved to Paris in 1753. He is known to have had schooling in the gentlemanly arts (especially fencing and riding) and must have been trained too in those musical. In 1769 he played in the orchestra of the Concert des Amateurs under Gossec; three years later he appeared as soloist under the same auspices in his Op.2 pair of concertos. He was musical director and leader of the ensemble from 1773 until its disbandment in 1781, after which he formed the Concert de la Loge Olympique and had a hand in commissioning Haydn's 'Paris' symphonies for that association. He also served the Duke of Orleans as musician and huntsman until the duke's death in 1785. In 1787 he visited London to take part in exhibition fencing matches, and he made another trip to England in 1789–90 in the wake of the French Revolution. Having returned again to Paris and been dismayed, he settled in the north of the country, where his activities were mostly military and unsuccessful. Periods of incarceration and wandering followed (including a trip back to the Caribbean in 1795–7), but he ended his days once more a musician in Paris. Most of his works were for his own instrument – violin concertos, *symphonies concertantes* for two violins, quartets – though he also wrote comic operas.

St John Passion (Ger. *Johannespassion*). The most celebrated setting is Bach's, first performed in Leipzig on Good Friday (7 April) 1724, and again in 1725 (with five new numbers), ?1732 and 1749, scored for voices with flutes, oboes, strings and continuo, the text adapted from Brockes. Pärt's setting is of the Latin text as *Passio Domini nostri Jesu Christi secundam Joannem* (t, bar, satb qt, ch, ob, vn, vc, bn, org; f.p. Munich, 27 Nov 1982). Other versions exist by Demantius, Schütz and Telemann.

St Louis. Midwest US city, with a symphony orchestra (founded 1881) and summer opera festival (Opera Theatre of St Louis, founded 1976).

St Luke Passion (Ger. *Lukaspassion*). There is a setting falsely attributed to Bach, and one correctly ascribed to Penderecki.

St Mark Passion (Ger. *Markuspassion*). Lost work by Bach, which several musicians have made efforts to reconstruct from numbers the composer used elsewhere.

St Martial. Abbey at Limoges, in southwest France, which held a rich collection of liturgical books from the 9th to the 12th centuries. These provide important sources for the early history of musical notation and polyphony.

St Matthew Passion (Ger. *Matthäuspassion*). Bach's is pre-eminent, with words by Picander, first performed in Leipzig on Good Friday (11 April) 1727, and again in 1729, 1736 and later. The 1736 score is the standard version, for two choirs, each with flutes, oboes, strings and continuo. At the centre of the work is the alto aria 'Erbarme Dich', with obbligato violin. There are also settings by Davy, Lassus, Schütz, etc.

St Paul (*Paulus*). Oratorio by Mendelssohn to words by Julius Schubring, on the saint's conversion and missionary life. First performance: Düsseldorf, 22 May 1836.

St Petersburg (Sankt Peterburg). Russian city founded by Peter I in 1703 as the capital, which it remained until 1918. It was known as Petrograd (1914–24) and Leningrad (1924–91). The chief theatre for opera and ballet is the MARIINSKY; a second opera company, the Maly, was established in 1920. The main concert orchestra is the Philharmonic, founded in 1921, whose principal conductors have included Mravinsky (1938–88), Sanderling (jointly with Mravinsky 1941–60) and Yuri Temirkanov (from 1988).

Saint-Saëns, (Charles) Camille (b. Paris, 9 Oct 1835; d. Algiers, 16 Dec 1921). French composer, who – in music ripely Romantic or elegantly Classical, dramatic or entertaining – maintained an untroubled mastery.

Born into the petit bourgeoisie, he lost his father when he was a few months old and was brought up by his mother and her aunt, who gave him piano lessons. He took to music immediately. By the age of seven he was having professional instruction and playing in public; at 10 he made his formal debut at the Salle Pleyel, in concertos by Mozart and Beethoven. In 1848 he entered the Conservatoire, where he studied the organ and composition (with Halévy). He produced his Op.1 (three harmonium pieces) in 1852 and his Op.2, his First Symphony, the next year, when he also became organist of St Merry. From there he moved to the Madeleine (1857–76). He had, too, a teaching position at the Ecole Niedermeyer (1861–5), where his pupils included Fauré, a lifelong friend. In addition, as conductor, pianist and organizer, he worked to promote music he cared about: Wagner and Liszt, but also Mozart and Bach, as well as new

French music, for which he founded the Société Nationale de Musique in 1871. Meanwhile, he continued to compose, producing music, he said, 'as an apple tree produces apples'. Works of his 20s and 30s include another symphony, three Lisztian symphonic poems (among them the *Danse macabre*), several concertos, songs, chamber pieces and sacred music.

In 1875, against his mother's wishes and despite his homosexual inclinations, he married 19-year-old Marie Laure Emilie Truffot; two sons were born and died in infancy, and he left his wife in 1881. It was during and after this turbulent period that he created or completed one of his strongest works, *Samson et Dalila*, as well as one of his most ostentatious, the Third Symphony, with organ, and, perhaps most remarkably, one of his most delightful, *Le Carnaval des animaux*. He suffered another trauma in 1888 when his mother died. Having contemplated suicide, he survived by composing and travelling. Algeria and Egypt were favourite destinations; he also journeyed through much of Europe and as far as Uruguay. Music came out of these tours, prompted by the love of the exotic he had already expressed in *Samson*.

He lived to enjoy the status of a grand old man – not so much in France, but certainly in England (whence came commissions for his Third Symphony, a coronation march for Edward VII and an oratorio, *The Promised Land*) and the USA (which he visited in 1915). With that status went conservatism: he vilified the young Debussy and was appalled by *The Rite of Spring*. Yet the continuing apple harvest of sonatas, choral music, songs and operas saw a certain updating of style and subject matter: leaner textures, modal colourings, Greek topics. He was also the first notable composer to write a film score, for *L'Assassinat du Duc de Guise* (1908).

Brian Rees *Camille Saint-Saëns* (1999)

Operas: *La Princesse jaune* (1 act; Louis Gallet), f.p. Paris, 1872; *Samson et Dalila* (see SAMSON), 1859–77; *Le Timbre d'argent* (Barbier and Carré), f.p. Paris, 1877; *Etienne Marcel* (Gallet), f.p. Lyons, 1879; *Henry VIII* (Léonce Détroyat and Armand Silvestre), f.p. Paris, 1883; *Proserpine* (Gallet), f.p. Paris, 1887; *Ascanio* (Gallet, after Paul Meurice), f.p. Paris, 1890; *Phryné* (Lucien Augé de Lassus), f.p. Paris, 1893; *Frédégonde* (Gallet), f.p. Paris, 1895 (completion of work left unfinished by Guiraud); *Les Barbares* (Victorien Sardou and Pierre Barthélemy Gheusi), f.p. Paris, 1901; *Hélène* (1 act; Saint-Saëns), f.p. Monte Carlo, 1904; *L'Ancêtre* (Augé de Lassus), f.p. Monte Carlo, 1906; *Déjanire* (Gallet), f.p. Monte Carlo, 1911

Symphonies: No.1, E♭, Op.2, 1853; No.2, A minor, Op.55, 1859; No.3 'Organ', C minor, Op.78, 1886

Concertos: Piano Concerto No.1, D, Op.17, 1858; No.2, G minor, Op.22, 1868; No.3, E♭, Op.29, 1869; No.4, C minor, Op.44, 1875; No.5 'Egyptian', F, 1896; Violin Concerto No.1, A, Op.20, 1859; No.2, C, Op.58, 1858; No.3, B minor, Op.61, 1880; Cello Concerto No.1, A minor, Op.33, 1872; No.2, D minor, 1902

Other concertante works: *Rhapsodie d'Auvergne*, Op.73, pf, orch, 1884; *Wedding Cake*, Op.76, pf, str, 1885; *Africa*, Op.89, pf, orch, 1891; Introduction and Rondo capriccioso, Op.28, vn, orch, 1863; Romance, E, Op.67, hn/vc, orch, 1866; Romance, Op.37, fl/vn, orch, 1871; Romance, F, Op.36, hn/vc, orch, 1874; *Allegro appassionato*, Op.43, vc, orch, 1875; *Morceau de concert*, Op.62, vn, orch, 1880; *Havanaise*, Op.83, vn, orch, 1887; *Morceau de concert*, Op.94, hn, orch, 1887; *Caprice andalous*, Op.122, vn, orch, 1904; *La Muse et le poète*, Op.132, vn, vc, orch, 1910; *Morceau de concert*, Op.154, hp, orch, 1918; *Odelette*, Op.162, fl, orch, 1920

Other orchestral works: *Le ROUET D'OMPHALE*, Op.31, 1872; *Phaéton* (see PHAETON), Op.39, 1873; *Danse macabre*, Op.40, 1874; *La Jeunesse d'Hercule*, Op.50, 1877; *Suite algérienne*, Op.60, 1880 (No.4 *Marche militaire française*); etc.

Sacred: *Oratorio de Noël*, Op.12, soli, ch, str qt, hp, org, 1858; *Ave Maria*, s, org, 1859; *Le Déluge* (oratorio), Op.45, 1875; *Requiem*, Op.54, soli, ch, orch, 1878; etc.

Chamber: *Le CARNAVAL DES ANIMAUX*, 2 pf, ens, 1886; Septet, E♭, Op.65, pf, tpt, str qt, db, 1880; Piano Quintet, A minor, Op.14, *c*.1855; String Quartet No.1, E minor, Op.112, 1899; No.2, G, Op.153, 1918; Serenade, vn, va/vc, pf, org, 1866; Piano Quartet, B♭, Op.41, 1875; *Caprice sur des airs danois et russes*, Op.79, pf, fl, ob, cl, 1887; Piano Trio No.1, F, Op.18, 1863; No.2, E minor, Op.92, 1892; etc.

Instrumental: Violin Sonata No.1, D minor, Op.75, 1885; No.2, E♭, Op.102, 1896; Cello Sonata No.1, C minor, Op.32, 1872; No.2, F, Op.123, 1905; Oboe Sonata, D, Op.166, 1921; Clarinet Sonata, E♭, Op.167, 1921; Bassoon Sonata, G, Op.168, 1921; *Fantaisie*, Op.95, hp, 1893; *Fantaisie*, Op.124, vn, hp, 1907; *Cavatine*, D♭, Op.144, trbn, pf, 1915; reductions of concertante pieces, etc.

Piano: Variations on a Theme of Beethoven, Op.35, duo, 1874; 6 Etudes, Op.52, 1877 (No.6 *En forme de valse*); 6 Etudes, Op.135, left hand, 1912; etc.

Organ: *Fantaisie*, E♭, 1857; *Trois rapsodies sur des cantiques bretons*, Op.7, 1866; etc.

Songs (those obelisked orchestrated by the composer): 'Rêverie'[†] (Hugo), 1851; 'Le Pas d'armes du roi Jean'[†] (Hugo), 1852; 'L'Attente'[†] (Hugo), *c*.1855; 'La Cloche'[†] (Hugo), *c*.1855; 'La Mort d'Ophélie' (Legouvé), *c*.1857; 'Clair de lune' (Catulle Mendès), 1865; 'Si vous n'avez rien à me dire' (Hugo), 1870; 'Une Flûte invisible' (Hugo), with fl, 1885; 'Guitares et mandolines' (Saint-Saëns), 1890; 'Le Rossignol' (Théodore Banville), 1892; etc.

Saite (Ger., pl. *Saiten*). String; hence *Saiteninstrumente* (string instruments).

Salicet, Salicional. Organ stop (from Lat. *salix*, willow) producing delicate tones from narrow pipes.

Salieri, Antonio (b. Legnago, 18 Aug 1750; d. Vienna, 7 May 1828). Italian composer, probably not responsible for Mozart's death, even if his career in Vienna, where he arrived as a 15-year-old student of Gassmann, exposed him to a genius with whom he could not compete. His earlier studies took place in his home town and Venice, where Gassmann acquired him. While still in his teens he met Metastasio, became Gluck's protégé and had his first comic opera staged. In 1774 he succeeded Gassmann as court composer and conductor of the Italian opera, and the next year he married Theresia Helferstorfer, by whom he had eight children. With the emperor's leave, he spent two years in Italy mounting new operas (1778–80), and in 1784–7 he was several times in Paris for the same purpose, having taken over from Gluck at the Opera. His third and last work for Paris, *Tarare*, was his masterpiece, which he revised for Vienna with the help of Da Ponte. Later works were less successful, and in 1804 he wrote a *Requiem*, which he intended should be his last composition – though he could not stop himself writing canons and more sacred music. He retired, as he acknowledged, because his style – mixing Italian and French elements, with a simplicity in texture and form that makes his music sound rudimentary against the more familiar Mozart – had become outmoded. But he continued his work as a teacher, numbering Beethoven, Schubert and Liszt among his pupils.

John A. Rice *Antonio Salieri and Viennese Opera* (1998)

Operas: *Armida* (Marco Coltellini), f.p. Vienna, 1771; *Les Danaïdes* (Jean-Baptiste de Tschudy and François Louis du Roullet, after Calzabigi), f.p. Paris, 1784; *Prima la musica e poi le parole* (1 act; Giovanni Battista Casti), f.p. Vienna, 1786; *Tarare* (Beaumarchais), f.p. Paris, 1787, rev as *Axur, re d'Ormus* (Da Ponte), f.p. Vienna, 1788; *Falstaff* (Carlo Prospero Defranceschi, after Shakespeare), f.p. Vienna, 1799; *L'Angiolina* (Defranceschi, after Jonson *Epicoene*), f.p. Vienna, 1800; about 35 others
Other works: 2 keyboard concertos, C, B♭, 1773; Concerto, C, fl, ob, orch, 1774; *Requiem*, C minor, 1804; etc.

Sallinen, Aulis (Heikki) (b. Salmi, 9 Apr 1935). Finnish composer. He studied with Merikanto and Kokkonen at the Sibelius Academy (1955–60), and began by blending avant-garde elements into music of solid Sibelian continuity, as in his First Symphony (1970–71), which begins and ends in F

minor but meets Ligeti and others in between. His first opera, *The Horseman*, revealed a talent for dramatic music, sharpened almost to a Janáček-like intensity in his second, *The Red Line*.

Operas: *The Horseman* (Paavo Haavikko), Op.32, f.p. Savonlinna, 1975; *The Red Line* (Sallinen, after Ilmari Kianto), Op.46, f.p. Helsinki, 1978; *The King Goes Forth to France* (Haavikko), Op.53, f.p. Savonlinna, 1984; *Kullervo* (Sallinen, after the Kalevala and Aleksis Kivi), Op.61, f.p. Los Angeles, 1992; *The Palace* (Irene Dische and Enzensberger), Op.68, f.p. Savonlinna, 1995; *King Lear* (Sallinen, after Shakespeare), Op.76, f.p. Helsinki, 2000
Orchestral: Violin Concerto, Op.18, 1968; Chamber Music I, Op.38, str, 1975; II, Op.41, a fl, str, 1976; III 'The Nocturnal Dances of Don Juanquixote', Op.58, vc, str, 1986; 8 symphonies, etc.
Other works: String Quartet No.3 'Aspects of Peltoniemi Hintrik's Funeral March', Op.19, 1969; *Winter was hard*, Op.20:1, children's ch, pf, 1969; etc.

salmo (It., pl. *salmi*). Psalm.

Salome. Opera by Strauss to Hedwig Lachmann's translation of Wilde's play, itself based on a New Testament episode. At the court of the decadent Herod (tenor) and Herodias (mezzo-soprano), Salome (soprano) performs her Dance of the Seven Veils, an exotic waltz sequence, and is rewarded with the head of Jokanaan (John the Baptist, formerly baritone). First performance: Dresden, 9 Dec 1905.

There are also treatments of the subject by Massenet (*Hérodiade*), Glazunov (music for the Wilde play, Op.90), Schmitt, Davies, etc.

Salomon, Johann Peter (baptized Bonn, 20 Feb 1745; d. London, 28 Nov 1815). German impresario and violinist, active in London from 1781. An oboist's son, he joined his father in service to the Bonn court when he was 13, then worked for Prince Heinrich of Prussia. In Berlin he met C.P.E. Bach, who introduced him to J.S. Bach's solo violin music. He began presenting regular concerts in London in 1781, brought Haydn to participate in 1790–91 and 1794–5, and was honoured by the composer's writing important violin solos for him in the symphonies and quartets intended for his concerts. The symphonies he arranged for chamber performance; he also wrote symphonies of his own, besides violin music and songs. Later he was a founder member of the Philharmonic Society (subsequently Royal), whose first concert he led, under three years before his death as a result of a riding accident. Beethoven wrote to a friend of his distress at the loss of 'a noble-minded man whom I well remember since my childhood'.

salon. Domestic artistic gathering. It was the custom, particularly in late-19th-century Paris, for patrons and established artists to hold weekly open-house sessions at which music would often be performed and discussed.

Salonen, Esa-Pekka (b. Helsinki, 30 June 1958). Finnish composer-conductor. He studied at the Sibelius Academy as a horn player, conductor (with Jorma Panula) and composer (with Rautavaara), and formed a composing-performing group with fellow students, including Lindberg. In 1983, at short notice, he led the Philharmonia Orchestra in Mahler's Third Symphony in London, and an international career opened before him; he became music director of the Los Angeles Philharmonic in 1992. His creative output, limited by his success as a conductor, includes *L.A. Variations* for orchestra (1996) and *Dichotomie* for piano (2000).

salon music. Songs, piano pieces and instrumental items of a lighter sort, made for home performance in the decades around 1900 – by no means necessarily at salons, which could be highly sophisticated.

salon orchestra. Ensemble performing light music in a café or similar environment, centred on a piano trio, generally with additional players. Schoenberg's *Pierrot lunaire* alludes to the sound.

salsa. Variety of popular music that emerged in Cuba in the 1940s, defined by exuberant cross-metres and syncopations against a basic 4/4 pattern divided into durational units of three–three–two. Taken to New York in the 1940s and 1950s, it gave rise to Latin jazz. It also has an abundant life back home and in other Latin American countries.

saltando (It., leaping). Direction for the bow to bounce on the strings; also given as *sautillé* or *spiccato*.

saltarello (It., little hop). Italian Renaissance dance, fast and commonly in 6/8, first mentioned around 1400. In 16th-century dance collections a saltarello would normally follow a slow piece, either a pavan or a passamezzo; in its role, and sometimes its music, it was equivalent to the French or English galliard. Its popularity declined in the 17th century, leaving the term available for a folkdance that appeared in the late 18th century and was heard by Mendelssohn, to be recalled in the finale of his 'Italian' Symphony.

Salve regina (Hail Queen). MARIAN ANTIPHON, probably dating from the 11th century. It had a big place in the Renaissance cult of the Virgin and was set by Ockeghem, Obrecht, Josquin, La Rue and many others. There are later settings by Schubert, Poulenc, etc.

Salzburg. Austrian city at the northern edge of the Alps, an ancient settlement that St Rupert in 582 chose as the site for an abbey of St Peter. Until 1816 the city and its environs formed an ecclesiastical domain, ruled by the archbishop. Music was important for both church and court, and the 18th-century archbishops employed some distinguished composers, including Biber, Caldara, Michael Haydn and, finally, Mozart.

The memory of Mozart's connections with the city resulted in the foundation in 1841 of the Mozarteum (an institution providing concerts and education that developed into a conservatory in 1914) and the next year of a music festival. In 1880 Mozart's birthplace was opened as a museum.

In 1920 the Salzburg Festival was re-established as an annual summer event, offering plays, operas and concerts, with the participation of the Vienna Philharmonic, visiting ensembles and many of the most noted soloists, conductors and directors in successive generations. Performances take place in three theatres built into the former stables and riding school, as well as in churches, at the Mozarteum and outdoors. In the 1950s, 1960s and 1970s the festival was dominated by Karajan, and then by Gerard Mortier (1992–2001). It has been responsible for the first performances of operas by Strauss, Henze, Berio, Saariaho, etc.

Salzédo, Carlos (Léon) (b. Arcachon, 6 Apr 1885; d. Waterville, Maine, 17 Aug 1961). French–US harpist-composer. Son of a singing teacher, he studied at the Bordeaux and Paris conservatoires before emigrating in 1909 to become a prominent performer, teacher and organizer (co-founder with Varèse of the International Composers' Guild). His compositions took the harp from the world of Ravel to that of Hindemith.

samba. Afro-Brazilian dance with song.

samisen. Japanese lute. The term was wrongly used for a gong in the scores of Japanese operas by Puccini and Mascagni.

Sammartini. Italian family of musicians, founded by Alexis Saint-Martin, a French oboist who settled in the country and was the father of Giovanni Battista and Giuseppe.

(1) **Giovanni Battista** (b. ?Milan, 1700/1; d.

Milan, 15 Jan 1775). Italian composer, a pioneer of the symphony. He and his brother studied with their father and started their careers in the Milan opera orchestra. In the mid 1720s he began acquiring positions in Milanese churches, for which he wrote oratorios, cantatas and masses. He also had some success in the 1730s and 1740s in opera. But he was most active and most famed as a composer of instrumental music, being pre-eminent among the early symphonists working in Milan; indeed, he wrote the first symphonies with a known date (1732). Remaining in the city all through his professional life, he taught Gluck and welcomed other visitors: J.C. Bach, Boccherini and the boy Mozart. He was twice married.

His early works show an emergence from the Vivaldi tradition into the preliminary Classical style that he fully achieved in his 40s and 50s and later enriched. Most of his 68 symphonies are in three movements: a sonata-form piece with vital motivic development continuing in the recapitulation, an expressive slow movement and a concluding minuet or witty presto. He also wrote concertos and some of the earliest string quartets and quintets, and was widely published, performed, admired and imitated.

(2) **Giuseppe (Francesco Gaspare Melchiorre Baldassare)** (b. Milan, 6 Jan 1695; d. London, Nov 1750). Italian composer, who was resident from the end of the 1720s in London. There he won renown as an oboe virtuoso, playing in concerts and operas; Handel wrote solos for him, notably in the aria 'Quella fiamme' in *Arminio*. Burney praised his compositions – concertos and sonatas, of which only one concerto features the oboe – as 'full of science, originality, and fire'. Most often played are a concerto grosso in G minor (from his Op.5, published in 1747) and a recorder concerto in F.

sampler. Electronic instrument that allows digitally recorded sounds to be played, usually by means of a keyboard. It is normally used as part of an ensemble, as in Benjamin's *Antara* and Reich's *City Life*.

Samson. Ancient Jewish hero (see Judges 13–16). Works based on his story include:

(1) Handel's oratorio to a text by Newburgh Hamilton drawn from John Milton. Samson (tenor) is beset by the worthy hopes of his father Manoa (bass) and friend Micah (soprano), and by the tempting of Dalila (soprano) and mocking of Harapha (bass), with terrible consequences. A soprano in the finale has the air 'Let the bright seraphim'. First performance: London, 18 Feb 1743.

(2) Saint-Saëns's opera *Samson et Dalila* to a libretto by Ferdinand Lemaire. With the Hebrews in bondage to the Philistines, Delilah (mezzo-soprano) seduces Samson (tenor) into betraying the secret of his strength; the last and most seductive of her three arias is 'Mon coeur s'ouvre à ta voix'. There is a Bacchanale of triumphant hedonism before Samson, his power restored, pulls down the pillars of the heathen temple. First performance: Weimar, 2 Dec 1877.

Samuel, Harold (b. London, 23 May 1879; d. London, 15 Jan 1937). British pianist, who trained at the RCM with Edward Dannreuther and Stanford and was notable for having brought Bach's keyboard music into regular performance. He gave week-long series including virtually all Bach's keyboard works in London (1921) and New York (1924), and also taught at the RCM.

San Carlo. The principal opera house of NAPLES.

Sanctus. Section of the ORDINARY of the MASS, comprising the acclamations *Sanctus* and *Benedictus*, each followed by a *Hosanna* (normally set to the same music both times).

Sanderling, Kurt (b. Arys, East Prussia, 19 Sep 1912). German conductor. He began as a répétiteur in Berlin in 1931 while studying privately and in 1936 sought refuge in the Soviet Union, where he conducted the Moscow Radio Symphony Orchestra (1936–41) and then the Leningrad Philharmonic, jointly with Mravinsky. In 1960 he returned to Berlin as conductor of the East Berlin Symphony Orchestra, a post he kept until 1977, when he began appearing more frequently internationally. A notable, gritty interpreter of the German and Russian classics from Beethoven to Shostakovich, he remained active into his 90s.

Sandström, Sven-David (b. Borensberg, 30 Oct 1942). Swedish composer. He studied at the conservatory in Stockholm with Lidholm, Ligeti and Nørgård (1968–72), and returned as a teacher (1985–98). In 1999 he took a post at the University of Indiana. A prolific composer, he caused a stir in the late 1980s when he moved into an extravagant neo-Romantic style.

San Francisco. Californian city with a symphony orchestra (founded 1911) and opera company (1923). Music directors of the former have included Monteux (1935–52), Krips (1963–9), Ozawa (1969–77), Edo de Waart (1977–85), Herbert Blomstedt (1985–95) and Tilson Thomas (from 1995). In the area are major educational institutions, including Stanford University, the University of California at Berkeley and Mills College, Oakland, all musically important.

Sankey, Ira David (b. Edinburg, Penn., 28 Aug 1840; d. Brooklyn, 13 Aug 1908). US singer and, with Dwight L. Moody, compiler of hymn books wildly popular in their time.

Sankt-Bach-Passion. Work by Kagel, a Passion on the life of J.S. Bach, setting documents from his life to music tenuously and beautifully abstracted from his chorales.

Sant' Alessio, Il (St Alexis). Opera by Landi to a libretto by Giulio Rospigliosi. Alexis (treble) returns secretly to his family in Rome after many years as a holy man in Palestine. But they have heard of his presence there and want to go. In his dilemma, and tempted by the Devil (bass) to reveal himself, he appeals to heaven, is sent an Angel (treble) and dies. First performance: Palazzo Barberini, Rome, 1631/2.

Santa Croce, Francesco (b. Padua, c.1487; d. Loreto, ?1556). Italian composer, who was active largely in Treviso and was an early exponent of music for double choir, possibly influential on Willaert.

Santa Cruz (Wilson), Domingo (b. La Cruz, Valparaiso, 5 Jul 1899; d. Santiago, 6 Jan 1987). Chilean composer, the dominant figure in his country's musical life in the middle decades of the 20th century. He studied with Enrique Soro in Santiago and del Campo in Madrid (1922–4), where he was attached to the Chilean embassy. Back in Chile he directed a choir, reformed the National Conservatory, taught there, and exerted himself in numerous other ways, besides producing a compact output including choral music, symphonies and string quartets, in a Hindemithian style with a Latin flavour.

Santa Fe. City in New Mexico whose summer opera festival was founded by the conductor John Crosby in 1957. The repertory has regularly featured Strauss and new works, by composers including Floyd, Berio, Weir and Saariaho.

Santoro, Cláudio (b. Manaus, 23 Nov 1919; d. Brasília, 27 Mar 1989). Brazilian composer. He studied with the German composer Hans Joachim Koellreutter, who introduced him to serialism, and in Paris with Boulanger. In 1948 he attended the Prague Congress of Progressive Composers, whose condemnation of serialism affected him. He began studying Brazilian folk music, which was the root of his style until around 1960, when he started to reintroduce more advanced principles. As a teacher he has held positions both in Brazil and in Germany.

santūr. Turkish–Iranian dulcimer.

sarabande [saraband]. Dance of 16th-century Latin American origin – it was then sung and lively – that became a standard element in the Baroque suite, now slow and the centre of gravity. The faster kind had a continued life, especially in Italian guitar music, while the slow sarabande developed in France, with a characteristic weight on the second beat in triple time. There are sarabandes of this type in keyboard and stage works by Lully, Lalande, the Couperins and Rameau, and in suites by numerous German composers, notably Handel and Bach. Apart from a lone example in Auber's *Les Diamants de la couronne* (1841), the form then lapsed, to be taken up by Debussy ('Hommage à Rameau'), Satie, Busoni, etc.

Saracini, Claudio (b. Siena, 1 Jul 1586; d. Mirandola, 20 Sep 1630). Italian composer. Born into a noble and musical family, he was proficient as a singer and lutenist and wrote keenly expressive and sometimes charming songs.

Sarasate (y Navascuéz), Pablo (Martín Melitón) de (b. Pamplona, 10 Mar 1844; d. Biarritz, 20 Sep 1908). Spanish violinist-composer. The son of a military bandmaster, he started on the violin at five and was giving concerts at eight. Patronage took him on for further studies in Madrid and at the Paris Conservatoire with Alard (1856–9); he then set out on the path of a touring virtuoso, though he also performed in quartets. Carl Flesch remembered his 'aesthetic moderation, euphony, and technical perfection'. Composers who wrote for him included Lalo (F minor Concerto and *Symphonie espagnole*), Bruch (G minor Concerto and Scottish Fantasy), Saint-Saëns (First Concerto, Third Concerto and Introduction and Rondo capriccioso), and Wieniawski (Second Concerto), and he composed showpieces himself, notably a fantasy on *Carmen*. Whistler's portrait of him is at the Carnegie Institute, Pittsburgh.

sardana. The national dance of Catalonia, performed in solemn circles to the accompaniment traditionally of flute and drum with shawms. It has naturally appealed to Catalan composers, such as Gerhard.

Sargent, (Harold) Malcolm (Watts) (b. Ashford, Kent, 29 Apr 1895; d. London, 3 Oct 1967). British conductor, knighted in 1947. The son of an organist-choirmaster, he came to the attention of

Henry Wood, who encouraged him. He held appointments with the Hallé and the Liverpool Philharmonic, but is remembered especially as chief conductor from 1948 of the Proms, to which he brought an astute sense of occasion.

Šárka. Legendary heroine of pagan Bohemia, subject of one of Smetana's symphonic poems *Má vlast* and of operas by Janáček and Fibich.

Śārngadeva (*fl.* first half of the 13th century). Indian theorist, author of the monumental *Saṅgītaratnākara* (Ocean of Music), in Sanskrit verse.

Sarri, Domenico Natale (b. Trani, Apulia, 24 Dec 1679; d. Naples, 25 Jan 1744). Italian composer, resident in Naples from boyhood and trained at the San Onofrio conservatory. He was at the peak of his fame and expertise as an opera composer around 1720, and made the first setting of Metastasio's earliest important libretto, *Didone abbandonata* (1724). Then he was eclipsed by Vinci and Pergolesi.

sarrusophone. Double-reed keyed brass instrument designed in 1856 by Pierre Louis Gautrot and named after Pierre Auguste Sarrus, a French army bandmaster. Gautrot planned a whole family – soprano in B♭, alto in E♭, tenor in B♭, baritone in E♭, bass in B♭ and contrabass in E♭ – to take the place of oboes and bassoons in bands, though the sound is more saxophone-like but thinner. The instruments failed to win lasting acceptance, but the contrabass survived in symphony orchestras, as a replacement for the contrabassoon, especially in France: it has a part in scores by Saint-Saëns, Massenet, Ravel (*Rapsodie espagnole*) and Stravinsky (*Threni*).

Sarti, Giuseppe (baptized Faenza, 1 Dec 1729; d. Berlin, 28 Jul 1802). Italian composer. The son of a jeweller-violinist, he studied with Padre Martini in Bologna and started his career as an opera composer in 1752. A visit to Copenhagen the next year resulted in a protracted stay and a string of 30 operas in Italian, French and Danish. In 1775 he returned to Italy, where he gained new triumphs with *Giulio Sabino* (1781) and *Fra i due litiganti* (1782, libretto by Goldoni). Invited by Catherine II, he went to St Petersburg in 1784, stopping in Vienna, where his *Litiganti* was in vogue. He met Mozart, who quoted from the *Litiganti* in the supper scene of *Don Giovanni* – a mark of dubious honour to which he responded by writing a paper attacking the complexity of the quartets his colleague had dedicated to Haydn.

In St Petersburg he composed more Italian operas and a *Requiem* for Louis XVI besides collaborating on an opera in Russian, *The Early Reign of Oleg*, to a libretto by the empress. This was a moment in the long history of attempts by opera composers to recapture the spirit of ancient Greek drama: Euripides's *Alcestis* is performed as a play within a play, before Oleg in Constantinople, with choruses in Greek modes and rhythms accompanied by a flute (standing in for the ancient tibia) and solos with accompaniment for harp and pizzicato strings (similarly representing the lyre). In 1801 he left Russia to return again to Italy, but he died in Berlin, visiting one of his daughters.

Sartorio, Antonio (b. Venice, 1630; d. Venice, 30 Dec 1680). Italian composer, chiefly of operas for his native city, though he was employed as well at the ducal court in Hanover (1666–75). His operas commonly have a profusion of arias, perhaps 70 or more, often including a lament over a repeating bass and one or more heroic numbers with trumpet. His brother, Gasparo (1625/6–80), was also an opera composer in Venice.

Sarum rite. Liturgical tradition in use from the 13th century to the 16th at the cathedral of Salisbury (Sarum) and more widely in England in the latter part of this period. It thereby provided context and material for composers in the great age of English polyphony that culminated in Taverner and Tallis.

Sáry, László (b. Györ, 1 Jan 1940). Hungarian composer. Following studies with Szervánszky at the Liszt Academy (1961–6) he became interested in the western European and US avant-garde and in 1970 formed the New Music Studio with two colleagues, Jeney and Vidovszky. Insistent pattern-making – and breaks away from the pattern – characterize his art.

sassofono (It., pl. *sassofoni*). Saxophone.

SATB [satb]. Abbreviation indicating the make-up of a mixed choir or quartet, with soprano, alto, tenor and bass voices.

Satie, Erik [Eric Alfred Leslie] (b. Honfleur, 17 May 1866; d. Paris, 1 Jul 1925). French composer. Radically simple, his music exuded a calm trust in the old church modes and floating dissonances, in both respects influencing his friend Debussy. Self-denying and self-dismissive, it yet survived to convey its message of messagelessness to Cage.

He lost his Scots mother when he was six, and spent his childhood partly with his shipbroker father in Paris and partly with his grandparents in Honfleur. In 1878 his father got married again, to a pianist who dabbled in composition: Satie disliked her, not least because she sent him to the Conservatoire in 1879. Lazy, he stumbled on with his studies, and in his early 20s produced his first important compositions: sets of three Sarabandes (1887), *Gymnopédies* (1888) and *Gnossiennes* (1890), all for piano. The Sarabandes are remarkable for their unresolved chords, the other pieces, with fanciful titles, for their serene modal melodies, evocative of ancient Greece and the orient.

In 1891, enjoying a growing friendship with Debussy, he began living a bohemian existence in Montmartre and associating with the artistic rosicrucian sect led by the writer Joséphin Péladan. Though he publicly broke with Péladan the next year, he maintained his involvement in the esoteric and formed his own church. Most of his music of 1891–5 was intended for ritual dramas and is appropriately hieratic, but often also eccentric, raising the question – as so much of his music does – whether the oddity was personal expression, an identification with the destitute (for which the *Messe des pauvres* would provide evidence), a disguise, the result of incompetence, or the fruit of some abstract system, zealously followed. To take an extreme example, *Vexations*, a strange piano phrase directed to be repeated 840 times, could be regarded just as a joke or as a real challenge to Western musical norms. Also during this period, a legacy enabled him to buy 12 identical grey velvet suits.

With Montmartre growing posher, he moved out in 1898, to the southern industrial suburb of Arcueil-Cachan. But he was still working in Montmartre as a café pianist and walked the several kilometres there and back daily. Composition came virtually to a halt. The only works he completed between 1900 and 1910 were a few café items, some piano exercises and the *Trois pièces en forme de poire* for piano duet, around which the fictitious story arose that he called them 'pear-shaped' because Debussy had suggested he give more attention to form. He did, though, recognize that he needed further instruction, and enrolled in classes in counterpoint and orchestration given by d'Indy and Roussel at the Schola Cantorum (1905–8).

Any effect on his productivity was delayed until 1911, when Ravel played the Sarabandes in a recital and there was a performance of Debussy's orchestral version of two *Gymnopédies*. Suddenly given smart attention – or anxious to prove he was not only the revolutionary precursor of almost a quarter-century ago but a living, breathing composer – he started writing more abundantly than ever, mostly in the form of piano pieces with bizarre titles: *Four Flabby Preludes (for a dog)*, *Three Real Flabby Preludes (for a dog)*, *Sketches and Teases of a Large Good Fellow in Wood*, *Old Sequins and Old Cuirasses*. Under such names came music as plain and puzzling as before – and as private. The masterpiece of this period is *Sports et divertissements*, where the composer's calligraphy and marginal comments are available only to the performer.

In 1915 he was taken up by the young Cocteau, who created a craze for his music and got him the plum opportunity of the time: a commission from Diaghilev. The result was *Parade* (1917), after which came his supreme expression of musical cool, *Socrate* (1918), a classical cantata right outside the usual French academic mode, not antiquated but, as he said, 'white and pure, like antiquity'. Cocteau's promotion also gained him a following among younger composers, especially those grouped as *Les* SIX, of whom Milhaud was particularly close. The two composers worked together on *Musique d'ameublement* (Furniture Music), designed to be ignored, after which his main achievements were two more ballets in 1924. His health now was giving way, probably a result of heavy drinking. When he died, Milhaud and some others at last pushed open the door on the room in Arcueil that none but the composer had entered for nearly 30 years, and were astonished by its bareness.

Nigel Wilkins, ed. *The Writings of Erik Satie* (1980); Robert Orledge *Satie the Composer* (1990)

Orchestral: *Cinq grimaces* (for *A Midsummer Night's Dream*), 1915; PARADE (ballet), 1916–17; *Trois petites pièces montées*, 1919; *Le Piège de méduse*, 1921; *Musique d'ameublement*, 1918–23; *Mercure* (ballet), 1924; *Relâche* (ballet), 1924

Vocal: *Messe des pauvres*, ch, org, 1893–5; *Geneviève de Brabant* (miniature marionette opera), 1899–1900; SOCRATE, s/4 women's voices, pf/chbr orch, 1917–18

Chamber: *Choses vues à droite et à gauche (sans lunettes)*, vn, pf, 1914; *Marche de Cocagne*, 2 tpt, 1919; *Sonnerie pour réveiller le bon gros roi des singes*, 2 tpt, 1921

Piano duet: *Trois morceaux en forme de poire*, 1903; *En habit de cheval*, 1911; *Aperçus désagréables*, 1908–12; *Trois petites pièces montées*, 1919; *La Belle Excentrique* (3 dances), 1920

Piano solo: *Quatre ogives*, 1886; *Trois sarabandes*, 1887; *Trois* GYMNOPEDIES, 1888; *Trois gnossiennes*, 1890–93; *Le Fils des étoiles*, 1891; *Trois sonneries de la Rose+Croix*, 1892; *Uspud*, 1892; *Danses gothiques*, 1893; *Vexations*, 1893; *Pièces froides*, 1897; *Jack in the Box* (ballet), 1899; *Poudre d'or*, ?1901–2; *Prélude en tapisserie*, 1906; *Passacaille*, 1906; *Quatre préludes flasques (pour un chien)*, 1912; *Véritables préludes flasques (pour un chien)*, 1912; *Chapitres tournés en tous sens*, 1913; *Croquis et agaceries d'un gros bonhomme en bois*, 1913; *Descriptions automatiques*, 1913; *Embryons dessechés*, 1913; *Enfantillages pittoresques*, 1913; *Menus propos enfantins*, 1913; *Les Pantins dansent*, 1913; *Peccadilles importunes*, 1913; *Le Piège de méduse*, 1913; *Vieux sequins et vieilles cuirasses*, 1913; *Heures séculaires et instantanées*, 1914; *Sports et divertissements*, 1914; *Les Trois Valses du précieux dégoûté*, 1914; *Avant-dernières pensées*, 1915; *Sonatine bureaucratique*, 1917; *Cinq nocturnes*, 1919; *Rêverie de l'enfance de Pantagruel*, 1919; *Premier menuet*, 1920; etc.

Songs: 'Chanson', 'Elégie', *Trois mélodies* (all Latour), 1887; 'Bonjour Biqui!' (Satie), 1893; *Trois poèmes d'amour* (Satie), 1914; *Trois mélodies* (Fargue, Godebska, Chalupt), 1916; *Quatre petites mélodies* (Lamartine, Cocteau, 18th-century, Radiguet), 1920; *Ludions* (5; Fargue), 1923

Café songs: 'Je te veux', ?1901; 'Tendrement', 1902; 'La Diva de l'empire', 1904; etc., all in various versions

Satoh, Somei (b. Sendai, 19 Jan 1947). Japanese composer. Self-taught, he draws influences from minimalism and Feldman into slow, exquisite pieces for solo voice with electronics and for orchestra.

Satz (Ger., pl. *Sätze*). Movement (of a work), though the term, derived from *setzen* (to set) can have other meanings.

Sauguet, Henri (b. Bordeaux, 18 May 1901; d. Paris, 21 Jun 1989). French composer, originally Jean Pierre Poupard. He studied in Bordeaux with Canteloube and others, became interested in Stravinsky and Satie, and corresponded with Milhaud, who encouraged his move to Paris in 1923. Almost immediately he became a member of a secondary Les Six formed around Satie, this time a Les Quatre known as the Ecole d'Arcueil and including Henri Cliquet-Pleyel, Max Jacob and Roger Désormière. He swam easily in the ironic-sentimental, neoclassical waters of Paris, and won particular esteem as a ballet composer (*La Chatte*, 1927; *Les Forains*, 1945), though his large output also includes operas (*La Chartreuse de Parme*, 1927–36), symphonies, concertos, chamber pieces for all kinds of combination, sacred music, secular cantatas, songs and even electronic music.

Saul. Ancient Jewish king (see 1 Samuel 9–31). Works based on his story include:

(1) Purcell's cantata *In guilty night*, on his visit to the Witch of Endor.

(2) Handel's oratorio to a text by Charles Jennens. The drama centres on David (tenor; soprano castrato and contralto in revivals), Saul (bass) and David's relationships with Saul's three unalike children: the loving Michal (soprano), the despising Merab (soprano) and the noble bosom friend Jonathan (tenor), within choral frames. The celebrated Dead March is for Jonathan. First performance: London, 16 Jan 1739.

(3) Nielsen's opera *Saul og David* to a libretto by Einar Christiansen that again features Saul (bass-baritone) in the company of David (tenor), Jonathan (tenor), Mikal (soprano) and the Witch of Endor (mezzo-soprano). First performance: Copenhagen, 28 Nov 1902.

Other Sauline works include a song by Musorgsky, an oratorio by Parry, a symphonic poem by Wagenaar and a ballet by Schuman.

sautillé (Fr., springing). Direction for the bow to bounce on the strings, also given as *saltando* or *spiccato*.

Savall, Jordi (b. Igalada, Barcelona, 1 Aug 1941). Catalonian viol player and conductor, the founder director with his wife, the soprano Montserrat Figueras, of the group Hespèrion XX, whose repertory has ranged from medieval music to Bach. He studied the viol with August Wenzinger in Basle.

Savinio, Alberto (b. Athens, 25 Aug 1891; d. Rome, 6 May 1952). Italian composer and painter, originally Andrea del Chirico; the painter Giorgio was his brother. He studied in Athens and with Reger in Munich, but was most influenced by Parisian neoclassicism. His musical works are all dramatic: operas, radio operas, ballets, mostly to his own librettos and scenarios.

Savioni, Mario (b. Rome, 1606–8; d. Rome, 22 Apr 1685). Italian singer-composer. As a boy and as a man he sang in Rome in church music and opera. His madrigals and cantatas came out of the sophisticated Roman musical culture of the time.

Savonlinna. City in Finland, where in 1967 an annual summer opera festival was founded within the castle of Olavinlinna.

Savoy. Medieval–Renaissance duchy incorporating parts of present-day France, Italy and Switzerland. The 15th-century dukes and duchesses were great patrons, vying with their Burgundian neighbours. Du Fay and Brumel were among the composers they invited.

Savoy operas. Term for the works of Gilbert and Sullivan, many of which were introduced at the Savoy Theatre in London.

saw, musical. Instrument, specially made or else obtained from an ironmonger, played in a sitting position, with the handle between the knees and the further end held by one hand while the other applies a fiddle bow. Flexing the blade changes the pitch: the effect is curiously vocal. Used by folk musicians in the mid 19th century, it was taken up by music-hall performers, usually in rather maudlin items. Sauguet's *Plainte* (1949) is a rare example of a piece specially conceived for it.

Sawallisch, Wolfgang (b. Munich, 26 Aug 1923). German conductor. He studied at the Munich Academy and began his career as répétiteur at Augsburg in 1947. Appointments followed in Aachen (1953–8), Wiesbaden (1958–60) and Cologne (1960–63); he also conducted at Bayreuth and was principal conductor of the Vienna Symphony (1960–70) and Hamburg Philharmonic (1961–73). He then devoted himself to the Bavarian Staatsoper in Munich (1971–93), where his performances, especially of Strauss, were exemplary. After that he brought new glory in the German repertory to the Philadelphia Orchestra (1993–2003).

Sawer, David (Peter) (b. Stockport, 14 Sep 1961). British composer, trained at York University and in Cologne with Kagel. Notable works include music-theatre pieces and *Byrnan Wood* for orchestra (1992).

sax. Abbreviation for saxophone.

Sax, Adolphe (Antoine Joseph) (b. Dinant, 6 Nov 1814; d. Paris, 4 Feb 1894). Belgian inventor and maker of wind instruments, following his father in that trade. He studied flute and clarinet at the Brussels Conservatoire, began work as a teenager and moved in 1842 to Paris, where he soon met Berlioz. In 1845 an official enquiry resulted in the adoption of his instruments for French military bands. That same year he patented his saxhorns, and the next his saxophones. He taught saxophone at the Paris Conservatoire (1858–71) and directed the stage band at the Opera (1858–94), while engaging vigorously in legal action against challenges to his patents.

saxhorn. Family of valved brass instruments, developed by Sax in 1842–5 as a homogeneous ensemble, unlike the existing (and continuing) mixture of cornets, trumpets, tubas and euphoniums used by bands. Saxhorns have a tube of conical bore, normally wound so that the bell rises perpendicularly to the mouthpiece. Originally they were made in a full range of sizes, from soprano and alto (in trumpet territory) down to contrabass, but the only ones to survive in British and US bands (and occasionally orchestras) are the tenor and baritone, often simply called tenor horn and baritone.

saxophone. Single-reed keyed brass instrument invented by Sax around 1840. Saxophones have clarinet-like mouthpieces (which means that clarinettists can easily play them) and conical tubes, rather stout, with a U-bend and an outward-pointing, flared bell, though the higher members of the family are customarily made straight. They have a normal range of two and a half octaves, extended to three or even four by some makers. The commonest sizes are the soprano in B♭, alto in E♭, tenor in B♭ and baritone in E♭; less common are the sopranino, bass and contrabass. Sax also created a second family of instruments in C and F for orchestral use, but these are obsolete: the band instruments, popularized by Sousa and others at the end of the 19th century, spread into the symphony orchestra, and gained a further boost when they were taken up by jazz musicians after the First World War.

Saxophones – most commonly the alto, but also the tenor and soprano – appear in orchestral scores by Bizet (*L'Arlésienne*), Strauss (*Symphonia domestica*), Bartók (*The Wooden Prince*), Berg (*Lulu*), Ravel (*Boléro*, *Pictures at an Exhibition*), Prokofiev (*Romeo and Juliet*) and Birtwistle (*The Triumph of Time*), among others. Solo pieces include Debussy's Rhapsody (with piano) and Birtwistle's *Panic* (with drummer and wind orchestra). There are also works for saxophone quartet.

Paul Harvey *Saxophone* (1995); Richard Ingham, ed. *The Cambridge Companion to the Saxophone* (1998)

saxophone quartet. Ensemble of soprano, alto, tenor and baritone saxophones.

Saxton, Robert (Louis Alfred) (b. London, 8 Oct 1953). British composer. He studied privately with Lutyens, at Cambridge with Holloway (1972–5), at Oxford (1975–6) and with Berio, an influence on his earlier music. Later works are more concerned with harmonic progression, often achieved through textures of ecstatic liveliness, and include the chamber symphony *The Circles of Light* (1985–6), many works for large orchestra, choral pieces and chamber music. He has taught at the Guildhall School, the RAM and (since 1999) Oxford.

Saygun, Ahmet Adnan (b. Izmir, 7 Sep 1907; d. Istanbul, 6 Jan 1991). Turkish composer, trained in

Paris at the Conservatoire and the Schola Cantorum (under d'Indy). He collected Turkish folk music, acting as Bartók's host in this endeavour. His most important works are the oratorio *Yunus Emre* (1946) and opera *Köroğlu* (1973).

Sayings of Péter Bornemisza, The (*Bornemisza Péter mondasai*). Work by Kurtág for soprano and piano, a musically imposing and morally challenging 'concerto' (in the sense of a Baroque sacred concerto). First performance: Darmstadt, 5 Sep 1968.

Sayve, Lambert de (b. 1548/9; d. Linz, Feb 1614). Netherlandish composer. He joined the Austrian imperial chapel as a choirboy in 1562 and spent the rest of his life in service to various members of the imperial family. His works include motets, masses and German songs, stylistically indebted to his teacher Monte or to the Venetian polychoral style.

Scala, La. Common way of referring to the Teatro alla Scala of Milan, so called because it was built – in 1778 – on the site of the church of Santa Maria alla Scala (i.e. stairway). Always one of the principal opera houses of Italy, it became in the late 19th century one of the three or four most prestigious houses internationally. Works created there include – besides Salieri's *L'Europa riconosciuta*, which opened the theatre – *La gazza ladra*, *Nabucco*, *Otello* (Verdi), *Falstaff*, *Donnerstag* and *La vera storia*.

scala di seta, La (The Silken Ladder). Opera by Rossini to an adaptation by Giuseppe Foppa of a recent French libretto. The heroine uses wit and love to get out of an arranged marriage that would – since she has secretly married her sweetheart – be bigamous. First performance: Venice, 9 May 1812.

scala enigmatica. Scale Verdi found in a journal and used in his *Ave Maria*: C–D♭–E–F♯–G♯–A♯–B–C. Nono also based works on it.

scale. Sequence of notes played or notated in ascending or descending order through one or more octaves. The scales available on the white notes of the piano are:

Major (Ionian) C–D–E–F–G–A–B–C
Dorian D–E–F–G–A–B–C–D
Phrygian E–F–G–A–B–C–D–E
Lydian F–G–A–B–C–D–E–F
Mixolydian G–A–B–C–D–E–F–G
Natural minor (Aeolian) A–B–C–D–E–F–G–A
Locrian (Hyperaeolian) B–C–D–E–F–G–A–B
These may be transposed onto any degree,

generating, say, D major (D–E–F♯–G–A–B–C♯–D) or B♭ Phrygian (B♭–C♭–D♭–E♭–F♭–G♭–A♭–B♭).

Two other minor scales are important. The melodic minor includes the notes commonest in minor-key melodies, rising A–B–C–D–E–F♯–G♯–A and falling A–G–F–E–D–C–B–A. The harmonic minor has the notes of the minor triad (A–C–E), the dominant in major form (E–G♯–B) and the subdominant in minor form (D–F–A), hence A–B–C–D–E–F–G♯–A and the same in descent.

Piano exercises normally include also the chromatic scale, through all 12 notes of the octave.

Among other scales are the whole-tone, proceeding only through whole tones, the OCTATONIC scale of alternating whole tones and semitones, the 'acoustic scale' found in Romanian folk music and beloved of Bartók, with a Lydian lower segment and a Mixolydian upper (e.g. C–D–E–F♯–G–A–B♭–C), and various PENTATONIC scales.

Scales are ways of lining up the notes in a KEY or MODE. A piece of music may be said to be in a key (Symphony No.29 in A major, C minor Mass) or in a mode if it is freely transposable (thus 'Greensleeves' is in the Dorian mode) but not in a scale.

Nicolas Slonimsky *Thesaurus of Scales and Melodic Patterns* (1947)

Scandello, Antonio (b. Bergamo, 17 Jan 1517; d. Dresden, 18 Jan 1580). Italian composer. He began his career as a cornettist in Bergamo and Trent, then in 1549 was recruited by the Elector Moritz of Saxony for the Dresden court. There he remained, and branched out into composition, his works including masses, motets, a St John Passion and German songs. Converted to Protestantism, he was court chapelmaster from 1568.

Scardanelli-Zyklus (Scardanelli Cycle). Concert-length sequence of works by Holliger, principally comprising choral settings of poems from Hölderlin's later, deranged years, when Scardanelli was one of his pseudonyms. Also included are pieces for small orchestra and a flute solo, *(t)air(e)*. First performance: Donaueschingen, 18 Oct 1985.

Scarlatti. Italian family of musicians.

(1) **(Pietro) Alessandro (Gaspare)** (b. Palermo, 2 May 1660; d. Naples, 22 Oct 1725). Composer, widely admired in his time for his vocal music, and remembered, if largely in the abstract, as continuing the formalization of opera seria. He belonged to a musical family: three of his younger siblings were professional singers in Naples, another (Francesco) was a composer and violinist

who went to London, and two of his sons became composers, one very minor (Pietro Filippo), the other not (Domenico).

Alessandro and his two sisters who became singers were sent to Rome when he was 12 to stay with relatives. Possibly he studied briefly with Carissimi, but the details of his education are unknown. He married at 17 and had 10 children in quite rapid succession, of whom five survived to adulthood. His continuing concern for them, long past their reaching maturity, could be regarded as an attempt at control or, more positively, as the response of one who had been obliged to take on family responsibilities when very young. At 18 he produced his first opera, *Gli equivoci nel sembiante*, which was a great success in Rome and was repeated in several Italian cities and abroad. More operas, cantatas and oratorios followed, for patrons including Queen Christina of Sweden and the artistic cardinals Benedetto Pamphili and Pietro Ottoboni.

In 1683 he accepted an appointment as chapelmaster to the viceroy of Naples, where he remained for nearly 20 years, though he often returned to Rome to oversee performances of new works – even while maintaining an extraordinary output of operas, oratorios and cantatas for the viceroy. He is known to have written 30 or so operas for Naples; the real figure may have been double that. Several of them were widely produced, especially *Il Pirro e Demetrio*, which travelled as far as Brunswick and London. In *Dal male il bene* (1687), a revision of *Tutto il mal non vien per nuocere* (1681), he introduced the fast–slow–fast overture and so sowed the first seed of the symphony.

He left Naples in 1702, tried unsuccessfully for a position with Prince Ferdinando de' Medici in Florence (though the prince had been and was to remain his patron) and returned to Rome. There was now no opportunity for opera in the city, but he composed an abundance of oratorios, serenatas and cantatas for Pamphili, Ottoboni and other patrons, as well as operas for Ferdinando and for Venice (*Il Mitridate Eupatore*). He was also chapelmaster at Santa Maria Maggiore.

In 1708 he accepted an invitation to return to the Neapolitan viceregal court. More operas, serenatas and cantatas were the result, as well as some essays in the comic vein (intermezzos in serious operas and a full-scale operatic comedy) and instrumental music. He went back to Rome for the period 1718–21, then spent his last years in Naples in virtual retirement.

The typical Scarlatti opera concerns the loves of dignified rulers, includes around 50 short arias, almost exclusively in da capo form from the late

1690s onwards, and has little space for ensembles other than a brief closing chorus for all the characters. Arias are lightly accompanied, with fuller orchestral punctuation; they are effectively concerto movements for solo voice, impelled by a remarkable ability to keep up freshness of musical invention, despite the frequent repetition of emotional stances (doubt, decision, leave-taking, rejoicing, lament) from one work to another. The serenatas and oratorios are opera-like, while the more than 600 cantatas represent the apogee of the Roman form of sophisticated vocal chamber music.

Though a few arias and cantatas have been kept alive by singers, he alone, of all the great Baroque composers, eluded anything but sporadic revival in the second half of the 20th century.

Edward J. Dent *Alessandro Scarlatti* (1905, [2]1960); Donald Jay Grout *Alessandro Scarlatti: An Introduction to his Operas* (1979)

Operas: *L'honestà negli amori* (F. Parnasso), f.p. Rome, 1680 (includes aria 'Gia il sole del Gange'); *Il Pompeo* (Nicolò Minato), f.p. Rome, 1683; *Il Pirro e Demetrio* (Adriano Morselli), f.p. Naples, 1694 (includes aria 'Le violette'); *La donna ancora è fedele* (Domenico Filippo Contini), f.p. Naples, 1698 (includes aria 'Se Florindo è fedele'); *Il Mitridate Eupatore* (Girolamo Frigimelica), f.p. Venice, 1707; *Il Tigrane* (Domenico Lalli), f.p. Naples, 1715; *La Griselda* (after Zeno), f.p. Rome, 1721; about 60 others, plus serenatas (*Il giardino d'amore*, c.1702) and insert arias

Cantatas: *Oh di Betlemme altera povertà* (*Cantata pastorale per la nascità di Nostro Signore*), s, str qt, lute; *Su le sponde del Tebro*, s, 2 vn, tpt, con; etc.

Other works: sacred, orchestral, chamber and keyboard music

(2) (Giuseppe) Domenico (b. Naples, 26 Oct 1685; d. Madrid, 23 Jul 1757). Composer and keyboard performer, son of Alessandro and born in the same year as Bach and Handel. He spent most of his adult life in Portugal and Spain, devoting himself to the keyboard sonata and creating well over 500 pieces of acute inventiveness, spirit and technical perfection.

Presumably trained by his father, he gained an appointment as organist and composer in the Neapolitan court chapel when he was 15. In 1702 he accompanied Alessandro to Florence, where he may have encountered Cristofori and the emergent piano. He then returned to Naples, but in 1705 was ordered by his father back to Rome so that the two of them could proceed to Venice, where he would more likely find appropriate opportunities (probably including lessons with Gasparini). What he achieved in Venice is not known. In 1709 he returned to Rome and wrote operas for the exiled Polish queen Maria Casimira, besides consorting with Handel, Corelli and others at the home of the musical cardinal Pietro Ottoboni. He also gained a church appointment and one with the Portuguese ambassador. Alessandro was now back in Naples but evidently exerting influence, and in 1717 Domenico obtained a legal document asserting his independence. He was 31, unmarried and only modestly successful.

The pattern began to change when in 1719 he left for Lisbon, having accepted a post as cathedral chapelmaster. He made three return trips to Italy during the next few years, notably to see his father one last time in 1725 and three years later to be married in Rome: he was 42. After that he seems never to have left the Iberian peninsula.

One of his tasks in Lisbon was to teach the king's daughter, Maria Barbara, and he remained in her service when, in 1728, she moved to Madrid as wife of the Spanish crown prince (later Ferdinand VI). In 1739 his wife died, and he remarried. Four of his nine children survived infancy; none of them inherited the family's musical bent. How his life passed at the Spanish court for almost three decades is unknown. He had written some vocal music in Lisbon but now seems to have concentrated entirely on keyboard sonatas, though there are no dates of composition to indicate how many were written in Italy or Lisbon. He may have worked with Farinelli, who was in Madrid from 1737; he may not. A quiet life is possible, and an active mind.

The sonatas are as far removed as possible, within the confines of Baroque music, from Alessandro's operas: compact, abstract, private, making experience (feelings, foibles, sounds of the guitar and other Spanish traits) into a play of fingers. In another way, though, Domenico in his sonatas faced the same challenge as Alessandro in his arias: that of finding new musical ideas to support the same form time and again (the sonatas are all single BINARY movements) and of developing those ideas consistently and brilliantly. The performances he was receiving two centuries and more later, by such unlike pianists as Horowitz and Pletnev, partly measure his success.

Ralph Kirkpatrick *Domenico Scarlatti* (1953, ²1983); Malcolm Boyd *Domenico Scarlatti* (1986)

Sonatas: 555 in Kirkpatrick's catalogue, of which 8 include a second instrument and 7 are of doubtful attribution, the most popular including those in D minor, K.1 (Allegro); G minor, K.8 (Allegro); D minor, K.9 (Allegro); C minor, K.11; G, K.13 (Presto); G, K.14 (Presto); E, K.20 (Presto); A, K.24 (Presto); B minor, K.27 (Allegro); D, K.29 (Presto); 'The Cat's Fugue', G minor, K.30 (Moderato); D minor, K.32 (Aria); F, K.44 (Allegro); B minor, K.87; D, K.96 (Allegrissimo); D, K.119 (Allegro); G,

K.125 (Vivo); D minor, K.141 (Allegro); G, K.146; C, K.159 (Allegro); A minor, K.175 (Allegro); A, K.208 (Andante è cantabile); D minor, K.213 (Andante); C♯ minor, K.247 (Allegro); A, K.322 (Allegro); B minor, K.377 (Allegrissimo); E, K.380 (Andante commodo); F minor, K.466 (Andante moderato); F minor, K. 481 (Andante è cantabile); D, K.491 (Allegro); F minor, K.519 (Allegro assai); E, K.531 (Allegro)

Sacred: *Salve regina*, s, str, con, 1756–7; *Stabat mater*, ch, con; etc.

Other works: operas, cantatas, serenatas, arias, sinfonias

(3) **Giuseppe** (b. Naples, *c*.1720; d. Vienna, 17 Aug 1777). Italian composer. He was a cousin of Domenico Scarlatti, whom he probably visited in Spain, though he was mostly active in Vienna and Venice, writing opera. He was helped by Gluck, and himself gave some musical advice to the young Salieri. The high point of his career came with the operas he produced in Vienna around 1757–60, including settings of Goldoni (*L'isola disabitata*, *Il mercato di Malmantile*) and Metastasio (*L'Issipile*).

scat. Jazz style of singing flurries of nonsense syllables.

Scelsi, Giacinto (b. La Spezia, 8 Jan 1905; d. Rome, 9 Aug 1988). Italian composer, noted for his concentration on steadily evolving sounds. Of noble birth and independent means, he travelled widely during his 20s and 30s, and studied with the Scriabin disciple Egon Koehler in Geneva and the serialist Walter Klein in Vienna (1935–6). His works of this period go in various directions. In the early 1950s he settled in Rome, where he began exploring a radically new style, based on a sustained approach – through microtonal neighbours and changes of timbre – to a single note as an image of focused contemplation. The classic upshot was his *Quattro pezzi* for chamber orchestra (1959), each based on one note. He also wrote solo vocal pieces suggestive of shamanic delivery, and big scores evoking the ritual practices of vanished civilizations: many of these larger works were not performed until shortly before his death, when his work at last gained recognition. Much of his music was improvised, in moments prepared by meditation, and then set down by an amanuensis.

Orchestral: *Quattro pezzi su una nota sola*, chbr orch, 1959; *Hurqualia*, 1960; *Aion*, 1961; *Chukrum*, str, 1963; *Nomos*, 1963; *Anahit*, vn, chbr orch, 1965; *Uaxactum*, with ch, 1966; *Konx-Om-Pax*, with ch, 1969; *Pfhat*, with ch, 1974

Chamber: String Quartet No.1, 1944; No.2, 1961; No.3,

1963; No.4, 1964; No.5, 1985; *Kya*, cl, septet, 1959; *Khoom*, s, hn, str qt, perc, 1962; *Trilogy*, vc, 1957–65; *Okanagon*, hp, tam tam, db, 1968; many other pieces, especially for solo instrument

Piano: Suite No.8 'Bot-Ba', 1952; No.9 'Ttai', 1953; No.10 'Ka', 1954; No.11, 1956

Vocal: *Canti del Capricorno*, v, 1962–72; many other solo and choral pieces

scena (It., scene, pl. *scene*, though in Eng. 'scenas'). Normally part of an opera, an extended dramatic solo. The term can also be applied to a concert piece of a similar sort, such as Mozart's *Popoli di Tessaglia*.

Schack, Benedikt (Emanuel) (b. Mirotice, 7 Feb 1758; d. Munich, 10 Dec 1826). Czech tenor and composer, for whom Mozart wrote the role of Tamino in *Die Zauberflöte*; since he was also a flautist, he probably played the title instrument as well. His wife was the Third Lady in the same production. The son of a schoolteacher, he had joined Schikaneder's company in 1786, after studies in Prague and Vienna followed by various kinds of musical employment. Having contributed music to many of Schikaneder's shows, he moved to Graz in 1793, to end his singing career at the court theatre in Munich (1796–1814). He was not only Mozart's performer but his friend, and is said to have taken part (on the soprano line) in a bedside sing-through of the unfinished *Requiem* on the composer's last night – an event which (if it happened) he might have recalled when writing sacred music in his own final years.

Schaeffer, Pierre (Henri Marie) (b. Nancy, 14 Aug 1910; d. Aix-en-Provence, 19 Aug 1995). French composer, creator of the earliest music made by altering recorded sounds – or MUSIQUE CONCRETE, to use the term he invented. He trained at the Ecole Polytechnique and joined French radio as a technician in 1936. Six years later he was one of the founding members of the Studio d'Essai, where he worked towards what he eventually achieved in 1948: compositions made from sound recordings. In 1951 he became head of an electronic composition department under radio auspices, the Groupe de Recherche de Musique Concrète, and invited outside composers to work there – notably Messiaen, Boulez and Barraqué – alongside such homegrown colleagues as Henry. In 1953 he left the department in Henry's charge, but he returned to create a few works in 1958–9, now avoiding the surrealist effects of his first pieces and focusing on connections and transformations dependent purely on qualities of sound. He then abandoned composition to concentrate on research into the nature and experience of timbre. He also taught at the Conservatoire from 1968.

Works made alone: *Etude aux chemins de fer*, 1948; *Etude pathétique*, 1948; *Etude au piano*, 1948; *Etude aux tourniquets*, 1948; *Etude violette*, 1948; *Etude aux allures*, 1958; *Etude aux sons animés*, 1958; *Etude aux objets*, 1959

Works made with Henry: *Bidule en ut*, 1950; *Symphonie pour un homme seul*, 1950, rev 1953; *Orphée 53*, 1953

Schafer, R(aymond) Murray (b. Sarnia, Ont., 18 Jul 1933). Canadian composer and writer on music. He studied with Weinzweig at the conservatory in Toronto, travelled and studied informally in Europe (1956–61), then returned to Canada, where he held various teaching positions, notably at the communications centre of Simon Fraser University (1965–75). During this period he contemplated the place of sound in education and in society, work that resulted in such widely noted texts as *The Composer in the Classroom* (1965) and *The Tuning of the World* (1977). His compositions range from mixed-media pieces to string quartets.

Schäfer, Christine (b. Frankfurt, 3 Mar 1965). German soprano whose skills of cool agility with expressive intensity, of extraordinary range with a sense of self-determination, have made her a model Lulu (at Salzburg in 1995, Glyndebourne in 1996, etc.) and an exceptional singer also of music from Mozart to Boulez. She studied with Ingrid Figur at the conservatory in Berlin.

Schäffer, Boguslaw (Julian) (b. Lwów, 6 Jun 1929). Polish composer. He was a pupil of Artur Malawski at the Kraków Conservatory, where he gained an appointment in 1963. By that time he had produced the first serial piece in post-war Poland (Music for Strings – Nocturne, 1953) and the first essays in indeterminacy (1955). His colossal output covers all genres.

Schallplatte (Ger., pl. *Schallplatten*). Gramophone record.

scharf (Ger.). Sharp (direction).

Scharwenka, (Franz) Xaver (b. Samter/ Szamotuły, 6 Jan 1850; d. Berlin, 8 Dec 1924). German pianist-composer. In 1865 his family moved to Berlin, where he and his brother Ludwig Philipp (1847–1917) studied at the New Academy of Music. He started touring as a pianist on both sides of the Atlantic in 1874, married in 1877 and opened a conservatory in Berlin in 1881. His works, mostly for piano, include four concertos (in B♭ minor, C minor, C♯ minor and F minor), two sonatas and 25 Polish dances, of which the first, Op.3:1, is a popular item. Philipp Scharwenka was also a composer, though overshadowed.

Schat, Peter (b. Utrecht, 5 Jun 1935; d. Amsterdam, 3 Feb 2003). Dutch composer. He studied with Van Baaren at the Utrecht Conservatory (1952–8), with Seiber in London and with Boulez in Basle (1960–61). In his Improvisations and Symphonies for wind quintet (1960) he introduced the notion of having performers move. Later works express left-wing sympathies and a desire, too, for a new musical harmony, achieved since the early 1980s with reference to a 'tone clock' of 12 tonalities.

Schauspieldirektor, Der (The Impresario). Short operatic entertainment by Mozart to a libretto by Gottlieb Stephanie. A comic portrayal of theatre life, the work includes arias for rival sopranos. First performance: Schönbrunn, 7 Feb 1786.

Scheherazade. German form of SHEHERAZADE. Rimsky-Korsakov's suite was published by a German house and this spelling is still sometimes used.

Scheidemann, Heinrich (b. Wöhrden, Holstein, *c*.1595; d. Hamburg, 1663). German organist-composer. He studied with Sweelinck in Amsterdam (1611–14) and succeeded his father as organist of the Catharinenkirche in Hamburg. Developing Sweelinck's style through the medium of the German Baroque organ, his chorales, chorale fantasias and other works were foundation stones of the north German organ school.

Scheidt, Samuel (baptized Halle, 3 Nov 1587; d. Halle, 24 Mar 1654). German organist-composer. The son of a city official, he studied with Sweelinck in Amsterdam when he was around 20 and returned to Halle to become court organist. There he remained, through vicissitudes of war, plague (which carried off all four of his young children in 1636; he and his wife, whom he had married when close on 40, later had more) and civic disputes. He also travelled for musical purposes, and met the other leading German musicians of his time, Schütz, Schein and Praetorius. His works include contrapuntal chorale settings and other music for organ, as well as motets and sacred concertos.

Schein, Johann Hermann (b. Grünhain, near Annaberg, 20 Jan 1586; d. Leipzig, 19 Nov 1630). German composer. After the death of his schoolmaster father in 1593, the family returned to Dresden, where he sang in the court chapel as a treble. With the Elector's support he had a serious education at Schulpforta, near Naumburg, and Leipzig University. In 1616 he was appointed cantor of St Thomas's in Leipzig (later Bach's post). Twice married, he lost several of his offspring in early childhood. Scheidt was godfather to one; Schütz, another friend, visited him on his deathbed and wrote a memorial piece for him. Like Schütz he was indebted to Italian music, especially to Viadana in his many sacred works and German madrigals (to his own words), most of which are for several voices with continuo. He also wrote suites in four movements (pavan, galliard, courante, allemande).

Schelle (Ger., pl. *Schellen*). Small bell, especially sleighbell.

Schelle, Johann (baptized Geising, Thuringia, 6 Sep 1648; d. Leipzig, 10 Mar 1701). Another of Bach's predecessors as cantor of the Thomaskirche in Leipzig (1677–1701), he succeeded Knüpfer, who, with Schütz, had been among his teachers. He wrote cantatas and psalm settings, sometimes lavishly and brilliantly polychoral.

Schelomo. See SOLOMON.

Schenk, Johann Baptist (b. Wiener Neustadt, 30 Nov 1753; d. Vienna, 29 Dec 1836). Austrian composer, notably of singspiels, among which *Der Dorfbarbier* (1796) was one of the hits of its time. He was also a friend of Mozart's and in 1793 helped an aspirant with his counterpoint exercises: Beethoven.

Schenker, Heinrich (b. Wisniowczyki, Galicia, 19 Jun 1868; d. Vienna, 13 Jan 1935). Austrian theorist. He studied with Bruckner at the Vienna Conservatory and gained attention from Brahms for his compositions. It was, though, as a theorist and private teacher that he made his career. His analyses, for which he introduced new technical terms and a concise way of graphically representing whole musical movements, were concerned with several levels of harmonic-melodic-contrapuntal process in tonal works. The deep background might be a rather simple formula, variously elaborated, extended and contradicted in the middleground and foreground. This view has been enormously influential, not least on composers (e.g. Babbitt) right outside the tonal tradition.

Scherchen-Hsiao, Tona (b. Neuchâtel, 12 Mar 1938). Swiss–French composer. The daughter of the conductor Hermann Scherchen (1891–1966) and composer Hsiao Shu-sien, she studied in China and in Europe with Henze (Salzburg, 1961–3), Messiaen (Paris, 1963–5) and Ligeti (Vienna, 1966–7). Her works make sophisticated crossings between the oriental (in a feeling for time and gesture, not material) and the contemporary French.

scherzando (It.). Playfully. The marking *allegretto scherzando* appears in Beethoven's Eighth Symphony and Bartók's Concerto for Orchestra. Also to be found are *scherzoso* and *scherzevole*.

scherzi, Gli (The Scherzos/Jokes). Name given to Haydn's Op.33 quartets, which pioneered such movements.

scherzo (It., joke, pl. *scherzi*, though in Eng. normally 'scherzos'). A quick movement of humorous or lively character, normally in triple time and minuet form, with two sections and a gentler middle passage, the trio. It was used to replace the minuet in four-movement works, first by Haydn in his Op.33 quartets (1781), then by Beethoven and many other composers. Most often the scherzo takes the minuet's third place in the scheme, following the slow movement, but it may precede the slow movement, as in Beethoven's Ninth Symphony and Bruckner's Eighth and Ninth Symphonies. The general custom, again as with the minuet, is to repeat each of the first two sections, then play the trio twice, and finish with the opening sections again, now not repeated.

Musical use of the term started in the early 17th century, when it was applied to madrigals of an amusing sort (e.g. Monteverdi's *Scherzi musicali*, 1607). It spread to instrumental music in the later Baroque, but rarely, Bach's lone example coming in his A minor Partita. Haydn established the Classical form and Beethoven made it ubiquitous, in works from his early wind octet (1792) to his late quartets, where scherzo character is projected into music in 2/4 or 4/4. In his symphonies he variously expanded the scale and weight of the scherzo, bringing the trio back twice (Nos.4 and 7), joining the scherzo into the finale (No.5), making the movement richer and grander (No.9).

With Schubert the two sections of the scherzo could become a full sonata form, while Mendelssohn made the type light and brilliant, a model for Berlioz (Queen Mab scherzo in *Roméo et Juliette*) and Schumann. Beethovenian energy was restored by Brahms and Bruckner, but the 20th-century scherzo, from Mahler through Shostakovich to Davies, is often grotesque or parodic.

Chopin wrote four independent scherzos for piano, and the term has also been used in titles and subtitles for free-standing works by Dukas (*The Sorcerer's Apprentice*), Stravinsky, etc.

Schick, Steven (Edward) (b. Mason City, Iowa, 8 May 1954). US percussionist, an artist of extraordinary sensitivity. He studied at the University of Iowa and the conservatory in Freiburg, and has taught regularly at Darmstadt, San Diego and the Manhattan School. Besides giving enthralling solo recitals (with Ferneyhough's *Bone Alphabet*, written for him, and Feldman's *The King of Denmark* among his pièces de résistance), he appears with his own percussion group, red fish blue fish.

Schickele, Peter (Johann) (b. Ames, Iowa, 17 Jul 1935). US composer and creator of P.D.Q. Bach, 'last and least of the sons of J.S. Bach', whose works began appearing in concerts and recordings in 1965. Trained at Swarthmore College and the Juilliard School, he has also put out music under his own name.

Schiff, András (b. Budapest, 21 Dec 1953). Hungarian pianist. He studied at the Liszt Academy in Budapest, and made his debut there in 1972. Prizes at the Tchaikovsky (1974) and Leeds (1975) competitions helped further his international career, and in 1979 he settled in the West. He was influential in wresting Bach from the exclusive grasp of harpsichordists.

Schiff, Heinrich (b. Gmunden, 18 Nov 1951). Austrian cellist and conductor. He studied with Tobias Kühne in Vienna and André Navarra in Detmold. A superb musician, as much in new works written for him by Henze and Casken as in Bach, he began a second career as a conductor in 1984 and was appointed artistic director of the Northern Sinfonia of England in 1990.

Schikaneder, Emanuel (Johann Joseph) (b. Straubing, 1 Sep 1751; d. Vienna, 21 Sep 1812). Austrian playwright and showman. He was educated at the Jesuit school in Regensburg and sang in the cathedral choir. By 1774 he was in work as an actor and author of singspiels, both words and music. He was regularly on tour, with his own company and others, before he settled at the Freihaus-Theater auf der Weiden in Vienna (1789–1801). There he produced a succession of musical fantasy plays including *Die Zauberflöte*, in which he created Papageno, with his brother and niece also in the cast. Misfortune dogged his later career in Vienna (at the Theater an der Wien, 1801–6), Brno and Budapest, and he died poor and mad.

Kurt Honolka *Papageno: Emanuel Schikaneder* (1990)

Schiller, (Johann Christoph) Friedrich von (b. Marbach, 10 Nov 1759; d. Weimar, 9 May 1805). German poet and playwright, whose verse entered Beethoven's Ninth Symphony, as well as songs and choral pieces by Schubert, and whose dramas provided material for operas by Rossini (*William Tell*), Donizetti (*Maria Stuarda*), Verdi (*Giovanna d'Arco, I masnadieri, Luisa Miller, Don Carlos*) and Tchaikovsky (*The Maid of Orleans*).

Schillinger, Joseph (Moiseyevich) (b. Kharkiv, 31 Aug 1895; d. New York, 23 Mar 1943). Ukrainian–US theorist. He studied at the Petrograd Conservatory (1914–18) and began a career in the Soviet Union as educationist, composer, ethnologist and jazzman. In 1928 he left for New York, where he taught a system of composition, notionally based on mathematical principles, to Gershwin and Earle Brown among others.

Schillings, Max von (b. Düren, 19 Apr 1868; d. Berlin, 24 Jul 1933). German composer-conductor. While studying at Munich University he came under Strauss's influence, though not sufficiently to drown out his early operas' Wagnerism, learned when he was on the music staff at Bayreuth in 1892. He scored a much bigger success with the melodramatic *Mona Lisa* (1915), introduced during his period conducting at the Stuttgart Opera (1908–18). Later he conducted at the Berlin Staatsoper (1918–25), on tour and in the recording studio. His non-operatic works, nearly all predating *Mona Lisa*, include a violin concerto (1910), other orchestral pieces, songs and chamber music. His second wife was a soprano, Barbara Kemp, who sang *Mona Lisa* at the Met in 1923.

Schindler, Anton (Felix) (b. Meedl, Moravia, 13 Jun 1795; d. Bockenheim, near Frankfurt, 16 Jan 1864). Austrian musician, who moved to Vienna in 1813 and met Beethoven the next year. From 1820 he was working regularly for the composer in musical and household matters. He was also responsible for keeping the conversation books in which the deaf master's thoughts were recorded, – though he destroyed many of these and altered others.

Schirmer, G. US music publishing firm founded in New York in 1866 by Gustav Schirmer (1829–93) in succession to an earlier company. It published the Library of Musical Classics (beginning in 1892), started a libretto series in 1911 and has had associations with composers including Schoenberg, Schuman, Menotti and Kirchner. It was acquired by Music Sales in 1986.

schisma [skhisma]. Extremely small interval, of 1.95 cents, being the difference between the Pythagorean and syntonic commas.

Schl. Ger. abbreviation for *Schlagwerk* (percussion).

Schlag (Ger., pl. *Schläge*). Beat; hence also *Schlagwerk*, *Schlagzeug* or *Schlaginstrumente* as terms for percussion.

schleppend (Ger.). Dragging, unsurprisingly more often found in the negative form *nicht schleppend*.

Schluss (Ger., pl. *Schlüsse*). Conclusion, as in *Schluss-Satz*, finale.

Schlüssel (Ger., pl. *Schlüssel*). Clef.

Schmelzer, Johann Heinrich (b. Scheibbs, Lower Austria, *c*.1620–23; d. Prague, Mar 1680). Austrian composer. The son of a baker, he somehow arrived in Vienna as a musician, perhaps when still in his teens. He joined the court orchestra as a violinist in 1649 and was appointed chapelmaster just a few months before his death, from plague. For court dramas and festivities he wrote 150 ballet suites, incorporating old dances and character pieces, sometimes with a local tinge. He also wrote sonatas and sacred music. His three sons became violinists under his training.

Schmidt, Franz (b. Pressburg/Bratislava, 22 Dec 1874; d. Perchtoldsdorf, near Vienna, 11 Feb 1939). Austrian composer, of music belatedly and splendidly tonal. In 1888 his family moved to Vienna, and he helped support them by playing the piano in dance schools. In 1890 he entered the conservatory, where his teachers included Bruckner, Fuchs and Hellmesberger (for cello); he also studied with Leschetizky. As a cellist in the opera orchestra (1896–1911), he played for Mahler. Then in 1914 he began a teaching career at the conservatory, of which he became director (1925–7) and rector (1927–31).

As a composer he was slow to enter his stride. *Notre Dame*, his Quasimodo opera, has some characteristically rich orchestral writing, erotic and wistful with elements of gypsy music, but his best works date from his last dozen years – from a time when the sunset of Viennese Romanticism could be recalled with an elegiac glow but also a remarkable fresh energy. His relationship to Brahms and Bruckner parallels Rachmaninoff's to Tchaikovsky.

Harold Truscott *The Music of Franz Schmidt* (1984)
www.franzschmidtgesellschaft.at

Operas: *Notre Dame* (Schmidt and Leopold Wilk, after Hugo), 1902–4, f.p. Vienna, 1914; *Fredigundis* (Bruno Warden and Ignaz Welleminsky), 1916–21, f.p. Berlin, 1922.

Oratorio: *Das Buch mit sieben Siegeln* (Revelation), 1935–7

Orchestral: Symphony No.1, E, 1896–9; No.2, E♭, 1911–13; No.3, A, 1927–8; No.4, C, 1932–3; Concertante Variations on a Theme of Beethoven, pf left hand, orch, 1923; Variations on a Hussar Song, 1930–31; Piano Concerto, E♭, left hand, 1934

Chamber: String Quartet, A, 1925; Piano Quintet, G, 1926; String Quartet, G, 1929; Quintet, B♭, cl, pf, str trio, 1932; Quintet, A, cl, pf, str trio, 1938

Other works: Toccata, D minor, pf left hand, 1938; org music

Schmitt, Florent (b. Blâmont, Meurthe-et-Moselle, 28 Sep 1870; d Neuilly-sur-Seine, 17 Aug 1958). French composer. He studied at the Paris Conservatoire, notably with Massenet, and won the Prix de Rome in 1900. Close to Ravel, he made his name with three big works composed during the next few years: Psalm 47 for soprano, choir and orchestra (1904), the exotic ballet *La Tragédie de Salomé* (1907, revised as a symphonic poem in 1910) and the Piano Quintet (1902–8), all melding influences from Debussy and Strauss. He then worked as a music critic and administrator while amassing a large output of orchestral, large-scale choral and chamber music.

Schnabel, Artur (b. Lipnik, 17 Apr 1882; d. Axenstein, Switzerland, 15 Aug 1951). Austrian–US pianist. The family settled in Vienna when he was seven, and he studied there with Leschetizky and the musicologist Eusebius Mandyczewski. In 1900 he moved to Berlin, and in 1905 he married the contralto Therese Behr, with whom he gave many recitals. He also appeared with some of the great string players of his time, though the centre of his repertory was in Beethoven's piano sonatas, which he played in Berlin in their entirety in the centenary year of 1927 and began recording soon after. For many later musicians his Beethoven was exemplary, as too were his Schubert and Mozart recordings: 'Schnabel represented a way of looking almost directly at the music and bypassing the instrument' (Gould). He had the insight of a composer, one whose works embrace Schoenbergian serialism and include three symphonies, five quartets and a Duodecimet for mixed ensemble. In 1933 he left Berlin; thereafter he worked in Switzerland and the USA.

Artur Schnabel *My Life and Music* (1961, ʳ1988)

Schnebel, Dieter (Wolfgang) (b. Lahr, Baden, 14 Mar 1930). German composer, a persistent ques-

tioner. He studied at the conservatory in Freiburg (1949–52), where Metzger was a classmate; he also went to the Darmstadt summer courses in 1950 and 1951. Then he read music and theology at Tübingen University (1952–5) and was ordained a Lutheran pastor, active as such while also teaching in Kaiserslautern (1955–63), Frankfurt (1963–70), Munich (1970–76) and at the Hofschule der Künste in Berlin (1976–95). A central and influential member of the post-1945 avant-garde, he has been an unusually low-profile one, partly because his interests have been so unconventional, particularly since the late 1960s, when the political situation and his wife's death lent steel to his questioning spirit. His works come in groups, including *für stimmen (... missa est)* (some samples of church music for an atheist age, 1956–68), *Modelle* (music-theatre pieces of 1961–6, e.g. *nostalgie* for conductor), *Räume* (e.g. *MO-NO*, a book of music to be read), *Produktionsprozesse* (e.g. *Maulwerke* for voices and electronics, 1968–74) and *Re-Visionen* (adaptations of Webern, Schubert, etc., 1972–89).

Schneewittchen (Snow-White). Opera by Holliger setting Robert Walser's play. The characters – principally Snow-White (soprano) and the Queen (contralto) – recount the story as long in the past, but as something that still exhausts and disturbs them. First performance: Zurich, 17 Oct 1998.

schnell (Ger.). Fast. Also *schneller*, faster.

Schnittke, Alfred [Schnitke, Alfred Garriyevich] (b. Engels, 24 Nov 1934; d. Hamburg, 3 Aug 1998). Russian composer of colossal, varied and disquieting output. He began his musical studies in Vienna (1946–8), where his German Jewish father was working as a journalist. (His mother was a Volga German.) Then he studied with Nikolay Rakov and Yevgeny Golubev at the Moscow Conservatory (1953–61), where he remained as a teacher until 1972; he also encountered the Second Viennese School through Herschkowitz. His exposure to the traditions of Shostakovich and Schoenberg precipitated a crisis around 1970, an eruption of quotes and references he described as 'polystylistic'. In later works he found different ways to resolve or transcend the conflict between frank expression and modernist subversion, sometimes leaning towards Mahler. After 1985, when he suffered the first in a series of strokes, he became more and more productive. In 1989 he moved to Hamburg.

Alexander Ivashkin *Alfred Schnittke* (1996); Alexander Ivashkin, ed. *A Schnittke Reader* (2002)

www.schnittke.de

Operas: *Life with an Idiot* (Viktor Yerofeyev), 1990–92, f.p. Amsterdam, 1992; *Historia von D. Johann Fausten* (Jörg Morgener and Schnittke), 1981–93, f.p. Hamburg, 1995; *Gesualdo* (Richard Bletschacher), 1992–4, f.p. Vienna, 1995

Symphonies: No.1, 1969–72; No.2 'St Florian', with ch, 1979; No.3, 1981; No.4, ch, chbr orch, 1984; No.5 (Concerto Grosso No.4), 1988; No.6, 1992; No.7, 1993; No.8, 1994; No.9, 1997–8, unfinished

Concerti grossi: No.1, 2 vn, kbds, chbr orch, 1977; No.2, vn, vc, orch, 1981–2; No.3, 2 vn, chbr orch, 1985; No.4 (Symphony No.5), 1988; No.5, vn, orch, 1991; No.6, pf, vn, str, 1993

Other concertos: Piano Concerto, 1960; Music for Piano and Chamber Orchestra, 1964; Concerto, pf, str, 1979; Concerto, pf duet, chbr orch, 1988; Violin Concerto No.1, 1957, rev 1962; No.2, 1966; No.3, 1978; No.4, 1984; Sonata, vn, chbr orch, 1968; *Quasi una sonata*, vn, chbr orch, 1987; Viola Concerto, 1985; *Monologue*, va, str, 1989; Cello Concerto No.1, 1985–6, No.2, 1990; Double Concerto, ob, hp, str, 1971; Concerto for Three, str trio, str, 1994

Other orchestral works: *Pianissimo*, 1968; Passacaglia, 1979–80; *Gogol Suite*, 1980; *(K)ein Sommernachtstraum*, 1985; *Music to an Imagined Play*, 1985; *Peer Gynt* (ballet), 1986; *4 Aphorisms*, chbr orch, 1988; *For Liverpool*, 1994; *Symphonic Prelude*, 1994; etc.

Choral: *Requiem*, soli, ch, ens, 1975; *'Seid nüchtern und wachet ...'* (Faust Cantata), 1982; Concerto, 1984–5; etc.

Chamber and solo: Piano Quintet, 1972–6; String Quartets Nos.1–4, 1966, 1980, 1983, 1989; Piano Quartet, 1988; String Trio, 1985; Piano Trio, 1992; Violin Sonatas Nos.1–3, 1963, 1968, 1994; *Suite in the Old Style*, vn, pf, 1972; Cello Sonatas Nos.1–2, 1978, 1994; *A Paganini*, vn, 1982; Piano Sonatas Nos.1–3, 1987, 1990, 1992; etc.

Cadenzas: to Beethoven's Violin Concerto and several Mozart concertos

Schnorr von Carolsfeld, Ludwig (b. Munich, 2 Jul 1836; d. Dresden, 21 Jul 1865). German tenor. The son of the painter Julius Schnorr von Carolsfeld, he studied at the Leipzig Conservatory and made his debut with the Karlsruhe Opera in 1855. Also in the company was the soprano Malvina Garrigues (1825–1904), whom he married in 1860, the year they moved to Dresden. After much preparation and some doubts they created the central roles in *Tristan und Isolde*. He died six weeks later, and she abandoned her career.

Schobert, Johann (b. ?Silesia, c.1735; d. Paris, 28 Aug 1767). German harpsichordist-composer, author of sonatas and concertos that influenced Mozart. He arrived in Paris in 1760 or 1761. Almost nothing is known of where he came from, and a few years later he was dead, along with his wife and one of his children, from having eaten poisonous mushrooms.

Schoeck, Othmar (b. Brunnen, 1 Sep 1886; d. Zurich, 8 Mar 1957). Swiss composer. He studied at the conservatories of Zurich (1905–7) and Leipzig (with Reger, 1907–8), then returned to Switzerland to work as a composer, conductor and piano accompanist. Working in a late Romantic style, he devoted himself largely to songs, setting words by the German Romantics and his friend Hermann Hesse. Of about 400 such compositions, most were composed before the First World War, including 'Nachruf' (Uhland) and 'Dämmrung senkte sich von oben' (Goethe). His other works include operas on subjects from Holberg (*Don Ranudo*, f.p. Zurich, 1919), Kleist (*Penthesilea*, f.p. Dresden, 1927), Eichendorff (*Das Schloss Dürande*, f.p. Berlin, 1943), etc., and a horn concerto (1951).

Schoenberg [Schönberg], **Arnold (Franz Walter)** (b. Vienna, 13 Sep 1874; d. Los Angeles, 13 Jul 1951). Austrian–US composer. He was, with Stravinsky, one of the essential creators of 20th-century music: he led the way in abandoning tonality (1908). But he was no firebrand revolutionary. His great effort was to change music from within: to respond to pressures coming out of the great Austro–German tradition, and to maintain the guardian criteria of that tradition – in particular its high respect for thematic and harmonic coherence. As a result, his second great innovation, the serialism he introduced in the early 1920s, was in some ways a step back, into orderliness again. In expressive terms he was concerned with extreme psychological states, precisely defined, and with the transcendent, both before and after his formal return to Judaism in 1933, the year he was obliged to leave Berlin.

He was the eldest of three children in an Orthodox Jewish family of modest means. After the death of his father, who had kept a shoe shop, he had to work in a bank to support the family (1891–5). But he pursued his musical interests: he played chamber music with friends, among whom Zemlinsky gave him some lessons, and he composed. His D major String Quartet (1897), unpublished until after his death, is closer to Dvořák than to Brahms (his parents were of Hungarian–Czech origin), but the string sextet *Verklärte Nacht* (1899) is already more earnest, combining a Brahmsian imperative for development (and a Brahmsian medium) with *Tristan* harmony and a Straussian richness of colour. It was as if all the currents of late Romanticism were coming together, in music ripe and effulgent, and he pursued that style in songs, not least the *Gurrelieder* he later orchestrated.

In 1901 he married Zemlinsky's sister Mathilde and moved to Berlin, where he worked in the

Überbrettl cabaret theatre and wrote the symphonic poem *Pelleas und Melisande* (1902–3), a gorgeous, impassioned story of love and jealousy close to Strauss. Strauss was impressed, and got him his first teaching job, at the Stern Conservatory; he now had a child to support, Gertrud (b. 1902), but in 1903 he returned to Vienna, where he taught privately, Berg and Webern becoming his pupils the next year. Also in 1903 *Verklärte Nacht* was performed for the first time and his music began to be published.

His style now developed rapidly, within his preferred sphere of chamber music. In his First Quartet (1905) and First Chamber Symphony (1906) – for a radically compact orchestra of 15 soloists – the music presses through the usual four movements in one continuous span, with harmonic progress sometimes so fast the sense of key is endangered. The line against chaos is being held, but only just. Then in 1908, in the last movement of his Second Quartet and song cycle *Das Buch der hängenden Gärten*, he took what seemed the inevitable next step, relinquished tonality altogether, and discovered that what happened was not chaos but luminous calm and intensity of experience, not the rapid flux of his earlier music but stopped time. In both cases the break came to words by Stefan George, in the quartet (with soprano) at the opening line 'I feel air from other planets'.

He found his new musical air thoroughly breathable. Within little more than a year he completed the song cycle and composed sets of pieces for piano (Op.11) and orchestra (Op.16), as well as a short solo opera, *Erwartung*. Forms from the past, all dependent on repetition, were replaced by rushes of constant change or moments of stillness, with superb freedom of orchestral sound in *Erwartung* and the Op.16 pieces. The music spoke of creative exuberance and adventure – exuberance and adventure that splashed out also into painting (often of staring faces) and writing (visionary texts for music). It spoke too of the emotional turbulence in which its composer was living. Having given birth to a son, Georg, in 1906, his wife began an affair with the painter Richard Gerstl. Schoenberg demanded an end to the liaison, Mathilde complied, and Gerstl killed himself.

After the first wave of atonal pieces Schoenberg's productivity slowed. He returned with his family to Berlin (1911–15), where he wrote *Pierrot lunaire* and made his conducting debut at its first performance. He then served in the Austrian army (1915–16) before starting his oratorio *Die Jakobsleiter*, the unfinished testimony to the religious direction his thoughts were taking. Meanwhile, now back in Vienna, he was working his way towards the principles of serialism while teaching and running a concert series devoted to new music, the SOCIETY FOR PRIVATE MUSICAL PERFORMANCES, staffed by his growing circle of pupils and former pupils. In 1923, after a decade of slack compositional achievement, he completed his first serial works, Opp.23–5. That same year Mathilde died, and 10 months later he married Gertrud Kolisch, again a sister of a musical friend, the quartet leader Rudolf Kolisch.

In 1925 he was called back again to Berlin to take over Busoni's master classes at the Prussian Academy of the Arts. There he worked with confidence, producing chamber works, orchestral pieces, choruses and a comic opera, all in the 12-note system and with strong references to the past: his Third Quartet, for instance, is in the usual four movements, and his orchestral masterpiece of this period is a set of symphonic variations. He also wrote the first two acts of his opera *Moses und Aron*.

This productive period came to an end in 1933, when his Jewishness became a political issue. He immediately left the academy for Paris, where he reaffirmed his Jewish faith. Within the year he moved on to the USA, and in 1934 settled in Los Angeles for health reasons. His second family by now included a daughter, Nuria (b. 1932), later the wife of Luigi Nono; two sons, Ronald and Lawrence, were born in California.

He remained in Los Angeles for the rest of his life, for by the end of the war he was too ill to accept the invitations that came to return to Europe or settle in Israel. He continued to teach, at UCLA (1936–44), and to compose, now more variously. In 1932–4 he had returned to tonal composition, first in updating Baroque concertos, then in writing original pieces (the Suite in G for strings), and from this point tonal and serial compositions alternated in his output. He was able to go back to an earlier style in belatedly completing his Second Chamber Symphony, and his serial pieces began to admit strongly tonal elements (*Ode to Napoleon*) or at least to embrace smoother harmony and a more traditional feeling for continuity (Piano Concerto). There was also a return to the expressive intensity of 1908–9, especially in the String Trio and *A Survivor from Warsaw*. Several other late works he voiced as prayers, whether on liturgical texts (*Kol nidre*) or with his own words, as in his unfinished last piece, *Modern Psalm*.

Throughout his career he was faced with rejection and hostility; even *Verklärte Nacht* was at first turned down because it contained an inadmissible chord, and a public concert he conducted in Vienna in 1913, with works of his own and his pupils, was disrupted by the outraged audience (surely including many people who, just five weeks before, had cheered the première of *Gurrelieder*). But opposition only confirmed his sense of mission. He saw a task, that of passing on to the future what he had received from the masters he revered (Mozart and Brahms above all): a musical language continuously and organically developing, capable of sustaining formal complexity and richness of expression. He undertook that task. And if the resulting music can be craggy and defensive, it is much more often generous and sure. It is not comfortable. But it speaks with a rare certainty.

Charles Rosen *Schoenberg* (1975); Arnold Schoenberg *Style and Idea*, ed. Leonard Stein (1975); Allen Shawn *Arnold Schoenberg's Journey* (2002)

www.schoenberg.at

Operas: ERWARTUNG, Op.17, 1909; *Die* GLÜCKLICHE HAND, Op.18, 1910–13; VON HEUTE AUF MORGEN, Op.32, 1928–9; *Moses und Aron* (see MOSES), 1926–32

Vocal orchestral: 6 Songs (Heinrich Hart, Des Knaben Wunderhorn, Petrarch), Op.8, s, orch, 1903–5; GURRELIEDER, soli, ch, orch, 1900–11; *Lied der Waldtaube* (*Song of the Wood Dove*) from *Gurrelieder*, mez, chbr orch, arr 1922; 4 Songs (Stefan George, Rilke), Op.22, mez, orch, 1913–16; *Die* JAKOBSLEITER, soli, ch, orch, 1916–17; KOL NIDRE, Op.39, speaker, ch, orch, 1938; Prelude 'Genesis', Op.44, ch, orch, 1945; *A* SURVIVOR FROM WARSAW, Op.46, speaker, ch, orch, 1947; MODERN PSALM, Op.50c, speaker, ch, orch, 1950

Orchestral (full): *Pelleas und Melisande* (see PELLEAS ET MELISANDE), Op.5, 1902–3; Chamber Symphony No.1, Op.9, arr 1922, rev 1935; 5 Pieces, Op.16, 1909; Variations, Op.31, 1926–8; *Begleitmusik zu einer Lichtspielszene* (*Accompaniment to a Film Scene*), Op.34, 1929–30; CELLO CONCERTO (after G.M. Monn), 1932–3; String Quartet Concerto (after Handel), 1933; Violin Concerto, Op.36, 1935–6; Chamber Symphony No.2, 1906–39; PIANO CONCERTO, Op.42, 1942; Theme and Variations, Op.43a, concert band, 1943, arr orch, Op.43b, 1943

Orchestrations: songs (Beethoven, Loewe, Schubert), 1912; 2 Chorale Preludes (Bach), 1922, Prelude and Fugue, E♭ (Bach), 1928; Piano Quartet, G minor (Brahms), 1937

Orchestral (strings): Gavotte and Musette, 1897; VERKLÄRTE NACHT, Op.4, arr 1917, rev 1943; String Quartet No.2, Op.10, with s, arr ?1919; Suite, G, 1934

Choral (small-scale): 2 Canons (Goethe), 1905; *Friede auf Erden* (C.F. Meyer), Op.13, 1907; *Der deutsche Michel* (Ottokar Kernstock), men's ch, 1915–16; 4 Pieces (Schoenberg, Bethge), Op.27, 1925; 3 Satires (Schoenberg), Op.28, 1925; 3 Folksongs, 1929; 6 Pieces (Schoenberg), men's ch, Op.35, 1929–30; 3 Folksongs, Op.49, 1948; *Dreimal tausend Jahre*

(D.D. Runes), Op.50a, 1949; *De profundis* (Psalm 130 in Hebrew), Op.50b, 1950; other canons

String quartets: D, 1897; No.1, D minor, Op.7, 1904–5; No.2, F♯ minor, with s in movts 3–4 (George), Op.10, 1907–8; No.3, Op.30, 1927; No.4, Op.37, 1936

Other chamber works: VERKLÄRTE NACHT, str sextet, Op.4, 1899; CHAMBER SYMPHONY No.1, E, Op.9, 15 insts, 1906; 3 Pieces, 12 insts, 1910; *Die eiserne Brigade*, pf qnt, 1916; Serenade, Op.24, cl, b cl, mand, gtr, str trio, with b in song (Petrarch), 1920–23; *Weihnachtsmusik*, 2 vn, vc, hmnm, pf, 1921; Suite, Op.29, 3 cl, pf, str trio, 1925–6; String Trio, Op.45, 1946; Phantasy, Op.47, vn, pf, 1949; canons

Chamber arrangements: *Kaiser-Walzer* (Johann Strauss II), fl, cl, pf qnt, 1925; other works by Johann Strauss II and Schubert

Songs: Op.1 (2; Karl von Levetzow), ?1898; Op.2 (4), 1899; *Brettl Lieder* (8, for cabaret; Hugo Salus, Gustav Falke, Colly, Gustav Hochstetter, Otto Julius Bierbaum, Wedekind, Schikaneder), 1901; Op.3 (6; Des Knaben Wunderhorn, Gottfried Keller, Dehmel, Jacobsen, Hermann Lingg), 1899–1903; Op.6 (8; Julius Hart, Dehmel, Paul Remer, Hermann Conradi, Keller, John Henry Mackay, Kurt Aram, Nietzsche), 1903–5; Op.12 (2; Heinrich Ammann, Viktor Klemperer), 1907; Op.14 (2; George, Georg Henckel), 1907; *Das* BUCH DER HÄNGENDEN GÄRTEN, Op.15, 1908–9; 'Am Strande' (Rilke), 1909; *Herzgewächse* (Maeterlinck), Op.20, s, cel, hp, hmnm, 1911; 4 Folksongs, 1929; Op.48 (3; Jakob Haringer), 1933; other early songs

Recitations: PIERROT LUNAIRE, Op.21, 1912; *Ode to Napoleon* (Byron), Op.41, with pf qnt, 1942

Piano: 3 Pieces, Op.11, 1909; 6 Little Pieces, Op.19, 1911; 5 Pieces, Op.23, 1920–23; Suite, Op.25, 1921–3; Piece, Op.33a, 1928–9; Piece, Op.33b, 1931

Organ: Variations on a Recitative, Op.40, 1941

Schoenberg Ensemble. Amsterdam modern-music ensemble founded in 1974 by Reinbert de Leeuw, its continuing chief conductor.

schola cantorum (Lat., school of singers). Term used of the papal choir in the early Middle Ages and often assumed by later choirs, as well as by the college founded by d'Indy and others in Paris in 1894.

Scholl, Andreas (b. Eltville, 10 Nov 1967). German countertenor of supreme accomplishment. Following family tradition, he began singing in the ancient choir of Kiedrich, after which he studied with Jacobs in Basle (1987–93), where he began teaching in 2000. He has performed with the leading early music groups, in solo recital and occasionally in opera.

schöne Müllerin, Die (The Fair Maid of the Mill). Song cycle by Schubert to 20 poems by Wilhelm

Müller, comprising a narrative of love and loss. The songs are delivered mostly in the voice of a wayfaring young man. Beginning with a simple paean to the travelling life in 'Das Wandern', he follows a brook, comes to a mill, enjoys a love affair with a girl there, loses her to a rival, and returns away, with some bitterness in his heart that sleep will heal as the last song is sung by the brook (often prominent in the accompaniment). As published, the music supposes a tenor voice, but the work is often sung in transposition by baritones and basses, much less often by women, since the persona is so particularly male. There was no precedent for a song cycle on this scale – though there was soon a successor, in Schubert's own *Winterreise*.

school music. Music to be performed in music class, usually by children with limited training. See also CHILDREN'S MUSIC; EDUCATION.

Schoolmaster, Der (*Der Schulmeister*). Name given to Haydn's Symphony No.55, possibly with his approval, on account of the dotted figure in the slow movement that suggests the teacher's cautioning finger.

Schopenhauer, Arthur (b. Danzig, 22 Feb 1788; d. Frankfurt, 21 Sep 1860). German philosopher, author of *The World as Will and Representation* (1818), in which he held that reality is a single will to existence, and that music uniquely expresses that will: 'the composer reveals the innermost nature of the world, and expresses the profoundest wisdom in a language that his reasoning faculty does not understand.' Wagner's reading of Schopenhauer in 1854 was crucial.

Schöpfung, Die. See *The* CREATION.

Schöpfungsmesse (Creation Mass). Fifth of Haydn's late masses, which quotes from *The Creation*. First performance: Eisenstadt, 13 Sep 1801.

Schott. Music publishing firm founded in Mainz, probably in 1780, by Bernard Schott (1748–1809) and continued by his sons Johann Andreas (1781–1840) and Johann Joseph (1782–1855); hence the official name B. Schott's Söhne. During its first half century the company had connections with Mozart (first vocal score of *Don Giovanni*) and Beethoven (*Missa solemnis*, Ninth Symphony, Op.127 and Op.131 quartets). Johann Andreas's son Franz Philipp (1811–74) and his heir Ludwig Strecker (1853–1943) published Wagner's *Ring*, *Meistersinger* and *Parsifal*. Later composers to have been associated closely with the house include Hindemith, Henze and Ligeti. The company also publishes periodicals and records (on the Wergo label).

Schottische (Ger., Scottish). Ballroom dance in 2/4, having connections with the polka, the waltz and possibly also the écossaise (which would provide the only link of any kind with Scotland). It was introduced to Britain in 1848.

Schreier, Peter (b. Meissen, 29 Jul 1935). German tenor, of such style and grain that he excelled in Mozart, Bach and lieder. He studied from 1959 at the school of the Dresden Staatsoper, where he made his debut in 1961. His Met debut in 1967 (Tamino) came near the start of his international career. In 1970 he began conducting, and this activity became more important as he reduced his vocal appearances, retiring from opera in 2000.

Schreker, Franz (August Julius) (b. Monaco, 23 Mar 1878; d. Berlin, 21 Mar 1934). Austrian composer, creating music of dappled decadence alongside and distinct from both Strauss and Schoenberg. A court photographer's son, he studied with Fuchs at the Vienna Conservatory (1892–1900) and taught from 1912 at the academy there. Also a conductor, he gave the first performance of Schoenberg's *Gurrelieder* in 1913. His own creative powers were established by his opera *Der ferne Klang*, which draws on Strauss, Mahler and Debussy to create a rich milieu for the dramatization of sensuality. (Berg made the piano score and learned something.) The more Wagnerian *Die Gezeichneten* and *Der Schatzgräber* confirmed his reputation, and in 1920 he was invited to Berlin to direct the conservatory. His later operas took on some Hindemith-style neoclassicism, but, as a Jew in an increasingly Nazi environment, he suffered attack, and when the Nazis came to power he was dismissed from his teaching post. His music remained in eclipse until the time of his centenary.

Christopher Hailey *Franz Schreker* (1993)

www.schreker.org

Operas (all but the first to his own librettos):
  Flammen (Dora Leen), Op.10, 1901–2; *Der* FERNE KLANG, *c.*1903–10; *Das Spielwerk und die Prinzessin*, 1908–12, f.p. Frankfurt and Vienna, 1913; *Die Gezeichneten*, 1913–15, f.p. Frankfurt, 1918; *Der Schatzgräber*, 1915–18, f.p. Frankfurt, 1920; *Irrelohe*, 1919–22, f.p. Cologne, 1924; *Der singende Teufel*, 1924–8, f.p. Berlin, 1928; *Christophorus*, 1925–9, f.p. Freiburg, 1978; *Der Schmied von Gent*, 1929–32, f.p. Berlin, 1932
Orchestral: *Ekkehard* (overture), Op.12, 1902–3; Romantic Suite, Op.14, 1903; Fantastic Overture,

Op.15, 1904; *Der Geburtstag der Infantin* (ballet), chbr orch, 1908; *Valse lente*, *c*.1908; Chamber Symphony, 23 insts, 1916; etc.

Other works: songs, partsongs, piano pieces

Schröder-Devrient, Wilhelmine (b. Hamburg, 6 Dec 1804; d. Coburg, 26 Jan 1860). German soprano. The daughter of a baritone and an actress, she was on stage when she was 11 and made her operatic debut as Pamina in Vienna at 16. During the period of her greatest success, from 1822 into the mid 1830s, she appeared in major houses from Vienna and Dresden to Paris and London, and was remarked upon for her dramatic vividness, notably as Beethoven's Leonore (a performance for which she received his thanks). Later, in the few years before she retired from the stage at 43, she was the first Adriano (in *Rienzi*), Senta and Venus for Wagner in Dresden. Her husbands were an actor, an officer and a baron; with the first of these she had four children.

Schroeter, Johann Samuel (b. ?Güben, *c*.1752; d. London, 2 Nov 1788). German pianist-composer. He and his siblings were encouraged by their father, a professional oboist. Corona Elisabeth Wilhelmine Schröter (1751–1802) was a singer-actress who impressed Goethe and was close to Schiller; she set poems by both men as songs. Johann Heinrich Schröter was a violinist who mysteriously vanished in his mid-20s, and Marie Henriette Schröter a singer at the Darmstadt court. Corona, Johann Samuel and Johann Heinrich all appeared in London in 1772, and Johann Samuel stayed on when the others left. He was introduced at court by J.C. Bach, whom he succeeded in 1782 as music master to Queen Charlotte – though only briefly, until he eloped to Scotland with one of his students. That did not prevent him from gaining the favour of the Prince of Wales, but this time death intervened. Rebecca, the eloper made widow, studied with Haydn during his first London visit and became his passionate friend, if not his mistress; she was rewarded with the dedication of three piano trios. Her late husband was noted as a light and graceful pianist, and was credited by Burney with bringing the true art of the piano to England. He wrote 12 concertos (for three of which Mozart composed cadenzas) and sonatas.

Schubart, Christian Friedrich Daniel (b. Obersontheim, Swabia, 24 Mar 1739; d. Stuttgart, 10 Oct 1791). German writer and composer. After a failed attempt by his parents to have him study theology, he embarked on an artistic career of fitful success. The Duke of Württemberg, whose court he had served in various musical capacities since 1769, banished him in 1773 and had him imprisoned in 1777, apparently for insulting the ducal mistress. He spent 10 years in confinement and wrote much, then ended his days in poor health as court and theatre poet in Stuttgart. His study of musical aesthetics, published in Vienna in 1806, was widely read, not least by Beethoven and Schubert (who set four of his poems, including 'Die Forelle' and 'An mein Klavier'). His compositions, chiefly songs to his own words, show his proto-Romantic spirit and admiration for folksong.

Schubert, Franz (Peter) (b. Vienna, 31 Jan 1797; d. Vienna, 19 Nov 1828). Austrian composer. Music flowed from him. In a creative life of only 15 years or so, he must have completed a song or instrumental movement every few days on average. And the effortlessness can be heard. His music makes itself felt with an unusual intimacy, even, at most times, quietness. He had no success with genres requiring rhetorical force, notably opera (which he repeatedly attempted) and the concerto (which he did not). But his peerlessness as a song writer has long been acknowledged, and he found his own ways – around the immense presence of Beethoven in the same city – to address large-scale instrumental form.

The son of a schoolmaster, he grew up in an affectionate family with three elder brothers and a younger sister. His first lessons came from his father and eldest brother, but by the age of nine or 10 he had progressed so far that his father placed him with a professional organist, Michael Holzer. In 1808 he was admitted to the imperial chapel choir, and so to a boarding place at the city's principal school. There he was encouraged by Josef von Spaun, a young student who became a lifelong friend; some compositions survive from when he was 13 or 14. When he was 15 his mother died. Also that year his voice broke, though he was able to remain at school. By this time he was writing songs and quartets (for a family ensemble), besides exercises for Salieri, his teacher from June 1812.

In the autumn of 1813 he left school for a year at a teacher-training college, after which he began teaching alongside his father: he had been exempted from military service on grounds of height – he was under the minimum of five feet (1.5m) – and was already wearing glasses. He went on seeing Salieri until the end of 1816, but by the autumn of 1814, when he wrote 'Gretchen am Spinnrade', he was his own man as a composer, still only 17.

Important works of 1815 include his Third Symphony and Mass in B♭, as well as 150 songs, including 'Erlkönig'. There were days when he wrote eight songs; 5 July, though not so prodigious, saw three notable Goethe settings: 'Wandrers Nachtlied', 'Der Fischer' and 'Erster Verlust'. The same year he was befriended by Franz von Schober, a law student, who helped supply him with song texts, as did another youthful friend, Johann Mayrhofer. Schober also kept encouraging him to give up teaching in order to devote himself to composition.

His first step, in May 1816, was to move out of the family home into lodgings with another friend. Spaun, meanwhile, had sent a bunch of his Goethe songs to the poet, but the latter was not impressed, and his music continued to have a private, domestic circulation, most importantly at the evenings ('Schubertiads' they came to be called) when friends would gather around the composer at his piano. By the end of 1816 – when he left his teaching job and moved in with Schober's mother – the Schubertiad repertory included a host more songs and three violin sonatas, while other works of the year had included the Fourth and Fifth Symphonies.

In 1817 Schober introduced to Schubert the operatic baritone Johann Michael Vogl, who became his first eminent performer. Now 20 and at liberty, he wrote numerous songs that year, including 'Der Tod und das Mädchen' (Death and the Maiden) and 'Die Forelle' (The Trout), as well as piano sonatas and other instrumental works. But by November he had returned to his father's home and school. Around the same time he reacted to the Rossini craze in Vienna by writing two overtures 'in the Italian style', the second of which brought him his first concert performance, in March 1818. In the meantime he had moved with his father to a new house and a new school, and for once his productivity slowed down.

Escape came in July 1818 with the offer of a position as music master to the two daughters of Count Johann Esterházy at Zseliz, the family's summer residence in Hungary. He returned with them to Vienna in November, and took lodgings with Mayrhofer. Nearness intensified their collaboration. The following summer he spent three months with Vogl in Steyr and the surrounding countryside, where he began the 'Trout' Quintet to a commission from a local patron. A year later, in June 1820, he had his first big public performance when his one-act opera Die Zwillingsbrüder was staged. As a result he was asked to write incidental music for Die Zauberharfe, presented two months later and projecting in its score a new, fuller orchestral voice. By the end of the year he had found a similar combination of lyrical urgency and harmonic depth in the 'Quartettsatz', the first movement of an unfinished

quartet in C minor. Leaving works incomplete was something of a habit, encouraged by the unusually private nature of his creative life, and by the fact that he was almost always writing for himself, not to a commission or for a forthcoming concert.

Early in 1821 he left Mayrhofer's place; he also found new friends – the young painter Moritz von Schwind and later the writer Eduard von Bauernfeld – with whom he formed a close trio. In February 1821 came the magnificent setting of Goethe's Gesang der Geister über den Wassern for men's voices and low strings., followed by his first publications, instigated by a group of his friends: 'Erlkönig' started the series, on 31 March 1821, to be followed by 19 more songs by the end of the year. (Publications of the following year included the Variations on a French Song dedicated to Beethoven 'by his admirer and worshipper Franz Schubert'.) But he was composing far faster than the presses could run. Schober took him to stay with relations in the summer at Atzenbrugg (where he wrote waltzes) and in September–October at Ochsenburg, near St Pölten (where the two of them worked at an opera, Alfonso und Estrella). He then moved in with Schober from the start of 1822, and Alfonso was finished, but turned down by the theatres to which it was submitted.

More songs were published that year, and more composed. There were also bigger achievements: the Mass in A♭ (September), the 'Unfinished' Symphony (October) and the work for which that work was set aside, the 'Wanderer' Fantasy for piano (November). But at the end of the year he fell ill with syphilis, and left Schober's for his father's house. The following summer he was in Linz and Steyr again, recuperating. When he returned to Vienna he completed a new opera, Fierrabras, which again was rejected. By the end of 1823 he had composed the song cycle Die schöne Müllerin and incidental music for Rosamunde.

Early in 1824 came a return to chamber music with the Octet and the quartets in A minor and D minor ('Death and the Maiden'). Some of his youthful friends were moving away, geographically and personally, and their absence, together with his illness, turned him towards regret and nostalgia. Going to Zseliz again that summer with the Esterházy family did not help, though some works for piano duet resulted. The following summer, that of 1825, he spent with Vogl again in and around Steyr, composing the Piano Sonata in D, starting the 'Great C major' Symphony, and completing a group of songs from Walter Scott's The Lady of the Lake.

Works of the next year, 1826, include Shakespeare songs, the Piano Sonata in G and the extraordinarily intense String Quartet in G. He applied for a post as vice-director of the imperial chapel, but failed to get it. Happier occasions were the convivial evenings with friends, making music or spending time in cafés and inns. With some of his friends he visited the dying Beethoven on 19 March 1827; this was their only meeting. At Beethoven's funeral he was one of the 36 torch bearers. In September he visited Graz with a friend, then returned to Vienna to complete *Winterreise* and compose the Piano Trio in E♭.

The first part of *Winterreise* was published in January 1828, the second in the following December, posthumously. As his syphilitic condition worsened he dived on with tireless creative energy. On 26 March 1828 he and his friends put on a public concert of his works in Vienna, including mostly new music: songs, choruses, the E♭ trio. The event made little stir. Soon afterwards he completed the Fantasy in F minor for piano duet, and in the summer he started the E♭ Mass and some songs to new poets: Ludwig Rellstab and Heine. In September he moved in with his brother Ferdinand, and as his health declined further, so his creativity only quickened, to an almost unbelievable degree. Three last piano sonatas date from the month of his move, and the String Quintet must have been written around the same time. In October he went on a short walking tour with Ferdinand and a couple of friends. Shortly after their return his syphilis entered its terminal stage.

He was buried near Beethoven. In the months of grief following his death, his friends clubbed together to raise money for a monument, to bear an epitaph by Franz Grillparzer: 'The art of music here entombed a rich possession, but even fairer hopes.'

Those hopes – dashed hopes for what Schubert might have achieved if he had lived another 40 years, like his near contemporaries Rossini and Berlioz – remain maddening and bewildering. In practical terms, though, the supply of his music did continue during this period, as publishers began bringing out songs and chamber pieces, while Schumann promoted the 'Great C major' Symphony. Even so, a lot of compositions were printed for the first time only in the complete edition of 1884–97, and it was left to the 20th century to discover the weight of the late piano sonatas – and the delightfulness of the early symphonies.

As for the obscurities in the biographical record, they began to be examined more thoroughly around the time of his bicentenary. In particular, his long record of warm male friendships and his links (albeit indirect) with homosexual circles could now be discussed, and the possible effect on his music considered.

Crucial to that music is melody, in his instrumental music as much as his songs – and in the instrumental music within the songs, i.e. the piano accompaniments, which often have their own lyrical persona, at once within and outside the fictional character who sings. Schubert's melody was manifold. It could be fresh and short-phrased, like a folksong, or dramatic and declamatory, or rolling on. But it always suggested a voice, a person feeling and expressing.

This essentially vocal manner gives Schubert's great instrumental works (essentially those written in or after 1820) an unusual character. They are the reports of an imaginary being – one with whom the composer surely identified – exposed to a world that may be comforting or hostile, conveying its comfort or hostility in harmonic terms. Schubert was a great innovator in this respect, capable of luxuriant support but also of alarming dissonances and of progressions into remote keys, thanks to his way of switching from major to minor or moving between tonalities separated by the interval of a third. Complicated and often lengthened by such procedures, movements and works rarely have their ends fully in sight. Rather, each piece is a journey, made by a composer who found his reflection in so many song texts as the wanderer.

John Reed *The Schubert Song Companion* (1985, '1997); Elizabeth Norman McKay *Franz Schubert* (1996); Brian Newbould *Schubert* (1997)

Schubert's works are often identified by D numbers, from the catalogue originated by Otto Erich Deutsch.

Theatre music

Operas: *Des Teufels Lustschloss* (August von Kotzebue), D.84, 1813–14; *Die Bürgschaft*, D.435, 1816, unfinished; ALFONSO UND ESTRELLA, D.732, 1821–2; FIERRABRAS, D.796, 1823; other sketches and fragments

Singspiels: *Der vierjährige Posten* (1 act; Theodor Körner), D.190, 1815; *Fernando* (1 act; Albert Stadler), D.220, 1815; *Claudine von Villa Bella* (Goethe), D.239, 1815, acts 2–3 lost; *Die Freunde von Salamanka* (Johann Mayrhofer), D.326, 1815–16; *Die Zwillingsbrüder* (Georg von Hofmann), D.647, 1818–19; *Die Verschworenen* (Ignaz Castelli), D.787, 1822–3

Incidental music: *Die* ZAUBERHARFE, D.644, 1820; ROSAMUNDE, D.797, 1823

Orchestral music

Symphonies: No.1, D, D.82, 1813; No.2, B♭, D.125, 1814–15; No.3, D, D.200, 1815; No.4 'Tragic', C minor, D.417, 1816; No.5, B♭, D.485, 1816; No.6, C, D.589, 1817–18; No.7, E, draft, 1821; No.8 'UNFINISHED', B minor, D.759, 1822; No.9 'GREAT C MAJOR', D.944, ?1825–8; D, sketches, ?1828

Other works: *Konzertstück*, D, D.345, vn, orch, 1816;

Rondo, A, D.438, vn, str, 1816; Overture, B♭, D.470, 1816; Overture, D, 1817; Polonaise, B♭, vn, orch, 1817; Overture in the Italian Style, D, D.590, 1817; Overture in the Italian Style, C, D.591, 1817; Overture, E minor, D.648, 1819

Choral music

Oratorio: LAZARUS, D.689, 1820, unfinished

Masses (all for soli, ch, orch): No.1, F, D.105, 1814; No.2, G, D.167, 1815; No.3, B♭, D.324, 1815; No.4, C, D.452, 1816; No.5, A♭, D.678, 1819–22; No.6, E♭, D.950, 1828

Other church music: *Salve regina*, B♭, D.106, t, orch, 1814; *Totus in corde langueo*, C, D.136, s/t, orch, ?1815; *Stabat mater*, G minor, D.175, ch, orch, 1815; *Magnificat*, C, D.486, soli, ch, orch, 1815; *Stabat mater*, F major-minor, D.383, soli, ch, orch, 1816; *Salve regina*, B♭, D.386, ch, 1816; *Salve regina*, A, D.676, s, str, 1819; *Salve regina*, C, D.811, men's ch, 1824; *Deutsche Messe*, D.872, ch, orch, 1827; *Tantum ergo*, E♭, D.962, soli, ch, orch, 1828; *Intende voci*, B♭, D.963, t, ch, orch, 1828; etc.

Secular choral (mixed voices, with piano except where stated): *Hymne an den Unendlichen* (Schiller), D.232, 1815; *An die Sonne* (Johann Peter Uz), D.439, 1816; *Gebet* (Friedrich de la Motte Fouqué), D.815, 1824; *Gott im Ungewitter* (Uz), D.985, ?1827; *Gott der Weltschöpfer* (Uz), D.986, ?1827; *Mirjams Siegesgesang* (Franz Grillparzer), D.942, 1828; Psalm 92 (Hebrew), D.953, unaccompanied, 1828; etc.

Secular choral (women's voices, with piano): Psalm 23 (Ger.), D.706, 1820; *Gott in der Natur* (Ewald Kleist), D.757, 1822; *Coronach* (Adam Storck, after Scott), D.836, 1825; *Ständchen* (Grillparzer), D.920, with solo a, 1827; etc.

Secular choral (men's voices, with instrumental ensemble): GESANG DER GEISTER ÜBER DEN WASSERN (Goethe), D.714, with low str, 1821; *Nachtgesang im Walde* (Johann Gabriel Seidl), D.913, with hn qt, 1827

Secular choral (men's voices, with piano): *La pastorella al prato* (Goldoni), D.513, ?1817; *Das Dörfchen* (Gottfried August Bürger), D.598, 1818; *Im gegenwärtigen Vergangenen* (Goethe), D.710, ?1821; *Die Nachtigall* (Johann Karl Unger), D.724, 1821; *Frühlingsgesang* (Franz von Schober), D.740, 1822; *Geist der Liebe* (Friedrich von Matthisson), D.747, 1822; *Gondelfahrer* (Mayrhofer), D.809, 1824; *Wiederspruch* (Seidl), D.865, ?1826; *Mondenschein* (Schober), D.875, 1826; *Nachthelle* (Seidl), D.892, 1826; *Ständchen* (Grillparzer), D.920, with solo a, 1827; etc.

Secular choral (men's voices, unaccompanied): *Die Einsiedelei* (Johann Gaudenz von Salis-Seewis), D.337, c.1816; *Sehnsucht* (Goethe), D.656, 1819; *Grab und Mond* (Seidl), D.893, 1826; *Liebe* (Schiller), D.983a, ?1822; *Die Nacht*, D.983c, ?1822; etc.

Chamber music

String quartets: No.1, G minor-B♭, D.18, 1812; No.2, C, D.32, 1812; No.3, B♭, D.36, 1812–13; No.4, C, D.46, 1813; No.5, B♭, D.68, 1813, first movement

and finale; No.6, D, D.74, 1813; No.7, D, D.94, 1811/12; No.8, B♭, D.112, 1814; No.9, G minor, D.173, 1815; No.10, E♭, D.87, 1813; No.11, E, D.353, 1816; No.12 'Quartettsatz', C minor, D.703, 1820, unfinished; No.13 'ROSAMUNDE', A minor, D.804, 1824; No.14 'DEATH AND THE MAIDEN', D minor, D.810, 1824; No.15, G, D.887, 1826

Violin sonatas: D, D.384, 1816; A minor, D.385, 1816; G minor, D.408, 1816 (these 3 pubd as sonatinas); A, D.574, 1817; Rondo brillant, B minor, D.895, 1826; Fantasy, C, D.934, 1827

Other works: 'TROUT' Quintet, A, D.667, pf, vn, va, vc, db, 1819; Octet, F, D.803, cl, hn, bn, str qt, db, 1824; 'ARPEGGIONE' Sonata, D.821, arpeggione, pf, 1824 (usually played on cello); Notturno, E♭, D.897, pf trio, ?1828; Piano Trio, B♭, D.898, ?1828; Piano Trio, E♭, D.929, 1827; String Quintet, C, D.956, str qt and vc, 1828; etc.

Piano music

Sonatas: E, D.157, 1815, unfinished; C, D.279, 1815; E, D.459, 1816; A minor, D.537, 1817; A♭, D.557, 1817; E minor, D.566, 1817; E♭, D.568, 1817; B, D.575, 1817; F minor, D.625, 1818, unfinished; A, D.664, 1819/25; A minor, D.784, 1823; C 'Reliquie', D.840, 1825, unfinished; A minor, D.845, 1825; D, D.850, 1825; G, D.894, 1826; C minor, D.958, 1828; A, D.959, 1828; B♭, D.960, 1828

Other solo pieces: 12 Waltzes, D.145, 1815–21; 2 Scherzos, B♭, D♭, D.593, 1817; 'Grazer' Fantasy, C, D.605a ?1818; March, E, D.606, ?1818; Adagio, E, D.612, 1818; Variation on a Waltz by Diabelli, C minor, D.718, 1821; 'WANDERER' Fantasy, C, D.760, 1822; *Valses sentimentales* (34), D.779, c.1823; 6 Moments Musicaux, C, A♭, F minor, C♯ minor, F minor, A♭, D.780, 1823–8; German Dances (16), D.783, 1823–4; Hungarian Melody, D.817, 1824; German Dances (6), D.820, 1824; 4 Impromptus, C minor, E♭, G♭, A♭, D.899, 1827; Allegretto, C minor, D.915, 1827; 4 Impromptus, F minor, A♭, B♭, F minor, D.935, 1827; 3 Piano Pieces (Impromptus), E♭ minor, E♭, C, D.946, 1828; *Valses nobles* (12), D.969, 1827; etc.

Duets: Rondo, D, D.608, 1818; Sonata, B♭, D.617, 1818; 8 Variations on a French Song, E minor, D.624, 1818; *Trois marches militaires*, D.733, ?1818; Sonata 'Grand Duo', C, D.812, 1824; Variations on an Original Theme, A♭, D.813, 1824; 4 Ländler, D.814, 1824; *Divertissement à l'hongroise*, D.818, ?1824; *Six grandes marches*, D.819, ?1824; *Divertissement sur des motifs originaux français*, E minor, D.823, c.1825; *Grande marche héroïque*, D.885, 1826; Fantasy, F minor, D.940, 1828; Allegro 'Lebensstürme', A minor, D.947, 1828; Rondo, A, D.951, 1828; Introduction, Variations on an Original Theme and Finale, B♭, D.968a, ?1824; *Deux marches caractéristiques*, D.968b, ?1826; etc.

Songs

Cycles: *Die SCHÖNE MÜLLERIN*, D.795, 1823; WINTERREISE, D.911, 1827.

Collection: SCHWANENGESANG, D.957, 1828

Others: 'Abendstern' (Mayrhofer), D.806, 1824; 'Die

abgeblühte Linde' (István Széchényi), D.514, 1817;
'Ach um deine feuchten Schwingen' (*Suleika II*;
?Marianne von Willemer), D.717, 1821; 'Die
Allmacht' (Ladislaus Pyrker), D.852, 1825; 'Am
Bach im Frühlinge' (Franz von Schober), D.361,
1816; 'Am Grabe Anselmos' (Matthias Claudius),
D.504, 1816; 'An den Mond' (Goethe), D.259, 1815;
'An den Mond' (Goethe), D.296, 1816; 'An die
Entfernte' (Goethe), D.765, 1822; 'An mein Klavier'
(Schubart), D.342, c.1816; 'An die Laute' (Johann
Friedrich Rochlitz), D.905, 1827; 'An die Leier'
(Franz von Bruchmann), D.737, 1822; 'An die
Musik' (Schober), D.547, 1817; 'An die Nachtigall'
(Ludwig Hölty), D.497, 1816; 'An die Türen will
ich schleichen' (*Harfenspieler II*; Goethe), D.479,
1816, rev 1822; 'An die untergehende Sonne'
(Gotthard Ludwig Kosegarten), D.457, 1816; 'An
eine Quelle' (Claudius), D.530, 1817; 'An schwager
Kronos' (Goethe), D.369, 1816; 'An Sylvia' ('Who is
Sylvia?'; Eduard von Bauernfeld, after
Shakespeare), D.891, 1826; 'Auf der Bruck' (Ernst
Schulze), D.853, 1825; 'Auf der Donau' (Mayrhofer),
D.553, 1817; 'Auf dem See' (Goethe), D.543, 1817;
'Auf dem Strom' (Ludwig Rellstab), D.943, with hn
obbligato, 1828; 'Auf dem Wasser zu singen'
(Friedrich Leopold zu Stolberg), D.774, 1823;
'Auflösung' (Mayrhofer), D.807, 1824; 'Ave Maria'
(*Ellens Gesang III*; Adam Storck, after Scott),
D.839, 1825; 'Bei dir allein' (Johann Gabriel Seidl),
D.866:2, ?1828; 'Beim Winde' (Mayrhofer), D.669,
1819; 'Bertas Lied in der Nacht' (Franz Grillparzer),
D.653, 1819; 'Blanka' (Friedrich von Schlegel),
D.631, 1818; 'Der blinde Knabe' (Jakob Nikolaus
von Craigher, after Colley Cibber), D.833, 1825;
'Die Blumensprache' (?Eduard Platner), D.519,
?1817; 'Dass sie hier gewesen' (Rückert), D.775,
?1823; 'Du bist die Ruh'' (Rückert), D.776, 1823;
'Der Einsame' (Karl Gottlieb Lappe), D.800, 1825;
ERLKÖNIG (Goethe), D.328, 1815; 'Erster Verlust'
(Goethe), D.226, 1815; 'Der Fischer' (Goethe),
D.225, 1815; 'Des Fischers Liebesglück' (Karl
Gottfried von Leitner), D.933, 1827; 'Fischerweise'
(Franz Xaver von Schlechta), D.881, 1826; 'Der
Fluss' (Friedrich von Schlegel), D.693, 1820; 'Die
Forelle' (Schubart), D.550, 1817; 'Frühlingsglaube'
(Uhland), D.686, 1820; 'Ganymed' (Goethe),
D.544, 1817; 'Geheimes' (Goethe), D.719, 1821;
'Geheimnis' (Mayrhofer), D.491, 1816; 'Die Götter
Griechenlands' (Schiller), D.677, 1819;
'Greisengesang' (Rückert), D.778, 1823; 'Gretchen
am Spinnrade' (Goethe), D.118, 1814; 'Gruppe aus
dem Tartarus' (Schiller), D.583, 1817;
'Heidenröslein' (Goethe), D.257, 1815; 'Heimliches
Lieben' (Karoline von Klenke), D.922, 1827; 'Heiss
mich nicht reden' (*Gesänge aus Wilhelm Meister II*;
Goethe), D.877:2, 1826; 'Herrn Josef Spaun'
(Matthäus von Collin), D.749, 1822; Der HIRT AUF
DEM FELSEN (Wilhelm Müller), D.965, with cl
obbligato, 1828; 'Horch, horch! die Lerch' ('Hark,
hark the lark'; August Wilhelm von Schlegel, after
Shakespeare), D.889, 1826; 'Im Abendrot' (Lappe),
D.799, 1824/5; 'Im Frühling' (Schulze), D.882, 1826;
'Im Haine' (Bruchmann), D.738, ?1822/3;

'Iphigenia' (Mayrhofer), D.573, 1817; 'Jäger, ruhe
von der Jagd!' (*Ellens Gesang II*; Storck, after
Scott), D.838, 1825; 'Die junge Nonne' (Craigher),
D.828, 1825; 'Der Jüngling an der Quelle' (Johann
Gaudenz von Salis-Seewis), D.300, c.1817; 'Der
Jüngling und der Tod' (Josef von Spaun), D.545,
1817; 'Kennst du das Land?' ('Mignon'; Goethe),
D.321, 1815; 'Der Knabe' (Friedrich von Schlegel),
D.692, 1820; 'Der König in Thule' (Goethe), D.367,
1816; 'Lachen und Weinen' (Rückert), D.777, ?1823;
'Licht und Liebe' (Collin), D.352, ?1816; 'Die
Liebende schreibt' (Goethe), D.673, 1819;
'Liebhaber in allen Gestalten' (Goethe), D.558,
1817; 'Lied der Delphine' (Christian Wilhelm von
Schütz), D.857, 1825; 'Das Lied im Grünen'
(Johann Anton Friedrich Reil), D.917, 1827; 'Lied
eines Schiffers an die Dioskuren' (Mayrhofer),
D.360, 1816; 'Litanei auf des Fest aller Seelen'
(Johann Georg Jacobi), D.343, 1816; 'Das
Mädchen' (Friedrich von Schlegel), D.652, 1819;
'Die Männer sind méchant' (Seidl), D.866:3,
?1828; 'Meeresstille' (Goethe), D.216, 1815; 'Der
Musensohn' (Goethe), D.764, 1822; 'Nacht und
Träume' (Collin), D.827, ?1822; 'Nachtgesang'
(Kosegarten), D.314, 1815; 'Nachtviolen'
(Mayrhofer), D.752, 1822; 'Nähe des Geliebten'
(Goethe), D.162, 1815; 'Nur wer die Sehnsucht
kennt' (*Gesänge aus Wilhelm Meister I*; Goethe),
D.877:1, 1826; 'Nur wer die Sehnsucht kennt'
(*Gesänge aus Wilhelm Meister IV*; Goethe),
D.877:4, 1826; 'La pastorella al prato' (Goldoni),
D.528, 1817; 'Prometheus' (Goethe), D.674, 1819;
'Raste, Krieger' (*Ellens Gesang I*; Storck, after
Scott), D.837, 1825; 'Rastlose Liebe' (Goethe), D.138,
1815, rev 1821; 'Die Rose' (Friedrich von Schlegel),
D.745, 1822; 'Schäfers Klagelied' (Goethe), D.121,
1814; 'Schlaflied' ('Schlummerlied', Mayrhofer),
D.527, 1817; 'Der Schiffer' (Mayrhofer), D.536, 1817;
'Der Schmetterling' (Friedrich von Schlegel),
D.633, c.1819; 'Schwanengesang' (Senn), D.744,
1822; 'Schwestergruss' (Bruchmann), D.762, 1822;
'Sei mir gegrüsst' (Rückert), D.741, 1821/2;
'Seligkeit' (Hölty), D.433, 1816; 'Sprache der Liebe'
(August Wilhelm von Schlegel), D.410, 1816; 'Die
Sterne' (Leitner), D.939, 1828; 'Der Tod und das
Mädchen' (Claudius), D.531, 1817; 'Totengräbers
Heimwehe' (Craigher), D.842, 1825; 'Über
Wildemann' (Schulze), D.884, 1826; 'Dem
Unendlichen' (Klopstock), D.291, 1815; 'Versunken'
(Goethe), D.715, 1821; 'Die Vögel' (Friedrich von
Schlegel), D.691, 1820; 'Der Wanderer' (Georg
Philipp Schmidt von Lübeck), D.489, 1816; 'Der
Wanderer' (Friedrich von Schlegel), D.649, 1819;
'Der Wanderer an den Mond' (Seidl), D.870, 1826;
'Wanderers Nachtlied' (Goethe), D.224, 1815;
'Wanderers Nachtlied' (Goethe), D.768, by 1824;
'Was bedeutet die Bewegung?' (*Suleika I*;
?Willemer), D.720, 1821; 'Wehmut '(Collin), D.772,
?1822/3; 'Wer nie sein Brot' (*Harfenspieler III*;
Goethe), D.480, 1816, rev 1822; 'Wer sich der
Einsamkeit gibt' (*Harfenspieler I*; Goethe), D.478,
1816, rev 1822; 'Wiegenlied' (anon.), D.498, 1816;
'Wiegenlied' (Seidl), D.867, ?1826; 'Der

Winterabend '(Leitner), D.938, 1828; 'Der zürnende Barde' (Bruchmann), D.785, 1823; 'Der Zwerg' (Collin), D.771, 1822/3; etc.

Schubertiad. Concert devoted to music by Schubert, the term deriving from musical evenings the composer enjoyed with his friends.

Schulhoff, Erwin (b. Prague, 8 Jun 1894; d. Wülzburg, 18 Aug 1942). Czech composer. He was born into a German Jewish family and studied during the decade 1904–14 in Prague, Vienna, Leipzig (with Reger) and Cologne. Seriously marked then by his wartime experience as a soldier, he settled in Germany (1919–23), where he associated with left-wing artists, notably George Grosz and Otto Dix. Jazz, he felt, would provide a radical disjunction from traditional music, but he was also powerfully attracted by Schoenberg and Stravinsky. He then went back again to Czechoslovakia, to lead an active and diverse career as a pianist, jazzman and composer. In this last capacity he was now at his most prolific, wielding the diverse influences on him (including the Czech tradition) with agility and brilliance. But, as a communist, he was a keen observer of artistic currents in the Soviet Union, and from 1932 onwards he made his music more regular. After the Munich agreement (1938) he obtained Soviet citizenship and considered emigrating, but he waited too long, was arrested and died in a concentration camp.

Stage: *Ogelala* (ballet), f.p. Dessau, 1925; *Flammen* (opera; Max Brod, after Karel Josef Beneš), f.p. Brno, 1932; etc.

Orchestral: Symphony No.1, 1924–5; No.2, 1932; No.3, 1935; No.4, 1936–7; No.5, 1938; No.6 (Symphony of Freedom), 1940–41; Piano Concerto, Op.11, 1913–14; Piano Concerto, with chbr orch, 1923; Double Concerto, fl, pf, chbr orch, 1927; Suite, chbr orch, 1921; etc.

Vocal: *Die Wolkenpumpe* (Hans Arp), bar, 4 wind, 3 perc, 1922; *H.M.S. Royal Oak* (jazz oratorio; Otto Rombach), 1930; etc.

Chamber: String Sextet, 1920–24; String Quartet, G, Op.25, 1918; 5 Pieces, str qt, 1923; String Quartet No.1, 1924; No.2, 1925; Duo, vn, vc, 1925; Violin Sonata, Op.7, 1913; Violin Sonata, 1927; Cello Sonata, Op.17, 1914; *Bassnachtigall*, dbn, 1922; Flute Sonata, 1927; *Hot-Sonate*, a sax, pf, 1930; etc.

Piano: 10 Pieces, Op.30, 1919; *Cinq études de jazz*, 1926; etc.

Schuller, Gunther (Alexander) (b. New York, 22 Nov 1925). US composer. The son of a New York Philharmonic violinist, he studied horn and composition at the St Thomas Choir School (1937–42), and at 17 was appointed principal horn of the Cincinnati Symphony. Two years later he moved to a similar position at the Metropolitan Opera, from which he resigned in 1959 to concentrate on composition. He has also been vigorously active as a teacher (notably at Tanglewood since 1963), conductor, broadcaster and record producer. His numerous compositions, written with a strong feeling for instrumental character, draw on US and European modernism, in some cases with a jazz–classical fusion for which he coined the term THIRD-STREAM MUSIC. Among his works are a full-length opera, *The Visitation* (after Kafka, f.p. Hamburg, 1966), several concertos (including three for horn) and other orchestral pieces, songs, a lot of music for ensemble or solo instrument, and arrangements of compositions by ragtime or jazz composers.

Schulz, Johann Abraham Peter (b. Lüneburg, 31 Mar 1747; d. Schwedt an der Oder, 10 Jun 1800). German composer. His baker father intended him for the church, but at 15 he visited C.P.E. Bach and Kirnberger in Berlin, and three years later he returned as Kirnberger's pupil. He then travelled in the retinue of a Polish princess, meeting Grétry, Haydn and Johann Reichardt, a lifelong friend. He also helped his old teacher by writing the S–Z music articles for an encyclopedia. Appointments followed at the courts of Prussia (1776–87) and Copenhagen (1787–95), where he was responsible for lifting Danish musical life into the modern age. He retired in poor health, having made an important contribution to the lied with settings of folksong-like simplicity.

Schuman, William (Howard) (b. New York, 4 Aug 1910; d. New York, 15 Feb 1992). US composer, notably of streamlined symphonies. After a youth devoted to baseball and popular music (including the composition of numerous songs), he went unwillingly to an orchestral concert in 1930 and immediately enrolled at the Malkin Conservatory. From there he progressed to Columbia University (1933–7) and to studies with Roy Harris (1936–8). During this time he began teaching at Sarah Lawrence College, got married and started to make a reputation. His Third Symphony (1941) brought him national attention (he withdrew its predecessors and other early works), and in 1943 he received the first Pulitzer Prize for music, for *A Free Song*. Two years later he was appointed president of the Juilliard School, where he revitalized the syllabus and had the Juilliard Quartet formed as an ensemble in residence. So successful was he as an administrator that he was invited to move on to the presidency of Lincoln Center (1962–9), from which he retired after suffering a heart attack. Neither official business nor endangered health did much to sap his creative strength, expressed in 'vitality, optimism, enthusiasm, long lyrical line, rhythmic impetuosity, bristling counterpoint, brilliant textures, dynamic tension' (Bernstein).

www.williamschuman.org

Operas: *The Mighty Casey* (Jeremy Gury, after Ernest L. Thayer), f.p. Hartford, 1953, rev as *Casey at the Bat* (cantata), 1976; *A Question of Taste* (J.D. McClatchy, after Roald Dahl), f.p. Cooperstown, 1989

Ballets (for Martha Graham): *Night Journey*, 1947; *Judith*, 1949; *Voyage for a Theater*, 1953; *The Witch of Endor*, 1965

Orchestral: Symphony No.3, 1941; No.4, 1941; No.5 (Symphony for Strings), 1943; No.6, 1948; No.7, 1960; No.8, 1962; No.9 'Le Fosse ardeatine', 1968; No.10 'American Muse', 1976; Piano Concerto, 1938–42; Violin Concerto, 1947, rev 1954, 1958–9; *New England Triptych*, 1956; etc.

Orchestration: Variations on 'America' (Ives), 1963

Other works: *A Free Song* (Whitman), ch, orch, 1942; *Carols of Death* (Whitman), ch, 1958; chamber music, piano works, songs ('Orpheus and his lute', 1944), etc.

Schumann. German composers, husband and wife.

(1) **Robert (Alexander)** (b. Zwickau, Saxony, 8 Jun 1810; d. Endenich, near Bonn, 29 Jul 1856). He was the born Romantic: much of his music has that rapturous spring of urgency and emotional frankness, coming in short lyric forms he perfected for the piano. But he also shared other passions with the German Romantic writers he avidly read, passions for historical romance, fantasy and masquerade. And in his 30s he turned the Romantic impulse to refashioning the great Classical archetypes of symphony and oratorio.

His voracious reading started when he was a boy, for his father was a bookseller and publisher, whose stock supplemented the education the young Schumann was receiving at the Zwickau Lyceum (1820–28). In parallel he pursued music, with special zeal after hearing Moscheles play in Karlsbad – he was just nine – and being taken to *Die Zauberflöte* around the same time. Through his school years he composed and versified in equal measure. Then, obedient to the wishes of his mother and guardian (his father had died in 1826), he became a law student, switching between the universities of Leipzig (1828–9) and Heidelberg (1829–30), and thoroughly neglecting his classes in favour of musical and literary composition, coupled with conscientious piano practice. Schubert's death affected him greatly; Hummel and Moscheles were important to him too, and among writers Jean Paul. Meanwhile, he began to have fears for his sanity. His father had died at 45

after years of suffering from weak nerves, and his physically and mentally impaired sister Emilie had gone before, at 19.

In Leipzig he became the pupil of Friedrich Wieck, at whose behest his mother allowed him to give up his legal training for six months and devote himself to music. He moved in with the Wiecks in October 1830, and the trial period never ended. Wieck, though, was preoccupied with his daughter Clara, with whom he was away on concert tours in the winter of 1830–31 and then for seven months from September 1831. At this point Schumann moved out. He was having theory lessons briefly with the theatre conductor, Heinrich Dorn, and his music was starting to appear in print, beginning with the 'Abegg' Variations (written in 1829–31 on the name of a girlfriend) and *Papillons*. Also in 1831 he published his first article – on Chopin, a new discovery. At the same time he continued writing fiction, planning a phantasmagorical novel in which people he knew – Wieck, Clara, Christel (another girlfriend), Paganini (whom he had heard in 1830) – would appear transformed. So would he. He developed two characters as self-projections, the spontaneous Florestan and the pensive Eusebius. They made their first appearance in his Chopin article and remained guiding figments of his inner life.

His hopes as a virtuoso began to dissolve, owing to trouble with the middle and index fingers of his right hand (possibly the result of using a mechanical device to strengthen them, possibly the effect of mercury treatment for syphilis). As a composer, though, he was on course. Among works he completed in 1832–3 were the Toccata in C and the Paganini transcriptions; he also began a symphony in G minor, which he abandoned the next year with the finale only sketched, and which was his last effort at anything but piano music until 1838.

In October 1833, unbalanced by the death of his sister-in-law, he came close to throwing himself from the window of his fourth-floor flat – an experience that left him with a dread of heights, resolved temporarily by moving to an apartment on the ground floor. This he was soon sharing with another young composer, Ludwig Schunke, whose presence helped restore his mental condition (until poor Schunke died of consumption a year later). But more works were dropped and none finished in 1834, even if that was partly because he was occupied with a new twice-weekly musical paper, the *Neue Zeitschrift für Musik*, which he helped found, contributed to regularly and edited from 1835. There was also the diversion of a love affair with Ernestine von Fricken, memorialized in *Carnaval*. They were even betrothed.

Her charms, though, began to fade in his mind in April 1835, when Clara, now 15½, came back from a five-month concert tour. Later that year he met Mendelssohn, the new director of the Leipzig Gewandhaus concerts, as well as Chopin and Moscheles. On New Year's Day 1836 he broke off his engagement to Ernestine, but his new affair did not run smoothly. Wieck was stoutly against it. Clara was having composition lessons now not with Schumann but with her father's preferred spousal candidate. So Schumann returned to the ever-compliant Christel.

Composition, too, absorbed him. He worked at his *Etudes symphoniques* and at sonatas, including a Beethoven memorial originally entitled *Ruins, Trophies, Palms* and eventually published, with its grand gestures less advertised, as the Fantasy in C. Visiting friends (Chopin, Sterndale Bennett) distracted him, as did Robena Laidlaw, a young Scottish pianist on his arm in June–July 1837, while he was composing the solo *Fantasiestücke* for her. Then in August Clara wrote to him for the first time in more than a year, and the next month they met again. When he asked Wieck for permission to marry, Wieck's response was to take Clara away on another seven-month tour, during which Schumann wrote the *Noveletten, Kinderscenen* and *Kreisleriana*.

When Clara returned, in May 1838, his creativity deserted him; when she left again, in July, he became suicidal. In September he moved to Vienna, where he hoped to settle with Clara. He visited Schubert's brother Ferdinand, and retrieved the score of the unplayed 'Great C major' Symphony, before the mortal illness of his own brother Eduard brought him back to Leipzig in April 1839. In June he and Clara began legal proceedings to allow them to marry without her father's consent. It was more than a year before the case was resolved, in their favour, and they were married in a village church near Leipzig on 12 September 1840.

This was Schumann's year of song. He had achieved relatively little in 1839, but early in 1840 he wrote his first song since his schooldays, and more than 100 followed: solo songs (including the Heine and Eichendorff *Liederkreis* cycles, *Dichterliebe* and *Frauenliebe und -leben*), duets and partsongs. Piano music was swept aside until the end of the decade, except for pieces that came out of contrapuntal endeavours he undertook with Clara in 1845.

After all the songs came his year of orchestral music. At this time creative events could happen with speed: he started the 'Spring' Symphony on 23 January 1841, finished it four weeks later and heard Mendelssohn conduct the first performance on 31 March. Encouraged, he moved on to the Overture,

Scherzo and Finale in E (April–May, effectively a symphony without a slow movement), a fantasy for piano and orchestra (May, this became the first movement of the Piano Concerto), a symphony in D minor (May–September, revised as the Fourth Symphony) and one in C minor (September, discarded). Clara tried out the fantasy in August, two and a half weeks before giving birth to their first child, and the works in E and D minor were both performed before the end of the year.

As if working his way deliberately through the genres, in 1842, after some fallow months, he turned to chamber music, producing three string quartets (June–July), a piano quintet (September–October), a piano quartet (October–November) and a piano trio (*Fantasiestücke*, December). Next, in 1843, was choral music: *Das Paradies und die Peri*, an opera project rescued as an oratorio. The urge towards opera remained, and in 1844, while on a four-month tour of the Baltic and Russia with Clara, he made some sketches for a *Faust*; this too developed into a concert work, nearly a decade later. Back in Leipzig, he resigned the editorship of the *Neue Zeitschrift* to work fitfully on various opera subjects, but he was in low spirits and was not revived either by a holiday in the Harz mountains in September 1844 or by a move to Dresden the following month.

The only important achievements of the next two years were the definitive version of the Piano Concerto and the Symphony in C. More opera ideas were considered, and rejected. Then, after concerts with Clara in Vienna, Brno, Prague and Berlin during the winter of 1846–7, he regained his creative energy and enjoyed a triumphant return to his home town in July. There were sadnesses: the death of his youngest child and only son at 16 months, and then of Mendelssohn. But he moved forward through more piano trios and songs to an opera at last: *Genoveva*, composed between December 1847 and August 1848, during a period of revolutionary unrest that he observed with enthusiasm, writing three *Freedom Songs* for men's voices and wind band.

His political engagement was equivocal. When revolution came to Dresden in May 1849, the Schumanns fled to the country. They returned when monarchical stability had been restored, but Schumann's first effort was a set of marches, which he at first asked his publisher to bring out with the date 1849 in large type, a provocation he later quietly let slip. It would be hard to read any political feeling into the rest of his abundant output from the 12 months after *Genoveva*: the incidental music for Byron's *Manfred*, most of the long-delayed *Scenen aus Goethes Faust*, other Goethe settings (the *Requiem für Mignon* and some songs and choruses), various instrumental pieces (including sets of poetic miniatures for clarinet and for cello), the *Spanisches Liederspiel* and the *Album für die Jugend* for young pianists. By the end of 1849 there were more miniatures (for oboe), more Spanish songs and more children's pieces: duets, among them a 'Birthday March' which he and his eldest daughter, just eight, played for Clara as a 30th birthday surprise. (There were now three small girls and two baby boys in the family. Two more children came later, a girl in 1851 and a boy in 1854.)

At the end of March 1850, after various concert trips with Clara, he accepted the post of city music director in Düsseldorf. First, though, came the rehearsals and performances of *Genoveva* in Leipzig in May–June, attended by Liszt, Hiller, Spohr and Moscheles among other distinguished friends. The move to Düsseldorf took place at the beginning of September, and though Schumann did not like the people or the locality (with the exception of Cologne Cathedral), he was soon bounding into new works: the Cello Concerto, the 'Rhenish' Symphony, two tragic overtures (*Die Braut von Messina* and *Julius Cäsar*) and two choral-orchestral works (*Der Rose Pilgefahrt* and *Der Königssohn*), all finished before the 1851 summer holiday.

Works of the next season included the revised version of the D minor Symphony, the Mass and the *Requiem*. But in early April 1852, while working on the *Requiem*, he began to decline into illness. Summer cures, at Bad Godesberg and Schevenin- gen (for sea bathing) were ineffective, and he had to relinquish the first two concerts of the 1852–3 Düsseldorf season to his deputy – much to every- one's relief, for he was a weak conductor.

He nevertheless resumed his position on the podium in December 1852 and conducted success- fully at the Lower Rhine Music Festival in May. There he heard Joachim, for whom he wrote a fantasy and a concerto in September–October. An- other new young friend, made through Joachim, was Brahms, who visited the Schumanns while the concerto was in progress, and on whom Schu- mann wrote one of his last articles, alongside the *Märchenerzählungen* for mixed trio, in early October 1853. After that came just a few more instrumental pieces in the next month: the *Gesänge der Frühe* for piano, Third Violin Sonata and cello Romances. There was also the fiasco of his last Düsseldorf concert on 27 October, though concerts in the Netherlands in December went well.

In February 1854 his condition slipped, and the rest of his life makes a distressing story. He wrote a theme dictated by angels, and five variations on it – his last music, except for accompaniments to solo violin works by Bach and Paganini. He asked to be admitted to an asylum, but was dissuaded by Clara. He threw himself from a bridge into the Rhine, but was rescued by fishermen. At last he had his wish, and was committed to the care of a Dr Richarz in Endenich. Clara was not allowed to visit, though Schumann was able to correspond with her (and others) during a remission that lasted from September 1854 to May 1855. After a silence of more than a year she was summoned, and spent his last two days with him. He seemed to recognize her.

Eric Sams *The Songs of Robert Schumann* (1969, ³1993); Eric Frederick Jensen *Schumann* (2001)

Orchestral and vocal orchestral music

Symphonies: G minor, 1832–3; No.1 'Spring', B♭, Op.38, 1841, f.p. Leipzig, 31 Mar 1841 (Mendelssohn); No.2, C, Op.61, 1845–6, f.p. Leipzig, 5 Nov 1846 (Mendelssohn); No.3 'RHENISH', E♭, Op.97, 1850, f.p. Düsseldorf, 6 Feb 1851; No.4, D minor, Op.120, 1841, f.p. Leipzig, 6 Dec 1841 (Ferdinand David), rev 1851, f.p. Düsseldorf, 30 Dec 1852

Concertos: PIANO CONCERTO, A minor, Op.54, 1841–5; Conzertstück, Op.86, hn qt, orch, 1849; Introduction and Allegro appassionato, Op.92, pf, orch, 1849; Cello Concerto, A minor, Op.129, 1850; Fantasy, C, Op.131, vn, orch. 1853; Introduction and Allegro, D minor-major, Op.134, pf, orch, 1853; Violin Concerto, D minor, 1853

Overtures, etc.: Overture, Scherzo and Finale, Op.52, 1841, rev 1845; *Die Braut von Messina* (overture), Op.100, 1850–51; *Julius Cäsar* (overture), Op.128, 1851; *Hermann und Dorothea* (overture), Op.136, 1851

Opera: GENOVEVA, Op.81, 1847–8

Incidental music: MANFRED, Op.115, 1848–9

Choral orchestral: *Das PARADIES UND DIE PERI*, Op.50, 1843; *Scenen aus Goethes Faust* (see FAUST), 1844–9, ov 1853; *Requiem für Mignon*, Op.98b, soli, ch, orch, 1849; *Der Rose Pilgerfahrt* (Moritz Horn), Op.112, soli, ch, orch, 1851; *Der Königssohn* (Uhland), Op.116, soli, ch, orch, 1851; *Des Sängers Fluch* (Richard Pohl, after Uhland), Op.139, soli, ch, orch, 1852; *Vom Pagen und der Königstochter* (Emanuel Geibel), Op.140, soli, ch, orch, 1852; *Requiem*, Op.148, ch, orch, 1852; Mass, Op.147, ch, orch, 1852–3; *Das Glück von Edenhall* (Hasenclever, after Uhland), Op.143, soli, ch, orch, 1853

Chamber music

Quintets and quartets: Piano Quintet, E♭, Op.44, 1842; Andante and Variations, 2 pf, 2 vc, hn, 1843; String Quartets Nos.1–3, Op.41, A minor, F, A, 1842; Piano Quartet, E♭, Op.47, 1842

Trios: *Fantasiestücke* (4), Op.88, pf trio, 1842; Piano Trio No.1, D minor, op.63, 1847; No.2, F, Op.80, 1847; No.3, G minor, Op.110, 1851; *Märchenerzählungen* (4), Op.132, cl/vn, va, pf, 1853

Duos: Adagio and Allegro, Op.70, hn/vn/vc, pf, 1849;

Fantasiestücke (3), Op.73, cl/vn/vc, pf, 1849; 3
Romances, Op.94, ob/vn/cl, pf, 1849; 5 Pieces in
Folk Style, Op.102, vc/vn, pf, 1849; Violin Sonata
No.1, A minor, Op.105, 1851; No.2, D minor, Op.121,
1851; No.3, A minor, 1853; *Märchenbilder* (4),
Op.113, va/vn, pf, 1851; 5 Romances, vc, pf, 1853

Piano music

Solo works: ABEGG Variations, Op.1, 1830;
PAPILLONS, Op.2, 1830–31; Allegro, B minor, Op.8,
1831; Toccata, C, Op.7, 1829–33; Etudes after
Paganini's Caprices (12 in 2 sets), Op.3 and Op.10,
1832–3; 6 Intermezzos, Op.4, 1832; Impromptus on
a Theme by Clara Wieck (10), Op.5, 1833; Sonata
No.1, F♯ minor, Op.11, 1832–5; CARNAVAL, Op.9,
1834–5; *Concert sans orchestre* Op.14, 1835–6, rev as
Sonata No.3, F minor, 1853; *Etudes symphoniques*
(12), Op.13, 1834–7; *Fantasiestücke* (8), Op.12, 1837;
DAVIDSBÜNDLERTÄNZE, Op.6, 1837; Sonata No.2,
G minor, Op.22, 1833–8; Fantasy, C, Op.17, 1836–8;
Noveletten (8), Op.21, 1838; KINDERSCENEN,
Op.15, 1838; KREISLERIANA, Op.16, 1838; *Arabeske*,
Op.18, 1838–9; *Humoreske*, Op.20, 1838–9; Piano
Pieces (4), Op.32, 1838–9; *Blumenstück*, Op.19, 1839;
3 Romances, Op.28, 1839; *Nachtstücke* (4), Op.23,
1839–40; FASCHINGSSCHWANK AUS WIEN,
Op.26, 1839–40; *Albumblätter* (20), Op.124,
1832–45; Studies for the Pedal Piano (6), Op.56,
1845; Sketches for the Pedal Piano (4), Op.58, 1845;
Fugues on B–A–C–H (6), Op.60, org/pedal pf,
1845; Fugues (4), Op.72, 1845; *Album für die Jugend*,
Op.68, 1848; *Waldscenen* (9), Op.82, 1848–9; *Bunte
Blätter* (14), Op.99, 1838–49; Marches (4), Op.76,
1849; *Fantasiestücke* (3), Op.111, 1851; Piano Pieces
in Fughetta Form (7), Op.126, 1853; *Sonaten für die
Jugend* (3), Op.118, 1853; *Gesänge der Frühe* (5),
Op.133, 1853; Theme and Variations, 1854

Duets: Polonaises (8), 1828; *Bilder aus Osten* (6
impromptus), Op.66, 1848; *Klavierstücke für
kleine und grosse Kinder* (12), Op.85, 1849;
Ballscenen (9), Op.109, 1851; *Kinderball* (6 pieces),
Op.130, 1853

Duo: Andante and Variations, Op.46, 1843 (originally
with 2 vc and hn)

Songs

Sets and cycles: LIEDERKREIS (Heine), Op.24, 1840;
Myrthen (26), Op.25, 1840; *Lieder und Gesänge I*
(5), Op.27, 1840; *Drei Gedichte* (Emanuel Geibel),
Op.29, 1840; *Drei Gedichte* (Geibel), Op.30, 1840;
Drei Gesänge (Adelbert von Chamisso), Op.31,
1840; *Zwölf Gedichte* (Justinus Kerner), Op.35,
1840; *Sechs Gedichte* (Robert Reinick), Op.36, 1840;
Zwölf Gedichte aus Liebesfrühling (Rückert, Nos.2,
4 and 11 by Clara), Op.37, 1840; LIEDERKREIS
(Eichendorff), Op.39, 1840; FRAUENLIEBE UND
-LEBEN (Chamisso), Op.42, 1840; *Romanzen und
Balladen I* (3), Op.45, 1840; DICHTERLIEBE
(Heine), Op.48, 1840; *Romanzen und Balladen II*
(3), Op.49, 1840; *Romanzen und Balladen III* (3),
Op.53, 1840; *Vier Gesänge*, Op.142, 1840;
Romanzen und Balladen IV (3), Op.64, 1841–7;
Lieder und Gesänge II (5), Op.51, 1840–49;
Spanisches Liederspiel (Geibel; Nos.6–7 and 10 are

solo songs), Op.74, 1849; *Lieder-Album für die
Jugend* (28), Op.79, 1849; *Lieder und Gesänge aus
Wilhelm Meister* (Goethe), Op.98a, 1849;
Minnespiel (Rückert; Nos.1–2, 4 and 6 are solo
songs), Op.101, 1849; *Drei Gesänge* (Körner, after
Byron), Op.95, with hp, 1849; *Lieder und Gesänge
III* (5), Op.77, 1840–50; *Fünf Lieder und Gesänge*,
Op.127, 1840–50; *Drei Gesänge*, Op.83, 1850; *Der
Handschuh* (Schiller), Op.87, 1850; *Sechs Gesänge*
(Wilfred von der Neun), Op.89, 1850; *Sechs
Gedichte* (Lenau), Op.90, 1850; *Lieder und Gesänge
IV*, Op.96, 1850; *Fünf heitere Gesänge*, Op.125,
1850–51; *Sieben Lieder* (Elisabeth Kulmann),
Op.104, 1851; *Sechs Gesänge*, Op.107, 1851; *Vier
Husarenlieder* (Lenau), Op.117, 1851; *Drei Gedichte*
(Gustav Pfarrius), Op.119, 1851; *Gedichte der
Königin Maria Stuart* (5), Op.135, 1852; *Spanische
Liebeslieder* (Geibel: Nos.2–3, 5 and 7–8 are solo
songs), Op.138, 1849

Individual songs: *Opp.24, 39, 42 and 48 are normally
performed complete. Among popular numbers from
the other publications are the following:* 'Der arme
Peter' (Heine), Op.53:3; 'Aufträge' (Christian
L'Egru), Op.77:5; 'Aus den östlichen Rosen'
(Rückert), Op.25:25; 'Die beiden Grenadiere'
(Heine), Op.49:1; 'Belsatzar' (Heine), Op.57, 1840;
'Blondels Lied' (Johann Gabriel Seidl), Op.53:1;
'Dein Angesicht' (Heine), Op.127:2; 'Du bist wie
eine Blume' (Heine), Op.25:24; 'Er ist's' (Mörike),
Op.79:23; 'Erstes Grün', Op.35:4; 'Es leuchtet meine
Liebe' (Heine), Op.127:3; 'Heiss mich nicht reden',
Op.98a:5; 'Kennst du das Land?' (Goethe),
Op.79:28; 'Kennst du das Land?', Op.98a:1; 'Lehn
deine Wang' (Heine), Op.142:2; 'Lied der Suleika'
(Goethe), Op.25:9; 'Loreley' (Wilhelmine Lorenz),
Op.53:2; 'Die Lotosblume' (Heine), Op.25:7;
'Marienwürmchen' (Des Knaben Wunderhorn),
Op.79:13; 'Die Meerfee' (Julius Buddeus), Op.125:1;
'Mein Wagen rollet langsam' (Heine), Op.142:4;
'Meine Rose', Op.90:2; 'Nur wer die Sehnsucht
kennt', Op.98a:3; 'Der Nussbaum' (Julius Mosen),
Op.25:3; 'Der Page', Op.30:2; 'Der Sandmann'
(Hermann Kletke), Op.79:12; 'Schneeglöckchen'
(Rückert), Op.79:26; 'Des Sennen Abschied'
(Schiller), Op.79:22; 'Talismane' (Goethe), Op.25:8;
'Tragödie' (Heine), Op.64:3; 'Widmung' (Rückert),
Op.25:1

Duets and ensembles: *Vier Duette*, Op.34, 1840; *Drei
zweistimmige Lieder*, Op.43, 1840; *Spanisches
Liederspiel* (Geibel: Nos.1–4 and 8 are duets, Nos.5
and 9 quartets), Op.74, 1849; *Vier Duette*, Op.78,
1849; *Minnespiel* (Rückert; Nos.3 and 7 are duets,
Nos.5 and 8 quartets), Op.101, 1849; *Drei Lieder*,
Op.114, trios, 1849–50; *Mädchenlieder* (3,
Kulmann), Op.103, 1851; *Spanische Liebeslieder*
(Geibel: Nos.4 and 9 are duets, No.10 is a quartet),
Op.138, 1849

Recitations (for speaker, pf): *Schön Hedwig*
(Hebbel), Op.106, 1849; *Zwei Balladen*, Op.122,
1852–3

Partsongs for mixed voices: *Fünf Lieder* (Wilhelm
Gerhard, after Burns), Op.55, 1846; *Vier Gesänge*,
Op.59, 1846; *Romanzen und Balladen* (20 in 4 sets),

Opp.67, 75, 145 and 146, 1849–51; *Vier doppelchörige Gesänge*, Op.141, 1849

Partsongs for women's voices: *Romanzen* (12 in 2 sets), Opp.69 and 91, 1849

Partsongs for men's voices: *Sechs Lieder*, Op.33, 1840; *Drei Gesänge*, Op.62, 1847; *Ritornelle in canonischen Weisen* (8; Rückert), Op.65, 1847; *Drei Freiheitsgesänge*, wind ad lib, 1848; *Verzweifle nicht im Schmerzenstal* (motet; Rückert), Op.93, 1849; *Fünf Gesänge* (Heinrich Laube), Op.137, 1849

(2) **Clara** (Josephine) [née Wieck] (b. Leipzig, 13 Sep 1819; d. Frankfurt, 20 May 1896). She was the eldest child of Friedrich Wieck, who destined her for musical glory and began giving her the appropriate training when she was five. Fully according with his expectations, she made her debut at the Leipzig Gewandhaus when she was just nine, gave her first complete recital two years later and went with him on a long concert tour in the 1831–2 season. By 1835 she had appeared throughout Europe and been praised by Goethe, Chopin and Paganini; soon Liszt and Franz Grillparzer (who wrote a poem in her honour) joined her admirers. But there was also one nearer home, and less pleasing to her father. Robert Schumann, nine years older, had lodged with the Wiecks in 1830–31, and in 1837 he formally asked her father for her hand. The response was negative, and became violently so, obliging the young couple to seek legal redress that allowed them to marry on the day before her 21st birthday.

The burdens of a heavy father were replaced by those of a young family, as she gave birth to eight children between 1841 and 1854, seven of them surviving infancy. But she went on performing (even as far afield as Russia in 1844) and teaching, and she continued to compose – especially in 1853, when a move into a new house gave her private space. Then her husband's illness and death made creative thought impossible, and afterwards Brahms became the vessel of her compositional hopes, as also of her affections, which he warmly reciprocated.

Her children she brought up with her long-divorced mother in Berlin (1857–63; see BARGIEL) and in Baden-Baden (1863–73). Two of them died in their mid 20s; another was committed to an asylum; and during this same decade of the 1870s she lost her father. Through all that she went on performing, until 1891. From 1878 she also headed the piano department at the Hoch Conservatory in Frankfurt.

What she might have achieved as a composer remains a tantalizing unknown. Her early works show facility, and an imagination that was deepened by studies with her husband. Just when her music was becoming more personal she stopped.

Nancy B. Reich *Clara Schumann* (1985, ²2001)

Orchestral: Piano Concerto, A minor, Op.7, 1833–6
Chamber: Piano Trio, G minor, Op.17, 1846; 3 Romances, Op.22, vn, pf, 1853
Piano: Scherzo, D minor, Op.10, 1838; 3 Romances, Op.11, 1839; Scherzo No.2, C minor, Op.14, pub 1845; *Quatre pièces fugitives*, Op.15, 1841–4; 3 Preludes and Fugues, Op.16, 1845; Variations on a Theme by Robert Schumann, F♯ minor, Op.20, 1853; 3 Romances, Op.21, 1853; many earlier pieces, cadenzas for concertos by Mozart and Beethoven
Songs: Poems from Rückert's *Liebesfrühling*, Op.12, 1841, pub in Robert's Op.37; 6 Songs (Heine, Geibel, Rückert), Op.13, 1840–43; 6 Songs (Hermann Rollett *Jucunde*), Op.23, 1853; etc.
Partsongs: 3 Mixed Choruses (Geibel), 1848

Schumann, Elisabeth (b. Merseburg an der Saale, 13 Jun 1888; d. New York, 23 Apr 1952). German soprano. She studied in Dresden, Berlin and Hamburg, where she made her debut (as the Shepherd in *Tannhäuser*, 1909) and remained a member of the company. Strauss drew her to Vienna (1919–38); she then settled in New York. She made many lieder recordings, pure and affecting, and was valued, too, in Mozart roles and as Sophie in *Der Rosenkavalier*.

Schuppanzigh, Ignaz (b. Vienna, 20 Nov 1776; d. Vienna, 2 Mar 1830). Austrian violinist, associated with Beethoven and Schubert. A professor's son, he took to music in his teens and was soon leading a string quartet that had the benefit of having Haydn and, later, Beethoven present at rehearsals. He also led orchestral concerts. Count Razumovsky supported him in a new quartet (1808–14); he then settled in St Petersburg (1816–23), where he continued his work on Beethoven's behalf – as he did after his return to Vienna. He took part in the first performances of all the Beethoven quartets except Op.74 and Op.131, as well as the Septet, the 'Archduke' Trio and the Ninth Symphony. He also led the premières of Schubert's Octet and A minor Quartet. Schubert dedicated the latter work to him; Beethoven made jokes (including musical ones: 'Lob auf den Dicken', the canon 'Falstafferel') about his obesity.

Schurmann, (Edward) Gerard (b. Kertosono, Dutch East Indies, 19 Jan 1928). Dutch–British composer, of impassioned and big-gestured music. He was brought to England as a child, though not before he had imbibed the sounds of the Indonesian gamelan and of his Hungarian mother's folksongs. Soon after the Second World War he began making a career as a pianist and conductor, but he decided to devote himself to composition, in which he had some lessons with

Rawsthorne, and to support himself by writing film scores. In 1981 he settled in Hollywood. His works include *Six Studies of Francis Bacon* (1968, the painter was a friend), concertos for piano, violin and cello, and a concerto for orchestra (1994–6).

Schusterfleck (Ger., cobbler's patch). Dismissive term for a motif presented in simple ascending or descending sequence – music requiring no thought.

Schütz, Heinrich (baptized Köstritz, 9 Oct 1585; d. Dresden, 6 Nov 1672). German composer, the pre-eminent master of the early Baroque in his country, venerated as the head of the river that led to Bach.

An innkeeper's son, he was heard singing by the visiting Landgrave Moritz of Hessen-Kassel, who took him into service in 1599 and, a decade later, sent him to train with Gabrieli in Venice. He stayed until 1613, leaving only after Gabrieli's death, with a thorough grounding in traditional counterpoint, the newer Venetian style and organ playing. Dutifully he returned to Kassel, but he had only been there a year when the Elector Johann Georg I of Saxony called him to Dresden. A brief visit in the autumn of 1614 turned into a connection with the leading court in Protestant Germany that lasted almost six decades. By 1619 he was formally the Dresden chapelmaster, and on 1 June that year he was married, to the daughter of a court official. Two daughters were born before his wife's death in 1625; he placed them with their grandmother and never remarried.

Other events of 1619 were the unveiling of an organ in Bayreuth, where he met Scheidt and Praetorius, and the publication of a first volume of psalms in elaborate settings for two or three choirs with continuo and, in some cases, groups of strings and brass. The music of his next collection, the *Cantiones sacrae*, is for smaller resources but with the expressive richness of Italian monody. His wife's death then left him temporarily incapable of either musical magnificence or vivid emotion, and he concentrated instead on simple four-part harmonizations for which he found words in a devotional book, the Becker Psalter.

Two years after his bereavement he produced the first German opera, *Dafne*, to a libretto adapted from Rinuccini; the score is lost. Returning to Venice for musical refreshment in 1628–9, he remade contact with Monteverdi, was impressed by the new way of doing opera and published a book of Latin sacred music. In 1631 Saxony's entry into the Thirty Years War drew resources from the musical establishment in Dresden, and he wel-comed an invitation to Copenhagen (1633–5). The following winter he wrote his most important funerary monument, the *Musikalische Exequien*. With conditions in Dresden worsening, he tried unsuccessfully to return to Copenhagen in 1637. He also began agitating for copyrights to cover his works, which were starting to appear in pirated editions. Like other German masters of the time, notably Praetorius, he seems to have recognized that publication could provide an income independent of the vagaries of princes, and between 1636 and 1650 he assembled five volumes of sacred music, all less lavish than the psalms of 1619, in accord with the times and his continent character.

In 1638 his elder daughter died, at 16. After that he spent long periods away, notably in Wolfen-büttel, where he enjoyed the warm favour of the Duchess Sophie Elisabeth, herself a composer, and her husband August, a man his own age. In the spring of 1645 he asked to retire from his Dresden post; he was nearing 60, and wanted to return to Weissenfels to live with his sister. But though the Elector allowed him annual leave, his services were still required. In 1651–3 he again several times asked to retire, and in January 1655 his remaining daughter died. However, only after the death in 1657 of Johann Georg I was he at last given liberty to settle more permanently in Weissenfels, though music was still expected of him in Dresden and Wolfenbüttel, and he produced some of his finest works for the new Elector, Johann Georg II: the Christmas oratorio *Historia der Geburt Jesu Christi* probably in 1660, the St John Passion for Good Friday 1665 and the Matthew and Luke passions the following year. The Christmas work is again for a full array of vocal and instrumental choirs, while the passions achieve extreme acuity in austerity.

He spent his last few years back in Dresden, living soberly and quietly as he always had, and working on his last composition, a grand setting of the longest psalm.

Basil Smallman *Schütz* (2000)

Larger sacred works: *Historia der Auferstehung Jesu Christi* (Easter Oratorio), 10 v, viol qt, con, pub 1623; MUSIKALISCHE EXEQUIEN, 9 v, con, pub 1636; *Die sieben Wortten unsers lieben Erlösers*, 5 v, insts, con; *Historia der Geburt Jesu Christi* (Christmas Oratorio), 12 v, chbr orch, pub 1664; *Magnificat*, 4 v, insts, con, before 1665; St Matthew Passion, 9 v, 1666; St Luke Passion, 7 v, 1666; St John Passion, 6 v, 1666; *Meine Seele erhebt den Herren* (Ger. *Magnificat*), 8 v, con (in *Schwanengesang*)

Collections (with publication dates): *Primo libro de madrigali*, 1611; *Psalmen Davids*, 8–20 v, con, some with insts, 1619; *Cantiones sacrae*, 4 v, con, 1625; Becker Psalter, 4 v, con, 1628, rev 1661; *Kleiner geistliche Konzerten*, 2 Vols., 1–5 v, con, 1636 (includes *Bringt her den Herren, Erhöre mich*), 1639; *Symphoniae sacrae* 3 Vols., 1–6 v, insts, con, 1629, 1647, 1650; *Geistliche Chormusik*, 1–6 v, con, some with insts, 1648 (includes *Selig sind die Toten, Das ist je gewisslich wahr* – rev of elegy for Schein); *Zwölf geistliche Gesänge*, 3–8 v, con, 1657; *Schwanengesang* (Psalm 119, Ger. *Magnificat*), voices, con, 1671

schwach (Ger.). Weak.

Schwanda the Bagpiper (Švanda dudák). Opera by Weinberger to a libretto by Miloš Kareš after an old Czech tale. Schwanda (baritone) accompanies the robber Babinski (tenor) on exploits involving a queen, a magician and the devil, then returns to his wife. The polka and fugue are favourite items. First performance: Prague, 27 Apr 1927.

Schwanengesang (Ger.). SWANSONG. Publisher's title for a collection of late Schubert songs comprising 'Liebesbotschaft', 'Kriegers Ahnung', 'Frühlingssehnsucht', 'Ständchen', 'Aufenthalt', 'In der Ferne', 'Abschied' (all Ludwig Rellstab), 'Der Atlas', 'Ihr Bild', 'Das Fischermädchen', 'Die Stadt', 'Am Meer', 'Der Doppelgänger' (all Heine) and 'Die Taubenpost' (Johann Gabriel Seidl). Unlike *Die schöne Müllerin* and *Winterreise*, the group was not planned as a cycle and has no narrative consistency. The same title was used for Schütz's last collection.

Schwantner, Joseph (b. Chicago, 22 Mar 1943). US composer. He trained at the Chicago Conservatory and Northwestern University (1964–8), then embarked on a teaching career, first at the Eastman School and latterly at Yale. His works, expressively full and vigorous, include concertos and ensemble pieces.

schwärmend (Ger.). Dreamy.

Schwartz, Elliott (Shelling) (b. Brooklyn, 19 Jan 1936). US composer. He studied at Columbia University (1954–62) and began teaching at Bowdoin College, Maine, in 1964. His works make lively and colourful use of sometime avant-garde techniques.

Schwarzkopf, (Olga Maria) Elisabeth (Friederike) (b. Jarotschin, Posen province, 9 Dec 1915). German soprano, one of the most esteemed lieder artists of her generation, gifted with a radiant voice and a punctilious care for expression, as well as an aristocratic bearing on stage. She studied and sang during the Second World War in Berlin and Vienna, and enjoyed an international career from

1947. In 1953 she married Walter Legge, the record producer. Her operatic roles included Mozart characters, the Marschallin in *Der Rosenkavalier* and Anne in *The Rake's Progress*, a part she created. She withdrew (though not entirely) from singing in 1975 to embark on a second career giving master classes.

schwebend (Ger.). Soaring.

schweigen (Ger.). Keep silence.

schweigsame Frau, Die (The Silent Woman). Opera by Strauss to a libretto by Stefan Zweig after Ben Jonson's play *Epicoene*, the plot resembling that of *Don Pasquale*. Sir Morosus (bass) is tricked by his nephew Henry (high tenor) into a mock marriage with Aminta (coloratura soprano), who is in fact already married to Henry. The idea is that she will turn distinctly unsilent after the ceremony, whereupon Henry will procure his uncle a divorce and the grateful old man will leave his nephew all his money. With Strauss's ebullient help it pretty much works out that way. First performance: Dresden, 24 Jun 1935.

Schweinitz, Wolfgang von (b. Hamburg, 7 Feb 1953). German composer, a pupil of Ligeti at the conservatory in Hamburg (1973–5). He was associated with the neo-Romantic reaction in German music (Mozart Variations for orchestra, 1976), and drew attention again with his opera *Patmos* (f.p. Munich, 1990), setting the Apocalypse. The work was written during a period he spent in the north German countryside; he then moved to Weimar and on to Berlin.

Schweitzer, Albert (b. Kaysersberg, Upper Alsace, 14 Jan 1875; d. Lambaréné, Gabon, 4 Sep 1965). Alsatian humanitarian and organist. The son of a Lutheran pastor, he studied the organ as a boy and developed enthusiasms for Bach and Wagner. He trained for the Lutheran ministry at Strasbourg University (1893–9), where he taught after ordination. He also published an influential book on Bach and a complete edition of the organ music. In 1913 he founded a mission hospital at Lambaréné, but he continued to give recitals in Europe when on leave.

schwer (Ger.). Heavy.

Schwertsik, Kurt (b. Vienna, 25 Jun 1935). Austrian composer. He studied at the Vienna Academy (1949–57) as a composer and horn player, and in 1958 was co-founder with Cerha of the new-music ensemble Die Reihe. He was then a pupil of

Stockhausen in Cologne and Darmstadt, but under the influence of Cage and of his friend Cardew he distanced himself from the current avant-garde. In 1965, with Otto Zykan, he founded a new concert series in Vienna, now seeking 'more amusement, more tolerance and fewer ethical ambitions'. That meant retrieving the qualities of gentleness, humour and benignity he found in light music – qualites to be treated with as much irony as affection. He has performed and recorded song programmes with his wife Christa.

Operas: *Das Märchen von Fanferlieschen Schönefüsschen* (The Wondrous Tale of Fanferlizzy Sunnyfeet; Karin and Thomas Korner, after Clemens von Brentano), Op.42, f.p. Stuttgart, 1983; etc.
Orchestral: *Draculas Haus- und Hofmusik*, 1968; Alphorn Concerto, Op.27, hn, orch, 1975; Violin Concerto No.1, Op.31, 1977; No.2 'Albayzin and Sacromonte', Op.81, 2000; *Irdische Klänge*, Op.37, Op.45, Op.60 and Op.64, 1980–92; etc.
Other works: ballets, chamber music, ensemble pieces, songs

schwungvoll (Ger.). Buoyantly.

Sciarrino, Salvatore (b. Palermo, 4 Apr 1947). Italian composer, of music often impalpable yet expressively immediate. He taught himself to compose through an actively creative boyhood, and his catalogue includes music he wrote at 19. Since that time he has been finding poetry and expressive precision in a nocturnal world of soft, fluttering, marginal sounds, breathy and fragile, with occasional unpredictable ventures into quite different areas within the widening sphere of his works and musical interests. An international figure in his early 20s, he withdrew to Città di Castello in order to devote himself to composition, producing a large output strong in chamber music and, latterly, opera.

Operas: *Perseo e Andromeda* (1 act; after Laforgue), f.p. Stuttgart, 1991; LUCI MIE TRADITRICI, 1997–8; MACBETH, 2002; etc.
Orchestral: *Un'immagine di Arpocrate*, pf, ch, orch, 1974–9; *Autoritratto nella notte*, 1982; *Il clima dopo Harry Partch*, pf, orch, 2000; etc.
Chamber: *Sei capricci*, vn, 1975–6; Quintettino No.1, cl qnt, 1976; No.2, wind qnt, 1977; *Introduzione all'oscuro*, 12 insts, 1981; *Lo spazio inverso*, 5 insts, 1985; *Sei quartetti brevi*, str qt, 1967–92; *Infinito nero*, mez, 8 insts, 1997–8; *Cantare con silenzio*, 6 v, fl, perc, elec, 1999; String Quartet No.7, 2000; etc.
Piano: Sonata No.1, 1976; No.2, 1983; No.3, 1987; No.4, 1991–2; No.5, 1994–5; etc.

scoop. A fault in singing, or at least an exaggerated expressive device, whereby the singer reaches the note from below with some effort.

scordatura (It., mistuning). Abnormal tuning of a string instrument – for example, anything other than the customary tuning of the violin (in ascending fifths, G–D–A–E).

The practice and the term were introduced in the early 16th century in lute music that had the lowest string or strings tuned down in order to extend the instrument's range. Downward retunings may similarly be applied to the bowed strings, as may upward ones, to enhance brilliance and penetration. A scordatura may alternatively be used to facilitate particular harmonies or for an unusual effect. Always the tone of the instrument is changed, estranged.

Baroque composers were fond of scordatura for the violin, Biber especially so. But then, like so many things, it faded out until the 20th century, when it was revived for various purposes. The upward scordatura for a solo violin in Mahler's Fourth Symphony produces a grotesque sound of the kind that had appealed to Baroque composers, too, for different reasons. Stravinsky in *The Firebird* used a downward retuning of the violin's top string, from E to D, to produce D major arpeggios in natural harmonics. In Ligeti's *Ramifications* for strings, half the musicians play instruments tuned a quarter-tone sharp, so that the ensemble harmony is besmirched. Ligeti also made scordatura a route to exquisite harmonic effects in his Violin Concerto.

score. Notation of music for multiple performers with the parts layered in orderly alignment. The parts in a score are scored through, by barlines; hence the term, which originally was not applied to solo music (except in the special case of polyphonic keyboard music presented in OPEN SCORE). But this nicety is lapsing.

Used as a verb, though, the term retains its ensemble associations. To score music is to set it for larger forces, whether chamber group, voices or orchestra. This may be a matter of taking an existing piece and arranging it, as with Ravel's scoring of Musorgsky or Holliger's of Liszt. Equally, the term can be used of an original work, whether or not there was a stage when a physical sketch or draft was scored. And it can mean either the act ('Messiaen began scoring *Saint François d'Assise* in 1979', which definitely implies a preliminary draft) or the art ('Stravinsky's scoring is always lucid', which does not). Very often scoring will be synonymous with orchestration, but one may also speak – particularly if discussing the art – of the scoring of a string quartet, a Renaissance mass or even a piece of piano music. Scoring in such cases refers to artistry in matters of sonority, texture and the placement of lines and chords.

Scores are necessary to people composing, playing, singing, rehearsing, conducting and studying – six quite different activities, often requiring different kinds of score. Composers may work with a SKETCH SCORE, SHORT SCORE or DRAFT SCORE at an intermediate stage of composition. Instrumentalists will generally each have a PART to perform from, though in more complex chamber pieces the part may be replaced by a PLAYING SCORE. Singers, whether soloists or choir members, will have a VOCAL SCORE, showing them the accompaniment, their cues and, for choristers, their place in the ensemble. Vocal scores are also used by pianists at rehearsals of operas and choral works, while a pianist rehearsing a non-vocal work, such as a ballet, will have a PIANO REDUCTION. Conductors will need a display of all the parts, a FULL SCORE – so will students and scholars, but perhaps one made for closer inspection: a MINIATURE SCORE or STUDY SCORE. A large work may well be published in three of these forms, most commonly full score, vocal or piano score, and miniature or study score. That has been the stable practice since around 1800.

Manuscript notation in score goes back to the 12th century, but was commonly replaced by the PARTBOOK arrangement around 1225. Medieval composers probably wrote their music one part after another, so that at no stage was there a score. But the development of polyphony in the Renaissance is unimaginable without score notation, so that while music was still copied and distributed in partbooks, it must have been composed in score drafts now lost. The only scores that survive from the 14th and 15th centuries record polyphonic music laid out so that it could be read at the keyboard.

With the blossoming of music printing in the mid 16th century, choral music began to be published in score. Manuscript sources from the same period show passages and whole pieces copied in score for the purposes of instruction and study. The invariable rule was for parts to be presented on the page in descending order of register.

That rule had to be compromised in the Baroque period, with the introduction of combinations of instruments and voices. The parts within a family (voices, strings) would still be placed in descending order, but the families would be kept together, normally with vocal parts between the strings and the continuo (at the bottom), and with brass, timpani and woodwinds (in that order) above. Scores published during this period were generally for presentation rather than performance, and included such modern features as the naming of each instrument or voice in a space to the left of its opening.

The reordering of instrumental families with woodwind at the top began in the late Classical period, but, in an inheritance from the Baroque period, 19th-century scores still have the voices between the violas and the cellos. That changed in the 20th century when the regular pattern became: woodwinds (flutes, oboes, clarinets, saxophones, bassoons), brass (horns, trumpets, trombones, tuba), harp, piano, percussion, timpani, voices, strings (violins, violas, cellos, basses).

Just as uniformity was achieved, though, so new diversities began, especially in the 1950s. Stravinsky gave some of his last works a visual appearance in keeping with their spareness by omitting staves not actively in use. Barraqué and Boulez reorganized orchestral seating and made changes accordingly to the disposition of parts on the page. Stockhausen's electronic *Studie II* was published in the form of a score that theoretically could be used to recreate the piece, but that most readers would treat as an aid to listening, as with the later 'listening score' of Ligeti's *Artikulation*.

scorrevole (It.). Flowingly.

Scotch. See SCOTTISH.

Scotch snap. Division of a beat into a short accented note and a longer unaccented one, normally semiquaver and dotted quaver in a small rising or falling interval. The figure is found in folk music other than Scottish; it was called Lombard in 18th-century France and Italy, and is a characteristic of Hungarian music. But it has distinctly Scots connections in, for example, Purcell and Debussy.

Scotch tune. English Baroque genre imitative of Scottish folksong.

Scotland. Musical survivals are fragmentary before Carver in the early 16th century. Flamboyant polyphony was then briskly dispatched by the Scottish Reformation (1560), and the transfer of the monarchy to London (1603) left Scottish culture without a head. There was a brief Enlightenment revival, coupled with a fashion for Scots folksongs arrangements (by Haydn and Beethoven among others). Then came the even keener vogue for the novels of Walter Scott, though as a creative stimulus this was felt mostly outside Scotland. Within the country composition started to flourish again at the end of the 19th century (Mackenzie, MacCunn), with further boosts after the Second World War (Hamilton, Musgrave) and in the late 20th century (Weir, MacMillan).

John Purser *Scotland's Music* (1992)

Scott, Cyril (Meir) (b. Oxton, Cheshire, 27 Sep 1879; d. Eastbourne, 31 Dec 1970). British pianist-composer. He was sent at 12 to study for a year and a half with Humperdinck at the Hoch Conservatory in Frankfurt, and returned in 1895, now for studies with Knorr. Friends he made included Grainger, Quilter and others of the Frankfurt Group, and also the poet Stefan George. In 1898 he went back to England to start a career as a composer-pianist, his opulent, luxuriating music given an appropriate embodiment in his romantic good looks. Apart from two symphonies, his earlier works feature the piano and include his Piano Quartet (1900), First Sonata (1910), Concerto (1915) and many smaller solo pieces. Later he became very much occupied with the occult and more various in his genres. He married Rose Allatini, a novelist, in 1921.

Scott, Walter (b. Edinburgh, 15 Aug 1771; d. Abbotsford, 21 Sep 1832). Scottish writer, created baronet in 1818. His works went rapidly into operas by Rossini (*La donna del lago*), Donizetti (*Lucia di Lammermoor*), Boieldieu and Bishop, songs by Schubert and overtures by Berlioz (*Waverley, Rob Roy*). Later Scottiana include Bizet's *La Jolie Fille de Perth*.

Scottish. Name given to Mendelssohn's Third Symphony, originally 'Scotch', prompted by a visit to Holyrood House, and dedicated to Queen Victoria. First performance: Leipzig, 3 Mar 1842.

Scriabin [Skryabin, Scriabine], **Aleksandr (Nikolayevich)** (b. Moscow, 6 Jan 1872; d. Moscow, 27 Apr 1915). Russian pianist-composer, whose rhapsodic music pressed to the borders of atonality and, he hoped, mystic communication.

His father was a lawyer and consular official of aristocratic family; his mother a pianist who had studied with Leschetizky. She died when he was just over a year old, and he was brought up by an aunt, a grandmother and a great aunt in a warm atmosphere of female affection and admiration. He showed musical gifts from early childhood, and met Rachmaninoff, a lasting friend and colleague, in Nikolay Zverev's class when he was 12. The following year he began lessons with Taneyev, who remained his teacher, together with Arensky, at the Moscow Conservatory (1888–92).

He then started out on a career as a concert pianist, concentrating on Chopin. From 1894 he was promoted and published by Belyayev, and in 1897 he married Vera Isaakovich, a fellow pianist who was devoted to him and his art. Five years later he abandoned her, their four young children and Russia to live in Italy, Switzerland and Brussels with a new young admirer, Tatyana Schloezer, who encouraged his egocentricity and his music. His Fourth Sonata (1903) marks a turning point in his development from a Chopinesque early style towards a new luxuriance and vehemence, impelled by his identification with Nietzsche's philosophy. From this he turned in 1905 to theosophy, and his music became still more individual: the harmony tends to remain static for long periods, held so by adherence to non-tonal features (the tritone, the whole-tone scale, the diminished seventh chord), leaving the music to grow in profuse ornamentation, to surge forward, to hover.

In 1908 Koussevitzky brought him back to Russia, and increasingly he focused on two expressive types, the demonic and the voluptuous, in short pieces interspersed with the occasional longer movement sustained as a mounting series of waves (*Le Poème de l'extase, Prométhée*, Sonatas Nos.5–10). Much that he wrote after 1910 relates to his 'mystic chord': C–F♯–B♭–E–A–D, from the bass up. He became convinced of the spiritual purpose of art and felt himself to be working towards a *Mysterium*, for which he left fragments of an *Acte préalable* (1914–15) and which he intended would appeal to all the senses – COLOUR projections were foreseen, along with scents – and trigger some kind of cataclysm. His Messianic leanings were furthered by the knowledge he had been born on Christmas Day according to the old Russian calendar. With many plans barely sketched or merely announced, he died of septicaemia.

Faubion Bowers *Scriabin* (1969, ²1996)

Orchestral: Symphony No.1, E, Op.26, with choral finale (Scriabin), 1899–1900; No.2, C minor, Op.29, 1901; No.3 'Le DIVIN POEME', Op.43, 1902–4; *Le POEME DE L'EXTASE* (Symphony No.4), Op.54, 1905–8; Piano Concerto, F♯ minor, Op.20, 1896–7; *Rêverie*, Op.24, 1898; *Prométhée* (see PROMETHEUS), Op.60, pf, orch, 1909–10

Piano sonatas: No.1, F minor, Op.6, 1892; No.2, G♯ minor, Op.19, 1892–7; No.3, F♯ minor, Op.23, 1897; No.4, F♯, Op.30, 1903; No.5, Op.53, 1907; No.6, Op.62, 1911–12; No.7 'White Mass', Op.64, 1911–12; No.8, Op.66, 1912–13; No.9 'Black Mass', Op.68, 1912–13; No.10, Op.70, 1912–13

Piano preludes: Op.2:2, 1886–9; Op.9:1, left hand, 1894; 24, Op.11, 1888–96; 6, Op.13, 1895; 5, Op.15, 1895–6; 5, Op.16, 1894–5; 7, Op.17, 1895–6; 4, Op.22, 1897; 2, Op.27, 1900; 4, Op.31, 1903; 4, Op.33, 1903; 3, Op.35, 1903; 4, Op.37, 1903; 4, Op.39, 1903; Op.45:3, 1904; 4, Op.48, 1905; Op.49:2, 1905; Op.51:2, 1906; Op.56:1, 1908; Op.59:2, 1910; 2, Op.67, 1912–13; 5, Op.74, 1914

Piano études: Op.2:1, 1886–9; 12, Op.8, 1894; 8, Op.42, 1903; Op.49:1, 1905; Op.56:4, 1908; 3, Op.65, 1911–12;

Other piano works: 10 Mazurkas, Op.3, 1889;

Nocturne, Op.9:2, left hand, 1894; 9 Mazurkas, Op.25, 1898–9; 2 Mazurkas, Op.40, 1903; Fantasie, Op.28, 1900; *Deux poèmes*, Op.32, 1903; *Feuillet d'album*, *Poème fantasque*, Op.45:1–2, 1904; *Rêverie*, Op.49:3, 1905; *Fragilité*, *Poème ailé*, *Danse languide*, Op.51:1, 3–4, 1906; *Poème*, *Enigme*, *Poème languide*, Op.52, 1907; *Ironies*, *Nuances*, Op.56:2–3, 1908; *Désir*, *Caresse dansée*, Op.57, 1908; *Feuillet d'album*, Op.58, ?1911; *Poème*, Op.59:1, 1910; *Poème-Nocturne*, Op.61, 1911–12; *Deux poèmes* (*Masque*, *Etrangeté*), Op.63, 1911–12; *Deux poèmes*, Op.69, 1912–13; *Deux poèmes*, Op.71, 1914; *Vers la flamme*, Op.72, 1914; *Deux danses* (*Guirlandes*, *Flammes sombres*), Op.73, 1914

Scribe, (Augustin) Eugène (b. Paris, 24 Dec 1791; d. Paris, 20 Feb 1861). French writer, enormously prolific with plays and librettos, influential on the course of grand opera through his collaborations with Auber (*La Muette de Portici*), Rossini (*Le Comte Ory*), Halévy (*La Juive*), Meyerbeer (*Les Huguenots*) and Verdi (*Les Vêpres siciliennes*). *Un ballo in maschera* and *L'elisir d'amore* are among operas based on adaptations of his librettos.

Sculthorpe, Peter (Joshua) (b. Launceston, Tasmania, 29 Apr 1929). Australian composer, who has found a sense of place in aboriginal music, but more in a poetic response to the outback landscape, influenced also by Balinese and Japanese music. Trained at Melbourne University and at Oxford with Wellesz and Rubbra (1958–61), he joined the staff at Sydney University in 1963. Varèse and Bartók were important to him in his youth, and though he subsequently forsook European modernism in search of a positively Australian style, he kept a commitment to strong, clear forms and new sounds, and to finding a place for exotica in the high citadel of musical classicism, the string quartet. His *Rites of Passage* (1974) was the first new work staged in the Sydney Opera House.

Michael Hannan *Peter Sculthorpe* (1982)

Orchestral: *Irkanda IV*, vn, str, per, 1961; *Sun Music I–IV*, 1965–9; *Music for Japan*, 1970; Piano Concerto, 1982; *Earth Cry*, 1986; *Kakadu*, 1988; *Nourlangie*, gtr, str, perc, 1989; *Great Sandy Island*, 1998; etc.
Percussion quartet: *Djilele*, 1981–90 (arr pf, etc.); *Jabiru Dreaming*, 1989–92
String quartets: No.5 'Irkanda II', 1959; No.8, 1969; No.11 'Jabiru Dreaming', 1990 (arr of perc work); etc.
Other works: *Irkanda I*, vn, 1955; *Night Pieces*, pf, 1971; choral and vocal music, operas and ballets, etc.

sdegnoso (It.). Indignant.

sea. Natural phenomenon whose fluctuations and, by poetic extension, moods have made it a favourite metaphor for music since the Romantic period – though not for composers who spent their lives in central Europe and so never saw it (e.g. Beethoven). There is sea music in works by Mendelssohn (*Meeresstille und glückliche Fahrt*), Wagner (*Der fliegende Holländer*), Rimsky-Korsakov (*Sheherazade*), Elgar (*Sea Pictures*), Debussy (*La Mer*), Sibelius (*The Oceanides*), Vaughan Williams (A *Sea Symphony*), Bridge (*The Sea*), Britten (*Peter Grimes*), Barraqué, etc.

Sea Pictures. Song cycle by Elgar, with orchestra, comprising 'Sea Slumber Song' (Roden Noel), 'In Haven' (Alice Elgar), 'Sabbath Morning at Sea' (Elizabeth Barrett Browning), 'Where Corals Lie' (Richard Garnett) and 'The Swimmer' (Adam Lindsay Gordon). First performance: Norwich, 5 Oct 1899.

Searle, Humphrey (b. Oxford, 26 Aug 1915; d. London, 12 May 1982). British composer. After his education at Winchester and Oxford, he studied at the RCM (1937) and with Webern in Vienna (1937–8). Back in London he worked for various musical organizations before and after the Second World War, during which he participated in the intelligence service. Webern and Schoenberg influenced his works; he was, with Lutyens, one of the first British composers to make contact with central European modernism. His works include the one-act operas *The Diary of a Madman* (f.p. Berlin, 1959) and *The Photo of the Colonel* (f.p. Frankfurt, 1964), and the full-length HAMLET, as well as cantatas and five symphonies. He also wrote a book on Liszt.

season. Annual phase of musical activity, usually starting in early autumn (September in the northern hemisphere) and ending as spring turns into summer (in May–June). Season openings may be important musical and social events, especially for US institutions. In earlier times the season was more limited: the practice started with public opera, which was generally confined to the carnival season, running from the day after Christmas to Shrove Tuesday – a period, therefore, of around two months.

seasons. Being the longest instance of cyclical time evident within a human lifespan, the wheel of the seasons has prompted a lot of music, including Vivaldi's Le QUATTRO STAGIONI (a set of four violin concertos), Haydn's oratorio The SEASONS, Spohr's Ninth Symphony, a set of piano pieces by Tchaikovsky, Cage's String Quartet and ballets by Verdi (in *Les Vêpres siciliennes*), Glazunov and, again, Cage. Among works pertaining to just one of the seasons are the following.

Spring: polyphonic songs by Landini and Le Jeune; violin pieces by Beethoven and Milhaud; symphonies by Schumann, Raff, Paine, Langgaard and Britten; symphonic poems by Debussy, Glazunov, Sibelius, Delius, Roussel, Koechlin and Bridge; cantatas by Rachmaninoff and Nielsen; dance music by Stravinsky, Copland and Johann Strauss II. There are also innumerable spring songs (Mozart, Schubert, Schumann, Mendelssohn, Gounod, Tchaikovsky, Wolf, Debussy, Strauss) and vernal piano pieces (Mendelssohn, Grieg, Sinding). The popularity of spring may be ascribed to natural optimism but also to the growth that music can embody. But where Schumann's, Debussy's and Bridge's springs are indeed bounding and regenerative, Stravinsky hears also the violence.

Summer: 'Sumer is icumen in'; songs by Berlioz, Mahler and Ligeti; symphonies by Raff, Melartin and Langgaard; symphonic poems by Webern, d'Indy, Suk, Delius, Honegger and Bridge; other pieces by Montéclair, Glinka, Schoenberg (*The Summer Wind's Wild Ride* from *Gurrelieder*), Prokofiev and Barber, as well as the midsummer music of Mendelssohn, Tippett and Britten.

Autumn: symphonies by Raff and Langgaard; other works by Grieg, Fauré, Prokofiev, Bax, Takemitsu, Stockhausen, Tippett and Ligeti.

Winter: songs by Schubert, Mendelssohn, Strauss, Britten, Kurtág and Benjamin; symphonies by Tchaikovsky and Raff; other works by Bax, Prokofiev, Cage, Cardew, Takemitsu, Henze and Dufourt; seasonal operas by Rimsky-Korsakov; see also CHRISTMAS MUSIC.

Seasons, The (*Die Jahreszeiten*). Oratorio by Haydn (for s, t, b, ch, orch) to a text by Gottfried van Swieten after James Thomson; in this case, unlike *The Creation*, Haydn set only German words. The four parts form a kind of peasant cantata, following the human and natural cycle from spring to winter. First performance: Vienna, 24 Apr 1801.

seating plan. How an ORCHESTRA or other ensemble is disposed in SPACE.

sec (Fr.). Dry, a brief, light attack.

secco (It.). (1) As SEC.

(2) Abbreviation of *recitativo secco*, i.e. dry recitative.

Sechter, Simon (b. Friedberg, Bohemia, 11 Oct 1788; d. Vienna, 10 Sep 1867). Austrian teacher. He went to Vienna in 1804 to study further, and by the 1820s was making a reputation as a teacher himself. Schubert had a lesson with him shortly before

dying; Bruckner was his pupil. He composed copiously, allegedly writing a fugue a day.

Sechzehntel(-Note) (Ger.). 16th-note, semi-quaver.

second. (1) Note in second position in a diatonic system, e.g. D in C major.

(2) Interval equivalent to that between tonic and second. The interval may be a major second (two semitones, e.g. C–D) or a minor (one semitone, e.g. E–F). Chromatic alteration may produce an augmented second (three semitones, e.g. C–D♯, enharmonically a minor third).

(3) Instruments or groups normally playing below the first section or principal, e.g. second violins, second clarinet.

seconda (It.). Second; the interval, or as in *seconda volta* (second time).

seconda pratica. See PRIMA PRATICA.

seconde (Fr.). Second (interval); hence *seconde majeure*, *seconde mineure*.

second inversion. Vertical rearrangement of a triad so that the fifth is in the bass, e.g. G–C–E.

secondo (It.). Second, as in the marking on the lower part of a piano duet.

second subject. Idea conventionally introduced in the dominant key in a sonata-form exposition.

Second Viennese School. Umbrella term for Schoenberg, Berg and Webern, sometimes understood to include other Schoenberg pupils – even those who, like Skalkottas, studied with him in Berlin. The school was not, then, strictly Viennese, nor was it strictly second, unless one accepts that Haydn, Mozart and Beethoven constituted a First Viennese School.

Secret, The (*Tajemství*). Opera by Smetana to a libretto by Eliška Krásnohorská. The discovery of a secret tunnel leads Kalina (baritone) to his long-beloved Miss Róza (contralto), against the background of a younger match between the latter's niece Blaženka (soprano) and Vít (tenor). First performance: Prague, 18 Sep 1878.

section. (1) Orchestral department, e.g. the woodwind section.

(2) Informal term for part of a work or movement, generally longer than a passage.

secular music. All that is not SACRED MUSIC.

secundal. Term used of harmony rich in seconds.

Seefried, Irmgard (b. Köngetried, Swabia, 9 Oct 1919; d. Vienna, 24 Nov 1988). German–Austrian soprano. She studied with her father and at the Augsburg conservatory, and joined the Aachen Opera under Karajan in 1939. In 1943 she moved to the Vienna Staatsoper, with which she remained until her retirement in 1976, a superb lyric soprano. She was married to the violinist Wolfgang Schneiderhan (1915–2002); Henze wrote *Ariosi* for the two of them.

Seeger, Charles (Louis) (b. Mexico City, 14 Dec 1886; d. Bridgewater, Conn., 7 Feb 1979). US proponent of modernism and, later, folk music. He graduated from Harvard in 1908, spent some time in Europe, then taught at Berkeley (1912–19) and in New York (1921–35), where he was a guiding, goading presence for Cowell and others. Among his pupils was Ruth Crawford, later his second wife. He went to Washington as a musical adviser in the wake of the Depression and subsequently redirected his vigour into folk music. Two of his children, Pete and Peggy, became popular folksingers.

Seeger, Ruth Crawford. See Ruth CRAWFORD.

Segerstam, Leif (Selim) (b. Vaasa, 2 Mar 1944). Finnish conductor and composer. Training at the Sibelius Academy and the Juilliard School (1963–5) was followed by a busy international career, including posts with opera companies and orchestras in Finland, Germany and Scandinavia. His performances and compositions alike are exuberant and impulsive, his catalogue including almost an annual symphony along with concertos and quartets.

segno (It., sign). Typographical character,

used as a signpost in repetitions, which the performer may be asked to make *dal segno* (from the sign) or *al segno* (up to the sign), often abbreviated A.S. and D.S. The reprise closes at *Fine* (It., end). The *dal segno* thus readily produces an X–ABA form, as in a recitative and aria, or a ternary form with an introduction.

Segovia, Andrés (b. Linares, 21 Feb 1893; d. Madrid, 2 Jun 1987). Spanish guitarist. He studied in Granada, where he made his debut in 1909. In the 1920s he embarked on a long international career that vastly boosted the prestige of the guitar

as a classical instrument. Falla, Rodrigo and Turina were among the composers to write for him.

segue (It., follows). Instruction to continue without interruption; *attacca*.

seguidilla. Spanish song-dance in vivacious triple time, taken up by Spanish composers from the 16th century through Sor to Falla, but most famously by Bizet in *Carmen*.

Seiber, Mátyás (György) (b. Budapest, 4 May 1905; d. Kruger National Park, South Africa, 24 Sep 1960). Hungarian–British composer, who showed, through a diverse output, a consistently alert and agile response to Bartók, Schoenberg and jazz. He studied with Kodály at the Budapest Academy of Music (1919–24) and taught at the Hoch Conservatory in Frankfurt (1928–33), where he put jazz on the syllabus. Making London his refuge in 1935, he wrote film music and worked in adult education at Morley College (1942–57). He died in a car crash; Ligeti dedicated *Atmosphères* to his memory.

Cantatas: *Ulysses* (Joyce), t, ch, orch, 1946–7; *Choral Suite from Faust*, s, t, ch, orch, 1950; etc.
Chamber: String Quartet No.1, 1924; No.2, 1934–5; No.3, 1948–51; Concert Piece, vn, pf, 1953–4; Violin Sonata, 1960; etc.
Other works: orchestral pieces, songs, etc.

seises (Sp., sixes). Sixsomes of choirboys instituted in Spanish cathedrals in the 15th century. The Seville group is extant.

Seixas, (José António) Carlos de (b. Coimbra, 11 Jun 1704; d. Lisbon, 25 Aug 1742). Portuguese composer, who succeeded his father as organist of Coimbra Cathedral at 14 and was called to the same post in the royal chapel at 16. He was therefore a colleague of Scarlatti's, but went his own way in the 88 keyboard sonatas that are his most important surviving works.

seizième de soupir (Fr.). Hemidemisemiquaver (64th-note) rest.

Sekunde (Ger.). Second (interval).

Semele. Oratorio by Handel to an anonymous adaptation of an opera libretto Congreve had written for John Eccles. The vain Semele (soprano), taken up into celestial luxury by Jupiter (tenor), is easily tricked by Juno (contralto) into bringing about her own destruction, a story to which the chorus responds with appropriate joy or dismay. Jupiter sings his enchanting 'Where'er you walk' as he creates an arcadian landscape for

Semele. First performance: London, Covent Garden, 10 Feb 1744; staged Cambridge, 1925, and thereafter often done as an opera.

semibiscroma (It.). Hemidemisemiquaver, 64th-note.

semibreve (UK; It. *semibreve*). Whole note (US). Introduced in the 13th century as the shortest DURATION (a division of the breve), it has been since the Renaissance the longest in common use.

semi-chorus. Smaller group given its own music in a choral work, often a solo quartet, but placed and functioning as part of the chorus.

semicroma (It.). Semiquaver, 16th-note.

semi-opera. Play with substantial musical episodes, current in London for just four decades – from 1674, the date of *The Tempest* with music by Locke, Humfrey and others – but instanced by important works from Purcell.

semiotics. The study of signs and of languages as systems of signs, which has brought into musical analysis a breadth of cultural reference, especially to linguistics and anthropology. Important in this field is the work of Nicolas Ruwet and Jean-Jacques Nattiez.

semiquaver (UK). 16th-note (US). See DURATION.

Semiramis. Legendary queen of Assyria and prominent operatic character, central to the following:
(1) Metastasio's libretto *Semiramide riconosciuta*, set by Vinci and Porpora in 1729 and later by Jommelli, Hasse, Gluck, Sarti, Sacchini, Salieri and Meyerbeer.
(2) Mozart's lost (or possibly only projected) *Semiramis* for actors with orchestral music.
(3) Rossini's opera *Semiramide* to a libretto by Gaetano Rossi after a play by Voltaire. Having gained the throne of Babylon by the murder of her husband, Semiramis (soprano) is destroyed, with her co-conspirator Assur (bass), through the arrival of moral strength and legitimacy in the form of her son Arsace (contralto). The overture is a grand dramatic piece; also celebrated is Semiramide's brilliant cavatina 'Bel raggio lusinghier'. First performance: Venice, 3 Feb 1823.

semiseria. See OPERA SEMISERIA.

semitone. The smallest interval in nearly all Western music. The equal-tempered scale has 12 semitone steps. All smaller divisions fall under the heading MICROTONE.

Semper Oper (Semper Opera). The opera house in Dresden, named after Gottfried Semper, who designed the original building of 1841 that was rebuilt and reopened in 1985.

semplice (It.). Simply. Marking implying an absence of ornamentation in Baroque music or a straightforward manner of performance elsewhere. Nielsen titled his Sixth Symphony with the term.

sempre (It., always). Term used to indicate – or remind the performer of – a long-standing style or tempo, as in *sempre legato*, *sempre allegro*.

Semyon Kotko. Opera by Prokofiev to a libretto he wrote with Valentin Katayev after the latter's novella *I am a Son of the Labouring Masses*. The soldier Semyon (tenor) returns to his village, becomes a hero of the revolution and wins his beloved Sofya (soprano) against the bourgeois wishes of her father, Tkachenko (bass-baritone). First performance: Moscow, 23 Jun 1940.

Senesino. Pseudonym of Francesco Bernardi (b. Siena, *c*.1690; d. Siena, ?1759). Italian castrato called thus from his place of birth. Vastly lauded and vastly paid (1,400 guineas was his salary in 1730), he sang in London regularly between 1720 and 1736. Among 17 Handel roles he created were Julius Caesar and Bertarido (*Rodelinda*).

Senfl, Ludwig (b. ?Basle, *c*.1486; d. Munich, 1542/3). Swiss composer. He was a member of Emperor Maximilian I's court chapel from 1496 (as a choirboy) until the monarch's death in 1519. As such he was close to Isaac. In 1523 he joined the court chapel of Duke Wilhelm IV of Bavaria. He sympathized with the Reformation and, though at least in minor orders, married in 1529. The next year, however, he wrote a motet exhorting church unity, to be sung at a congress in Augsburg. Other works include masses, mass propers, motets and polyphonic German songs.

Senleches, Jaquemin de (*fl.* late 14th century). French composer of ARS SUBTILIOR songs, notably *La harpe de melodie*. In 1382–3 he moved from the court of the queen of Castile to that of the Cardinal of Aragon.

sennet. Flourish for trumpets or cornetts indicated in an Elizabethan–Jacobean play, e.g.

Macbeth Act 3, scene 1: 'Sennet sounded. Enter Macbeth as King.'

sentence. Alternative term for PERIOD (1).

senza (It., without). Term used in markings such as *senza sordino* (without mute).

sepolcro (It., sepulchre). Genre of oratorio given in Baroque Vienna by costumed singers in front of a representation of Christ's tomb. Composers involved included Bertali, Cesti and Emperor Leopold I.

sept. Seventh (as interval).

septet (Fr. *septuor*, Ger. *Septett*, It. *septetto*). Group of seven instruments or voices, or group of seven performers on such, or genre of music for that medium, or work of that genre. The best known septets are those by Beethoven, Schoenberg (Op.29) and Stravinsky. An operatic example appears in *Les Troyens*.

Sept haïkaï (Seven Haiku). Work by Messiaen for solo piano, woodwind, percussion and eight violins, offering impressions of Japanese landscapes, birds and GAGAKU music. First performance: Paris, 30 Oct 1963.

septième (Fr.). Seventh (interval), hence *septième majeure, septième mineure*.

septimal. (1) Term used of harmony rich in sevenths.
(2) Using frequency ratios involving the number 7, especially 7:4 (the HARMONIC SEVENTH), 7:5 (a little under an equal-tempered tritone), 7:6 (under a minor third) and 9:7 (over a minor third). Some theorists, notably Mersenne and Leonhard Euler, argued for the inclusion of such intervals, especially the harmonic seventh, but generally they were rejected until the 20th century. Partch was among those who then rejoiced in them.

Septime (Ger.). Seventh (interval).

septimole. SEPTUPLET.

septuor (Fr.). Septet.

septuplet. Group of seven equal notes to be played in the time of some other number, most usually four or six.

sequence. (1) Chant added to the mass, with new words, during the period 850–1250, so called because it came in succession (Lat. *sequentia*) after the gradual and alleluia. The sequences most often reset are *Veni Sancte Spiritus* (Whitsun), *Stabat mater* and *Dies irae* (*Requiem*).
(2) Series of repetitions of a melodic or harmonic idea, moving scalewise up or down.

Séquence. Work by Barraqué setting poems by Nietzsche as a monodrama for soprano with an ensemble of strings and percussion (quasi-solo pf, vn, vc, hp, 5 perc). First performance: Paris, 10 Mar 1956.

Sequenza. Member of a series of 14 solo pieces by Berio, studies in virtuosity and physical engagement with different instruments (including the human voice).

Serafin, Tullio (b. Rottanova di Cavarzere, near Venice, 1 Sep 1878; d. Rome, 2 Feb 1968). Italian conductor, revered for his sense of style and strong influence on the careers successively of Ponselle, Callas and Sutherland. He trained at the Milan Conservatory and made his conducting debut at Ferrara in 1898. After a spell as principal conductor of La Scala (1909–18, with a wartime break) he worked at the Met (1924–34), in Rome (1934–43) and then internationally, into his 80s.

Seraglio, The. See *Die* ENTFÜHRUNG AUS DEM SERAIL.

serenade (Fr. *sérénade*, Ger. *Serenade, Ständchen*, pl. *Serenaden, Ständchen*, It. *serenata*, pl. *serenate*). Originally a song sung from beneath a beloved's window under a clear night sky (It. *sereno*). The term was first used in the late 16th century, but the practice is much older. Serenading, to use the verb form, also appears in opera – notably in *Don Giovanni* and *Die Meistersinger*, in both cases ironically and with the traditional plucked-string accompaniment. Melodies with pizzicato backing in instrumental works often evoke serenades of a romantic kind, as in the quartet published as Haydn's Op.3:5 and known by the nickname 'Serenade'.

There is, though, another class of serenades, performed by instrumental groups and with an intended audience of more than one. Works of this sort were commissioned to enhance an evening's entertainment and could be written for outdoor ensembles (often of wind instruments) or indoor ones. The genre began in the late 17th century and reached its glory in the works of Mozart, whose serenades, nocturnes and cassations may each include a march, a sonata allegro, one or two slow movements with contrasting minuets (this part sometimes featuring a soloist) and a finale. Beethoven's two serenades are chamber pieces.

In the second half of the 19th century the serenade was reinvented again, now as a concert piece of an engagingly melodious character, often featuring ensembles characteristic of the Classical form (string orchestra, winds with or without lower strings); there are examples by Brahms, Dvořák, Tchaikovsky, Elgar and Strauss. Schoenberg's Serenade looks back to both Classical and Renaissance types. Stravinsky seemingly chose the title for its provocative boast of amiability, as later did Berio and Maderna.

serenata. Serenade (It.), but also in Eng. (pl. serenatas) a distinct kind of musical festivity current from the mid 17th century to the end of the 18th. Serenatas were shorter than operas (about an hour long, usually with a break), performed by singers in costume but reading from their parts, within or against elaborate scenery. They might be given, with respect to the etymology, outdoors (one in Dresden in 1719 was delivered from a barge on the Elbe), in theatres or in palaces. The excuse was generally a state occasion – a monarch's birthday, a princely marriage, a royal birth, a victory – to which the text might allude in the shape of a classical allegory. Originating in Italy and Vienna, the form spread to Germany and Britain (taking over the court ode in the 18th century), and was practised by Cesti, Alessandro Scarlatti, Albinoni, Vivaldi, Bach, Handel, Boyce, Haydn, etc.

Serenata notturna. Tautologous title of a serenade for strings by Mozart, K.239.

serial. Having to do with, or based on, the principles of SERIALISM.

serialism. Compositional technique in which all 12 notes of the chromatic scale are used, arranged in a ROW or SET. This was the most important and influential example of the use of an ALGORITHM in 20th-century music, alternatively known as 12-note composition, 12-tone composition or dodecaphony. Sometimes, though, the word 'serialism' is reserved for the European phenomenon of post-1945, and these other terms are preferred for prior and alternative traditions.

Though there are 12-note themes in the last of Berg's *Altenbergleider* (1912), in Schoenberg's *Die Jakobsleiter* from a little later, and even in Liszt's Faust Symphony from long before, the systematic use of 12-note sets was introduced by Schoenberg and Hauer around 1920, with the same aim of reasserting order within the unbounded world of atonality.

Schoenberg, right from the first, worked with rows in four forms: the original or prime (e.g. B♭–E–F♯–E♭–F–A–D–C♯–G–A♭–B–C), the retrograde or reversion (C–B–A♭, etc.), the inversion, with every interval switched in direction (B♭–E–D–F–E♭–B–F♯–G–C♯–C–A–A♭), and the retrograde inversion (A♭–A–C etc.). Each of these may be transposed to any level, so that altogether 48 forms are available.

Effectively the rules of serialism end there. Nothing is said about the vexed question of serial harmony (about, for example, how to set out segments of the row in chords or create harmonic ambiences and progressions some other way) or further matters of form and style. According to Schoenberg's own pronouncement, 'one uses the row and then one composes as before' – and indeed, his elaboration of serialism was accompanied by a full-scale return to traditional forms and genres.

Of Schoenberg's pupils, Berg never kept to a single row for a whole movement. Instead of using retrogrades and inversions he preferred to alter the row order, in that way following Hauer's TROPE system rather than his teacher's usual row technique (though Schoenberg later followed suit in his *Ode to Napoleon*). Also, he introduced non-serial material (such as the Bach chorale in his Violin Concerto) and emphasized diatonic features in his harmony.

Webern, by contrast, wrote consistently in counterpointed row forms after 1924 (whereas Schoenberg by 1935 was creating the occasional tonal piece again). In his case, too, serialism was responsible for a change of style. There was no thought of composing 'as before', unless that phrase is understood in larger historical terms, for with him serialism opened up the possibility of densely organized polyphony of a kind unknown since Bach. In his last works he also moved towards applying algorithms to rhythmic motifs and orchestrational choices.

Other composers to adopt serialism before 1945 included not only Eisler, Gerhard and Skalkottas, who were Schoenberg pupils, but also Martin, Dallapiccola and Krenek, who were not.

After 1945, in a climate of positivism and reconstruction, serialism enjoyed an enormous second growth on both sides of the Atlantic in the hands of young or very young composers – Babbitt, Barraqué, Boulez, Nono, Stockhausen – and at least one older one, Stravinsky. The effort to extend serial procedures to rhythm, timbre and dynamics, and even to create forms resulting from serial rules, resulted in TOTAL SERIALISM at the beginning of the 1950s.

Though the period of absolute adherence to

such practices was rather brief (except in the case of Babbitt, who was far more thoroughgoing in establishing the theoretical groundwork), the heritage of serialism remained: total chromaticism with close attention to the individual interval, the disruption of norms in rhythm, form and ensemble, the application of algorithms and other rules. Even composers who have worked with rows very little or not at all – Ligeti, Kurtág, Birtwistle and many of younger generations – have taken on that inheritance. For others since the 1960s, 'serialism' has been the code word for everything they wanted to reject in radically simplifying music or restoring traditional ways.

George Perle *Serial Composition and Atonality* (1962, ⁶1991)

series. See ROW; SET.

serinette. Small barrel organ, often with just 10 notes above the treble staff, made in the 17th, 18th and early 19th centuries to imitate birdsong and encourage caged birds to sing (as used by George III, both the British monarch and the character in Davies's *Eight Songs for a Mad King*). See also BIRDSONG.

serioso (It.). Serious. Beethoven called his Op.95 *Quartetto serioso* to distinguish it from the light quartet repertory of the time.

Serkin. US pianists, father and son.

(1) **Rudolf** (b. Eger, 28 Mar 1903; d. Guilford, Vermont, 8 May 1991). Austro-Hungarian by birth, he studied with Richard Robert in Vienna, where he met Adolf Busch, the dominant influence on his musical life. Busch drew him to Berlin; they made important recordings together; and they continued working with each other in the USA after 1939. He also married Busch's daughter and became the guiding spirit of the Marlboro Festival. As a player he could be severe, but he could be revelatory, too, especially in Mozart concertos.

(2) **Peter (Adolf)** (b. New York, 24 Jul 1947). He studied with his father and at Curtis with Horszowski, and was also influenced by the leading musicians he heard – and, as a boy, performed with – at Marlboro. Luminous and elevated, his playing suits Messiaen and Takemitsu, but also Schoenberg and Wolpe, and indeed Beethoven: he has maintained a mixed repertory, and pursued a career slightly outside the norms. Goehr, Knussen and Lieberson are among composers to have written for him.

Serly, Tibor (b. Losonc, 25 Nov 1901; d. London, 8 Oct 1978). Hungarian–US composer, remembered especially for his completion of Bartók's Viola Concerto. His family moved to the USA in 1905, but he returned to Budapest to study (with Kodály, Hubay and Weiner at the Liszt Academy, 1922–5). He then played in the Cincinnati Symphony (1926–7), the Philadelphia Orchestra (1928–35) and the NBC Symphony (1937–8), after which he devoted himself to composition and theory – and to Bartók, whom he helped assiduously in New York.

Sermisy, Claudin de (b. *c*.1490; d. Paris, 13 Oct 1562). French composer, associated with the royal chapel, for which he wrote masses, but most popular in his time and best remembered for his polyphonic songs, which include 22 to poems by his contemporary Clément Marot.

Serocki, Kazimierz (b. Toruń, 3 Mar 1922; d. Warsaw, 9 Jan 1981). Polish composer, among the leaders of the avant-garde and founders of the Warsaw Autumn Festival. A pupil of Kazimierz Sikorski in Łódź and Boulanger in Paris, he wrote orchestral pieces and a Percussions de Strasbourg classic (*Continuum*, 1966).

Serov, Aleksandr (Nikolayevich) (b. St Petersburg, 23 Jan 1820; d. St Petersburg, 1 Feb 1871). Russian composer. He was largely self-taught, and became an influential critic before getting down to work as an opera composer. If eclectic and overblown, his operas – *Judith* (1863), *Rogneda* (1865) and the posthumously completed *The Power of the Fiend* (1871), all introduced in St Petersburg – influenced such younger composers as Musorgsky and Tchaikovsky.

serpent. Bass CORNETT, owing its name to its sinuous shape, and having a range from the C below the bass stave (or thereabouts) up through three octaves. Made of wood, usually walnut, with metal fittings and an ivory or horn mouthpiece, it was invented in France *c*.1590 and spread to England after 1660. In both countries it was most often used in church to support the choir. It reached Germany in the 18th century and joined the army band. Cumbersome, it needed judicious handling. If played badly it could sound, according to Burney, like 'a great hungry, or rather angry, Essex calf'.

serré (Fr., tightened). Intensified. Often found in the form *de plus en plus serré* (more and more intense).

Serse (Xerxes). Opera by Handel to an anonymous revision of Silvio Stampiglia's libretto.

Xerxes (mezzo-soprano castrato), King of Persia, unwittingly causes not only despair and confusion among the good but also bad faith among the wicked by falling in love with Romilda (soprano), the beloved of his brother Arsamene (mezzo-soprano). But true love prevails. Xerxes' aria 'Ombra mai fù' ('Handel's Largo') opens the action. First performance: London, 15 Apr 1738.

serva padrona, La (The Maid as Mistress). Opera by Pergolesi to a libretto by Gennaro Antonio Federico. It was originally given as an intermezzo in two parts, which together can make a one-acter for two singing characters. The maid Serpina (soprano) frustrates the efforts of her master-guardian Uberto (bass) to find a wife, a role she wants for herself. Enormously successful all over Europe, from Malta to St Petersburg, the opera in Paris helped spark the QUERELLE DES BOUF-FONS. First performance: Naples, 5 Sep 1733.

service. Regular act in a synagogue or church. In a musical context a service is normally a setting of items with a permanent place in the Anglican liturgy, including music for different services: the canticles for Matins and Evensong, sometimes with the Communion ordinary (i.e. the mass ordinary in English) and the funeral sentences. The Elizabethan terms 'short service' and 'great service' refer to degrees of musical splendour not numbers of items. There are examples from this period by Tallis, Byrd, Parsons, Mundy and Morley, and from later centuries by Child, Blow, Purcell, S.S. Wesley, Stanford, Howells, etc.

sesquialtera (Lat.). 3:2 ratio in frequency (therefore a perfect fifth) or rhythm. Also an organ mutation stop containing the third and fifth.

Sessions, Roger (Huntington) (b. Brooklyn, 28 Dec 1896; d. Princeton, 16 Mar 1985). US composer, who followed a resolute path from neoclassicism into atonality. He studied at Harvard (1910–15) and with Parker at Yale (1915–17), then taught at Smith College (1917–21) and as Bloch's assistant in Cleveland (1921–5). The next several years he spent largely in Italy and Berlin, though he worked with Copland on presenting concerts of contemporary music in New York. He resumed permanent residence in the USA in 1933 and continued his work as a teacher, notably at Princeton (1935–65, except for some years at Berkeley immediately after the Second World War). His works of the 1920s were influenced by Stravinsky and Bloch, but Schoenberg became increasingly important to him, and in his Violin Sonata (1953) he turned to serialism. In

all periods his music avoids national colour while having an energetic density that speaks of the USA.

Roger Sessions *Questions about Music* (1970); Frederik Prausnitz *Roger Sessions* (2002)

Operas: *The Trial of Lucullus* (Brecht), f.p. Berkeley, 1947; *Montezuma* (Giuseppe Antonio Borgese), 1935–63, f.p. Berlin, 1964

Orchestral: Symphony No.1, 1926–7; No.2, 1944–6; No.3, 1957; No.4, 1958; No.5, 1964; No.6, 1966; No.7, 1966–7; No.8, 1968; No.9, 1975–8; Piano Concerto, 1955–6; Violin Concerto, 1927–35; Double Concerto, vn, vc, orch, 1970–71; *The Black Maskers* (suite), 1928; Divertimento, 1959–60; Rhapsody, 1970; Concertino, chbr orch, 1971–2; Concerto for Orchestra, 1981

Vocal: *Idyll of Theocritus*, s, orch, 1954; *When Lilacs Last in the Door-yard Bloom'd* (Whitman), soli, ch, orch, 1964–70; etc.

Chamber and instrumental: String Quintet, 1957–8; String Quartet No.1, 1936; No.2, 1950–51; Piano Sonata No.1, 1927–30; No.2, 1946; No.3, 1964–5; Solo Violin Sonata, 1953; etc.

sesta (It.). Sixth (interval).

sestetto (It.). Sextet.

set. (1) Put (words) to music. An opera composer sets a libretto; a song is a setting of a poem.

(2) Group of musical elements – often the 12 notes of the chromatic scale as used in SERIALISM or some other 12-note compositional technique, though smaller sets have been identified in analysing atonal or near-atonal music by Scriabin, Schoenberg, Bartók, etc. The term was borrowed from set theory (a branch of mathematics) by Babbitt and has the advantage of being more general than 'row' or 'series'. A set is not necessarily a linear succession. In particular, a 12-note set may be a partition into two halves, each a HEXACHORD having no fixed internal order.

settima (It.). Seventh (interval).

Seven Last Words. Those of Christ on the Cross, as recorded in the Gospels. The words are inevitably crucial in Passions; Schütz devoted a work specifically to them. Orchestral music was commissioned from Haydn to be interspersed with sermons on them at Cadiz Cathedral, and the composer subsequently made quartet and cantata arrangements. There are also settings by Gounod and Gubaidulina.

Seven Stars' Symphony. Work by Koechlin with movements devoted to Douglas Fairbanks, Lilian Harvey, Greta Garbo, Clara Bow, Marlene Dietrich, Emil Jannings and Charlie Chaplin.

seventh. (1) Note in seventh position in a diatonic system, e.g. B in C major.

(2) Interval between that note and the (lower) tonic, hence the largest diatonic interval before the octave. A major seventh comprises 11 semitones (e.g. C–B), a minor seventh 10 (e.g. C–B♭). Chromatic alteration can produce a diminished seventh (e.g. C–B♭♭, enharmonically a sixth) or an augmented seventh (e.g. C–B♯, enharmonically an octave).

seventh chord. A triad with added seventh, most commonly a DOMINANT SEVENTH. See also DIMINISHED SEVENTH CHORD.

Sévérac, (Marie Joseph Alexandre) Déodat de (b. St Félix-Camaran, now St Félix-Lauragais, Haute-Garonne, 20 Jul 1872; d. Céret, Pyrénées-Orientales, 24 Mar 1921). French composer. Of long aristocratic lineage, he studied at the Toulouse Conservatory (1893–6) and with d'Indy and Magnard at the Schola Cantorum (1896–1907). Though he made many artistic friendships in Paris (with Roussel, Picasso and Marie Laurencin among others), he preferred to live in the southern lands, whose music and landscapes entered his piano pieces and songs.

sex. Human music may be younger than human reproduction, but the link between the two is thousands of years old. In no culture is marriage entirely without music, with the single exception of the modern register office. There is also a copious literature of love songs and fertility rituals from around the world.

But music's connection with sex is more than a matter of use. Both sway the mind without (before) words; both are rich evokers of fantasy. Also, music itself may be the love object, seducer or overwhelmer. And the relationship between performer and listener can be a quasi-sexual one of giving and receipt. It should be no surprise, then, that outstanding performers have had for their audiences an erotic charge; especially has this been true of singers. And of course, a great deal of opera is sexual drama.

Music's sexuality, though, is ambiguous: it both penetrates (trips into the ear, right into the mind, even seems to be taking place within the mind) and embraces. It comes, most often, from male composers, but is voiced most often in a female vocal range, whether by women singers, violins or a pianist's right hand. It is infinitely supple, a promise to all.

sexes and sexualities. For much of its history Western music was the prerogative of men composers, and orchestras were dominated by men – often exclusively, and by regulation. Increasing equality of the sexes in the 20th century not only brought an end to overt discrimination (except in the case of the Vienna Philharmonic, which maintained its all-male recruiting policy to the end of the century) but opened the way for such composers as Ruth Crawford, Galina Ustvolskaya and Sofia Gubaidulina. Later came interest in those exceptional women who had composed in earlier times, from Hildegard of Bingen to Clara Schumann. Intense argument continues as to whether women's music is, will be or should be different from men's. Some think it is, inevitably. Some see a need for women composers to deviate consciously from aspects of music they regard as male, such as progression towards a goal or the composer–musician–listener hierarchy, and to discover quite new forms of music and music-making.

Much the same discussion goes on with regard to the music of male homosexual composers, except that the forebears are more prestigious (from Corelli and Lully to Cage and Henze), and some have become battlegrounds all their own. Tchaikovsky has been seen as a man burdened by – and expressing – homosexual guilt or as an artist thoroughly comfortable with (and expressing) his appetites, while the claiming of Schubert and Handel as homosexual remains uncertain and controversial.

One further difference is that the portrayal of homosexual characters or situations in music was extremely rare before the works of Britten, Vivier and others in the 1970s, whereas women characters are fully represented in the repertories of opera and song. That women can interpret such male-created characters as Susanna and the Countess with full conviction, that another female role in *Le nozze di Figaro* – Cherubino – is a character of delightfully duple sex (an adolescent boy enacted by a woman), and that spectators of all kinds can be drawn into and touched by the drama of these people must make us wary of analyses that invoke some fundamental difference between the sexes and sexualities.

Susan McClary *Feminine Endings* (1991, ²2002); Philip Brett, Elizabeth Wood and Gary C. Thomas ed. *Queering the Pitch* (1994)

sext. Sixth (as interval).

Sexte (Ger.). Sixth (interval).

sextet (Fr. *sextette, sextuor*, Ger. *Sextett*, It. *sestetto*). Group of six instruments or voices, or group of six performers on such, or genre of music for that medium, or work of that genre. The most common such ensemble is the string sextet (2 vn, 2 va, 2 vc), whose repertory includes works by Brahms, Tchaikovsky, Schoenberg, Strauss (opening of *Capriccio*), etc. Other sextet combinations include the horns and strings of an early work by Beethoven and – the most familiar operatic example – the shocked voices at a moment in *Lucia di Lammermoor*.

sextuplet. Group of six equal notes to be played in the time of some other number, most usually four.

sf, sfz. Abbreviations for *sforzando* or *sforzato*.

sfogato (It., airy). Direction for light tone, delicate touch (in Chopin, for example).

sforzando, sforzato (It.). Enforcing, enforced, implying a forceful attack on a single note or chord, abbreviated *sf, sfz*.

Sgambati, Giovanni (b. Rome, 28 May 1841; d. Rome, 14 Dec 1914). Italian composer. In 1862 he was taken up by Liszt, with whom he studied and travelled, though Rome remained his base, and he helped establish the school there attached to the Accademia di Santa Cecilia. He was one of the first Italian composers since the 18th century to concentrate on instrumental music, his works including two piano quintets, a string quartet, orchestral music and many piano pieces.

Shadow of Night, The. Orchestral work by Birtwistle, alluding to Dowland and melancholy. First performance: Cleveland, 10 Jan 2002.

shake. 17th-century Eng. term for trill.

Shakespeare, William (baptized Stratford-on-Avon, 26 Apr 1564; d. Stratford-on-Avon, 23 Apr 1616). English playwright and poet. There are around 100 songs in the plays, some adapting popular tunes, others leaving scope to composers down the centuries, including Arne, Birtwistle, Carter, Chausson, Finzi, Haydn, Johnson, Morley, Poulenc, Schubert, Strauss, Stravinsky, Tippett, Vaughan Williams and Warlock. For larger musical treatments see BEATRICE ET BENEDICT; FALSTAFF; HAMLET; KING LEAR; *Die* LUSTIGEN WEIBER VON WINDSOR; MACBETH; *A* MIDSUMMER NIGHT'S DREAM; OTHELLO; ROMEO AND JULIET and *The* TEMPEST. There are additional Shakespeare operas by Barber, Boesmans, Castelnuovo-Tedesco, Goetz, Harbison, Henze, Nabokov, Stanford, Storace, Wagner and Wolf-Ferrari.

shakuhachi. Japanese bamboo flute.

Shalyapin, Fyodor. See Fyodor CHALIAPIN.

Shankar, Ravi (b. Benares, 7 Apr 1920). Indian sitarist and composer. He first toured Europe and the USA in 1956–7, and in the next decade formed fruitful contacts with Yehudi Menuhin and George Harrison (of the Beatles). His compositions include two sitar concertos (1971, 1976).

shanty [chanty]. Sea song, as sung by British and US sailors in the 19th century.

shape note. Note with shaped head, a different shape for each degree of the scale. Introduced in 1801 and exclusive to the USA (especially the South and Midwest), shape notes provided a way into conventional notation for singers versed in tonic sol-fa, since each solmization syllable had its equivalent shape.

Shapero, Harold (Samuel) (b. Lynn, Mass., 29 Apr 1920). US composer. He studied with Slonimsky at the Malkin Conservatory in Boston (1936–8), with Krenek and Piston at Harvard, and with Hindemith and Boulanger. In 1951 he joined the Brandeis faculty. His works, deliciously witty and fluent in their Classical modelling, include a Symphony for classical orchestra (1947) and three short piano sonatas (1944).

Shapey, Ralph (b. Philadelphia, 12 Mar 1921; d. Chicago, 13 Jun 2002). US composer, who flourished in adamant apartness from New York musical life. The son of Russian Jewish immigrants, he had lessons with Wolpe from 1938 but attended no college or conservatory and made his way largely alone, developing his own atonal harmonic system. His circle in New York was that of the abstract expressionist painters, whose vividness and energy he emulated in such works as *Rituals* for orchestra (1959) and *Incantations* for wordless soprano and 10-piece ensemble (1961). He then taught at the University of Chicago (1964–92), where he was founder director of the Contemporary Chamber Players. In 1992 he was awarded a Pulitzer Prize for his big orchestral *Concerto fantastique* (1989–91), but the award was scandalously withdrawn. His large output, chiefly of instrumental music, also includes nine quartets.
Patrick D. Finley *A Catalogue of the Works of Ralph Shapey* (1997)

Shaporin, Yury (Aleksandrovich) (b. Glukhov, 8 Nov 1887; d. Moscow, 9 Dec 1966). Russian composer. He studied with Steinberg and Tcherepnin at the St Petersburg Conservatory (1913–18), then worked in the theatre with Gorky, Blok, Mayakovsky and others. After the disbandment of the Association for Contemporary Music, of which he had been a member, he concentrated on major works fully within the Russian tradition, notably his opera *The Decembrists* (1920–53).

sharp. Raised in pitch, normally by a semitone. Thus C♯ (to use the sharp sign) is a semitone above C; a further semitone sharpening produces C double sharp (Cx). See also ACCIDENTAL.

sharpen. Raise in pitch, usually by a semitone. Thus a sharpened fourth is an augmented fourth.

sharp key. Key with a sharp or sharps in its signature, e.g. A major and F♯ minor, both of which have three sharps.

Shaw, George Bernard (b. Dublin, 26 Jul 1856; d. Ayot St Lawrence, Herts., 2 Nov 1950). British playwright and music critic. He was a regular critic – forceful, funny and often acute – from soon after his arrival in London (in 1876) until 1894, latterly under the pseudonym Corno di Bassetto.

Shaw, Robert (Lawson) (b. Red Bluff, Cal., 30 Apr 1916; d. New Haven, Conn., 25 Jan 1999). US conductor, valued especially as a trainer of choirs. Having been diverted in his studies at Pomona College from theology into music, he retained a religious conviction in his work. He was also principal conductor of the Atlanta Symphony (1967–88).

shawm. Double-reed woodwind instrument, with variants widely distributed in Europe (until supplanted by the oboe and bassoon in the 17th century), North Africa and Asia. Shawms are distinguished from their European successors by a more conical shape and a reed shield, the pirouette, against which players can place their lips and thereby achieve a more robust sound.

The earliest shawms in Europe were shorter than the oboe and correspondingly higher. They may have been introduced from the Islamic world, though the instrument's history is also bound up with that of the bagpipe chanter. The treble shawm (ancestral oboe) and the alto (or bombarde) were developed in the first half of the 14th century, and followed in the 16th century by tenor and bass instruments. By this time shawms were being played in court and civic bands, alongside cornetts and sackbuts. Their rapid decline in the 17th century took place before they could be recorded in any orchestral score, but they survived as folk instruments.

Shchedrin, Rodion (Konstantinovich) (b. Moscow, 16 Dec 1932). Russian composer, a colourful postmodernist. A music scholar's son, he had a thorough musical training from an early age and was ultimately Shaporin's pupil at the Moscow Conservatory (1951–5). By the time he graduated he had won professional esteem and official backing, to which the Bolshoy production of his ballet *The Little Humpbacked Horse* in 1960 added popularity. Still close to Prokofiev at this point, he later brought touches of modernism and jazz – or Bizet in his unashamed *Carmen Suite* for percussion and strings (1967) – into his eclectic mix. Other works include five piano concertos, three symphonies, four concertos for orchestra (No.1 'Naughty Limericks', 1963) and piano music (24 Preludes and Fugues, 1964–70; *Polyphonic Notebook*, 1972).

Shcherbachev, Vladimir (Vladimirovich) (b. Warsaw, 25 Jan 1889; d. Leningrad, 5 Mar 1952). Russian composer. He was the nephew of the composer Nikolay Vladimirovich (1853–?), who is said to have died in Monte Carlo after losing all his money and working as a croupier. The younger Shcherbachev studied with Steinberg and Lyadov at the St Petersburg Conservatory (1908–14), during which time he travelled to western Europe as a pianist with Diaghilev's company. A member of the Association for Contemporary Music, he was an important teacher at his alma mater (1923–31). He alone refused to condemn Shostakovich's *Lady Macbeth* when the work was discussed by the Leningrad Composers' Union in 1936. His own compositions include five symphonies.

Shebalin, Vissarion (Yakovlevich) (b. Omsk, 11 Jun 1902; d. Moscow, 28 May 1963). Russian composer. He spent his life at the Moscow Conservatory, first as a student (1923–8), then immediately after as a teacher and eventually as director (1942–8), a post he lost in the purge of 'formalists', though he was reinstated as professor in 1951. Musically indebted to his teacher Myaskovsky and a close friend to Shostakovich, he wrote five symphonies, nine quartets and an operatic *Taming of the Shrew* (1946–56).

Sheep may safely graze (*Schafe können sicher weiden*). Recitative and aria in Bach's secular cantata *Was mir behagt ist nur die munter Jagd!* Much arranged.

sheet music. Printed music.

Sheherazade. Narratrix of the *1001 Nights*. Works named in her honour include:

(1) The rapturous and hedonistic orchestral suite by Rimsky-Korsakov in four movements: 1 *The Sea and Sindbad's Ship*, 2 *The Tale of the Kalender Prince* (i.e. prince disguised as a beggar), 3 *The Young Prince and the Young Princess*, 4 *The Festival at Baghdad – The Sea – Shipwreck on a Rock Surmounted by a Bronze Warrior – Conclusion*. First performance: St Petersburg, 15 Dec 1888.

(2) An early overture by Ravel.

(3) The orchestral song cycle by Ravel (to words by Tristan Klingsor), full of exotic and erotic suggestions. The songs are: 1 'Asie', 2 'La Flûte enchantée', 3 'L'Indifférent'. First performance: Paris, 17 May 1904.

(4) The first of Szymanowski's *Masques* for piano.

(5) Gerhard's song cycle *L'infantament meravellós de Shahrazada*.

sheng. Chinese mouth organ with a vertical cluster of pipes. The Japanese equivalent is the SHŌ.

Sheng, Bright [Zong Liang] (b. Shanghai, 6 Dec 1955). Chinese composer. He studied at the Shanghai Conservatory and, from 1982, in New York, where his teachers included Chou, Perle and Davidovsky. A Chinese atmosphere is combined in his music with mainstream modernism. He made his name with *H'un* (Lacerations) for orchestra (1988), since followed by many other orchestral pieces, chamber scores and operas.

Shepherd on the Rock, The. See *Der* HIRT AUF DEM FELSEN.

Sheppard, John (b. *c*.1515; d. Dec 1568). English composer. He was choirmaster at Magdalen College, Oxford (1543–8), and then a member of the Chapel Royal. Most of his vigorously contrapuntal music seems to have been written for the restored Catholic liturgy under Mary I, including his six-voice *Cantate* mass and numerous hymns, psalms and responsories.

Sheriff, Noam (b. Ramat-Gan, 7 Jan 1935). Israeli composer. He studied with Ben-Haim and in Berlin with Blacher (1960–62), and has taught in Jerusalem and Tel-Aviv since 1966–7. His works, mostly instrumental, combine features from classical and Jewish traditions.

Sherman, Russell (b. New York, 25 Mar 1930). US pianist of exemplary virtuosity and grace, who in latter years has been lured out of his teaching studio (at the New England Conservatory) only for occasional recitals and recordings, playing Haydn, Beethoven, Liszt and contemporary US works. He studied with Steuermann.

Shield, William (b. Swalwell, Co. Durham, 5 Mar 1748; d. London, 25 Jan 1829). British composer. The son of a music master, he was orphaned at nine and apprenticed to a boat builder, from whose trade he escaped to study with Avison and become a jobbing musician. He moved to London in 1772 and won success as a theatre composer, though not until he was 30 (*The Flitch of Bacon*, 1778). He was also late marrying – over 40 – but enjoyed happiness in that state, without children. By the age of 50 he had virtually retired, but, made Master of the King's Music in 1817, he wrote the last British court ode the next year.

Shifrin, Seymour (b. Brooklyn, 28 Feb 1926; d. Boston, 26 Sep 1979). US composer. He studied with Schuman at Juilliard, Luening at Columbia and Milhaud in Paris (1951–2), then taught at Berkeley (1952–66) and Brandeis (1966–79). Working in a fine, highly chromatic style, he favoured chamber music, his output including five quartets and *Satires of Circumstance* for mezzo and mixed sextet (1964).

shift. Change of left-hand position on the violin, from first to second (half shift), third (whole shift) or fourth (double shift), etc.

shipelcurb (Ir.). Irish sheep bell. Peirse Cibber's priceless supper-club piece *Cruel Bliss, ipse Sir Perrie Pip's Erreur* uses shipelcurbs (Bubbles's 'Her cherub lips sure pull his purple curlicue': 'pure rubbish' – Culpepper). See PUBLISHER.

shō. Japanese mouth organ played in GAGAKU, equivalent to the Chinese SHENG.

shofar. Jewish liturgical instrument, a trumpet made from a ram's horn that has been heated and twisted to give it an upward turn near the wide end. It is played at Rosh ha-Shanah and Yom Kippur services. Elgar included it in *The Apostles*, though the part is normally played on flugelhorn.

short octave. Altered tuning of the bottom octave of keyboard instruments to reduce the number of little-used notes. For example, a whole octave (C–C) might be crammed into the keys that would normally cover only a sixth (E–C), leaving out the C♯, E♭, F♯ and A♭. The practice was common in the 16th century, and though the increasing chromaticization of music made it less useful, it continued into the 19th century.

short score. Composing draft of a work for large forces, usually on two or four staves with some indications of proposed instrumentation.

Shostakovich, Dmitry (Dmitriyevich) (b. St Petersburg, 25 Sep 1906; d. Moscow, 9 Aug 1976). Russian composer. As the most gifted composer to emerge in the new Soviet state, he was subject to extraordinary and often contradictory pressures: to add to the great repertory and yet to express the dynamic difference of a revolutionary society, to write both symphonies and film scores, and – most arduous of all – to adapt to the corruption of values that took place under Stalin. His creative survival is remarkable, his achievement even more so.

He studied with Steinberg and Glazunov at the Petrograd Conservatory (1919–25); his graduation piece was his First Symphony, which was already entirely individual and gained him a reputation in Russia and abroad. Then immediately he stopped, and when he got going again steered a middle course between the rival musical organizations of the time. He assimilated the modernism espoused by the Association for Contemporary Music, especially that of Stravinsky and Prokofiev, but he also accepted the need voiced by the Russian Association of Proletarian Musicians for useful music (film scores, teaching material). Between 1927 and 1932 he produced two more symphonies with explicitly revolutionary choral finales but almost nothing else for the concert hall. Rousing celebration would always appeal less to him than satire and the grotesque, but at this point he wrote from a position of sympathy with the government and found opportunities to exercise his preferences in music for the theatre: two operas and two full-length ballets besides a variety of scores for plays and films.

His second opera, *The Lady Macbeth of the Mtsensk District*, was an outstanding success at home and abroad; by January 1936 it had been seen in western Europe and the Americas and was playing in Moscow in three different productions. Then it was visited by Stalin. A vulgar denunciation in the party newspaper *Pravda* followed, the work was taken from the stage, and his Fourth Symphony was withdrawn after rehearsals. His Fifth, written the next year, he called 'a composer's reply to just criticism' – with how much sarcasm it is difficult to know. The finale is ostensibly triumphant, but can equally be heard as a forced paean. Previously he had used irony with bright dexterity against specific external targets; now it was internal, as in Mahler, creating a tense atmosphere of self-doubt and self-contradiction. Often the meaning is hard to read. In his Sixth Symphony (1939), for instance, the weight of a long tragic adagio at the start is not displaced by the two fast movements that follow, joky and brittle. However, the Piano Quintet (1940) marks the beginning of a franker kind of expression coming in chamber music.

His next symphony, No.7, brought him back to public concerns, for it was an immediate response to the 1941 German siege of Leningrad. Like other artists, he was evacuated, in his case to Moscow. While away he started another opera – *The Gamblers*, after Gogol – but abandoned it. Then came two more symphonies, in which he failed to maintain the expectations aroused by the Seventh that he would accept the responsibilities of a state artist: the Eighth was too pessimistic for a time of struggle, the Ninth too flippant to be a victory celebration. Ultimately, in 1948, he and his leading colleagues came under official attack (see POLITICS). He put his new violin concerto aside for less restrictive times, and devoted himself on the public front to approved subject matter – such as the cantata *The Song of the Forests*, celebrating Stalin's afforestation of the steppe – while writing more personal music in string quartets, songs and a volume of preludes and fugues for piano.

In 1953, after Stalin's death, he was able to resume his compositional life as before, notably with his Tenth Symphony, a work of victorious negativity that has been construed as a portrait of the late dictator. Other works that had been held in reserve – the violin concerto and the song cycle *From Jewish Folk Poetry* – could now be heard. But any feeling of liberation was short lived, and there were also personal problems. In 1954 he lost his wife, Nina, to whom he had been married in 1932. Their marriage had been an open one, and he was on intimate terms with a pupil who had become a fellow composer, Galina Ustvolskaya. But Nina's death was a blow, and he was left with two teenage children, Galina (b. 1936) and Maxim (b. 1938). In 1956 he remarried, but his creativity remained depressed. His next two symphonies, Nos.11 and 12, were programme pieces – film scores without films – and again he found a more immediate, more personal outlet in chamber music, especially in his Eighth Quartet (1960), in which he included quotations from other works as well as his musical monogram D–S–C–H (in German note names, i.e. D–E♭–C–B).

The relaxation of artistic constraints during Khrushchev's later years in power made it possible for him to restore *The Lady Macbeth* to the stage, albeit under a new title, and address the hot theme of anti-Semitism hotly in his Symphony No.13 (1961). But again this was a brief flare in a creative life that had largely gone underground, into chamber music and film scores (notably for the *Hamlet* directed by his old friend and colleague Grigory Kozintsev). That life emerged prominently again in his Fourteenth Symphony, a symphonic song cycle on poems of death, and his Fifteenth, with its puzzling quotations from Rossini's *Guillaume Tell* overture and Wagner's *Ring*. Other works of this late period were similarly concerned with mortality and disintegration – not least the Fifteenth Quartet, a sequence of six slow movements.

The posthumous publication of *Testimony* (1979), in which Solomon Volkov purported to present the composer's views, was widely greeted in the West as revealing the 'real' Shostakovich. But the authenticity of Volkov's account has been questioned, and, in any event, there could never be an easy explanation of music so riven and masked.

Elizabeth Wilson *Shostakovich* (1994); Laurel E. Fay *Shostakovich* (2000)

Theatre and film music

Operas: *The* NOSE, Op.15, 1927–8; *The* LADY MACBETH OF THE MTSENSK DISTRICT, Op.29, 1930–32, rev as KATERINA IZMAYLOVA, Op.114, 1954–63; *The Gamblers* (Gogol), 1941–2, unfinished; *Moscow – Cheryomushki* (operetta; Vladimir Mass and Mikhail Chervinsky), Op.105, 1958, f.p. Moscow, 1959

Ballets: *The Golden Age*, Op.22, 1927–30; *The Bolt*, Op.27, 1930–31; *The Limpid Stream*, Op.39, 1934–5

Film scores (with directors): *New Babylon* (Grigory Kozintsev and Leonid Trauberg), Op.18, 1928; *Alone* (Kozintsev and Trauberg), Op.26, 1930–31; *Golden Hills* (Sergey Yutkevich), Op.30, 1931; *The Counterplan* (Lev Arnshtam and Fridrikh Ermler), Op.33, 1932; *The Tale of the Priest and his Servant Blockhead* (Mikhail Tsekhanovsky), Op.36, 1934; *Love and Hate* (Albert Gendelstein), Op.38, 1934; *The Youth of Maxim* (Kozintsev and Trauberg), Op.41, 1934; *Girl Friends* (Arnshtam), Op.41a, 1934–5; *The Return of Maxim* (Kozintsev and Trauberg), Op.45, 1936–7; *Volochayev Days* (Georgy and Sergey Vasilyev), Op.48, 1936–7; *Viborg District* (Kozintsev and Trauberg), Op.50, 1938; *Friends* (Arnshtam), Op.51, 1938; *The Man with a Gun* (Yutkevich), Op.53, 1938; *The Great Citizen* (Ermler), 2 series, Op.52, 1937, Op.55, 1938–9; *The Silly Little Mouse* (Tsekhanovsky), Op.56, 1939; *The Adventures of Korzinkina* (Klimenty Mints), Op.59, 1940–41; *Zoya* (Arnshtam), Op.64, 1944; *Simple People* (Kozintsev and Trauberg), Op.71, 1945; *The Young Guard* (Sergey Gerasimov), Op.75, 1947–8; *Pirogov* (Kozintsev), Op.76, 1947; *Michurin* (Aleksandr Dovzhenko), Op.78, 1948; *Encounter at the Elbe* (Grigory Aleksandrov), Op.80, 1948; *The Fall of Berlin* (Mikhail Chiaureli), Op.82, 1949; *Belinsky* (Kozintsev), Op.85, 1950; *The Unforgettable Year 1919* (Chiaureli), Op.89, 1951; *The Song of the Great Rivers* (Ivens), Op.95, 1954; *The Gadfly* (Aleksandr Faintsimmer), Op.97, 1955; *The First Echelon* (Mikhail Kalatozov), Op.99, 1956; *Five Days – Five Nights* (Arnshtam), Op.111, 1960; *Hamlet* (Kozintsev), Op.116, 1963–4; *A Year is Like a Lifetime* (Grigory Roshal), Op.120, 1965; *Sofiya*

Perovskaya (Arnshtam), Op.132, 1967; *King Lear* (Kozintsev), Op.137, 1970

Incidental music and other theatre scores: *The Bedbug* (play; Mayakovsky), Op.19, 1929; *Poor Columbus* (entr'acte and finale for opera by Erwin Dressel), Op.23, 1929; *The Shot* (play; Aleksandr Bezymensky), Op.24, 1929; *Rule, Britannia* (play; Adrian Piotrovsky), Op.28, 1931; *Hypothetically Murdered* (revue; Vsevolod Voyevodin and Yevgeny Ryss), Op.31, 1931; *Hamlet*, Op.32, 1931–2; *La Comédie humaine* (play; Sukhotin, after Balzac), Op.37, 1933–4; *Salute to Spain* (show; Aleksandr Afinogenov), Op.44, 1936; *King Lear*, Op.58a, 1941; *The Fatherland* (show), Op.63, 1942; *The Russian River* (show), Op.66, 1944

Orchestrations: BORIS GODUNOV (Musorgsky), Op.58, 1939–40; KHOVANSHCHINA (Musorgsky), Op.106, 1952–8

Orchestral music

Symphonies: No.1, F minor, Op.10, 1923–5, f.p. Leningrad, 12 May 1926 (Malko); No.2 'To October', B, Op.14, with ch in finale (Bezymensky), 1927, f.p. Leningrad, 5 Nov 1927 (Malko); No.3 'The First of May', E♭, Op.20, with ch in finale (Semyon Kirsanov), 1929, f.p. Leningrad, 21 Jan 1930 (Gauk); No.4, C minor, Op.43, 1935–6, f.p. Moscow, 30 Dec 1961 (Kondrashin); No.5, D minor, Op.47, 1937, f.p. Leningrad, 21 Nov 1937 (Mravinsky); No.6, B minor, Op.54, 1939, f.p. Leningrad, 21 Nov 1939 (Mravinsky); No.7 'Leningrad', C, Op.60, 1941, f.p. Kuybïshev, 5 Mar 1942 (Samosud); No.8, C minor, Op.65, 1943, f.p. Moscow, 4 Nov 1943 (Mravinsky); No.9, E♭, Op.70, 1945, f.p. Leningrad, 3 Nov 1945 (Mravinsky); No.10, E minor, Op.93, 1953, f.p. Leningrad, 17 Dec 1953 (Mravinsky); No.11 'The Year 1905', G minor, Op.103, 1957, f.p. Moscow, 30 Oct 1957 (Rakhlin); No.12 'The Year 1917', D minor, Op.112, 1961, f.p. Leningrad, 1 Oct 1961 (Mravinsky); No.13 'Babi Yar' (Yevtushenko), B♭ minor, Op.113, b, ch, orch, 1962, f.p. Moscow, 18 Dec 1962 (Kondrashin); No.14 (Apollinaire, Wilhelm Küchelbecker, Lorca, Rilke), Op.135, s, b, str, perc, 1969, f.p. Leningrad, 29 Sep 1969 (Barshay); No.15, A, Op.141, 1971, f.p. Leningrad, 8 Jan 1972 (Maxim Shostakovich)

Concertos: Piano Concerto No.1, C minor, Op.35, with tpt and str, 1933; No.2, F, Op.102, 1957; Violin Concerto No.1, A minor, Op.77, 1947–8, rev 1955; No.2, C♯ minor, Op.129, 1967; Cello Concerto No.1, E♭, Op.107, 1959; No.2, G, Op.126, 1966

Vocal orchestral: 2 Fables (Ivan Krylov), Op.4, mez, ch, orch, 1922; 6 Romances (Jap. poets), Op.21, t, orch, 1928–32; 6 Romances (Pasternak, after Raleigh, Shakespeare; Samuil Marshak, after Burns, Eng. trad), Op.62a, b, orch, 1942, rev as Op.140, 1971; Poem of the Motherland (cantata), Op.74, 1947; From Jewish Folk Poetry, 1948–?64; *The Song of the Forests* (oratorio; Yevgeny Dolmatovsky), Op.81, 1949; *The Sun Shines on our Motherland* (cantata, Dolmatovsky), Op.90, 1952; *The Execution of Stepan Razin* (Yevtushenko), Op.119, b, ch, orch, 1964; 6 Verses (Tsvetayeva),

Op.143a, a, chbr orch, 1974; Suite (Michelangelo), Op.145a, b, orch, 1975

Other works: Scherzo No.1, F♯ minor, Op.1, 1919; No.2, E♭, Op.7, 1923–4; Theme and Variations, B♭, Op.3, 1921–2; Prelude and Scherzo, str, 1924–5; Jazz Suite No.1, 1934, No.2, 1938; 8 Preludes, 1934; 5 Fragments, Op.42, chbr orch, 1935; Festive Overture, Op.96, 1947; Overture on Russian and Kyrgyz Folk Themes, Op.115, 1963; Funeral–Triumphal Prelude in Memory of the Heroes of Stalingrad, Op.130, 1966; *October*, Op.131, 1967; March of the Soviet Militia, Op.139, 1970

Orchestrations: *Tahiti Trot* (*Tea for Two*), Op.16, 1928; 2 Pieces (Domenico Scarlatti), Op.17, wind band, 1928; *Songs and Dances of Death* (Musorgsky), 1962; 2 Choruses (Davidenko), Op.124, 1963; Cello Concerto (Schumann), Op.125, 1963

Chamber and instrumental music

String quartets: No.1, C, Op.49, 1935; No.2, A, Op.68, 1944; No.3, F, Op.73, 1946; No.4, D, Op.83, 1949; No.5, B♭, Op.92, 1952; No.6, G, Op.101, 1956; No.7, F♯ minor, Op.108, 1960; No.8, C minor, Op.110, 1960; No.9, E♭, Op.117, 1964; No.10, A♭, Op.118, 1964; No.11, F minor, Op.122, 1966; No.12, D♭, Op.133, 1968; No.13, B♭ minor, Op.138, 1970; No.14, F♯, Op.142, 1973; No.15, E♭ minor, Op.144, 1974

Other chamber works: Piano Trio No.1, Op.8, 1923; No.2, E minor, Op.67, 1944; 2 Pieces, str octet, Op.11, 1924–5; Cello Sonata, D minor, Op.40, 1934; Piano Quintet, G minor, Op.57, 1940; Violin Sonata, Op.134, 1968; Viola Sonata, Op.147, 1975

Piano solo: 3 Fantastic Dances, Op.5, 1922; Sonata No.1, Op.12, 1926; No.2, Op.61, 1942; *Aphorisms*, Op.13, 1927; 24 Preludes, Op.34, 1932–3; *Children's Notebook*, Op.69, 1944–5; 24 Preludes and Fugues, Op.87, 1950–51; 7 *Dolls' Dances*, 1952 (from ballets)

Piano duo: Suite, F♯ minor, Op.6, 1922; Concertino, Op.94, 1954

Songs and choruses

Songs (with piano except where stated): 4 Romances (Pushkin), Op.46, b, 1936; 6 Romances, Op.62, b, 1942; *Victorious Spring* (Mikhail Svetlov; 2 songs for show), Op.72, 1945; *From Jewish Folk Poetry*, Op.79, s, a, t, 1948; 2 Romances (Lermontov), Op.84, 1950; 4 Songs (Dolmatovsky), Op.86, 1951; 4 Monologues (Pushkin), Op.91, b, 1952; 5 Romances (Dolmatovsky), Op.98, b, 1954; Spanish Songs, Op.100, mez, 1956; *Satires* (Chorny), Op.109, s, 1960; 5 Romances (*Krokodil*), Op.121, b, 1965; Preface to the Complete Edition of My Works, Op.123, b, 1966; 7 Romances (Blok), Op.127, s, pf trio, 1967; 'Spring, spring' (Pushkin), Op.128, 1967; 6 Verses (Tsvetayeva), Op.143, a, 1973; Suite (Michelangelo), Op.145, b, 1974; 4 Verses by Captain Lebyadkin (Dostoyevsky *The Devils*), Op.146, b, 1974

Choruses: 10 Poems, Op.88, 1951; 2 Russian Folksong Arrangements, Op.104, 1957; *Loyalty* (8 ballads: Dolmatovsky), Op.136, 1970

Shudi. Family of harpsichord makers founded by Burkat Shudi (1702–73), who arrived in London from his native Switzerland in 1718 and learned the craft from Hermann Tabel. In 1739 he set up by himself, to be joined by John BROADWOOD and succeeded by his son, also Burkat.

si (Fr., It., Sp.). The note or key of B.

Sibelius, Jean [Johan Julius Christian] (b. Hämeenlinna (Tavastehus), 8 Dec 1865; d. Järven-pää, 20 Sep 1957). Finnish composer. His achievement of a resilient personal style paralleled (but preceded) his country's gaining its independence, and national themes were important to him – not so much folksongs as the myths and landscapes he put into his tone poems and symphonies. But his music triumphantly overflowed his country's borders. His quest for an ancient, bardic kind of utterance brought forth new possibilities for tonality, with inflections from the old modes. And the cool changelessness of the typical Finnish vista – water and a line of trees – became reflected in new kinds of ostinato texture and consistent form, where steady growth is more important than dynamic argument.

Having as a small boy lost his doctor father to cholera, he was brought up with his two siblings by his mother and grandmother. He copied an uncle in assuming the French form of his first name. The family was Swedish-speaking, and though he attended a Finnish-speaking school he was not fluent in the language until he was a young man. Meanwhile, he played the violin in chamber music at home and began composing. In 1885 he went to Helsinki to study both the law and the violin, but the former discipline he dropped after a year to enrol at the music institute run by Martin Wegelius, who gave him composition lessons. He then went abroad for two years (1889–91), studying with Albert Becker in Berlin and with Goldmark and Fuchs in Vienna.

While in Berlin he heard Robert Kajanus's *Aino* symphony, which prompted him, once back in Helsinki, to write a symphony of his own on the *Kalevala*, the Finnish national epic: *Kullervo* (1892). That same year he married Aino Järnefelt, and in 1897 a state pension freed him from occasional teaching to concentrate on composition. The chronology of his works from this period is complicated, because some were revised – though not his Tchaikovskian First Symphony of 1898–9, whose success was soon capped by that of *Finlandia*, warmly greeted as an outburst of national pride.

Now generally regarded as Finland's leading composer, he began to gain international esteem in the early years of the new century, and he travelled widely in Europe. At home, though, he was inclined to nights of heavy drinking with his friends, until, at his wife's behest, in 1904 he had a villa built at Järvenpää, outside the city. There he lived for the rest of his life (the house is now a museum), and there he moved towards a more classical style in his Third Symphony (1904–7).

His Fourth (1911) brought a darkening of mood: it is his bleakest, most dissonant, insisting on the tonally disruptive tritone. In 1914 he made his only visit to the USA, and the next year wrote his Fifth Symphony, which in its final revision gained the unusual but compelling three-movement form of allegro becoming scherzo (originally these were separate movements), andante, and finale of struggling heroism. This version arrived during a period of turmoil for the nation that resulted in an independent Finland. After that came an interlude of minor works, followed by the pure and elusive Sixth Symphony (1923). The Seventh (1924), compressed into one powerful movement, was followed by music for *The Tempest* (1925) and by *Tapiola* (1926), a further step into compact force and rigorous strangeness. That was all. He lived another three decades and may have written – and burned – an eighth symphony. But from his long old age at Järvenpää nothing more emerged.

Glenda Dawn Goss, ed. *The Sibelius Companion* (1996); Guy Rickards *Sibelius* (1997)

Orchestral and vocal orchestral music

Symphonies (all first performances conducted by the composer): *Kullervo* (Kalevala), s, bar, ch, orch, 1892, f.p. Helsinki, 28 April 1892; No.1, E minor, Op.39, 1898–9, f.p. Helsinki, 26 Apr 1899; No.2, D, Op.43, 1901–2, f.p. Helsinki, 8 Mar 1902; No.3, C, Op.52, 1904–7, f.p. Helsinki, 24 Mar 1906; No.4, A minor, Op.63, 1911, f.p. Helsinki, 3 Apr 1911; No.5, E♭, Op.82, 1915, f.p. Helsinki, 8 Dec 1915, rev 1916–19; No.6, D minor, Op.104, 1923, f.p. Helsinki, 19 Feb 1923; No.7, C, Op.105, 1924, f.p. Stockholm, 24 Mar 1924

Concerto: VIOLIN CONCERTO, D minor, Op.47, 1903, rev 1905

Tone poems: EN SAGA, Op.9, 1892, rev 1902; *Spring Song*, Op.16, 1894, rev 1895, 1902; *The Wood Nymph*, Op.15, 1895; LEMMINKÄINEN SUITE, Op.22, 1893–5, rev 1897, 1900, 1939; FINLANDIA, Op.26, 1900; POHJOLA'S DAUGHTER, Op.49, 1905–6; NIGHTRIDE AND SUNRISE, Op.55, 1908; *The Dryad*, Op.45:1, 1910; LUONNOTAR (Kalevala), Op.70, s, orch, 1913; The BARD, Op.64, 1913, rev 1914; *The* OCEANIDES, Op.73, 1914; TAPIOLA, Op.112, 1926

Incidental scores (suites from most): *King Kristian II* (Adolf Paul), Op.27, 1898; *Kuolema* (Arvid Järnefelt), 1903; *Pelléas et Mélisande* (Maeterlinck), Op.46, 1905; *Belshazzar's Feast* (Hjalmar Procopé), Op.51, 1906; *Swanwhite* (Strindberg), Op.54, 1908;

The Lizard (Mikael Lybeck), Op.8, 1909; *Twelfth Night* (Shakespeare), Op.60, 2 songs ('Come away, death'; 'Hey ho, the wind and the rain'), 1909; *Scaramouche* (Poul Knudsen), Op.71, 1913; *Everyman* (Hofmannsthal), Op.83, 1916; *The* TEMPEST, Op.109, 1925

Opera: *The Maiden in the Tower* (1 act; Rafael Hertzberg), 1896

Choral orchestral: *Cantata for the University Ceremonies of 1894* (Kasimir Lönnbohm), 1894; *Cantata for the Coronation of Nicholas II* (Paavo Cajander), 1896; *Cantata for the University Ceremonies of 1897* (Forsman), 1897; *A Song for Lemminkäinen* (Yrjö Weijola), Op.31:1, ?1896; *Sandels* (Runeberg), Op.28, 1898; *The Breaking of the Ice on the Oulu River* (Zachris Topelius), Op.30, 1899; *Impromptu* (Viktor Rydberg), Op.19, 1902; *Snöfrid* (Rydberg), Op.29, 1900; *The Origin of Fire* (Kalevala), Op.32, 1902; *Do you have courage?* (Josef Julius Wecksell), Op.31:2, 1904; *The Captive Queen* (Cajander), Op.48, 1906; *Jäger March* (Heikki Nurmio), Op.91a, 1917–18; *Our Native Land*, Op.92, 1918; *Song of the Earth* (J. Hemmer), Op.93, 1919; *Hymn to the Earth* (Eino Leino), Op.95, 1920; *Scout March* (Jalmari Finne), Op.91b, 1921; *Väinö's Song* (Kalevala), Op.110, 1926; Masonic Ritual Music, Op.113, 1926–46

Orchestral song: 'The Rapid-Shooter's Brides' (August Ahlqvist-Oksanen), Op.33, 1897

Suites and lighter pieces: KARELIA, Op.10 (overture), Op.11 (suite), 1893; Romance, C, Op.42, str, 1903; *Cassazione*, Op.6, 1904; *Valse triste*, Op.44:1, 1904; *Scene with Cranes*, Op.44:2, 1906; Dance Intermezzo, Op.45:2, 1907; *Pan and Echo*, Op.53a, 1906; *In memoriam*, Op.59, 1909, rev 1910; *Canzonetta* and *Valse romantique*, Op.62, 1911; *The Lover*, Op.14, str, 1911–12; *Scènes historiques I*, Op.25, 1911; *Scènes historiques II*, Op.66, 1912; 2 Serenades, D, G minor, Op.69, vn, orch, 1912–13; 2 Pieces, Op.77, vn/vc, orch, 1914–15; 6 Humoresques, Opp.87 and 89, vn, orch, 1917; *Autrefois* (*Scène pastorale*), Op.96b, 1919; *Valse lyrique*, Op.96a, 1920; *Valse chevaleresque*, Op.96c, 1921; *Suite mignonne*, Op.98a, 2 fl, str, 1921; *Suite caractéristique*, Op.100, hp, str, 1922; *Suite champêtre*, Op.98b, str, 1923; etc.

Other music

Chamber: *Malinconia*, Op.20, vc, pf, 1900; String Quartet 'Voces intimae', D minor, Op.56, 1909; 4 Pieces, Op.78, vn/vc, pf, 1915–17; 6 Pieces, Op.79, vn, pf, 1915–17; Violin Sonatina, E, Op.80, 1915; 5 Pieces, Op.81, vn, pf, 1915–18; *Novelette*, Op.102, vn, pf, 1922; *Andante festivo*, str qt, 1922; *Cinq danses champêtres*, Op.106, vn, pf, 1924; 4 Pieces, Op.115, vn, pf, 1929; 3 Pieces, Op.116, vn, pf, 1929; etc.

Piano: 6 Impromptus, Op.5, 1893; Sonata, F, Op.12, 1893; 10 Pieces, Op.24, 1895–1903; *Kyllikki*, Op.41, 3 pieces, 1904; 10 Pieces, Op.58, 1909; *The Bells of Kallio Church*, Op.65b, 1912; 3 Sonatinas, Op.67, 1912; 2 Rondinos, Op.68, 1912; *Pensées lyriques*, Op.40, 1912–16; Little Pieces, Op.34, 1913–16; 4 Lyric Pieces, Op.74, 1914; *Cinq morceaux*, Op.75,

1914; 13 Pieces, Op.76, 1911–19; 5 Pieces, Op.85, 1916–17; 6 Pieces, Op.94, 1914–19; 6 Bagatelles, Op.97, 1920; 8 Pieces, Op.99, 1922; 5 Romantic Pieces, Op.101, 1924; 5 Characteristic Impressions, Op.103, 1924; 5 Esquisses, Op.114, 1929; etc.

Organ: 2 Pieces, Op.111, org, 1925, 1931

Songs (mostly in Swedish; those obelisked orchestrated by the composer): 'Arioso'[†] (Runeberg), Op.3, 1911; 'Black Roses' (Ernst Josephson), Op.36:1, 1899; 'The Diamond on the March Snow'[†] (Wecksell), Op.36:6, 1900; 'Driftwood' (Ilman Calamnius), Op.17:7, 1902; 'The Echo Nymph' (Larin Kyösti; Finn.), Op.72:4, 1915; 'To Evening' (A.V. Forsman; Finn.), Op.17:6, 1898; 'The First Kiss' (Runeberg), Op.37:1, 1900; 'The Maiden's Tryst' (Runeberg), Op.37:5, 1901; 'The North' (Runeberg), Op.90:1, 1917; 'On a balcony by the sea'[†] (Rydberg), Op.38:2, 1902; 'Reed, reed, rustle' (Gustaf Fröding), Op.36:4, 1900; 'Row, row, duck' (Forsman; Finn.), 1899; '6 Flower Songs' (Frans M. Franzén, Runeberg), Op.88, 1917; 'Spring is flying'[†] (Runeberg), Op.13:4, 1891; 'Then I questioned no further'[†] (Runeberg), Op.17:1, 1891–2; 'Was it a dream?' (Wecksell), Op.37:4, 1902; etc.

Partsongs: The Lover (Finn., trad), Op.14, 1894; Hymn (Fridolf Gustafsson), Op.21, 1896; 9 songs, Op.18, 1893–1904; 10 movements from 1897 university cantata, Op.23, ?1899; 2 songs, Op.65, 1911–12; 5 songs, Op.84, men's ch, 1914–17; 2 songs, Op.108, 1924–5

Sibelius Academy. The principal Finnish conservatory, founded as the Helsinki Music Institute (1882) and operating under its present name since 1939.

siciliana, siciliano (Fr. *sicilienne*). Kind of aria or instrumental movement in slow 6/8 or 12/8 time, often with a gentle melancholy or pastoral feeling. There are many examples in the operas, oratorios and cantatas of Alessandro Scarlatti, Handel and Bach, and in instrumental works by Handel, Bach, Domenico Scarlatti and François Couperin. Classical instances occur in Mozart (slow movement of the Piano Concerto in A, K.488) and Haydn, and there are revivals and reminiscences of the style in Stravinsky and Henze.

side drum (Fr. *caisse claire, tambour militaire*, Ger. *kleine Trommel, Militärtrommel*, It. *tamburo militare, tamburo piccolo*). DRUM 14–16 inches (35–40cm) in diameter and 4–12 inches (10–30cm) deep, so called because in marching bands it would be slung across the shoulder to rest slantwise at waist height on the player's side, though orchestral musicians would expect to have it on a stand, with its flat sides tilted slightly from the horizontal. The top is beaten with sticks; the bottom has snares (strings of gut, metal or wire-covered silk)

stretched over it, to add fizzing sympathetic vibrations. A descendant of the medieval tabor, it kept its association with the fife in military bands, while for the navy it was a signalling device. Sporadically used by Handel (*Royal Fireworks Music*), Rossini (*La gazza ladra*), etc., it became a standard orchestral instrument in the early 20th century, with a starring role in Ravel's *Boléro*.

Siege of Rhodes, The. Opera by Charles Coleman, Henry Cooke, George Hudson, Henry Lawes and Locke to a libretto by William Davenant, the first all-sung English opera. The music is lost. First performance: London, Sep 1656.

Siegfried. Opera by Wagner to his own libretto after German myth, the third part of *The Ring*. Siegfried (tenor) reforges the sword of his father Siegmund (singing his mighty Forging Song), retrieves the ring and magic helmet from the dragon Fafner (bass) deep in the woods (orchestral Forest Murmurs), gains help from the Woodbird (soprano), kills his slippery foster-father Mime (tenor) and finds his mate in Brünnhilde (soprano) on the rock where she was left at the end of the previous opera. First performance: Bayreuth, 16 Aug 1876.

Siegfried Idyll. Work for chamber orchestra by Wagner, based on themes from *Siegfried* and designed as a birthday gift for his wife Cosima, to be played on the stairway below her bedroom on Christmas morning 1870. Their son Siegfried had been born the year before.

Siegmeister, Elie (b. New York, 15 Jan 1909; d. Manhasset, NY, 10 Mar 1991). US composer. He studied with Riegger and in Paris with Boulanger (1927–31), then returned to New York to work as a conductor, pianist and teacher. During this period he espoused a simpler and distinctly US style, but during his years at Hofstra University (1949–76) his music became more complex again. He wrote eight symphonies, concertos, quartets, violin sonatas, piano sonatas, songs and cantatas.

Sierra, Roberto (b. Vega Baja, 9 Oct 1953). Puerto Rican composer. He studied at the University of Puerto Rico and in Hamburg with Ligeti (1979–82), whom he introduced to Caribbean folk music. He, too, gained a lot in adapting his heritage to a sophisticated style. He returned to Puerto Rico to teach, and in 1992 was appointed to the Cornell faculty.

Siface. Pseudonym of Giovanni Francesco Grossi (b. Chiesina Uzzanese, near Pescia, 12 Feb 1653; d.

near Ferrara, 29 May 1697). Italian castrato, so called from his debut role (in Cavalli's *Scipione affricano*, Rome, 1671). In 1679 he joined the service of the Duke of Modena, and in 1687 he sang in London for the duke's sister, who was queen. Evelyn admired 'his holding out and delicateness in extending and loosing a note, with that incomparable softness, and sweetness'. Purcell wrote a *Sefauchi's Farewell* for harpsichord. Boasting of an affair, he was murdered at the behest of his lover's family.

sight reading. Playing music at first sight, unprepared. The equivalent term for vocalists is 'sight singing'.

signature. See KEY SIGNATURE; TIME SIGNATURE.

Signor Bruschino, Il. Opera by Rossini to a libretto by Giuseppe Foppa after a French play. Signor Bruschino (bass) bests his old enemy Gaudenzio (bass) by conniving in a marriage between the latter's ward Sofia (soprano) and Florville (tenor). There is a witty overture. First performance: Venice, 27 Jan 1813.

Sigurbjørnsson, Thorkell (b. Reykjavík, 16 Jul 1938). Icelandic composer. He studied at the Reykjavík College of Music, in the USA and at Darmstadt, and has been active in Reykjavík and abroad as a teacher and pianist. His music is stylistically diverse.

Silbermann. Leading family of German organ builders in the 18th century. The business was started in Strasbourg around the beginning of the century by the brothers Andreas (1678–1734) and Gottfried (1683–1753). Andreas worked in Paris for a while; Gottfried also made clavichords and pianos. They were succeeded by Andreas's son Johann Andreas (1712–83).

silence. A necessary part of music, by no means only as a frame. Busoni pointed out that silences between movements are not blank periods but filled with memory and expectation. Mahler's Second Symphony was perhaps the first work in which such silences are measured. Silences at the end may also be significant, and are sometimes closely defined in Ligeti's music, so that the conductor has to hold off applause while counting a certain number of beats. Silences within the musical continuity may be pauses for breath or expressions of shock, the latter especially in opera or quasi-operatic music. They may also be more frequent, helping to create the musical continuity as a dialectic of sound and silence (Webern) or

threatening the onward urge (Barraqué's Sonata). Then again, silence may be taken as music's ideal condition, as in Cage's *4′ 33″*.

Silence has also been the condition in which many composers since around 1900 have found themselves, either permanently (Wolf, Duparc, Dukas, Elgar, Sibelius, Ives) or for long periods (Varèse, Barraqué). For many composers since the late 20th century, from Pärt to Takemitsu, silence has been not the absence of music but its goal.

Silja, Anja (b. Berlin, 17 April 1935). German soprano, one of the great singing actresses. She made an early start, and had sung a wide repertory before being engaged in 1960 by Wieland Wagner, her mentor and consort. With him she sang most of the leading female parts in Wagner and evolved an intense veracity of character projection. Her other great roles included Cassandra in *Les Troyens* and, in later years, Janáček's older women.

silofono (It., pl. *silofoni*). Xylophone.

Siloti, Alexander. See Aleksandr ZILOTI.

Silvestrov, Valentyn (Vasilevich) (b. Kiev, 30 Sep 1937). Ukrainian composer. He studied engineering before becoming a pupil of Lyatoshynsky at the Kiev Conservatory (1958–64), where he began working with serialism in an intense lyrical manner. Feeling keenly the presence of the past, he would often mingle or alternate styles, as in his First Symphony (1963), until in the 1970s he reestablished homogeneity, in music with a strong sense of loss in adverting to the amplitude and rhetoric of the late Romantic period. Cadence, almost always impending, is immensely protracted. Notable works include his Fifth Symphony (1980–82), violin concerto *Widmung* (1990–91) and two string quartets (1974, 1988).

SIMC (Société Internationale de la Musique Contemporaine). See ISCM.

similar motion. The movement of two or more contrapuntal parts in the same direction at the same time. Keyboard scales may be played by the hands in similar motion.

simile (It.). Similar. Used to indicate that a bar, phrase or whatever is to be performed in like manner to its predecessor.

Simon Boccanegra. Opera by Verdi to a libretto by Piave after a play by Antonio García Gutiérrez; for the revised version Boito altered the libretto. In an unusually male-dominated and political drama, Boccanegra (baritone), doge of Genoa, is the victim of a plot led by Fiesco (bass), the unknowing grandfather of Boccanegra's daughter Maria/Amelia (soprano), who finds her true love in Gabriele (tenor). The most celebrated number is Fiesco's grief-stricken romanza 'Il lacerato spirito'. First performance: Venice, 12 Mar 1857; rev Milan, 24 Mar 1881.

simple interval. An octave or less, as opposed to a COMPOUND INTERVAL.

simple time. Metre in which the main beats can be divided in half (e.g. 2/4, where the crotchet beat can contain two quavers, or similarly 3/2 and 4/8), as opposed to COMPOUND TIME.

Simpson, Christopher (b. ?Egton, Yorks., c.1605; d. ?Holborn, London, summer 1669). English musician, the author of two widely used handbooks: *The Division-Violist* (1659) and *The Principles of Practical Music* (1665). He also wrote music for viols.

Simpson, Robert (Wilfred Levick) (b. Leamington Spa, 2 Mar 1921; d. Tralee, Co. Kerry, 21 Nov 1997). British composer. He studied with Howells (1942–6), then worked for the BBC (1951–80) while writing music galvanized by three composers on whom he wrote books: Nielsen, Bruckner and Beethoven. Most of his works are in traditional instrumental genres (11 symphonies, 15 string quartets), though not at all in traditional forms: the form is, rather, very actively created by a strongly willed process dependent on tonal conflict.

simultaneity. Term preferred to 'chord' by some 12-note composers on the grounds that it avoids implying diatonic function.

Sinding, Christian (August) (b. Kongsberg, 11 Jan 1856; d. Oslo, 3 Dec 1941). Norwegian composer. He was set on a career as a violinist when he went to the Leipzig Conservatory in 1874, but by the time he left four years later he had swerved to composition, taught by Jadassohn. Wagner, Liszt and Strauss influenced him strongly, and he spent much of his time in Germany. He wrote an opera, four symphonies, concertos, chamber music, numerous songs and many piano pieces, these last including the popular *Rustle of Spring* (1896).

sine tone. Sound of one pure FREQUENCY, so called because its SPECTRUM follows a sine curve.

sinfonia (It., symphony, overture, pl. *sinfonie*). The normal Italian term for symphony, extending to

Mahler and beyond, but used in English most usually for Baroque and pre-Classical orchestral pieces that belong to the symphony's infancy, whether they were written as opera overtures or concert items.

Sinfonia. Orchestral work by Berio incorporating amplified vocal octet (originally the Swingle Singers) and including as its third movement a swathe of quotations around the scherzo from Mahler's Second Symphony. First performance: New York, 10 Oct 1968; with fifth movement, Donaueschingen, 18 Oct 1969.

Sinfonia antartica (Antarctic Symphony). Vaughan Williams's Symphony No.7, so named by him, being based on his score for the film *Scott of the Antarctic* (1948).

sinfonia concertante (It., symphony in concerto style, pl. *sinfonie concertante*, Fr. *symphonie concertante*, pl. *symphonies concertantes*). Concerto with more than one soloist. There was a vogue for works of this kind in the Classical and early Romantic periods, especially in Paris. Three remain in the repertory: Mozart's for violin and viola (K.364) and for wind quartet (K.297b), and Haydn's for violin, oboe, cello and bassoon. For other works with multiple soloists see DOUBLE CONCERTO and TRIPLE CONCERTO.

Sinfonie (Ger., pl. *Sinfonien*). Symphony.

Sinfonies pour les soupers du roi (Symphonies for the king's suppers). Title given in the manuscript sources of 18 suites by Lalande.

sinfonietta. Symphonic piece of reduced pretensions. The term seems to have been coined around 1880 by Rimsky-Korsakov, as *Symphoniette*, but it is particularly associated with the work by Janáček, in compact five-movement form but for large forces (including 12 trumpets). Used, though, in the name of an ensemble, the word implies a grouping of soloists specializing in contemporary music, thanks to the prestige of the London Sinfonietta.

sing. Perform with the VOICE, normally at a definite pitch (in contrast with speaking, where pitch is less well defined). Singing, coming from within and requiring no instrument, can be practised by all, and surely is. Universal, it is also an individual expression – for the singer and also for those who hear, since the auditory function is finely attuned to vocal qualities. An experienced listener can easily recognize hundreds of different singers, almost at the first note, whereas such discrimination is unimaginable in the case of pianists or violinists.

To sing is generally to sing words (the alternative is VOCALIZE). Words are removed from their everyday currency – elevated, as it may seem, and singing is therefore found worldwide in the exercise of religion and drama. Words may also be remembered better, and communicated better, when sung: songs – work songs and wedding songs, laments and lullabies, intoned epics and genealogies – travel down the eons in all human cultures, spoken texts only in the briefest form of proverbs.

Words, and their sounds, will also influence styles of singing. The French language, for instance, favours a high tessitura, the Russian a low one. Beyond that, singing styles can only be ascertained with any reliability when supported by notation and a pitch standard – for music, therefore, after 1600. (The appropriateness of FALSETTO, for example, in medieval and Renaissance music remains controversial.) Ways to sing music since 1800 become clearer, thanks to the increasing definition of voice types in opera scores, and the evidence of treatises on singing. Bellini's scores, for instance, are handbooks in bel canto singing, whereas Wagner's are guides to another style. Later composers have been more or less exact in indicating their wishes, especially for new techniques achieved either naturally (e.g. SPRECH-GESANG) or with electronic enhancement. Also, some 19th-century singers made recordings, and few 20th-century artists failed to do so; these can provide powerful further information about style and tradition.

And yet, because the art is so personal, all singers have ultimately to find their own ways to sing – shower singers as well as opera stars, for: 'Since singing is so good a thing, I wish all men would learn to sing' (Byrd, preface to *Psalms, Sonnets and Songs*).

Johan Sundberg *The Science of the Singing Voice* (1987); J.B. Steane *Singers of the Century*, 3 Vols. (1996–2000)

Singakademie (Ger.). German choral organization, as founded in many cities in the 19th century; some were alternatively called *Singverein* or *Gesangverein*.

singer. Vocal performer. Singers are normally classified by range of VOICE as SOPRANO, MEZZO-SOPRANO, CONTRALTO, TREBLE, TENOR, BARITONE or BASS. Solo singers may be involved in several different kinds of musical event, including recitals (normally with just piano), concerts of new or old music (with appropriate ensembles), orchestral concerts and opera. Some specialize in one or another; some essay all. Opera singers, especially, have been among the most lavishly valued musicians since Handel's time.

singhiozzando (It.). Sobbing; a marking used especially in vocal music, though strings too can sob.

single reed. Characteristic of clarinets and saxophones; see REED.

singspiel (Ger., sing-play, pl. *Singspiele*). German play with songs and perhaps more elaborate numbers, emerging in the 1760s on the model of ballad opera and opéra comique. The genre is sometimes considered to include *Die Zauberflöte* and *Fidelio*, but generally a consistently lighter musical style and simpler dramatic themes are expected, as in Schubert's *Die Zwillingsbrüder*.

Singverein (Ger., sing society). German choral organization, as founded in many cities (e.g. Munich, Kiel) in the 19th century; some were alternatively called *Gesangverein*.

Sinigaglia, Leone (b. Turin, 14 Aug 1868; d. Turin, 16 May 1944). Italian composer. In 1894 he went to Vienna, where he studied with Eusebius Mandyczewski and met Brahms and Dvořák, of whom the latter gave him lessons in 1900–1 and was a decisive influence. Back home he collected Piedmontese folksongs and used them in his compositions, which include picturesque orchestral pieces and chamber works, besides folksong arrangements.

siren. Mythological songstress, of a species mentioned by Homer, Sophocles, Plato, Ovid, etc. Classical sirens were airborne: female beings with wings, feathered legs and bird feet. Later they became semi-fish, mermaids, as memorialized in Debussy's *Sirènes*, the middle movement of his *Nocturnes*. Other siren songs include the first of Szymanowski's *Métopes* for piano.

sirventes. Troubadour term for a satirical song.

Sisask, Urmas (b. Rapla, 9 Sep 1960). Estonian composer. He studied at the music school and conservatory in Tallinn, and has composed instrumental and sacred choral music in a contemplative style, influenced by observing the night sky.

sistrum. Ancient Egyptian and later Roman handheld jingles, associated with the worship of Isis. The instrument was revived in *Double Music* by Cage and Harrison.

sitār. Indian–Pakistani long-necked lute with sympathetic strings, popularized in the West by Ravi Shankar.

Sitsky, Larry [Lazarus] (b. Tianjin, China, 10 Sep 1934). Russian–Australian composer. He studied at the New South Wales State Conservatorium and at the San Francisco Conservatory (1959–61), where he imbibed Busoni's influence from Egon Petri. Asian music has also been important to him. As well as composing, he has worked in Australia as a university lecturer and piano teacher.

Sivori, (Ernesto) Camillo (b. Genoa, 25 Oct 1815; d. Genoa, 19 Feb 1894). Italian violinist-composer, a protégé of Paganini and his successor on the international circuit. He mastered Paganini's most challenging works but was a different kind of artist, noted for his sweetness; he led the first performance of Verdi's quartet, at the composer's request. His own compositions include two concertos and exhibition pieces, notably 12 *Etudes-caprices* (1867).

Six, Les. French group of composers, comprising Auric, Durey, Honegger, Milhaud, Poulenc and Tailleferre, named as such by the critic Henri Collet in January 1920, though the six had been giving concerts together since June 1917 as Les Nouveaux Jeunes (The New Youngsters). They were indeed young: Auric was 18 at the time of their first concert, Durey, the oldest, 29. Most of them were fresh out of the Conservatoire, ready to take their musical ideals from the distinctly unacademic Satie and their smart aesthetics from Cocteau. The German tradition was out; café music, sophistication and frivolity were in. The group collaborated on two ventures: an *Album des Six*, containing piano pieces by all of them, and Cocteau's playlet-ballet *Les Mariés de la Tour Eiffel* (1921). Durey opted out of this, and the other members, too, soon went their own ways. But the spirit of Les Six – iconoclastic, unpretentious – lived on in some of Poulenc's and Milhaud's later music, and had an effect on other composers of the time in Paris and elsewhere.

six-four chord. Major or minor triad in second inversion – e.g. G–C–E, reading from the bottom. The chord consists of a sixth and a fourth over its lowest note, and is written in figured bass $^6_4$. In tonal harmony a six-four chord must resolve to a root-position triad, which it can most easily do through scalewise descent of the upper notes (G–C–E then goes to G–B–D). A six-four chord commonly sets off the cadenza in the first movement of a Classical concerto.

sixième, sixte (Fr.). Sixth (interval); hence *sixte majeure, sixte mineure*.

sixteen-foot (16'). Term used of organ stops, and by extension of other instruments (e.g. double basses), to indicate their range. The derivation is from pipes: an 8' pipe will produce low C (the C below the bass staff), and is taken as the norm. Music for a 16' pipe or instrument is commonly notated in the octave above, i.e. as if for the 8' version.

sixteenth-note (US). Semiquaver (UK). See DURATION.

sixth. (1) Note in sixth position in a diatonic system, e.g. A in C major.

(2) Interval equivalent to that between tonic and sixth. The interval may be a major sixth (nine semitones, e.g. C–A) or a minor (eight semitones, e.g. A–F). Chromatic alteration may produce an augmented sixth (ten semitones, e.g. C–A♯, enharmonically a seventh) or a diminished sixth (seven semitones, e.g. A–F♭, enharmonically a fifth).

The sixth was a dissonance in medieval times, but with the third, its inversion, became a consonance at the beginning of the Renaissance. As the note at the limit of the HEXACHORD, it was normally the largest melodic interval that could appear in medieval and Renaissance music.

sixth chord, six-three chord. Major or minor triad in first inversion – e.g. E–G–C, reading from the bottom. The chord consists of a sixth and a third over its lowest note, and is written in figured bass $^6_3$. In tonal harmony such chords are normally consonant; they are frequent in early Renaissance music.

sixty-fourth-note (US). Hemidemisemiquaver (UK). See DURATION.

Skalkottas, Nikos [Nikolaos] (b. Halkis, Eubea, 21 Mar 1904; d. Athens, 20 Sep 1949). Greek composer, nationalist and Schoenbergian. He trained as a violinist at the Athens Conservatory (1914–20) and from 1921 in Berlin, where he also had composition lessons with Jarnach (1925–7), Weill (1928–9) and Schoenberg (1927–31). Playing in cafés and cinemas kept him afloat until, in 1928, he gained the support of a patron. That arrangement came to an end in 1931, and financial insecurity, combined with unhappiness in love, sent him into a depression. In 1933 he returned to Athens to work as a back-desk violinist, his pessimism maintained by his solitariness in

Greece as a follower of Schoenberg. He essayed the more popular local style masterfully in his 36 Greek Dances for orchestra (1931–6), but devoted most of his free time to big orchestral and chamber works that had no immediate prospect of performance or publication, including the overture *The Return of Ulysses* (1942–3), several concertos and quartets. Their formal models are conventional, but the dimensions may be larger, and often the textures are dense, multi-thematic and multi-serial. He married in 1946; his death came as the result of a strangulated hernia he had ignored.

Skempton, Howard (b. Chester, 31 Oct 1947). British composer. He studied with Cardew and was influenced also by US experimental composers in achieving music that is outwardly simple – but not so simple that it cannot also be extremely individual, whether in tones of wistfulness or wit. Apart from many piano pieces, he has written orchestral, chamber and choral music.

sketch (Fr. *esquisse*, Ger. *Skizze*). (1) Note towards a composition. A sketch may be a memory aid or a working document – a means of putting ideas in order, trying different possibilities, etc. After use, sketches may be destroyed or kept: if kept, they will provide evidence for scholars interested in the creative process. The sketches of Beethoven, most notably, have been so used.

(2) As part of a title (MacDowell's *Woodland Sketches*, Boulez's *Messagesquisse*) the word implies something composed spontaneously.

sketch score. Compositional outline for a larger work, implying more sketchiness than in a DRAFT SCORE or SHORT SCORE.

skhisma. See SCHISMA.

Skizze (Ger., pl. *Skizzen*). Sketch.

slancio, con (It.). With dash, impetuously. The marking is most common for the violin.

slapstick. Variant of the WHIP.

slargando (It.). Broadening, slowing.

slått (pl. *slåtter*). Genre of Norwegian folk music, a Hardanger fiddle tune, used in titles by Grieg and other Norwegian composers.

Slavonic Dances. Works by Dvořák in folk style for piano duet, later orchestrated. There are two sets of eight, each a pan-Slavonic medley, from which those most often heard are the Furiant (No.1, C), Dumka (No.2, E minor), Polka (No.3, A♭) and Furiant (No.8, G minor) from the first set, and the Odzemek (No.1, B♭), Dumka (No.2, E minor), Sribske (No.7, C) and Sousedska (No.8, A♭) from the second.

Slavonic Rhapsodies. Three orchestral works by Dvořák in folk style, in D, G minor and A♭.

Sleeping Beauty, The (*La Belle au bois dormant*, *Spyashchaya krasavitsa*). Full-length ballet score by Tchaikovsky to a scenario by Marius Petipa and Ivan Vsevolozhsky, choreographed by Petipa. Perrault's fairytale is told, with divertissements, in the sumptuous masterpiece of Russian imperial ballet. First performance: St Petersburg, 16 Jan 1890.

sleighbells. Small jingling bells, round and with a slit, used in Mozart's German Dance K.605:3 ('The Sleigh Ride'), Mahler's Fourth Symphony, etc.

slentando (It.). Slowing.

slide. (1) As an ornament, a two-note scalewise approach to the note, usually from below.

(2) Continuous movement from one note to another, a GLISSANDO or PORTAMENTO.

(3) Physical object that renders a slide in the second sense possible, though its main purpose is to make notes other than natural harmonics available: a U-shaped tube that can be slid in and out, as in a trombone. Organ pipes and wind instruments are sometimes fitted with a tuning slide.

slide trumpet. Trumpet with a slide. It was introduced around 1400, fell out of use when the valve trumpet appeared in the later 18th century, and was reinvented in the 19th, without lasting success. Purcell used slide trumpets of a particular English kind – known as 'flat trumpets', with a slide moving back over the player's shoulder – in his music for the funeral of Mary II.

Slippers, The (*Cherevichki*). Opera by Tchaikovsky, a revision of his *Vakula the Smith*, to a libretto by Yakov Polonsky after Gogol's *Christmas Eve*. The Devil (baritone) flirts with the witch Solokha (mezzo-soprano) but is forced by her son Vakula (tenor) to help the young man win his beloved Oxana (soprano). Rimsky-Korsakov's *Christmas Eve* is based on the same story. First performance: St Petersburg, 6 Dec 1876 (*Vakula*); Moscow, 31 Jan 1887 (*Slippers*).

Slonimsky, Nicolas [Nikolay Leonidovich] (b. St Petersburg, 27 Apr 1894; d. Los Angeles, 25 Dec 1995). Russian–US musician and writer. He studied at the St Petersburg Conservatory, went to Paris in 1920 and arrived in the USA as Koussevitzky's secretary. In 1927 he began his own career as a conductor, specializing in new US works, which he presented at home and also in Europe: he gave the first performances of Ives's *Three Places in New England*, Varèse's *Ionisation*, etc. After the early 1940s he mostly taught, lectured, amused and compiled reference books, including several editions of *Baker's Biographical Dictionary of Music* and of his own *Music since 1900*, as well as his *Lexicon of Musical Invective* (1952, ²1965). His nephew, Sergey Mikhaylovich (b. 1932) is a Leningrad-trained composer.

Nicolas Slonimsky *Perfect Pitch: A Life Story* (1988)

slur. Close linking of two or more notes in playing or singing. This may be achieved by performing the notes in one breath, with one bowstroke or, in the case of keyboard instruments, with a more or less imperceptible overlap. The effect is notated by means of a line curving over the notes, a sign for which the term also serves. Slurs are nearly always marked in vocal music when one syllable is stretched over more than one note.

Smalley, Dennis (Arthur) (b. Nelson, 16 May 1946). New Zealand composer. After a university education in New Zealand he continued his training in Paris, where he studied with Messiaen and in the Groupe de Recherches Musicales, and at York University (from 1971). He then taught at the University of East Anglia (1976–94) and the City University in London (from 1994). His works, all of which involve electronic means, include one of the classics of tape music, *Pentes* (1974).

Smalley, (John) Roger (b. Swinton, Manchester, 26 Jul 1943). British–Australian composer. He studied with Fricker, Goehr and John White in London, and with Stockhausen in Cologne (1965–6). Strongly infleunced by Stockhausen in such works as *Pulses* for brass, percussion and electronics (1969) and *Accord* for two pianos (1974–5), he was a founder member of the live electronic group Intermodulation (1970–76). In 1976 he took a post at the University of Western Australia in Perth, and his music soon became more laid back, embracing tonal harmonies and the Australian scene.

smanioso, smaniato, smaniante (It.). Frenziedly.

Smareglia, Antonio (b. Pola, Istria, 5 May 1854; d. Grado, Istria, 15 Apr 1929). Italian composer. He studied with Faccio at the Milan Conservatory and was an ardent Wagnerian in his youth: at the La Scala première of *Lohengrin*, in 1873, he locked arms with a combatant and tumbled with him all the way down the stairs from the top balcony. His strongest opera was *Nozze istriane* (f.p. Trieste, 1895), which Joyce admired.

Smart, George (Thomas) (b. London, 10 May 1776; d. London, 23 Feb 1867). British musician, knighted in 1811. The son of a music publisher and trained in the Chapel Royal choir, he played the violin and (less successfully) timpani at Salomon's Haydn concerts and was subsequently a founder member of the Philharmonic Society, for which he directed the local première of Beethoven's Ninth Symphony in 1826. Late in his long life he was able to pass on to singers the Handel tradition he had inherited from his father, who a century before had seen the composer conduct.

Smetana, Bedřich [Friedrich] (b. Litomyšl, 2 Mar 1824; d. Prague, 12 May 1884). Czech composer. He was a keen and vigorous musical nationalist, and his determination to avoid Vienna-centred conventions led him not only to outbursts of stirring pride and joviality but also to persistent innovation in form and gesture, by which he gained a rare expressive intensity.

The son of a master brewer who was also an amateur violinist, he rapidly outstripped his father and local teachers. Wider opportunities opened during his school years in Prague (1838–40) and Plzeň (1840–43), including opportunities to accompany dancing and to dance himself, which is how he met Kateřina Kolářová, who later became his wife. Back in Prague he supported himself as a private teacher while studying with the blind composer-teacher Josef Proksch (1844–6). His ambitions were high: he had heard Liszt in Prague in 1840 and now initiated a correspondence with the master. He tried to launch himself as a virtuoso; he founded a music institute. Both projects failed. Also, the collapse of the 1848 Prague Revolution left the political climate depressing, and he and Kateřina lost three of their four young daughters in 1854–6.

From 1856 he was based largely in Gothenburg, conducting, playing and composing, with visits to Prague and to Liszt. During this time he also started writing letters in Czech, though German remained his principal language until 1861. Kateřina died in 1859, and the next year he married a family connection. By now prospects for music and independence were brighter in Prague, but though he decisively returned in 1861, key posts went to others: he was, musically and politically, too radical. That view changed when two operas by him, *The Brandenburgers in Bohemia* and *The Bartered Bride*, were mounted in quick succession in 1866. He was appointed principal conductor of the Provisional Theatre that same year, and there presented two more operas: *Dalibor*, on a Czech chivalric legend, and the comedy *The Two Widows*.

In 1874 he began to notice signs of deafness, among other symptoms of syphilis, and he relinquished his place at the theatre. Specialists were consulted, fruitlessly. Nevertheless, he went on composing at a rapid pace, producing during the next five years two further operas (*The Kiss* and *The Secret*), five symphonic poems to complete his *Má vlast* cycle, and his First Quartet 'From My Life', whose finale poignantly includes the whistling sound that was in his ears every evening. In 1881 his opera *Libuše*, a patriotic pageant, received its delayed première as the work chosen to open the new Provisional Theatre, but his condition was worsening and composition becoming harder, especially in the last year, following his haunted Second Quartet.

John Clapham *Smetana* (1972)

Operas: *The Brandenburgers in Bohemia* (Karel Sabina), 1862–3, f.p. Prague, 1866; *The* BARTERED BRIDE, 1863–6, rev 1869–70; *Dalibor* (Josef Wenzig, translated into Czech by Ervín Špindler), 1865–7, f.p. Prague, 1868, rev 1870; *Libuše* (Josef Wenzig, translated into Czech by Ervín Špindler), 1869–72, f.p. Prague, 1881; *The* TWO WIDOWS, 1873–4, rev 1877; *The* KISS, 1875–6; *The* SECRET, 1877–8; *The Devil's Wall* (Krásnohorská), 1879–82, f.p. Prague, 1882; *Viola* (Krásnohorská, after Shakespeare), 1874, 1883–4, unfinished
Symphonic poems: *Richard III*, 1857–8; *Wallenstein's Camp*, 1858–9; *Hakon Jarl*, 1860–61; MÁ VLAST, c.1872–9
Other orchestral: *Jubel Overture*, 1848–9; *Triumphal Symphony*, 1853–4; *March for Shakespeare Festival*, 1864; *Ceremonial Prelude*, 1868; *Libuše's Judgment*, 1869; *The Peasant Woman*, polka, 1879; *Prague Carnival*, 1883; etc.
Chamber: String Quartet No.1 'FROM MY LIFE', E minor, 1876; No.2, D minor, 1882–3; Piano Trio, G minor, 1855, rev 1857; *From the Homeland*, vn, pf, 1880; etc.
Piano: *Six morceaux caractéristiques*, c.1847–8; *Wedding Scenes*, 1849; *Album Leaves*, 2 sets and others, 1848–56; 3 Polkas, c.1852–3; *Trois polkas de salon*, ?1854; *Trois polkas poétiques*, ?1854; Sketches (8), 2 sets, 1856–7; *Scherzo Etude*, 1858; *Bal vision: polka rapsodie*, 1858; Polka, C, 1858; *Macbeth and the Witches*, 1859; *Bettina Polka*, 1859, rev 1883; *Souvenir de Bohème en forme de polka*, 1859–60; *Am Seegestade*, 1861; *Fantasie concertante sur des chansons nationales tchèques*, 1862; *Motives from*

the Opera *Dalibor*, 1873; *Dreams* (6), 1875; *Czech Dances* (10), 2 sets, 1877, 1879; Andante, F minor, 1880; Romanza, G minor, 1881; etc.
Other works: songs, men's choruses, women's choruses, organ preludes

Smith, 'Father' (Bernard) (b. *c.*1630; d. London, 1708). English organ builder of Dutch or German origin. He arrived in England in 1666, was elected organist of St Margaret's, Westminster, and was appointed King's Organ Maker in 1681, precipitating rivalry with Renatus Harris. Remarked on for their sweetness and brilliance, all his organs have been altered, with the exception of a chamber organ at Compton Wynyates, Northants.

Smith, John Stafford (baptized Gloucester, 30 Mar 1750; d. London, 21 Sep 1836). British musician, son of the Gloucester Cathedral organist. He studied with Boyce and served the Chapel Royal as boy treble, adult singer and organist from 1761 to 1817. Meanwhile, he amassed an extraordinary collection of old music, including the Old Hall manuscript and the Mulliner Book. He also wrote songs, one of which, 'To Anacreon in Heaven', later had its tune fitted to 'The Star-Spangled Banner'.

smorzando (It.). Dying away; abbreviated *smorz.*, the same as *morendo*.

Smyth, Ethel (Mary) (b. London, 22 Apr 1858; d. Woking, 9 May 1944). British composer, created dame in 1922. Born into a prosperous military family, she had to make her own fight: to compose. In 1877 she went to the Leipzig Conservatory for tuition from Jadassohn and Reinecke, whom she left to take private lessons with the Austrian pianist and composer Heinrich von Herzogenberg. Meetings with Brahms, Clara Schumann, Tchaikovsky and others gave her encouragement, and she began to make a flourishing career in Germany. Back in England she was active in the suffragette movement. She wrote her own librettos, in German, French and English, and in her later years, having retired from composition on account of deafness, she published autobiographical volumes. Her musical voice, if not particularly individual, was strong.

Ronald Crichton, ed. *The Memoirs of Ethel Smyth* (1987)

Operas: *The Wreckers* (Henry Brewster and Smyth), 1902–4, f.p. Leipzig, 1906; *The Boatswain's Mate* (1 act; Smyth), 1913–14, f.p. London, 1916; etc.
Orchestral: Serenade, 1890; Mass, soli, ch, orch, 1891, rev 1925; *The March of the Women*, women's ch, orch, 1911; Concerto, vn, hn, orch, 1927; etc.

Chamber: String Quintet, E, 1884; String Quartet, E minor, 1902–12; etc.

snare drum. SIDE DRUM.

Snow Maiden, The (*Snegoruchka*). Verse play by Aleksandr Ostrovsky. The Snow Maiden, love child of Spring and Frost, wants to live among human beings to enjoy their songs and games. She thereby keeps the land under the lock of winter, until she learns love and melts. Musical responses include:

(1) Tchaikovsky's score for the first production. First performance: Moscow, 23 May 1873.

(2) Rimsky-Korsakov's opera. First performance: St Petersburg, 10 Feb 1882.

SO. Abbreviation, in orchestras' names, for Symphony Orchestra.

soave, soavamente, soavemente, con soavità (It.). Gently.

SOCAN. Société Canadienne des Auteurs, Compositeurs et Editeurs de Musique, Canadian performing rights agency.

socialist realism. Official Soviet aesthetic promulgated in 1932, the underlying idea being that artists should portray the real world but bend their portraits towards the socialist future. Quite what this meant for music was never very clear; hence the problems of 1936 and 1948 (see POLITICS). The term has sometimes been used pejoratively, of works deemed bland and insincere, such as Shostakovich's *Song of the Forests*. However, the essential idea – that art is entrammelled in life, especially national life – had a long history in Russian culture and a distinguished one elsewhere. What was new, and problematic, was the required optimism.

Société des Concerts du Conservatoire. Principal institution for giving orchestral concerts in Paris, founded in 1828 and active until replaced by the Orchestre de Paris in 1967.

Society for Private Musical Performances (Verein für Musikalische Privataufführungen). Organization set up by Schoenberg in Vienna in November 1918 to present concerts of new and recent music under idealistic conditions, in response both to post-war financial stringency and the bruising the composer had experienced in Viennese public concert life. Programmes were not divulged in advance, critics were not invited, subscriptions were according to means, and applause was not required: music was no longer to function as entertainment or social lubricant. The repertory included works by Schoenberg and his pupils but ranged further, to embrace Reger, Ravel, Stravinsky, Scriabin, Bartók, etc., orchestral scores being reduced for keyboard or small ensemble. Arrangers and performers came from within Schoenberg's circle. Inflation brought activities to an end in 1922, though a sister organization established by Zemlinsky in Prague continued from 1921 to 1924.

sociology of music. The study of music as a social phenomenon; the study, therefore, of how, when, where and by whom in different societies music is heard, performed, evaluated and composed. This study may be focused on gathering information about musical practices: patterns of home music-making and concert attendance, means of selecting and training performers, the RECEPTION of new works, etc. Alternatively, music sociologists may be more concerned with analysing such data, especially in terms of the relationship between music and social structure. When done from a Marxist point of view, an analysis of this kind may seek to make not only descriptive but prescriptive statements, to find a new place for music – and no doubt a new kind of music – in a new society. See POLITICS.

Sociological investigation has deepened understanding of how music is embedded in a society, and takes its meaning partly from that embedding. A Bach cantata heard as the local cantor's contribution to this Sunday's service is, for example, something very different from the same cantata heard from a record as the work of a great master dead for a quarter of a millennium. On a larger level, links have been explored between general aspects of musical language and social context – how, for example, the Renaissance came with a change from a feudal to a bourgeois society, the Baroque style spread with emergent capitalism, Romanticism was the music of the Industrial Revolution, and the global capitalism of the late 20th century marginalized classical music in favour of pop.

Sociologists by inclination tend to be critical of the society in which they find themselves – especially of, in the case of modern society, the disadvantaging of women, the power of class interests and the persistence of assumptions about art. The challenge is to make this scepticism – which at its baldest would see Beethoven's greatness as a fiction of 19th-century middle-class values – constructive.

Theodor W. Adorno *Introduction to the Sociology of Music* (1976); John Shepherd *Whose Music?* (1977); Richard Leppert and Susan McClary, ed. *Music and Society* (1987)

Socrate. Concert piece by Satie for solo soprano or four women's voices with piano or chamber orchestra, describing the death of Socrates to words from Victor Cousin's translation of Plato. First performance: Paris, 7 Jun 1920.

Sofronitsky, Vladimir (Vladimirovich) (b. St Petersburg, 8 May 1901; d. Moscow, 29 Aug 1961). Russian pianist, of desperate intensity – glittering, tumultuous and large – especially in the music of Scriabin, whose daughter he married. He studied in Warsaw and with Leonid Nikolayev at the Petrograd Conservatory (1916–21), where he also attended Steinberg's composition classes. After some years of touring and two in Paris, he settled back in Russia, teaching at the conservatories of Leningrad (from 1936) and Moscow (from 1942). Drink and drugs precipitated his death.

soft pedal. Left pedal on the piano; see UNA CORDA.

soggetto (It.). Subject, of a fugue. Term introduced by Zarlino.

soh. In tonic sol-fa the fifth degree of the scale.

Sohal, Naresh (Kumar) (b. Harsipind, Hoshiarpur district, Punjab, 18 Sep 1939). Indian composer. The son of an Urdu poet, he studied sciences and mathematics at Punjab University before moving to Britain in 1962. He studied composition with Jeremy Dale Roberts in London (1965–6), and did research into quarter-tones at Leeds University (1972–4). These he has used in works combining European modernism with certain Indian features, while also gaining a reputation as a photographer and television director.

Soir, Le (Evening). Name given to Haydn's Symphony No.8, which forms a trilogy with No.6 'Le Matin' and No.7 'Le Midi'. Its fourth movement, 'La tempesta', quotes a Gluck air.

Soirées musicales (Musical Evenings). Set of songs and duets by Rossini, transcribed by Liszt for piano and orchestrated by Respighi and Britten.

Sokolov, Grigory (b. Leningrad, 18 Apr 1950). Russian pianist. He studied at the Leningrad Conservatory and won the Tchaikovsky Competition in 1966, though it was not until the 1990s that he gained widespread renown for his phenomenal virtuosity, depth of musical understanding and particular feeling for character and counterpoint in Baroque music (he has recorded *Die Kunst der*

Fuge twice) as much as Beethoven, Chopin, Franck and Scriabin.

sol (Fr., It., Sp.). The note or key of G; see SOLMIZATION.

sola (It., alone, only). Feminine form of SOLO used in Italian expressions – e.g. *per voce sola* (for unaccompanied voice).

Solage (*fl.* 1370–90). French composer, known for 10 polyphonic songs in the CHANTILLY manuscript. He may have served Jean, Duke of Berry, and been associated with a circle of connoisseurs able to appreciate his rhythmic ingenuities and the harmonic surprise of his spectacular 'Joieux de cuer' and bizarre 'Fumeux fume par fumee'.

Soldaten, Die (The Soldiers). Opera by Zimmermann to his own libretto after the play by Jakob Lenz. With a large cast – plus chorus, dancers, full orchestra and tape – as well as stylistic diversity and complex staging (sometimes with three scenes proceeding simultaneously), the opera presents a busy, fragmented and ultimately destructive world, in which the principal victim is Marie (dramatic soprano). First performance: Cologne, 15 Feb 1965.

Soldier's Tale, The. See HISTOIRE DU SOLDAT.

solenne, solennamente (It.). Solemnly.

Soler (Ramos), Padre Antonio (Francisco Javier José) (baptized Olot, Gerona, 3 Dec 1729; d. El Escorial, 20 Dec 1783). Catalan composer, notably of keyboard sonatas. Trained at the choir school of Montserrat from the age of six, he entered the royal monastery of El Escorial in 1752 and became chapelmaster there in 1757. He continued his studies with the Royal organist-composer José de Nebra and Domenico Scarlatti, and published a theory of modulation (1762), which drew him into lively debate. Though he wrote a great deal of sacred music – masses, psalms, festival villancicos – he is remembered almost exclusively for his 120 sonatas, many of them written in the course of his work as keyboard instructor to the Infante Gabriel. He also wrote six concertos for two keyboards and six quintets for organ and strings.

Solera, Temistocle (b. Ferrara, 25 Dec 1815; d. Milan, 21 Apr 1878). Italian librettist, a published poet before he started work with Verdi, on *Oberto*. He then provided texts for *Nabucco*, *I lombardi*, *Giovanna d' Arco* and *Attila* before moving to Spain with his soprano wife.

sol-fa. See TONIC SOL-FA.

solfège. The basic musical skills, imparted in the French tradition with an emphasis on aural training through solfeggio.

solfeggio. The singing of scales and exercises to tonic sol-fa syllables, developed as part of the education of singers in Italy in the first half of the 18th century.

soli (It., pl. of *solo*). Solos, soloists.

Sollberger, Harvey (Dene) (b. Cedar Rapids, Iowa, 11 May 1939). US composer and flautist. He studied at the University of Iowa and with Beeson and Luening at Columbia (1960–64). Remaining in New York to teach, he was a founder member of the GROUP FOR CONTEMPORARY MUSIC and rapidly emerged as a strongly imaginative creator, bringing new sounds into the tradition of Varèse, Shapey and Wolpe. In 1982 he moved to the University of California at San Diego, where he has continued his work as composer and performer.

solmization. The association of syllables with notes, as a memory aid, found in many different cultures. The European system is attributed to Guido of Arezzo and originally used the syllables ut-re-mi-fa-sol-la for the notes of any HEXA-CHORD. Those syllables were derived from the opening notes of the first six lines of the hymn *Ut queant laxis*, which may have been composed for the purpose. They also provided the note names common in Latin countries, with the addition of *si* for the seventh, and offered a basis for TONIC SOL-FA.

solo (It., alone, only). Piece or passage for one performer. The word may be used adjectivally without gender agreement, as in 'solo sonata', a term useful to distinguish works for solo strings (by Bach, Reger, Bartók, Ligeti, etc.) from sonatas with piano accompaniment. As a marking in a score, the word may indicate a passage where one performer has a solo role. Alternatively, it may require that just one performer plays or sings while the others reading from that line remain silent, until the counter-direction 'tutti'.

Solomon. Ancient Jewish king (see 1 Kings 3–11). Works based on his story include:

(1) Handel's oratorio to an anonymous text. Solomon (mezzo-soprano) is praised by the high priest Zadok (tenor) and Pharoah's Daughter (soprano), makes his celebrated judgement between two harlots (sopranos), and entertains the Queen of Sheba (soprano), after her bustling orchestral Arrival. First performance: London, 17 Mar 1749.

(2) Bloch's cello rhapsody *Schelomo* (the Hebrew name in German transliteration). First performance: New York, 3 May 1917.

solo quartet. Group of four soloists (s, a, t, b) featured in a large-scale choral work, e.g. Beethoven's Ninth Symphony or *Missa solemnis*.

Solti, Georg (b. Budapest, 21 Oct 1912; d. Antibes, 5 Sep 1997). Hungarian–British conductor (originally György Stern), knighted in 1971. Educated at the Liszt Academy in Budapest, with Dohnányi, Bartók and Kodály among his teachers, he joined the Budapest Opera as a répétiteur, worked with Toscanini at Salzburg (1936–7) and made his conducting debut in Budapest with *Figaro* (1938). Facing discrimination as a Jew, he left the next year for Switzerland. His career took off rapidly after the war: he was music director of the Bavarian Staatsoper (1946–52), the Frankfurt Opera (1952–61), Covent Garden Opera (1961–71), the Chicago Symphony (1969–91) and the LPO (1979–81). Fiery and brilliant, he also made numerous recordings, including the first gramophone *Ring* (1958–65).

Georg Solti and Harvey Sachs *Solti on Solti* (1997)

sombrero de tres picos, El (The Three-cornered Hat, *Le tricorne*). Ballet score by Falla to a scenario by Martínez Sierra after the Alarcón play that also served for Wolf's Der CORREGIDOR, originally choreographed by Massine and designed by Picasso. There are two suites. First performance: London, 22 Jul 1919.

Somers, Harry (Stewart) (b. Toronto, 11 Sep 1925; d. Toronto, 9 Mar 1999). Canadian composer. He studied with Weinzweig at the conservatory in Toronto (1942–9) and Milhaud in Paris (1949–50), then returned to Canada and took various jobs. His works, strenuous and modernist, include the opera *Louis Riel* (f.p. Toronto, 1967).

Somervell, Arthur (b. Windermere, 5 Jun 1863; d. London, 2 May 1937). British composer, knighted in 1929. He studied at Cambridge, in Berlin and in London, his teachers including Stanford and Parry. His works include song cycles to poems by Tennyson (*Maud*, 1898), Housman (*The Shropshire Lad*, 1904), etc., as well as church music and orchestral works.

sommo, somma (It.). Ultimate, as in *con somma passione* (with the utmost passion).

son (Fr.). Sound.

sonagli (It.). Jingles.

sonance. Place of an interval on a scale from consonance to dissonance, within a particular musical context. Compare CORDANCE.

sonata (It., something sounded, played, pl. *sonate*, though in Eng. 'sonatas'; Fr. *sonate*, Ger. *Sonate*). An instrumental composition, normally in three or four movements and for one or two players. In Classical and later sonatas the first movement, at least, will usually be in SONATA FORM.

The term can be traced to 13th-century Provence, but its use was sporadic until the growth of instrumental music in the 16th century. Throughout the Baroque period its meaning remained unsettled and confused with that of other terms (sinfonia, canzona, concerto). It could imply relatively large forces, as in Monteverdi's *Sonata sopra 'Sancta Maria'* from his Vespers, but it was also regularly applied to more modestly scored pieces of two kinds for which Corelli provided models: the SONATA DA CHIESA and the SONATA DA CAMERA, to be performed respectively in church and in courtly, or at least genteel, households. The two genres did not stay distinct for long in the rich, multifarious and multi-centred activities of Baroque composers, though certain stabilities can be discerned, including the scoring and texture of the TRIO SONATA.

In the Classical period the sonata began to belong more to the performer, whether adept or amateur, and became firmly a solo or duo item. It also acquired a regular – though not invariable – shape: opening movement in sonata form, slow movement, finale. Solo keyboard sonatas had been written by earlier composers, notably Domenico Scarlatti and Soler, but with Haydn and Mozart – and, especially, Beethoven and Schubert – the PIANO SONATA had a new scale and weight. All these composers also favoured the VIOLIN SONATA, and Beethoven pioneered sonatas for cello and horn.

Early Romantic composers, notably Schumann and Chopin, went on writing sonatas, but the emphasis shifted to miniatures, character pieces and dance forms. Liszt's Sonata (1852–3) was in every way exceptional: a single capacious movement in dramatic virtuoso style. Towards the end of the 19th century, the duo sonata suited a general reflective mood, felt by Brahms, Fauré and others, while Scriabin took the piano sonata in new directions.

Sonatas since Scriabin have been diverse, not least in colour. Hindemith wrote sonatas for most of the normal instruments, including tuba, cor anglais, harp and double bass. There were also in the first half of the 20th century sonatas for flute, viola and harp (Debussy), violin with cello (Ravel), and two pianos with percussion (Bartók). The sonata implied an appeal to tradition, but it could be restorative (Prokofiev) or progressive (Barraqué), and if the former, it could be dimly remembering Scarlatti more than Beethoven (Cage). Even if it remembered Beethoven, it might recall much else besides (Ives). And soon there were works – Davies's 'St Michael' Sonata for wind (1957), Ferneyhough's Sonatas for string quartet (1967) – that curved back to review the sonatas of four centuries before.

William S. Newman *The Sonata in the Baroque Era* (1959, ⁴1983), *The Sonata in the Classic Era* (1963, ³1983), *The Sonata since Beethoven* (1969, ³1983)

sonata allegro. Opening movement, of a symphony, quartet or sonata, in SONATA FORM, or a synonym for that form.

sonata da camera (It., chamber sonata). Mid-Baroque genre, normally a TRIO SONATA, comprising a prelude and two or three dance movements. After 1700 such works were generally called by another name, e.g. suite, partita, ordre.

sonata da chiesa (It., church sonata). Mid-Baroque genre, normally a TRIO SONATA with four movements in the pattern slow–fast (fugato)–slow–fast (gigue). After 1700 the 'da chiesa' denotation tended to be dropped as different schemes took over: slow–fast–fast or – commonest of all, thanks to influence from the sinfonia and concerto – fast–slow–fast. But the term 'sonata da chiesa form' has been retained for much later works on the old slow–fast–slow–fast model, such as Haydn's F minor Quartet or Bartók's Third.

sonata form. Musical form developed in, and most characteristic of, the Classical period, when it suited an Enlightenment principle that music's inner workings should be accessible to the listener. Various ways were found to achieve this, and they all came together in sonata form: having themes that are clear and memorable; giving two of those themes prominence and contrast, so that the music can unfold as an argument between them; progressively varying or intensifying a theme so as to heighten tension; and restoring the status quo – or, preferably, arriving at a deeper rest, implied but not expressed at the start, where some degree of agitation or awkwardness was needed to get the music going.

Sonata form was originally, and remained, the form of choice for first movements. It gradually emerged during the middle decades of the 18th century from Baroque binary form, i.e. from a form in which the first part leads from the tonic to the dominant, and the second part duly leads back from the dominant to the tonic. In sonata form this basic harmonic design was dynamized. The dominant in the first part (or relative major in the case of a minor-key movement) was given its own theme, the 'second subject', and the rearrival of the tonic in the second part became a dramatic moment, coming now after a period of restlessness. Also, the sense of homecoming was prolonged by having the entire first part, including the second subject, heard now in the tonic. This produced a form in three large sections, for which there are conventional names:

Exposition: first subject (tonic) – transition – second subject (dominant) – codetta
Development: development (harmonically unstable) – retransition
Recapitulation: first subject (tonic) – transition – second subject (tonic) – coda

The division into two repeated parts (exposition, development-recapitulation) was retained from the Baroque form, but the second repetition was probably never observed, and exposition repeats went out in middle-period Beethoven.

Fully at work in Haydn's music by 1770, these fundamental principles provided not so much a recipe as a pattern of growth. It may be significant that no adequate description of sonata form was published until after the death of Mozart: composers had been working not from a textbook but from their material, and their interpretations of sonata form were correspondingly various. The whole form might be prefaced by a call to attention or slow introduction. The two subjects could be opposed in character – often the second would be more lyrical – but they might be virtually identical (hence the term 'monothematic sonata form'). The codetta might introduce a new theme. The development could employ all kinds of techniques of distortion, complication and intensification, and the retransition could lead through witty feints at the expected event that most defined the form: the 'double return', thematic and harmonic (of the first subject and of the tonic key). After that moment the order of the two subjects might be reversed, and the coda could be expanded almost into a section in its own right.

It was so expanded by Beethoven, who also developed the form by exploring other possibilities for the key of the second subject (especially keys a third from the tonic), extending the development and expanding the entire scale. The first movement of his 'Eroica' Symphony is three times the length of symphonic opening movements that Haydn – and Beethoven himself – had been writing only a few years before.

Tenacious as an idea – one of the great memes of music – sonata form swept through other musical forms and held its place through all the changes of the Romantic and later periods. Even in the Classical period it infiltrated the other movements of symphonies, quartets and sonatas: a minuet or scherzo would often be a miniature sonata form, the slow movement a sonata form without development (a form also frequent in overtures), and the finale a sonata rondo. The first movements of Mozart's and Beethoven's concertos combine sonata form with the solo-ritornello form of the Baroque concerto, and shades of sonata form can also be found in their operatic and sacred music. Beethoven in his last years had sonata form driving in vigorous harness with fugue (*Grosse Fuge*) or variation form (Diabelli Variations).

After Beethoven sonata form became what it had not been before, indeed a recipe, if one followed with enormous variety and virtuosity by later composers. One notable innovation was the embracing of the four conventional movement types – opening allegro, slow movement, scherzo and finale – within one sonata form, as in Liszt's Sonata and Schoenberg's First Chamber Symphony. But it could be argued, too, that the essence of sonata form – the persuasive growth of music out of the potential of its material – was perpetuated by composers who broke the mould: Debussy and Barraqué.

Charles Rosen *Sonata Forms* (1980, ²1988)

sonata rondo. RONDO displaying elements of sonata form.

Sonatas and Interludes. Work by Cage for prepared piano. There are 16 sonatas, in binary form with repetitions, and four interludes, placed after sonatas IV (1), VIII (2 and 3) and XII (4). Sonatas XIV and XV make a pair with the title *Gemini*, after a sculpture by Richard Lippold, one of the composer's artist friends in New York. The dedication is to Maro Ajemian, who probably gave the first performance in 1949.

sonata style. Style of composition in which sonata form is a guiding principle. A piece may be in sonata style (e.g. having tonal-thematic conflict and development) without being strictly in sonata form.

Sonate (Ger., Fr., sonata, Ger. pl. *Sonaten*). Sonata.

sonatina (It., little sonata, pl. *sonatine*, though in Eng. 'sonatinas'; Fr. *sonatine*, Ger. *Sonatine*). Genre liked by minor composers of the Classical period (Clementi, Dussek) and their publishers – but there is nothing too little about Schubert's violin sonatinas. Busoni, Ravel, Bartók, Boulez and others revived the title for small-scale sonatas.

song. Vocal piece normally delivered by one person and short. But this definition is at once too inclusive and too exclusive. For example, for most operatic solo numbers the term ARIA is more appropriate, though arias are commonly called songs where they seem to be delivered as such within the context of the drama (e.g. Don José's Flower Song in *Carmen*, Marguerite's Jewel Song in *Faust*). Liturgical pieces, too, commonly go by other names (hymn, antiphon, etc.). On the other hand, the chief medium of secular vocal composition in the later Middle Ages was the POLYPHONIC SONG, normally for three or four voices, and in Romantic Germany and England the choral PARTSONG had a hold. Brevity, too, is not indispensable – witness Mahler's *Song of the Earth*. Nor even is the voice necessary, for instruments can sing both songs (Mendelssohn's Songs without Words) and song themes. Nevertheless, in what follows song will be considered in its basic form, as individual vocal expression.

But what individual is expressing? Composed song has always gained some of its life from a multiple assumption of roles, a polyphony within the one person. The words, presuming them to come first at least in order of creation, already speak with two voices, those of poet and imaginary narrator. The composer will not only amplify, colour, characterize and take over those voices but probably add another, in the accompaniment. And singers, now, will want to recreate the two poetic voices as their own. Fischer-Dieskau in *Winterreise* is singing for himself, for Schubert, for Wilhelm Müller and for a nameless wanderer. The great singer will also make the song ours, something we recognize but previously had no song for.

The earliest songs with musical notation, those of the TROUBADOUR tradition that reached its peak in the 12th century, are less complex in this regard, in that the same person was both poet and composer, accepting identification also with the imaginary narrator, who would normally sing of the pains of love. This is true also of the slightly later TROUVERE and MINNESINGER songs (unaccompanied, like those of the troubadours). And indeed, the inexhaustible topic of love has remained song's principal theme down through the ages, maintained most immediately in the polyphonic songs of the later Middle Ages.

With the Renaissance a new kind of song – the LUTE SONG, for a singer accompanying himself (the sex implied) – began to appear in Italy, and later in France (as the AIR DE COUR) and England (Dowland). Song was re-established as individual expression, and it continued to hold an important place throughout the first half of the Baroque period, up to the time of the abundantly songful Purcell.

Then it passed from composers' first preoccupations, to return with the first inklings of Romanticism and folksong revival towards the end of the 18th century. The piano-accompanied LIED led the way, from Reichardt through Beethoven to Schubert, Schumann and Brahms. Only in the later 19th century did its record begin to be matched by the Russian song (Musorgsky), the French MELODIE (Fauré, Duparc, Debussy) and the songs of British, Scandinavian, US and central European composers. Even then the lied energetically continued its existence, in the works of Wolf, Mahler, Strauss and Berg.

After about 1930 it becomes necessary to speak of 'art song', as distinct from the new forms of popular song that had begun with a whisper (Foster, Sullivan) and become a clamour (Gershwin, Porter, etc., and afterwards rock). The price – and the pride – of confinement was sophistication, in the output of such composers as Poulenc, Britten and Rorem.

But there were alternatives: to transgress the boundaries of popular culture, as Schoenberg had already done by wildly alienating the cabaret song in *Pierrot lunaire*, or to find radically new kinds of lyricism – perhaps with unusually wide intervals and novel instrumental combinations, as in works by Webern, Boulez and Kurtág.

Denis Stevens, ed. *A History of Song* (1960, ²1970)

song cycle (Ger. *Liederkreis*). Sequence of songs (usually four or more) devised to be performed and heard as a unity. Normally another criterion is implied: narrative continuity, or at least consistency. Otherwise one is dealing with a song collection or set. Beethoven's *An die ferne Geliebte* (1816) is the first notable example, but it had many predecessors, German and British. Its successors include Schubert's *Die schöne Müllerin* and *Winterreise*, Schumann's two works with the title *Liederkreis*, as well as his *Dichterliebe* and *Frauenliebe und -leben*, Musorgsky's *The Nursery*, *Sunless* and *Songs and Dances of Death*, and Fauré's *La Bonne Chanson*. Janáček's *Diary of One who Disappeared* and Schoenberg's *Pierrot lunaire* extend the genre.

song form. TERNARY form.

Song of the Earth, The. See *Das* LIED VON DER ERDE.

Song of the Flea. Sung by Mephistopheles in Goethe's *Faust*, set by Beethoven, Berlioz and Musorgsky.

Songs and Dances of Death (*Pesni i plyaski smerti*). Song cycle by Musorgsky to words by Arseny Golenishchev-Kutuzov, comprising four numbers in which Death addresses its victims. There are orchestrations by Rimsky-Korsakov and Glazunov, and by Shostakovich.

Songs my mother taught me. Song by Dvořák, his Op.55:4.

Songs without Words (*Lieder ohne Worte*). Eight volumes of lyric piano pieces by Mendelssohn, six in each volume, the last two collections being posthumous. The title (in German) was introduced with the second volume, the first having been published in London as 'Original Melodies'. The most popular items are the Andante con moto in E (1:1), Hunting Song (1:3), Venetian Gondola Songs in G minor (1:6), F♯ minor (2:6) and A minor (5:5), Duetto in A♭ (3:6), Adagio in F (4:4), Andante espressivo (May Breezes) in G (5:1), Spring Song in A (5:6) and Spinning Song (The Bees' Wedding) in C (6:4). (Titles given in brackets here are among those added by later wellwishers.)

sonnambula, La (The Sleepwalker). Opera by Bellini to a libretto by Romani. The somnambulist is Amina (soprano, a Pasta role), whose night-time wanderings lead her to compromise herself, but she is ultimately vindicated, sleepwalking again, and able to save her beloved Elvino (tenor) from the alternative of Lisa (soprano). The score includes Amina's entrance cavatina and cabaletta 'Come per me – Sovra il sen', the Amina–Elvino betrothal duet 'Prendi, l'anel' and Amina's somnambulatory cantabile 'Ah! non credea'. First performance: Milan, 6 Mar 1831.

sonnerie (Fr., sounding). A military or hunting signal, or the arrangement of bells in a tower, or a peal of bells.

sonoramente (It.). Sonorously; abbreviated *sonore*.

sonority. (1) Single sound, an alternative to 'note' where the latter's suggestion of pitch is inappropriate (e.g. in percussion or electronic music).

(2) Quality of sound, embracing harmony and timbre, as in 'Ligeti is a master of orchestral sonority'.

Sony. Japanese electronics company founded in 1946, at first manufacturing only hardware. It entered the record market in 1968 as the Japanese partner of CBS, which it bought in 1988. The CD operation, based in New York, maintained the CBS catalogue and roster of artists while becoming more involved in crossover projects.

Sonzogno. Italian publishing house, active in music from 1874 under Edoardo Sonzogno (1836–1920), who ran competitions for one-act operas four times between 1883 and 1902, winning *Cavalleria rusticana* in the process. He became the publisher not only of Mascagni but also of Leoncavallo, Giordano and Cilea.

sop. Abbreviation for soprano.

sopra (It.). On or above, as in the markings *sopra una corda* (on one string) and *come sopra* (as above).

Sopran (Ger.). Soprano.

sopranino. Used of instruments higher than the soprano of the family, e.g. sopranino recorder.

soprano (Fr. *soprano*, Ger. *Sopran*, It. *soprano*, pl. *soprani*). Used by itself the word denotes a female voice of high range, or a singer with that voice. The range is normally from middle C to high A, though often with upward (and downward) extensions required from soloists. With qualification it can indicate high register in other voices (e.g. boy soprano, soprano castrato, male soprano, i.e. falsettist) or instruments (e.g. soprano saxophone). Cognate with 'supreme' and 'sovereign', the term derives from the Latin *superius*, which was applied to the top voice in 15th-century polyphony.

Women sang in the Middle Ages, all the way from convents to whorehouses, but the solo soprano was a jewel of the late Renaissance, and in particular of opera and its associated genres. In the Baroque period the voice grew more flamboyant: Carissimi's cantata *Apritevi, inferni* was one of the first pieces to exploit the high C. As composers came to write ever more closely for particular singers, so different kinds of soprano voice became manifest in their music. Mozart provides the outstanding example. Roles he wrote for Josepha Hofer (the Queen of the Night in *Die Zauberflöte*) and Louise Villeneuve (Dorabella in *Così fan tutte*) are radically different, the one having a lot of rapid figuration reaching up to a high F, the other much lower and warmer (a MEZZO-SOPRANO part in modern terminology). Different again are the kinds of voice presumed by the Countess and Susanna in *Figaro*: dignified and spirited. In the next century bel canto required a new combination of brilliance and expressive power, and Wagner's principal soprano roles demanded a new force. Even so, 19th-century singers could essay an extraordinary range of roles: Schröder-Devrient, for example, sang bel canto (Bellini's Romeo), Wagner (Senta) and Classical bravura (Donna Anna in *Don Giovanni*).

Specialization increased during the later 19th and 20th centuries, and separate categories of soprano voice were distinguished, including COLORATURA, DRAMATIC SOPRANO, FALCON, LIGHT SOPRANO, LYRIC SOPRANO, SOUBRETTE and SPINTO. But the boundaries are flexible, and every soprano has to find the music that will resonate with her unique voice.

soprano clef. C CLEF on the bottom line (obsolete).

Sor, (Joseph) Fernando (Macari) (baptized Barcelona, 14 Feb 1778; d. Paris, 10 Jul 1839). Catalan guitarist-composer. He was trained at the Montserrat choir school and had an opera produced in Barcelona when he was 19. During the next decade, with support from administrative sinecures, he wrote symphonies, quartets and songs. He then joined the fight against the French in 1808 (he had attended military academy), but later worked for the foreign regime, and so had to leave Spain when it fell in 1813. The rest of his life he spent mostly in London and Paris, writing ballets (*Cendrillon* was a huge success, which he followed to Moscow), songs and a great deal of guitar music, fantasias, sonatas, variations and divertimentos, influenced by Mozart and Haydn, which he played in concert. He also published a guitar method.

Brian Jeffery *Fernando Sor* (1977)

Sorabji, Kaikhosru Shapurji (b. Chingford, 14 Aug 1892; d. Winfrith Newburgh, 15 Oct 1988). British pianist-composer, born Leon Dudley Sorabji. His father was Parsi, his mother Spanish–Sicilian. Privately educated and largely self-taught in music, he had a dazzling intellect, which he was not afraid to flash at those he perceived as enemies. He was also reclusive. At the beginning of the 1930s he withdrew from concert giving, stopped publishing his music, banned performances even of pieces in print (which included his almost-four-hour *Opus clavicembalisticum*, 1929–30), and retired to the small Dorset town of Corfe Castle. There he went on producing works of enormous scale and textural complexity, for piano alone or with orchestra, influenced by the composers he championed in his writings – Busoni and Szymanowski especially – but unique in their formidableness. In 1976 he again allowed some carefully chosen performances and recordings, and after his death his music began to gain its place at the extremes of virtuoso monumentalism.

Kaikhosru Shapurji Sorabji *Around Music* (1932), *Mi contra fa* (1947)

Sorcerer's Apprentice, The. See L'APPRENTI SORCIER.

sordino (It.). Mute, as in *con sordino* (with the mute), *senza sordini* (without mutes).

sordun. Double-reed instrument that had a short life from the 1590s into the early decades of the 17th century. Its tube was folded back within a wooden casing, so that it was effectively a shortened bassoon.

Sørensen, Bent (b. Borup, 18 Jul 1958). Danish composer, pupil of Nørholm and Nørgård. His music characteristically suggests states of misty reminiscence, redolent of a lost past. *Alman* for string quartet (1983–4) was his breakthrough piece, followed by other quartets, chamber works and larger compositions (*The Echoing Garden*, s, t, ch, orch, 1990–92).

Sorochintsy Fair (*Sorochinskaya yarmarka*). Unfinished opera by Musorgsky to his own libretto after a story by Gogol. The work is a comic-fantastic love story Ukrainian-style, and was left by the composer far from complete. Lyadov and others made the first score, superseded in 1930 by Shebalin's version. First performance: Moscow, 21 Oct 1913.

Sosnovsky. See Maxim BEREZOVSKY.

sospirando (It., sighing). Plaintive.

sospiro (It., sigh). Crotchet rest.

sospiro, Un. Concert étude by Liszt.

sostenuto (It., sustained). Projected evenly and authoritatively, probably more slowly, with the notes given their full rhythmic values; abbreviated *sost.*

sostenuto pedal. Middle pedal on the piano, invented by Claude Montal in Paris in 1862. Depressing it causes notes undamped at the moment to remain so, while others are unaffected –

unlike the left, sustaining pedal, which takes the dampers off all notes.

sotto voce (It.). In an undertone, aside, a direction applicable as much to instruments as voices.

soubrette (Fr., little kitten). Light, agile soprano voice, or role for such a voice – usually a canny servant, e.g. Despina in *Così fan tutte*.

sound. The substance or the medium of music. Music is an art of sound unfolding through TIME, and an art of time unfolding through sound.

Sound is vibration, transmitted from the sounding body to the ear by means of fluctuations in air pressure. These fluctuations are of three essential kinds: they may vary in FREQUENCY (i.e. how many times a second the pressure goes through a cycle of peaking and declining), in complexity (i.e. how smooth or irregular the pressure variations, or sound waves, are: no matter how complex, they will be analysable into a number of components, for which the term PAR-TIAL is used) and in AMPLITUDE (i.e. how much the pressure varies through its cycle of change). The EAR registers these different variables as PITCH, TIMBRE and LOUDNESS, while also responding to changes in them through time, i.e. to the sound's ENVELOPE. In particular, the onset of a sound – the starting TRANSIENT – may be a complex event that affects how the whole sound is heard. Also important is the FORMANT, the mode of vibration favoured by the body of the instrument (the physiology of the vocal cavity in the case of a singer) and by the ACOUSTICS of the space in which the music is taking place.

Almost all musical instruments (including the voice) generate sound from some vibrating system, intimately connected with another that will amplify the sound and project it. This is clearly seen in the violin, whose strings alone would make only a very faint and thin sound, which the body of the instrument loudens and embellishes. Most musical instruments allow variation of pitch, achieved by changing the length of string or air column in play; if not, then like the piano they will generally provide a number of fixed pitches. Most instruments also provide for variation of timbre, loudness and envelope. These matters of connection, amplification, projection and control have absorbed instrument makers since the earliest times.

Musical instruments may thus be seen as highly developed machines – among the oldest machines in use in modern civilization – for creating sounds in determined and variable ways.

Musicians, though, may be more used to thinking of their material not as sound but as tones, an idealized equivalent. Indeed, Western music throughout much of its history was concerned to standardize sounds, and to distinguish the musical from the 'non-musical' – a category that would include microtonal deviations from the customary pitches, all but a very few varieties of vocal or instrumental timbre, and nearly all unpitched sounds, with the exception only of a few percussion instruments let in for emphasis (and even they might be treated with extreme restraint: percussionists have a quiet time in Brahms).

In the early 20th century this attitude began to change, partly because of developments in compositional technique, partly for social reasons that made the sounds of the factory as admissible as those of the drawing room, and partly because of changes in the sound environment. To the trains of the 19th century were added cars in the street and then electrical appliances in the home: noise became part of the hum of life, and its continuing exclusion from music impossible.

Acknowledging the change – indeed, relishing it – Varèse coined the term 'organized sound' for his work, in deliberate distinction from the more restrictive 'music'. Not only did he greatly enlarge the scope of percussion instruments in his scores, he also looked forward to having electronic means that would allow the musical use of any sound. Later composers who have regularly worked with electronics, like Stockhausen, have been very aware of the nature and qualities of sound, and have brought that awareness into their music. But the same awareness may be there in the output of composers working with traditional instruments and voices, such as Lachenmann. With Cage, as early as *4'33"* (1952), any and every sound could be music, and no sound too.

Hermann L.F. Helmholtz *On the Sensations of Tone* (1875, ⁶1948); John R. Pierce *The Science of Musical Sound* (1983)

soundboard. The under part of a keyboard instrument (or back of an upright piano), a sheet of wood that vibrates in sympathy with the strings and adds much to the power and richness of the sound.

soundhole. An opening in the belly of a string instrument, there to enhance the quality and distribution of the sound. In contact with the outside, the air inside the instrument can now resonate independently of the body. Soundholes in instruments of the violin family are *f*-shaped, in lutes and guitars round, often with decoration, in which case they are known as rose holes.

soundpost. Interior stick that connects the belly of a string instrument to the back and brings both structural and acoustic benefits: it eases the pressure placed on the belly by the strings in tension, and it transmits vibrations to the back. Its importance to the sound is recognized by its name in French (*âme*), German (*Seele*) and Italian (*anima*): soul.

soupir (Fr., sigh). Crotchet (quarter-note) rest.

source. Record of a composition from which copies and editions are made. Written records are most usual, though sound recordings may also be significant sources for music since 1900 (e.g. the piano music of Bartók or Ives, as played by the composer), and digital data for music since the late 20th century.

Sources are judged by their closeness to the composer, with autographs of chief importance, followed by copies and editions near the composer in time and space. There may be several autograph sources, dating from the process of composition (from SKETCH to fair copy) and after (corrected proofs, revisions marked in printed copies, etc.), all of which will be of interest to a modern editor. Their evaluation will depend on matters of scholarship and policy, notably on whether the editor wants to establish the first completed version of the piece (the *Fassung erster Hand*) or the last (the *Fassung letzter Hand*). Questions that have to be resolved include those of notational practice (personal and period), of competence on the composer's part, and of whether differences between the first edition and the corresponding autograph are to be considered as the composer's changes or as misprints.

sourdine (Fr.). Mute.

Sousa, John Philip (b. Washington, 6 Nov 1854; d. Reading, Penn., 6 Mar 1932). US composer-conductor, the son of Iberian and Bavarian immigrants. Following his father, he joined the US Marine Band as an apprentice of 13. He then worked as a theatre violinist in Philadelphia before returning to the marine band as a conductor (1880–92), resigning to form his own band, Sousa's Band. With them he stormed Europe four times (1900–5), went on a world tour (1910–11) and continued in action until 1931, except for a break for navy service during the First World War. He wrote all kinds of light music, including operettas and songs, but is remembered for his marches, especially *The Washington Post* (1889), *The Liberty Bell* (1893) and *The Stars and Stripes Forever* (1897).

sousaphone. Bass tuba, commissioned by Sousa in the 1890s and worn by the player, with the tubing around the chest. Sousa asked for the bell to be pointed up, so that it 'projected the sound upward and mushroomed it over the entire band and audience', but a forward-pointing bell is generally preferred.

soutenu (Fr.). Sustained; equivalent to *sostenuto*.

South Bank Centre. The principal musical venue in London, embracing three auditoria: the Royal Festival Hall (opened 1951, seating 2,900), the Queen Elizabeth Hall (opened 1967, seating 917) and the Purcell Room (opened 1967, seating 370).

Souzay (Tisserand), Gérard (Marcel) (b. Angers, 8 Dec 1918; d. Antibes, 17 Aug 2004). French baritone. He studied at the Paris Conservatoire and with Pierre Bernac, Claire Croiza and Lotte Lehmann, and was particularly esteemed for his sophistication as a recitalist, in German song as much as French.

Sowerby, Leo (b. Grand Rapids, Mich., 1 May 1895; d. Port Clinton, Ohio, 7 Jul 1968). US composer. He studied in Chicago and had his violin concerto played by the symphony orchestra in 1913. In 1921 he was the first recipient of the US Prix de Rome. He then returned to Chicago, to teach at the American Conservatory (1925–62) and serve as organist and choirmaster at the Episcopal cathedral (1927–62). Besides church and organ music he wrote five symphonies and two organ concertos.

space. The use of space in music – prescribing how performers are positioned – is as old as ANTIPHONY and the PROCESSIONAL. There is also a special category of outdoor music. Moving inside again, separation of groups gained a wider importance in the POLYCHORAL music of the late Renaissance and early Baroque, but declined in the 18th century to be revived in the 19th for dramatic interventions by OFFSTAGE instruments, groups and choirs. The grail scenes of *Parsifal*, with voices above the audience on different levels, offer a particularly full-scale vivification of the auditorium as dramatic space. Meanwhile, offstage effects on a smaller scale were occasionally taken over into the concert repertory, as by Berlioz and Mahler. But these extensions into space, whether in opera or concert music, depended on the norm of having the orchestra in its usual place, in the pit or on the platform.

That norm, like so many others, was questioned by Ives, who in his *Unanswered Question* imagined most of the ensemble out of sight. Alternatively, the layout of the orchestra onstage could be changed in conformity with the musical design, as it was by Bartók with the double orchestra, antiphonally placed, of his Music for Strings, Percussion and Celesta.

Ives's example was followed multifariously by Henry Brant, while in Europe the development of separated sources came via electronic music. At a time when technicians were developing stereo reproduction, Stockhausen produced *Gesang der Jünglinge* (1955–6) for five groups of loudspeakers and *Gruppen* for three orchestras placed around the audience (1955–7). Most later electronic music is for at least two sound channels and more often four, with the potential for artificial spaces as enveloping as Wagner's grail chapel and for movements of sound in space – a possibility realized by Stockhausen with instruments in *Licht* and other works for players as characters on stage. The concert space can also be enlivened by having players move between different positions, as in Birtwistle's *Verses for Ensembles* and Boulez's *Domaines*, or by dispersing the orchestra around the hall, a powerful and versatile technique used to create effects of exuberance, drama or estrangement in works by Carter, Nono, Kurtág, Lachenmann, Rihm and Kyburz.

Other works produced since *Gruppen*, by Barraqué, Berio, Birtwistle, Boulez and Xenakis, have found other possibilities by reseating the ORCHESTRA onstage – not that a normal seating plan is without spatial consequences, determining, for instance, how brass and percussion instruments will sound from further back, or a flute solo will be less visible than one played by the principal cello, or the whole orchestral sound will be formed in balance and perspective by how the players are arranged.

spacing. The layout of chords in terms of register. See POSITION (3).

spagnoletta. Late Renaissance dance on a more or less fixed ground and characterized also by an opening melodic formula. Musical versions appear from 1581 almost to the end of the 17th century, including two by Farnaby in the Fitzwilliam Virginal Book.

Spain (España). The country had its own chant by the mid 7th century, but this was largely displaced in favour of Gregorian by the Council of Burgos (1080), to survive only in Toledo as MOZARABIC CHANT. In any event, much more influential on the national musical character was the period of Moorish rule, which began in 711 and withstood progressive Christian reconquest until the fall of Granada in 1492. Moorish musicians performed at

Christian courts and even in churches. Their instruments – especially the lute, ancestor of the guitar and vihuela – and their melodic style became deeply ingrained in the country's songs, dances and dance songs.

In the 16th century some of the gold from the New World was converted into sacred polyphony, at an excellent exchange rate. Ockeghem had visited earlier, and Low Countries music helped stimulate the native tradition that developed in the music of Peñalosa, Morales, Guerrero and Victoria. Simultaneously Spain acquired songs (in the genres of romance and VILLANCICO) and instrumental music, for the vihuela and keyboards.

Morales and Victoria had been admired in Rome, but Spanish music in the 17th century became more provincial. A local kind of opera, the ZARZUELA, was introduced, and the vihuela gave way to the guitar. A notable outsider, Domenico Scarlatti, devoted himself to private music, for a solo performer at the keyboard, as did Soler. Among subsequent native composers, Martín y Soler in the Classical period and Sor in the early 19th century found their opportunities abroad.

A belated national-Romantic surge came around 1900 in the music of Albéniz, Granados, Falla and Turina – so belated it was rapidly followed by modernism, in Falla and Gerhard (though not Rodrigo). It was further complicated by a growing sense of regional identity, especially among composers from CATALONIA. Spanish musical nationalism, rooted in dance, had also been somewhat pre-empted by the international Hispanic style cultivated especially by Frenchmen (Bizet, Lalo, Chabrier, Ravel, Debussy) and Russians (Glinka, Rimsky-Korsakov). And though the resulting familiarization may have helped Spanish composers gain a hearing abroad – where most of them made their careers (though again not Rodrigo) – their emigration left home institutions somnolent. The Spanish Civil War (1936–9) was a further dampener, though in the 1950s and 1960s an ambitious new generation arrived, led by Cristóbal Halffter and Luis de Pablo.

Gilbert Chase *The Music of Spain* (1941, [2]1959)

Spanisches Liederbuch (Spanish Songbook). Collection of songs by Wolf to translations of Spanish poems by Paul Heyse and Emanuel Geibel.

Sparrow (*Spatzenmesse*). Name given to Mozart's Mass in C, K.220, for the violins' chirps in the *Sanctus* and *Osanna*.

Spartacus (*Spartak*). Full-length ballet score by

Khachaturian, originally to a scenario by Nikolay Volkov concerning the slaves' revolt of 73 BC. (f.p. Leningrad, 26 Dec 1956), definitively restaged by Yuri Grigorovich at the Bolshoy (f.p. Moscow, 1968). It includes a spacious Romantic adagio.

Spaur. Name given to Mozart's Mass in C, K.258, though this may not in fact have been the mass sung at the consecration of Count Friedrich Franz Joseph von Spaur.

speaker. See LOUDSPEAKER.

species. One of five varieties of counterpoint identified in music theory by 1532 and definitively expounded by Fux in his influential treatise *Gradus ad Parnassum* (1725). A given melody in even notes may be joined by a line moving at the same speed (first species, note-against-note), at double or triple speed, depending on the metre (second species), at quadruple or sextuple speed (third species), at the same speed as the first but with syncopations (fourth species), or at changing speeds, including very small values (fifth species).

specification. The details of an organ's stops and other accoutrements.

spectral. Term introduced by Dufourt for music in which the composition of timbres (i.e. of a SPECTRUM for each sound), whether by electronic or natural means, is a prime concern. Spectral composition came out of work undertaken at IRCAM in the late 1970s by Dufourt, Grisey and Murail, though it had been anticipated by Radulescu and Stockhausen. Others associated with it include Saariaho and Vivier.

Spectre de la rose, Le (The Spirit of the Rose). Poem by Théophile Gautier set by Berlioz in *Nuits d'été*. Also a ballet by Fokine to Weber's *Aufforderung zum Tanze*, first and famously performed by Vaslav Nijinsky and Tamara Karsavina.

spectrum. The frequencies present in a sound, so named by analogy with the visual spectrum. These frequencies may be determined by spectral analysis, for which there are digital procedures.

speech. Everyday mode of vocal delivery, as distinct from song. Speech was long regarded as extraneous to music, and even when the two happened in the same context – a liturgy, a play with songs, a semi-opera – they did so separately, until the arrival in the late 18th century of MELODRAMA. A more intimate fusion came in the early 20th century, when composers might specify

the rhythms of speech (*The Soldier's Tale, Façade*) or even the melodic contours (*Pierrot lunaire*), in this case creating an intermediate between speech and song, SPRECHGESANG. Another innovation of the period was the speaking chorus, in Milhaud's *Choëphores* and many works by Vogel. Other composers, including Strauss in *Ariadne auf Naxos* and Berg in *Lulu*, specifically exploited how speaking characters remain in their own domain, not properly part of the music's space and action.

speech-song. See SPRECHGESANG.

Spem in alium nunquam habui (In no other is my hope). Motet by Tallis in 40 parts, probably commissioned c.1570 by the Duke of Norfolk to match Striggio's similarly scored *Ecce beatam lucem*.

spheres. See MUSIC OF THE SPHERES.

spianato (It., planed). Smoothened. The term was introduced by Chopin for his Andante spianato.

spiccato (It., separated). Equivalent to staccato in music before 1750, later indicating a bouncing bowstroke – i.e. the same as *saltando* and *sautillé*.

Spiel (Ger., pl. *Spiele*). Play, manner of performance, hence *spielen* (to play), *spielend* (playful), *Spieler* (player).

Spieloper (Play-opera). Singspiel.

Spies, Claudio (b. Santiago, 26 Mar 1925). Chilean–US composer. He studied with Boulanger at the New England Conservatory and with Fine and Piston at Harvard, where he began his career in academic teaching, moving on to Swarthmore and Princeton. A member of Stravinsky's circle, he was influenced by the serial works.

spinet. A small harpsichord. The name comes from the Latin *spinetta* (little thorn) with reference to the instrument's quills, and in France the word *épinette* was used for all quill-plucked keyboard instruments into the 17th century. In modern English the term is generally restricted to domestic instruments having a limited compass and, for further space-saving, strings set obliquely to the keys.

Spinner, Leopold (b. Lemberg/Lviv, 26 Apr 1906; d. London, 12 Aug 1980). Austrian composer. He studied in Vienna with Paul Pisk (1926–30) and Webern (1935–8), a decisive influence. In 1938 he settled in England, where he later found work as an editor at Boosey & Hawkes, working on Stravinsky's scores.

spinto (It., pushed on). Lyric voice, tenor or soprano, capable of extra force, e.g. Alvaro and Leonora in *La forza del destino*.

spirito, con (It.). With spirit, lively.

spiritoso, spirituoso (It., spirited). It may mean 'with soul, with judgment and discretion' (Brossard, 1703) but the more common implication is of liveliness, as with *con spirito*.

spiritual. Kind of sacred song that developed among ex-African slaves in the USA in the 18th and 19th centuries as an expression of sadness and hope, e.g. 'Nobody Knows the Trouble I Seen' and 'Michael, Row the Boat Ashore'. After the Civil War (1861–5) spirituals (short for 'spiritual songs') were made more widely known by publishers, touring choirs and solo performers. They appealed to Dvořák and appear in works by Tippett and Zimmermann.

split note. An unfortunate attack on a brass or woodwind instrument, resulting in a split between two notes.

Spohr, Louis (b. Brunswick, 5 Apr 1784; d. Kassel, 22 Oct 1859). German composer and violinist, a prolific master of the pleasing. A doctor's son, he was brought up in a musical home and put to the violin; he also started composing before he was 10. The family had moved out to Seesen, and he was sent back to Brunswick for serious lessons. At 15 he was taken on by the local duke, in whose orchestra he discovered Mozart (his 'idol and model') and who enabled him to study with Franz Eck. He was also influenced by the playing of Pierre Rode. From Brunswick he moved to Gotha as concertmaster (1805–12), and in 1806 he married the harp virtuoso Dorette Scheidler (1787–1834). With her he went on tour as far afield as Vienna, Rome, London and Paris, in between fulfilling his obligations in Gotha and later in Vienna (as orchestra director at the Theater an der Wien, 1813–15) and Frankfurt (as opera director, 1817–19).

In 1822 he was appointed music director in Kassel, where he spent the rest of his life. Apart from presenting his own works, he was important in the Bach revival and in furthering Wagner's operas. His second wife, whom he married in 1836, was a pianist, Marianne Pfeiffer, and with her he resumed touring in Germany. He also paid four visits to London (1843–53), where his music was favoured only just below Mendelssohn's.

Assiduous in his duties, he was much loved, too, in Kassel. His music, though, failed to make the leap into the canon that was being established around the time of his death, for charm, melodiousness and felicity – the qualities that had endeared him to the bourgeoisie of the first half of the 19th century – were not those most important to the connoisseurs who now stood at the gates of history. Only his Octet and Nonet were not forgotten until his bicentenary, when his violin concertos, symphonies and other chamber works began to be appreciated again and pre-echoes of Wagner could be noted in his Indian opera *Jessonda*.

Clive Brown *Louis Spohr* (1984)

Operas: FAUST, f.p. Prague, 1816, rev London, 1852; *Jessonda* (Eduard Gehe, after Antoine Marin le Mierre), f.p. Kassel, 1823; etc.
Symphonies: No.1, E♭, Op.20, 1811; No.2, D minor, Op.49, 1820; No.3, C minor, Op.78, 1828; No.4 'The Power of Tones', F, Op.86, 1832; No.5, C minor, Op.102, 1837; No.6 'Historical Symphony in the Style and Taste of Four Different Periods', G, Op.116, 1840; No.7 'The Earthly and the Divine in Human Life', C, Op.121, 1841; No.8, G, Op.137, 1847; No.9 'The Seasons', B minor, Op.143, 1850; No.10, E, Op.156, 1857
Violin concertos: No.1, A, Op.1, 1802–3; No.2, D minor, Op.2, 1804; No.3, C, Op.7, 1806; No.4, B minor, Op.10, 1805; No.5, E♭, Op.17, 1807; No.6, G minor, Op.28, 1809; No.7, E minor, Op.38, 1814; No.8 'in the manner of an operatic scene', A minor, Op.47, 1816; No.9, D minor, Op.55, 1820; No.10, A, Op.62, 1810; No.11, G, Op.70, 1825; No.12, A, Op.79, 1828; No.13, E, Op.92, 1835; No.14 'Then and Now', A minor, Op.110, 1839; No.15, E minor, Op.128, 1844
Other orchestral works: Clarinet Concerto No.1, C minor, Op.26, 1808; No.2, E♭, Op.57, 1810; No.3, F minor, 1821; No.4, E minor, 1828; String Quartet Concerto, A minor, Op.131, 1845; etc.
Chamber: Nonet, Op.31, wind qnt, vn, va, vc, db, 1813; Octet, Op.32, cl, 2 hn, vn, 2 va, vc, db, 1814; Septet, Op.147, fl, cl, hn, bn, vn, vc, pf, 1853; Quintet, Op.52, fl, cl, hn, bn, pf, 1820; 4 double string quartets, 7 string quintets, 36 string quartets, 5 piano trios, 7 sonatas for vn and hp, etc.
Other works: sacred music, songs, virtuoso violin pieces, etc.

Spontini, Gaspare (Luigi Pacifico) (b. Maiolati, near Iesi, 14 Nov 1774; d. Maiolati, 24 Jan 1851). Italian–French composer of grand opera. Of poor family, he was a late student at the Turchini conservatory in Naples (1793–5) and won only modest success before he moved to Paris in 1803. There, by contrast, he soon gained the patronage of Empress Joséphine – and gained, too, a triumph with *La Vestale* (1807). In 1810 he married, and in 1814 he adroitly switched his allegiance to Louis

XVIII. Following the failure of his *Olimpie* (1819), though, he moved the next year to Berlin, where his embroilment in musical politics and his blind self-certainty did him no favours. In 1842, with little to show for his two decades and more in Germany, he retired to Paris, and from there returned to his birthplace the year before his death. The power his works exerted in the theatre may have owed a lot to his fearsome authority, as conductor and stage director, but there was something, too, in the scores: an expansion of Gluck's grandeur into spectacle and an infusion of Romantic directness.

Operas: *La* VESTALE; *Fernand Cortez* (Etienne de Jouy and Joseph Alphonse Esménard), f.p. Paris, 1809, rev 1817, rev Berlin, 1824, 1832; *Olimpie* (Michel Dieulafay and Charles Brifaut, after Voltaire), f.p. Paris, 1819, rev Berlin, 1821, Paris, 1826; *Nurmahal* (Carl Alexander Herklots, after Moore), f.p. Berlin, 1822; *Alcidor* (Théaulon de Lambert), f.p. Berlin, 1825; *Agnes von Hohenstaufen* (Ernst Raupach), f.p. Berlin, 1829, rev 1837; etc.
Other works: choral music, songs, etc.

sprechgesang (Ger., speech-song). Kind of vocal delivery between speech and song, first defined by Humperdinck in his opera *Königskinder* (1897), with the instruction that performers should approximate the given notes. Schoenberg took up the idea in his *Gurrelieder* (1911) and several immediately following works, including most notably *Pierrot lunaire*, in which he introduced what became the standard notation, with an 'x' on the note stem. However, the performance of sprechgesang was never standardized. In his preface to *Pierrot* Schoenberg asked that the performer should 'give the pitch exactly, but then immediately leave it in a fall or rise'. But this has been taken as meaning anything from virtual singing to nightclub crooning or expressionist dramatization.

Schoenberg returned to sprechgesang (for which his terms were *Sprechstimme*, speaking voice, *Sprechmelodie*, speech melody, or *Rezitation*) for the part of Moses in *Moses und Aron* and, with simplified notation, in the *Ode to Napoleon* and *A Survivor from Warsaw*. Berg in *Wozzeck* followed Schoenberg's practice and added a new shade, 'half sung', between sprechgesang and song.

sprechstimme. See SPRECHGESANG.

sprezzatura (It., pride). Term introduced by Caccini in the preface to his *Euridice* (1600) to indicate a speech-like freedom and fullness of expression.

springer (Ger. *Nachschlag*). Ornament; an extra note, notated in smaller type, played within the time of its predecessor. For example, a crotchet plus springer would be played as a dotted quaver plus semiquaver. There are examples in Chopin.

springs. Natural subject for imitation at the piano, as in Liszt's *Au bord d'une source* and Szymanowski's *La Fontaine d'Aréthuse*.

spurious work. Composition not written by its supposed composer. Misattribution may be due to difficulties in distinguishing one composer from another (particularly with works of the 14th and 15th centuries, which may be variously attributed in sources), to a deliberate wish to mislead, or to obliviousness to the facts of the matter – concerning, for example, the pieces by which Albinoni, Allegri and others are best known. Music's great forgeries have been motivated only partly by commercial opportunism (as when 18th-century publishers cheerfully borrowed the names of Pergolesi and Haydn); much more misdirection has come from whim, the search for amusement (e.g. Kreisler's 'old masters'), and ignorance. Scholarship since the late 19th century has been concerned to weed out spurious works, but some (notably 'by' Bach and Mozart) have taken on lives of their own.

square. 15th- and 16th-century English term for a bottom part taken from a piece of polyphony and reused, again within polyphony.

square dance. 19th-century US dance for eightsomes each of four couples beginning as if on the sides of a square. Movements are cried out by a caller.

square piano. Domestic PIANO of rectangular shape, manufactured in abundance in the late 18th century and early 19th, then supplanted by the upright.

Sri Lanka. See INDIA.

Staatskapelle (Ger.). State opera orchestra, notably those of Berlin and Dresden.

Staatsoper (Ger.). State opera. Companies in Berlin, Dresden, Hamburg, Munich and Vienna are so called.

Stabat mater. Poem of 13th-century Franciscan origin, describing the sorrows of Christ's mother at the foot of the Cross, and sung as a sequence, hymn, votive antiphon or concert piece. There are settings by Browne, Josquin, Palestrina, Pergolesi, Rossini, Verdi, Szymanowski, etc.

staccato (It., detached). Style of playing in which notes are clipped of some of their time and given a little separate emphasis. Notation is by means of a dot, short line or wedge, above or below the note, the dot being commonest:

These forms are all found from the early Baroque period onwards and do not necessarily have different connotations. Where both are found together, the short line or wedge will probably indicate a more extreme staccato, or *staccatissimo*, even more clipped. Conversely, the degree of detachment may be limited by combining staccato notation with a slur.

Staden, Sigmund Theophil (baptized Kulmbach, 6 Nov 1607; buried Nuremberg, 30 Jul 1655). German organist-composer. His father, Johann Staden (1581–1634), was the leading musician of his time in Nuremberg, visited Bayreuth in 1618 to try out the new organ with Michael Praetorius, Scheidt and Schütz, and produced sacred and secular choral music and instrumental pieces, as well as four musical sons. Sigmund Theophil, trained by his father and by Jakob Paumann in Augsburg, took over the family's musical responsibilities in Nuremberg, where in 1643 he conducted what was billed as 'an outline of the origin, continuation, developments, use and misuse of the noble art of music'. This concert included music of the angels, music that sounded at the beginning of the world and music of the Hebrews, most of it dreamed up by the conductor, who the next year published the earliest singspiel, *Seelewig*.

Stadler, Anton (Paul) (b. Bruck an der Leitha, 28 Jun 1753; d. Vienna, 15 Jun 1812). Austrian clarinettist. He and his brother Johann, also a clarinettist, played in Vienna from 1773, and he formed an attachment to Mozart, his fellow in freemasonry as well as music. He played alongside the composer in the first performance of the quintet for piano and wind. Enjoying the clarinet's low register, he developed the BASSET CLARINET, for which Mozart wrote his clarinet quintet and concerto. Mozart also composed obbligatos for him on clarinet and basset horn in *La clemenza di Tito*.

Stadtpfeifer (Ger.). Town piper, a municipal appointment in Germany and neighbouring countries from the 14th century until around 1800. Depending on the size and importance of the city, the piper might be just a signaller and watchman or have charge of a band and larger musical resources. Musicians who held such posts include Susato, Hassler, Staden, Pezel, Telemann and various Bachs.

Städtische Oper (Ger., city opera). Municipal opera house.

staff, stave (pl. staves). Set of horizontal lines, normally five, on which music is notated. Staves appeared in the treatise known as MUSICA ENCHIRIADIS but became widespread only in the later 11th century, through the influence of Guido of Arezzo's teaching. Four-line staves became standard for plainsong in NEUMES; five-line staves were introduced in the early 13th century. Staves with larger numbers of lines are used for TABLATURE.

The normal staff has a CLEF and KEY SIGNATURE, with notes of the key placed on the lines or in the spaces between them, from low at the bottom to high at the top. A note foreign to the key will have an ACCIDENTAL; one beyond the compass of the staff will require at least one LEGER LINE. Two or more staves may be joined by a BRACE to form a SYSTEM.

stage. Area in a theatre or other auditorium, generally raised. The rule in opera is for the singers to be on the stage, with the orchestra in the pit. In a concert hall, or venue serving as such, all the performers will normally be on the stage. But there may be OFFSTAGE musicians, in opera a stage band, and in some works since the mid 1950s a wider use of SPACE.

stage band (It. *banda*). Wind ensemble playing on stage or in the wings, a fixture in Italian and French opera of the 19th century, there to add to the excitement and also to create an illusion of music as part of the action, as at the march bringing on the wooden horse in *Les Troyens*. Ensembles of other kinds are used for the latter purpose on stage in operas both earlier (*Don Giovanni*) and later (*Wozzeck*).

Staggins, Nicholas (d. Windsor, 13 Jun 1700). English composer, at court from 1670 and appointed Master of the King's Music in 1674.

stagione (It., season, pl. *stagioni*). System of opera-house planning, in which works are presented during short seasons of from two to four weeks, normally with performances of several pieces intercalated. This method works when singers are coming together for a particular production, as is normally the case at the more prestigious houses. Smaller theatres, with a permanent ensemble, can run productions in repertory – i.e. spreading performances throughout their annual programme.

Stainer, John (b. London, 6 Jun 1840; d. Verona, 31 Mar 1901). British church musician, knighted in 1888. Trained as a chorister at St Paul's and later educated at St Michael's College, Tenbury, and Oxford, he remained in Oxford as an organist and conductor, became organist of St Paul's (1872–88) and then returned to Oxford as professor of music. He wrote church music, including the popular oratorio *The Crucifixion* (1887), and was a pioneer in the study of music before Palestrina.

Stainer & Bell. British music publishing firm founded in London in 1907 by a group of investors; the name was a fabrication. Initially the company specialized in new British music, but it soon became a place for early music, publishing the *Musica Britannica* series (from 1951), etc.

Stamitz. Czech–German dynasty of composers associated with the powerhouse of pre-Classical music at Mannheim.

(1) **Johann (Wenzel Anton)** (baptized Německý Brod, now Havlíčkův Brod, 19 Jun 1717; buried Mannheim, 30 Mar 1757). The son of an organist-choirmaster, he was educated at a Jesuit school. He joined the Mannheim court probably in 1741, rose to become director of instrumental music in 1750 and developed the orchestra into the most formidable of its time. In his many symphonies he made use of the crescendo that was a Mannheim speciality (borrowed from opera overtures by Jommelli and others) as well as forward-looking features: four-movement form (which he was the first to use), four-bar phrasing, wind solos and a larger orchestra, with flutes, oboes or clarinets as well as horns and sometimes trumpets and timpani. His clarinet concerto was probably the first; he also wrote concertos for flute and violin. In 1754–5 he visited Paris, where several volumes of symphonies, concertos and chamber pieces by him were published during the years immediately after his death. His Mass in D was, too, widely admired.

(2) **Carl (Philipp)** (baptized Mannheim, 8 May 1745; d. Jena, 9 Nov 1801). Elder son of Johann, his first teacher. After his father's death he continued his training with other Mannheim musicians and joined the orchestra as a second fiddle (1762–70). He and his brother Anton then based themselves in Paris until in 1777 he left for a life of travel, spending time in London, The Hague (where in 1783 he played alongside the boy Beethoven) and

several German cities. Everywhere he composed, producing a copious output of symphonies, of wind music and of *symphonies concertantes*, concertos and chamber works, these featuring a range of solo instruments: clarinet, oboe, flute, cello and bassoon as well as his own violin, viola and viola d'amore, a particular favourite. Much of this busy output was published. By 1790 he was married, and after that his life was more settled – geographically, at least. Several children died in infancy, he also lost his wife, and he contracted debts, for though he continued to compose, taste had moved on. (Two centuries later it returned, at least to re-embrace some concertos, including those for flute in G, clarinet and bassoon in B♭ and bassoon in F, the 10 for clarinet and the typically melodious slow movement – Romance – of one for cello.)

(3) **Anton (Thadäus Johann Nepomuk)** (b. Německý Brod, 27 Nov 1750; d. France, 1796–1809). Younger son of Johann. Trained at Mannheim under his brother Carl and Christian Cannabich, he joined Carl in the orchestra's second fiddles (1764–70) and went with him to Paris, but stayed on as a violin teacher, royal musician and husband. He published a rather smaller quantity of symphonies, *symphonies concertantes*, concertos (including nine for violin) and chamber music.

Stanchinsky, Aleksey (Vladimirovich) (b. Obolsunovo, Vladimir region, 9 Mar 1888; d. near Logachevo, Smolensk region, 6 Oct 1914). Russian composer of piano music. He studied the piano with Lhévinne and composition with Nikolay Zhilyayev and Taneyev. In his teens he became a Scriabinist, but the death of his father in 1908 precipitated a psychological breakdown, and he spent a year in a clinic. Discharged as incurable, he turned against his old music, which he tried to destroy, and embarked on a new style, contrapuntal and constructivist. He was found dead after having disappeared for several days.

Ständchen (Ger.). Serenade, in the sense of a song, for soloist or chorus. There are examples by Schubert, Brahms, Strauss, etc.

Stanford, Charles Villiers (b. Dublin, 30 Sep 1852; d. London, 29 Mar 1924). Irish composer, knighted in 1902. The son of a distinguished lawyer, he grew up in a cultivated, musical home. In 1870 he went up to Cambridge, and in 1873 was appointed organist of Trinity College, gaining leave for periods of study abroad in 1874–6. He had lessons with Reinecke in Leipzig, met Brahms and was in Bayreuth for the first festival. Meanwhile he began to make a reputation at home as a composer and conductor, and in 1878 he married. While still in his 30s he gained the pre-eminent appointments in British musical education, as professor of composition at the new RCM (1883) and professor of music at Cambridge (1887). Among his pupils were Vaughan Williams, Holst and Bridge; another, Ivor Gurney, recalled: 'He was a stiff master, though a very kind man; difficult to please and most glad to be pleased.' Increasingly little in contemporary music pleased him, and his output declined after 1912. His virtues were those of the Brahmsian world in which he had grown up, and yet he spoke Brahms with an Irish accent and had, too, a strong attachment to English cathedral music, which he restored to glory.

Charles Villiers Stanford *Studies and Memories* (1908), *Pages from an Unwritten Diary* (1914)

Choral: Services, B♭, Op.10, 1879; A, Op.12, 1880, 1895; F, Op.36, 1889; G, Op.81, 1904; C, Op.115, 1909; *The Lord is my Shepherd*, 1886; Three Motets, Op.38, pub 1905 (*Justorum animae, Coelos ascendit hodie, Beati quorum via*); *Songs of the Sea* (Newbolt), Op.91, bar, men's ch, orch, 1904; partsongs (*Blue Bird*, Op.119:3, 1910); etc.

Other works: *Much Ado About Nothing* (opera; Julian Sturgis, after Shakespeare), Op.76a, f.p. London, 1901; Symphony No.3 'Irish', F minor, Op.28, 1887; Clarinet Concerto, A minor, Op.80, 1902; 6 other symphonies, 3 piano concertos, 2 violin concertos, 6 Irish rhapsodies, etc.; 8 string quartets, etc.; 5 organ sonatas, etc.; songs

Stanley, John (b. London, 17 Jan 1712; d. London, 19 May 1786). British organist-composer. Blinded by accident at two, he made great strides as a musician under Maurice Greene's tuition and began gaining appointments as an organist when he was 12. At 17 he received the Oxford BMus, the youngest person ever to do so. In 1738 he married, and his sister-in-law served as his amanuensis, allowing him to set down (and publish) volumes of instrumental solos, concertos for strings, cantatas and organ voluntaries – works that count among the finest of Handel's time.

star. See NIGHT.

Starer, Robert (b. Vienna, 8 Jan 1924; d. Kingston, NY, 22 Apr 2001). Austrian–US composer. He studied at the Vienna Academy (1937–8), the Jerusalem Conservatory and the Juilliard School (1947–9), and taught at Juilliard and Brooklyn College. His works include ballets for Martha Graham (*Samson Agonistes*, 1961), concertos, three string quartets, piano music and biblical cantatas.

stark (Ger.). Strong, implying an emphatic or exposed manner of projection.

Star-Spangled Banner, The. National anthem of the USA, though not adopted officially until 1931. Francis Scott Key (1779–1843) wrote the words, to a tune by the British composer John Stafford Smith (1750–1836).

Starzer, Josef (baptized Vienna, 5 Jan 1728; d. Vienna, 22 Apr 1787). Austrian composer, especially of ballet music for the Viennese and Russian courts (he was in Russia for several years from 1759). He also wrote string quartets, wind music and a setting of Metastasio's Passion.

Stasov, Vladimir (Vasilyevich) (b. St Petersburg, 14 Jan 1824; d. St Petersburg, 23 Oct 1906). Russian critic. An architect's son, he spent his working life in the St Petersburg Public Library. As a critic he vigorously promoted the Balakirev circle, for whom his name *moguchaya kuchka* (MIGHTY HANDFUL) stuck. He also jumped into his friends' creative lives before the fact, pushing and guiding. Later, attached to Belyayev, he became stiffly conservative in his views.

Staud, Johannes Maria (b. Innsbruck, 17 Aug 1974). Austrian composer, of music that, whether rugged or fragile, has precise accomplishment and poetry. After a conservatory education in Vienna (1994–6) he continued his studies with Kyburz and Ferneyhough, and gained an international reputation in his mid 20s. His works include an opera after Poe, *Berenice* (f.p. Munich, 2004).

stave. See STAFF.

steel band. Ensemble of metal drums, first made from oildrums in Trinidad in the 1930s, now custom-built. Each drum, or pan, is tuned to several notes, from three (in the case of bass instruments) to 20 or so (the tune-carrying 'tenor pans'). The notes come from striking specific areas, arranged ringwise around the top, with adjacent notes wherever possible an octave, fifth or fourth apart, because hitting one area will tend to stimulate those on either side.

steel pan (steel drum). Steel band instrument, occasionally used by composers in the classical tradition.

Steffani, Agostino (b. Castelfranco, near Venice, 25 Jul 1654; d. Frankfurt, 12 Feb 1728). Italian composer admired especially for his chamber duets. At 13 he was recruited by the Elector of Bavaria, probably as a singer, and he stayed in Munich for 21 years, except for a period studying composition with Ercole Bernabei in Rome

(1672–4). In 1677 he was joined by his elder brother Ventura Terzago, who had taken an uncle's surname and become a librettist; they worked together on Steffani's first opera, *Marco Aurelio*, and others. The year before his operatic debut he had been ordained priest, and he became increasingly occupied with ecclesiastical and diplomatic affairs. He accepted an invitation to Hanover (1688–1703), where he had charge of the new, short-lived Italian opera. While there, in 1702, he began making a complete, revised collection of the chamber duets that were the main beneficiaries of his skills in vocal writing and counterpoint. After a period in Düsseldorf he returned to Hanover, now as apostolic vicar in northern Germany. Eight months before his death he was elected president of the Academy of Vocal Music in London, which prompted him to return to composition and produce a *Stabat mater*, among other works.

Colin Timms *Polymath of the Baroque* (2003)

Steg (Ger.). Bridge, on a string instrument; hence *Am Steg*, equivalent to *sul ponticello*.

Steibelt, Daniel (Gottlieb) (b. Berlin, 22 Oct 1765; d. St Petersburg, 20 Sep 1823). German pianist-composer, of renowned arrogance. Daring to compete with Beethoven at Count Fries's home in Vienna in 1800, he was beaten off, and continued his chequered career mostly in Paris, London and St Petersburg, where his limitations were perhaps less audible.

Steinberg, Maximilian [Shteynberg, Maksimilian Oseyevich] (b. Vilna, 4 Jul 1883; d. Leningrad, 6 Dec 1946). Russian composer, a pupil and son-in-law of Rimsky-Korsakov. He graduated from the St Petersburg Conservatory in 1908 and remained there as a teacher to the end of his life. His works include five symphonies.

Stein der Weisen, Der (The Philosopher's Stone). Opera by various hands to a libretto by Schikaneder, including one number possibly by Mozart (the duet 'Nun, liebes Weibchen', K.625). First performance: Vienna, 11 Sep 1790.

Steinway. US piano firm founded in New York in 1853 by Heinrich Engelhard Steinway (originally Steinweg, 1797–1871) and rapidly at the forefront of the industry. The founder's sons, Theodore (1825–89) and William (1836–96), carried the firm to international pre-eminence, where it has remained.

Richard K. Lieberman *Steinway and Sons* (1995)

stem [tail]. Thin vertical line attached to the head of a minim or smaller value as notated.

Stenhammar, (Karl) Wilhelm (Eugen) (b. Stockholm, 7 Feb 1871; d. Stockholm, 20 Nov 1927). Swedish composer who achieved an unusual combination of opulence with fineness. The son of an architect-composer, he grew up in a cultivated household and had private musical tuition, completed by piano studies with Heinrich Barth in Berlin (1892–3). From 1902 he appeared regularly as a pianist with the Aulin Quartet. He was also active as a conductor, notably with the Gothenburg orchestra (1906–22). Like his colleagues Nielsen and Sibelius, he moved out from Nordic Romanticism, but more towards Strauss and earlier German masters, drawn by his work as a chamber musician and the exhaustive contrapuntal studies he began in 1909.

Orchestral: Symphony No.1, F, 1902–3; No.2, G minor, Op.34, 1911–15; Piano Concerto No.1, B♭ minor, Op.1, 1893; No.2, D minor, Op.23, 1904–7; 2 Sentimental Romances, Op.28, vn, orch, 1910
Other works: *Ett folk* (Verner von Heidenstam), Op.22, bar, ch, orch, 1904–5; *Sången*, Op.44, soli, ch, orch, 1922; 6 quartets, piano music, songs, etc.

stentato, stentando (It.). Labouring, a marking especially associated with Verdi's vocal writing but much older.

step. Scalewise melodic interval, hence a major or minor second (sometimes called whole or full step and half step).

Stephan, Rudi (b. Worms, 29 Jul 1887; d. Tarnopol, Galicia, 29 Sep 1915). German composer. He studied in Frankfurt and Munich and wrote some striking orchestral pieces in late Romantic style but abstract (Music for Orchestra, 1912; Music for Violin and Orchestra, 1913) before his early death in action.

Stephanie, (Johann) Gottlieb (b. Breslau/Wrocław, 19 Feb 1741; d. Vienna, 23 Jan 1800). German–Austrian man of the theatre. A soldier in the Seven Years War (1756–63), he was in the theatre from 1768, notably as director of the National Singspiel in Vienna (1779–86) – and notably there as librettist of Mozart's *Entführung* and *Schauspieldirektor*.

sterbend (Ger.). Dying away, *morendo*.

Stern, Isaac (b. Kremenets, 21 Jul 1920; d. New York, 22 Sep 2001). Russian–US violinist. Taken to San Francisco when he was a year old, he studied with Naoum Blinder (1932–7), of the Russian school, and made his debuts as a recitalist in 1935 and concerto soloist (with the San Francisco Symphony and Monteux) the next year. From soon after the war he was appearing all over the world – though not in Germany, where he declined to perform. In 1960 he formed a trio with Eugene Istomin and Leonard Rose, and that same year he took the lead in saving Carnegie Hall from demolition. Concertos were written for him by Bernstein, Schuman and Dutilleux.

Isaac Stern and Chaim Potok *My First 79 Years* (1999)

stesso, stessa (It.). Same, as in *lo stesso tempo* (at the same tempo) or the more common *L'*ISTESSO TEMPO.

Steuermann, Edward [Eduard] (b. Sambor, 18 Jun 1892; d. New York, 11 Nov 1964). Polish–US pianist-composer. He studied in Berlin with Busoni and Schoenberg, whose circle he joined, and whom he followed to Vienna. In 1938 he moved to New York, continuing to play, teach, compose and enjoy Schoenberg's confidence. He was involved in the first performances of many Schoenberg works, from *Pierrot lunaire* to the Fantasy by way of the Piano Concerto.

Stevens, Bernard (George) (b. London, 2 Mar 1916; d. Great Maplestead, Essex, 6 Jan 1983). British composer. He studied at Cambridge (1934–7) and with R.O. Morris at the RCM (1937–40), where he taught (1948–81) while adding to an output of serious, solid and often sombre works that included two symphonies, concertos for violin and piano, and cantatas.

Stevenson, Ronald (b. Blackburn, 6 Mar 1928). British pianist-composer. He studied in Manchester and Rome, settled in Scotland in 1952, and associated himself deeply with Busoni's music. His works include a Passacaglia on DSCH for piano (1960–62) and two piano concertos.

stick. Percussion beater, as used on drums, triangles, tam tams and other instruments, normally wooden and lacking the hard head of a MALLET. There may be almost no head at all, or one covered with felt, sponge, etc.

Stierhorn (Ger., bull horn). See COWHORN.

stile antico (It., ancient style). Term applied to Renaissance polyphony as it was passing, and so virtually synonymous with PRIMA PRATICA, though longer lived.

stile concitato (It., agitated style). Term coined by Monteverdi for the musical expression of excitement, especially martial, as in his *Combattimento*. It is distinguished above all by sequences of rapid repeated notes.

stile moderno (It., modern style). Used by contrast with *stile antico*.

stile rappresentativo (It., representing style). See RAPPRESENTATIVO.

Still, William Grant (b. Woodville, Miss., 11 May 1895; d. Los Angeles, 3 Dec 1978). US composer. He had a mixed and spasmodic musical education, working with masters as different as W.C. Handy and Varèse, but settled into a secure diatonic language, expressed in five symphonies, symphonic poems and choral music. Several works address his African–US heritage.

Stimme (Ger., pl. *Stimmen*). Voice, in the sense of singing voice or instrumental/vocal part.

Stimmung (Ger., pl. *Stimmungen*). Mood or tuning. Both senses are implied in the title of Stockhausen's *Stimmung* (1968) for six singers using Asian vocal techniques and electronic amplification to project the harmonics of a low B♭.

stochastic (from Gk *stochos*, goal). Term borrowed by Xenakis from probability theory, where it denotes a process whose steps are governed by rules of probability, a process that leads, therefore, to a goal. Xenakis used probability calculations to determine musical quantities in his stochastic music, but the term has also been applied more loosely to music in which detail seems much less important than general effect.

Stockhausen, Karlheinz (b. Mödrath, near Cologne, 22 Aug 1928). German composer. His works of the 1950s and 1960s were full of new ideas for composing, performing and listening to music, both electronic (in which he was a pioneer) and live. This fecundity of invention, coupled with personal magnetism, made him a commanding presence, with an influence on fellow musicians from Carter to the Beatles.

Self-supporting from the age of 16, he studied at the conservatory in Cologne (1947–51) and, crucially, at the 1951 DARMSTADT summer course, where, with Nono and Goeyvaerts, he discussed possibilities opened by Messiaen's recent piano piece *Mode de valuers et d'intensités* – possibilities for TOTAL SERIALISM. He went back to Cologne and wrote a work of this kind, *Kreuzspiel* (Cross-play; his musical thinking, though abstract, was deeply imbued with Catholic spirituality). Then in January 1952 he left to study with Messiaen in Paris, where he also met Boulez, worked in Schaeffer's studio and began the ensemble work *Kontrapunkte*, which, with its fluid gestures and striking creation of form by erasure, the instruments falling silent one by one, marked him as one of the leaders of the new avant-garde. He returned to Cologne in spring 1953 at Herbert Eimert's invitation to co-direct the new West German Radio studio for ELECTRONIC MUSIC, where he made some of the first compositions with synthesized sounds. Also in 1953 he married Doris Andreae (who became the mother of his first four children) and started teaching at Darmstadt, returning almost every summer for the next two decades.

His work in electronic music prompted him to a fruitful study of the science of sound. In *Gesang der Jünglinge* (1955–6) he created an interplay of vocal and electronic sounds, while *Zeitmasze* for woodwind (1955–6) works with varieties of strict and supple time, and *Gruppen* (1955–7) was developed as a study in rhythm, tempo and vibration. This last work's three-part counterpoint of tempos required three orchestras, each with its own conductor, and each producing complex textures to imitate, in their harmony and polymetre, the complexity an oscilloscope would show in a natural sound wave. But though the basis was strongly theoretical, his sense of occasion also came into play. *Gesang* had been an early stereo spectacular, originally requiring five banks of loudspeakers, and *Gruppen* has bold and thrilling effects of sounds thrown from one orchestra to another.

All his concerns – with composing sounds as well as music, with making connections between live and electronic realms, with inventing everything afresh, with sound drama – came together in *Kontakte* (1959–60), especially in the version where a pianist and a percussionist play along with the recorded electronic part. This electronic music starts out from a uniform source – pulses – to achieve elaborate and multifarious images, which the live performers attempt to catch, imitate, overtake, observe, outdo. Perpetual surprise becomes an alternative to narrative form, in which, with its rooting in the affective and in a progressive view of time, he never had any interest, his world being one of perception and the eternal.

He made non-progressive form an item of policy in his notion of the musical MOMENT, with its exemplary work *Momente* (1961–4). This was originally an hour-long song of love and harmony,

addressed partly to a new woman in his life: Mary Bauermeister, with whom he had two more children. A revision in 1972 made it more theatrical, more warmly ecstatic, and brought it to full concert length, for by now he was preferring not to share programmes with other composers. Accordingly he has, since 1966, generally written pieces that would either stand alone or join other compositions of his, designed for his own performing group in concerts restricted to his music.

That group arose around *Mikrophonie I* (1964), one of the earliest examples of live electronic music, in which six musicians provoke, detect and manipulate vibrations from a large tam tam – the same instrument that was an imposing sonic and visual feature of *Kontakte* and *Momente*. He continued to compose fixed electronic music, exploring the INTERMODULATION of transcontinental recordings to create music of the world in *Telemusik* and *Hymnen*. But the group was his focus. Working with players he knew, and in the mood of the time, he gradually moved away from standard notation towards diagrams and even, in *Aus den sieben Tagen* (1968), brief texts devised to stimulate intuitive performance. Concurrently he took a deepening interest in spiritual practices from India and Japan.

Only the title, then, was unsurprising when he produced *Mantra* for two pianists (1969–70) – a precipitate return to traditional notation, and even to a polytonal language, not without shades of Hindemith and Busoni: the whole hour-long work is a sequence of transformations of a 12-note modal melody, unashamedly presented at the outset. Yet this volte-face turned out to be a new beginning. Nearly all his subsequent works have similarly used FORMULA composition, including, most immediately, two orchestral works, *Trans* and *Inori*. Both are powerfully dramatic, not only by action, now, but by enaction, by what they convey: a dream symbolic of death and a ritual of prayer.

In that way they led naturally to opera – though in embarking on the genre he was characteristically ambitious, for *Licht* (1977–2002) is a sequence of seven full-length theatre works. Many of its moments, scenes and acts were made for separate performance, by a new performing ensemble including members of his family and entourage: his sons Markus (trumpet) and Simon (electronic keyboards), as well as Suzanne Stephens (basset horn) and Kathinka Pasveer (flute). During the *Licht* period he also became his own publisher and record producer, creating at the home he designed for himself near Cologne a workplace perfectly isolated from the rest of the world.

Jonathan Cott *Stockhausen: Conversations with the Composer* (1973); Robin Maconie, ed. *Stockhausen on Music* (1989); Michael Kurtz *Stockhausen* (1992)

www.stockhausen.org

The composer's numbering does not use the term 'opus' or 'Op.'

Operas: LICHT, Nr.47–80, 1977–2003.

Large concert works: *Punkte*, Nr.½, orch, 1952, rev 1962–6; GRUPPEN, Nr.6, 3 orch, 1955–7; *Carré*, Nr.10, 4 ch-orch groups, 1959–60; MOMENTE, Nr.13, s, ch, brass, perc, 2 elec org, 1961–4, rev 1972; *Mixtur*, Nr.16, orch, elec, 1964; *Stop*, Nr.18, orch, 1965; *Dritte Region der Hymnen*, Nr.22⅔, orch, elec ens, tape, 1969; TRANS, Nr.35, orch, elec, tape, staging, 1971; INORI, Nr.38, orch, mime, 1973–4; *Jubiläum*, Nr.45, orch, 1977

Installations: *Fresco*, Nr.29, orch, 1969; *Sternklang*, Nr.34, park music, 1971; *Alphabet für Liège*, Nr.36, musical exhibition, 1972

Choral: *Mikrophonie II*, Nr.17, with elec, 1965; STIMMUNG, Nr.24, 6 solo v, 1968; *Atmen gibt das Leben*, Nr.39, 1974–7

Ensemble: *Kreuzspiel*, Nr.1/7, pf, ob, b cl, 3 perc, 1951; *Schlagtrio*, Nr.⅓, pf, timp, 1952, rev 1974; KONTRAPUNKTE, Nr.1, pf, 9 insts, 1952–3; ZEITMASZE, Nr.5, woodwind qnt, 1955–6; *Refrain*, Nr.11, pf, cel, vib, 1959; *Plus-Minus*, Nr.14, variable, 1963; *Mikrophonie I*, Nr.15, tam tam, elec, 1964; *Adieu*, Nr.21, wind qnt, 1966; HYMNEN, Nr.22½, elec ens, tape, 1966–7; *Prozession*, Nr.23, elec ens, 1967; *Kurzwellen*, Nr.25, elec ens, 1968; AUS DEN SIEBEN TAGEN, Nr.26, variable, 1968; *Expo*, Nr.31, variable, 1969–70; *Für kommende Zeiten*, Nr.33, variable, 1968–70; *Herbstmusik*, Nr.40, 4 players, 1974; *Musik im Bauch*, Nr.41, 6 perc, 1975; *Tierkreis*, Nr.41½, 12 zodiac melodies, various arrs, 1975; *Sirius*, Nr.43, s, b, basset hn, tpt, 1975–7

Duo: KONTAKTE, Nr.12½, pf, perc, tape, 1959–60; *Pole*, Nr.30, variable, 1969–70; *Mantra*, Nr.32, 2 pf, elec, 1969–70

Solo: Piano Pieces I–IV, Nr.2, 1952–3, V–X, Nr.4, 1954–61, XI, Nr.7, 1956 (others in *Licht*); *Zyklus*, Nr.9, perc, 1959; *Solo*, Nr.19, melody inst with tape recorders, 1965–6; *Spiral*, Nr.27, melody inst with shortwave radio, 1969; *Harlekin*, Nr.42, cl, 1975; *Amour*, Nr.44, cl, 1976; *In Freundschaft*, Nr.46, melody inst, 1977

Electronic: Etude, Nr.⅓, 1952; *Studie I–II*, Nr.3, 1953, 1954; GESANG DER JÜNGLINGE, Nr.8, 1955–6; KONTAKTE, Nr.12, 1959–60; *Telemusik*, Nr.20, 1966; HYMNEN, Nr.22, 1966–7

Stokowski, Leopold (Anthony) (b. London, 18 Apr 1882; d. Nether Wallop, Hants., 13 Sep 1977). British–US conductor. Having taken to music as a small boy, he entered the RCM at the then-unprecedentedly early age of 13. In 1902 he became organist and choirmaster of St James's, Piccadilly, and it was to take another church post that he first went to New York, in 1905. He soon returned,

though, for further study, after which he made his conducting debut in Paris in 1908. That brought an invitation to Cincinnati, and so led to his appointment with the Philadelphia Orchestra (1912–38), which he raised to world rank. He also introduced important new works, including *The Rite of Spring*, *Wozzeck* and compositions by Schoenberg, Ives, Rachmaninoff and Varèse. In his long later career – he conducted till the year of his death – he appeared throughout the USA and, from 1951 on, regularly in Europe. A resolute performer, and a commanding figure on stage (or on film, in Disney's *Fantasia*), he was not afraid to retouch scoring, and he also made majestic arrangements, notably of Bach's Toccata and Fugue in D minor.

William Ander Smith *The Mystery of Leopold Stokowski* (1990)

Stoltzer, Thomas (b. Schweidnitz, Silesia, *c*.1480–85; d. near Znaim, Moravia, 1526). German composer. Possibly a pupil of Finck, he was chapelmaster to the Hungarian court from 1522 until his death by drowning in the Taja. He wrote church music of all kinds but is particularly esteemed for his psalm motets, of which four, setting Luther's translations, are among the first instances of Renaissance polyphony setting the vernacular. In them he could give voice to his otherwise timid support for the Reformation.

Stolz, Teresa (b. Elbekosteletz, 5 Jun 1834; d. Milan, 23 Aug 1902). Czech soprano. Her twin elder sisters were the wife and mistress of Luigi Ricci, with whom she studied before making her debut in Tbilisi in 1857. Emerging as a great Verdi soprano, she worked with the composer on the newly revised *Forza del destino* in Milan in 1869, introduced Aida to Italy in 1872 and took part in the first performances of the *Requiem*, retiring in 1879. By all accounts her singing was powerful and secure, full of noble passion. Her great-nephew Robert Stolz (1880–1975) was a composer of operettas and film scores.

Stölzel, Gottfried Heinrich (b. Grünstädtel, near Schwarzenberg, Erzgebirge, 13 Jan 1690; d. Gotha, 27 Nov 1749). German composer. Trained by his father and at school in Gera, he passed his musical apprenticeship under Melchior Hofmann of the collegium musicum in Leipzig (1707–10), then went to Breslau/Wrocław. He left there for a tour of Italy (1713–15), during which he met Vivaldi, Domenico Scarlatti and other composers. Next came three years in Prague. In 1719 he married, and the following year became chapelmaster at the Saxe-Gotha court, where he remained. His works include operas and serenatas, oratorios, around 450 extant church cantatas (and almost as many lost), concertos and trio sonatas. Bach copied pieces by Stölzel into his notebooks for Anna Magdalena (including the popular aria 'Bist du bei mir') and Wilhelm Friedemann, and may also have performed some of the church music.

stop. Most of the word's distinct musical uses are in accord with its normal connotation of closure – though organ stops are openings.

(1) To place a finger on one of the strings of a string instrument, so changing the length in vibration and hence the note, to which, or to the action, the term can also be applied: you stop a string and so play a stop. The word is most commonly used in this sense when two or more notes are being played on an instrument of the violin family. Double stopping produces two notes at once, and a triple stop has three, irrespective of whether all the notes are actually stopped (i.e. one or more may be played on open strings).

(2) To close a pipe at one end. It is then said to be end-stopped, as flutes in many folk cultures are. An end-stopped pipe produces a note an octave lower than an open pipe of the same length.

There is a special meaning in the case of the horn, whose bell is conveniently placed and large enough that it can be stopped (not completely) by the player's hand. This technique enabled hornists in pre-valve days to find notes other than the instrument's natural harmonics, and has remained in use as a way of producing a tone at once veiled and pinched. Hand stopping of the trumpet is much more awkward and very rarely used.

(3) ORGAN STOP. By analogy the same word is used of the different mechanisms and knobs controlling the register and timbre of a harpsichord.

Storace. British musical siblings, with Mozart connections, the children of an Italian-born bass player and a theatre proprietor's daughter.

(1) **Nancy** [Anna Selina] (b. London, 27 Oct 1765; d. London, 24 Aug 1817). Soprano. She had singing lessons from Sacchini and Rauzzini, was performing in public when barely into double digits, and in 1778 accompanied her parents to Italy, so that she could be launched in opera. That duly happened, and in 1783 she was engaged as prima donna in Vienna, where she was the first Susanna in *Figaro*. Mozart also wrote a concert aria for her, 'Ch'io mi scordi di te', with a piano obbligato for himself. Her marriage, to an older man, was soon over. In 1787 the Storaces returned to London, and she sang in her brother's operas as well as Handel oratorios. In 1797 she took up with

a tenor, and though they could not regularize their relationship, she being already married, it lasted nearly 20 years.

(2) **Stephen** (**John Seymour**) (b. London, 4 Apr 1762; d. London, 19 Mar 1796). Composer. At the age of 14 or so he was sent to the San Onofrio conservatory in Naples, where he lodged with a bishop uncle. It was partly to check on his progress (limited, though he had climbed Vesuvius) that his parents went out in 1778, and he was dispatched back home. He published some songs and two quintets, and perhaps on the strength of these was invited to join his sister and mother in Vienna (his father had died) and write opera. Two comedies were the result: *Gli sposi malcontenti* (1785) and *Gli equivoci* (1786, with a libretto by Da Ponte after *The Comedy of Errors*). Mozart may have helped with and certainly influenced his career. After returning to London in 1787 he threw himself into writing English operas, mostly with spoken dialogue. They include *The Pirates* (1792) and *The Cherokee* (1794).

str. Abbreviation for string or strings.

Stradella, Alessandro (b. Rome, 1 Oct 1644; d. Genoa, 25 Feb 1682). Italian composer. Of gentle birth, he was protected as a page after the deaths of his parents in 1655–6. From 1658 he was a member of Queen Christina of Sweden's musical entourage, and by 1663 he was writing motets and sacred cantatas for her. Opportunities to compose for the theatre came from the Colonna family. In 1669 he had to leave Rome when he was discovered to have been involved in a plot to embezzle church funds, but he was soon back, writing theatre music, oratorios and instrumental works, including perhaps the earliest concerto grosso (though called a sonata, for two violins and lute with strings). In 1677, however, he was obliged to absent himself permanently, having infuriated a cardinal. He went to Venice, where he was engaged to teach a patrician's mistress, with whom he took off to Turin. Thither they were pursued, an attempt was made on his life, and he found himself departing alone for Genoa, where he wrote operas and, for Modena, the oratorio *Susanna* (1681). But he again got himself involved with a woman who had powerful friends, and this time the result was his murder, by a soldier. The opera his story resembles was duly composed by Flotow.

Carolyn Gianturco *Alessandro Stradella* (1994)

Stradivari, Antonio (b. ?Cremona, 1644–9; d. Cremona, 18 Dec 1737). Italian violin maker, whose instruments have been revered since the late 18th century as the greatest ever made. A pupil of

Nicolò Amati, he made his earliest known instrument in 1666 and continued to practise his art until he was around 90. He was joined by his sons Francesco (1671–1743), Omobono (1679–1742) and Paolo (1708–75), the last a child of his second marriage, but the leading hand was almost always his. Of the 650 or so Stradivari (or Stradivarius, to use the Latinized form) violins that survive, those of his late maturity (1700–20) are most prized. He also made much smaller numbers of cellos, violas and guitars.

W.H., A.F. and A.E. Hill *Antonio Stradivari* (1902, '1963)

straight mute. The classic mute for brass instruments, made of metal or other material and blocked at the wider end, though sound can filter out between the cork strips that hold it in place. See also CUP MUTE.

strain. Song, melody, period.

Stratas, Teresa (b. Toronto, 26 May 1938). Canadian lyric soprano, of dramatic conviction. She studied with Irene Jessner and made her debut as Mimì with Canadian Opera (1958), appearing soon after at the Met (1959) and Covent Garden (1961). In 1979 she took the lead in the first three-act *Lulu*, latterly devoting herself to relief work in Calcutta with Mother Teresa and in Romania.

strathspey. Scottish dance, a slower reel in common time.

Straus, Oscar (b. Vienna, 6 Mar 1870; d. Bad Ischl, 11 Jan 1954). Austrian operetta composer. Originally Strauss, he dropped an 's' to distinguish himself from colleagues. He studied with Hermann Grädener in Vienna and Bruch in Berlin, worked variously as a conductor and composer, and gained his first big successes with the songs he wrote for the Überbrettl cabaret in Berlin (1900–4). Then he returned to Vienna to write operettas, including *Ein Walzertraum* (A Waltz Dream, 1907) and *Der tapfere Soldat* (The Chocolate Soldier, 1908). Between 1939 and 1948 he was in France and the USA.

Strauss. Dynasty of Viennese waltz maestros largely responsible for the sway of 3/4 that began in the 1820s, soon became international and has continued ever since.

(1) **Johann (Baptist) I** (b. Vienna, 14 Mar 1804; d. Vienna, 25 Sep 1849). An innkeeper's son, he played the violin from boyhood and joined Lanner's band in 1819. In 1825 he married (his first child, Johann II, was on the way) and founded his own orchestra, which was engaged at Zum Sperl, a beer garden

and dance hall, from 1829. Chopin and Wagner were among innumerable visitors. In 1833 he began making international tours, and in 1846 the post of court ball-music director was created for him (even though he had left his family for his mistress in 1842). He wrote around 150 waltzes, as well as galops, quadrilles and marches (*Radetzky March*, Op.228, 1848).

Besides his two eldest children, his successors included his third son, Eduard (1835–1916), and Eduard's son Johann III (1866–1939). His court appointment passed to Johann II (1862–71) and Eduard (1872–1901).

(2) **Johann (Baptist) II** (b. Vienna, 25 Oct 1825; d. Vienna, 3 Jun 1899). Eldest son of Johann Strauss I. He wrote a scrap of waltz music when he was six, but his father was against him going into music, and his serious musical education began only after Johann I had left the family. His studies, with Anton Kohlmann and Joseph Drechsler, progressed so well that in 1844 he was able to set up his own orchestra in competition with his father (though playing his father's waltzes as well as his own). After his father's death the bands merged under his leadership, and between 1856 and 1886 he took his musicians on tour, including to the USA in 1872. Meanwhile, he was thrice married. Welcomed everywhere, his music embodied the giddy joy in pleasure and the sentimental yearning of a culture in magnificent decadence. The waltzes were admired by Brahms at the time, and later arrranged by Schoenberg and imitated by Ravel and Strauss (Richard).

Joseph Wechsberg *The Waltz Emperors* (1973)

Operettas: *Die* FLEDERMAUS; *Eine Nacht in Venedig* (A Night in Venice; Friedrich Zell and Richard Genée), f.p. Berlin, 1883; *Der Zigeunerbaron* (The Gypsy Baron; Ignaz Schnitzer), f.p. Vienna, 1885; etc.

Waltzes: *Liebeslieder*, Op.114, 1852; *Accelerationen*, Op.234, 1860; *Morgenblätter* (Morning Papers), Op.279, 1864; *Wiener Bonbons*, Op.307, 1866; *An der schönen blauen Donau* (The Blue Danube), Op.314, 1867; *Künstlerleben*, Op.316, 1867; *Geschichten aus dem Wienerwald* (Tales from the Vienna Woods), Op.325, 1868; *Wein, Weib und Gesang* (Wine, Women and Song), Op.333, 1869; *Tausend und eine Nacht*, Op.346, 1871; *Wiener Blut*, Op.354, 1873; *Wo die Citronen blüh'n*, Op.364, 1874; *Du und Du*, Op.367, 1874; *Rosen aus dem Süden*, Op.388, 1880; *Frühlingsstimmen* (Voices of Spring), Op.410, 1883; *Lagunen-Walzer*, Op.411, 1883; *Schatz-Walzer* (Treasure Waltz), Op.418, 1885; *Kaiser-Walzer* (EMPEROR Waltz), Op.437, 1889; over 200 others

Polkas: *Explosions-Polka*, Op.43, 1847; *Annen-Polka*, Op.117, 1852; *Champagner-Polka*, Op.211, 1858; *Tritsch-Tratsch*, Op.214, 1858; *Unter Donner und Blitz* (Thunder and Lightning), Op.324, 1868;

Pizzicato-Polka, 1870 (with Josef Strauss); over 100 others
Other works: quadrilles, marches, etc.

(3) Josef (b. Vienna 20 Aug 1827; d. Vienna, 22 Jul 1870). Second son of Johann Strauss I. Though he studied music as a boy, he began his adult life in architecture and engineering, and only gradually, during the 1850s, began to work alongside his elder brother, conducting and composing. Melancholic by nature, he was unfit for life in the limelight and on the road, but he brought to his compositions (e.g. the waltz *Sphären-Klänge*, Op.235, 1868) an unusual depth of expression and an awareness of Berlioz, Liszt and Wagner.

Strauss, Richard (Georg) (b. Munich, 11 Jun 1864; d. Garmisch-Partenkirchen, 8 Sep 1949). German composer and conductor. With its grand sweep and gorgeous detailing, his music continued the triumph of the Austro–German Romantic style right into the mid 20th century. But his was also a new kind of Romanticism, propelled less by self-expression than by one strong urge: to give pleasure.

His father was a horn player in the Munich Court Orchestra who had married well, and could therefore provide him with comfort and the best musical education – including the education he received attending the orchestra's rehearsals. He began composing at six, had his first professional performances when he was 16, and by the age of 20 had heard his music conducted by one of the leading musicians of the time, Hans von Bülow. During this period he was discovering Wagner and modifying the conservatism he had inherited from his father, but his works were still in traditional forms and genres: concertos, pieces for wind ensemble, songs, sonatas and quartets.

Change came when he was working as von Bülow's assistant in Meiningen (1885–6), where a friend, Alexander Ritter, deepened his interest in Liszt and Wagner, Schopenhauer and Nietzsche. He moved through a picturesque symphony, *Aus Italien*, into the first of his dynamic and atmospheric tone poems: *Macbeth* and *Don Juan*. At the same time he progressed in his career as a conductor, through posts in Munich (1886–9) and Weimar (1889–94). He then returned to Munich, where he became principal conductor in 1896, and two years later transferred to a similar post with the Berlin Court Opera. Meanwhile, in September 1894, he married Pauline de Ahna, a soprano with whom he had been working since 1887; their son was born in 1897.

His first opera, *Guntram* (1894), was deeply indebted to Wagner, which was curious when he was so soon bursting with original imagination and accomplishment in songs and, especially, tone poems – the rondo-scherzo *Till Eulenspiegel* and the symphonic-scale *Also sprach Zarathustra*, *Don Quixote* and *Ein Heldenleben*. These four works are all portraits of heroes: the trickster, the prophet, the dreamer and, finally, the composer, for *Ein Heldenleben* (A Hero's Life, 1897–8) is a magnificent and knowing piece of self-dramatization in which he displayed extraordinary skills of musical narrative and depiction achieved through gesture, timing and orchestration. He virtually invented the film score before the fact, and indeed these works were crucial examples to composers of film music in the 1930s and later.

For his next big works he again drew on his personal situation. His second opera, *Feuersnot* (1901), is a satire in which he appears as the apprentice to Wagner's sorcerer, and his *Symphonia domestica* is a sequel to *Ein Heldenleben* in which the hero withdraws from the professional hurly-burly to enjoy the contentments of family life. (He conducted its first performance in New York in 1904, during his first visit to the USA.) But revelation goes only so far. To place these autobiographical works beside Mahler's symphonies of the same period is to see how far he was from the confessional mode: the persona of his music is robust, good-humoured and at ease.

Turning from his own family to that of 1st-century Judaean royalty in his third opera, *Salome* (1903–5), he produced the first of many works to find, at whatever distance of time or space, a mirror for contemporary psychologizing. Herod is the weak father, Herodias the strong and cynical mother, Salome the daughter who has so much of everything that all she can seek is sexual gratification, obsessively. These decadent sensualists are strikingly portrayed, and the work – no doubt helped by a Dance of the Seven Veils in which Salome divests herself – was an instant hit, produced by 50 companies within two years. Its success enabled him to build a villa in the Bavarian mountains at Garmisch, where he and his wife lived thereafter.

From this point he was almost constantly occupied with one opera after another for three and a half decades. *Elektra*, a first collaboration with the poet-dramatist Hugo von Hofmannsthal, went further in expressing extreme emotional states by means of dissonance: anger, daughterly love, guilt. After that he wanted to try something different, and Hofmannsthal obliged him with a lavish human comedy set in 18th-century Vienna, *Der Rosenkavalier* (1909–10). Loaded with charm, sentiment, character and waltzes, this work moved decisively away from the modernist direction of

Elektra, though under its sumptuous surface the harmony is at times as unsettled and strident. The piece set the tone for the operas to come: the style would be regressive but not merely imitative. In particular, the flood of nostalgia would not overwhelm definition of character: even the tiniest roles would be real musical personages. So it was in *Ariadne auf Naxos*, whose second version (1916) is an opera within an opera, providing opportunities for reflection on the genre and self-mockery. Lesser works of this period include a ballet for Diaghilev (*Josephslegende*), a nature symphony for a colossal orchestra (*Eine Alpensinfonie*) and a fairytale opera in which, for once, Strauss was flummoxed by Hofmannsthal's conceits (*Die Frau ohne Schatten*).

Having maintained his base in Berlin as a conductor until the end of the First World War, he was then joint director of the Vienna Staatsoper (1919–24), during which time his major creative achievement was another slice from his own life, *Intermezzo*, an opera of marital discord overcome by sophisticated understanding. He then resumed his partnership with Hofmannsthal in their favoured genres of mythology (*Die ägyptische Helena*) and period comedy (*Arabella*), both finely adapted to bourgeois sensibilities. Hofmannsthal died during work on *Arabella*, and he found a new librettist in Stefan Zweig, with whom he wrote another comedy, after Ben Jonson, *Die schweigsame Frau* (1933–4).

Germany now was a different country. He seems not to have understood this: he at first accepted official appointments and commissions from the Nazis, and when his assistance began to be deemed superfluous – partly as a result of his association with Zweig, a Jew – he buried his head in work. He kept Zweig on as literary adviser, supervising the librettos Joseph Gregor wrote for the war drama *Friedenstag* and a further essay in post-Freudian mythology, *Daphne*. That work was followed by yet another in the same vein, *Die Liebe der Danae*, for which Gregor worked up a draft by Hofmannsthal. In all these works of the 1920s and 1930s there is often a sense of freewheeling mastery, of music pouring forth with a superb obliviousness. The works of his last decade, though, include some of his finest. *Capriccio* was a farewell to opera in the form of another, deeper musing on the genre, again with a novel-like richness of characterization. After that came orchestral works revisiting his classicism of six decades before, as well as a meditation-lament for strings written from a Germany exhausted and destroyed (*Metamorphosen*) and the glorious autumnal relinquishment of the Four Last Songs.

His estimation of himself, voiced in London two years before his death, was frank and unabashed, like his music: 'I may not be a first-rate composer, but I am a first-class second-rate composer.' This seems just. His tone poems from *Don Juan* to *Ein Heldenleben*, his operas from *Salome* to *Der Rosenkavalier* and several of his songs have been central to the repertory since the moment they were written, but there is a quality – vision – they lack. Still, for sheer contentment with the world and enjoyability at a supreme level of expertise, his music has few equals.

Michael Kennedy *Richard Strauss* (1976, [2]1995); Bryan Gilliam *The Life of Richard Strauss* (1999)
www.richard-strauss.com

Theatre and orchestral music

Operas: GUNTRAM, Op.25, 1892–3, rev 1934–9; FEUERSNOT, Op.50, 1900–1; SALOME, Op.54, 1903–5; ELEKTRA, Op.58,1906–8; *Der* ROSENKAVALIER, Op.59, 1909–10; *Ariadne auf Naxos* (see ARIADNE), Op.60, 1911–12, rev 1916; *Die* FRAU OHNE SCHATTEN, Op.65, 1914–18; INTERMEZZO, Op.72,1918–23; *Die* ÄGYPTISCHE HELENA, Op.75, 1923–7; ARABELLA, Op.79, 1929–32; *Die* SCHWEIGSAME FRAU, Op.80, 1933–4; FRIEDENSTAG, Op.81, 1935–6; DAPHNE, Op.82, 1936–7; *Die* LIEBE DER DANAE, Op.83, 1938–40; CAPRICCIO, Op.85, 1940–41

Other dramatic works: *Der Bürger als Edelmann* (incidental music; Hofmannsthal, after Molière), Op.60, 1912, suite 1918; *Josephslegende* (ballet), Op.63, 1912–14; *Schlagobers* (ballet), Op.70, 1921–2, suite 1932; *Der Rosenkavalier* (film adaptation), 1925

Stage arrangements: *Die Feen* (Wagner), 1888; *Iphigénie en Tauride* (Gluck), 1899; *Die Ruinen von Athen* (Beethoven), 1924; *Idomeneo* (Mozart), 1930

Orchestral: Symphony No.1, D minor, 1880; No.2, F minor, Op.12, 1883–4; Serenade, E♭, Op.7, 13 wind, 1881; Violin Concerto, D minor, Op.8, 1880–82; Horn Concerto No.1, E♭, Op.11, 1882–3; Suite, B♭, Op.4, 13 wind, 1884; *Burleske*, D minor, pf, orch, 1885–6; *Aus Italien*, Op.16, 1886; MACBETH, Op.23, 1886–8; DON JUAN, Op.20, 1888–9; *Tod und Verklärung*, Op.24, 1888–9; TILL EULENSPIEGEL, Op.28, 1894–5; ALSO SPRACH ZARATHUSTRA, Op.30, 1895–6; DON QUIXOTE, Op.35, 1896–7; *Ein* HELDENLEBEN, Op.40, 1897–8; *Symphonia domestica*, Op.53, 1902–3; *Eine* ALPENSINFONIE, Op.64, 1911–15; *Parergon zur Symphonia domestica*, Op.73, pf left hand, orch, 1924; *Panathenäenzug*, Op.74, pf left hand, orch, 1927; Divertimento, Op.86, chbr orch, 1940–41; Horn Concerto No.2, E♭, 1942; Sonatinas Nos.1–2, F, E♭, 16 wind, 1943, 1944–5; METAMORPHOSEN, 23 str, 1943–5; Oboe Concerto, 1945; Duett-Concertino, cl, bn, str, hp, 1947; etc.

Songs

Orchestral songs: *Vier Gesänge*, Op.33, 1896–7 ('Verführung', John Henry Mackay; 'Gesang der Apollopriesterin', Emanuel von Bodman;

'Hymnus', Schiller; 'Pilgers Morgenlied', Goethe);
Zwei grössere Gesänge, Op.44, 1899 ('Notturno',
Dehmel; 'Nächtlicher Gang', Rückert); *Zwei
Gesänge*, Op.51 ('Der Thal', Uhland, 1902; 'Der
Einsame', Heine, 1906); *Drei Hymnen von Friedrich
Hölderlin*, 1921 ('Hymne an die Liebe', 'Rückkehr
in die Heimat', 'Die Liebe'); VIER LETZTE LIEDER,
1948
Song cycles: *Krämerspiegel* (Alfred Kerr), Op.66,
1918; *Drei Lieder der Ophelia* (Karl Simrock, after
Shakespeare), Op.67:1–3, 1918
Other songs (those obelisked orchestrated by the
composer): 'Ach Lieb' (Felix Dahn), Op.21:3,
1887–8; 'Ach weh' (Dahn), Op.21:4, 1887–8; 'All'
mein Gedanken' (Dahn), Op.21:1, 1887–8;
'Allerseelen' (Hermann von Gilm), Op.10:8, 1885;
'Als mir dein Lied erklang'[†] (Brentano), Op.68:4,
1918; 'Amor'[†] (Brentano), Op.68:5, 1918; 'An die
Nacht'[†] (Brentano), Op.68:1, 1918; 'Der
Arbeitsmann'[†] (Dehmel), Op.39:3, 1898; 'Das
Bächlein'[†], Op.88:1, 1933; 'Befreit'[†] (Dehmel),
Op.39:4, 1898; 'Breit über mein Haupt' (Adolf
Friedrich von Schack), Op.19:2, 1885–7; 'Cäcilie'[†]
(Heinrich Hart), Op.27:2, 1894; 'Des Dichters
Abendgang'[†] (Uhland), Op.47:2, 1900; 'Du meines
Herzens Krönelein' (Dahn), Op.21:2, 1887–8;
'Einerlei' (Arnim), Op.69:3, 1918; 'Freundliche
Vision'[†] (Otto Julius Bierbaum), Op.48:1, 1900;
'Frühlingsfeier'[†] (Heine), Op.56:5, 1903–6; 'Geduld'
(Gilm), Op.10:5, 1885; 'Gefunden' (Goethe),
Op.56:1, 1903; 'Die Georgine' (Gilm), Op.10:4, 1885;
'Die heiligen drei Könige'[†] (Heine), Op.56:6,
1903–6; 'Heimkehr' (Schack), Op.15:5, 1884–6;
'Heimliche Aufforderung' (Mackay), Op.27:3, 1894;
'Himmelsboten' (Des Knaben Wunderhorn),
Op.32:5, 1896; 'Ich liebe dich'[†] (Detlev von
Liliencron), Op.37:2, 1898; 'Ich trage meine Minne'
(Karl Henckell), Op.32:1, 1896; 'Ich wollt' ein
Sträusslein binden'[†] (Brentano), Op.68:2, 1918;
'Liebeshymnus'[†] (Henckell), Op.32:3, 1896; 'Lied
der Frauen'[†] (Brentano), Op.68:6, 1918; 'Mein
Auge'[†] (Dehmel), Op.37:4, 1898; 'Meinem Kinde'[†]
(Gustav Falke), Op.37:3, 1897; 'Mit deinen blauen
Augen' (Heine), Op.56:4, 1903–6; 'Mohnblumen'
(Dahn), 1888; 'Morgen'[†] (Mackay), Op.27:4, 1894;
'Muttertändelei'[†] (Gottfried August Bürger),
Op.43:2, 1899; 'Die Nacht' (Gilm), Op.10:3, 1885;
'Nachtgang' (Bierbaum), Op.29:3, 1895; 'Nichts'
(Gilm), Op.10:2, 1885; 'Das Rosenband'[†]
(Klopstock), Op.36:1, 1897; 'Ruhe, meine Seele'[†]
(Henckell), Op.27:1, 1894; 'Säusle, liebe Myrthe'[†]
(Brentano), Op.68:3, 1918; 'Schlagende Herzen'
(Bierbaum), Op.29:2, 1895; 'Schlechtes Wetter'
(Heine), Op.69:5, 1918; 'Seitdem dein Aug''
(Schack), Op.17:1, 1885–7; 'Ständchen' (Schack),
Op.17:2, 1885; 'Traum durch die Dämmerung'
(Bierbaum), Op.29:1, 1895; 'Die Verschwiegenen'
(Gilm), Op.10:6, 1885; 'Waldseligkeit'[†] (Dehmel),
Op.49:1, 1901; 'Wiegenlied'[†] (Dehmel), Op.41:1,
1899; 'Wie sollten wir' (Schack), Op.19:4, 1885–8;
'Winterliebe'[†] (Henckell), Op.48:5, 1900;
'Winterweihe'[†] (Henckell), Op.48:4, 1900; 'Die
Zeitlose' (Gilm), Op.10:7, 1885; 'Zueignung'[†]

(Gilm), Op.10:1, 1885; etc.
Orchestrations: *Ganymed* (Schubert), 1897; *Ich liebe
dich, Wonne der Wehmut* (Beethoven), 1898

Other music

Choral orchestral: *Taillefer* (Uhland), Op.52, soli, ch,
orch, 1903; etc.
Unaccompanied choral: *Deutsche Motette* (Rückert),
Op.62, 1913; *Die Göttin in Putzzimmer* (Rückert),
1935; *An den Baum Daphne* (Gregor), 1943; etc.
Recitations (for speaker, pf): *Enoch Arden* (Adolph
Strodtmann, after Tennyson), Op.38, 1897; *Das
Schloss am Meere* (Uhland), 1899
Chamber and instrumental: String Quartet, A, Op.2,
1880; Cello Sonata, F, Op.6, 1880–83; Piano
Quartet, C minor, Op.13, 1883–4; Violin Sonata,
E♭, Op.18, 1887
Piano: 5 Pieces, Op.3, 1880–81; Sonata, B minor, Op.5,
1880–81; *Stimmungsbilder*, Op.9, 1882–4; etc.

stravaganza (It., extravagance). Exuberance in
fantasy and virtuosity, a condition of Italian
Baroque music, especially for the violin, though
Vivaldi's 12 concertos entitled *La stravaganza* are
not of this kind.

Stravinsky [Strawinsky], **Igor (Fyodorovich)** (b.
Oranienbaum, 5 Jun 1882; d. New York, 6 Apr 1971).
Russian composer. With his ballet score *The Rite of
Spring* (1910–13) Western music changed. The
piece is for a large orchestra similar to that being
used at the same time by Mahler and Strauss, but
the sounds are quite new, with wind instruments
and drums to the fore. Rhythm – especially the
rhythm of insistent pulsation – becomes primary
and elemental, in keeping with the ballet's subject
of savage ritual. Also new, and far-reaching, was
the approach to form he had taken in his preceding ballet, *Petrushka* (1910–11). Where Western
composers since the Renaissance had aimed for a
harmonious integration of parts and a continuous
flow, he worked with abruptness and discontinuity. The term 'mechanical', hitherto oppro-
brious, became a fair description of music
delighting in layered textures, dissimilar sections
and odd harmonic progressions, all held in place
by a consistent pulse. He challenged, too, the idea
of musical history as one smooth path to the
present. Beethoven was less important to him than
the 18th century and jazz. He freely arranged,
quoted or imitated music that appealed to him,
from Gesualdo to Webern, making everything his
own. He was also able to change course radically
several times during his composing life of more
than 60 years.

Third in a family of four sons, he had a
comfortable upbringing in St Petersburg, where
his father was a principal bass at the Mariinsky
Theatre. Summers would be spent on the family

estate at Ustilug, in the west of the country, where the composer continued to spend holidays after his marriage in 1906 to his cousin Ekaterina Nossenko. He studied law at the university in St Petersburg (1901–6), while beginning to find himself as a composer. In 1902 he started lessons with Rimsky-Korsakov, under whose guidance he progressed from songs and piano pieces to a symphony (1905–7). He and his wife also started a family: their elder son was born in 1907 and their elder daughter the next year. In 1909 a performance of his orchestral *Fireworks* caught the attention of Serge Diaghilev, manager of the Ballets Russes, who in the autumn of that year commissioned his first major work, *The Firebird*.

After the first performance of *The Firebird*, in Paris in June 1910, he and his family stayed in western Europe, settling in Switzerland, where the two younger children were born in 1910 and 1914. This was also a time of prodigious musical change. Where *The Firebird* had taken its colourful fairytale plumage from Rimsky-Korsakov, his second ballet was the strikingly original *Petrushka*, a portrait of human beings behaving like machines, bustling and dancing at a fair, and of a puppet, Petrushka, who has the emotional life of a person, raging and lovelorn. The role was taken by Vaslav Nijinsky, who two years later choreographed *The Rite of Spring* for its première in Paris on 29 May 1913, the occasion of uproar among the audience. Stravinsky was now a figure of world renown.

He had been going back to Russia occasionally, but after the outbreak of the First World War in the summer of 1914, that became impossible, and the October Revolution of 1917 effectively sealed him off from his homeland, to which he returned only for an eightieth-birthday visit in 1962. His response was to create a rural Russia of the mind, in songs, instrumental items and theatre pieces that were based on Russian folklore but also extended the pulsed, harmonically acerbic style of *Petrushka* and *The Rite*. Wartime stringency encouraged him to write for smaller forces, as in the farmyard ballet *Renard* for four singers and small orchestra (1916) or *Histoire du soldat* for four actors/dancers and seven instrumentalists (1918). With such reduced ensembles he developed an extraordinary gift for instrumental colour and character, while the score to the peasant-wedding ballet *Les Noces* (1914–23), accompanying vocal soloists and a chorus with four pianos and percussion, intensified his music's mechanical aspects. The Symphonies of Wind Instruments (1920) is a similar musical machine, but scored for orchestral winds and formed of refrains and choruses, like a litany.

During the long period of working on *Les Noces* he changed home and style again. His first post-war effort for the Ballets Russes, *Pulcinella* (1919–20), was based on 18th-century Neapolitan music, and it opened the door to many further reworkings of found material, as well as to a whole neoclassical period, at the start of which his ideal was Bach. Relevant pieces include the Octet (1923), the Concerto for piano and wind (1924) and the opera-oratorio *Oedipus Rex* (1926–7), set to a text by Jean Cocteau, translated into Latin, and achieving an unexpected fusion of Baroque stylization with Verdian pathos. Meanwhile, from 1921 onwards, he spent much of his time in Paris and on tour with his mistress Vera Sudeikina, while his wife, mother and children lived elsewhere in France.

His last work for Diaghilev's Ballets Russes – *Apollo* (1928), whose score for string orchestra creates another odd marriage, this time of suave café music with the discipline of French Baroque style – was also his first collaboration with George Balanchine, who became his preferred choreographer. Sharing a way of giving a modern spin to classical ideals, the two artists worked together again on *Jeu de cartes* (1935–6), *Orpheus* (1946–7) and *Agon* (1954–7), as well as on danced realizations of some of the concert pieces to which he increasingly devoted himself.

Up to the end of the 1920s his big works were nearly all for the theatre (including the nine works he had produced by Diaghilev), the main exceptions being the two pieces he wrote to provide himself with concert dates as a pianist: the Concerto with wind and Capriccio (1928–9). By contrast, large-scale abstract works began to dominate his output after 1930, partly because such works were commissioned. He wrote the *Symphony of Psalms* (1930) for the Boston Symphony, the Symphony in C (1937–40) for the Chicago Symphony and the Symphony in Three Movements (1942–5) for the New York Philharmonic. But the return to canonical forms – symphony, concerto – may also have been associated in his mind with his reawakened religious observance. In 1926 he composed his first sacred piece, a Russian 'Our Father'. *Oedipus Rex* was on one level a Passion of Christ in the guise of a classical drama. Then came the *Symphony of Psalms*, a kind of liturgy for the concert hall, followed in the 1940s, 1950s and 1960s by more sacred cantatas in increasingly rapid succession.

In 1938–9, within little more than six months, he lost his elder daughter, his wife and his mother. The Second World War brought another uprooting. In September 1939 he sailed to New York with Vera, whom he married the following March; three months later they settled in Los Angeles. Proximity there to the film industry occasioned some projects, all of which faltered at an early stage, their material to be re-used in concert pieces: *Four Norwegian Moods* (1942) and *Ode* (1943). A need for money also produced a rather miscellaneous output around this time, including a dance for elephants (*Circus Polka*), a piece for a theatrical revue (*Scènes de ballet*), a contribution to a set of scenes from Genesis (*Babel*) and works for jazz band (*Scherzo à la russe, Ebony Concerto*). After the end of the war, though, he was able to make a healthy living as a composer and conductor of his works, in the concert hall and for recordings – though his abilities on the podium were limited.

In 1947 he embarked on his biggest work: a full-length opera, *The Rake's Progress*, to a libretto written for him by Auden and Kallman. Their models were the operas of Mozart, right down to the presence of harpsichord-accompanied recitative, with passing homages also to other features of the opera repertory, from Monteverdi to Donizetti and Verdi. But the classical elegance is, as always with Stravinsky, ironic – sometimes jarring, sometimes anxious, sometimes a joke. The score was finished in 1951 and performed that year in Venice, during his first return visit to Europe since 1939. The city became his spiritual home and the setting for several later premières.

Two years after starting the opera he was visited by a young conductor, Robert Craft, who soon moved into the house and became his musical-intellectual associate. With Craft at his side he began to interest himself in Schoenberg (of whose music he had probably stayed rather ignorant since attending a performance of *Pierrot lunaire* in Berlin in 1912), in Webern and in their serial techniques. The change was drastic. Within three years of the *Rake* première he had worked out a serial style in his Three Shakespeare Songs for mezzo and mixed trio (1953) and *In memoriam Dylan Thomas* for tenor with quartets of strings and trombones (1954). But his music retained all its essential character: its rhythmic alertness, its harmonic bite and its access to the past. As he himself observed, he had always enjoyed working with small groups of intervals: serialism was, in a sense, waiting for him.

Work on *Agon* – a brilliant product of French Renaissance dances and the new serial Stravinsky – was interrupted by a second work for Venice, the *Canticum sacrum* for vocal soloists, chorus and orchestra (1955–6), a musical homage to the city's patron, St Mark. Another sacred choral work – *Threni* (1957–8), Stravinsky's biggest piece after *The Rake's Progress* – also had a Venetian première. By now he was thoroughly familiar not only with

Schoenberg and Webern but with the music of the new generation of European composers led by Boulez and Stockhausen – music that had an affect on the supple rhythms and sparkling textures of his miniature piano concerto *Movements* (1958–9).

The year of his 80th birthday, 1962, brought a dinner at the White House with the Kennedys, a new biblical parable for television (*The Flood*), and trips to South Africa, Israel, western Europe and South America as well as Russia. There were just a few more works in his early 80s, including *Requiem Canticles* for soloists, choir and orchestra (1965–6). This was, of course, performed at his funeral, in Venice.

When he died, in 1971, Stravinsky was honoured as the world's foremost composer. He had long outlived his close contemporaries – Bartók, Berg, Webern – and his influence had been unequalled. Debussy had been touched by his early works, and in the 1920s and 1930s, as the leader of the Paris school, he had been an example to such diverse younger composers as Messiaen and Honegger, Poulenc and Prokofiev, Milhaud and Szymanowski, Copland and Carter, Hindemith and Weill. At that time he had seemed to be championing an alternative to the atonality of Schoenberg, but his adoption of serialism in the 1950s closed the gap. After that he was an inspiration to all.

But though he must be counted the dominant composer of the 20th century, his works have entered the repertory unequally. *The Firebird* (usually in the form of one of the suites he drew from it), *Petrushka* and *The Rite of Spring* recur regularly in ballet theatres, concert halls and recording studios, but other works are infrequent visitors and some are rarely heard at all. Soloists seem to prefer the concertos of Prokofiev and Rachmaninoff, conductors the symphonies of Shostakovich. Stravinsky's works, each an individual, do not so easily fall into a pattern, and he remains the least known of the great composers.

Stephen Walsh *The Music of Stravinsky* (1988), *Stravinsky*, Vol.1 (1999); Louis Andriessen and Elmer Schönberger *The Apollonian Clockwork* (1989)

Dramatic and orchestral music

Operas: *The* NIGHTINGALE, 1908–14; MAVRA, 1921–2; *Oedipus Rex* (see OEDIPUS), 1926–7; *The* RAKE'S PROGRESS, 1948–51

Other dramatic works with voices: *Les* NOCES (ballet), 1914–23; RENARD (ballet), 1915–16; HISTOIRE DU SOLDAT (musical play), 1918; PULCINELLA (ballet), 1919–20; *Perséphone* (ballet; Gide), woman speaker, t, ch, orch, 1933–4; *The* FLOOD (musical play for television), 1961–2

Orchestral (full): Symphony No.1, E♭, 1905–7; *Scherzo fantastique*, 1907–8; *Feu d'artifice* (*Fireworks*), 1908; *The* FIREBIRD (ballet), 1909–10, also suite; PETRUSHKA (ballet), 1910–11; *The* RITE

OF SPRING (ballet), 1910–13; *Chant du rossignol* (ballet from *The* NIGHTINGALE), 1916–17; 4 Studies, 1914–18, No.4 1928; *Le* BAISER DE LA FEE (ballet), 1928; Capriccio, pf, orch, 1928–9; Violin Concerto, D, 1931; Divertimento (from *Le Baiser de la fée*), 1934; *Jeu de cartes* (ballet), 1936; SYMPHONY IN C, 1939–40; *The Star-Spangled Banner* (arr), 1941; *Circus Polka*, 1942; *4 Norwegian Moods*, 1942; *Ode*, 1943; *Scherzo à la russe*, 1943–4; *Scènes de ballet*, 1944; SYMPHONY IN THREE MOVEMENTS, 1942–5; ORPHEUS (ballet), 1947; AGON (ballet), 1953–7; *Greeting Prelude*, 1955; MOVEMENTS, pf, orch, 1958–9; *Monumentum pro Gesualdo*, 1960; Variations, 1963–4; Canon on a Russian Popular Tune, 1965

Orchestral (reduced): *Song of the Volga Boatmen*, wind, timp, perc, 1917; *Rag-time*, 11 insts, 1918; SYMPHONIES OF WIND INSTRUMENTS, 23 wind, 1920, rev 1945–7; Suites Nos.1–2, chbr orch, 1917–25; *Pulcinella* (suite), chbr orch, *c*.1922; PIANO CONCERTO, with wind, timp, dbs, 1923–4; *Apollon musagète* (see APOLLO) (ballet), str, 1927–8; Concerto 'DUMBARTON OAKS', Eb, chbr orch, 1937–8; *Bluebird Pas-de-deux* (arr of Tchaikovsky), chbr orch, 1941; *Danses concertantes*, chbr orch, 1940–42; Concerto in D, str, 1946; Concertino, 12 insts, 1952; 8 Instrumental Miniatures, chbr orch, 1962

Jazz band: *Praeludium*, 1936–7; *Scherzo à la russe*, 1944; *Ebony Concerto*, with solo cl, 1945; Tango, 1953

Vocal orchestral: *Faun and Shepherdess* (Pushkin), mez, orch, 1906; *2 Songs of the Flea* (arrs of Beethoven and Musorgsky), b, orch, 1910; *The King of the Stars* (*Zvezdolikiy*, *Le Roi des étoiles*; Balmont), men's ch, orch, 1911–12; *Tilimbom* (Russ. trad), s, orch, 1923; 3 Little Songs 'Recollections of My Childhood' (Russ. trad), s, chbr orch, 1929–30; SYMPHONY OF PSALMS, ch, orch, 1930; *Babel*, man speaker, men's ch, orch, 1944; 2 Poems (Verlaine), bar, chbr orch, 1951; CANTICUM SACRUM, t, bar, ch, orch, 1955; *Choral-Variationen über das Weihnachtslied 'Vom Himmel hoch'* (arr of Bach), ch, orch, 1955–6; THRENI, soli, ch, orch, 1957–8; *A Sermon, a Narrative and a Prayer*, speaker, a, t, ch, orch, 1960–61; *Abraham and Isaac*, bar, chbr orch, 1962–3; *Introitus*, men's ch, pf, hp, perc, low str, 1965; REQUIEM *Canticles*, a, b, ch, orch, 1965–6

Other music

Smaller choral works: 4 Russian Peasant Songs (*Saucers*; Russ. trad), women's ch, 1914–17, rev with hn qt, 1954; *Our Father* (*Pater noster*), ch, 1926, rev 1949; *Creed* (*Credo*), ch, 1932, rev 1949; *Blessed Virgin* (*Ave Maria*), ch, 1934, rev 1949; Mass, ch, 10 wind, 1944–8; Cantata (Renaissance Eng.), s, t, women's ch, wind qt, vc, 1951–2; *Tres sacrae cantiones* (completion of settings by Gesualdo), ch, 1957–9; *The Dove Descending* (anthem;T.S. Eliot), ch, 1962

Songs with ensemble: 3 Japanese Lyrics, s, wind qt, pf, str qt, 1912–13; *Pribaoutki* (Russ. trad), bar, 8 insts, 1914; *Berceuses du chat* (Russ. trad), a, 3 cl, 1915–16; *Pastorale* (wordless), s, wind qt, 1923; 3 Shakespeare Songs, mez, fl, cl, ca, 1953; 4 Songs (Russ. trad), v, fl, hp, gtr, 1953–4; *In memoriam Dylan Thomas* (Dylan Thomas), t, str qt, trbn qt, 1954; 2 Poems (Balmont), s, wind qt, pf, str qt, 1954; *Elegy for J.F.K.* (Auden), bar, 3 cl, 1964; 2 Sacred Songs (arr of Wolf), mez, 9 insts, 1968

Songs with piano: *Pastorale*, 1907; 2 Songs (Sergey Gorodetsky), 1908; 2 Poems (Verlaine), 1910; 2 Poems (Balmont), 1911; 3 Little Songs 'Recollections of My Childhood', 1913; *Trois histoires pour enfants* (Russ. trad), 1915–17; 4 Russian Songs (trad), 1918–19; *The Owl and the Pussy-Cat* (Edward Lear), 1966

Chamber: 3 Pieces, str qt, 1914; *Histoire du soldat* (suite), septet, 1918, arr vn, cl, pf, 1919; *La Marseillaise* (arr), vn, 1919; 3 Pieces, cl, 1919; Concertino, str qt, 1920; Octet, wind, 1922–3; *Duo concertante*, vn, pf, 1931–2; *Suite italienne* (from *Pulcinella*), vc/vn, pf, 1932; *Elégie*, va, 1944; *Lied ohne Name*, 2 bn, 1949; Septet, 1952–3; *Epitaphium*, fl, cl, hp, 1959; Double Canon, str qt, 1959; *Lullaby*, 2 rec, 1960; Canzonetta (arr of Sibelius), 8 insts, 1963; *Fanfare for a New Theatre*, 2 tpt, 1964; other arrs for vn and pf

Piano (solo unless otherwise stated): 4 Studies, 1908; *The Rite of Spring*, duet, 1910–13; *Valse des fleurs*, duet, 1914; 3 Easy Pieces, duet, 1914–15; *Souvenir d'un marche boche*, 1915; 5 Easy Pieces, duet, 1916–17; *Valse pour les enfants*, 1916–17; Etude, pianola, 1917; *Piano-Rag-Music*, 1919; *Les Cinq Doigts*, 1921; 3 Movements from *Petrushka*, 1921; Sonata, 1924; Serenade in A, 1925; Concerto, 2 pf, 1931–5; Tango, 1940; Sonata, 2 pf, 1943–4; other arrs of own works for pf solo, pf duet, 2 pf, pianola

street cry. Call made by a pedlar or market trader to promote business. Parisian street cries were incorporated into motets in the 13th and 14th centuries; London cries appear in works from around 1600 by Dering, Gibbons and Weelkes. The genre was imitated by Auden and Stravinsky in *The Rake's Progress*.

Streich (Ger., pl. *Streiche*). Stroke, such as that of a bow on a string. Hence *Streicher* (string instruments), *Streichquartett* (string quartet).

streng (Ger.). Strict.

strepitoso (It.). Noisy, often with a sense of bounding onwards.

stretto (It., constricted). (1) Part of a FUGUE where voices sound the subject in quick succession.

(2) Climactic concluding section of a piece, marked by an increase in tempo. The form *stretta* is also used.

Strich (Ger.). Stroke of a bow, as in *Strich für Strich* (with a bowstroke for each note, detached).

strict canon. Canon in which the intervals in every line are always the same, whereas 'free canon' allows chromatic alteration in order to fit the harmony.

strict counterpoint. Counterpoint obedient to rules, especially those of the SPECIES.

Striggio, Alessandro (b. Mantua, c.1536–7; d. Mantua, 29 Feb 1592). Italian composer. He served the Medicis of Florence (for whom he visited England in 1567), the d'Estes of Ferrara and the Gonzagas of his native city, to which he returned in 1584. Apart from music for court intermedi he wrote madrigals and a motet for 40 voices – music that was appreciated and imitated in England, not least by Tallis. His son of the same name (?1573–1630) was also a court musician-diplomat, but is chiefly remembered as the librettist of Monteverdi's *Orfeo*.

string (Fr. *corde*, Ger. *Saite*, It. *corda*). Vibrating part of many orchestral instruments, including not only the orchestral instruments known as strings but also pianos and harpsichords, guitars and lutes, harps and dulcimers. Strings have been made of gut, silk, metal or plastic, or some combination (see GIMPING). Instruments of the violin family were traditionally fitted with gut strings made from lamb guts, treated in alkaline solutions, wound together and polished. In the 20th century it became normal to cover the gut with metal, to replace it with plastic or to use pure wire strings.

In the context of European classical music, the term 'string instruments' customarily refers to members of the violin family: the VIOLIN itself, the VIOLA, the CELLO and the DOUBLE BASS. From these come the strings of the ORCHESTRA and the instruments of the string quartet and other groupings. With their ability to mimic the human voice – though over a wider range and without the need to pause for breath – and by virtue also of their homogeneity of sound, the strings have formed the foundation of instrumental ensemble music since the start of the 17th century.

string drum. Drum with a string passing through its skin. Rubbing the string produces a roaring sound; hence the term lion's roar for the instrument.

stringendo (It.). Increasing in speed and tension.

string orchestra. Orchestra of strings alone (violins, violas, cellos, basses). Such an ensemble can play a lot of Baroque and pre-Classical music (perhaps with continuo), and also a later repertory including works by Dvořák, Tchaikovsky, Elgar, Schoenberg, Berg, Webern, Bartók, Stravinsky, Boulez and Birtwistle.

string piano. Term introduced by Cowell for a piano that the performer plays with hands inside, plucking or hammering the strings.

string quartet (Fr. *quatuor à cordes*, Ger. *Streichquartett*, It. *quartetto d'archi*). Group of instruments comprising two violins, viola and cello, or group of players on those instruments, or genre of music for that medium, or work of that genre.

Since Haydn the string quartet has been regarded by composers, performers and listeners as one of instrumental music's ultimate challenges, alongside the symphony and the piano sonata, with which, as a genre, it shares some central features: seriousness, abstraction and compelling unity achieved through several movements. These features – along with the distinction of the quartet as a group of soloists from the four-part string orchestra – appeared here and there from early in the 18th century, but they came together definitively and were developed with unparallelled authority and imagination by Haydn in his Opp.9, 17, 20 and 33 (1771–81). Haydn pursued the genre to the end of his creative life, and his example was followed by Mozart and Beethoven.

Mozart found the quartet an unusually trying medium, and unlike Haydn and Beethoven (but like many other composers at the time) he enriched its texture in his string quintets, piano quartets, flute quartets and clarinet quintet – though he also wrote a remarkable string trio. Beethoven returned to the quartet in his last years to produce a series of works that not only awed and perplexed his contemporaries but have remained among the most highly regarded works in the repertory. Near them in date and importance stand the last three quartets of Schubert.

The quartet was, from the first, directed to audiences of two kinds. It was a convenient medium of amateur music-making, but it was also made for public concerts. From this mixing of impulses came gains. As private music, companionable, the quartet evolved qualities of wit, ease and friendly dialogue. As public music it became also forthright: the four instruments had to address not only each other but an audience, and their equality was tilted in favour of concert-like display for the first violinist, or leader. Spohr's quartets are especially of this kind; he also invented the double quartet (or string octet, an innovation notably taken up by Mendelssohn) and the string quartet concerto (an exceedingly awkward genre, requiring four conversationalists to project against a crowd; there are later examples by Schoenberg and Ross Lee Finney).

Like the symphony, the quartet moved into a period of decline in the middle of the 19th century, but then experienced a revival in the 1870s, thanks partly to the new classicism of such composers as Brahms, Dvořák, the young Debussy and – in his one important instrumental work – Verdi, and also partly to the growth in touring ensembles, among which Joachim's quartet was the most important. That revival has never stopped, nor have the activities of virtuoso performing groups, those of the 20th century including the Kolisch, Juilliard, Quartetto Italiano, Arditti, Kronos and Emerson. The role of the amateur musician now was largely over, except to listen.

In keeping with the medium's elevated status, the quartet repertory – unlike the piano or orchestral repertories – contains exceedingly few miniatures, illustrative pieces or lighter works, and its formal standards of scale (20–30 minutes), continuity and seriousness have proved extraordinarily durable, through a quarter-millennium of musical revolutions. It follows that most string quartets are called just that. Smetana added a subtitle to his first quartet, but evocative titles (e.g. those of Xenakis, Dutilleux, Nono, Reich) are all from a much later stage in the quartet's history, which is quickly traced below. The number of quartets written by particular composers in particular periods is indicated, with no number for composers who wrote only one quartet.

1769–1826: Haydn (58), Boccherini (78), Mozart (10), Gyrowetz (45), Beethoven (16), Reicha (23), Spohr (22), Onslow (15), Cherubini (1), Schubert (15), Arriaga (3)

1827–57: Mendelssohn (6+), Cherubini (5), Spohr (14), Onslow (20), Berwald (3), Schumann (3)

1862–95: Dvořák (14), Tchaikovsky (3), Verdi, Brahms (3), Smetana (2), Grieg, Borodin (2), Wolf (2), Franck, Debussy

1895–1939: Zemlinsky (4), Ives (2), Chausson, Reger (5), Ravel, Schoenberg (4), Bartók (6), Sibelius, Webern (3), Berg (2), Stravinsky (2), Szymanowski (2), Elgar, Cowell (5), Hindemith (6), Janáček (2), Fauré, Bridge (4), Prokofiev (1), Crawford

1935–: Shostakovich (15), Barber, Tippett (4), Prokofiev (1), Britten (3), Perle (5), Babbitt (6), Boulez, Cage (4), Carter (5), Feldman (4), Ligeti (2), Gerhard (2), Berio (3), Goehr (4), Davies, Xenakis (3), Lutosławski, Schnittke (4),

Sciarrino (7), Ferneyhough (4), Rihm (12), Wuorinen (3), Holliger, Dutilleux, Nono, Dillon (2), Reich, Glass (5)

string quintet. Group of five string instruments, or group of players on those instruments, or genre of music for that medium, or work of that genre. There are two common types of string quintet, depending on whether the instrument added to the regular quartet is a second viola (Mozart, Beethoven, Mendelssohn, Dvořák, Brahms) or a second cello (Boccherini, Schubert). Dvořák wrote a quintet with double bass.

strings. Term normally implying bowed instruments, and among those the regular orchestral family of violins, violas, cellos and basses.

string trio. Group of instruments comprising violin, viola and cello, or group of players on those instruments, or genre of music for that medium, or work of that genre. There are notable string trios by Mozart, Webern, Schoenberg, Young, Schnittke and Ferneyhough.

stromento (It., pl. *stromenti*). Instrument. Hence *recitativo stromentato*, or simply *stromentato* (accompanied recitative), *stromenti a fiato* (wind instruments).

strophic. Song or other vocal piece having the same music repeated for each strophe (i.e. stanza, verse). The alternative kind of song, where the music is in continuous change, is said to be 'through-composed'.

Stroppa, Marco (b. Verona, 8 Dec 1959). Italian composer. After studies at the Verona, Milan and Venice conservatories he started work at IRCAM in 1982 and returned there as head of musical research (1987–90) after a period at MIT. In 1997 he took a teaching post at the conservatory in Stuttgart. His works include pieces with electronics (*Traiettoria* for piano and tape, 1982–4) and for spaced ensembles.

Strozzi, Barbara (b. Venice, 1619; d. Padua, 11 Nov 1677). Italian singer-composer. She belonged to an artistic family; her adoptive father Giulio (1583–1652) was a poet whose librettos were set by Monteverdi, Cavalli and others, and an earlier relation, Piero (*c*.1550–1609), was among the Florentines who created opera. Cavalli was her teacher, and she sang regularly at musical gatherings at her father's house. She was also one of the first women to publish compositions: volumes of madrigals, cantatas and ariettas.

structure. 'One of the key words of our time', according to one of Boulez's early essays, and indeed the whole period since the First World War has seen an unusual concern with musical structure, with the mechanisms by which moments are connected and forms built. For example, there has been a shift in the study of music from criticism (directed at meaning) to analysis (concerned with material structure and form). At the same time composers have been inclined to distrust any imaginative enterprise not backed by the creation of evident structure, whether in a neoclassical revival of sonata, fugue and other structural types from the 18th and 19th centuries, in the pursuit of serialism and other algorithmic procedures, or in the synthesis of music by electronic means, often requiring the structure of each sound to be determined in advance.

strumento (It., pl. *strumenti*). Instrument. Also to be found is the older form STROMENTO.

Stück (Ger., pl. *Stücke*). Piece.

Stucky, Steven (Edward) (b. Hutchinson, Kansas, 7 Nov 1949). US composer. He studied with Husa at Cornell, where he joined the faculty in 1980. An authority on Lutosławski, he has achieved in his own music a comparable balance of colourful late modernism with symphonic drive.

study (Fr. *étude*, Ger. *Etüde*, *Studie*, pl. *Etüden*, *Studien*, It. *studio*, pl. *studi*). Composition designed to provide practice in some technical difficulty. Studies are, accordingly, most often solo pieces, and keyboard studies are the commonest. They originated in the 18th century, as studies, lessons and exercises for the harpsichord, and burgeoned in the early 19th century, when Cramer, Clementi and others published volumes of studies for the home pianist. Liszt, Chopin and Schumann, all in the 1830s, made the study a concert item, and their initiative was followed by Scriabin, Rachmaninoff and Debussy. Stravinsky's Four Studies for orchestra (1914–28) are studies more in matters of compositional style, structure and technique, as are Messiaen's *Quatre études de rythme* for piano (1949–50) and Stockhausen's electronic *Studien* (1953–4).

study score. Full score meant for perusal rather than performance, and so often in a smaller format, though not as small as a miniature score.

Sturm und Drang (Ger., storm and stress). German literary movement emphasizing fierce and wild emotion, as expressed by Goethe and other writers in the 1770s. The term has also been applied to some music of the period or earlier, especially by Haydn, Mozart, C.P.E. Bach, Benda and Vogler.

style. General characteristics of a composer, a period, a form, or a country, region or city. For example, Debussy's style is something carrying over from *La Mer* to his Etudes for piano, early Baroque style is to be found in Monteverdi and Schütz, sonata style is important in Beethoven and Henze, and elements of Spanish style may be found in Domenico Scarlatti and Falla. Clearly the term is nebulous, but, equally clearly, it is useful and meaningful. For performers, an understanding of style is crucial. A pianist playing a Mozart concerto, for example, may benefit from studying other works by the composer (to provide insights into his style), other piano music and theoretical writings of his time (as evidence of period style), and so on. The resulting performance may thereby become more stylish.

style period. See PERIOD (2).

su, sul, sulla, sulle (It.). On or at, as in *sul G*, a direction in violin music to play on the G string.

subdominant. The note or key a fifth below the tonic of a major or minor key. In C major or minor, therefore, the subdominant is F and the subdominant tonality F major or minor.

subito (It.). Suddenly, immediately, as in *allegro subito*, at once fast.

subject. Theme worked in a fugue or sonata form, the latter normally having two subjects, first and second. The term is not generally used of musical ideas developed in other forms, such as themes in sets of variations or leitmotifs in Wagner operas.

subject group. Term coined by Tovey to deal with sonata-form movements in which there is more than one theme in one or both of the two exposition sections.

submediant. The note or key a third below the tonic of a major or minor key. In C major or minor, therefore, the submediant is A and the submediant tonality A major or minor.

Subotnick, Morton (b. Los Angeles, 14 Apr 1933). US composer, mostly of electronic music. He studied with Milhaud and Kirchner at Mills College (1957–9), where he immediately joined the faculty (1959–66). After a period at New York

University (1966–9) he returned to the west coast to teach at the CalArts. Though he has worked most often with live singers (including his wife, Joan LaBarbara) and instrumentalists, he has also produced purely electronic pieces, of which *Silver Apples of the Moon* (1967) was the first made for release on record.

succentor. Assistant to a PRECENTOR.

Suchoň, Eugen (b. Pezinok, 25 Sep 1908; d. Bratislava, 5 Aug 1993). Slovak composer. He studied in Bratislava and in Prague with Novák (1931–3), then returned to Bratislava to teach. His works of the next two decades draw Slovak folk music into a style of expanded tonality, after which he was affected by serialism; hence the difference between his operas *The Whirlpool* (f.p. Bratislava, 1949) and *Svätopluk* (f.p. Bratislava, 1960).

suitcase aria. Favourite aria that a travelling singer would bring along to insert in a certain opera wherever the performance was taking place. The practice survived from the Baroque period to the 20th century, to fall victim to a doctrine of authenticity that valued individual works above the actual conditions into which they were born.

suite (Fr., succession). Composition in several movements, distinguished by its sense of being more a choice selection than a compelling unity (the hallmark of the symphony and sonata). There are, in essence, two kinds of suite, different in time and nature: the Baroque suite, which died with Bach, and the suite as a sequence of excerpts, generally from a stage work. In the later 19th century original suites began to appear again, partly in emulation of Bach.

The term was first used in 1557 on one of Pierre Attaingnant's publications, which included several suites of dances by Estienne du Tertre, but one of the basic features of the early suite – placing a lively dance after a slow one – is found in 14th-century manuscripts. During the first half of the 17th century, in a ferment of suite-making throughout France, Germany, Italy and Britain, the suite slipped away from the dance floor to become a purely musical object, for playing and listening. Suites were written for viol consort (William Lawes) or other chamber grouping, orchestra, lute or keyboard (Froberger) and began to gain a regular pattern of allemande (slow), courante (fast), sarabande (slow, the centre of gravity) and gigue (fast), perhaps with a prelude to begin. All movements would normally be in the same key.

This was the form followed by Bach in works for soloist (cello, keyboard, violin) or orchestra that he called suites or partitas, sometimes with additional movements (especially after the sarabande, though the D minor partita for violin ends with an immense chaconne) or with the omission of the prelude (French suites). Among others writing in this golden age of the suite were Couperin, Rameau and Handel. After 1750 the suite was rapidly submerged in the incoming tide of sonata-style Classicism, though Mozart began a suite as an exercise in an archaic mode (K.399). The form was then revived by Saint-Saëns and Tchaikovsky, followed in the 20th century by Schoenberg and Hindemith.

The extract suite comes from the same historical stem as the original suite, since 17th-century dance selections would often be drawn from court theatrical entertainments. It came into its own when composers wanted to give a concert life to incidental music and ballet scores, examples including the suites from Grieg's *Peer Gynt* music, Tchaikovsky's *Nutcracker*, Stravinsky's *Firebird*, Ravel's *Daphnis et Chloé* and Prokofiev's *Romeo and Juliet*. The extract model also prompted original suites made as sequences of picturesque movements, such as Holst's *Planets*.

Suk, Josef (b. Křečovice, 4 Jan 1874; d. Benešov, near Prague, 29 May 1935). Czech composer, a late Romantic, and violinist. He began his music studies with his father, a village schoolmaster, and continued with Foerster, Hanuš Wihan and Dvořák at the Prague Conservatory (1885–92). While still a student he joined Wihan's quartet as second violin; the group was soon known as the Czech Quartet, and it enjoyed a distinguished career until he retired in 1933. His connections with another of his teachers were as deep, for he was Dvořák's favourite pupil, and in 1898 he married the composer's daughter Otilie. Out of grief at Dvořák's death in 1904, followed by Otilie's the next year, he produced his greatest work, *Asrael* (1906–7), a symphony of Mahlerian expressive power. After 1912 he became much less productive as a composer, perhaps less because of his teaching duties at the Prague Conservatory (from 1922) than as a result of the complex new directions in which he was trying to develop his style. His grandson, also Josef Suk (b. 1929), is a violinist.

Orchestral: Serenade, E♭, Op.6, str, 1892; *A Winter's Tale* (overture), Op.9, 1894, rev 1926; *Fairy Tale*, Op.16, 1899–1900; Fantasy, Op.24, vn, orch, 1902–3; Fantastic Scherzo, Op.25, 1903; *Prague*, Op.26, 1904; *Asrael* (symphony), Op.27, 1905–6; *A Summer's Tale*, Op.29, 1907–9; *The Ripening*, Op.34, 1912–17; *Towards a New Life* (march),

Op.35c, ch, orch, 1920; *Epilogue*, Op.37, soli, ch, orch, 1920–32; etc.

Chamber: Piano Quartet, A minor, Op.1, 1891; String Quartet, B♭, Op.11, 1896; String Quartet, Op.31, 1911; Meditation on an Old Czech Hymn 'St Wenceslas', Op.35a, str qt, 1914; Elegy, Op.23, pf trio, 1902; 4 Pieces, Op.17, vn, pf, 1900 (No.4 *Burlesca*); etc.

Other works: piano music (6 Pieces, Op.7, 1891–3; *About Mother*, Op.28, 1907), songs, partsongs

sul. See SU.

Sullivan, Arthur (Seymour) (b. Lambeth, 13 May 1842; d. London, 22 Nov 1900). British composer, especially of operettas, knighted in 1883. The son of an Irish army bandmaster, he began his training as a Chapel Royal chorister (1854–8) and had a sacred song published in 1855. He then studied with Sterndale Bennett at the RAM (1856–8) and Julius Rietz at the Leipzig Conservatory (1858–61), after which he returned to London to work as an organist, teacher and composer of parlour songs. But he was also making a reputation for more ambitious music, notably his incidental score for *The Tempest*. He began moving in distinguished circles: he knew Millais (who painted his portrait), Tennyson, the musical encylopedist George Grove and members of the royal family.

In 1866–7 he wrote his first operetta, but it was not until 1871 that he formed his partnership with W.S. Gilbert – a partnership that, from his point of view, was a mixed blessing, since it diverted him from more serious work. The judgement of generations, though, is that he made the right choice. The combination of his blithe, tuneful melodies (an English answer to Offenbach) with Gilbert's witty rhymes and sharp characterizations produced works that tempered irony with sentiment and naivety with sophistication. Produced by Richard D'Oyly Carte, from 1881 at the new Savoy Theatre, the 'Savoy Operas' were an enormous success until the relationship between their creators began to break down in 1890, and the nine works from *HMS Pinafore* to *The Gondoliers* have remained part of English-language popular culture.

Sullivan held various conducting posts while working with Gilbert and leading a somewhat raffish life in high society: he regularly wintered in Monte Carlo and spent the last 20 years of his life with a married woman from the USA, Mrs Mary Frances Ronalds, with whom he brought up his nephew.

Arthur Jacobs *Arthur Sullivan* (1984, ²1992)

Operettas with Gilbert: *Thespis*, f.p. London, 1871, lost/reused; *Trial by Jury*, f.p. London, 1875; *The*
Sorcerer, f.p. London, 1877, rev 1884; *HMS Pinafore*, f.p. London, 1878; *The Pirates of Penzance*, f.p. Paignton, 1879; *Patience*, f.p. London, 1881; *Iolanthe*, f.p. London, 1882; *Princess Ida*, f.p. London, 1884; *The Mikado*, f.p. London, 1885; *Ruddigore*, f.p. London, 1887; *The Yeomen of the Guard*, f.p. London, 1888; *The Gondoliers*, f.p. London, 1889; *Utopia Limited*, f.p. London, 1893; *The Grand Duke*, f.p. London, 1896

Other stage works: *Cox and Box* (operetta; F.C. Burnand), f.p. London, 1867; *Ivanhoe* (opera; Julian Sturgis, after Scott), f.p. London, 1891; *The Rose of Persia* (operetta; Basil Hood), f.p. London, 1899; etc.

Orchestral: *The Tempest* (incidental music), 1861; 'Irish' Symphony, E, 1866; Overture 'In memoriam', 1866; Cello Concerto, D, 1866; *Overture di ballo*, 1870; etc.

Other works: oratorios, anthems, hymns ('Onward Christian Soldiers'), songs ('The Lost Chord', 1877), early chamber and instrumental music

sul ponticello. See PONTICELLO.

sul tasto. See TASTO.

Sumer is icumen in (Middle Eng., Summer is coming in). Extraordinary composition probably written in Reading around 1250, a seasonal song to words beginning 'Sumer is icumen in: lhude sing cuccu' set as a ROUND for four voices while two others sing a bass.

summation tone. See COMBINATION TONE.

summer. See SEASONS.

Sun. Name given to Haydn's Op.20 quartets, for the motif on the title page of the first edition.

Sunless (*Bez solntsa*). Song cycle by Musorgsky to words by Arseny Golenishchev-Kutuzov, outlining a narrative of depressed withdrawal from the world at the end of an unhappy affair, and of suicide.

Sunrise. Name given to Haydn's Quartet Op.76:4. There are also musical sunrises in Strauss (*Eine Alpensinfonie*), Schoenberg (*Gurrelieder*), Sibelius, Messiaen, etc.

Suor Angelica. See *Il* TRITTICO.

supertonic. The note a whole tone above the tonic of a major or minor key, i.e. the second degree of the scale.

Supervia, Conchita (b. Barcelona, 9 Dec 1895; d. London, 30 Mar 1936). Spanish mezzo-soprano, of vibrant voice and engaging personality. She made her debut with a Spanish company at the Teatro Colón in Buenos Aires in 1910, and from the mid-1920s was internationally in demand as Carmen, Rosina (*The Barber of Seville*) and the heroines of other Rossini operas she helped revive (*The Italian Girl in Algiers*, *La Cenerentola*). She died in childbirth.

Suppé, Franz von [Suppé Demelli, Francesco Ezechiele Ermengildo, Cavaliere] (b. Spalato/Split, 18 Apr 1819; d. Vienna, 21 May 1895). Austrian composer of operettas. Born into a family of civil servants, he was taught and encouraged locally, and then studied with Ignaz Xaver Seyfried and Sechter in Vienna. In 1840 he began his career as a composer-conductor in the city's operetta theatres, including the Theater an der Wien (1845–62). He is remembered especially for the overtures to *Ein Morgen, Mittag und Abend in Wien* (Morning, Noon and Night in Vienna, 1844), *Dichter und Bauer* (Poet and Peasant, 1846) and *Leichte Cavallerie* (Light Cavalry, 1866).

supper music. See TAFELMUSIK.

Surinach, Carlos (b. Barcelona, 4 Mar 1915; d. New Haven, 12 Nov 1997). Catalan–US composer. He studied in Barcelona and in Germany, and in 1951 settled in the USA, where he won particular success as a composer of music for dance, working with Martha Graham (*Embattled Garden*, 1958; *Acrobats of God*, 1960) and the Joffrey Ballet (*Feast of Ashes*, 1963, set to his *Doppio concertino* for violin, piano and nonet of 1954 and *Ritmo jondo* of 1953).

sur la touche, sur le chevalet. Fr. equivalents to *sul* TASTO, *sul* PONTICELLO.

Surprise. Name given to Haydn's Symphony No.94. The surprise is the loud drumstroke in the slow movement. First performance: London, 23 Mar 1792.

surtitles. Means of conveying the libretto to an opera audience, on a screen at the top of the proscenium arch. The technique was first used by the Canadian Opera Company for a performance of *Elektra* (21 Jan 1983) and was rapidly taken up by other theatres.

Survivor from Warsaw, A. Work by Schoenberg, his last completed orchestral score. A narrator, in sprechgesang, speaks the composer's words, adapted from the testimonies of Jewish survivors of the Nazi terror, dramatically preparing the

expression of continuing faith that comes from a men's choir. First performance: Albuquerque, New Mexico, 4 Nov 1948.

Susato, Tylman (b. Soest, near Dortmund, *c*.1510–15; d. ?Sweden, 1570 or later). Netherlandish composer and publisher. He was active in Antwerp as a calligrapher and trumpeter from around 1530, and from 1543 had charge of the first important music press in the Low Countries, bringing out volumes of masses, metrical psalms and secular songs, including compositions of his own.

Suslin, Viktor (Yevseyevich) (b. Miass, Ural region, 13 Jun 1942). Russian composer whose music tends to the extremely sparse. He studied at the Kharkov Conservatory (1961–2) and the Gnesin Institute in Moscow (1962–6). In 1975 he formed the improvisation group Astraea with Artyomov and Gubaidulina, and in 1981 he moved to Germany.

suspension. A chord progression in which what is suspended is a dissonant note held over from a previous chord. This normally then resolves by stepwise descent.

Süssmayr, Franz Xaver (b. Schwanenstadt, Upper Austria, 1766; d. Vienna, 17 Sep 1803). Austrian composer, close to Mozart. He studied first with his teacher-choirmaster father, then in Kremsmünster (1779–87). In 1788 he settled as a music teacher in Vienna, where in 1790 or 1791 he became acquainted with Mozart. He helped his friend both in life, by writing secco recitatives for *La clemenza di Tito*, and posthumously, by completing the *Requiem*. His own works include singspiels and cantatas.

sustaining pedal. The right pedal of the piano, which, when depressed, causes the dampers to be raised, so that all the strings will vibrate freely. The notes that are being played thus go on sounding after the hands have been removed from the keys, and other strings can vibrate in sympathy. The effect is to make the sound louder and more resonant, though care is needed to avoid harmonic confusion.

Sutermeister, Heinrich (b. Feuerthalen, Schaffhausen, 12 Aug 1910; d. Morges, 16 Mar 1995). Swiss composer. He was a pupil of Orff and author of operas (*Die schwarze Spinne*, f.p. Radio Beromünster, 1936; *Romeo und Julia*, f.p. Dresden, 1940) and choral music.

Sutherland, Joan (b. Sydney, 7 Nov 1926).

Australian soprano, created dame in 1979. She began training with her mother and continued in Sydney and at the RCM (1951–2) before making her Covent Garden debut as the First Lady in *Die Zauberflöte* in 1952. Two years later she married a fellow Australian in London, Richard Bonynge, and he became her preferred conductor. He also encouraged her towards the bel canto repertory, and her first Lucia (in *Lucia di Lammermoor*) at Covent Garden in 1959 was her breakthrough. She repeated the role at the Met (1960) and La Scala (1961), going on to tour the world in this and other parts by Donizetti, Bellini (Norma), Handel, Massenet, etc. Her vocalism was brilliant and sure, if at the expense of verbal communication. She retired in 1990.

Norma Major *Joan Sutherland* (1987)

Suzuki, Shin'ichi (b. Nagoya, 18 Oct 1898; d. Matsumoto, 26 Jan 1998). Japanese music educationist. The son of a violin manufacturer, he began developing his method of violin teaching, based on drilled repetition by pupils in groups, in the 1930s.

Svadebka. See *Les* NOCES.

Svendsen, Johan (Severin) (b. Christiania, now Oslo, 30 Sep 1840; d. Copenhagen, 14 Jun 1911). Norwegian composer, especially of orchestral music. The son of a military musician, he was playing the violin in professional orchestras while still in his teens. He then studied at the Leipzig Conservatory (1863–7), during which time he began his career as a composer. In October 1867 he conducted a concert of his music in Christiania, gaining a warm review from Grieg, who dedicated a violin sonata (No.2) to him. But he soon left Norway again for wider opportunities in Paris and Germany, and to marry. He went back to Christiania in 1872 to conduct, at first alongside Grieg. He was abroad again in 1877–80, and in 1883 was appointed conductor of the Royal Opera in Copenhagen, where he remained following his retirement in 1908. As a composer he complemented Grieg (as Grieg acknowledged), with his mastery of orchestration and large form, his works including two symphonies (D, Op.4, 1865–6; B♭, Op.15, 1874), a Romance for violin and orchestra (Op.26, 1881) and four Norwegian rhapsodies. He wrote little in Copenhagen, possibly because his wife, so it is said, angrily threw his Third Symphony into the fire in 1887, providing Ibsen with an episode for *Hedda Gabler*. They were divorced in 1901 and he married a ballerina.

swanee whistle. Whistle with a sliding stopper to vary the pitch continuously. A toy instrument of the 19th century, it was used by early jazz bands and so came to the ear of Ravel (*L'Enfant et les sortilèges*). Since the 1960s it has been quite common in the orchestra. The same slide-whistle principle has been used since c.1768–70 in the manufacture of mechanical singing birds. See also BIRDSONG.

Swan Lake (*Le lac des cygnes, Lebedinoye ozero*). Ballet score by Tchaikovsky to a scenario by V.P. Begichev and Vasily Heltser after German folktales, choreographed by Julius Wenzel Reisinger. Odette, who has been changed into a swan by Rothbart, draws the attention of Prince Siegfried, who is subsequently seduced by Rothbart's daughter Odile, as a black swan. First performance: Moscow, 4 Mar 1877.

Swan of Tuonela, The (*Tuonelan joutsen*). Symphonic poem by Sibelius (1893), written as prelude to a projected opera, *The Building of the Boat*, but included in the LEMMINKÄINEN SUITE. A solo cor anglais depicts the swan gliding on the still waters of the Finnish underworld.

swansong (Ger. *Schwanengesang*). An artist's final composition or performance, from the legend that a swan, on the point of death, utters a beautiful melody. The term was applied by publishers to Schütz's last work and Schubert's ultimate songs.

Swayne, Giles (Oliver Cairnes) (b. Hitchin, 30 Jun 1946). British composer. He studied with Maw and others at Cambridge and the RAM, and attended some of Messiaen's classes in Paris (1976–7). His extended and passionate *Cry* for chorus (1979) widened his stylistic embrace, as did a study visit to West Africa (1982–3) followed by a period living in Ghana (1990–96). Later works include *Havoc* for countertenor, flute, choir and instrumental groups (1999).

Sweden (Sverige). Archaeological evidence of ancient music includes some bronze trumpets from around 1000 BC. Two millennia later Christianization bore the country into the mainstream of European culture, and then the Vasa kings of the 16th century established court music; Erik XIV (r. 1560–68) was himself a composer. War and royal patronage brought German, French and Italian musicians to Stockholm in the 17th century, though no Swedish monarch was more munificent to the arts than Gustav III (r. 1771–92), who rebuilt the DROTTNINGHOLM theatre. Also from his time, the satiric-sentimental songs of Carl Michael Bellman (1740–95) are dear to Swedes. In the 19th century responsibility for cultural life passed, as elsewhere, from the court to the bourgeoisie, with the concomitant foundation of music societies, orchestras and conservatories. Important native composers came more sporadically: Crusell and Berwald in the early Romantic period. The continuous history of Swedish composition begins around 1900 with Stenhammar and Alfvén, followed by Atterberg, Rosenberg, Wirén, Blomdahl, Pettersson, Hambraeus and Sandström.

Sweelinck, Jan Pieterszoon (b. Deventer, ?May 1562; d. Amsterdam, 16 Oct 1621). Dutch organist-composer. The son and grandson of organists, he grew up in Amsterdam, where his father became organist of the Oude Kerk in 1564. He lost his father when he was 11, then probably completed his training in Haarlem, and by 1580 had succeeded to his father's post. Music was not part of Calvinist worship: he was employed by the city, and played for an hour in the morning and an hour in the evening, before or after services. In 1590 he married. Four years later, on the title page of his first publication (a volume of polyphonic songs in French), he began using his mother's sur-name. He also published polyphonic settings of the psalms – similarly in French, designed for a circle of musical amateurs in Amsterdam – and motets for Catholic use (*Hodie Christus natus est*, from his 1619 collection). Among his keyboard works are settings of chorales and secular melodies (*Mein junges Leben hat ein End*), as well as fantasias and toccatas, bringing traditions in English, Italian and Iberian music to a consummation. His fame as an organist and teacher drew pupils from north Germany, including Scheidt and Scheidemann, through whom his influence passed down to Bach. Another student was his son, Dirck Janszoon Sweelinck (1591–1652), who followed him at the Oude Kerk.

Frits Noske *Sweelinck* (1988)

swell. Mechanism allowing an organ to produce a crescendo. In most cases some pipes are enclosed in a box that partly opens when a pedal is depressed. Swell devices were also applied to some harpsichords in the third quarter of the 18th century.

Swieten, Gottfried (Bernhard) Baron **van** (b. Leiden, 29 Oct 1733; d. Vienna, 29 Mar 1803). Dutch–Austrian courtier and musical amateur. The family moved to Vienna in 1745, and he followed a diplomatic career that culminated in his posting to Berlin as ambassador (1770–77), after which he returned to the imperial capital. Already an amateur composer, in Berlin he developed a taste for Bach and Handel, whose works he promoted in Vienna: Mozart made arrangements of several Handel scores for him. He also commissioned symphonies from C.P.E. Bach, adapted the texts for Haydn's *Die sieben letzten Worte*, *The Creation* and *The Seasons*, and helped the young Beethoven, whose First Symphony was dedicated to him.

Switzerland (Schweiz, Suisse, Svizzera). The Benedictine monastery of St Gallen was one of the leading musical centres of the 9th, 10th and 11th centuries. Later times witnessed visitors including Wagner in Lucerne and Stravinsky in Morges, the foundation of orchestras, conservatories and opera companies, the work of notable conductors (Ansermet, Sacher, Dutoit) and the arrival of important native composers, among them Schoeck, Martin, Huber and Holliger.

SWR. Südwestrundfunk (South West Radio), formed in 1998 from the merging of the Südwest-funk (SWF, Baden-Baden) with the Süddeutscher Rundfunk (SDR, Stuttgart), and maintaining the orchestras of both. Conductors of the former have included Rosbaud (1948–62), Ernest Bour (1964–79), Gielen (1986–99) and Sylvain Cambreling (from 1999), and of the latter Celibidache (1971–7) and Norrington (from 1998). The SWF/SWR has been notably active in new music, in Baden-Baden, at its experimental studio in Freiburg (where Nono worked) and at the Donaueschingen Festival.

syllabic. Setting one note to each syllable. The alternatives are melisma (many notes to one syllable) and reciting note (many syllables to one note).

Sylphides, Les (The Sylphs). Ballet to orchestral arrangements of pieces by Chopin, choreographed by Fokine and first performed in St Petersburg in 1907, then brought to Paris two years later by Diaghilev. The original version had five pieces orchestrated by Glazunov. Diaghilev's production had further numbers scored by Stravinsky, Lyadov and Tcherepnin. Other hands have been involved in subsequent revivals.

Sylvia. Full-length ballet score by Delibes to a scenario by Jules Barbier and Baron de Reinach, choreographed by Louis Mérante. The action, based on Tasso, concerns the love of the shepherd Aminta for the nymph Sylvia, who is trapped by Orion and released by Eros. First performance: Paris Opera, 14 Jun 1876.

symbolism. An artistic encoding of feelings or abstractions (e.g. death, love, desire, glory) in specific symbols. In music the great example is Wagner, whose use of leitmotifs had an enormous influence on what became an artistic movement known as symbolism; there were symbolist painters and poets, especially in France, Belgium, Scandinavia and Russia. During the time symbolism was its peak, 1890–1910, the influence went back into music, not least in responses to Maeterlinck from Debussy, Fauré, Sibelius, Schoenberg and Dukas.

sympathetic string. String on a musical instrument, not stimulated itself but placed so that it will vibrate in sympathy with strings that are bowed, plucked or struck, enriching the tone. The viola d'amore has sympathetic strings, as do various Indian instruments, including the sitār.

symphonia (medieval Lat., from the Gk *syn*, together, + *phone*, sounding). The ancestor of the word SYMPHONY, to which any of the following meanings can also apply.

(1) Consonance, in medieval music theory.

(2) An instrument, in writings from the Middle Ages to the 17th century. Most usually it was the hurdy-gurdy that was meant, but different authors at different times had different ideas, across the range from drum (Isidore of Seville, early 7th century) to keyboard instrument (Praetorius, a thousand years later).

(3) A synonym for sinfonia in the 17th century. Carter revived the term as a title.

symphonic. Having the qualities of a symphony, in the sense of a composition or an orchestra. A work for symphonic forces uses full orchestra. The term appears in titles to indicate a symphony-like approach to other forms, as in Franck's Symphonic Variations, Rachmaninoff's Symphonic Dances and Hindemith's Symphonic Metamorphosis. Usage can, though, be more metaphorical, so that one may speak of the symphonic qualities of Beethoven's 'Hammerklavier' Sonata, meaning its scale, strength of development and compelling unity. Hence also Schumann's *Etudes symphoniques* for piano.

Symphonic Metamorphosis on Themes by Carl Maria von Weber (*Symphonische Metamorphosen über Themen von Carl Maria von Weber*). Orchestral work by Hindemith on themes from piano duets by Weber and from his *Turandot*. First performance: New York, 20 Jan 1944.

Symphonic Movement. See MOUVEMENT SYMPHONIQUE.

symphonic poem (Fr. *poème symphonique*, Ger. *Symphonische Dichtung*). An orchestral composition that depicts a scene or story, often (and originally) by means of a PROGRAMME. The term was first used by Liszt in 1854, though he had been writing symphonic poems as overtures since 1848. Strauss introduced the alternative 'tone poem' (Ger. *Tondichtung*).

The symphonic poem answered two great needs of the Romantic period: for music to be explicit in its meanings, and for the different aspects of a work in several movements (introduction, reflection, exhilaration, conclusion) to be combined in one. Its roots were in the descriptive piano piece, of the kind Liszt had been writing since the 1830s, and in a tradition of dramatic or illustrative orchestral writing that went back to Beethoven's third *Leonore* overture (1806). Beethoven had gone on to compose a free-standing overture, *Namensfeier*, and both Berlioz and Mendelssohn had made the overture more picturesque; examples include the former's *Waverley* (1827–8) and *Rob Roy* (1832), and the latter's *Midsummer Night's Dream* (1826) and *Hebrides* (1830). The programme symphonies of Beethoven ('Pastoral') and Berlioz ('Fantastique') were also important in the symphonic poem's pedigree, since from them composers could learn how to be symphonic and poetic at the same time.

Normally the answer involved some adjustment on both sides. Many of the basic elements of symphony composition would be retained: the introduction near the outset of contrasting themes – normally two, though there might be just one theme and a conflicting or withholding harmonic atmosphere – to be followed by prominent development, more reflective music and some concluding resolution, whether calm or victorious. But there could also be dramatic interventions (as there had been in *Leonore* No.3). Those apart, the poetic programme would be one that lent itself to quasi-symphonic phases of exposition, followed by struggle or disagreement, contemplation and dénouement. However, the symphonic poems of Liszt and, especially, Smetana are often far from conventional in form and character.

The repertory of symphonic poems is, therefore, heterogeneous, and it includes works for which composers preferred to use the old term 'overture' (Tchaikovsky, Elgar) or cast as a suite (Rimsky-Korsakov, Holst) or scherzo (Dukas). With the rise of the ballet as a genre of interest to composers, and particularly after Diaghilev's investment in the one-act ballet, a lot of symphonic poems were made for dancing. After the late 1920s the symphonic poem went into a steep decline as

Romanticism gave way generally to forms of neo-classicism and modernism. Perhaps, too, the rise of the film score, which flourished on the conventions of the symphonic poem, encouraged composers of concert music to look sharply in other directions, though Schoenberg created a piece of movie music for the orchestral auditorium. Around 1960, with a reassertion of the poetic (if not yet the symphonic), a revival began. Ligeti's *Atmosphères*, from near the beginning of this period, might be regarded as an abstract symphonic poem, lacking an illustrative intent but powerfully suggestive – a symphonic poem from which the observer, so palpable in the works of Liszt or Tchaikovsky, has withdrawn.

Examples that fit more obviously into the genre are listed below.

1848–69: Liszt: *Tasso, Les Préludes, Orpheus, Prometheus, Mazeppa, Hamlet, Hunnenschlacht, Die Ideale*; Smetana: *Richard III, Wallenstein's Camp, Hakon Jarl*; Tchaikovsky: *Romeo and Juliet*

1872–88: Smetana: *Má vlast*; Saint-Saëns: *Le Rouet d'Omphale, Danse macabre*; Duparc: *Lénore*; Tchaikovsky: *Francesca da Rimini, Hamlet*; Franck: *Les Eolides, Le Chasseur maudit, Psyché*; Balakirev: *Tamara*; Chausson: *Viviane*; Wolf: *Penthesilea*; Rimsky-Korsakov: *Sheherazade*

1888–1910: Strauss: *Macbeth, Don Juan, Tod und Verklärung, Till Eulenspiegel, Also sprach Zarathustra, Don Quixote, Ein Heldenleben*; Sibelius: *En saga, Swan of Tuonela, Finlandia, Pohjola's Daughter*; Debussy: *Prélude à 'L'Après-midi d'un faune', Nocturnes*; Dukas: *L'Apprenti sorcier*; Schoenberg: *Verklärte Nacht, Pelleas und Melisande*; Elgar: *Cockaigne, In the South*; Ives: *Central Park in the Dark*; Zemlinsky: *Die Seejungfrau*; Scriabin: *Le Poème de l'extase, Prométhée*; Rachmaninoff: *The Isle of the Dead*

1910–28: Sibelius: *The Dryad, The Bard, The Oceanides, Tapiola*; Stravinsky: *The Firebird, Petrushka, The Rite of Spring, Chant du rossignol, Le Baiser de la fée*; Debussy: *Images, Jeux*; Delius: *Summer Night on the River, On Hearing the First Cuckoo in Spring*; Ravel: *Daphnis et Chloé, La Valse*; Elgar: *Falstaff*; Ives: *Three Places in New England*; Vaughan Williams: *The Lark Ascending*; Holst: *The Planets*; Janáček: *Taras Bulba, The Ballad of Blaník*; Bax: *Tintagel*; Varèse: *Amériques*; Ireland: *Mai-Dun*; Bartók: *The Miraculous Mandarin*; Honegger: *Pacific 231, Rugby*; Bridge: *Enter Spring*

1930–59: Schoenberg: *Accompaniment to a Film Scene*; Ruggles: *Sun-treader*; Messiaen: *Les Offrandes oubliées, Réveil des oiseaux*; Revueltas: *Sensemayá*; Koechlin: *Les Bandar-log*; Copland: *Appalachian Spring*; Stravinsky: *Orpheus*; Varèse: *Déserts*

1960–: Takemitsu: *Green, Winter*; Birtwistle: *The Triumph of Time, Melencolia I, The Shadow of Night*; Henze: *Heliogabalus Imperator, Tristan, Le*

Miracle de la rose; Xenakis: *Eridanos*; Messiaen: *Chronochromie*; Lumsdaine: *Hagoromo*; Davies: *A Mirror of Whitening Light*; Tippett: *The Rose Lake*; Goehr: *Colossos or Panic*

Symphonic Variations (*Variations symphoniques*). Work for piano and orchestra by Franck. First performance: Paris, 1 May 1886.

Symphonie (Fr., Ger., Ger. pl. *Symphonien*). Symphony.

symphonie concertante. See SINFONIA CONCERTANTE.

Symphonie espagnole (Spanish Symphony). Violin concerto by Lalo, written for Sarasate. First performance: Paris, 7 Feb 1875.

Symphonie fantastique (Fantastic Symphony). Orchestral work by Berlioz based on a programme in which he dramatized his desires and fears under the subtitle 'Episode in the Life of an Artist'. A melody, which he called 'idée fixe', stands for his musing, observing self within the work. The movements are: 1 *Rêveries, passions* (Dreams, Passions), 2 *Un Bal* (A Ball), 3 *Scène aux champs* (Field Scene), 4 *Marche au supplice* (March to the Scaffold), 5 *Songe d'une nuit du Sabbat* (Dream of a Witches' Sabbath). First performance: Paris, 5 Dec 1830.

Symphonie funèbre et triomphale. See GRANDE SYMPHONIE FUNEBRE ET TRIOMPHALE.

Symphonies of Wind Instruments (*Symphonies d'instruments à vent*). Work by Stravinsky for orchestral woodwind and brass, composed as a memorial to Debussy and rescored in 1945–7 without the rare alto clarinet of the original version. First performance: London, 10 Jun 1921.

Symphonische Dichtung (Ger., pl. *Symphonische Dichtungen*). Symphonic poem.

symphony (Fr. *symphonie*, Ger. *Symphonie*, It. *sinfonia*). A substantial orchestral composition, traditionally in four movements, the term being used either for an individual example or generically ('the Romantic symphony'). The same word can denote an orchestra that would have such works in its repertory (e.g. the Boston Symphony). Before and after the great age of symphony composition – which began around 1760 and barely survived the double hammer blows of the 20th century's two world wars – the term could be used in different ways: Handel's oratorios have symphonies as interludes and Galina Ustvolskaya's symphonies are unlike anything in the symphonic literature. For other, earlier meanings of the term see SYMPHONIA.

In concert life since Beethoven the symphony has been widely regarded as the pre-eminent form, surpassing the quartet or sonata by virtue of size, above opera or song as music needing no words, and exceeding the concerto by its seriousness, its gravity that eschews outward display. This view is certainly open to argument: the inferiority of quartets and opera, for instance, is by no means obvious. Besides, there is another history of the symphony that took a different route from Beethoven, towards incorporating elements of opera, song and concerto, as Berlioz and Mahler did. Still, the symphony has kept its aura. And once the concert had settled into something like its present form, in the 1870s, the symphony gained its normal place alone in the second half, the evening's culminative experience. The later symphonies that do not make high claims – such as Stravinsky's Symphony in C or Shostakovich's Ninth – are few and provocative. Symphonies are supposed to be major statements, and even composers distant from any symphonic tradition – Liszt, Berio – have seen the genre in this light.

But that is not at all how the symphony began, and the post-Beethoven image has inevitably distorted impressions of the 18th-century symphony. The works that are most admired, performed and recorded are those that approximate to the Beethoven model – chiefly the later symphonies of Haydn and Mozart, which overshadow not only the earlier Haydn but also the many other symphony composers of the Classical period and immediately before.

By the time Haydn wrote his first symphonies, around 1757, the form had been awakening through a quarter-century, and its prehistory stretched back to 1687, when Alessandro Scarlatti introduced a new kind of overture, fast–slow–fast. This became the standard pattern for overtures in the 18th century, and overtures supplied material for concerts, which at this time were private affairs in princely surroundings. The earliest known symphony made specifically for concert use, in the same three-movement form, came from Sammartini in Milan in 1732, followed soon by composers in Vienna and Paris. Also important in the genre's early history were the opera overtures of Jommelli, for their liveliness of colour and dynamics. But the chief research laboratory of the early symphony was at the Mannheim court, where Johann Stamitz created effective four-movement symphonies in the 1740s and 1750s.

Haydn composed his first symphonies in or near the year of Stamitz's death and, so far from standing alone, belonged to an extraordinary new generation that included the second-generation Mannheim composers Cannabich, Filtz and Beck, the Parisian Gossec, the London Bach (J.C.) and, in his own city of Vienna, Ordonez, Leopold Hofmann, Dittersdorf and Wanhal, all born in the 1730s. The symphonies they wrote as young men had three or four movements, very occasionally with a slow introduction (pioneered, it would seem, by Hofmann). Their orchestra was growing from the ensemble of strings with pairs of oboes and horns plus continuo that had at first served Sammartini: bassoons were added regularly, flutes sometimes, and trumpets and timpani occasionally for works in D major. Haydn's symphonies of this period explore diverse possibilities, including not only what would become his and the genre's standard form (slow introduction leading into sonata-form allegro, slow movement, minuet and trio, and finale – a scheme he first used in No.15) but also patterns with a slow movement first (Nos.5, 11, 15 and 21) or the minuet in second place (No.25), programme symphonies (Nos.6–8), and works with cors anglais instead of oboes (No.22) or concertante instruments, such as quartets of horns (Nos.13 and 31).

Widely distributed, Haydn's symphonies challenged his contemporaries and aroused his juniors – notably Mozart, whose first important symphonies date from the mid-1770s: the 'Little' G minor and No.29 in A. Haydn went on producing two or three symphonies a year, whether for his Esterházy patrons or for the new public concerts in Paris (Nos.82–7, 1785–6) and London (Nos.93–104, 1791–5). The rise of the symphony was accelerated by the arrival of public concert-giving, and several of Haydn's contemporaries, among them Cannabich and Gossec, were also vigorously active in these years of their comparative maturity. Mozart's symphonies were more single and special, prompted by concerts in Paris (No.31, 1778), Linz (No.36, 1783), Prague (No.38, 1786) and Vienna (Nos.39–41, 1788), or by the wish to retrieve music from a serenade (No.35, 1782). As with the string quartet, he may have felt uncharacteristically cautious in a genre that his great compeer had virtually invented. But he found his own ways to make it work, more lyrically and perhaps more privately.

Haydn's last symphonies came after Mozart's death, but now there was a new young colleague in Vienna, Beethoven. With rather few exceptions Beethoven wrote for the Classical ORCHESTRA that had served Haydn and Mozart since around 1780, with pairs of woodwind, horns and trumpets, timpani and strings. But the sound was new –

fuller and richer and larger in its harmonic implications, suggesting development over a longer span and calling for grand extensions of the coda to provide suitable closing weight. In the 'Eroica' (No.3, 1803–4) Beethoven created an opening movement as long as an entire Haydn symphony. He also made the symphony not only more imposing but more directly personal. Where Haydn's symphonies share feelings, intimations and jokes with their audience, Beethoven's state, give and address. And where Mozart wrote a symphony when he had to give a concert, Beethoven put on a concert when he had a symphony to impart. Beethoven was surely also the first composer to view his symphonies as a cycle, a set making up a larger composition. Yet each work was different: the elusive Fourth (1806), the intensely dramatic Fifth (1804–8), with its insistent opening image and its drive from the scherzo right through into the finale, the pictorial 'Pastoral' (1807–8), the spacious Seventh (1811–12), the compact and humorous Eighth (1812), and then the Ninth (1817–23), unprecedented in drawing the voices of pan-human celebration into the substance of the symphony.

Most of Beethoven's contemporaries were amazed into silence – or have been silenced by the judgement of history: the outstanding exception is Schubert, who discovered a symphonic mastery all his own in his 'Unfinished' (1822) and 'Great C major' (1825). For those who came after, Beethoven was the single, unavoidable and awesome model, to which they could respond with either a new classicism or a wild Romantic leap: on the one hand Mendelssohn's brilliant 'Italian' Symphony (1833), on the other Berlioz's *Symphonie fantastique* (1830), with its exuberant and macabre images. Mendelssohn's example was a help to Schumann, who in his Fourth went some way towards unifying the four movements by giving them motivic connections and playing them without a break. Liszt placed himself rather in the Berlioz line, following literary programmes (his are Dante and Faust symphonies, where Berlioz's later two took their subjects from Byron and Shakespeare) and including voices, as Berlioz had in his 'dramatic symphony' *Roméo et Juliette*.

Liszt's symphonies came from a moribund period, the 1850s. But then in the next two decades the genre gained new leases of life in the works of Bruckner, Dvořák, Tchaikovsky and, after a long hesitation, Brahms. Brahms's delay is significant. From his point of view there had been no symphony since Beethoven's to approach Beethoven's thoroughness and depth in the unification of contrasts. His First Symphony (1855–76) was both a conscious homage to Beethoven and a

release, a fresh beginning, after which his three further symphonies followed quickly. Dvořák and Bruckner found their own directions with less sense of historical obligation – several directions in Dvořák's case, several approaches to one symphonic ideal in Bruckner's. As for Tchaikovsky, he also looked back to Beethoven, but to the combination of sovereign formal control with psychological detail and scene painting that he found in Beethoven's Fifth and Sixth, and emulated in the last three of his six numbered symphonies, as well as in his programme symphony, *Manfred* (1885).

In the next generation Tchaikovsky's example was crucial to Rachmaninoff, Sibelius and Mahler, all of whom profited from his achievement of an ultimate in the Romantic symphony: the symphony as song, as the quasi-vocal expression of feeling. Mahler's symphonies may not be more subjective, but they certainly provide subjectivity with a larger field of operation. All have durations of an hour or more; many include solo songs or choral movements; and in each case the plan is overtly dramatic, as it had been in Berlioz and Liszt. Mahler's Third Symphony (1895–6) ends with an adagio of love music, while the concluding slow movements of his *Song of the Earth* (1907–9) and Ninth Symphony (1909–10) come even nearer their prototype, Tchaikovsky's Sixth (1893), in that their mood is one of death-haunted farewell. Sibelius, meanwhile, went precisely the opposite way from Mahler, towards objectivity, concision and single-movement form, all potently reached in his Seventh (1924).

By this time the symphony was in crisis. Its claim to be the highest repository of musical thought had been questioned by Strauss's symphony-length tone poems and, still more insidiously, by Debussy's *La Mer* (1903–5) This was in many respects a symphony, following the three-movement form with thematic transformation that Franck had established in his otherwise so different, solid D minor Symphony. But it was not called a symphony. It opened the possibility that the much-venerated symphony might be, after all, just a title, and that works of the greatest virtue and value might now be found elsewhere. The suspicion of the symphony shown by so severe a traditionalist as Schoenberg is also indicative of a problem. At a time when Mahler was writing symphonies for huge forces, Schoenberg produced a 'chamber symphony' for just 15 musicians (1906). That was as near as he came to writing a symphony, an undertaking that became still more unlikely when he moved into atonality, and so left behind the forces of major-minor tonality that had given purpose and amplitude to symphonies from

Haydn to Mahler. Berg produced two atonal symphonies, but both operatic: the second act of *Wozzeck* (1917–22) composed in the form of a symphony, and the suite from *Lulu* (1934). Webern wrote just one, in two short movements for chamber orchestra (1928). Distant from the Second Viennese School but sharing their viewpoint, Bartók preferred to write symphonic works in other forms (Music for Strings, Percussion and Celesta; Concerto for Orchestra).

The symphony was beginning to seem like a thing of the past, and could be created as such: Prokofiev's 'Classical' Symphony (1916–17) was one of the first examples of 20th-century neoclassicism. But neoclassicists found it hard to sustain their chosen period constraints and their irony. Even Stravinsky, who wrote a manifestly non-symphonic *Symphony of Psalms* (1930), was drawn into the rhetorical power and heft of the symphony by the time of his Symphony in Three Movements (1942–5), while Prokofiev moved from 18th-century pastiche through recyclings of stage works to his magniloquent Fifth (1944). Thus neoclassicism became, in the 1930s and 1940s, a new Romanticism, to be encountered also in the symphonies of Honegger and Shostakovich. Changes in the wider world at this time – economic depression, the increasing power of dictatorships, world war – were of course not irrelevant. On artists with direct experience of Stalin's Russia or the Nazi territories they impinged very directly, and the insistent call to seriousness was felt by many as a call to symphonism.

For some time after 1945 the symphony lived on by a hair's breadth. Shostakovich's Tenth (1953) was his last traditional symphony before his puzzling and final Fifteenth (1971); those in the interim were loose programme symphonies (Nos.11–12) and powerful vocal works (Nos.13–14). There were similar interruptions, totally blank, in the symphonic outputs of Rosenberg, Rubbra and Tippett (though not of Schuman and Henze). And perhaps for the symphonies of this period one should look right outside the ostensible genre – to Barraqué's … *au delà du hasard*, for example, with its symphonic feeling for the rush of energy through notes, for the placing of climaxes and for the union of fury and repose. Ustvolskaya – another composer who wrote no symphonies in the sixties – kept the term for works that have very little to do with the symphonic convention, whereas Gerhard's symphonies and Lutosławski's Second are remarkable adventures in using the extremely disrupted and disruptive musical language of the time in a more orthodox symphonic manner. The major symphonies of the late

20th century came from Russian composers, but also again from others, notably Birtwistle, whose orchestral works were symphonic in scope.

As for the postmodern symphony, it found its supreme example at once in Berio's *Sinfonia* (1968–9), where, around a middle movement made of quotations playing while the scherzo from Mahler's Second is unfolding, voices and instruments warble from the present day and from the beginning of time.

Robert Simpson, ed. *The Symphony*, 2 Vols. (1967); Michael Steinberg *The Symphony* (1995)

Pre-Classical, 1732–57: Sammartini (68), Johann Stamitz, C.P.E. Bach

Classical, 1757–1800: Haydn (104), Cannabich, Filtz, Gossec, Beck, Ordonez, Hofmann, Dittersdorf, Wanhal, Carl Stamitz, Mozart (41)

Beethoven-period, 1800–1825: Beethoven (9), Spohr (Nos.1–2), Schubert (7½)

Early Romantic, 1826–57: Spohr (Nos.3–9), Berlioz (3), Schumann (4), Berwald (4), Liszt (2), Bizet

High Romantic, 1865–96: Dvořák (9), Bruckner (9), Borodin (2), Tchaikovsky (7), Brahms (4), Saint-Saëns (No.3), Franck

Late Romantic, 1888–1925: Mahler (9), Chausson, Nielsen (6), Rachmaninoff (Nos.1–2), Dukas, Schmidt (4), Ives (4), Sibelius (7), Stenhammar (2), Ropartz (No.3), Suk, Szymanowski (Nos.1–3), Elgar (2), Vaughan Williams (Nos.1–3)

Post-Romantic, 1916–: Prokofiev (7), Rosenberg (8), Roussel (Nos.2–4), Bax (7), Shostakovich (15), Sessions (8), Webern, Copland (3), Honegger (5), Stravinsky (3), Vaughan Williams (Nos.4–9), Szymanowski (No.4), Koechlin, Harris (16), Hindemith (5), Walton (2), Rachmaninoff (No.3), Barber (2) Rubbra (11), Schuman (10), Lutosławski (4), Carter, Martinů (6), Bernstein (3), Tippett (4), Henze (10), Messiaen, Zimmermann, Dutilleux (2), Gerhard (4), Nørgård (6), Ustvolskaya (5), Wolpe, Silvestrov (6), Knussen (3), Berio, Goehr, Schnittke (8), Davies (8)

Symphony in C. Work by Stravinsky for Beethoven-scale orchestra in four movements, commissioned by the Chicago Symphony to mark its 50th anniversary. The 'in C' is part of the title, at least partly because it is such an odd C – ungrounded, often suspended on the dominant – that this symphony is in. First performance: Chicago, 7 Nov 1940.

Symphony in Three Movements. Work by Stravinsky commissioned by the New York Philharmonic to mark its 100th anniversary. This was Stravinsky's war symphony and, though he did not number them, his fourth, following a student symphony in E♭, the Symphony of Psalms and the Symphony in C. First performance: New York, 24 Jan 1946.

Symphony of a Thousand. Unofficial name for Mahler's Eighth Symphony, current in his time and causing him mixed feelings. The work is for eight vocal soloists, choir, boys' choir and massive orchestra, and did indeed involve more than a thousand at its première.

Symphony of Psalms (*Symphonie de psaumes*). Work by Stravinsky for chorus and orchestra with no violins, violas or clarinets, commissioned by Koussevitzky to mark the 50th anniversary of his Boston Symphony. The psalms, sung in Latin but sounding Orthodox, are *Exaudi orationem meam*, *Expectans expectavi* and *Laudate Dominum*. First performance: Brussels, 13 Dec 1930.

syncopation. A particularly pointed kind of CROSS-RHYTHM, so that accents fall regularly on weak beats, and strong beats are unmarked (i.e. silent). The metrical frame is shifted, which may produce the effect of music running ahead of time, and be exciting. Known in Western music since the Ars Nova, it is particularly associated with ragtime and jazz and with composers touched by those forms, such as Stravinsky.

synthesizer. Electronic instrument that synthesizes sounds from an array of devices for producing, modifying and combining regular waves. The synthesizer thus puts all the utensils of the 1950s electronic music studio into one box, which can be used in the studio to create music on tape, or performed (usually by means of a keyboard) as a concert instrument. The first example, the RCA Synthesizer, was an enormous contrivance donated to the Columbia-Princeton Electronic Music Center and only suitable for creating tape pieces: Babbitt used it in Composition for Synthesizer (1961) and later works. Commercial synthesizers, produced by Robert Moog, Donald Buchla and other makers, became available in the mid-1960s, were popularized by Carlos, and rapidly gained use in studios, rock bands and classical ensembles (for works by Adams, Harvey, etc.). In the 1980s they were largely ousted by more versatile – and increasingly portable – computer technology.

syntonic comma. See COMMA.

syrinx (Gk). Panpipes. See PAN.

system. (1) Set of two or more staves needed to show music that has more than one line. For example, piano music is normally written and printed on systems of two staves, one for each hand. Usually there is a brace at the left edge of each system, and barlines may also link some or all of the staves.

(2) ALGORITHM, in most cases a repetitive element. The term was introduced by British musicians in the early 1970s describing early forms of MINIMALISM.

Szalonek, Witold (b. Czechowice, 2 Mar 1927; d. Berlin, 14 Oct 2001). Polish composer. He studied at the Katowice Conservatory with Boleslaw Woytowicz (1949–56), at Darmstadt and in Paris with Nadia Boulanger (1962–3). After a time back at the conservatory in Katowice (1967–74) he succeeded Blacher as professor at the Academy of the Arts in Berlin. In his music he brought a particular expressive intensity to bear on avant-garde techniques.

Székely, Zoltán (b. Kocs, 8 Dec 1903; d. Banff, Canada, 5 Oct 2001). Hungarian–US violinist. He studied in Budapest with Hubay and gave recitals with Bartók, who wrote a rhapsody and a concerto for him (in both cases No.2). In 1950, with his colleagues in the Hungarian Quartet, he moved to the USA.

Szell, George [Georg] (b. Budapest, 7 Jun 1897; d. Cleveland, 29 Jul 1970). Hungarian–US conductor. He grew up in Vienna, where he studied composition with Foerster and Reger. At 17 he conducted the Berlin Philharmonic in a work of his own and was taken up by Strauss. He held conducting posts in various cities, including Berlin (1924–9) and Prague (1929–37), before leaving for Britain (1937–9) and then the USA. His long period as chief conductor of the Cleveland Orchestra (1946–70) gave him the opportunity to create a front-rank ensemble responsive to his meticulousness and disicpline. He also conducted regularly in Salzburg.

Szene (Ger., pl. *Szenen*). Scene, scena.

Szervánszky, Endre (b. Budatétény, 1 Jan 1911; d. Budapest, 25 Jun 1977). Hungarian composer. He studied as a clarinettist at the academy in Budapest (1922–7), returned for composition studies with Albert Siklós (1931–6), and returned again in 1948 to teach composition. Close to Bartók and Kodály in his earlier works, he began to explore a more modern style in his Six Orchestral Pieces (1959). By his example, and in person, he offered encouragement and support to younger composers at a time when avant-garde music met with official disfavour. One of those composers, Kurtág, expressed gratitude in a memorial (*Officium breve*) quoting from his Serenade for strings (1947–8). Other works include a *Requiem* to words by Pilinszky (1963).

Szeryng, Henryk (b. Warsaw, 22 Sep 1918; d. Kassel, 3 Mar 1988). Polish–Mexican violinist. A supreme virtuoso, he studied with Carl Flesch in Berlin (from 1928) and started his international career in 1933. He gave concerts for anti-Nazi troops during the Second World War and settled in Mexico in 1946. Arthur Rubinstein restored him to world audiences in 1954.

Szigeti, Joseph (b. Budapest, 5 Sep 1892; d. Lucerne, 19 Feb 1973). Hungarian–US violinist. His father and uncle, both professional musicians, gave him his first lessons, and he was then a pupil of Hubay at the Budapest Academy. He made his debut at 10, and from 1907 was largely abroad, playing in Britain (until 1913), teaching in Geneva (1917–24), then performing again internationally, with increasing frequency in the USA. Bartók wrote a rhapsody (No.1) and *Contrasts* for him, and gave a recital with him at the Library of Congress. Other works he introduced included concertos by Harty (1909), Bloch (1938) and Martin (1952). In 1960 he settled in Switzerland and gradually retired, leaving some exemplary recordings – especially those of the Beethoven sonatas with Arrau.

Szőllősy, András (b. Szászváros, Transylvania, 27 Feb 1921). Hungarian composer and scholar. He studied at Budapest University, at the Liszt Academy with Kodály and in Rome with Petrassi. In 1966 he published the standard catalogue of Bartók's compositions.

Szpilman, Władysław (b. Sosnowiec, 5 Dec 1911; d. Warsaw, 6 Jul 2000). Polish pianist and composer, whose memoir of surviving the ghetto in Nazi-occupied Warsaw became the subject of Roman Polanski's film *The Pianist* (2002). He studied in Berlin with Schnabel and Schreker, and worked for Polish radio before and after the war.

Szymanowski, Karol (Maciej) (b. Tymoszówka, Ukraine, 6 Oct 1882; d. Lausanne, 29 Mar 1937). Polish composer, valued especially for the luxuriant and evocative music he produced during and immediately after the First World War.

He was born into the Polish landed gentry of Ukraine and enjoyed a cultured upbringing: his sister Zofia became a poet, whose words he set, and the three other children of the family also made their lives as artists. At 13 he first heard Wagner's music, in Vienna, and was transfixed. He studied privately with Noskowski in Warsaw (1901–4), but

soon became dissatisfied with musical life in what was, at that time, a provincial Russian city. In 1905 he got together with three contemporaries (Fitelberg, Ludomir Różycki and Apolinary Szeluto) under the banner 'Young Poland in Music' to found a music publishing company and a concert series. Performers who became involved included Arthur Rubinstein and Pawel Kochański. Their ideals were nationalist and innovatory, yet Szymanowski's output of this period was still deeply indebted to recent German music (Wagner, Strauss, Reger) – though that did not stop it gaining him international attention.

In 1911–12 he was in Vienna, which bored him as much as Warsaw. But he visited other places that did not: Italy (1909), Sicily (1910), north Africa (1914). These journeys south, to where ancient Mediterranean culture was still alive, were combined with musical discoveries (Debussy's *Pelléas*, Stravinsky's *Firebird* and *Petrushka*) to provide the seeds for a stylistic transformation. He returned to the family home in Tymoszówka immediately before the outbreak of war in the summer of 1914, and sank himself into studies of Italian and Byzantine art, Islam and the ancient Greeks. At the same time he produced a great florescence of music: his Third Symphony, First Violin Concerto, First Quartet, instrumental pieces including the triptychs of *Mythes*, *Métopes* and *Masques*, and songs. Enraptured in mood, rich in harmony and colour, and led most often by airy ornamental melody, these works brought influences from Scriabin and Debussy into a delirious consummation.

There came a sudden stop in 1917, when the Tymoszówska house was destroyed. The family moved to Elisavetgrad, and Szymanowski turned from music to literature. The problems he felt as a homosexual, sensually confident but morally uncertain, he examined first in a novel (of which the manuscript was lost in 1939) and then, returning to composition, in an opera, *King Roger*, continuing his wartime style. In 1919 he returned with his family to Poland, now independent, and while continuing work on *King Roger* he began in the early 1920s writing music more assertively Polish. He made two visits to London and the USA in 1920–21 with Kochański and Rubinstein, but unlike them was determined to make his career at home. With the example of Stravinsky's *Rite* and *Les Noces* in mind, he created evocations of ancient Polish music in the song cycle *Słopiewnie* and the resonant choral-orchestral *Stabat mater* (1925–6). He also rented a house in Zakopane, in the Tatra mountains, whence came his choral ballet *Harnasie* and piano mazurkas.

His last decade was unsettled by professional

frustrations and illness. He had high hopes of transforming music education in his position as head of the Warsaw Conservatory, where he started in 1927, but in 1929 he was obliged to go to Switzerland for almost a year to recover from tuberculosis, and in 1932, blocked by conservatism within the school, he resigned. He completed a few last works in 1932–4, including his Fourth Symphony, with a solo piano part he wrote for himself in order to secure concert engagements and so survive. But then his health worsened again, and he died shortly after settling into a sanatorium in Lausanne.

Jim Samson *The Music of Szymanowski* (1980)

Operas: *Hagith* (Felix Dormann), Op.25, 1912–13, f.p. Warsaw, 1922; KING ROGER, Op.46, 1920–24

Ballets: *Mandragora*, Op.43, 1920; *Harnasie*, Op.55, 1923–31

Orchestral: Symphony No.1, F minor, Op.15, 1906–7; No.2, B♭, Op.19, 1909–10; No.3 'The Song of the Night' (Rumi), Op.27, t/s, ch, orch, 1914–16; No.4 (*Symphonie concertante*), Op.60, pf, orch, 1932; Violin Concerto No.1, Op.35, 1916; No.2, Op.61, 1933; Concert Overture, Op.12, 1904–5; *Prince Potemkin* (incidental music), Op.51, 1925

Orchestral songs: *Love Songs of Hafiz*, Op.26, arr 1914 (from Op.24:1,4–5); *Songs of a Fairytale Princess*, Op.31, arr 1933; *Songs of an Infatuated Muezzin*, Op.42, arr 1934; *Słopiewnie*, Op.46b, arr 1928; etc.

Choral: *Demeter* (Zofia Szymanowska), Op.37b, a, women's ch, orch, 1917, rev 1924; *Stabat mater* (Pol.), op.53, soli, ch, orch, 1925–6; Kurpie Songs, ch, 1928–9; *Veni Creator* (Pol.), Op.57, s, ch, orch, 1930; *Litany to the Virgin Mary* (Pol.), Op.59, s, ch, orch, 1930–33

String quartets: No.1, C, Op.37, 1917; No.2, Op.56, 1927

Violin and piano: Sonata, D minor, Op.9, 1904; Romance, Op.23, 1910; Nocturne and Tarantella, Op.28, 1915; *Mythes*, Op.30, 1915 (*La Fontaine d'Aréthuse, Narcisse, Dryades et Pan*); 3 Paganini Caprices, Op.40, 1918; *La Berceuse d'Aitacho Enia*, Op.52, 1925

Piano: Sonata No.1, C minor, Op.8, 1904; No.2, A, Op.21, 1911; No.3, Op.36, 1917; 4 Etudes, Op.4, 1902; *Métopes*, Op.29, 1915 (*L'Ile des sirens, Calypso, Nausicaa*); 12 Etudes, Op.33, 1916; *Masques*, Op.34, 1916 (*Shéhérazade, Tantris le bouffon, Sérénade de Don Juan*); etc.

Songs: *Love Songs of Hafiz* (Bethge), Op.24, 1911; *Songs of a Fairytale Princess* (Szymanowska), Op.31, 1915; 3 Songs (Dymitr Davidov), Op.32, 1915; 4 Songs (Tagore), Op.41, 1918; *Songs of an Infatuated Muezzin* (Jarosław Iwaszkiewicz), Op.42, 1918; *Słopiewnie* (Julian Tuwim), 1921; 4 Songs (Joyce), Op.54, 1926; etc.

t. Abbreviation for tenor.

Tabarro, Il. See *Il* TRITTICO.

tabla. Small drum pair. Several kinds are distributed throughout the Islamic world and beyond, the most familiar in the West being the Indian sort, which the seated player holds in the lap and pats with fingers. This instrument has been used by Berio (*Circles*) and others.

tablature. Form of notation other than the conventional one on staves. Tablatures often come closer than staff notation to the mechanics of the instrument, showing how to place the fingers on the strings or, in the case of wind instruments, holes. Often chords will be represented by letters or figures, and durations may be indicated by separate symbols. Specific forms of tablature have been in use for keyboard instruments (in Germany and Spain from the early 14th century to the mid 18th) and the lute (universally). FIGURED BASS notation is a form of tablature, as is the notation of guitar music with chord symbols.

table (Fr.). BELLY.

tablebook. Variety of PARTBOOK with the parts facing in different directions, so that they could be read by performers around a table. The tablebook was a common form of publication for English lute airs and ensemble pieces.

table music. See TAFELMUSIK.

tabor. Small medieval drum, as played by a musician on pipe and tabor.

Tábor. See MA VLAST.

tacet (Lat., is silent). Instruction to keep silence.

tactus (Lat., beat). Cycle of downbeat and upbeat in Renaissance music theory.

Taddei, Giuseppe (b. Genoa, 26 Jun 1916). Italian baritone, one of the leading singers of the 1950s–60s, especially in Verdi. He studied in Rome, made his debut there in 1936 and came to international prominence soon after the war. His warm, expressive singing made him a valued presence in recordings.

Tafelmusik (Ger., table music). Music performed at mealtimes, a practice going back to the Middle Ages (if not before) and made a regular part of court life in the late Renaissance and Baroque periods. Examples include Lalande's *Musique pour les soupers du roi* and Telemann's three volumes of *Musique de table*, each a set of several works.

Taffanel, (Claude) Paul (b. Bordeaux, 16 Sep 1844; d. Paris, 22 Nov 1908). French flautist, the father of the French school. A pupil of Louis Dorus, he played from 1864 in the Paris Opera orchestra and succeeded to his teacher's position at the Conservatoire in 1893.

tail. See STEM.

taille. French Renaissance–Baroque term for an instrument, voice or part of tenor range. The standard five-part string ensemble of the

Lully–Rameau period had a *haute-taille*, a *taille* and a *basse-taille* between a *dessus* and a *basse-contre*.

Tailleferre, (Marcelle) Germaine (b. Parc-St-Maur, near Paris, 19 Apr 1892; d. Paris, 7 Nov 1983). French composer. Her fellow students at the Conservatoire included Honegger, Milhaud and Auric, and with them she became a member of Les Six. Later her graceful individuality emerged in a variety of piano and chamber works, songs, choral items and stage pieces. 'A Marie Laurencin for the ear' Cocteau called her, for the fluent, light touch she shared with that painter contemporary.

tailpiece. The bottom part of a string instrument, to which the strings are attached. Generally it is made of ebony.

Takács Quartet. Ensemble of Hungarian origin, at the international forefront in the 1980s. Founded by students of Mihály at the Liszt Academy, it won the Evian Competition (1977) and moved to the USA in 1983. Its original leader was Gábor Takács-Nagy, who left in 1993 to return to Hungary, where he has maintained a career as a chamber musician, forming a Takács Piano Trio.

Takemitsu, Tōru (b. Tokyo, 8 Oct 1930; d. Tokyo, 20 Feb 1996). Japanese composer, master of the floating sound. He began occasional lessons with Yasuji Kiyose in 1948, but attended no conservatory and largely felt his own way forward. In 1950–52 he was a member of a group headed by Kiyose, and a piano piece of his (revised as *Litany*) was played at one of their concerts. Its dissonance, unusual in Japanese music at the time, made an impression on other young composers, including Jōji Yuasa, with whom he formed a new group, Experimental Workshop. For their concerts he composed his first larger score, the Chamber Concerto (1955); his second, *Requiem* for strings (1957), gained praise from Stravinsky and was widely performed. Increasingly in contact with Western contemporaries, he was particularly attracted to those whose music had approached the oriental, especially Boulez and Cage. Their work helped stimulate his most freely imaginative period, when he ventured into electronic music and produced aleatory scores (e.g. the original version of *Arc*, whose six movements may be played in any order). Meanwhile, in *Ring*, *Sacrifice* and *Valeria*, he worked with combinations that were unusual in Western music but perfectly normal if considered as equivalents of Japanese groupings (flute for shakuhachi, lute for biwa, guitar for koto, accordion for shō).

Soon he was writing for Japanese instruments directly, notably in *November Steps* (1967), which was commissioned by the New York Philharmonic, enjoyed worldwide success and marked the start of his mature career as a creator of evocative drifts of sound. The sharp intensity and individuality expressed in *Winter* (1971) tended to become submerged later in gorgeous homages to Messiaen and Debussy, but each score is superbly accomplished. Many refer to natural phenomena (trees, stars, the sea); many, too, have soloists as lyrical central figures in their landscapes.

Tōru Takemitsu *Confronting Silence* (1995); Peter Burt *The Music of Tōru Takemitsu* (2001)

Full orchestral: *Coral Island*, s, orch, 1962; *Arc*, pf, orch, 1963–6, rev 1976; *Green*, 1967; *November Steps*, shakuhachi, biwa, orch, 1967; *Asterism*, pf, orch, 1968; *Crossing*, pf, vib, gtr, hp, v, orch, 1970; *Cassiopeia*, perc, orch, 1971; *Winter*, 1971; *Autumn*, shakuhachi, biwa, orch, 1973; *Gitimalya*, mar, orch, 1974; *Quatrain*, cl, vn, vc, pf, orch, 1975; *A Flock Descends into the Pentagonal Garden*, 1977; *Far Calls, Coming, Far!*, vn, orch, 1980; *riverrun*, pf, orch, 1984; *Vers, l'arc-en-ciel, Palma*, gtr, ob d'amore, orch, 1984; *Gémeaux*, ob, trbn, 2 orchs, 1971–86; *From Me Flows What You Call Time*, 5 perc, orch, 1990; *My Way of Life* (Ryuichi Tamura), bar, ch, orch, 1990; *Fantasma/Cantos*, cl, orch, 1991; *Spectral Canticle*, vn, gtr, orch, 1995; etc.

Chamber orchestral: Chamber Concerto, 12 wind, 1955; *Requiem*, str, 1957; *Dorian Horizon*, str, 1966; *Eucalypts I*, fl, ob, hp, str, 1970; *In an Autumn Garden*, gagaku ens, 1973–9; *Rain Coming*, 1982; *Nostalghia*, vn, str, 1987; *Tree Line*, 1988; *Archipelago S*, chbr orch, 1993; etc.

Ensemble: *Le Son calligraphié I–III*, str octet, 1958–60; *Landscape*, str qt, 1960; *Ring*, fl, gtr, lute, 1961; *Sacrifice*, a fl, lute, vib, 1962; *Valeria*, 2 fl, 2 acdn, gtr, vn, vc, 1965; *Stanza I*, v, pf, gtr, hp, vib, 1969; *Eucalypts II*, fl, ob, hp, 1971; *Waves*, cl, hn, 2 trbn, perc, 1976; *Quatrain II*, cl, vn, vc, pf, 1977; *Waterways*, 8 insts, 1978; *A Way a Lone*, str qt, 1981; *Rain Tree*, 3 perc, 1981; *Between Tides*, pf trio, 1993; etc.

Duo or solo: *Distance de fée*, vn, pf, 1951, rev 1989; *Masque I–III*, 2 fl, 1959–60; *Eclipse*, shakuhachi, biwa, 1966; *Cross Talk*, 2 acdn, tape, 1968; *Season*, perc, 1970; *Munari by Munari*, perc, 1971; *Stanza II*, hp, tape, 1971; *Voice*, fl, 1971; *Toward the Sea*, a fl, gtr, 1981; *From Far Beyond Chrysanthemums and November Fog*, vn, pf, 1983; *Rocking Mirror Daybreak*, 2 vn, 1983; *Paths*, tpt, 1994; *Air*, fl, 1995; etc.

Piano: *Litany*, 1950, rev 1990; *At the Circus*, 1952; *Uninterrupted Rest I–III*, 1952–9; *Piano Distance*, 1961; *Corona*, 1962; *Crossing*, 1962; *For Away*, 1973; *Les Yeux clos*, 1979; *Rain Tree Sketch*, 1982; *Les Yeux clos II*, 1988; *Rain Tree Sketch II*, 1990

Tape: *Vocalism A.I.*, 1956; *Sky, Horse and Death*, 1958; *Water Music*, 1960; etc.

Other works: choral pieces, film scores, theatre music

Takt (Ger., pl. *Takte*). Bar, beat or tempo. Hence *Taktstock* (baton).

talea (Lat., cutting). 14th-century term for a sequence of rhythmic values repeated in the tenor of an motet or other polyphonic composition showing ISORHYTHM.

Talens lyriques, Les. Baroque ensemble founded in 1991 by the harpsichordist Christophe Rousset, and taking its name from Rameau's *Les Fêtes d'Hébé*.

Tale of Tsar Saltan, The (*Skazka o Tsare Saltane*). Opera by Rimsky-Korsakov to a libretto by Vladimir Belsky after Pushkin, titled in full *The Tale of Tsar Saltan, of his Son the Famous and Mighty Hero Gvidon Saltanovich and of the Beautiful Swan Princess*. After that, a synopsis is redundant: the piece is a fairytale. The celebrated Flight of the Bumblebee is made by Gvidon, transformed by the swan princess, on a magic island, so that he can rejoin his father. First performance: Moscow, 3 Nov 1900.

Tales from the Vienna Woods (*Geschichten aus dem Wienerwald*). Waltz by Johann Strauss II.

Tales of Hoffmann, The. See *Les* CONTES D'HOFFMANN.

Talich, Václav (b. Kroměříž, 28 May 1883; d. Beroun, 16 Mar 1961). Czech conductor, remarkable for the lean drive and tonal beauty of his performances. He studied at the Prague Conservatory (1897–1903) and began his career as a violinist in the Berlin Philharmonic under Nikisch. After taking various kinds of musical employment and studying further he was chief conductor of the Czech Philharmonic (1919–41), with whom he appeared and recorded again after the Second World War, though his health now was poor.

Tallis, Thomas (b. c.1505; d. Greenwich, 20/23 Nov 1585). English composer, one of the supreme masters of late Renaissance polyphony. Little is known of his life. He enters recorded history as an organist at a Dover monastery in 1532, and five years later he was in London, perhaps already associated with the Chapel Royal. Certainly he was a member by 1545, and he remained so until his death. He therefore lived through the early Protestantism of Henry VIII and Edward VI, the revived Catholicism of Mary I (1553–8) and the Protestant re-establishment of Elizabeth I.

Such a career involved changes of tack. For example, his music for Mary has a triumphal splendour quite different from the quiet, largely chordal style he adopted as one of the first composers to set texts from the 1547 Anglican prayer book. Regular liturgical music under Elizabeth was limited to the simple. Some psalm tunes he wrote in 1567 include 'Tallis's Canon' (later given the words 'Glory to Thee, my God, this Night') and the melody Vaughan Williams took for his Tallis Fantasia. But the monopoly of music printing that Elizabeth granted him and Byrd in 1575 allowed them to publish a collection of Latin motets. His Elizabethan works also include the extraordinary 40-part motet *Spem in alium*, the Lamentations (a matchless fusion of English modal plangency with continental imitative techniques), and two elaborations of the *Felix namque* plainsong for organ, pieces that perhaps record his virtuosity as a performer. Through all the vicissitudes of a long life he kept in his music an essential serenity, slightly melancholic, and a grace of ingenuity concealed – qualities that permanently marked English church music.

He was married for more than 40 years, apparently without children. To quote from his epitaph: 'As he did lyve, so also did he dy, In myld and quyet Sort (O! happy Man).'

Paul Doe *Tallis* (1968, ²1976)

?before 1547 (Henry VIII): *Salve intemerata Virgo* a 5; Mass a 4; *Sancte Deus, sancte fortis* a 4; *Audivi vocem* a 4

?1547–53 (Edward VI): Short Service a 4; *Hear the voice and prayer* a 4; *I call and cry to Thee* a 5; *If ye love me* a 4; *Remember not* a 4

?1553–8 (Mary I): *Gaude gloriosa Dei mater* a 6; Mass *Puer natus est nobis* a 7

?1553–85 (Elizabeth I): CANTIONES, QUAE AB ARGUMENTO SACRAE VOCANTUR (*Absterge Domine* a 5; *Derelinquat impius* a 5; *In jejunio et fletu* a 5; *In manus tuas* a 5; *O nata lux de lumine* a 5; *O sacrum convivium* a 5; *Salvator mundi* a 5; *Te lucis ante terminum* a 5; etc.); Lamentations a 5; *Loquebantur variis linguis* a 7; *Laudate Dominum* a 5; SPEM IN ALIUM NUNQUAM HABUI a 40
Instrumental: 2 In Nomines a 4, keyboard pieces

Tallis Scholars. British group formed by Peter Phillips in 1973 to perform Renaissance polyphony.

Talma, Louise (b. Arcachon, 31 Oct 1906; d. Yaddo, NY, 13 Aug 1996). French–US composer. Brought to New York by her widowed mother in 1914, she studied in the city and spent her teaching career at Hunter College (1928–79). During the period 1928–39 she visited Fontainebleau regularly, to study with Boulanger and later to teach. Boulanger's influence was crucial, and the later impact of serialism did not deeply disturb her style. She wrote mostly songs, choral music and piano works, but also some orchestral pieces and an opera (*The Alcestiad*, 1955–8, to a libretto by Thornton Wilder).

talon (Fr.). End of the bow known in Eng. as frog, heel or nut, hence *au talon* (play with the heel of the bow).

tambour (Fr.). Drum, as in *tambour militaire* (side drum), *tambour de Basque* (tambourine), etc.

tambourin. Lively 18th-century French dance in duple time, imitating a pipe and tabor. There are infectious examples in Rameau's operas.

tambourine. Instrument comprising a wooden ring with a drumskin on one side and jingles set in holes around the edge. Played by patting, shaking or rubbing, it was known in ancient Mesopotamia and Egypt, and spread around the world. The first composers to include it in the orchestra were Gluck (*Echo et Narcisse*, 1779) and Mozart (German Dances, K.571, 1787), and it became a standard member of the percussion department after Rimsky-Korsakov and Tchaikovsky.

Tamburini, Antonio (b. Faenza, 28 Mar 1800; d. Nice, 8 Nov 1876). Italian baritone, renowned for his sweet, strong voice going down into bass territory. He began his career in Cento (1818) and was an international star from the 1820s until his retirement in 1855, creating roles in operas by Bellini (*Il pirata, I puritani*) and Donizetti (*Marino Faliero, Don Pasquale*).

tamburo (It., pl. *tamburi*). Drum, as in *tamburo basco* (tambourine), *tamburo grosso* (bass drum), etc.

Tamerlano (Tamburlaine). Opera by Handel to a libretto by Haym of Agostino Piovene's libretto. The extravagant bad behaviour of the conqueror Tamburlaine (alto castrato) creates the circumstances for an elaborate chain of misdirections, but finally the noble couple Asteria (soprano) and Andronicus (alto castrato) are united, Tamburlaine meets his match in Irene (contralto), and the Turkish emperor, Bajazet (tenor), is the only victim, self-poisoned. First performance: London, 31 Oct 1724.

tampon. Double-headed drumstick.

tam tam. Large gong up to 3 feet (1m) across, sometimes to 5 feet (1·5m), with a shallow rim, making a crashing sound. Imported from China, the instrument first appears in a wind-band piece from the French Revolution, Gossec's *Marche lugubre* (1790). It was then used intermittently (notably in Tchaikovsky's 'Pathétique' Symphony) before becoming a standard part of the orchestra in the 20th century.

Tanada, Fuminori (b. Okayama, 12 Jan 1961). Japanese composer. He trained in Tokyo and with Ballif, Jolas, Paul Méfano and Nigg in Paris (1984–7), where he has remained as a composer and pianist. His works, mostly on a chamber scale, include a fine Flute Quartet (2001).

Tancredi (Tancred). Opera by Rossini to a libretto by Gaetano Rossi after Voltaire's play. Set in Sicily in 1005, amid strife between Christians and Arabs, the opera concerns the faithful love of Amenaide (soprano) for Tancred (contralto), though through most of the piece she is unable to exonerate herself from suspicions of treachery. The work ends happily with the lovers united (original version) or unhappily with them dying together (Ferrara revision, closer to Voltaire). Only the hero's name is a link with Tasso and thereby with Monteverdi's *Il combattimento di Tancredi e Clorinda*. First performance: Venice, 6 Feb 1813; rev Ferrara, Mar 1813.

Tan Dun (b. Si Mao, Hunan, 18 Aug 1957). Chinese–US composer. Sent to the countryside during the Cultural Revolution (1966–76), he was, from 1978, one of the first students at the reopened Beijing Conservatory and rapidly made a stir with his innovatory imagination. In 1986 he moved to New York, at first to study at Columbia. His works include operas (*Marco Polo*, f.p. Munich, 1996), experimental pieces, orchestral music and film scores.

Taneyev, Sergey (Ivanovich) (b. Vladimir, 25 Nov 1856; d. Dyudkovo, near Zvenigorod, 19 Jun 1915). Russian composer, a follower of Tchaikovsky but with an unusual interest in Renaissance and Bachian counterpoint. Born into the upper bourgeoisie, he studied at the Moscow Conservatory (1866–75), notably with Tchaikovsky. In 1878 he began teaching at the conservatory, from which he resigned in 1905 in protest at the disciplining of students who had sympathized with the revolutionary movement. He died of pneumonia, which he contracted after attending the funeral of his pupil Scriabin, leaving an opera (*The Oresteia*, f.p. St Petersburg, 1895), four symphonies (No.4, C minor, Op.12, 1896–8) and much chamber music. His uncle Aleksandr

Sergeyevich (1850–1918) was a civil servant who wrote operas, three symphonies and salon music.

tangent. The brass tip of a clavichord key that touches the string to make a sound.

Tanglewood. Estate in southwest Massachusetts where summer concerts and courses have been given annually since 1940 with the participation of the Boston Symphony.

tango. Sultry Argentinian dance, developed in the early 20th century from the habanera and other Latin American forms, in syncopated 2/4 time. It was popular in Europe before the First World War, and enjoyed an international revival in the late 20th century, centred on the work of Piazzolla. More classically inclined composers who wrote tangos include Stravinsky.

Tannhäuser. Opera by Wagner, titled in full *Tannhaüser und der Sängerkrieg auf Wartburg* (Tannhäuser and the Singing Contest on the Wartburg), to his own libretto after earlier Romantic treatments of real events and medieval legends. The historical Tannhäuser (*c*.1205–70) was a MINNESINGER who went on crusade. Wagner's hero (tenor) is a man torn between the voluptuous, represented by Venus (soprano), and the chaste, in the person of Elisabeth (soprano), the former quality being extended and intensified in the revised version. Having revealed, at the Wartburg contest, his experience of Venus's allures, he is obliged to go on pilgrimage, from which he returns to die, his soul saved by the intercession of the already deceased Elisabeth. The imposing overture contrasts fizzing exuberance with the solemn melody of the Pilgrims' Chorus; also sometimes heard as orchestral items are the Venusberg Music (Bacchanal) and the Entrance of the Guests (for the Act 2 song contest). Other numbers include Elisabeth's exuberant greeting song 'Dich, teure Halle' and her Prayer, the Hymn to the Evening Star sung by Tannhäuser's companion Wolfram (baritone) and Tannhäuser's Rome Narration. First performance: Dresden, 19 Oct 1845 (Dresden version); rev Paris Opera, 13 Mar 1861 (Paris version, rev Vienna, 22 Nov 1875).

Tansman, Alexandre [Aleksander] (b. Łódź, 12 Jun 1897; d. Paris, 15 Nov 1986). Polish–French composer. He studied in his home town and with Piotr Rytel in Warsaw before moving to Paris in 1919. There he married, and there he remained, apart from a period in California during the Second World War, close to his idol Stravinsky – though his allegiance to Parisian neoclassicism

was modified by his Polish Jewish heritage. His works include operas and ballets, nine symphonies, concertos, the oratorio *Isaïe, le prophète* (1951), a *Stèle* in memory of Stravinsky for voice and ensemble (1972), eight quartets and guitar pieces.

tanto (It., so much). Found in such markings as *allegro ma non tanto*, implying some restraint on the speed.

Tantum ergo. Final section of the hymn *Pange lingua*, used separately at the evening office of Benediction, and set by Schubert, etc.

Tanz (Ger., pl. *Tänze*). Dance.

Tapiola. Symphonic poem by Sibelius (1926), his last big work, devoted to Tapio, god of the Finnish forests. First performance: New York, 26 Dec 1926.

tarantella. Lively Italian folkdance in 6/8 named after the city of Taranto in Apulia. The tarantula gets its name from the same place: hence the legend (medically unfounded) that the dance would cure the spider's bite. There are piano tarantellas by Chopin and Liszt, and orchestral ones by Mendelssohn (finale of the 'Italian' Symphony, combining tarantella and saltarello themes) and Stravinsky (*Pulcinella*).

Taras Bulba. Orchestral rhapsody by Janáček after Gogol's story of the Cossack leader who loses two sons to his quest for military glory and honour. The movements are: *The Death of Andri, The Death of Ostap, Prophecy and Death of Taras Bulba*. First performance: Brno, 9 Oct 1921.

tardo (It., slow). Tempo marking found in music from Monteverdi to Schütz, thereafter extinct, except in terms for slowing: *tardando* and the more common *ritardando*.

Tarnopolski, Vladimir [Tarnopolsky, Vladimir Grigoryevich] (b. Dnepropetrovsk, 30 Apr 1955). Russian composer, of polystylistic music that may be searching, playful, grotesque or all three. He studied with Nikolay Sidelnikov, Denisov and Yuri Kholopov at the Moscow Conservatory (1973–8), where he was appointed professor in 1992. Among his works are the cantata *Brooklyn Bridge* (1988), *Kassandra* for ensemble (1991) and the opera *Wenn die Zeit über die Ufer tritt* (f.p. Munich, 1999).

tárogató. Hungarian clarinet, used by Mahler in Budapest for the shepherd's piping in Act 3 of *Tristan*, and after him by Richter in Bayreuth.

Tárrega, Francisco (b. Villareal, Castellón, 21 Nov 1852; d. Barcelona, 15 Dec 1909). Spanish guitarist-composer, who did much to promote the instrument through his concert tours, compositions and arrangements (of Beethoven, Chopin, his friends Albéniz and Granados, etc.). He studied guitar and piano as a child, was trained at the Madrid Conservatory and made his Paris and London debuts in 1880.

Tartini, Giuseppe (b. Pirano, Istria, 8 Apr 1692; d. Padua, 26 Feb 1770). Italian violinist-composer. Intended for the Church, he escaped in his teens to music and marriage. In his 20s he heard Veracini and retired for some years to perfect his playing; he also seems to have discarded his wife at this point. From 1721 he was employed at St Anthony's Basilica in Padua, attracting many pupils. He composed numerous sonatas and concertos for his instrument, including the 'DEVIL'S TRILL' Sonata, as well as a D major concerto often appropriated by trumpeters, but probably not including one of the works published as his in his lifetime: *L'arte del arco*, a giant sequence of variations on a Corelli gavotte. Also a theorist, he provided the first description of a COMBINATION TONE.

Tasso, Torquato (b. Sorrento, 11 Mar 1544; d. Rome, 25 Apr 1595). Italian poet. Personally acquainted with Wert and other composers, he wrote verse for madrigals. Later his epic *Gerusalemme liberata* was delved into by opera composers from Monteverdi (*Il* COMBATTI-MENTO DI TANCREDI E CLORINDA) to Dvořák (ARMIDA), his pastoral play *Aminta* both influenced an early librettist (Rinuccini) and provided material for a ballet classic (*Sylvia*), and his life story was treated by Goethe in a play for which Liszt wrote an overture (f.p. Weimar, 28 Aug 1849) he made into his symphonic poem, *Tasso: lamento e trionfo*.

Taste (Ger., pl. *Tasten*). Key on a keyboard, hence *Tasteninstrument* (keyboard instrument).

tastiera (It.). Keyboard, fingerboard. See TASTO.

tasto (It., pl. *tasti*). Key on a keyboard or fingerboard on a bowed string instrument. The direction *sul tasto* (or *sulla tastiera*) indicates playing over or near the fingerboard, producing a fluting tone.

Tauber, Richard (b. Linz, 16 May 1891; d. London, 8 Jan 1948). Austrian–British tenor, son of an actor-manager. He made his debut at 11 as Tamino in *Die Zauberflöte* at his father's theatre in Chemnitz and was soon singing in Dresden,

Berlin, Munich and Salzburg. In the mid 1920s he turned more to operetta and to recording, his sweet voice earning him a large following.

Tausig, Carl (b. Warsaw, 4 Nov 1841; d. Leipzig, 17 Jul 1871). Polish pianist. He studied with his father and, from the age of 14, with Liszt, who said he had 'fingers of steel'. One of the great virtuosos of his time, playing everything from Scarlatti (in his own versions) to Liszt, he died of typhoid.

Tavener, John (Kenneth) (b. London, 28 Jan 1944). British composer, knighted in 2000. Noted especially for solemn religious works, he studied at the RAM (1961–5) and scored an early success when his cantata *The Whale*, telling the story of Jonah, was performed at the London Sinfonietta's first concert in 1968. This and other early works achieved a distinctive fusion of hieratic late Stravinsky with a tonal sweetness and childlike simplicity, and won the attention of the Beatles, who put out two records of his music. Subsequently he encountered difficulties both personal (a failed marriage) and creative, difficulties mitigated when he joined the Russian Orthodox Church in 1977 and thoroughly resolved a few years later when he found a spiritual and artistic guide in Mother Thekla, a Russian–British nun. Nearly all his many subsequent concert works, liturgical pieces and operas have expressed Orthodox spirituality and used Orthodox modes, albeit with a personal warmth and spaciousness. Widely regarded as his masterpiece, *The Veil of the Temple* is an eight-hour ceremony of chants spiralling towards the heavenly.

John Tavener, ed. Brian Keeble *The Music of Silence* (1999)

Large works: *The Whale*, mez, b, speaker, ch, orch, 1966; *Ultimos ritos*, soli, ch, orch, tape, 1972; *Akhmatova: Requiem*, s, b, orch, 1980; *Ikon of Light*, ch, str trio, 1984; *Akathist of Thanksgiving*, soli, ch, ens, 1987; *The Protecting Veil*, vc, str, 1988; *Resurrection*, soli, ch, ens, 1989; *We shall see Him as He is*, soli, ch, orch, 1992; *The Apocalypse*, soli, ch, orch, 1993; *Fall and Resurrection*, s, ct, b, ch, orch, 1997; *Total Eclipse*, sax, treble, t, ct, orch, 1999; *Ikon of Eros*, vn, s, ch, orch, 2000; *Lamentations and Praises*, ch, ens, 2000; *Lament for Jerusalem*, s, ct, ch, orch, 2002; *The Veil of the Temple*, s, ch, ens, 2002; *Supernatural Songs* (Yeats), ct, str, perc, 2003; etc.

Smaller choral works: *Funeral Ikos*, 1981; *The Lamb* (Blake), 1982; *Hymn to the Mother of God*, 1985; *Hymn for the Dormition of the Mother of God*, 1985; *Magnificat* and *Nunc dimittis*, 1986; *God is with us*, 1987; *The Tyger* (Blake), 1987; *Today the Virgin*, 1989; *Annunciation*, 1992; *Song for Athene*, 1993; *As one who has slept*, 1996; *Butterfly Dreams*, 2002; etc.

Other works: chamber music, songs, piano pieces

Taverner. Opera by Davies to his own libretto. Based on the myth of the 16th-century composer's renunciation of music, the piece contrasts fanaticism with faith in the persons of Taverner (tenor) and the White Abbot (baritone). First performance: London, 12 Jul 1972.

Taverner, John (b. Lincs., c.1490; d. Boston, Lincs., 18 Oct 1545). English composer, outstanding representative of the flamboyant local style of polyphony at its pre-Reformation climax. There are no records of him before 1524–5, when he was in the choir of the collegiate church at Tattershall in Lincolnshire. He was then instructor of the choristers at Cardinal College, Oxford (1526–30; the college was later refounded as Christ Church), before returning to Lincolnshire to join the choir at St Botolph's in Boston. By 1537 he had retired, apparently because he could afford to do so. That his silence was an act of Protestant repentance appears to be a myth, emanating from Foxe's *Book of Martyrs*, though it provided Davies with material for an opera.

His three six-part masses are imposing and glorious, with long-spanning melodies, an effortless handling of large proportions, variety of texture and high contrapuntal expertise; each is based on a plainsong cantus firmus. Rather similar in style are his three *Magnificat* settings. But there are other works, such as the *Western Wind* and *Mean* masses, that handle the text in a more syllabic and more chordal manner, and that may be later in date. A section from the *Gloria Tibi Trinitas* mass gave rise to the IN NOMINE tradition.

Colin Hand *John Taverner* (1978)

Masses: *Corona spinea* a 6; *Gloria Tibi Trinitas* a 6;
  Mater Christi a 5; *Mean* a 5; *O Michael* a 6;
  Plainsong a 4; *Small Devotion* a 5; *Western Wind*
  a 4
Other works: *Dum transisset sabbatum* a 5;
  Magnificat settings, votive antiphons, etc.

Taylor, (Joseph) Deems (b. New York, 22 Dec 1885; d. New York, 3 Jul 1966). US composer and popularizer. After studies at New York University followed by further musical training and various jobs in publishing and journalism, he worked as a critic in the 1920s and as a broadcaster from 1931 onwards. Meanwhile he had great success as a composer: his Met performances (14 for *The King's Henchman* in 1927–9 and 16 for *Peter Ibbetson* in 1931–5) set a record for US composers that still stands. He was also the presenter in the Disney film *Fantasia*.

Tchaikovsky [Chaykovsky], **Petr (Ilyich)** (b. Kamsko-Votkinsk, Vyatka governorate, 7 May 1840; d. St Petersburg, 6 Nov 1893). Russian composer. Of all the great composers, he perhaps commands the widest affection. That must be due partly to his open self-expression, and in particular to his willingness to present himself not as heroic, like other Romantics, but as vulnerable. Yet though many of his works reveal a person beset by the problems of existence, many realize ideal worlds – the Mediterranean, the 18th century, the ballet stage – with consummate charm and supreme technique.

He was the second of six children in the family of a mining engineer-manager and enjoyed a comfortable early childhood, learning the piano and French. Family ties remained strong, and in adulthood he was to be specially close to three of his younger siblings: Alexandra, and the twins Modest and Anatoly. He was also an emotionally fragile boy, keenly aware that a spell had been broken when he was sent to board at the School of Jurisprudence in St Petersburg in September 1850. The death of his mother, when he was just 14, was another blow. Music helped. Outside school he had some piano and singing lessons, though when he graduated in May 1859 to take a civil service post he was no more than a gifted amateur.

He was determined to become more. In 1861 he began lessons with Nikolay Zaremba, and with Anton Rubinstein's encouragement he enrolled full time at the new St Petersburg Conservatory in 1863, relieved to be devoting himself to music at last. He produced his first important work, the overture *The Storm*, and began making his mark within the small world of Russian music, to the extent that he was invited by Nikolay Rubinstein, Anton's brother, to teach at what was soon to become the Moscow Conservatory. Starting there right after his graduation in January 1866, he lived in Nikolay's home and worked on his First Symphony under guidance from both Rubinsteins: soliciting help from elder colleagues was not unusual in Russian culture, but with him it was also a sign of insecurity. He then moved on to his first opera, *The Voyevoda*, which was performed at the Bolshoy in February 1869 but failed to satisfy the critics, the public or its restless composer, who reused some of the material in a new opera, *The Oprichnik*.

Meanwhile, late in 1867, he had met Balakirev, who was in Moscow for Berlioz's concerts and already the leader of a circle of nationalist composers in St Petersburg, the MIGHTY HANDFUL. Tchaikovsky rapidly added Balakirev to his bench of mentors, along with the Rubinsteins, and Balakirev, whether by luck or intuition, steered him towards the central dramatic subject of his creative life: tragic love. To Balakirev's programme he composed the fantasy overture *Romeo and Juliet* (autumn 1869), his first triumph in creating music that is highly charged emotionally and at the same time finely balanced in form and execution. The ideas are at once sharply expressive and full of musical promise, and what they promise is in accord with the programme. Most particularly, the love music, rapturous, foreshadows catastrophe right from the start and carries the music forward naturally into turbulence and conflict. Soon afterwards he produced his first volume of songs, including 'None but the lonely heart', which is typical of his song output in its sentimental softness but unique in its melodic appeal.

While still close to Balakirev he composed a symphony on folktunes (No.2), an opera in one of the Balakirev-approved genres, that of magical fantasy Russian-style (*Vakula the Smith*), and incidental music in the same vein for *The Snow Maiden*. But his adherence to Balakirev's nationalist aesthetic was never absolute. During this period (1872–4) he also wrote more parlour songs and the second of his three string quartets, works of a classicizing tendency. In all this music there was little of the impassioned lyricism – the orchestral or instrumental song – he had discovered in *Romeo and Juliet*. That came in his First Piano Concerto (winter 1874–5), the epitome of the concerto as the drama of the Romantic individual, but a work initially deemed unplayable by Nikolay Rubinstein. Tchaikovsky accordingly passed it to Hans von Bülow, who gave the first performance in Boston in October 1875.

By that time the composer had completed his Third Symphony and was at work on his first ballet score, *Swan Lake*. The symphony owes its nickname of 'Polish' not to folk material but to its *Tempo di polacca* finale, the musical influences on it coming rather from Schumann and Mendelssohn. While working on the ballet, which he completed in April 1876, he also produced his third quartet, began *Les Saisons* (an attractive calendar of piano pieces, one for each month) and visited Paris, where he was bowled over by Bizet's *Carmen*. He made another journey west in August 1876 to attend the première in Bayreuth of Wagner's *Ring*, which he enjoyed less. *Carmen*, with its compelling expression of tragic fate, was the piece he wanted to emulate, and in his symphonic fantasia *Francesca da Rimini* (autumn 1876) he initiated an engagement with destiny and passion that grew still more intense the next year, when he started work simultaneously on his Fourth Symphony and opera *Eugene Onegin*.

At this point his personal life became closely and even uncannily intertwined with what was on his work table. *Eugene Onegin* is the story of a man who rejects a younger woman's protestation of love and is destroyed by his pride. Just as Tchaikovsky was setting to work on his treatment, he found himself in the same situation, receiving a love letter from a conservatory student, Antonina Milyukova. By now he was 37 and well settled into a bachelor existence. He had enjoyed a brief love affair with a French singer, Désirée Artôt, in 1868, but otherwise his experience seems to have been entirely homosexual and therefore discreet. Such a life involved a certain degree of risk, and probably also some guilt, and he may have thought that marriage would free him from both, while also settling the minds of his family (excepting his brother Modest, whose inclinations were also homosexual). He therefore married Antonina, on 18 July 1877, and almost immediately regretted it. After only a few days with her in Moscow, he departed alone for Kamenka, his sister's family's estate and his regular summer home. In late September he returned to Moscow for the start of the conservatory term, but again he spent just a few days connubially, this time suffering a nervous collapse from which he was salvaged when his brother Anatoly took him to western Europe once more, now for several months. He spent time in Switzerland and Italy, revisited Paris, saw and admired Delibes's *Sylvia* in Vienna, and completed the symphony and opera that had been with him through these bizarre months. Meanwhile, a separation from Antonina was agreed, and he never saw her again.

If *Eugene Onegin* is the portrait of a character and a case not unlike his own, the Fourth Symphony sounds like autobiography at full throttle, its first movement tearing with hope and pain. Yet this movement is also ingeniously constructed. It uses its driving first theme not only as an image of fate but also as a motive force to push the music through an unusual yet highly effective harmonic progression. The normal increase then relaxation of tension is replaced by a ladder that is also a wheel, the harmony rising by minor-third steps from F minor through A♭ minor, C♭ and D minor to F minor again, re-established with all its unruly force remaining. By casting the middle movements as escapes (into an idealized world, close to ballet) and by bringing back his fate theme in the finale, Tchaikovsky made an important contribution to the unification that composers since Beethoven had been seeking in the symphony. This was a project to which he returned in his three further essays in the form.

The symphony's psychological programme he

divulged (and perhaps exaggerated) to someone who had entered his life a few months before his luckless wife and was, in stark contrast, the woman he wanted: emotionally forthcoming (their correspondence was intimate in all but sexual matters), physically remote (by her wish they never met) and wealthy, giving him a pension that released him from the conservatory. She was Nadezhda von Meck, the widow of a railway proprietor, and she remained his patron and communicant for 14 years.

While still abroad – in Switzerland in the spring of 1878 – he was visited by a friend, the young violinist Iosif Kotek, and prompted into writing a concerto. But the story of this sunny and melodious work was the same as that of the First Piano Concerto. He offered it to a great Russian virtuoso, Leopold Auer, who turned it down, leaving another musician, Adolf Brodsky, to give the first performance abroad. More immediately, he travelled back from Switzerland to Kamenka, where he composed the first of two extended settings for the Russian church, his *Liturgy of St John Chrysostom*. In September he returned to Moscow and to the conservatory, only to resign the next month and leave again for western Europe. This was the pattern of his life for several years: summers at Kamenka and elsewhere in Russia, winters or springs in the West. Largely absent now from Moscow and St Petersburg, he continued to enjoy a more cosmopolitan vision than his Russian contemporaries, and a more cosmopolitan reputation.

Some of his most attractive, but also some of his most neglected works date from this period, the latter including two operas: *The Maid of Orleans* (1878–9), in the Meyerbeer mode of grand pageantry, and the more streamlined *Mazeppa* (1881–3), on an episode from Russian history. He discovered a relaxed alternative to the symphony in the orchestral suite, which could contain character pieces and impressions of older styles. He also produced the superb Serenade for strings (1880) and, in the same year, the 1812 overture – an effective picture of Russia's defiance of Napoleon, with clashing national anthems and military effects – as well as a lively piece in the Russian tradition of musical travel writing, the *Capriccio italien*. Then, as a memorial to Nikolay Rubinstein, he composed perhaps his finest chamber work, the Piano Trio in A minor.

In 1882 Balakirev renewed contact with him, and again was soon pressing a musical proposal on him: a programme symphony based on Byron's dramatic poem *Manfred*. This drew him back into a sphere of musical expression he had left since his previous symphony, No.4, a sphere of anxiety,

oppression and alienation complemented by dream visions of calm and of intricate delight. After that came an operatic melodrama, *The Enchantress*, whose first performance, at the Mariinsky in St Petersburg on 1 November 1887, he conducted himself. He then devoted part of his usual winter break in the West to conducting concerts, and returned to spend the summer writing his Fifth Symphony, which, like *Manfred*, has a fate theme running through all four movements. Again he conducted the première, in St Petersburg on 17 November 1888, as he did also that of the third of his musical tales from Shakespeare, *Hamlet*, a week later.

He was now thoroughly a master, honoured at home and internationally acclaimed – even by Brahms, despite reservations on both sides – and the creative uncertainty that had followed his dive into marriage and precipitate leap out again was over. In *The Sleeping Beauty* he provided a lasting musical memento of the imperial Russian ballet, resplendent and sumptuous. Soon after the first performance, at the Mariinsky in January 1890, he was at work on an opera for the same theatre, produced there before the end of the year: *The Queen of Spades*, another story of fate, and of a man bewildered by his desires, with Pushkin's story adapted for the stage by the composer's brother Modest. The extraordinary score includes a divertissement in pastiche rococo style, one product of Tchaikovsky's continuing love affair with the period. (Another was his Fourth Suite, made of Mozart arrangements, and yet another the cello concerto Variations on a Rococo Theme, which he had written on the brink of the fateful year of 1877.)

When von Meck broke with him – in the autumn of 1891, for reasons unclear – his pride was hurt but not his pocket, for he could well afford now to live on his earnings as a composer. Earlier that year he had made a short tour of the north east of the USA, including concerts in the new Carnegie Hall, and he was at work on a double bill of fairytales for the Mariinsky: the opera *Iolanta* and ballet *The Nutcracker*. Immediately after finishing the latter score, in the spring of 1892, he launched into a symphony in E♭, but this he abandoned, transforming part of it into his one-movement Third Piano Concerto the next year. By then he had satisfied his symphonic urges with a work in B minor, drafted in February–April 1893 before what turned out to be his last trip abroad – to England, where he received an honorary doctorate at Cambridge along with Saint-Saëns, Boito and Bruch.

The new symphony (No.6), with the unusual device of a slow finale, in place of the triumphal march that sounded a forced note in the Fifth, was completed during the summer and first performed in St Petersburg on 28 October 1893. The next day Modest suggested the subtitle 'Pathétique' for it, and eight days after that its composer was dead, of cholera contracted by drinking unboiled water. The nearness of that event to the 'Pathétique', with its descent into stillness and silence, has led many to see here a connection between art and life as fierce as that of 1877. According to one theory, Tchaikovsky wrote the symphony against the background of brewing homosexual scandal and was ordered by old schoolfriends to commit suicide rather than face public humiliation. But this may be fanciful. The 'Pathétique' is certainly a tragic piece and a personal one, and it completes the composer's career disquietingly. But a four-movement symphony, set to an original plan and scored with scrupulous precision, cannot just be read as a suicide note.

In the 'Pathétique' Symphony, as in all his great works, the messages are various, and they have been variously read. For some his music is autobiography, written in blood, or else it fails. For others he is the supreme professional, dealing expertly with matters of form and instrumentation, an objective master of diverse musical genres. For two of his greatest admirers in the next generation he was a master of melody (Rachmaninoff) or of style (Stravinsky). And still there are works that, like *Iolanta* or others among the operas, have slipped through everyone's nets and remained almost ignored, yet part of the multifarious real Tchaikovsky.

David Brown *Tchaikovsky*, 4 Vols. (1978–91); Alexander Poznansky *Tchaikovsky* (1991), *Tchaikovsky Through Other's Eyes* (1999)

Theatre and orchestral music

Operas: *The Voyevoda* (Tchaikovsky, after Ostrovsky), Op.3, 1867–8, f.p. Moscow, 1869, destroyed; *The Oprichnik* (Tchaikovsky, after Ivan Lazhechnikov), 1870–72; *Vakula the Smith*, Op.14, 1874, f.p. St Petersburg, 1876, rev as The SLIPPERS, 1885; EUGENE ONEGIN, Op.24, 1877–8; *The Maid of Orleans* (see JOAN OF ARC), 1878–9; MAZEPPA, 1881–3; *The Enchantress* (Ippolit Shpazhinsky), 1885–7, f.p. St Petersburg, 1887; *The* QUEEN OF SPADES, Op.68, 1890; IOLANTA, Op.69, 1891

Ballets: SWAN LAKE, Op.20, 1875–6; *The* SLEEPING BEAUTY, Op.66, 1888–9; *The* NUTCRACKER, Op.71, 1891–2

Incidental music: *The* SNOW MAIDEN, Op.12, 1873; HAMLET, Op.67a, 1891

Symphonies: No.1 'Winter Daydreams', G minor, Op.13, 1866, f.p. Moscow, 15 Feb 1868, rev 1874, f.p. Moscow, 1 Dec 1883; No.2 'LITTLE RUSSIAN', C minor, Op.17, 1872, f.p. Moscow, 7 Feb 1873, rev 1880, f.p. St Petersburg, 12 Feb 1881; No.3 'Polish', D, Op.29, 1875, f.p. Moscow, 19 Nov 1875; No.4, F minor, Op.36, 1877–8, f.p. Moscow, 22 Feb 1878; MANFRED, Op.58, 1885; No.5, E minor, Op.64, 1888, f.p. St Petersburg, 17 Nov 1888; No.6 'Pathétique', B minor, Op.74, 1893, f.p. St Petersburg, 28 Oct 1893

Concertos: PIANO CONCERTO No.1, B♭ minor, Op.23, 1874–5; No.2, G, Op.44, 1879–80; No.3, E♭, Op.75, 1893; Concert Fantasia, Op.56, pf, orch, 1884; VIOLIN CONCERTO, D, Op.35, 1878; *Sérénade mélancolique*, Op.26, vn, orch, 1875; *Valse-scherzo*, Op.34, vn, orch, 1877; Variations on a Rococo Theme, Op.33, vc, orch, 1876; *Pezzo capriccioso*, Op.62, vc, orch, 1887

Suites: No.1, D, Op.43, 1878–9; No.2, C, Op.53, 1883; No.3, G, Op.55, 1884; No.4 'Mozartiana', G, Op.61, 1887

Other orchestral works: *The Storm* (overture), Op.76, 1864; Overture, F, 1865–6; Concert Overture, C minor, 1865–6; Festival Overture, Op.15, 1866; *Fatum* (symphonic poem), Op.77, 1868; ROMEO AND JULIET (fantasy overture), 1869, rev 1870, 1880; Serenade, small orch, 1872; *The* TEMPEST (symphonic fantasia), Op.18, 1873; Slavonic March, Op.31, 1876; FRANCESCA DA RIMINI (symphonic fantasia), Op.32, 1876; *Capriccio italien*, Op.45, 1880; Serenade, C, Op.48, str, 1880; *1812* (EIGHTEEN-TWELVE; festival overture), Op.49, 1880; Festival Coronation March, 1883; HAMLET (fantasy overture), Op.67, 1888; *The Voyevoda* (symphonic ballad), Op.78, 1890–91; *The* NUTCRACKER (suite), Op.71a, 1892

Chamber and piano music

Chamber: *Souvenir de Florence*, Op.70, str sextet, 1890; String Quartet No.1, D, Op.11, 1871; No.2, F, Op.22, 1874; No.3, E♭ minor, Op.30, 1876; Piano Trio, A minor, Op.50, 1881–2; *Souvenir d'un lieu cher*, Op.42, vn, pf, 1878

Piano: Romance, Op.5, 1868; *Valse-scherzo*, Op.7, 1870; Capriccio, Op.8, 1870; *Deux morceaux*, Op.10, 1871 (No.2 Humoresque); *Six morceaux*, Op.19, 1873 (No.4 Nocturne, C♯ minor); *Six morceaux sur un seul thème*, Op.21, 1873; *Les Saisons*, Op.37b, 1875–6; *Album pour enfants*, Op.39, 1878; *Douze morceaux*, Op.40, 1878 (No.2 *Chanson triste*); Sonata, G, Op.37, 1878; *Six morceaux*, Op.51, 1882 (No.6 *Valse sentimentale*); *Dumka*, Op.59, 1886; *Valse-scherzo*, 1889; *Dix-huit morceaux*, Op.72, 1893

Choral music and songs

Choral: *Liturgy of St John Chrysostom*, Op.41, ch, 1878; *Vesper Service*, Op.52, ch, 1881–2; cantatas, etc.

Songs (those obelisked orchestrated by the composer): 'Again, as before' (Daniil Rathaus), Op.73:6, 1893; 'Amid the din of the ball' (A.K. Tolstoy), Op.38:3, 1878; 'Cradle Song' (Apollon Maykov), Op.16:1, 1872; 'Do not believe, my friend' (A.K. Tolstoy), Op.6:1, 1869; 'Does the day reign?' (Apukhtin), Op.47:6, 1880; 'Don Juan's Serenade' (A.K. Tolstoy), Op.38:1, 1878; 'Frenzied Nights' (Apukhtin), Op.60:6, 1886; 'I bless you, forests'

(A.K. Tolstoy), Op.47:5, 1880; 'If only I had known' (A.K. Tolstoy), Op.47:1, 1880; 'I'll tell you nothing' (Fet), Op.60:2, 1886; 'It was in early spring' (A.K. Tolstoy), Op.38:2, 1878; 'Legend'[†] (Aleksey Pleshcheyev), Op.54:6, 1883; 'The Nightingale' (Pushkin), Op.60:4, 1886; 'None but the lonely heart' (Mey, after Goethe), Op.6:6, 1869; 'Not a word, o my friend' (Pleshcheyev), Op.6:2, 1869; 'O, if only you could' (A.K. Tolstoy), 1878; 'Pimpinella' (Tchaikovsky), Op.38:6, 1878; 'Softly the spirit flew up to heaven' (A.K. Tolstoy), Op.47:2, 1880; 'Was I not a little blade of grass?'[†] (Ivan Surikov), Op.47:7, 1880; 'Why did I dream of you?' (Mey), Op.28:3, 1875; etc.

Tchaikovsky Competition. One of the major music competitions, held in Moscow every four years since 1958. It includes contests for pianists, violinists, cellists and singers, but the piano competition is the most prestigious.

Tchaikovsky Conservatory. Formal name of the Moscow Conservatory.

Tcherepnin [Cherepnin, Tcherepnine]. Russian–French–US family of composers.

(1) **Nikolay (Nikolayevich)** (b. St Petersburg, 15 May 1873; d. Paris, 26 Jun 1945). He studied at the St Petersburg Conservatory with Rimsky-Korsakov, who influenced him strongly. Diaghilev engaged him to conduct the first Ballets Russes season in Paris, in 1909, and his ballet *Le Pavillon d'Armide* was included. Other orchestral works of this period, similarly rich and fantastical, include his prelude to *La Princesse lointaine* and *Le Royaume enchanté*. He fled the Bolsheviks to direct the conservatory and conduct at the opera in Tbilisi (1918–21) before settling with his family in Paris.

(2) **Aleksandr (Nikolayevich)** (b. St Petersburg, 21 Jan 1899; d. Paris, 29 Sep 1977). The son of Nikolay, he shared his father's busy musical life and completed his education in Paris. In 1934–7 he travelled in the Far East, hearing music that would influence him and meeting his future wife, Lee Hsien Ming. Then in 1948 he and his family moved to the USA, where he was active as a teacher, pianist and conductor. His large and various output includes operas, ballets, six piano concertos and four symphonies.

(3) **Serge (Aleksandrovich)** (b. Paris, 2 Feb 1941). The elder son of Aleksandr, he studied at Harvard with Billy Jim Layton and Kirchner (1958–63), at Princeton and in Europe. He has worked as a college teacher and composer, chiefly of electronic music.

(4) **Ivan (Aleksandrovich)** (b. Paris, 5 Feb 1943; d. Boston, 11 Apr 1998). The younger son of Aleksandr, he joined his brother at Harvard (1960–64) and also studied in Europe, returning to Harvard in 1972 to teach. His works make versatile use of avant-garde techniques.

Tcherepnin scale. Name coined by Nicolas Slonimsky for a scale with a repeating unit of semitone–tone–semitone (e.g. C–Db–Eb–E–F–G–Ab–A–B–C) found in Aleksandr Tcherepnin's music. This is one form of the third of Messiaen's MODES OF LIMITED TRANSPOSITIONS.

te. In tonic sol-fa the seventh degree of the scale.

teaching. See EDUCATION.

Tear, Robert (b. Barry, 8 Mar 1939). Welsh tenor, of distinctively reedy and highly expressive voice coupled with dramatic intelligence. He was a choral scholar at King's College, Cambridge, and made his stage debut with the English Opera Group in 1963 (Male Chorus in *The Rape of Lucretia*). Britten wrote for him in *The Burning Fiery Furnace* and *The Prodigal Son*; Tippett did so in *The Knot Garden*. Throughout the 1970s–90s he was regularly at Covent Garden, in a repertory from Handel to Berio.

Tebaldi, Renata (b. Pesaro, 1 Feb 1922; d. San Marino, 19 Dec 2004). Italian soprano, of commanding vocal beauty, the chief rival to Callas and, in respect of superb tonal richness, the antithesis. She studied in Parma, where she made her debut in 1944. Two years later she was chosen by Toscanini to take part in the reopening of La Scala, and her international career began in 1950 with appearances in London, Paris and San Francisco. Specially treasured in the spinto repertory (Tosca, Desdemona, etc.), she retired from opera in 1973 and gave her last concert in 1976.

tecla (Sp.). Key on a keyboard.

tedesca, tedesco (It.). German. Thus *alla tedesca* is an indication of German style, usually the style of a GERMAN DANCE.

Te Deum. Ancient Christian hymn of praise, believed in the Middle Ages to have sprung spontaneously from the lips of St Ambrose and St Augustine at the latter's baptism. It is a regular part of Matins and may also be used on special occasions of celebration. There are notable settings of the original Latin text by Haydn, Berlioz, Bruckner and Verdi, and of the Anglican translation by Purcell and Handel.

Teil (Ger., pl. *Teile*). Part, in the sense of section.

Te Kanawa, Kiri (b. Gisborne, Auckland, 6 Mar 1944). New Zealand soprano, of opulent voice, created dame in 1982. She completed her training at the London Opera Centre and made a big impression with her performance as the Countess in *Figaro* at Covent Garden in 1971. Soon she was appearing internationally. In 1981 she sang at Prince Charles's wedding.

Teldec. German company, releasing records from 1935 as Telefunken, with a notable early-music series Das Alte Werk founded in 1958. The Teldec name was formed in 1950 from an alliance with Decca, but used as a label only after the company had been acquired by Warner in 1988.

Telefunken. See TELDEC.

Telemann, Georg Philipp (b. Magdeburg, 14 Mar 1681; d. Hamburg, 15 Jun 1767). German composer of remarkable fecundity. The chief musician in Hamburg for almost half a century, he produced annual settings of the Passion and over a thousand cantatas, besides innumerable concertos, overtures and sonatas. He also published a good deal of his music, thereby reaching audiences unfamiliar with Bach and Handel, and so became the most successful German composer of his day. As the work of his great contemporaries became better known, his star dimmed, to brighten again in the late 20th century.

Born into a family of pastors and pastors' daughters, he gained a quick interest in music at school, against the wishes of his widowed mother. Obedient to her intentions, he went to Leipzig in 1701 to study law but soon became deeply involved in musical activities. He founded a collegium musicum, wrote operas and gained a post as organist, annoying the incumbent director of music, Kuhnau, but surely gearing up the city's musical life in preparation for Kuhnau's successor, Bach. In 1705 he was appointed chapelmaster to the court at Sorau/Żary, where he delightedly discovered Polish folk music. Three years later he moved to Eisenach, which is probably where he met Bach; in 1714 he was godfather to the Bach son who duly took one of his names, Carl Philipp Emmanuel. By then he was a father himself, and a widower, having married a lady-in-waiting at the Sorau court, who died in 1711 after the birth of their daughter.

In 1712 he moved to Frankfurt as city director of music, and in 1714 he remarried, to gain in due course eight sons and two more daughters. With his reputation similarly growing, he received several offers of visiting or permanent appointments; the one he accepted, in 1721, took him to Hamburg. His main duties there were ecclesiastical and educational, involving the composition and performance of two cantatas each Sunday, a Passion every year and other oratorios, but he also involved himself, as he had in Leipzig, in opera (as musical director of the local company, 1722–38) and public concerts. Besides all that, he engraved the plates for his numerous publications, and in his old age maintained a correspondence with Handel, whom he had known since 1701.

He moved forward with the times, and learned from the generation of his godson, bringing galant features into his style and elements of French music, but even some of his earlier works (notably *Seliges Erwägen*, his dramatic Passion to his own words) enjoyed repeated performances in Hamburg to the end of the century.

Richard Petzoldt *Georg Philipp Telemann* (1974)

Operas: *Der geduldige Socrates* (Johann Ulrich von König, after Nicolò Minato), f.p. Hamburg, 1721; *Pimpinone* (intermezzo; Johann Philipp Praetorius, after Pietro Pariati), f.p. Hamburg, 1725; *Orpheus* (Telemann, after Michel du Boullay), f.p. Hamburg, 1726; etc.

Other vocal works: passions, oratorios, over 1,000 church cantatas, about 50 secular cantatas, masses, psalms, motets, hymns, *Magnificat* settings, songs, etc.

Instrumental: *Musique de table* (3 sets, each including an orchestral suite, a concerto, a quartet, a trio sonata and a solo sonata), pub 1733; *c.*130 other orchestral suites (A minor, rec, str), over 100 other concertos (D, tpt, str; E minor, rec, fl, str; G, va, str), many other quintets, quartets, sonatas, fantasias (12, fl), etc.

television. Where music on RADIO made a natural fit – an aural art for a medium of sound – music on television has been more problematic. Unlike the roving, capricious eye in the concert hall, the camera has to make prepared choices and linger. Some musicians sit more happily under its gaze than others, for reasons that have little to do with musical prowess. More than that, the speaking voice – a reassuring constancy of television – is generally banished. And quality of sound, from a standard television receiver, will be poor. Music enters here an awkward, even alien environment.

The successes of music on television have tended to come less from concert relays than from educational and documentary programmes, and from efforts to visualize musical performance in new ways particular to the medium. Many of these successes came between the late 1950s and early 1970s: the CBS recordings of Bernstein's Young People's Concerts with the New York Philharmonic, Ken Russell's BBC biographies of Elgar, Delius and other composers, innumerable master classes, and a realization of Boulez's *Le Marteau sans maître* as *Tele-Marteau*, with inventive lighting and camera work.

Opera on television has also had its difficulties, since television – so commonplace a feature of the living room – does not easily become a window into the strange and spectacular: its mode is more that of everyday naturalism, and the most renowned operas made for television, notably Menotti's *Amahl and the Night Visitors* (f.p. NBC, 1951) and Britten's *Owen Wingrave* (f.p. BBC, 1971), have taken that into account. Stravinsky's *The Flood* (f.p. CBS, 1962) is an exception, but one that has failed to generate the repeated productions that should have accrued to a classic. And studio productions of repertory operas (common from the first beginnings of television, in London in 1936) became extremely rare after the 1970s, though that was partly because of technical developments that smoothened transmission of opera from the theatre.

Is television an eye into the world or a world in itself? Innovatory studio productions of opera and concert music implied the latter. Their decline suggests an acceptance of the medium's neutrality – an acceptance that may or may not be warranted but tends to take away the vision and leave the telly.

Brian G. Rose *Television and the Performing Arts* (1986); Jeremy Tambling *A Night in at the Opera* (1994)

tema (It., pl. *temi*). Theme.

temperament. Tuning arranged so that intervals sound roughly the same in whatever key. Some adjustment is necessary because, for example, three pure major thirds, of frequency ratio 5:4, add up to a frequency ratio of $5^3:4^3$, i.e. 125:64, just a little less than the 2:1 of the pure octave. If, therefore, F–A and A–C♯ are tuned on a keyboard instrument as pure intervals, D♭(C♯)–F will be sharp. That can be avoided by distributing the discrepancy, making all the major thirds a little wide. If this is done evenly, the result is EQUAL TEMPERAMENT, which gradually replaced MEANTONE TEMPERAMENT and other systems in the 18th century. Untempered tuning, with pure frequency ratios, is known as JUST INTONATION. See also Johann Philipp KIRNBERGER, Andreas WERCKMEISTER.

Stuart M. Isacoff *Temperament* (2001)

Tempest, The. Shakespeare's last play on his own, a fantasy of love found, betrayal revenged, folly thwarted and magic relinquished. Robert Johnson's songs probably graced the first performance. Later musical versions include:

(1) Semi-opera long attributed to Purcell but now thought to be the work of John Weldon (1712), incorporating earlier music. The text was an adaptation of 1667 by William D'Avenant and Dryden, revised in 1674 by Thomas Shadwell for a production with music by Humfrey, Locke and others. Characters are added, together with masques and comedy. Weldon's score (if indeed it was his) was repeatedly revived until 1750.

(2) Singspiel libretto, *Die Geisterinsel*, by Friedrich Wilhelm Gotter and Friedrich Hildebrand von Einsiedel, which they wrote for Mozart, but too late. The project passed to Friedrich Fleischmann (1796), followed by Reichardt (1798) and Zumsteeg (1798). In its characters and plot the piece stays close to the source.

(3) Beethoven's D minor piano sonata Op.31:2. The connection was recorded by Schindler, and is therefore unreliable.

(4) Symphonic fantasia by Tchaikovsky. First performance: Moscow, 19 Dec 1873.

(5) Incidental music by Chausson, comprising songs and interludes with an ensemble of flute, harp, celesta (very early in the instrument's history) and string trio. Ariel is a tenor. First performance: Paris, 5 Nov 1888.

(6) Opera *La tempesta* by Felice Lattuada to a libretto by Arturo Rossato. The vengeance motif is to the fore, with the King of the Island (baritone) killing Calibano (bass) and compelling obedience from the Usurper (bass) before the marriage of Miranda (soprano) and Fernando (tenor). First performance: Milan, 23 Nov 1922.

(7) Incidental music by Sibelius. First performance: Copenhagen, 16 Mar 1926.

(8) Orchestral piece *Prosperos Beschwörungen* by Wellesz (1934–6).

(9) Opera *Der Sturm* by Martin. The libretto is based on Johann Elias Schlegel's translation, Ariel a dancer speaking in rhythm. First performance: Vienna, 17 Jun 1956.

(10) Incidental music by Wolpe. First performance: New York, 1960.

(11) Incidental music by Tippett. First performance: London, Apr 1962.

(12) Opera Un RE IN ASCOLTO by Berio (1984), including elements from (2).

(13) Opera *The Tempest* by John Eaton, to Andrew Porter's conflation of the play. Among more predictable vocal dispositions, Caliban is a female jazz singer. First performance: Santa Fe, 27 Jul 1985.

(14) Opera *The Tempest* by Adès, to a verse transformation by Meredith Oakes. Caliban (tenor) moves into the centre as a wounded angel, finally left in peace on his island with Ariel

(coloratura soprano). First performance: London, 10 Feb 2004.

There are also musical responses by Sullivan, Fibich, Bainbridge and Benjamin.

temple block. Spherical wooden drum, with a slit, usually made of camphor wood and brightly painted. Such drums entered Western classical music through ragtime and jazz, and are available in a range of sizes and therefore pitches.

tempo (It.). Musical speed. The plural forms 'tempi' and 'tempos' are both in common use.

Before 1600 tempo could be indicated only by means of time signatures and standard durational values, and to some extent this usage has persisted. Music in 2/2 will generally be slow, music in 4/16 fast. Historically the next alternative, introduced with the Baroque period, was a verbal indication – generally one of the Italian forms that rapidly became normal, though variable through time in their meanings. By the Classical era there were five standard degrees – PRESTO, ALLEGRO, ANDANTE, ADAGIO and LARGO – plus additional possibilities, such as *prestissimo, allegretto, andantino*, MODERATO, LENTO and GRAVE. French, German and English equivalents began to become frequent in the late 19th century, by which time the case had long been complicated by the METRONOME. This notionally allowed a greater precision, since composers could indicate the number of beats per minute. On the other hand, there is a big difference between reading a piece in one's study and having it performed in a concert hall. The value of Beethoven's metronome markings has been persistently questioned – and persistently upheld. Composers' own recordings of their music (Stravinsky and Boulez provide examples) often run wildly counter to their metronomically indicated speeds.

The confusion should not be disconcerting. Tempo may justly vary with the nature of the instruments and the size and acoustics of the hall; there may also be a need for unquantifiable RUBATO. See also A TEMPO.

tempo giusto (It.). Strict time. As a marking it may indicate absence of rubato, especially after a freer passage.

tempo primo (It., first time). An indication to return to the opening speed.

Tempora mutantur (Lat., Changing Times). Title given to Haydn's Symphony No.64, for no known reason.

temps (Fr.). (1) Beat, hence *temps faible* (weak beat), *temps fort* (strong beat), *à deux temps* (duple time), etc.

(2) Tempo.

Temps restitué, Le (Time Restored). Work by Barraqué for soprano, choir and orchestra, the first part he drafted of his *La Mort de Virgile*. First performance: Royan, 4 Apr 1968.

tempus. In ARS NOVA notation the division of the breve into three breves (perfect) or two (imperfect).

Tenducci, Giusto Ferdinando (b. Siena, *c.*1735; d. Genoa, 25 Jan 1790). Italian castrato active largely in England, Ireland and Scotland. He created roles in Arne's *Artaxerxes* and J.C. Bach's *Adriano in Siria*, and Mozart wrote an aria for him, now lost. Married in Cork in 1766, he is said to have fathered two children.

tenebrae (Lat., darkness). Evening service peculiar to the Thursday, Friday and Saturday of Holy Week. There is music for it by Gesualdo, Victoria, Charpentier, Couperin, Zelenka and the many composers who have made LAMENTATIONS settings.

tenebroso (It.). Sombre.

teneramente, tenero, teneroso, con tenerezza (It.). Tenderly.

Tenney, James (Carl) (b. Silver City, New Mexico, 10 Aug 1934). US composer. He studied the piano with Steuermann at Juilliard, gained a master's degree in composition under Kenneth Gaburo and Lejaren Hiller at the University of Illinois (1958–61), and worked briefly with Partch. He then moved to New York, where he developed his interests in computer sound synthesis and unconventional tunings, of which the latter was to prove the more profitable and lifelong pursuit. Most of his works are for small instrumental ensemble or soloist. After teaching at York University, Toronto (1976–2000), he moved to CalArts.

Tennstedt, Klaus (b. Merseburg, 6 Jun 1926; d. Kiel, 11 Jan 1998). German conductor, specially valued in Mahler. After conservatory studies in Leipzig he began his career as an orchestra leader, but a growth on his left hand caused him to divert to conducting. He then held principal posts at theatres in Chemnitz (1954–7), Dresden (1958–62) and Schwerin (1962–71), defected to the West in 1971 and continued his career at the Kiel Opera

(1972–6). His international career began in 1974 with the Toronto Symphony and blossomed rapidly. He was the first German to conduct the Israel Philharmonic (1978) and became music director of the LPO (1983–7). Declining health led him then to reduce his activities and to retire in 1994.

tenor (Lat., holder). (1) Used by itself the word denotes a man's voice of high range (singing without falsetto), or a singer with that voice. The normal range and extensions are those of the soprano, but an octave lower; and since tenor parts are conventionally notated on the treble clef, to be read an octave below, they look like soprano parts. As an adjective the term can also indicate an instrument or clef of similar register (e.g. tenor saxophone).

In medieval and early Renaissance polyphony the tenor was the fundamental and lowest voice (see below). By the 15th century the term was also being applied to a high man's voice, of the kind that surely had been heard in churches for centuries before, singing the more florid chants.

The tenor voice is implied by much of the song literature of the 16th century and went on being valued by early Baroque composers, until it was supplanted in the later 17th century by the castrato (and in France by the haute-contre). With the exception of the title role in *Idomeneo*, Mozart's tenors are secondary characters. The heroic tenor is a creature of the 19th century, forged in the operas of Rossini and the voices of such singers as Duprez.

Certain kinds of tenor voice are commonly distinguished, including the LYRIC TENOR, the SPINTO, the LIGHT TENOR (*tenore di grazia*), the DRAMATIC TENOR (*tenore robusto, tenore di forza*), the HELDENTENOR and the CHARACTER tenor. But voices are too fuzzy and personal to be easily classified.

(2) The fundamental voice in medieval and early Renaissance polyphony, often giving the plainsong or secular melody on which other parts are built.

tenor clef. C CLEF on the fourth line up, used for cellos and trombones. Parts for tenor singers conventionally use the treble clef, with an implicit downward transposition by an octave. In older music the treble clef may be doubled, or fitted with an '8' in its tail.

tenor drum (Fr. *caisse roulante*, Ger. *Rührtrommel*, It. *cassa rullante*). Rather larger than a side DRUM – 18 inches (45cm) in diameter and 15 inches (36cm) deep – lacking snares, and with a correspondingly softer sound, it was absorbed from army bands by Berlioz and Wagner, to become a frequent orchestral instrument in the 20th century.

tenore di forza. Dramatic tenor, as in Donizetti.

tenore di grazia. Light tenor.

tenore robusto. Dramatic tenor, as in later Verdi.

tenorino. Light-voiced, youthful tenor.

tenor horn. Saxhorn in E♭, a band instrument.

tenoroon. Tenor bassoon, a fifth above the normal instrument, used mostly in teaching.

tenor viola [tenor violin]. Large viola of the 16th and 17th centuries, made by the Amatis, Stradivari, etc., and sometimes indicated in scores as distinct from the alto viola.

tenth. Note an octave above the third, or interval an octave wider than a third.

tenuto (It.). Held, i.e. sustained for its entire durational value, or occasionally more, abbreviated *ten*.

Terezín. See THERESIENSTADT.

Terfel (Jones), Bryn (b. Pwllheli, 9 Nov 1965). Welsh baritone, strong and beguiling. He trained at the Guildhall School in London, won the lieder prize at the 1989 Singer of the World competition in Cardiff and was soon embarked on an international career in song and opera, his roles including the Mozart baritones, Jokanaan and Falstaff.

ternary. Form in three sections, of which the last is a repetition of the first, perhaps varied. In musical writing the form is often indicated as ABA, or ABA' to show an altered repetition. Such forms are common in songs and short lyric movements, in slow movements and in minuets and scherzos.

Terpsichore. The muse of choral lyric and dance, sometimes shown with a lyre.

terraced dynamics. Changes of loudness in discrete steps, thought appropriate in the mid 20th century for Baroque music.

Tertian, Terzian. Organ mutation stop sounding at the third and fifth.

Tertis, Lionel (b. West Hartlepool, 29 Dec 1876; d.

London, 22 Feb 1975). British viola player, a pioneer of the instrument as an honorable speciality. He studied at the RAM, introduced many works by British composers and transcriptions of his own, and retired in 1936.

Terz (Ger., pl. *Terzen*). Third (as interval), also used as a prefix in naming instruments pitched a third above (*Terzgeige*) or below (*Terzposaune*) the norm.

terza (It.). Third (interval).

terzet (Ger. *Terzett*, It. *terzetto*). Composition for three singers.

tessitura (It., texture). The range most frequently used in a vocal role (or, by extension, solo instrumental part) or most comfortable for a voice. Either a role or a voice may be described as having a high or low tessitura.

testo (It., text). Role of narrator in 17th-century Italian works, e.g. Monteverdi's *Combattimento*.

tetrachord. In ancient Greek music theory a set of four notes bounded by a perfect fourth. Three types, or genera, were distinguished: the diatonic (semitone–tone–tone), the chromatic (semitone–semitone–minor third) and the enharmonic (quarter-tone–quarter-tone–major third). Early medieval theorists added a variant diatonic type, tone–semitone–tone.

tetralogy. Set of four works, usually Wagner's *Ring*.

Tetrazzini, Luisa (b. Florence, 29 Jun 1871; d. Milan, 28 Apr 1940). Italian soprano, renowned for agility and lustre. She studied in Florence and with her sister Eva, also a soprano, and made her debut in Rome in 1890. Her spectacular international career began with debuts at Covent Garden in 1907 and the Met the next year; during the next few years she also made some recordings.

Tetzlaff, Christian (b. Hamburg, 29 Apr 1966). German violinist, a virtuoso of dazzling precision. A pupil of Üwe-Martin Haiberg at the conservatory in Lübeck and of Walter Levine in Cincinnati (1985–6), he plays a repertory from Bach to Ligeti and has three musician siblings: Angela (flute), Tanja (cello) and Stephan (double bass).

Teutscher (Ger.). GERMAN DANCE.

Textbuch (Ger.). Libretto.

texture. Informal term for the feel of sound, a matter of contrapuntal density, harmony and timbre. 'Texture music' was a term coined in the 1960s for works by composers (e.g. Penderecki) whose primary concern was with this aspect.

Teyte, Maggie (b. Wolverhampton, 17 Apr 1888; d. London, 26 May 1976). British soprano, preeminent as Mélisande, created dame in 1958. She studied at the RCM and with Jean de Reszke in Paris, and in 1908 was picked by Debussy for her greatest role, which she sang until 1948 while pursuing an international career in opera and concerts.

Thaïs. Opera by Massenet to a libretto by Louis Gallet after a novel by Anatole France. The *Méditation* is an orchestral intermezzo with solo cello, covering the protagonist's conversion from life as a courtesan in Alexandria. First performance: Paris, 16 Mar 1894, rev Paris, 13 Apr 1898.

Thalberg, Sigismond (Fortuné François) (b. Pâquis, near Geneva, 8 Jan 1812; d. Posillipo, near Naples, 27 Apr 1871). Pianist of uncertain parentage, possibly Austrian aristocratic and illegitimate. He studied in Vienna with Sechter and Hummel, and started his international career in 1830, becoming Liszt's chief rival. Mostly he played his own music, consisting chiefly of fantasies and variations on operatic themes and popular melodies.

Thalia. The muse of comedy, light poetry and idyll.

Thamos, König in Ägypten (Thamos King of Egypt). Music by Mozart for a play by Tobias Philipp Freiherr von Gebler, comprising three choruses and five orchestral pieces. The play concerns the magnanimity of Menes, the pharaoh deposed by Rameses, in securing the throne for the latter's son Thamos. Mozart wrote his score for one or more productions in Salzburg, 1773–9.

Thayer, Alexander Wheelock (b. South Natick, Mass., 22 Oct 1817; d. Trieste, 15 Jul 1897). US biographer of Beethoven. After completing studies at Harvard in 1848, he devoted his life to collecting eyewitness testimony and other material for the definitive life of the composer, published first in German with the help of Hermann Deiters.

theatre organ. See CINEMA ORGAN.

Theile, Johann (b. Naumburg, 29 Jul 1646; buried Naumburg, 24 Jun 1724). German composer, pupil of Schütz. Renowned in his time as 'the father of contrapuntists' and as a pious, honest man, he wrote some of the earliest choral fugues in his masses. These and other liturgical settings (psalms, motets, a St Matthew Passion) form the bulk of his output; he also wrote a treatise with examples on canonic composition, *Das musikalische Kunstbuch*, which Bach knew, as well as the first score for the Hamburg opera (*Adam und Eva*, 1678, lost).

Thema (Ger., pl. *Themen*). Theme.

thematic catalogue. Ordered list, often in book form, of compositions, including in each case the opening (incipit) in musical notation. Down the centuries such catalogues have served different purposes, from reminding monks of chant melodies to alerting customers to the full range of a publisher's stock, but they are most likely to be encountered as guides to the outputs of individual composers. Haydn and Mozart kept such catalogues of their own. As a scholarly achievement, the thematic catalogue began with Köchel's documentation of Mozart's music, published in 1862. Important among the many cataloguers since 1950 are Deutsch (Schubert) and Hoboken (Haydn).

thematic material. Group of ideas, interlocking or appearing in quick succession, functioning as a theme. Or a theme with several definable components.

theme. Melodic idea that a composition develops, consisting of anything from a bar or two (anything shorter has to be called a MOTIF) to a whole tune in several phrases.

Derived from the ancient study of rhetoric, where it meant a subject for discussion, the term was first applied to music by Zarlino in 1558, with very much the sense it has retained. The nature of the theme, though, has changed with the nature of music. In the Renaissance and Baroque eras it was an idea for contrapuntal elaboration, used synonymously with 'point' and 'subject'. Classical musicians still used the word for opening material: the melodic start of a movement (discounting any introduction), which might be a full-scale melody in the case of a THEME AND VARIATIONS. In the 19th century the term was extended to ideas that by definition must come later, such as second themes in sonata movements and reminiscence themes in operas. With Beethoven's example so important, thematic working – DEVELOPMENT, TRANSFORMATION – came to be highly valued, though interpreted in very different ways by, for example, Liszt, Franck and Brahms. Concomitantly – and

also for expressive purposes – the theme needed to be deeply imbued with character.

But there is also music in which a theme may be hard to discern (the overture to *Così fan tutte*) or in which the thematic principle is deliberately averted (much that has been written since 1945).

theme and variations (Fr. *thème et variations*, Ger. *Thema mit Variationen*, It. *tema con variazioni*). Form comprising a theme of song or dance character, classically in two sections, each repeated, followed by a sequence of variations on the melody of the theme and, possibly, a final repetition of the theme unadorned or a coda. The more convenient but less explicit term 'variation form' is also used.

Characteristic of the Classical–Romantic age, though with a background in such Baroque types as passacaglia and chorale variations, the form arose in the work of C.P.E. Bach and other mid-18th-century composers. J.S. Bach's Goldberg Variations, not based on an omnipresent theme, do not belong in this tradition. Haydn made important use of the form for movements in symphonies, quartets and sonatas, and also for independent works – notably his Variations in F minor for piano (1793), exemplifying his favoured variety of 'double variations', alternately on themes in major and minor modes. Mozart's variation movements are more brilliant, and Beethoven combined the showiness and solidity of his great predecessors (notably in his sets in F and C minor, and EROICA Variations), going on far into unknown territory in the late absorption with variation form that gave rise to his DIABELLI VARIATIONS (1819–23) and other works. More generally by this time the form had become an excuse for freewheeling virtuosity: 'lots of words and little sense', as Monsigny, a French encyclopedist, described it in 1818. Schubert's variations, though, represent another exception.

The formal variation set was re-established as a strong medium by Brahms (sets on themes by Schumann, Handel, Paganini and Haydn), though in other works of his period and later – by Dvořák (Symphonic Variations), Tchaikovsky (Variations on a Rococo Theme), Franck (Symphonic Variations), Strauss (*Don Quixote*), Schoenberg, etc. – the sections are more or less obscured. Brahms also reintroduced the passacaglia (finale of the Fourth Symphony), an antiquarian initiative taken up by Webern in his Op.1. Webern's later variations for piano (Op.27) and orchestra (Op.30) are based on themes that are themselves miniature sets of variations, so that the distinction between theme (fixed) and variations (momentary) dissolves.

Theodora. Oratorio by Handel to a text by Thomas Morell after Robert Boyle. Theodora (soprano) and Irene (mezzo-soprano) are Christians at the time of the persecution of the emperor Valens (bass). Didymus (alto castrato), a Roman soldier, loves Theodora and decides to share her fate. First performance: London, 16 Mar 1750.

Theodorakis, Mikis (b. Chios, 29 Jul 1925). Greek composer, on the borders of popular music. He studied in Athens and, following political exile, in Paris with Messiaen. Having begun to make a name for film and ballet scores, he returned to Greece in 1960, but was arrested and exiled again for the duration of the military regime (1967–74). His works include numerous songs, symphonies with voices, and continuing film scores (*Zorba the Greek*, 1964).

theorbo. Lute with an elongated neck to support bass strings, invented in Italy in the late 16th century and in use until the end of the 17th. It is commonly used as a continuo instrument. See also ARCHLUTE.

theory. The fundamentals of knowledge and hypothesis concerning the nature and realization of music. Music theory is generally distinguished from music history, though it overlaps with matters of acoustics, aesthetics, analysis, notation, philosophy, psychology and sociology. It also has a history of its own, beginning, in the Western tradition, with Aristoxenus (4th century BC), whose writings consider scales, consonance and tuning – matters of abiding interest to theorists. The latest millennium or so of music theory is represented by Hucbald, Guido, Jehan des Murs, Tinctoris, Zarlino, Rameau and Schenker.

theremin. Electronic instrument developed in Petrograd in the 1920s by Lev Sergeyevich Termen (Léon Thérémin, 1896–1993). It produces a wailing tone that players can vary in pitch and volume by moving their hands in relation to an antenna and a loop. Regularly used in film scores for its weirdness, the instrument has also seen the concert hall, and enjoyed a revival in its long-lived inventor's last years. A remarkable documentary film, *Theremin: An Electronic Odyssey* (1993), tells the story. See also ONDES MARTENOT.

Theresienmesse (Theresa Mass). Fourth of Haydn's late masses, named in honour of Maria Theresa (1772–1807), wife of Emperor Franz II, because she sang in the first performance: she was a professional singer. First performance: Eisenstadt, ?8 Sep 1799.

Theresienstadt (Terezín). Concentration camp set up by the Nazis in Czechoslovakia as a purported model of an artistic society. Among composers who were interned and worked there were Haas, Krása and Ullmann, all of whom perished at Auschwitz in 1944.

thesis. See ARSIS.

Thibaud, Jacques (b. Bordeaux, 27 Sep 1880; d. Mont Cemet, near Barcelonette, 1 Sep 1953). French violinist. Trained at the Paris Conservatoire, he is particularly remembered for the trio he formed with Cortot and Casals in the 1920s and 1930s.

Thibaut IV Count of Champagne and Brie and King of Navarre (b. Troyes, 30 May 1201; d. Pamplona, 7 Jul 1253). Trouvère, represented by more surviving songs than any of his colleagues. He went on crusade (1239–40) and quarrelled with the Church, which necessitated from him a pilgrimage to Rome in 1248. His songs cover various topics: courtly love, crusading, apostrophes to the Virgin Mary.

Thieving Magpie, The. See *La* GAZZA LADRA.

Thill, Georges (b. Paris, 14 Dec 1897; d. Paris, 17 Oct 1984). French tenor, esteemed as the noblest French heroic tenor of the early gramophone age. After war service he studied at the Paris Conservatoire (1918–20) and with De Lucia in Naples (1920–22), then made his debut at the Paris Opera in 1924. From 1928 he was active internationally, in an enormous repertory that encompassed Samson, Calaf, Aeneas and Wagner heros, but also lyrical French roles. He made his farewell stage appearance at the Paris Opera in 1953 and retired altogether three years later.

third. (1) Note in third position in a diatonic system, e.g. E in C major.

(2) Interval between that note and the tonic. A major third comprises four semitones (e.g. C–E), a minor third three (e.g. C–E♭). Chromatic alteration can produce a diminished third (e.g. C–E♭♭, enharmonically a major second) or an augmented third (e.g. C–E♯, enharmonically a fourth).

third inversion. Vertical rearrangement of a four-note chord so that the fourth note is in the bass, e.g. the dominant seventh G–B–D–F becomes F–B–G–D, or any other placing with F lowest.

third-stream music. Term coined by Schuller in

the late 1950s for music hybridizing classical and jazz traditions.

thirty-second-note (US). Demisemiquaver (UK). See DURATION.

Thomas, (Charles Louis) Ambroise (b. Metz, 5 Aug 1811; d. Paris, 12 Feb 1896). French composer, renowned for his MIGNON and HAMLET. A musician's son, he studied with Le Sueur at the Paris Conservatoire (1828–32), won the Prix de Rome and returned from Italy to embark on a career as an opera composer. From 1851 he also taught at the Conservatoire, which from 1871 he directed. Influenced by Rossini and Donizetti, he had a string of modest successes and failures at the Opéra-Comique before the triumph there in 1866 of his *Mignon*, followed two years later by *Hamlet* at the Opera. Disturbed by changes in musical composition and taste, he then went into virtual creative retirement, to return for one last misadventure, *Françoise de Rimini* (f.p. Opera, 1882). He held Wagner, Debussy, Fauré and instrumental music in general all in his ample low esteem.

Thomas, Augusta Read (b. Glen Cove, NY, Apr 1964). US composer, admired for the poetry of her fluent, colourful music and of her titles (*Air and Angels, Eclipse Musings, Orbital Beacons*). She studied at Northwestern, Yale (with Druckman) and the RAM, and gained posts at the Eastman School (1995) and with the Chicago Symphony (1997). In 1994 she married Rands.

Thomas, Michael Tilson (b. Los Angeles, 21 Dec 1944). US conductor, noted for his wide sympathies and flair. With grandparents in Yiddish theatre (under the original family name of Tomashevsky), he studied at University of Southern California with Ingolf Dahl. Even before graduating, in 1967, he was working with a young musicians' orchestra in Los Angeles and making international contacts. He became assistant conductor to William Steinberg at the Boston Symphony in 1969, then was music director of the Buffalo Symphony (1971–9), the LSO (1988–95) and the San Francisco Symphony (from 1995).

Thomas, Theodore (Christian Friedrich) (b. Esens, East Friesland, 11 Oct 1835; d. Chicago, 4 Jan 1905). German–US conductor. His father, a city musician, took the family to the USA in 1845, when his education effectively ceased. After working as a jobbing violinist, he began conducting in 1858, energetically introducing New York audiences to the great masters. He was conductor of the New York Philharmonic (1877–91) and then founder conductor of the Chicago Symphony.

Thompson, Randall (b. New York, 21 Apr 1896; d. Boston, 9 Jul 1984). US composer. He studied at Harvard and with Bloch in New York (1920–21), then worked as a teacher, notably at Harvard (1948–65). Valued for his choral music (*The Testament of Freedom*, 1943; *Frostiana*, 1959), he also wrote three symphonies and two quartets.

Thomson, George (b. Limekilns, Fife, 4 Mar 1757; d. Leith, 18 Feb 1851). Scottish publisher. A civil servant and amateur musician, he devoted much of his free time and money to commissioning arrangements of Scots and Welsh folksongs with piano trio accompaniment – and he went to the best composers he could find: Haydn and Beethoven, as well as Pleyel, Kozeluch, Weber and Hummel. He also had contacts with distinguished writers. Burns and Scott rewrote texts for him, and his granddaughter married Charles Dickens.

Thomson, Virgil (Garnett) (b. Kansas City, Mo., 25 Nov 1896; d. New York, 30 Sep 1989). US composer and critic. He played the organ during his schooldays, then studied at Harvard with Edward Burlingame Hill and Archibald T. Davison (1919–23), taking a year in Paris for lessons with Boulanger (1920–21). In 1925 he returned to Paris for a longer period, during which he met Gertrude Stein and set her incantatory libretto to curiously blithe, homespun music in *Four Saints in Three Acts*. This had a camp first production in Hartford in 1934. In 1940 he returned to New York as music critic of the *Herald Tribune*, where he remained for 14 years, showing no lack of the self-expression he abjured in his music. His enormous output includes a long series of portraits of friends, each composed in the subject's presence.

Anthony Tommasini *Virgil Thomson* (1997)

Operas: FOUR SAINTS IN THREE ACTS, 1927–33; *The Mother of Us All* (Gertrude Stein), f.p. New York, 1947; *Lord Byron* (Jack Larson), f.p. New York, 1972

Orchestral: Symphony on a Hymn Tune, 1928; Symphony No.2, 1931; *The Plow that Broke the Plains* (suite), 1936; *Louisiana Story* (suite), 1948

Other works: *Capital Capitals* (Stein), men's voices, pf, 1927; sacred music, songs, chamber music, piano pieces, etc.

thoroughbass. Obsolete English term equivalent to CONTINUO. The study of thoroughbass was the study of harmony.

Three Choirs Festival. The oldest music festival, held annually since 1715 (in all probability) except for wartime breaks, rotating from one to another of three cathedrals in western England –

Gloucester, Hereford, Worcester – and involving their choirs. Handel was regularly featured almost from the first, followed in the 19th century by Spohr and Mendelssohn, then Bach, Brahms, Dvořák and English composers of the late Romantic renaissance: Parry, Elgar, Vaughan Williams (whose Tallis Fantasia had its first performance at the 1910 festival), etc.

Three-cornered Hat, The. See *El* SOMBRERO DE TRES PICOS.

Threepenny Opera, The. See *Die* DREI-GROSCHENOPER.

Three Places in New England. Orchestral work by Ives comprising: 1 *The Saint-Gaudens in Boston Common* (a meditation on a monument to the revolutionary Colonel Shaw and his regiment of black soldiers), 2 *Putnam's Camp, Redding, Connecticut* (a musical anecdote, depicting a young boy wandering away on a holiday outing and having a vision of another revolutionary incident), 3 *The Housatonic at Stockbridge* (a slow winding of dense harmony for strings, recalling a time when the composer and his wife walked beside the river). The work is also triple in its versions: for full orchestra (the original score, pub 1976, ed. James B. Sinclair), for chamber orchestra (Ives's 1929 arrangement for the first performances), and the latter as adapted by him for publication in 1935. First performance: New York, 10 Jan 1931.

Three Sisters. Opera by Eötvös to a Russian libretto he drew in collaboration with C.H. Henneberg from the Chekhov play. In a work at once elegantly strange and passionately forceful, events are shuffled to focus on the characters, among whom the three sisters are sung by countertenors. First performance: Lyons, 13 Mar 1998.

Three Tenors, The. Phenomenon involving José Carreras, Plácido Domingo and Luciano Pavarotti in collective concerts (beginning at the Baths of Caracalla in Rome, 7 July 1990) and recordings.

Threni (Threnodies). Work by Stravinsky, titled in full *Threni: id est Lamentationes Jeremiae Prophetae*. His first fully 12-note composition, it has abutting short sections for different choices from the ensemble of six soli, choir and orchestra. First performance: Venice, 23 Sep 1958.

through-composed. Song in which the music does not repeat from stanza to stanza, as it does in a strophic song.

Thuille, Ludwig (b. Bolzano, 30 Nov 1861; d. Munich, 5 Feb 1907). Austrian composer. He studied at the monastic school in Kremsmünster, in Innsbruck and with Rheinberger in Munich (1879–82), where he befriended Richard Strauss and Alexander Ritter, and remained after graduating to teach. His works include chamber pieces (Sextet for piano and wind, 1886–8) as well as operas, choral music, songs and a symphony.

Thunder and Lightning (*Donner und blitzen*). Polka by Johann Strauss II.

thunder machine. Device for imitating thunder. Various contrivances were used in 19th-century theatres: a large rotatable drum filled with pebbles or metal balls, a heavy sphere of stone or lead to be rolled down a ramp, etc. A later alternative is the thunder sheet: a large sheet of metal, suspended and shaken. Thunder effects are required in Strauss's *Alpensinfonie* and other works.

Thus Spake Zarathustra. See ALSO SPRACH ZARATHUSTRA.

Tibbett, Lawrence (Mervil) (b. Bakersfield, Cal., 16 Nov 1896; d. New York, 15 Jul 1960). US baritone, a vivid actor (his first profession) and noble singer. He studied in New York, made his debut in Los Angeles in 1923 and appeared regularly at the Met (1923–50) and internationally.

tibia. Ancient Roman double pipe, equivalent to the Greek aulos. According to Ovid, 'the tibia sang in the temples, it sang in the games, it sang at mournful funeral rites'. To play it was an honoured profession.

tie. Extension of a note from one metrical unit into another, marked by a curved line joining two note heads. For example, the last quaver of one bar may be tied to the first crotchet of the next, producing an unbroken duration of a dotted crotchet.

tief (Ger.). Deep, by itself and as in *tiefgespannt* (deep-stretched), implying a loosely fitted drum head.

tiento (Sp., touch). Renaissance–Baroque term (with the Portuguese equivalent *tento*) for a contrapuntal invention such as Italians would have called a *ricercare*.

tierce (Fr.). (1) Third (interval), hence *terce majeure, tierce mineure*.

(2) An organ stop sounding at the third.

tierce de Picardie (Fr., Picardy third). A major third placed in the final chord of a movement in the minor. The term, of unknown derivation, was introduced by Rousseau in 1767, by which time the usage was virtually obsolete.

Till Eulenspiegel (Till Owlglass). Tone poem by Strauss, titled in full *Till Eulenspiegels lustige Streiche, nach alter Schelmenweise – in Rondeauform – für grosses Orchester gesetzt* (Till Eulenspiegel's Merry Pranks – in Rondo Form – Set for Large Orchestra), the hero being a trickster from German folklore. First performance: Cologne, 5 Nov 1895.

timbales. (1) Pair of tunable drums, adopted from Latin American dance bands.
(2) (Fr.). Timpani.

timbre. Colour of sound: what distinguishes a clarinet from a trumpet playing the same note at the same volume for the same length of time. The phenomenon depends on the starting TRANSIENT, the ENVELOPE and the harmonic SPECTRUM. Variation of timbre is possible on nearly all instruments, and hybrid timbres can be obtained by skilful orchestration. Events since 1900 – the arrival of many new percussion instruments and of electronic sound synthesis – vastly increased possibilities of timbre composition.

time. (1) Dimension of music, which is the art of sound in time. The human experience of time is one of change leading ultimately to death. One of the great consolations of Western music since the Renaissance is that it projects a time that is ameliorative, restorative, progressive, and in which the ending is an affirmation, even a triumph. Beethoven is the central and archetypal Western composer partly because his music achieves this so magnificently, time and again. Music fills out the listener's temporal consciousness and provides a positive image of time that most people probably experience rather rarely in everyday life: when solving a problem, settling an argument, accomplishing a task.

But there are other sorts of time in music – even in Beethoven. Indeed, no music would be able to absorb the listener's whole awareness of time if it did not have some complexity. The sense of continuous progress, principally embodied in harmony, may be countered by recollection (of themes, especially), by tendencies to race ahead (in rhythm, perhaps), by braking devices (sustained notes or chords) and by references to musical situations outside the present piece (e.g., in the case of Beethoven, Baroque forms). Time may fork

in the very substance of the piece, where, for instance, rapid rhythmic change is combined with slower harmonic evolution, or where different tempos are simultaneously in play. Where these and other non-progressive factors are strongly developed – in Schubert, Debussy, Ligeti – the music may seem to correspond to mental states of fantasy or dream, states in which the flow of imagination is sufficient to itself and seeks no endpoint. In some cases, too, the temporal sense is not flooded; instead there is some distance between the listener and the music, so that the listener can observe how the music proceeds. This can be a matter of attitude, but certain music – Stravinsky's, for example – makes a position of distance inescapable.

When it unfolds in its own time, not ours, music may also provide an experience very remote from the everyday: an experience of infinite time, of eternity. That, too, was not unknown to Beethoven.

(2) Metre, as in waltz time, common time, 6/8 time, etc.

time point. Concept introduced by Babbitt in 1957 as a rhythmic equivalent to pitch class. Time points are regular zero-time instants within the bar. For example, in 3/4 time, with the semiquaver as smallest unit, there are 12 time points: zero (beginning of first beat), one (beginning of second semiquaver of first beat), etc. The distance between two time points is a duration, just as the distance between two pitches is an interval.

time signature. Indication of metre, notated at the start of a composition, after the clef and key signature (if any). A change of metre will probably necessitate a new time signature, normally preceded by a double bar. In a convention dating back to the 15th century, most time signatures consist of two numbers, one over the other. The bottom one indicates the metrical unit, in terms of how many are contained in a semibreve (whole note); the top one shows how many units are contained in each bar. Thus 3/4 sets out a metre of three crotchet beats. There are also two time signatures surviving from medieval practice: C (4/4) and ¢ (2/2, or ALLA BREVE).

time–space notation. Simplified rhythmic notation introduced by Earle Brown in 1953. Durations are indicated not by the usual symbols but by distances along the staff: the note head may become a horizontal line, or the distance may simply be one of space between attacks. This is especially convenient for percussion notation, and has been occasionally adopted by Berio,

Stockhausen, etc. It is also useful in the layout of scores or parts designed as aids to listening rather than instructions for performance – tape parts in ensemble pieces, for instance. Of course, it buys ease at the price of precision.

timp. Abbreviation for timpani.

timpani (It., sing. *timpano*, Fr. *timbales*, Ger. *Pauken*). Large bowl-shaped copper drums with membranes of calfskin or synthetic material, played with two sticks, one in each hand. A range of sticks is used, from soft (with large heads covered with felt or sponge) to hard (small wooden heads), for different qualities of sound. The instrument can be tuned by means of screws that change the tension in the membrane, and its sound can be muted by placing a cloth on it. Timpani made since the beginning of the 20th century have included pedals to change the note. The derivation of the word is from the Latin *tympanum* (drum), from which comes the occasional spelling *tympani*. The term 'kettle-drums' is obsolescent.

The earliest representation of the instrument is on a Babylonian plaque of *c.*700 BC. Pairs of timpani, mounted on horseback, were used as war drums by Persians in the 1st century AD and by Islamic armies, whence their adoption in Europe during the crusades and later. The instrument in its current form was inherited from the Ottomans in the 15th century and used in church music from the early 17th century, along with trumpets, also brought in from the battlefield; the earliest score to specify timpani was Lully's *Thésée* (1675). The association of trumpets and timpani continued to the time of Mozart, and their connection with war is still keenly felt in Beethoven's Ninth Symphony.

From Lully to Beethoven the standard set-up was a pair of timpani (as with the ancestral cavalry), one tuned to the tonic, the other, larger, to the dominant a fourth below, perhaps with changes of tuning between movements. But other tunings were possible, and there were such wonderful oddities as Johann Wilhelm Hertel's Sinfonia for eight timpani and orchestra (*c.*1748). Berlioz wrote for 10 players on 16 timpani in his *Requiem*; two or three players are common in scores since Mahler, increasing the timpani's versatiliy and making chords possible. By this stage the norm was a set of three timpani per player, sometimes with an additional very high (small) or low (big) drum. The introduction of pedal timpani allowed such effects as a rising whole-tone scale (Strauss's *Salome*) and glissandos (Nielsen's Fourth Symphony, Stravinsky's *Renard*).

The inevitably tiny repertory for timpanists as soloists and ensemble players includes Stockhausen's *Schlagtrio* and Carter's Eight Pieces.

Jeremy Montagu *Timpani and Percussion* (2002)

Tinctoris, Johannes (b. Braine l'Alleud, near Nivelles, *c.*1435; d. ?1511). Netherlandish theorist, author of the first published music dictionary, *Terminorum musicae diffinitorium* (Treviso, 1495), with 299 entries. He also wrote several treatises covering the aesthetics and uses of music, notation, practical musicianship, consonance and counterpoint. His learning he employed, too, in his compositional works: masses, motets and songs. A student in Orleans, he was in service to the king of Naples from around 1472.

tinnitus. Whistling in the ear, suffered by Schumann and Smetana.

Tiomkin, Dimitri (b. Kremenchuk, 10 May 1894; d. London, 12 Nov 1979). Ukrainian–US composer. He trained as a pianist in St Petersburg and Berlin (with Egon Petri and Busoni) before he started a second career as a film composer after moving to Hollywood in 1929. His three Oscars he won for *High Noon* (1952), *The High and the Mighty* (1954) and *The Old Man and the Sea* (1958).

Tippett, Michael (Kemp) (b. London, 2 Jan 1905; d. London, 8 Jan 1998). British composer, remarkable for the abundance and variety of his energies and enthusiasms, knighted in 1966. Brought up in a comfortable, not particularly musical family, he studied with Charles Wood and C.H. Kitson at the RCM (1923–8). He then settled in Oxted, Surrey, where he activated local music while continuing his training privately with R.O. Morris (1930–32) and starting out as a composer. It was a slow process. His earliest unrevised works date from the end of the 1930s and show a fusion of contemporary European music (Stravinsky, Bartók, Hindemith) with the sprung rhythm and polyphonic exuberance he admired in English madrigals and jazz. Meanwhile he was developing a sense of himself as an artist in society, conducting for socialist organizations.

All the factors in his creative make-up – sympathy with the oppressed (and their music), delight in the distant past, freshness – came together in his oratorio *A Child of Our Time* (1939–41). Sparked off by a recent incident in 1938 in which a Jewish boy had killed a Nazi diplomat only to unleash a new phase in the German persecution of the Jews, the work is modelled on Handel's *Messiah* and Bach's Passions, with spirituals in place of chorales. It was first performed in 1944, after Tippett had spent two months in prison as a conscientious objector.

His next project of similar scope was the opera *The Midsummer Marriage* (1946–52), where again the issue is the reconciliation of opposing traits in the human psyche: male and female, manual and intellectual, spontaneous and reflective. The theme is treated in a parable on the preparation of two young people for union, and draws on Jung, *Die Zauberflöte*, Celtic myth, Shaw's metaphysical plays and T.S. Eliot. The range of sources was typical, but the music burst through them with rapturous lyricism and exultant dance, and those qualities spilled over into Tippett's orchestral works of the next five years. Early audiences were bemused, and it was not until the end of the 1960s that the opera found its moment.

By then he had long changed his style. His opera *King Priam* (1958–61) was a sculptured myth set in Messiaen-style blocks, and again there were strong echoes in ensuing works (the Concerto for Orchestra and Second Piano Sonata). Then in the heady cantata *The Vision of St Augustine* (1963–5) and the modern psychological drama *The Knot Garden* (1966–9) he started to weld small fragments into larger, swinging continuities. His Third Symphony (1970–72) specifically returns to the juncture in Beethoven's Ninth at which a singing voice appears, but what follows, as solace for modern woes, is a soprano singing the blues.

Though disabled by failing eyesight, he lived into a happy old age of acclaim and creative buoyancy. Later works – notably his Triple Concerto, *Byzantium*, last two quartets and symphonic poem *The Rose Lake* – resumed all aspects of his creative history in a glorious fusion and effusion.

Michael Tippett *Those Twentieth Century Blues: An Autobiography* (1991); Meirion Bowen, ed. *Tippett on Music* (1995)

www.michael-tippett.com

Operas (all librettos by the composer): *The* MIDSUMMER MARRIAGE, 1946–52; KING PRIAM, 1958–61; *The* KNOT GARDEN, 1966–9; *The Ice Break*, 1973–6, f.p. London, 1977; *New Year*, 1986–8, f.p. Houston, 1989
Vocal orchestral: *A* CHILD OF OUR TIME (Tippett), soli, ch, orch, 1939–41; *Crown of the Year* (Christopher Fry), women's ch, ens, 1958; *The Vision of St Augustine* (St Augustine, Bible), bar, ch, orch, 1963–5; *The Shires Suite*, ch, orch, 1965–70; *Songs for Dov* (Tippett), t, chbr orch, 1969–70; *The Mask of Time* (Tippett), soli, ch, orch, 1977–82; *Byzantium* (Yeats), s, orch, 1989–90
Orchestral: Symphony No.1, 1944–5; No.2, 1956–7; No.3, s, orch, 1970–72; No.4, 1976–7; Concerto, double str, 1938–9; Fantasia on a Theme of Handel, pf, orch, 1939–41; Little Music, str, 1946; Suite, D, 1948; Fantasia concertante on a Theme of Corelli, str, 1953; Divertimento on Sellinger's Round, chbr orch, 1953–4; Piano Concerto, 1953–5;

Praeludium, brass, perc, 1962; Concerto for Orchestra, 1962–3; Triple Concerto, str trio, orch, 1978–9; Festal Brass with Blues, brass band, 1983; *The Rose Lake*, 1991–3
Smaller choral works: 2 Madrigals (Hopkins, Edward Thomas), 1942; *Plebs angelica*, 1943; *The Weeping Babe* (Edith Sitwell), 1944; *Dance, Clarion Air* (Fry), 1952; 4 Songs from the British Isles, 1956; *Lullaby* (Yeats), 1960; *Music* (Shelley), 1960; *Magnificat* and *Nunc dimittis*, 1961
Chamber: String Quartet No.1, 1934–5, rev 1943; No.2, 1941–2; No.3, 1945–6; No.4, 1977–8; No.5, 1990–91; Sonata, 4 hn, 1955; *Music for Words, Perhaps*, 6 insts, 1960
Instrumental: Piano Sonata No.1, 1938, rev 1942; No.2, 1962; No.3, 1972–3; No.4, 1984; *Preludio al Vespro di Monteverdi*, org, 1945; *The Blue Guitar*, gtr, 1982–3; *Prelude: Autumn*, ob, pf, 1991
Songs: *Boyhood's End* (W.H. Hudson), t, pf, 1943; *The Heart's Assurance* (Sidney Keyes, Alun Lewis), s/t, pf, 1950–51; *Songs for Achilles* (Tippett), t, gtr, 1961; *Songs for Ariel* (Shakespeare), v, pf/hpd, 1962

Titan. Name given by Mahler to his First Symphony. He changed his mind, but the name has stuck to a limited degree. The Titans were deities of ancient Greece held to have ruled before the Olympian Gods; PROMETHEUS was one of them.

Titelouze, Jehan (b. St Omer, 1562/3; d. Rouen, 24 Oct 1633). French organist-composer, a founder of the French school of organ composition. Where he trained is unknown; he was organist of Rouen Cathedral from 1588 to the end of his life. In correspondence with Mersenne, he also involved himself actively in practical and theoretical matters concerning music and the organ. He published two volumes of organ music in the 1620s, each providing contrapuntal elaborations of chants (for various hymns and the *Magnificat*) to be played in alternation with the choir.

toccata (It., touched). Generally a keyboard piece in fast, regular rhythm, a study in velocity and even touch – though Baroque toccatas could be in several sections, as extended as sonatas but distinguished by free form. The term has also been used in other circumstances, as by Monteverdi for the fanfare-like opening of his *Orfeo*.

The first use of the word came in a 1536 collection of lute pieces, after which there was a delay before it suddenly became normal for keyboard works, applied in the 1590s to compositions by the Gabrielis, Merulo, etc. Important composers of toccatas in the next century included Frescobaldi, Michelangelo Rossi, Pasquini, Froberger and Muffat. Bach's toccatas include works of the old sort, in multiple sections (often including a fugue, not necessarily at the end), and pieces marked by rapid even motion, providing models for the toccatas of his successors.

Those successors, some time in coming, included Schumann, Widor, Debussy, Ravel and Prokofiev.

Toch, Ernst (b. Vienna, 7 Dec 1887; d. Santa Monica, Cal., 1 Oct 1964). Austrian–US composer. Self-taught, he first took Mozart and Brahms as his models, and he retained a firm belief in tradition after accepting more modern impulses (especially from Hindemith) in the 1920s. He moved from a position at the conservatory in Mannheim (1913–29) to Berlin, which he left at Hitler's arrival in 1933 for London, New York and California, his home from 1936. There he continued to teach, at USC, and to compose, his large output including much chamber music and seven late symphonies.

Tod und das Mädchen, Der (Death and the Maiden). Song by Schubert to words by Matthias Claudius: the Maiden asks Death to pass her by; instead he requires her hand. The name has also accrued to the composer's D minor quartet, which has variations on the song's introduction as its slow movement and which, altogether, is itself a dialogue with death.

Toeschi, Carl Joseph (baptized Ludwigsburg, 11 Nov 1731; d. Munich, 12 April 1788). German composer. The son of an Italian violinist who had settled in Germany, he grew up in Mannheim, where he studied with Johann Stamitz and Anton Filtz. He spent his career with the orchestra as violinist, leader and composer, and was among the many musicians who went with the Elector from Mannheim to Munich in 1778. Trips to Paris brought him a French wife and an elegant lightening of his melodic style. His works include symphonies, flute concertos, numerous chamber pieces and ballets.

Togni, Camillo (b. Gussago, Brescia, 18 Oct 1922; d. Brescia, 28 Nov 1993). Italian composer. His initial training was in Brescia, and with Casella in Siena and Rome (1939–42), but what marked him most was first hearing Schoenberg's music in 1938, thanks to Michelangeli. He completed his piano studies with that master in Brescia (1943–50), wrote a dissertation on Croce's aesthetics under Luigi Rognoni at Milan University (1942–7), and made a deep study of Schoenberg. A regular at Darmstadt in the 1950s, he followed new developments from a position that was already solid, authoritative and self-critical. He taught, notably at the Parma Conservatory (1977–88), and

produced a relatively small output, of works mostly compact and dark. They include two one-act operas after Trakl (*Blaubart*, 1972–5; *Barabbas*, 1981–5) and six piano capriccios (Nos.1–3, Op.38, 1954–7; No.4, 1969; No.5, 1987; No.6, 1991).

Tomášek, Václav Jan Křtitel [Tomaschek, Wenzel Johann] (b. Skuteč, 17 Apr 1774; d. Prague, 3 Apr 1850). Czech composer, an early Romantic. A self-made man, he paid for his education – which went as far as legal studies at Prague University – by singing as a chorister and later by playing and teaching the piano. After a time in service to Count Georg Buquoy (1806–22), he lived independently in Prague with his wife, whom he married in 1824. He is remembered chiefly for his lyric piano pieces, which include 42 eclogues and 15 rhapsodies. Among his many songs are settings of Goethe, with whom he was in contact, and some of the earliest Czech art songs.

Tomasi, Henri (b. Marseilles, 17 Aug 1901; d. Paris, 13 Jan 1971). French composer, who produced a large output of theatre and other works, but is remembered especially for his jazz-flavoured trumpet concerto (1948). He studied conducting with Philippe Gaubert at the Paris Conservatoire, and worked as an opera conductor.

tombeau (Fr., tomb, monument, pl. *tombeaux*). French memorial genre, originally literary, the earliest musical example being Ennemond Gaultier's *tombeau* for the lutenist Mesengeau (d. 1638). Further *tombeaux* came from Marais, Louis Couperin, D'Anglebert, Froberger and others, generally in the form of a slow dance: allemande or pavan. The tradition was revived by Ravel, and then by composers commemorating Debussy, Dukas, etc.

Tombeau de Couperin, Le (Couperin's Monument). Suite by Ravel. The original piano version has six movements – Prelude, Fugue, Forlane, Rigaudon, Menuet, Toccata – of which he orchestrated four, to be played in the order 1–3–5–4. First performance: Paris, 11 Apr 1919 (pf), 28 Feb 1920 (orch).

Tomkins, Thomas (b. St David's, 1572; buried Martin Hussingtree, Worcs., 9 Jun 1656). Welsh composer. The son of a cathedral musician, he was himself appointed inspector of the choristers at Worcester Cathedral in 1592, possibly after studying with Byrd. Almost certainly he had a connection with the Chapel Royal from long before he became its second organist in 1621, contributing anthems for the coronation of

James I in 1603 (*Be Strong and of a Good Courage* for seven-part choir and organ) and the funeral of Prince Henry in 1612 (*Know ye not*). In 1622 he published a book of madrigals, each dedicated to a member of his family (including three half-brothers who were also members of the Chapel Royal, and his son Nathaniel, who became a canon of Worcester) or a musical or clerical friend in Worcester or London; the book includes *When David heard that Absalom was slain* and *Too much I once lamented*. Three years later he was largely responsible for the coronation music for Charles I, but he seems to have spent most of his later years in Worcester. Following in the tradition of Byrd, his works include five services and numerous anthems, as well as consort and keyboard music: fantasias (Fancy 'for two to play' at one keyboard), In Nomines, pavans and other dances.

Denis Stevens *Thomas Tomkins* (1957)

Tomlinson, John (b. Oswaldtwistle, 22 Sep 1946). British bass, a powerful vocal actor, using shades of rawness and gravity in his voice to summon lived expression. He studied in Manchester and made his debut with Glyndebourne Touring Opera in 1972. Among his notable roles are Wotan (Bayreuth, 1988), the Green Knight (in the first *Gawain*, Covent Garden, 1991) and Schoenberg's Moses (Met, 1999).

Tommasini, Vincenzo (b. Rome, 17 Sep 1878; d. Rome, 23 Dec 1950). Italian composer, remembered especially for his orchestration of Scarlatti sonatas to make a ballet score for Diaghilev, *Le donne di buon umore* (1917). His other works – orchestral pieces, operas, string quartets – reflect his admiration for Debussy, though he had received his professional education under Bruch in Berlin. Enjoying family wealth, he was also able to devote himself to the study of aesthetics.

tom-toms. Small, wood-framed drums with membranes of calfskin or plastic, commonly played in pairs.

ton (Fr.). Tone.

Ton (Ger., pl. *Töne*). Tone.

tonadilla (Sp., little song). Genre of short popular opera that developed in Spain in the third quarter of the 18th century, declined early the next century and was replaced by a revival of the form it had displaced, the ZARZUELA.

tonal. Descriptive of music adhering to a key or mode, or at least having some central pitch.

tonal answer. An ANSWER in a FUGUE where the subject is altered to preserve the tonality.

tonality. (1) An umbrella term for musical systems defined by keys, modes or central pitches. It has been most used in contrast with ATONALITY or POLYTONALITY.

(2) Term used to indicate the key, mode or pitch centre of a passage, as in 'tonality of E'. This meaning is closer to that for which the word was coined, in 1821 by the composer François Castil-Blaze, who used it to mean the tonic, fifth and fourth of a key.

Tonart (Ger., pl. *Tonarten*). Key.

tonary. Liturgical book in which antiphons and other chants are grouped by TONE (5).

Tondichter (Ger., tone poet, pl. *Tondichter*). Composer.

Tondichtung (Ger., pl. *Tondichtungen*). Tone poem.

tone. (1) Sound, usually with an emphasis on frequency, as in 'combination tone'.

(2) Quality of sound, i.e. timbre. A violin is judged by its tone.

(3) US equivalent to the UK 'note', as in 12-tone music.

(4) Interval of one sixth of an octave, i.e. two semitones, often called a 'whole tone' to be clear. The precise size of the tone depends on the TEMPERAMENT; some temperaments have two, slightly different.

(5) MODE used in plainsong. Gregorian chant has eight numbered tones in authentic-plagal pairs: DORIAN and HYPODORIAN (on D), PHRYGIAN and HYPOPHRYGIAN (on E), LYDIAN and HYPOLYDIAN (on F), and MIXOLYDIAN and HYPOMIXOLYDIAN (on G).

tone colour. TIMBRE.

tone poem. Term introduced by Strauss in preference to SYMPHONIC POEM.

tone row. See ROW.

tonguing. Technique used in playing wind instruments to give a staccato or a sharp attack. The tongue is placed against the reed or palate, depending on the instrument, and pulled back, as when making the 't' or 'd' sound. Runs may require double tonguing (t-k or d-g attacks) or triple tonguing (t-k-t, d-g-d). See also FLUTTERTONGUE.

Tonhalle Orchestra (Tonhalle-Orchester). The oldest Swiss orchestra (1868), based in Zurich. Through its first 71 years it had two principal conductors: Friedrich Hegar and then Volkmar Andreae. Later incumbents have included Rosbaud, Kempe, Eschenbach and David Zinman (from 1995).

tonic [keynote]. The principal note in the major-minor system, e.g. C in C major or minor. This is the note on which a major or minor scale starts and ends, the note towards which a melody in that system is drawn to find completion.

tonic accent. Accent that a note or chord acquires by virtue of higher pitch.

tonic sol-fa. Method of notation and instruction in which notes are given names according to their position in the scale. Thus any major scale is represented as *doh–re–mi–fa–soh–la–te–doh*, with other syllables for chromatic notes. To simplify matters, minor scales start on *la*. The system was first formalized by Sarah Glover (1785–1867), a Norwich schoolteacher, in the 1830s and vastly popularized by John Curwen (1816–80), a Congregationalist minister. For both its purpose was to facilitate the teaching of tunes to sing.

Tonkunst (Ger., tone art). Music. Hence *Tonkünstler*, musician.

tono (It., pl. *toni*). Tone.

Tonreihe (Ger., tone row). Row.

tonus peregrinus (Lat., wandering tone). TONE (5) where the reciting pitch is mobile. It seems to have been an addition to the regular eight tones, and is found in rather few chants, notably that of the psalm *In exitu Israel*.

topos (Gk, place, pl. *topoi*). Sphere of reference to which a work may appeal. The topoi of Debussy's *Prélude à 'L'Après-midi d'un faune'*, for example, would include the pastoral (call signals from solo flute and oboe suggestive of a shepherd's piping), Greek antiquity (modal features, plus of course the title), Mallarmé's poem (as again proclaimed by the title), the expression of languorous sensuality (through rhythmic-harmonic metaphors established at least since Berlioz) and a French tradition of picturesque orchestral miniature.

torculus. Kind of NEUME.

Torelli, Giuseppe (b. Verona, 22 Apr 1658; d. Bologna, 8 Feb 1709). Italian composer. Brought up in a large family, comfortably off, he must have had training in Verona before moving to Bologna, where in 1684 he was admitted to the Accademia Filarmonica. He played the violin in the orchestra at San Petronio there (1686–96), then seems to have travelled with the castrato Francesco Antonio Pistocchi to Ansbach and Vienna (1699–1700) before they both returned to Bologna and San Petronio. Described at the time as 'a man not only of docile and humble habits but also erudite and eloquent', he produced numerous trio sonatas, concerti grossi and sonatas for strings with trumpet for use at San Petronio.

Torke, Michael (b. Milwaukee, 22 Sep 1961). US composer. He studied at the Eastman School and Yale (1984–5) and rapidly gained note for bright, colourful orchestral pieces (e.g. *Ecstatic Orange*, 1985–7) coming out of minimalism and rock.

Toronto. Canadian city, whose musical institutions include the Toronto Symphony – founded in 1916, with conductors including Ernest MacMillan (1931–56) and Andrew Davis (1975–88) – and the Toronto Conservatory (1886, renamed Royal Conservatory in 1947).

Tortelier, Paul (b. Paris, 21 Mar 1914; d. Villarceaux, Val d'Oise, 18 Dec 1990). French cellist, noted for his forward, grainy sound and expressive vitality. He studied with Gerard Hekking at the Paris Conservatoire and became an international virtuoso after playing the solo part in Strauss's *Don Quixote* (a favourite vehicle) with Beecham in London in 1947, besides maintaining a busy teaching career. His son is the conductor Yan Pascal Tortelier (b. 1947).

Tosca. Opera by Puccini to a libretto by Giacosa and Illica after Victorien Sardou's play. In one of the most emphatic of love-triangle dramas, Tosca (soprano), a singer in Rome in 1800, and her lover, the painter Cavaradossi (tenor), appear to be at the mercy of the police chief, Scarpia (baritone), but all three are ruled by passion, and all three die within the 24-hour period of the action. The work is the source of popular arias: Tosca's 'Vissi d'arte' and Cavaradossi's 'Recondita armonia' and 'E lucevan le stelle'. First performance: Rome, 14 Jan 1900.

Toscanini, Arturo (b. Parma, 25 Mar 1867; d. New York, 16 Jan 1957). Italian conductor. Incisive, driven, regularly brilliant, he was at the peak of his career in the early decades of the microphone, and his recordings of certain works (Verdi's *Requiem* and *Falstaff*) are classics. He was a tailor's son, who showed musical promise from an early age and was sent to the Parma Conservatory when he was nine. On graduating, in 1885, he began his career as a cellist: he was in the orchestra at La Scala for the première of Verdi's *Otello* in 1887. But he had already made his debut as a conductor (with *Aida* in Rio de Janeiro in 1886), and at the premières of *Pagliacci* (1892) and *La Bohème* (1896) he held the baton. He was then artistic director of La Scala (1898–1913) and the Met (1908–15), exerting his formidable energy and refusal to compromise. During a second period at La Scala (1920–29, including the première of *Turandot*) he came into conflict with the fascist government, which resulted in a period of self-exile he ended only in 1946. In 1930 he became the first non-German to conduct at Bayreuth (Wagner had long been among his passions), but he broke his connections with Germany and then Austria as fascism spread there. Increasingly he was based in New York, as chief conductor of the Philharmonic (1928–36) and the NBC Symphony (1937–54), with which he made most of his recordings. His daughter Wanda married Horowitz.

Joseph Horowitz *Understanding Toscanini* (1987)

Tost. Name given to Haydn's quartets Opp.54, 55 and 64, dedicated to the violinist Johann Tost.

Tosti, (Francesco) Paolo (b. Ostano sul Mare, 9 Apr 1846; d. Rome, 2 Dec 1916). Italian–British composer of parlour songs ('Goodbye', 'Mattinata'), knighted in 1908. He studied in Naples with Mercadante and others, and settled in London in 1880 as singing teacher to the royal family.

total serialism. The organization of all possible musical parameters according to serial principles, also known as 'integral serialism' or 'general serialism'. Webern, though not Schoenberg, would seem to have been working in this direction, for example in his use not only of 12-note pitch sets but of duration sets, 2–2–1–2 (e.g. crotchet, crotchet, quaver, crotchet) and 3–1–2–6, with their retrograde forms, in his Variations Op.30 (1940). Babbitt went further in his Three Compositions for piano (1947), where the duration set 5–1–4–2 is not only reversed but 'inverted' (by complementing the values to 6: 1–5–2–4), and in his Composition for 12 Instruments (1948), which uses not only a 12-fold ensemble but 12-note sets of 'chromatic' durations (durations of from one to 12 units, e.g. demisemiquaver, semiquaver, dotted semiquaver, etc., up to dotted crotchet). Similar rhythmic scales were introduced around the same

time independently by Messiaen and Boulez, and the latter's *Structures Ia* (1951) applied serial organization not only to such durations but also to dynamic levels and to modes of attack (or at least to their symbolic representations). Stockhausen did something similar in his *Kreuzspiel* of the same year, taking, as Boulez had, the model of Messiaen's *Mode de valeurs et d'intensités* (1949). Total serialism as thus practised meant treating each note by itself, and because the resultant scattering of points was limiting as a musical texture, the technique was soon abandoned by European composers.

The ideal, though, was not. Stockhausen in his electronic *Studien* (1953–4) sought to create entirely consistent musical worlds in which similar rules governed the treatment of pitch, rhythm and timbre, and in his *Gruppen* (1955–7) he worked with tempo sets. Even composers who wrote little or no serial music, such as Ligeti and Birtwistle, have continued to be fascinated by the concept of music as a construction in several different domains of sound and time.

M.J. Grant *Serial Music, Serial Aesthetics* (2001)

Totentanz (Ger.). DANCE OF DEATH.

To the Distant Beloved. See AN DIE FERNE GELIEBTE.

touch. The finger pressure applied to a keyboard instrument. An instrument may be described as having a heavy or light touch, depending on how much pressure is needed to make a sound. Alternatively, the term may be used of the player – of how the key's speed of descent is controlled. Qualities of touch in this sense will affect loudness and timbre, and thereby phrasing. In older English other instruments may be touched (as the recorder offered by Hamlet was not by Guildenstern), and the term occasionally appeared as a title.

touche (Fr.). Key on a keyboard or fingerboard on a bowed string instrument.

Tournai Mass. Grouping of movements from the 13th century (*Kyrie, Sanctus, Agnus Dei*) and the early 14th (*Gloria, Credo*) preserved at Tournai Cathedral.

Tournemire, Charles (Arnould) (b. Bordeaux, 22 Jan 1870; d. Arcachon, 4 Nov 1939). French organist-composer. He studied with Widor at the Paris Conservatoire and with Franck, whom he succeeded at Ste Clotilde in 1898. His large output includes four operas and eight symphonies, but he is remembered almost exclusively for his organ music, which consists mostly of plainsong elaborations in a style of absorbed piety that influenced Messiaen. His *L'Orgue mystique* (published 1927–32) is a set of 51 organ masses for the liturgical year.

Tourte, François Xavier (b. Paris, 1747/8; d. Paris, 25 Apr 1835). French bowmaker, 'the Stradivari of the bow'. He and his brother Léonard probably learned the art from their father, and were responsible for the shape of the modern bow, François's being articles of superb craftsmanship.

Tovey, Donald (Francis) (b. Eton, 17 Jul 1875; d. Edinburgh, 10 Jul 1940). British educator, knighted in 1935. The son of an Eton master, he began his career as a pianist while reading classics at Oxford (1894–8). In 1914 he was appointed professor of music at Edinburgh University, and after that he concentrated on educational work – not only with his students but through the medium of the programme note, which he made into a forum for close, insightful analysis voiced in common language. His notes for the Reid Orchestra, which he founded in 1917, became the basis of his *Essays in Musical Analysis* (1935–44). He also composed, especially before his Edinburgh appointment, his most notable later work being a concerto for Casals (1935).

Toward the Unknown Region. Song for choir and orchestra by Vaughan Williams, setting Whitman. First performance: Leeds, 1907.

Tower, Joan (Peabody) (b. New Rochelle, NY, 6 Sep 1938). US composer. Brought up in South America, where her father was a mining engineer, she absorbed indigenous music before returning to the USA for formal studies at Bennington and Columbia. In 1969 she was the pianist co-founder of the Da Capo Players, a chamber group specializing in new music for the *Pierrot lunaire* quintet, including her own *Petroushkates* (1980). While playing with them (until 1984) she developed a new vibrancy, energy and colour in her music without spurning its avant-garde origins, and her first orchestral piece, *Sequoia* (1981), set her on a course of continuing large-scale commissions, among which *Silver Ladders* (1986) won her the Grawemeyer Award. Other works include concertos and a series of five *Fanfares for the Uncommon Woman* (1986–93), as well as numerous chamber and instrumental pieces. She has also taught at Bard College since 1972 and served as composer-in-residence with several orchestras.

tower music (Ger. *Turmmusik*). Music played from the tower of a church or town hall by bands of cornetts, trumpets and trombones in Germany during the period from the late 16th century to the early 18th. Holliger's *Turmmusik* alludes to the tradition.

toy [toye]. Simple lute or keyboard piece, common type in English music of *c.*1590–1660.

toy instruments. Whistles, small percussion instruments, etc., played as children's toys. Berchtesgaden, near Salzburg, was a centre of their manufacture in the 18th century; hence, among other such works, the 'Toy Symphony' usually attributed to Leopold Mozart. Of more recent invention are toy pianos, with a range of an octave and a half or so. Cage wrote for one.

tpt. Abbreviation for trumpet.

tr. Abbreviation for TRILL in notation.

tracker. Wooden strip connecting an organ key to its respective pallet. An organ may thus have tracker action, as distinct from electric or pneumatic action.

tract. Mass chant associated with Lent and other penitential seasons, normally sung antiphonally.

tradition. Body of ideas and practices that has had some consistency through time; thus an attachment to instrumental colour in Rameau and Boulez could be seen as characteristic of the French tradition. One may also speak of the symphonic tradition, the violin tradition, etc. When used without qualification, the term is often being used to disqualify, to place a work or composer as outside 'the tradition' – a problematic notion, not least because views on this can differ. Barraqué's Sonata, for example, can be heard as a thoroughly traditional piece or a thoroughly iconoclastic one, which will partly depend on whether one understands the essential quality of the tradition as conservatism or self-renewal. Also, 'the tradition' (of Western art music) can no longer be considered in lone and superior independence from traditions of non-Western music, popular music, etc. Traditions are best understood plurally, and as interacting gusts of achievement and principle moving through history rather than as walled alleys. See also HISTORY.

Traetta, Tommaso (Michele Francesco Saverio) (b. Bitonto, near Bari, 30 Mar 1727; d. Venice, 6 Apr 1779). Italian composer, a proponent of REFORM

OPERA before and alongside Gluck. He studied with Porpora and Durante at the Loreto conservatory in Naples (1738–48) and began his career as an opera composer locally, influenced by contact with Jommelli. Appointed to the Parma court in 1758, he was expected to unite French tastes for drama, dancing and choral splendour with Italian lyricism in setting adaptations of librettos from Rameau's operas (*Ippolito ed Aricia*, 1759). His achievement in that made his reputation and gave him the opportunity to write operas for Mannheim (*Sofonisba*, 1762) and Vienna (the Gluckian *Ifigenia in Tauride*, 1763). He then worked in Venice (1765–8) before being called to St Petersburg by Catherine II (*Antigona*, 1772). In 1775 he left Russia in poor health, went to London (where Sacchini's popularity was an obstacle) and spent his last two years or so in Venice.

tragédie lyrique. French serious opera of the century from Lully through Rameau to Gluck.

Tragic. Name given by Schubert to his Fourth Symphony and by Brahms to an overture. Mahler's Sixth is also sometimes known thus.

Trampler, Walter (b. Munich, 25 Aug 1915; d. Port Joli, Nova Scotia, 27 Sep 1997). German–US viola player, a warm and virtuoso exponent of a repertory from classic chamber music to solo works by Berio and Henze. Taught by his father and at the academy in Munich, he made his debut as a violinist in 1933 and as a violist in 1935 (Berlin, Mozart's Sinfonia Concertante). In 1939 he moved to New York and into a long career as a performer and teacher.

Trans. Orchestral work by Stockhausen with dream imagery. Strings play in purple light behind a gauze; wind and percussion are amplified, as is the recorded sound of a weaving shuttle; and soloists appear. First performance: Donaueschingen, 16 Oct 1971.

Transcendental Etudes. See ETUDES D'EXECUTION TRANSCENDANTE.

transcription. Arrangement. The term is most often used of piano versions, whether of orchestral scores or of simpler originals (e.g. those of Liszt and Godowsky), or else of arrangements made in the reverse direction, from keyboard to orchestra (e.g. those of Elgar and Webern after Bach). It can also be applied to the copying of music from one notational system into another (e.g. from lute tablature to staff notation).

Transfiguration de Notre Seigneur Jésus-Christ, La (The Transfiguration of Our Lord Jesus Christ). Work by Messiaen for seven instrumental soloists (pf, fl, cl, vc, vib, mar, xyl), a choir of 100 and an orchestra of 109. It is a concert liturgy in two septenaries, or sequences of seven movements, each including two gospel narratives, four meditations and a concluding chorale. First performance: Lisbon, 7 Jun 1969.

Transfigured Night. See VERKLÄRTE NACHT.

transformation. Alteration of a theme so that it has a new identity, while maintaining a resemblance to its original form. The technique is particularly associated with Romantic music, beginning with Beethoven (e.g. finale of the Ninth Symphony, with its martial transformation of the main theme). Thematic transformation was most often used to generate different, related characters in a piece of musical narrative (Liszt's symphonic poems or Wagner's operas, where different leitmotifs often have a common source) or to create connection between the movements of a symphonic work (Franck, Tchaikovsky). There are also sporadic instances in Baroque and Classical music: different dances drawn from the same thematic material, or the theme of a slow introduction reconfigured in the ensuing allegro (Haydn's Symphony No.103).

transient. Momentary feature of a sound, especially its starting transient, which often has an important part in defining timbre. Recorded piano sounds that have been deprived, by editing, of their starting transients resemble organ tones.

transition [bridge]. Passage whose structural function is to lead from one section to another, especially in a sonata form.

transpose. Change pitch level. A piece may be transposed from E major to C major; a theme may be transposed down a fourth.

transposing instruments. Instruments whose parts are notated at a different pitch level from that at which they sound. Music for the cor anglais, for example, is frequently notated a fifth higher than it should sound, because this allows the player to handle the instrument as if it were an oboe (which indeed sounds a fifth higher than the cor anglais), keeping fingerings that are familiar. The player sees C, plays C, and the F below is heard. The cor anglais is thus said to be 'in F'.

Again with the original intention of keeping oboe fingering, the standard clarinet, in B♭, sounds a major second below the notated pitch. There are also clarinets in A, E♭, etc. Other transposing instruments include the alto flute (in G), the oboe d'amore (in A), saxophones (in B♭ and E♭), the horn (in F) and trumpets (in B♭ and D).

Parts for instruments of extreme range are conventionally notated in a different octave, for convenience. The piccolo, for instance, sounds an octave higher than written, the double bass an octave lower. But these are not regarded as transposing instruments.

Scores, especially of music from before 1950, will generally maintain the conventional way of writing for transposing instruments. Thus a C major chord might show a horn on G, a tenor saxophone on F♯, an alto flute on D and a high trumpet on B♭. But scores and parts may also be written and published 'in C', i.e. with all transposing instruments notated at sounding pitch. Performers therefore have to cope with reading their music either with or without the traditional transposition.

transposition. Changing the pitch level. Keyboard players have to be adept at transposition so that they can, for instance, change the level of an accompaniment in response to the needs of a solo singer or a congregation. Almost any composition will include the transposition of a melody or harmony, sometimes with a slight adjustment of intervals to suit the new harmonic context.

transverse flute. Former name for the standard flute, distinguishing it from the recorder, played in vertical position.

traps. DRUM KIT.

tratto (It.). Dragged, a term normally used in the negative, as in *grave ma non troppo tratto* (Beethoven's Op.135 quartet).

Trauer (Ger.). Mourning. Hence *Trauermarsch* (funeral march), *Trauermusik* (funeral music), *traurig* (mournful).

Trauersinfonie. See MOURNING.

Traum, Ein (A Dream). Name given to the slow movement of Haydn's Quartet Op.50:5.

Träumerei (Reverie). Piano piece by Schumann, No.7 of his *Kinderscenen*.

traurig (Ger.). Sad.

trautonium. Electronic instrument built by Friedrich Trautwein (1888–1956) and first exhibited by him in Berlin in 1930. Its pitch was controlled by moving a finger along a wire. Hindemith wrote a Konzertstück for it.

traverso. Shortening of *flauto traverso* (It., transverse flute).

travesti (It.). Cross-dressed. The term is used of operatic roles requiring women to appear as boys or young men, e.g. Cherubino (*Le nozze di Figaro*) and Oktavian (*Der Rosenkavalier*), but not normally of cases where the cross-dresser is male, such as Arnalta (*L'incoronazione di Poppea*).

Traviata, La (The Fallen Woman). Opera by Verdi to a libretto by Piave after the younger Dumas's play *La Dame aux camélias*. Violetta (soprano) abandons the Paris demi-monde to settle with Alfredo (tenor), but leaves him at the insistence of his father Germont (baritone) and dies, both men at her bedside. Notable numbers include Violetta's Act 1 soliloquy 'Ah fors'è lui – Di quell'amor – Sempre libera' and Act 3 farewell 'Addio del passato', Alfredo's brindisi 'Libiamo ne' lieti calici' (seconded by Violetta and the chorus) and lyrical 'Dei miei bollenti spiriti', Germont's aria 'Di Provenza il mar' and the Violetta–Alfredo duets 'Un dì felice' and 'Parigi, o cara'. First performance: Venice, 6 Mar 1853.

trbn. Abbreviation for trombone.

treble. (1) Upper part of the pitch range, as opposed to bass.

(2) A voice of high range, usually a boy's before the change into the adult male register that comes at puberty, or a singer with that voice. Used adjectivally, the word can indicate an instrument of similar register (e.g. treble recorder).

The term originated in early polyphony, denoting a third voice, the TRIPLUM. Its persistence as a word is unique to English, other languages having forms of the word 'soprano' for the register and for the voice – and 'boy soprano' is the usual US term for the latter.

Boy choristers were singing in churches in the Middle Ages, and most of the great Renaissance composers, from Du Fay to Palestrina, began their musical careers as trebles. So in later periods did Purcell, Haydn and Schubert. The western European tradition of the all-male liturgical choir began to change around 1600 with the admission of women singers in church, but it has remained strong in England and Vienna to the present. Boy choirs also appear occasionally in concert works (Mahler's Eighth Symphony) and operas

(*Carmen*), and there are solo treble roles in operas by Landi and Britten.

treble clef. G CLEF on the second line up, the standard clef for higher instruments and voices (violin, oboe, soprano, etc.), for the right hand at a keyboard, and for other voices and instruments reading with transposition (e.g. tenor sounding an octave lower, horn sounding a fifth lower).

Trebor (*fl. c.*1380–1400). Probably French composer, author of songs in the CHANTILLY manuscript that include references to lords of Foix and Aragon.

tre corde (It., three strings). Direction to release the left (UNA CORDA) pedal on a piano.

Tremblay, Gilles (b. Arvida, Quebec, 6 Sep 1932). Canadian composer. He studied at the Montreal Conservatory (1949–54) and at the Paris Conservatoire (1954–8), where Messiaen's teaching was crucial to him. After remaining in Europe a while, working in the French radio electronic music studio and attending the Darmstadt courses, in 1962 he returned to the Montreal Conservatory to teach composition. His works include *Les Vêpres de la Vierge* for soprano, choir and ensemble (1986).

tremblement (Fr.). Trill (obsolete).

tremolando (It., tremblingly). Quick oscillation between notes in the prevailing harmony, e.g. a third or an octave apart.

tremolo (It., trembling). Rapid repetition of a note, as distinct from the trill and vibrato, where the note changes. These distinctions were not always made in older sources, but Monteverdi specified the single-note tremolo for the voice in the preface to his eighth book of madrigals (1638). String instruments can readily produce a similar effect; as with voices, the repeated notes may be clearly articulated or the tremolo may be a wavering of volume. Wind instruments and the piano can imitate the device by means of a tremolando.

trepak. Russian Cossack dance in lively 2/4, typically performed by men kicking their legs out from a squatting position. There is an example in Tchaikovsky's *Nutcracker* suite.

triad. Three-note chord which, in close position, would embrace two thirds. A major triad has a major third below a minor (e.g. C–E–G). A minor triad has a minor third below a major (e.g. C–Eb–G). These two chords are fundamental to the major-minor system, and nearly all compositions in that system end on one or other of them. Among important dissonances, in major-minor harmony, are the diminished triad, with two minor thirds (e.g. C–Eb–Gb), and the augmented triad, with two major thirds (e.g. C–E–G♯).

Trial, Antoine (b. Avignon, 1737; d. Paris, 5 Feb 1795). French tenor. He followed his composer brother Jean Claude (1732–71) to Paris, where, with his thin voice and acting skills, he specialized in peasant characters and simpletons. Having been active in the Terror, he lost his career with Robespierre's fall and poisoned himself, but his name survived to describe the kind of singer he had been.

triangle. Percussion instrument, a steel rod bent into triangular shape, held on a loop of gut or plastic, and struck with a steel beater or drumstick. Mentioned and depicted regularly from the 10th century onwards, it entered the opera orchestra in the early 18th century and was used in imitations of JANISSARY music by Mozart, Haydn and Beethoven. Liszt made it a solo instrument in his First Piano Concerto, and at that time its form became stable: earlier triangles had sometimes had loose jingling rings slipped around the rod.

trichord. Three-note chord of any kind, unlike the TRIAD.

tricinium. Three-part Renaissance or early-Baroque composition.

trill. Rapid alternation of the notated pitch with the note a second above, major or minor depending on the harmony or on the composer's indication, notated and realized thus:

Trille du diable, Le. See DEVIL'S TRILL.

trio. (1) Group of three instruments or voices, or group of performers on such, or genre of music for that medium, or work of that genre. There are trios in operas; the commonest instrumental forms are the PIANO TRIO and STRING TRIO.

(2) Alternate section of a dance or (later) other movement. Trios figure in suites and other dance-style music of the Baroque. Originally they were in three parts, and though that etymological necessity was soon abandoned, the trio generally retained a contrasting quietness. Placed between two

unfoldings of a minuet, it became a regular part of the symphony and string quartet from the time those genres arose, and kept its place in the new context of the scherzo.

(3) Three-part contrapuntal composition for keyboard, as in examples by Bach.

trio sonata. Sonata for two instruments with continuo, the main chamber genre of the Baroque. The two instruments would usually be violins, but other combinations were possible (violin and flute, two flutes, etc.). Four performers, not three, are needed, since the continuo part generally implies a keyboard plus low string instrument.

triple concerto. Concerto with three soloists, most notably Beethoven's for piano, violin and cello, first performed in Vienna in May 1808. Other examples include Mozart's Concerto K.242 for three pianos, Martin's PETITE SYMPHONIE CONCERTANTE and Tippett's work with string trio soloists.

triple counterpoint. INVERTIBLE COUNTERPOINT in three parts.

triple croche (Fr.). 32nd-note, demisemiquaver.

triple fugue. Fugue on three subjects.

triple stop. Threesome of notes played simultaneously on a string instrument with three fingers on different strings, i.e. by triple stopping. A lot of Baroque composers presumed arpeggiation of the three notes, but some – and many in the 20th century – did not.

triplet. Group of three equal notes to be played in the time of two.

triple time. Three beats to the bar.

triple wind. Three each of flutes, oboes, clarinets and bassoons, the standard line-up in Brahms, Dvořák and Tchaikovsky.

triplum (Lat., triple). Term used in the 13th–15th centuries for a third voice in polyphony, added to the tenor and duplum.

Triptych. Set of three music-theatre pieces for voices and ensemble by Goehr, more or less benign looks at human folly. *Naboth's Vineyard*, Op.25 (f.p. London, 1966), is a biblical parable of greed and retribution, *Shadowplay*, Op.30 (f.p. London, 1970) a treatment of Plato's image of the man in a cave for whom shadows are reality, and *Sonata*

about Jerusalem, Op.31 (f.p. Tel-Aviv, 1971) the story of a false messiah.

Tristan chord. Chord of the same kind as the first in *Tristan und Isolde*: F–B–D♯–G♯. It appeared in earlier music (e.g. the slow movement of Mozart's Quartet in E♭, K.428), but Wagner's opera made it a crux, its harmonic meaning endlessly debated.

Tristan Schalmei (Tristan shawm). Instrument (now extinct) made by Wilhelm Heckel in the late 19th century for the shepherd's piping in Act 3 of *Tristan*.

Tristan und Isolde (Tristram and Yseult). Opera by Wagner to his own libretto after the *Tristan* of the medieval German poet Gottfried von Strassburg. Isolde (soprano), being borne by ship in the company of Tristan (tenor) as bride for his king, resolves on death for herself and her captor, but her companion Brangäne (soprano) provides them instead with a love potion. The second act is a long love scene, watched over by Brangäne and ended by the arrival of the king, Marke (bass). Tristan, wounded in the ensuing scuffle, retires to his coastal castle with his faithful Kurwenal (baritone), waiting for Isolde to come, then dying in her arms, after which she sings herself into death in her LIEBESTOD. Wagner provided a concert ending for the prelude, and also a version in which the *Liebestod* is affixed. First performance: Munich, 10 Jun 1865.

tritone. Interval of three whole tones, or half an octave, which may be considered an augmented fourth (e.g. C–F♯) or diminished fifth (e.g. C–G♭). Used harmonically, it introduced a tonal confusion that caused medieval musicians to be wary of it and give it the nickname *diabolus in musica* (devil in music). It retained its aura of uncertainty and untrustworthiness in later music, and began to transcend its reputation only in Liszt, Debussy and Scriabin. Messiaen made it precisely what it had not been in the Middle Ages: a cadencing interval.

trittico, Il (The Triptych). Triple bill of one-act operas by Puccini. *Il tabarro*, to a libretto by Giuseppe Adami, is a tragedy of jealousy and revenge. *Suor Angelica* and *Gianni Schicchi*, to librettos by Giovacchino Forzano, are a melodrama set in a convent and a bubbling family comedy – though deriving from Dante's *Inferno* – in which Gianni Schicchi (baritone) contrives at one stroke to get wealth for himself and peace for his daughter, Lauretta (soprano), with her beloved Rinuccio (tenor). Lauretta has the sweet solo 'O mio babbino caro'. First performance: New York, Met, 14 Dec 1918.

Triumph of Time, The. Orchestral work by Birtwistle, with imagery of time that returns (a soprano saxophone call) and does not. First performance: London, 1 Jun 1972.

Triumphs of Oriana, The. Volume of English madrigals edited by Morley (1601), in honour of Elizabeth I. There are 26 pieces by 23 composers, including Weelkes, Wilbye and Morley himself.

trobairitz. Female troubadour.

Trois petites liturgies de la Présence Divine (Three Little Liturgies of the Divine Presence). Work by Messiaen for solo piano with women's choir (singing his own text), ondes martenot, celesta, vibraphone, percussion and string orchestra. First performance: Paris, 21 Apr 1945.

Trojahn, Manfred (b. Cremlingen, near Brunswick, 22 Oct 1949). German composer, associated with the expressionist–Romantic revival of the 1970s. He studied with de la Motte and Ligeti in Hamburg (from 1971), and caused a stir with his frankly retro First Symphony (1973–4). Later works include two operas: *Enrico* (f.p. Schwetzingen, 1991) and *Was ihr wollt* (f.p. Munich, 1998).

Trojan War. Greek–Trojan combat whose historical reality was in ancient times completely subsumed by poetry: the *Iliad* of Homer and, dealing with the aftermath, his *Odyssey* and works by Aeschylus, Sophocles, Euripides and Virgil. Operas drawing on this heroic material include ELEKTRA, IDOMENEO, IPHIGENIE EN AULIDE, IPHIGENIE EN TAURIDE, KING PRIAM and *Les* TROYENS.

tromba (It., pl. *trombe*). Trumpet; hence *tromba a chiavi* (keyed trumpet), *tromba da tirarsi* (slide trumpet), *tromba marina* (trumpet marine), *trombone* (big trumpet).

Tromboncino, Bartolomeo (b. ?Verona, 1470; d. ?Venice, 1535 or later). Italian composer. The son of a court piper and himself a trombonist (whence his name), he seems to have spent his early years largely in Mantua. In 1499 he killed his wife after discovering her with her lover, and though he was pardoned, he fled the city in 1501. Soon after he was in Lucrezia Borgia's service in Ferrara, and by 1521 he was in Venice. He was particularly a master of the frottola, which he helped make a more serious genre, setting some Petrarch.

trombone (Fr., It. *trombone*, pl. *tromboni*, Ger. *Posaune*). BRASS instrument, differing from the trumpet in three features: its lower range, its larger mouthpiece and its slide to vary the length of the tube and hence the pitch of the sound. In nomenclature the range is the most crucial factor, since there are valve trombones without slides. Even when such an instrument is known as a 'bass trumpet', it will generally be played by a trombonist.

The modern trombone – successor to the original tenor trombone – has a tube 9 feet (2·7m) long, with the slide fully extended, providing fundamentals, or pedals, going down from B♭ below the bass staff as the slide is pushed out. The slide enables the player to cover the fifth from the third harmonic (F on the bass staff) down to the second, and so has seven positions for the notes descending in semitones, though being continuously movable it can also produce smaller intervals and glissandos. By changing the embouchure the player can reach different harmonics, up to the 12th (F in the soprano register). Modern trombones also have valve-controlled attachments: an extra coil that lowers the pitch by a fourth (effectively converting a tenor into a bass trombone, originally a distinct instrument, and still often treated as such in modern scores), and a further device allowing descent by a semitone or more. Pitch and sonority can also be changed with a mute. The instrument thus has a continuous range of three and a half octaves, up from B below the bass staff, with pedal notes in the octave below (but these used only as special effects, in Berlioz and some later music).

Other, uncommon members of the family include the soprano or treble trombone (an octave above the tenor), the alto (a fifth above the tenor) and the contrabass (an octave below the tenor). Soprano and alto trombones (or slide trumpets) appeared in Baroque music, and the alto was revived in the 20th century, notably by Stravinsky (*Threni*, *The Flood*). The contrabass featured in German and Italian opera houses, and was used by Wagner (in the *Ring*) and Verdi (as CIMBASSO).

Trombones were first made in the mid 15th century; the earliest surviving example is a tenor of 1551. The instrument was heard in town bands and in church, in which context it was used by composers from the Gabrielis to Mozart (*Requiem*, including a solo in the 'Tuba mirum'). A set of three trombones was also normal in the orchestra for serious opera at the time of Gluck and Mozart, and became a standard part of the symphony orchestra with Beethoven. So it has remained. Solo music for the instrument is limited: much of it was written for Vinko Globokar, including Berio's *Sequenza V*.

David M. Guion *The Trombone* (1988)

Trommel (Ger., pl. *Trommeln*). Drum.

Trompete (Ger., pl. *Trompeten*). Trumpet.

trope. (1) Version of a chant with interpolations of extra words with extra music. Such liturgical accretions were largely removed by the Council of Trent (1545–63). But the form, of addition by parenthesis, was reinterpreted by Messiaen and Boulez.

(2) Term used by Hauer for a row in which the order of notes within each hexachord is undefined. Schoenberg and Berg also occasionally worked with tropes.

troper. Manuscript collection of tropes.

troppo (It.). Too much. Term usually found in negative forms, as in *allegro non troppo* (fast, not too much so).

troubadour (Fr., from Provençal *trobador*, finder). Poet-composer of a southern French tradition flourishing in the 12th and early 13th centuries. Some troubadours were princes, others of plebeian birth who followed princes: they were, in any event, a cut above the jobbing musician of their period (*joglar*, or in northern France JONGLEUR). Their usual subject was courtly love, but some troubadour songs are laments and some satirical. They survive as unaccompanied melody, and were probably meant to be performed that way. Notable troubadours included Arnault Daniel, Guillaume IX of Aquitaine, Raimbaut de Vaqeiras, Raimon de Miraval, Guiraut Riquier, Jaufre Rudel and Bernart de Ventadorn. All the surviving repertory comes from two volumes copied *c*.1300 or later, almost a century after the last troubadour had sung.

Elizabeth Aubrey *The Music of the Troubadours* (1996)

trousers role. TRAVESTI part.

Trout. Name given to Schubert's Quintet for piano and strings, whose fourth movement (of five) is a set of variations on his song 'Die Forelle' (The Trout).

trouvère (Fr., from Old Fr. *trover*, find). Poet-composer of a northern French tradition flourishing in the very late 12th and 13th centuries, a musician comparable in status and art with the troubadours of the south. Notable trouvères

included Adam de la Halle, Blondel de Nesle, Chrétien de Troyes, Gace Brulé and Thibaut IV of Navarre.

Trovatore, Il (The Troubadour). Opera by Verdi to a libretto by Cammarano after a play by Antonio García Gutiérrez. The troubadour is Manrico (tenor), rival of the Count di Luna (baritone) for the love of Leonora (soprano). As a result of jealousy, and of vengeance sought by the gypsy Azucena (mezzo-soprano), the Count is alone at the end, having executed Manrico (revealed by Azucena to have been his long-lost brother) and seen Leonora die from self-administered poison. The famously convoluted plot (to which Berio and Calvino made reference in *La* VERA STORIA) is endowed with a striking number of forceful utterances from the principals (Leonora's 'Tacea la notte – Di tale amor' and 'D'amor sull'ali rosee – Tu vedrai', Azucena's 'Stride la vampa' and 'Condotta ell'era', Manrico's 'Mal reggendo' and 'Ah si, ben mio – Di quella pira', di Luna's 'Il balen del suo sorriso – Per me ora fatale'), and indeed from the chorus (Anvil Chorus, Soldiers' Chorus). First performance: Rome, 19 Jan 1853.

Troyens, Les (The Trojans). Opera by Berlioz to his own libretto after Virgil's *Aeneid*. The first two acts show the destruction of Troy, as foreseen by Cassandra (soprano). The remaining three concern the grand amour between the escaped Trojan prince Aeneas (tenor) and Dido (soprano), queen of Carthage, who kills herself when he has left her to found Rome. The great numbers include Cassandra's opening recitative and aria 'Les Grecs ont disparu! – Malheureux roi', the septet 'Tout n'est que paix', the duet for Dido and Aeneas 'Nuit d'ivresse', Dido's death scene 'Ah! Je vais mourir' and two orchestral moments: the Trojan March and ROYAL HUNT AND STORM. First performance: Paris, 4 Nov 1863 (Acts 3–5); Karlsruhe, 6 Dec 1890 (complete).

trumpet (Fr. *trompette*, Ger. *Trompete*, It. *tromba*). BRASS instrument with a cup mouthpiece and a largely cylindrical bore widening into a bell. More generally the word can be used of all basically cylindrical wind instruments blown with vibrating lips, conical types being horns. In the form of conch shells, animal horns and instruments of wood or ceramic, the trumpet has origins receding into prehistory.

Even in metal form it is ancient. Trumpets of silver and bronze were placed in the tomb of Tutankhamun (1327 BC), and there are records of the instrument among the Assyrians, Hebrews and Greeks. Roman trumpets (Lat. *tuba, buccina*, etc.)

derived from the Etruscans and were close to the Greek model in form and function. The Eng. word comes from the Old High German *trumba*; as *trombetta* it first appears in Dante's *Inferno*.

Early trumpets were straight, but a century after Dante, around 1400, makers began to produce the instrument in the looped form it has kept. At the same time the trumpet moved from the battlefield to become a ceremonial instrument, fanfaring the comings of princes or used by the municipal STADTPFEIFER in independent German towns.

The basic trumpet provides just the notes of its harmonic series, from which the player selects by adjusting the embouchure. A 4-foot (1·2m) trumpet has a fundamental of C on the bass staff, though the fundamental is not normally played, the practical range beginning with the second partial. Medieval trumpeters used no partial beyond the fourth, thus limiting their calls and signals to intervals of an octave, fifth and fourth; this came to be known as the PRINCIPALE register. In the 16th century the range was extended into the CLARINO register, as far as the 13th partial. Schütz, in one of his *Symphoniae sacrae* of 1629, asked for the 16th partial (three octaves above the second partial), required also by later Baroque composers of church music and opera, especially in such centres of trumpet excellence as Bologna (Gabrielli, Torelli) and Kremsier/Kroměříž (Vejvanovský). Bach wrote splendidly for the instrument, and Leopold Mozart composed a concerto for it, as did Haydn and Hummel after the invention of the KEYED TRUMPET. A pair of trumpets, normally introduced with timpani, became standard in the Classical orchestra.

Around 1815 the trumpet took its modern form, when the VALVE was introduced, allowing different lengthenings of the tube and therefore different lowerings of the fundamental. Used singly or in combination, three valves made the trumpet a fully chromatic instrument: with all three valves open, the lowest practical note is depressed by a tritone, i.e. to E below middle C for the trumpet in B♭, which gradually during the 19th century became the most usual orchestral instrument, with the trumpet in C next in line. Even the most virtuoso music rarely goes much beyond the three-octave range of Schütz's trumpeters.

Wagner had a bass trumpet in C made for *The Ring*; at the other extreme, and around the same time, piccolo trumpets in B♭ or D (especially) were introduced for Baroque music. The brilliant, high D trumpet gained a new repertory, in Stravinsky's *Petrushka*, Davies's Sonata, etc., and the bass trumpet (normally played by a trombonist) also found a place on the fringes of the regular orchestra. Among 20th-century trumpet concertos are works by Zimmermann and Birtwistle; the instrument also personifies the hero Michael in Stockhausen's *Licht*, and its prominence in jazz has made more kinds of MUTE available.

Philip Bate *The Trumpet and Trombone* (1966, ²1972); Don L. Smithers *The Music and History of the Baroque Trumpet before 1721* (1973, ²1988)

trumpet marine. Large Renaissance–Baroque bowed instrument with one string, so called because, like a trumpet, it was used to produce natural harmonics – though the 'marine' part of its name remains mysterious.

trumpet tune. Piece with a melody in trumpet style, common in the Baroque period, especially in England.

Trumpet Voluntary. Misnomer (usually with a misattribution to Purcell) for Jeremiah Clarke's *Prince of Denmark's March*.

tuba. (1) BRASS instrument with a deep cup mouthpiece and wide conical bore, introduced in 1835 to provide bass reinforcement to the trombones in place of the ophicleide. It is commonly associated with the trombones in orchestral scores, though it gains an independent existence in those of late-20th-century composers such as Carter and Birtwistle (who in *Earth Dances* and other works has two tubas instead of the regular one). Standard types include the contrabass in 16' C (US orchestras), the bass tuba in F (continental Europe) or E♭ (Britain), the tenor tuba in B♭ (known as the euphonium in band circles) and the French six-valved tuba in 8' C (for which Ravel wrote a solo in his *Pictures at an Exhibition* orchestration). The instrument's normal range is from the A below the bass staff to the G♯ almost four octaves higher, and its small solo literature includes concertos by Vaughan Williams and Birtwistle.

R. Winston Morris and Edward R. Goldstein *The Tuba Source Book* (1996)

(2) Ancient Roman trumpet.

Tubin, Eduard (b. Kallaste, 18 Jun 1905; d. Stockholm, 17 Nov 1982). Estonian–Swedish composer, who in his late years found an international audience for his symphonies, along a line between Sibelius and Prokofiev. He studied with Kapp at the Tartu Conservatory and Kodály in Budapest, worked as a theatre conductor in Tartu (1931–44) and then settled in Stockholm.

Symphonies: No.1, C minor, 1931–4; No.2, 1937; No.3, D minor, 1940–42; No.4 (*Sinfonia lirica*), A, 1942–3; No.5, B minor, 1946; No.6, 1952–4; No.7, 1956–8; No.8, 1965–6; No.9 (*Sinfonia semplice*), 1969; No.10, 1973
Other works: concertos, choral music, operas, sonatas, etc.

tubular bells (Fr. *cloches tubes*, Ger. *Röhrenglocken*, It. *campane, campanelle*). Hollow cylinders of brass or steel suspended within a frame, introduced to the orchestra in the late 19th century and welcomed by many composers from Mahler to Boulez. The standard set-up has a range from C on the treble staff up through an octave and a fourth, though bells down to middle C are not uncommon. See also BELL.

tucket. Flourish of trumpets: 'Then let the trumpets sound the tucket sonnance' (*Henry V*, Act 4, Scene 2). The term is cognate with, but not derived from, toccata.

Tuckwell, Barry (Emmanuel) (b. Melbourne, 5 Mar 1931). Australian horn player, of fine tone and expert virtuosity. After conservatory studies in Sydney he moved to Britain in 1950 and became principal in the LSO (1955–68). Then, until his retirement in 1996, he appeared widely as a soloist and with his own Tuckwell Wind Quintet. Banks, Musgrave and Knussen wrote concertos for him.

Tudor. Welsh–English dynasty ruling from 1485 to 1603. Much of the history of the period has been told in opera, relevant works including Saint-Saëns's *Henry VIII*, Donizetti's *Anna Bolena*, Davies's *Taverner*, Pacini's *Maria, regina d'Inghilterra*, Gomes's *Maria Tudor*, Rossini's *Elisabetta, regina d'Inghilterra* and Donizetti's *Maria Stuarda*. Though the Church was in turmoil, this was a glorious era for polyphony in England, represented by the generations of Fayrfax and Cornyshe, Taverner and Tallis, and Parsons and Byrd.

Tudor, David (Eugene) (b. Philadelphia, 20 Jan 1926; d. Tomkins Cove, NY, 13 Aug 1996). US pianist and composer. He started his career in 1938 as an organist, later studying the piano with Irma Wolpe and composition with her husband Stefan. Through them he came to know Feldman and so in 1950 to join the circle around Cage, who wrote *Music of Changes*, *4' 33"* and many later works for him. With Cage he performed for Merce Cunningham's dance company and toured Europe, where Stockhausen, Bussotti and others composed pieces exploiting his startling, incisive energy and adven-

turousness with regard to sonority. After 1960 he devoted himself largely to live electronic music, in which field he was an innovatory composer.

Tudway, Thomas (b. *c*.1650; d. Cambridge, 23 Nov 1726). British church musician. A chorister at the Chapel Royal and then, from 1670, organist of King's College, Cambridge, he compiled a monumental collection of English church music from Tye to Handel, including anthems and an evening service of his own.

Tunder, Franz (b. Bannesdorf, near Burg, Fehmarn, 1614; d. Lübeck, 5 Nov 1667). German organist-composer. A musician's son, he was appointed court organist in 1632 at Gottorf, where he probably came under the wing of Johann Heckelauer and thereby made the acquaintance of Italian music. From 1641 until his death he was organist at the Marienkirche in Lübeck, not only performing at services but leading concerts, with a repertory including his Latin motets, chorale fantasias, etc. He was succeeded by his son-in-law, Buxtehude.

tune. (1) MELODY that is singable (or whistlable) and self-sufficient.

(2) To change the pitch of an instrument; or the correct pitching – an instrument is tuned to make it in tune. Woodwind and brass instruments have devices to adjust tuning; string instruments have knobs to tighten or slacken the strings and so vary the pitch. Orchestras customarily tune to the A above middle C as played by the principal oboe, or on the piano in the case of a piano concerto. Pianos and other keyboard instruments require the offices of professional tuners, who make adjustments with the help of tuning forks, electronic appliances and their ears (to detect, for example, the beats of mistuned octaves). Normally pianos are tuned with slightly stretched octaves (up to 1 per cent above the 2:1 frequency ratio) to take account of inharmonicity in the instrument's sound.

tuning. See TEMPERAMENT; TUNE (2).

tuning fork. Two-pronged metal object producing a fixed pitch when struck, invented in 1711 by the British trumpeter John Shore (1662–1752). The pitch can be altered by filing at the tips of the prongs (to sharpen) or adding adhesive material (to flatten). Electronic devices began to supplant the tuning fork for some purposes in the 1970s.

tuning slide. Device on a wind instrument or organ pipe to vary the length of the tube and therefore the pitch.

Turandot. Opera by Puccini to a libretto by Giuseppe Adami and Renato Simoni after the play by Gozzi. Calaf (tenor), a foreign prince in legendary China, survives various trials – the playful antics of Ping (baritone), Pang (tenor) and Pong (tenor), the suicide of Liù (soprano), who loves him, the pain of his father, Timur (bass) – to win, finally, the love of the vengeful princess Turandot (soprano). Left incomplete at the composer's death, the score was finished by Alfano. Toscanini abbreviated this effort for the opening performances, though at the very first he let the work end where the composer had left it. A version by Berio arrived in 2002 to challenge the standard Alfano–Toscanini ending. Turandot's 'In questa reggia' is among the most startling arias for dramatic soprano, Calaf's 'Nessun dorma' one of the most beguiling melodies for hefty tenor. Liù sings 'Signore, ascolta' (to which Calaf replies with 'Non piangere, Liù') and 'Tu che di gel'. First performance: Milan, La Scala, 25 Apr 1926.

Other musical treatments of the play include Weber's overture and marches for the Schiller translation (1809) and an opera by Busoni to his own libretto (1917).

Turangalîla. Symphony by Messiaen, who explained the Sanskrit title as composed of two elements: *turanga* ('time which runs') and *lîla* ('divine action in the cosmos … the play of life and death … love'). Scored for large orchestra with solo piano and ondes martenot, the work has 10 movements: 1 *Introduction*, 2 *Chant d'amour 1*, 3 *Turangalîla 1*, 4 *Chant d'amour 2*, 5 *Joie du sang des étoiles* (Joy of the Blood of the Stars), 6 *Jardin du sommeil d'amour* (Garden of Love's Sleep), 7 *Turangalîla 2*, 8 *Développement de l'amour*, 9 *Turangalîla 3*, 10 *Final*. The whole forms the centrepiece of the composer's Tristan trilogy, between his *Cinq rechants* and *Harawi*. First performance: Boston, 2 Dec 1949.

turba (Lat., crowd). Group represented by a chorus in a Passion.

turca, alla. See ALLA TURCA.

turco in Italia, Il (The Turk in Italy). Opera by Rossini to a libretto by Romani after one by Mazzolà. Overseen by a poet, Prosdocimo (bass), who stands partly outside the action, Selim the Turk (bass) is reunited with his faithful Zaida (soprano) despite romantic intrigues Italian-style. First performance: Milan, 14 Aug 1814.

Tureck, Rosalyn (b. Chicago, 14 Dec 1914; d. New York, 17 Jul 2003). US pianist, an esteemed Bach exponent. She began concentrating on Bach in 1937, two years after graduating from Juilliard. After the Second World War her career became international, and though she occasionally played on period (as well as electronic) instruments, the piano remained home to her clarity. She also lectured widely and established the Tureck Bach Institute in New York (1967), succeeded by the Tureck Bach Research Foundation in Oxford (1993).

Turina (y Perez), Joaquin (b. Seville, 9 Dec 1882; d. Madrid, 14 Jan 1949). Spanish composer. After studying locally he moved to Madrid, where he met Falla, and in 1905 to Paris, where he maintained his friendship with Falla, took lessons from d'Indy at the Schola Cantorum and was fascinated by Debussy. In 1914 he returned to Madrid with Falla, and there he largely remained, as professor of composition at the conservatory (from 1930), critic and composer. His works include a *Sinfonia sevillana* (1920), *La oración del torero* (1925) for string quartet or orchestra, numerous piano pieces descriptive of the Spanish scene and songs.

Turkey. An uneasy relationship with Europe (large parts of which it ruled from the 16th century until the late 19th) had its diverse musical echoes: in the imitations of JANISSARY music by Classical composers and in the simultaneous myth of the noble Turk, exemplified in Mozart's *Entführung*. Giuseppe Donizetti, the composer's brother, had charge of a short-lived palace opera theatre in Istanbul (1859–64). 20th-century modernization was reflected in the foundation of the Ankara Conservatory (1936) and in the arrival of composers, notably Saygun, adapting the Western classical tradition to local circumstances.

Turkish crescent [Jingling Johnny, Chinese pavilion] (Fr. *chapeau chinois, pavillon chinois*, Ger. *Schellenbaum*). Military standard with jingles, inherited by European regiments from the janissaries and used by Berlioz in his *Symphonie funèbre et triomphale*.

Turmmusik (Ger.). TOWER MUSIC.

turn. Undulating figure around the marked note, notated and realized thus (though the rhythm will vary with style and context):

Turnage, Mark-Anthony (b. Corringham, Essex, 10 Jun 1960). British composer, whose music has an urban contemporaneity that comes from his urgent instrumental lyricism, closeness to jazz and focus on current social issues. He studied at the RCM with Oliver Knussen and John Lambert, and gained early attention with his orchestral *Night Dances* (1980–81). In 1983, at Tanglewood, he met Henze, who helped foster his early career. He was composer-in-residence with the CBSO (1989–93), and was appointed associate composer with the BBC Symphony in 2000.

Andrew Clements *Mark-Anthony Turnage* (2000)

Operas: *Greek* (Steven Berkoff), f.p. Munich, 1988; *The Silver Tassie* (Amanda Holden, after Sean O'Casey), f.p. London, 2000
Orchestral: *Three Screaming Popes*, 1988–9; *Drowned Out*, 1992–3; *Your Rockaby*, s sax, orch, 1993–4; *Evening Songs*, 1998; *Silent Cities*, 1998; *Another Set To*, trbn, orch, 2000; etc.
Ensemble: *Blood on the Floor*, jazz trio, large ens, 1993–6; *About Time*, modern ens, Classical orch, 1999; etc.

Turner, Eva (b. Oldham, 10 Mar 1892; d. London, 16 Jun 1990). British soprano, outstanding as Turandot, created dame in 1962. She studied with Albert Richards Broad in Bristol, and began her career with the Carl Rosa Opera (1916–24). Discovered by Toscanini's assistant, she was among the first to sing Turandot (Brescia, 1926), a role she took to Covent Garden (1928) and La Scala (1929); her fiercely precise and majestic utterance of 'In questa reggia' was recorded in 1930. But she was also heard internationally as Aida, Santuzza, Tosca, etc. She taught at the University of Oklahoma (1950–59) and then at the RAM, and in her late years was beamingly present at many Covent Garden performances.

Turn of the Screw, The. Opera by Britten to a libretto by Myfanwy Piper after Henry James's story. The Governess (soprano) witnesses the tantalizing and ultimately fatal hold that the ghosts of former employees – Quint (tenor) and Miss Jessel (soprano) – have over her charges Miles (treble) and Flora (soprano). The work is scored for a 14-piece ensemble and constructed as a spiral of 15 variations on a 12-note theme. First performance: Venice, 14 Sep 1954.

tutte le corde (It., all the strings). Direction to release the left (UNA CORDA) pedal on a piano.

tutti (It., all). (1) A whole group of performers, as opposed to soloists.
(2) Direction for all the players of an instrument

to join in, following a passage for just one or two of them.
(3) Direction for all the players of a section to come together, after a *divisi* passage.
(4) An orchestral passage in which most players are active.

Tüür, Erkki-Sven (b. Kärdla, Hiiumaa, 16 Oct 1959). Estonian composer, with a background in rock (as vocalist of the group In Spe) and classical music. He studied with Jann Rääts (at the Tallinn Conservatory, 1980–84), with Lepo Sumera and at Darmstadt, and began to be known internationally in the early 1990s. His works include symphonies, violin and cello concertos, choral music, an *Architectonics* series of instrumental scores and the opera *Wallenberg* (f.p. Dortmund, 2001).

Tveitt, (Nils) Geirr (b. Oslo, 19 Oct 1908; d. Oslo, 1 Feb 1981). Norwegian composer. After studies at the conservatory in Leipzig (1928–32) he spent a year in Paris and Vienna, and his music brings European mainland influences – Ravel, Bartók, Prokofiev – into the Norwegian nationalist tradition.

twelfth. Note an octave above the fifth, or interval an octave wider than a fifth.

Twelfth Mass. Spurious Mozart mass popular with choirs in the 19th and early 20th centuries, the 12th in Vincent Novello's series of Mozart masses (others of which were also inauthentic).

twelve-note composition, twelve-tone composition. Alternative terms for SERIALISM, preferred in the USA by composers and theorists who felt 'serialism' had been hijacked by the young post-1945 Europeans.

twelve-tone tonality. Term introduced by Perle for a body of analytical and compositional tools allowing an understanding of 12-note harmony.

Twilight of the Gods. See GOTTERDAMMERUNG.

Two Widows, The (*Dvě vdovy*). Opera by Smetana to a libretto by Emanuel Züngel after a French play. One of the widows, Karolina (soprano), uses her wiles to persuade the other, Anežka (soprano), to accept a new husband in Ladislav (tenor). First performance: Prague, 27 Mar 1874 (with spoken dialogue); 15 Mar 1878 (with recitatives).

Tye, Christopher (b. *c.*1505; d. ?1572). English composer. After studying at Cambridge he was master of the choristers at Ely Cathedral from 1543, probably spent some years with the Chapel Royal, returned to Ely (1558–61) and passed his last years as a comfortable country parson, having been ordained in 1560. His surviving works include masses (*Western Wind* a 4; *Euge bone* a 6), Latin motets, English anthems and consort music, including 21 In Nomines.

tympani. See TIMPANI.

Tzigane (Gypsy). Showpiece by Ravel for violin with piano or orchestra, dedicated to Jelly d'Aranyi. First performance: Paris, 30 Nov 1924 (orchestral version).

Überbrettl. Early 20th-century Berlin cabaret run by the writer Ernst von Wolzogen with high aesthetic ideals. Schoenberg, Oscar Straus and Zemlinsky were among composers associated with it.

übermässig (Ger.). Augmented.

Übung (Ger., pl. *Übungen*). Exercise.

u.c. Abbreviation for UNA CORDA.

Uchida, Mitsuko (b. Atami, near Tokyo, 20 Dec 1948). Japanese pianist, of extraordinary deftness and fine control. She studied in Tokyo and with Richard Hauser in Vienna, and became internationally known in the 1980s as a Mozart performer, later broadening the range of her reputation to include Bartók, Debussy, Schubert and Schoenberg.

'ūd (Arabic, wood). Arab instrument, recorded from the 7th century, adopted in Europe under the same name: *al-'ūd* = lute.

uguale (It.). Equal, alike.

Uitti, Frances-Marie (information not disclosed). US cellist, famed especially for her use of two bows and her relationships with Scelsi, Kurtág, Harvey, etc. She completed her training with André Navarra and has spent much of her professional life in Rome and, latterly, Amsterdam.

ukelele, ukulele (from Hawaiian, leaping flea). Small guitar taken in the late 19th century from Madeira to Hawaii, and in the early 20th century from there to the world.

Ukraine. Even during the period of subjection to Russia (1654–1991), Kiev had the status of a mother city of the eastern Slavs. Its academy (1615–1915) was a centre of religious music. The country had its Romantic nationalist in Mykola Lysenko (1842–1912), who founded a music institute in Kiev. Boris Lyatoshynsky (1895–1968) steered Ukrainian music into the post-Romantic period and was the teacher of Silvestrov and others.

Ullmann, Viktor (b. Teschen/Těšín, 1 Jan 1898; d. Auschwitz, 17 Oct 1944). Czech composer. After studies with Schoenberg in Vienna, he returned to Prague, where he worked at the New German Theatre and followed Hába's quarter-tone course at the conservatory (1935–7). In 1942 he was arrested as a Jew and interned at Theresienstadt (Terezín), where he composed a one-act opera, *Der Kaiser von Atlantis* (1943). This was put into rehearsal in September 1944, but fell victim to censorship and to the transport of inmates, including the composer, to Auschwitz. The eventual staging of the work (Amsterdam, 1975) was one of the first acts in the re-establishment of Jewish composers who had been Nazi victims.

ultrachromatic. Including MICROTONE intervals.

ultramodern. Term current in the USA in the 1920s for music (e.g. by Cowell, Bartók) perceived as going beyond the first wave of MODERNISM.

Ulysses. See ODYSSEY.

Umfang (Ger.). Compass.

Umkehrung (Ger.). Inversion.

Umlauf, Ignaz (b. Vienna, 1746; d. Meidling, 8 Jun 1796). Austrian composer who directed the German opera company in Vienna (1778–83), for which he wrote *Die Bergknappen* (1778) and other works. His son Michael (1781–1842) was a conductor admired by Beethoven, whose 1814 *Fidelio* and Ninth Symphony he steered through their first performances.

Umstimmung (Ger.). SCORDATURA.

unaccompanied. Lacking keyboard accompaniment. The term can apply to a choir or soloist.

una corda (It., one string). Effect on the piano controlled by the left pedal, abbreviated *u.c.* Beethoven, the first to notate the effect, was familiar with pianos in which the pedal shifted the action so that only one (with the pedal fully depressed) or two (pedal half-depressed) of the three strings were struck. Since the middle of the 19th century pianos have lost this subtlety, the pedal having only one position, causing one string (of the two in the middle-bass) or two (of the three in the treble) to be sounded. On upright pianos the pedal works in a different way, reducing the gap between hammers and strings.

Unanswered Question, The. Work by Ives. Offstage strings sound soft sustained chords, representing the silence of the seers; a trumpet (or ob, cl or cor anglais) asks the meaning of life, to which four flutes (or 2 fl, ob, cl) respond with vain scurryings. Both the original (1908) and the revised (*c*.1930–35) scores have been published. First performance: New York, 11 May 1946.

Unda Maris (Lat., sea wave). Organ stop producing an undulating effect from pipes tuned slightly sharp or flat.

underlay. How words fit music, which may be unclear in medieval and Renaissance sources.

understand. To understand music is to deduce some reason why it is as it is, structurally. A great deal of Western classical music invites understanding, doing so by such means as harmonic progression, melodic imitation, metrical consistency, thematic development and appeal to formal models. For many listeners, the deepening of understanding is a primary goal of listening, and performers may be praised for the understanding they reveal. Deeper understanding is even identified with increased closeness to the expressive essence. However, there is also music that actively frustrates understanding in any terms outside itself – i.e. it does not exemplify particular progressions or have distinct themes – and yet is powerfully expressive: Barraqué's music, for instance, or Birtwistle's, or Ockeghem's.

understudy. Person ready to take on a role if the billed artist is indisposed, or, as a verb, to prepare for that eventuality. Understudies in opera are normally rehearsed by the assistant director.

Undine (Ondine). Water nymph who encounters a mortal man, with tragic consequences to them both. The classic telling of her story is by Friedrich de la Motte Fouqué, who created the libretto for Hoffmann's opera (f.p. Berlin, 1816). Lortzing wrote both words and music for his version, and there are also treatments by Ravel and Debussy for piano and by Henze as a ballet score for Frederick Ashton to choreograph and Margot Fonteyn to dance (f.p. London, 1958).

Unfinished. Name given to Schubert's Symphony in B minor, of which he completed just the first two movements, leaving sketches for a third. Why he stopped work on the piece is unknown. In the case of other unfinished works – Mozart's *Requiem*, Puccini's *Turandot*, Busoni's *Doktor Faust*, Berg's *Lulu* – the evident cause was death, though in the 20th-century examples incompleteness may also have been wished on the scores by their creators. Composers may be seduced or intrigued by the vibrant potentiality of something not yet finished. They may have reasons for wanting to stay in a particular world, not leave it. They may also, like Barraqué, choose the grand fragmentary as their artistic domain.

unica. Composers who confined themselves to a single work may only be imagined, though Duparc, Dukas, Decaux and Barraqué (all French) came close. Dukas is a notable case of the composer widely known for just one work, a category that also includes Mouret, Sinding, Albéniz and Rodrigo.

Composers who completed only one opera make a distinguished group: Beethoven, Schumann, Borodin, Sibelius, Debussy, Chausson, Dukas, Bartók, Fauré, Gershwin, Ligeti, Messiaen, Lachenmann, Carter. More are known for a singleton from a larger output: Cimarosa, Halévy, Flotow, Nicolai, Smetana, Ponchielli, Saint-Saëns, Delibes, Mascagni, Leoncavallo, Humperdinck, Dvořák, Zandonai, Pfitzner, Busoni, Szymanowski. A special case of the one-opera composer is the one-aria composer, Gustave Charpentier.

union. Orchestral musicians, like other workers, have the protection of trade unions, including in Britain the MUSICIANS' UNION and in North America the AMERICAN FEDERATION OF MUSICIANS and AMERICAN GUILD OF MUSICAL ARTISTS.

unison. Agreement on the same note by two or more musical lines. A string quartet may play a melody in unison (Wuorinen's Fourth Quartet); a mixed choir singing 'in unison' will normally in fact be singing in parallel octaves, between men and women.

unisono, all' (It., at the unison). (1) See ALL'UNISONO.

(2) Direction placed over a figured bass, requiring no harmony at this point, only movement at the unison or octave.

unisson (Fr.). Unison.

United Kingdom. Country formed by the union of ENGLAND (plus WALES) and SCOTLAND from 1707 and the incorporation of IRELAND from 1801 to 1921, after which only Ulster remained in the union. With England so much the dominant partner, the others have been able to maintain cultural independence largely by expressing their difference. England, having no such battle to wage, perhaps for that reason needed native artists less (except in literature, where foreigners could not compete). The audience valued music highly – public concerts and concert halls started in England – but viewed it as an import commodity. Thus Handel, Haydn, Mendelssohn and Dvořák all enjoyed far more success than any native composer, and they all contributed to the most English of genres, the concert oratorio, drawing on what were the strongest continuities in English musical life: church music and the amateur choir.

By absorbing the keynotes of English church music – modality, polyphony, hymn-like melody, an expression of radiance – Elgar and Vaughan Williams around 1900 came forward as composers of abstract, secular music. Many more followed: Bax and Bridge, Tippett and Britten, Birtwistle and Davies, Hopkins and Ferneyhough, forming not so much a continuous tradition as a succession of individual responses to the same background. Essential to that background were Tudor music, choral singing and a feeling for landscape. Though LONDON dominates the country's musical life, many composers have sought rural surroundings.

But most British composers have also felt a fascination with abroad, no longer as an alien realm from which artists come, but as a source of revivifying ideas. As Britain's political superiority waned, so its music flowered.

United States of America. Founded largely by religious refugees, the country resounded to their psalms before there was much other music from new arrivals. The *Bay Psalm Book* (1640) was the first volume printed in the British colonies; its ninth edition (1698) included the first printed music. Even a century later the first notable US composer, William Billings, was a psalmodist, though secular music had started to make inroads with performances of ballad operas in Charleston, New York and Williamsburg in the 1730s.

In the early 19th century musical life began to be more thoroughly established, if almost entirely as an import business: the organization founded in Boston in 1815 was the Handel and Haydn Society (which survives), while in the operatically alive city of New Orleans the repertory was French and Italian. US composers of the period – Heinrich, Gottschalk – tended to be brilliant eccentrics on the sidelines. They and their successors – Fry, Bristow – were still largely ignored when US orchestras were founded, beginning with the ancestor of the New York Philharmonic in 1842. Nor was native music of much interest to the impresarios who brought in European stars to perform to immense audiences.

Certain traits in US music were thus well established before the Civil War (1861–5). Like any society of colonizers and immigrants, the country found itself with a mish-mash of traditions: from Britain came psalms and theatre songs, from the Mediterranean opera, from central Europe orchestral life, from all these places folk music of many kinds, and from Africa the less well recorded inheritances of slaves. NEW YORK – the main port of entry and internally a magnet by virtue of its work opportunities – had a particularly diverse culture. Moreover, as citizens of the first colonized territory to have established its independence, US musicians faced the questions of whether and how their music should be nationally distinctive. Also, as democrats, they had to consider how a musical culture of aristocratic origin could be made widely available. Education and showmanship were immediate issues.

More orchestras, opera companies, conservatories and concert societies date from the late 19th century, when a new generation of US composers appeared: Paine, MacDowell, Parker, Chadwick. All were trained in Germany and artistically stamped there. Dvořák, teaching in New York in the early 1890s, encouraged his pupils to listen to music nearer home, and his views were echoed in the work of Farwell, Cadman, Gilbert and, most extraordinarily, Ives. But indigenous music was already taking on a life of its own in ragtime, and the immense growth of POPULAR MUSIC in the 20th century – through jazz, show tunes and rock – gave forceful answers to the old questions, for here was music that could not have come from anywhere else and was universal in its appeal.

Indeed, the components of what is generally held to sound 'American' come largely from popular music: jazz rhythms, strong melody and emotional frankness, bold scoring and vigorous presentation, but also at times the quieter affirmations of hymns and blues.

Yet many US composers persisted in seeking other solutions, outside the commercial realm and in music of more ambitious scale. Coinciding with the emergence of the USA as a world power, around the time of the First World War, varieties of radical modernism began yielding results particular to the USA. Ives was godfather to this multifarious tradition, which embraced Varèse, Cowell and Ruggles, with Charles Seeger an important instigator.

But where Varèse had come from Europe to start afresh in New York, many composers in the 1920s and 1930s went in the reverse direction, not only to Germany but now also to Paris, where Boulanger taught Carter, Copland, Harris and others. Their music became marked by Stravinsky and the French tradition, while ties with Europe were further strengthened by the arrival of composers fleeing Nazism and war, among them Schoenberg, Stravinsky and Wolpe, though all worked differently in the USA, responding to popular music, opportunities for change and democratic ideals.

Stravinsky, Copland and Harris were among the last composers to be embraced by the country's mass culture, before that culture found its match in rock 'n' roll in the 1950s. The remaining (if diminishing) prestige of classical music as an educational good allowed many composers subsequently to find a place in academia; others gained support from patrons and foundations, and from working with dance or theatre companies. Babbitt and Cage are the cardinal examples of these alternatives, the one fizzing with ideas to impart, the other quietly going on saying he had none.

US music during the Cold War, from the late 1940s into the 1980s, grew in exuberant variety partly as an expression of individual liberty, in opposition to the state-led artistic policy of the Soviet Union. Composers espoused not only 12-note music (Babbitt) and chance (Cage) but also minimalism (Reich) and styles of more local reverberation, including tonal symphonism (Schuman) and post-Romantic opera (Barber), while Partch and Nancarrow continued the line of resolute independents and Carter created modernist summations. The later lack of cultural direction is sagely reflected in the postmodernism of Bolcom.

John Rockwell *All American Music* (1983); Richard Crawford *America's Musical Life: A History* (2001)

Universal Edition. Music publishing firm founded in Vienna in 1901. Emil Hertzka (managing director 1907–32) signed contracts with Bartók (1908), Mahler and Schoenberg (1909), Webern and Zemlinsky (1910), Szymanowski (1912) and Janáček (1917) among others, and later the firm took on Stockhausen, Boulez, Berio, Birtwistle, Pärt, etc.

Universal Music Group. Company formed in 1996 to hold the musical interests of the Canadian group Seagram, acquiring the Decca, Deutsche Grammophon and Philips labels in 1998.

Universe Symphony. Projected work by Ives for a large orchestra in many independent groups. Versions by Larry Austin and Johnny Reinhard were performed in the mid-1990s.

unpitched. See UNTUNED.

unprepared suspension. Holding over from one chord to another of a note dissonant in the first as well as the second.

Unterhaltungsmusik (Ger.). Entertainment music. See also KUNSTMUSIK.

untuned. Term used of percussion instruments whose sound has no definite pitch, e.g. cymbals. They may alternatively be called 'unpitched' or 'noise' instruments.

upbeat. Gesture in a weak rhythmic position anticipating another more strongly placed, the downbeat. This gesture may be silent, as when a conductor gives an upbeat before the start of a piece, or it may be sounded by one or more notes. Often the upbeat will come late in a bar, for a downbeat at the start of the next. Music in regular metre is an orderly succession of upbeats and downbeats, though interesting music will vary and disturb the orderliness, for instance by placing upbeats slightly differently in different parts, by separating the rhythmic upbeat from melodic and harmonic upbeats, etc.

upbow. Action of the bow from point to nut, i.e. rising in the case of the violin. Upbows often go with upbeats, though part of good bowing technique is to make the upbow as strong as the downbow.

upper mordent. See MORDENT.

upright piano. Domestic piano in which the strings run vertically, first made by John Isaac Hawkins in Philadelphia in 1800.

Upshaw, Dawn (b. Nashville, 17 Jul 1960). US soprano, of natural sound and candid expression. She studied at the Manhattan School, joined the Met's young artists programme and was singing internationally by the late 1980s. Notable roles include the Angel in *Saint François d'Assise*, parts in new operas by Adams, Harbison and Golijov, and the purer heroines of Mozart and Handel.

Upupa und der Triumph der Sohnesliebe, L' (The Hoopoe and the Triumph of a Son's Love). Opera by Henze to his own libretto after Arabian tales. Al Kasim (baritone) gains the precarious help of the Demon (tenor) in fulfilling the task set by his father and going on to more. First performance: Salzburg, 12 Aug 2003.

Urania. The muse of astronomy.

Uraufführung (Ger., original performance). World première.

Urlinie (Ger., original line). Term in Schenkerian analysis, usually understood to refer to the melody that slowly proceeds in the deep background through the whole length of a work or movement.

Urtext (Ger., original text). Edition presenting a work as left by its composer, without the accretions of later editors. Problems arise because most composers leave their works in multitudinous forms – manuscripts, revised manuscripts, printed editions, corrected editions, recordings and other kinds of SOURCE – so that editorial questions remain.

Ussachevsky, Vladimir (Alexis) (b. Hailar, Manchuria, 3 Nov 1911; d. New York, 2 Jan 1990).

Russian–US composer. He moved to California in 1930 and studied there and at the Eastman School (with Hanson and Rogers, 1935–9). After war service he continued his education under Luening at Columbia, where he joined the faculty in 1947. He and Luening were pioneers of electronic music – his *Of Wood and Brass* (1964–5) boldly swings recorded sounds around – but he also wrote choral music indebted to Orthodox traditions.

Ustvolskaya, Galina (Ivanovna) (b. Petrograd, 17 Jun 1919). Russian composer. She studied at the Leningrad Conservatory, first in the junior department (1937–9), then with Shostakovich (1939–47, apart from wartime hospital work). The affair she had with her teacher was musical as well as personal, and he quoted from her 1949 trio not only in his Fifth Quartet (1952) but also in one of his last works, the Michelangelo Suite. As for his influence on her, she drew away, inwards. What she kept was the fierce expressive utterance. Its context was changed – often undeveloped (she went on using the title of symphony for works radically non-symphonic), in an atmosphere of sudden contrast – and so was its meaning, which would often evoke spiritual drama. She has spent her entire life in the city of her birth, teaching in the conservatory junior department (1947–75) and living in total privacy.

Symphonies: No.1 (Gianni Rodari), boys' choir, orch, 1955; No.2 'True and Eternal Bliss!' (Hermannus Contractus), boy speaker, orch, 1979; No.3 'Jesus, Messiah, Save Us!' (Hermannus), boy speaker, orch, 1983; No.4 'Prayer' (Hermannus), ct, tpt, tam tam, pf, 1985–7; No.5 'Amen', man speaker, vn, ob, tpt, tuba, perc, 1989–90
Other ensemble works: Trio, vn, cl, pf, 1949; Composition No.1 'Dona nobis pacem', pic, tuba, pf, 1970–71; No.2 'Dies irae', 8 db, perc, pf, 1972–3; No.3 'Benedictus qui venit', 4 fl, 4 bn, pf, 1974–5; etc.
Piano sonatas: No.1, 1947; No.2, 1949; No.3, 1952; No.4, 1957; No.5, 1986; No.6, 1988

ut (Fr.). The note or key of C; see SOLMIZATION.

utility music (Ger. GEBRAUCHSMUSIK). Music made for purposes other than listening: dances, marches, table music, music for gymnastic displays, etc.

va. Abbreviation for viola.

Vaccai, Nicola (b. Tolentino, 15 Mar 1790; d. Pesaro, 5/6 Aug 1848). Italian composer. Born into a medical family, he studied in Rome and Naples (with Paisiello), and had only mixed success before the brief triumph he enjoyed with *Zadig ed Astartea* (f.p. Naples, 1825) and *Giulietta e Romeo* (f.p. Milan, 1825). The latter was soon superseded by Bellini's *I Capuleti ed i Montecchi*, though its penultimate scene was often inserted into Bellini's score, following a suggestion Rossini made to Malibran in Paris in 1832. Other than that, he won respect as a singing teacher, in Paris, England and, from 1833, back in Italy, where he belatedly married and had children. His vocal exercises are still used.

vagans (Lat., wanderer). Fifth part in Renaissance polyphony, which might be in any of the four normal registers, soprano, alto, tenor or bass, though the tenor was the usual choice.

Vaillant, Jehan (*fl.* ?1360–90). French composer of five polyphonic songs in the CHANTILLY manuscript, including *Par maintes foys*, a virelai with birdcalls.

Vainberg, Moisey (Samuilovich) [Weinberg, Mieczysław] (b. Warsaw, 8 Dec 1919; d. Moscow, 26 Feb 1996). Polish–Russian composer, close to Shostakovich. He trained as a pianist before settling in the Soviet Union and studying composition with Vasily Zolotarev at the Minsk Conservatory (1939–41). His determining encounter with Shostakovich came soon after. In 1948 he refused to recant his modernist inclinations, and his life became arduous: in 1953 he spent three months in prison. But he was rehabilitated. His works include 19 symphonies, four chamber symphonies, numerous concertos, 17 string quartets, operas and ballets.

Valen, (Olav) Fartein (b. Stavanger, 25 Aug 1887; d. Haugesund, 14 Dec 1952). Norwegian composer who, in isolation, developed a style of luminous dissonance conveyed in clear counterpoint. His parents were missionaries, and he was with them in Madagascar between the ages of two and six. The family then returned to Stavanger, which he left to study in Copenhagen (1906–9) with Elling and at the Berlin Conservatory (1909–11) with Bruch. He stayed in Berlin studying independently until 1916, when he went back to Norway and settled in the fishing port of Valevåg. There, dissatisfied with the late Romantic style of his first compositions, he searched for a new manner but completed only two scores. In 1924 he moved to Oslo, where he worked as a university music librarian and taught theory; a winter on Mallorca (1932–3) was creatively important. Now he was composing more regularly, perhaps partly because Schoenberg's serialism offered him confirmation. But in Oslo he found little support, and he took advantage of a state pension to return to Valevåg in 1938 and cultivate his music (four symphonies, concertos for violin and piano, etc.) and his roses.

Vallotti, Francesco Antonio (b. Vercelli, 11 Jun 1697; d. Padua, 10 Jan 1780). Italian church musician. Trained as a boy in his home town, he was ordained in 1720 and became chapelmaster of St

Anthony's in Padua in 1730. There, heading a choir and an orchestra led by Tartini, he wrote concerted pieces and others looking back to Renaissance polyphony.

Valls, Francesc [Francisco] (b. ?Barcelona, ?1665; d. Barcelona, 3 Feb 1747). Catalan composer, chapelmaster of Barcelona Cathedral (1709–40). An unprepared ninth in his *Scala aretina* mass (1702) sparked a long-lasting controversy into which Alessandro Scarlatti entered (against).

valse (Fr.). Waltz. Notable *valses* include:

(1) Schubert's *Valses sentimentales* and *Valses nobles*.

(2) Sibelius's *Valse triste* for strings, originally part of his incidental score for Arvid Järnefelt's play *Death*.

(3) Ravel's *Valses nobles et sentimentales* for piano or orchestra. First performance: Paris, 9 May 1911, 22 Apr 1912 (orch, as ballet *Adélaïde*).

(4) Ravel's 'choreographic poem' for orchestra *La Valse*, a dance of death almost certainly prompted by Poe's 'Masque of the Red Death'. First performance: Paris, 12 Dec 1920.

valve. Device to open and close an additional loop of tubing in a brass instrument, and so change the pitch. Valves were introduced around 1814 by Heinrich Stölzel, a German horn player, and by the 1830s were standard on trumpets, horns and the new tubas. Previously a player could produce only notes of the harmonic series defined by the instrument's length; valves made several different lengths available, and therefore several different harmonic series. For example, the trumpet (from which the fundamental is not normally required) could fill the gap between its second harmonic (e.g. C on the bass stave) and its third (the G above) by the use of three valves, depressing its pitch by one, two and three semitones respectively. With all three valves open, the fundamental falls a tritone and the third harmonic is now C♯ on the bass stave. Other combinations of open and closed valves will produce D, E♭, E, F and F♯.

If fundamental tones are required, as they may be from horns and tubas, there is an octave gap between the first and second harmonics to be filled. A fourth valve, offering a depression of five semitones, will accommodate this: with all four valves open the pitch falls 11 semitones (so that the second harmonic is a semitone above the original fundamental), with just the first closed it falls 10, and so on.

However, the effects of valves do not sum up exactly, and having three or four open will produce discrepant intonation. That can be adjusted by the player to some degree, but often extra valves are added – a fourth on the trumpet, fifth and sixth on tubas – so that any interval can be covered by just one or two.

vamp. Improvise simple chords at the piano in preparation for a song or instrumental solo.

Vampyr, Der (The Vampire). Opera by Marschner to a libretto by Wilhelm August Wohlbrück stemming from a story drafted by Byron. The vampire is Lord Ruthven (baritone), whose career of murder and vein-sucking is ended by Aubry (tenor), who thereby saves Malwina (soprano) and is given her hand by a grateful father. First performance: Leipzig, 29 Mar 1828.

van Dam, José (b. Brussels, 25 Aug 1940). Belgian bass-baritone, born Joseph van Damme. After studies in Brussels he began his career in Paris and in the 1970s advanced to the international stage as Escamillo. In 1983 he created the title role in *Saint François d'Assise*, for which he was well suited by his stamina, resonant power and persuasive honesty of expression.

Vanhal, Jan. See Johann Baptist WANHAL.

Varesco, Giovanni Battista (baptized Trent, 26 Nov 1735; d. Salzburg, 25 Aug 1805). Italian librettist, Mozart's collaborator on *Idomeneo*. Educated by the Jesuits, he became chaplain and musician to the archbishop of Salzburg in 1766. He was Mozart's choice for *Idomeneo*, being on hand, and again for *L'oca del Cairo*.

Varèse, Edgard [Edgar] **(Victor Achille Charles)** (b. Paris, 22 Dec 1883; d. New York, 6 Nov 1965). French–US composer. An extreme radical in a radical generation, he pressed on with the modernist adventure in the 1920s, when most of his contemporaries were retrenching, and pursued strident dissonance, complex rhythm, percussion sounds and free form. Even then he was not satisfied. He foresaw a musical liberation that could come only from electronic means, and when those means became available he produced, in his *Poème électronique*, one of the early masterpieces of electronic music.

His childhood was divided between Paris and Burgundy, where his mother's family lived and where he was lastingly impressed by the big-blocked Romanesque architecture. Intemperate from his youth, he broke with his father to study music, first with Roussel at the Schola Cantorum (1904–5), then with Widor at the Conservatoire (1905–7). Moving to Berlin, he met Busoni, whose recently published ideas on musical innovation struck a chord, and Strauss, who arranged a performance of his symphonic poem *Bourgogne*. In 1913 he returned to Paris, and at the end of 1915 he embarked for New York. Most of his music had been lost in war and travel, except for a single published song and *Bourgogne*, which he took with him but later destroyed.

The move to the USA was an opportunity for a new beginning. He worked as a conductor, married, helped found and run an organization for new music, the International Composers Guild, and was at his most creatively productive. In the decade 1918–27 he wrote six works, whereas after that, though he lived almost another 40 years, came only five more.

He remembered the music he had heard in Europe – Debussy, the atonal Schoenberg, Stravinsky's *Petrushka* and *Rite* – but he listened, also, to the sounds of the New York streets, in a city where skyscrapers were going up like modern versions of the Burgundian Romanesque. Though long reflective melodies sometimes appear, his early US pieces are marked by brief signals, often reiterating a single note and so generating a tension that explodes in fierce dissonant chords for winds or rampant polyrhythms from percussion. In his 'organized sound' (a term he preferred to 'music'), all the qualities of sound were thoroughly involved, timbre, rhythm and intensity as much as pitch.

In 1928–33 he was back in Paris, where he extended his exploration of new resources, writing one of the earliest Western classical works for percussion alone (*Ionisation*) and one of the first to include electronic instruments (*Ecuatorial*, for which in different versions he tried the theremin and the ondes martenot). With its text from pre-Columbian ritual, evoking an ancient world as important to him as modern technology, *Ecuatorial* was finished in the USA and shortly followed by a long period of frustration. He tried to get help from film companies in extending the possibilities of music, and he dreamed of a work (*Espace*) that would involve simultaneous radio broadcasts from around the world. The tape recorder allowed him to make progress again, most spectacularly in his *Poème électronique*. Other late works are more sombre. Where *Amériques* had been a celebration of new worlds, vital with life and energy, *Déserts* was a tone poem of emptiness and desolation, and though in his last years he was hailed as a modern master by Boulez and Stockhausen, he was haunted by themes of night and death.

Louise Varèse *Varèse* (1972); Jonathan W. Bernard *The Music of Edgard Varèse* (1987)

Orchestral: *Amériques*, ?1918–21; ARCANA, 1925–7
Ensemble: *Offrandes* (Vicente Huidobro, José Juan Tablada), s, chbr orch, 1921; HYPERPRISM, 9 wind, 7 perc, 1922–3; OCTANDRE, 7 wind, db, 1923; INTEGRALES, 11 wind, 4 perc, 1924–5; IONISATION, 13 perc, 1929–31; *Ecuatorial*, b, 8 brass, pf, org, 2 ondes martenot, 6 perc, 1932–4; *Etude pour 'Espace'*, chorus, 2 pf, perc, 1947; DESERTS, 14 wind, pf, 5 perc, tape, ?1950–54; *Nocturnal*, s, b chorus, chbr orch, 1961 (completed Chou Wen-chung)
Other works: *Un Grand Sommeil noir* (song; Verlaine), pub 1906; DENSITY 21.5, fl, 1936; POEME ELECTRONIQUE, tape, 1957–8

variable metres. Systematic succession of metres – e.g. 3/8–4/8–5/8 in consecutive bars – introduced by Blacher in 1950 and also used by Hartmann.

variation. Form of a melody altered by decoration, change of rhythm, change of mode, elision, omission, etc. Variation is essential to almost all music, since repetition and change are in constant play. The art of writing formal variations arrived with the first independent instrumental music in the Renaissance and early Baroque (see DIVISION (1), DOUBLE (1), CHORALE VARIATIONS, CHACONNE, PASSACAGLIA) and was continued in the THEME AND VARIATIONS.

Variations on a Theme of Haydn (*Variationen über ein Thema von Haydn*). Orchestral work by Brahms (who also made a two-piano version), based on the second movement, 'Chorale St Antoni', of a wind divertimento in B♭ now thought to be by Pleyel. The work is therefore sometimes retitled 'Variations on the St Antoni Chorale', but this obscures Brahms's homage. First performance: Vienna, 2 Nov 1873.

Variationen über einen Kinderlied (Variations on a Nursery Song). Work for piano and orchestra by Dohnányi, on 'Ah! vous dirai-je maman?', a tune more familiar to an anglophone audience as 'Twinkle, twinkle, little star'.

Vasks, Peteris (b. Aizpute, 16 Apr 1946). Latvian composer. He studied the double bass in Vilnius and composition with Velntins Utkins at the conservatory in Riga, graduating in 1978. His works are mostly instrumental, slow and meditative.

Vasquez, Juan (b. Badajoz, c.1500; d. ?Seville, c.1560). Spanish composer. He served the cathedral of Badajoz from before 1530 until 1550, except for a time at Palencia Cathedral around 1540 and a visit to Madrid. In 1551 he joined the service of a nobleman in Seville, where he published a volume of music for all the offices of the dead (*Agenda defunctorum*) and another of lively, tuneful songs that spread through the courts of Spain.

vaudeville. Chameleon term apparently arising from two kinds of French Renaissance song: the *vau de Vire* (valley of the Vire, its Norman place of origin) and the *voix de ville* (city voices). In the 17th and 18th centuries it meant a topical or lowbrow song of a kind used in popular theatre, particularly as a closing number, in which all the main characters would sing verses in turn. This sort of vaudeville finale enjoyed a more distinguished and extended life in works by Mozart (*Die Entführung, Don Giovanni*), Stravinsky (*The Rake's Progress*) and Carter (*What Next?*). Meanwhile the term attached itself – especially in the USA at the end of the 19th century and into the 20th – to a genre of theatrical entertainment that included songs, chorus girls, comic sketches and novelty acts.

Vaughan Williams, Ralph (b. Down Ampney, Glos., 12 Oct 1872; d. London, 26 Aug 1958). British composer. Through English folksong and late Tudor music he found a path into a glowing harmony beyond the sunset years of the major-minor system. He lived all his life in England, appealed strongly to English sensibilities in his natural religion of landscape and myth, and was revered by English audiences partly as an antithesis to the modernism of Bartók, Stravinsky and Schoenberg.

He lost his father, a Church of England clergyman, when he was two and was brought up in the London area by his mother, who came from the Wedgwood family. A Wedgwood aunt taught him music, which he then studied at the RCM (1890–92), Cambridge (1892–5) and the RCM again (1895). His teachers included Parry, Stanford and Charles Wood, and his fellow pupils Holst, a lasting friend. In 1897 he went to Berlin for further study with Bruch and took a job as church organist. He also began making a name as a composer of songs and partsongs, and produced his first orchestral scores after he had started collecting folksongs in 1902. In 1905 he became conductor of an amateur music festival in Dorking, with which he remained associated until 1953 and where his Bach performances were deeply admired. He also followed his philosophy of musical citizenship in lecturing and in editing the *English Hymnal* (1906), to which he contributed some tunes, though his creed was more Blake's and Bunyan's than that of his father's church.

In 1908 – into his mid 30s and dissatisfied with his progress so far – he went to Paris briefly to acquire, as he put it, some 'French polish' from Ravel. Soon after returning he produced his first major works, including the song cycle *On Wenlock Edge* (1908–9) and the radiantly euphonious Fantasia on a Theme by Thomas Tallis for strings (1910). These two scores embodied two of his principal expressive types, pastoral and transcendent, with their respective allusions to folksong and 16th-century music – both sources that helped him re-create consonant harmony with an ear for modal relations. Other works of this burgeoning time include the first two of his nine symphonies (unnumbered by him, except for the Ninth), his first opera (not a genre in which he triumphed, though it was an opera, *The Pilgrim's Progress*, on which he laboured deepest and longest), the *Wasps* overture and the idyll *The Lark Ascending*.

Service in the First World War in France and Greece brought an interruption. He then started teaching at the RCM (1919–39) and became more widely active as a conductor, especially of his own works, which came plentifully. Among them were many sacred pieces, including the Mass (an unaccompanied Latin setting for Westminster Cathedral, in which he made himself a colleague of Tallis and Byrd) and *Sancta civitas*, expressing a visionary serenity also found in the one-act Bunyan opera *The Shepherds of the Delectable Mountains*, the chamber concerto for viola *Flos campi* and the ballet *Job*. But the turbulent F minor Symphony (1931–4) and cantata *Dona nobis pacem* (1936) suggest he was by no means out of touch with what was happening, musically and politically, in continental Europe. He received the honour of having his music banned by the Nazis in 1939 on account of his activity in support of refugees.

During the Second World War he wrote some patriotic music and a first film score (for *49th Parallel*), but his main creative direction now was inwards. Working on *The Pilgrim's Progress*, and not expecting to finish it, he drew on it for his luminous Symphony in D (1938–43, dedicated to Sibelius), whose mood overlapped into his A minor quartet and oboe concerto. That mood did not extend, though, into his Symphony in E minor (1944–7), whose bleakness he maintained in its successor, the *Sinfonia antartica* (1949–52) based on his score for *Scott of the Antarctic*. Meanwhile *The Pilgrim's Progress* was produced at Covent Garden in 1951. Two years later, into his 80s, he married his secretary and literary associate Ursula Wood, after which he went on, in full creative strength, exploring the further reaches within him of buoyancy (Symphony in D minor, utilizing again the tuned percussion of the Antarctic music) and glowing meditation (Symphony No.9).

Michael Kennedy *The Works of Ralph Vaughan Williams* (1964, ²1980); Wilfrid Mellers *Vaughan Williams and the Vision of Albion* (1989)

www.rvwsociety.com

Operas (most librettos by the composer): *Hugh the Drover* (Child), 1910–14, f.p. London, 1924; *The Shepherds of the Delectable Mountains* (after Bunyan), 1921, f.p. London, 1922; *Sir John in Love* (after Shakespeare), 1924–8, f.p. London, 1929; *The Poisoned Kiss* (Evelyn Sharp and Vaughan Williams, after Richard Garnett), 1927–9, f.p. Cambridge, 1936; *Riders to the Sea* (after Synge), 1925–32, f.p. London, 1937; *The Pilgrim's Progress* (after Bunyan, incorporating *The Shepherds*), 1921–51, f.p. London, 1951

Symphonies: *A Sea Symphony* (No.1; Whitman), s, bar, ch, orch, 1903–9; *A London Symphony* (No.2), 1911–13; *Pastoral Symphony* (No.3), 1916–21; No.4, F minor, 1931–4; No.5, D, 1938–43; No.6, E minor, 1944–7; SINFONIA ANTARTICA (No.7), s, women's ch, orch, 1949–52; No.8, D minor, 1953–5; No.9, E minor, 1956–7

Other choral orchestral works: TOWARD THE UNKNOWN REGION (Whitman), ch, orch, 1905–6; *5 Mystical Songs* (Herbert), bar, ch, orch, 1911; Fantasia on Christmas Carols, bar, ch, orch, 1912; *Lord, Thou hast been our Refuge* (Psalm 90), ch, orch/org, 1921; *Sancta civitas* (oratorio; Revelation), t, bar, ch, orch, 1923–5; *Te Deum*, G, ch, orch/org, 1928; *5 Tudor Portraits* (Skelton), mez, bar, ch, orch, 1935; *Dona nobis pacem* (cantata; Whitman, etc.), s, bar, ch, orch, 1936; *Serenade to Music* (Shakespeare), 16 soli, orch, 1938; *The Old Hundredth Psalm Tune*, ch, orch, 1953; *Hodie* (Christmas cantata), s, t, bar, ch, orch, 1953–4; etc.

Other orchestral works: *In the Fen Country*, 1904; *Norfolk Rhapsody* No.1, 1906; *The Wasps* (overture and suite), 1909; FANTASIA ON A THEME BY THOMAS TALLIS, str, 1910; *The Lark Ascending*, vn, orch, 1914; Concerto (accademico), D minor, vn, str, 1924–5; *Flos campi*, va, small ch, small orch, 1925; *Job* (ballet), 1927–30; Prelude and Fugue, C minor, 1930 (from org piece); Piano Concerto, C, 1926–31; *The Running Set*, 1933; Fantasia on 'Greensleeves', 1934 (arr Ralph Greaves from *Sir John*); Suite, va, small orch, 1934; 2 Hymn Tune Preludes, small orch, 1936; *5 Variants of 'Dives and Lazarus'*, str, hp, 1939; Concerto, A minor, ob, str, 1944; Partita, str, 1946–8; Concerto grosso, str, 1950; Romance, D♭, harmonica, str, pf, 1951; Tuba Concerto, F minor, 1954; etc.

Film scores: *49th Parallel*, 1940–41; *Scott of the Antarctic*, 1948; etc.

Band: English Folksong Suite, 1923; Sea Songs, 1923; *Toccata marziale*, 1924; Prelude on 3 Welsh Hymn Tunes, 1955; Variations, 1957

Smaller choral works: 3 Elizabethan Songs (Herbert, Shakespeare), 1890–1902; *O clap your hands*, 1920; Mass, G minor, 1920–21; Services, D minor, 1939;

Valiant for Truth (Bunyan), 1940; *The Souls of the Righteous* (Solomon), 1947; *Prayer to the Father of Heaven* (Skelton), 1948; 3 Shakespeare Songs, 1951; *O taste and see*, 1952; *A Vision of Aeroplanes* (Ezekiel), 1956; partsongs, folksong arrs, carols, hymn tunes, etc.

Chamber and instrumental: Phantasy Quintet, str, 1912; String Quartet, G minor, 1908–9; A minor, 1942–4; 6 Studies in English Folksong, vc/vn/va/cl, pf, 1926; Violin Sonata, A minor, 1954; etc.

Organ: 3 Preludes on Welsh Hymn Tunes, 1920; Prelude and Fugue, C minor, 1921; 2 Preludes on Welsh Folksongs, 1956

Songs: 'Linden Lea' (William Barnes), 1901; 'Orpheus with his Lute' (Shakespeare), 1901; *The House of Life* (6; D.G. Rossetti), 1903; *Songs of Travel* (9; Stevenson), 1901–4; *On Wenlock Edge* (6; Housman), t, pf qnt, 1908–9; 3 Songs from Shakespeare, 1925; 4 Poems by Fredegond Shove, 1925; *Along the Field* (8; Housman), v, vn, 1927; 7 Songs from 'The Pilgrim's Progress' (Bunyan), 1952; 10 Blake Songs, v, ob, 1957; 4 Last Songs (Ursula Vaughan Williams), 1954–8; 3 Vocalises, s, cl, 1958; folksong arrs, etc.

Vautor, Thomas (*fl.* 1600–1620). English madrigalist, in service to the Duke of Buckingham and an Oxford BMus (Lincoln College, 1616), influenced by Italian as well as English models. His single volume, published *c*.1620, includes madrigals both light (*Sweet Suffolk owl, Mother, I will have a husband*) and searching (*Cruel madam, Fairest are the words, Sweet thief*).

vc. Abbreviation for violincello. See CELLO.

Vecchi, Orazio (Tiberio) (baptized Modena, 6 Dec 1550; d. Modena, 19 Feb 1605). Italian composer, best known for L'AMFIPARNASSO, a comedy designed to be told (but not staged) in madrigals. He was trained as a musician and churchman in his native city, and held posts as chapelmaster at the cathedral there and more briefly at other cathedrals while also making visits to Venice, where he published several volumes of canzonettas, madrigals and sacred works.

Végh, Sándor (b. Koloszvar/Cluj, 17 May 1912; d. Freilassing, 7 Jan 1997). Hungarian–French violinist. He studied with Hubay, Leo Weiner and Kodály at the Liszt Academy (1924–30), and played with the Hungarian Quartet (1935–8) before founding his own Végh Quartet (1940–78), whose recordings of Mozart, Beethoven and Bartók convey rare qualities of intimacy with the music. He was also a much sought-after teacher, notably at the Salzburg Mozarteum (1970–87) and Prussia Cove in Cornwall (from 1972).

Vejvanovský, Paul Josef (b. *c*.1633–9; buried Kremsier/Kroměříž, 24 Sep 1693). Moravian trumpeter-composer. He studied at the Jesuit college in Troppau/Opava (1656–60), where he met Biber, and in 1661 was appointed trumpeter to the prince-bishop's court in Kremsier/Kroměříž. There he remained, writing masses, motets, litanies, psalms and sonatas, almost all with groups of strings and brass.

Velluti, Giovanni Battista (b. Montolmo, now Corridonia, Ancona, 28 Jan 1780; d. Dolo, Venice, 22 Jan 1861). Italian castrato, the last to appear on the stage. He studied in Bologna and Ravenna, made his debut in Forli in 1801 and created roles in Rossini's *Aureliano in Palmira* and Meyerbeer's *Il crociato in Egitto*. His appearances were mostly in northern Italy, but he also sang abroad (London, 1825), before retiring in 1830.

veloce (It.). Swiftly.

velocity. Speed of execution at the piano; see, for example, Czerny's *School of Velocity*, Op.299.

Venezia e Napoli. See ANNEES DE PELERINAGE.

Venice (Venezia). Maritime republic at the head of the Adriatic. With sporadic exceptions (a motet by Ciconia for a doge's coronation in 1400) the city was not musically important until the early 16th century, when it became one of the principal centres of music publishing. Willaert, chapelmaster at the state basilica of St Mark's from 1527 to 1562, was the first major composer active there, starting a tradition of polychoral music. His successor, Zarlino (chapelmaster 1565–90), established a fine ensemble of singers and instrumentalists (including Merulo and Andrea Gabrieli as organists), preparing for the glory of Giovanni Gabrieli.

During Monteverdi's time in the city (1613–43), musical magnificence slipped from the church to the new opera houses, for which Cavalli and later Legrenzi wrote. In the 18th century music also found a home in the hospitals (foundations that cared not only for the sick but for bastards and orphans), where charity often displayed itself in sumptuous entertainment. Lotti, Albinoni, the Marcellos, Vivaldi and Galuppi, all Venetian-born, contributed to the rich swathe of musical activity the city enjoyed – with operas also by such visitors and immigrants as Porpora, Jommelli, Traetta, Sarti and Hasse – at a time when its political power was declining.

The only important musical institution to survive the city's loss of independence (1797) was the opera house *La* FENICE, which had opened five years earlier, and which was one of several theatres swept by a Rossini craze in the 1810s. Wagner wrote a large part of *Tristan* in Venice in 1858–9, and, with a fine sense for artistic inevitability, returned there in 1882 to die. His musical obsequies were written by Liszt (*La lugubre gondola, R.W. – Venezia*) and the theme of Venice as the watery home of decay and death was established.

There was continuing life there as well. The founding of the conservatory in 1877 made possible a rebirth of Venetian music in the work of Malipiero and his pupils Nono and Maderna, and Stravinsky became a frequent visitor. His *Rake's Progress* was first performed at La Fenice, and he wrote his *Canticum sacrum* and *Threni* specifically for the city. But his, too, was the lugubrious gondola, ferrying his coffin out to the cemetery island of San Michele, where he was buried alongside Diaghilev.

H.C. Robbins Landon and John Julius Norwich *Five Centuries of Music in Venice* (1991)

Veni Creator Spiritus. Whitsun hymn, set by Mahler in his Eighth Symphony.

Veni Sancte Spiritus. Whitsun sequence, set by Dunstable (in combination with *Veni Creator Spiritus*), Du Fay, Josquin, Victoria, etc.

vent (Fr.). Wind, as in *instruments à vent* (wind instruments).

Venus and Adonis. Title of two notable operas:

(1) Blow's, the first all-sung opera in English. Adonis (baritone) leaves Venus (soprano) to a teasing scene with Cupid (soprano) and returns fatally wounded by the Aedalian boar. First performance: London or Windsor, *c*.1683.

(2) Henze's, to a libretto by Hans-Ulrich Treichel after Shakespeare, a madrigal-opera-ballet in which the love of Venus (soprano) and Adonis (tenor) provokes Mars (baritone) to kill the latter. First performance: Munich, 11 Jan 1997.

Vêpres siciliennes, Les (The Sicilian Vespers, *I vespri siciliani*). Opera by Verdi to a libretto by Scribe and Charles Duveyrier, often performed in Italian. Hélène/Elena (soprano) and Henri/Arrigo (tenor), loving each other, are torn by conflicting attitudes to Montfort/Montforte (baritone), the French governor of Sicily: she wants revenge on the man he discovers to be her father, while Procida (bass) urges them both to take part in the Sicilian uprising against the governor. The ball scene in the third act includes a ballet of the Four Seasons; among the arias are Hélène's virtuoso 'Merci, jeunes amies' ('Mercè, dilette amiche') and Procida's 'Et toi, Palerme' ('O tu, Palermo'). First performance: Paris Opera, 13 Jun 1855.

Veracini, Francesco Maria (b. Florence, 1 Feb 1690; d. Florence, 31 Oct 1768). Italian violinist-composer. The grandson and nephew of Florentine violinists, he studied with his uncle and with the cathedral organist, Giovanni Maria Casini. Much of his life he spent as an independent virtuoso, visiting Venice, London and Dresden with periodic returns to Florence (where he had a wife), never staying long in one place. He was arrogant, possibly mad, but he was an outstanding performer: Burney noted that 'the peculiarites of his performance were his bow-hand, his shake, his learned arpeggios, and a tone so loud and clear, that it could be distinctly heard through the most numerous band of a church or theatre'. In 1755 he settled back in Florence as a church musician. His surviving works include operas for London, cantatas, sonatas and concertos.

Veränderungen (Ger.). Variations, as in Bach's and Beethoven's titles for their Goldberg and Diabelli sets, though *Variationen* became the commoner term.

vera storia, La (The True Story). Opera by Berio to a libretto by Italo Calvino. The true story is that, punningly, of *Il trovatore*, remade into a true story. In the first act the elements are presented: four characters, a chorus, love, rivalry, betrayal. In the second, both more continuous and more sombre, these elements are reworked into a poetry of recollection. First performance: La Scala, Milan, 9 Mar 1982.

verbunkos (from Ger. *Werbung*, recruiting). Dance originally executed by hussars, accompanied by gypsy musicians and hoping to impress potential recruits into the Austrian army. Conscription rendered it unnecessary after 1849, but it survived, though functionless, typically alternating between slow music (*lassu*) and fast (*friss*). It was essential to the Hungarian style of Liszt and Brahms, as well as Bartók (especially in his frequent slow-fast forms) and Kodály.

Verdelot, Philippe (b. Verdelot, Les Loges, Seine-et-Marne, c.1480–85; d. ?Florence, ?1530–32). French composer, who spent most of his adult life in Italy (in Florence from 1521), where he was one of the earliest madrigalists. He was the major contributor to the first published volume of madrigals (1530), and his works in the form went on being reprinted until 1566. He also wrote motets; as with his madrigals, most are for four voices, some for five or six.

Verdi, Giuseppe (Fortuno Francesco) (b. Roncole, near Busseto, 9/10 Oct 1813; d. Milan, 27 Jan 1901). Italian composer. A master of robust melodrama and expressive melody, he kept those popular elements strong in his style while continuously developing his range and sophistication. Some of his operas were instantly successful and have remained favourites of the repertory.

The son of a tavern-keeper, he showed musical aptitude as a young boy and had lessons with the village priests before going to school in Busseto in 1823. There he gained a patron (and future father-in-law) in Antonio Barezzi, who helped finance his studies in Milan with Vincenzo Lavigna (1832–5: he was refused admittance to the conservatory). He returned to Busseto as local music master, published his first songs in 1838 and left the next year for Milan, where his first opera, *Oberto*, was produced at La Scala, resulting in a commission for three more. But these beginnings of his public success were accompanied by private grief: both his children died before reaching the age of 18 months, and Margherita, his wife of four years, followed them in May 1840. He was at work on a comedy, *Un giorno di regno*, which failed.

He returned to full creative vigour with *Nabucco* (1842), which established him as an international figure; by 1847 it had been seen from Constantinople to Havana, as well as in London, Paris and Berlin. The resulting pressure of commissions, and his own immense drive, resulted then in constant productivity at a rate of an opera every nine months on average during what he called the 'galley years' that lasted until he achieved the extraordinary hat trick of *Rigoletto*, *Il Trovatore* and *La Traviata* (1851–3). Meanwhile, he absorbed Donizetti's influence alongside Rossini's, and he kept their standard forms for arias, duets and ensembles in three or four sections: an opening *tempo d'attacco* (not used in arias), an adagio, a *tempo di mezzo* (involving some dramatic change) and a concluding presto (a cabaletta in the case of arias, a stretta in ensembles). But he added a rude orchestral strength and dramatic incisiveness all his own, insisting on the passionate appeal made by his characters and situations. He also set some store by the *tinta* (his term) of each score: its particular and characteristic colour, which might come from intervallic correspondences, choice of vocal registers or background musical allusions (to the waltz, for example, in *La traviata*). As his success brought him greater control over his work, he tackled a variety of themes and settings, from historical epic (*Attila*, *La battaglia di Legnano*) to personal drama (*Luisa Miller, Stiffelio*). Also, as the composer of *Nabucco*, he had come into contact with the Milanese cultural élite, and thereby been encouraged to find his subjects in more dignified authors (Schiller, Shakespeare, Hugo, Byron).

Soon he gained a new stability in his private life. In 1847, in Paris preparing *Jérusalem*, he set up home with Giuseppina Strepponi, whom he had known as a singer since 1839 and who was now a teacher of singing – though they did not marry until 1859. In 1848 he bought a house at Sant'Agata, ancestral territory, but he and Strepponi stayed largely in Paris until the next year, and went back for protracted visits prompted by his two later works for the Opera: *Les Vêpres siciliennes* (1855) and *Don Carlos* (1867). The city's tradition of grand opera fascinated him and fed into the scores he was writing for other houses, including *Un ballo in maschera* (1859).

Released from the relentless schedule of his 30s, he was becoming ever more a national hero, his name a rallying cry in the late 1850s, when 'Viva Verdi!' meant long life to Vittorio Emanuele Re d'Italia, the Savoyard monarch who did indeed become the united country's first ruler. In 1861 the reluctant composer accepted a seat in the first Italian parliament, from which he resigned in 1865. Meanwhile, the worldwide success of his works, and his ability to drive a hard bargain, had brought him great wealth, and he was settling into semi-retirement. In the 1860s he worked on only two operas: *La forza del destino*, for St Petersburg, and *Don Carlos*. After that, in 1868–9, he wrote a contribution to a collaborative *Requiem* he had proposed for Rossini; he completed the setting of the funeral mass in 1874 as a memorial to the novelist Alessandro Manzoni, having written *Aida* for the opening of the Suez Canal (1871) and a string quartet (1873).

There his creative career might have ended, except that in 1879 his publisher Giulio Ricordi tweaked his interest in working with the much younger Arrigo Boito on a version of Shakespeare's *Othello*. The two tried out their partnership in substantially revising *Simon Boccanegra* (1881) and then, after the further delay of creating a new version of *Don Carlos* for the Italian stage (1882–4), they proceeded to *Otello* and so to *Falstaff*, at last a triumphant comedy. In both these scores the orchestration has a new richness and subtlety, and the old Rossini–Donizetti forms are melting into a more continuous dramatic flow, though always allowing for moments of vigorous lyrical expression. After that there was talk of a *King Lear*, a project he had long cherished, but he was now in his 80s. He completed a set of four sacred pieces (though he had never had much time for the church) and returned to silence. His wife died in November 1897, he in the early days of the 20th century.

Julian Budden *The Operas of Verdi*, 3 Vols. (1973–81, ²1992); Mary Jane Phillips-Matz *Verdi* (1993)

www.giuseppeverdi.org

Operas: *Oberto, Conte di San Bonifacio* (Solera), f.p. Milan, 1839; *Un giorno di regno* (Romani), f.p. Milan, 1840; NABUCCO, f.p. Milan, 1842; *I LOMBARDI ALLA PRIMA CROCIATA*, f.p. Milan, 1843, rev as *Jérusalem*, f.p. Paris, 1847; ERNANI, f.p. Venice, 1844; *I DUE FOSCARI*, f.p. Rome, 1844; *Giovanna d' Arco* (see JOAN OF ARC), f.p. Milan, 1845; *Alzira* (Cammarano, after Voltaire), f.p. Naples, 1845; ATTILA, f.p. Venice, 1846; MACBETH, f.p. Florence, 1847, rev, f.p. Paris, 1865; *I masnadieri* (Andrea Maffei, after Schiller), f.p. London, 1847; *Il corsaro* (Piave, after Byron), f.p. Trieste, 1848; *La battaglia di Legnano* (Cammarano), f.p. Rome, 1849; LUISA MILLER, f.p. Naples, 1849; *Stiffelio* (Piave), f.p. Trieste, 1850, rev as *Aroldo* (Piave), f.p. Rimini, 1857; RIGOLETTO, f.p. Venice, 1851; *Il TROVATORE*, f.p. Rome, 1853; *La TRAVIATA*, f.p. Venice, 1853; *Les VEPRES SICILIENNES*, f.p. Paris, 1855; SIMON BOCCANEGRA, f.p. Venice, 1857, rev, f.p. Milan, 1881; *Un BALLO IN MASCHERA*, f.p. Rome, 1859; *La FORZA DEL DESTINO*, f.p. St Petersburg, 1862; DON CARLOS, f.p. Paris, 1867, rev, f.p. Milan, 1884; AIDA, f.p. Cairo, 1871; *Otello* (see OTHELLO), f.p. Milan, 1887; FALSTAFF, f.p. Milan, 1893

Choral and vocal orchestral: *Inno delle nazioni* (Boito), v, ch, orch, 1862; REQUIEM, 1874; *Pater noster*, ch, 1880; *Ave Maria*, s, str, 1880; QUATTRO PEZZI SACRI, 1889–97

Instrumental: String Quartet, E minor, 1873

Songs (with publication dates): *Sei romanze*, 1838; 'L'esule' (Solera), 1839; *Sei romanze*, 1845; 'Il poveretto', 1847; 'Stornello', 1869; etc.

Veress, Sándor (b. Kolozsvár/Cluj, 1 Feb 1907; d. Berne, 4 Mar 1992). Hungarian–Swiss composer, combining lucidity with a speculative cast of mind that led to an individual serial style: the Hungarian tradition is taken into clear Alpine air. He studied with Bartók and Kodály at the Liszt Academy in Budapest (1923–7) and worked with Lajtha on folk music (1929–33). From 1934 he was Bartók's assistant in folk-music research, and from 1943 he taught at the Liszt Academy, where Ligeti and Kurtág were among his students. His interests in music education and his work as a composer took him on frequent travels, and in 1949 he settled permanently in Berne, where he taught at the conservatory (1950–77) and the university (1968–77), his pupils including Holliger. Among his works are pieces for string orchestra, sonatas for solo violin (1935) and cello (1967), and *Diptychon* for wind quintet (1968).

verismo (It., realism). Term first applied to Italian operas with an everyday setting, such as *Cavalleria rusticana* (1889), but extended to cover other operas of the next two decades or so – by Leoncavallo, Puccini, Zandonai, etc. – in which the emotional temperature is consistently high even though the ambience may be exotic or historical. The inelegant adjective 'veristic' is sometimes used in a wider context.

Verklärte Nacht (Transfigured Night). Work by Schoenberg for string sextet (2 vn, 2 va, 2 vc), arranged by him for full orchestral strings. It follows the narrative of a poem by Richard Dehmel in which two lovers are walking through a moonlit wood. She confesses she is pregnant by another man, and he embraces both her and the child to come. The work was rejected for performance by the Vienna Composers' Union on the grounds of an inadmissible chord. First performance: Vienna, 18 Mar 1902.

Verlaine, Paul (b. Metz, 30 Mar 1844; d. Paris, 8 Jan 1896). French poet, a most musical writer whose verse's easy slide into song was overseen by Chabrier, Debussy, Fauré, Hahn and, less expectedly, Varèse and Stravinsky.

verlöschend (Ger.). Dying away.

Vermeulen, Matthijs (b. Helmond, 8 Feb 1888; d. Laren, 26 Jul 1967). Dutch composer (originally Mattheus Christianus Franciscus Van der Meulen). His seven symphonies – driven by long melodies, often polyphonically entwined – engage a late-Romantic expressive vigour in an enriched harmonic language. A blacksmith's son, he began training for the priesthood but in 1907 accepted his musical fate and took lessons with Daniël de Lange in Amsterdam. After two years he started work as a music critic, and Diepenbrock became his compositional mentor. In 1920, frustrated by what he saw as Mengelberg's excessively German programming at the Concertgebouw, he moved with his family to France, supported by friends. Still, though, he lacked performances. He began writing Paris sketches for a newspaper in the Dutch East Indies (1926–40) and for several years gave up composition. In 1939 one of his symphonies, No.3 (1921–2), was at last performed, by the Concertgebouw under van Beinum. Buoyed up, he returned to creative work, through years in which he lost his wife and a son involved in the Resistance. He remarried in 1946 and returned to Amsterdam and to criticism. Further performances followed, but his music was little known, even in the Netherlands, until the 1980s, when its frank, independent spirit began to be recognized.

Symphonies: No.1 (*Symphonia carminum*), 1912–14; No.2 'Prélude à la nouvelle journée', 1919–20; No.3 'Thrène et péan', 1921–2; No.4 'Les Victoires', 1940–41; No.5 'Les Lendemains chantants', 1931–5; No.6 'Les Minutes heureuses', 1956–8; No.7 'Dithyrambes pour le temps à venir', 1963–5
Other works: chamber music, songs

vermindert (Ger.). Diminished.

Verona. City in northeast Italy, home to a Renaissance ACADEMY and, since 1913, an annual summer opera festival in the Arena (Roman amphitheatre).

verratene Meer, Das (The Treacherous Sea). Opera by Henze to a libretto by Hans-Ulrich Treichel after Mishima's novel *The Sailor who Fell from Grace with the Sea*. Noburo (tenor), a boy living with his widowed mother, Fusako (soprano), hero-worships her sailor lover, Ryuji (baritone). When Ryuji protests his ordinariness, Noburo goes along with other boys in planning his execution. First performance: Berlin, 5 May 1990.

verschwindend (Ger.). Disappearing.

verse. Part of a song or hymn where the same music returns to different words, as opposed to a refrain, or chorus, in which both words and music are the same at each repetition.

verse anthem. Anglican form of the 16th and 17th centuries, in which verses for a soloist or soloists alternate with others for the choir.

Verses for Ensembles. Work by Birtwistle, his first commissioned by the London Sinfonietta, for wind quintet, brass quintet and three percussionists. The block structure and call-response elements are dramatized by having the musicians move among different stations. First performance: London, 12 Feb 1969.

verset (Fr., little verse). Organ piece generally replacing a line in a psalm or other sung text.

versicle. Part of a liturgical dialogue, said or sung by the priest, eliciting a response from the choir or congregation – e.g. 'The Lord be with you' followed by 'And with thy spirit'. Pre-Reformation formulae for versicles and responses were the source for Merbecke's settings, in common Anglican use.

Verstovsky, Aleksey (Nikolayevich) (b. Seliverstovo, Tambov governate, 1 Mar 1799; d. Moscow, 17 Nov 1862). Russian composer, a pupil of Steibelt and Field. He worked as inspector and then director of theatres in Moscow while creating some of the earliest Russian operas, in a style deriving from Weber: *Pan Twardowski* (1828), *Vadim* (1832) and *Askold's Grave* (1835). But these were all outshone by Glinka.

vertical. Pertaining to things happening at the same time, which are therefore vertically aligned in a score. One may speak of music's vertical dimension, of heavy verticals (strong chords), etc.

Verzeichnis (Ger.). Catalogue.

vespers. Evening service, so called from the Latin *vesper* (evening). In the Western Church it includes several psalms (with antiphons), a hymn and the *Magnificat*. Settings include:

(1) Monteverdi's *Vespro della Beata Vergine* (Vespers of the Blessed Virgin). As published in 1610 the work comprises the following items: *Domine ad adiuvandum*, ch a 6, insts, con; *Dixit Dominus*, ch a 6, insts, con; *Nigra sum*, t, con; *Laudate pueri*, ch a 8, org; *Pulchra es*, 2 s, con; *Laetatus sum*, ch a 6, con; *Duo seraphim*, 3 t, con; *Nisi Dominus*, 2 ch a 5, con; *Audi coelum*, t, ch a 6, con; *Lauda Jerusalem*, ch a 7, con; *Sonata sopra 'Sancta Maria, ora pro nobis'*, s, insts, con; *Ave maris stella*, 2 ch a 5, insts, con; *Magnificat*, ch a 7, insts, org; *Magnificat*, ch a 6, org

(2) Mozart's *Vesperae de Dominica* (Sunday Vespers), K.321, and *Vesperae solennes de confessore* (Solemn Vespers of a Confessor), K.339, both for solo qt, ch, orch, and both with the same sequence: *Dixit Dominus, Confitebor, Beatus vir, Laudate pueri, Laudate Dominum, Magnificat*.

Settings of the Russian Orthodox vespers include Tchaikovsky's.

vespri siciliani, I. See *Les* VEPRES SICILIENNES.

Vestale, La (The Vestal). Opera by Spontini to a libretto by Etienne de Jouy. The vestal virgin is Julia (soprano), torn by the love she retains for Licinius (tenor), whom she is due to crown in his triumph. Meeting him at night, she lets the vestal flame go out, is condemned to death, but at the last moment is saved when lightning relights the flame. The work has occasionally been revived for an outstanding diva (Ponselle, Callas, Caballé). First performance: Paris Opera, 15 Dec 1807.

via (It.). Away, as in *via sordini* (take off mutes).

Via Crucis (The Way of the Cross). Work by Liszt for choir with piano or organ, to texts (Christ's words, Latin hymns, German chorales) selected by Princess Carolyne Sayn-Wittgenstein. First performance: Budapest, Good Friday 1929.

Viadana, Lodovico (b. Viadana, near Parma, c.1560; d. Gualtieri, near Parma, 2 May 1627). Italian composer. A Franciscan friar, he served various cathedrals as chapelmaster and was a pioneer of the new expressive monody in church music: his second book of *Concerti ecclesiastici* (1607) includes a mass for soloist and continuo. Besides his large output of liturgical music he produced some canzonettas and sinfonias.

viaggio a Reims, Il (The Journey to Rheims). Opera by Rossini to a libretto by Luigi Balocchi after Mme de Staël's novel *Corinne*. Written on the occasion of the coronation of Charles X, it features a variety of characters caught together at a hotel on their way to the event. Rossini reused some of the music in *Le Comte Ory*. First performance: Paris, 19 Jun 1825.

Viardot, (Michelle Ferdinande) Pauline [née García] (b. Paris, 18 Jul 1821; d. Paris, 18 May 1910). French mezzo-soprano, daughter of Manuel García and sister of Maria Malibran. She studied singing with her mother, the piano with Liszt and composition with Reicha, then started her career as Rossini's Desdemona in London (1838) and Paris (1839). In 1840 she married Louis Viardot, with whom she set up one of the foremost intellectual salons in Paris. But she continued her career. In 1843 she visited Russia and captivated Turgenev, who joined her household; she befriended Schumann, who dedicated his Heine *Liederkreis* to her; and she enjoyed spectacular success in Paris in Meyerbeer's *Le Prophète* (1849) and Gluck's *Orfeo* (1859). She also gave the first performance of Brahms's Alto Rhapsody. In later years she taught singing and composed.

vib. Abbreviation for vibraphone.

vibraharp. Obsolete name for the vibraphone.

vibraphone. Percussion instrument, a metallophone with a pedal to undamp the keys (as on the piano), tubular resonators and rotatable discs at the tops of the resonators. These discs, driven by an electric motor, produce the vibrato effect from which the instrument gained its name, though the motor may be turned off, and indeed many composers request this. The normal range is three octaves, from the F below middle C up.

Developed in the USA during and after the First

World War for dance bands, the instrument began its classical career with Milhaud's *L'Annonce faite à Marie* (1933) and Berg's *Lulu* (1934). Immediately after the Second World War it became a standard part of the percussion section, used by composers from Vaughan Williams to Boulez.

vibrato. More or less rapid oscillation in pitch. This is an essential part of singing and instrumental technique, though it requires a keen exercise of taste and historical judgement. An almost subliminal vibrato brings warmth to the sound and is almost ubiquitous among modern singers and string players, who may then exaggerate the vibrato to make an expressive point. For singers, an uncontrolled or excessive vibrato becomes a fault: wobble. For string players, whose vibrato comes from quivering the finger on the string, there are questions about the appropriateness of the effect in music of different periods; treatises and some very early recordings suggest it may not always have been so widespread. Exaggerated vibrato has been required as an effect in some scores since the 1960s, notated by a wavy line over the music. Generous vibrato on wind instruments used to be partly responsible for the character of French and Russian orchestras, though it died out with the internationalization of orchestral sound in the late 20th century.

Vicentino, Nicola (b. Vicenza, 1511; d. Milan, *c*.1576). Italian theorist-composer. He probably studied with Willaert in Venice; he was also an ordained priest. In the 1540s he joined the household of Cardinal Ippolito II d'Este and published a volume of madrigals, but he was and is renowned chiefly for his treatise *L'antica musica ridotta alla moderna prattica* (1555), in which he addressed the new problems of TEMPERAMENT introduced by chromatic music.

Vickers, Jon(athan Stewart) (b. Prince Albert, Saskatchewan, 29 Oct 1926). Canadian tenor, of extraordinary expressive frankness and force. He studied with George Lambert at the conservatory in Toronto and began his career in Canada before making his debuts at Covent Garden (1957) and Bayreuth (1958). He excelled in roles of heroic suffering: Handel's Samson, Tristan, Florestan, Peter Grimes.

Victoria, Tomás Luis de (b. Ávila, 1548; d. Madrid, 20 Aug 1611). Spanish composer, one of the great masters of Renaissance polyphony in its golden sunset years. He was the seventh of 11 children in a family that lost its father in 1557 and came under the protection of a priest uncle. When his voice

broke he moved from the choirstalls of Ávila Cathedral to the Collegio Germanico, a Jesuit institution in Rome, where he may have had lessons with Palestrina. He stayed on to teach at the Collegio (1571–6) while holding other musical posts, and after his ordination as a priest (1575) joined St Philip Neri's oratorians. In 1587 he returned to Spain as chaplain to the Dowager Empress María at the convent of Las Descalzas Reales in Madrid. There he remained until his death, except for a second visit to Rome (1592–5), which he undertook to oversee the printing of a volume of masses, but which also allowed him to assist at Palestrina's funeral.

His music, exclusively for the church, shows emergent major-minor tonality assuring purposeful movement and defining moments of keen piety – sorrowing or exultant – expressed in chromatic harmonies or contours. These give his music a particularly Spanish fervour, which was appreciated in his lifetime. Several collections of masses and motets were published and republished between 1572 and 1600, and he ended his public career with a volume devoted to his magnificent six-part *Missa pro defunctis* for the dowager empress.

Eugene Casjen Cramer *Studies in the Music of Tomás Luis de Victoria* (2001)

Masses (with publication dates): *Ave maris stella* a 4, 1576; *Gaudeamus* a 6, 1576; *O quam gloriosium* a 4, 1583; *O magnum mysterium* a 4, 1592; *Ave regina coelorum* a 8, 1600; *Missa pro defunctis* (REQUIEM) a 6, 1605; 16 others
Other works: Lamentations, pub 1585; 18 *Magnificat* settings, motets (*O magnum mysterium* a 4), etc.

vida breve, La (Life is Short). Opera by Falla to a libretto by Carlos Fernández Shaw. Set in Granada against a background of indigenous song and dance, the opera centres on Salud (soprano) who, betrayed by Paco (tenor), turns up at his wedding and falls dead. The score includes the popular Spanish Dance No.1. First performance: Nice, 1 Apr 1913.

Vidal, Peire (*fl. c*.1183–1205). Troubadour, said to have travelled with Richard Coeur-de-Lion to Cyprus. 12 songs by him survive, including *Pos tornatz sui en Proensa* (*c*.1189).

vide (Fr.). Empty, open, as in *corde à vide* (open string).

Vidovszky, László (b. Békéscsaba, 25 Feb 1944). Hungarian composer, of ironic character and theatrical inclinations. He studied with Farkas at the Liszt Academy (1962–7), co-founded the New

Music Studio with Jeney and Sáry (1970), and spent a year in Paris at Messiaen's classes and the Groupe de Recherches Musicales (1970–71), returning to teach in the teacher-training department of the Liszt Academy (1972–84) and then Pécs University.

vielle (Fr.). Medieval fiddle or hurdy-gurdy.

Vienna (Wien). The centre of Austro–German music in the Classical and Romantic periods, home to Haydn, Mozart, Beethoven, Schubert, Brahms, Bruckner, Mahler, Schoenberg, Berg and Webern. The city began to become musically important under Maximilian I, who reorganized the imperial chapel there in 1498. Ferdinand II (r. 1619–37) made Vienna the capital of the Holy Roman Empire, with territories covering much of central Europe and north Italy, and began the practice of importing Italian music and musicians, including Giovanni Priuli and Giovanni Valentini, two pupils of Gabrieli. Cesti's opera *Il pomo d'oro* was lavishly staged for the wedding of Leopold I in 1668; Fux and Caldara at the court of Charles VI (r. 1711–40) brought the age of Baroque musical Vienna to an end.

Italians remained central at court until Salieri retired in 1824, though Gluck was director of the opera house, the Burgtheater (1755–70). Mozart's operas are now remembered as dominating Vienna during his decade in the city (1781–91), but at the time works by Paisiello, Sarti and Martín y Soler were more popular. A German company was installed briefly at the Burgtheater around 1780, and at the same time Joseph II allowed other theatres to open in the suburbs. One of the first to do so was Schikaneder's Theater auf der Wieden (1787), where *Die Zauberflöte* had its première. Meanwhile, in the centre, aristocratic patronage supported a rich supply of music in salons, concert rooms, dance halls and chapels. Music publishing also took off, and it was possible for a composer – Haydn – to lead a hectic creative life independent of the imperial court.

Beethoven did that too, and so did Schubert, as support for music shifted in the early 19th century from wealthy individuals to bourgeois institutions, notably the Gesellschaft der Musikfreunde (Association of Musical Amateurs), which was founded in 1812 and opened a conservatory five years later. Schikaneder's new suburban theatre, the Theater an der Wien (1801), became the principal venue for opera (*Fidelio*), plays with music (*Rosamunde, Die Zauberharfe*) and concerts (including that at which Beethoven's Fifth and Sixth Symphonies and Fourth Piano Concerto were first performed). In cafés and inns the waltz

began its reign, a reign which virtually coincided with that of Franz Josef I (1848–1916), though it had been in preparation since the 1820s.

Brahms arrived in Vienna in 1862, at a time of urban expansion and rebuilding. The medieval city walls were being demolished to make way for a circular boulevard, the Ringstrasse, on or near which arose a new opera house, for what was still the court company, and a concert hall, the Musikverein. The Vienna Philharmonic started giving concerts regularly in 1860; other concert societies and choirs date from the same period. For half a century Vienna was musically awhirl, with Brahms and Bruckner at work, Johann Strauss II and Franz Lehár writing operettas, and, near the end of the period, Mahler directing the opera (1897–1907), to acclaim from a new generation that included Schoenberg and his pupils. In these years immediately before the First World War the city was also witnessing revolutions in architecture, painting and psychology (Freud).

With the collapse of the Austro-Hungarian empire at the end of the First World War, Vienna became merely a national, not an imperial, capital, with catastrophic effects on its economy, prestige and creative energy. Further material damage came with the Second World War, and the opera house (now the Staatsoper) had to be rebuilt. The city has remained, though, a centre of performing excellence. Opera is given at the liberally funded Staatsoper and the Volksoper, concerts in the Musikverein (with a Grosser Saal and a recital room, the Brahmssaal) and the Konzerthaus (with a large auditorium, a medium-size Mozartsaal and a small Schubertsaal).

Carl E. Schorske *Fin-de-siècle Vienna* (1980); Franz Endler *Vienna: A Guide to its Music and Musicians* (1989); Raymond Erickson *Schubert's Vienna* (1997)

Vienna Boys Choir (Wiener Sängerknaben). Institution of around 150 boys, from whom are drawn choirs for the Hofmusikkapelle (Court Chapel) and touring.

Vienna Philharmonic Orchestra (Wiener Philharmoniker). Founded in 1842 and regularly active since 1860, it is supreme in its finesse and unusual in being at once a concert and an opera orchestra, playing at the Vienna Staatsoper, the Musikverein and the Salzburg Festival. Its former principal conductors included Richter (1875–98), Mahler (1898–1901), Weingartner (1908–27) and Furtwängler (1933–54). Latterly it has had no chief conductor but has worked regularly with Karajan, Abbado, Boulez, Rattle, etc.

Vier ernste Gesänge (Four Serious Songs). One of

Brahms's last works, for bass and piano, setting biblical texts: meditations on death and St Paul's praise of charity. The prompt, more than the composer's own mortality, was the final illness of Clara Schumann.

Vier letzte Lieder (Four Last Songs). Strauss's glowing sunset masterpiece, setting three poems by Hermann Hesse ('Frühling', 'September', 'Beim Schlafengehen') and one by Joseph von Eichendorff ('Im Abendrot'). First performance: London, 22 May 1950.

Vierne, Louis (Victor Jules) (b. Poitiers, 8 Oct 1870; d. Paris, 2 Jun 1937). French organist-composer. Having limited sight, he studied at the Institution des Jeunes Aveugles (1880–90) and with Franck and Widor at the Conservatoire (1890–93), where he was soon engaged as a teacher (1894–1911). In 1900 he became organist at Notre Dame, and he died, as he had wished, playing there. His organ works include six symphonies and *Pièces de fantaisie* (1926–7), a collection of 24 pieces including *Carillon de Westminster*, *Clair de lune* and an Impromptu.

vierstimmig (Ger.) Four-part.

Viertel(-Note) (Ger.). Quarter-note, crotchet.

Viertelton (Ger.). Quarter-tone.

Vierundsechzigstel(-Note) (Ger.). 64th-note, hemidemisemiquaver.

Vieuxtemps, Henry (b. Verviers, 17 Feb 1820; d. Mustapha, Algeria, 6 Jun 1881). Belgian violinist-composer. He began his training with his father, who propelled him into a performing career: he made his debut at six, and at nine, now a pupil of de Bériot, appeared in Paris in a Rode concerto. In 1833–4 he was in Vienna, where he studied counterpoint with Sechter and revived Beethoven's almost forgotten concerto. He went on to London, where he met Paganini, and Paris (1835–6), where he had lessons with Reicha. After that he travelled widely, making trips to the USA (1843–4, 1857–8, 1870–71) and Russia (1840, 1846–51). From 1871 he devoted his energies to teaching at the Brussels Conservatory, where Ysaÿe was among his pupils, but poor health obliged him to resign in 1879. He wrote seven violin concertos (No.4, Op.31, D minor, *c*.1850; No.5, A minor, Op.37, 1861), other virtuoso showpieces (*Souvenir d'Amérique*, on 'Yankee Doodle', vn, pf) and two cello concertos.

vif (Fr.). In a lively manner.

vihuela. Plucked instrument with frets and six or seven strings, tuned like the lute in its sequence of intervals (fourth-fourth-major third-fourth-fourth for a six-string instrument) but with a guitar-like shape. It had a place in Spain in the 16th century comparable with that of the lute elsewhere in Europe, as a solo instrument (in fantasias, variations and arrangements of sacred polyphony) and an accompaniment to the voice. Important composer-practitioners included Luys Milán and Miguel de Fuenllana.

Villa-Lobos, Heitor (b. Rio de Janeiro, 5 Mar 1887; d. Rio de Janeiro, 17 Nov 1959). Brazilian composer. He was the first to show classical music the colour and rhythm of Latin America, in an exuberantly vast and various output. His father, a librarian and keen amateur musician, introduced him to the cello. After his father's death in 1899, he was brought up by his mother and intended for medicine, but he neglected his studies to play the guitar with popular musicians, and between the ages of 18 and 25 travelled all over Brazil and beyond, as far as Barbados. His reminiscences (about being captured by cannibals, for instance) may stray from dry fact, but they appropriately reflect his music's lust for life.

Back in Rio he devoted himself to playing in cafés and composing. In 1913 he married Lucilia Guimarães, a pianist, who appeared in the first concert devoted to his music (1915) and helped him build a local reputation. Also crucial were his contacts in Rio in 1917–18 with Milhaud and Arthur Rubinstein, who championed his music. In 1922 his participation in a festival of contemporary art in São Paulo made him a national figure and intensified his sense of himself as a modernist. The following year, with state and private support, he left for Paris. He stayed seven years, though he made visits home and also travelled several times to Dakar, in search of African music. The music he presented in Paris created a sensation, especially the orchestral *Chôros*, with their tropical luxuriance (the *chôros* being a Brazilian popular genre) treated in a manner out of Rimsky-Korsakov and early Stravinsky. Varèse became a friend, Messiaen an admirer.

On his return to Brazil, in 1930, he took on the task of advising the government on music education and performance, and in 1942 set up a conservatory in Rio. Patriotism seems to have overridden any doubts he may have had about serving a far-right regime, though his status as an official composer may have influenced his retreat from radicalism. In 1936 he parted amicably from his wife for another woman. His travels at this time were mostly within South America, but after the end of the Second World War he resumed his wider wanderings, making almost annual trips to the USA and France to conduct. In 1952 he settled in Paris again, but he returned to Brazil shortly before his death.

Gerard Béhague *Heitor Villa-Lobos* (1994)

Orchestral: *Uirapuru*, 1917; *Chôros* No.6, 1926; *Chôros* No.8, 2 pf, orch, 1925; *Chôros* No.10, ch, orch, 1926; *Chôros* No.11, pf, orch, 1928; *Chôros* No.14, ch, band, orch, 1928; Introduction to the *Chôros*, gtr, orch, 1929; *Chôros* No.9, 1929; *Chôros* No.12, 1929; *Chôros* No.13, 2 orchs, band, 1929; BACHIANAS BRASILEIRAS No.2 'O trenzinho do Caipira', 1930; *Bachianas brasileiras* No.4, 1930–36; *Bachianas brasileiras* No.3, pf, orch, 1938; *O papagaio do Moleque*, 1932; *Descobrimento do Brasil*, 4 suites, 1937; *Bachianas brasileiras* No.7, 1942; *Bachianas brasileiras* No.8, 1944; *Bachianas brasileiras* No.9, str, 1945; Guitar Concerto, 1951; *Dawn in a Tropical Forest*, ov., 1953; 12 symphonies, etc.

Choral: *Chôros* No.3, men's ch, 6 wind, 1925; *Bachianas brasileiras* No.9, 1945; etc.

Chamber: *Chôros* No.2, fl, cl, 1924; *Chôros* No.7, 8 insts, 1924; *Chôros* No.4, 4 brass, 1926; *2 chôros bis*, vn, vc, 1928; Woodwind Quartet, 1928; *Quinteto em forma de chôros*, wind qnt, 1928; *Bachianas brasileiras* No.1, at least 8 vc, 1930; *Bachianas brasileiras* No.6, fl, bn, 1938; *Bachianas brasileiras* No.5, s, at least 8 vc, 1938–45; 17 string quartets, etc.

Guitar: *Chôros* No.1, 1920; 12 Etudes, 1929; 5 Preludes, 1940

Piano: *Prole do bebê*, 2 sets, 1918, 1921; *Chôros* No.5, 1925; *Bachianas brasileiras* No.4, 1930–36; etc.

Other works: operas, ballets, songs, sacred music, film scores

villancico (Sp., little peasant). Renaissance–Baroque genre that, throughout its twisting career, kept its roots in lively dance-song and its form of a refrain with several stanzas (*coplas*). The Spanish villancico of the late 15th and early 16th centuries was a polyphonic song treating themes of love or ribaldry, and was practised by composers including Encina, Peñalosa and Morales. Solo villancicos, with vihuela or keyboard, were cultivated a little later, but near the end of the 16th century the villancico became a religious song, used in church particularly at Christmas and Corpus Christi (though there were objections). As such it enjoyed a new life in Latin America.

villanella. Variety of lively homophonic song that emerged in Naples in the 1530s and 1540s, in pointed contrast with the more sophisticated madrigal. It was taken up by high-art composers elsewhere, including Willaert, Lassus and Maren-zio, and the distinction from the madrigal was lost.

Viñao, Alejandro (Raul) (b. Buenos Aires, 4 Sep 1951). Argentinian–British composer. After studies with Jacobo Ficher in Buenos Aires, he left in 1975 for further training at the RCM and City University in London. There he stayed, working principally with computer technology in live performance, as in *Son entero* for four singers (1985–8) and the opera *Rashomon* for soloists and chorus (1995–9). Something of South America remains in the heat of his music.

Vinci, Leonardo (b. Strongoli, Calabria, *c.*1696; d. Naples, 27/28 May 1730). Italian composer. He studied with Gaetano Greco at the Poveri conservatory in Naples (1708–18) and began his career writing comedies in Neapolitan dialect (1719–24) before moving on to opera seria in 1722. After the success of *Didone abandonnata* (1726), his first Metastasio opera, he set six new librettos by the poet. He also worked at the royal chapel (from 1726) and in the summer of 1728 taught at his old conservatory, where Pergolesi was among his pupils. His music, with its elegant melody in regular phrases, simply accompanied, was something fresh. Accordingly he was much commissioned, and wrote three operas a year during his short career, which ended, according to gossip, when he was poisoned by a rival in love.

Vinci, Pietro (b. Nicosia, Sicily, *c.*1535; d. Nicosia or Piazza Armerina, ?15 Jun 1584). Italian composer. He may have moved to the mainland around 1560 and was chapelmaster at Santa Maria Maggiore in Bergamo (1568–80), where he married. He also wrote madrigals for a Milanese patron, Antonio Londonio, before returning in 1581 to Sicily. His published works include 10 volumes of madrigals (in a style emanating from Rore), masses and motets.

Vine, Carl (Edward) (b. Perth, 8 Oct 1954). Australian composer who sprang to note in the late 1970s as a composer of vital, colourful dance music close to the US minimalist tradition. He had piano and composition lessons while studying sciences at the University of Western Australia, and in 1979 co-founded the ensemble Flederman; his sextet *Café Concertino* (1984) is a classic of their repertory. His other works include symphonies, concertos and string quartets.

Viñes, Ricardo (b. Lérida, 5 Feb 1875; d. Barcelona, 29 Apr 1943). Spanish pianist. He studied with Bériot at the Paris Conservatoire (1887–94) and led an international career, but is specially remembered for his associations with contemporary French and Spanish composers. Works dedicated to him include Debussy's *Poissons d'or*, Ravel's *Miroirs* and Falla's *Noches en los jardines de España*. He also composed songs and piano pieces.

Vingt-quatre violons du roi (The King's 24 Violins). String orchestra forming a five-part ensemble (6–4–4–4–6) at the French court from 1618, at the latest, until abolished in 1761.

Vingt regards sur l'Enfant-Jésus (20 Views of the Child Jesus). Piano work by Messiaen of recital length: 1 *Regard du Père*, 2 *Regard de l'étoile*, 3 *L'Echange*, 4 *Regard de la Vierge*, 5 *Regard du Fils sur le Fils*, 6 *Par Lui tout a été fait*, 7 *Regard de la Croix*, 8 *Regard des hauteurs*, 9 *Regard du Temps*, 10 *Regard de l'Esprit de joie*, 11 *Première communion de la Vierge*, 12 *La Parole toute puissante*, 13 *Noël*, 14 *Regard des anges*, 15 *Le Baiser de l'Enfant-Jésus*, 16 *Regard des prophètes, des bergers et des mages*, 17 *Regard du silence*, 18 *Regard de l'onction terrible*, 19 *Je dors, mais mon coeur veille*, 20 *Regard de l'église d'amour*. First performance: Paris, 26 Mar 1945.

Vinteuil. See IMAGINARY COMPOSERS.

viol. Bowed string instrument with frets, commonly played in a vertical position, held on the lap (for smaller instruments) or between the legs. This method of playing had been applied to the medieval fiddle and rebec, and though it had died out in Europe, it continued in the Arab world. When viols emerged in Spain in the late 15th century, therefore, the stimulus may have been Islamic, though with some influence too from the vihuela; their tuning replicates that of the vihuela and lute. They faded out of musical life in the 18th century, except for the largest of them – the contrabass, or VIOLONE, a continuo instrument – which survived as the double bass. Their revival started in the second half of the 19th century, when a few cellists began taking up the bass viol, or VIOLA DA GAMBA, and was speeded up by Arnold Dolmetsch. By the end of the 20th century many viol consorts were at work again, with a repertory including new compositions by Benjamin, Tavener, etc.

Viols come in several different sizes, of which the commonest are treble (usually with six strings tuned D–G–middle C–E–A–D), tenor (a fifth below the treble) and bass (a fourth below the tenor). Any of these can be played as a solo instrument, but most commonly they are used together in a consort, or CHEST. Instruments of all sizes are normally made in the same form, with flat backs and sloping shoulders. Light and strung at low tension, they have a soft, reedy and resonant quality and are played with a bow that is convex, like an archery bow.

The instrument seems to have spread from Spain to Italy around 1500 and from there to the Holy Roman Empire, France and England by the 1520s. English amateurs took a particular fancy to it and kept the viol consort fully alive: for an important line of 17th-century composers, notably Jenkins and William Lawes, it was the preferred medium, long after it had fallen into desuetude on the continent. In France and Germany the bass viol survived largely as a solo instrument. Its French virtuosos included Marin Marais and Antoine Forqueray, while Bach wrote sonatas for it, obbligatos (notably in his St Matthew and St John Passions) and parts in his Sixth Brandenburg Concerto.

Ian Woodfield *The Early History of the Viol* (1984); Alison Crum *Play the Viol* (1989, ²1992)

viola (Fr. *alto*, Ger. *Bratsche*). Bowed instrument, the alto-tenor relative and companion of the violin, tuned a fifth lower (C–G–D–A), its lowest note being the C below middle C. This difference in pitch would imply a 3:2 ratio in size between the viola and the violin, but all modern violas are smaller than this, and some very much smaller, hardly bigger than a violin: the instrument has to be miniaturized somewhat so that it can be held by an outstretched arm, like the violin, but it is unlike the violin in its range of sizes. Being relatively compact, the viola is less resonant than the violin, gentler and darker as well as lower. That is reflected in its repertory.

The viola arrived soon after the violin, in the early 16th century. The earliest depiction of it is in a fresco in Saronno Cathedral from around 1535. At that time the Italian word *viola* could indicate any member of the viol (*viola da gamba*) or violin (*viola da braccio*) families. Only gradually did the nomenclature clarify, and then not altogether. Baroque scores often distinguished two or three viola parts: alto viola and tenor viola (Handel's Op.3:1) or *haute-contre*, *taille* and *quinte* (French music). These indicated instruments with the usual viola tuning but differing in register and therefore presumably in size – and indeed large violas, with bodies up to 19 inches (48cm) long, survive from this period, by makers including Stradivari. By the middle of the 18th century, however, violas were known as such and had been reduced to one part in the string ensemble – except in France – regaining their two on such rare and beautiful occasions as Mozart's quintets.

Mozart was also among the first composers to write exposed solo music for the viola, in his Sinfonia Concertante, K.364 and Trio, K.498. Works generous to the viola in the 19th century include Berlioz's *Harold en Italie* as well as the quartets of Brahms and Dvořák. But the viola really came into its own after 1920, in concertos by Hindemith (himself a violist), Walton, Bartók, Kurtág, Druckman, Berio (*Voci*), Eötvös (*Replica*), etc., in sonatas by Shostakovich and Ligeti, and in several works by Boulez (*Le Marteau sans maître*, *Eclat/Multiples*).

The VIOLA JOKE is a classic form of musical humour, no doubt because the viola was traditionally an option for underachieving violinists. But Mozart, Dvořák and Schoenberg were not too proud to play the instrument, or to treat it with admiration and affection in their music.

Yehudi Menuhin and William Primrose *Violin and Viola* (1976); David Dalton *Playing the Viola: Conversations with William Primrose* (1988)

viola da braccio (It., arm bowed-string instrument). Term used in the 16th and early 17th centuries for instruments of the violin family, including the cello.

viola da gamba (It., leg bowed-string instrument). The term was used in the 16th and early 17th centuries for instruments of the viol family, but became restricted in the mid 17th century to the bass viol. The abbreviation gamba is common.

viola d'amore (It., viola of love; Fr. *viole d'amour*, Ger. *Liebesgeige*). Sensuous offspring of a *ménage à trois* involving the viola (which the instrument resembles in size and playing position), the viol (which it recalls in shape and decoration) and Islamic instruments (with which it shares its sympathetic strings). The last was the third partner to arrive, around 1730. At that time the instrument was tuned in accordance with the tonality of the piece, but by the end of the 18th century a tuning in D major had become standard: A–D–A–D (above middle C)–F♯–A–D, with the sympathetic strings tuned similarly or an octave higher. The instrument was used by Bach, Vivaldi, Carl Stamitz and many others in the 18th century but since then has been brought out only on special occasions, as in *Les Huguenots*, *Madama Butterfly*, Janáček's *Katya Kabanova*, Hindemith's *Kammermusik* No.6 and Prokofiev's *Romeo and Juliet*.

viola joke. Standard genre of musical humour. Examples include:

How is lightning like a violist's fingers? Neither strikes in the same place twice.

What's the definition of a minor second? Two violists playing in unison.
What's the definition of 'perfect pitch'? Throwing a viola into a skip without hitting the rim.
What do a viola and a law suit have in common? Everyone's happy when the case is closed.
What's the range of a viola? As far as you can kick it.
What's the longest viola joke? *Harold en Italie*.

viole. (1) (Fr.) Viol.
(2) (It. pl.) Violas.

violin (Fr. *violon*, Ger. *Geige*, *Violine*, It. *violino*). The highest pitched bowed instrument of its family, dominant in Western classical music from the Baroque to modern times. The glory of the violin is that it can rival the human voice (specifically the soprano voice) in expressive nuance and carrying power, but over a greater range, with more agility and without having to pause for breath. The construction of violins is an art compounded of science and mythology; the playing of the instrument requires an exceedingly rare combination of skills and aptitudes – and, even then, a great deal of hard work, for professional violinists would expect to spend several hours each day alone with their instrument, practising. The violin demands, from its makers and from its performers, an almost religious dedication, which it rewards with the purest song of which human beings have yet been capable.

The instrument has the form of an hourglass-shaped resonating box, to which four strings are attached, supported by a neck with fingerboard and tuning pegs, a bridge in the middle and a tailpiece at the end. These are attachments to the belly, a convex plate usually made from spruce. The corresponding back plate, also convex, and the sides of the box ('ribs') are commonly of maple, as are the bridge and the neck with its scroll at the end, while ebony is used for modern fingerboards and tailpieces. Soundholes, *f*-shaped, punctuate the belly, which inside is connected to the back plate by a soundpost. The strings may be played open (normally tuned G–D–A–E, the lowest note being the G below middle C) or stopped, i.e. shortened by finger pressure from the left hand, reducing the vibrating length and so heightening the pitch. Ever higher notes are reached by ever higher positions of the left hand, from first position to tenth or beyond.

Violins first appeared in northern Italy and had three strings (as shown in the earliest representation, dating from 1508–9), soon replaced by four. Their antecedents were the rebec, the fiddle and the *lira da braccio*, all of which they soon superseded, while the unrelated viols went on in parallel. At first the term *viola da braccio* was used for all instruments of the violin family, giving way to the French *violon* and Italian *violino* from the 1520s to the 1530s.

For several decades the violin was an instrument of dance musicians, while the viols pursued their more dignified course. But then, with the movement from Renaissance polyphony to Baroque monody, the violin was well placed to assume a prominent role. It became an apt accompaniment and spur to the voice in the operas and madrigals of Monteverdi, while both he and his contemporary Marini began exploring its individual character. Meanwhile the early school of Brescian violin makers was being overtaken by the artist-craftsmen of Cremona – the Amatis, Stradivaris and Guarneris – whose instruments have remained most valued. Those instruments (suitably adapted) will now be heard playing the great concertos of Beethoven, Tchaikovsky and Berg, but the music for which they were made was that of Corelli and Vivaldi, and of the first virtuoso violinists: Tartini and Locatelli. In Austria there was another tradition of violin making (Jacob Stainer) and composing (Biber).

Around 1800 various changes to the instrument and its technique wre introduced. The BOW was standardized by François Xavier Tourte; the fingerboard was lengthened and other modifications were made to support stronger strings at higher tensions providing greater brilliance; and the chin rest was added (by Spohr, c.1820). Since then the instrument has been little altered, though there have been strong efforts to reverse history and restore the instruments and bows of Mozart's time or Bach's in order to play their music. As for technique, many of the possibilities had been explored by Paganini by 1830, leaving only *sul ponticello* and *sul tasto* sonorities, snap pizzicatos and microtones to be added by Schoenberg, Bartók and others a century later, followed by still more marginal sounds in Lachenmann's music.

After Paganini the mingled stream of great violinists has included numerous lineages. Charles-Auguste de Bériot, inspired by Viotti, taught Vieuxtemps, who taught Ysaÿe. Rodolphe Kreutzer (of the 'Kreutzer' Sonata) taught Joseph Massart, who taught Wieniawski and Kreisler. Spohr taught Ferdinand David, who taught Joseph Joachim, who taught Leopold Auer, who taught Heifetz. Throughout the 19th century and into the 20th virtuosos were expected to offer wildly difficult display pieces, but latterly the active repertory has settled around a rather small group of concertos and sonatas, with additions commissioned by adventurous soloists (such as Anne

Sophie Mutter and Thomas Zehetmair) or rediscovered in the past by others equally spirited (e.g. Andrew Manze).

Robin Stowell, ed. *The Cambridge Companion to the Violin* (1992); Richard Dawes, ed. *The Violin Book* (1999); Patricia and Allen Strange *The Contemporary Violin* (2001)

violin concerto. Work for solo violin and orchestra, usually titled thus (e.g. Mendelssohn's Violin Concerto), though the term may be used generically, as in 'Gubaidulina's violin concerto *Offertorium*'.

After several each by Bach, Vivaldi and Mozart, the central repertory includes works by Beethoven (f.p. Vienna, 23 Dec 1806, Clement), Mendelssohn (f.p. Leipzig, 13 Mar 1845, David), Bruch (No.1, f.p. Koblenz, 24 Apr 1866, Otto von Königslow), Lalo (SYMPHONIE ESPAGNOLE), Brahms (f.p. Leipzig, 1 Jan 1879, Joachim), Tchaikovsky (f.p. Vienna, 4 Dec 1881, Adolf Brodsky), Dvořák (f.p. Prague, 14 Oct 1883, František Ondříček), Sibelius (f.p. Helsinki, 8 Feb 1904, Ottokar Nováček), Elgar (f.p. London, 10 Nov 1910, Kreisler), Prokofiev (No.1, f.p. Paris, 18 Oct 1923, Marcel Darrieux; No.2, f.p. Madrid, 1 Dec 1935, Robert Soëtens), Stravinsky (f.p. Berlin, 23 Oct 1931, Dushkin), Berg (f.p. Barcelona, 19 Apr 1936, Krasner), Bartók (No.2, f.p. Amsterdam, 23 Mar 1939, Székely) and Ligeti (f.p. Cologne, 3 Nov 1990, Saschko Gawriloff).

The closely successive works by Bruch, Lalo, Brahms, Tchaikovsky and Dvořák represent the high noon of the Romantic violin concerto; equally remarkable is the crop of the 1930s, including, besides the Stravinsky, Berg, Prokofiev Second and Bartók, works by Szymanowski, Sessions, Schoenberg, Walton, Britten and Barber. Among other notable concertos are those of Haydn, Spohr, Paganini, Vieuxtemps, Schumann, Wieniawski, Strauss, Glazunov, Nielsen, Weill, Hindemith, Schuman, Martin, Shostakovich, Henze, Bernstein (Serenade), Schnittke, Gubaidulina (*Offertorium*), Dutilleux (*L'Arbre des songes*), Lutosławski (*Chain 2*), Carter, Rihm (*Gesungene Zeit*) and Adams, as well as shorter pieces for violin and orchestra by Saint-Saëns, Chausson, Ravel, Vaughan Williams and Dutilleux.

violino (It., pl. *violini*). Violin.

violino piccolo (It.). Small violin, a Baroque instrument usually tuned a fourth above the regular violin, though Bach's First Brandenburg Concerto has one tuned a third above.

violin sonata. Normally a SONATA for violin and piano, though Baroque sonatas (Corelli, Geminiani, Tartini, Biber, Leclair) may be accompanied by continuo or strings, and there are unaccompanied sonatas by Bach, Hindemith, Honegger, Prokofiev, Bartók, Zimmermann, Sessions and Henze.

Haydn and Mozart described their sonatas as for piano and violin, the piano having the main continuity. With Beethoven and Schubert the two instruments became more evenly matched and the genre intensified its dual personality, not favouring virtuosity from either partner. Later composers to have contributed to it include Schumann, Grieg, Brahms, Saint-Saëns, Franck, Strauss, Ives, Fauré, Roussel, Debussy, Respighi, Honegger, Elgar, Janáček, Bartók, Ravel, Prokofiev, Hindemith, Copland, Poulenc, Wolpe, Zimmermann, Seiber, Schnittke and Shostakovich. There are also works of sonata weight by Stravinsky (*Duo concertant*), Schoenberg (Phantasy) and Carter (Duo).

violist. Player on viol or viola.

violon (Fr.). Violin.

violoncello. Full and formal name for the CELLO.

violone (It., large viol). A term of confusingly various application in the 17th and 18th centuries but now reserved for the contrabass viol, tuned a fifth below the bass of the species. Instruments of this kind were used to support orchestral bass lines and were the direct ancestors of the double bass.

Viotti, Giovanni Battista (b. Fontanetto da Po, 12 May 1755; d. London, 3 Mar 1824). Italian violinist-composer. Apparently of humble origin, he gained the protection of a Turinese nobleman by virtue of the musical talent he displayed as a boy, and became the pupil of Pugnani, heir to a tradition going back to Corelli. He served his apprenticeship in the orchestra of the royal chapel of Turin (1755–80), then set out with Pugnani on a tour through Switzerland, Germany and Russia (1780–81), after which he made his way alone to Paris. There he settled, at first giving public concerts, then working as a court musician and opera impresario. In July 1792, as the French Revolution proceeded, he moved to London, where he again coupled performance with commerce. Suspected as a Jacobin, he was exiled in 1798, and though he returned around two years later, he kept a lower musical profile, now working in the wine business. Having failed at that, he went back to Paris and was briefly director of the Opera (1819–21). In 1823 he returned to the home of friends in London. Accounts of his playing stress strength and fullness of tone, along with a powerful cantabile style. He wrote 29 concertos (No.22, A minor) and much chamber music for his instrument.

Vir, Param (b. Delhi, 6 Feb 1952). Indian–British composer, known specially for a double bill of chamber operas, *Snatched by the Gods* (1990) and *Broken Strings* (1992), in a sensitive East–West style. He studied philosophy at Delhi University and composition in Britain in the mid 1980s with Davies and Knussen.

Virdung, Sebastian (b. ?Amberg, *c*.1465; d. *c*.1515). German theorist, author of the first printed manual dealing with (and illustrating) musical instruments, *Musica getutscht* (Music Germanized, 1511). The son of an innkeeper, he studied in Heidelberg, where he remained as a court musician and chaplain until 1505 or 1506, when his career became more erratic.

virelai. One of the three fixed forms (with the BALLADE and RONDEAU) of French song in the 14th and 15th centuries. The word comes from the Old Fr. *virer* (turn, twist), suggesting that this was originally a dance song, though opinions differ as to whether its deeper ancestry was Arabic or in the liturgical production of such French centres as St Martial. Within an invariable ABBA pattern the sections could include different patterns and numbers of lines, often with seven-syllable lines offset by lines of three or four syllables, perhaps all governed by just two rhymes. Most of Machaut's virelais are monophonic, and the exceptions add only parts probably intended for instruments.

virga. Kind of NEUME.

virginals. Keyboard instrument with plucked strings. The term's etymology is uncertain (perhaps the connection was with young women players, or with the sound of a girl's voice) and its early applications were various: in English, well into the 17th century, it could mean any plucked keyboard instrument. Now it indicates one with the strings perpendicular to the keys, i.e. in a wide box (rectangular or wing-shaped) rather than a long one, as with harpsichords and spinets. The plural form of the word perhaps derives from double instruments, a 'mother' with a smaller 'child' an octave higher that could be linked or detached; whether single or double the instrument can also be called the 'virginal'. Its importance in domestic music in the 16th and 17th centuries is attested by many paintings, especially Dutch.

virtuosity. Extreme skill in performance, whether shown by a player or required by a composer. The term can be used in an admiring sense or to disparage ('mere virtuosity', suggesting empty display). There can also be compositional virtuosity – in contrapuntal writing, for instance, or orchestration.

virtuoso (It., one showing excellence, pl. *virtuosi*, though in Eng. normally 'virtuosos'). (1) Exceptional performer, though when the term was adopted into English, in the early 18th century, it could signify high accomplishment in any field of thought or artistry. In English it is applied to people of either sex, though the female form *virtuosa* is also found. As with virtuosity, the term can have negative associations.

(2) Used adjectivally, as in 'virtuoso passage', it indicates brilliance and agility.

Visée, Robert de (b. *c.*1655; d.1732–3). French guitarist-composer. He was in royal service *c.*1680–1720 and published 12 suites and other pieces for guitar.

Vishnegradsky, Ivan. See Ivan WYSCHNE-GRADSKY.

Visions de l'Amen. Work by Messiaen for two pianos, which he wrote for Loriod and himself as seven images of concurrence with the divine plan: 1 *Amen de la Création*, 2 *Amen des étoiles, de la planète à l'anneau*, 3 *Amen de l'agonie de Jésus*, 4 *Amen du désir*, 5 *Amen des anges, des saints, du chant des oiseaux*, 6 *Amen du jugement*, 7 *Amen de la consommation*. First performance: Paris, 10 May 1943.

Visitatio sepulchri (The Visitation of the Sepulchre). Eastertide liturgical drama.

visual art. Artists see music in many different ways. Some leave portraits of great composers: examples include Courbet (Berlioz), Renoir (Wagner, though the image flatters neither party), Picasso (Stravinsky) and Schiele (Schoenberg, Webern). Some work for opera and ballet as designers: Picasso again, Matisse, Hodgkin, Hockney, Robert Wilson. Some are drawn to musical subjects, especially and repeatedly Klee. Some create music (Duchamp), joining composers who draw or paint (Schoenberg, Ruggles, Cage) along with others known equally for work in both fields (Russolo, Čiurlionis).

Vitali, Giovanni Battista (b. Bologna, 18 Feb 1632; d. Bologna, 12 Oct 1692). Italian composer. He was active in Bologna (where he was taught by Cazzati) as a singer and instrumentalist at San Petronio and member of the Accademia Filarmonica; then in 1684 he joined the Este court in Modena. Besides several volumes of sonatas and suites, he published *Artificii musicali* (1689), a book of canons, contrapuntal inventions and exemplary works in different forms. He also wrote oratorios and cantatas, including one for the coronation of Mary of Modena as Queen of England. His son Tommaso Antonio Vitali (1663–1745) was a violinist-composer who played in the Este court orchestra through nearly seven decades (1674–1742) and also wrote sonatas. A Chaconne in G minor for violin, performed only in imaginative 19th-century restorations (by Ferdinand David and Léopold Charlier), is ascribed to him probably unwarrantedly.

vite (Fr.). Quickly. Tempo designation current in French music since the time of François Couperin.

Vitry, Philippe de (b. ?Champagne, 31 Oct 1291; d. Paris, 9 Jun 1361). French theorist-composer, the principal architect of the ARS NOVA, named after a treatise he wrote in the early 1320s. A man of formidable intellectual powers, he served successive French kings as secretary, adviser and diplomat, and was admired by his contemporaries (including Petrarch) as poet and philosopher, mathematician and musician. His compositions surely encompassed much more than the 12 motets ascribed to him by modern scholars. These few motets, though, are of the first importance: they sparkle with a sophistication both musical and literary (being political attacks and theological tracts in poetic form), and were significant historically in establishing a texture of two lively voices over a slow tenor.

Vittori, Loreto (baptized Spoleto, 5 Sep 1600; d. Rome, 23 Apr 1670). Italian castrato-composer. He sang at Spoleto Cathedral as a boy and was taken up by a succession of distinguished patrons, including the cardinals Lodovico Ludovisi (in the 1620s) and Antonio Barberini, while also singing in the papal choir (1622–47). One of the first star castratos (with Pasqualini), he wrote operas and arias.

Vittoria. See VICTORIA.

vivace (It.). In a lively manner. Generally speed is implied, whether the term is used alone as a tempo marking or in some combination (e.g. *allegro vivace*), but in the 18th century *vivace* could be moderately paced and considered. Also found is *vivacissimo*.

Vivaldi, Antonio (Lucio) (b. Venice, 4 Mar 1678; d. Vienna, 28 Jul 1741). Italian composer. Unique in the spirited brilliance he brought to the Baroque concerto, he displayed his gifts with extraordinary fecundity. His music was known across Europe, by such contemporaries as Bach, Telemann and Tartini, but he spent most of his life in Venice, and his music has the city's lightness, playfulness and architectural clarity.

His father, Giovanni Battista (c.1655–c.1729), was a violinist at St Mark's, perhaps also a composer and surely his first teacher. The young Vivaldi trained, however, for the Church, was ordained in March 1703 and gained the sobriquet of 'the red priest', on account of his hair colour – though he soon stopped exercising his priestly function, for reason, he said, of chronic illness (possibly asthma or angina). He also had other business. In September 1703 he was appointed violin teacher at the Pio Ospedale della Pietà, an institution for orphaned and abandoned girls who, wherever possible, were trained to take part in lavish services, where congregations of nobility and distinguished visitors came to hear sonatas and concertos as well as settings of the liturgy. There he remained, with brief interruptions, while making a wider reputation as a composer through his publications. His Op.1 and Op.2, comprising sonatas, were followed in 1711 by his vastly admired first collection of concertos, *L'estro armonico*. By 1713 he was also writing operas, sometimes two or three a year; many were produced for the San Angelo theatre in Venice, where he had interests as an impresario.

The pursuit of his operatic career took him to Mantua (1718–20) and Rome (1723–?5), but he went on providing music for the Pietà: the place was evidently depending on him for its musical prestige. Anna Giraud, possibly one of his pupils, became a professional singer, and she and her sister joined his household in the 1720s, creating a scandal, though he denied any impropriety. He continued writing parts for her into the 1730s, when operas by him were staged in Prague, Florence and Vienna; very possibly he assisted at those premières. Ferrara, too, he visited, to exert himself again as an opera manager, and he was on another journey when he died.

He continued writing concertos all his life: among those documented as late are one for Amsterdam (for a visit he made in 1738) and several for the Pietà in 1740. Diverse as his almost 500 such works are in scoring and internal structure, they formalized a three-movement pattern, fast–slow–fast, with ritornello form in the first movement: a lively passage for the full ensemble starts the piece and recurs, with alterations

and in other keys, while soloists lead the thread in between. A few other works besides *Le quattro stagioni* (The Four Seasons) have descriptive titles and illustrative effects.

Through his various activities – as independent composer for various princely patrons (to whom he dedicated his published volumes), opera creator-promoter and disseminator of his own wildly popular concertos – he was among the first composers to take advantage of the developing commerce in music. Around 1730 he stopped publishing his concertos, because he could make more money selling manuscript copies. He had little doubt of his worth and none of his speed, boasting that he could compose a concerto faster than it could be copied. It was his music's immediacy, perhaps, that made it rapidly dispensable but that contributed to its revival in the 20th century. He was virtually forgotten within two or three decades of his death, to become ubiquitous – at least on account of four works – after the Second World War.

Michael Talbot *Vivaldi* (1978, ²1993); H.C. Robbins Landon *Vivaldi* (1993)

Operas: *Ottone in Villa* (Domenico Lalli), f.p. Vicenza, 1713; *Dorilla in Tempe* (Antonio Maria Lucchini), f.p. Venice, 1726; *Farnace* (Lucchini), f.p. Venice, 1727; *Orlando furioso* (Grazio Braccioli), f.p. Venice, 1727; *L'Atenaide* (Zeno), f.p. Florence, 1728; *La fida ninfa* (Scipione Maffei), f.p. Verona, 1732; *L'Olimpiade* (Metastasio), f.p. Venice, 1734; *Il Tamerlano* (Agostino Piovene), f.p. Verona, 1735; *Griselda* (Goldoni, after Zeno), f.p. Venice, 1735; etc.

Sacred: *Juditha triumphans* (oratorio; Giacomo Cassetti), f.p. Venice, 1716; other choral items (*Beatus vir*, C; *Dixit Dominus*, D; *Gloria*, D, 2 settings; *Magnificat*, G minor, several versions; etc.); solo pieces (*Nisi Dominus*, G minor, a, str, con; *Stabat mater*, F minor, a, str, con; etc.)

Violin concertos: *L'ESTRO ARMONICO*, Op.3 (12); *La stravaganza*, Op.4 (12); *Il CIMENTO DELL'ARMONIA E DELL'INVENTIONE*, Op.8 (12, including *Le QUATTRO STAGIONI*); *La CETRA*, Op.9 (12); about 180 others

Other works: about 250 other concertos, 110 chamber pieces, 30 cantatas

Vives, Amadeo (b. Collbató, near Barcelona, 18 Nov 1871; d. Madrid, 2 Dec 1932). Catalan composer, a pupil of Ribera and Pedrell. He co-founded the Orfeó Català (1891), the leading Catalan choir, and worked briefly as a convent choirmaster before injury and illness disabled his right arm. After that he moved to Madrid and wrote for the theatre, his works including the opera *Maruxa* (1914) and zarzuelas *Bohemios* (1904) and *Doña Francisquita* (1923).

Vivier, Claude (b. Montreal, 14 Apr 1948; d. Paris, 12 Mar 1983). Canadian composer. He studied with Tremblay in Montreal, Koenig in Utrecht (1971–2) and Stockhausen – a crucial influence – in Cologne (1972–4). After two years back in Canada he journeyed through Japan, Bali and Iran in 1976, and returned with a refreshed sense of musical possibility. Parisian spectralism was also important to the mature style he discovered in *Lonely Child*, music of incantatory melody floated in shadowy clouds of tone. He spent his last year in Paris, living a dangerous existence in the homosexual underworld, and was the victim of a brutal murder.

Works: *Shiraz*, pf, 1977; *Lonely Child*, s, chbr orch, 1980; *Zipangu*, 13 str, 1980; *Bouchara*, s, 11 insts, 1981; *Prologue pour un Marco Polo* (Paul Chamberland and Vivier), soli, chbr orch, 1981; *Samarkand*, wind qnt, pf, 1981; *Glaubst Du an die Unsterblichkeit der Seele*, ch, 3 synth, 2 perc, 1983; etc.

vivo (It.). In a lively manner.

Vlad, Roman (b. Cernăuți, 29 Dec 1919). Romanian–Italian composer-scholar. He studied in his home city and, from 1938, in Rome, remaining in Italy as a composer, teacher, writer and administrator. Drawn by serialism since 1943, he has embraced diverse styles.

Vltava. See MA VLAST.

vn. Abbreviation for violin.

vocal cords. See VOICE.

vocalise. Singing without words, or wordless composition for voice. 19th-century vocalises, with such rare exceptions as Spohr's Sonatina for voice and piano (1848), were exercises. They became concert pieces with Fauré, Ravel and Rachmaninoff, etc. Choral vocalise appears in Debussy's *Sirènes*, Holst's *Planets* and Bartók's *Miraculous Mandarin*.

vocalize. Verb used to indicate some kind of vocal delivery unlike conventional singing.

vocal score. Score of an opera, or other large-scale vocal work, in which the vocal parts are given in full with the accompaniment reduced for solo piano.

voce (It., pl. *voci*). Voice, part. The direction *colla voce* indicates that the accompanist must follow the singer's rhythm.

Voces intimae (Lat., intimate voices). Name Sibelius gave his String Quartet, Op.56.

Vogel, Wladimir (Rudolfovich) (b. Moscow, 29 Feb 1896; d. Zurich, 19 Jun 1984). Russian–German–Swiss composer, famed for works with speaking chorus, notably *Wagadu's Untergang durch die Eitelkeit* (1930) and *Thyl Claes*, an oratorio in two concert-length parts (1938–45). Guided by Scriabin in his youth, he was interned during the First World War as a German national (his father was German, his mother Russian) and in 1918 departed for Berlin. There he studied with Heinz Tiessen (1919–21) and Busoni (until 1924), took note of Schoenberg, and taught at the conservatory. In 1933 he was obliged to move to Switzerland.

Vogelweide. See WALTHER VON DER VOGELWEIDE.

Vogl, Johann Michael (b. Ennsdorf, near Steyr, 10 Aug 1768; d. Vienna, 19 Nov 1840). Austrian baritone, remembered as Schubert's friend and interpreter. He was a schoolfriend in Kremsmunster of Süssmayr, with whom he went to Vienna in 1786 (to study law) and who drew him into opera in 1795. His roles included Orestes in *Iphigénie en Tauride*, the Count in *Figaro* and Pizarro in the 1814 *Fidelio*. Close to Schubert from 1817, he retired in 1834.

Vogler, Abbé Georg Joseph (b. Pleichach, near Würzburg, 15 Jun 1749; d. Darmstadt, 6 May 1814). German theorist, organist and composer. The son of a violinist and instrument maker, he studied law and theology at the universities of Würzburg and Bamberg, and in 1771 gained a position as almoner at the Electoral court of Mannheim. The next year he was appointed chaplain, but Elector Carl Theodor gave him leave and support to pursue his musical studies in Italy (1773–5), notably with Vallotti. On his return he founded a music school in Mannheim and began a series of publications bringing a systematic approach to the study and practice of harmony. He recalculated the frequency ratios of intervals, analysed all chords as related to one or another root-position triad and defined a complete network of modulations. Carl Theodor called him to Munich in 1784, but he left in 1786 for the court of Gustav III of Sweden. Again he was able to travel, and in 1792–3 journeyed through southern Spain, Greece and North Africa in search of the origins of Western chant. His last appointment, in 1807, was to the grand ducal court of Darmstadt, where he continued his work as a theorist and teacher, his pupils including Weber and Meyerbeer. He wrote operas, much sacred music, cantatas and symphonies, but was most valued as an improviser on the organ – at least by some: Mozart in 1777 heard only 'an unintelligible muddle'.

voice (Fr. *voix*, Ger. *Stimme*, It. *voce*). (1) The human instrument of singing and speech. Animals can make noises but are not normally said to have voices: the voice is one of the determining features of a person.

Like most other musical instruments, the voice is composed of two parts: an oscillator, which produces vibrations, and a resonator, which amplifies and colours them. The oscillator in this case is the set of vocal folds (or cords) in the back of the throat, regulated by muscles that can tighten or loosen them, so raising or lowering the frequency of their vibrations. These vibrations resonate within the pharynx and mouth, and the singer (or speaker) can affect the sound by muscle action on these cavities.

What counts as a musical voice has changed through history (see SING; SINGER). Key works in the 20th-century extension of vocal possibilities include Schoenberg's *Pierrot lunaire*, Kagel's *Anagrama*, Ligeti's *Aventures*, Stockhausen's *Momente* and Berio's *Epifanie* and *Sinfonia*.

(2) Part, in the sense of contrapuntal line.

voice leading. The US term for PART WRITING (UK).

voice production. The art and technique of amplifying and controlling the singing voice, a matter of lively debate, much mystique and dubious expertise on the part of singing teachers.

voicing. Adjustment of an organ, harpsichord, piano or other keyboard instrument in manufacture to produce full, even tone.

Voir Dit, Le (The True Tale). Epistolary romance by Machaut, written in his early 60s, concerning the love of a young woman, Peronne, for an ageing poet. The affair rekindles the poet's artistic impulses, and the two characters exchange poems and songs.

voix (Fr.). Voice(s), part(s).

Volans, Kevin (b. Pietermaritzburg, 26 Jul 1949). South African–Irish composer. He studied at Witwatersrand and in Cologne (1973–81), where he had lessons with Stockhausen and Kagel, besides working at the electronic music studio. After a period at the University of Natal (1981–5) he settled in Ireland. His works of the 1980s adapt African notions of rhythmic pattern-making, but as his music developed so it came to embrace other connections (with Stravinsky, for example) and settle into an alert calm all its own. A continuing delicate intricacy of pulsed rhythm has led to many collaborations with dance companies. His works include *White Man Sleeps* for two harpsichords, viola da gamba and percussion (1982, arranged as String Quartet No.1, 1986), other string quartets, concertos and an opera on Rimbaud, *The Man with Footsoles of Wind* (f.p. London, 1993).

www.kevinvolans.com

volante (It.). Flying.

Volkonsky, Andrey (Mikhaylovich) (b. Geneva, 14 Feb 1933). Russian composer, avant-garde dissident. Born into the princely family that appears in *War and Peace*, he studied in Paris (1945–7) with Boulanger and Lipatti. In 1947 the family returned to Russia, and he continued his education at the Tambov Music School and, with Shaporin, the Moscow Conservatory (1950–54), where his background and interests (in Stravinsky) caused mistrust. That mistrust turned into hostility after he adopted serialism, in his *Musica stricta* for piano (1956). The intensity and the playfulness alike of his avant-garde leanings were irritating to Soviet officialdom, and he was allowed to maintain his public career only as a harpsichordist and leader of the early-music ensemble Madrigal. However, *Les Plaintes de Shchaza* for soprano and mixed quintet (1961) came to the attention of Boulez, who conducted performances in western Europe. In 1973 he moved to France to continue his work as a composer and early music specialist.

Volkslied (Ger.). Folksong. Also *volkstümlich* (folk style), *Volkstanz* (folk dance), *Volksweise* (folk tune).

volta (It., turn). (1) Renaissance dance in triple time, characterized by a turn in which the man lifts his partner high. It was popular at the French court under Henry IV (r. 1589–1610) and enjoyed the favour of composers around the same time; there are examples by Byrd and Morley in the Fitzwilliam Virginal Book.

(2) Term used in markings of repeats: *prima volta* (or *1*) is placed over the music to be performed first time round, leading back to the beginning for a reprise at the end of which the *seconda volta* (or *2*) option is chosen.

volti subito (It.). Turn over quickly, abbreviated V.S.

volume. See LOUDNESS.

voluntary. Organ composition or improvisation played in church, usually after the service. The term, having no equivalents in other languages, was used as a title by British composers from Richard Alwood (in the Mulliner Book) through Tallis, Byrd, Locke, Blow, Purcell, Croft, Roseingrave, Greene and Boyce to Samuel Wesley.

Von der Wiege bis zum Grabe (From the Cradle to the Grave). Symphonic poem by Liszt.

Von Heute auf Morgen (From One Day to the Next). One-act opera by Schoenberg to a libretto by his wife under the pseudonym of Max Blonda. Husband (bass-baritone) and Wife (soprano) are tempted by sexual adventures but ultimately opt for happy domesticity. First performance: Frankfurt, 1 Feb 1930.

Voříšek, Jan Václav [Worzischek, Johann Hugo] (b. Vamberk, northeast Bohemia, 11 May 1791; d. Vienna, 19 Nov 1825). Czech composer, follower of Beethoven. The son of a schoolmaster and church musician, he was appearing as a piano virtuoso before, at the age of 10, he won a scholarship to the classical gymnasium in Prague. He went on to study law at the university there (1810–13) but slid towards music under instruction from Tomášek. Enthusiasm for Beethoven then took him to Vienna, where he worked as a civil servant, conductor and court organist, and duly won the admiration of his hero, who sent his own doctor to try to cure the younger man's chronic illness. He also knew and possibly influenced Schubert: his impromptus extend from Tomášek's manner towards an early Romantic piano style. Among his other works are a violin sonata, a piano sonata in B♭ minor and a symphony in D.

Vorschlag (Ger., forestroke). Appoggiatura.

Vorspiel (Ger.). Prelude.

vorwärts (Ger.). Forwards.

votive. Adjective derived from the Lat. *votum* (prayer) and used to indicate a liturgical act with a particular intention, e.g. a *Requiem* mass or a MARIAN ANTIPHON.

Vox Humana (Lat., human voice). Organ stop imitating the human voice.

Voynich Cipher Manuscript, The. Work by Kyburz for 24 singers and 17 instrumentalists in spatially separated ensembles, sparked off by a 16th-century book that describes an entire imaginary world in indecipherable script. First performance: Donaueschingen, 22 Oct 1995.

V.S. Abbreviation for VOLTI SUBITO or VOCAL SCORE.

Vučković, Vojislav (b. Pirot, 18 Oct 1910; d. Belgrade, 25 Dec 1942). Yugoslav composer. He studied with Suk and others at the Prague Conservatory, and returned to Belgrade in 1934 to work as a teacher, critic, broadcaster, conductor and composer. His early commitment to modernism was later moderated by his active communist sympathies, which led to his being shot during the Nazi occupation.

Vulpius, Melchior (b. Wasungen, near Meiningen, *c*.1570; buried Weimar, 7 Aug 1615). German church musician. Born to poor parents (he latinized the family name of Fuchs), he worked as a schoolmaster and church musician in Schleusingen (1589–96) and then Weimar. His works include about 400 hymns, about 200 motets and a St Matthew Passion.

vuoto, vuota (It., empty). Confirming indication placed over a silent bar.

Vycpálek, Ladislav (b. Prague, 23 Feb 1882; d. Prague, 9 Jan 1969). Czech composer. He studied literature at Prague University (1901–6) and worked in the library there (1907–42) while taking lessons with Novák (1908–12) and coming to prominence as a composer. His works, strongly contrapuntal, include three cantatas: *Cantata on the Last Things of Man* (1920–22), *Blessed is this Man* (1933) and *Czech Requiem* (1940).

Vyšehrad. See MA VLAST.

Waelrant, Hubert (b. 1516/17; d. Antwerp, 19 Nov 1595). Netherlandish composer-editor. He worked with the printer Jean de Laet in producing 16 volumes of mostly sacred music (1554–8), including motets and psalms of his own that suggest he was a Protestant. Later he wrote secular songs and madrigals.

Wagenaar, Johan (b. Utrecht, 1 Nov 1862; d. The Hague, 17 Jun 1941). Dutch composer, matching Romanticism with ironic humour. He studied in Utrecht with Richard Hol, whom he succeeded at the school of music (1887–1919) before becoming director of the Hague Conservatory (1919–39). His works include orchestral pieces (overture *Cyrano de Bergerac*, 1905; symphonic poem *Saul and David*, 1906) and operas. His son Bernard (1894–1971) was also a composer, who settled in the USA in 1920, taught at what became the Juilliard School (1925–68) and wrote four symphonies and four quartets.

Wagenseil, Georg Christoph (b. Vienna, 29 Jan 1715; d. Vienna, 1 Mar 1777). Austrian composer. The son of a court official, he studied with Fux and Matteo Palotta (1735–8), and in 1739, with Fux's backing, gained a lifetime position as composer to the court. He was an all-round musician – keyboard virtuoso (until discommoded by illness in his last decade or so), teacher, composer – and internationally respected: he had operas presented in Italy, symphonies and concertos published in Paris, and keyboard works played by the boy Mozart. His output also included masses, oratorios and chamber music, all in a galant style.

Wagner. German musical dynasty founded by Richard and his wife Cosima (1837–1930). Their formidable heritage – genes from Liszt (through Cosima) as well as Wagner, and control of the BAYREUTH festival – passed to their son Siegfried and then to his sons Wieland (1917–66) and Wolfgang (b. 1919).

(1) **(Wilhelm) Richard** (b. Leipzig, 22 May 1813; d. Venice, 13 Feb 1883). German composer. Controversial in his lifetime and deeply paradoxical, he is still, in Nietzsche's words, 'a case'. Nietzsche's reaction was extreme – adoration turning into loathing without a pause – but Wagner has always tended to elicit extreme responses. Overwhelming, his music can excite rapture or mistrust. His operas (and he wrote little else) have been seen and discussed as uniquely profound studies of human psychology and existence, treating central themes of love, salvation and society, but they have also had more worrisome supporters. He was a genius who had to (and did) transcend his own ignobility. He was a showman who held (and achieved) the highest artistic ambitions.

His paternity has never been resolved. When he was six months old his mother lost her husband, Friedrich Wagner; nine months later she married Ludwig Geyer, a court actor and painter in Dresden, who may have been the composer's natural father. He duly started his education in Dresden, until in 1828 his mother moved the family back to Leipzig (Geyer had died in 1821). There, in his teens, he was drawn to the theatre and music, wrote a verse tragedy, began harmony studies with Christian Gottlieb Müller and was elated by two Beethoven experiences: Wilhelmine

Schröder-Devrient in *Fidelio* in 1829 and, the next year, the score of the Ninth Symphony, completed only seven years before. He finished his education at St Thomas's school (1830–31) and, with the teacher-composer Christian Theodor Weinlig, at the university (1831–2). During this period he wrote piano music and a symphony, then began an opera, *Die Hochzeit*. Already, as in all the stage works he was to complete, he was setting his own words.

In January 1833 he started a year as chorus master at the Würzburg theatre, a year in which he wrote *Die Feen*, his first completed opera. Turned down by the Leipzig company, this was not performed until after his death. In June 1834 he set to work on his second opera, *Das Liebesverbot*, after Shakespeare's *Measure for Measure*. The next month he found a new job as music director of a travelling company, which he left for the Magdeburg theatre, so that he could stay near Minna Planer, an actress with whom he was in love. In Magdeburg *Das Liebesverbot* had its first and (during his lifetime) only performance. He followed Minna to Königsberg in July 1836 and married her there on 24 November. Six months later she ran off, and by the time she returned, after four and a half months, he was music director at the theatre in Riga.

While there, between July 1837 and March 1839, he conducted operas and concerts; he also started a new stage work, *Rienzi*. After leaving Riga he and Minna crossed the Baltic to London (encountering a storm that provided memories for *Der fliegende Holländer*) and went on to Paris (1839–42). Here he was at the centre of the modern world, as he saw it. Performances of Beethoven and Berlioz exhilarated him, and helped gear him up to complete *Rienzi*, go on to his *Faust* overture (one of his very few important concert works) and *Der fliegende Holländer*, and begin to dream of further operas based on the legends to which he had been introduced by a fellow German in Paris, Samuel Lehrs: *Tannhäuser* and *Lohengrin*. In a few years – indeed, in a few months, between finishing *Rienzi* in November 1840 and starting the composition of *Der fliegende Holländer* in July 1841 – he transformed himself from a mediocre artist into a great one. Material success, though, eluded him.

He left Paris with Minna for Dresden, where *Rienzi* had been accepted. It triumphed, and the company hastily put on his *Holländer*, then engaged him as conductor in February 1843. *Tannhäuser*, already in train, had its première under his direction in 1845, and the next year he conducted Beethoven's Ninth for the first time. *Lohengrin* was not performed. Increasingly revolutionary in his ideals, political and artistic, he began a work that would show the ending of a decayed and decadent order – *Siegfrieds Tod*, the eventual *Götterdämmerung* – and he lent support to the 1849 uprising in Dresden, soon suppressed.

Needing to flee, he found refuge in Zurich, with the help of Liszt, who presented *Lohengrin* in Weimar the next year. He went on with *Siegfrieds Tod*, began to think of building his own festival theatre, wrote a long essay on the theory of opera (*Oper und Drama*) and completed the texts of the four operas of *Der Ring des Nibelungen*, creating a trilogy on the model of Greek drama (a crucial ideal) plus a 'fore-evening'. The project was to engage him for a quarter of a century. Supported by loans from a local businessman, Otto Wesendonck, he proceeded through the composition of *Das Rheingold* (1853–4), *Die Walküre* (1854–6) and the first two acts of *Siegfried* (1856–7), vitally influenced by reading Schopenhauer's philosophy. By now he was in love with Wesendonck's wife, Mathilde, and he stopped work on the *Ring* in favour of a story of immense, doomed love: *Tristan und Isolde*, begun in a cottage ('Asyl') Wesendonck had provided for him. Minna put a stop to the strange recompense he was offering his patron, and the couple left for Venice (1858–9), Lucerne and Paris again (1859–61). This time he arrived as a European figure (though the two completed *Ring* operas had not yet been performed), and he revised *Tannhäuser* for a performance at the Opera that had bourgeois patrons protesting and Baudelaire writing vigorously in support.

An amnesty allowed him to return to German–Austrian lands and settle in Vienna 1861–4, where he worked on *Die Meistersinger* in between concert tours undertaken to make money (also the motive for his London concerts of 1855). But the financial gains were limited, and an invitation to Munich, coming in 1864 from Ludwig II, the 18-year-old king of Bavaria, was a godsend. *Tristan* was produced in the city, with Hans von Bülow conducting, and Wagner was granted a handsome annuity. He also began an affair with von Bülow's wife (and Liszt's daughter) Cosima. This, and his luxurious way of life, gained him enemies, and in December 1865 he had to leave the Bavarian capital. The following month he learned that Minna, from whom he had been separated since 1862, had died in Dresden. In April he moved into the Villa Tribschen, near Lucerne, where Cosima joined him permanently in November 1868; she brought their two daughters, Isolde (aged three and a half) and Eva (almost two), and arrived pregnant with their son Siegfried. Divorced from von Bülow, she married Wagner on 25 August 1870, and he composed the *Siegfried Idyll* to greet her on her first birthday as his wife.

In April 1871 he paid his first visit to BAYREUTH, in northern Bavaria, drawn by an encyclopedia picture of the margravial opera house. Finding this an unsuitable home for his schemes, he decided to build a new theatre on the edge of the town. He moved there the next year – to temporary quarters, while his villa, Wahnfried, was being built – and laid the foundation stone of his theatre on his 59th birthday, when he also conducted Beethoven's Ninth. During the next three years he worked to complete the building (with the help of receipts from concert tours and a grant from Ludwig), choose singers and finish *Götterdämmerung*. Then in August 1876 the *Ring* was given in full for the first time in the new festival house, to international audiences that included Grieg, Nietzsche, Saint-Saëns and Tchaikovsky.

The long-awaited première created an enormous stir, and left an enormous deficit. To help cover the losses he again gave concerts in London, in May 1877, but much of the remaining debt was covered by Ludwig. The theatre was then dark until it reopened in the summer of 1882 for the first performances of *Parsifal*, the composer's last work. He wrote some of this final score during travels in Italy (in the autumn of 1876, most of 1880 and the winter of 1881–2) and returned with his family to Venice soon after the initial run, taking an apartment in the Palazzo Vendramin. There he died, and his body was returned by rail to Bayreuth for interment in the Wahnfried garden.

Wagner saw himself primarily as a composer, and a dramatist because he was a composer. For him the highest ideal was not absolute music but rather music drama (his coinage: any consideration of his work is bound to be guided by terms he invented himself). Music drama was the fulfilment of music's destiny; it was 'deeds of music made visible'. It restored the artistic wholeness known to the ancient Greeks, whose drama was sung. It also took up the challenge thrown to the future by the predecessor he valued above all: Beethoven, whose last symphony had reached its culmination with an inrush of words and implicit drama, and whose single opera had brought symphonic music to the stage. His means would be Beethoven's. The orchestra's function would not just be to support the voices and colour the backgrounds but to maintain a full, rich and dense musical continuity ('unending melody'), thanks in large measure to a strong sense of thematic development, based on the LEITMOTIF, and of harmonic goal. Leitmotifs would lead the way, not as signals of characters and situations (though they have been named and understood in that way) but rather as powerful, persuasive and adaptable musical entities, making

possible spans of two hours and more (Act 1 of *Götterdämmerung*), unparallelled not only in their length but in their capacity to engross.

In differentiating music drama from opera Wagner was not primarily making a value judgement. He had used the term 'romantic opera' to describe his own three works of the 1840s leading up to the *Ring* – *Der fliegende Holländer*, *Tannhäuser* and *Lohengrin* – all of which he wanted performed at Bayreuth. But music drama was different. It had fewer incidents and simpler dramatic shapes, and it eschewed the set pieces of opera (quartets, quintets, etc.), for its expressive aims were long range: it dived into the inner lives of its characters, and it stayed there.

It quickly found its model in *Tristan*, whose two central characters are people who explicitly turn their regard from the outward to an interior world of feeling and being. These two figures virtually fill the score; others come on for relatively brief 'operatic' moments or provide background (and vocal relief) for the principal couple. Each act is composed as one long span reaching towards a climax that is either an interruption (acts 1 and 2) or a culmination (act 3), and the entire work can be heard as a striving to resolve the dissonance – the '*Tristan* chord' – introduced at the start of the prelude. This musical action is the base of the piece. And because the action is essentially musical it is also, as Wagner saw it, essential, dealing with the ultimate things, which music alone of the arts can touch. A wound in the fabric of the world – a dissonance, an unassuageable longing – is explored and intensified, in motivic development, self-recognition and love, and finally healed, in ecstatic consonance and death.

Wagner's preoccupation with redemption stories, of which all his mature operas and music dramas are examples, echoed both the musical language of his time – with its possibilities of highly elaborated and circuitous harmonic routes reaching towards final concord – and his age's concerns with how social justice and personal completion could be achieved outside the promises of religion. His political ideals are hard to gauge. In life he veered from revolutionary socialism (Dresden, 1849) to divine-right monarchism (Munich, 1869), consistent only in seeking the best opportunities for his art. His most overtly political work, the *Ring*, has been interpreted in countless ways, and can be so because, as much as *Der fliegende Holländer* or *Tristan*, it looks for fulfilment beyond – both beyond the finale, in a new order to follow the burning of Valhalla, and beyond the visible action, in music. The importance of nostalgia to his thinking also has to be recognized. His perfect society, as mirrored in *Die*

Meistersinger, was an idealized Renaissance Germany led by an artist-craftsman. And his most vaunting attempt to elicit a religious response to art, in *Parsifal*, drew on the fundamental mysteries of what was being displaced, Christianity. Like his own Wotan – the primary agent of the *Ring* and his most fully developed character – he was both utopian and pessimist.

He was contradictory, too, in his other opinions. Unerring in his musical judgement, he was capable of grotesque views on race – views made more noisome by subsequent German history. For some, his failings of humanity must damn him. For others, his works count as colossal acts of atonement.

Bryan Magee *Aspects of Wagner* (1968, ²1988); Barry Millington *Wagner* (1984); Barry Millington, ed. *The Wagner Compendium* (1992)

Operas: *Die Feen* (Wagner, after Gozzi), 1833–4; *Das Liebesverbot* (Wagner, after Shakespeare), 1834–6, f.p. Magdeburg, 1836; RIENZI, 1837–40; *Der* FLIEGENDE HOLLÄNDER, 1841; TANNHÄUSER, 1842–5, rev 1860–61; LOHENGRIN, 1845–8; *Das* RHEINGOLD (*Ring* 1), libretto 1851–2, music 1853–4; *Die* WALKÜRE (*Ring* 2), libretto 1851–2, music 1854–6; TRISTAN UND ISOLDE, 1856–9; *Die* MEISTERSINGER VON NÜRNBERG, 1861–7; SIEGFRIED (*Ring* 3), libretto 1851, music 1856–7, 1869; GÖTTERDÄMMERUNG (*Ring* 4), libretto 1848–9, music 1869–74; PARSIFAL, 1876–82

Orchestral: Symphony, C, 1832; *Columbus* (overture), 1835; *Polonia* (overture), 1836; *Rule Britannia* (overture), 1837; *Eine Faust-Ouvertüre* (see FAUST), 1840, rev 1855; SIEGFRIED IDYLL, small orch, 1870; *Kaisermarsch* (Wagner), men's ch, orch, 1871; *Grosser Festmarsch* (*Centennial March*), 1876; etc.

Choral: *Das Liebesmahl der Apostel* (Wagner), men's ch, orch, 1843; *Hebt an den Sang* (*An Webers Grabe*) (Wagner), men's ch, 1844; *Kinderkatechismus zu Kosels Geburtstag* (Wagner), 4 high v, orch, 1873–4; etc.

Songs: *Sieben Kompositionen zu Goethes Faust*, 1831, rev 1832; 'Der Tannenbaum' (Georg Scheurlin), 1838; WESENDONCK-LIEDER, 1857–8; etc.

Piano: Albumblatt, E, 1840; *Eine Sonate für das Album von Frau M.W.*, 1853; Albumblatt, C, 1861; *Ankunft bei den schwarzen Schwänen* (Albumblatt), A♭, 1861; Albumblatt, E♭, 1875; etc.

Editions, etc.: Gluck: *Iphigénie en Aulide* (performing version), 1846–7; insert arias, vocal scores, etc.

(2) **Siegfried (Helferich Richard)** (b. Tribschen, near Lucerne, 6 Jun 1869; d. Bayreuth, 4 Aug 1930). German composer and composer's son. His fate as Richard Wagner's offspring was to be overshadowed, not only by his father but by his mother, whom he outlived by only four months. He studied with Humperdinck, travelled in India and China as a young man and served from 1892 as

his mother's assistant at Bayreuth. From 1896 he conducted there and from 1906 produced. Meanwhile, he pursued his own career as a composer of fairytale operas, closer to his teacher in manner than to his father.

www.siegfried-wagner.org

Operas (librettos by the composer): *Der Bärenhäuter*, Op.1, 1898, f.p. Munich, 1899; *Herzog Wildfang*, Op.2, 1900, f.p. Munich, 1901; *Der Kobold*, Op.3, 1903, f.p. Hamburg, 1904; *Bruder Lustig*, Op.4, 1904, f.p. Hamburg, 1905; *Sternengebot*, Op.5, 1905, f.p. Hamburg, 1908; *Banadietrich*, Op.6, 1909, f.p. Karlsruhe, 1910; *Schwarzschwanenreich*, Op.7, 1910, f.p. Karlsruhe, 1918; *Sonnenflammen*, Op.8, 1912, f.p. Darmstadt, 1918; *Der Heidenkönig*, Op.9, 1913, f.p. Cologne, 1933; *Der Friedensengel*, Op.10, 1914, f.p. Karlsruhe, 1926; *An allem ist Hütchen schuld!*, Op.11, 1915, f.p. Stuttgart, 1917; *Der Schmied von Marienburg*, Op.13, 1920, f.p. Rostock, 1923; *Rainulf und Adelasia*, Op.14, 1922, f.p. Metzingen, 2003; *Die heilige Linde*, Op.15, 1927, f.p. Cologne, 2001; a few unfinished

Other works: orchestral compositions, songs

Wagner-Régeny, Rudolf (b. Szász-Régen, Transylvania, 28 Aug 1903; d. Berlin, 18 Sep 1969). Romanian–German composer. He moved to Berlin in 1920 to study with Schreker and Friedrich Koch at the conservatory, and stayed on as an opera composer. *Der Günstling* (f.p. Dresden, 1935) brought him official favour, which evaporated after he had moved closer to Weill and criticized militarism and tyranny in *Die Bürger von Calais* (f.p. Berlin, 1939) and *Johanna Balk* (f.p. Vienna, 1941), both written in collaboration with the German theatre man Caspar Neher. After a period of personal and creative collapse came a renewal in 1950 with the help of serialism and metrical subtleties learned from his friend Blacher, but his last works are again freer.

Wagner tuba. Brass instrument of which Wagner required a quartet in each of his *Ring* operas. Their parts were to be doubled by the fifth to eighth hornists, two on instruments in F (like the orchestral horn), two on instruments a fourth higher. Wagner tubas differ from horns in their elliptically wound and more continuously widening tube, less wide than an ordinary tuba's. Their sound is noble, heroic. For a while they became almost a regular part of the large symphony orchestra, used by Bruckner, Strauss and Stravinsky.

wait. English town musician, equivalent to the German *Stadtpfeifer*. In the 13th and 14th centuries the word signified a watchman; it was applied to the musicians instituted by many towns in the 15th century because they, like watchmen, played shawms (and a slide trumpet). They acquired a wider range of instruments in the 16th and 17th centuries, and some survived into the 19th.

Waldesrauschen (Forest Noise). Concert étude by Liszt.

Waldhorn (Ger., forest horn). HAND HORN.

Waldstein. Name given to Beethoven's Piano Sonata in C Op.53, which he dedicated to his patron Count Ferdinand Waldstein (1762–1823).

Waldteufel, (Charles) Emile (b. Strasbourg, 9 Dec 1837; d. Paris, 12 Feb 1915). French composer. Born, as Charles Emile Lévy, into a family of dance composers and instrumentalists, he wrote waltzes for Paris and London, including *Les Patineurs* (1882).

Wales (Cymru). Traditions of singing and of harp and crwth playing reach back into the first milllennium AD. Gerald of Wales (12th century) and others record music flourishing at the courts of the Welsh princes, but local culture was diminished by the English conquest (1282) and further undermined after the Act of Unification (1536). Rebirth came in the mid 18th century with the development of Welsh Methodism, which strongly favoured communal hymns, and with the re-emergence of the harpist (in John Parry of Ruabon and others). Choral singing and harp playing have been encouraged since then by the EISTEDDFOD tradition, while the country has gained a more international sort of art music thanks to music education at the University of Wales (from 1905), a permanent orchestra in the capital Cardiff (from 1928) and an opera company, Welsh National Opera (from 1946). Composers working in this new tradition have included Grace Williams, Daniel Jones and Alun Hoddinott.

walking bass. Line moving in regular patterns of 4/4 crotchets, each note a little detached. Such basses are particularly associated with Baroque music and jazz.

Walküre, Die (The Valkyrie). Opera by Wagner to his own libretto after German myth, the second part of *The Ring*. Siegmund (tenor) is given shelter by Sieglinde (soprano), to whom he tells his story ('Wintersturme') and in whom he finds both sister and mate. Wotan (bass-baritone), in deference to his wife Fricka (soprano), has to let Sieglinde's husband, Hunding (bass), kill Siegmund: his daughter – the valkyrie, or warrior goddess, Brünnhilde (soprano) – conveys the news to the hero in the awesome 'Todesverkündigung' (Annunciation of Death). She then goes against her father's wishes in trying to help Sieglinde and Siegmund; her sisters gather in anxiety (RIDE OF THE VALKYRIES); and he regretfully punishes her by leaving her lying on a mountaintop surrounded by fire (Wotan's Farewell, followed by Magic Fire Music). First performance: Munich, 26 Jun 1870.

Wallace, (William) Vincent (b. Waterford, 11 Mar 1812; d. Château de Haget, Vieuzos, Hautes-Pyrénées, 12 Oct 1865). Irish composer. The son of an army bandmaster, he was active in musical life in Dublin, where he was notably impressed by Paganini before emigrating with his wife to Australia in 1835. He left there for Chile in 1838, and worked his way up through the Americas to arrive in New York in 1843. Two years later he turned up in London, where his opera *Maritana* was enthusiastically received. Failing to equal this triumph, he returned to South America in 1849, then spent several years in New York and contracted a bigamous marriage. He was back in London in 1860, continuing to try for operatic success.

Walmisley, Thomas Attwood (b. London, 21 Jan 1814; d. Hastings, 17 Jan 1856). British church musician. He was the son of a church musician and godson of Thomas Attwood, with whom he studied. In 1833 he was appointed organist of Trinity and St John's colleges, Cambridge, and in 1836 he became university professor of music. He wrote services (notably an Evening Service in D minor) and anthems.

Walsh, John (b. c.1665; d. London, 13 Mar 1736). British music publisher, succeeded in the trade by his son, also John (1709–66). Both published Handel.

Walter, Bruno (b. Berlin, 15 Sep 1876; d. Beverly Hills, 17 Feb 1962). German–US conductor, originally named Bruno Walter Schlesinger. He started at the Stern Conservatory in Berlin when he was eight and determined on his career after hearing von Bülow conduct in 1889. His first jobs were with the opera companies in Cologne (1893), where he made his debut, and Hamburg (1894), where he worked under Mahler. Following a sequence of other positions he returned to Mahler's side in Vienna in 1901: he conducted the first performances of Mahler's *Das Lied von der Erde* and Ninth Symphony, and later promoted the composer by means of his recordings, combining strength with intimacy. His next post was as music director of the Munich opera (1913–22), after which he conducted widely before becoming director of the Leipzig Gewandhaus in 1929. Forced to return to Vienna in 1933, he had to leave there in 1938 and settled in the USA the next year. He conducted the major orchestras and at the Met, while returning regularly to Europe after the war. Besides Mahler, Mozart was specially close to him.

Erik Ryding and Rebecca Pechefsky *Bruno Walter* (2001)

Walther, Johann Gottfried (b. Erfurt, 18 Sep 1684; d. Weimar, 23 Mar 1748). German organist-composer and lexicographer. Related to Bach through his mother, he studied in Erfurt before travelling around Germany (1703–7) to meet leading musicians. He then settled permanently in Weimar, where Bach joined him and in 1712 stood godfather to his first son. Besides publishing the first comprehensive music encyclopedia (1732), he wrote over 100 fine chorale preludes.

Walther von der Vogelweide (b. *c*.1170; d. *c*.1230). Minnesinger, the foremost lyric poet of medieval Germany. He began his artistic life at court in Vienna, where Reinmar von Hagenau was his model. In 1198 he left Vienna and moved from court to court, protected by emperors and local sovereigns. More than 200 poems by him survive, but only one reliably authentic melody, the *Palästinalied*.

Walton, William (Turner) (b. Oldham, 29 Mar 1902; d. Ischia, 8 Mar 1983). British composer, knighted in 1951, an iconoclast who became Elgar's natural successor. Brought up in a musical family of modest circumstances, he won a place as a chorister at Christ Church, Oxford, when he was 10. He started to compose there, and stayed on as an undergraduate, but left in 1920 without taking a degree. By now he was part of the smart set: he lived with the three siblings Osbert, Sacheverell and Edith Sitwell, the arbiters of British modernity, visited Italy with them (a vital experience of sunshine and ease), collaborated with Edith on *Façade* (1922–9) and shared their urbane cosmopolitanism. Emboldened by Bartók and Schoenberg, he wrote a string quartet that impressed Berg when it was played at the first ISCM Festival (1923), but *Façade* was a more cavalier response to Schoenberg, eschewing the angst of *Pierrot lunaire* for a bright, smart world nearer Poulenc, yet English in its sentimental irony. Other society friends helped support him (some of them, the women, his lovers), through more works that drew on tangy continental in-

fluences, notably the breezy overture *Portsmouth Point*, Viola Concerto (first played by Hindemith) and exuberant cantata *Belshazzar's Feast* (1930–31), with its Handel–Elgar choruses set in an exotic orchestral score indebted to Stravinsky. But his commitment to the English tradition was deepening, and shades of Sibelius and Hindemith in his First Symphony (1932–5) are outmatched by those of Elgar, whose noble manner he echoed fully in his 1937 coronation march *Crown Imperial*.

The Second World War drew him closer to his home country and to films. Like Prokofiev, he found a perfect niche for a modern Romantic style behind the screen. Then in 1948, on a visit to Argentina, he met and spontaneously married Susana Gil Passo, with whom he set up home on Ischia. If his new location had its effect on his grand opera *Troilus and Cressida* (f.p. Covent Garden, 1954), it perhaps also encouraged a cheerful indolence. Larger works emerged at increasingly longer intervals, to be met with criticism that they repeated or betrayed his earlier achievements. He seemed not to mind, and in his last years returned to the musical world of his boyhood, that of the Anglican cathedral.

Michael Kennedy *Portrait of Walton* (1989)

Operas: *Troilus and Cressida* (Christopher Hassall), f.p. London, 1954, rev 1975–6; *The Bear* (1 act; Paul Dehn, after Chekhov), f.p. Aldeburgh, 1967
Ballets: *The Wise Virgins*, 1940 (after Bach); *The Quest*, 1943
Orchestral: Symphony No.1, B♭ minor, 1932–5; No.2, 1959–60; Sinfonia Concertante, orch, pf, 1926–7, rev 1943; Viola Concerto, 1928–9; Violin Concerto, 1938–9; Cello Concerto, 1956; *Portsmouth Point* (overture), 1925; *Siesta*, small orch, 1926; *Façade* (2 suites), 1926, 1938; *Crown Imperial* (coronation march), 1937; *Scapino* (overture), 1940; *Music for Children*, 1940–41; *Spitfire Prelude and Fugue*, 1942 (from *The First of the Few*); 2 Pieces, str, 1944 (from *Henry V*); *Orb and Sceptre* (coronation march), 1953; *Johannesburg Festival Overture*, 1956; *Partita*, 1957; Variations on a Theme by Hindemith, 1962–3; *Capriccio burlesco*, 1968; Improvisations on an Impromptu of Benjamin Britten, 1969; Sonata, str, 1971 (arr of String Quartet); *Varii capricci*, 1975–6 (arr of 5 Bagatelles for gui); *Prologo e fantasia*, 1981–2; etc.
Film scores: *Escape Me Never*, 1934; *As You Like It*, 1936; *The First of the Few*, 1942; *Henry V*, 1943–4; *Hamlet*, 1947; *Richard III*, 1955; etc.
Choral orchestral: *Belshazzar's Feast* (see BELSHAZZAR), bar, ch, orch, 1930–31; *Coronation Te Deum*, ch, orch, 1952–3;
Smaller choral works: *A Litany*, ch, 1916, rev 1930; *Make we joy*, ch, 1931; *Set me as a seal*, 1938; *Where does the uttered music go?*, 1945–6; *What cheer*, ch, 1961; *The Twelve* (Auden), ch, org, 1964–5; *Missa brevis*, ch, org, 1965–6; *All this time*, ch, 1970;

Jubilate, ch, org, 1971–2; *Cantico del sole* (St Francis), ch, 1973–4; *Magnificat, Nunc dimittis*, ch, org, 1974; *Antiphon* (Herbert), ch, org, 1977; *King Herod and the Cock*, ch, 1977; etc.

Recitation: *Façade* (Edith Sitwell), reciter, fl, cl, sax, tpt, vc, perc, 1922–9

Songs: *Anon in Love* (6), t, gui/orch, 1959; *A Song for the Lord Mayor's Table* (6), s, pf/orch, 1962; etc.

Chamber and instrumental: String Quartet, A minor, 1945–6; Piano Quartet, 1918–21; Violin Sonata, 1947–9; 2 Pieces, vn, pf, 1948–50; *Duets for Children*, pf, 1940; 5 Bagatelles, gtr, 1971; Passacaglia, vc, 1979–80

waltz (Fr. *valse*, Ger. *Walzer*). Dance in triple time for couples holding each other and gliding in circles. The German verb *walzen* appears from the mid 18th century, and features of waltz style are implicit in the GERMAN DANCE, of which Mozart wrote many. But the waltz became a recognized type only around the time of his death, distinguished musically by its lilting metre and general harmonic rhythm of one chord per bar, and choreographically by its close embrace, which won it both scandalized alarm (Byron, in 'The Waltz', wrote of 'hands which may freely range in public sight where ne'er before') and enormous popularity across Europe and North America. Schubert and Weber, around 1820, were among the first composers to explore the waltz as a musical genre, a little before Joseph Lanner and Johann Strauss I became the rival waltz kings of Viennese ballrooms, establishing forever the link between the dance and the imperial capital.

From there the waltz became ubiquitous, found in concert music (Chopin, Liszt, Brahms, Tchaikovsky, Ravel) and opera (from *Parsifal* and *La Bohème* to *Salome* and *Der Rosenkavalier*) as well as in the operettas and dances of the later Strausses and their successors (Waldteufel, Lehár). The spin came to an end with the First World War, as marked by Ravel's *La Valse*, and later waltzes (by Prokofiev, Shostakovich, etc.) tend to have something spectral about them.

Walzer (Ger., pl. *Walzer*). Waltz.

Wand, Günter (b. Elberfeld, 7 Jan 1912; d. Ulmiz, Switzerland, 14 Feb 2002). German conductor, much revered in his later years: he made his US debut (with the Chicago Symphony) at 77, and the recordings of Beethoven and Bruckner that came from his 70s and 80s were hailed for their thoroughness and conviction. Orchestras with which he was associated at this time included the NDR and BBC symphonies. He had studied in Cologne and Munich, though was largely self-taught as a conductor, and had a whole earlier

career in German theatres and as chief conductor of the Gürzenich Orchestra of Cologne (1946–74).

Wanderer. Name given to Schubert's Fantasy in C for piano, which includes variations on a theme from his song 'Der Wanderer', D.489. Liszt made arrangements of the work for piano and orchestra and for two pianos.

Wanhal, Johann Baptist [Vanhal, Jan Křtitel] (b. Nové Nechanice, 12 May 1739; d. Vienna, 20 Aug 1813). Czech composer. Of peasant origin, he had local teaching and began his career in 1757 as an organist. Countess Schaffgotsch, impressed by his talent, took him to Vienna, and there he had lessons with Dittersdorf, though he still had to buy himself out of serfdom with his earnings as a composer and teacher. Another patron, Baron Riesch, enabled him to visit Venice (1769–70) and other Italian cities. After that he lived largely in Vienna, one of the first composers to support himself independently. This he did ably, producing over 700 works for publication (symphonies, concertos, string quartets and other chamber music, sonatas and pictorial pieces for piano), even though he seems to have suffered some mental instability. He also wrote much for the church, including around 60 masses. Michael Kelly left an irresistible record of a quartet gathering when he played the cello with Haydn, Dittersdorf and Mozart.

war. See BATTLE.

War and Peace (*Voyna i mir*). Opera by Prokofiev to a libretto by him and Mira Mendelson after Tolstoy's novel. Lyrical scenes involving Natasha Rostova (soprano) with the men in her life – Prince Andrey Bolkonsky (high baritone), Pierre Bezukhov (tenor) and Anatol Kuragin (tenor) – contrast with choral tableaux featuring Field Marshal Kutuzov (bass) and his fellow generals as they frustrate Napoleon's invasion. First performance: Prague, 1948 (first staging, preceded by partial concert performances in Moscow, 1944–5); Moscow, Bolshoy, 15 Dec 1959 (first relatively complete presentation).

Ward, John (b. *c*.1589; d. ?1638). English composer. He was trained in the cathedral choir (1597–1604) and grammar school (1604–7) of Canterbury, then served the Fanshawes. Tending to the expressively serious and densely worked, his music includes a volume of madrigals (1613), fantasias and In Nomines for viols, and sacred items.

Ward, Robert (b. Cleveland, 13 Sep 1917). US

composer. He studied with Hanson and Bernard Rogers at the Eastman School, and with Jacobi at Juilliard, where he stayed on to teach until 1956, when he left to go into music publishing. His opera after Arthur Miller's play *The Crucible* was presented by New York City Opera in 1961 and much acclaimed. In 1967 he returned to teaching, at the North Carolina School of the Arts.

Warlock, Peter (b. London, 30 Oct 1894; d. London, 17 Dec 1930). British composer and – under his original name, Philip Heseltine – music scholar. Of affluent family, he was educated at Eton and while there gained an enthusiasm for the music of Delius, who helped him. Failing to settle at university, he worked on Elizabethan music at the British Museum and made important friendships with D.H. Lawrence (1915) and Bernard van Dieren (1916). He also married an artist's model who was already the mother of his son. His songs disclose a passionate lyrical intensity, together with a swagger not unrelated to his erratic, combative nature.

Barry Smith *Peter Warlock* (1994)

Songs with ensemble: 'The Curlew' (Yeats), t, fl, cor ang, str qt, 1920–22
Songs with piano: 'Adam lay ybounden', 1922; 'Balulalow' (Luther), ?1919; 'Passing by', 1928; 'Pretty ring time' (Shakespeare), 1925; 'Sigh no more ladies' (Shakespeare), 1927; 'Sleep' (Fletcher), 1922; 'Sweet and twenty' (Shakespeare), 1924; 'Take, o take those lips away' (Shakespeare), 1918; 'Yarmouth Fair' (Hal Collins), 1924; etc.
Choral: 3 Carols, ch, orch, 1923; 3 Dirges of Webster, ch, 1923–5; *Bethlehem Down* (Blunt), ch, 1927; etc.
Other works: Serenade, str orch, 1921–2; CAPRIOL SUITE, pf duet/str orch, 1926, arr full orch 1928

warm up. Prepare to play or sing. Wind instruments have to be warmed and hydrated by the player's breath before they will respond at their best, but human beings, too, need to warm up, to flex their minds and muscles, and in this sense the term is used of all musicians. Most will have warm-up exercises they regularly use; singers and orchestral players can often be heard warming up before a concert.

War Requiem. Oratorio-style work by Britten setting the Latin mass for the dead interleaved with songs for tenor and baritone on war poetry by Wilfred Owen. First performance: Coventry Cathedral, 30 May 1962.

Warsaw Autumn. Annual festival of contemporary music instituted in 1956. Through the 1960s and 1970s it was one of the few meeting points for composers across the Iron Curtain. Barraqué, Boulez, Stockhausen and Xenakis were among Western artists who appeared there, and the festival played a crucial role in encouraging and promoting the music of Lutosławski, Penderecki, Gorecki, etc.

Warsaw Concerto. See Richard ADDINSELL.

water. The sounds of water have often been imitated, as rain (Debussy's *Jardins sous la pluie*), mountain spray (Messiaen's *Chronochromie*), FOUNTAINS, RIVERS, SEA or SPRINGS. Gerhard and Le Caine are among composers to have made electronic music from recordings of water; Tan Dun has often used water in live performance. See also the following entries.

water gong. Gong lowered into a vessel of water after it has been struck, thus flattening the pitch; it may then be raised out again. Cage introduced the effect in his *First Construction* (1939).

Water Music. Set of three suites by Handel (F, 2 ob, bn, 2 hn, str, con; D, 2 ob, bn, 2 hn, 2 tpt, str, con; G, rec, fl, str, con) written for a royal barge party. Harty arranged six movements for symphony orchestra. First performance: River Thames, 17 Jul 1717.

water organ. Organ powered by falling water, which sucks air into the pipes. Such instruments were described by Hellenistic writers (notably Hero of Alexandria, 1st century AD), and knowledge of them had passed through Arab and Byzantine channels to western Europe by the late 13th century. Spectacular examples, playing by themselves, were placed in some of the great gardens of the 16th and 17th centuries, e.g. at the Villa d'Este, Richmond and Versailles.

wave. Means by which sound is disseminated, as pressure vibrations travelling through air or some other medium.

wavelength. Distance between adjacent peaks (or troughs) in a wave. Since the speed of sound is the same for all frequencies, the wavelength is inversely proportional to the frequency; thus high sounds have short wavelengths and low sounds long ones.

wa-wa mute. See HARMON MUTE.

Waxman [Wachsmann], **Franz** (b. Königshütte, 24 Dec 1906; d. Los Angeles, 24 Feb 1967). German–US composer. While studying in Dresden and Berlin he supported himself as a nightclub pianist and thereby gained an entrée to the film studios. In 1934 he moved to Los Angeles, where he worked on films from *The Bride of Frankenstein* (1935) to *The Nun's Story* (1959). His *Carmen Fantasie* for violin and orchestra (1947) came from a movie score (*Humoresque*); other concert pieces he wrote directly.

WDR. Westdeutscher Rundfunk (West German Radio), founded in 1956, formerly the Cologne station of Nordwestdeutscher Rundfunk. The Cologne radio established an orchestra (1947) and one of the first and most important electronic music studios (1951).

Webbe, Samuel (b. ?London, 7 Oct 1740; d. London, 25 May 1816). British composer. He served an apprenticeship as a cabinet maker before gaining his musical education with the organist of the Bavarian chapel in London. In 1775 he became organist himself of the Sardinian chapel. He wrote glees and catches, and Catholic church music.

Weber. German musical family. Three of the four daughters of Fridolin Weber (1733–79), a singer-violinist, became singers close to Mozart. Carl Maria von Weber was their cousin, the son of Fridolin's brother Franz Anton (1734–1812), a composer and string player.

(1) **(Maria) Josepha** (b. Zell, 1758; d. Vienna, 29 Dec 1819). She married the Viennese court musician Franz de Paula Hofer and was the first Queen of the Night in *Die Zauberflöte*.

(2) **(Maria) Aloysia (Louise Antonia)** (b. *c.*1760; d. Salzburg, 8 Jun 1839). Mozart fell in love with her before her marriage to the actor-painter Joseph Lange, and went on writing arias for her (K.294, 316, 418–9) that suggest a voice of extraordinary range, agility and expressiveness.

(3) **(Maria) Constanze (Caecilia Josepha Johanna Aloisia).** See MOZART (4).

(4) **Carl Maria (Friedrich Ernst) von** (b. Eutin, ?19 Nov 1786; d. London, 5 Jun 1826). German composer. Among the early Austro–German Romantics he stood nearest the flame of theatrical life, to which he contributed boldly and by which he got singed. His operas, except for *Der Freischütz*, have their brilliant musical invention undercut by ramshackle librettos and period expectations that have kept them from regular performance, and his concert pieces were achieved in the same way against the practical circumstances in which he worked, those of the emerging musical marketplace.

He spent his childhood on the road, with the family company, presenting plays and operas. Along the way he picked up a musical education,

notably in Salzburg in 1797 with Michael Haydn, to whom he returned in 1801. He also studied in Vienna with Vogler (1803–4), who recommended him for his first post, as music director at the theatre in Breslau/Wrocław (1804–6). From there he moved to Carlsruhe/Pokój and then Stuttgart (1807–10), where he was encouraged by Franz Danzi and wrote his first mature opera, the heroic-comic *Silvana*. He travelled on, and had a profitable stay in Munich in 1811: his *1001 Nights* singspiel *Abu Hassan* was put on there, and he wrote two concertos for the clarinettist Heinrich Baermann. He was also thinking about an opera based on a recently published ghost story: *Der Freischütz*.

Early in 1813 he became director of the opera in Prague, where he threw himself into performing (he was a pioneer of the conductor's baton and also busied himself with all matters of staging), leaving himself little time to compose. In October 1816 he left with Caroline Brandt, a singer he was soon to marry, and by the end of the year he had been appointed director of the German opera in Dresden. There he had to combat the rivalry of the Italian company under Morlacchi; he also had the troubles of tuberculosis and an unhappy family life. Yet he was able to return to creative work, and specifically to the *Freischütz* project. The resulting opera was produced in Berlin in 1821 and triumphed.

Later that year he received a new opera commission from Vienna, which led to *Euryanthe*, a grand drama in the popular chivalric mode that won only modest success. Exhausted and increasingly ill, he fell silent again until another commission arrived, from Charles Kemble for Covent Garden. In February 1826 he travelled to London to complete and supervise the new work, the fantastical *Oberon*, and there he died.

By an accident of timing, he grew up under the spell of Mozart, relatively unaware of Beethoven. That gave him the freedom to develop independently, but it also limited his historical reputation, at least until the late 20th century, when alternatives to the Beethoven direction began to be taken seriously. However, the verve, colour and dramatic prowess of his music had appealed to some of his colleagues and successors before that – not least Berlioz (who orchestrated his *Auffor-derung zum Tanze*), Wagner (who idolized him as progenitor of German opera) and Mahler (who made a performing version of his unfinished opera *Die drei Pintos*).

John Warrack *Carl Maria von Weber* (1968, ²1976); Carl Maria von Weber, ed. John Warrack *Writings on Music* (1981)

Operas: *Peter Schmoll und seine Nachbarn* (Joseph Türk), f.p. Augsburg, 1803; *Silvana*, f.p. Frankfurt,

1810; ABU HASSAN, 1810–11; *Der* FREISCHÜTZ, 1817–21; *Die drei Pintos* (Theodor Hell), 1820–21, unfinished; EURYANTHE, 1822–3; OBERON, 1825–6; etc.

Incidental music: TURANDOT, Op.37, 1809; *Preciosa*, Op.78, 1820–21; etc.

Orchestral without soloists: Symphony No.1, Op.19, 1806–7; No.2, 1807; *Grande ouverture*, 1807; *Der Beherrscher der Geister* (overture), Op.27, 1811; *Jubel-Ouvertüre*, Op.59, 1818; etc.

Orchestral with soloists: Piano Concerto No.1, C, Op.11, 1810; No.2, E♭, Op.32, 1811–12; *Concert-Stück*, F minor, Op.79, pf, orch, 1821; Clarinet Concertino, C minor/E♭, Op.26, 1811; Clarinet Concerto No.1, F minor, Op.73, 1811; No.2, E♭, Op.74, 1811; Bassoon Concerto, F, Op.75, 1811, rev 1822; *Andante e rondo ungarese*, C minor, Op.35, bn, orch, 1813; Horn Concertino, E minor, Op.45, 1815

Chamber: Variations on a Theme from *Silvana*, Op.33, cl, pf, 1811; Clarinet Quintet, B♭, Op.34, 1811–15; *Grand duo concertant*, E♭, Op.48, cl, pf, 1815–16; Trio, G minor, Op.63, fl, vc, pf, 1818–19; etc.

Piano: Sonata No.1, C, Op.24, 1812; No.2, A♭, Op.39, 1814–16; No.3, D minor, Op.49, 1816; No.4, E minor, Op.70, 1819–22; *Rondo brillante*, Op.62, 1819; *Aufforderung zum Tanze*, Op.65, 1819; *Polacca brillante*, Op.72, 1819; etc.

Other works: choral music, arias, duets, vocal ensembles, songs, piano duets, arrangements

Weber, Ben [William Jennings Bryan] (b. St Louis, 23 Jul 1916; d. New York, 16 Jun 1979). US composer, a 12-note Romantic. Largely self-taught, he was encouraged by Schnabel and Schoenberg, and began using serialism in 1938, one of the first US composers to do so. (Virgil Thomson is said to have been astonished by the incongruity of a 12-note composer who was also a homosexual – or a homosexual who was also a 12-note composer.) In 1945 he settled in New York as a composer, teacher and copyist, a role in which he was a virtuoso. Some of his finest works come from soon after, including the Fantasy for piano (1946), Concert Aria after Solomon for soprano and mixed octet (1949) and Symphony on Poems of William Blake for baritone and chamber orchestra (1950).

Webern, Anton (Friedrich Wilhelm von) (b. Vienna, 3 Dec 1883; d. Mittersill, 15 Sep 1945). Austrian composer. Everything he wrote has the dimensions and the lyrical intensity of a song. In his pursuit also of highly imbricated structure he was at once a modernist and a reviver of polyphonic techniques from Bach and before. And he was deeply Austrian in his love of music (Schubert, Bruckner, Mahler) and of the mountain things – flowers, crystals, clear air – he emulated in his brief and intimate works. In the

words of his teacher Schoenberg, what he offered was 'a novel in a single gesture, a joy in a breath'.

He began lessons with Schoenberg in Vienna in 1904, while also studying with Guido Adler for a doctorate, which he gained in 1906 for an edition of Isaac's music. At Schoenberg's he met Berg: the two pupils became firm friends, and both of them remained devoted to their master. In 1908, on completing his lessons, he began a fitful career as a conductor, abandoning his posts after no more than a few months. His mother's death in 1906 had unsettled him; all his music, he said, was related to that loss, until his love for his cousin Wilhelmine gave him a new subject in the summer of 1910. They were married early in 1911, with the first of their four children on the way.

Keeping close to Schoenberg musically as well as personally, he had moved into atonality in 1908–9, setting poems by Stefan George. Always short, his compositions reached an extreme of brevity in 1911–14, the last of the Op.11 cello pieces being a Mahlerian adagio in just 20 notes. After an interruption due to army service (1915–16) he concentrated on songs, often with accompaniment for a small mixed ensemble that he could use for strands and flecks of colour. In his choice of poems he gradually moved away from chinoiserie and expressionist visions towards liturgical texts and rhymes of homely piety – though paradoxically his style became increasingly astringent, the voice swinging in Opp.16–18 through sevenths, ninths and wider intervals.

In 1922 he became conductor of the Workers' Symphony Concerts in Vienna, his longest and most fruitful conducting appointment. Two years later he followed Schoenberg on the path to serialism, from which he never turned back. The new method made it possible for him to write instrumental scores again, and with his Symphony (1927–8) he discovered the aptness of serialism to strict canon (first movement) and symmetrically patterned variation (second), music of perfection and clarity. Thereafter his style changed little, and he found an ideal mirror for his music in the gently pantheist poetry of his friend and neighbour Hildegard Jone.

As the culture around him collapsed – and he lost all his appointments, as well as the freedom to travel to conduct for the BBC in London, a regular engagement between 1929 and 1936 – he kept to his work. He was shot in error by a US soldier at the liberation.

Kathryn Bailey *The Life of Webern* (1998)

www.antonwebern.com

Orchestral: *Im Sommerwind*, 1904; Passacaglia, Op.1, 1908; 5 Movements, Op.5, str, arr 1928; 6 Pieces,

Op.6, 1909, rev 1928; 5 Pieces, Op.10, chbr orch, 1911–13; 5 Pieces, 1913; Symphony, Op.21, chbr orch, 1927–8; Variations, Op.30, 1940

Orchestrations: German Dances, D.820 (Schubert), 1931; *Fuga (ricercata) a 6 voci* (Bach, *Das musikalische Opfer*), 1934–5

Choral: *Entflieht auf leichten Kähnen* (George), Op.2, ch, 1908; 2 Songs (Goethe), Op.19, ch, vn, cl, b cl, gtr, cel, 1925–6; *Das Augenlicht* (Jone), Op.26, ch, orch, 1935; Cantata No.1 (Jone), Op.29, s, ch, orch, 1938–9; Cantata No.2 (Jone), Op.31, s, b, ch, orch, 1941–3

Songs with orchestra/ensemble: 2 (Rilke), Op.8, v, 8 insts, 1910; 'Schmerz immer, Blick nach oben' (Webern), v, str qt, 1913; 3 (Webern, George), s, orch, 1913–14; 4 (Karl Kraus, Bethge, Trakl), Op.13, v, chbr orch, 1914–18; 6 (Trakl), Op.14, s, cl, b cl, vn, vc, 1917–22; 5 Sacred Songs (trad), Op.15, s, fl, cl, tpt, vn and va, hp, 1917–22; 5 Canons on Latin Texts (missal, Des Knaben Wunderhorn), Op.16, v, cl, b cl, 1923–4; 3 Folk Texts, Op.17, s, cl, b cl, vn and va, 1924–5; 3 (trad, missal), Op.18, v, cl, gtr, 1925

Songs with piano: 5 (Dehmel), 1906–8; 5 (George), Op.3, 1908–9; 5 (George), Op.4, 1908–9; 4 (George), 1908–9; 4 (trad, Bethge, Strindberg, Goethe), Op.12, 1915–17; 3 (Jone), Op.23, 1933–4; 3 (Jone), Op.25, 1934

Chamber: Slow Movement, str qt, 1905; String Quartet, 1905; Rondo, str qt, 1906; Piano Quintet, 1907; 5 Movements, Op.5, str qt, 1909; 4 Pieces, Op.7, vn, pf, 1910; 6 Bagatelles, Op.9, str qt, 1911–13; 3 Little Pieces, Op.11, vc, pf, 1914; Cello Sonata, 1914; Movement, str trio, 1925; String Trio, Op.20, 1926–7; Quartet, Op.22, vn, cl, sax, pf, 1928–30; Concerto, Op.24, fl, ob, cl, hn, tpt, trbn, vn, va, pf, 1931–4; String Quartet, Op.28, 1936–8

Chamber arrangements: *Schatzwalzer* (Johann Strauss II), str qnt, pf, hmnm, 1921; Chamber Symphony No.1 (Schoenberg), fl, cl, vn, vc, pf, 1922–3

Piano: Movement, 1906; Sonata Movement, 1906; *Kinderstück*, 1924; Piece, 1925; Variations, Op.27, 1935–6

Weckman, Matthias (b. Niederdorla, near Mühlhausen, ?1616; d. Hamburg, 24 Feb 1674). German composer. His clergyman father took him to Schütz in Dresden when he was about 12, and he trained under Schütz as a boy chorister and young composer. In 1655 his spectacular organ playing won him an appointment in Hamburg. He was twice married and had at least 11 children. His surviving compositions – concerted sacred items, chamber sonatas, keyboard pieces – are not much more numerous and show a fine handling of the influences to which he was exposed: Schütz, the Sweelinck school through Jacob Praetorius, and Froberger.

We Come to the River. Opera by Henze to a

libretto by Edward Bond. Unfolding on three musical-dramatic planes simultaneously, the work is a portrait of a nameless empire in decadence and revolt. The General (baritone) comes to see the pity of war, but his voice is unheard and he becomes a Lear-like figure of tragic disillusionment. First performance: London, 12 Jul 1976.

Wedding Cantata. See WEDDING MUSIC.

wedding music. The Baroque wedding cantata was a secular piece, to be enjoyed after the church ceremony. Bach wrote two: *Weichet nur*, often called the Wedding Cantata, and *O holder Tag*. Grander nuptials, royal and princely, were often the occasion for an opera or serenata in the 17th and 18th centuries. There are onstage weddings in several ballets, including *The Sleeping Beauty* and *Les Noces*. Weddings portrayed within operas are rarer; they tend to come afterwards, or not at all. The marriage of Lohengrin and Elsa, for instance, is aborted – though that has not stopped brides taking its music for their entry into the church. The wedding march from Mendelssohn's *Midsummer Night's Dream* music often provides the exit.

Wedge. Name given to Bach's E minor Fugue, BWV 548 for organ on account of its subject's shape on the page: it alternates through gradually widening intervals.

Weelkes, Thomas (b. ?Elsted, Sussex, ?1576; buried London, 1 Dec 1623). English composer. Likely a rector's son, he was evidently trained in the English polyphonic tradition, which in a novel way underpins the madrigals he published in three volumes of 1597–1600 – settings of superb craft and vivid, sometimes intense expression. In 1598 he became organist of Winchester College, moving on three or four years later to the post of cathedral choirmaster and organist in Chichester, where he married. There was a lighter madrigal collection in 1608; otherwise he devoted himself to church music, often with the same splendid effect as in his earlier madrigals. In his last few years his drunken ways brought him criticism.

David C. Brown *Thomas Weelkes* (1969)

Madrigals: *As Vesta was, from Latmos hill descending; Aye me alas; Cease sorrows now; Come sirrah Jack ho; Death hath deprived me of my dearest friend (A Remembrance of my Friend M. Thomas Morley); Hark all ye lovely saints above; Like two proud armies; The nightingale the organ of delight; O care thou wilt dispatch me; To shorten winter's sadness; Sing we at pleasure; Strike it up tabor; Sweet heart arise; Three virgin nymphs; Thule the period of* cosmography; What have the gods; When Thoralis delights to walk

Anthems: Alleluia, I heard a voice; Christ rising; Give ear, O Lord; Give the king thy judgements, O God; Gloria in excelsis Deo; Hosanna to the son of David; O Lord, arise; When David heard

Other works: services (Service for Trebles a 5), keyboard pieces, consort music

Weerbeke, Gaspar von (b. Oudenaarde, c.1445; d. c.1520). Netherlandish composer of church music. He spent much of his life in Italy, at the musically splendid Sforza court in Milan through the 1470s, in Rome the next decade, associated again with Milan and also Burgundy in the 1490s, and then in Rome once more. Compère and Josquin were among his colleagues. In his music, much of which was printed by Petrucci, he brought an Italian suavity into the northern polyphonic tradition.

weich (Ger.). Soft and open.

Weigl, Joseph (b. Vienna, 6 Feb 1881; d. New York, 11 Aug 1949). Austrian–US composer. He studied at the Vienna Academy and with Zemlinsky, and had a distinguished career as a teacher himself before the Nazi annexation of Austria in 1938. Moving to the USA, he continued that career at various institutions in the northeast. His works, strongly rooted in the Viennese tonal tradition, include six symphonies and eight quartets.

Weihe des Hauses, Die (The Consecration of the House). Overture by Beethoven for the play by Carl Meisl that opened the new theatre in the Viennese suburb of Josefstadt. Meisl had adapted his *Ruinen von Athen* for the occasion, and some of Beethoven's music for that piece was reused. But the overture was new, as was a chorus. First performance: Vienna, 3 Oct 1822.

Weill, Kurt (Julian) (b. Dessau, 2 Mar 1900; d. New York, 3 Apr 1950). German–US composer. His social ideals and his musical intuitions alike led him to a kind of music – and a kind of career – on the edge. He had a thorough classical background and was evidently at ease with the idioms of his distinguished senior contemporaries Schoenberg and Stravinsky, but he went another way, not wanting to abjure the musical richness, the contemporaneity and the dramatic possibilities of the new popular music of his time. In Europe he brought the echo of that music into opera houses and concert halls; in the USA, his home for the second half of his adult life, he applied his classical experience to Broadway.

The son of a synagogue cantor, he received musical encouragement from an early age, though his training was spasmodic on account of his impatience with tradition and his lack of means: he spent just a year at the conservatory in Berlin (1918–19) and began work as a theatre musician before being accepted as Busoni's pupil in Berlin (1921–4). He progressed rapidly. In 1922–3 two of his works were played by the Berlin Philharmonic, and in 1926 his one-act opera *Der Protagonist* established him as a theatre composer. The next year he began his collaboration with Brecht, which led to fast and simultaneous work on two operas: *Die Dreigroschenoper* (*The Threepenny Opera*, first given with his wife, Lotte Lenya, in the lead) and *Mahagonny*. His music here – Bach meets the 1920s dance band, with canons and chorales brought into critical contact with popular rhythms and song styles – he had been developing in previous works, but in Brecht's caustic lyricism it found its ideal match. The two artists went on to work together on other, shorter pieces, before parting company with some acrimony in 1930.

These were difficult years in Germany. Jewish and leftist, Weill was doubly irritating to the Nazis, and in March 1933 he left Berlin for Paris, where his projects included a final piece with Brecht (*Die sieben Todesünden*), a farewell to the concert world (Symphony No.2) and shows for the commercial theatre. One of these, *The Eternal Road*, took him to New York with Lenya in December 1935, and there they stayed. His reputation as the composer of *The Threepenny Opera* gained him entry to the highest Broadway circles, and he found new collaborators who shared his dissatisfaction with the state of the world and his dream that popular theatre might help change it. He worked on a rapid succession of musicals, producing some hit tunes (notably 'September Song', from *Knickerbocker Holiday*) but also stretching the genre to embrace longer, more sophisticated musical items and weightier subjects. *Lady in the Dark* (1940), for instance, portrays a character under psychoanalysis and is largely composed of musically continuous dream sequences. As for its composer he had a long-standing cardiac condition, and his heart failed before his optimism.

For many years after his death he was remembered chiefly as Brecht's musician who became a Broadway songwriter. The consistency of his vision – not diminished by his unfussy willingness to adapt himself to circumstances – became clear only when the full range of his work re-entered performance.

David Drew *Kurt Weill: A Handbook* (1987); Ronald Taylor *Kurt Weill* (1991)

www.kwf.org

Full-length stage works: *Die* DREIGROSCHENOPER, 1928; AUFSTIEG UND FALL DER STADT MAHAGONNY, 1927–9; *Happy End* (Elisabeth Hauptmann and Brecht), 1929, f.p. Berlin, 1929; *Die Bürgschaft* (Caspar Neher), 1930–31, f.p. Berlin, 1932; *Der Silbersee* (Georg Kaiser), 1932–3, f.p. Leipzig, 1933 (simultaneous premières in Erfurt and Magdeburg); *Der Kuhhandel* (Robert Vambery) 1934, rev as *A Kingdom for a Cow* (Reginald Arkell and Desmond Carter), f.p. London, 1935; *Der Weg der Verheissung* (Werfel), 1934–5, rev as *The Eternal Road*, 1935–6, f.p. New York, 1937; *Johnny Johnson* (Paul Green), 1936, f.p. New York, 1936; *Knickerbocker Holiday* (Maxwell Anderson), 1938, f.p. New York, 1938; *Lady in the Dark* (Moss Hart and Ira Gershwin), 1940, f.p. Boston, 1940; *One Touch of Venus* (S.J. Perelman and Ogden Nash), 1943, f.p. New York, 1943; *The Firebrand of Florence* (Justus Mayer and Ira Gershwin), 1944, f.p. New York, 1944; *Street Scene* (Elmer Rice and Langston Hughes), 1946, f.p. Philadelphia, 1946; *Love Life* (Lerner), 1947–8, f.p. New York, 1948; *Lost in the Stars* (Anderson), 1949, f.p. New York, 1949

Shorter theatre and radio works: *Der Protagonist* (Kaiser), f.p. Dresden, 1926; *Royal Palace* (Iwan Goll), 1925–6, f.p. Berlin, 1927; *Mahagonny* (songspiel; Brecht), 1927, f.p. Baden-Baden, 1927; *Der Zar lässt sich photographieren* (Kaiser), 1927, f.p. Leipzig, 1928; *Das Berliner Requiem* (radio cantata; Brecht), 1928; *Der Jasager* (Brecht, after Noh), 1930, f.p. Berlin, 1930; *Die sieben Todesünden* (Brecht), 1933, f.p. Paris, 1933; *Railroads on Parade* (Edward Hungerford), 1938–9, f.p. New York, 1939; *Down in the Valley* (Arnold Sundgaard), 1945–8, f.p. Bloomington, 1948; etc.

Concert works: Symphony No.1, 1921; No.2, 1933–4; String Quartet, 1923; *Recordare*, ch, 1923; Concerto, vn, wind, 1924; *Das neue Orpheus* (Goll), s, vn, orch, 1925; *Kleine Dreigroschenmusik*, wind, 1928–9; *Der Lindberghflug* (Brecht), t, bar, ch, orch, 1929; etc.

Songs (with source shows): 'Alabama-Song' (*Mahagonny*), 'Die Ballade von der sexuellen Hörigkeit' (*Dreigroschenoper*), 'Denn wie man sich bettet' (*Mahagonny*), 'Fennimores Lied' (*Silbersee*), 'I'm a stranger here myself' (*Venus*), 'Das Lied von der unzulänglichkeit menschlichen Strebens' (*Dreigroschenoper*), 'Morität von Mackie Messer' (*Dreigroschenoper*), 'Pollys Lied' (*Dreigroschenoper*), 'Salomon-Song' (*Dreigroschenoper*), 'September Song' (*Knickerbocker*), 'Speak low' (*Venus*), 'Surabaya Johnny' (*Happy End*), etc.

Weinberg, Mieczysław. See Moisey VAINBERG.

Weinberger, Jaromir (b. Prague, 8 Jan 1896; d. St Petersburg, Fla., 8 Aug 1967). Czech–US composer, who was cursed with an early success: his appealing folksy opera SCHWANDA THE BAGPIPER (1926). Before that he had studied with Novák in Prague and Reger in Leipzig. After it he maintained some success as a composer, but in 1939 he left for the USA and became increasingly depressed. He committed suicide.

Weinen, klagen, sorgen, zagen. Cantata by J.S. Bach. Liszt wrote a prelude on the bass of the opening chorus and, following the death of his daughter Blandine, a set of variations for piano or organ.

Weingartner, (Paul) Felix, Edler von Münzberg (b. Zara/Zadar, 2 Jun 1863; d. Winterthur, 7 May 1942). Austrian conductor. He studied in Graz and Leipzig and became a protégé of Liszt, who had his opera *Sakuntala* staged in Weimar in 1884. After that he started work as a conductor in German theatres, becoming director of the Berlin court opera (1891–8) and concerts (1891–1907). In 1908 he succeeded Mahler in Vienna, where he stayed with the Philharmonic until 1927, after which his base was in Switzerland. Touchy, he was five times married. But as a conductor – one of the earliest to make recordings – he moved with sure purpose, flexible in his tempos but refined in temperament. He remained active as a composer, producing operas and seven symphonies, despite little appreciation.

Felix Weingartner *Weingartner on Music and Conducting* (1969)

Weinzweig, John (Jacob) (b. Toronto, 11 March 1913). Canadian composer. Born to poor Polish Jewish immigrants, he studied at Toronto University (1934–7) and with Rogers at the Eastman School (1937–9). He returned to Toronto to work as a teacher, notably at the university (1951–78), and composer. In both fields he did much to bring Canada musically into the 20th century; he was the first Canadian to write serial music. His works include a series of orchestral divertimentos.

Weir, Judith (b. Cambridge, 11 May 1954). Scottish composer. She studied with Tavener while still at school and with Holloway while at King's College, Cambridge (1973–6). Since then she has held residencies with educational institutions and orchestras. From the first her music was lively and ironic, as is sometimes reflected in her titles, e.g. *Music for 247 Strings* (for violin and piano, 1981). Her slantwise approach to bright tonal harmony suggests an amused admirer of Messiaen and Ligeti, while folk music often enlivens her strict sense of form, as with Janáček and Stravinsky. Among her works are three operas to her own librettos – the brilliant and disturbing *A NIGHT AT THE CHINESE OPERA* (1987), *The Vanishing*

Bridegroom (1990) and *Blond Eckbert* (1993) – as well as an excellent carol written for her old college, *Illuminare, Jerusalem* (1985).

Weisgall, Hugo (David) (b. Ivancice, near Brno, 13 Oct 1912; d. Long Island, 11 Mar 1997). US composer. The son of a Jewish cantor, Adolph Joseph Weisgal (1885–1981), who brought the family to the USA in 1920, he studied at Peabody (1927–32), with Scalero at the Curtis Institute (1934–9) and intermittently with Sessions (1932–41). His language skills made him an effective cultural diplomat in the army in Europe (1941–7), and he became a powerful cultural administrator in his own country. He was also a prominent teacher, at the Juilliard School (1957–70) and Queens College (1961–83), and a composer of harmonically dark, vigorously lyrical operas, notably *Six Characters in Search of an Author* (1953–6).

Weiss, Silvius Leopold (b. Breslau/Wrocław, ?12 Oct 1686; d. Dresden, 16 Oct 1750). German lutenist-composer, like his father before him (and, indeed, his son after him). After starting out in service to the local count, he was in Italy in 1710–14 with the Polish prince Alexander Sobiesky and worked alongside Domenico Scarlatti at the Roman court of the prince's mother, the exiled queen Maria Casimira. By 1717 he had joined the court in Dresden, where he stayed, though he also travelled to Prague, Vienna, Berlin and Leipzig, gaining general praise as the outstanding lutenist of his era (though he nearly met his end as a performer in 1722, when a French violinist tried to bite off the top joint of his right thumb). He met Bach, who arranged one of his many lute sonatas for violin and harpsichord.

Weissenberg, Alexis (Sigismond) (b. Sofia, 26 Jul 1929). Bulgarian–French pianist, a virtuoso whose recordings of Bach and Stravinsky are extraordinary. Warmly encouraged by his mother, he studied with Olga Samaroff at Juilliard (1946–9) and won the Leventritt Competition in 1947, the start of his international career, which he interrupted for a decade of further study (1956–66).

Weldon, John (b. Chichester, 19 Jan 1676; d. London, 7 May 1736). British composer, trained at Eton and with Purcell (1693). He was organist of New College, Oxford (1694–1702), before settling in London as an organist (notably with the Chapel Royal from 1708) and composer, probably responsible for the semi-opera *The* TEMPEST long attributed to Purcell.

Welitsch [Veličkova], Ljuba (b. Borissovo, 10 Jul 1913; d. Vienna, 31 Aug 1996). Bulgarian–Austrian soprano. Trained in Vienna by Theodor Lierhammer, she was with the companies in Graz, Hamburg and Munich before joining the Vienna Staatsoper in 1946. Her recordings show thrilling dramatic utterance combined with warm tonal beauty. She was specially admired as Salome, with which she made her Met debut in 1949.

Wellesz, Egon (Joseph) (b. Vienna, 21 Oct 1885; d. Oxford, 9 Nov 1974). Austrian composer, a Schoenberg pupil and echt-Viennese. Born into the prosperous bourgeoisie, he heard Mahler conduct *Der Freischütz* on his 13th birthday and determined on a life in music. Like his friend Webern, he studied musicology under Guido Adler and was a composition pupil of Schoenberg (1905–6), but unlike Webern he remained a scholar, doing pioneer work on Byzantine chant and Baroque opera, while his musical relationship with Schoenberg was more ambivalent: in some works he returned to tonality, and Strauss and Bruckner were dear to him. In 1938 he and his wife moved to Oxford, where he was a genial and much respected member of the music faculty, but his creative heart remained in Vienna. His works include two collaborations with Hofmannsthal – the ballet *Achilles auf Skyros* (1921) and opera *Alkestis* (1922–3) – as well as a set of orchestral character pieces after *The* TEMPEST and nine symphonies (1945–71).

Wellingtons Sieg, oder Die Schlacht bei Vittoria (Wellington's Victory, or The Battle of Vitoria). Orchestral work by Beethoven, written at the behest of Maelzel for his mechanical panharmonicon and immediately made available for human performers. Loudly expressing satisfaction at the British victory of 21 June 1813, it was received with great enthusiasm (four performances in four months) but has been an embarrassment to some later admirers of the composer. First performance: Vienna, 8 Dec 1813 (human).

Wendling, Johann Baptist (baptized Rappoltsweiler/Ribeauville, 17 Jun 1723; d. Munich, 27 Nov 1797). Alsatian flautist-composer with Mozart connections. Born into a family of musicians, he settled at the Mannheim court in 1752 and was joined there three years later by his violinist brother Franz Anton (1733–86). They both married singers – his wife was Dorothea (1736–1811), Franz Anton's Elisabeth (1746–86) – and they both had daughters who were named after their aunts and also became singers. Mozart was close to the family in Mannheim in 1777–8: he wrote flute music for Johann Baptist and vocal pieces for the flautist's wife ('Basta vincesti', K.386) and daughter Elisabeth (1752–94). The latter, a great beauty, had preferred to stay the Elector's mistress rather than marry J.C. Bach. Later her mother and aunt were Ilia and Electra in *Idomeneo*.

Werckmeister, Andreas (b. Benneckenstein, Harz mountains, 30 Nov 1685; d. Halberstadt, 26 Oct 1706). German organ builder and theorist of temperament. 'Werckmeister III', advocated in his *Musicalische Temperatur* (1691) and based on some narrow perfect fifths (C–G–D–A and B–F♯) with the rest just, is used by some modern performers.

Wert, Giaches de (b. ?Ghent, 1535; d. Mantua, 6 May 1596). Netherlandish composer, especially of madrigals showing a new dramatic sensibility. He was taken to Naples as a boy singer and remained in Italy all his life, associated from the 1550s with the Gonzagas in Mantua, Ferrara and Novellara. In 1565 he became chapelmaster at the new Gonzaga chapel of Santa Barbara in Mantua, where he had to deal with the professional and (as it turned out) sexual rivalry of Agostino Bonvicino, discovered in 1570 as his wife's lover. After their separation she was accused of political intrigues and died in prison, while beginning to compose also for the Este court in Ferrara. His output is evenly divided between sacred music and madrigals, though it was the latter for which he was most renowned. Among the poets he set was Tasso, with whom he was acquainted.

Werther. Opera by Massenet to a libretto by Edouard Blau, Paul Milliet and Georges Hartmann after Goethe's novel. Charlotte (mezzo-soprano) chooses duty over love, and Werther (tenor), the love object set aside, kills himself. The score includes his 'Pourquoi me reveilles'. First performance: Vienna, 16 Feb 1892.

Wesendonck-Lieder (Wesendonck Songs). Set of songs by Wagner (1857–8) to poems by Mathilde Wesendonck, the wife of his patron of the time, and the woman with whom he was conducting an affair of the heart while working on *Tristan*, for which the third and fifth songs were studies. The complete set comprises: 1 'Der Engel' (The Angel), 2 'Stehe still!' (Remain still), 3 'Im Treibhaus' (In the Greenhouse), 4 'Schmerzen' (Agonies), 5 'Träume' (Dreams). Wagner approved an orchestration by Mottl; there is also a more seductive and nuanced version for chamber orchestra by Henze.

Wesley. British family of preachers and church musicians descended from Samuel (1662–1735), an Anglican clergyman, among whose 18 children were John (1703–91), the founder of Methodism, and Charles (1707–88), hymn writer.

(1) **Samuel** (b. Bristol, 24 Feb 1766; d. London, 11 Oct 1837). Organist-composer, son of Charles the hymn writer. Tales are told of his extraordinary musical precocity (which he shared with his brother Charles, nine years older): that he could play a tune before he was three, taught himself to read at four from the score of Handel's *Samson* and wrote an oratorio of his own, *Ruth*, when he was eight. In 1776 the family moved to London, and the father began to accept that he had musicians on his hands, despite his misgivings – misgivings that proved to be well justified in Samuel's case, for he was lured by the music of the Roman Catholic embassy chapels and in 1784 converted, marking the occasion with a grand mass he dedicated to the pope, to the chagrin of his father and uncle. However, his enthusiasm was short lived, though he went on writing Latin church music (*In exitu Israel* for double choir and organ, 1810), as well as Anglican settings. His erratic religious adherence may have been a product of his severe manic-depressive condition, though he was, too, robustly independent in behaviour: he married his wife only when she became pregnant, and, after the marriage came to an end in 1810, he lived with a younger woman who had been his housekeeper. He also found it hard to settle into institutional employment, though he was widely regarded as the outstanding British organist of his day. His vigorous presence in London concert life (he was a pioneer promoter of Bach; hence the naming of his son) is recorded in his symphonies, concertos and quartets.

Michael Kassler and Philip Olleson *Samuel Wesley* (2001)

(2) **Samuel Sebastian** (b. London, 14 Aug 1810; d. Gloucester, 19 Apr 1876). Organist-composer, son of Samuel. He received his training as a Chapel Royal chorister and began his career as an organist in London in 1826, moving on to appointments at Hereford Cathedral (1832–5), Exeter Cathedral (1835–42), Leeds Parish Church (1842–9), Winchester Cathedral (1849–65) and Gloucester Cathedral (1865–76). In 1850 he was also made first organ professor at the RAM. Everywhere he had difficulties, by virtue of his irascibility and inconsistency, but everywhere he was admired. He roused Anglican church music (which had slept through the Classical period) into the Romantic age and left pieces that choirs still love singing, including his Service in E (1842–3) and anthems *Blessed be the God and*

Father (1833–4) and *Thou wilt keep him in perfect peace* (c.1850).

Wessel, David (b. Belleville, Ill., 6 Oct 1942). US composer. He studied mathematics and psychology at the University of Illinois (1960–64) and Stanford (1964–8). His work on timbre perception at Michigan State University (1969–79) bore fruit in the elegant and fascinating *Antony* (1977) for massed synthesized tones. He was then prominent at IRCAM (1979–88) before moving to the Center for New Music and Audio Technologies at Berkeley. His later works involve live performance and improvisation.

When Lilacs Last in the Door-yard Bloom'd. Elegy by Whitman for Lincoln, set by Hindemith and Sessions. Hindemith made his version after the Second World War as a 'Requiem for those we love', to quote the subtitle.

whip. Percussion instrument made from two flat pieces of wood, hinged in a V so that they can be slapped together to give a sharp report, like a whipcrack. The sound comes at the start of Ravel's Piano Concerto in G and in many other 20th-century scores.

whistle. (1) Simple wind instrument that comes in many kinds, including the tin or penny whistle (straight with holes, like a recorder), SWANEE WHISTLE and policeman's or referee's whistle (bulbous). Whistles were traditionally distinguished from flutes and recorders on grounds of function: they were not for music, or only for very modest music. That changed in the 20th century, with, for example, the use of the swanee whistle by Ravel (nocturne of *L'Enfant et les sortilèges*) and Ligeti. Still, in keeping with their lowly status whistles are normally played by percussionists.

(2) To produce pitched sound by blowing through pursed lips. This is not something singers like to do, and whistling in opera is very rare (except from the audience).

White, John (b. Berlin, 5 Apr 1936). British composer. He studied at the RCM (1955–9) and began his teaching career there, becoming a genial influence on English experimentalism through his contacts with Cardew, Smalley and others. He has also worked a great deal in the theatre. Modest in every respect except quantity, his Satie-esque music is at once cosy and disturbing. Running through his output is a line of about 150 piano sonatas.

White, Robert (b. c.1538; d. London, Nov 1574).

English composer. After studying at Trinity College, Cambridge, he was choirmaster at Ely (1562–6), Chester and Westminster Abbey (1570–74). He died of plague. His works include Latin psalms and Lamentations, settings of keen expressive force.

White Mass. Name Scriabin gave to his Piano Sonata No.7.

white noise. Noise that contains a full range of frequencies at randomly varying amplitudes; if not, it is 'coloured'. The effect is of a continuous hissing. White noise is one of the basic components of electronic music.

white note. Note played on a white key on the piano; hence white-note scale for a scale through such notes.

white tone. Sound produced by a singer or instrumentalist without vibrato, giving an effect of purity.

whole note (US). Semibreve (UK). See DURATION.

whole tone, whole step. Interval of two semitones, as the adjective emphasizes. The whole-tone scale (e.g. C–D–E–F♯–A♭–B♭–C) is particularly associated with Debussy.

Whythorne, Thomas (b. Ilminster, 1528; d. London, c.31 July 1596). English lutenist-composer. He published the first collection of partsongs in England (1571) but is more remarkable as the author of the first autobiography in the language, discovered in 1955 and published in 1961. This tells how he studied at Oxford and worked as a musician in great households before and after the visit he made to Naples in his mid-20s.

Widor, Charles Marie (Jean Albert) (b. Lyons, 21 Feb 1844; d. Paris, 12 Mar 1937). French organist-composer. Born into a family of organ builders, he studied in Brussels with Fétis and with Lemmens, heir to the teaching of Bach. He became organist at St Sulpice in Paris in 1860 and stayed 64 years, while also working as a music critic, conductor and teacher. In 1890 he succeeded Franck as organ professor at the Conservatoire, and in 1896 he became professor of composition as well. He wrote operas (*Maître Ambros*, 1886), symphonies and concertos, and chamber music, but is remembered mostly for his 10 organ symphonies, of which the first eight came out in two volumes of four (1872, 1887), followed by the *Symphonie gothique* (1895) and *Symphonie romane* (1900). The Fifth Symphony ends with a celebrated toccata, but his music can also be massive or intimate as well as brilliant.

Andrew Thomson *The Life and Times of Charles-Marie Widor* (1987)

Wieck, (Johann Gottlob) Friedrich (b. Pretzsch, near Torgau, 18 Aug 1785; d. Loschwitz, near Dresden, 6 Oct 1873). German music teacher. He studied theology before starting work as a teacher. In 1813 or 1814 he settled in Leipzig, where he stayed until 1840, the year his daughter Clara married Schumann against his opposition. By now divorced and remarried, he moved to Dresden.

Wiegenlied (Ger., rocking song). LULLABY.

Wieniawski, Henryk (b. Lublin, 10 July 1835; d. Moscow, 31 Mar 1880). Polish violinist-composer. The son of a pianist, he studied with Lambert Massart at the Paris Conservatoire (1843–6) and made his debut in Paris in January 1848, accompanied by his 10-year-old brother Józef. They then went back to Poland, giving concerts on the way, but Henryk, now determined to compose as well, returned to the Conservatoire for harmony studies with Henri Collet (1849–50). The Wieniawski brothers spent 1851–3 playing in Russia; after that Henryk led a virtuoso career all over Europe and married (in 1860). At Anton Rubinstein's invitation he returned to Russia (1860–72), where his work as a teacher, soloist and quartet player had a determining effect on the country's violin school. He then went back to a life of international touring, to the detriment of his health. By all accounts an exciting and outgoing performer, with a warm tone and plentiful vibrato, he left two concertos (in F♯ minor and the more popular work in D minor, 1862), as well as virtuoso concert studies.

Wilbye, John (baptized Diss, 7 Mar 1574; d. Colchester, autumn 1638). English composer. He spent 30 years in service to Lady Elizabeth Kytson at Hengrave Hall, Suffolk, and published two books of madrigals (1598, 1609) generally lighter in texture than those of his contemporary Weelkes, whose life was the more varied and rumbustious. Yet he could find and sustain intimate pathos. Among his madrigals are *Adieu, sweet Amaryllis, Draw on sweet night* (one of the finest English madrigals), *Flora gave me fairest flowers, Happy, o happy he, Lady when I behold* (two settings, a 6 and a 4) and *Of joys and pleasing pains*. He wrote little else.

David C. Brown *Wilbye* (1974)

Wilder, Philip van (b. ?Willam, near Wormhout, *c*.1500; d. London, 24 Feb 1553). Netherlandish–English lutenist-composer, resident in England from around 1520 and much favoured by Henry VIII. In his music he combined the Josquin tradition with the English, his works including songs and a 12-voice *Deo gratias*, which might have been written for the meeting between Henry and François I of France at the Field of the Cloth of Gold (1532).

Wilkinson, Robert (b. *c*.1475–80; d. 1515 or later). English composer. His contributions to the Eton Choirbook include two imposing works: a *Salve regina* a 9 and a 13-part canon setting the Apostle's Creed. He was probably a scholar at the college, and remained as a choirman and master of the choristers (*c*.1500–15), after which he may have died or become a priest elsewhere.

Willaert, Adrian (b. ?Bruges, *c*.1490; d. Venice, 7 Dec 1562). Netherlandish composer and one of the great masters of polyphony between Josquin and the generation of Palestrina. He went to Paris for legal training but instead studied music with Mouton. He then left for Rome, where he is said to have heard his motet *Verbum bonum* being sung in the papal chapel as a work of Josquin's: when they were told the piece was his, the singers lost all interest in it. He had more luck with Cardinal Ippolito I d'Este, whom he accompanied to Esztergom (1517–19). On his return he transferred to the court of the cardinal's brother Alfonso, Duke of Ferrara, until in 1527 he was appointed chapelmaster of St Mark's, Venice, his position for the rest of his life. Evidently a meticulous and learned composer, he was the teacher of the theorist Zarlino, and possibly of his successor Rore. His *Musica nova* (1559), a collection of motets and madrigals remarkable for contrapuntal expertise and rich expressive colouring, was much debated in its time, and has been since. He also wrote masses, psalms and many other motets, including some for double choir, though he came before the full flowering of the Venetian polychoral tradition.

Willan, (James) Healey (b. Balham, 12 Oct 1880; d. Toronto, 16 Feb 1968). British–Canadian composer. He emigrated in 1913 to teach at the conservatory in Toronto, where he was also a distinguished university professor (1936–50), organist and composer, valued especially for his church music in the Anglican tradition: Latin and English masses, motets and anthems.

Williams, Alberto (b. Buenos Aires, 23 Nov 1862; d.

Buenos Aires, 17 Jun 1952). Argentinian composer and pianist, invigorator of his country's music. A scholarship took him to Paris (1882–9), where he studied at the Conservatoire and with Franck. Back in Buenos Aires he was active as an administrator and teacher (at his own conservatory), besides composing and giving concerts; he also made return trips to Europe. His works include nine symphonies.

Williams, Grace (Mary) (b. Barry, 19 Feb 1906; d. Barry, 10 Feb 1977). Welsh composer. She studied with Gordon Jacob and Vaughan Williams at the RCM, and with Wellesz in Vienna (1930). After a period teaching in London she returned to Wales in 1947, and with her orchestral *Penillion* (1955) started to draw more from Welsh traditions into her lyrical symphonic style.

Williams, John (Towner) (b. New York, 8 Feb 1932), US composer. He was a pupil of the pianist-arranger Bobby Van Eps in Los Angeles, of Rosina Lhevinne at Juilliard and of Castelnuovo-Tedesco back in Los Angeles. In 1956 he began work in films and television, rising steadily to become, by the mid 1970s, one of the most successful movie composers (*Close Encounters of the Third Kind*, *Star Wars*, both 1977). He has also produced concert works, including several concertos.

Williamson, Malcolm (Benjamin Graham Christopher) (b. Sydney, 21 Nov 1931; d. Cambridge, 2 Mar 2003). Australian composer. He studied with Eugene Goossens at the conservatory in Sydney (1949–50), then travelled to London, where his teachers included Elisabeth Lutyens and Erwin Stein. In the 1960s he won acclaim especially for his operas (*Our Man in Havana*, 1963; *English Eccentrics*, 1964; *The Violins of Saint-Jacques*, 1966) and orchestral music (symphonies, piano concertos) in a style alluding variously to Stravinsky, Messiaen and Britten. He also wrote Roman Catholic church music. In 1975 he was appointed Master of the Queen's Music.

William Tell. See GUILLAUME TELL.

Willis, Henry (b. London, 27 Apr 1821; d. London, 11 Feb 1901). British organ builder, supreme in his time. Around 1848 he went to Paris to learn from Cavaillé-Coll; he later provided instruments for numerous cathedrals. Willis organs survive at St Paul's, Salisbury, Hereford, etc.

Wilson, John (b. Faversham, 5 Apr 1595; d. Westminster, 22 Feb 1674). English composer, especially of lute songs. He began as a theatre musician at the

end of Shakespeare's career and became Oxford professor of music (1656–61).

Winchester Troper. Book containing the earliest notated polyphony; two-part organa of *c*.1000.

wind (Ger. *Bläser*). Collective term for blown instruments, including both WOODWIND and BRASS, though often confined to the former. The plural form is 'winds', but one can equally speak of 'five wind', i.e. five wind instruments.

wind machine. A theatre device, incorporated into concert works by Strauss (*Don Quixote*), Ravel (*Daphnis*), Messiaen (*Des Canyons*), etc. A barrel is rotated inside a close-fitting canvas cover, producing a wind effect that can be raised in pitch and amplitude by speeding up the rotation.

wind quintet (Fr. *quintette à vents*, Ger. *Bläser-quintett*). Group of instruments comprising flute, oboe, clarinet, horn and bassoon, or group of players on those instruments, or genre of music for that medium, or work of that genre. The wind quintet evolved in imitation of the string quartet from the regular eight-piece wind ensemble of Mozart's Vienna: two each of oboes, clarinets, horns and bassoons, as in his C minor Serenade, K.388. His Quintet for piano and wind (no flute) must have been a particular stimulus. The medium's important history began in the early 19th century with Reicha and Danzi, and for a long while ended there, for otherwise the repertory dates from the 1920s and later, including works by Hindemith, Nielsen and Schoenberg, followed by Carter, Ligeti, Kurtág and Birtwistle.

Wine, Women and Song (*Wein, Weib und Gesang*). Waltz by Johann Strauss II.

winter. See SEASONS.

Winter, Peter (baptized Mannheim, 28 Aug 1754; d. Munich, 17 Oct 1825). German composer. Brought up in the lively musical atmosphere of Mannheim, he was playing violin in the court orchestra when he was 10, and received a permanent position in 1776. Two years later he moved with the court to Munich, where he soon became director of the orchestra. As such he met Mozart on the occasion of *Idomeneo* (and later); Mozart was not impressed. Nonetheless, he provided a bridge from Mozart's world to Weber's. He wrote quantities of operas and other theatre works, and chamber music.

Winter Daydreams (*Zimnie grezy*). Name Tchaikovsky gave his First Symphony.

Winterreise (Winter Journey). Song cycle by Schubert to 24 poems by Wilhelm Müller, the colossus of the song repertory, lasting more than an hour in performance. The cycle was published in two parts, which are somewhat distinct. In the first the singing persona sees his distress – lost love – mirrored with varying degrees of sympathy, bitter mockery and disregard in the winter landscape through which he is travelling, while in the second his wandering mind is taken over by dreams and nightmares, to come to uneasy rest at a weird encounter with a musician ('Der Leiermann', The Hurdy-Gurdy Man). As published, the music supposes a baritone voice, but the work is often sung in transposition by tenors, and latterly has been performed, too, by women (and countertenors), for its expressive soul is universal.

Winter Wind. Name given to Chopin's Etude in A minor, Op.25:11.

Wirbel (Ger.). Drumroll; also *Wirbeltrommel* (tenor drum).

wirebrush. See BRUSH.

Wirén, Dag (Ivar) (b. Striberg, Narke, 15 Oct 1905; d. Stockholm, 19 Apr 1986). Swedish composer. He studied with Ellberg at the conservatory in Stockholm (1926–31) and with Sabaneyev in Paris (1932–4), where encounters with Stravinsky and Prokofiev confirmed his neoclassical orientation. Back in Stockholm he worked as a music administrator and critic. His works include a popular Serenade for strings (1937), five symphonies and five quartets.

Wise, Michael (b. Salisbury, c.1647; d. Salisbury, 24 Aug 1687). English composer. He was a chorister in the immediate post-Restoration Chapel Royal and a composer there from 1676, while maintaining his position as organist and choirmaster at Salisbury Cathedral (1668–87). He met his death at the hands of the watch, to whom he had given 'stubborn and refractory language'. Anthems and services (Evening Service in D minor) make up his works.

Wishart, Trevor (b. Leeds, 11 Oct 1946). British composer. He studied at Oxford (1965–8), Nottingham and York, and has worked particularly with electronic and unconventional media. His *Vox* series (six works for voices and tape, 1981–9) is impressively abundant with new vocal sounds, used with intriguing spirit.

wit. See HUMOUR.

Witches' Minuet. Name given to the minuet of Haydn's D minor quartet, Op.76:2.

Wittgenstein, Paul (b. Vienna, 5 Nov 1887; d. Manhasset, NY, 3 Mar 1961). Austrian–US pianist, brother of the philosopher Ludwig. He lost his right arm in the First World War and commissioned left-hand concertos from Ravel, Strauss, Prokofiev, etc.

Wohltemperirte Clavier, Das (The Well-Tempered Clavier). J.S. Bach's title for a set of 24 preludes and fugues in all the major and minor keys he put together in 1722. Suitably adjusted in TEMPERAMENT, a clavier (i.e. keyboard) could cope with music in any key. Many composers produced showpieces to demonstrate the fact, though none at the level of Bach's. Precisely what he meant by 'wohltemperirte', though, is unclear – equal temperament is only one possibility. He put together a second volume over a longer period, and this, without his authority, got subsumed under the same name. The two sets, also collectively called 'The 48', were used by Bach in his teaching and have been touchstones for keyboard performers and composers since Beethoven.

wolf. Unpleasant disintonation, supposed to resemble a wolf's howling. It may be caused by the tuning of an instrument other than in equal temperament, leaving one particular fifth too sharp or too flat. Or the wolf may howl because a string instrument resonates at a pitch just off the note the player is trying to produce.

Wolf, Hugo (Filipp Jakob) (b. Windischgraz/ Slovenjgradec, 13 Mar 1860; d. Vienna, 22 Feb 1903). Austrian composer, especially of songs that convey late-Romantic passion – intense, amused, lusting for life – on a smaller platform. Of German–Slovene parentage, he began music lessons with his father, took to the art with a will and studied with Robert Fuchs at the Vienna Conservatory (1875–7). He was a troublesome student and left abruptly – though only after he had been awestruck by Wagner: the music and the man. After a few months back home he returned to Vienna, now to earn his living as a music teacher while teaching himself to compose. His emotional life remained intense, and was shared with friends (including Mahler) and a sweetheart. For her he composed numerous songs (though by far the most important work of this period is his powerful quartet), while the more mundane exercise of sex, with a prostitute, gained him the syphilis that would lead him through insanity to death.

He worked briefly as a music critic (1884–7),

forcibly expressing his likes (Wagner, Liszt, Chopin, Schubert) and dislikes (Brahms), and thereby probably doing himself more harm than good. A rehearsal of his symphonic poem *Penthesilea* by the Philharmonic was a disaster, though he did at last find a publisher in 1887 for some of his songs. Possibly his love affair with Melanie Köchert, wife of the court jeweller, played a part in gearing up his creative powers and resolve. In February 1888 he began an extraordinary spree of composition, and later that year the resulting songs started being heard in public in Vienna. Many were published in 1889–90, in what he ensured were splendidly produced volumes devoted to settings of Eichendorff, Mörike and Goethe. Meanwhile he was setting translations of Spanish and then Italian poems while searching for an opera subject he could find compelling. Lacking that, he lost the will or ability to compose in 1892–4, and only returned to work when he had found his libretto, *Der Corregidor*.

After this came more songs and the beginning of a second opera, *Manuel Venegas*, but his mind was giving way, and in the autumn of 1897 he was committed to an asylum. Köchert went on visiting him thrice weekly to the end, and threw herself out of a fourth-floor window three years after his death.

Eric Sams *The Songs of Hugo Wolf* (1961, ²1983); Susan Youens *Hugo Wolf: The Vocal Music* (1992)

Stage: *Das Fest auf Solhaug* (incidental music; Ibsen), 1890–91; *Der* CORREGIDOR (opera), 1895.

Orchestral: *Penthesilea*, 1883–5; ITALIENISCHE SERENADE, str, 1892 (arr of qt)

Choral: *Sechs geistliche Lieder* (Eichendorff), unaccompanied, 1881; *Christnacht* (August von Platen), soli, ch, orch, 1886–9; *Elfenlied* (August Wilhelm von Schlegel, after Shakespeare), s, women's ch, orch, 1889–91; many arrangements of songs, etc.

Chamber: String Quartet, D minor, 1878–84; Intermezzo, E♭, str qt, 1886; ITALIENISCHE SERENADE, str qt, 1887

Song collections: *Sechs Lieder für eine Frauenstimme*, 1877–82; *Sechs Gedichte*, 1883–7; *Gedichte von Joseph v. Eichendorff* (20), 1880–88; *Gedichte von Eduard Mörike* (53), 1888; *Gedichte von J.W. v. Goethe* (51), 1888–9; SPANISCHES LIEDERBUCH (44), 1889–90; *Alte Weisen* (6), 1890; *Drei Gesänge aus Ibsens Das Fest auf Solhaug*, 1891; *Italienisches Liederbuch*, Vol.1 (22), 1890–91, Vol.2 (24), 1896; *Drei Gedichte von Robert Reinick*, 1888–96; *Vier Gedichte*, 1888–96; *Drei Gedichte von Michelangelo*, 1897

Individual songs (those obelisked orchestrated by the composer; the initial letters indicate those coming from the Eichendorff, Goethe, Italian, Mörike and Spanish collections): 'Alles endet' (Michelangelo), 'An die Äolsharfe' (M), 'An die Türen will ich schleichen'† (*Harfenspieler I*; G), 'Anakreons Grab'† (G), 'Auch kleine Dinge' (I), 'Auf ein altes Bild'† (M), 'Auf eine Wanderung' (M), 'Bedeckt mich mit Blumen' (S), 'Begegnung' (M), 'Bei einer Trauung' (M), 'Die Bekehrte' (G), 'Blumengruss' (G), 'Denk' es, o Seele!'† (M), 'Elfenlied' (M), 'Epiphanias' (G), 'Er ist's'† (M), 'Der Freund' (E), 'Frühling übers Jahr' (G) 'Fühlt meine Seele' (Michelangelo), 'Fussreise' (M), 'Ganymed'† (G), 'Der Gärtner' (M), 'Gebet'† (M), 'Der Genesene an die Hoffnung' (M), 'Gesang Weylas'† (M), 'Heimweh' (M), 'Heiss mich nicht reden' (*Mignon I*; G), 'Herr was trägt' (S), 'Im Frühling' (M), 'In dem Schatten'† (S), 'In der Frühe'† (M), 'Kennst du das Land' † (*Mignon*; G), 'Lebe wohl' (M) 'Mögen alle bösen Zungen' (S), 'Der Musikant' (E), 'Nein, junger Herr' (I), 'Nimmersatte Liebe' (M), 'Nun lass uns' (I), 'Nun wandre, Maria' (S), 'Nur wer die Sehnsucht kennt' (*Mignon II*; G), 'Phänomen' (G), 'Der Rattenfänger'† (G), 'Schlafendes Jesuskind'† (M), 'Der Schreckenberger' (E), 'So lasst mich scheinen' (*Mignon III*; G), 'Die Spröde' (G), 'Storchenbotschaft' (M), 'Verborgenheit' (M), 'Das verlassene Mägdlein' (M), 'Verschwiegene Liebe' (E), 'Wer nie sein Brot'† (*Harfenspieler II*; G), 'Wer sich der Einsamkeit ergibt'† (*Harfenspieler I*; G), 'Wie lange schon' (I), 'Wohl denk ich oft' (Michelangelo); etc.

Wolff, Christian (b. Nice, 8 Mar 1934). US composer. He studied classics at Harvard (1951–63) and remained there on the faculty until 1971, when he moved to Dartmouth College as professor of classics and music. While still in his teens he became a member of Cage's circle. Right away his pieces were very spare. In 1957 he introduced performer choice, and from this came a clear socialist engagement, whether in the very open *Burdocks* (1970–71) or in later pieces drawing material from labour songs.

Wolf-Ferrari, Ermanno (b. Venice, 12 Jan 1876; d. Venice, 21 Jan 1948). Italian composer. His father was a Bavarian painter, to whose surname he added his mother's. He studied with Rheinberger in Munich (1892–5), where he spent much of the rest of his life, except when he was director of the music school in Venice (1903–9). That was also the period of his sprightly reinventions of 18th-century opera buffa in *Le donne curiose*, *I quattro rusteghi* and *Il segreto di Susanna*, of which the first two he based on plays by Goldoni. He stayed in Zurich during the First World War, but, with his mixed inheritance, was by no means untouched by the conflict, which virtually stopped him composing for a decade.

Operas: *Le donne curiose* (after Goldoni), f.p. Munich, 1903; *I quattro rusteghi* (after Goldoni), f.p. Munich, 1906; *Il segreto di Susanna* (1 act), f.p. Munich, 1909; *I gioielli della Madonna*, f.p. Berlin, 1911; *Sly* (after Shakespeare *The Taming of the Shrew*), f.p. Milan, 1927; *La vedova scaltra* (after Goldoni), f.p. Rome, 1931; *Il campiello* (after Goldoni), f.p. Milan, 1936; etc.

Other works: cantatas, concertos, chamber music, etc.

Wolpe, Stefan (b. Berlin, 25 Aug 1902; d. New York, 4 Apr 1972). German–US composer, whose later works blend avant-garde openness and a jazz feel in fluid and characterful instrumental designs. He studied with Juon at the conservatory in Berlin (1920–21), gained encouragement from Busoni and immediately joined in the iconoclastic and socialist endeavours of artists in post-war Berlin. A little later he found those endeavours modelled at the Bauhaus in Weimar, and he began, characteristically, to find the universal and human in new and abstract compositional techniques, his taste for popular music sometimes helping him. Under pressure from events, however, he devoted himself in 1929–33 almost exclusively to theatre and propaganda work against the rising Nazis. His inevitable flight, when they came to power, took him to Vienna, where he studied with Webern, but only for a few months before moving on to Palestine. In the calmer environment there he taught (at the conservatory in Jerusalem, 1936–8) and composed, now drawing on local folk music, Arab as well as eastern Jewish.

In 1938 he settled in New York, where he taught at various institutions, for college students (Philadelphia Academy of Music, 1949–52; Black Mountain College, 1952–6) and adults. He began writing music of great dynamism, partly informed by jazz and powerfully conveyed in such works as *Battle Piece* and the Violin Sonata. Their qualities he best described himself, in his refugee's – but highly expressive – language: 'I very much like to maintain the flexibility of sound structures (as one would try to draw on water). That leads me to the promotion of a very mobile polyphony in which the partials of the sound behave like river currents and a greater orbit spread-out is guaranteed to the sound, a greater circulatory agility (a greater momentum too).' Contact with Cage, Tudor and others at Black Mountain College brought some experimental features into his music, such as the choreographed foot-stamping of his quartet with oboe (which is nevertheless keyed into the rhythmic drive), and he also learned something while teaching at Darmstadt in the 1950s. His music became leaner, more agile and more colourful, while keeping its firm sense of character and dramatic pacing. In his last years he was beset by Parkinson's diease.

www.wolpe.org

Orchestral: *The Man from Midian* (ballet), 1942; Symphony, 1955–6; Piece in 3 Parts, pf, 16 insts, 1961; Chamber Piece No.1, 14 insts, 1964; No.2, 13 insts, 1967

Larger vocal works: Hebrew Choral Songs, 2 sets, 1931–44; *Yigdal* (Maimonides), bar, ch, org, 1945; 4 Pieces (Hebrew Bible, Gershon Shofman), ch, 1954; *Dust of Snow* (Frost), ch, 1958; *Street Music* (Wolpe), bar, speaker, 5 insts, 1962; Cantata for Voice, Voices and Instruments (Hölderlin, Herodotus, Robert Creeley), mez, 3 women's v, 10 insts, 1963; etc.

Chamber: *Musik zu Hamlet*, fl, cl, vc, 1929; *Suite im Hexachord*, ob, cl, 1936; Oboe Sonata, 1938–41; Violin Sonata, 1949; Quartet, t sax, tpt, pf, perc, 1950, rev 1954; Quartet, ob, vc, pf, perc, 1955; Quintet with Voice (Hilda Morley), bar, 5 insts, 1957; Piece in 2 Parts, fl, pf, 1960; In 2 Parts, 6 insts, 1962; Piece for 2 Instrumental Units, 7 insts, 1963; Piece in 2 Parts for Violin Alone, 1964; Trio in 2 Parts, fl, vc, pf, 1964; Solo Piece for Trumpet, 1966; Second Piece for Violin Alone, 1966; String Quartet, 1969; *From Here on Farther*, vn, cl, b cl, pf, 1969; Piece for Trumpet and 7 Instruments, 1971; etc.

Songs: 'To the Dancemaster' (Chaim Nochman Bialik), mez, cl, pf, 1938; *Drei Lieder* (Brecht), 1943; *Zwei Lieder* (Berthold Viertel), 1945; 3 Songs, 1946; 'Lazy Andy Ant' (Helen Fletcher), s, 2 pf, 1947; *Excerpts from Dr Einstein's Address about Peace in the Atomic Era*, 1950; 6 Songs for *The Good Woman of Setzuan*, 1953; 6 Songs from the Hebrew, 1936–54; Songs for *Peer Gynt*, 1954; Songs for *The Tempest*, 1960; 6 Songs, 1955–61; 16 Songs from *The Domestic Breviary* (Brecht), 1965; etc.

Piano: Passacaglia, 1935–6; Toccata, 1941; *Battle Piece*, 1943–7; Music for a Dancer, 1950; 7 Pieces, 3 pf, 1951; *Enactments*, 3 pf, 1953; *Form*, 1959; *Form IV: Broken Sequences*, 1969; etc.

Woman from Arles. See L'ARLESIENNE.

WoO. Abbreviation for *Werk ohne Opuszahl* (work without opus number), used in catalogues of music by composers who normally used opus numbers, such as Beethoven and Schumann. For example, Beethoven's set of C minor Variations for piano is WoO 80 in the catalogue by Kinsky and Halm.

Wood, Charles (b. Armagh, 15 Jun 1866; d. Cambridge, 12 Jul 1926). Irish composer. He studied at the RCM with Stanford (1883–7) and at Cambridge (1888–90), and from 1888 taught at both institutions, succeeding Stanford as Cambridge professor in 1924. His works include Anglican church music, partsongs and string quartets.

Wood, Henry (Joseph) (b. London, 3 Mar 1869; d. Hitchin, 19 Aug 1944). British conductor, founder of the Proms, knighted in 1911. Brought up in a musical home, he studied at the RAM (1886–8) and began his career with touring opera companies. In 1895 he was appointed conductor of the summer promenade concerts at the Queen's Hall, where, modelling his style and appearance on Nikisch, he rapidly made his reputation. With six concerts a week to prepare, he found the time to include new works, by composers from Rimsky-Korsakov through Debussy, Mahler and Schoenberg to Shostakovich. He also conducted energetically elsewhere in Britain and abroad (he made his US debut with the New York Philharmonic in 1904), and made some bold and skilful orchestrations – notably his *Fantasia on British Sea Songs*, regularly played at the Last Night of the Proms, the festival he established and that still carries his mark.

Arthur Jacobs *Henry J. Wood* (1994)

Wood, Hugh (Bradshaw) (b. Parbold, Lancs., 27 Jun 1932). British composer. He read history at Oxford and studied privately with Mátyás Seiber, Iain Hamilton and others while teaching at Morley College (1958–67). His *Scenes from Comus*, performed at the 1965 Proms, established his reputation but by no means fixed his style: though finding his roots in the Viennese tradition from Beethoven to Schoenberg, he has also been touched by Gerhard, Messiaen and Tippett, and has maintained a robust independence. He taught at Cambridge (1977–99). His works include a symphony (1982), concertos for cello, violin and piano, four quartets and numerous songs.

Wood, James (b. Barton-on-Sea, 27 May 1953). British composer, percussionist and choirmaster, concerned in his creative work with ritual and microtonality. He studied with Boulanger and at Cambridge.

woodblock. Instrument of teak or other wood, in block form with a slit. It is laid on a surface, or suspended, and struck, producing a sharp, hollow retort of indeterminate pitch.

Wooden Prince, The (*A fából faragott királyfi*). Ballet score by Bartók to a scenario by Béla Balázs. The wooden prince is a puppet made by a prince to attract a princess, who is more taken with the image than the real thing until he forsakes the magic of his guardian fairy. First performance: Budapest, 12 May 1917.

Woodward, Roger (b. Sydney, 20 Dec 1942). Australian pianist, a searching virtuoso concerned with new music (Barraqué, Feldman) as much as

old. He studied in Sydney from 1957 with the Rachmaninoff pupil Alexander Sverjensky, and in Warsaw from 1965 with Zbigniew Drzewiecki. By the end of the 1970s he was appearing internationally. He has also taught, and in 2002 became director of the school of music and dance at San Francisco State University.

woodwind. Family of instruments including flutes (and piccolos), oboes (and cors anglais), clarinets and bassoons, all traditionally wind instruments made from wooden pipes, even if flutes are now most often of metal. Saxophones, though played by clarinettists, do not belong to the woodwind family (nor to the brass). The plural form is 'woodwinds', or more commonly 'woodwind'. A woodwind quintet (US, obsolete) is a wind quintet.

Woolrich, John (b. Cirencester, 3 Jan 1954). British composer. He studied with Edward Cowie at Lancaster University (1975–7) and has led a threefold career as a teacher at various institutions, performer (especially with his Composers Ensemble, commissioning songs and small instrumental pieces) and composer. Many of his works are touched by the imprint of mythic figures, including Mozart, Monteverdi and other composers of the past, in a fine balance of fantasy and irony.

Worcester Fragments. Collection of around 100 polyphonic settings attributable to a school of composers in the English city in the 13th and first half of the 14th centuries.

word painting. Setting of a word so that the meaning is reflected in the vocal line. This may be virtual onomatopoeia with such a word as 'arise', 'sigh', 'troubled', etc., but the term can also be extended to cases where there is no such direct cue for melodic gesture and the musical response is more to expressive connotations ('mournful', 'love'). Word painting can be emphasized, minimized or added by the singer.

Wordsworth, William (Brocklesby) (b. London, 17 Dec 1908; d. Kingussie, Scotland, 10 Mar 1988). British composer, descended from the poet's brother. He studied at Edinburgh with Tovey (1934–6), a powerful influence on his eight symphonies and six quartets, though he also absorbed Bartók and electronic music (Symphony No.7 'Cosmos', with tape, 1980).

work (Fr. *oeuvre*, Ger. *Werk*, It. *opera*). Composition. The notion of musical works as abiding entities seems to date from around 1800, when compositions began to be maintained and revived in performance. A work is not generally to be identified with its representation on paper (which is the SCORE of the work) nor with its realization in sound (which is a PERFORMANCE of the work). There is therefore room for argument as to what it is, and what contributions are made to it by the composer's invention, by preceding history and by the later accretions of performers and commentators. Differing views on these points may well alter performance and perception. Even electronic works, of fixed constitution, may change in the living history of reinterpretation.

Roman Ingarden *The Work of Music and the Problem of its Identity* (1986); Lydia Goehr *The Imaginary Museum of Musical Works* (1992)

world music. Term of late-20th-century currency for music outside the categories of Western classical and popular, embracing therefore Hungarian folksong, Burmese court music and Afro-Caribbean dance forms. The usefulness of the term is proportional to what these have in common.

Worzischek, Johann Hugo. See Jan Václav VOŘÍŠEK.

Wozzeck. Opera by Berg to his own libretto after Georg Büchner's play. Wozzeck (baritone) is a simple soldier and a human figure beset by caricatures: the Captain (tenor) and the manic Doctor (bass). His salvation might have come from his mistress Marie (soprano), but she has her own failings, of fidelity. The composer drew from the score *Drei Bruchstücke aus 'Wozzeck'* (Three Fragments from *Wozzeck*, s, orch), being a portrait of Marie. First performance: Berlin, 14 Dec 1925.

Wranitzky, Paul (b. Nova Rise, Moravia, 30 Dec 1756; d. Vienna, 26 Sep 1808). Moravian composer and conductor. He studied in Olomouc and Vienna, where he arrived in 1777 and may have been Haydn's pupil. In 1787 he joined the Burgtheater orchestra, and in 1790 he produced a popular singspiel, *Oberon*, which prompted and partly influenced Mozart's *Die Zauberflöte*. His other works include symphonies and quartets. As a conductor he was respected by his great contemporaries, and had charge of the first performances of Haydn's *Creation* and Beethoven's Fifth Symphony. His brother Anton (1761–1820) was also active in Viennese musical life as a composer and violinist.

wrest pin. Screw on a keyboard instrument or harp to which one of the strings is attached, and which can be turned in order to change the tension in the string and therefore the tuning.

wrong note. Mistake in performance – though 'mistakes' may be deliberate in harmonically complex music. The term 'wrong-note music' was a response to neoclassicism; Ives assured his copyists that his wrong notes were right.

Wunderhorn. See *Des* KNABEN WUNDERHORN.

Wunderkind. See CHILD PRODIGY.

Wunderlich, Fritz (b. Kusel, Rheinland-Pfalz, 26 Sep 1930; d. Heidelberg, 17 Sep 1966). German tenor. He studied at the conservatory in Freiburg and made his debut in Stuttgart as Tamino in 1955. Mahler (*Das Lied von der Erde*) and Bach's Evangelists were also in his repertory. A fine artist, much beloved, he died as the result of a fall.

Wuorinen, Charles (b. New York, 9 Jun 1938). US composer. He studied with Luening, Beeson and Ussachevsky at Columbia, and while a graduate student there was pianist and co-founder of the Group for Contemporary Music (1962). Already a prolific composer, he absorbed the influences of Wolpe and Babbitt into a flexible style, sometimes already showing a richness of imagery that was to become characteristic. His electronic piece *Time's Encomium* (1969) won him a Pulitzer Prize, but not tenure at Columbia, where he had been teaching since 1964. He accordingly moved to the Manhattan School and, in 1984, to Rutgers University. By that time his music had become less flamboyantly exuberant in its surface detailing, though not in its underlying rhythmic and harmonic energies – energies that have suited it to the ballet stage as much as to chamber ensembles of all kinds.

www.charleswuorinen.com

Opera: *Haroun and the Sea of Stories* (Fenton, after Rushdie), f.p. New York, 2004
Ballets: *The Mission of Virgil*, 1993; *The Great Procession*, 1995; *The River of Light*, 1996
Orchestral: *Grand Bamboula*, str, 1971; *A Reliquary for Igor Stravinsky*, 1975; *The Golden Dance*, 1986; Symphony Seven, 1997; 3 piano concertos, etc.
Chamber: String Quartet No.1, 1971; No.2, 1979; No.3, 1987; No.4, 2000; chamber concertos, etc.
Other works: *Time's Encomium*, tape, 1969; *The Blue Bamboula*, pf, 1980; sacred choral music, songs, other keyboard pieces

Wurlitzer. US company of instrument manufacturers, founded by Rudolph Wurlitzer (1831–1914), who emigrated from Saxony in 1853, tracing his ancestry back to a 16th-century lute maker. Under his three sons the company won enormous success in the marketing of cinema organs (from around 1910) and jukeboxes (from the 1920s).

Wynne (Thomas), David (b. Penderyn, Glam., 2 Jun 1900; d. Maesycwmmer, Glam., 23 Mar 1983). Welsh composer. He was a miner before training at University College, Cardiff (1925–8), and going on to a career in music education. Spurred by Bartók's example, he wrote four symphonies and four quartets, growing from Welsh song.

Wyschnegradsky [Vishnegradsky], **Ivan (Aleksandrovich)** (b. St Petersburg, 14 May 1893; d. Paris, 29 Sep 1979). Russian composer. Under guidance from Nikolay Sokolov in 1911–14 he became a follower of Scriabin's ideas, mystical and musical. He moved to Paris after the Revolution and began working with microtones, especially in a variety of works for two (or four) pianos tuned a quarter-tone apart.

Xenakis, Iannis (b. Braila, Romania, 29 May 1922; d. Paris, 4 Feb 2001). Greek–French composer, who used mathematical principles to create sounds in a state of raw nature. His father was a businessman; he lost his mother when he was a young boy. In 1940 he entered the Athens Polytechnic, but the school closed soon afterwards in response to the Italian invasion. He joined the Resistance and was severely wounded in 1945. Nevertheless, he completed his education, then left in 1947 for Paris. There he started work in the studio of the architect Le Corbusier, for whom he elaborated some designs (including that for the Philips pavilion at the 1958 Brussels Exposition). He also followed Messiaen's courses at the Conservatoire (1951–3), married (1953), made his professional debut with the orchestral *Metastasis* (1955) and joined the MUSIQUE CONCRETE studio (also 1955).

In 1959 he completed his apprenticeship with Le Corbusier, but by now his creative life was entirely in music – though music conceived on the same lines as his architectural projects. Planes of sound were created from layers of glissandos; complex patterns were worked out according to STO- CHASTIC principles, sometimes with computer calculations. In solo pieces the density of events would result in music of high virtuosity. Though his thinking was radically new, it also linked back to ancient Greek considerations of the links between music and number, as he recognized in so often titling his works in classical or pre-classical Greek. Rapidly gaining attention for the novelty of his sounds and ideas, he began travelling all over the world to attend performances, lecture and teach, while keeping an institutional basis in Paris at his Equipe de Mathématique et d'Automatique

Musicales (EMAMu), founded in 1966. In 1974 he was able to make the first of many return visits to Greece.

He became extraordinarily prolific: in 1991 alone, for instance, he completed three works for large orchestra, totalling 50 minutes of music, as well as an electronic piece. And perhaps because of the speculative way he worked, setting up algo- rithmic procedures that would govern whole stretches of music, there might be sharp diver- gences of style and substance between adjacent works. In some pieces he aimed for the energy, and even the modality, of folk music, and his per- cussion works – among his best – have an elemental strength.

Iannis Xenakis *Formalized Music* (1971, ²1992); Bálint András Varga *Conversations with Iannis Xenakis* (1996)

www.iannis-xenakis.org

Orchestral: *Metastasis*, 1953–4; *Pithoprakta*, 1955–6; *Polla ta dhina*, children's ch, orch, 1962; *Terretektorh*, 1965–6; *Kraanerg*, 1968–9; *Synaphai*, pf, orch, 1969; *Erikhthon*, pf, orch, 1974; *Jonchaies*, 1977; *Aïs*, bar, perc, orch, 1980; *Nekuia*, ch, orch, 1981; *Keqrops*, pf, orch, 1986; *Ata*, 1987; *Dox-Orkh*, vn, orch, 1991; etc.

Mixed ensemble: *Atrées*, 1956–62; *Thallein*, 1984; *Jalons*, 1986; *Waarg*, 1988; *Echange*, b cl, ens, 1989; *O-mega*, perc, ens, 1997; etc.

Percussion (with numbers of players): *Persephassa*, 6, 1969; *Psappha*, 1, 1975; *Plëiades*, 6, 1978; *Idmen B*, 6, 1985; *Kassandra*, bar, 1, 1987; *Rebonds*, 1, 1987–8; *Okho*, 3, 1989; *Zythos*, trbn, 6, 1996; etc.

Chamber: *ST/4*, str qt, 1956–62; *Eonta*, pf, 5 brass, 1963–4; *Nomos alpha*, vc, 1965–6; *Anaktoria*, cl, hn, bn, str qt, db, 1969; *Charisma*, cl, vc, 1971; *N'Shima*, 2 mez, 5 insts, 1975; *Dmaathen*, ob, perc, 1976; *Akanthos*, s, 8 insts, 1977; *Dikhthas*, vn, pf, 1979;

Tetras, str qt, 1983; *Tetora*, str qt, 1990; etc.
Choral: *Oresteia*, ch, ens, 1965–6; *Nuits*, ch, 1967–8;
  Pour la paix, ch, tape ad lib, 1981
Piano: *Herma*, 1961; *Evryali*, 1973; *Mists*, 1981
Electronic: *Orient-Occident*, 1960; *Bohor*, 1962;
  Persépolis, 1971; *La légende d'Eer*, 1977;
  Taurhiphanie, 1987; *Gendy3*, 1991

xyl. Abbreviation for xylophone.

xylophone (Fr. *xylophone*, Ger. *Xylophon*, pl.
Xylophone, It. *silofono*). Percussion instrument
with tuned bars of wood (Gk *xylon*; rosewood is
preferred) laid out in the manner of a piano
keyboard and struck with one beater or two in
each hand. Modern instruments generally have
tuned brass resonators beneath the keys. Probably
of Far Eastern origin, the instrument was known
in Europe by 1511, and Rameau owned an example,
but the first score to include it was Ferdinand
Kauer's Six Variations (*c*.1810), and the first to
survive in the active repertory is Saint-Saëns's
Danse macabre (1872). Since the beginning of
the 20th century it has been a regular member
of the orchestra, usually in the form of a four-
octave instrument whose lowest note is middle C
(though its parts are commonly notated an octave
lower).

xylorimba. Instrument with the five-octave range
of the MARIMBA but the thicker, narrower keys –
and therefore more penetrating sound – of the
xylophone. Boulez requires two in *Pli selon pli*,
though by 'xylorimba' in *Le Marteau sans maître*
he intended a four-octave xylophone.

Yale School of Music. Institution at Yale University, New Haven, Conn., originating in 1890, when the chair of music was founded.

Yamada, Kōsaku (b. Tokyo, 9 Jun 1886; d. Tokyo, 29 Dec 1965). Japanese composer. He studied at the Tokyo Music School (1904–8) and at the conservatory in Berlin from 1910 with Leopold Carl Wolff. In 1914 he returned to Tokyo, where the next year he gave the first concert in Japan by a Western-style orchestra. He also appeared as a conductor in the USA (1917–19) and Europe (1930s), later devoting himself to composition. Strauss was a central figure to him, but Debussy also left a mark on his large output of operas, tone poems, choral music and songs.

Yamaha. Japanese instrument firm founded when Torakusu Yamaha (1851–1916) built a harmonium in 1887. Since the 1970s the company, in Hamamatsu, has been the world leader in the production of pianos, synthesizers, electric guitars, wind instruments, etc.

Yanov-Yanovsky, Feliks (b. Tashkent, 28 May 1934). Uzbek composer of Russophone family. He studied at the Tashkent Conservatory, where he began teaching in 1961. His works – symphonies, violin concertos, Latin sacred works – explore East–West communications. So do those of his son, Dmitry Feliksovich (b. Tashkent, 24 Apr 1963), who studied with his father and began making an international reputation in the 1990s, especially through performances by the Kronos Quartet.

Years of Pilgrimage. See ANNEES DE PELERI-NAGE.

Yellow River Concerto. Celebrated example of collective composition from the period of the Cultural Revolution in China. The work, which emerged in 1969 from a four-man team including the pianist Yin Chengzong, was an arrangement for piano and orchestra of the cantata *Yellow River* (1939) by the prototypical Chinese communist composer Xian Xinghai (1905–45).

Yevgeny Onegin. See EUGENE ONEGIN.

Young, La Monte (Thornton) (b. Bern, Ida., 14 Oct 1935). US composer. With the encouragement of family members he learned to play the clarinet in popular groups; he then had more formal studies with Leonard Stein (1955–6), at UCLA (1957–8) and with Seymour Shifrin at Berkeley (1958–60). His String Trio (1958) showed his originality: it is a 12-note composition but made with unusually few and long notes (lasting a minute or more), one of the ancestral works of minimalism. (Terry Riley was a fellow student.) In 1959, at Darmstadt, he encountered Stockhausen and, more decisively, Cage. He moved to New York in 1960, studied with Richard Maxfield at the New School (1960–61) and became a founder of the FLUXUS movement. In 1963 he established the Theatre of Eternal Music, an ensemble with which he has given often lengthy performances involving drones, repetitive figures, just intonation (since 1964), strong amplification and patterned lighting by his wife Marin Zazeela. Also since 1964 he has been working on a growing project for solo pianist, *The Well-Tuned Piano*, again choosing just intonation in lengthily elaborating fundamental harmonic relations.

www.melafoundation.org

Young, William (d. Innsbruck, 23 Apr 1662). English viol player-composer, serving the arch-ducal court in Innsbruck by 1652, and highly esteemed there. He was the first English composer to publish sonatas (1653).

Young Person's Guide to the Orchestra, A. Work by Britten made for a 1946 documentary film on the orchestra, with variations (on the hornpipe from Purcell's *Abdelazer* music) focusing on the different instrumental families.

Yradier. See IRADIER.

Ysaÿe, Eugène (Auguste) (b. Liège, 16 Jul 1858; d. Brussels, 12 May 1931). Belgian violinist-composer. A violinist's son, he studied with Rodolphe Massart at the Liège Conservatory (1872–4), with Wieniawski in Brussels and with Vieuxtemps in Paris. Anton Rubinstein promoted him as a soloist, and from 1883 he and his quartet (founded in 1886) were pre-eminent, playing new works by Franck (Sonata), Chausson (*Concert*, *Poème*), Debussy (Quartet), etc. Though regarded as the outstanding virtuoso of his generation, he concentrated on works of substance: the programmes he gave with Raoul Pugno comprised mostly sonatas. His compositions, too, combine difficulty with exploratory passion – especially his six solo sonatas (published in 1924).

Yu, Julian (b. Beijing, 2 Sep 1957). Chinese composer. He studied at the Beijing Conservatory, with Yuasa in Tokyo (1980–82), and from 1985 at the Queensland Conservatorium, where he stayed on to teach. His works include elaborations of figures from Bach.

Yuasa, Jōji (b. Koriyama, 12 Aug 1929). Japanese composer. He abandoned medical studies in 1951 to join the Experimental Workshop with Takemitsu and others. His works often involve electronic means and spatial configurations.

Yun, Isang (b. Duk San, San Chun Gun, Tong-yong, now Chung Mu, 17 Sep 1917; d. Berlin, 3 Nov 1995). Korean–German composer. The son of a poet, he studied in Japan (with Ikenouchi) before the Second World War, then returned to Korea, where he was active in the anti-Japanese resistance and imprisoned. In 1955 he travelled to Europe for further study in Paris, Berlin and Darmstadt. He remained in Germany until 1967, when he was abducted by the South Korean authorities and again imprisoned, as a communist. International pressure brought his release two years later and his return in 1970 to Berlin, to teach at the conservatory. His large output (especially in orchestral and chamber forms) conveys melodic and cultural traditions from the Far East into the European, and specifically German, late 20th century.

www.yun-gesellschaft.de

Orchestral: Symphony No.1, 1983; No.2, 1984; No.3, 1985; No.4 'In dunkelen singen', 1986; No.5 (Nelly Sachs), bar, orch, 1987; concertos for vn (3), vc, fl, ob, cl; etc.

Chamber: *Loyang*, 9 insts, 1962; Clarinet Quintet No.1, 1984; No.2, 1994; String Quartet No.3, 1959; No.4, 1988; No.5, 1990; No.6, 1992; etc.

Solo: *Piri*, ob, 1971; *Sori*, fl, 1988; etc.

Other works: *Sim Tjong* (opera), f.p. Munich, 1972; other operas, choral and vocal music

Zabaleta, Nicanor (b. San Sebastian, 7 Jan 1907; d. San Juan, Puerto Rico, 31 Mar 1993). Spanish harpist. He placed his instrument centre-stage through a career from 1926 (Paris debut, following tuition there with Marcel Tournier) to 1992 (final concert in Madrid), giving the first performances of concertos by Ginastera, Josef Tal, etc.

Zadok the Priest. Coronation anthem by Handel, one of four he wrote for George II, beginning with a notable example of Baroque minimalism, into which the choir comes crashing. First performance: Westminster, 11 Oct 1727.

Zaide. Customary title for an unfinished opera by Mozart to a libretto by Johann Andreas Schachtner. Zaide (soprano) tries to help Gomatz (tenor), a Christian slave, escape from the Sultan Soliman (tenor), with the help of Allazim (bass). The abduction is foiled, but the outcome is uncertain: the score stops. Its numbers include Zaide's calming aria 'Ruhe sanft' and Mozart's only surviving pieces of MELODRAMA. First performance: Frankfurt, 27 Jan 1866.

Zajc, Ivan (b. Rijeka, 3 Aug 1832; d. Zagreb, 16 Dec 1914). Croatian composer. He studied with Lauro Rossi and others at the Milan Conservatory (1850–55), worked in operetta in Vienna as a composer and conductor (1862–70), and returned to Croatia to revitalize musical life. His enormous output, reaching Op.1202, embraced all genres.

Zandonai, Riccardo (b. Sacco di Rovereto, Trentino, 30 May 1883; d. Pesaro, 5 Jun 1944). Italian composer. He studied with Mascagni in Pesaro (1898–1901), and in 1907 was introduced by Boito to Giulio Ricordi, who groomed him as Puccini's successor. That mantle he duly accepted, his *Francesca da Rimini* (1914) being a gloriously heady response to d'Annunzio's rich text. His other operas include *Conchita* (1911), *Giulietta e Romeo* (1922) and *I cavalieri di Ekebù* (1922).

Zappa, Frank (b. Baltimore, 21 Dec 1940; d. Laurel Canyon, Los Angeles, 4 Dec 1993). US composer. Active largely in the rock field, he was influenced by 20th-century classical music (Ives, Varèse, Stockhausen) and made albums with the Ensembles InterContemporain (*The Perfect Stranger*, 1984) and Modern (*The Yellow Shark*, 1993). In these he dissolved barriers, creating situations (high modernism meets movie music) that are funky and provocative.

Zarlino, Gioseffo (b. Chioggia, *c*.1517; d. Venice, 4 Feb 1590). Italian theorist. Brought up by the Franciscans, he was a singer at Chioggia Cathedral by 1536 and was ordained priest, probably in 1540. In 1541 he moved to Venice, where he continued his studies in music (under Willaert), philosophy and ancient languages. His *Le istitutioni harmoniche*, published in 1558, was a groundbreaking effort to provide a rational basis for the new harmony (based on major and minor triads) in frequency ratios and a reconfiguration of the modes, with the scale on C now fundamental. He used his harmonic understanding to address matters of tuning and counterpoint, and responded to criticisms in susbequent treatises. From 1565 he was chapelmaster at St Mark's; he also composed motets and madrigals.

zarzuela. Kind of Spanish opera with spoken dialogue, tracing its origins to court entertainments in the 1650s at the Palacio Real de la Zarzuela (i.e. little bramble bush), a hunting lodge outside Madrid. In the early 18th century the zarzuela entered the public theatres, but it was ousted in the 1770s by newer, shorter, more comic forms, notably the TONADILLA. Its rebirth is dated from Rafael Hernando's *Colegiales y soldados* (1849), which was followed by a rush of activity. The Teatro de la Zarzuela was opened in Madrid in 1856 and staged the works of Joaquín Gaztambide, Francisco Asenjo Barbieri, Pascual Emilio Arrieta and others. In the 1860s the influence of French operetta began to be felt (Viennese following at the start of the 20th century), and a new type of one-acter, the *género chico*, emerged. Zarzuela composers of the first half of the 20th century included Amadeo Vives, Pablo Sorozábal and Federico Moreno Torroba, whose *María Manuela* (1957) shines from the twilight of the genre.

Zauberflöte, Die (The Magic Flute). Opera by Mozart to a libretto by Emanuel Schikaneder. The prince Tamino (tenor), accompanied by the plebeian Papageno (baritone), through trials wins Pamina (soprano), and by his virtue assures the triumph of light – the rule of Sarastro (bass) – over darkness in the person of the captivating Queen of the Night (coloratura soprano). The score is a colourful community of different styles: fearsome coloratura brilliance in the Queen of the Night's arias 'O zitt're nicht' and 'Der Hölle Rache', quasi-folksongs in Papageno's 'Der Vogelfänger bin ich, ja' and 'Ein Mädchen oder Weibchen', warm sentiment in Tamino's 'Dies Bildnis ist bezaubernd schön' (sung to Pamina's portrait) and Pamina's G minor 'Ach, ich fühl's', hymn-like gravity in Sarastro's 'O Isis und Osiris' and 'In diesen heil'gen Hallen'. Even the orchestra has personality, in the Overture and March of the Priests. And any audience will range from children witnessing a lively fairytale to older people savouring again the work's music and humanity (both together in the Pamina–Papageno duet 'Bei Männern, welche Liebe'). First performance: Vienna, 30 Sep 1791.

Zauberharfe, Die (The Magic Harp). Music by Schubert for Georg von Hofmann's play, comprising an overture and other numbers. First performance: Vienna, 19 Aug 1820.

Zehetmair, Thomas (b. Salzburg, 23 Nov 1961). Austrian violinist of intense virtuosity and exploratory keenness. He studied at the Mozarteum with his father, Helmut Zehetmair, and later with Max Rostal and Nathan Milstein; he also studied period performance practice with Harnoncourt. In 1978 he made his debut in Vienna, since when he has been particularly admired for his playing of Bach and contemporary music (Holliger, Schnebel, etc.). He also leads a quartet.

Zeitmass (Ger., time-measure, pl. *Zeitmasse, Zeitmasze*). Tempo.

Zeitmasze (Tempos). Work by Stockhausen for five woodwind (fl, ob, cor anglais, cl, bn) – a bundle of temporal ribbons that are fixed (regular in speed) or flexible, metronomic or corporeal (determined by how fast or how slowly the music can be played), played by the instruments as helter-skelter soloists or as an ensemble. First performance: Paris, 15 Dec 1956 (Domaine Musical).

Zeitoper (Ger., opera of the age). Variety of opera produced in Germany in the last years of the Weimar Republic (*c.*1927–33), dealing with contemporary characters. There are examples by Krenek (*Jonny spielt auf*), Hindemith (*Neues vom Tage*), Brand (*Maschinist Hopkins*) and Schoenberg (*Vom heute auf morgen*).

Zelenka, Jan (Lukas Ignatius) Dismas (baptized Louňovice pod Blanikem, 16 Oct 1679; d. Dresden, 22/23 Dec 1745). Czech composer, Baroque individualist. He probably had his first lessons with his father, the local church musician, and may have had a Jesuit education. In 1710/11 he joined the Dresden court as a violone player, and there he remained, apart from a period of travel and study that took him possibly to Italy and certainly to Vienna (1717–19), where Fux was his teacher. From Fux he learned the art of fugue, splendidly employed in many of his sacred works, along with a keen expressiveness and colourful orchestration, while his rather few instrumental pieces display those qualities along with eccentric humour. By report he was reserved and devout; he never married. His music was admired by his contemporaries, including Bach, but then fell into oblivion until the latter part of the 20th century.

Janice B. Stockigt *Jan Dismas Zelenka* (2000)

Sacred: 21 masses, 2 *Requiem* settings (in C minor and D minor), Lamentations and responsories for Holy Week, litanies, psalms (*Miserere*, C minor), hymns, antiphons, etc., all for soli, ch, insts
Instrumental: 6 sonatas, 2 ob, bn, con, *c.*1721–2; concerto, *Hipocondrie*, overture, symphony, all 1723; 5 capriccios, *c.*1717–29

Zelter, Carl Friedrich (b. Berlin, 11 Dec 1758; d. Berlin, 15 May 1832). German composer and teacher. He worked alongside his father as a mason, with music his hobby until he had composition lessons (1784–6) with C.F.C. Fasch, later founder of the Berlin Singakademie. In 1800 he succeeded Fasch as conductor of this institution; he also became professor of music at the Academy of the Arts (1809) and founded his own music institute (1822). Mendelssohn and Meyerbeer were among his pupils. He had an important correspondence with Goethe, and gained the poet's approval for his song settings, which are rather simple and strophic.

Zemlinsky, Alexander (von) (b. Vienna, 14 Oct 1871; d. Larchmont, NY, 15 Mar 1942). Austrian composer, in the ripest late-Romantic style yet touchingly intimate. He studied with Robert and J.N. Fuchs at the Vienna Conservatory (1886–92) and won Brahms's attention with his chamber music. In 1895 he met Schoenberg and gave him some advice; the two young men remained friends and musical allies, and in 1901 Schoenberg married Zemlinsky's sister. That same year Zemlinsky had an affair with his pupil Alma Schindler, who rejected him for Mahler. He may have found consolation in professional success. His second opera, *Es war einmal*, had been presented (by Mahler) at the court opera, and he was embarked on a career as a theatre conductor.

He took over the musical direction of the German theatre in Prague (1911–27), where he won respect for his performances (from Stravinsky among others), gave the première of Schoenberg's *Erwartung* and founded a new-music series like Schoenberg's Society for Private Musical Performances. Much as he admired his friend, though, he took a different course, remaining closer to Mahler and Strauss. Rich and lyrical, his music also delights at times in the unusual. He was very aware (Schindler had made him so) of his faults of physique, and some of his finest works are those that, like *Der Zwerg*, give voice to the malformed and rejected. Other achievements of his Prague period include his Second Quartet and Lyric Symphony.

In 1927 he moved to Berlin as Klemperer's assistant at the Kroll Opera, and there he began to absorb the new influences of Hindemith and Weill. He then fled the Nazis successively to Vienna again (1933–8) and the USA, where a stroke in 1939 put an end to his active life. He died almost forgotten, and remained so until a revival began around the time of his centenary.

Antony Beaumont *Zemlinsky* (2000)

Operas: *Sarema* (Zemlinsky, after Rudolf von Gottschall), 1893–5, f.p. Munich, 1897; *Es war einmal* (Maximilian Singer, after Holger Drachmann), 1897–9, f.p. Vienna, 1900; *Der*

Traumgörge (Leo Feld), 1904–6, f.p. Nuremberg, 1980; *Kleider machen Leute* (Feld, after Keller), 1907–9, f.p. Vienna, 1910, rev 1922, f.p. Prague, 1922; *Eine florentinische Tragödie* (Max Meyerfeld, after Wilde), Op.16, 1915–16, f.p. Stuttgart, 1917; *Der* ZWERG, Op.17, 1921; *Der Kreidekreis* (Zemlinsky, after Klabund), 1930–32, f.p. Zurich, 1933; *Der König Kandaules* (Zemlinsky, after Gide), 1935–8, f.p. Hamburg, 1996

Orchestral and vocal orchestral: Psalm 83, soli, ch, orch, 1900; *Die Seejungfrau*, 1902–3; Psalm 23, Op.14, ch, orch, 1910; 6 Songs (Maeterlinck), v, orch, 1913; LYRIC SYMPHONY, Op.18, s, bar, orch, 1922–3; Symphonic Songs, v, orch, 1929; Sinfonietta, Op.23, 1934; Psalm 13, Op.24, ch, orch, 1935; etc.

Chamber: String Quartet No.1, Op.4, 1896; No.2, Op.15, 1913–15; No.3, Op.19, 1924; No.4, Op.25, 1936; Trio, D minor, Op.3, cl/vn, vc, pf, 1896; etc.

Other works: songs, piano pieces (*Fantasien über Gedichte von Richard Dehmel*, Op.9, 1898), etc.

Zender, Hans (b. Wiesbaden, 22 Nov 1936). German composer-conductor. He studied at the conservatories in Frankfurt and Freiburg, and has held posts with the Saarbrücken Radio Symphony (1971–84), the Hamburg Staatsoper and the Südwestfunk (from 1999). Some of his works turn to the Far East, others to Western masterpieces (e.g. his elaboration of *Winterreise* for tenor and ensemble), but always from a contemporary German point of view.

Zeno, Apostolo (b. Venice, 11 Dec 1668; d. Venice, 11 Nov 1750). Italian librettist. He wrote from 1696 for the principal Venetian composers – Carlo Francesco Pollarolo, Ziani, Gasparini, etc. – sometimes in collaboration with Pietro Pariati. He was then court poet in Vienna (1718–29), writing opera and oratorio texts mostly for Caldara. Relieved of the clamorous obligations of the public theatre, he hoped to put on the stage models of noble behaviour, but he wondered about his success and devoted his later years to scholarship. Nevertheless, some of his librettos remained current throughout the 18th century and even beyond: *Lucio Vero* (1700), often retitled *Vologeso*, was set by Albinoni, Keiser, Galuppi, Jommelli, Sarti, Sacchini, Traetta and Martín y Soler.

Ziani, Marc'Antonio (b. Venice, c.1653; d. Vienna, 22 Jan 1715). Italian composer. He was a nephew of Pietro Andrea Ziani (?1616–84), a church musician and opera composer with whom he may have studied, and who certainly helped him in his career. By the mid 1680s he was one of the most successful opera composers in Venice. In 1700 he was appointed imperial vice-chapelmaster in Vienna, promoted to chapelmaster in 1712 (and succeeded in that position by Fux). There he continued his abundant output of operas and also wrote church music. His fame was European (some sonatas were published in London in 1703), and his operas were still being performed in Vienna 30 years after his death.

ziehen (Ger.). Draw out.

Zigeuner (Ger.). Gipsy, as in Brahms's *Zigeunerlieder* (Gipsy Songs).

Zildjian. Turkish–US family of cymbal makers, whose metallurgical secret was discovered by Avedis Zildjian in Constantinople in 1623 and has been jealously guarded by the family ever since. There are branches at work in Istanbul, Massachusetts and Canada.

Zillig, Winfried (b. Würzburg, 1 Apr 1905; d. Hamburg, 18 Dec 1963). German composer. He studied in Vienna and Berlin with Schoenberg (1925–8), worked as a conductor with German theatres and (after the Second World War) radio services, and composed in a Schoenberg–Stravinsky style. He made a performing version of his teacher's *Jakobsleiter*.

Ziloti, Aleksandr (Ilich) (b. near Kharkov/Kharkiv, 9 Oct 1863; d. New York, 8 Dec 1945). Russian conductor and pianist. He studied with Nikolay Rubinstein, Taneyev and Tchaikovsky at the Moscow Conservatory (1871–81), and, after working with Liszt in Weimar (1883–6), returned there to teach (1887–91), his cousin Rachmaninoff being among his pupils. For most of the next decade he was in western Europe and the USA. He then founded the Ziloti Concerts in St Petersburg (1903–17), presenting outstanding artists and new works by Stravinsky, Scriabin, Prokofiev, Rachmaninoff, etc. In 1919 he left for England, and then New York, where he taught at Juilliard.

Zimbalist, Efrem (Aleksandrovich) (b. Rostov on the Don, 9 Apr 1890; d. Reno, Nev., 22 Feb 1985). Russian–US violinist. Taught by his violinist-conductor father and by Auer in St Petersburg (1901–7), he made his US debut in 1911 and stayed, performing and teaching, from 1928, at the Curtis Institute, of which he was director (1941–68).

Zimbelstern (Ger., cymbal-star). An organ stop; a revolving star atop the case, with bells attached.

Zimerman, Krystian (b. Zabrze, 5 Dec 1956). Polish pianist, remarkably fluent and refined in his control of colour and character. He studied with Andrzeij Jasinski and in 1975 won the Chopin Competition, the youngest to do so. Nevertheless, he devoted time the next year to working with Rubinstein and has remained careful in the frequency of his concerts and recordings. His repertory includes Chopin, Liszt, Brahms, Debussy and the Lutosławski concerto, written for him.

Zimmermann, Bernd Alois (b. Bliesheim, near Cologne, 20 Mar 1918; d. Grosskönigsdorf, now Pulheim, near Cologne, 10 Aug 1970). German composer. Unlike so many of the composers who achieved prominence after 1945, he had come to adulthood before the war, and his participation in the avant-garde was always more circumspect. He was called up into the army from his studies in Cologne and Bonn, and served in France, where he first came across the music of Stravinsky and Milhaud. In 1942 he was able to continue his studies with Heinrich Lemacher and Jarnach in Cologne, and in 1948–50 he attended courses given by Fortner and Leibowitz at Darmstadt. He then taught in Cologne at the university (1950–52) and conservatory (1957–70).

His first published works, dating from his early 30s, bring together elements from Schoenberg, Bartók, Stravinsky and, sometimes, jazz, but *Perspektiven* for two pianos (1955–6) is much closer to Webern's symmetrical patterning. It was also one of several works he described as imaginary ballets: in its successors the needs of character might involve him in quotation – from Bach and Messiaen, for instance, in another two-piano work, *Monologe* (1964). In this he was ahead of his time. He developed an aesthetic of 'pluralism', of the multi-layering of different materials, different times, and in his opera *Die Soldaten* he used quotation along with diversity of musical style, going further in the *Requiem für einen jungen Dichter* (Requiem for a Young Poet) to embrace 20th-century news on tape. Meanwhile, any playfulness in his technique was being overtaken by pessimism. His works for cello constitute almost an autobiography through the instrument, and the last of them came shortly before he committed suicide.

Opera: *Die* SOLDATEN, 1958–64

Vocal orchestral: *Omnia tempus habent*, s, 17 insts, 1957–8; *Requiem für einen jungen Dichter*, soli, ch, jazz group, orch, tape, 1967–9; *Ich wandre mich und sah an alles Unrecht, dass geschah unter der Sonne*, 2 speakers, b, orch, 1970

Orchestral: Violin Concerto, 1950; Oboe Concerto, 1952; Trumpet Concerto 'Nobody knows de trouble I see', 1954; *Alagoana*, 1950–55; *Canto di speranza*, vc, orch, 1957; *Antiphonen*, va, small orch, 1961–2; *Dialoge*, 2 pf, orch, 1960–65; *Musique pour les soupers du roi Ubu*, 1962–6; Cello Concerto 'en forme de pas de trois', 1965–6; *Photoptosis*, 1968; *Stille und Umkehr*, 1970

Instrumental: Violin Sonata, 1950; Solo Violin Sonata, 1951; *Enchiridion*, pf, 1949–52; *Metamorphosen*, pf, 1954; Solo Viola Sonata, 1955; *Perspektiven*, 2 pf, 1955–6; *Konfigurationen*, pf, 1956; Solo Cello Sonata, 1960; *Présence*, pf trio, 1961; *Tempus loquendi*, fl, 1963; *Monologe*, 2 pf, 1964; *Intercomunicazione*, vc, pf, 1967; 4 Short Studies, vc, 1970

Tape: *Tratto*, 1965–7; *Tratto II*, 1970

Zimmermann, Frank Peter (b. Duisburg, 27 Feb 1965). German violinist of fine virtuosity and classic demeanour, specially admired in Mozart and the most challenging music: Paganini, Ysaÿe and Ligeti. He studied with Valery Gradov in Essen, Saschko Gawriloff in Berlin and Hermann Krebbers in Amsterdam. His sister Tabea (b. 1966) is an outstanding violist and the destined performer of Ligeti's solo sonata.

Zimmermann, Udo (b. Dresden, 6 Oct 1943). German composer, a pupil of Johannes Paul Thilman at the Dresden conservatory (1962–8) and of Gunther Kochan in Berlin (1968–70). His first opera, *Die weisse Rose* (1966–7), won him early respect for its vivid portrayal of the anti-Hitler resistance, and he remained prominent, and prolific, among the younger composers of East Germany. He then turned his energies to administration, as artistic director of the Leipzig Opera (1990–2001) and Deutsche Oper, Berlin (from 2001).

Zingarelli, Niccolò Antonio (b. Naples, 4 Apr 1752; d. Torre del Greco, near Naples, 5 May 1837). Italian composer. He studied with Anfossi and Sacchini at the Loreto conservatory in Naples, and worked as an organist and violin teacher before starting to win favour as a composer of opera seria in 1785. Melodious and undemanding, his operas emerged at a rate of roughly two a year until 1803. Meanwhile he was also active in church music, as chapelmaster of the Holy House of Loreto (1796–1804) and St Peter's in Rome (1804–11). In the latter capacity he crossed swords with Napoleon, but redeemed himself by writing a solemn mass that was over in 20 minutes. He returned to Naples as director of the newly unified conservatory in 1813, his pupils including Mercadante and Bellini. His operas, he felt, had been displaced by Rossini's, but it was Bellini's work that superseded his most successful piece, *Giulietta e Romeo* (1796).

zingarese, alla. See ALLA ZINGARESE.

Zink (Ger., pl. *Zinken*). Cornett.

Zipoli, Domenico (b. Prato, 16/17 Oct 1688; d. Santa Catalina, near Cordoba, Argentina, 2 Jan 1726). Italian organist-composer, latterly in South America. He studied in Florence, Naples, Bologna and Rome (with Pasquini), where he stayed until leaving for Spain in 1716 to become a Jesuit missionary in what were known as the Paraguay reductions. Having arrived the next year, he completed his training for the priesthood but died of tuberculosis before ordination. His church music lived on in South America for half a century and more, while his reputation in Europe was maintained by his keyboard sonatas, published in 1716.

zither. Alpine folk instrument of the psaltery type; a box of tuned strings having frets and plucked with a plectrum.

znamenny. Corpus of Russian chant probably going back to the mid 15th century.

zoppa, alla. See ALLA ZOPPA.

Zorn, John (b. New York, 2 Sep 1953). US composer. He studied at Webster University, St Louis, and has been active in downtown music in New York since 1974, first as an improvising saxophonist, later as a record producer and composer, drawing on a wide variety of models and refusing to draw any line between his work for classical ensembles and that with rock bands. His works include the piano concerto *Aporias* (1998).

Zoroastre. Opera by Rameau to a libretto by Louis de Cahusac. Zoroastre (haute-contre) – i.e. Zarathustra, the Persian prophet – wins the hand of Amélite (soprano), heiress to the throne of Bactria, and at the same time foils the sorcerer Abramane (bass). First performance: Paris Opera, 5 Dec 1749; rev Paris Opera, 19 Jan 1756.

Zumsteeg, Johann Rudolf (b. Sachsenflur, near Mergentheim, 10 Jan 1760; d. Stuttgart, 27 Jan 1802). German composer. He followed his father in service to the Duke of Württemberg, and was particularly admired for his operas and songs. The former, including *Die Geisterinsel* (1798, after *The Tempest*), were influenced by his admiration for Mozart; the latter in turn influenced Schubert.

Zurich (Zürich). See TONHALLE ORCHESTRA.

zurückhaltend (Ger.). Holding back, slowing.

zweistimmig. Two-part.

Zweiunddreissigstel(-Note) (Ger.). 32nd-note, demisemiquaver.

Zwerg, Der (The Dwarf). One-act opera by Zemlinsky to a libretto by Georg Klaren after Oscar Wilde's story *The Birthday of the Infanta*. Donna Clara (soprano), the Infanta, plays at love with her new birthday present, the Dwarf (tenor), who is really smitten with her. Catching sight of himself in a mirror, and realizing the gulf between his ugliness and her beauty, he becomes desperate. She will not save him. First performance: Cologne, 28 May 1922.

Zwilich, Ellen Taaffe (b. Miami, 30 Apr 1939). US composer. She trained as a violinist and played in the American Symphony under Stokowski before studying composition with Carter and Sessions and gaining a doctorate at Juilliard (1975). Her firm curve away from modernism is documented in her three symphonies, numerous concertos and chamber pieces.

Zwölftonmusik (Ger.). 12-note music.